Inverness
the Northe
Highlands & Is
p883

Stirling &
Central Scotland
p824

⭐ Edinburgh p751

Glasgow &
Southern
Scotland
p783

The Lake District
& Cumbria
p575

Newcastle &
Northeast England
p609

Manchester, Liverpool
& Northwest England
p537

Yorkshire
p479

Snowdonia &
North Wales
p711

Birmingham,
the Midlands
& the Marches
p392

Hay-on-Wye
& Mid-Wales
p687

Cambridge
& East Anglia
p353

Pembrokeshire
& South Wales
p659

Cardiff (Caerdydd)
p641

Southwest
England
p224

⭐ London p58

Canterbury &
Southeast England
p146

Oxford,
Cotswolds
& Around p181

Transport

THIS EDITION WRITTEN AND RESEARCHED BY
David Else, Oliver Berry, Fionn Davenport, Marc Di Duca,
Belinda Dixon, Peter Dragicevich, Damian Harper, Anna Kaminski,
Catherine Le Nevez, Fran Parnell, Andy Symington, Neil Wilson

welcome to Great Britain

Variety Packed

From the graceful architecture of Canterbury Cathedral in the south to the soaring ramparts of Edinburgh Castle in the north, via the mountains of Wales or the picture-postcard landscape of the Cotswolds, Britain's astounding variety is a major reason to travel here. The cities tempt with top-class shops and restaurants, and some of the world's finest museums, while cutting-edge clubs and world-famous theatres provide endless nights to remember. Next day, you're deep in the countryside, high in the hills or enjoying a classic seaside resort. In Britain, there really is something for everyone, whether you're eight or 80, going solo or travelling with your friends, your kids or your grandma.

Time Travel

A journey through Britain is a journey through history – but not history that's dull and dusty. This is history you can feel and re-live. You can lay your hands on the megaliths of a 5000-year-old stone circle, or walk the battlements of a medieval fortress – just as they were patrolled by knights in armour many centuries ago. Fast-forward to the future and you're admiring 21st-century architecture in Glasgow or exploring the space-age domes of Cornwall's Eden Project.

Edinburgh Castle, Buckingham Palace, Stonehenge, Manchester United, The Beatles – Britain does icons like no other place on earth, and travel here is a fascinating mix of famous names and hidden gems.

(left) Big Ben (p63), Houses of Parliament (p63) and the London Eye (p83)
(below) Stourhead (p268), England

English Spoken Here

While Britain boasts complex traditions and culture, on the surface, at least, it's familiar to many visitors thanks to a vast catalogue of British film and TV exports. And for most visitors, Britain's national language – English – is equally recognisable, and one more reason why travel here is a breeze. Of course Wales and Scotland have their own languages, but everyone speaks English too – and all outsiders get a little confused by local accents in places such as Devon, Snowdonia and Aberdeen.

Easy Does It

A final thing to remember while you're planning a trip to Britain: getting from place to place is pretty straightforward. Although the locals may grumble (in fact, it's a national pastime), public transport is pretty good, and a train ride through the British landscape can be a highlight in itself. Whichever way you get around, in this compact country you're never far from the next town, the next pub, the next restaurant, the next national park or the next impressive castle on your hitlist of highlights. The choice is endless, and we've hand-picked the best places for you. Use it to steer yourself from place to place, and mix it with making your own discoveries. You won't be disappointed.

Great Britain

Top Experiences

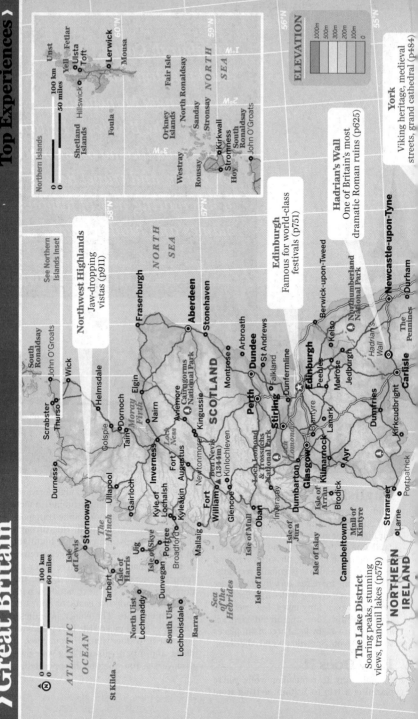

Northwest Highlands
Jaw-dropping vistas (p911)

Edinburgh
Famous for world-class festivals (p751)

Hadrian's Wall
One of Britain's most dramatic Roman ruins (p625)

York
Viking heritage, medieval streets, grand cathedral (p484)

The Lake District
Soaring peaks, stunning views, tranquil lakes (p579)

ELEVATION

1000m
500m
300m
200m
100m
0

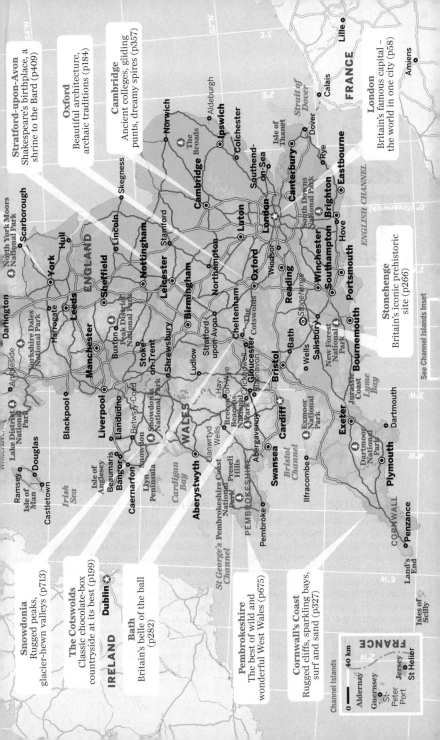

Stratford-upon-Avon
Shakespeare's birthplace, a shrine to the Bard (p409)

Oxford
Beautiful architecture, archaic traditions (p184)

Cambridge
Ancient colleges, gliding punts, dreamy spires (p357)

London
Britain's famous capital – the world in one city (p58)

Stonehenge
Britain's iconic prehistoric site (p266)

Snowdonia
Rugged peaks, glacier-hewn valleys (p713)

The Cotswolds
Classic chocolate-box countryside at its best (p199)

Bath
Britain's belle of the ball (p282)

Pembrokeshire
The best of wild and wonderful West Wales (p675)

Cornwall's Coast
Rugged cliffs, sparkling bays, surf and sand (p327)

25 TOP EXPERIENCES

Stonehenge

1 Mysterious and compelling, Stonehenge (p266) is Britain's most iconic ancient site. People have been drawn to this myth-rich ring of bluestones for the last 5000 years, and we're still not sure why it was built. Most visitors get to gaze at the 50-ton megaliths from behind the perimeter fence, but with enough planning you can book an early-morning or evening tour and walk around the inner ring. In the slanting sunlight, away from the crowds, it's an ethereal place – an experience that certainly stays with you.

Edinburgh

2 Edinburgh (p751) is a city of many moods – famous for its festivals and especially lively in summer. It's also worth visiting out of season for sights such as the castle silhouetted against a blue spring sky with a yellow haze of daffodils misting the slopes below the esplanade. Or a chill December morning with the fog snagging the spires of the Old Town, the ancient streets and alleyways more mysterious than ever, rain on the cobblestones and a warm glow beckoning from the window of a pub.
Edinburgh Castle (p754), right

JOHN FREEMAN/GETTY IMAGES ©

Oxford

3 For centuries, the brilliant minds and august institutions of Oxford University have made Oxford (p184) famous across the globe. You'll get a glimpse of this revered world as you stroll hushed college quads and cobbled lanes roamed by cycling students and dusty academics. The beautiful buildings and archaic traditions have changed little over the years, leaving Oxford much as alumni such as Einstein or Tolkien would have found it. All Souls College (p190), top left

Isle of Skye

4 Of all Scotland's many islands, Skye (p918) is one of the most famous and best loved by visitors, thanks to a mix of history (the island's link to Bonnie Prince Charlie is forever remembered by 'The Skye Boat Song'), accessibility (the ferry from the mainland has been replaced by a bridge) and sheer beauty. With jagged mountains, velvet moors and towering sea cliffs, Skye's scenery never fails to impress. And for those days when the mist comes in, there are plenty of castles and local museums to explore, and cosy pubs to enjoy. Portree (p922), top right

The Cotswolds

5 The most wonderful thing about travel in the Cotswolds (p199) is that no matter where you go or how lost you get, you'll still end up in an impossibly picturesque village complete with rose-clad cottages, an ancient church of honey-coloured stone, a pub with sloping floors and fine ales, and a view of the lush green hills. It's easy to leave the crowds behind and find your very own slice of medieval England – and some of the best boutique hotels in the country.

Snowdonia

6 The rugged northwest corner of Wales has rocky mountain peaks, glacier-hewn valleys, sinuous ridges, sparkling lakes and rivers, and charm-infused villages. The busiest part is around Snowdon (p719) itself, where many people hike to the summit, and many more take the jolly cog railway, while to the south and west are rarely trod areas perfect for off-the-beaten-track exploration. And just nearby sit the lovely Llŷn Peninsula (p727) and Isle of Anglesey (p732), where the sun often shines, even if it's raining on the mountains.

Bath

7 Britain boasts many great cities, but Bath (p282) stands out as the belle of the ball. Thanks to the natural hot water that bubbles to the surface, the Romans built a health resort here. The waters were rediscovered in the 18th century, and Bath became the place to see and be seen by British high society. Today, the stunning Georgian architecture of grand town houses and sweeping crescents (not to mention Roman remains, a beautiful cathedral and a cutting-edge 21st-century spa) means Bath demands your undivided attention.
Roman Baths (p283), bottom

PAUL THOMPSON/GETTY IMAGES ©

SIMON GREENWOOD/GETTY IMAGES ©

JULIAN FINNEY/GETTY IMAGES ©

Football

8 In some parts of the world it's called 'soccer', but here in Britain it's definitely 'football' (p1020). Despite what the fans may say in Italy or Brazil, the English Premier League has some of the world's finest teams. Big names include the globally renowned Arsenal, Liverpool and Chelsea, plus *the* most famous club on the planet: Manchester United. North of the border, Scotland's best-known teams are Glasgow Rangers and Glasgow Celtic – and their 'old firm' rivalry is legendary – while in Wales the national sport is most definitely rugby.

The Lake District

9 William Wordsworth and his Romantic chums were the first to champion the charms of the Lake District (p579), and it's not hard to see what stirred them. With soaring mountains, whaleback fells, razor-edge valleys and – of course – glistening lakes (as well as England's highest peak), this craggy corner of northwest England has some of the country's finest vistas. Come for the comfortable lakeside hotels, or come for the hardy hiking – whatever you choose, inspiration is sure to follow. Windermere (p579), top right

Hadrian's Wall

10 Hadrian's Wall (p625) is one of Britain's most revealing and dramatic Roman ruins, its sturdy line of battlements, forts, garrisons, towers and castles disclosing much about the everyday life of the international battalions posted along its length almost 2000 years ago. But this great wall was always about more than mere fortification. Hadrian's edge-of-empire barrier symbolised the boundary of civilised order. To the south was the orderly Roman world of tax-paying, bathhouses and underfloor heating, while to the north was the unruly land of the marauding Celts.

Castles & Stately Homes

11 Britain's turbulent history is nowhere more apparent than in the mighty castles that dot the landscape, from clifftop ruins such as Corfe (p250) or fortresses such as Caernarfon (p726), to formidable Stirling (p828) and still-inhabited Windsor (p220). And when the aristocracy no longer needed castles, they built mansions known as 'stately homes' at the heart of their country estates. Classics of the genre include Blenheim Palace (p193) and Chatsworth House (p478) in England, Powis Castle (p709) in Wales and Scone Palace (p862) in Scotland. Blenheim Palace (p193), below

Cornwall

12 At Britain's far southwestern extremity, the former kingdom of Cornwall (p327) boasts endless miles of unbroken coastline, with rugged cliffs, sparkling bays, scenic fishing ports and white sandy beaches favoured by everyone from bucket-and-spade families to sun-bronzed surfers. Above the cliffs, the towers of former tin mines now stand like dramatic castles, while inland from the coast is a tranquil landscape of lush farmland and picturesque villages, crowned by the domes of the Eden Project (p349)– a stunning symbol of Cornwall's renaissance. Polperro (p348), bottom

Cambridge

13 Abounding with exquisite architecture and steeped in tradition, Cambridge (p357) is a university town extraordinaire. The tightly packed core of ancient colleges, the picturesque riverside 'Backs' (college gardens) and the surrounding meadows give Cambridge a more tranquil appeal than its historic rival Oxford. Highlights include the intricate vaulting of King's College Chapel, and no visit is complete without an attempt to steer a punt (flat-bottomed boat) along the river and under the quirky Mathematical Bridge. You'll wonder how you could have studied anywhere else.

Stratford-upon-Avon

14 The pretty English Midlands town of Stratford-upon-Avon (p409) is famed around the world as the birthplace of the nation's best-known dramatist, William Shakespeare. Today, the town's tight knot of Tudor streets form a living map of Shakespeare's life and times, while crowds of fans and would-be thespians come to enjoy a play at the theatre or visit the five historic houses owned by Shakespeare and his relatives, with a respectful detour to the old stone church where the Bard was laid to rest. Hall's Croft (p409), bottom

Cardiff

15 The exuberant capital of Wales, compact Cardiff (p641) has recently emerged as one of Britain's leading urban centres. After a mid-20th-century decline, the city has entered the new millennium with vigour and confidence, flexing architectural muscles and revelling in a sense of style. From the historic castle to the ultramodern waterfront, from lively street cafes to infectious nightlife, from Victorian shopping arcades to the gigantic rugby stadium that is the pulsating heart of the city on match days, Cardiff undoubtedly has buzz.
Castle Arcade (p655), top left

Whisky

16 After tea, Britain's best-known drink is whisky (p991). And while this amber spirit is made in England and Wales, it is always most associated with Scotland. With more than 2000 whisky brands available, there are distilleries dotted across Scotland, many open to visitors, with Speyside one of the main concentrations and a favourite spot for connoisseurs. Before enjoying your tipple, heed these warnings: never spell whisky with an 'e' (that's the Irish variety); and when ordering at the bar, never ask for 'Scotch'. What else would you drink in Scotland?

Afternoon Tea

17 Afternoon tea is a very British tradition, an in-between-meals snack elevated to national institution, served in country hotels and teashops. It consists of sandwiches (with the bread cut wafer-thin and filled with something light, such as cucumber) and something sweet (again, the emphasis is on something light, so expect sponge cake) plus, of course, a cup of tea, poured from a silver teapot and sipped politely from fine bone china cups.

York

18 With its Roman remains and Viking heritage, ancient city walls and maze of medieval streets, York (p484) is a living showcase for the highlights of English history. For a great introduction, join one of the city's many walking tours through the snickleways (narrow alleys), each the focus of a ghost story or historical character, then admire the intricacies of York Minster, the biggest medieval cathedral in all of Northern Europe, or explore history of another age at the National Railway Museum, the world's largest collection of historic locomotives. The Shambles (p489), below

Scotland's Northwest Highlands

19 In the Highlands of Scotland you're never far from a breathtaking view, but the far northwest (p911) is awe-inspiring even by these high standards, with the rugged mountainscapes of Assynt, the desolate beauty of Torridon, the piercing incisions of sea lochs and the remote cliffs of Cape Wrath. Add to this Britain's finest whale-watching, polished off with some warm Highland hospitality – romantic hotels, gourmet restaurants, classic pubs – and you've got an unforgettable corner of the country. Cuillin Hills (p921), bottom

Pembrokeshire

20 Perched at the tip of wild and wonderful West Wales, the county of Pembrokeshire (p675) boasts one of Britain's most beautiful and dramatic stretches of coast, with sheer cliffs, natural arches, blowholes, sea stacks, and a wonderful hinterland of tranquil villages and secret waterways. It's a landscape of Norman castles, Iron Age hill forts, holy wells and Celtic saints – including the nation's patron, St David – and the remnants of prehistoric inhabitants that left behind intriguing stone circles.
Tenby (p675), top left

Liverpool

21 For many visitors, Liverpool (p558) will forever be associated with The Beatles, but a visit here proves the city now has much more to offer. After a major redevelopment, the waterfront is once again the heart of Liverpool, with Albert Dock declared a World Heritage Site of iconic and protected buildings, a batch of top museums, ensuring all sides of the city's history are not forgotten, and the Tate Liverpool gallery and Beatles Story museum, celebrating popular culture and those (still) most famous musical sons. Albert Dock (p561), top right

Britain's Pubs

22 The pub (p991) is the centre of British social life – whether it's a congenial evening with friends or a 'swift half' after work. And pubs are an equally ideal place for visitors to relax after a hard day of sightseeing, whether it be in the heart of the city or out in the countryside.

Tower of London

23 With its ancient towers and battlements overlooking the Thames, the Tower of London (p75) is an icon of the capital. The walls are nearly 1000 years old, established by William the Conqueror in the 1070s. Since then, the Tower has been a fortress, a royal residence, a treasury, a mint, an arsenal and a prison. Today it's home to the Crown Jewels, the famous red-coated Yeoman Warders (known as Beefeaters) and a flock of ravens that – legend says – must never leave.

Golf

24 It may be a 'good walk spoilt', but golf is one of the most popular sports in Britain, for participants of all levels and (especially when it comes to major tournaments) for thousands of spectators too. With courses across the country, including some in the most scenic locations, visitors to Britain with a penchant for the little white ball will surely want to try their skill. A highlight for aficionados is a round on the Old Course at St Andrews (p857), the venerable home of golf.

23

ENTRY TO THE TRAITORS' GATE

Canterbury Cathedral

25 Few other English cathedrals come close to Canterbury (p150), the top temple of the Anglican Church and a place of worship for over 15 centuries. Its intricate tower dominates the Canterbury skyline, its grandeur unsurpassed by later structures. At its heart lies a 12th-century crime scene, the very spot where Archbishop Thomas Becket was put to the sword – an epoch-making event that launched a million pilgrimages and still pulls in the crowds today. A lone candle mourns the gruesome deed, the pink sandstone before it smoothed by 800 years of devout kneeling.

need to know

Currency
» Pound; also called 'pound sterling' (£)

Language
» English; also Scottish Gaelic and Welsh

When to Go

Warm to hot summers, mild winters

Fort William•
GO May or Sep

•Aberdeen
GO May–Sep

•Edinburgh
GO May–Sep

Brecon
GO May–Sep

•Norwich
GO May–Sep

•London
GO Any time

•Exeter
GO Apr–Oct

High season
(Jun–Aug)
» Weather at its best. Accommodation rates at their peak – especially for August school holidays.

» Roads are busy, especially in seaside areas, national parks and popular cities such as Oxford, Bath, Edinburgh and York.

Shoulder
(Mar–May & Sep–Oct)
» Crowds reduce. Prices drop.

» March to May is a mix of sunny spells and sudden showers; September to October can be balmy. May and September are best for much of Scotland's outdoors.

Low season
(Nov–Feb)
» Wet and cold. Snow falls in mountain areas, especially up north.

» Opening hours reduced October to Easter; some places shut for winter. Big-city sights (particularly London's) operate all year.

Your Daily Budget

Budget less than

£50

» Dorm beds: £10–25

» Cheap meals in cafes and pubs: £5–9

» Long-distance coach: £10–30 (200 miles)

Midrange

£50–100

» Midrange hotel or B&B: £60–130 (London £90–180) per double room

» Main course in midrange restaurant: £9–18

» Long-distance train: £15–50 (200 miles)

» Car rental: from £30 per day

Top end more than

£100

» Four-star hotel room: from £130 (London £180)

» Three-course meal in a good restaurant: around £40 per person

Money
» Exchange bureaux and ATMs widely available, especially in cities and major towns.

Visas
» Not required for most citizens of Europe, Australia, NZ, USA and Canada.

Mobile Phones
» Phones from most other countries operate in Britain but attract roaming charges. Local SIM cards cost from £10; SIM and basic handset around £30.

Driving
» Traffic drives on the left; steering wheels are on the right side of the car. Most rental cars have manual gears (stick shift).

Websites
» **BBC** (www.bbc.co.uk) News and entertainment from the national broadcaster.

» **Visit Britain** (www .visitbritain.com) Comprehensive official tourism website.

» **Lonely Planet** (www.lonelyplanet .com/great-britain) Destination info, hotel bookings, traveller forum and more.

» **Traveline** (www .traveline.org.uk) Great portal site for public transport in all parts of Britain.

» **British Arts Festivals** (www .artsfestivals.co.uk) Listing hundreds of festivals – art, literature, dance, folk and more.

Exchange Rates

Australia	A$1	63p
Canada	C$1	62p
Europe	€1	80p
Japan	¥100	77p
New Zealand	NZ$1	49p
USA	US$1	62p

For current exchange rates, see www.xe.com.

Important Numbers
Area codes vary in length (eg ☏020 for London, ☏01225 for Bath). Omit the code if you're inside that area. Drop the initial 0 if you're calling from abroad.

Britain (& UK) country code	☏+44
International access code	☏00
Emergency (police, fire, ambulance, mountain rescue or coastguard)	☏999

Arriving in Britain
» **Heathrow airport**
Train to central London (London Paddington station) every 15 minutes (from £18)

» **Gatwick airport**
Train to central London (London Victoria station) every 15 minutes (from £16)

» **Eurostar trains from Paris or Brussels**
Arrive at London St Pancras International station in central London

» **Buses from Europe**
Arrive at London Victoria Coach Station in central London

» **Taxis from airports**
Trips to central London from Heathrow £40-50; from Gatwick £70-90 (more at peak hours)

Great Britain on a Shoestring
If you're on a tight budget, there's no getting away from it – Britain isn't cheap. Public transport, admission fees, restaurants and hotel rooms all tend to be expensive compared with their equivalents in many other European countries. But with some careful planning, a trip here doesn't have to break the bank. You can save money by staying in B&Bs instead of hotels, or hostels instead of B&Bs. Motels along motorways and outside large towns are soulless, but who cares? Most of the time you'll be asleep. You can also save by prebooking long-distance coach or train travel – and by avoiding times when everyone else is on the move (like Friday afternoon). Many attractions are free (or offer discounts on quiet days, such as Monday). And don't forget that you won't have to stump up a penny to enjoy Britain's best asset: the wonderful countryside and coastline.

first time

Everyone needs a helping hand when they visit a country for the first time. There are phrases to learn, customs to get used to and etiquette to understand. The following section will help demystify Britain so your first trip goes as smoothly as your fifth.

Top Tips for Your Trip

» At major London airports, tickets for the express trains into central London are usually available from official transport staff in the baggage arrivals hall; this saves queuing or dealing with unfamiliar machines on the station platform.

» The best way to get local currency is usually from an ATM, but this term is rarely used in England; the colloquial term 'cash machine' is more common.

» If staying more than a few days in London, get an Oyster, the travel card the locals use (p144).

» Pickpockets and hustlers lurk in the more crowded tourist areas, especially in London. No need to be paranoid, but do be on your guard.

» Britain's electrical plugs are unlike those in the rest of Europe, so bring (or buy) a UK-specific plug adaptor (p1030).

Booking Ahead

Whatever your budget, book accommodation in advance for the first few nights of your trip – especially during peak season. If you're on a longer or more flexible trip, booking in advance is not essential; when arriving in a new area, the tourist office usually has a list of local hotels and B&Bs with availability.

Booking ahead and avoiding peak periods will generally get you a better rental car deal and is highly recommended for major journeys by public transport. For more details, see the Transport chapter (p1035).

What to Wear

Britain's weather is notoriously changeable. A rain jacket is essential, as is a small backpack to carry it in when the sun comes out. You'll also need sunscreen and an umbrella; you're bound to use both – possibly on the same day.

When sightseeing at castles, cathedrals, museums and galleries, remember what your granny told you: comfortable shoes can make or break a trip. If you plan to enjoy Britain's great outdoors, suitable hiking gear is required in higher/wilder areas, but not for casual strolls in the countryside.

Some smarter pubs, bars and restaurants have dress codes banning jeans, T-shirts and trainers (sneakers or runners).

What to Pack

» Passport
» Credit card
» Drivers licence
» Phrasebook
» Electrical plug adaptor (UK-specific)
» Personal medicines
» Mobile (cell) phone and charger
» Earplugs
» Toiletries
» Sunscreen
» Sunhat
» Sunglasses
» Waterproof jacket
» Umbrella
» Comfortable shoes
» Padlock
» Torch
» Camera, memory cards and charger
» Pen and paper
» Taste for warm beer

Checklist

» Check the validity of your passport

» Check any visa or entry requirements

» Make any necessary bookings (sights, accommodation, travel)

» Check the airline baggage restrictions

» Put all restricted items (eg hair gel, pocketknife) in hold baggage

» Inform your credit/debit card company of your trip

» Organise travel insurance

» Check mobile (cell) phone compatibility

» Check rental car requirements

Etiquette

» **Manners**
The British have a – sometimes overstated – reputation for being polite, but good manners are still considered important in most situations. When asking directions, 'Excuse me, can you tell me the way to...' is a better tactic than 'Hey, where's...'

» **Queues**
In Britain, queues ('lines' to Americans), whether to board a bus, buy tickets at a kiosk or enter the gates of an attraction, are sacrosanct. Any attempt to 'jump the queue' will result in an outburst of tutting and hard stares – which is about as angry as most locals get in public.

» **Escalators**
If you take an escalator or a moving walkway (especially at tube stations in London), be sure to stand on the right, so folks in a hurry can pass on the left.

» **Bargaining**
If you're in a market, bargaining or haggling over the price of goods (but not food) is OK; politeness is still the key though. Bargaining in shops is very rare.

Tipping

» **Restaurants**
Around 10% in restaurants and teashops with table service. Nearer 15% at smarter restaurants. Tips may be added to your bill as a 'service charge'. Paying a tip or a service charge is not obligatory.

» **Pubs & Bars**
If you order drinks (or food) and pay at the bar, tips are not expected. If you order at the table, your meal is brought to you, and you pay afterwards, then 10% is usual.

» **Taxis**
Around 10%, or rounded up to the nearest pound, especially in London.

Money

Paper money comes in £5, £10, £20 and £50 denominations; some shops don't accept £50s because fakes circulate. Other currencies are rarely accepted, although some gift shops in London may take euros, US dollars and yen. ATMs (usually called 'cash machines') are common in cities and towns, but watch out for tampering; a common ruse is to attach a card-reader to the slot. Visa and MasterCard credit and debit cards are widely accepted in Britain, except at some small-scale B&Bs which take cash or cheque only. Other credit cards, such as AmEx, are not so widely accepted. Cities and larger towns have banks and exchange bureaux for changing your money into pounds, but some bureaux offer poor rates so check first. You can change money at some post offices, which is very handy in country areas; exchange rates are fair.

what's new

For this new edition of Great Britain, our authors have hunted down the fresh, the transformed, the hot and the happening. These are some of our favourites. For up-to-the-minute recommendations, see lonelyplanet.com/great-britain.

Queen Elizabeth Olympic Park, London

1 In 2012, a huge swathe of East London was transformed into the Queen Elizabeth Olympic Park, where iconic sporting architecture combined with landscaped grounds to create a legacy for the future. (p105)

Emirates Air Line Cable Car, London

2 Initially a public transport solution linking Olympic venues, the spectacular cable car across the River Thames is destined to become an attraction in its own right. (p107)

St Pancras Renaissance London Hotel, London

3 Renaissance may be a hotel brand, but the name is appropriate here at St Pancras, a famous Victorian Gothic masterpiece now restored to its former glory. (p117)

Riverside Museum, Glasgow

4 Glasgow's rapidly developing waterfront has been graced with an extraordinary new building; the wave-like roof symbolises the city's shipbuilding heritage, and there's more historical transport inside. (p791)

Turner Contemporary, Margate

5 This landmark gallery stands proud on the south coast, bathed in the sea-refracted light so loved by the artist JMW Turner, for whom it is named. (p157)

Doctor Who Experience, Cardiff

6 The huge success of reinvented TV classic *Doctor Who,* made in Cardiff, is celebrated with this new attraction – complete with TARDIS and Daleks, of course. (p646)

Mary Rose Museum, Portsmouth

7 England's most famous shipwreck gets a new home, showing Henry VIII's flagship in a new light, and reuniting the vessel with artefacts raised from the deep. (p233)

M Shed, Bristol

8 Lodged in a massive old dockside warehouse, Bristol's new museum is a treasure trove of memorabilia – from slave-trade reminders to Massive Attack record decks. (p273)

Museum of Liverpool

9 Liverpool's multilayered past is celebrated at this interactive exploration of cultural and historical milestones: poverty, wealth, football (soccer), plus – of course – The Beatles. (p563)

Hepworth Wakefield, Wakefield

10 An award-winning gallery of contemporary sculpture, anchored by a world-class collection of works by local artist Barbara Hepworth. (p528)

Wales Coast Path

11 Britain's newest hiking trail is also its longest (870 miles). Come for a month or a day – you don't have to walk it all in one go. (p670)

if you like...

Castles

Britain's turbulent history bequeaths a landscape dotted with defensive masterpieces of the medieval era, complete with moats, keeps, battlements, dungeons and all the classic features we know from history books or legends of knights and maidens in distress.

Tower of London Landmark of the capital, patrolled by famous Beefeaters and protected by mythical ravens (p75)

Caerphilly Castle The second-largest castle in Britain, its former moat now a scenic lake (p658)

Edinburgh Castle The focal point of the Scottish capital, and its very reason for being (p754)

Warwick Castle Preserved enough to be impressive, ruined enough to be romantic (p406)

Stirling Castle Classic fortress atop volcanic crag, with stunning views from the battlements (p828)

Beaumaris Wales is the land of castles; imposing Beaumaris, along with nearby Conwy, Caernarfon and Harlech, is a jointly listed World Heritage Site (p732)

Carreg Cennen The most dramatically positioned fortress in Wales, standing guard over a lonely stretch of Brecon Beacons National Park (p695)

Royal Britain

Queen Elizabeth II, a national icon, celebrated her Diamond Jubilee in 2012 after 60 years on the throne. With a monarch at the top for centuries, it's no surprise that many reminders of Britain's regal heritage dot the country today.

Buckingham Palace The Queen's official London residence, best known for its royal-waving balcony and the Changing of the Guard (p65)

Windsor Castle The largest and oldest occupied fortress in the world, a majestic vision of battlements and towers, and the Queen's weekend retreat (p220)

Westminster Abbey Where English monarchs are crowned and married – most recently William and Kate (p63)

Royal Yacht Britannia The royal family's floating home during foreign travels, now retired and moored near Edinburgh (p766)

Balmoral Castle Built for Queen Victoria in 1855 and still a royal Highland hideaway (p879)

Royal Pavilion Opulent palace built for playboy prince, later King George IV (p170)

Althorp House Ancestral home and burial place of Diana, Princess of Wales (p454)

Cathedrals

Along with castles, the cathedrals of Britain are the country's most impressive and inspiring historic structures. Many were works in progress for centuries, so display an eclectic mix of styles, with solid Norman naves later enjoying the addition of graceful Gothic arches or soaring spires, and – most beautiful of all – vast extents of stained-glass windows.

St Paul's Cathedral A symbol of the city for centuries, and still an essential part of the London skyline (p79)

York Minster One of the largest medieval cathedrals in all of Europe, especially renowned for its windows (p484)

Canterbury Cathedral The mother ship of the Anglican Church, still attracting pilgrims and visitors in their thousands (p150)

St Davids Cathedral An ancient place of worship in Britain's smallest city (p681)

Glasgow Cathedral A shining example of Gothic architecture, and the only mainland Scottish cathedral to have survived the Reformation (p788)

» Brighton Pier (p170), England

Ruined Abbeys

Thanks to the work of industrious monks from the 12th to the 14th centuries, great abbeys are a feature of the British landscape. Thanks to Henry VIII's spat with the Catholic Church around 1540, many are now in ruins – but they're no less impressive for today's visitor.

Fountains Abbey Extensive ruins set in more recently landscaped water gardens – one of the most beautiful sites in Britain (p502)

Rievaulx Abbey Tranquil remains of columns and arches hidden away in a secluded valley (p506)

Melrose Abbey The finest of all the great Border abbeys; the heart of Robert the Bruce is buried here (p809)

Whitby Abbey Stunning clifftop ruin with an eerie atmosphere that inspired the author of *Dracula* (p508)

Glastonbury Abbey The legendary burial place of King Arthur and Queen Guinevere (p294)

Tintern Abbey Riverside ruins that inspired generations of poets and artists (p662)

Stately Homes

While France has endless chateaux, and Germany a *schloss* on every corner, Britain boasts a raft of stately homes – vast mansions where the landed gentry have lived for generations, but now open their doors so the rest of us can admire the fabulous interiors.

Blenheim Palace A monumental baroque fantasy and one of Britain's greatest stately homes (p193)

Castle Howard Another stunning baroque edifice, best known as the setting for *Brideshead Revisited* (p496)

Powis Castle Rising above a fantastical cloud of manicured yew trees, this one-time fortress was enriched by generations of aristocratic families (p709)

Chatsworth House The quintessential stately home, a treasure trove of heirlooms and works of art (p478)

Village Idylls

If you want to see the Britain you've always imagined, or the Britain you know so well from period movies and TV costume dramas, you'll absolutely love the country's villages, all very different in character, but all a reminder of a simpler age.

Lavenham A wonderful collection of exquisitely preserved medieval buildings virtually untouched since the 15th century (p376)

Lacock Well-preserved medieval village, essentially free of modern development and – unsurprisingly – a frequent set for movies and TV period dramas (p269)

Hutton-le-Hole One of Yorkshire's most attractive villages, with sheep grazing on a wide green amid a scattering of cottages (p506)

Mousehole Southwest England overflows with picturesque pint-sized ports, but this is one of the best (p337)

Beddgelert A conservation village of rough grey stone buildings in the heart of Snowdonia National Park (p718)

Cromarty At the northeastern tip of the Black Isle, with a fine collection of 18th-century sandstone houses (p891)

If you like... clifftop drama, the Minack is a unique theatre (p342), carved into vertiginous cliffs overlooking the Atlantic in Cornwall. The classic play to catch is *The Tempest*, but any performance is spellbinding.

Great Outdoors

Beyond its towns and cities, Britain boasts vasts swaths of countryside, some of it surprisingly high and wild – a playground for hikers, bikers, and other fans of outdoor activity.

Lake District A feast of mountains, valleys, views and – of course – lakes; the landscape that inspired William Wordsworth and entices hikers today (p579)

Northumberland National Park The dramatically empty landscape of England's far north is remote and off the beaten track (p631)

Snowdonia The best-known slice of nature in Wales, with the grand but surprisingly accessible peak of Snowdon at its heart (p713)

Yorkshire Dales A compact collection of moors, hills, valleys, rivers, cliffs and waterfalls, perfect for easy strolls or hardy treks (p512)

Ben Nevis Every year thousands of people aim for the summit of Scotland's famous (and Britain's highest) mountain (p903)

Industrial Heritage

Britain's history is not all about big castles or twee cottages; the nation also drove the world's industrialisation in the 18th and 19th centuries, and this golden (though rather grimy) era is celebrated at several sites around the country.

Ironbridge Gorge The place where it all started, the crucible of the Industrial Revolution, where 10 museums for the price of one give fascinating insights (p430)

Blaenavon A World Heritage Site of well-preserved ironworks and the fascinating Big Pit coal mine (p663)

New Lanark Once the largest cotton-spinning complex in Britain and a testament to enlightened capitalism (p806)

National Railway Museum A cathedral to Britain's great days of steam; for railway fans of all ages it's the perfect place to go loco (p485)

Roman Remains

For 400 years the province of Britannia was part of the Roman Empire, a legacy still visible at various sites around the country – from sturdy defences for soldiers to fancy houses for wealthy citizens.

Roman Baths The city of Bath takes its name from these famous Roman remains – a complex of bathhouses around natural thermal waters, with additions from the 17th century when restorative waters again became fashionable (p283)

Hadrian's Wall Snaking coast-to-coast across lonely hills, this 2000-year-old fortified line once marked the northern limit of imperial Roman jurisdiction (p625)

Caerleon One of three legionary forts in Britain, with impressive remains of barracks, baths and an amphitheatre (p664)

Corinium Museum The sleepy Cotswold town of Cirencester was once Corinium, the second-largest Roman city in Britain; this excellent museum recalls those days, including beautiful mosaics (p210)

If you like... kooky collections, Portmeirion (p731) is a private village built in a mix of styles from Moorish to Ancient Greek; it's most famous as the set for cult TV show *The Prisoner*.

Outdoor Art

Many of the great stone sculptures by well-known British artists are from, and of, the earth, so it's fitting that we can now admire many of them in a natural setting. Works in steel and other materials complete the picture.

Yorkshire Sculpture Park England's biggest outdoor sculpture collection, dominated by the works of Henry Moore and Barbara Hepworth (p527)

Tout Quarry An unsung artistic gem: around 50 rock-carved sculptures still in situ, including works by Antony Gormley and Dhruva Mistry (p256)

Angel of the North England's best-known public work of art spreads its rusty wings and stands sentinel near Newcastle (p620)

Grizedale Forest A maze of walking and biking routes, passing around 90 outdoor sculptures created by local and international artists (p590)

Shopping

For every identikit mega-store in Britain there's an independent shop with soul and character – whether you're looking for books, clothes, jewellery, arts and crafts, retro handbags or 1960s vinyl.

Portobello Rd, London Britain's biggest city has shopping galore, with Portobello Rd one of the best-known street markets, surrounded by quirky boutiques and gift stores (p140)

Victoria Quarter, Leeds Lovely arcades of wrought ironwork and stained glass, and home to several top fashion boutiques (p525)

North Laine, Brighton Narrow streets lined with shops selling books, antiques, collectables, vintage clothing and more (p176)

Cardiff Arcades Half a dozen ornate arcades branch off the city centre main streets, all with speciality shops and cafes (p654)

Hay-on-Wye The self-proclaimed secondhand-book capital of the world boasts over 30 bookshops and millions of volumes, attracting browsers, collectors and academics from around the world (p704)

Galleries

Fans of the visual arts are spoilt for choice in Britain. Galleries abound, from long-standing classics and famous works in the larger cities, to quirky and offbeat locations featuring experimental and up-and-coming artists.

Tate Britain One of the best-known galleries in London, full to the brim with the finest local works (p88)

Tate Modern London's other Tate focuses on modern art in all its wonderful permutations (p82)

BALTIC Newcastle's very own 'Tate of the North' with work by some of contemporary art's biggest show-stoppers (p616)

National Museum Cardiff An excellent collection of Welsh artists, plus works by Monet, Renoir, Matisse, Van Gogh, Francis Bacon and David Hockney (p644)

Kelvingrove Art Gallery & Museum A national landmark in Glasgow – a great collection, and a cracking spot to learn about Scottish art (p792)

Barber Institute of Fine Arts With works by Rubens, Turner and Picasso, this Birmingham gallery is no lightweight (p399)

SCULPTURE, ANTONY GORMLEY. PHOTOGRAPHER: JERRY HARDMAN-JONES/COURTESY WHITE CUBE ©

» *Angel of the North* sculpture (p620), England

Arts & Music Festivals

Whatever your taste in music or the arts, there's a festival for you somewhere in Britain.

Edinburgh International Festival The world's biggest festival of art and culture. 'Nuff said (p773)

Glastonbury Britain's biggest and best-loved music festival (p296)

Hay Festival A world-class celebration of all things literary at Britain's bookshop capital (p703)

Notting Hill Carnival London's Caribbean community shows the city how to party (p111)

Pride Gay and lesbian street parade through London culminating in a concert in Trafalgar Sq (p111)

Artsfest A cultural Birmingham extravaganza featuring everything from ballet and bhangra to rhythm and blues (p400)

Latitude Festival An eclectic mix of music, literature, dance, drama and comedy, in a stunning location and of a manageable size (p381)

Coastal Beauty

It won't have escaped your notice that Britain is an island. Surrounded by the sea, the country boasts a nautical heritage and a long coastline with many beautiful spots.

Jurassic Coast An exhilarating 3D geology lesson, with towering rock stacks, sea-carved arches and fossils aplenty (p251)

Pembrokeshire Towering cliffs, rock arches, clean waters and perfect sandy beaches at the tip of West Wales (p675)

Tongue Sea lochs penetrate the rocky coast in this wild stretch of Scotland's north (p911)

Holkham Bay A pristine expanse of sand with giant skies stretching overhead (p387)

Gower Peninsula Family-friendly beaches and surfer hang-outs, backed by sand dunes and tranquil farmland (p670)

Beachy Head & Seven Sisters Where the South Downs plunge into the sea, these mammoth chalk cliffs provide a dramatic finale (p169)

Classic Seaside Resorts

For a view of Britain's coast at its most quirky and nostalgic you have to sample a traditional seaside resort. This is the place for buckets and spades, a dip in the waves and a stroll along the prom-prom-prom...

Scarborough The original British beach resort, where 'sea-bathing' first began, way back in the 17th century (p499)

Southwold Genteel old-style seaside town with lovely beach, charming pier and famous rows of colourful beach huts (p380)

Brighton Alongside ubercool bars and boutiques there are still plenty of naughty postcards and kiss-me-quick hats in 'London-by-the-Sea' (p169)

Llandudno Beachside Punch-and-Judy shows, a step-back-in-time pier and a classic esplanade (p741)

Bournemouth Seven miles of sandy beach, 3000 deckchairs and a pair of Edwardian cliff-lifts (p245)

month by month

Top Events

1 **Edinburgh International Festival and Fringe**, August

2 **Glyndebourne**, late May–August

3 **Trooping the Colour**, mid-June

4 **Glastonbury Festival**, late June

5 **Abergavenny Food Festival**, September

January

January is mid-winter in Britain. Festivals and events to brighten the mood are thin on the ground, but luckily some include fire – lots of it.

London Parade

A ray of light in the gloom, the New Year's Day Parade in London (to use its official title; www.london parade.co.uk) is one of the biggest events of its kind in the world, featuring marching bands, street performers, classic cars, floats and displays winding their way through the streets, watched by over half a million people.

Up Helly Aa

Half of Shetland dresses up with horned helmets and battleaxes in this spectacular re-enactment of a Viking fire festival (p950), with a torchlit procession leading the burning of a full-size Viking longship.

Celtic Connections

Glasgow plays host to a celebration of Celtic music, dance and culture (www .celticconnections.com),

with participants from all over the globe.

February

Britain may be scenic under snow and sunshine, or more likely grey and gloomy under dark skies. Hang in there…

Jorvik Viking Festival

The ancient Viking capital of York becomes home once again to invaders and horned helmets galore, with the intriguing addition of longship races (p491).

Fort William Mountain Festival

Britain's capital of the outdoors celebrates the peak of the winter season with ski workshops, mountaineering films and talks by famous climbers (www.mountain festival.co.uk).

March

Spring finally arrives. There's a hint of better weather, and some classic sporting fixtures grace the calendar. Many locals

stay hunkered down at home, though, so hotels offer special rates.

Six Nations Rugby Championship

Highlight of the rugby calendar (www.rbs6nations .com), with the home nations playing at London's Twickenham, Edinburgh's Murrayfield and Cardiff's Millennium Stadiums.

University Boat Race

Annual race down the River Thames in London between the rowing teams from Cambridge and Oxford Universities (p110), an institution since 1856 that still enthrals the country.

April

The weather slowly improves, with warmer and drier days bringing out spring blossoms. Attractions that close for the low season open around the middle of the month or at Easter.

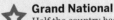

Grand National

Half the country has a flutter on the highlight of the three-day horse race meeting at Aintree on the first Saturday of the month (p564) – a steeplechase with a testing course and notoriously high jumps.

London Marathon
Super-fit athletes cover 26.22 miles in just over two hours, while others dress up in daft costumes and take considerably longer (p110).

Camden Crawl
Your chance to spot the next big thing in the music scene or witness a secret gig by an established act, with 40 of Camden's venues given over to live music for two full days (p110).

Beltane
Thousands of revellers climb Edinburgh's Calton Hill for this modern revival of a pagan fire festival marking the end of winter (www.beltane.org).

Spirit of Speyside
Based in Dufftown, a Scottish festival of whisky, food and music (p881), with five days of art, cooking, distillery tours and outdoor activities.

May
The weather is usually good, with more events to enjoy. There are two public holidays this month (first and last Mondays) so traffic is very busy over the corresponding long weekends.

FA Cup Final
Grand finale of the football (soccer) season for over a century. Teams from across England battle it out over the winter months, culminating in this heady spectacle at Wembley Stadium – the home of English football.

Brighton Festival
Lively three-week arts fest taking over the streets of buzzy south-coast resort Brighton (p171) – and alongside the mainstream performances there's a festival fringe as well.

Chelsea Flower Show
The Royal Horticultural Society flower show at Chelsea (p110) is the highlight of the gardener's year.

Hay Festival
The ever-expanding 'Woodstock of the mind' brings an intellectual influx to book-town Hay-on-Wye (p703).

Glyndebourne
Famous festival (www.glyndebourne.com) of world-class opera in the pastoral surroundings of East Sussex, running until the end of summer.

June
Now it's almost summer. You can tell because this month sees the music-festival season kick off properly, while sporting events, from rowing to racing, fill the calendar.

Derby Week
Horse-racing, people-watching and clothes-spotting are on the agenda at this week-long meeting in Epsom, Surrey (www.epsomderby.co.uk).

Cotswold Olimpicks
Welly-wanging, pole-climbing and shin-kicking are the key disciplines at this traditional Gloucestershire sports day (p206), held every year since 1612.

Trooping the Colour
Military bands and bear-skinned grenadiers march down London's Whitehall in this martial pageant (p110) to mark the monarch's birthday.

Royal Ascot
It's hard to tell which matters more, the fashion or the fillies, at this highlight of the horse-racing year in Berkshire (p223).

Wimbledon Tennis
The world's best-known grass-court tennis tournament (p110), attracting all the big names, while crowds cheer or eat tons of strawberries and cream.

Glastonbury Festival
One of Britain's favourite pop and rock gatherings (p296) is invariably muddy and a rite of passage for every self-respecting British teenager.

Meltdown Festival
London's Southbank Centre hands over the reins to a legend of contemporary music (past curators include David Bowie and Patti Smith) to create a program of concerts, talks and films (p110).

Royal Regatta
Boats of every description take to the water for Henley's upper-crust river jamboree (p199).

Pride
Highlight of the gay and lesbian calendar (p111), this technicolour street parade heads through London's West End.

Glasgow's West End Festival
Scotland's second city hosts a major celebration of music and arts (p795).

July

Proper summer. Festivals every week. Schools break up at the end of the month, so there's a holiday tingle in the air, dulled only by busy roads on Friday, because everyone's going somewhere for the weekend.

Great Yorkshire Show
Harrogate plays host to one of Britain's largest county shows (p497). This is the place for Yorkshire grit, Yorkshire tykes, Yorkshire puddings, Yorkshire beef…

T in the Park
World-class acts since 1994 ensure this major music festival (www.tinthepark.com) is Scotland's answer to Glastonbury.

Latitude
Relaxed festival (p381) in the seaside town of Southwold, with theatre, cabaret, art and literature, plus top names from the alternative music scene.

International Musical Eisteddfod
Festival of international folk music at Llangollen (p739), with eclectic fringe and big-name evening concerts.

(Above) London Eye lit up for Pride night
(Below) Notting Hill Carnival

Royal Welsh Show

Prize bullocks and local produce at this national farm and livestock event (p706) in Builth Wells.

Cowes Week

Britain's biggest yachting spectacular (p242) on the choppy seas around the Isle of Wight.

Womad

Roots and world music take centre stage at this festival (www.womad.org) in a country park in the south Cotswolds.

Truck

Indie music festival (www.thisistruck.com) in Oxfordshire, known for its eclectic acts.

Port Eliot Festival

Beginning life as a literary festival, now branched out into live music, theatre and outdoor art (p349).

August

Schools and colleges are closed, parliament is in recess, the sun is shining (hopefully), most people go away for a week or two, and the nation is in holiday mood.

Edinburgh Festivals

Edinburgh's most famous August happening is the International Festival and Fringe, but this month the city also has an event for anything you care to name – books, art, theatre, music, comedy, marching bands... (www.edinburghfestivals.co.uk)

Notting Hill Carnival

London's famous multicultural Caribbean-style street carnival in the district of Notting Hill (p111). Steel drums, dancers, outrageous costumes.

Reading Festival

Venerable rock and pop festival (p221), always a good bet for big-name bands.

Leeds Festival

Reading's northern sister (p521). Same weekend, same line-up, with bands shuttling between the two.

National Eisteddfod of Wales

The largest celebration of native Welsh culture, steeped in history, pageantry and pomp (p740); held at various venues around the country.

Brecon Jazz Festival

Smoky sounds at one of Europe's leading jazz festivals (p699), in the charming mid-Wales town of Brecon.

September

The first week of September is still holiday time, but then schools reopen, traffic returns to normal, and the summer party's over for another year. Ironically, the weather's often better than in August, now everyone's back at work.

Bestival

Quirky music festival (p241) on the Isle of Wight with a different fancy-dress theme every year.

Great North Run

Tyneside plays host to the one of the biggest half marathons in the world (www.greatrun.org), with the greatest number of runners in any race at this distance.

Abergavenny Food Festival

The mother of all epicurean festivals (p702) and the champion of Wales' burgeoning food scene.

Ludlow Food & Drink Festival

Great foodie town and a great foodie festival (p439).

Braemar Gathering

The biggest and most famous Highland Games (p879) in the Scottish calendar, traditionally attended by members of the royal family. Highland dancing, caber-tossing and bagpipe-playing.

October

October means autumn. The leaves are falling from the trees, attractions start to shut down for the low season, and accommodation rates drop as hoteliers try to entice a final few guests before winter.

Horse of the Year Show

The country's major indoor horse event (www.hoys.co.uk), with dressage, show-jumping and other equine activities, at the NEC arena near Birmingham.

Dylan Thomas Festival

A celebration of the Welsh laureate's work with readings, events and talks in Swansea (p667).

Falmouth Oyster Festival

The Westcountry port of Falmouth marks the start of the traditional oyster-catching season (www.falmouthoysterfestival.co.uk) with a celebration of local food from the sea and fields of Cornwall.

November

Winter's here, and November is a dull month. The weather is often cold and damp, summer is a distant memory and Christmas is still too far away.

Guy Fawkes Night

Also called Bonfire Night (www.bonfirenight.net); on 5 November fireworks fill Britain's skies in commemoration of a failed attempt to blow up parliament, way back in 1605.

Remembrance Day

Red poppies are worn and wreaths are laid in towns and cities around the country on 11 November, in commemoration of fallen military personnel (www.poppy.org.uk).

December

Schools break up earlier, but shops and businesses keep going until Christmas Eve; the last weekend before Christmas Day is busy on the roads as people visit friends and family, or head for the airport.

Stonehaven Fireball Festival

The Scottish fishing town of Stonehaven celebrates Hogmanay with a spectacular procession of fireball-swinging locals (www.stonehavenfireballs.co.uk).

New Year Celebrations

The last night of December sees fireworks and street parties in town squares across the country. London's Trafalgar Sq is where the city's largest crowds gather to herald the New Year.

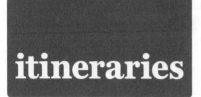

itineraries

Whether you've got six days or 60, these itineraries provide a starting point for the trip of a lifetime. Want more inspiration? Head online to lonelyplanet .com/thorntree to chat with other travellers.

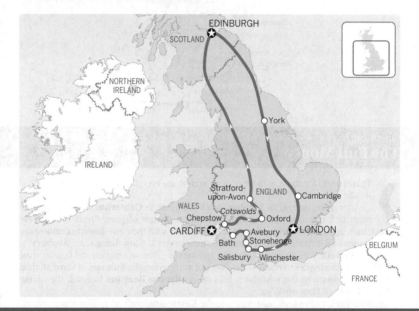

Two Weeks
Best of Britain

Start with a full day in Britain's greatest city, **London**, simply walking the streets to admire the world-famous sights: Buckingham Palace, Tower Bridge, Trafalgar Sq and more. Then head southwest to the grand cathedral cities of **Winchester** and **Salisbury**, across to the iconic menhirs of **Stonehenge** and its less well-known counterpart **Avebury Stone Circle**, then onwards to the beautiful historic city of **Bath**.

Loop over to **Chepstow** for its impressive castle, and then continue to **Cardiff**, the Welsh capital. Retrace slightly, then cruise across the classic English countryside of the **Cotswolds** to reach the university city of **Oxford**. Not far away is **Stratford-upon-Avon**, for everything Shakespeare.

Strike out north to Scotland's capital, **Edinburgh**, for another great castle, before crossing down to **York** for its glorious cathedral and historic city walls. Keep going south to reach **Cambridge**, another landmark university city. Then enjoy the last few days back in **London**, immersed in galleries, museums, luxury shops, street markets, West End shows, East End cafes – or whatever takes your fancy.

One Month
The Full Monty

This is a trip for those with time, or an urge to see everything. So brace yourself, and let's be off.

After a day or two in **London**, head southeast to **Canterbury**, then along the coast to hip and happening **Brighton**. For a change of pace, divert to the **New Forest**, then up to historic **Winchester** and **Salisbury** with their awe-inspiring cathedrals. Next, religion of a different kind: the ancient stone circles at **Stonehenge** and **Avebury**.

Go west to **Bath**, with its grand Georgian architecture, Roman remains and famous spas, and then over the border to reach Wales. Stop off at the energetic little city of **Cardiff**, then head north through to the whaleback hills of the **Brecon Beacons** to reach the quirky book-mad town of **Hay-on-Wye**.

Then it's back to England, and east into the **Cotswolds**, with its rolling hills, quintessential rural scenery and chocolate-box towns like **Chipping Norton**. Not far away is the famous university town of **Oxford**, as well as the ancient town of **Warwick**, with its spectacular castle, and Shakespeare's birthplace **Stratford-upon-Avon**.

Continue north to **Chester**, for its famous city walls, diverting into North Wales for the grand castles at **Conwy** and **Caernarfon**, and the stunning mountains of **Snowdonia**. If time allows and the weather's good, you can take a train to the top of the highest peak.

Then ferry across the Mersey to **Liverpool**, with its famous musical heritage and revitalised waterfront, or to **Manchester** for a taste of big-city life, followed by a total change of scenery in the tranquil mountains of the **Lake District**. To the north is the sturdy border town of **Carlisle**, and one of Britain's most impressive Roman remains, **Hadrian's Wall**.

Hop across the border to Scotland, via the tranquil **Southern Uplands**, to reach good-time **Glasgow**. Then trek to **Fort William** (and maybe up **Ben Nevis**, Britain's highest mountain), from where it's easy to reach the beautiful **Isle of Skye**.

Then it's time to head south again, via **Stirling Castle** to **Edinburgh**, and on through the historic abbey towns of **Melrose** and **Jedburgh**.

Back in England, you can marvel at the castle and cathedral of **Durham** and the ancient Viking capital of **York**, before taking in the ancient university city of **Cambridge** and enjoying the last few days of your trip in **London**.

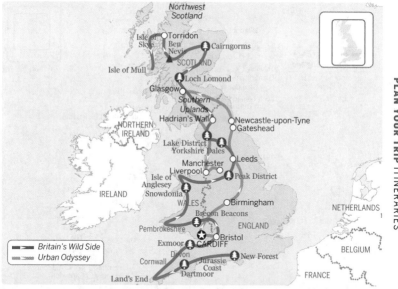

Britain's Wild Side

Urban Odyssey

Three to Four Weeks
Britain's Wild Side

This tour takes you through the best of Britain's natural landscape. Start in the **New Forest**, then go west via Dorset's fossil-ridden **Jurassic Coast** to reach granite-topped **Dartmoor**. Stop off at **Land's End**, then traverse the stunning **Cornwall** coast and rich farmland of **Devon** to reach the gorse-clad hills of **Exmoor**.

Cross into Wales to hike the **Brecon Beacons** or stroll the beaches of **Pembrokeshire**, then head north to explore mountainous **Snowdonia** and the nearby **Isle of Anglesey**. Then it's back to England, through the hills and moors of the **Peak District** and **Yorkshire Dales** to reach the peaks and grand scenery of the **Lake District**.

Head north again, across (or along) the Roman remains of **Hadrian's Wall**, and over the border into Scotland. Saunter through the delightful **Southern Uplands**, then continue via **Loch Lomond** to the mountain wilderness of the **Cairngorms**.

The top of Britain is crowned by the famous highlands and islands of **Northwest Scotland**, where jewels include peaks like **Ben Nevis** and remote mountain ranges such as **Torridon**, while out to sea the lovely isles of **Skye** and **Mull** bask in the afternoon sun.

Two to Three Weeks
Urban Odyssey

To dig a little under Britain's skin, take this ride through some of its less well-known and revitalised cities.

Kick off in **Bristol**, a city with fierce pride and a rich historic legacy, then cross over to **Cardiff**, once a provincial backwater but now the lively Welsh capital.

Next stop is **Birmingham**, oozing transformation, with a renovated waterside, energised museums and a space-age shopping centre. Onwards to **Leeds**, where rundown factories and warehouses have been turned into loft apartments, ritzy boutiques and stylish department stores.

Shopping not your thing? No problem. Head for **Newcastle-upon-Tyne** and twin-city **Gateshead**; both have given up on heavy industries in favour of art and architecture – and are famous for to-the-hilt partying.

Still want more? It's got to be **Glasgow**, Scotland's other great city, boasting fabulous galleries and welcoming pubs. Then it's south to **Liverpool**, which has reinvented itself as a cultural hot spot, with a famous musical heritage and very lively current scene. Finish your tour in **Manchester**, a long-time stage for artistic endeavour, with dramatic new architecture and a rather well-known football club.

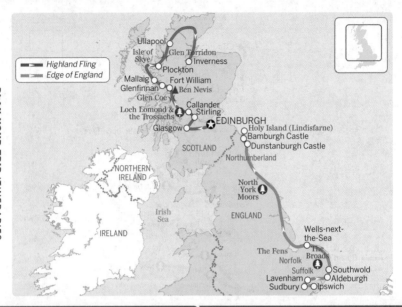

One to Two Weeks
Highland Fling

This itinerary is a tour of Scotland's finest and most famous sights, and naturally starts in **Edinburgh**, where highlights include the renowned castle, as well as the Royal Mile, the new parliament and the haunts of the Old Town. For a change of pace, hop over to **Glasgow** for a day or two as well. Then head northeast to see Scotland's other great castle at **Stirling**. Next stop is **Callander**, a good base for exploring the **Trossach mountains**, part of Loch Lomond and the Trossachs National Park, for a first taste of Highland scenery.

Continue north and the landscape becomes ever more impressive, culminating in the grandeur of **Glen Coe**. Keen hill-walkers will pause for a day at **Fort William** to trek to the top of **Ben Nevis** (plus another day to recover!) before taking the 'Road to the Isles' past glorious **Glenfinnan** to the lovely little port of **Mallaig**.

Take the ferry to the **Isle of Skye**, then head back to the mainland to reach pretty **Plockton** and magnificent **Glen Torridon**. Onwards, via the outpost of **Ullapool**, takes you into the British mainland's furthest reaches, the remote mountain landscape of Scotland's far Northwest, before looping south to finish your tour at **Inverness**.

One to Two Weeks
Edge of England

If you like the outdoors, and prefer flocks of birds to crowds of people, try this backwater route along England's eastern fringe. Start in **Ipswich**, then head out into the sleepy county of **Suffolk**, where quaint villages and market towns such as **Sudbury** and **Lavenham** dot the landscape, while along the coast are wildlife reserves, shingly beaches, fishing ports such as **Aldeburgh**, and the delightfully retro seaside resort of **Southwold**.

Things get even quieter in **Norfolk**, especially around the misty lakes and windmill-lined rivers of the **Broads**. For beach strolls or historic country pubs, head for the coastal villages near **Wells-next-the-Sea**.

Across the border in Lincolnshire lies the eerie, pan-flat landscape of the **Fens**, now a haven for otters and birdlife.

Continue into the heather-clad **North York Moors** where humpbacked hills roll all the way to the coast to drop dramatically into the choppy waters of the North Sea.

Enjoy a blustery stroll on the wild coast of Northumberland near the landmark castles of **Bamburgh** and **Dunstanburgh**, then end your tour at the historic island of **Lindisfarne**.

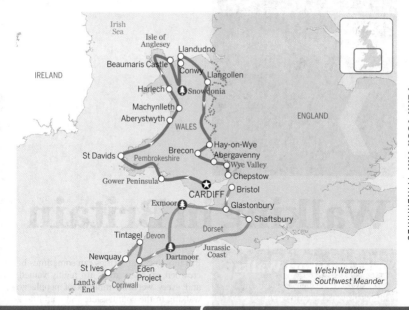

One to Two Weeks
Welsh Wander

> The coast and countryside of Wales has long been a favourite with visitors, and this tour includes most of the hot spots. Combine it with the Southwest Meander for a longer jaunt along part of Britain's Celtic fringe.

Start in **Cardiff**, with its fantastical castle, gigantic rugby stadium, revitalised waterfront and stunning Millennium Centre. Head west via the beautiful **Gower Peninsula** to reach the clear waters and sandy beaches of **Pembrokeshire**. Don't miss the ancient cathedral at **St Davids** – Britain's smallest city. Continue up the coast to **Aberystwyth**, then through 'alternative' **Machynlleth** to reach **Harlech** and its ancient castle. Divert to the tranquil **Isle of Anglesey** and historic **Beaumaris Castle**, then strike through the mountains of **Snowdonia** to reach **Conwy** (another stunning castle) and the seaside resort **Llandudno**.

Southwards takes you to **Llangollen**, with its jolly steam trains and vertiginous aqueduct, then along the England-Wales borderlands to book-mad **Hay-on-Wye**. Loop inland to peaceful **Brecon** and foodie **Abergavenny**, then saunter down the **Wye Valley** to finish at the frontier town of **Chepstow** – and yet another amazing castle.

One to Two Weeks
Southwest Meander

> The southwest of England takes a bit of effort to reach but repays in full with a rich green landscape dotted with hills and moors, surrounded by glistening seas.

Start in **Bristol**, the capital of the Westcountry, then saunter south to reach **Glastonbury**. It's famous for its annual music festival and the best place to stock up on candles or crystals at any time of year.

West leads to heathery **Exmoor**. South leads to **Dorset**, where highlights include picturesque **Shaftsbury** and the fossil-strewn Jurassic Coast.

Onwards into **Devon**, and there's a choice of coasts, as well as **Dartmoor**, the highest and wildest hills in southern Britain.

Cross into **Cornwall** to explore the space-age biodomes of the **Eden Project**. Nearby, but in another era entirely, is **Tintagel Castle**, the legendary birthplace of King Arthur. Depending on your tastes, you can hang-ten in surf-flavoured party-town **Newquay**, or browse the galleries at **St Ives**.

The natural finish to this wild west tour is **Land's End**, where the British mainland comes to a final full stop. Sink a drink in the First and Last pub, and promise yourself a return trip some day...

Walking in Britain

Best for Short Walks
Yorkshire Dales, Cotswolds, South Downs, Brecon Beacons, Southern Uplands

Best for Coast Walks
Devon and Cornwall, Northumberland, Norfolk and Suffolk, Pembrokeshire, Isle of Skye

Best Long-Distance Walks
Coast to Coast Walk, Hadrian's Wall Path, Cotswold Way, South West Coast Path, West Highland Way, Offa's Dyke Path

Best Seasons
Summer (Jun–Aug) Weather usually warm and dry; plenty of daylight, too.
Late spring (May) and early autumn (Sep) Fewer crowds; days often mild and sunny.

Best Maps
Ordnance Survey UK's national mapping agency; Explorer series 1:25,000 scale.
Harvey Maps Specially designed for walkers; Superwalker series 1:25,000 scale.

Best Websites
www.nationaltrail.co.uk Great for specifics on some longer routes.
www.ramblers.org.uk Comprehensive website of Britain's leading organisation for walkers; includes walker-friendly accommodation across the country.

Britain's towns and cities can sometimes be crowded, so open areas are highly valued, and every weekend millions of people go walking in the countryside. You could do a lot worse than join them. You can choose between an easy stroll through tranquil woods and farmland for an hour or two, or an all-day hike over moors and mountains, or a week-long trek on a national trail – or anything in between.

Unlike hiking and trekking in some other parts of the world, walking in Britain is not usually about serious expeditions in vast wilderness areas. The nature of the country means you're rarely more than a couple of hours from human habitation (maybe a bit more in remote parts of Scotland), although you can still get a great feeling of peace and solitude.

In Britain, walking is not just for hardy or sporty types. How much you do and how far you go is totally your choice. There's something for young and old, and walking is often perfect for families too.

Whatever option you go for, walking in Britain will help you appreciate the landscape and understand the country, and you might even learn a bit about the friendly natives as well.

Planning

Walking is the most popular outdoor activity in Britain – for locals and visitors alike – firstly, because it opens up some beautiful corners of the country, and secondly, because it can be done virtually on a whim. In fact, compared to hiking and trekking in some other parts of the world, it doesn't take much planning at all.

Getting Started

An established infrastructure for walkers already exists in Britain, so everything is easy for visitors or first-timers. Most villages and country towns in areas where walking is popular have shops selling maps and local guidebooks, while the local tourist office can provide leaflets and other information. In the national parks, suggested routes or guided walks are often available. (For more on Britain's national parks, see p1015.) This all means you can arrive in a place for the first time, pick up some info, and within an hour you'll be walking through some of Britain's finest landscape. No fees. No permits. No worries. It really is almost effortless.

Britain's Footpath Network

Britain is covered in a vast network of footpaths, many of which are centuries old, dating from the time when walking was the only way to get from farm to village, from village to town, from town to coast, or from valley to valley. Any walk you do today will follow these historic paths. Even Britain's longest walks simply link up many shorter paths. You'll also sometimes walk along 'bridleways' originally used for horse transport, and old unsurfaced roads called 'byways'.

Rights of Way

The absolute pleasure of walking in Britain is mostly thanks to the 'right of way' network – public paths and tracks across private property, especially in England and Wales. In Britain, nearly all land (including in national parks) is privately owned, but if there's a right of way you can follow it through fields, pastures, woods, even farmhouse yards, as long as you keep to the route and do no damage. In some mountain and moorland areas, walkers can move freely beyond the rights of way and explore at will. Known as 'freedom to roam', where permitted it's clearly advertised with markers on gates and signposts. For more information see www.countrysideaccess.gov.uk.

Scotland has a different legal system, so there aren't as many actual rights of way, but the Scottish Outdoor Access Code allows walkers to cross most private land

WEATHER WATCH

While walking in Britain, it's always worth remembering the fickle nature of the British weather. The countryside can appear gentle and welcoming, and often is, but sometimes conditions can turn nasty – especially on the higher ground. At any time of year, if you're walking on the hills or open moors, it's vital to be well equipped. You should carry warm and waterproof clothing (even in summer); a map and compass (that you know how to use); and drink and food, including high-energy stuff such as chocolate. If you're really going off the beaten track, leave details of your route with someone.

providing they act responsibly. There are restrictions during lambing time, birth-nesting periods and grouse- and deer-hunting seasons (p40).

Experience Required

When deciding which area of Britain to visit for walking, a lot may depend on your own experience.

Generally speaking, the lower and more cultivated the landscape, the easier the walking, with clear paths and signposts – ideal for beginners. As the landscape gets higher, conditions tend to get more serious. In mountain and moorland areas, if the route is popular there will be a path (but sometimes it is faint), but not many signposts. This option is suitable if you already have a bit of walking experience. In remote areas, if the route is rarely trodden, there may be no visible path at all, and absolutely no signposts, so you'll need to know what you're doing – as well as know how to use a detailed map and compass for navigation.

Britain's Best Walking Areas

Although you can walk just about anywhere in Britain, some areas are better than others. Here's a rundown of favourite places, suitable for short walks of a couple of hours, or longer all-day outings. For information on multiday hikes see the Long-Distance

HILL WALKING IN SCOTLAND: A MATTER OF TIMING

Walking in the hills and mountains of Scotland tends to be a more serious undertaking than walking in most parts of England and Wales. As well as the remote landscape, there are some important dates to consider. For more details and up-to-date information see www.outdooraccess-scotland.com and www.midgeforecast.co.uk.

October–March Winter conditions. Ice axe and crampons are usually required for higher hills; for experienced mountaineers only.

Mid-April–end May Lambing season. Walkers are asked to avoid areas where sheep are lambing.

Mid-June–August Midge season (flying, biting insects).

12 August–third week in October Grouse shooting season. Walkers should avoid areas where shooting takes place.

1 July–15 February Deer stalking (hunting) season; especially busy August to October. Walkers should avoid areas where stalking takes place.

Walking section (p42). For more pointers on each region, see the introductory Walking sections at the start of each chapter in this book; more ideas are given throughout the chapters as well.

Southern England

The chalky hills of the South Downs stride across the counties of West Sussex and East Sussex, while the New Forest in Hampshire is great for easy strolls and the nearby Isle of Wight has excellent walking options. The highest and wildest area in southern England is Dartmoor, dotted with Bronze Age remains and granite outcrops called 'tors' – looking for all the world like abstract sculptures. Exmoor has heather-covered hills cut by deep valleys and a lovely stretch of coastline, while the entire coast of the southwest peninsula from Dorset to Somerset offers dramatic walking conditions – especially along the beautiful cliff-lined shore of Cornwall.

Central England

The gem of central England is the Cotswold hills, classic English countryside with gentle paths through neat fields, mature woodland and pretty villages of honey-coloured stone. The Marches, where England borders Wales, are similarly bucolic with more good walking options. For something higher, aim for the Peak District, divided into two distinct areas: the White Peak, characterised by limestone, farmland and verdant dales, ideal for gentle strolls; and the Dark Peak, with high peaty moorlands, heather and gritstone outcrops, for more serious hikes.

Northern England

The Lake District is the heart and soul of walking in England, a wonderful area of soaring peaks, endless views, deep valleys and, of course, beautiful lakes. On the other side of the country, the rolling hills of the Yorkshire Dales make it another popular walking area. Further north, keen walkers love the starkly beautiful hills of Northumberland National Park, while the nearby coast is less daunting but just as dramatic – perfect for wild seaside strolls.

South & Mid-Wales

The Brecon Beacons is a large range of gigantic rolling whaleback hills with broad ridges and table-top summits, while out in the west is Pembrokeshire, a wonderful array of beaches, cliffs, islands, coves and harbours, with a hinterland of tranquil farmland and secret waterways, and a relatively mild climate year-round.

North Wales

For walkers, North Wales *is* Snowdonia, where the remains of ancient volcanoes bequeath a striking landscape of jagged peaks, sharp ridges and steep cliffs. There are challenging walks on Snowdon itself – at 1085m, the highest peak in Wales – and many more on the nearby Glyder and Carneddau ranges, or further south around Cader Idris.

Southern & Central Scotland

This extensive region embraces several areas just perfect for keen walkers, including Ben

» (above) Yorkshire Dales National Park
   (p512), England
» (left) Walking near the Cuillin Hills
   (p921) on the Isle of Skye, Scotland

Lomond, the best-known peak in the area, and the nearby Trossachs range, now within the new Loch Lomond and the Trossachs National Park. Also here is the splendid Isle of Arran, with a great choice of coastal rambles and high-mountain hikes.

Northern & Western Scotland

For serious walkers, heaven is the northern and western parts of Scotland, where the forces of nature have created a mountainous landscape of utter grandeur, including two of Scotland's most famous place names, Glen Coe and Ben Nevis (Britain's highest mountain at 1344m). Off the west coast lie the dramatic mountains of the Isle of Skye.

Keep going north and west, and things just keep getting better: a remote and beautiful area, sparsely populated, with scenic glens and lochs, and some of the largest, wildest and finest mountains in Britain.

Long-Distance Walking

As well as enjoying walks that take a few hours, avid hikers savour the chance of completing one of Britain's famous long-distance routes – many of which are specifically named and signposted as national trails, such as the Pennine Way National Trail and Offa's Dyke Path National Trail.

BRITAIN'S BEST LONG ROUTES

Although Britain's long-distance trails have official start and finish points, you don't have to do the whole thing end-to-end in one go. Many people walk just a section for a day or two, or use the main route as a basis for loops exploring the surrounding area.

» **Coast to Coast Walk** (190 miles) A top-quality trail across northern England, through three national parks and a spectacular mix of valleys, plains, mountains, dales and moors.

» **Cotswold Way** (102 miles) A delightful walk through classic picture-postcard countryside with fascinating smatterings of English history along the way.

» **Cumbria Way** (70 miles) A wonderful Lake District hike, keeping mainly to the valleys, with breathtaking views of the mountains on either side.

» **Hadrian's Wall Path** (84 miles) A new national trail following the famous Roman structure all the way across northern England, and giving the Coast to Coast a run for its money in the popularity stakes.

» **Pennine Way** (256 miles) The granddaddy of them all, Britain's oldest national trail; an epic hike along the mountainous spine of northern England.

» **South West Coast Path** (630 miles) A roller-coaster romp round England's southwest peninsula, past beaches, bays, shipwrecks, seaside resorts, fishing villages and clifftop castles.

» **Thames Path** (173 miles) A journey of contrasts beside England's best-known river, from rural Gloucestershire to the heart of London.

» **Pembrokeshire Coast Path** (186 miles) Marking the line where West Wales drops suddenly into the sea, passing popular beaches and isolated clifftop stretches.

» **Offa's Dyke Path** (178 miles) Following Britain's longest archaeological monument, the 8th-century ditch that still largely marks the boundary between Wales and England.

» **Great Glen Way** (73 miles) A largely level walk on paths and forest tracks beside Loch Ness and the Caledonian Canal.

» **St Cuthbert's Way** (62 miles) Following the footsteps of the 6th-century missionary through southern Scotland and northern England.

» **Southern Upland Way** (212 miles) Scotland's 'coast to coast', a tough and committing trek through remote hills and moorlands.

» **West Highland Way** (96 miles) One of Britain's top favourites, through glens and beside lochs with spectacular scenery at every step.

THE ANCIENT ART OF MUNRO BAGGING

At the end of the 19th century an eager hill walker named Sir Hugh Munro published a list of 545 Scottish mountains measuring over 3000ft (914m) – a height at which he believed they gained special significance. Of these summits, he classified 277 as mountains in their own right (new surveys have since revised this to 283), the rest being satellite peaks of lesser consequence (known as 'tops'). Today any Scottish mountain over the magical 3000ft mark is called a Munro, and many keen hill walkers now set themselves the target of summiting (or 'bagging') all 283.

Munro bagging started soon after the list was published. By 1901 the Reverend AE Robertson had become the first person to bag the lot, and between 1901 and 1981 another 250 people managed to climb all the Munros, but the huge increase in hill walking from the 1980s saw the number of 'Munroists' soar; by 2010 the total was 4500.

To the uninitiated it may seem odd that Munro baggers see their obsession as time well spent, but the quest is, of course, more than merely ticking names on a list – it takes walkers to some of the wildest, most beautiful parts of Scotland.

Most long-distance routes take between one and two weeks to complete, although some are longer. There are so many to choose from you'd easily wear out your boots trying to do them all, but it's easy to pick a route (or part of a route) that suits your experience and the time you have available.

Famous Long Routes

Some long-distance walking routes – such as the Pennine Way, the West Highland Way and the Pembrokeshire Coast Path – are well known and well maintained, with signposts and route-markers along the way, as well as being highlighted on Ordnance Survey maps. The most high-profile of these are the national trails, usually very clearly marked on the ground and on the map – ideal for beginners or visitors from overseas (although they're easy to follow, they're not necessarily easy underfoot). A downside of these famous routes is that they can be crowded in holiday times, making accommodation harder to find. An upside is the great feeling of camaraderie with other walkers on the trail.

Other Long Routes

In addition to the national trials and other high-profile routes, Britain has many other long-distance routes that are 'made up' (by joining many existing paths into a single entity) and exist only in dedicated guidebooks – with no equivalent sign-posting or markings on maps. This doesn't mean the obscure routes aren't enjoyable or spectacular – one of Britain's most popular long-distance routes, the Coast to Coast Walk, started out as just one man's idea, jotted down and published in a homespun volume – but it does mean you need to be a bit more experienced to follow them. For more information, see p670.

The latest addition to Britain's portfolio of long-distance routes is the Wales Coast Path, an 870-mile jaunt between Chepstow and Queensferry – making Wales the only country in the world with a footpath of this type along its entire coastline.

Where to Stay

Because Britain doesn't have the endless tracts of wilderness found in some other countries, you're never more than a few miles from a village – even in the national parks. This means your overnight stops can be at inns or B&Bs, and camping equipment is not required. (In fact, long-distance walkers carrying their own camping kit in true backpacking style are relatively rare in Britain.)

Baggage Transfer

To make your walking in Britain really easy, you don't even have to carry your pack if you don't want to. Baggage-transfer services operate on most of the main long-distance routes, carrying your kit between each night's accommodation. It may be the soft option, but it certainly makes the walking far more enjoyable. Most long routes are served by at least one baggage-transfer service. The main players include the following:

AMS (www.amsscotland.co.uk)
Luggage Transfers (www.luggagetransfers.co.uk)
Sherpa Van (www.sherpavan.com)
Walkers Bags (www.walkersbags.co.uk)

Travel with Children

Best Regions for Kids

London
The capital has children's attractions galore; many are free.

Devon, Cornwall & Wessex
Lovely beaches and reliable weather, though crowded in summer.

The Midlands
Caverns and 'show caves', plus former railways now traffic-free cycle routes.

Oxford & the Cotswolds
Oxford has Harry Potter connections; the Cotswolds is ideal for little-leg strolls.

Lake District & Cumbria
Zip wires and kayaks for teenagers; boat rides and Beatrix Potter for youngsters.

Wales
Long coast of beaches and pony-trekking in the hill country. And loads of castles...

Southern Scotland
Kid-friendly museums in Edinburgh and Glasgow; Southern Uplands mountain biking.

Scottish Highlands & Islands
Hardy teenagers plunge into outdoor activities; there are also dolphin-spotting boat trips.

Britain is great for travel with children because it's compact, with a lot of attractions in a small area. So when the kids in the back of the car say 'are we there yet?' your answer can often be 'yes'. To point you in the right direction, we've highlighted many family-friendly attractions here. With a bit of planning, and some online research to get the best bargains, having the kids on board can make your trip even more enjoyable.

Britain for Kids

Many places of interest cater for kids as much as adults. At historic castles, for example, mum and dad can admire the medieval architecture, while the kids will have great fun striding around the battlements. In the same way, many national parks and holiday resorts organise specific activities for children. It goes without saying that everything ramps up in the school holidays.

Bargain Hunting

Most visitor attractions offer family tickets – usually two adults plus two children, for less than the sum of the individual entrance charges. Most offer cheaper rates for solo parents and kids, too. Be sure to ask, as these are not always clearly displayed.

On the Road

If you're going by public transport, trains are great for families: intercity services have plenty of room for luggage and extra stuff like buggies (strollers), and the kids can move about a bit when bored. In contrast, they need to stay in their seats on long-distance coaches.

If you're hiring a car, most (but not all) rental firms can provide child seats – but you'll need to check this in advance. Most will not actually fit the child seats; you need to do that yourself, for insurance reasons.

Dining, not Whining

When it comes to refuelling, most cafes and teashops are child-friendly. Restaurants are mixed: some offer high chairs and kiddy portions; others say 'no children after 6pm'.

Children under 18 are usually not allowed in pubs serving just alcohol. Pubs also serving meals generally allow children of any age (with their parents) in England and Wales, but in Scotland they must be over 14 and must leave by 8pm. If in doubt, simply ask the bar staff.

And finally, a word on another kind of refuelling: Britain is still slightly buttoned up about breastfeeding. Older folks may tut-tut a bit if you give junior a top-up in public, but if done modestly it's usually considered OK.

Children's Highlights

Best Fresh-Air Fun

If the kids tire of castles and museums, you're never far from a place for outdoor activities to blow away the cobwebs.

» **Wildlife Cruises, Scotland's west coast**
What child could resist a boat trip to see seals, porpoises and dolphins, maybe even a whale?

» **Puzzle Wood, Forest of Dean** Wonderful woodland playground with mazy paths, weird rock formations and eerie passageways.

» **Whinlatter Forest Park, Cumbria** Highlights include a Go Ape adventure park and excellent mountain-bike trails, plus live video feeds from red squirrel cams.

» **Bewilderwood, Norfolk** Zip wires, jungle bridges, tree houses, marsh walks, boat trips, mazes and all sorts of old-fashioned outdoor adventure.

BABY-CHANGING FACILITIES

Most museums and other attractions in Britain usually have good baby-changing facilities (cue old joke: I swapped mine for a nice souvenir). Elsewhere, some city-centre public toilets have baby-changing areas, although these can be a bit grimy; your best bet for clean facilities is an upmarket department store. On the road, baby-changing facilities are generally bearable at motorway service stations and OK at out-of-town supermarkets.

» **Lyme Regis, Dorset** Guided tours to find your very own prehistoric fossil.

» **Cotswold Farm Park** Child-friendly introduction to the world of farm animals.

» **Tissington Trail, Derbyshire** Cycling this former railway is fun and almost effortless. You can hire kids' bikes, tandems and trailers. Don't forget to hoot in the tunnels!

Best Hands-On Action

Please do not touch? No chance. Here are some places where grubby fingers and enquiring minds are positively welcomed.

» **Science Museum, London** Seven floors of educational exhibits, at the mother of all science museums.

» **Enginuity, Ironbridge** Endless hands-on displays at the birthplace of the Industrial Revolution.

» **National Waterfront Museum, Swansea** Great interactive family fun.

» **Glasgow Science Centre** Bringing science and technology alive through hundreds of engaging exhibits.

» **Discovery Museum, Newcastle** Tyneside's rich history on display; highlights include a buzzers-and-bells science maze.

Best Rainy-Day Distractions

For those inevitable gloomy days, head for the indoor attractions. Don't forget the nation's great collection of museums. Alternatively, try outdoor stuff like coasteering in Pembrokeshire or canyoning in the Lake District. It's always fun – wet or dry.

PLANNING

When to Go

The best time for families to visit Britain is pretty much the best time for everyone else: from April/May to the end of September. It's worth avoiding August – the heart of school summer holidays – when prices go up and roads are busy, especially near the coast. Other school holidays are two weeks around Easter Sunday, and mid-December to early January, plus three week-long 'half-term' breaks – usually late February (or early March), late May and late October.

Places to Stay

Some hotels welcome kids (with their parents) and provide cots, toys and babysitting services, while others maintain an adult atmosphere. Many B&Bs offer 'family suites' of two adjoining bedrooms with one bathroom, and an increasing number of hostels (YHA, SYHA and independent) have family rooms with four or six beds – some even with private bathroom attached. If you want to stay in one place for a while, renting a holiday cottage is ideal. Camping is very popular with British families, and there are lots of fantastic campsites, but you'll usually need all your own gear.

Handy Websites

Baby Goes 2 (www.babygoes2.com) Advice, tips and encouragement (and a stack of adverts) for families on holiday.

Mums Net (www.mumsnet.com) No-nonsense advice on travel and more from a gang of UK mothers.

» **Cadbury World, Birmingham** Dentists may cry, but kids love the story of chocolate. And yes, there are free samples.

» **Underground Edinburgh** Take a guided tour of the haunted vaults beneath the medieval Old Town.

» **Eden Project, Cornwall** It may be raining outside, but inside these giant domes it's forever tropical forest or Mediterranean climate.

» **Cheddar Gorge Caves, Wessex** Finally nail the difference between stalactites and stalagmites in the Westcountry's deep caverns.

» **Underground Passages, Exeter** Explore medieval catacombs – the only system of its kind open to the public in England.

Best Stealth Learning

Across the country are many excellent museums, where young minds can be exercised while the kids think they are 'just' having fun.

» **At-Bristol** One of Britain's best interactive science museums, covering space, technology and the human brain.

» **Riverside Museum, Glasgow** Top-class interactive museum with a focus on transport.

» **Jorvik Centre, York** Excellent smells-and-all Viking settlement reconstruction.

» **Natural History Museum, London** Highlights include the life-size blue whale and animatronic dinosaurs.

» **Thinktank, Birmingham** Every display comes with a button or a lever at this 'edutaining' science museum.

» **National Space Centre, Leicester** Spacesuits, zero-gravity toilets and mini-astronaut training – guaranteed to boost little brains.

» **Centre for Alternative Technology, Machynlleth** Educational, fun and truly green – great for curious kids.

regions at a glance

London

History ✓✓✓
Entertainment ✓✓✓
Museums ✓✓✓

Historic Streets

London's ancient streets contain many of Britain's most famous and history-steeped landmarks. The echoes of the footfalls of monarchs, poets, whores and saints can still be detected in places like the Tower of London, Westminster Abbey and St Paul's Cathedral, as well as the pubs and coaching inns that once served Dickens, Shelley, Keats and Byron.

Entertainment

From West End theatres to East End clubs, from Camden's rock venues to Covent Garden's opera house, from tennis at Wimbledon to cricket at Lord's or football at Wembley, London's world-famous venues and arenas offer a perpetual clamour of entertainment.

Museums & Galleries

While the British Museum is the big crowd-puller, the capital has museums and galleries of every shape and size – and many of the very best are free.

p58

Canterbury & Southeast England

Cathedral ✓✓✓
History ✓✓
Food & Drink ✓✓✓

Canterbury Cathedral

A major reason to visit southeast England, this is one of the finest cathedrals in Europe. Write your own Canterbury tale as you explore its atmospheric chapels, cloisters and crypts.

Invasion Heritage

The southeast has always been a gateway for Continental arrivals, some more welcome than others. Castles and fortresses, the 1066 battlefield and Dover's wartime tunnels tell the region's story of invasion and defence.

Food & Drink

Kent is deservedly known as the Garden of England, celebrated for hops, fruit, fish and vineyards. Sussex isn't far behind, with England's finest sparkling wine giving the French stuff a run for its euro.

p146

Oxford, Cotswolds & Around

Architecture ✓✓✓
Homes ✓✓✓
Villages ✓✓✓

Architecture

Oxford's architecture will never leave you indifferent, whether you gaze across the 'dreaming spires' from the top of Carfax Tower, or explore the medieval streets on foot, or simply admire the fantastic gargoyles on the college facades.

Stately Homes

Favoured by the rich and powerful for centuries, this region is scattered with some of the finest stately homes and country houses in Britain. Top of the pile is the baroque masterpiece of Blenheim Palace.

Villages

Littered with picturesque 'chocolate box' scenes of honey-coloured stone cottages, thatched roofs, neat greens and cobbled lanes, the villages of the Cotswolds are a charming snapshot of rural England.

p181

Southwest England

Coastline ✓✓✓
History ✓✓✓
Activities ✓✓✓

Beaches
Britain's southwest peninsula juts determinedly into the Atlantic and an almost endless chain of sandy beaches – some big, some small, some brash, some tranquil – offer something for everyone.

Stone Circles
The ancient landscape of Wessex is nowhere more epitomised than the mysterious stone circle of Stonehenge. Nearby is Avebury, even bigger than Stonehenge, surrounded by many other reminders of the past.

Outdoor Activities
If you like to take it nice and easy, come to walk the moors or tootle along cycle trails. If you prefer life fast and furious, come to surf the best waves in England or learn to dive or kitesurf.

p224

Cambridge & East Anglia

History ✓✓✓
Coastline ✓✓
Waterways ✓✓

Historic Buildings
From the magnificent cathedrals of Ely, Norwich and Peterborough to Cambridge's King's College Chapel, Trinity's Great Court and the New Court at St John's, East Anglia's architectural splendour is second to none.

Coastline
With wide sandy beaches, great seafood, delightful old pubs, globally important bird reserves, villages still proud of their nautical heritage and classic seaside resorts, the coastline of East Anglia is rich and varied.

The Broads
The Norfolk and Suffolk Broads is a tranquil area of lakes and rivers, and an ideal spot for boating, birding, canoeing, cycling or walking, or just getting back to nature at a leisurely pace.

p353

Birmingham, the Midlands & the Marches

Activities ✓✓✓
Homes ✓✓✓
Food & Drink ✓✓

Outdoor Activities
The Peak District National Park, Cannock Chase, the Shropshire Hills, the Roaches, the Malvern Hills, Offa's Dyke Path, the Tissington Trail and the Pennine Cycleway all make this region great for hiking and biking.

Stately Homes
Grand houses like Haddon Hall, Burghley House and Chatsworth promise sprawling deer-filled grounds and grand interiors full of priceless heirlooms and oil paintings.

Food & Drink
Foodies take note: Birmingham is the curry capital of the country (and, increasingly, a magnet for Michelin-starred chefs), while the tiny town of Ludlow is an epicentre of gastronomic exploration.

p392

Yorkshire

Activities ✓✓✓
Food & Drink ✓✓✓
History ✓✓✓

Outdoor Activities
With rolling hills, scenic valleys and high moors and a cliff-lined coast all protected by national parks, Yorkshire is a natural adventure playground for hiking, biking, surfing and rock climbing.

Food & Drink
Lush pasture means Yorkshire beef and lamb is sought after, while the famous breweries of Masham turn out excellent real ales, always best sampled in one of Yorkshire's equally excellent traditional pubs.

History
From York's Viking heritage and the abbeys of Rievaulx, Fountains and Whitby, to the archaeology of Leeds, Bradford and Sheffield, follow some of Britain's most important historical narratives here.

p479

Manchester, Liverpool & Northwest England

Museums ✓✓✓
Sport ✓✓✓
Seaside ✓✓

Museums
The northwest's collection of heritage sites, from the wonderful People's History Museum in Manchester to the International Slavery Museum in Liverpool, is testament to the region's rich history and its ability to keep it alive.

Football
Two cities, Liverpool and Manchester, give the world four famous clubs, including the two most successful in English history. Manchester's National Football Museum is just another reason for fans to visit this region.

Blackpool
The queen of England's classic seaside resorts keeps going, thanks to the rides of the Pleasure Beach amusement park, where adrenalin junkies can always find a fix.

p537

The Lake District & Cumbria

Mountains ✓✓✓
Lakes ✓✓✓
Activities ✓✓✓

Mountains
Cumbria is the most mountainous part of England, a stunningly beautiful region that famously moved William Wordsworth to write his ode to 'a host of golden daffodils'.

Lakes
Dotted between the mountains are numerous lakes, some big and famous – Windermere, Coniston, Ullswater – others small, hidden and little known. The Lake District National Park protects this striking and valuable landscape.

Walking
If anywhere is the heart and soul of walking in England, it's the Lake District. Casual strollers find gentle routes through foothills and valleys, while serious hikers tackle high peaks and fells.

p575

Newcastle & Northeast England

History ✓✓✓
Landscapes ✓✓✓
Castles ✓✓✓

Hadrian's Wall
One of the world's premier Roman Empire sites, this potent symbol of power and defence strides its way for over 70 miles across the neck of England, from Tyneside to the Solway Firth. You can travel its length, stopping off at forts along the way.

Big Landscapes
If it's widescreen vistas you're after, the northeast never fails to please. From the golden beaches of Northumberland to the high moors of the Pennine uplands, great views are guaranteed.

Castles
Northumberland's vast expanse is dotted with some of Britain's finest castles, all acting as reminders of the centuries-long scrap between the Scots and the English over these remote borderlands.

p609

Cardiff (Caerdydd)

Architecture ✓✓
Sport ✓✓
Nightlife ✓✓

Architecture
From the medieval battlements of Caerphilly Castle and the fantastical structures of Cardiff Castle, to Victorian shopping arcades and Cardiff Bay's ultramodern waterfront, the Welsh capital has plenty to keep building buffs interested.

Sport
Cardiff is the home of Welsh sport, with the Millennium Stadium dominating the centre. The city is never more alive than during a rugby international, when the singing from the stands resonates through the streets.

Nightlife
A lively music scene, some swish bars and a swathe of old-fashioned pubs attract hordes of generally good-humoured lads and ladettes every weekend.

p641

Pembrokeshire & South Wales

Coastline ✓✓✓
Castles ✓✓✓
Countryside ✓✓

Hay-on-Wye & Mid-Wales

Wildlife ✓✓
Towns ✓✓
Food ✓✓✓

Snowdonia & North Wales

Mountains ✓✓✓
History ✓✓✓
Coastline ✓✓

Edinburgh

History ✓✓✓
Culture ✓✓✓
Food ✓✓✓

Coastal Scenery

South Wales boasts two of Britain's most beautiful stretches of coast – the Gower Peninsula and Pembrokeshire – between them offering clifftop walks, family-friendly beaches, surfing hot spots and watery adventures such as sea-kayaking and coasteering.

Castles

South Wales has some of the best castles, including Chepstow and Pembroke, while remote Carreg Cennen, in the Brecon Beacons, is the most spectacularly positioned of them all.

Countryside

Inland and away from the towns and cities, South Wales is carpeted with bucolic green pastures, most notably in Monmouthshire and Carmarthenshire.

p659

Wildlife

In the mountains and moors of the Brecon Beacons and many other parts of the region you can spot birds of prey – most famously the once-rare red kites, and most easily at feeding stations such as Gigrin Farm in Rhyader – while coastal Ceredigion shelters important wetland habitats.

Market Towns

From book-obsessed Hay-on-Wye and food-obsessed Abergavenny to quirky Llanwrtyd Wells and quaint Llandrindod Wells, these market towns are full of charm.

Food

Restaurants, inns and country gastropubs throughout the region are at the forefront of a new Welsh gastronomy, focusing on the finest fresh, locally grown, organic ingredients.

p687

Mountains

Home to some of Britain's finest mountain scenery south of the Scottish Highlands – and for most visitors much more accessible – Snowdonia's imposing peaks provide a scenic backdrop for innumerable outdoor pursuits.

Industrial Heritage

Welsh slate once roofed much of the world and the region's quarries and caverns bear witness to the lives of generations of workers, while railways now shunt tourists through spectacular terrain.

Beaches

From the North Coast's popular resort towns to the surf spots and quiet bays of Anglesey and the Llŷn Peninsula, North Wales has plenty of beach to go round.

p711

History

Perched on a brooding black crag overlooking the city centre, Edinburgh Castle has played a pivotal role in Scottish history. And on the edge of the city lies medieval Rosslyn Chapel, Scotland's most beautiful and enigmatic church.

Culture

Dubbed the Athens of the North, the Scottish capital is a city of high culture and lofty ideals, of art and literature, philosophy and science.

Food

The last decade has seen a boom in the number of restaurants in Edinburgh, while Scottish cuisine has been given a makeover by inventive chefs using top-quality local produce.

p751

Glasgow & Southern Scotland

Museums ✓✓✓
Abbeys ✓✓
Homes ✓✓

Museums & Galleries

Glasgow's mercantile, industrial and academic history has left the city with a wonderful legacy of museums and art galleries, dominated by the grand Victorian cathedral of culture that is the Kelvingrove.

Historic Abbeys

Rolling countryside and ruined abbeys are the big draws along the country's southern border, where you'll find the Gothic ruins of Melrose, Jedburgh and Dryburgh abbeys.

Stately Homes

The peace that followed the Act of Union saw landowners build luxurious homes for their families. Highlights of this region include Culzean Castle, Paxton House, Floors Castle and Mellerstain House.

p783

Stirling & Central Scotland

Castles ✓✓✓
Islands ✓✓✓
Whisky ✓✓

Castles

Central Scotland is home to the greatest concentration of castles in the country, from regal Stirling and the turreted splendour of Craigievar to the more restrained elegance of Crathie and Balmoral.

Islands

Island-hopping is a great way to explore Scotland's western seaboard, and the islands of this region – wild Jura, scenic Mull and the jewel of Iona – are a brilliant introduction.

Whisky

No trip to Scotland is complete without a visit to a whisky distillery – the Speyside region and the isle of Islay are epicentres of the industry.

p824

Inverness & the Northern Highlands & Islands

Activities ✓✓✓
Scenery ✓✓✓
History ✓✓

Outdoor Activities

Between them, Aviemore, gateway to winter snow sports and summer hill-walking, and Fort William, 'Outdoor Capital of the UK', offer enough adventure to keep you busy for a year.

Mountain Scenery

Landscape photographers are spoilt for choice, with classic views ranging from the mountain beauty of Glen Coe and the snow-patched summits of the Cairngorms to the rock pinnacles of the Cuillin Hills.

History

The region is rich in prehistoric remains, including the standing stones of Callanish and the neolithic settlement of Skara Brae. Abandoned rural communities are a sombre reminder of the Clearances.

p883

> Every listing is recommended by our authors, and their favourite places are listed first

> Look out for these icons:

 TOP CHOICE Our author's top recommendation

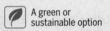 A green or sustainable option

FREE No payment required

On the Road

England

England Highlights

1 Spending more time than you'd planned in England's (and Britain's) endlessly entertaining capital, **London** (p58)

2 Being a Jane Austen character for a day in elegant **Bath** (p282)

3 Wandering lonely as a cloud in the idyllic **Lake District** (p579)

4 Exploring medieval walls, Viking sights and the soaring Gothic minster in historic **York** (p484)

5 Falling in love with the impossibly quaint villages of the **Cotswolds** (p199)

6 Getting some higher education among the dreamy spires of **Oxford** (p184)

7 Punting along the river in **Cambridge** (p357)

8 Seeing wild scenery and ancient engineering at **Hadrian's Wall** (p625)

9 Catching a Shakespeare play or visit the Bard's grave in **Stratford-upon-Avon** (p409)

10 Marvelling at one of Europe's greatest cathedrals in **Canterbury** (p147)

London

☎ 020 / POP: 7.82 MILLION / AREA: 609 SQ MILES

Best Places to Eat

» Bistrot Bruno Loubet (p127)

» Gordon Ramsay (p124)

» Hakkasan (p126)

» Laughing Gravy (p123)

» Poppies (p129)

Best Places to Stay

» Haymarket Hotel (p114)

» Hazlitt's (p114)

» Hoxton (p120)

» Zetter Hotel (p120)

» St Pancras Renaissance London Hotel (p117)

Why Go?

Everyone comes to London with a preconception shaped by a multitude of books, movies, TV shows and songs. Whatever yours is, prepare to have it exploded by this endlessly fascinating, amorphous city. You could spend a lifetime exploring it and find that the slippery thing's gone and changed on you. One thing is constant: that great serpent of a river enfolding the city in its sinuous loops, linking London both to the green heart of England and the world.

From Roman times the world has come to London, put down roots and whinged about the weather. There is no place on earth that is more multicultural; any given street yields a rich harvest of languages, and those narrow streets are also steeped in fascinating history, magnificent art, imposing architecture and popular culture. When you add an endless reserve of cool to this mix, it's hard not to conclude that London is one of the world's great cities, if not the greatest.

When to Go

Spring in the city sees daffodils in bloom, costumed marathon runners and London's edgiest music event, the Camden Crawl. In June you'll find the parks filled with people, Trooping the Colour, summer arts festivals, gay pride and Wimbledon.

London in December is all about Christmas lights on Oxford and Regent Sts, and perhaps a whisper of snow.

That said, London is a place that you can visit any time of the year.

History

London first came into being as a Celtic village near a ford across the River Thames, but the city only really took off after the Roman invasion in AD 43. The Romans enclosed their Londinium in walls that still find refrain in the shape of the City (with a capital 'C') of London today.

By the end of the 3rd century AD, Londinium was almost as multicultural as it is now, with 30,000 people of various ethnic groups and temples dedicated to a host of cults. Internal strife and relentless barbarian attacks took their toll on the Romans, who abandoned Britain in the 5th century, reducing the conurbation to a sparsely populated backwater.

The Saxons then moved in to the area, establishing farmsteads and villages. Their 'Lundenwic' prospered, becoming a large, well-organised town divided into 20 different wards. As the city grew in importance, it caught the eye of Danish Vikings, who launched many invasions and razed the city in the 9th century. The Saxons held on until, finally beaten down in 1016, they were forced to accept the Danish leader Knut (Canute) as King of England, after which London replaced Winchester as its capital. In 1042 the throne reverted to the Saxon Edward the Confessor, whose main contribution to the city was the building of Westminster Abbey.

The Norman Conquest saw William the Conqueror marching into London, where he was crowned king. He built the White Tower (the core of the Tower of London), negotiated taxes with the merchants, and affirmed the city's independence and right to self-government. From then until the late 15th century, London politics were largely taken up by a three-way power struggle between the monarchy, the church and city guilds.

The greatest threat to the burgeoning city was that of disease caused by unsanitary living conditions and impure drinking water. In 1348 rats on ships from continental Europe brought the bubonic plague, which wiped out a third of London's population of 100,000 over the following year.

London was consolidated as the seat of law and government in the kingdom during the 14th century. An uneasy political compromise was reached between the factions, and the city expanded rapidly in the 16th century under the House of Tudor.

The Great Plague struck in 1665 and by the time the winter cold arrested the epidemic, 100,000 Londoners had perished. Just as the population considered a sigh of relief, another disaster struck. The mother of all blazes, the Great Fire of 1666, virtually razed the place. One consequence was that it created a blank canvas upon which master architect Sir Christopher Wren could build his magnificent churches.

London's growth continued unabated, and by 1700 it was Europe's largest city, with 600,000 people. An influx of foreign workers brought expansion to the east and south, while those who could afford it headed to the more salubrious environs of the north and west, divisions that still largely shape London today.

Georgian London saw a surge in artistic creativity, with the likes of Dr Johnson, Handel, Gainsborough and Reynolds enriching the city's culture while its architects fashioned an elegant new metropolis. At the same time the gap between rich and poor grew ever wider, and lawlessness was rife.

In 1837, 18-year-old Victoria ascended the throne. During her long reign (1837–1901), London became the fulcrum of the expanding British Empire, which covered a quarter of the earth's surface. The Industrial Revolution saw the building of new docks and railways (including the first underground line in 1863), while the Great Exhibition of 1851 showcased London to the world. The city's population mushroomed from just over two million to 6.6 million during Victoria's reign.

Although London suffered relatively minor damage during WWI, it was devastated by the Luftwaffe in WWII, when huge swathes of the centre and East End were flattened and 32,000 people were killed. Ugly housing and low-cost developments were hastily erected in postwar London, and immigrants from around the world flocked to the city and once again changed its character. On 6 December 1952 the Great Smog descended, a lethal combination of fog, smoke and pollution caused by residential coal fires, vehicle exhausts and industry, killing some 4000 people.

Prosperity gradually returned, and the creative energy that had been bottled up in the postwar years was suddenly unleashed. London became the capital of cool in fashion and music in the 'Swinging Sixties', a party followed by the hangover of the harsh economic climate of the 1970s. Since then

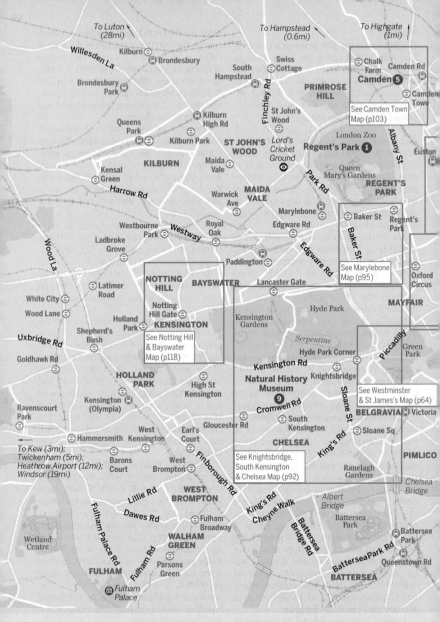

London Highlights

1 Watching the world pass by on a sunny day in **Regent's Park** (p95) or any of London's other green oases

2 Admiring the booty of an empire at the **British Museum** (p97)

3 Losing your head in history at the **Tower of London** (p75)

4 Sizing up the awe-inspiring architecture of **Westminster Abbey** (p63)

5 Discovering the next cool thing in one of Camden's **live music venues** (p135)

See Islington Map (p128)

See Hoxton, Shoreditch & Spitalfields Map (p104)

See North Central London Map (p100)

See West End Map (p70)

See The City Map (p78)

See South Bank Map (p84)

BARNSBURY

Highbury & Islington

Caledonian Rd & Barnsbury

York Way

Upper St

New North Rd

KINGSLAND

HACKNEY

London Fields

Haggerston

Mare St

Victoria Park

To Olympic Park (700m); Stratford (1mi)

KING'S CROSS

King's Cross St Pancras

ST PANCRAS

Euston Sq

Russell Sq

BLOOMSBURY

Goodge St

2

British Museum

SOHO

Piccadilly Circus

Covent Garden

ST JAMES'S

Westminster

4

Westminster Abbey

PENTONVILLE

FINSBURY

CLERKENWELL

Farringdon

Kingsway

HOLBORN

Temple

Barbican

Moorgate

Old St

City Rd

6

Hoxton

Hoxton

SHOREDITCH

SPITALFIELDS

Shoreditch High St

Liverpool St

Cambridge Heath

Bethnal Green Rd

Bethnal Green

Bethnal Green

Whitechapel

Stepney Green

Mile End

To Docklands (1.5mi); London City Airport (5mi)

WHITECHAPEL

Aldgate

Commercial Rd

Limehouse DLR

St Paul's Cathedral

7

Blackfriars

Bank

Mansion House Cannon St

Monument

Tower Hill

3

Tower of London

Shadwell DLR

The Highway

WAPPING

Wapping

ROTHERHITHE

Tate Modern

Waterloo East

Waterloo

London Bridge

BOROUGH

Long La

Grange Rd

Design Museum

Rotherhithe

Bermondsey

Southwark Park

Lower Rd

Canada Water

Nature Reserve

Surrey Quays

Evelyn Rd

To Greenwich (1.5mi)

WESTMINSTER

Tate Britain

Pimlico

Vauxhall Bridge

Vauxhall

LAMBETH

Elephant & Castle

Kennington La

Walworth Rd

Old Kent Rd

South Bermondsey

DEPTFORD

Kennington

Oval

Kennington Park

Burgess Park

Queens Rd (Peckham)

New Cross Gate

NINE ELMS

VAUXHALL

Wandsworth Rd

Clapham Rd

Brixton Rd

Denmark Rd

Peckham Rd

PECKHAM

Denmark Hill

Peckham Rye

Nunhead

STOCKWELL

To Brixton (600m); Brixton Windmill (1.5mi); Gatwick Airport (25mi)

2 km

1 miles

6 Seeing the locals through beer goggles on a Hoxton **bar hop** (p132)

7 Getting closer to God at the top of the dome of **St Paul's Cathedral** (p79)

8 Embarking on an eye-opening tour of modern and contemporary art at **Tate Modern** (p82)

9 Revelling in the astounding stonework and displays at the **Natural History Museum** (p90)

the city has surfed up and down the waves of global economics, hanging on to its position as the world's leading financial centre even during the recent international banking crisis.

In 2000, the modern metropolis won its first mayor of London (as distinguished from the Lord Mayor of the City of London), an elected role covering the City and all 32 urban boroughs. Bicycle-riding, shapeless-suit-wearing Boris Johnson, a Conservative with a shock of blond hair and a large, affable persona was elected in 2008 and has proved a popular mayor. In the 2012 mayoral election, he retained his post by defeating arch rival Ken Livingstone.

In August 2011, numerous London boroughs were rocked by riots – characterised by looting and arson – which were initially met by a mild police response. Analysts still debate the causes of the riot, pointing at single-parent families, gang culture, unemployment, criminal opportunism and social moral decay.

Both the Olympics and the Queen's Diamond Jubilee concocted a year of royal pageantry and sporting glory for London in 2012. The countdown to 2012 saw new Overground train lines opening, a cable car flung across the Thames, the massive regeneration of a rundown and once-polluted area of East London for the Olympic Park and a spruce up, tidy and facelift for numerous squares and gardens across town.

 Sights

The city's main geographical feature is the murky Thames, which snakes around but roughly divides the city into north and south. The old City of London (note the big 'C') is the capital's financial district, covering roughly a square mile bordered by the river and the many gates of the ancient (long-gone) city walls: Newgate, Moorgate etc. The areas to the east of the City are collectively known as the East End. The West End, on the City's other flank, is effectively the centre of London nowadays. It actually falls within the City of Westminster, which is one of London's 32 boroughs and has long been the centre of government and royalty.

Surrounding these central areas are dozens of former villages (Camden Town, Islington, Clapham etc), each with its own High St, which were long ago swallowed by London's sprawl.

When the sun shines make like a Londoner and head to the parks.

WESTMINSTER & ST JAMES'S
Purposefully positioned outside the old City (London's fiercely independent burghers preferred to keep the monarch and parliament at arm's length), Westminster has been the centre of the nation's political power for nearly a millennium. The area's many landmarks combine to form an awesome display of authority, pomp and gravitas.

LONDON IN...

Two Days

Only two days? Start in **Trafalgar Square** and see at least the outside of all the big-ticket sights – **London Eye**, **Houses of Parliament**, **Westminster Abbey**, **St James's Park Palace**, **Buckingham Palace**, **Green Park**, **Hyde Park**, **Kensington Gardens and Palace** – and then motor around **Tate Modern** until you get booted out. In the evening, explore **Soho**. On day two, race around the **British Museum**, then head to the City. Start with our **walking tour** and finish in the **Tower of London**. Head to the East End for an evening of **foreign food** and **hip bars**.

Four Days

Take the two-day itinerary but stretch it to a comfortable pace, spending extra time in Tate Modern, British Museum and the Tower of London. Stop at the **National Gallery** while you're in Trafalgar Sq and explore inside **Westminster Abbey** and **St Paul's Cathedral**. On your extra evenings, check out **Camden** and **Islington** or enjoy a slap-up dinner in **Kensington** and **Knightsbridge**.

One Week

As above, but add in a day each for **Greenwich**, **Kew Gardens** and **Hampton Court Palace**.

St James's is an aristocratic enclave of palaces, famous hotels, historic shops and elegant buildings, with some 150 historically noteworthy buildings in its 36 hectares.

Westminster Abbey
CHURCH

(Map p64; ☑020-7222 5152; www.westminster -abbey.org; 20 Dean's Yard; adult/child £15/6, tours £3; ◉9.30am-4.30pm Mon, Tue, Thu & Fri, to 7pm Wed, to 2.30pm Sat; ◉Westminster) Westminster Abbey is simply one of London's most imposing treasures. The abbey is not only a sublime place of worship, but is etched with enough history and architectural detail to fill several days' exploration. The abbey serves up the country's history on cold slabs of stone; for centuries, the country's greatest have been interred here, including most of the monarchs from Henry III (died 1272) to George II (1760).

Westminster Abbey has never been a cathedral (the seat of a bishop). It's what is called a 'royal peculiar' and is administered directly by the Crown. Every monarch since William the Conqueror has been crowned here, with the exception of a couple of unlucky Eds who were murdered (Edward V) or abdicated (Edward VIII) before the magic moment. Look out for the strangely underwhelming Coronation Chair.

The building itself is an arresting sight. Though a mixture of architectural styles, it is considered the finest example of Early English Gothic in existence. The original church was built in the 11th century by King (later Saint) Edward the Confessor, who is buried in the chapel behind the main altar. Henry III began work on the new building in 1245 but didn't complete it; the French Gothic nave was finished in 1388. Henry VII's astonishing Late Perpendicular–style Lady Chapel was consecrated in 1519 after 16 years of construction.

Apart from the royal graves, keep an eye out for the many famous commoners interred here, especially in Poets' Corner, where you'll find the resting places of Chaucer, Dickens, Hardy, Tennyson, Dr Johnson and Kipling as well as memorials to the other greats (Shakespeare, Austen, Brontë etc). Elsewhere you'll find the graves of Handel and Sir Isaac Newton.

The octagonal Chapter House dates from the 1250s and was where the monks would meet for daily prayer before Henry VIII's suppression of the monasteries in 1536. Used as a treasury and 'Royal Wardrobe', the cryptlike Pyx Chamber dates

from about 1070. The neighbouring Abbey Museum has as its centrepiece the death masks of generations of royalty.

Parts of the Abbey complex are free to visitors. This includes the Cloister and the 900-year-old College Garden. Free concerts are held here from 12.30pm to 2pm on Wednesday from mid-July to mid-August. Adjacent to the abbey is St Margaret's Church (Map p64; ◉9.30am-3.30pm Mon-Sat, 2-4.45pm Sun), the House of Commons' place of worship since 1614. There are windows commemorating churchgoers Caxton and Milton, and Sir Walter Raleigh is buried by the altar.

Verger-led tours are held several times a day (except Sunday) and are limited to 25 people per tour; call ahead to secure your place. Of course, admission to the Abbey is free if you wish to attend a service. On weekdays, Matins is at 7.30am, Holy Communion at 8am and 12.30pm, and Choral Evensong at 5pm. There are services throughout the day on Sunday. You can sit and soak in the atmosphere, even if you're not religious.

Houses of Parliament
HISTORIC BUILDING

(Map p64; www.parliament.uk; Parliament Sq; ◉Westminster) Coming face to face with one of the world's most recognisable landmarks is always a surreal moment, but in the case of the Houses of Parliament it's a revelation. Photos just don't do justice to the ornate stonework and golden filigree of Charles Barry and Augustus Pugin's neo-Gothic masterpiece (1840).

Officially called the Palace of Westminster, the oldest part is Westminster Hall (1097), which is one of only a few sections that survived a catastrophic fire in 1834. Its roof, added between 1394 and 1401, is the earliest known example of a hammerbeam roof and has been described as the greatest surviving achievement of medieval English carpentry.

The palace's most famous feature is its clock tower, aka Big Ben (Map p64). Ben is actually the 13-ton bell, named after Benjamin Hall, who was commissioner of works when the tower was completed in 1858.

At the business end, parliament is split into two houses. The green-hued House of Commons is the lower house, where the 650 elected Members of Parliament sit. Traditionally the home of hereditary bluebloods, the scarlet-decorated House of Lords now has peers appointed through various means. Both houses debate and vote on legislation,

Westminster & St James's

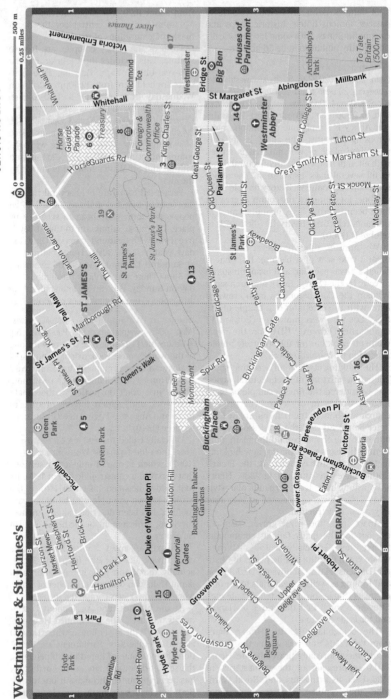

0 0 500 m
0 0.25 miles

River Thames

Victoria Embankment

Houses of Parliament

Big Ben

17

Whitehall

Richmond Tce

Westminster Bridge St

St Margaret St

Abingdon St

Millbank

2

Treasury

Foreign & Commonwealth Office

King Charles St

8

6

Horse Guards Parade

Horse Guards Rd

3

Great George St

Parliament Sq

14

Westminster Abbey

Great College St

Tufton St

Whitehall Pl

Old Queen St

Great SmithSt

Marsham St

Monck St

7

Carlton Gardens

19

St James's Park Lake

St James's Park

St James's Park

Birdcage Walk

Tothill St

Great Peter St

Medway St

Broadway

Caxton St

Old Pye St

ST JAMES'S

Pall Mall

The Mall

Marlborough Rd

13

Petty France

St James's St

12

4

Buckingham Gate

Castle La

Victoria St

Howick Pl

Ashley Pl

16

11

Queen's Walk

Queen Victoria Monument

Spur Rd

Buckingham Palace Rd

Palace St

Stag Pl

Piccadilly

Green Park

5

Buckingham Palace

9

18

Bressenden Pl

Victoria St

Victoria

Green Park

Duke of Wellington Pl

Constitution Hill

Buckingham Palace Gardens

10

Lower Grosvenor Pl

Eaton La

BELGRAVIA

Hobart Pl

Curzon St

Market Mews

Shepherd St

Hertford St

Brick St

Old Park La

Hamilton Pl

20

Memorial Gates

Grosvenor Pl

Grosvenor Cres

Halkin St

Chapel St

Chester St

Wilton St

Upper Belgrave St

Belgrave Pl

Eaton Pl

Hyde Park

Serpentine Rd

Rotten Row

Park La

Hyde Park Corner

1

15

Belgrave Sq

Belgrave Square

Eaton Sq

Lyall Mews

Eaton Mews

Westminster & St James's

which is then presented to the Queen for her Royal Assent (in practice, this is a formality; the last time Royal Assent was denied was 1708). At the annual State Opening of Parliament (usually in November), the Queen takes her throne in the House of Lords, having arrived in the gold-trimmed Irish State Coach from Buckingham Palace. It's well worth lining the route for a gawk at the crown jewels sparkling in the sun.

When parliament is in session, visitors are admitted to the House of Commons Visitors' Gallery. Expect to queue for at least an hour and possibly longer during Question Time (at the beginning of each day). The House of Lords Visitors' Gallery can also be visited.

Parliamentary recesses (ie MP holidays) last for three months over summer and a couple of weeks over Easter and Christmas. When parliament is in recess there are guided tours (☎0844 847 1672; www.ticketmaster.co.uk /housesofparliament; 75-min tours adult/child £15/6) of both chambers and other historic areas. UK residents can approach their MPs to arrange a free tour and to climb the clock tower.

Buckingham Palace PALACE
(Map p64; ☎020-7766 7300; www.royalcollection .org.uk; Buckingham Palace Rd; adult/child £17/9.75; ◷late Jul-Sep, changing of the guard 11.30am May-Jul, alternate days rest of yr; ◉Victoria) With so many imposing buildings in the capital, the Queen's palatial London pad can come as

a bit of an anticlimax. Built in 1703 for the Duke of Buckingham, Buckingham Palace replaced St James's Palace as the monarch's official London residence in 1837. When she's not giving her famous wave to far-flung parts of the Commonwealth, Queen Elizabeth II divides her time between here, Windsor and Balmoral. To know if she's at home, check whether the yellow, red and blue standard is flying.

Nineteen lavishly furnished State Rooms – hung with artworks by the likes of Rembrandt, van Dyck, Canaletto, Poussin and Vermeer – are open to visitors when HRH (Her Royal Highness) takes her holidays. The two-hour tour includes the Throne Room, with his-and-hers pink chairs initialed 'ER' and 'P'. Access is by timed tickets with admission every 15 minutes (audio guide included).

Your ticket to Buckingham Palace is good for a return trip if bought direct from the palace ticket office (ask to have it stamped). *A Royal Day Out* is a combined ticket including the State Rooms, Queen's Gallery and Royal Mews (adult/child £31.95/18.20).

Changing of the Guard
At 11.30am daily from May to July (on alternate days, weather permitting, for the rest of the year), the old guard (Foot Guards of the Household Regiment) comes off duty to be replaced by the new guard on the forecourt of Buckingham Palace. Highly popular, the show lasts about half an hour (brace for crowds). If you're here in November,

the procession leaving the palace for the State Opening of Parliament is much more impressive.

Queen's Gallery

Originally designed by John Nash as a conservatory, the gallery (Map p64; www.royalcollection.org.uk; Buckingham Palace Rd, southern wing, Buckingham Palace; adult/child £9/4.50; ⊙10am-5.30pm) showcases some of the palace's treasures on a rotating basis, through temporary exhibitions. Entrance to the gallery is through Buckingham Gate.

Royal Mews

Indulge your Cinderella fantasies while inspecting the exquisite state coaches in the Royal Mews (Map p64; www.royalcollection.org.uk; Buckingham Palace Rd; adult/child £8/5; ⊙10am-5pm Apr-Oct, to 4pm Mon-Sat Nov-Dec), a working stable looking after the immaculately groomed horses and opulent vehicles the royals use for getting from A to B. Highlights include the magnificent gold coach of 1762 and the 1910 Glass Coach (Prince William and Catherine Middleton actually used the 1902 State Landau for their wedding in 2011).

St James's Park & Palace   PARK

(⊖St James's Park, Green Park) With its manicured flower beds and ornamental lake, St James's Park is wonderful for strolling and taking in the surrounding palaces. The striking Tudor gatehouse of St James's Palace (Map p64; Cleveland Row; Green Park), begun by the palace-mad Henry VIII in 1530, is best approached from St James's St, to the north of the park. This was the residence of Prince Charles and his sons before they shifted

---

THE FOURTH PLINTH

Three of the four plinths located at Trafalgar Square's corners are occupied by notables: King George IV on horseback, and military men General Sir Charles Napier and Major General Sir Henry Havelock. The remaining plinth, originally earmarked for a statue of William IV, has remained largely vacant for the past 150 years. The Royal Society of Arts conceived the Fourth Plinth Project (www.london.gov.uk/fourthplinth) in 1999, opting to use the space for works by contemporary artists. The Mayor's office has since taken over the project, continuing with the contemporary art theme.

---

next door to Clarence House (1828), following the death of its previous occupant, the Queen Mother, in 2002. It's supreme for photo opportunities with one of the resolutely unsmiling royal guards.

Green Park   PARK

(Map p64; ⊖Green Park) Green Park's 47-acre expanse of meadows and mature trees links St James's Park to Hyde Park and Kensington Gardens, creating a green corridor from Westminster all the way to Kensington. Once a duelling ground, the park became a vegetable garden during WWII. Although it doesn't have lakes, fountains or formal gardens, it's blanketed with daffodils in spring and semi-naked bodies whenever the sun shines.

Westminster Cathedral   CATHEDRAL

(Map p64; www.westminstercathedral.org.uk; Victoria St; tower adult/child £5/2.50; ⊙7am-7pm; ⊖Victoria) Begun in 1895, this neo-Byzantine cathedral is still a work in progress, with new sections completed as funds allow. Look out for Eric Gill's highly regarded stone Stations of the Cross (1918). The Chapel of St George and the English Martyrs displays the body of St John Southwark, a priest who was hanged, drawn and quartered in 1654 for refusing to reject the supremacy of the Pope. The Chapel of the Blessed Sacrament and other parts of the interior are ablaze with Eastern Roman mosaics and ornamented with 100 types of marble; other areas are just bare brick. The distinctive 83m red-brick and white-stone tower offers splendid views of London and, unlike St Paul's dome, you can take the lift.

Banqueting House   PALACE

(Map p64; www.hrp.org.uk/banquetinghouse; Whitehall; adult/child £5/free; ⊙10am-5pm Mon-Sat; ⊖Westminster) The beautiful, classical design of the Banqueting House was conceived by Inigo Jones for James I in 1622. It's the only surviving part of Whitehall Palace after the Tudor bit went skywards in a 1698 conflagration. The chief attraction is the ceiling, painted by Rubens in 1635 at the behest of Charles I. The king didn't get to savour it for long; in 1649 he was frogmarched out of the 1st-floor balcony to lose his head for treason. An audioguide is included in the price.

No 10 Downing Street   HISTORIC BUILDING

(Map p64; www.number10.gov.uk; 10 Downing St; ⊖Westminister) It's typically British that the official seat of the prime minister is a nondescript Georgian town house in Whitehall.

The street was cordoned off with a rather large iron gate during Margaret Thatcher's tenure, so you can't get up close.

Churchill Museum & Cabinet War Rooms
MUSEUM

(Map p64; www.iwm.org.uk/cabinet; Clive Steps, King Charles St; adult/child £15/free; ☺9.30am-6pm; ⊜Westminster) Winston Churchill co-ordinated the Allied resistance against Nazi Germany on a Bakelite telephone from this underground military HQ during WWII. The Cabinet War Rooms remain much as they were when the lights were flicked off in 1945, capturing the drama and dogged spirit of the time, while the museum affords intriguing insights into the resolute, cigar-smoking wartime leader.

FREE Institute Of Contemporary Arts
ART GALLERY

(Map p64; www.ica.org.uk; The Mall; ☺noon-11pm Wed, to 1am Thu-Sat, to 9pm Sun; ⊜Charing Cross) A one-stop contemporary-art bonanza, the excitingly cerebral program at the ICA includes film, photography, theatre, installations, talks, performance art, DJs, digital art and book readings. Stroll around the galleries, watch a film, browse the left-field bookshop, then head to the bar for a beer.

Spencer House
HISTORIC HOME

(Map p64; ✆020-7499 8620; www.spencerhouse.co.uk; 27 St James's Pl; adult/child £12/10; ☺10.30am-5.45pm Sun Feb-Jul & Sep-Dec; ⊜Green Park) The ancestral home of Princess Diana's family, Spencer House was built in the Palladian style between 1756 and 1766. It was converted into offices after the Spencers moved out in 1927, but 60 years later an £18 million restoration returned it to its former glory. Visits are by guided tour.

Apsley House
HISTORIC HOME

(Map p64; www.english-heritage.org.uk; 149 Piccadilly; adult/child £6.30/3.80, with Wellington Arch £8.20/4.90; ☺11am-5pm Wed-Sun Apr-Oct, to 4pm Wed-Sun Nov-Mar; ⊜Hyde Park Corner) This stunning house, containing exhibits devoted to the life and times of the Duke of Wellington, was designed by Robert Adam for Baron Apsley in the late 18th century. It was later sold to the first Duke of Wellington, who cut Napoleon down to size in the Battle of Waterloo and lived here for 35 years until his death in 1852. With 10 of its rooms open to the public, the house has a stairwell dominated by Antonio Canova's staggering

3.4m-high statue of a fig-leafed Napoleon with titanic shoulders. Don't miss the elaborate Portuguese silver service.

Wellington Arch
MUSEUM

(Map p64; www.english-heritage.org.uk; Hyde Park Corner; adult/5-15yr £4/2.40, with Apsley House £8.20/4.90; ☺10am-5pm Wed-Sun Apr-Oct, 10am-4pm Wed-Sun Nov-Mar; ⊜Hyde Park Corner) Throttled by the Hyde Park Corner roundabout, this is London's answer to the Arc de Triomphe (except this one commemorates France's *defeat* at the hands of the Duke of Wellington). Erected in 1826, the monument is topped with Europe's largest bronze sculpture: *Peace Descending on the Quadriga of War* (1912). Until the 1960s, part of the monument served as the capital's smallest police station (complete with pet moggy); the arch now houses a three-floor exhibition space. The open-air balconies (accessible by lift) afford unforgettable views of Hyde Park, Buckingham Palace and the Houses of Parliament.

WEST END

A strident mix of culture and consumerism but more a concept than a fixed geographical area, the West End is synonymous with roof-raising musicals, bright lights, outstanding restaurants and indefatigable bag-laden shoppers. It casts its net around Piccadilly Circus and Trafalgar Sq to the south, Regent St to the west, Oxford St to the north and Covent Garden to the east and the Strand to the southeast.

Named after the elaborate collars (picadils) that were the sartorial staple of a 17th-century tailor who lived nearby, Piccadilly became the fashionable haunt of the well-heeled (and collared), and still boasts establishment icons such as the Ritz hotel and Fortnum & Mason department store. It meets Regent St, Shaftesbury Ave and Haymarket at the neon-lit swirl of Piccadilly Circus, home to the ever-popular and ever-misnamed Eros statue (really Anteros).

Mayfair, west of Piccadilly Circus, hogs all of the most expensive streets from the Monopoly board, including Park Lane and Bond St, which should give you an idea of what to expect: lots of pricey shops, Michelin-starred restaurants, society hotels and gentlemen's clubs. The elegant bow of Regent St and frantic Oxford St are the city's main shopping strips. At the heart of the West End lies Soho, a boho grid of

(Continued on page 72)

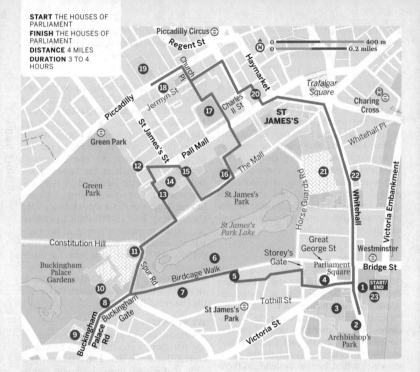

START THE HOUSES OF PARLIAMENT
FINISH THE HOUSES OF PARLIAMENT
DISTANCE 4 MILES
DURATION 3 TO 4 HOURS

Walking Tour
Royal London Walk

❯ Start at the heart of it all, emerging from Westminster underground station to cross Bridge St to the Palace of Westminster, aka the **❶ Houses of Parliament**. Originally built in 1097, **Westminster Hall** is the oldest surviving part of the original palace – seat of the English monarchy from the 11th to the 16th century – much of which burned down in October 1834. Note the statue of Oliver Cromwell standing outside, controversially erected in 1899. Following the length of the Houses of Parliament along Abingdon St (which becomes Old Palace Yard) brings you to the **❷ Jewel Tower**, the only other still-extant chunk of the old palace, built in the 14th century for storing Edward III's royal treasures. Constructed largely from Kentish ragstone, the tower contains intriguing medieval historical features, an exhibition on the history of Parliament and a small cafe.

Exit the Jewel Tower to the breathtaking majesty of **❸ Westminster Abbey**, London's West Minster (as distinct from the minster in the east – St Paul's Cathedral) and traditional

venue of coronation for the English monarchy. Amid great pomp and ceremony, Prince William married Catherine Middleton here on 29 April 2011. Walking around Parliament Sq, note the **❹ Supreme Court of the United Kingdom**, within the ornate Middlesex Guildhall, dating from 1913. Observe the statue of **Abraham Lincoln**, a copy of an effigy sculpted by Augustus Saint-Gaudens which stands in Lincoln Park, Chicago.

Round the corner and walk west (left) along Great George St, with the **HM Treasury** on the far side of the road. Turn left down Storey's Gate and then right into Old Queen St, before trotting down **❺ Cockpit Steps** (a surviving part of the former Royal Cockpit, where cockfights were held), said to be haunted by a headless woman dressed in red! The steps lead down to lovely **Birdcage Walk**, named after the royal Aviary, which was once situated here. Cross over the road and walk into **❻ St James's Park** (which used to be the royal gardens) to walk alongside the lake. As you near the western end of the park, you will pass the **7 Guards Museum** on the far side of Birdcage Walk. Get here for 10.50am any day from April to August to catch the guards getting into formation outside the museum for their march up to Buckingham Palace.

Walk up Buckingham Gate to the **8 Queen's Gallery** and the **9 Royal Mews** before walking back to **10 Buckingham Palace** and the **11 Queen Victoria Memorial**, dating from 1911, with its grumpy looking monarch staring down the Mall. Follow the ceremonial route of the Mall (rhymes with 'shall') and cross into **Green Park** (another of London's Royal Parks) to head up Queen's Walk to grand **12 Spencer House** before retracing your steps back to the Mall and **13 Clarence House**, residence of Prince Charles and former home of Queen Elizabeth the Queen Mother. Five rooms of the house are usually opened up to the public for pre-booked tours each year between August and October. The unflinching guards on Stable Yard Road are an impressive sight.

Continuing east along the Mall to walk north up Marlborough Road to **14 St James's Palace** and the **15 Queen's Chapel** opposite. Open during services only, the church interior has exquisite 17th-century fittings, atmospherically illuminated by light streaming in through the large windows above the altar. Return to the Mall and keep walking east to climb the steps alongside a **16 bronze statue of Queen Elizabeth II** (unveiled in 2009) with King George VI behind her. On the corner at **No 4 Carlton Gardens** is the house where General Charles de Gaulle set up the headquarters of the Free French Forces in 1940. Ahead you can see the towering **Duke of York Column** rising up in Waterloo Place.

Take the first left and cross over the pedestrian crossing in Pall Mall to walk into **17 St James's Square**, surrounded by good-looking Georgian architecture. With a statue of King William III at its centre, the private gardens at the heart of the square are open from 10am to 4.30pm on weekdays. **The Naval and Military Club** at No 4 in the northeast corner of the square is known as the 'In and Out', reflected in the words on the entrance; on the northwest corner at No 14 is the **London Library**, established by Thomas Carlyle: a private library with 15 miles of shelving.

Head up Duke of York St towards the side-on form of **St James's Piccadilly**, designed by Christopher Wren, and walk up colonnaded Piccadilly Arcade to exit into Piccadilly. On the far side of the road is the impressive entrance of the **18 Royal Academy of Arts**, founded by George III in 1768, and located within Burlington House. Explore the impressive stone-paved piazza of the main courtyard. Head back across the road and walk a short distance east to mint-green **19 Fortnum & Mason**, London's oldest grocery store and holder of many royal warrants.

Walk east along Piccadilly and turn right down Church Pl just west of St James's Piccadilly and onto Jermyn St. Head east and go right to Regent St, turn left onto King Charles II St and walk down **20 Royal Opera Arcade**, London's oldest shopping arcade. From Pall Mall, walk along Cockspur St to pass Trafalgar Sq and head down Whitehall. Walking past the old Admiralty Building, you will reach **21 Horse Guards Parade**, where the mounted troopers of the Household Cavalry change guard daily at 11am daily (10am Sunday) and a lite-pomp version takes place at 4pm when the dismounted guards are changed. Open daily, the **Household Cavalry Museum** is here as well. On the far side of Whitehall stands **22 Banqueting House**, with its bust of Charles I on the corner above the door, while continuing south along Whitehall takes you past **No 10 Downing Street** and returns you to the Houses of Parliament.

West End

BLOOMSBURY

FITZROVIA

Great Portland St

Foley St

Riding House St

Goodge St

39

32

Charlotte St

Charlotte Pl

62

Windmill St

Bayley St

Morwell St

Tottenham Court Rd

Percy St

10

Rathbone Pl

Gresse St

29

Hanway Pl

Hanway St

Tottenham Court Rd

Mortimer St

Little Portland St

Margaret St

Eastcastle St

Great Titchfield St

Wells Mews

Wells St

Berners Mews

Berners St

Newman St

17

52

55

Berners St

75

Oxford St

Falconberg Ct

Sutton Row

Great Castle St

Winsley St

Regent St

80

Oxford Circus

Ramillies St

Great Marlborough St

Poland St

Berwick St

Noel St

D'Arblay St

16

70

38

Carlisle St

St Anne's Court

43

21

Soho Square

Soho St

Great Chapel St

60

Manette St

Greek St

14

67

Frith St

Dean St

Bateman St

Manette St

34

76

Ganton St

Broadwick St

Ingestre Pl

19

Richmond Mews

42

30

12

23

35

59

65

Meard St

SOHO

Hanover St

Maddox St

Kingly St

Carnaby St

Beak St

Golden Sq

Birdie La

26

54

58

Old Compton St

45

31

Romilly St

22

Wardour St

To Wild Honey (25m)

Conduit St

78

Boyle St

Clifford St

Old Burlington St

Savile Row

Heddon St

Regent St

Warwick St

Sherwood St

Brewer St

Great Windmill St

Archer St

25

37

Rupert St

Shaftesbury Ave

Gerrard St

Wardour St

Rupert St

Lexington St

Denman St

48

Piccadilly Circus

Coventry St

56

Oxendon St

Whitcomb St

Panton St

Orange St

Glasshouse St

Anteros (Eros) statue

5

Royal Academy of Arts

40

Swallow St

Sackville St

Vigo St

Burlington Gdns

1

77

81

Piccadilly

Eagle Pl

Jermyn St

Regent St

St Alban's St

Haymarket

13

Suffolk Pl

New Bond St

Albemarle St

Dover St

Stafford St

Old Bond St

Cork St

9

Royal Arcade

Burlington Arcade

73

Jermyn St

Duke of York St

Britain & London Visitor Centre

Charles II St

Pall Mall

ST JAMES'S

Piccadilly

Arlington St

St James's St

71

Bury St

Duke St

Ryder St

King St

St James's Square

Waterloo Pl

Carlton House Tce

Green Park

Green Park

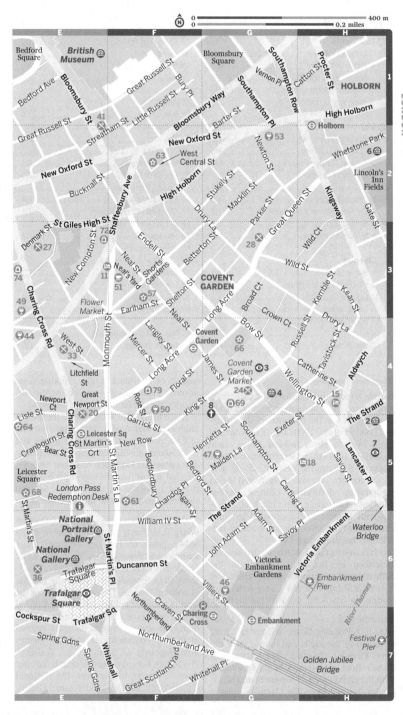

West End

(Continued from page 67)

narrow streets and squares hiding gay bars, strip clubs, cafes and advertising agencies. Carnaby St was the epicentre of the swinging London of the 1960s but is now largely given over to chain fashion stores. Lisle St and, in particular, Gerrard St (north of Leicester Sq) form the heart of Chinatown, a convergence of reasonably priced Asian restaurants, decorative Chinese arches and busy Cantonese supermarkets. Heaving with tourists and dominated by huge cinemas (with occasional star-studded premieres), neighbouring Leicester Sq (*lester*) has undergone a much-needed facelift. Described by Benjamin Disraeli in the 19th century as Europe's finest street, the Strand still boasts a few classy hotels, including the Savoy, but its lustre has dimmed.

Piccadilly Circus   SQUARE
(Map p70; Piccadilly Circus; ⊖Piccadilly Circus) Designed in the 1820s and named after the street Piccadilly (heading west to Hyde Park Corner from the square) at its confluence with the grand sweep of Regent St and Shaftesbury Avenue, Piccadilly Circus is today a tumult of stop-start traffic, blinking neon advertisement panels and camera-toting visitors from all four corners of the globe.

At the heart of the action stands the famous aluminium statue of Anteros, twin brother of Eros, dedicated to the philanthropist and child-labour abolitionist Lord Shaftesbury. The statue has long been mistaken for Eros, the God of Love, and the misnomer has stuck (it's even marked on the London A-Z and signs for 'Eros' lead from the underground).

Trafalgar Square   LANDMARK
(Map p70; ⊖Charing Cross) Trafalgar Sq is the public heart of London, hosting rallies, marches and feverish New Year's festivities. Londoners congregate here to celebrate anything from football victories to the ousting of political leaders. The square is one of the world's grandest public places, with Admiral Nelson surveying his fleet from the 43.5m-high Nelson's Column at its heart, erected in 1843 to commemorate his 1805 victory over Napoleon off Spain's Cape Trafalgar. The square is flanked by splendid buildings: Canada House to the west, the National Gallery (p73) and National Portrait Gallery

(p73) to the north, South Africa House and the church of St Martin-in-the-Fields to the east. Further south stands Admiralty Arch, built in honour of Queen Victoria in 1910 (and with a mysterious stone nose around seven foot up from the ground on one of the northernmost arches), and beyond that, the Mall (rhymes with 'shall', not 'shawl') is the ceremonial route leading to Buckingham Palace.

FREE National Gallery ART GALLERY
(Map p70; www.nationalgallery.org.uk; Trafalgar Sq; ⊙10am-6pm Sat-Thu, to 9pm Fri; ◉Charing Cross) Gazing grandly over Trafalgar Sq through its Corinthian columns, the National Gallery is the nation's most important repository of largely pre-modern art. Four million visitors flock annually to admire its 2300-plus Western European paintings, spanning the eras from the 13th to the early 20th centuries. Highlights include Turner's *The Fighting Temeraire*, Botticelli's *Venus and Mars* and van Gogh's *Sunflowers*. The medieval religious paintings in the Sainsbury Wing are delightful, but for more modern zest, the works by Monet, Cézanne and Renoir

are crowd-pullers. The comprehensive audio guides (£3.50) are recommended, as are the free introductory tours, while for sustenance nothing beats the National Dining Rooms (p121) in the Sainsbury Wing.

FREE National Portrait Gallery ART GALLERY
(Map p70; www.npg.org.uk; St Martin's Pl; ⊙10am-6pm Sat-Wed, to 9pm Thu & Fri; ◉Charing Cross) The fascinating National Portrait Gallery is like stepping into a picture book of English history. Founded in 1856, the permanent collection (around 11,000 works) starts with the Tudors on the 2nd floor and descends to contemporary figures (from pop stars to scientists), including Marc Quinn's *Self*, a frozen self-portrait of the artist's head cast in blood and recreated every five years. An audiovisual guide (£3) will lead you through the gallery's most famous pictures.

Royal Academy of Arts GALLERY
(Map p70; ☎020-7300 8000; www.royalacademy .org.uk; Burlington House, Piccadilly; admission depending on exhibition £6-20; ⊙10am-6pm Sun-Thu, to midnight Fri, 9am-midnight Sat; ◉Green Park) Hosting high-profile exhibitions and a small

display from its permanent collection, the crafty academy made it a condition of joining its exclusive club of 80 artists for new members to donate one of their artworks. The collection embraces works from such masters as Constable, Turner and Sir Norman Foster while the Summer Exhibition showcases contemporary art. Free tours of the John Madesjki Fine Rooms are held.

Covent Garden Piazza HISTORIC AREA
(Map p70; ⊖Covent Garden) Hallowed turf – or cobbles – for opera fans descending on the esteemed Royal Opera House, Covent Garden is one of London's biggest tourist hot spots. London's first planned square, Covent Garden Piazza now hosts bands of tourists shopping in quaint old arcades and ringing street entertainers and buskers. On its western flank rises St Paul's Church (Map p70; www.actorschurch.org; Bedford St; ⊙8.30am-5.30pm Mon-Fri, 9am-1pm Sun), with a lovely courtyard at the back, ideal for a picnic in the sun.

London Transport Museum MUSEUM
(Map p70; www.ltmuseum.co.uk; Covent Garden Piazza; adult/child £13.50/free; ⊙10am-6pm Sat-Thu, 11am-6pm Fri; ⊖Covent Garden) Kids and adults alike can tick off all manner of vehicles at this refurbished museum, from sedan chairs to train carriages, trams and taxis along with original advertising posters, photos and a fab shop for tube-map boxers shorts or a pair of 'Mind the Gap' socks.

Sir John Soane's Museum MUSEUM
(Map p70; www.soane.org; 13 Lincoln's Inn Fields; tours £5; ⊙10am-5pm Tue-Sat, 6-9pm 1st Tue of month; ⊖Holborn) One of the most atmospheric and intriguing of London's museums, this was the remarkable home of architect and collector extraordinaire Sir John Soane (1753–1837). Now a rewarding museum, the house has been left largely as it was when Sir John was taken out in a box. Among his eclectic acquisitions are an Egyptian sarcophagus, dozens of Greek and Roman antiquities and the original *Rake's Progress,* William Hogarth's set of caricatures telling the story of a late-18th-century London cad. Soane was clearly a bright spark – check out the ingenious folding walls in the picture gallery. Tours (£10) are held at 11am on Saturdays but bookmark the evening of the first Tuesday of each month when the house is candlelit and even more magical (queues are long). The museum is currently undergoing an ambitious expansion.

Somerset House GALLERIES
(Map p70; www.somersethouse.org.uk; Strand; ⊙7.30am-11pm; ⊖Temple) The first Somerset House was built for the Duke of Somerset, brother of Jane Seymour, in 1551. For two centuries it played host to royals (Elizabeth I once lived here), foreign diplomats, wild masked balls, peace treaties, the Parliamentary army (during the Civil War) and Oliver Cromwell's wake. Having fallen into disrepair, it was pulled down in 1775 and rebuilt in 1801 to designs by William Chambers. Among other weighty organisations, it went on to house the Royal Academy of the Arts, the Society of Antiquaries, the Navy Board and, that most popular of institutions, the Inland Revenue.

The tax collectors are still here, but that doesn't dissuade Londoners from attending open-air events in the grand central courtyard, such as films over 12 days in summer and ice skating in winter. The riverside terrace is a popular spot for caffeine with views of the Thames.

Near the Strand entrance, the Courtauld Gallery (Map p70; www.courtauld.ac.uk; adult/child £6/free, admission free 10am-2pm Mon; ⊙10am-6pm) displays a wealth of 14th- to 20th-century art, including a room of Rubens and works by van Gogh, Renoir and Cézanne. Downstairs, the Embankment Galleries are devoted to temporary exhibitions; prices and hours vary.

Handel House Museum MUSEUM
(Map p95; www.handelhouse.org; 25 Brook St; adult/child £5/2; ⊙10am-6pm Tue, Wed, Fri & Sat, 10am-8pm Thu, noon-6pm Sun; ⊖Bond St) George Frideric Handel's pad from 1723 until his death in 1759 is now a moderately interesting museum dedicated to his life. He wrote some of his greatest works here, including the *Messiah,* and music still fills the house during live recitals (see the website for details).

From songs of praise to *Purple Haze,* Jimi Hendrix lived next door at number 23 many years (and genres) later.

Burlington Arcade SHOPPING ARCADE
(Map p70; 51 Piccadilly; ⊖Green Park) The well-to-do Burlington Arcade, built in 1819, is famously patrolled by the Burlington Beadles, uniformed guards who constitute one of the world's smallest private police forces.

THE CITY
Packed with beguiling churches, intriguing architecture, hidden gardens and atmospheric

LOCAL KNOWLEDGE

ALAN KINGSHOTT: CHIEF YEOMAN WARDER AT THE TOWER

What is the best way to tackle the Tower? To understand the Tower's full history, I suggest visitors take a guided tour (in English) by a Yeoman Warder. With such a vast amount of history within the walls, you should allow at least three hours to fully enjoy your experience.

What of the Crown Jewels? The new presentation of the Crown Jewels is a must-see with a new layout, which will help visitors easily explore our sometimes complex history and ceremonies. Just ask a member of the Jewel House staff about any item: you will be amazed at their wealth of knowledge and it will enhance your visit.

How many Ravens are there in the Tower? We must have six ravens at the Tower at any one time by a Royal Decree put in place by Charles II. According to an old legend, should the birds leave, the Monarchy and the White Tower will crumble and fall. We tend not to provoke legends so generally we have eight birds.

Any ceremonies you can recommend? There are many ceremonies at the Tower of London, most of which can be viewed by visitors. However, many happen around royal events such as the Queen's Birthday and the State Opening of Parliament. Alternatively there is the Ceremony of the Keys (the locking up of the Tower of London), which takes place, as it has done for 700 years, at 9.30pm every night. (Note: attendance is free but requires that you apply by post at least two months in advance and supply a return-address envelope.)

lanes, you could spend weeks exploring the City of London, which, for most of its history, *was* London. Its boundaries have changed little since the Romans first founded their gated community here two millennia ago.

It's only in the last 250 years that the City has gone from being the very essence of London and its main population centre to just its central business district. But what a business district it is – despite the hammering its bankers have taken in recent years, the 'square mile' remains at the very heart of world capitalism.

Currently fewer than 10,000 people actually live here, although some 300,000 descend on it each weekday, when they generate almost three-quarters of Britain's entire GDP before squeezing back onto the tube. On Sundays the City becomes a virtual ghost town; it's a good time to poke around but come with a full stomach – most shops and eateries are closed.

Tower of London FORTRESS
(Map p78; ☎0844 482 7777; www.hrp.org.uk; Tower Hill; adult/child £20.90/10.45, audio guides £4/3; ⊙9am-5.30pm Tue-Sat, from 10am Sun & Mon, until 4.30pm Nov-Feb; ⊕Tower Hill) One of London's four World Heritage Sites (joining Westminster Abbey, Kew Gardens and Maritime Greenwich), the Tower offers a window on to a gruesome and quite compelling history.

In the 1070s, William the Conqueror started work on the White Tower to replace the castle he'd previously had built here. By 1285, two walls with towers and a moat were built around it and the defences have barely been altered since. A former royal residence, treasury, mint and arsenal, it became most famous as a prison when Henry VIII moved to Whitehall Palace in 1529 and started meting out his preferred brand of punishment.

The most striking building is the central White Tower, with its solid Romanesque architecture and four turrets. Today it houses a collection from the Royal Armouries, including Henry VIII's commodious suit of armour. On the 2nd floor is St John's Chapel, dating from 1080 and therefore the oldest church in London. To the north stands Waterloo Barracks, which now contains the spectacular and newly redisplayed Crown Jewels, including the platinum crown of the late Queen Mother, set with the 105-carat Koh-i-Noor (Mountain of Light) diamond and the Imperial State Crown. Slow-moving travelators shunt visitors past the collection. On the far side of the White Tower rises the Bloody Tower, where the 12-year-old Edward V and his little brother were held 'for their own safety' and later murdered, probably by their uncle, the future Richard III. Sir Walter Raleigh did a 13-year stretch here, when he wrote his *History of the World*.

Tower of London

TACKLING THE TOWER

Although it's usually less busy in the late afternoon, don't leave your assault on the Tower until too late in the day. You could easily spend hours here and not see it all. Start by getting your bearings with the hour-long Yeoman Warder (Beefeater) tours; they are included in the cost of admission, entertaining and the only way to access the **Chapel Royal of St Peter ad Vincula** , which is where they finish up.

When you leave the chapel, the **Tower Green scaffold site** is directly in front. The building immediately to your left is Waterloo Barracks, where the **Crown Jewels** are housed. These are the absolute highlight of a Tower visit, so keep an eye on the entrance and pick a time to visit when it looks relatively quiet. Once inside, take things at your own pace. Slow-moving travelators shunt you past the dozen or so crowns that are the treasury's centrepiece, but feel free to double-back for a second or even third pass – particularly if you ended up on the rear travelator the first time around. Allow plenty of time for the **White Tower** , the core of the whole complex, starting with the exhibition of royal armour. As you continue onto the 2nd floor, keep an eye out for **St John's Chapel** . The famous **ravens** can be seen in the courtyard around the White Tower. Head next through the towers that formed the **Medieval Palace** , then take the **East Wall Walk** to get a feel for the castle's mighty battlements. Spend the rest of your time poking around the many, many other fascinating nooks and crannies of the Tower complex.

BEAT THE QUEUES

» **Buy** your fast-track ticket in advance online or at the City of London Information Centre in St Paul's Churchyard.

» **Palacepalooza** An annual Historic Royal Palaces membership allows you to jump the queues and visit the Tower (and four other London palaces) as often as you like.

Chapel Royal of St Peter ad Vincula
This chapel serves as the resting place for the royals and other members of the aristocracy who were executed on the small green out front. Several notable identities are buried under the chapel's altar.

Tower Green scaffold site
Seven people, including three queens (Anne Boleyn, Catherine Howard and Jane Grey), lost their heads here during Tudor times, saving the monarch the embarrassment of public executions on Tower Hill. The site now features a sculpture by Brian Catling.

Beauchamp Tower

Main Entrance

Bell Tower

White Tower
Much of the White Tower is taken up with this exhibition of 500 years of royal armour. Look for the virtually cuboid suit made to match Henry VIII's bloated body, complete with an oversized armoured pouch to protect his, ahem, crown jewels.

St John's Chapel
Kept as plain and unadorned as it would have been in Norman times, the White Tower's 2nd-floor chapel is the oldest surviving church in London, dating from 1080.

Crown Jewels
When they're not being worn for affairs of state, Her Majesty's bling is kept here. Among the 23,578 gems, look out for the 530-carat Cullinan diamond at the top of the Royal Sceptre, the largest part of what was (until 1985) the largest diamond ever found.

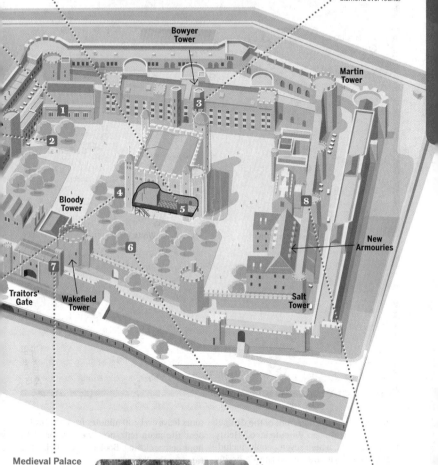

Bowyer Tower

Martin Tower

1

2

3

Bloody Tower

4

5

8

6

New Armouries

7

Traitors' Gate

Wakefield Tower

Salt Tower

Medieval Palace
This part of the Tower complex was commenced around 1220 and was home to England's medieval monarchs. Look for the recreations of the bedchamber of Edward I (1272–1307) in St Thomas' Tower and the throne room on the upper floor of the Wakefield Tower.

Ravens
This stretch of green is where the Tower's famous ravens are kept, fed on raw meat and blood-soaked bird biscuits. According to legend, if the birds were to leave the Tower, the kingdom would fall.

East Wall Walk
Follow the inner ramparts, starting from the 13th-century Salt Tower, passing through the Broad Arrow and Constable Towers, and ending at the Martin Tower, where the Crown Jewels were once stored.

The City

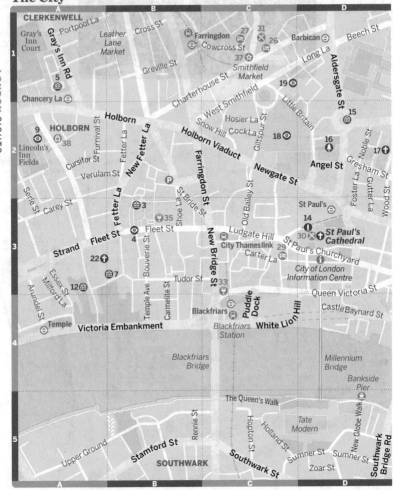

On the small green in front of the **Chapel Royal of St Peter ad Vincula** stood Henry VIII's **scaffold**, where seven people, including Anne Boleyn and her cousin Catherine Howard (Henry's second and fifth wives) were beheaded.

Look out for the latest in the Tower's long line of famous ravens, which legend says could cause the White Tower to collapse should they leave (their wings are clipped in case they get any ideas).

To get your bearings, take the hugely entertaining free guided tour with any of the Beefeaters (Yeoman Warders). Hour-long tours leave every 30 minutes from the bridge near the main entrance; the last tour's an hour before closing. Book online for cheaper rates for the Tower.

Tower Bridge   BRIDGE
(Map p78; ⊖Tower Hill) London was still a thriving port in 1894 when elegant Tower Bridge was built. Designed to be raised to allow ships to pass (it still lifts around 1000 times a year), electricity has now replaced the original steam power. A lift leads up from the northern tower to the **Tower Bridge Exhibition** (Map p78; www.towerbridge.org.uk;

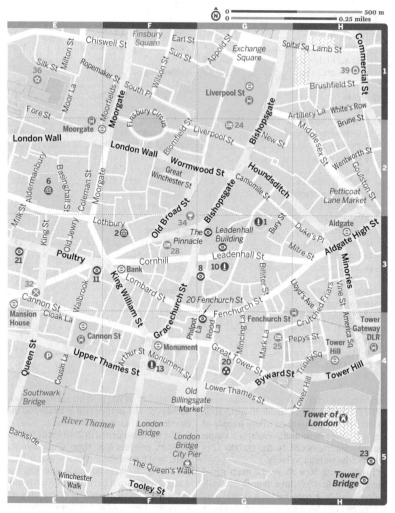

adult/child £7/3; ⊙10am-5.30pm Apr-Sep, 9.30am-5pm Oct-Mar; ⊜Tower Hill) 42m above the water, from where you can walk along the east- and west-facing walkways. The same ticket gets you into the engine rooms below the southern tower, for the real mechanical lowdown. Below the bridge on the City side is Dead Man's Hole, where corpses that had made their way into the Thames (through suicide, murder or accident) were regularly retrieved.

St Paul's Cathedral CHURCH
(Map p78; www.stpauls.co.uk; St Paul's Churchyard; adult/child £12.50/4.50; ⊙8.30am-4pm Mon-Sat;

⊜St Paul's) Dominating the City with one of the world's largest church domes (around 65,000 tons worth), St Paul's Cathedral was designed by Christopher Wren after the Great Fire and built between 1675 and 1710. The site is ancient hallowed ground with four other cathedrals preceding Wren's masterpiece here, the first dating from 604. As part of the 300th anniversary celebrations, St Paul's underwent a £40 million renovation project that gave the church a deep clean.

The dome is famed for sidestepping Luftwaffe incendiary bombs in the 'Second Great Fire of London' of December 1940,

The City

becoming an icon of dogged London resilience during the Blitz. Outside the cathedral, to the north, a **monument to the people of London** (Map p78; north of St Paul's) is a simple and elegant memorial to the 32,000 Londoners who weren't so lucky.

Inside, some 30m above the main paved area, is the first of three domes (actually a dome inside a cone inside a dome) supported by eight huge columns. The walkway around its base, 257 steps up a staircase on the western side of the southern transept, is called the **Whispering Gallery** because if you talk close to the wall, your words will carry to the opposite side 32m away. A further 119 steps brings you to the **Stone Gallery**, 152 iron steps above which is the **Golden Gallery** at the very top, which rewards you with unforgettable views of London.

The **Crypt** has memorials to up to 300 military demigods, including Wellington, Kitchener and Nelson, whose body lies below the dome. But the most poignant memorial is to Wren himself. On a simple slab bearing his name, a Latin inscription translates as: 'If you seek his memorial, look about you'. Also in the crypt is a cafe and the excellent **Restaurant at St Paul's**.

The **Oculus**, opened in 2010 in the former treasury, projects four short films onto its walls (you'll need the mp3 audiotour to hear the sound). If you're not up to climbing the dome, experience it here (in recorded form). Free mp3 audio tours lasting 45 minutes are available. Free guided tours leave the tour desk four times daily at 10.45am, 11.15am, 1.30pm and 2pm (90 minutes). Evensong takes place at 5pm (3.15pm on Sunday).

FREE **Museum of London**   MUSEUM
(Map p78; www.museumoflondon.org.uk; 150 London Wall; ⊘10am-6pm; ⊖Barbican) Catching this riveting museum early on in your stay helps peel back the layers of historical London for valuable perspectives on this great city. The first gallery, **London before London**, illustrates the settlements predating Roman era. The Roman section explores the ancient roots of the modern city as we know it while Saxon, medieval, Tudor and

Stuart London is intriguingly brought to life. The museum's new £20 million Galleries of Modern London encompases everything from 1666 (the devastating Great Fire of London) to the present day. While the Lord Mayor's ceremonial coach is the centrepiece, an effort has been made to create an immersive experience: you can enter reconstructions of an 18th-century debtors' prison, a Georgian pleasure garden and a Victorian street.

FREE Guildhall   HISTORIC BUILDING
(Map p78; ☏020-7606 3030; www.guildhall.cityof london.gov.uk; Gresham St; ⊙9am-5pm unless closed for events, closed Sun Oct-Apr; Clockmakers' Museum 9.30am-4.45pm Mon-Sat, Guildhall Art Gallery 10am-5pm Mon-Sat, noon-4pm Sun; ⊖Bank) Plumb in the middle of the 'square mile', the Guildhall has been the seat of the City's local government for eight centuries. The present building dates from the early 15th century.

Visitors can see the Great Hall, where the city's mayor is sworn in and where important fellows such as the Tsar of Russia and the Prince Regent celebrated beating Napoleon. It's an impressive space decorated with the shields and banners of London's 12 principal livery companies, carved galleries (the west of which is protected by disturbing statues of giants Gog and Magog) and a beautiful oak-panelled roof. There's also a lovely bronze statue of Churchill sitting in a comfy chair. Beneath it is London's largest medieval crypt (visit by free guided tour only, bookings essential), with 19 stained-glass windows displaying the livery companies' coats of arms.

The Clockmakers' Museum charts 500 years of horology with an intriguing collection of more than 700 clocks, including a decimal watch from 1852, with anti-clockwise-sweeping hands, and the Guildhall Art Gallery displays around 250 artworks. Included in the art gallery admission is entry to the remains of an ancient Roman amphitheatre, which lay forgotten beneath this site until 1988.

FREE Bank of England Museum   MUSEUM
(Map p78; www.bankofengland.co.uk/museum; Bartholomew Lane; ⊙10am-5pm Mon-Fri; ⊖Bank) Guardian of the country's current shaky financial system, the Bank of England was established in 1694 when the government needed to raise cash to support a war with France. It was moved here in 1734 and largely renovated by Sir John Soane. The surprisingly interesting museum traces the history of the bank and banking system. Audioguides are free and you even get to pick up (and leave behind) a £230,000 gold bar.

Monument   MONUMENT
(Map p78; www.themonument.info; Monument St; adult/child £3/1; ⊙9.30am-5.30pm; ⊖Monument) Designed by Wren to commemorate the Great Fire, the towering Monument is 60.6m high, the exact distance from its base to the bakery on Pudding Lane where the blaze began. Corkscrew your way up the 311 tight spiral steps (claustrophobes beware) for some of London's best wraparound views and twist down again to collect a certificate commemorating your climb.

Dr Johnson's House   MUSEUM
(Map p78; www.drjohnsonshouse.org; 17 Gough Sq; adult/child £4.50/1.50; ⊙11am-5pm Mon-Sat; ⊖Chancery Lane) The Georgian house where Samuel Johnson and his assistants compiled the first English dictionary (between 1748 and 1759) is full of prints and portraits of friends and intimates, including the good doctor's Jamaican servant to whom he bequeathed this grand residence.

Inns of Court   HISTORIC BUILDINGS
All London barristers work from within one of the four atmospheric Inns of Court, positioned between the walls of the old City and Westminster. It would take a lifetime working here to grasp all the intricacies of their arcane protocols, originating in the 13th century. It's best just to soak up the dreamy ambience of the alleys and open spaces and thank your lucky stars you're not one of the bewigged barristers scurrying about. A roll call of former members would include the likes of Oliver Cromwell, Charles Dickens, Mahatma Gandhi and Margaret Thatcher.

Lincoln's Inn (Map p78; www.lincolnsinn.org .uk; Lincoln's Inn Fields; ⊙grounds 9am-6pm Mon-Fri, chapel & gardens noon-2.30pm Mon-Fri; ⊖Holborn) still has some original 15th-century buildings. It's the oldest and most attractive of the bunch, with a 17th-century chapel and pretty landscaped gardens.

Gray's Inn (Map p78; www.graysinn.org.uk; Gray's Inn Rd; ⊙grounds 10am-4pm Mon-Fri; Chancery Lane) was largely rebuilt after the Luftwaffe levelled it.

Middle Temple (Map p78; www.middletemple .org.uk; Middle Temple Lane; ⊙10-11.30am & 3-4pm Mon-Fri; Temple) and Inner Temple (Map p78; www.innertemple.org.uk; King's Bench Walk;

⊙10am-4pm Mon-Fri; ⊜Temple) both sit between Fleet St and Victoria Embankment. The former is the best preserved, while the latter is home to the intriguing 12th-century Temple Church (Map p78; ☑020-7353 8559; www.templechurch.com; ⊙hours vary), built by the Knights Templar and featuring nine stone effigies of knights in its round chapel. Check the church's website or call ahead for opening hours.

Fleet St
FAMOUS THOROUGHFARE

(Map p78; ⊜Temple) As 20th-century London's 'Street of Shame', Fleet St was synonymous with the UK's scurrilous tabloids until the mid-1980s, when the press barons embraced computer technology, ditched a load of staff and largely relocated to the Docklands. It's named after the River Fleet, which it once crossed.

St Katharine Docks
HARBOUR

(⊜Tower Hill) A centre of trade and commerce for 1000 years, St Katharine Docks is now a buzzing waterside area of pleasure boats, shops and eateries. It was badly damaged during the war, but survivors include the popular Dickens Inn, with its original 18th-century timber framework, and Ivory House (built 1854) which used to store ivory, perfume and other precious goods.

SOUTH BANK

Londoners once crossed the river to the area controlled by the licentious Bishops of Southwark for all manner of bawdy frolicking frowned upon in the City. It's a much more seemly area now, but the frisson of theatre and entertainment remains. While South Bank only technically refers to the area of river bank between Westminster and Blackfriars Bridges (parts of which are actually on the east bank due to the way the river bends), we've used it as a convenient

ST DUNSTAN-IN-THE-EAST

For a lovely escape from the hurly-burly of the City's streets, track down this lovely bombed out church (Map p78; ⊙7am-dusk; ⊜Monument or Tower Hill) off St Dunstan's Hill, lovingly arranged with a garden and greenery. Overlooked by its surviving Wren-designed steeple, it's a sublime and tranquil spot for a breather.

catch-all for those parts of Southwark and Lambeth that sit closest to the river.

FREE Tate Modern
GALLERY

(Map p84; www.tate.org.uk; Queen's Walk; ⊙10am-6pm Sun-Thu, to 10pm Fri & Sat; ⊜Southwark) One of London's most popular attractions, this outstanding modern and contemporary art gallery is housed in the creatively revamped Bankside Power Station south of the Millennium Bridge. A spellbinding synthesis of funky modern art and capacious industrial brick design, the eye-catching result is one of London's must-see sights. Tate Modern has also been extraordinarily successful in bringing challenging work to the masses while a stunning extension is under construction, aiming for a 2016 completion date.

The multimedia guides (£3.50) are worthwhile and there are free 45-minute guided tours of the collection's highlights (Level 3 at 11am and midday; Level 5 at 2pm and 3pm). Note the late-night opening hours on Friday and Saturday.

Shakespeare's Globe
HISTORIC THEATRE

(Map p84; ☑020-7401 9919; www.shakespeares-globe.org; 21 New Globe Walk; adult/child £11/7; ⊙10am-5pm; ⊜London Bridge) Today's Londoners may flock to Amsterdam to misbehave but back in the bard's day they'd cross London Bridge to Southwark. Free from the city's constraints, men could settle down to a diet of whoring, bear-baiting and heckling of actors. The most famous theatre was the Globe, where a genius playwright was penning box-office hits such as *Macbeth* and *Hamlet*.

The original Globe – known as the 'Wooden O' after its circular shape and roofless centre – was erected in 1599. Rival to the Rose Theatre, all was well but did not end well when the Globe burned down within two hours during a performance in 1613 (a stage cannon ignited the thatched roof). A tiled replacement fell foul of the party-pooping Puritans in 1642, who saw the theatre as the devil's workshop, and it was dismantled two years later. Its present-day incarnation is the vision of American actor and director Sam Wanamaker, who sadly died before the opening night in 1997.

Admission includes the exhibition hall and guided tour (departing every 15 to 30 minutes) of the theatre, faithfully reconstructed from oak beams, handmade bricks, lime plaster and thatch. Tours shift to the nearby

LONDON'S NEW SKYSCRAPERS

A recent scramble for high-altitude, futuristic towers – given further lift by the Olympics – has shaken up the otherwise rather staid, low-lying London skyline. Most famous is The Shard, rising over London Bridge like a vast glass splinter. The City of London's tallest building, the straight-edged Heron Tower (100 Bishopsgate) was completed just up the road from 30 St Mary Axe (The Gherkin; Map p78; ☎7071 5008; www.30stmaryaxe.co.uk; St Mary Axe; ⊖Aldgate or Bank) (nicknamed the Gherkin) in 2011. Aiming for a 2014 completion date, the top-heavy 20 Fenchurch St (Walkie Talkie) will be topped with a vast sky garden boasting magnificent views over town. Further construction on the concrete stub of the radical looking Pinnacle (22-24 Bishopsgate) – nicknamed the Helter Skelter due to its cork-screwing top – was on hold at the the time of writing. The wedge-shaped 48-storey, 225m-high Leadenhall Building (nicknamed the Cheese Grater) is aiming for a 2014 completion date.

Rose Theatre instead when matinees are being staged in season.

Between April and October plays are performed, and while Shakespeare and his contemporaries dominate, modern plays are also occasionally staged (see the website for upcoming performances). As in Elizabethan times, seatless 'groundlings' can watch in all-weather conditions (£5; seats are £15 to £39) for the best views. There is no protection from the elements and you'll have to stand, but it's an unforgettable experience.

London Eye
VIEWS

(Map p84; ☎0871 781 3000; www.londoneye.com; adult/child £18/9.50; ⊙10am-8pm; ⊖Waterloo) This 135m-tall, slow-moving Ferris-wheel-like attraction is the tallest in the western hemisphere. Passengers ride in enclosed egg-shaped pods; the wheel takes 30 minutes to rotate completely, offering 25-mile views on clear days. Drawing 3.5 million visitors annually, at peak times (in July and August and school holidays), it can seem like they are all in the queue with you. Save money and shorten queues by buying tickets online, or cough up an extra £10 to show off your fast-track swagger. Alternatively, visit before 11am or after 3pm to avoid peak density. Add sparkle with priority boarding and a glass of champers (£35) and eyeball the huge choice of ticket combinations.

The Shard
LANDMARK

(Map p84; www.the-shard.com; 32 London Bridge St; ⊖London Bridge) Puncturing the skies above London, the dramatic splinter-like form of The Shard – the tallest building in Western Europe – has rapidly become an icon of the town. Approaching completion at the time of writing, the tower will boast the rooms-with-a-view, five-star Shangri-La Hotel, restaurants and a 360-degree viewing gallery in the clouds, accessible via high-speed lifts.

FREE Imperial War Museum
MUSEUM

(Map p84; www.iwm.org.uk; Lambeth Rd; ⊙10am-6pm; ⊖Lambeth North) Fronted by a pair of intimidating 15in naval guns that could lob a 1938lb shell more than 16 miles, this riveting museum is housed in what was once Bethlehem Royal Hospital, known as Bedlam. There's not just Lawrence of Arabia's 1000cc motorbike here, but a German V-2 rocket, a Sherman tank, a lifelike replica of Little Boy (the atom bomb dropped on Hiroshima), a P-51 Mustang, a Focke-Wulf Fw 190 and other classic fighter planes dangling from the ceiling plus a recreated WWI trench and WWII bomb shelter as well as a Holocaust exhibition.

Old Operating Theatre Museum & Herb Garret
MUSEUM

(Map p84; www.thegarret.org.uk; 9A St Thomas St; adult/child £5.80/3.25; ⊙10.30am-4.45pm; ⊖London Bridge) The highlight of this unique museum, 32 steps up the spiral stairway of the Tower of St Thomas Church (1703), focuses on the nastiness of 19th-century hospital treatment. A fiendish array of amputation knives presages the operating theatre, where doctors operated in rough-and-ready (pre-ether, pre-chloroform, pre-antiseptic) conditions. Contact the museum for details of their spooky Surgery by Gaslight evenings and other events. Also browse the natural remedies in the herb garret, including snail water for venereal disease and bladderwrack for goitre and tuberculosis.

South Bank

0 500 m
0 0.25 miles

River Thames

Victoria
Embankment
Gardens

Embankment
Pier

Festival
Pier

Waterloo
Bridge

Blackfriars
Bridge

Millennium
Pier

Bankside
Pier

London
Bridge
City Pier

Old Billingsgate
Market

Lower Thames St

Tower of
London

To Design
Museum
(500m)

William
Curtis
Park

City Hall

Tooley St

Druid St

Crucifix La

Tower Bridge Rd

Bermondsey St

Tanner St

BERMONDSEY

Abbey St

Bermondsey
Market

Grange Rd

Rothsay St

Law St

Great Dover St

Harper Rd

Newington Causeway

Elephant
& Castle

London Rd

Garden Row

Imperial
War Museum

St George's Rd

Lambeth Rd

Cosser St

LAMBETH

Kennington Rd

Archbishop's
Park

Lambeth Palace Rd

Carlisle La

Lower Marsh

Bayliss Rd

Baylis Rd

Westminster
Bridge

Westminster
Bridge Rd

York Rd

Addington St

London Eye

Hungerford
Bridge

Golden Jubilee
Bridge

Jubilee
Gardens

Millennium
Pier

Westminster
Pier

SOUTH
BANK

Waterloo

Waterloo Rd

Belvedere Rd

Tenison Way

Upper Ground

Stamford St

Coin St

Rennie
St

Paris Garden

Hatfields St

Duchy St

Theed St

Roupell St

Meymott St

Joan
St

The Cut

Mitre Rd

Coral St

Pearman St

Morley St

Waterloo Rd

Blackfriars Rd

Southwark St

Southwark
Bridge

Great Guildford St

New
Globe
Walk

Tate
Modern

Hopton St

Holland St

Sumner St

Park St

Bankside

Southwark
Bridge

London
Bridge

Stoney St

Bankside

Borough High St

Southwark Bridge Rd

Union St

Copperfield St

Great Suffolk St

Glasshill St

Webber St

Lancaster St

Surrey Row

Lant St

Redcross
Way

Ayres St

Borough

Swan St

Trinity St

Borough Rd

Waterloo Rd

Westminster Bridge Rd

Lambeth
North

SOUTHWARK

BOROUGH

Great Dover St

Tabard
St

Long La

Guy St

Weston St

Snowsfields

St Thomas St

Kipling St

Crosby
Row

Newcomen St

Railway App

The Queen's Walk

London Bridge

London
Bridge

1
2
3
4
5
6
7
8
9
10
11
12
13
14
15
16
17
18
19
20
21
22
23
24
25
26
27
28
29
30
31
32
33
34
35

South Bank

Southwark Cathedral　　CATHEDRAL
(Map p84; ☏020-7367 6700; Montague Close; suggested donation £4-6.50; ⊙8am-6pm Mon-Fri, 9am-6pm Sat & Sun, Evensong 5.30pm Tue, Thu & Fri, 4pm Sat, 3pm Sun; ⊖London Bridge) The earliest surviving chunks of this relatively small cathedral are the retrochoir at the eastern end, some ancient arcading by the southwest door, 12th-century wall cores in the north transept and an arch that dates to the original Norman church, although most of the cathedral is Victorian. In the south aisle of the nave, hunt down the green alabaster monument to William Shakespeare, next to which is a plaque to Sam Wanamaker (1919–93); nearby hangs a splendid icon of Jesus Christ illuminated by devotional candles. Do hunt down the exceedingly fine Elizabethan sideboard in the north transept.

City Hall　　LANDMARK
(Map p84; www.london.gov.uk; Queen's Walk; ⊙8.30am-6pm Mon-Fri; ⊖London Bridge) Home to the Mayor of London, bulbous City Hall was designed by Foster and Partners. The 45m, glass-clad building has been compared to a litany of surprising objects, from Darth Vader's helmet to a woodlouse and a 'glass gonad'. Visitors can view the mayor's meeting chamber and attend debates, while the scoop amphitheatre outside is the venue for a variety of free entertainment, from music to theatre in warmer weather.

Design Museum　　MUSEUM
(www.designmuseum.org; 28 Shad Thames; adult/child £8.50/5; ⊙10am-5.45pm; ⊖Tower Hill) Housed in a 1930s-era warehouse, the rectangular galleries here stage a revolving program of special exhibitions devoted to contemporary design, host the annual *Brit Insurance Design Awards* competition for design innovations, and display a permanent collection of modern British design. The museum is moving to a new site in the former Commonwealth Institute south of Holland Park in 2014.

HMS Belfast　　SHIP
(Map p84; http://hmsbelfast.iwm.org.uk; Queen's Walk; adult/child £13/free; ⊙10am-5pm; ⊖London Bridge) White ensign flapping on the

The River Thames

A FLOATING TOUR

London's history has always been determined by the Thames. The city was founded as a Roman port nearly 2000 years ago and over the centuries since then many of the capital's landmarks have lined the river's banks. A boat trip is a great way to experience the attractions.

There are piers dotted along both banks at regular intervals where you can hop on and hop off the regular services to visit places of interest. The best place to board is Westminster Pier, from where boats head downstream, taking you from the City of Westminster, the seat of government, to the original City of London, now the financial district and dominated by a growing band of skyscrapers. Across the river, the once shabby and neglected South Bank now bristles with as many top attractions as its northern counterpart.

In our illustration we've concentrated on the top highlights you'll enjoy at a fish's-eye

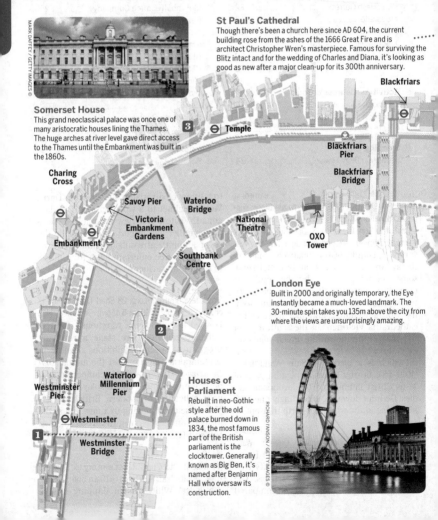

St Paul's Cathedral
Though there's been a church here since AD 604, the current building rose from the ashes of the 1666 Great Fire and is architect Christopher Wren's masterpiece. Famous for surviving the Blitz intact and for the wedding of Charles and Diana, it's looking as good as new after a major clean-up for its 300th anniversary.

Blackfriars

Somerset House
This grand neoclassical palace was once one of many aristocratic houses lining the Thames. The huge arches at river level gave direct access to the Thames until the Embankment was built in the 1860s.

Temple

Blackfriars Pier

Blackfriars Bridge

Charing Cross

Savoy Pier

Waterloo Bridge

Victoria Embankment Gardens

National Theatre

OXO Tower

Embankment

Southbank Centre

London Eye
Built in 2000 and originally temporary, the Eye instantly became a much-loved landmark. The 30-minute spin takes you 135m above the city from where the views are unsurprisingly amazing.

Waterloo Millennium Pier

Westminster Pier

Westminster

Houses of Parliament
Rebuilt in neo-Gothic style after the old palace burned down in 1834, the most famous part of the British parliament is the clocktower. Generally known as Big Ben, it's named after Benjamin Hall who oversaw its construction.

Westminster Bridge

view as you sail along. These are, from west to east, the **Houses of Parliament** 1, the **London Eye** 2, **Somerset House** 3, **St Paul's Cathedral** 4, **Tate Modern** 5, **Shakespeare's Globe** 6, the **Tower of London** 7 and **Tower Bridge** 8.

Apart from covering this central section of the river, boats can also be taken upstream as far as Kew Gardens and Hampton Court Palace, and downstream to Greenwich and the Thames Barrier.

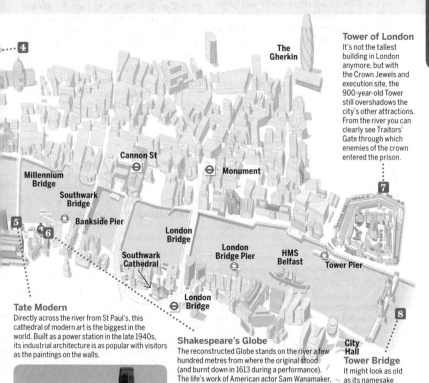

Tower of London
It's not the tallest building in London anymore, but with the Crown Jewels and execution site, the 900-year-old Tower still overshadows the city's other attractions. From the river you can clearly see Traitors' Gate through which enemies of the crown entered the prison.

Tate Modern
Directly across the river from St Paul's, this cathedral of modern art is the biggest in the world. Built as a power station in the late 1940s, its industrial architecture is as popular with visitors as the paintings on the walls.

Shakespeare's Globe
The reconstructed Globe stands on the river a few hundred metres from where the original stood (and burnt down in 1613 during a performance). The life's work of American actor Sam Wanamaker, the theatre runs a hugely popular season from April to October each year.

Tower Bridge
It might look as old as its namesake neighbour but one of the world's most iconic bridges was only completed in 1894. Not to be confused with London Bridge upstream, this one's famous raising bascules allowed tall ships to dock at the old wharves to the west and are still lifted up to 1000 times a year.

City Hall

DOUG MCKINLAY / GETTY IMAGES ©

DOUG MCKINLAY / GETTY IMAGES ©

Thames breeze, HMS *Belfast* is a magnet for naval-gazing kids. This large, light cruiser served in WWII, helping sink the German battleship *Scharnhorst* and shelling the Normandy coast on D-Day. Explore the nine decks and see the engine room, gun decks, galley, chapel, punishment cells, canteen and dental surgery. An audioguide is available.

Britain at War Experience   MUSEUM
(Map p84; www.britainatwar.co.uk; 64-66 Tooley St; adult/child £13/5.50; ⊙10am-5pm Apr-Oct, to 4.30pm Nov-Mar; ☻London Bridge) Here, you can pop down to the London Underground air-raid shelter, look at gas masks and ration books, stroll around Southwark during the Blitz and learn about the battle on the home front. It's crammed with fascinating WWII memorabilia.

London Dungeon   FRIGHT EXPERIENCE
(Map p84; ☎020-7403 7221; www.thedungeons.com; 28-34 Tooley St; adult/child £20/15; ⊙10.30am-5pm, extended hours during holidays; ☻London Bridge) Older kids love the London Dungeon, as the terrifying queues during school holidays and weekends attest. It's all spooky music, macabre hangman's drop-rides, fake blood and actors dressed up as torturers and gory criminals (including Jack the Ripper and Sweeney Todd). The best bits are the fairground-ride boat to Traitor's Gate, the Extremis Drop Ride to Doom and Vengeance – a spookily entertaining '5D laser ride'.

London Bridge Experience & London Tombs   FRIGHT EXPERIENCE
(Map p84; www.thelondonbridgeexperience.com; 2-4 Tooley St; adult/child £23/17; ⊙10am-5pm Mon-Fri, 10am-6pm Sat & Sun; ☻London Bridge) Another coronary-inducing attraction, similar to but not related to nearby London Dungeon. This one starts with the relatively tame London Bridge Experience, where actors bring to life the bridge's history with the assistance of plenty of severed heads. Once the entertaining educational bit is out the way, the London Tombs turns up the terror. Adding to the general creepiness is the knowledge that these were once plague pits and therefore actual tombs. The experience takes about 45 minutes, with the tombs an optional additional 25 minutes. It's all great, occasionally heart-in-the-mouth entertainment and you save up to 50% by buying online.

Sea Life   AQUARIUM
(Map p84; ☎0871 663 1678; www.sealife.co.uk/london; County Hall; adult/child £18/13; ⊙10am-6pm; ☻Waterloo) Within imposing County Hall, this is one of the largest aquariums in Europe, with all sorts of aquatic (many endangered) creatures from the briny deep grouped into different zones (coral cave, rainforest, River Thames), culminating with the shark walkway. Check the website for shark-feeding times and book online for a 10% discount.

Hayward Gallery   ART MUSEUM
(Map p84; www.southbankcentre.co.uk; Belvedere Rd; ⊙10am-6pm Sat-Thu, to 10pm Fri; ☻Waterloo) The 1968 Brutalist architecture is as opinion-dividing as you can get but the popular international contemporary art shows held here constitute a further rich seam of culture in the Southbank Centre. Facilities include the upstairs Waterloo Sunset Pavilion, a Dan Graham–designed 'drop-in centre for children and old people and a space for viewing cartoons' with onto London's Brutalist horizons.

PIMLICO

The origins of its name highly obscure, Pimlico is a grand part of London, bordered by the Thames but lacking a strong sense of neighbourhood and becoming prettier the further you stray from Victoria station.

FREE **Tate Britain**   ART MUSEUM
(www.tate.org.uk; Millbank; ⊙10am-5.40pm; ☻Pimlico) The more elderly and venerable of the two Tate siblings, this riverside Portland stone edifice celebrates paintings from 1500 to the present, with works from Blake, Hogarth, Gainsborough, Barbara Hepworth, Whistler, Constable and Turner – in particular – whose light-infused visions dominate the Clore Gallery. It doesn't stop there and vibrant modern and contemporary art finds expression in pieces from Lucian Freud, Francis Bacon and Tracey Emin while the controversial Turner Prize (inviting annual protests outside the gallery) is held here every year between October and January. Free one-hour thematic tours are held at 11am, noon, 2pm and 3pm from Monday to Friday (noon and 3pm on Saturday and Sunday) are eye-opening but don't overlook Late at Tate night (first Friday of the month), when the gallery stays open till 10pm.

TATE MODERN HIGHLIGHTS

More than 40 million eager art-goers poured through Tate Modern (p82) in its first decade since opening, making it one of the most-visited of London's sights. The ambitiously run exhibition space is getting even bigger with the recent conversion of two of the former power station's underground oil tanks, while a funky 11-storey extension is slated for a 2016 opening date.

Before tackling Tate Modern, note that special exhibitions are held in levels 2 and 4. Free 45-minute guided highlights tours run on Level 3 (11am and noon) and Level 5 (2pm and 3pm) – no booking is required. Handy multimedia guides are also available. Don't forget that Tate Modern is open till 10pm on Friday and Saturday, so you can make an evening of it.

The collection is in perpetual rotation so while the essential themes of the various galleries remain constant, the paintings and art works that represent each concept may vary.

A major highlight of Tate Modern is the architecture and its splendid conversion into a space housing and displaying art. The 4.2 million bricks of the Sir Gilbert Scott–designed Bankside Power Station – generating its last watt in 1981 when rising oil prices finally switched off its turbines – were ambitiously transformed into this modern and contemporary art gallery in 2000.

You can't exactly miss the cavernous 3300-sq-m Turbine Hall, but try to join everyone else streaming down the ramp from Holland St to maximise its impact. Originally housing the power station's colossal turbines, the hall is the jaw-dropping venue for large-scale, temporary exhibitions from October to April. Past exhibits have included Doris Salcedo's dramatic *Shibboleth* fissure cracking the floor and Ai Weiwei's thoughtful and compelling *Sunflower Seeds* – a huge carpet of hand-painted, ceramic seeds.

To give a sense of continuity to the displays, the permanent collection is grouped thematically on levels 3 and 5. For surrealist creations from the lucid minds of Paul Delvaux, Yves Tanguy, Max Ernst and other artists, immerse yourself in Poetry and Dream on Level 3. Also on Level 3, Material Gestures focuses on European and American painting and sculpture of the 1940s and 1950s, including abstract expressionism and embracing works by Barnett Newman, Victor Pasmore, Alberto Giacometti, Mark Rothko and other artists.

The dramatic pairing of Italian futurist Umberto Boccioni's *Unique Forms of Continuity in Space* and Roy Lichtenstein's pop icon *Whaam!* kicks off States of Flux on Level 5. These two pieces are separated by half a century, divided by two World Wars, a Cold War and the arrival of the nuclear age, but both share a common dynamism and iconic power. The gallery proceeds to explore the signature avant-garde art movements of the 20th century, including cubism, futurism, vorticism and pop art, featuring works from Picasso, Georges Braque, Wassily Kandinsky, Piet Mondrian, Juan Gris, Gino Severini and others. Also on Level 5, Energy and Process takes Art Povera, the revolutionary art of the 1960s, as its focus.

After you have had your fill of modern art, cap your visit with a trip to the restaurant and bar on Level 7 for sublime views of St Paul's and the River Thames. A popular cafe can be found on Level 2.

CHELSEA & KENSINGTON

Known as the royal borough, Chelsea and Kensington lays claim to the highest income earners in the UK (shops and restaurants will presume you are among them). Kensington High St has a lively mix of chains and boutiques while even the charity shops along King's Rd resemble fashion outlets. If the sun obliges, lie supine on the grass in splendid Hyde Park but don't forget that some of London's most beautiful and fascinating museums, clustered together in South Kensington, are must-sees come rain or shine.

FREE Victoria & Albert Museum   MUSEUM
(V&A; Map p92; www.vam.ac.uk; Cromwell Rd; ⊙10am-5.45pm Sat-Thu, to 10pm Fri; ⊖South Kensington) This outstanding museum boasts an unparalleled collection specialising in decorative art and design with some 4.5

ℹ️ LONDON'S TOP VIEWPOINTS

Not a predominantly flat city as is Bĕijīng, for example, London has a host of natural high points and hills yielding long and spectacular views over town. Throw in panoramas from architectural and skyscraping elevations and you've more than enough choice for the wide-angle perspective on London.

London Eye (p83) Does what it says on the packet, but brace for queues.

The Shard (p83) Superb views of London in all directions from the high-altitude viewing platform.

Monument (p81) Wraparound views of London reward climbs to the top.

St Paul's Cathedral (p79) Clamber up to the top of the dome for some divine views.

Parliament Hill (p107) Choose a sunny day, pack a picnic and enjoy the view from this Hampstead Heath highpoint.

Greenwich Park (📞8858 2608; www .royalparks.gov.uk; King George St; ⊘dawn-dusk, cars from 7am; ℝGreenwich or Maze Hill, DLR Cutty Sark) The views from the Royal Observatory are some of London's most supreme.

million objects from Britain and around the globe. The museum setting and gorgeous architecture is as inspiring as the sheer diversity and rarity of its exhibits. Part of Albert's legacy to Londoners in the wake of the Great Exhibition of 1851, the museum is a bit like the nation's attic, spread generously through nearly 150 galleries. Highlights of the world's greatest collection of decorative arts include the **Ardabil Carpet** (Room 42, Level 1), the sumptuous **China Collection** and **Japan Gallery** (Rooms 44 and 47e, Level 1), **Tipu's Tiger** (Room 41, Level 1) the astonishing **Cast Courts** (Room 46a, Level 1), the **Raphael Cartoons** (Rooms 48a, Level 1), the hefty **Great Bed of Ware** (Room 57, Level 2) and the stunning **Jewellery Gallery** (Rooms 91-93, Level 3). You'll need to plan as the museum is epic, but it's open late on Friday evenings, for less crowds. For food and drink, make for the V&A Cafe in the magnificent Refreshment Rooms, dating from the 1860s, or the garden cafe in the John Madesjki Garden in summer.

FREE Natural History Museum   MUSEUM
(Map p92; www.nhm.ac.uk; Cromwell Rd; ⊘10am-5.50pm; ⊜South Kensington) This ornate building itself is one of London's finest and a work of art: pale blue and honey-coloured stone, broken by Venetian arches decorated with all manner of carved critters.

A sure-fire hit with kids of all ages, this splendid museum is crammed with fascinating discoveries, starting with the giant **Diplodocus** skeleton that greets you in the main hall. In the **dinosaur gallery**, the fleshless fossils are brought to robotic life with the roaring 4m-high animatronic **Tyrannosaurus Rex**.

The other galleries are equally impressive. An escalator slithers up and into a hollowed-out globe where two exhibits – The Power Within and Restless Surface – explain how wind, water, ice, gravity and life itself impact on the earth. The **mock-up of the Kobe earthquake** is a bone-rattling lesson in plate tectonics.

The **Darwin Centre** houses a team of biologists and a staggering 20-million-plus animal and plant specimens. Take a lift to the top of the Cocoon, a seven-storey egg-shaped structure encased within a glass pavilion, and make your way down through the floors of interactive displays. Glass windows allow you to watch the scientists at work.

Finally, don't overlook **Sensational Butterflies** by the East Lawn and the charming **Wildlife Garden**, a slice of English countryside in SW7.

FREE Science Museum   MUSEUM
(Map p92; www.sciencemuseum.org.uk; Exhibition Rd; ⊘10am-6pm; ⊜South Kensington) With seven floors of interactive and educational exhibits, this scientifically spellbinding museum will mesmerise even the most precocious of young Einsteins. Some children head straight for voice warpers, lava lamps, boomerangs, bouncy globes and alien babies in the ground-floor shop, and stay put. Highlights include the **Energy Hall** on the ground floor, the riveting **Flight Gallery** on the 3rd floor and the **flight simulator**. There's also a 450-seat **Imax cinema**. If you've kids under the age of five, pop down to the basement for **The Garden**, where there's a fun-filled play zone, including a water-play area, besieged by tots in red waterproof smocks.

Hyde Park
PARK

(Map p92; ☉5.30am-midnight; ⊖Marble Arch, Hyde Park Corner or Queensway) At 145 hectares, Hyde Park is central London's largest open space. Henry VIII expropriated it from the Church in 1536, when it became a hunting ground and later a venue for duels, executions and horse racing. The 1851 Great Exhibition was held here, and during WWII the park became an enormous potato field. These days, it serves as an occasional concert venue and a full-time green space for fun and frolics. There's boating on the Serpentine for the energetic, while Speakers' Corner (Map p92; Park Lane; ⊖Marble Arch) is for oratorical acrobats on Sundays, maintaining a tradition begun in 1872 as a response to rioting. Just north of here, Marble Arch (Map p95; ⊖Marble Arch) was designed by John Nash in 1828 as the entrance to Buckingham Palace and moved here in 1851; it once served as a police lookout. The infamous Tyburn Tree, a three-legged gallows, once stood nearby. It is estimated that up to 50,000 people were executed here between 1196 and 1783.

Kensington Palace
PALACE

(Map p118; www.hrp.org.uk/kensingtonpalace; Kensington Gardens; adult/child £14.50/free; ☉10am-6pm; ⊖High St Kensington) Kensington Palace (1605) became the favourite royal residence under the joint reign of William and Mary and remained so until the death of George II (in 1762 George III bought Buckingham Palace for his wife, Charlotte). It still contains private apartments where various members of the royal extended family live. In popular imagination it's most associated with three intriguing princesses: Victoria (who was born here in 1819 and lived here with her domineering mother until her accession to the throne), Margaret (sister of the current queen, who lived here until her 2002 death) and, of course, Diana. The building underwent magnificent restoration work totalling £12 million and reopened in early 2012.

Kensington Gardens
PARK

(Map p118; ☉dawn-dusk; ⊖High St Kensington) Blending in with Hyde Park, these royal gardens are part of Kensington Palace and hence popularly associated with Princess Diana. Diana devotees can visit the Diana, Princess of Wales Memorial Fountain (Kensington Gardens; Knightsbridge), a soothing structure fashioned from 545 pieces of Cornish granite, channeling a circular stream drawn from chalk aquifers more than 100m underground which cascades gently and flows together in a pool at the bottom; paddling is encouraged. The astonishing Albert Memorial (Map p92; ☑7495 0916; 45min tours adult/concession £6/5; ☉tours 2pm & 3pm 1st Sun of the month Mar-Dec; ⊖Knightsbridge or Gloucester Rd) is a unique chunk of Victorian bombast, a lavish marble, mosaic and gold affair opposite the Royal Albert Hall, built to honour Queen Victoria's husband, Albert (1819–61).

The gardens also house the Serpentine Gallery (Map p92; www.serpentinegallery.org; admission free; ☉10am-6pm), one of London's edgiest contemporary art spaces; the recently opened Serpentine Sackler Gallery (Map p92; The Ring) is on the far side of the Serpentine Bridge, in the former Magazine. The Sunken Garden, near the palace, is at its prettiest in summer, while tea in the Orangery (Map p118; www.hrp.org.uk; Kensington Palace, Kensington Gardens; mains £9.50-14; ☉10am-6pm Mar-Sep, to 5pm Oct-Feb; ⊖Queensway, Notting Hill Gate or High St Kensington) is a treat any time of the year.

King's Road
STREET

(⊖Sloane Square) Named after King Charles II who would return to Hampton Court Palace along a farmer's track here after amorous interludes with Nell Gwyn, this street was almost synonymous with London fashion during the '60s and '70s. The road and surrounding streets are excellent for retail therapy and look-ins on some of the city's best-dressed neighbourhoods. Near the Sloane Sq end, the Saatchi Gallery (Map p92; www.saatchi-gallery.co.uk; Duke of York's HQ, King's Rd; ☉10am-6pm) serves up stimulating temporary exhibitions of contemporary art.

TATE-A-TATE

Whisking art lovers between London's Tate galleries, the colourful Tate Boat (Map p84; www.thamesclippers.com) stop en route at the London Eye. Services from Bankside Pier run from 9.57am to 4.44pm daily at 40-minute intervals (10.20am to 4.27pm from Millbank Pier). One-way tickets are £5.50 (children £2.80), with discounts available for Travelcard holders.

Knightsbridge, South Kensington & Chelsea

N
0   500 m
0   0.25 miles

G1

MAYFAIR

Charles St
Hay's Mews
Farm St
Hill St
Mount Row
Grosvenor Sq
Adam's Row
Mount St
Aldford St
South St
Culross St
Upper Grosvenor St
Grosvenor St
Woods Mews

To Marble Arch (150m)

Park La

Park La
Deanery St

Curzon Sq
Curzon St
Market Mews
Shepherd St
Hertford St
Brick St

21 ✕ G

25 ✕

Green Park

Piccadilly

Memorial Gates ● 1

Buckingham Palace Gardens

Grosvenor Pl
Chapel St
Chester St

Halkin St

Hyde Park Corner ✪

Belgrave Square

Knightsbridge
18 ✕

Kinnerton St

Motcomb St

20 ✕

Lowndes St

Serpentine Rd

South Carriage Dr

Knightsbridge
15 ✕
30 ✪
✪ Knightsbridge

Sloane St
Basil St

11 🏨

Brompton Rd
29

● 6 E

Park La

● 1
Hyde Park

North Ride

The Serpentine

Rotten Row

Knightsbridge

KNIGHTSBRIDGE

Montpelier St

Rutland Gate

Ennismore Gdns

Kensington Rd

Bayswater Rd

Lancaster Gate ✪

To easyHotel (Paddington) (350m)

To Paddington Train Station (300m)

Lancaster Gate

Bayswater Rd

Leinster Tce
Porchester Tce

Buck Hill Walk

5 🏛

The Ring

Diana, Princess of Wales Memorial Fountain

The Long Water

Kensington Gardens

Lancaster Walk

Budge's Walk

Round Pond

4 🏛

Albert Memorial ●

Kensington Gore

26 ●

Prince Consort Rd

9 🏨

Exhibition Rd

Kensington Rd

The Flower Walk

Kensington Rd

Palace Gate

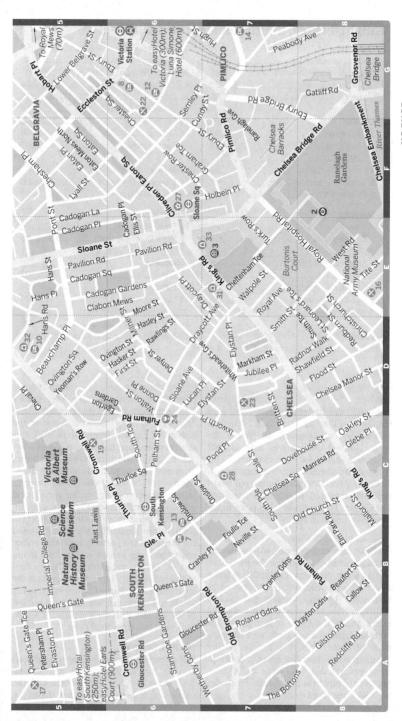

Knightsbridge, South Kensington & Chelsea

FREE **Royal Hospital
Chelsea** HISTORIC BUILDINGS
(Map p92; www.chelsea-pensioners.co.uk; Royal
Hospital Rd; ⊗10am-noon Mon-Sat & 2-4pm daily;
⊖Sloane Square) Designed by Wren, the
Royal Hospital Chelsea was built in 1692
to provide shelter for ex-servicemen. Today
it houses hundreds of war veterans known
as Chelsea Pensioners, charming old chaps
generally regarded as national treasures.
The Chelsea Flower Show takes place in the
hospital grounds in May.

Chelsea Physic Garden GARDEN
(www.chelseaphysicgarden.co.uk; 66 Royal Hospital
Rd; adult/child £8/5; ⊗noon-5pm Tue-Fri, to 10pm
Wed Jul & Aug, noon-6pm Sun Apr-Oct; ⊖Sloane
Square) This gorgeous botanical enclave was
established by the Apothecaries' Society
in 1676 for students working on medicinal
plants and healing. One of Europe's oldest
of its kind, the small grounds are a compen-
dium of botany from carnivorous pitcher
plants to rich yellow flag irises, a cork oak
from Portugal, delightful ferns and a treasure trove of rare trees and shrubs. Free tours
are held three times daily.

FREE **Fulham Palace** HISTORIC BUILDING
(www.fulhampalace.org; Bishop's Ave; ⊗palace
& museum 1-4pm Sat-Wed, gardens dawn to dusk
daily; ⊖Putney Bridge) Summer home of the
bishops of London from 704 to 1975, this
genteel palace near the Thames has an adorable courtyard which draws watercolourists
on sunny days, a splendid cafe in the drawing room at the rear (looking out on a magnificent lawn), a pretty walled garden and
a Tudor Revival chapel. There's also an informative museum and historical tours (£5)
several times a month, while hiking around
the extensive and partially excavated palace
moat (once the longest in England) is enjoyable. Events and garden walks are held
at the palace and films are screened on the
lawn in summer. Putney Bridge is just to the
south, where you can link up with a section
of the Thames Path for the pleasant 4-mile
walk west to Barnes footbridge.

MARYLEBONE

Not as exclusive as its southern neighbour
Mayfair, hip Marylebone has one of London's most pleasant high streets and the
famous, if rather disappointing, Baker St,

immortalised in the hit song by Gerry Raffer-ty and strongly associated with Victoria-era sleuth Sherlock Holmes (there's a museum and gift shop at his fictional address, 221b).

Regent's Park PARK
(◉Regent's Park) A former royal hunting ground, Regent's Park was designed by John Nash early in the 19th century, although what was actually laid out is only a frac-tion of the celebrated architect's grand plan. Nevertheless, it's one of London's most lovely open spaces – at once serene and lively, cos-mopolitan and local – with football pitches,

tennis courts, a boating lake, London Zoo, and Regent's canal along its northern side. **Queen Mary's Gardens**, towards the south of the park, are particularly pretty, with spectacular roses in summer. **Open Air Theatre** (☑0844 826 4242; www.openairtheatre .org) hosts performances of Shakespeare and other classics here on summer evenings, along with comedy and concerts.

London Zoo ZOO
(www.londonzoo.co.uk; Outer Circle, Regent's Park; adult/child £18/14; ◉10am-5.30pm Mar-Oct, to 4pm Nov-Feb; ◉Camden Town) These famous

Marylebone

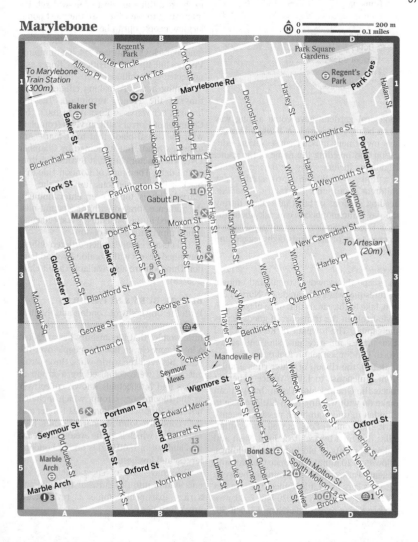

Marylebone

zoological gardens have come a long way since being established in 1828, with massive investment making conservation, education and breeding the name of the game. Highlights include Penguin Beach, Gorilla Kingdom, Animal Adventure (the new childrens' zoo) and Butterfly Paradise. Feeding sessions or talks take place during the day. Arachnophobes can ask about the zoo's Friendly Spider Programme, designed to cure fears of all things eight-legged and hairy.

Regent's Canal CANAL

To escape the crowded streets and enjoy a picturesque, waterside angle on North London, take to the canals that once played such a vital role in the transport of goods across the capital. The towpath of Regent's Canal also makes an excellent shortcut across North London, either on foot or by bike.

In full, the ribbon of water runs 9 miles from Limehouse to Little Venice (where it meets the Grand Union Canal) but you can make do with walking from Little Venice to Camden in under an hour, passing Regent's Park and London Zoo, as well as beautiful villas designed by architect John Nash and redevelopments of old industrial buildings. Allow 15 to 20 minutes between Camden and Regent's Park, and 25 to 30 minutes between Regent's Park and Little Venice. The London Waterbus Company (☏020-7482 2660; www.londonwaterbus.com; single/return £7.20/10.30)

and Jason's Trip (www.jasons.co.uk; opposite 42 Blomfield Rd; single/return £8/9) run canal boats between Camden Lock and Little Venice.

Madame Tussauds WAXWORKS
(Map p95; ☏0870 400 3000; www.madame-tussauds.co.uk; Marylebone Rd; adult/child £26/22; ⏰9.30am-5.30pm; ⦿Baker Street) Tickets may cost a (wax) arm and a (wax) leg and the crowds can be as awesome as the exhibits, but the opportunity to pose beside Posh and Becks has clear-cut kudos. Most of the life-size wax figures – such as Leonardo Di Caprio – are fantastically lifelike and as close to the real thing as most of us will get. It's interesting to see which are the most popular; few people opt to be snapped with Mohamed Al-Fayed, but queues for the Queen (and Barack Obama) can get leg-numbing. Visitors line up to give Hitler the finger as a neglected Churchill looks on.

Honing her craft making effigies of victims of the French revolution, Tussaud brought her wares to England in 1802. Her Chamber of Horrors still survives (complete with the actual blade that took Marie Antoinette's head), but it's joined by Chamber Live, where actors lunge at terrified visitors in the dark. The Spirit of London ride in a black cab is tremendous fun and the 4-D Marvel film is top-drawer entertainment, the audience sprayed with air jets and mist and jabbed in the back during a spectacular action film centred on London.

Tickets are cheaper when ordered online; combined tickets with London Eye and London Dungeon are also available (adult/child £65/48).

BLOOMSBURY & ST PANCRAS

With the University of London and the British Museum within its genteel environs, it's little wonder that Bloomsbury has attracted a lot of very clever, bookish people over the years. Between the world wars, these pleasant streets were colonised by a group of artists and intellectuals known collectively as the Bloomsbury Group, which included novelists Virginia Woolf and EM Forster and the economist John Maynard Keynes. Russell Square, which is at the area's very heart, was laid out in 1800 and is one of London's largest and loveliest.

The conversion of spectacular St Pancras station into the Eurostar terminal and a ritzy apartment complex is reviving the area's fortunes.

TREASURES OF THE BRITISH MUSEUM

The British Museum (p97) is colossal, so it pays to make a judicious selection of the collection's star highlights instead of being laid low by the demands of exploration. Consider joining one of the free Eye Opener tours of individual galleries or 'spotlight' highlight tours, which target individual pieces for a summary lowdown. Don't overlook the big-ticket exhibitions which regularly pitch up (some of which will in future be displayed in the World Conservation and Exhibitions Centre under construction in the northwest corner, due to open in 2014), for which you may need to book tickets in advance.

Covered with a magnificent, Norman Foster–designed glass-and-steel roof, the Queen Elizabeth II Great Court is the largest covered public square in Europe. It surrounds the famous Reading Room, where users have included Karl Marx, Lenin, Mahatma Gandhi and Bram Stoker (although not simultaneously).

A broken chunk of a larger granite slab found near the village of Rosetta in Egypt, the Rosetta Stone in Room 4 on the ground floor west of the Reading Room proved invaluable as the key to deciphering Egyptian hieroglyphics.

Not far away, the Parthenon Sculptures (also known as the Elgin Marbles) can be admired in the Ancient Greece gallery (Room 18). The sculptures once decorated the outside of the Parthenon, a temple dedicated to Athena, with events from Greek mythology and a frieze portraying a sacred procession.

Also on the ground floor, the Feather bonnet of Yellow Calf is a tremendous headdress from the North America Gallery (Room 26). Next door in the Mexico Gallery (Room 27), the Mosaic Mask of Tezcatlipoca (Skull of the Smoking Mirror) – a human skull decorated with bands of turquoise mosaic and black lignite – is an astonishing sight, believed to represent a creator deity. The oldest room in the museum, the 1820 King's Library is a marvellous neoclassical space, retracing how such disciplines as biology, archaeology, linguistics and geography emerged during the 18th century Enlightenment.

On the upper floor, the artefacts from the Sutton Hoo Ship-Burial (see p; Room 41) constitute a highly significant Anglo-Saxon hoard from a burial site in Suffolk dating from the 7th century, excavated in 1938. Objects from the largest of the grassy mounds in Suffolk include coins and the highly elaborate and well-known helmet, complete with face mask, eye sockets and eyebrows inlaid with silver wire and garnets; the helmet was painstakingly rebuilt from hundreds of damaged fragments.

The leathery remains of the Lindow Man (Room 50) – a 1st-century man aged around 25 at the time of his violent death – were astonishingly well-preserved in a peat bog near Manchester and dug up in the 1980s. The beautiful Oxus chariot model and gold figurines in the Ancient Iran Gallery (Room 52) are glittering highlights of the Oxus Treasure, a glorious collection of metalwork from the ancient Persian capital of Persepolis. The artefacts from the Royal Tombs of Ur (from modern-day Iraq) are nearby in room 56.

On the upper floor, the Mummy of Katebet from Thebes is a tremendous highlight of the Egyptian Death and Afterlife Gallery (Room 63), with its splendidly painted mummy mask. During her lifetime, the mummified woman was an elderly Chantress of Amun (a performer for temple rituals).

When museum fever strikes you down, pop across the way to the lovely Museum Tavern (49 Great Russell St) where Karl Marx used to polish off a drink or two after a hard day's graft in the Reading Room of the British Library.

FREE British Museum   MUSEUM
(Map p70; ☏020-7323 8000; www.britishmuseum.org; Great Russell St; ☺10am-5.30pm Sat-Wed, to 8.30pm Thu & Fri; ⊖Russell Square) The country's largest museum and one of the oldest and finest in the world, this famous museum boasts vast Egyptian, Etruscan, Greek,

Roman, European and Middle Eastern galleries, among many others.

Begun in 1753 with a 'cabinet of curiosities' bequeathed by Sir Hans Sloane to the nation on his death, the collection mushroomed over the ensuing years partly through plundering the empire. The grand

Right Royal Britain

Royalty has long been a British institution, with dynasties of Scottish kings, Welsh princes and, of course, the English monarchs that dominated the scene for centuries. Queen Elizabeth II celebrated 60 years of rule in 2012, and the public displays of loyalty and affection show the institution is still going strong.

Hampton Court Palace

1 Hampton Court Palace (p108) was used by King Henry VIII – he of the famous six wives – as a retreat from the affairs of state (but not the affairs of the heart). Today, it's Britain's grandest Tudor structure, and you can still relax in the extensive gardens, but don't get lost in the 300-year-old maze.

1. Hampton Court Palace (p108) **2.** Changing of the guard, Buckingham Palace (p65) **3.** Balmoral Castle (p879)

Buckingham Palace

2 Buckingham Palace (p65) has been the monarch's residence in London since 1837. If the Queen is at home, the 'royal standard' flag flies on the roof. If she's away, you can take a tour inside. Either way, don't miss the parade of soldiers at the famous Changing of the Guard.

Balmoral Castle

3 Deep in the Highlands of Scotland, Balmoral Castle (p879) is the Queen's holiday home. Built for Queen Victoria in 1855 as a private residence for the royal family, it popularised the style of architecture known as Scottish Baronial – slender towers, conical-topped turrets, stepped gables, narrow windows, fake battlements and heraldic symbols – that characterises so many of Scotland's 19th-century country houses.

Tower of London

4 The Tower of London (p75) is a world-famous monument with a 1000-year-old history. Over the centuries it's been a royal residence, treasury, mint, prison and arsenal. Today it's home to the spectacular Crown Jewels, as well as red-coated Beefeaters and ravens with mythical power.

North Central London

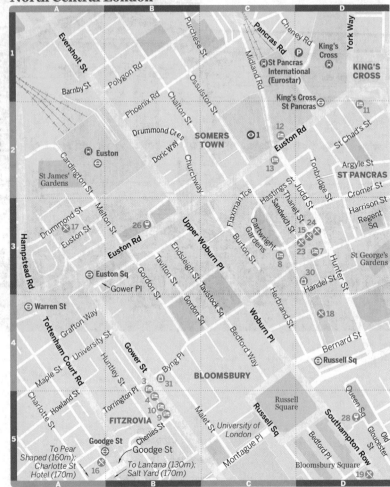

Enlightenment Gallery was the first section of the redesigned museum to be built (in 1820).

Among the must-sees are the **Rosetta Stone**, the key to deciphering Egyptian hieroglyphics, discovered in 1799; the controversial **Parthenon Sculptures**, stripped from the walls of the Parthenon in Athens by Lord Elgin (the British ambassador to the Ottoman Empire), and which Greece wants returned; the stunning **Oxus Treasure** of 7th- to 4th-century-BC Persian gold; and the Anglo-Saxon **Sutton Hoo** burial relics.

The **Great Court** was restored and augmented by Norman Foster in 2000 and now has a spectacular glass-and-steel roof, making it one of the most impressive architectural spaces in the capital. In the centre is the **Reading Room**, with its stunning blue-and-gold domed ceiling, where Karl Marx wrote the *Manifesto of the Communist Party*.

You'll need multiple visits to savour even the highlights here; happily there are 15 half-hour free 'Eye Opener' tours between 11am and 3.45pm daily, focussing on different parts of the collection. Other tours

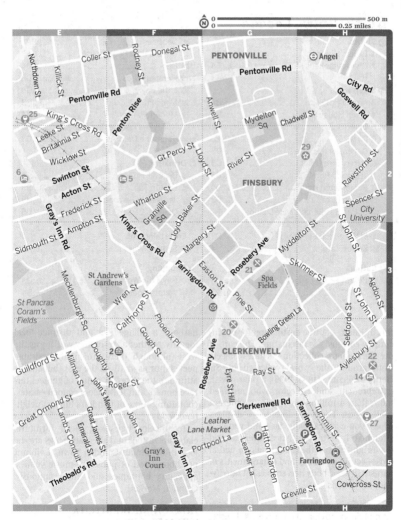

include the 90-minute highlights tour at 10.30am, 1pm and 3pm daily (adult/child £8/5), and audioguides are available (£4.50).

British Library LIBRARY
(Map p100; www.bl.uk; 96 Euston Rd; ⊗9.30am-6pm Mon & Wed-Fri, to 8pm Tue, to 5pm Sat, 11am-5pm Sun; ⊜King's Cross St Pancras) For visitors, the real highlight is a visit to the Sir John Ritblat Gallery where the most precious manuscripts, spanning almost three millennia, are held. Here you'll find the *Codex Sinaiticus* (the first complete text of the New Testament), a Gutenberg Bible (1455),

the stunningly illustrated Jain sacred texts, Leonardo da Vinci's notebooks, a copy of the *Magna Carta* (1215), explorer Captain Scott's final diary, Shakespeare's First Folio (1623) and the lyrics to 'A Hard Day's Night' (scribbled on the back of Julian Lennon's birthday card) plus original scores by Handel, Mozart and Beethoven.

FREE **Wellcome Collection** MUSEUM
(Map p95; www.wellcomecollection.org; 183 Euston Rd; ⊗10am-6pm Tue, Wed, Fri & Sat, 10am-10pm Thu, 11am-6pm Sun; ⊜Euston Square) Focussing on the interface of art, science and medicine,

North Central London

this museum – 'A free destination for the incurably curious' – is fascinating. The core of the permanent collection includes objects from around the world collected by Sir Henry Wellcome (1853–1936), a pharmacist, entrepreneur and collector who amassed more than a million objects from different civilisations. There are interactive displays where you can scan your face and watch it stretched into the statistical average and downright creepy things such as an actual cross-section of a body and enlargements of parasites (fleas, body lice, scabies) at horrifying proportions.

Charles Dickens Museum   MUSEUM
(Map p100; www.dickensmuseum.com; 48 Doughty St; adult/child £6/3; ⊙10am-5pm Mon-Sat, 11am-5pm Sun; ⊖Russell Square) The handsome four-storey house narrowly escaped demolition and opened as a museum in 1925. Shut for most of 2012 for much-needed refurbishment, Dickens' sole surviving London residence is where his work really flourished – *The Pickwick Papers, Nicholas Nickleby* and *Oliver Twist* were all written here.

CAMDEN TOWN
Once well outside the city limits, the former hamlets of North London were long ago gobbled up by the metropolis, yet they still harbour a village feel and distinct local identity. Neither as resolutely wealthy as the west (although there are highly desirable pockets) or as gritty as the east (but there's attitude), the 'Norf' is a mix of genteel terrace houses and featureless council estates, containing some of London's hippest neighbourhoods.

Technicolor hairstyles, facial furniture, elaborate tattoos and alternative togs are the look of bohemian Camden Town, a vibrant neighbourhood of pubs, live-music venues, appealing boutiques and, most famously, Camden Market.

HOXTON, SHOREDITCH & SPITALFIELDS
These revitalised and hip areas northeast of the city have enough sightseeing allure to keep daytime travellers occupied, but things really get going in the evening, when the late-night pubs, clubs and restaurants come into their own. Vibrant Hoxton and Shoreditch form the centre of gravity for nightlife, while Sunday is optimum for strolling at leisure through Spitalfields after a Saturday night out. Over the centuries, waves of immigrants have left their mark here, and it's a great place to come for diverse cuisine and vibrant nightlife.

Camden Town

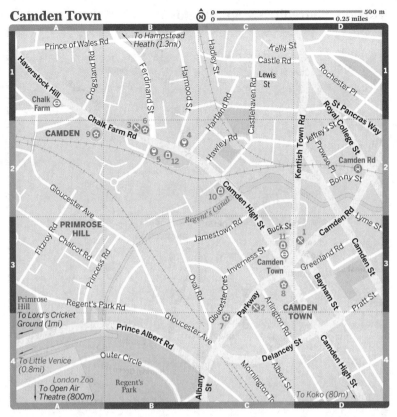

Camden Town

🍴 Eating

🍷 Drinking

⭐ Entertainment

🛍 Shopping

FREE Dennis Severs' House   MUSEUM
(Map p104; ☎020-7247 4013; www.dennissevers house.co.uk; 8 Folgate St; ⊖Liverpool St) This extraordinary Georgian house is set up as if its occupants (a family of Huguenot silk weavers) had just walked out the door, with half-drunk cups of tea, lit candles and, with perhaps more detail than we need, a full chamber pot by the bed. More than a museum, it's an opportunity to meditate on the minutiae of everyday Georgian life through silent exploration.

Bookings are required for the Monday evening candlelit sessions (£14; 6pm to 9pm) and the same on Wednesdays (£14; 6pm to 9pm, October to March), but you can just show up on Sundays (£10; noon to 4pm) or Mondays (£7; noon to 2pm) following the first and third Sundays of the month.

Hoxton, Shoreditch & Spitalfields

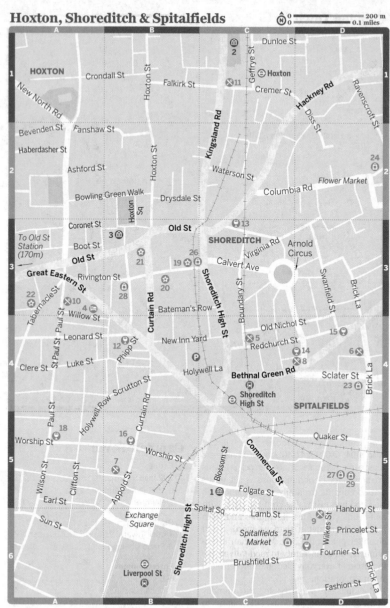

FREE **Geffrye Museum** MUSEUM
(Map p104; www.geffrye-museum.org.uk; 136 Kingsland Rd; ☺10am-5pm Tue-Sat, noon-5pm Sun; ⊖Hoxton or Old Street) If you like nosing around other people's homes, you'll love this museum. Devoted to middle-class domestic interiors, these former almshouses (1714) have been converted into a series of living rooms dating from 1630 to the current Ikea generation. On top of the interiors, the back garden has been transformed into period garden 'rooms' and a lovely walled herb garden (April to October only).

Hoxton, Shoreditch & Spitalfields

FREE **White Cube Gallery** GALLERY
(Map p104; www.whitecube.com; 48 Hoxton Sq; ⊙10am-6pm Tue-Sat; ⊜Old Street) Set in an industrial building with an impressive glazed-roof extension, White Cube hosts an intriguing program of contemporary-art exhibitions, from sculptures to video, installations and painting.

EAST END & DOCKLANDS
A huge area, the East End and Docklands are not rich in sights, but a dramatic new focus has emerged in the Olympic Park, while recently opened Overground lines make transport a breeze.

The Docklands' Canary Wharf and Isle of Dogs are an island of tower blocks, rivalling those of the City itself. London's port was once the world's greatest, the hub of the enormous global trade of the British Empire. Since being pummelled by the unpleasant Luftwaffe in WWII, its fortunes have been topsy-turvy, but massive development of Canary Wharf replaced its crusty seadogs with battalions of dark-suited office workers.

FREE **Museum of London Docklands** MUSEUM
(www.museumoflondon.org.uk/docklands; Hertsmere Rd, West India Quay; ⊙10am-6pm; ⊠DLR West India Quay) Housed in a heritage-listed warehouse, this museum uses a combination of artefacts and multimedia to chart the history of the city through its river and docks. There's a lot to see here, including an affecting section on the slave trade. The museum faces West India Quay; head west (towards the city) from the DLR station.

Olympic Park PARK, OLYMPIC VENUE
(www.london2012.com/olympic-park; ⊜Stratford) From 2008, a huge, once-contaminated and largely neglected swath of industrial East London was ambitiously regenerated and transformed into London's Olympic Park for the 2012 Games. Complementing its iconic sporting architecture, the Olympic Park was thoughtfully designed with a diverse mix of wetland, woodland, meadow and other wildlife habitats as an environmentally fertile legacy for the future. The signature buildings are the sustainably-built Olympic Stadium, the uplifting Aquatics Centre and the cutting-edge Velodrome. The twisted, abstract tangle of metal overlooking everything is the ArcelorMittal Orbit, aka the 'Hubble Bubble Pipe', a 115m-high observation tower which opened during the games. Now that the games are over, the parkland has been renamed the Queen Elizabeth Olympic Park. Panoramic views of the Olympic Park can also be had from the View Tube (www.theviewtube.co.uk; The Greenway; ⊙9am-5pm; Pudding Mill Lane) on the Greenway, next to the park.

LONDON SIGHTS

BRIXTON WINDMILL

Built for one John Ashby in 1816, the lovely Brixton Windmill (www.brixton windmill.org; Blenheim Gardens; ⊖Brixton, then bus 45 or 59) is the closest one to central London still in existence and a reminder that much of London is made up of once pastoral villages. Recently restored and open for exploration in the afternoons a few weekends a month, it's an astonishing sight.

Mudchute Park & Farm   FARM, SANCTUARY
(www.mudchute.org; Mudchute; ⊙farm 9am-5pm Tue-Sun; 🚻) This marvellous and fun-filled inner city farm on the Isle of Dogs has loads of well-kept animals and rare breeds (including the ever-popular llamas), with views of Canary Wharf reinforcing the urban/pastoral context. There's also a neat cafe, serving excellent breakfasts and wholesome lunches.

GREENWICH
Greenwich (*gren*-itch) straddles the hemispheres and the ages, retaining its own sense of identity based on historic associations with the sea and science and possessing an extraordinary cluster of buildings that have earned 'Maritime Greenwich' its place on Unesco's World Heritage list.

Greenwich is easily reached on the DLR or via train from London Bridge. Thames River Services (www.thamesriverservices.co.uk;

single/return £9.50/12.50) has boats departing from Westminster Pier (single/return £10/13, one hour, every 40 minutes), or alternatively take the cheaper Thames Clippers ferry.

FREE Old Royal Naval College   HISTORIC BUILDINGS
(www.oldroyalnavalcollege.org; 2 Cutty Sark Gardens; ⊙10am-5pm; 🚇DLR Cutty Sark) Designed by Wren, the Old Royal Naval College is a magnificent example of monumental classical architecture. Parts are now used by the University of Greenwich and Trinity College of Music, but you can visit the chapel and the extraordinary Painted Hall, which took artist Sir James Thornhill 19 years to complete.

The complex was built on the site of the 15th-century Palace of Placentia, the birthplace of Henry VIII and Elizabeth I. This Tudor connection, along with Greenwich's industrial and maritime history, is explored in the Discover Greenwich (www.ornc.org; The Pepys Building, King William Walk; ⊙10am-5pm) centre. The tourist office is based here, along with a cafe/restaurant and microbrewery. Yeomen-led tours of the complex leave at 2pm daily, taking in areas not otherwise open to the public (£6, 90 minutes).

FREE National Maritime Museum   MUSEUM
(☎020-8858 4422; www.nmm.ac.uk; Romney Rd; ⊙10am-5pm; 🚇DLR Cutty Sark) With its newly opened Sammy Ofer Wing, the National Maritime Museum houses a splendid collection of nautical paraphernalia recount-

RICHARD LIDDLE, LONDON BLACK CABS (TAXI) DRIVER

Celebrity-spotting suggestions? All of London is good for celebrity spotting, but if you want a chance to meet Madonna or see the stars of stage and screen going for workouts or rehearsals then Covent Garden is the main area.

The best-but-least-known part of town? This has to be Southwark. Just across the River Thames over London Bridge you will stumble across the Borough Market, an area you can find food and drink from all over the world. Wander through the market and you enter Southwark. Take a walk along by the Thames, where the shops, restaurants, places of interest and views will amaze you.

The best view of London from a cab? Get the driver to take you over Lambeth Bridge from the north to the south side and as he turns left off of the bridge get him to stop. Look out of the window and there is the Houses of Parliament in all its splendour – the best view in the whole of London

Your favourite part of London and why? Camden Market. The area is huge and you can find every possible type of merchandise. Grab a seat in a cafe, buy a coffee and watch the whole of humanity pass you by. Just fantastic.

ing Britain's brine-soaked seafaring history. Exhibits range from Miss Britain III (the first boat to top 100mph on open water) from 1933, the 19m-long golden state barge built in 1732 for Frederick, Prince of Wales, humdingers such as Cook's journals and Nelson's uniform, complete with bullet hole and interactive plus educational displays. An ambitious new gallery in the Sammy Ofer Wing narrates the history of Britain partly by way of the Wave, an innovative audio-visual installation.

Royal Observatory   HISTORIC BUILDING
(☑0208-858 4422; www.rmg.co.uk; adult/child £7/2; ☺10am-5pm ; ⊠DLR Cutty Sark) Rising south of Queen's House, idyllic Greenwich Park climbs up the hill, affording stunning views of London from the Royal Observatory, which Charles II had built in 1675 to help solve the riddle of longitude.

Success was confirmed in 1884 when Greenwich was designated as the prime meridian of the world, and Greenwich Mean Time (GMT) became the universal measurement of standard time.

In the north of the observatory is lovely Flamsteed House and the Meridian Courtyard (where you can stand with your feet straddling the western and eastern hemispheres); admission is by ticket. The southern half contains the highly informative and free Astronomy Centre and the Peter Harrison Planetarium (adult/child £6.50/4.50).

Queen's House   HISTORIC BUILDING
(www.rmg.co.uk/queens-house; Romney Rd; ☺10am-5pm; ⊠DLR Cutty Sark) Looking directly to the Thames between the domes of the Old Royal Naval College (p106), the elegant Palladian Queen's House was designed by Inigo Jones in 1616 for the wife of Charles I. Don't miss the ceremonial Great Hall and the delightful helix-shaped Tulip Staircase.

Greenwich Guided Walks   WALKING TOUR
(☑0757-577 2298; www.greenwichtours.co.uk; adult £7; ☺12.15pm & 2.15pm) Tours leave from the tourist office.

O2   VENUE
(www.theo2.co.uk; Peninsula Sq; ⊖North Greenwich) The world's largest dome (365m in diameter) opened on 1 January 2000, at a cost of £789 million, as the Millennium Dome. Renamed the O2, it's now a 20,000-seat sports and entertainment arena surround-

EMIRATES AIR LINE CABLE CAR

Destined to become a sight in its own right and capable of ferrying 2400 people per hour across the Thames in either direction, the new Emirates Air Line Cable Car (adult/child single £4.30/2.20, return £8.60/4.40; ☺7am-9pm Mon-Fri, from 8am Sat, from 9am Sun Apr-Sep, shorter hours rest of the year) links together the Greenwich Peninsula and the Royal Docks in a five- to 10-minute journey. Expected to help regenerate both sides of the river around each embarkation point, the UK's first urban cable car system will have cabins available every half minute; Oyster card and Travelcard holders get a discount for journeys, which are bike-friendly too. Arriving at Royal Docks, you can hop on the DLR at Royal Victoria DLR station while in Greenwich, the underground interchange is with North Greenwich Station.

ed by shops and restaurants. The Arena also houses the British Music Experience (☑0844 847 1761; www.britishmusicexperience.com; Millennium Way; adult/child £12/6; ☺11am-7.30pm; North Greenwich), which entertainingly traces the history of British popular music from 1945 to the present day. O2 conducts regular guided climbs of the dome's exterior (£22 to £28). There are ferry services from central London on concert nights.

HAMPSTEAD & HIGHGATE

These quaint and well-heeled villages, perched on hills north of London, are home to a litany of celebrities.

Hampstead Heath   PARK
(⊠Gospel Oak or Hampstead Heath) With its 320 hectares of rolling meadows and wild woodlands, Hampstead Heath is a million miles away – well, approximately four – from central London. A walk up Parliament Hill affords one of the most spectacular views of the city, and on summer days it's a choice spot for picnickers. Also bewilderingly popular are the murky brown waters of the single-sex and mixed bathing ponds (basically duck ponds with people splashing about in them), although most folk are content just to sun themselves around London's 'beach'.

FREE **Kenwood House**   HISTORIC BUILDING
(www.english-heritage.org.uk; Hampstead Lane; admission free; ⊙11.30am-4pm; ⊞Gospel Oak or Hampstead Heath) Kenwood House is a magnificent neoclassical mansion (1764) on the northern side of the heath that houses a collection of paintings by English and European masters including Rembrandt, Vermeer, Turner and Gainsborough. Closed for renovations until autumn 2013, the grounds remain accessible.

Highgate Cemetery   CEMETERY
(☎020-8340 1834; www.highgate-cemetery.org; Swain's Lane; West Cemetery adult/child £7/3, East Cemetery adult/child £3/2; ⊙West Cemetery tours 2pm Mon-Fri Mar-Nov, hourly 11am-3pm Sat & Sun year-long, East Cemetery 10am-5pm Mon-Fri, 11am-5pm Sat & Sun Mar-Oct, to 4pm Nov-Feb; ⊖Archway) Weaving their Gothic magic, the shrouded urns, obelisks, broken columns, sleeping angels, classical tomb porticoes and overgrown graves make this boneyard a sublime Victorian Valhalla. On the eastern side you can pay your respects to the graves of Karl Marx and George Eliot (Mary Ann Evans), but the highlight is the overgrown West Cemetery, where a maze of winding paths leads to the Circle of Lebanon, rings of tombs flanking a circular path and topped with a majestic cedar of Lebanon tree. Admission to the West Cemetery is by tour only and bookings are essential for weekday tours. From Archway station, walk up Highgate Hill until you reach Waterlow Park on the left. Go through the park; the cemetery gates are opposite the exit.

WORTH A TRIP

ESTORICK COLLECTION OF MODERN ITALIAN ART

The outstanding concentration of art in the Estorick Collection of Modern Italian Art (Map p128; ☎7704 9522; www.estorickcollection.com; 39a Canonbury Sq; adult/concession/student £5/3.50/free; ⊙11am-6pm Wed-Sat, noon-5pm Sun; Highbury & Islington) in Islington boasts one of the world's leading collections of futurist painting, from such gifted artists as Umberto Boccioni, Giacomo Balla and Gino Severini.

OUTSIDE CENTRAL LONDON

Kew Gardens   BOTANIC GARDENS
(www.kew.org.uk; Kew Rd; adult/child £14/free, Kew Explorer adult/child £4/1; ⊙9.30am-6.30pm Apr-Aug, earlier closing other months; ⊞Kew Bridge, ⊖Kew Gardens) In 1759 botanists began rummaging around the world for specimens they could plant in the 3-hectare plot known as the Royal Botanic Gardens. They never stopped collecting, and the gardens, which have bloomed to 120 hectares, provide the most comprehensive botanical collection on earth (including the world's largest collection of orchids). The beautiful gardens are now recognised as a Unesco World Heritage Site.

No worries if you don't know your golden slipper orchid from your fengoky or your quiver tree from your alang-alang; a visit to Kew is a journey of discovery for everyone. You can easily spend a whole day wandering around, but if you're pressed for time, the Kew Explorer (adult/child £4/1) is a hop-on/hop-off road train that leaves from Victoria Gate and takes in the gardens' main sights.

Highlights include the enormous early Victorian Palm House, a hothouse of metal and curved sheets of glass; the impressive Princess of Wales Conservatory; the red-brick, 1631 Kew Palace (www.hrp.org.uk/kew palace; adult/child £5.30/free; ⊙11am-5pm Easter-Sep), formerly King George III's country retreat; the celebrated Great Pagoda designed by William Chambers in 1762; the Temperate House, the world's largest ornamental glasshouse; and the very enjoyable Rhizotron and Xstrata Treetop Walkway, where you can survey the tree canopy from 18m up in the air.

The gardens are easily reached by tube, but you might prefer to take a cruise on a riverboat from the Westminster Passenger Services Association (☎020-7930 2062; www.wpsa.co.uk), which runs several daily boats from April to October, departing from Westminster Pier (return adult/child £18/9, 90 minutes).

Hampton Court Palace   PALACE
(www.hrp.org.uk/HamptonCourtPalace; adult/child £14/7; ⊙10am-6pm Apr-Oct, to 4.30pm Nov-Mar; ⊞Hampton Court) Built by Cardinal Thomas Wolsey in 1514 but coaxed from him by Henry VIII just before Wolsey (as chancellor) fell from favour, Hampton Court Palace is England's largest and grandest Tudor structure.

POUND SAVERS

As many of London's very best sights are free, you can easily spend a busy week without paying much on admission charges. However, if you're hanging around for longer and have particular attractions that you're keen to see, there are options for saving a few pounds.

The London Pass (www.londonpass.com; per 1/2/3/6 days £46/61/66/89) is a smart card that gains you fast-track entry to 55 different attractions, including pricier ones such as the Tower of London and St Paul's Cathedral. You'd have to be racing around frantically to get real value from a one-day pass, but you could conceivably save quite a bit with the two- or three-day version. Passes can be booked online and collected from the London Pass Redemption Desk (11a Charing Cross Rd; ⊜Leicester Square) (check online for opening hours) opposite the Garrick Theatre. It also sells a version with a preloaded Transport For London (TFL) travel pass, but it's cheaper to buy this separately.

If you're a royalty buff, taking out an annual membership to the Historic Royal Palaces (www.hrp.org.uk; individual/joint membership £43/65) allows you to jump the queues and visit the Tower of London, Kensington Palace, Banqueting House, Kew Palace and Hampton Court Palace as often as you like. If you were intending to visit all five anyway, membership will save you more than £18 (£58 for a couple). There can be a lengthy wait for membership cards, but temporary cards are issued immediately.

It was already one of the most sophisticated palaces in Europe when, in the 17th century, Wren was commissioned to build an extension. The result is a beautiful blend of Tudor and 'restrained baroque' architecture.

Take a themed tour led by costumed historians or, if you're in a rush, visit the highlights: Henry VIII's State Apartments, including the Great Hall with its spectacular hammer-beamed roof; the Tudor Kitchens, staffed by 'servants'; and the Wolsey Rooms. You could easily spend a day exploring the palace and its 60 acres of riverside gardens, especially if you get lost in the 300-year-old maze.

Hampton Court is 13 miles southwest of central London and is easily reached by train from Waterloo. Alternatively, the riverboats that head from Westminster to Kew continue here (return adult/child £22.50/11.25, three hours).

Richmond Park   PARK
(⊙7am-dusk Mar-Sep, from 7.30am Oct-Feb; ⊜Richmond) London's wildest park – and the largest urban parkland in Europe – spans more than 1000 hectares and is home to all sorts of wildlife, most notably herds of red and fallow deer. It's a terrific place for birdwatching, rambling and cycling.

To get there from Richmond tube station, turn left along George St then left at the fork that leads up Richmond Hill.

☞ Tours

One of the best ways to orient yourself when you first arrive in London is with a 24-hour hop-on/hop-off pass for the double-decker bus tours. The buses loop around interconnecting routes throughout the day, providing a commentary as they go, and the price includes a river cruise and three walking tours. Save a few pounds by booking online.

Original Tour   BUS TOUR
(www.theoriginaltour.com; adult/child/family £26/13/91; ⊙every 20min 8.30am-5.30pm)

Big Bus Tours   BUS TOUR
(☑020-7233 9533; www.bigbustours.com; adult/child £26/10)

Citisights   WALKING TOURS
(☑020-8806 3742; www.chr.org.uk/cswalks.htm) Focuses on the academic and the literary.

London Beatles Walks   WALKING TOURS
(☑07958 706329; www.beatlesinlondon.com; adult/child £6/free) Following the footsteps of the Fab Four.

London Walks   WALKING TOURS
(☑020-7624 3978; www.walks.com) Harry Potter tours, ghost walks and the ever popular Jack the Ripper tours.

London Mystery Walks   WALKING TOURS
(☑07957 388280; www.tourguides.org.uk)

WORTH A TRIP

ABBEY ROAD

Beatles aficionados can't possibly visit London without making a pilgrimage to Abbey Road Studios (3 Abbey Rd) in St John's Wood. The fence outside is covered with decades of fans' graffiti. Stop-start local traffic is long accustomed to groups of tourists lining up on the zebra crossing to reenact the cover of the fab four's 1969 masterpiece and penultimate swan song *Abbey Road*. In 2010, the crossing received the accolade of Grade II listed status. For an entertaining live view of the crossing and highlights of the day's action, check out the fun webcam at www.abbeyroad. com/crossing. To get here, take the tube to St John's Wood, cross the road, follow Grove End Rd to its end and turn right.

City Cruises FERRY TOURS
(Map p64; ☎020-7740 0400; www.citycruises.com; single/return trips from £8/10.50, day pass £13.50) Ferry service between Westminster, Waterloo, Tower and Greenwich piers.

Capital Taxi Tours TAXI TOURS
(☎020-8590 3621; www.capitaltaxitours.co.uk; two-hour day tour £165 per taxi, by night 2½ hour tour £235 per taxi) Takes up to five people on a variety of tours with Blue Badge, City of London and City of Westminster registered guides/drivers, cheeky Cockney Cabbie option and foreign language availability.

London Bicycle Tour CYCLING TOURS
(Map p84; ☎020-7928 6838; www.londonbicycle.com; 1A Gabriel's Wharf, 56 Upper Ground; tour incl bike from £18.95; ⊖Waterloo) Themed 2½- to 3½-hour tours of the 'West End', 'East', 'Central' or 'Royal West'.

City Jogging Tours JOGGING TOURS
(☎0845 544 0433; www.cityjoggingtours.co.uk; tours £26) Combine sightseeing with keeping fit on a 6km route, graded for 'gentle joggers' or 'recreational runners'.

London Duck Tours AMPHIBIOUS-VEHICLE TOURS
(Map p84; ☎020-7928 3132; www.londonduck tours.co.uk; County Hall; ⊖Waterloo) Cruise the streets in the same sort of amphibious landing craft used on D-Day before making a dramatic plunge into the Thames.

★✰ Festivals & Events

Chinese New Year CULTURAL CELEBRATION
Late January or early February sees Chinatown snap, crackle and pop with fireworks, a colourful street parade, lion dances and *dim sum* aplenty.

University Boat Race BOAT RACE
(www.theboatrace.org) A posh-boy grudge match held annually since 1829 between the rowing crews of Oxford and Cambridge Universities (late March).

London Marathon RUNNING RACE
(www.london-marathon.co.uk) Up to half a million spectators watch the whippet-thin champions and bizarrely clad amateurs take to the streets in late April.

Camden Crawl MUSIC FESTIVAL
(www.thecamdencrawl.com; 1-/2-day pass £39/62) Your chance to spot the next big thing on the music scene or witness a secret gig by an established act, with 40 of Camden's venues given over to live music for two full days (late April/early May).

Chelsea Flower Show HORTICULTURAL SHOW
(www.rhs.org.uk/chelsea; Royal Hospital Chelsea; admission £19-42) Held in May, arguably the world's most renowned horticultural show attracts green fingers from near and far.

Trooping the Colour ROYAL PARADE
Celebrating the Queen's official birthday (in June), this ceremonial procession of troops, marching along the Mall for their monarch's inspection, is a pageantry overload.

Royal Academy Summer Exhibition ART EXHIBITION
(www.royalacademy.org.uk; adult/child £9.50/5) Running from mid-June to mid-August, this is an annual showcase of works submitted by artists from all over Britain, mercifully distilled to 1200 or so pieces.

Meltdown Festival MUSIC FESTIVAL
(www.southbankcentre.co.uk) The Southbank Centre hands over the curatorial reigns to a legend of contemporary music (such as David Bowie, Morrissey or Patti Smith) to pull together a full program of concerts, talks and films in late June.

Wimbledon Lawn Tennis Championships TENNIS TOURNAMENT
(www.wimbledon.org) Held at the end of June, the world's most prestigious tennis event is

as much about strawberries, cream and tradition as smashing balls.

Pride   GAY & LESBIAN
(www.pridelondon.org) The big event on the gay and lesbian calendar, a Technicolor street parade heads through the West End in late June or early July, culminating in a concert in Trafalgar Sq.

Lovebox   MUSIC FESTIVAL
(www.lovebox.net) London's contribution to the summer music festival circuit, held in Victoria Park in mid-July.

Notting Hill Carnival   STREET PARADES
(www.nottinghillcarnival.biz) Held over two days in August, this is Europe's largest and London's most vibrant outdoor carnival, where London's Caribbean community shows the city how to party. Unmissable and truly crazy.

🛏 Sleeping

When it comes to finding a place for a good night's kip, London is one of the most expensive places in the world. 'Budget' is pretty much anything below £90 per night for a double; at the top end, how does a £14000-per-night suite on Hyde Park Corner sound? Double rooms ranging between £90 and £180 per night are considered midrange; more expensive options fall into the top-end category.

London, however, has a delightful selection of characterful hotels, whether brimming with history, zany modern decor or all-stops-out charm. Most of the ritzier places offer substantial discounts on the weekends, for advance bookings and at quieter times.

Public transport is good, so you don't need to be sleeping at Buckingham Palace to be at the heart of things.

Budget accommodation is scattered about, with good options in Bloomsbury, St Pancras, Earl's Court and the South Bank. For something a little nicer, check out Bayswater, Notting Hill Gate or Belgravia. To splash the cash, consider the West End, Clerkenwell, Kensington and Knightsbridge. Most budget and midrange places offer free wi-fi (expensive places may charge).

Prices listed here include 20% VAT, when it applies.

WESTMINSTER & ST JAMES'S

A bed in the Queen's own hood can be as ritzy as the Ritz, but won't necessarily cost you a king's ransom.

Rubens at the Palace   HOTEL ££
(Map p64; ☎020-7834 6600; www.rubenshotel.com; 39 Buckingham Palace Rd; @🛜; ⊖Victoria) Right by Buckingham Palace, Rubens is a firm favourite with US visitors looking for that quintessential royal experience. Rooms are monarchist chic: heavy patterned fabrics, dark wood, thick drapes and crowns above the beds.

WEST END

Like in Monopoly, land on a Mayfair hotel and you may have to sell your house, or at least remortgage. This is the heart of the action, and a couple of hostels cater for would-be Soho hipsters of more modest means.

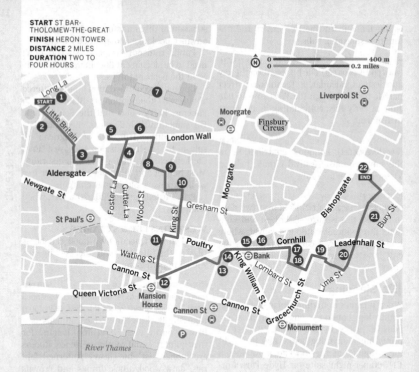

Walking Tour
City of London

❭ The City of London has as much history
and intriguing architecture in its square
mile as the rest of London put together. This
tour traces some of the City's hidden gems
(secluded parks, charming churches) in a
journey from ancient to ultramodern.

It's fitting to start at ❶ **St Bartholomew-
the-Great**, as this fascinating 12th-century
church was once a pilgrimage stop for travellers to London. In more recent times, it's been
used for scenes in *Four Weddings & A Funeral*,
Shakespeare in Love and *Sherlock Holmes*.

Head out through the Tudor gatehouse. In
the distance you'll see the Victorian arches
of Smithfield's meat market, which has occupied this site just north of the old city walls
for 800 years. Executions were held here,
most famously the torching of Protestants
under Mary I and the grisly killing of Scottish
hero William Wallace (Braveheart) in 1305; a
plaque on the front of ❷ **St Bartholomew's
Hospital** commemorates him. Also note the
shrapnel damage to the wall – the legacy of
an attack in 1916 by a German Zeppelin.

Head back towards the gate and turn right
into Little Britain. Follow it as it curves to the
right and look out for the large tree marking
the entrance to ❸ **Postman's Park**. This
lovely space includes a touching legacy of
Victorian socialism: a tiled wall celebrating
everyday heroes.

Turn right at the end of the park, then left
and left again into Noble St. You're now inside
what was once the old City's ❹ **walls**,
remnants of which you'll pass on your left.
Commenced in Roman times, the fortifications were demolished in the 18th and 19th
centuries, but the shape of them can be
traced in street names such as Newgate,
Moorgate, Bishopsgate and Aldgate. This section was only uncovered after WWII bombs
destroyed the buildings covering it. Take the
stairs up to the footbridge crossing the street
called London Wall towards the ❺ **Museum
of London**. The museum's Roman section
will give you a feel for the layout of the City.

Turn left when leaving the museum and follow the Highwalk. On your left you'll see **6 ruins** of the barbicans (defensive towers) that once guarded the northwestern corner of the walls, with the **7 Barbican Centre** behind them. Filling a space bombed out during WWII and once revolutionary, parts of it are extraordinarily ugly, particularly the forbidding high-rise tower blocks (romantically named Shakespeare, Cromwell and Lauderdale). At its heart is an arts centre consisting of concert halls, cinemas, galleries, eateries, a library and a school.

Follow the painted lines on the Highwalk for a closer look, or turn right at Pizza Express, take the escalator down to Wood St and head towards the remaining tower of **8 St Alban's**, a Wren-designed church destroyed in WWII. Turn left and you'll find a sweet garden on the site of **9 St Mary Aldermansbury**, capped by a bust of Shakespeare. The 12th-century church was ruined in the war then shipped to Missouri where it was re-erected.

Turn right on to Aldermansbury and head to the **10 Guildhall**. Take King St down to Cheapside, cross the road and head right to elegant **11 St Mary-le-Bow**. The church was rebuilt by Wren after the Great Fire, and then rebuilt again after WWII. The term 'Cockney' traditionally refers to someone born within the sound of this church's bell.

Backtrack to Bow Lane and follow this narrow path to beautiful **12 St Mary Aldermary**, rebuilt in the Perpendicular Gothic style in 1682 following the fire. Turn left on to Queen Victoria St and then right into Bucklersbury, where you'll see **13 St Stephen's Walbrook** directly in front of you. In the 3rd century, a Roman temple stood here, and in the 7th century a Saxon church. Rebuilt after the Great Fire, the current St Stephen's is

one of Wren's greatest masterpieces, with elegant Corinthian columns supporting a beautifully proportioned dome. Henry Moore sculpted the round central altar from travertine marble in 1972.

Leaving the church, you'll pass **14 Mansion House**, built in 1752 as the official residence of the Lord Mayor. As you approach the busy Bank intersection, lined with neoclassical temples to commerce, you might think you've stumbled into the ancient Roman forum (the actual forum was a couple of blocks east). Head for the **15 equestrian statue of the Iron Duke**, behind which a metal pyramid details the many significant buildings here. Directly behind you is the **16 Royal Exchange**; walk through it and exit through the door on the right, then turn left onto Cornhill.

If you're still not churched out, cross the road to **17 St Michael's**, a 1672 Wren design which still has its box pews. Hidden in the warren of tiny passages behind the church is its **18 churchyard**. Head through to Gracechurch St, turn left and cross the road to wonderful **19 Leadenhall Market**. This is roughly where the ancient forum once stood. As you wander out the far end, the famous **20 Lloyd's of London** displays its metallic innards for all to see.

Once you turn left onto Lime St, you'll see ahead of you Norman Foster's 180m **21 30 St Mary Axe**. Its dramatic curved shape has given spawned many nicknames (the Crystal Phallus, the Towering Innuendo), but it's as the Gherkin that it is fondly known. Built nearly 900 years after St Bartholomew-the-Great, it's testimony to the City's ability to constantly reinvent itself for the times. A short walk away, the **22 Heron Tower** was completed in 2011 and is currently the tallest building in the City.

ⓘ WHEN RIGHT IS RIGHT

Vehicles entering Savoy Ct off the Strand for the Savoy (p114) tradition-ally drive on the right-hand side of the road, *not* the left. This is the only road in the UK where you can legally drive on the 'wrong' side of the road (Savoy Ct being a private road and not a public thoroughfare).

TOP CHOICE Haymarket Hotel
HOTEL £££

(Map p70; ☎020-7470 4000; www.haymarket hotel.com; 1 Suffolk Pl; r £318-408, ste from £492; @🖵🏊; ⊖Piccadilly Circus) An exquisite place to hang your well-trimmed hat, the Tim and Kit Kemp–designed Haymarket is a super-stylish and eye-catching treat, with a knock-out swimming pool bathed in serene mood lighting.

Hazlitt's
HOTEL £££

(Map p70; ☎020-7434 1771; www.hazlittshotel .com; 6 Frith St; s £206, d/ste from £259/646; @🖵; ⊖Tottenham Court Road) Envelop yourself in Georgian finery at this lovely 1718 house and journey back to the days of four-poster beds, claw-foot baths and panelled walls. Each of the 30 individually-decorated rooms over-flows with Georgian antiques and days-gone-by charm (plus up-to-the-minute mod cons).

Dean Street Townhouse
BOUTIQUE HOTEL £££

(Map p70; ☎0207-434 1775; www.deanstreet townhouse.com; 69-71 Dean St; r £160-310; 🏊🖵) This Soho gem of a 39-bedroom boutique hotel enjoys a de-lightful boudoir atmosphere with choice rooms – everything faultlessly in its place – from 'tiny' options upwards.

One Aldwych
HOTEL £££

(Map p70; ☎020-7300 1000; www.onealdwych .com; 1 Aldwych; d/ste from £195/440; @🖵🏊; ⊖Covent Garden) Granite bathrooms, long swimming pool with underwater music, ma-jestic bar and restaurant, modern art, and a lift that changes colour to literally lift your mood.

Savoy
HOTEL £££

(Map p70; ☎020-7836 4343; www.fairmont.com/ savoy-london; Strand; 🖵🏊; ⊖Charing Cross) A night surrounded by the Edwardian and art deco grandeur of the iconic Savoy is never a casual choice, considering the sudden stu-pefying hole in your bank balance, but as one of life's memorable treats, you can't go wrong. The £100 million refit has injected fizz back into a classic glass of champers and it's all here: river views, sumptuous rooms, pre-eminent restaurants and the much-loved American Bar. There's a charge for parking and wi-fi.

Brown's Hotel
HOTEL £££

(Map p70; ☎020-7493 6020; www.brownshotel .com; 30 Albemarle St; r/ste from £485/915; @🖵; ⊖Green Park) A stunner of a five-star number, this 117-room hotel was created in 1837 from 11 houses joined together, where lovely old-world traditional features (Edwardian oak panelling, working fireplaces) complement individually decorated rooms.

Soho Hotel
HOTEL £££

(Map p70; ☎020-7559 3000; www.sohohotel .com; 4 Richmond Mews; r/ste from £354/516; @🖵; ⊖Oxford Circus) A converted car park may sound unglamorous, but Kit Kemp's signature touches, bold colours and im-agination are all over the place, from the Botero-designed cat in the lobby to the 91 individually-designed rooms, each a modish triumph. Wi-fi costs £20.

Covent Garden Hotel
HOTEL £££

(Map p70; ☎020-7806 1000; www.coventgarden hotel.co.uk; 10 Monmouth St; d/ste from £312/492; 🏊@🖵; ⊖Covent Garden) Well-positioned and classy Firmdale hotel housed in an old French hospital.

Oxford St YHA
HOSTEL £

(Map p70; ☎0845 371 9133; www.yha.org.uk; 14 Noel St; dm/tw from £18/44; @🖵; ⊖Oxford Circus) This recently refurbed hostel is a tip-top choice for its central (albeit noisy) location, bright and colourful complexion, cleanliness and manageable 93-bed size plus decent view over London's rooftops from some rooms.

THE CITY

While it's bristling with bankers during the week, you can often pick up a considerable bargain in the City on weekends.

Threadneedles
HOTEL £££

(Map p78; ☎020-7657 8080; www.theeton collection.com; 5 Threadneedle St; r weekend/ weekday from £175/345; @🖵; ⊖Bank) The hand-painted glass dome in the circular lobby recalls Threadneedle's former stand-ing as a bank HQ. It's elegant and chic, with an unruffled air, pleasantly presented rooms and an understated modernity.

Apex City of London HOTEL ££
(Map p78; ☎020-7702 2020; www.apexhotels.co.uk; 1 Seething Lane; r from £100; 📶; ⊖Tower Hill) Business-focussed but close enough to the Tower to hear the heads roll, the Apex offers particularly enticing weekend rates, a gym, huge TVs, free wi-fi and a rubber ducky in every room.

YHA London St Paul's HOSTEL £
(Map p78; ☎0845 371 9012; www.yha.org.uk; 36 Carter Lane; dm £20-25, d £50; ⊖St Paul's) Perfectly placed for hoovering up the sights of the City and the South Bank, this elegantly housed 208-bed hostel is just down the road from St Paul's (the bells, the bells!). There's no self-catering, no lift and a seven-night maximum stay.

SOUTH BANK

Immediately south of the river is a great spot for reaching the central sights, while gauging the personality of London south of the river.

TOP CHOICE **Kennington B&B** B&B ££
(☎020-7735 7669; www.kenningtonbandb.com; 103 Kennington Park Rd; d £120-150; ⊖Kennington) With gorgeous bed linen and well-preserved Georgian features, this lovely B&B is very tasteful in virtually every regard, from the shining, tiled shower rooms and Georgian shutters to the fireplaces and cast-iron radiators. It's a short walk from Kennington underground station.

Park Plaza Westminster Bridge HOTEL £££
(Map p84; ☎0844-415 6780; www.parkplaza.com; 220 Westminster Bridge Rd; d £159-238; ❄📶🏊; ⊖Waterloo) This snazzy fresh hotel offers contemporary, stylish and comfortable rooms. Skimp on it and you'll end up with a room facing into the atrium; splash out and you get a studio or penthouse gazing onto the Thames, Westminster Bridge, Big Ben or the London Eye.

Premier Inn London County Hall HOTEL ££
(Map p84; ☎0871 527 8648; www.premierinn.com; County Hall, Belvedere Rd; rm £112-160; 📶; ⊖Waterloo) Location, location, location: and a choice positioning within a landmark historic building and a few steps from the London Eye, Westminster and Big Ben. All other crucial boxes come ticked – service is congenial, rooms are decently sized and the tariff is low (but there's a £3 wi-fi charge daily).

Captain Bligh House B&B ££
(Map p84; ☎020-7928 2735; www.captainblighhouse.co.uk; 100 Lambeth Rd; s/d £63-75/85-90; 📶; ⊖Lambeth North) With helpful but non-intrusive owners, this late-18th-century property opposite the Imperial War Museum has shipshape and quiet rooms with kitchen. The downside is there's a minimum four-night stay policy, no credit cards, one night's nonrefundable deposit and you'll need to book way ahead. No lift.

St Christopher's Village HOSTEL £
(Map p84; ☎020-7939 9710; www.st-christophers.co.uk; 163 Borough High St; dm/r from £14/62; @📶; ⊖London Bridge) The Village – a huge, up-for-it party hostel, with a club hopping till 4am at weekends and a roof terrace bar – is the main hub of three locations on the same street. It's either heaven or hell, depending on what side of 30 you're on. The other locations are much smaller, quieter and, frankly, more pleasant. **St Christopher's Inn** (Map p84; 121 Borough High St) is above a very nice pub, while **Oasis** (Map p84; 59 Borough High St) is women-only.

PIMLICO & BELGRAVIA

Lime Tree Hotel B&B ££
(Map p92; ☎020-7730 8191; www.limetreehotel.co.uk; 135-137 Ebury St; s £99, d £150-175; @📶; ⊖Victoria) A smartly renovated Georgian town house hotel with a beautiful back garden to catch the late afternoon rays. The three 'C's: cosy, congenial and clean.

Luna Simone Hotel B&B ££
(☎020-7834 5897; www.lunasimonehotel.com; 47-49 Belgrave Rd; s £70-75, d £95-120; @📶; ⊖Pimlico) Rooms are quite compact but clean and calming at this central, welcoming hotel; the ones at the back are quieter. Belgrave Rd follows on from Eccleston Bridge, directly behind Victoria Station.

B+B Belgravia B&B ££
(Map p92; ☎020-7259 8570; www.bb-belgravia.com; 64-66 Ebury St; s/d/tw £99/135/145; @📶; ⊖Victoria) This lovely place marries contemporary chic with Georgian elegance; rooms are neat and although not very spacious, fine studio rooms with compact kitchens are along the road at No 82.

Windermere Hotel B&B ££
(Map p92; ☎020-7834 5163; www.windermere-hotel.co.uk; 142-144 Warwick Way; s £105-155, d £129-165; @📶; ⊖Victoria) The attractive and newly refurbished Windermere has 19 small,

BOOKING SERVICES

At Home in London (☎020-8748 1943; www.athomeinlondon.co.uk) For B&Bs.

GKLets (☎020-7613 2805; www.gklets .co.uk) Apartments.

British Hotel Reservation Centre (☎020-7592 3055; www.bhrconline.com) Hotels.

London Homestead Services (☎020-7286 5115; www.lhslondon.com) B&Bs.

LondonTown (☎020-7437 4370; www .londontown.com) Hotels and B&Bs.

Uptown Reservations (☎020-7937 2001; www.uptownres.co.uk) Upmarket B&Bs.

Visit London (☎per min 10p 0871 222 3118; www.visitlondonoffers.com) Hotels.

bright and individually designed rooms in a white mid-Victorian town house, with a recently installed lift and a reasonably priced restaurant.

KNIGHTSBRIDGE
Named after a bridge over the River Westbourne, Knightsbridge is where you'll find some of London's best-known department stores and some top hotels.

Levin Hotel HOTEL £££
(Map p92; ☎020-7589 6286; www.thelevinhotel. co.uk; 28 Basil St; r from £305; ❅☏; ❸Knightsbridge) As close as you can get to sleeping in Harrods, the 12-room Levin knows its market. Despite the baby-blue colour scheme, there's a subtle femininity to the decor, although it's far too elegant to be flouncy.

Knightsbridge Hotel HOTEL £££
(Map p92; ☎020-7584 6300; www.knights bridgehotel.com; 10 Beaufort Gardens; s/d from £235/282; @☏; ❸Knightsbridge) Another Firmdale property, the six-floor Knightsbridge is on a quiet, tree-lined cul-de-sac very close to Harrods.

CHELSEA & KENSINGTON
Well-turned-out Chelsea and Kensington offer easy access to the museums, natty shopping choices and some of London's best-looking streets.

Number Sixteen TOP/CHOICE HOTEL £££
(Map p92; ☎020-7589 5232; www.numbersixteen hotel.co.uk; 16 Sumner Pl; s from £168, d £222-360; @☏; ❸South Kensington) It's four properties in one delightful whole and a stunning place to stay, with 42 individually designed rooms, a cosy drawing room, a fully stocked library and a simply idyllic back garden.

Gore HOTEL ££
(Map p92; ☎020-7584 6601; www.gorehotel.com; 190 Queen's Gate; r from £135; @☏; ❸Gloucester Road) A short stroll from the Royal Albert Hall, the Gore serves up British grandiosity (antiques, carved four-posters, polished mahogany, a secret bathroom in the Tudor room) in 50 individually furnished, magnificent rooms.

Aster House B&B ££
(Map p92; ☎0207-581 5888; www.asterhouse.com; 3 Sumner Pl; s/d £144/216-300; ❅☏; ❸South Kensington) The Singaporean owners certainly know how to keep things clean and shipshape at this charming and well-priced house hotel with a delightful plant-filled orangerie and ducks in the garden.

Vicarage Private Hotel B&B ££
(Map p118; ☎020-7229 4030; www.londonvicarage hotel.com; 10 Vicarage Gate; s/d £95/125, without bathroom £56/95; @☏; ❸High St Kensington) On the corner with Palace Gardens Terrace (with its astonishing cherry trees in spring), this place is all about location (between Notting Hill Gate and Kensington High St) and value for money. Rooms are nothing special, with the cheapest (non–en suite) on floors three and four. Breakfast is included and rates fall in winter.

EARL'S COURT & FULHAM
West London's Earl's Court is lively, cosmopolitan and so popular with travelling Antipodeans it's been nicknamed Kangaroo Valley. There are no real sights, but it has inexpensive digs and an infectious holiday atmosphere.

Barclay House B&B ££
(☎020-7384 3390; www.barclayhouselondon.com; 21 Barclay Rd; s/d £69/89; @☏; ❸Fulham Broadway) A proper homestay B&B with a handful of rooms with en suite in a charming Victorian town house. It's so popular there's now a four-night minimum stay requirement, unless they can shoehorn you in between slots. From the tube station head west on

Fulham Broadway and then look out for Barclay Rd on your left.

Twenty Nevern Square
HOTEL **££**

(☏020-7565 9555; www.20nevernsquare.com; 20 Nevern Sq; r from £95; @☎; ⊖Earl's Court) An Ottoman theme runs through this Victorian town house hotel, where a mix of wooden furniture, luxurious fabrics and natural light helps maximise space – even in the excellent-value cheaper rooms.

Base2stay
APARTMENT HOTEL **££**

(☏020-7244 2255; www.base2stay.com; 25 Court-field Gardens; s/d from £93/99; @☎; ⊖Earl's Court) With comfort, smart decor, power showers, flatscreen TVs with internet access, artfully concealed kitchenettes, neat rooms and a sustainable credo, this boutique establishment feels like a four-star hotel without the wallet-emptying price tag.

easyHotel
BUDGET HOTEL **£**

(www.easyhotel.com; r from £25; @☎; ⊖) Earls Court (44 West Cromwell Rd, Earl's Court; ⊖Earl's Court); Paddington (10 Norfolk Pl, Paddington; ⊖Paddington); South Kensington (14 Lexham Gardens, South Kensington; ⊖Gloucester Rd) This no-frills chain has tiny rooms with even tinier bathrooms, all bedecked in the company's trademark garish orange.

NOTTING HILL, BAYSWATER & PADDINGTON
Don't be fooled by Julia Roberts and Hugh Grant's shenanigans, Notting Hill and the areas immediately north of Hyde Park are as shabby as they are chic. There are some gorgeous gated squares surrounded by Georgian town houses, but the area is better exemplified by the Notting Hill Carnival.

Scruffy Paddington has lots of cheap hotels, with a major strip of unremarkable ones along Sussex Gardens that may be worth checking out if you're short on options.

Vancouver Studios
APARTMENT HOTEL **££**

(Map p118; ☏020-7243 1270; www.vancouver studios.co.uk; 30 Prince's Sq; apt £89-170; @☎; ⊖Bayswater) It's the addition of kitchenettes and a self-service laundry that differentiate these smart, reasonably priced studios and three-bedroom apartment (sleeping from one to six people) from a regular Victorian town house hotel. In spring, the garden is filled with colour and fragrance.

New Linden Hotel
HOTEL **££**

(Map p118; ☏020-7221 4321; www.newlinden .co.uk; Herford Rd, near Leinster Sq; s/d from £79/105; @☎; ⊖Bayswater) Cramming in a fair amount of style for little whack, this terrace house hotel exudes a modern and cool feel. The quiet location, helpful staff and monsoon shower heads in the deluxe rooms make this an excellent proposition.

FITZROVIA

Sanderson
HOTEL **£££**

(Map p70; ☏020-7300 1400; www.sanderson london.com; 50 Berners St; r from £253; @☎; ⊖Goodge Street) Liberace meets Philippe Starck in an 18th-century French bordello – and that's just the reception. A 3-D space scene in the lift shuttles you into darkened corridors leading to blindingly white rooms complete with sleigh beds, oil paintings hung on the ceiling, en suites behind glass walls and pink silk curtains.

Charlotte Street Hotel
HOTEL **£££**

(Map p70; ☏020-7806 2000; www.charlotte streethotel.com; 15-17 Charlotte St; d/ste from £300/492; @☎; ⊖Goodge Street) Another of the Firmdale clan, this one's a favourite with media types, with a small gym and a screening room.

London Central YHA
HOSTEL **£**

(☏0845 371 9154; www.yha.org.uk; 104-108 Bolsover St; dm £21-32, q from £70; @☎; ⊖Great Portland Street) One of London's new breed of YHA hostels, most of the four- to six-bed rooms have en suites. There's a flash cafe-bar attached to reception and a wheelchair-accessible kitchen downstairs.

BLOOMSBURY & ST PANCRAS
One step from the West End and crammed with Georgian town-house conversions, these are more affordable neighbourhoods. A stretch of lower-priced hotels runs along Gower St and on the pretty Cartwright Gardens crescent. While hardly a salubrious location, St Pancras is handy with some excellent budget options.

TOP CHOICE St Pancras

Renaissance London Hotel
HOTEL **£££**

(Map p100; ☏020-7841 3540; www.marriott.co.uk; Euston Rd; d from £295; P☎♿; ⊖King's Cross St Pancras) Staying in this iconic George Gilbert Scott–designed Gothic masterpiece is an alluring (but expensive) proposition. The

Notting Hill & Bayswater

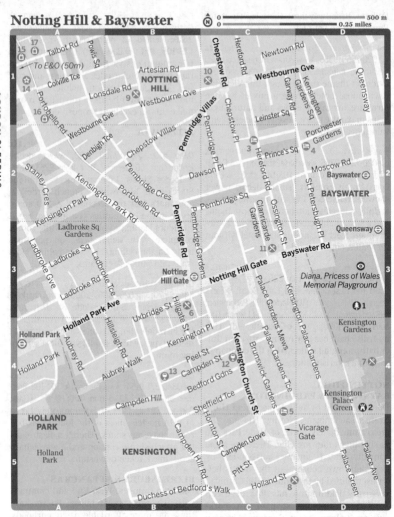

architecture is a redbrick Victorian fantasy, the lobby a magnificent conversion of the former train station taxi rank with a splendid double-staircase. Rooms are stylishly modern, dining in the Marcus Wareing–run restaurant is excellent and you can toast the former booking office architecture from the 29m-long bar.

Rough Luxe BOUTIQUE HOTEL **£££**
(Map p100; ☎0207-837 5338; www.roughluxe .co.uk; 1 Birkenhead St; r £200, with shared bathroom £179; ☎; ☺King's Cross St Pancras) Half rough, half luxury goes the blurb, and the

compelling blend of shabby and chic at this Grade II listed property is a compelling formula. Rooms treat you to the finest quality bed linen, eclectic art works cling to walls, you may get a free-standing copper bath and the service is top-notch, but the wallpaper is fetchingly distressed and the 1970s TV doesn't quite work.

Arran House Hotel B&B **££**
(Map p100; ☎020-7636 2186; www.arranhotel -london.com; 77-79 Gower St; s/d/tr/q £70/110/ 128/132, without bathroom £60/80/105/111; @☎; ☺Goodge Street) Period features such as

Notting Hill & Bayswater

cornicing and fireplaces, gorgeous gardens out back for a summer drink and a cosy lounge with two computers pushes this welcoming hotel from the average to the appealing. Squashed en suites or shared bathrooms are the trade-off for these reasonable rates.

Arosfa Hotel
B&B ££

(Map p100; ☎020-7636 2115; www.arosfalondon .com; 83 Gower St; s £60-65, d/tr/q £90/102/110; @🖧; ⊖Goodge Street) While the decor of the immaculately presented rooms is more understated, Arosfa's guest lounge is blinged up with chandeliers and clear plastic chairs. Recent refurbishments have added en suites to all 15 bedrooms, but they're tiny (putting the 'closet' back into water closet).

Jesmond Hotel
B&B £

(Map p100; ☎0207-636 3199; www.jesmonhotel .org.uk; 63 Gower St; s/d/tr/q £60/100/130/145, shared bathroom £50/80/105/135; @🖧; ⊖Goodge Street) This family-run B&B in Bloomsbury is a charmer of a place with a very handy location and fab breakfasts. Rooms may be basic and rather small but are clean and everyone is made to feel welcome. Quieter rooms face the pretty garden.

YHA London St Pancras
HOSTEL £

(Map p100; ☎020-7388 9998; www.yha.org.uk; 79 Euston Rd; dm/r from £20/61; @🖧; ⊖Kings Cross) Recent renovations have made this 185-bed hostel a dependable central London choice – despite the busy road. Rooms range from private doubles to six-bed dorms; most have bathrooms. There's a good bar and cafe but no kitchen.

Ridgemount Hotel
B&B ££

(Map p100; ☎020-7636 1141; www.ridgemounthotel .co.uk; 65-67 Gower St; s/d/tr/q £55/78/96/108, without bathroom £43/60/81/96; @🖧; ⊖Goodge Street) There's a comfortable, welcoming feel at this old-fashioned, slightly chintzy place that's been in the same family for 40 years.

Harlingford Hotel
B&B ££

(Map p100; ☎020-7387 1551; www.harlingfordhotel .com; 61-63 Cartwright Gardens; s/d/tr £86/115/130; @🖧; ⊖Russell Square) This family-run Georgian 43-room hotel sports refreshing, upbeat decor: bright-green mosaic-tiled bathrooms (with trendy sinks), fuchsia bedspreads and colourful paintings in a neighbourhood of stiff competition. It's all stairs and no lift; request a 1st-floor room.

Clink78
HOSTEL £

(Map p100; ☎020-7183 9400; www.clinkhostel .com; 78 Kings Cross Rd; dm/r from £12/60; @🖧; ⊖Kings Cross) If anyone can think of a more right-on London place to stay than the courthouse where The Clash went on trial, please let us know. You can watch TV from the witness box or sleep in the converted cells, but the majority of the rooms are custom-built and quite comfortable.

Clink261
HOSTEL £

(Map p100; ☎020-7833 9400; www.clinkhostels. com; 261-265 Grays Inn Rd; dm/r £14.60-65; @🖧; ⊖Kings Cross) Lacking the history of its sister perhaps, but this brightly refurbished hostel has had a makeover into a funky, welcoming and cheery hostel with very neat dorms, fantastically designed self-catering kitchen, fun TV lounge and internet room.

Generator
HOSTEL £

(Map p100; ☑020-7388 7666; www.generator
hostels.com/London; 37 Tavistock Pl; dm/r from
£18/55; @ 🛜; ⊖Russell Square) Lashings of primary colours and shiny metal are the hallmarks of this huge hostel. This former police
barracks has 820 beds; a bar that stays open
until 2am and hosts quizzes, pool competitions, karaoke and DJs; safe-deposit boxes;
and a large eating area (but no kitchen).
Come to party.

CLERKENWELL & FARRINGDON

In these now fashionable streets, it's hard
to find an echo of the notorious 'rookeries'
of the 19th century, where families were
squeezed into damp, fetid basements, living
in possibly the worst conditions in the city's
history. This is the London documented so
vividly by Dickens.

The availability of accommodation hasn't
kept pace with Clerkenwell's revival, but it's
still a great area to stay in. The best pickings
aren't exactly cheap.

TOP CHOICE Zetter Hotel
HOTEL £££

(Map p100; ☑020-7324 4444; www.thezetter.com;
86-88 Clerkenwell Rd; d from £222, studio £294-
438; @ 🛜; ⊖Farringdon) Guided by a sustainable ethos (water is supplied by its own bore
hole), the 59-room Zetter is lovely, from the
fine furnishings to the cutting-edge facilities. The rooftop studios with private patios
and long views are the icing on this cake.
Bistrot Bruno Loubet (p127) takes care of
the fine food end.

Rookery
LUXURY HOTEL £££

(Map p78; ☑020-7336 0931; www.rookery
hotel.com; 12 Peter's Lane, Cowcross St; s £222, d
£282-612; @ 🛜; ⊖Farringdon) Taking its name
from London's notorious slums (Fagin's
house in *Oliver Twist* was nearby), this
antique-strewn luxury hotel recreates an
18th-century ambience with none of the
attendant grime or crime. For a bird's-eye
view of St Paul's, book the two-storey Rook's
Nest, but be warned: Fagin never had a lift.

Fox & Anchor
BOUTIQUE HOTEL

(Map p78; ☑0121-616 3614; www.foxandanchor
.com; 115 Charterhouse St; r £222-246, ste £324,
weekend rate r £138-162, ste £234; ❋ 🛜; ⊖Far-
ringdon or Barbican) Each of the six rooms
at this characterful choice above a handsome pub near Smithfield Market is unique:
thoughtfully and sumptuously decorated,
some with clawfoot baths, but all with up-
to-the-minute mod cons and real panache.
Rooms are cheaper at weekends.

HOXTON, SHOREDITCH & SPITALFIELDS

Its rough-edged reputation well-smoothed
by gentrification and the arrival of moneyed
twenty-somethings, this is a knockout area
to stay for some of London's best bars and
nightlife.

TOP CHOICE Hoxton
HOTEL £

(Map p104; ☑020-7550 1000; www.hoxtonhotels
.com; 81 Great Eastern St; d & tw £59-199; @ 🛜;
⊖Old Street) A revolutionary pricing structure means that while all the rooms are
identical, the hotel aims at constantly full
occupancy. Book three months ahead (sign
up on the website) and you can, if fortunate,
nab a room for £1; you'll also need to book
early for £49 to £69 deals. The reasonably
sized rooms all have comfy beds, quality
linen and TVs that double as computers.

Andaz
HOTEL ££

(Map p78; ☑020-7961 1234; www.london.liverpool
street.andaz.com; 40 Liverpool St; r from £145;
@ 🛜; ⊖Liverpool Street) The former Great
Eastern Hotel is now the London flagship
for Hyatt's youth-focussed Andaz chain.
There's no reception here, just black-clad
staff who check you in on laptops. Rooms
are a little generic but have free juice, snacks
and wi-fi.

EAST END & DOCKLANDS

40 Winks
GUESTHOUSE ££

(www.40winks.org; 109 Mile End Rd; s/d £105/175;
⊖Stepney Green) This fun Queen Anne town
house spills over with charm, eclectic style
and whimsy, so much so that the two bedrooms (one single) are devoid of TVs. Fash-
ionistas coming to London make this their
first port of call, so book way ahead.

GREENWICH

If you'd rather keep the bustle of central
London at arm's length and nightclubbing is
your idea of hell, Greenwich offers a village-
like ambience and some great old pubs to
explore.

Number 16
B&B ££

(☑020-8853 4337; www.st-alfeges.co.uk; 16 St
Alfege Passage; s/d £75/125; @ 🛜; ⊠DLR Greenwich) This one-time sweet (candy) shop has
two well-appointed doubles and a single, individually decorated in shades of blue, green
or yellow and all with bathroom or shower
room. The amiable owners make everyone
feel at home, with chats and cups of tea in
the charming basement kitchen. From the

DLR station head up Greenwich High St and look for St Alfege Passage on your left – it's the lane that skirts the church.

HAMPSTEAD & HIGHGATE

A little further out but still in transport Zone 2, the following are excellent options within walking distance of Hampstead Heath.

Palmers Lodge   HOSTEL £

(☎020-7483 8470; www.palmerslodge.co.uk; 40 College Cres; dm £18-38; P @ 중; ❻Swiss Cottage) Reminiscent of a period murder mystery (in a good way), this former children's hospital has bags of character. Listed by English Heritage, it's stuffed with cornicing, moulded ceilings, original fireplaces and imposing wooden panelling. Ceilings are high, rooms are spacious, and there's a chapel bar with pews, a grand stairway and a roomy lounge. From Swiss Cottage tube station, cross Finchley Rd, turn left and take College Cres, which heads straight up the hill.

Hampstead Village Guesthouse   B&B ££

(☎020-7435 8679; www.hampsteadguesthouse .com; 2 Kemplay Rd; s £55-75, d £80-95, apt £100-175; @ 중; ❻Hampstead) Eclectic and thoroughly charming, this grand Victorian house has an easygoing hostess, comfy beds and a delightful back garden. There's also a studio flat, which can accommodate up to five people. From the tube station, turn left down Hampstead High St. After a few streets and lanes turn left into Willoughby Rd and then first right into Kemplay Rd.

AIRPORTS

Yotel   BUDGET HOTEL £

(☎020-7100 1100; www.yotel.com; s/d £69/85, or per 4hr £29/45 then per additional hr £8; @ 중) Gatwick (South Terminal); Heathrow (Terminal 4) The best news for early-morning flyers since coffee-vending machines, Yotel's smart 'cabins' offer pint-sized luxury: comfy beds, soft lights, internet-connected TVs, monsoon showers and fluffy towels. Swinging cats isn't recommended, but when is it ever?

✗ Eating

Dining out in London has become so fashionable that you can hardly open a menu without banging into some celebrity chef or other. The range and quality of eating options has increased exponentially over the last few decades. Waves of immigrant flavours have deeply infused London cuisine and the expectations of modern-day Londoners are much more demanding.

In this section we have sieved out choice restaurants and cafes noted for their location, value for money, unique character, ambience and, of course, good food. Vegetarians needn't fret; London has a host of dedicated meat-free joints, while most others have veggie offerings. Supermarkets are everywhere in central London. Look out for the big names: Waitrose, Tesco, Sainsbury's, Marks & Spencer, Morrisons and Asda.

WESTMINSTER & ST JAMES'S

Inn the Park   BRITISH ££

(Map p64; ☎0207-451 9999; www.innthepark.com; St James's Park; mains £9.50-18.50; ⊙8am-6pm, till 11pm in spring and summer; ❻Charing Cross or St James's Park) Enjoying a fine location within one of London's best-looking and grandest parks, this Oliver Peyton wooden restaurant rewards diners with fine cuisine and delicious views (especially from the terrace). Book ahead for dinner.

WEST END

Mayfair, Soho and Covent Garden are the gastronomic heart of London, with a blinding choice of restaurants and cuisines at budgets to suit booze hounds, theatre-goers or determined grazers.

Tamarind   INDIAN ££

(Map p92; ☎020-7629 3561; www.tamarind restaurant.com; 20 Queen St; mains £6.95-28; ⊙lunch Sun-Fri, dinner daily; ❻Green Park) A mix of spicy Moghul classics and new creations keep this award-winning Michelin-starred Indian basement restaurant a popular and refreshingly authentic choice.

TOP CHOICE **National Dining Rooms**   BRITISH £££

(Map p70; ☎020-7747 2525; www.peytonand byrne.co.uk; Sainsbury Wing, National Gallery; mains £14.50-19.50; ⊙10am-5pm Sat-Thu, 10am-8.30pm Fri; ❻Charing Cross) It's fitting that this acclaimed restaurant should celebrate British food, being in the National Gallery and overlooking Trafalgar Sq. For a much cheaper option with the same views, ambience, quality produce and excellent service, try a salad, pie or tart at the adjoining bakery.

Great Queen Street   BRITISH ££

(Map p70; ☎020-7242 0622; 32 Great Queen St; mains £9-19; ⊙lunch daily, dinner Mon-Sat; ❻Holborn) Her claret-coloured walls and mismatched wooden chairs convey cosiness and tie-loosening informality, but the daily-changing, seasonal menu is still the very best of British, and booking is a must.

Veeraswamy
INDIAN ££

(Map p70; ☑020-7734 1401; www.veeraswamy .com; 99 Regent St, enter Swallow St; mains £15-30, pre- & post-theatre 2-/3-course £18/21; ⊖Piccadilly Circus) Since 1926 Veeraswamy has occupied this prime 1st-floor location, with windows overlooking Regent St – making it Britain's longest-running Indian restaurant. The excellent food, engaging service and exotic, elegant decor make for a memorable eating experience. The entrance is on Swallow St.

Mooli's
INDIAN £

(Map p70; www.moolis.com; 50 Frith St; roti wrap £5; ⊙noon-10pm Mon-Wed, to 11.30pm Thu-Sat, closed Sun; ⊖Tottenham Court Road) This snacktastic Soho 'Indian street food' eatery will have you drooling over the home-made rotis packed with scrumptious fillings (meat, paneer, chickpeas), graded through the chilli spectrum.

Wild Honey
MODERN EUROPEAN ££

(☑020-7758 9160; www.wildhoneyrestaurant.co.uk; 12 St George St; mains £15-24; ⊖Oxford Circus) If you fancy a relatively affordable meal within the oak-panelled ambience of a top Mayfair restaurant, Wild Honey offers excellent lunch and pre-theatre set menus (respectively, £21.95 and £22.95 for three courses).

L'Atelier de Joël Robuchon
FRENCH ££

(Map p70; ☑020-7010 8600; www.joel-robuchon .com; 13 West St; mains £16-34; ⊖Leicester Square) Superchef Robuchon has 25 Michelin stars to his name – and two of them are derived from this, his London flagship. A wall of living foliage adds lushness to the dimly lit dining room, with a sparkling open kitchen as its showcase. Degustation (£125) and set lunch and pre-theatre menus (two/three courses £22/27) are available.

Ben's Cookies
BAKERY £

(Map p70; www.benscookies.com; 13a The Piazza, Covent Garden; cookie £1.50; ⊙10am-8pm Mon-Sat, 11am-7pm Sun; ⊖Covent Garden) Simply fantastic – gooey and often warm – freshly baked cookies in 18 delectable varieties. You won't want to leave.

Dean Street Townhouse
TEAHOUSE ££

(Map p70; www.deanstreettownhouse.com; 69-71 Dean St; afternoon tea £16.75; ⊖Tottenham Court Road) Serene afternoon tea in the parlour of this fine boutique hotel is the perfect place to unwind on cosy, upholstered furniture with little to occupy you but tea served with finger sandwiches, pastries, scones, crumpets, clotted cream and jam.

Giaconda Dining Room
MODERN EUROPEAN ££

(Map p70; ☑020-7240 3334; www.giacondadining .com; 9 Denmark St; mains £13.50-33; ⊙Tue-Fri lunch & dinner, dinner Sat; ⊖Tottenham Court Road) Blink and you'll miss this 10-table restaurant (we did at first). It's well worth hunting down for quality British, French and Italian dishes and attentive service. Pig trotters are a specialty but for those less au fait with offal, there's always a choice of fish dishes.

Abeno Too
JAPANESE £

(Map p70; www.abeno.co.uk; 17-18 Great Newport St; mains £8-13; ⊖Leicester Square) This restaurant specialises in soba (noodles) and okonomi-yaki (Japanese-style pancakes), which are cooked in front of you on a hotplate. Sit at the bar or by the window and feast.

Yauatcha
CHINESE ££

(Map p70; ☑020-7494 8888; www.yauatcha.com; 15 Broadwick St; dishes £4-16; ⊖Piccadilly Circus or Oxford Circus) Dim sum restaurants don't come much cooler than this, housed in Richard Rogers–designed Ingeni building, with a choice of light-filled ground-floor tables or hip basement zone. The dim sum is outstanding.

Arbutus
MODERN EUROPEAN ££

(Map p70; ☑020-7734 4545; www.arbutusrestaurant .co.uk; 63-64 Frith St; mains £14-20; ⊖Tottenham Court Road) Focussing on seasonal produce, inventive dishes and value-for-money set meals, Anthony Demetre's Michelin-starred brainchild just keeps getting better.

Nordic Bakery
SCANDINAVIAN £

(Map p70; www.nordicbakery.com; 14a Golden Sq; snacks £4-5; ⊙8am-8pm Mon-Fri, 9am-7pm Sat, 11am-6pm Sun; ⊖Piccadilly Circus) As straightforward and stylish as you'd expect from the Scandinavians, this small cafe has bare wooden walls and uncomplicated Nordic snacks, such as sticky Finnish cinnamon buns, salmon served on dark rye bread and tosca cake.

Fernandez & Wells
DELICATESSEN, CAFE £

(Map p70; www.fernandezandwells.com; 73 Beak St; mains £4-5; ⊖Piccadilly Circus) A wonderful West End mini-chain, this is one of the four branches of Fernandez & Wells, each occupying small, friendly and elegant spaces. Both the cafe and the espresso bar do sandwiches and incredibly good coffee.

Bocca di Lupo ITALIAN ££

(Map p70; ☑020-7734 2223; www.boccadilupo
.com; 12 Archer St; mains £11-25; ⊖Piccadilly Circus) Hidden on a dark Soho backstreet, Bocca radiates elegant sophistication, setting
taste buds a quiver with a mouth-watering
menu spanning Italy's culinary regions.

Barrafina SPANISH ££

(Map p70; ☑020-7813 8016; www.barrafina.co.uk;
54 Frith St; tapas £5-13; ⊖Tottenham Court Road)
The tapas here may not be as reasonably
priced as you'd get in Spain, but they are
simply infused with quality.

Bar Shu CHINESE ££

(Map p70; www.bar-shu.co.uk; 28 Frith St; mains
£8-20; ⊖Piccadilly Circus or Leicester Square) Authentic Sìchuān food long eluded the sweet-
toothed Cantonese chefs of Chinatown, but
Bar Shu concocts all the right flavours with
dishes steeped in smoked chillies and the
crucial aromatic peppercorn.

🖉 **Hummus Bros** CAFE £

(www.hbros.co.uk; mains £4-8; ☎) Soho (Map p70;
88 Wardour St; Piccadilly Circus); Holborn (Map
p100; 37-63 Southampton Row; Holborn); Cheapside (128 Cheapside; St Pauls) Don't come here if
you're chickpea-challenged, because this informal place is hummus heaven. It comes in
small or regular bowls with a choice of meat
or veggie toppings and a side of pita bread.

THE CITY

You'll be sorely dismayed if you've got an
empty belly on a Sunday morning in the
City. Even during the busy weekdays, the
chain eateries are often your best option.

[TOP CHOICE] **Sweetings** SEAFOOD ££

(Map p78; www.sweetingsrestaurant.com; 39 Queen
Victoria St; mains £12.50-32; ⊙lunch Mon-Fri;
⊖Mansion House) Serving customers since
1889, Sweetings is a massively popular fixture on the culinary map of the City, serving delicious and sustainably sourced fish
(grilled, fried or poached), fried whitebait,
smoked trout and the standout chef's pie
(£13.50).

Restaurant at St Paul's MODERN BRITISH £££

(Map p78; www.restaurantatstpauls.co.uk; Crypt,
St Paul's Cathedral; 2/3 course lunch £21.95/24.95;
⊙noon-3pm; ⊖St Paul's) Dine in the crypt of
St Paul's Cathedral at this choicely located
restaurant with a short and simple but
regularly changing menu offering two- or
three-course lunches and a good-value express lunch, as well as afternoon tea.

SOUTH BANK

Popular restaurants make the most of the
iconic riverside views but scouting around
turns up gems all over the place. For a feed
with a local feel, head to Borough Market
(p140) or Bermondsey St.

[TOP CHOICE] **Laughing Gravy** BRITISH ££

(Map p84; ☑020-7998 1707; www.thelaughing
gravy.co.uk; 154 Blackfriars Rd; mains £8.50-17.50;
⊙11am-late Mon-Fri, 5.30pm-late Sat, noon-6pm
Sun; ⊖Southwark) Recently steered in a lu-
crative fresh direction by new owners, this
restaurant is a Southwark gem, with a sure-
fire menu combining locally sourced food
and culinary talent, plus splendid roasts on
Sunday and attentive service all round.

Oxo Tower Brasserie FUSION £££

(Map p84; ☑020-7803 3888; www.harveynichols
.com/restaurants/oxo-tower-london; Barge House
St; mains £18-26; ⊖Waterloo) The extravagant
views are the big drawcard, so skip the
restaurant and head for the slightly less
extravagantly priced brasserie, or if you're
not hungry, the bar. The food is excellent,
combining European and East Asian flavours. Set-price menus (two/three courses
£22.50/26.50) are offered at lunchtime, before 6.15pm and after 10pm.

Magdalen MODERN BRITISH ££

(Map p84; ☑020-7403 1342; www.magdalen
restaurant.co.uk; 152 Tooley St; mains £14-18, lunch
2/3 course £16/19; ⊙lunch Mon-Fri, dinner Mon-
Sat; ⊖London Bridge) This lovely Tooley St restaurant hits the spot for anyone determined
to savour some of London's best Modern
British fare. With a focus on charcuterie, lovingly cooked and presented, it's not the place
to bring a vegetarian or a weight-conscious
waif on a date.

Anchor & Hope GASTROPUB ££

(Map p84; 36 The Cut; mains £12-17; ⊙lunch Tue-
Sun, dinner Mon-Sat; ⊖Southwark) The hope is
that you'll get a table without waiting hours
because you can't book at this quintessential
gastropub, except for Sunday lunch at 2pm.
The anchor is gutsy, unashamedly carnivorous British food.

BELGRAVIA

Thomas Cubitt BRITISH ££

(Map p92; ☑020-7730 6060; www.thethomascubitt
.co.uk; 44 Elizabeth St; mains £17-23; ⊖Victoria)
The bar below gets rammed to the impressively high rafters with the swanky Belgravia set, and upstairs is this excellent,

---

WORTH A TRIP

THE BURGERS OF BRIXTON

Honest Burgers (020-7733 7963; www.honestburgers.co.uk; Unit 12, Brixton Village; burgers from £6.50; noon-4pm Sun-Wed, noon-4pm & 6-10pm Thu-Sat; Brixton), an excellent-value burger outfit in the trendy and enterprising Brixton Village, has won serious plaudits for its juicy and tender burgers and glorious rosemary-seasoned triple-cooked chips. It's well worth waiting for a table, which you could well have to do (it's titchy and only seats around 30; no bookings).

---

elegant dining room. The culinary focus is thoroughly British and deftly executed. The downstairs menu is cheaper (£10 to £17).

Kazan　　　　　　　　　　　TURKISH ££
(www.kazan-restaurant.com; 93-94 Wilton Rd; mains £11.95-15.95; Victoria) Kazan received repeated accolades for its set *meze* platters, *shish* kebabs and *karniyarik* (lamb-stuffed aubergines). Flavours are rich and full, service attentive and the refreshingly unaffected setting allows diners to concentrate on the culinary aromas. Seafood and vegetarian options also available.

KNIGHTSBRIDGE

Dinner by Heston Blumenthal　　　　MODERN BRITISH £££
(Map p92; 0207-201 3833; www.dinnerbyheston.com; Mandarin Oriental Hyde Park, 66 Knightsbridge; set lunch £28, mains £32-72; Knightsbridge) The eagerly awaited opening of sumptuously presented Dinner is a gastronomic tour de force, ushering diners on a tour of British culinary history (with inventive modern inflections). The interior design is a similar triumph, from the glass-walled kitchen and its overhead clock mechanism to the large windows onto the park.

Marcus Wareing at the Berkeley　　　　　　　　FRENCH £££
(Map p92; 020-7235 1200; www.marcus-wareing.com; Berkeley Hotel, Wilton Pl; 3-course lunch/dinner £38/80; Knightsbridge) Wareing runs this one-time Gordon Ramsay restaurant under his own name, and its reputation for exquisite food and exemplary service has only been enhanced.

CHELSEA & KENSINGTON

These highbrow neighbourhoods harbour some of London's very best (and priciest) restaurants.

Tom's Kitchen　　　　MODERN EUROPEAN ££
(Map p92; 020-7349 0202; www.tomskitchen.co.uk; 27 Cale St; breakfast £4-15, mains £13.90-30; breakfast Mon-Fri, lunch & dinner daily; South Kensington) Celebrity chef Tom Aikens' restaurant keeps the magic flowing through the day, with award-winning breakfasts and pancakes drawing acclaim and crowds to its informal, but engaging, dining setting.

L'Etranger　　　　　FRENCH, JAPANESE ££
(Map p92; 020-7584 1118; www.etranger.co.uk; 36 Gloucester Rd; mains £15-29; Gloucester Road) A refined grey and burgundy interior (echoed in waitress uniforms that are part kimono, part Parisian runway) sets the tone for a romantic formal dining experience. While most of the menu is French, it's also possible to blow the budget on sashimi and five types of caviar. The two-/three-course weekday set lunch and pre-6.45pm dinner are £17/20.

Orsini　　　　　　　　　　　ITALIAN ££
(Map p92; www.orsiniristorante.com; 8a Thurloe Pl; snacks £2-6, mains £9-16; 8am-10pm; South Kensington) Marinated in authentic Italian charm, this tiny family-run eatery serves excellent espresso and deliciously fresh baguettes stuffed with Parma ham and mozzarella. More substantial fare is offered in the evenings.

Gordon Ramsay　　　　　　　FRENCH £££
(Map p92; 020-7352 4441; www.gordonramsay.com; 68 Royal Hospital Rd; 3-course lunch/dinner £45/90; Sloane Square) One of Britain's finest restaurants and London's longest-running with three coveted Michelin stars, you'll need to book ahead and hop into your best togs: jeans and T-shirts don't get past the door. And if you've seen the chef in action, you'll know not to argue.

NOTTING HILL, BAYSWATER & PADDINGTON

Notting Hill teems with good places to eat, from cheap takeaways to atmospheric pubs and restaurants worthy of the fine-dining tag. Queensway has the best strip of Asian restaurants this side of Soho.

Taquería
MEXICAN £

(Map p118; www.taqueria.co.uk; 139-143 Westbourne Grove; tacos from £4.10; ⏳lunch & dinner; ⊖Notting Hill Gate) Its sustainable credentials are as exacting and appealing as its authentic soft-corn, freshly-made tortillas – this place instantly elbows other Mexican restaurants into the Tex-Mex shade. Fish is all sustainably sourced and the pork, chicken and eggs come free range.

Geales
SEAFOOD ££

(Map p118; ☎020-7727 7528; www.geales.com; 2 Farmer St; 2-course lunch £10, mains £10-18; ⏳closed lunch Mon; ⊖Notting Hill Gate) Frying fish since 1939, Geales' fish is highly succulent, although chips disappointingly cost extra (outside of the set lunch) in what should be a classic combination. The corner location, tucked away off energetic Notting Hill Gate, is a big draw, with tables spilling out onto a quiet street.

Electric Brasserie
FRENCH ££

(Map p118; ☎020-7908 9696; www.electric brasserie.com; 191 Portobello Rd; breakfasts £5.50-13.50, mains £9-36; ⊖Ladbroke Grove) The leather-and-cream look is coolly suited to this brasserie attached to the Electric Cinema (p137). And the food's excellent as well, whether it's breakfast, weekend brunches, hearty lunches or dinner. If you're feeling decadent, lobster and chips (£36) is the way to go.

E&O
ASIAN ££

(www.rickerrestaurants.com; 14 Blenheim Crescent; mains £9.50-28; ⊖Ladbroke Grove) This splendid-looking restaurant off Portobello Road lures crowds with its ever-popular Japanese-Chinese Pan-Asian fusion fare, sleek black-and-white minimalism and cool bar.

Satay House
MALAYSIAN £

(☎020-7723 6763; www.satay-house.co.uk; 13 Sale Pl; mains £5-19; ⊖Edgware Road) Authentic Malaysian cuisine, including some dishes that will blow your head off, have been served here for nearly 40 years. Book ahead for an upstairs table, although the communal tables in the basement can be fun. Sale Pl is one block along Sussex Gardens from Edgware Rd.

MARYLEBONE
You won't go too far wrong planting yourself on a table anywhere along Marylebone's charming High St.

Providores & Tapa Room
FUSION £££

(Map p95; ☎020-7935 6175; www.theprovidores. co.uk; 109 Marylebone High St; 2/3/4/5 courses £30/43/53/60; ⊖Baker Street) New Zealand's most distinctive culinary export since kiwi fruit, chef Peter Gordon works his fusion magic here, matching his creations with NZ wines. Downstairs, in a cute play on words, the Tapa Room (as in the Polynesian bark-cloth) serves sophisticated tapas, along with excellent breakfasts.

La Fromagerie
CAFE £

(Map p95; www.lafromagerie.co.uk; 2-6 Moxon St; mains £6-13; ⊖Baker Street) This deli-cafe has bowls of delectable salads, antipasto, peppers and beans scattered about the long communal table. Huge slabs of bread invite you to tuck in, and all the while the heavenly waft from the cheese room beckons.

Locanda Locatelli
ITALIAN ££

(Map p95; ☎020-7935 9088; www.locandalocatelli. com; 8 Seymour St; mains £11-30; ⊖Marble Arch) Known for its sublime but pricey pasta dishes, this dark but quietly glamorous restaurant in an otherwise unremarkable hotel is one of London's hottest tables.

BLOOMSBURY & ST PANCRAS

Dabbous
MODERN EUROPEAN ££

(Map p100; ☎0207-323 1544; www.dabbous.co.uk; 39 Whitfield St; mains £11-14, 3/4-course set lunch £21/24; ⊖Goodge Street) An innovative approach to flavour and healthy ingredients lies behind this restaurant's growing popularity. The rather stark and pared down ambience may not suit all tastes, but it's offset by an inventive menu full of surprises and ideas; the basement cocktail bar is just the place for a pre-meal libation.

North Sea Fish Restaurant
FISH & CHIPS £

(Map p100; www.northseafishrestaurant.co.uk; 7-8 Leigh St; mains £9-20; ⏳closed Sun; ⊖Russell Square) Every day is fryday except Sunday at the North Sea, a classic chippie for eat-in or takeaway with jumbo-sized plaice or halibut steaks, deep-fried or grilled, and large servings of chips.

Pâtisserie Deux Amis
FRENCH £

(Map p100; ☎020-7383 7029; 63 Judd St; baguettes from £2.90; ⊖Russell Square or King's Cross St Pancras) If you crave scrummy croissants, pain au chocolate, fine coffee, filled baguettes and all the gourmand trappings of Gallic breakfasts and snacks, this bijou patisserie is a delight, with a few tables flung out front and excellent service all round.

Chilli Cool
CHINESE £

(Map p100; www.chillicool.com; 15 Leigh St; mains £4.80-19.80; ⊖Russell Square) Don't judge a Chinese book by its cover – what Chilli Cool (Chinese name Lao Chengdu, referring to the capital of Sichuan) lacks in gloss is more than heartily compensated for by its sure-fire Sichuan menu, which spills forth all the classics: *dan dan* noodles, *ma po tofu* (tofu with nuggets of mince in a spicy sauce) and sliced beef Sicchuan style.

Diwana Bhel Poori House
INDIAN £

(Map p100; 121-123 Drummond St; mains £7-9; ⏚; ⊖Euston or Euston Square) This ace Indian vegetarian eatery specialises in *bhel poori* (sweet-and-sour, soft and crunchy 'party mix' snacks), *dosas* (filled rice-flour pancakes), *thali* and the all-you-can-eat, value lunchtime buffet is a legendary blowout.

FITZROVIA
Tucked away behind busy Tottenham Court Rd, Fitzrovia's Charlotte and Goodge Sts form one of central London's most vibrant eating precincts.

TOP CHOICE Hakkasan
CHINESE £££

(Map p70; ☎7927 7000; www.hakkasan.com; 8 Hanway Pl; mains £9.50-42; ⊖Tottenham Court Road) Michelin-starred Hakkasan – hidden down a lane like all fashionable haunts should be – elegantly pairs fine Chinese dining with stunning design and some persuasive cocktail chemistry. The low lighting hits all the right romantic notes and the all-embracing menu ranges from Sichuan *ma po doufu* to grilled Shanghai dumplings, Peking duck and beyond.

Salt Yard
SPANISH, ITALIAN ££

(Map p70; ☎020-7637 0657; www.saltyard.co.uk; 54 Goodge St; tapas £4-8; ⊖Goodge Street) Named after the place where cold meats are cured, this softly lit joint serves delicious Spanish and Italian tapas. Try the roasted chicken leg with gnocchi, wild garlic and sorrel, or flex your palate with courgette flowers stuffed with cheese and drizzled with honey.

🍃 Lantana
CAFE £

(Map p70; www.lantanacafe.co.uk; 13 Charlotte Pl; mains £4-10; ⊙breakfast & lunch Mon-Sat; ⊖Goodge Street) Excellent coffee and substantial, inventive brunches induce queues on Saturday mornings outside this Australian-style cafe.

CAMDEN TOWN
Camden's great for cheap eats, while neighbouring Chalk Farm and Primrose Hill are salted with gastropubs and upmarket restaurants.

CHAIN-CHAIN-CHAIN, CHAIN OF FOODS

It's an unnerving, but not uncommon, experience to discover the idiosyncratic cafe or pub you were so proud of finding on your first day in London popping up on every other high street. But among the endless Caffe Neros, Pizza Expresses and All-Bar-Ones are some gems, or, at least, great fallback options. The following are some of the best:

GBK (Map p100; www.gbk.co.uk) Gourmet Burger Kitchens, dishing up creative burger constructions, including lots of vegetarian options.

Konditor & Cook (Map p70; www.konditorandcook.com) London's best bakery chain, serving excellent cakes, pastries, bread and coffee.

Leon (Map p70; www.leonrestaurants.co.uk) Focussing on fresh, seasonal food (salads, wraps and the like).

Nando's (Map p103; ☎020-7424 9040; www.nandos.co.uk; 57-58 Chalk Farm Rd; Camden Town) Loved by Londoners for fantastic value, mouthwatering spicy chicken *a la portuguesa* – with some blindingly hot peri-peri sauces.

Ping Pong (Map p95; www.pingpongdimsum.com; ⊙lunch & dinner) Chinese dumpling joints.

Pizza Express (Map p70; ☎020-7437 9595; www.pizzaexpress.com; 10 Dean St; mains £6.95-11.50) Excellent pizza, neat ambience and standout locations across London.

Wagamama (Map p70; www.wagamama.com; 4 Streatham St, Bloomsbury) Japanese noodles taking over the world from their London base.

Zizzi (Map p118; www.zizzi.co.uk) Wood-fired pizza.

TOP CHOICE Market Restaurant   MODERN BRITISH ££

(Map p103; 020-7267 9700; www.market restaurant.co.uk; 43 Parkway; 2-course lunch £10, mains £10-14; lunch & dinner Mon-Sat, lunch Sun; Camden Town) In a simple, forthright but at the same time appealing setting of bare brick walls and basic wooden chairs, this fantastic and uncomplicated restaurant does a magnificent job of preparing wholesome British cuisine, with the occasional European nod.

Mango Room   CARIBBEAN ££

(Map p103; 020-7482 5065; www.mangoroom .co.uk; 10-12 Kentish Town Rd; mains £11-14; Camden Town) Mango Room is an upmarket Caribbean experience serving a mix of modern and traditional dishes: Creole snapper, goat curry, jerk chicken etc set to a ska and reggae musical backdrop.

ISLINGTON

Allow at least an evening to explore Islington's Upper St, along with the lanes leading off it.

TOP CHOICE Le Mercury   FRENCH £

(Map p128; 020-7354 4088; www.lemercury .co.uk; 140a Upper St; mains £7-10; Highbury & Islington) A cosy Gallic haunt ideal for cash-strapped Casanovas, given that it appears much more expensive than it is. Sunday lunch by the open fire upstairs is a treat, although you'll have to book.

Ottolenghi   BAKERY, MEDITERRANEAN ££

(www.ottolenghi.co.uk; mains £10-15;) Islington (Map p128; 020-7288 1454; 287 Upper St; 8am-11pm Mon-Sat, 9am-7pm Sun; Angel); Belgravia (Map p92; 13 Motcomb St; 8am-8pm Mon-Fri, 8am-7pm Sat, 9am-6pm Sun; Knightsbridge); Kensington (Map p118; 1 Holland St; 8am-8pm Mon-Fri, 8am-7pm Sat, 9am-6pm Sun; High St Kensington); Notting Hill (Map p118; 63 Ledbury Rd; 8am-8pm Mon-Fri, 8am-7pm Sat, 8.30am-6pm Sun; Notting Hill Gate) Mountains of meringues draw you through the door, where a sumptuous array of bakery treats and salads greets you. Meals are as light and tasty as the lovely white interior design. Vegetarians are well catered for. The Islington branch is open till later – until 11pm, and 7pm on Sundays.

CLERKENWELL & FARRINGDON

Clerkenwell's hidden gems are well worth digging for. Pedestrianised Exmouth Market is a good place to start.

TOP CHOICE Bistrot Bruno Loubet   FRENCH ££

(Map p100; 020-7324 4455; www.bistrotbruno loubet.com; 86-88 Clerkenwell Rd; mains £12-17; breakfast, lunch & dinner; Farringdon) Facing onto St John's Sq, this elegant restaurant from Bruno Loubet at the Zetter (p120) matches top quality ingredients and inventive taste combinations with impeccable execution, in the food, cocktails and the home-infused aperitifs.

St John   BRITISH ££

(Map p78; 020-7251 0848; www.stjohnrestaurant .com; 26 St John St; mains £14-22; Farringdon) Bright whitewashed brick walls, high ceilings and simple wooden furniture keep diners free to concentrate on the world-famous nose-to-tail offerings. Expect chitterlings and ox tongue.

Little Bay   EUROPEAN £

(Map p100; 020-7278 1234; www.little-bay .co.uk; 171 Farringdon Rd; mains before/after 7pm £6.45/8.45; Farringdon) The crushed-velvet ceiling, handmade twisted lamps that improve around the room (as their creator got better at making them) and elaborately painted bar and tables showing nymphs frolicking are weird but fun. The hearty food is very good value.

Modern Pantry   FUSION ££

(Map p100; 020-7553 9210; www.themodern pantry.co.uk; 47-48 St John's Sq; mains £15-22; breakfast, lunch & dinner; Farringdon) One of London's most talked-about eateries, this three-floor Georgian town house in the heart of Clerkenwell has a cracking innovative, all-day menu.

Medcalf   BRITISH ££

(Map p100; 020-7833 3533; www.medcalfbar .co.uk; 40 Exmouth Market; mains £10-16; closed dinner Sun; Farringdon) The stylish Medcalf is one of the best value hang-outs right in the heart of Exmouth Market. Housed in a beautifully converted 1912 butcher's shop, it serves up interesting and well-realised British fare.

HOXTON, SHOREDITCH & SPITALFIELDS

From the hit-and-miss Bangladeshi restaurants of Brick Lane to the Vietnamese strip on Kingsland Rd, and the Jewish, Spanish, French, Italian and Greek eateries in between, the East End's cuisine is as multicultural as its residents.

Islington

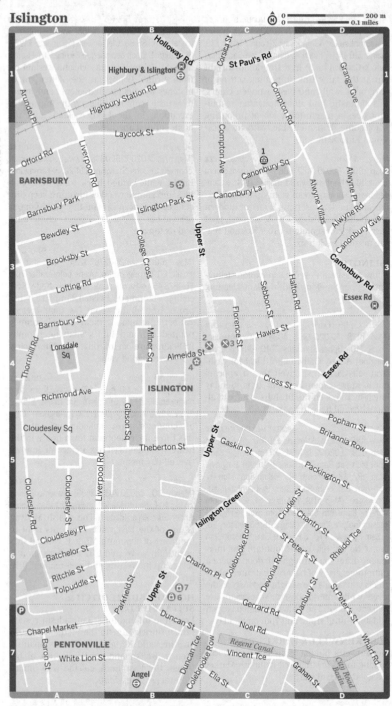

Islington

◎ Sights

✖ Eating

◎ Entertainment

◎ Shopping

TOP CHOICE Poppies   FISH & CHIPS £

(Map p104; www.poppiesfishandchips.co.uk; 6-8 Hanbury St; mains £6-11; ⊘11am-11pm, to 10.30pm Sun; ⊠Shoreditch High Street, ⊜Shoreditch High Street) Frying since 1945, this fantastic Spitalfields chippie is a retro delight, a throwback to the 1950s with iconic jukebox, wall-to-wall memorabilia, waitresses in pinnies and hairnets and classic fish and chips (plus jellied eels).

Fifteen   ITALIAN ££

(☎0871 330 1515; www.fifteen.net; 15 Westland Pl; breakfast £2-8.50, trattoria £6-11, restaurant £11-25; ⊘breakfast, lunch & dinner; ⊜Old Street) Jamie Oliver's culinary philanthropy started at Fifteen, set up to give unemployed young people a shot at a career. The Italian food is beyond excellent, and, surprisingly, even those on limited budgets can afford a visit. From Old Street tube station, take City Rd and after 300m turn right into Westland Place.

Sông Que   VIETNAMESE £

(Map p104; www.songque.co.uk; 134 Kingsland Rd E2; mains £6-9; ⊜Hoxton) Arrive after 7.30pm and you can expect to queue: this humble eatery is one of the best Vietnamese restaurants in London and you'll be shunted out shortly after your last bite. Sông Que is 300m along Kingsland Rd, the continuation of Shoreditch High St.

Princess of Shoreditch   GASTROPUB ££

(Map p104; ☎020-7729 9270; www.theprincessof shoreditch.com; 76 Paul St; pub mains £10-18.50; ⊜Old Steet) Perfect for a drink or a meal, the Princess can get busy thanks to its excellent gastropub menu, fine wine list, choice ales

and particularly good-looking interior. Upstairs is the slightly more expensive dining room.

L'Anima   ITALIAN ££

(Map p104; ☎020-7422 7000; www.lanima.co.uk; 1 Snowden St; mains £15-32.50; ⊘lunch Mon-Fri, dinner Mon-Sat; ⊜Liverpool Street) Sleek design meets accomplished cooking – what could be more Italian? The capacious space is divided into a formal dining room and a bar/lounge where you can drop in for a quick pasta fix.

Albion   BRITISH ££

(Map p104; www.albioncaff.co.uk; 2-4 Boundary St; mains £9-13; ⊜Old Street) For those wanting to be taken back to Dear Old Blighty's cuisine but with rather less grease and stodge, this self-consciously retro 'caff' serves up top-quality bangers and mash, steak-and-kidney pies, devilled kidneys and, of course, fish and chips.

Les Trois Garçons   MODERN FRENCH £££

(Map p104; ☎7613 1924; www.lestroisgarcons.com; 1 Club Row; 2/3 courses £39.50/45.50; ⊘closed dinner Sun; ⊜Shoreditch High Street) A virtual menagerie of stuffed or bronze animals fills every surface, while chandeliers dangle between a set of suspended handbags. The food is great, if overpriced, and the small army of bow-tie-wearing waiters unobtrusively delivers complimentary bread and tasty gifts from the kitchen.

Brick Lane Beigel Bake   BAGELS £

(Map p104; 159 Brick Lane; most bagels less than £2; ⊘24hr; ⊜Liverpool Street) Always busy, this relic of London's Jewish East End is more takeaway than cafe and sells dirt-cheap bagels, a top late-night snack on a bellyful of booze.

EAST END

TOP CHOICE Formans   BRITISH ££

(☎020-8525 2365; www.formans.co.uk; Stour Rd, Fish Island; mains £11.50-20; ⊘dinner Thu & Fri, brunch & dinner Sat, lunch Sun; ⊜Hackney) Curing fish since 1905, riverside Formans boasts prime views over the Olympic stadium alongside a delectable choice of smoked salmon (including the signature London cure) and seafood plus a choice of other mouthwatering British dishes. A viewing gallery into the smokery and a lounge bar rounds out an attractive picture.

GREENWICH & SOUTH LONDON

Tai Won Mein   NOODLES £

(39 Greenwich Church St; mains from £4.95; ⊙11.30am-11.30pm; ℞DLR Cutty Sark) This busy Cantonese restaurant serves epic portions of steaming noodles to those overcoming Greenwich's titanic sights. Flavours are simple, but fresh, and the namesake *tai won mein* (big bowl of noodles) seafood noodles may have you applauding (but put your chopsticks down first).

 Drinking

As long as there's been a city, Londoners have loved to drink – and, as history shows, often immoderately. The pub is the hub of social life and, despite depleting numbers, there's always one near at hand. When the sun shines, drinkers spill out into the streets, parks and squares.

Boho Soho is undoubtedly the heart of bar culture, with enough variety to cater to all tastes. Still great for grungy boozers and rock kids, Camden has lost ground on the bohemian-cool front to Hoxton and Shoreditch.

Neighbourhoods such as Clerkenwell, Islington, Southwark, Notting Hill and Earl's Court are bursting at their beer-addled seams with pub-crawl potential.

Mirroring its worker-base, the City is a Monday to Friday spot and several of its historic pubs shut up shop at weekends or on Sundays. South London has some fine historic pubs near the river.

The price of beer in pubs is enough to drive you to drink – expect to pay upwards of £3.25 per pint of lager.

WEST END

Gordon's Wine Bar   BAR

(Map p70; www.gordonswinebar.com; 47 Villiers St; ⊖Embankment) What's not to love about this cavernous, candlelit wine cellar that's been practically unchanged for the last 120 years? Get here before the office crowd (generally around 6pm) or forget about getting a table.

TOP CHOICE French House   BAR

(Map p70; 49 Dean St; ⊖Leicester Square) French House, the meeting place of the Free French Forces during WWII, is Soho's legendary boho boozer with a history to match: De Gaulle is said to have knocked back shots here, while Dylan Thomas, Peter O'Toole, Brendan Behan and Francis Bacon all conspired to drink the place dry. The no-mobile phones, no-music and no-TV ruling only amplifies the mystique.

LAB   COCKTAIL BAR

(Map p70; www.lab-townhouse.com; 12 Old Compton St; ⊖Leicester Square) The decor of the London Academy of Bartending has been left behind, but a frisson of creativity runs through the cocktail menu and LAB's mixologists can have your tastebuds singing.

Princess Louise   PUB

(Map p70; 208 High Holborn; ⊖Holborn) This late-19th-century Victorian boozer is arguably London's most beautiful pub. Spectacularly decorated with fine tiles, etched mirrors, plasterwork and a gorgeous central horseshoe bar, it gets packed with the after-work crowd.

Coach & Horses   PUB

(Map p70; www.coachandhorsessoho.co.uk; 29 Greek St; ⊖Leicester Square) Regulars at this no-nonsense Soho institution have included Francis Bacon, Peter O'Toole and Lucien Freud. The Wednesday and Saturday night singalongs are tops.

Lamb & Flag   PUB

(Map p70; 33 Rose St; ⊖Covent Garden) Everyone's Covent Garden 'find', this historic pub is often as jammed with punters as it is packed with history. Built in 1623 and formerly (and evocatively) called the 'Bucket of Blood', inside it's all brass fittings and creaky wooden floors.

Galvin at Windows   BAR

(Map p64; www.galvinatwindows.com; The Hilton, 22 Park Lane; ⊖Hyde Park Corner) Be stunned by both the views and the cocktail prices at this 28th-floor eyrie at the Hilton, overlooking Hyde Park.

Jewel   COCKTAIL BAR

(www.jewelbar.com) Piccadilly Circus (Map p70; 4-6 Glasshouse St; ⊖Piccadilly Circus); Covent Garden (Map p70; 29-30 Maiden Lane; ⊖Covent Garden) Chandeliers, banquettes, cocktails and, in Piccadilly, sunset views.

Monmouth Coffee Company   CAFE

(⊙Mon-Sat) Covent Garden (Map p70; 27 Monmouth St; ⊖Covent Garden); Borough (Map p84; 2 Park St; ⊖London Bridge) There's an array of treats on the counter, but it's the coffee that's the star, nay god, here. Chat to a caffeinated stranger on one of the tight tables at the back, or grab a takeaway and slink off to a nearby lane for your fix.

THE CITY

Vertigo 42
BAR

(Map p78; ☑020-7877 7842; www.vertigo42.co.uk; Tower 42, Old Broad St; ⊖Liverpool St) Book a two-hour slot in this 42nd-floor champagne bar (no shorts, caps or flipflops) with stunning vertiginous views across London from the former National Westminster Tower. Reservations only.

Ye Olde Cheshire Cheese
PUB

(Map p78; Wine Office Crt, 145 Fleet St; ⊖Holborn) Rebuilt six years after the Great Fire, this hoary pub was popular with Dr Johnson, Thackeray, Dickens and the visiting Mark Twain. Touristy but always atmospheric and enjoyable for a pub meal.

Black Friar
PUB

(Map p78; 174 Queen Victoria St; ⊖Blackfriars) With its fabulous Arts and Crafts interior and a strong choice of ales and bitters, this pub is a pleasant surprise, flung up on the site of a Dominican monastery, a theme that finds constant echo throughout.

SOUTH BANK

[TOP CHOICE] Rake
PUB

(Map p84; 14 Winchester Walk; ⊙noon-11pm Mon-Fri, from 10am Sat; ⊖London Bridge) The only pub actually within Borough Market and London's smallest boozer, the Rake crams a superlative choice of bitters and real ales into pea-sized premises. There's valuable elbow space on the bamboo-decorated decking outside.

George Inn
PUB

(Map p84; www.nationaltrust.org.uk/main/w -georgeinn; 77 Borough High St; ⊖London Bridge) This glorious old boozer is London's last surviving galleried coaching inn, dating from 1676 and now a National Trust property. Getting a mention in Dickens' *Little Dorrit*, it also stands on the site of the Tabard Inn, where the pilgrims in Chaucer's *Canterbury Tales* gathered before hitting the road to Canterbury.

Anchor
PUB

(Map p84; 34 Park St; ⊖London Bridge) This 18th-century riverside boozer replaced the 1615 original where Samuel Pepys witnessed the Great Fire. Trips to the terrace are rewarded with fine views, but brace for a constant deluge of drinkers. Dr Samuel Johnson was once a regular.

CHELSEA & KENSINGTON

Bibendum Oyster Bar
BAR

(Map p92; www.bibendum.co.uk; 81 Fulham Rd; ⊖South Kensington) Slurp up some bivalves and knock back a champers in the glorious foyer of the standout art nouveau/deco Michelin House (1911). The Michelin Man is everywhere: in mosaics, stained glass (the originals disappeared in WWII), crockery and the architecture itself.

BLOOMSBURY & ST PANCRAS

[TOP CHOICE] Newman Arms
PUB

(Map p70; www.newmanarms.co.uk; 23 Rathbone St; ⊖Tottenham Court Road) One of the few family-run pubs in central London, this tiny one-room affair with upstairs pie room has a big history; George Orwell and Dylan Thomas drank here and a scene from Michael Powell's *Peeping Tom* was filmed in the passageway alongside the pub in 1960.

Euston Tap
BAR

(Map p100; www.eustontap.com; 190 Euston Rd; ⊙from noon; ⊖Euston Square) Housed in a 19th century Portland stone lodge, this small two-floor place squeezes in an impressive range of real ales and bottled beers for specialist drinkers and beer obsessives; if cider is more your calling, head opposite to the Cider Tap for a mouthwatering range.

Queen's Larder
PUB

(Map p100; www.queenslarder.co.uk; 1 Queen Sq; ⊖Russell Square) This small and supremely cosy pub in a gorgeous square gets its name from Queen Charlotte, wife of 'Mad' king George III, who rented part of the pub's cellar to store special foods for him while he was undergoing treatment nearby. Poets Sylvia Plath and Ted Hughes married in the church opposite.

Big Chill House
BAR, DJS

(Map p100; www.bigchill.net; 257-259 Pentonville Rd; ⊖King's Cross) Come the weekend, the only remotely chilled-out space in this busy bar, split over two levels, is its first-rate and generously proportioned rooftop terrace.

NOTTING HILL, BAYSWATER & PADDINGTON

[TOP CHOICE] Churchill Arms
PUB

(Map p118; 119 Kensington Church St; ⊖Notting Hill Gate) Adorned with a gob-smacking array of flower baskets and Union Jacks, this magnificent old boozer on Kensington Church St is a London classic, famed for its atmosphere, Winston memorabilia, knick-knacks and attached conservatory serving fine Thai food.

Windsor Castle PUB
(Map p118; www.thewindsorcastlekensington.co.uk; 114 Campden Hill Rd; ⊖Notting Hill Gate) A fine pub with oak partitions separating the original bars at the crest of Campden Hill Rd. One of the loveliest walled gardens of any pub in London is tucked away through the side entrance. The bones of Thomas Paine (*Rights of Man* writer) are rumoured to be in the cellar.

MARYLEBONE

TOP CHOICE Purl COCKTAIL BAR
(Map p95; ☑020-7935 0835; www.purl-london .com; 50-54 Blandford St; ⊖5-11.30pm Mon-Thu, till midnight Fri & Sat; ⊖Baker Street) Coined after an old English early morning drink of warm beer, gin, wormwood and spices, Purl is all warm, low lighting, subterranean mellowness and some magnificently presented and unusual cocktails. If you're a group, book an alcove table. On the musical menu is swing and jazz. Book ahead.

Artesian BAR
(www.artesian-bar.co.uk; Langham Hotel, 1c Portland Pl; ⊖Oxford Circus) For doses of colonial glamour with a touch of the Orient, the sumptuous bar at the Langham hits the mark. Rum is the speciality here – award-winning cocktails (from £14) are concocted from the 60 varieties on offer.

CAMDEN TOWN

Lock Tavern PUB, LIVE MUSIC
(Map p103; www.lock-tavern.co.uk; 35 Chalk Farm Rd; ⊖Camden Town) The archetypal Camden pub, the Lock has both a rooftop terrace and a beer garden and attracts an interesting crowd with its mix of ready conviviality and regular live music.

Proud Camden BAR, LIVE MUSIC
(Map p103; www.proudcamden.com; The Horse Hospital, Stables Market; admission free-£10; ⊖Camden Town) Proud occupies a former horse hospital within Stables Market, with booths in the stalls, ice-cool rock photography on the walls and hip locals. Spin around the gallery during the day, enjoy bands at night and hit the terrace in summer.

CLERKENWELL & FARRINGDON

Jerusalem Tavern PUB
(Map p100; www.stpetersbrewery.co.uk; 55 Britton St; ⊖Farringdon) Pick a wood-panelled cubbyhole to park yourself in at this tiny 1720 coffee shop–turned-inn (named after the Priory of St John of Jerusalem) and choose from a selection of St Peter's fantastic beers and ales, brewed in North Suffolk.

HOXTON, SHOREDITCH & SPITALFIELDS
Good stops on a Hoxton hop:

TOP CHOICE Book Club BAR, CLUB
(Map p104; ☑020-7684 8618; www.wearebtc .com; 100 Leonard St; ⊖8am-midnight Mon-Wed, 8am-2am Thu & Fri, 10am-2am Sat & Sun; ⊖Old Street) A cerebral/creative vibe animates this fantastic one-time Victorian warehouse in Shoreditch that hosts cultural events (life drawing, workshops, dance lessons) and DJ nights to complement the drinking, enthusiastic ping pong games and pool-playing shenanigans. Early birds can catch breakfast from 8am weekdays and food continues through the day.

TOP CHOICE Loungelover COCKTAIL BAR
(Map p104; ☑020-7012 1234; www.lestroisgarcons .com; 1 Whitby St; ⊖6pm-midnight Sun-Thu, to 1am Fri & Sat; ⊖Liverpool Street) Book a table, sip a cocktail and admire the Louis XIV chairs, the huge hippo head, the cage-turned-living room, the jewel-encrusted stag's head and the loopy chandeliers. Utterly fabulous.

Mason & Taylor BAR
(Map p104; www.masonandtaylor.co.uk; 51-55 Bethnal Green Rd; ⊖5pm-midnight Mon-Thu, 5pm-1am Fri, noon-1am Sat, noon-midnight Sun; ⊖Shoreditch High Street) Ale aficionados can migrate to this bar which overflows with a seasoned and expertly selected choice of cask and bottled beers. There's a strong showing of microbrewery beers, including the Camden Town Brewery and the Redchurch Brewery. Sample the range of draught beers in taster flights of three or six one-third pints.

Ten Bells PUB
(Map p104; cnr Commercial & Fournier Sts; ⊖Liverpool Street) The most famous Jack the Ripper pub, Ten Bells was patronised by his last victim before her grisly end, and possibly by the slayer himself. Admire the wonderful 18th-century tiles and ponder the past over a pint.

Queen of Hoxton BAR
(Map p104; www.queenofhoxton.com; 1-5 Curtain Rd; ⊖5pm-midnight Mon-Wed, 5pm-2am Thu & Fri,

6pm-2am Sat; ⊖Liverpool Street) All comers – drinkers, clubbers, film fans – should find things to royally rave about at the graffiti-clad Queen, with its games room, DJ nights and rooftop bar, which comes into its own come summer and open-air film nights (www.rooftopfilmclub.com).

Worship St Whistling Shop   COCKTAIL BAR
(Map p104; www.whistlingshop.com; 63 Worship St; ⊖Old Street) The busy master mixologists in this drinking den are content to visit the more unexplored outer regions of cocktail chemistry and aromatic science, concocted within the on-site lab and its rotary evaporators. Many of the ingredients are made in-house.

GREENWICH

TOP CHOICE **Greenwich Union**   PUB
(www.greenwichunion.com; 56 Royal Hill; ⎅DLR Cutty Sark) The award-winning and handsome Greenwich Union peddles six or seven local microbrewery beers, including raspberry and wheat varieties, and a strong list of ales, bottled international brews, duffed up leather armchairs and a conservatory and beer garden at the rear.

Cutty Sark Tavern   PUB
(www.cuttysarktavern.co.uk; 4-6 Ballast Quay; ⎅DLR Cutty Sark) Housed in a delightful bow-windowed, wood-beamed Georgian building facing the Thames, this historic gem has half a dozen cask-conditioned ales on tap, and riverside seating outside.

HAMPSTEAD & HIGHGATE

Spaniard's Inn   PUB
(www.thespaniardshampstead.co.uk; Spaniards Rd; ⊙11am-11pm; ⊖Hampstead then take bus 21) An enigmatic tavern dating from 1585, complete with dubious claims that Dick Turpin, the dandy highwayman, was born here and used it as a hideout. Literary luminaries such as Dickens, Shelley, Keats and Byron also availed themselves of its charms, which extends to a big, blissful garden and a large choice of specialty beers.

Holly Bush   PUB
(22 Holly Mount; ⊖Hampstead) Dating from the early 19th century, this beautiful pub has a secluded hilltop location, open fires in winter and a knack for making you stay a bit longer than you had intended. It's above Heath St, reached via the Holly Bush Steps.

☆ Entertainment

From West End luvvies to East End geezers, Londoners have always loved a spectacle. With bear-baiting and public executions long on the no-no list, they've fallen back on what London does well: some of the world's best theatre, nightclub and live-music scenes.

For a comprehensive list of what to do on any given night, check out *Time Out.* The listings in the free tube papers, *Evening Standard* and *Metro,* are also handy.

Theatre

London is a world capital for theatre across the spectrum from mammoth musicals to thoughtful drama for the highbrow crowd. Blockbuster musicals run and run, with mindboggling longevity. *Les Miserables* and *Phantom of the Opera* lead the pack, with *Mamma Mia!, Blood Brothers, Chicago* and *The Lion King* in hot pursuit. But the theatrical biscuit goes to Agatha Christie's *The Mousetrap,* keeping audiences guessing since 1952.

On performance days, you can buy half-price tickets for West End productions (cash only) from the official agency **tkts** (Map p70; www.tkts.co.uk; ⊖Leicester Sq; ⊙10am-7pm Mon-Sat, noon-4pm Sun; Leicester Square) on the south side of Leicester Sq. The booth is the one with the clocktower; beware of touts selling dodgy tickets. For a comprehensive look at what's being staged and where, visit www.officiallondontheatre.co.uk, www.theatremonkey.com or http://london.broadway.com.

The term 'West End' – as with Broadway – generally refers to the big-money productions such as musicals, but also includes other heavyweights. Some recommended options:

National Theatre   THEATRE
(☎020-7452 3000; www.nationaltheatre.org.uk; Upper Ground; ⊖Waterloo) Flagship South Bank venue with three theatres and excellent-value tickets for classic and contemporary productions.

Royal Court Theatre   THEATRE
(Map p92; ☎020-7565 5000; www.royalcourttheatre.com; Sloane Sq; ⊖Sloane Square) Progressive theatre and champion of new talent.

Old Vic   THEATRE
(Map p84; ☎0844 871 7628; www.oldvictheatre.com; The Cut; ⊖Waterloo) Kevin Spacey continues his run as artistic director (and

GAY & LESBIAN LONDON

The West End, particularly Soho, is the visible centre of gay and lesbian London, with numerous venues clustered around Old Compton St and its surrounds. However, Soho doesn't hold a monopoly on gay life. Vauxhall is a hub for the hirsute, hefty and generally harder-edged sections of the community. The railway arches are now filled with dance clubs, leather bars and a sauna. Clapham (South London), Earl's Court (West London), Islington (North London) and Limehouse (East End) have their own miniscenes.

Generally, London's a safe place for lesbians and gays. It's rare to encounter any problem with sharing rooms or holding hands in the inner city, although it would pay to keep your wits about you at night and be conscious of your surroundings.

The easiest way to find out what's going on is to pick up the free press from a venue (*Pink Paper, Boyz, QX*). The gay section of *Time Out* is useful, as are www.gaydarnation. com (for men) and www.gingerbeer.co.uk (for women). The hard-core circuit club nights run on a semiregular basis at a variety of venues: check out DTPM, Fiction (both at www.dtpmevents.co.uk), Matinee, SuperMartXé (both at www.loganpresents.com) and Megawoof!.

Some venues to get you started:

Candy Bar (Map p70; www.candybarsoho.co.uk; 4 Carlisle St; Tottenham Court Rd) Long-running lesbian hang-out.

Friendly Society (Map p70; 79 Wardour St; Piccadilly Circus) Soho's quirkiest gay bar, this Bohemian basement is bedecked in kid's-room wallpaper and Barbie dolls.

G-A-Y (www.g-a-y.co.uk) Bar (Map p70; 30 Old Compton St; ⊖Leicester Square); G-A-Y Late (Map p70; 5 Goslett Yard; ☺11pm-3am; ⊖Tottenham Court Rd); G-A-Y Club@Heaven (The Arches, Villiers St; ☺11pm-4am Thu-Sat; ⊖Charing Cross) Too camp to be restricted to one venue, G-A-Y now operates a pink-lit bar on the strip, a late-night bar a few streets away and club nights at one of gaydom's most internationally famous venues, Heaven.

Gay's the Word (Map p100; 66 Marchmont St; ⊖Russell Square) Books and magazines.

George & Dragon (Map p104; 2 Hackney Rd; ⊖Old St) Appealing corner pub where the crowd is often as eclectically furnished as the venue.

Popstarz (Map p70; www.popstarz.org; The Den, 18 West Central St; ☺10pm-4am Fri; ⊖Tottenham Court Rd) London's legendary indie pop club night. The online flyer gets you in free.

Royal Vauxhall Tavern (RVT; www.rvt.org.uk; 372 Kennington Lane; admission free-£9; ⊖Vauxhall) Much-loved pub with crazy cabaret and drag acts. Head under the arches from Vauxhall tube station onto Kennington Lane, where you'll see the tavern immediately to your left.

Two Brewers (www.thetwobrewers.com; 114 Clapham High St; admission free-£5; ⊖Clapham Common) Popular bar with regular acts and a nightclub out the back. From the tube station, head north along Clapham High St (away from the common).

Village (Map p70; www.village-soho.co.uk; 81 Wardour St; Piccadilly Circus) Glitzy gay bar with excellent, lengthy happy hours.

occasional performer) at this venue, which features classic, highbrow drama.

Donmar Warehouse THEATRE
(Map p70; ☎0844 871 7624; www.donmarwarehouse.com; 41 Earlham St; ⊖Covent Garden) A not-for-profit company that has forged itself a West End reputation.

Off West End is where you'll generally find the most original works. Some venues to check out:

Almeida THEATRE
(Map p128; ☎020-7359 4404; www.almeida.co.uk; Almeida St; ⊖Highbury & Islington) A plush Islington venue that can be relied on to provide the city with an essential program of imaginative theatre, under its creative artistic director, Michael Attenborough.

Young Vic THEATRE
(Map p84; ☎020-7922 2922; www.youngvic.org; 66 The Cut; ⊖Waterloo) One of the capital's most respected theatre troupes – bold, brave and

talented – the Young Vic stages winning performances. There's a lovely two-level bar-restaurant with an open-air terrace upstairs.

Nightclubs

The volume and variety of venues in today's city is staggering. Clubland is no longer confined to the West End, with megaclubs scattered throughout the city wherever there's a venue big enough, cheap enough or quirky enough to hold them. Some run their own regular weekly schedule, while others host promoters on an ad hoc basis. The big nights are Friday and Saturday, although some of the most cutting-edge sessions are midweek. Admission prices vary widely; it's often cheaper to arrive early or prebook tickets.

Fabric
CLUB

(Map p78; www.fabriclondon.com; 77a Charterhouse St; admission £8-18; ⏰10pm-6am Fri, 11pm-8am Sat, 11pm-6am Sun; ⊖Farringdon) Consistently rated by DJs as one of the world's greatest, Fabric's three dance floors occupy a converted meat cold-store opposite the Smithfield meat market. Friday's FabricLive offers drum and bass, breakbeat and hip hop, Saturdays see house, techno and electronica, while hedonistic Sundays are delivered by the Wetyourself crew.

Plastic People
CLUB

(Map p104; www.plasticpeople.co.uk; 147-149 Curtain Rd; admission £5-10; ⏰10pm-3.30am Fri & Sat, to 2am Sun; ⊖Old Street) Taking the directive 'underground club' literally, Plastic People provides a low-ceilinged subterranean den of dubsteppy, wonky, funky, no-frills fun times.

Xoyo
CLUB

(Map p104; www.xoyo.co.uk; 32-37 Cowper St; ⊖Old Street) This roomy Shoreditch warehouse club throws together a pulsingly popular mix of gigs, club nights and art events.

Pulse
CLUB

(Map p84; ☎020-7261 0981; http://pulseclub .co.uk; 1 Invicta Plaza; ⊖Southwark) A siren-call to hedonists city-wide, this vast, superclub just south of Blackfriars Bridge hops with a mind-boggling 4500-clubber capacity.

Ministry of Sound
CLUB

(Map p84; www.ministryofsound.com; 103 Gaunt St; admission £13-22; ⏰11pm-6.30am Fri & Sat; ⊖Elephant & Castle) Where the global brand started, it's London's most famous club and still packs in a diverse crew with big local and international names.

Cargo
CLUB

(Map p104; www.cargo-london.com; 83 Rivington St; admission free-£16; ⊖Old Street) A popular club with a courtyard where you can simultaneously enjoy big sounds and the great outdoors. Also hosts live bands.

Rock, Pop & Jazz

It goes without saying that London is a crucible of musical talent, with young bands gigging around venues citywide. Big-name gigs sell out quickly, so check www.seetickets.com before you travel.

Koko
CONCERT VENUE

(www.koko.uk.com; 1a Camden High St; ⏰7-11pm Sun-Thu, to 4am Fri & Sat; ⊖Mornington Crescent) Occupying the grand Camden Palace theatre, Koko hosts live bands most nights and the regular Club NME (New Musical Express; £5) on Friday.

O2 Academy Brixton
LIVE MUSIC

(☎0844 477 2000; www.o2academybrixton.co.uk; 211 Stockwell Rd; ⊖Brixton) This Grade II–listed art deco venue is always winning awards for 'best live venue' (something to do with the artfully sloped floor, perhaps) and hosts big-name acts in a relatively intimate setting (5000 capacity).

Dublin Castle
LIVE MUSIC, PUB

(Map p103; ☎020-7485 1773; www.thedublincastle .com; 94 Parkway; ⊖Camden Town) There's live punk or alternative music most nights in this pub's back room (cover usually £6).

Jazz Café
LIVE MUSIC

(Map p103; www.jazzcafe.co.uk; 5 Parkway; ⊖Camden Town) Jazz is just one part of the picture at this intimate club that stages a full roster of rock, pop, hip hop and dance, including famous names.

Barfly
PUB

(Map p103; ☎0207-691 4245; www.barflyclub.com; 49 Chalk Farm Rd; ⊖Chalk Farm) This grungy, indie-rock Camden venue hosts small-time artists looking for their big break. The Killers, Kasabian and Franz Ferdinand have all been on the billing. The lean is clearly towards rock from the US and UK, with alternative-music radio station Xfm hosting regular nights.

Ronnie Scott's
JAZZ, CLUB

(Map p70; ☎020-7439 0747; www.ronniescotts .co.uk; 47 Frith St; ⊖Leicester Square) London's legendary jazz club has been pulling in jazz titans since 1959.

100 Club
LIVE MUSIC, CLUB

(Map p70; ☎020-7636 0933; www.the100club .co.uk; 100 Oxford St; ⊖Oxford Circus) Hosting live music for 70 years, this legendary London venue once showcased the Stones and was at the centre of the punk revolution. It now divides its time between jazz, rock and even a little swing.

606 Club
BLUES, JAZZ

(☎7352 5953; www.606club.co.uk; 90 Lots Rd; Mon-Thu £10, Fri & Sat £12, Sun £10; ⊖Fulham Broadway or Earl's Court) Named after its old address on the King's Road, which cast a spell over jazz lovers London-wide back in the 1980s, this tucked-away basement jazz club and restaurant gives centre stage to contemporary British-based jazz musicians nightly. The club frequently opens until 2am, although at weekends you have to dine to gain admission (booking is advised).

Hope & Anchor
LIVE MUSIC, PUB

(Map p128; ☎020-7700 0550; 207 Upper St; admission free-£6; ⊖Angel) There is a scarcity of decent pubs in Islington, where the offerings are overwhelmingly cocktail lounges or DJ bars, but this rough-round-the-edges boozer with a famous musical past (U2, Dire Straits, Joy Division and Keane have all played here) attracts a muso cross-section of the neighbourhood and is a lot of fun.

Roundhouse
LIVE MUSIC, THEATRE

(Map p103; ☎0844 482 8008; www.roundhouse. org.uk; Chalk Farm Rd; ⊖Chalk Farm) Built in 1847 as a railway shed, Camden's Roundhouse has been an iconic concert venue since the 1960s (capacity 3300), hosting the likes of the Rolling Stones, Led Zeppelin and The Clash. Theatre and comedy are also staged.

Classical Music

With four world-class symphony orchestras, two opera companies, various smaller ensembles, brilliant venues, reasonable prices and high standards of performance, London is a classical capital. Keep an eye out for the free (or nearly so) lunchtime concerts held in many of the city's churches.

Royal Albert Hall
CONCERT HALL

(Map p92; ☎020-7589 8212; www.royalalberthall. com; Kensington Gore; ⊖South Kensington) This landmark elliptical Victorian arena – classically based on a Roman ampitheatre – hosts classical concerts and contemporary artists, but is best known as the venue for the annual classical music festival, the Proms.

Barbican
ARTS CENTRE

(Map p78; ☎0845 121 6823; www.barbican.org.uk; Silk St; ⊖Barbican) Home to the excellent London Symphony Orchestra (www.lso.co.uk), this famously hulking complex (named after a Roman fortification) has a rich program of film, music, theatre, art and dance including concerts. In the City, the arts centre is well signposted from both the Barbican and Moorgate tube stations.

Southbank Centre
CONCERT HALLS

(Map p84; ☎0844 875 0073; www.southbank centre.co.uk; Belvedere Rd; ⊖Waterloo) Home to the London Philharmonic Orchestra (www.lpo.co.uk), Sinfonietta (www.london sinfonietta.org.uk) and the Philharmonia Orchestra (www.philharmonia.co.uk), among others, this centre hosts classical, opera, jazz and choral music in three premier venues: the Royal Festival Hall, the smaller Queen Elizabeth Hall and the Purcell Room. Look out for free recitals in the foyer.

Opera & Dance

Royal Opera House
OPERA, BALLET

(Map p70; ☎020-7304 4000; www.roh.org.uk; Bow St; tickets £5-195; ⊖Covent Garden) Covent Garden is synonymous with opera thanks to this world-famous venue, which is also the home of the Royal Ballet, Britain's premier classical ballet company. Backstage tours take place three times a day on weekdays and four times on Saturdays (£10.50, book ahead).

Sadler's Wells
DANCE

(Map p100; ☎0844 412 4300; www.sadlers-wells .com; Rosebery Ave; tickets £10-49; ⊖Angel) A glittering modern venue that was, in fact, first established in the 17th century, Sadler's Wells has been given much credit for bringing modern dance to the mainstream.

London Coliseum
OPERA

(Map p70; ☎0871 911 0200; www.eno.org; St Martin's Lane; tickets £10-87; ⊖Leicester Square) Home of the progressive English National Opera; the English National Ballet also performs here.

Comedy

When London's comics aren't being outrageously funny on TV, you might find them doing stand-up somewhere in your neighbourhood. There are numerous venues to choose from (with pubs in on the act).

Comedy Store
CLUB

(Map p70; ✆0844 847 1728; www.thecomedy
store.co.uk; 1A Oxendon St; admission from £20;
⊖Piccadilly Circus) One of London's first
comedy clubs, featuring the capital's most
famous improvisers, the Comedy Store
Players, on Wednesdays (8pm) and Sundays (7.30pm).

Comedy Cafe
CLUB

(Map p104; ✆020-7739 5706; www.comedycafe
.co.uk; 68 Rivington St; admission free–£15; ⊗Wed-
Sat; ⊖Old Street) Have dinner and watch
comedy; free New Act Night on Wednesday
is good for toe-curling entertainment.

99 Club
MULTI VENUE CLUB

(✆0776 048 8119; www.the99club.co.uk; admission £10-30) Not quite the famous 100 Club,
this virtual venue takes over various bars
around town nightly, with three rival clones
operating on Saturdays.

Soho Theatre
THEATRE

(Map p70; ✆020-7478 0100; www.sohotheatre
.com; 21 Dean St; tickets around £10-20; ⊖Totten-
ham Court Road) This is where grown-up comedians graduate to once crowds start paying attention.

Pear Shaped
COMEDY NIGHT

(Map p70; www.pearshapedcomedy.com; Fitzroy
Tavern, 16a Charlotte St; admission £5; ⊗8.30pm
Wed; ⊖Goodge Street) Advertising themselves
as 'London's second-worst comedy club', Pear
Shaped has open spots for comic hopefuls.

Cinemas

Glitzy premieres usually take place in one of
the mega multiplexes in Leicester Sq.

Electric Cinema
CINEMA

(Map p118; ✆020-7908 9696; www.electriccinema
.co.uk; 191 Portobello Rd; tickets £8-15; ⊖Ladbroke
Grove) Getting Londoners buzzing since 1911,
the Electric can help you grab a glass of wine
from the bar, head to your leather sofa (£30)
and snuggle down for a flick. Check out the
Electric Brasserie (p125) next door.

BFI Southbank
CINEMA, MEDIATHEQUE

(Map p84; ✆020-7928 3232; www.bfi.org.uk; Belvedere Rd; tickets £9; ⊗11am-11pm; ⊖Waterloo)
A film-lover's fantasy, screening some 2000
flicks a year, from classics to foreign art
house. There's also the Mediatheque viewing stations, for exploring the British Film
Institute's extensive archive of movies and
watching whatever you like for free.

BFI IMAX
IMAX CINEMA

(Map p84; ✆020-7199 6000; www.bfi.org.uk/imax;
Waterloo Rd; tickets £9-16; ⊖Waterloo) Watch 3-D
movies and cinema releases on the UK's biggest screen: 20m high (nearly five double-
decker buses) and 26m wide.

Prince Charles
CINEMA

(Map p70; www.princecharlescinema.com; Leicester
Pl; ⊖Leicester Square) West End cinema ticket
prices are eye-watering, so wait till the first-
runs have finished and come here, central
London's cheapest picturehouse. Completing the score are mini-festivals, old classics
and sing-along screenings.

Sport

As the capital of a football-mad nation, you
can expect London to be brimming over
with sporting spectacles during the cooler
months. The Wimbledon Lawn Tennis
Championships (p110) is one of the biggest
events on the city's summer calendar.

FOOTBALL (SOCCER)

The home ground for England's national
football team, and the venue for the FA Cup
final, is Wembley Stadium (www. wembley
stadium.com). Tickets for Premier League
football matches are like gold dust, but you
could try your luck. Contacts for London's
Premier League clubs:

Arsenal Emirates Stadium
STADIUM

(✆7704 4040; www.arsenal.com; 75 Drayton Park;
self-guided tour £17.50, guided tour £35; ⊖Arsenal,
Finsbury Park or Highbury & Islington) Arsenal
Emirates Stadium is the third largest in the
England. Many were sorry to see the old stadium go, with its old tea ladies and working-
class atmosphere, but most have learned to
love it. Daily tours available.

Chelsea
STADIUM

(www.chelseafc.com; stadium tours adult/child
£18/12; ⊖Fulham Broadway)

Fulham
STADIUM

(www.fulhamfc.com; Craven Cottage, Stevenage Rd;
tours adult/child £10.50/7.50; ⊖Putney Bridge)

Tottenham Hotspur
STADIUM

(www.tottenhamhotspur.com; White Hart Lane, 748
High Rd; ☒White Hart Lane)

RUGBY

Twickenham (www.rfu.com; Rugby Rd; Twickenham) is the home of English rugby union,
but as with football, tickets for international
matches are difficult to get unless you have

contacts. The ground also has the World Rugby Museum (020-8892 8877; adult/child £7/5; 10am-5pm Tue-Sat, 11am-5pm Sun), which is worth combining with a tour of the stadium (adult/child £15/9, bookings recommended).

CRICKET

Cricket is as popular as ever in the land of its origin. Test matches take place at two venerable grounds: Lord's Cricket Ground (which also hosts tours) and the Brit Oval (0871 246 1100; www.britoval.com; Oval). Tickets cost from £20 to £80, but if you're a fan it's worth it. If not, it's an expensive and protracted form of torture.

Lord's Cricket Ground · CRICKET GROUND

(020-7616 8595; www.lords.org; St John's Wood Rd; tours adult/child £15/9; St John's Wood) The next best thing to watching a test at Lord's is the absorbingly anecdotal 100-minute tour of the ground and facilities, held when there's no play. It takes in the famous (members only) Long Room and the MCC Museum, featuring evocative memorabilia, including the tiny Ashes trophy.

HORSE RACING

Epsom · HORSE RACING

(01372 470 047; www.epsomderby.co.uk; admission from £7; Epsom Downs) With much more racing credibility than Ascot, this famous racetrack's star turn is Derby Day in June, but it has meets all year.

Shopping

From world-famous department stores to quirky backstreet retail revelations, London is a mecca for shoppers with an eye for style and a card to exercise.

London's famous department stores are a tourist attraction in themselves and if there's a label worth having, you'll find it in central London. The capital's most famous designers (Paul Smith, Vivienne Westwood, Stella McCartney, the late Alexander McQueen) have their own stores scattered about and are stocked in major department stores. Look out for dress agencies that sell second-hand designer clothes, bags and shoes – there are particularly rich pickings in the wealthier parts of town.

Nick Hornby's book *High Fidelity* may have done for London music-store workers what *Sweeney Todd* did for barbers, but those obsessive types still lurk in wonderful independent stores all over the city.

WEST END

Oxford St is the place for high street fashion, while Regent St cranks it up a notch. Carnaby St is nowhere near the hip hub it was in the 1960s, but the lanes around it still have some interesting boutiques. Bond St has designers galore, Savile Row is all about bespoke tailoring and Jermyn St is the place for smart clobber (particularly shirts). For musical instruments, visit Denmark St (off Charing Cross Rd).

Also check out these stores:

Selfridges · DEPARTMENT STORE

(Map p95; www.selfridges.com; 400 Oxford St; Bond St) Famed for its innovative window displays – especially at yuletide – the funkiest of London's one-stop shops bursts with fashion labels and tempts with an unparalleled food hall and Europe's largest cosmetics department.

Fortnum & Mason · DEPARTMENT STORE

(Map p70; www.fortnumandmason.com; 181 Piccadilly; Piccadilly Circus) It's the byword for quality and service from a bygone era, steeped in 300 years of tradition. The old-world basement food hall is where Britain's elite come for their pantry provisions and epicurean morsels.

Liberty · DEPARTMENT STORE

(Map p70; www.liberty.co.uk; Great Marlborough St; Oxford Circus) An irresistible blend of contemporary styles and indulgent pampering in a mock-Tudor fantasyland of carved dark wood.

Topshop Oxford Circus · CLOTHES

(Map p70; www.topshop.com; 216 Oxford St; Oxford Circus) Billed as the 'world's largest fashion store', the Topshop branch on Oxford Circus is a frenzy of shoppers searching for the latest look at reasonable prices. It's home to a range by London's favourite local supermodel rock chick, Kate Moss. Topman is upstairs.

Grays Antiques · ANTIQUES

(Map p95; www.graysantiques.com; 58 Davies St; Bond St) Top-hatted doormen welcome you to this wonderful building full of specialist stallholders. Make sure you head to the basement where the Tyburn River still runs through a channel in the floor.

HMV · MUSIC

(Map p70; www.hmv.com; 150 Oxford St; Oxford Circus) Giant store selling music, DVDs and magazines.

Foyle's
BOOKS

(Map p70; www.foyles.co.uk; 113-119 Charing Cross Rd; ⊜Tottenham Court Road) Flogging books since 1906, Foyles is a bookselling institution and retail landmark. Great to get lost in.

Ray's Jazz
JAZZ, BLUES

(www.foyles.co.uk; Foyles, 113-119 Charing Cross Rd; ⊜Tottenham Court Road) Where jazz anoraks find those elusive back catalogues from their favourite jazz and blues artists. It's inside Foyle's.

Stanfords
BOOKS, MAPS

(Map p70; www.stanfords.co.uk; 12-14 Long Acre; ⊜Covent Garden) A wonderland of travel titles and maps, with 150 years of experience.

DR Harris
BEAUTY PRODUCTS

(Map p70; www.drharris.co.uk; 29 St James's St; ⊙closed Sun; ⊜Green Park) Chemist and perfumer since the 18th century and the Prince of Wales' royal pharmacist, this is the place for moustache wax or the restorative and right royal Dr Harris Pick-me-up, to take the sting out of hangovers.

Minamoto Kitchoan
CONFECTIONARY

(Map p70; www.kitchoan.com; 44 Piccadilly; ⊙closed Sun; ⊜Piccadilly Circus) Delectable Japanese Wagashi confectionary made from red beans, rice, sweet potatoes and other natural ingredients, delightfully shaped into tasty morsels and served with a cup of green tea. Charming.

Waterstones
BOOKS

(www.waterstones.com) Piccadilly (Map p70; 203-206 Piccadilly; ⊜Piccadilly Circus); Bloomsbury (Map p100; 82 Gower St; ⊜Goodge St) The Piccadilly branch is the largest bookstore in Europe, boasting knowledgeable staff, regular author readings and signings. Check out the 5th View bar in the Piccadilly store; it is well worth a visit.

Benjamin Pollock's Toy Shop
TOYS

(Map p70; www.pollocks-coventgarden.co.uk; 1st fl, Covent Garden Market; ⊜Covent Garden) You can turn up all sorts of treasures at this gem of a traditional toy shop selling Victorian paper toy theatres, children's masks, spinning tops, finger puppets, antique teddy bears, dolls and more.

Rigby & Peller
LINGERIE

(www.rigbyandpeller.com) Mayfair (Map p70; 22A Conduit St; ⊜Oxford Circus); Knightsbridge (Map p92; 2 Hans Rd; ⊜Knightsbridge); Chelsea (Map p92; 13 Kings Rd; ⊜Sloane Square); Westfield mall (Westfield Mall, Ariel Way; ⊙10am-10pm Mon-Sat, 11am-9pm Sun; ⊜Wood Lane) Get into some right royal knickers with a trip to the Queen's corsetière.

Butler & Wilson
JEWELLERY

(www.butlerandwilson.co.uk) Mayfair (Map p95; 20 South Moulton St; ⊜Bond St); Chelsea (Map p92; 189 Fulham Rd; ⊜South Kensington) Camp jewellery, antique baubles and vintage clothing.

BM Soho
DANCE MUSIC

(Map p70; www.bm-soho.com; 25 D'Arblay St; ⊜Oxford Circus) Your best bet for dance music – if they haven't got what you're after, they'll know who has.

Forbidden Planet
COMICS, SCI-FI

(Map p70; 179 Shaftesbury Ave; ⊜Tottenham Court Rd) Need a set of light sabre chopsticks fast? Forbidden Planet is a mecca for collectors of comics, manga, Star Trek figurines, horror and fantasy literature, sci-fi and Star Wars memorabilia.

KNIGHTSBRIDGE, KENSINGTON & CHELSEA

Knightsbridge draws the hordes with quintessentially English department stores.

Harrods
DEPARTMENT STORE

(Map p92; www.harrods.com; 87 Brompton Rd; ⊜Knightsbridge) Simultaneously stylish and garish, Harrods is an obligatory stop for visitors, cash-strapped and big, big spenders alike. The spectacular food hall is a sight in itself.

John Sandoe Books
BOOKS

TOP CHOICE

(Map p92; www.johnsandoe.com; 10 Blacklands Tce; ⊜Sloane Square) This atmospheric little bookshop is a treasure trove of literary gems and hidden surprises. In business for decades, loyal customers swear by it and the knowledgeable booksellers spill forth with well-read pointers.

Harvey Nichols
DEPARTMENT STORE

(Map p92; www.harveynichols.com; 109-125 Knightsbridge; ⊜Knightsbridge) London's temple of high fashion, jewellery and perfume.

NOTTING HILL, BAYSWATER & PADDINGTON

Portobello Rd and the lanes surrounding it are the main focus, both for the famous market and the quirky boutiques and gift stores.

ROLL OUT THE BARROW

London has more than 350 markets selling everything from antiques and curios to flowers and fish. Some, such as Camden and Portobello Road, are tourist-packed, while others are just for locals.

Columbia Road Flower Market (Map p104; Columbia Rd; ⊘8am-2pm Sun; ⊜Old St) The best place for East End barrow boy banter ('We got flowers cheap enough for ya muvver-in-law's grave'). Unmissable.

Borough Market (Map p84; Southwark St) A farmers' market sometimes called London's Larder, it has been here in some form since the 13th century. It's wonderfully atmospheric; you'll find everything from organic falafel to boars' heads.

Camden Market (Map p103; www.camdenmarkets.org; Camden High St; ⊘10am-5.30pm; ⊜Camden Town) London's most famous market is actually a series of markets spread along Camden High St and Chalk Farm Rd. Despite a major fire in 2008, the **Camden Lock Market** (Map p103; www.camdenlockmarket.com; 54-56 Camden Lock Pl; ⊜Camden Town, Chalk Farm) and **Camden Stables Market** (Map p103; Camden High St; ⊜Chalk Farm) are still the places for punk fashion, cheap food, hippy chic and a whole lotta craziness.

Portobello Road Market (Map p118; www.portobellomarket.org; Portobello Rd; ⊘8am-6.30pm Mon-Sat, to 1pm Thu; ⊜Notting Hill Gate or Ladbroke Grove) One of London's most famous street markets, in Notting Hill. New and vintage clothes are its main attraction, with antiques at its south end and food at the north.

Old Spitalfields Market (Map p78; www.oldspitalfieldsmarket.com; 105a Commercial St; ⊘10am-4pm Mon-Fri, 11am-5pm Sat, 9am-5pm Sun; ⊜Liverpool St) It's housed in a Victorian warehouse, but the market's been here since 1638. Thursdays are devoted to antiques and vintage clothes, Fridays to fashion and art, but Sunday's the big day, with a bit of everything.

Broadway Market (www.broadwaymarket.co.uk; London Fields; ⊘9am-5pm Sat; ⊜Bethnal Green) Graze from the organic food stalls, choose a cooked meal and then sample one of the 200 beers on offer at the neighbouring Dove Freehouse. It's a bit of a schlep from the tube. Head up Cambridge Heath Rd until you cross the canal. Turn left, following the canal and you'll see the market to the right after a few short blocks.

Brixton Market (www.brixtonmarket.net; Electric Ave; ⊘10.30am-6pm Mon-Wed, to 10pm Thu-Sat, 10.30am-5pm Sun; ⊜Brixton) Immortalised in the Eddie Grant song, Electric Ave is a cosmopolitan treat that mixes everything from reggae music to exotic foods and spices.

Brixton Village (www.brixtonmarket.net; Electric Ave; ⊘10.30am-6pm Mon-Wed, to 10pm Thu-Sat, 10.30am-5pm Sun; ⊜Brixton) Revitalised and hip transformation of Granville Arcade near Brixton Market, with a host of inventively inclined shops and fantastic restaurants and cafes.

Sunday (Up)market (Map p104; www.sundayupmarket.co.uk; The Old Truman Brewery, Brick Lane; ⊘10am-5pm Sun; ⊜Liverpool St) Handmade handbags, jewellery, new and vintage clothes and shoes, plus food if you need refuelling.

Brick Lane Market (Map p104; www.visitbricklane.org; Brick Lane; ⊘8am-2pm Sun; ⊜Liverpool St) An East End pearler, this is a sprawling bazaar featuring everything from fruit and veggies to paintings and bric-a-brac.

Camden Passage Market (Map p128; www.camdenpassageislington.co.uk; Camden Passage; ⊘10am-2pm Wed, to 5pm Sat; ⊜Angel) Get your fill of antiques and trinkets galore. Not in Camden (despite the name).

Greenwich Market (www.greenwichmarket.net; College Approach; ⊘10am-5.30pm Wed-Sun) Rummage through antiques, vintage clothing and collectables (Thursday and Friday) or arts and crafts (Wednesday and weekends), or just chow down in the food section.

Petticoat Lane Market (Wentworth St & Middlesex St; ⊘9am-2pm Sun-Fri; ⊜Aldgate) A cherished East End institution overflowing with cheap consumer durables and jumble-sale ware.

Ceramica Blue
HOMEWARES

(Map p118; www.ceramicablue.co.uk; 10 Blenheim Cres; ⊖Ladbroke Grove) A wonderful place for original and eye-catching crockery and coloured glass imported from more than a dozen countries, with Japanese eggshell-glaze teacups, serving plates with traditional South African designs and more.

Rellik
VINTAGE THREADS

(www.relliklondon.co.uk; 8 Golborne Rd; ⊖West-bourne Park) Located at the foot of one of London's most notorious Brutalist tower blocks – the 31-storey Ernő Goldfinger–designed shocker called the Trellick Tower – Rellik stocks vintage classic threads for those in the know.

MARYLEBONE

Daunt Books
BOOKS

(Map p95; 83 Marylebone High St; ⊖Baker Street) An exquisitely beautiful store, with guidebooks, travel literature, fiction and reference books, all sorted by country.

ISLINGTON

Curios, baubles and period pieces abound along Camden Passage. Upper and Cross Sts have an interesting mix of stores.

Laura J London
WOMEN'S SHOES

(Map p128; www.laurajlondon.com; 114 Islington High St; ⊖Angel) A girlie boutique stocking shoes and accessories from a local designer.

CLERKENWELL & FARRINGDON

London Silver Vaults
SILVER

(Map p78; www.thesilvervaults.com; 53-63 Chancery Lane; ⊖Chancery Lane) Thirty subterranean shops forming the world's largest retail collection of silver under one roof.

HOXTON, SHOREDITCH & SPITALFIELDS

Rough Trade
ALTERNATIVE, PUNK, INDIE

(www.roughtrade.com) East (Map p104; www.roughtrade.com; 91 Brick Lane, Dray Walk, Old Truman Brewery; ☉8am-8pm Mon-Fri, 11am-7pm Sat & Sun; ⊖Liverpool St); West (Map p118; 130 Talbot Rd; ⊖Ladbroke Grove) At the forefront of the punk explosion of the 1970s, it's the best place to come for anything of an indie or alternative music bent.

Present
MEN'S CLOTHES

(Map p104; www.present-london.com; 140 Shoreditch High St; ⊖Old Street) Hip men's designer duds.

Start
CLOTHES

(Map p104; www.start-london.com; 42-44 Rivington St; ⊖Old Street) Spilling over three stores on the same lane (womenswear, menswear and men's formal), your quest for designer jeans starts here.

ⓘ Information

Dangers & Annoyances

Considering its size and wealth disparities, London is generally safe. That said, keep your wits about you and don't flash your cash unnecessarily. A contagion of youth-on-youth knife crime is cause for concern, so walk away if you sense trouble brewing and take care at night. When travelling by tube, choose a carriage with other people in it and avoid deserted suburban stations. Following reports of robberies and sexual attacks, shun unlicensed or unbooked minicabs.

Nearly every Londoner has a story about a wallet/phone/bag being nicked from under their noses – or arses, in the case of bags on floors in bars. Watch out for pickpockets on crowded tube trains, night buses and streets.

When using ATMs, guard your PIN details carefully. Don't use an ATM that looks like it's been tampered with as there have been incidents of card cloning.

Emergency

Police/Fire/Ambulance (☑999)

Rape & Sexual Abuse Support Centre (☑0808 802 9999)

Samaritans (☑08457 90 90 90)

Internet Access

You'll find free wireless (wi-fi) access at many bars, cafes and hotels. Large tracts of London, notably Canary Wharf and the City, are covered by pay-as-you-go wi-fi services that you can sign up to in situ – and London's mayor has promised blanket wi-fi coverage of this sort for all of London by 2012. You'll usually pay less at the numerous internet cafes (about £2 per hour).

Internet Resources

BBC London (www.bbc.co.uk/london)

Evening Standard (www.thisislondon.com)

Londonist (www.londonist.com)

Time Out (www.timeout.com/london)

Urban Path (www.urbanpath.com)

View London (www.viewlondon.co.uk)

Walk It (www.walkit.com) Enter your destination and get a walking map, time estimate and information on calories burnt and carbon dioxide saved.

WANT MORE?

For in-depth information, reviews and recommendations at your fingertips, head to the Apple App Store to purchase Lonely Planet's *London City Guide* iPhone app.

Alternatively, head to Lonely Planet (www.lonelyplanet.com/london) for planning advice, author recommendations, traveller reviews and insider tips.

Media

Two free newspapers bookend the working day – *Metro* in the morning and the *Evening Standard* in the evening – both available from tube stations. All of the national dailies have plenty of London coverage. Published every Wednesday, *Time Out* (£2.99) is the local listing guide par excellence.

Medical Services

To find a local doctor, pharmacy or hospital, consult the local telephone directory or call ☑0845 46 47.

Hospitals with 24-hour accident and emergency units include the following:

St Thomas' Hospital (☑020-7188 7188; Lambeth Palace Rd; ⊖Waterloo)

University College Hospital (☑0845 155 5000; 235 Euston Rd ; ⊖Euston Square)

Toilets

If you're caught short around London, public toilets can be elusive. Only a handful of tube stations have them, but the bigger National Rail stations usually do (often coin operated). If you can face five floors on an escalator, department stores are a good bet.

Tourist Information

For a list of all tourist offices in London and around Britain, see www.visitmap.info/tic.

Britain & London visitor centre (www.visitbritain.com; 1 Regent St; ⊙9am-6.30pm Mon-Fri, 10am-4pm Sat & Sun; ⊖Piccadilly Circus) Books accommodation, theatre and transport tickets; has *bureau de change*, international telephones and internet terminals. Longer hours in summer.

City of London information centre (☑020-7332 1456; www.visitthecity.co.uk; St Paul's Churchyard; ⊙9.30am-5.30pm Mon-Sat, 10am-4pm Sun; ⊖St Paul's) Tourist information, fast-track tickets to City attractions and guided walks (adult/child under 12 £7/free).

Greenwich tourist office (www.greenwich.gov.uk; Pepys House, 2 Cutty Sark Gardens; ⊙10am-5pm; ℝDLR Cutty Sark) Information plus guided tours.

ⓘ Getting There & Away

London is the major gateway to England.

AIR There are a number of London airports; see Getting Around for details.

BUS Most long-distance coaches leave London from Victoria Coach Station.

CAR Check reservation numbers of the main car-hire firms, all of which have airport and various city locations. Also see Car & Motorcycle, p1038.

TRAIN London's main-line terminals are all linked by the tube and each serves different destinations. Most stations have left-luggage facilities (around £4) and lockers, toilets (20p) with showers (around £3), newsstands and bookshops, and a range of eating and drinking outlets. St Pancras, Victoria and Liverpool St stations all have handy shopping centres attached.

If you can't find your destination in the list of main-line terminals below, consult the journey planner at www.nationalrail.co.uk.

Charing Cross Canterbury.

Euston Manchester, Liverpool, Carlisle, Glasgow.

King's Cross Cambridge, Hull, York, Newcastle, Scotland.

Liverpool Street Stansted airport, Cambridge.

London Bridge Gatwick airport, Brighton.

Marylebone Birmingham.

Paddington Heathrow airport, Oxford, Bath, Bristol, Exeter, Plymouth, Cardiff.

St Pancras Gatwick and Luton airports, Brighton, Nottingham, Sheffield, Leicester, Leeds, Paris.

Victoria Gatwick airport, Brighton and Canterbury.

Waterloo Windsor, Winchester, Exeter, Plymouth.

ⓘ Getting Around

To/From the Airports

GATWICK There are **National Rail** (www.nationalrail.co.uk) services between Gatwick's South Terminal and Victoria station (from £13.50, 37 minutes), running every 15 minutes during the day and hourly through the night. Other trains head to London St Pancras International (from £10, 66 minutes). Fares are cheaper the earlier you book. If you're racing to make a flight, the **Gatwick Express** (☑0845 850 1530; www.gatwickexpress.com; one way/return £17.90/30.80, 30 minutes, every 15 minutes) departs Victoria every 15 minutes from 5am to 11.45pm (one way/return £18.90/33.20, 30 minutes, first/last train 3.30am/12.32am).

Prices start from £2, depending on when you book, for the **EasyBus** (www.easybus.co.uk)

minibus service between Gatwick and Earls Court (£10, allow 1¼ hours, every 30 minutes from 4.25am to 1am). You'll be charged extra if you have more than one carry-on and one check-in bag. Book online for the cheapest deals.

Gatwick's taxi partner, **Checker Cars** (www .checkercars.com), has a counter in each terminal. Fares are quoted in advance (about £95 for the 65-minute ride to Central London).

HEATHROW The transport connections to Heathrow are excellent, and the journey to and from the city is usually painless. The cheapest option is the Underground (the tube). The Piccadilly line is accessible from every terminal (£5.30, one hour to central London, departing from Heathrow every five minutes from around 5am to 11.30pm). If it's your first time in London, it's a good chance to practice using the tube as it's at the beginning of the line and therefore not too crowded when you get on. If there are vast queues at the ticket office, use the automatic machines instead; some accept credit cards as well as cash. Keep your bags near you and expect a scramble to get off if you're hitting the city at rush hour (7am to 9am and 5pm to 7pm weekdays).

You might save some time on the considerably more expensive Heathrow Express, an ultra-modern train to Paddington station (one way/return £18/34, 15 minutes, every 15 minutes 5.12am to 11.48pm). You can purchase tickets on board (£5 extra), from self-service machines (cash and credit cards accepted) at both stations, or online.

There are taxi ranks for black cabs outside every terminal; a fare to the centre of London will cost between £50 and £85.

LONDON CITY The Docklands Light Railway connects London City Airport to the tube network, taking 22 minutes to reach Bank station (£4.30). A black taxi costs around £25 to/from central London.

LUTON There are regular **National Rail** (www .nationalrail.co.uk) services from St Pancras (£13, 29 to 39 minutes) to Luton Airport Parkway station, where a shuttle bus (£1.50) will get you to the airport within 10 minutes. EasyBus minibuses head from Victoria, Earl's Court and Baker St to Luton (from £2, walk-on £10, allow 1½ hours, every 30 minutes). A taxi costs around £65.

STANSTED The Stansted Express connects with Liverpool Street station (one way/return £21.50/29.50, 46 minutes, every 15 minutes 6am to 12.30am).

EasyBus also has services between Stansted and Baker St (from £2, £10 walk-on, 1¼ hours, every 20 minutes). The Airbus A6 links with Victoria Coach Station (£11, allow 1¾ hours, at least every 30 minutes). National Express also runs

buses to Stansted from Liverpool Street Station (£9 one way, 80 mins, every 30 mins).

A taxi cab to/from central London costs about £100.

Bicycle

The central city is flat and relatively compact and the traffic moves slowly – all of which make it surprisingly good for cyclists. It can get terribly congested though, so you'll need to keep your wits about you – and lock your bike (including both wheels) securely. Operating 24 hours a day and already clocking in over 11 million cycle hires, the excellent **Barclays Cycle Hire Scheme** (www.tfl.gov.uk) allows you to hire a bike from one of 400 docking stations around London. The access fee is £1 for 24 hours or £5 per week; after that, the first 30 minutes is free (making the bikes perfect for short hops), or £1/4/6/15 for one hour/90 minutes/two hours/three hours. Cycle as often as you like, but leave five minutes between each trip. Visitors to London can pay either on-line or or using a credit or debit card at a docking station. The minimum age for buying access is 18; the minimum age for riding a Barclays bike is 14.

Car

The M25 ring road encompasses the 609 sq miles that is broadly regarded as Greater London. For motorists it's the first circle of hell; London's streets can be congested beyond belief. Traffic is heavy, roadwork continuous, parking is either impossible or expensive, and wheel-clampers are diligent. If you drive into central London from 7am to 6pm on a weekday, you'll need to pay a £10 per day congestion charge (visit www.tfl.gov.uk for payment options) or face a hefty fine. If you're hiring a car to continue your trip from London, take the tube to Heathrow and pick it up from there.

Public Transport

Although complaining about it is a local sport, London's public transport is excellent, with tubes, trains, buses and boats conspiring to get you anywhere you need to go. **TFL** (www.tfl.gov .uk), the city's public transport provider, is the glue that binds the network together. Its website has a handy journey planner and information on all services, including cabs. As a creature of leisure, you'll hopefully be able to avoid those bits that Londoners hate (especially the sardine

LONDON GETTING AROUND

MAPS

No Londoner would be without a pocket-size *London Mini A-Z*, which lists nearly 30,000 streets. Worth getting if you're in London for more than a few weeks.

LONDON'S OYSTER DIET

To get the most out of London, you need to be able to jump on and off public transport like a local, not scramble to buy a ticket at hefty rates each time. The best and cheapest way to do this is with an Oyster card, a reusable smartcard on which you can load either a season ticket (weekly/monthly £29/112) or prepaid credit. The card itself is £5, which is fully refundable when you leave.

London is divided into concentric transport zones, although most places are in Zones 1 and 2. The season tickets will give you unlimited transport on the tube, buses and rail services within these zones. All you need to do is touch your card to the yellow sensors on the station turnstiles or at the front of the bus.

If you opt for pay as you go, the fare will be deducted from the credit on your card at a much lower rate than if you were buying a one-off paper ticket. An Oyster bus trip costs £1.35 as opposed to £2.30 for an individual fare, while a Zone 1 tube journey is £2 as opposed to £4.30. Even better, in any single day your fares will be capped at the equivalent of the Oyster day-pass rate for the zones you've travelled in (Zones 1-2 peak/off-peak £8.40/7).

Assuming you avoid peak hours (6.30am to 9.30am and 4pm to 7pm), this ready reckoner gives the cheapest options for your length of stay:

» **1-4 days**: prepay
» **5-24 days**: weeklies topped up with prepay for any remaining days
» **25-31 days**: monthly

squash of rush-hour tubes), so get yourself an Oyster card and make the most of it.

BOAT

The myriad boats that ply the Thames are a great way to travel, avoiding traffic jams while affording great views. Passengers with daily, weekly or monthly travelcards (including on Oyster) get a third off all fares. London has some 40 miles of inner-city canals, mostly built in the 19th century.

Thames Clippers runs regular commuter services between Embankment, Waterloo, Blackfriars, Bankside, London Bridge, Tower, Canary Wharf, Greenwich, North Greenwich and Woolwich piers (adult/child £6/3) from 7am to midnight (from 9.30am weekends).

Leisure services include the Tate-to-Tate boat and Westminster–Greenwich services. There are also boats to Kew Gardens and Hampton Court Palace.

London Waterbus Company (p96) and Jason's Trip (p96) both run canal boat journeys between Camden Lock and Little Venice; see websites for times.

BUS

Travelling around London by double-decker bus is a great way to get a feel for the city, but it's usually slower than the tube. Heritage 'Route-master' buses with conductors operate on route 9 (from Aldwych to Royal Albert Hall) and 15 (between Trafalgar Sq and Tower Hill); these are the only buses without wheelchair access. In 2012

a brand new fleet of freshly designed hybrid diesel/electric hop-on/hop-off (and wheelchair-accessible) Routemasters began running on route 38 between Victoria and Hackney.

Buses run regularly during the day, while less frequent night buses (prefixed with the letter 'N') wheel into action when the tube stops. Single-journey bus tickets (valid for two hours) cost £2.30 (£1.35 on Oyster, capped at £4.20 per day); a weekly pass is £18.80. Children ride for free. At stops with yellow signs, you must buy your ticket from the automatic machine (or use an Oyster) before boarding. Buses stop on request, so clearly signal the driver with an outstretched arm.

LONDON UNDERGROUND, DLR & OVERGROUND

'The tube', as it's universally known, extends its subterranean tentacles throughout London and into the surrounding counties, with services running every few minutes from roughly 5.30am to 12.30am (from 7am to 11.30pm Sunday).

It's easy to use. Tickets (or Oyster card top-ups) can be purchased from counters or machines at the entrance to each station using either cash or credit card. They're then inserted into the slot on the turnstiles (or you touch your Oyster card on the yellow reader), and the barrier opens. Once you're through you can jump on and off different lines as often as you need to get to your destination.

Also included within the network are the driverless Docklands Light Railway (DLR), and the train lines shown on tube maps as 'Overground'. The DLR links the City to Docklands, Greenwich and London City Airport.

The tube map itself is an acclaimed graphic design work, using coloured lines to show how the 14 different routes intersect. However, it's not remotely to scale. The distances between stations become greater the further from central London you travel, while Leicester Square and Covent Garden stations are only 250m apart.

TRAIN

Particularly south of the river, where tube lines are in shorter supply, the various rail companies are an important part of the public transport picture. Most stations are now fitted with Oyster readers and accept TFL travelcards. If you travel outside your zone you'll need to have enough prepay credit on your Oyster card to cover the additional charge. As not all stations have turnstiles, it's important to remember to tap-in and tap-out at the Oyster reader at the station or your card will register an unfinished journey and you're likely to be charged extra. You can still buy a paper ticket from machines or counters at train stations.

Taxi

London's famous black cabs are available for hire when the yellow light above the windscreen is lit. To get an all-London licence, cabbies must do 'The Knowledge', which tests them on up to 25,000 streets within a 6-mile radius of Charing Cross and all points of interest from hotels to churches. Fares are metered, with flag fall of £2.20 and the additional rate dependent on time of day, distance travelled and taxi speed. A one-mile trip will cost between £5.20 and £8.40. To order a black cab by phone, try **Dial-a-Cab** (☎020-7253 5000; www.dialacab.co.uk); you must pay by credit card and will be charged a premium.

Licensed minicabs operate via agencies (most busy areas have a walk-in office with drivers waiting). They're a cheaper alternative to black cabs and quote trip fares in advance. To find a local minicab firm, visit www.tfl.gov.uk.

There have been many reports of sexual assault and theft by unlicensed minicab drivers. Only use drivers from proper agencies; licensed minicabs aren't allowed to tout for business or pick you up off the street without a booking, so avoid the shady characters who hang around outside nightclubs or bars.

LONDON GETTING AROUND

Canterbury & Southeast England

Best Places to Eat

» Deeson's (p154)
» Allotment (p162)
» Eddie Gilbert's (p159)
» Terre à Terre (p174)
» Town House (p177)

Best Places to Stay

» Abode Canterbury (p153)
» Jeake's House (p164)
» Wallett's Court (p161)
» Reading Rooms (p157)
» Hotel Una (p171)

Why Go?

Rolling chalk hills, venerable Victorian resorts, fields of hops and grapes sweetening in the sun – welcome to England's southeast, four soothing counties' worth of country houses, fairy-tale castles and the country's finest food and drink. That fruit-ripening sun shines brightest and longest on the southeast, warming a string of seaside towns wedged between formidable chalk cliffs. There's something for everyone here, from the understated charm of Whitstable to the bohemian spirit of hedonistic Brighton and the more genteel Eastbourne.

The southeast is also pock-marked with reminders of darker days. The region's position as the front line against Continental invaders has left a wealth of turbulent history, including the 1066 battlefield, Dover Castle's secret war tunnels and scattered Roman ruins.

England's spiritual heart is Canterbury, its cathedral and ancient Unesco-listed attractions essential viewing for any 21st-century pilgrim.

When to Go

May is a good time to get creative at Great Britain's second-largest arts festival in Brighton. During June, don your top hat and breeches to revel in frilly Victoriana at Dickens festivals in Broadstairs and Rochester.

Any time between May and October is ideal for a hike along the South Downs Way, running the length of England's newest national park. In November head to Lewes for one of the most spectacular Guy Fawkes Night celebrations in all of England.

Activities

The southeast of England may be Britain's most densely populated corner, but there are still plenty of off-the-beaten-track walking and cycling routes to enjoy.

Cycling

Finding quiet roads for cycle touring takes a little extra perseverance in the southeast of England, but the effort is richly rewarded. Long-distance routes that form part of the National Cycle Network (NCN; www.sustrans .org.uk):

» **Downs & Weald Cycle Route** (110 miles; NCN Routes 2, 20 & 21) London to Brighton and on to Hastings.

» **Garden of England Cycle Route** (165 miles; NCN Routes 1 & 2) London to Dover and then Hastings.

You'll also find less demanding routes on the NCN website. Meanwhile, there are plenty of uppers and downers to challenge mountain bikers on walking trails, such as the South Downs Way National Trail (100 miles), which takes hard nuts two days but mere mortals about four.

Walking

Two long-distance trails meander steadily westward through the region, but there are plenty of shorter ambles to match your schedule, stamina and scenery wishlist.

» South Downs Way (www.nationaltrail.co .uk/southdowns) This 100-mile National Trail through England's newest national park is a beautiful roller-coaster walk along prehistoric droveways between the ancient capital, Winchester, and the seaside resort of Eastbourne.

» North Downs Way (www.nationaltrail.co .uk/Northdowns) This popular 153-mile walk begins near Farnham in Surrey, but one of its most beautiful sections runs from near Ashford to Dover in Kent; there's also a loop that takes in Canterbury near its end. History buffs will appreciate the 1066 Country Walk, which connects with the South Downs Way.

ⓘ Information

Kent Attractions (www.kentattractions.co.uk)
Tourism South East (www.visitsoutheast england.com) The official website for south and southeast England.
Visit Kent (www.visitkent.co.uk)
Visit Surrey (www.visitsurrey.com)
Visit Sussex (www.visitsussex.org)

ⓘ Getting There & Around

The southeast is easily explored by train or bus, and many attractions can be visited in a day trip from London. Contact the National Traveline (www.travelinesoutheast.org.uk) for comprehensive information about public transport in the region.

Bus

Explorer Tickets (adult/child £6.50/4.50) provide unlimited day-long travel on most buses throughout the region. You can buy them at bus stations or on the first bus you take.

Train

Secure 33% discounts on most rail fares in the southeast by purchasing a **Network Railcard** (www.railcard.co.uk/network; per year £28). Three adults can travel with you for the same discounted fare, and you save 60% on fares for children under 15.

KENT

Kent isn't described as the garden of England for nothing. Within its sea-lined borders you'll find a fragrant landscape of gentle hills, fertile farmland, cultivated country estates and fruit-laden orchards. It could also be described as the beer garden of England, producing the world-renowned Kent hops, some of the country's finest ales and wines from its numerous vineyards. At its heart is spellbinding Canterbury, crowned by its enthralling cathedral.

Here, too, are beautiful coastal stretches dotted with beach towns and villages, from old-fashioned Broadstairs to gentrified Whitstable and the aesthetically challenged port town of Dover.

Canterbury
POP 43,400

Canterbury tops the charts for English cathedral cities and is one of southern England's top attractions. Many consider the World Heritage-listed cathedral that dominates its centre to be one of Europe's finest,

WANT MORE?

Head to Lonely Planet (www.lonely planet.com/england/southeast-england) for planning advice, author recommendations, traveller reviews and insider tips.

Canterbury & Southeast England Highlights

1 Shopping, tanning and partying in **Brighton & Hove** (p169), hedonist capital of the southeast

2 Making a pilgrimage to **Canterbury** (p150), one of England's most important religious sites

3 Wandering the cobbled lanes of **Rye** (p164), one of England's prettiest towns

A127
Stanford-le-Hope
Grays
Thurrock
Canvey Island
Southend-on-Sea
Tilbury
Gravesend
A2
Rochester
Gillingham
Chatham
Sheerness
Isle of Sheppey
Leysdown-on-Sea
Herne Bay
Whitstable
Birchington
Margate
Isle of Thanet 6
Broadstairs
Ramsgate
M2
Sittingbourne
Faversham 7
Richborough Roman Fort
Sandwich
Maidstone
Bearsted
Canterbury 2
Leeds Castle 4
Howlett's Wild Animal Park
Chilham
Deal
Sutton
Ringwould
Westcliffe
Staplehurst
KENT
A28
A2
M20
St Margaret's Bay
Dover 8
Biddenden Vineyards 7
Ashford
Sissinghurst
A21
Chapel Down Vinery 7
Tenterden
Folkestone
Capel-le-Ferne
A259
Hythe
Channel Tunnel
Hawkhurst
Romney Marsh
Burwash
Bodiam Castle
New Romney
St Mary's Bay
Bateman's
A268
EAST SUSSEX
A21
Rye 3
Lydd
Lydd-on-Sea
Battle
Pevensey Castle
Bexhill
A259
Hastings
Strait of Dover

NORTH SEA

N
0 _____ 20 km
0 _____ 10 miles

4 Kicking back at the moated marvel that is **Leeds Castle** (p155)

5 Scrambling up **Beachy Head** (p169), a spectacular headland in snow-white chalk

6 Shaking out your beach towel for some seaside fun on the **Isle of Thanet** (p157)

7 Packing your thirst for a **vineyard** or **brewery** tour (p165)

8 Exploring the atmospheric WWII tunnels beneath sprawling **Dover Castle** (p161)

THE CANTERBURY TALES

If English literature has a father figure, then it is Geoffrey Chaucer (1342–1400). Chaucer was the first English writer to introduce characters – rather than 'types' – into fiction, and he did so to greatest effect in his best-known work, *The Canterbury Tales*.

Written between 1387 and his death, in the now hard-to-decipher Middle English of the day, Chaucer's *Tales* is an unfinished series of 24 vivid stories told by a party of pilgrims journeying between London and Canterbury. Chaucer successfully created the illusion that the pilgrims, not Chaucer (though he appears in the tales as himself) are telling the stories, which gave him unprecedented freedom as an author. *The Canterbury Tales* remains one of the pillars of the literary canon, but more than that it's a collection of rollicking good yarns of adultery, debauchery, crime and edgy romance, and filled with Chaucer's witty observations about human nature.

and the town's narrow medieval alleyways, riverside gardens and ancient city walls are a joy to explore. But Canterbury isn't just a showpiece for the past – it's a spirited place with an energetic student population and a wide choice of contemporary bars, restaurants and arts. Book ahead for the best hotels and eateries: pilgrims may no longer flock here in their thousands, but tourists certainly do.

History

Canterbury's past is as rich as it comes. From AD 200 there was a Roman town here, which later became the capital of the Saxon kingdom of Kent. When St Augustine arrived in England from Africa in 597 to bring the Christian message to the pagan hordes, he chose Canterbury as his *cathedra* (primary seat) and set about building an abbey on the outskirts of town. Following the martyrdom of Thomas Becket, Archbishop of Canterbury, the town became northern Europe's most important centre of pilgrimage, which in turn prompted Geoffrey Chaucer's *The Canterbury Tales,* one of the most outstanding poetic works in English literature.

Despite its blasphemous murders and rampant tourism, the city of Canterbury still remains the primary seat for the Church of England.

◎ Sights

Canterbury Cathedral   CATHEDRAL
(www.canterbury-cathedral.org; adult/concession £8/7, tour adult/child £5/3, audiotour adult/concession £3.50/2.50; ⊙9am-5pm Mon-Sat, 12.30pm-2.30pm Sun) A rich repository of more than 1400 years of Christian history, the Church of England's mother ship is a truly extraordinary place with an absorbing history. This Gothic cathedral, the highlight of the city's World Heritage Sites, is the southeast's top tourist attraction as well as a place of worship. Allow at least two hours to do it justice.

The cathedral is an overwhelming edifice crammed with enthralling stories, arresting architecture and a very real and enduring sense of spirituality – although visitors can't help but pick up on the ominous undertones of violence and bloodshed that whisper from its walls.

This ancient structure is packed with monuments commemorating the nation's battles. Also here are the grave and heraldic tunic of one of the nation's most famous warmongers, Edward the Black Prince (1330–76). The spot in the northwest transept where Archbishop Thomas Becket met his grisly end has drawn pilgrims for more than 800 years and is marked by a flickering candle and striking modern altar.

The doorway to the crypt is beside the altar. This cavernous space is the cathedral's highlight, the only survivor from the cathedral's last devastating fire in 1174, which destroyed the rest of the building. Look for the amazingly well-preserved carvings among the forest of pillars.

The wealth of detail in the cathedral is immense and unrelenting, so it's well worth joining a one-hour tour (three daily, Monday to Saturday from Easter to October), or taking a 40-minute self-guided audiotour.

Canterbury Heritage Museum   MUSEUM
(www.canterbury-museums.co.uk; Stour St; adult/child £8/free; ⊙10am-5pm daily) A fine 14th-century building, once the Poor Priests' Hospital, now houses the city's captivating museum, which houses a jumble of exhibits dating from pre-Roman times to the assassination of Becket, and from the likes of Joseph Conrad to locally born celebs. The kids' room is excellent, with a memorable

glimpse of real medieval poo among other fun activities. Choo-choo fans can admire the *Invicta* loco, which ran on the world's third passenger railway, the Crab & Winkle line between here and Whitstable. The building also houses the **Rupert Bear Museum** (Rupert's creator, Mary Tourtel, was born in Canterbury) and a gallery celebrating another old-time children's favourite, Bagpuss.

St Augustine's Abbey

RUIN

(EH; adult/child £4.90/2.90; ⊘10am-6pm Jul & Aug, to 5pm Wed-Sun Apr-Jun) An integral but often overlooked part of the Canterbury World Heritage Site, St Augustine's Abbey was founded in AD 597, marking the rebirth of Christianity in southern England. Later requisitioned as a royal palace, it fell into disrepair and only stumpy foundations remain. A small museum and a worthwhile free audiotour do their best to underline the site's importance and put flesh back onto its now-humble bones.

FREE St Martin's Church

CHURCH

(North Holmes Rd; ⊘11am-3pm Tue, Thu & Sat Apr-Sep) This stumpy little building just off the road to Sandwich is thought to be England's oldest parish church in continuous use, and where Queen Bertha (wife of the Saxon King Ethelbert) welcomed St Augustine when he arrived in England in the 6th century. The original Saxon church has been swallowed up by a medieval refurbishment, but is still worth the 900m walk east of the abbey.

Eastbridge Hospital

HISTORIC BUILDING

(www.eastbridgehospital.org.uk; 25 High St; adult/child £2/1; ⊘10am-5pm Mon-Sat) A 'place of hospitality' for pilgrims, soldiers and the elderly since 1180, Eastbridge Hospital of St Thomas the Martyr is the last of many such buildings in the city still open to the public. It's worth a visit for the Romanesque undercroft and historic chapel. The 16th-century almshouses, still in use, sit astride Britain's oldest road bridge, dating back more than 800 years.

Roman Museum

MUSEUM

(Butchery Lane; adult/child £6/free; ⊘10am-5pm) This fascinating subterranean archaeological site was recently saved from a council attempt to convert it into a restaurant. Visitors can walk around a reconstructed Roman marketplace and rooms, including a kitchen, as well as view Roman mosaic floors.

West Gate Towers

MUSEUM

(St Peter's St) The city's only remaining medieval gateway has become Canterbury's most-discussed sight in recent years. Threatened with closure due to council cuts in 2011, it was taken over by a local businessman who spent large sums turning it into a real family attraction. His sudden death in early 2012 left the towers closed (again) and their future uncertain. Double-decker buses only ceased edging their way through the narrow 14th-century archway, wing mirrors flattened, in spring 2012.

FREE Greyfriars Chapel

CHURCH

(⊘2-4pm Mon-Sat Easter-Sep) You'll find Greyfriars Chapel in serene riverside gardens behind Eastbridge Hospital. The first monastery built in England by Franciscan monks in 1267, its grounds are a tranquil spot to unfurl the picnic blanket.

Canterbury Tales

INTERPRETATION CENTRE

(www.canterburytales.org.uk; St Margaret's St; adult/child £7.75/5.75; ⊘10am-5pm Mar-Oct) This ambitious three-dimensional interpretation of Chaucer's classic tales using jerky

CANTERBURY & SOUTHEAST ENGLAND CANTERBURY

THE MARTYRDOM OF THOMAS BECKET

Not one to shy away from nepotism, in 1162 King Henry II appointed his good mate Thomas Becket to the highest clerical office in the land, figuring it would be easier to force the increasingly vocal religious lobby to fall into line if he was pals with the archbishop. Unfortunately for Henry, he underestimated how seriously Thomas would take the job, and the archbishop soon began to disagree with almost everything the king said or did. By 1170 Henry had become exasperated with his former favourite and 'suggested' to four of his knights that Thomas was too much to bear. The dirty deed was done on 29 December. Becket's martyrdom – and canonisation in double-quick time (1173) – catapulted Canterbury Cathedral to the top of the league of northern European pilgrimage sites. Mindful of the growing criticism of his role in Becket's murder, Henry arrived in Canterbury in 1174 for a dramatic *mea culpa* and, after allowing himself to be whipped and scolded, was granted absolution.

Canterbury

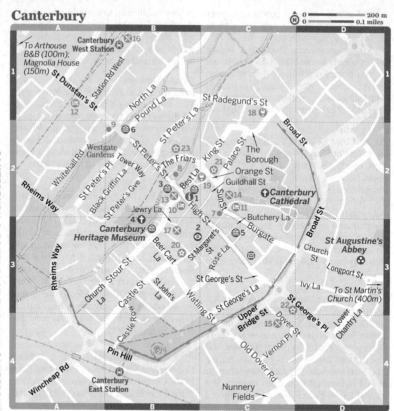

animatronics and audioguides is certainly entertaining, but could never do full justice to the original work. However, it does provide a lighthearted introduction for the young or uninitiated.

Beaney House of Art & Knowledge
MUSEUM

(☎01227-378100; 18 High St; ⊙ 9am-5pm Mon-Wed, Fri & Sat, 9am-7pm Thu, 10am-5pm Sun) This mock-Tudor edifice is the grandest on the main shopping thoroughfare, if not the most authentic. Formerly called the Royal Museum & Art Gallery, it has housed Canterbury's main library, a museum and an art gallery since 1899, but it closed in 2009 for renovation and expansion. The whole caboodle reopened in 2012 with a new name (in honour of the 19th-century benefactor who funded the original building), a much larger exhibition space, much improved library and a new tenant, the tourist office.

👉 Tours

Canterbury Historic River Tours
BOAT TOUR

(☎07790-534744; www.canterburyrivertours.co.uk; adult/child £8/4.50; ⊙10am-5pm Mar-Oct) Knowledgeable guides double up as energetic oarsmen on these fascinating River Stour mini cruises, which depart from behind the Old Weaver's House on St Peter's St.

Canterbury River Navigation Company
BOAT TOUR

(☎07816-760869; www.crnc.co.uk; Westgate Gardens; adult/child from £8/4; ⊙Apr-Oct) Weather permitting – and subject to demand – this company offers relaxing punt trips on the River Stour.

Canterbury Guided Tours
WALKING TOUR

(☎01227-459779; www.canterburyguidedtours.com; adult/child/concession £6.50/4.50/6; ⊙11am Feb-Oct, plus 2pm Jul-Sep) Guided walking tours leave from opposite the Cathedral entrance.

Canterbury

⊙ Top Sights
Canterbury Cathedral C2
Canterbury Heritage Museum B3
St Augustine's Abbey D3

⊙ Sights
1 Beaney House of Art & Knowledge B2
2 Canterbury Tales B3
3 Eastbridge Hospital B2
4 Greyfriars Chapel B3
5 Roman Museum C3
6 West Gate Towers B2

Activities, Courses & Tours
7 Canterbury Guided Tours C2
8 Canterbury Historic River Tours B2
9 Canterbury River Navigation
   Company B2

Sleeping
10 Abode Canterbury B2

11 Cathedral Gate Hotel C2
12 House of Agnes A1

⊗ Eating
13 Boho B2
14 Deeson's C2
15 Farmhouse C4
16 Goods Shed B1
17 Veg Box Cafe B3

Drinking
18 Parrot C1
19 Thomas Becket C2

Entertainment
20 Alberry's Wine Bar B3
21 Ballroom C2
22 Chill Nightclub C3
23 New Marlowe Theatre B2

Check the website or tourist office, as this may change.

🎉 Festivals & Events

Myriad musicians, comedians, theatre groups and other artists from around the world come to party at the Canterbury Festival (☎01227-787787; www.canterburyfestival.co.uk) over two weeks in October.

🛏 Sleeping

TOP CHOICE Abode Canterbury   HOTEL £££
(☎01227-766266; www.abodehotels.co.uk; 30-33 High St; r from £135; ☻🛜) The 72 rooms at this super-central sleepery, the only boutique hotel in town, are graded from 'comfortable' to 'fabulous', and for the most part live up to their names. They come with little features such as handmade beds, cashmere throws, velour bathrobes, beautiful modern bathrooms and little tuckboxes of locally produced snacks. There's a splendid champagne bar, restaurant and tavern, too.

House of Agnes   HOTEL ££
(☎01227-472185; www.houseofagnes.co.uk; 71 St Dunstan's St; r from £83; @🛜) Situated near the West Gate, this rather wonky 13th-century beamed inn, mentioned in Dickens' *David Copperfield*, has eight themed rooms bearing such names as 'Marrakesh' (Moorish), 'Venice' (carnival masks), 'Boston'

(light and airy) and 'Canterbury' (antiques and heavy fabrics). If you prefer your room to have straight lines and right angles, there are eight less exciting, but no less comfortable, rooms in an annex in the walled garden.

Arthouse B&B   B&B ££
(☎01227-453032; www.arthousebandb.com; 24 London Rd; r £60-65; 🅿🛜) A night at Canterbury's newest and most laid-back digs, housed in a 19th-century fire station, is a bit like sleeping over at a really cool art student's pad. The theme is funky and eclectic, with furniture by local designers and artwork by the instantly likeable artist owners, who have a house-studio out back. The organic continental breakfast is laid out in the guest kitchen, with a hostel-like vibe. Only one of the three rooms has an en suite.

Cathedral Gate Hotel   HOTEL ££
(☎01227-464381; www.cathgate.co.uk; 36 Burgate; s/d £70/105, without bathroom £48/80; 🛜) Predating the spectacular cathedral gate it adjoins, this quaint 15th-century hotel is a medieval warren of steep staircases and narrow passageways leading to 27 pleasingly old-fashioned rooms with angled floors, low doors and cockeyed walls. Some have cathedral views, while others overlook pretty Buttermarket. There's no lift.

Magnolia House
B&B ££

(☎01227-765121; www.magnoliahousecanterbury.co.uk; 36 St Dunstan's Tce; s/d from £50/95; P@⊗) An alluringly cosy Georgian guesthouse, Magnolia House comes complete with beautifully appointed if slightly overfilled rooms, lovely gardens and big, cooked-just-for-you breakfasts. Head up St Dunstan's St from the West Gate for about 400m until you reach a roundabout, then turn left and St Dunstan's Terrace is the second on the left.

Kipp's Independent Hostel
HOSTEL £

(☎01227-786121; www.kipps-hostel.com; 40 Nunnery Fields; dm/s/d £16/22/36; @) Occupying a red-brick town house in a quietish residential area less than a mile from the city centre, these superb backpacker digs enjoy a homely atmosphere, clean (though cramped) dorms and rave reviews.

Yew Tree Park
CAMPSITE £

(☎01227-700306; www.yewtreepark.com; Stone St; tent & 2 adults £14.50-19.20; ☺Apr-Sep; P@⊗⊜) This is a family-run campsite set in gentle rolling countryside 5 miles southeast of the city. Phone ahead for directions and transport information.

✖ Eating

TOP CHOICE Deeson's
BRITISH ££

(☎01227-767854; 25-27 Sun St; mains £4.50-16) Put the words 'local', 'seasonal' and 'tasty' into a make-believe restaurant search engine and this superb British eatery would magically pop up first for Canterbury. Local fruit and veg and award-winning wines, beers and ciders, fish from Kent's coastal waters and the odd ingredient from the proprietor's own allotment are all served in a straightforward, contemporary setting just a Kentish apple's throw from the Cathedral gates.

Boho
INTERNATIONAL £

(43 St Peter's St; snacks £3-10; ☺9am-6pm Mon-Sat, 10am-5pm Sun) This hip eatery in a prime spot on the main drag is extraordinarily popular and you'd be lucky to get a table on busy shopping days. The coolest sounds on CD lilt through the chic retro dining space while chilled diners chow down on humungous burgers, full-Monty breakfasts and imaginative, owner-cooked international mains. Boho doesn't do bookings, so be prepared to queue.

Farmhouse
MODERN BRITISH ££

(www.thefarmhousecanterbury.co.uk; 11 Dover St; mains £10-16; ☺9am-11pm Tue-Thu, to 2am Fri & Sat, 11am-5pm Sun; ⊗) This multi-purpose venue just outside the city centre is Canterbury's coolest retreat morning, noon and night. The daytime restaurant plates up cooked-to-order mains, all bursting with seasonal Kentish flavour, amid '60s cabinets, wireless sets and other retro fittings. After dark the focus switches to the moody bar, which at weekends pounds to live bands.

Goods Shed
MARKET, RESTAURANT ££

(☎01227-459153; Station Rd West; mains £12-20; ☺market 9am-7pm Tue-Sat, 10am-4pm Sun, restaurant breakfast, lunch & dinner Tue-Sat, lunch Sun) Farmers market, food hall and fabulous restaurant rolled into one, this converted warehouse by the Canterbury West train station is a hit with everyone from self-caterers to sit-down gourmets. The chunky wooden tables sit slightly above the market hubbub but in full view of its appetite-whetting stalls, and daily specials exploit the freshest farm goodies the Garden of England has to offer.

Veg Box Cafe
VEGETARIAN £

(1 Jewry Lane; soups/specials £4.95/6.95; ☺breakfast & lunch Mon-Sat; ⊘) Perched above Canterbury's top veggie food store, this laid-back and welcoming spot uses only the freshest, locally sourced organic ingredients for its dishes.

▯ Drinking

Parrot
PUB

(1-9 Church Lane) Built in 1370 on Roman foundations, Canterbury's oldest boozer has a snug, beam-rich pub downstairs and a much-lauded dining room upstairs under yet more ageing oak. Needless to say, many a local microbrewed ale is pulled in both venues.

Thomas Becket
PUB

(21 Best Lane) A classic English pub with a garden's worth of hops hanging from its timber frame, Thomas Becket has several quality ales to sample and traditional decor of copper pots, comfy seating and a fireplace to cosy up to on winter nights. It also serves decent pub grub.

☆ Entertainment

Alberry's Wine Bar
CLUB

(St Margaret's St) An after-hours music bar that puts on everything from smooth live jazz to DJ-led drum and bass to commercial pop. It's a two-level place where you can relax over a French Kiss (cocktail or otherwise) above, and party in the basement bar below.

Chill Nightclub CLUB
(www.chill-nightclub.com; St George's Pl) Canterbury's most visible nightclub is a large, fun, cheesy place with a popular student night on Mondays and house anthems and 'old skool' at weekends.

Ballroom LIVE MUSIC
(www.theballroom.co; 15 Orange St) The eclectic events calendar here features everything from a resident DJ to open mic nights, cabaret and live music in a listed 18th-century ballroom.

New Marlowe Theatre THEATRE
(☑01227-787787; www.newmarlowetheatre.org.uk; The Friars) The old Marlowe Theatre was bulldozed in 2009, and this spanking new, state-of-the-art building bolted together in its place opened in late 2011. Established from day one as the southeast's premier venue for performing arts, the New Marlowe attracts top companies and fast-selling productions. Check out the bizarre auditorium, with its dark faux veneers contrasting sharply with the lifejacket-orange seating.

❶ Information

Kent & Canterbury Hospital (☑01227-766877; Etherbert Rd) Located a mile south from the town centre, the hospital has a minor-injuries emergency unit.

PC Repairs Kent (19-21 St Dunstan's St; per hr £3; ☺10am-6pm Mon-Sat) A nine-machine cyber cafe near Canterbury West train station.

Post Office (19 St George's St)

Tourist office (☑01227-378100; www.canterbury .co.uk; 18 High St; ☺9am-5pm Mon-Wed, Fri & Sat, to 7pm Thu, 10am-5pm Sun) Recently relocated to the Beaney House of Art & Knowledge. Staff can help book accommodation, excursions and theatre tickets.

---

❶ CANTERBURY ATTRACTIONS PASSPORT

The Canterbury Attractions Passport (adult/child £19/15.25) gives entry to the cathedral, St Augustine's Abbey, the Canterbury Tales and any one of the city's museums. It's available from the tourist office.

---

❶ Getting There & Away

The city's bus station is just within the city walls on St George's Lane. There are two train stations, Canterbury East for London Victoria and Canterbury West for London's Charing Cross and St Pancras stations.

Bus
Canterbury connections:

Dover National Express £5.40, 40 minutes, hourly
London Victoria National Express, £15.20, two hours, hourly
Margate £4.70, 50 minutes, three per hour
Ramsgate £4.70, 45 minutes, hourly
Sandwich £3.10, 40 minutes, three hourly
Whitstable £2.80, 30 minutes, every 10 min

Train
Canterbury connections:

Dover Priory £7.50, 25 minutes, every 30 minutes
London St Pancras High-speed service, £31.80, one hour, hourly
London Victoria/Charing Cross £26.80, 1¾ hours, two to three hourly

❶ Getting Around

Canterbury's centre is mostly set up for pedestrians. Car parks are dotted along and just inside the walls, but to avoid heavy traffic day trippers may prefer to use one of three Park & Ride sites, which cost £2.50 per day and connect to the centre by bus every eight minutes (7am to 7.30pm Monday to Saturday).

Taxi
Cabwise (☑01227-712929)
Canterbury Cars (☑01227-453333)

Leeds Castle

For many people, the immense moated Leeds Castle (www.leeds-castle.com; adult/child £19.75/12.50; ☺10am-6pm Apr-Sep, to 5pm Oct-Mar) is the world's most romantic castle, and it's certainly one of the most-visited in Britain. While it looks formidable enough from the outside – a hefty structure balancing on two islands amid a large lake and sprawling estate – it's actually known as something of a 'ladies' castle'. This stems from the castle having been home to a who's who of medieval queens in its more than 1000 years of history, most famously Henry VIII's first wife, Catherine of Aragon.

The castle was transformed over the centuries from fortress to lavish palace. Its last owner, the high-society hostess Lady

Baillie, modernised some rooms for use as a princely family home and party pad, to entertain the likes of Errol Flynn, Douglas Fairbanks and JFK. Highlights include Queen Eleanor's medieval bathroom, King Henry VIII's ebony-floored banquetting hall and the boardroom where, in 1978, Israeli and Egyptian negotiators met for talks prior to the Camp David Accords. Since Lady Baillie's death in 1974, a private trust has managed the property. This means some parts of the castle are periodically closed for private events.

The castle's vast estate offers enough attractions of its own to justify a daytrip: peaceful walks, an aviary, falconry demonstrations and a restaurant. You'll also find plenty of kiddie and toddler attractions, as well as a hedge maze, overseen by a grassy bank from where fellow travellers can shout encouragement or misdirections.

Leeds Castle is just east of Maidstone. Trains run from London Victoria to Bearsted (£19.60, one hour) and from there you catch a special shuttle coach to the castle (£5 return), but only between March and October and on winter weekends.

Whitstable

POP 30,195

Perhaps it's the oysters, harvested since Roman times… Maybe it's the weatherboard houses and shingle beach… Perhaps it's the pleasingly old-fashioned main street with petite galleries, been-there-forever outfitters and emporia of vintage frillies… But most likely it's for all of these reasons and more that Whitstable has become a weekend mecca for metropolitan types, looking for refuge from the city hassle. Between waves of Londoners, the town lapses back into fishing-town mode, with its busy harbour and ice-chilled fish market supplying Kent's restaurants.

◎ Sights

Whitstable Museum & Gallery   MUSEUM
(www.whitstable-museum.co.uk; 5 Oxford St; adult/concession £3/1; ⊙10am-4pm) This modest museum has glass cases examining Whitstable's oyster industry, the Crab & Winkle Railway which once ran from Canterbury, and the local fishing fleet, as well as a corner dedicated to actor Peter Cushing, star of several Hammer Horror films and the town's most famous resident, who died in 1994.

🛏 Sleeping & Eating

Hotel Continental   HOTEL ££
(☑01227-280280; www.hotelcontinental.co.uk; 29 Beach Walk; r/huts from £80/75; ℗) The late-'90s quarters in this seaside art-deco building are nothing special – come instead for the converted clapboard fishermen's cottages (huts) right on the beach, which need to be booked well in advance.

Wheeler's Oyster Bar   SEAFOOD £££
(☑01227-273311; 8 High St; mains £18.50-22.50; ⊙lunch & dinner Thu-Tue) Squeeze onto a stool by the bar or into the four-table Victorian dining room of this baby-blue and pink restaurant, choose from the seasonal menu and enjoy the best seafood in Whitstable. This place knows its stuff, as it's been serving oysters since 1856. Bookings are highly recommended unless you're travelling solo. Cash only.

Samphire   MODERN BRITISH ££
(☑01227-770075; 4 High St; mains £10-18; ⊙10am-10pm) The shabby-chic jumble of tables and chairs, large-print wallpaper and blackboard menus create the perfect stage for meticulously crafted mains containing East Kent's most flavour-packed ingredients. An interesting side dish is the namesake samphire, an asparagus-like plant that grows on sea-sprayed rocks and cliffs and is often found on menus in these parts.

❶ Information

Whitstable has no tourist office, but you can pick up maps and other information at the **library** (31-33 Oxford St; ⊙9am-6pm Mon-Fri, to 5pm Sat, 10am-4pm Sun).

❶ Getting There & Away

Bus 4 departs for Canterbury (30 minutes) every 10 minutes.

Margate

POP 40,400

A popular resort for more than two centuries, Margate's late-20th-century slump was long and bleak as British holiday-makers ditched Victorian frump for the carefree *costas* (shores) of Spain. But this grand old seaside dame, with her fine-sand beaches and artistic associations, has bounced off the bottom. Major cultural regeneration projects – including the spectacular new Turner Contemporary art gallery – are slowly reversing the town's fortunes and on busy days even the odd non-English speaker can be overheard in the newly minted cafes and rejuvenated old town.

◎ Sights

TOP CHOICE Turner Contemporary

ART GALLERY

(www.turnercontemporary.org; Rendezvous (Seafront); ⊙10am-6pm Tue-Sun) This state-of-the-art gallery, bolted together on the site of the seafront guest house where master painter JMW Turner used to stay, finally opened in 2011 after much delay. Instantly one of East Kent's top attractions, its strikingly featureless shell and minimalist interior never fails to impress. The only thing distracting the eye, apart from the artwork on display, is the sea view from the floor-to-ceiling windows. These allow you to appreciate the very thing Turner loved so much about Margate – the sea, sky and refracted light of the north Kent coast. The gallery is attracting top-notch contemporary installations by high-calibre artists such as Tracey Emin (who grew up in Margate) and Alex Katz, so be sure to catch a free gallery tour (weekends at 11am).

Shell Grotto

GROTTO, CAVE

(www.shellgrotto.co.uk; Grotto Hill; adult/child £3/1.50; ⊙10am-5pm Apr-Oct) Margate's unique attraction is this mysterious subterranean grotto, discovered in 1835. It's a claustrophobic collection of rooms and passageways embedded with millions of shells arranged in symbol-rich mosaics. It has inspired feverish speculation over the years but presents few answers; some think it a 2000-year-old pagan temple, others an elaborate 19th-century hoax. Either way, it's an exquisite place worth seeing.

🛏 Sleeping & Eating

TOP CHOICE Reading Rooms

B&B £££

(☑01843-225166; www.thereadingroomsmargate .co.uk; 31 Hawley Sq; r £180; 🛜) Occupying an 18th-century Georgian town house on a tranquil square just five minutes on foot from the sea, this luxury boutique B&B is as stylish as they come. Generously cut rooms with waxed wooden floors and beautiful French antique reproduction furniture contrast with the 21st-century bathrooms fragrant with Ren cosmetics. Breakfast is served in your room. Booking essential.

ISLE OF THANET

Margate, Ramsgate and Broadstairs are all towns on the Isle of Thanet, but you won't need a wetsuit or a ferry to reach them – the 2-mile-wide Wantsum Channel dividing the island from the mainland silted up in the 16th century, transforming the East Kent landscape forever. In its island days, Thanet was the springboard for several epoch-making episodes in English history. It was here that the Romans kicked off their invasion in the 1st century AD and where St Augustine landed in AD 597 to launch his conversion of the pagans.

Mad Hatter

CAFE £

(9 Lombard St; mains £4-8; ⊙11am-5.30pm Sat, from noon Sun) Insanely unmissable, this completely cuckoo eatery run by a top-hatted proprietor packs two rooms of a 1690s house with bonkers regalia and knick-knackery from down the ages. Christmas decorations stay up all year and the toilets are original Victorian porcelain. The yummy cakes and snacks are all homemade.

ℹ Information

Tourist Office (☑01843-577577; www.visit thanet.co.uk; Droit House, Stone Pier; ⊙10am-5pm Easter-Oct, 10am-5pm Tue-Sat, to 4pm Sun Nov-Easter) Serving all of Planet Thanet (as locals call the Isle of Thanet), this office stands next to the Turner Contemporary. Pick up a copy of *The Isle,* a glossy magazine crammed with listings and Thanet essentials.

ℹ Getting There & Away

Bus

Canterbury Bus 8, £4.70, 45 minutes, four hourly

London Victoria National Express, £16, 2½ hours, four daily

Train

London St Pancras High-speed service, £37.20, 1½ hours, hourly

London Victoria £31.90, one hr 50 minutes, two hourly

Broadstairs

POP 24,370

While its bigger, brasher neighbours seek to revive and regenerate themselves, quaint little Broadstairs just quietly gets on with what it's done best for the past 150 years – wowing visitors with its tight sickle of reddish sand and sun-warmed lapping sea. Dickens certainly thought Viking Bay a pretty spot, making several visits between 1837 and 1859. The resort now plays the Victorian nostalgia card at every opportunity and names every second business after the works of its most famous holidaymaker.

The large clifftop house dominating the northern end of Viking Bay is where Dickens stayed while in Broadstairs and where he wrote parts of *David Copperfield*. Today it's a private residence and not open to the public.

Sights

Dickens House Museum   MUSEUM
(2 Victoria Pde; adult/child £3.60/2; ⊘2pm-5pm Easter-May, 10am-5pm Jun-Sep) Given a fresh lick of paint for Dickens' 200th birthday in 2012, this quaint museum is Broadstairs' top attraction and the former home of Mary Pearson Strong – Dickens' inspiration for the character of Betsey Trotwood in *David Copperfield*. Diverse Dickensiana on display includes letters from the author.

✲ Festivals & Events

Broadstairs' biggest bash is the annual, nine-day Dickens Festival (www.broadstairs dickensfestival.co.uk) in late June, which culminates in a banquet and ball in Victorian fancy dress.

🛏 Sleeping & Eating

Copperfields Guest House   B&B **££**
(☏01843-601247; www.copperfieldsbb.co.uk; 11 Queen's Rd; s/d £50/75; ☏) This vegetarian B&B offers three homely rooms with en suites, and a warm welcome from the owners and pet Yorkie. It also caters for vegans, and all products in the bathrooms are cruelty free. Just a short hop away from the seafront, with space to store muddy bikes.

Oscar's Festival Cafe   CAFE **£**
(www.oscarsfestivalcafe.co.uk; 15 Oscar Rd; snacks £4-6.50; ⊘10.30am-5pm Wed-Sun) Just back from the bandstand at the southern end of Viking Bay, this hidden gem successfully recreates the buttered-toast-and-railways brand of 1950s austerity that the British find so comforting.

Tartar Frigate   PUB **££**
(42 Harbour St; mains £14.50-18) In summer tourists and locals alike spill out onto the beach from this 18th-century harbourside pub. Top-notch local seafood and regular live folk music.

Getting There & Away

The Thanet Loop bus runs every eight to 10 minutes to Ramsgate (10 to 15 minutes) and Margate (15 to 25 minutes). Other services:

Bus

The Thanet Loop bus runs every eight to 10 minutes to Ramsgate (10 to 15 minutes) and Margate (15 to 25 minutes). Other services:
Canterbury Bus 8A/9, £4.70, 1½ hours, up to three times an hour
London Victoria National Express, £14.70, three hours, four daily

Train

London St Pancras High-speed service, £36, one hour 20 minutes, hourly
London Victoria £21, two hours, twice hourly

Ramsgate

POP 40,000

The most varied of Thanet's towns, Ramsgate has a friendlier feel than rival Margate and is more vibrant than its quaint little neighbour Broadstairs. A forest of sails whistles serenely in the breeze below the handsomely curved walls of Britain's only royal harbour, and the seafront is surrounded by bars and cosmopolitan street cafes. Just one celebrity chef away from being described as 'up and coming', Ramsgate retains a shabbily undiscovered charm. Its sweeping, environmentally sanctioned Blue Flag beaches, some spectacular Victorian architecture and a few welcoming places to stay and eat make it worth the trip.

◉ Sights & Activities

FREE Spitfire Memorial Museum   MUSEUM
(www.spitfiremuseum.org.uk; Manston Rd; ⊘10am-5pm Apr-Oct, to 4pm Nov-Mar) Located about 4 miles northwest of the town centre at Manston Airport (aka Kent International), the main aim at this purpose-built museum is to get up close and personal with two real WWII planes, one a Spitfire, the other a Hurricane. Both look factory-fresh but are surprisingly delicate and so, sadly, there's no clambering on board. Gathered around the planes are myriad flight-associated exhibits, many relating to Manston's role as an airfield during the Battle of Britain. To get here, take

the hourly bus 38 from King St and alight at the airport. The museum is about 10 minutes' walk along Manston Rd.

🛏 Sleeping & Eating

Glendevon Guesthouse
B&B **££**

(✆01843-570909; www.glendevonguesthouse.co.uk; 8 Truro Rd; s/d from £55/85; ⓟ🐾) Run by energetic and outgoing young hosts, this comfy guest house takes the whole ecofriendly thing very seriously, with guest recycling facilities, ecoshowers and even energy-saving hairdryers. The hallways of this grand Victorian house, a block back from the seafront, are decorated with watercolours by local artists. All rooms have kitchenettes, and breakfast is a convivial affair taken around a communal table.

Eddie Gilbert's
SEAFOOD **££**

(✆01843-852123; 32 King St; mains £8.50-21; ⊙lunch & dinner Mon-Sat, lunch Sun) Indulge in England's favourite aroma of battered fish and chips at East Kent's best seafood restaurant, located above a traditional fishmonger's. The beamed dining space decorated with lobster cages, fish nets and sea charts is the ideal setting for platters of locally caught fish, prepared in some very inventive ways by a Michelin-trained chef.

ℹ Information

Tourist office (✆01843-598751; Customs House, Harbour Parade; ⊙10am-2pm Mon-Sat) A small visitor centre with out-of-hours brochure stands.

ℹ Getting There & Away

Boat

Euroferries (✆0844 414 5355; www.euroferries.co.uk) High-speed ferries to Boulogne (1¼ hours, from £49 per car, four times daily).

Transeuropa Ferries (✆01843-595522; www.transeuropaferries.com) Ferries to Ostend in Belgium (five hours, from £52 per car, three times daily).

Bus

Ramsgate is linked to Margate, Broadstairs and Sandwich by frequent local bus services, and to London (Victoria) by National Express (£13.90, three hours, four times daily).

Train

London Charing Cross £31.20, two hours, hourly

London St Pancras High-speed service, £36.20, 1¼ hours, hourly

Sandwich

POP 4500

As close as you'll get to a living museum, Sandwich was once England's fourth city (after London, Norwich and Ipswich), a fact hard to grasp as you ponder its drowsy medieval lanes, ancient churches, Dutch gables, crooked peg-tiled roofs and overhanging timber-framed houses. Once a port to rival London, Sandwich began its decline when the entrance to the harbour silted up in the 16th century, and this once-vital gateway to and from the Continent spent the next 400 years retreating into quaint rural obscurity. Preservation is big here, with huge local interest in period authenticity. The tiny 100-seat cinema is preserved as an art-deco museum piece and the 1920s garage deals more in classic cars than modern vehicles. Within the town's historical core, unlisted buildings are the exception.

Of course, Sandwich indirectly gave the world its favourite snack when the Fourth Earl of Sandwich called for his meat to be served between two slices of bread, thus freeing him to gamble all night without leaving the table or smudging his cards. From then on, it became *de rigueur* to ask for meat 'like Sandwich' and the rest is fast-food history, although the town makes precious little of it.

◉ Sights & Activities

Sandwich's web of medieval and Elizabethan streets is perfect for ambling through and getting pleasantly lost (many do). **Strand Street** in particular has one of the country's highest concentrations of half-timbered buildings. Ornate brickwork on some houses betrays the strong influence of 350 Protestant Flemish refugees (referred to as 'the Strangers'), who settled in the town in the 16th century at the invitation of Elizabeth I.

Guildhall Museum
MUSEUM

(adult/child £1/50p; ⊙10.30am-12.30pm & 2-4pm Tue, Wed, Fri & Sat, 2-4pm Thu & Sun Apr-Nov) Sandwich's small but thorough museum is a good place to start. Exhibitions examine the town's rich past as a Cinque Port, its role in various wars and the gruesome punishments meted out to felons, fornicators and phoney fishermen.

Sandwich Quay
WATERFRONT

Several attractions line the River Stour. First up is a cute little flint-chequered Barbican tollgate built by Henry VIII, which controls

CINQUE PORTS

Due to their proximity to Europe, southeast England's coastal towns were the frontline against raids and invasion during Anglo-Saxon times. In the absence of a professional army and navy, these ports were frequently called upon to defend themselves, and the kingdom, on land and at sea.

In 1278 King Edward I formalised this ancient arrangement by legally defining the Confederation of Cinque Ports. The five original ports – Sandwich, Dover, Hythe, Romney and Hastings – were awarded numerous perks and privileges in exchange for providing the king with ships and men. At their peak, the ports were considered England's most powerful institution after crown and church.

The ports' importance eventually evaporated when the shifting coastlines silted up several Cinque Port harbours and a professional navy was based at Portsmouth. But still the pomp and ceremony remain. The Lord Warden of the Cinque Ports is a prestigious post now bestowed on faithful servants of the crown. The Queen Mother was warden until she passed away, succeeded by Admiral Lord Boyce. Previous incumbents include the Duke of Wellington and Sir Winston Churchill.

The old south coast saying 'Who names us sank and not sink is a foreigner and foe' describes a faux pas committed today by many unknowing tourists, both foreign and British. Cinque, as in Cinque Port, should be pronounced 'sink', and not 'sank' as the French would say.

traffic flow over the river's only road bridge. Nearby rises Fishergate, built in 1384 and once the main entrance to the town, through which goods from the Continent and beyond once passed. On fair-weather days, hop aboard the **Sandwich River Bus** (☎07958 376183; www.sandwichriverbus.co.uk; adult/child 30min trip £7/5, 1hr £12/8; ⊗every 30-60min 11am-6pm Thu-Sun Apr-Sep) beside the toll bridge for seal-spotting trips along the River Stour and in Pegwell Bay, or an interesting way to reach Richborough.

Salutation Gardens   GARDENS
(www.the-secretgardens.co.uk; adult/child £6.50/3; ⊗10am-5pm) Just along from Fishergate is Sandwich's top attraction, a set of exquisite gardens laid out behind a 1912 mansion by leading early 20th-century garden designers Jekyll and Lutyens. There's a superb tearoom in the grounds.

🛌 Sleeping & Eating

TOP CHOICE **Bell Hotel**   HOTEL ££
(☎01304-613388; www.bellhotelsandwich.co.uk; The Quay; s/d from £95/110; P🐾🛜) Today the haunt of celebrity golfers, the Bell Hotel has been sitting on the town's quay since Tudor times, though much of the remaining building is from the 19th century. A splendid sweeping staircase leads to luxurious rooms, some with pretty quay views. The Old Dining Room restaurant is one of East Kent's poshest nosh spots.

King's Arms   INN ££
(☎01304-617330; cnr Church St St Mary's & Strand St; light meals £3-8.50, mains £9.75-21; 🐾) This 15th-century inn opposite St Mary's church serves quality English food and very popular Sunday lunches in a beamed dining room heated by large fireplaces. There are six B&B rooms upstairs.

ℹ Information

Tourist office (☎01304-613565; www.open-sandwich.co.uk; Guildhall, Cattle Market; ⊗10am-4pm Mon-Sat Apr-Oct) Located in the historic Guildhall.

ℹ Getting There & Away

Trains run from Dover Priory train station (22 minutes, hourly), Ramsgate (12 minutes, hourly) and London Charing Cross (£21.20, two hours and 20 minutes, hourly).

Buses also go to Ramsgate (26 minutes, hourly), Dover (41 minutes, hourly) and Canterbury (40 minutes, three hourly).

Richborough

Roman Britain began here amid the windswept ruins of **Richborough's Roman Fort** (EH; adult/child £4.90/2.90; ⊗10am-6pm Apr-Sep, to 4pm Sat & Sun Oct-Mar), just 2 miles north of Sandwich. This is where the successful AD 43 invasion of Britain was launched. To celebrate their victory, the Romans planted a colossal triumphal arch here, the base of which remains. The fort's clearest features today – high walls and scores of deep defensive ditches that give it the appearance of a vast jelly mould – came later when the Romans were forced to stave off increasingly vicious seaborne attacks.

There's a small onsite museum and an audiotour to steer you through the rise and fall of Roman Richborough. To arrive as the Romans did, by boat, take the Sandwich River Bus from Sandwich Quay.

Dover

POP 39,078

Down-in-the-dumps Dover has certainly seen better days and its derelict postwar architecture and shabby town centre of vacant shops is a sad introduction to Blighty for travellers arriving from the Continent, most of whom pass through quickly. Lucky, then, that the town has a couple of stellar attractions to redeem it. The port's vital strategic position so close to mainland Europe gave rise to a sprawling hilltop castle, with some 2000 years of history to its credit. The spectacular white cliffs, as much a symbol of English wartime resilience as Winston Churchill or the Battle of Britain, rear in chalky magnificence to the east and west.

A recent development is Dover's rise as a top stopover for cruise ships, with almost 160 vessels calling at the West Docks in 2012 alone.

◉ Sights & Activities

TOP
CHOICE Dover Castle   CASTLE
(EH; www.english-heritage.org.uk; adult/child £16.50/9.90; ☺10am-6pm Apr-Jul & Sep, from 9.30am Aug, to 5pm Oct, 10am-4pm Sat & Sun Nov-Mar; P) Occupying top spot, literally and figuratively, in Dover's townscape, this most impressive of castles was built to bolster the country's weakest point at the shortest sea crossing to mainland Europe. It sprawls across the city's hilltop, commanding a tremendous view of the English Channel as far as the French coastline. There's lots to see here, so allow at least three hours.

The site has been in use for as many as 2000 years. On the vast grounds are the remains of a Roman lighthouse, which dates from AD 50 and may be the oldest standing building in Britain. Beside it lies the restored Saxon Church of St Mary in Castro.

The robust 12th-century Great Tower, with walls up to 7m thick, is a medieval war-

ren filled with interactive exhibits and light-and-sound shows that take visitors back to the times of Henry II.

The biggest draw of all is the network of secret wartime tunnels. The claustrophobic chalk-hewn passageways were first excavated during the Napoleonic Wars and then expanded to house a command post and hospital in WWII. The highly enjoyable 50-minute guided tour (every 20 minutes) tells the story of one of Britain's most famous wartime operations, code-named Dynamo, which was directed from here in 1940 and saw hundreds of thousands of men evacuated from the beaches at Dunkirk. The story is told in a very effective way, with video projected sharply onto the tunnel walls and sounds rumbling through the rock. At one point the entire passageway is consumed in flames and at others visitors are plunged into darkness.

Dover Museum   MUSEUM
(www.dovermuseum.co.uk; Market Sq; adult/child £3.50/2.25; ☺10am-5pm Mon-Sat year-round, 10am-3pm Sun Apr-Sep) By far the most enthralling exhibit in the town's three-storey museum is an astonishing 3600-year-old Bronze Age boat, discovered here in 1992. Vaunted as the world's oldest-known seagoing vessel, it measures a thumping 9.5m by 2.4m and is kept in a huge, low-lit, climate-controlled glass case.

Roman Painted House   RUINS
(New St; adult/child £3/2; ☺10am-5pm Tue-Sun Jun-Sep) A crumbling 1960s bunker is the unlikely setting for some of the most extensive, if stunted, Roman wall paintings north of the Alps. Several scenes depict Bacchus (god of wine and revelry), which makes perfect sense as this large villa was built around AD 200 as a *mansio* (hotel) for travellers needing a little lubrication to unwind.

⌂ Sleeping

B&Bs are clustered along Castle St, Maison Dieu Rd and Folkestone Rd.

TOP
CHOICE Wallett's Court   HOTEL £££
(☎01304-852424; www.wallettscourt.com; Westcliffe, St Margaret's-at-Cliffe; d from £170; P� ☎≋) The weekend haunt of de-stressing London high-flyers, romantic couples and the odd moneyed cliff walker, this place is just a bit special. Digs at this country house set in rolling farmland range from spacious Jacobean guestrooms to beamed converted barns to a canvas wigwam. Add to that a soothing spa,

Dover

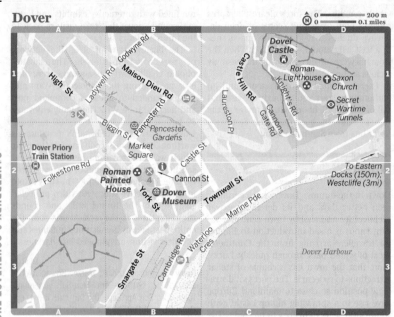

a first-rate restaurant and perky service, and you have yourself one very relaxing country retreat. Heading towards Deal, turn right off the A258 after almost 2 miles for Westcliffe.

Dover Marina Hotel   HOTEL **££**

(☎01304-203633; www.dovermarinahotel.co.uk; Waterloo Cres; r £69-107; ☎) Just a few steps from Dover's beach, this newly revamped hotel crams 81 rooms of varying dimensions into a gently curving 1870s edifice. The undulating corridors show the building's age, but there's nothing wonky about the rooms with their trendy ethno-fabrics, big-print wallpaper and contemporary artwork. Half the rooms have unrivalled sea views and 10 boast much-sought-after balconies.

East Lee Guest House   B&B **££**

(☎01304-210176; www.eastlee.co.uk; 108 Maison Dieu Rd; d £60; P☎) This lovely terracotta-shingled town house impresses with its grand, elegantly decorated communal areas, recently renovated rooms, energetic hosts and excellent, varied breakfasts.

✖ Eating

TOP CHOICE **Allotment**   BRITISH **££**

(www.theallotmentdover.com; 9 High St; mains £7.50-16; ☺Tue-Sat) Dover's best dining spot

Dover

◎ Top Sights

🛏 Sleeping

⊗ Eating

plates up local fish and meat from around Canterbury for breakfast, lunch and dinner, seasoned with herbs from the tranquil garden out back, in a relaxed, understated setting. Swab the decks with a Kentish wine as you admire the view of the Maison Dieu (13th-century pilgrims' hospital) directly opposite, through the exquisite stained-glass frontage.

La Salle Verte   CAFE **£**

(14-15 Cannon St; snacks £2-5.50; ☺breakfast & lunch Mon-Sat) A much-loved coffee or lunch halt with fascinating black and white images of old Dover lining the walls, a rockin' jukebox and friendly proprietors. Fills up at lunch even on winter Wednesdays.

❶ Information

Post office (68-72 Pencester Rd)

Tourist office (☑01304-205108; www.white cliffscountry.org.uk; Market Sq; ⊙9.30am-5pm Mon-Sat year-round, 10am-3pm Sun Apr-Sep) Located in the town's museum.

❶ Getting There & Away

Boat

Ferries depart for France from the Eastern Docks below the castle. Fares vary according to season and advance purchase. With the demise of SeaFrance, services are in a state of flux.

DFDS (☑0871 574 7235; www.dfdsseaways .co.uk) Services to Dunkirk (two hours, every two hours).

LD Lines (☑0800 917 1201; www.ldlines.co.uk) Services to Boulogne (50 minutes, up to seven times daily).

MyFerryLink (☑0844 2482 100; www.my ferrylink.com) Services to Calais (1 hour 20 minutes; eight times daily).

P&O Ferries (☑0871 664 2020; www.poferries .com) Runs to Calais (1½ hours, every 40 to 60 minutes).

Bus

Dover connections:

Canterbury Bus 15, £4.50, 45 minutes, twice hourly

London Victoria Coach 007, £14.80, 2½ to 3½ hours, 19 times daily

Sandwich Bus 87/88, £5, 45 minutes, hourly

Train

Dover connections:

London Charing Cross £21.10, two hours, twice hourly

London St Pancras High-speed service, £36.20, one hour, hourly

Ramsgate Via Sandwich, £8.70, 35 minutes, hourly

❶ Getting Around

Between 7am and 11pm, a **port shuttle bus** (£2, five minutes, every 20 minutes) runs between the Eastern Docks and train station, as they're a long walk apart.

Around Dover

THE WHITE CLIFFS

Immortalised in song, literature and film, these resplendent cliffs are embedded in the British national consciousness, acting as a big, white 'Welcome Home' sign to g tions of travellers and soldiers.

The cliffs rise 100m high and extend miles either side of Dover, but it is the 6-m stretch east of town – properly known as the Langdon Cliffs – that especially captivates visitors' imaginations. The chalk here is about 250m deep and the cliffs are about half a million years old, formed when the melting icecaps of northern Europe gouged a channel between France and England.

The Langdon Cliffs are managed by the National Trust, which has a tourist office (☑01304-202756; ⊙9.30am-5.30pm Mar-Oct, 10.30am-4pm Nov-Feb) and carpark (nonmembers £3 per park per day) 2 miles east of Dover along Castle Hill Rd and the A258 road to Deal, or off the A2 past the Eastern Docks. From the tourist office, follow the stony path east along the clifftops for a bracing 2-mile walk to the stout Victorian South Foreland Lighthouse (NT; www.nationaltrust.org .uk; adult/child £4/2; ⊙guided tours 11am-5.30pm Fri-Mon mid-Mar–Oct). This was the first lighthouse to be powered by electricity and is the site of the first international radio transmissions, in 1898.

A mile further on the same trail brings you to delightful St Margaret's Bay, a gap in the chalk with a sun-trapping shingle beach and the welcoming Coastguard Pub (www.thecoastguard.co.uk; mains £10-20). This is the closest point to France and many a cross-Channel swimmer has stepped into the briny here. From the top of the hill, bus 15 shuttles back to Dover or onward to Deal every hour.

To see the cliffs in all their full-frontal glory, Dover White Cliffs Tours (☑01303-271388; www.doverwhiteclifftours.com; adult/child £8/4; ⊙daily Jul & Aug, Sat & Sun Apr-Jun & Sep-Oct)) runs 40-minute sightseeing trips at least three times daily from the Western Docks.

EAST SUSSEX

Home to rolling countryside, medieval villages and gorgeous coastline, this inspiring corner of England is besieged by weekending Londoners whenever the sun pops out. And it's not hard to see why as you explore the cobbled medieval streets of Rye, wander around historic Battle where William the Conqueror first engaged the Saxons in 1066, and peer over the edge of the breathtaking Seven Sisters chalk cliffs and Beachy Head

home from 1842 until his death in 1882, **Down House** (EH; Luxted ...ult/child £9.90/5.90; ☺11am-5pm daily Jul & Aug, Wed-Sun Apr-Jun & Sep-Oct, ...pm Sat & Sun Nov-Mar) witnessed the development of Darwin's theory of evolution by natural selection. The house and gardens have been restored to look much as they would have in Darwin's time, including Darwin's study where he undertook much of his reading and writing, the drawing room where he conducted some of his indoor experiments; and the gardens and greenhouse where some of his outdoor experiments are recreated. Three self-guided trails in the area let you follow in the great man's footsteps.

Down House is in Downe, off the A21. Take bus 146 from Bromley North or Bromley South railway station, or service R8 from Orpington.

near the genteel seaside town of Eastbourne. Brighton, a highlight of any visit, offers some kicking nightlife, offbeat shopping and British seaside fun. Off the beaten track, you can stretch your legs on the South Downs Way, which traverses England's newest national park, the South Downs National Park.

Rye

POP 4200

Often described as England's quaintest town, Rye is a little nugget of the past, a medieval settlement that looks like it's been dunked in formaldehyde and left on the shelf for all to admire. Even the most hard-boiled cynic can't fail to be softened by Rye's cobbled lanes, mysterious passageways and crooked half-timbered Tudor buildings. Tales of resident smugglers, ghosts, writers and artists abound.

Rye was once one of the Cinque Ports, occupying a high promontory above the sea. Today the town rises 2 miles from the briny; sheep graze where the Channel's strong tides once swelled.

◉ Sights

A short walk from the Rye Heritage Centre, most start their exploration of Rye in the famous **Mermaid St**, bristling with 15th-century timber-framed houses with quirky house names such as 'The House with Two Front Doors' and 'The House Opposite'.

Ypres Tower MUSEUM

(www.ryemuseum.co.uk; adult/child £3/free; ☺10.30am-5pm Apr-Oct, to 4pm Nov-Mar) Just off Church Sq stands the sandcastle-esque Ypres Tower (pronounced 'wipers'), one part of Rye Museum. You can scramble through the 13th-century building to learn about its long history as a fort, prison, mortuary and museum (the last two at overlapping times), but it's the views of Rye Bay, Dungeness nuclear power station and even France on very clear days, that will hold your attention longest. The star attraction at the other branch of the **museum** (3 East St; adult/child £1.50/free; ☺10.30am-5pm Sat & Sun Apr-Oct), a short stroll away, is a well preserved 18th-century fire engine complete with its leather hoses and lead buckets.

Lamb House HOUSE, MUSEUM

(NT; West St; adult/child £4.60/2.35; ☺2-6pm Tue & Sat late Mar-Oct) This Georgian town house is a favourite stomping ground for local apparitions, but not that of its most famous resident, American writer Henry James, who lived here from 1898 to 1916, during which time he wrote *The Wings of the Dove*.

Church of St Mary the Virgin CHURCH

(Church Sq; tower adult/child £2.50/1; ☺9.15am-5.30pm Apr-Sep) Rye's church is a hotchpotch of medieval and later styles and its turret clock is the oldest in England (1561) still working with its original pendulum, which swings above your head as you enter. Climb the tower for panoramic views of the town and surroundings.

⌷ Sleeping

TOP CHOICE **Jeake's House** HOTEL ££

(☎01797-222828; www.jeakeshouse.com; Mermaid St; s/d from £70/90; P🖘) Superbly situated on cobbled Mermaid St, this labyrinthine 17th-century town house once belonged to US poet Conrad Aitken. The 11 rooms are named after writers who actually stayed here, though the decor was probably slightly less bold back then, minus the beeswaxed antiques and lavish drapery. You can literally take a pew in the snug book-lined bar and, continuing the theme, breakfast is served in an 18th-century former Quaker chapel.

Mermaid Inn
HOTEL **££**

(☏01797-223065; www.mermaidinn.com; Mermaid St; d from £90; 🅿) Few inns can claim to be as atmospheric as this ancient hostelry, dating from 1420. Every room is different – but each is thick with dark beams and lit by leaded windows, and some are graced by secret passageways that now act as fire escapes. Small wonder it's such a popular spot – these days you're as likely to spot a celeb or a minor royal as the resident ghost.

George in Rye
HOTEL **£££**

(☏01797-222114; www.thegeorgeinrye.com; 98 High St; d from £135; @☎) This old coaching inn has managed to reinvent itself as a contemporary boutique hotel while staying true to its roots. Downstairs, an old-fashioned wood-panelled lounge is warmed by roaring log fires, while the guestrooms in the main building, created by the set designer from the film *Pride & Prejudice*, are chic and understated.

 Eating

Haydens
CAFE **£**

(108 High St; snacks/meals from £3/9; ⊙10am-5pm) Staunch believers in organic and fair-trade produce, these guys dish up delicious omelettes, ploughman's lunches, salads and bagels in their light, breezy cafe. There's a wonderful ele... great views ov... countryside.

Ypres Castle In...
(Gun Gardens; meal... family-friendly Su... Mediterranean and... a big beer garden fo...

ⓘ Information

Post office (Unit 2, Stat... ...acn)

Rye Heritage Centre (☏01797-226696; www.ryeheritage.co.uk; Strand Quay; ⊙10am-5pm Apr-Oct, reduced hours Nov-Mar) See a town-model audiovisual history for £3.50 and, upstairs, a freaky collection of penny-in-the-slot novelty machines.

Rye internet cafe (46 Ferry Rd; per hr £2; ⊙10am-8pm Tue-Thu, to 7pm Fri, to 6pm Sat)

Tourist office (☏01797-229049; www.visit1066country.com; 4/5 Lion St; ⊙10am-5pm Apr-Sep, to 4pm Oct-Mar) Help available with accommodation bookings and train and bus tickets.

ⓘ Getting There & Away

Bus

Dover Bus 100, £5.80, two hours, hourly

Hastings Bus 344 or 100, £4.80, 40 minutes, two per hour

London Charing Cross change in Ashford, £29.60, two hours, hourly

---

A SWIG OF KENT & SUSSEX

With booze cruises over to Calais now almost a thing of the past, many Kent and Sussex drinkers are rediscovering their counties' superb home-grown beverages. Both counties produce some of the most delicious ales in the country and the southeast's wines are even outgunning some traditional Continental vintners.

Kent's Shepherd Neame Brewery (☏01795-542016; www.shepherdneame.co.uk; 10 Court St, Faversham; tours £11.50; ⊙call ahead or see website for tour times) is Britain's oldest and cooks up aromatic ales brewed from Kent-grown premium hops. Sussex's reply is Harveys Brewery (☏01273-480209; www.harveys.org.uk; Bridge Wharf, Lewes; per person £2.50; ⊙evenings three times a week Jun-Jul & Sep-Nov) which perfumes Lewes town centre with a hop-laden scent. Book in advance for tours of either brewery.

Mention 'English wine' not too long ago and you'd likely hear a snort of derision. Not any more. Thanks to warmer temperatures and determined winemakers, English wine, particularly of the sparkling variety, is developing a fan base all of its own.

Award-winning vineyards can be found in both Sussex and Kent, whose chalky soils are likened to France's Champagne region. Many vineyards now offer tours and wine tastings. Some of the most popular are Biddenden Vineyards (☏01580-291726; www.biddendenvineyards.com; 1.2 miles from Wealden; admission free; ⊙tours 10am Wed & Sat) and Chapel Down Vinery (☏01580-766111; www.englishwinesgroup.com; admission £9; ⊙tours daily Jun-Sep, weekends May & Oct), located 2.5 miles south of Tenderden on the B2082.

ring Cross (£29.60, two
Change in Ashford.

ttle

POP 5190

'If there'd been no battle, there'd be no Battle', goes the saying in this unassuming village, which grew up around the hillside where invading French duke William of Normandy, aka William the Conqueror, scored a decisive victory over local King Harold in 1066. The epicentre of 1066 country, visitors flock here to see the spot where Harold got it in the eye, with the biggest crowd turning up mid-October to witness the annual re-enactment on the original battlefield.

◉ Sights

Battle Abbey   HISTORIC SITE
(EH; adult/child £7.50/4.50; ◷10am-6pm Apr-Sep) Another day, another photogenic ruin? Hardly. On this spot raged the pivotal battle in the last successful invasion of England in 1066: an event with unparalleled impact on the country's subsequent social structure, architecture and well...pretty much everything. Four years after, the conquering Normans began constructing an abbey in the middle of the battlefield, a penance ordered by the Pope for the loss of life incurred here.

Only the foundations of the original church remain, the altar's position marked by a plaque – also supposedly the spot England's King Harold famously took an arrow in his eye. Other impressive monastic buildings survive and make for atmospheric explorations.

The battlefield's innocently rolling lush hillsides do little to evoke the ferocity of the event, but high-tech interactive presentations and a film at the visitors centre, as well as blow-by-blow audiotours, do their utmost to bring the battle to life.

Yesterday's World   MUSEUM
(www.yesterdaysworld.co.uk; 89-90 High St; adult/child £7.25/5.25; ◷10am-5.30pm Apr-Sep) Overshadowed literally and figuratively by the abbey, this growing museum is an incredible repository of England's retail past. The first building houses entire streets of quaint old shops where costumed dummies proffer long-discontinued brands, every space in between stuffed with yester-year products, enamel advertising signs, battered toys, wartime memorabilia and general nostalgia-

inducing knick-knackery. The second building houses the Royalty Room where a cardboard cut-out illustrates just how tiny Queen Victoria was (1.40m).

❶ Getting There & Away

Bus 304/305 goes to Hastings (26 minutes, hourly).

Trains travel to Hastings (£3.90, 15 minutes, twice hourly) and to London Charing Cross (£20.90, one hour and 20 minutes, twice hourly).

Bodiam Castle

Surrounded by a square moat teeming with oversized goldfish, archetypal Bodiam Castle (NT; adult/child £7/3.50; ◷10.30am-5pm mid-Feb–Oct) makes you half expect a fire-breathing dragon to appear at one of its four towers or a golden-haired princess to lean over its walls. It is the legacy of the 14th-century soldier of fortune (the polite term for knights who slaughtered and pillaged their way around France) Sir Edward Dalyngrigge, who married the local heiress and set about building a castle to ensure everybody knew who was boss.

Parliamentarian forces left the castle in ruins during the English Civil War, but in 1917 Lord Curzon, former viceroy of India, bought it and restored the exterior. Much of the interior remains unrestored, but it's possible to climb to the battlements for some sweeping views.

While here, you'll most likely hear the tooting of the nearby Kent & East Sussex steam railway (www.kesr.org.uk; day ticket adult/child £15/10), which runs from Tenterden in Kent through 11 miles of gentle hills and woods to Bodiam village, from where a bus takes you to the castle. It operates three to five services on most days from May to September, and in the weekend and school holidays in October, December and February.

The castle is 9 miles northeast of Battle off the B2244. Bus 349 from Hastings (40 minutes) stops at Bodiam once every two hours, Monday to Saturday.

Hastings

POP 86,900

Forever associated with the Norman invasion of 1066 (even though the crucial events took place 6 miles away), Hastings thrived as one of the Cinque Ports (see p160) and, in its Victorian heyday, was one of the country's most fashionable resorts. After a period of steady decline, the town is enjoying a mini-renaissance and these days is an intriguing mix of tacky resort, fishing port and arty New Age hangout.

◉ Sights

Stade NEIGHBOURHOOD

(Rock-A-Nore Rd) The seafront area known as the Stade (below East Hill) is home to distinctive black clapboard structures known as Net Shops. These were built to store fishing gear back in the 17th century, but some now house fishmongers who sell off the catch of Europe's largest beach-launched fishing fleet, usually hauled up on the shingle behind.

The Stade is very much a working place, where the combined pong of diesel and fish guts scents the air, but there are a couple of attractions here, too. Housed in a former church, the Fishermen's Museum (www .hastingsfish.co.uk; Rock-A-Nore Rd; ⊙10am-5pm Apr-Oct) has shoals of barnacled exhibits, all swimming around the huge 1912 fishing boat *Enterprise*. Nearby, the fishy theme continues at the Blue Reef Aquarium (www .bluereefaquarium.co.uk/hastings; Rock-A-Nore Rd; adult/child £8.20/6.10; ⊙10am-5pm), though its exotically goggle-eyed inhabitants probably wouldn't taste that great with chips.

A controversial addition to the Stade is the Jerwood Gallery (www.jerwoodgallery.org; Rock-A-Nore Rd; adult/concession £7/5; ⊙11am-4pm Tue-Fri, to 6pm Sat & Sun), opened in 2012, a large purpose-built venue for contemporary British art. Howls of local disapproval were ignited when the complex clipped the end off the historic Stade where coaches used to park.

Hastings Castle CASTLE, RUIN

(www.discoverhastings.co.uk; Castle Hill Rd; adult/ child £4.25/3.50; ⊙10am-5pm Easter-Sep) Half the fun of reaching the clifftop ruins of Hastings' Norman castle is the journey up there on the West Hill Cliff Railway (George St; adult/child £2.50/1.50; ⊙10am-5.30pm Mar-Sep), a late-Victorian funicular. The fortress was built by William the Conquerer, and an exhibition in the grounds tells the story of the castle and Battle of Hastings in 1066.

Also on West Hill, a short walk east of the castle, is the Smugglers Adventure (www.smugglersadventure.co.uk; St Clement Caves; adult/child £7.40/5.40; ⊙10am-5pm Easter-Sep), where you can explore underground caverns and hear smuggling yarns from the Sussex coast.

Hastings Country Park NATURE RESERVE

This 267-hectare clifftop nature reserve, reached by another 19th-century contraption, the East Hill Cliff Railway (Rock-A-Nore Rd; adult/child £2.50/1.50; ⊙10am-5.30pm Apr-Sep), is a dog-walkers' and picknickers' paradise.

🛏 Sleeping & Eating

Swan House B&B ££

(☎01424-430014; www.swanhousehastings.co.uk; 1 Hill St; s/d from £70/115; @☎) Inside its 15th-century timbered shell, this place blends

---

THE LAST INVASION OF ENGLAND

The most famous battle in the history of England took place in 1066, a date seared into every English schoolchild's brain. The Battle of Hastings began when King Harold's army arrived on the scene on 14 October and created a three-ringed defence consisting of archers, then cavalry and massed infantry at the rear. William marched north from Hastings and took up a position about 400m south of Harold and his troops. He tried repeatedly to break the English cordon, but Harold's men held fast. William's knights then feigned retreat, drawing some of Harold's troops after them. It was a fatal mistake. Seeing the gap in the English wall, William ordered his remaining troops to charge through, and the battle was as good as won. Among the English casualties was King Harold who, as tradition has it, was hit in the eye by an arrow and struck down by Norman knights as he tried to pull it out. At news of his death, the last English resistance collapsed.

In their wonderfully irreverent parody of British history, *1066 And All That* (1930), WC Sellar and RJ Yeatman suggest that 'the Norman conquest was a Good Thing, as from this time onward England stopped being conquered and thus was able to become top nation...' When you consider that England hasn't been successfully invaded since, it's hard to disagree.

contemporary and vintage chic to perfection. Rooms feature organic toiletries, fresh flowers, hand-painted walls and huge beds. The guest lounge, where pale sofas, painted floorboards and striking modern sculpture rub shoulders with beams and a huge stone fireplace, is a stunner.

Dragon Bar BAR, RESTAURANT ££
(71 George St; mains £11.50-21.50; ⊗lunch & dinner Mon-Sat, lunch Sun) The younger end of the alternative old-town crowds are attracted to this atmospheric, laid-back bar. It's full of dark walls, mismatched furniture and beaten leather sofas and the eclectic menu features everything from Thai curry to Winchelsea lamb and pizzas.

❶ Information

Tourist office (☑01424-451111; Queen's Sq; ⊗8.30am-6pm Mon-Fri, 9am-5pm Sat, 10.30am-4pm Sun)

❶ Getting There & Away

Bus

Eastbourne Bus 99, £4, one hour 20 minutes, three per hour

London Victoria National Express, £14.40, 2½ to four hours, two daily

Rye Buses 100 & 344, £4.80, 40 minutes, twice hourly

Train

Brighton Via Eastbourne, £13.10, one hour to one hour 20 minutes, twice hourly

London Charing Cross £21.10, 1½ hours, twice hourly

London Victoria £15.90, two hours, hourly

Eastbourne

POP 97,000

This classic seaside resort has long brought to mind images of octogenarians dozing in deckchairs. While many of Eastbourne's seafront hotels still have that retirement-home feel, in recent years an influx of students and one of the southeast's largest new Polish communities have given the town a more sprightly feel.

The creation of the new South Downs National Park to the west also means Eastbourne's pebbly beaches, scrupulously snipped seaside gardens and picturesque arcade-free promenade are likely to host increasing numbers of walkers and cyclists, finishing or embarking on a trip along the South Downs Way.

◉ Sights & Activities

FREE **Towner Art Gallery** ART GALLERY
(☑01323-434660; www.townereastbourne.org.uk; Devonshire Park, College Rd; ⊗10am-5pm, tours 11.30am Tue-Sun) One of the southeast's most exciting exhibition spaces, this purpose-built building has temporary shows of contemporary work on the ground and second floors, while the first floor is given over to rotating themed shows created from the gallery's 4000-piece collection. Building tours include a peek inside the climate-controlled art store.

Pier WATERFRONT
(www.eastbournepier.com) Eastbourne's ramshackle pier is a lovable piece of Victoriana jutting into the chilly Channel. All its tearooms, fish and chip counters, twopence machines and fortunetellers are firmly in place, and there's a popular student nightclub at the very tip.

Museum of Shops MUSEUM
(20 Cornfield Tce; adult/child £5/4; ⊗10am-5pm) This small museum is swamped by an obsessive collection of how-we-used-to-live memorabilia.

☞ Tours

City Sightseeing BUS TOUR
(www.city-sightseeing.co.uk; adult/child £7.50/4.50; ⊗every 30min 10am-5pm) Open-top bus tours around local sights and up to Beachy Head.

Sussex Voyages BOAT TOUR
(☑01293-888780; www.sussexvoyages.co.uk; Sovereign Harbour Marina Village; adult/child/concession £26/23/15) Two-hour Beachy Head and Seven Sisters boat tours leaving from Sovereign Harbour (take bus 51 or 99) on rigid-hulled inflatables. Reservations essential.

🛏 Sleeping

The Big Sleep HOTEL £
(☑01323-722676; www.thebigsleephotel.com; King Edward's Pde; s/d from £45/59; 🐾) Hip, fresh and friendly, this seafront hotel has 50 gobsmacking rooms with big-print wallpaper, retro furnishings and curtains that look as though they might have been grazing on Beachy Head just a few hours prior. A trendy bar, big basement games room and Channel views make this BN21's coolest kip.

Albert & Victoria B&B ££
(☑01323-730948; www.albertandvictoria.com; 19 St Aubyns Rd; s/d from £35/75; 🐾) Book ahead

to stay at this delightful Victorian terraced house, whose fragrant rooms, canopied beds, crystal chandeliers and secluded walled garden for summer breakfasts are mere paces from the seafront promenade. The four rooms are named after four of Queen Victoria's offspring.

Eating & Drinking

Lamb Inn
PUB ££

(36 High St; mains £7-13; ⊙11am-11.30pm) This Eastbourne institution located less than a mile northwest of the train station in the undervisited Old Town has been plonking Sussex ales on the bar for eight centuries, and now also serves gourmet British pub grub. A holidaying Dickens also left a few beer rings and smudged napkins here when he stayed across the road. Buses 1 and 1A stop nearby.

Belgian Cafe
SEAFOOD ££

(11-23 Grand Pde; mains £11-17) You might not know that Belgian beer can taste of fruit, the national dish is mussels and chips, and Tintin hails from its capital, Brussels. But you will once you've experienced this popular cafe near the pier.

Shopping

Camilla's Bookshop
BOOKS

(www.camillasbookshop.com; 57 Grove Rd) Literally packed to the rafters with musty volumes, this incredible secondhand-book repository, an interesting amble from the train station, fills three floors of a crumbling Victorian town house.

Information

Tourist office (☑0871 663 0031; www.visiteastbourne.com; Cornfield Rd; ⊙9.15am-5.30pm Mon-Fri, to 5pm Sat Apr-Oct)

Getting There & Away

Bus

Brighton Bus 12, £3.50, one hour 15 minutes, up to four hourly

Hastings Bus 99, £4, one hour 20 minutes, three per hour

Train

Brighton £9.50, 30 to 40 minutes, twice hourly

London Victoria £27.70, 1½ hours, twice hourly

Around Eastbourne

After decades of campaigning, planning and deliberation, the South Downs National Park, over 600 sq miles of rolling chalk downs stretching west from Eastbourne for about 100 miles, finally came into being in March 2010.

BEACHY HEAD

The famous cliffs of Beachy Head are the highest point of the chalky rockfaces that slice across the rugged coastline at the southern end of the South Downs. It's a spot of thrilling beauty – at least until you remember this is also officially one of the world's top suicide spots!

From Beachy Head, the stunning Seven Sisters Cliffs undulate their way west. A clifftop path (a branch of the South Downs Way) rides the waves of chalk as far as picturesque Cuckmere Haven. Along the way, you'll stumble upon the tiny seaside hamlet of Birling Gap, where you can stop for a drink, snack or ice cream at the Birling Gap Hotel (Seven Sisters Cliffs). The secluded beach is a suntrap popular with locals and walkers taking a breather.

Beachy Head is off the B2103, from the A259 between Eastbourne and Newhaven. Eastbourne's City Sightseeing tour bus stops at the clifftop.

PEVENSEY CASTLE

The ruins of William the Conqueror's first stronghold, Pevensey Castle (EH; adult/child £4.90/2.90; ⊙10am-6pm Apr-Sep), sit 5 miles east of Eastbourne, just off the A259. Picturesquely dissolving into its own moat, the castle marks the point where William the Conqueror landed in 1066, just two weeks before the Battle of Hastings. After his victory, Old Bill wasted no time in building upon sturdy Roman walls to create a castle, which was used time and again through the centuries, right up to WWII. You can roam about its decaying husk with an enlightening audioguide, free with entry.

Regular train services between London Victoria and Hastings via Eastbourne (10 minutes) stop at Westham, half a mile from Pevensey.

Brighton & Hove

POP 247,800

Raves on the beach, Graham Greene novels, mods and rockers in bank-holiday fisticuffs, naughty weekends for Mr and Mrs Smith, classic car runs from London, the United Kingdom's biggest gay scene and the Channel's best clubbing – this city by the sea evokes many images for the British. One thing is certain: with its bohemian, cosmopolitan, hedonistic vibe, Brighton is where England's seaside experience goes from cold to cool.

Brighton is without doubt Britain's most colourful and outrageous city, and one with many faces. Here, bosomy burlesque meets contemporary design, Spanish students leave Starbucks to rub shoulders with stars in Spanish bars, the southeast's grottiest hostels share thin walls with kinky boutique hotels, microbrew ales costing £4 a pint occupy bar space with £1 buckets of 'sex on the beach', and stags watch drag. This is the city that returned the country's first Green Party MP in 2010, where Valentine's Day is celebrated with more gusto than Christmas, and the place, according to the 2001 census, with the highest UK population of Jedi.

Brighton rocks all year round, but really comes to life during the summer months when tourists, language students and revellers from London pour into the city, keen to explore the city's legendary nightlife, summer festivals and quirky shops. The highlight for the sightseeing visitor is, without doubt, the weird and wonderful Royal Pavilion, a 19th-century party palace built by the Prince Regent, who kicked off Brighton's enduring love of the outlandish.

◉ Sights

Royal Pavilion   PALACE
(www.royalpavilion.org.uk; Royal Pavilion Gardens; adult/child £9.80/5.60; ☉9.30am-5.45pm Apr-Sep, 10am-5.15pm Oct-Mar) The city's must-see attraction is the Royal Pavilion, the glittering party pad and palace of Prince George, later Prince Regent and then King George IV. It's one of the most opulent buildings in England, certainly the finest example of early 19th-century chinoiserie anywhere in Europe and an apt symbol of Brighton's reputation for decadence.

The entire palace is an eye-popping spectacle, but some interiors stand out even amid the riot of decoration. The dragon-themed banqueting hall must be the most incredible in all England; more dragons and snakes writhe in the music room, with its ceiling of 26,000 gold scales; and the then state-of-the-art kitchen must have wowed Georgians with its automatic spits and hot tables. Prince Albert carted away all of the furniture, some of which has been loaned back by the current queen. An unimpressed Queen Victoria called the Royal Pavilion 'a strange, odd Chinese place' but for visitors to Brighton it's an unmissable chunk of Sussex history.

FREE Brighton Museum & Art Gallery   MUSEUM, GALLERY
(www.brighton-hove-museums.org.uk; Royal Pavilion Gardens; ☉10am-5pm Tue-Sun) Set in the Royal Pavilion's renovated stable block, this museum and art gallery has a glittering collection of 20th-century art and design, including a crimson Salvador Dalí sofa modelled on Mae West's lips. There's also an enthralling gallery of world art, an impressive collection of Egyptian artefacts and an 'images of Brighton' multimedia exhibit containing a series of oral histories and a model of the defunct West Pier.

Brighton Pier   AMUSEMENT PARK
(www.brightonpier.co.uk; Madeira Dr) This grand, century-old pier is the place to experience Brighton's tackier side. There are plenty of stomach-churning fairground rides and dingy amusement arcades to keep you amused, and candy floss and Brighton rock to chomp on while you're doing so.

Look west and you'll see the sad remains of the West Pier (www.westpier.co.uk), a skeletal iron hulk that attracts flocks of starlings at sunset. It's a sad end for this Victorian marvel, on which the likes of Charlie Chaplin and Stan Laurel once performed.

So far there's no sign of the i360 observation tower ('Hurray!' some may cry), a spectacularly space-age piece of architecture from the creators of the London Eye that may one day loom 150m above the seafront. The venue would include a West Pier Heritage Centre – a pavilion with audiovisual exhibits relating the pier's history.

☞ Tours

City Sightseeing   BUS TOUR
(www.city-sightseeing.co.uk; adult/child £10/3; ☉every 30 mins May–mid-Sep) Open-top hop-on/hop-off bus tours leaving from Grand Junction Rd near Brighton Pier.

Tourist Tracks   MP3 TOUR
(www.tourist-tracks.com) MP3 audioguides are downloadable from the website (£5) or available on a preloaded MP3 player at the tourist office (£6 per half-day).

✦✦ Festivals & Events

There's always something fun going on in Brighton, from Gay Pride (www.brightonpride.org) to food and drink festivals. The showpiece is May's three-week-long Brighton Festival (01273-709 709; www.brightonfestival.org). The biggest arts festival in Britain after Edinburgh, it draws theatre, dance, music and comedy performers from around the globe.

🛏 Sleeping

Despite a glut of hotels in Brighton, prices are relatively high and you'd be wise to book well ahead for summer weekends and for the Brighton Festival in May. Expect to pay up to a third more across the board at weekends.

Amsterdam
HOTEL ££££

(01273-688825; www.amsterdam.uk.com; 11-12 Marine Pde; d £85-160) A popular gay-run hotel that also welcomes straights, with tastefully decorated, bright and spacious rooms and wonderful sea views. Request a room on a higher floor if you're a light sleeper.

TOP CHOICE Hotel Una
BOUTIQUE HOTEL ££

(01723-820464; www.hotel-una.co.uk; 55-56 Regency Sq; s £55-75, d £115-150; ❄🛜) All of the 19 generous rooms here wow guests with their bold-patterned fabrics, supersized leather sofas, in-room free-standing baths and vegan/veggie/carnivorous breakfast in bed. Some, such as the two-level suite with its own mini-cinema, and the under-pavement chambers with their own spa and jacuzzi, are truly showstopping and not as expensive as you might expect. All this plus a cool cocktail bar and lots of timewarp period features make the Una our numero uno.

Hotel Pelirocco
THEME HOTEL ££

(01273-327055; www.hotelpelirocco.co.uk; 10 Regency Sq; s £59-65, d £99-145, ste from £249; 🛜) One of Brighton's sexiest and nuttiest places to stay, the Pelirocco takes the theme concept to a new level and has become the ultimate venue for a flirty rock 'n' roll weekend. Flamboyant rooms, some designed by artists, others by local sponsors, include the Soviet-chic room with vodka bottles frozen into the walls, the Pin-up Parlour dedicated to Diana Dors, and the Pretty Vacant double, a shrine to the Sex Pistols. But the one everyone wants is the Play Room suite with its 3m circular bed, mirrored ceiling and pole-dancing area.

Neo Hotel
BOUTIQUE HOTEL ££

(01273-711104; www.neohotel.com; 19 Oriental Pl; d from £100; 🛜) You won't be surprised to learn the owner of this gorgeous hotel is an interior stylist. The nine rooms could have dropped straight from the pages of a design magazine, each finished in rich colours and tactile fabrics, with bold floral and Asian motifs and black-tiled bathrooms. Wonderful breakfasts include homemade smoothies and fruit pancakes. Reception is not open 24 hours.

Baggies Backpackers
HOSTEL £

(01273-733740; www.baggiesbackpackers.com; 33 Oriental Pl; dm/d £13/35; 🛜) A warm, familial atmosphere, worn-in charm, attentive onsite owners and clean, snug dorms have made this long-established hostel an institution. It's also blessed with a homely kitchen, inexpensive laundry, cosy basement music and chill-out room, and a TV lounge piled high with video cassettes. The hostel only takes phone bookings and is a stag- and hen-free zone. Cash only.

Snooze
HOTEL ££

(01273-605797; www.snoozebrighton.com; 25 St George's Tce; s/d from £55/65; @🛜) This eccentric Kemptown pad's retro styling encompasses vintage posters, bright '60s and '70s patterned wallpaper, flying wooden ducks, floral sinks and mad clashes of colour. It's more than just a gimmick – the rooms are comfortable and spotless, and there are great meat-free breakfasts. You'll find it just off St James' St, about 500m east of New Steine.

myhotel
HOTEL ££

(01273-900300; www.myhotels.com; 17 Jubilee St; r from £89; P@🛜) With trendsetting rooms looking like space-age pods with curved white walls, floor-to-ceiling observation windows and suspended flatscreen TVs, enlivened by the odd splash of neon orange or pink, there's nothing square about this place. You can even hook up your iPod and play music through speakers in the ceiling. There's a cocoon-like cocktail bar downstairs and, if you've currency to ignite, a suite with a steamroom and harpooned vintage carousel horse.

Motel Schmotel
B&B ££

(01273-326129; www.motelschmotel.co.uk; 37 Russell Sq; s/d from £50/60; 🛜) If you can overlook the petite rooms and miniscule bathrooms, this 11-room B&B in a Regency town house, a

Brighton & Hove

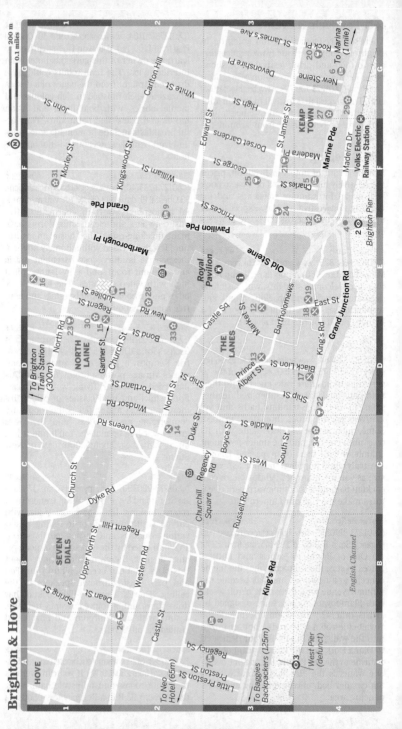

HOVE

SEVEN DIALS

NORTH LAINE

KEMP TOWN

THE LANES

Royal Pavilion

Churchill Square

Regency Sq

English Channel

Brighton Pier

West Pier (defunct)

To Marina (1 mile)

To Brighton Train Station (300m)

To Neo Hotel (65m)

To Baggies Backpackers (125m)

0   200 m
0   0.1 miles

Brighton & Hove

short stroll from virtually anywhere, is a sound and central place to hit the sack. Rooms are accented with colourful oversized prints and an uncluttered design, and guests heap praise on the breakfast cooked by the always-there-to-help couple who run things.

 Paskins Town House B&B **£**
(☏01273-601203; www.paskins.co.uk; 18-19 Charlotte St; r from £45; @🛜) Around a kilometre east of the pier along the seafront, this environmentally friendly B&B is spread between two elegant town houses. Paskins prides itself on using ecofriendly products such as recycled toilet paper, low-energy lightbulbs and biodegradable cleaning materials. The individually designed rooms are beautifully maintained, and excellent organic and vegetarian breakfasts are served in the art deco-inspired breakfast room.

Drakes BOUTIQUE HOTEL **£££**
(☏01273-696934; www.drakesofbrighton.com; 43-44 Marine Pde; r £115-295; P✳@🛜) This stylishly minimalist boutique hotel oozes understated class. So understated is the entrance, in fact, you could easily miss it. All rooms have similar decor in bold fabrics

and funky European elm panelling, but it's the feature rooms everyone wants – their giant freestanding tubs are set in front of full-length bay windows with widescreen Channel views. The basement restaurant is Brighton's best.

Kipps Brighton HOSTEL **£**
(☏01273-604182; www.kipps-brighton.com; 76 Grand Pde; dm/d from £15/40; @🛜) The owners of Canterbury's award-winning hostel have created equally commendable budget digs here in Brighton. There's a real cafe vibe around reception, and facilities include a communal kitchen. Free movie, pizza and pub nights successfully separate guests from their wi-fi-enabled devices.

✖ Eating

Brighton easily has the best choice of eateries on the south coast, with cafes, diners and restaurants to fulfil every whim. It's also one of Britain's best destinations for vegetarians, and its innovative meat-free menus are terrific value for anyone on a tight budget. For food from the former British Empire and beyond, head for Preston St, which has an incredible concentration of ethnic eateries.

Terre à Terre
VEGETARIAN ££

(☏01273-729051; www.terreaterre.co.uk; 71 East St; mains £14; ⊙lunch & dinner Tue-Sun; ✍) Even staunch meat eaters will rave about this legendary vegetarian restaurant. A sublime dining experience, from the vibrant modern space to the entertaining menus and inventive dishes packed with rich, robust flavours.

Iydea
VEGETARIAN £

(www.iydea.co.uk; 17 Kensington Gardens; mains £5.50-7; ⊙9am-5.30pm Mon-Sat, from 9.30am Sun; 🛜✍) Even by Brighton's lofty standards, the food at this new vegetarian cafe is a treat. The daily changing choices of curries, lasagnes, falafel, enchiladas and quiches swamp the tastebuds with flavour and can be washed down with a selection of vegan wines, organic ales and homemade lemonades. On the hop, you can take any dish away in environmentally friendly packaging. The award-winning veggie breakfast is one of Britain's best.

The Gingerman
MODERN EUROPEAN £££

(☏01273-326688; 21a Norfolk Sq; 3-course menu £18; ⊙lunch & dinner Tue-Sun) Seafood from Hastings, Sussex beef, Romney Marsh lamb, local sparkling wines and countless other seasonal, local and British treats go into the adroitly flash-fried and slow-cooked dishes served at this snug, 32-cover eatery. Reservations are advised. Norfolk Square is a short walk west along Western Rd from the Churchill Sq shopping centre.

Infinity Foods Cafe
VEGETARIAN £

(50 Gardner St; mains £3.50-7.50; ⊙10.30am-5pm Mon-Fri, from 10am Sat, noon-4pm Sun; 🛜✍) The sister establishment of Infinity Foods wholefoods shop (health-food cooperative and Brighton institution) serves a wide variety of vegetarian and organic food, with many vegan and wheat- or gluten-free options including tofu burgers, mezze plates and falafel.

JB's American Diner
BISTRO £

(31 King's Rd; burgers £7, mains £6.50-12) The waft of hotdogs as you push open the door, the shiny red-leather booths, the stars and stripes draped across the wall, the '50s soundtrack twanging in the background and the colossal portions of burgers, fries and milkshakes – in short, a hefty slab of authentic Americana teleported to the Brighton seafront.

Food for Friends
VEGETARIAN ££

(www.foodforfriends.com; 17-18 Prince Albert St; mains £11-13; ✍) An ever-inventive choice of vegetarian and vegan food keeps bringing locals back for seconds and thirds at this place to see and be seen – literally, by every passerby through the huge streetside windows.

English's Oyster Bar
SEAFOOD ££

(www.englishs.co.uk; 29-31 East St; mains £11-25) An almost 70-year-old institution and celebrity haunt, this Brightonian seafood paradise dishes up everything from Essex oysters to locally caught lobster and Dover sole. It's converted from fishermen's cottages, with shades of the elegant Edwardian era inside and alfresco dining on the pedestrian square outside.

Foodilic
BUFFET £

(www.foodilic.com; 60 North St; buffet £6.45; ⊙8am-9.30pm Mon-Sat, to 6pm Sun; 🛜) It's as good for breakfast (£2) as for a late dinner, but it's the eat-till-you-burst buffet of scrumptious healthy fare that packs out this funky place all day long.

Scoop & Crumb
ICE CREAM £

(5-6 East St; snacks £3-5, sundaes £2.50-6; ⊙10am-6pm Sun-Fri, to 7pm Sat) This ice-cream parlour belongs to the city's artisan ice-cream producer, and the sundaes (more than 50 types) are second to none. Freshly cut sandwiches and monster toasties are also available.

🍷 Drinking

Outside London, Brighton's nightlife is the best in the south, with its unique mix of seafront clubs and bars. On West St, drunken stag and hen parties and charmless, tacky nightclubs rule. For more ideas, visit www .drinkinbrighton.co.uk.

Brighton Rocks
BAR

(www.brightonrocksbar.co.uk; 6 Rock Pl; 🛜) Incongruously located in an alley of garages and used-car lots, this cocktail bar is firmly established on the Kemptown gay scene, but welcomes all comers. 'Shocktails' and the 'man wall' aside, there's a mighty fine 'grazing' menu, and theme parties and other events bring in the punters.

Dorset
GASTROPUB

(www.thedorset.co.uk; 28 North Rd; 🛜) In fine weather this laid-back Brighton institution throws open its doors and windows and spills tables onto the pavement. You'll be just as welcome for a morning coffee as for an evening pint here, and should you not leave between the two, there's a decent gastropub menu.

Talk of Tea TEAHOUSE
(www.talkoftea.co.uk; 26 Spring St; ☺8.30am-6pm Mon-Sat, 10am-4pm Sun; ☏) This sparkling new teahouse will leave you with a classic black, white, green, herbal or fruit dilemma, as it stocks Brighton's biggest selection of teas (almost 60). Its early opening, freshly made sarnies and cakes, and free wi-fi make this a superb spot to start the day.

Coalition BAR
(171-181 Kings Rd Arches) On a summer's day, there's nowhere finer to sit and watch the world go by than at this popular beach bar, diner and club. All sorts happen here, from comedy to live music, to club nights.

Entertainment

Brighton offers the best entertainment line-up on the south coast, with clubs to rival London and Manchester for cool. Keep tabs on what's hot and what's not by searching out publications such as *The List*, *Source* and *What's On*.

Nightclubs
When Britain's top DJs aren't plying their trade in London, Ibiza or Aya Napia, chances are you'll spy them here. All of Brighton's clubs open until 2am, and many as late as 5am.

Tube NIGHTCLUB
(Kings Rd Arches) Twin giant brick subterranean tunnels, with bars at the front and back, playing funky house, '70s, R&B and disco to a stylish and attitude-free crowd.

Psychosocial NIGHTCLUB
(www.psychosocialbrighton.com; 1-2 Morley St) This club specialises in everything and nothing, from punk to tropical nights, stand-up comedy to live music, and rap to lesbian satire.

Audio NIGHTCLUB
(www.audiobrighton.com; 10 Marine Pde) Some of the city's top club nights are held at this ear-numbing venue. The music's top priority here, attracting a young, up-for-it crowd.

Concorde 2 NIGHTCLUB
(www.concorde2.co.uk; Madeira Dr) Brighton's best-known and best-loved club is a disarmingly unpretentious den, where DJ Fatboy Slim pioneered the Big Beat Boutique and still

---

GAY & LESBIAN BRIGHTON

Perhaps it's Brighton's longtime association with the theatre but the city has been a gay haven for more than 100 years. With upwards of 25,000 gay men and about 15,000 lesbians living here, it is the most vibrant queer community in the country outside London.

Kemptown (aka Camptown), on and off St James' St, is where it's all at. The old Brunswick Town area of Hove is a quieter alternative to the traditionally cruisy (and sometimes seedy) scene in Kemptown.

For up-to-date information on gay Brighton, check out www.gay.brighton.co.uk and www.realbrighton.com, or pick up the free monthly magazine *Gscene* (www.gscene .com) from the tourist office.

For Drinking...

Poison Ivy (129 St James' St) In-your-face pub featuring drag acts and camp karaoke.

A Bar (www.amsterdam.uk.com; 11-12 Marine Pde; ☺noon-2am) Extremely hip bar and sauna above the pier in the Amsterdam hotel; its sun terrace is a particular hit.

Bulldog (www.bulldogbrighton.com; 31 St James' St) Longest-running gay bar in Brighton, mostly frequented only by men.

Queen's Arms (www.queensarmsbrighton.com; 7 George St; ☺3pm-late) And they don't mean Victoria or Elizabeth! Plenty of camp cabaret and karaoke at this pub.

For Dancing...

Revenge (www.revenge.co.uk; 32-34 Old Steine) Nightly disco with occasional cabaret.

Basement Club (31-34 Marine Pde) Located beneath the Legends Hotel, arguably the best gay hotel in town and 2009 winner of the Golden Handbag award.

occasionally graces the decks. Each month there's a huge variety of club nights, live bands and concerts by international names.

Theatre

Brighton Dome THEATRE
(☑01273-709709; www.brightondome.org; 29 New Rd) Once the stables and exercise yard for King George IV's horses, this art-deco complex houses three theatre venues within the Royal Pavilion estate. ABBA famously won the 1974 Eurovision Song Contest here.

Theatre Royal THEATRE
(☑08448 717 650; New Rd) Built by decree of the Prince of Wales in 1806, this grand venue hosts musicals, plays and operas.

Komedia Theatre COMEDY
(☑0845 293 8480; www.komedia.co.uk; 44-47 Gardner St) A stylish comedy, theatre and cabaret venue attracting some of the brightest stars on the stand-up circuit.

🛍 Shopping

In the market for a pair of vegetarian shoes, a gauche portrait of a Lego man or a letter opener in the shape of a...? Whatever item you yearn for, old or new, you'll probably find it in Brighton. The tightly packed Lanes is the most popular shopping district, its every twist and turn jam-packed with jewellers and gift shops, coffee shops and boutiques selling everything from antique firearms to hard-to-find vinyls. There's another, less-claustrophobic shopping district in North Laine, a series of partially pedestrian thoroughfares north of the Lanes, including Bond, Gardner, Kensington and Sydney Sts, lined with retro-cool boutiques and bohemian cafes. Mainstream chains gather within the Churchill Square Shopping Centre and along Western Rd.

❶ Information

Brighton City Guide (www.brighton.co.uk)
City Council (www.brighton-hove.gov.uk) A mine of information about every aspect of the city.

Jubilee Library (Jubilee St; ⊙10am-7pm Mon & Tue, to 5pm Wed, Fri & Sat, to 8pm Thu, 11am-4pm Sun) Bring ID to sign up for free internet access.

Post office (2-3 Churchill Sq) Located within the WH Smiths bookstore.

Royal Sussex County Hospital (☑01273-696955; Eastern Rd) Has an accident and emergency department, 2 miles east of the centre.

Tourist office (☑01273-290337; www.visit brighton.com; Royal Pavilion Shop; ⊙9.30am-5.30pm) Superbly run office with an accommodation booking service (£1.50), train and bus ticketing and a highly recommended (free) greeter scheme that offers expert guides who show visitors around the city.

Visit Brighton (www.visitbrighton.com)

Wistons Clinic (☑01273-506263; 138 Dyke Rd) For general medical consultations, less than a mile from the centre.

❶ Getting There & Away

Brighton is 53 miles from London and transport between the two is fast and frequent. If arriving by car, parking is plentiful but pricey, and the city-centre traffic, bus-clogged lanes and road layouts are confusing.

Bus

Standard connections:
Arundel Bus 700, £4.20, two hours, at least hourly
Chichester Bus 700, £4.40, 2¾ hours, at least hourly
Eastbourne Bus 12, £3.50, one hour 10 minutes, up to every 10 minutes
London Victoria National Express, £11, 2¼ hours, hourly

Train

All London-bound services pass through Gatwick Airport (£9.50, 30 to 40 minutes, up to five hourly).
Chichester £11.60, 50 minutes, half-hourly
Eastbourne £9.50, 30 to 40 minutes, half-hourly
Hastings £13, one hour 10 minutes, half-hourly
London St Pancras £15.40, 1¼ hours, half-hourly
London Victoria £16, 50 minutes, three-hourly
Portsmouth £15, 1½ hours, hourly

❶ Getting Around

Most of Brighton can be covered on foot. Alternatively, buy a day ticket (£4.40) from the driver of all Brighton and Hove buses, or a £2 PlusBus ticket on top of your rail fare, which gives unlimited bus travel for the day.

Parking can be expensive. The city operates a pay-and-display parking scheme. In the town centre, it's usually £3.50 per hour for a maximum stay of two hours. Alternatively, there's a Park & Ride 2.5 miles northwest of the centre at Withdean, from where bus 27 zips into town.

Cab companies include **Brighton Streamline Taxis** (☑01273-747474) and **City Cabs** (☑01273-205205), and there's a taxi rank at the junction of East St and Market St.

WEST SUSSEX

After the fast-paced adventures of Brighton and East Sussex, West Sussex offers a welcome respite. The serene hills and valleys of the South Downs ripple across the county, fringed by sheltered coastline. Beautiful Arundel and cultured Chichester make good bases from which to explore the county's winding country lanes and remarkable Roman ruins.

Arundel

POP 3408

Arguably the prettiest town in the county, Arundel is clustered around a vast fairy-tale castle and its hillside streets overflow with antique emporiums, teashops and a host of eateries. While much of the town appears medieval – the whimsical castle has been home to the Dukes of Norfolk for centuries – most of it dates back to Victorian times.

◉ Sights & Activities

Arundel Castle CASTLE
(www.arundelcastle.org; adult/child £17/8; ☉10am-5pm Tue-Sun Apr-Oct) Originally built in the 11th century, all that's left of the early structure are the modest remains of the keep at its core. It was thoroughly ruined during the English Civil War, and most of what you see today is the result of passionate reconstruction by the eighth, 11th and 15th dukes of Norfolk between 1718 and 1900. The current duke still lives in part of the castle, whose highlights include the atmospheric keep, the massive Great Hall and the library, which has works by the painters Thomas Gainsborough and Hans Holbein. The castle does a good impression of Windsor Castle and St James' Palace in the popular 2009 film *The Young Victoria,* and occasionally is closed for other film shoots.

Arundel Cathedral CATHEDRAL
(www.arundelcathedral.org; ☉9am-6pm Apr-Oct) Arundel's ostentatious 19th-century Catholic cathedral is the other dominating feature of the town's impressive skyline. Commissioned by the 15th duke in 1868, this impressive structure was designed by Joseph Aloysius Hansom (inventor of the Hansom cab) in the French Gothic style, but shows much Victorian economy and restraint. Although small for a cathedral – it only holds 500 worshippers – Hansom's clever layout makes the building seem a lot bigger.

A 1970s shrine in the north transept holds the remains of St Philip Howard, a canonised Catholic martyr who was banged up in the Tower of London by Elizabeth I until his death in 1595 for reverting to Catholicism.

🛏 Sleeping & Eating

Arundel House BOUTIQUE B&B ££
(☎01903-882136; www.arundelhouseonline.com; 11 High St; d/ste from £85/110; ☎) The contemporary rooms at this lovely 'restaurant with rooms' may be slightly low-ceilinged, but they're clean-cut and very comfortable, with showers big enough for two. The restaurant downstairs serves some of the best food in Arundel, which, happily, extends to breakfast.

Arden Guest House B&B ££
(☎01903-882544; www.ardenguesthouse.net; 4 Queens Lane; s/d £55/75, without bathroom £45/65; P☎) For the classic British B&B experience, head to this eight-room guest house just over the river from the historical centre. Rooms are freshly decorated and tick all the boxes, the hosts are amiable and the breakfasts cooked. No pets or children under 14.

TOP CHOICE Town House BRITISH £££
(☎01903-883847; 65 High St; set lunch/dinner from £15.50/23.50; ☉lunch & dinner Tue-Sat) The only thing that rivals the 16th-century Florentine gilded-walnut ceiling in this compact and very elegant eatery is the sparkling atmosphere and acclaimed British cuisine with a European twist. Book ahead.

❶ Getting There & Away

Trains run to London Victoria (£15.90, 1½ hours, twice hourly) and to Chichester (£4.20, 20 minutes, twice hourly); change at Barnham. There are also links to Brighton (£8.80, one hour 20 minutes, twice hourly); again, change at Barnham. Bus 700 (£4.40, two hours, twice hourly) is a slower option to Brighton.

Chichester

POP 23,700

A lively Georgian market town still almost encircled by its medieval town walls, the administrative capital of West Sussex keeps watch over the plains between the South Downs and the sea. Visitors flock to its splendid cathedral, streets of handsome 18th-century town houses, famous theatre and annual arts festival. A Roman port garrison in its early days, the town is also a launch pad to other fascinating Roman remains, as well as to Arundel and the coast.

◎ Sights

Chichester Cathedral CATHEDRAL
(www.chichestercathedral.org.uk; West St; ☉7.15am-7pm) This understated cathedral was begun in 1075 and largely rebuilt in the 13th century. The freestanding church tower, now in fairly bad shape, went up in the 15th century and the spire dates from the 19th century when its predecessor famously toppled over. Inside, three storeys of beautiful arches sweep upwards and Romanesque carvings are dotted around. Interesting features to track down include a smudgy stained-glass window added by artist Marc Chagall in 1978 and a glassed-over section of Roman mosaic flooring.

Free guided tours lasting 45 minutes start at 11.15am and 2.30pm Monday to Saturday, Easter to October, and the excellent cathedral choir is guaranteed to give you goosebumps during the daily evensong (5.30pm).

Pallant House Gallery ART GALLERY
(www.pallant.org.uk; 9 North Pallant; adult/concession £9/5.50; ☉10am-5pm Tue, Wed, Fri & Sat, to 8pm Thu, from 11am Sun) A Queen Anne mansion built by a local wine merchant, handsome Pallant House and a 21st-century wing host this superb gallery , which focuses on 20th-century, mostly British, art. Showstoppers such as Patrick Caulfield, Lucian Freud, Graham Sutherland, Frank Auerbach and Henry Moore are interspersed with international names such as Emil Filla, Le Corbusier and RB Kitaj. Most of these older works are in the mansion, while the newer wing is packed with pop art and temporary shows of modern and contemporary work.

Novium MUSEUM
(www.thenovium.org; Tower St; adult/concession £7/6; ☉ 10am-5pm Mon-Sat, to 4pm Sun Apr-Oct, closed Mon & Tue Nov-Mar) Opened in mid-2012, Chichester's purpose-built museum provides a home for the eclectic collections of the now-defunct District Museum as well as many artefacts from Fishbourne and a huge mosaic from Chilgrove Roman villa. The highlight is the set of Roman baths discovered in the 1970s, around which the six-million-pound museum was designed.

⌑ Sleeping

Accommodation is very thin on the ground in the city centre. Beds fill when there are goings-on at Goodwood racecourse, just to the north of Chichester.

Ship Hotel HOTEL ££
(☏01243-778000; www.theshiphotel.net; North St; r from £110; ☏) The grand central staircase in this former Georgian town house climbs to 36 fairly spacious rooms of commanding period chic. It's the most enticing option in the city centre and also boasts an excellent all-day brasserie. Book well ahead.

Trents B&B ££
(☏01243-773714; www.trentschichester.co.uk; 50 South St; s/d from £68/90; ☏) Right in the central city, the five snazzy rooms above this trendy bar-restaurant are understandably popular.

✕ Eating

St Martin's Tearooms TEAHOUSE £
(3 St Martins St; mains £4-10; ☉10am-6pm Mon-Sat) A little cocoon of nooks and crannies tucked away in a part-18th-century, part-medieval town house, this organic cafe serves freshly ground coffee with wholesome, mostly vegetarian, food and a sinful selection of desserts. There's also a guest piano with which to shatter the tranquil scene, if you so wish. St Martin's St is off East St.

Comme Ça FRENCH ££
(☏01243-788724; 67 Broyle Rd; mains £9-16; ☉lunch Wed-Sun, dinner Tue-Sat; P) Run by a Franco-English couple, this friendly French place does traditional Normandy cuisine in a converted Georgian inn, with a lovely vine-covered alfresco area. It's located a short walk north of the centre.

☆ Entertainment

Chichester Festival Theatre THEATRE
(☏01243-781312; www.cft.org.uk; Oakland's Park) This somewhat Soviet-looking playhouse was built in 1962 and has a long and distinguished history. Sir Laurence Olivier was the theatre's first director, and Ingrid Bergman, Sir John Gielgud and Sir Anthony Hopkins are some of the other famous names to have played here.

❶ Information

Post office (10 West St)

Tourist office (☏01243-775888; www.visit chichester.org; Novium, Tower St; ☉10am-5pm Mon-Sat, to 4pm Sun)

❶ Getting There & Away

Bus

Brighton Bus 700, £4.40, 2½ hours, twice hourly

London Victoria National Express, change at Gatwick Airport, £15.20, three hours 40 minutes, every two hours

Portsmouth Bus 700, £4.20, one hour, twice hourly

Train

Chichester has train connections to the following:

Arundel Change at Barnham, £4.30, 20 to 30 minutes, twice hourly

Brighton £12.80, 50 minutes, twice hourly

London Victoria £15.90, 1½ hours, half hourly

Portsmouth £7.50, 30 to 40 minutes, twice hourly

Around Chichester

FISHBOURNE PALACE & MUSEUM

Mad about mosaics? Then head for Fishbourne Palace (www.sussexpast.co.uk; Roman Way; adult/child £8.20/4.20; ⊙10am-5pm Mar-Oct, reduced hours & days rest of the year), the largest-known Roman residence in Britain. Happened upon by labourers in the 1960s, it's thought that this once-luxurious mansion was built around AD 75 for a Romanised local king. Housed in a modern pavilion are its foundations, hypocaust (ancient Roman central heating system) and painstakingly re-laid mosaics. The centrepiece is a spectacular floor depicting Cupid riding a dolphin, flanked by sea horses and panthers. There's also a fascinating little museum and replanted Roman gardens.

Fishbourne Palace is 1½ miles west of Chichester, just off the A259. Bus 700 leaves from outside Chichester Cathedral and stops at the bottom of Salthill Rd (five minutes' walk away; four hourly). The museum is a 10-minute amble from Fishbourne train station.

SURREY

Surrey is the heart of commuterville, preferred by well-off Londoners when they spawn, move out of the city and buy a country pad. For the most part, though, it's made up of uninspiring towns and dull, sprawling suburbs. Further away from the roaring motorways and packed rush-hour trains, the county reveals some inspiring landscapes made famous by authors Sir Arthur Conan Doyle, Sir Walter Scott and Jane Austen.

Farnham

POP 37,055

Nudging the border with Hampshire and joined at the hip with the garrison settlement of Aldershot, affluent Farnham is Surrey's prettiest town and its most worthwhile destination. Blessed with lively shopping streets of Georgian symmetry, a 12th-century castle and some soothing river walks, this easy-going market town makes for an undemanding day trip from the capital just an hour away.

Farnham has no tourist office, but maps and leaflets are available from the library (28 West St), museum (38 West St) and town hall (South St).

◉ Sights

Farnham Castle CASTLE

(☑01252-721194; www.farnhamcastle.com; palace adult/child £3.50/2.50, keep free; ⊙ palace 2-4pm Wed only, keep 9am-5pm Mon-Fri, 10am-4pm Sat & Sun, closed Jan) Constructed in 1138 by Henry de Blois, the grandson of William the Conqueror, there's not much left of the castle keep today except the beautiful old ramparts. Even if the keep is closed, it's worth walking around the outside for the picturesque views.

A residential palace house, Farnham Castle was built in the 13th century as a stopover for the bishops of Winchester on London journeys. From 1926 to the 1950s, it was taken over by the bishops of Guildford. It's now privately owned, but you can visit one afternoon a week with an audioguide.

Farnham Castle is located up the old steps at the top of Castle St.

FREE **Museum of Farnham** MUSEUM

(38 West St; ⊙10am-5pm Tue-Sat) This engaging little museum is located in the splendid Willmer House, a Georgian mansion built in 1718 for the wealthy hop merchant and maltster John Thorne.

Themed rooms trace Farnham's history from flint-tool days to Bakelite nostalgia. A corner is dedicated to William Cobbett, the town's most famous son, a 19th-century reformer, radical MP, writer and journalist who established *Hansard* (the official record of what is said in Parliament). Cobbett's bust takes pride of place in the peaceful garden out back, where you'll also find a timber gallery housing temporary exhibitions.

Sleeping & Eating

Bush Hotel   HOTEL **££**

(☑01252-715237; www.mercure-uk.com; The Borough; r from £94; P❋☎) You'll like 'beating about the bush' once you've slept at this 17th-century inn right in the heart of the action. Rolling renovations keep things fresh, and there's a snug beamed bar and highly recommended restaurant that spills into the pretty courtyard.

Plough Inn   PUB **£**

(74 West St; mains £6-11; ⊙noon-11.30pm) Tasty pub fare with a few nods to vegetarians and the Continent, plus Kentish ale, await at this friendly pub. Once popular with a student mob, it's a haven now for all folks.

❶ Getting There & Away

BUS National Express bus to **London Victoria** (£9.50, two hours, daily)

TRAIN **London Waterloo** £14.30, one hour, twice hourly; change trains at Woking.

Winchester £18, one hour, twice hourly; change trains at Woking.

Hindhead

The tiny hamlet of Hindhead, 8 miles south of Farnham off the A287, lies in the middle of the largest area of open heath in Surrey. During the 19th century a number of prominent Victorians bought up property in the area, including Sherlock Holmes' mastermind Sir Arthur Conan Doyle (1859–1930). One of three founders of the National Trust, Sir Robert Hunter, lived in nearby Haslemere, and today much of the area is administered by the foundation.

The most beautiful part of the area is to the northeast, where you'll find a natural depression known as the Devil's Punchbowl. There are a number of excellent trails and bridleways here. To get the best view, head for Gibbet Hill (280m), which was once an execution ground.

The Hindhead YHA Hostel (☑0845 371 9022; www.yha.org.uk; Devil's Punchbowl, Thursley, Godalming; dm £16.95) is a completely secluded cottage run by the National Trust on the northern edge of the Punchbowl – perfect digs for walkers.

Bus 19 runs hourly to Hindhead from Farnham.

Oxford, Cotswolds & Around

Best Places to Eat

» Le Champignon Sauvage (p217)

» Prithvi (p217)

» Chef's Table (p212)

» Edamame (p195)

» 5 North St (p208)

Best Places to Stay

» Old Swan & Minster Mill (p201)

» Malmaison (p194)

» Cotswold88 (p214)

» Ellenborough Park (p216)

» Lamb Inn (p204)

Why Go?

Dotted with gorgeous little villages, this part of the country is as close to the old-world English idyll as you'll get. It's a haven of lush rolling hills, rose-clad cottages, graceful stone churches and thatched roofs. Add to the mix the legendary university city of Oxford, with its splendid architecture and lively student vibe, and it's easy to see why the region is a magnet for visitors.

Although the roads and the most popular villages are busy in summer, it's easy to get off the tourist trail. The Cotswolds are at their best when you find your own romantic refuge and discover the fire-lit inns and grandiose manors that persuade A-list celebrities and the merely moneyed to buy property here.

Most of the area is an easy day trip from London, but Oxford and the Cotswolds deserve at least a couple of leisurely days.

When to Go

On 1 May you can welcome the dawn with Oxford's Magdalen College Choir, which sings hymns from the college tower. In July you can sip champagne and watch the rowing at Henley's Royal Regatta (p199) and Festival. September is the best time to sample England's finest ales at the four-day St Albans Beer Festival. The best time for rambling in the Cotswolds is in spring, early summer and September, with the weather in your favour but without the July and August crowds.

Oxford, Cotswolds & Around Highlights

1 Following in the footsteps of Lyra, Tolkien, CS Lewis and Inspector Morse as you tour the **Oxford colleges** (p185)

2 Meandering around **Painswick**, one of the most beautiful and unspoilt towns in the Cotswolds (p214)

3 Getting a glimpse of the high life at the Queen's weekend hideaway, **Windsor Castle** (p220)

4 Touring the elegant cloisters at the magnificent **Gloucester Cathedral** (p215)

5 Country driving near **Stow-on-the-Wold and Upper and Lower Slaughter** (p209)

6 Sampling the superb food at the many fine restaurants in **Cheltenham** (p215)

7 Touring **Blenheim Palace** (p193), one of the country's greatest stately homes

8 Exploring the anthropological treasure trove that is the **Pitt Rivers Museum** (p190) in Oxford

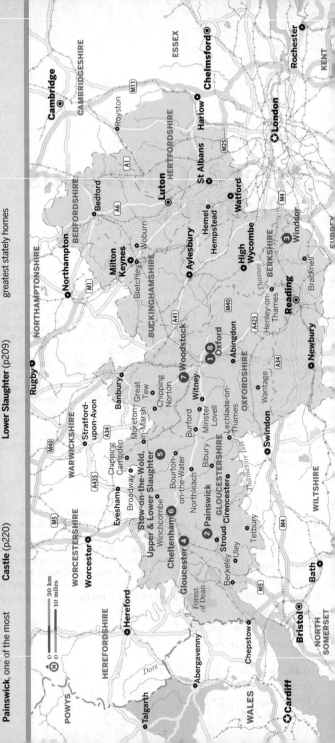

History

In Roman times, the region was traversed by a network of roads, some of which still exist today. By the 11th century, the wool and grain trade of these fertile valleys had made the locals rich and William the Conqueror had built his first motte and bailey in Windsor. In the 12th century, Henry II fortified the royal residence at Windsor, and in the 13th century, Oxford's first colleges were established.

Meanwhile, the Cotswolds flourished by supplying London with corn, wool and clothing. By the 14th century, the wool merchants were content to show off their good fortune by building the beautiful villages and graceful wool churches (built with the wealth made from the sale of wool) that are still scattered around the area today.

The region's proximity to London made it a popular retreat for wealthy city dwellers. The nobility and aristocracy flocked to Hertfordshire and Buckinghamshire, building country piles as retreats from the city.

Activities

Walking or cycling through the Cotswolds or Buckinghamshire's Chiltern Hills is an ideal way to get away from the crowds and discover some of the lesser-known vistas and villages of the region.

Cycling

Gentle gradients and scenic vistas make the Cotswolds ideal for cycling, with only the steep western escarpment offering a challenge to the legs. Plenty of quiet country lanes and byways criss-cross the region, or you can follow the signposted Thames Valley Cycle Way (NCN Routes 4, 5).

Mountain bikers can use a variety of bridleways in the Cotswolds and Chilterns, and in the west of the region, the Forest of Dean has many dirt-track options and some dedicated mountain-bike trails.

Walking

The Cotswold Hills offer endless opportunities for day hikes, but if you're looking for something more ambitious, the 102-mile Cotswold Way (www.nationaltrail.co.uk/cotswold) from Bath to Chipping Campden takes about a week to walk.

Alternatively, the Thames Path (www.nationaltrail.co.uk/thamespath) follows the river downstream from its source near Cirencester to London, with a particularly enjoyable five-day section from near Cirencester to Oxford.

Finally, the picturesque 87-mile Ridgeway National Trail (www.nationaltrail.co.uk/ridgeway) meanders along the chalky grassland of the Wiltshire downs near Avebury, down into the Thames Valley and then along the spine of the Chilterns to Ivinghoe Beacon near Aylesbury in Buckinghamshire.

ℹ️ Getting There & Around

Frequent trains and buses connect the region to London. Driving around the Cotswolds gives you the most freedom, though you can make the most of the regional public transport with the **Cotswolds Discoverer pass** (www.escapeto thecotswolds.org.uk/discoverer).

Traveline (☑️0871 200 22 33; www.traveline eastanglia.org.uk) provides timetables for all public transport across the country.

BUS Major bus routes are run by **Stagecoach** (www.stagecoachbus.com) and **Arriva** (www.arrivabus.co.uk), with a host of smaller companies offering services to local towns and villages.

TRAIN Services in the region are limited, with the exception of the area immediately outside London. For general rail information, call **National Rail** (www.nationalrail.co.uk).

OXFORDSHIRE

The long history of academic achievement and genteel living distinguish Oxfordshire from other parts of the country. Rustic charm and grand attractions are in abundant supply here, with a host of delightful villages surrounding the world-renowned university town.

Oxford is a highlight on any itinerary, with more than 1500 listed buildings, a choice of excellent museums and an air of refined sophistication. Between the gorgeous colleges and hushed quads, students cycle along cobbled lanes little changed by time.

Yet there is a lot more to the county. Just to the north is Blenheim Palace, an extravagant baroque pile that's the birthplace of Sir Winston Churchill, while to the south is the elegant riverside town of Henley, famous for its ever-so-posh Royal Regatta.

WANT MORE?

Head to Lonely Planet (www.lonely planet.com/england/oxfordshire/oxford) for planning advice, author recommendations, traveller reviews and insider tips.

🏃 Activities

Walkers may be interested in the Oxfordshire Way, a scenic, 65-mile signposted trail running from Bourton-on-the-Water to Henley-on-Thames, and the Wychwood Way, a historic, 37-mile route from Woodstock, which runs through an ancient royal forest. The routes are divided into manageable sections, described in leaflets available at most local tourist offices.

The quiet roads and gentle gradients also make Oxfordshire good cycling territory. The main signposted route through the county is the Oxfordshire Cycleway, which takes in Woodstock, Burford and Henley. If you don't have your own wheels, you can hire bikes in Oxford.

You'll find more information at www.oxfordshire.gov.uk/countryside.

ℹ️ Getting Around

Pick up bus and train timetables for most routes at local tourist offices. The main train stations are in Oxford and Banbury and have frequent connections to London Paddington and London Euston, Hereford, Birmingham, Bristol and Scotland.

The main bus operators are the **Oxford Bus Company** (☑01865-785400; www.oxfordbus.co.uk), **Stagecoach** (☑01865-772250; www.stagecoachbus.com/oxfordshire) and Swanbrook (p198).

Oxford

POP 134,248

Oxford is a privileged place, one of the world's most famous university towns. It is steeped in history, studded with august buildings and yet it maintains the feel of a young town, thanks to its large student population. The elegant honey-coloured buildings of the 39 colleges that make up the university wrap around tranquil courtyards along narrow cobbled lanes, and inside their grounds, a studious calm reigns. Just as in Cambridge, the existence of 'town' beside 'gown' makes it more than simply a bookish place of learning.

Oxford is a wonderful place to ramble: the oldest colleges date back almost 750 years, and little has changed inside the hallowed walls since then. But along with the rich history, tradition and lively academic life, there is a whole other world beyond the college walls. Oxford has a long industrial past and

---

ℹ️ VISITING THE COLLEGES

If you have your heart set on visiting Oxford's iconic buildings, remember that not all are open to the public. For the colleges that are, visiting hours change with the term and exam schedule; check www.ox.ac.uk/colleges for full details of visiting hours and admission before planning your visit.

---

the working majority still outnumber the academic elite.

The university buildings are scattered throughout the city, with the most important and architecturally significant in the centre. Jericho, in the northwest, is the trendy, artsy end of town, with slick bars, restaurants and an art-house cinema, as well as the wonderfully tranquil Port Meadow, while Cowley Rd, southeast of Carfax, is the gritty, ethnically diverse area packed with cheap places to eat and drink. Further out, in the salubrious northern suburb of Summertown, you'll find more upmarket restaurants and bars.

History

Strategically placed at the confluence of the Rivers Cherwell and Thames (called the Isis here, from the Latin *Tamesis*), Oxford was originally a key Saxon town heavily fortified by Alfred the Great during the war against the Danes.

By the 11th century, the Augustinian abbey in Oxford had begun training clerics, and when Anglo-Norman clerical scholars were expelled from the Sorbonne in 1167, the abbey began to attract students in droves. Alongside Oxford's growing prosperity grew the enmity between the new students and the local townspeople, culminating in the St Scholastica's Day Massacre in 1355, which started as an argument over beer. Thereafter, the king ordered that the university be broken up into colleges, each of which then developed its own traditions.

The university, largely a religious entity at the time, was rocked by the Reformation and then by the public trials and burning at the stake of Protestant heretics under 'Bloody' Mary. As the Royalist headquarters, Oxford backed the losing side during the Civil War, but flourished after the restoration of the monarchy, with some of its most iconic buildings constructed at that time.

The arrival of the canal system in 1790 had a profound effect on the rest of Oxford. By creating a link with the Midlands' industrial centres, work and trade suddenly expanded beyond the academic core. This development was further strengthened by the construction of the railways. However, the city's real industrial boom came when William Morris began producing cars here in 1913. With the success of his Bullnose Morris and Morris Minor, his Cowley factory went on to become one of the largest motor plants in the world. Although the works have been scaled down since their heyday, Minis still run off BMW's Cowley production line today.

As for the colleges, the first ones (Balliol, Merton and University) were built in the 13th century, with at least three more being added in each of the following three centuries. Newer colleges, such as Keble, were added in the 19th and 20th centuries to cater for an ever-expanding student population. However, tradition dies hard at Oxford, and it wasn't until 1877 that lecturers were allowed to marry, and another year before female students were admitted. Even so, it took another 42 years before women were granted degrees. Today, there are 39 colleges catering to about 20,000 students and in 2008 the last all-female college, St Hilda's, finally opened its door to male students.

⊙ Sights

University Buildings & Colleges

Much of the centre of Oxford is taken up by graceful university buildings and elegant colleges, each one individual in its appearance and academic specialities.

TOP CHOICE **Christ Church** COLLEGE
(www.chch.ox.ac.uk; St Aldate's; adult/child £8/6.50; ⊙9am-5pm Mon-Sat, 2-5pm Sun) The largest of all of Oxford's colleges and the one with the grandest quad, Christ Church is also its most popular. Its magnificent buildings, illustrious history and latter-day fame as a location for the *Harry Potter* films have tourists coming in droves.

Woe betide you should you display your outsider status by referring to Christ Church as Christ Church College. It's simply Christ Church – full stop. The Queen's College is not to be confused with Queens' College in Cambridge, and High St and Broad St are referred to as 'the High' and 'the Broad', respectively.

The college was founded in 1524 by Cardinal Thomas Wolsey, who suppressed the monastery existing on the site to acquire the funds for his lavish building project. Over the years numerous luminaries have been educated here, including philosopher John Locke, poet WH Auden, Charles Dodgson (Lewis Carroll), and no less than 13 British prime ministers!

OXFORD ODDITIES

It should not surprise you that a fount of creativity such as Oxford would have more than its fair share of architectural oddities and bizarre rituals. Here are a select few.

» **The Gandhi ceiling boss** Inside the pleasant but otherwise unremarkable University Church of St Mary the Virgin (www.university-church.ox.ac.uk; High St; tower adult/child £3/2.50; ⊙9am-5pm), there's a ceiling boss in the shape of Mahatma Gandhi. Why Gandhi? No one knows exactly, though he did speak at the church in the 1930s.

» **The Headington Shark** If you happen to be passing along the main street in nearby Headington, you may notice a giant shark sticking out of an ordinary suburban house, apparently having crashed through the roof.

» **The Tolkien gravestone** JRR Tolkien is buried with his wife Edith at the Wolvercote Cemetery. The names Beren and Luthien are carved on their gravestone, a reference to the love between a mortal man and an immortal elf maiden who gave up her immortality to be with him.

» **New College ritual** Every three years, the Lord Major of Oxford has to walk along the ruins of the city wall which is part of New College (p189) to fulfil a medieval obligation that the wall would be repaired if need be (the walk is merely symbolic).

» **Exam attire** Oxford students have to wear their academic dress to take their exams.

Oxford

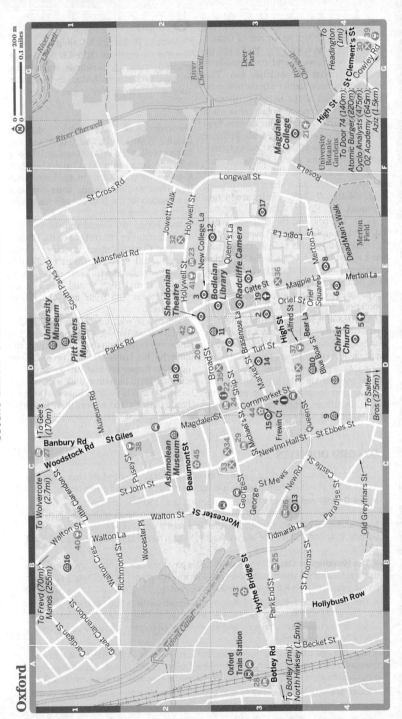

200 m
0.1 miles

To Headington
(1mi)

St Clement's St

To Door 74 (140m);
Atomic Burger (220m);
Cyclo Analysts (475m);
O2 Academy (645m);
Aziz (1.5km)

Cowley Rd

High St

University
Botanic
Gardens

Roselа

Magdalen
College

Deer
Park

River Cherwell

River Cherwell

River Cherwell

Longwall St

St Cross Rd

Jowett Walk

Holywell St

New College La

Merton Field

DeadMan's Walk

Logic La

Merton St

Merton La

Mansfield Rd

South Parks Rd

Sheldonian
Theatre

Holywell St

Bodleian
Library

Radcliffe Camera

Queen's La

Catte St

Magpie La

Oriel
Square

Merton St

University
Museum

Pitt Rivers
Museum

Parks Rd

Broad St

Brasenose La

Market St

Turl St

High St

Oriel St

Alfred St

Bear La

Blue Boar St

Christ
Church

Museum Rd

Ship St

Cornmarket St

St Michael's St

Frewin Ct

Queen St

New Inn Hall St

St Ebbes St

New Rd

Castle St

Paradise St

Old Greyfriars St

To Salter
Bros (375m)

Gee's
(170m)

Banbury Rd

Woodstock Rd

St Giles

Pusey St

St John St

Ashmolean
Museum

Beaumont St

Magdalen St

George St

George St Mews

Worcester St

Walton St

Walton Pl

Walton St

Walton La

Walton Cres

Richmond St

Worcester St

Tidmarsh La

St Thomas St

Hollybush Row

Hythe Bridge St

Park End St

Oxford Canal

Becket St

Oxford
Train Station

Botley Rd

To Botley (1mi);
North Hinksey (1.5m)

To Freud (70m);
Manos (255m)

To Wolvercote
(2.7mi)

Great Clarendon St

Little Clarendon St

Cardigan St

Great Clarendon St

Oxford

The main entrance is below the imposing Tom Tower, the upper part of which was designed by former student Sir Christopher Wren. Great Tom, the 7-ton tower bell, still chimes 101 times each evening at 9.05pm (Oxford is five minutes west of Greenwich) to sound the curfew imposed on the original 100 students (plus the one added in 1663).

Visitors must go further down St Aldate's to the side entrance. Immediately on entering is the 15th-century cloister, a relic of the ancient Priory of St Frideswide, whose shrine was once a focus of pilgrimage. From here, you go up to the Great Hall, the college's magnificent dining room, with its hammerbeam roof and imposing portraits of past scholars; it was replicated in the film studios as the dining hall at Hogwarts for the *Harry Potter* films.

Coming down the grand staircase, you'll enter Tom Quad, Oxford's largest and arguably most impressive quadrangle, and from here, Christ Church Cathedral, the smallest cathedral in England. Why the smallest? Because it was simply the college chapel that was declared a cathedral by Henry VIII when he broke with the Church of Rome, suppressed more monasteries and convents, and gave the college its current name (it used to be Cardinal's College). Inside, brawny Norman columns are topped by elegant vaulting, and beautiful stained-glass windows illuminate the walls. Look out for the rare depiction of the murder of Thomas Becket, dating from 1320.

You can also explore another two quads and the Picture Gallery, with its modest collection of Renaissance art. To the south of the college is Christ Church Meadow, a leafy expanse bordered by the Rivers Cherwell and Isis, ideal for leisurely walking.

The hall often closes between noon and 2pm and the cathedral in late afternoon.

Bodleian Library
LIBRARY

(www.bodley.ox.ac.uk; Broad St; Divinity School adult/child £1/free, audioguide £2.50, tours £6.50; ⊙9am-5pm Mon-Fri, to 4.30pm Sat, 11am-5pm Sun, tours 10.30am, 11.30am, 1pm & 2pm Mon-Sat, 11.30am, 2pm & 3pm Sun) Oxford's Bodleian Library is one of the oldest public libraries in the world, the first of England's three copyright libraries (the other two are the British Library and the Cambridge University library) and quite possibly the most impressive library you'll ever see. It currently holds more than 11 million items, 117 miles of shelving and has seating space for up to 2500 readers, with a staggering 4000 books and articles arriving *every week*, all of which need to be catalogued and stored.

The Bodleian Library has its roots in a 15th-century collection of books and its present state is largely due to the efforts of Sir Thomas Bodley, a 16th-century Fellow of Merton College who came to the agreement with the Stationers' Company of London that the library would receive a copy of every single book published in the UK – an agreement that still stands today.

The oldest part of the library surrounds the stunning Jacobean-Gothic Old Schools Quadrangle, which dates from the early 17th century and sports some of Oxford's odder architectural gems. On the eastern side of the quad is the Tower of Five Orders, an ornate building depicting the five classical orders of architecture. On the west side is the Divinity School, the university's first teaching room. It is renowned as a masterpiece of 15th-century English Gothic architecture and has a superb fan-vaulted ceiling; it featured as the Hogwarts hospital wing in the Harry Potter films.

Most of the rest of the library is closed to visitors, but library tours allow access to the medieval Duke Humfrey's library, where, the library proudly boasts, no fewer than five kings, 40 Nobel Prize winners, 25 British prime ministers and such writers as Oscar Wilde, CS Lewis and JRR Tolkien studied amid rows filled with grand ancient tomes chained to the shelves. Those wishing to read here (the books may not be borrowed) still have to swear Bodley's Oath, which involves vowing 'not to bring into the Library or kindle therein any fire or flame'. You'll also get to see the 17th-century Convocation House and Court, where parliament was held during the Civil War. The tour takes about an hour and is not suitable for children under 11 (for fear that they will run amok).

Magdalen College
COLLEGE

(www.magd.ox.ac.uk; High St; adult/child £5/4; ⊙noon-7pm) Set amid 40 hectares of lawns, woodlands, river walks and deer park, Magdalen (*mawd*-len), founded in 1458, is one of the wealthiest and most beautiful of Oxford's colleges.

An elegant Victorian gateway leads into a medieval chapel (with its glorious 15th-century tower) and on to the remarkable cloisters (with strange animals perching on the buttresses), some of the finest in Oxford. The fantastic gargoyles and grotesques along the frontage here are said to have inspired CS Lewis' stone statues in *The Chronicles of Narnia*. Behind the cloisters, the lovely Addison's Walk leads through the grounds and along the banks of the River Cherwell for just under a mile. Were you here in the mid-1870s, you would have encountered Oscar Wilde taking his pet lobster for a walk.

Magdalen has a reputation as an artistic college, and some of its other famous students and fellows have included TE Lawrence 'of Arabia', Poet Laureate Sir John Betjeman, Nobel Laureate Seamus Heaney and explorer Wilfred Thesiger, not to mention seven other Nobel Prize winners.

The college also has a fine choir that sings *Hymnus Eucharisticus* at 6am on May Day (1 May) from the top of the 42m bell tower. The event now marks the culmination of a solid night of drinking for most students as they gather in their glad rags on Magdalen Bridge to listen to the dawn chorus.

Opposite the college and sweeping along the banks of the River Cherwell is the beautiful Botanic Garden (www.botanic-garden.ox.ac.uk; adult/child £4/free; ⊙9am-6pm May-Aug), founded in 1621 for the study of medicinal plants. The bench that Lyra and her extra-universal lover Will intend to haunt in Phillip Pullman's *His Dark Materials* is usually well-attended by mooning adolescents.

Radcliffe Camera
LIBRARY

(Radcliffe Sq; extended tours £13) The Radcliffe Camera is the quintessential Oxford landmark and one of the city's most photographed buildings. The spectacular circular library/reading room, filled with natural light, was built between 1737 and 1749 in grand Palladian style, and has Britain's third-largest dome. In case you're wondering: no, you cannot enter disguised as a student; the only way to see the interior is to join one of the extended tours of the Bodleian Library. These tours no longer explore the underground tunnels and passages leading to the library's vast book stacks, as these were sealed in 2012 with the rebuilding of the New Bodleian Library. Tours take place at 9.15am Wednesday and Saturday and at 11.15am and 1.15pm most Sundays. They last about 90 minutes.

For excellent views of the Radcliffe Camera and surrounding buildings, climb the 14th-century tower in the beautiful University Church of St Mary the Virgin (p185). On Sunday the tower does not open until about noon, after the morning service. At the time of writing, the tower was undergoing restoration, and should reopen again in 2013. Look for a peculiar architectural feature inside.

Sheldonian Theatre
CEREMONIAL HALL

(www.sheldon.ox.ac.uk; Broad St; adult/child £2.50/1.50; ⊘10am-12.30pm & 2-4.30pm Mon-Sat) The monumental Sheldonian Theatre, built in 1663, was the first major work of Christopher Wren, at that time a professor of astronomy. Inspired by the classical Theatre of Marcellus in Rome, it has a rectangular front end and a semicircular back, while the ceiling of the main hall is blanketed by a fine 17th-century painting of the triumph of truth over ignorance. What's remarkable about the ceiling is its length, made possible by ingenious braces made of shorter timbers for want of trees adequate in length. The Sheldonian is now used for college ceremonies and public concerts, but you can climb to the cupola for good views of the surrounding buildings.

New College
COLLEGE

(www.new.ox.ac.uk; Holywell St; admission £3; ⊘11am-5pm Mar-Sep) From the Bodleian, stroll under the Bridge of Sighs (New College Lane) – sometimes erroneously referred to as a copy of the famous bridge in Venice, but the only thing this bridge has in common with its Venetian namesake is its name). The bridge links the two halves of Hertford College to New College. This 14th-century college was the first in Oxford for undergraduates and is a fine example of the glorious Perpendicular style. The chapel here is full of treasures, including superb stained glass, much of it original, and Sir Jacob Epstein's disturbing statue of Lazarus.

During term time, visitors may attend beautiful Evensong, a choral church service held nightly at 6pm. Access for visitors is through the New College Lane gate from Easter to early October, and through the Holywell St entrance the rest of the year.

William Spooner was once a college warden here, and his habit of transposing first consonants of words gave rise to the term 'spoonerism'. Local lore suggests that he once reprimanded a student by saying, 'You have deliberately tasted two worms and can leave Oxford by the town drain'. Spooner aside, other famous alumni include Hugh Grant and Kate Beckinsale, and New College is also famous for a bizarre medieval ritual.

Merton College
COLLEGE

(www.merton.ox.ac.uk; Merton St; admission £2, guided tour £2; ⊘2-5pm Mon-Fri, 10am-5pm Sat & Sun, guided tour 45 min) From High St, follow the wonderfully named Logic Lane to Merton College, one of Oxford's original three colleges. Founded in 1264, Merton is the oldest college and was the first to adopt collegiate planning, bringing scholars and tutors together into a formal community and providing a planned residence for them. Its distinguishing architectural features include the large gargoyles whose expressions suggest that they're about to throw up, and the charming 14th-century Mob Quad – the first of the college quads.

Just off the quad is a 13th-century chapel and the Old Library (admission on guided tour only), the oldest medieval library in use (look for the chained books). It is said that Tolkien spent many hours here writing *The Lord of the Rings* and that the trees in the Fellows' Garden inspired the walking trees of Middle Earth. Other literary giants associated with the college include TS Eliot and Louis MacNeice.

During the summer months it may be possible to join a guided tour of the college grounds. If you're visiting in summer, look out for posters advertising candlelit concerts in the chapel.

Behind Merton College is the ominously named Dead Man's Walk, so called because the Jews, who were not allowed to bury their dead within the city, would take the bodies along there to the Jewish cemetery (now the Botanic Garden).

FREE **All Souls College** COLLEGE
(www.all-souls.ox.ac.uk; High St; ⊘2-4pm Mon-Fri) One of the wealthiest Oxford colleges and one of several graduate colleges, though it doesn't accept just any old Oxford graduate. Each year, the university's top finalists sit a fellowship exam, with an average of only two making the grade annually. All Souls was founded in 1438 as a centre of prayer and learning, and today fellowship of the college is one of the highest academic honours in the country.

Much of the college facade dates from the 1440s and, unlike other older colleges, the front quad is largely unchanged in five centuries. It also contains a beautiful 17th-century sundial designed by Christopher Wren. Most obvious though, are the twin mock-Gothic towers on the north quad. Designed by Nicholas Hawksmoor in 1710, they were lambasted for ruining the Oxford skyline when first erected.

Oxford Union LIBRARY
(www.oxford-union.org; Frewin Crt; admission £1.50; ⊘9.30am-5pm Mon-Fri) Oxford's legendary members' society is famous for its feisty debates, heavyweight international speakers (as well as odder guests, such as Kermit the Frog) and Pre-Raphaelite murals. Although most of the building is off-limits to nonmembers, you can visit the library to see the murals, which were painted between 1857 and 1859 by Dante Gabriel Rossetti, William Morris and Edward Burne-Jones. The murals depict scenes from the Arthurian legends but are very difficult to see on bright days, as they surround the windows.

Brasenose College COLLEGE
(www.bnc.ox.ac.uk; Radcliffe Sq; admission £1.50; ⊘noon-4pm) Small and select, this elegant 16th-century place is named after a 'brass nose', or a brass door knocker, to be precise. The door knocker in question resides above the high table in the dining hall and is very well travelled: in 1533, it made it all the way to Stamford, Lincolnshire, only to be returned in 1890, along with the house to which it was attached at the time.

Trinity College COLLEGE
(www.trinity.ox.ac.uk; Broad St; adult/child £1.75/1; ⊘10am-noon & 2-4pm Sun-Fri, 2-4pm Sat) This small 16th-century college is worth a visit to see its exquisitely carved chapel, one of the most beautiful in the city, and the lovely garden quad designed by Christopher Wren. An Oxford legend says that the back gates of Trinity will only be opened for a ruler from the previous Stuart dynasty. Not surprisingly, the visitor will find them welded shut.

St Edmund Hall COLLEGE
(www.seh.ox.ac.uk; Queen's Lane; ⊘10am-4pm) St Edmund Hall ('Teddy Hall' to its residents) is the sole survivor of the original medieval halls, the teaching institutions that preceded colleges in Oxford. The Mohawk chief Oronhyatekha studied here in 1862 (and eloped with the principal's daughter) but it is best known for its small chapel decorated by William Morris and Edward Burne-Jones.

FREE **Corpus Christi College** COLLEGE
(www.ccc.ox.ac.uk; Merton St; ⊘1.30-4.30pm) Reputedly the friendliest and most liberal of Oxford's colleges, Corpus Christi is small but strikingly beautiful. The bizarre pelican sundial in the front quad calculates the time by the sun and the moon, although it is always five minutes fast.

FREE **Exeter College** COLLEGE
(www.exeter.ox.ac.uk; Turl St; ⊘2-5pm) Exeter is known for its elaborate 17th-century dining hall and ornate Victorian Gothic chapel housing *The Adoration of the Magi,* a William Morris tapestry.

OTHER SIGHTS

TOP CHOICE **University & Pitt Rivers Museums** MUSEUM
(www.oum.ox.ac.uk; Parks Rd; admission free; ⊘University Museum 10am-5pm, Pitt Rivers Museum 10am-4.30pm Tue-Sun, noon-4.30pm Mon; ⊕) Housed in a glorious Victorian Gothic building with slender, cast-iron columns, ornate capitals and a soaring glass roof, the University Museum (www.oum.ox.ac.uk; Parks Rd; entry by donation; ⊘10am-5pm; ⊕) is worth a visit for its architecture alone. However, the real draw is the mammoth natural history collection of more than five million exhibits, ranging from exotic insects and fossils to a towering *T. Rex* skeleton and the remains of the first dinosaur ever to be mentioned in a written text, in 1677.

LOCAL KNOWLEDGE

BILL RITCHIE: BILL SPECTRE GHOST TRAILS

Most Haunted Spots

» The cross in the centre of Broad St outside Balliol College where Nicholas Ridley, Hugh Latimer and Thomas Cranmer were burnt at the stake in the 16th century for heresy.

» Oxford Castle (p192): the Empress Matilda escaped from the castle by abseiling down St George's tower in 1142, and Mary Blandy was hanged there in 1752 for poisoning her father 'by mistake'!

» Brasenose Lane: the Devil himself is said to have made an appearance in the 19th century.

Inspirational Oxford

» The doorway opposite the west entrance of the University Church of St Mary the Virgin (p185) inspired CS Lewis to write *The Lion, The Witch and The Wardrobe*.

» Christopher Wren, who, although mainly remembered for St Paul's Cathedral, first designed the chapel at Pembroke College and the Sheldonian Theatre (p189) on Broad St.

Hidden Gem

» Witch in a bottle and witch's ladder at the Pitt Rivers Museum.

Things the University Would Rather You Didn't Know

» In medieval times, Magpie Lane was Oxford's red light district where the 'nymphs of the pavement' would tout for business. Its name in those days – Gropecunt Lane – was indicative of the trade plied there.

Hidden away through a door at the back of the main exhibition hall, the wonderful Pitt Rivers Museum (www.prm.ox.ac.uk; Parks Rd; admission by donation; ☺10am-4.30pm Tue-Sun, noon-4.30pm Mon; 🚻) is an anthropologist's wet dream – a treasure trove of objects from around the world to satisfy any armchair adventurer and a place where you can spend days on end. The dim light inside the hall lends the glass cases stuffed with Victorian explorers' prized booty an air of mystery, and one of the reasons this museum is so brilliant is because there are no computers here or shiny modern gimmicks. Among this circus of feathered cloaks, necklaces of teeth, blowpipes, magic charms, Noh masks, totem poles, fur parkas, musical instruments and shrunken heads, you may spot ceremonial headgear from Uganda worn during circumcision ceremonies, a Naga skull with buffalo horns surmounted by a German Pickelhaube, blowpipes from South America and Borneo, a porcupine fish helmet from Kiribati, a whalebone ivory war paddle from the South Pacific, an aboriginal cradle made from a single piece of bark, ancient dental implements, ceremonial masks and costume and more, so much more.

Both museums run workshops for children almost every weekend.

FREE Ashmolean Museum MUSEUM (www.ashmolean.org; Beaumont St; ☺10am-6pm Tue-Sun; 🚻) Britain's oldest public museum, second in repute only to London's British Museum, was established in 1683 when Elias Ashmole presented the university with the collection of curiosities (which came be to known as Tradescant's Ark) amassed by the well-travelled John Tradescant, gardener to Charles I.

Its collections, displayed in bright, spacious galleries within one of Britain's best examples of neo-Grecian architecture, span the world and include everything from Egyptian mummies and sarcophagi, Islamic and Chinese art, Japan's 'floating world' and examples of the earliest written languages to rare porcelain, tapestries and silverware, priceless musical instruments and extensive displays of European art (including works by Raphael and Michelangelo).

The Ashmolean has recently undergone a makeover, leaving it with new interactive features, a giant atrium, glass walls revealing galleries on different levels, and a beautiful rooftop restaurant. New basement displays include 'Ark to Ashmolean', featuring such gems as the death mask of Oliver Cromwell, Lawrence of Arabia's

Arab robes, the lantern Guy Fawkes was carrying when arrested on 5 November 1605, Powhatan's mantle, said to belong to the father of Pocohontas, and 'Exploring the Past', aimed at younger visitors, as well as the fascinating exhibit focusing on money around the world and what it could have bought in its particular historical period and place.

Oxford Castle Unlocked   PRISON

(www.oxfordcastleunlocked.co.uk; 44-46 Oxford Castle; adult/child £9/6; ⊙from 10am, last tour 4.20pm; ⊛) Oxford Castle Unlocked explores the 1000-year history of Oxford's castle and prison. Your entertaining costumed guide begins the tour in the 11th-century Crypt of St George's Chapel, possibly the first formal teaching venue in Oxford, and continues into the Victorian prison cells and the 18th-century Debtors' Tower, where you learn about the inmates' grisly lives, daring escapes and cruel punishments. The tour also takes you up the Saxon St George's Tower, which has excellent views of the city, while outside the castle you can clamber up the original medieval motte.

Modern Art Oxford   ART GALLERY

(www.modernartoxford.org.uk; 30 Pembroke St; entry by donation; ⊙10am-5pm Tue-Sat, noon-5pm Sun; ⊛) Far removed from Oxford's hallowed hallways of history, this is one of the most refreshing contemporary art museums outside London, with a rota of changing heavyweight exhibitions, a wonderful gallery space and plenty of activities for children.

Museum of the History of Science   MUSEUM

(www.mhs.ox.ac.uk; Broad St; admission by donation; ⊙noon-5pm Tue-Fri, 10am-5pm Sat, 2-5pm Sun) Science, art, celebrity and nostalgia come together at this fascinating museum, where the exhibits include everything from a blackboard used by Einstein to the world's finest collection of historic scientific instruments, all housed in a beautiful 17th-century building.

Oxford Covered Market   MARKET

(www.oxford-covered-market.co.uk; Market St; ⊙9am-5.30pm) A haven of traditional butchers, fishmongers, cobblers, barbers, delis, little eateries and independent shops, this is the place to go for Sicilian sausage, handmade chocolates, traditional pies, funky T-shirts and wacky hats for wed-

dings and/or the Ascot. If you're in Oxford at Christmas, it's a must for its traditional displays of freshly hung deer, wild boar, ostrich and turkey. Otherwise, it's a good spot for lunch.

FREE Museum of Oxford   MUSEUM

(www.museumofoxford.org.uk; St Aldate's; ⊙10am-5pm Tue-Sat) Though it often gets overlooked in favour of Oxford's other museums, this is an absorbing romp through the city's history, from the Roman and Saxon eras to the Victorian era and 20th-century industries (such as marmalade-making and car manufacture). The reconstructions of period interiors, such as a 19th-century Jericho kitchen, are particularly good.

Carfax Tower   TOWER

(cnr Cornmarket & Queen Sts; adult/child £2.50/1.30; ⊙10am-5.30pm) Oxford's central landmark, towering over what has been a crossroads for 1000 years, is the sole reminder of medieval St Martin's Church and offers good views over the city centre.

🏃 Activities

A quintessential Oxford experience, punting is all about sitting back and quaffing Pimms (the quintessential English summer drink) as you watch the city's glorious architecture float by. Which, of course, requires someone else to do the hard work – punting is far more difficult than it appears.

Punts are available from mid-March to mid-October, 10am to dusk, and hold five people including the punter (£16/20 per hour weekdays/weekends, £70 deposit).

The most central location to rent punts is Magdalen Bridge Boathouse (www.oxford punting.co.uk; High St). From here, you can punt downstream around the Botanic Garden and Christ Church Meadow or upstream around Magdalen Deer Park. Alternatively, head for the Cherwell Boat House (www.cherwellboathouse.co.uk; Bardwell Rd) for a countryside amble, where the destination of choice is the busy boozer, the Victoria Arms (Mill Lane). To get to the boathouse, take bus 2 or 7 from Magdalen St to Bardwell Rd and follow the signposts.

Salter Bros (www.salterssteamers.co.uk; Folly Bridge; boat trips adult/child £11.60/6.20; ⊙9.15am & 2.30pm Jun-mid-Sep) offer a range of trips along the Isis from Oxford. The most popular is the scenic journey to the historic market town of Abingdon. The trip takes 1¾

BLENHEIM PALACE

Blenheim Palace (www.blenheimpalace.com; adult/child £20/10; ⏱10.30am-5.30pm mid-Feb–Oct) One of the country's greatest stately homes, Blenheim Palace is a monumental baroque fantasy designed by Sir John Vanbrugh and Nicholas Hawksmoor between 1705 and 1722. The land and funds to build the house were granted to John Churchill, Duke of Marlborough, by a grateful Queen Anne after his decisive victory at the 1704 Battle of Blenheim. Now a Unesco World Heritage Site, Blenheim (pronounced *blen-num*) is home to the 11th duke and duchess.

Inside, the house is stuffed with statues, tapestries, ostentatious furniture and giant oil paintings in elaborate gilt frames. Highlights include the Great Hall, a vast space topped by 20m-high ceilings adorned with images of the first duke in battle; the opulent Saloon, the grandest and most important public room; the three state rooms, with their plush decor and priceless china cabinets; and the magnificent Long Library, 55m in length.

From the library, you can access the Churchill Exhibition, which is dedicated to the life, work and writings of Sir Winston, who was born at Blenheim in 1874. For an insight into life below stairs, the Untold Story exhibition explores the family's history through the eyes of the household staff.

If the crowds in the house become too oppressive, retire to the lavish gardens and vast parklands, parts of which were landscaped by Lancelot 'Capability' Brown. To the front, an artificial lake sports a beautiful bridge by Vanbrugh, and a minitrain is needed to take visitors to a maze, adventure playground and butterfly house. For a quieter and longer stroll, glorious walks lead to an arboretum, cascade and temple.

hours and passes the college boathouses and several popular riverside pubs en route.

👉 Tours

The tourist office can also advise on a number of self-guided (brochure or audio) tours of the city and there are themed tours to suit all tastes.

Tourist Office WALKING TOUR
(☎01865-252200; www.visitoxfordandoxfordshire.com; 15-16 Broad St; tours from adult/child £6/3.75; ⏱9.30am-5pm Mon-Sat, 10am-4pm Sun) Runs tours of Oxford city and colleges (10.45am and 2pm year-round, 11am and 1pm July and August), Inspector Morse tours (1.30pm Saturday), family walking tours (1.30pm during school holidays), and a bewildering array of themed tours, including *Alice in Wonderland* and *Harry Potter*; check the website for exact dates.

Bill Spectre's Ghost Trails WALKING TOUR
(☎07941 041811; www.ghosttrail.org; adult/child £7/4; ⏱6.30pm Fri & Sat; 👪) For a highly entertaining and informative look at Oxford's dark underbelly, join Victorian undertaker Bill Spectre on a tour of the city's most haunted sites. The tour lasts 1¾ hours and departs from Oxford Castle Unlocked and the tourist office. Audience participation likely.

Blackwell WALKING TOURS
(☎01865-333606; oxford@blackwell.co.uk; 48-51 Broad St; adult/child £7/6.50; ⏱mid-Apr–Oct) Oxford's most famous bookshop runs 1½-hour guided walking tours, including a literary tour (2pm Tuesday and 11am Thursday), a tour devoted to 'The Inklings' – an informal literary group whose membership included CS Lewis and JRR Tolkien (11.45am Wednesday), and a Historic Oxford tour (2pm Friday). Book ahead.

Oxon Carts PEDICAB TOURS
(☎07747 024600; www.oxoncarts.com; tour £25) Flexible hour-long tours conducted by a fleet of pedicabs. Passengers receive a copy of a 1904 map of the city and a personal guide to its buildings and history.

City Sightseeing BUS TOURS
(www.citysightseeingoxford.com; 24hr ticket adult/child £13/6; ⏱9.30am-6pm Apr-Oct) Hop-on/hop-off bus tours depart every 10 to 15 minutes from the bus and train stations and the 20 dedicated stops around town.

🛏 Sleeping

Book ahead between May and September. If you're stuck, you'll find a string of B&Bs along Iffley, Abingdon, Banbury and Headington Rds.

THE BRAINS BEHIND THE OED

In 1879, Oxford University Press began an ambitious project: a complete re-examination of the English language. The four-volume work was expected to take 10 years to complete. Recognising the mammoth task ahead, editor James Murray issued a circular appealing for volunteers to pore over their books and make precise notes on word usage. Their contributions were invaluable, but after five years, Murray and his team had only reached the word 'ant'.

Of the thousands of volunteers who helped out, the most prolific of all was Dr WC Minor, a US Civil War surgeon. Over the next 20 years, he became Murray's most valued contributor, providing tens of thousands of illustrative quotations and notes on word origins and usage. Murray received all of the doctor's contributions by post from Broadmoor, a hospital for the criminally insane. When he decided to visit the doctor in 1891, however, he discovered that Minor was not an employee but the asylum's longest-serving inmate, a schizophrenic committed in 1872 for a motiveless murder. Despite this, Murray was deeply taken by Minor's devotion to his project and continued to work with him, a story told in full in Simon Winchester's 1998 book *The Surgeon of Crowthorne*.

Neither Murray nor Minor lived to see the eventual publication of *A New English Dictionary on Historical Principles* in 1928. Almost 40 years behind schedule and 10 volumes long, it was the most comprehensive lexicographical project ever undertaken, and a full second edition did not appear until 1989.

Today, the updating of such a major work is no easier, and the public were again asked for help in 2006. This time, the BBC ran a TV programme, *Balderdash and Piffle*, encouraging viewers to contact the publisher with early printed evidence of word use, new definitions and brand-new entries for the dictionary. A second edition was broadcast a year later.

For a full history of the famous dictionary and the development of printing, arrange a visit to the **Oxford University Press Museum** (☎01865-267527; Great Clarendon St; ⊙by appointment).

TOP CHOICE Malmaison
HOTEL £££

(☎01865-268400; www.malmaison-oxford.com; Oxford Castle; d/ste from £125/275; P@☎) This is one place you'd wish would lock you up and throw away the key. This former Victorian prison next to Oxford Castle was converted into a sleek hotel with plush interiors, sultry lighting and giant beds, with each room made from three cells. For a treat, book the Governor's Suite, with four-poster bed and minicinema. Great online deals.

TOP CHOICE Bath Place Hotel
BOUTIQUE HOTEL ££

(☎01865-791812; www.bathplace.co.uk; 4-5 Bath Pl, Holywell St; s/d from £95/120) Comprising several 17th-century weavers' cottages surrounding a tiny, plant-filled courtyard right in the shadow of New College, this is one of Oxford's more unusual hotels. Inside it's all creaky floors, exposed beams, canopied beds and soothing cream walls. The cheapest doubles are on the small side, but the great service and good buffet breakfast make up for it.

Oxford Rooms
STUDENT ROOMS ££

(www.oxfordrooms.co.uk; s/d from £50/90; @) You can sleep inside hallowed colleges and breakfast in a grand hall by staying in student rooms. Most rooms are functional singles with basic furnishings and shared bathrooms, though there are some en suite, twin and family rooms available. Some have views over college quads, though more modern ones are in a nearby annexe. Available during university holidays.

Old Parsonage Hotel
BOUTIQUE HOTEL £££

(☎01865-310210; www.oldparsonage-hotel.co.uk; 1 Banbury Rd; d from £225; P@☎) Wonderfully quirky, the Old Parsonage is a small boutique hotel in a 17th-century stone building covered with wisteria, with just the right blend of period charm and modern luxury. Inside, there's a contemporary art collection, artfully mismatched furniture and chic bedrooms with handmade beds and marble bathrooms. Oscar Wilde once made it his home.

Ethos Hotel   BOUTIQUE HOTEL **££**
(☎01865-245800; www.ethoshotels.co.uk; 59 Western Rd; d from £125; @☎) Hidden away off Abingdon Rd, this funky new hotel has bright, spacious rooms with bold patterned wallpaper, enormous beds and marble bathrooms. It's aimed at independent travellers: you get a minikitchen with a microwave, and breakfast is delivered to your room in a basket. To get here, cross Folly Bridge to Abingdon Rd and take the first right onto Western Rd.

Buttery Hotel   HOTEL **££**
(☎01865-811950; www.thebutteryhotel.co.uk; 11-12 Broad St; s/d from £65/115; @) Right in the heart of the city and with views over the college grounds, the Buttery is Oxford's most central hotel. The rooms are spacious but rather modest, so it's the location that you're paying for. Ask for a room at the back to avoid being woken up by revellers on weekends.

Oxford YHA   HOSTEL **£**
(☎0845 371 9131; www.yha.org.uk; 2a Botley Rd; dm/d from £23/50; @☎) Particularly convenient for budget travellers ridin' the rails, this is Oxford's best budget option, with simple but comfortable four- and six-bed en suite dorms, private rooms and loads of facilities, including a restaurant, library, garden, laundry and a choice of lounges (though internet is not free).

Burlington House   B&B **££**
(☎01865-513513; www.burlington-house.co.uk; 374 Banbury Rd, Summertown; s/d from £66/92; P@☎) Twelve big, bright and elegant rooms with brightly patterned wallpaper and splashes of colour are available at this Victorian merchant house. The fittings are luxurious, the service attentive, the bathrooms immaculate and breakfast comes complete with organic eggs and granola. It has good public transport links to town.

Remont Guesthouse   B&B **££**
(☎01865-311020; www.remont-oxford.co.uk; 367 Banbury Rd, Summertown; s/d from £90/120; P☎) All modern style, subtle lighting and plush furnishings, this 25-room guesthouse has rooms decked out in cool neutrals with silky bedspreads and abstract art. Rooms come with huge plasma-screen TVs and a sunny garden. To get here, head up St Giles St and when the road branches continue for 2km up Banbury Rd.

St Michael's Guest House   B&B **£**
(☎01865-242101; 26 St Michael's St; s/d from £42/55; ☎) Expect creaky stairs, narrow corridors and spick-and-span rooms with shared bathrooms at this super-central guesthouse, presided over by friendly Margaret. Full English breakfast is included in the price.

Central Backpackers   HOSTEL **£**
(☎01865-242288; www.centralbackpackers.co.uk; 13 Park End St; dm £19-22; @☎) A friendly budget option right in the centre of town, this small hostel has basic, bright and simple rooms that sleep four to 12 people, a rooftop terrace and a small lounge with satellite TV – all in a right-on-top-of-a-nightclub location.

🍴 Eating

Oxford offers plenty of choice when it comes to eating out; head to Walton St in Jericho, to Summertown, St Clements or up Cowley Rd for a good selection of independent restaurants. Look out for local chain G&D's for excellent ice cream and cakes.

TOP CHOICE Edamame   JAPANESE **£**
(www.edamame.co.uk; 15 Holywell St; mains £6-8; ⊙lunch Wed-Sun, dinner Thu-Sat) The queue out the door speaks volumes about the quality of the food here. This tiny joint, all light wood and friendly bustle, is the best place in town for genuine Japanese – bento boxes, tempura, noodle dishes and even the love-it-or-hate-it *natto*, and the sushi (Thursday night, £2.70 to £4.30) is divine. Arrive early and be prepared to wait.

Gee's   MODERN BRITISH **££**
(☎01865-553540; www.gees-restaurant.co.uk; 61 Banbury Rd; mains £12-19) Set in a Victorian conservatory, this top-notch restaurant is popular with the visiting parents of university students, thanks to its creative menu of modern British and European dishes. The two-/three-course lunch menu is a great bet at £17/21 and the setting is stunning, though the atmosphere is rather formal. Book ahead.

Atomic Burger   AMERICAN **£**
(www.atomicburger.co.uk; 96 Cowley Rd; mains £7-11; ⊙closed breakfast Mon-Fri) Fast food, but not as you know it. Atomic comes with the Fallout Challenge, which involves consuming a triple burger stack complete with fear-inducing ghost chilli hot sauce. Not keen on killing your taste buds? Try the inventive Messy Jessie, Dead Elvis, the barbeque ribs or nachos and curly fries, all washed down with mega shakes. Everything's freshly made.

Door 74
MODERN BRITISH ££

(☎01865-203374; www.door74.co.uk; 74 Cowley Rd; mains £9-15; ⊙closed Mon & Sun dinner) This cosy little place woos its fans with a rich mix of British and Mediterranean flavours and friendly service. The menu is limited and the tables tightly packed, but the food is consistently good and weekend brunches (full English breakfast, pancakes etc) supremely filling. Book ahead.

Missing Bean
CAFE £

(www.themissingbean.co.uk; 14 Turl St; mains £3-6; ⊙8am-6.30pm Mon-Fri, 10am-6.30pm Sat, 10.30am-5.30pm Sun;) The Brazilian medium roast and cappuccino art at this independent coffee shop is a daily staple for many students, and there are loose-leaf teas, shakes and smoothies for the less caffeine-dependent. The fresh muffins, cakes and ciabatta sandwiches make this a great lunchtime stop.

Quod
MODERN BRITISH ££

(www.quod.co.uk; 92 High St; mains £13-17) Bright, buzzing and decked out with modern art and beautiful people, this joint dishes up modern brasserie-style food to the masses. It's always bustling and, at worst, will tempt you to chill by the bar with a cocktail while you wait. The two-course set lunch (£12.95) is great value.

Fishes
MODERN BRITISH ££

(☎01865-249796; www.fishesoxford.co.uk; North Hinksey; mains £11-19;) Old and quaint on the outside but sleek and modern inside, this popular summer haunt west of the city centre is gastropubbery at its best, with ingredients such as quinoa sitting comfortably alongside great bangers and mash. The pub is 3 miles out of town; head south along the A34 and follow the sign after the Botley junction.

Chiang Mai Kitchen
THAI £

(www.chiangmaikitchen.co.uk; 138 High St; mains £8.50-10;) Authentic Thai cuisine in the heart of Oxford, complete with tear-jerkingly spicy *som tum* (spicy papaya salad), a range of curries (including, unusually, venison), noodle dishes and standout classics such as chicken with cashew nuts. There's an extensive separate menu for vegetarians.

Fire & Stone
PIZZA £

(www.fireandstone.com; 28 George St; pizza £10) The wood-fired pizzas from this slick, colourful place take their inspiration from five continents. Try the Marrakesh, with ground lamb and mint-and-cucumber yoghurt, the sweet potato and yellow curry Koh Samui or the classic New York, with crispy smoked bacon and mozzarella.

Manos
GREEK £

(www.manosfoodbar.com; 105 Walton St; mains £6-8;) For delicious home-cooked tastes of the Med, head for this Greek deli and restaurant, where you'll find the likes of spinach and feta tart, chicken souvlaki and a great selection of meze. The ground floor has a cafe and deli, serving inexpensive wraps and salads, while downstairs has more style and comfort.

Jamie's Italian
ITALIAN ££

(www.jamiesitalian.com; 24-26 George St; mains £9-19) Celebrity chef Jamie Oliver's restaurant serves up some excellent rustic Italian dishes at affordable prices, with the antipasti served on their trademark wooden planks. Decor is modern (all graffitied walls and exposed brick), dishes such as linguini with clams and wild mushroom *panzerotti* are great, and the service efficient.

Café Coco
MEDITERRANEAN ££

(www.cafe-coco.co.uk; 23 Cowley Rd; mains £6-10.50) This Cowley Rd institution is a hip hang-out, with classic posters on the walls and a bald plaster-cast clown in an ice bath. The food combines Mediterranean mains with waffles and pecan pie, and most people come for the atmosphere.

Aziz
INDIAN £

(www.aziz.uk.com; 230 Cowley Rd; mains £6-9; ⊙closed Fri lunch;) An award-winning curry house attracting vegans, vegetarians and curry-lovers in hoards. Standout items on the extensive menu include lamb *razalla* and *murgh kaliya* (black-pepper chicken in creamy sauce), and portions are generous enough to ensure you'll be rolling out the door.

Drinking

Oxford is blessed with some wonderful traditional pubs (www.oxfordpubguide.co.uk), as well as a good selection of funky bars.

TOP CHOICE Turf Tavern
TRADITIONAL PUB

(4 Bath Pl) Hidden down a narrow alleyway, this tiny medieval pub is one of the town's best loved and bills itself as 'an education in intoxication' (it's where president Bill

Clinton 'did not inhale'). Home to 11 real ales, it's always packed with a mix of students, professionals and the lucky tourists who manage to find it. Plenty of outdoor seating.

Bear   PUB
(6 Alfred St) Arguably Oxford's oldest pub (there's been a pub on this site since 1242), this atmospherically creaky place requires the vertically challenged to duck their heads when passing through doorways. There's a great tie collection on the walls and ceiling (though you can no longer exchange yours for a pint), and there are usually a couple of worthy guest ales.

White Horse   TRADITIONAL PUB
(www.whitehorseoxford.co.uk; 52 Broad St) This tiny old-world place – Oxford's smallest pub – was a favourite retreat for TV detective Inspector Morse, and it can get pretty crowded in the evening. It makes a great place for a quiet afternoon pint of Hobgoblin or whatever the guest beer happens to be.

Eagle & Child   TRADITIONAL PUB
(49 St Giles) Affectionately known as the 'Bird & Baby', this atmospheric place, dating from 1650, was once the favourite haunt of Tolkien and CS Lewis. Its wood-panelled rooms and good selection of real ales still attract a mellow crowd.

Trout   PUB
(www.thetroutoxford.co.uk; 195 Godstow Rd, Wolvercote) This charming old-world pub, 2½ miles north of the city centre, has been a favourite hangout of town and gown for many years. Immortalised by Inspector Morse, it's generally crammed with happy diners enjoying the riverside garden, though if you wish to eat, come armed with patience.

Kazbar   BAR
(www.kazbar.co.uk; 25-27 Cowley Rd; ⊘5pm-midnight Mon-Fri, noon-midnight Sat & Sun) This funky Moroccan-themed bar has giant windows, low lighting, warm colours and a cool vibe. It's buzzing most nights with hip young things sipping cocktails and filling up on the Spanish and North African tapas (£4 to £6).

Frevd   PUB
(119 Walton St) A cavernous neoclassical church-turned-bar with quirky art and great cocktails. It's popular with a young style-conscious crowd.

Raoul's   COCKTAIL BAR
(www.raoulsbar.co.uk; 32 Walton St; ⊘4pm-midnight) Perfectly mixed cocktails and funky music at Jericho's finest retro-look bar.

☆ Entertainment

Despite its large student population, Oxford's club scene is fairly limited, with several cattle-mart clubs in the centre of town and a lot of crowd-pleasing music. If you're a fan of classical music, however, you'll be spoilt for choice, with a host of excellent venues and regular concerts throughout the year. See www.dailyinfo.co.uk or www.music atoxford.com for listings.

Creation Theatre   THEATRE
(www.creationtheatre.co.uk) Performing in a variety of nontraditional venues, including city parks, the BMW plant and Oxford Castle, this theatre company produces highly original, mostly Shakespearean shows featuring plenty of magic and special effects.

O2 Academy   LIVE MUSIC
(www.o2academyoxford.co.uk; 190 Cowley Rd) Oxford's best club and live-music venue hosts everything from big-name DJs and international touring artists to indie bands, hard rock and funk nights across three performance spaces. Expect a mixed crowd of students, professionals and academics.

Bridge   CLUB
(www.bridgeoxford.co.uk; 6 Hythe Bridge St; ⊘closed Sun) The three floors of this club heave with revellers almost every night of the week, with resident DJs playing a mix of dance anthems, funk, hip hop and R'n'B, while those needing to rest their feet can retire to the lounge for the signature cocktails.

Cellar   LIVE MUSIC
(www.cellaroxford.co.uk; Frewin Crt, off Cornmarket St; ☎) There's live music nightly at this independent venue. From local DJs to indie rock, reggae, funk, hip hop, and drum and bass, to even the odd play, the Cellar's got all angles covered.

Oxford Playhouse   THEATRE
(www.oxfordplayhouse.com; Beaumont St) The city's main stage for quality drama also hosts an impressive selection of touring music, dance and theatre performances, and the Burton Taylor Studio has quirky student productions.

OXFORD, COTSWOLDS & AROUND OXFORD

ⓘ Information

All accommodation options reviewed offer wi-fi and/or internet access. You'll find that every major bank and ATM is handily represented on or close to Cornmarket St.

Daily Info (www.dailyinfo.co.uk) Daily listings for events, gigs, performances and accommodation.

John Radcliffe Hospital (☎01865-231405; Headley Way, Headington) Three miles east of the city centre in Headington.

Oxford City (www.oxfordcity.co.uk) Accommodation and restaurant listings, as well as entertainment, activities and shopping.

Oxford Online (www.visitoxford.org) Oxford's official tourism website.

Post office (102 St Aldate's; ◷9am-5.30pm Mon-Sat)

Tourist office (☎01865-252200; www.visit oxford.org; 15-16 Broad St; ◷9.30am-5pm Mon-Sat, 10am-4pm Sun)

ⓘ Getting There & Away

Bus

Oxford's main bus/coach station is at **Gloucester Green**. Services to **London** (£18 return) run up to every 15 minutes, day and night, and take about 90 minutes.

Airline (www.oxfordbus.co.uk) Runs to **Heathrow** (£24, 90 minutes) half-hourly from 4am to 10pm and at midnight and 2am, and **Gatwick** (£29, two hours) hourly from 5.15am to 8.15pm, and every two hours from 10pm to 4am.

National Express (www.nationalexpress.com) Runs buses to Birmingham, Bath and Bristol, but all are easier to reach by train.

Stagecoach (www.stagecoachbus.com) Serves most of the small towns in Oxfordshire and runs the X5 service to **Cambridge** (£12, 3½ hours) roughly every half-hour.

Swanbrook (www.swanbrook.co.uk) Services to Cheltenham and Gloucester via Witney and Burford (£8, three to four daily Monday to Saturday, one daily Sunday, 1½ hours).

Car

Driving and parking in Oxford is a nightmare. Use the five Park & Ride car parks on major routes leading into town. Parking is free and buses (10 to 15 minutes, every 10 minutes) cost £2.50.

Train

Oxford's train station is conveniently placed at the western end of Park End St. There are half-hourly services to **London Paddington** (£23, one hour) and roughly hourly trains to **Birmingham** (£16, 1¼ hours). Hourly services also run to **Bath** (£16, 1¼ hours) and **Bristol** (£22, one to two hours), but require a change at Didcot Parkway.

ⓘ Getting Around

Bicycle

Cyclo Analysts (☎01865-424444; 150 Cowley Rd; per day/week £19/55) Rents hybrid bikes.

Bus

Buses 1 and 5 go to Cowley Rd from St Aldate's, 2 and 7 go along Banbury Rd from Magdalen St, and 16 and 35 run along Abingdon Rd from St Aldate's.

A multi-operator **Plus Pass** (per day/week £6/19) allows unlimited travel on Oxford's bus system.

FOOD, FESTIVALS AND FARMERS' MARKETS

When the locally sourced, seasonal food movement took off a few years ago, the Cotswolds were already there. Organic, ethically produced produce has long been a staple in its villages. In the delis and independent food shops all over the region, visiting foodies will make tempting discoveries. Edible goodies to look out for include Simon Weaver Organic (www.simonweaver.net), from a farm near Upper Slaughter, organic beef from LoveMyCow (www.lovemycow.com) in Bourton-on-the-Water, smoked fish and meats from Upton Smokery (www.uptonsmokery.co.uk) in Burford and fantastic ice cream from the Cotswold Ice Cream Company (www.cotswoldicecream.net).

The feast doesn't stop there. Each calendar year sees a smattering of food festivals all over the Cotswolds, with independent producers bringing their wares and chefs showing off their stuff. These include the Stroud Food & Drink Festival (www.stroud valleysfestivals.co.uk) in September, the Wild Thyme Food Festival (www.wildthyme restaurant.co.uk) in Chipping Norton in April, and the brand new Food & Farming Festival (http://cotswoldfarmpark.co.uk) at Cotswold Farm Park in May.

Finally, weekly farmers markets (www.farmersmarkets.net) take place in several villages, with a multitude of local producers selling their seasonal delights to the general public. The biggest ones are held in Stroud, Bourton-on-the-Water, Stow-on-the-Wold, Lechlade-on-Thames and Cirencester. What are you waiting for? Go forth and sample!

Taxi

There are taxi ranks at the train station and bus station, as well as on St Giles and at Carfax. For a green alternative, call **Oxon Carts** (☏07747 024600), a pedicab service.

HENLEY-ON-THAMES

POP 10,646

The attractive commuter town of Henley is synonymous with the Henley Royal Regatta (www.hrr.co.uk), a world-famous rowing tournament that sees the town bursting into action in July. The five-day regatta has grown into a major fixture in the social calendar of the upwardly mobile, and although rowers of the highest calibre take part, the main event is rather overshadowed by the champagne-fuelled antics of the wealthy who come here to see and be seen. Still, picnicking in the public enclosure (tickets £15 to £19) and watching the rowers' straining muscles as the boats whizz by makes for a good day out in sunny weather.

The week following the regatta is taken up by the Henley Festival (www.henley -festival.co.uk), a vibrant black-tie affair that features everything from opera to rock, jazz, comedy and swing, the main events taking place on a floating stage on the Thames.

Trains to London Paddington (£14.20, hourly) take about one hour though you have to change twice – at Reading/Slough and Twyford.

THE COTSWOLDS

Glorious villages riddled with beautiful old mansions of honey-coloured stone, thatched cottages, atmospheric churches and rickety almshouses draw crowds of visitors to the Cotswolds. The booming medieval wool trade brought the area its wealth and left it with such a proliferation of beautiful buildings that its place in history is secured for evermore. If you've ever craved exposed beams or lusted after a cream tea in the mid-afternoon, there's no finer place to fulfil your fantasies.

Activities

The gentle hills of the Cotswolds are perfect for walking, cycling and riding. The 102-mile Cotswold Way (www.nationaltrail .co.uk/cotswold) gives walkers a wonderful overview of the area. The route meanders

---

ℹ️ THE COTSWOLDS DISCOVERER

If you're planning on seeing much of the Cotswolds in a short space of time and don't have your own wheels, your best bet is the Cotswolds Discoverer (www.escapetothecotswolds.org .uk/discoverer; 1-/3-day bus pass £10/25, train pass £8.50/20), which gives you unlimited travel on participating bus or train routes.

---

from Chipping Campden to Bath, passing through some lovely countryside and tiny villages, with no major climbs or difficult stretches, and is easily accessible from many points en route if you fancy tackling a shorter section.

Away from the main roads, the winding lanes of the Cotswolds make fantastic cycling territory. Again, the local tourist offices are invaluable in helping to plot a route.

ℹ️ Information

For information on attractions, accommodation and events:

Cotswolds (www.the-cotswolds.org)
Cotswolds Tourism (www.cotswolds.com)
Oxfordshire Cotswolds (www.oxfordshirecots wolds.org)

ℹ️ Getting Around

The Cotswolds have been well and truly discovered, and the most popular villages can be besieged by tourists and traffic in summer. Travel by public transport requires careful planning and patience; for the most flexibility, and the option of getting off the beaten track, your own car is unbeatable. Plan to visit the main centres early in the morning or late in the evening, focus your attention on the south or take to the hills on foot or by bike to avoid the worst of the crowds. Better still, just leave the crowds behind and meander down deserted country lanes and bridleways until you discover your very own bucolic village seemingly undisturbed since medieval times.

Alternatively, **Cotswold Roaming** (☏01865-308300; www.cotswold-roaming.co.uk) runs guided bus tours from Oxford between April and October. Half-day tours of the Cotswolds (£30) include Minster Lovell, Burford and Bibury, while full-day tours of the North Cotswolds (£45) feature Bourton-on-the-Water, Lower Slaughter, Chipping Campden and Stow-on-the-Wold.

The Cotswolds

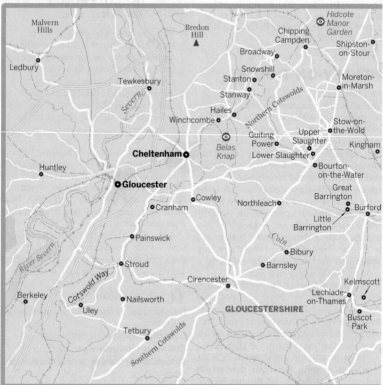

Witney

POP 22,765

The sleepy town of Witney is firmly on Oxford's commuter belt, but make your way through the traffic and new housing developments to the centre of town and you'll find a charming village green flanked by pretty stone houses. At one end is a glorious wool church and 18th-century almshouses, at the other a 17th-century covered market. Witney built its wealth through blanket production, its main trade from the Iron Age until 2002! Its mills, wealthy merchants' homes and blanket factories can still be seen today. The baroque, 18th-century Blanket Hall dominates genteel High St, while at Wood Green you'll find a second village green and a cluster of stunning old stone cottages.

Pick up a copy of the *Witney Wool & Blanket Trail* from the tourist office (☑01993-775802; www.oxfordshirecotswolds.org; 3 Welch Way; ⏰9am-5.30pm Mon-Thu, 9am-5pm Fri, 9.30am-5pm Sat) to guide you around the town.

Your best bet for a meal is the Fleece (☑01993-892270; www.fleecewitney.co.uk; 11 Church Green; P), a contemporary pub, restaurant and B&B on the main village green. The spacious brasserie has an ambitious seasonal menu, with some wonderful smoked fish, Aberdeenshire steak and a roast of the day (£12.50). If you wish to stay, the rooms here are sleek and stylish (single/double £80/90).

Stagecoach bus S1 runs from Oxford to Witney every 20 minutes Monday to Saturday, hourly on Sunday (30 minutes). Swanbrook runs between Cheltenham (£8, one hour, one to three daily) and Oxford (30 minutes) via Witney.

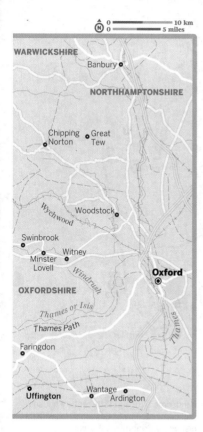

Minster Lovell

POP 1348

Set on a gentle slope leading down to the meandering River Windrush, Minster Lovell is a gorgeous village with a cluster of stone cottages nestled beside an ancient pub and riverside mill. One of William Morris' favourite spots, the village has changed little since medieval times. It's divided into two halves: Old Minster, recorded in the Domesday Book (1086) and the rather newer Minster Lovell, across the river.

The main sight in Old Minster is Minster Lovell Hall, the 15th-century manor house that was home to Viscount Francis Lovell. Lovell fought with Richard III at the Battle of Bosworth in 1485 and joined Lambert Simnel's failed rebellion after the king's defeat and death. Lovell's mysterious disappearance was never explained, and when a skeleton was discovered inside a secret vault

in the house in 1708, it was assumed he had died while in hiding. The manor is now in ruins; you can peek past the blackened walls into the roofless great hall and the interior courtyard, the wind whistling eerily through the gaping windows.

The revamped, luxurious Old Swan & Minster Mill (☑01993-774441; www.oldswan andminstermill.com; d from £165-350; [P][🛜]) has charming period-style rooms in the 17th-century Old Swan or sleek, contemporary design in the 19th-century converted mill, covered with creepers. Windrush Spa is due to open alongside the river in late 2012, with full-scale pampering complete with a range of treatments and an outdoor pool. The Old Swan serves excellent gastropub food, with doorstep sandwiches for lunch and handmade sausages, daily fish and game for dinner (mains £15 to £23).

Swanbrook coaches stop here on the Oxford to Cheltenham run (one to three daily). Stagecoach bus 233 between Witney and Burford stops here Monday to Saturday (10 minutes each way, 10 daily).

Burford

POP 1340

Slithering down a steep hill to a medieval crossing point on the River Windrush, the remarkable village of Burford is little changed since its glory days at the height of the wool trade. It's a stunningly picturesque place with higgledy-piggledy stone cottages, fine Cotswold town houses and the odd Elizabethan or Georgian gem. Antique shops, tearooms and specialist boutiques peddle nostalgia to the hordes of visitors who make it here in summer, but despite the crowds it's easy to get off the main drag and wander along quiet side streets seemingly lost in time.

The helpful tourist office (☑01993-823558; www.oxfordshirecotswolds.org; Sheep St; ⊗9.30am-5.30pm Mon-Sat, until 4pm Nov-Feb) provides the Burford Trail leaflet (50p), with information on walking in the local area.

◉ Sights & Activities

Burford's main attraction lies in its incredible collection of buildings, including the 16th-century Tolsey House (Toll House; High St; admission free; ⊗2-5pm Mon-Fri, 11am-5pm Sat & Sun Apr-Oct), where the wealthy wool merchants held their meetings. This quaint building perches on sturdy pillars and now houses a small museum on Burford's history.

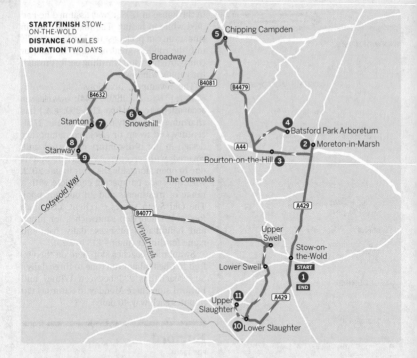

Driving Tour
Cotswolds Highlights

❯ Given its vast network of winding, secluded country lanes, magnificent stately homes, timeless villages with crooked half-timbered houses and independent food markets, it's impossible to cover all of the Cotswold highlights in one go. This circular tour focuses on one of the most picturesque cross-sections of classic villages, markets, stately houses and ruins.

Begin your tour at ❶ **Stow-on-the-Wold**, the highest of the Cotswold villages at 244m and a market town since the 12th century. Though some feel that its attractive narrow streets, lined with antique stores and book-shops, have a somewhat contrived feel to them, this is still very much a trading centre; in May and October, the village comes alive with the two annual Charter Fairs, with many beautiful equine specimens and Romany horse traders camping on the outskirts of town.

In the centre of the village, take your time to admire the Market Square, lined with handsome 17th- and 18th-century houses and dominated by St Edward's Hall with its distinctive Corinthian pilasters.

From Stow, take the A429 4 miles north to ❷ **Moreton-in-Marsh**, its wide main street sitting atop what used to be the Roman Fosse Way. Though the town is essentially a busy crossroads, there are appealing coaching inns facing each other across the main street, and the White Hart Royal Hotel is where Charles I stayed on 2 July 1644. Moreton's main street is also known for its excellent local food shops and delis, where you can stock up on produce to take with you.

From Moreton, take the A44 west, passing through tiny ❸ **Bourton-on-the-Hill**, lined with attractive 17th- and 18th-century cottages and famous for two things: the gibbeting cage in which the bodies of dead highwaymen were hung in the 19th century, and horse training, with several stud farms in the vicinity of the village. This is a good spot to pause for lunch before turning north onto the B4479 and taking the first right to **4 Batsford Park Arboretum**, exotic woodlands unrivalled elsewhere in Britain, with more than 3300 labelled trees, bamboos and shrubs from Nepal, China, North America and Japan, as well as bronze statues brought over by Bertie Mitford, Lord Redesdale, who created this enchanted wood in 1880. Highlights here include the vast American redwoods, the flowering Japanese cherries (at their best in spring) and the strangely churchlike 'cathedral' lime.

Follow the signs that will take you back to the B4479 and then head north for 3 miles to **5 Chipping Campden**. While the village's name derives from the Old English *ceapen*, meaning 'market', 'Chippy's' visible prosperity derives from its past as a successful wool town. As you drive down the elegant, S-shaped High St, take in the Jacobean, Georgian and Tudor houses that line it, with their crooked half-timbered facades, bumpy roofs, twisted beams and honey-coloured stone walls. One of the most prominent landmarks here is Grevel House. Dating from the 14th century, it was the home of the highly successful wool merchant William Grevel, and has a splendid Perpendicular-style gabled window.

In the middle of the main street stands the iconic 17th-century Market Hall, an open-sided building where dairy farmers used to sell their produce. It looks like a cross between a barn and a chapel, with its simple arches and uneven stone floors.

Take Cidermill Lane up from the main street to the church of St James; if you peek through the gates next to it, you'll see the remains of Campden House, a grand 17th-century merchant's pad that was burned down by Royalist soldiers during the Civil War. While one of its pavilions has since been restored, it's not open to the public.

After an overnight stay at Chipping Campden, follow the B4081 south out of town, going straight over the A44 and following the signposts along the unnamed, winding country lane for a couple of miles to the village of **6 Snowshill**. If the narrow lanes, the church, the gable-windowed houses and slate roofs looks familiar, that's because they featured in the film *Bridget Jones's Diary*, with a local house used as Bridget's parents' house.

Dominating the village is **Snowshill Manor** (www.nationaltrust.org.uk; noon-5pm Wed-Sun mid-Mar-Oct; adult/child £9.70/4.90), a shrine to the obsessive collecting of its owner, the poet and architect Charles Wade.

From the manor, take Snowshill Rd towards Broadway for 2 miles, but bypass it by taking West End Lane and then the B4632 south towards Cheltenham. Three miles down, take the left turn-off to **7 Stanton**. A tiny stunner of a village, its houses are crafted out of that golden stone that the Cotswolds are known for, with not a shop or quaint tearoom in sight. The buildings most likely to catch your eye are the Jacobean Stanton Court, belonging to architect Sir Philip Stott, who was responsible for the restoration of the other Stanton houses, and the fine Perpendicular tower of the church of St Michael, which has an absolutely beguiling medieval interior.

You'll undoubtedly see walkers passing through the village, heading south along the Cotswold Way to the village of **8 Stanway**, just a mile south; follow the road that runs parallel to the trail. There is little more to Stanway than a few thatched-roofed cottages, a church and the most magnificent Jacobean structure that is **Stanway House** (www.stanwayfountain.co.uk; 2-5pm Tue & Thu Jun-Aug; adult/child £7.50/2.50), which is hidden behind a triple-gabled gatehouse and home to Britain's tallest fountain, which erupts, geyser-like, to a height of 300ft. The manor is a private home and open to the public only on select days.

Just south of Stanway, at a crossroads overlooked by a **9 war memorial** featuring a bronze St George and the Dragon by Alexander Fisher, take the B4077 east for around 8 miles, before turning south at Upper Swell, passing through Lower Swell and following the signs south to **10 Lower Slaughter**, a picture-perfect village lined with houses made of golden stone. You'll have to leave the car behind for the five-minute stroll to the former village mill (now a museum) set on the River Eye, though it's more a babbling brook than a river. Head 1km west along the narrow lanes to **11 Upper Slaughter**, less visited than its neighbour but no less attractive due to its idyllic setting between a small ford and the hills. Stop for lunch at the sumptuous Lords of the Manor, a 17th-century mansion and award-winning restaurant, before following the signposts to the A429 and driving the remaining 4 miles back to Stow.

THE GOOD LIFE

The Cotswolds' mellow charms attract moneyed city folk, A-list celebrities and wealthy downsizers in equal measure, but mere mortals can get a slice of the good life at one of the numerous luxury hotels in the area. Here are just a few to whet your fancy.

Barnsley House (☎01285-740000; www.barnsleyhouse.com; Barnsley; d £300-525; P@☎🖥🖥) For funky chic and indulgent sophistication, this hideout for the rich and famous is just the spot for a romantic weekend.

Cowley Manor (☎01242-870900; www.cowleymanor.com; Cowley; d £180-500; P☎🖥) Handmade furniture and fabrics by young British designers adorn the simple but elegant rooms at this super-sleek hotel.

Lygon Arms (☎0800 652 8413; www.barcelo-hotels.co.uk; High St, Broadway; d £152-390; P@☎🖥) Choose medieval splendour or modern chic at this 16th-century inn in the heart of Broadway.

Just off the main street, you'll find the town's 14th-century almshouses and the Church of St John the Baptist (www .burfordchurch.org). The Norman tower here is topped by a 15th-century steeple, and inside you'll find a fine fan-vaulted ceiling and several mausolea that have somehow survived the Reformation. Look for a plaque beside the entrance that commemorates the execution of three Levellers (Roundhead soldiers who mutinied due to their leaders' failure to uphold the notion of equality of all men before the law) by Cromwell's army.

Younger visitors will enjoy a visit to the hugely popular Cotswold Wildlife Park (☎01993-823006; www.cotswoldwildlifepark.co.uk; adult/child £13/9; ☺10am-6pm), 3 miles south of Burford and home to a vast menagerie of penguins, zebras, white rhinos, Amur leopards and much more. A miniature train (£1) and petting zoo take the excitement up a notch. Last admission is 1½ hours before closing time.

There are several delightful walks from Burford, including the one along the picturesque river path to the untouched and rarely visited village of Swinbrook (3 miles), where the 12th-century church of St Mary has the remarkable tombs of the Fettiplace family who dominated the area for 500 years.

🛏 Sleeping & Eating

Burford has a wonderful choice of atmospheric, upmarket hotels but far fewer options at more affordable prices.

TOP CHOICE Lamb Inn   INN **£££**
(☎01993-823155; www.cotswold-inns-hotels .co.uk/lamb; Sheep St; s/d from £120/160; P☎)

At this atmospheric 15th-century inn, expect flagstone floors, beamed ceilings, creaking stairs, a laid-back vibe downstairs, and luxurious period-style rooms with antique furniture upstairs. The restaurant caters both to vegetarians and the carnivorously inclined with its top-notch modern British food (two-/three-course dinner £32.50/39, eight-course tasting menu £49); there's less formal dining in the bar (mains £11 to £18).

Bull   HOTEL **££**
(☎01993-822220; www.bullatburford.co.uk; High St; s/d from £70/75) You'll be following in the footsteps of guests as illustrious as Charles II if you stay at this distinguished hotel. The plusher rooms feature four-poster beds and antique furniture, and the restaurant is pure gourmet, with beautifully executed dishes making the most of local ingredients.

Angel   MODERN BRITISH **££**
(☎01993-822714; www.theangelatburford.co.uk; 14 Witney St; mains £15.50-19) Set in a lovely 16th-century coaching inn, this atmospheric brasserie serves up an innovative menu of modern British and European food. Dine in by roaring fires in winter, or eat al fresco in the lovely walled garden in warmer weather. There are three traditionally decorated rooms (double £100) upstairs if you wish to linger.

Huffkins   TEAROOM
(www.huffkins.com; 98 High St; afternoon tea £16; ☺8am-5pm Mon-Sat, 10am-5pm Sun) Superb tearoom serving some of the most memorable scones you're likely to have. Also a great place to stock up on local chutneys and other produce.

ℹ️ Getting There & Away

From Oxford, Swanbrook runs three buses a day (one on Sunday) to Burford (45 minutes) and on to Cheltenham. Stagecoach bus 233 runs between Witney and Burford 10 times a day, Monday to Saturday (20 minutes).

Chipping Norton

POP 5972

The sleepy but attractive town of Chipping Norton ('Chippy' to locals) has plenty of quiet side streets to wander and none of the Cotswold crowds. Handsome Georgian buildings and old coaching inns cluster around the market square, while on Church St you'll find a row of beautiful honey-coloured almshouses built in the 17th century. Further on is the secluded Church of St Mary, a classic example of the Cotswold wool churches, with a magnificent 15th-century Perpendicular nave and clerestory.

Chippy's most enduring landmark, however, is the arresting Bliss Mill on the outskirts of town. This monument to the industrial architecture of the 19th century is more like a stately home than a factory, topped by a domed tower and chimney stack of the Tuscan order.

For lunch or dinner your best bet is Wild Thyme (☎01608-645060; www.wildthymerestaurant.co.uk; 10 New St; mains £9-19, s/d from £40/60; ⊗Tue-Sat), thrilling the palate with top-notch dishes such as goat's-cheese soufflé with red-onion marmalade or roast pork belly with truffle mash. The desserts are nothing short of sublime, and the three upstairs rooms have feather duvets and Egyptian cotton bedding. Look out for the annual food festival (p198) hosted here in May.

Alternatively, head 4 miles southwest of town to the pretty village of Kingham, home of the Kingham Plough (☎01608-658327; www.thekinghamplough.co.uk; The Green, Kingham; mains £13-18, s/d from £85/115; ⊗closed Sun dinner) – a city slicker's dream of a country pub. Its hearty seasonal dishes are cobbled together from very local ingredients, be it pheasant in winter or new season lamb in spring. The three stylish rooms are largely unadorned but comfortable.

Stagecoach bus S3 runs between Chippy and Oxford (55 minutes) roughly every half-hour.

Moreton-in-Marsh

POP 3198

Home to some beautiful buildings but plagued by heavy traffic that clogs up its broad High St (built on top of the Roman Fosse Way) Moreton-in-Marsh is a major transport hub also known for its excellent food shops stocking Cotswold produce; try Warner's Budgens (High St) or the Cotswold Cheese Company (www.cotswoldcheesecompany.co.uk). On Tuesdays, the town bursts into life for its weekly market, and if you're here in September, don't miss the one-day Moreton Show (www.moretonshow.co.uk), the ultimate agricultural extravaganza, attracting up to 20,000 people with the best of local food and gussied-up livestock competitions.

Just east of Moreton, Chastleton House (NT; www.nationaltrust.org.uk; adult/child £9.10/4.30; ⊗1-5pm Wed-Fri Mar-Oct) is one of England's finest and most complete Jacobean houses. Full of rare tapestries, family portraits and antique furniture, its Long Gallery is particularly resplendent. Outside, there's a classic Elizabethan topiary garden.

Pulham's Coaches (www.pulhamscoaches.com) runs hourly bus 801 between Moreton and Cheltenham (1¼ hours, Monday to Saturday) via Stow-on-the-Wold (15 minutes) and Bourton-on-the-Water (20 minutes).

There are trains to Moreton from London Paddington (£30, 1¾ hours, every two hours) via Oxford (£8.90, 35 minutes) and on to Worcester (£11, one hour) and Hereford (£16.90, one hour 45 minutes).

Chipping Campden

POP 2206

An unspoiled gem in an area full of pretty villages, Chipping Campden is a glorious reminder of life in the Cotswolds in medieval times. The graceful curving main street is flanked by a picturesque array of wayward stone cottages, fine terraced houses, ancient inns and historic homes, many made of that honey-coloured stone that the Cotswolds is so famous for. Despite its obvious allure, the town remains relatively unspoiled by tourist crowds, though it is very popular with walkers rambling along the Cotswold Way.

◎ Sights & Activities

Standing out from the splendour of other historic buildings along the High St is the

THE COTSWOLDS OLIMPICKS

The medieval sport of shin-kicking lives on in Chipping Campden, where each year the townspeople gather to compete at the Cotswold Olimpicks (www .olimpickgames.co.uk), a traditional country sports day first celebrated in 1612. It is one of the most entertaining and bizarre sporting competitions in England, and many of the original events, such as welly wanging (throwing), the sack race and climbing a slippery pole, are still held. It is held annually at the beginning of June.

highly photogenic 17th-century Market Hall, with multiple gables and an elaborate timber roof; this is where dairy produce used to be sold. Chipping Campden made its fortune during the wool boom, so it's little wonder that one of the most prominent buildings in town is the 14th-century Grevel House, former home of successful wool merchant William Grevel. Nearby on Church St is a remarkable row of almshouses dating from the 17th century, and the Jacobean lodges and gateways of the now-ruined Campden House, a large and lavish 15th-century house, the remains of which you can see clearly from the Shipston Rd. At the western end of the High St is the 15th-century St James' (⊙10am-5pm Mon-Sat, 2-6pm Sun Mar-Oct); built in the Perpendicular style, it has a magnificent tower and some graceful 17th-century monuments.

The surviving Court Barn Museum (☑01386-841951; www.courtbarn.org.uk; Church St; adult/child £3.75/free; ⊙10am-5pm Tue-Sun Apr-Sep) is now a craft and design museum featuring work from the Arts and Crafts Movement, such as silverwork, pottery and hand-dyed cloth. Down Sheep St you'll find the former Silk Mill, taken over by galleries of local art, ceramics and silver, with Hart Gold & Silversmiths (www.hartsilversmiths .co.uk) upstairs.

About 4 miles northeast, Hidcote Manor Garden (NT; www.nationaltrust.org.uk; Hidcote Bartrim; adult/child £10/5; ⊙10am-6pm) is one of the finest examples of Arts and Crafts landscaping in Britain, with outdoor 'rooms' filled with flowers and rare plants for the arboreally inclined.

🛏 Sleeping & Eating

TOP CHOICE Cotswold House Hotel   BOUTIQUE HOTEL £££
(☑01386-840330; www.cotswoldhouse.com; The Square; r £120-670; ℗@) This chic Regency town-house-turned-boutique hotel has bespoke furniture, ultra-comfortable king-sized beds, Frette linens, cashmere throws, private gardens and hot tubs. You can indulge in some treatments at the Temple Spa, dine in style at Juliana's (three-course set dinner £52) or take an informal approach at Hick's Brasserie (mains £12 to £20).

Eight Bells Inn   B&B ££
(☑01386-840371; www.eightbellsinn.co.uk; Church St; s/d from £65/85) This 14th-century inn is an atmospheric B&B featuring bright, modern rooms with iron bedsteads, soothing neutral decor and warm accents. The pub downstairs wins points for its flagstone floors and good, no-nonsense pub grub (two-/three-course menu £18/22) such as pork medallions with caramelised applies.

Volunteer Inn   B&B £
(☑01386-840688; www.thevolunteerinn.net; Lower High St; s/d from £35/50) This is the favourite haunt of walkers and cyclists travelling along the Cotswold Way. It's a clutch of simple rooms atop a friendly, busy pub.

Maharaja   INDIAN £
(www.thevolunteerinn.net; Lower High St; mains £7-11; ⌖) Popular Indian restaurant covering all the classics, as well as the more unusual *shazni* prawns and spiced venison.

❶ Information

Pop into the helpful **tourist office** (☑01386-841206; www.chippingcampdenonline.org; High St; ⊙9.30am-5pm) to pick up a town trail guide (£1) for information on the most historic buildings and to get you off the main drag and down some of the gorgeous back streets. If you're visiting on a Tuesday between July and September, it's well worth joining a **guided tour** at 2.30pm (suggested donation £3) run by the Cotswold Wardens.

❶ Getting There & Around

Between them, buses 21 and 22 run almost hourly to Stratford-upon-Avon or Moreton-in-Marsh. Bus 21 also stops in Broadway. No Sunday services.

You can hire bikes from **Cotswold Country Cycles** (www.cotswoldcountrycycles.com; Longlands Farm Cottage; per day £15).

Broadway

POP 2496

This pretty village, a quintessentially English place with a smattering of antique shops, tearooms and art galleries, has inspired writers, artists and composers in times past with its graceful, golden-hued cottages set at the foot of a steep escarpment. Take the time to wander down to the lovely 12th-century Church of St Eadburgha, a signposted 1-mile walk from town. Near here, a path leads uphill for 2 miles to Broadway Tower (www.broadwaytower.co.uk; adult/child £4.50/2.50; ◎10.30am-5pm), a crenulated, 18th-century Gothic folly on the crest of the escarpment for the all-encompassing views from the top.

For modern comfort within a 300-year-old exterior, try the wonderfully friendly Crown & Trumpet (✆01386-853202; www .cotswoldholidays.co.uk; Station Rd; d £60; P✿), the Broadway 'local' with five en suite rooms (complete with sloped floors, exposed beams and low ceilings) above the lively pub. Downstairs is a good bet for real ales and a proper roast dinner. Sleek and stylish Russells (✆01386-853555; www .russellsofbroadway.co.uk; 20 High St; 2-/3-course menu £15/18) is known for its award-winning modern British fare, with everything beautifully executed, from the gnocchi to the saddle of rabbit. Upstairs there are seven spacious, individually designed rooms (doubles £105 to £203), combining exposed beams and four-poster beds with modern luxuries such as iPod docks.

Bus 21 goes to Moreton-in-Marsh, Chipping Campden and Stratford (50 minutes, four daily Monday to Saturday). Bus 606 goes to Cheltenham (50 minutes, four daily Monday to Saturday).

Around Broadway

About 3 miles south of Broadway is Snowshill Manor (p203), a wonderful Cotswold mansion once home to the marvellously eccentric Charles Paget Wade. The house contains Wade's extraordinary collection of crafts and design (inspired by his grandmother's antique lacquered Chinese cabinet), including everything from musical instruments to Victorian perambulators and Japanese samurai armour. Outside, the lovely gardens (maintained organically, without any pesticides) were designed as an exten-

sion of the house, with pools, terraces and wonderful views.

Nearby is the splendid Jacobean mansion, Stanway House (p203). Inhabited by the same family (that of the Earl of Wemyss) for more than 450 years, it has a delightful, lived-in charm with much of its original furniture and character intact. The house is surrounded by wonderful, baroque water gardens, home to the world's highest gravity fountain.

Winchcombe

POP 4379

Winchcombe is very much a working, living place, with butchers, bakers and small independent shops lining the main street. It was capital of the Saxon kingdom of Mercia and one of the most important towns in the Cotswolds until the Middle Ages. Today, the remnants of its illustrious past can still be seen.

The helpful tourist office (✆01242-602925; www.winchcombe.co.uk; High St; ◎10am-5pm Mon-Sat, to 4pm Sun Apr-Oct, to 4pm Sat & Sun rest of year) can assist with planning an itinerary.

◉ Sights & Activities

Don't miss the picturesque cottages on Vineyard St and Dents Tce and look out for the hideous gargoyles that adorn St Peter's Church.

TOP
CHOICE Sudeley Castle   CASTLE
(www.sudeleycastle.co.uk; adult/child £11/4.20; ◎10.30am-5pm) The town's main attraction, this magnificent castle was a favoured retreat of Tudor and Stuart monarchs. It once served as the home of Katherine Parr (Henry VIII's widow) and her second husband, Thomas Seymour, with Princess Elizabeth (before she became Elizabeth I) part of the household for a time until, finally, Seymour's inappropriate displays of affection towards Elizabeth prompted Katherine to banish her from the premises. It's worth paying extra to visit the South Hall exhibition, detailing the history of the intricate knot garden, and a splendid portrait of Elizabeth I. Just outside are the beautiful remains of the banquet hall, covered with creepers. The house is still used as a family home and much of the interior is off-limits to visitors, but you can get a glimpse of its grand proportions

while visiting the exhibitions of costumes, memorabilia and paintings, and the surrounding gardens. For insight into real life in the castle, join one of the 'Connoisseur Tours' (£15, at 11am, 1pm and 3pm Tuesday, Wednesday and Thursday).

Walking Trails
WALKING
(www.winchcombewelcomeswalkers.com) Winchcombe is ideally situated for walkers, with a spider's web of trails branching out in every direction. The Cotswold Way passes through here, touching on Belas Knap, and there's the Gloucestershire Way to Tewkesbury and Stow, the Warden's Way and Windrush Way leading to Bourton-on-the-Water, and the long-distance Worcestershire-bound St Kenelm's Way and Wychavon Way.

Belas Knap
BURIAL CHAMBER
There's easy access to the Cotswold Way from Winchcombe, and the 2½-mile hike to Belas Knap is one of the most scenic short walks in the region. Five-thousand-year-old Belas Knap is the best-preserved Neolithic burial chamber in the country. Visitors are not allowed inside, but the views down to Sudeley Castle and across the surrounding countryside are breathtaking.

Hailes Abbey
RUIN
(EH; www.english-heritage.org.uk; adult/child £4.40/2.20; ☉10am-5pm) Just outside the town are the evocative ruins of this Cistercian abbey, once one of the country's main pilgrimage centres, due to a long-running medieval scam. The abbey was rumoured to possess a vial of Christ's blood, which turned out to be merely coloured water. Before the deception came to light, thousands of credulous pilgrims contributed to the abbey's wealth.

🍴 Sleeping & Eating

TOP CHOICE 5 North St
MODERN EUROPEAN £££
(☎01242-604566; www.5northstreetrestaurant.co.uk; 5 North St; 2-/3-course lunch £23/27, 7-course tasting menu £64; ☉lunch Wed-Sun, dinner Tue-Sat) From its splendid 400-year-old timbered exterior to what you eventually find on your plate, this Michelin-starred restaurant is a treat from start to finish. Chef Marcus' cooking is rooted in traditional ingredients but with exotic influences creeping in to create the likes of pigeon with cherry jus or bayleaf-infused rice pudding with Guinness ice cream. Superb.

White Hart Inn
HOTEL ££
(☎01242-602359; www.whitehartwinchcombe.co.uk; r £79-119) An appealing central inn that caters well to walkers; choose one of the three cheaper 'rambler' rooms, with shared bathrooms and iron bedsteads, or go for greater luxury in a superior room. The attached 'wine and sausage' restaurant (mains £10 to £18) serves a good selection of brasserie dishes, as well as seven types of the aforementioned sausages.

Westward at Sudeley Lodge
B&B ££
(☎01242-604372; www.westward-sudeley.co.uk; Sudeley; s/d from £45/90; ℗) At this robust 18th-century hunting lodge that doubles as a warm family home, you get to stay in one of three rooms with sweeping views of the valley. Decor is muted and deliberately dated, the owners hospitable without being intrusive, and the breakfasts ample.

❶ Getting There & Away

Bus 606 runs from Broadway (65 minutes, four daily Monday to Saturday) to Cheltenham via Winchcombe; bus 559 runs daily (Monday to Saturday only) from Broadway.

Stow-on-the-Wold
POP 2794
The highest town in the Cotswolds (244m), Stow is anchored by a large market square surrounded by handsome buildings and steep-walled alleyways, originally used to funnel the sheep into the fair. It's still an important market town and has long held a strategic place in Cotswold history, standing as it does on the Roman Fosse Way and at the junction of six roads. Today, it's famous for its twice-yearly Stow Horse Fair (May and October) and attracting a disproportionate number of people from passing coach tours.

Go Stow (www.go-stow.co.uk; 12 Talbot Ct; ☉10am-5pm Mon-Sat, 11am-4pm Sun) has information on local attractions, makes accommodation bookings and rents audio tours to the town.

🍴 Sleeping & Eating

Number 9
B&B ££
(☎01451-870333; www.number-nine.info; 9 Park St; s/d from £45/65; 🤍) Centrally located and wonderfully atmospheric, this friendly B&B is all wonderfully sloping floors and exposed

COTSWOLD FARM PARK

Cotswold Farm Park (www.cotswoldfarmpark.co.uk; adult/child £7.95/6.50; ☺10.30am-5pm Mar-Sep; ⊞), halfway between Stow and Winchcombe, near Guiting Power, is a wonderful day out for the family. The farm, owned by TV presenter Adam Henson, is designed to introduce little ones to the world of farm animals. There are milking and shearing demonstrations, an adventure playground and a 2-mile wildlife walk, not to mention the new food festival that started in May 2012 and is set to become an annual event.

beams. The three rooms are cosy but spacious, and have gleaming bathrooms and low ceilings that somehow manage not to make the rooms seem oppressive. Full English breakfast included.

Stow-on-the-Wold YHA   HOSTEL £

(☎0845 371 9540; www.yha.org.uk; The Square; dm £18; P@☎) In a you-can't-get-more-central-than-this location on the market square, the Cotswolds' only hostel is located in a wonderful 16th-century town house, with compact dorms, a children's play area and its own on-site cafe, offering inexpensive hot meals.

Old Butchers   MODERN EUROPEAN ££

(☎01451-831700; www.theoldbutchers.com; 7 Park St; mains £15-26; ☺closed Mon & Sun dinner) Simple, smart and sophisticated, this is Stow's top spot for dining, serving robust, local ingredients whipped up into sublime dishes with big flavours. It's mostly fine modern British cuisine, with chef Peter both drawing inspiration from Continental Europe and not shying away from bone marrow and calves' brains – which make an offally good meal in themselves!

Vine Leaf   BRITISH ££

(☎01451-832010; www.thevineleaf.co.uk; 10 Talbot Court; sandwiches £6.50-7.50, 2-/3-course set menu £11/14; ☺closed alternate Thu) A wonderful little catch-all cafe, serving hearty breakfasts (including pancakes with maple syrup), chunky lunchtime sandwiches with locally baked bread, burgers and more substantial mains crafted from locally sourced produce.

❶ Getting There & Away

Pullhams bus 855 links Stow with Moreton, Bourton, Northleach and Cirencester (eight daily Monday to Saturday). Bus 801 runs to Cheltenham, Moreton and Bourton (four daily Monday to Friday, nine on Saturday).

The Slaughters

POP 400

The picture-postcard villages of Upper and Lower Slaughter manage to maintain their unhurried medieval charm in spite of receiving a multitude of visitors. The village names have nothing to do with abattoirs; they are derived from the Old English 'sloughtre', meaning slough or muddy place, but today the River Eye is contained within limestone banks and meanders peacefully through the village past the 17th-century Lower Slaughter Manor to the Old Mill (www.oldmill-lowerslaughter.com; admission £2; ☺10am-6pm), which houses a small museum and an ice-cream parlour, famous for its fantastic organic ice cream.

Upper Slaughter is less visited than Lower Slaughter, and it's a pleasant stroll between the two villages. Take time to linger in the timeless streets of Upper Slaughter, taking in the peaceful atmosphere. For eating or sleeping, you can do no better than Lords of the Manor (☎01451-820243; www.lordsofthemanor.com; Upper Slaughter; d £199-495; P). 'Countryside splendour' is what comes to mind when you clap your eyes on this 17th-century mansion. The rooms are spacious and tasteful in the traditional sense of the word, the fittings luxurious, but you won't find TV or wi-fi here; the idea is to rest and take in the beautiful countryside and partake in traditional pastimes of horse riding and clay-pigeon shooting. The Michelin-starred restaurant is one of the best around (three-course menu £69), with imaginative, beautifully presented dishes.

To see the Slaughters at their best, arrive on foot from Bourton (a 1-mile walk) across the fields. From here you can continue for another mile across the fields to Upper Slaughter, with its own fine manor house and glorious cottages.

Northleach

POP 1855

Little visited and underappreciated, Northleach has been a little market town since 1227 and comprises late-medieval cottages, imposing merchants' stores and half-timbered Tudor houses. A wonderful mix of architectural styles cluster around the market square and the narrow laneways leading off it, but the highlight is the Church of St Peter & St Paul, a masterpiece of Cotswold Perpendicular style, its grandeur and architectural complexity testimony to its wool-era wealth. Its large traceried stained-glass windows and collection of memorial brasses are unrivalled in the region.

Near the square is Oak House, a 17th-century wool house that contains Keith Harding's World of Mechanical Music (www.mechanicalmusic.co.uk; adult/child £8/3.50; ◎10am-5pm), a fascinating museum of lovingly restored self-playing musical instruments where you can hear Rachmaninoff's works played on a reproducing piano.

Escape to the Cotswolds (www.cotswolds aonb.co.uk; ◎10am-4pm Wed-Sun Apr-Oct; admission free) is an excellent visitors' centre with displays on local conservation efforts and a plethora of tourist info. It's housed in the Old Prison (an attraction in itself), its cells initiating you into the world of Gloucestershire's crime and punishment through the ages.

Just outside town is Chedworth Roman Villa (NT; www.nationaltrust.org.uk; Yanworth; adult/child £9.40/4.70; ◎10am-5pm), one of the largest Roman villas in England. Built as a stately home in about AD 120, it contains some wonderful mosaics illustrating the seasons (some of which were only excavated in 2011), bathhouses and, a short walk away, a temple by the River Coln. It's 3 miles northwest of Fossebridge, off the A429.

For overnight stays, Wheatsheaf (☎01451-860244; www.cotswoldswheatsheaf.com; West End; d £100-130; @☎), a former coaching inn, is a favourite of those who love hunting, riding and other countryside pursuits. Its 14 rooms blend nice period touches, such as free-standing baths, with modern comforts, and the restaurant serves an excellent menu of hearty British dishes (£7 to £16).

❶ Getting There & Away

Swanbrook runs six buses a day Monday to Saturday between Cheltenham (30 minutes) and Northleach, and three to Oxford (one hour).

Pullham's bus 855 runs to Stow, Moreton, Bourton and Cirencester (eight daily Monday to Saturday).

Cirencester

POP 18,324

Refreshingly unpretentious, with narrow, winding streets and graceful town houses, charming Cirencester (siren-sester) is an affluent, elegant town. The lovely market square – the heart of the town – is surrounded by Victorian architecture, and the nearby streets showcase a harmonious medley of buildings from various eras.

It's difficult to believe that under the Romans (who called the town Corinium), Cirencester was second only to London in terms of size and importance and, although little of this period remains, you can still see the grassed-over ruins of one of the largest amphitheatres in the country. The medieval wool trade was also good to the town, with wealthy merchants funding the building of a superb church.

Today, Cirencester is the most important town in the southern Cotswolds, with lively Monday and Friday markets as important as the expensive boutiques and trendy delis that line its narrow streets.

The tourist office (☎01285-654180; www .cotswold.gov.uk; Park St; ◎10am-5pm Mon-Sat, 2-5pm Sun Apr-Oct, to 4pm rest of year) is in the museum and has a leaflet detailing a guided walk around the town and its historic buildings.

◉ Sights & Activities

TOP CHOICE Corinium Museum   MUSEUM

(www.cotswold.gov.uk/go/museum; Park St; adult/child £5/2.50; ◎10am-5pm Mon-Sat, 2-5pm Sun; ☞) This is a romp through Cirencester's extensive history up until the 19th century. The largest part of this modern, well-presented, partly interactive museum is, understandably, dedicated to its Roman past and covers everything from Roman forts and armies, daily life in an affluent household, health and beauty according to the Romans and funereal rites and religion; all brought to life through innovative displays and computer reconstructions. You can dress as a Roman soldier, meet an Anglo-Saxon princess and discover what Cirencester was like during its heyday as a wealthy medieval wool town. Highlights of the Roman collection include the beautiful

Hunting Dogs and Four Seasons floor mosaics, and a reconstructed Roman kitchen and butcher's shop.

Church of St John the Baptist   CHURCH
(www.cirenparish.co.uk; Market Sq; suggested donation £3; ⊙10am-5pm) The cathedral-like St John's, one of England's largest parish churches, boasts an outstanding Perpendicular-style tower (open Sat May to September) with wild flying buttresses, but it is the majestic three-storey south porch that is the real highlight. Built as an office by late-15th-century abbots, it subsequently became the medieval town hall.

Soaring arches, magnificent fan vaulting and a Tudor nave adorn the light-filled interior, where you'll also find a 15th-century painted stone pulpit – one of the few surviving pre-Reformation pulpits in Britain. The east window contains fine medieval stained glass, and a wall safe displays the Boleyn Cup, made for Anne Boleyn in 1535.

FREE **New Brewery Arts Centre**   ARTS CENTRE
(www.newbreweryarts.org.uk; Brewery Ct; ⊙9am-5pm Mon-Sat, 10am-4pm Sun) Home to over a dozen resident craft workers and host to regular exhibitions, workshops and classes, this arts centre is set in a beautifully converted Victorian brewery.

Cirencester Park   PARK
(Cecily Hill; ⊙8am-5pm) The extensive baroque-landscaped grounds of the Bathurst Estate, with a lovely walk along Broad Ride. No bicycles allowed.

🛏 Sleeping & Eating

No 12   B&B ££
(☎01285-640232; www.no12cirencester.co.uk; 12 Park St; d £100) This Georgian town house right in the centre of Cirencester has four gloriously unfussy rooms kitted out with a tasteful mix of antiques and modern furnishings. Think piles of feather pillows, merino blankets, extra-long beds, slick modern bathrooms and a host of little extras to make you smile.

Old Brewhouse   B&B ££
(☎01285-656099; www.theoldbrewhouse.com; 7 London Rd; s/d from £60/75; P🐾) Set in a charming 17th-century town house, this lovely B&B has pretty rooms with cast-iron beds and country-style florals or patchwork quilts. The courtyard rooms are newer and larger, with wooden floors, and the beautiful garden room even has its own patio.

Jesse's Bistro   MODERN BRITISH ££
(☎01285-641497; www.jessesbistro.co.uk; Black Jack St; mains £14-24; ⊙lunch Tue-Sun, dinner Wed-Sat) Hidden away in a cobbled stable yard with its own fishmonger and cheese shop, Jesse's is a great little place, with flagstone floors, wrought-iron chairs and mosaic tables. The great dishes feature local, seasonal produce, such as Cornish crab and Cotswold beef, but the real treat is the fresh fish and meat cooked in the wood-burning oven.

Made by Bob   MODERN BRITISH £
(www.foodmadebybob.com; 6 Corn Hall, Marketplace; mains £9-18; ⊙7.30am-6.30pm Mon-Sat; 🐾) Part deli, part hip brasserie, with a casual atmosphere and inventive, sophisticated fare on the daily changing menu. Lighter bites include doorstop sandwiches, and breakfast is better than in most other cafes: muesli, eggs benedict and, of course, the full English. Bob, you have done well.

Lick the Spoon   CAFE £
(www.lickthespoon.co.uk; 3 Black Jack St; drinks £3; ⊙9.30am-5pm Mon-Fri, 9am-5.30pm Sat, 11am-4pm Sun) One word: chocolate. It comes both in award-winning solid form, all boxed up for you to take away, and in glorious liquid form. Coffee is roasted on the premises for those desiring a caffeine kick alongside the sugar rush.

❶ Getting There & Away

Stagecoach bus 51 runs to Cheltenham Monday to Saturday (40 minutes, hourly). National Express buses run roughly hourly from Cirencester to Cheltenham Spa (30 minutes), Gloucester (one hour) and London (£14, 2½ hours).

Bibury

POP 1235
Once described by William Morris as 'the most beautiful village in England', Bibury is a Cotswold gem with a cluster of gorgeous riverside cottages and tangle of narrow streets flanked by wayward stone buildings. The main attraction is Arlington Row, a stunning sweep of cottages, now thought to be the most photographed street in Britain. Also worth a look is the 17th-century Arlington Mill, just a short stroll away across Rack Isle, a wildlife refuge once used as a cloth-drying area.

Few visitors make it past these two sights, but for a glimpse of the real Bibury, venture into the village proper behind

Arlington Row, where you'll find the Saxon Church of St Mary. Although much altered since its original construction, many 8th-century features are still visible among the 12th- and 13th-century additions. You can also fish for your supper at the Bibury Trout Farm (www.biburytroutfarm.co.uk; entry £3.75; ⊙9am-7pm Mon-Sat), a fishery with attractive picnic spots and smoked fish for sale.

Bibury's accommodation choices are underwhelming. The best place to stay is in the nearby village of Coln, where the jasmine-clad New Inn (✆0844 815 3434; www.new-inn .co.uk; Coln-St-Aldwyns; s/d from £135/145) offers quirky luxury in 16th-century surroundings. It's also the best bet in the area for food, with a particularly imaginative modern British menu (mains £12 to £20).

Buses 860, 865, and 866 pass through Bibury en route to Cirencester (15 minutes) at least once daily from Monday to Saturday.

Kelmscott

POP 101

Three miles east of Lechlade along the A417 lies the gorgeous Tudor pile Kelmscott Manor (✆01367-252486; www.kelmscottmanor. org.uk; adult/child £9/4.50; ⊙11am-5pm Wed & Sat Apr-Oct), once the summer home of William Morris, the poet, artist and founder of the Arts and Crafts Movement. The interior is true to his philosophy that one should not own anything that is neither beautiful nor useful, and the house contains many of Morris' personal effects, as well as fabrics and furniture designed by him and his associates.

From here it's well worth making a detour to the village of Southrop to dine at the Swan (✆01367-850205; www.theswanatsouthrop .co.uk; 2-/3-course menu £15/19; ⊙closed dinner-Sun), a 17th-century inn with stone floors, exposed beams and extremely sophisticated food at reasonable prices.

Tetbury

POP 5250

Once a prosperous wool-trading centre, Tetbury's busy streets are lined with medieval cottages, sturdy old town houses and Georgian Gothic gems. Prince Charles has an estate near here (Highgrove), as does the Princess Anne.

Tetbury is also a great place for antiques fans, with a shop of old curios on almost every corner. A good time to visit is the last Monday in May for the Woolsack Races (www .tetburywoolsack.co.uk) – a nod to the town's past – or in August, for the Festival of British Eventing (www.gatcombe-horse.co.uk).

Look out for the row of gorgeous medieval weavers' cottages that line the steep hill at Chipping Steps, leading up to the Chipping (market), surrounded by graceful 17th- and 18th-century town houses. From here, it's a short stroll to Market Sq, where the 17th-century Market House stands as if on stilts. Close by, the Georgian Gothic Church of St Mary the Virgin has a towering spire and wonderful interior.

If staying overnight, the Ormond (✆01666-505690; www.theormond.co.uk; 23 Long St; s/d from £79/110; 🅿🛜) is a central, modern hotel with a range of individually styled rooms sporting subtle but striking fabrics and funky wallpapers, and with some big, bold flavours served up at the award-winning restaurant. The Snooty Fox (✆01666-502436; www.snooty-fox.co.uk; s/d from £70/80), named by a rather sore owner who was snubbed by the local hunting community, is a pleasant old coaching inn with three brightly decorated rooms and a menu of solid Modern British classics (mains £10 to £22). The best place to eat in town is undoubtedly the French-inspired Chef's Table (✆01666-504466; www.thechefstable.co.uk; 49 Long St; mains £9-13; ⊙closed dinner Sun-Tue), a fantastic deli and bistro serving up a mouth-watering lunch of local organic ingredients rustled up into hearty rustic dishes, such as bouillabaisse and crispy pork belly.

Cotswold Green bus 29 runs between Tetbury and Stroud (30 minutes, six daily Monday to Saturday). Wessex Connect bus 620 goes to Bath (1¼ hours, six daily Monday to Friday, four on Saturday), stopping at Westonbirt Arboretum en route.

Uley

POP 1100

This lovely little hamlet, with its quaint village green and jumble of pretty houses, sits below the overgrown remains of the largest Iron Age hill fort in England, Uley Bury. Dating from about 300 BC, the fort and its 2-mile perimeter walk provide spectacular views over the Severn Vale; follow the steep path that runs from the village church.

If you're driving, access to the car park is off the B4066, north of the village.

Virtually untouched since the mid-1870s, Woodchester Mansion (www.woodchester mansion.org.uk; adult/child £6.50/free; ⊘11am-4pm Sat & Sun Easter-Oct) is an incredible place, formerly belonging to the Leigh family and abandoned before it was finished, yet amazingly grand and graceful. Doors open to nowhere, fireplaces are stuck halfway up walls, and corridors end at ledges with views of the ground below. The house also features an impressive set of gruesome gargoyles and is home to one of England's most important colonies of horseshoe bats and several resident ghosts. It's a mile north of Uley on the B4066.

Bus 20 runs between Uley and Stroud (55 minutes, four times daily Monday to Saturday).

Berkeley

POP 1865

An astounding relic from medieval times, Berkeley Castle (www.berkeley-castle.com; adult/child £9.50/5; ⊘11am-5.30pm Thu, Sun & bank hols Apr-Oct) has remained virtually untouched since it was built as a sturdy fortress in Norman times, though it has been the home of the Berkeleys for nearly 900 years. Edward II was imprisoned and then murdered here in 1327 (allegedly with a hot poker up his rectum) on the order of his wife, Queen Isabella, and her lover. You can still see the King's Gallery, with its cell and dungeon. You can also visit the castle's state rooms, as well as the medieval Great Hall, Picture Gallery and kitchen. Regular jousting events and medieval banquets are held here in summer.

Berkeley is also home to a man who's had a great impact on our lives; Jenner Museum (www.jennermuseum.com; Church Lane; adult/child £6/3.50, incl Berkeley Castle £14/7.50; ⊘12.30-5.30pm select days Apr-Oct, check website) honours the life and works of Edward Jenner, country doctor who discovered the principle of vaccination. The museum is in the beautiful Queen Anne house, where the doctor performed the first smallpox vaccination in 1796. Follow the path from the castle through St Mary's churchyard.

Bus 207 plies the route between Berkeley and Gloucester (55 minutes, three times daily Monday to Saturday).

Stroud

POP 13,058

Stroud once hummed with the sound of more than 150 cloth mills operating around the town, but when the bottom fell out of the market, the town went into decline. Although a handful of the handsome old mills are still operating, the pleasant town has become a bohemian enclave known for its fair-trade shops, delis and independent stores. This is still one of the most important market towns in the Cotswolds, with four dozen or so independent stallholders converging every Saturday on the town for the farmers' market. Another great place for organic food, books and more is the Shambles Market (www.shamblesmarket stroud.co.uk), which takes place in the historic Shambles on Friday and Saturday.

In the centre of town, the Subscription Rooms are home to the tourist office (☑01453-760960; www.visitthecotswolds.org.uk; George St; ⊘10am-5pm Mon-Sat).

The main attraction is the diverting Museum in the Park (www.stroud.gov.uk/museum; Stratford Pk; ⊘10am-5pm Tue-Fri, 11am-5pm Sat & Sun; ♿), set in an 18th-century mansion surrounded by parkland. The bright, well-lit museum tells the history of the town and its cloth-making, and there are interactive displays of everything from dinosaurs to Victorian toys and Stroud's female artists. A separate gallery hosts eclectic contemporary art exhibitions.

The nicest place to stay is in nearby Nailsworth at the 16th-century Egypt Mill (☑01453-833449; www.egyptmill.com; s/d £95/105; P🐾), where you can fall asleep to the sound of the water gurgling over the weir. This is also one of the best restaurants in town, serving the likes of great fish and chips and goat's cheese and onion marmalade tart, with a lovely waterside location.

For a relaxed meal, head for Star Anise (www.staraniseartscafe.com; Gloucester St; mains £6-8; ⊘8am-5pm Mon-Fri, 8.30am-5pm Sat, 10am-2pm Sun; 🖉), a vegetarian cafe serving inventive dishes (including a couple of fish ones) featuring local produce. It's a popular spot for Sunday brunch, and often hosts live music and other community events.

Another good bet is Woodruffs Organic Cafe (www.woodruffsorganiccafe.co.uk; 24 High St; mains £5.50-9; ⊘8.30am-5pm Mon-Sat), a small, cheerful place with a schizophrenic menu

OXFORD, COTSWOLDS & AROUND BERKELEY

of salads, soups, tapas, fruit smoothies and even vegan ice cream.

Bus 46 runs hourly to Painswick (10 minutes) and Cheltenham (40 minutes) from Monday to Saturday, while bus 54 serves Cirencester (20 minutes, one to four daily Monday to Saturday). Trains run roughly hourly to London (£18, 1½ to two hours), Gloucester (20 minutes) and Cheltenham (40 minutes).

Painswick

POP 1666

One of the most beautiful and unspoilt towns in the Cotswolds, hilltop Painswick is an absolute gem. Despite its obvious charms, Painswick sees only a trickle of visitors, so you can wander the narrow winding streets and admire the picture-perfect cottages, handsome stone town houses and medieval inns in your own good time.

◉ Sights & Activities

Running downhill beside and behind the church is a series of gorgeous streetscapes. Look out for Bisley St, the original main drag, which was superseded by the now ancient-looking New St in medieval times. Just south of the church, rare iron stocks stand in the street.

St Mary's Church   CHURCH

The village centres on a fine, Perpendicular wool church, its pointy steeple fingering the sky, surrounded by tabletop tombs and exactly 99 clipped yew trees that resemble giant lollipops. Legend has it that if the 100th yew tree were allowed to grow, the devil would appear and shrivel it. They planted it anyway, to celebrate the millennium and –

CHEESE OF VICTORY

Cooper's Hill in Cranham, near Painswick, is the location of the Cotswolds' most dangerous sport: the annual Cheese-Rolling (www.cheese-rolling.co.uk; ⊙last bank hol May). Laugh if you will, but this 200-year-old tradition sees locals running, tumbling and sliding down a steep hill in pursuit of a 7lb round of Double Gloucester cheese; it's only a 90m run, but people get hurt every year. The prize? The cheese itself, and the glory of catching it.

lo and behold! – one of the trees toppled several years later, making the number an odd 99 again. The work of the Horned One, perhaps?

Painswick Rococo Garden   GARDEN

(www.rococogarden.co.uk; adult/child £6.50/3; ⊙11am-5pm mid-Jan–Oct; ⊞) Just a mile north of town, the ostentatious Painswick Rococo Garden is the area's biggest attraction and the only garden of its type in England, designed by Benjamin Hyett in the 1740s and now restored to its former glory. Winding paths soften the otherwise strict geometrical precision, bringing visitors around the central vegetable garden to the many Gothic follies dotted in the grounds. There's also a children's nature trail and maze.

⌑ Sleeping

TOP CHOICE Cotswolds88   BOUTIQUE HOTEL £££

(☑01452-813688; www.cotswolds88.com; Kemps Lane; d £110-280; ⓟ🐾) This is a happy marriage of 18th-century architecture and a modern interior. With avant-garde furnishings, everything here is over the top – from the wallpaper to the psychedelic lighting. Spacious, individually decorated rooms come with every creature comfort, and the suites have four-poster beds and spas. The restaurant is one of the region's best, featuring sophisticated yet playful fare.

Cardynham House   HOTEL £££

(☑01452-814006; www.cardynham.co.uk; Tibbiwell St; s/d from £65/87; ⊙closed Mon & dinner Sun; 🐾) Each of the rooms at 15th-century Cardynham House has a different theme, four-poster beds and heavy patterned fabrics. Choose the Shaker-style New England room, the opulent Arabian Nights room, the chintzy Old Tuscany room or for a private pool and garden, the Pool Room. Downstairs, the Bistro (mains £10 to £20) serves modern British cuisine.

❶ Getting There & Away

Bus 46 connects Cheltenham (30 minutes) and Stroud (10 minutes) with Painswick hourly Monday to Saturday.

GLOUCESTERSHIRE

Gloucestershire's greatest asset is the elegant Regency town of Cheltenham, with its tree-lined terraces, upmarket boutiques and a tempting collection of dining options.

DON'T MISS

GLOUCESTER CATHEDRAL

Gloucester (*glos*-ter), originally a settlement for retired Roman soldiers, came into its own in medieval times, when the pious public flocked to see the grave of Edward II and financed the building of what remains one of England's most beautiful cathedrals.

The cathedral (www.gloucestercathedral.org.uk; College Green; suggested donation £5; ⊘7.30am-6pm; guided tours: 10.30am-4pm Mon-Sat, noon-2.30pm Sun; tower tours: adult/child £4/1.50; 2.30pm Wed-Fri, 1.30pm & 2.30pm Sat) is the first and best example of Gothic Perpendicular style. Originally the site of a Saxon abbey, a Norman church was built here by a group of Benedictine monks in the 12th century, and when Edward II was murdered in 1327, the church was chosen as his burial place. Edward's tomb proved so popular that Gloucester became a centre of pilgrimage.

Inside, the best of Norman and Gothic design are skillfully combined with sturdy columns, creating a sense of gracious solidity. From the elaborate 14th-century wooden choir stalls, you'll get a good view of the imposing Great East Window, one of the largest in England. Upstairs, if you stand at one end of the curving Whispering Gallery, a person at the other end will hear your words reverberating across the wonderfully elaborate lierne vaulting.

Beneath the window in the northern ambulatory is Edward II's magnificent tomb, and nearby is the late 15th-century Lady Chapel, a glorious patchwork of stained glass. One of the cathedral's treasures is the exquisite Great Cloister (used in the first two *Harry Potter* films). Completed in 1367, it is the first example of fan vaulting in England and only matched in beauty by Henry VIII's Chapel at Westminster Abbey.

National Express has buses roughly every two hours to London (£6, 3¼ hours). Buses 94 and 98 run to Cheltenham (30 minutes) every 10 minutes Monday to Saturday, and every 20 minutes on Sunday.

The London-bound train stops at Cheltenham (11 minutes, every 20 minutes).

The county capital, Gloucester, is well worth a visit for its magnificent Gothic cathedral, while to the west, the picturesque Forest of Dean is a leafy backwater perfect for cycling and walking.

Cheltenham

POP 110,013

Cheltenham is a city oozing an air of gracious refinement, its streetscapes largely left intact since its heyday as a spa resort in the 18th century. At the time, it rivalled Bath as the place for the sick, hypochondriac and merely moneyed to go, and today it is still riddled with historic buildings, beautifully proportioned terraces and manicured squares.

◉ Sights

FREE Cheltenham Art
Gallery & Museum   MUSEUM
(www.cheltenhammuseum.org.uk; Clarence St) Cheltenham's excellent museum depicts Cheltenham life through the ages and has wonderful displays on William Morris and the Arts and Crafts Movement, as well as Dutch and British art, rare Chinese and English ceramics and a section on Scott's ill-fated expedition to Antarctica.

FREE Pittville Pump Room   CONCERT HALL
(www.pittvillepumproom.org.uk; Pittville Park; ⊘9am-noon) Built in 1830 as a centrepiece to a vast estate, the Pittville Pump Room is Cheltenham's finest Regency building, originally used as a spa. Wander into the main auditorium and sample the pungent spa waters from the fountain, or just explore the vast parklands and the lake it overlooks.

Holst Birthplace Museum   MUSEUM
(www.holstmuseum.org.uk; 4 Clarence Rd; adult/child £4.50/4; ⊘10am-5pm Tue-Sat, 1.30-5pm Sun) The composer Gustav Holst was born in Cheltenham in 1874, and the rooms of his childhood home are laid out in typical period fashion. They feature many of Holst's personal possessions, including the piano on which most of *The Planets* was composed, as well as photos of the notoriously camera-shy composer.

Cheltenham

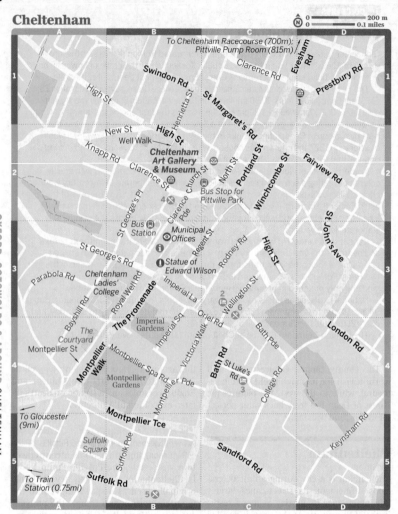

Cheltenham Racecourse RACECOURSE
(www.cheltenham.co.uk) Cheltenham's race-course can attract up to 40,000 people a day during the National Hunt Festival in mid-March. This is England's premier steeple-chase event and is attended by droves of breeders, trainers, riders and spectators. The racecourse is about a mile north of the city centre, via Evesham Rd.

🛌 Sleeping

Book as far in advance as possible during the festivals – especially for race week.

TOP CHOICE Ellenborough Park BOUTIQUE HOTEL £££
(☎ 01242-807541; www.ellenboroughpark.com; Southam Rd; d from £230; P@☎) If you like style in the traditional sense of the word, this majestic country house, sitting amid landscaped grounds, will appeal. Each of the 62 rooms and suites is individually de-signed; decorative fireplaces are mixed and matched with modern features, such as iPod docks. Take the Prestbury Rd/B4632 northeast from the city centre; the hotel is signposted off it.

Cheltenham

Big Sleep HOTEL **££**

(☏01242-696999; www.thebigsleephotel.com; Wellington St; r £55-160, f £90-300; P@ᗙ) This place is all designer looks, thoroughly modern rooms and no-frills minimalism. The family studios have their own kitchenette, and breakfast is included in the price. A brilliant option if you're travelling with family or friends.

Brennan B&B **£**

(☏01242-525904; www.brennanguesthouse.co.uk; 21 St Luke's Rd; s/d £30/50; Pᗙ) Just five compact rooms with sinks, all decked out in creams, a convenient central location overlooking St Luke's church, and an attentive, congenial host make this the pick of the budget B&B bunch. Full English breakfast included.

✗ Eating

  Le Champignon
Sauvage FRENCH **£££**

(☏01242-573449; www.lechampignonsauvage.co.uk; 24-26 Suffolk Rd; 2-/3-course set menu £48/59; ☉Tue-Sat) For nearly a quarter of a century this Cheltenham institution has been delighting visitors and locals alike with chef David's finely executed dishes and pairing of flavours, such as cured pigeon breast with fig compote and inspired and unlikely sounding desserts such as the chocolate and olive tart with fennel ice cream.

TOP CHOICE **Prithvi** INDIAN **££**

(☏01242-226229; www.prithvirestaurant.com; 37 Bath Rd; 5-course taster menu £25; ☉dinner Tue, lunch & dinner Wed-Sun) A brand new Indian restaurant, Prithvi's top-notch service matches its immaculate dishes. Each mouthwatering offering is presented with great attention to detail, and the superb five-course taster menu is one of the biggest treats in Cheltenham.

Dfly ASIAN FUSION **££**

(1a Crescent Pl; mains £7-13; ☉Tue-Sat) Bar, restaurant and hip hang-out rolled into one, Dfly is a friendly place with an eclectic menu of well-executed Thai, Malaysian and Chinese dishes, as well great sushi.

ℹ Information

Tourist office (☏01242-522878; www.visitcheltenham.info; 77 The Promenade; ☉9.30am-5pm Mon-Sat) The tourist office will move into the Cheltenham Art Gallery & Museum once it reopens in 2013.

ℹ Getting There & Away

Bus

National Express runs buses to **London** (£7, 2½ hours, hourly). Other bus routes include:

Cirencester Bus 51 (40 minutes, hourly).

Gloucester Bus 94 (30 minutes, every 10 minutes Monday to Saturday, every 20 minutes on Sunday).

Oxford Bus 853 (£7.50, 1½ hours, three daily Monday to Saturday, one Sunday).

Train

Trains run to **London** (£31, 2¼ hours), **Bristol** (£7.30, 50 minutes), **Gloucester** (£3.60, 11 minutes) and **Bath** (£11.60, 1¼ hours) roughly every half-hour.

ℹ Getting Around

Bus D runs to Pittville Park and the train station from Clarence St every 10 minutes.

Forest of Dean

POP 79,982

The Forest of Dean is the oldest oak forest in England and a wonderfully scenic place to walk, cycle or paddle. The 42-sq-mile woodland, designated England's first National Forest Park in 1938, was formerly a royal hunting ground and a centre of iron and coal mining, and its mysterious depths supposedly inspired Tolkien's forest of Middle Earth in *The Lord of the Rings* and JK Rowling's Forbidden Forest in the *Harry Potter* adventures.

Sights & Activities

TOP CHOICE Puzzle Wood   ADVENTURE PARK
(www.puzzlewood.net;adult/child£6/4.50; ⊙10am-5pm; ⊕) A pre-Roman, open-cast ore mine, overgrown with eerie lichen-covered trees, this place has a maze of paths, weird rock formations, tangled vines and dark passageways, so the potential for adventure is immense. If it seems familiar, that's because a recent *Dr Who* episode and the BBC1 *Merlin* series were shot here. Puzzle Wood is 1 mile south of Coleford on the B4228.

Clearwell Caves   CAVES
(www.clearwellcaves.com;adult/child£6/4; ⊙10am-5pm) To explore iron mining – one of the oldest professions of the residents of the Forest of Dean – descend into a damp subterranean world, comprising a warren of dimly-lit passageways, caverns and pools and home to several species of bats. The caves are signposted off the B4228 a mile south of Coleford.

Dean Heritage Centre   MUSEUM
(www.deanheritagemuseum.com; Camp Mill, Soudley; adult/child£6/3; ⊙10am-5pm; ⊕) This entertaining museum looks at everything from the forest's geology to Roman occupation, medieval hunting laws, free mining, cottage crafts and coal mining. There are plenty of sights for kids, too, from a mini-zoo with pigs, rabbits and weasels, to the current pride and joy – the Gruffalo Trail, featuring life-size wooden carvings from Julia Donaldson's classic picture book.

Cycling   CYCLING
There is a number of excellent cycling trails around the Forest of Dean, varying from tranquil family-friendly jaunts to more demanding circuits. You can hire both leisure bikes and full suspension mountain bikes (£16 to £26 per day) and get advice on cycling routes at Pedalabikeaway (p426) near Coleford.

✗ Eating

Three Choirs Vineyard   MODERN BRITISH **££**
(☎01531-890223; www.threechoirs.com; Newent; mains £15-17) This bright and airy restaurant serves classic brasserie dishes using locally sourced produce if possible. You can also take a guided tour of the working vineyard (£7.50) and try the award-winning wines before departing with a few bottles from the gift shop.

⊕ Getting There & Away

From Gloucester, buses 30 and 31 run to Coleford (one hour, twice hourly) via Cinderford and there are trains to Lydney (20 minutes, hourly).

BEDFORDSHIRE & BUCKINGHAMSHIRE

The sweeping valleys and forested hills of Bedfordshire and Buckinghamshire once attracted the rich and famous, who used them as a rural hideaway for their majestic stately homes and grand gardens, many of which are still intact today.

Woburn Abbey & Safari Park

Once a Cistercian abbey but dissolved by Henry VIII and awarded to the earl of Bedford, Woburn Abbey (www.woburn.co.uk; adult/child £13.50/6.50; ⊙11am-4pm Apr-Sep) is a wonderful country pile set within a 1200-hectare deer park. The opulent house displays paintings by Gainsborough, van Dyck and Canaletto. Highlights include the bedroom of Queen Victoria and Prince Albert; the beautiful wall hangings and

---

DON'T MISS

STOWE GARDENS

The Stowe Gardens (NT; www.national trust.org.uk; adult/child £9/5; ⊙10am-5.30pm Wed-Sun Mar-Oct), worked on by the greatest British landscape gardeners, including Charles Bridgeman, William Kent and 'Capability' Brown on behalf of the supremely wealthy Temple family in the 18th century, are the most impressive you're ever likely to see. The 400-hectare property comprises 32 temples and structures, spread throughout the themed landscapes – from the column-studded Western Garden with its statuary and the South Vista with its symmetrical Lake Pavilions and splendid Corinthian Arch, to the intricately designed temples of Eastern Garden and the tranquillity of the Elysian Fields, where you can imagine the souls of dead warriors resting in peace for all eternity.

Stowe is 3 miles northwest of Buckingham off the A422.

ST ALBANS

A bustling market town with a host of crooked Tudor buildings and elegant Georgian town houses, St Albans was founded as Verulamium after the Roman invasion of AD 43 but was renamed in the 3rd century after a Roman soldier, Alban, who became England's first Christian martyr.

St Albans Cathedral (www.stalbanscathedral.org.uk; admission by donation; ⊙8.30am-5.45pm; tours 11.30am & 2.30pm Mon-Fri, 11.30am & 2pm Sat, 2.30pm Sun), built around the tomb of St Alban by King Offa of Mercia in 793, is a magnificent melange of Norman and Gothic architecture. The longest medieval nave in the country gives way to ornate ceilings, semi-lost wall paintings, an elaborate nave screen and, of course, the shrine of St Alban, hiding behind a stone reredos. There are free guided tours daily.

The town's other attraction is the Verulamium Museum (www.stalbansmuseums.org.uk; St Michael's St; adult/child £3.80/2; ⊙museum 10am-5.30pm Mon-Sat, 2-5.30pm Sun, hypocaust 10am-4.30pm Mon-Sat, 2-4.30pm Sun), a fantastic expose of everyday life under the Romans, the displays including household objects, legionnaires' armour, statuary, jewellery, glassware and grave goods.The highlight, however, is the Mosaic Room, where five superb mosaic floors, uncovered between 1930 and 1955, are laid out, the most splendid of which is the Shell Mosaic.

Grab some lunch at Lussmanns Eatery (☑01727-851941; www.lussmans.com; Waxhouse Gate; mains £12-17), a bright, modern restaurant serving a changing monthly menu of creative British dishes with Mediterranean touches.

The tourist office (☑01727-864511; www.stalbans.gov.uk; Market Pl; ⊙10am-4.30pm Mon-Sat) can book entertaining themed guided walks of the city.

Trains run between St Pancras and St Albans (£10.60, 20 minutes) every 10 minutes.

cabinets of the Chinese Room, plus the mysterious story of the Flying Duchess.

On an equally grand scale is Woburn Safari Park (www.woburn.co.uk/safari; adult/child £20/15; ⊙10am-5pm), the country's largest drive-through animal reserve. Rhinos, tigers, lions, zebras, bison, monkeys, elephants and giraffes roam the grounds, while in the 'foot safari' area, you can see sea lions, penguins and lemurs.

For both attractions, buy a Passport Ticket (adult/child £22.50/15.50), which can be used on two separate days within any 12-month period.

The abbey and safari park are easily accessible by car off the M1 motorway. Trains run from London King's Cross to Flitwick, a 15-minute taxi trip (£17 to £22) to Woburn.

Bletchley Park

Once England's best-kept secret, Bletchley Park (www.bletchleypark.org.uk; The Manor, Bletchley; adult/child £12/6; ⊙9.30am-5pm) was the scene of a huge code-breaking operation during WWII, dramatised in the 2001 film Enigma. Almost 8500 people worked here in total secrecy – intercepting, decrypting, translating and interpreting enemy correspondence. Joining one of the guided tours (www.bletchleypark.org.uk; ⊙2 daily Mon-Fri, hourly weekends) gives you a real insight into the complex code-breaking process and the hard work, frustration and successes that shaped this secret war effort, while inside Station X you can also see the Enigma machine itself – crucial to the breaking of the code.

Bletchley is just south of Milton Keynes off the B4034. Trains run from London Euston to Bletchley (£15, 40 minutes, hourly).

BERKSHIRE

Long known as the 'Royal County of Berkshire', this rather posh and prosperous part of the world acts as a country getaway for some of England's most influential figures. Within easy reach of London and yet entirely different in character, the pastoral landscape features handsome villages and historic houses, as well as some of the top attractions in the country. Few visitors make it past the historic towns of Windsor and Eton, home to the Queen's favourite castle and the world-renowned public school, but wander further afield and you'll be rewarded with tranquil rural countryside and exquisitely maintained villages.

Windsor & Eton

POP 30,568

Dominated by the massive bulk of Windsor Castle, these twin towns have a rather surreal atmosphere, with the morning pomp and ceremony of the changing of the guards in Windsor, and the sight of school boys dressed in formal tailcoats wandering the streets of tiny Eton.

Windsor town centre is full of expensive boutiques, grand cafes and trendy restaurants. Eton, by comparison, is far quieter, its one-street centre lined with antique shops and art galleries. Both are easily doable as a day trip from London.

◉ Sights

Windsor Castle   CASTLE
(www.royalcollection.org.uk; adult/child £17/10; ◷9.45am-5.15pm) The largest and oldest occupied fortress in the world, Windsor Castle is a majestic vision of battlements and towers used for state occasions and as the Queen's weekend retreat.

William the Conqueror first established a royal residence in Windsor in 1070; since then successive monarchs have rebuilt, remodelled and refurbished the castle complex to create the massive and sumptuous palace that stands here today. Henry II replaced the wooden stockade in 1165 with a stone round tower and built the outer walls to the north, east and south; Charles II gave the state apartments a baroque makeover; George IV swept in with his preference for Gothic style; and Queen Victoria refurbished a beautiful chapel in memory of her beloved Albert.

Join a free guided tour (every half-hour) or take a multilingual audio tour of the lavish state rooms and beautiful chapels. The State Apartments and St George's Chapel are closed at times during the year. If the Queen is in residence, you'll see the Royal Standard flying from the Round Tower.

Windsor & Eton

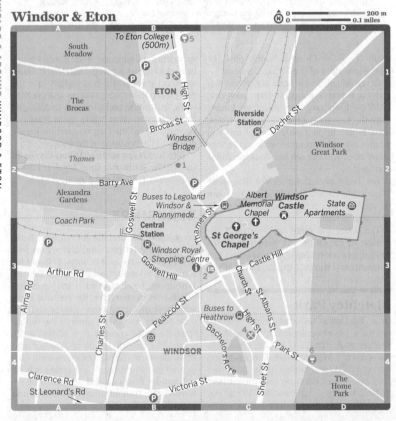

Queen Mary's Dolls' House
Your first sight will be an incredible dolls' house, designed by Sir Edwin Lutyens for Queen Mary in 1924. The attention to detail is spellbinding – there's running water, electricity and lighting, tiny Crown Jewels and vintage wine in the cellar!

State Apartments
The Grand Staircase sets the tone for the rooms, and highlights include **St George's Hall**: on the ceiling, the shields of the Knights of the Garter (originally from George IV's time here) were re-created after the fire of 1992. The blank shields indicate knights who had fallen out of favour.

For intimate gatherings (just 60 people), the Queen entertains in the Waterloo Chamber, its paintings commemorating the victory over Napoleon.

The King's Dressing Room has some of the most important Renaissance paintings in the royal collection. Alongside Sir Anthony van Dyck's magnificent Triple Portrait of Charles I, you will see works by Hans Holbein, Rembrandt and Peter Paul Rubens.

St George's Chapel
This elegant chapel, commissioned for the Order of the Garter by Edward IV in 1475, is one of Britain's finest examples of Perpendicular Gothic architecture. The nave and fan-vaulted roof were completed under Henry VII, but the final nail was struck under Henry VIII in 1528.

The chapel – along with Westminster Abbey – serves as a royal mausoleum. The most recent royal burial occurred in April 2002, when the body of George VI's widow,

Windsor & Eton

⊙ Top Sights

⊙ Activities, Courses & Tours

⊙ Sleeping

⊗ Eating

⊙ Drinking

READING FESTIVAL

Each August Bank Holiday weekend, about 80,000 revellers descend on the industrial town of Reading for one of the country's biggest rock music events. The Reading Festival (www .readingfestival.com) is a three-day extravaganza that features the likes of Kasabian, Foo Fighters, the Maccabees, and Florence and the Machine. Tickets will set you back about £85 per day or £198 for a three-day pass.

the Queen Mother (1900–2002), was transported here in a splendid and sombre procession and interred alongside her husband. In April 2005, Prince Charles and Camilla Parker-Bowles were blessed here following their civil marriage in the town's Guildhall.

St George's Chapel closes on Sunday, but time your visit well and you can attend Evensong at 5.15pm daily except Wednesday.

Albert Memorial Chapel
Originally built in 1240 and dedicated to Edward the Confessor, this small chapel was the place of worship for the Order of the Garter until St George's Chapel snatched that honour. After the death of Prince Albert at Windsor Castle in 1861, Queen Victoria ordered its elaborate redecoration as a tribute to her husband. A major feature of the restoration is the magnificent vaulted roof, whose gold mosaic pieces were crafted in Venice. There's a monument to the prince, although he's actually buried with Queen Victoria in the Frogmore Royal Mausoleum in the castle grounds.

Windsor Great Park
Stretching behind Windsor Castle almost all the way to Ascot, Windsor Great Park covers about 40 sq miles and features a lake, walking tracks, a bridleway and gardens. The Savill Garden (www.theroyallandscape .co.uk; adult/child £8.50/3.75; ⊙10am-6pm) is particularly lovely and located about 4 miles south of Windsor Castle. Take the A308 out of town and follow the brown signs.

The Long Walk is a 3-mile jaunt along a tree-lined path from King George IV Gate to the Copper Horse statue (of George III) on Snow Hill, the highest point of the park. The Queen can occasionally be spotted driving down the Long Walk, accompanied only by a bodyguard.

OXFORD, COTSWOLDS & AROUND WINDSOR & ETON

Changing of the Guard

A fabulous spectacle, with triumphant tunes from a military band and plenty of foot stamping, the changing of the guard (⊙11am Mon-Sat Apr-Jul, alternate days Aug-Mar) draws crowds to the castle gates each day to watch the smartly attired lads in red uniforms and bear-fur hats do their thing. Stay to the right of the crowd for better views.

Eton College   PUBLIC SCHOOL

(www.etoncollege.com; adult/child £7/5.50; ⊙guided tours 2pm & 3.15pm daily during school hols, Wed, Fri-Sun during term time) Eton's main street here is surprisingly hushed as you make your way down to the most enduring and illustrious symbol of England's class system, Eton College.

Those who have studied here include 18 prime ministers, countless princes, kings and maharajahs, famous explorers, authors, and economists – among them the Duke of Wellington, Princes William and Harry, George Orwell, Ian Fleming, Aldous Huxley, Sir Ranulph Fiennes, John Maynard Keynes and Bear Grylls.

Eton is the largest and most famous public (meaning very private) school in England; it's only under the current headmaster that Eton has begun to accept applicants from state schools rather than just private schools.

It was founded by Henry VI in 1440 with a view towards educating 70 highly qualified boys awarded a scholarship from a fund endowed by the king. Every year since then, 70 King's Scholars (aged 12 to 14) have been chosen based on the results of a highly competitive exam; these pupils are housed in separate quarters from the rest of the 1300 or so other students, known as Oppidans.

All the boys are boarders and must wear formal tailcoats, waistcoats and white collars to lessons (though the top hats went out in 1948). Fencing, shooting, polo and beagling are on the list of school sporting activities, and Eton very much embodies the old ideal of *mens sana in corpore sano* (a healthy mind in a healthy body).

Tours of Eton take in the chapel, the cloisters, the Museum of Eton Life – with a feature on Eton's star sport of rowing – the lower school, with names etched into its ancient desks by bored students, and the school yard, with a memorial to Etonians who died in the two world wars. You may recognise some of the buildings, as *Chariots of Fire*, *The Madness of King George*, *Mrs Brown* and *Shakespeare in Love* are just some of the movies that have been filmed here.

Buy tickets in advance at the tourist office, as they cannot be purchased at Eton itself.

Legoland Windsor   AMUSEMENT PARK

(www.legoland.co.uk; Winkfield Rd; adult/child £43/34; ⊙from 10am Mar-early Nov) A fun-filled theme park of white-knuckle rides, Legoland is more about the thrills of scaring yourself silly than the joys of building your own castle from the eponymous bricks: the professionals have already done this for you, with almost 40 million Lego bricks transformed into some of the world's greatest landmarks. Book online to save £9 off the ticket prices.

The Legoland shuttle bus departs opposite the Theatre Royal from 10am, with the last bus returning 30 minutes after the park has closed.

Tours

French Brothers   BOAT TOURS

(www.frenchbrothers.co.uk; Clewer Court Rd; ⊙11am-5pm Easter-Oct) French Brothers runs a variety of boat trips to Runnymede (adult/child £5.20/2.60, 45 minutes) and around Windsor and Eton (adult/child £8.40/4.20, two hours). Boats leave from just next to Windsor Bridge. If you fancy doing the hop-on/hop-off bus plus a 35-minute boat trip, a combined boat and bus ticket costs £12.50/6 per adult/child.

RUNNYMEDE: A WORLD FIRST

In June 1215, King John met his barons and bishops in a large field 3 miles southeast of Windsor, and over the next few days they hammered out an agreement on a basic charter of rights guaranteeing the liberties of the king's subjects and restricting the monarch's absolute power. The document they signed was the Magna Carta, the world's first constitution. It formed the basis for statutes and charters throughout the world's democracies. (Both the national and state constitutions of the United States, drawn up more than 500 years later, paraphrase this document.)

Today, the field remains pretty much as it was, except that it now features two lodges (1930) designed by Sir Edward Lutyens. In the woods behind the field are two memorials.

Runnymede is on the A308, 3 miles southeast of Windsor. Bus 71 stops near here on the Windsor–Egham route.

Tourist Office

(☎01753-743900; www.windsor.gov.uk; adult/child £6/3; ☺11.30am Sat & Sun) Themed guided walks of the city.

🛏 Sleeping

Windsor and Eton are easily doable as a day trip from London. If you wish to remain after the hordes of visitors have gone home, there's a good selection of quality hotels and B&Bs, but few budget options.

Harte & Garter Hotel & Spa

HOTEL **££**

(☎01753-863426; www.foliohotels.com/harteandgarter; High St; d from £99; ☎) Right opposite the castle, this Victorian hotel blends period style with modern furnishings. High ceilings, giant fireplaces, decorative cornices and dark woods seamlessly combine with contemporary fabrics, plasma-screen TVs and traditional, cast-iron baths. Some rooms enjoy wonderful views over the castle and all guests can enjoy the luxurious spa in the converted stable block.

76 Duke Street

B&B **££**

(☎01753-620636; www.76dukestreet.co.uk; 76 Duke St; s/d £80/100; P☎) Two immaculate, centrally located double rooms, presided over by a welcoming hostess who cooks up a superb breakfast. The second bedroom is only available if booked along with the first, so it's ideal for a family or two couples. Head west along Arthur Rd, turn right into Vansittart Rd, then right, and right again into Duke St.

✖ Eating & Drinking

Windsor and Eton are packed with pubs and brasseries, with a cluster of good sandwich chains situated under the railway arches of the central station.

Gilbey's

MODERN BRITISH **££**

(☎01753-854921; www.gilbeygroup.com; 82-83 High St, Eton; 2-/3-course menu £18.50/24) Small but perfectly formed, this restaurant is one of the area's finest. Terracotta tiling and a sunny courtyard garden and conservatory give Gilbey's a Continental cafe feel, complemented by a superb modern British menu. Expect the likes of chicken with wild mushroom risotto, and roast lamb. There's an extensive choice of wine.

Green Olive

GREEK **£**

(www.green-olive.co.uk; 10 High St; 2-/3-course lunch £10-13; ✎) A great spot for a light lunch, Green Olive dishes up generous portions of traditional Greek *mezedhes* in bright,

---

ROYAL ASCOT

Get out your Sunday best and join the glitterati at Royal Ascot (www.ascot.co.uk) for the biggest racing meet of the year. The royal family, A-list celebrities and the rich and famous gather here to show off their Jimmy Choos and place the odd bet. The four-day festival takes place in mid-June, and it's essential to book tickets well in advance. You can soak up the atmosphere from the Silver Ring for a mere £20 per day, or head for the Grandstand and Paddock, where you can rub shoulders with the great and the good for £60 per day. Just make sure you dress to impress (ridiculously over-the-top hats are de rigeur for the ladies).

---

simple surroundings, as well as some interesting dessert choices.

Two Brewers

PUB

(34 Park St) This 17th-century inn perched on the edge of Windsor Great Park is near the castle's tradesmen's entrance and supposedly frequented by castle staff. Think low beamed ceilings, dim lighting and royal photographs with irreverent captions on the wall.

Henry VI

PUB

(37 High St) This old pub mixes low ceilings and subtle lighting with leather sofas and modern design. It's the kind of place where you can sit back with an afternoon pint and read the paper. There's a nice garden for al fresco dining and live music on weekends.

ℹ Information

Royal Windsor information centre (www.windsor.gov.uk; Old Booking Hall, Windsor Royal Shopping Arcade; ☺9.30am-5pm Mon-Sat, 10am-4pm Sun) Has information on a self-guided heritage walk around town.

ℹ Getting There & Away

Bus 702 connects Windsor with **London Victoria** coach station (£9.50, one hour, hourly), and bus 77 connects Windsor with **Heathrow** (one hour, hourly).

Trains from Windsor Central station go to Slough, with regular connections to **London Paddington** (30 to 45 minutes). Trains from Windsor Riverside station go to **London Waterloo** (one hour). Services run half-hourly from both and tickets cost £8.50.

Southwest England

Includes »

Why Go?

England's southwest is simply spectacular. Here the past is ever present – prepare for close encounters with iconic stone circles, Iron Age hillforts and Roman baths. Blockbuster stately homes border romantic castles and serene cathedrals frame sumptuous Georgian cityscapes. The landscape immerses you in the myths of Kings Arthur and Alfred the Great, and the writings of Thomas Hardy, Jane Austen and Daphne du Maurier.

But the southwest also has an eye to the future. Here you can tour counter-culture ecotowns, pioneering restaurants and cool surfer hang-outs, and sleep in campsites peppered with chic yurts and retro campervans. Then there are three wildlife-rich national parks, fossil-studded shores, England's best surf spots and a coastline flecked with exquisite bays, towering rock formations and tranquil sweeps of sandy beach. It all gives you a bit of a dilemma. With the southwest it's not so much why go, as what to do first.

Best Places to Eat

» Paul Ainsworth at No 6 (p330)
» Seahorse (p312)
» Menu Gordon Jones (p288)
» Bell's Diner (p279)

Best Places to Stay

» Scarlet (p331)
» Gidleigh Park (p324)
» Queensberry (p287)
» Urban Beach (p246)

When to Go

This region appeals at any time of year, but spring, summer and early autumn enjoy better weather; they're also when most sights are open. In April and May, cliffs, hillsides and formal gardens burst into a profusion of fragrance and blooms. June offers the chance to catch music festival fever at ultracool Glastonbury and on the funky Isle of Wight, while the quirky Port Eliot Festival brings a feast of music, performance and literature to east Cornwall in mid-July.

In July and August coastal areas and blockbuster city sights can get overwhelmed by visitor numbers. But early September brings the end of school summer holidays, cheaper sleeps, quieter beaches and warmer seas.

Activities

Cycling

Cycling the southwest is a superb, if sometimes taxing, way to experience England's great outdoors. National Cycle Network (NCN) routes that cross the region include the West Country Way (NCN Route 3), a 250-mile jaunt from Bristol to Padstow via Glastonbury, Taunton and Barnstaple, and the Devon Coast to Coast Cycle Route (NCN Route 27), which travels for 102 miles between Exmoor and Dartmoor.

The 160-mile circular Wiltshire Cycleway runs along the county's borders. In Hampshire, the New Forest has hundreds of miles of cycle paths which snake through a historic, wildlife-rich environment, while the Isle of Wight has 62 miles of bike-friendly routes and its very own cycling festival.

Off-road mountain-biking highlights include the North Wessex Downs, Exmoor National Park and Dartmoor National Park. Many cycle trails trace the routes of old railway lines, including Devon's 11-mile Granite Way between Okehampton and Lydford, and Cornwall's popular Camel Trail linking Padstow with Wadebridge.

For further information on cycling trails, contact Sustrans (www.sustrans.org.uk) or local tourist offices.

Walking

Often called the 630-mile adventure, the South West Coast Path (www.southwestcoastpath.com) is Britain's longest national walking trail, and stretches west from Minehead on Exmoor, via Land's End to Poole in Dorset. You can pick it up at many points along the coast for a short (and spectacular) day's stroll, or tackle longer stretches. The South West Coast Path Association (www.swcp.org.uk) publishes an annual guide.

For wilderness hikes, the national parks of Dartmoor and Exmoor are hard to beat. Dartmoor is bigger and more remote; Exmoor's ace in the pack is a cracking 34 miles of precipitous coast. The region's third national park, the New Forest, is an altogether gentler affair, but still offers hundreds of miles of trails.

Other hiking highlights are Exmoor's Coleridge Way (www.coleridgeway.co.uk), the Isle of Wight and Bodmin Moor.

In northeast Wiltshire, the Ridgeway National Trail (www.nationaltrail.co.uk/ridgeway) starts near Avebury and winds 44 miles through chalk hills to meet the River Thames at Goring. The trail then continues another 41 miles (another three days) through the Chiltern Hills.

Water Sports

Testing your mettle in washing-machine waves may draw you to the southwest's coasts. North Cornwall and to a lesser extent north Devon, serve up the best surf in England. Party-town Newquay is the epicentre; other top spots are Bude in Cornwall and Croyde in Devon; while Bournemouth is trying to boost its waves with a new artificial surf reef. Region-wide surf conditions can be found at www.magicseaweed.com.

For sailing, highlights includes Britain's 2012 Olympic sailing venues at Weymouth and Portland, the yachting havens of the Isle of Wight, and the watery playgrounds of Poole, where you can try your hand at everything from sailing to powerboating.

Other Activities

The southwest is also prime territory for kitesurfing, windsurfing, sea kayaking, diving and wakeboarding; while plenty of firms also offer caving, coasteering, mountain boarding, climbing and kitebuggying. We give details of providers throughout; www.visitsouthwest.co.uk has further options.

❶ Getting Around

It is possible to travel the southwest using public transport, but services to more remote areas are limited; using your own wheels gives you more flexibility. **Traveline South West** (☎0871 200 2233; www.travelinesw.com) provides region-wide bus and train timetable info.

Bus

The region's bus network is fairly comprehensive, but becomes increasingly patchy further away from main towns. **National Express** (www.nationalexpress.com) usually provides the quickest bus link between cities and larger towns. **PlusBus** (www.plusbus.info) adds local bus travel to your train ticket (from £2 per day). Participating cities include Bath, Exeter, Plymouth, Portsmouth, Taunton, Truro and Weymouth. Buy tickets at train stations.

Key bus providers include:

First (www.firstgroup.com) The region's largest bus company. The FirstDay Southwest ticket (adult/child/family £8/6/19) is valid for one day on many First buses. Weekly (adult/child from £37/23) passes are also available.

Stagecoach (www.stagecoachbus.com) A key provider in Hampshire and Devon. Does one-day tickets (adult/child from £5/3).

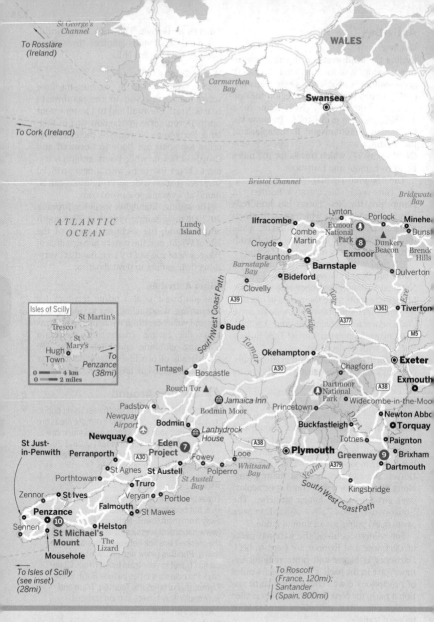

Southwest England Highlights

❶ Bagging a place on an early-morning walk inside the massive sarsen ring at **Stonehenge** (p266)

❷ Strolling along England's most breathtakingly beautiful street, Bath's **Royal Crescent** (p283)

❸ Foraging for 200-million-year-old fossils in Dorset's constantly crumbling **Jurassic Coast** (p251)

❹ Seeing the massive remains of Henry VIII's favourite warship in the historic dockyard at **Portsmouth** (p233)

❺ Falling in love with the utterly romantic ruin of **Corfe Castle** (p250)

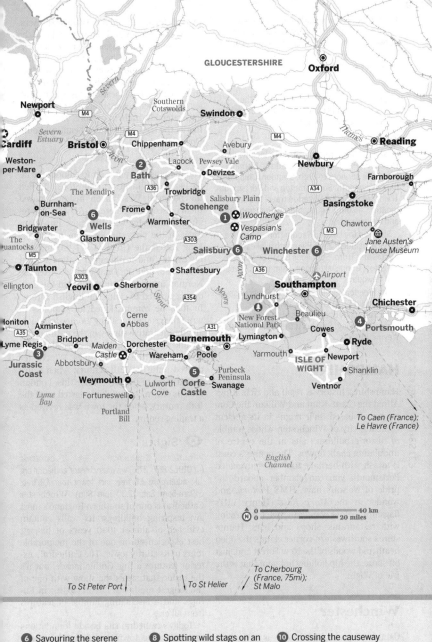

GLOUCESTERSHIRE

◉ **Oxford**

Newport

Southern
Cotswolds

M4

Bristol ◉

◉ **Reading**

Severn
Estuary

Cardiff

Chippenham

Avebury

M4

Weston-
per-Mare

Lacock

Pewsey Vale

Newbury

Farnborough

Bath ❷

Devizes

A36

Trowbridge

A34

The Mendips

Frome

Salisbury Plain

Stonehenge

Warminster

Basingstoke

Burnham-
on-Sea

❻

Wells

Salisbury Plain

Stonehenge ❶ ☢ *Woodhenge*

☢ *Vespasian's
Camp*

M3

Chawton

Bridgwater

The
Quantocks

Glastonbury

A303

Salisbury ❻

Winchester ❻

*Jane Austen's
House Museum*

M5

Taunton

Shaftesbury

A36

ellington

Yeovil

A303

Sherborne

A354

Moors

Southampton

Airport

Chichester

oniton

Axminster

Cerne
Abbas

A31

New Forest
National Park

Beaulieu

Portsmouth ❹

Bridport

Lyme Regis

A35

❸

Maiden
Castle

Dorchester

Wareham

Poole

Lymington

Cowes

Ryde

Newport

**Jurassic
Coast**

Abbotsbury

Bournemouth

Yarmouth

**ISLE OF
WIGHT**

Shanklin

Weymouth

Lulworth
Cove

Corfe
Castle ❺

Purbeck
Peninsula

Swanage

Ventnor

*Lyme
Bay*

Fortuneswell

Portland
Bill

To Caen (France);
Le Havre (France)

*English
Channel*

0 ──── 40 km
0 ──── 20 miles

To St Peter Port

To St Helier

To Cherbourg
(France, 75mi);
St Malo

❻ Savouring the serene
cathedrals at **Salisbury** (p262),
Winchester (p228) and **Wells**
(p291)

❼ Marvelling at the ecological
ingenuity of the **Eden Project**
(p349)

❽ Spotting wild stags on an
early-morning Exmoor **wildlife
safari** (p297)

❾ Cracking the clues to
Agatha Christie's life at her
enchanting holiday home,
Greenway (p311)

❿ Crossing the causeway
to **St Michael's Mount**
(p337)

Wilts & Dorset (www.wdbus.co.uk) Useful service across Wiltshire and Dorset. Seven-day network tickets (£22) can be used on all buses.

Western Greyhound (www.westerngreyhound .com) Key operator in Cornwall.

Car

The main car-hire firms have offices at the region's airports and main-line train stations; rates are similar to elsewhere in the UK.

Train

Bristol is a main train hub; its links include those to London Paddington, Scotland and Birmingham, plus services to Bath, Swindon, Chippenham, Weymouth, Southampton and Portsmouth. Trains from London Waterloo travel to Bournemouth, Salisbury, Southampton, Portsmouth and Weymouth.

Stops on the London Paddington–Penzance service include Exeter, Plymouth, Liskeard, St Austell and Truro. Spur lines run to Barnstaple, Paignton, Gunnislake, Looe, Falmouth, St Ives and Newquay.

The Freedom of the South West Rover pass (adult/child £100/50) allows eight days' unlimited travel over 15 days in an area west of, and including, Salisbury, Bath, Bristol and Weymouth.

HAMPSHIRE

Hampshire's history is regal and rich. Kings Alfred the Great, Knut and William the Conqueror all based their reigns in its ancient cathedral city of Winchester, whose jumble of historic buildings sits in the centre of undulating chalk downs. The county's coast is awash with heritage too – in rejuvenated Portsmouth you can clamber aboard the pride of Nelson's navy, HMS *Victory,* and wonder at the *Mary Rose* (Henry VIII's flagship), before wandering wharfs buzzing with restaurants, shops and bars. Hampshire's southwestern corner claims the open heath and woods of the New Forest and, just off shore, the hip holiday hot-spot that is the Isle of Wight.

Winchester

POP 45,000

Calm, collegiate Winchester is a mellow must-see for all visitors. The past still echoes strongly around the flint-flecked walls of this ancient cathedral city. It was the capital of Saxon kings and a power base of bishops, and its statues and sights evoke two of England's mightiest myth-makers: Alfred the Great and King Arthur (he of the round table). Winchester's architecture is exquisite, from the handsome Elizabethan and Regency buildings in the narrow winding streets to the wondrous cathedral at its core. Thanks to its location, nestled in a valley of the River Itchen, there are also charming waterside trails to explore, and the city marks the beginning of the beautiful South Downs Way.

History

The Romans first put their feet under the table here, but Winchester really took off when the powerful West Saxon bishops moved their episcopal see here in AD 670. Thereafter, Winchester was the most important town in the powerful kingdom of Wessex. King Alfred the Great (r 871–99) made it his capital, and it remained so under Knut (r 1016–35) and the Danish kings. After the Norman invasion of 1066, William the Conqueror arrived to claim the English throne. In 1086 he commissioned local monks to write the ground-breaking *Domesday Book,* an administrative survey of the entire country and the most significant clerical accomplishment of the Middle Ages. Winchester thrived until the 12th century, when a fire gutted most of the city – after this, London took its crown. A long slump lasted until the 18th century, when the town was revived as a trading centre.

◉ Sights

Winchester Cathedral   CATHEDRAL
(☑01962-857 275; www.winchester-cathedral .uk; adult/child £6/free, incl tower tour £9/free; ◷9am-5pm Sat, 12.30-3pm Sun) Winchester Cathedral is one of southern England's most awe-inspiring buildings. Its walls contain evidence of almost 1000 years of history, best experienced on one of the memorable tours of its sturdy tower. The Cathedral's exterior features a fine Gothic facade, but it's the inside that steals the show with one of the longest medieval naves (164m) in Europe, and a fascinating jumble of features from all eras.

Today's cathedral sits beside foundations that mark the town's original 7th-century minster church. The cathedral was begun in 1070 and completed in 1093, and was subsequently entrusted with the bones of its patron saint, St Swithin (Bishop of Winchester from 852 to 862). He is best known for the

Winchester

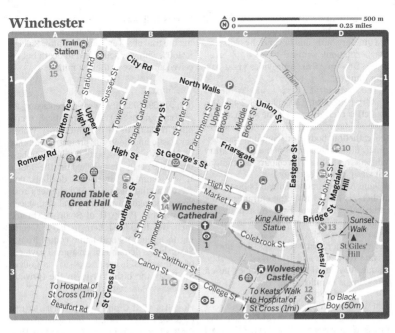

Winchester

proverb stating if it rains on St Swithin's Day (15 July), it will rain for a further 40 days and 40 nights.

Soggy ground and poor workmanship spelled disaster for the early church; the original tower collapsed in 1107 and major restructuring continued until the mid-15th century. Look out for the monument at the far end of the building to diver William Walker; he saved the cathedral from collapse by delving repeatedly into its waterlogged underbelly from 1906 to 1912 to bolster rotting wooden foundations with vast quantities of concrete and brick.

The intricately carved medieval choir stalls are another highlight, sporting everything from mythical beasts to a mischievous green man.

Choral evensong (5.30pm Monday to Saturday, 3.30pm Sunday) is intensely atmospheric; Sunday services also take place at 7.40am, 8am and 10am.

The cathedral's tree-fringed lawns are a tranquil spot to take time out, especially on the quieter south side beyond the cloisters; the permanent second-hand book stall in the Deanery Porch provides great bargain hunting.

The Cathedral Library and Triforium Gallery (☺10.30am-3.30pm Tue-Sat, 2-4pm Mon Apr-Oct) is tucked away on the south side of the nave. It provides a fine elevated view of the cathedral body and contains the dazzlingly illuminated pages of the 12th-century Winchester Bible – its colours as bright as if it was painted yesterday.

Jane Austen, one of England's best-loved authors, is buried near the entrance in the cathedral's northern aisle. Austen died a stone's throw from the cathedral in 1817 at Jane Austen's House (8 College St), where she spent her last six weeks. It's now a private residence and is marked by a slate plaque. Another of her former homes, now a museum, is 18 miles away.

Cathedral body tours (free; ☺hourly 10am-3pm Mon-Sat) last one hour. Tower and roof tours (tickets £6; ☺11.30am Sat & 2.15pm Mon, Wed, Fri & Sat Jun-Aug, 11.30am Sat & 2.15pm Wed & Sat Sep-May) see you clambering 213 steps up narrow stairwells, navigating an interior gallery high above the nave, visiting the bell chamber and going onto the roof for views as far as the Isle of Wight. For safety reasons these tours are only open to those aged 12 to 70. They're popular – book well in advance. Crypt Tours (free; ☺10.30am, 12.30pm & 2.30pm Mon-Sat Apr-Oct) aren't always available because of flooding. If the crypt is open, look out for *Sound II*, a poignant sculpture by Anthony Gormley.

FREE Round Table
& Great Hall   HISTORIC BUILDING
(☏01962-846476; www.hants.gov.uk/greathall; Castle Ave; suggested donation £2; ☺10am-5pm) Winchester's cavernous Great Hall is the only part of 11th-century Winchester Castle that Oliver Cromwell spared from destruction. Crowning the wall like a giant-sized dartboard of green and cream spokes is what centuries of mythology has dubbed King Arthur's Round Table. It's actually a 700-year-old copy, but is fascinating nonetheless. It's thought to have been constructed in the late 13th century and then painted in the reign of Henry VIII (King Arthur's image is unsurprisingly reminiscent of Henry's youthful face).

This hall was also the stage for several gripping English courtroom dramas, including the trial of adventurer Sir Walter Raleigh in 1603, who was sentenced to death but received a reprieve at the last minute.

FREE Wolvesey Castle   CASTLE
(EH; ☏02392-378291; www.english-heritage.org.uk; ☺10am-5pm Apr-Sep) The fantastical, crumbling remains of early-12th-century Wolvesey Castle huddle in the protective embrace of the city's walls, despite the building having been partly demolished in the 1680s. It was completed by Henry de Blois, and served as the Bishop of Winchester's residence throughout the medieval era. Queen Mary I and Philip II of Spain celebrated their wedding feast here in 1554. According to legend, its odd name comes from a Saxon king's demand for an annual payment of 300 wolves' heads. Access is via College St. Today the bishop lives in the (private) Wolvesey Palace next door.

Hospital of St Cross   HISTORIC BUILDING
(☏01962-853525; www.stcrosshospital.co.uk; St Cross Rd; adult/child £3/1; ☺9.30am-5pm Mon-Sat, 1-5pm Sun) Monk, bishop, knight, politician and grandson of William the Conqueror, Henry de Blois was a busy man. But he found time to establish this still-impressive hospital in 1132. As well as healing the sick and housing the needy, the hospital was built to feed and house pilgrims and crusaders en route to the Holy Land. It's the oldest charitable institution in the country, and is still roamed by 25 elderly black- or red-gowned brothers in pie-shaped trencher hats, who continue to hand out alms. Take a peek into the stumpy church, the brethren hall, the kitchen and the peaceful gardens. The best way to arrive is via the 1-mile Keats' Walk. Upon entering, claim the centuries-old Wayfarer's Dole – a crust of bread and horn of ale (now a small swig of beer) from the Porter's Gate.

Military Museums   MUSEUM
Of Winchester's clutch of army museums, the pick is the Royal Green Jackets Museum (The Rifles; ☏01962-877826; www.winchester militarymuseums.co.uk; Peninsula Barracks, Romsey Rd; adult/child £3/1.50; ☺10am-5pm), which has a mini rifle-shooting range, a room of 6000 medals and an impressive blow-by-blow diorama of Napoleon's downfall, the Battle of Waterloo. The Gurkha Museum

JANE AUSTEN'S HOUSE MUSEUM

There's more than a touch of the period dramas she inspired about the former home of Jane Austen (1775–1817) in Chawton village. This appealing red-brick house, where the celebrated English novelist lived with her mother and sister from 1809 to 1817, is now a museum ([☎]01420-83262; www.jane-austens-house-museum.org.uk; Chawton; adult/child £7/2; [☉]10.30am-4.30pm mid-Feb–Dec). While here she wrote *Mansfield Park*, *Emma* and *Persuasion*, and revised *Sense and Sensibility*, *Pride and Prejudice* and *Northanger Abbey*.

The interior depicts a typical well-to-do Georgian family home, complete with elegant furniture and copper pans in the kitchen. Highlights include the occasional table Austen used as a desk, first editions of her novels and the delicate handkerchief she embroidered for her sister.

The museum is 18 miles east of Winchester; take bus 64 from Winchester to Alton Butts (45 minutes, half-hourly Monday to Saturday, five on Sunday) then walk 800m to Chawton village.

([☎]01962-843659; www.thegurkhamuseum.co.uk; Peninsula Barracks, Romsey Rd; adult/child £2/free; [☉]10am-5pm Mon-Sat, noon-4pm Sun) features the regiment's history, combining a jungle tableau with a history of Gurkha service to the British crown. Horsepower (www.horsepowermuseum.co.uk; Peninsula Barracks, Romsey Rd; admission free; [☉]10am-4pm Tue-Fri, noon-4pm Sat & Sun) gallops through the combat history of the Royal Hussars, from the Charge of the Light Brigade to armour-clad vehicles.

🏃 Activities

Winchester has a tempting range of walks. The 1-mile Keats' Walk meanders through the water meadows to the Hospital of St Cross. Its beauty is said to have prompted the poet to pen the ode 'To Autumn'. Pick up the trail near Winchester College; alternatively, head down Wharf Hill, through the water meadows to St Catherine's Hill (1 mile). The tranquil Riverside Walk trails a short distance from the castle along the bank of the River Itchen to High St.

👉 Tours

Winchester College   SCHOOL
([☎]01962-621100; www.winchestercollege.org; College St; tours adult/child £6/5; [☉]10.45am & noon Mon-Sat, plus 2.15pm & 3.30pm Wed, Fri-Sun) Winchester College gives you a rare chance to nosey around a prestigious English private school. It was set up by William Wykeham, Bishop of Winchester in 1393, 14 years after he founded Oxford's New College. Hour-long guided tours trail through the school's medieval core, taking in the 14th-century Gothic chapel, complete with wooden vaulted roof, the dining room (called College Hall), and a vast 17th-century open classroom (called School), where exams are still held. It's all deeply atmospheric and unshakably affluent; a revealing insight into how the other half learns. Tours start from the Porter's Lodge; access to the college is by guided tour only.

Guided Walks   HERITAGE WALKS
(adult/child £4.50/free; [☉]11am & 2.30pm Mon-Sat Apr-Oct, 11.30am Sun May-Aug, 11am Sat only Nov-Mar) These 90-minute walks include Kings and Castles, Mitres and Mortarboards, and City Highlights. They leave from the tourist office (p232).

🛏 Sleeping

Wykeham Arms   HISTORIC INN ££
([☎]01962-853834; www.fullershotels.com; 75 Kingsgate St; s/d/ste £70/119/150; [P][?]) At 250-odd years old, the Wykeham bursts with history – it used to be a brothel and also put Nelson up for a night (some say the events coincided). Creaking stairs lead to plush bedrooms that manage to be both deeply established but also on-trend; brass bedsteads meet jazzy throws, oak dressers sport stylish lights. Each room has its own teddy bear too.

St John's Croft   BOUTIQUE B&B ££
([☎]01962-859976; www.st-johns-croft.co.uk; St John's St; s/d £40/70; [P][?]) A B&B to fall in love with. Supremely but oh-so-casually stylish, this rambling Queen Anne town house teams rattan carpets with bulging bookcases, and Indian art with shabby-chic antiques. The rooms are vast, the garden is tranquil and breakfast is served beside the Aga in the country-house kitchen.

5 Clifton Terrace
BOUTIQUE B&B ££

(☏01962-890053; cliftonterrace@hotmail.co.uk; 5 Clifton Tce; s/d/f £60/75/110; ☎) At this elegant Georgian town house family heirlooms sit beside candy-striped rugs and peppermint-green claw-footed baths. It's delightful, easy-going and great value too.

Hotel du Vin
HISTORIC HOTEL £££

(☏01962-841414; www.hotelduvin.com; Southgate St; r £145-230; P@☎) A glamorous, gorgeous oasis, boasting luxurious furnishings, ornate chaises longues and extravagant stand-alone baths.

No 21
B&B ££

(☏01962-852989; St John's St; s/d £45/90) Atmospheric cathedral views, a flower-filled cottage garden and rustic rooms (think painted wicker and woven bedspreads) make this art-packed house a peaceful city bolt-hole.

Eating

TOP CHOICE **Black Rat**
MODERN BRITISH ££

(☏01962-844465; www.theblackrat.co.uk; 88 Chesil St; mains £17-20; ☼dinner daily, lunch Sat & Sun) The decor here is casually countrified, the food is anything but. Accomplished cooking has won it a Michelin star – partly down to the intense flavours conjured from ingredients such as braised beef cheek, lamb rump and oxtail.

Chesil Rectory
BRITISH ££

(☏01962-851555; www.chesilrectory.co.uk; 1 Chesil St; mains £16) Flickering candles and low beams lend this 15th-century restaurant a romantic feel. Locally sourced delicacies include carpaccio of Hampshire venison with mushrooms, and smoked trout with watercress. The two-course lunch and early-evening menu (£16, 6pm to 7pm) is a steal.

Wykeham Arms
PUB ££

(☏01962-853834; www.wykehamarmswinchester.co.uk; 75 Kingsgate St; mains £14-21; ☼lunch & dinner Mon-Sat, lunch Sun; ☎☏) Local fare packs this super-quirky pub's menu. Dishes range from creative to comfort; try salt-baked beetroot with spicy lentils or slow-cooked lamb cassoulet. The aged Hampshire beef is a carnivore's delight.

Old Vine
PUB ££

(☏01962-854616; www.oldvinewinchester.com; 8 Great Minster St; mains £11-15) At this mellow old English inn an eclectic menu darts from mushrooms with paprika, to pear and blue-cheese tart. It's all best enjoyed at a window table overlooking Cathedral Green. Bookings recommended.

Drinking & Entertainment

TOP CHOICE **Wykeham Arms**
PUB

(www.wykehamarmswinchester.co.uk; 75 Kingsgate St; ☎) Somehow reminiscent of an endearingly eccentric old uncle, this is the sort of pub you'd love as your local: thousands of tankards and school canes hang from the ceiling, worn school desks lend pint-supping an illicit air. At 6pm perfect bar snacks emerge: sizzling sausages (75p), served with mustard and a fork.

Black Boy
PUB

(www.theblackboypub.com; 1 Wharf Hill) This adorable old boozer is filled with a happy band of drinkers and sometimes-obsessive collections, from pocket watches to wax facial features; bear traps to sawn-in-half paperbacks. The pumps produce five locally brewed real ales.

Railway Inn
LIVE MUSIC

(www.railwaylive.co.uk; 3 St Paul's Hill; ☼5pm-midnight Sun-Thu, to 2am Fri, to 1am Sat) As eclectic and alternative as you get; bands span folk, rock, roots and blues; or there's Dr Strangelove's Burlesque Discotheque every Friday.

ℹ Information

Discovery Centre (www3.hants.gov.uk/wdc; Jewry St; ☼9am-7pm Mon-Fri, 9am-5pm Sat, 10am-3pm Sun; ☎) Free internet access.

Tourist office (☏01962-840500; www.visitwinchester.co.uk; High St; ☼10am-5pm Mon-Sat, plus 11am-4pm Sun May-Sep)

ℹ Getting There & Away

Winchester is 65 miles west of London.

Bus

Regular, direct National Express buses shuttle to London Victoria (£12, 1¾ hours).

Train

Trains leave every 30 minutes for London Waterloo (£30, 1¼ hours) and hourly for Portsmouth (£10.20, one hour). There are also fast links to the Midlands.

ℹ Getting Around
Car

The **Park & Ride** (£2 to £3 per day) is signed off junctions 10 and 11 of the M3.

Taxi

Ranks for taxis are at the train station and outside the tourist office, or you can phone **Wintax Taxis** (☑01962-878727).

Portsmouth

POP 207,100

Prepare to splice the main brace, hoist the halyard and potter around the poop deck – Portsmouth is one of the principal ports of Britain's Royal Navy, and the sights of its historic dockyard rank alongside London's Greenwich. Here you can jump aboard Lord Nelson's warship *HMS Victory,* which led the charge at Trafalgar, and see the evocative hulk of Henry VIII's flagship, the *Mary Rose.*

Portsmouth was bombed heavily during WWII and chunks of the city feature soulless postwar architecture, but the cobbled streets of the Point still provide a tangible taste of the past. Regeneration at the glitzy shopping enclave of Gunwharf Quays includes the spectacular Spinnaker Tower, which provides jaw-dropping views. Add some superb restaurants and chic sleep spots, and you have plenty of reasons for an overnight stay. The suburb of Southsea, which begins a mile southeast of Gunwharf Quays, is rich in good hotels and eateries.

◉ Sights & Activities

TOP CHOICE Portsmouth Historic Dockyard   HISTORIC SHIPS
(☑02392-728060; www.historicdockyard.co.uk; adult/child/family £21/16/62; ⊙10am-6pm) Portsmouth's blockbuster attraction comprises three stunning historic ships and an impressive cluster of museums. They sit in the heart of one of Britain's most important modern-day naval ports in a site peppered with red-brick Georgian warehouses, vast wooden boatsheds, statues and painted ships' figureheads. The ticket price also includes a boat trip (p235) round the harbour. Together it makes for a full day's outing; the last admission is 1½ hours before closing.

As resplendent as she is venerable, the dockyard's star sight is HMS Victory (www .hms-victory.com), Lord Nelson's flagship at the Battle of Trafalgar (1805) and the site of his infamous dying words 'Kiss me, Hardy', after victory over the French had been secured. This remarkable ship is topped by a forest of ropes and masts, and weighted by a swollen belly filled with cannon and paraphernalia for an 850-strong crew. Clam-

bering through the low-beamed decks and crew's quarters is an evocative experience.

The raising of the 16th-century warship *Mary Rose* was an extraordinary feat of marine archaeology. This 700-tonne floating fortress was Henry VIII's favourite vessel, but she sank suddenly off Portsmouth while fighting the French in 1545. Of a crew of 400, it's thought 360 died. The ship was only raised from her watery grave in 1982. Now the new £35-million, boat-shaped Mary Rose Museum (www.maryrose.org) that's been built around her showcases the massive hull. This can be seen from tiered galleries which reconstruct life on each deck, using some of the 19,000 artefacts that were raised with her. They range from the military, including scores of cannons and hundreds of longbows, to the touchingly prosaic: water jugs, hair combs and even leather shoes.

Anywhere else, the magnificent warship HMS Warrior (www.hmswarrior.org), built in 1860, would grab centre stage. This stately dame was at the cutting edge of technology in her day, riding the transition from wood to iron and sail to steam. The gleaming upper deck, vast gun deck and the dimly lit cable lockers conjure up vivid pictures of life in the Victorian navy.

Expect model ships, battle dioramas, medals and paintings in the Royal Naval Museum (www.royalnavalmuseum.org). Audiovisual displays recreate the Battle of Trafalgar, one gallery is devoted to Lord Nelson and others let you take command of a warship – see if you can cure the scurvy and avoid mutiny.

The Trafalgar Sail Exhibition is a small museum showcasing the only *HMS Victory* sail to survive the Battle of Trafalgar. Clearly bearing the scars of conflict, it's riddled with the holes made by Napoleonic cannon; a telling illustration of the battle's ferocity.

Stroll into Action Stations!, a warehouse full of interactive gadgets, and you'll soon be piloting a replica Merlin helicopter, controlling an aircraft carrier, upping periscope or jumping aboard a ship simulator. The whole set-up is a thinly disguised recruitment drive for the modern navy, but it's fun nonetheless.

The Point   HISTORIC AREA
Some 500m south of Gunwharf Quays, the Point (also known as Spice Island) is home to characterful cobbled streets dotted with higgledy-piggledy houses and salty sea-dog

Portsmouth

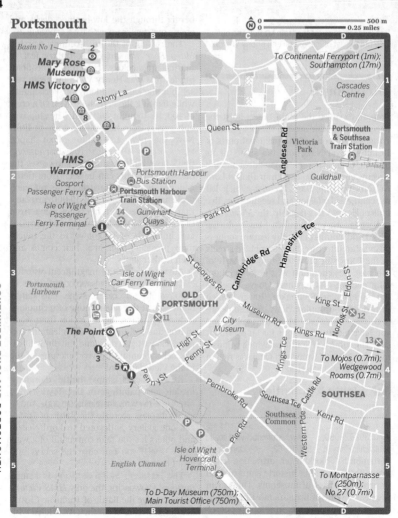

N 0 —————— 500 m
0 —————— 0.25 miles

Basin No 1

Mary Rose Museum

HMS Victory

Stony La

HMS Warrior

Gosport Passenger Ferry

Isle of Wight Passenger Ferry Terminal

Portsmouth Harbour

Portsmouth Harbour Bus Station

Portsmouth Harbour Train Station

Gunwharf Quays

Isle of Wight Car Ferry Terminal

OLD PORTSMOUTH

The Point

Queen St

Anglesea Rd

Victoria Park

Portsmouth & Southsea Train Station

Guildhall

Park Rd

Cambridge Rd

Hampshire Tce

St Georges Rd

Museum Rd

King St

Eldon St

Norfolk St

Kings Tce

Kings Rd

City Museum

High St

Penny St

Penny St

Pembroke Rd

Southsea Tce

Castle Rd

Western Pde

SOUTHSEA

Kent Rd

Southsea Common

Pier Rd

Isle of Wight Hovercraft Terminal

English Channel

To Continental Ferryport (1mi); Southampton (17mi)

Cascades Centre

To Mojos (0.7mi); Wedgewood Rooms (0.7mi)

To D-Day Museum (750m); Main Tourist Office (750m)

To Montparnasse (250m); No 27 (0.7mi)

pubs; their waterside terraces are top spots to gaze at the passing parade of ferries and navy ships. You can clatter up the steps of the Round Tower (originally built by Henry V) and stroll along the old fort walls to the Square Tower, which was built in 1494. Underneath, cavernous vaults frame Sally Ports; openings in the defences that gave historic captains access to the sea, and give modern sun worshippers access to a strip of shingle beach.

To walk to the Point, follow the chain link design set into the pavement from Gunwharf Quays.

Spinnaker Tower   TOWER

(☎02392-857520; www.spinnakertower.co.uk; Gunwharf Quays; adult/child £8.50/7; ◷10am-6pm) The Spinnaker Tower soars 170m above Gunwharf Quays – an unmistakable symbol of Portsmouth's new-found razzle-dazzle. Its two sweeping white arcs resemble a billowing sail from some angles, and a sharp skeletal ribcage from others.

It's one of the UK's tallest publicly accessible structures, offering 23-mile views over Portsmouth, the Isle of Wight and the South Downs. Observation Deck 1 has a hair-raising view through the glass floor, while

Portsmouth

the roofless **Crow's Nest** on Deck 3 allows you to feel the wind on your face. Tickets are 15% cheaper when booked online.

Royal Navy Submarine Museum   MUSEUM
(☑02392-510354; www.submarine-museum.co.uk; Haslar Jetty Rd, Gosport; adult/child £12/9; ⊙10am-5.30pm) The tour of this bona-fide ex-service submarine leads from the torpedo compartments via the galley (kitchen) to the heads (toilets), providing a revealing insight into the claustrophobic conditions. To visit, catch the Gosport Passenger Ferry then walk 500m along the waterfront.

D-Day Museum   MUSEUM
(☑02392-827261; www.ddaymuseum.co.uk; Clarence Esplanade, Southsea; adult/child £6.50/4.50; ⊙10am-5pm) The exhibits here recount the assault mounted by Allied D-Day forces in 1944 and Portsmouth's key role in the operation.

Explosion!   MUSEUM
(☑02392-505600; www.explosion.org.uk; Priddy's Hard, Gosport; adult/child £10/5; ⊙10am-5pm daily Apr-Oct, 10am-4pm Sat & Sun Nov-Mar) A 1771 powder magazine packed full of ordinance that traces the story of naval munitions from gunpowder to Exocet missiles.

☞ Tours

Boat Trips   BOAT TOUR
(☑01983-864602; Historic Dockyard; adult/child £6/3, or incl with dockyard ticket ; ⊙10.30am-4pm Apr-Oct, 11am-3pm Nov-Mar) These weather-permitting, 45-minute harbour tours pro-vide salt-sprayed views of *Warrior*, *Victory* and Gunwharf Quays; you'll go past modern warships as well.

Walking Tours   HERITAGE WALKS
(adult/child £3/1; ⊙2.30pm Sat & Sun Apr-Oct) Themes for these guided walks include Nelson, Henry VIII and Old Fortifications. Tours run on some summer weekdays as well – the tourist office (p236) has more information.

🛏 Sleeping

^{TOP}_{CHOICE} **Florence House**   BOUTIQUE HOTEL **££**
(☑02392-751666; www.florencehousehotel.co.uk; 2 Malvern Rd, Southsea; d £75-145; ℗@⌨) Definitely in the easy-to-check-into-hard-to-leave category. Enjoy vast beds piled artfully high with bathrobes, and retro-chic bathrooms in black-and-white tiles. The pamper dial is set to high – picnic baskets can even be provided on demand.

Fortitude Cottage   B&B **££**
(☑02392-823748; www.fortitudecottage.co.uk; 51 Broad St; s £45, d £65-135; ℗⌨) A combination

ℹ HMS VICTORY

In the summer, tours of Nelson's flagship are self-guided. But between autumn and spring, hugely popular 40-minute **guided tours** are held. Arrive early to bag a place – you can't book in advance.

of swish rooms (think dark brown and dull gold), a superb location and thoughtful touches (chocolates on the tea tray) make this a near-perfect B&B. The penthouse is magnificent; its private roof terrace has wicker chairs and binoculars, better to experience expansive harbour views.

Somerset House
BOUTIQUE HOTEL ££££

(02392-753555; www.somersethousehotel.co.uk; 10 Florence Rd, Southsea; d £100-200;) An achingly tasteful make over has turned this late-Victorian town house into a haven of designer calm. Stained glass, dark woods and polished floors cosy up to Balinese figurines and the very latest luxury bathrooms.

Oyster Cottage
B&B ££

(02392-823683; www.theoystercottage.co.uk; 9 Bath Sq; d £70-90;) A real delight, from the blue-and-white candy-striped bed linen to the warm, funny owner Carol ('I actually *like* guests'). The views, from the Isle of Wight on the left to Portsmouth Harbour on the right, might make you linger longer in your room.

Southsea Backpackers
HOSTEL £

(02392-832495; www.portsmouthbackpackers.co.uk; 4 Florence Rd, Southsea; dm £15, d £34-38;) A cheerful if grungy hostel, where a pool table, patio and BBQ compensate for the well-worn rooms.

Eating

Kitsch'n d'or
FRENCH ££

(02392-861519; www.kitschndor.com; 37 Eldon St; mains £15, 4 courses £23; lunch & dinner Tue-Sat, lunch Mon & Sun) Prepare to be transported to rural Provence. Rustic dishes are rich with hearty flavours, from duck with wild mushrooms and truffle cream, to a meltingly tender shin of beef with red wine sauce. The *fruits de mer* platter is epic: the mounds of local lobster, scallops and steaming clams are so fresh it needs to be ordered a day in advance.

A Bar
BAR, BISTRO ££

(www.abarbistro.co.uk; 58 White Hart Rd; mains £11;) A place to sample local produce and soak up local life: the menu is strong on fish that's been landed just yards away – look out for cider-drinking fishermen from mid-afternoon. Food is served until 10.30pm. The 200-strong wine list includes local Stopham and sparkling Nyetimber, prices span £15 to £1000 a bottle.

No 27
MODERN BRITISH £££

(02392-876272; www.restaurant27.com; 7a South Parade, Southsea; 3-course lunch/dinner £27/40; lunch Sun, dinner Wed-Sat) One of Portsmouth's newest classy eateries, 27 has been impressing local foodies with its creative cuisine. The decor is ultrasmart but discrete; the flavour combinations are surprising: look out for oxtail pudding, and warm rosemary and fig jelly.

Rosie's Vineyard
BISTRO ££

(www.rosies-vineyard.co.uk; 87 Elm Grove, Southsea; mains £11; 6-11pm Mon-Sat, noon-11pm Sun) From the rickety cane bar stools to the vast list of vintages chalked up on the wall (from £2.70 a glass), this is the epitome of a snug little wine bar. Bistro classics include chicken and chorizo cassoulet and huge mounds of local sausages and mash.

Drinking

Rows of bars and trendy balconied eateries line Gunwharf Quays.

King St Tavern
PUB

(www.thekingstreettavern.co.uk; 70 King St) Just what a British pub should be: friendly and un-messed-about with. Buffed wood and old mirrors frame long tables around which to share a pint; it's home to jazz and folk sessions, too.

Mojos
BAR

(02392-873471; 92 Albert Rd, Southsea;) Ready-to-party people of all ages are drawn to this purple-and-red venue in the heart of Southsea's bar strip.

Entertainment

Southsea is thick with nightclubs and live-music venues.

Wedgewood Rooms
LIVE MUSIC

(www.wedgewood-rooms.co.uk; 147b Albert Rd) One of Portsmouth's best live-music venues; also hosts DJs and comedians.

Vue
CINEMA

(www.myvue.com; Gunwharf Quays) Big screen, multiplex.

Information

Online Cafe (www.online-cafe.co.uk; 163 Elm Grove; per 10min/1hr 50p/£3; 9am-9pm Mon-Fri, 10am-8pm Sat & Sun) Internet access.
Tourist office (02392-826722; www.visit portsmouth.co.uk; Clarence Esplanade;

⊙10am–5pm) Now in the D-Day Museum in Southsea.

ⓘ Getting There & Away

Portsmouth is 100 miles southwest of London.

Boat

Ferries link the Isle of Wight (p242) and Portsmouth.

Several routes run from Portsmouth to France. Prices vary wildly depending on times and dates of travel – an example fare is £280 return for a car and two adults on the Portsmouth–Cherbourg route. Book in advance, be prepared to travel off-peak and look out for special deals.

Brittany Ferries (www.brittanyferries.co.uk) Services run regularly from Portsmouth to St Malo (10¾ hours), Caen (four hours) and Cherbourg (three hours) in France, and twice-weekly to Santander (13 hours) in Spain.

Condor Ferries (www.condorferries.co.uk) Runs a weekly car-and-passenger service from Portsmouth to Cherbourg (6½ hours) between June and September.

LD Lines (www.ldlines.co.uk) Shuttles daily to Le Havre (five to eight hours) in France.

Bus

There are 13 National Express buses from London (£15, 2¼ hours) daily; some go via Heathrow Airport (£16, 3½ hours). Bus 700 runs to Chichester (one hour) and Brighton (four hours) at least hourly.

Train

Trains run every 30 minutes from London Victoria (£30, two hours) and Waterloo (£30, 1¾ hours) stations. For the Historic Dockyard get off at the final stop, Portsmouth Harbour.

Departures include:
Brighton (£15, 1½ hours, hourly)
Chichester (£7, 40 minutes, twice an hour)
Southampton (£9, 1¼ hours, three hourly)
Winchester (£10, one hour, hourly)

ⓘ Getting Around

Bus

Bus 6 runs every 15 minutes between Portsmouth Harbour bus station and South Parade Pier in Southsea, via Old Portsmouth.

Taxi

Ranks for taxis are near the bus station. Or call **Aquacars** (☎02392-666666) in Southsea.

NEW FOREST

With typical, accidental English irony, the New Forest is anything but new – it was first proclaimed a royal hunting preserve in 1079. It's also not much of a forest, being mostly heathland ('forest' is from the Old French for 'hunting ground'). Today the forest's combined charms make it a joy to explore. Wild ponies mooch around pretty scrubland, deer flicker in the distance and rare birds flit among the foliage. Genteel villages dot the landscape, connected by a web of walking and cycling routes.

Activities

Cycling

The New Forest makes for superb cycling country, with 200 miles of trails linking the main villages and the key railway station at Brockenhurst.

Cycling in the New Forest (£2) shows the approved off-road and quieter 'on-road' routes. The *New Forest Cycle Experience Route Pack* (£4) features seven trips, ranging from a 4-mile glide through the forest to a 24-mile leg test round the cliffs of the Isle of Wight. The *Forest Leisure Cycling Route Pack* (£4) has six circular trails for all abilities – all start from the village of Burley.

Maps and guides can be bought from Lyndhurst tourist office or via its website.

CAMPING IN THE NEW FOREST

The New Forest is a haven for campers. The Forestry Commission runs eight relatively rural sites. Lyndhurst's tourist office has a free brochure detailing other designated areas; see also www. thenewforest.co.uk

To rent bikes you'll need to pay a deposit (usually £20) and provide identification.

AA Bike Hire — BICYCLE RENTAL
(☑02380-283349; www.aabikehirenewforest.co.uk; Fern Glen, Gosport Lane, Lyndhurst; adult/child per day £10/5)

Country Lanes — BICYCLE RENTAL
(☑01590-622627; www.countrylanes.co.uk; Train Station, Brockenhurst; adult/child per day £16/9)

New Forest Cycle Hire — BICYCLE RENTAL
(☑01590-624204; www.newforestcyclehire.co.uk; Train Station, Brockenhurst; adult/child per day £14/7)

Forest Leisure Cycling — BICYCLE RENTAL
(☑01425-403584; www.forestleisurecycling.co.uk; The Cross, Burley; adult/child per day £15/6)

Horse Riding

Stables welcoming beginners:

Arniss Equestrian Centre — HORSE RIDING
(☑01425-654114; www.arnissequestrian.co.uk; Godshill, Fordingbridge; per hour £35)

Burley Villa — HORSE RIDING
(☑01425-610278; www.burleyvilla.co.uk; near New Milton; per hour £32)

Forest Park — HORSE RIDING
(☑01590-623429; www.forestparkridingstables .co.uk; Rhienfield Rd, Brokenhurst; per hour £33)

Other Activities

The forest is prime hiking territory. Ordnance Survey (OS) produces a detailed, 1:25,000 Explorer map (*New Forest*; No 22, £8); Crimson Publishing's *New Forest Short Walks* (£8) features 20 day hikes.

Ranger Walks — WALKING TOUR
(☑02380-286840; www.forestry.gov.uk; per person £5-10) Memorable dusk deer-watching safaris and wild-food-foraging trips.

New Forest Activities — CANOEING, ARCHERY
(☑01590-612377; www.newforestactivities.co.uk; High St, Beaulieu) Runs canoeing (adult/child

per two hours £28/22), kayaking (per two hours £28) and archery (adult/child per 1½ hours £20/15) activities.

Getting There & Around

Bus

Regular services run to Bournemouth and Southampton.

New Forest Tour (www.thenewforesttour.info; 1-day adult/child £10/4, 5-day £20/8; ☺hourly 10am-5pm mid-Jun–mid-Sep) The hop-on/hop-off bus passes through Lyndhurst's main car park, Brockenhurst station, Lymington, Beaulieu and Exbury.

Train

Two trains an hour run to Brockenhurst from London Waterloo (£40, two hours) via Winchester (£11, 30 minutes) and on to Bournemouth (£7, 25 minutes). Local trains also shuttle twice an hour between Brockenhurst and Lymington.

Lyndhurst & Brockenhurst

POP 6532

The quaint country villages of Lyndhurst and Brockenhurst are separated by just 4 miles and make for atmospheric bases from which to explore the rest of the national park. Both boast picturesque sleeping spots; Brockenhurst can lay claim to a superb eatery, while Lyndhurst is home to an evocative museum.

The New Forest Centre, in Lyndhurst, contains a tourist office (☑02380-282269; www.thenewforest.co.uk; High St, Lyndhurst; ☺10am-5pm) with a wealth of information, including camping guides and walking and cycling maps. The centre also houses the New Forest Museum (www.newforest centre.org.uk; High St, Lyndhurst; adult/child £4/free; ☺10am-4pm), which features a local labourer's cottage (complete with socks drying beside the fire), potato dibbers and a cider press. Listen out for recordings of the autumn pony sales, which take place after the annual drifts (roundups).

Just across the car park, the library (☺9.30am-1pm Mon, Wed & Sat, 2-5.30pm Tue & Fri) has free internet access.

Sleeping

TOP CHOICE Pig — BOUTIQUE HOTEL £££
(☑01590-622354; www.thepighotel.co.uk; Beaulieu Rd, Brockenhurst; r £125-185; ℙ🛜) What a delight: log baskets, croquet mallets and ranks of guest gumboots give this restaurant-

with-rooms a country-house air; espresso machines and minilarders lend bedrooms a luxury touch. In fact, all this effortless elegance makes it feel like you're easing into life at a friend's (very stylish) rural retreat.

Daisybank Cottage   BOUTIQUE B&B **££**
(⏲01590-622086; www.bedandbreakfast-new forest.co.uk; Sway Rd, Brockenhurst; s £75, d £90-135; P🐾🐕) A wealth of little flourishes make a huge difference here: range-baked cakes on arrival; local goodie-packed breakfasts (think strawberry and champagne jam); iPod docks in gorgeous bedrooms. Feeling romantic? The Garden Room, apparently, prompts the most proposals.

Little Hayes   B&B **££**
(⏲02380-283816; www.littlehayes.co.uk; 43 Romsey Rd, Lyndhurst; d £80-90; P🐕) Moulded ceilings, old oak banisters and the odd chandelier speak of this Edwardian guesthouse's age. The breakfasts are full of New Forest produce.

✕ Eating & Drinking

TOP
CHOICE **The Pig**   MODERN BRITISH **££**
(⏲01590-622354; www.thepighotel.co.uk; Beaulieu Rd, Brockenhurst; mains £14-26; ⊙lunch & dinner daily, pizzas 2-6pm Fri-Sun; 🐕) Add this to your must-do list. Home-grown and own-reared produce packs this hotel's imaginative menu, including rarities such as crayfish, quail, and smoked sea salt. Eat inside in style or enjoy a flat-bread pizza on the terrace beside the roaring wood oven – toppings include tomatoes, smoked chilli and home-cured ham. The rooms here are an excellent place to stay the night.

Waterloo Arms   PUB **£**
(www.waterlooarmsnewforest.co.uk; Pikes Hill, Lyndhurst; mains £11) This cosy 17th-century thatched pub serves hearty grub and excellent ales in a snug, wood-beamed interior.

ℹ Getting There & Away

Bus

Bus 6 shuttles between Lyndhurst, Brockenhurst and Lymington (hourly Monday to Saturday, five on Sunday); so does the New Forest Tour.

Train

Trains run twice an hour between Brockenhurst and Lymington.

Around Lyndhurst

Petrol-heads, historians and ghost-hunters all gravitate to Beaulieu (www.beaulieu.co.uk; adult/child £19/9.50; ⊙10am-6pm) – pronounced *bew*-lee – an all-in-one vintage car museum, stately home and tourist complex based on the site of what was once England's most important 13th-century Cistercian monastery. Following Henry VIII's monastic land-grab of 1536, the abbey fell to the ancestors of current proprietors, the Montague family.

Motor-maniacs will be in raptures at Lord Montague's National Motor Museum, a splendid collection of vehicles that will sometimes leave you wondering if they really are cars, or strange hybrid planes, boats or metal bubbles with wheels. It's hard to resist the romance of the early classics, or the oomph of winning F1 cars. Here, too, are several jet-powered land-speed record-breakers including *Bluebird,* which famously broke the record (403mph, or 649km/h) in 1964. There are even celebrity wheels – look out for Mr Bean's Austin Mini and James Bond's whizz-bang speed machines.

Beaulieu's grand but indefinably homely palace began life as a 14th-century Gothic abbey gatehouse, but received a 19th-century Scottish Baronial makeover from Baron Montague in the 1860s. Don't be surprised if you hear eerie Gregorian chanting or feel the hairs on the back of your neck quiver – the abbey is supposedly one of England's most haunted buildings.

The New Forest Tour bus stops directly outside the complex on its circular route via Lyndhurst, Brockenhurst and Lymington.

Buckler's Hard

For such a tiny place, this picturesque huddle of 18th-century cottages, near the mouth of the River Beaulieu, has a big history. It started life in 1722, when one of the dukes of Montague decided to build a port to finance an expedition to the Caribbean. His dream was never realised, but when the war with France came, this embryonic village with a sheltered gravel waterfront became a secret boatyard where several of Nelson's triumphant Battle of Trafalgar warships were built. In the 20th century it played its part in more clandestine wartime manoeuvrings – the preparations for the D-Day landings.

The hamlet is now a fascinating heritage centre – Buckler's Hard Story (☎01590-616203;www.bucklershard.co.uk;adult/child £6.20/4.40; ☺10am-5pm) – which features immaculately preserved 18th-century labourers' cottages. The maritime museum charts the inlet's shipbuilding history and its role in WWII – for a little light relief, seek out Nelson's dinky baby clothes.

The luxurious Master Builder's House Hotel (☎0844-815 3399; www.themasterbuilders.co.uk; d from £130; P) is also part of the complex. This beautifully restored 18th-century hotel has 25 grandly chic rooms, featuring soft lighting, burnished trunks and plush fabrics. The gorgeous restaurant (mains £12 to £20) overlooks the river, while the wood-panelled Yachtsman's Bar serves classy pub grub from £5.

Buckler's Hard is 2 miles downstream from Beaulieu; a picturesque riverside walking trail links the two.

Lymington

POP 15,383

Yachting haven, New Forest base and jumping-off point to the Isle of Wight – the appealing Georgian harbour town of Lymington has several strings to its tourism bow. This former smuggler's port offers great places to eat and sleep, plenty of nautical shops and, in Quay St, an utterly quaint cobbled lane.

◉ Sights & Activities

St Barbe Museum   MUSEUM
(☎01590-676969; www.stbarbe-museum.org.uk; New St; adult/child £4/2; ☺10am-4pm Mon-Sat) Explores tales of boat-builders, sailing ships, contraband and farming through a mix of models and artefacts.

Puffin Cruises   BOAT TOUR
(☎07850-947618; www.puffincruiseslymington.com) Your chance to ride the waves without having to buy a yacht. The best trip (adult/child £17/7, Sunday to Friday, May to October) is an exhilarating surge across the Solent to the Isle of Wight, where the Needles lighthouse and towering chalk stacks loom from the water. There is also a two-hour sunset cruise in high summer.

⌷ Sleeping

TOP CHOICE Mill at Gordleton   BOUTIQUE HOTEL £££
(☎01590-682219; www.themillatgordleton.co.uk; Silver St, Hordle; s/d/ste £125/165/245; P🖥)

Step inside here and know, instantly, you're going to be looked after beautifully. Wicker, velvet and gingham dot exquisite rooms, while the garden is a magical mix of rushing water, fairy lights and modern sculpture. The acclaimed restaurant (mains £6 to £18) focuses firmly on the homemade and the home-grown. The Mill is 4 miles west of Lymington.

Stanwell House   BOUTIQUE HOTEL £££
(☎0844-7046820; www.stanwellhouse.com; 14 High St; s £99, d £140-180, ste £220; @🖥) The epitome of discreet luxury; cane chairs grace the elegant conservatory, eclectic bedrooms boast stand-alone baths, gently distressed furniture and plush throws. The Drydock bar has nautical twinges, while the seafood menu (noon to 9.30pm) features everything from tapas (£6) to vast shellfish platters for two (£50).

Havenhurst House   B&B £
(☎01590-671130;www.havenhurstbedandbreakfast.co.uk; Milford Rd; s/d £35/50; P) Sleep spots this cheap are normally nowhere near this nice. This roomy modern family home has underfloor heating, tasteful bedrooms, stylish bathrooms and top-quality breakfasts. It's a mile from the centre of town.

✗ Eating

Ship Inn   PUB ££
(www.theshiplymington.co.uk; The Quay; mains £5-15; ☺food 11am-10pm) A pub for all seasons: knock back summertime drinks on the waterside terrace, while in winter a toasty log burner will get you warm. Hearty food ranges from French onion soup to slow-roast lamb; drinks totter from tangy real ales to vintage champagne.

Egan's   EUROPEAN ££
(☎01590-676165; Gosport St; 2-/3-course lunch £15/18, mains £16-24; ☺Tue-Sat) The wooden tables here are highly polished and so is the food. Rich local ingredients are transformed by well-travelled flavours – the local cod comes with chorizo, the guinea fowl with porcini mushroom risotto.

ⓘ Information

Library (North Close; ☺9.30am-5pm Mon, Thu & Sat, to 7pm Tue & Fri, to 1pm Wed) Free internet access.

ISLE OF WIGHT MUSIC FESTIVALS

The isle's festival tradition stretches back to the early 1970s, when 600,000 hippies came to see the Doors, the Who, Joni Mitchell and rock icon Jimi Hendrix's last performance. Decades later the gatherings are still some of England's top musical events. The Isle of Wight Festival (www.isleofwightfestival.org), held in mid-June, has been headlined by the likes of Muse, Pearl Jam, the Foo Fighters and the Rolling Stones, while Bestival (www.bestival.net), in early to mid-September, delights in an eclectic, counter-culture feel, drawing the Super Furry Animals, Scissor Sisters, Fatboy Slim and more.

ⓘ Getting There & Away

Boat
Wightlink Ferries (☑0871 376 1000; www .wightlink.co.uk) Car and passenger ferries run hourly to Yarmouth on the Isle of Wight.

Train
Lymington has two train stations: Lymington Town and Lymington Pier. Isle of Wight ferries connect with Lymington Pier. Trains run to Southampton (£9, 30 minutes), via Brockenhurst, every half hour.

ISLE OF WIGHT

On the Isle of Wight these days there's something groovy in the air. For decades this slab of rock anchored off Portsmouth has been a magnet for family holidays, and it still has seaside kitsch by the bucket and spade. But now the proms and amusement arcades are framed by pockets of pure funkiness. A brace of music festivals draws the party crowd, you can feast on just-caught seafood in cool fishermen's cafes, and 'glamping' (camping's more glamorous cousin) rules – here campsites are dotted with ecoyurts and vintage campervans. Yet still the isle's principal appeal remains: a mild climate, myriad outdoorsy activities and a 25-mile shore lined with beaches, dramatic white cliffs and tranquil sand dunes.

🏃 Activities

Cycling
With 200 miles of cycle routes, the Isle of Wight makes pedal-pushers smile. The island's official visitor website has a range of suggested trips, complete with maps. A Cycling Festival (☑01983-203891; www.sun seaandcycling.com) is held every September.

Bike rentals start at around £12 per day, or £45 per week. Many firms deliver and collect on orders over £30.

Tavcycles BICYCLE RENTAL
(☑01983-812989; www.tavcycles.co.uk; 140 High St, Ryde)

Wight Cycle BICYCLE RENTAL
(☑0800 112 3751; www.thewightcycle.com; Zigzag Rd, Ventnor)

Wight Cycle Hire BICYCLE RENTAL
(☑01983-761800; www.wightcyclehire.co.uk; Station Rd, Yarmouth)

Walking
This is one of the best spots in southern England for rambling, with 500 miles of well-marked walking paths, including 67 miles of coastal routes. The island's Walking Festival (www.isleofwightwalkingfestival.co.uk), held over two weeks in May, is billed as the UK's largest.

Other Activities
Water sports are serious business on the Isle of Wight. Cowes is the sailing centre, surfers and wind- and kitesurfers flock to the south west, especially around Compton Bay, while power boats run trips out to the Needles (p245).

ⓘ Information
Useful websites include www.islandbreaks.co.uk and www.isleofwight.com.

The Isle of Wight closed its tourist offices as part of spending cuts and replaced them with a council-run **tourist information call centre** (☑01983-813813; www.islandbreaks.co.uk; ☺8am-6pm Mon-Fri, 9am-1pm Sat). There are small-scale info points at the Newport, Ryde and Yarmouth bus stations.

ⓘ Getting There & Away
Hovertravel (☑08434-878887; www.hover travel.co.uk; day-return adult/child £18/8; ☺hourly) Shuttles foot passengers between Southsea (a Portsmouth suburb) and Ryde.
Red Funnel (☑08448-449988; www.redfunnel .co.uk) Operates car-and-passenger ferries

Isle of Wight

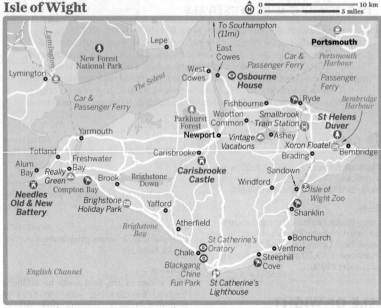

between Southampton and East Cowes (day-return adult/child £15/8, from £45 with car, 55 minutes, hourly) and high-speed passenger ferries between Southampton and West Cowes (day-return adult/child £21/11, 25 minutes, twice hourly).

Wightlink Ferries (☎08713-761000; www.wight link.co.uk) Operates passenger ferries every half hour from Portsmouth to Ryde (day-return adult/child £16/8, 20 minutes). It also runs half-hourly car-and-passenger ferries from Portsmouth to Fishbourne (40 minutes) and from Lymington to Yarmouth (30 minutes). For both, an adult/child day return costs £13/7. Car fares start at around £55 for a short-break return.

ⓘ Getting Around

Bus
Southern Vectis (www.islandbuses.info) Runs buses between the eastern towns roughly every 30 minutes; regular services to the remoter southwest, especially sections between Blackgang Chine and Brook, are less frequent. Between April and September, the Island Coaster makes one return circuit a day along the southern shore from Ryde to Alum Bay in the far southwest. Rover Tickets are available for a day (adult/child £10/5) or a week (adult/child £20/12).

Car
1st Call (☎01983-400055; www.1stcallcarsales.com; 15 College Close,

Sandown; per day/week from £30/130) Collects and delivers island wide.

Train
Island Line (www.island-line.com) Trains run twice-hourly from Ryde to Shanklin, via Sandown, Brading and Smallbrook Junction (25 minutes). Day rover tickets are available (adult/family £5.50/14).

Isle of Wight Steam Railway (☎01983-882204; www.iwsteamrailway.co.uk; ⊙Apr-Sep) Chugs regularly from Smallbrook Junction to Wootton Common (return adult/child £9.50/5, 1st class £14.50/10, one hour).

Cowes & Around

Pack your yachting cap – the hilly Georgian harbour town of Cowes is famous for Cowes Week (www.skandiacowesweek.co.uk), one of the longest-running and biggest annual sailing regattas in the world. Started in 1826, the regatta still sails with as much gusto as ever in late July or early August. Fibreglass playthings and vintage sailboats line Cowes' waterfronts, which are lopped into East and West Cowes by the River Medina; a chain ferry shuttles regularly between the two (foot passengers free, cars £2).

The island's capital, Newport, is 5 miles south.

⦿ Sights

TOP CHOICE **Osborne House**   STATELY HOUSE
(EH; ☎01983-200022; www.english-heritage.org.uk; East Cowes; adult/child £13/8; ⊙10am-5pm Apr-Oct ; **P**) This lemon-frosted, Italianate palace exudes the kind of pomp that defines the Victorian era. Built in the 1840s at the behest of Queen Victoria, the monarch grieved here for many years after her husband's death, and died here herself in 1901. The extravagant rooms include the opulent Durbar Room; another highlight is a carriage ride to the Swiss Cottage where the royal ankle-biters would play. Between November and March, visits are by pre-booked tours only.

Carisbrooke Castle   CASTLE
(EH; ☎01983-522107; www.english-heritage.org.uk; adult/child £7.50/4.50; ⊙10am-5pm Apr-Oct; **P**) Charles I was imprisoned here before his execution in 1649. Today you can clamber the sturdy ramparts and play bowls on the very green the doomed monarch used.

🛏 Sleeping

Fountain   HOTEL **££**
(☎01983-292397; www.fountaininn-cowes.co.uk; High St, West Cowes; s £90, d £100-120; ☏) American President Thomas Jefferson and France's King Charles X have both stayed at this cosy harbour-side inn. Today it's creaky rather than swish, but sash windows and irregular walls bestow an old-fashioned charm. Enjoy espressos and pastries in the cool cafe, pub grub (mains £9) in the snug bar; and boat-watching from the seafront patio.

🖊 **Anchorage**   B&B **££**
(☎01983-247975; www.anchoragecowes.co.uk; 23 Mill Hill Rd, West Cowes; s £40-60, d £60-85; **P**☏) These spic-and-span rooms are named after compass points: East is spacious, while North has a brass bedstead and Victorian fireplace. Breakfasts are rich in island produce.

Ryde to Shanklin

The nippiest foot-passenger ferries between Wight and Portsmouth alight in Ryde, a workaday Victorian town rich in all the cheap and cheerful trimmings of the classic British seaside. Next come the cutesy village of Brading, with its fine Roman villa; photogenic Bembridge Harbour, fringed by sandy beaches; and the twin resort towns of Sandown and Shanklin, boast-ing promenades and hordes of families wielding buckets and spades. The area also features unique places to doze off – including a decommissioned warship and vintage Airstream trailers.

⦿ Sights

⦿ Sights

Brading Roman Villa   RUIN
(☎01983-406223; www.bradingromanvilla.org.uk; Morton Old Rd, Brading; adult/child £6.50/3.50; ⊙9.30am-4pm) The exquisitely preserved mosaics here (including a famous cockerel-headed man) make this one of the finest Romano-British sites in the UK. Wooden walkways lead over rubble walls and brightly painted tiles, allowing you to gaze right down onto the ruins below.

St Helens Duver   NATURE RESERVE
(NT; www.nationaltrust.org.uk; ⊙24hr; **P**) Head for this idyllic sand-and-shingle spit bordering the mouth of the River Yar, and walk trails snaking past swathes of sea pink, marram grass and rare clovers. It's signed from the village of St Helens, near Bembridge Harbour.

🛏 Sleeping & Eating

TOP CHOICE **Vintage Vacations**   CAMPGROUND **£**
(☎07802-758113; www.vintagevacations.co.uk; Ashey, near Ryde; 4-person caravans per week £450-650; ⊙Apr-Oct; **P**) The bevy of 1960s Airstream trailers on this farm are retro chic personified. The gleaming aluminium shells shelter lovingly selected furnishings ranging from cheerful patchwork blankets to vivid tea cosies. Alternatively, opt for a beach-shack retreat, a 1930s Scout Hut, or the Mission: a late-Victorian tin chapel.

Xoron Floatel   FLOATING B&B **££**
(☎01983-874596; www.xoronfloatel.co.uk; Bembridge Harbour; d £60; **P**) Your chance to go to sleep on a gunboat – this former WWII warship is now a cheery, bunting-draped houseboat. Comfy cabins come complete with

ℹ **CAR FERRY COSTS**

The cost of car ferries to the Isle of Wight can vary enormously. Make savings by booking ahead, asking about special offers and travelling off-peak. Some deals include admission to island attractions. Booking online can be around £20 cheaper.

STEEPHILL COVE

You can't drive to Steephill Cove, which makes it all the more special. Its tiny, sandy beach is fringed by buildings that range from stone cottages to rickety-looking shacks. Beach finds festoon porches dotted with driftwood furniture and draped with fishing nets; a tiny clapper-board lighthouse presides over the scene. It's let out as a fabulous self-catering apartment (☎07801-899747; www.theboathouse-steephillcove.co.uk; Steephill Cove; per week £1100-1800) sleeping six; a couple of other gorgeous options are nearby. Two great places to eat, the Boathouse and the Crab Shed, add to the appeal.

Steephill Cove is 1 mile west of Ventnor. Walk from the Botanical Gardens, or hike from the hillside car park 200m west of Ventnor Esplanade, then follow the (steep) coast path until you arrive.

snug bathrooms, while the views from the flower-framed sun deck are simply superb.

Kasbah
B&B ££

(☎01983-810088; www.kasbahryde.com; 76 Union St, Ryde; d £65-85; @🕏) More North Africa than East Wight, Kasbah brings a funky blast of the Mediterranean to Ryde. Intricate lanterns, stripy throws and furniture fresh from Marrakesh dot the chic rooms; tapas (£3.50) are on offer in the chilled-out bar.

Crab & Lobster
PUB ££

(www.crabandlobsterinn.co.uk; 32 Forelands Field Rd, Bembridge; mains £11) Unsurprisingly, seafood is the speciality here – from crab and lobster soup (£6) to shellfish platters to share (£60).

Ventnor & Around

The Victorian town of Ventnor slaloms so steeply down the island's southern coast that you'd be forgiven for mistaking it for the south of France. The winding streets are home to a scattering of quirky boutiques, while local hotels, eateries and the atmospheric Steephill Cove are well worth a detour.

To the west, the island's southernmost point is marked by the stocky 19th-century St Catherine's Lighthouse and its 14th-century counterpart: St Catherine's Oratory. Nearby, kid-friendly Blackgang Chine Fun Park (☎01983-730330; www.blackgangchine.com; admission £10.50; ☺10.30am-4.30pm Mar-Oct), features water gardens, animated shows and a hedge maze.

🛏 Sleeping

Hambrough
BOUTIQUE HOTEL £££

(☎01983-856333; www.thehambrough.com; Hambrough Rd, Ventnor; d £170-280; P🕏) It's hard to say which views are better: the 180-degree

vistas out to sea, or those of super-sleek rooms where espresso machines and heated floors keep luxury levels set sky-high.

St Augustine Villa
B&B ££

(Harbour View; ☎01983-852285; www.harbourviewhotel.co.uk; Esplanade, Ventnor; s £81-94, d £88-103; P🕏) Crisp white linen graces bedrooms which look onto expansive seascapes – watch the sun set from a sofa, or the waves roll from a four-poster bed. The window-seated Tower Room sees light and views pour in from three sides.

✕ Eating

TOP CHOICE Boathouse
SEAFOOD ££

(☎01983-852747; www.theboathouse-steephillcove.co.uk; Steephill Cove; mains £16-32; ☺lunch Thu-Tue Jun–early Sep) Arrive early enough, and you'll see Steephill Cove's fishermen (Jimmy and Mark) landing your lunch – the sanded wooden tables here are just steps from the sea. It makes a spellbinding spot to sip some chilled wine, sample succulent lobster and revel in Wight's new-found driftwood chic.

Pond Cafe
MODERN BRITISH ££

(☎01983-855666; www.robert-thompson.com; Bonchurch; mains £8-25) This smart little bistro brims with local produce, from the beef carpaccio starter to the island cheeses (soft and blue) for dessert. In-the-know locals book a terrace table for super-value three-course lunches (£18) or early-evening meals (two-courses £15).

Crab Shed
CAFE £

(Steephill Cove; snacks £4; ☺noon-3pm Apr-Sep) Lobster pots and fishing boats line the slipway outside a shack that's a riot of sea-smoothed spas, cork floats and faded buoys. Irresistible treats include meaty crab salads, mackerel ciabatta and crumbly crab pasties.

West Wight

Rural and remote, Wight's westerly corner is where the island really comes into its own. Sheer white cliffs rear from a surging sea and the stunning coastline peels west to Alum Bay and the most famous chunks of chalk in the region: the Needles. These jagged rocks rise shardlike out of the sea, forming a line like the backbone of a prehistoric sea monster. West Wight is also home to arguably the isle's best beach: sandy, windswept Compton Bay.

⊙ Sights & Activities

Needles Old Battery   FORT

(NT; ☎01983-754772; www.nationaltrust.org.uk; adult/child £4.60/2.30; ⊙10.30am-5pm mid-Mar–Oct) Established in 1862, this remote gun emplacement was used as an observation post during WWII – today you can explore the Victorian cartridge store, trek down a 60m cliff tunnel to a searchlight lookout and drink in extraordinary views.

New Battery (⊙11am-4pm Tue, Sat & Sun Apr-Oct) is on the same site. Displays in its vaults outline the clandestine space-rocket testing carried out here in the 1950s.

Walk to the battery along the cliffs from Alum Bay (1 mile) or hop on the tourist bus (www.islandbuses.info; adult/child £10/5; ⊙Apr-Sep) that runs twice-hourly between battery and bay.

Needles Pleasure Cruises   BOAT TOUR

(☎01983-761587; www.needlespleasurecruises.co .uk; Alum Bay; adult/child £5/3; ⊙10.30am-4.30pm Apr-Oct) Twenty-minute voyages from Alum Bay beach to the Needles, providing close-up views of those towering white cliffs.

🛏 Sleeping

⧋TOP CHOICE⧋ Really Green   GLAMPING £

(☎07802-678591; www.thereallygreenholiday company.com; Blackbridge Rd, Freshwater Bay; yurt per week £345-595; ⊙Apr-Oct; ℗) The epitome of 'glamping' (glamorous camping), the five-person, fully furnished yurts on this tree-shaded site feature four-poster beds, futons, wood-burning stoves and time-worn antiques. You can even have continental breakfast delivered to your tent flap – roughing it has never been so smooth.

Totland Bay YHA   HOSTEL £

(☎08453-719348; www.yha.org.uk; Hirst Hill, Totland Bay; dm £17; ℗) Family-friendly Victorian house overlooking the water, with a maximum of eight beds per room.

DORSET

For many, Dorset conjures up the kind of halcyon holiday memories found in flickering 1970s home movies, and the county does still deliver arcade-loads of seaside kitsch. But it also offers so much more. Here you can hike, kayak or swim beside the sea-carved bays and rock arches of the stunning Jurassic Coast, then scour fossil-packed beaches for your own prehistoric souvenir. Immerse yourself in Thomas Hardy's lyrical landscape, then discover massive Iron Age hill forts, rude chalk figures, must-see stately homes and fairy-tale castles. Hang out in resorts packed with party animals then chill-out on beaches beloved by multi-millionaires. Or learn to harness the wind in 2012 Olympic sailing waters. These days there's a whole new side of Dorset waiting to be explored.

❶ Information

Jurassic Coast (www.jurassiccoast.com) World Heritage site website.

Visit Dorset (www.visit-dorset.com) The county's official tourism website.

❶ Getting Around

Bus

A key provider is **First** (www.firstgroup.com). Rural and urban areas in Dorset and Wiltshire are linked by Wilts & Dorset (p228).

Train

One mainline runs from Bristol and Bath through Dorchester West to Weymouth. The other connects London with Weymouth, via Southampton, Bournemouth, Poole and Dorchester South.

Bournemouth

POP 163,600

If one thing has shaped Bournemouth it's the beach. This glorious, 7-mile strip of soft sand first drew holiday-makers in the Victorian days. Today, as well as grey-haired coach parties, the resort attracts boozed-up stag parties, and on Saturday nights fancy-dress is everywhere; angels in L-plates meet men in mankinis. But Bournemouth is more than just a bright 'n' breezy party town. It also boasts the area's best surf spot, some hip hideaways, great restaurants and boat trips to the start of Dorset's spectacular Jurassic Coast.

◉ Sights & Activities

Bournemouth Beach   BEACH
Backed by 3000 deckchairs, Bournemouth's sandy shoreline regularly clocks up seaside awards. It stretches from Southborne in the far east to Alum Chine in the west – an immense promenade backed by ornamental gardens, kid's playgrounds and cafes. The resort also prides itself on two piers (Bournemouth and Boscombe). Around Bournemouth Pier you can hire brightly painted beach huts (☑08450-550968; per day/week £25/95), deckchairs (per day £2), windbreaks (£2.50) and parasols (£4).

At the East Cliff Lift Railway (☑01202-451781; Undercliff Dr; adult/child £1.20/80p; ⊙Easter-Oct), cable cars on rails wiz up bracken-covered slopes, cutting out the short, steep hike up the zigzag paths.

Alum Chine   GARDEN
(Mountbatten Rd; ⊙24hr) This award-winning subtropical enclave dates from the 1920s, providing a taste of Bournemouth's golden age. Set 1.5 miles west from Bournemouth Pier, its plants include those from the Canary Islands, New Zealand, Mexico and the Himalayas; their bright-red bracts, silver thistles and purple flowers frame views of a glittering sea.

In the centre of Bournemouth, the Pleasure Gardens stretch back for 1.5 miles from behind Bournemouth Pier in three colourful sweeps.

Russell-Cotes   MUSEUM
(☑01202-451858; www.russell-cotes.bournemouth.gov.uk; Russell-Cotes Rd; adult/child £5/4; ⊙10am-5pm Tue-Sun) This ostentatious mix of Italianate villa and Scottish baronial pile was built at the end of the 1800s for Merton and Annie Russell-Cotes as somewhere to showcase the remarkable range of souvenirs gathered on their world travels. Look out for a plaster version of the Parthenon frieze, Maori woodcarvings and Persian tiles. Paintings include those by Rossetti, Edwin Landseer and William Frith.

Rib Experience   BOAT TRIP
(☑01202-496772; www.bournemouthribexperience.co.uk; Bournemouth Pier; adult/child £25/20) Dorset's extraordinary World Heritage Jurassic Coast starts some 5 miles west of Bournemouth at the Old Harry Rocks. These spray-dashed, 40-minute trips aboard 8m rigid inflatable boats blast past Sandbanks and across the mouth of Poole Harbour, providing up-close views of the chalky columns. The stacks used to be massive arches before erosion brought the tops tumbling down – huge scooped-out sections of cliff clearly show how the sea begins the erosion process.

🛏 Sleeping

Bournemouth has huge concentrations of budget B&Bs, especially around the central St Michael's Rd and to the east of the train station.

TOP CHOICE Urban Beach   BOUTIQUE HOTEL ££
(☑01202-301509; www.urbanbeach.co.uk; 23 Argyll Rd; d £60-180; P@⊜) Bournemouth's finest hipster hotel combines a kooky counter-culture vibe with luxury lodgings and top-notch service. Rooms are achingly but casually stylish and you can borrow everything from brightly coloured wellingtons to toothpaste and iPods. There's a cool bistro downstairs, a heated deck for pre-dinner cocktails and Boscombe Beach is just 5 minutes' walk away.

Langtry Manor   HOTEL ££
(☑01202-553887; www.langtrymanor.com; Derby Rd; s from £102, d £102-240; P⊜) Prepare for

---

SURF REEF

Bournemouth boasts Europe's first ever artificial surf reef, a clump of 70m-long sandbags that's submerged 220m off Boscombe Pier. It's designed to create faster, more challenging breaks, but teething troubles and propeller damage have set debate swirling around whether it's delivered on its aims.

The reef itself isn't for beginners, but you can learn nearby. The Sorted Surf School (☑01202-300668; www.bournemouth-surfschool.co.uk; Overstrand Building, Undercliff Dr), right beside Boscombe Pier, does lessons (£30 for two hours) and hires out wetsuits (two/eight hours £10/30), surfboards (two/eight hours £10/30), bodyboards (two/eight hours £5/15) and kayaks (one/four hours £15/45).

a delicious whiff of royal indiscretion – this minimansion was built by Edward VII for his mistress Lillie Langtry. Opulent grandeur is everywhere, from the red-carpeted entrance to immense chandeliers. Modern flourishes include artful lighting and spas, while the King's Suite is a real jaw-dropper: a monumental, climb-up-to-get-in four-poster bed; the fireplace is big enough to feature a couple of chairs.

Balincourt　　　　　　　　　　　　B&B **££**
(☑01202-552962;　www.balincourt.co.uk;　58 Christchurch Rd; s £53-60, d £86-120; P ☎) This Victorian guesthouse is a labour of love – even the china on the tea tray is hand painted to match each room's colour scheme. Decor is refined and lightly floral, elegant umbrella stands and ticking grandfather clocks add to the heritage feel.

Amarillo　　　　　　　　　　　　　B&B **££**
(☑01202-553884;　www.amarillohotel.co.uk;　52 Frances Rd; s £45, d £60-70; P ☎) Minimalist decor, beige throws and clumps of twisted willow make this a real find – an inexpensive Bournemouth sleep spot with style.

Bournemouth Backpackers　　　　　HOSTEL **£**
(☑01202-299491; www.bournemouthbackpackers .co.uk; 3 Frances Rd; dm £14; ☎) Plain dorms in a small (19-bed) suburban house. It's for non-UK citizens only; reservations by email, or by phone between 5.30pm and 6.30pm, Sunday to Friday in summer (5pm to 7pm Sundays only in winter).

✖ Eating

West Beach　　　　　　　　　　SEAFOOD **££**
(☑01202-587785; www.west-beach.co.uk; Pier Approach; mains £13-20; ☺breakfast, lunch & dinner) A firm favourite with Bournemouth's foodie crowd, this bustling eatery delivers both award-winning dishes and the best views in town. Try Dorset sea bass with braised fennel or a seafood platter for two (£50) crammed with crab, oysters, langoustines, clams and cockles – best enjoyed on the decked dining terrace that juts out over the sand.

Urban Reef　　　　　　　　BAR, BISTRO **££**
(www.urbanreef.com; Undercliff Dr, Boscombe; mains £10-18; ☺breakfast, lunch & dinner, closed Sun & Mon dinner Oct-Mar) Join Bournemouth's surf riders and urban trendsetters at this hip haunt, watching the waves pound to a chilled soundtrack on the seafront deck or

in the deli-cum-cafe-bar. Alternatively head upstairs for succulent sustainable fish dishes, panoramic views and warming log fires.

Print Room　　　　　　　　　　FRENCH **££**
(☑01202-789669;　www.theprintroom-bourne mouth.co.uk; Richmond Hill; mains £14-18; ☺breakfast, lunch & dinner) This charismatic brasserie exudes Parisian chic, from the black-and-white tiled floors to the burnished wooden booths. Gallic-influenced dishes include twice-baked Gruyere soufflé and a deeply decadent rich chocolate mousse. Or try that most excellent French tradition: the *plat du jour*, including wine, for only £8.

Drinking & Entertainment

Most of the main entertainment venues are clustered around Firvale Rd, St Peter's Rd and Old Christchurch Rd. The gay scene kicks off around the Triangle.

TOP CHOICE Sixty Million Postcards　　　　PUB
(www.sixtymillionpostcards.com; 19 Exeter Rd) An indie crowd inhabits this quirky drinking den, where worn wooden floors and fringed lampshades frame events ranging from DJ sets (expect 70s vinyl, soul and punk) and cinema screenings, to pub quizzes and pop-up Sunday jumble sales.

Lava Ignite　　　　　　　　　NIGHTCLUB
(www.lavaignite.com; Firvale Rd) Four-room megaclub playing R&B, pop, house, hip hop and dubstep.

❶ Information

Cyber Place (☑01202-290099; 25 St Peter's Rd; per 10min/hr 50p/£2; ☺10am-8pm)
Tourist office (☑08450-511700; www.bourne mouth.co.uk; Westover Rd; ☺9.30am-5.30pm Mon-Sat, 11am-3pm Sun)

❶ Getting There & Away

Bus
National Express routes:
Bristol (£20, four hours, one daily)
London (£23, 2½ hours, half-hourly)
Oxford (£15, three hours, two daily)
Southampton (£6, 50 minutes, half-hourly)

Local buses:
Poole (15 minutes, every 10 minutes) Bus M1/M2.
Salisbury (£6, 1¼ hours, at least hourly) Bus X3.

The **Getting About Card** (adult/child £5/3) gives a day's unlimited bus travel in Poole, Bournemouth and neighbouring Christchurch.

Train

Destinations include Dorchester South (£11, 45 minutes, hourly), London Waterloo (£25, 2¾ hours, half-hourly), Poole (£4, 11 minutes, half-hourly) and Weymouth (£13, one hour, hourly).

Poole

POP 144,320

Just a few miles west of Bournemouth, Poole was once the preserve of hard-drinking sailors and sunburned day trippers. But these days you're as likely to encounter super-yachts and Porsches because the town borders Sandbanks, one of the most expensive chunks of real estate in the world. But you don't have to be knee-deep in cash to enjoy Poole's quaint old harbour, excellent eateries and nautical pubs. The town is also the springboard for some irresistible boat trips and a tempting array of water sports.

◉ Sights

Brownsea Island   ISLAND

(NT; ☎01202-707744; www.nationaltrust.org.uk; adult/child £5.60/2.80; ☉10am-5pm late Mar-Oct) This small, wooded island in the middle of Poole Harbour played a key role in a global movement famous for three-fingered salutes, shorts and toggles – Lord Baden-Powell staged the first ever scout camp here in 1907. Today trails weave through heath and woods, past peacocks, red squirrels, red deer and a wealth of birdlife.

Free guided walks (at 11.30am and 2pm) focus on the wartime island, smugglers and pirates.

Half-hourly boats, run by Brownsea Island Ferries (☎01929-462383; www.brownseaislandferries.com; Poole Quay), start at 10am, leaving from Poole Quay (adult/child return £9.50/6) and Sandbanks (adult/child return £5.75/4.50). Services operate when the island is open only, the last boat is at 4.30pm.

Poole Old Town   HISTORIC AREA

The attractive historic buildings on Poole Quay range from the 15th to the 19th century, and include the Tudor King Charles pub on Thames St; the cream Old Harbour Office (1820s) next door; and the impressive red-brick Custom House (1813) opposite, complete with Union Jack and gilded coat of arms. The tourist office sells the *Poole Cockle Trail* guide to the old town (30p).

FREE **Waterfront Museum**   MUSEUM

(☎01202-262600; 4 High St; ☉10am-5pm Mon-Sat, noon-5pm Sun) This engrossing museum, set in a beautifully restored 15th-century warehouse, is home to a 2300-year-old Iron Age logboat dredged up from Poole Harbour. At 10m long and 14 tonnes, it's the largest to be found in southern Britain and probably carried 18 people. It was hand-chiselled from a single tree; millennia later you can still see the blade marks in the wood.

Sandbanks   BEACH

A 2-mile, wafer-thin peninsula of land that curls around the expanse of Poole Harbour, Sandbanks is studded with some of the most expensive houses in the world. But the golden beaches that border them are free, and have some of the best water-quality standards in the country. They're also home to a host of watersport operators.

Brownsea Island Ferries shuttle between Poole Quay and Sandbanks every half hour (adult/child £8.50/5.50) from 10am to 5pm, between April and October.

⌂ Sleeping

TOP CHOICE **Saltings**   BOUTIQUE B&B ££

(☎01202-707349; www.the-saltings.com; 5 Salterns Way; d £85; P☎) You can almost hear the strains of the Charleston in this utterly delightful 1930s guesthouse. Charming art deco flourishes include curved windows, arched doorways and decorative uplighters. Immaculate rooms feature dazzling white, spearmint and pastel blue, plus fresh flowers, digital radios and fridges stocked with chocolate bars. Plump for the minisuite for your own seating area, pocket-sized balcony and view of a blue lagoon. Saltings is halfway between Poole and Sandbanks.

Corkers   B&B ££

(☎01202-681393; www.corkers.co.uk; 1 High St; s £61-78, d £83-94; ☎) A superb, central location and cheery rooms (think yellow and blue checks) make this bijou B&B a top hideaway. Rooms 4 and 5 have their own roof terrace with grandstand views over bustling Poole Quay.

Antelope   INN ££

(☎01202-672029; www.antelopeinn-poole.co.uk; 8 High St; s £85, d £99-135; P☎) A creaking old

WATER SPORTS – POOLE HARBOUR

Poole Harbour's sheltered coasts may inspire you to get on the water. Operators cluster near the start of the Sandbanks peninsula. Pool Harbour Watersports (01202-700503; www.pooleharbour.co.uk; 284 Sandbanks Rd) does lessons in windsurfing (per three hours £45) and kitesurfing (per day £99), as well as kayak tours (per three hours £40). FC Watersports (01202-707757; www.fcwatersports.co.uk; 19 Banks Rd, Sandbanks) provides similarly priced kitesurfing lessons, as does Watersports Academy (01202-708283; www.thewatersportsacademy.com; Banks Rd), which also runs windsurfer taster sessions (per hour £25), plus sailing courses (per two hours/two days £55/165) and wakeboarding and water-skiing (per 15 minutes £20).

coaching inn with rich colours, dark woods and ministereos right in the heart of old Poole.

Eating & Drinking

Guildhall Tavern   FRENCH ££
(01202-671717; www.guildhalltavern.co.uk; 15 Market St; mains £19, 2-course lunch/dinner £12/17; ⊙Tue-Sat; 🅿) More Provence than Poole, the food at this brasserie is Gallic gourmet charm at its best: unpretentious and first class. Flavour sensations include halibut with Chablis hollandaise, and duck with Grand Marnier. Exquisite aromas fill the dining room, along with the quiet murmur of people enjoying very good food.

Storm   SEAFOOD ££
(01202-674970; www.stormfish.co.uk; 16 High St; mains £17; ⊙lunch & dinner daily Apr-Oct, dinner Mon-Sat Nov-Mar) The superbly cooked seafood served here depends on what Pete, the fisherman-owner, has caught. It might be intense Goan fish curry, whole flounder with herbs or roast red gurnard with lemon and sea salt.

Poole Arms   PUB ££
(www.localbiztoday.com/poole-arms; The Quay; mains £6-17) The grub at this ancient pub is strong on locally landed seafood – try the rich fish soup, herring roe or Lyme Bay cod with pesto. Order some New Forest beer, then settle in the snug wood-lined bar with the locals, or on the terrace overlooking the quay.

ℹ️ Information

Tourist office (08452-345560; www.poole tourism.com; Poole Quay; ⊙10am-5pm) Opens to 6pm in July and August.

ℹ️ Getting There & Around

Bus
London (£24, 3¼ hours, twice-hourly) National Express.

Bournemouth (15 minutes, six per hour) Bus M1/M2.

Sandbanks (15 minutes, hourly Monday to Saturday) Bus 52.

Boat
Brittany Ferries (www.brittany-ferries.com) Sails between Poole and Cherbourg in France (2½ to 6½ hours, one to three daily May to September). Prices range from around £80 for foot passengers to £250 for a car and two adults.

Sandbanks Ferry (www.sandbanksferry.co.uk; per pedestrian/car £1/3.50; ⊙7am-11pm) Takes cars from Sandbanks to Studland every 20 minutes. It's a short cut from Poole to Swanage, Wareham and the Isle of Purbeck, but the summer queues can be horrendous.

Taxi
Dial-a-Cab (01202-666822)

Train
Rail connections are as for Bournemouth; just add 15 minutes to times to London Waterloo (£25).

Southeast Dorset

With its string of glittering bays and towering rock formations, the southeast Dorset shoreline is the most beautiful in the county. Also known as the 'Isle' of Purbeck (although it's actually a peninsula), it's also the start of the Jurassic Coast and the scenery and geology, especially around Lulworth Cove, make swimming irresistible and hiking memorable. The hinterland harbours the immense, fairy-tale ruins of Corfe Castle, while Wareham sheds light on the mysterious figure of Lawrence of Arabia.

WAREHAM & AROUND
POP 2568

Saxons established the sturdy settlement of Wareham on the banks of the River Frome in the 10th century, and their legacy lingers in the remains of their defensive walls and

SOUTHWEST ENGLAND SOUTHEAST DORSET

one of Dorset's last remaining Saxon churches. Wareham is also famous for its links to the enigmatic TE Lawrence, the British soldier immortalised in the 1962 David Lean epic *Lawrence of Arabia*.

Sights

TOP CHOICE Clouds Hill HISTORIC HOME
(NT; ☎01929-405616; www.nationaltrust.org.uk; near Bovington; adult/child £5/2; ⊙11am-5pm Wed-Sun mid-Mar–Oct; P) This tiny cottage was home to TE Lawrence (1888–1935), the British scholar, military strategist and writer made legendary for his role in helping unite Arab tribes against Turkish forces in WWI. The house's four rooms provide a compelling insight into a complex man; they're also much as he left them – he died at the age of 46 after a motorbike accident on a nearby road.

Highlights include the deeply evocative photos Lawrence took during his desert campaign and his sketches of French crusader castles. There's also a surprisingly comfortable cork-lined bathroom, an aluminium foil-lined bunk room and a heavily beamed music room, which features the desk where Lawrence abridged *Seven Pillars of Wisdom*.

Clouds Hill is 7 miles northeast of Wareham on an unclassified road.

St Martin's on the Walls CHURCH
(North St, Wareham; ⊙9am-5pm) This 11th-century church features a 12th-century fresco on the northern wall, and a marble effigy of TE Lawrence. If it's locked in normal shop hours, get the key from Joy's Outfitters in North St.

Monkey World ZOO
(☎01929-462537; www.monkeyworld.co.uk; Longthorns; adult/child £11/7.75; ⊙10am-5pm; P) An appealing sanctuary for rescued chimpanzees, orang-utans, gibbons, marmosets and some utterly adorable ring-tailed lemurs.

Sleeping & Eating

Red Lion INN ££
(☎01929-550099; www.redlionwareham.co.uk; 1 North St, Wareham; d £120) A supremely stylish makeover of this old inn's vast rooms sees them sporting brass bedsteads, sweet armchairs and wind-up alarm clocks. The locally sourced menu includes home-cured gravlax, while Sunday roast trimmings include Dorset Blue Vinny cauliflower cheese.

Trinity B&B ££
(☎01929-556689; www.trinitybnb.co.uk; 32 South St, Wareham; s/d £45/65; 🛜) This 15th-century cottage oozes so much character, that you half expect to bump into a chap in doublet and hose. The staircase is a swirl of ancient timber, floors creak under plush rugs, and bathrooms glint with yellow and green tiles and smart new fittings.

Information
Purbeck tourist office (☎01929-552740; www.visitswanageandpurbeck.com; Holy Trinity Church, South St, Wareham; ⊙9.30am-4pm Mon-Sat, plus 10am-4pm Sun Jul & Aug)

Getting There & Away
BUS Bus 40 runs hourly between Poole (35 minutes) and Swanage (30 minutes) via Wareham and Corfe Castle.

TRAIN Wareham is on the main railway line from London Waterloo (£20, 2½ hours, hourly) to Weymouth (£9, 30 minutes, hourly).

CORFE CASTLE
The massive, shattered ruins of Corfe Castle loom so dramatically from the landscape it's like blundering into a film set. The defensive fragments tower over an equally photogenic village, which bears the castle's name, and makes for a romantic spot for a meal or an overnight stay.

Sights & Activities

TOP CHOICE Corfe Castle CASTLE
(NT; ☎01929-481294; www.nationaltrust.org.uk; adult/child £7.72/3.86; ⊙10am-6pm Apr-Sep, 10am-4pm Oct-Mar) One of Dorset's most iconic landmarks, these towering battlements were once home to Sir John Bankes, right-hand man and attorney general to Charles I. The castle was besieged by Cromwellian forces during the Civil War – for six weeks the plucky Lady Bankes directed the defence and the castle fell only after being betrayed from within. The Bankes decamped to Kingston Lacy (NT; ☎01202-883402; www.nationaltrust.org.uk; house adult/child £11.70/5.85, grounds only £6.30/3.15; ⊙house 11am-5pm Wed-Sun, grounds daily mid-Mar–Oct; P) and the Roundheads gunpowdered Corfe Castle apart, an action that's still startlingly apparent today: turrets and soaring walls sheer off at precarious angles; the gatehouse splays out as if it's just been blown up. Today you can roam over most of the site, peeping through slit windows and prowling the fractured defences.

Swanage Steam Railway HERITAGE RAILWAY
(☎01929-425800; www.swanagerailway.co.uk;
adult/child return £10.50/7; ☺daily Apr-Oct, Sat &
Sun Nov-Mar) Vintage steam trains run (hourly) between Swanage and Norden (25 minutes), stopping at Corfe Castle.

🛏 Sleeping & Eating

Mortons House HOTEL £££
(☎01929-480988; www.mortonshouse.co.uk; East
St; d £160-215; ℗🐾) This is a place to break
open the Bollinger: a romantic, luxurious
16th-century, minibaronial pile. The rooms
are festooned with red brocade and gold
tassels; an occasional chaise longue adds to
the effect.

Ammonite B&B £
(☎01929-480188; www.ammonite-corfecastle.co
.uk; 88 West St; s £50, d £55-75; ℗🐾) The pleasing rooms at this tranquil edge-of-village
B&B feature pastels and pine; the aga-
cooked breakfast includes local eggs, homemade jams and crusty bread from Corfe
Castle's bakery.

Castle Inn PUB ££
(www.castleinncorfe.com; 63 East St; mains £10-15)
With its flagstone floors and ancient beams
draped with fairy lights, this is the locals'
choice. Prepare for tasty pub classics, plus
some surprises: try the Poole Harbour oysters or roast local duck.

❶ Getting There & Away

Bus 40 shuttles hourly between Poole, Wareham, Corfe Castle and Swanage.

LULWORTH COVE & AROUND

South of Corfe Castle the coast steals the
show. For millions of years the elements
have been creating an intricate shoreline of
curved bays, caves, stacks and weirdly wonderful rock formations – most notably the
massive natural arch at Durdle Door.

At Lulworth Cove, a pleasing jumble of
thatched cottages and fishing gear leads
down to a perfect circle of white cliffs. It's a
charismatic place to stay; inevitably, it draws
coach party crowds in the height of summer.

◉ Sights & Activities

TOP CHOICE Durdle Door NATURAL FEATURE
(℗) This immense, 150-million-year-old
Portland stone arch plunges into the sea
near Lulworth Cove. Part of the Jurassic
Coast, it was created by a combination of
massive earth movements and then erosion.
Today it's framed by shimmering bays –
bring a swimsuit and head down the hundreds of steps for an unforgettable dip.

There's a car park at the top of the cliffs,
but it's best to hike along the coast from
Lulworth Cove (1 mile), passing the delightfully named Lulworth Crumple, where layers of rock have been forced into dramatically zigzagging folds.

Lulworth Castle CASTLE
(EH; ☎08454-501054; www.lulworth.com; adult/
child £5/3; ☺10.30am-5pm Sun-Fri) A creamy,
dreamy white, this baronial pile looks more
like a French chateau than a traditional English castle. Built in 1608 as a hunting lodge,
it's survived extravagant owners, extensive

SOUTHWEST ENGLAND SOUTHEAST DORSET

JURASSIC COAST

The kind of massive, hands-on geology lesson you wish you had at school, the Jurassic
Coast is England's first natural World Heritage site, putting it on a par with the Great Barrier
Reef and the Grand Canyon. This striking shoreline stretches from Exmouth in East Devon
to Swanage in Dorset, encompassing 185 million years of the earth's history in just 95
miles. It means you can walk, in just a few hours, many millions of years in geological time.

It began when layers of rocks formed; their varying compositions determined by different climates: desert-like conditions gave way to higher then lower sea levels. Massive earth
movements then tilted all the rock layers to the east. Next, erosion exposed the different
strata, leaving most of the oldest formations in the west and the youngest in the east.

The differences are very tangible. Devon's rusty-red Triassic rocks are 200 to 250 million years old. Lyme Regis has fossil-rich, dark-clay Jurassic cliffs 190 million years old.
Pockets of much younger, creamy-coloured Cretaceous rocks (a mere 140 to 65 million
years old) also pop up, notably around Lulworth Cove, where erosion has sculpted a
stunning display of bays, stacks and rock arches.

The coast's website (www.jurassiccoast.com) is a great information source; also look
out locally for the highly readable Official Guide to the Jurassic Coast (£4.95), or buy it
at www.jurassiccoasttrust.org.

remodelling and a disastrous fire in 1929. It has been extensively restored – check out the reconstructed kitchen and cellars, then climb the tower for sweeping coastal views.

Secondwind Watersports KAYAK TOUR
(📞01305-834951; www.jurassic-kayaking.com; Lulworth Cove; per person £50; ☺up to 2 tours daily) This three-hour paddle offers jaw-dropping views of Dorset's heavily eroded coast. Starting at Lulworth Cove, you glide through Stair Hole's caves and stacks, across Man O'War Bay then under the stone arch at Durdle Door, stopping for swims and picnics along the way.

🛏 Sleeping & Eating

Lulworth Cove Inn INN ££
(📞01929-400333; www.lulworth-coveinn.co.uk; Main Rd; d £80-110; 🅿) The decor may be super-simple (think block prints and pine), but the setting is superb – ask for one of the balcony rooms and sit watching seagulls swoop over the cove from your own tiny terrace.

Rose Cottage B&B ££
(📞01929-400253; www.lulworthcove.co.uk; Main Rd; s/d £50/90; 🅿🏊) The quintessential 18th-century English cottage – from the thatched roof to the roses round the door. The aged rooms are truly lilliputian (some share bathrooms), the doors are hobbit-sized (duck) and you can use the pool of the hotel next door.

Durdle Door Holiday Park CAMPGROUND £
(📞01929-400200; www.lulworth.com; sites from £25; ☺Mar-Oct; 🅿) Clifftop site, just minutes from the famous rock arch.

Cove Fish SEAFOOD £
(📞01929-400807; Lulworth Cove; ☺10am-4pm Tue-Sun Easter-Oct, Sat & Sun Nov-Easter) Set right beside the path to the beach, this shed is piled high with seafood caught by the owner, ninth generation fisherman Joe. Bag a fish kebab for the BBQ, or settle at the wobbly table outside and tuck into Lulworth Cove crab – a meal that's travelled yards, not miles.

ⓘ Information
Lulworth Cove Heritage Centre (📞01929-400587; www.lulworth.com; ☺10am-5pm) Excellent displays outline how geology and erosion have combined to shape the area's remarkable shoreline.

Dorchester
POP 16,171

With Dorchester, you get two towns in one: a real-life, bustling county town, and Thomas

Hardy's fictional Casterbridge. The Victorian writer was born just outside Dorchester and clearly used it to add authenticity to his writing – so much so that his literary locations can still be found amid the town's white Georgian terraces and red-brick buildings. You can also visit his former homes here and see his original manuscripts. Add incredibly varied museums and some attractive places to eat and sleep, and you get an appealing base for a night or two.

◉ Sights

Dorset County Museum MUSEUM
TOP CHOICE
(📞01305-262735; www.dorsetcountymuseum.org; High West St; adult/child £6/free; ☺10am-5pm Mon-Sat) The Thomas Hardy collection here is the biggest in the world, offering extraordinary insights into his creative process – reading his cramped handwriting, it's often possible to spot where he's crossed out one word and substituted another. There's also an atmospheric reconstruction of his study at Max Gate and a letter from Siegfried Sassoon, asking Hardy if Sassoon can dedicate his first book of poems to him.

As well as the superb Hardy exhibits, look out for Jurassic Coast fossils, especially the huge ichthyosaur and the 6ft fore paddle of a plesiosaur. Bronze and Iron Age finds from Maiden Castle (p254) include a treasure trove of coins and neck rings, while Roman artefacts include 70 gold coins, nail cleaners and (toe-curlingly) ear picks.

Max Gate HISTORIC BUILDING
(Hardy Country; NT; 📞01297-489481; www.nationaltrust.org.uk; Alington Ave; adult/child £4/2; ☺11am-5pm Wed-Sun mid-Mar–Oct; 🅿) Thomas Hardy was a trained architect and designed this attractive house, where he lived from 1885 until his death in 1928. *Tess of the D'Urbervilles* and *Jude the Obscure* were both written here, and the house contains several pieces of original furniture. It's a mile east of Dorchester, on the A352.

Hardy's Birthplace HISTORIC BUILDING
(Hardy Country; NT; 📞01305-262366; www.nationaltrust.org.uk; adult/child £5/2.20; ☺11am-5pm Wed-Sun mid-Mar–Oct; 🅿) This picturesque cob-and-thatch house is the birthplace of Thomas Hardy. It's perhaps a little short on attractions, but makes an evocative stop for Hardy completists. It's in Higher Bockhampton, 3 miles northeast of Dorchester.

Hardy Literary Locations   NOTABLE BUILDINGS

Mayor of Casterbridge locations hidden amongst modern Dorchester include **Lucetta's House**, a grand Georgian affair with ornate door posts near the tourist office, while in parallel South St, a red-brick mid-18th-century building (now a bank) is named as the inspiration for the house of the mayor himself. The tourist office sells book location guides.

FREE **Roman Town House**   HISTORIC BUILDING
(www.romantownhouse.org; High West St; ⊙24hr) The knee-high flint walls and beautifully preserved mosaics here powerfully conjure up the Roman occupation of Dorchester (then Durnovaria). Peek into the summer dining room to see the underfloor heating system (hypocaust), where charcoal-warmed air circulated around pillars to produce a toasty 18°C.

Tutankhamen   MUSEUM
(☑01305-269571; www.tutankhamun-exhibition.co.uk; High West St; adult/child £8/6; ⊙10am-4pm) Recreates the sounds, smells and sights of ancient Egypt, including a fake-gold mock-up of a pharaoh's tomb.

⊨ Sleeping

TOP CHOICE **Beggars Knap**   BOUTIQUE B&B ££
(☑01305-268191; www.beggarsknap.co.uk; 2 Weymouth Ave; s £50-60, d £65-100, f £75-120; P) Despite the name, this altogether fabulous, vaguely decadent guesthouse is far from impoverished. Opulent rooms drip with chandeliers and gold brocades; beds draped in fine cottons range from French sleigh to four-poster. You could pay much, much more and get something half as nice.

Westwood   B&B ££
(☑01305-268018; www.westwoodhouse.co.uk; 29 High West St; s/d/f £70/95/125; 🛜) Colours from a Georgian palette grace the walls of this elegant 18th-century town house. Plush bedrooms feature wicker furniture, cast iron bedsteads and dainty cushions, while the conservatory is home to a superb breakfast spread.

Slades Farm   B&B ££
(☑01305-264032; sladesfm@btinternet.com; North St, Charminster; d £65-75; P) A subtle barn conversion with airy rooms, breakfasts full of farmers market produce, riverside paddocks and three cute alpacas to befriend. It's 2 miles north of Dorchester.

✖ Eating

Surf & Turf at Shelley's Plaice   SEAFOOD ££
(☑01305-757428; Trinity St; mains £12-18; ⊙lunch Tue-Sat, dinner Thu-Sat) Lobster pots and lifebelts dangle from the rafters at this kooky bistro, where the chalked-up menu depends entirely on what local fishermen have caught. Flavoursome delights range from fish soup to perfectly cooked cod, monkfish or lemon sole; or get cracking on a whole Portland crab.

Sienna   MODERN BRITISH £££
(☑01305-250022; www.siennarestaurant.co.uk; 36 High West St; 2-course lunch/dinner £26/37; ⊙lunch Wed-Sat, dinner Tue-Sat) Dorchester's Michelin-starred eatery casts a culinary spell over seasonal produce. Look out for wild garlic and pungent truffles; duck might be teemed with spiced blackberry purée. The cheeseboard bears the very best of the west, served with apple chutney and homemade digestives. Booking is required.

No 6   FRENCH ££
(☑01305-267679; www.no6-restaurant.co.uk; 6 North Sq; mains £13-20; ⊙lunch & dinner Tue-Fri, dinner Sat) Much of the fish at this cosmopolitan bistro comes straight off a Weymouth trawler. The French chef specialises in giving local produce a continental makeover – look out for lamb's kidney on brioche, and crab baked Creole-style.

❶ Information

Tourist office (☑01305-267992; www.visit-dorset.com; Antelope Walk; ⊙9am-5pm Mon-Sat)

❶ Getting There & Around

Bicycle
Dorchester Cycles (☑01305-268787; 31 Great Western Rd; adult/child per day £12/8; ⊙9am-5pm Mon-Sat)

Bus
London (£24, four hours, one daily) National Express.

Lyme Regis (1¾ hours, hourly) Bus 31.

Poole (1¼ hours, three daily Monday to Saturday) Bus 347/387.

Sherborne (one hour, four to seven daily Monday to Saturday) Bus 216; via Cerne Abbas.

Weymouth (35 minutes, three per hour Monday to Saturday, six on Sunday) Bus 10/210.

Train
Hourly trains from Dorchester South:
Bournemouth (£11, 45 minutes)

London Waterloo (£25, 2¾ hours)
Southampton (£22, 1½ hours)
Weymouth (11 minutes)

Services, every two hours, from Dorchester West head to Bath (£16, two hours) and Bristol (£17, 2½ hours).

Around Dorchester

CERNE ABBAS & THE CERNE GIANT

If you had to describe an archetypal sleepy Dorset village, you'd come up with something a lot like Cerne Abbas: its houses run the gamut of England's architectural styles, roses climb countless doorways, and half-timbered houses frame a honey-coloured, 12th-century church.

But this village also packs one heck of a surprise – a real nudge-nudge, wink-wink tourist attraction in the form of the Cerne Giant (admission free; ⊙24hr; P). Nude, full frontal and notoriously well endowed, this chalk figure is revealed in all his glory on a hill on the edge of town. And he's in a stage of excitement that wouldn't be allowed in most magazines. The giant is around 60m high and 51m wide and his age remains a mystery; some claim he's Roman but the first historical reference comes in 1694, when three shillings were set aside for his repair. The Victorians found it all deeply embarrassing and allowed grass to grow over his most outstanding feature. Today the hill is grazed by sheep and cattle, though only the sheep are allowed to do their nibbling over the giant – the cows would do too much damage to his lines.

The village has the swish New Inn (☎01300-341274; www.newinncerneabbas.com; 14 Long St; d £95-160; mains £13-20.), plus Abbots (☎01300-341349; www.abbotsbedandbreakfast.co.uk; 7 Long St; s/d/f £45/85/120; ⊙cafe 10am-

5pm; 🤶), a B&B-cum-cafe, where atmospheric rooms are either stone, lemon or blue, and wooden attic ceilings slope just above head-height. The cafe's cakes are real diet-busters.

Dorchester is 8 miles to the south. Bus 216 (four to seven daily Monday to Saturday) connects Cerne Abbas with Dorchester (30 minutes) and Sherborne (30 minutes).

Weymouth & Around

A 3-mile sandy beach and an immense harbour ensured this strip of Dorset coast was the 2012 Olympic sailing venue – a state-of-the-art water-sports centre and a soaring viewing tower are among the legacies. Otherwise, the area's core character remains: Weymouth's billowing deckchairs and candy-striped beach kiosks signal a sometimes faded Georgian resort, while the pock-marked central plateau of the neighbouring Isle of Portland still proudly proclaims a rugged, quarrying past. Portland also offers jaw-dropping views down on to 17-mile Chesil Beach, which is backed by the Fleet, Britain's biggest tidal lagoon – a home to 600 nesting swans.

WEYMOUTH

POP 51,130

Weymouth has been a popular seaside spot since King George III (the one with a 'nervous disorder') took an impromptu dip here in 1789. Some 200-plus years later, the town is still popular with holidaymakers, drawn by a curling, golden beach, a revitalised historic harbour and oodles of seaside kitsch.

☉ Sights & Activities

Weymouth Beach   BEACH

Weymouth's fine sandy shore is perfect for a stroll down seaside memory lane. Here you can rent a deckchair, sun-lounger or pedalo

SOUTHWEST ENGLAND AROUND DORCHESTER

WORTH A TRIP

MAIDEN CASTLE

Occupying a massive slab of horizon on the southern fringes of Dorchester, Maiden Castle (EH; www.english-heritage.org.uk; admission free; ⊙24hr; P) is the largest and most complex Iron Age hill fort in Britain. The huge, steep-sided chalk ramparts flow along the contour lines of the hill and surround 48 hectares – the equivalent of 50 football pitches. The first hill fort was built on the site around 500 BC and in its heyday was densely populated with clusters of roundhouses and a network of roads. The Romans besieged and captured it in AD 43 – an ancient Briton skeleton with a Roman crossbow bolt in the spine was found at the site. The sheer scale of the ramparts is awe-inspiring, especially from the ditches immediately below, and the winding complexity of the west entrance reveals just how hard it would be to storm. Finds from the site are displayed at Dorset County Museum (p252). Maiden Castle is 1½ miles southwest of Dorchester.

(per hour £6), watch Punch and Judy shows and take a donkey ride. Alternatively, go all Californian and join a volleyball game.

Nothe Fort
FORT

(☑01305-766626; www.nothefort.org.uk; Barrack Rd; adult/child £6/1; ⊙10.30am-5.30pm Apr-Oct) Crowning the headland beside Weymouth Harbour, these photogenic 19th-century defences are studded with cannons, searchlights and 12-inch coastal guns. Exhibits detail the Roman invasion of Dorset, a Victorian soldier's drill, and Weymouth in WWII. Commanding an armoured car and clambering around the magazine prove popular with regiments of children.

Sea Life
AQUARIUM

(☑01305-761070; www.sealife.co.uk; Lodmoor Country Park; admission £20; ⊙10am-5pm; P) Profiles sharks, penguins and seahorses in a 3-hectare aquatic park. To save £8 per ticket, buy online, 24 hours in advance.

White Motor Boats
BOAT TRIP

(☑01305-785000; www.whitemotorboat.freeuk.com; adult/child return £8/6; ⊙3-4 boats daily Apr-Oct) This wind-blown 40-minute jaunt crosses Portland Harbour's vast Olympic sailing waters, before dropping you off at Portland Castle. Boats leave from Cove Row on Weymouth Harbour.

🛏 Sleeping

B+B
B&B ££

(☑01305-761190; www.bb-weymouth.com; 68 The Esplanade; s £60, d £75-115; P 🛜) Cool, sleek B+B deposits a dollop of boutique glamour amid Weymouth's B&B scene. Minimalist lines, monogrammed bed linen and own-brand toiletries grace the bedrooms, while the 1st-floor lounge sports espresso machines, leather sofas and panoramic views of the bay.

Old Harbour View
B&B ££

(☑01305-774633; www.oldharbourviewweymouth.co.uk; 12 Trinity Rd; s/d £76/96; P 🛜) In this spruce Georgian terrace you get boating themes in the fresh, white bedrooms and boats right outside the front door – one room overlooks the busy quay, the other faces the back.

Chatsworth
B&B ££

(☑01305-785012; www.thechatsworth.co.uk; 14 The Esplanade; s £35-50, d £80-120; P 🛜) A sunny waterside terrace lets you watch yachts cast off just metres away while you eat breakfast. Inside crisp colours define compact rooms, with either a harbour or sea view.

🍴 Eating & Drinking

Clusters of bars line the old harbour; ice-cream kiosks dot the prom.

Perry's
EUROPEAN ££

(☑01305-785799; www.perrysrestaurant.co.uk; 4 Trinity Rd; mains £13-24) Weymouth's top table is a genteel, relaxed Georgian town house which consistently delivers irresistible dishes – try the locally landed whole grilled fish of the day. The cognoscenti book the 1st-floor window table (complete with fabulous harbour view) for a two-course set lunch, a bargain at £14.

Marlboro
CAFE £

(46 St Thomas St; mains £8; ⊙noon-9.45pm) This traditional chippy is just yards from Weymouth's quay so the seafood is super-fresh. Order your supper to take away, or tuck into mounds of crisp chips and succulent fish in the bay-windowed, licensed cafe (open till 8pm).

ℹ Information

Tourist office (☑01305-785747; www.visitweymouth.co.uk; Pavilion Theatre, The Esplanade; ⊙9.30am-5pm Apr-Oct, 9.30am-4pm Nov-Mar)

ℹ Getting There & Away

BUS

London (£21, 4¼ hours, one daily) National Express.

Axminster (two hours, hourly) Bus 31.

Dorchester (35 minutes, three per hour to six daily) Bus 10/210.

Fortuneswell (Isle of Portland; 30 minutes, half-hourly) Bus 1.

Lyme Regis (1¾ hours, hourly) Bus 31.

Portland Bill (Isle of Portland; 45 minutes, four daily to one per hour May to September only) Bus 501.

The Jurassic Coast Bus X53 (two to six daily) travels from Weymouth to Wareham (50 minutes), Poole (1½ hours), Abbotsbury (35 minutes) and Lyme Regis (1¾ hours). Between Monday and Saturday it goes on to Exeter (three hours).

BOAT

Condor Ferries (www.condorferries.co.uk) At time of writing the Weymouth–Channel Island ferry service had been relocated to Poole; check the website for details.

TRAIN

Hourly services:

Bournemouth (£13, one hour)
Dorchester South (11 minutes)
London Waterloo (£56, 3½ hours)

WORTH A TRIP

ABBOTSBURY SWANNERY

Every May some 600 free-flying swans choose to nest at the Abbotsbury Swannery (☎01305-871858; www.abbotsbury-tourism.co.uk; New Barn Rd, Abbotsbury; adult/child £10.50/7.50; ☺10am-5pm late Mar–Oct), which shelters in the Fleet lagoon, protected by the ridge of Chesil Beach. The swannery was founded by local monks about 600 years ago, and feathers from the Abbotsbury swans are still used in the helmets of the Gentlemen at Arms (the Queen's official bodyguard). Wandering the network of trails that wind between the swans' nests is an awe-inspiring experience that is punctuated by occasional territorial displays (think snuffling cough and stand-up flapping), ensuring that even the liveliest children are stilled.

The swannery is at the picturesque village of Abbotsbury, 10 miles from Weymouth off the B3157.

Services every two hours:
Bath (£15.60, two hours)
Bristol (£17.40, 2½ hours)

ISLE OF PORTLAND

The 'Isle' of Portland is really a hard, high comma of rock fused to the rest of Dorset by the ridge of Chesil Beach. Its strip of waste waterfront land now features a new sailing centre and a glitzy apartment block. But inland, on the 500ft central plateau, a quarrying past still holds sway, evidenced by huge craters and large slabs of limestone. Proud, and at times bleak and rough around the edges, Portland is decidedly different from the rest of Dorset, and is all the more compelling because of it. Its industrial heritage, water-sport facilities, rich bird life and starkly beautiful cliffs make it worth at least a day trip.

The key population clusters of Fortuneswell and Chiswell are towards the north of the isle; Portland Bill is 4 miles south at the tip.

☉ Sights

TOP CHOICE Tout Quarry PUBLIC ART

(☺24hr) Portland's unique white limestone has been quarried for centuries, and has been used in some of the world's finest buildings, such as the British Museum and St Paul's Cathedral. The disused workings at Tout Quarry now house 53 sculptures that have been carved into the rock in situ. The result is a fascinating combination of the raw material, the detritus of the quarrying process and the beauty of chiselled works. Labyrinthine paths snake through hacked-out gullies and around jumbled piles of rock, revealing the half-formed bears, bison and lizards that emerge out of stone cliffs. Highlights include

Still Falling by Antony Gormley, *Woman on Rock* by Dhruva Mistry and the well-hidden *Green Man*. Tout Quarry is signed off the main road, just south of Fortuneswell.

Portland Lighthouse LIGHTHOUSE

(☎01255-245156; www.trinityhouse.co.uk; Portland Bill; adult/child £4/3; ☺11am-5pm Sun-Thu Apr-Sep; ℗) For a real sense of the isle's remote nature, head to its southern tip, Portland Bill. Then climb the 13m-high, candy-striped lighthouse for breathtaking views of rugged cliffs and the Race, a surging vortex of conflicting tides.

Portland Castle CASTLE

(EH; ☎01305-820539; www.english-heritage.org.uk; Liberty Rd, near Chiswell; adult/child £5/3; ☺10am-5pm Apr-Oct) A particularly fine product of Henry VIII's castle-building spree, with expansive views over Portland harbour. Open until 6pm in July and August.

✗ Eating

Crab House Cafe SEAFOOD ££

(☎01305-788867; www.crabhousecafe.co.uk; Portland Rd, Wyke Regis; mains £16-21; ☺lunch & dinner Wed-Sat, lunch Sun) This is the place to come for as-fresh-as-it-gets seafood and beach-shack-chic. The funky cabin has views onto its own oyster beds in the Fleet Lagoon, and the waterside terrace makes a top spot to enjoy dishes such as clam and cockle spaghetti or cracked whole crab, best washed down with a glass of lip-smacking Somerset cider from Bridge Farm.

Cove House PUB £

(Chiswell Seafront; mains £10) Extraordinary Chesil Beach views, memorable sunsets and great grub (try the Lyme Bay scallops) in a history-rich fishermen's inn.

❶ Information

Tourist office (☎01305-861233; www.visit weymouth.co.uk; Portland Bill; ⊙11am-5pm Easter-Sep)

❶ Getting There & Away

BUS Bus 1 runs from Weymouth to Fortuneswell (half-hourly, 20 minutes). Between May and September bus 501 goes from Weymouth to Portland Bill (four daily to one per hour).

BOAT White Motor Boats (p255) runs ferries to Portland Castle from Weymouth.

CHESIL BEACH

One of the most breathtaking beaches in Britain, Chesil is 17 miles long, 15m high and moving inland at the rate of 5m a century. This mind-boggling, 100-million-tonne pebble ridge is the baby of the Jurassic Coast. A mere 6000 years old, its stones range from pea-sized in the west to hand-sized in the east.

The Chesil Beach Visitors Centre (☎01305-759692; www.chesilbeach.org; Ferrybridge; admission free; ⊙10am-4pm), just over the bridge to Portland, is a great gateway to the beach. The pebble ridge is at its highest around this point – 15m compared to 7m at Abbotsbury. From the car park an energy-sapping hike up sliding pebbles leads to the constant surge and rattle of waves on stones and dazzling views of the sea, with the thin pebble line and the expanse of the Fleet behind. The centre details an ecosystem that includes ringed plover, redshank and oyster catchers, as well as drifts of thrift and sea campion. There's also a sustainable seafood cafe (⊙9am-5pm daily, plus dinner Thu-Sat Jul & Aug), plus glass-bottom boat trips run by Fleet Observer (☎01305-759692; adult/child £7/4) on the Fleet Lagoon.

Lyme Regis

POP 3570

Fantastically fossiliferous, Lyme Regis packs a heavyweight historical punch. Rock-hard relics of the past pop out repeatedly from the surrounding cliffs – exposed by the landslides of a retreating shoreline. Now a pivot point of the Unesco-listed Jurassic Coast, fossil fever is definitely in the air and everyone, from proper palaeontologists to those out for a bit of fun, can engage in a spot of coastal rummaging.

Lyme was also famously the setting for *The French Lieutenant's Woman,* the film version – starring Meryl Streep – immortalised the iconic Cobb harbour defences in movie history. Add sandy beaches and some delightful places to sleep and eat, and you get a charming base for explorations.

◉ Sights & Activities

Lyme Regis Museum   MUSEUM
(☎01297-443370; www.lymeregismuseum.co.uk; Bridge St; adult/child £3.75/free; ⊙10am-5pm Mon-Sat, 11am-5pm Sun Apr-Oct, 11am-4pm Wed-Sun Nov-Mar) In 1814 a local teenager called Mary Anning found the first full ichthyosaurus skeleton near Lyme Regis, propelling the town onto the world stage. An incredibly famous fossilist in her day, Miss Anning did much to pioneer the science of modern-day palaeontology. The museum, on the site of her former home, tells her story and exhibits spectacular fossils and other prehistoric finds.

Dinosaurland   FOSSIL MUSEUM
(☎01297-443541; www.dinosaurland.co.uk; Coombe St; adult/child £5/4; ⊙10am-5pm mid-Feb–Nov) This joyful, mini, indoor Jurassic Park overflows with fossilised remains – look out for belemnites, plesiosaurus and an impressive

---

WATER SPORTS – PORTLAND HARBOUR

The 890-hectare Portland Harbour, just south of Weymouth, lets you glide in the wake of sailors at the 2012 Olympics. The new Weymouth & Portland National Sailing Academy (☎08453-373214; www.wpnsa.org.uk; Portland Harbour) is home to SailLaser (www.sail-laser.com; Osprey Quay, Portland), which runs lessons (two/four days £190/330) and hires lasers (two hours/day £45/95). Meanwhile, Windtek (☎01305-787900; www.windtek.co.uk; 109 Portland Rd, Wyke Regis; ⊙Thu-Mon) runs lessons in windsurfing (four hours/day £45/90) and kitesurfing (per day £95).

Local waters offer superb diving, with a huge variety of depths, seascapes and wrecks. Operators include Underwater Explorers (☎01305-824555; www.underwaterexplorers.co.uk; 15 Castletown, Portland) and Fathom & Blues (☎01305-766220; www.fathomandblues.co.uk; 262 Portland Rd, Wyke Regis). Lessons start at around £95 a day; some operators shuttle qualified divers to a site (around £20) and rent equipment sets (from £60).

locally found ichthyosaur. Lifelike dinosaur models will thrill youngsters – the rock-hard tyrannosaurus eggs and 73kg dinosaur dung will have them in raptures.

Cobb
HARBOUR WALL

(⊙24hr) First built in the 13th century, this curling, protective barrier has been strengthened and extended over the years, so it doesn't present the elegant line it once did, but it's still hard to resist wandering its length for a wistful, sea-gazing Meryl Streep moment at the tip.

🛏 Sleeping

TOP CHOICE 1 Lyme Townhouse
BOUTIQUE B&B ££

(☏01297-442499; www.1lymetownhouse.co.uk; 1 Pound St; d £100-110, ste £135; 🛜) With its witty designer decor, luxury flourishes and in-town location, this 18th-century terrace is hard to resist. Swanky wrought-iron beds, coffee machines and Molton Brown toiletries dot the bedrooms, while breakfast is a gourmet hamper delivered directly to your door. Book room 5 for a don't-want-to-leave double with gorgeous sea views.

Coombe House
B&B ££

(☏01297-443849; www.coombe-house.co.uk; 41 Coombe St; s/d £36/68, 5-person flat per week £350-610; 🅿) Easygoing and stylish, the airy bedrooms in this fabulous value guesthouse are full of bay windows, wicker and white wood. Breakfast is delivered to your room on a trolley, complete with home-made bread and a toaster – perfect for a lazy lie-in in Lyme.

Old Lyme
B&B ££

(☏01297-442929; www.oldlymeguesthouse.co.uk; 29 Coombe St; d £82-90, tr £120; 🅿) Simple, blue-and-yellow rooms, patterned curtains and china trinkets define this quaint, 17th-century cottage.

✗ Eating

TOP CHOICE Hix Oyster & Fish House

SEAFOOD ££

(☏01297-446910; www.hixoysterandfishhouse.co.uk; Cobb Rd; mains £12-21; ⊙noon-10pm Tue-Sun) Expect sweeping views of the Cobb and dazzling food at this super-stylish open-plan cabin. Ink-cooked spelt comes with Devon squid, scallops with black pudding and steak with scrumpy-fried onions. Perhaps start by slurping some oysters: Brownsea Island or Falmouth molluscs come at £2.25 to £3.50 a pop.

Town Mill
CAFE, BAKERY £

(www.townmillbakery.com; 2 Coombe St; mains £5; ⊙8.30am-3.30pm Mon-Sat, from 10am Sun) More like a friend's front room than a cafe, this is Lyme's top snacking spot. Brunch sees you carving slices off huge loaves to toast them yourself, before asking the stranger sitting next to you to please pass the jam. Lunch tempts with soups and flans, while the pizza suppers (5pm to 8pm) in the summer holidays are worth arriving early for.

Alexandra
TEAROOM ££

(www.hotelalexandra.co.uk; Pound St; afternoon tea £5-21; ⊙2.30-5.30pm) Head to this grand, 18th-century hotel's sea-view lawns for the ultimate English experience: afternoon tea, complete with scones, clotted cream and cucumber sandwiches.

Harbour Inn
PUB £

(Marine Pde; mains £9-14) Stone walls, wooden settles, a harbour-side beer garden and the best pub grub in town.

FOSSIL HUNTING

Fossil fever is catching. Lyme Regis sits in one of the most unstable sections of Britain's coast, and regular landslips mean nuggets of prehistory constantly tumble from the cliffs. If you are bitten by the bug, the best cure is one of the regular fossil walks staged locally.

In the village of Charmouth, 3 miles east of Lyme, the Charmouth Heritage Coast Centre (☏01297-560772; www.charmouth.org; adult/child £7/3) runs one to seven trips a week. Or, in Lyme itself, Lyme Regis Museum (☏01297-443370; adult/child £10/5) offers three to seven walks a week; local expert Brandon Lennon (☏07944-664757; www.lymeregisfossilwalks.com; adult/child £7/5; ⊙Sat-Mon) also leads expeditions. Book early – places fill up weeks in advance.

For the best chances of a find, time your trip to Lyme to within two hours of low water. If you choose to hunt by yourself, official advice is to check tide times and collect on a falling tide, observe warning signs, keep away from the cliffs, only pick up from the beach and always leave some behind for others. Oh, and tell the experts if you find a stunner.

ℹ Information

Tourist office (☏01297-442138; www.west dorset.com; Church St; ⊙10am-5pm Mon-Sat, 10am-4pm Sun)

ℹ Getting There & Away

Bus 31 runs to Dorchester (1¼ hours) and Weymouth (1¾ hours) hourly. Bus X53 (two to six daily) goes west to Exeter (1¾ hours) and east to Weymouth (1¾ hours).

Sherborne

POP 9590

Sherborne gleams with a mellow, orangey-yellow stone – it's been used to build a central cluster of 15th-century buildings and the impressive abbey church at their core. This serene town exudes wealth. The five local fee-paying schools include the famous Sherborne School, and its pupils are a frequent sight as they head off to lessons around the town. Ranks of clothing boutiques and shops selling antiques reinforce the well-heeled feel. Evidence of splashing the cash 16th- and 18th-century style lies on the edge of town with two castles: one a crumbling ruin, the other a marvellous manor house, complete with a Capability Brown lake.

⊙ Sights & Activities

FREE Sherborne Abbey   CHURCH
(☏01935-812452; www.sherborneabbey.com; suggested donation £3.50; ⊙8am-6pm) At the height of its influence, the magnificent Abbey Church of St Mary the Virgin was the central cathedral of the 26 Saxon bishops of Wessex. Established early in the 8th century, it became a Benedictine abbey in 998 and functioned as a cathedral until 1075. The church has mesmerising fan vaulting that's the oldest in the country; a central tower supported by Saxon-Norman piers; and an 1180 Norman porch. Its tombs include the elaborate marble effigy belonging to John Lord Digby, Earl of Bristol, and those of the elder brothers of Alfred the Great, Ethelred and Ethelbert.

On the edge of the abbey lie the beautiful 15th-century St John's Almshouses (admission £2; ⊙2-4pm Tue & Thu-Sat May-Sep); look out, too, for the six-sided conduit now at the foot of Cheap St. This arched structure used to be the monks' lavatorium (wash house), but was moved to provide the townsfolk with water when the abbey was disbanded.

Sherborne Old Castle   CASTLE
(EH; ☏01935-812730; www.english-heritage.org.uk; adult/child £3.40/2; ⊙10am-5pm Apr-Oct) These days the epitome of a picturesque ruin, Sherborne's Old Castle was built by Roger, Bishop of Salisbury, in around 1120. Elizabeth I gave it to her one-time favourite Sir Walter Raleigh in the late 16th century. He spent large sums of money modernising it before opting for a new-build instead – moving across the River Yeo to start work on Sherborne New Castle. The old one became a Royalist stronghold during the English Civil War, but Cromwell reduced the 'malicious and mischievous castle' to rubble after a 16-day siege in 1645, leaving just the fractured southwest gatehouse, great tower and north range.

Sherborne New Castle   CASTLE
(☏01935-812072; www.sherbornecastle.com; house adult/child £10/free, gardens only £5/free; ⊙11am-4.30pm Tue-Thu & weekends Apr-Oct; ℗) Having had enough of the then 400-year-old Sherborne Old Castle, Sir Walter Raleigh began building the New Castle in 1594. Raleigh got as far as the central block before falling out of favour with the royals and ending up back in prison – this time at the hands of James I. In 1617 James sold the castle to Sir John Digby, Earl of Bristol, who added the wings we see today. Some 130 years later, the grounds received a mega-makeover at the hands of landscape-gardener extraordinaire Capability Brown; visit today and marvel at the massive lake he added, along with the remarkable 12-hectare waterside gardens.

Walking Tours   HERITAGE TOURS
(£4; ⊙11am Fri Jul-Sep) These 90-minute trips explore the photogenic old town, leaving from the tourist office (p260).

🛏 Sleeping

Cumberland House   B&B ££
(☏01935-817554; www.bandbdorset.co.uk; Green Hill; s £50-65, d £65-85; ℗🖥) There are few straight lines in this 17th-century cottage; instead, walls undulate towards each other in charming rooms finished in oatmeal, fresh lemon and terracotta. Breakfast is either continental (expect tangy home-made compote) or full English – there's freshly squeezed orange juice either way.

FORDE ABBEY

A former Cistercian monastery, Forde Abbey (☑01460-220231; www.fordeabbey.co.uk; Chard; abbey adult/child £10.50/free, gardens £8.50/free; ⊙abbey noon-4pm Tue-Fri & Sun Apr-Oct, gardens 10am-4.30pm) was built in the 12th century, updated in the 17th century, and has been a private home since 1649. The building boasts magnificent plasterwork ceilings and fine tapestries but it's the gardens that are the main attraction: 12 hectares of lawns, ponds, shrubberies and flower beds with many rare and beautiful species.

It's 10 miles north of Lyme Regis; public transport is a nonstarter.

Stoneleigh Barn   B&B ££

(☑01935-389288; www.stoneleighbarn.co.uk; North Wootton; s/d/f £60/80/90; P🖥) Outside, this gorgeous 18th-century barn delights the senses – it's smothered in bright, fragrant flowers. Inside, exposed trusses frame spacious rooms delicately decorated in lilac and turquoise. Stoneleigh is 3 miles southeast of Sherborne.

Eastbury   HOTEL £££

(☑01935-813131; www.theeastburyhotel.co.uk; Long St; s £70, d £140-190; P🖥) The best rooms here have real 'wow' factor – black-and-gold lacquer screens frame minimalist freestanding baths; shimmering fabrics swathe French sleigh beds. The standard rooms are less exotic but still swish, boasting fresh-baked biscuits, luxury smellies and linen bathrobes.

Eating

Green   MODERN BRITISH ££

(☑01935-813821; www.greenrestaurant.co.uk; 3 The Green; mains £7-14; ⊙Tue-Sat) The contented chatter of Sherborne's food fans lends this restaurant a vibrant air, while creative flavour combos keep taste buds tingling: pheasant breast is teamed with mulled wine, local scallops are paired with blood-orange butter. On Friday and Saturday there's a sumptuous set dinner (two/three courses £32/37).

Three Wishes   CAFE, BISTRO ££

(www.thethreewishes.co.uk; 78 Cheap St; mains £6-12; ⊙9.30am-5.30pm Mon-Thu, dinner Fri & Sat, lunch Sun) Imaginative uses of top-notch Dorset produce keeps customers happy at this buzzing eatery – favourites include the flavoursome seared beef and blue-cheese salad, or the fragrant kiln-roasted local salmon risotto.

ℹ Information

Tourist office (☑01935-815341; www.visit-dorset.com; Digby Rd; ⊙9am-5pm Mon-Sat) Stocks the free *Sherborne: Famous Abbey Town* leaflet, which has a map and town trail.

ℹ Getting There & Away

Bus

Dorchester (one hour, two-hourly Monday to Saturday) Bus 216, via Cerne Abbas (30 minutes).

Shaftesbury (£5.30, 30 minutes, daily) National Express.

Yeovil (30 minutes, hourly Monday to Saturday) Buses 57 and 58.

Train

Hourly services to Exeter (£17, one hour), London Waterloo (£30, 2½ hours) and Salisbury (£12, 40 minutes).

Shaftesbury & Around

POP 6640

Crowning a ridge of hogbacked hills and overlooking pastoral meadows, the agreeable market town of Shaftesbury circles around its historic abbey ruins. The medieval faith community that lived here was nationally significant, and the names of its key players – Kings Alfred and Knut - still evoke a rich heritage. Shaftesbury's other big landmark is Gold Hill. This often-photographed, painfully steep, quaint cobbled slope is lined by chocolate-box cottages and starred in a famous TV advert for Hovis bread.

◉ Sights

Shaftesbury Abbey   RUINS

(☑01747-852910; www.shaftesburyabbey.org.uk; Park Walk; adult/child £3/free; ⊙10am-5pm Apr-Oct) These hilltop ruins mark the site of what was England's largest and richest nunnery. It was founded in 888 by King Alfred the Great, and was the first religious house in Britain built solely for women; Alfred's daughter, Aethelgifu, was its first abbess. It Edward is thought to have been buried here, and King Knut died at the abbey in 1035. Most of the buildings were dismantled by Henry VIII in the Dissolution of 1539, but you can still wander around its foundations with a well-devised audioguide and hunt out statuary and illuminated manuscripts in the museum.

Old Wardour Castle
CASTLE

(EH; ☏01747-870487; www.english-heritage.org.uk; adult/child £4/2.40; ☺10am-5pm Apr-Oct, 10am-4pm Sat & Sun Nov-Mar; P) The six-sided Old Wardour Castle was built around 1393 and suffered severe damage during the English Civil War, leaving these imposing remains. The views from the upper levels are fabulous while its grassy lawns make a fine spot for a picnic. It's open until 6pm in July and August and is 4 miles west of Shaftesbury.

🛏 Sleeping & Eating

Fleur de Lys
HOTEL **£££**

(☏01747-853717; www.lafleurdelys.co.uk; Bleke St; s£80-90,d£110-150; P@🛜) For a delicious dollop of luxury, immerse yourself in the world of Fleur de Lys. Fluffy bathrobes, minifridges and laptops ensure you click into pamper mode. The restaurant (lunch pre-booked Wednesday to Sunday, dinner Monday to Saturday, two/three courses £27/33) rustles up elegant dishes such as crab consommé, and local Dover sole with caviar.

Updown
COTTAGE **£**

(☏07710-307202; www.updowncottage.co.uk; 12 Gold Hill; per week from £500; P🛜) This whitewashed, four-bedroom cottage clinging to Gold Hill is a supremely picturesque place to sleep. Snug, beam-lined rooms, open fires and a hillside garden make it one to remember, the boutique bathrooms make it hard to leave.

Mitre
PUB **££**

(23 High St; mains £6-10) Expect drink-them-in views over Blackmore Vale from this atmospheric old inn's decked terrace, and a menu crammed with classy pub classics – try the Cumberland bangers 'n' mash or pork and cider casserole.

ⓘ Information

Tourist office (☏01747-853514; www.shaftesburydorset.com; 8 Bell St; ☺10am-5pm)

ⓘ Getting There & Away

Bus

London Victoria (£20, four hours, one daily) National Express, goes via Heathrow.

Salisbury (one hour, three to four Monday to Saturday) Bus 26/27.

Sherborne (£5.30, 30 minutes, one daily) National Express.

WILTSHIRE

Wiltshire is rich in the reminders of ritual and packed with not-to-be-missed sights. Its verdant landscape is littered with more mysterious stone circles, processional avenues and ancient barrows than anywhere else in Britain. It's a place that teases and tantalises the imagination – here you'll experience the prehistoric majesty of Stonehenge and the atmospheric stone ring at Avebury. Then there's the serene 800-year-old cathedral at Salisbury – a relatively modern religious monument. Add the supremely stately homes at Stourhead and Longleat and the impossibly pretty village of Lacock, and you have a county crammed full of English charm waiting to be explored.

ⓘ Information

There are tourist offices in Salisbury (p265) and **Bradford-on-Avon** (☏01225-865797; www.bradfordonavon.co.uk; 50 St Margaret's St; ☺10am-5pm), but council-run offices in Devizes and Avebury have been closed.

Visit Wiltshire (www.visitwiltshire.co.uk)

ⓘ Getting Around

Bus

The bus coverage in Wiltshire can be patchy, especially in the northwest of the county. There are two main operators.

First (www.firstgroup.com) Serves west Wiltshire.

Wilts & Dorset Buses (www.wdbus.co.uk) Covers Salisbury and many rural areas. It sells one-day Explorer Tickets (£8) and seven-day Passes (Salisbury area £13, network-wide £22).

Train

Rail lines run from London Waterloo to Salisbury and beyond to Exeter and Plymouth, branching off north to Bradford-on-Avon, Bath and Bristol, but most of the smaller towns and villages aren't served by trains.

Salisbury

POP 39,730

Centred on a majestic cathedral that's topped by the tallest spire in England, the gracious city of Salisbury makes a charming base from which to discover the rest of Wiltshire. It's been an important provincial city for more than a thousand years, and its streets form an architectural timeline ranging from medieval walls and half-timbered Tudor town houses to Georgian mansions and Victorian villas. Salisbury is also a lively, modern town, boasting plenty of bars, restaurants and terraced cafes, as well as a concentrated cluster of excellent museums.

☉ Sights

FREE Salisbury Cathedral   CATHEDRAL
(☎01722-555120; www.salisburycathedral.org.uk; requested donation adult/child £5/3; ☉7.15am-6.15pm) England is endowed with countless stunning churches, but few can hold a candle to the grandeur and sheer spectacle of Salisbury Cathedral. Built between 1220 and 1258, the structure bears all the hallmarks of the early English Gothic style, with an elaborate exterior decorated with pointed arches and flying buttresses, and a sombre, austere interior designed to keep its congregation suitably pious.

Beyond the highly decorative West Front, a small passageway leads into the 70m-long nave, lined with handsome pillars of Purbeck stone. In the north aisle look out for a fascinating medieval clock dating from 1386, probably the oldest working timepiece in the world. At the eastern end of the ambulatory the glorious Prisoners of Conscience stained-glass window (1980) hovers above the ornate tomb of Edward Seymour (1539–1621) and Lady Catherine Grey. Other monuments and tombs line the sides of the nave, including that of William Longespée, son of Henry II and half-brother of King

Salisbury

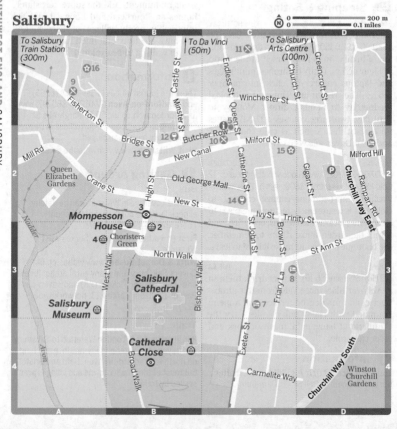

John. When the tomb was excavated a well-preserved rat was found inside Longespée's skull.

The cathedral really comes into its own during evensong, which takes place at 5.30pm Monday to Saturday and 3pm on Sunday, during term time only.

Salisbury's 123m crowning glory, its spire, was added in the mid-14th century, and is the tallest one in Britain. It represented an enormous technical challenge for its medieval builders; it weighs around 6500 tons and required an elaborate system of cross-bracing, scissor arches and supporting buttresses to keep it upright. Look closely and you'll see that the additional weight has buckled the four central piers of the nave.

Sir Christopher Wren surveyed the cathedral in 1668 and calculated that the spire was leaning by 75cm. A brass plate in the floor of the nave is used to measure any shift, but no further lean was recorded in 1951 or 1970. Despite this, reinforcement of the notoriously 'wonky spire' continues to this day.

Salisbury Cathedral's Chapter House (⊙10am-4.30pm Mon-Sat, 12.45-4.30pm Sun) is home to one of only four surviving original copies of the Magna Carta, the historic agreement made between King John and his barons in 1215 that acknowledged the fundamental principle that the monarch was not above the law. It's a still-powerful document; beautifully written and remarkably well preserved.

The best way to experience the cathedral, is on a 90-minute tower tour (☑01722-555156; adult/child £8.50/6.50; ⊙11am-2.30pm Apr-Sep, 1 per day Mon-Sat Nov-Mar); these see you climbing 332 vertigo-inducing steps to the base of the spire for jaw-dropping views across the city and the surrounding countryside. Bookings are required.

Cathedral Close
HISTORIC AREA

Salisbury's medieval cathedral close, a hushed enclave surrounded by beautiful houses, has an other-worldly feel. Many of the buildings date from the same period as the cathedral, although the area was heavily restored during an 18th-century clean-up by James Wyatt.

The close is encircled by a sturdy outer wall, constructed in 1333; the stout gates leading into the complex are still locked every night. Just inside the narrow High St Gate is the College of Matrons, founded in 1682 for widows and unmarried daughters of clergymen. South of the cathedral is the Bishop's Palace, now the private Cathedral School, parts of which date back to 1220. The close is also home to three museums and historic buildings – Salisbury Museum, Mompesson House, and the Rifles.

Salisbury Museum
MUSEUM

(☑01722-332151; www.salisburymuseum.org.uk; 65 Cathedral Close; adult/child £5.40/1.80; ⊙10am-5pm Mon-Sat year-round, plus noon-5pm Sun Jun-Sep) The hugely important archaeological finds here include the Stonehenge Archer; the bones of a man found in the ditch surrounding the stone circle – one of the arrows found alongside probably killed him. Add gold coins dating from 100 BC and a Bronze Age gold necklace, and it's a great introduction to Wiltshire's prehistory.

Mompesson House
HISTORIC BUILDING

(NT; ☑01722-335659; www.nationaltrust.org.uk; Cathedral Close; adult/child £5.30/2.65; ⊙11am-5pm Sat-Wed mid-Mar–Oct) Built in 1701, this fine Queen Anne building boasts magnificent plasterwork ceilings, exceptional period furnishings and a wonderful carved staircase. All that made it the perfect location for the 1995 film *Sense and Sensibility*.

Rifles   MUSEUM
(The Wardrobe; ☎01722-419419; www.thewardrobe.org.uk; 58 Cathedral Close; adult/child £4/1; ☺10am-5pm Mon-Sat, noon-4.30pm Sun, closed Dec & Jan) Collections include a cannonball from the American War of Independence, Victorian redcoat uniforms and displays on 19th- and 21st-century conflicts in Afghanistan.

Tours

Salisbury Guides   HERITAGE TOURS
(☎07873-212941; www.salisburycityguides.co.uk; adult/child £4/2; ☺11am daily Apr-Oct, 11am Sat & Sun Nov-Mar) These 90-minute trips leave from the tourist office. There's an 8pm ghost walk on Fridays from May to September.

✨ Festivals

Salisbury Festival   ARTS FESTIVAL
(www.salisburyfestival.co.uk) A prestigious, eclectic event running from late May to early June, encompassing classical, world and pop music, plus theatre, literature and art.

🛏 Sleeping

TOP CHOICE St Ann's House   BOUTIQUE B&B ££
(☎01722-335657; www.stannshouse.co.uk; 32 St Ann St; s/d £60/110) For some perfectly priced indulgence head to this sumptuous Georgian terrace, which overflows with antiques, fine silk and linen direct from Istanbul. The gourmet breakfast buffet includes *ashera* (a cinnamon-scented Turkish pudding), roll mops and baked goat's cheese. The chef-proprietor has spent decades cooking for the rich and famous – ask about former clients and prepare for some great stories.

CANAL TRIPS

The 87-mile-long Kennet & Avon (www.katrust.org) runs all the way from Bristol to Reading. Sally Boats (☎01225-864923; www.sallyboats.ltd.uk) hires out narrowboats. Weekly rates for a four-berth boat range from around £680 in the winter to £950 in high-summer.

Spire House   B&B ££
(☎01722-339213; www.salisbury-bedandbreakfast.com; 84 Exeter St; s £65-75, d £80, f £95-100; ℗) Breakfast tables here groan with home-made goodies: Dorset apple cakes, muffins, bread and jam. The comfy rooms have four-poster beds, Georgian-themed wallpaper and, at the front, cracking cathedral views.

Old Rectory   B&B ££
(☎01722-502702; www.theoldrectory-bb.co.uk; 75 Belle Vue Rd; s £45-55, d £70-85; ℗ 🛜) This B&B's serene, airy rooms are decked out in cream and shades of blue, the delightful walled garden is framed by roses and the Australian owner, Trish, will make you feel right at home. The Old Rectory is a mile north of the cathedral.

Rokeby   B&B ££
(☎01722-329800; www.rokebyguesthouse.co.uk; 3 Wain-a-long Rd; s £40-70, d £60-95; ℗ 🛜) Glinting bathrooms, satin cushions and gauzy throws lift this late-Victorian B&B above the rest. Stand-alone baths, wrought-iron fireplaces and the decking overlooking the lawn help too. Rokeby is a mile northeast of the cathedral.

Salisbury YHA   HOSTEL £
(☎0845-371 9537; www.yha.org.uk; Milford Hill; dm £18; ℗ @) A real gem: neat rooms in a rambling, listed Victorian building. Choose from doubles or dorms, a cafe-bar, laundry and dappled gardens add to the appeal.

Eating

Anokaa   INDIAN
(☎01722-414142; www.anokaa.com; 60 Fisherton St; mains £11-32; ✎) Sophisticated, contemporary Indian cuisine makes this the top table in town. Expect char-grilled halibut to be flavoured with curry leaves, and asparagus to come with cheese and roast strawberries. Wise locals head for the bargain buffet lunches (£9 per person).

Da Vinci   ITALIAN ££
(☎01722-328402; www.davinciofsalisbury.co.uk; 68 Castle St; mains £8-26; ☺lunch & dinner Mon-Sat) The Da Vinci *ristorante* brings a dash of southern Europe to south Wiltshire. Here risottos come infused with saffron, meats are wrapped in rich hams and cheese, and the pasta comes laced with flavour-packed sauces.

Pheasant
GASTROPUB ££

(☑01722-322866; www.restaurant-salisbury.com; 19 Salt Lane; mains £7-15; ☺food noon-9.30pm) Flying the flag for great British bar food, this chilled-out gastropub does the basics well; try the pheasant stuffed with bacon and leeks, and the gooey, crumbly Eton mess. To drink? Perhaps a pint of Pigswill (honestly – it's a local ale).

Bird & Carter
DELI, CAFE £

(3 Fish Row, Market Sq; snacks from £5; ☺8.30am-6pm Mon-Sat, 10am-4pm Sun) This heavily beamed deli-cafe is piled high with local meats and cheeses – the New Forest Blue, Old Sarum and Nanny Williams come from just a few miles away. Grab a wedge of quiche and chunky potato salad to go, or duck upstairs to eat alongside weathered wood, stained glass and old church pews.

 Drinking

Haunch of Venison
PUB

(www.haunchofvenison.uk.com; 1 Minster St) Featuring wood-panelled snugs, spiral staircases and wonky ceilings, this 14th-century drinking den is packed with atmosphere – and ghosts. One is a cheating whist player whose hand was severed in a game – look out for his mummified bones on display inside.

Spirit
BAR

(46 Catherine St) Hip hang-out with a multi-coloured light-up floor, crowd-pleasing tunes on the decks and a choice of vivid cocktails.

Moloko
BAR

(www.themolokobar.co.uk; 5 Bridge St) Black and red decor, Soviet stars and hot-coloured vodkas create a cold war theme.

☆ **Entertainment**

Salisbury Arts Centre
ARTS CENTRE

(www.salisburyartscentre.co.uk; Bedwin St) Housed in the converted St Edmund's church some 800m northeast of the cathedral, this innovative arts centre showcases cutting-edge theatre, indie films, dance and live gigs.

Salisbury Playhouse
THEATRE

(www.salisburyplayhouse.com; Malthouse Lane) A major producing theatre that also hosts top touring shows and musicals.

Chapel
NIGHTCLUB

(www.chapelnightclub.com; 34 Milford St) Buzzing bar with adjoining club where the DJ sets range from urban to chart and cheese.

ⓘ **Information**

Library (Market Pl; ☺10am-7pm Mon,Tue & Fri, to 5pm Wed, Thu & Sat) Internet access (free; maximum use 30 minutes per day).

Tourist office (☑01722-334956; www.visit wiltshire.co.uk/salisbury; Fish Row, Market Sq; ☺9.30am-6pm Mon-Sat, 10am-4pm Sun Jun-Sep, 9.30am-5pm Mon-Sat Oct-Apr)

ⓘ **Getting There & Away**

Bus

National Express services include Bath (£11, 1¼ hours, one daily), Bristol (£10, 2¼ hours, daily) and London (£10, three hours, three daily) via Heathrow.

Local services include Bus 26/27 to Shaftesbury (one hour, three to four Monday to Saturday) and bus 2 to Devizes (one hour, hourly Monday to Saturday).

Tour buses leave Salisbury for Stonehenge regularly (p268).

Train

Trains run half-hourly from London Waterloo (£35, 1½ hours).

Hourly connections include:

Bath (£9, one hour)
Bradford-on-Avon (£11.60, 40 minutes)
Bristol (£11, 1¼ hours)
Exeter (£30, two hours)
Portsmouth (£17, 1½ hours)
Southampton (£8.40, 30 minutes)

Around Salisbury

OLD SARUM

The huge ramparts of Old Sarum (EH; ☑01722-335398; www.english-heritage.org.uk; adult/child £3.50/1.80; ☺10am-5pm; ℗) sit on a grassy rise about 2 miles from Salisbury. It began life as a hill fort during the Iron Age, and was later occupied by both the Romans and the Saxons. By the mid-11th century it was a town – one of the most important in the west of England; William the Conqueror convened one of his earliest councils here, with the first cathedral being built in 1092, snatching the bishopric from nearby Sherborne Abbey. But Old Sarum always had problems: it was short on water and exposed to the elements, and in 1219 the bishop was given permission to move the cathedral to a new location beside the River Avon, founding the modern-day city of Salisbury. By 1331 Old Sarum's cathedral had been demolished for building materials and the settlement was practically abandoned.

Today you can wander the grassy ramparts, see the stone foundations of the original cathedral, and look across the Wiltshire countryside to the spire of Salisbury's new cathedral. Medieval tournaments, open-air plays and mock battles are held on selected days. There are free guided tours at 3pm in June, July and August. Old Sarum stays open longer in July and August (9am to 6pm).

Between them, buses 5 and 8 run twice an hour from Salisbury to Old Sarum (hourly on Sundays).

WILTON HOUSE

Stately Wilton House (☏01722-746700; www.wiltonhouse.com; house adult/child £14/7.50; ☉11.30am-4.30pm Sun-Thu May-Aug; P) provides an insight into the exquisite, rarefied world of the British aristocracy. One of the finest stately homes in England, the Earls of Pembroke have lived here since 1542, and it's been expanded, improved and embellished by successive generations since a devastating fire in 1647. The result is quite staggering and delivers a whistle-stop tour of the history of European art and architecture: magnificent period furniture, frescoed ceilings and elaborate plasterwork frame paintings by Van Dyck, Rembrandt and Joshua Reynolds. Highlights are the Single and Double Cube Rooms, designed by the pioneering 17th-century architect Inigo Jones. The fine landscaped grounds (adult/child £5.50/4; ☉11am-5pm daily May-Aug) were largely laid out by Capability Brown.

All that architectural eye candy makes the house a favoured film location: *The Madness of King George*, *Sense and Sensibility* and *Pride and Prejudice* were all shot here. But Wilton was serving as an artistic haven long before the movies – famous guests include Ben Jonson, Edmund Spenser, Christopher Marlowe and John Donne. Shakespeare's *As You Like It* was performed here in 1603, shortly after the bard had written it.

Wilton House is 2½ miles west of Salisbury; bus R3 runs from Salisbury (10 minutes, two hourly).

Stonehenge

This compelling ring of monolithic stones (EH; ☏0870-333 1181; www.english-heritage.org.uk; adult/child £6.90/3.50; ☉9am-7pm) has been attracting a steady stream of pilgrims, poets and philosophers for the last 5000 years and is easily Britain's most iconic archaeological site.

The landscape around Stonehenge is undergoing a two-year revamp which should dramatically improve the experience of those visiting. But even before the changes, and despite the huge numbers of tourists who traipse around the perimeter, Stonehenge still manages to be a mystical, ethereal place – a haunting echo from Britain's forgotten past, and a reminder of the people who once walked the many ceremonial avenues across Salisbury Plain. Even more intriguingly, it's still one of Britain's great archaeological mysteries: despite countless theories about what the site was used for, ranging from a sacrificial centre to a celestial timepiece, in truth, no one knows for sure what drove prehistoric Britons to expend so much time and effort on its construction.

Admission to Stonehenge is free for both EH and NT members.

TOP
CHOICE **Stone Circle**
Access Visits   WALKING TOUR
(☏01722-343830; www.english-heritage.org.uk; adult/child £14.50/7.50) Circle-access visits are an unforgettable experience. Visitors normally have to stay outside the stone circle itself, but on these self-guided walks, you get to wander around the core of the site, getting up-close views of the iconic bluestones and trilithons. They take place in the evening or early morning so the quieter atmosphere and the slanting sunlight add to the effect. Each visit only takes 26 people; to secure a place book at least two months in advance.

THE SITE

The first phase of construction at Stonehenge started around 3000 BC, when the outer circular bank and ditch were erected. A thousand years later, an inner circle of granite stones, known as bluestones, was added. It's thought that these mammoth 4-ton blocks were hauled from the Preseli Mountains in South Wales, some 250 miles away – an almost inexplicable feat for Stone Age builders equipped with only the simplest of tools.

Stonehenge

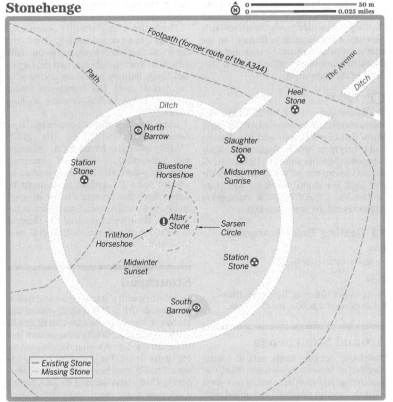

0 ————— 50 m
0 ————— 0.025 miles

Footpath (former route of the A344)

Path

The Avenue

Ditch

Heel Stone

Ditch

North Barrow

Slaughter Stone

Station Stone

Bluestone Horseshoe

Midsummer Sunrise

Altar Stone

Sarsen Circle

Trilithon Horseshoe

Midwinter Sunset

Station Stone

South Barrow

☐ Existing Stone
☐ Missing Stone

Although no one is entirely sure how the builders transported the stones so far, it's thought they probably used a system of ropes, sledges and rollers fashioned from tree trunks – Salisbury Plain was still covered by forest during Stonehenge's construction.

Around 1500 BC, Stonehenge's main stones were dragged to the site, erected in a circle and crowned by massive lintels to make the trilithons (two vertical stones topped by a horizontal one). The sarsen (sandstone) stones were cut from an extremely hard rock found on the Marlborough Downs, 20 miles from the site. It's estimated that dragging one of these 50-ton stones across the countryside would require about 600 people.

Also around this time, the bluestones from 500 years earlier were rearranged as an inner bluestone horseshoe with an altar stone at the centre. Outside this the trilithon horseshoe of five massive sets of

stones was erected. Three of these are intact; the other two have just a single upright. Then came the major sarsen circle of 30 massive vertical stones, of which 17 uprights and six lintels remain.

Much further out, another circle was delineated by the 58 Aubrey Holes, named after John Aubrey, who discovered them in the 1600s. Just inside this circle are the South and North Barrows, each originally topped by a stone. Like many stone circles in Britain (including Avebury (p270), 22 miles away) the inner horseshoes are aligned to coincide with sunrise at the midsummer solstice, which some claim supports the theory that the site was some kind of astronomical calendar.

Prehistoric pilgrims would have entered the site via the Avenue, whose entrance to the circle is marked by the Slaughter Stone and the Heel Stone, located slightly further out on one side.

A marked pathway leads around the site, and although you can't walk freely in the circle itself, it's possible to see the stones fairly close up. An audioguide is included in the admission price, and can be obtained from the Stonehenge tourist office, which is 50m north of the main circle.

 Tours

The Stonehenge Tour (☑01722-336855; www.thestonehengetour.info; return adult/child £11/5) leaves Salisbury's railway and bus stations half-hourly from June to August, and hourly between September and May. Tickets last all day, so you can hop off at Old Sarum on the way back. For guided tours, try Salisbury Guided Tours. (☑07775-674816; www.salisburyguidedtours.com; per person from £72).

❶ Getting There & Around

Bus

No regular buses go to the site.

Taxi

Taxis charge £40 to go to Stonehenge from Salisbury, wait for an hour and come back.

Around Stonehenge

Stonehenge actually forms part of a huge complex of ancient monuments. North of Stonehenge and running roughly east–west is the Cursus, an elongated embanked oval; the slightly smaller Lesser Cursus is nearby. Theories abound as to what these sites were used for, ranging from ancient sporting arenas to processional avenues for the dead. Two clusters of burial mounds, the Old and New Kings Barrows, sit beside the ceremonial pathway the Avenue, which originally linked Stonehenge with the River Avon, 2 miles away.

The National Trust website (www.nationaltrust.org.uk) has a downloadable 3½-mile circular walk that traces tracks across the chalk downland from Stonehenge, past the Cursus and Kings Barrows and along a section of the Avenue itself. The Stonehenge visitor centre also has leaflets detailing walking routes.

Some 1½ miles east of Stonehenge, near Amesbury, is Woodhenge (EH; ☑0870 3331181; www.english-heritage.org.uk; admission free; ☺dawn-dusk), a series of concentric rings that would once have been marked by wooden posts. It's thought there might be some correlation between the use of wood and stone in both henges. Excavations in the 1970s at Woodhenge revealed the skeleton of a child with a cloven skull, buried near the centre.

Stourhead

Overflowing with vistas, temples and follies, Stourhead (NT; ☑01747-841152; www.nationaltrust.org.uk; house or garden adult/child £7.50/4.10, house & garden £12.50/6.20; ☺house 11am-5pm Fri-Tue mid-Mar–Sep; ℗) is landscape gardening at its finest. The Palladian house has some fine Chippendale furniture and paintings by Claude and Gaspard Poussin, but it's a sideshow to the magnificent 18th-century gardens (☺9am-dusk year-round), which spread out across the valley. A picturesque 2-mile circuit takes you past the most ornate follies, around the lake and to the Temple of Apollo; a 3½-mile side trip can be made from near the Pantheon to King Alfred's Tower (adult/child £3/1.50; ☺noon-4pm school

---

CHANGING STONEHENGE

Ancient Stonehenge is undergoing significant change. For decades debate has raged over the impact of the modern world on the jewel in Britain's archaeological crown. Framed by busy roads, bound by wire fences, crowded with visitors and underscored by traffic noise, it's been a long way from the haven of spiritual tranquillity some expected to find.

But work is now underway to reconnect this stirring monument with its surrounding ritual landscape. The busy A344, which cut the henge off from its processional Avenue, is being closed (in April 2013) and turned into a grassy footpath which will provide the main access to the site. Close to the stones, the visitor centre and car park is being removed and the land returned to grassland. A new visitor centre, due for completion in October 2013, is being built 1½ miles to the west. It'll have an archaeology gallery with Stonehenge finds, plus a cluster of recreated Neolithic houses. The hoped for result? Dignity and mystery returned to an archaeological gem in a much more fitting setting.

holidays only), a 50m-high folly with wonderful views.

Stourhead is off the B3092, 8 miles south of Frome (in Somerset).

Longleat

Half ancestral mansion and half safari park, Longleat (☑01985-844400; www .longleat.co.uk; all-inclusive ticket adult/child £27/20, house & grounds £13.50/8.50; ☺10am-7.30pm Jul & Aug, to 5pm Apr-Jun, to 4pm Mar, Sep & Oct; Ⓟ) became the first stately home in England to open its doors to the public, in 1946. It was prompted by finance: heavy taxes and mounting post-WWII bills meant the house had to earn its keep. The estate was transformed into Britain's first safari park in 1966, turning Capability Brown's landscaped grounds into an amazing drive-through zoo, populated by a menagerie of animals more at home in the African wilderness than the fields of Wiltshire. Longleat also has a throng of attractions, including a narrow-gauge railway, a Dr Who exhibit, a Postman Pat village, pets' corner and a butterfly garden.

Under all these tourist trimmings it's easy to forget the house itself, which contains fine tapestries, furniture and decorated ceilings, as well as seven libraries containing around 40,000 tomes. The highlight, though, is an extraordinary series of paintings and psychedelic murals by the present-day marquess, who was an art student in the '60s and upholds the long-standing tradition of eccentricity among the English aristocracy – check out his website (www.lordbath .co.uk).

Longleat House is just off the A362, 3 miles from both Frome and Warminster.

Malmesbury

The mellow hilltop town of Malmesbury is peppered with ancient buildings constructed out of honey-coloured Cotswold stone. It's the oldest borough in England, having been awarded that civic status in AD 880, and boasts one of the county's finest market crosses – a 15th-century crown-like structure built to shelter the poor from the rain.

The town's big draw is Malmesbury Abbey (☑01666-826666; www.malmesbury abbey.info; suggested donation £2; ☺10am-5pm), a wonderful blend of ruin and living church, with a somewhat turbulent history. It be-

gan life as a 7th-century monastery, which was later replaced by a Norman church. By the mid-15th century the abbey had been embellished with a spire and twin towers, but in 1479 a storm toppled the east tower and spire, destroying the eastern end of the church. The west tower followed suit in 1662, destroying much of the nave. The present-day church is about a third of its original size, and is flanked by ruins at either end. Notable features include the Norman doorway decorated with biblical figures, the Romanesque Apostle carvings and a four-volume illuminated bible dating from 1407. A window at the western end of the church depicts Elmer the Flying Monk, who in 1010 strapped on wings and jumped from the tower. Although he broke both legs during this leap of faith, he survived and became a local hero.

Just below the abbey are the Abbey House Gardens (☑01666-822212; www.abbey housegardens.co.uk; adult/child £8/3; ☺11am-5.30pm mid-Mar–Oct), which include a herb garden, river, waterfall and 2 hectares of colourful blooms.

Bus 31 runs to Swindon (45 minutes, hourly Monday to Saturday), while bus 91 heads to Chippenham (35 minutes, hourly Monday to Saturday).

Lacock

With its geranium-covered cottages, higgledy-piggledy rooftops and idyllic location next to a rushing brook, pockets of the medieval village of Lacock seem to have been preserved in aspic since the mid-19th century. The village has been in the hands of the National Trust since 1944, and in many places is remarkably free of modern development – there are no telephone poles or electric street lights, and although villagers drive around the streets, the main car park on the outskirts keeps it largely traffic-free. Unsurprisingly, it's also a popular location for costume dramas and feature films – the village and its abbey pop up in the Harry Potter films, *The Other Boleyn Girl* and BBC adaptations of *Moll Flanders* and *Pride and Prejudice*.

◉ Sights

Lacock Abbey ABBEY
(NT; ☑01249-730459; www.nationaltrust.org.uk; adult/child £10.70/5.30; ☺10.30am-5.30pm Mar-Oct, 11am-4pm Nov-Feb) Lacock Abbey was founded as an Augustinian nunnery in 1232

by Ela, Countess of Salisbury. After the Dissolution the abbey was sold to Sir William Sharington in 1539, who converted the nunnery into a home, demolished the church, built a tower and added a brewery. Highlights are the deeply atmospheric medieval rooms, while the stunning Gothic entrance hall is lined with bizarre terracotta figures; spot the scapegoat with a lump of sugar on its nose. Some of the original 13th-century structure is evident in the cloisters and there are traces of medieval wall paintings. The recently restored botanic garden is also worth a visit.

On Tuesdays year-round and on winter weekdays, access to the abbey is limited to the cloisters. A cheaper ticket (adult/child £7.90/4) will get you into the grounds, museum and abbey cloisters, but not the abbey building itself.

The ticket into the abbey also includes admission to the Fox Talbot Museum of Photography, which profiles the man who pioneered the photographic negative: William Henry Fox Talbot (1800–77). A prolific inventor, he began developing the system in 1834 while working at the abbey. The museum details his ground-breaking work and displays a superb collection of his images.

🛏 Sleeping & Eating

Sign of the Angel   B&B **£££**
(📞01249-730230; www.lacock.co.uk; 6 Church St; s £85, d £130-165; 🅿) If you want to slumber amid a superb slice of history, check into this 15th-century beamed bolt-hole. Packed with antique beds, tapestries and buffed chests, comfort levels are brought up to date with free-standing sinks and slipper baths. The restaurant revels in English classics – try the pigeon, Stilton and walnut pâté, then squeeze in treacle tart with clotted cream.

King John's Hunting Lodge   B&B **££**
(📞01249-730313; www.kingjohnslodge.2day.ws; 21 Church St; s/d/f £80/100/130; 🅿) Lacock's oldest building is a picturesque venue for a quintessentially English afternoon tea (£7 to £16) of cucumber sandwiches, scones, clotted cream and home-made jam. Upstairs, snug, resolutely old-fashioned bedrooms are crammed with creaky furniture and Tudor touches.

Lacock Pottery   B&B **££**
(📞01249-730266; www.lacockbedandbreakfast .com; d £84-94; 🅿🛜) A serene, airy former workhouse featuring peat fires, organic breakfasts and, appropriately, fine ceramics.

George Inn   PUB **£**
(4 West St; mains from £10) A 14th-century, horse brass–hung pub dispensing good grub and local ales.

❶ Getting There & Away

Bus 234 runs hourly, Monday to Saturday, from Chippenham (15 minutes).

Avebury

While the tour buses head straight for Stonehenge, prehistoric purists make for the massive stone circle at Avebury. Though it undoubtedly lacks the dramatic trilithons of its sister site across the plain, Avebury is arguably a more rewarding place to visit. It's bigger, older and a great deal quieter, and a large section of the village is actually inside the stones – footpaths wind around them, allowing you to really soak up the extraordinary atmosphere. Avebury also boasts a surrounding landscape that's rich in prehistoric sites, and a unique attraction: a manor house where extensively restored rooms span five completely different eras.

◉ Sights

TOP CHOICE **Avebury Stone Circle**   MONUMENT
(NT; 📞01672-539250; www.nationaltrust.org.uk; ☺24hr) With a diameter of about 348m, Avebury is the largest stone circle in the world. It's also one of the oldest, dating from around 2500 to 2200 BC, between the first and second phase of construction at Stonehenge. The site originally consisted of an outer circle of 98 standing stones of up to 6m in length, many weighing 20 tons, which had been carefully selected for their shape and size. The stones were surrounded by another circle delineated by a 5m-high earth bank and ditch up to 9m deep. Inside were smaller stone circles to the north (27 stones) and south (29 stones).

In the Middle Ages, when Britain's pagan past was an embarrassment to the church, many of the stones were buried, removed or broken up. In 1934, wealthy businessman and archaeologist Alexander Keiller supervised the re-erection of the stones, and planted markers to indicate those that had disappeared; he later bought the site for posterity using funds from his family's marmalade fortune.

Self-Guided Tour

Modern roads into Avebury neatly dissect the circle into four sectors. Starting at High St, near the Henge Shop, and walking round the circle in an anticlockwise direction, you'll encounter 11 standing stones in the southwest sector. They include the Barber Surgeon Stone, named after the skeleton of a man found under it – the equipment buried with him suggests he was a barber-cum-surgeon.

The southeast sector starts with the huge portal stones marking the entry to the circle from the West Kennet Avenue. The southern inner circle stood in this sector and within this ring was the obelisk and a group of stones known as the Z Feature. Just outside this smaller circle, only the base of the Ring Stone remains.

In the northern inner circle in the northeast sector, three sarsens remain of what would have been a rectangular cove. The northwest sector has the most complete collection of standing stones, including the massive 65-ton Swindon Stone, one of the few never to have been toppled.

Avebury Manor HISTORIC BUILDING
(NT; ☏01672-539250; www.nationaltrust.org.uk; adult/child £9/4.50; ☺11am-5pm Thu-Tue Apr-Oct) This 16th-century manor house had the mother of all heritage makeovers as part of the BBC TV series *The Manor Reborn*. It used original techniques and materials to recreate interiors spanning five periods, so now you can sit on beds, play billiards and listen to the grammar phone in rooms that range from Tudor, through Georgian to the 1930s. In the garden, the topiary and box hedges create a series of rooms that inspired Vita Sackville-West, creator of Sissinghurst gardens in Kent. Visits are by timed tickets only; arrive early to bag a slot.

Silbury Hill PREHISTORIC SITE
(www.english-heritage.org.uk) This huge mound rises abruptly from the surrounding fields just west of Avebury. At more than 40m high, it's the largest artificial earthwork in Europe and was built in stages from around 2500 BC. No significant artefacts have been found at the site, and the reason for its construction remains unclear. A massive project to stabilise the hill took place in 2008 after a combination of erosion and damage caused by earlier excavations caused part of the top to collapse. Direct access to the hill isn't allowed, but you can view it from a lay-by on the A4. For more atmospheric views, take the footpath across the fields from Avebury (1½ miles each way) to the hill's north side.

FREE **West Kennet Long Barrow** BURIAL MOUND
(EH; ☏01672-539250; www.english-heritage.org.uk; ☺dawn-dusk) Set in the fields south of Silbury Hill, this is England's finest burial mound and dates from around 3500 BC. Its entrance is guarded by huge sarsens and its roof is made out of gigantic overlapping capstones. About 50 skeletons were found when it was excavated; finds are on display at the Wiltshire Heritage Museum (☏01380-727369; www.wiltshireheritage.org.uk; 41 Long St; adult/child £5/4; ☺10am-5pm Mon-Sat, noon-4pm Sun) in Devizes. A footpath just to the east of Silbury Hill leads to West Kennet (500m).

🍽 Sleeping & Eating

TOP CHOICE **Manor Farm** B&B ££
(☏01672-539294; www.manorfarmavebury.com; High St; s £75-85, d £75-95; P) A rare chance to sleep in style inside a stone circle – this red-brick farmhouse snuggles just inside Avebury henge. The elegant, comfy rooms blend old woods with bright furnishings, there's a splendid free-standing claw-foot bath, and the windows provide spine-tingling views of those 4000-year-old standing stones.

Circle CAFE £
(mains from £7; ☺10am-6pm; 🖋) A veggie and wholefood cafe beside the Great Barn

SOUTHWEST ENGLAND AVEBURY

RITUAL LANDSCAPE

Avebury is surrounded by a network of ancient monuments, including Silbury Hill and West Kennet Long Barrow. To the south of the village, the West Kennet Avenue stretched out for 1½ miles, lined by 100 pairs of stones. It linked the Avebury circle with a site called the Sanctuary. Post holes indicate that a wooden building surrounded by a stone circle once stood at the Sanctuary, although no one knows quite what the site was for.

The Ridgeway national trail starts near Avebury and runs eastwards across Fyfield Down, where many of the sarsen stones at Avebury (and Stonehenge) were collected.

Avebury

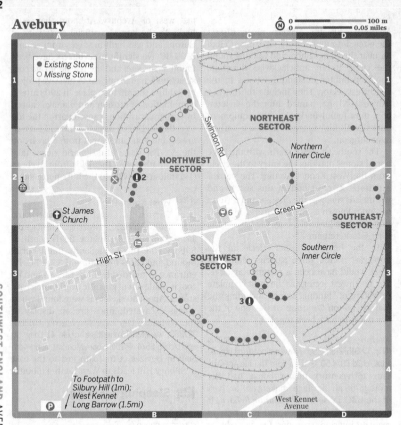

- Existing Stone
- Missing Stone

Swindon Rd

NORTHEAST SECTOR

Northern Inner Circle

NORTHWEST SECTOR

St James Church

Green St

SOUTHEAST SECTOR

High St

Southern Inner Circle

SOUTHWEST SECTOR

To Footpath to
Silbury Hill (1mi);
West Kennet
Long Barrow (1.5mi)

West Kennet Avenue

Avebury

⊙ Sights
1 Avebury Manor A2
2 Avebury Stone Circle B2
3 West Kennet Avenue C3

⊜ Sleeping
4 Manor Farm B3

⊗ Eating
5 Circle B2

⊜ Drinking
6 Red Lion C2

serving homemade quiches and cakes, chunky sandwiches and afternoon teas.

🍷 Drinking

Red Lion   PUB
(Swindon Rd; mains from £7) Having a pint here means downing a drink at the only pub in the world inside a stone circle. It's also haunted by Flori, who was killed during the Civil War when her husband threw her down a well – its plunging shaft now forms the centrepiece of the dining room.

ℹ️ Getting There & Away

Bus 49 runs hourly between Avebury, Swindon (30 minutes) and Devizes (25 minutes; change for Salisbury).

BRISTOL

POP 393,300

Bristol might just be Britain's most overlooked city. While most visitors speed past en route to Bath without giving the southwest's biggest metropolis so much as a second glance, they're missing out on one of Britain's quirkiest and coolest cities. Once dominated by heavy industry and badly damaged during WWII, over the last decade or so Bristol has reinvented itself as a hub of culture and creativity, with a wealth of art galleries, theatres, design studios and media companies dotted around the much-revitalised centre. With a revamped waterfront, a flashy new shopping centre at Cabot Circus and a landmark new history museum at M Shed – not to mention its status as the UK's first-ever Bike City – there's a definite buzz about Brizzle these days.

History

The city began as a small Saxon village and the medieval river-port of Brigstow. Bristol developed as a trading centre for cloth and wine, before 'local hero' John Cabot (actually a Genoese sailor called Giovanni Caboto) really put the city on the map, when he set sail from Bristol to discover Newfoundland in 1497. Over the following centuries, Bristol became one of Britain's major ports, and grew rich on the proceeds of the transatlantic slave trade, and from dealing in cocoa, sugar and tobacco.

By the 18th century Bristol was suffering from competition from other UK ports, especially London and Liverpool. The city repositioned itself as an industrial centre, becoming an important hub for shipbuilding and the terminus for the pioneering Great Western Railway line from London. During the 20th century Bristol also played a key role in Britain's burgeoning aeronautics industry: many key components of Concorde were developed in the nearby suburb of Filton.

During WWII the city's heavy industry became a key target for German bombing, and much of the city centre was reduced to rubble. The postwar rush for reconstruction left Bristol with plenty of concrete eyesores, but over the last decade the city has undergone extensive redevelopment, especially around the dockside.

In 2006, the city celebrated the bicentenary of the birth of Isambard Kingdom Brunel, the pioneering Victorian engineer responsible (among many other things) for developing the Great Western Railway, the Clifton Suspension Bridge and SS *Great Britain*.

⊙ Sights

TOP CHOICE **SS Great Britain** SHIP
(www.ssgreatbritain.org; Great Western Dock, Gas Ferry Rd; adult/child/family £12.50/6.25/33.50; ⊙10am-5.30pm Apr-Oct) Bristol's pride and joy is the mighty steamship SS *Great Britain*, designed by the genius engineer Isambard Kingdom Brunel in 1843. Built from iron and driven by a revolutionary screw propeller, this massive vessel was one of the largest and most technologically advanced steamships ever built, measuring a mighty 322ft (98m) from stern to tip, and capable of completing the Transatlantic crossing between Bristol and New York in just 14 days. She served as a luxury liner until 1886, but enormous running costs and mounting debts eventually led her towards an ignominious end: she was sold off and served variously as a troop vessel, quarantine ship, emigration transport and coal-hulk, before finally being scuttled near Port Stanley in the Falklands in 1937.

Happily, that wasn't the end for the SS *Great Britain*. The ship was towed back to Bristol in 1970, and a painstaking 30-year restoration program has since brought her back to stunning life. You can wander around the ship's impeccably refurbished interior, including the galley, surgeon's quarters, dining saloon and the great engine room, but the highlight is the amazing 'glass sea' on which the ship sits, enclosing an airtight dry dock that preserves the delicate hull and allows visitors to see the ground-breaking screw propeller up close.

Tickets also allow admission to the neighbouring Maritime Heritage Centre (☑0117-927 9856; Great Western Dockyard, Gas Ferry Rd; ⊙10am-5.30pm Apr-Oct, 10am-4.30pm Nov-Mar), which has exhibits on the ship's illustrious past and the city's boat-building heritage.

During autumn and winter, a replica of John Cabot's ship, the Matthew (☑0117-927 6868; www.matthew.co.uk), is moored nearby, the same design of ship in which the explorer made his landmark voyage from Bristol to Newfoundland in 1497. When the ship's docked in Bristol, it runs regular cruises around the harbour (adult/child £10/8); see the website for the next sailing dates.

FM Shed MUSEUM
(www.mshed.org; Princes Wharf; ⊙10am-5pm Tue-Fri, 10am-6pm Sat & Sun; ⊕) It's taken four years and £27m to build, but Bristol's brand-new museum is finally open – and it's really rather brilliant. Lodged in a massive old warehouse overlooking the docks, it's a treasure trove of weird-and-wonderful memorabilia rummaging through the city's past. The 3000-odd exhibits are divided into three sections (People, Place and Life), and

Bristol

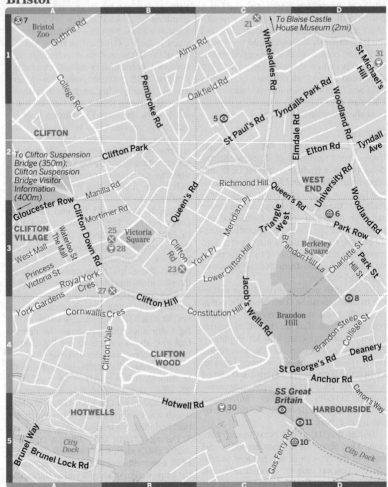

provide a panoramic overview of Bristol's history – from slaves' possessions and vintage double-decker buses to Wallace and Gromit figurines and a set of bright-pink decks once used by Massive Attack. Multimedia displays and background panels make everything enormously accessible, and you're absolutely guaranteed to walk away with a deepened understanding of the city. Best of all, it's free – although well worth the £2 suggested donation.

Clifton Village   HISTORIC AREA

During the 18th and 19th centuries, wealthy Bristol merchants transformed the former spa resort of Clifton into an elegant hilltop suburb packed with impressive Georgian mansions. Some of the finest examples can be seen along Cornwallis Cres and Royal York Cres. These days, Clifton is still the poshest postcode in Bristol, with a wealth of streetside cafes and designer shops, and a villagey atmosphere that's far removed from the rest of the city.

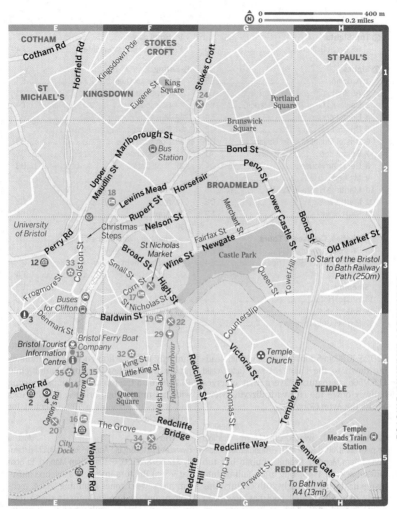

Clifton Suspension Bridge BRIDGE

(www.cliftonbridge.org.uk) Clifton's most famous (and photographed) landmark is another Brunel masterpiece, the 76m-high Clifton Suspension Bridge, which spans the Avon Gorge from Clifton over to Leigh Woods in northern Somerset. Construction began in 1836, but sadly Brunel died before the bridge's completion in 1864. It was mainly designed to carry light horse-drawn traffic and foot passengers, but these days around 12,000 cars cross it every day – testament to the quality of the construction and the vision of Brunel's design.

It's free to walk or cycle across the bridge; car drivers pay a 50p toll. There's a **visitor information point** (visitinfo@clifton-suspension -bridge.org; ☺10am-5pm) near the tower on the Leigh Woods side. Free guided tours of the bridge take place at 3pm on Saturdays and Sundays from Easter to October.

The Downs PARKS

Near the bridge, the grassy parks of Clifton Down and Durdham Down (often referred to as just the Downs) make a fine spot for a picnic. Nearby, a well-worn observatory houses a **camera obscura** (adult/child

Bristol

£2/1; ⊙10.30am-5.30pm) and a tunnel leading down to the **Giant's Cave** (adult/child £1.50/50p), a natural cavern that emerges halfway down the cliff with dizzying views across the Avon Gorge.

Bristol Lido   BATHHOUSE
(☑01179-339530; www.lidobristol.com; Oakfield Pl; pool adult/child £20/7.50; ⊙nonmembers sessions 1-4pm Mon-Fri) Bristol's public hot tub dates back to 1849, but after falling into disrepair during the early 20th century, this lovely naturally heated pool has now been fully restored and is back to its steamy best (with a balmy water temperature of around 24°C). Spa treatments and massage sessions are also available, and there's a rather good bar and restaurant where you can relax once you're done. Priority is given to members; on weekends and busy days the lido is closed for day visitors, so phone ahead to make sure there's space.

Bristol Zoo   ZOO
(www.bristolzoo.org.uk; adult/child £14.50/8.75; ⊙9am-5.30pm) The city's award-winning zoo occupies a huge site on the north side of Clifton. Highlights include gorilla and gibbon islands, a reptile and bug house, a

butterfly forest, a lion enclosure, a monkey jungle and the new **Zooropia** (adult/child £7.70/6.70), a treetop adventure park strung with net ramps, rope bridges, hanging logs and a zip-line. There's a 10% discount for online tickets.

At-Bristol   MUSEUM
(www.at-bristol.org.uk; Anchor Rd; adult/child/family £12.50/8/35.50; ⊙10am-5pm Mon-Fri, to 6pm Sat & Sun) Bristol's interactive science museum has several zones spanning space, technology and the human brain. In the Curiosity Zone you get to walk through a tornado, spin on a human gyroscope and strum the strings of a virtual harp. It's fun, imaginative and interactive, and should keep kids entertained for a few hours.

Bristol Aquarium   AQUARIUM
(www.bristolaquarium.co.uk; Harbourside; adult/child/family £12.50/8.75/38.50; ⊙10am-5pm Mon-Fri, to 6pm Sat & Sun) Bristol's harbourside aquarium has been newly renovated, with underwater habitats including a Bay of Rays, a Coral Sea, a Shark Tank and an Amazon River Zone. There's also an informative section about Britain's native habitats and an impressive underwater tunnel, as well

as a new star resident, Velcro the Pacific Octopus. There's a £2 discount for buying in advance online.

Arnolfini GALLERY
(www.arnolfini.org.uk; 16 Narrow Quay; ⊙10am-6pm Tue-Sun) The city's avant-garde art gallery occupies a hulking redbrick warehouse by the river, and remains the top venue in town for modern art, as well as occasional exhibitions of dance, film and photography.

FREE **Bristol Museum & Art Gallery** MUSEUM
(Queen's Rd; ⊙10am-5pm) Housed in a stunning Edwardian baroque building, the city museum and art gallery has an excellent collection of British and French art; galleries dedicated to ceramics and decorative arts; and archaeological, geological and natural history wings. Renovation works are currently in progress, so some galleries may be closed.

FREE **Georgian House** HISTORIC BUIDLING
(7 Great George St; ⊙10am-4pm Tue-Sun Apr-Aug) This 18th-century house provides an evocative illustration of aristocratic life in Bristol during the Georgian era. The six-storeyed house belonged to West India merchant John Pinney, along with his slave Pero (after whom Pero's Bridge across the harbour is named). It's decorated throughout in period style, typified by the huge kitchen (complete with cast-iron roasting spit), the book-lined library and the grand drawing rooms. Look out for Pinney's cold-water plunge-pool in the basement.

FREE **Red Lodge** HISTORIC BUILDING
(Park Row; ⊙10am-4pm Tue-Sun Apr-Aug) Built in 1590 but remodelled in 1730, this red-brick house is a mix of Elizabethan, Stuart and Georgian architecture. The highlight is the Great Oak Room, which still features its original Elizabethan oak panelling, plaster-work ceiling and carved chimney piece.

FREE **Blaise Castle House Museum** MUSEUM
(Henbury Rd; ⊙10am-5pm Wed-Sat) In the northern suburb of Henbury is this late-18th-century house and social-history museum. Displays include vintage toys, costumes and other Victorian ephemera. Bus 42/42A (45 minutes, every 15 minutes) passes the castle from Colston Ave; bus 1 (20 minutes, every 10 minutes) from the station and St Augustine's Pde doesn't stop quite as close, but is quicker.

☞ Tours

Bristol Highlights Walk WALKING TOUR
(www.bristolwalks.co.uk; adult/under 12yr £3.50/ free; ⊙11am Sat Apr-Sep) Tours the old town, city centre and Harbourside. It's run every Saturday at 11am; just turn up outside the tourist office. Themed tours for groups exploring Clifton, Brunel and the history of Bristol traders are run on request.

THE TRIANGULAR TRADE

It's a sobering thought that much of Bristol's 18th-century wealth and splendour was founded on human exploitation. In the late 1600s, the first slave ship set sail from Bristol harbour, kick-starting the city's connections with the so-called 'triangular trade', in which Africans had been kidnapped from their homes (or traded, usually for munitions) before being shipped across the Atlantic and sold into a life of slavery in the New World. Conditions on the boats were horrific; it was expected that one in 10 of those captured would die en route – in reality, many more did. Their human cargo unloaded, the merchants stocked their vessels with luxury goods such as sugar, rum, indigo, tobacco and cotton, and sailed back to Britain.

Bristol, London and Liverpool were the three main British ports engaged in the practice. By the time the slave trade (not slavery itself) was finally abolished in the British Empire in 1807, it's thought that 500,000 Africans were enslaved by Bristol merchants – a fifth of all people sold into slavery by British vessels.

The financial profits for Bristol's traders were immense, and that legacy lingers. Many of the grand houses in Clifton were built on the proceeds of the 'trade', and several of the city's most elegant edifices – such as the Bristol Old Vic theatre – were partly financed by slave-trading investors.

For further insights, download the MP3 audio tour from the Visit Bristol (www.visit bristol.co.uk) website, or pick up the Slave Trade Trail leaflet (£3) from the tourist office.

WORTH A TRIP

TYNTESFIELD

Formerly the aristocratic home of the Gibbs family, Tyntesfield (NT; ☎01275-461900; www.nationaltrust.org.uk/tyntesfield; adult/child £12.60/6.20, gardens only £7.50/4.10; ⊙11am-5pm Sat-Wed Mar-Oct) is an ornate Victorian pile that prickles with spiky turrets and towers. The house was built in grand Gothic Revival style by the architect John Norton, and is crammed with Victorian decorative arts, a working kitchen garden and a magnificent private chapel. The house has undergone extensive (and very expensive) renovation since being acquired in 2001, and has now regained something very close to its former splendour. Work is still underway to renovate the house's ornate orangery and walled gardens.

Tyntesfield is 7 miles southwest of Bristol, off the B3128.

FREE MP3 Tours   WALKING TOUR
(www.visitbristol.co.uk/about-bristol/video-and-audio/audio-tours) Free downloadable MP3 guides covering the slave trade, Brunel, pirates, heritage architecture, historic churches and the city's literary connections.

Bristol Packet Boat Trips   BOAT TOUR
(www.bristolpacket.co.uk; ⊙11am-4.15pm Sat & Sun) This boat company runs regular cruises around the harbour area (adult/child £5.50/3.50, departures every 45 minutes, daily during school holidays). There are also weekly cruises along the Avon from May to October (adult/child £15/13) and a regular Sunday afternoon trip to Beese's Tea Gardens (£9.90/6.25). Cruises to Bath (£26/15) run once a month from May to September.

 Festivals & Events

Bristol Shakespeare Festival   THEATRE
(www.bristolshakespeare.org.uk) Britain's biggest outdoor festival devoted to the Bard, held between May and September.

Bristol Harbour Festival   COMMUNITY FESTIVAL
(www.bristolharbourfestival.co.uk) Bands, events and historic ships take over the city's docks in early August.

International Balloon Fiesta   HOT-AIR BALLOONS
(www.bristolballoonfiesta.co.uk) Hot-air balloons fill the skies at Ashton Court in August.

Encounters   FILM FESTIVAL
(www.encounters-festival.org.uk) Bristol's largest film-fest is in November.

Sleeping

Bristol's hotels tend to be geared towards the business crowd, but there are a couple of great-value chains and a handful of intriguing new B&Bs dotted around the city centre.

TOP CHOICE Number 38   B&B £££
(☎0117-946 6905; www.number38clifton.com; 38 Upper Belgrave Rd, Clifton; d £138; P☎) Perched on the edge of the Downs, this super new B&B puts most of the city's hotels to shame in terms of designer decor. The 10 rooms are huge, contemporary and very cool – sombre greys and smooth blues dictate the colour palette, while waffle bathrobes and REN bath goodies await in the power showers, and city views unfold from the roof terrace. The two suites even have old-fashioned tin baths. It's really handy for Clifton and Whiteladies roads, but a long walk from the centre, so it might not be ideal for everyone.

TOP CHOICE Hotel du Vin   HOTEL £££
(☎0117-925 5577; www.hotelduvin.com; Narrow Lewins Mead; r £145-215; P☎) If expense is no object, there's only one choice in Bristol, and that's this indulgently elegant warehouse conversion. Occupying an old sugar store, it's a mix of industrial chic and sleek minimalism, complete with giant futon beds, clawfoot baths and frying-pan showerheads. All the rooms are named after vintage champagnes; the best are the split-level suites with mezzanines. The bistro is a beaut, too.

Brooks Guest House   B&B ££
(☎0117-930 0066; www.brooksguesthousebristol.com; Exchange Ave; d £70-99; ☎) Bristol has been crying out for a smart, modern B&B near the city centre for years – and at long last it has one, and in a fantastic spot right next door to St Nick's Market too. Rooms are a tad boxy, but pleasantly finished with flock wallpaper, John Lewis bedlinen and Hansgröhe power showers. Downstairs, there's a contemporary lounge with leather chairs and wood floors, and a cute city garden for breakfast or afternoon tea. Parking is available for £9.50 at the nearby Queen Charlotte St car park.

Greenhouse — B&B ££

(0117-902 9166; www.thegreenhousebristol.co.uk; 61 Greenbank Rd, Southville; s/d £60/99; P) No bells and whistles here – just a lovely, friendly, quiet B&B in Southville, a few minutes' stride to the river and the centre. Cream rooms, white sheets and an excellent all-organic breakfast make it well worth considering.

Bristol Hotel — HOTEL ££

(0117-923 0333; www.doylecollection.com/locations/bristol_hotels/the_bristol_hotel.aspx; Prince St; d £95-155) This newly redone hotel (formerly the Jury's Inn) has lots in its favour – riverside location, luxurious rooms, bistro – but it's pretty pricey and frequented by a businessy crowd. The downstairs River Grille restaurant is a popular spot for dinner with the city's suits. No car park, but there's an NCP next door.

Bristol YHA — HOSTEL ££

(bristol@yha.org.uk; 14 Narrow Quay; dm/s/d £22/37/74) Few hostels can boast a position as good as this one, right beside the river in a red-brick warehouse. Facilities are great, including kitchens, cycle store, games room and the excellent Grainshed coffee lounge – but the dorms are pretty functional, and the doubles are expensive.

Mercure Brigstow Hotel — HOTEL ££

(0117-929 1030; H6548@accor.com; Welsh Back; d £63-125) Despite the concrete-and-glass facade, this Mercure hotel's surprisingly cool inside. Bedrooms boast floating beds, curved panel walls and tiny TVs set into bathroom tiles (gimmicky, yes, but fun).

Eating

Eating out in Bristol is a real highlight – the city is jammed with restaurants of every description, ranging from classic British 'caffs' to designer dining emporiums.

TOP CHOICE Bell's Diner — BRITISH ££

(0117-924 0357; www.bellsdiner.com; 1-3 York Rd; dinner mains £14.50-21, tasting menu £49.50; lunch Wed-Fri, dinner Tue-Sat) Run by one of the city's most respected chefs, Christopher Wicks, Bell's is very probably Bristol's best – and certainly most daring – bistro. Wicks is known for his adventurous flavour combinations, and the menu is full of exotic-sounding ingredients (pink fur potato, onion soubise, seaweed, toasted hay). But at its core, his food is all about celebrating the very best of British – best experienced on the eight-course tasting menu – an ethos that seems perfectly suited to the restaurant's setting in a converted grocer's shop in lively Montpelier. Bookings are essential.

Muset by Ronnie — BRITISH ££

(0117-973 7248; www.ronnies-restaurant.co.uk; 12-16 Clifton Rd; 2-/3-course lunch menu £13/16, dinner menu £19/22, mains £13-21) Chef Ron Faulkner has a new Clifton establishment, in addition to his original, much-vaunted address in Thornbury. Faulkner trained under big names including Anton Mosimann and Ed Baines, and his Brit-meets-Mediterranean blend has earned him local fans as well as critical acclaim. Expect rich, hearty fare such as smoked eel, lamb shank and roast duck, served with a contemporary side of steamed kohlrabi or brown shrimp butter.

Riverstation — BRITISH ££

(0117-914 4434; www.riverstation.co.uk; 2-/3-course lunch £12.75/15.50, dinner mains £14.50-19.75) It's been around for many years now, but this riverside bistro is as reliable as ever. It's a split-level affair, with a downstairs cafe for coffee, cake and light lunches, and

SOUTHWEST ENGLAND BRISTOL

BRISTOL IN...

Two Days

Begin your time in Bristol by exploring the city's historic **Floating Harbour.** Devote a morning to the magnificent **SS Great Britain**, followed by lunch at **Riverstation**. In the afternoon, check out the latest exhibition at the **Arnolfini art gallery**, and then spend some time exploring Bristol's history at its excellent new city museum, **M Shed**. Finish up with dinner at **Glassboat**, and indulge yourself with a night at the swanky **Hotel du Vin**.

On day two, head up the hill to stately Clifton. Factor in a walk across the **suspension bridge**, a stroll across the **Downs**, and lunch at one of the area's many cafes and restaurants – we particularly like **Thali Café**. Spend the afternoon talking to the animals at **Bristol Zoo** or swimming at the **Bristol Lido**, then catch a cab to **Bell's Diner** or **Muset by Ronnie** for supper before retiring to bed at **Number 38**.

a more refined bistro on the 1st floor that turns out some of the city's best European cuisine. Ask for a window table to make the most of the harbour views.

Cowshed
BRITISH ££

(☎0117-973 3550; www.thecowshedbristol.com; 46 Whiteladies Rd; 3-course lunch £10, dinner mains £12.95-21.50) Country dining in a city setting. The feel's half-rustic, half-contemporary – big windows and modern murals contrast with exposed stone and pine furniture – and the menu's all about hearty flavours: lamb shoulder with root-veg mash, or roast quail and pigeon with bubble-and-squeak. The Sunday roast is an institution.

Cafe Maitreya
VEGETARIAN ££

(☎0117-951 0100; www.cafemaitreya.co.uk; 89 St Marks Rd; mains £8.95-10.95; ☺10am-11.30pm Tue-Sat, 10am-4pm Sun; ☒) This Easton eatery has won a raft of awards for its innovative veggie food, and it's recently branched out with a funky new arts-space-cum-music-venue. The vibe is deliberately casual, and the all-veggie food is universally good, whether you choose the nettle risotto or the root-veg *tarte tatin*.

Thali Café
INDIAN £

(☎0117-974 3793; www.thethalicafe.co.uk; 1 Regent St; meals £7.95-10.50) Bristol has some great Indian restaurants, but few are as beloved as this minichain of canteens, which now has four outlets, including this one in Clifton. It specialises in fresh, authentic thalis (multicourse Indian meals), as well as regional dishes ranging from Goan fish fries to Chompatti beach snacks. For dining-on-a-budget, there's really nowhere better in Bristol.

Glassboat
FRENCH ££

(☎0117-929 0704; www.glassboat.co.uk; Welsh Back; 2-/3-course lunch menu £15/20, dinner mains £15.50-22; ☺lunch Tue-Fri & Sun, dinner Mon-Sat) You couldn't ask for a more romantic place for dinner than this double-decked river barge, with its candlelit tables and watery views. The food is solid rather than spectacular, revolving around French standards such as fish soup, rabbit hotpot and tarragon chicken with *pommes dauphinoises*.

Primrose Café
BISTRO ££

(☎0117-946 6577; www.primrosecafe.co.uk; 1-2 Boyce's Ave; dinner mains £13.50-17.50; ☺breakfast & lunch Mon-Sat, dinner Tue-Sat) A Clifton classic, perfect for morning coffee spent with the papers, a quick lunchtime snack

or a proper sit-down dinner. The food is British with a French accent, served up in a cosy candlelit dining room full of wooden furniture and chalkboard menus, and if the weather's sunny, the pavement tables are perfect for watching Clifton life mosey by. It's right next door to one of Bristol's oldest shopping arcades.

Pieminister
PIES £

(24 Stokes Croft; pies around £4.50; ☺10am-7pm Sat, 11am-4pm Sun) Bristol's beloved pie shop turns out imaginative creations such as Thai Chook (chicken with green curry sauce) and Chicken of Aragon (chicken, bacon, garlic and vermouth), all drowned in lashings of gravy (meat-free if you wish). The main shop is on Stokes Croft, but there's another outlet in St Nick's market.

Bordeaux Quay
MEDITERRANEAN ££

(☎0117-943 1200; www.bordeaux-quay.co.uk; Canon's Way; brasserie mains £8.50-13.50, dinner mains £13.50-25) This ecoconscious restaurant is housed in a converted dock warehouse, and offers a choice of settings: a downstairs cafe for cake, coffee and bistro lunches, and a more formal upstairs for Mediterranean-style dining. The same open-plan industrial feel runs throughout, but standards can be variable, especially considering the prices and 12.5% service charge. There's a cookery school if you'd like to brush up your own skills.

Drinking

Apple
THEME BAR

(Welsh Back) Cider-lovers won't want to miss this converted barge on Welsh Back, which offers over 40 varieties, including raspberry, strawberry and six different perries (pear ciders).

Grain Barge
PUB

(www.grainbarge.com; Mardyke Wharf, Hotwell Rd) Built in 1936, overhauled in 2007, this barge near SS *Great Britain* is owned by the city's renowned microbrewery, the Bristol Beer Factory. Gaze across the harbour while downing a pint of traditional No. 7 Bitter or dark Exhibition ale.

Highbury Vaults
PUB

(164 St Michaels Hill) This endearingly scruffy boozer has a warren of wood-panelled rooms and hallways, and a choice of at least eight real ales on tap. There's a delightful little beer garden, too – look out for the little train running through the greenery.

Albion
PUB

(Boyce's Ave) Lovely old-fashioned place that's popular with evening drinkers from Clifton's well-heeled streets.

 Entertainment

The Bristol club scene moves fast; so check the latest listings at *Venue* (www.venue. co.uk; £1.50). The freebie mag *Folio* is published monthly.

Watershed
CINEMA, MEDIA CENTRE

(www.watershed.co.uk; 1 Canon's Rd) Bristol's digital media centre hosts regular art-house programs and film-related events, including the Encounters Festival in November.

Bristol Old Vic
THEATRE

(www.bristololdvic.org.uk; 103 The Cut) Bristol's stately theatre (one of England's oldest) hosts big touring productions in its ornate auditorium, plus more experimental work in its smaller studio.

Thekla
CLUB

(www.thekla.co.uk; The Grove) Bristol's venerable club-boat has nights for all moods: electropunk, indie, disco and new wave, plus regular live gigs.

Colston Hall
LIVE MUSIC

(www.colstonhall.org; Colston St) Bristol's historic concert hall tends to attract the best bands and big-name comedy acts.

ⓘ Information

Bristol tourist information centre (☑0333-321 0101; www.visitbristol.co.uk; E-Shed, 1 Canons Rd; ◷10am-6pm)

Bristol Royal Infirmary (Marlborough St; ◷24hr)

ⓘ Getting There & Away

The **Travel Bristol** (www.travelbristol.org) website lists comprehensive information on public transport in and around Bristol city.

Air

Bristol International Airport (☑0871-3344344; www.bristolairport.co.uk) Bristol's airport is 8 miles southwest of the city. Destinations include UK airports such as London Gatwick, Leeds, Manchester, Edinburgh and Glasgow (mainly handled by Ryanair and Easyjet) as well as direct flights to many European cities (handled by many different carriers).

Parking at the airport is expensive (starting at around £30 in the cheapest Silver Zone), but substantial discounts are available online.

Bus

Bristol has excellent bus and coach connections. Timetables are available from the bus station on Marlborough Rd.

National Express coaches go to Birmingham (£21.30, two hours, six to eight daily), London (£21, 2½ hours, hourly), Cardiff (£8.70, 1¼ hours, every two hours) and Exeter (£15, two hours, four daily).

Useful local buses:

Bath (50 minutes, several per hour) Express bus X39/339.

Wells (one hour, half-hourly Monday to Saturday, hourly on Sunday) Bus 376, with onward connections to Glastonbury (1¼ hours).

Weston-super-Mare (one hour, every half hour Monday to Saturday) Bus X1.

Train

Bristol is an important rail hub, with regular services to London Paddington provided by **First Great Western** (www.firstgreatwestern.co.uk) and services to northern England and Scotland mainly covered by **CrossCountry.** (www.crosscountrytrains.co.uk)

DESTINATION	FARE (ONE WAY)	DURATION (HR)	FREQUENCY
Birmingham	£47	1½	hourly
Edinburgh	£136	6½	hourly
Exeter	£25	1	hourly
Glasgow	£136	6½	hourly
London	£39	1¾	hourly
Penzance	£42	5½	hourly
Truro	£42	5	hourly

ⓘ Getting Around

To/From the Airport

Bristol International Flyer (http://flyer.bristolairport.co.uk) Runs shuttle buses (one way/return £10/7, 30 minutes, every 10 minutes at peak times) from the bus station and Temple Meads.

Boat

Bristol Ferry Boat Company (☑0117-927 3416; www.bristolferry.com; adult/child return £3.80/3.20, day pass £7/5) Regular ferry service around the harbour which runs from its city centre base near the tourist office. There are two hourly routes: the red route runs west towards Hotwells, with stops including Millennium Sq and the *SS Great Britain*; the blue route runs east to Temple Meads, with stops including Castle Park (for Cabot Circus), Welsh Back, Millennium Sq, the *SS Great Britain* and Bathurst Basin. Single hops from the City

BANKSY

Bristol's artistic antihero, Banksy, may be a world-famous name these days, but his heart's still very much rooted in the city. Known for his guerrilla graffiti and stencil street art, Banksy's true identity is a closely guarded secret, but it's generally believed he was born in 1974 in Yate, 12 miles from Bristol, and cut his artistic teeth in a graffiti outfit.

He's since become known across the globe for his anti-establishment, anti-authoritarian artworks, which frequently take a wry view of 21st-century culture (especially capitalism, consumerism and the cult of celebrity). Banksy's most notorious works include the production of spoof banknotes (featuring Princess Diana's head instead of the Queen's), a series of murals on Israel's West Bank barrier (depicting people digging holes and climbing ladders over the wall) and a painting of a caveman pushing a shopping trolley at the British Museum (which the museum promptly claimed for their permanent collection).

More recently, Banksy's made forays into the film world: his documentary *Exit Through The Gift Shop*, about an LA street artist, was nominated for an Oscar in 2011.

Long despised by the city's authorities, Banksy's become a real tourist magnet for Bristol. Though many of his works have been washed away, a few still survive: look out for the love triangle stencil (Frogmore St, visible from Park St) featuring an angry husband, a two-timing wife, and a naked man dangling from a window; stencils of the Grim Reaper on the side of the Thekla (p281) and a SWAT marksman opposite the Children's Hospital on Kingsdown; and the Mild Mild West mural (featuring a Molotov cocktail-wielding teddy bear) on Cheltenham Rd.

For more on the artist's latest antics, check out www.banksy.co.uk.

Centre to M Shed and Temple Meads to Castle Park cost £1.

Bus

Useful city buses:

Bus 8/9 to Clifton (10 minutes), Whiteladies Rd and Bristol Zoo Gardens every 15 minutes from St Augustine's Pde. Add another 10 minutes from Temple Meads.

Bus 73 Runs from Parkway Station to the centre (30 minutes).

Taxi

The taxi rank on St Augustine's Pde is a central but rowdy place on weekend nights. There are plenty of companies; try **Streamline Taxis** (☎0117-926 4001). If you're taking a non-metered cab, agree on the fare in advance.

BATH

POP 90,144

Britain's littered with beautiful cities, but precious few can hold a candle to Bath. Home to some of the nation's grandest Georgian architecture and stateliest streets – not to mention one of the world's best-preserved Roman bathhouses – this slinky, sophisticated, snooty city has been a tourist draw for nigh-on 2000 years. Founded on top of a network of natural hot springs, Bath's heyday really began during the 18th century,

when local entrepreneur Ralph Allen and his team of father-and-son architects, John Wood the Elder and Younger, turned this sleepy backwater into the toast of Georgian society, and constructed fabulous landmarks such as the Circus and Royal Crescent.

But while its architecture seems to have been pickled in time, Bath is very much a cosmopolitan, 21st-century city, with a wealth of modern cafes, bistros and boutiques dotted along its streets, as well as the huge new shopping centre SouthGate, seamlessly designed to blend in with the rest of Bath's period buildings. It has its drawbacks – it's pricey, poncy and plagued by teeth-grindingly awful traffic – but even the most perfect of princesses has to have her flaws; no matter how hard you try, you still find yourself falling for her all the same.

History

Prehistoric peoples probably knew about the hot springs; legend has it King Bladud, a Trojan refugee and father of King Lear, founded Bath some 2800 years ago when his pigs were cured of leprosy by a dip in the muddy swamps. The Romans established the town of Aquae Sulis in AD 44 and built the extensive baths complex and a temple to the goddess Sulis-Minerva.

Long after the Romans decamped, the Anglo-Saxons arrived, and in 944 a monastery was founded on the site of the present abbey. Throughout the Middle Ages, Bath was an ecclesiastical centre and a wool-trading town, but it wasn't until the early 18th century that Ralph Allen and the celebrated dandy Richard 'Beau' Nash made Bath the centre of fashionable society. Allen developed the quarries at Coombe Down, constructed Prior Park and employed the two John Woods (father and son) to create some of Bath's most glorious buildings.

During WWII, Bath was hit by the Luftwaffe during the so-called Baedeker raids, which deliberately targeted historic cities in an effort to sap British morale. Several houses on the Royal Crescent and the Circus were badly damaged, and the city's Assembly Rooms were gutted by fire, although all have since been carefully restored.

In 1987, Bath became the only city in Britain to be declared a Unesco World Heritage site in its entirety, leading to many subsequent wrangles over construction and development, most recently concerning the design of the redeveloped Thermae Bath Spa and SouthGate shopping centre.

◉ Sights & Activities

Roman Baths · MUSEUM

(www.romanbaths.co.uk; Abbey Churchyard; adult/child £12/7.80; ◷9am-6pm) Ever since the Romans arrived in Bath, life in the city has revolved around the three geothermal springs that bubble up near the abbey. In typically ostentatious style, the Romans constructed a glorious complex of bathhouses above these thermal waters to take advantage of their natural temperature, which emerge at a constant 46°C. Situated alongside an important temple dedicated to the healing goddess Sulis Minerva, the baths are believed to have attracted tourists from right across the Empire, and now form one of the best-preserved ancient Roman spas in the country.

The heart of the complex is the Great Bath, a large lead-lined pool filled with steaming, geothermally-heated water from the so-called 'Sacred Spring' to a depth of 1.6m. Though it's now open to the air, the bath would originally have been covered by a vast 45m-high barrel-vaulted roof. Further bathing pools and changing rooms are situated to the east and west, with excavated sections revealing the hypocaust system that would have kept the bathing rooms balmy.

One of the most picturesque corners of the complex is the 12th-century King's

DRIVING IN BRISTOL

Heavy traffic and pricey parking make driving in Bristol a headache. If you do decide to drive, make sure your hotel has parking, or use the Park & Ride buses (☑01179-222910; return before 10am Mon-Fri £3.50, after 10am Mon-Fri £2.50, Sat £2.50; ◷every 10min Mon-Sat) from Portway, Bath Rd and Long Ashton. Note that overnight parking is not permitted at the Park & Ride car parks.

Bath, built around the original sacred spring; 1.5 million litres of hot water still pour into the pool every day. Beneath the Pump Room are the remains of the Temple of Sulis-Minerva; look out for the famous gilded head of Minerva herself and the engraved Haruspex stone on which the statue would originally have stood.

Even though the baths are off-limits to modern-day bathers, they remain a fascinating window into everyday Roman life, and unsurprisingly get very busy. You can usually avoid the worst crowds by buying tickets in advance online, visiting early on a midweek morning, and by avoiding July and August. Admission includes an audioguide in a choice of eight languages, featuring a special commentary by the bestselling author Bill Bryson.

Bath Abbey · CHURCH

(www.bathabbey.org; requested donation £2.50; ◷9am-6pm Mon-Sat, 1-2.30pm & 4.30-5.30pm Sun) Looming above the centre of the city, Bath's huge abbey church was built between 1499 and 1616, making it the last great medieval church raised in England. Its most striking feature is the west facade, where angels climb up and down stone ladders, commemorating a dream of the founder, Bishop Oliver King. Among those buried here are Sir Isaac Pitman (who devised the Pitman method of shorthand) and the celebrated *bon viveur* Beau Nash.

On the abbey's southern side, the small Vaults Heritage Museum (◷10am-4pm Mon-Sat) explores the abbey's history and its links with the nearby baths.

Royal Crescent · HISTORIC AREA

Bath is rightly celebrated for its glorious Georgian architecture, and it doesn't get

Bath

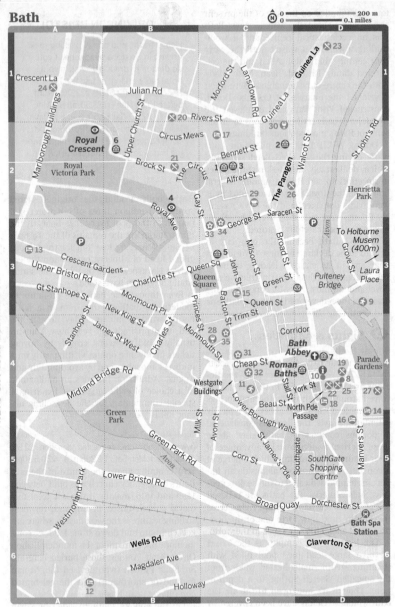

N 0 ————— 200 m
0 ————— 0.1 miles

SOUTHWEST ENGLAND BATH

any grander than on **Royal Crescent**, a semicircular terrace of majestic town houses overlooking the green sweep of Royal Victoria Park. Designed by John Wood the Younger (1728–82) and built between 1767 and 1775, the houses were designed to appear perfectly symmetrical from the outside, but the original owners were allowed to design the interiors to their own specifications; consequently no two houses on the Crescent

Bath

are quite the same. They would originally have been rented for the summer season by wealthy socialites, who descended on Bath to indulge in a whirlwind programme of masquerades, dances, concerts and tea parties.

For a glimpse into the splendour and razzle-dazzle of Georgian life, head for the beautifully restored house at No 1 Royal Crescent (www.bath-preservation-trust.org.uk; 1 Royal Cres; adult/child £6.50/2.50; ⊙10.30am-5pm Tue-Sun late Feb–mid-Dec), given to the city by the shipping magnate Major Bernard Cayzer, and since restored using only 18th-century materials. Among the rooms on display are the drawing room, several bedrooms and the huge kitchen, complete with massive hearth, roasting spit and mousetraps.

A walk east along Brock St from the Royal Crescent leads to the Circus, a ring of 33 houses divided into three terraces. Plaques on the houses commemorate famous residents such as Thomas Gainsborough, Clive of India and David Livingstone.

To the south along Gravel Walk is the Georgian Garden, restored to resemble a typical 18th-century town house garden.

Assembly Rooms HISTORIC BUILDING
(www.nationaltrust.org.uk/main/w-bathassembly rooms; 19 Bennett St; adult/child £2/free; ⊙10.30am-6pm) Opened in 1771, the city's glorious Assembly Rooms were where fashionable Bath socialites once gathered to waltz, play cards and listen to the latest chamber music. You're free to wander around the rooms, as long as they haven't been reserved for a special function; rooms open to the public include the card room, tearoom and the truly splendid ballroom, all of which are lit by their original 18th-century chandeliers. The Assembly Rooms were all but gutted by incendiary bombs during WWII but have since been carefully restored.

FREE **Holburne Museum** ART GALLERY
(www.holburne.org; Great Pulteney St; temporary exhibitions incur fee; ⊙10am-5pm) Sir William Holburne, the 18th-century aristocrat, aesthete and art fanatic, amassed a huge collection which now forms the core of the Holburne Museum, in a lavish mansion at the end of Great Pulteney St. Fresh from a three-year refit, the museum houses an impressive roll-call of works by artists including

Turner, Stubbs, William Hoare and Thomas Gainsborough, as well as a fine collection of 18th-century majollica and porcelain.

Jane Austen Centre · MUSEUM

(www.janeausten.co.uk; 40 Gay St; adult/child £7.45/4.25; ⊙9.45am-5.30pm) Bath is known to many as a location in Jane Austen's novels, including *Persuasion* and *Northanger Abbey*. Though Austen only lived in Bath for five years from 1801 to 1806, she remained a regular visitor throughout her life, as well as a keen student of the city's social scene. This museum houses a small collection of memorabilia relating to the writer's life in Bath, and costumed guides bring the era to life. There's also a Regency tearoom which serves crumpets and cream teas in suitably frilly surrounds.

Building of Bath Museum · MUSEUM

(www.bath-preservation-trust.org.uk; The Vineyards, The Paragon; adult/child £4/2; ⊙10.30am-5pm Tue-Sun mid-Feb–Nov) This museum explores the story of Bath's architecture, with antique tools, displays on Georgian construction methods and a 1:500 scale model of Bath.

Fashion Museum · MUSEUM

(www.fashionmuseum.co.uk; Assembly Rooms, Bennett St; adult/child £7.25/5.25; ⊙10.30am-5pm) In the basement of the Assembly Rooms, this museum contains a wonderful collection of costumes worn from the 16th to late 20th centuries. Exhibitions are changed annually, so check the website for the latest shows.

American Museum in Britain · MUSEUM

(www.americanmuseum.org; Claverton Manor; adult/child £8/4.50; ⊙noon-5pm) Britain's largest collection of American folk art, including Native American textiles, patchwork quilts and historic maps, is housed in a fine mansion a couple of miles from the city centre. Several rooms have been recreated in period style, including a 17th-century Puritan house, an 18th-century tavern and a New Orleans boudoir c 1860. Catch bus 18/418/U18 from the bus station.

Boat Trips · CRUISES

Various cruise operators offer boat trips up and down the River Avon from the landing station underneath Pulteney Bridge, including the open-top Pulteney Cruisers (☎01225-312900; www.bathboating.com; adult/child £8/4), the Pulteney Princess (☎07791-910650; www.pulteneyprincess.co.uk; adult/child £8/3) or Bath City Boat Trips (☎07974-

560197; www.bathcityboattrips.com; adult/child £6.95/4.95).

You can also pilot your own vessel down the Avon from the Bathwick Boating Station (☎01225-312900; www.bathboating.co.uk; Forrester Rd; 1st hr per adult/child £7/3.50, additional hr £3/1.50; ⊙10am-6pm Easter-Oct), which rents out traditional skiffs, rowboats and Canadian canoes. The jetty is in the suburb of Bathwick, a 20-minute walk southeast from the city centre.

Tours

Mayor's Guide Tours · WALKING TOUR

(☎01225-477411; www.bathguides.co.uk; ⊙10.30am & 2pm Sun-Fri, 10.30am Sat) Excellent historical tours proXvided free by the Mayor's Corp of Honorary guides. Leave from outside the Pump Rooms. Extra tours at 7pm on Tuesdays and Thursdays May to September. They cover about 2 miles and are wheelchair accessible.

Jane Austen's Bath Walking Tours · WALKING TOUR

(☎01225-443000; adult/child £6/5; ⊙11am Sat & Sun) A guided tour of the Georgian city, organised by the Jane Austen Centre. Tours leave from the Abbey Churchyard.

Bizarre Bath Comedy Walk · WALKING TOUR

(☎01225-335124; www.bizarrebath.co.uk; adult/student £8/5; ⊙8pm Mar-Oct) Daft city tour mixing street theatre and live performance. Leaves from outside the Huntsman Inn on North Parade Passage. The walk is usually wheelchair accessible, but construction work has made access to one area impossible, so they're not currently charging wheelchair visitors.

Bath City Sightseeing · BUS TOUR

(☎01225-330444; www.city-sightseeing.com; adult/child £12.50/7.50; ⊙9.30am-6.30pm Mar-Nov) Hop-on/hop-off city tour on an open-topped bus, with a commentary in seven languages. Buses stop several times an hour at various points around town. A second route, the Skyline tour, also travels out to Prior Park; the same tickets are valid on both routes.

Festivals & Events

Bath has lots of festivals. All bookings are handled by Bath Festivals (☎01225-463362; www.bathfestivals.org.uk; 2 Church St; ⊙9.30am-5.30pm Mon-Sat).

Bath Literature Festival   BOOK
(www.bathlitfest.org.uk) Annual book festival in late February or early March.

Bath International Music Festival   MUSIC
(www.bathmusicfest.org.uk) Mainly classical and opera, plus smaller gigs of jazz, folk and world. Mid-May to early June.

Bath Fringe Festival   THEATRE
(www.bathfringe.co.uk) Major theatre festival around mid-May to early June.

🛌 Sleeping

Bath gets incredibly busy, especially in the height of summer and at weekends, when prices are at a premium. Very few hotels have parking, although some offer discounted rates at municipal car parks.

TOP CHOICE Queensberry Hotel   HOTEL £££
(☎01225-447928; www.thequeensberry.co.uk; 4 Russell St; d £150-270, ste £460; ☜) It's a budget-buster, but the quirky Queensberry is undoubtedly one of Bath's best boutique spoils. Four Georgian town houses have been combined into one seamlessly stylish whole, but all the rooms are subtly different: some are cosy in gingham checks and country creams, others feature zesty upholstery, original fireplaces and freestanding tubs. The basement Olive Tree Restaurant is one of the town's top tables, too. Parking is available at a nearby private garage. Rates don't include breakfast.

TOP CHOICE Halcyon   HOTEL ££
(☎01225-444100; www.thehalcyon.com; 2/3 South Pde; d £125-145; ☜) Just what Bath needed: a smart, stylish city-centre hotel that doesn't break the bank. Situated on a listed terrace off Manvers St, the heavily renovated Halcyon is all about style on a budget: white-washed rooms, bright bed linen, Philippe Starck bath fittings and White Company smellies, along with a smart basement breakfast room and the brand new Circo

cocktail bar. The drawbacks? Rooms are spread out over three floors and there's no lift. They're also very variable in size: front rooms have the views, and the ones on the top floor avoid late-night bar noise.

Henry   B&B ££
(☎01225-424052; www.thehenry.com; 6 Henry St; d £80-120, f £145-165) This tall, slim town house has an absolutely superb position, literally steps from the centre, and offers a good choice of clean, uncluttered rooms finished in crisp whites and smooth beiges. It's decent value considering the location, but there's no parking and it can feel very cramped when it's full. More space is available at the 'Below Stairs' self-catering apartment nearby. Two-night minimum stay at weekends.

139 Bath   B&B ££
(☎01225-314769; www.139bath.co.uk; 139 Wells Rd; r £120-195; ℗☜) It's a bit out of the centre, but this swish B&B really sets the pace. It's been thoughtfully designed throughout, with swirly fabrics, contemporary colour schemes and supremely comfy beds, plus lots of little spoils such as cafetière coffee, Molton Brown bath products and a generous buffet breakfast (two four-poster rooms even have spas). Posh it certainly is, but it's still a touch pricey for a B&B.

Brooks   HOTEL ££
(☎01225-425543; www.brooksguesthouse.com; 1 & 1a Crescent Gardens; s £59-89, d £80-150, f £120-160; ☜) On the west side of Bath, this town house blends heritage fixtures attractively with snazzy finishes. The owners have focused on the details: goosedown duvets, pocket-sprung mattresses, DAB radios and breakfast choices including smoked salmon brioche and homemade muesli. Parking's problematic.

Haringtons Hotel   HOTEL ££
(☎01225-461278; www.haringtonshotel.co.uk; Queen St; d £88-168) Bath's classical trappings

THERMAE BATH SPA

Taking a dip in the Roman Baths might be off the agenda, but you can still sample the city's curative waters at **Thermae Bath Spa** (☎0844-888 0844; www.thermaebathspa. com; Bath St; ☉9am-10pm, last entry 7.30pm). Here the old **Cross Bath**, incorporated into an ultramodern shell of local stone and plate glass, is now the setting for a variety of spa packages. The New Royal Bath ticket includes steam rooms, waterfall shower and a choice of bathing venues – including the jaw-dropping open-air rooftop pool, where you can swim in the thermal waters in front of a backdrop of Bath's stunning cityscape.

aren't to everyone's taste, so things are kept modern and minimal at this city-centre crash pad: clean lines, crisp colour schemes and LCD TVs, although some of the rooms are shoebox-sized.

Three Abbey Green B&B ££

(📞01225-428558; www.threeabbeygreen.com; 3 Abbey Green; d £90-140, f £140-220; 🖥) Considering the location, this place is a steal – tumble out of the front door and you'll find yourself practically on the abbey's doorstep. It's on a leafy square, and though the rooms lack sparkle, the suites have adjoining singles – ideal for family travellers.

Georgian Stables APARTMENT ££

(📞01225-465956; 41 Sydney Buildings; d £85) This deliciously quirky apartment is a find: it's in a lovely canalside location 10 minutes walk from the city, and offers unusual accommodation inside a converted stableblock, accessed by the original cobbled ramp. The apartment itself is all clean lines and white walls, but patches of exposed stone in the bedroom and shower room provide reminders of its heritage.

Bath YHA HOSTEL £

(www.yha.org.uk; Bathwick Hill; dm £20.40, d from £59; 🅿@) Lodged inside an Italianate mansion and a more modern annexe, a steep climb (or a short hop on bus 18) from the city centre, this hostel offers decent rooms, spacious kitchens and lovely grounds.

 Eating

TOP CHOICE **Menu Gordon Jones** GOURMET BRITISH ££

(📞01225-480871; www.menugordonjones.co.uk; 2 Wellsway; 5-course lunch £30, 6-course dinner £40) Gordon Jones is the name to watch in Bath. Previously head honcho at the über-expensive Royal Crescent Hotel, he's since branched out with his own pocket-sized restaurant, which has already earned him critical plaudits aplenty. The multicourse 'surprise menus' are dreamt up by Jones on the day, and showcase his taste for experimentation, both in terms of ingredients (smoked eel, seagull's eggs, samphire) and presentation (test-tubes, edible cups, slate plates). The pop soundtrack and minuscule dining room won't please everyone, but the menus are incredible value considering the skill. Jones is destined for big things: book now while you can.

Circus MODERN BRITISH ££

(📞01225-466020; www.thecircuscafeandrestaurant .co.uk; 34 Brock St; mains lunch £5.50-10, dinner £11-14; ⏰10am-midnight Mon-Sat) It's not quite the locals' secret it once was, but the Circus is still one of Bath's best. Installed in a converted town house between the Circus and the Royal Crescent, it's the model of a modern Brit bistro: chef Ali Golden has a taste for hearty dishes such as rabbit pie and roast guinea-fowl, all seasonally inspired, impeccably presented and reassuringly generous. The dining rooms cellar feels cramped when it's full, so aim for an upstairs table and reserve ahead.

Marlborough Tavern GASTROPUB ££

(📞01225-423731; www.marlborough-tavern.com; 35 Marlborough Buildings; mains £12-17) Bath certainly isn't short on gastropubs, but the Marlborough is still very much top of the class. It's half cosy boozer, half contemporary bistro, with big wooden tables, deep seats, and a crackling fire on winter nights. Chef Richard Knighting previously worked in Michelin-starred restaurants, and it shows: his menu is a mix of heartwarming classics and cheffy showiness, and rarely fails to hit the mark.

Chequers GASTROPUB

(📞01225-360017; www.thechequersbar.com; 50 Rivers St; mains £10.50-£19) Big, bold flavours are the order of the day at the Chequers: chunky pork chops, venison bangers and braised beef cheek, dished up perhaps with a classy champ mash or a rich red wine jus. It's scooped multiple awards for its food, and it's usually packed out for Sunday lunch. The pub's 18th-century, but feels designer-modern.

Demuth's VEGETARIAN ££

(📞01225-446059; www.demuths.co.uk; 2 North Pde Passage; lunch £4.95-11, dinner £14.50-17; 🍴) Even the most committed of carnivores can't fail to fall for this long-established veggie restaurant, which consistently turns out some of the city's most creative food – from cheddar soufflé served with figs, walnut purée and spring greens, to a port-poached pear baked with fennel seeds and ewe's cheese.

Sotto Sotto ITALIAN ££

(📞01225-330236; 10a North Pde; pasta £9, mains £13-17) Authentic Italian food served in a lovely cellar setting complete with barrel-brick roof. Ingredients are shipped in direct and everything's just like mama made, from the *osso bucco* (veal shank) to the *orecchiette mare e monti* (top-hat pasta with seafood, beans and pancetta).

Hudson Steakhouse STEAKHOUSE £££
(☎01225-332323; www.hudsonbars.com; 14 London St; steaks £22-34; ⊗dinner Mon-Sat) Steak, steak and more steak is this place's *raison d'être*. Top-quality cuts take in everything from porterhouse to prime fillet, all sourced from a Staffordshire farmers' co-op.

Sam's Kitchen Deli CAFE £
(www.samskitchendeli.co.uk; 61 Walcot St; lunch £8-10; ⊗8am-6pm Mon-Sat, every 2nd Fri 8am-10pm) This eclectic cafe is a fantastic place for lunch, offering a choice of set dishes (including a daily roast), served straight from the pans on the counter. With its dilapidated piano, cast-iron staircase and reclaimed furniture, it's vintage shabby-chic Bath, and very popular. Look out for supper clubs and live gigs every other Friday.

Café Retro CAFE £
(18 York St; mains £5-11; ⊗breakfast, lunch & dinner Tue-Sat, breakfast & lunch Mon) This place is a poke in the eye for the corporate coffee chains. The paint job's scruffy, the crockery's ancient and none of the furniture matches, but that's all part of the charm: this is a cafe from the old school, and there's nowhere better for a burger, cake or hot mug of tea. Takeaways available from Retro to Go next door.

Sally Lunn's TEAROOM £
(4 North Pde Passage; lunch mains £5-6, dinner mains from £8) This fabulously frilly tearoom occupies one of Bath's oldest houses, and makes the perfect venue for classic cream tea (served in proper bone china), accompanied by finger sandwiches, dainty cakes and the trademark Sally Lunn's Bun.

☕ Drinking

Same Same But Different CAFE, BAR
(7a Prince's Buildings, Bartlett St; ⊗8am-6pm Mon-Wed, 8am-11pm Thu-Sat, 10am-5pm Sun) Boho hang-out for the town's trendies, tucked down an alley off George St. Savour wine by the glass, snack on a plate of tapas or sip a cappuccino with the Sunday papers.

Door 34 COCKTAIL BAR
(www.door34.co.uk; 34 Monmouth St; cocktails from around £8; ⊗from 7pm) This cocktail bar touts itself as a 'liquid alhemist's lounge', and

it certainly mixes a mean martini. The town house decor and paperback menus add a touch of class, and the mixologists will happily give you some cocktail tips if you smile sweetly. Look out for the weekly rum club.

Star Inn PUB
(www.star-inn-bath.co.uk; 23 The Vineyards, off The Paragon) Not many pubs are registered relics, but the Star is – it still has many of its 19th-century bar fittings. It's the brewery tap for Bath-based Abbey Ales; some ales are served in traditional jugs, and you can even ask for a pinch of snuff in the 'smaller bar'.

☆ Entertainment

Venue magazine (www.venue.co.uk) has comprehensive listings of Bath's theatre, music and gig scenes.

Moles LIVE MUSIC
(www.moles.co.uk; 14 George St) Bath's historic music club is the place to catch live gigs by big-name bands.

Porter Cellar Bar LIVE MUSIC
(George St) Run by the folk at Moles, this student favourite lays on the acts who aren't yet big enough to play the main venue: it's Bath's only veggie pub, too.

Theatre Royal THEATRE
(www.theatreroyal.org.uk; Sawclose) This is one of the southwest's classiest regional theatres. Major touring productions go in the main auditorium, while smaller shows appear in the Ustinov Studio.

Komedia CABARET, COMEDY
(www.komedia.co.uk; 22-23 Westgate St) Live comedy and cabaret at this Bath offshoot of the Brighton-based original.

Little Theatre Cinema CINEMA
(St Michael's Pl) Bath's excellent art-house cinema screens fringe films and foreign-language flicks.

ℹ Information

Bath visitor centre (www.visitbath.co.uk; Abbey Churchyard; ⊗9.30am-5pm Mon-Sat, 10am-4pm Sun) Sells the Bath City Card (£3), which is valid for three weeks and offers discounts at many local shops, restaurants and attractions.

Main post office (27 Northgate St)
Police station (Manvers St; ⊗7am-midnight)
Royal United Hospital (☎01225-428331; Combe Park)

ⓘ Getting There & Away

Bus

Bath's bus and coach station is on Dorchester St near the train station.

National Express coaches run direct to London (£20.70, 3½ hours, eight to 10 daily) via Heathrow (£20.70, 2¾ hours). Services to most other destinations require a change at Bristol or Heathrow.

Local buses include:

Bath (50 minutes, four per hour Monday to Saturday, half-hourly on Sunday) Bus X39/339.

Bradford-on-Avon (30 minutes, half-hourly, eight on Sunday) Bus 264/265.

Frome (hourly Monday to Saturday) Bus 184.

Wells (1 hour 10 minutes, hourly Monday to Saturday, five on Sunday) Bus 173.

Train

Bath Spa station is at the end of Manvers St. Many services connect through Bristol (£9.90, 20 minutes, two or three per hour), especially to the north of England.

Direct services include:

Bradford-on-Avon (£3.90, 11 to 15 minutes, two per hour)

Cardiff Central (£18, one hour, hourly)

Exeter (£27.50, 1¼ hours, hourly)

London Paddington (£39, 1½ hours, half-hourly)

London Waterloo (£39, 1½ hours, half-hourly)

Salisbury (£15.70, one hour, hourly)

ⓘ Getting Around

Bicycle

Bath's hills make getting around by bike challenging, but the canal paths along the Kennet and Avon Canal and the 13-mile **Bristol & Bath Railway Path** (www.bristolbathrailwaypath.org. uk) offer great cycling.

Bus

Bus 18 runs from the bus station, High St and Great Pulteney St up Bathwick Hill past the YHA to the university every 10 minutes. Bus 4 runs every 20 minutes to Bathampton from the same places.

Car & Motorcycle

Bath has serious traffic problems (especially at rush hour). **Park & Ride services** (☎01225-464446; return Mon-Fri £3, Sat £2.50; ◷6.15am-7.30pm Mon-Sat) operate from Lansdown to the north, Newbridge to the west and Odd Down to the south. It takes about 10 minutes to the centre; buses leave every 10 to 15 minutes. If you brave the city, the best value car park is underneath the new SouthGate shopping centre (two/eight hours £3/13, after 6.30pm £2).

SOMERSET

Sleepy Somerset provides the type of pleasing pastoral wanderings that are reminiscent of a simpler, calmer, kinder world. Its landscape of hedgerows, hummocks and russet-coloured fields is steeped in ancient rites and scattered with ancient sites. The cloistered calm of the cathedral city of Wells acts as a springboard for the limestone caves and gorges around Cheddar; while the hippie haven of Glastonbury provides an ancient abbey, mud-drenched festival and masses of Arthurian myth.

Somerset hugs the coast of the Bristol Channel and includes much of Exmoor National Park, which we cover separately. Glastonbury and Wells make good bases.

ⓘ Information

Somerset visitor centre (☎01934-750833; www.visitsomerset.co.uk; Sedgemoor Services M5 South; ◷9.15am-5pm daily Easter-Oct, 9.15am-5pm Mon-Fri Nov-Easter)

Visit South Somerset (www.visitsouthsomer set.co.uk)

ⓘ Getting Around

Most buses in Somerset are operated by **First** (☎08456-064446; www.firstgroup.com), supplemented by smaller operators. For timetables and general information contact Traveline South West (p225).

Key train services link Bath, Bristol, Bridgwater, Taunton and Weston-super-Mare. The M5 heads south past Bristol, to Bridgwater and Taunton, with the A39 leading west across the Quantocks to Exmoor.

Wells

POP 10,406

With Wells, small is beautiful. This tiny, picturesque metropolis is England's smallest city, and only qualifies for the 'city' title thanks to a magnificent medieval cathedral, which sits in the centre beside the grand Bishop's Palace. Wells has been the main seat of ecclesiastical power in this part of Britain since the 12th century, and is still the official residence of the Bishop of Bath and Wells. Medieval buildings and cobbled streets radiate out from the cathedral green to a marketplace that has been the bustling heart of Wells for some nine centuries (Wednesday and Saturday are market days). A quiet provincial city, Wells' excellent restaurants and busy shops help make it a good launching pad for exploring the Mendips and northern Somerset.

◉ Sights

Wells Cathedral   CATHEDRAL
(www.wellscathedral.org.uk; Cathedral Green; requested donation adult/child £6/3; ⊙7am-7pm) Wells' gargantuan Gothic cathedral (officially known as the Cathedral Church of St Andrew) sits plum in the centre of the city, sorrounded by one of the largest cathedral closes anywhere in England. It was built in several stages between 1180 and 1508, and consequently showcases a range of different Gothic styles.

Dominated by its squat towers, the cathedral's most famous asset is its west front, an immense sculpture gallery decorated with more than 300 figures, built in the 13th century and restored in 1986. The facade would once have been painted in vivid colours, but has long since reverted to its original sandy hue. Apart from the figure of Christ, installed in 1985 in the uppermost niche, all the figures are original.

Inside, the cathedral's famous scissor arches separate the nave from the choir. Though they appear purely decorative, they were actually built to counter the subsidence of the central tower.

High up in the north transept is a mechanical clock dating from 1392 – the second-oldest in England after the one at Salisbury Cathedral – which shows the position of the planets and the phases of the moon.

Other highlights include the elegant Lady Chapel (1326), the fan-vaulted Chapter House (1306) and the celebrated chained library, which contains books and manuscripts dating back to 1472. Outside, the cathedral's Chain Bridge enabled clerics to reach the cathedral without getting their robes wet.

Free guided tours usually run every hour from Monday to Saturday, but you'll need a photography permit (£3) to take pictures.

Cathedral Close   HISTORIC AREA
Wells Cathedral forms the centrepiece of a cluster of ecclesiastical buildings dating back to the Middle Ages. Facing the west front, on the left are the 15th-century Old Deanery and the Wells & Mendip Museum (www.wellsmuseum.org.uk; 8 Cathedral Green; adult/child £3/1; ⊙10am-5.30pm Easter-Oct, 11am-4pm Wed-Mon Nov-Easter), with exhibits on lo-

cal life, cathedral architecture and the infamous Witch of Wookey Hole.

Further along, Vicars' Close is a stunning 14th-century cobbled street, with a chapel at the end; members of the cathedral choir still live here. It is thought to be the oldest complete medieval street in Europe.

Penniless Porch, a corner gate leading onto Market Sq, is so-called because beggars asked for alms here.

Bishop's Palace   HISTORIC BUILDING
(www.bishopspalacewells.co.uk; adult/child £6.35/2.70; ⊙palace 10am-6pm Apr-Dec, gardens Feb-Dec) Built for the bishop in the 13th century, this moat-ringed palace is purportedly the oldest inhabited building in England. Inside, the palace's state rooms and ruined great hall are worth a look, but it's the shady gardens that are the real draw. The natural springs after which Wells is named bubble up in the palace's grounds. The swans in the moat have been trained to ring a bell outside one of the windows when they want to be fed.

🛏 Sleeping

🏆 **Babington House**   LUXURY HOTEL £££
(☑01373-812266; www.babingtonhouse.co.uk; near Frome; r £340-530; P🐾🛜) It's eye-poppingly pricey, but this lauded design hotel is without doubt one of Britain's most luxurious places to stay. It's somewhere between *Homes & Gardens* and *Wallpaper*: heritage beds, antique dressers and period fireplaces sit side-by-side with minimalist furniture, sanded wood floors and retro lamps. There's a top-class restaurant, cool library, private 45-seat cinema and, of course, a spa in the old cow-shed. It's 14 miles east of Wells.

Beryl   B&B ££
(☑01749-678738; www.beryl-wells.co.uk; Hawkers Lane; d £100-150; P🐾) This grand gabled mansion offers a delicious taste of English eccentricity. Every inch of the house is crammed with antique atmosphere, and the rooms boast grandfather clocks, chaises longues and four-posters galore. It's about a mile from Wells.

Ancient Gate House Hotel   HOTEL ££
(☑01749-672029; www.ancientgatehouse.co.uk; Browne's Gate; d £106-131; 🛜) This old hostelry is as central as you can get – it's partly built right into the cathedral's west gate. Rooms are prettily decorated in regal reds and

duck-egg blues; the best have four-poster beds and knockout views of the cathedral through their latticed windows.

Number Twelve B&B ££
(☎01749-679406; www.numbertwelve.info; 12 North Rd; d £80-95; P☎) An Arts and Crafts house offering two pleasant bedrooms. Number 1 is the nicest, with freestanding bath and a small balcony with cathedral views. You'll be treated to tea and cake on arrival.

✗ Eating

Goodfellows BISTRO, CAFE ££
(☎01749-673866; www.goodfellows.co.uk; 5 Sadler St; 3-course bistro dinner £39) Two eateries in one, both excellent. The continental-style cafe (menus £10-17; ☻8.30am-4pm Mon & Tue, 8.30am-5pm & 6-10pm Wed-Sat) serves quick lunch food and patisseries made by the inhouse pastry chef. For something more sophisticated, the seafood **bistro** (mains £11.50-23; ☻noon-2pm Tue-Sat, 6.30-9.30pm Wed-Sat) offers a full line-up of fishy delights plus a choice of settings (downstairs for open-plan dining, upstairs for intimacy). Hard-core fish-fans should plump for the six-course tasting menu (£55).

Old Spot BRITISH ££
(☎01749-689099; www.theoldspot.co.uk; 12 Sadler St; 2-/3-course lunch £15.50/18.50, dinner mains £14-18.50; ☻lunch Wed-Sun, dinner Tue-Sat) Hale and hearty classics form the core of Ian Bates's bistro. It's heavy on rich, meaty dishes such as duck terrine, pork fillet with lentils and black pudding, or guinea fowl with mushroom pithivier. The interior is attractive, too: rough wood tables and big glass windows.

Cafe Romna INDIAN ££
(☎01749-670240; 13 Sadler St; mains £5-16) Some unusual flavours are on offer alongside classic curries at this Bangladeshi fusion restaurant.

❶ Information

Tourist office (☎01749-672552; www.wellstourism.com; Market Pl; ☻9.30am-5.30pm Apr-Oct, 10am-4pm Nov-Mar) Stocks the *Wells City Trail* leaflet (30p) and sells discount tickets to Wookey Hole and Cheddar Gorge.

❶ Getting There & Away

The bus station is south of Cuthbert St, on Princes Rd. Useful services:

Bath (1¼ hours, hourly Monday to Saturday, five on Sunday) Bus 173.

Bristol (one hour, half-hourly Monday to Saturday, hourly on Sunday) Bus 376.

Cheddar (25 minutes, hourly Monday to Saturday, four on Sunday) Bus 126; continues to Weston-super-Mare (1½ hours).

Glastonbury (15 minutes, several per hour) Bus 377.

Taunton (1¼ hours, hourly Monday to Saturday) Bus 29, stops in Glastonbury.

Wookey Hole & Cheddar Gorge

Wookey Hole CAVE
(www.wookey.co.uk; adult/child £16/11; ☻10am-5pm Apr-Oct, 10.30am-4pm Nov-Mar) Two miles from Wells on the southern edge of the Mendip Hills, the River Axe has carved out a series of deep limestone caverns collectively known as Wookey Hole. They're famous for their ornate stalagmites and stalactites, one of which is supposedly the legendary Witch of Wookey Hole, who was turned to stone by a local priest. There are also many subterranean lakes and rivers, some of which are astonishingly deep – Britain's deepest cave dive was made here in September 2004, when divers descended more than 45m.

Admission to the caves is by guided tour. The rest of the complex is disappointingly tacky, with attractions including a mirror maze, an Edwardian penny arcade, a paper mill and a valley populated by giant plastic dinosaurs. During weekends, you might even be greeted by the witch herself, Carla Calamity (real name Carole Bonahan, a former estate agent).

Tickets remain valid for the whole day, and there's a 15% discount for booking online.

Cheddar Gorge CAVE
(www.cheddarcaves.co.uk; Explorer Ticket adult/child £18.50/12; ☻10am-5.30pm) Only marginally less touristy than their Wookey cousins, the massive cliffs of Cheddar Gorge are nonetheless a dramatic sight. This is England's deepest natural canyon, and in places the limestone cliffs tower 138m above the twisting road.

The gorge is famous for its bewildering network of subterranean caves, a few of which are open to the public. Cox's Cave and Gough's Cave, both lined with

CHEDDAR CHEESE

As well as its caves, Cheddar is also famous as the spiritual home of the nation's favourite cheese. Cheddar's strong, crumbly, tangy cheese is the essential ingredient in any self-respecting ploughman's lunch, and has been produced in the area since at least the 12th century; Henry II boldly proclaimed cheddar to be 'the best cheese in Britain', and the king's accounts from 1170 record that he purchased 10,240lbs (around 4644kg) of the stuff. In the days before refrigeration, the Cheddar caves made the ideal cool store for the cheese, with a constant temperature of around 7°C. However, the powerful smell attracted rats and the practice was eventually abandoned.

These days most cheddar cheese is made far from the village, but if you're interested in seeing how the genuine article is made, head for the Cheddar Gorge Cheese Company (☑01934-742810; www.cheddargorgecheeseco.co.uk; adult/child £2.25/free; ☉10am-5pm Easter-Oct). You can take a guided tour of the factory from Easter to October, and pick up some tangy, whiffy souvenirs at the on-site shop.

stalactites and stalagmites, are subtly illuminated to bring out the spectrum of colours in the rock. To explore the more remote caverns, you'll need to organise a caving trip with X-Treme (☑01934-742343; www.cheddargorge.co.uk/x-treme; 1½-hr trip adult/child £21/19); be prepared to get cold, wet and very muddy. Rock-climbing sessions are also available.

The Cheddar caves have been inhabited by prehistoric people since the last ice age; a 9000-year-old skeleton (imaginatively named Cheddar Man) was discovered here in 1903, although carbon dating has suggested Gough's Cave was inhabited several thousand years earlier. Rumours of prehistoric cannibalism also seem to have been confirmed by recent discoveries of polished human skulls that are believed to have been used as drinking vessels.

Cheddar gets extremely busy during summer and school holidays, when the gorge road turns into one long traffic jam. You can normally escape the worst crowds by climbing the 274-step staircase known as Jacob's Ladder, which leads to a spectacular viewpoint and a 3-mile cliff trail.

There's a 10% discount for online booking.

Glastonbury

POP 8429

Ley lines converge, white witches convene and every shop is filled with the aroma of smouldering joss-sticks in good old Glastonbury, the southwest's undisputed capital of alternative culture. Now famous for its annual musical mudfest held on Michael Eavis' farm in nearby Pilton, Glastonbury

has a much older and more mysterious past: the town's iconic Tor was an important pagan site, and is rumoured by some to be the mythical Isle of Avalon, King Arthur's last resting place. It's also allegedly one of the world's great spiritual nodes, marking the meeting point of many mystical lines of power – so if you feel the need to get your chakras realigned, this is definitely the place. Whatever the truth of the various legends swirling round Glastonbury, one thing's for certain – watching the sunrise from the top of the Tor is an experience you definitely won't forget in a hurry.

◉ Sights

TOP CHOICE Glastonbury Tor   LANDMARK
(NT; www.nationaltrust.org.uk) The iconic hump of Glastonbury Tor looms up from flat fields to the northwest of town. This 160m-high grassy mound provides glorious views over the surrounding countryside, and a focal point for a bewildering array of myths. According to some it's the home of a faery king, while an old Celtic legend identifies it as the stronghold of Gwyn ap Nudd (ruler of Annwyn, the Underworld) – but the most famous legend identifies the tor as the mythic Isle of Avalon, where King Arthur was taken after being mortally wounded in battle by his nephew Mordred, and where Britain's 'once and future king' sleeps until his country calls again.

Whatever the truth of the legends, the tor has been a site of pilgrimage for many years, and was once topped by the medieval chapel of St Michael, although today only the tower remains.

Glastonbury

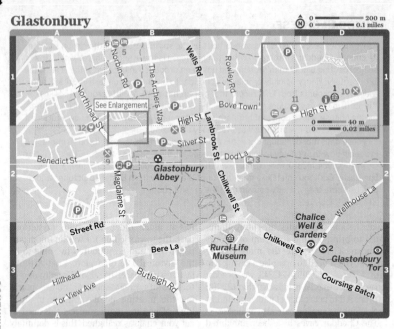

It takes about 45 minutes to walk up and down the tor, plus an extra half-hour to walk from town. The regular **Tor Bus** (adult/child £3/1.50; ☉half-hourly Apr-Sep) from Dunstan's car park stops at Chalice Well, near the start of the main trail on Well House Lane.

Glastonbury Abbey   RUINS
(www.glastonburyabbey.com; Magdalene St; adult/child £6/4; ☉9am-8pm) The scattered ruins of Glastonbury Abbey give little hint that this was once one of England's great seats of ecclesiastical power. Legend has it that the first abbey here was founded by Joseph of Arimathea, Jesus' great uncle, although the present-day ruins largely date from the 12th century.

The abbey was torn down following Henry VIII's Dissolution of the monasteries in 1539, when the last abbot Richard Whiting was hung, drawn and quartered on the tor. Precious little remains of the original building, except for the nave walls, the ruined St Mary's chapel, and the remains of the crossing arches, which may have been scissor-shaped like those in Wells Cathedral. The grounds also contain a museum, cider orchard and herb garden, as well as the Holy Thorn tree, which supposedly sprung from

Joseph's staff and mysteriously blooms twice a year, at Christmas and Easter.

In the 12th century, monks supposedly uncovered a tomb in the abbey grounds inscribed *Hic iacet sepultus inclitus rex arturius in insula avalonia*, or 'Here lies buried the renowned King Arthur in the Isle of Avalon'. Inside the tomb were two entwined skeletons, supposedly those of Arthur and his wife Guinevere; the bones were reburied beneath the altar in 1278, but were lost following the abbey's destruction.

Chalice Well & Gardens   GARDENS
(www.chalicewell.org.uk; adult/child £3.70/1.90; ☉10am-6pm) Shaded by yew trees and crisscrossed by quiet paths, the Chalice Well and Gardens have been sites of pilgrimage since the days of the Celts. The iron-red waters from the 800-year-old well are rumoured to have healing properties, good for everything from eczema to smelly feet; some legends also identify the well as the hiding place of the Holy Grail. In fact, the reddish waters are caused by iron deposits in the soil. You can drink the water from a lion's-head spout, or rest your feet in basins surrounded by flowers.

The Chalice Well is also known as the 'Red Spring' or 'Blood Spring'; its sister, **White Spring**, surfaces across Wellhouse Lane.

Glastonbury

FREE **Rural Life Museum**　　　　　MUSEUM
(Abbey Farm, Chilkwell St; ⊘10am-5pm Tue-Sat)
This modest museum explores Somerset's agricultural heritage, with a restored farmhouse detailing the life of local farmer John Hodges, and a wonderful barn containing vintage tools relating to local industries such as willow growing, peat digging, cider making and cheese making. Try to time your visit with one of the regular craft displays.

Lake Village Museum　　　　　MUSEUM
(The Tribunal, 9 High St; adult/child £2/1.50; ⊘10am-5pm) Upstairs from Glastonbury's tourist office, the Lake Village Museum displays finds from a prehistoric bog village discovered in nearby Godney. The houses were clustered in about six groups and built from reeds, hazel and willow. It's thought they were occupied by summer traders who lived the rest of the year around Glastonbury Tor.

⊨ Sleeping

Chalice Hill　　　　　B&B ££
(☑01458-838828; www.chalicehill.co.uk; Dod Lane; d £100; ℗) This grand Georgian B&B has been renovated with flair by its artistic owner Fay Hutchcroft. A sweeping staircase circles up through the house, leading to three

spacious rooms: try Phoenix for its modern art, or Sun and Moon for its handsome cast-iron bed. Breakfast is served communally in the book-lined lounge.

Lantern Tree　　　　　B&B ££
(☑01458-833455; www.thelanterntree.co.uk; 19 Manor House Rd; s/d/tr £55/65/85) Lovely B&B offering a brace of rooms: Amethyst has a brass bedstead and fluffy pillows, while the Green Room has a roll-top bath and two-bed layout (ideal for families). Fridges, fruit teas and memory-foam mattresses are nice additions. There is a £10 supplement for one-night stays.

Glastonbury White House　　　　　B&B ££
(☑01458-830886; www.theglastonburywhitehouse.com; 21 Manor House Rd; d £50-60; ℗) There are only two rooms here, but owner Carey has made them super-cosy, with extra touches such as fridges, fresh milk and bottles of White Spring water. Breakfast is extra (£5 continental, £7.50 cooked). It's about five minutes' walk from High St.

Parsnips　　　　　B&B ££
(☑01458-835599; www.parsnips-glastonburyco.uk; 99 Bere Lane; s/d £55/70; ℗@) Modern it may be, but this red-brick B&B is a solid bet, with bright rooms in gingham and cream, complimentary coffee on arrival, and a range of holistic treatments by arrangement.

Crown Glastonbury Backpackers　　HOSTEL £
(☑01458-833353; www.glastonburybackpackers.com; 4 Market Pl; dm £16.50, d £35-60; ℗@) Basic hostel above the old Crown pub. Rooms are spartan, and the pub's proximity can make things noisy. Kitchen and laundry available.

✕ Eating & Drinking

Rainbow's End　　　　　CAFE £
(17a High St; mains £4-8; ⊘breakfast & lunch; ☑) This psychedelic cafe sums up the spirit of Glastonbury, with its all-veggie food, potted plants and mix-and-match furniture. Tuck into homity pie or a hot quiche, and follow up with a scrumptious homemade cake. There's a small patio out back.

Hundred Monkeys Cafe　　　　　BISTRO ££
(52 High St; mains £8-15; ⊘lunch Mon-Wed & Sun, lunch & dinner Thu-Sat) Surprisingly sleek bistro, decked out with leather sofas, pine tables and a big blackboard listing fresh pastas, salads and mains. If you've a spare half-hour ask about the origin of the name – the original 100th monkey.

GLASTONBURY FESTIVAL

To many people, the village of Glastonbury is synonymous with the Glastonbury Festival of Contemporary Performing Arts (www.glastonburyfestivals.co.uk), a majestic (and frequently mud-soaked) extravaganza of music, street theatre, dance, cabaret, carnival, ecology, spirituality and general all-round weirdness that's been held on and off on farmland in Pilton, just outside Glastonbury for the last 40 years.

The first event was held in 1970, when young dairy farmer Michael Eavis decided to stage his own British version of Woodstock on his land at Worthy Farm in Pilton, a few miles outside Glastonbury. Eavis borrowed £15,000 and invited some bands to play on a couple of makeshift stages in his field. Entry was £1, which included a pint of milk from Eavis' dairy herd; among the acts who performed was Marc Bolan of T-Rex, who arrived in typically flamboyant style in his own velvet-covered Buick.

Forty years later, the festival has become the world's longest-running performing-arts festival, attracting crowds of more than 120,000 (more like 180,000 once you factor in the bands, technical staff, caterers and media types). Glastonbury is more a way of life than a music festival, and it's a rite of passage for every British teenager. It's even had a feature-length film made about it, directed by Julien Temple.

Eavis' daughter Emily has since taken over the day-to-day-running of the festival, and her decision to give headline slots to commercial artists such as Jay-Z and U2 has inevitably led many people to grumble that Glastonbury's gone mainstream. But at the very least, the festival's future is relatively stable – it was recently granted its first-ever six-year licence by Mendip District Council, which finally seems to have recognised, after years of wrangling, that the festival really is a national treasure after all.

Mocha Berry   CAFE £
(14 Market Pl; mains £4-8; ⊙Sun-Wed) Ideal for a quick cappuccino, sandwich or stack of pancakes.

Who'd a Thought It Inn   PUB
(17 Northload St) In keeping with Glastonbury's outsider spirit, this town pub is brimming with wacky character, from the vintage signs and upside-down bike on the ceiling to the reclaimed red telephone box tucked in one corner. Locals pack in for its superior food and ales; Glastonbury kingpin Michael Eavis has even been known to pop in for a pint.

George & Pilgrim   PUB
(1 High St; mains £7-15) Partly 15th-century inn with one of the town's most convincingly historic interiors, timbers, flagstones and all. There's a wide choice of southwest ales, and a solid if unremarkable pub menu (lunch daily, dinner Monday to Saturday).

ⓘ Information

Glastonbury tourist office (☑01458-832954; www.glastonburytic.co.uk; The Tribunal, 9 High St; ⊙10am-5pm)

ⓘ Getting There & Away

There is no train station in Glastonbury, so buses are the only public transport option.

The frequent Bus 377 (several times per hour) travels north to Wells (15 minutes) and south to Street (10 minutes) and Yeovil (50 minutes). Bus 29 travels to Taunton (50 minutes, hourly Monday to Saturday).

EXMOOR NATIONAL PARK

Barely 21 miles across and 12 miles north to south, Exmoor might be the little sister of England's national parks, but what she lacks in scale she more than makes up in scenery. Part wilderness expanse, part rolling fields, dotted with bottle-green meadows, wooded combes and crumbling cliffs, Exmoor seems to sum up everything that's green and pleasant about the English landscape. Waymarked paths criss-cross the moor, and a dramatic section of the South West Coast Path runs from Minehead (a family-fun resort just outside the park) all the way to Padstow in Cornwall.

It's a haven for ramblers, mountain-bikers and horse-riders, and it's also home to lots of rare wildlife, including some of England's largest herds of wild red deer; best spotted on a dawn safari.

🏃 Activities

Active Exmoor
(☎01398-324599; www.activeexmoor.com) Comprehensive info on outdoor activities.

Cycling

Cycling is popular on Exmoor, despite the formidable hills. Several sections of the National Cycle Network (NCN; www.sustrans.org.uk) cross the park, including the West Country Way (NCN route 3) from Bristol to Padstow, and the Devon Coast to Coast Cycle Route (NCN route 27) between Exmoor and Dartmoor.

For off-road cycling, popular trails travel through the Brendon Hills, the Crown Estate woodland and along the old Barnstaple railway line. Exmoor & Quantocks MTB Experiences (☎01643-705079; www.exqumtb.co.uk) runs weekend mountain-biking courses from £75 to £150.

For bike hire, try one of the following companies:

Fremington Quay   BICYCLE RENTAL
(☎01271-372586; www.biketrail.co.uk; per day adult/child £16.75/8.50; ⏰10am-5pm Wed-Sun) Delivers bikes to your door, including tandems, tag-a-longs, choppers and dog trailers.

Pompys   BICYCLE RENTAL
(☎01643-704077;www.pompyscycles.co.uk;⏰9am-5pm Mon-Sat) Standard bikes £14 per day, full-suspension £30.

Pony Trekking & Horse Riding

Exmoor is popular riding country and lots of stables offer pony and horse treks from around £40 to £45 for a two-hour hack – see the *Exmoor Visitor* free newspaper for full details.

Brendan Manor Stables   HORSE RIDING
(☎01598-741246) Near Lynton.

Burrowhayes Farm   HORSE RIDING
(☎01643-862463; www.burrowhayes.co.uk)

Knowle Riding Centre   HORSE RIDING
(☎01643-841342; www.knowleridingcentre.co.uk)

Outovercott Stables   HORSE RIDING
(☎01598-753341; www.outovercott.co.uk)

Walking

The open moors and profusion of marked bridleways make Exmoor an excellent area for hiking. The best-known routes are the Somerset & North Devon Coast Path, which is part of the South West Coast Path (www.southwestcoastpath.com), and the Exmoor section of the Two Moors Way, which starts in Lynmouth and travels south to Dartmoor and beyond.

Other routes include the Coleridge Way (www.coleridgeway.co.uk) which winds for 36 miles through Exmoor, the Brendon Hills and the Quantocks. Part of the 180-mile Tarka Trail also cuts through the park; join it at Combe Martin, hike along the cliffs to Lynton/Lynmouth, then head across the moor towards Barnstaple.

Organised walks run by the NPA are held throughout the year. Its autumn dawn safaris to see rutting stags are superb, as are its summertime evening deer-watching hikes.

EXMOOR SAFARIS

If you're a nature-lover or keen photographer, you definitely won't want to miss taking your very own wildlife safari. The national park is home to a wonderful range of unusual birds and beasts, from endangered bats to stubby Exmoor ponies, but it's best known for its large populations of wild red deer. These skittish creatures are very elusive, however, so if you want to see them, your best bet is to rely on the skills of a local guide (and, of course, get up nice and early).

Several companies offer 4WD 'safari' trips across the moor: the best season to visit is autumn, especially from October onwards, when the annual autumn 'rutting' season begins, and stags can be seen bellowing, charging and clashing horns in an attempt to impress their prospective mates.

Standard 2½-hour safari trips cost around £25, although longer expeditions can usually be arranged with plenty of advance notice. Experienced companies include:

Barle Valley Safaris (☎01643-851386; www.exmoorwildlifesafaris.co.uk; safari £30)

Discovery Safaris (☎01643-863080; www.discoverysafaris.com; safari £20)

Exmoor Safari (☎01643-831229; www.exmoorsafari.co.uk; safari £30)

Red Stag Safari (☎01643-841831; www.redstagsafari.co.uk; safari £25-38)

Exmoor National Park

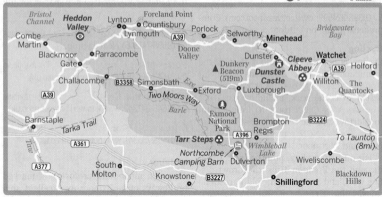

Pick up the *Exmoor Visitor* for full details – NPA walks are highlighted in green.

ℹ Information

Tourist Information

There are three tourist offices NPA Centres around the park – the main one is in Dulverton. All are open from 10am to 5pm daily.

Dulverton (☎01398-323841; NPCDulverton@ exmoor-nationalpark.gov.uk; 7-9 Fore St)

Dunster (☎01643-821835; NPCDunster@ exmoor-nationalpark.gov.uk)

Lynmouth (☎01598-752509; NPCLynmouth@ exmoor-nationalpark.gov.uk)

Websites

Exmoor National Park (www.exmoor-national park.gov.uk) The official NPA site.

Exmoor Tourist Association (www.exmoor .com) Accommodation and activities.

Visit Exmoor (www.visit-exmoor.info) Useful advice on activities, events, accommodation and eating out.

What's On Exmoor (www.whatsonexmoor.com) Local event listings.

ℹ Getting Around

Various buses serve Exmoor's main towns and villages, all of which are listed at the useful ExploreMoor **website** (www.exploremoor.co.uk). Other useful services:

300 Coastal Link Runs along the coast from Minehead to Lynmouth via Allerford and Porlock.

400 Exmoor Explorer Cross-moor bus via Minehead, Allerford, Porlock, Exford, Wheddon Cross and Dunster.

MoorRover On-demand minibus that can take you anywhere on Exmoor for £6; it will also carry bikes and provide a luggage transfer service. You need to book at least a day ahead.

Dulverton

Dulverton is the southern gateway to Exmoor National Park, and sits at the base of the Barle Valley near the confluence of two key rivers, the Exe and Barle. It's a no-nonsense sort of country town, home to a collection of gun-sellers, fishing-tackle stores and gift shops.

There's a lovely 12-mile circular walk along the river from Dulverton to Tarr Steps – an ancient stone clapper bridge haphazardly placed across the River Barle and shaded by gnarled old trees. The bridge was supposedly built by the devil for sunbathing. It's a four- to five-hour trek for the average walker. You can add another three or four hours to the walk by continuing from Tarr Steps up Winsford Hill for distant views over Devon.

🛌 Sleeping

Tarr Farm HOTEL **££**
(☎01643-851507; www.tarrfarm.co.uk; s/d £90/ 150; P) This is the place to really lose yourself: a charming farmhouse nested amongst the woods near Tarr Steps, 7 miles from Dulverton. The nine rooms are spacious and luxurious, with nice extras such as organic bath goodies and homemade biscuits. The restaurant (mains £11 to £20) is especially good on game, fish and local lamb.

Town Mills
B&B **££**

(☎01398-323124; www.townmillsdulverton.co.uk; High St; s/d £65/90; **P**🛜) The top choice if you want to stay within walking distance of town. It's in a riverside mill, and the rooms are thoroughly contemporary, with creamy carpets, magnolia walls and bits of floral artwork.

Three Acres
B&B **££**

(☎01398-323730; www.threeacrescountryhouse .co.uk; d £90-120; **P**) If you don't mind a drive, this sweet farmhouse is lost amongst the narrow lanes around Dulverton. It's scooped lots of B&B awards, and with good reason: the six prim rooms overlook rolling Exmoor hills, and there's a different daily special for breakfast, from Exe trout to homemade bangers. Lovely.

🍴 Eating

Woods
BISTRO **££**

(☎01398-324007; 4 Bank Sq; mains £11-16.50) This cute bistro is a far more sophisticated affair than you'd expect to find in out-of-the-way Dulverton. Generous portions of corn-fed chicken, confit duck and stuffed sea-bream are served up in a cosy dining room, full of wooden furniture and black-and-white photos. But it's the 'Famous Steak-And-Chips' that really pulls in the punters – don't be surprised if you need a friend to finish yours.

Lewis' Tea Rooms
CAFE **££**

(☎01398-323850; 13 High St; mains £5-18; ☺breakfast & lunch Mon-Sat, plus dinner Thu-Sat Jul & Aug) Top-class teas (including many rare estate varieties) are the order of the day at this delightful tearoom, but it's worth leaving room for the Welsh rarebits and crumbly cakes too. It's charmingly frilly and floral, and it opens late for suppers in summer, too.

BUSHCRAFT

For budding backcountry adventurers, Mountains+Moor (☎01643-841610; www.mountainsandmoor.co.uk) offers navigation lessons (from £80 per two days) and summer mountain-craft courses (two/five days £110/270), which include camp-craft, rope work and river crossings, and take the form of mini-expeditions.

Farthings Farm Shop
DELI **£**

(☎01398-323878; www.exmoor-farm-shop.co.uk; 5 Bridge St; ☺9am-5pm Mon-Sat) The place to stock up on moor goodies, from big slabs of Exmoor Blue Cheese to locally made jams and chutneys. There's a great choice of meat cuts, too.

Lynton & Lynmouth

Nestled on the northern edge of the moor, these twin coastal towns are quite different in feel: bustling Lynmouth is a busy harbour lined with pubs, souvenir sellers and fudge shops, while its clifftop cousin of Lynton feels much more genteel and well-to-do. The two areas are linked by a cliffside railway that's powered by the rushing waters of the West Lyn River, which feeds numerous cascades and waterfalls nearby.

👁 Sights

Cliff Railway
HERITAGE RAILWAY

(www.cliffrailwaylynton.co.uk; single/return adult £2.25/3, child £1.40/2; ☺10am-6pm Easter-Oct) This extraordinary piece of Victorian engineering was designed by George Marks, believed to be a pupil of Brunel. Two cars linked by a steel cable descend or ascend the slope according to the amount of water in the cars' tanks. It's been running like clockwork since 1890, and certainly makes an interesting way to commute between Lynton and Lynmouth.

Glen Lyn Gorge
GORGE

(☎01598-753207; adult/child £5/3; ☺10am-5pm Easter-Oct) Halfway between the two towns, this shady gorge offers some delightful riverside walks and a small exhibition centre devoted to hydroelectric power.

Lyn & Exmoor Museum
MUSEUM

(St Vincent's Cottage, Market St; adult/child £1/20p; ☺10am-12.30pm & 2-5pm Mon-Fri, 2-5pm Sun Apr-Oct) This small harbourside museum contains background on the Lynmouth Flood, a devastating flash flood which swept through the town in 1952 and claimed 34 lives.

🥾 Activities

There are some beautiful short walks in and around the two villages, as well as access to some longer routes: the South West Coast Path, the Coleridge Way and the Tarka Trail all pass through Lynmouth, and it is the official starting point of the Two Moors Way.

HOSTELS & CAMPING BARNS

The only YHA hostel inside the national park is at Exford (☎0845-3719634; exford@yha.org.uk; Exe Mead; dm £14; P), although for more basic accommodation, there's also Pinkery Bunkhouse (☎01643-831437; pinkery@exmoor-national park.gov.uk) near Simonsbath and camping barns at Mullacott Farm (☎01629-592700) near Ilfracombe and Northcombe Farm (☎01629-592700) near Dulverton.

Prices start at around £8.50 per night and you'll need all the usual camping supplies.

The most popular hike is to the stunning Valley of the Rocks, described by poet laureate Robert Southey as 'rock reeling upon rock, stone piled upon stone, a huge terrifying reeling mass'. It's just over a mile west of Lynton, and is believed to mark the original course of the River Lyn. Many of the tortuous rock formations have been named over the years – look out for the Devil's Cheesewring and Ragged Jack – the valley is also home to a population of feral goats.

Other popular trails wind to the lighthouse at Foreland Point, east of Lynmouth, and Watersmeet, 2 miles upriver from Lynmouth, where a handily placed National Trust teashop is housed in a Victorian fishing lodge.

📟 Sleeping

There are plenty of mid-price B&Bs dotted along Lee Rd in Lynton.

North Walk House
B&B ££

(☎01598-753372; www.northwalkhouse.co.uk; Lynton; d £50-78; P🛜) This smart cliffside house is refreshingly frill-free, with five colour-themed rooms decked out with stripy bedspreads, wood floors, pine furniture and the odd sea view. Ecofriendly toiletries and an all-organic breakfast ensure the green factor stays high, too.

Castle Hill
B&B

(☎01598-752291; www.castlehill.biz; Castle Hill, Lynton; d £60-95, f £120-130) This slender Victorian house occupies a prime position in Lynton, literally steps from the shops and clifftops. It's a trad, value-focused B&B, with

six decent rooms in tones of cream and beige: go for one of the two balcony suites if you prefer to sleep with a view.

St Vincent House
B&B ££

(☎01598-752244; www.st-vincent-hotel.co.uk; Castle Hill, Lynton; d £75-80; P🛜) Grade-II listed and built by a compatriot of Nelson, this sea-captain's house has history by the bucketload. All the rooms are named after famous battleships, and though the decor is a touch flouncy, they're very comfortable. Top-floor Victory feels suspiciously like a ship's cabin, with its low ceiling and tiny windows.

Old Rectory
HOTEL £££

(☎01598-763368; www.oldrectoryhotel.co.uk; Martinhoe; d £215-250) Cheap it most certainly isn't, but this swish hotel along the coast in Martinhoe beats seven bells out of Lynton's B&Bs in terms of style. Rooms are supremely plush (elegant baths, silky fabrics) and the hotel hosts regular wine-tasting sessions in its *table d'hôte* restaurant.

✖ Eating

Rising Sun
PUB ££

(☎01598-753223; www.risingsunlynmouth.co.uk; mains £11.25-18) It's only a quick walk uphill from the touristy Lynmouth seafront, but this thatched pub is a world away from pasties-from-a-bag. Head chef Paul Sage has turned this into the town's most enticing eatery, making maximum use of the meat, seafood and game on his doorstep – try the lobster for an absolute treat. The building itself has plenty of smugglers' character, with higgledy-piggledy floors and hefty beams.

🛈 Information

Lynton tourist office (☎01598-752225; info@ lyntourism.co.uk; Lynton Town Hall, Lee Rd; ⊙10am-4pm Mon-Sat, to 2pm Sun)

Porlock & Around

The coastal village of Porlock is one of the prettiest on the north Exmoor coast; the huddle of thatched cottages lining its main street is framed on one side by the sea, and on the other by a jumble of houses that cling to the steeply sloping hills behind. Winding lanes lead to the picturesque breakwater of Porlock Weir, 2 miles to the west, with a fine shingly beach and lovely coastal views.

The village of Selworthy, 2½ miles southeast of Porlock, forms part of the

50-sq-km Holnicote Estate (NT; www.national trust.org.uk/holnicote-estate), the largest area of National Trust land on Exmoor. Though its cob-and-thatch cottages look ancient, the village was almost completely rebuilt in the 19th century by local philanthropist Thomas Acland to provide housing for elderly workers on his estate.

🛏 Sleeping & Eating

Culbone
PUB

(📞01643-862259; www.theculbone.com; mains £12.50-22) On the A39 between Porlock and Lynmouth, this smart pub-with-rooms offers 28-day aged steaks (there's a choice of five different cuts, as well as a huge *côte de boeuf* for two), but the seafood and veggie choices are both good, too. It's in a country location but the setting is contemporary, with slate floors and black leather chairs, a vibe which runs into the upstairs rooms. Chef Jack Scarterfield also runs cooking courses.

Cafe Porlock Weir
RESTAURANT, HOTEL £££

(📞01643-863300; www.thecafeporlockweir.co.uk; Porlock Weir; mains £11.50-14.50) Chef Andrew Dixon has renamed his seaside establishment, but its selling points are the same: classic dishes and a sea-blown spot beside Porlock Weir. The restaurant's more good value than gourmet these days, so while the flavours are still rich, the price tag's much leaner. The upstairs rooms are looking tired, though.

Ship Inn
PUB £

(www.shipinnporlock.co.uk; High St; mains £8.50-12.50; 🅿) Coleridge and pal Robert Southey both downed pints in this thatched Porlock pub – you can even sit in 'Southey's Corner'. Substantial pub food – mainly steaks, roasts and stews – are served in the bar, and there are 10 surprisingly light rooms in pine and cream.

❶ Information

Porlock tourist office (📞01643-863150; www.porlock.co.uk; West End, High St; ⏱10am-5pm Mon-Sat, 10am-1pm Sun)

❶ Getting There & Away

If you're driving, the most scenic route to Porlock is the steep, twisting **toll road** (car/motorbike/bicycle £2.50/1.50/1) that hugs the coast all the way from Lynmouth. Better still, you get to avoid the 1:4 gradient on Porlock Hill.

Dunster

Centred around a scarlet-walled castle and a medieval yarn market, Dunster is one of Exmoor's oldest villages, an attractive muddle of cobbled streets, bubbling brooks and packhorse bridges.

◉ Sights

Dunster Castle
CASTLE

(NT; www.nationaltrust.org.uk/dunstercastle; castle adult/child £8.80/4.40, garden & park only £4.80 /2.20; ⏱11am-5pm Mar-Oct) This impressive red-brick castle was originally owned by the Luttrell family, whose manor encompassed much of northern Exmoor. Although it served as a fortress for around 1000 years, the present castle was heavily remodelled during Victorian times, so little remains of the original Norman stronghold, save for the 13th-century gateway. Its grand rooms are full of Tudor furnishings, ornate plasterwork and ancestral portraits, and the terraced gardens offer sweeping coastal views, as well as an important collection of strawberry trees.

St George's Church
CHURCH

Dating mostly from the 15th century, this church boasts a wonderfully carved fanvaulted rood screen. Just behind the church is a 16th-century dovecote, which would have housed squab pigeons destined for the Luttrell's dinner table.

Watermill
MILL

(www.dunsterwatermill.co.uk; Mill Lane; adult/child £3.50/2; ⏱11am-4.45pm Apr-Oct) This working 18th-century mill still has most of its original cogs, wheels and grinding stones. There's also a sweet riverside tearoom.

🛏 Sleeping & Eating

Dunster Castle Hotel
HOTEL ££

(📞01643-823030; www.thedunstercastlehotel .co.uk; 5 High St; r £90-125; 🛜) Right in the heart of the village, this former coaching inn has been expensively refurbished and now has a good choice of light, uncluttered rooms – the superior kingsize rooms are definitely worth the extra outlay (£125), especially rococo-style Grabbist and spacious Conyger. The restaurant (mains £14.95 to £17.95) specialises in rich, chunky fare: belly pork with lyonnaise potatoes, or rump of lamb with minted jelly.

Spears Cross
B&B **££**

(☎01643-821439; www.spearscross.co.uk; 1 West St; d £89-99) If you like your floral fabrics, puffy armchairs and china crockery, you'll be thoroughly happy at this four-room B&B, which is still flying the flag for the old-fashioned style of British B&B. The house is 15th century, and the rooms are squeezed into all kinds of awkward spaces, but luxuries such as Penhaligon's toiletries are a welcome surprise. Savour rare-breed bangers and traditional 'Dunster Toast' at the brekkie table.

Luttrell Arms
PUB **££**

(☎01643-821555; www.luttrellarms.co.uk; High St; d £120-150; **P**) In medieval times this glorious old coaching inn was the guesthouse of the Abbots of Cleeve. Huge flagstones, heavy armchairs and faded tapestries dot the lounge – a perfect fit for the hearty bar food. The rooms have period curios too: four-poster beds, brass plates, beams or perhaps a plaster fireplace.

Reeve's
BRITISH **££**

(☎01643-821414; www.reevesrestaurantdunster.co.uk; dinner £12.25-16.25; ◷lunch Sat & Sun, dinner Tue-Sat) This surprisingly swanky restaurant dishes up Dunster's best food in an attractive dining room full of fairy lights and stripped-wood floors. Its dishes are complex and satisfying: think delicate stacks of monkfish, venison marinated in port and juniper or Exmouth scallops in chive butter.

Cobblestones Cafe
CAFE **££**

(High St; mains £5-14; ◷lunch daily, dinner Wed-Sat) Plump for the daily roast or potted shrimps on toast at this village cafe, or better still just drop in for a superior cream tea.

❶ Getting There & Away

Bus 29 stops at Dunster on its way between Taunton and Minehead (half-hourly Monday to Saturday, hourly on Sunday).

The **West Somerset Railway** (☎01643-704996; www.west-somerset-railway.co.uk; 24hr rover ticket adult/child £17/8.50) stops at Dunster during the summer.

DEVON

Devon offers freedom. Freedom from and freedom to. Its rippling, beach-fringed landscape is studded with historic homes, vibrant cities and wild, wild moors. So here you can swap the commute for a boat trip. Step off the treadmill and step onto a rugged coast path. Ditch schedules and to-do lists and get lost in hedge-lined lanes that aren't even on your map. Go surfing, cycling, kayaking, horse-riding or sea-swimming. Or simply drink in surroundings that make you smile. Explore a rich heritage, from Tudor townscapes to art deco delights. Discover collegiate Exeter, touristy Torquay, yachting haven Dartmouth and counter-culture Totnes. Or escape to wilderness Dartmoor and the remote, surf-dashed north coast. Sample wine made from the vines beside you and food that's fresh from field, furrow or sea. It's a place to rediscover, recharge or reconnect. Because in offering freedom, Devon can help shine a little sunshine on your soul.

❶ Information

Visit South West (www.visitsouthwest.co.uk)

❶ Getting Around

Traveline South West (www.travelinesw.com) Details all bus and train routes and times; tourist offices also stock timetables.

Bus

The Devon interactive bus **map** (www.journeydevon.info) helps in route-planning. Central Dartmoor is covered by a fleet of smaller operators.

First (www.firstgroup.com) A key operator in south and east Devon.

Stagecoach Devon (www.stagecoachbus.com) Operates local services, especially in Exeter, north Devon and around Torquay.

BUS PASSES

Firstday Southwest (adult/child/family £7.60/6.20/18.70) A day's unlimited bus travel on First buses in Devon and Cornwall.

First Seven Day (adult/child/family £37/23/56) Week-long pass for most First buses in Devon.

Stagecoach Explorer (adult/child/family £7/5/15) One day's travel on Stagecoach's southwest network.

Train

Devon's main line skirts southern Dartmoor, running from Exeter to Plymouth and on to Cornwall. Branch lines include the 39-mile Exeter–Barnstaple Tarka Line; the 15-mile Plymouth–Gunnislake Tamar Valley Line and the scenic Exeter–Torquay Paignton line.

Freedom of Devon & Cornwall Rover Allows unlimited train travel in Devon and Cornwall for three days out of seven (adult/child £42/21), or eight days out of 15 (£64/32).

Exeter

POP 119,600

Well heeled and comfortable, Exeter exudes evidence of its centuries-old role as the spiritual and administrative heart of Devon. The city's Gothic cathedral presides over stretches of cobbled streets, fragments of the terracotta Roman city wall and a tumbling of medieval and Georgian buildings. A snazzy new shopping centre brings bursts of the modern, thousands of university students ensure a buzzing nightlife and the vibrant quayside acts as a launch pad for cycling or kayaking trips. Throw in some stylish places to stay and eat and you have a relaxed but lively base for explorations.

History

Exeter's past can be read in its buildings. The Romans marched in around AD 55 – their 17-hectare fortress included a 2-mile defensive wall, crumbling sections of which remain, especially in Rougemont and Northernhay Gardens. Saxon and Norman times saw growth: a castle went up in 1068, the cathedral 40 years later. The Tudor wool boom brought Exeter an export trade, riches and half-timbered houses; prosperity continued into the Georgian era when hundreds of merchants built genteel homes. The Blitz of WWII brought devastation. In 1942 in just one night, 156 people died and 12 hectares of the city were flattened. In the 21st century the £220 million Princesshay shopping centre added shimmering glass and steel lines to the architectural mix.

◉ Sights

Exeter Cathedral   CATHEDRAL
(☑01392-285983; www.exeter-cathedral.org.uk; The Close; adult/child £5/free; ⊙9.30am-4.45pm Mon-Sat) Magnificent in warm, honey-coloured stone, Exeter's Cathedral Church of St Peter is framed by lawns and wonky half-timbered buildings – a quintessentially English scene peopled by picnickers snacking to the sound of the bells.

The site has been a religious one since at least the 5th century but the Normans started the current building in 1114; the towers of today's cathedral date from that period. In 1270 a 90-year remodelling process began, introducing a mix of Early English and Decorated Gothic styles.

Above the Great West Front scores of weather-worn figures line a once brightly painted screen that now forms England's largest collection of 14th-century sculpture. Inside, the ceiling is mesmerising – the longest unbroken Gothic vaulting in the world, it sweeps up to meet ornate ceiling bosses in gilt and vibrant colours. Look out for the 15th-century Exeter Clock in the north transept: in keeping with medieval astronomy it shows the earth as a golden ball at the centre of the universe with the sun, a fleur-de-lys, travelling round. Still ticking and whirring, it chimes on the hour.

The huge oak canopy over the Bishop's Throne was carved in 1312, while the 1350 minstrels' gallery is decorated with 12 angels playing musical instruments. Cathedral staff will point out the famous sculpture of the lady with two left feet and the tiny St James Chapel, built to repair the one destroyed in the Blitz. Look out for its unusual carvings: a cat, a mouse and, oddly, a rugby player.

In the Refectory (mains £6; ⊙10am-5pm Mon-Sat) you can tuck into cakes, quiches and soups at trestle tables surrounded by vaulted ceilings, stained glass and busts of the great, the good and the dead.

Free guided tours (⊙11am & 12.30pm Mon-Sat, plus 2.30pm Mon-Fri) last 45 minutes. Evocative evensong services are held at 5.30pm Monday to Friday, and 3pm on Saturday, with choral evensong on Sunday at 3pm.

Underground Passages   TUNNELS
(☑01392-665887; www.exeter.gov.uk/passages; Paris St; adult/child £5.50/4; ⊙9.30am-5.30pm Mon-Sat, 10am-4pm Sun Jun-Sep, 11.30am-4pm Tue-Sun Oct-May) Prepare to crouch down, don a hard hat and possibly get spooked in

---

CATHEDRAL ROOF TOURS

For a sensational view of Exeter Cathedral book one of these high-rise guided walks (☑01392-285983; www.exeter-cathedral.org.uk; adult/child £10/5; ⊙2pm Tue-Thu, 11am Sat Apr-Sep). Climb 251 steps up a spiral staircase, head out onto the sweeping roof to stroll its length, then gaze down on the city from the top of the North Tower. They're popular so book two weeks ahead.

Exeter

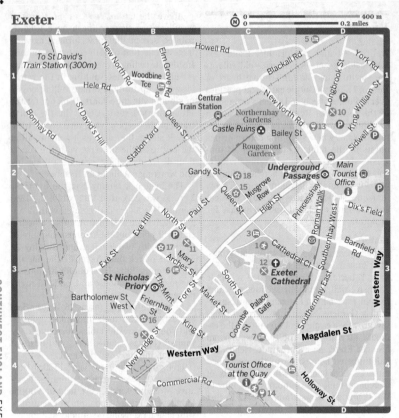

Exeter

◉ Top Sights
Exeter Cathedral	C3
St Nicholas Priory	B3
Underground Passages	D2

◉ Activities, Courses & Tours
1	Redcoat Tours	C3
2	Saddles & Paddles	C4

◉ Sleeping
3	Abode at the Royal Clarence	C3
4	Globe Backpackers	C4
5	Raffles	D1
6	St Olaves	B3
7	White Hart	C4
8	Woodbine	B1

◉ Eating
9	@Angela's	B4
10	Harry's	D1
11	Herbies	B3
	MC Cafe, Bar & Grill	(see 3)
	Michael Caines	(see 3)
12	Refectory	C3

◉ Drinking
13	Old Firehouse	D2
14	On the Waterfront	C4

◉ Entertainment
15	Cavern Club	C2
16	Exeter Picturehouse	B4
17	Mamma Stone's	B3
18	Phoenix	C2

what is the only publicly accessible system of its kind in England. These medieval vaulted passages were built to house pipes bringing fresh water to the city. Unlike modern utility companies, the authorities opted to have permanent access for repairs, rather than dig up the streets each time – genius. Guides lead you on a scramble through the network telling tales of ghosts, escape routes and cholera. The last tour is an hour before closing; they're popular – book ahead.

St Nicholas Priory   MONASTERY, MUSEUM
(☑01392-665858; www.exeter.gov.uk/priory; The Mint; adult/child £3/1; ☺10am-5pm Sat, plus Mon-Fri school holidays) This 900-year-old former Benedictine monastery is built of beautiful russet stone and vividly recreates life inside a late-Elizabethan town house. Expect brightly coloured furnishings, elaborate plaster ceilings and intricate oak panelling.

FREE **Bill Douglas Centre**   MUSEUM
(☑01392-724321; www.billdouglas.org; Old Library, Prince of Wales Rd; ☺10am-5pm Mon-Fri) A delightful homage to film and fun, the Bill Douglas Centre is a compact collection of all things celluloid, from magic lanterns to Mickey Mouse. Inside discover just what the butler did see and why the flicks are called the flicks. Among the mass of movie memorabilia are Charlie Chaplin bottle stoppers, Ginger Rogers playing cards, James Bond board games and Star Wars toys.

🏃 Activities

The River Exe and the Exeter Canal are framed by foot and cycle paths which wind south from the Quay, past pubs, beside an ever broadening estuary towards the sea, 10 miles away.

Saddles & Paddles   OUTDOORS
(☑01392-424241; www.sadpad.com; Exeter Quay; ☺9.30am-5.30pm) Rents out bikes (adult per hour/day £6/15), kayaks (per hour/day £10/35) and Canadian canoes (per hour/day £15/50); the tourist office stocks maps.

👉 Tours

FREE **Redcoat Tours**   WALKING TOURS
(☑01392-265203; www.exeter.gov.uk/visiting; ☺2-4 daily Apr-Oct, 2-3 daily Nov-Mar) For an informed and entertaining introduction to Exeter's history, tag along on one of these 1½-hour tours. Themes range from murder and trade to Romans and religion – there are

even torchlit prowls through the catacombs and night-time ghost walks. Tours leave from Cathedral Yard or the Quay; pick up a program from the tourist office.

🛏 Sleeping

TOP CHOICE **Abode at the Royal Clarence**   HOTEL ££
(☑01392-319955; www.abodehotels.co.uk/exeter; Cathedral Yard; r £120-300; ☎) This is the epitome of sink-into-it luxury. Exquisite rooms are categorised as Comfortable, Desirable, Enviable or Fabulous – either way they're a drop-dead gorgeous blend of Georgian grandeur and minimalist chic. Expect bespoke beds, roll-topped baths and a complementary tuckbox of local treats. Breakfast is not included.

Raffles   B&B ££
(☑01392-270200; www.raffles-exeter.co.uk; 11 Blackall Rd; s/d £42/72; ℗) The antique dealer owner has peppered each room of this late-Victorian town house with heritage features – look out for Bakelite radios, wooden plant stands and creaking trunks. Largely organic breakfasts and a walled garden add to the appeal.

White Hart   INN ££
(☑01392-279897; www.whitehartpubexeter.co.uk; 66 South St; s £50-70, d £50-80; ℗☎) They've been putting people up here since the Plantagenets were on the throne in the 1300s. The courtyard is a wisteria-fringed bobble of cobbles and the bar is book-lined and beamed. Rooms are tasteful modern affairs with suede chairs, honey and gold hues and glinting bathrooms. The Sunday night doubles (£50) are a steal.

St Olaves   HOTEL ££
(☑01392-217736; www.olaves.co.uk; Mary Arches St; d £80-125, ste £95-155, f £165; ℗☎) This hotel's swirling spiral staircase is so beautiful it's tempting to sleep beside it. But if you did, you'd miss out on the 18th-century-with-contemporary-twist bedrooms: think rococo mirrors, brass bedsteads and plush furnishings.

Globe Backpackers   HOSTEL £
(☑01392-215521; www.exeterbackpackers.co.uk; 71 Holloway St; dm/d £16.50/42; ☎) Rightly a firm favourite among budget travellers, this spotlessly clean, relaxed, rambling house boasts three doubles, roomy dorms and wet room showers that are positively luxurious.

Wood Life
CAMPGROUND £

(☎01392-832509; www.thewoodlife.org; The Linhay, near Kenn; 5/7 nights from £550/730; ☻Apr-Oct; ℗) Your chance to get back to nature without getting grubby, this cavernous, six-person tent has decked floors, wicker chairs and brass bedsteads; the highlights though are the wood-burning stove and campfire – you can even chop your own logs. Exeter, Dartmoor and the beach are each about 5 miles away.

Woodbine
B&B £££

(☎01392-203302;www.woodbineguesthouse.co.uk; 1 Woodbine Tce; s/d £38/66; ☎) A surprise sits behind this archetypal flower-framed terrace: fresh, modish rooms with low beds and burgundy flashes – there's even under-floor heating in the bathrooms.

✕ Eating

Michael Caines
FINE DINING ££

(☎01392-223638; www.michaelcaines.com; Cathedral Yard; mains £25) Run by the eponymous, double Michelin-starred chef, the food here is a complex blend of prime West-country ingredients and full-bodied French flavours. Gastronomes linger over the seven-course tasting menu (£72), but the three-course set lunches (£23) are a comparative bargain.

MC Cafe, Bar & Grill
CAFE, BISTRO ££

(Cathedral Yard; mains £12, 2-course lunch/dinner £10/11; ☻9am-10pm) The MC in the title stands for TV chef Michael Caines, so prepare for bistro classics with creative twists: beef burgers with onion confit; fish encased in a local Otter Ale batter. Leave room though for the devilishly dark chocolate tart.

BLACKDOWN YURTS

Organic bedding, fresh spring water, thick rugs and blazing log burners make this the epitome of cushy camping (☎01884-266699; www.blackdownyurts.co.uk; nr Exeter; four-person yurt per week £375-460; ℗). There's a field kitchen, fire pit and an endless supply of logs too. The four, cosy, ecofriendly yurts are tucked away on a sleepy smallholding around 15 miles east of Exeter.

@Angela's
MODERN BRITISH ££

(☎01392-499038; www.angelasrestaurant.co.uk; 38 New Bridge St; dinner mains £19; ☻lunch Wed-Sat, dinner Tue-Sat) Dedication to sourcing local ingredients sometimes sees the chef at this smart bistro rising before dawn to bag the best fish at Brixham Market; his steamed John Dory with seared scallops is worth the trip alone. The beef has grazed Devon fields, while local duck is made memorable by a rich Grand Marnier sauce. Wise foodies opt for the pre-booked lunch (two-/three-courses £19/23).

Herbies
VEGETARIAN £

(15 North St; mains £5-9; ☻lunch Mon-Sat, dinner Tue-Sat; ✓) Cosy and gently groovy, Herbies has been cheerfully feeding Exeter's veggies for more than 20 years. It's *the* place in town to tuck into delicious sundried tomato and mushroom risotto or a hearty Greek vegetable pie. it's strong on vegan dishes too.

Harry's
BISTRO ££

(www.harrys-exeter.co.uk; 86 Longbrook St; mains £8-12; ☻closed Sun) Harry's is the kind of welcoming neighbourhood eatery you wish was on your own doorstep but rarely is. The decor is all wooden chairs, blackboard menus and gilt mirrors; the food includes seared tuna, Spanish ham with marinated figs, and a hearty three-bean chilli.

🍷 Drinking

On the Waterfront
BAR

(www.waterfrontexeter.co.uk; The Quay) In 1835 this was a warehouse; now its red-brick, barrel-vaulted ceilings stretch back from a thoroughly modern bar. The tables outside are a popular spot for a riverside pint.

Old Firehouse
PUB

(www.oldfirehouseexeter.co.uk; 50 New North Rd) A candlelit Exeter institution, often crowded with students and famous for its buzzing atmosphere, sunny terrace and impressive range of real ales and ciders.

☆ Entertainment

Mamma Stone's
LIVE MUSIC

(www.mamastones.com; 1 Mary Arches St; ☻6pm-midnight, 9pm-3am when bands play) This boho hangout is a riot of painted wood and showcases everything from acoustic sets to pop, folk and jam nights. Mamma Stone's daughter, Joss (yes, *the* Joss Stone), plays sometimes too. Roll up about 11pm and see them pull back the tables so the crowd can groove away.

Phoenix ARTS CENTRE
(www.exeterphoenix.org.uk; Gandy St; ⊘closed Sun; 🛜) The city's art and soul; Phoenix is a hub of exhibitions, performance, music, dance, film, classes and workshops. There's a buzzing cafe-bar too.

Exeter Picturehouse CINEMA
(www.picturehouses.co.uk; 51 Bartholomew St West) An intimate, independent cinema, screening mainstream and art-house movies.

Cavern Club LIVE MUSIC
(www.cavernclub.co.uk; 83 Queen St; ⊘11am-5pm Mon-Sat, 8pm-1am Sun-Thu, 11am-2am Fri & Sat) Prepare for a sweaty, hectic melee when bands take to the stage at this long-standing indie club, famous for big-name DJs and breaking acts from the counter-culture scene.

❶ Information

Exeter library (Castle St; ⊘9am-6pm Mon, Tue, Thu & Fri, 10am-5pm Wed 9am-4pm Sat; 🛜) Internet (per 30 minutes £2.20), plus free wi-fi.

Police station (☑08452-777444; Heavitree Rd; ⊘24hr)

Royal Devon & Exeter Hospital (Barrack Rd) Accident and emergency.

Main tourist office (☑01392-665700; www.heartofdevon.com; Dix's Field; ⊘9am-5pm Mon-Sat Apr-Sep, 9.30am-4.30pm Oct-Mar)

Tourist office at the Quay (☑01392-271611; www.heartofdevon.com; The Quay; ⊘10am-5pm Apr-Sep, 11am-4pm Sat & Sun Oct-Mar)

❶ Getting There & Away

Air

Exeter International Airport (www.exeter -airport.co.uk) Flights connect with cities in Europe and the UK, including Glasgow, Manchester and Newcastle, plus the Channel Islands and the Isles of Scilly.

Bus

Services include:

Bude (£6.50, two hours, five Monday to Saturday) Bus X9; runs via Okehampton.

Moretonhampstead (one hour, six daily Monday to Saturday) Bus 359.

Plymouth (£6.50, 1¼ hours, two-hourly Monday to Saturday, three on Sunday) Bus X38.

Sidmouth (one hour, one to three per hour) Bus 52A/B.

Totnes (50 minutes, seven daily Monday to Saturday, two on Sunday) Bus X64.

The **Jurassic Coastlinx** (Bus X53) runs three to seven services daily to Lyme Regis, Weymouth and Poole.

On Sundays between June and mid-September Bus 82, the **Transmoor Link**, makes five trips from Exeter to Plymouth via Moretonhampstead, Postbridge, Princetown and Yelverton.

Train

Main-line and branch-line trains run from Exeter St David's and Exeter Central stations:

Barnstaple (£9, 1¼ hours, one to two hourly)

Bristol (£15, 1¼ hours, half-hourly)

Exmouth (£4, hourly, 40 minutes)

London Paddington (£35, 2½ hours, half-hourly)

Paignton (£6, 50 minutes, half-hourly)

Penzance (£15, three hours, hourly)

Plymouth (£5, one hour, half-hourly)

Torquay (£6, 45 minutes, half-hourly)

Totnes (£6, 35 minutes, half-hourly)

❶ Getting Around

To/From the Airport

Bus 56 runs from the bus station and Exeter St David's train station to Exeter Airport (30 minutes, hourly 7am to 6pm).

Bicycle

Saddles & Paddles (p305) rents out bikes, kayaks and canoes.

Bus

Bus H links St David's train station with Central Station and the High St, passing near the **bus station**.

Car

Hire options include **Europcar** (www.europcar .co.uk). Park & Ride buses (adult/child £2.25/ 1.50) operate every 10 minutes, running from Sowton (near M5, junction 30) and Matford (near M5, junction 31) Monday to Saturday, and from Honiton Rd (near M5, junction 29) daily.

Taxi

Ranks at St David's train station and on High and Sidwell St.

Capital Taxis (☑01392-434343; ⊘24hr)

Club Cars (☑01392-213030; ⊘24hr)

Gemini (☑01392-666666; ⊘24hr)

Around Exeter

Powderham Castle HISTORIC BUILDING

(☎01626-890243; www.powderham.co.uk; adult/child £10.50/8.50; ⊙11am-4.30pm Sun-Fri Apr-Oct; P) The historic home of the Earl of Devon, Powderham is a stately but still friendly place. Built in 1391, it was damaged in the Civil War and remodelled in the Victorian era. A visit takes in a fine wood-panelled Great Hall, parkland with 650 deer and glimpses of life 'below stairs' in the kitchen. The earl and family are still resident and, despite its grandeur, for disarming, fleeting moments it feels like you're actually wandering through someone's sitting room.

Powderham is on the River Exe near Kenton, 8 miles south of Exeter. Bus 2 runs from Exeter (30 minutes, every 20 minutes Monday to Saturday).

A La Ronde HISTORIC BUILDING

(NT; ☎01395-265514; www.nationaltrust.org.uk; Summer Lane; adult/child £7.20/3.70; ⊙11am-5pm Sat-Wed Feb-Jun, Sep & Oct, 11am-5pm daily Jul & Aug; P) This quirky 16-sided cottage was built in 1796 so two spinster cousins could display a mass of curiosities acquired on their 10-year European grand tour. Its glass alcoves, low lintels and tiny doorways mean it's like clambering through a doll's house – highlights are a delicate feather frieze in the drawing room and a gallery smothered with a thousand seashells. In a fabulous collision of old and new, this can only be seen via remote control CCTV from the butler's pantry. The house is 10 miles south of Exeter, near Exmouth; bus 57 (30 minutes, every 15 minutes) runs close by.

Torquay & Around

POP 110.370

It may be south Devon, not the south of France, but Torquay has long been dubbed the English Riviera, thanks to palm trees, plentiful beaches and steep hills. The town is the quintessential, sometimes faded, English resort, torn between targeting elderly vacationers and young party animals. But an azure circle of bay and a mild microclimate have also drawn a smarter set, and the bay now competes with Devon's finest foodie hubs in terms of top eateries. Add an intriguing Agatha Christie connection and attractions ranging from an immense aviary to an impressive ecozoo, and it all adds up to some grand days out beside the sea.

Torquay's neighbouring resort, Paignton, sits 3 miles south; the fishing port of Brixham is 5 miles further south again.

◉ Sights & Activities

Beaches BEACH

Torquay boasts no fewer than 20 beaches and a surprising 22 miles of coast. Holidaymakers flock to the central (but tidal) Torre Abbey Sands; locals head for the sand-and-shingle beaches beside the 240ft red-clay cliffs around Babbacombe. A steep, narrow road leads to the beach; better still hop on the glorious 1920s funicular railway (☎01803-328750; www.babbacombecliffrailway.co.uk; adult/child return £1.90/1.30; ⊙9.30am-5pm Feb-Oct, to 6pm Jun-Sep); a memorable trip in a tiny wooden carriage that shuttles up and down rails set into the cliff.

Paignton Zoo ZOO

(☎0844-474 2222; www.paigntonzoo.org.uk; Totnes Rd, Paignton; adult/child £13/9; ⊙10am-5pm; P) This 80-acre site is dotted with spacious

---

RIVER COTTAGE CANTEEN

TV chef Hugh Fearnley-Whittingstall campaigns hard on sustainable food, so it's fitting that his east Devon canteen (☎01297-631862; www.rivercottage.net; Trinity Sq, Axminster; mains £5-16; ⊙9am-5pm daily, dinner Tue-Sat; ☑) champions local, seasonal and organic ingredients. Hearty flavours include pollock with bacon, and a deeply satisfying Dorset mushroom and Ticklemoor goat's cheese risotto; try the Stinger Beer, brewed from (carefully) handpicked Dorset nettles; it's spicy with just a hint of tingle. Alternatively, book a four-course gastronomic delight at the nearby River Cottage HQ (☎01297-630313; www.rivercottage.net; 4 courses £60-70; ⊙lunch Sun, dinner Fri & Sat, booking required). There's another River Cottage Canteen in Plymouth (p317).

Axminster is 30 miles east of Exeter. Trains (£8.40, 40 minutes, hourly) leave from Exeter's St David's station.

enclosures recreating habitats as varied as savannah, wetland, tropical forest and desert. Highlights are the crocodile swamp, orang-utan island, a huge glass-walled lion enclosure and a lemur wood, where you walk over a plank suspension bridge as the primates leap around in surrounding trees. Buses 81 and 12A run at least hourly from Torquay (25 minutes).

Living Coasts
ZOO

(☑0844-474 3366; www.livingcoasts.org.uk; Beacon Quay; adult/child £10/7.45; ⊙10am-5pm) An enormous open-plan aviary bringing you up close to free-roaming penguins, punk-rocker style tufted puffins and disarmingly cute bank cormorants.

Babbacombe
Model Village
MINIATURE VILLAGE

(☑01803-315315; www.model-village.co.uk; Hampton Ave; adult/child £9.50/7.50; ⊙10am-dusk) Prepare for a fabulously eccentric, 4-acre world in miniature, complete with tiny Stonehenge, football stadium, beach and lilliputian population.

Ferry to Brixham
FERRY

(☑01803-882811; www.greenwayferry.co.uk; Princess Pier; adult/child return £5/3; ⊙12 sailings daily Apr-Oct) This blast across Tor Bay offers spray-dashed views of beaches, crumbling cliffs and grand Victorian hotels.

🛏 Sleeping

TOP CHOICE Cary Arms
BOUTIQUE HOTEL £££

(☑01803-327110; www.caryarms.co.uk; Babbacombe Beach; d £230-270, ste £370) The great British seaside goes seriously stylish at this oh-so-chic bolt-hole. Neutral tones are jazzed up by candy-striped cushions, balconies directly overlook the beach and there's even a stick of rock with the hotel's name running through it on your pillow.

Headland View
B&B ££

(☑01803-312612; www.headlandview.com; Babbacombe Downs; s/d £57/72; ℗☎) Set high on the cliffs at Babbacombe, this charming terrace is peppered with subtle nautical flourishes, from jaunty model lighthouses to boat motifs on the curtains. The wicker chairs on the tiny balconies have five-star views of a cracking stretch of sea.

Lanscombe House
B&B ££

(☑01803-606938; www.lanscombehouse.co.uk; Cockington Lane; d £70-115; ℗) Laura Ashley herself would love the lashings of tasteful fabrics, four-poster beds and free-standing slipper baths on show here. This serene hideaway is in a country park a mile south west of central Torquay – in its English cottage garden you can hear owls hoot at night.

Torquay Backpackers
HOSTEL £

(☑01803-299924; www.torquaybackpackers.co.uk; 119 Abbey Rd; dm/d £16/34; @☎) Photos of grinning past guests plaster noticeboards; flags of all nations drape the walls at this budget stalwart. There are luxuries too: great showers, a DVD den and a decked, alfresco pool table terrace.

Hillcroft
B&B ££

(☑01803-297247; www.thehillcroft.co.uk; 9 St Lukes Rd; s £75-80, d £75-90, ste £115-130; ℗@☎) The swish rooms range from boutique Bali to Moroccan chic; the top-floor suite (think exposed stone, beams and antique beds) is smashing.

🍴 Eating & Drinking

Room in the Elephant
FINE DINING £££

(☑01803-200044; www.elephantrestaurant.co.uk; 3 Beacon Tce; 2/3/7 courses £46/56/70; ⊙dinner Tue-Sat) A restaurant to remember. Torquay' Michelin-starred eatery is defined by imaginative cuisine: smoked beef tartare, pickled turnips, wild garlic and quail eggs dot the menu. Dessert might be bitter chocolate fondant topped by salted caramel ice cream or a raid on a platter packed with prime Westcountry cheeses.

Number 7
SEAFOOD ££

(☑01803-295055; www.no7-fish.com; 7 Beacon Tce; mains £14; ⊙lunch Wed-Sat year-round, dinner daily Jul-Sep, Tue-Sat Oct-Jun) Fabulous smells fill the air at this bustling harbourside bistro, where the chalked-up menus are packed with crab, lobster and fish fresh from the boats. Try it grilled or baked; accompaniments range from oil and herbs, through to garlic and brandy, and Moroccan spices.

Elephant Brasserie
MODERN BRITISH ££

(☑01803-200044; www.elephantrestaurant.co.uk; 3 Beacon Tce; 2/3 courses £23/27; ⊙Tue-Sat) The setting may be less formal, but the bistro below Torquay's Michelin-starred Room in the Elephant is still super-stylish. Innovative treatments include lovage and apple vichyssoise, and a squid-and-mackerel burger with sea-salted fries.

AGATHA CHRISTIE

Torquay is the birthplace of the 'Queen of Crime', Agatha Christie (1890–1976), author of 75 novels and 33 plays, and creator of Hercule Poirot, the moustachioed, immodest Belgian detective, and Miss Marple, the surprisingly perceptive busybody spinster. Born Agatha Miller, she grew up, courted and honeymooned in Torquay and also worked as a hospital dispenser here during WWI, thus acquiring her famous knowledge of poisons.

The tourist office stocks the free Agatha Christie Mile leaflet, which guides you round significant local sites, while Torquay Museum (01803-293975; www.torquaymuseum. org; 529 Babbacombe Rd; adult/child £5.15/3.25; 10am-5pm Mon-Sat year-round, 1.30-5pm Sun Jul-Sep) has a huge collection of photos, handwritten notes and displays devoted to her famous detectives. The highlight, though, is Greenway, her summer home near Dartmouth. The Agatha Christie Cruise (01803-882811; www.greenwayferry.co.uk; adult/child £14/10; daily Wed-Sun Apr-Oct) sails there from Torquay's Princess Pier – it's best to book. Boats also go from Dartmouth and Totnes; a steam train runs from Paignton.

Orange Tree   EUROPEAN ££
(01803-213936; www.orangetreerestaurant.co.uk; 14 Park Hill Rd; mains £17; dinner Mon-Sat) This award-winning brasserie adds a dash of Continental flair to local fish, meat and game. Ingredients and flavours are rich; in the vein of pan-seared Devon beef laced with Madeira, mushrooms and white-truffle oil.

Hole in the Wall   PUB
(6 Park Lane) A heavily beamed, Tardis-like boozer with a tiny terrace; an atmospheric spot for a pint.

ℹ Information
Tourist office (0844 474 2233; www.the englishriviera.co.uk; Vaughan Pde, the Harbour; 9.30am-5pm Mon-Sat, daily Jun-Sep)

ℹ Getting There & Away
Bus
Services include:
Brixham (50 minutes, every 15 minutes) Bus 12, via Paignton.
Totnes (one hour, hourly to four a day) Bus X80.
Dartmouth (1¼ hours, hourly Monday to Friday) Bus X81.

Ferry
Regular ferries shuttle between Torquay and Brixham (p309).

Train
Trains run from Exeter via Torquay (£6, 50 minutes, hourly) to Paignton (£6, 52 minutes).
Dartmouth Steam Railway & Riverboat Co (www.dartmouthrailriver.co.uk; Paignton Station; adult/child return £10.50/7.50; Mar-Nov) These steam trains puff from Paignton via Greenway Halt to Kingswear (adult/child return £10.50/7.50, 30 minutes, four to nine trains a day), which is linked by ferry to Dartmouth (p313).

Brixham
POP 17,460
An appealing, pastel-painted tumbling of fishermen's cottages leads down to Brixham's horseshoe harbour, signalling a very different place from Torquay. Here arcades and gift shops coexist with winding streets, brightly coloured boats and one of England's busiest fishing ports. Although picturesque, Brixham is far from a neatly packaged resort, and its brand of gritty charm offers an insight into work-a-day life along Devon's coast.

◉ Sights
Golden Hind   SAILING SHIP
(01803-856223; www.goldenhind.co.uk; The Quay; adult/child £4/3; 10am-4pm Mar-Sep) Devon explorer Sir Francis Drake carried out a treasure-seeking circumnavigation of the globe aboard the *Golden Hind*, in the late 1500s. This replica is full-sized, but it's a remarkably small vessel for such a voyage. Cross the gangplank and see how 60 men crammed in below decks, before peering into the captain's cabin and prowling around the poop deck.

Brixham Heritage Museum   MUSEUM
(01803-856267; www.brixhamheritage.org.uk; Bolton Cross; adult/child £2/free; 10am-4pm Tue-Sat Apr-Oct, to 1pm Nov-Mar) The town's salty history is explored here, with an eclectic collection of exhibits on sailboats, smuggling, shipbuilding and sea rescues.

✕ Eating & Drinking

David Walker   FISH MARKET **£**
(Unit B, Fish Market; ⊘9am-3pm Mon-Fri, to 1pm Sat) *The* place to connect with Brixham's fishing industry and stock up for your BBQ – the counters are piled high with the day's catch. Picnic goodies include huge, cooked shell-on prawns (per 500g £8) and dressed crab (from £5 each).

Beamers   BISTRO **££**
(☎01803-854777; www.beamersrestaurant.co.uk; 19 The Quay; mains £12-23; ⊘dinner Wed-Mon; ☑) The superbly cooked fish is from the market just round the corner, the meat and veg comes from Devon's rolling hills. Samphire, saffron and Pernod spring some menu surprises, while bagging a window table secures an absorbing harbour view.

Maritime   PUB
(79 King St) Eccentric old boozer smothered in thousands of key rings, stone jugs and chamber pots, presided over by a chatty parrot called Mr Tibbs.

ℹ Information

Tourist office (☎08444-742233; www.the englishriviera.co.uk; The Quay; ⊘9.30am-5pm Mon-Sat Apr-Oct, plus Sun late Jul to Sep)

ℹ Getting There & Away

Bus
Bus 22 shuttles to Kingswear (20 minutes, three-per-hour to hourly); where you can catch the ferry to Dartmouth (p313). Bus 12 (every 15 minutes) runs to Torquay via Paignton.

Ferry
Regular ferries shuttle between Brixham and Torquay (p309).

Dartmouth & Around

POP 9555

A bewitching blend of primary-coloured boats and delicately shaded houses, Dartmouth is hard to resist. Buildings cascade down steep, wooded slopes towards the River Dart while 17th-century shops with splendidly carved and gilded fronts line narrow lanes. Its popularity with a trendy sailing set risks imposing too many boutiques and up-market restaurants, but Dartmouth is also a busy port and the constant traffic of working boats ensures an authentic tang of the sea. Agatha Christie's summer home and a

captivating art-deco house are both nearby, adding to the town's appeal.

Dartmouth hugs the quay on the west side of the Dart estuary, it's linked to the village of Kingswear on the east bank by a string of car and foot ferries, providing a key transport link to Torquay.

◉ Sights & Activities

TOP CHOICE ⊘ **Greenway**   HISTORIC BUILDING
(NT; ☎01803-842382; www.nationaltrust.org.uk; Greenway Rd, Galmpton; adult/child £9/5; ⊘10.30am-5pm Wed-Sun Mar-Oct, plus Tue Aug) The enchanting summer home of crime writer Agatha Christie sits beside the River Dart near Dartmouth. Here you wander between rooms where the furnishings and knick-knacks are much as she left them; check out her hats in the lobby; the books in her library and the clothes in her wardrobe; and listen to her speak (via replica radio) in the drawing room.

Woods speckled with splashes of magnolias, daffodils and hydrangeas frame the water, while the planting creates intimate, secret spaces – the boathouse provides not-to-be-missed views over the river. In Christie's book *Dead Man's Folly*, Greenway doubles as Nasse House, with the boathouse making an appearance in a murder scene.

Greenway's few parking spaces have to be pre-booked. It's more fun to go by the **Greenway Ferry** (☎01803-882811; www.greenway ferry.co.uk), which runs from Dartmouth (adult/child return £7/4.50, eight daily), Totnes (adult/child return £12/9, one daily) and Torquay (p310). It only operates when the house is open – booking is advised. Alternatively, take the Dartmouth Steam Railway from Paignton to Greenway Halt (adult/child £7.50/5) then walk a mile through the woods, or hike along the picturesque **Dart Valley Trail** from Kingswear (4 miles).

Coleton Fishacre   HISTORIC BUILDING
(NT; ☎01803-752466; www.nationaltrust.org.uk; Brownstone Rd, near Kingswear; adult/child £9/5; ⊘10.30am-5pm Sat-Thu Apr-Sep, Sat-Wed Mar & Oct; ℗) For an evocative glimpse of Jazz Age glamour, drop by this former home of the D'Oyly Carte family of theatre impresarios. Built in the 1920s, its faultless art-deco embellishments include original Lalique tulip uplighters, comic bathroom tiles and a stunning saloon – complete with tinkling piano. The croquet terrace leads to deeply shelved

SOUTHWEST ENGLAND DARTMOUTH & AROUND

subtropical gardens and suddenly revealed vistas of the sea. Hike the 4 miles along the cliffs from Kingswear, or drive.

Dartmouth Castle
CASTLE

(EH; ☑01803-833588; www.english-heritage.org.uk; adult/child £5/3; ⊙10am-5pm Apr-Sep, to 4pm Oct, 10am-4pm Sat & Sun Nov-Mar) Encounter mazy passages, atmospheric guardrooms and great views from the battlements. Get there via the tiny, open-top Castle Ferry (return ticket £1.40; ⊙10am-4.45pm Apr-Oct).

Blackpool Sands
BEACH

Sun-loving locals head 3 miles south of Dartmouth to this long curl of coarse sand, lured by beautiful views, kayaking (per hour/day £15/40) and a licensed cafe (⊙8am-5pm, later in Jul & Aug) stacked with organic, local produce. Take bus 93 from Dartmouth (25 minutes, hourly Monday to Saturday).

🛏 Sleeping

Brown's
BOUTIQUE HOTEL ££

(☑01803-832572; www.brownshoteldartmouth.co.uk; 29 Victoria Rd; s £75, d £95-165; ℗) With leather armchairs and white painted shutters, Browns somehow conjures the feel of a contemporary, unstuffy London club. Rooms are snug but luxurious, designer smellies dot the bathrooms and sketches by local cartoonist Simon Drew line the walls. The cocktail bar is casually cool and the free Friday tapas (5pm to 7pm) draw the crowds.

Just B
GUESTHOUSE £

(☑01803-834311; www.justbdartmouth.com; reception 17 Fosse St; r £62-90) The 11 chi-chi options here range from bedrooms with bathrooms to mini-apartments, all featuring snazzy furnishings, crisp cottons and comfy beds. They're scattered over three central properties, and the 'just B' policy (no '&B' means no breakfast) keeps the price down.

Charity House
B&B ££

(☑01803-832176; Collaford Ln; s/d £60/80) Quirky collectibles pepper this 17th-century guesthouse in an artful array of driftwood, Panama hats and gleaming bits of boats. Classy bedrooms team stylish fabrics and modern bathrooms with views of a historic church – it's right in the heart of town too.

🍴 Eating

TOP CHOICE Seahorse
SEAFOOD £££

(☑01803-835147; www.seahorserestaurant.co.uk; 5 South Embankment; mains £17-28; ⊙lunch Wed-Sun, dinner Tue-Sat) Only when chefs really know their stuff do they dare to cook food this simply. The house speciality is revelatory – fish grilled over a charcoal fire, and finished with herbs and oil. Super-fresh seafood comes largely from Brixham (7 miles away) or Dartmouth Embankment (10 paces), the atmosphere is relaxed; definitely one not to miss. Canny locals opt for the set lunch (two/three courses £15/20).

Rockfish
SEAFOOD ££

(☑01803-832800; www.rockfishdevon.co.uk; 8 South Embankment; mains £9-17; ⊙noon-9.30pm) Weathered boarding and a chilled soundtrack lend this award-winning fish 'n' chip shop the air of a beatnik boathouse. The menu is a cut above your average chippy; along with cod and haddock there's also monkfish, scallops, oysters and good wine. Eat in (enjoy the atmosphere) or take away (fight the seagulls).

Alf Resco
CAFE, B&B £

(☑01803-835880; www.cafealfresco.co.uk; Lower St; mains from £6; ⊙7am-2pm; 🐾) Tucked under a huge canvas awning, this hip hangout brings a dash of cosmopolitan charm to town. Rickety wooden chairs and old street signs are scattered around the front terrace, making a great place for brunch alongside

---

ON THE WATER

The River Dart is so beautiful it's hard to resist the urge to get on the water. Totnes Kayaks (☑07799-403788; www.totneskayaks.co.uk; The Quay, Stoke Gabriel; per 1/3/6 hrs £10/23/35; ⊙9am-5pm Apr-Oct), in the placid village of Stoke Gabriel offers you the chance to do just that, with their sit-on-top boats. Owner Tom will advise on the best routes depending on the tide – so going with the flow might take you up river to Sharpham Vineyard and Totnes, or down river to Greenway (p311) and Dartmouth. Stoke Gabriel is 9 miles up river from Dartmouth, on the Kingswear side.

TV marine biologist Monty Halls is also setting up boat trips from a new Dartmouth base – see his website (☑01803-431858; www.montyhalls.co.uk/great-escapes/trips/boat-trips; per person £30) for the latest.

the riverboat crews. The B&B rooms (£75) are pure shabby-chic.

ⓘ Information

Tourist office (☏01803-834224; www.discover dartmouth.com; Mayor's Ave; ◉10am-5pm Mon-Sat, to 2pm Sun Apr-Oct, 10am-4.30pm Mon, Tue, Thu-Sat Nov-Mar)

ⓘ Getting There & Away

Boat

Dartmouth Steam Railway & River Boat Co (☏01803-555872; www.dartmouthrailriver. co.uk; adult/child £12/7.50) Cruises along the River Dart to Totnes (1¼ hours, two to four daily April to September).

Bus

Services include:

Plymouth (£6.25, two hours, hourly Monday to Saturday) Bus 93; runs via Kingsbridge (one hour).

Torquay (1¼ hours, hourly Monday to Friday) Bus X81.

Totnes (50 minutes, hourly, Monday to Saturday) Bus 81.

Ferry

Dartmouth–Kingswear Ferries (www.dart mouthhigherferry.com; car/pedestrian £4/1; ◉7am-10.20pm) Dartmouth's **Higher** and **Lower Ferries** both take cars and foot passengers, shuttling across the river to Kingswear every six minutes.

Train

Regular steam trains (p310) link Kingswear with Paignton.

Totnes & Around

POP 8336

Totnes has such a reputation for being alternative that local jokers wrote 'twinned with Narnia' under the town sign. For decades famous as Devon's hippie haven, eco-conscious Totnes also became Britain's first 'transition town' in 2005, when it began trying to wean itself off a dependence on oil. Sustainability aside, Totnes boasts a tempting vineyard, a rare 1930s house, a gracious Norman castle and a mass of fine Tudor buildings.

◉ Sights & Activities

High Cross House   HISTORIC BUILDING
(☏01803-842382; www.nationaltrust.org.uk; Dartington Estate; adult/child £7.20/3.70; ◉10.30am -5pm Mar-Dec; P) This exquisite blue-and-

white creation is one of the most important Modernist-era houses in England. Designed by William Lescaze in 1932, its rectilinear and curved lines are deeply evocative of the period, as is the interior of paired down furniture and smooth wood. It was created as a 'machine for living' and mirroring that, today you're encouraged to experience the space: play the piano, sit on the chairs and browse the art books. But be warned, having settled into one of the streamlined 1930s sofas, it is rather hard to leave. It's all tucked away on the Dartington Estate.

Totnes Castle   CASTLE
(EH; ☏01803-864406; www.english-heritage.org .uk; Castle St; adult/child £3.50/2.10; ◉10am-5pm Apr-Sep, to 6pm July & Aug, to 4pm Oct) The outer keep of Totnes' Norman motte-and-bailey fortress crowns a hill at the top of town, providing engrossing views over higgledy-piggledy rooftops and the river valley. Hunt out the medieval loo, too.

TOP CHOICE ⟩ Sharpham Wine & Cheese   VINEYARD
(☏01803-732203; www.sharpham.com; ◉10am-5pm Apr-Sep) Here row upon row of vines line up on sloping hills more reminiscent of Chablis than south Devon. Tours and tastings range from self-guided rambles (£2.50), via sampling wines and cheeses (£7 to £10), to full blown tours and tutored tastings (£15 to £55). The award-winning alfresco cafe dishes up gourmet air-dried hams, smoked fish and (inevitably) superb cheese and wine – book. The vineyard is 3 miles south of Totnes, signed off the A381. A more atmospheric option is to hike from town along the Dart Valley Trail.

Canoe Adventures   CANOEING
(☏01803-865301; www.canoeadventures.co.uk; adult/child £22/17) Voyages in 12-seater Canadian canoes – the monthly moonlit paddles are a treat.

⊨ Sleeping

TOP CHOICE ⟩ Dartington Hall   B&B ££
(☏01803-847000; www.dartington.org; Dartington Estate; s £39-104, d £99-209; P) The wings of this idyllic, ancient manor house have been carefully converted into rooms that range from heritage-themed to deluxe-modern. Ask for one overlooking the grassy, cobble-fringed courtyard and settle back for a truly tranquil night's sleep.

Steam Packet INN ££

(✆01803-863880; www.steampacketinn.co.uk; St Peters Quay; s/d/f £60/80/95; 🅿) It's almost as if the minimalist bedrooms of this wharf-side former warehouse have been plucked from the pages of a design magazine; expect painted wood panels, willow arrangements and neutral tones. Opt for a river-view room, then watch the world float by.

Old Forge B&B ££

(✆01803-862174; www.oldforgetotnes.com; Seymour Pl; s £60, d £72-92, f £105; 🅿🛜) This 600-year-old B&B used to be a smithy and the town jail – thankfully comfort has now replaced incarceration: deep red and sky-blue furnishings cosy up to bright throws and spa baths. The family room has its own decked sun terrace and there's a hot tub and a walled garden too.

✕ Eating & Drinking

TOP CHOICE **Riverford Field Kitchen** BRITISH ££

(✆01803-762074; www.riverford.co.uk; Wash Barn; 2/3 courses £20/27; ⊗lunch daily, dinner Mon-Sat; 🍴) At this futuristic farm-bistro vegetables are plucked to order from the fields in front of you and the meats are organic and locally sourced. Eating is a convivial affair – sitting at trestle tables you pass platters laden with food to your neighbours. Rich flavours and creative treatments might include garlic chargrilled chicken plus British veg that's transformed by saffron, cumin, pistachio and pecan. Planning laws require you to book, and take a free tour of the fields. The farm is 3 miles west of Totnes.

 Rumour PUB, RESTAURANT ££

(✆01803-864682; www.rumourtotnes.com; 30 High St; mains £7-15; ⊗dinner daily, lunch Mon-Sat) It's so friendly here it's almost like dining in a friend's front room. The menu includes favourites such as sea bass with samphire, south Devon steak, and roast beetroot and goats' cheese, as well as seriously good pizzas and irresistible puds.

Willow VEGETARIAN £

(87 High St; mains £8; ⊗lunch Mon-Sat, dinner Wed, Fri & Sat; 🍴) A long-time hang-out for Totnes' New Agers. Tuck into couscous, quiches, hotpots and homemade cakes – look out for the curry nights, too.

ⓘ Information

Tourist office (✆01803-863168; www.totnes information.co.uk; Coronation Rd; ⊗9am-5pm Mon-Fri & 10am-4pm Sat Apr-Oct, 10am-4pm Mon-Fri & to 1pm Sat Nov-Mar)

ⓘ Getting There & Away

Boat

Boats shuttle down river to Dartmouth (p313).

Bus

Services include:

Dartmouth (50 minutes, hourly, Monday to Saturday) Bus X81.

Torquay (one hour, hourly Monday to Saturday, four on Sunday) Bus X80.

Train

Trains go at least hourly to Exeter (£6, 35 minutes) and Plymouth (£6, 30 minutes). The privately run **South Devon Steam Railway** (www.southdevonrailway.org; adult/child return £12/7; ⊗4-9 trains daily Apr-Oct) chuffs to Buckfastleigh, on the edge of Dartmoor.

Plymouth

POP 258,700

Plymouth is decidedly different from the rest of Devon. The county's biggest city is an important Royal Navy port, thanks to its location beside a vast, sheltered bay. For decades, some have dismissed Plymouth as sprawling and ugly, pointing to architectural eyesores and sometimes palpable poverty. But the arrival of two celebrity chefs and ongoing waterfront regeneration begs a re-think. Because Plymouth is also packed with possibilities: swim in an art-deco lido; tour a gin distillery; learn to kayak; roam an aquarium; take a boat trip across the bay; then see a show and party till dawn. And the ace in the pack? Plymouth Hoe – a cafe-dotted, wide, grassy headland offering captivating views of a boat-studded bay.

History

Plymouth's history is dominated by the sea. The first recorded cargo left in 1211 and by the late 16th century it was the port of choice for explorers and adventurers. It's waved off Sir Francis Drake, Sir Walter Raleigh, the fleet that defeated the Spanish Armada, the pilgrims who founded America, Charles Darwin, Captain Cook and countless boats carrying emigrants to Australia and New Zealand.

DARTINGTON HALL

Henry VIII gave this beguiling 800-acre estate (☑01803-847000; www.darting ton.org; Dartington, near Totnes) to two of his wives (Catherines Howard and Parr); now it's home to B&B accommodation (p313), the 1930s High Cross House (p313), the Barn art-house cinema, a mellow pub (☑01803-847111; www.dartingtonhall.com; Dartington Estate; mains £12-17; ☑), landscaped grounds and a medieval great hall that hosts events ranging from classical music to literature festivals. The estate is 1½ miles northwest of Totnes.

During WWII Plymouth suffered horrendously at the hands of the Luftwaffe – more than 1000 civilians died in the Blitz, which reduced the city centre to rubble. The 21st century has brought regeneration to waterfront areas, a £200-million Drake Circus shopping centre and a growing university sector, bringing a burst of new buildings and 30,000 students to the heart of town.

◉ Sights & Activities

Plymouth Hoe   HEADLAND

Francis Drake supposedly spied the Spanish fleet from this grassy headland overlooking Plymouth Sound (the city's wide bay); the fabled bowling green on which he finished his game was probably where his statue now stands. Later the Hoe became a Victorian holiday spot and the wide promenade is backed by an array of multistoreyed villas and once-grand hotels.

The red-and-white-striped former lighthouse, Smeaton's Tower (☑01752-304774; The Hoe; adult/child £2.50/1; ☑10am-noon & 1-3pm Tue-Sat Apr-Oct), was built 14 miles offshore on the Eddystone Rocks in 1759, then moved to the Hoe in 1882. Climbing its 93 steps provides an illuminating insight into lighthouse keepers' lives and stunning views of the city, Dartmoor and the sea. Evidence of Plymouth's martial past comes in the form of the Citadel, a huge 17-century fortress (still an army base), and scores of war memorials; the largest bears the names of 23,186 Commonwealth sailors who were lost at sea during WWI and WWII.

Barbican   NEIGHBOURHOOD

(www.plymouthbarbican.com) To get an idea of what Plymouth was like before the Blitz, head for the Barbican, a district of cobbled streets and Tudor and Jacobean buildings, many now converted into galleries, antiques shops and restaurants.

The Pilgrim Fathers' *Mayflower* set sail for America from here on 16 September 1620. The Mayflower Steps mark the approximate embarcation point – track down the passenger list displayed on the side of Island House nearby. Scores of other famous departures are also commemorated at the steps, including Captain James Cook's 1768 voyage of discovery, and the first emigrant ships to New Zealand.

Plymouth Gin Distillery   DISTILLERY

(☑01752-665292; www.plymouthgin.com; 60 Southside St; tours £6; ☑half-hourly 10.30am-4.30pm Mon-Sat, 11.30am-3.30pm Sun) They've been making gin here since 1793, making it the world's oldest producer. The Royal Navy ferried it round the world in countless officers' messes and the brand was specified in the first recorded recipe for a dry martini in the 1930s. Tours wind past the stills and take in a tutored tasting before depositing you in the heavily beamed medieval bar for a free tipple.

National Marine Aquarium   AQUARIUM

(☑0844 893 7938; www.national-aquarium.co.uk; Rope Walk; adult/child £12/8; ☑10am-5pm daily, to 6pm Apr-Sep) The sharks here swim in coral seas that teem with moray eels and vividly coloured fish – there's even a loggerhead turtle called Snorkel who was rescued from a Cornish beach. Walk-through glass arches ensure huge rays glide over your head, while the gigantic Atlantic reef tank reveals just what's lurking a few miles offshore.

Boat Trips   BOAT TOUR, FERRY

Plymouth Boat Trips (☑01752-253153; www .plymouthboattrips.co.uk; Barbican Pontoon) offers a wide range of options – the pick is a 30-minute blast-across-the-bay to the quaint, pub-packed Cornish fishing villages of Kingsand and Cawsand (adult/child £8/4, four daily April to October). It also does one-hour harbour cruises (adult/child £6.50/3.50, four daily) to the warships at Plymouth's naval base, and fishing trips (per 3 hours £20) – have your catch turned into a meal at the funky Boathouse Cafe (2 Commercial

Plymouth

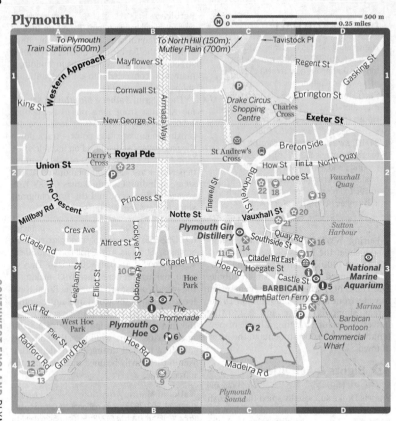

Plymouth

Wharf; dishes £2-8; ⊙9am-5pm Sun-Thu, 8am-9pm Fri & Sat) for £10 extra.

The little yellow **Mount Batten Ferry** (www.mountbattenferry.com; adult/child return £3/2) shuttles from the Barbican Pontoon across to the Mount Batten Peninsula.

Mount Batten Centre BOATING

(☑01752-404567; www.mount-batten-centre.com; 70 Lawrence Rd, Mount Batten Peninsula) Two-hour taster sessions include those in sail dingys (£20) and sit-on-top kayaks (£17). Two-day courses include kayaking (£86), sailing (£160) and windsurfing (£136).

🛏 Sleeping

Fertile B&B hunting grounds are just back from Hoe, especially around Citadel Rd.

 St Elizabeth's House BOUTIQUE HOTEL **£££**

(☑01752-344840; www.stelizabeths.co.uk; Longbrook St, Plympton St Maurice; d £90-199; P 🛜) This pamper palace overflows with jaw-dropping bathrooms, from free-standing tubs and wetrooms, to waterfall baths with a TV above your toes. Bedrooms are the size of suites and suites are the size of apartments. It's all set amid sloping lawns in the suburb-village of Plympton St Maurice, 5 miles east of Plymouth.

Sea Breezes B&B **££**

(☑01752-667205; www.plymouth-bedandbreakfast .co.uk; 28 Grand Pde; s/d/f £40/70/95) At this deeply comfortable guesthouse fresh decor ranges from subtle gingham to groovy swirls. The bathrooms gleam, the towels are fluffy and the breakfasts feature melon, strawberries and hand-cut toast. Bag a front-facing bedroom (go for the one with the window seat) for smashing sea views.

Bowling Green HOTEL **££**

(☑01752-209090; www.thebowlinggreenplymouth .com; 10 Osborne Pl; s/d/f £50/70/80; P 🛜) Some of the airy cream-and-white rooms in this family-run hotel look out onto the modern incarnation of Drake's famous bowling green. If you tire of watching people throw woods after jacks you can play chess in the conservatory.

Four Seasons B&B **£**

(☑01752-223591; www.fourseasonsguesthouse.co .uk; 207 Citadel Rd East; s £32-8, d £48-64) Treats are everywhere here, from the big bowls of free sweets to the mounds of Devon bacon for breakfast. They've got the basics right,

too: tasteful rooms decorated in gold and cream.

Rusty Anchor B&B **££**

(☑01752-663924; www.therustyanchor-plymouth .co.uk; 30 Grand Pde; s/d £35/70) Decorative driftwood and shells lend this relaxed B&B a flavour of the sea; four rooms have views of Plymouth Sound's wide waters. Owner Jan will try to meet your breakfast requests – be they kippers, pancakes or home-made rolls.

🍴 Eating

The arrival of two celebrity chefs is changing Plymouth's eating scene. As well as Hugh Fearnley-Whittingstall's new gaff, Gary Rhodes' Hoe-side eatery (www.rhodes atthedome.co.uk) is set to make a splash from 2013.

TOP CHOICE **River Cottage Canteen & Deli** MODERN BRITISH **££**

(☑01752-252702; www.rivercottage.net; Royal William Yard; mains £7-15; ⊙breakfast, lunch & dinner Tue-Sat, breakfast & lunch Sun; 🖉) Hugh Fearnley-Whittingstall's TV programs have long campaigned for local, sustainable, seasonal, organic produce, and that's exactly what you get here. Expect meats to be roasted in front of an open fire, fish to be simply grilled and familiar veg to be given a revelatory makeover.

Barbican Kitchen MODERN BRITISH **££**

(☑01752-604448; www.barbicankitchen.com; 60 Southside St; mains £5-18; 🖉) In this busy bistro the stone interior fizzes with bursts of shocking pink and lime. The food is attention grabbing, too – try the confit duck salad or the herb gnocchi with mushrooms, garlic and pine nuts. The beef medallions, with Devon blue-cheese sauce, are divine.

Royal William Bakery CAFE, BAKERY **£**

(www.royalwilliambakery.com; Royal William Yard; mains £5; ⊙8.30am-4.30pm Tue-Sun) Piles of huge, just-cooked loaves, tureens full of soup, crumbly pastries and irresistible cakes – this is a bakery like few others. The serve-yourself style is so laid-back you don't get a bill – just tell them what you've eaten and they'll tot it up at the end.

Rock Salt MODERN BRITISH **££**

(☑01752-225522; www.rocksaltcafe.co.uk; 31 Stonehouse St; mains £7-20 ; ⊙breakfast, lunch & dinner Tue-Sat; 🕿) They bill it as good honest food, and it is: great ingredients and creative flavour combos delivered with flair in a

SOUTHWEST ENGLAND PLYMOUTH

DON'T MISS

TINSIDE LIDO

Tucked between the Hoe and the shore, Tinside Lido (01752-261915; www .everyoneactive.com; Hoe Rd; adult/child £3.65/2.40; ⊙10am-6pm Jun-Sep) is an outdoor, saltwater art-deco pool which was first opened in 1935. During its heyday in the '40s and '50s, thousands of Plymouthians flocked to the pool on summer days, to swim to the soothing strains of a string orchestra. In the '70s and '80s the pool fell into disrepair before closing in 1992. It's since been restored to its former glory thanks to a hefty £3.4 million refurbishment and now it's packed throughout summer with school kids and sun worshippers; sadly, though, there's no sign of the string orchestra returning just yet.

chilled-out brasserie. It's set slightly south of Plymouth's edgy nightclub strip, Union St.

Cap'n Jaspers CAFE £
(www.capn-jaspers.co.uk; Whitehouse Pier, Quay Rd; snacks £3-5; ⊙7.30am-midnight) Unique and slightly insane, this cabin-kiosk has been delighting bikers, tourists, locals and fishermen for decades with motorised gadgets and teaspoons attached by chains. Try the crab rolls, the filling could have been caught by the bloke sitting next to you.

Drinking

Like any Navy city, Plymouth has a more than lively nightlife. Union St is clubland; Mutley Plain and North Hill have a studenty vibe, while the Barbican has more restaurants amid the bars. All three areas get rowdy, especially at weekends.

Dolpin PUB
(14 The Barbican) This wonderfully unreconstructed Barbican boozer is all scuffed tables, padded bench seats and an authentic, no-nonsense atmosphere. Feeling peckish? Get a fish 'n' chip takeaway from next-door-but-one, then settle down with your pint.

View 2 BAR
(www.view2barbican.co.uk; Vauxhall Quay; ⊙10am-midnight Sun-Thu, 10am-3am Fri, 10am-2am Sat) Just round from the heart of the Barbican, this cool venue's flagstone terrace is ideal for a waterside drink. Expect comedy, quiz nights, soul, funk and R&B.

Minerva PUB
(www.minervainn.co.uk; 31 Looe St) Stone walls, wooden benches, chunks of sailing ships, real ales, live music and Thursday night jam sessions make this 16th-century drinking den a locals' favourite.

☆ Entertainment

Annabel's CABARET, CLUB
(www.annabelscabaret.co.uk; 88 Vauxhall St; ⊙8.30am-2am Thu-Sat) The stage spots in this quirky venue are filled by an eclectic collection of acts (expect anything from comedy to burlesque). Crowd-pleasing tunes fill the dance floor while classy cocktails fill your glass.

Barbican Live Lounge NIGHTCLUB
(www.barbicanlivelounge.com; 11 The Parade; ⊙8pm-4am Wed-Sat) The live music in this buzzing, barrel-roofed club ranges from rock and jazz, to indie, blues and soul.

Plymouth Arts Centre CINEMA
(www.plymouthac.org.uk; 38 Looe Street; ⊙10am-8.30pm Tue-Sat, 4-8.30pm Sun) This cultural hot-spot combines an independent cinema, modern-art exhibitions, and a licensed, vegetarian-friendly cafe.

Theatre Royal THEATRE
(www.theatreroyal.com; Royal Pde) Plymouth's main theatre stages large-scale touring and home-grown productions; its studio space, the Drum, is renowned for featuring new writing.

🛈 Information

Plymouth library (Drake Circus; per 30 min £2; ⊙9am-7pm Mon & Fri, to 5pm Tue-Thu & Sat) Internet access.

Police station (Charles Cross; ⊙24hr)

Tourist office (01752-306330; www.visit plymouth.co.uk; 3 The Barbican; ⊙9am-5pm Mon-Sat, 10am-4pm Sun Apr-Oct, 9am-5pm Mon-Fri, 10am-4pm Sat Nov-Mar)

🛈 Getting There & Away

Bus

Services include:

Birmingham (£53, 5½ hours, four daily)

Bristol (£31, three hours, four daily)

Exeter (£6.50, 1¼ hours, two-hourly Monday to Saturday, three on Sunday) Bus X38.

London (£33, five to six hours, four daily)

Penzance (£9, 3½ hours, four daily)

On Sundays between June and mid-September the Transmoor Link, bus 82, makes five cross-Dartmoor trips from Plymouth to Exeter, via Yelverton, Princetown, Postbridge and Moretonhampstead.

Train

Services include:

Bristol (£25, two hours, two or three per hour)

Exeter (£8, one hour, two or three per hour)

London Paddington (£45, 3¼ hours, half-hourly)

Penzance (£8, two hours, half-hourly)

Totnes (£5, 30 minutes, half-hourly)

Around Plymouth

Buckland Abbey   HISTORIC BUILDING
(NT; ☎01822-853607; www.nationaltrust.org.uk; near Yelverton; adult/child £8/4; ◷10.30am-5.30pm Mar-Oct, 11am-4.30pm Fri-Sun Nov-Dec & Feb; P) Buckland Abbey was originally a Cistercian monastery and 13th-century abbey church, but was transformed into a family residence by Sir Richard Grenville before being purchased in 1581 by his cousin and nautical rival Sir Francis Drake. Its displays include Drake's Drum, said to beat by itself when Britain is in danger of being invaded. Look out for the fine Elizabethan garden and estate walks too.

Buckland Abbey is 11 miles north of Plymouth. You'll need your own transport to get here.

Dartmoor National Park

Dartmoor is an ancient, compelling landscape, so different from the rest of Devon that a visit feels like falling straight into Tolkien's *Return of the King*. Exposed granite hills (called tors) crest on the horizon, linked by swathes of honey-tinged moors. On the fringes, streams tumble over moss-smothered boulders in woods of twisted trees. The centre of this 368-sq-mile wilderness is the higher moor; an elemental, treeless expanse. Moody and utterly empty, you'll either find its remote beauty exhilarating or chilling, or quite possibly a bit of both.

Dartmoor can be picture-postcard pretty and on sunny summer days it's idyllic; ponies wander at will and sheep graze beside the road. But peel back the picturesque and there's a core of hard reality – stock prices mean many farmers struggle to make a profit. In this mercurial place the urban illusion of control over our surroundings is stripped away and the elements are in charge. Steven Spielberg chose to film part of his WWI epic *War Horse* in this landscape; a century earlier it inspired Sir Arthur Conan Doyle to write *The Hound of the Baskervilles*. In sleeting rain and swirling mists you suddenly see why – the moor morphs into a bleak wilderness where tales of a phantom hound can seem very real indeed.

Dartmoor is also a natural breakout zone with a checklist of charms: superb walking, cycling, riding, climbing and white-water kayaking; rustic pubs and fancy restaurants; wild camping nooks and country-house hotels – perfect bolt-holes when the fog rolls in.

Dartmoor is administered by the Dartmoor National Park Authority, DNPA (www.dartmoor-npa.gov.uk).

🏃 Activities

Walking

Some 730 miles of public footpaths snake across Dartmoor's open heaths and rocky tors. Crimson's *Dartmoor Walks* (£12) has 28 hikes of up to 9 miles, their *Dartmoor Short Walks* (£8) focuses on family-friendly treks. Tourist offices can advise on trails and guided walks (www.dartmoor.gov.uk/visiting;

ROYAL WILLIAM YARD

This cluster of 1830s waterfront warehouses once supplied stores for countless Royal Navy vessels. Today it's home to sleek apartments, a couple of art galleries, a relaxed pub and a string of eateries; the best being River Cottage Canteen (p317) and the Royal William Bakery (p317). A simple exhibition (◷9am-4pm Mon-Thurs, to noon Fri) outlines the yard's history; roaming past the former slaughterhouse, bakery, brewery and cooperage underlines just how big this victualling operation was. The yard is 2 miles west of the city centre, hop on bus 34 (8 minutes, one-to-two hourly), Better still, catch the ferry (www.royalwilliamyardharbour.co.uk; adult/child single £2.50/1.50; ◷10.30am-6pm Apr-Sep) that runs from the Barbican Pontoon.

Dartmoor National Park

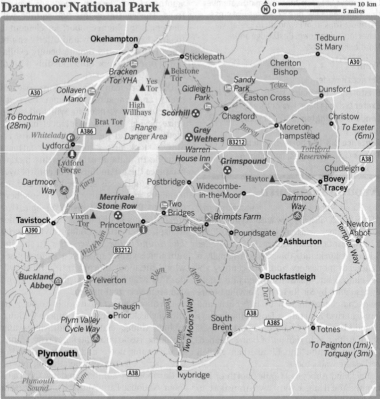

guided walk per person £4) – themes include War Horse, Sherlock Holmes, myths, geology, industry and archaeology; highlights are the memorable moonlit rambles amid stone rows.

CYCLING

Routes include the 11-mile Granite Way, which runs along a former railway line between Okehampton and Lydford. The 13-mile Princetown & Burrator Mountain Bike Route is a challenging moorland circuit along tracks and bridleways taking in Princetown, Sheepstor village and Burrator Reservoir. Tourist offices also sell the Dartmoor Cycling Map (£13).

Devon Cycle Hire   BICYCLE RENTAL
(☎01837-861141; www.devoncyclehire.co.uk; Sourton Down, near Okehampton; per half/full day £12/14; ☺9am-5pm Apr-Sep) On the Granite Way.

HORSE RIDING

Riding costs around £20/36 per hour/half-day.

Babeny Farm   HORSE RIDING
(☎01364-631296; Poundsgate, near Ashburton) All experience levels.

Cholwell   HORSE RIDING
(☎01822-810526; www.cholwellridingstables.co.uk; near Mary Tavy) Caters for novices and experts.

Shilstone Rocks   HORSE RIDING
(☎01364-621281; www.dartmoorstables.com; Widecombe-in-the-Moor) Beginners welcome.

WHITE WATER

The raging River Dart makes Dartmoor a top spot for thrill seekers. Experienced kayakers can get permits from the DNPA (www.dartmoor-npa.gov.uk). For a range of white-water activities (per four people £180), try

CRS Adventures (☑01364-653444; www.crs
adventures.co.uk) near Widecombe-in-the-
Moor. Rivers are only open in the winter.

CLIMBING

Adventure Okehampton   OUTDOORS
(☑01837-53916; www.adventureokehampton.com;
Klondyke Rd, Okehampton; per half day £15;
⊙school holidays only) Runs both wall- and
rock-climbing sessions, plus activities including archery, abseiling and bushcraft.

ⓘ Information

Dartmoor visitor website (www.dartmoor
.co.uk)

Higher Moorland tourist office (DNPA Princetown; ☑01822-890414; www.dartmoor.gov.
uk; ⊙10am-5pm Apr-Sep, to 4pm Mar & Oct,
10.30am-3.30pm Thu-Sun Nov-Feb)
Dartmoor's main tourist office also stocks
walking guides, maps and clothes.

DNPA Haytor (☑01364-661520; ⊙10am-
4pm daily Apr-Oct, 10.30am-3.30pm Thu-Sun
Nov-Mar)

DNPA Postbridge (☑01822-880272; ⊙10am-
5pm Apr-Sep, to 4pm Oct)

ⓘ Getting There & Around

Public transport is an option, but planning is
needed. Tourist offices stock bus timetables; see
also www.journeydevon.co.uk.

Bus

The **Dartmoor Sunday Rover** (adult/child/
family £7.50/5/16; ⊙Jun-Sep) offers unlimited
Sunday travel on most moorland bus routes; buy
from drivers or at Plymouth train station.

  Key routes onto the moor:

Bus 83/84/86 (hourly) From Plymouth to
Tavistock, via Yelverton.

Bus 118 (one to four daily) From Barnstaple to
Tavistock (2¼ hours), via Lydford and Okehampton.

Bus 359 (two hourly Monday to Saturday)
From Exeter to Moretonhampstead.

There are several key routes around the Moor, be
warned: some are seasonal.

Bus 98 (three daily, Monday to Saturday) A
year-round service, which runs from Tavistock
to Merrivale and Princetown; one bus a day
goes onto Two Bridges and Postbridge.

Haytor Hoppa Runs on summer Saturdays
only (April to October), providing four buses
between Newton Abbot, Haytor, Widecombe-in-
the-Moor and Bovey Tracey.

Transmoor Link (Bus 82; ☑0871 200 22
33; www.traveline.org.uk) Runs on summer
Sundays only (June to mid-September) with
five buses shuttling between Plymouth and
Exeter (2½ hours) via Yelverton, Princetown,
Two Bridges, Postbridge, Warren House Inn and
Moretonhampstead.

PRINCETOWN

Set in the heart of the remote, higher moor,
Princetown is dominated by the grey, fore-
boding bulk of Dartmoor Prison. When the
jail stopped housing American and French
prisoners of war in the early 1800s, the town
fell into decline and on bad weather days it
can still have a bleak feel. But it's also a useful insight into the harsh realities of moorland life and makes an atmospheric base for
some excellent walks.

  The prison reopened as a convict jail in
1850 and just up from its looming gates
the **Dartmoor Prison Heritage Centre**
(☑01822-322130; www.dartmoor-prison.co.uk;
adult/child £3/2; ⊙9.30am-12.30pm & 1.30-4pm)
provides a chilling glimpse of life inside –
look out for straitjackets, manacles and
mock-up cells, and the escape tale of Frankie
'the mad axeman' Mitchell, supposedly
sprung by 1960s gangster twins the Krays.
The centre also sells the bizarrely cheery
garden ornaments made by today's inmates.

  The tourist office has worth-seeing displays; it also used to be Princetown's main
hotel and is where Arthur Conan Doyle

SOUTHWEST ENGLAND DARTMOOR NATIONAL PARK

WARNING

The military uses three adjoining areas of Dartmoor as training ranges where live am-
munition is used. Tourist offices can explain their locations; they're also marked on Ordnance Survey (OS) maps. You're advised to check if the route you're planning falls within
a range; if it does, find out if firing is taking place when you want to walk via the Firing
Information Service (☑0800 458 4868; www.dartmoor-ranges.co.uk). During the day red
flags fly at the edges of in-use ranges, while red flares burn at night. Even when there's
no firing, beware of unidentified metal objects lying in the grass. Don't touch anything
you find: note its position and report it to the Commandant (☑01837-650010).

DARTMOOR HIKES

The 18-mile Templer Way is a two- to three-day leg stretch from Haytor to Teignmouth, while the West Devon Way forms a 36-mile trek linking Okehampton and Plymouth. The 90-mile Dartmoor Way circles from Buckfastleigh in the south, through Moretonhampstead, northwest to Okehampton and south through Lydford to Tavistock. The 102-mile Two Moors Way runs from Ivybridge, across Dartmoor and Exmoor to Lynmouth, on the north Devon coast.

Be prepared for Dartmoor's notoriously fickle weather and carry a map and compass as many trails are not way-marked. The Ordnance Survey (OS) Explorer 1:25,000 map No 28, *Dartmoor* (£7.99), is the most comprehensive and shows park boundaries and Ministry of Defence firing-range areas.

began *The Hound of the Baskervilles*. Staff can point you towards the real-life locations that inspired the book, such as nearby Foxtor Mires, which appear as Grimpen Mire.

The Prince of Wales (☎01822-890219; www.theprinceofwalesprincetown.co.uk; Tavistock Rd; dm £12, breakfast £5) pub runs the pick of Dartmoor's bunkhouses, boasting central heating and double-glazing (on the moor, this matters), snazzy showers, a cool communal lounge and (joy-of-joys) a drying room. The bar is famous for its three open fires, mixed-grill platters the size of tea trays and pints of full-bodied, Princetown-brewed Jail Ale.

❶ Getting There & Away

Bus 98 runs from Tavistock to Princetown (three daily, Monday to Saturday), one service a day goes on to Two Bridges and Postbridge. For summer Sunday services east across the moor, see the Transmoor Link (p321).

POSTBRIDGE

There's not much to the quaint village of Postbridge apart from a couple of shops, pubs and whitewashed houses. It's best known for its 13th-century clapper bridge across the East Dart, made of large granite slabs supported by stone pillars.

There's a tourist office (p321) in the car park, and a post office and shop nearby.

🛏 Sleeping & Eating

Two Bridges   HOTEL £££
(☎01822-890581; www.twobridges.co.uk; Two Bridges; s £95-125, d £140-190; P🅿🛜) Polished wood panels, hand-hewn furniture and the sense of entering a cocoon-like country house define this elegant moorland hotel. Squishy leather sofas frame huge inglenook fireplaces in the bar, former guests Wallis Simpson, Winston Churchill and Vivien Leigh probably enjoyed sitting here too. It's 3 miles southwest of Postbridge.

Brimpts Farm   B&B £
(☎0845-0345968; www.brimptsfarm.co.uk; site per person £2.50, s/d £30/55; ☀cafe: 11.30am-5.30pm weekends & school holidays; P) The brightly painted, country-cottage bedrooms above this farmhouse have views over *War Horse* location, Combestone Tor. Converted barns provide another batch of rooms and there's back-to-nature camping too. Brimpts is also one of the best moorland cream tea venues, offering freshly baked scones, homemade jams and utterly gooey clotted cream (£4.50). The farm is signed off the B3357, Two Bridges–Dartmeet road.

Runnage YHA   CAMPING BARN £
(☎0800 0191 700; www.yha.org.uk; dm £9; P) Set in a working farm, this converted hayloft sees you bedding down to a soundtrack of bleating sheep. It's 1½ miles east of Postbridge: take the 'Widecombe' turning off the Moretonhampstead road.

Bellever YHA   HOSTEL £
(☎0845-371 9622; www.yha.org.uk; dm £18; P) A characterful former farm on the edge of a conifer plantation, with a huge kitchen, lots of rustic stone walls and cosy dorms. It's a mile south of Postbridge.

[TOP CHOICE] Warren House Inn   PUB £
(www.warrenhouseinn.co.uk; mains £6-12; ☀bar 11am-11pm, food noon-8.30pm) Marooned amid miles of open moor, this former tin miners' haunt exudes the kind of hospitality you only get in a pub in the middle of nowhere. A Dartmoor institution, its stone floors, trestle tables and hearty food are warmed by a fire that's reputedly been crackling since 1845. The Warreners' Pie (local rabbit) is legendary. Between November and March the pub closes at 5pm on Monday and Tuesday. It's on the B3212, about 2 miles northeast of Postbridge.

① Getting There & Away

Bus 98 runs to Princetown (one per day Monday to Saturday). Postbridge is also served by the Transmoor Link (p321).

WIDECOMBE-IN-THE-MOOR
POP 566

This is archetypal Dartmoor, down to the ponies grazing on the village green. Widecombe's honey-grey, 15th-century buildings circle a church whose 40m tower has seen it dubbed the Cathedral of the Moor. Inside search out the boards telling the fire-and-brimstone tale of the violent storm of 1638 – it knocked a pinnacle from the roof, killing several parishioners. As ever on Dartmoor, the devil was blamed, said to be in search of souls.

The village is commemorated in the traditional English folksong of 'Widecombe Fair'; the event itself takes place on the second Tuesday of September.

🛏 Sleeping & Eating

Higher Venton Farm   B&B ££
(☎01364-621235; www.ventonfarm.com; s/d £32/65; ℗) This 16th-century farmhouse could be used to define the architectural style 'picture-postcard thatch'. With low lintels and a tightly winding staircase, there's not a straight line in the place.

Rugglestone Inn   PUB £
(www.rugglestoneinn.co.uk; mains £5-9) You'll find plenty of locals in front of this intimate old pub's wood-burning stove. Its stone floor and low beams set the scene for hearty dishes; pies are a speciality, including fishermen's, beef in ale, and a rich steak and stilton.

① DRIVING ON DARTMOOR

Dartmoor's roads are exciting to drive, but large stretches have unfenced grazing so you'll come across Dartmoor ponies, sheep and even cows in the middle of the road. Many sections have a 40mph speed limit. Car parks on the moor can be little more than lay-bys; their surface can be rough to very rough.

① Getting There & Away

Bus connections to Widecombe are not good. Year-round, bus 672 stops once a week (Wednesdays) en route to Buckfastleigh (40 minutes) and Newton Abbot (one hour). On summer Saturdays it's served by the Haytor Hoppa (p321).

CHAGFORD & AROUND
POP 1479

With its wonky thatches and cream-and-white-fronted buildings, Chagford gathers round a busy square, apparently every inch a historic moorland town. But along with the staid shops selling waxed jackets and hip flasks, there's also a dash of the modern: contemporary pottery galleries, snazzy delis and some supremely stylish places to eat and sleep.

In a steep gorge 4 miles northeast of Chagford, hunt out an enchanting architectural oddity: the stately but cosy, Lutyens-designed **Castle Drogo** (NT; ☎01647-433306; www.nationaltrust.org.uk; nr Drewsteignton; adult/child £8.40/4.20; ◷mid-Mar to Oct 11am-5pm; ℗).

SOUTHWEST ENGLAND DARTMOOR NATIONAL PARK

PREHISTORIC DARTMOOR

With an estimated 11,000 monuments Dartmoor is ripe for archaeological explorations. It has the largest concentration of Bronze Age (c 2300–700 BC) remains in the country, 75 stone rows (half the national total), 18 stone circles and 5000 huts.

The **Merrivale Stone Rows**, near Princetown, are a handy one-stop-shop for most monument types. The site has a parallel stone row, a stone circle, a menhir, burial chambers and dozens of hut circles. To the north east, near Chagford, the **Grey Wethers** stone circles stand side by side on a stretch of open moor; another stone circle is 400m away near Fernworthy. Also nearby, at Gidleigh, **Scorhill** stone circle is sometimes called the Stonehenge of Dartmoor, although only half of the original stones remain. The biggest site is the Bronze Age village of **Grimspound**, just off the B3212, where you can wander inside the circular stone wall that once surrounded an entire village, and the ruins of several granite roundhouses.

You can buy guides to some sites (£4), while the DNPA (www.dartmoor-npa.gov.uk) runs archaeology-themed walks.

ENJOY DARTMOOR MAGAZINE

The DNPA's *Enjoy Dartmoor* magazine is packed with details of activities, attractions, campsites and the full diary of guided walks. Pick it up at tourist offices and venues across the moor.

🛏 Sleeping & Eating

Gidleigh Park   HOTEL £££

(☎01647-432367; www.gidleigh.com; near Gidleigh; d £325-1175; 🅿🛜) This sumptuous oasis of ultimate luxury teams crests, crenellations and roaring fires with shimmering sanctuaries of blue marble, waterproof TVs and private saunas. Culinary alchemy occurs in the double Michelin-starred restaurant, where a three-course dinner costs £105 – thrifty cognoscenti opt for the £40 two-course lunch instead. This dollop of utter extravagance is 2 miles west of Chagford.

22 Mill Street   B&B ££

(☎01647-432244; www.22millst.com; 22 Mill St; d £89-109; 🕑Tue-Sun) The elegant rooms of this sleek retreat feature exposed stone walls, wooden floorboards, satin cushions and bursts of modern art. Its intimate restaurant (two-course lunch/dinner £17/36) delivers creative dishes packed with produce from the moors and the shores – look out for wild garlic-infused Dartmoor lamb, and hand-dived local scallops.

🖉 Sparrowhawk   HOSTEL £

(☎01647-440318; www.sparrowhawkbackpackers .co.uk; 45 Ford St; dm/d/f £17/38/46) At this long-standing backpacker's favourite, primary colours meet beams, exposed stone and hand-painted lampshades. Light dorms overlook a central courtyard that's ringed by rickety outbuildings – a great spot to swap travellers' tales. It's 5 miles southeast of Chagford, in market-town Moretonhampstead.

Sandy Park   INN ££

(☎01647-433267; www.sandyparkinn.co.uk; Sandy Park; mains £8-12; 🅿) Part pub, part chic place to stay, at this 17th-century thatch you can sip a pint of real ale in a comfy, exposed-beam bar, sample cracking Dartmoor fare in the restaurant, then totter upstairs to sleep amid plump pillows and bright furnishings (single/double £59/79).

ℹ Getting There & Away

Bus 178 runs to Okehampton (one hour, two daily Monday to Saturday). Between Monday and Saturday bus 173 runs from Chagford to Moretonhampstead (twice daily) and Exeter (five daily).

OKEHAMPTON & LYDFORD
POP 7831

Okehampton huddles on the edge of an uninhabited tract of bracken-covered slopes and granite tors – the mind-expanding landscape known as the higher moor. The town has a staging post feel, and its traditional shops and pubs are good places to prepare for a foray into the wilderness.

Some 9 miles southwest, the village of Lydford has an archetypal inn, a string of weathered granite cottages, castle ruins and a stunning gorge.

◉ Sights & Activities

Okehampton Castle   CASTLE

(EH; ☎01837-52844; www.english-heritage.org.uk; Castle Lodge, Okehampton; adult/child £3.80/2.30; 🕑10am-5pm Apr-Jun & Sep, to 6pm Jul & Aug) Clinging to a wooded spur, the ruined Norman motte and keep of what was once Devon's largest castle set the scene for some picturesque rampart clambering.

Finch Foundry   HISTORIC SITE

(NT; ☎01837-840046; www.nationaltrust.org.uk; Sticklepath; adult/child £4.70/2.40; 🕑11am-5pm mid-Mar-Oct; 🅿) The last working water-powered forge in England sits at the end of a 4-mile (3½-hour) walk east along the Tarka Trail from Okehampton.

Lydford Gorge   WATERFALL

(NT; ☎01822-820320; www.nationaltrust.org.uk; Lydford; adult/child £6/3; 🕑10am-5pm mid-Mar-Sep, to 4pm Oct) The 1½-mile rugged riverside hikes here snake past a series of bubbling whirlpools (including the fearsome Devil's Cauldron) to the thundering, 30m-high White Lady waterfall.

🛏 Sleeping & Eating

Collaven Manor   B&B ££

(☎01837-861522; www.collavenmanor.co.uk; Sourton; s £55-65, d £98-146; 🅿) For a delightful dollop of old England, head to this exquisite, 15th-century minimanor house. A baronial hall, ancient beams and sumptuous furnishings reinforce the heritage-meets-modern comforts feel. It's 5 miles southwest of Okehampton.

Bracken Tor YHA
HOSTEL **£**

(☑0844 293 0555; www.yha.org.uk; Saxongate; dm £19; [P]@) A perfect base for hikes or an adventurous break – this 100-year-old country house sits in 4 acres of grounds on the fringe of the higher moor. It's a mile south of Okehampton, and is also a YHA activity centre, offering climbing, canoeing and bike hire.

Castle
INN **££**

(☑01822-820241; www.castleinndartmoor.co.uk; Lydford; d £60-95; [P]📶) This Elizabethan inn's bedrooms range from small-ish 'n' simple to spacious and luxurious – bag room 1 for a double shower, private deck and 13th-century castle views. The bar is the ultimate snug: lamp-light bathes bow ceilings and high-backed benches, while the food (mains £9) is hearty Dartmoor pub-grub fare.

❶ Information

Tourist office (☑01837-53020; www.okehampton devon.co.uk; Museum Courtyard, 3 West St, Okehampton; ☺10am-5pm Mon-Sat Easter-Oct, 10am-4.30pm Mon,Tue, Fri & Sat Nov-Easter)

❶ Getting There & Away

Bus X9 (five daily Monday to Saturday) Runs to Exeter and Bude via Okehampton.

Bus 178 (one daily Monday to Saturday) Goes from Okehampton to Chagford (30 minutes) and Moretonhampstead (one hour).

Bus 118 (two to five daily) Runs from Tavistock to Barnstaple via Lydford and Okehampton.

Croyde & Braunton

POP 8360

The cheerful, chilled village of Croyde is Devon's surf central. Here olde worlde meets new wave: thatched roofs peep out over racks of wetsuits; crowds of cool guys in board shorts sip beer outside 17th-century inns.

Four miles inland, Braunton boasts Britain's first surf museum and a tourist office (☑01271-816400; www.brauntontic.co.uk; Caen St, Braunton; ☺10am-3pm Mon-Fri, 10am-2pm Sat).

☉ Sights & Activities

Museum of British Surfing
MUSEUM

(☑01271-815155; www.museumofbritishsurfing.org .uk; Caen St, Braunton; adult/child £3.75/2.75; ☺10am-5pm Tue-Sun) Few museums are this cool. Vibrant surfboards and vintage wetsuits line the walls, sepia images catch your eye. The stories are compelling: 18th-century British sailors riding Hawaiian waves; England's 1920s home-grown surf pioneers – here heritage meets hanging ten.

Surfing
SURFING

The water's hard to resist. Ralph's (☑01271-890147; Hobbs Hill, Croyde; surfboard & wetsuit per 4/24hrs £12/18, bodyboard & wetsuit per 4/24 hours £10/15; ☺mid-Mar–Dec 9am-dusk) is among those hiring equipment. Lessons are provided by Surf South West (☑01271-890400; www.surfsouthwest.com; Croyde Beach; per half/full day £28/54; ☺Mar-Nov) and Surfing Croyde Bay (☑01271-891200; www.surfing croydebay.co.uk; 8 Hobbs Hill; per half day adult/child £40/35).

🍴 Sleeping & Eating

Croyde gets very busy in the summer – book ahead, even for campsites.

Thatch
B&B **££**

(☑01271-890349; www.thethatchcroyde.com; 14 Hobbs Hill, Croyde; d £50-110, f £130) This cavernous, thatched pub is a legendary surfers' hang out. Its trendy bedrooms feature delicate creams, browns and subtle checks; the owners also run similar rooms above another wave-riders' pub and in the cottage opposite. The pick though are at the nearby (quieter) Priory, where elegant beams, frame exposed stone.

Chapel Farm
B&B **££**

(☑01271-890429; www.chapelfarmcroyde.co.uk; Hobbs Hill, Croyde; s/d/tr £35/70/90; [P]📶) Walls and ceilings shoot off at atmospherically random angles in this thatched cob farmhouse. It used to be a home to monks – now it's a study in light, pretty bedrooms, finished with bursts of pine.

Bay View Farm
CAMPGROUND **£**

(☑01271-890501; www.bayviewfarm.co.uk; Croyde; site per 2 adults £24; [P]) One of the area's best campsites, with laundry, showers and surf-view pitches. Often requires a week's minimum booking in summer.

Mitchum's
CAMPGROUND **£**

(☑07875-406473; www.croydebay.co.uk; site per 2 adults £29-63; ☺Jun-Aug; [P]) Mitchum's has superb facilities at two sites, one next to Croyde village, the other overlooking the sandy beach. There's a two-night minimum booking in July and August.

❶ Getting There & Away

Services include:

Bus 308 (hourly Monday to Saturday, five on Sunday) Goes from Barnstaple to Braunton, Saunton Sands and Croyde (40 minutes).

SOUTHWEST ENGLAND CROYDE & BRAUNTON

Bus 3 (half-hourly Monday to Saturday, hourly Sunday) Runs between Ilfracombe and Barnstaple (40 minutes), via Braunton.

Ilfracombe & Around

POP 19,136

Ilfracombe's geology is startling. Precipitous headlands plunge down to pint-sized beaches; waterfront walkways cling to the sides of sheer cliffs. It seems at first a classic, well-worn Victorian watering hole. Steep streets slope to a historic harbour lined by touristy shops; formal gardens, crazy golf and ropes of twinkling lights line the promenade. But the resort also has a snazzier side, as evidenced by a string of smart eateries and places to sleep, a Damien Hirst connection and an utterly unusual heritage swim spot.

◎ Sights & Activities

Ilfracombe Aquarium AQUARIUM
(☑01271-864533; www.ilfracombeaquarium.co.uk; The Pier; adult/child £3.50/2.50; ◷10am-4.30pm, to 5.45pm late-Jul & Aug) This bijou but beautifully executed aquarium recreates aquatic environments from Exmoor to the Atlantic, via estuary, rock pool and harbour (hunt out the fearsome lobster and graceful rays).

TOP CHOICE Tunnelsbeaches SWIMMING
(☑01271-879882; www.tunnelsbeaches.co.uk; Granville Rd; adult/child £2.50/1.95; ◷10am-5pm or 6pm Easter-Oct, to 7pm Jul & Aug) These Victorian tidal swimming pools beautifully evoke Ilfracombe's heyday. Passageways hacked out of solid rock lead to a strip of beach where you can still plunge into the sea. Sepia photos depict the pools in the 19th century, conveying a world of woollen bathing suits, segregated swimming and boating etiquette ('Gentlemen who cannot swim should never take ladies upon the water').

🛌 Sleeping & Eating

TOP CHOICE Westwood B&B ££
(☑01271-867443; www.west-wood.co.uk; Torrs Park; d £80-125; ᴘ🛜) Modern, minimal and marvellous; this ultrachic guesthouse is a study of neutral tones and dashes of vivid colour. It's graced by pony-skin chaises longues and stand-alone baths; some rooms have sea glimpses.

Olive Branch & Room B&B ££
(☑01271-879005; www.olivebranchguesthouse.co.uk; 56 Fore St; s £42-75 d £70-95; 🛜) Artful decor, ritzy bathrooms and bay windows with armchairs and sea views, make this a swish in-town retreat. Its bistro (mains £14) echoes to cool tunes and the chatter of happy diners. Try the squash, spinach and pine-nut lasagne, or sea bream with salsa verde – either way there's prosecco by the glass.

Ocean Backpackers HOSTEL £
(☑01271-867835; www.oceanbackpackers.co.uk; 29 St James Pl; dm/d £15/38; ᴘ@🛜) Brightly painted en suite dorms, a convivial kitchen and free coffee lend this long-established indie hostel a laid-back vibe; the giant world map in the lounge is a real travel conversation kick-starter.

11 The Quay EUROPEAN ££
(☑01271-868090; www.11thequay.com; 11 The Quay; mains £6-25; ◷lunch & dinner daily Apr-Oct, Wed-Sun Nov-Mar) Ilfracombe's hippest harbourside hang-out by far is owned by the glamour boy of British art, Damien Hirst (he of the cut-in-half cows). His creations line the walls, so you get to tuck into risotto nero, shellfish bisque and Lundy Island lobster while gazing at his dot paintings, *Pharmacy* installation and, with delicious irony, fish in formaldehyde.

ⓘ Information

Tourist office (☑01271-863001; www.visit ilfracombe.co.uk; Landmark Theatre, the Seafront; ◷9am-5pm Mon-Fri, 10.30am-4.30pm Sat & Sun Apr-Oct, closed Sun Nov-Mar)

ⓘ Getting There & Away

Bus 3 (40 minutes, every half-hour Monday to Saturday, hourly Sunday) runs to Barnstaple, via Braunton. Bus 300 heads to Lynton (45 minutes, one to three daily), with connections on to Minehead (40 minutes).

Clovelly

POP 450

Clovelly is the quintessential, picture-postcard Devon village. Its cottages cascade down cliffs to meet a curving crab claw of a harbour, which is lined with lobster pots and set against a deep-blue sea. Clovelly's cobbled streets are so steep that cars can't negotiate them, so supplies are brought in by sledge – you'll see these big bread baskets on runners leaning outside homes. Clovelly is often branded artificial, but this is a real community – 98% of the houses are occupied; in some Westcountry villages more than half the properties are holiday homes.

Entry to the privately owned village is via the **visitor centre** (☎01237-431781; www .clovelly.co.uk; adult/child £6.50/4; ☉9am-6.30pm Jun-Sep, 9.30am-5pm Apr-May & Oct, 10am-4pm Nov-Mar).

Charles Kingsley, author of the children's classic *The Water Babies,* spent much of his early life in Clovelly. You can visit his former house, as well as a highly atmospheric fisherman's cottage and the village's twin chapels. Right on the waterfront, the **Red Lion** (☎01237-431237; www.clovelly.co.uk; d £145-175) has gorgeous bedrooms with either harbour or sea views, a quality restaurant (two/three courses £25/30), and a welcoming bar (mains £8). Half way up the hill, **Donkey Shoe Cottage** (☎01237-431601; www .donkeyshoecottage.co.uk; 21 High St; s/d £30/60) has country-style B&B rooms, with stripped floorboards and raspberry-red walls.

Bus 319 (four to six Monday to Saturday) runs between Clovelly, Hartland Village, Bideford (40 minutes) and Barnstaple (one hour).

Hartland Abbey

This 12th-century **former monastery** (☎01237-441234; www.hartlandabbey.com; adult/child £10.50/4; ☉11.30am-5pm, house Sun-Thu Jun-Sep, Wed-Thu & Sun Apr-May, gardens Sun-Fri Apr-Sep; **P**) was another post-Dissolution handout, given to the sergeant of Henry VIII's wine cellar in 1539. Now a stately home, it boasts fine murals, ancient documents, paintings by English masters, Victorian photos, and bewitching **gardens**.

Hartland Abbey is 5 miles west of Clovelly, off the A39 between Hartland and Hartland Quay.

CORNWALL

You can't get further west than the ancient Celtic kingdom of Cornwall (or Kernow, as it's known around these parts). Blessed with the wildest coastline and most breathtakingly beautiful beaches in England, this proudly independent land has always been determined to march to its own tune.

While the staple industries of old – mining, fishing and farming – have all but disappeared, Cornwall has since reinvented itself as one of the nation's creative corners. Whether it's exploring the space-age domes of the Eden Project, sampling the culinary creations of a celebrity chef or chilling out on a deserted sweep of sand, this is one

place where you're guaranteed to feel the itch of inspiration. Time to let a little Kernow into your life.

❶ Getting Around

Bus, train and ferry timetables can be found on the **Traveline South West** (☎0871 200 2233; www.travelinesw.com) website.

Bus

Cornwall has two main bus operators.

First (☎customer service 0845 600 1420, timetables 0871-200 2233; www.firstgroup.com/ukbus/devon_cornwall)

Western Greyhound (☎01637-871871; www .westerngreyhound.com)

Train

Cornwall's main railway line follows the coast as far as Penzance, with spurs to Gunnislake, Looe, Falmouth, St Ives and Newquay.

CrossCountry (☎0844 811 0124; www.cross countrytrains.co.uk) Operates services to the north of England, the Midlands and Scotland.

First Great Western (☎08457-000125; www .firstgreatwestern.co.uk) Operates the main line from London Paddington via Exeter, Plymouth, St Austell, Truro and Penzance, as well as the regional branch lines.

Bude

POP 9242

Just a scant few miles across the Devon border, Bude might not be the prettiest town on the north Cornish coast, but it has a bevy of impressive beaches.

◎ Sights & Activities

Beaches   BEACH

Bude's beaches are definitely its main asset. Closest is **Summerleaze**, a bucket-and-spade affair with lots of space at low tide, and a 1930s saltwater **sea pool**. North across Summerleaze Down is **Crooklets**, offering golden sand and rock pools at low tide.

To reach Bude's other beaches requires either a car or a hike along the coast path. Three miles south of town is **Widemouth Bay** (pronounced *widmouth*), a broad, sandy beach good for both families and surfers. Two miles further is the shingly beach of **Millook**, followed by cliff-backed **Crackington Haven**.

Three miles north of town are the National Trust–owned **Northcott Mouth** and **Sandymouth**. A mile further on is pebbly **Duckpool**, often quiet even in summer.

PUBLIC TRANSPORT PASSES

Several passes are available covering public transport in Cornwall.

Bus

The Firstday Southwest pass (adult/child/family £7.60/6.20/18.70) offers a day's unlimited bus travel on First buses in Devon and Cornwall.

Western Greyhound Day Explorer (adult/child £7/4.50)

Train

The Freedom of Devon & Cornwall Rover pass allows unlimited train travel in Devon and Cornwall for three days out of seven (adult/child £42/21), or eight days out of 15 (£64/32).

Bus & Train

Ride Cornwall (adult/child £10/7.50) One day's travel on all rail and bus services within Cornwall. Valid after 9am Monday to Friday and weekends.

Bude Castle MUSEUM
(www.thecastlebude.org.uk; The Castle; adult/child £3.50/2.50; ⊙10am-5pm Easter-Oct, 10am-4pm Nov-Easter) Housed in a peculiar folly behind Summerleaze Beach, Bude Castle was built by local inventor Sir Goldsworth Gurney, whose creations included theatrical limelight and steam carriages. The building now houses the Castle Restaurant and a small heritage centre which roves through Bude's maritime, geological and social history.

🛌 Sleeping

Dylan's Guesthouse B&B £
(☎01288-354705; www.dylansguesthouseinbude.co.uk; Downs View; s £40-50, d £50-70; ℗) This snazzy B&B has rooms decked out in white linen, chocolate throws, pine throws and quirky curios. Most look across the town's golf course and downlands.

Elements Hotel HOTEL ££
(☎01288-275066; www.elements-life.co.uk; Marine Dr; s £52.50, d £89-109; ℗🤶) Smart clifftop hotel with 11 rooms in whites and creams, big views from the outdoor deck, a gym and Finholme sauna, and surf packages courtesy of nearby Raven Surf School.

✗ Eating

Life's a Beach CAFE ££
(www.lifesabeach.info; Summerleaze; lunch mains £4-6, dinner mains £16-21.50; ⊙Mon-Sat) This beachside bistro overlooking Summerleaze has a split personality: by day it's a beach caff serving coffees, panini and ice creams, by night it's a smart seafood restaurant.

Castle Restaurant EUROPEAN ££
(☎01288-355222; www.thecastlerestaurantbude.co.uk; Bude Castle; lunch mains £8.50-10, dinner mains £14.50-18) Inside the town's 'castle', Kit Davis's restaurant serves European-style food taking in everything from roast ling to rack of lamb. Aim for one of the balcony tables if the weather's good.

❶ Information

Bude tourist office (☎01288-354240; www.visitbude.info; The Crescent; ⊙10am-5pm Mon-Sat, plus 10am-4pm Sun summer) Beside the main car park near the Castle.

❶ Getting There & Away

Bus 594/595 (six daily Monday to Saturday, four on Sunday in summer) travels to Boscastle via Widemouth and Crackington Haven.

Boscastle

Precious few Cornish harbours can match Boscastle in the beauty stakes. Nestled in the crook of a steeply wooded coombe (valley) at the confluence of three rivers, Boscastle's seagoing heritage stretches back to Elizabethan times, and with its quaint cottages, steep cliffs, tinkling streams and sturdy quay, it's an almost impossibly photogenic spot.

But the peaceful setting belies some turbulent history: in 2004 Boscastle was devastated by one of Britain's largest-ever flash floods, which carried away cars, bridges and buildings. The village has since been rebuilt, but look closely and you'll still spot reminders of the floods dotted around.

◎ Sights

Museum of Witchcraft   MUSEUM
(☎01840-250111; www.museumofwitchcraft.com;
The Harbour; adult/child £4/3; ⊙10.30am-6pm
Mon-Sat, 11.30am-6pm Sun Mar-Nov) This oddball museum claims to house the world's
largest collection of witchy memorabilia,
from haunted skulls to hags' bridles and
voodoo dolls. It's half-tacky, half-spooky, and
some of the more 'controversial' exhibits
definitely aren't suitable for kids of a sensitive disposition (or adults, for that matter).

⌂ Sleeping & Eating

For good pub grub, try the cosy Cobweb
(☎01840-250278; www.cobwebinn.co.uk; The
Bridge; mains £5-14) and the old-time Napoleon (☎01840-250204; High Street; mains £6-12).

Boscastle House   B&B ££
(☎01840-250654; www.boscastlehouse.com;
Tintagel Rd; s/d £55/120; P☎) The fanciest of
Boscastle's B&Bs, in a Victorian house overlooking the valley, with six rooms named
after Cornish legends. Charlotte has bay
window views, Nine Windows has his-and-
hers sinks and a freestanding bath, Trel-
awney has ample space and its own sofa.

Orchard Lodge   B&B £
(☎01840-250418; www.orchardlodgeboscastle.
co.uk; Gunpool Lane; d £75-104; P☎) A short
walk uphill, this is a thoroughly modern
B&B, crisply finished in slinky fabrics and
cool colours and run with efficiency by
owners Geoff and Shirley Barratt. Rates get
cheaper the longer you stay.

Boscastle YHA   HOSTEL £
(boscastle@yha.org.uk; dm £14; ⊙Apr-Nov)
Boscastle's shoebox-sized hostel was all but
washed away by the floods, but it's been
completely renovated. It's in one of the village's oldest buildings beside the harbour,
but be prepared for small dorms.

❶ Information

Boscastle tourist office (☎01840-250010;
www.visitboscastleandtintagel.com; The
Harbour; ⊙10am-5pm Mar-Oct, 10.30-4pm
Nov-Feb)

Tintagel

POP 1822

The spectre of King Arthur looms large over
Tintagel and its spectacular clifftop castle
(EH; ☎01840-770328; adult/child £5.20/2.60;
⊙10am-6pm Apr-Sep, 10am-5pm Oct, 10am-4pm
Nov-Mar). Though the present-day ruins
mostly date from the 13th century, archaeological digs have revealed the foundations of
a much earlier fortress, fuelling speculation
that Arthur may indeed have been born at
the castle as locals like to claim.

Whatever the truth of the legend, it's
certainly a fine spot for a fortress. Though
much of the structure has crumbled away,
it's still possible to make out several walls
and much of the original layout. Part of the
castle stands on a rocky outcrop cut off from
the mainland, and is accessed via a wooden
bridge and a very steep staircase (vertigo
sufferers beware).

The village itself is a bit of a letdown in
comparison. Its touristy shops and tearooms
make the most of the King Arthur connection, but the only worthwhile sight is the
Old Post Office (NT; ☎01840-770024; Fore St;
adult/child £3.20/1.60; ⊙11am-5.30pm mid-Mar–
Sep, 11am-4pm Oct), a 16th-century longhouse
that was used as a post office during the
19th century.

❶ Getting There & Away

Tintagel is on the route for the 594/595 bus (six
daily Monday to Saturday), with connections to
Bude, Boscastle and Newquay.

Padstow

POP 3162

If anywhere symbolises Cornwall's recent
renaissance, it's Padstow. This once-sleepy
fishing port has been transformed into one
of the county's most cosmopolitan corners
thanks to celebrity chef Rick Stein, whose
property portfolio encompasses several restaurants, shops and hotels around town, as
well as a seafood school and fish-and-chip
outlet.

The 'Stein Effect' has certainly changed
the place: Padstow feels more Kensington-
chic than Cornish-quaint these days, with a
rash of fancy restaurants, fashion boutiques
and chi-chi shops sitting alongside the old
pubs and pasty shops.

Whether the town's managed to hold on
to its soul in the process is debatable, but it's
still hard not to be charmed by the quayside
setting – especially once the summer crowds
have left for home.

⊙ Sights & Activities

⬛ National Lobster Hatchery
NATURE DISPLAY

(www.nationallobsterhatchery.co.uk; adult/child £3.50/1.50; ⊙10am-7.30pm Jul & Aug, 10am-5pm Apr-Jun & Sep-Oct, earlier closing Nov-Mar) To combat falling lobster stocks, this harbourside hatchery rears baby lobsters in special tanks before returning them to the wild. Displays detail the crustaceans' life cycle, and there are viewing tanks where you can watch the residents.

Beaches
BEACH

Padstow is surrounded by fine beaches, including the so-called Seven Bays: Trevone, Harlyn, Mother Ivey's, Booby's, Constantine, Treyarnon and Porthcothan. Bus 556 runs close to most of them.

Camel Trail
CYCLING

The old Padstow–Bodmin railway was closed in the 1950s, and has now been turned into Cornwall's most popular bike trail. The main section starts in Padstow and runs east through Wadebridge (5¾ miles), but the trail runs on all the way to Poley Bridge on Bodmin Moor (18.3 miles). The views of coast and countryside are grand, but it gets busy – book bikes well in advance, or bring your own.

Bikes can be hired from Padstow Cycle Hire (☑01841-533533; www.padstowcyclehire.com; South Quay; ⊙9am-5pm, to 9pm in summer) or Trail Bike Hire (☑01841-532594; www.trailbikehire.co.uk; Unit 6, South Quay; ⊙9am-6pm) at the Padstow end, or from Bridge Bike Hire (☑01208-813050; www.bridgebikehire.co.uk) at the Wadebridge end, for around £12 to £15 per day. Tagalongs, tandems and kids' trailers cost extra.

Boat Trips
BOAT TOUR

Between Easter and October, cruise boats including the Jubilee Queen (☑07836-798457; adult/child £10/5) and Padstow Sealife Safaris (☑01841-521613; www.padstowsealifesafaris.co.uk; 2-hour cruise adult/child £39/£25) run trips to local seal and seabird colonies.

Padstow Boat Trips (www.padstowboattrips.com) keeps listings of all the local operators.

🛏 Sleeping

Treann House
B&B

(☑01841-553855; www.treannhousepadstow.com; 24 Dennis Rd; d £95-125) This stylish number makes a fancy place to stay. The three rooms are finished with stripped floors, crisp sheets and antique beds, and the Estuary Room has its own dinky balcony with a panorama over Padstow's rooftops.

Treverbyn House
B&B £

(☑01841-532855; www.treverbynhouse.com; Station Rd; d £85-120; ℗) This town house offers four colour-themed rooms (pink, green, lilac or yellow) plus an extra-romantic turret hideaway. The style is classic – oriental rugs, brass bedsteads, traditional tea trays – but the rooms are huge, and breakfast includes home-made jams and smoked kippers.

Treyarnon Bay YHA
HOSTEL £

(treyarnon@yha.org.uk; Tregonnan; dm £14; ℗@) A super 1930s-built beach hostel on the bluffs above Treyarnon Bay. Rooms are big and there's a good cafe, plus barbecues in summer. Bus 556 stops nearby at Constantine.

✕ Eating

TOP CHOICE Paul Ainsworth at No 6
BRITISH £££

(☑01840-532093; www.number6inpadstow.co.uk; 6 Middle St; dinner mains £22-27) Paul Ainsworth is the name to watch in Padstow – partly thanks to his recent TV appearances, but mainly because he's one of Cornwall's most talented young chefs. His flagship restaurant blends classic British and modern European, focusing on local goodies such as just-landed seafood, ham knuckle, squab pigeon and Cornish lamb. Don't miss his signature dessert, 'A Trip to the Fairground', which scooped top honours on BBC2's *Great British Menu* in 2011.

TOP CHOICE Seafood Restaurant
SEAFOOD £££

(☑01841-532700; www.rickstein.com; Riverside; £22.50-62.50) Rick Stein's much-vaunted seafooderie needs no introduction – it's one of Britain's foremost fish addresses, with an expensive menu offering treats such as fresh Padstow lobster and sumptuous *fruits de mer*. You'll generally need to book months in advance – although last-minute lunch tables sometimes crop up, so it might be worth trying your luck.

Margot's Bistro
BRITISH ££

(☑01840-533441; margotspadstow.blogspot.com; 11 Duke St; mains £14.50-17.50; ⊙dinner Tue-Sat year-round, lunch Wed-Sat summer) While the food snobs head for Stein's, Margot's is where you'll be sent by the locals. Run by madcap chef Adrian Oliver, known for his chaotic style and homely, seasonal food, it's a fantastically convivial place – but it's tiny and the tables are packed in sardine-tight.

Rick Stein's Cafe
EUROPEAN ££

(☑01841-532700; Middle St; mains £10-18; ☺closed Sun) Stein's backstreet bistro offers stripped-down samples of his trademark cuisine at more reasonable prices (you'll probably still need to book, though).

Rojano's in the Square
ITALIAN ££

(www.rojanos.co.uk; 9 Mill Sq; pizzas & pastas £6.95-10.95) Authentic pizza and pasta joint, with a tiny streetside terrace and a buzzy modern dining room. It's now run by Paul Ainsworth, so standards are high.

ⓘ Information

Padstow tourist office (☑01841-533449; www.padstowlive.com; North Quay; ☺10am-5pm Mon-Sat)

ⓘ Getting There & Away

Services include:

Newquay Bus 556 (hourly Monday to Saturday, five on Sunday) Runs via Padstow's main beaches along the coast to Newquay.

Bude Bus 594/595 (six daily Monday to Saturday) via Wadebridge, Boscastle and Tintagel.

Newquay

POP 19,423

Bright, breezy and brash: that's Newquay, Cornwall's premier party town and the spiritual home of British surfing. Perched above a cluster of golden beaches, Newquay's clifftop setting is fabulous, but the town's become better known for its after-dark antics – it's a favourite summer getaway for surfers, clubbers and stag parties, creating a drink-till-dawn atmosphere that's more Costa del Sol than Cornwall. The drab, concrete-heavy town centre doesn't do it any favours, either – but if it's white sand and wild nights you're after, Newquay definitely fits the bill.

◎ Sights & Activities

Newquay Beaches
BEACH

Newquay is set amid some of North Cornwall's finest beaches. The best known is Fistral, England's most famous surfing beach and the venue for the annual Boardmasters surfing festival. It's nestled on the west side of Towan Head, a 10-minute walk from the town centre.

To the east of Towan Head are Newquay's other main beaches. Just below town are Towan, Great Western and Tolcarne, followed by nearby Lusty Glaze. All offer good swimming and lifeguard supervision throughout the summer.

You'll need transport to reach Newquay's other beaches. North of Lusty Glaze is Porth, a long, narrow beach that's popular with families, followed a couple of miles later by the massive curve of Watergate Bay, home to Jamie Oliver's much-vaunted restaurant, Fifteen Cornwall (p332). Two miles north brings you to Mawgan Porth, a horseshoe-shaped bay which often stays quieter than its neighbours.

You'll find even more beaches to the southwest of Newquay, including the large, sandy beaches of Crantock (about 3 miles from town) and Holywell Bay (6 miles from town).

O'Neill Surf Academy
SURFING

(☑01841-520052; www.oneillsurfacademy.co.uk/) Organised school on Watergate Bay, affiliated with the O'Neill surfing brand.

Adventure Sports
ADVENTURE SPORTS

Newquay has several outdoor activity centres where you can try out sports such as kitebuggying, paddle surfing and coasteering (a mix of rock-climbing, scrambling and wild swimming).

Two of the best are Adventure Centre (☑01637-872444; www.adventure-centre.org) on Lusty Glaze, and EboAdventure (☑0800 781 6861; www.penhaleadventure.com) on Holywell Bay.

🛏 Sleeping

TOP CHOICE Scarlet
HOTEL £££

(☑01637-861600; www.scarlethotel.co.uk; r from winter/summer £195/295; P🐾🏊) For out-and-out luxury, Cornwall's fabulously chic new ecohotel takes the crown. In a regal location above Mawgan Porth, it screams designer style, from the huge seaview rooms with their funky furniture and minimalist decor to the luxurious spa, complete with meditation lounge, outdoor hot tubs and wild swimming pool. The restaurant's a beauty, too.

Carnmarth Hotel
HOTEL ££

(☑01637-872519; www.carnmarth.com; Headland Rd; r £95-130; P) This decent mid-range hotel is a short walk uphill from Fistral Beach, overlooking the golf course. Rooms aren't spectacular, but neutral tones, plain furniture and distant coast views make the prices seem reasonable, even in season.

Newquay Townhouse B&B £
(☎01637-620009; www.newquaytownhouse.co.uk; 6 Tower Rd; d £50-70; P �☎) Near the town centre, with bright rooms livened up with stripy cushions and wicker furniture. Some have window seats, but only one has bay views.

✗ Eating

TOP CHOICE **Fifteen Cornwall** ITALIAN £££
(☎01637-861000; www.fifteencornwall.com; lunch/dinner menu £28/60) Jamie Oliver's social enterprise restaurant on Watergate Bay is where everyone wants to eat. Underprivileged youngsters learn their trade in the kitchen preparing Oliver's trademark zesty, Italian-influenced food, while diners soak up the views and the buzzy, beachy vibe. It's a red-hot ticket: bookings essential.

Beach Hut BISTRO ££
(☎01637-860877; Watergate Bay; mains £9.75-19.95; ⊙breakfast, lunch & dinner) If you can't get a table at Fifteen, head downstairs to this bistro by the sand. It's similarly beachy in feel, and the menu's simple surf 'n' turf: sticky pork ribs, 'extreme' burgers and a different fish every day.

Café Irie CAFE £
(☎01637-859200; www.cafeirie.co.uk; 38 Fore St; lunch £3-8; ⊙breakfast & lunch Mon-Sat) A surfer's favourite in the centre of Newquay, perfect for hot chocolate, sticky cakes and jacket spuds after hitting the waves. The decor's cool too, with mix-and-match furniture, a psychedelic piano and surfy murals.

🍷 Drinking & Entertainment

Chy BAR
(www.thekoola.com/the-chy-bar; 12 Beach Rd) Chrome, wood and leather dominate this cafe-bar overlooking Towan Beach. The action continues till late at the Koola nightclub downstairs.

Central PUB
(11 Central Sq) As its name suggests, this rowdy pre-club pub is in the heart of town, and the outside patio is always packed on summer nights.

❶ Information

Newquay tourist office (☎01637-854020; www.visitnewquay.com; Marcus Hill; ⊙9.30am-5.30pm Mon-Sat, 9.30am-12.30pm Sun)

❶ Getting There & Away

Air
Newquay Airport (☎01637-860600; www.newquaycornwallairport.com) Regular flights to London, Belfast, Birmingham, Cardiff, Edinburgh and the Isles of Scilly.

Bus 556 (22 minutes, hourly Monday to Saturday, five on Sunday) runs from the bus station.

Bus
The 585/586 is the fastest service to Truro (50 minutes, twice hourly Monday to Saturday), while the hourly 587 follows the coast via Crantock (14 minutes), Holywell Bay (25 minutes) and Perranporth (50 minutes).

Train
There are trains every couple of hours on the branch line between Newquay and Par (£4.30, 45 minutes) on the main London–Penzance line.

St Ives
POP 9870

Even if you've seen St Ives many times before, it's still hard not to be dazzled as you gaze across its jumble of slate roofs, church towers and turquoise bays. Once a busy pilchard harbour, St Ives later became the centre of Cornwall's arts scene in the 1920s and '30s, and the town's cobbled streets are crammed with quirky galleries and crafts shops – although the outsider edge has been somewhat dulled by the steady dribble of chain stores and generic restaurants.

A ghost town in winter, St Ives is one of Cornwall's crown jewels, despite the crowds and traffic jams in summer.

◉ Sights & Activities

Tate St Ives ART MUSEUM
(☎01736-796226; www.tate.org.uk/stives; Porthmeor Beach; adult/child £5.75/3.25; ⊙10am-5pm Mar-Oct, to 4pm Tue-Sun Nov-Feb) Hovering like a concrete curl above Porthmeor Beach, this far-westerly outpost of the Tate focuses mainly on the work of the artists of the so-called 'St Ives School'. Key works by Terry Frost, Patrick Heron, Naum Gabo, Ben Nicholson and Barbara Hepworth are all on show, as well as the naive paintings of fisherman-turned-artist Alfred Wallis, who didn't start painting until the ripe old age of 67. On the top floor there's a stylish cafe-bar which has a memorable panorama across St Ives.

A joint ticket with the Barbara Hepworth Museum costs adult/child £10/5.50.

TRERICE

Built in 1751, the charming Elizabethan manor of Trerice (NT; ☑01637-875404; www.
nationaltrust.org.uk/trerice; adult/child £7.20/3.60; ⊗house 11am-5pm, gardens 10.30-5pm
mid-FebOct) is famous for the elaborate barrel-roofed ceiling of the Great Chamber, but
has plenty of other intriguing features, including ornate fireplaces, original plasterwork
and a fine collection of period furniture. There's also an amusing lawnmower museum
in the barn, with over 100 grass-cutters going back over a century.

Trerice is 3 miles southeast of Newquay. Bus 527 runs from Newquay to Kestle Mill,
about a mile from the manor house.

Barbara Hepworth Museum　MUSEUM
(☑01736-796226; Barnoon Hill; adult/child £5.50/
3.25; ⊗10am-5pm Mar-Oct, 10am-4pm Tue-Sun
Nov-Feb) Barbara Hepworth (1903–75) was
one of the leading abstract sculptors of the
20th century and a key figure in the St Ives
art scene. Her studio on Barnoon Hill has
remained almost untouched since her death
and the adjoining garden contains several
of her most notable sculptures. Hepworth's
work is scattered throughout St Ives; look
for works outside the Guildhall and inside
the 15th-century parish church of St Ia.

A joint ticket with the Tate St Ives costs
adult/child £10/5.50.

Beaches　BEACH
The largest town beaches are Porthmeor
and Porthminster, both of which have sand
aplenty and good cafes.

Between them juts the grassy promontory known as The Island, topped by the tiny
pre-14th-century Chapel of St Nicholas. On
the peninsula's east side is the little cove of
Porthgwidden, which is often a good place
to escape the crowds.

Boat Trips　BOAT TOUR
From the harbourfront, several operators
including St Ives Boats (☑0777 300 8000;
www.stivesboats.co.uk; adult/child £10/8) offer
fishing trips and scenic cruises, including to
the grey seal colony on Seal Island. If you're
really lucky, you might even spot a porpoise
or a basking shark in summer.

🛏 Sleeping

TOP CHOICE **Boskerris**　HOTEL £££
(☑01736-795295; www.boskerrishotel.co.uk; Boskerris Rd; d £130-195; P⌂) It's a bit out of St
Ives in nearby Carbis Bay, but this flashy
guesthouse is worth the trip. It's a favourite
with the weekend supplements: cool mono-
tones contrast with bespoke wallpaper, scat-

ter cushions, shell-shaped chandeliers and
curvy lamps, and bay views extend in grandstand style from the floaty patio.

No 1 St Ives　B&B ££
(☑01736-799047; www.no1stives.co.uk; 1 Fern
Glen; d £85-125; P⌂) This renovated granite
cottage bills itself as 'shabby chic', but it's
nothing of the sort. It's a model of a modern B&B, and full of spoils – filtered water,
goose-down duvets, iPod docks and White
Company bath-stuffs. Rooms vary in size,
but all sport the same palette of whites,
creams and cappuccinos.

Blue Hayes　HOTEL £££
(☑01736-797129; www.bluehayes.co.uk; Trelyon
Ave; r £110-240) Riviera luxury in a St Ives
stunner, with manicured grounds, a balus-
traded breakfast terrace and five suite-sized
rooms, most of which provide a memorable
perspective along the St Ives coastline.

Treliska　B&B ££
(☑01736-797678; www.treliska.com; 3 Bedford Rd;
d £60-80; ⌂) The smooth decor at this B&B is
attractive – chrome taps, wooden furniture,
cool sinks – but it's the position that sells it,
just steps from the town centre.

Little Leaf Guest House　B&B
(☑01736-795427; www.littleleafguesthouse.co.uk;
Park Ave; r £80-115; ⌂) A tiny five-roomer, on
a hill uphill from town. Rooms are sweet
and simple, finished in creamy colours and
pine furniture. Ask for Room 2 or 5 if you're
a sucker for a seaview.

🍴 Eating

TOP CHOICE **Porthminster Beach Café**　BISTRO ££
(☑01736-795352; www.porthminstercafe.co.uk;
Porthminster Beach; lunch £10.50-16.50, dinner
£10-22; ⊗9am-10pm) For a seaside lunch
there's nowhere better than this designer

SOUTHWEST ENGLAND ST IVES

St Ives

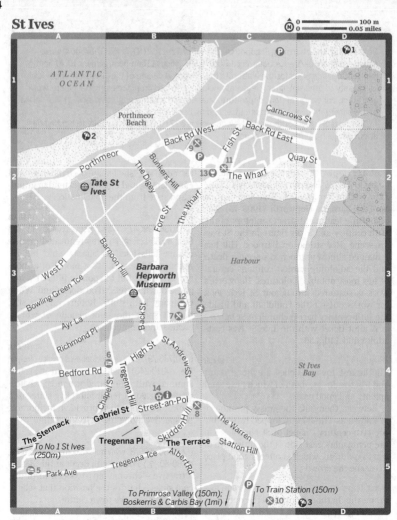

beach cafe, with its gorgeous suntrap terrace and Mediterranean-influenced menu. Tuck into rich bouillabaisse or Provençal fish soup, accompanied by beachy vistas.

Seagrass MODERN BRITISH ££
(📞01736-793763; www.seagrass-stives.com; Fish St; dinner mains £13.25-19.95; ⊙Tue-Fri) This vaunted restaurant on the 'front is overseen by Lee Groves, an ex-semifinalist on *Masterchef: The Professionals*. His elegant food and flavours have earned him plenty of plaudits: seafood and Cornish game figure heavily, often with an adventurous

twist. The two-/three-course menu (served from Sunday to Thursday) is fab value at £15.95/19.95.

Alba SEAFOOD ££
(📞01736-797222; Old Lifeboat House; mains £11-18) Split-level sophistication next to the lifeboat house, serving top-quality seafood. With its banquette seats and sharp decor, it's stylish – especially if you get one of the prime tables next to the panoramic window.

Loft RESTAURANT ££
(📞01736-794204; www.theloftrestaurantandterrace .co.uk; Norway Lane; dinner £12.95-22.95) Tucked

St Ives

⊙ Top Sights

⊙ Sights

⊙ Activities, Courses & Tours

⊜ Sleeping

⊗ Eating

⊙ Drinking

⊛ Entertainment

away in the old artists' quarter and housed in a converted net loft, this relaxed bistro is a good bet. The menu has a choice of meat, seafood and veggie options, although standards are solid rather than spectacular.

🍴 **Blas Burgerworks**   CAFE £
(The Warren; burgers £5-10; ⊙dinner Tue-Sun) Imaginative burger-joint with an ecofriendly, Fair Trade, 100% home-made manifesto. Traditionalists go for the 6oz, 100%-beef Blasburger, while veggies could plump for a halloumi stack or a ginger, coriander and chilli tofu-burger.

🍷 Drinking

Hub   CAFE, BAR
(www.hub-stives.co.uk; The Wharf) The openplan Hub is the heart of St Ives' (limited) nightlife: frothy lattes by day, cocktails afterdark, concertina doors onto the harbour.

Sloop Inn   PUB
(The Wharf) A classic fishermen's boozer, complete with tankards behind the bar and a comprehensive selection of Cornish ales.

The quayside tables go fast, so arrive early if it's sunny.

☆ Entertainment

Guildhall   CONCERT VENUE
(1 Street-an-Pol) Regularly hosts music and theatre, especially during the annual St Ives September Festival (www.stivesseptember festival.co.uk).

ⓘ Information

St Ives tourist office (☏01736-796297; www .stivestic.co.uk; Street-an-Pol; ⊙9am-5.30pm Mon-Fri, 9am-5pm Sat, 10am-4pm Sun) Inside the Guildhall.

ⓘ Getting There & Away

Bus

The quickest bus to Penzance is bus 17 (30 minutes, twice hourly Monday to Saturday, hourly on Sunday). In summer the open-top bus 300 takes the scenic route via Zennor, Land's End and St Just.

Train

The gorgeous branch line from St Ives is worth taking just for the coastal views: trains terminate at St Erth (£3, 14 minutes, half-hourly), where you can catch connections along the Penzance–London Paddington main line.

Zennor

POP 217

The twisting B3306 from St Ives to the windswept village of Zennor is a coastal rollercoaster of a road, winding through a landscape of ancient drystone walls, barren moorland and rocky bluffs.

The village itself clusters around the medieval church of St Senara. Inside, a famous carved chair depicts the legendary Mermaid of Zennor, who is said to have fallen in love with the singing voice of local lad Matthew Trewhella. Locals say you can still sometimes hear them singing down at nearby Pendour Cove – and even if you don't, the coast path here is gloriously wild.

Downhill from the church, the Wayside Folk Museum (admission £3; ⊙10.30am-5pm Sun-Fri May-Sep, 11am-5pm Sun-Fri Apr & Oct) houses a treasure trove of artefacts gathered by inveterate collector Colonel 'Freddie' Hirst in the 1930s. The displays range from blacksmiths' hammers and cobblers' tools to an 18th-century kitchen and two reclaimed watermills.

DON'T MISS

CHAPEL PORTH

The rugged cliffs around the village of St Agnes, 12 miles southwest of Newquay, were once a mining heartland, and the coastline is littered with the remains of crumbling minestacks and engine houses.

One of the most famous (and photogenic) is above the rocky cove of Chapel Porth, a National Trust–owned beach 2 miles from St Agnes. From the NT car park, it's a steep, mile-long walk to the ruined engine stack of Wheal Coates, which teeters above the cliffs and still boasts its original chimney and winding house.

From here, the coast path winds along the cliffs around Tubby's Head and St Agnes Head, both offering wonderfully wild views.

After the walk, you can reward yourself with fresh flapjacks, hot chocolates and bacon butties from the Chapel Porth Cafe (⊙10am-5pm), where the house special is a 'hedgehog' ice cream (vanilla covered in clotted cream and hazelnuts).

Between the church and museum is the marvellous Tinner's Arms (☎01736-792697; www.tinnersarms.com; mains £10.50-16.50, s/d £55/95), a classic Cornish inn with a rambling bar, roaring hearth and a refreshing lack of TVs and fruit-machines. Four rooms are available at the White House if you feel like prolonging your visit.

The village also has an attractive hostel (☎01736-798307; zennorbackpackers@btinternet.com; dm/f £12/50; P) housed in a converted chapel, with four- to six-bed dorms and a cafe serving sandwiches and cream teas.

St Just-in-Penwith

Beyond Zennor, the Penwith landscape starts to feel big, wild and empty. Blustery cliffs, lonely fields and heather-clad hills unfurl along the horizon en route to the stern granite mining town of St Just and the rocky promontory of Cape Cornwall, a notorious shipwreck spot, now guarded by the blinking lighthouse at Pendeen Watch.

⊙ Sights

It's hard to imagine today, the St Just area was once at the heart of Cornwall's booming tin and copper mining industry.

TOP CHOICE Geevor Tin Mine   MINE
(www.geevor.com; adult/child £9.95/6; ⊙9am-5pm Sun-Fri Mar-Oct, to 4pm Nov-Feb) Just north of St Just near Pendeen, this historic mine closed in 1990 and now provides a memorable insight into the dark, dingy and dangerous conditions in which Cornwall's miners worked. Above ground, you can view the dressing floors and the original machinery used to sort the minerals and ores, before taking a guided tour into some of the underground shafts. Claustrophobes need not apply.

Levant Mine & Beam Engine   INDUSTRIAL HERITAGE
(www.nationaltrust.org.uk/main/w-levantmineandbeamengine; adult/child £6.30/3.10; ⊙11am-5pm Sun-Thu) At this National Trust–owned site, one of the world's only working beam engines is still in thunderous action. Built in 1840, this great engine design was the powerhouse behind the Cornish mining boom, powering mineral trains and pumping water from the shafts. Lovingly restored by a team of enthusiasts, it's a sight to behold when it's in full steam.

Botallack Mine   RUIN, MINE
Clinging to the cliffs near Levant, this dramatic engine house has abandoned mine shafts extending right out beneath the raging Atlantic waves. It's a treacherous climb down, so it's best viewed from a distance from nearby Botallack Head.

ⓘ Getting There & Away

St Just is 6 miles north of Land's End. Buses 17/17A/17B travel from St Ives (1¼ hours) via Penzance (half-hourly Monday to Saturday, five on Sunday).

Sennen & Land's End

In the far west, the coastline peaks and plunges all the way into the sandy scoop of Sennen, which overlooks one of Penwith's most stunning stretches of sand on Whitesand Bay (pronounced Whitsand).

From here, there's a wonderful stretch of coast path that leads for about a mile-and-a-half along the clifftops all the way to Land's

End, the westernmost point of mainland England, where the coal-black cliffs plunge dramatically down into the pounding surf, and the views stretch all the way to the Isles of Scilly on a clear day.

Unfortunately, the decision to build the Legendary Land's End (www.landsend -landmark.co.uk; adult/child £10/7; ☉10am-5pm Mar-Oct) theme park just behind the headland in the 1980s hasn't done much to enhance the view. Take our advice: just pay for the car park, skip the tacky multimedia shows and opt for an exhilarating clifftop stroll instead.

Land's End is 9 miles from Penzance. Bus 1/1A travels from Penzance (one hour, six daily Monday to Saturday) to Land's End; half the buses go via Sennen, the other half via Treen and Porthcurno.

In summer, the open-top 300 bus runs five times daily taking in Penzance, Land's End, Sennen and St Ives.

Mousehole

With a tight tangle of slate-roofed cottages and alleyways gathered behind the granite breakwater, Mousehole (pronounced mow-zle) looks like something from a children's storybook. In centuries past this was Cornwall's busiest pilchard port, but the fish dried up at the turn of the century, and the village now survives almost entirely on tourist traffic.

Packed in summer and deserted in winter, the village is ripe for a wander, with a maze of tiny sloops, slips, netlofts and courtyards. It's also famous for its annual display of Christmas lights, and as the home of 'stargazey pie', a pilchard pie in which the fish-heads are left poking up through the pie's crust. It's traditionally eaten on Tom Bawcock's Eve (23 December), named after a

local lad who reputedly rescued the town from a famine by braving stormy seas to land a bumper haul of pilchards.

To stay the night, set yourself up at the Old Coastguard Hotel (☎01736-731222; www .oldcoastguardhotel.co.uk; d £110-195; P☎🎀), a swish seaside hotel with jaw-dropping sea views on the edge of Mousehole. Seafood takes prominence in the restaurant, and there's a cliff garden for soaking up the rays.

Bus 6 makes the 20-minute journey to Penzance half-hourly.

Penzance

POP 21,168

Overlooking the sweep of Mount's Bay, the old harbour of Penzance has a salty, sea-blown charm that feels altogether more authentic than many of Cornwall's polished-up ports.

It's resisted the urge to prettify itself simply to cater to the summer trade, and feels all the better for it: its streets and shopping arcades still feel real and a touch ramshackle, and there's nowhere better for a windy-day walk than the town's stately seafront prom.

◉ Sights

Penlee House Gallery & Museum GALLERY (www.penleehouse.org.uk; Morrab Rd; adult/child £4.50/3; ☉10am-5pm Mon-Sat Easter-Sep, 10.30am-4.30pm Mon-Sat Oct-Easter) Penzance's historic art gallery displays paintings by artists of the Newlyn School (including Stanhope Forbes) and hosts regular exhibitions. Admission is free on Saturday.

St Michael's Mount LANDMARK (NT; ☎01736-710507; www.stmichaelsmount.co.uk; castle & gardens adult/child £8.75/4.25; ☉house

SOUTHWEST ENGLAND MOUSEHOLE

WORTH A TRIP

GURNARD'S HEAD

Pubs don't get much more remote than the Gurnard's Head (☎01736-796928; www .gurnardshead.co.uk; lunch £5.50-12, dinner £12.50-16.50). It's 6 miles out along the Zennor coast road, but don't fret about missing it – it's the only building for miles and has its name spelled out in huge white letters on the roof. Having been taken over by renowned hoteliers the Inkin brothers (who also run the Old Coastguard near Mousehole), it's now one of Cornwall's loveliest rural retreats.

Book-lined shelves, sepia prints, scruffy wood and stone walls create a reassuringly lived-in feel, and the menu's crammed with comfort food – pheasant, braised beef, or beetroot risotto, followed perhaps by figgy tart or cinnamon sponge. Upstairs rooms are simple and stylish, with checked throws and sunny colours: standard rates are £97.50 to £167.50, but the dinner-plus-B&B rates (£142.50 to £212.50 for two people) offer the best value.

West Cornwall

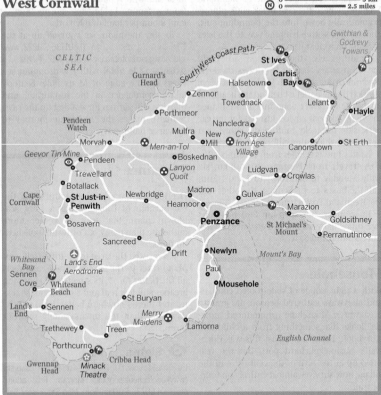

10.30am-5.30pm Sun-Fri late Mar-Oct, gardens open Mon-Fri Apr-Jun, Thu & Fri Jul-Sep) Looming from the waters of Mount's Bay, this abbey-crowned, tidal island is one of Cornwall's most iconic sights. There's been a monastery on the island since at least the 5th century, but the present abbey was mostly built during the 12th century by the Benedictine monks of Mont St Michel. The abbey later became the family seat of the St Aubyns (who still reside here), and is now under the stewardship of the National Trust.

Highlights include the rococo drawing room, the original armoury, the 14th-century priory church and the abbey's subtropical cliff gardens. Recent excavations have also uncovered important Bronze Age finds, including an axe-head, dagger and metal clasp, now on display inside the castle. You can also see one of the island's three remaining pillboxes, built during WWII when fears of German invasion were at their height.

St Michael's Mount is connected to the mainland and the small seaside town of Marazion by a cobbled causeway. You can catch a ferry (adult/child £2/1) at high tide, but it's worth timing your arrival for low tide so you can walk across on the causeway, just as the monks and pilgrims did centuries ago.

The 513 bus covers the 3 miles between Marazion and Penzance, three times a day.

Jubilee Pool   SWIMMING
(www.jubileepool.co.uk; adult/child £4.30/3.20, family day-ticket £14; ⊙10.30am-6pm May-Sep) At the eastern end of the town's 19th-century promenade, this 1930s lido is open throughout the summer – just don't expect the water to be warm. Entry is half-price after 3.30pm.

🛌 Sleeping

Penzance has lots of low-price B&Bs, especially along Alexandra Rd and Morrab Rd.

TOP CHOICE Artist Residence Penzance B&B ££

(☎01736-365664; www.arthotelcornwall.co.uk; Chapel St; d £80-120; ☎) This deliciously different new hotel on Chapel St is like sleeping inside an art gallery. All the rooms have their own bespoke design courtesy of a local artist: cartoony murals by Matt MacIvor, pop-art doves by Pinky Vision, butterfly wallpapers by Dolly Divine. They're furnished with hand-picked bits of retro furniture and most peep across Penzance's rooftops. Bold, imaginative and brilliant fun.

Hotel Penzance HOTEL ££

(☎01736-363117; www.hotelpenzance.com; Briton's Hill; d £109-125; ☎) Perched on a hill with views across Mount's Bay, this town house hotel makes a pleasant Penzance base. Bedrooms are staid in style, with cream-and-magnolia colours, varnished desks and vintage lamps: the best have bay windows looking out to sea. The hotel's restaurant, The Bay, serves quality food.

Camilla House B&B ££

(☎01736-363771; www.camillahouse.co.uk; 12 Regent Tce; s £35, d £75-85; P) The pick of the heritage B&Bs on Regent's Terrace, worth considering for its period architecture and views over the prom. Hardly cutting edge, but cosy.

Penzance YHA HOSTEL £

(☎0845 371 9653; penzance@yha.org.uk; Castle Horneck, Alverton; dm from £14; P@) Penzance's YHA is inside an 18th-century house on the edge of town. It's a rambling place, with a cafe, laundry and four- to 10-bed dorms. It's a 15-minute walk from the front; buses 5 and 6 stop nearby.

Eating

Bakehouse MEDITERRANEAN ££

(☎01736-331331; www.bakehouserestaurant.co.uk; Chapel St; mains £8.95-19.50; ☺lunch Wed-Sat, dinner daily) This attractive double-floored diner is tucked away down an alley off Chapel St. Food is filling and unpretentious: fish served with Med-style marinades, or steaks with a choice of sauces or spicy rubs. The dining room has A-frame beams and art, or there's a small palm-filled courtyard.

Archie Brown's CAFE £

(☎01736-362828; Bread St; mains £4-10; ☺breakfast & lunch Mon-Sat) Archie Brown's has long been a favourite lunch-spot for Penzance's artists and earth-mothers: it's perched above a health shop, and serves quiches, salads and homebaked cakes with a wholefood ethos.

Assay House BISTRO ££

(☎01736-369729; 12-13 Chapel St; mains £14-17; ☺breakfast & lunch daily, dinner Fri & Sat) This glass-fronted establishment keeps changing hands, but its current guise is this streetside bistro, serving crispy fish goujons and tapas-style platters.

Drinking & Entertainment

Turk's Head PUB

(Chapel St) They pull a fine pint of ale at Penzance's oldest boozer. The bar's covered in maritime memorabilia, and it's said a secret smugglers' tunnel still links the pub to the harbour.

Zero Lounge BAR

(Chapel St) More urban chic than olde worlde, this open-plan bar also boasts the town's best beer garden.

SOUTHWEST ENGLAND PENZANCE

CORNISH MINING SITES

Since 2006, Cornwall and West Devon's historic mining areas have formed part of the UK's newest Unesco World Heritage site, the Cornwall & West Devon Mining Landscape (www.cornish-mining.org.uk).

The Cornish Mines & Engines (☎01209-315027; cornishmines@nationaltrust.org.uk; adult/child £6.30/3.10) centre in Poole, near Redruth, makes an ideal place to get acquainted with this once great industry. At the heart of the complex are two working beam engines, both once powered by steam boilers designed by local lad Richard Trevithick (who was born in Redruth in 1771, and whose cottage at Penponds is now open to the public). Films, photos and artefacts trace the area's rich mining history, while you can see more mining gear in action at King Edward Mine (☎01209-614681; www.kingedwardmine.co.uk; adult/child £6/1.50; ☺10am-5pm May-Sep).

It's also well worth making a visit to the historic beam engine at Levant (p336) and the mine at Geevor (p336), where you can take an underground tour into the old mineshafts.

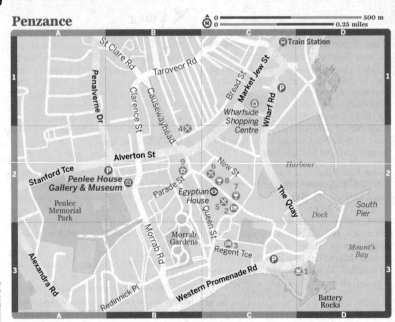

Penzance

Acorn Arts Centre THEATRE
(www.acornartscentre.co.uk; Parade St) The town's arts centre has been through troubled times, but it's now up and running again. Check the website for film, theatre, comedy and gigs.

⊙ Getting There & Away

Bus

Destinations include:

Helston & Falmouth Bus 2/2A (hourly Monday to Saturday, six on Sunday) via Marazion, Praa Sands.

St Ives (30 minutes, half-hourly Monday to Saturday, hourly on Sunday) Buses 17/17A/17B.

Truro (one hour, three or four daily Monday to Saturday) Bus X18.

Train

Penzance is the last stop on the line from London Paddington. Trains run roughly hourly. Sample fares:

Exeter (£39.50, three hours)

London Paddington (£56, hourly, 5½ hours)

St Ives (£3.80, 30 minutes)

Truro (£9.50, 30 minutes)

The Lizard

For a taste of Cornwall's stormier side, head for the ink-black cliffs, rugged coves and open heaths of the Lizard Peninsula. Windlashed in winter, in summer it bristles with wildflowers, butterflies and coves that are perfect for a secluded swim.

The Lizard used to be at the centre of Cornwall's smuggling industry and is still alive with tales of Cornish 'free-traders', contraband liquor and the government's preventive boats. The most notorious excise dodger was John Carter, the so-called King of Prussia – Prussia Cove near Marazion is named after him. These shores were also a graveyard for ships – more vessels have come to grief on the Lizard's treacherous reefs than almost anywhere else in Britain.

The Lizard's main town is Helston, which is famous for its annual street party, Flora Day, held on 8 May.

⊙ Sights & Activities

Lizard Lighthouse Heritage Centre MUSEUM
(www.lizardlighthouse.co.uk; adult/child £6/3; ⊙11am-5pm Mon-Fri Mar-Oct) Housed in a 1751 landmark lighthouse at the south of the Lizard Peninsula, this museum contains exhibits on local seafaring and shipwrecks – you

Penzance

can also take a guided tour into the tower to see the lamp room.

National Seal Sanctuary WILDLIFE RESERVE
(☏0871-423 2110; www.sealsanctuary.co.uk; adult/child £14.40/12; ⊙10am-5pm May-Sep, 9am-4pm Oct-Apr) Towards the northwest of the Lizard Peninsula, this sanctuary on the Helford River cares for sick and orphaned seals washed up along the Cornish coastline before returning them to the wild.

🛏 Sleeping

Lovelane Caravans CARAVAN, CAMPGROUND
(www.lovelanecaravans.com; Tregallast Barton; caravan per week £340-475) The lovingly restored retro beauties on offer here come complete with lino floors, charity-shop china and antique kettles. As there's no electricity, the only light comes from paraffin lamps and wood-stoves (ideal for star-spotting), and there's space for pitching your own tent too. It's near St Keverne, some 12 miles southeast of Helston.

Lizard YHA HOSTEL £
(☏0845 371 9550; www.yha.org.uk; dm £22; ⊙Apr-Oct) Wow – this absolutely marvellous hostel commands the kind of sea view you'd normally have to pay through the nose for. Housed in former lighthouse-keepers' cottages, it's quite simply one of the most spectacularly situated hostels anywhere in England.

✖ Eating

Kota RESTAURANT ££
(☏01326-562407; www.kotarestaurant.co.uk; mains £12-20; ⊙Tue-Sat) This adventurous fusion restaurant hunkers under the hefty beams of an old harbourside mill and serves some of Cornwall's most exotic flavours, with Szechuan, Thai and Malaysian spices all finding their way into the mix. It's in Porthleven, 3 miles south of Helston.

Halzephron Inn PUB ££
(☏01326-240406; www.halzephron-inn.co.uk; mains £10.95-18.50) At this hugger-mugger cliffside inn, forget fancy furnishings and designer food. Instead expect a proper old Cornish local, full of old-time charm, with real ales, filling food and a homely atmosphere. It's at Gunwalloe, 5 miles south of Helston.

Ann's Pasties BRITISH £
(☏01326-290889; www.annspasties.co.uk; pasties £2.85; ⊙9am-3pm Mon-Sat) Looking for Cornwall's best pasties? Head for Ann Muller's shop, attached to her house near Lizard Point. The recipes are 100% authentic and the ingredients are 100% Cornish – little wonder Rick Stein's given them his seal of approval.

❶ Getting There & Away

Services include:

Bus 2 Penzance to Falmouth, with stops at Porthleven and Helston (eight to ten Monday to Saturday, six on Sunday).

Bus 32 Helston to Gunwalloe, Gweek, Coverack and St Keverne (two on Sundays only).

Bus 33 Helston to Poldhu, Mullion and the Lizard (three daily Monday to Friday).

Bus 82 Helston to Truro (hourly Monday to Saturday, five on Sunday).

Falmouth & Around

POP 20,775

Nestled at the head of the Fal River, the harbour town of Falmouth made its fortune during the 18th and 19th centuries, when clippers, trading vessels and mail packets from across the world stopped off to unload their cargoes. The town is still an important centre for shipbuilding and repairs, although these days it's also a lively student hang-out thanks to the nearby campus of University College Falmouth.

SOUTHWEST ENGLAND FALMOUTH & AROUND

MINACK THEATRE

In terms of theatrical settings, the Minack (☎01736-810181; www.minack.com) really has to take top billing. Carved directly into the crags overlooking Porthcurno Bay and the azure-blue Atlantic, this amazing clifftop amphitheatre was the lifelong passion of local lady Rowena Cade, who dreamt up the idea in the 1930s and oversaw the theatre until her death in 1983. It's now a hugely popular place for alfresco theatre, with a 17-week season running from mid-May to mid-September: regulars bring wine, picnic supplies, wet-weather gear and – most importantly of all, considering the seats are carved out of granite – a very comfy cushion.

Above the theatre, the visitor centre (adult/child £3.50/1.40; ◉9.30am-5.30pm Apr-Sep, 10am-4pm Oct-Mar) recounts the theatre's history; it's closed when there's a matinee.

The Minack is 3 miles from Land's End and 9 miles from Penzance. Bus 1/1A from Penzance stops several times daily.

It's also a great base for venturing along Cornwall's south coast, with a wealth of bars and bistros, a trio of beaches and the nation's foremost maritime museum on its doorstep.

◉ Sights & Activities

National Maritime Museum   MUSEUM
(www.nmmc.co.uk; Discovery Quay; adult/child £10.50/7.20; ◉10am-5pm) This is the sister outpost to the National Maritime Museum in Greenwich, London. It focuses on Falmouth's history as a seafaring port, with varied exhibitions exploring everything from the underwater environment of the Fal Estuary to the town's groundbreaking nautical mail service, the Falmouth Packet.

At the heart of the complex is the Flotilla Gallery, where a collection of important vessels are suspended from the ceiling on steel wires. From the top floor of the Look Out tower, there's a 360-degree panorama right across Falmouth Bay.

Pendennis Castle   CASTLE
(EH; ☎01326-316594; adult/child £5.40/2.70; ◉10am-6pm Jul & Aug, 10am-5pm Apr-Jun & Sep,

10am-4pm Oct-Mar) Falmouth's been an important port since the Middle Ages. This Tudor castle on the promontory of Pendennis Point was built by Henry VIII to protect the harbour in tandem with its sister fortress at St Mawes, on the opposite side of the estuary.

Highlights include the atmospheric Tudor gun deck, a WWI guard house and the WWII-era Half-Moon Battery. The Noonday Gun rings out at noon sharp daily in July and August.

Beaches   BEACH
Falmouth has three lovely beaches. Nearest to town is busy Gyllyngvase, a short walk from the town centre, where there's lots of sand and the lively Gylly Beach Café. Just around the headland is little Swanpool, while Maenporth is another mile further west. The 500 bus stops at all three in season.

🛏 Sleeping

Falmouth has plenty of B&Bs and hotels, especially around Melvill Rd and Avenue Rd.

Falmouth Townhouse   HOTEL ££
(☎01326-312009; www.falmouthtownhouse.co.uk; d £85-120; 🛜) The choice for the design-conscious, in a town house halfway between the high street and Discovery Quay. Despite the heritage building, the feel is studiously modernist: slate greys, retro furniture and minimal clutter throughout. Go for a top-floor room to avoid bar noise.

Highcliffe Contemporary B&B   B&B ££
(☎01326-314466; www.falmouth-hotel.co.uk; 22 Melvill Rd; d £92-130) Does what it says on the tin – contemporary B&B rooms, all with their own different decorative touch, and luxuries such as iPod docks, retro radios and pocket-sprung mattresses. Go for spacious Room 2 or the light, white Attic Suite (Room 7).

St Michael's Hotel   HOTEL £££
(☎01326-312707; www.stmichaelshotel.co.uk; r £118-248; 🅿🛜🏊) The pick of the seafront hotels, with checks, stripes and slatted wood for that essential maritime feel. It's not worth skimping here: go for the biggest room you can afford, and indulge at the spa, swimming pool and the smart Flying Fish Restaurant (two/three courses £25/29).

Falmouth Backpacker's   HOSTEL £
(☎01326-319996; www.falmouthbackpackers.co.uk; 9 Gyllyngvase Tce; dm/s £19/25, d £50-60)

This indie hostel has been brightened up with primary colours and the odd funky print. There's an Aga in the kitchen and a DVD lounge, and owner Judi is full of fun and activity ideas.

Greenbank HOTEL **£££**
(☑01326-312440; www.greenbank-hotel.co.uk; Harbourside; s £99-129, d £185-225; P 🐾) A Falmouth classic and still a good choice for heritage and harbour views. Public rooms have maritime touches – nautical knick-knacks and ships in cabinets – but the rooms stick to safe beiges and creams. 'Executive Harbour' rooms offer the most space and the choicest sea views.

✖ Eating

Wheelhouse SEAFOOD
(☑01326-318050; Upton Slip; ⊗dinner Wed-Sat) This backstreet shellfish bar has become a red-hot recommendation since opening in 2011. Tables are crammed into the tiny dining-room, and the chalkboard menu's deliberately simple: fresh crab, scallops, mussels or lobsters, all eaten hands-on and served with either matchstick fries or crusty bread. It's only open four nights a week, and is always packed out – book well ahead.

Cove BRITISH **££**
(☑01326-251136; www.thecovemaenporth.co.uk; Maenporth; 3-course menu £20, mains £13.95-24.50) Maenporth's beach-view restaurant is run by chef Arty Williams, who's stock-in-trade is giving a zesty fusion spin to traditional Brit cuisine. It's a bit of a trek, but worth the journey – and the 3-course *prix fixe* menu is super value.

Oliver's BISTRO **££**
(☑01326-218138; www.oliverstheeatery.com; 33 High St; mains £12.95-19.95; ⊗lunch Tue-Sat, dinner Tue-Sun) The decor feels stark at this streetside diner – plain white walls, plain wood furniture – but the food is simple and reliable. The menu has a strong French influence, with a surfeit of meaty dishes, seafood and foraged ingredients.

Gylly Beach Café CAFE **££**
(☑01326-312884; www.gyllybeach.com; Gyllyngvase Beach; mains £10.95-15.95; ⊗breakfast, lunch & dinner) The Gylly Beach is definitely the choice for a sundowner – it has a lovely patio deck overlooking the sands, and serves cold beers and killer cocktails. The menu's great too: quality steak, seafood and pasta after dark, and fry-ups and pancakes for brekkie.

Indaba on the Beach SEAFOOD **£££**
(☑01326-311886; www.indabafish.co.uk; Swanpool; mains £11-18; ⊗lunch daily, dinner Mon-Sat) Seafood-specific restaurant, perched on a rock above Swanpool. Go for classic mussels or splash out on a full-blown *fruits de mer* platter.

Stein's Fish & Chips FISH & CHIPS **££**
(☑01841-532700; Discovery Quay; fish £7.85-9.25; ⊗12-2.30pm & 5-9pm) Rick Stein's posh Falmouth fish-and-chips shop batters unusual species including lemon sole and sea bream alongside the usual cod and hake – but be prepared to pay the premium. Sit-down dishes are served at the oyster bar (open 5pm to 9pm) upstairs.

Boathouse GASTROPUB **££**
(Trevethan Hill; mains £6-12) This groovy gastropub has the atmosphere of a ship's galley, with a deck overlooking the river to Flushing. There's usually a good choice of mains chalked on the blackboard.

Harbour Lights FISH & CHIPS **£**
(Arwenack St; fish & chips £4-6) Falmouth's classic chippie, sustainably sourced and much cheaper than Stein's.

SOUTHWEST ENGLAND FALMOUTH & AROUND

KYNANCE COVE

Cornwall's littered with photogenic coves, but it's hard to find a more picture-perfect spot than Kynance Cove, a National Trust–owned beach. It's a showstopper, studded with offshore islands and blessed with some of the most dazzlingly turquoise water in Cornwall. It's also known for its unusual geology: the cliffs around the cove are rich in serpentine, a red-green rock popular with Victorian trinket-makers.

The cove is a mile north of Lizard Point. There's a large NT car park on the cliffs (free for NT members), about half-a-mile uphill. Light lunches, coffees and cream teas are available at the Kynance Cove Cafe (www.kynancecovecafe.co.uk; mains £8-14), right beside the beach.

TREBAH & GLENDURGAN GARDENS

Two of Cornwall's great gardens sit side by side along the northern bank of the Helford River. They're about 4 miles' drive from Falmouth: head for Mawnan Smith and follow the signs.

First planted in 1840, Trebah ([✆]01326-252200; www.trebahgarden.co.uk; adult/child £8.50/2.50; ⊙10.30am-4.30pm Mar-Oct) is one of Cornwall's finest subtropical gardens, dramatically situated in a steep ravine filled with giant rhododendrons, huge Brazilian rhubarb plants and jungle ferns.

Next-door Glendurgan (NT; [✆]01326-250906; www.nationaltrust.org.uk/glendurgan -garden; adult/child £6.80/3.50; ⊙10.30am-5.30pm Tue-Sat) was established around the same time by the wealthy Fox family, and is now owned by the National Trust. It's known for its stunning views of the River Helford, as well as an impressive maze and secluded beach near Durgan village.

 Drinking

Top spots for a pint include: the Front (Arwenack St) for well-kept beers; Quayside (Arwenack St), with outside seating on the harbour; and the Chain Locker (Quay St), crammed with maritime atmosphere.

 Getting There & Away

Bus

Services include:

Glendurgan, Gweek & the Helford Passage (hourly Monday to Saturday, four to seven on Sunday) Bus 500 only runs as far as the Helford Passage; bus 35 continues to Helston.

Truro (hourly) Bus 88 is the fastest; bus 88A continues to Newquay.

Train

Falmouth is at the end of the branch line from Truro (£3.80, 20 minutes), which also stops at Penryn.

Truro

POP 17,431

Cornwall's capital has been at the centre of the county's fortunes for eight centuries. Truro grew up around a now-vanished hilltop castle, and later became rich as a busy river port and one of Cornwall's five stannary towns. The town was granted its own bishop in 1877, and the soaring three-spired cathedral followed soon after.

These days it's a busy commercial city, with a selection of shops, galleries and restaurants, as well as Cornwall's main county museum.

◉ **Sights**

FREE Royal Cornwall Museum   MUSEUM
([✆]01872-272205; www.royalcornwallmuseum.org.uk; River St; ⊙10am-5pm Mon-Sat) Collections at the county's archaeological museum encompass everything from geological specimens to Celtic torques and a ceremonial carriage. Upstairs there's an Egyptian section and a little gallery with some surprising finds: a Turner here, a van Dyck there, and several works by Stanhope Forbes.

Truro Cathedral   CHURCH
(www.trurocathedral.org.uk; High Cross; suggested donation £4; ⊙7.30am-6pm Mon-Sat, 9am-7pm Sun) Built on the site of a 16th-century parish church in soaring Gothic Revival style, Truro Cathedral was completed in 1910, making it the first cathedral built in England since St Paul's. Inside, the vast nave contains some fine Victorian stained glass and the impressive Father Willis Organ.

Trelissick Gardens   GARDENS
(NT; www.nationaltrust.org.uk/trelissick-garden; adult/child £7.20/3.60; ⊙10.30am-5.30pm Feb-Oct, 11am-4pm Nov-Jan) At the head of the Fal estuary, 4 miles south of Truro, Trelissick is one of Cornwall's most beautiful estates, with a formal garden filled with magnolias and hydrangeas, and a huge expanse of fields and parkland criss-crossed by walking trails.

🛏 **Sleeping**

Mannings Hotel   HOTEL ££
([✆]01872-270345; www.manningshotels.co.uk; Lemon St; s £79, d £99-109; [P][🛜]) The city's best option is this efficient city-centre pad

(formerly the Royal Hotel), geared heavily towards the business crowd. Bold colours, wall-mounted TVs and sleek furniture keep things uncluttered, and there are 'apart-hotels' for longer stays (£129).

Townhouse
B&B ££

(01872-277374; www.trurotownhouse.com; 20 Falmouth Rd; s £59-69, d £69-79) A practical, businessy B&B uphill from the town centre. Snug rooms feature colourful throws, work desks and angle-poise lamps; some have four-posters. Rooms are all on the small side.

Eating

Saffron
BRITISH ££

(01872-263771;www.safronrestauranttruro.co.uk; 5 Quay St; mains £13.50-16.50; ⊙lunch Mon-Fri, dinner Tue-Sat) This stalwart restaurant remains as reliable as ever. Its generous menu is Cornish-meets-Mediterranean – spider crab bisque, seared cod with saffron potatoes – and the dining room's sunny tones make it feel warm and inviting.

Bustopher's
BISTRO ££

(01872-279029; www.bustophersbarbistro.com; 62 Lemon St; mains £10-18) Another longstander that's been modernised to cater for the city's changing tastes. Cosy candles, sash windows and stripped-wood floors give things an intimate ambience, ideal for bistro fare such as creamy cider mussels or Toulouse sausage with pomme purée.

Indaba Fish
SEAFOOD ££

(01872-274700; Tabernacle St; mains £14-18; ⊙dinner) The 'city' sister to Indaba's beachside establishment at Swanpool. Again, the emphasis is on classic seafood – Falmouth oysters, Newlyn lobsters, North Coast fish – although the backstreet location is nothing like as sexy.

Drinking

Old Ale House
PUB

(Quay St) Burnished wood 'n' beer mats sum up the vibe at the OAH – there's a different choice of daily ales chalked up behind the bar, and live jazz at weekends. You're even encouraged to throw your peanut shells on the floor.

Old Grammar School
PUB

(19 St Mary St; ⊙10am-late) Open-plan drinking den with big tables and soft sofas to sink into. Lunch is served from noon to 3pm; later it's cocktails, candles and imported Belgian and Japanese beers.

Vertigo
BAR

(15 St Marys St; ⊙10am-late) Stylish late-night bar, worth a look for its metro decor and sweet walled garden.

 Entertainment

Hall for Cornwall
THEATRE

(01872-262466; www.hallforcornwall.co.uk; Lemon Quay) The county's main venue for touring theatre and music.

ⓘ Information

Tourist office (01872-274555; tic@truro.gov.uk; Boscawen St; ⊙9am-5.30pm Mon-Fri, 9am-5pm Sat)

ⓘ Getting There & Away

Bus

Truro's bus station is beside Lemon Quay. Useful lines:

Falmouth (hourly) Bus 88.

Helston (one hour, hourly, five on Sunday) Bus 82.

Penzance (hourly Monday to Saturday, six on Sunday) Bus X18. Express service via Redruth and Camborne.

St Agnes (hourly Monday to Saturday) Bus 85/85A.

St Ives (1½ hours, hourly Monday to Saturday) Bus 14/14A.

Train

Truro is on the main London Paddington–Penzance line and the branch line to Falmouth. Destinations:

Bristol (£42, 3½ hours)

Exeter (£16.90, 2¼ hours)

Falmouth (£3.80, 30 minutes)

London Paddington (£56, 4½ hours)

Penzance (£9.50, 30 minutes)

Around Truro

THE ROSELAND

Stretching into the sea south of Truro, this beautiful rural peninsula gets its name not from flowers but from the Cornish word *ros*, meaning promontory. Highlights include the coastal villages of Portloe, a wreckers' hang out on the South West Coast Path, and Veryan, awash with daffodils in spring and framed by two thatched roundhouses. Nearby are the beaches of Carne and Pendower, which join at low tide to form one of the best stretches of sand on Cornwall's south coast.

Picture-postcard pretty St Mawes has a beautifully preserved clover-leaf castle (EH; ☑01326-270526; adult/child £4.60/2.40; ☺10am-6pm Sun-Fri Jul-Aug, 10am-5pm Sun-Fri Apr-June & Sep, earlier closing at other times), commissioned by Henry VIII and designed as the sister fortress to Pendennis across the estuary. The St Mawes Ferry (adult/child return £8/4.50) shuttles pedestrians across from Falmouth several times an hour.

St Just-in-Roseland boasts one of the most beautiful churchyards in the country, tumbling down to a creek filled with boats and wading birds.

LOST GARDENS OF HELIGAN

Cornwall's own real-life secret garden (☑01726-845100; www.heligan.com; adult/child £10/6; ☺10am-6pm Mar-Oct, 10am-5pm Nov-Feb). Formerly the family estate of the Tremaynes, the gardens fell into disrepair following WWI (when many staff were killed) and have since been restored to their former splendour by Tim Smit (the man behind the Eden Project) and a huge army of gardeners, horticultural specialists and volunteers. Among the treats in store at Heligan are a working kitchen garden, formal terraces, a secret grotto and a wild jungle valley – as well as the world's largest rhododendron, measuring an impressive 82 feet from root to tip.

Heligan is 7 miles from St Austell. Bus 526 (30 minutes, hourly, 10 on Sunday) links Heligan with Mevagissey and St Austell train station.

Fowey
POP 2273

Nestled on the steep tree-covered hillside overlooking the River Fowey, opposite the old fishing harbour of Polruan, Fowey (pronounced Foy) is a pretty tangle of pale-shaded houses and snaking lanes. Its long maritime history includes being the base for 14th-century raids on France and Spain; to guard against reprisals Henry VIII constructed St Catherine's Castle above Readymoney Cove, south of town.

It later became the area's key port for transporting china-clay, although the heavy industry is long gone, and these days Fowey has become another of Cornwall's most chi-chi seaside getaways.

The author Daphne du Maurier lived in Fowey, and every May the town hosts the Daphne du Maurier Literary Festival (www.dumaurier.org) in her honour.

BODMIN MOOR

It can't quite boast the wild majesty of Dartmoor, but Bodmin Moor has a bleak beauty all of its own.

Cornwall's 'roof' is a high heath pock-marked with bogs, ancient remains and lonely granite hills, including Rough Tor (pronounced *row-tor*, 400m) and Brown Willy (419m), Cornwall's highest points. It's a desolate place that works on the imagination; for years there have been reported sightings of the Beast of Bodmin, a large, black cat-like creature, although no one's ever managed to snap a decent picture.

The wild landscape offers some superb walking, and there are some great trails suitable for hikers and mountain-bikers around Cardinham Woods (www.forestry.gov.uk/cardinham) on the moor's eastern edge. Other landmarks to look out for are Dozmary Pool, at the centre of the moor, said to have been where Arthur's sword, Excalibur, was thrown after his death. Nearby is Jamaica Inn (☑01566-86250; www.jamaicainn.co.uk; s £65, d £80-110; ℗), made famous by Daphne du Maurier's novel of the same name (although it's been modernised since du Maurier's day).

The Bodmin & Wenford Railway (www.bodminandwenfordrailway.co.uk; rover pass adult/child £11.50/6; ☺Mar-Oct) is the last standard-gauge railway in Cornwall plied by steam locomotives. Trains are still decked out in original 1950s livery and chug from Bodmin Parkway and Bodmin General station to Boscarne Junction, where you can join the Camel Trail cycle route. There are two to four return trips daily depending on the season.

For general information on the moor, contact Bodmin tourist office (☑01208-76616; www.bodminlive.com; Mount Folly; ☺10am-5pm Mon-Sat).

PANDORA INN

One of Cornwall's oldest and loveliest creekside pubs, the Pandora Inn (☑01326-372678; www.pandorainn.com; Restronguet Creek; mains £10-16) is nestled in a beautiful river setting. Inside, blazing hearths, snug alcoves and ships in cabinets; outside, thatched roof, cob walls and a pontoon snaking out onto Restronguet Creek. The location really has the wow factor, but the pub hit the headlines in 2011 when a stray ember set fire to the roof and burned it to the ground – not that you'd ever know it, as it's since been impeccably rebuilt.

The Pandora sits at the bottom of a steep hill near the village of Mylor, roughly equidistant from Truro and Falmouth. It's signed off the A39, but it's still tricky to find, so a decent map will come in handy.

🛏 Sleeping

🏆 Upton House   B&B £££

(☑01726-832732; www.upton-house.com; 2 Esplanade; d £140-180) An utterly bonkers B&B that's gone all-out for decorative overload: the four rooms are full of tongue-in-cheek touches, from neon-pink flamingos and cat-skin mats to antique baths and skull-meets-fleur-de-lys wallpaper. Owner Angelique holds regular soirées, too: supper clubs, craftwork sessions and drawing-room drinks parties. Mad, but marvellous.

🍃 Coriander Cottages   B&B ££

(☑01726-834998; www.foweyaccommodation.co.uk; Penventinue Lane; r £90-120; P🐾) A delightfully rural complex on the outskirts of Fowey, with ecofriendly accommodation in a choice of open-plan self-catering barns, all with quiet country views. Unusually, nightly and weekly rates are available.

Old Quay House   HOTEL £££

(☑01726-833302; www.theoldquayhouse.com; 28 Fore St; d £255-395; 🐾) The epitome of Fowey's upmarket trend, this exclusive quayside hotel is all natural fabrics, rattan chairs and tasteful tones, and the rooms are a mix of estuary-view suites and attic penthouses. Very Kensington, not very Cornish.

Golant YHA   HOSTEL £

(☑0845 371 9019; golant@yha.org.uk; Penquite House; dm from £14; P@) A few miles north of Fowey, this rural hostel sits amongst 16 hectares and is reached by its own kilometre-long drive. The architecture's Georgian, and many rooms have estuary views.

🍴 Eating & Drinking

Bistro   FRENCH ££

(☑01726-832322; www.thebistrofowey.co.uk; 24 Fore St; 2-/3-course menu £15.95/18.95) Sparkling bistro dining on Fowey's main street, with a seasonal menu offering Cornish interpretations of Gallic classics: bouillabaisse, fish soup, roast cod loin, sole menunière. Mosaic floors and monochrome prints keep the dining area sleek and chic.

Sam's   BISTRO ££

(www.samsfowey.co.uk; 20 Fore St; mains £9.95-14.95) Comfortable as an old pair of flip-flops, this Fowey diner just keeps pulling in the punters. It's deliberately laid-back – booth seats, day-glo menus, sauce bottles on the tables – and offers solid seafood and burgers in starter or main sizes. There's a beachside outpost beside Polkerris Beach. No bookings.

King of Prussia   PUB

(www.kingofprussia.co.uk; Town Quay) Fowey's awash with pubs, but you might as well go for one with a harbour view – this one also takes its name from the local 'free trader' John Carter.

ℹ Getting There & Away

Bus

Buses to Fowey all stop at Par Station, with onward connections on the Penzance–London Paddington mainline. For services to St Austell try First's bus 25 (45 minutes, hourly Monday to Saturday) and Western Greyhound's bus 525 (45 minutes, 10 or 11 daily in summer).

Ferry

Bodinnick Ferry (car with 2 passengers/pedestrian/bicycle £4.50/1.30/1.60; ⏱last ferry around 8.45pm Apr-Oct, 7pm Nov-Mar) Car ferry crossing the river to Bodinnick.

Polruan Ferry (adult/child/bicycle £1.60/80p/1) Foot-passenger ferry across the estuary to Polruan village, starting point for some lovely coastal walks. Depending on the time of year, boats leave from either Town Quay or Whitehouse slip, just off the Esplanade.

Polperro

The ancient fishing village of Polperro is a picturesque muddle of narrow lanes and cottages set around a tiny harbour, best approached along the coastal path from Looe or Talland Bay. It's always jammed with day trippers and coach tours in summer, so arrive in the evening or out of season if possible.

Polperro was once heavily involved in pilchard fishing by day and smuggling by night; the displays at the small Heritage Museum (☑01503-272423; The Warren; adult/child £1.75/50p; ⊙10am-6pm Mar-Oct) include sepia photos, pilchard barrels and fascinating smuggling memorabilia.

Looe

POP 5280

Perched on the long curve of south coast between the Fowey River and Plymouth Sound, Looe is a breezy blend of historic fishing port and bucket-and-spade resort. Split into East and West Looe and divided by the broad river, it's a pleasant base for exploring Cornwall's southeastern reaches, and has some good beaches nearby.

◉ Sights & Activities

Wild Futures
Monkey Sanctuary   WILDLIFE RESERVE
(☑01503-262532; www.monkeysanctuary.org; St Martins; adult/child £8/5; ⊙11am-4.30pm Sun-Thu Easter-Sep) Half a mile west of town, this wildlife centre is guaranteed to raise some 'aaahhhhs' over its woolly and capuchin monkeys, many of which were rescued from illegal captivity.

Boat Trips   BOAT TOUR
Half a mile offshore is tiny Looe Island, a 22-acre nature reserve run by the Cornwall Wildlife Trust. The boat Islander (☑07814-139223; adult/child return £6/4, plus £2.50/1 landing fee) crosses to the island in summer.

Other boats set out from Buller Quay for destinations along the coast, including Polperro (£19) and Fowey (£12). Check the signs on the quayside for the next sailings.

⌶ Sleeping

Barclay House   B&B £££
(☑01503-262929; www.barclayhouse.co.uk; St Martins Rd; d £125-165; P❀✆) This detached Victorian villa sits on 6-acre gardens and has the best bedrooms in East Looe, with wraparound river views and graceful shades of peach, pistachio and aquamarine.

Beach House   B&B ££
(☑01503-262598; www.thebeachhouselooe.co.uk; Hannafore Point; d £100-130; P) Smart B&B in a modern house overlooking Hannafore Point. The compact rooms are named after Cornish bays: top of the pile is Kynance, with a massive bed and private balcony.

❶ Information

Looe tourist office (☑01503-262072; www.visit-southeastcornwall.co.uk; Fore St; ⊙10am-5pm Easter-Oct,) In the Guildhall. Open occasional days November to Easter.

❶ Getting There & Away

Bus

Bus 572 travels to Plymouth (1¼ hours, seven daily Monday to Saturday).

Train

The scenic **Looe Valley Line** (every two hours Monday to Saturday, eight on Sunday, day ranger adult/child £3.90/1.95) trundles to Liskeard on the London–Penzance line.

Around Looe

Lanhydrock   HISTORIC BUILDING
(NT; ☑01208-265950; www.nationaltrust.org.uk/lanhydrock; adult/child £10.70/5.30, grounds only £6.30/3.40; ⊙house 11am-5pm Tue-Sat, grounds 10am-6pm daily) This huge house provides a fascinating insight into the 'upstairs, downstairs' lives of the Cornish gentry, namely the Robartes family. Extensively rebuilt after a fire in 1881, it's the quintessential Victorian manor, complete with gentlemen's smoking room, toy-strewn nursery and antique-filled dining room – as well as a network of enormous kitchens where the family's lavish dinner parties would have been prepared.

Also look out for the impressive plasterwork ceiling of the Long Gallery, which was created by 17th-century Italian artists and miraculously escaped the great fire.

The house is about 2½ miles southeast of Bodmin.

THE EDEN PROJECT

The giant biomes of the Eden Project – the largest greenhouses in the world – have become one of Cornwall's most celebrated landmarks. Tropical, temperate and desert environments have been recreated inside the biomes, so a single visit can carry you from the steaming rainforests of South America to the dry deserts of Northern Africa.

In summer the biomes become a spectacular backdrop to a series of gigs known as the Eden Sessions (artists have included José Gonzalez, Goldfrapp and The Magic Numbers) and from November to February Eden transforms itself into a winter wonderland for the Time of Gifts festival, complete with a full-size ice-rink.

It's informative, educational and enormous fun, but it does get busy. Booking online avoids the queues and gets a 10% to 15% discount.

There are regular buses from St Austel. If you're driving, just follow signs from the A38.

Port Eliot
HISTORIC BUILDING

(01503-230211; www.porteliot.co.uk; house & grounds adult/child £8/4, grounds only £4/2; 2-6pm Sat-Thu Mar-Jun) Stretching across the eastern end of Cornwall is the 6000-acre estate of Port Eliot, the seat of the Earl of St Germans. Since March 2008 the house and grounds have been opened to the public for a hundred days every year, and every July the estate hosts a major outdoor bash, the Port Eliot Festival (www.porteliotfestival.com), which began life as a literary festival but has now branched out into live music, theatre and outdoor art.

Occasional trains from Plymouth stop at the tiny station of St Germans; otherwise you'll need your own transport to get to the estate.

Antony House
HISTORIC BUILDING

(01752-812191; www.nationaltrust.org.uk/antony; adult/child £8.10/5.10, grounds only £4.10/2.10; house 1-5pm Tue-Thu & Sun Jun-Aug, gardens open from midday) Owned by the National Trust and occupied by the Carew-Pole family, this house's main claim to fame are its decorative gardens, designed by the 18th-century landscape architect Humphry Repton and filled with outlandish topiary, some of which featured in Tim Burton's big-screen adaptation of *Alice in Wonderland*.

The house is 9 miles east of Looe or 6 miles west from Plymouth – the Torpoint Ferry (www.tamarcrossings.org.uk/index.aspx?articleid=36386; cars £2.50, pedestrians & cyclists free; 24hr) stops a couple of miles away. Opening days vary throughout the year, so phone ahead or check the website.

ISLES OF SCILLY

Twenty-eight miles southwest of mainland Cornwall lie the tiny Isles of Scilly, a miniature archipelago of more than 140 islands, five of which are inhabited. Nurtured by the Gulf Stream and blessed with a balmy subtropical climate, the Scillys have long survived on the traditional industries of farming, fishing and flower-growing, but these days tourism is by far the biggest moneyspinner. St Mary's is the largest and busiest island, closely followed by Tresco, while only a few hardy souls remain on Bryher, St Martin's and St Agnes.

With a laid-back island lifestyle, a strong community spirit and some of the most glorious beaches anywhere in England, it's hardly surprising that many visitors find themselves drawn back to the Scillys year after year. While life moves on at breakneck speed in the outside world, time in the Scillys seems happy to stand still.

The islands get very busy in summer, while many businesses shut down completely in winter. Hotels are expensive, so most people choose to stay in self-catering cottages – the two main companies are Island Properties (01720-422082; www.scillyhols.com) and Sibley's Island Homes (01720-422431; www.sibleysonscilly.co.uk). All of the inhabited islands (except Tresco) have a basic campsite.

ℹ Information

Isles of Scilly tourist board (01720-422536; tic@scilly.gov.uk; St Mary's; 8.30am-6pm Mon-Fri, 9am-5pm Sat, 9am-2pm Sun May-Sep, shorter hrs in winter)
Simply Scilly (www.simplyscilly.co.uk)

ℹ Getting There & Away

Air
British International (📞01736-363871; www.isleofscillyhelicopter.com) Helicopters run to St Mary's and Tresco from Penzance heliport. Full return fares are adult/child £190/110. Saver fares (for travel Monday to Friday) and day-trip fares are much cheaper.

Isles of Scilly Skybus (📞0845 710 5555; www.islesofscilly-travel.co.uk) Several daily flights from Land's End (adult/child return £120/93) and Newquay (£150/118), plus at least one from Exeter, Bristol and Southampton daily in summer.

Boat
Scillonian III (📞0845 710 5555; www.islesofscilly-travel.co.uk; ⊙Mar-Oct) Scilly's ferry plies the notoriously choppy waters between Penzance and St Mary's (adult/child return £95/43). There's at least one daily crossing in summer (except on Sundays), dropping to four a week in the shoulder months.

ℹ Getting Around

Boat
Inter-island launches run by the **St Mary's Boatmen Association** (📞01720-423999; www.scillyboating.co.uk) sail regularly from St Mary's to the other islands. Trips cost a flat rate adult/child £8.20/4.10, or you can take a 'circular' return via another island for £12/6.

Bus
The only bus services are on St Mary's. The airport bus (£3) departs from Hugh Town 40 minutes before each flight, while the **Island Rover** (📞01720-422131; www.islandrover.co.uk; £8) offers a twice-daily sightseeing trip in a vintage bus in summer.

Taxi
For taxis, try **Island Taxis** (📞01720-422126), **Scilly Cabs** (📞01720-422901) or **St Mary's Taxis** (📞01720-422555).

St Mary's

The largest and busiest island in the Scillys is St Mary's, which contains most of the islands' big hotels, B&Bs, restaurants and shops. The Scillonian ferry and most flights from the mainland arrive on St Mary's, but the other main islands (known as the 'off-islands') are easily reached via regular inter-island launches.

The traditional sport of gig racing is still hugely popular in the Scillys. These six-oared wooden boats were originally used to race out to secure valuable pilotage of sailing ships. You can often see gig racing around the shores of St Mary's between May and September, and every May the island hosts the World Pilot Gig Championships, which attracts teams from as far away as Holland and the USA.

◉ Sights

Hugh Town   NEIGHBOURHOOD
About a mile west of the airport is the main settlement of Hugh Town, home to most of the island's hotels, shops and guesthouses, as well as the main harbour. The small **Isles of Scilly Museum** (Church St; adult/child £3.50/1; ⊙10am-4.30pm Mon-Fri, 10am-noon Sat Easter-Sep, 10am-noon Mon-Sat Oct-Easter or by arrangement) explores the islands' history, with a collection of artefacts recovered from shipwrecks (including muskets, a cannon and a ship's bell), Romano-British finds and a fully rigged 1877 pilot gig.

Beaches   BEACH
The small inlets scattered around the island's coastline are best reached on foot or by bike. Porth Hellick, Watermill Cove and the remote Pelistry Bay are particularly worth seeking out.

🏃 Activities

Scilly Walks   WALKING TOUR
(📞01720-423326; www.scillywalks.co.uk; adult/child £5/2.50) Three-hour archaeological and historical tours, as well as visits to the off-islands.

Island Wildlife Tours   WALKING TOUR
(📞01720-422212; www.islandwildlifetours.co.uk; half-/full day £6/12) Regular birdwatching and wildlife walks.

Island Sea Safaris   BOAT TOUR
(📞01720-422732; www.islandseasafaris.co.uk) Trips to see local seabird and seal colonies (adult/child £32/22). Also rents wetsuits and snorkelling gear.

🛏 Sleeping

Isles of Scilly Country Guesthouse B&B ££
(📞01720-422440; www.scillyguesthouse.co.uk; High Lanes; d £88-100; 📶) Set back from the Hugh Town hustle, this charming rural guesthouse is one of the comfiest on St Mary's. The large rooms are completely chintz-free and look out across St Mary's fields, and there's an on-site conservatory Kaffeehaus serving Bavarian goodies such

THE CHANNEL ISLANDS

Clustering just off the coast of France, Jersey, Guernsey, Sark, Herm and Alderney are crammed full of old-world charm. These slabs of granite boast exquisite coastlines, beautiful harbours and forgotten, shaded lanes. The warm Gulf of St Malo ensures sub-tropical plants and colourful flowers; it also gifts sublime local seafood and attracts an incredible array of bird life.

The larger islands of Guernsey and Jersey are the main entrypoints, with a plethora of flights and ferries from both England and France. Air links between Guernsey, Jersey and Alderney are good, while fleets of ferries also connect them and the other islands. Accommodation options abound – even the smaller islands have a wide range. For transport, accommodation and eating options, see the islands' websites, below.

During WWII, the Channel Islands were the only British soil to be occupied by the Nazis, and poignant museums – some housed in old war tunnels and bunkers – provide an insight into the islanders' fortitude.

The islands are proudly independent, self-governing British Crown dependencies and sport a wealth of quirky anachronisms. English is the main language and although place names may look French, local pronunciation is very different. The islands print their own version of the British pound – you can't use it on the mainland, but you can use British money on the islands. The Channel Islands aren't covered by NHS or EHIC cards, so make sure your travel insurance includes medical treatment. Tourist entry requirements are the same as for the UK.

Jersey

At 9 miles by 5 miles, Jersey (www.jersey.com) is the biggest of the Channel Islands. An offshore finance centre with a rugged north coast, key sights are the Durrell Wildlife Park (www.durrell.org) and the thought-provoking Jersey War Tunnels (www.jerseywartunnels.com), a former WWII underground military hospital.

Guernsey

The second largest island, Guernsey (www.visitguernsey.com) features a captivating capital, St Peter Port and stunning sea-cliffs and sandy bays. Victor Hugo's former home, Hauteville House (www.victorhugo.gg), and Castle Cornet (www.museums.gov.gg) are the big draws.

Sark

On steep-sided Sark (www.sark.info) transport is by bike, tractor or horse and cart – the island (measuring 3 miles by 1.5 miles) has a magical, castaway feel.

Herm

Tiny, traffic-free Herm (www.hermisland.com) is just 1.5 miles long and half a mile wide. Flower-strewn hills are framed by white sandy shores – Shell Beach is a superb spot for a swim.

Alderney

Remote Alderney (www.visitalderney.com) is the third largest island. Its village capital St Anne is picture-perfect; its wealth of bird and wildlife includes blonde hedgehogs and 7000 squawking seabirds.

as *apfelstrudel* and German breads baked by owner Sabine.

Wingletang   B&B **££**
(☏01720-422381; www.wingletangguesthouse.co.uk; s £32-42, d £72-88) This granite-fronted cottage in the heart of Hugh Town is well over 200 years old, but the accommodation is surprisingly light inside. Sea-blue curtains, magnolia walls and simple furnishings make it feel like a family home, and

THE OFF-ISLANDS

If St Mary's feels like a beautifully remote, castaway island, wait till you experience the other inhabited chunks of rock scattered just offshore. Each has its own character and appeal.

Tresco

The main attraction of Scilly's second largest island is the magical Tresco Abbey Garden (☑01720-424105; www.tresco.co.uk/stay/abbey-garden; adult/child £12/free; ☺10am-4pm), which boasts more than 5000 subtropical plants. One of the most affordable places to stay is the New Inn (☑01720-422849; contactus@tresco.co.uk; d £110-240), the island's popular pub, which also has pleasant pastel sea-view rooms.

Bryher

Only around 70 people live on Bryher, Scilly's smallest and wildest inhabited island. Covered by rough bracken and heather, it takes the full force of Atlantic storms; Hell Bay in a winter gale is a truly powerful sight. Bryher is home to the exquisite Hell Bay Hotel (☑01720-422947; www.hellbay.co.uk; d £190-320), a cheery pub-cafe called Fraggle Rock (☑01720-422222; ☺10.30am-4.30pm & 7-11pm; ☎) and a campsite (☑01720-422886; www.bryhercampsite.co.uk; sites from £10).

St Martin's

The northernmost of the main islands, St Martin's is renowned for stunning beaches. Lawrence's Bay on the south coast becomes a broad sweep of sand at low tide; Great Bay on the north is arguably Scilly's finest beach; and the secluded cove of Perpitch is in the southeast.

St Martin's has a small village shop and Scilly Diving (☑01720-422848; www.scillydiving.com; Higher Town), which offers snorkelling trips and diving courses. Accommodation is limited; there's one super-expensive hotel, St Martin's on the Isle (☑01720-422090; www.stmartinshotel.co.uk; d £300-560), a campsite (☑01720-422888; www.stmartinscampsite.co.uk; sites £9-10.50; ☺Mar-Oct) and a handful of B&Bs, the pick of which is bijou Polreath (☑01720-422046; Higher Town; d £100-110, weekly stays only May-Sep).

St Agnes

England's most southerly community somehow transcends even the tranquillity of the other islands, with its cloistered coves, coastal walks and a scattering of prehistoric sites. If you're staying over try the sea-view rooms in Covean Cottage (☑01720-422620; http://st-agnes-scilly.org/covean.htm; d £60-80) or camp at Troytown Farm (☑01720-422360; www.troytown.co.uk; sites £7.50-8.50, tents £1-7 depending on size); while England's most southwesterly pub, the Turk's Head (☑01720-422434; mains £7-12), will keep you well fed and watered.

---

you're welcome to browse the little library of nature books.

Garrison Campsite CAMPGROUND £
(☑01720-422670; tedmoulson@aol.com; Tower Cottage, Garrison; sites £8.15-11) A 9.5-acre, sea-view site with good facilities.

Eating

Juliet's Garden Restaurant RESTAURANT, CAFE ££
(☑01720-422228; www.julietsgardenrestaurant.co.uk; mains £8-16; ☺summer) A converted barn 15 minutes' walk from town serving light lunches by day and candlelit fare by night.

Cambridge & East Anglia

Best Places to Eat

» Midsummer House (p366)

» Great House (p377)

» Company Shed (p371)

» Pea Porridge (p378)

» Roger Hickman's (p385)

Best Places to Stay

» Lavenham Priory (p377)

» Cley Windmill (p387)

» Varsity Hotel & Spa (p365)

» Angel Hotel (p378)

» Sutherland House (p381)

Why Go?

Unfurling gently eastwards to the sea, the vast flatlands of East Anglia are a rich web of lush farmland, melancholy fens and sparkling rivers. The area is justly famous for its sweeping sandy beaches, big skies and the bucolic landscape that once inspired Constable and Gainsborough.

It's not all rural idyll though: rising out of the fens is the world-famous university town of Cambridge, with its stunning classical architecture and earnest attitude, and to the east is the cosmopolitan city of Norwich. Around them magnificent cathedral cities, pretty market towns and implausibly picturesque villages are testament to the enormous wealth amassed here during medieval times, when the wool and weaving industries flourished.

Meanwhile, the meandering coastline is peppered with pretty fishing villages and traditional bucket-and-spade resorts, while inland is the languid, hypnotic charm of the Norfolk Broads, an ideal location for serious relaxation.

When to Go

Aldeburgh swings into action with its classical music festival in June. You can chill out and tune in at the Latitude Festival in Southwold in July. On 24 December the King's College Chapel is at its best at the Festival of Nine Lessons and Carols. East Anglia is at its best between late spring and early autumn, when the weather is still pleasant but the crowds haven't arrived yet, but during the months of July and August, the Norfolk coast beaches and seaside towns tend to be busiest with visitors.

Cambridge & East Anglia Highlights

❶ Dreaming of your student days while **punting** (p364) past Cambridge's historic colleges

❷ Soaking up the medieval atmosphere in topsy-turvy **Lavenham** (p376)

❸ Marvelling at the exquisite rib vaulting at **Norwich Cathedral** (p381)

❹ Walking the prom, dining on sublime food and just chilling out in understated **Aldeburgh** (p379)

❺ Enjoying the heavenly sounds of Evensong at **King's College Chapel** (p358)

❻ Canoeing your way through the tranquil waterways of the **Norfolk Broads** (p381)

❼ Wandering aimlessly along the pristine sands of **Holkham beach** (p387)

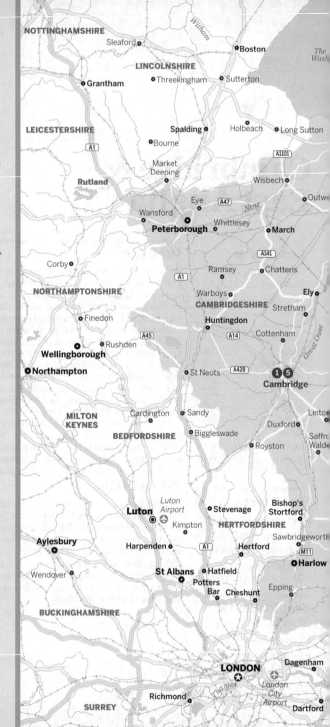

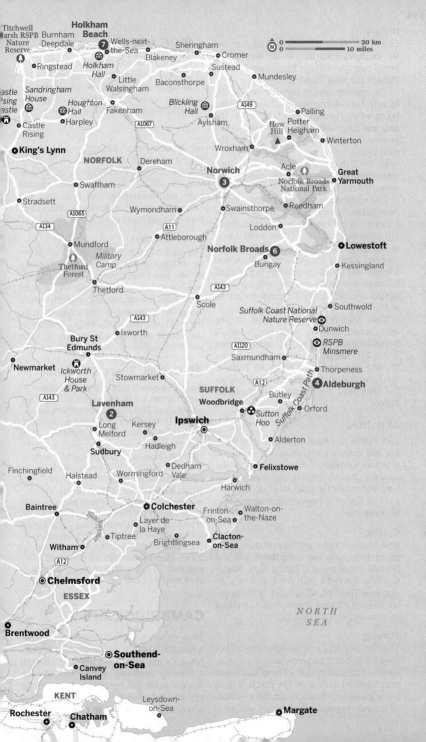

History

East Anglia was a major Saxon kingdom and the treasures unearthed in the Sutton Hoo burial ship proved that they enjoyed something of the good life here.

The region's heyday, however, was in the Middle Ages, during the wool and weaving boom, when Flemish weavers settled in the area and the grand churches and the world-famous Cambridge University began to be established.

By the 17th century much of the region's marshland and bog had been drained and converted into arable land.

The emergence of a work-happy urban bourgeoisie coupled with a strong sense of religious duty resulted in the parliamentarianism and Puritanism that would climax in the Civil War. Oliver Cromwell, the uncrowned king of the parliamentarians, was a small-time merchant residing in Ely when he answered God's call to take up arms against the fattened and corrupt monarchy of Charles I.

East Anglia's fortunes waned in the 18th century, however, when the Industrial Revolution got under way up north. During WWII East Anglia became an ideal base for the RAF and the United States Air Force in the fight against Nazi Germany, due to its flat open land and proximity to mainland Europe.

Activities

East Anglia is a great destination for walking and cycling enthusiasts, with miles of coastline to discover, vast expanses of flat land for leisurely touring and plenty of inland waterways for quiet boating. Try Visit East of England (www.visiteastofengland.com) for more info.

Cycling

East Anglia is famously flat and there's gorgeous riding to be had along the Suffolk and Norfolk coastlines and in the Fens. Mountain bikers should head for Thetford Forest, near Thetford, while much of the popular on- and off-road Peddars Way walking route is also open to cyclists.

Walking

The Peddars Way and Norfolk Coast Path (www.nationaltrail.co.uk/peddarsway) is a six-day, 93-mile national trail from Knettishall Heath near Thetford to Cromer. The first half trails along an ancient Roman road, then finishes by meandering along the beaches, sea walls,

WANT MORE?

Head to Lonely Planet (www.lonely planet.com/england/eastern-england/cambridge) for planning advice, author recommendations, traveller reviews and insider tips.

salt marshes (great for bird watching) and fishing villages of the coast.

Curving round further south, the 50-mile Suffolk Coast Path (www.suffolkcoastand heaths.org) wanders between Felixstowe and Lowestoft, via Snape Maltings, Aldeburgh, Dunwich and Southwold.

Other Activities

The coast and the Norfolk Broads are popular destinations for sailing, as you can easily hire boats and arrange lessons. It's also possible to just putt-putt your way around the Broads in motorboats or gently canoe along the slow-moving rivers. Alternatively, the wide and frequently empty beaches of the Norfolk coast make great spots for land yachting and kitesurfing.

🛈 Getting There & Around

There are excellent public transport links between London, the Midlands and East Anglia and getting about East Anglia is straightforward. Consult **Traveline** (www.travelineeastanglia.org .uk) for all public transport information.

BUS **Stagecoach** (www.stagecoachbus.com) and **First Group** (www.firstgroup.com), along with a host of smaller companies, offer bus services across the region.

TRAIN **National Express East Anglia** (www .nationalexpresseastanglia.com) offers the handy **Anglia Plus Pass** (one day/three days out of seven £13.50/27), which allows you to explore Norfolk, Suffolk and parts of Cambridgeshire. The pass is valid for unlimited regional travel after 8.45am on weekdays and anytime at weekends. Up to four accompanying children can travel for £2 each.

CAMBRIDGESHIRE

Many visitors to Cambridgeshire never make it past the beautiful university town of Cambridge, where august old buildings, student cyclists in academic gowns and glorious chapels await. But beyond the breathtaking city, the flat reclaimed fen, lush farmland and myriad waterways make perfect walking and cycling territory, while the extraordinary cathedral at Ely and the rip-roaring Imperial War Museum at Duxford would be headline attractions anywhere else.

ℹ Getting Around

The region's public transport radiates from Cambridge, which is a mere 55-minute train ride from London. This line continues north through Ely to King's Lynn in Norfolk. From Ely, branch lines run east through Norwich and southeast into Suffolk.

Cambridge

POP 108,860

Abounding with exquisite architecture, steeped in history and tradition and renowned for its quirky rituals, Cambridge is a university town extraordinaire. The tightly packed core of ancient colleges, the picturesque 'Backs' (college gardens) leading on to the river and the leafy green meadows that seem to surround the city give it a far more tranquil appeal than its historic rival Oxford.

Like 'the Other Place', as Oxford is known, the buildings here seem unchanged for centuries, and it's possible to wander the college buildings and experience them as countless prime ministers, poets, writers and scientists have done. The sheer academic achievement seems to permeate the very walls, with cyclists loaded down with books negotiating narrow cobbled passageways, students relaxing on manicured lawns and great minds debating life-changing research in historic pubs. Meanwhile, first-time punters zigzag erratically across the river, shoppers stroll unhurriedly through the Grand Arcade, and those long past their student days wonder what it would have been like to study in such splendid surroundings.

History

Despite roots stretching back to the Iron Age, Cambridge was little more than a rural backwater until the 11th century, when an Augustinian order of monks set up shop here – the first of the religious institutions that eventually became the colleges. When the university town of Oxford exploded in a riot between town and gown in 1209, a group of scholars, fed up with the constant brawling between locals and students, upped and joined what was to become the university of Cambridge. Cambridge wasn't spared by the riots, and brawls between

ℹ VISITING THE COLLEGES

Most colleges close to visitors for the Easter term and all are closed for exams from mid-May to mid-June. Also, opening hours vary from day to day, so if you have your heart set on visiting a particular college, contact it in advance to avoid disappointment.

town and gown took place with disturbing regularity here as well.

The first Cambridge college, Peterhouse (never Peterhouse *College*), was founded in 1284, and in 1318 the papal bull by Pope John XXII declared Cambridge to be an official university.

By the 14th century, royalty, nobility, churches, trade guilds and anyone rich enough could court prestige by founding their own colleges, though the system was shaken up during the Reformation with the dissolution of the monasteries. It was 500 years before female students were allowed into the hallowed grounds, though, and even then they were only allowed into women-only colleges Girton and Newnham, founded in 1869 and 1871 respectively. By 1948 Cambridge minds had broadened sufficiently to allow women to actually graduate.

The honour roll of famous Cambridge graduates reads like an international who's who of high achievers: 87 Nobel Prize winners (more than any other institution in the world), 13 British prime ministers, nine archbishops of Canterbury, an immense number of scientists, and a healthy host of poets and authors. This is the town where Newton refined his theory of gravity, Whipple invented the jet engine, Crick and Watson discovered DNA, and Stephen Hawking was, until 2009, a professor of mathematics. William Wordsworth, Lord Byron, Vladimir Nabokov and John Cleese all studied here.

Today the university remains one of the best for research worldwide. Thanks to some of the earth-shaking discoveries made here, Cambridge is inextricably linked to the history of learning.

◉ Sights

CAMBRIDGE UNIVERSITY
Cambridge University comprises 31 colleges, though not all are open to the public.

CAMBRIDGE & EAST ANGLIA CAMBRIDGE

Cambridge

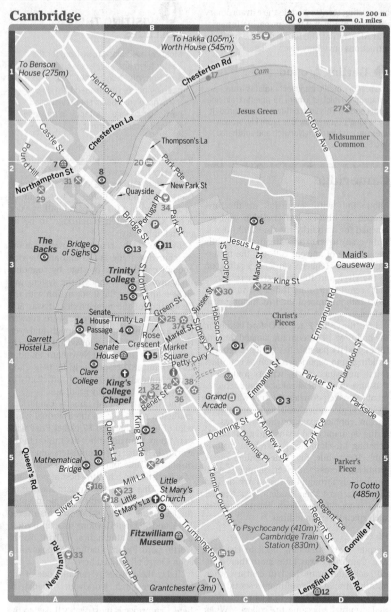

King's College Chapel CHAPEL
(www.kings.cam.ac.uk/chapel; King's Pde; adult/child £7.50/free, Evensong free; ⏲9.45am-4.30pm Mon, from 9.30am Tue-Sun, Evensong 5.30pm Mon-Sat, 10.30am & 3.30pm Sun, term time only) In a city crammed with show-stopping architecture, this is the scene-stealer. Chances are you will already have seen it on a thousand postcards, tea towels and choral CDs before you catch your first glimpse of the grandiose King's College Chapel, but still it inspires awe. It's one of the most extraordinary examples of Gothic

Cambridge

architecture in England, begun in 1446 as an act of piety by Henry VI and finished by Henry VIII around 1516. Its steeples have long been a magnet for night climbers.

While you can enjoy stunning front and back views of the chapel from King's Parade and the river, the real drama is within. Mouths drop open upon first glimpse of the inspirational fan-vaulted ceiling, its intricate tracery soaring upwards before exploding into a series of stone fireworks. This vast 80m-long canopy is the work of John Wastell and is the largest expanse of fan vaulting in the world.

The chapel is also remarkably light, its sides flanked by lofty stained-glass windows that retain their original glass, rare survivors of the excesses of the Civil War in this region. It's said that these windows were ordered to be spared by Cromwell himself, who knew of their beauty from his own studies in Cambridge.

The antechapel and the choir are divided by a superbly carved wooden screen, designed and executed by Peter Stockton for Henry VIII. The screen bears his master's initials entwined with those of Anne Boleyn. Look closely and you may find an angry human face (possibly Stockton's) amid the elaborate jungle of mythical beasts and symbolic flowers. Above is the magnificent bat-wing organ, originally constructed in 1686, though much altered since.

The thickly carved wooden stalls just beyond the screen are a stage for the chapel's world-famous choir. You can hear them in full voice during the magnificent Evensong. If you happen to be visiting at Christmas, it is also worth queuing for admission to the incredibly popular Festival of Nine Lessons and Carols on Christmas Eve.

Beyond the dark-wood choir, light suffuses the high altar, which is framed by Rubens' masterpiece *Adoration of the Magi* (1634) and the magnificent east window. To the left of the altar in the side chapels, an exhibition charts the stages and methods of building the chapel.

The chapel is open for reduced hours during term time, and charges an entry fee for non-members of the University.

Trinity College COLLEGE

(www.trin.cam.ac.uk; Trinity St; adult/child £1.50/1; ⊙10.30am-4.30pm) The largest of Cambridge's colleges, Trinity is entered through an impressive Tudor gateway first created in 1546. As you walk through, have a look at the statue of the college's founder, Henry VIII, that adorns it. His left hand holds a golden orb, while his right grips not the original sceptre but a table leg, put there by student pranksters and never replaced. It's a wonderful introduction to one of Cambridge's most venerable colleges, and a reminder of who really rules the roost.

As you enter the Great Court, scholastic humour gives way to wonderment, for it is the largest of its kind in the world. To the right of the entrance is a small tree, planted in the 1950s and reputed to be a descendant of the apple tree made famous by Trinity alumnus Sir Isaac Newton. Other alumni include Francis Bacon, Lord Byron, Tennyson, HRH Prince Charles (legend has it that his bodyguard scored higher in the exams than he did), at least nine prime ministers (British and international) and some 32 Nobel Prize winners.

The college's vast hall has a dramatic hammerbeam roof and lantern, and beyond this are the dignified cloisters of Nevile's Court and the renowned Wren Library (⊙noon-2pm Mon-Fri). It contains 55,000 books dated before 1820 and more than 2500 manuscripts, including AA Milne's original *Winnie the Pooh*. Both Milne and his son, Christopher Robin, were graduates.

Henry VIII would have been proud to note, too, that his college would eventually come to throw the best party in town, the lavish May Ball in June, though you will need a fat purse, and a friend on the inside, to get an invitation.

St John's College COLLEGE

(www.joh.cam.ac.uk; St John's St; adult/child £4/free; ⊙10am-5.30pm) Alma mater of six prime ministers, three saints and Douglas Adams (author of *The Hitchhiker's Guide to the Galaxy*), St John's is one of the city's most photogenic colleges, and is also the second-biggest after Trinity. Founded in 1511 by Henry VII's mother, Margaret Beaufort, it sprawls along both banks of the river, joined by the Bridge of Sighs, a masterpiece of stone tracery and a focus for student pranks. Over the bridge is the 19th-century New Court, an extravagant neo-Gothic creation, and out to the left are stunning views of the Backs. Parts of the college are much older and the chapel, though smaller than King's, is one of Cambridge's hidden gems.

Christ's College COLLEGE

(www.christs.cam.ac.uk; St Andrew's St; admission free, Darwin room £2.50; ⊙9.30am-noon, Darwin room 10am-noon & 2-4pm) Over 500 years old and a grand old institution, Christ's is worth visiting if only for its gleaming Great Gate emblazoned with heraldic carving of spotted Beaufort yale (antelope-like creatures), Tudor roses and portcullis. Its founder, Lady Margaret Beaufort, hovers above like a guiding spirit. A stout oak door leads into First Court – one of Cambridge's more picturesque Front Courts and the only circular one. Pressing on through the Second Court there is a gate to the Fellows' Garden, which contains a mulberry tree under which 17th-century poet John Milton reputedly wrote *Lycidas*. Charles Darwin also studied here and his room has been restored as it would have been when he lived in it. You can buy a guided-walk brochure (£1.20) to Darwin-related sites in the college from the porter's lodge. Other controversy-generating alumni include Sacha Baron Cohen (aka Ali G and Borat) and historian Simon Schama.

Corpus Christi College COLLEGE

(www.corpus.cam.ac.uk; King's Pde; admission £2.50; ⊙10am-4.30pm) Entry to this illustrious college is via the so-called New Court, which dates back a mere 200 years. To your right is the door to the Parker Library, which holds the finest collection of Anglo-Saxon manuscripts in the world. As you enter, take a look at the statue on the right, that of the eponymous Matthew Parker, who was college master in 1544 and Archbishop of Canterbury to Elizabeth I. Mr Parker was known for his curiosity, and his endless questioning gave rise to the term 'nosy parker'. Meanwhile, a monastic atmosphere still radiates from the inner Old Court, which retains its medieval form. Look out for the fascinating sundial and plaque to playwright and past student Christopher Marlowe (1564–93), author of *Doctor Faustus* and *Tamburlaine*.

On the corner of Benet St you'll find the college's new Corpus Clock. Made from 24-carat gold, it displays the time through a series of concentric LED lights. A hideous-looking insect 'time-eater' crawls across the top. The clock is only accurate once every five minutes. At other times it slows or stops and then speeds up, which according to its creator, JC Taylor, reflects life's irregularity.

Trinity Hall College   COLLEGE
(www.trinhall.cam.ac.uk; Trinity Lane; admission by donation) Henry James once wrote of the delightfully diminutive Trinity Hall ('Tit Hall' to students), 'If I were called upon to mention the prettiest corner of the world, I should draw a thoughtful sigh and point the way to the gardens of Trinity Hall.' Wedged cosily among the great and the famous, but unconnected to better-known Trinity, it was founded in 1350 as a refuge for lawyers and clerics escaping the ravages of the Black Death, thus earning it the nickname, the 'Lawyers' College'. The college's 16th-century library has original Jacobean reading desks and chained books (an early antitheft device) on the shelves, while the chapel is one of the most beautiful of the colleges. You can attend Evensong here at 6.30pm Thursday and 6pm Sunday during term time. Writer JB Priestley, astrophysicist Stephen Hawking and actor Rachel Weisz are among Trinity Hall's graduates.

FREE Gonville & Caius College   COLLEGE
(www.cai.cam.ac.uk; Trinity St) Known locally as Caius (pronounced 'keys'), Gonville and Caius was founded twice, first by a priest called Gonville, in 1348, and then again in 1557 by Dr Caius (his given name was Keys – it was common for academics to use the Latin form of their names), a brilliant physician who supposedly spoilt his legacy by insisting in the statutes that the college admit no 'deaf, dumb, deformed, lame, chronic invalids, or Welshmen'! Fortunately for the college, his policy didn't last long, and the megastar of astrophysics, Stephen Hawking, is now a fellow here. Other notable ex-students include Francis Crick (of Crick and Watson, who discovered DNA) and Edward Wilson, of the tragic Scott expedition to the Antarctic.

The college is of particular interest thanks to its three fascinating gates: Virtue, Humility and Honour. They symbolise the progress of the good student, since the third gate (the *Porta Honoris,* a fabulous domed and sundial-sided confection) leads to the Senate House and thus graduation.

FREE Peterhouse   COLLEGE
(www.pet.cam.ac.uk; Trumpington St) The oldest and smallest college, Peterhouse is a charming place founded in 1284. Much of the college was rebuilt or added to over the years, including the exceptional little chapel built in 1632, but the main hall is bona fide 13th century and has been beautifully restored.

Just to the north is Little St Mary's Church, which has a memorial to Peterhouse student Godfrey Washington, great-uncle of George. His family coat of arms was the stars and stripes, the inspiration for the US flag. Rumours abound among undergrads – vigorously denied by college authorities – of tales of hauntings and spectral happenings on the site. Three Nobel Prize winners count themselves among Peterhouse's alumni.

Queens' College   COLLEGE
(www.queens.cam.ac.uk; Silver St; adult/child £2.50/free; ☺10am-4.30pm) The gorgeous 15th-century Queens' College sits elegantly astride the river and has two enchanting medieval courtyards: Old Court and Cloister Court. Here, too, is the beautiful half-timbered President's Lodge and the tower in which famous Dutch scholar and reformer Desiderius Erasmus lodged from 1510 to 1514. He had plenty to say about Cambridge: the wine tasted like vinegar, the beer was slop and the place was too expensive, but he did note that the local women were good kissers. Don't forget to have a look at the Mathematical Bridge.

FREE Magdalene College   COLLEGE
(www.magd.cam.ac.uk; Magdalene St) Originally a Benedictine hostel, riverside Magdalene has the dubious honour of being the last college to allow women students; when they were finally admitted in 1988, male students wore black armbands and flew the college flag at half-mast. Its greatest asset is the Pepys Library, housing the magnificent collection of books bequeathed by the famous mid-17th-century diarist to his old college.

FREE Emmanuel College   COLLEGE
(www.emma.cam.ac.uk; St Andrew's St) The 16th-century Emmanuel College ('Emma' to students) is famous for its exquisite chapel designed by Sir Christopher Wren. The college has a prodigious collection of ducks, who freely roam the area and in early spring produce armies of bright yellow ducklings. Here, too, is a plaque commemorating John Harvard (BA 1632), a scholar here who later settled in New England and left his money to a certain Cambridge College in Massachusetts – now Harvard University.

FREE Jesus College   COLLEGE
(www.jesus.cam.ac.uk; Jesus Lane) This tranquil 15th-century college was once a nunnery of

St Radegund before the Bishop of Ely, John Alcock, expelled the nuns for 'improvidence, extravagance and incontinence'. Highlights include a Norman arched gallery, a 13th-century chancel and art nouveau features by Pugin, William Morris (ceilings), Burne-Jones (stained glass) and Ford Madox Brown. Illustrious alumni include Thomas Cranmer, burnt for his faith in Oxford during the Reformation, and long-running (58 years!) BBC radio journalist Alistair Cooke. And no, in spite of what some tour guides may tell you, Jesus did not attend Jesus College.

OTHER SIGHTS

The Backs   PARKLANDS

Behind the grandiose facades, stately courts and manicured lawns of the city's central colleges lies a series of gardens and parklands butting up against the river. Collectively known as the Backs, these tranquil green spaces and shimmering waters offer unparalleled views of the colleges and are often the most enduring image of Cambridge for visitors. The picture-postcard snapshots of college life, graceful bridges and weeping willows can be seen from the pathways that cross the Backs, from the comfort of a chauffeur-driven punt or from the lovely pedestrian bridges that criss-cross the river.

The fanciful Bridge of Sighs (built in 1831) at St John's is best observed from the stylish bridge designed by Wren just to the south. The oldest crossing is at Clare College, built in 1639 and ornamented with decorative balls. Its architect was paid a grand total of 15p for his design and, feeling aggrieved at such a measly fee, it's said he cut a chunk out of one of the balls adorning the balustrade so the bridge would never be complete. Most curious of all is the flimsy-looking wooden construction joining the two halves of Queen's College known as the Mathematical Bridge, first built in 1749. Despite what unscrupulous guides may tell you, it wasn't the handiwork of Sir Isaac Newton (he died in 1727), originally built without nails, or taken apart by academics who then couldn't figure how to put it back together.

TOP CHOICE Fitzwilliam Museum   MUSEUM

(www.fitzmuseum.cam.ac.uk; Trumpington St; entry by donation, guided tour £5; ⊙10am-5pm Tue-Sat, noon-5pm Sun) Fondly dubbed 'the Fitz' by locals, this colossal neoclassical pile was one of the first public art museums in Britain, built to house the fabulous treasures that the seventh Viscount Fitzwilliam had bequeathed to his old university. An unabashedly over-the-top building, it sets out to mirror its contents in an ostentatious jumble of styles that mixes mosaic with marble, Greek with Egyptian, and more. It was begun by George Basevi in 1837, but he did not live to see its completion: while working on Ely Cathedral he stepped back to admire his handiwork, slipped and fell to his death.

The lower galleries are filled with priceless treasures spanning the ancient world; look out for a Roman funerary couch, an inscribed copper votive plaque from Yemen (c AD 100-200), a figurine of Egyptian cat goddess Bastet, some splendid Egyptian sarcophagi and mummified animals, plus some dazzling illuminated manuscripts. The Chinese ceramics section was closed at the

PRANKSTERS, NIGHT CLIMBERS AND CUBES

In a city with so much concentrated mental prowess, it is perhaps inevitable that the student community would excel at all kinds of mischief. The most impressive prank ever to take place in Cambridge – lifting an Austin Seven van onto the roof of the landmark Senate House in 1958 – involved a great deal of planning from four Mechanical Sciences students and spawned a number of copycat pranks, including suspending another Austin Seven from the Bridge of Sighs.

King's College has long been a target of night climbers – students who get their thrills by scaling the lofty heights of out-of-bounds buildings at night. The sport is taken very seriously – to the point where a Trinity College student, Geoffrey Winthrop Young, wrote the *Roof Climber's Guide to Trinity* in 1900. If you're in Cambridge after a particularly spectacular climber excursion, you may find some out-of-place object atop the pinnacles of King's College Chapel – anything from a traffic cone to a Santa hat.

Finally, we have the Cubes (Cambridge University Breaking and Entering Society) whose objective is to get someplace where they shouldn't be and leave a distinctive calling card – the most famous being the wooden mallard in the rafters of Trinity's Great Hall.

time of writing due to a robbery. The upper galleries showcase works by Leonardo da Vinci, Titian, Rubens, the Impressionists, Gainsborough and Constable, right through to Rembrandt and Picasso; standout works include the tender *Pietà* by Giovanni del Ponte and Salvator Rosa's dark and intensely personal *L'Umana Fragilita*. You can join a one-hour guided tour of the museum at 2.30pm Saturday.

FREE Kettle's Yard   GALLERY
(www.kettlesyard.co.uk; cnr Northampton & Castle Sts; ☉house 2-4pm Tue-Sun, gallery 11.30am-5pm Tue-Sun) If you like snooping around other people's houses (let's face it, most of us do!), you'll love this very personal glimpse into the incredible home of HS 'Jim' Ede, a former curator at the Tate Gallery in London. Ring the bell of this deceptively small cottage (which turns out to be much bigger on the inside, like the TARDIS) and then wander around the rooms at your leisure, where all the furniture, ceramics and art – such as the collection of 20th-century works by the likes of Miró, Henry Moore and others – is arranged just so, allowing you a real sense of the man's personality. Look out for the pebble spiral and don't forget to peek into the attic. There are also exhibitions of contemporary art in the modern gallery next door.

FREE Scott Polar
Research Institute   MUSEUM
(☑guide Kay Smith 01223-336573, museum 01223-336540; www.spri.cam.ac.uk/museum; Lensfield Rd; ☉10am-4pm Tue-Sat) The Scott Polar Institute, founded with part of the relief fund set up in the wake of the ill-fated Scott expedition to the South Pole, these days takes a lead role in climate change research and has an excellent museum that focuses on polar exploration, charting the feats of the likes of Amundsen, Nansen and Scott himself. Regardless of whether you see Scott as a valiant explorer or a vain, poorly prepared expedition leader whose bad decisions led to the demise of his team, it's difficult not to be moved by the collection of artefacts, such as paintings, photographs, clothing, equipment and maps, journals and last messages left for loved ones by Scott's polar crew.

Other engaging exhibits include models of ships that ventured into the frigid Arctic and Antarctic waters, innovative equipment such as the 'Nansen cooker', and interactive displays on ice and climate change. In the

CHARIOTS OF FIRE

The Trinity College Great Court is the scene of the run made famous by the film *Chariots of Fire* – a 350m-sprint around the quadrangle in 43 seconds (the time it takes the clock to strike 12). Although many students attempt it, Harold Abrahams (the hero of the film) never did, and the run in the movie was filmed at Eton. If you fancy your chances, remember that you'll need Olympian speed to even come close.

section devoted to the people of the Arctic, you can examine Inuit carvings and scrimshaw (etched bones), a Sámi knife with a carved reindeer-horn sheath, a walrus tusk with walrus hunt scenes etched on it, and particularly fine examples of *tupilaat* (carved caribou horn figures with ancestor souls captured inside) from Greenland. For an entertaining free guided tour, contact independent tour guide Kay Smith in advance.

Great St Mary's Church   CHURCH
(www.gsm.cam.ac.uk; cnr King's Pde & Market St, Senate House Hill; tower adult/child £3.50/2; ☉9am-5pm Mon-Sat, 12.30-5pm Sun) Cambridge's staunch university church was built between 1478 and 1519 in the late-Gothic Perpendicular style and is one of few churches to boast two organs. Climb the 123 steps of the tower for superb vistas of the dreamy spires, albeit marred by wire fencing.

The beautiful classical building directly across King's Pde is the Senate House, designed in 1730 by James Gibbs; graduations are held here in summer, when gowned and mortar-boarded students parade the streets.

Round Church   CHURCH
(www.christianheritageuk.org.uk; Bridge St; adult/child £2.20/free; ☉10am-5pm Tue-Sat, 1-5pm Sun) The beautiful Round Church is another of Cambridge's gems and one of only four such structures in England. It was built by the mysterious Knights Templar in 1130 and shelters an unusual circular nave ringed by chunky Norman pillars. Its proximity to Bridge St reminds you of its original role; that of a chapel for pilgrims crossing the river.

Cambridge University
Botanic Garden   GARDENS
(www.botanic.cam.ac.uk; entrance on Bateman St; adult/child £4.50/free, with guided tour £7;

⊙10am-6pm) Founded by Charles Darwin's mentor, Professor John Henslow, the beautiful Botanic Garden is home to 8000 plant species, a wonderful arboretum, glasshouses (home to carnivorous pitcher plants as well as the delicate slipper orchid), a winter garden and flamboyant herbaceous borders. You can take an hour-long guided tour of the garden at 11am on the first Saturday of the month and on some Wednesdays. The gardens are 1200m south of the city centre via Trumpington St.

 ## Activities

PUNTING

Gliding a self-propelled punt along the Backs is a blissful experience once you've got the knack, though it can also be a manic challenge to begin. If you wimp out you can always opt for a relaxing chauffeured punt.

Punt hire costs £14 to £16 per hour, chauffeured trips of the Backs cost £10 to £12, and a return trip to Grantchester will set you back £20 to £30. All companies offer discounts if you pre-book tickets online.

Cambridge Chauffer Punts   PUNTING

(www.punting-in-cambridge.co.uk; Silver St Bridge) One of the biggest punting companies in Cambridge, with regular chauffered punting tours.

Granta   PUNTING

(www.puntingincambridge.com; Newnham Rd) Conveniently located punt rental company for those looking to head towards Grantchester.

Scudamore's   PUNTING

(www.scudamores.com; Granta Pl) Also hires rowboats, kayaks and canoes.

☞ Tours

Check out **Visit Cambridge** (www.visit cambridge.org) for information on self-guided walking and audio tours of the city.

Walking Tours   GUIDED TOUR

(☑01223-457574; tours@cambridge.gov.uk; Wheeler St; ⊙1.30pm daily, sometimes extra tours at 10.30am, 11.30am & 14.30pm) The tourist office arranges these, as well as other less frequent tours, such as colourful 'Ghost Tours' and 'Punt and Pint Tours'. The tourist office has more details; book in advance.

Riverboat Georgina   BOAT TOUR

(☑01223-307694; www.georgina.co.uk) One-/two-hour cruises (£6/12), with the option of including lunch or a cream tea.

City Sightseeing   BUS TOUR

(www.city-sightseeing.com; adult/child £13/7; ⊙every 20 min 10am-4.40pm) Hop-on/hop-off bus tours.

⚝ Festivals & Events

Cambridge has a jam-packed schedule of almost continual events, of which the tourist office has exhaustive listings; also, check the notices on the fence around St Mary's church to see what's happening.

Bumps   BOAT RACE

(www.cucbc.org/bumps; ⊙Mar & May) Traditional rowing races along the Cam (or the Granta as the Cambridge stretch is called),

---

 HOW TO PUNT

Punting looks pretty straightforward but, believe us, it's not. We thought we'd share a few tips with you to prevent you from zigzagging wildly across the river, losing your pole and falling in.

» Standing at the back end of the punt, lift the pole out of the water at the side of the punt.

» Let the pole slide through your hands to touch the bottom of the river.

» Tilt the pole forward (that is, in the direction of travel of the punt) and push down to propel the punt forward.

» Twist the pole to free the end from the mud at the bottom of the river, and let it float up and trail behind the punt. You can then use it as a rudder to steer.

» If you haven't fallen in yet, raise the pole out of the water and into the vertical position to begin the cycle again.

» Hold on to the pole, particularly when passing under Clare Bridge, as students sometimes snatch them for a giggle.

in which college boat clubs compete to 'bump' the crew in front.

Beer Festival
BEER
(www.cambridgebeerfestival.com; ⊙May) Hugely popular week-long beer and cider extravaganza on Jesus Green, featuring brews from all over the country as well as a great range of British cheeses.

Folk Festival
MUSIC
(www.cambridgefolkfestival.co.uk; ⊙late Jul) Popular three-day music fest in neighbouring Cherry Hinton, which has hosted the likes of Elvis Costello, Paul Simon, kd lang and Joan Armatrading in recent years.

May Balls
FORMAL BALLS
(⊙early Jun) These formal balls are the biggest student event of the year. Why *May* Ball in June? Because they were originally held in May until the college authorities decided that booze-fuelled revelry just before the exams is not a great idea, so now they take place after the exams.

Cambridge Shakespeare Festival
THEATRE
(www.cambridgeshakespeare.com; ⊙Jul & Aug) The famous playwright's best-loved works played out in outdoor settings.

🛏 Sleeping

TOP CHOICE Varsity Hotel & Spa
HOTEL £££
(✐01223-306030; www.thevarsityhotel.co.uk; Thompson's Lane; d/ste from £225/385; �🛜) A celebration of Cambridge's august intellectual heritage, this hotel has an unparalleled location. The decor is understated, with lovely touches such as four-poster beds and floor-to-ceiling glass, monsoon showers and iPod docks. From the roof terrace there's a splendid view of the city.

TOP CHOICE Hotel du Vin
HOTEL £££
(✐01223-227330; www.hotelduvin.com; Trumpington St; d from £150; @🛜) This hotel chain really knows how to do things right. Its Cambridge offering has all the usual trademarks, from quirky but stylish rooms with monsoon showers and luxurious Egyptian cotton sheets, to the vaulted cellar bar and the French-style bistro (mains £15 to £22).

Cambridge Rooms
COLLEGE ROOMS ££
(www.cambridgerooms.co.uk; s/d from £41/78) If you wish to experience life inside the hallowed college grounds, you can stay in a student room in one of several colleges.

Accommodation varies from functional singles (with shared bathroom) overlooking college quads to more modern, en-suite rooms in nearby annexes.

Hotel Felix
BOUTIQUE HOTEL £££
(✐01223-277977; www.hotelfelix.co.uk; Whitehouse Lane, Huntingdon Rd; s/d from £165/200; P@🛜) Occupying a lovely grey-brick Victorian villa in landscaped grounds the 52 rooms here embody designer chic, with minimalist style and touches such as Egyptian cotton bedding and rain showers in many rooms. The slick restaurant offers modern Mediterranean cuisine (mains £13 to £23). Follow Castle St and then Huntingdon Rd out of the city for about 1.5 miles.

Worth House
B&B £
(✐01223-316074; www.worth-house.co.uk; 152 Chesterton Rd; s/d from £44/55; P🛜) A pleasant 20-minute walk from the centre across Jesus Green, this warm and welcoming B&B has five spacious, carpeted rooms with all the comforts and placid decor. Full English breakfast is included, and the owners go out of their way to be helpful.

Rosa's Bed and Breakfast
B&B ££
(✐01223-512596; www.rosasbedandbreakfast.co.uk; 53 Roseford Rd; s £45-60; 🛜) Ideal for solo travellers, this friendly family-run B&B has four cosy en-suite singles – all creams and pale wood – and the hosts are engaging without being intrusive. Well connected to the centre by the Citi 7 bus. Head up Castle St for 300m, turn right into Histon Rd, follow it for 1.2km and turn right into Roseford Rd.

Benson House
B&B ££
(✐01223-311594; www.bensonhouse.co.uk; 24 Huntingdon Rd; d from £90; P🛜) Just a 15-minute walk from the city centre, the rooms at this B&B range from monochrome minimalism to muted classical elegance, and breakfast includes kippers. To get here follow Castle St north of the city centre into Huntingdon Rd.

City Roomz
HOTEL ££
(✐01223-304050; www.cityroomz.co.uk; Station Rd; s/d from £52.50/67.50; @🛜) This converted-granary-cum-budget-hotel features compact en suites with exposed brick walls and bunk beds in the twins. Avoid like the proverbial plague on Friday and Saturday nights when last-minute guests too drunk to catch the last train home raise the barn.

Cambridge YHA HOSTEL £
(☑0845-371 9728; www.yha.org.uk; 97 Tenison Rd; dm/tw £19/45; @🛜) Busy, popular hostel with compact dorms and good facilities near the railway station.

 Eating

TOP CHOICE **Midsummer House** MODERN BRITISH £££
(☑01223-369299; www.midsummerhouse.co.uk; Midsummer Common; 3-/4-/5-course set menu £40/50/60, tasting menu £95; ⊘lunch Wed-Sat, dinner Tue-Sat) In a Victorian villa backing onto the river, this place is sheer gastronomic delight. Chef Daniel's Michelin-starred creations are distinguished by depth of flavour, great technical skill and expert pairings of ingredients. Expect the likes of slow roast duck with sweet potato and grapefruit and sea bass with truffle. The service is exemplary, and free of pretention.

Cotto INTERNATIONAL ££
(www.cottocambridge.co.uk; 183 East Rd; lunch mains £9-23, 3-course dinner £45; ⊘9am-3pm Tue-Fri, dinner Thu-Sat; ☑) The popularity of this spot is due to chef Hans' ability to coax wonderful flavours out of simple ingredients, most of them seasonal and locally sourced. For lunch you can expect risotto with mushrooms and veggies, and hearty soup, whereas the evening menu is more sophisticated, giving you veal kidneys à la dijonaise, salt marsh lamb and beautiful desserts.

Oak Bistro MODERN BRITISH ££
(☑01223-323361; www.theoakbistro.co.uk; 6 Lensfield Rd; mains £12-20, 2-/3-course set lunch £12/15; ⊘Mon-Sat) This great local favourite serves up simple, classic dishes with modern flair, such as tuna nicoise salad and slow-roasted lamb. The atmosphere is relaxed and welcoming, the decor minimalist and there's even a hidden walled garden for alfresco dining. Reservations essential even for lunch, due to its size and popularity.

Hakka CHINESE ££
(☑01223-568988; www.hak-ka.co.uk; 24 Milton Rd; mains £7.50-11.50; ⊘closed lunch; ☑) Chef Daniel's mother has taught him the secrets of Hakka cooking and once you've tasted his signature salt and chilli chicken, you'll be inclined to give her a hug and a kiss. The menu is extensive but the sizzling dishes stand out. Service can be slow on busy nights.

Thanh Binh VIETNAMESE ££
(☑01223-362456; www.thanhbinh.co.uk; 17 Magdalene St; mains £11-14, 2-course lunch menu £9) Cambridge's only Vietnamese restaurant has some wonderfully flavourful dishes on the menu – from the sublime pork balls to beef pho and tilapia steamed in lemongrass. Dinner on weekends requires a reservation and can feel a bit rushed, but it's perfect for lunch.

Stickybeaks CAFE £
(www.stickybeakscafe.co.uk; 42 Hobson St; mains £3-7; ⊘8am-5.30pm Mon-Fri, 9am-5.30pm Sat, 10am-5pm Sun; ☑) Sip creamy hot chocolate, nibble on an array of cakes or tuck into some imaginative salads (couscous with pomegranate, Puy lentils with goat's cheese) and sausage rolls with unusual chutney at this popular new cafe.

Chop House TRADITIONAL BRITISH ££
(http://www.cambscuisine.com/cambridge-chop-house; 1 Kings Pde; mains £9.50-24) This place has wooden floors, windows overlooking the street, and – true to the name – a menu of classic, meat-heavy English cuisine. If you're craving sausage and mash, a sizzling steak, suet pudding, fish pie or potted ham, look no further. Sister restaurant St John's Chop House (http://www.cambscuisine.com/st-johns-chop-house; 21-24 Northampton St) is located near the rear entrance to St John's College.

Jamie's Italian ITALIAN ££
(www.jamieoliver.com/italian; Old Library, Wheeler St; mains £9-19) Set in the city's Guildhall, the celebrity chef's 'neighbourhood Italian' is popular with the city's young trendsters. The building itself has loads of character, the antipasti arrives on the signature wooden planks and the mains are simple, filling and unpretentious.

Dojo ASIAN £
(www.dojonoodlebar.co.uk; 1-2 Miller's Yard, Mill Lane; mains £5-8.50) Favoured by students from Queens and noodle lovers in general, this brisk spot serves generous portions of Chinese, Thai, Japanese, Vietnamese and Malaysian noodle and rice dishes within a compact, bright interior.

Fitzbillies BAKERY, CAFE ££
(www.fitzbillies.co.uk; 52 Trumpington St; cafe mains £8-19; ⊘closed dinner Mon) Cambridge's oldest bakery, beloved by generations of students for its ultrasticky buns and quaint wood

shopfront, makes a good stop for breakfast, while its cafe next door serves good British food in simple surroundings.

Gardenia   GREEK £
(2 Rose Cres; mains £4-6.50) 'Gardi's' is responsible for the late-night nutrition of a large chunk of the student population, its walls plastered with photos of happy customers munching on the lamb souvlaki and doner kebabs.

Clowns   CAFE £
(54 King St; coffee £1.70, mains £4.50-8; ⊙8am-11pm) A Cambridge institution, run by a friendly Italian family, decked out with pictures of clowns. Great for a cooked breakfast, homemade lasagne, or simply lingering over a good coffee and a newspaper.

 Drinking

While cocktail bars are still low on the ground, Cambridge has plenty of pubs – from no-frills joints with sticky floors and pool tables to idyllic riverside spots serving the best of British cuisine alongside your beer.

Maypole   PUB
(www.maypolefreehouse.co.uk; 20a Portugal Pl) This friendly, locally popular traditional pub has hit on a winning formula: serve a good selection of real ales, not forgetting lesser-known beers from smaller breweries, throw in some great cocktails, and then, when it seemed that things couldn't get any better, add a successful beer festival in 2012 (set to become an annual event).

Eagle   PUB
(Benet St) Cambridge's most famous pub has loosened the tongues and pickled the grey cells of many an illustrious academic; among them Nobel Prize–winning scientists Crick and Watson, who discussed their research into DNA here. It's a traditional 17th-century pub with five cluttered, cosy rooms (the back one has WWII airmen's signatures on the ceiling) and good pub grub.

Portland Arms   PUB
(www.theportlandarms.co.uk; 129 Chesterton Rd) The best spot in town to catch a gig and see the pick of up-and-coming bands, the Portland is a popular student haunt and music venue. Its wood-panelled interior and spacious terrace make it a good bet any day of the week and there's a monthly comedy night as well.

Granta   PUB
(☑01223-505016; Newnham Rd) If the exterior of this picturesque waterside pub, overhanging a pretty mill pond, looks strangely familiar, it could well be because it is the darling of many a TV director. Its terrace sits right beside the water, and when your Dutch courage has been sufficiently fuelled, there are punts for hire alongside the terrace.

☆ **Entertainment**

In spite of being a lively student town, Cambridge has few nightclubs. There are, however, several good venues for live music.

Junction   LIVE MUSIC
(www.junction.co.uk; Cambridge Leisure Park, Clifton Way) Theatre, dance, comedy, live bands and club nights at Cambridge's youth venue near the railway station. To get here follow Regent St, then Hills Rd south out of the city for about a mile before turning left onto Clifton Way.

PsychoCandy   NIGHTCLUB
(www.clubpsychocandy.com; Station Rd; ⊙bi-monthly) This quirky basement club is by no means mainstream and you won't find any rowdy townies here. It's a wonderful gamer nerdfest-meets-club heaven and you're guaranteed a fun night with the likes of Legend of Zelda techno, and club remixes of the Teenage Mutant Ninja Turtles theme tune.

Corn Exchange   THEATRE
(www.cornex.co.uk; Wheeler St) The city's main centre for arts and entertainment, attracting the top names, from pop and rock to ballet.

Lola Lo   NIGHTCLUB
(www.lolalocambridge.com; 1-6 Guildhall Chambers, Corn Exchange St; ⊙8pm-3am Thu-Mon) Bringing a South Pacific vibe to the centre of Cambridge, Lola Lo specialises in cocktails and themed nights, featuring disco, current hits, club anthems and not-so-big-name DJs. Grass skirts are de rigueur for ladies (though we might be lying).

Fez   NIGHTCLUB
(www.cambridgefez.com; 15 Market Passage) Hip-hop, dance, R&B, techno, funk, top-name DJs and club nights – you'll find it at Cambridge's most popular club, the Moroccan-themed Fez, strewn with Turkish rugs and cushions.

ℹ Information

You'll find all the major banks and a host of ATMs around St Andrew's St and Sidney St. The going rate for internet access is about £1 per hour.

Addenbrooke's Hospital (☎01223-245151; Hills Rd) Southeast of the centre.

Budget Internet Cafe (30 Hills Rd; ⊙10am-9pm Mon-Sat, 11am-7pm Sun)

Police station (☎01223-358966; Parkside)

Post office (St Andrew's St)

Tourist office (☎0871-266 8006; www.visitcambridge.org; Old Library, Wheeler St; ⊙10am-5.30pm Mon-Fri, to 5pm Sat, 11am-3pm Sun) Pick up a guide to the Cambridge colleges (£4.99) in the gift shop or a leaflet (£1.20) outlining two city walks. Download audio tours from the website or book slots on tours. Rudimentary Cambridge map costs £1.

ℹ Getting There & Away

BUS From Parkside there are regular **National Express** (www.nationalexpress.com) buses to the following destinations:

Gatwick £37, 3½ to four hours

Heathrow £31, 2½ to three hours

Luton £15, 1½ hours, every two hours

Oxford £11, 3¼ to 3½ hours, every 30 minutes

Stansted £13, 50 minutes

CAR Cambridge's centre is largely pedestrianised and the car parks are expensive. Use one of the five free **Park & Ride** car parks on major routes into town. Buses (tickets £2.70) serve the city centre every 10 minutes between 7am and 7pm daily, then every 20 minutes until 10pm.

TRAIN The train station is off Station Rd, which is off Hills Rd. Destinations:

Birmingham New Street £30, three hours, hourly

Bury St Edmunds £9, 40 minutes, two hourly

Ely £4,15 minutes, three hourly

King's Lynn £9, 45 minutes, hourly

London Kings Cross £19, 50 to 75 minutes

Stansted £11, 30 minutes, hourly

ℹ Getting Around

BICYCLE Cambridge is very bike-friendly, and two wheels provide a great way of getting about town.

Cambridge Station Cycles (www.stationcycles .co.uk; Station Building, Station Rd; per half-day/day/week £7/10/25) Near the train station.

City Cycle Hire (www.citycyclehire.com; 61 Newnham Rd; per half-/full day from £6/10, per week £17-22)

BUS A free gas-powered City Circle bus runs around the centre, stopping every 15 minutes from 9am to 5pm, on Downing St, King's Pde and Jesus Lane. City bus lines run around town from Drummer St bus station; C1, C3 and C7 stop at the train station. Dayrider passes (£3.30) offer unlimited travel on all buses within Cambridge for one day.

Around Cambridge

GRANTCHESTER

Old thatched cottages with gardens covered in flowers, breezy meadows and classic cream teas aren't the only reason to make the pilgrimage along the river to the picture-postcard village of Grantchester. You'll also be following in the footsteps of some of the world's greatest minds on a 3-mile walk, cycle or punt that has changed little since Edwardian times.

The journey here is idyllic on a sunny day, and once you arrive you can flop into a deck chair under a leafy apple tree and wolf down calorific cakes or light lunches at the quintessentially English Orchard Tea Garden (www.orchard-grantchester.com; Mill Way; lunch mains £6-8; ⊙9.30am-7pm). This was the favourite haunt of the Bloomsbury Group who came to camp, picnic, swim and discuss their work.

IMPERIAL WAR MUSEUM

The romance of the winged war machine is alive and well at Europe's biggest aviation museum (http://aam.iwm.org.uk/; Duxford; adult/child £17/free; ⊙10am-6pm; 🚗), where almost 200 lovingly waxed vintage aircraft are housed in several enormous hangars. The vast airfield showcases everything from dive bombers to biplanes, Spitfire and Concorde. Make this a day trip, especially if you're bringing your kids, who'll want to try their hand at the interactive rocket launchers and flight simulators.

The awe-inspiring American Air Museum hangar, designed by Norman Foster, pays homage to the daring of the American servicemen in WWII and hosts the largest collection of American civil and military aircraft outside the USA, while the slick Air-Space hangar houses an exhibition on British and Commonwealth aviation.

The winged machines are not here just to look pretty; a number of the lovingly restored planes, such as the legendary 'Flying Fortress', take to the skies during the ultrapopular June/July Winged Legends airshow – an exhilarating spectacle not least because there's considerable risk involved for the pilot.

Duxford is 9 miles south of Cambridge at Junction 10 of the M11. Bus C7 runs from Emmanuel St in Cambridge to Duxford (45 minutes, every half-hour daily, less frequently on Sundays).

Ely

POP 15,100

A small but charming city dominated by a jaw-dropping cathedral, Ely (*ee*-lee), named after the eels that once inhabited the undrained fens surrounding the town, makes an excellent day trip from Cambridge. From the Middle Ages onwards, Ely was one of the biggest opium-producing centres in Britain, with high-class ladies holding 'poppy parties' and mothers in the Fens sedating their children with 'poppy tea'. Today, beyond the dizzying heights of the cathedral towers, Ely is a cluster of medieval streets lined with traditional tearooms and pretty Georgian houses.

◉ Sights

Ely Cathedral CATHEDRAL
(www.elycathedral.org; tower tour £6 Mon-Sat, £8.50 Sun; ⊙7am-6.30pm, Evensong 5.30pm Mon-Sat, 4pm Sun, choral service 10.30am Sun) Dominating the town, the stunning silhouette of Ely Cathedral is locally dubbed the 'Ship of the Fens' due to its visibility across the flat fenland for vast distances.

Walking into the early 12th-century Romanesque nave (with some Gothic arches added later to support the weight of the mighty walls) you're immediately struck by its clean, uncluttered lines and lofty sense of space. The cathedral is renowned for its entrancing ceiling, painted by two artists (Henry Le Strange and Thomas Gambier), the masterly 14th-century Octagon (the most impressive of all of England's churches) and lantern towers that soar upwards in shimmering colours.

The vast 14th-century Lady Chapel is filled with eerily empty niches that once held statues of saints and martyrs. They were hacked out unceremoniously by iconoclasts during the English Civil War. However, the astonishingly delicate tracery and carving remain, overseen by a rather controversial statue of Holy Mary by David Wynne, unveiled in 2000 to mixed reviews.

The cathedral's incredible architecture and light have made it a popular film location: you may recognise some of its fine details from scenes in *Elizabeth: The Golden Age* and *The Other Boleyn Girl*.

Ely has been a place of worship and pilgrimage since at least 673, when Etheldreda, daughter of the king of East Anglia, founded a nunnery here (shrugging off the fact that she had been twice married in her determination to become a nun) and was canonised shortly after her death. The nunnery was sacked by the Danes, rebuilt as a monastery, demolished and then resurrected as a church after the Norman Conquest. In 1109 Ely became a cathedral, to leave mere mortals in no doubt about the power of the church.

For more insight into the fascinating history of the cathedral join a free guided tour, or a tower tour of the Octagon Tower or the West Tower. Try to time your visit to attend the spine-tingling Evensong or choral service.

Oliver Cromwell's House MUSEUM
(www.olivercromwellshouse.co.uk; adult/child £4.50/4, joint ticket with Ely Museum £6.80; ⊙10am-5pm;) By St Mary's Green stands the attractive half-timbered house where England's only dictator lived with his family from 1636 to 1647, when he was the local tithe collector. This entertaining museum challenges you to answer one question: was this complex character a hero or a villain? The interactive exhibits keep children happily occupied throughout.

Ely Museum MUSEUM
(www.elymuseum.org.uk; Market St; adult/child £3.50/1; ⊙10.30am-5pm Mon-Sat, 1-5pm Sun;) Housed in the Old Gaol House, this quirky little museum appropriately features gruesome prison tableaux inside prisoners' cells, as well as historical displays on Romans, Anglo-Saxons, the Long Barrow burial ground at nearby Haddlington and the formation of the Fens. You are also initiated into the mysteries of old Ely trades such as eel-catching and leatherwork, as well as the local role in the World Wars.

✗ Eating

TOP CHOICE Peacocks Tearoom TEAROOM £
(www.peacockstearoom.co.uk; 65 Waterside; cream teas £7; ⊙10.30am-4.30pm Wed-Sun;) Consistently voted one of Britain's top teashops, this award-winning, family-run, wisteria-clad

OLIVER CROMWELL – THE SCOURGE OF KINGS

Well, one king, at any rate. While some believe that the enigmatic Cromwell was a regicidal dictator, others hail him as a hero of liberty, although the truth is much more complex than that.

East Anglia's most notorious son was born in Huntingdon in 1599. His first 40 years or so as a smallholder were spent in obscurity, but after he underwent a religious conversion and became a militant Puritan there was no stopping him, driven as he was by ambition and clarity of purpose before God. After a spell as a Member of Parliament for Huntingdon and then Cambridge, 'Old Ironsides' excelled as a military commander during the English Civil War, fighting on the side of the victorious Republicans. Despite the fact that he was only one of several signatories of the death warrant of Charles I, he is the one largely held responsible.

Though modern interpretation suggests that Cromwell allowed Jews back into Britain to 'stimulate the economy', the fact that he used the full weight of his office as Lord Protector to force through this unpopular decision shows how firmly he believed that the conversion of the Jews to Christianity was the essential precondition to the establishment of Christ's rule on earth: 'Was it not our duty in particular to encourage them to settle here, where alone they could be taught the truth?'

His other major achievements were the conquests of Ireland and Scotland, acts that – together with the death of Charles I – won him widespread posthumous animosity, to the point where his body was exhumed from Westminster Abbey after Restoration and then treated as if he had been a live rebel: hanged at Tyburn and decapitated. The body was almost certainly thrown into the common pit at Tyburn (the present-day site of Marble Arch), while the head was stuck on Westminster Hall and remained there for several decades, blowing down in a storm in the early 18th century. Picked up, it passed into private ownership and was occasionally exhibited as a curiosity. A descendant of its last owner deeded it to Sidney Sussex College in 1960 – Cromwell's alma mater – and it was buried in the chapel. There is a plaque on the wall by the door but the exact location is kept secret, lest self-proclaimed Royalists dig it up and defile it.

place serves a vast selection of leaf teas – from black-tea mixes named after Sherlock Holmes characters to delicate, citrus-infused green teas, and luscious homemade cakes, scones, soups, salads and sandwiches – try the brie and bacon with homemade blueberry chutney.

Old Fire Engine House TRADITIONAL BRITISH ££
(☎01353-662582; www.theoldfireenginehouse.co.uk; 25 St Mary's St; 2-/3-course set lunch £15/20, mains £15-18; ⊙closed dinner Sun) Backed by beautiful gardens and showcasing a variety of artwork, this delightfully homey place, which has been run by the same husband-and-wife team for over 40 years, serves classic English food, prepared from seasonal local ingredients, and excellent afternoon teas. Expect the likes of steak-and-kidney pie or rabbit with prunes and bacon, washed down with a carefully chosen wine.

ⓘ Information

Tourist office (☎01353-662062; www.visitely.org.uk; 29 St Mary's St; ⊙10am-5pm) Stocks leaflets (£0.50) on the 'Eel Trail' town walk and organises guided walking tours of the city, as well as ghost tours and other events.

ⓘ Getting There & Away

The easiest way to get to Ely is by train.

Cambridge (£4, 20 minutes, every 20 minutes)
King's Lynn (£6, 30 minutes, hourly)
Norwich (£18, one hour, every 20 minutes)

Following the Fen Rivers Way (map available from tourist offices), it's a lovely 17-mile towpath walk from Cambridge to Ely.

ESSEX

The county's inhabitants have been the butt of some of England's cruellest jokes and snobbery for years due to the chav stereotypes (young people who favour designer sportswear together with lots of gold bling), but beyond the fake Burberry bags and slots 'n' bumper car resorts, there's a rural idyll of sleepy medieval villages and rolling countryside where one of England's best-loved painters, Constable, found inspiration. Here, too, is the historic town of Colchester, and even Southend-on-Sea, the area's most popular resort, have a softer side in the traditional cockle-sellers and cobbled lanes of sleepy suburb Leigh.

Colchester

POP 104,390

Dominated by its sturdy castle and ancient walls, Colchester is Britain's oldest recorded city, with settlement noted here as early as the 5th century BC. Centuries later, in AD 43, the Romans came, saw, conquered and constructed their northern capital Camulodunum here, which was razed by Boudica in AD 60. A thousand years later, the invading Normans built the monstrous war machine that is the castle. Today, amid the maze of narrow streets in the city centre you'll find a few half-timbered gems, the fine castle and a striking new art space.

Sights

TOP CHOICE firstsite ARTS CENTRE
(www.firstsite.uk.net; St Botolph's; admission free; ⊙10am-5pm Tue, Wed, Sat & Sun, to 7pm Thu & Fri; ⊕) Opinion has been divided about Colchester's newest attraction – an arts centre housed inside a stunning curved-glass and copper building. Inside, it's also visually striking – lots of space, lots of light, installations flowing seamlessly into one another, and seats to perch on if you wish to leaf through some art books. The contemporary visual art on display is carefully chosen to be presented alongside historical works for context, and most exhibitions are temporary, with the exception of the magnificent Berryfield Mosaic – a Roman artefact found on firstsite's location in 1923, and now under glass in the centre of the gallery space. Love it or hate it, firstsite will not leave you indifferent.

TOP CHOICE Colchester Castle CASTLE
(www.colchestermuseums.org.uk; adult/child £6.25/4; ⊙10am-5pm Mon-Sat, from 11am Sun; ⊕) Built upon the foundations of the Roman Temple of Claudius, England's largest surviving Norman keep (bigger even than that of the Tower of London) was first established in 1076 and now houses an exceptional interactive museum that brings the Romano-British archaeological exhibits to life through a combination of artefacts, videos and hands-on displays. There are guided tours of the Roman vaults, Norman rooftop chapel and castle walls. The museum will be closed for redevelopment between January 2013 and Easter 2014.

FREE Hollytrees Museum MUSEUM
(www.colchestermuseums.org.uk; High St; ⊙10am-5pm Mon-Sat, from 11am Sun; ⊕) This museum trawls through 300 years of domestic life of the wealthy and their servants, with quirky exhibits that include a shipwright's baby carriage in the shape of a boat, make-your-own Victorian silhouette feature and an intricate, envy-inducing dolls' house. One room is dedicated to the art of clock-making – a prestigious trade that Colchester was once famous for.

Dutch Quarter HISTORIC NEIGHBOURHOOD
The best of the city's half-timbered houses and rickety roof lines are clustered together in this Tudor enclave just a short stroll north of High St. The area remains as a testament to the 16th-century Protestant weavers who fled here from Holland.

Sleeping & Eating

Colchester is easily doable as a day trip from London, but if you're staying there are some excellent B&Bs that give the town's ancient hotels a run for their money.

Trinity Townhouse B&B ££
(☎01206-575955; www.trinitytownhouse.co.uk; 6 Trinity St; s/d from £85/100; ☎) This central Tudor town house has five lovely rooms, each with its own character. Go for four-poster Wilbye, cottage-style Darcy or the more modern Furley. Each has period features, king-size beds, flatscreen TV and a designer bathroom. No children under five.

TOP CHOICE Company Shed SEAFOOD ££
(☎01206-382700; www.the-company-shed.co.uk; 129 Coast Rd, West Mersea; mains £4-12; ⊙9am-5pm Tue-Sat, from 10am Sun) It's a simple idea: bring your own bread and wine, perch on one of the seats inside this seaside shack, and tuck into the mussels, Colchester oysters, prawns and smoked fish, courtesy of the Howard family – eighth-generation oystermen. The seafood platter (£11.95) lets you

sample a good cross-section. West Mersea is on Mersea Island, 9 miles south of town.

Green Room   MODERN BRITISH **££**
(☑01206-574001; 50-51 North Hill; lunch mains £7-9, dinner mains £14-17) This easygoing bistro has simple wooden tables, bright artwork and some of the best food in town. Locally sourced meats, fish and oysters feature heavily on the seasonal menu, and it buzzes with happy diners lapping up the likes of seared cod cheeks, and pork belly and black-pudding salad.

ⓘ Information

Tourist office (☑01206-282920; www.visit colchester.com; 1 Queen St; ◷9.30am-5pm Mon-Sat)

ⓘ Getting There & Away

The bus station is on Queen St. There are three daily National Express buses to London Victoria (£15, 2½ hours).

Mainline services stop at Colchester North, about half a mile north of the centre. Trains run to London Liverpool St (£25, one hour, every 15 minutes).

Dedham Vale

Born and bred in East Bergholt, John Constable's romantic visions of country lanes, springtime fields and babbling creeks were inspired by and painted in this serene vale. The area has hung on to its rural charm despite the intervening centuries, and although you may not see the rickety old cart pictured in his renowned painting *The Hay Wain,* the background of picturesque cottages, rolling countryside and languid charm remains.

Now known as Constable country, Dedham Vale centres on the picturesque villages of Dedham, East Bergholt and Flatford. With leafy lanes, arresting pastoral views and graceful old churches, it's a glorious area to explore on foot or by bike. There's a tourist office (☑01206-299460; www.dedham valestourvalley.org; Flatford Lane, East Bergholt; ◷10am-5pm Easter-Oct, 11am-4pm Sat & Sun Nov–mid-Mar) beside the vale's top attraction, the riverside Flatford Mill, once owned by the artist's family and now used as an education centre. Constable fans will recognise the picturesque red-brick mill immediately, as it features in many of his paintings and remains as idyllic a setting today.

Near the mill is thatched Bridge Cottage (NT; ☑01206-298260; www.nationaltrust .org.uk; Flatford Lane, East Bergholt; parking £3; ◷10.30am-5.30pm May-Sep), which has an exhibition on the artist but none of his works. Call ahead about the organised tours (£6) which feature the Flatford Mill, Willy Lott's Cottage (which features in *The Hay Wain*) and other sites of Constable's paintings.

If you'd like to base yourself here, try Dedham Hall (☑01206-323027; www.dedham hall.co.uk; Dedham; s/d £65/110), an atmospheric 15th-century manor house where you can also take painting courses (nonresidents 3-/7-day £245/310) if you wish to follow in Constable's footsteps.

Alternatively, pamper yourself at the luxurious Maison Talbooth (☑01206-322367; www.milsomhotels.com; Stratford Rd, Dedham; ste £235-350; P🐾), with its individually decorated suites and outdoor hot tub, and chow on down at the Sun Inn (www.thesuninn dedham.com; mains £13-19), featuring a changing seasonal menu of expertly prepared British and Italian dishes, as well as a good selection of real ales.

Buses 247 and 87A run regularly from Colchester to Dedham (40 minutes); buses 93 and 93A run to East Bergholt (35 minutes). If coming by train, the mill is a lovely 2-mile walk from Manningtree.

Saffron Walden

POP 14,310

The little market town of Saffron Walden, around since 1141, is a delightful knot of half-timbered houses, narrow lanes, crooked roofs and ancient buildings. The town gets its curious title from the saffron crocus (the purple flower responsible for the most expensive spice on earth), which was cultivated in the surrounding fields from the 15th century until 1717.

The ultrahelpful tourist office (☑01799-524002; www.visitsaffronwalden.gov.uk; 1 Market Pl; ◷9.30am-5pm Mon-Sat Apr-Oct) provides a useful town trail leaflet with information on the town's historic buildings.

⊙ Sights

The town's most famous building is the 14th-century Old Sun Inn (Church St), an ornate wooden structure once used as Cromwell's HQ. Don't miss the stunning 17th-century pargeting (decorative plaster work).

AUDLEY END HOUSE

Positively palatial in its scale, style and the all-too-apparent ambition of its creator, the first earl of Suffolk, the fabulous early-Jacobean Audley End House (EH; www.english -heritage.org.uk; adult/child £13/7.80; ☉house noon-5pm Wed-Sun) eventually did become a royal palace when it was bought by Charles II in 1668.

Today, the enormous building is only one-third of its original size, but it's still magnificent. Its lavishly decorated rooms glitter with silverware, priceless furniture and paintings, making it one of England's grandest country homes. The sumptuous interior was remodelled in Gothic style by the third Baron Braybrooke in the 19th century, and much of his creations are what remain today.

The house is surrounded by a landscaped park (☉10am-6pm Wed-Sun) designed by Lancelot 'Capability' Brown and host to concerts throughout the summer months.

Audley End House is 1 mile west of Saffron Walden off the B1383. Audley End train station is 1.25 miles from the house. Taxis from the town marketplace cost around £5.

Nearby is the Church of St Mary the Virgin (www.stmaryssaffronwalden.org; Church St) with a 59m-tall tower, its oldest parts dating back to 1250. A symbol of the town's saffron-inspired golden age, it is one of the largest churches in the county and sports some impressive Gothic arches and Lord Audley's tomb.

In the excellent museum (www.saffronwaldenmuseum.org; Museum St; adult/child £1.50/free; ☉10am-5pm Mon-Sat, from 2pm Sun;) itself dating from 1835, you'll find an eclectic collection of artefacts covering everything from local history and 18th- and 19th-century costume to geology, a partially interactive natural-history exhibit, Victorian toys and ancient Egyptian items. There's a sandpit for young archaeologists and a fascinating 'Worlds of Man' collection, ranging from West African carvings and weaponry to Inuit bone harpoons. The bramble-covered ruins of Walden Castle Keep, built about 1125, lie in the grounds.

Tucked down at the end of quiet lanes off Bridge St and Castle St is the restored Victorian Bridge End Garden (www.bridgeendgarden.org; admission free; ☉dawn-dusk), with a proliferation of fruit trees and roses.

On the eastern side of the town, across the common, is the Turf Maze, thought to be 800 years old and the largest of its kind.

Eating

Saffron Walden is easily doable as a day trip from Cambridge.

Eight Bells　　　　PUB ££
(www.8bells-pub.co.uk; 18 Bridge St; mains £12-18; ☉closed dinner Sun;) A warm mix of medieval character and contemporary style, this 16th-century gastropub serves up the likes of roast pork tenderloin with sage-infused apple and home-cured gravadlax. Scrubbed wooden floors, half-timbered walls, abstract art, deep leather sofas and roaring fires make it a great place to sip on a pint or enjoy a top-notch meal.

Cafe Coucou　　　　CAFE £
(17 George St; mains £7-10; ☉9am-5pm Mon-Sat) Delicious homemade quiches, huge scones, chunky doorstop sandwiches and salads sell like hotcakes at this cheerful family-run cafe.

❶ Getting There & Around

The C7 bus runs into Cambridge (one hour, hourly). Buses 301 and 59 run from Audley End station into Saffron Walden (15 minutes) regularly on weekdays, less often on weekends.

Audley End train station is 2.5 miles west of town. Train services:

Cambridge £6, 20 minutes, every 20 minutes
London Liverpool Street £19, one hour, twice hourly Monday to Saturday, hourly Sunday

Southend-on-Sea

POP 160,260

Full of flashing lights and fairground rides, Southend is London's weekend playground, with gaudy amusements and nightclubs bordering on seedy. Beyond all this there's a glorious stretch of sandy beach, an absurdly long pier and in the suburb of Old Leigh, a traditional fishing village.

◎ Sights & Activities

Southend's main attraction is the world's longest pier (☎01702-215620; pier train adult/child £3.50/2, pier walk & ride £2.50/1.50; ☉8.15am-8pm), a staggering 1.34 miles, to be precise, built in 1830 and a magnet for boat crashes, storms and fires, the last of which ravaged its tip in 2005. In spite of that, at the time of writing, a new cultural centre had just been lowered onto the end of the pier. It houses a cafe, artists' studios and an auditorium. It's a peaceful if windy stroll to the head of the pier, and you can hop on the Pier Railway to save the long slog back.

Afterwards, dip beneath the pier's entrance to see the antique slot machines at the museum (www.southendpiermuseum.co.uk; adult/child £1.50/free; ⊙11am-5pm Sun-Wed).

Just west along the seafront, Southend morphs seamlessly into the suburbs of Westcliff-on-Sea, Chalkwell and Leigh-on-Sea, reachable by a long stroll or short hops on the local train. Wander the cobbled streets, cockle sheds, art galleries and craft shops of Old Leigh for a taste of life before the amusement arcades took over.

🛏 Sleeping & Eating

Roslin Beach Hotel   HOTEL ££
(☑01702-586375; www.roslinhotel.com; Thorpe Esplanade; s/d from £87/115; P🛜🐾) This delightful, low-key hotel is a little out of the way – a 30-minute walk from the pier – but its location right on the waterfront and its bright, unfussy rooms decked out in subtle pastel shades make it worthwhile. The adjoining restaurant is a sure bet for well-executed Modern British dishes, too.

Beaches   B&B ££
(☑01702-586124; www.beachesguesthouse.co.uk; 192 Eastern Esplanade; s/d from £40/70; 🛜) A welcome respite from violent florals and heavy swag curtains, rooms at Beaches are bright, simple and tasteful, with white Egyptian-cotton bed linen, feather duvets and subtle individual colour schemes.

TOP CHOICE Simply Seafood   SEAFOOD ££
(☑01702-716645; www.simplyseafood.co.uk; High St, Leigh-on-Sea; lunch mains £8-13, dinner mains £11-20; ✈) Tucked away under a flyover just east of the heart of Old Leigh, the strength of this light, bright little is undoubtedly seafood. The crispy whitebait is so fresh it may as well have leapt out of the sea onto your plate, the scallops are perfectly seared and the emperor's seafood platter is fit for royalty. The service is wonderfully attentive and there's even an extensive vegetarian menu for the nonpescatarians.

Azurro   ITALIAN ££
(☑01702-435845; www.azzurrosouthend.com; 326 London Rd, Westcliff-on-Sea; 2-course early dinner £9.95; ✈) The guys at this fabulous Italian joint know their stuff: their professional pride won't allow them to grill a fine piece of meat to oblivion, so don't ask for your venison to be 'well done'. Apart from the grilled carnivorous offerings, the array of pizzas and pastas is simple, but very nicely done.

ℹ Information

Tourist office (☑01702-618747; www.visit southend.co.uk; Southend Pier, Western Esplanade; ⊙8.15am-8pm) At the entrance to the pier.

ℹ Getting There & Around

The easiest way to arrive is by train. There are trains roughly every 15 minutes from London Liverpool St to Southend Victoria, and from London Fenchurch St to Southend Central (£10.60, 55 minutes). Southend Central is a 10-minute walk from the sea, whereas Southend Victoria is a 15-minute walk away. Trains leave Southend Central for Leigh-on-Sea (10 minutes, every 10 to 15 minutes).

SUFFOLK

Dotted with picturesque villages seemingly lost in time, Suffolk built its wealth and reputation on the back of the medieval wool trade, and although the once-busy coastal ports little resemble their former selves, the inland villages remain largely untouched, with magnificent wool churches and lavish medieval homes attesting to the once-great might of the area. To the west are the picture-postcard villages of Lavenham and Long Melford; further north the languid charm and historic buildings attract visitors to Bury St Edmunds; and along the coast the genteel seaside resorts of Aldeburgh and Southwold seem miles away from their more brash neighbours to the north and south.

ℹ Getting Around

Consult **Suffolk County Tourism** (www.suffolk onboard.com) or **Traveline** (www.travelineeast anglia.co.uk) for local transport information. The two main bus operators in rural areas are **Constable** (www.constablecoachesltd.co.uk) and **Chambers** (www.chamberscoaches.co.uk).

Ipswich is the main transport hub of the region. Trains from Ipswich include the following services:

DON'T MISS

SUTTON HOO

Somehow missed by plundering grave robbers and left undisturbed for 1300 years, the hull of an enormous Anglo-Saxon ship (guided tour adult/child £2.50/1.25; ⊘guided tour 11.30am & 12.30pm) was discovered here in 1939, buried under a mound of earth. The ship was the final resting place of Raedwald, King of East Anglia until AD 625, and was stuffed with a fabulous wealth of Saxon riches. The massive effort that went into his burial gives some idea of just how important an individual he must have been.

Many of the original finds and a full-scale reconstruction of his ship and burial chamber can be seen in the visitor centre (NT; www.nationaltrust.org.uk/suttonhoo; Woodbridge; adult/child £7.50/3.90; ⊘10.30am-5pm; ⊞). The finest treasures, including the king's exquisitely crafted helmet, shields, gold ornaments and Byzantine silver, are displayed in London's British Museum, but replicas are on show here.

Access to the original burial mounds is restricted, but you can join a one-hour guided tour (adult/child £2.50/1.25; ⊘11.30am & 12.30pm), which explores the area and does much to bring this fascinating site back to life. The site is open year-round but has restricted opening hours in low season. Check the website.

Sutton Hoo is 2 miles east of Woodbridge and 6 miles northeast of Ipswich off the B1083. Buses 71 and 73 go to Sutton Hoo 10 times per day Monday to Saturday, passing through Woodbridge (10 minutes) en route to Ipswich (40 minutes).

Bury St Edmunds £8, 35 minutes, twice hourly
London Liverpool St £26, 1¼ hours, every 20 minutes
Norwich £13.40, 45 minutes, twice hourly

Stour Valley

Both Constable and Gainsborough grew up or worked among the soft, pastoral landscape and comely villages of the Stour Valley, and the timber-framed houses and elegant churches that date all the way back to the region's 15th-century boom in the weaving trade are still very much as they were then. This now-quiet backwater once produced more cloth than anywhere else in England, but in the 16th century production gradually shifted elsewhere and the valley reverted to a rustic idyll.

Long Melford

POP 3675

At one end is a sprawling village green lorded over by the magnificent Holy Trinity Church (⊘9am-6pm) – more cathedral-sized than church-sized. Though its present incarnation is a spectacular example of a 15th-century wool church, its roots date back to the 11th century and its defining features are its stained-glass windows and distinctive flushwork.

From outside, the romantic Elizabethan mansion of Melford Hall (NT; www.nationaltrust.org.uk/melfordhall; adult/child £7/3.50; ⊘1-5pm Wed-Sun May-Oct) seems little changed since it entertained the queen in 1578. Inside, there's a panelled banqueting hall, much Regency and Victorian finery, and a display on Beatrix Potter, who was a cousin of the Parker family, which owned the house from 1786 to 1960.

There's a noticeably different atmosphere at Long Melford's other red-brick Elizabethan mansion, Kentwell Hall (www.kentwell.co.uk; adult/child £9.95/6.50; ⊘noon-4pm Apr-Sep; ⊞). Despite dating back to the Domesday Book and being full of Tudor pomp and centuries-old ghosts, it is still used as a private home by the Phillips family and has a wonderfully lived-in feel. It's surrounded by a rectangular moat, plus there's a Tudor-rose maze and a rare-breeds farm that'll keep the kids happy. Kentwell hosts special events throughout the year, including several full Tudor recreations. when the whole estate bristles with bodices and hose, and Scaresville – a costumed Halloween extravaganza.

🛏 Sleeping & Eating

Black Lion Hotel & Restaurant HOTEL £££
(⊘01787-312356; www.blacklionhotel.net; The Green; s/d from £102/125; ⊞) Discover your favourite vintage at this small hotel on the village green, its flamboyant rooms named after

different types of wine. The decor, all serious swag curtains, four-poster and half-tester beds and rich fabrics, is a creative combination of contemporary style and traditional elegance, and the same can be said of the dishes served at its restaurant (mains £13 to £21).

High Street Farmhouse   B&B **££**
(☎01787-375765; www.highstreetfarmhouse.co.uk; High St; d £70; P) This 16th-century farmhouse offers a choice of cosy (read: room to swing only a small cat) but bright rooms full of rustic charm. Expect patchwork quilts, pretty florals, knotty pine and cast-iron bedsteads. There's a lovely mature garden outside and cooked breakfast included.

Scutcher's Bistro   BRITISH **£££**
(☎01787-310200; www.scutchers.com; Westgate St; mains £19-22; ⊘Tue-Sat) With its rather mismatched decor, this unpretentious place is renowned throughout the Stour Valley for its beautiful takes on traditional dishes such as fish and chips and roast lamb (though the prices are a tad high) that leave locals coming back regularly for more. It's just off the Green.

Tiffins Tea Emporium   TEAROOM **£**
(Drury House, Hall St; tea £2.50; ⊘9am-5pm) A great favourite for its extensive range of cakes, perfectly brewed tea, and savoury pies and sandwiches.

❶ Getting There & Away

Buses from High St outside the post office run to Bury St Edmunds (50 minutes, hourly Monday to Saturday) and Sudbury (10 minutes, twice hourly Monday to Saturday).

Sudbury

Besides giving us the celebrated portrait and landscape painter Thomas Gainsborough (1727–88) and being the model for Charles Dickens' fictional town Eatanswill in *The Pickwick Papers* (1836–37), Sudbury is a bustling market town that prospered during the wool trade, with small-scale silk weaving surviving to this day.

Most visitors come here to see Gainsborough's House (www.gainsborough.org; 46 Gainsborough St; adult/child £5/2; ⊘10am-5pm Mon-Sat), the birthplace of the town's most famous export. It showcases the largest collection of his work in the world. The 16th-century house and gardens feature a Georgian facade built by Thomas Gainsborough's father in the 18th century. Inside,

look for his earliest surviving portrait, *A Boy and a Girl in a Landscape,* the exquisite *Portrait of Harriett, Viscountess Tracy,* celebrated for its delicate portrayal of drapery, and the landscapes that were his passion.

Sudbury has a train station with an hourly service to London (£24, 1¼ hours). There are regular buses to Ipswich (one hour), Long Melford, Lavenham, Bury St Edmunds and Colchester.

Lavenham

POP 1740

One of East Anglia's most beautiful and rewarding towns, the former wool trade centre of Lavenham is home to a wonderful collection of exquisitely preserved medieval buildings that lean and lurch to dramatic effect. Lavenham's 300 half-timbered and pargeted houses and thatched cottages have been left virtually untouched since the town's heyday in the 15th century, thanks to the zealous preservation efforts of the locals.

◉ Sights

Lavenham's most enchanting buildings are clustered along High St, Water St and around the unusually triangular Market Pl, dominated by the early-16th-century whitewashed Guildhall of Corpus Christi (NT; www.nationaltrust.org.uk/lavenham; adult/child £4.30/1.80; ⊘11am-5pm), a superb example of a close-studded, timber-framed building. It is now a local-history museum with displays on the wool trade and medieval guilds, and in its tranquil garden you can see dye plants that produced the typical medieval colours.

Also on Market Pl, the caramel-coloured 14th-century Little Hall (www.littlehall.org.uk; Market Pl; adult/child £3/free; ⊘2-5.30pm Wed, Thu, Sat & Sun Apr-Oct) was once home to a successful wool merchant. Inside, the rooms of this medieval gem had been restored to period splendour through the efforts of the Gayer-Anderson twins who made it their home in the 1920s and 1930s.

At the village's high southern end rises the Church of St Peter & St Paul (⊘8.30am-5.30pm), a late Perpendicular edifice that seems to lift into the sky, with its beautifully proportioned windows, soaring flint tower and gargoyle waterspouts. Built between 1485 and 1530, it was one of Suffolk's last great wool churches, completed on the eve of the Reformation, and now a lofty testament to Lavenham's past prosperity.

If you're visiting at a weekend it's well worth joining a guided village walk (tour £3; ⊙2.30pm Sat, 11am Sun) run by the tourist office (☎01787-248207; www.discoverlavenham .co.uk; Lady St; ⊙10am-4.45pm mid-Mar–Oct, Sat & Sun only Nov–mid-Mar).

🛏 Sleeping & Eating

TOP
CHOICE **Lavenham Priory**　　　B&B ££
(☎01787-247404;　www.lavenhampriory.co.uk; Water St; s/d from £87/120; P⊗) A rare treat, this sumptuously restored 15th-century B&B steals your heart as soon as you walk in the door. Each of the six Elizabethan rooms is a classic in its own right, with cavernous fireplaces, leaded windows, oak floors, original wall paintings, canopied four-poster beds and exquisite period features throughout. Book well in advance.

Swan Hotel　　　HOTEL £££
(☎01787-247477;　www.theswanatlavenham.co.uk; High St; d from £195; P⊗) A warren of stunning timber-beamed 15th-century buildings now shelters one of the region's best-known hotels. Rooms are suitably spectacular, some with immense fireplaces, colossal beams and magnificent four-posters, all without eschewing plasma-screen TVs. The Great Hall is an atmospheric place to try the modern English cuisine (three-course set dinner £38).

Guinea House　　　B&B ££
(☎01787-249046; www.guineahouse.co.uk; 16 Bolton St; d from £75) Wonderfully snug, salmon-coloured B&B with just two en-suite doubles with sloped ceilings and floral patterns. Full English breakfast included but credit cards are not accepted.

TOP
CHOICE **Great House**　　　FRENCH ££
(☎01787-247431; www.greathouse.co.uk; Market Pl; 3-course lunch/dinner £21/32; ⊙lunch Wed-Sat, dinner Tue-Fri; ⊗) Chic design blends effortlessly with 15th-century character at this much-loved restaurant in the centre of town. The decor in the five rooms is an effortless marriage between classic period features and contemporary design, with funky wallpaper, sleek furniture and plasma-screen TVs. The restaurant serves classic French dishes (three-course lunch/dinner £21/32) with a modern flourish.

❶ Getting There & Away

Regular bus 743 connects Lavenham with Bury St Edmunds (30 minutes) and Sudbury (20 minutes) hourly until 6pm Monday to Saturday.

Bury St Edmunds
POP 36,220

Bury has long attracted travellers for its powerful history: St Edmund, last Saxon king of East Anglia, was decapitated by the Danes in 869, and in 903 the martyr's body was reburied here, his grave becoming a site of pilgrimage and the core of one of the most powerful monasteries in medieval Europe. Then in 1214 the English barons chose the abbey as the place to draw up a petition that would form the basis of the Magna Carta, making it a 'Cradle of the Law' and setting the country on the road to a constitutional government.

These days, the town is a genteel kind of place, with atmospheric ruins, handsome Georgian architecture, tranquil gardens, a newly completed cathedral and the famous Greene King brewery.

⊙ Sights

Abbey & Park　　　RUIN
(⊙dawn-dusk) Now a picturesque ruin residing in beautiful gardens behind the cathedral, the once all-powerful abbey still impresses despite the townspeople having made off with much of the stone after the Dissolution. The Reformation also meant an end to the veneration of relics, and St Edmund's grave and bones have long since disappeared.

You enter the park via one of two well-preserved old gates: opposite the tourist office, the staunch mid-14th-century Great Gate is intricately decorated and ominously defensive, with battlements, portcullis and arrow slits. The other entrance sits further up Angel Hill, where a gargoyle-studded early 12th-century Norman Tower looms.

Just beyond the Great Gate is a peaceful garden where the Great Court was once a hive of activity, and further on a dovecote marks the only remains of the Abbot's Palace. Most impressive, however, are the remains of the western front, where the original abbey walls were burrowed into in the 18th century to make way for houses. The houses are still in use and look as if they have been carved out of the stone like caves. Nearby is Samson Tower and in front of it a beautiful statue of St Edmund by Dame Elisabeth Frink (1976). The rest of the abbey spreads eastward like a ragged skeleton, with various lumps and pillars hinting at its immense size.

St Edmundsbury Cathedral　　　CATHEDRAL
(www.stedscathedral.co.uk; St James, Angel Hill; requested donation £3; ⊙8.30am-6pm) Completed

in 2005, the 45m-high Millennium Tower is a vision in Lincolnshire limestone, and its traditional Gothic-style construction gives a good idea of how the towers of many other English cathedrals must have looked fresh from the stonemason's chisel.

Most of the rest of the building is from the early 16th century, though the eastern end is postwar 20th-century, and the northern side was completed in 1990. The overall effect is light and lofty, with a gorgeous hammerbeam roof and a striking sculpture of the crucified Christ by Dame Elisabeth Frink in the north transept. The impressive entrance porch has a tangible Spanish influence, a tribute to Abbot Anselm (1121–48), who opted against pilgrimage to Santiago de Compostela in favour of building a church dedicated to St James (Santiago in Spanish) right here.

Stop by the Treasury (Angel Hill; ⊙10am-4pm) in the cellar for a glimpse of church silver and ornate medieval Bibles.

For a more in-depth insight into the church's history and heritage join one of the guided tours (www.stedscathedral.co.uk; Angel Hill; ⊙11.30am Mon-Sat Apr-Sep) of the cathedral.

St Mary's Church
CHURCH

(www.stmarystpeter.net/stmaryschurch; Honey Hill; entry by donation; ⊙10am-4pm) With the longest nave of any parish church in England, St Mary's contains the tomb of Mary Tudor (Henry VIII's sister and a one-time queen of France). Built around 1430, it also has a host of vampire-like angels swooping from its roof, and a bell is still rung to mark curfew, as it was in the Middle Ages.

Greene King Brewery
BREWERY

(www.greeneking.co.uk; Crown St; tours day/evening £8/10, museum free; ⊙museum 10.30am-4.30pm Mon-Sat) Churning out some of England's favourite booze since Victorian times, this famous brewery runs popular daily tours, after which you can appreciate what all the fuss is about in its brewery bar. Even if you don't make the tour, you can check out the scale model of the brewery at the on-site museum, and learn about the history of beer.

Moyse's Hall Museum
MUSEUM

(www.stedmundsbury.gov.uk/moyseshall; Cornhill; adult/child £7.30/5.30; ⊙10am-5pm Mon-Sat, noon-4pm Sun; 🖫) In an impressive 12th-century undercroft, this enjoyable museum covers the important episodes in Bury's history, such as the Bury witch trials. There are also medieval dressing-up clothes to engage the kids and the ticket also allows entry to the West Stow Anglo-Saxon Village (Icklingham Rd; adult/child £6/4; ⊙10am-5pm), complete with actors in period costume.

🛏 Sleeping

TOP CHOICE Angel Hotel
HOTEL ££

(☎01284-714000; www.theangel.co.uk; 3 Angel Hill; r from £100; 🅿🖭) This famous old coaching inn has hosted dignitaries such as Charles Dickens (the 'Dickens room' remaining as it was, complete with four-poster bed). Rooms are split between a contemporary wing, with retro 'Impression' rooms, and a traditional Georgian building, with 'Classic' rooms. The modern restaurant has a stylish menu (mains £14 to £18), plus organic wines.

Fox Inn
HOTEL ££

(☎01284-705562; www.thefoxinnbury.co.uk; 1 Eastgate St; s/d from £89/95; 🖭) In a courtyard barn attached to Bury's oldest inn, the luxurious rooms here blend the warmth of exposed brick and beams with minimalist contemporary styling. The Fox is 600m from the cathedral. Head up Angel Hill, bear right at the end into Mustow St and on to Eastgate St.

🍴 Eating & Drinking

TOP CHOICE Pea Porridge
MODERN BRITISH ££

(☎01284-700200; www.peaporridge.co.uk; 28-29 Cannon Street; mains £13-20; ⊙Tue-Sat) Set in a 19th-century former bakery, this exciting newcomer on the Bury scene is responsible for some of the most memorable dishes in town, executed with imagination and flair. Expect the likes of curried sweetbreads with sweet potato, and grilled mackerel with Yorkshire champagne rhubarb, with attentive service to boot and beautiful presentation. All lunchtime mains are £11.95.

TOP CHOICE Maison Bleue
FRENCH £££

(☎01284-760623; www.maisonbleue.co.uk; 31 Churchgate St; mains £16-22; ⊙Tue-Sat) Muted colours, leather banquettes, white linen and contemporary style merge with a fish-heavy menu in this excellent French restaurant. The food, from the Colchester oysters to the Gressingham duck, is superb but not fussy, the service impeccable and the setting stylish yet relaxed. The three-course set lunch/dinner menu (£21/32) is a great way to enjoy it.

Old Cannon
MODERN BRITISH ££

(www.oldcannonbrewery.co.uk; 86 Cannon Street; mains £8-13) This working brewery serves some fantastic ales, such as the award-winning Black Pig and Gunner's Daughter. The 'cannon fodder' to accompany your brew comprises brasserie dishes such as deep-fried whitebait, poached smoked haddock and sausages with colcannon, with the ingredients sourced locally.

Nutshell PUB
(The Traverse) See how many of your friends you can squeeze into this thimble-sized timber-framed pub, recognised by the *Guinness Book of Records* as Britain's smallest (we think probably six people or so).

ℹ Information

Tourist office (☎01284-764667; tic@stedsbc .gov.uk; 6 Angel Hill; ☺9.30am-5pm Mon-Sat, 10am-3pm Sun)

ℹ Getting There & Around

BUS The central bus station is on St Andrew's St North.
Cambridge Stagecoach; bus 11, 65 minutes, hourly Monday to Saturday
London National Express; £16, 2½ hours, daily

TRAIN The train station is 900m north of the tourist office, with frequent buses to the centre.
Cambridge £9, 45 minutes, hourly
Ely £9, 30 minutes, every two hours

Aldeburgh

POP 2790
One of the region's most charming, time-warped towns, the small fishing and boat-building village of Aldeburgh has an understated charm. Handsome pastel-coloured houses, independent shops, art galleries and ramshackle fishing huts selling fresh catch line the High St, while a sweeping shingle beach stretches along the shore offering tranquil big-sky views.

Aldeburgh also has a lively cultural scene. Composer Benjamin Britten and lesser-known poet George Crabbe both lived and worked here; Britten founded East Anglia's primary arts and music festival, the Aldeburgh Festival (www.aldeburgh.co.uk; ☺Jun), which has been taking place for over 60 years at the Snape Maltings (www.snapemaltings .co.uk), a former malthouse turned concert hall 5 miles west of town. Britten's legacy is commemorated by Maggi Hambling's controversial 13ft-high steel *Scallop* sculpture, a short stroll north along the seashore.

In late September/early October, the Aldeburgh Food & Drink Festival (www.aldeburgh foodanddrink.co.uk) celebrates the best of Suffolk cooking at nearby Snape Maltings.

Aldeburgh's other photogenic gem is the intricately carved and timber-framed 16th-century Moot Hall (www.aldeburghmuseum .org.uk; adult/child £1/free; ☺2.30-5pm), which now houses a local history museum.

Information can be found at the tourist office (☎01728-453637; www.suffolkcoastal.gov .uk/tourism; 152 High St; ☺9am-5.30pm Mon-Sat, 10am-4pm Sun)

🛏 Sleeping & Eating

TOP CHOICE Ocean House B&B ££
(☎01728-452094; www.oceanhousealdeburgh.co .uk; 25 Crag Path; s/d £70/90) Right on the seafront and with only the sound of the waves to lull you to sleep at night, this beautiful Victorian guest house has three wonderfully cosy, period-style rooms. Expect pale pastels, subtle florals and tasteful furniture. There's a baby grand piano on the top floor, a gaily painted rocking horse, and bikes to borrow.

Dunan House B&B ££
(☎01728-452486; www.dunanhouse.co.uk; 41 Park Rd; d from £75; P🐾) Set well back off the street in lovely gardens, this charming B&B has a range of rooms mixing contemporary and traditional elements. With friendly hosts, and breakfast made from local, wild and home-grown produce, it's a real treat.

TOP CHOICE Lighthouse MODERN EUROPEAN ££
(☎01728-453377; www.lighthouserestaurant.co.uk; 77 High St; mains £11-16; 🍴) Rightly deserving the accolade of Aldeburgh's best restaurant, this unassuming bistro with casual decor welcomes you with friendly and knowledgeable service, and a menu looking to the sea for inspiration. The catch of the day is always a good bet, but the likes of slow-cooked pork belly with chilli jam and lentils don't lag far behind.

Regatta Restaurant SEAFOOD ££
(☎01728-452011; www.regattaaldeburgh.com; 171 High St; mains £13-21; ☺noon-2pm & 6-10pm) Sleek, contemporary restaurant where local fish is the main attraction. The celebrated owner-chef supplements his wonderful seafood with meat and vegetarian options and regular gourmet nights. Book ahead.

Fish & Chip Shop FISH & CHIPS £
(226 High Street; fish & chips £5-6; ☺noon-2pm & 5-8pm Mon-Sat, noon-7pm Sun) Aldeburgh has a

DUNWICH & RSPB MINSMERE

Strung along the coastline north of Aldeburgh is a poignant trail of serene and little-visited coastal heritage towns that are gradually succumbing to the sea. Most dramatically, the once-thriving port town of Dunwich is now an eerie village, its 12 medieval churches lost under the waves.

The region is a favourite haunt of the binocular-wielding birdwatcher brigade, and RSPB Minsmere (www.rspb.org.uk; Westleton; adult/child £5/1.50; ☉9am-dusk) flickers with feathered activity year-round. The reserve is home to one of England's rarest birds, the bittern, with hundreds of migrant birds paying a visit in autumn. Binoculars are available for rent and there are hides along the trails to facilitate bird-spotting.

With public transport lacking you'll need your own wheels, or the will to walk or bike this stretch of peaceful and varied coastline.

reputation for the finest fish and chips in the area, and this is the place that kick-started it.

❶ Getting There & Away

There are frequent bus services to Ipswich (1¼ hours), where you can make connections to the rest of the country.

Orford

Secluded and seductive, the gorgeous village of Orford, 6 miles south of Snape Maltings, is well worth a detour. It's a laid-back place littered with pretty houses and dominated by the odd polygonal keep of Orford Castle (EH; www.english-heritage.org.uk; adult/child £5.80/3.50; ☉10am-6pm Apr-Oct, Sat & Sun only Nov-Mar). The 12th-century castle is remarkably intact and has an innovative, 18-sided drum design with three square turrets. From the roof there are glorious views of Orford Ness (NT; www.nationaltrust.org.uk/orfordness; incl ferry crossing adult/child £7.50/4; ☉10am-2pm Tue-Sat Jul-Sep), the largest vegetated shingle spit in Europe. Once used as a secret military testing ground, it is now home to a nature reserve and many rare wading birds, animals and plants. Ferries run from Orford Quay: the last ferry departs at 2pm and returns from the reserve at 5pm.

On your return, make a beeline for the Butley Orford Oysterage (www.butleyorford oysterage.co.uk; mains £8-13), lauded locally for the fish and seafood they catch and smoke themselves, and get some goodies to take home with you from Pinney's, their shop by the harbour.

Southwold

POP 3860

Southwold's reputation as a well-heeled holiday getaway has earned it the nickname

'Kensington-on-Sea' after the upmarket London borough, and its lovely sandy beach, pebble-walled cottages, cannon-dotted clifftop and rows of beachfront bathing huts are all undeniably picturesque. Over the years the town has attracted many artists, including JMW Turner, Charles Rennie Mackintosh, Lucian Freud and Damien Hirst.

For most visitors Southwold's shorefront is the main attraction. Take time to amble along the promenade and admire the squat 19th-century lighthouse before ending up at the little pier (www.southwoldpier.co.uk), first built in 1899 but recently reconstructed. In the 'under the pier' show you'll find a quirky collection of slot machines, the likes of which you're not likely to have seen elsewhere.

The Coastal Voyager (www.coastalvoyager.co.uk) is on hand to whisk you off on a range of boat trips, including a 30-minute high-speed fun trip (adult/child £22/12), a leisurely river cruise to nearby Blythburgh, and a three-hour trip to Scroby Sands to see a seal colony and wind farm.

Inland, the Church of St Edmund (Church St; ☉9am-6pm) is worth a peek for its fabulous medieval screen and 15th-century bloodshot-eyed 'Southwold Jack' effigy (believed to be part of a clock), grumpily overlooking the church's rear. A mere stone's throw away is an old weavers' cottage that now houses the Southwold Museum (www.southwoldmuseum.org; 9-11 Victoria St; requested donation £3; ☉10.30am-noon & 2-4pm Aug, 2-4pm Apr-Oct), exploring Southwold's 1000-year old fishing industry, the explosive 132-ship and 50,000-men Battle of Solebay (1672), fought just off the coast, and the role of the sea – Southwold's livelihood and its destroyer.

You can also take an hour-long tour (£10) of the town's very own **Adnams Brewery** (www.adnams.co.uk; Adnams Pl), producer of six types of beer, as well as vodka and gin, followed by a 30-minute tutored beer tasting.

Southwold's liveliest event is the **Latitude Festival** held in Henham Park (5 miles west of town), combining an eclectic mix of music, literature, dance, drama and comedy with a stunning location.

The **tourist office** (☑01502-724729; www.visit-sunrisecoast.co.uk; 69 High St; ☺10am-5pm Mon-Sat, 11am-4pm Sun) has extensive accommodation listings.

🛏 Sleeping & Eating

TOP CHOICE/ **Sutherland House** HOTEL £££
(☑01502-724544; www.sutherlandhouse.co.uk; 56 High St; d £140-180; 🅿🛜) Each of the three individually styled boudoirs at this 15th-century house has its own unforgettable feature, be it pargeted ceilings, exposed beams or a free-standing bathtub. In contrast to the decor, gadgets are ultramodern and the top-notch restaurant (mains £11 to £19), reputedly the town's best, specialises in fish, with catch-of-the-day dishes reinvented daily.

Swan HOTEL £££
(☑01502-722186; www.adnams.co.uk; Market Sq; s/d from £110/165; 🐾) There's a timeless elegance to the public rooms at the Swan, where large fireplaces, grandfather clocks and old-fashioned lamps induce a kind of soporific calm within a splendid Georgian exterior. You can choose between similarly period-style rooms or the newly refurbished Lighthouse Rooms with garden views. The atmospheric restaurant serves a mainly fishy menu (mains £15 to £22).

Coasters MODERN BRITISH ££
(☑01502-724734; www.coastersofsouthwold.co.uk; 12 Queen St; mains £8-15; ☺closed Mon) Right on the main drag, this unassuming restaurant has a great reputation and a loyal local following. The menu is short but sweet, and every dish, from Thai green curry mussels to braised pork belly, is memorable. There is also a range of sandwiches and cakes for a light lunch. Book ahead for dinner.

❶ Getting There & Away

Bus connections are limited: catch one of the hourly services to Lowestoft (45 minutes) or Halesworth train station (30 minutes) and continue from there.

NORFOLK

Big skies, sweeping beaches, windswept marshes, meandering inland waterways and pretty flint houses make up the county of Norfolk. They say the locals have 'one foot on the land, and one in the sea' and you're never far from water here, whether it's the tranquil setting of rivers and windmills in the **Norfolk Broads** (☑610 734; www.broads-authority.gov.uk) or the wide sandy beaches, fishing boats and nature reserves along the coast. Meanwhile, in Norwich, the county's bustling capital, you'll find a remarkable cathedral and castle, medieval churches, a lively market and an excellent choice of pubs, clubs and restaurants.

Norwich

POP 121,550

The affluent and easygoing city of Norwich (pronounced 'norr-ich') is a rich tapestry of meandering laneways liberally sprinkled with architectural gems – spoils of the city's heyday at the height of the medieval wool boom. Though Norwich's history stretches back well over a thousand years, the city's golden age was during the Middle Ages, when it was England's most important city after London. A magnificent cathedral lords over it all from one end of the city centre and a sturdy Norman castle from the other. Around these two landmarks a series of leafy greens, grand squares, quiet lanes, crooked half-timbered buildings and a host of medieval churches pan out across this compact and artsy city. Meanwhile thriving markets, modern shopping centres, contemporary-art galleries and a young student population give the city an easygoing vibe that makes it one of the most appealing places in East Anglia. Add easy access to the Broads and sweeping beaches along the coast and you have an excellent base for touring the area.

⊙ Sights

Norwich is a fantastic city for sightseeing on foot, with winding laneways and narrow passageways criss-crossing the centre of town.

TOP CHOICE/ **Norwich Cathedral** CATHEDRAL
(www.cathedral.org.uk; admission by donation; ☺7.30am-6pm, Hostry 9.30am-4.30pm Mon-Sat) Norwich's most stunning landmark is the

Norwich

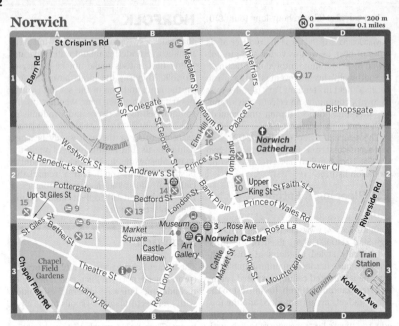

magnificent Anglican cathedral, its barbed spire soaring higher than any in England except Salisbury, while the size of its cloisters is second to none.

Begun in 1096, the cathedral is one of the finest Anglo-Norman abbey churches in the country, rivalled only perhaps by Durham. The sheer size of its nave is impressive, but its most renowned feature is the superb Gothic rib vaulting added in 1463. Among the spidery stonework are 1200 sculpted roof bosses depicting Bible stories. Together they represent one of the finest achievements of English medieval masonry.

Similar bosses can be seen in closer detail in the cathedral's remarkable cloisters. Built between 1297 and 1430, the two-storey cloisters are unique in England today and were originally built to house a community of about 100 monks.

Some features that perhaps you won't have been expecting: in the centre of the nave, above the bronze font (which came from a nearby chocolate factory), you'll find a 21st-century touch – Censing Angel (2012) – a suspended celestial figure woven out of willow branches by sculptor Joy Whiddett, trailing the words 'peace', 'hope' and 'love'.

Outside the cathedral's eastern end is the grave of the WWI heroine Edith Cavell, a Norfolk-born nurse who was executed for helping hundreds of Allied soldiers escape from German-occupied Belgium. The cathedral close also contains handsome houses and the old chapel of King Edward VI School (where English hero Admiral Nelson was educated). Its current students make up the choir, which performs in at least one of the three services held daily.

The visitor entrance to the cathedral is through the stunning new Hostry building – all glass and light – which rises within the walls of its original equivalent. Inside you can learn about the history and role of the cathedral. For a deeper insight join one of the guided tours (⊙10.45am, 12.30pm & 2.15pm); the tours are free but a donation is expected.

TOP CHOICE **Norwich Castle**   CASTLE
(www.museums.norfolk.gov.uk; castle & exhibitions adult/child £7/5; ⊙10am-5pm Mon-Sat, 1-5pm Sun; ♠) Perched on a hilltop overlooking central Norwich, this massive Norman castle keep is a sturdy example of 12th-century aristocratic living. The castle is one of the best-preserved examples of Anglo-Norman military architecture in the country.

Norwich

A gaol for five centuries, it's now home to an art gallery and superb interactive museum, approached across a bridge on which hangings were staged throughout Norwich's existence. The museum crams in a wealth of history, including lively exhibits on Boudica and the Iceni, the Anglo-Saxons and Vikings, natural history displays and even an Egyptian gallery. Every room is enlivened with plenty of fun for kids, but best of all is the atmospheric keep itself, which sends shivers down the spine, with graphic displays on grisly punishments meted out in its days as a medieval prison. Guided tours (adult/child £2.40/1.80) also run around the battlements (minimum age eight) and the creepy dungeons.

Meanwhile the art gallery houses paintings of the acclaimed 19th-century Norwich School of landscape painting founded by John Crome, and even if displays of ceramics normally make you glaze over, don't miss the world's largest collection of novelty teapots.

The Royal Norfolk Regimental Museum (www.rnrm.org.uk; Shirehall, Market Ave), which details the history of the local regiment since 1830, was in the process of being refurbished and moved at the time of writing.

Tombland & Elm Hill　HISTORIC NEIGHBOURHOOD
In the heart of the city, near the cathedral, lies leafy Tombland, where the market was originally located ('tomb' is an old Norse word for empty, hence space for a market). Cross over and follow Princes St to reach Elm Hill, Norwich's prettiest street, with its medieval cobblestones, crooked timber beams and doors, intriguing shops and tucked-away cafes.

FREE Sainsbury Centre for Visual Arts　GALLERY
(www.scva.org.uk; University of East Anglia; ◎10am-5pm Tue-Sun) Housed in the first major building by Norman Foster, in the University of East Anglia grounds, the Sainsbury Centre is the most important centre for the arts in East Anglia. It is filled with an eclectic collection of works by Picasso, Moore, Degas and Bacon, displayed beside an extensive collection of objects and curios from Africa, the Pacific and the Americas. Equally worthwhile are the temporary offerings, ranging from local heritage to international art movements.

The gallery is about 2 miles west of the city centre. To get here take bus 25, 26 or 35 from Castle Meadow (20 minutes).

Bridewell Museum　MUSEUM
(www.museums.norfolk.gov.uk; Bridewell Alley; adult/child £4.40/2.70; ⚐) The 14th-century bridewell, or 'prison for women, beggars and tramps', housed in a former merchant's house, has reopened after a grand facelift in July 2012. The museum focuses on key points in the city's history, such as its prominence as England's second city in the Middle Ages and its 19th-century industrial heritage. The displays include some wonderfully eccentric objects, such as the snake-proof boot, and the interactive displays in the Pharmacy are proving a hit with younger visitors.

CAMBRIDGE & EAST ANGLIA NORWICH

Dragon Hall
HISTORIC BUILDING

(www.dragonhall.org; 115-123 King St; adult/child £4.50/3.50; ⏱10am-4pm Tue-Thu, from noon Sun Apr-Oct) A remarkable medieval building, this magnificent trading hall dates from 1430 and is the only building of its kind to have belonged to one man – Robert Toppes – rather than a guild, suggesting that he was a successful 15th-century entrepreneur. The 1st-floor great hall has a stunning crown-post roof with a carved dragon figure, which gave the building its name, and the displays in the cellars, together with the audio guide, introduce you to the building's various incarnations. Guided tours are available at 2pm Tuesdays.

☞ Tours

Tourist Office
WALKING TOUR

(☏01603-213999; www.visitnorwich.co.uk; adult/child £4.50/1.80; ⏱11.30am or 2pm Thu-Sat Easter-Oct) The tourist office organises a dizzying array of guided tours, departing from outside the Forum, and has free downloadable pdf and audio city tours on its website.

Ghost Walks
WALKING TOUR

(☏07831-189985; www.ghostwalksnorwich.co.uk; adult/child £6/4; ⏱7.30pm Mon, Tue & Thu) A wonderful immersion in Norwich's haunted history; tours depart from the Adam & Eve pub.

Olde Norwich
HISTORICAL TOUR

(☏07917-664472; www.oldenorwich.co.uk; adult/child £6/3; ⏱2pm May-Oct) A 12-seater open-top charabanc drives you around town, taking in all 12 of Norwich's iconic buildings (www.norwich12.co.uk). Tours depart from Castle Meadow, outside Waterstones.

🛏 Sleeping

Gothic House
B&B ££

(☏01603-631879; www.gothic-house-norwich.com; Magdalen St, King's Head Yard; s/d £65/95; P🛜) This faithfully restored Grade II Regency house hidden away in a quiet courtyard in the heart of the city has just two rooms, but if period style is your thing, they are *the* place to be. From the fabrics and furnishings to the ornaments and mirrors, it's flush with character and charm. The rooms are bright and spacious, immaculately kept and each private bathroom is stocked with Molton Brown toiletries. To get here follow Wensum St north across the river into Magdalen St for 300m.

38 St Giles
B&B £££

(☏01603-662944; www.38stgiles.co.uk; 38 St Giles St; s/d from £90/130; P) Ideally located, beautifully styled and friendly, this boutique B&B is a gem. There are no airs and graces, just three handsome rooms with wooden floors, handmade rugs, fireplaces and a contemporary feel. Your gracious hosts prepare a sure contender for the best breakfast in Norwich – featuring granola, local and organic meats and eggs, and cinnamon pancakes.

St Giles House Hotel
HOTEL £££

(☏01603-275180; www.stgileshousehotel.com; 41-45 St Giles St; d £120-210; 🛜) In the heart of the city in a stunning 19th-century building, this large hotel has individually styled rooms. Rooms range from fashionably art deco to less personal modern decor. A good restaurant serves modern British menu (mains £13.50 to £22), plus there's a spa and terrace for cocktails. Light sleepers, ask for a room away from the road.

THE HAUNTING OF BLICKLING HALL NORWICH

Largely remodelled in the 17th century for Sir Henry Hobart, James I's chief justice, Blickling Hall (NT; www.nationaltrust.org.uk/blickling; Blickling; adult/child £10.95/5.35, garden only £7.65/3.85; ⏱house noon-5pm Wed-Mon, gardens 10am-5pm) began life in the 11th century as a manor house and bishop's palace. Today it is a grand Jacobean mansion set in vast parklands and as famous for its ghostly sightings as its spectacular Long Gallery.

In 1437 the isolated house was claimed by the Boleyn family and passed through the generations to Thomas, father of Anne Boleyn. Poor old Anne was executed by her husband Henry VIII in 1533, and it's said that on the anniversary of her death a coach drives up to the house, drawn by headless horses, driven by headless coachmen and containing the queen with her head on her lap.

If you're not around to witness the spectacle that day, there's still quite a lot to see. The grand state rooms are stuffed with fine Georgian furniture, pictures and tapestries, and the Long Gallery has an impressive Jacobean plaster ceiling.

Blickling Hall is 15 miles north of Norwich off the A140. Buses run twice hourly from Castle Meadow and Tombland in Norwich. Aylsham is the nearest train station, 1.5 miles away.

By Appointment HOTEL ££
(☑01603-630730; www.byappointmentnorwich.co.uk; 25-29 St George's St; s/d from £95/125; @) This fabulously theatrical and delightfully eccentric B&B occupies three heavy-beamed 15th-century merchants' houses, and is also home to a labyrinthine restaurant well known for its classic English fare. Its antique furniture, creaky charm and superb breakfasts make this well worth booking in advance.

No 15 B&B ££
(☑01603-250283; www.number15bedandbreakfast.co.uk; 15 Grange Rd; s/d £50/70; 🛜☑) There are just two cosy but uncluttered bedrooms at this serene B&B in a leafy residential street. The pastel-shade rooms have period satinwood furniture, white linens and good bathrooms; breakfasts are ample, vegetarian, organic and local; holistic massage is on offer; and your congenial host Ian makes the whole experience a home away from home. No 15 is about a mile west of the city centre. Bus 25 passes nearby.

Caversham House B&B ££
(☑01603-412726; www.caversham-house.co.uk; 108 Constitution Hill; s/d £42/75; 🛜) Though this friendly, understated guesthouse is a brisk 20-minute walk north of the centre, it's worth it for the warm welcome from June and Don, who gladly share their knowledge of Norwich. The three rooms are snug en-suites decked out in neutral shades, and a continental breakfast is included. Follow Magdalen St north of the centre and keep going straight.

✕ Eating

Roger Hickman's MODERN BRITISH £££
TOP CHOICE
(☑01603-633522; www.rogerhickmansrestaurant.com; 79 Upper St Giles St; 2-/3-course set menu lunch £18/21, dinner £33/38; ☉Tue-Sat) Understated, classic elegance is what this place is all about: pale floorboards, white linen, bare walls and professional, unobtrusive service. In fact, there's nothing to distract you from the top-quality dishes such as smoked venison with fig chutney or spring lamb with sweetbreads, made with flair, imagination and a simple dedication to quality.

Farmer Browns MODERN BRITISH ££
TOP CHOICE
(☑01603-628542; www.farmerbrowns.co.uk; 22 Tombland; mains £10-18) This excellent newcomer is making quite a reputation for itself, thanks to its commitment to Norfolk ingredients and an ever-changing, creative menu. The lunchtime menu is a bargain, the service is friendly and efficient, and you can expect the likes of Bingham blue and apricot gnocchi, pigeon breast with Turkish delight, or anything else that Stuart the chef concocts.

Library MODERN EUROPEAN ££
(www.thelibraryrestaurant.co.uk; 1a Guildhall Hill; mains £10-15; ☉closed dinner Sun) We don't normally encourage people to eat in a library, but for this 19th-century library, housing a chilled-out brasserie, we'll make an exception. The menu is heavy on imaginative meat and fish dishes using locally sourced produce, such as Lowestoft haddock and oysters, but there are few dishes to tempt vegetarians. No one should skip out on the Eton Mess.

BamBam ASIAN ££
(☑01603-665660; www.mybambam.co.uk; 27-28 Tombland; mains £12-15; ☉dinner Tue-Sat) Part glam bar, part innovative Asian restaurant, BamBam still seems to be trying to establish its identity. The eccentric menu sounds like a concoction of a mad genius: how about a 16-course spoon-tasting menu of bite-sized delights? Or sweetcorn soup with tuna terrine and ice cream? Whatever you pick, it's guaranteed to be memorable.

Greenhouse VEGETARIAN £
(www.greenhousetrust.co.uk; 42-48 Bethel St; snacks & mains £4-7.50; ☉10am-5pm Tue-Sat;☑) This organic, free-trade, vegetarian/vegan cafe is bound to leave you feeling wholesome, with a menu of simple dishes such as hearty soups, noticeboards crammed with posters for community events, and a lovely vine-covered, herb-planted terrace.

Mustard CAFE £
(Bridewell Alley; breakfast £4.50-6; ☉9am-6pm Tue-Sat) On the very spot where the original Colman's Mustard shop once stood, this funky little cafe proudly carries on with the theme, with flashes of bright yellow throughout. The coffees are decent, the breakfast menu features some unusual items, such as *huevos rancheros* (Mexican-style eggs with salsa), and the changing daily lunch items include the likes of hearty lasagne.

Tea House TEAROOM £
(5 Wrights Crt, Elm Hill; tea £2.50; ☉9am-5pm Mon-Sat) This compact, friendly tearoom in a tiny courtyard makes a great stop for tea and scones.

Drinking

It was once said that Norwich had a pub for every day of the year, and although that may not be completely true, there's certainly plenty of choice. Start your quest in Tombland or St Benedict's St for a taste of what's on offer.

Adam & Eve   PUB

(www.adamandevenorwich.co.uk; Bishopsgate) Norwich's oldest-surviving pub, Adam & Eve have been on that same spot since biblical times (OK, since at least 1249, when it was built to quench the thirst of the cathedral builders). It's a tiny place with a sunken floor and a mixed clientele of regulars, choristers and ghost hunters. There's even a 'spooky' meal-and-ghost-walk deal, to top the already enticing selection of ales, bitters and malt whiskies.

Fat Cat   PUB

(49 West End St) There are 32 real ales here, including their own Marmalade Cat and lesser-known gems like Spectrum Trip Hazard and Burton Bridge Stairway to Heaven. Head west from the centre along St Benedict's St, which merges into Dereham Rd at the junction. Follow the road for another 600m, then turn right into Nelson St and right again into West End St.

Information

Tourist office (☑01603-213999; www.visit norwich.co.uk; The Forum; ☺9.30am-6pm Mon-Sat, to 2.30pm Sun) Just inside the Forum.

Getting There & Around

Norwich has free parking at six Park & Ride locations. Buses (£2.30) run to the city centre up to every 15 minutes from 6.40am to 7.50pm.

AIR **Norwich International Airport** (www .norwichinternational.com), four miles north of town; has cheap flights to Europe and several British destinations.

BUS The bus station is on Queen's Rd 400m south of the castle. Follow Red Lion St into Stephen's St and then turn left onto Surrey St. **National Express** (www.nationalexpress.com) and **First Eastern Counties** (www.firstgroup .com) run services:

Cromer £5, one hour, hourly

King's Lynn £8.60, 1½ hours, hourly

London £18, three hours, seven daily

TRAIN The train station is off Thorpe Rd, 600m east of the castle.

Cambridge £21, 1¼ hours, twice hourly

Ely £15, one hour, twice hourly

London Liverpool Street £30, two hours, twice hourly

North Coast Norfolk

The north coast of Norfolk has something of a split personality, with a string of busy seaside towns with brash attractions and hordes of people clustering along the eastern end, and a collection of small villages with trendy gastropubs and boutique hotels scattered about the western end. In between sit vast sandy beaches and the marshy coast that attracts numerous bird species, including oystercatchers, plovers, curlews and brent geese.

The Coasthopper bus (www.coasthopper .co.uk) runs from Cromer to Hunstanton, serving Cley, Blakeney, Wells, Holkham, Burnham Deepdale and (with a connection) King's Lynn.

CROMER
POP 3800

Once a thriving medieval port, taking the place of the village of Shipden which was claimed by the sea (ships have been wrecked here on underwater church spires!), and then a fashionable Victorian coastal resort, Cromer is slowly becoming gentrified again after years of degeneration into a glut of fish-and-chip shops and trashy amusement arcades. Its main attractions are Cromer crabs, the atmospheric pier and its appealing stretch of sandy beachfront.

The Rocket Cafe (The Gangway; mains £4-10; ☺10am-5pm daily, dinner Sat), which shares the new RNLI building on the waterfront with the Lifeboat Museum, has an airy interior and outdoor terrace overlooking the water, nicely complementing the heaped Cromer crab platters, soups and sandwiches.

Just 2 miles southwest of town off the B1436 is Felbrigg Hall (NT; www.nationaltrust. org.uk; adult/child £7.80/3.65; ☺11am-5pm Sat-Wed Mar-Oct), an elegant Jacobean mansion that once belonged to the Windham family, with a fine Georgian interior and splendid facade. The walled gardens and orangery are particularly lovely, with access to the Weavers Way running through the estate.

Cromer has direct trains to Norwich hourly Monday to Saturday and services every two hours on Sunday (£6, 45 minutes). The Coasthopper bus runs from Cromer west along the coast roughly every half-hour in summer.

CLEY MARSHES

One of England's premier birdwatching sites, the Cley Marshes Nature Reserve (pronounced 'cly') is a mecca for twitchers, with more than 300 bird species recorded here – numerous waders, as well as plentiful migrant species passing through – and a network of walking trails leading to a series of hides hidden amid the golden reed beds. There's a visitor centre (www.norfolkwildlifetrust.org.uk; adult/child £5/free; ◑10am-5pm) built on high ground across the A149, where you pay the entrance fee, pick up trail maps and rent binoculars.

You can pick up some fantastic picnic food in the village of Cley, just west of the reserve. The renowned Cley Smokehouse (◑01263-740282; ◑9am-5pm) is the place for all manner of locally smoked fish and meats, while the Picnic Fayre (◑9am-5pm) across the road, is a superb deli featuring great breads, cheeses, homemade pork pies and cakes, Norfolk ice cream, jams and chutneys. If you don't suffer from the Don Quixote syndrome, a substantial dinner is to be had at the 17th-century Cley Windmill (◑01263-740209; www.cleymill.co.uk; set dinner menu £32, d £89-189), with the chef working wonders with seasonal produce. One of the most unique places to sleep (◑01263-740209; www.cleymill.co.uk; d £80-165) in East Anglia, it has nine bedrooms with four-poster, half-tester or cast-iron beds (the room at the top reached by ladder alone), a circular living room, and views across the marshes.

BLAKENEY POINT

The pretty village of Blakeney was once a busy fishing and trading port before its harbour silted up. These days it has an inviting seafront walk, lined with yachts, and is a good place to jump aboard boat trips out to a 500-strong colony of common and grey seals that live, bask and breed on nearby Blakeney Point. Several companies, including Bishop's Boats (www.norfolksealtrips.co.uk; Blakeney Harbour), and Beans Boat Trips (www.beansboattrips.co.uk; Morston) run hour-long trips (adult/child £9/5) daily from April to October, but the best time to come is between June and August when the common seals pup.

The best place to eat in town is the Moorings (www.themoorings.co.uk; High St; sandwiches £6, dinner mains £14-20; ◑closed dinner Sun & Mon), with cheery decor suggestive of summer and beaches, wonderfully attentive service and a menu featuring Poseidon's subjects (though the likes of seared pigeon breast

sneak in too); don't miss the puddings. The Kings Arms (◑01263-740341; www.blakeneykingsarms.co.uk; Westgate St; d £75), a traditional pub, sits just back from the quay, and its seven modest en-suite rooms with low, beamed ceilings make for a peaceful stay.

WELLS-NEXT-THE-SEA
POP 2450

Thronged with crowds on holiday weekends, what used to be an important port in the 16th and 17th centuries is now a tranquil old town a mile or so from the water, with curio shops lining its tiny main drag, Staithe St, attractive Georgian houses and flint cottages surrounding a large green, and a long stretch of beach flanked by pine-covered dunes.

The steam train that plies this 10¼ narrow-gauge railway (www.wellswalsingham railway.co.uk; adult/child return £8.50/7; ◑3-5pm daily Apr-Oct) – the longest of its kind in the world – huffs its way for 5 miles to Little Walsingham (www.walsingham.org.uk), where there are shrines and a ruined abbey that used to rival Canterbury and Bury St Edmunds for the most important pilgrimage site in England, due to the popularity of its Chapel of Our Lady of Walsingham. The picturesque journey takes 45 minutes.

If staying overnight, the Wells YHA (◑0845-371 9544; www.yha.org.uk; Church Plains; dm £17; [P]) has simple rooms in an ornately gabled early 20th-century church hall. If you prefer to rough it right by the beach, Pinewoods Holiday Park (◑01328-710439; www.pinewoods.co.uk; per tent site £20; 4-bed lodge per week £1290; [P]) has attractive tent sites and rudimentary beach huts (with no facilities) scattered among the pines and assorted shrubbery. Bike hire and water sports are available and a tiny railway connects the site to Wells. In Wells proper, the Crown (www.thecrownhotelwells.co.uk), a former coaching inn, is renowned locally for its robust dishes made from locally sourced ingredients.

The small tourist office (◑01328-710885; www.visitnorthnorfolk.com; Staithe St; ◑10am-5pm Mon-Sat, to 1pm Sun Apr-Oct) can help with all inquiries.

The Coasthopper bus goes through Wells roughly half-hourly in summer on its way between Cromer (one hour) and King's Lynn (1½ hours).

HOLKHAM

The pretty village of Holkham is dominated by Holkham Hall and Estate (www.holkham.co.uk; adult/child £12/6, parking £2.50; ◑noon-4pm

EXPLORING THE NORFOLK BROADS

Why Should I Wish To Visit a Swamp?

These vast wetlands, formed when the Rivers Wensum, Bure, Waveney and Yare flooded the big gaping holes inland, dug by 12th-century crofters looking for peat, comprise fragile ecosystems and, protected as a national park, are home to some of the UK's rarest plants and birds, so the appeal to twitchers and naturalists is obvious. Apart from that, if you've ever envisioned yourself captaining your own boat and living as a 'boat person', there are 125 miles of lock-free waterways to explore. And if you enjoy paddling a solitary canoe and losing yourself in the hypnotic lapping of the water away from the rest of humanity, there's plenty of scope for that, too.

What Is There to See and Do That Doesn't Involve Water?

The Museum of the Broads (www.northnorfolk.org/museumofthebroads; Staithe; adult/child £4/3.50; ☺10.30am-5pm Easter-Oct), 5 miles north of Potter Heigham off the A149, teaches you about the marshmen who lived in the area, their traditional lifestyles, peat extraction and modern conservation.

If you want to delve deeper into the life of a fen dweller, the tiny Toad Hole Cottage (How Hill; ☺9.30am-6pm Jun-Sep, 10.30am-1pm & 1.30-5pm Apr, May & Oct) shows how the eel-catcher's family lived and the tools they used to work the marshes around them.

The more frivolous Bewilderwood (www.bewilderwood.co.uk; Hornig Rd, Hoveton; adult/child £13.50/10.50; ☺10am-5.30pm Mar-Oct) is a forest playground for children and adults alike, with zip wires, jungle bridges, tree houses and all sorts of old-fashioned outdoor adventure involving plenty of mud, mazes and marsh walks.

The Broads' most impressive ecclesiastical attraction is the 14th-century St Helen's Church (Ranworth; ☺8am-7pm), known locally as the 'Cathedral of the Broads', and which dominates the pretty village of Ranworth and features a magnificent painted medieval rood screen and a 15th-century antiphoner – a rare illustrated book of prayers.

Finally, siderodromophiles will love the Bure Valley Steam Railway (www.bvrw.co.uk; adult/child £8.50/6; ☺Feb-Oct) – a narrow-gauge steam train that runs between Aylsham and Wroxham.

How Do I Get There?

Driving around the Broads is missing the point and pretty useless. The main centres in the Broads – Wroxham, on the A1151 from Norwich, and Potter Heigham, on the A1062 from

Sun, Mon & Thu Apr-Oct), a somewhat severe Palladian mansion, largely unadorned on the outside, set in a vast deer park designed by William Kent. This is the ancestral seat of the original Earl of Leicester and still belongs to his descendants.

The interior is sumptuous yet restrained by the standards of the day, with a red velvet-lined saloon, copies of Greek and Roman statues, the fluted columns of the Marble Hall and the luxury of the Green State Bedroom where kings and queens have stayed.

You can also visit the Bygones Museum (museum only adult/child £7/3.50; ☺10am-5pm Apr-Oct) in the stable block. It has over 4000 exhibits – everything from mechanical toys to vintage cars and steam engines.

For many, Holkham's true delight is the other part of the estate – the Holkham National Nature Reserve, comprising the vast expanse of almost pristine beach of Holkham Bay, its air permeated with the aroma of pine forest, and a chunk of woodland with ribboning pathways leading to hides where you can spot some of the shy wildlife. Regularly voted one of England's best, the reserve is a popular spot with walkers and you can reach nearby villages by following the signposted seafront paths. The only place to park for access to the beach is Lady Anne's Drive (parking per hr from £2).

The Coasthopper bus goes through Holkham roughly half-hourly in summer.

BURNHAM DEEPDALE

In-the-know backpackers and walkers flock to this lovely coastal spot, with its tiny twin villages of Burnham Deepdale and Brancaster Staithe strung along a rural road. Stroked by the beautiful Norfolk Coastal

Wroxham – are reachable by bus from Norwich and Great Yarmouth, respectively, and from there you can either take to the water or to the trails.

Exploring By Boat

Taking to the water gives you the most freedom and you'll find numerous boat rental outlets.

You can hire a variety of launches (full tuition given), from large cabin cruisers to little craft with outboards, for anything from a couple of hours' gentle messing about on the water to a week-long trip. Depending on boat size, facilities and season, a boat costs from around £65 for four hours, £110 for one day, from £650 to £1300 for a week, including fuel and insurance. If you don't want to drive your own, you can choose anything from hour-long jaunts on the water to multiday boat holidays. Broads Tours (www.broads.co.uk) takes care of both, while Boats for the Broads (www.dayboathire.com) and Barnes Brinkcraft (www.barnesbrinkcraft.co.uk) arrange short-term rental from Wroxham, and Blakes (www.blakes.co.uk) arranges all manner of boating holidays.

Exploring by Canoe

Solitary paddlers can find canoes for hire in different spots around the Broads for around £38 per day; Rowan Craft (www.rowancraft.com; Geldeston) and Waveney River Centre (www.waveneyrivercentre.co.uk; Burgh St Peter) come recommended. Mark the Canoe Man (www.thecanoeman.com; half-day trip £25-45) knows the secrets of the Broads and arranges day and overnight guided trips to areas the cruisers can't reach, as well as canoe and kayak hire, weekend camping canoe trails (two nights £70), bushcraft courses (two days £140) and the paddle steamer – paddling one way, then taking the steam train back (from £50).

Exploring by Foot/Bike

Walkers and cyclists will also find a web of trails crossing the region, including the 56-mile Weavers' Way that stretches from Cromer to Great Yarmouth, taking in some choice parts of the landscape along the way. The Broads' highest point, How Hill, is just 12m above sea level, so superhero levels of fitness are not required. There are numerous bike rental points along the way; these include Broadland Cycle Hire (www.norfolkbroadscycling.co.uk; Bewilderwood, Hoveton) and Clippesby (www.clippesby.com; Clippesby). Bikes cost about £16 per day (you can also hire child seats and tandems).

Path, surrounded by beaches and reedy marshes, alive with bird life and criss-crossed by cycling routes, Burnham Deepdale is also a base for a whole host of water sports.

Ecofriendly, well-run Deepdale Farm (☏01485-210256; www.deepdalefarm.co.uk; site per adult/child £9/5, dm/d £15/60, 2-person tepees/yurts £80/95; P@🖳) is a backpacker haven. It has spotless en-suite rooms set in converted 17th-century stables, as well as camping space and glamping options in the form of Native American–style tepees and Mongolian yurts. There's a large kitchen and lounge area, picnic tables, a barbecue and a laundry and cafe next door.

The hostel also operates a tourist office (☏01485-210256; ⊙10am-4pm), the best place to go to organise kitesurfing or windsurfing on nearby beaches. Bike hire is also available (half-/full day £10/16).

Just west of the hostel is the award-winning White Horse (☏01485-210262; www.whitehorse brancaster.co.uk; mains £10-14, s/d from £95/150; P🖳), a gastropub with a menu strong on seafood; the tapas-style dishes, featuring brown potted shrimp, seared tuna, tempura mackerel and more set it apart from its competitors. The guest rooms upstairs embody the seaside with their subtle colour scheme.

The Coasthopper bus stops outside Deepdale Farm roughly half-hourly in summer.

King's Lynn

POP 34,570

Once one of England's most important ports, King's Lynn was long known as 'the Warehouse on the Wash'. It was said you could cross from one side of the River Great Ouse to the other by simply stepping from boat to boat in its heyday. Something of the salty port-town tang can still be felt in old King's Lynn, with its cobbled lanes, narrow streets flanked by old merchants' houses and vibrant weekly markets.

◉ Sights

St Margaret's Church   CHURCH
(www.stmargaretskingslynn.org.uk; Margaret Plain) A patchwork of architectural styles, this church is worth a look for its two extraordinarily elaborate Flemish brasses. You can also see a remarkable 17th-century moon dial, which tells the tide, not the time. You'll find historic flood-level markings by the west door. Opposite is the 1421 Trinity Guildhall, with an attractive stone facade.

Old Gaol House   MUSEUM
(Saturday Market Pl; adult/child £3.20/2.20, Regalia Room free; ⊙10am-4pm Wed-Sat Apr-Oct; 🚹) Explore the old cells and hear grisly tales of smugglers, witches and highwaymen in the town's old jail. The Regalia Room houses the town civic treasures, including the 650-year-old King John Cup, exquisitely decorated with scenes of hunting and hawking.

Lynn Museum   MUSEUM
(www.museums.norfolk.gov.uk; Market St; adult/child £3.60/2; ⊙10am-5pm Tue-Sat; 🚹) The town's main museum features displays on maritime life in Lynn and West Norfolk history; highlights include a large hoard of Iceni gold coins and the Seahenge gallery, which showcases a 4000-year-old timber circle which has miraculously survived intact and explores the lives of the Bronze Age people who created it.

Green Quay   MUSEUM
(www.thegreenquay.co.uk; South Quay; admission free; ⊙9am-5pm; 🚹) This fantastic interactive museum introduces you to the wildlife, flora and fauna of the area through a mix of displays, videos and freshwater tank holding some denizens of the Wash (the estuary),

with sensitive exhibitions on the effects of climate change and how to preserve the fragile local ecosystems.

True's Yard   MUSEUM
(www.truesyard.co.uk; North St; adult/child £3/1.50; ⊙10am-4pm Tue-Sat) Housed in two restored fishermen's cottages – the only remainder of the bustling, fiercely independent fishing community that once lived in this part of the city – this museum looks at the traditions and difficult life of the fishermen and their families, who were packed into cottages such as these like sardines.

✯✯ Festivals & Events

Festival Too   MUSIC
(www.festivaltoo.co.uk; ⊙Jul) A free rock-and-pop bash featuring the likes of Lemar, The Stranglers and Atomic Kitten, and attracting upwards of 10,000 people.

King's Lynn Festival   CULTURE
(www.kingslynnfestival.org.uk; ⊙Jul) East Anglia's most important cultural gathering, with a diverse program of concerts and recitals of all kinds, from medieval ballads to opera, as well as literary talks.

🛏 Sleeping & Eating

🍴 Bank House   B&B ££
(☎01553-660492; www.thebankhouse.co.uk; King's Staithe Sq; s/d from £80/100; 🅿⚡) Overlooking the water, the 18th-century former bank is now an elegantly furnished townhouse with five luxurious rooms, mixing exposed beams with modern furnishings and nice touches, such as Molton Brown toiletries. There's also a lovely, modern brasserie (mains £8 to £17) serving seriously good British food, including hefty lunchtime sandwiches (£5), made from locally sourced ingredients.

🍴 Market Bistro   MODERN BRITISH ££
(☎01553-771483; www.marketbistro.co.uk; 11 Saturday Market Pl; 2-/3-course lunch menu £12/15;

WORTH A TRIP

TITCHWELL MARSH NATURE RESERVE

Just west of Burnham Deepdale is tiny Titchwell, whose primary attraction is the Titchwell Marsh Nature Reserve (parking £4; ⊙dawn-dusk) comprising some choice marshland, sandbars and lagoons which attract numerous sea birds and waders. If you wish to linger, Titchwell Manor (☎01485-210221; www.titchwellmanor.com; Titchwell; d £130-250, mains £10-18; 🅿⚡) is a slick contemporary hotel set in a grand Victorian house with modern British cuisine, and there's a large garden popular with children.

SANDRINGHAM HOUSE

Royalists and those bemused by the English sovereigns will have plenty to mull over at this, the Queen's country estate (www.sandringhamestate.co.uk; adult/child £11.50/5.50, gardens & museum only £8.50/4.50; ⊘11am-4.30pm Apr-Oct), set in 25 hectares of beautifully landscaped gardens, and open to the public when the royal family is not in residence.

Queen Victoria bought the 8000-hectare estate in 1862 for her son, the Prince of Wales (later Edward VII), but he promptly had it overhauled in the style later named Edwardian.

Visitors can wander around the ground-floor rooms – all regularly used by the royal family, from the sumptuous dining room and the royal rifle room, to the Big Game Room, which represents the royal family's contribution to the demise of various endangered species. Head out to the old stables, which house a flag-waving museum filled with diverse royal memorabilia. The superb royal vintage-car collection includes the very first royal motor from 1900 and the buggy in which the Queen Mother would bounce around race tracks.

There are guided tours (⊘ 11am & 2pm Wed & Sat) of the gardens. The shop is also worth a visit for the organic goodies produced on the sprawling estate.

Sandringham is 6 miles northeast of King's Lynn off the B1440. Take Hunstanton-bound bus 10 or 11 from the bus station (30 minutes, hourly).

⊘Mon-Sat) This friendly, family-run place has been winning a lot of fans with its commitment to Norfolk ingredients such as Cromer crab, locally smoked fish and samphire from the marshes, not to mention their inventive seasonal dishes. These all-rounders make their own ice cream too.

❶ Information

Tourist office (☎01553-763044; www.visit westnorfolk.com; Purfleet Quay; ⊘10am-5pm Mon-Sat, from noon Sun) Housed in the lovely 17th-century Custom House, the tourist office arranges guided walks (adult/child £4.50/1.50) at 2pm Tuesdays, Fridays and Saturdays in high season. There's an engaging exhibition here (£1.50) on King's Lynn's maritime days.

❶ Getting There & Away

There are hourly trains from Cambridge (£9, 50 minutes) via Ely and London Kings Cross (£31, 1¾ hours). **Coasthopper 1** (www.coasthopper. co.uk) bus runs to Hunstanton (35 minutes, hourly) and connects with the Coasthopper 2 service, which runs along the north Norfolk coast. Services are frequent from April to September, less so the rest of the year.

Around King's Lynn

CASTLE RISING CASTLE

There's something bordering on ecclesiastical about the beautifully embellished keep of this castle (www.castlerising.co.uk; adult/child £4/2.50; ⊘10am-6pm Apr-Nov), built in 1138

and set in the middle of a massive earthwork upon which pheasants scurry about like guards. So extravagant is the stonework that it's no surprise to learn that it shares stonemasons with some of East Anglia's finest cathedrals. It was once the home of Queen Isabella, who (allegedly) arranged the gruesome murder of her husband, Edward II.

It's well worth the trip 4 miles northeast of King's Lynn off the A149. Bus 41 runs here (15 minutes) hourly from the King's Lynn bus station.

HOUGHTON HALL

Built for Britain's first de facto Prime Minister Sir Robert Walpole in 1730, the grand Palladian-style Houghton Hall (www.houghton hall.com; adult/child £10/3.50; ⊘house 1.30-5pm, grounds 11.30am-5.30pm Wed, Thu & Sun Easter-Sep) is worth seeing for the ornate staterooms alone. The sumptuous interiors are overflowing with gilt, tapestries, velvets and period furniture, but the most remarkable thing about Houghton Hall is not actually there: Sir Robert Walpole's grandson sold the estate's splendid art collection to Catherine the Great of Russia as part of the estate's accumulated debt, and those paintings formed part of the basis for the world-renowned collection at the State Hermitage in St Petersburg.

Even when the house is closed, the surrounding grounds, home to 600 deer, make for pleasant rambling. Houghton Hall is just off the A148 on the way from Kings Lynn to Cromer.

Birmingham, the Midlands & the Marches

Best Places to Eat

» Chequers Inn (p451)

» Simpsons (p401)

» Church Street Townhouse (p412)

» Reform (p450)

» Hammer & Pincers (p463)

Best Places to Stay

» Hotel du Vin (p400)

» Hart's (p441)

» Hotel Maiyango (p459)

» George Hotel (p452)

» Hambleton Hall (p462)

Why Go?

Few other places in the country come so close to the dream of England as the country's heart. If you're searching for green valleys and chocolate-box villages of wonky timbered houses, the legend surrounding Nottingham's Robin Hood, or stately homes that look like the last lord of the manor just clip-clopped out of the stables, you'll find them here. You'll also find the relics of centuries of industrial history, best exemplified by the World Heritage–listed mills of Ironbridge and the Derwent Valley; dynamic cities including England's second-largest, Birmingham, an industrial crucible reinvented as cultural melting pot; and tumbling hills where the air is so clean you can taste it. Walkers and cyclists flock to these areas, particularly the Peak District National Park and the Shropshire Hills, to vanish into the vastness of the landscape.

When to Go

February and March see the wonderful chaos of Shrovetide football in Ashbourne. Literary buffs take note: Shakespeare takes a back seat to contemporary wordsmiths at Stratford's Literary Festival in April/May. If you're up for a belt-loosening, belly-stretching good time, head to Ludlow's famous Food and Drink Festival in September.

On weekends from April to September, Shropshire Hills Shuttles provides access to wonderful walking trails on the Long Mynd and the Shropshire Hills, and June to September is the peak season for walking and cycling in the Peak District.

Activities

The rugged hills of the Peak District are the Midlands' number-one spot to get in touch with nature. Famous walking trails such as the Pennine Way and Limestone Way struggle across the hills, while cyclists pit determination and muscle against such challenging routes as the Pennine Cycleway (NCN 68) from Derby to Buxton. Other activities include caving and rock-climbing.

Tracing the border between England and Wales, the lush green hills of the Marches are scattered with ruined castles, and the exposed summits of the highest hills offer views to match anything in the Peak and Lakes. Top spots for walking and cycling include the Long Mynd and Stiperstones in Shropshire, the Malvern Hills in Worcestershire and the area around Symonds Yat in Herefordshire.

Sailors, windsurfers and water babies of all ages and levels of experience flock to Rutland Water near Leicester, while canoeing and kayaking are popular diversions in Hereford and Symonds Yat, and hang-gliders and paragliders launch from the hills above Church Stretton in Shropshire.

ℹ️ Getting There & Around

Birmingham Airport (☎0871 222 0072; www .birminghamairport.co.uk) and **East Midlands Airport** (☎0871 919 9000; www.eastmidlands airport.com) near Derby are the main air hubs.

There are excellent rail connections to towns across the Midlands. **National Express** (☎08718 81 81 81; www.nationalexpress.com), at Birmingham Coach Station, and local bus companies connect larger towns and villages, though services are reduced in the low season. For general route information, consult **Traveline** (☎0871 200 2233; www.travelinemidlands. co.uk) or visit www.networkwestmidlands.com. Ask locally about discounted all-day tickets.

BIRMINGHAM

POP 977,087

Once a byword for bad town planning, England's second-largest city – known to locals as 'Brum' – is shaking off the legacy of industrial decline, and spending some serious money replacing its drab 1960s concrete architecture with gleaming glass and steel. The town centre looks better than it has done in decades, helped in no small part by the revitalised Bullring shopping mall and the iconic Selfridges building, which looks out over the city like the compound eye of a giant robot insect.

With its industrial legacy and chaotic road network, Birmingham might not leap out as a tourist attraction, but there's a lot to see, including some fine museums and galleries, while the nightlife and food are the best in the Midlands. Sleek Modern British restaurants dominate in the centre, while the 'burbs were the birthplace of the balti – England's unique contribution to the world of curry, invented by Pakistani workers who moved here in the 1970s.

History

Birmingham was first mentioned in the Domesday Book of 1086, where it was described as a small village, home to a handful of villagers and two ploughs, with a total value of £1. From these humble beginnings, Brum exploded into a bustling industrial and mercantile hub, building its fortunes first on the wool trade and then on metalworking from the 16th century.

In the mid-18th century, the Lunar Society brought together the leading geologists, chemists, scientists, engineers and theorists of the age and Birmingham became the world's first industrialised town, attracting a tide of workers from across the nation.

A degree of salvation came in the mid-1800s, when enlightened mayors such as Joseph Chamberlain (1836–1914) cleaned out the slums and filled the centre with grand civic buildings. Sadly, little evidence of this golden age remains today thanks to WWII bombers and overzealous town planning. Vast swaths of the centre were demolished in a bid to transform Birmingham into 'Britain's Motor City'.

Whatever the mistakes of the past, recent years have seen a series of successful regeneration projects as part of the 'Big City Plan', with 21st-century landmarks appearing all over the city.

🔵 Sights

Every Sunday from May to October, a free history bus runs around Birmingham's museums, stopping at the Birmingham Museum & Art Gallery, Soho House, Aston Hall and Sarehole Mill, as well as several smaller museums. Contact any of the museums for details. For information on all of Birmingham's museums, visit www.bmag.org.uk.

Birmingham, the Midlands & the Marches Highlights

1 Hiking or cycling the rugged trails of the **Peak District National Park** (p467)

2 Contemplating the apple tree that inspired Isaac Newton's theories on gravity at his birthplace, **Woolsthorpe Manor** (p451)

3 Enjoying England's great contribution to the world of curry in the balti restaurants of **Birmingham** (p403)

4 Walking in the footsteps of the Bard in Shakespeare-obsessed **Stratford-upon-Avon** (p409)

5 Drinking in the history of **Ye Olde Trip to Jerusalem** (p443), allegedly England's oldest inn, carved into the cliff below Nottingham Castle

6 Stepping back into Jane Austen's England in the stone-lined streets of **Stamford** (p452)

7 Getting lost in the grandeur of **Chatsworth House** (p478), one of the nation's stateliest homes

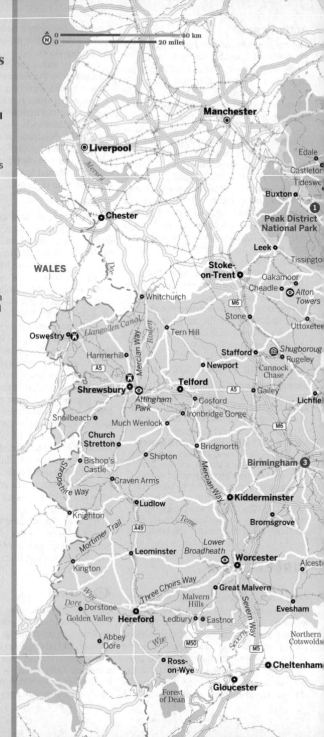

City Centre

Birmingham's grandest civic buildings are clustered around pedestrianised Victoria Sq, at the western end of New St, dominated by the stately facade of Council House, built between 1874 and 1879. The square was given a facelift in 1993, with modernist sphinxes and a fountain topped by a naked female figure, nicknamed 'the floozy in the jacuzzi' by locals, overlooked by a disapproving statue of Queen Victoria.

Further west, Centenary Sq is bookended by the art deco Hall of Memory War Memorial, the International Convention Centre (ICC) and Symphony Hall. The impressive and inventively designed new £189-million Birmingham Library building will open on the north side of the square in 2013.

FREE Birmingham Museum & Art Gallery   MUSEUM
(☎0121-303 2834; www.bmag.org.uk; Chamberlain Sq; ☉10am-5pm Mon-Thu & Sat, 10.30am-5pm Fri, 12.30-5pm Sun; 🖪) Housed in the annexe at the back of Council House, the delightful Birmingham Museum & Art Gallery houses an impressive collection of ancient treasures and Victorian art, including an important

Birmingham

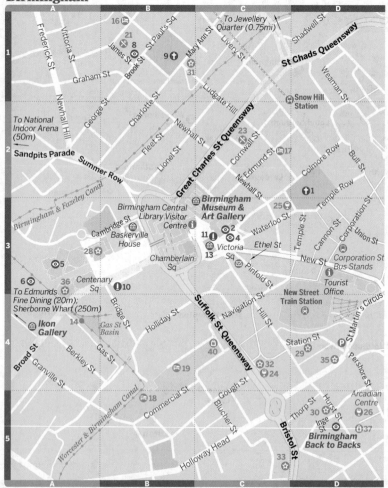

collection of major Pre-Raphaelite works by Rossetti, Edward Burne-Jones and others.

Birmingham Back to Backs   NEIGHBOURHOOD
(NT; ☎0121-666 7671; 55-63 Hurst St; tour adult/child £6.30/3.20; ☺10am-5pm Tue-Sun) On the other side of the Bullring, this cluster of restored back-to-back terraced houses can be visited by a quirky tour that takes you through four working-class homes, telling the stories of those who lived here between the 1840s and the 1970s.

Town Hall   HISTORIC BUILDING
(☎0121-780 3333; www.thsh.co.uk) The west side of Victoria Sq is marked out by the neoclas-sical Town Hall, constructed in 1834 and styled after the Temple of Castor and Pollux in Rome, and now used as a venue for classi-cal concerts and stage performances.

Cathedral Church of St Philip   CATHEDRAL
(☎0121-262 1840; Colmore Row; entry by dona-tion; ☺7.30am-6.30pm Mon-Fri, 8.30am-5pm Sat & Sun) North of the New St shopping pre-cinct, the small but perfectly formed Cath-edral Church of St Philip was constructed in a neoclassical style between 1709 and 1715. The Pre-Raphaelite artist Edward Burne-Jones was responsible for the magnificent stained-glass windows.

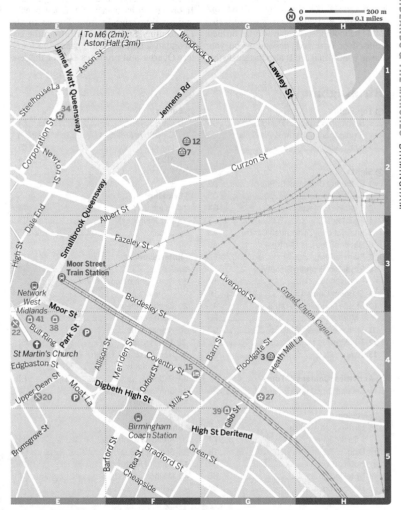

Birmingham Canals

During the industrial age, Birmingham was a major hub on the English canal network (the city technically has more miles of canals than Venice), and visiting narrow boats still float into Gas St Basin in the heart of the city, passing a string of swanky wharfside developments.

FREE **Ikon Gallery**   GALLERY

(☎0121-248 0708; www.ikon-gallery.co.uk; 1 Oozells Sq; ⊙11am-6pm Tue-Sun) Across the canal from the International Convention Centre and Symphony Hall, the glitzy Brindley Pl development contains banking offices, designer restaurants and the cutting-edge Ikon Gallery, housed in a stylishly converted Gothic schoolhouse. Prepare to be thrilled, bemused or outraged, depending on your take on conceptual art. It also has a cafe that serves great tapas and sherry to refuel between cultural hot spots.

National Sea Life Centre   AQUARIUM

(☎0121-643 6777; www.visitsealife.com; 3a Brindley Pl; adult/child £18/14.40; ⊙10am-5pm Mon-Fri, to 6pm Sat & Sun) The Sir Norman Foster–designed National Sea Life Centre is the largest inland aquarium in England, its tanks teeming with exotic marine life including razor-jawed hammerhead sharks, turtles and otters. Prepurchase tickets online for fast-track entry during school holidays.

Jewellery Quarter

Birmingham has been a major player on the British jewellery scene ever since Charles II brought back a taste for fancy buckles and sparkly brocade from France in the 17th century. Stretching north from the last Georgian square in Birmingham, the Jewellery Quarter still produces 40% of the jew-

Birmingham

BIRMINGHAM IN...

Two Days

Start off in the centre, dropping into Victoria Sq and the eclectic **Birmingham Museum & Art Gallery**. Go west through Centenary Sq to reach the Birmingham Canals, where you can while away an afternoon at the **National Sea Life Centre** or **Ikon Gallery**, before dining at **Simpsons**. On day two, indulge your inner shopaholic at the gleaming shopping malls of the **Bullring** and **Mailbox**, which both have good options for lunch. In the afternoon, catch up on some social history at the museum **Birmingham Back to Backs**. After dark, roam south to the **Balti Triangle** to sample Birmingham's unique contribution to the world of curry.

Four Days

Follow the two-day itinerary, but add a **canal cruise**. On day three, head north from the centre to **Aston Hall** and **Soho House**, or south to the famous **Barber Institute**, then take in a show at the **Repertory Theatre** or a concert at **Symphony Hall**. Use day four to explore the fascinating **Jewellery Quarter**, have a long lunch sampling Modern British cuisine at one of Birmingham's up-and-coming restaurants, and spend the afternoon reliving *Charlie and the Chocolate Factory* fantasies at **Cadbury World**.

ellery manufactured in the UK, and dozens of workshops are open to the public. The tourist office provides a free booklet, *Jewellery Quarter: The Essential Guide*, or you can take a virtual tour at www.jewellery quarter.net.

The Jewellery Quarter is three-quarters of a mile northwest of the centre; take bus 101 or ride the metro from Snow Hill or the train from Moor St to Jewellery Quarter station.

St Paul's Church CHURCH
St Paul's Sq is dominated by the 18th-century St Paul's Church, where Matthew Boulton and James Watt came to pray.

FREE **Royal Birmingham Society of Artists** ARTS CENTRE
(☑0121-236 4353; www.rbsa.org.uk; ⊙10.30am-5.30pm Mon-Fri, 10.30am-5pm Sat, 1-5pm Sun) At the northwest corner of the pretty Georgian St Paul's Sq, the Royal Birmingham Society of Artists has been exhibiting the work of local artists and artisans since 1814.

FREE **Museum of the Jewellery Quarter** MUSEUM
(☑0121-554 3598; 75-79 Vyse St; ⊙10.30am-4pm Tue-Sun) The Smith & Pepper jewellery factory is preserved in the museum as it was on its closing day in 1981 after 80 years of operation. You can explore the long history of the trade in Birmingham and watch master jewellers at work.

Outlying Areas

Thinktank MUSEUM
(☑0121-202 2222; www.thinktank.ac; Millennium Point, Curzon St; adult/child £12.25/8.40; ⊙10am-5pm, last admission 4pm) A 10-minute walk northeast of the centre, surrounded by the footprints of vanished factories, the Millennium Point development contains this entertaining and ambitious attempt to make science accessible to children. There's also a digital Planetarium (Curzon St; admission £1, advance booking required), covered by the same ticket, and an Imax cinema.

FREE **Barber Institute of Fine Arts** GALLERY
(☑0121-414 7333; www.barber.org.uk; ⊙10am-5pm Mon-Fri, 11am-5pm Sat & Sun) Around 2.5 miles south of the centre at the University of Birmingham, the Barber Institute of Fine Arts displays Renaissance masterpieces; European masters such as Rubens and Van Dyck; British greats including Gainsborough, Reynolds and Turner; and classics from modern titans Picasso, Magritte and others. Take the train to University station, or buses 61, 62 or 63.

Cadbury World MUSEUM
(☑0844 880 7667; www.cadburyworld.co.uk; Linden Rd; adult/child £14.75/10.75, under 3yr free) The next best thing to Willy Wonka's Chocolate Factory, Cadbury World is about 4 miles south of Birmingham in the village of Bournville. It aims to educate visitors about the history of cocoa and the Cadbury family, but sweetens the deal with free samples,

displays of chocolate-making machines, and chocolate-themed rides. Surrounding the chocolate works, pretty **Bournville Village** was built by the philanthropic Cadbury family to accommodate early 20th-century factory workers. Opening hours vary through the year; bookings are essential in July and August. Trains run to Bournville from Birmingham New St Station.

Aston Hall HISTORIC BUILDING
(☎0121-675 4722; Trinity Rd; house adult/child £4/ free, grounds free; ⊙noon-4pm Tue-Sun Apr-Oct) About 3 miles north of the centre in Aston (of Aston Villa fame), this well-preserved hall was built in extravagant Jacobean style between 1618 and 1635. The lush grounds are a wonderful retreat from the city streets, and the sumptuous interiors are full of friezes, moulded ceilings and tapestries. To get to Aston Hall, take bus 65 or a train to Aston station from New St station.

☞ Tours

Birmingham Tours WALKING TOUR
(☎0121-427 2555; www.birmingham-tours.co.uk) Runs popular walking tours and the hop-on/hop-off **Big Brum Buz** (day ticket adult/ child £12/5; ⊙Sat & Sun May-Sep).

Second City Canal Cruises BOAT TOUR
(☎0121-236 9811; www.secondcityboats.co.uk) Narrow-boat tours of Birmingham's canals lasting anything from one hour to two days, leaving from the Gas St Basin.

Sherborne Wharf BOAT TOUR
(☎0121-455 6163; www.sherbornewharf.co.uk; Sherborne St; adult/child £6.50/5; ⊙11.30am,1pm, 2.30pm & 4pm daily mid-Apr–Oct, Sat & Sun Nov–mid-Apr) Nostalgic narrow-boat cruises from the quayside by the International Convention Centre.

✯ Festivals & Events

Crufts Dog Show DOG SHOW
(www.crufts.org.uk) The world's greatest collection of pooches on parade, held every March at the National Exhibition Centre.

Birmingham Pride GAY
(www.birminghampride.com) One of the largest and most colourful celebrations of gay and lesbian culture in the country, held in May.

Artsfest ARTS
(www.artsfest.org.uk) The UK's largest free arts festival features visual arts, dance and music in venues across the city in September.

⌐ Sleeping

Most Birmingham hotels are aimed at business travellers, ensuring high prices during the week. Look out for cheap deals at weekends or for longer stays. B&Bs are concentrated outside the centre in Acocks Green (to the southeast) or Edgbaston and Selly Oak (to the southwest).

TOP CHOICE Hotel du Vin HOTEL ££
(☎0121-200 0600; www.hotelduvin.com; Church St; s/d from £99; P@⊛) Housed in the handsome Victorian precincts of the former Birmingham Eye Hospital, this spiffing red-brick hotel has real class, with wrought-iron balustrades, classical murals and seasoned charms. Art deco–inspired rooms have spectacular bathrooms, there's a pampering spa, a bistro with shabby-chic worn floorboards and a stellar wine list, plus a lounge bar with comfy, duffed-up leather furniture. Parking is extra.

Malmaison HOTEL ££
(☎0121-246 5000; www.malmaison.com; 1 Wharfside St; d from £99; P@⊛) Within tickling distance of Harvey Nichols and the smart

BIRMINGHAM BRAINS

The Industrial Revolution was a great time for entrepreneurs, and nowhere more so than in Birmingham, where the industrialists, philosophers and intellectuals of the Lunar Society came together to swap ideas for the greatest technological leap forward since the invention of the wheel. As well as engineers such as Matthew Boulton, James Watt and gaslight mogul William Murdoch, the society drew in such great thinkers as philosopher and naturalist Erasmus Darwin, oxygen discoverer Joseph Priestley, pottery boss Josiah Wedgwood, botanist Joseph Banks (who sailed to Australia with Captain Cook) and US founding father Benjamin Franklin. Between 1765 and 1813, this esteemed company held regular meetings at **Soho House** (☎0121-554 9122; Soho Ave, Handsworth; ⊙11.30am-4pm Tue-Sun Apr-Oct), now an engaging museum, to thrash out their groundbreaking ideas. There's a gleaming golden **statue of Boulton, Watt and Murdoch** near Centenary Sq.

WORTH A TRIP

THE CUSTARD FACTORY

Drop by Digbeth to the **Custard Factory** (☎0121-224 7777; www.custardfactory.co.uk; Gibb St), a hip art and design enclave set in the converted buildings of the factory that once churned out Britain's favourite custard. It's full of small galleries, quirky design boutiques, offbeat cafes, skateboard shops and vintage clothes outlets. Adding to the neighbourhood's artistic frisson is nearby **Eastgate Projects** (www.eastsideprojects.org; 86 Heath Mill Lane; ⏲noon-6.30pm Thu, noon-5pm Fri & Sat).

eateries of the Mailbox, mood lighting and Regency tones set the scene in the stylish rooms, which offer floor-to-ceiling views. Indulgences include a brasserie, champagne bar and miniature spa. Wheelchair accessible.

Birmingham Central Backpackers HOSTEL £
(☎0121-643 0033; www.birminghamcentralbackpackers.com; 58 Coventry St; dm from £13; @📶) Despite the railway-bridge-right-next-door setting in down-at-heel Digbeth, Birmingham's purple and turquoise backpacker hostel is handy for the bus station, and guests have a choice of clean, multicoloured dorms or funky Japanese-style pods. The excellent facilities include a lounge with DVD movies and Playstation, a guest kitchen and a bar.

Hotel Indigo HOTEL ££
(☎0121-643 2010; www.hotelindigo.com; The Cube, Wharfside St; d £100; P📶🏊) A stylish and zesty core operation on the 23rd and 24th floors of standout The Cube, Hotel Indigo marries a handy location with chic boutique exuberance and great views from its rooms. There's a small swimming pool and parking is extra. Panoramic vistas continue on the floor above with the Marco Pierre White Steakhouse Bar & Grill.

Bloc BOUTIQUE HOTEL £
(☎0121-212 1223; www.blochotels.com; St Paul's, Caroline St; r from £45; 📶) Doing what it says on the packet, this Jewellery Quarter hotel excels in sharp, contemporary pod-design. Rooms are tiny but space is cleverly stretched – flatscreen TVs are built into walls, storage is under-bed, and bathrooms are compact but with luxe shower-heads. Rooms come window or no-window. Discount parking nearby.

Westbourne Lodge B&B ££
(☎0121-429 1003; www.westbournelodge.co.uk; Fountain Rd; s/d from £49.50/69; P@📶) This popular B&B is conveniently located about 2 miles out in the suburb of Edgbaston (follow the A456). Rooms are a little chintzy but spacious, and there's a pleasant terrace to enjoy in summer.

Eating

Birmingham is best known for its brilliant baltis but the city has a growing reputation for fine dining and gastronomy. For cheap eats, look to the myriad Asian eateries in Chinatown, just south of the centre.

TOP CHOICE **Simpsons** MODERN BRITISH £££
(☎0121-454 3434; www.simpsonsrestaurant.co.uk; 20 Highfield Rd; 3-course set lunch £38; ⏲closed dinner Sun) Simpsons is far from the centre in a gorgeous Victorian house in Edgbaston, but it's worth making the journey for the imaginative creations sliced and diced by Michelin-starred chef Andreas Antona. You could even stay the night in one of the four luxurious bedrooms upstairs (£180-225; Tuesday to Saturday only). Reservations recommended.

Lasan INDIAN ££
(☎0121-212 3664; www.lasangroup.com; 3-4 Dakota Buildings, James St; mains £16-20; ⏲lunch Sun-Fri, dinner daily) Expletive-loving chef Gordon Ramsay gave his endorsement to this elegant and upscale Indian as Britain's best local restaurant. From our experience, the service and style are spot on and the North and South Indian dishes here are masterpieces.

Purnells MODERN BRITISH £££
(☎0121-212 9799; www.purnellsrestaurant.com; 55 Cornwall St; 2-/3-course lunch £22/27, dinner £36/42; ⏲lunch Tue-Fri, dinner Tue-Sat) Exquisite, inventive dishes (such as ox cheek with lentils cooked in toffee) are served in an airy Victorian red-brick building with a striking modern interior. Run by celebrated chef Glynn Purnell.

Edmunds Fine Dining MODERN BRITISH £££
(☎0121-633 4944; www.edmundsbirmingham.com; 6 Brindley Pl; 2-/3-course lunch/preconcert

dinner from £19.50/24.50; ☺lunch Tue-Fri, dinner Tue-Sat) Michelin-starred chef Andy Waters' sleek place is where traders from the surrounding banking houses come to spend their bonuses. Expect lots of locally sourced meats, fish and farm-fresh produce balanced with an enticing vegetarian menu. The restaurant is just back from the river in the Brindley Pl precinct.

Mount Fuji
JAPANESE ££
(☏0121-633 9853; www.mountfuji.co.uk; Bullring; mains £7-14) Put retail therapy on hold and sashay to this minimalist Japanese sushi cafe for sashimi, bento boxes and sake.

Cafe Soya
ASIAN £
(☏0121-622 3888; Upper Dean St; mains £6.50-9) Excellent cafe serving tasty dim sum, rice dishes and filling bowls of noodles (vermicelli, wheat noodles or *ho fun*, thick rice noodles). There's a Cafe Soya (Hurst St, Arcadian Centre; ☺ Thu-Tue) in the Arcadian Centre.

🍷 Drinking

The pub scene in the centre is sadly dominated by bland commercial chains, but some diamonds glint in the Birmingham rough.

Old Joint Stock
PUB
(☏0121-200 1892; www.oldjointstocktheatre.co.uk; 4 Temple Row West; ☺11am-10.30pm Mon-Sat, noon-5pm Sun; ☎) A vast high-ceilinged temple of a pub, housed in a former bank and appealing to a high-spirited after-work crowd. There's an 80-seat theatre upstairs that puts on plays and comedy shows.

Island Bar
BAR
(☏0121-632 5296; www.bar-island.co.uk; 14-16 Suffolk St Queensway; ☺5pm-late Mon-Sat) Locals rave about the cocktails at this funky nightspot, where you can sit in perspex chairs in front of giant blow-ups of Hawaiian beaches and groove to rock and roll.

Sobar
BAR
(☏0121-693 5084; www.sobar.co.uk; Arcadian Centre, Hurst St; ☺5pm-late Tue & Wed, noon-2am Thu, noon-3am Fri & Sat) A glammed-up, shirted and booted crowd packs out this black-and-red bar to the strains of mainstream dance and house.

☆ Entertainment

Tickets for most Birmingham events can be purchased through the entertainment megacorp TicketWeb (☏0870 060 0100; www.ticketweb.co.uk).

Free listings magazines available at venues around town include the fortnightly *What's On* and monthly *Birmingham 24seven* magazine, which cover everything from exhibitions to club nights.

NIGHTCLUBS
The main party district is south of New St station, where a series of defunct warehouses and pubs have found new life as bars and clubs. Chinatown's Arcadian Centre (www.thearcadian.co.uk; Hurst St) is the gateway to this hedonistic quarter, with numerous party bars and dancing spots.

Air
CLUB
(www.airbirmingham.com; Heath Mill Lane) This superclub is home to the renowned Godskitchen night (www.godskitchen.com), where some of the country's top DJs whip the crowd into a frenzy.

Q Club
CLUB
(www.qclub.co.uk; 212 Corporation St; ☺from 8.30pm or 10pm) The old brick Central Hall that houses this legendary club is on its last legs, but the 'Q' is still going strong. DJs pump out boisterous electro, house, jungle and old-school club classics.

LIVE MUSIC
As well as the following venues, the National Indoor Arena (☏0121-780 4141; www.thenia.co.uk; King Edwards Rd), north of Brindley Pl, and the National Exhibition Centre Arena (☏0121-780 4141; www.thenec.co.uk; off the M42), near Birmingham Airport, host stadium-fillers from the world of rock and pop.

Sunflower Lounge
LIVE MUSIC
(☏0121-632 6756; www.twitter.com/Sunflowerlounge; 76 Smallbrook Queensway; ☺to 2am Fri & Sat) Tucked away on the dual carriageway near New St train station, this quirky little mod bar matches a magnificent alternative soundtrack with a regular program of live gigs and DJ nights.

Jam House
LIVE MUSIC
(www.thejamhouse.com; 3-5 St Paul's Sq; ☺6pm-midnight Tue & Wed, 6pm-1am Thu, 6pm-2am Fri & Sat) Pianist Jools Holland was the brains behind this moody smart-casual music venue in posh St Paul's Sq. Acts range from jazz big bands to famous soul crooners. Over 21s only.

Symphony Hall
CLASSICAL MUSIC
(www.symphonyhall.co.uk; Broad St) For top talent from the classical music world, head to

THE BEAUTIFUL BALTI

If curry is the unofficial national dish of England, then the balti is its finest interpretation. First cooked up in the curry houses of Sparkbrook in southern Birmingham, this one-pot curry is prepared in a cast-iron wok with plenty of onion and chilli. Tracing its origins back to Baltistan in northern Pakistan, the balti is traditionally served with a giant *karack* naan bread that's big enough to feed the whole table.

The best place to sample this Brummie delicacy is in the so-called Balti Triangle about 2.5 miles southeast of the centre, formed by Ladypool Rd, Stoney Lane and Stratford Rd. Reflecting the religious sensibilities of local residents, restaurants serve soft drinks, fruit juices and *lassis* (yoghurt shakes) instead of alcohol, but diners are welcome to bring their own beer and wine. To get here, take bus 2, 5, 5A or 6 from Corporation St and ask the driver for Ladypool Rd. Top Birmingham balti picks:

Grameen Khana (📞0121-449 9994; www.grameenkhana.com; 310-312 Ladypool Rd; meals £15) Multicoloured lights and Bollywood movies provide a backdrop to one of the city's best baltis.

Saleem's Restaurant & Sweet House (📞0121-449 1861; 256-258 Ladypool Rd) Long established and understandably popular for its tasty milk-based Indian sweets and generous portions of balti.

Al Faisal's (📞0121-449 5695; www.alfaisal.co.uk; 136-140 Stoney Lane; mains from £6.50) Serves delicious dishes from the mountains of Kashmir, as well as classic Birmingham baltis.

the ultramodern Symphony Hall, the official home of the City of Birmingham Symphony Orchestra. Shows also take place in the handsome auditorium at the Town Hall.

O2 Academy   LIVE MUSIC
(www.o2academybirmingham.co.uk; 16-18 Horsefair, Bristol St) Birmingham's leading venue for big-name rockers and tribute bands.

THEATRE & CINEMA

Birmingham Repertory Theatre   THEATRE
(www.birmingham-rep.co.uk; Centenary Sq, Broad St) Reopening in September 2013 after a two-year redesign, 'the Rep' will have three performance spaces – the Main House, the more experimental Door and a new 300-seat studio theatre (as part of the new Library development next door), presenting edgy drama and musicals, with an emphasis on contemporary work.

Electric Cinema   CINEMA
(www.theelectric.co.uk; 47-49 Station St; deluxe seats £12) Topped with its art deco sign, this is the oldest working cinema in the UK (screening since 1909) enjoy a mix of mainstream and art-house cinema. Be waited upon in plush two-seater sofas or have a drink in the small bar.

Giant Screen   CINEMA
(📞0121-202 2222; www.thinktank.ac; Millennium Point, Curzon St; tickets from adult/child £9.60/

7.60) Coming into its own in the age of the 3D blockbuster, Birmingham's Giant Screen is housed in the same building as the Thinktank.

Hippodrome   THEATRE
(📞0844 338 5000; www.birminghamhippodrome. com; Hurst St) The place to come to see stars off the telly, plus highbrow entertainment from the Birmingham Royal Ballet.

New Alexandra Theatre   THEATRE
(www.alexandratheatre.org.uk; Suffolk St Queens way) This Brummie institution has been around even longer than the veteran comedians and touring stage shows walking its boards.

 Shopping

The workshops of the Jewellery Quarter are well worth a browse and there are several bustling markets selling cheap imported clothes in the pedestrian precincts surrounding the Bullring.

Bullring   MALL
(www.bullring.co.uk; St Martin's Circus; ⊙10am-8pm Mon-Fri, 9am-8pm Sat, 11am-5pm Sun) Split into two vast retail spaces – the East Mall and West Mall – the Bullring has all the international brands and chain cafes you could ask for, plus the standout architectural wonder of Selfridges.

GAY & LESBIAN BIRMINGHAM

Birmingham's loud and lively gay scene is centred on the streets south of the Bullring, which throng with the bold, bright and beautiful on weekend nights. For up-to-the-minute information on the Brummie scene, check www. visitgaybrum.com, or ask the crowds during May's Birmingham Pride (p400) festivities.

Mailbox   MALL

(www.mailboxlife.com; Wharfside St; ☺10am-6pm Mon-Wed, to 7pm Thu-Sat, 11am-5pm Sun) Birmingham's stylish waterside shopping experience, the redevelopment of the former Royal Mail sorting office, comes complete with designer hotels, a fleet of upmarket restaurants, the luxury department store Harvey Nichols, designer names and a super snazzy metallic extension called The Cube.

Information

Dangers & Annoyances

As in most large cities, it's wise to avoid walking alone late at night in unlit areas. The area around Digbeth bus station can be quite rough after dark – stick to the High St if you are walking to central Birmingham.

Emergency

Police station (☎0845 113 5000; Steelhouse Lane)

Medical Services

Birmingham Children's Hospital (☎0121-333 9999; www.bch.nhs.uk; Steelhouse Lane)

Heartlands Hospital (☎0121-424 2000; www .heartofengland.nhs.uk; Bordesley Green East) Catch bus 15, 17, 97 or 97A.

Money

Thomas Cook (☎0121-643 5057; Middle Mall, Bullring; ☺10am-8pm Mon-Fri, 9am-8pm Sat, 11am-5pm Sun) Bureau de change.

Post

Central post office (1 Pinfold St; ☺9am-5.30pm Mon-Sat) With bureau de change.

Tourist Information

Heart of England tourist board (☎01905-761100; www.visitheartofengland.com)

Tourist office (☎0121-202 5115; www.visit birmingham.com; cnr Corporation & New Sts; ☺9am-5pm Mon-Sat, 10am-4pm Sun) With racks of brochures, maps and info on activities, transport and sights. There's also a branch in the Birmingham Central Library (Chamberlain Sq; ☺10am-6pm Mon-Fri, 9am-5pm Sat).

Getting There & Away

Air

Birmingham Airport (p393) is about 8 miles east of the centre, with flights to destinations around the UK and Europe, plus a few long-haul connections to America and Dubai.

Bus

Most intercity buses run from **Birmingham Coach Station** (Digbeth High St), but the X20 to Stratford-upon-Avon (1¼ hours, hourly, every two hours at weekends) leaves from a stop on Moor St, just north of the Pavilions mall. **National Express** (www.nationalexpress.com) runs coaches between Birmingham and major cities across the country, including:

London £15.70, 2¾ hours, every 30 minutes

Manchester £12.60, 2½ hours, 12 daily

Oxford £11.60, 1½ to two hours, five daily

Train

Most long-distance trains leave from New St station, beneath the Pallasades shopping centre, but Chiltern Railways runs to London Marylebone (£31.90, 2½ hours, twice hourly) from Birmingham Snow Hill, and London Midland runs to Stratford-upon-Avon (£6.30, one hour, hourly) from Snow Hill and Moor St station. Useful services from New St include Derby (£13.80, 45 minutes, four per hour), Leicester (£13.10, one hour, two per hour), London Euston (£40.90, 1½ hours, every 30 minutes), Manchester (£30.50, 1¾ hours, every 15 minutes) and Shrewsbury (£11.70, one hour, two per hour).

Getting Around

To/From the Airport

Fast and convenient trains run regularly between New St and Birmingham International station (20 minutes, every 10 minutes), or take bus 58 or 900 (45 minutes, every 20 minutes) from Moor St Queensway. A taxi from the airport to the centre costs about £20.

Car

All the big car-hire companies have town offices:

Avis (☎0844 544 6038; www.avis.co.uk; 17 Horse Fair)

Enterprise Rent-a-Car (☎0121-782 5158; www .enterprise.co.uk; 9-10 Suffolk St Queensway)

Public Transport

Local buses run from a convenient hub on Corporation St, just north of the New St junction. For routes, pick up a free copy of the *Network Birmingham Map & Guide* from the tourist office. Commuter trains to destinations in the north of Birmingham (including Aston) operate from Moor St train station, close to Selfridges. Birmingham's single tram line, the **Metro** (www.travelmetro.co.uk), runs from Snow Hill to Wolverhampton via the Jewellery Quarter, West Bromwich and Dudley.

Special saver tickets covering all the buses and trains are available from **Network West Midlands** (☑0121-214 7214; www.networkwestmidlands.com; ⊙9am-5.30pm Mon-Fri, to 5pm Sat) on the lower ground floor of the Pavilions mall.

TOA Taxis (☑0121-427 8888; www.toataxis.net) are a reliable black-cab taxi firm.

WARWICKSHIRE

Warwickshire could have been just another picturesque English county of rolling hills and market towns were it not for the birth of a rather well-known wordsmith. William Shakespeare was born and died in Stratford-upon-Avon, and the sights linked to his life are a magnet for tourists from around the globe. Famous Warwick Castle attracts similar crowds. Elswhere visitor numbers dwindle but Kenilworth has atmospheric castle ruins and Coventry claims two fine cathedrals and an excellent motoring museum.

ⓘ Information

Shakespeare Country (www.shakespeare-country.co.uk)

ⓘ Getting There & Around

The Warwickshire transport site (www.warwickshire.gov.uk/transport) covers all aspects of travel in the county, including bus and train timetables. Coventry is the main transport hub, with frequent rail connections to London Euston and Birmingham New St.

Coventry

POP 300,848

Dominated today by its twin spires and identikit tower blocks, Coventry was once a bustling hub for the production of cloth, clocks, bicycles, automobiles and munitions. It was this last industry that drew the German Luftwaffe in WWII: on the night of 14

November 1940, the city was so badly blitzed that the Nazis coined a new verb, *coventrieren*, meaning 'to flatten'. Postwar planners filled in the gaps with dull concrete developments, and the city faced a further setback with the collapse of the British motor industry in the 1980s. A handful of medieval streets escaped the bombers, offering a taste of old Coventry.

⊙ Sights

TOP CHOICE **Coventry Transport Museum**   MUSEUM
(☑024-7623 4270; www.transport-museum.com; Hales St; free admission; ⊙10am-5pm) This stupendous museum has hundreds of 'cars' through the ages, from horseless carriages to jet-powered, land-speed record breakers. There's a brushed stainless steel DeLorean DMC-12 (of *Back to the Future* fame) with gull-wing doors, alongside a gorgeous Jaguar E-type, a Daimler armoured car and, for specialists of 1970s British design oddities, a Triumph TR7 and an Austin Allegro 'Special'. View the Thrust SCC, the current holder of the World Land Speed Record and the Thrust 2, the previous record holder. Kids will be engrossed by the atmospheric 'Coventry Blitz Experience' and the Thrust speed simulator (£1).

Coventry Cathedral   CATHEDRAL
(☑024-7652 1200; www.coventrycathedral.org.uk; Priory Row; adult/child under 7 £7/5; 9am-5pm Mon-Sat, noon-3.45pm Sun) The evocative ruins of St Michael's Cathedral (spire adult/child £2.50/1), built around 1300 but destroyed by Nazi incendiary bombs in the Blitz, stand as a permanent memorial to Coventry's darkest hour and as a symbol of peace and reconciliation. Climb the 180 steps of its Gothic spire for panoramic views.

Symbolically adjoining the old cathedral's sandstone walls is the Sir Basil Spence-designed Coventry Cathedral, a modernist architectural masterpiece, with a futuristic organ, stained glass and a Jacob Epstein statue of the devil and St Michael.

FREE **Herbert Art Gallery & Museum**   GALLERY
(☑024-7683 2386; www.theherbert.org.uk; ⊙10am-4pm Mon-Sat, noon-4pm Sun) Behind Coventry's twin cathedrals, the Herbert has an eclectic collection of paintings and sculptures (including work by TS Lowry and Stanley Spencer), a delightful cafe, and lots

of exhibitions and activities aimed at kids. The intriguing gallery on peace and reconciliation and the history gallery are worth a look-in.

FREE **St Mary's Guildhall**   HISTORIC BUILDING
(☑024-7683 3328; Bayley Lane; ☺10am-4pm) This hall is where the town's trades came together in the Middle Ages to discuss town affairs. As one of England's finest guildhalls, it was chosen to be a jail for Mary Queen of Scots. Stained-glass windows glorify the kings of England; further down the hall stands WC Marshall's statue of Lady Godiva. Look out for the medieval tapestry depicting Henry VI.

🛏 Sleeping & Eating

Spire View Guest House   B&B £
(☑024-7625 1602; www.spireviewguesthouse.co.uk; 36 Park Rd; s/tw from £25/51; ☎) Rooms are a bit tired but the location in a quiet street (with several other guesthouses nearby) just minutes' walk from the train station is handy, and the hosts are eager to please.

Playwrights   CAFE ££
(☑024-7623 1441; www.playwrightsrestaurant.co.uk; 4-6 Hay Lane; mains £6-20; ☺9am to late) On the lovely cobbled lane leading from Earl St to the cathedral, this bright, inviting cafe, bar and bistro is as good for breakfast as it is for lunch or an intimate dinner, with tables flung out on the cobbles in warmer weather.

ℹ Information

Tourist office (☑024-7622 5616; www.visitcoventry.co.uk; ☺9.30am-4.30pm Mon-Fri, 10am-4.30pm Sat, 10am-noon & 1-4.30pm Sun) Housed in the restored tower of St Michael's Cathedral.

ℹ Getting There & Away

From the main bus station, National Express buses serve most parts of the country. Bus X17 (every 20 minutes) goes to Kenilworth (25 minutes), Leamington Spa (40 minutes) and Warwick (1¼ hours).

Trains go south to London Euston (£42.60; 1¼ hours, every 10-20 minutes) and you will rarely have to wait for a train to Birmingham (30 minutes, every 10 minutes).

Warwick

POP 25,434

Regularly name-checked by Shakespeare, Warwick was the ancestral seat of the Earls of Warwick, who played a pivotal role in the Wars of the Roses. Despite a devastating fire in 1694, Warwick remains a treasure-house of medieval architecture with rich veins of history and charming streets, dominated by the soaring turrets of magnificent Warwick Castle.

👁 Sights

Warwick Castle   CASTLE
(☑0870 442 2000; www.warwick-castle.co.uk; castle adult/child £27.45/19.45; ☺10am-6pm Apr-Sep, to 5pm Oct-Mar; ℗) Founded in 1068 by William the Conqueror, the stunningly preserved Warwick Castle is the biggest show in town. The ancestral home of the Earls of Warwick, this castle remains impressively intact, and the Tussauds Group has filled the interior with noisy attractions that bring the castle's rich history to life in a flamboyant but undeniably family-friendly way.

As well as waxworks populating the private apartments there are jousting tournaments, daily trebuchet-firings, themed evenings and a dungeon. Tickets discounted if you buy online.

FREE **Collegiate Church of St Mary**   CHURCH
(☑01926-492909; Old Sq; church entry by £2 donation, clock tower adult/child £2.50/1; ☺10am-6pm Apr-Oct, to 4.30pm Nov-Mar) Founded in 1123, this magnificent Norman church was badly damaged in the Great Fire of Warwick in 1694 and is packed with 16th- and 17th-century tombs. Highlights include the Norman crypt with a 14th-century extension, the impressive Beauchamp Chapel (built between 1442 and 1464 to enshrine the mortal remains of the Earls of Warwick), and the **clock tower**, for supreme views over town.

Lord Leycester Hospital   HISTORIC BUILDING
(☑01926-491422; www.lordleycester.com; High St; adult/child £4.90/3.90, garden only £2; ☺10am-5pm Tue-Sun Apr-Sep, to 4pm Oct-Mar) Charmingly leaning against the Westgate and a survivor of the 1694 fire, the wonderfully wonky Lord Leycester Hospital has been used as a retirement home for soldiers (but not as a hospital) since 1571. Visitors can wander round the chapel, guildhall, regimental museum and restored walled garden, which includes a knot garden and a Norman arch.

FREE **Warwickshire Museum**   MUSEUM
(☑01926-412501; Market Pl; ☺10am-5pm Tue-Sat year-round, 11.30am-5pm Sun Apr-Sep) Housed in

Warwick

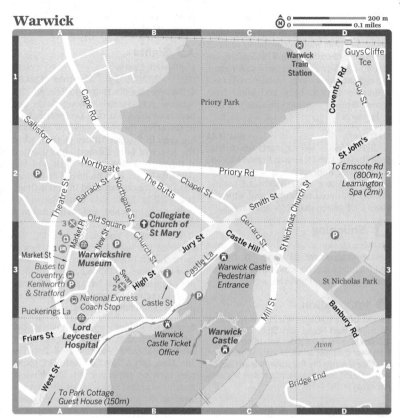

Warwick's striking 17th-century market hall, Warwickshire Museum has some entertaining displays on local history and the Warwick sea dragons (Jurassic-era sea creatures).

🛏 Sleeping

Reasonably priced B&Bs line Emscote Rd, which runs northeast towards Leamington Spa, a genteel spa town that is almost a suburb of Warwick, 2 miles to the east.

Rose & Crown   PUB ££
(☎01926-411117; www.roseandcrownwarwick.co.uk; 30 Market Pl; mains from £10.75; r incl breakfast from £75; ⓟ@☎☎) This convivial gastropub enjoys a congenial location on the town square, with five lovely, spacious and tastefully decorated rooms, as well as great beer and superior food.

Park Cottage Guest House   B&B ££
(☎01926-410319; www.parkcottagewarwick.co.uk; 113 West St; s/d £52.50/70; ⓟ) Southwest of

the centre, this stand-alone 16th-century wattle-and-daub building once served as the dairy for the castle, with seven pretty rooms, each with a teddy bear, original floors and a courtyard garden.

✖ Eating

Tailors MODERN BRITISH £££
(☎01926-410590; www.tailorsrestaurant.co.uk; 22 Market Pl; 2-/3-course dinner £28/32.50; ⊙Tue-Sat) Set in a former gentlemen's tailor shop, this elegant eatery serves prime ingredients – guinea fowl, pork belly and lamb from named farms – presented delicately in neat little towers.

Merchants BRASSERIE £
(☎01926-403833; www.merchantswarwick.co.uk; Swan St; mains from £5; ⊙lunch & dinner Mon-Sat) With a neat and appealing layout, stylish leather furniture and chalkboard menus, this black-fronted restaurant and wine bar offers a fab selection of £5 main courses.

🔒 Shopping

Warwick Books BOOKS
(www.warwickbooks.net; 24 Market Pl) Helpful and friendly small bookshop with great recommendations and first-rate service.

ℹ Information

Tourist Office (☎01926-492212; www.warwick-uk.co.uk; Court House, Jury St; ⊙9.30am-4.30pm Mon-Fri, from 10am Sat, 10am-4pm Sun) Near the junction with Castle St, the tourist office is within the flagstone-floored Court House (1725) and sells the informative *Warwick Town Trail* leaflet (45p).

ℹ Getting There & Away

National Express (www.nationalexpress.com) coaches operate from Puckerings Lane. Stagecoach X17 runs to Coventry (1¼ hours, every 15 minutes Monday to Saturday), via Kenilworth (30 minutes). Stagecoach bus 16 goes to Stratford-upon-Avon (40 minutes, hourly) in one direction, and Coventry in the other. The main bus stops are on Market St.

Trains run to Birmingham (£7, 45 minutes, half-hourly), Stratford-upon-Avon (£5.20, 30 minutes, hourly) and London (£25, 1¾ hours, every 20 minutes), from the station northeast of the centre.

Kenilworth

POP 23,219

It's well worth deviating from the A46 between Warwick and Coventry to visit the spine-tinglingly atmospheric ruins of Kenilworth Castle. A refreshing counterpoint to the commercialism of Warwick's royal ruin, the castle was the inspiration for Walter Scott's *Kenilworth*, and it still feels pretty inspiring today.

◉ Sights

Kenilworth Castle CASTLE
(EH; ☎01926-852078; adult/child £8/4.80; ⊙10am-5pm Mar-Oct, to 4pm Nov-Feb; P) This sublime ruin sprawls among fields and hedges on the outskirts of Kenilworth. Built in the 1120s, the castle survived the longest siege in English history in 1266, when the forces of Lord Edward (later Edward I) threw themselves at the moat and battlements for six solid months. The fortress was dramatically extended in Tudor times, but it fell in the English Civil War and its walls were breached and water defences drained.

The excellent audioguide will tell you all about the relationship between former owner Robert Dudley and the 'Virgin Queen', who was wined and dined here at tremendous expense, almost bankrupting the castle. Don't miss the magnificent and recently restored Elizabethan gardens.

Stoneleigh Abbey HISTORIC HOME
(☎01926-858535; www.stoneleighabbey.org; adult/child £8/3.50; ⊙tours noon & 2pm Tue-Thu, 11am, 1pm & 3pm Sun Easter-Oct, garden open 11am-5pm same days; P) The kind of stately home that makes movie directors go weak at the knees, this 850-year-old country house by the River Avon name-drops Charles I and Jane Austen among its roll call of visiting celebrities. The original abbey was founded by Cistercian monks in 1154, but the house was massively expanded by the wealthy Leigh family (distant cousins of the Austens) in the 16th century. Completed in 1726 and only viewable on tours (included in admission), the splendid Palladian west wing contains richly detailed plasterwork ceilings and wood-panelled rooms, and the landscaped grounds are fine picnic territory. Stoneleigh is 2 miles east of Kenilworth, off the B4115.

🛏 Sleeping & Eating

Numerous pubs and eateries line the High St (just north of the castle) and Warwick Rd (just south).

The Old Bakery B&B ££
(☎01926-864111; www.theoldbakery.eu; 12 High St; s/d from £75/95; P🛜) Located down the High St east of the castle, this quiet and

popular B&B has attractively attired and modern rooms and a cosy and welcoming bar serving real ales on the ground floor.

Loweridge Guest House B&B ££
(☎01926-859522; www.loweridgeguesthouse.co.uk /links.php; Hawkesworth Dr; s/d from £75/90; P@) This handsome Victorian house has a grand staircase and elegant guest lounge straight out of *Country Life* magazine. There are four huge rooms with swish, modern bathrooms and three have their own private sun-trap patio. The guesthouse is a short walk northeast from the High St, off Coventry road.

Clarendon Arms PUB ££
(☎01926-852017; www.clarendonarmspub.co.uk; 44 Castle Hill; mains £8-13) Almost opposite the castle, this bright and homely alehouse has home-cooked food, a warm ambience and a cosy little beer garden.

ℹ Information

For tourist information, browse the brochures at the town **library** (☎01926-852595; 11 Smalley Pl; ⊙9am-7pm Mon & Thu, to 5.30pm Tue & Fri, 10.30am-5.30pm Wed, 9.30am-4pm Sat).

ℹ Getting There & Away

From Monday to Saturday, bus X17 runs every 15 minutes from Coventry to Kenilworth (25 minutes) and on to Leamington Spa (from Kenilworth, 15 minutes) and Warwick (20 minutes). On Sunday, take bus U17 (half-hourly) for Coventry or bus 18A (hourly) for Warwick.

Stratford-upon-Avon

POP 22,187

The author of some of the most quoted lines ever written in the English language, William Shakespeare was born in Stratford in 1564 and died here in 1616, and the five houses linked to his life form the centrepiece of a tourist attraction that verges on a cult of personality.

Experiences in this unmistakably Tudor town range from the touristy (medieval re-creations and Bard-themed tearooms) to the humbling (Shakespeare's modest grave in Holy Trinity Church) and the sublime (taking in a play by the world-famous Royal Shakespeare Company).

◎ Sights & Activities

Shakespeare's Birthplace HISTORIC HOME
(Henley St) Start your Shakespeare adventure at the house where the world's most popular playwright supposedly spent his childhood days. In fact, the jury is still out on whether this really was Shakespeare's birthplace, but devotees of the Bard have been dropping in since at least the 19th century, leaving their signatures scratched onto the windows. Set behind a modern facade, the house contains restored Tudor rooms, live presentations from famous Shakespearean characters, and an engaging exhibition on Stratford's favourite son.

Nash's House & New Place HISTORIC SITE
(☎01789-292325; www.shakespeare.org.uk; cnr Chapel St & Chapel Lane) When Shakespeare retired, he swapped the bright lights of London for a comfortable town house at New Pl, where he died of unknown causes in April 1616. The house was demolished in 1759, but an attractive Elizabethan knot garden occupies part of the grounds. Archaeologists are digging beneath the plot in search of Shakespearean treasures (see www.digforshakespeare.com). Recent finds are displayed in the adjacent Nash's House, where Shakespeare's granddaughter Elizabeth lived. Displays describe the town's history and there's a collection of 17th-century furniture and tapestries.

Hall's Croft HISTORIC HOME
(☎01789-292107; Old Town) Shakespeare's daughter Susanna married respected doctor John Hall, and their handsome Jacobean town house stands south of the centre en route to Holy Trinity Church. Deviating from the usual Shakespearean theme, the exhibition offers fascinating insights into medicine in the 16th and 17th centuries. The lovely walled garden sprouts with aromatic herbs employed in medicinal preparations.

Holy Trinity Church CHURCH
(☎01789-266316; www.stratford-upon-avon.org; Old Town; church admission free, Shakespeare's grave adult/child £1.50/50p; ⊙8.30am-6pm Mon-Sat, 12.30-5pm Sun Apr-Sep, shorter hours Oct-Mar) The final resting place of the Bard is said to be the most visited parish church in all of England. Inside are handsome 16th- and 17th-century tombs (particularly in the Clopton Chapel), some fabulous carvings on the choir stalls and, of course, the grave of

Stratford-upon-Avon

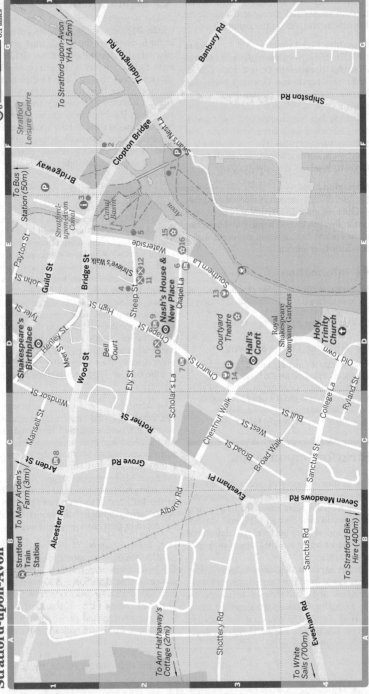

0 0.1 miles
0 200 m

To Stratford-upon-Avon YHA (1.5mi)

Tiddington Rd
Banbury Rd
Shipston Rd

Stratford Leisure Centre

Swan's Nest La
Clopton Bridge

Bridgeway
To Bus Station (50m)

Payton St
John St
Guild St
Tyler St
Bridge St
High St
Sheep St

Stratford-upon-Avon Canal
Canal Basin
Shrieve's Walk
Waterside
Avon
Southern La

Shakespeare's Birthplace
Henley St
Meer St
Wood St
Bell Court
Chapel St
Ely St
Chapel La

Nash's House & New Place
Courtyard Theatre
Hall's Croft
Royal Shakespeare Company Gardens
Holy Trinity Church
Old Town
College La
Ryland St

Windsor St
Mansell St
Arden St
Grove Rd
Rother St
Scholar's La
Chestnut Walk
West St
Broad St
Broad Walk
Bull St
Church St
Sanctus St

Alcester Rd
To Mary Arden's Farm (3mi)
Evesham Pl
Albany Rd
Seven Meadows Rd
Sanctus Rd

Stratford Train Station

To Ann Hathaway's Cottage (2mi)
Shottery Rd
To White Sails (700m)
Evesham Rd
To Stratford Bike Hire (400m)

Stratford-upon-Avon

William Shakespeare, with its ominous epitaph: 'cvrst be he yt moves my bones'.

Anne Hathaway's Cottage   HISTORIC HOME
(☑01789-292100; Cottage La, Shottery; adult/child £9/5) Before tying the knot with Shakespeare, Anne Hathaway lived in Shottery, a mile west of the centre, in this delightful thatched farmhouse. As well as period furniture, there are the gorgeous gardens and an orchard and arboretum, with examples of all the trees mentioned in Shakespeare's plays. A footpath (no bikes allowed) leads to Shottery from Evesham Pl.

Mary Arden's Farm   HISTORIC HOME, FARM
(☑01789-293455; Station Rd, Wilmcote; adult/child £9.50/6.50) Shakespeare genealogists can trace the family tree to the childhood home of the Bard's mother at Wilmcote, 3 miles west of Stratford. Aimed squarely at families, the working farm has exhibits tracing country life over the centuries, with nature trails, falconry displays and a collection of rare-breed farm animals. You can get here on the City Sightseeing bus, or cycle via Anne Hathaway's Cottage, following the Stratford-upon-Avon Canal towpath.

Falstaff's Experience   GHOST TRAIN
(☑01789-298070; www.falstaffsexperience.co.uk; 40 Sheep St; adult/child £5/2.50; ⊙10.30am-5.30pm) Set in an old timbered building, Falstaff's Experience offers a ghost-train take on Shakespeare's tales, with oldey-worldey walk-throughs, mannequins of Tudor celebs and live actors hamming it up like Olivier. Night-time ghost tours (adults only) are led by famous mediums.

👉 Tours

Options include the popular and informative two-hour **guided town walks** (☑01789-292478; adult/child £5/2; ⊙11am Mon-Wed, 2pm Thu-Sun) that depart from Waterside, opposite Sheep St, which is also the starting point for the spooky **Stratford Town Ghost Walk** (adult/child £6/3; ⊙7.30pm Mon, Thu, Fri & Sat).

City Sightseeing   BUS TOUR
(☑01789-412680; www.citysightseeing-stratford.com; adult/child £11.75/6; ⊙every 30min Apr-Sep, less frequently Oct-Mar) Open-top, hop-on/hop-off bus tours leave from the tourist office on Bridge Street, rolling to each of the Shakespeare properties. Tickets are valid for 24 hours (48-hour tickets also exist) and can be bought from the driver; on-board commentary in seven languages.

Avon Boating   BOAT TOUR
(☑01789-267073; www.avon-boating.co.uk; The Boathouse, Swan's Nest Lane; 30min river cruises adult/child £4.50/3) Runs river cruises that depart every 20 minutes from either side of the main bridge.

Bancroft Cruisers   BOAT TOUR
(☑01789-269669; www.bancroftcruisers.co.uk; 45min river cruise adult/child £5.50/3.50; ⊙daily Apr-Oct) These fun trips leave from the riverbank by the Holiday Inn, off Bridgeway.

ℹ️ SHAKESPEARE HISTORIC HOMES

Five of the most important buildings associated with Shakespeare contain museums that form the core of the visitor experience at Stratford, run by the Shakespeare Birthplace Trust . You can buy individual tickets to the Shakespeare Houses (☎01789-204016; www.shakespeare.org.uk; all 5 properties adult/child £21.50/13.50, 3 in-town houses £14/9; ⊙9am-5pm Apr-Oct, hours vary Nov-Mar), but it's more cost-effective to buy a combination ticket either covering the three houses in town, or all five properties. Expect long queues throughout the summer.

⭐ Festivals & Events

The top event on Stratford's cultural calendar is the **Stratford Literary Festival** (☎01789-207100; www.stratfordliteraryfestival.co.uk) in April/May, which attracts literary big-hitters of the calibre of John Simpson and Jonathan Miller.

🛏️ Sleeping

B&Bs are plentiful, particularly along Grove Rd and Evesham Pl, but vacancies can be hard to find during the high season – the tourist office can help with bookings for a fee.

Church Street Townhouse   BOUTIQUE HOTEL £££

(☎01789-262222; www.churchstreettownhouse.com; 16 Church St; r £110-180; 🛜) The 12 rather decadent rooms at this exquisite boutique hotel are divine and very plush, some with free-standing bath and all with iPod dock, flatscreen TVs and luxurious furnishings. The building itself is a centrally located 400-year-old gem with a first-rate restaurant and bar, rounding out an excellent stay. Rooms pricier at weekends.

Stratford-upon-Avon YHA   HOSTEL £

(☎0845 371 9661; www.yha.org.uk; Hemmingford House, Alveston; dm from £16; P@) Set in a large 200-year-old mansion, 1.5 miles east of the town centre along Tiddington Rd, this superior hostel attracts travellers of all ages. There's a canteen, bar and kitchen. Buses 18 and 18A run here from Bridge St.

Shakespeare Hotel   HOTEL £££

(☎01789-294997; www.mercure.com; Chapel St; s/d £135/150; P@) With rooms named after the Bard's plays or characters and a hearty fire crackling in the hearth, the gorgeous Shakespeare offers the full Tudor inn experience in a timbered medieval charmer on the main street. Rooms – some with four-poster beds and wood panels – are tasteful but a wee tired at this Mercure property, but staff are helpful and there's an undeniable historic appeal. Car parking is £10 per guest.

Arden Hotel   HOTEL £££

(☎01789-298682; www.theardenhotelstratford.com; Waterside; r incl breakfast from £125; P@) Formerly the Thistle, this elegant property facing the Swan Theatre has been stylishly revamped, with a sleek brasserie and champagne bar, and rooms featuring designer fabrics and bathrooms full of polished stone.

White Sails   GUESTHOUSE ££

(☎01789-264326; www.white-sails.co.uk; 85 Evesham Rd; r from £95) Plush fabrics, framed prints, brass bedsteads and shabby-chic tables and lamps set the scene at this gorgeous, intimate guesthouse on the edge of the countryside. The five individually furnished rooms come with flatscreen TVs, climate control and glamorous bathrooms.

Emsley Guesthouse   B&B ££

(☎01789-299557; www.theemsley.co.uk; 4 Arden St; d from £64; P🛜) This lovely five-bedroom Victorian property has a personable owner, very clean and attractive accommodation and a large, pretty family room at the top with an exposed beam ceiling.

🍴 Eating

Sheep St is clustered with upmarket eating options, mostly aimed at theatregoers (look out for good-value pre-theatre menus).

TOP CHOICE Church Street Townhouse   BISTRO ££

(☎01789-262222; www.churchstreettownhouse.com; 16 Church St; mains from £11.50; ⊙8am-10pm; 🛜) Open all day, this lovely restaurant is a fantastic place for immersing yourself in Stratford's historic charms, whether for breakfast, lunch or dinner. The food is delightful and the ambience impeccably congenial and well presented. Music students from Shakespeare's old grammar school across the way tinkle the piano ivories daily at 5.30pm.

Lambs MODERN EUROPEAN **££**

(☑01789-292554; www.lambsrestaurant.co.uk; 12 Sheep St; mains £10.25-18.75; ⊘lunch Wed-Sun, dinner daily) Lambs swaps Shakespeare chintz in favour of Venetian blinds and modern elegance but throws in authentic 16th-century ceiling beams for good measure. The menu embraces Gressingham duck, deep-fried goat's cheese and slow-roasted lamb shank, backed up by a strong wine list.

The Oppo BISTRO **££**

(☑01789-269980; www.theoppo.co.uk; 13 Sheep St; mains £11.50-24.50; ⊘closed lunch Sun) Inviting, charming and atmospheric Sheep St bistro with well prepared and tasty dishes, perfect for putting paid to pre-theatre munchies.

Edward Moon's MODERN BRITISH **££**

(☑01789-267069; www.edwardmoon.com; 9 Chapel St; mains £10-15) Named after a famous travelling chef who cooked up the flavours of home for the British colonial service, this snug and just refurbished eatery serves delicious, hearty English dishes, many livened up with herbs and spices from the East.

 Drinking

Dirty Duck PUB

(Waterside) Officially called the 'Black Swan', this enchanting riverside alehouse is a favourite thespian watering hole, boasting a roll call of former regulars (Olivier, Attenborough etc) that reads like an actors' *Who's Who*.

Windmill Inn PUB

(Church St) Ale was flowing here at the same time as rhyming couplets gushed from Shakespeare's quill – this pub with low ceilings has been around a while.

☆ **Entertainment**

Royal Shakespeare Company THEATRE

(RSC; ☑0844 800 1110; www.rsc.org.uk; Waterside; tickets £8-38) Coming to Stratford without seeing a production of Shakespeare would be like going to Beijing and bypassing the Great Wall. The three theatre spaces run by the world-renowned Royal Shakespeare Company have witnessed performances by such legends as Lawrence Olivier, Richard Burton, Judi Dench, Helen Mirren, Ian McKellan and Patrick Stewart.

There are two grand stages in Stratford – **Royal Shakespeare Theatre** and the **Swan**

Theatre on Waterside (both were extensively redeveloped between 2007 and 2010). Contact the RSC for the latest news on performance times at the three venues. There are often special deals for under 25-year-olds, students and seniors and a few tickets are held back for sale on the day of the performance, but eager backpackers tend to snap these up fast. Wise theatregoers book well ahead.

🛈 Information

For local information, turn to the helpful Town Hosts, who stroll around Stratford in yellow jerseys helping confused tourists find their way to sights, hotels and restaurants.

Tourist office (☑0870 160 7930; www.shakespeare-country.co.uk) Just west of Clopton Bridge on the corner with Bridgeway.

🛈 Getting There & Away

If you drive to Stratford, be warned that town car parks charge high fees, 24 hours a day.

BUS National Express (www.nationalexpress.com) coaches and other bus companies run from Stratford's Riverside bus station (behind the Stratford Leisure Centre on Bridgeway). Services include:

Birmingham National Express £8.80, one hour, twice daily

London Victoria National Express £17.60, three to four hours, five daily

Moreton-in-Marsh bus 21/22, one hour, hourly

Oxford National Express £11.20, one hour, twice daily

Warwick bus 16, 40 minutes, hourly.

TRAIN From Stratford train station, London Midland runs to Birmingham (£6.80, one hour, hourly), Chiltern Railways runs to London Marylebone (£25, 2¼ hours, four daily). The nostalgic **Shakespeare Express** (☑0121-708 4960; www.shakespeareexpress.com) steam train chugs twice every Sunday in July and August between Stratford and Birmingham Snow Hill; journey time is one hour.

🛈 Getting Around

A bicycle is handy for getting out to the outlying Shakespeare properties. **Stratford Bike Hire** (☑07711-776340; www.stratfordbikehire.com; 7 Seven Meadows Rd; per half-day/day from £7/13) will deliver to your accommodation.

Punts, canoes and rowing boats are available for hire from Avon Boating (p411) near Clopton Bridge.

Around Stratford-upon-Avon

CHARLECOTE PARK

A youthful Shakespeare is said to have poached deer in the grounds of **Charlecote Park** (NT; ☎01789-470277; adult/child £8.90/4.45; ⏲noon-5pm Fri-Tue Mar-Oct, noon-4pm Sat & Sun Dec), a lavish Elizabethan pile backing onto the River Avon. Fallow deer still roam the grounds today, and the interiors were restored from Georgian chintz to Tudor splendour in 1823. Highlights include Victorian kitchens, filled with culinary-moulds, and an original Tudor gatehouse unaltered since 1551. Charlecote is around 5 miles east of Stratford-upon-Avon. Bus 18 (18A on Sunday) runs to Charlecote hourly from Stratford (30 minutes), continuing to Leamington Spa (30 minutes).

STAFFORDSHIRE

Despite being wedged between the ever-expanding conurbations of Birmingham and Manchester, Staffordshire is surprisingly green, and the northern half of the county rises to meet the rugged hills of the Peak District.

Information

Staffordshire Tourism (www.enjoystaffordshire.co.uk)

Getting There & Around

Regular trains and National Express (www.nationalexpress.com) buses serve Stafford and other major towns. The main local bus operator is **First Group** (☎0870 850 0868; www.firstgroup.com). For details of services, browse the public transport pages at www.staffordshire.gov.uk/transport.

THEME PARK SHENANIGANS

Staffordshire is rightly famous for its theme parks, which resound with the screams of adrenalin junkies lured here by fast and furious thrill rides such as Thirteen, the world's first vertical drop roller coaster. Buckle up, it's going to be a bumpy ride...

Alton Towers

The phenomenally popular **Alton Towers** (☎0870 444 4455; www.altontowers.com; adult/under 12yr £45/36, water park £14/10; ⏲10am-5.30pm, open later for school holidays, weekends & high season, closed Nov-Mar) offers maximum G-forces for your buck. Rollercoaster fans are well catered for – as well as the vertical drop-ride Thirteen, you can ride lying down, sitting down or suspended from the rails on the Nemesis, Oblivion, Air and Rita. Gentler thrills include log flumes, carousels, stage shows, a pirate-themed aquarium and a splashtastic water park. For discounted entry fees, book online.

The **Dimmingsdale YHA** (☎0845 371 9513; www.yha.org.uk; dm from £14) is a miniature hostel 2 miles northwest of the park, set in pleasant walking country.

Alton Towers is east of Cheadle off the B5032. Most large towns in the area offer package coach tours (enquire at tourist offices), or you can ride the Alton Towers bus from Stoke-on-Trent, Nottingham and Derby (see the Alton Towers website for details).

Drayton Manor

Alton Towers' closest rival, **Drayton Manor** (☎0844 472 1950; www.draytonmanor.co.uk; adult/child £36/25; ⏲10.30am-5pm Easter-Oct, longer hours May-Sep) has been serving up screams since 1949. Crowd-pleasers include the Apocalypse free-fall tower, voted Britain's scariest ride, and Shockwave, Europe's only stand-up roller coaster. Younger kids will be just as thrilled by Thomas Land, dedicated to the animated steam-train character.

The park currently has no on-site accommodation, but Tamworth is just 2 miles away, with plenty of B&Bs and hotels – contact **Tamworth Tourist Information** (☎01827-709581; Market St) for recommendations. Drayton Manor is on the A4091, between junctions 9 and 10 of the M42. Package coach tours run from Birmingham, or you can take bus 110 from Birmingham Bull St to Fazeley (one hour, every 20 minutes) and walk the last 15 minutes.

Stafford

POP 63,681

The capital of Staffordshire is a quiet little place that seems somewhat overshadowed by Lichfield and other towns around the county. The main shopping street has some handsome Georgian and medieval buildings, but little evidence remains that this was once the capital of the Anglo-Saxon kingdom of Mercia. For local info, drop into the tourist office (201785-619619; www .visitstafford.org; Eastgate St; ⊗9.30am-5pm Mon-Fri, 9am-4pm Sat) at the Stafford Gatehouse Theatre.

Surrounded by high-street shops, the Ancient High House (201785-619131; Greengate St; ⊗10am-4pm Tue-Sat) is the largest timber-framed town house in the country, artistically assembled in 1595. Creaking stairways lead to carefully restored rooms, and to displays on the history of the town and medieval construction techniques.

The hilltop remains of Stafford Castle (201785-257698; www.staffordbc.gov.uk/live/cme50.htm; Newport Rd; admission free; ⊗visitor centre 11am-4pm Wed-Sun Apr-Oct, 11am-4pm Sat & Sun Nov-Mar), a classic Norman moat and bailey, sit romantically in a forest glade about 1 mile southwest of town, just off the A518.

Buses X1 (1¼ hours, hourly) and 101 (1¼ hours, hourly) run between Stafford and Hanley (Stoke-on-Trent). Trains run to Birmingham (£9.60, 40 minutes, every 20 minutes), Manchester (£20, one hour, every 30 minutes) and London Euston (£55, 1½ hours, hourly).

Around Stafford

The regal, neoclassical mansion of Shugborough (201889-881388; www.shugborough .org.uk; adult/child £12/7, parking £3; ⊗11am-5pm Tue-Sun Mar-Oct) is the ancestral home of renowned royal photographer Lord Lichfield and, accordingly, a good proportion of the wall space is devoted to his work. Unless you're an ardent monarchist, a more compelling reason to visit is the collection of exquisite Louis XV and XVI furniture in the staterooms.

Shugborough is 6 miles east of Stafford on the A513; bus 825 from Stafford to Lichfield runs nearby (20 minutes, half-hourly Monday to Saturday).

Lichfield

POP 27,900

Even without its magnificent Gothic cathedral (one of the most spectacular in the country) this quaintly cobbled market town would be worth a visit to tread in the footsteps of lexicographer and wit Samuel Johnson, and natural philosopher Erasmus Darwin, grandfather of Charles. Johnson once described Lichfield folk as 'the most sober, decent people in England', which was generous considering that this was the last place in the country to stop burning people at the stake!

◉ Sights

FREE Lichfield Cathedral CATHEDRAL
(201543-306100; www.lichfield-cathedral.org; entry by donation; ⊗7.30am-6.15pm daily, to 5pm Sun low season) Crowned by three dramatic towers, Lichfield Cathedral is a stunning Gothic fantasy, constructed in stages from 1200 to 1350. The enormous vaulted nave is set slightly off line from the choir, creating a bizarre perspective when viewed from the west door, and carvings inside the cathedral still bear signs of damage caused by Civil War soldiers sharpening their swords.

In the octagonal Chapter House, you can view the illuminated *Chad Gospels,* created around AD 730, an ornate Anglo-Saxon bas-relief known as the Lichfield Angel and a faded but glorious medieval wall painting above the door.

The grand west facade positively bows under the weight of 113 statues of bishops, saints and kings of England. Do stroll around delightful, once-fortified **Cathedral Close**, ringed with imposing 17th- and 18th-century houses.

Erasmus Darwin House HISTORIC HOME
(201543-306260; www.erasmusdarwin.org; Beacon St; adult/child £3/1; ⊗noon-5pm Tue-Sun) After turning down the job of royal physician to King George III – perhaps a lucky escape, considering the monarch's descent into madness – Erasmus Darwin became a leading light in the Lunar Society, debating the origins of life with such luminaries as Wedgwood, Boulton and Watt decades before his grandson Charles came up with the theory of evolution. The former house of the 'Grandfather of Evolution' contains some intriguing personal effects, and at the back is

a fragrant herb garden leading to Cathedral Close.

FREE **Samuel Johnson Birthplace Museum** MUSEUM, HISTORIC HOME
(☑01543-264972; www.samueljohnsonbirthplace.org.uk; Breadmarket St; ☉10.30am-4.30pm Apr-Sep, 11am-3.30pm Oct-Mar) A short walk south of Erasmus Darwin House, this absorbing museum charts the life of the pioneering lexicographer, wit, poet and critic Samuel Johnson, who moved to London from his native Lichfield and devoted nine years to producing the first dictionary of the English language. Johnson was later immortalised in James Boswell's famous biography *The Life of Samuel Johnson*. Ten years in the making, Johnson's first dictionary helped define the word 'dull' with this example: 'to make dictionaries is dull work'. On the first floor of the museum a short dramatised film narrates Johnson's life story. It's a lovely property to explore.

Lichfield Heritage Centre INTERPRETATION CENTRE
(☑01543-256611; www.lichfieldheritage.org.uk; Market Sq; adult/child £2.50/1, tower adult/child £2.75/1.25; ☉9.30am-4pm Mon-Fri, 9.30am-5pm Sat, 10am-4pm Sun) A nicely presented series of exhibits covering 1300 years of Lichfield history, set in the old St Mary's Church. Climb the tower for sweeping city views.

🛌 Sleeping

The Bogey Hole B&B £
(☑01543-264303; www.thebogeyhole.co.uk; 23 Dam St; s/d £40/60) A sweet little place near the cathedral with bright and rather feminine en suite rooms, lounge with TV, and kitchen at top and laundry room below. Without signage, it's the cream-coloured quaint house at No 23.

George Hotel HOTEL ££
(☑01543-414822; www.thegeorgelichfield.co.uk; 12-14 Bird St; s/d £89/99; P@☎) Part of the Best Western chain, this old Georgian pub has been upgraded into a comfortable midrange hotel, scoring points for location rather than atmosphere.

🍴 Eating & Drinking

Chandlers' Grande Brasserie MODERN EUROPEAN ££
(☑01543-416688; www.chandlersrestaurant.co.uk; Bore St; mains £11-24; ☉closed dinner Sun; ☎) Set in the old Corn Exchange and decked out

with natural wood and polished brass, this is where locals go for a big night out, as much for the ambience as for the Mediterranean-inspired main courses.

Chapters Cathedral Coffee Shop CAFE £
(☑01543-306125; 19 The Close; sandwiches & salads £3-6; ☉breakfast & lunch) A fine 18th-century house with a lovely big window onto the cathedral, and views onto a 13th-century walled garden, serving morning and after-noon tea and Sunday lunches.

Damn Fine Cafe CAFE £
(16 Bird St; mains £6; ☉9am-4pm Tue, Thu & Fri, 9am-3.30pm Wed, 9am-5pm Sat, 10am-4pm Sun) Popular and teeming with locals, this cafe (order and pay at the counter) is a handy place to load up on sandwiches, soup, or fill-ing and full-on bacon-and-sausage breakfast or vegetarian toad-in-the-hole.

ℹ️ Information

The **tourist office** (☑01543-412112; www.visitlichfield.co.uk; Lichfield Garrick; ☉10am-4pm Mon-Sat) doubles as the box office for the Lichfield Garrick theatre.

ℹ️ Getting There & Away

The bus station is opposite the main train sta-tion on Birmingham Rd. Bus 112 runs to Birming-ham (1¼ hours, hourly), while the 825 serves Stafford (1¼ hours, hourly).

Lichfield has two stations. Trains to Birming-ham (40 minutes, every 20 minutes) leave from Lichfield City station in the centre. Trains to London Euston (£19.90, 2¼ hours) run from Lichfield Trent Valley station.

Stoke-on-Trent

POP 240,636

At the heart of the Potteries – the famous pottery-producing region of Staffordshire – Stoke-on-Trent is famed for its ceramics, but don't expect cute little artisanal producers. This was where pottery shifted to mass pro-duction during the Industrial Revolution, and Stoke is a sprawl of industrial town-ships tied together by flyovers and bypasses. There are dozens of active potteries that you can visit, including the famous Wedgwood factory; the town museum presents a good overview. Hanley is the official 'city centre' with the main bus station, surrounded by the suburbs of Tunstall, Burslem, Fenton, Longton and Stoke (with the train station).

CHEADLE

About 11 miles from Stoke-on-Trent, the sleepy market town of Cheadle merits a detour for the simply astonishing St Giles Church (📞01538-753130; www.stgilescatholicchurch .co.uk; 18 Charles St; ⏰8am-3pm), fashioned by the Gothic-revivalist Augustus Welby Pugin (1812–52). Famous for adding the Gothic flourishes to London's Houses of Parliament, Pugin filled St Giles with extravagant gilded murals of angels and medieval motifs that cover every square inch of walls, ceiling and pillars. Despite its 200-foot spire, the less flamboyant exterior hardly prepares you for the church interior, which is exactly like stepping into an illuminated manuscript. With its riot of gold, green, red and blue paintwork and splendid tiled floor, it's a work of art. To admire the interior in all its glory, there's a box to switch on the lights (£1 for 15 minutes).

The church is a 10-minute walk south from Cheadle High St; buses 32 and 32A run to Cheadle every 20 minutes from the Hanley bus stand (30 minutes).

⊙ Sights

The tourist office has leaflets on all the potteries that are open to the public.

Wedgwood Visitor Centre   INTERPRETATION CENTRE

(📞0870 606 1759; www.wedgwoodvisitorcentre .com; adult/child £10/8; ⏰10am-5pm Mon-Fri, 10am-4pm Sat & Sun) Set in attractive parkland, the modern production centre for Josiah Wedgwood's porcelain empire displays an extensive collection of historic pieces, including plenty of Wedgwood's delicate, neoclassical blue-and-white jasperware. The fascinating industrial process is revealed and there's an interesting film on Josiah's life and work, including his involvement in canal-building and opposition to slavery.

FREE Potteries Museum & Art Gallery   MUSEUM

(📞01782-232323; Bethesda St; ⏰10am-5pm Mon-Sat & 2-5pm Sun) This museum houses an extensive ceramics display, from Toby jugs and jasperware to outrageous ornamental pieces such as the Minton Peacock. You can also see treasures from the outstanding Staffordshire Hoard, displays on the WWII Spitfire (created by the Stoke-born aviator Reginald Mitchell) and artworks by TS Lowry and Sir Henry Moore.

🛏 Sleeping & Eating

Hanley is well-stocked with chain eateries and pubs.

Verdon Guest House   B&B £

(📞01782-264244; www.verdonguesthouse.co.uk; 44 Charles St; s/d from £28/44; 🅿@🛜) The area's not an oil painting, but this central and lovingly kept Victorian B&B has comfy rooms a few short steps from the bus station. Breakfast £5 extra.

Kenwood Guest House   B&B £

(📞01782-765787; www.kenwoodguesthousestoke .co.uk; 14 Stoke Rd; 🅿🛜) There's a warm welcome, very clean and well-equipped rooms plus filling breakfasts at this well-located family-run B&B.

ⓘ Information

Tourist office (📞01782-236000; www.visit stoke.co.uk; Victoria Hall, Bagnall St; ⏰9am-5pm Mon-Fri, 10am-2pm Sat)

ⓘ Getting There & Away

From Stoke-on-Trent station in Stoke, trains run to Stafford (20 minutes, half-hourly) and London (£53.50, 1½ hours, two hourly). The Hanley bus station is on Lichfield St. National Express (www .nationalexpress.com) runs to London (£23.80, four hours, seven daily) and Manchester (£6.50, 1½ hours, eight daily). Other services include Bus 32A to Alton Towers (one hour, every two hours) and First bus 101 to Stafford (1¼ hours, hourly).

WORCESTERSHIRE

Probably best known for its famous condiment, invented by two Worcester chemists in 1837, Worcestershire marks the transition from the industrial heart of the Midlands to the peaceful countryside of the Welsh Marches. The southern and western fringes of the county burst with lush countryside and sleepy market towns, while the capital is a classic English county town, whose magnificent cathedral inspired the composer Elgar to write some of his greatest works.

🏃 Activities

The longest riverside walk in the UK, the 210-mile Severn Way winds its way through Worcestershire en route from Plynlimon in Wales to the sea at Bristol. A shorter challenge is the 100-mile Three Choirs Way, linking Worcester to Hereford and Gloucester. The Malvern Hills are also prime country for walking, cycling and paragliding, though there are no official cycling routes.

ℹ️ Information

Visit Worcestershire (www.visitworcester shire.org)

ℹ️ Getting Around

Worcester is a convenient rail hub, and Kidderminster is the southern railhead of the quaint **Severn Valley Railway** (☑01299-403816; www.svr.co.uk; ⊘daily May-Sep, Sat & Sun Oct-Apr). Buses connect larger towns, but services to rural areas can be frustratingly infrequent – search the transport pages at www.worcester shire.gov.uk for bus companies and timetables.

Worcester

POP 94,029

Worcester (*woos*-ter) has enough historic treasures to forgive the architectural eyesores from the postwar love affair with all things concrete. The home of that famous sauce (an unlikely combination of fermented tamarinds and anchovies), this ancient cathedral city was the site of the last battle of the Civil War. The defeated Charles II only narrowly escaped the pursuing Roundheads by hiding in an oak tree, an event still celebrated in Worcester every 29 May, when government buildings are decked out with oak sprigs.

👁️ Sights

Worcester Cathedral CATHEDRAL
(☑01905-732900; www.worcestercathedral.org.uk; entry by £5 donation, tower adult/child £4/2, tours £3/free; ⊘7.30am-6pm, tower 11am-5pm Sat Apr-Oct, tours 11am & 2.30pm Mon-Sat Apr-Sep, Sat Oct-Mar, evensong 5.30pm Mon-Wed, Fri & Sat, 4pm Sun; 🐾) Rising beautifully above the River Severn, Worcester's majestic cathedral is best known as the final resting place of Magna Carta signatory King John.

With its colossal Gothic arches, stained glass creating a kaleidoscope of colour and the exquisitely painted vaulted-ceiling of the Choir, the cathedral interior is magnificent. John's tomb is just one of many grand memorials dotted around, from the ostentatious mausoleums of bishops and earls to the worn graves of forgotten Crusader knights. Beneath it all is an atmospheric Norman crypt, constructed in 1084 by St Wulfstan, the only Saxon bishop to hang on to his seat after the Norman invasion. Other highlights include a charming cloister and a 12th-century circular chapterhouse.

The strong-legged can tackle the 249 steps to the top of the tower where Charles II surveyed his troops during the disastrous Battle of Worcester. Hour-long cathedral tours run from the gift shop. Composer Edward Elgar was a local lad, and several of his works had their first public outings at the cathedral – to appreciate the acoustics, come for evensong.

Commandery MUSEUM
(☑01905-361821; www.worcestercitymuseums.org .uk; College St; adult/child £5.40/2.30; ⊘10am-5pm Mon-Sat, 1.30-5pm Sun) The town's history museum is housed in a splendid Tudor building that served as King Charles II's headquarters during the battle of Worcester. Engaging audioguides and interactive exhibits tell the story of Worcester during key periods in its history. Be sure to visit the 'painted chamber', covered with intriguing 15th-century religious frescos.

Royal Worcester Porcelain Works MUSEUM
(☑01905-21247; www.worcesterporcelainmuseum .org.uk; Severn St; adult/concession £6/5; ⊘10am-5pm Mon-Sat Easter-Oct, 10.30am-4pm Tue-Sat Nov-Easter) Up there with Crown Derby and Wedgwood, the Royal Worcester porcelain factory gained an edge over its rivals by picking up the contract to provide fine crockery to the English monarchy. An entertaining audio tour reveals some quirkier sides to the Royal Worcester story, including its brief foray into porcelain dentures and 'portable fonts' designed for cholera outbreaks. The shop has some splendid pieces, from monk-shaped candle-snuffers to decorated thimbles and pill boxes.

👣 Tours

Worcester Walks WALKING TOUR
(☑01905-726311; www.worcesterwalks.co.uk; adult £5; ⊘11am Mon-Fri Apr-Sep) Offers popular

half-hour walking tours from April to September.

Worcester River Cruises BOAT TOUR
(📞01905-611060; www.worcesterrivercruises.co.uk; adult/child £5.50/3.50; ⏰hourly 11am-5pm) Runs 45-minute cruises on the Severn.

Discover History
Walking Tours WALKING TOUR
(📞07949 222137; www.discover-history.co.uk; adult £5) Various themed historic tours with costumed guides.

🛏 Sleeping

Barrington House B&B ££
(📞01905-422965; www.barringtonhouse.eu; 204 Henwick Rd; r £80-90; P@🛜) A lovely Georgian house by the river with wonderful views, a pretty walled garden, three plush bedrooms full of brocade and trim, and hearty breakfasts served with eggs from the owners' hens.

Diglis House Hotel HOTEL ££
(📞01905-353518; www.diglishousehotel.co.uk; Severn St; s/d from £70/105; P🛜) This rambling and cosy 28-room Georgian house next to the new boathouse enjoys a lovely setting by the water, a short stroll from the cathedral. The best rooms have four posters, luxe bathrooms and river views.

Ye Olde Talbot Hotel HOTEL ££
(📞01905-235730; www.oldenglishinns.co.uk; Friar St; s/d from £40/69; 🛜) Attached to a popular bar and bistro right in the centre, this tasteful inn dates back to the 13th century, but many of the rooms are housed in a modern extension. Discounted parking in multistorey car park.

🍴 Eating

Phat Nancy's CAFE £
(📞01905-612658; www.phatnancys.co.uk; 16 New St; sandwiches from £3; ⏰9am-4pm Mon-Sat) Nancy's has a punk diner vibe and 'custombuilt' sandwiches (gluten-free bread available). It's takeaway only, and busy, busy at lunchtime.

 Little Ginger Pig BISTRO £
(📞01905-338913; www.littlegingerpig.co.uk; 9-11 Copenhagen St; dishes from £6; ⏰9.30am-4pm Mon-Thu, 9.30am-5pm Fri, 8.30am-5pm Sat) The focus is on local produce and independent labels at this pleasant and frequently busy cafe, bistro and bar.

Mac & Jacks DELI, CAFE £
(44 Friar St; mains from £4.95; ⏰10am-4pm Tue-Thu, 10am-5pm Fri & Sat) This Friar St outfit has a lovely deli downstairs for quality titbits and a relaxing cafe upstairs for caffeine, sandwiches and a wholesome menu of hot dishes.

🍷 Drinking & Entertainment

Cardinal's Hat PUB
(31 Friar St) Despite looking as English as Tudor ruffs and claiming a resident ghost, this atmospheric Worcester institution sells Austrian beers in traditional steins and serves authentic Austrian delicacies at lunchtime.

Marr's Bar LIVE MUSIC
(📞01905-613336; www.marrsbar.co.uk; 12 Pierpoint St; ⏰from 8pm) The best live-music venue for miles around, Marr's still has its original sprung dance floors from its days as a dance studio. There's a lively schedule of gigs, acts, comedy shows, acoustic and jamming evenings most nights.

ℹ Information

The **tourist office** (📞01905-726311; www.visitworcester.com; Guildhall, High St; ⏰9.30am-5pm Mon-Sat) has stacks of brochures.

ℹ Getting There & Around

BUS The bus station is inside the Crowngate Centre on Friary Walk.
Birmingham Bus 144, 1¾ hours, every 20 minutes (hourly Sunday)
Great Malvern Bus 44, 30 minutes, twice hourly
Ledbury Bus 417, 50 minutes, five daily Mon-Sat
London National Express £20.60, four hours, three daily
Upton-upon-Severn Bus 363, 30 minutes, hourly

TRAIN Worcester Foregate is the main rail hub, but services also run from Worcester Shrub Hill. Regular trains run to:
Hereford £8.30, 50 minutes, hourly
London Paddington £28.60, 2½ hours, twice hourly

Great Malvern

POP 35,558

Tumbling down the side of a forested ridge about 7 miles southwest of Worcester, the picturesque spa town of Great Malvern is

DON'T MISS

ELGAR BIRTHPLACE MUSEUM

England's most popular classical composer is celebrated with appropriate pomp and circumstance at Elgar Birthplace Museum (☎01905-333224; www.elgarmuseum.org; Lower Broadheath; adult/child £7.50/3.50; ☉11am-5pm Feb-late Dec), housed in the humble cottage where Edward Elgar was born in 1857. Admission includes an audioguide with musical interludes so that you can appreciate what all the fuss is about.

Buses 308 and 310 go from Worcester to Broadheath Common (15 minutes, three daily Monday to Saturday), a short walk from the museum.

the gateway to the Malverns, a soaring range of volcanic hills that rise unexpectedly from the surrounding meadows. In Victorian times, the medicinal waters were prescribed as a panacea for everything from gout to 'sore eyes' – should you wish to test the theory, you can sample Malvern water straight from the ground at a series of public wells dotted around the town. In May/June, classical musicians flock to town for the biannual Elgar Festival, celebrating the life and works of great English composer Edward Elgar, who lived nearby at Malvern Link.

◉ Sights

Great Malvern Priory   MONASTERY

(☎01684-561020; www.greatmalvernpriory.org.uk; Church St; entry by £3 donation; ☉9am-5pm Apr-Oct, reduced hours Nov-Mar) The 11th-century Great Malvern Priory is packed with remarkable features, from original Norman pillars to surreal modernist stained glass. The choir is enclosed by a screen of 15th-century tiles and the monks' stalls are decorated with delightfully irreverent 14th-century misericords, depicting everything from three rats hanging a cat to the mythological reptile, the basilisk.

Malvern Museum of Local History   MUSEUM

(☎01684-567811; www.malvernmuseum.co.uk; Priory Gatehouse, Abbey Rd; adult/child £2/50p; ☉10.30am-5pm daily Mar-Oct, closed Wed during school terms) Straddling Abbey Rd in the

grand Priory Gatehouse (c 1470), the town museum offers a thorough exploration of the things for which Great Malvern is renowned, including spring waters, medieval monasteries, the Malvern Hills and Morgan Motors.

FREE **Morgan Motor Company**   MUSEUM

(☎01684-584580; www.morgan-motor.co.uk; Pickersleigh Rd; tours £10; ☉8.30am-3pm Mon-Thu, to noon Fri) The Morgan Motor Company has been handcrafting elegant and beautiful sports cars since 1909, and you can still see the mechanics at work on guided tours of the factory (pre-booking essential). The museum has a fine fleet of vintage classics. Bus 44 from Church St runs past the factory.

☞ Tours

Walking tours (adult/child £3/1.50) leave from the tourist office at 10.30am Saturday and 2.30pm Sunday, exploring the town's medieval and Victorian history.

⛏ Sleeping

Bredon House   HOTEL **££**

(☎01684-566990; www.bredonhouse.co.uk; 34 Worcester Rd; s/d from £45/70; **P⊛**) A short saunter from the centre, this genteel family- and pet-friendly Victorian hotel backs onto a stunning vista. Rooms are decorated in a quirky but tasteful mix of new and old, and the books, magazines and family photographs dotted around the place make it feel like staying with relatives.

Como House   B&B **££**

(☎01684-561486; www.comohouse.co.uk; Como Rd; s/d £42/65; **P⊛@⊜**) This handsome Malvern-stone house benefits from a quiet location away from the central bustle. Rooms are snug, the garden is a delight and the mood is restoratively calm. The owners will pick you up from the station and drop you off by the walking trails.

Abbey Hotel   HOTEL **£££**

(☎01684-892332; www.sarova.co.uk; Abbey Rd; s/d from £170/180; **P⊛**) Tangled in vines like a Brother's Grimm fairy-tale castle, this stately property offers decent enough rooms in a prime location by the museum and priory.

✕ Eating

St Ann's Well Cafe   CAFE **£**

(☎01684-560285; www.stannswell.co.uk; snacks from £2; ☉10am-4pm daily Easter-Sep, Fri-Sun Oct-Easter) A steep climb above St Ann's Rd (check opening times beforehand with the tourist office), this quaint cafe is set in a handsome early-19th-century villa, with mountain-fresh spring water bubbling into a carved basin by the door.

Anupam INDIAN ££
(☎01684-573814; www.anupam.co.uk; 85 Church St; mains £9-15) Hidden in an arcade just off the main road, this stylish place has a menu that roams the subcontinent, from hearty Mughlai curries to Keralan treats such as tandoori kingfish.

Priors Croft MODERN BRITISH ££
(☎01684-891369; www.priorscroft.com; Grange Rd; mains £7.50-16) A grand folly opposite the theatre with quality pub-style food, which can be enjoyed inside or out in the sunny garden.

☆ Entertainment

Malvern Theatres THEATRE
(www.malvern-theatres.co.uk; Grange Rd) One of the country's best provincial theatres, this long-established cultural hub packs in a lively program of classical music, dance, comedy, drama and cinema. Several nearby restaurants offer good value pre-theatre menus.

Theatre of Small Convenience THEATRE
(www.wctheatre.co.uk; Edith Walk) Set in a converted Victorian public lavatory decked out with theatrical Italianate flourishes, this unusual place has just 12 seats and a program running from puppet shows to poetry and opera.

ℹ Information

The **tourist office** (☎01684-892289; www.malvernhills.gov.uk; 21 Church St; ⊙10am-5pm) is a mine of walking and cycling information. The post office on the square has a bureau de change.

ℹ Getting There & Around

National Express (www.nationalexpress.com) runs one bus daily to London (£20.40, 3½ to 4 hours). For Worcester (30 minutes, twice hourly), take bus 44 or 362/363 (the Malvern Link).

The train station is east of the centre, off Ave Rd. Trains run to Hereford (£7, 35 minutes, hourly), Worcester (15 to 20 minutes, two or three hourly) and Ledbury (13 minutes, hourly).

HEREFORDSHIRE

Slumbering in the English countryside, Herefordshire is a patchwork of fields, hills and cute little black-and-white villages, many dating back to the Tudor era and beyond. Getting around is complicated by infrequent bus services and meandering country lanes, but taking the scenic route is part of the appeal of this laid-back rural idyll.

🏃 Activities

As well as the famous Offa's Dyke Path, walkers can follow the Herefordshire Trail (www.herefordshiretrail.com) on a 150-mile circular loop through Leominster, Ledbury, Ross-on-Wye and Kington. Only slightly less ambitious is the 107-mile Wye Valley Walk (www.wyevalleywalk.org), which runs from Chepstow in Wales through Herefordshire and back out again to Rhayader. Then there's the Three Choirs Way, a 100-mile route connecting the cathedrals of Hereford, Worcester and Gloucester. Cyclists can trace the Six Castles Cycleway (NCN Route 44) from Hereford to Leominster and Shrewsbury, or NCN Route 68 to Great Malvern and Worcester. Climbers and canoeists make a beeline for the gorge of the River Wye at Symonds Yat.

ℹ Information

Visit Herefordshire (www.visitherefordshire.co.uk)

WALKING IN THE MALVERN HILLS

The jack-in-the-box Malvern Hills, which dramatically pop up out of the Severn plains on the boundary between Worcestershire and Herefordshire, rise to the lofty peak of the Worcester Beacon (419m), reached by a steep 3-mile climb above Great Malvern. More than 100 miles of trails traipse over the various summits, which are mostly capped with exposed grassland, offering the kind of views that inspire orchestral movements.

The tourist office has racks of pamphlets covering popular hikes, including a map of the mineral-water springs, wells and fountains dotted around the town and the surrounding hills. The enthusiast-run website www.malverntrail.co.uk is also a goldmine of useful walking information.

❶ Getting Around

For bus timetables, search for 'bus' at www.herefordshire.gov.uk. Alternatively, pick up the chunky Bus and Train Timetable from any tourist office (50p). Trains run frequently to Hereford, Leominster and Ledbury, with regular bus connections on to the rest of the county.

Hereford

POP 56,353

Best known for prime steaks, cider and the Pretenders (three of the original band members were local boys), Hereford dozes in the midst of apple orchards and rolling pastures at the heart of the Marches, straddling the River Wye.

◉ Sights

Hereford Cathedral   CATHEDRAL
(☏01432-374200; www.herefordcathedral.org; 5 College Cloisters; cathedral entry by £5 donation, Mappa Mundi £6; ⊙9.15am to evensong, Mappa Mundi 10am-5pm Mon-Sat May-Sep, to 4pm Mon-Sat Oct-Apr, evensong 5.30pm Mon-Sat, 3.30pm Sun) After Welsh marauders torched the original Saxon cathedral, the Norman rulers of Hereford erected a larger, grander cathedral on the same site, which was subsequently remodelled in a succession of medieval architectural styles.

The signature highlight is the magnificent **Mappa Mundi**, a single piece of calfskin vellum intricately painted with some rather fantastical assumptions about the layout of the globe in around 1290. The same wing contains the world's largest surviving chained library of rare manuscripts manacled to the shelves, kept in a moisture and temperature controlled room. The collection includes a first edition of Dr Johnson's *A Dictionary of the English Language,* a first edition of the King Jame's Bible, a polyglot Bible from the 16th century, a 1217 copy of the revised *Magna Carta* and the illuminated 8th-century *Hereford Gospels.*

Heated by four impressive Gurney stoves, the magnificent cathedral comes alive with **evensong**, and every three years in August it holds the famous **Three Choirs Festival** (www.3choirs.org), shared with Gloucester and Worcester Cathedrals.

FREE **Old House**   MUSEUM
(☏01432-260694; ⊙10am-5pm Tue-Sat year-round, to 4pm Sun Apr-Sep) This gloriously creaky black-and-white, three-storey wooden house was built in 1621. Climb upstairs for beautifully kept medieval rooms with period furniture (including 17th-century cradles), carved wood panelling and antique cast-iron firebacks.

FREE **Hereford Museum & Art Gallery**   MUSEUM
(☏01432-260692; Broad St; ⊙10am-5pm Tue-Sat year-round, to 4pm Sun Apr-Sep) The quirky collection at the town museum has displays on just about everything from 19th-century witches' curses to Roman antiquities.

Cider Museum & King Offa Distillery   BREWERY
(☏01432-354207; www.cidermuseum.co.uk; 21 Ryelands St; adult/child £5/3; ⊙10am-5pm Tue-Sat Apr-Oct, 11am-3pm Tue-Sat Nov-Mar) The name is the giveaway at this brewery and museum. Displays cover cider-making history and you can sample the delicious modern brews. Look for the fine *costrels* (minibarrels) used by agricultural workers to carry their wages, which were partially paid in cider. Follow Eign St west from the centre and turn south along Ryelands St.

☞ Tours

Guided walks (adult/child £3.50/free; ⊙11am Mon-Sat, 3pm Sun May-Sep) start from the tour-

---

THE WORLD AS VIEWED FROM HEREFORD

There are many medieval *mappa mundi* (maps of the world) in existence, but the vellum map held by Hereford Cathedral is perhaps the most intricate. Created by a Lincolnshire monk named Richard de Bello in the 13th century, the map is a pictorial representation of the total world knowledge of the most informed men in England at the time it was created – which was based largely on hearsay, rumours and the exaggerations of drunken seafarers. Consequently, the oceans are populated by mermaids and sea serpents, and landmasses play host to dragons, half-plant–half-human mandrakes and sciapods, mythical inhabitants of India, with one giant foot used to shelter their heads from the sun. Author CS Lewis drew inspiration from this map for some of the more outlandish creatures in his *The Chronicles of Narnia* series.

SIPPING YOUR WAY AROUND CIDER COUNTRY

Crisp, dry ciders have been produced in Herefordshire since medieval times. The **Herefordshire Cider Route** (www.ciderroute.co.uk) drops in on numerous local cider producers, where you can try before you buy, and then totter off to the next cidery. Putting road safety first, tourist offices have maps and guide booklets to help you explore by bus or bicycle.

If you only have time to visit one cider-maker, make it **Westons Cider Mills** (📞01531-660233; www.westons-cider.co.uk; The Bounds; ⏰9am-4.30pm Mon-Fri, 10am-4pm Sat & Sun), whose house brew is even served in the Houses of Parliament! Informative **tours** (adult/child £7.50/4, 1¼ hours) start at 11am, 12.30pm and 2.30pm, with free cider and perry tastings for the grown-ups. Westons is just under a mile west of the tiny village of Much Marcle.

---

ist office, exploring less-well-known historic sights in the centre.

If you fancy guiding yourself along the River Wye, you can rent open canoes from **Ultimate Left Bank** (📞01432-360057; www.leftbankcanoehire.com; Bridge St; canoe hire half-day/day £15/20) at the Left Bank centre.

🛏 Sleeping

TOP CHOICE Castle House   HOTEL ££££
(📞01432-356321; www.castlehse.co.uk; Castle St; s/d/ste from £130/150/195; 🅿@🛜) This award-winning boutique hotel is tranquilly set in a regal Georgian town house that was once the luxurious digs of the Bishop of Hereford. There's a highly sophisticated restaurant, the sun-kissed garden spills down to the river, and suites and rooms are magnificent (with eight new rooms a short walk away at No 25 Castle St). Wheelchair accessible.

Charades   B&B ££
(📞01432-269444; www.charadeshereford.co.uk; 34 Southbank Rd; s/d £50/65; 🅿🛜) This imposing Victorian house has five inviting rooms with high ceilings, big and bright windows and some with soothing countryside views. The house itself has character in spades – look for old service bells in the hall and the plentiful Titanic memorabilia. It's handy for the bus station, but just over half-a-mile walk from the cathedral.

Norfolk Guest House   B&B ££
(📞01432-340900; www.norfolkhousehereford.co.uk; 23 St Martins St; s/d £50/70; 🅿🛜) Charming and welcoming guest house in a lovely Georgian house on the far side of the Old Bridge. Parking on road.

Alberta Guest House   B&B £
(📞01432-270313; www.thealbertaguesthouse.co.uk; 5-13 Newtown Rd; s/d £35/50; 🅿🛜) Simple but warm and welcoming; in the north of town.

✕ Eating & Drinking

The Stewing Pot   BRITISH ££
(📞01432-265233; www.stewingpot.co.uk; 17 Church St; mains £14-17; ⏰lunch & dinner Tue-Sat) This popular restaurant opposite the Mousetrap cheese shop has a decidedly simple ambience but its forte is particularly wholesome and appetising dishes using seasonal, locally produced ingredients (roast pork loin in cider) and refreshingly good service.

Cafe@All Saints   CAFE £
(📞01432-370414; www.cafeatallsaints.co.uk; High St; mains £6-9; ⏰8am-5pm Mon-Sat) This neatly designed offering inside the renovated nave of All Saint's Church on the High St has wholesome daily specials, kicking off from 8am with bacon butties, eggy bread and breakfasts; you can even enjoy a beer, cider or glass of wine. There's outside seating for warmer days.

Black Lion   PUB
(www.theblacklionhereford.co.uk; 31 Bridge St) The more real ales and local ciders you knock back in this traditional pub, the more you may believe the tales of resident ghosts from the site's history as a monastery, an orphanage, a brothel and even a Chinese restaurant.

Jailhouse   CLUB
(http://thejailhouse.wordpress.com; Gaol St; ⏰to 3am Wed, Fri & Sat) Edgy, underground DJs and alternative sounds are constantly on the billing at Hereford's leading club. Look out for secret sets by big-name spinners.

ℹ️ Information

Tourist office (☎01432-268430; www.visit herefordshire.co.uk; 1 King St; ⊗9.30am-5pm Mon-Sat) Opposite the cathedral.

ℹ️ Getting There & Around

BUS The bus station is on Commercial Rd, northeast of the town centre. National Express (www.nationalexpress.com) goes to London (£20.60, 4½ hours, four daily) and Gloucester (£6.90, 1¼ hours, five daily). Local services:

Ledbury Bus 476, 30 minutes, hourly (five Sunday services)

Ludlow Bus 492, 1¼ hours, twice hourly (three Sunday services)

Ross-on-Wye Bus 38, 45 minutes, hourly (six Sunday services)

Worcester Bus 420, one hour, twice hourly (four services Sunday)

TRAIN The train station is northeast of the centre, with hourly trains to Birmingham (£14.20, 1½ hours) and London Paddington (£46.50, three hours), either direct or with a change in Newport, South Wales.

Ross-on-Wye

POP 10,085

Laid-back Ross-on-Wye, which sits prettily on a red sandstone bluff over a kink in the River Wye, is an easy paddle from Symonds Yat, but there are enough sights to warrant a trip by road. The town was propelled to fame in the 18th century by Alexander Pope and Samuel Taylor Coleridge, who penned tributes to philanthropist John Kyrle, Man of Ross, who dedicated his life and fortune to the poor of the parish.

◉ Sights

The 17th-century Market House (☎01989-260675; ⊗10am-5pm Mon-Sat, 10.30am-4pm Sun Apr-Oct, 10.30am-4pm Tue-Sun Nov-Mar) sits atop weathered sandstone columns in Market Pl;

inside the salmon-pink building is an agreeably hand-crafted heritage centre with local history displays.

Crowning the hilltop, pin-straight St Mary's Church (Church St; ⊗9am-5pm) is a 13th-century construction with a fine east window and grand alabaster memorials, including the grave of John Kyrle and the outrageously ostentatious tombs of the noble Rudhall family. Behind the church, Royal Parade runs to the edge of the bluff, lined with realistic-looking but ersatz castle ruins, constructed in 1833.

🛏️ Sleeping & Eating

White House Guest House   B&B ££
(☎01989-763572; www.whitehouseross.com; Wye St; s/d £45/65; P@☎) This 18th-century stone house has a great location across the road from the River Wye. Vivid window boxes give it a splash of colour and the quiet and comfortable rooms are decorated in shades of burgundy and crisp white.

Bridge at Wilton   B&B ££
(☎01989-562655; www.bridge-house-hotel.com; s/d from £80/98; P) A distinguished Georgian country house, a mile west of Ross, with smart rooms and a highly praised restaurant featuring Modern British food.

Pots and Pieces   CAFE £
(www.potsandpieces.com; 40 High St; mains from £5; ⊗breakfast & lunch) The best of the tearooms around the market place, with ceramics and crafts to browse while you sip a coffee or munch on a cupcake or sandwich.

ℹ️ Information

Tourist office (☎01432-260675; tic-ross@herefordshire.gov.uk; Market House, Market Pl; ⊗10.30am-4.30pm Wed-Mon Apr-Sep, to 4pm Sun Oct-Mar) Has information on sights and walks – ask for the *Ross-on-Wye Heritage Trail* booklet (50p).

BLACK-AND-WHITE VILLAGES

A triangle of Tudor England survives almost untouched in northwest Herefordshire, where higgledy-piggledy black-and-white houses cluster round idyllic village greens, seemingly oblivious to the modern world. A delightful 40-mile circular drive follows the Black-and-White Village Trail, meandering past the most handsome timber-framed buildings, starting at Leominster and looping round through Eardisland and Kington, with Kington being the southern terminus of the Mortimer Trail (www.mortimercountry .co.uk) from Ludlow. You can pick up guides to exploring the villages by car, bus or bicycle from any tourist office.

GOLDEN VALLEY

Nudging the foot of the Black Mountains, this lush valley was made famous by children's author CS Lewis, of Narnia acclaim. Following the meandering River Dore, the valley is peppered with historic relics, including Arthur's Stone, a 5000-year-old Neolithic dolmen (chamber-tomb) near the village of Dorestone, and the handsome 12th-century Dore Abbey (www.doreabbey.org.uk; ☉daylight hours) in the appropriately named village of Abbey Dore. Bus 39 between Hereford and Hay-on-Wye (five daily, Monday to Saturday) follows the valley, stopping at Dorestone and Peterchurch. For accommodation and dining ideas, visit www.herefordholidays.co.uk.

❶ Getting There & Around

The bus stand is on Cantilupe Rd. From Monday to Saturday, bus 38 runs hourly to Hereford (45 minutes), and bus 33 runs hourly to Gloucester (40 minutes). For Monmouth, take bus 34 (45 minutes, every two hours Monday to Saturday).

Forest of Dean

The Forest of Dean spills over the Gloucestershire border near the village of Goodrich, just off the A40 between Ross-on-Wye and Monmouth. The River Wye skirts the edge of the forest, offering glorious views to canoeists who paddle out from the delightful village of Symonds Yat.

GOODRICH

Seemingly part of its craggy bedrock, Goodrich Castle (EH; ☎01600-890538; adult/child £6/3.60; ☉10am-5pm Apr-Oct, to 6pm Jul & Aug, 10am-4pm Wed-Sun Nov-Mar) is a fabulously complete medieval castle, topped by a superb 12th-century keep that affords spectacular views. A small exhibition tells the story of the castle from its 11th-century origins to its demise in the 1600s.

Welsh Bicknor YHA (☎0845 371 9666; www.yha.org.uk; dm from £10; ☉Apr-Oct; Ⓟ) is an austere-looking former Victorian rectory surveying a grand sweep of countryside from its lovely riverside grounds. It's on the Wye Valley Walk, 1.5 miles from Goodrich; follow the signed road near Goodrich Castle and take the right fork where the road splits.

Bus 34 stops here every two hours on its way between Ross (20 minutes) and Monmouth (20 minutes), except on Sundays.

SYMONDS YAT

Right on the edge of the forest, squeezed between the River Wye and the towering limestone outcrop known as Symonds Yat Rock, Symonds Yat East is an endearing tangle of pubs and guesthouses, with great walks and an excellent canoeing centre and campsite right in the middle of the village.

An ancient hand-hauled ferry (adult/child/bicycle £1/50p/50p) crosses the Wye to Symonds Yat West on the other side of the valley, where you'll find a riverside caravan park and some family-friendly amusements for campers.

🕊 Activities

This area is renowned for canoeing and rock climbing and there's also good hiking and cycling in the nearby Forest of Dean – the scenic Peregrine Path follows the riverbanks from Symonds Yat East to Monmouth.

The most popular walk from Symonds Yat East picks its way up the side of the 504m Symonds Yat Rock, affording fabulous views of river and valley. In July and August, you may be lucky enough to spot peregrine falcons soaring by the drop-off.

A kiosk atop the rock sells drinks and snacks, and peaceful walking trails continue east through the forest into Gloucestershire.

Rock climbers follow a series of mainly trad routes directly up the face of the cliff, but routes in the easier grades tend to be very polished, and rock falls are common – bring a varied rack and wear your helmet. *Symonds Yat* by John Willson is the definitive guidebook.

The Wyedean Canoe Centre (☎01594-833238; www.wyedean.co.uk; half-day hire from £28; ☉8.30am-8.30pm) hires out canoes and kayaks, and also organises multiday kayaking trips, white-water trips, caving and climbing. Several companies offer a similar service in Symonds Yat West. Strong currents make the river dangerous for swimming. Fair-weather water-babies can enjoy the Wye without the hard work on a sedate, 40-minute gorge cruise run by Kingfisher Cruises (☎01600-891063; adult/child £5.50/3) leaving from beside the ferry crossing.

🛏 Sleeping & Eating

Garth Cottage
B&B ££

(📞01600-890364; www.garthcottage-symondsyat .com; per person £40.50; ⊙mid-March–Oct; P🛆) The pick of accommodation on the east side, this friendly, family-run B&B sits by the riverside near the ferry crossing, and has spotlessly maintained, bright rooms with river views. Good deals for longer stays.

Old Court Hotel
HOTEL ££

(📞01600-890367; www.oldcourthotel.co.uk; r £85-155; P🛆) A striking 16th-century manor house set in lovely gardens on the outskirts of Symonds Yat West, complete with Elizabethan dining room. Choose from spic-and-span contemporary rooms, timbered charmers with four-posters or a barn apartment.

Wyedean Canoe
Centre Campsite
CAMPSITE £

(📞01600-890238; www.wyedean.co.uk; sites per adult/child £10/6; ⊙Apr-Oct) Open April to October, this popular canoe centre has a lovely campsite with a clean bathroom block, set right by the river. Rates drop by 25% from Monday to Thursday.

ℹ Getting There & Away

There is no direct public transport, but bus 34 between Ross-on-Wye and Monmouth can drop you off on the main road 1.5 miles from the village (services run every two hours). Bikes are available for hire from **Pedalabikeaway** (📞01594-860065; www.pedalabikeaway.co.uk; Cannop Valley, near Coleford; per day £16-26; ⊙9am-6pm).

Ledbury

POP 8491

An atmospheric little town creaking with history and dotted with antique shops, Ledbury is a favourite destination for day trippers. The best way to pass the time is to wander the crooked black-and-white streets, which zero in on a delightfully leggy medieval Market House. The timber-framed structure is precariously balanced atop a series of wooden posts supposedly taken from the wrecked ships of the Spanish Armada.

Almost impossibly cute Church Lane runs its cobbled way from the High St to the town church, crowded with tilting timber-framed buildings.

At the top of the lane lies the 12th-century church of St Michael and All Angels (www .ledburyparishchurch.org.uk; ⊙8.30am-6pm, to 4pm low season) with a splendid 18th-century

spire and tower divided from its medieval nave.

🛏 Sleeping & Eating

The town pubs offer reasonably priced meals, but budget travellers will struggle to find cheap accommodation.

Verzon House Hotel
HOTEL £££

(📞01531-670381; www.verzonhouse.com; s/d from £110/185; P@🛆) The ultimate country-chic retreat, this lovely Georgian farmhouse has eight luxuriously appointed rooms with tactile fabrics, free-standing baths, goose-down pillows, and toe-tickling deep-pile carpets. There's also a very smart brasserie. Verzon House is 3 miles west of Ledbury on the A438.

Feathers Hotel
HOTEL £££

(📞01531-635266; www.feathers-ledbury.co.uk; High St; mains £10-17, s/d from £95/140; P🛆) This charming black-and-white Tudor hotel looms over the main road in Ledbury. Rooms in the oldest part of the building come with slanting floorboards, painted beams and much more character than the modern rooms. There's an atmospheric wood-panelled restaurant and a swimming pool.

Cameron & Swan
CAFE £

(📞01531-636791; www.cameronandswan.co.uk; 15 The Homend; mains £6-7; ⊙breakfast & lunch Mon-Sat) A bustling cafe serving tasty deli sandwiches, giant meringues and other tasty homemade treats in a bright, airy dining room.

ℹ Information

Tourist office (📞01531-636147; www.visit ledbury.co.uk; 3 The Homend; ⊙10am-5pm Mon-Sat Apr-Oct, to 4pm Nov-Mar) Just off the High St, behind St Katherine's Chapel, this helpful office has information on town tours.

ℹ Getting There & Away

Bus 476 runs to Hereford (40 minutes, hourly Monday to Saturday, every two hours Sunday); bus 132 runs to Gloucester (one hour, hourly Monday to Saturday). Trains run to Great Malvern (15 minutes, hourly), Hereford (£5.70, 20 minutes, hourly), Worcester (£6, 30 minutes, hourly) and further afield.

SHROPSHIRE

Sleepy Shropshire is a glorious scattering of hills, castles and timber-framed villages tucked against the Welsh border. Highlights include food-obsessed Ludlow, industrial Ironbridge and the beautiful Shropshire Hills, which offer the best walking and cycling in the Marches.

Activities

Walking

The towering Shropshire Hills call out to walkers like a siren. Between Shrewsbury and Ludlow, the landscape rucks up into dramatic folds, with spectacular trails climbing the flanks of Wenlock Edge and the Long Mynd near Church Stretton. The county is also crossed by long-distance trails, including the famous Offa's Dyke Path and the popular Shropshire Way, which meanders around Ludlow, Craven Arms and Church Stretton. For general information on walking in the county, visit www.shropshire walking.co.uk.

Cycling

Mountain bikers head for the muddy tracks that scramble over the Long Mynd near Church Stretton, or the rugged forest trails of Hopton Wood, near Craven Arms, while road riders aim for the Six Castles Cycleway (NCN 44), which runs for 58 miles from Shrewsbury to Leominster.

Tourist offices sell copies of *Cycling for Pleasure in the Marches,* a pack of five maps and guides covering the entire county. Alternatively, you can download cycling pamphlets free from www.shropshirecycling .co.uk.

Information

Secret Shropshire (www.secretshropshire .org.uk)
Shropshire Tourism (www.shropshiretourism .co.uk)

Getting Around

Shrewsbury is the local transport hub, and handy rail services go to Church Stretton, Craven Arms and Ludlow. The invaluable *Shropshire Bus & Train Map,* available free from tourist offices, shows useful routes. **Shropshire Hills Shuttles** (www.shropshirehillsshuttles.co.uk) runs useful bus services along popular hiking routes on weekends and bank holidays.

Shrewsbury

POP 67,126

A delightful jumble of winding medieval streets and timbered Tudor houses leaning at precarious angles, Shrewsbury (*shroos-bree*) was a crucial front in the conflict between English and Welsh in medieval days and the birthplace of Charles Darwin (1809–82). Even today, the road bridge running east towards London is known as the English Bridge to mark it out from the Welsh Bridge leading northwest towards Holyhead.

Sights

The most handsome buildings can be found on the narrow lanes surrounding St Alkmond's Church, particularly along Fish St and amorously named Grope Lane. At the bottom of the High St on Wyle Cop, the seriously overhanging Henry Tudor House was where Henry VII stayed before the Battle of Bosworth.

At the other end of the High St in a cute cobbled square is Shrewsbury's 16th-century Old Market Hall (www.oldmarkethall .co.uk), whose upper levels contain the town's pocket-sized cinema.

St Mary's Church   CHURCH
(St Mary's St; ⊙10am-4pm Mon-Sat) The interior of this tall-spired medieval church contains a fabulous interior, graced with an impressive collection of stained glass, including a 1340 window depicting the Tree of Jesse, a Biblical representation of the lineage of Jesus, and a magnificent oak ceiling in the nave which largely all collapsed in a huge gale in 1894 when the top of the spire blew off. Much of the glass in the church is sourced from Europe, including some outstanding Dutch glass from 1500. There's a small cafe at the rear.

Shrewsbury Abbey   CHURCH
(☑01743-232723; www.shrewsburyabbey.com; Abbey Foregate; entry by £2 donation; ⊙10.30am-3pm Mon-Sat, 11.30am-2.30pm Sun) Famous as the setting for Ellis Peters' *Chronicles of Brother Cadfael,* the lovely red-sandstone Shrewsbury Abbey is all that remains of a vast, cruciform Benedictine monastery founded in 1083. Twice the setting for meetings of the English parliament, the Abbey church lost its spire and two wings when the monastery was dissolved in 1540. It sustained further damage in 1826 when engineer Thomas Telford ran the London–Holyhead road right through the grounds. Nevertheless, you can still see some impressive Norman, Early English and Victorian features, including an exceptional 14th-century west window.

Shrewsbury

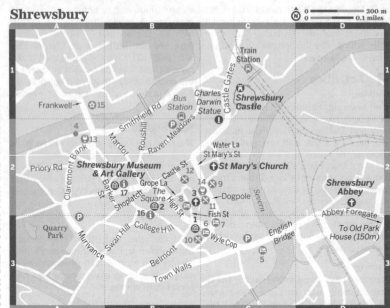

FREE Shrewsbury Museum & Art Gallery
MUSEUM
(☎01743-281205; www.shrewsburymuseums.com; Barker St; ◉10am-5pm Mon-Sat, to 4pm Sun May-Sep) The town museum is currently housed in the timbered Rowley's House from the 1590s (next to the lovely brick appendage of Rowley's Mansion from 1618), with exhibits from Roman treasures to Shropshire gold, including the bronze age Perry bracelet. The museum and tourist office is undergoing a slow move (due in 2013) to the Music Hall on the Square.

Shrewsbury Castle
CASTLE
(☎01743-358516; adult/child £2.50/1.50; ◉10am-5pm Mon-Sat, to 4pm Sun May-Sep, 10am-4pm Tue-Sat Feb-Apr) Hewn from flaking red Shropshire sandstone, the town castle contains the Shropshire Regimental Museum, plus fine views from Laura's Tower and the battlements. The lower level of the Great Hall dates from 1150.

☞ Tours

Guided walking tours (adult/child £4/2.50; ◉2.30pm Mon-Sat, 11am Sun Nov-Apr) leave from the tourist office.

Alternatively, enjoy Shrewsbury from the water on board the Sabrina (☎01743-369741; www.sabrinaboat.co.uk; from £3.50), which cruises the River Severn. Trips leave roughly hourly between 11am and 4pm (March to October) from Victoria Quay near the Welsh Bridge. Ghost cruises every Thursday evening.

🛏 Sleeping

Pretty Abbey Foregate is lined with B&Bs.

Old House Suites
HISTORIC HOTEL **££**
(☎07974-099119; www.theoldhousesuites.com; The Old House, 20 Dogpole; ste £85-135; **P@**) Shrewsbury's most historic place to hang your tricorn, the Old House has three lavish suites, all with views of the garden from a gloriously crooked timbered Tudor town house that was once owned by one of Catherine of Aragon's courtiers. Looking like a medieval oil painting brought to life, the main suite is glorious with its own Tudor-styled loo with bath, shower in passage and lounge (where breakfast is served). The owner conducts (voluntary) hour-long history tours of the property for guests. There's no sign, but it's up the steps from the Dogpole bus stop.

Lion Hotel
HOTEL **££**
(☎01753-353107; www.thelionhotelshrewsbury.co.uk; Wyle Cop; s/d from £80/98; **P**) A gilded wooden lion crowns the doorway of this

Shrewsbury

BIRMINGHAM, THE MIDLANDS & THE MARCHES SHREWSBURY

famous 16th-century coaching inn, decked out inside with portraits of lords and ladies in powdered wigs. Charles Dickens was a former guest and the lounge is warmed by a grand stone fireplace. Rooms are lovely, down to the period-pattern fabrics and ceramic water jugs. Breakfast included.

Lion & Pheasant BOUTIQUE HOTEL ££
(☑01743-770345; www.lionandpheasant.co.uk; 50 Wyle Cop; d £95-175) There's more than a dash of pizazz at this stylish town house offering crisp, neat, bright and well-designed boutique accommodation in a former coaching inn with 22 individually styled rooms. The hotel also owns two nearby cottages for nightly or weekly rates. Breakfast is included.

Tudor House B&B ££
(☑01743-351735; www.tudorhouseshrewsbury.com; 2 Fish St; s/d from £69/79; @☎) A bowing frontage festooned with hanging baskets and window boxes sets the scene at this delightful Tudor cottage. It's handy for everything in the centre, and rooms are adorned with shimmery fabrics and flowery trim. Not all rooms have an en suite.

 Eating

Drapers Hall FRENCH £££
(☑01743-344679; www.drapershallrestaurant.co.uk; St Mary's Pl; mains £12.50-24.50, s/d from £95/

120; P☎) The sense of history is palpable in this beautifully preserved 16th-century hall, fronted by an elegant Elizabethan facade. Award-winning Anglo-French haute cuisine is served in rooms adorned with wood panelling and artwork, and upstairs there are spectacular heirloom-filled bedrooms.

No 4 Butcher Row CAFE £
(☑01743-366691; www.number-four.com; 4 Butcher Row; mains £4-8.50; ☺8.30am-4pm Mon-Fri, 8.30am-5pm Sat, dinner from 6.30pm Fri only) Tucked away next to the Bull Inn near St Alkmond's Church, this neat, modern and very popular outfit is just the ticket for fantastic breakfasts, from eggs Benedict to bacon baguettes or a Full English; lunch mains are excellent and affordable.

Mad Jack's MODERN EUROPEAN ££
(☑01743-358870; www.madjacks.uk.com; 15 St Mary's St; mains £11-16, s/d/ste from £70/80/90; ☎) Mad Jack's is a classy place that straddles the boundary between cafe, restaurant and bar, with an elegant dining room and a plant-filled courtyard. The menu features inventive Modern European cuisine prepared with locally sourced ingredients. There are four swish contemporary bedrooms upstairs.

**Good Life Wholefood
Restaurant** VEGETARIAN £
(☏01743-350455; Barracks Passage; mains £3.50-7; ☺lunch Mon-Sat) Wholesome, freshly prepared vegetarian food is on the cards at this healthy refuge off Wyle Cop. Favourites include quiches, nut loaf, salads, soups, veggie lasagne and a lovely spinach moussaka.

🍷 Drinking

Armoury PUB
(www.armoury-shrewsbury.co.uk; Victoria Ave) Despite being a modern creation, the Armoury feels like it has been here for generations. It's cavernous, with long wooden tables, floor-to-ceiling bookshelves, assorted collectibles and the aromas of fine cooking.

Loggerheads PUB
(1 Church St; ☺11am-11pm Mon-Sat, noon-10.30pm Sun) With its traditional charms and 17th-century architecture, Loggerheads has a crop of small, cosy corners including the Poet's Room hung with portraits of Samuel Beckett, Ted Hughes and Sylvia Plath, and other luminaries of verse.

Three Fishes PUB
(4 Fish St) The quintessential creaky Tudor alehouse, with a jolly publican, mellow regulars and hops hanging from the 15th-century beamed ceiling.

☆ Entertainment

To view mainstream and art-house movies in a charming Elizabethan setting, visit the Old Market Hall Film & Digital Media (☏01743-281 281; www.oldmarkethall.co.uk; The Square).

Theatre Severn THEATRE
(www.theatresevern.co.uk; Frankwell Quay) This much-acclaimed and expansive new riverside theatre and music venue hosts everything from pop gigs and comedy nights to plays and classical concerts.

🔒 Shopping

Appleyards Delicatessen DELI
(☏01743-240180; 85 Wyle Cop) Fantastic, traditional shop simply stuffed with a cornucopia of cheeses and beers.

ℹ Information

Tourist office (☏01743-281200; www.visit shrewsbury.com; Barker St; ☺10am-5pm Mon-Sat year-round, 10am-4pm Sun May-Sep)

ℹ Getting There & Away

BUS The **bus station** (Smithfield Rd) is beside the river. Bus 435 runs to Ludlow (1½ hours, hourly Monday to Saturday), via Church Stretton. Other useful services:

Birmingham National Express, £6.70, 1½ hours, twice daily

Ironbridge Bus 96, 35 minutes, every two hours Monday to Saturday

London National Express, £19.80, 4½ hours, twice daily

TRAIN From the train station at the bottom of Castle Foregate, trains run half-hourly to Ludlow (£12.90, 30 minutes, hourly at weekends). Trains also go direct to London Euston (£52, 2¾ hours, every 20 mins). Or take one of the regular trains to Birmingham or Crewe and change.

If you're bound for Wales, **Arriva Trains Wales** (☏0845 900 0773; www.arrivatrainswales.co.uk) runs to Swansea (£33.80, 3¾ hours, hourly) and Holyhead (£39.80, three hours, hourly).

ℹ Getting Around

You can hire bikes at **Dave Mellor Cycles** (www.davemellorcycles.com; 9a New St, Frankwell).

Attingham Park

The most impressive of Shropshire's stately homes, Attingham Park (NT; ☏01743-708123; NT; house & grounds adult/child £9/5.25, grounds only £4.05/2.15; ☺house 11am-5.30pm mid-Mar–early-Nov, grounds 9am-6pm year-round) was built in imposing neoclassical style in 1785. With its grand columned facade and manicured lawns, and a stagecoach turning-circle in the courtyard, the house could have been plucked straight from a bodice-ripping period drama. Inside you can see an elegant picture gallery by John Nash, plus two wings, decorated in very different Regency styles – highlights include the cherub-filled ladies' boudoir and the grand dining room, laid out as if the banquet guests could arrive any minute. Home to some 300 fallow deer, the landscaped grounds swirl around an ornamental lake.

Attingham Park is 4 miles southeast of Shrewsbury at Atcham – take bus 81 or 96 (18 minutes, six daily Monday to Friday, less frequent at weekends).

Ironbridge Gorge

Strolling or cycling through the woods, hills and villages of this peaceful river gorge, it's hard to believe such a sleepy enclave could really have been the birthplace of the Industrial Revolution. Nevertheless, it was here that Abraham Darby perfected the art of smelting iron ore with coke in 1709, making it possible to mass-produce cast iron for the first time.

Abraham Darby's son, Abraham Darby II, invented a new forging process for producing single beams of iron, allowing Abraham Darby II to astound the world with the first-ever iron bridge, constructed in 1779. The bridge remains the focal point of this World Heritage Site, and 10 very different museums tell the story of the Industrial Revolution in the very buildings where it took place.

◉ Sights

The Ironbridge museums are administered by the Ironbridge Gorge Museum Trust (☏01952-884391; www.ironbridge.org.uk), and all are open from 10am to 5pm from late March to early November, unless stated otherwise. You can buy tickets as you go, but the good-value passport ticket (adult/child £23.25/15.25) allows year-round entry to all of the sites.

Museum of the Gorge   MUSEUM
(☏01952-433424; The Wharfage; adult/child £3.60/2.35) Kick off your visit at the Museum of the Gorge, which offers an overview of the World Heritage Site using film, photos and 3D models. Housed in a Gothic warehouse by the river, it's filled with entertaining, hands-on exhibits.

Iron Bridge   BRIDGE
(toll house admission free) The flamboyant, arching and gravel-strewn Iron Bridge, which gives the area its name, was constructed to flaunt the new technology invented by the inventive Darby family. At the time of its construction in 1779, nobody could believe that anything so large – its weight is 384 tonnes – could be built from cast iron without collapsing under its own weight. There's

a small exhibition on the bridge's history at the former toll house.

Blists Hill Victorian Town   MUSEUM
(☏01952-433424; Legges Way; adult/child £14.95/9.95) Set at the top of the Hay Inclined Plane (a cable lift that once transported coal barges uphill from the Shropshire Canal), Blists Hill is a lovingly restored Victorian village repopulated with townsfolk in period costume, busy with day-to-day chores. There's even a bank, where you can exchange your modern pounds for shillings to use at the village shops. In summer, a Victorian fair is an added fun attraction for young ones.

Coalbrookdale Museum of Iron   MUSEUM
(Wellington Rd; adult/child, £7.40/4.95) Set in the brooding buildings of Abraham Darby's original iron foundry, the Museum of Iron contains some excellent interactive exhibits. As well as producing the girders for the Ironbridge, the factory became famous for heavy machinery and extravagant ornamental castings, including the gates for London's Hyde Park. Combined tickets with Darby Houses also available.

Darby Houses   MUSEUM
(☏01952-433522; adult/child £4.75/3.25; ☺Apr-Oct) Just uphill from the Museum of Iron are these beautifully restored 18th-century homes, which housed generations of the Darby family in gracious but modest Quaker comfort.

Coalport China Museum &
Tar Tunnel   MUSEUM
(museum adult/child £7.60/5.10, Tar Tunnel £2.60/2; ☺Tar Tunnel Apr-Sep) As ironmaking fell into decline, Ironbridge diversified into manufacturing china pots, using the fine clay mined around Blists Hill. Dominated by a pair of towering bottle kilns, the atmospheric old china works now contains an absorbing museum tracing the history of the

---

COSFORD ROYAL AIR FORCE MUSEUM

About 13 miles east of Ironbridge, this famous aerospace museum (☏01902-376200; www.rafmuseum.org.uk; Shifnal; ☺10am-6pm Mar-Oct, 10am-5pm Nov-early Jan & mid-Jan–Feb) is run by the Royal Air Force, whose pilots once steered many of these winged wonders across the skies. Aircraft on display range from fearsome war machines such as the Vulcan bomber (which once carried Britain's nuclear deterrent) to strange experimental aircraft such as the FA330 Bachstelze, a tiny helicopterlike glider towed behind German U-boats to warn them of enemy ships. The museum is a half-mile walk from Cosford train station, on the Birmingham–Shrewsbury line. Visit in June for the annual Cosford Air Show (www.cosfordairshow.co.uk), when the Red Arrows stunt team paint the sky with coloured smoke.

Ironbridge Gorge

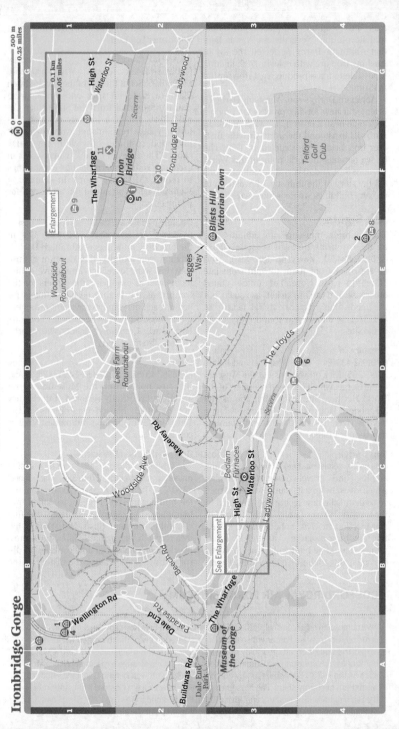

Ironbridge Gorge

Top Sights

Blists Hill Victorian Town........E3
Iron Bridge........F2
Museum of the Gorge........A3

Sights

1 Coalbrookdale Museum of Iron........A1
2 Coalport China Museum & Tar Tunnel........E4
3 Darby Houses........A1
4 Enginuity........A1
5 Iron Bridge Tollhouse........F2
6 Jackfield Tile Museum........D4

Sleeping

7 Calcutts House........D3
8 Coalport YHA........E4
9 Library House........F1

Eating

10 D'arcys at the Station........F2
11 Restaurant Severn........F1

industry, with demonstrations of traditional pottery techniques.

A short stroll along the canal brings you to the 200-year-old **Tar Tunnel**, an artificial watercourse that was abandoned when natural bitumen started trickling from its walls.

Jackfield Tile Museum MUSEUM
(☎01952-433424; adult/child £7.60/5.10) Once the largest tile factory in the world, Jackfield was famous for its encaustic tiles, with ornate designs produced using layers of different coloured clay (the tiles are still produced here today for period restorations). Gas-lit galleries re-create ornately tiled rooms from past centuries, from Victorian public conveniences to fairy-tale friezes from children's hospital wards. The museum is on the south bank of the Severn, near the footbridge to the Coalport China Museum. To reach it, cross the footbridge at the bottom of the Hay Inclined Plane. Tours of the factory are held every Tuesday at 11.30am.

Enginuity MUSEUM
(Wellington Rd; adult/child £7.85/6.75) If the kids are starting to look glazed, recharge their batteries at this levers-and-pulleys science centre beside the Museum of Iron, where you can control robots, move a steam locomotive with your bare hands (and a little engineering know-how) and power up a vacuum cleaner with self-generated electricity.

Broseley Pipeworks MUSEUM
(adult/child £4.75/3.10; ⌚1-5pm mid-May–Sep) This was once the biggest clay tobacco pipemaker in the country, but the industry took a nose-dive after the introduction of prerolled cigarettes in the 1880s, and the factory was preserved much as the last worker left it when the last lights were turned off in 1957. The pipeworks is a 1-mile walk south of the river (cross the Ironbridge and follow the signs) on a winding lane that passes the old workers' cottages (ask the tourist office for the *Jitties* leaflet).

Sleeping

Rooms are everywhere in Ironbridge, even the post office can house you (d £42). There are two YHA hostels at Ironbridge, but the imposing and good-looking Coalbrookdale hostel is reserved for groups.

TOP CHOICE **Library House** B&B ££
(☎01952-432299; www.libraryhouse.com; 11 Severn Bank; s/d from £65/80; P@) Up an alley off the main street, this lovingly restored Georgian library building is hugged by vines, backed by a beautiful garden and decked out with stacks of vintage books, curios, prints and lithographs. There are three charmingly well-preserved, individually decorated rooms, named Milton, Chaucer and Eliot. The affable dog whipping around is Fizz.

Coalport YHA HOSTEL £
(☎0845 371 9325; www.yha.org.uk; High St; dm/f from £16/50; P) This superior hostel is set in a converted china factory next to the China Museum and canal. Rooms are modern and functional; the big drawcards are the facilities, including a laundry, kitchen and licensed cafe, and its location in the quietest, prettiest corner of Ironbridge.

Calcutts House B&B ££
(☎01952-882631; www.calcuttshouse.co.uk; Calcutts Rd; s/tw/d from £50/70/55; P) This former ironmaster's pad dates from the 18th century, tucked away on the south bank around the corner from the Jackfield Tile Museum, about a mile east of the bridge. Its traditionally decorated rooms have heaps

of character, one furnished with an outsize two-hundred-year-old four-poster bed.

✗ Eating & Drinking

Most places to eat line the High St, but old-fashioned pubs dot both banks of the River Severn.

TOP CHOICE Restaurant Severn BRITISH, FRENCH **£££**
(✆01952-432233; www.restaurantsevern.co.uk; 33 High St; 2-/3-course dinner from £23.95/25.95; ⊙dinner Wed-Sat, lunch Sun; P) The highly praised food at this small but busy riverside restaurant is a winning hybrid of English and French. The simple decor and laid-back service merely emphasises the quality of the cooking, and the delectable, locally sourced menu changes weekly.

D'arcys at the Station MEDITERRANEAN **££**
(✆01952-884499; www.darcysironbridge.co.uk; Ladywood; mains £11.25-13.50; ⊙dinner Tue-Sat) Just over the bridge and finely housed in the handsome old station building by the river, this restaurant has recently relocated to Ironbridge, bringing with it flavoursome Mediterranean dishes from Basque chicken to Cypriot kebabs and piri piri trout.

ℹ Information

Tourist office (✆01952-884391; www.visit ironbridge.co.uk; The Wharfage; ⊙10am-5pm) Located at the Museum of the Gorge.

ℹ Getting There & Away

The nearest train station is 6 miles away at Telford, but you can continue on to Ironbridge on bus 96 (20 minutes, every two hours, Monday to Saturday). The same bus continues from the Visitor Centre to Shrewsbury (40 minutes). Bus 9 runs from Bridgnorth (30 minutes, four daily, no Sunday service) and bus 39 runs to Much Wenlock (30 minutes, four daily, no Sunday service).

ℹ Getting Around

At weekends and on bank holidays from Easter to October, the Gorge Connect bus (free to Museum Passport holders) runs from Telford bus station to all of the museums on the north bank of the Severn. A Day Rover pass costs £2.50/1.50 per adult/child.

Bikes can be rented from Bicycle Hub (✆01952-883249; rental per day from £15; ⊙10am-5pm Mon-Sat) in the Fusion centre, behind the Jackfield Tile Museum.

Much Wenlock

POP 1959

With one of those quirky names that abound in the English countryside, Much Wenlock is as charming as it sounds. Surrounding the time-worn ruins of Wenlock Priory, the streets are studded with Tudor, Jacobean and Georgian houses, and locals say hello to everyone. As well as being a perfect English village, Much Wenlock also claims to have jump-started the modern Olympics.

◉ Sights

Across from the tourist office, the wonky Guildhall (✆01952-727509; admission £1; ⊙10.30am-1pm & 2-4.30pm Mon-Sat & 2-4.30pm Sun Apr-Oct), built in classic Tudor style in 1540, features some splendidly ornate wood-carving. A short walk north, the ancient, eroded Holy Trinity Church (www.muchwenlock church.co.uk; ⊙9am-5pm) was built in 1150 over Saxon foundations.

Wenlock Priory RUINS
(EH; ✆01952-727466; adult/child incl audioguide £4/2.40; ⊙10am-5pm daily May-Aug, 10am-5pm Wed-Sun Apr, Sep & Oct, 10am-4pm Sat & Sun Nov-Mar; P) The maudlin Cluniac ruins of Wenlock Priory rise up from vivid green lawns, sprinkled with animal-shaped topiary. Raised by Norman monks over the ruins of a Saxon monastery from AD 680, the hallowed remains include a finely decorated chapterhouse and an unusual carved lavabo, where monks came to ceremonially wash before eating.

⌂ Sleeping & Eating

Raven Hotel HOTEL **££**
(✆01952-727251; www.ravenhotel.com; Barrow St; mains £10-20; s/tw/d £85/120/130; P) Much Wenlock's finest, this 17th-century coaching inn and converted stables has oodles of historical charm and rich country-chic styling throughout. Overlooking a flower-filled courtyard, the excellent restaurant serves classic Mediterranean and British fare.

The Washhouse B&B **££**
(✆01952-728334; 12 Back Lane; s/d £50/65) There's a grand total of two en suite rooms in the detached cottage at this great B&B tucked away just off the High St. The upstairs room has more character, but both are pleasant.

GRANDADDY OF THE MODERN OLYMPICS

All eyes were on London for the Olympic Games in 2012, but tiny Much Wenlock held its own Olympic Games in July the same year, as it has annually since 1850. The idea of holding a sporting tournament based on the games of ancient Greece was the brainchild of local doctor William Penny Brookes, who was looking for a healthy diversion for bored local youths. Accordingly, he created a tournament for 'every kind of man', with running races, high and long jumps, tilting, hammer throwing and wheelbarrow races – plus glee singing, knitting and sewing so every kind of woman wasn't left out!

The games soon piqued the interest of Baron Pierre Coubertin, who visited Much Wenlock in 1890 and consulted Brookes extensively before launching the modern Olympic Games in Athens in 1896. Unfortunately, Brookes was effectively airbrushed out of the Olympic story until 1994, when International Olympic Committee President Juan Antonio Samaranch visited Much Wenlock to pay his respects to 'the founder of the Modern Olympic Games'.

The Much Wenlock Olympics are still held every July, with events that range from the triathlon to volleyball. You can find details at www.wenlock-olympian-society.org.uk.

The Fox PUB ££
(☏01952-727292; www.the-fox-inn.co.uk; 46 High St; mains £13.50-23.50, s/d from £65/85; ☉dinner Tue-Sat, lunch Tue-Sun; P@🖥) Warm yourself by the massive fireplace, then settle down in the dining room to savour locally sourced venison, pheasant and beef, swished down with a pint of Shropshire ale. Candlelit dinners here are lovely. It also has five contemporary rooms.

ⓘ Information

The **tourist office** (☏01952-727679; www.muchwenlockguide.info; The Square; museum admission free; ☉10.30am-1pm & 1.30-5pm daily Apr-Oct, 10.30am-1pm & 1.30-5pm Tue & Fri, 10.30am-1pm Sat Nov-Mar) has stacks of brochures on local sights and walks, and a modest **museum** of local history.

ⓘ Getting There & Away

Buses 436 and 437 run from Shrewsbury to Much Wenlock (35 minutes, hourly, every two hours Sunday) and on to Bridgnorth (20 minutes). Bus 39 runs to Ironbridge (30 minutes, four daily, no Sunday service).

Around Much Wenlock

The spectacular limestone escarpment of Wenlock Edge swells up like an immense petrified wave, breaking over the Shropshire countryside. Formed from limestone that once lined the bottom of Silurian seas, the ridge sprawls for 15 miles from Much Wenlock to Craven Arms along the route of the B4371, providing a fantastic hiking backroute from Ludlow and Ironbridge Gorge.

For a bite, a beer or a bed, point your hiking boots towards the 17th-century Wenlock Edge Inn (☏01746-785678; www.wenlockedgeinn.co.uk; s/d £50/75, mains £9-18; P), perched atop the Edge about 4.5 miles southwest of Much Wenlock. It's a down-to-earth place with above-average pub grub and five chintzy but cosy rooms.

Alternatively, ramble out to remote Wilderhope Manor YHA (☏0845 371 9149; www.yha.org.uk; Longville-in-the-Dale; dm/f £13.95/44.95; ☉Fri, Sat & school holidays; P), a gloriously atmospheric gabled greystone Elizabethan manor, with spiral staircases, wood-panelled walls, an impressive stone-floored dining hall and spacious, oak-beamed rooms. This is hostelling for royalty!

Bus 155 from Ludlow and buses 153/154 from Bridgnorth run infrequently to Shipton, a half-mile walk from Wilderhope – call the hostel for the latest timetable.

Bridgnorth & Around

POP 11,891

Cleaved into two by a dramatic sandstone bluff that tumbles down to the River Severn, Bridgnorth is one of Shropshire's finest-looking historic towns, with a wealth of architectural charm despite much of the high town succumbing to fire in 1646 during the Civil War.

The adorable St Leonard's Close, around its namesake church, contains some of the most attractive buildings and almshouses in town, including a splendid six-gabled house, once part of the grammar school.

Jump aboard the Bridgnorth Cliff Railway (01746-762052; www.bridgnorthcliff railway.co.uk; return £1; 8am-8pm Mon-Sat & noon-8pm Sun May-Sep, to 6.30pm Oct-Apr) the steepest inland railway in Britain, trundling up the cliff since 1892. At the top of the route, a pedestrian walkway (affording astonishing nighttime panoramas) curves around the bluff to a pretty park dotted with scattered masonry, some leaning at an incredible angle – all that remains of Bridgnorth Castle – passing the grand and imposing Thomas Telford–designed and cupola-topped St Mary's Church.

Bridgnorth is also the northern terminus of the Severn Valley Railway (01299-403816; www.svr.co.uk; adult one-way/return £11.50/16.50, child £5.75/8.25; daily May-Sep, Sat & Sun Oct-Apr), whose trains chug down the valley to Kidderminster (one hour), starting from the station on Hollybush Rd. Cyclists can follow a beautiful 20-mile section of the Mercian Way (NCN Route 45) beside the railway line towards the Wyre Forest.

On the High St, Northgate is the last surviving of five gates, containing a small museum. Several narrow lanes drop down from the High Town to the Low Town, including the very steep pedestrian Cartway, at the bottom of which is Bishop Percy's House, dating from 1580.

Just south of town, Daniels Mill (01746-762753; www.danielsmill.co.uk; adult/child £4/3; 11am-4pm Easter-Oct) is the largest working water-powered mill in the country, and is still produces flour for local bakers. Visitors get a personal tour of the working machinery from the resident miller.

Near the top of the Cartway, the licensed Cinnamon Cafe (01746-762944; Waterloo House, Cartway; mains £5-8; 9am-6pm Mon-Wed & Fri, 10am-4pm Sat & Sun) serves up savoury bakes (many vegetarian and vegan) plus quiches and homemade muesli and cakes, which you can munch indoors or in front of the views from the terrace. Not far from the Town Hall on the High St, the well-stocked Bridgnorth Delicatessen (45 High St; 9am-5pm Mon-Sat, 11am-4pm Sun) does business from a lovely old shop, full of gleaming jars.

Based at the town library, the tourist office (01746-763257; www.visitbridgnorth.co.uk; 9.30am-5pm Mon-Sat Apr-Oct, Mon-Wed, Fri & Sat Nov-Mar) can advise on local B&Bs.

❶ Getting There & Away

Buses 436 and 437 run hourly from Shrewsbury to Bridgnorth (one hour, five Sunday services), via Much Wenlock (25 minutes). Bus 9 runs to Ironbridge (30 minutes, four daily, no Sunday service).

Church Stretton & Around

POP 3841

Set in a deep valley formed by the Long Mynd and the Caradoc Hills, Church Stretton is an ideal base for walks or cycle tours through the Shropshire Hills. Although black-and-white timbers are heavily in evidence, most of the buildings in town are 19th-century fakes, built by the Victorians who flocked here to take the country air. The Norman-era St Laurence's Church features an exhibitionist sheila-na-gig over its north door.

🏃 Activities

Walking

Church Stretton clings to the steeply sloping sides of the Long Mynd, Shropshire's most famous hill, which rises to 517m. Dubbed 'Little Switzerland' by the Victorians, this desolate but dramatic bluff is girdled by walking trails that offer soaring views over the surrounding countryside. Most people start walking from the National Trust car park at the end of the Carding Mill Valley (www.cardingmillvalley.org.uk), half a mile west of Shrewsbury Rd – a small tearoom (11am-5pm) provides refreshments.

A maze of single-track roads climbs over the Long Mynd to the adjacent ridge of Stiperstones, which is crowned by a line of spooky-looking crags where Satan is said to hold court. You can continue right over the ridge to the village of Snailbeach, with its intriguing mining relics, passing the Bog (01743-792484; www.bogcentre.co.uk; 10am-5pm Wed-Sun Easter-Oct), a cosy cafe and tourist office next to the ruins of an abandoned mining village.

Other Activities

The tourist office has maps of local mountain-biking circuits and details of local horse-riding stables.

Plush Hill Cycles   BICYCLE RENTAL
(01694-720133; www.plushhillcycles.co.uk; 8 The Square; per day from £20) Handy range of mountain bikes and electric bikes.

🛏 Sleeping

Bridges Long Mynd YHA   HOSTEL £
(📞01588-650656; www.yha.org.uk; Bridges; dm from £16; 🅿) On the far side of the Long Mynd, this superior YHA property is housed in a former school in the tiny hamlet of Bridges near Ratlinghope. Popular with hikers, the hostel is wonderfully isolated, but meals and liquid refreshment are available at the nearby Horseshoe Inn pub. To get here, cross the Mynd to Ratlinghope, or take the Long Mynd shuttle bus.

Mynd House   B&B ££
(📞01694-722212; www.myndhouse.com; Ludlow Rd; s/d from £45/75; 🅿@🛜) South of Church Stretton in Little Stretton, this inviting, family-friendly guesthouse has splendid views across the valley and backs directly onto the Mynd. The lovely rooms are named after local hills, there's a small bar and lounge stocked with local books, and a room for drying your boots.

🍴 Eating & Drinking

There are several cosy pubs along the High St.

Berry's Coffee House   CAFE £
(📞01694-724452; www.berryscoffeehouse.co.uk; 17 High St; meals £6-8; ⏲9am-5pm, later Fri & Sat; 🚼) A particularly homely and delightful cafe with loads of rooms in an 18th-century house, just off the main street, offering an organic, free-range, fair-trade home-cooked menu, including Shropshire breakfasts and wicked desserts. No credit cards.

Studio   MODERN EUROPEAN £££
(📞01694-722672; www.thestudiorestaurant.net; 59 High St; 2/3 courses £25.50/28.50; ⏲dinner Wed-Sat) A former artist's studio, not far from the church, sets the scene for the town's most intimate restaurant, featuring an award-winning menu of modern English and traditional French food.

ℹ Information

The **tourist office** (📞01694-723133; www.churchstretton.co.uk; Church St; ⏲9.30am-5pm Mon-Sat, closed 12.30-1.30pm in winter), adjoining the library, has abundant walking information as well as free internet access.

ℹ Getting There & Around

Trains between Ludlow and Shrewsbury stop here every hour, taking 20 minutes from either end. Alternatively, take bus 435 from Shrews-

bury or Ludlow (40 minutes, hourly Monday to Saturday).

From April to September, the **Long Mynd & Stiperstones Shuttle** (www.shropshirehills shuttles.co.uk; day ticket adult/child £7/2.50; ⏲seven daily Sat & Sun Apr-Sep) runs from the Carding Mill Valley in Church Stretton to the villages atop the Long Mynd, passing the YHA at Bridges, the Stiperstones and the Snailbeach mine.

Bishop's Castle

POP 1630

Set amid blissfully peaceful Shropshire countryside, Bishop's Castle is a higgledy-piggledy tangle of timbered town houses and Old Mother Hubbard cottages. Lined with surprisingly posh boutiques, the High St climbs from the town church to the adorable Georgian town hall abutting the crooked 16th-century House on Crutches (📞01588-630075; admission free; ⏲2-5pm Sat & Sun Apr-Sep), which also houses the town museum.

The pleasingly potty Old Time (📞01588-638467; www.oldtime.co.uk; 29 High St; ⏲10am-6pm Mon-Sat, to 2pm Sun) is part furniture workshop and part tourist information office.

🏃 Activities

Walkers can hike from north Bishop's Castle along the Shropshire Way, which joins up with the long-distance Offa's Dyke Path and Kerry Ridgeway to the west. The northern sections of the Shropshire Way climb to the high country of the Stiperstones and the Long Mynd near Church Stretton. Bishop's Castle also lies on the popular Six Castles Cycleway (NCN Route 44) between Shrewsbury and Leominster.

🛏 Sleeping & Eating

Rooms are more expensive at weekends.

Poppy House   B&B ££
(📞01588-638443; www.poppyhouse.co.uk; 20 Market Sq; s/d from £40/70, dishes from £6; ⏲cafe 10am-5pm Wed-Fri & Sun, to 10pm Sat; 🛜) This sweet guesthouse has lovely, individual rooms with latch-doors (and all with bath), loads of old beams and is attached to a friendly cafe that upgrades to fine dining on Saturday nights.

Castle Hotel   HOTEL ££
(📞01588-638403; www.thecastlehotelbishops castle.co.uk; The Square; s/d/f incl breakfast

£60/85/125;) This solid-looking 18th-century coaching inn was built with stones from the now-vanished Bishop's Castle, which also contributed the gorgeous wood panelling in the dining room. All eight en suite rooms are lovely, with modern fabrics meeting old antique furniture. The pub bar in the hotel is decidedly cosy and the garden delightful. Rates increase at the weekends.

Porch House   B&B ££
(01588-638854; www.theporchhouse.com; High St; s/d from £50/75;) Part of a terrace of timbered 16th-century buildings, this gem has two charming rooms with mod-cons: one a suite with a vast bath, the other carrying a discernible list courtesy of the ancient timber work.

Yarborough House   CAFE, BOOKS £
(www.yarboroughhouse.com; The Square; 10am-5pm Tue & Thu-Sun) Excellent coffee and cakes in an excellent secondhand bookshop with a simply vast collection of secondhand classical music CDs and LPs.

Drinking

Three Tuns   PUB
(www.thethreetunsinn.co.uk; Salop St) Bishop's Castle's finest watering hole is attached to the tiny Three Tuns Brewery (www.threetunsbrewery.co.uk), which has been rolling barrels of nut-brown ale across the courtyard since 1642. It's a cosy local and the ales are delicious.

Six Bells Inn   PUB
(Church St; mains £8-13; lunch Tue-Sun, dinner Wed-Sat) This historic 17th-century coaching inn is alive with loyal locals and ramblers who come to sample ales from its adjoining brewery.

Getting There & Away

Bus 553 runs to and from Shrewsbury (one hour, six daily). On Saturdays and bank holiday weekends, you can jump on the Secret Hills Shuttle from Craven Arms (40 minutes, four per day).

Ludlow

POP 9548

Quite why this genteel market town fanning out from the rambling ruins of a fine Norman castle became a national gastronomic phenomenon is not entirely clear, but today Ludlow's delightful muddle of narrow streets are crammed with independent butchers, bakers, grocers, cheesemongers and exceptional restaurants.

Sights & Activities

Ludlow Castle   CASTLE
(01584-873355; www.ludlowcastle.com; Castle Sq; adult/child £5/2.50; 10am-7pm daily Aug, to 5pm Apr-Jul & Sep, to 4pm Oct, Nov, Feb & Mar, Sat & Sun only Dec & Jan) Perched in an ideal defensive location atop a cliff above a crook in the river, the town castle was built to ward off the marauding Welsh – or to enforce the English expansion into Wales, according to those west of the border. Founded after the Norman conquest, the castle was dramatically expanded in the 14th century.

The Norman chapel in the inner bailey is one of the few surviving round chapels in England, and the sturdy keep (built around 1090) offers wonderful views over the hills.

Church of St Laurence   CHURCH
(www.stlaurences.org.uk; King St; entry by £2 donation; 10am-5.30pm Apr-Sep, 11am-4pm Oct-Mar) One of the largest parish churches in Britain, the church of St Laurence contains grand Elizabethan alabaster tombs and some delightfully cheeky medieval misericords carved into its medieval choir stalls, including a beer-swilling chap raiding his barrel. The Lady Chapel contains a marvelous Jesse Window originally dating from 1330 (although much of the glass is Victorian). Four windows in St John's Chapel date from the mid-15th century, including the delightful, honey-coloured Golden Window. Climb the tower (£3) for stunning views.

Walking & Cycling

Ludlow is ringed by wonderful landscapes. Starting just outside the castle entrance, the waymarked Mortimer Trail runs for 30 miles through idyllic English countryside to Kington in Herefordshire. The tourist office has various leaflets describing the route, or visit www.mortimercountry.co.uk.

Another fine walking or cycling route is the Shropshire Way, which runs northwest to Craven Arms, or northeast to Wenlock Edge over the dramatic summit of Clee Hill (540m), the highest point in the county. The hill affords awe-inspiring views south to Worcestershire's Malvern Hills.

For something more leisurely, simply stroll around town. A scenic path drops behind Ludlow Castle and crosses the River Teme via the Dinham Bridge, following the south bank east to Ludford Bridge. Climbing the hill, duck through the narrow Broadgate (the sole survivor of seven medieval gates, with its slots for the portcullis still intact) marking the medieval town limits, and stroll past the Georgian town houses of Broad St to reach the Buttercross, Ludlow's medieval butter market.

Tours

Popular town tours (☎01584-874205; www .ludlowhistory.co.uk;adult/child£2.50/free; ☺2.30pm Sat & Sun Apr-Oct) leave from the Cannon in Castle Sq. Alternatively, search for spooks on the ghost walk (www.shropshireghostwalks .co.uk; per person £4; ☺8pm Fri), which leaves from outside the Church Inn on the Buttercross.

Festivals & Events

The town's busy calendar peaks with the Ludlow Festival (www.ludlowfestival.co.uk), a fortnight of theatre and music in June and July that uses the castle as its dramatic backdrop. The Ludlow Food & Drink Festival (www.foodfestival.co.uk) is one of Britain's best foodie celebrations, spanning a long weekend in September.

Sleeping

 Feathers Hotel   HOTEL ££
(☎01584-875261; www.feathersatludlow.co.uk; Bull Ring; s/d from £85/105, 2/3 courses £32.50/39.95; ℗) Stepping through the almost impossibly ornate timbered Jacobean facade, it's all tapestries, creaky wood furniture, timber beams and stained glass: you can almost hear the cavaliers toasting the health of King Charles. The best rooms are in the old building – rooms in the newer wing lack the character and romance. Prices creep up at weekends. The restaurant is also highly recommended.

De Grey's   B&B ££
(☎01584-872764; www.degreys.co.uk; 5 Broad St; s/d from £95/110, light meals from £4; ℗☎) Above the swooningly nostalgic tearooms of the same name, this smart B&B has nine comfy and twee rooms with low ceilings, beams, leaded windows, reassuringly solid oak beds and four-posters in the suites. Higher rates Friday and Saturday.

Dinham Hall Hotel   HOTEL £££
(☎01584-876464; www.dinhamhall.co.uk; s/d from £105/145; ℗) A resplendent 18th-century country manor with views of the castle and the river from gorgeous rooms full of heirloom furniture, plus a superb fine-dining restaurant and afternoon teas.

Eating

Almost every pub and restaurant in town has caught the local-produce-and-deli-ingredients bug.

La Bécasse   MODERN FRENCH £££
(☎01584-872325; www.labecasse.co.uk; 17 Corve St; 2-/3-course lunch £26/30; ☺lunch Wed-Sun, dinner Tue-Sat) Artistically presented and bursting with inventive flavours, meals are served in an oak-panelled, exposed-brick dining room in the 17th-century coach house. Michelin-starred chef Will Holland has created some remarkable dishes.

Mr Underhill's   MODERN BRITISH £££
(☎01584-874431; www.mr-underhills.co.uk; Dinham Weir; 8-course set menu from £62.50, ste from £235; ☺dinner Wed-Sun) This dignified and award-winning restaurant is set in a converted corn mill that dips its toes in the river. The Modern British food is exquisitely prepared, using market-fresh ingredients in a menu that changes daily. Should you be too full to walk home, one of the four particularly elegant suites can oblige.

Drinking

Real ales are the order of the day in flavour-obsessed Ludlow. The Ludlow Brewing Company (www.theludlowbrewingcompany.co.uk; 105 Corve St; ☺10am-5pm Mon-Fri, to 1pm Sun) produces award-winning brews, and sells directly from the brewery.

Of the many pubs, the hop-strewn Church Inn (Buttercross) is a cosy little escape with a pulpit at the bar, tucked away on the narrow lane beside the old butter market. The quiet little Wheatsheaf Inn (Lower Broad St), under the medieval Broadgate, has a good choice of local ales.

Overlooking the market square, Ludlow Assembly Rooms (☎01584-878141; www.ludlow assemblyrooms.co.uk; adult/child £5/3) also double as the town cinema.

Shopping

The best of the delis, independent butchers and artisanal bakers are clustered around the market square and the surrounding lanes.

Ludlow Market takes place on the Market Sq on Mondays, Wednesdays, Fridays and Saturdays on the site of the old Victorian town hall, demolished overnight in 1986.

❶ Information

Tourist office (☏01584-875053; www.ludlow .org.uk; Castle Sq; ⊙10am-5pm Mon-Sat, 10.30am-5pm Sun) This well-stocked office contains an inside-out museum (☏01584-813666; admission free; ⊙10am to 5pm Mon-Sat year-round, Sun Jun-Aug) featuring the town and surrounding area.

❶ Getting There & Around

You can also reach Shrewsbury on bus 435 (1½ hours, hourly Monday to Saturday), which runs via Craven Arms (20 minutes) and Church Stretton (40 minutes). Trains run frequently from the station on the north edge of town to Hereford (£8.70, 25 minutes, half hourly) and Shrewsbury (£11.20, 30 minutes, half hourly) via Church Stretton (20 minutes).

You can hire bikes from **Wheely Wonderful** (☏01568-770755; www.wheelywonderful cycling.co.uk; Petchfield Farm; adult bike per day from £18; ⊙9am-5pm Mon-Sat Apr-Oct), 5 miles west of Ludlow.

NOTTINGHAMSHIRE

Say Nottinghamshire and people think of one thing – Robin Hood. Whether the hero woodsman existed is hotly debated, but the county plays up its connections to the outlaw. Storytelling seems to be in Nottinghamshire's blood – local wordsmiths include provocative writer DH Lawrence, of *Lady Chatterley's Lover* fame, and hedonist poet Lord Byron. The city of Nottingham is the bustling hub, but venture into the surrounding countryside and you'll discover historic towns and stately homes surrounding the green bower of Sherwood Forest.

❶ Information

Experience Nottinghamshire (www .experiencenottinghamshire.com)

❶ Getting There & Around

National Express (www.nationalexpress.com) and **Trent Barton** (☏01773-712265; www .trentbarton.co.uk) buses provide the majority of bus services. See www.nottinghamshire.gov. uk/buses for timetables. Trains run frequently to most large towns, and many smaller villages in the Peak District.

Nottingham

POP 266,988

Forever associated with men in tights and a sheriff with anger-management issues, Nottingham is a dynamic county capital with big-city aspirations, fascinating historical sights and a buzzing music and club scene thanks to its spirited student population.

◉ Sights & Activities

Nottingham Castle & Art Gallery   CASTLE, GALLERY

(☏0115-915 3700; www.nottinghamcity.gov.uk/ nottinghamcastle; adult/child £5.50/4, Mortimer's Hole tours £2.50/1.50; ⊙10am-5pm Tue-Sun Mar-Oct, to 4pm Nov-Feb, Mortimer's Hole tours 11am & 2pm Mon-Sat, noon, 1pm, 2pm, 3pm Sun) Nottingham's famous castle sits atop a sandstone outcrop worm-holed with caves and tunnels. The original castle was founded by William the Conqueror and held by a succession of English kings before falling in the English Civil War. Its 17th-century replacement now contains a diverting local-history museum and art gallery.

Burrowing through the bedrock beneath the castle, the underground passageway Mortimer's Hole emerges at Brewhouse Yard. In 1330 supporters of Edward III used the tunnel to breach the castle security and capture Roger Mortimer, the machiavellian Earl of March, who briefly appointed himself ruler of England after deposing Edward II.

Castle admission includes entry to the charming Museum of Nottingham Life at Brewhouse Yard (Castle Blvd), housed in five atmospheric 17th-century cottages.

City of Caves   CAVE

(☏0115-988 1955; www.cityofcaves.com; adult/ child £6.50/5.50; ⊙10.30am-5pm) Over the centuries, the sandstone underneath Nottingham has been carved into a veritable Swiss cheese of caverns and passageways. From the top level of the Broadmarsh shopping centre, audio tours (or performance tours at weekends and during school holidays – book ahead) lead you through a WWII air-raid shelter, a medieval underground tannery, several pub cellars and a mock-up of a Victorian slum dwelling. A joint ticket with the Galleries of Justice costs adult/child £12/9.75.

Galleries of Justice   MUSEUM

(☏0115-952 0555; www.galleriesofjustice.org. uk; High Pavement; adult/child £9.50/7.50;

⊙10.30am-5pm) In the grand Georgian Shire Hall, the Galleries of Justice offers a ghoulish stroll through centuries of British justice, including medieval trials by fire and water. Audio tours run on Monday and Tuesday; live-action tours with 'gaolers' run Wednesday to Sunday (daily during school holidays).

FREE **Nottingham Contemporary** GALLERY (☑0115-948 9750; www.nottinghamcontemporary .org; Weekday Cross; ⊙10am-7pm Tue-Fri, 10am-6pm Sat, 11am-5pm Sun) Behind its lace-patterned concrete facade, this sleek gallery holds edgy, design-oriented exhibitions of paintings, prints, photography and sculpture.

National Ice Centre SKATING (☑0843 373 3000; www.national-ice-centre.com; Bolero Sq; skating £6, skate hire £2) On Bolero Sq (named for Nottingham skaters Jayne Torvill and Christopher Dean's iconic 1984 gold-medal-winning routine), this was the UK's first ice centre with twin Olympic-sized (60m x 30m) rinks. The complex incorporates the East Midland's premier entertainment venue, the **Capital FM Arena**, hosting sporting fixtures, competitions and performances. Daily skating session times are posted online.

☞ Tours

Ezekial Bone Tours WALKING TOUR (☑07941 210986; www.bonecorporation.co.uk; tours adult/child £8/4; ⊙Sat May-Sep) Entertaining history tours are led by Nottingham's 'modern day Robin Hood' Ezekial Bone aka Ade Andrews. In addition to the two-hour Robin Hood town tours, Andrews runs Robin Hood Sherwood Forest tours and various other walks year-round by request.

Nottingham Princess CRUISE (☑0115-910 0400; www.princessrivercruises.co.uk; 2/3hr cruises from £13.95/15.45) Lunch and dinner (and dance) cruises along the River Trent.

Original Nottingham Ghost Walk WALKING TOUR (www.ghost-walks.co.uk; adult/child £5/3; ⊙7pm Sat Jan-Nov) Tours lasting 1¼ hours depart from **Ye Olde Salutation Inn** (Maid Marian Way) – descend into the medieval caves if you dare...

DON'T MISS

WOLLATON HALL

Built in 1588 for land owner and coal mogul Sir Francis Willoughby, **Wollaton Hall** (www.nottinghamcity.gov.uk; Wollaton Park, Derby Rd; admission free, parking per 3hr/day £2/4; tours adult/child £5/3; ⊙11am-5pm Mar-Oct, to 4pm Nov-Feb) has more frills and ruffs than an Elizabethan banquet hall. This fabulous manor was created by avant-garde architect Robert Smythson. As well as extravagant rooms from the Tudor, Regency and Victorian periods, the hall incorporates a natural history museum, and sits within 200 hectares of grounds roamed by herds of fallow and red deer.

Wollaton Hall is 2.5 miles west of the city centre; take bus 30 or 2 from Victoria bus station (15 minutes).

☆☆ Festivals & Events

Nottingham hosts an intriguing selection of festivals – search events online at the website www.nottinghamcity.gov.uk.

The city's biggest live music festival, **Splendour**, takes place in July, while the Caribbean community celebrates its **Carnival** in August. October's medieval **Goose Fair** has evolved from a travelling market to a modern funfair; the **Robin Hood Beer Festival**, featuring over 1000 beers and 200 ciders, and the family-friendly **Robin Hood Pageant** take place in the same month.

⌑ Sleeping

TOP CHOICE **Hart's** BOUTIQUE HOTEL ££ (☑0115-988 1900; www.hartsnottingham.co.uk; Standard Hill, Park Row; d from £125; ☐@☎) Within the Nottingham General Hospital compound, the city's swishest hotel's ultracontemporary rooms are in a striking modernist building, while its renowned restaurant is housed in an historic red-brick wing. Work out in the small gym or unwind in the private garden.

Lace Market Hotel BOUTIQUE HOTEL ££ (☑0115-852 3232; www.lacemarkethotel.co.uk; 29-31 High Pavement; s/d incl breakfast from £59/79; ☐☎) Within an elegant Georgian town house in the heart of the trendy Lace Market, sleek rooms have state-of-the-art furnishings and amenities. Its fine-dining

Nottingham

Ⓝ 0 ——— 200 m
0 ——— 0.1 miles

To Victoria Bus Station (350m)
Igloo Backpackers Hostel (540m)

Wollaton St

Upper Parliament St

Cannon Ct

Sky Mirror

E Circus St

Angel Row

Maid Marian Way

Market St

Queen St

King St

Clumber St

Lincoln St

George St

Broad St

Heathcote St

Carlton St

Woolpack La

Long Row
Old Market Square

Smithy Row

Pelham St

Victoria St

St Mary's Gate

To National Ice Centre (150m)

South Pde

Bridlesmith Walk

St Peter's Gate

Bridlesmith Gate

Fletcher Gate

Pilcher Gate

Broadway

Park Row

Mount St

St James's St

Friar La

Spaniel Row

Wheeler Gate

Hounds Gate

St James's Tce

Castlegate

Low Pavement

Listergate

LACE MARKET

Weekday Cross

City of Caves

Middle Hill

Cliff Rd

High Pavement

Popham St

Lenton Rd

Castle Rd

Nottingham Castle & Art Gallery

Collin St

Peveril Dr

Greyfriar Gate

Canal St

Trent St

Nottingham Canal

Castle Blvd

Wilford St

Carrington St

Nottingham Train Station

Station St

Eating

Nottingham reputedly has more restaurants, pubs and bars per square mile than anywhere else in Europe.

restaurant, Merchants, and adjoining genteel pub, the Cock & Hoop (☎0115-852 3231; 25 High Pavement), are both excellent.

Greenwood Lodge City
Guest House   B&B ££
(☎0115-962 1206; www.greenwoodlodgecityguesthouse.co.uk; Third Ave, Sherwood Rise; s/d from £51.50/86.50; P🐾) A gorgeous B&B set in a large Victorian house north of the centre. The location is quiet, and the house and frilly rooms are full of period character, and there's a pretty courtyard garden. Children under 10 aren't permitted.

Igloo Backpackers Hostel   HOSTEL £
(☎0115-947 5250; www.igloohostel.co.uk; 110 Mansfield Rd; dm/s/d £16/38/48; 🐾) A favourite with international backpackers, this independent hostel is opposite the Golden Fleece pub and a 24-hour supermarket.

TOP
CHOICE Hart's Restaurant   MODERN BRITISH £££
(☎0115-988 1900; www.hartsnottingham.co.uk; Standard Hill, Park Row; mains £17.50-29; 🐾) Adjacent to Hart's boutique hotel, its contemporary restaurant has plush booths, ultra-attentive service and surprisingly affordable prices considering it offers central Nottingham's finest cuisine (deconstructed prawn cocktail, bacon-wrapped monkfish and so on).

Delilah Fine Foods   DELI, CAFE £
(www.delilahfinefoods.co.uk; 15 Middle Pavement; dishes £3.95-8.95; ⊘8am-7pm Mon-Fri, 9am-7pm Sat, 11am-5pm Sun) Impeccably selected cheeses, pâtés, meats and more from artisan

Nottingham

producers are available to sample, take away or eat on-site at this gourmands' dream.

Restaurant Sat Bains MODERN EUROPEAN ₤₤₤
(www.restaurantsatbains.com; Lenton Lane; tasting menus ₤75-99; ☺dinner Tue-Sat; ☝) Two miles southwest of the centre off the A52, Nottingham's top table recently gained a second Michelin star for its wildly inventive Modern European cooking. Book well in advance and beware of hefty cancellation charges. It also has eight chic guest rooms (double from ₤129).

The Walk Cafe CAFE, SEAFOOD ₤₤
(☎0115-950 1502; www.thewalkcafe.co.uk; 12 Bridlesmith Walk; mains ₤7.20-11.90; ☺11am-6pm Sun-Wed, to 10pm Thu-Sat) Hidden off a pedestrian walkway, this local secret serves some of the best seafood around, including premium fish and triple-cooked chips and succulent crab platters.

Memsaab INDIAN ₤₤
(☎0115-957 0009; www.mem-saab.co.uk; 12-14 Maid Marian Way; mains ₤7.50-17.50; ☺dinner) The best of the glamorous modern Indian eateries on Maid Marian Way, serving fabulous regional specialities in dinner-date friendly surroundings.

Alley Cafe Bar VEGETARIAN ₤
(☎01159-551013; www.alleycafe.co.uk; Cannon Ct; mains ₤5.50-6.85; ☺11am-9pm Mon & Tue, 11am-late Wed-Sat, noon-5pm Sun; ☝) Down a narrow alleyway, this beat-spinning hippie haven serves dishes such as tofu, tempeh and hemp-seed burgers and organic beers, wines and ciders, hosts events such as open-mic nights, and exhibits local art.

Drinking

Weekends in Nottingham are boisterous affairs, when the streets throng with lads on stag nights, girls on hen parties, student revellers and intoxicated grown-ups who should really know better, but there are plenty of low-key alternatives.

TOP CHOICE Ye Olde Trip to Jerusalem PUB
(☎0115-947 3171; www.triptojerusalem.com; Brewhouse Yard, Castle Rd) Wedged into the cliff below the castle, this atmospheric alehouse claims to be England's oldest pub. Founded in 1189, it supposedly slaked the thirst of departing crusaders and its rooms and cobbled courtyards are still the most ambient place in Nottingham for a pint. Informal tours (per person ₤2.50) of its cellars can be arranged by booking at least two weeks ahead.

Pitcher & Piano
BAR, RESTAURANT

(www.pitcherandpiano.com; Unitarian Church, High Pavement) A deconsecrated 19th-century church with soaring ceilings, glorious stained glass and flickering candles make this chain bar/restaurant branch one of a kind.

Pit & Pendulum
PUB

(www.eerie-pubs.co.uk/pit-pendulum; 17 Victoria St; 🐱) Local goths flock to this dimly lit pub for the vampire vibe and theatrical decor (push the floor-to-ceiling basement 'bookcase' to reach the toilets), as well as 'seven deadly sins' cocktails and occasional live music.

Brass Monkey
BAR

(www.brassmonkeybar.co.uk;HighPavement;⊙4pm-1am Mon-Sat, till midnight Sun) Nottingham's original cocktail bar rocks the Lace Market with DJ sets and quirky takes on favourites such as elderflower mojitos. The roof terrace gets packed on summer evenings.

Rocket @ Saltwater
BAR

(📞0115-924 2664; www.rocketrestaurants.co.uk; The Cornerhouse, Forman St) Slick hipster rooftop bar and restaurant.

Canal House
PUB

(📞0115-955 5060; http://thecanalhouse.co.uk; 48-52 Canal St) The best of the canal-front pubs, run by the independent Castle Rock Brewery and split in two by a watery inlet.

Malt Cross
PUB

(www.maltcross.com; 16 St James's St) A fine place for a pint in a stately old Victorian music hall.

⭐ Entertainment

For musicals, touring theatre shows and veteran music acts, try the Royal Concert Hall and Theatre Royal, which share the same building and booking office (📞0115-989 5555; www.royalcentre-nottingham.co.uk; Theatre Sq). Tours backstage can be arranged (£5.50, 90 minutes).

Rock City
LIVE MUSIC

(📞0115-950 6547; www.rock-city.co.uk; 8 Talbot St) This monster venue hosts everything from Goth rock and Midlands metal to Northern Soul.

Nottingham Playhouse
THEATRE

(📞0115-941 9419; www.nottinghamplayhouse.co.uk; Wellington Circus) Beside Anish Kapoor's enormous *Sky Mirror* dish, the Playhouse puts on serious theatre, from stage classics to the avant-garde. Arty types hang out at its attached restaurant and bar.

Stealth
CLUB

(📞0845 413 4444; www.stealthattack.co.uk; Masonic Pl, Goldsmith St) An underground club for those who like their bass heavy and their drums supercharged. The attached Rescue Rooms (📞0115-828 3173; www.rescuerooms.com) has a varied line-up of live bands and DJs.

NG1
CLUB

(📞0115-958 8440; www.ng1club.co.uk; 76-80 Lower Parliament St; ⊙11pm-4am Wed, 10pm-5am Fri, to 6am Sat, 11pm-4am Sun) Nottingham's favourite gay club, NG1 is unpretentious,

---

LOCAL KNOWLEDGE

EZEKIAL BONE AKA ADE ANDREWS

What's your background? I did a history degree and worked as a Heritage Ranger at Sherwood Forest, then set up Ezekial Bone Tours (p441) to deconstruct the Robin Hood myths and focus on the historic building blocks.

Did Robin Hood actually exist? He's a composite hero: many real outlaws in the medieval period were woven together over time by minstrels and storytellers. St Mary's Church (📞guided tours 0115-948 3658; www.stmarysnottingham.org; High Pavement; ⊙10.30am-2.30pm Tue-Sat) is mentioned in the 1450 *Ballad of Robin Hood and the Monk*, and Old Market Sq in *Robin Hood and the Potter* circa 1500. It was only at the end of the 16th century that playwright Antony Munday elevated Robin Hood from a yeoman to a displaced Saxon Earl as a symbol of the gentry's dissatisfaction with the crown.

What is Hood's relevance in the 21st century? Robin Hood was an original eco-warrior in harmony with the land. I want to put him on the pedestal he deserves – as a figurehead of culture and the environment.

What are the best places to experience Nottingham's history? The Lace Market area, the caves, Nottingham Castle and Ye Olde Trip to Jerusalem.

Ade Andrews is a writer, actor, producer and tour guide.

hedonistic fun, with two dance floors belting out funky house, pop and '80s classics.

Broadway Cinema CINEMA
(www.broadway.org.uk; 14-18 Broad St) Artistic hub with an independent cinema, media arts gallery and a cafe/bar where you can actually hear yourself talk.

ℹ Information

Post office (Queen St) Has a bureau de change.

Tourist office (☎0844 477 5678; www .experiencenottinghamshire.com; The Exchange, 1-4 Smithy Row; ☺9.30am-5.30pm Mon-Sat year-round, 11am-5pm Sun late Jul-Aug & mid-late Dec) Friendly office with racks of info and Robin Hood merchandise.

ℹ Getting There & Away
Air

East Midlands Airport (p393) is about 18 miles south of Nottingham; Skylink buses pass the airport (one hour, hourly, 24 hours).

Bus

Local services run from the Victoria bus station, behind the **Victoria Shopping Centre** (Lower Parliament St) on Milton St. Bus 100 runs to Southwell (50 minutes, every 20 minutes Monday to Saturday, four Sunday services) and bus 90 to Newark (55 minutes, hourly, every two hours Sunday).

Long-distance buses operate from the dingy **Broadmarsh bus station** (Collin St). For the Peaks, the hourly Transpeak service runs to Derby (40 minutes), Matlock Bath (1¼ hours), Bakewell (two hours) and Buxton (2½ hours).

Frequent National Express services:

Birmingham £9.90, 1¼ hours, seven daily
Leicester £3.80, 45 minutes, 10 daily
London £6.50, 3½ hours, 10 daily
Sheffield £7.90, one hour 20 minutes, hourly

Train

The train station is just south of the town centre. Useful services:

Derby £6.30, 25 minutes, three hourly
Lincoln £10.20, one hour, hourly
London £27, two hours, three hourly
Manchester £20.60, two hours, every 40 minutes
Sheffield £8, one hour, half-hourly

ℹ Getting Around

For information on buses within Nottingham, call **Nottingham City Transport** (☎0115-950 6070; www.nctx.co.uk). A Kangaroo ticket gives you unlimited travel on buses and trams within the city for £4.

The single tram line operated by **Nottingham Express Transit** (www.thetram.net; single/day from £1.90/3.50) runs from Nottingham train station to Hucknall, passing close to Broadmarsh bus station, the tourist office and Theatre Royal.

Bunneys Bikes (☎0115-947 2713; www .bunneysbikes.com; 97 Carrington St; per day £12.99; ☺9am-5.30pm Mon, Thu & Fri, 8am-5.30pm Tue, 9am-7pm Wed, 10am-5pm Sat) is near the train station. Hire bicycles are also available from Nottingham Tourism Centre and Broadmarsh Bus Station for £4 per day through a Nottingham City Council bike-share scheme. A bonus is that hire includes unlimited use of Nottingham city buses, trams and trains.

Around Nottingham
NEWSTEAD ABBEY

The evocative lakeside ruins of News-tead Abbey (☎01623-455900; www.newstead abbey.org.uk; adult/child £10/8, gardens only £4/3; ☺house noon-5pm Fri-Mon Apr-Sep, garden 9am-dusk year-round) are inextricably associated with the original tortured romantic, Lord Byron (1788–1824), who owned the house until 1817. Founded as an Augustinian priory in around 1170, the building was converted into a residence in 1539. Byron's old living quarters are full of suitably eccentric memorabilia, and the landscaped grounds include a monument to his yappy dog, Boatswain.

Newstead Abbey is 12 miles north of Nottingham, off the A60. Pronto buses run from Victoria bus station, stopping at Newstead Abbey gates (30 minutes, every 20 minutes Monday to Saturday, half-hourly Sunday), a mile from the house and gardens. Trains run to Newstead station, 2.5 miles from the abbey.

SHERWOOD FOREST NATIONAL NATURE RESERVE

If Robin Hood wanted to hide out in Sherwood Forest today, he'd have to disguise himself and the Merry Men as day-trippers on mountain bikes. Now covering just 182 hectares of old growth forest, it's nevertheless a major destination for Nottingham city dwellers.

Until a proposed new visitor centre opens, the Sherwood Forest visitor centre (www.sherwoodforest.org.uk; Swinecote Rd, Edwinstowe; parking £3; ☺10am-5pm), on the B6034, is an uninspiring collection of faded late-20th-century buildings housing cafes, gift shops and 'Robyn Hode's Sherwode', with wooden cut-outs, murals and mannequins telling the tale of the famous woodsman. It's the departure point for walking trails passing such Sherwood Forest landmarks as the Major Oak (1 mile return), a broad-boughed oak tree (propped up by supporting rods) alleged to have sheltered Robin of Locksley. For informative guided walks try Ezekial Bone Tours (p441). The week-long Robin Hood Festival (www.nottinghamcity.gov.uk) is a massive medieval re-enactment that takes place here every August.

An arrow's flight from the visitor centre, Sherwood Forest YHA (☎0845 371 9139; www.yha.org.uk; Forest Corner; dm £12.40-24.90; ℗) is a modern hostel with comfortable dorms, a bar, self-catering kitchen and meals.

From Nottingham, take the Sherwood Arrow (bus 33, 30 minutes, four daily Monday to Saturday, two Sunday services).

Southwell

POP 6285

A graceful scattering of grand, wisteria-draped country houses, Southwell is straight out of the pages of a novel from the English Romantic period. Rising from the village centre, the awe-inspiring Southwell Minster (www.southwellminster.org; suggested donation £3, photo permit £5; ⊙8am-7pm), built over Saxon and Roman foundations, blends 12th- and 13th-century features including zigzag doorframes and curved arches. Its chapterhouse features some unusual stained glass and detailed carvings of faces, animals and leaves of forest trees.

On the road to Newark, Southwell Workhouse (NT; Upton Rd; adult/child £7/3.50; ⊙noon-5pm Wed-Sun Mar-Oct, closed Nov-Feb) is a sobering reminder of the tough life faced by paupers in the 19th century. You can explore the factory floors and workers' chambers accompanied by an audioguide narrated by 'inmates' and 'officials'.

By the main junction, the rambling, timbered coaching inn Saracen's Head Hotel (☎01636-812701; www.saracensheadhotel.net; s/d incl breakfast from £75/95, 2-/3-course meals £15.95/19.95; ☎) has 27 beautifully refurbished rooms and an oak-panelled restaurant. Enticing gourmet delis and tearooms line the village streets.

Bus 100 runs from Nottingham (50 minutes, every 20 minutes, four services Sunday). For Newark-on-Trent, take bus 28 or 29 (30 minutes, hourly or better) or the less frequent bus 3.

Newark-on-Trent

POP 25,376

Dominated by the ruins of Newark Castle (www.newark-sherwooddc.gov.uk/newarkcastle; Castlegate; tours adult/child £3/1.50; ⊙9am-6pm), the delightful riverside town of Newark paid the price for backing the wrong side in the English Civil War. After surviving four sieges by Cromwell's men, the town was ransacked by Roundheads when Charles I surrendered in 1646. The helpful tourist office (☎01636-655765; www.visitnewarkandsherwood.co.uk; Gilstrap Centre, Castlegate; ⊙10am-4pm), in the castle grounds, has details of castle tours and events, and can also find accommodation in Newark.

Southwest of the castle along the river, the family-friendly Millgate Museum (☎01636-655730; 48 Millgate; ⊙10.30am-4.30pm) is packed with old agricultural and industrial machinery, but the highlight is the walk-through re-creation of a Victorian shopping street.

Newark Air Museum (☎01636-707170; www.newarkairmuseum.org; adult/child £7/4; ⊙10am-5pm), 2 miles east of town, by the Winthorpe Showground, has an impressive collection of aircraft, including a fearsome Vulcan bomber.

Everything is baked fresh on the premises at The Old Bakery Tea Rooms (☎01636-611501; www.oldbakerytearooms.co.uk; 4 Queens Head Ct; mains £5.95-8.95; ⊙9.30am-5pm Mon-Sat; ☎), The Old Bakery Tea Rooms, housed in an enchanting Hansel and Gretel–like timber-framed Tudor building dating from the 15th century. Lunch specials include soups, frittata, bruschetta and smoked salmon brioche.

Newark has two stations. Trains on the East Coast Main Line between London and the north stop at Newark North Gate, while East Midlands trains between Leicester, Nottingham and Lincoln stop at Newark Castle station. Bus 90 runs hourly to Nottingham (55 minutes, every two hours Sunday).

LINCOLNSHIRE

One of the most sparsely populated corners of England, Lincolnshire's farmland unfolds over low hills and the pancake-flat Fens, and is dotted with windmills and, more recently, wind turbines. Surrounding its charming county town of Lincoln you'll find seaside resorts, scenic waterways, serene nature reserves and stone-built towns tailor-made for English period dramas.

Activities

The 140-mile Viking Way walking trail snakes across the gentle hills of the Lincolnshire Wolds from the banks of the River Humber to Oakham in Leicestershire.

Cyclists can find information on routes across the county in any of the local tourist offices; the Water Rail Way is a flat, sculpture-lined on-road cycling route that follows the River Witham through classic Fens countryside between Lincoln and Boston.

Information

Visit Lincolnshire (www.visitlincolnshire.com)

Getting There & Around

East Midlands trains connect Lincoln, Newark Castle and Nottingham, and Newark North Gate and Grantham lie on the East Coast Main Line between London and Edinburgh. Local buses link Lincolnshire's towns but services are slow and infrequent. Check the transport pages at www.lincoln shire.gov.uk, which also has cycling route info.

Lincoln

POP 85,595

A bustling metropolis by Lincolnshire standards, but a sleepy backwater compared with almost anywhere else, Lincolnshire's county town is a tangle of cobbled medieval streets surrounding its colossal 12th-century cathedral. Ringed by historic city gates – including the Newport Arch on Bailgate, a relic from the original Roman settlement – this is one of the Midlands' most beautiful cities: the lanes that topple over the edge of Lincoln Cliff are lined with Tudor town houses, ancient pubs and quirky independent stores.

Flanking the River Witham at the base of the hill, the new town is less absorbing, but the revitalised Brayford Waterfront development by the university is an idyllic spot to watch the boats go by.

Sights

Lincoln Cathedral CHURCH
(http://lincolncathedral.com; Minster Yard; adult/child £6/1; ⊙7.15am-8pm Mon-Fri, to 6pm Sat & Sun, evensong 5.30pm Mon-Sat, 3.45pm Sun) Towering over Lincoln like a medieval skyscraper, Lincoln's magnificent cathedral is a breathtaking representation of divine power on earth. The great tower rising above the crossing is the third-highest in England at 83m, but in medieval times, a lead-encased wooden spire added a further 79m, topping even the great pyramids of Giza.

The first Lincoln cathedral was constructed between 1072 and 1092, but it fell in a devastating fire in 1141, and the second cathedral was destroyed by an earthquake in 1185. Bishop Hugh of Avalon (St Hugh) rebuilt and massively expanded the cathedral, creating one of the largest Gothic buildings in Europe.

On the fabulous exterior, restored Norman friezes show Adam and Eve bringing sin into the world, and Jesus making the ultimate sacrifice to undo the damage.

The vast interior of the church is too large for modern congregations – services take

---

LINCOLNSHIRE: BOMBER COUNTY

Following WWI the Royal Air Force (RAF) was formed in 1918 and two years later its college was established in Lincolnshire. During WWII, England's 'Bomber County' was home to numerous squadrons and by 1945 had more airfields (49) than any other in the country. US Navy flying boats flew antisubmarine patrols and B-29 bombers were based here.

Lincoln's tourist office has details of the county's aviation legacies including the Spitfires and four-engined Lancaster *City of Lincoln* on display at the Battle of Britain Memorial Flight Visitor Centre (☑01522-782040; www.lincolnshire.gov.uk/bbmf; Dogdyke Rd, Coningsby; admission free, hangar tours adult/child £6/4; ⊙10am-5pm Mon-Fri), as well as Lincolnshire Aviation Heritage Centre (☑01790-763207; www.lincsaviation.co.uk; East Kirkby, near Spilsby; adult/child £7/3; ⊙10am-5pm Mon-Sat Easter-Oct, to 4pm Mon-Sat Nov-Easter), sited on an orginal WWII Bomber Command airfield complete with its original wartime control tower. The RAF's Waddington Air Show (www.waddingtonair show.co.uk) takes place 3 miles south of Lincoln on the first weekend in July.

Lincoln

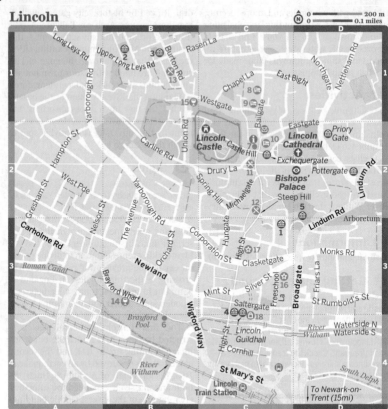

place in St Hugh's Choir, a church within a church running east from the crossing. The choir stalls are accessed through a magnificent carved stone screen; look north to see the stunning rose window known as the Dean's Eye (c 1192), mirrored to the south by the floral flourishes of the Bishop's Eye (1330). There's more stained glass in the three Services Chapels in the North Transept.

The glory of Lincoln cathedral is in the detail. Beyond St Hugh's Choir, the Angel Choir is supported by 28 columns topped by carvings of angels and foliate scrollwork. Tucked atop one of the columns is the official emblem of Lincoln, the tiny Lincoln Imp – a cheeky horned pixie, allegedly turned to stone by the angels after being sent by the devil to vandalise the church.

Other interesting details include the 10-sided chapterhouse – where Edward I held his parliament and where the climax of *The Da Vinci Code* was filmed in 2005.

Don't miss the one-hour guided tours, which take place at least twice a day plus less-frequent tours of the roof and the tower. All are included in the admission price. The best time to hear the organ resounding through the cathedral is during evensong.

Lincoln Castle   CASTLE
(www.lincolnshire.gov.uk/lincolncastle; adult/child £6/4; ⊙10am-6pm) One of the first castles erected by the victorious William the Conqueror to keep his new kingdom in line, Lincoln Castle offers awesome views over the city and miles of surrounding countryside. Highlights include the chance to view one of the four surviving copies of the Magna Carta (dated 1215), and the grim Victorian prison chapel, dating back to the days when this was the county jailhouse and execution ground.

Lincoln

Free guided tours of the castle run once or twice daily (weekends only in December and January).

Bishops' Palace HISTORIC SITE
(EH; ☎01522-527468; www.english-heritage.org.uk; adult/child £4.50/2.70; ☺10am-5pm Thu-Mon Apr-Oct, 10am-4pm Sat & Sun Nov-Mar) Beside Lincoln Cathedral are the time-ravaged but still imposing ruins of the 12th-century Bishops' Palace, gutted by parliamentary forces during the Civil War. From here, the local bishops once controlled a diocese stretching from the Humber to the Thames. Entertaining audioguides are included in admission.

FREE Collection MUSEUM
(www.thecollectionlincoln.org; Danes Tce; ☺10am-4pm daily, from 10.45am 1st Sun of month) Archaeology bursts into life with loads of hands-on displays where kids can handle artefacts and dress up in period costume. Check out the crushed skull of a 4000-year-old 'yellowbelly' (the local term for, well, the locals), pulled from a Neolithic burial site near Sleaford.

FREE Usher Gallery GALLERY
(www.thecollectionlincoln.org; Lindum Rd; ☺10am-5pm Tue-Sat, 1-5pm Sun) A handsome Edwardian building decorated with carvings of cow skulls houses an impressive collection of works by such greats as Turner, Lowry and English watercolourist, Peter de Wint (1784–1849).

FREE Museum of Lincolnshire Life MUSEUM
(Old Barracks, Burton Rd; ☺10am-4pm daily Apr-Sep, closed Sun Oct-Mar) In an old Victorian barracks, displays at this charming community museum span everything from Victorian farm implements to the tin-can tank built in Lincoln for WWI. Around the corner from the museum is the cute little Ellis Mill (Mill Rd; admission free; ☺2-5pm Sat & Sun Apr-Sep, 2pm-dusk Sun Oct-Mar), the windmill that ground the town's flour in the 18th century.

☞ Tours

History-focused 90-minute guided walking tours (☎01522-521256; www.lincolnguidedtours.co.uk; adult/child £4/free; ☺tours 11am daily Jul & Aug, Sat & Sun Jun, Sep & Oct) run from outside the tourist office. Genuinely spooky 75-minute ghost walks (☎01522-874056; adult/child £4/2; ☺7pm Wed-Sat year-round) depart adjacent to the tourist office in Castle Sq.

Boat trips along the River Witham and Fossdyke Navigation, a canal system dating back to Roman times, start from Brayford Waterfront. The Brayford Belle (☎01522-881200; www.lincolnboattrips.com; adult/child £6.50/4) runs five times daily from Easter to September, and weekends only in October. No credit cards.

See **Tour Lincoln** for bus tours.

TOP LINCOLN TIPS

Walking between Lincoln's old and new towns can feel like an Everest expedition. Fortunately, Lincoln's 'Little Green Bus', the Walk & Ride (all-day pass adult/child £3/1.60) service runs every 20 minutes from the Stonebow at the corner of High St and Saltergate to the cathedral and Newport Arch, then back via Brayford Waterfront and the train station.

To tour the city in comfort, hop aboard the new Tour Lincoln (adult/child/family £10/4/25) bus. Tickets are sold at the tourist office; tours last one hour and tickets are valid all day. The tourist office also sells the three-day Visit Lincoln Pass (adult/family £12/35), giving access to several heritage sites including the castle, cathedral and Bishops' Palace; and the three-day Explore Lincoln Pass (adult/family £20/50), which includes both the Tour Lincoln bus and the Visit Lincoln Pass.

🛏 Sleeping

TOP CHOICE Castle Hotel BOUTIQUE HOTEL ££

(☎01522-538801; www.castlehotel.net; Westgate; s £90, d £110-120, incl breakfast; P🐾) Each of the 18 rooms at this boutique hotel have been exquisitely refurbished in olive, truffle and oyster tones. Built on the site of Lincoln's Roman forum in 1852, the red-brick building's incarnations variously include a school and WWII lookout station. Take advantage of the great-value dinner, bed and breakfast deals linked to its award-winning new restaurant Reform.

Bail House B&B ££

(☎01522-541000; www.bailhouse.co.uk; 34 Bailgate; r from £89; P@🐾🏊) Stone walls, worn flagstones, secluded gardens and one room with an extraordinary timber-vaulted ceiling are just some of the charms of this lovingly restored Georgian town house in central Lincoln. There's even a seasonal heated outdoor swimming pool.

White Hart Hotel HOTEL ££

(☎01522-526222; www.whitehart-lincoln.co.uk; Bailgate; s/d from £70/90; P@🐾) You can't get more venerable than this grand dame of Lincoln hotels, sandwiched between castle and cathedral, with a history dating back 600 years and flowing countrified rooms.

🍴 Eating

Tearooms are dotted along Steep Hill. Restaurant reservations are generally recommended in the evenings.

TOP CHOICE Reform MODERN BRITISH ££

(☎01522-538801; www.castlehotel.net; The Castle Hotel, Westgate; mains £11.95-22.95; ⊗breakfast, lunch & dinner) Inside the stylised Castle Hotel, the menu of its sophisticated restaurant, Reform, is inspired by local, seasonal produce. Starters such as Stilton mousse or crispy pig cheeks with polenta are followed by mains such as confit of pork belly or seared scallops and pigeon, but the real showstoppers are desserts such as warm plum and raspberry crumble tart with white-chocolate ice cream and quince purée.

Brown's Pie Shop BRITISH ££

(☎01522-527330; www.brownspieshop.co.uk; 33 Steep Hill; takeaway pies £1.50-3, lunch mains £8.95-11.95, dinner mains £9.95-24.95; ⊗lunch & dinner Mon-Sat, noon-8pm Sun) This long-established pie shop is one of Lincoln's top tables, encompassing a smart upstairs dining room and cosy brick-lined basement. Its hearty pies are stuffed with locally sourced beef, rabbit and game.

Jew's House MODERN EUROPEAN ££

(☎01522-524851; www.jewshouserestaurant.co.uk; 15 The Strait (Steep Hill); 2-/3-course lunch menus £13.50-17.50, mains £14.75-26; ⊗lunch & dinner Tue-Sat) Set in one of England's oldest houses, the Romanesque Jew's House, constructed in around 1160. This local favourite serves up gourmet fare in atmospheric surrounds. For the ultimate indulgence, go for the six-course tasting menu (£49.50).

Wig & Mitre PUB ££

(www.wigandmitre.com; 30 Steep Hill; mains £10-15; ⊗breakfast, lunch & dinner; 👶) Civilised pub-restaurant the Wig & Mitre has an excellent menu yet retains the ambience of a friendly local. Food is served throughout the day, from morning fry-ups to lunchtime sandwiches and filling evening roasts. Bookings not necessary.

Old Bakery
MODERN BRITISH ££

(☎01522-576057; www.theold-bakery.co.uk; 26-28 Burton Rd; mains £14-20.95; ☻lunch Tue-Sun, dinner Tue-Sat) The menu at this eccentric foodie haven is built around impeccably presented local produce and – appropriately – freshly baked bread. It also has a deli, offers regular half-day cookery lessons (£90), and has four quaint guest rooms upstairs.

Drinking

Bland chain pubs crowd the High St, but there are a few worthy independent public houses.

Strugglers Inn
PUB

(83 Westgate) A sunny walled-courtyard beer garden out back, cosy interior and superb selection of real ales on tap make this the pick of Lincoln's independent pubs.

Electric Bar & Restaurant
BAR

(☎01522-565182; www.electricbarandrestaurant .co.uk; 5th fl, DoubleTree by Hilton Lincoln, Brayford Wharf North; ☎) Opened in 2012 on the top floor of Lincoln's snazzy new four-star DoubleTree Hilton Hotel, this swish spot with glittering river views has streamlined decor, a great cocktail list, regular live jazz, and a restaurant serving sophisticated British dishes with a retro twist (eg ham-hock terrine and iced peanut-butter parfait).

☆ Entertainment

Check www.lovelincoln.co.uk or www.visit lincolnshire.com for events listings.

Lincoln Drill Hall
ARTS CENTRE

(www.lincolndrillhall.com; Freeschool Lane) Downhill near the station, this stern-looking building hosts bands, orchestras, stage shows, comedy and daytime festivals.

Lola Lo
CLUB

(www.lolalolincoln.com; 280-281 High St; ☻10pm-3am Mon-Thu, from 8pm Fri & Sat) Lincoln might be a long way from the Pacific, but this Tiki bar and club goes all out to convince revellers otherwise, with tropical cocktails and themed nights such as Tuesday's millionaire-style Decorus nights, Wednesday's Naughty Disko and Thursday's Kitsch.

❶ Information

Post office (90 Bailgate) With bureau de change.

Tourist office (☎01522-545458; www.visit lincoln.com; 9 Castle Hill; ☻10.30am-4pm Mon-Sat) Friendly office in a handsome 16th-century building by the castle.

❶ Getting There & Away

BUS National Express (www.nationalexpress. com) runs direct bus services from Lincoln to London (£24.90, 5¼ hours, daily) and Birmingham (£6.60, three hours, daily). Local Stagecoach buses mainly run Monday to Saturday; useful services include the following:

Grantham Bus 1, 1¼ hours, half-hourly (also five Sunday services)

Louth Bus 10, one hour, six daily

Newark-on-Trent Bus 46, 1¼ hours, four to five daily

TRAIN Getting to and from Lincoln by rail usually involves changing trains.

Boston £12.30, 1¼ hours, every two hours, change at Sleaford

Cambridge £26.50, 2½ hours, hourly, change at Peterborough and Ely

Sheffield £13.10, one hour 20 minutes, hourly

Grantham & Around

Grantham would be just another country town were it not for two famous 'yellow-bellies' (as Lincolnshire locals call themselves) – Isaac Newton and former prime minister Margaret Thatcher, the daughter of a humble Grantham greengrocer, who plied his trade at 2 North Pde.

The town itself has just a few sights, but there are some fascinating country houses in the surrounding countryside, including Newton's birthplace, 17th-century Woolsthorpe Manor (NT; Water Lane; adult/child £6.65/3.35; ☻11am-5pm Wed-Sun), 8 miles south. The apple that inspired the theory of gravity allegedly fell from the tree in the garden. There's a nifty kids science room and a cafe. Take Centrebus 9 from Grantham (20 minutes, five to six daily, Monday to Saturday).

At the exceptional Chequers Inn (☎01476-870701; www.chequersinn.net; Main St, Woolsthorpe by Belvoir; mains £10.50-19.50), some 7 miles southwest of Grantham, dine on some of the finest food in the Midlands on the sunny patio overlooking Belvoir Castle (☎01476-871002; www.belvoircastle.com; adult/child £15/8, gardens only £8/5; ☻castle tours generally 11.15am, 1.15pm & 3.15pm, gardens 11am-5pm Sun & Mon May-Aug), in the rambling garden bordering a sheep-filled paddock or inside by the open fire. A fabulous range of ciders and real ales are on tap and, across the lane, the former stables house four simple but stylish guest rooms.

Stamford

POP 19,525

One of England's prettiest towns, Stamford seems frozen in time, with elegant streets lined with honey-coloured limestone buildings and hidden alleyways dotted with hearty alehouses, interesting eateries and small independent boutiques. A forest of historic church spires rises overhead and the gently gurgling River Welland meanders through the town centre. Unsurprisingly, the town is a top choice for filmmakers looking for the postcard vision of England, appearing in everything from *Pride and Prejudice* to *The Da Vinci Code*.

Sights

The town's top attraction is nearby Burghley House, but just strolling the streets is a delight. Drop in on St Mary's Church (St Mary's St), with its charmingly wonky broach spire, or explore the 15th-century chapel and chambers of the William Browne Hospital (Broad St; adult/child £2.50/1; ☉11am-4pm Sat & Sun May-Sep).

Sleeping

TOP CHOICE George Hotel   HISTORIC HOTEL £££
(☏01780-750750; www.georgehotelofstamford.com; 71 St Martin's; s/d from £95/175, 4-poster d £230; P@🅿️🛜) Stamford's luxurious landmark inn opened its doors in 1597 and its rooms impeccably blend period charm and modern elegance, while its restaurant serves superior Modern British cuisine.

The William Cecil at Stamford   HISTORIC HOTEL £££
(☏01780-750070; www.thewilliamcecil.co.uk; High St, St Martins; s/d midweek £100/110, weekends £120/130; P🛜) Within the Burghley Estate, rooms at this stunningly renovated hotel are inspired by Burghley House, with period furnishings and luxuries such as claw-foot baths. The smart restaurant opens to a wicker-chair furnished patio.

Stamford Lodge   B&B ££
(☏01780-482932; www.stamfordlodge.co.uk; 66 Scotgate; s/d £65/85; 🛜) Centrally situated, this 18th-century former bakehouse has five fresh, modern rooms and excellent breakfasts.

Eating

The finest meals in town are served at the George Hotel and The William Cecil.

Tobie Norris   PUB ££
(www.tobienorris.com; 12 St Pauls St; mains £9.95-15.95; ☉lunch daily, dinner Mon-Sat) A wonderful stone-walled, flagstone-floored pub with a warren of rooms and a sunny courtyard, serving international dishes such as wasabi chicken with crushed plum potatoes and wholesome local ales.

Jim's Yard   MODERN BRITISH ££
(☏01780-756080; www.jimsyard.biz; 3 Ironmonger St; mains £13-19; ☉lunch & dinner Tue-Sat) Tucked away in a courtyard off a narrow laneway, Jim's upmarket fare is sourced from local producers.

Entertainment

Stamford Arts Centre   ARTS CENTRE
(☏01780-763203; www.stamfordartscentre.com; 27 St Mary's St) The centre hosts everything from live jazz and art-house cinema to stand-up comedy.

Getting There & Away

Kimes Bus 4 runs to Grantham (1¼ hours, three daily Monday to Saturday) and National Express to London (£15.30, three hours, one daily).

DON'T MISS

BURGHLEY HOUSE

Lying just a mile south of Stamford, flamboyant Burghley House (www.burghley.co.uk; adult/child incl sculpture garden £13.80/7; ☉11am-5pm Sat-Thu mid-Mar–late Oct) – pronounced bur-lee – was built by Queen Elizabeth's chief adviser William Cecil, whose descendants have lived here ever since.

Set in more than 810 hectares of grounds, landscaped by the famous Lancelot 'Capability' Brown, the house bristles with cupolas, pavilions, belvederes and chimneys, and the staterooms are a treasure-trove of ormolu clocks, priceless oil paintings, Louis XIV furniture and magnificent murals painted by the 17th-century Italian master Antonio Verrio.

The renowned Burghley Horse Trials take place in early September. Follow the marked path for 15 minutes through the park by Stamford train station.

453

Cross-country trains run to Birmingham (£14, 1½ hours, hourly) and Stansted Airport (£17, 1¾ hours, hourly) via Cambridge (£9, 1¼ hours) and Peterborough (£7.30, 15 minutes).

Boston

POP 35,124

It's hard to believe that sleepy Boston was the inspiration for its larger and more famous American cousin. Although no Boston citizens sailed on the *Mayflower,* the town became a conduit for persecuted Puritans fleeing Nottinghamshire for religious freedom in the Netherlands and America. In the 1630s, the fiery sermons of Boston vicar John Cotton inspired many locals to follow their lead, among them the ancestors of John Quincy-Adams, the sixth American president. These pioneers founded a namesake town in the new colony of Massachusetts and the rest, as they say, is history.

◉ Sights

Built in the early 14th-century, St Botolph's Church (church free, tower adult/child £3/1; ⊙church 8am-4.30pm daily, tower 10am-4pm Mon-Sat, last climb 3pm) – the name Boston is a corruption of 'St Botolph's Stone' – is known locally as the Stump in reference to the truncated appearance of its 88m-high tower. Puff your way up the 365 steps on a clear day and you'll see to Lincoln, 32 miles away.

Before escaping to the New World, the Pilgrim Fathers were briefly imprisoned in the 14th-century Guildhall (⊘01205-365954; www.bostonguildhall.co.uk; South St; ⊙10.30am-3.30pm Wed-Sat), one of Lincolnshire's oldest brick buildings, dating from the 1390s. Inside are fun, interactive exhibits, as well as a restored 16th-century courtroom, and a recreated Georgian kitchen.

About 800m northeast of Market Pl, the Maud Foster Windmill (⊘01205-352188; www.maudfoster.co.uk; adult/child £4/2; ⊙10am-5pm Wed & Sat) is the tallest working windmill in the country, with seven floors that creak and tremble with every turn of the sails.

⌂ Sleeping & Eating

White Hart   PUB ££
(⊘01205-311900; www.whitehartboston.com; 1-5 High St; s/d £78/98, mains £6.95-16.95; [P] @) Right in the middle of town, this handsome pub-hotel has tastefully modernised rooms and a decent menu in the Modern British mould.

ⓘ Information

Tourist office (⊘01205-365954; www.boston guildhall.co.uk; South St; ⊙10.30am-3.30pm Wed-Sat) Inside the Guildhall.

ⓘ Getting There & Away

Trains connect Boston with Lincoln (£12.30, 1¼ hours) via a change at Sleaford.

NORTHAMPTONSHIRE

Dotted with villages full of pincushion cottages with thatched rooves and Tudor timbers, Northamptonshire also has a string of stately manors, including the ancestral homes of George Washington and Diana, Princess of Wales.

ⓘ Information

Northamptonshire: Britain on Show (www .britainonshow.co.uk; ☏)

ⓘ Getting Around

Northampton is the hub for bus services around the county; see the 'Transport & Streets' pages at www.northamptonshire.gov.uk for routes and timetables. Trains run by London Midland are useful for getting to/from Northampton; Corby and Kettering are on the East Midlands line.

Northampton

POP 194,458

Rebuilt after a devastating fire in 1675, Northamptonshire's county town was one of the prettiest in the Midlands before WWII bombers and postwar town planners wreaked havoc. Today navigating the one-way road system is a nightmare not helped by poor signage, but the city's heart retains some grand architecture. Northampton played a significant role in the Wars of the Roses and the English Civil War, before shifting its attention to manufacturing shoes.

◉ Sights

All Saints' Church   CHURCH
(www.allsaintsnorthampton.com; George Row; ⊙9am-6pm) Constructed after the 1675 fire, All Saints' Church owes an obvious debt to the churches built by Sir Christopher Wren after the Great Fire of London, with an ornate barrel-vaulted ceiling and dark-wood organ and reredos. For more fine architecture, take a peek at the handsome Sessions

House (containing the tourist office) and the Guildhall on George Row.

Northampton Museum & Art Gallery
MUSEUM, GALLERY

(www.northampton.gov.uk/museums; Guildhall Rd; ◎10am-5pm Tue-Sat, 2-5pm Sun) Even those without a shoe fetish will get a kick out of the impressive displays, where you can learn about the history of shoemaking and footwear fashions.

St Peter's Church
CHURCH

West of the central Market Sq, St Peter's Church – collect the key from the nearby ibis hotel (☎01604-608900; www.ibishotel.com; Sol Central, Marefair) – is a marvellous Norman edifice built in 1150 and adorned with ancient carvings.

Church of the Holy Sepulchre
CHURCH

(◎2-4pm Wed, 11am-3pm Sat May-Sep) North of the centre, beyond the eyesore bus station, Church of the Holy Sepulchre is one of the few surviving round churches in the country, founded when the first Earl of Northampton returned from the Crusades in 1100.

🛏 Sleeping & Eating

The tourist office can advise on B&Bs in the area.

Church Bar & Restaurant
MODERN EUROPEAN ££

(☎01604-603800; www.thechurchrestaurant.com; 67-83 Bridge St; mains £13-15; ◎lunch & dinner Mon-Sat) At this superbly converted old church, you can feast on modern European cooking (bookings recommended), or sip a cocktail under the stained-glass windows in the bar.

ℹ Information

Tourist office (☎01604-367997; www.britain onshow.co.uk; Sessions House, George Row; ◎8am-5.30pm Mon-Fri year-round, 10am-2pm Sat Apr-Sep)

ℹ Getting There & Away

BUS Greyfriars bus station is on Lady's Lane, just north of the Grosvenor shopping centre. National Express (www.nationalexpress.com) coach services:

Birmingham £7.40, one hour 40 minutes, three daily

London £6.50, 2¼ hours, five daily

Nottingham £13.20, 2½ hours, one daily

TRAIN Northampton has good rail links with Birmingham (£12, one hour, half-hourly) and London Euston (£13, one hour, three hourly). The train station is about half a mile west of town along Gold St.

Around Northampton

Northamptonshire has a cache of ancient churches, some dating back to Saxon times. Many open only from May to September; Northhampton's tourist office has information including bus schedules.

ALTHORP

The ancestral home of the Spencer family, Althorp House (☎bookings 01604-770107; www.althorp.com; adult/child £13/6, incl upper floors £15.50/8.50; ◎11am-5pm Jul & Aug, last entry 4pm, closed Sep-Jun) – pronounced altrup – is the final resting place of Diana, Princess of Wales, who is commemorated by a memorial and museum. You don't have to be a Di devotee to enjoy the outstanding art collection, with works by Rubens, Gainsborough and Van Dyck. Tickets are limited and must be booked by phone or online; profits go to charities supported by the Princess Diana Memorial Fund.

Althorp is off the A428, 5.5 miles northwest of Northampton. Stagecoach bus 96 (hourly, Monday to Saturday) runs from Northampton to Rugby, passing the gates to the Althorp estate, where you can call to arrange a pick up.

STOKE BRUERNE
POP 395

About 8 miles south of Northampton, brightly painted barges frequent this charming little village nestled against the Grand Union Canal, the main drag of England's canal network. From here, you can follow the waterways all the way to Leicester, Birmingham or London. Set in a converted corn mill, the entertaining National Waterways Museum (www.nwm.org.uk/stoke; adult/child £4.75/3.10; ◎11am-3pm Wed-Fri, 11am-5pm Sat & Sun) charts the history of the canal network and its bargemen, lock keepers and pit workers.

Several other boat owners offer summertime cruises and charters including 25-minute trips aboard the Boat Inn's Indian Chief (☎01604-862428; adult/child £3/2.50; ◎Sun).

For overnight stays, try Waterways Cottage (☎01604-863865; www.waterwayscottage. co.uk; Bridge Rd; d incl breakfast £75), an adorable thatched cottage right off the front of a biscuit box.

Meals and brews are served up at the canalside Boat Inn (01604-862428; www.boatinn.co.uk; mains £6.75-17.95; lunch & dinner).

Buses 86 and 87 both run between Stoke Bruerne and Northampton (30 minutes, six daily Monday to Saturday).

SULGRAVE MANOR

The impressively preserved Tudor mansion Sulgrave Manor (www.sulgravemanor.org.uk; adult/child £8.25/4; 11am-4pm Tue-Sun May-Oct, closed Nov-Apr) was built by Lawrence Washington in 1539 and the Washington family lived here for almost 120 years before Colonel John Washington, the great-grandfather of America's first president George Washington, sailed to Virginia in 1656.

Sulgrave Manor is southwest of Northampton, just off the B4525 near Banbury. Trains run to Banbury, from where you can take a taxi.

LEICESTERSHIRE

Leicestershire was a vital creative hub during the Industrial Revolution, but its factories were a major target for German air-raids in WWII and most towns in the county still bear the scars of war-time bombing. Nevertheless, there are some impressive remains from Elizabethan castles to Roman ruins, while the busy capital Leicester offers a taste of India with its temples and curry houses.

ℹ Information

Leicestershire Tourism (www.goleicestershire.com)

ℹ Getting There & Around

Leicester is well served by buses and trains. For bus routes and timetables, visit the 'Roads & Transport' pages at www.leics.gov.uk. Regular buses connect Rutland to Leicester, Stamford and other surrounding towns.

Leicester

POP 279,923

Built over the buried ruins of two millennia of history, Leicester (*les*-ter) suffered at the hands of the Luftwaffe and postwar planners. However, a massive influx of textile workers from India and Pakistan since the 1960s has transformed the city into a bustling global melting pot. Modern Leicester is alive with the sights, sounds and flavours of the subcontinent. Its Indian community has established dozens of mosques and temples, including several right in the centre.

Historical treasures include one of England's finest medieval guildhalls.

◉ Sights

Apart from the National Space Centre, all of Leicester's museums (www.leicester.gov.uk/museums) are free.

FREE New Walk Museum & Art Gallery   MUSEUM, GALLERY
(New Walk; 10am-5pm Mon-Sat, from 11am Sun) Highlights of this grand Victorian museum include the revamped dinosaur galleries, the painting collection (with works by Francis Bacon, TS Lowry and Stanley Spencer) and the Egyptian gallery, where real mummies rub shoulders with displays on Boris Karloff's *The Mummy*.

FREE Guildhall   HISTORIC BUILDING
(Guildhall Lane; 11am-4.30pm Mon-Wed & Sat, 1-4.30pm Sun Feb-Nov, closed Dec & Jan) Leicester's perfectly preserved 14th-century guildhall is reputed to be the most haunted building in Leicester. You can search for spooks in the magnificent Great Hall, the wood-panelled 'Mayor's Parlour' and the old police cells, which contain a reconstruction of a 19th-century gibbet.

National Space Centre   MUSEUM
(www.spacecentre.co.uk; adult/child £13/11; 10am-5pm Tue-Sun, last entry 3.30pm) Although British space missions usually launch from French Guiana or Kazakhstan, Leicester's space museum is still a fascinating introduction to the mysteries of the spheres. The ill-fated Beagle 2 mission to Mars was controlled from here and fun, kid-friendly displays cover everything from astronomy to the status of current space missions. The centre is off the A6 about 1.5 miles north of the city centre. Take bus 54 from Charles St in the centre.

FREE Newarke Houses Museum   MUSEUM
(The Newarke; 10am-5pm Mon-Sat, from 11am Sun) Sprawling over two 16th-century mansions, this entertaining museum has exhibits detailing the lifestyles of local people through the centuries. Don't miss the walk-through re-creation of a WWI trench, and the trophies of the Royal Leicestershire

The Art & Soul of Britain

Britain's artistic heritage is astoundingly rich and globally renowned. As the English language spread around the world in the colonial period, so too did English literature, meaning writers like Charles Dickens and Jane Austen are enjoyed far from their original homeland. In more recent times, the same happened with British cinema and pop music.

If theatre's your thing, you're spoilt for choice in London's West End. For a flavour of the past, take in a play by Shakespeare at Shakespeare's Globe in London, or in the Bard's hometown of Stratford-upon-Avon.

For a broader selection, try one of Britain's many arts, music and culture festivals. The Edinburgh Festival is one of the best known, while others, including Glyndebourne (opera), Hay-on-Wye (literature) and Glastonbury (pop and rock) add extra colour to the countryside.

For the visual arts, Britain has fabulous galleries, from big-hitters like the Tate in London to impressive collections in the other cities around the country, as well as open-air sculpture parks and public art.

Whatever your taste in the arts, Britain cannot disappoint.

LITERARY LOCATIONS

- » **Bath** (p282) Grandeur that never tired Jane Austen's heroines.
- » **Canterbury** (p147) Forever associated with Chaucer and his famous Tales.
- » **Haworth** (p529) Home for the Brontë sisters, surrounded by wuthering moors.
- » **Lake District** (p579) Source of inspiration for William Wordsworth.
- » **Laugharne** (p674) Dylan Thomas lived here, on the 'heron-priested shore'.
- » **The Trossachs** (p834) Setting for Sir Walter Scott's historical novel *Rob Roy*.
- » **Stratford-upon-Avon** (p409) Immortalised by William Shakespeare.

Clockwise from top left
1 Edinburgh Festival Fringe (p773) 2 Glastonbury Festival (p296) 3 Shakespeare's Globe (p82), London

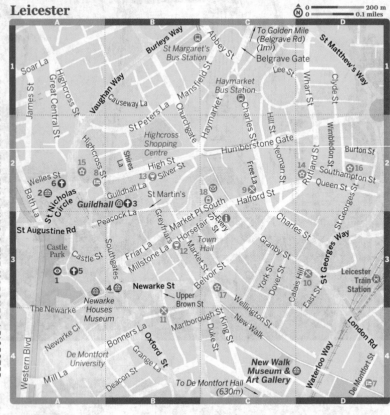

Leicester

◉ Top Sights

Guildhall	B2
New Walk Museum & Art Gallery	D4

◉ Sights

1	Great Hall	A3
2	Jewry Wall Museum	A2
3	Leicester Cathedral	B2
4	Magazine	B3
5	St Mary de Castro	A3
6	St Nicholas Church	A2

⊜ Sleeping

7	Belmont House Hotel	D4
8	Hotel Maiyango	A2

⊗ Eating

9	Good Earth	C2

10	Kayal	D3
11	Tinseltown Diner	B4

⊜ Drinking

12	Firebug	B3
13	The Globe	B2

⊕ Entertainment

14	Curve Theatre	D2
15	Mosh	A2
16	Phoenix Square	D2
17	Superfly	C3

⊜ Shopping

18	Leicester Market	C2

Regiment, including an outrageous snuff box made from a tiger's head.

Leicester Castle   CASTLE

Scattered around the Newarke Houses Museum are the ruins of Leicester's medieval castle, where Richard III spent his final days before the Battle of Bosworth. The most impressive chunk of masonry is the monumental gateway known as the Magazine (Newarke St), once a storehouse for cannonballs and gunpowder. Clad in Georgian brickwork, the 12th-century Great Hall (Castle Yard), stands behind a 15th-century gate near the church of St Mary de Castro (Castle St), where Geoffrey Chaucer was married in 1336. The hall was closed at the time of writing due to structural damage; contact the tourist office for updates including tours.

FREE Jewry Wall Museum   MUSEUM

(St Nicholas Circle; ⊙11am-4.30pm Feb-Oct, closed Nov-Jan) You can see fine Roman mosaics and frescos in this museum exploring the history of Leicester from Roman times to the modern day. In front of the museum is the Jewry Wall, part of Leicester's Roman baths. Tiles and masonry from the baths were incorporated in the walls of neighbouring St Nicholas Church.

FREE Leicester Cathedral   CHURCH

(www.cathedral.leicester.anglican.org; 21 St Martin's; ⊙8am-6pm Mon-Sat, 7am-5pm Sun) In the midst of the shopping district on Guildhall Lane, this substantial medieval church features some striking carvings on its roof supports. Inside, you can see a memorial to Richard III, who rode out from Leicester to fatal defeat at the Battle of Bosworth.

⭐ Festivals & Events

Leicester Comedy Festival   COMEDY

(☎0116-2616812; www.comedy-festival.co.uk; ⊙Feb) England's longest-running comedy festival draws big names as well as fresh talent.

Leicester Caribbean Carnival   CULTURAL

(www.leicestercarnival.com; ⊙1st Sat Aug) The biggest Caribbean celebration in the country after London's Notting Hill Carnival, with colourful costumes galore.

Diwali   RELIGIOUS

(⊙Oct or Nov) Leicester's Hindu community celebrates the Festival of Lights with fireworks, parades and ornate street lights on Belgrave Rd. Dates vary according to the lunar calendar.

🛏 Sleeping

TOP CHOICE Hotel Maiyango   HOTEL ££

(☎0116-251 8898; www.maiyango.com; 13-21 St Nicholas Pl; d incl breakfast from £99; @🖳🛜) Attached to Leicester's funkiest bar at the end of the pedestrian High St, this sophisticated pad has spacious rooms, decorated with handmade Asian furniture, contemporary art and massive plasma TVs. In addition to its candlelit Maiyango Restaurant & Bar, it also has a fabulous new Kitchen Deli gourmet cafe and store.

Belmont House Hotel   HOTEL ££

(☎0116-254 4773; www.belmonthotel.co.uk; De Montfort St; s/d from £59/79; 🅿@🛜) In a quiet location near De Montfort Hall, the 19th-century Belmont has been owned and run by the same family for four generations and recently received a stylish contemporary makeover.

🍴 Eating

A visit to Leicester isn't complete without singeing your tastebuds on a curry along the Golden Mile. Self-caterers should head to the fabulous Leicester Market (p460). The glitzy High Cross shopping centre on Shires Lane has upmarket chain restaurants.

Tinseltown Diner   AMERICAN ££

(www.tinseltown.co.uk; 5-9 Upper Brown St; mains £6.99-14.99; ⊙11.30am-2am Sun-Thu, 11.30am-3.30am Fri & Sat; 🚼) Craving a triple-decker chilli burger or an Oreo-cookie-and-peanut-butter milkshake? This being Leicester, Tinseltown's effect is more Bollywood than Hollywood, but kids will love the menu and razzmatazz.

Kayal   INDIAN ££

(☎0116-255 4667; www.kayalrestaurant.com; 153 Granby St; mains £8.99-14.99; ⊙lunch & dinner Mon-Fri, noon-11pm Sat, noon-10pm Sun) This small, upmarket Midlands chain trades the chicken tikka masala clichés for the spicy flavours of Kerala. Menu highlights include delicious dosas (lentil-flour pancakes) and zingy crab and kingfish curries.

Good Earth   VEGETARIAN £

(☎0116-262 6260; 19 Free Lane; mains £3.50-6.50; ⊙noon-3pm Mon-Fri, 10am-4pm Sat; 🖉) Justifiably popular for its wholesome veggie bakes, huge, fresh salads and homemade cakes.

DON'T MISS

THE GOLDEN MILE

Lined with sari stores, jewellery emporiums and pure-veg curry houses, Belgrave Rd – aka the Golden Mile – is *the* place to come for authentic Indian vegetarian food. Menus are built around the spicy flavours of the south, with delicious staples such as dosas (lentil-flour pancakes), *idli* (steamed rice cakes) and huge thalis (plate meals), with vegetable curries, flatbreads, rice and condiments. Belgrave Rd is about 1 mile northeast of the centre – follow Belgrave Gate and cross Burleys Flyover.

There are more top-notch eateries on the Golden Mile than you can shake a chapatti at. Our top pick is **Bobby's** (☎0116-266 0106; www.eatatbobbys.com; 154-156 Belgrave Rd; dishes £4.50-5.95; ✈), famed for its *namkeen* – lentil-flour snacks that come in myriad shapes and sizes. After dining, stop in at the shops along the strip selling *mithai* (Indian sweets), sugary combinations of nuts, fruit and milk curds.

Drinking

The Maiyango hotel's Moroccan-style bar mixes Leicester's best cocktails.

The Globe   PUB
(www.theglobeleicester.co.uk; 43 Silver St) In the atmospheric Lanes – a tangle of alleys south of the High St – this old-fashioned boozer offers fine draught ales and a crowd who rate their drinks by quality rather than quantity.

Firebug   BAR
(www.firebugbar.co.uk; 1 Millstone Lane; ⊙noon-2am Mon & Tue, noon-4am Wed-Sat, 1pm-2am Sun) A lava lounge for the student crowd, with a great selection of beers on tap, as well as theme nights, stage shows and gigs.

☆ Entertainment

Leicester's new Cultural Quarter development centres on Rutland St. Mainstream clubs cluster around Churchgate and Gravel St.

Curve Theatre   THEATRE
(☎0116-242 3595; www.curveonline.co.uk; Rutland St; backstage tours adult/child £3/2) A sleek artistic space with big-name shows and some innovative modern theatre; call the ticket office to book backstage tours. The bar is a sophisticated place for lunch or a sundowner.

Phoenix Square   CINEMA
(☎0116-242 2803; www.phoenix.org.uk; Midland St) Leicester's premier venue for art-house films and digital media.

De Montfort Hall   LIVE MUSIC
(☎0116-233 3111; www.demontforthall.co.uk; Granville Rd) Big orchestras and big song-and-dance performances are on the bill at this huge venue near Leicester University.

Mosh   NIGHTCLUB
(www.moshleicester.com; 37 St Nicholas Pl; ⊙11pm-3am Tue, Fri & Sat) Unleash your inner indie kid at this loud and lively rock joint.

Superfly   NIGHTCLUB
(www.superfly-city.com; 2 King St) Behind a towering mock-Tudor facade, Superfly serves up four floors of diverse beats, with guest DJs and gigs.

Shopping

Leicester Market   MARKET
(www.leicestermarket.co.uk; Market Pl; ⊙outdoor market 7am-6pm Mon-Sat, indoor market 8am-5pm Tue-Sat) More than 300 stalls at Leicester's indoor and outdoor markets sell everything from organic vegetables to aromatic spices, fish and shellfish, new and secondhand clothes and homewares, electronic goods, cosmetics, jewellery, flowers and fabrics.

ℹ Information

Post office (39 Gallowtree Gate) On the ground floor of WH Smith bookshop; has a bureau de change.

Tourist office (☎0844 888 5181; www.goleicestershire.com; 7-9 Every St; ⊙10am-5.30pm Mon-Fri, 10am-5pm Sat) Helpful office with reams of city and county info.

ℹ Getting There & Away

BUS Buses operate from **St Margaret's bus station** (Gravel St), located north of the centre. The useful Skylink bus runs to East Midlands airport (£6.20, 50 minutes, every 30 minutes, 24 hours). Bus 440 runs to Derby (£7, one hour, 10 daily); one bus a day continues to Buxton (£13.40, 2¼ hours).

National Express services:

Coventry £6.50, 45 minutes, four daily

London £6.50, 2¾ hours, one or two hourly

Nottingham £3.80, 45 minutes, two hourly

TRAIN East Midlands trains run to:

Birmingham £11.70, one hour, twice hourly

London St Pancras £45, 1¼ hours, two to four hourly

❶ Getting Around

The centre is cut off from the suburbs by a tangle of underpasses and flyovers, but downtown Leicester is easy to get around on foot. For unlimited transport on local buses, buy a Flexi Day Ticket (£5).

Around Leicester

BOSWORTH BATTLEFIELD

Given a few hundred years, every battlefield ends up simply a field, but the site of the Battle of Bosworth – where Richard III met his maker in 1485 – is enlivened by an entertaining Heritage Centre (☑01455-290429; www.bosworthbattlefield.com; adult/child £7.50/4.50; ☺10am-5pm Apr-Oct, to 4pm Nov-Mar) full of skeletons and musket-balls. The best time to visit is in August, when the battle is re-enacted by enthusiasts in period costume.

Although it lasted just a few hours, the Battle of Bosworth marked the end of the Plantagenet dynasty and the start of the Tudor era. This was where the mortally wounded Richard III famously proclaimed 'A horse, a horse, my kingdom for a horse'...actually, he didn't. The quote was invented by that great Tudor propagandist William Shakespeare, who also painted the able-bodied Richard as a cruel, calculating hunchback with a withered arm.

The battlefield is 16 miles southwest of Leicester at Sutton Cheny, off the A447. Arriva (☑0844 800 4411; www.arrivabus.co.uk) bus 153 runs hourly from Leicester to Market Bosworth, a 3-mile walk from the battlefield. Alternatively, book a taxi with Bosworth Gold Cars (☑01455-291999).

CONKERS & THE NATIONAL FOREST

The National Forest (www.forestry.gov.uk/nationalforest) is an ambitious project to generate new areas of sustainable woodland by planting 30 million trees in Leicestershire, Derbyshire and Staffordshire. More than seven million saplings have already taken root, and all sorts of visitor attractions are springing up in the forest, including Conkers (☑01283-216633; www.visitconkers.com; Rawdon Rd; adult/child £8.95/6.95; ☺10am-6pm Easter–mid-Oct, to 5pm mid-Oct–Easter), a family-oriented nature centre, with interactive displays, indoor and outdoor playgrounds and lots of hands-on activities. Conkers is 20 miles northwest of Leicester off the A444; bus 23 from Ashby-de-la-Zouch to Moira passes this way.

Nearby, bike trails run through the forest, including a flat 2km path around the lake, from the brand-new cycle centre Hicks Lodge (☑01751-460011; www.purplemountain.co.uk; Willesley Wood Side; bike rental per day adult/child £30/15; ☺trails 8am-dusk, bike hire 10am-4pm Mon-Fri, 9am-5pm Sat & Sun), which rents wheels and has a cafe, and also organises guided tours and night rides.

National Forest YHA hostel (☑0845 371 9672; www.yha.org.uk; dm £10-18, d £38-58; P@☎), 300m west of Conkers visitor centre along Bath Lane, has loads of ecofriendly features (such as greywater and solar biomass boiler usage), en suite rooms, and a restaurant serving local produce and organic wines.

DERBYSHIRE

The Derbyshire countryside is painted in two distinct tones – the lush green of rolling valleys, criss-crossed by dry stone walls, and the barren mottled brown hilltops of the high moorlands. The big attraction here is the Peak District National Park, which preserves some of England's most evocative scenery, attracting legions of hikers, climbers, cyclists and cave enthusiasts.

🏃 Activities

The Peak District National Park is the hub for outdoor enthusiasts.

STEAMING AROUND LEICESTER

A fun jaunt rather than a serious way to get from A to B, the classic Great Central Railway (☑01509-632323; www.gcrailway.co.uk; return adult/child £14/9) operates steam locomotives from Leicester North station on Redhill Circle to Loughborough Central, following the 8-mile route along which Thomas Cook ran the original package tour in 1841. The locos chug several days a week from June to August and weekends for the rest of the year – check timetables online. To reach Leicester North station, take bus 25 from the Haymarket bus station on Charles St (bus 26 to return).

ℹ Getting There & Around

East Midlands Airport (p393) is the nearest air hub, and Derby is well served by trains, but connecting services to smaller towns are few. In the Peak District, the Derwent Valley Line runs from Derby to Matlock. Edale and Hope lie on the Hope Valley Line from Sheffield to Manchester. For a comprehensive list of Derbyshire bus routes, visit the 'Transport' pages at www .derbyshire.gov.uk.

Derby

POP 229,407

Derby was one of the crucibles of the Industrial Revolution. Almost overnight, a sleepy market town was transformed into a major manufacturing centre, producing everything from silk to bone china, and later locomotives and Rolls-Royce aircraft engines. The city suffered the ravages of industrial decline in the 1980s, but has bounced back with some impressive cultural developments and a rejuvenated riverfront.

◉ Sights

FREE **Derby Cathedral** CHURCH
(www.derbycathedral.org; 18 Irongate; ⊙9.30am-4.30pm Mon-Sat & services Sun) Founded in AD 943, but reconstructed in the 18th century, Derby Cathedral's vaulted ceiling towers over a fine collection of medieval tombs, including the opulent grave of the oft-married Bess of Hardwick, who at various times held court at Hardwick Hall, Chatsworth House and Bolsover Castle. Peregrine falcons nest in the tower – follow their progress at www .derbyperegrines.blogspot.co.uk.

FREE **Derby Museum & Art Gallery** MUSEUM
(www.derby.gov.uk; The Strand; ⊙10am-5pm Tue-Sat, 1-4pm Sun) Local history and industry displays include fine ceramics produced by Royal Crown Derby and an archaeology gallery.

SPLASHING ABOUT ON RUTLAND WATER

Tiny Rutland was merged with Leicestershire in 1974, but in 1997 regained its 'independence' as England's smallest county.

Rutland centres on Rutland Water, a vast artificial reservoir created by the damming of the Gwash Valley in 1976. Covering 1255 hectares, the reservoir attracts numerous bird species, including ospreys – best viewed from the hides at the Rutland Water Nature Reserve (www.rutlandwater.org.uk; adult/child £5.50/3.20; ⊙9am-5pm) near Oakham.

At Skyes Lane near Empingham, the Rutland Water Visitor Centre (☑01780-686800; www.anglianwater.co.uk; ⊙10am-4pm) has a snack kiosk, walking and cycling trails and information on the area.

Within the Whitwell Centre, Rockblok (☑01780 460 060; www.rutlandcycling.com; Whitwell Leisure Park, Bull Brigg Lane, Whitwell; ⊙9am-6pm) has a vertigo-inducing high-ropes course, an outdoor climbing wall and bikes for hire (adult/child per day from £9.99/6.99) for a gentle pedal around the lakeshore. In the same compound, Rutland Watersports (☑01780-460154; www.anglianwater.co.uk/leisure) offers aquatic activities, including sailing and windsurfing. You can rent gear, take lessons or do certified courses.

The Rutland Belle (☑01572-787630; www.rutlandwatercruises.com; adult/child £8/5; ⊙Sat & Sun Apr & Oct, daily May-Sep, closed Nov-Mar) offers afternoon cruises from Whitwell to Normanton on the southern shore of the reservoir, where a stone causeway leads out across the water to Normanton Church (☑01780-686800; www.anglianwater.co.uk; adult/child £3/2; ⊙tours 12.30pm, 1.30pm & 2.30pm Sun-Wed Apr-Sep, 12.30pm, 1.30pm & 2.30pm Sun Oct, closed Nov-Mar), saved from inundation by a limestone barrier wall. Inside are displays on the history of the reservoir.

Close to the boat jetty, the Normanton Centre (☑01780-720888) offers bike hire at the same rates as the Whitwell Centre; see also www.rutlandcycling.com. Just down the road at Edith Weston, Rutland Sailing School (☑01780-721999; www.rutlandsailing school.co.uk) rents out boats and runs sailing courses.

Easily the best place to stay in the area is Hambleton Hall (☑01572-756991; www .hambletonhall.com; s/d incl breakfast from £215/270, mains £33-39; ℗), one of England's finest country hotels, which surveys the countryside from a peninsula jutting out into Rutland Water, 3 miles east of Oakham. Its luxuriant floral rooms and Michelin-starred restaurant are surrounded by gorgeous gardens.

WORTH A TRIP

WYMESWOLD

The cute village of Wymeswold, 16 miles north of Leicester via the A46, warrants a detour for a sensational meal. Hammer & Pincers (☎01509-880735; 5 East Rd; mains £14-31; ☺lunch Tue-Sun, dinner Tue-Sat; ☒) is set in bucolic gardens at the edge of the village. Everything – down to the breads and condiments – is homemade and steaks are a speciality. There are also gourmet menus (6-/8-courses £37.50/45), and cookery demonstrations by arrangement.

Wymeswold is best reached by your own wheels; buses from Leicester require changing at Loughborough or Ashfordby.

Quad   GALLERY, CINEMA
(☎01332-290606; www.derbyquad.co.uk; Market Pl; gallery & BFI Mediatheque free; ☺gallery 11am-6pm, from noon Sun, BFI Mediatheque 11am-8pm, from noon Sun) A striking modernist cube on Market Pl, Quad contains a futuristic art gallery, cinema and mediatheque – an archive of films and TV covering decades of broadcasting, run by the British Film Institute (BFI).

Royal Crown Derby Factory   CERAMICS
(☎01332-712833; www.royalcrownderby.co.uk; Osmaston Rd; tour & museum adult/child £5/4.75; ☺10am-5pm Mon-Sat, tours 11am & 1.30pm Tue-Fri by reservation) Derby's historic potteries still turn out some of the finest bone china in England, from edgy Asian-inspired designs to the kind of stuff your grandma used to collect. Children must be aged over 10 to join tours.

🛏 Sleeping

Chuckles   B&B £
(☎01332-367193; www.chucklesguesthouse.co.uk; 48 Crompton St; s/d £32/54; ☎) The friendliest of several cosy B&Bs just south of the centre, Chuckles is run by an arty couple and is renowned for its bountiful breakfasts. Take Green Lanes and turn onto Crompton St by the church.

Cathedral Quarter Hotel   HOTEL ££
(☎01332-546080; www.thefinessecollection.com/ cathedralquarter; 16 St Mary's Gate; s/d incl breakfast from £90/110; @☎) A bell's peal from the cathedral, this grand Georgian edifice houses Derby's finest digs. The service is as polished as the grand marble staircase and there's an on-site spa and fine-dining restaurant.

✖ Eating

For atmospheric and inexpensive dining, also try Derby's pubs.

TOP
CHOICE   Jack Rabbits   CAFE, DELI £
(☎01332-349966; www.jackrabbitskitchen.co.uk; 50 Queen St; mains £4.95-8.95; ☺9.30am-3pm Mon, 9.30am-6pm Tue-Fri, 9am-5pm Sat; ☒) Jack Rabbits' gourmet sandwiches, quiches and ready-to-eat meals (perfect for a riverside picnic) and its deli goods (including homemade jams and chutneys) have proved so popular that it's opened an adjoining sunlit cafe for lazy grazing on platters, cheeseboards and scrumptious cakes and slices.

European Restaurant
& Bistro   MODERN EUROPEAN ££
(☎01332-368732; www.theeuropeanrestaurant.co .uk; 22 Irongate; mains £9.50-19.90; ☺lunch Tue-Sat, dinner Mon-Sat) 'European' generally translates to Italian on the menu of this smart restaurant and bistro opposite the cathedral, which serves top-quality fare with pride.

Darleys   MODERN BRITISH £££
(☎01332-364987; www.darleys.com; Waterfront, Darley Abbey; mains £19.20-21.50; ☺lunch daily, dinner Mon-Sat) Two miles north of the centre, this upmarket restaurant has a gorgeous setting in a bright converted mill overlooking the river. Classy fare includes warm fig tart, goats'-cheese mousse and toasted hazelnuts.

🍷 Drinking & Entertainment

Derby has a wonderful selection of historic real ale pubs, many of which have live music.

Catch art-house films at Quad, or check what's showing at the two theatre spaces run by Derby Live (☎01332-255800; www .derbylive.co.uk; Market Pl).

Ye Olde Dolphin   PUB
(☎01332-267711; 5a Queen St) Dating from 1530, Derby's oldest pub has a hearty menu, live music in the beer garden on weekends, and organises ghost tours.

Brunswick Inn   PUB
(www.brunswickinn.co.uk; 1 Railway Tce) Set at the end of a working-class terrace near the station, this award-winning inn is a warren of cosy rooms where you can enjoy the nut-brown ales created by the house brewery.

Brewery Tap   PUB
(www.brewerytap-dbc.co.uk; 1 Derwent St) Serves its own brews and guest ales in elegant Victorian surrounds.

Old Silk Mill   PUB
(19 Full St) Live music several times a week including Sunday afternoon jazz.

❶ Information

Tourist office (☎01332-255802; www.visit derby.co.uk; Market Pl; ⊗9.30am-5pm Mon-Thu, to 5.30pm Fri & Sat) Under the Assembly Rooms in the main square.

❶ Getting There & Away

AIR About 8 miles northwest of Derby, East Midlands Airport (p393) is served by regular Skylink buses (30 minutes, half-hourly, hourly 8.20pm to 6.20am).

BUS Local and long-distance buses run from Derby's bus station, immediately east of the Westfield shopping mall. From Monday to Saturday, Transpeak has hourly buses between Derby and Buxton (2½ hours), via Matlock (1½ hours) and Bakewell (two hours). Five buses continue to Manchester (3½ hours).

Other services:

Leicester National Express, £7.40, 1 hour (7 daily)

Nottingham Red Arrow, 30 minutes, half-hourly

TRAIN The train station is about half a mile southeast of the centre on Railway Tce. Services:

Birmingham £12.20, 45 minutes, four hourly

Leeds £20, 1½ hours, every 30 minutes

London £53.30, 1¾ hours, two hourly

Sheffield £10.10, 30 minutes, every 15 minutes

Around Derby

KEDLESTON HALL

Sitting pretty in vast landscaped grounds, Kedleston Hall (NT; house & gardens adult/child £9.90/4.90, gardens only £4.40/2.20; ⊗house noon-5pm Sat-Wed Feb-Nov, gardens 10am-6pm Feb-Nov, house & gardens closed Dec & Jan) is a must for fans of stately homes. The Curzon family has lived here since the 12th century, but the current wonder was built by Sir Nathaniel Curzon in 1758. Meanwhile, the poor old peasants in Kedleston village had their humble dwellings moved a mile down the road, as they interfered with the view!

Entering the house through a grand portico, you'll reach the breathtaking Marble Hall with massive alabaster columns and statues of Greek deities. Other highlights include Indian treasures amassed by Viceroy George Curzon and a domed, circular saloon modelled on the Pantheon in Rome, as well as 18th-century-style pleasure gardens.

Kedleston Hall is 5 miles northwest of Derby, off the A52. Arriva (☎0844 800 4411; www.arrivabus.co.uk) bus 109 between Derby and Ashbourne passes the Smithy, about 1 mile from Kedleston (25 minutes, every two hours Monday to Saturday). On summer Saturdays, the bus goes right to the hall.

CALKE ABBEY

Like an enormous, long-neglected cabinet of wonders, Calke Abbey (NT; ☎01332-863822; Ticknall; house & park adult/child £11/5.50, park only £6.80/3.40; ⊗house 12.30-5pm Sat-Wed, park 7.30am-7.30pm daily) is not your average stately home. Built around 1703, the house was occupied by a dynasty of eccentric and reclusive baronets. The result is a ramshackle maze of rooms crammed with ancient furniture, mounted animal heads, dusty books, stuffed birds and bric-a-brac spanning three centuries. Some rooms are in fabulous condition, while others are left much as they were found, with crumbling plaster and peeling wallpaper.

Other highlights include the chilly brewhouse tunnels and the ancient oak forests of Calke Park, preserved as a National Nature Reserve.

Calke is 10 miles south of Derby off the A514, close to the village of Ticknall. Arriva bus 61 from Derby to Swadlincote stops at Ticknall, a mile-and-a-half walk from the house.

ASHBOURNE
POP 7600

Perched at the southern edge of the Peak District National Park, Ashbourne is a pretty spread of steeply slanting stone streets, lined with cafes, pubs and antique shops. The main attraction, however, is the chance to walk or cycle along the Tissington Trail, part of NCN Route 68, which runs north for 13 miles to Parsley Hay, connecting with the

Pennine Cycleway (NCN Route 68) and the High Peak Trail towards Buxton or Matlock. The track climbs gently along the tunnels, viaducts and cuttings of the disused railway line which once transported local milk to London.

🛏 Sleeping & Eating

Compton House   B&B **££**
(☎01335-343100; www.comptonhouse.co.uk; 27-31 Compton; s/d/f from £40/60/85; 🅿🛜) Fresh, clean, frilly rooms, a warm welcome and central location make this the pick of Ashbourne's B&Bs.

Bramhalls   CAFE **£**
(☎01335-342631; 22 Market Pl; dishes £3.25-7.95; ◷8am-5pm Mon-Sat) A great little deli and cafe with posh light meals and sandwiches, and excellent homemade pastries, breads, cold meats and 70 varieties of cheese.

🍷 Drinking

Smith's Tavern   PUB
(36 St John's St) A tiny pub on the main shopping street, with a big selection of real ales and an old piano at the back.

❶ Getting There & Away

Bus services include the following:

Buxton Bowers 42, 35 minutes, Bowers 442 one hour, 20 minutes; every one to two hours

Derby Arriva bus 109/Trent Barton Swift service, 40 minutes, hourly

Leek Cowes 108, 50 minutes, six daily

❶ Getting Around

About a mile above town, the **Cycle Hire Centre** (☎01335-343156; www.peakdistrict.gov.uk/visiting/cycle; Mapleton Lane; half-day/day from £12.50/15.50; ◷9am-5.30pm Mar-Oct, reduced hours Nov-Feb) is right on the Tissington Trail, at the end of a huge and atmospheric old railway tunnel leading under Ashbourne. You can also rent children's bikes, bikes with baby seats, trailers for buggies and tandems.

Matlock Bath

POP 2202

Unashamedly tacky, Matlock Bath (not to be confused with the larger, work-a-day town of Matlock 2 miles north) looks like a seaside resort that somehow lost its way and ended up at the foot of the Peak District National Park. Following the River Derwent through a sheer-walled gorge, the main promenade is lined with amusement arcades, tearooms, fish-and-chippers, pubs and shops catering to the bikers who congregate here on summer weekends. Outside summer, the town is considerably quieter and many lodgings and eateries shut.

◉ Sights & Activities

Steep paths climb the eastern side of the gorge, reached by pedestrian bridges from the A6. The tourist office has details of longer, more challenging walks in the hills. Note that many of the lanes up the side of the valley are too narrow for cars, with no space for turning.

Gulliver's Kingdom   AMUSEMENT PARK
(☎01925-444888; www.gulliversfun.co.uk; admission £13.95) This old-fashioned amusement park offers plenty of splashing, churning, looping attractions for anyone as tall as the signs at the start of the rides. Call for opening days and times or check the seasonal schedule online.

Heights of Abraham   AMUSEMENT PARK
(☎01629-582365; www.heightsofabraham.com; adult/child £13/9; ◷10am-5pm daily mid–late Feb, Sat & Sun late Feb–mid-Mar, daily mid-Mar–early Nov, closed rest of year) A spectacular cable-car ride (included in admission ticket only) from the bottom of the gorge brings you to this hilltop leisure park, whose atmospheric cave and mine tours and fossil exhibitions are a winner with kids.

ROYAL SHROVETIDE FOOTBALL

Some people celebrate Shrove Tuesday (the last day before Lent) by eating pancakes or dressing up in carnival finery, but Ashbourne marks the occasion with a riotous game of football where the ball is wrestled as much as kicked from one end of town to the other by crowds of revellers. Following 12th-century rules, villagers are split into two teams – those from north of the river and those living to the south – and the 'goals' are two mill-stones, set 3 miles apart. Participants are free to kick, carry or throw the ball, though it's usually squeezed through the crowds like a rugby scrum. Sooner or later, both players and ball end up in the river. Local shops board up their windows and the whole town comes out to watch or play. Fearless visitors are welcome to participate in the melee but under a quirk of the rules, only locals are allowed to score goals.

Peak District Mining Museum & Temple Mine
MUSEUM

(www.peakmines.co.uk; The Pavilion; museum adult/child £3.50/2.50, mine £3.50/2.50, combined tickets £6/4; ⊙10am-5pm daily Apr-Oct, 11am-3pm Wed-Sat Nov-Mar) An educational introduction to the mining history of Matlock is provided by this enthusiast-run museum. Set in an old Victorian dancehall, kids can wriggle through its maze of tunnels and shafts while adults browse historical displays. At noon and 2pm daily (weekends only November to March) you can go into the workings of the Temple Mine and pan for 'gold' (well, shiny minerals).

Peak Rail
HERITAGE RAILWAY

(www.peakrail.co.uk; adult/child £7.50/4) From a tiny platform just north of Sainsbury's supermarket on the outskirts of Matlock village, nostalgic steam trains trundle along a 4-mile length of track to the nearby village of Rowsley, home to Caudwell's Mill (☑01629-734374; www.caudwellsmillcraftcentre.co .uk; admission free, mill tours adult/child £4.50/2; ⊙9.30am-4.30pm), which includes a craft centre. Tickets include unlimited travel on the day of purchase. Services run five times a day Saturday and Sunday (and some weekdays) from May to October, and some weekends at other times of the year – check timetables online.

🛏 Sleeping & Eating

Despite its inland location, the official breakfast, lunch and dinner of Matlock Bath is fish and chips, served at dozens of cafes, tearooms and pubs along the strip.

Hodgkinson's Hotel & Restaurant
HOTEL ££

(☑01629-582170; www.hodgkinsons-hotel.co.uk; 150 South Pde; s/d incl breakfast from £41/77, 2-/3-course meals £29.50/34; ⊙restaurant dinner; P🐾🛜) Right in the thick of things on the parade, rooms at this hotel conjure up Matlock's golden age with antique furnishings, flowery wallpaper and cast-iron fireplaces.

🌱 Ashdale Guest House
B&B £

(☑01629-57826; www.ashdaleguesthouse.co.uk; 92 North Pde; s/d from £35/60; P) A tall stone house just beyond the tacky part of the promenade, with smart, tasteful rooms and organic breakfasts.

Temple Hotel
HOTEL ££

(☑01629-583911; www.templehotel.co.uk; Temple Walk; s/d incl breakfast from £65/80, mains

£7.95-9.50; P🛜) The views from this hillside inn are so lovely that Lord Byron once felt inspired to etch a poem on the restaurant window. It's a little dated, but the rooms are comfy and the Chatsworth Bar turns out filling meals and real ales.

🛍 Shopping

For arts, crafts and discounted clothing brands, check out the Derwent Valley mills.

Scarthin Books
BOOKS

(www.scarthinbooks.com; The Promenade, Cromford; ⊙9am-6pm Mon-Sat, noon-6pm Sun) More than 100,000 new and secondhand books cram 12 rooms in this biblioparadise, which hosts regular literary events. Its vegetarian cafe, wedged in amongst the clutter, serves organic pizza.

ℹ Information

Tourist office (☑01629-761103; www.visit peakdistrict.com; The Pavilion; ⊙10am-5pm Apr-Oct, 11am-3pm Nov-Mar) Visitor information point at the Peak District Mining Museum.

ℹ Getting There & Away

BUS Matlock is a hub for buses around the Peak District.

Bakewell Bus 172, one hour, hourly, Monday to Saturday

Chesterfield Bus 17, 35 minutes, two daily

Derby Transpeak, 1½ hours, hourly

Sheffield Bus 214, 1¼ hours, hourly

TRAIN Trains run hourly between Matlock Bath and Derby (£5, 30 minutes, hourly).

Chesterfield

POP 100,879

The eastern gateway to the Peaks, Chesterfield is worth a visit to see the astonishing crooked spire that rises atop St Mary & All Saints Church (☑0246-206506; www .chesterfieldparishchurch.org.uk; admission free, spire tours adult/child £3.50/1.50; ⊙spire tours 11.30am & 2pm Tue & Thu, 11.30am & 2.30pm Mon, Wed, Fri & Sat). Dating from 1360, the 68m-high spire is twisted in a right-handed corkscrew and it leans several metres southwest as a result of buckling of the south-facing side of the spire's lead casing in the sun. Learn more at the engaging Chesterfield Museum & Art Gallery (☑01246-345727; www.chesterfield.gov .uk; St Mary's Gate; ⊙10am-4pm Mon-Tue & Thu-Sat).

DERWENT VALLEY MILLS

Unlikely as it may sound, the industrial mills that line the Derwent Valley are ranked up there with the Taj Mahal on the Unesco World Heritage list. Founded in the 1770s by Richard Arkwright, the Cromford Mill (☑01629-825995; www.arkwrightsociety.org.uk; Mill Lane, Cromford; tour adult/child £3.50/2.50; ☺9am-5pm, tours by reservation), 3 miles south of Matlock Bath, was the first modern factory, producing cotton on automated machines, powered by a series of waterwheels along the River Derwent. This prototype inspired a succession of mills, ushering in the industrial age. The Arkwright Society runs atmospheric tours; buses 140 and 141 run here hourly from Matlock Bath (15 minutes, no Sunday service).

Other fascinating industrial relics include Strutt's North Mill (www.belpernorthmill .org; adult/child £3.50/2; ☺1-5pm Wed-Sun Mar-Oct, 1-5pm Sat & Sun Nov-Feb) at Belper, accessible on the Transpeak bus between Derby and Matlock; Masson Mills (☑01629-581001; www.massonmills.co.uk; Derby Rd; adult/child £3/2; ☺10am-4pm Mon-Fri, 11am-5pm Sat, to 4pm Sun, closed Dec), 1 mile south of Matlock Bath, where a museum tells the story of the valley's textile mills (and an attached shopping village is full of outlet stores for big clothing brands); and Caudwell's Mill, near Rowsley, a chugging, grinding, water-powered mill that still produces flour the old-fashioned way, with various craft workshops and a tearoom. You can get to Rowsley direct from Matlock Bath by bus on the route to Bakewell, or take the Peak Rail steam train and follow the riverside path from the station.

The Chesterfield tourist office (☑012246-345777; www.visitchesterfield.info; Rykneld Sq; ☺9am-5.30pm Mon-Sat Easter-early Nov, to 5pm Mon-Sat early Nov-Easter) is directly opposite the crooked spire.

Chesterfield lies on the main rail line between Nottingham/Derby (30 minutes) and Sheffield (10 minutes), with hourly services in both directions. The station is just east of the centre. The Chesterfield Coach Station is on Beetwell St – useful local services include bus 170 to Bakewell (45 minutes, hourly) and bus 66 to Buxton (45 minutes, five daily, four Sunday services).

Hardwick Hall

One of the most complete Elizabethan mansions in the country, Hardwick Hall (NT; house & garden adult/child £11.50/5.80, garden only £5.80/free; ☺house noon-4.30pm Wed-Sun, garden 9am-6pm daily) was home to the 16th century's second-most powerful woman, Elizabeth, Countess of Shrewsbury – known to all as Bess of Hardwick – who amassed a staggering fortune by marrying wealthy noblemen with one foot in the grave. Hardwick Hall was constructed using her inheritance from hubby number four, who shuffled off his mortal coil in 1590.

Designed by eminent architect Robert Smythson, the hall featured all the latest mod-cons of the time, including fully glazed windows – a massive luxury in the 16th century. The atmospheric interiors are decked out with magnificent tapestries and oil paintings of forgotten dignitaries. Set aside some time to explore the formal gardens or longer walking trails of Hardwick Park.

Next door to the manor is Bess' first house, Hardwick Old Hall (EH; adult/child £5/3, combined Hardwick Hall ticket £14/7; ☺10am-5pm Wed-Sun Apr-early Nov, 10am-5pm Sat & Sun early Nov-Mar), now a romantic ruin administered by English Heritage.

Hardwick Hall is 10 miles southeast of Chesterfield, just off the M1. Stagecoach Chesterfield–Nottingham buses stop at Glapwell, from where it's a 1½-mile walk to Hardwick Hall.

PEAK DISTRICT

Rolling across the southernmost hills of the Pennines, the Peak District is one of the most beautiful parts of the country. Ancient stone villages are folded into creases in the landscape and the hillsides are littered with famous stately homes and rocky outcrops that attract hordes of walkers, climbers and cavers. No one knows how the Peak District got its name – certainly not from the landscape, which has hills and valleys, gorges and lakes, wild moorland and gritstone escarpments, but no peaks. The most popular theory is that the region was named for the Pecsaetan, the Anglo-Saxon tribe who once populated this part of England.

Founded in 1951, the Peak District National Park was England's first national park and is Europe's busiest. But escaping the crowds is easy if you avoid summer weekends. Even at the busiest times, there are 555 sq miles of open English countryside in which to find your own viewpoint to soak up the glorious scenery.

Locals divide the Peak District into the Dark Peak – dominated by exposed moorland and gritstone 'edges' – and the White Peak, made up of the limestone dales to the south.

Although there are several YHA hostels in the Peak District, they're often booked out in advance by groups, so contact them before turning up.

🏃 Activities

Caving & Climbing

The limestone sections of the Peak District are riddled with caves and caverns, including a series of 'showcaves' in Castleton, Buxton and Matlock Bath. For serious caving (or potholing) trips, the first port of call should be the website www.peakdistrictcaving.info, run by the caving store Hitch n Hike (www.hitchnhike.co.uk; Mytham Bridge, Bamford), near Castleton, which has gear and advice for climbing.

The Peak District has long been a training ground for England's top mountaineers. In place of looming mountains, it offers glorious technical climbing on a series of limestone gorges, exposed tors (crags) and gritstone 'edges' that extend south into the Staffordshire Moorlands. Gritstone climbing in the Peaks is predominantly on old-school trad routes, requiring a decent rack of friends, nuts and hexes. Bolted sport routes are found on several limestone crags in the Peaks, but many use ancient pieces of gear and most require additional protection. The crags are best reached with your own transport; check seasonal bus services with Trent Barton (p440) or Buxton's tourist office.

Cycling

The plunging dales and soaring scarps are a perfect testing ground for cyclists, and local tourist offices are piled high with cycling maps and pamphlets. For easy traffic-free riding, head for the 17.5-mile High Peak Trail, which follows the old railway line from Cromford, near Matlock Bath, to Dowlow near Buxton. The trail winds through beautiful hills and farmland to Parsley Hay, where the Tissington Trail, part of NCN Route 68, heads south for 13 miles to Ashbourne.

Mirroring the Pennine Way, the Pennine Bridleway is another top spot to put your calves through their paces. Around 120 miles of trails have been created between Middleton Top and the South Pennines, and the route is suitable for horse riders, cyclists and walkers. You could also follow the Pennine Cycleway (NCN Route 68) from Derby to Buxton and beyond. Other popular routes include the Limestone Way, running south from Castleton to Staffordshire, and the Monsal Trail & Tunnels between Bakewall and Wyedale, near Buxton.

Peak Tours (www.peak-tours.com; mountain bike per day £20) delivers rental bikes anywhere in the Peak District, and offers guided cycling tours. From March to October, the Peak District National Park Authority (☎01629-816200; www.peakdistrict.gov.uk) operates several cycle-hire centres charging standard rates for a half/full day of £12.50/15.50 for adults and £8.50/10.50 for children.

Walking

The Peak District is one of the most popular walking areas in England, with awe-inspiring vistas of hills, dales and sky that attract legions of hikers in summer. The White Peak is perfect for leisurely strolls, which can start from pretty much anywhere (be sure to close gates behind you). When exploring the rugged territory of the Dark Peak, make sure your boots are waterproof and beware of slipping into rivulets and marshes.

The Peak's most famous walking trail is the Pennine Way, which runs north from Edale for more than 250 miles, finishing in the Scottish Borders. If you don't have three weeks to spare, you can reach the pretty town of Hebden Bridge in Yorkshire in three comfortable days.

The 46-mile Limestone Way winds through the Derbyshire countryside from Castleton to Rocester in Staffordshire, following footpaths, tracks and quiet lanes. Many people walk the 26-mile section between Castleton and Matlock in one long, tiring day, but two days is better. Tourist offices have a detailed leaflet.

Other popular routes include the High Peak Trail, Tissington Trail, and Monsal Trail & Tunnels, described under Cycling. Numerous short walks are available.

ℹ Information

Tourist offices or national park visitor centres include Buxton, Bakewell, Castleton and Edale. The Peak District National Park Authority website (www.peakdistrict.gov.uk) is a goldmine of

Peak District National Park

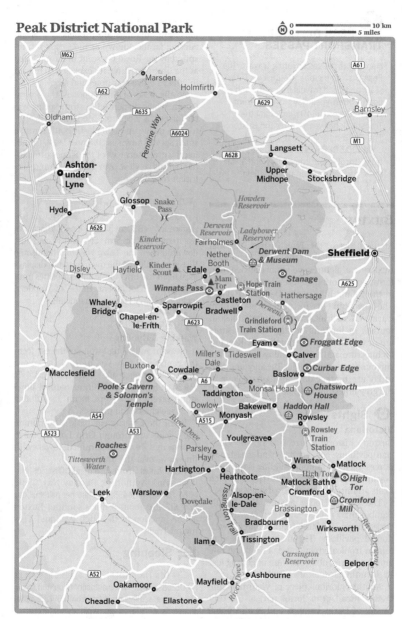

information on transport, activities and local events.

ⓘ Getting There & Away

Buses run from regional centres such as Sheffield and Derby to destinations across the Peak District. Be aware that buses are much more frequent at weekends, and many services close down completely in winter. Timetables are available from all the tourist offices, or online at www .derbyshire.gov.uk/buses. Trains run to Matlock Bath, Buxton, Edale and several other towns and villages.

ℹ PEAK DISTRICT TRANSPORT PASSES

Handy bus passes covering travel in the Peak District include the Zigzag Plus (£10, one child travels free with each adult), offering all-day travel on Trent Barton buses (p440), including the Transpeak between Derby and Buxton. The Derbyshire Wayfarer (adult/child £10.50/£5.25) covers buses and trains throughout the county and as far afield as Manchester and Sheffield.

Buxton

POP 24,112

At the heart of the Peak District National Park (albeit outside the park boundary) Buxton is a picturesque sprawl of Georgian terraces, Victorian amusements and parks in the rolling hills of the Derbyshire dales. The town built its fortunes on its natural warm-water springs, which attracted health tourists in Buxton's heyday. Today, visitors are drawn here by the flamboyant Regency architecture and the natural wonders of the surrounding countryside. Tuesday and Saturday are market days, bringing colour to the grey limestone market place.

◎ Sights

Victoriana

Buxton's historic centre is a riot of Victorian pavilions, concert halls and glasshouse domes. Its most famous building is the flamboyant, turreted Opera House (p472), which hosts an impressive variety of stage shows.

The Opera House adjoins the equally flamboyant Pavilion Gardens (www.paviliongardens.co.uk; ⊙9.30am-5pm), dotted with domed pavilions. The main building contains a tropical greenhouse, a nostalgic cafe and the tourist office. Beware of getting lost in the unlit gardens after dark.

Another glorious piece of Victoriana, the Devonshire Dome, forms part of the University of Derby campus and is also home to Devonshire Spa (⌨01332-594408; www.devonshire-spa.co.uk; 1 Devonshire Rd; treatments incl 1hr body spa £38, ocean wrap £49, day package from £65), which offers a full range of pampering treatments.

In Victorian times, spa activities centred on the extravagant Buxton Baths complex,

built in grand Regency style in 1854. The various bath buildings are fronted by a grand curving facade, known as the Crescent, inspired by the Royal Crescent in Bath. Closed at the time of writing, it's expected to reopen in 2014 as a five-star hotel and spa.

At the base of the Slopes is the Pump Room, which dispensed Buxton's spring water for nearly a century. Modern day health-tourists queue up to fill plastic bottles from a small spout known as St Ann's Well. Climbing the green terraces of the Slopes provides the definitive view over Buxton's grand Victorian rooftops.

FREE **Buxton Museum & Art Gallery** MUSEUM, GALLERY
(Terrace Rd; ⊙9.30am-5.30pm Tue-Fri, to 5pm Sat year-round, 10.30am-5pm Sun Easter-Sep) Just downhill from the Town Hall in a handsome Victorian building, the town museum displays local historical bric-a-brac and curiosities from Castleton's Victorian-era 'House of Wonders', including Harry Houdini's handcuffs.

🏃 Activities

Walking & Cycling

A pleasant mile-long stroll southwest from the centre will take you to Poole's Cavern (www.poolescavern.co.uk; adult/child £8/4.75; ⊙9.30am-5pm), a magnificent natural limestone cavern. Few steps mean it's suitable for wheelchairs and prams.

From the cavern's car park, a 20-minute walk leads up through Grin Low Wood to Solomon's Temple, a ruined tower with fine views over the town.

Rent bikes from the Peak District National Park Authority's Parsley Hay Cycle Hire (⌨01298-84493; bike hire per half-/full day from £12/15), about 8 miles south of Buxton at the junction of the High Peak and Tissington Trails.

🛏 Sleeping

TOP CHOICE **Old Hall Hotel** HISTORIC HOTEL ££
(⌨01298-22841; www.oldhallhotelbuxton.co.uk; The Square; s/d incl breakfast from £65/85; @🕏) There is a tale to go with every creak of the floorboards at this history-soaked establishment, supposedly the oldest hotel in England. Among other esteemed residents, Mary, Queen of Scots, stayed here from 1576 to 1578, albeit against her will. The rooms are still the grandest in town, and there are several bars, lounges and dining options.

Buxton

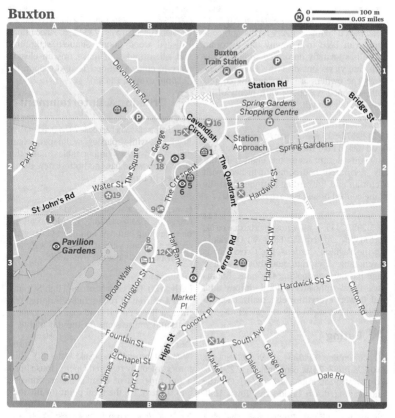

Buxton

◎ Top Sights
Pavilion Gardens...................................A3

◎ Sights
1	Buxton Baths	C2
2	Buxton Museum & Art Gallery	C3
3	Crescent	B2
4	Devonshire Dome	B1
5	Pump Room	B2
6	St Ann's Well	B2
7	Town Hall	B3

✿ Activities, Courses & Tours
Devonshire Spa...........................(see 4)

🛏 Sleeping
8	Grosvenor House	B3
9	Old Hall Hotel	B2
10	Roseleigh Hotel	A4
11	Victorian Guest House	B3

✕ Eating
12	Columbine Restaurant	B3
13	Green Pavilion	C2
14	Nat's Kitchen	C4
15	Simply Thai	B2

🍸 Drinking
16	Barbarella's	C2
17	Old Sun Inn	B4
18	Project X	B2

★ Entertainment
19	Opera House	B2

🔒 Shopping
Cavendish Arcade...........................(see 1)

Roseleigh Hotel
B&B **££**

(☑01298-24904; www.roseleighhotel.co.uk; 19 Broad Walk; d from £78; P@🖥) This gorgeous family-run B&B in a roomy old Victorian house has lovingly decorated rooms, many with fine views out over the Pavilion Gardens. The owners are a welcoming couple, both seasoned travellers, with plenty of interesting tales to tell.

Victorian Guest House
B&B **££**

(☑01298-78759; www.buxtonvictorian.co.uk; 3a Broad Walk; d from £82; P🖥) Overlooking the park, this elegant house has eight individually decorated bedrooms furnished with Victorian and Edwardian antiques, and the home-cooked breakfasts are renowned.

Grosvenor House
B&B **££**

(☑01298-72439; www.grosvenorbuxton.co.uk; 1 Broad Walk; s/d from £50/65; P🖥) Overlooking the Pavilion Gardens, the Grosvenor is a venerable Victorian guesthouse with a huge parlour overlooking the park. Rooms have floral upholstery, floral drapes and, well, flowery everything else, really. There's a minimum two-night stay at peak times.

Eating

Columbine Restaurant
MODERN BRITISH **££**

(☑01298-78752; 7 Hall Bank; mains £12.25-17.80; ⊙dinner Mon-Sat, closed Tue Nov-Apr) On the lane leading down beside the Town Hall, this understated restaurant is the top choice among in-the-know Buxtonites. The chef conjures up imaginative dishes using mainly local produce as well as sinful puddings. Bookings recommended.

Green Pavilion
CAFE **£**

(☑01298-77480; www.greenpavilion.co.uk; 6 Terrace Rd; dishes £3.50-8.95; ⊙8am-5pm; 🖊) A contemporary alternative to the Pavilion Gardens' old-fashioned tearooms, this funky little cafe brews Illy coffee, whips up gourmet burgers and wraps, and packs picnic hampers (including blankets for loan).

Nat's Kitchen
MODERN BRITISH **£££**

(☑01298-214642; www.natskitchen.co.uk; 9-11 Market St; 2-/3-course menus £21/27.50; ⊙9am-11pm) A relaxing dining room full of natural wood tones provides the backdrop to some inventive modern British cooking. Ingredients are sourced from local suppliers and there are some smart B&B rooms upstairs. Bookings recommended.

Simply Thai
THAI **££**

(☑01298-24471; www.simplythaibuxton.co.uk; 2-3 Cavendish Circus; mains £7.25-12.95; ⊙noon-11pm) Polished wood floors, Siamese sculptures and silk-attired staff make this an elegant place to enjoy a refined Thai afternoon tea (2.30pm to 5pm, £15.95).

Drinking & Entertainment

Barbarella's
WINE BAR

(www.barbarellaswinebar.co.uk; 7 The Quadrant; 🖥) Black-and-white paisley wallpaper, chandeliers and glossy timber tables make this sleek retro wine bar the hottest new drinking den in Buxton.

Project X
BAR

(www.project-x-cafe.com; The Old Court House, George St; ⊙8am-midnight; 🖥) Moroccan tables, hanging lanterns and deep-violet walls create a casbah vibe at this sultry cafe and bar, which hosts regular live music.

Old Sun Inn
PUB

(33 High St) The cosiest of the High St pubs, with a warren of rooms full of original features, a lively crowd that spans the generations and jam sessions on Tuesday nights.

Opera House
OPERA

(www.buxtonoperahouse.org.uk; Water St) Buxton's gorgeously restored Opera House hosts a full program of drama, dance, concerts and comedy. It's the focal point for Buxton's numerous festivals, including the Buxton Festival (www.buxtonfestival.co.uk; ⊙Jul) and International Gilbert & Sullivan Festival (www.gsfestivals.org; ⊙late Jul-early Aug).

Shopping

Retaining its original eggshell-blue art deco tiles, the Cavendish Arcade (Cavendish Circus) houses boutiques selling upmarket gifts.

Scrivener's Books & Bookbinding
BOOKS

(☑01298-73100; www.scrivenersbooks.co.uk; 42 High St; ⊙9am-5pm Mon-Sat, noon-4pm Sun) A delightfully chaotic bookshop, sprawling over five floors, where books are filed in piles and the Dewey system has yet to be discovered.

ⓘ Information

Post office (High St) With a bureau de change.

Tourist office (www.visitpeakdistrict.com; Pavilion Gardens; ⊙9.30am-5pm; 🖥) Has useful leaflets on walks in the area. Free hour-long Roman Buxton town walks depart at 11am and 2pm Saturday.

❶ Getting There & Away

Buses stop on both sides of the road at Market Pl. The hourly Transpeak runs to Derby (2½ hours), via Bakewell (one hour) and Matlock Bath (1½ hours). To reach Manchester by bus, take Skyline bus 199 (1½ hours, every 30 minutes Monday to Saturday). Other bus services:

Chesterfield Bus 66, 1¼ hours, five daily Monday to Saturday (four services Sunday)

Nottingham National Express £18, 2½ hours, one daily

Sheffield Bus 65, 1½ hours, five daily (three services Sunday)

Northern Rail has trains to and from Manchester (£9.10, one hour, hourly).

Castleton

POP 1200

Guarding the entrance to the forbidding Winnats Pass gorge, charming Castleton is a magnet on summer weekends for East Midlands visitors – come mid-week to enjoy the sights in relative peace and quiet. The village's streets are lined with leaning stone houses, walking trails criss-cross the surrounding hills, a wonderfully atmospheric castle crowns the ridge above, and the bedrock below is riddled with fascinating caves.

◉ Sights

Peveril Castle   CASTLE
(EH; adult/child £4.50/2.70; ⊙10am-5pm Apr-Oct, 10am-4pm Sat & Sun Nov-Mar) Topping the ridge to the south of Castleton, this evocative castle has been so ravaged by the centuries that it almost looks like a crag itself. Constructed by William Peveril, son of William the Conqueror, the castle was used as a hunting lodge by Henry II, King John and Henry III, and the crumbling ruins offer swooping views over the Hope Valley.

FREE **Castleton Museum**   MUSEUM
(☏01433-620679; Buxton Rd; ⊙9.30am-5.30pm) Attached to the tourist office, the cute town museum has displays on everything from mining and geology to rock climbing, hanggliding and the curious Garland Festival.

Peak Cavern   CAVE
(☏01433-620285; http://devilsarse.com; adult/child £8.75/6.75; ⊙10am-4pm daily Apr-Oct, Sat & Sun Nov-Mar) Castleton's most convenient cave is easily reached by a pretty streamside walk from the village centre. It has the largest natural cave entrance in England, known

(not so prettily) as the Devil's Arse. Dramatic limestone formations are lit with fibre-optic cables.

Speedwell Cavern   CAVE
(☏01433-621888; www.speedwellcavern.co.uk; adult/child £9.25/7.25; ⊙9.30am-4pm) About half a mile west of Castleton at the mouth of Winnats Pass, this claustrophobe's nightmare is reached via an eerie boat ride through flooded tunnels, emerging by a huge subterranean lake called the Bottomless Pit. New chambers are discovered here all the time by potholing expeditions.

Treak Cliff Cavern   CAVE
(☏01433-620571; www.bluejohnstone.com; adult/child £8.50/4.50; ⊙10am-5pm, last tour 4.20pm) A short walk across the fields from Speedwell Cavern, Treak Cliff is notable for its forest of stalactites and exposed seams of colourful Blue John Stone, which is still mined to supply the jewellery trade. Tours focus on the history of mining; kids can polish their own Blue John Stone during school holidays.

Blue John Cavern   CAVE
(☏01433-620638; www.bluejohn-cavern.co.uk; adult/child £9/4.50; ⊙10am-5.30pm) Up the side of Mam Tor, Blue John is a maze of natural caverns with rich seams of Blue John Stone that are still mined every winter. You can get here on foot up the closed section of the Mam Tor road.

🏃 Activities

At the base of 517m-high Mam Tor, Castleton is the northern terminus of the Limestone Way, which follows narrow, rocky Cave Dale, far below the east wall of the castle. The tourist office has maps and leaflets, including details of numerous easier walks.

🛏 Sleeping

Prices are often higher at weekends when booking ahead is advised.

Ye Olde Nag's Head Hotel   PUB £
(☏01433-620248; www.yeoldenagshead.co.uk; Cross St; d from £50; 🕾) The cosiest of the 'residential' pubs along the main road, offering comfortable, well-appointed rooms (some with four-poster beds and spas), ale-tasting trays and a popular restaurant, plus regular live music.

Causeway House   B&B ££
(☏01433-623921; www.causewayhouse.co.uk; Back St; s/d from £33/65) The floors within this

ancient character-soaked stone cottage are worn and warped with age, but the quaint bedrooms are bright and welcoming. Doubles have en suites but the two single rooms (one of which can be used as a twin) share a bathroom.

Rowter Farm CAMPSITE **£**
(☎01433-620271; sites per person £5; ☺Easter-Oct; **P**) A simple campsite about 1 mile west of Castleton in a stunning location up in the hills. Drivers should approach via Winnats Pass; on foot, follow the Cave Dale path.

Eating & Drinking

Teashops abound in Castleton. The village shop has limited stocks of provisions for walkers and is open seven days.

1530 ITALIAN **££**
(☎01433-621870; www.1530therestaurant.co.uk; Cross St; mains £9-21.95; ☺lunch & dinner Wed-Mon; ✐) Crispy thin-crust pizzas and fresh pastas such as king prawn, crab, crayfish and calamari linguine are the specialty of Castleton's swish new Italian flag-bearer.

Ye Olde Cheshire Cheese Inn PUB **£**
(☎01433-620330; www.cheshirecheeseinn.co.uk; How Lane; mains £7.95-10.95; ☜✐) Tradition is everything at this well-known alehouse, set in a fine, old timbered building on the main road. The pub menu is more exotic than most (try the wild boar casserole) and there are also comfy guest rooms.

Three Roofs Cafe CAFE **£**
(The Island; dishes £5.80-8.95; ☺10am-5pm; ☜) The most popular purveyor of cream teas, opposite the turn-off to the tourist office.

ℹ Information

Tourist Office (Buxton Rd; ☺9.30am-5.30pm Mar-Oct, 10am-5pm Nov-Feb) With a snack kiosk, museum and lots of leaflets on local walks.

ℹ Getting There & Away

BUS Services include the following:
Bakewell Bus 173, 50 minutes, three daily via Hope (10 minutes) and Tideswell (25 minutes)
Buxton Bus 68 and Bus 173, one hour, departs Castleton in the morning and returns in the afternoon (Monday to Saturday)
Edale Bus 260, 25 minutes, six services (Sunday only)
Sheffield Bus 272, 1¼ hours, hourly

TRAIN The nearest train station is at Hope, about 3 miles east of Castleton on the line between Sheffield and Manchester. On summer weekends, a bus runs between Hope station and Castleton to meet the trains, but it's an easy walk.

Derwent Reservoirs

North of the Hope Valley, the upper reaches of the Derwent Valley were flooded between 1916 and 1935 to create three huge reservoirs to supply Sheffield, Leicester, Nottingham and Derby with water. These man-made lakes soon proved their worth – the Dam-busters squadron carried out practice runs over Derwent Reservoir before unleashing their 'bouncing bombs' on the Ruhr Valley in Germany in WWII. Their exploits are detailed in the Derwent Dam Museum (www.derwentdammuseum.org; admission free; ☺10am-4pm Sun) in a tower atop the dam.

These days, the Ladybower, Derwent and Howden Reservoirs are popular destinations for walkers, cyclists and mountainbikers – and lots of ducks, so drive slowly! Fairholmes, near the Derwent Dam, has a tourist office (☺9.30am-5.30pm) dispensing

---

THE ANCIENT CASTLETON GARLAND FESTIVAL

Every 29 May – or on the 28th if the 29th is a Sunday – Castleton celebrates Oak Apple Day with the flamboyant village Garland Festival, which can trace its origins back to at least the 17th century, and possibly all the way back to Celtic times. Every year, two residents of the village are chosen to be Garland King and Queen and paraded through the village on horseback, with the Garland King buried under an enormous headdress woven with flowers. The strange behaviour of the Nettle Man, who whips anyone not wearing a sprig of oak leaves with a bunch of stinging nettles, adds to the surreal mood.

The tradition of wearing oak leaves dates back to the English Civil War, when it served as a badge of identification for supporters of Charles II, who escaped capture at the Battle of Worcester by hiding in an oak tree. However, scholars believe the festival may have its ultimate roots in the worship of the pagan fertility goddess Brigantia.

walking and cycling advice, a car park, a snack bar and a good cycle hire centre (☑01433-651261; ☺9.30am-5.30pm), charging the standard Peak rates.

Fairholmes is 2 miles north of the A57, the main road between Sheffield and Manchester. Bus 273 from Sheffield Interchange runs to Fairholmes in the morning, returning in the afternoon.

Edale

POP 316

Surrounded by majestic Peak District countryside, this cluster of stone houses set around a pretty parish church is an enchanting place to pass the time. Edale lies between the White and Dark Peak areas, and is the southern terminus of the Pennine Way. Despite the remote location, the Manchester–Sheffield line passes through the village, bringing throngs of weekend visitors.

Activities

Predictably, walking is the number one drawcard, and there are plenty of diverting strolls for less committed hill walkers.

As well as trips to Hollins Cross and Mam Tor, on the ridge dividing Edale from Castleton, you can walk north onto the Kinder Plateau, dark and brooding in the mist, gloriously high and open when the sun's out. This was the setting for a famous act of civil disobedience by ramblers in 1932 that paved the way for the legal 'right to roam' and the creation of England's national parks.

Weather permitting, a fine circular walk starts by following the Pennine Way through fields to Upper Booth, then up a path called Jacobs Ladder and along the southern edge of Kinder, before dropping down to Edale via the steep rocky valley of Grindsbrook Clough, or the ridge of Ringing Roger.

About 1.5 miles east of Edale, Ladybrook Equestrian Centre (☑01433-670205; www .ladybooth.co.uk; Nether Booth) offers horseback trips around the Peaks, lasting anything from one hour to a full day, plus pony farm rides for kids.

Sleeping

Upper Booth Farm   CAMPSITE £

(☑01433-670250; www.upperboothcamping.co.uk; sites per person/car £5/3; ☺Easter-Nov; P) Located along the Pennine Way about a mile from Edale, this peaceful campsite is set on a working farm and is surrounded by spectacular scenery. For hikers, there's a camping barn (per person £7) and small shop.

Edale YHA   HOSTEL £

(☑0870 770 5808; www.yha.org.uk; dm from £18.40; @☺) Spectacular views across to Back Tor unfold from this country-house hostel 1.5 miles east of Edale. The attached activity centre is very popular with student groups. Follow the signed road from the Hope road.

Stonecroft   B&B ££

(☑01433-670262; www.stonecroftguesthouse.co .uk; Grindsbrook; d from £80; P☺) This handsomely fitted-out stone house, built in the 1900s, has two comfortable bedrooms. Vegetarians and vegans are well catered for – host Julia is an award-winning chef and the organic breakfast is excellent.

Fieldhead Campsite   CAMPSITE £

(☑01433-670386; www.fieldhead-campsite.co.uk; sites per person/car from £5/2.50; P) Right next to the Moorland Centre, this pretty and well-equipped campsite spreads over six fields, with some pitches right by the river.

Eating

Old Nag's Head   PUB ££

(Grindsbrook; mains £7.55-12.95) Refurbished warm and welcoming walker-friendly pub.

Rambler Inn   PUB ££

(☑01433-670268; www.theramblerinn.com; Grindsbrook; mains £9.25-10.95; ☺) Cosy stone pub with real ales, hearty steaks, pies and casseroles, B&B rooms and occasional live music.

Cooper's Cafe   CAFE £

(☑01433-670401; Cooper's Camp; dishes £2.50-4.50; ☺8am-4pm; ☺) Load up on carbs at this cheerful cafe close to the village school.

ℹ Information

Moorland tourist office (☑01433-670207; www.edale-valley.co.uk; Grindsbrook; ☺9.30am-5pm Mon-Fri, to 5.30pm Sat & Sun Apr-Sep, shorter hours in low season) Visitor centre with maps, displays on the moors, a kiosk and a campsite.

ℹ Getting There & Away

From Monday to Friday, bus 200 runs between Edale and Castleton (20 minutes, three daily, school days only) via Hope. Trains run from Edale to Manchester (£10, every hour, 45 minutes) and Sheffield (£6.40, every two hours, 40 minutes) via Hope.

Eyam

POP 926

Quaint little Eyam (ee-em), a former lead-mining village, has a poignant history. In 1665, the town was infected by the dreaded Black Death plague, carried here by fleas on a consignment of cloth from London, and the village rector, William Mompesson, convinced villagers to quarantine themselves. Some 270 of the village's 800 inhabitants succumbed, while surrounding villages remained relatively unscathed. Today, Eyam's sloping streets of old cottages backed by rows of green hills are delightful to wander.

Sights

Eyam Parish Church   CHURCH
(◷9am-6pm Mon-Sat) Many of the plague victims were buried at Eyam's church. You can view stained-glass panels and moving displays telling the story of the outbreak. The churchyard contains a Celtic cross carved in the 8th century.

Eyam Hall   ARTS CENTRE
(www.eyamhall.co.uk; house & garden adult/child £7.50/4, craft centre admission free; ◷house & garden noon-4pm Wed, Thu & Sun Easter-early May & late Jul-Aug, craft centre 10.30am-5pm Tue-Sun Mar-Oct, to 4pm Nov-Feb) This solid-looking 17th-century manor house with stone windows and doorframes, home to a craft centre and several eateries, is surrounded by a traditional English walled garden.

Eyam Museum   MUSEUM
(www.eyammuseum.demon.co.uk; Hawkhill Rd; adult/child £2.50/2; ◷10am-4.30pm Tue-Sun late Mar-early Nov, closed early Nov-late Mar) The town's engaging museum has vivid displays on the Eyam plague, plus exhibits on the village's history of lead-mining and silk-weaving.

Activities

Eyam makes a great base for walking and cycling in the White Peak area. For an interesting short walk, follow Water Lane out of the village from the main square, then turn right and climb the hill to reach **Mompesson's Well**, where supplies were left during the plague time for Eyam folk by friends from other villages. The goods were paid for using coins sterilised in vinegar. To return to Eyam, retrace your steps down the lane, then take a path which leads directly to the church. This 2-mile circuit takes about 1½ hours.

Sleeping & Eating

Miner's Arms   PUB ££
(☏01433-630853; Water Lane; s £45, d £70-85, mains £8.45-14.95) Although its age isn't immediately obvious, this traditional village inn was built shortly before the plague hit Eyam. Inside you'll find beamed ceilings, affable staff, a cosy stone fireplace, comfy en suite rooms and good-value pub food.

Crown Cottage   B&B ££
(☏01433-630858; www.crown-cottage.co.uk; Main Rd; s/d from £50/70; P) Opposite the post office, this walker- and cyclist-friendly stone house full of pottery ornaments is crammed to the rafters most weekends, when there's a minimum two-night stay.

Eyam Tea Rooms   TEAHOUSE £
(The Square; dishes £1.25-4.95; ◷9.30am-4pm Wed-Mon) All chintz and doilies, this cute tearoom serves delicious homemade cakes and pastries as well as hearty lunches.

Peak Pantry   TEAHOUSE £
(The Square; dishes £2.10-3.50; ◷9am-5pm Mon-Sat, 10am-5pm Sun) This unpretentious place on the village square has a mouth-watering array of slices and decent coffee.

Getting There & Away

BUS Service include the following:
Buxton Bus 65/66, 40 minutes, five daily (four Sunday)
Chesterfield Bus 66/66A, 40 minutes, five daily (four Sunday)
Sheffield Bus 65, 40 minutes, five daily (three Sunday)

Bakewell

POP 3979

The second-largest town in the Peak District, pretty Bakewell is a great base for exploring the White Peak. The town is ringed by famous walking trails and stately homes, but it's probably best known for its famous pudding (of which the Bakewell Tart is just a poor imitation). Like other Peak towns, Bakewell is mobbed during the summer months – expect traffic jams and cut-throat competition for accommodation at weekends. The centre of town is Rutland Sq, the meeting point of the roads from Matlock, Buxton and Chesterfield.

◎ Sights

Up on the hill above Rutland Sq, All Saints Church (◎9am-4.45pm Apr-Oct, to 3.45pm Nov-Mar) is packed with ancient features, including a 14th-century font, a pair of Norman arches, some fine heraldic tombs and a collection of crude stone gravestones and crosses dating back to the 12th century.

Set in a time-worn stone house near the church, the Old House Museum (www.oldhousemuseum.org.uk; Cunningham Pl; adult/child £3.50/2; ◎11am-4pm Apr-early Nov, closed early Nov-Mar) explores local history. Check out the Tudor loo and the displays on wattle and daub, a traditional technique for building walls using woven twigs and cow dung. Nearby, its recently opened collection Spirit of the 1940s (www.oldhousemuseum.org.uk; Matlock St; adult/child £2/50p, combined ticket with Old House Museum £5/2; ◎10.30am-4pm Fri-Mon Apr-early Nov, closed early Nov-Mar) incorporates a '40s street scene, letters and photographs, and wartime memorabilia.

☆ Activities

Walking and cycling are, of course, the main activities. The scenic Monsal Trail follows the path of a disused railway line from Combs Viaduct on the outskirts of Bakewell to Topley Pike in Wye Dale, about 3 miles east of Buxton, including a number of re-opened old railway tunnels, covering 8½ miles in all.

For a rewarding shorter walk, follow the Monsal Trail for 3 miles to the dramatic viewpoint at Monsal Head, where you can pause for refreshment at the Monsal Head Hotel (☎01629-640250; www.monsalhead.com; s/d incl breakfast from £65/90, mains £11.20-16; P), serving real ales and outstanding Modern British cuisine. With more time to kill, continue to Miller's Dale, where viaducts give a rewarding vista across the steep-sided valley. The tourist offices at Bakewell and Buxton have full details.

Other walking routes go to the stately homes Haddon Hall (p478) and Chatsworth House (p478).

🛏 Sleeping

Rutland Arms Hotel HOTEL £££
(☎01629-812812; www.rutlandarmsbakewell.co.uk; The Square; s £88-118, d £140-165; P🛜) Jane Austen is said to have stayed in room 2 of this aristocratic, recently refurbished stone coaching inn while working on *Pride and Prejudice*. The more expensive of its 35 rooms have lots of florid Victorian flourishes.

Melbourne House B&B ££
(☎01629-815357; www.bakewell-accommodation.co.uk; Buxton Rd; d from £60; P) In a picturesque, creeper-covered building dating back more than three centuries, this inviting B&B is handily situated on the main road leading to Buxton.

🍴 Eating & Drinking

Bakewell's streets are lined with sweet tearooms and bakeries.

TOP CHOICE Piedaniel's FRENCH ££
(☎01629-812687; www.piedaniels-restaurant.com; Bath St; mains £16, 2-/3-course lunch £13/15 Tue-Fri; ◎Tue-Sat) Chefs Eric and Christiana Piedaniel's Modern French cuisine is the toast of local restaurants. A whitewashed dining room is the exquisite setting for dining on the likes of lobster bisque with *quenelles* (feather-light flour, egg and cream dumplings) followed by monkfish in salmon mousse. Weekday lunch menus are exceptional value. Ask about cooking classes and demonstrations.

Castle Inn PUB
(☎01629-812103; www.castle-inn-bakewell.co.uk; Bridge St; mains £7.50-17; 🛜🍴) The ivy-draped Castle Inn is one of the better pubs in Bakewell, with four centuries of practice in rejuvenating hamstrung hikers. Gourmet burgers are a menu highlight; it also has four adjacent guest rooms.

ⓘ Information

Tourist office (☎01629-813227; Bridge St; ◎9.30am-5pm Apr-Oct, from 10am Nov-Mar) Helpful place with racks of leaflets and books; can book accommodation. In the old Market Hall.

ⓘ Getting There & Away

Bakewell lies on the Transpeak bus route. Buses run hourly to Nottingham (1¾ hours), Derby (1¼ hours), Matlock Bath (30 minutes) and Buxton (50 minutes). Five services a day continue to Manchester (1¾ hours).

PUDDING OF CHAMPIONS

The Peak District's most famous dessert is – as any Bakewell resident will tell you – a pudding, not a tart. Invented following an accidental misreading of a recipe in around 1820, the Bakewell Pudding is a pastry shell, spread with jam and topped with frangipane, a paste of egg and ground almonds. If you've only ever seen the glazed version produced by commercial bakeries, the Bakewell original may look crude and misshapen, but is delicious. The Old Original Bakewell Pudding Shop (www.bakewellpuddingshop.co.uk; The Square) and Bloomers Original Bakewell Puddings (01629-814844; Water St) both claim to be the 'original' creator of the Bakewell Pudding – decide for yourself.

Around Bakewell

HADDON HALL

Glorious Haddon Hall (www.haddonhall.co.uk; adult/child £9.50/5.50; noon-5pm daily May-Sept, Sat-Mon Mar-Apr, Oct) looks exactly like a medieval manor house should – all stone turrets, time-worn timbers and walled gardens. The house was founded in the 12th century, and expanded and remodelled throughout medieval times. The 'modernisation' stopped when the house was abandoned in the 18th century, saving Haddon Hall from the more florid excesses of the Victorian period. It was used as a location for the period blockbusters *Jane Eyre* (1996 and 2011), *Elizabeth* (1998) and *Pride and Prejudice* (2005). Opening hours vary throughout the year outside peak season, check the website to confirm times.

The house is 2 miles south of Bakewell on the A6. You can get here on the Transpeak bus from Bakewell to Matlock and Derby (hourly) or walk along the footpath through the fields, mostly on the east side of the river.

CHATSWORTH HOUSE

Known as the 'Palace of the Peak', Chatsworth House (01246-582204; www.chatsworth.org; house & gardens adult/child £15/9, gardens only £10/6, playground £5, park free; 11am-5.30pm mid-Mar–late Dec, closed late Dec–mid-Mar) has been occupied by the earls and dukes of Devonshire for centuries. The manor was founded in 1552 by the formidable Bess of Hardwick and her second husband, William Cavendish, who earned grace and favour by helping Henry VIII dissolve the English monasteries. Mary, Queen of Scots, was imprisoned at Chatsworth on the orders of Elizabeth I in 1569.

While the core of the house dates from the 16th century, Chatsworth was altered and enlarged over the centuries. The current building has a Georgian feel, dating back to the last overhaul in 1820. Inside, the lavish apartments and mural-painted staterooms are packed with priceless paintings and period furniture. Look out for the portraits of the current generation of Devonshires by Lucian Freud.

The house sits in 25 sq miles of grounds and ornamental gardens, some landscaped by Lancelot 'Capability' Brown. Kids will love the farmyard adventure playground with loads of ropes, swings and slides, and farmyard critters.

Chatsworth is 3 miles northeast of Bakewell. Bus 214 from Sheffield Interchange to Matlock goes right to Chatsworth (hourly, 50 minutes) and bus 215 runs from Bakewell (20 minutes, hourly) on Sunday. On other days, take 214.

From Bakewell, walkers can take footpaths through Chatsworth Park via the mock-Venetian village of Edensor (en-sor), while cyclists can pedal via Pilsley.

Yorkshire

Best Places to Eat

» J Baker's Bistro Moderne (p493)
» Van Zeller (p498)
» Star Inn (p506)
» Gusto (p532)

Best Places to Stay

» Millgate House (p519)
» Devonshire Fell (p515)
» Hotel Helaina (p501)
» Middlethorpe Hall (p491)

Why Go?

With a population as big as Scotland's and an area half the size of Belgium, Yorkshire is almost a country in itself. It has its own flag, its own dialect and its own celebration, Yorkshire Day (1 August). While local folk are proud to be English, they're even prouder to be natives of 'God's Own County'.

What makes Yorkshire so special? First, there's the landscape – with its brooding moors and green dales rolling all the way to the dramatic coastline, Yorkshire has some of Britain's finest scenery. Second, there's the sheer breadth of history – every facet of the British experience is represented here, from Roman times to the 20th century.

But Yorkshire's greatest appeal lies in its people. Industrious and opinionated, they have a wry wit and shrewd friendliness. Stay here for a while and you'll come away believing, like the locals, that God is indeed a Yorkshirewoman.

When to Go

In February the week-long Jorvik Festival sees York taken over by a Viking invasion.

In July the Great Yorkshire Show happens in Harrogate, and at the same time of year Yorkshire's coastal sea cliffs become a frenzy of nesting seabirds.

The ideal time for hiking in the Yorkshire Dales is September, and the Walking Festival in Richmond also takes place in this month.

Yorkshire Highlights

❶ Exploring the medieval streets of **York** (p484) and its awe-inspiring cathedral

❷ Pulling on your hiking boots and striding out across the moors of the **Yorkshire Dales** (p512)

❸ Wandering among the atmospheric medieval ruins of **Fountains Abbey** (p502)

❹ Being beside the seaside at **Scarborough** (p499) with its traditional bucket-and-spade atmosphere

❺ Riding on the **North Yorkshire Moors Railway** (p507), one of England's most scenic train lines

❻ Discovering mining's dark side at the **National Coal Mining Museum for England** (p527)

❼ Enjoying the high-tech, hands-on exhibits at Bradford's **National Media Museum** (p526)

History

As you drive through Yorkshire on the main A1 road, you're following in the footsteps of the Roman legions who conquered northern Britain in the 1st century AD. In fact, many Yorkshire towns – including York, Catterick and Malton – were founded by the Romans, and many modern roads (including the A1, A59, A166 and A1079) follow the alignment of Roman roads.

When the Romans departed in the 5th century, native Britons battled for supremacy with invading Teutonic tribe the Angles and, for a while, Yorkshire was part of the Kingdom of Northumbria. In the 9th century the Vikings arrived and conquered most of northern Britain, an area which became known as the Danelaw. They divided the territory that is now Yorkshire into *thridings* (thirds), which met at Jorvik (York), their thriving commercial capital.

In 1066 Yorkshire was the scene of a pivotal showdown in the struggle for the English crown, when the Anglo-Saxon king, Harold II, rode north to defeat the forces of the Norwegian king, Harold Hardrada, in the Battle of Stamford Bridge, before returning south for his appointment with William the Conqueror – and a fatal arrow – in the Battle of Hastings.

The inhabitants of northern England did not take the subsequent Norman invasion lying down. In order to subdue them, the Norman nobles built a chain of formidable castles throughout Yorkshire, including those at York, Richmond, Scarborough, Pickering and Helmsley. They also oversaw the establishment of the great abbeys of Rievaulx, Fountains and Whitby.

The Norman land grab formed the basis of the great estates that supported England's medieval aristocrats. By the 15th century, the duchies of York and Lancaster had become so wealthy and powerful that they ended up battling for the English throne. Known as the Wars of the Roses (1455–87), the battles were a recurring conflict between the supporters of King Henry VI of the House of Lancaster (the red rose) and Richard, Duke of York (the white rose). They ended with the defeat of the Yorkist king, Richard III, by the earl of Richmond, Henry Tudor, in the Battle of Bosworth.

Yorkshire quietly prospered, with fertile farms in the north and the Sheffield cutlery business in the south, until the big bang of the Industrial Revolution transformed the landscape: south Yorkshire became a centre of coal mining and steelworks, while west Yorkshire was home to a massive textile industry and the cities of Leeds, Bradford, Sheffield and Rotherham flourished. By the late 20th century another revolution was taking place. The heavy industries had died out, and the cities of Yorkshire were reinventing themselves as shiny, high-tech centres of finance, higher education and tourism.

Activities

Yorkshire's varied landscape of wild hills, tranquil valleys, high moors and spectacular coastline offers plenty of opportunities for outdoor activities. See www.outdooryorkshire.com for more details.

Cycling

Yorkshire has a vast network of country lanes, although the most scenic areas also attract lots of motorists so even minor roads can be busy at weekends. Options include the following cycling trails.

North York Moors   MOUNTAIN BIKING (www.mtb-routes.co.uk/northyorkmoors) Off-road bikers can avail themselves of the network of bridleways, former railways and disused mining tracks now converted for two-wheel use. **Dalby Forest** (www.forestry.gov.uk/forestry/INFD-6Y6EWY), near Pickering, sports purpose-built mountain-biking trails of all grades from green to black.

Moor to Sea Cycle Route   CYCLING (www.moortoseacycle.net) A network of routes between Pickering, Danby and the coast includes a 20-mile traffic-free route that follows a disused railway line between Whitby and Scarborough.

White Rose Cycle Route   CYCLING (www.sustrans.org.uk; NCN Route 65) A 120-mile cruise from Hull to York and on to Middlesbrough, via the rolling Yorkshire Wolds and dramatic western scarp of the North York Moors, with a traffic-free section on the old railway between Selby and York.

Yorkshire Dales Cycleway   CYCLING (www.cyclethedales.org.uk) An exhilarating 130-mile loop, taking in the best of the national park. There's also lots of scope for off-road riding, with about 500 miles of bridleways and trails – for inspiration, check out www.mtbthedales.org.uk.

Walking

For shorter walks and rambles, the best area is the Yorkshire Dales, with a great selection of walks through scenic valleys or over wild hilltops and with a few higher summits thrown in for good measure. The East Riding's Yorkshire Wolds hold hidden delights, while the quiet valleys and dramatic coast of the North York Moors also offer many opportunities.

Cleveland Way   WALKING
(www.nationaltrail.co.uk/clevelandway) A venerable moor-and-coast classic that circles the North York Moors National Park on its 109-mile, nine-day route from Helmsley to Filey.

Coast to Coast Walk   WALKING
(www.wainwright.org.uk/coasttocoast.html) One of England's most popular walks: 190 miles across northern England from the Lake District through the Yorkshire Dales and North York Moors national parks. The Yorkshire section takes a week to 10 days and offers some of the finest walking of its kind in England.

Dales Way   WALKING
(www.dalesway.org.uk) A charming and not-too-strenuous amble from the Yorkshire Dales to the Lake District, following the River Wharfe through the heart of the Dales and finishing at Bowness-on-Windermere.

Pennine Way   WALKING
(www.nationaltrail.co.uk/pennineway) The Yorkshire section of England's most famous walk runs for more than 100 miles via Hebden Bridge, Malham, Horton-in-Ribblesdale and Hawes, passing near Haworth and Skipton.

White Rose Way   WALKING
(www.whiteroseway.co.uk) A new long-distance trail covering the 104 miles from Leeds city centre to Scarborough, taking in remote and picturesque Yorkshire villages along the way.

Wolds Way   WALKING
(www.nationaltrail.co.uk/yorkshirewoldsway) A beautiful but oft-overlooked walk that winds through the most scenic part of Yorkshire's East Riding district.

❶ Information

Yorkshire Tourist Board (www.yorkshire.com; 312 Tadcaster Rd, York YO24 1GS) Plenty of general leaflets and brochures are available, for postal and email enquiries only. For more detailed information, contact local tourist offices.

❶ Getting There & Around

The major north–south road transport routes – the M1 and A1 motorways – run through the middle of Yorkshire, serving the key cities of Sheffield, Leeds and York. If you're arriving by sea from northern Europe, Hull in the East Riding district is the region's main port.

Traveline Yorkshire (☑0871-200 22 33; www. yorkshiretravel.net) provides public transport information for all of Yorkshire.

BUS Long-distance coaches operated by **National Express** (☑08717-81 81 78; www. nationalexpress.com) serve most cities and large towns in Yorkshire from London, the south of England, the Midlands and Scotland.

Bus transport around Yorkshire is frequent and efficient, especially between major towns. Services are more sporadic in the national parks, but are still adequate for reaching most places, particularly in summer months (June to September).

TRAIN The main rail line between London and Edinburgh runs through Yorkshire, with at least 10 trains calling each day at York and Doncaster, where you can change trains for other Yorkshire destinations. There are also direct services between the major towns and cities of Yorkshire and other northern cities such as Manchester and Newcastle. For timetable information, contact National Rail Enquiries (p519).

NORTH YORKSHIRE

This, the largest of Yorkshire's four counties – and the largest county in England – is also the most beautiful. Unlike the rest of northern England, it has survived almost unscathed by the Industrial Revolution. Since the Middle Ages, North Yorkshire has been exclusively about sheep and the woolly wealth they produce.

Rather than closed-down factories, mills and mines, the artificial monuments dotting the landscape in these parts are of the magnificent variety – the great houses and wealthy abbeys that sit, ruined or restored, as a reminder that there was plenty of money to be made off the sheep's back.

All the same, North Yorkshire's biggest attraction is an urban one. While the genteel spa town of Harrogate and the bright and

WANT MORE?

Head to Lonely Planet (www.lonely planet.com/england/yorkshire/york) for planning advice, author recommendations, traveller reviews and insider tips.

YORKSHIRE

THE YORK PASS

If you plan on visiting a number of sights, you can save yourself some money by using a York Pass (www.yorkpass.com; 1/2/3 days adult £34/48/58, child £18/22/26). It gives you free access to more than 30 pay-to-visit sights in and around York, including York Minster, Jorvik and Castle Howard. You can buy it at York tourist office (p495) or online.

breezy seaside resorts of Scarborough and Whitby have many fans, nothing compares to the unparalleled splendour of York, England's most-visited city outside London.

York

POP 181,100

Nowhere in northern England says 'medieval' quite like York, a city of extraordinary cultural and historical wealth that has lost little of its pre-industrial lustre. A magnificent circuit of 13th-century walls enclose its medieval spider's web of narrow streets. At the heart of the city lies the immense, awe-inspiring minster, one of the most beautiful Gothic cathedrals in the world. York's long history and rich heritage is woven into virtually every brick and beam, and the modern, tourist-oriented city – with its myriad museums, restaurants, cafes and traditional pubs – is a carefully maintained heir to that heritage.

Try to avoid the inevitable confusion by remembering that around these parts, *gate* means street and *bar* means gate.

History

In AD 71 the Romans built a garrison called Eboracum, which in time became a large fort with a civilian settlement grown up around it. Hadrian used it as the base for his northern campaign, while Constantine the Great was proclaimed emperor here in AD 306. When the Roman Empire collapsed, the town was taken by the Anglo-Saxons, who renamed it Eoforwic and made it the capital of the independent kingdom of Northumbria.

In 625 a Roman priest, Paulinus, arrived and managed to convert King Edwin and all his nobles. Two years later they built the first wooden church here. For most of the next century, the city was a major centre of learning, attracting students from all over Europe. In 866 the next wave of invaders arrived, this time the Vikings, who gave the town a more tongue-friendly name, Jorvik. It was their capital for the next 100 years, and during that time they turned the city into an important trading port.

King Eadred of Wessex drove out the last Viking ruler in 954 and reunited Danelaw with the south, but trouble quickly followed. In 1066 King Harold II fended off a Norwegian invasion at Stamford Bridge, east of York, but was defeated by William the Conqueror a few months later in the Battle of Hastings.

After William's two wooden castles were captured by an Anglo-Scandinavian army, he torched the entire city (and Durham) and the surrounding countryside. The Normans then set about rebuilding it, adding a grand new minster. Over the next 300 years York (a contraction of the Viking name Jorvik) prospered through royal patronage, textiles, trade and the Church.

Throughout the 18th century the city was a fashionable social centre dominated by the aristocracy, who were drawn by its culture and new racecourse. When the railway was built in 1839, thousands of people were employed in new industries such as confectionery that sprang up around it. These industries went into decline in the latter half of the 20th century, but by then a new invader was asking for directions at the city gates, armed only with a guidebook.

⊙ Sights

York Minster   CHURCH
(www.yorkminster.org; Deangate; adult/child £9/free, combined ticket incl tower £14/3.50; ⊙9am-5.30pm Mon-Sat Apr-Oct, 9.30am-5.30pm Mon-Sat Nov-Mar, noon-5.30pm Sun year-round) Not content with being Yorkshire's most important historic building, the remarkable York Minster is also the largest medieval cathedral in all of Northern Europe. Seat of the archbishop of York, primate of England, it is second in importance only to Canterbury, home of the primate of *all* England – the separate titles were created to settle a debate over whether York or Canterbury was the true centre of the English church.

But that's where Canterbury's superiority ends, for this is without doubt one of the world's most beautiful Gothic buildings. If this is the only cathedral you visit in England, you'll still walk away satisfied – so long as you have the patience to deal with the constant flow of school groups and organised tours that will inevitably clog up your camera's viewfinder.

The first church on this site was a wooden chapel built for the baptism of King Edwin of Northumbria on Easter Day 627, whose location is marked in the crypt. It was replaced with a stone church built on the site of a Roman basilica, parts of which can be seen in the foundations. The first Norman minster was built in the 11th century and again, you can see surviving fragments in the foundations and crypt.

The present minster, built mainly between 1220 and 1480, manages to encompass all the major stages of Gothic architectural development. The transepts (1220–55) were built in Early English style; the octagonal chapter house (1260–90) and nave (1291–1340) in the Decorated style; and the west towers, west front and central (or lantern) tower (1470–72) in Perpendicular style.

Choir, Chapter House & Nave

Entrance to these features of York Minster is via the south transept, which was badly damaged by fire in 1984 but has been fully restored. To your right is the 15th-century choir screen depicting the 15 kings from William I to Henry VI. Facing you is the magnificent Five Sisters Window, with five lancets rising more than 15m high. This is the minster's oldest complete window; most of its tangle of coloured glass dates from about 1250. Just beyond it to the right is the 13th-century chapter house, a fine example of the Decorated style. Sinuous and intricately carved stonework (there are more than 200 expressive carved heads and figures) surrounds an airy, uninterrupted space.

Back in the main church, take note of the unusually tall and wide nave. From the aisles to the sides are roofed in stone, in contrast to the central roof, which is wood painted to look like stone. On both sides of the nave are painted stone shields of the nobles who met with Edward II at a parliament in York. Also note the dragon's head projecting from the gallery – it's a crane believed to have been used to lift a font cover. There are several fine windows dating from the early 14th century, but the most impressive is the Great West Window (1338), with its beautiful heart-shaped stone tracery.

Beyond the screen and choir is the lady chapel and, behind that, the high altar, dominated by the huge Great East Window

(1405). At 23.7m by 9.4m – roughly the size of a tennis court – it is the world's largest medieval stained-glass window and the cathedral's single-most important treasure. Needless to say, its epic size matches the epic theme it depicts: the beginning and end of the world, as described in *Genesis* and the *Book of Revelations.*

Undercroft, Treasury & Crypt

A set of stairs in York Minster's south transept leads down to the undercroft, where you'll also find the treasury and crypt – on no account should these be missed. In 1967 the foundations were shored up when the central tower threatened to collapse. As engineers worked frantically to save the building, archaeologists uncovered Roman and Norman remains that attest to the site's ancient history. One of the most extraordinary finds is a Roman culvert, still carrying water to the River Ouse. The treasury houses 11th-century artefacts, including relics from the graves of medieval archbishops.

The crypt contains fragments from the Norman cathedral, including the font showing King Edwin's baptism, which also marks the site of the original wooden chapel. Look out for the Doomstone, a 12th-century carving showing a scene from the Last Judgement with demons casting doomed souls into Hell.

Improved access and new exhibitions planned for the undercroft are scheduled to open some time in 2013.

Tower

(adult/child £6/3.50, combined ticket incl Minster £14/3.50) At the heart of York Minster is the massive tower, which is well worth climbing for its unparalleled views of York. You'll have to tackle a fairly claustrophobic climb of 275 steps and, most probably, a queue of people with cameras in hand. Access to the tower is near the entrance in the south transept, dominated by the exquisite Rose Window commemorating the union of the royal houses of Lancaster and York through the marriage of Henry VII and Elizabeth of York, which ended the Wars of the Roses and launched the Tudor dynasty.

FREE **National Railway Museum**   MUSEUM
(www.nrm.org.uk; Leeman Rd; ☉10am-6pm) While many railway museums are the sole preserve of lone men in anoraks comparing dog-eared notebooks and getting high on the smell of machine oil, coal smoke and

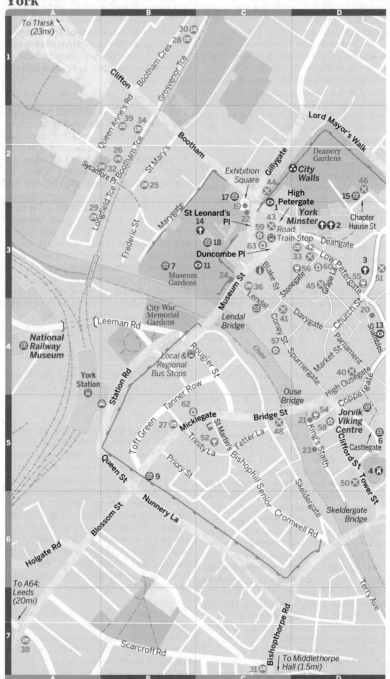

To Thirsk
(23mi)

Clifton

Bootham Cres
Grosvenor Tce

30
28

Queen Anne's Rd
39 34

26
Sycamore Pl 32
Bootham Tce
25
Longfield Tce
29
Frederic St

Bootham

St Mary's

Marygate

Lord Mayor's Walk

Deanery
Gardens

Exhibition
Square

Gillygate

44 City
Walls

46

15 Chapter
House St

17
19
22
St Leonard's
Pl
14 18
Duncombe Pl

7 11
Museum Gardens

Museum St

24

High
Petergate
1
York
Minster
2
43
59 Road
63 Train Stop

Deangate
42
33
56 60
45
Stonegate
Low Petergate
Grape La
Church St

Blake St
i 36
Lendal
41 Coney St
57 Spurriergate
Davygate
Parliament
Market St
20

3
55
51

13
Shambles

City War
Memorial
Gardens

Lendal
Bridge

Ouse

National
Railway
Museum

Leeman Rd

Rougier St

40
High Ousegate

York
Station

Station Rd

Local &
Regional
Bus Stops

Tanner Row
62

27 Micklegate
St Martin's
La
52
Trinity La

Fetter La

Ouse
Bridge

Bridge St
48

54
21 58
23

Jorvik
Viking
Centre

Castlegate
6
Clifford St

Tott Green

Bishophill Senior

King's Staith

Copperagte

Queen St

9

Priory St

Nunnery La

Skeldergate
Cromwell Rd

50

Tower St
4

Blossom St

Holgate Rd

Skeldergate
Bridge

To A64;
Leeds
(20mi)

38

Scarcroft Rd

Bishopthorpe Rd

Terry Ave

To Middlethorpe
Hall (1.5mi)
31

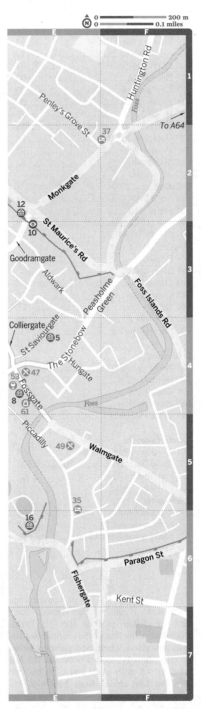

nostalgia, this place is different. York's National Railway Museum – the biggest in the world, with more than 100 locomotives – is so well presented and crammed with fascinating stuff that it's interesting even to folk whose eyes don't mist over at the thought of a 4-6-2 A1 Pacific class chuffing into a tunnel.

Highlights for the trainspotters among us include a replica of George Stephenson's *Rocket* (1829), the world's first 'modern' steam locomotive; the sleek and streamlined *Mallard,* which set the world speed record for a steam locomotive in 1938 (126mph); a 1960s Japanese *Shinkansen* bullet train; and the world-famous *Flying Scotsman,* the first steam engine to break the 100mph barrier (scheduled to return to the tracks eventually, but still undergoing restoration at the time of research). There's also a massive 4-6-2 loco from 1949 that's been cut in half so you can see how it works.

Even if you're not a rail nerd, you'll enjoy looking through the gleaming, silk-lined carriages of the royal trains used by Queen Victoria and Edward VII, or having a *Brief Encounter* moment over tea and scones at the museum's station platform cafe called, erm, Brief Encounter. Allow at least two hours to do the museum justice.

The museum is about 400m west of the train station and if you don't fancy walking you can ride the road train (adult/child £2/1) that runs between the minster and museum every 30 minutes from 11am to 4pm.

Jorvik Viking Centre MUSEUM
(www.jorvik-viking-centre.co.uk; Coppergate; adult/child £9.25/6.25; ⏱10am-5pm Apr-Oct, to 4pm Nov-Mar) Interactive multimedia exhibits aimed at bringing history to life often achieve exactly the opposite, but the much-hyped Jorvik – after the minster, the most-visited attraction in town – manages to pull it off with aplomb. It's a smells-and-all reconstruction of the Viking settlement unearthed here during excavations in the late 1970s, brought to you courtesy of a 'time-car' monorail that transports you through 9th-century Jorvik.

While some of the 'you will now travel back in time' malarkey is a bit naff, it's all done with a sense of humour tied to historical authenticity that will give you a pretty good idea of what life must have been like in Viking-era York. In the exhibition at the end of the monorail, look out for the Lloyds

York

Bank Turd, a fossilised human stool that measures an eye-watering nine inches long and half a pound in weight, and must be the only excrement in the world to have its own Wikipedia entry.

You can reduce time waiting in the queue by booking your tickets online and choosing the time you want to visit (it costs £1 extra).

FREE City Walls   ARCHAEOLOGICAL SITE
(⊙8am-dusk) If the weather's good, don't miss the chance to walk the City Walls, which follow the line of the original Roman walls and give a whole new perspective on the city. Allow 1½ to two hours for the full circuit of 4.5 miles or, if you're pushed for time, the short stretch from Bootham Bar

(Bootham) to Monk Bar (City Walls) is worth doing for the views of the minster.

Start and finish in the Museum Gardens or at Bootham Bar (on the site of a Roman gate), where a multimedia exhibit provides some historical context, and travel clockwise. Highlights include Monk Bar, which is the best-preserved medieval gate and still has a working portcullis, and Walmgate Bar, England's only city gate with an intact barbican.

At Monk Bar you'll find the Richard III Museum (www.richardiiimuseum.co.uk; adult/child £2.50/free; ☺9am-5pm Mar-Oct, 9.30am-4pm Nov-Feb), which sets out the case of the murdered 'Princes in the Tower' and invites visitors to judge whether their uncle, Richard III, killed them. Micklegate Bar Museum (www.micklegatebar.com; Micklegate; adult/child £3.50/free; ☺10am-4.30pm May-Sep, 11am-3.30pm Feb-Apr, Oct & Nov) charts the history of the city walls and the Battle of Towton, chief conflict in the Wars of the Roses.

You can download a free guide to the wall walk from www.visityork.org/explore/walls.html.

Yorkshire Museum · MUSEUM
(www.yorkshiremuseum.org.uk; Museum St; adult/child £7.50/free; ☺10am-5pm) Most of York's Roman archaeology is hidden beneath the medieval city, so the recently revamped displays in the Yorkshire Museum are invaluable if you want to get an idea of what Eboracum was like. There are maps and models of Roman York, funerary monuments, mosaic floors and wall paintings, and a 4th-century bust of Emperor Constantine.

There are excellent exhibits on Viking and medieval York as well, including priceless artefacts such as the beautifully decorated 9th-century York helmet and the exquisite 15th-century Middleham Jewel, an engraved gold pendant adorned with a giant sapphire. Kids will enjoy the dinosaur exhibit, centred around giant ichthyosaur fossils from Yorkshire's Jurassic coast.

In the grounds of the peaceful Museum Gardens (entrances on Museum St and Marygate; ☺dawn-dusk), you can see the Multangular Tower, a part of the City Walls that was once the western tower of the Roman garrison's defensive ramparts. The Roman stonework at the base has been built over with 13th-century additions.

On the other side of the gardens are the ruins of St Mary's Abbey dating from 1270 to 1294. The ruined Gatehall was its main entrance, providing access from the abbey to the river. The adjacent Hospitium dates from the 14th century, although the timber-framed upper storey is a much-restored survivor from the 15th century, used as the abbey guest house. St Mary's Lodge was built in about 1470 to provide VIP accommodation.

Shambles · STREET
(www.yorkshambles.com) The most-visited street in Europe is the narrow cobbled lane known as the Shambles, lined with 15th-century Tudor buildings that overhang so much they seem to meet above your head. Quaint and picturesque it most certainly is, and it hints at what a medieval street may have looked like – even if it's now overrun with people who've been told to buy a tacky souvenir and be back on the tour bus in 15 minutes. The Shambles takes its name from the Saxon word *shamel*, meaning 'slaughterhouse' – in 1862 there were 26 butcher shops on this street.

York Castle Museum · MUSEUM
(www.yorkcastlemuseum.org.uk; Tower St; adult/child £8.50/free; ☺9.30am-5pm) This excellent museum has displays of everyday life through the centuries, with reconstructed domestic interiors, a Victorian street and a less-than-homely prison cell where you can try out a condemned man's bed – in this case, that of highwayman Dick Turpin (he was imprisoned here before being hanged in 1739). There's a bewildering array of evocative objects from the past 400 years, gathered together by a certain Dr Kirk from the 1920s onwards for fear the items would become obsolete and disappear completely. He wasn't far wrong, which makes this place all the more interesting.

Treasurer's House · HISTORIC BUILDING
(NT; www.nationaltrust.org.uk; Chapter House St; adult/child £6.30/3; ☺11am-4.30pm Sat-Thu Apr-Oct, to 3pm Sat-Thu Nov) Home to York Minster's medieval treasurers, the Treasurer's House was substantially rebuilt in the 17th and 18th centuries. The 13 rooms house a fine collection of furniture and provide a clear insight into 18th-century life. The house is also the setting for one of the city's most enduring ghost stories: during the 1950s a plumber working in the basement swore he saw a band of Roman soldiers walking *through* the walls. His story remains popular, if unproven, and you can explore the cellar to find out for yourself.

Dig
MUSEUM

(www.digyork.com; St Saviour's Church, St Saviourgate; adult/child £5.50/5, Dig & Jorvik combined £13.25/10; ☉10am-5pm, last admission 4pm, closed 24-26 Dec) Under the same management as Jorvik, Dig cashes in on the popularity of archaeology programs on TV by giving you the chance to be an 'archaeological detective', unearthing the secrets of York's distant past as well as learning something of the archaeologist's world – what they do, how they do it, and so on. Aimed mainly at kids, it's much more hands-on than Jorvik and a lot of its merit depends on how good – and entertaining – your guide is.

Clifford's Tower
CASTLE

(EH; www.english-heritage.org.uk; Tower St; adult/child £4/2.40; ☉10am-6pm Apr-Sep, to 5pm Oct) There's precious little left of York Castle except for this evocative stone tower, a highly unusual figure-of-eight design built into the castle's keep after the original one was destroyed in 1190 during anti-Jewish riots. An angry mob forced 150 Jews to be locked inside the tower and the hapless victims took their own lives rather than be killed. There's not much to see inside, but the views over the city are excellent.

FREE Church of the Holy Trinity
CHURCH

(Goodramgate; ☉10am-5pm Tue-Sat May-Sep, 10am-4pm Tue-Sat Oct-Apr) Tucked away behind an inconspicuous gate and seemingly cut off from the rest of the town, the Church of the Holy Trinity is a fantastically atmospheric old building, having survived almost unchanged for the past 200 years. Inside are rare 17th- to 18th-century box pews, 15th-century stained glass and wonky walls that seem to have been built without plumb line or spirit level.

FREE York City Art Gallery
ART GALLERY

(www.yorkartgallery.org.uk; Exhibition Sq; ☉10am-5pm) Artists represented here include Joshua Reynolds, Paul Nash, Eugène Boudin, LS Lowry and the controversial York artist William Etty, who, back in the 1820s, was the first major British artist to specialise in painting nudes.

Merchant Adventurers' Hall
HISTORIC BUILDING

(www.theyorkcompany.co.uk; Fossgate; adult/child £6/free; ☉9am-5pm Mon-Thu, to 3.30pm Fri & Sat, 11am-4pm Sun Mar-Oct, reduced hours other times) Displays in this museum include oil paintings and antique silver, but the building itself is the star. Built between 1357 and 1361, it is one of the most handsome timber-framed buildings in Europe.

Fairfax House
HISTORIC BUILDING

(www.fairfaxhouse.co.uk; Castlegate; adult/child £6/free; ☉10am-5pm Tue-Sat, 12.30-4pm Sun, tours 11am & 2pm Mon) Built in 1762 by John Carr (of Harewood House fame), Fairfax House contains a superb collection of Georgian furniture.

☞ Tours

There's a bewildering range of tours on offer in York, from historic walking tours to ever more competitive night-time ghost tours (York is considered England's most haunted city). For starters, check the tourist office's own suggestions for walking itineraries at www.visityork.org/explore.

Ghost Hunt of York
WALKING TOUR

(www.ghosthunt.co.uk; adult/child £5/3; ☉tours 7.30pm) The kids will just love this award-winning and highly entertaining 75-minute tour laced with authentic ghost stories. It begins at the Shambles, whatever the weather (it's never cancelled) and there's no need to book, just turn up.

Yorkwalk
WALKING TOUR

(www.yorkwalk.co.uk; adult/child £5.50/3.50; ☉tours 10.30am & 2.15pm Feb-Nov) Offers a series of two-hour themed walks on an ever growing list of themes, from the classics – Roman York, the snickelways (narrow alleys) and City Walls – to specialised walks focused on chocolates and sweets, women in York, secret York and the inevitable graveyard, coffin and plague tour. Walks depart from Museum Gardens Gate on Museum St; there's no need to book.

YorkBoat
BOAT TOUR

(www.yorkboat.co.uk; King's Staith; adult/child £7.50/3.50; ☉tours 10.30am, noon, 1.30pm & 3pm) Hour-long cruises on the River Ouse, departing from King's Staith and, 10 minutes later, Lendal Bridge. Special lunch, dinner and evening cruises are also offered.

Original Ghost Walk of York
WALKING TOUR

(www.theoriginalghostwalkofyork.co.uk; adult/child £4.50/3; ☉tours 8pm) An evening of ghouls, ghosts, mystery and history, courtesy of a well-established group departing from the King's Arms pub by Ouse Bridge.

ANDY DEXTROUS: GHOST TOUR GUIDE

Things I love about York include its outstanding architecture, the maze of 'snickleways' (narrow alleys), the array of small independent shops, the street entertainment and festivals, and the central, green spaces like Museum Gardens (p489). All year round, the streets are full of appreciative visitors from all over the world enjoying the city, relaxing and adding to the atmosphere.

York's spookiest spots? Haunted pubs like the Old White Swan (p494), plus the Antiques Centre (p495) on Stonegate, which is also haunted. In the streets around the Minster you're always within a breath of a ghost tale.

Best of York? For beer and atmosphere, the Blue Bell (p494). For veggie and vegan food and a place that welcomes children, El Piano (p494). And for sheer ambience, Grays Court (p493).

Best of Yorkshire? Take the North Yorkshire Moors Railway (p507) to Goathland, then walk to Mallyan Spout waterfall. Include a drink at the Birch Hall Inn at Beck Hole. For a special meal, there's the Star Inn (p506) at Harome or the Stone Trough Inn (p497) at Kirkham; stroll down to the abbey ruins before or after your meal.

YORKSHIRE YORK

York Citysightseeing BUS TOUR
(www.city-sightseeing.com; day ticket adult/child £10/4; ⊙9am-5pm) Hop-on/hop-off route with 16 stops, calling at all the main sights. Buses leave every 10 minutes from Exhibition Sq near York Minster.

FREE **Association of Voluntary Guides** WALKING TOUR
(http://avgyork.co.uk; ⊙tours 10.15am & 2.15pm Apr-Oct, also 6.45pm Jun-Aug, 10.15am Nov-Mar) Two-hour walking tours of the city, setting out from Exhibition Sq in front of York City Art Gallery.

Festivals & Events

Check out the city's full calendar of events at www.yorkfestivals.com.

Jorvik Viking Festival HISTORY
(www.jorvik-viking-centre.co.uk/viking-festival) For a week in mid-February, York is invaded by Vikings once again as part of this festival, which features battle re-enactments, themed walks, markets and other bits of Viking-themed fun.

York Food Festival FOOD & DRINK
(www.yorkfoodfestival.com) For 10 days in September, all that's good to eat and drink in Yorkshire – food stalls, tastings, a beer tent, cookery demonstrations and more.

York Christmas SHOPPING
(www.visityork.org/christmas) Kicking off with St Nicholas Fayre market in late November, the run-up to Christmas is an extravaganza of street decorations, market stalls, carol singers and mulled wine.

Sleeping

Beds are hard to find in midsummer, even with the inflated prices of the high season. The tourist office's accommodation booking service charges £4, which might be the best four quid you spend if you arrive without a reservation.

Needless to say, prices get higher the closer you are to the city centre. However, there are plenty of decent B&Bs on the streets north and south of Bootham. Southwest of the town centre, B&Bs are clustered around Scarcroft Rd, Southlands Rd and Bishopthorpe Rd.

It's also worth looking at serviced apartments if you're planning to stay two or three nights. **In York Holidays** (☏01904-632660; www.inyorkholidays.co.uk) offers a good selection of places from about £100 a night for a two-person apartment.

TOP CHOICE **Middlethorpe Hall** HOTEL £££
(☏01904-641241; www.middlethorpe.com; Bishopthorpe Rd; s/d from £130/200; P🖥) York's top spot is this breathtaking 17th-century country house set in eight hectares of parkland, once the home of diarist Lady Mary Wortley Montagu. The rooms are divided between the main house, restored courtyard buildings and three cottage suites. Although we preferred the grandeur of rooms in the main house, every room is beautifully decorated with original antiques and oil paintings that have been carefully selected to reflect the period.

Abbeyfields
B&B ££

(☎01904-636471; www.abbeyfields.co.uk; 19 Bootham Tce; s/d from £49/79; ☎) Expect a warm welcome and thoughtfully arranged bedrooms here, with chairs and bedside lamps for comfortable reading. Breakfasts are among the best in town, with sausage and bacon from the local butcher, freshly laid eggs from a nearby farm and the aroma of newly baked bread.

Elliotts B&B
B&B ££

(☎01904-623333; www.elliottshotel.co.uk; 2 Sycamore Pl; s/d from £55/80; P@☎) A beautifully converted 'gentleman's residence', Elliotts leans towards the boutique end of the guesthouse market, with stylish and elegant rooms and high-tech touches, such as flatscreen TVs and free wi-fi. An excellent location, both quiet and central.

Hedley House Hotel
HOTEL ££

(☎01904-637404; www.hedleyhouse.com; 3 Bootham Tce; s/d/f from £75/95/110; P☎⛺) Run by a couple with young children, this smart red-brick terrace-house hotel could hardly be more family-friendly – plus it has a spa bath on the outdoor terrace at the back, private parking and is barely five minutes' walk from the city centre through the Museum Gardens.

Dairy Guesthouse
B&B ££

(☎01904-639367; www.dairyguesthouse.co.uk; 3 Scarcroft Rd; s/d from £55/75; ☎) A lovely Victorian home that has retained many of its original features, including pine doors, stained glass, and cast-iron fireplaces. But the real treat here is the flower- and plant-filled courtyard leading to the cottage-style rooms. Minimum two-night stay at weekends.

Guy Fawkes Inn
INN ££

(☎01904-623716; www.gfyork.com; 25 High Petergate; s/d/ste from £65/90/200) Directly opposite the minster is this comfortable and atmospheric hotel, complete with gas lamps and log fires. The premises include a cottage reputed to be the birthplace of Guy Fawkes himself. We're not convinced, but the cottage is still the most handsome room in the building, with a four-poster and lots of red velvet.

Mount Royale
HOTEL £££

(☎01904-628856; www.mountroyale.co.uk; The Mount; s/d from £95/125; P☎⛲) A grand, early 19th-century heritage-listed building converted into a superb luxury hotel, complete with a solarium, beauty spa and outdoor heated tub and swimming pool. The rooms in the main house are gorgeous, but the best of all are the open-plan garden suites, reached via an arcade of tropical fruit trees and bougainvillea.

Judges Lodgings Hotel
HOTEL £££

(☎01904-638733; www.judgeslodgings.com; 9 Lendal; s/d from £90/150) Despite being housed in an elegant Georgian mansion built for a wealthy physician, this is really a place for the party crowd to crash – it's within easy reach of city-centre pubs and the hotel's own lively courtyard bar rocks late into the night.

Arnot House
B&B ££

(☎01904-641966; www.arnothouseyork.co.uk; 17 Grosvenor Tce; r £80-88; P☎) With three beautifully decorated rooms (provided you're a fan of Victorian floral patterns), including two with impressive four-poster beds, Arnot House has an authentically old-fashioned look that appeals to a more mature clientele. No children allowed.

Brontë House
B&B ££

(☎01904-621066; www.bronte-guesthouse.com; 22 Grosvenor Tce; s/d/f from £45/80/100; P☎) The Brontë has five homely en-suite rooms, each individually decorated. Our favourite is the double with a carved 19th-century canopied bed, William Morris wallpaper and assorted bits and pieces from another era.

23 St Mary's
B&B ££

(☎01904-622738; www.23stmarys.co.uk; 23 St Mary's; s/d £55/90; P☎) A smart and stately town house with nine chintzy, country-house-style rooms. Some have hand-painted furniture for that certain rustic look, others are decorated with antiques, lace and polished mahogany.

York YHA
HOSTEL £

(☎0845-371 9051; www.yha.org.uk; 42 Water End, Clifton; dm £18-23; P@☎⛺) Originally the Rowntree (Quaker confectioners) mansion, this handsome Victorian house makes a spacious and child-friendly youth hostel, with most of its rooms four-bed dorms. It's about a mile northwest of the city centre; there's a riverside footpath from Lendal Bridge (poorly lit, so avoid after dark). Alternatively, take bus 2 from Station Ave or Museum St.

Ace Hotel
HOSTEL £

(☎01904-627720; www.acehotelyork.co.uk; 88-90 Micklegate; dm £18-30, tw £68; @☎) Housed in a Grade I Georgian building that was once home to the High Sheriff of Yorkshire, this is a large and well-equipped boutique hostel popular with school groups and stag and hen parties – don't come here looking for peace and quiet!

Briar Lea Guest House　　　　B&B **££**
(☑01904-635061; www.briarlea.co.uk; 8 Longfield Tce; s/d from £37/62; 🐾) Clean, basic rooms and a friendly welcome in a central location.

St Raphael　　　　B&B **££**
(☑01904-645028; www.straphaelguesthouse.co.uk; 44 Queen Anne's Rd; s/d from £65/78; P🐾) Historic house with that distinctive half-timbered look, a great central location and home-baked bread for breakfast.

Monkgate Guesthouse　　　　B&B **££**
(☑01904-655947; www.monkgateguesthouse.com; 65 Monkgate; s/d/f from £45/70/105; P🐾👪) Attractive guesthouse with a special family suite that has a separate bedroom for two kids.

Hotel 53　　　　HOTEL **££**
(☑01904-559000; www.hotel53.com; 53 Piccadilly; r from £95; P🐾) Modern and minimalist but very central, with secure parking just across the street.

✗ Eating

[TOP CHOICE] **J Baker's Bistro**
Moderne　　　　MODERN BRITISH **££**
(☑01904-622688; www.jbakers.co.uk; 7 Fossgate; 2-/3-course lunch £20/25, dinner £25/30; ⊙lunch & dinner Tue-Sat) Superstar chef Jeff Baker left a Michelin-starred eatery in Leeds to pursue his own vision of Modern British cuisine here. The ironic '70s-style decor (think chocolate/oatmeal/tango) with moo-cow paintings is echoed in the unusual menu, which offers witty gourmet interpretations of retro classics – try Olde York cheese and spinach pasties with dried grapes, capers and aged balsamic vinegar, or Whitby crab cocktail with apple 'textures' and curry-spiced granola. Wicked desserts include a separate chocolate menu.

📷 **Cafe No 8**　　　　CAFE, BISTRO **£**
(☑01904-653074; www.cafeno8.co.uk; 8 Gillygate; mains £7-10, 2-course lunch £14; ⊙11am-10pm Mon-Fri, from 10am Sat & Sun; 🐾👪) A cool little bistro with modern artwork mimicking the Edwardian stained glass at the front, No 8 offers a day-long menu of classic bistro dishes using fresh local produce, including smoked duck breast salad and cassoulet of

YORK YURTS

Only a 15-minute drive from York but half a world away in ambience, **York Yurts** (☑01759-380901; www.yorkyurts. com; Tadpole Cottage, Sutton Lane, Barmby Moor; d £70-80; P) offers the chance to sleep under canvas without having to rough it. There are four yurts (circular, wood-framed tents originating in Mongolia) in a field of about 1 hectare, complete with double beds, candles (no electricity), wood-burning stoves, cooking tents and barbecues (though you can have breakfast brought to you in bed if you put in an order). There's also a communal bathroom tent with a rolltop bath and hot tub.

Yorkshire pork and chorizo. It also does Sunday brunch. Booking is recommended.

Grays Court　　　　CAFE **£**
(www.grayscourtyork.com; Chapter House St; mains £6-10; ⊙lunch) An unexpected find in the heart of York, this 16th-century house has more of a country atmosphere. Enjoy gourmet coffee and cake in the sunny garden, or indulge in a light lunch in the historic setting of the oak-panelled Jacobean gallery (extra points if you grab the alcove table above the main door). The menu runs from smoked bacon with oatmeal pancakes and maple syrup to Yorkshire rarebit, and from lavender shortbread to lemon drizzle cake.

Ate O'Clock　　　　BISTRO **££**
(☑01904-644080; www.ateoclock.co.uk; 13a High Ousegate; mains £14-17; ⊙lunch Tue-Sat, dinner Mon-Sat) A tempting menu of classic bistro dishes (sirloin steak, pork tenderloin, pan-fried duck breast) made with fresh Yorkshire produce has made this place hugely popular with locals – best to book a table to avoid disappointment. A three-course dinner costs £18 from 6pm to 7.55pm, Tuesday to Thursday.

Bettys　　　　TEAHOUSE **££**
(www.bettys.co.uk; St Helen's Sq; mains £6-13, afternoon tea £18; ⊙9am-9pm; 👪) Old-school-style afternoon tea, with white-aproned waiters, linen tablecloths and a teapot collection ranged along the walls. The house speciality is the Yorkshire Fat Rascal, a huge fruit scone smothered in melted butter, but the smoked haddock with poached egg and

hollandaise sauce is our favourite lunch dish. No bookings – queue for a table at busy times, or head to the nearby Bettys Stonegate (www.bettys.co.uk; 46 Stonegate; mains £6-13; ◷10am-5.30pm Sun-Fri, from 9am Sat; ⊛).

Olive Tree
MEDITERRANEAN ££

(✆01904-624433; www.theolivetreeyork.co.uk; 10 Tower St; mains £10-17; ◷lunch & dinner) Local produce gets a Mediterranean makeover at this bright and breezy bistro, with a view across the street to Clifford's Tower. Classic pizza and pasta dishes are complemented by more ambitious recipes such as seared scallops with chorizo, and sea bass with asparagus, cherry tomatoes and saffron cream sauce. The lunchtime and early evening menu offers two courses for £13.

Café Concerto
CAFE, BISTRO ££

(✆01904-610478; www.cafeconcerto.biz; 21 High Petergate; snacks £5-10, mains £10-16; ◷8.30am-10pm) Walls papered with sheet music, chilled jazz on the stereo, and battered, mismatched tables and chairs set the bohemian tone in this comforting coffee shop-cum-bistro. Expect breakfasts, bagels and cappuccinos big enough to float a boat in during the day, and a sophisticated bistro menu in the evening.

El Piano
VEGAN £

(www.el-piano.com; 15 Grape Lane; meals £10-13; ◷11am-11pm Mon-Sat, noon-5pm Sun; ✍) With a menu that's 100% vegan, nut-free and gluten-free, this colourful, Hispanic-style spot is a vegetarian haven. Downstairs there's a lovely cafe and upstairs, three themed rooms. The menu offers dishes such as falafel, onion bhaji, corn fritters and mushroom-and-basil salad, either in tapas-size portions or as mixed platters. There's also a takeaway counter.

Melton's Too
BAR, BISTRO ££

(www.meltonstoo.co.uk; 25 Walmgate; mains £11-16; ◷10.30am-midnight Mon-Sat, to 11pm Sun; ☎) A comfortable, chilled-out cafe, bar and bistro, Melton's Too serves everything from cake and cappuccino to tapas-style snacks and three-course dinners (an early-bird special offers three courses for £12).

Living Room
INTERNATIONAL ££

(www.thelivingroom.co.uk; 1 Bridge St; mains £8-18; ◷11am-midnight; ☎) Balcony tables overlook the river and the menu focuses on quality versions of classic dishes from around the world. Sunday brunch is served noon to 6pm.

Siam House
THAI ££

(www.yorksiamhouse.co.uk; 63a Goodramgate; mains £9-15; ◷lunch Wed-Sat, dinner daily) Delicious Thai food in an atmosphere about as authentic as you could muster 3500 miles from Bangkok.

🍷 Drinking

With only a couple of exceptions, the best drinking holes in town are the older, traditional pubs. The area around Ousegate and Micklegate is popular with young drinkers and stag and hen parties, and can get a bit rowdy, especially at weekends.

⬛TOP CHOICE Blue Bell
PUB

(53 Fossgate) This is what a real English pub looks like – a tiny, wood-panelled room with a smouldering fireplace, decor (and beer and smoke stains) dating from c 1798, a pile of ancient board games in the corner, friendly and efficient bar staff, and Timothy Taylor and Black Sheep ales on tap. Bliss, with froth on top.

Ye Olde Starre
PUB

(40 Stonegate) Licenced since 1644, this is York's oldest pub – a warren of small rooms and small beer garden, with a half-dozen real ales on tap. It was used as a morgue by the Roundheads (supporters of parliament) during the Civil War, but the atmosphere has improved a lot since then.

Ackhorne
PUB

(9 St Martin's Lane) Tucked away off beery, sloppy Micklegate, this inn frequented by locals is as comfortable as old slippers – some of the old guys here look as though they've merged with the furniture. There's a pleasant beer garden at the back, and an open-mic night for local musicians on the first Tuesday of the month.

Old White Swan
PUB

(80 Goodramgate) Popular and atmospheric old pub with a small beer garden and a good range of guest real ales. And it's haunted...

King's Arms
PUB

(King's Staith) York's best-known pub in a fabulous riverside location, with tables spilling out onto the quayside. It's a perfect spot on a summer evening, but be prepared to share it with a few hundred other people.

☆ Entertainment

There are a couple of good theatres in York and an interesting art-house cinema, but as far as clubs are concerned, forget it: historic York is best enjoyed without them anyway.

York Theatre Royal
THEATRE
(www.yorktheatreroyal.co.uk; St Leonard's Pl) Well-regarded productions of theatre, opera and dance are staged here.

Grand Opera House
MUSIC, COMEDY
(www.grandoperahouseyork.org.uk; Clifford St) Despite the name, there's no opera here. Instead, there's a wide range of productions from live bands and popular musicals to stand-up comics and pantomime.

City Screen Picturehouse
CINEMA
(www.picturehouses.co.uk; 13-17 Coney St) An appealing modern building in a converted printing works, screening both mainstream and art-house films. There's also a nice cafe-bar on the terrace overlooking the river.

Shopping

Coney St, Davygate and the adjoining streets are the hub of York's central-city shopping scene, but the real treat are the antique, bric-a-brac and secondhand bookshops, concentrated in Colliergate, Micklegate and Fossgate.

Ken Spelman Booksellers
BOOKS
(www.kenspelman.com; 70 Micklegate) This fascinating shop has been selling rare, antiquarian and secondhand books since 1910. With an open fire crackling in the grate in winter, it's a browser's paradise.

Antiques Centre
ANTIQUES
(www.antiquescentreyorkeshop.co.uk; 41 Stonegate) A Georgian town house with a veritable maze of rooms and corridors, showcasing the wares of about 120 dealers selling everything from lapel pins and snuff boxes to oil paintings and longcase clocks. And the house is haunted as well...

Red House
ANTIQUES
(www.redhouseyork.co.uk; Duncombe Pl) The goods of about 60 antiques dealers are displayed in 10 showrooms spread over two floors, with items ranging from jewellery and porcelain to clocks and furniture.

Fossgate Books
BOOKS
(36 Fossgate) The place to buy cheap paperbacks and unusual books.

❶ Information

American Express (6 Stonegate; ⊘9am-5.30pm Mon-Fri, to 5pm Sat) Foreign exchange service available.

Post office (22 Lendal; ⊘8.30am-5.30pm Mon-Sat)

York District Hospital (☑01904-631313; Wiggington Rd) Located a mile north of the centre.

York tourist office (☑01904-550099; www.visityork.org; 1 Museum St; ⊘9am-6pm Mon-Sat, 10am-5pm Sun Apr-Sep, shorter hours Oct-Mar) Visitor and transport info for all of Yorkshire, plus accommodation booking, ticket sales and internet access.

❶ Getting There & Away

BUS For timetable information, call **Traveline Yorkshire** (☑0871-200 2233; www.yorkshiretravel.net) or check the computerised 24-hour information points at the train station and Rougier St. All local and regional buses stop on Rougier St, about 200m northeast of the train station.

There are National Express coaches to London (£28, 5½ hours, four daily), Birmingham (£28, 3¼ hours, one daily) and Newcastle (£15, 2¾ hours, four daily).

CAR A car is more hindrance than help in the city centre, so use one of the Park & Ride car parks at the edge of the city. If you want to explore the surrounding area, rental options include **Europcar** (☑01904-654040; www.europcar.co.uk; Train Station, Station Rd; ⊘8am-8.30pm Mon-Sat, from 9am Sun), located beside platform 1 in the train station; and **Hertz** (☑01904-612586; www.hertz.co.uk; Train Station, Station Rd), near platform 3 in the train station. Europcar also rents bicycles and stores luggage for £4 per bag.

TRAIN York is a major railway hub, with frequent direct services to Birmingham (£45, 2¼ hours), Newcastle (£15, one hour), Leeds (£11, 30 minutes), London King's Cross (£80, two hours), Manchester (£15, 1½ hours) and Scarborough (£10, 50 minutes). There are also trains to Cambridge (£60, 2¾ hours), changing at Peterborough.

❶ Getting Around

York is easy to get around on foot – you're never really more than 20 minutes' walk from any of the major sights.

BICYCLE The tourist office has a useful free map showing York's cycle routes, or visit **iTravel-York** (www.itravelyork.info/cycling). Castle Howard (15 miles northeast of York via Haxby and Strensall) is an interesting destination, and there's also a section of the **Trans-Pennine Trail cycle path** (www.transpenninetrail.org.uk) from Bishopthorpe in York to Selby (15 miles) along the old railway line.

You can rent bikes from **Giant York** (www.giant-york.co.uk; 13 Lord Mayor's Walk; ⊘9am-6pm Mon-Sat), outside Monk Bar; and Europcar (p495), by platform 1 in the train station; both charge around £15 per day.

BUS Local bus services are operated by **First York** (www.firstgroup.com/ukbus/york). Single fares range from £1.20 to £3, and a day pass valid for all local buses is £3.70 (available at Park & Ride car parks).

TAXI Station Taxis (⊘01904-623332; Train Station, Station Rd) has a kiosk outside the train station.

Castle Howard

Stately homes may be two-a-penny in England, but you'll have to try pretty damn hard to find one as breathtakingly stately as Castle Howard (www.castlehoward.co.uk; adult/child house & grounds £13/7.50, grounds only £8.50/6; ⊘house 11am-4.30pm Apr-Oct, grounds 10am-5.30pm Mar-Oct & 1st 3 weeks Dec, 10am-4pm Nov-Feb), a work of theatrical grandeur and audacity set in the rolling Howardian Hills. This is one of the world's most beautiful buildings, instantly recognisable from its starring role in the 1980s TV series *Brideshead Revisited* and, more recently, in the 2008 film of the same name (both based on Evelyn Waugh's 1945 novel of nostalgia for the English aristocracy).

When the earl of Carlisle hired his pal Sir John Vanbrugh to design his new home in 1699, he was hiring a bloke who had no formal training and was best known as a playwright. Luckily, Vanbrugh hired Nicholas Hawksmoor, who had worked as Christopher Wren's clerk of works – not only would Hawksmoor have a big part to play in the house's design, but he and Vanbrugh would later work wonders with Blenheim Palace. Today the house is still in the family, home to the Hon Simon Howard, great-grandson of the 9th earl of Carlisle, who can often be seen around the place.

If you can, try to visit on a weekday when it's easier to find the space to appreciate this hedonistic marriage of art, architecture, landscaping and natural beauty. As you wander about the peacock-haunted grounds, views open up over the hills, Vanbrugh's playful Temple of the Four Winds and Hawksmoor's stately mausoleum, but the great baroque house with its magnificent central cupola is an irresistible visual magnet. Inside, the house is full of treasures – the breathtaking Great Hall with its soaring Corinthian pilasters, Pre-Raphaelite stained glass in the chapel, and corridors lined with classical antiquities.

The entrance courtyard has a good cafe, a gift shop and a farm shop filled with foodie delights from local producers.

Castle Howard is 15 miles northeast of York, off the A64. There are several organised tours from York – check with the tourist office for up-to-date schedules. Stephenson's of Easingwold (www.stephensonsofeasingwold. co.uk) operates a bus service (£7.50 return, 40 minutes, three times daily Monday to Saturday) linking York with Castle Howard.

Harrogate

POP 85,128

The quintessential Victorian spa town, prim and pretty Harrogate has long been associated with a certain kind of old-fashioned Englishness – the kind that seems the preserve of retired army chaps and formidable dowagers who always vote Tory. They come to Harrogate to enjoy the flower shows and gardens that fill the town with magnificent displays of colour, especially in spring and autumn. It is fitting that the town's most famous visitor was Agatha Christie, who fled here incognito in 1926 to escape her broken marriage.

And yet, this picture of Victoriana redux is not quite complete. While it's undoubtedly true that Harrogate remains a firm favourite of visitors in their golden years, the town has plenty of smart hotels and trendy eateries catering to the boom in Harrogate's newest trade – conferences. All those dynamic young sales-and-marketing guns have to eat and sleep somewhere.

◉ Sights & Activities

Royal Pump Room Museum MUSEUM (www.harrogate.gov.uk; Crown Pl; adult/child £3.75/2.20; ⊘10.30am-5pm Mon-Sat, 2-5pm Sun Apr-Oct, to 4pm Nov-Mar) The ritual of visiting a spa town to 'take the waters' as a health cure became fashionable in the 19th century and peaked during the Edwardian era in the years before WWI. Charles Dickens visited Harrogate in 1858 and described it as 'the queerest place, with the strangest people in it, leading the oddest lives of dancing, newspaper-reading and dining' – sounds quite pleasant, really.

You can learn all about Harrogate's history as a spa town in the ornate Royal Pump Room, built in 1842 over the most famous of the sulphur springs. It gives an insight into how the phenomenon shaped the town and records the illustrious visitors it attracted. At the end, you get the chance to sample the spa water, if you dare.

Montpellier Quarter   NEIGHBOURHOOD

(www.montpellierharrogate.com) The most attractive part of town is the Montpellier Quarter, overlooking Prospect Gardens between Crescent Rd and Montpellier Hill. It's an area of pedestrianised streets lined with restored 19th-century buildings that are now home to art galleries, antique shops, fashion boutiques, cafes and restaurants – an upmarket annex to the main shopping area around Oxford and Cambridge streets.

Turkish Baths   SPA

(☎01423-556746; www.turkishbathsharrogate.co.uk; Parliament St; admission £14.50-20.50; ⊗check website) Plunge into Harrogate's past at the town's fabulously tiled Turkish Baths. This mock-Moorish facility is gloriously Victorian and offers a range of watery delights – hot rooms, steam rooms, plunge pools and so on. A visit is likely to last about 1½ hours. There's a complicated schedule of opening hours that are by turns ladies-only and mixed, so call or check online for details. If you prefer to stay dry, there are also guided tours (per person £3.50; ⊗9-10am Wed) of the building.

★ Festivals & Events

All three of Harrogate's major events are held at the Great Yorkshire Showground, just off the A661 on the southeastern edge of town.

Spring Flower Show   HORTICULTURE

(www.flowershow.org.uk; admission £14-15) The year's main event, held in late April. A colourful three-day extravaganza of blooms and blossoms, flower competitions, gardening demonstrations, market stalls, crafts and gardening shops.

Great Yorkshire Show   AGRICULTURE

(www.greatyorkshireshow.co.uk; adult/child £23/11) Staged over three days in mid-July by the Yorkshire Agricultural Society. Expect all manner of primped and prettified farm animals competing for prizes, and entertainment ranging from show jumping and falconry to cookery demonstrations and hot-air-balloon rides.

Autumn Flower Show   HORTICULTURE

(www.flowershow.org.uk; admission £14-15) Held in late September, this show has vegetable-

---

WORTH A TRIP

KIRKHAM PRIORY & STONE TROUGH INN

While crowds queue up to get into Castle Howard, you could turn off on the other side of the A64 along the minor road to the hamlet of Kirkham. Here, the picturesque ruins of Kirkham Priory (EH; www.english-heritage.org.uk; adult/child £3.40/2; ⊗10am-5pm Thu-Mon Apr-Sep, daily Aug) rise gracefully above the banks of the River Derwent, sporting an impressive 13th-century gatehouse encrusted with heraldic symbols.

After a stroll by the river, head up the hill on the far side to the Stone Trough Inn (www.stonetroughinn.co.uk; mains £12-18; ⊗lunch & dinner; 🛜📶🐾) for a spot of lunch. This traditional country inn serves gourmet-style pub grub (try the roast cod with creamed leek sauce) and its outdoor terrace has a great view over the valley.

---

and fruit-growing championships, a heaviest-onion competition, cookery demonstrations and children's events.

🛏 Sleeping

There are lots of excellent B&Bs and guesthouses just north of Harrogate town centre, on and around Franklin and Ripon Rds.

Bijou   B&B ££

(☎01423-567974; www.thebijou.co.uk; 17 Ripon Rd; s/d from £69/89; 🅿@🛜) Bijou by name and bijou by nature, this Victorian villa sits firmly at the boutique end of the B&B spectrum – you can tell that a lot of thought and care has gone into its design. The husband-and-wife team who own the place make fantastic hosts, warm and helpful but unobtrusive.

Hotel du Vin   BOUTIQUE HOTEL ££

(☎01423-856800; www.hotelduvin.com; Prospect Pl; r/ste from £110/180; 🅿@🛜) An extremely stylish boutique hotel that has made the other lodgings in town sit up and take notice. The loft suites with exposed oak beams, hardwood floors and designer bathrooms are among the nicest rooms we've seen in town, but even the standard rooms are spacious and very comfortable (though they can be noisy), each with a huge bed draped in soft Egyptian cotton.

Acorn Lodge
B&B ££

(☎01423-525630; www.acornlodgeharrogate.co.uk; 1 Studley Rd; s/d from £47/85; P🖳) Attention to detail makes the difference between an average and an excellent B&B, and the details at Acorn Lodge are spot on – stylish decor, crisp cotton sheets, powerful showers and perfect poached eggs for breakfast. The location is good too, just 10 minutes' walk from the town centre.

Harrogate Brasserie & Hotel
BOUTIQUE HOTEL ££

(☎01423-505041; www.harrogatebrasserie.co.uk; 26-30 Cheltenham Pde; s/d/f from £60/80/100; P🖳) Stripped pine, leather armchairs and subtle colour combinations make this one of Harrogate's most appealing places to stay. The cheerful and cosy accommodation is complemented by an excellent restaurant and bar, with live jazz every evening except Monday.

Arden House Hotel
B&B ££

(☎01423-509224; www.ardenhousehotel.co.uk; 69-71 Franklin Rd; s/d from £50/80; P🖳) This grand old Edwardian house has been given a modern makeover with stylish contemporary furniture, Egyptian-cotton bed linen and posh toiletries, but still retains some lovely period details, including tiled cast-iron fireplaces. Attentive service, good breakfasts and a central location are the icing on the cake.

✕ Eating

TOP CHOICE Van Zeller
MODERN BRITISH £££

(☎01423-508762; www.vanzellerrestaurants.co.uk; 8 Montpellier St; 2-course lunch £18, 3-course dinner £40; ⊙lunch & dinner Tue-Sat) Michelin-trained Yorkshire chef Tom van Zeller offers exquisite interpretations of classic British dishes, such as Yorkshire lamb served with tarragon gnocchi, globe artichoke and smoked almonds, in a refreshingly relaxed atmosphere. 'Fine food without the fuss' is his motto. Lunch and pre-theatre menu costs £25 for five courses.

Bettys
TEAROOM ££

(www.bettys.co.uk; 1 Parliament St; mains £6-13, afternoon tea £18; ⊙9am-9pm) A classic tearoom in a classic location with views across the park, Betty's is a local institution. It was established in 1919 by a Swiss immigrant confectioner who took the wrong train, ended up in Yorkshire and decided to stay. There are exquisite home-baked breads, scones and cakes, quality tea and coffee, and a gallery lined with art nouveau marquetry designs of Yorkshire scenes, commissioned by the founder in the 1930s.

Le D2
BISTRO ££

(www.led2.co.uk; 7 Bower Rd; 2-course lunch/dinner £13/18; ⊙Tue-Sat) This bright and airy bistro is always busy, with diners drawn back again and again by its relaxed atmosphere, warm and friendly service, and hearty menu that takes fresh local produce and adds a twist of French sophistication.

Tannin Level
BISTRO ££

(☎01423-560595; www.tanninlevel.co.uk; 5 Raglan St; mains £10-15; ⊙Tue-Sat) Old terracotta floor tiles, polished mahogany tables and gilt-framed mirrors and paintings create a relaxed yet elegant atmosphere at this popular neighbourhood bistro. A competitively priced menu based on seasonal British produce – think herb-crusted rump of lamb or pan-fried scallops – means you'd best book a table or face being turned away.

Le Jardin
BISTRO £

(☎01423-507323; www.lejardin-harrogate.com; 7 Montpellier Pde; lunch mains £5-9, 2-/3-course dinner £9/13; ⊙lunch Tue-Fri & Sun, dinner Tue-Sat) This cool little bistro has a snug atmosphere, especially in the evening when candlelight adds a romantic glow. During the day, locals throng to the tables to enjoy great salads, sandwiches and homemade ice cream.

Sasso
ITALIAN £££

(☎01423-508838; www.sassorestaurant.co.uk; 8-10 Princes Sq; mains £15-21; ⊙lunch & dinner Mon-Sat) A top-class basement trattoria where homemade pasta is served in a variety of traditional and authentic ways, along with a host of other Italian specialities.

☆ Entertainment

Harrogate Theatre
THEATRE

(www.harrogatetheatre.co.uk; Oxford St) A historic Victorian building that dates from 1900, staging variety, comedy, musicals and dancing.

Royal Hall
MUSIC

(www.royalhall.co.uk; Ripon Rd) A gorgeous Edwardian theatre that is now part of the conference and events venue Harrogate International Centre. The musical program covers orchestral and choral performances, piano recitals, jazz, and so on.

❶ Information

Post office (11 Cambridge Rd; ⊙9.30am-5.30pm Mon-Sat)

Tourist office (✉0845-389 3223; www.harrogate.gov.uk/tourism; Crescent Rd; ⊙9am-5.30pm Mon-Sat, 10am-1pm Sun Apr-Oct, reduced hours Nov-Mar)

❶ Getting There & Away

BUS National Express coaches run from Leeds (40 minutes, five daily). Bus 36 comes from Ripon (30 minutes, every 20 minutes) and continues on to Leeds.

TRAIN Trains run to Harrogate from Leeds (£7.40, 40 minutes, about half-hourly) and York (£7.40, 45 minutes, hourly).

Scarborough

POP 57,649

Scarborough is where the tradition of English seaside holidays began – and it began earlier than you might think. It was in the 1660s that a book promoting the medicinal properties of a local spring (now the site of Scarborough Spa) pulled in the first flood of visitors. A belief in the health-giving effects of sea bathing saw wheeled bathing carriages appear on the beach in the 1730s, and with the arrival of the railway in 1845

Scarborough's fate was sealed. By the time the 20th century rolled in, it was all donkey rides, fish and chips, and boat trips round the bay, with saucy postcards, beauty contests and slot-machine arcades only a decade or two away.

Like all British seaside towns, Scarborough suffered a downturn as people jetted off to the Costa Blanca in recent decades on newly affordable foreign holidays, but things are looking up again. The town retains all the trappings of the classic seaside resort, but is in the process of reinventing itself as a centre for the creative arts and digital industries. The Victorian spa is being redeveloped as a conference and entertainment centre, a former museum has been converted into studio space for artists, and there's free, open-access wi-fi along the promenade beside the harbour – an area being developed as the town's bar, cafe and restaurant quarter.

As well as the usual seaside attractions, Scarborough offers excellent coastal walking, a new geology museum, one of Yorkshire's most impressively sited castles, and a renowned theatre that is the home base for popular playwright Alan Ayckbourn, whose plays always premiere here.

WORTH A TRIP

BLACK SHEEP OF THE BREWING FAMILY

The village of Masham is a place of pilgrimage for connoisseurs of real ale – it's the frothing fountainhead of Theakston's beers, brewed here since 1827. The company's most famous brew, Old Peculier, takes its name from the Peculier of Masham, a parish court established in medieval times to deal with religious offences, including drunkenness, brawling and 'taking a skull from the churchyard and placing it under a person's head to charm them to sleep'. The court seal is used as the emblem for Theakston Ales.

To the horror of real-ale fans, and after much falling-out among Theakston family members, the Theakston Brewery was taken over by megabrewer Scottish & Newcastle in 1987. Five years later, Paul Theakston, who refused to go and work for S&N and was determined to keep small-scale artisan brewing alive, bought an old maltings building in Masham and set up his own brewery, which he named Black Sheep. He managed to salvage all kinds of traditional brewing equipment, including six Yorkshire 'stone square' brewing vessels, and was soon running a successful enterprise.

History came full circle in 2004 when Paul's four brothers took the Theakston brewery back into family ownership. Both Black Sheep Brewery (✉01765-680101; www.blacksheepbrewery.com; tours £5.95; ⊙10am-4.30pm Sun-Wed, to 11pm Thu-Sat) and Theakston's Brewery (✉01765-680000; www.theakstons.co.uk; tours £6.50; ⊙10.30am-5.30pm Jul & Aug, to 4.30pm May, Jun, Sep & Oct) have information centres and offer guided tours (best booked in advance).

Masham (pronounced 'Massam') is 9 miles northwest of Ripon on the A6108 to Leyburn. Bus 159 from Ripon to Richmond stops at Masham (30 minutes, every two hours Monday to Saturday).

Scarborough

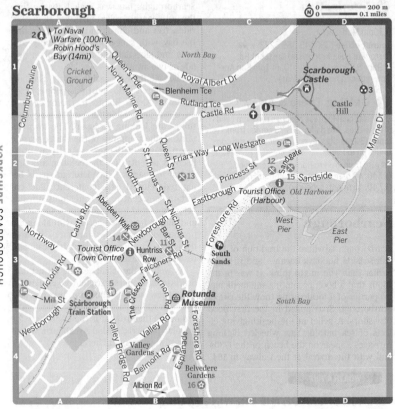

Sights

Scarborough Castle CASTLE
(EH; www.english-heritage.org.uk; adult/child
£4.90/2.90; ⊙10am-6pm Apr-Sep, to 4pm Thu-
Mon Oct & Sat-Sun Nov-Mar) Scarborough is not
exclusively about sandcastles, seaside rock
candy and walks along the promenade. The
massive medieval keep of Scarborough Castle occupies a commanding position atop its
headland. Legend has it that Richard I loved
the views from here so much that his ghost
just keeps coming back. Take a walk out to
the edge of the cliffs, where you can see the
2000-year-old remains of a Roman signal
station. Clearly the Romans appreciated
this viewpoint, too.

Rotunda Museum MUSEUM
(www.rotundamuseum.co.uk; Vernon Rd; adult/
child £4.50/free; ⊙10am-5pm Tue-Sun) The Rotunda Museum is dedicated to seaside rock
of a different kind – the coastal geology

of northeast Yorkshire, which has yielded
many of Britain's most important dinosaur
fossils. The strata in the local cliffs were also
important in deciphering England's geological history. Founded by William Smith, 'the
father of English geology', who lived in Scarborough in the 1820s, the museum has original Victorian exhibits as well as a hands-on
gallery for kids.

Sea Life Centre &
Marine Sanctuary AQUARIUM
(www.sealife.co.uk; Scalby Mills; adult/child/family
£15/11.40/46.80; ⊙10am-5pm) Of all the family-oriented attractions on the waterfront,
the best of the lot is the Sea Life Centre overlooking North Bay. You can see coral reefs,
turtles, octopuses, seahorses, otters and
many other fascinating creatures, though
the biggest draw is the Seal Rescue Centre
(feeding times 11.30am and 2.30pm). It's at
the far north end of North Beach and the

Scarborough

miniature **North Bay Railway** (www.nbr.org. uk; return adult/child £3.30/2.70; ⊙10.30am-3pm Apr-Sep, Sat & Sun year-round) runs the three-quarter-mile route. A lot of the attractions are outdoors, so it's not an ideal rainy-day refuge.

FREE **Peasholm Park** PARK
(www.peasholmpark.com; Columbus Ravine; ⊙24hr) Set back from North Bay, Scarborough's beautiful Edwardian pleasure gardens are famous for their summer sessions of **Naval Warfare** (adult/child £3.70/2.10; ⊙3pm selected dates Jun-Aug), when large model ships re-enact famous naval battles on the boating lake (check the website for dates).

FREE **St Mary's Church** CHURCH
(Castle Rd; ⊙10am-4pm Mon-Fri, 1-4pm Sun May-Sep) This church dates from 1180, and in the little cemetery across the lane is the **grave of Anne Brontë**.

🏃 Activities

There are some decent waves on England's northeast coast, supporting a growing surf scene. A top spot is **Cayton Bay**, 4 miles south of town, where you'll find **Scarborough Surf School** (www.scarboroughsurf school.co.uk; parking £2) offering full-day lessons for £45 per person and surfboard hire for £18 per day.

Back in town, you can get information and advice from the **Secretspot Surf Shop** (www.secretspot.co.uk; 4 Pavilion Tce) near the train station.

🛏 Sleeping

In Scarborough, if a house has four walls and a roof it will offer B&B. Competition is intense, and in such a tough market multi-night-stay special offers are a dime a dozen, which means single-night rates are the highest of all.

TOP CHOICE **Hotel Helaina** B&B ££
(☎01723-375191; www.hotelhelaina.co.uk; 14 Blenheim Tce; s/d from £59/79; ⊙daily Apr-Nov, Fri & Sat only Feb & Mar; 🛜) Location, location, location – you'd be hard pushed to find a place with a better sea view than this elegant guesthouse perched on the clifftop overlooking North Beach. And the view inside the rooms is pretty good too, with sharply styled contemporary furniture and cool colours. The standard rooms are a touch on the small side and it's well worth paying a bit extra for the deluxe sea-view room with bay window.

Beiderbecke's Hotel HOTEL £££
(☎01723-365766; www.beiderbeckes.com; 1-3 The Crescent; s/d from £85/130; P🛜) Set in an elegant Georgian terrace in the middle of town, on a quiet street overlooking gardens, this hotel combines stylish and spacious rooms with attentive but friendly and informal service. It's not quite boutique but, with its intriguing modern art on the walls and snazzy coloured toilet seats, it's heading in that direction.

Windmill B&B ££
(☎01723-372735; www.windmill-hotel.co.uk; Mill St; d £95; P) Quirky doesn't begin to describe

FOUNTAINS ABBEY

Nestled in the secluded valley of the River Skell are two of Yorkshire's most beautiful attractions, an absolute must on any northern itinerary. The alluring and strangely obsessive water gardens of the Studley Royal estate were built in the 18th century to enhance the picturesque ruins of 12th-century Fountains Abbey (NT; www.fountainsabbey.org.uk; adult/child £9/4.85; ⊙10am-5pm Apr-Sep, to 4pm Oct-Mar). Together, they present a breathtaking picture of pastoral elegance and tranquillity that have made them a Unesco World Heritage Site and the most visited of all the National Trust's pay-to-enter properties.

After falling out with the Benedictines of York in 1132, a band of rebel monks came here to establish their own monastery. Struggling to make it alone, they were formally adopted by the Cistercians in 1135. By the middle of the 13th century, the new abbey had become the most successful Cistercian venture in the country. After the Dissolution, when Henry III confiscated church property, the abbey's estate was sold into private hands, and between 1598 and 1611 Fountains Hall was built using stone from the abbey ruins. The hall and ruins were united with the Studley Royal estate in 1768.

Studley Royal was owned by John Aislabie, once Chancellor of the Exchequer, who dedicated his life to creating the park after a financial scandal saw him expelled from parliament. The main house of Studley Royal burnt down in 1946, but the superb landscaping, with its serene artificial lakes, survives almost unchanged from the 18th century.

A choice of scenic walking trails leads for a mile to the famous water gardens, designed to enhance the romantic views of the ruined abbey. Don't miss St Mary's Church above the gardens, a neogothic jewel designed by William Burgess, and ask the attendant to point out the trademark mouse carved into the stone of the mausoleum.

The remains of the abbey are impressively grandiose, gathered around the sunny Romanesque cloister, with a huge vaulted cellarium leading off the west end of the church. Here, the abbey's 200 lay brothers lived, and food and wool from the abbey's farms were stored. At the east end is the soaring Chapel of Nine Altars and on the outside of its northeast window is a Green Man carving (a pre-Christian fertility symbol).

Fountains Abbey is 4 miles west of Ripon off the B6265. Bus 139 travels from Ripon to Fountains Abbey visitor centre year-round (15 minutes, four times daily Monday to Saturday).

this place, a beautifully converted 18th-century windmill in the middle of town. There are two self-catering cottages and three four-poster doubles around a cobbled courtyard, but try to secure the balcony suite (£140 a night) in the upper floors of the windmill itself, with great views from the wrap-around balcony.

The Waves B&B ££
(☑01723-373658; www.scarboroughwaves.co.uk; 39 Esplanade Rd, South Cliff; per person £32-39; P☎) Crisp Egyptian cotton sheets and powerful showers make for comfortable accommodation at this B&B, but it's the second B that's the real star – the breakfasts range from vegetarian- and vegan-friendly fruit salads and smoothies to fry-ups, kippers and kedgeree. A unique selling point is the jukebox in the lounge, loaded with 1960s and '70s hits.

Interludes B&B ££
(☑01723-360513; www.interludeshotel.co.uk; 32 Princess St; s/d £45/68; ☎) Owners Ian and Bob have a flair for the theatrical and have enacted it with visible success on this lovely, gay-friendly Georgian home plastered with old theatre posters, prints and other thespian mementoes. The individually decorated rooms are given to colourful flights of fancy that are guaranteed to put a smile on your face. Children, alas, are not welcome.

Scarborough YHA HOSTEL £
(☑0845-371 9657; www.yha.org.uk; Burniston Rd; dm £19.50; P) An idyllic hostel set in a converted 17th-century water mill, 2 miles north of town along the A166 to Whitby. Take bus 3, 12 or 21.

Crown Spa Hotel HOTEL ££
(☑01723-357400; www.crownspahotel.com; Esplanade; s/d from £64/88; P☎) This grand old hotel opened its doors in 1845 and has been

going strong ever since, offering superb sea views and a luxurious modern spa.

Eating

Marmalade's BRASSERIE **££**

(☎01723-365766; 1-3 The Crescent; 2-/3-course dinner £18/22; ◷noon-9.30pm) The stylish brasserie in Beiderbecke's Hotel, offering cream and chocolate colours, art with a musical theme and cool jazz in the background (live on Thursday and Saturday), has a menu that adds a gourmet twist to traditional dishes such as roast pork, rack of lamb and steak and chips.

Glass House CAFE **£**

(☎01723-368791; www.glasshousebistro.co.uk; Burniston Rd; mains £4-8; ◷10am-5pm; 🛜👶) Homemade lasagne, steak-and-ale pie and filled baked potatoes pull in the lunchtime crowds at this appealing (and always busy) cafe beside the start of the North Bay Railway. Fried breakfasts, sandwiches, cakes and scones fill the menu for the rest of the day.

Lanterna ITALIAN **£££**

(☎01723-363616; www.lanterna-ristorante.co.uk; 33 Queen St; mains £15-21; ◷dinner Mon-Sat) A snug, old-fashioned Italian trattoria that specialises in fresh local seafood (including lobster, from £32) and classic dishes from the old country such as *stufato de ceci* (chickpea stew with oxtail) and white-truffle dishes in season (October to December, £30 to £45). As well as sourcing Yorkshire produce, the chef imports delicacies direct from Italy, including truffles, olive oil, prosciutto and a range of cheeses.

Golden Grid SEAFOOD **££**

(www.goldengrid.co.uk; 4 Sandside; mains £8-18; ◷11.30am-11pm) Whoever said fish and chips can't be eaten with dignity hasn't tried the Golden Grid, a sit-down fish restaurant that has been serving the best cod in Scarborough since 1883. Its starched white tablecloths and starched white aprons are staunchly traditional, as is the menu – as well as fish and chips there's freshly landed crab, lobster, prawns and oysters, plus sausage and mash, liver and bacon, and steak and chips.

Roasters CAFE **£**

(www.roasterscoffee.co.uk; 8 Aberdeen Walk; mains £5-7; ◷9am-5pm) A funky coffee shop with chunky pine tables, brown leather chairs and an excellent range of freshly ground coffees. There's a juice and smoothie bar too, and the lunch menu includes ciabatta sandwiches, salads and jacket potatoes.

Bonnet's TEAROOM **£**

(38-40 Huntriss Row; mains £5-9; ◷9am-5pm Mon-Sat, 11am-4pm Sun) One of the oldest cafes in town (established in 1880), Bonnet's serves delicious cakes and light meals in a quiet courtyard.

Tunny Club FISH & CHIPS **£**

(1 Sandgate; mains £4-7; ◷11am-11pm) A decent fish-and-chip shop whose upstairs dining room is a shrine to Scarborough's history of big-game fishing.

☆ Entertainment

Stephen Joseph Theatre THEATRE

(www.sjt.uk.com; Westborough) A good range of drama is staged here, including the premieres of plays by the renowned chronicler of middle-class mores, Alan Ayckbourn.

Scarborough Spa VARIETY

(www.scarboroughspa.co.uk; Foreshore Rd) The revitalised spa complex stages a wide array

---

THE TUNNY CLUB

Strange but true: in the 1930s Atlantic bluefin tuna (also known as tunny) started to follow the herring shoals into the North Sea, and Yorkshire became the hub of an American-style big-game fishery. Professional hunter Lorenzo Mitchell-Henry set the record for a rod-caught fish in British waters when he landed a 386kg monster in 1933, and Scarborough was soon home to the Tunny Club of Great Britain. Visiting millionaires and movie stars chartered local boats and vied with each other to smash the record.

Overfishing led to the disappearance of the herring shoals in the 1950s, and with them the tunny. However, in recent years the ocean giants have returned, attracted by warmer waters (a result of climate change) and recovering herring stocks. Meanwhile, the only evidence that remains of the fishery in Scarborough is the former premises of the Tunny Club at 1 Sandgate, now a fish-and-chip shop whose upstairs dining room is filled with big-game fishing memorabilia.

of entertainment, especially in the summer months – orchestral performances, variety shows, popular musicals and old-fashioned afternoon-tea dances.

ℹ Information

FreeBay Wifi (📶) Free wi-fi internet access along the harbourfront from West Pier to East Pier.

Post office (11-15 Aberdeen Walk; ⊙9am-5.30pm Mon-Fri, to 12.30pm Sat)

Tourist office (📞01723-383637; www.discover yorkshirecoast.com; Brunswick Shopping Centre, Westborough; ⊙9.30am-5.30pm Apr-Oct, 10am-4.30pm Mon-Sat Nov-Mar)

Tourist office (Sandside; ⊙10am-5.30pm Apr-Oct, to 9pm Jul & Aug)

ℹ Getting There & Away

BUS Bus 128 travels along the A170 from Helmsley to Scarborough (£6.50, 1½ hours, hourly) via Pickering, while buses 93 and X93 come from Whitby (£5.30, one hour, every 30 minutes) via Robin Hood's Bay (hourly).

Bus 843 goes to Scarborough from Leeds (£12, 2¾ hours, hourly) via York (£10, 1¾ hours, hourly).

TRAIN There are regular trains from Hull (£14, 1½ hours, hourly), Leeds (£26, one hour 20 minutes, hourly) and York (£18, 50 minutes, hourly).

ℹ Getting Around

Tiny Victorian-era **funicular railways** (per person 75p; ⊙Feb-Oct) rattle up and down Scarborough's steep cliffs between town and beach. Local **buses** leave from the western end of Westborough and outside the train station.

For a taxi, call **Station Taxis** (📞01723-366366); £5 should get you to most places in town.

NORTH YORK MOORS NATIONAL PARK

Inland from the north Yorkshire coast, the wild and windswept North York Moors rise in desolate splendour. Three-quarters of all the world's heather moorland is to be found in Britain, and this is the largest expanse in England. Ridge-top roads climb up from lush green valleys to the bleak open moors, where weather-beaten stone crosses mark the line of ancient roadways. In summer heather blooms in billowing drifts of purple haze.

This is classic walking country. The moors are criss-crossed with footpaths old and new, and dotted with pretty, flower-bedecked villages. The national park is also home to one of England's most picturesque steam railways.

North York Moors National Park

The park produces the very useful *Moors & Coast* visitor guide, available from tourist offices and hotels, with information on things to see and do. See also www.northyorkmoors.org.uk.

ⓘ Getting Around

The **Moorsbus** (www.northyorkmoors.org.uk/moorsbus) network covers all the main villages, operating only on Sunday and bank holiday Mondays from April to October. Pick up a timetable and route map from tourist offices or download one from the website. A standard day pass costs £6. (Note: a new service is planned to replace it in 2014.)

There's also a free public transport map, the *Moors Explorer Travel Guide*, available from tourist offices.

If you're planning to drive on the minor roads over the moors, beware of wandering sheep and lambs – hundreds are killed by careless drivers every year.

Helmsley

POP 1620

Helmsley is a classic North Yorkshire market town, a handsome place of old houses, historic coaching inns and – inevitably – a cobbled market square (market day is Friday), all basking under the watchful gaze of a sturdy Norman castle. Nearby are the romantic ruins of Rievaulx Abbey and a fistful of country walks.

⊙ Sights & Activities

The impressive ruins of 12th-century Helmsley Castle (EH; www.english-heritage.org.uk; adult/child £4.90/2.90; ⊙10am-6pm Apr-Sep, to 5pm Oct, to 4pm Sat & Sun Nov-Mar) are defended by a striking series of deep ditches and banks, to which later rulers added the thick stone walls and defensive towers. Only one tooth-shaped tower survives today, following the dismantling of the fortress by Sir Thomas Fairfax after the Civil War. The castle's tumultuous history is well explained in the tourist office.

Just outside the castle, Helmsley Walled Garden (www.helmsleywalledgarden.org.uk; adult/child £5.50/free; ⊙9.30am-5pm Mar-Oct) would be just another plant-and-produce centre were it not for its dramatic position and fabulous selection of flowers, fruits and vegetables (some of them rare), not to mention the herbs, including 40 varieties of mint. If you're into horticulture with a historical twist, this is Eden.

South of the castle stretches the superb landscape of Duncombe Park estate, with the stately home of Duncombe Park House (www.duncombepark.com; adult/child £5/free; ⊙11am-5.30pm Sun-Fri Jun-Aug) at its heart. From the house and formal gardens, wide grassy walkways and terraces lead through woodland to mock-classical temples, while longer walking trails are set out in the parkland, now protected as a nature reserve. The house is 1.5 miles south of town, an easy walk through the park. Guided tours of the house start hourly from 12.30pm to 3.30pm.

You could easily spend a day here, especially if you take in one of the many walks. Cream of the crop is the 3.5-mile route to Rievaulx Abbey (p506) – the tourist office can provide route leaflets and advise on buses if you don't want to walk both ways. This route is also the opening section of the Cleveland Way (p483).

🛏 Sleeping

Feversham Arms   HOTEL £££
(✆01439-770766; www.fevershamarms.com; High St; r from £130; P🐾🛜🌊) The Feversham Arms has recently had a designer makeover, creating a snug and sophisticated atmosphere where country charm meets boutique chic. Individually decorated bedrooms are complemented by an excellent restaurant, spa treatments and a heated outdoor pool in the central courtyard.

Feathers Hotel   INN ££
(✆01439-770275; www.feathershotelhelmsley.co.uk; Market Pl; s/d from £55/100) One of a number of old coach inns on Market Pl that offer B&B, half-decent grub and a pint of hand-pumped real ale. There are four-poster beds in some rooms and historical trimmings throughout.

Helmsley YHA   HOSTEL £
(✆0845-371 9638; www.yha.org.uk; Carlton Lane; dm £19.50; P) This hostel's location, 400m east of the market square at the start of the Cleveland Way, means it's often busy, so book in advance. It looks a bit like an ordinary suburban home.

Wrens of Ryedale   CAMPSITE £
(✆01439-771260; www.wrensofryedale.co.uk; Gale Lane; tent & 2 adults £10, with car £17; ⊙Apr-Oct) A sheltered campsite with more than a hectare of pristine parkland 3 miles east of Helmsley, just south of Beadlam.

✕ Eating

Helmsley is a bit of a foodie town, sporting a couple of quality delicatessens on the main square. There's Thomas of Helmsley (18 Market Pl; ⊗7.30am-5.30pm Mon-Sat, 10am-4pm Sun), a butcher and deli specialising in local produce, and Hunters of Helmsley (www.huntersofhelmsley.com; 13 Market Pl; ⊗8am-5.30pm), offering a cornucopia of locally made chutneys, jams, beers, cheeses, bacon, humbug sweets and ice cream – a great place to stock up for a gourmet picnic.

TOP CHOICE Star Inn   GASTROPUB £££
(☎01439-770397; www.thestaratharome.co.uk; mains £18-26; ⊗lunch Tue-Sun, dinner Mon-Sat; ☑) This thatch-roofed country gastropub is home to one of Yorkshire's best restaurants, with a menu specialising in top-quality produce from the surrounding countryside: Whitby cod with buttered marsh samphire, or Harome roe deer venison with wild mushrooms. There's also a gourmet vegetarian menu. It's the sort of place you won't want to leave, and the good news is you don't have to – the adjacent lodge has eight magnificent bedrooms (£180 to £260), each decorated in classic but luxurious country style. It's about 2 miles south of Helmsley just off the A170.

❶ Information

The **tourist office** (☎01439-770173; Castlegate; ⊗9.30am-5.30pm Mar-Oct, 10am-4pm Fri-Sun Nov-Feb) at the castle entrance sells maps and books, and can help with accommodation.

❶ Getting There & Away

All buses stop in the main square. Bus 31X runs from York to Helmsley (£7, 1¼ hours, twice daily Monday to Saturday). From Scarborough, take bus 128 (£7, 1½ hours, hourly Monday to Saturday, four times on Sunday) via Pickering.

Rievaulx

In the secluded valley of the River Rye, amid fields and woods loud with birdsong, stand the magnificent ruins of Rievaulx Abbey (www.english-heritage.org.uk; adult/child £5.80/3.50; ⊗10am-6pm Apr-Sep, reduced hours at other times). This idyllic spot was chosen by Cistercian monks in 1132 as a base for their missionary activity in northern Britain. St Aelred, the third abbot, famously described the abbey's setting as 'everywhere peace, everywhere serenity, and a marvellous free-

dom from the tumult of the world'. But the monks of Rievaulx (pronounced 'ree-voh') were far from unworldly and soon created a network of commercial interests ranging from sheep farms to lead mines. The extensive ruins give a wonderful sense of the size and complexity of the community that once lived here, and their story is fleshed out in a series of fascinating exhibits in the neighbouring tourist office.

In the 1750s landscape-gardening fashion favoured a Gothic look and many aristocrats had mock ruins built in their parks. The Duncombe family were able to go one better, as their lands contained a real medieval ruin, Rievaulx Abbey. They built Rievaulx Terrace & Temples (www.nationaltrust.org.uk; adult/child £5.50/3.10; ⊗11am-5pm Mar-Oct) so that lords and ladies could stroll effortlessly in 'the wilderness' and admire the abbey in the valley below. Visitors today can do the same, with views over Ryedale and the Hambleton Hills forming a perfect backdrop.

Rievaulx is located about 3 miles west of Helmsley. Note that there's no direct access between the abbey and the terrace. Their entrance gates are about a mile apart, though easily reached along a lane (steeply uphill if you're heading from the abbey to the terrace).

Hutton-le-Hole & Around

POP 210

With a scatter of gorgeous stone cottages, a gurgling brook and a flock of sheep grazing contentedly on the village green, Hutton-le-Hole must be a contender for the best-looking village in Yorkshire. The dips and hollows on the green may have given the place its name – it was once called simply Hutton Hole. Wannabe posh Victorians added the Frenchified 'le', which the locals defiantly pronounce 'lee'.

The **tourist office** (☎01751-417367; ⊗10am-5.30pm mid-Mar–early Nov) has leaflets about walks in the area, including a 5-mile circuit to the nearby village of Lastingham.

Attached to the tourist office is the largely open-air Ryedale Folk Museum (☎01751-417367; www.ryedalefolkmuseum.co.uk; adult/child £7/6; ⊗10am-6pm Feb-Oct), a constantly expanding collection of North York Moors buildings from different eras, including a medieval manor house, simple farmers' houses, a blacksmith's forge and a row of

1930s village shops. Demonstrations and displays give a fascinating insight into local life as it was in the past.

The Daffodil Walk is a 2.5-mile circular walk following the banks of the River Dove. As the name suggests, the main drawcard is the daffs, usually at their best in the last couple of weeks in April.

🛏 Sleeping

Lion Inn   PUB, B&B **££**
(📞01751-417320; www.lionblakey.co.uk; Blakey Ridge; s/d from £48/80; 🅿) From Hutton, the Blakey Ridge road climbs over the moors to Danby and, 6 miles on, passes one of the highest and most remote pubs in England (altitude 404m). With its low-beamed ceilings and cosy fireplaces, hearty grub (mains £11 to £23) and range of real ales, the Lion is a firm favourite with hikers and bikers.

Burnley House   B&B **££**
(📞01751-417548; www.burnleyhouse.co.uk; per person £36-45; 🅿🛜) This elegant Georgian home offers comfortable bedrooms and a hearty breakfast, but the best features are the lovely sitting room and garden where you can relax with a cup of tea and a book.

ℹ Getting There & Away

Hutton-le-Hole is 2.5 miles north of the main A170 road, about halfway between Helmsley and Pickering. Sunday-only Moorsbus services to Hutton-le-Hole include the M3 between Helmsley and Danby via the Lion Inn (five per day). On Mondays and Fridays, bus 174 runs to Hutton from Pickering (30 minutes, one daily).

Pickering

POP 6600

Pickering is a lively market town with an imposing Norman castle that advertises itself as the 'gateway to the North York Moors'. That gateway is the terminus of the wonderful North Yorkshire Moors Railway, a picturesque survivor from the great days of steam. The tourist office (📞01751-473791; The Ropery; ⊙9.30am-5.30pm Mon-Sat, to 4pm Sun Mar-Oct, 10am-4pm Mon-Sat Nov-Feb) has the usual details, as well as plenty of railway-related info.

◉ Sights

North Yorkshire Moors Railway   HERITAGE RAILWAY
(NYMR; www.nymr.co.uk; Pickering-Whitby day rover ticket adult/child £22.50/11.30) The privately owned North Yorkshire Moors Railway runs for 18 miles through beautiful countryside to the village of Grosmont. Lovingly restored steam locos pull period carriages resplendent with polished brass and bright paintwork, and the railway appeals to train buffs and day trippers alike. For visitors without wheels, it's excellent for reaching out-of-the-way spots.

Even more usefully, Grosmont is on the main railway line between Middlesbrough and Whitby, which opens up yet more possibilities for walking or sightseeing. Another useful website is www.nymr.demon.co.uk.

Pickering Castle   CASTLE
(EH; www.english-heritage.org.uk; adult/child £3.90/2.30; ⊙10am-5pm Jul & Aug, 10am-5pm Thu-Mon Apr-Jun & Sep) Pickering Castle is a lot like the castles we drew as kids: thick stone outer walls circle the keep, and the whole lot is perched atop a high motte (mound) with great views of the surrounding countryside. Founded by William the Conqueror, it was added to and altered by later kings.

🛏 Sleeping & Eating

There's a strip of B&Bs on tree-lined Eastgate (on the A170 to Scarborough) and a few more on Westgate (heading towards Helmsley). Decent options include Eleven Westgate (📞01751-475111; www.elevenwestgate.co.uk; 11 Westgate; s/d from £50/70; 🅿🛜), a pretty house with patio and garden, and the elegant Georgian town house at 17 Burgate (📞01751-473463; www.17burgate.co.uk; 17 Burgate; s/d £90/110; 🅿📧🛜).

There are several cafes and teashops on Market Pl, but don't overlook the tearoom (Pickering Station, Park St; mains £6; ⊙8.30am-4pm) at Pickering station, which serves excellent home-baked goodies and does a tasty roast-pork roll with apple sauce, crackling and stuffing.

🅣🅞🅟 **White Swan Hotel**   PUB, HOTEL **£££**
(📞01751-472288; www.white-swan.co.uk; Market Pl; r from £139; 🅿🛜) The top spot in town successfully combines a smart pub, a superb restaurant serving local produce cooked with a Continental twist (mains £13–23), and a luxurious boutique hotel. Nine modern rooms in the converted coach house up the ante, with flatscreen TVs and other stylish paraphernalia adding to the luxury found throughout the hotel.

❶ Getting There & Away

In addition to the NYMR trains, bus 128 between Helmsley (40 minutes) and Scarborough (50 minutes) runs hourly via Pickering. Bus 840 between Leeds and Whitby links Pickering with York (£8, 70 minutes, hourly).

Danby

POP 290

The Blakey Ridge road from Hutton-le-Hole swoops down steeply to Danby, a compact stone-built village set deep amid the moors at the head of Eskdale. It's home to the **Moors Centre** (☎01439-772737; www.north yorkmoors.org.uk; Lodge Lane; ◷10am-5pm Mar-Oct, 11am-4pm Nov-Feb), the national park's headquarters, which has interesting exhibits on the natural history of the moors as well as a cafe, an accommodation booking service and a huge range of local guidebooks, maps and leaflets.

You can reach Danby on the delightful **Esk Valley Railway** (www.eskvalleyrailway.co.uk). Whitby is a 20-minute ride east, Middlesbrough 45 minutes west, and there are four departures daily Monday to Saturday, two on Sunday.

Whitby

POP 13,600

Whitby is a town of two halves, split down the middle by the mouth of the River Esk. It's also a town with two personalities – on the one hand, a busy commercial and fishing port with a bustling quayside fish market; on the other, a traditional seaside resort, complete with sandy beach, amusement arcades and promenading holidaymakers slurping ice-cream cones in the sun.

It's the combination of these two facets that makes Whitby more interesting than your average resort. The town has managed to retain much of its 18th-century character, recalling the time when James Cook – Whitby's most famous adopted son – was making his first forays out at sea on his way to becoming one of the best-known explorers in history. The narrow streets and alleys of the old town hug the riverside, now lined with restaurants, pubs and cute little shops, all with views across the handsome harbour where colourful fishing boats ply their trade. Keeping a watchful eye over the whole scene is the atmospheric ruined abbey atop the East Cliff.

But Whitby also has a darker side. Most famously, it was the inspiration and setting for part of Bram Stoker's Gothic horror story *Dracula*. Less well known is the fact that Whitby is famous for the jet (fossilised wood) that has been mined from its sea cliffs for centuries. This smooth black substance was popularised in the 19th century when Queen Victoria took to wearing mourning jewellery made from Whitby jet. In recent years these morbid associations have seen the rise of a series of hugely popular goth festivals.

◉ Sights

Whitby Abbey RUINS
(EH; www.english-heritage.org.uk; adult/child £6.20/3.70; ◷10am-6pm Apr-Sep, reduced hours at other times) There are ruined abbeys and there are picturesque ruined abbeys, and then there's Whitby Abbey, dominating the skyline above the East Cliff like a great Gothic tombstone silhouetted against the sky. Looking as though it was built as an atmospheric film set rather than a monastic establishment, it is hardly surprising that this medieval hulk inspired the Victorian novelist Bram Stoker (who holidayed in Whitby) to make it the setting for Count Dracula's dramatic landfall.

From the end of Church St, which has many shops selling jet jewellery, the 199 steps of **Church Stairs** will lead you steeply up to Whitby Abbey, passing the equally atmospheric **St Mary's Church** (◷10am-5pm Apr-Oct, to 4pm Nov-Mar) and its spooky graveyard, a favourite haunt of courting goth couples.

Captain Cook Memorial Museum MUSEUM
(www.cookmuseumwhitby.co.uk; Grape Lane; adult/ child £4.50/3; ◷9.45am-5pm Apr-Oct, 11am-3pm Mar) This fascinating museum occupies the house of the ship owner with whom Cook began his seafaring career. Highlights include the attic where Cook lodged as a young apprentice, Cook's own maps and letters, etchings from the South Seas, and a wonderful model of the *Endeavour*, with the crew and stores all laid out for inspection.

Whitby Sands BEACH
Whitby's days as a seaside resort continue, with donkey rides, ice cream and bucket-and-spade escapades on Whitby Sands, stretching west from the harbour mouth. Atop the cliff on the harbour's west side, the **Captain Cook Monument** shows the great

Whitby

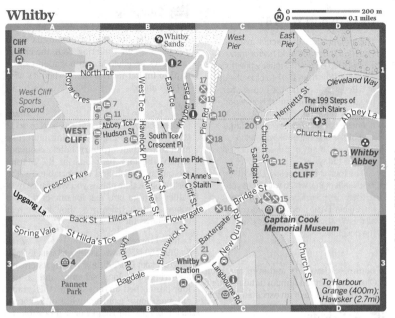

Whitby

⊙ Top Sights

⊙ Sights

⊙ Activities, Courses & Tours

⊙ Sleeping

⊗ Eating

⊙ Drinking

man looking out to sea, often with a seagull perched on his head. Nearby is the Whalebone Arch, which recalls Whitby's days as a whaling port. Whitby Sands can be reached from West Cliff via the cliff lift (per person 65p; ⊙May-Sep), an elevator that has been in service since 1931.

Whitby Museum   MUSEUM
(www.whitbymuseum.org.uk; Pannett Park; adult/child £4/1; ⊙9.30am-4.30pm Tue-Sun) Set in a park to the west of the town centre is the wonderfully eclectic Whitby Museum, with displays of fossil plesiosaurs and dinosaur footprints, Captain Cook memorabilia, ships

DRACULA IN WHITBY

The famous story of *Dracula*, inspiration for a thousand lurid horror movies, was written by Bram Stoker while holidaying in Whitby in 1897 (a blue plaque at 6 Royal Cres marks the house where he stayed). Although most Hollywood versions of the tale concentrate on deepest, darkest Transylvania, a large part of the original book was set in Whitby, and many of the sites can still be seen today.

The tourist office sells a *Dracula Trail* leaflet (£1), which will direct you to the Bram Stoker memorial seat on Khyber Pass. From here, you can see all the Whitby-based settings used in the novel.

in bottles, jet jewellery and even the 'Hand of Glory', a preserved human hand reputedly cut from the corpse of an executed criminal.

🏃 Activities

For a cracking day out, take a bus to Robin Hood's Bay, explore the village, have lunch, and then hike the 6-mile clifftop footpath back to Whitby (allow three hours).

First choice for a bike ride is the excellent 20-mile Whitby-to-Scarborough Coastal Cycle Trail, which starts a mile south of the town centre and follows the route of an old railway line via Robin Hood's Bay. Bikes can be hired for £15 to £22 a day from Dr Crank's Bike Shack (☎01947-606661; 20 Skinner St; ⊙10am-4.30pm Mon, Tue & Thu-Sat) in Whitby, or Trailways (www.trailways.info) at Hawsker.

⭐ Festivals & Events

Whitby Goth Weekends   COUNTER CULTURE
(www.whitbygothweekend.co.uk; tickets £50) Goth heaven, with gigs, events and the Bizarre Bazaar – dozens of traders selling goth gear, jewellery, art and music. Held twice yearly on the last weekends of April and October.

Whitby Spring Session   MUSIC & ARTS
(www.moorandcoast.co.uk; tickets from £35) Beards, sandals and real ale abound at this traditional festival of folk music, dance and dubious Celtic art on the May Bank Holiday weekend.

🛏 Sleeping

B&Bs are concentrated in West Cliff in the streets to the south and east of Royal Cres. If a house here ain't offering B&B, the chances are it's derelict. Accommodation can be hard to find at festival times when it's wise to book ahead.

TOP CHOICE Marine Hotel   INN ££££
(☎01947-605022; www.the-marine-hotel.co.uk; 13 Marine Pde; r £135-150; 🛜) Feeling more like mini-suites than ordinary hotel accommodation, the four bedrooms at the Marine are quirky, stylish and comfortable. It's the sort of place that makes you want to stay in rather than go out. Ask for one of the two rooms with a balcony – they have great views across the harbour.

Langley Hotel   B&B ££
(☎01947-604250; www.langleyhotel.com; 16 Royal Cres; s/d from £70/105; P🛜) With its cream-and-crimson colour scheme, and a gilt four-poster bed in one room, this grand old guesthouse exudes a whiff of Victorian splendour. Go for room 1 or 2, if possible, to make the most of the panoramic views from West Cliff.

Avalon Hotel   B&B ££
(☎01947-825315; www.avalonhotelwhitby.org.uk; 13-14 Royal Cres; d from £66) Just a few doors along from the house where Bram Stoker stayed during his holiday in 1897, the Avalon shares the same glorious sea views as those enjoyed by the author of *Dracula*. The rooms are clean and comfortable (many have recently been refurbished) and the owner is as friendly and helpful as you could hope for.

Shepherd's Purse   GUESTHOUSE ££
(☎01947-820228; www.theshepherdspurse.com; 95 Church St; r £60-75) This place combines a beads-and-baubles boutique and whole-food shop with guest accommodation in the courtyard at the back. The plainer rooms share a bathroom and are perfectly adequate, but we recommend the rustic en suite bedrooms situated around the courtyard. While the four-poster beds feel a bit as though they've been shoehorned in, the atmosphere is cute rather than cramped. Breakfast is not provided.

Whitby YHA   HOSTEL £
(☎0845-371 9049; www.yha.org.uk; Church Lane; dm £18-22; P@🛜) With an unbeatable po-

sition next to the abbey, this hostel doesn't need to try too hard, and it doesn't. You'll have to book well in advance to get your body into one of the basic bunks. Hike up the 199 steps from the town, or take bus 97 from the train station to Whitby Abbey (twice hourly Monday to Saturday).

Harbour Grange HOSTEL £
(☑01947-600817; www.whitbybackpackers.co.uk; Spital Bridge; dm from £17) Overlooking the harbour and less than 10 minutes' walk from the train station, this tidy hostel is conveniently located but has an 11.30pm curfew – just the ticket for a night when you don't want to paint the town red.

Trailways SELF CATERING ££
(☑01947-820207; www.trailways.info; Hawsker; for 3 nights from £290; P) If travelling on the North Yorkshire Moors Railway has given you a taste for trains, how about sleeping in one? Trailways has a beautifully converted InterCity 125 coach parked at the old Hawsker train station on the Whitby–Scarborough cycle route, offering luxurious self-catering accommodation with all mod cons for two to seven people.

Rosslyn House B&B ££
(☑01947-604086; www.guesthousewhitby.co.uk; 11 Abbey Tce; s/d from £40/58) Bright and cheerful with a friendly welcome.

Bramblewick B&B ££
(☑01947-604504; www.bramblewickwhitby.com; 3 Havelock Pl; s/d £35/70; P☎) Friendly owners, hearty breakfasts and abbey views from the top-floor room.

Argyle House B&B ££
(☑01947-602733; www.argyle-house.co.uk; 18 Hudson St; per person £28-35; ☎) Comfortable as old slippers, with kippers for breakfast.

✖ Eating & Drinking

Green's SEAFOOD ££
(☑01947-600284; www.greensofwhitby.com; 13 Bridge St; mains £13-20; ☺lunch & dinner) The classiest eatery in town is ideally situated to take its pick of the fish and shellfish freshly landed at the harbour. Grab a hearty lunch in the ground-floor bistro (mussels and chips, sausage and mash, fish and chips), or head to the upstairs restaurant for a sophisticated dinner date.

Moon & Sixpence BRASSERIE ££
(☑01947-604416; www.moon-and-sixpence.co.uk; 5 Marine Pde; mains £10-16; ☺10am-midnight; ☎)

This brasserie and cocktail bar has a prime position, with views across the harbour to the abbey ruins. The seafood-dominated menu concentrates on hearty, straightforward dishes such as chunky vegetable soup, seafood chowder, fish pie, homemade burgers, and mussels and chips.

Magpie Cafe SEAFOOD ££
(www.magpiecafe.co.uk; 14 Pier Rd; mains £5-16; ☺lunch & dinner) The Magpie flaunts its reputation for serving the 'World's Best Fish and Chips'. Damn fine they are too, but the world and his dog knows about it and summertime queues can stretch along the street. Fish and chips from the takeaway counter cost £5; the sit-down restaurant is dearer, but offers a wide range of seafood dishes, from grilled sea bass to paella.

Humble Pie 'n' Mash BRITISH £
(www.humblepienmash.com; 163 Church St; mains £5; ☺lunch & dinner Mon-Sat, lunch Sun) Superb homemade pies with fillings ranging from lamb, leek and rosemary to roast veg and goat's cheese, served in a cosy timber-framed cottage.

Java Cafe-Bar CAFE £
(2 Flowergate; mains £5-7; ☺8am-6pm; ☎) A cool little diner with stainless-steel counters and retro decor, music videos on the flatscreen and a menu of healthy salads, sandwiches and wraps washed down with excellent coffee.

YORKSHIRE WHITBY

CAPTAIN COOK – WHITBY'S ADOPTED SON

Although he was born in Marton (now a suburb of Middlesbrough), the renowned explorer Captain James Cook has been adopted by Whitby. Ever since the first tourists got off the train in Victorian times, local entrepreneurs have mercilessly cashed in on Cook's memory, as endless Endeavour Cafes and Captain Cook Chip Shops testify.

Still, Whitby played a key role in Cook's eventual success as a world-famous explorer. It was here that he first went to sea, serving his apprenticeship with local ship owners, and the design of ships used for his voyages of discovery – including the *Endeavour* – were based on the design of Whitby 'cats', flat-bottomed ships that carried coal from Newcastle to London.

Quayside   FISH & CHIPS ££

(www.whitbyfishandchips.com; 7 Pier Rd; mains £7-14; ☉lunch & dinner; 📶) Top-notch fish and chips minus the 'world's best' tag line – this place is your best bet if you want to avoid queues. Takeaway prices are £5.

Station Inn   PUB

(New Quay Rd) The best place in town for atmosphere and real ale, with its impressive range of cask-conditioned beers including Timothy Taylor's Golden Best and Ossett Silver King.

Duke of York   PUB

(www.dukeofyork.co.uk; Church St) A popular watering hole at the bottom of the Church Stairs, serving great views over the harbour and Timothy Taylor ales.

ℹ Information

Post office (Langbourne Rd; ☉8.30am-5.30pm Mon-Sat) Located inside the Co-op supermarket.

Tourist office (📞01947-602674; www.visit whitby.com; Langbourne Rd; ☉9.30am-6pm May-Sep, 10am-4.30pm Oct-Apr)

ℹ Getting There & Away

BUS Buses 93 and X93 run south to Scarborough (one hour, every 30 minutes), with every second bus going via Robin Hood's Bay (15 minutes, hourly), and north to Middlesbrough (one hour, hourly), with fewer services on Sunday. The Coastliner service 840 runs from Leeds to Whitby (£12.50, 3¼ hours, six times daily Monday to Saturday) via York and Pickering.

TRAIN Coming from the north, you can get to Whitby by train along the Esk Valley Railway from Middlesbrough (£5.30, 1½ hours, four per day), with connections from Durham and Newcastle. From the south, it's easier to get a train from York to Scarborough, and then a bus from Scarborough to Whitby.

Robin Hood's Bay

Picturesque Robin Hood's Bay (www.robin -hoods-bay.co.uk) is the end point of the Coast to Coast Walk (p483). It has nothing to do with the hero of Sherwood Forest – the origin of its name is a mystery, and the locals call it Bay Town or just Bay. But there's no denying that this fishing village is one of the prettiest spots on the Yorkshire coast.

Leave your car at the parking area in the upper village (minimum charge £3 for four hours), where 19th-century ships' captains built comfortable Victorian villas, and walk downhill to Old Bay, the oldest part of the village (don't even think about driving down). This maze of narrow lanes and passages is dotted with tearooms, pubs, craft shops and artists' studios (there's even a tiny cinema) and at low tide you can go down onto the beach and fossick around in the rock pools. The NT-listed Old Coastguard Station (www.nationaltrust.org.uk; The Dock; admission free; ☉10am-5pm Apr-Oct, to 4pm Sat & Sun Nov-Mar) houses an exhibition about local geology and natural history.

There are several pubs and cafes. The best pub for ambience and real ale is Ye Dolphin (King St), while the Swell Cafe (www.swell.org. uk; Chapel St; mains £5-7; ☉10am-4pm Mon-Fri, to 4.30pm Sat & Sun) does great coffee and has a terrace with a view over the beach.

Robin Hood's Bay is 6 miles south of Whitby. You can walk here along the coastal path in two or three hours, or bike to it along the cycle trail in 40 minutes. Bus 93 runs hourly between Whitby and Scarborough via Robin Hood's Bay – the bus stop is at the top of the hill, in the new part of town.

YORKSHIRE DALES NATIONAL PARK

The Yorkshire Dales – named from the old Norse word *dalr*, meaning 'valleys' – is the central jewel in the necklace of three national parks strung across northern England, with the dramatic fells of the Lake District to the west and the brooding heaths of the North York Moors to the east.

From well-known names such as Wensleydale and Ribblesdale to the obscure and evocative Langstrothdale and Arkengarthdale, the park's glacial valleys are characterised by a distinctive landscape of high heather moorland, stepped skylines and flat-topped hills. Down in the green valleys, patchworked with drystone dykes, are picture-postcard towns and hamlets where sheep and cattle still graze on village greens. And in the limestone country in the southern Dales, you'll find England's best examples of karst scenery (created by rainwater dissolving the underlying limestone bedrock).

The Dales have been protected as a national park since the 1950s, assuring their status as a walker's and cyclist's paradise. But there's plenty for nonwalkers as well, from

Yorkshire Dales National Park

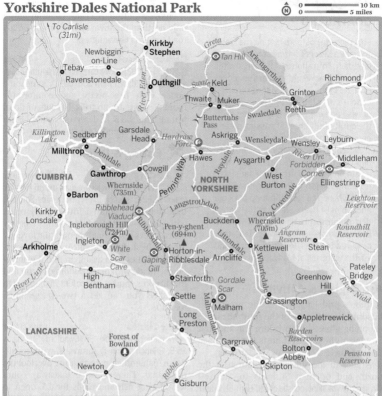

exploring the legacy of literary vet James Herriot of *All Creatures Great and Small* fame to sampling the favourite teatime snack of the British TV characters Wallace and Gromit at the Wensleydale Creamery.

The *Visitor* newspaper, available from tourist offices, lists local events and walks guided by park rangers, as well as many places to stay and eat. The official park website (www.yorkshiredales.org.uk) is also useful.

❶ Getting There & Around

About 90% of visitors to the park arrive by car, and the narrow roads can become extremely crowded in summer. Parking can also be a serious problem. If you can, try to use public transport as much as possible.

Pick up a Dales Bus Timetable from tourist offices, or consult the **Dalesbus** (www.dalesbus.org) website.

By train, the best and most interesting access to the Dales is via the famous **Settle–Carlisle Line** (www.settle-carlisle.co.uk). Trains run between Leeds and Carlisle, stopping at Skipton, Settle and numerous small villages, offering unrivalled access to the hills straight from the station platform.

Skipton

POP 14,300

This busy market town on the southern edge of the Dales takes its name from the Anglo-Saxon *sceape ton* (sheep town). There are no prizes for guessing how it made its money. Monday, Wednesday, Friday and Saturday are market days on High St, bringing crowds from all over and giving the town something of a festive atmosphere. The tourist office (☑01756-792809; www.skiptononline.co.uk; Town Hall, High St; ◷9.30am-4.30pm Mon-Sat Apr-Oct, to 4pm Nov-Mar) is in the town hall.

WORTH A TRIP

GOATHLAND

This picture-postcard halt on the North Yorkshire Moors Railway stars as Hogsmeade train station in the Harry Potter films, and the village appears as Aidensfield in the British TV series *Heartbeat*. It's also the starting point for lots of easy and enjoyable walks, often with the chuff-chuff-chuff of passing steam engines in the background.

One of the most popular hikes is to head northwest from the station (via a gate on the platform on the far side from the village) to the hamlet of Beck Hole, where you can stop for a pork pie and a pint of Black Sheep at the wonderfully atmospheric Birch Hall Inn (www.beckhole.info), where it's like stepping into the past. Return to Goathland via the waterfall at Mallyan Spout.

⊙ Sights & Activities

Skipton's pride and joy is the broad and bustling High St, one of the most attractive shopping streets in Yorkshire. On the first Sunday of the month it hosts the Northern Dales Farmers Market (www.ndfm.co.uk).

A gate to the side of the church at the north end of High St leads to Skipton Castle (www.skiptoncastle.co.uk; High St; adult/child £6.70/4.10; ⊙10am-6pm Mon-Sat, from noon Sun Mar-Sep, to 4pm Oct-Feb), one of the best-preserved medieval castles in England and a fascinating contrast to the ruins you'll see elsewhere.

No trip to Skipton is complete without a cruise along the Leeds–Liverpool Canal, which runs through the middle of town. Pennine Cruisers (www.penninecruisers.com; The Wharf, Coach St; adult/child £3/2; ⊙10.30am-dusk Mar-Oct) runs half-hour trips to Skipton Castle and back.

⊨ Sleeping

There's a strip of B&Bs just outside the centre on Keighley Rd. All those between numbers 46 and 57 are worth trying.

Park Hill B&B **££**
(☎01756-792772; www.parkhillskipton.co.uk; 17 Grassington Rd; d £75; P@☎) From the complimentary glass of sherry on arrival to the hearty breakfasts based on local produce, farm-fresh eggs and homegrown tomatoes, this B&B provides a real Yorkshire welcome. It enjoys an attractive rural location half a mile north of the town centre, on the B6265 road towards Grassington.

Carlton House B&B **££**
(☎01756-700921; www.carltonhouseskipton.co.uk; 46 Keighley Rd; s/d from £30/60) A handsome house with five pretty and comfortable rooms – there are no frills, but lots of floral prints. This B&B is deservedly popular on account of its friendly welcome.

✗ Eating & Drinking

Le Caveau FRENCH **££**
(☎01756-794274; www.lecaveau.co.uk; 86 High St; mains £13-23; ⊙lunch Tue-Fri, dinner Tue-Sat) Set in a stylishly decorated 16th-century cellar with barrel-vaulted ceilings, this friendly bistro offers a seasonal menu built lovingly around fresh local produce. Daily specials include dishes such as a light and flavourful quiche made with black pudding, bacon and mushrooms, and a succulent fish pie. On weekdays you can get a two-course lunch for £10.

Bizzie Lizzies FISH & CHIPS **£**
(www.bizzielizzies.co.uk; 36 Swadford St; mains £6-9; ⊙lunch & dinner) An award-winning sit-down fish-and-chip restaurant overlooking the canal. There's also a takeaway counter offering fish and chips for £5, open to 11.15pm.

Bean Loved CAFE **£**
(www.beanloved.co.uk; 17 Otley St; mains £5-9; ☎) This place just off High St serves the best coffee in town, along with good cakes and freshly prepared sandwiches.

Narrow Boat PUB
(38 Victoria St) A traditionally styled pub with a great selection of local ales and foreign beers, friendly service and bar meals.

❶ Getting There & Away

Skipton is the last stop on the Metro rail network from Leeds and Bradford (£8.40, 45 minutes, half-hourly, hourly on Sunday).

Grassington

The perfect base for jaunts around the south Dales, Grassington's handsome Georgian centre teems with walkers and visitors throughout the summer months, soaking up an atmosphere that – despite the odd touch of faux rusticity – is as attractive and traditional as you'll find in these parts.

The tourist office (☑01756-751690; Hebden Rd; ⏰9.30am-5pm Apr-Oct, Fri-Sun only Nov-Mar) is beside the big car park on the edge of town.

🛏 Sleeping & Eating

TOP CHOICE / Devonshire Fell   HOTEL **£££**

(☑01756-718111; www.devonshirefell.co.uk; Burnsall; s/d from £129/159; [P][@][🛜]) A sister property to Bolton Abbey's Devonshire Arms Country House Hotel, this former gentleman's club for mill owners has a much more contemporary feel, with beautiful modern furnishings crafted by local experts. The Conservatory Restaurant (also used as a breakfast room) has a stunning view over the valley. It's 3 miles southeast of Grassington on the B6160.

Ashfield House   B&B **££**

(☑01756-752584; www.ashfieldhouse.co.uk; Summers Fold; r from £96; [P][@][🛜]) A secluded 17th-century country house behind a walled garden, with exposed stone walls, open fireplaces and an all-round cosy feel. It's just off the main square.

Cobblestones Café   CAFE **£**

(3 The Square; mains £3-6; ⏰9.30am-5pm; 🌱) A cute little cafe, dog-friendly and popular with locals as well as visitors. In addition to cakes, coffee and Yorkshire tea, the menu includes lunch dishes such as fish and chips and steak-and-ale pie. A full English breakfast is served till noon.

Malham

POP 120

Stretching west from Grassington to Ingleton is the largest area of limestone country in England, a distinctive landscape dotted with dry valleys, potholes, limestone pavements and gorges. Two of the most spectacular features – Malham Cove and Gordale Scar – lie near the pretty village of Malham.

The national park centre (☑01969-652380; www.yorkshiredales.org.uk; ⏰10am-5pm daily Apr-Oct, to 4pm Sat & Sun only Nov-Mar) at the southern edge of the village has the usual wealth of information.

◉ Sights & Activities

A 0.75-mile walk north from Malham village leads to Malham Cove, a huge rock amphi-

theatre lined with 80m-high vertical cliffs. Peregrine falcons nest here in spring, when the Royal Society for the Protection of Birds (RSPB) sets up a birdwatching lookout. You can hike up the steep left-hand side of the cove (on the Pennine Way footpath) to see the extensive limestone pavement above the cliffs. Another 1.5 miles further north is Malham Tarn, a glacial lake and nature reserve.

A mile east of Malham along a narrow road (with very limited parking) is spectacular Gordale Scar, a deep limestone canyon with scenic cascades and the remains of an Iron Age settlement. The national park centre has a leaflet describing the Malham Landscape Trail, a 5-mile circular walk that takes in Malham Cove, Gordale Scar and the Janet's Foss waterfall.

The Pennine Way passes through Malham, with Horton-in-Ribblesdale a day's hike away to the northwest.

🛏 Sleeping

Beck Hall   HOTEL **££**

(☑01729-830332; www.beckhallmalham.com; s/d from £45/65; [P][🛜]) This rambling 17th-century country house on the edge of the village has 15 individually decorated rooms. We recommend the Green Room, with its old-style furnishings and four-poster bed. There's a gurgling stream flowing through the garden and a nice tearoom (open 11am to 6pm Tuesday to Sunday).

Malham YHA   HOSTEL **£**

(☑0845-371 9529; www.yha.org.uk; dm £19.50; [P][♿]) You will find this purpose-built hostel in the village centre. The facilities are top-notch and young children are well catered for.

❶ Getting There & Away

There are between two and five buses a day from Skipton to Malham. Check the Dalesbus (p513) website or ask at Skipton tourist office for details.

Note that Malham is reached via narrow roads that can get very congested in summer, so leave your car at the national park centre and walk into the village.

Ribblesdale & the Three Peaks

Scenic Ribblesdale cuts through the southwestern corner of the Yorkshire Dales National Park, where the skyline is dominated

THREE PEAKS CHALLENGES

Since 1968 more than 200,000 hikers have taken up the challenge of climbing Yorkshire's Three Peaks in less than 12 hours. The circular 25-mile route begins and ends at the Pen-y-Ghent Cafe in Horton-in-Ribblesdale (where you clock-in and clock-out to verify your time) and takes in the summits of Pen-y-ghent, Whernside and Ingleborough. Succeed and you become a member of the cafe's Three Peaks of Yorkshire Club. You can find details of the route at www.merseyventure.com/yorks and download a guide (£4) at www.walkingworld.com (walk ID 4228 and 4229).

Fancy a more gruelling test of your endurance? Then join the fell-runners in the annual Three Peaks Race (www.threepeaksrace.org.uk) on the last Saturday in April, and run the route instead of walking it. First held in 1954 when six people competed, it now attracts about 900 entries. The course record is two hours, 43 minutes and three seconds.

In the last week of September, cyclists get their chance in the Three Peaks Cyclo-Cross (www.3peakscyclocross.org.uk), which covers 38 miles of rough country and climbs 1524m.

by a trio of distinctive hills known as the Three Peaks – Whernside (735m), Ingleborough (724m) and Pen-y-ghent (694m). Easily accessible via the Settle–Carlisle railway line, this is one of England's most popular areas for outdoor activities, attracting thousands of hikers, cyclists and cavers each weekend.

SETTLE
POP 3621

The busy market town of Settle, dominated by its grand neogothic town hall, is the gateway to Ribblesdale and marks the beginning of the scenic part of the famous Settle–Carlisle railway line. Narrow cobbled streets lined with shops and pubs lead out from the central market square (Tuesday is market day), and the town offers plenty of accommodation options.

The tourist office (☎01729-825192; Town Hall, Cheapside; ⊙9.30am-4.30pm Apr-Oct, to 4pm Nov-Mar) has maps and guidebooks.

Around the main square are several good cafes, including Ye Olde Naked Man (Market Pl; mains £4-7), formerly an undertaker's (look for the 'naked man' on the outside wall, dated 1663), and the excellent Shambles (Market Pl; mains £6-8) fish-and-chip shop.

Trains from Leeds heading to Carlisle stop at Settle station near the town centre (£11, one hour, eight daily). Those heading for Morecambe (on the west coast) stop at Giggleswick, about 1.5 miles outside town.

HORTON-IN-RIBBLESDALE
POP 560

A favourite with outdoor enthusiasts, the little village of Horton and its railway station is 5 miles north of Settle. Everything centres

on the Pen-y-Ghent Cafe, which acts as the village tourist office, wet-weather retreat and hikers' information centre.

Horton is the starting point for climbing Pen-y-ghent and doing the Three Peaks Walk; it's also a stop on the Pennine Way. At the head of the valley, 5 miles north of Horton, is the spectacular 30m-high Ribblehead Viaduct, built in 1874 and, at 400m, the longest on the Settle–Carlisle line. You can hike there along the Pennine Way and travel back by train from Ribblehead station.

🛏 Sleeping & Eating

Horton is popular, so it's advisable to book accommodation in advance.

Golden Lion   INN £
(☎01729-860206; www.goldenlionhotel.co.uk; s/d from £40/65, dm £12) The Golden Lion is a lively pub that offers comfortable B&B rooms, a 40-bed bunkhouse, and three public bars where you can tuck into a bit of grub washed down with a pint of hand-pulled ale.

Holme Farm Campsite   CAMPSITE £
(☎01729-860281; per person £2, per tent £2) A basic, no-frills campsite next door to the Golden Lion pub, much used by Pennine Way hikers.

Pen-y-Ghent Cafe   CAFE £
(mains £3-6; ⊙9am-5.30pm Mon & Wed-Fri, 8.30am-5pm Sat & Sun) A traditional cafe run by the same family since 1965, the Pen-y-Ghent fills walkers' fuel tanks with fried eggs and chips, homemade scones and pint-sized mugs of tea. It also sells maps, guidebooks and walking gear.

INGLETON
POP 2000

The village of Ingleton, perched precariously above a river gorge, is the caving capital of England. It sits at the foot of one of the country's most extensive areas of limestone, crowned by the dominating peak of Ingleborough and riddled with countless potholes and cave systems.

The tourist office (☑01524-241049; www. visitingleton.co.uk; ☺10am-4pm Apr-Sep) is beside the main car park, while Bernie's Cafe (4 Main St; ☺9am-4pm Mon, Wed & Thu, to 6pm Fri-Sun) is the centre of the local caving scene.

Ingleton is the starting point for two famous Dales hikes. The shorter and easier of the two is the circular, 4.5-mile Waterfalls Walk (www.ingletonwaterfallstrail.co.uk; adult/child £5/2), which passes through native oak woodland on its way past a series of spectacular waterfalls on the Rivers Twiss and Doe. The more strenuous option is Ingleborough (724m). About 120,000 people climb this hill every year, but that doesn't make the 6-mile round trip any less of an effort. This is a proper hill walk, so pack waterproofs, food, water, a map and a compass.

Although most of the local caves are accessible only to experienced potholers, some are open to the general public. White Scar Cave (www.whitescarcave.co.uk; 80-min guided tours adult/child £8.50/5.50; ☺10am-4.30pm Feb-Oct, Sat & Sun only Nov-Jan) is the longest show cave in England, with a series of underground waterfalls and impressive dripstone formations leading to the 100m-long Battlefield Cavern, one of the largest cave chambers in the country. The cave is 1.5 miles northeast of the village on the B6255 road.

Gaping Gill, on the southeastern flank of Ingleborough, is one of the most famous caves in England. A huge vertical pothole 105m deep, it was the largest known cave shaft in Britain until the discovery of Titan in Derbyshire in 1999. Gaping Gill is normally off limits to noncavers, but twice a year on the May and August bank holiday weekends, local caving clubs set up a winch so that members of the public can descend into the depths in a special chair (£10 per person). For details, see www.bpc-cave.org. uk and www.cravenpotholeclub.org, and click on the Gaping Gill link.

Ingleton is 10 miles northwest of Settle. Take bus 581 from Settle train station (25 minutes, two daily).

Hawes
POP 700

Hawes is the beating heart of Wensleydale, a thriving and picturesque market town (market day is Tuesday) that has the added attraction of its own waterfall in the village centre. On busy summer weekends, however, Hawes' narrow arteries can get seriously clogged with traffic. Leave the car in the parking area beside the national park centre (☑01969-666210; Station Yard; ☺10am-5pm) at the eastern entrance to the village.

◉ Sights & Activities

Sharing a building with the park centre is the Dales Countryside Museum (☑01969-666210; Station Yard; adult/child £4/free; ☺10am-5pm, closed Jan), a beautifully presented social history of the area that explains the forces shaping the landscape, from geology to lead mining to land enclosure.

At the other end of town lies the Wensleydale Creamery (www.wensleydale.co.uk; tours £2.50; ☺9.30am-5pm Mon-Sat, 10am-4.30pm Sun), devoted to the production of the animated TV characters Wallace and Gromit's favourite crumbly white cheese. You can visit the cheese museum and then try-before-you-buy in the shop, which is free to enter. There are one-hour guided tours of the creamery between 10am and 3pm.

About 1.5 miles north of Hawes is 30m-high Hardraw Force, the highest unbroken waterfall in England, but by international standards not that impressive (except after heavy rain). Access is through the Green Dragon Inn, which levies a £2 admission fee.

⬛ Sleeping & Eating

Herriot's Guest House   B&B ££
(☑01969-667536; www.herriotsinhawes.co.uk; Main St; r per person from £40; ☎) A delightful guesthouse set in an old stone building close to the bridge by the waterfall, Herriot's has seven comfy en suite bedrooms set above an art gallery and coffee shop.

Green Dragon Inn   INN ££
(☑01969-667392; www.greendragonhardraw.co.uk; Hardraw; B&B per person £35-45, dm £15; ☎) A fine old pub with flagstone floors, low timber beams, ancient oak furniture and Theakston's on draught. The Dragon serves up a tasty steak-and-ale pie and offers bunkhouse accommodation or B&B in plain but adequate

YORKSHIRE HAWES

rooms, as well as a pair of larger, more comfortable suites.

Bainbridge Ings Caravan & Camp Site CAMPSITE £
(☑01969-667354; www.bainbridge-ings.co.uk; hikers & cyclists per person £5, car, tent & 2 adults £14; 🐾) An attractive site set around a spacious farmhouse in stone-walled fields about half a mile east of town. Gas, milk and eggs are sold on site.

Hawes YHA HOSTEL £
(☑0845-371 9120; www.yha.org.uk; Lancaster Tce; dm £19.50; P🐾) A modern place on the western edge of town, at the junction of the main A684 (Aysgarth Rd) and B6255, this is a family-friendly hostel with great views of Wensleydale.

Cart House TEAROOM £
(☑01969-667691; Hardraw; mains £6; ⊙Mar-Nov) Across the bridge from the Green Dragon, this craft shop and tearoom offers a healthier diet of homemade soup, organic bread and a 'Fellman's Lunch' of Wensleydale cheese, pickle and salad. There's a basic campsite at the back (£11 for two adults, tent and car).

ℹ Getting There & Away

Buses 156 and 157 run from Hawes to Leyburn (50 minutes, four daily Monday to Saturday), where you can connect with buses to or from Richmond.

From Garsdale station on the Settle–Carlisle Line, bus 113 runs to Hawes (20 minutes, three daily Monday to Friday). On Sundays and bank holidays from April to October, bus 831 goes to Hawes from Ribblehead station (25 minutes, one daily). Check bus times with Traveline Yorkshire (p483) or a tourist office before using these routes.

Richmond

POP 8200

The handsome market town of Richmond is one of England's best-kept secrets, perched on a rocky outcrop overlooking the River Swale and guarded by the ruins of a massive castle. A maze of cobbled streets radiates from the broad, sloping market square (market day is Saturday), lined with elegant Georgian buildings and photogenic stone cottages, with glimpses of the surrounding hills and dales peeking through the gaps.

◉ Sights

Top of the pile is the impressive heap that is **Richmond Castle** (www.english-heritage. org.uk; Market Pl; adult/child £4.70/2.80; ⊙10am-6pm Apr-Sep, reduced hours at other times), founded in 1070 and one of the first castles in England since Roman times to be built of stone. It's had many uses through the years, including a stint as a prison for conscientious objectors during WWI (there's a small and sobering exhibition about their part in the castle's history). The best part is the view from the top of the remarkably well-preserved 30m-high keep, which towers over the River Swale.

Military buffs will enjoy the **Green Howards Museum** (www.greenhowards.org. uk; Trinity Church Sq; adult/child £3.50/1; ⊙10am-4.30pm Mon-Sat, also 12.30-4.30pm Sun Apr-Oct, closed Jan), which pays tribute to the famous Yorkshire regiment. In a different vein, the **Richmondshire Museum** (www.richmond shiremuseum.org.uk; Ryder's Wynd; adult/child £3/free; ⊙10.30am-4pm Apr-Oct) is a delight, with local history exhibits including an early Yorkshire cave-dweller and displays about lead mining, which forever altered the Swaledale landscape a century ago. You can also see the original set that served as James Herriot's surgery in the TV series *All Creatures Great and Small*.

The **Georgian Theatre Royal** (www.georg iantheatreroyal.co.uk; Victoria Rd; tours per person £3.50; ⊙tours hourly 10am-4pm Mon-Sat Feb-Dec), built in 1788, is the most complete Georgian playhouse in Britain. Tours include a look at the country's oldest surviving stage scenery, painted between 1818 and 1836.

🏃 Activities

Walkers can follow paths along the River Swale both upstream and downstream from the town. A longer option is to follow part of the famous long-distance Coast to Coast Walk (p483) all the way to Reeth (11 miles) and take the bus back (see www.dalesbus. info/richmond).

In September/October the town hosts the **Richmond Walking & Book Festival** (www. booksandboots.org), 10 days of guided walks, talks, films and other events.

Cyclists can also follow Swaledale – as far as Reeth may be enough, while a trip along Arkengarthdale and then over the high wild moors to Kirkby Stephen via the Tan Hill Inn is a more serious (but very rewarding) 40-mile undertaking.

THE SETTLE–CARLISLE LINE

The 72-mile Settle–Carlisle Line (SCL), built between 1869 and 1875, offers one of England's most scenic railway journeys. The line's construction was one of the great engineering achievements of the Victorian era: 5000 navvies armed with picks and shovels built 325 bridges and 21 viaducts and blasted 14 tunnels in horrific conditions – nearly 200 of them died in the process.

Trains run between Leeds and Carlisle via Settle about eight times per day. The first section of the journey from Leeds is along the Aire Valley, stopping at Keighley, where the Keighley & Worth Valley Railway branches off to Haworth, Skipton (gateway to the southern Dales) and Settle. The train then labours up the valley beside the River Ribble, through Horton-in-Ribblesdale, across the spectacular Ribblehead Viaduct and then through Blea Moor Tunnel to reach remote Dent station, at 350m the highest mainline station in the country.

The line reaches its highest point (356m) at Ais Gill, where it leaves the Dales behind before easing down to Kirkby Stephen. The last halts are Appleby and Langwathby, just northeast of Penrith (a jumping-off point for the Lake District), before the train finally pulls into Carlisle.

The entire journey from Leeds to Carlisle takes two hours and 40 minutes and costs £26/32 for a single/day return. Various hop-on/hop-off passes are also available for one or three days. You can pick up a free SCL timetable – which includes a colour map of the line and brief details about places of interest – from most Yorkshire stations. For more information, contact National Rail Enquiries (☏08457-48 49 50; www.nationalrail.co.uk) or see www.settle-carlisle.co.uk.

🛏 Sleeping

There's a batch of pleasant places to stay along Frenchgate, and a couple more on Pottergate (the road into town from the east).

TOP CHOICE Millgate House   B&B £££

(☏01748-823571; www.millgatehouse.com; Market Pl; r £110-145; P@) Behind an unassuming grey door lies the unexpected pleasure of one of the most attractive guesthouses in England. While the house itself is a Georgian gem crammed with period details, it is overshadowed by the multi-award-winning garden at the back, which offers superb views over the River Swale and the Cleveland Hills. If possible, book the Garden Suite.

Frenchgate Hotel   HOTEL ££

(☏01748-822087; www.thefrenchgate.co.uk; 59-61 Frenchgate; s/d from £88/118; P) Nine elegant bedrooms occupy the upper floors of this converted Georgian town house, now a boutique hotel decorated with local art. The rooms have cool designer fittings that set off a period fireplace here, a Victorian roll-top bath there. Downstairs there's an excellent restaurant (three-course dinner £34) and a hospitable lounge with oak beams and an open fire.

Willance House   B&B ££

(☏01748-824467; www.willancehouse.com; 24 Frenchgate; s/d £55/71; ☏) This oak-beamed house, built in 1600, has three immaculate rooms (one with a four-poster bed) that combine old-fashioned charm and all mod cons.

66 Frenchgate   B&B ££

(☏01748-823421; www.66frenchgate.co.uk; 66 Frenchgate; s/d £70/94; ☏) Three of the six stylish bedrooms have superb river views.

Pottergate Guesthouse   B&B ££

(☏01748-823826; 4 Pottergate; d from £60) Compact and chintzy, with a friendly and helpful proprietor.

✗ Eating & Drinking

Rustique   FRENCH ££

(☏01748-821565; www.rustiqueyork.co.uk; Chantry Wynd, Finkle St; mains £10-16; ⊗10am-9pm Mon-Sat, from noon Sun) Tucked away in an arcade, this cosy bistro has consistently impressed with its mastery of French country cooking, from *confit de canard* (duck slow roasted in its own fat) to *paupiette de poulet* (chicken breast stuffed with brie and sun-dried tomatoes). Booking is recommended.

Cross View Tearooms   TEAROOM £
(www.crossviewtearooms.co.uk; 38 Market Pl; mains £4-7; ⊘9am-5.30pm Mon-Sat) So popular with locals that you might have to queue for a table at lunchtime, the Cross View is the place to go for a hearty breakfast, homemade cakes, a hot lunch, or just a nice cup of tea.

Seasons Restaurant & Cafe   INTERNATIONAL ££
(www.restaurant-seasons.co.uk; Richmond Station, Station Rd; mains £6-15; ⊘9am-9pm Mon-Sat, to 7pm Sun) Housed in the restored Victorian station building, this attractive open-plan eatery shares space with a boutique brewery, artisan bakery, ice-cream factory and cheesemonger – and yes, all this local produce is on the menu.

Barkers   FISH & CHIPS £
(Trinity Church Sq; mains £7-10; ⊘11am-9.30pm) The best fish and chips in town, sit-down or takeaway.

Black Lion Hotel   PUB
(Finkle St) Cosy bars, low beams and good beer and food.

Unicorn Inn   PUB
(2 Newbiggin) A determinedly old-fashioned free house, serving Theakston's and Old Speckled Hen.

❶ Information

The **tourist office** (☑01748-828742; www.richmond.org; Friary Gardens, Victoria Rd; ⊘9.30am-5.30pm Apr-Oct, to 4.30pm Nov-Mar) has the usual maps and guides, plus several leaflets showing walks in town and the surrounding countryside.

❶ Getting There & Away

From Darlington (on the railway between London and Edinburgh), it's easy to reach Richmond on bus 27 or X27 (30 minutes, every half hour, hourly on Sunday). All buses stop in Market Pl.

On Sundays and bank holiday Mondays only, from May to October, the Northern Dalesman bus 830 runs from Richmond to Hawes (1½ hours, one daily) via Reeth, and continues on to Ribblehead and Ingleton (2 hours, one daily).

WEST YORKSHIRE

It was the tough and unforgiving textile industry that drove West Yorkshire's economy from the 18th century onward. The woollen mills, factories and canals built to transport raw materials and finished products defined much of the county's landscape. But that's all in the past, and recent years have seen the transformation of this once hard-bitten area into quite the picture postcard.

Leeds and Bradford, two adjoining cities so big they've virtually become one, are the perfect case in point. Though both were founded amid the dark satanic mills of the Industrial Revolution, both are undergoing radical redevelopment and reinvention, prettifying their town centres and trying to tempt the more adventurous tourist with a host of new museums, galleries, restaurants and bars.

Beyond the cities, West Yorkshire is a landscape of bleak moorland dissected by deep valleys dotted with old mill towns and villages. The relics of the wool and cloth industries are still visible in the rows of weavers' cottages and workers' houses built along ridges overlooking the towering chimneys of the mills in the valleys – landscapes that were so vividly described by the Brontë sisters, West Yorkshire's most renowned literary export and biggest tourist draw.

❶ Getting Around

The Metro is West Yorkshire's highly efficient train and bus network, centred on Leeds and Bradford – which are also the main gateways to the county. For transport information, call **West Yorkshire Metro** (☑0113-245 7676; www.wymetro.com).

Day Rover (£7.10) tickets are good for unlimited travel on Metro buses and trains after 9.30am on weekdays and all day at weekends. A range of additional Rover tickets covering buses and/or trains, plus heaps of useful Metro maps and timetables, are available from bus and train stations and most tourist offices in West Yorkshire.

Leeds
POP 750,200

One of the fastest-growing cities in the UK, Leeds is the glitzy embodiment of rediscovered northern self-confidence. More than a decade of redevelopment has seen the city centre transform from near-derelict mill town into a vision of 21st-century urban chic, with skyscraping office blocks, glass-and-steel waterfront apartment complexes and renovated Victorian shopping arcades. The financial crisis of 2008–10 saw many flagship development projects grind to a halt, but tower cranes are beginning to sprout on the skyline again and the massive new entertainment venue, the Leeds Arena (www.leeds.gov.uk/arena; Clay Pit Lane), was scheduled to open in 2013.

Known as the 'Knightsbridge of the North', Leeds has made itself a shopping mecca, its streets lined with bustling malls sporting the top names in fashion. And when you've shopped till you've dropped, there's a plethora of pubs, clubs and excellent restaurants to relax in. From cutting-edge couture to contemporary cuisine, Leeds will serve it to you on a plate (or more likely in a stylishly designed bag). Amid all this fashion-conscious finery, it seems fitting that the network of city bus routes includes peach, mauve and magenta lines as well as the more humdrum red, orange and blue.

◉ Sights

FREE Royal Armouries   MUSEUM
(www.royalarmouries.org; Armouries Dr; ⊘10am-5pm) Leeds' most interesting museum is undoubtedly the Royal Armouries, beside the snazzy Clarence Dock residential development. It was originally built to house armour and weapons from the Tower of London, but was subsequently expanded to cover 3000 years' worth of fighting and self-defence. It all sounds a bit macho, but the exhibits are as varied as they are fascinating. The films, live-action demonstrations and hands-on technology may awaken interests you never thought you had, from jousting to Indian elephant armour – we dare you not to learn something! To get here, walk east along the river from Centenary Footbridge (10 minutes), or take bus 28 from Albion St.

Leeds Industrial Museum   MUSEUM
(www.leeds.gov.uk/armleymills; Canal Rd; adult/child £3.30/1.20; ⊘10am-5pm Tue-Sat, 1-5pm Sun) One of the world's largest textile mills has been transformed into a museum telling the story of Leeds' industrial past, both glorious and ignominious. The city became rich off the sheep's back, but at some cost in human terms – working conditions were Dickensian. As well as a selection of working machinery, there's a particularly informative display about how cloth is made. The museum is 2 miles west of the city centre; take bus 5 from the train station to get here.

FREE Leeds Art Gallery   GALLERY
(www.leeds.gov.uk/artgallery; The Headrow; ⊘10am-5pm Mon, Tue & Thu-Sat, noon-5pm Wed, 1-5pm Sun) The municipal gallery is packed with 19th-

and 20th-century British heavyweights – Turner, Constable, Stanley Spencer, Wyndham Lewis et al – along with contemporary pieces by more recent arrivals such as Antony Gormley, sculptor of the *Angel of the North*.

FREE Henry Moore Institute   GALLERY
(www.henry-moore.org; The Headrow; ⊘11am-5.30pm Thu-Mon, to 8pm Wed) Housed in a converted Victorian warehouse in the city centre, this gallery showcases the work of 20th-century sculptors but not, despite the name, anything by Henry Moore (1898–1986), who graduated from the Leeds School of Art. To see works by Moore, head to the Yorkshire Sculpture Park.

✻ Festivals

The August Bank Holiday (the weekend preceding the last Monday in August) sees 50,000-plus music fans converge on Bramham Park, 10 miles outside the city centre, for the Leeds Festival (www.leedsfestival.com). Spread across four stages, it's one of England's biggest rock-music extravaganzas.

⌂ Sleeping

There are no budget options in the city centre, and the midrange choices here are either chain hotels or places we wouldn't recommend. If you want somewhere cheapish you'll be forced to head for the suburbs, where there are plenty of decent B&Bs and smallish hotels.

TOP CHOICE Quebecs   BOUTIQUE HOTEL £££
(☎0113-244 8989; www.quebecshotel.co.uk; 9 Quebec St; d/ste from £180/300; @⊠) Victorian grace at its opulent best is the theme of our favourite hotel in town, a conversion from the former Leeds & County Liberal Club. The elaborate wood panelling and heraldic stained-glass windows in the public areas are matched by the contemporary design of the bedrooms. Booking online can get you a room for as little as half the rack rate.

Roomzzz   APARTMENTS ££
(☎0844-499 4888; www.roomzzz.co.uk; 10 Swinegate & 2 Burley Rd; 2-person apt from £79; @⊠) This outfit offers bright and modern luxury apartments complete with fitted kitchen, with the added advantage of 24-hour hotel reception. Roomzzz Leeds City is located at 10 Swinegate, right in the city centre;

Leeds

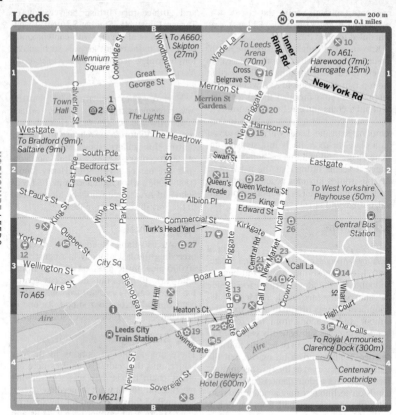

Roomzzz Leeds City West is half a mile west on Burley Rd.

42 The Calls
BOUTIQUE HOTEL **£££**

(☏0113-244 0099; www.42thecalls.co.uk; 42 The Calls; r/ste from £110/170; @☎) A snazzy boutique hotel in what was once a 19th-century grain mill overlooking the river, this place is a big hit with the trendy business crowd, who love its sharp, polished lines and designer aesthetic. The smaller 'study' rooms are pretty compact and breakfast is not included – it'll cost you an extra £15 for the full English.

Bewleys Hotel
HOTEL **££**

(☏0113-234 2340; www.bewleyshotels.com/leeds; City Walk, Sweet St; r from £64; P@☎) Bewleys is super-convenient for motorists, just off Junction 3 on the M621, but also just 10 minutes' walk from the city centre and with secure basement parking. Rooms are stylish and well appointed, with soundproofed walls and windows. The flat rate accommodates up to two adults plus two children under 12.

Moorlea
B&B **£**

(☏0113-243 2653; www.moorleahotel.co.uk; 146 Woodsley Rd; s/d from £40/50; ☎) Gay-friendly hotel northwest of the centre, near the University of Leeds.

Boundary Hotel Express
HOTEL **£**

(☏0113-275 7700; www.boundaryhotel.co.uk; 42 Cardigan Rd; s/d £42/54; P@☎) Basic but welcoming, the Express is 1.5 miles northwest of the centre, near Headingley cricket ground.

✗ Eating

The Leeds restaurant scene is constantly evolving, with new places springing up in the wake of new shopping and residential developments. The refurbished **Corn Exchange** (www.leedscornexchange.co.uk; ☎), a beautiful Victorian building with a spec-

Leeds

tacular domed roof, houses a branch of Anthony's, while celebrity chef James Martin's new restaurant, Leeds Kitchen, is in the recently opened Alea Casino at Clarence Dock.

Brasserie Blanc　　　　　　　FRENCH ££
(☏0113-220 6060; www.brasserieblanc.com; Victoria Mill, Sovereign St; mains £10-18; ⊙lunch & dinner Mon-Fri, noon-10.30pm Sat, noon-9pm Sun; ☝) Raymond Blanc manages to create a surprisingly intimate and romantic space amid the cast-iron pillars and red brick of an old Victorian warehouse, with a scattering of outdoor tables for sunny lunchtimes beside the river. The menu is unerringly French, from escargots (edible snails) to Toulouse sausage. The lunch and pre-7pm menu (6.30pm Saturday) offers three courses plus a glass of wine for £14.

Hansa's Gujarati　　　　　　　INDIAN £
(www.hansasrestaurant.com; 72-74 North St; mains £6-8; ⊙lunch Sun, dinner Mon-Sat; ✍) A Leeds institution, Hansa's has been dishing up wholesome Gujarati vegetarian cuisine for 20 years. The restaurant is plain and unassuming (save for a Hindu shrine), but the food is exquisite – specialities of the house include *samosa chaat*, a mix of spiced potato and chickpea samosas with a yoghurt and tamarind sauce.

Piazza by Anthony　　　　INTERNATIONAL ££
(www.anthonysrestaurant.co.uk; Corn Exchange, Call Lane; mains £10-18; ⊙10am-10pm Mon-Sat, to 9pm Sun; ☎) Leeds' landmark development is the refurbished Corn Exchange, with this cool and contemporary restaurant taking pride of place beneath a spectacular cast-iron Victorian roof. The all-day menu ranges from gourmet salads and sandwiches to pasta, meat, and fish dishes such as roast scallops with chorizo and butternut squash purée.

Pickles & Potter　　　　　DELI, CAFE £
(www.picklesandpotter.co.uk; 18-20 Queens Arcade; mains £4-5; ⊙9am-5pm Mon-Fri, to 6pm Sat, 10.30am-5pm Sun) This rustic cafe is famous for its superb sandwiches, especially the sumptuous roast-beef version complete with mustard, onion marmalade and fresh salad. There's also homemade soup, delicious cakes and a meat or vegetarian main course of the day.

Art's Cafe Bar & Restaurant　INTERNATIONAL ££
(www.artscafebar.co.uk; 42 Call Lane; mains £10-16; ⊙noon-11pm) Local art on the walls and a bohemian vibe throughout make this a popular place for quiet reflection, a chat and a really good cup of coffee. The dinner menu offers a half-dozen classic dishes, such as slow-cooked shoulder of venison and black pudding wrapped in Parma ham.

Anthony's
MODERN BRITISH £££

(☎0113-245 5922; www.anthonysrestaurant.co.uk; 19 Boar Lane; 2-/3-course dinner £36/45; ☺Tue-Sat) Anthony's serves top-notch Modern British cuisine to a clientele so eager that they'll think nothing of booking a month in advance. If you're going at any other time except Saturday evening, you'll get away with making your reservation a day or so in advance.

Create
MODERN BRITISH ££

(☎0113-242 0628; www.foodbycreate.co.uk/restaurant; 31 King St; 2-/3-course dinner £14/17; ☺11.30am-6pm Mon, to 10pm Tue-Sat) A new social-enterprise restaurant that not only serves superb British cuisine, it also provides jobs and work experience for homeless and marginalised people.

Leeds Kitchen
MODERN BRITISH ££

(☎0113-341 3266; www.theleedskitchen.co.uk; Alea Casino, Clarence Dock; mains £13-23; ☺lunch Sun, dinner Mon-Sat) Television celebrity chef James Martin's new restaurant serves the best of British produce with a gourmet twist. Close to the Royal Armouries museum.

Drinking

Leeds is renowned for its selection of pubs and bars. Glammed-up hordes of party animals crawl the cluster of venues around Boar and Call Lanes, where bars are opening (and closing) all the time. Most bars open till 2am and many turn into clubs after 11pm or midnight, with an admission charge.

Northbar
BAR

(www.northbar.com; 24 New Briggate) There's a Continental feel to this long and narrow, minimalist bar, enhanced by the unfamiliar beer labels, from Dortmunder and Duvel to Schneider and Snake Dog. In fact, Northbar is dedicated to the best of world beers, with more than a dozen ales on tap and dozens more in bottles.

Duck & Drake
PUB

(www.duckndrake.co.uk; 43 Kirkgate) A down-to-earth, traditional boozer with a well-worn atmosphere, a cast of regular pub characters and no fewer than 15 hand-pulled real ales to choose from. It also provides a stage for local rock and blues bands from Thursday to Sunday nights.

Whitelocks
PUB

(6-8 Turk's Head Yard) There's lots of polished wood, gleaming brass and colourful stained glass in this popular traditional pub, which dates from 1715. Theakston's, Deuchars IPA and several other real ales are on tap, and in summer the crowds spill out into the courtyard.

Baby Jupiter
BAR

(www.babyjupiter.co.uk; 11 York Pl) A retro gem with lots of purple velvet, hanging fishbowls and images from old sci-fi films, this basement bar sports a cool soundtrack that ranges from indie, funk and soul to punk, new wave and electro.

Sandinista
COCKTAIL BAR

(www.sandinistaleeds.co.uk; 5/5a Cross Belgrave St) This laid-back bar has a Latin look but a unifying theme, attracting an eclectic clientele with its mixed bag of music and unpretentious atmosphere. If you enjoy a well-mixed cocktail but aren't too fussed about looking glam, this is the spot for you.

Bar Fibre
BAR

(www.barfibre.com; 168 Lower Briggate) Leeds' most popular gay bar, which spills out onto the cleverly named Queen's Court, is where the beautiful set congregates. There's another cluster of gay bars downhill at the junction of Lower Briggate and The Calls.

Entertainment

In order to make sense of the ever-evolving scene, get your hands on the fortnightly *Leeds Guide* (www.leedsguide.co.uk; £1.50).

Nightclubs

The tremendous Leeds club scene attracts people from miles around. In true northern tradition, people brave the cold wearing next to nothing, even in winter, which is a spectacle in itself. Clubs charge a variety of admission prices, ranging from as little as £1 on a slow weeknight to £10 or more on Saturday.

HiFi Club
CLUB

(www.thehificlub.co.uk; 2 Central Rd) This intimate club is a good break from the hardcore sound of electronic dance: if it's Tamla Motown or the percussive beats of dance-floor jazz that shake your booty, this is the spot for you.

Cockpit
LIVE MUSIC

(www.thecockpit.co.uk; Swinegate) Snugly ensconced in a series of railway arches, the legendary Cockpit is the antidote to dance clubs. A live music venue of note (Coldplay, the White Stripes and the Flaming Lips have all cut their teeth here), it also hosts The Session on Friday nights, a superb indie/electro/guitar club night.

Mission CLUB

(www.clubmission.com; 8-13 Heaton's Ct) A massive club that redefines the term 'up for it'. Thursday sees the Full Moon Thai Beach Party student night, while Saturdays offer a range of house, dance and classic-anthem club nights, plus the Backdoor Disco gay club.

Wire CLUB

(www.wireclub.co.uk; 2-8 Call Lane; ⊘Thu-Sat plus some midweek nights) This small, atmospheric basement club, set in a forest of Victorian cast-iron pillars, throbs to a different beat every night, from rock and roll to drum and bass. Popular with local students.

Cinemas

Hyde Park Picture House CINEMA

(www.hydeparkpicturehouse.co.uk; Brudenell Rd) This Edwardian cinema shows a meaty range of art-house and mainstream choices. Take bus 56 from the city centre to get here.

Theatre & Opera

City Varieties MUSIC HALL

(www.cityvarieties.co.uk; Swan St) Founded in 1865, City Varieties is the world's longest running music hall, where the likes of Harry Houdini, Charlie Chaplin and Lily Langtry once trod the boards. Reopened after a major revamp, the program now features stand-up comedy, live music, pantomime and old-fashioned variety shows.

Grand Theatre &
Opera House MUSICALS, THEATRE

(www.leedsgrandtheatre.com; 46 New Briggate) Hosts musicals, plays and opera, including performances by the acclaimed Opera North (www.operanorth.co.uk).

West Yorkshire Playhouse THEATRE

(www.wyp.org.uk; Quarry Hill Mount) The Playhouse has a reputation for excellent live drama, from the classics to cutting-edge new writing. It's on the eastern edge of the city centre.

Sport

Leeds United Football Club FOOTBALL

(www.leedsunited.com; Elland Rd) Leeds supporters know all about pain: the team was relegated from the Premiership in 2004, and then from the Championship to League One in 2007. Loyal fans were rewarded with pro-

motion back to the Championship in 2010, and continue to pack the Elland Rd stadium in their masses. Take bus 93 or 96 from City Sq.

Yorkshire County Cricket Club CRICKET

(www.yorkshireccc.com; Headingley Carnegie Cricket Ground, St Michael's Lane) Headingley, the spiritual home of Yorkshire cricket, has been hosting cricket matches since 1890 and is still used for test matches. To get to the ground, take bus 18 or 56 from the city centre.

🛍 Shopping

Leeds' city centre has so many shopping arcades they all seem to blend into one giant mall. The latest development, Trinity Leeds (www.trinityleeds.com), scheduled to be open from 2013, is the city's biggest.

The mosaic-paved, stained-glass-roofed Victorian arcades of Victoria Quarter (www.v-q.co.uk), between Briggate and Vicar Lane, are well worth visiting for aesthetic reasons alone. Dedicated shoppers can join the footballers' wives browsing boutiques by Louis Vuitton, Vivienne Westwood and Swarovski. The flagship store here, of course, is Harvey Nichols (www.harveynichols.com; 107-111 Briggate).

Just across the street to the east, you'll find the opposite end of the retail spectrum in Leeds City Market (www.leedsmarket.com; Kirkgate; ⊘9am-5pm Mon-Sat, to 1pm Wed, open-air market Thu-Tue). Once the home of Michael Marks, who later joined forces with Spencer to become the retailing giant, this is Britain's largest covered market, selling fresh meat, fish and fruit and vegetables, as well as household goods.

ℹ Information

Gateway Yorkshire & Leeds visitor centre (☏0113-242 5242; www.visitleeds.co.uk; The Arcade, Leeds City Train Station; ⊘9am-5.30pm Mon-Sat, 10am-4pm Sun)

Post office (St John's Centre, 116 Albion St; ⊘9am-5.30pm Mon-Sat)

ℹ Getting There & Away

AIR Eleven miles northwest of the city via the A65, **Leeds Bradford International Airport** (www.leedsbradfordairport.co.uk) has flights to a range of domestic and international destinations. The Metroconnect 757 bus (£3.30, 40 minutes, every 30 minutes, hourly on Sunday) runs between Leeds bus station and the airport. A taxi costs about £20.

BUS National Express serves most major cities, including services from London (from £12, 4½ hours, hourly) and Manchester (from £5, 1¼ hours, every 30 minutes).

Yorkshire Coastliner (www.coastliner.co.uk) buses run from Leeds to York, Pickering, Goathland and Whitby (840); to York and Scarborough (843); and to Bridlington (845 and X45). A Freedom Ticket (£15) gives unlimited bus travel on all these services for a day.

TRAIN Leeds City Station has hourly services from London King's Cross (£50, 2½ hours), Sheffield (£13, one hour), Manchester (£15, one hour) and York (£12, 30 minutes).

Leeds is also the starting point for services on the famous Settle–Carlisle railway line.

ⓘ Getting Around

Leeds CityBus (www.wymetro.com; flat fare 50p) runs every few minutes from 6.30am to 7.30pm Monday to Saturday, linking the bus and train stations with all the main shopping areas in the city centre.

The various Day Rover passes covering trains and/or buses are good for reaching Bradford, Haworth and Hebden Bridge.

Bradford

Their suburbs may have merged into one sprawling urban conurbation, but Bradford remains far removed from its much more glamorous neighbour, Leeds. Thanks to its role as a major player in the wool trade, Bradford attracted large numbers of immigrants from Bangladesh and Pakistan during the 20th century. Despite occasional racial tensions, these new arrivals have helped reinvigorate the city and give it new energy (plus a reputation for superb curry restaurants). A high point of the year is the colourful Bradford Mela (www.bradfordmela. org.uk), a two-day celebration of Asian music, dance, arts, crafts and food in mid-June.

Bradford's top attraction is the National Media Museum (www.nationalmediamuseum. org.uk; off Little Horton Lane; ⊙10am-6pm, closed 25 Dec), an impressive glass-fronted building that chronicles the story of photography, film, TV, radio and the web from 19th-century cameras and early animation to digital technology and the psychology of advertising. There's lots of hands-on stuff too. You can film yourself in a bedroom scene, pretend to be a TV newsreader, or play 1970s and '80s video games. The IMAX cinema (adult/child £11/8.50) here shows the usual

combination of in-your-face nature films, space documentaries and 3D animations.

The museum looks out over City Park, Bradford's brand new central square, which is home to the Mirror Pool, the country's largest urban water feature.

Bradford is famous for its curries – it was voted the UK's Curry Capital in 2011 – so don't miss out on trying one of the city's hundred or so restaurants. A great help is the Bradford Curry Guide (www.visitbrad ford.com/food-and-drink/Bradford-Curry-Guide. aspx). Top recommendations include Bradford's oldest curry house, the Kashmir (27 Morley St; mains £4-6; ⊙dinner), for top Asian tucker served with no frills in very basic surroundings. At the opposite end of the spectrum is Zouk Tea Bar (www.zoukteabar.co.uk; 1312 Leeds Rd; mains £7-12; ⊙10am-midnight), a modern and stylish cafe-restaurant staffed by chefs from Lahore and serving everything from *chana puri* (curried chickpeas) for breakfast to legendary *lamb Nihari* (slow-cooked lamb with a thick and spicy sauce) for dinner.

Bradford is on the Metro train line from Leeds (£3.30, 20 minutes), with very frequent services every day.

Saltaire

A Victorian-era landmark, Saltaire was a model industrial village built in 1851 by philanthropic wool baron and teetotaller Titus Salt. The rows of neat, honey-coloured cottages – now a Unesco World Heritage Site – overlook what was once the largest factory in the world.

The factory is now Salts Mill (www.salt smill.org.uk; ⊙10am-5.30pm Mon-Fri, to 6pm Sat & Sun), a splendidly bright and airy building where the main attraction is a permanent exhibition of 1970s and '80s artworks by local boy David Hockney (1937–). In a fitting metaphor for the shift in the British economy from making things to selling them, this former engine of industry is now a shrine to retail therapy, with shops selling books, crafts and outdoor equipment, and a cafe and restaurant.

Saltaire's tourist office (✆01274-437942; www.saltairevillage.info; Salts Mill, Victoria Rd; ⊙10am-5pm) has maps of the village and runs hour-long guided walks (adult/child £4/3) through the town throughout the year.

Saltaire is 9 miles west of Leeds city centre and 3 miles north of Bradford centre, and is easily reached by Metro rail from either.

Harewood House

The great park, sumptuous gardens and mighty edifice of Harewood House (www.harewood.org; adult/child £14/7; ☉grounds 10am-6pm, house noon-3pm Apr-Oct) could easily fill an entire day trip from Leeds. It also makes a good port of call on the way to Harrogate.

A classic example of a stately English pile, the house was built between 1759 and 1772 by the era's superstar designers: John Carr designed the exterior, Lancelot 'Capability' Brown laid out the grounds, Thomas Chippendale supplied the furniture (the largest commission he ever received, costing the unheard-of amount of £10,000), Robert Adams designed the interior, and Italy was raided to create an appropriate art collection. The superb terrace was added 100 years later by yet another top name, Sir Charles Barry, best known for rebuilding the Houses of Parliament.

Many locals come to Harewood just to relax or saunter through the grounds (grounds-only ticket £10/6), without even thinking of going inside the house. Hours of entertainment can be had in the Bird Garden, with many exotic species including penguins (feeding time at 2pm is a highlight), and there's also a boating lake, cafe and adventure playground. For more activity, there's a network of walking trails around the lake or through the parkland.

Harewood is about 7 miles north of Leeds on the A61. Take bus 36 (20 minutes, at least half-hourly Monday to Saturday, hourly on Sunday), which continues on to Harrogate. Visitors coming by bus get half-price admission, so hang on to your ticket. From the main gate, it's a 2-mile walk through the grounds to the house and gardens, or you can use the free shuttle service.

National Coal Mining Museum for England

For close to three centuries, West and South Yorkshire were synonymous with coal production. The collieries shaped and scarred the landscape, while entire villages grew up around the pits, each male inhabitant and his descendants destined to spend their working lives underground. The industry came to a shuddering halt in the 1980s, but the imprint of coal is still very much in evidence, even if there's only a handful of collieries left. One of these, the former Caphouse Colliery, is now the National Coal Mining Museum for England (www.ncm.org.uk; Overton, near Wakefield; admission free; ☉10am-5pm, last tour 3.15pm), a superb testament to the inner workings of a coal mine.

The highlight of a visit is the underground tour (departing every 10 minutes): equipped with helmet and head-torch, you descend 140m in the 'cage', then follow subterranean passages to the coal seam where massive drilling machines now stand idle. Former miners work as guides and explain the details – sometimes with a suitably authentic and almost impenetrable mix of local dialect (known in Yorkshire as 'Tyke') and technical terminology.

Up on top, there are audiovisual displays, some fascinating memorabilia (including sketches by Henry Moore), and exhibits about trade unions, strikes and the wider mining communities – only a bit over-romanticised in parts. You can also stroll round the pit-pony stables (their equine inhabitants also now retired) or the slightly eerie bathhouse, unchanged since the miners scrubbed off the coal dust for the last time and emptied their lockers.

The museum is about 10 miles south of Leeds on the A642 between Wakefield and Huddersfield, which drivers can reach via Junction 40 on the M1. By public transport, take a train from Leeds to Wakefield (15 minutes, at least hourly), and then bus 232 towards Huddersfield (25 minutes, hourly).

Yorkshire Sculpture Park

One of England's most impressive collections of sculpture is scattered across the formidable 18th-century estate of Bretton Park, 200-odd hectares of lawns, fields and trees. A bit like the art world's equivalent of a safari park, the Yorkshire Sculpture Park (www.ysp.co.uk; Bretton Park, near Wakefield; admission free, parking £4; ☉10am-6pm Apr-Oct, to 5pm Nov-Mar) showcases the work of dozens of sculptors, both national and international. But the main focus of this outdoor gallery is the work of local kids Barbara Hepworth (1903–75), who was born in nearby Wakefield, and Henry Moore (1898–1986).

The rural setting is especially fitting for Moore's work, as the artist was hugely influenced by the outdoors and preferred his art to be sited in the landscape rather than indoors. Other highlights include pieces by Andy Goldsworthy and Eduardo Paolozzi. There's also a program of temporary exhibitions and installations by visiting artists, plus a bookshop and cafe.

The park is 12 miles south of Leeds and 18 miles north of Sheffield, just off Junction 38 on the M1 motorway. If you're on public transport, take a train from Leeds to Wakefield (15 minutes, at least hourly), or from Sheffield to Barnsley (20 minutes, at least hourly), and then take bus 9, which runs between Wakefield and Barnsley via Bretton Park (30 minutes, hourly Monday to Saturday).

Hepworth Wakefield

West Yorkshire's standing in the international arts scene got a boost in 2011 when the Yorkshire Sculpture Park was joined by this award-winning gallery of modern art, housed in a stunningly angular building on the banks of the River Calder. The Hepworth Wakefield (☎01924-247360; www.hepworthwakefield.org; Gallery Walk; admission free, parking £4.50; ◷10am-5pm Tue-Sun) has been built around the works of Wakefield-born sculptor Barbara Hepworth, perhaps best known for her work *Single Form*, which graces the United Nations Headquarters in New York. The gallery showcases more than a dozen Hepworth originals, as well as works by other 20th-century British artists including Ivon Hitchens, Paul Nash, Victor Pasmore, John Piper and Henry Moore. The Gott Collection of 19th-century art includes a 1793 painting of Wakefield Bridge and Chantry Chapel, which you can compare with the real thing by looking out the neighbouring window.

The gallery is near the centre of Wakefield, a 10-minute walk south of Wakefield Kirkgate train station.

Hebden Bridge

POP 4086

Tucked tightly into the fold of a steep-sided valley, Yorkshire's funkiest little town is a former mill town that refused to go gently with the dying of industry's light. Instead, it raged a bit and then morphed into an attractive little tourist trap with a distinctly bohemian atmosphere. The town is home to university academics, artists, die-hard hippies and a substantial gay community. All of this explains the abundance of craft shops, organic cafes and secondhand bookstores.

 Sights

From the town centre, a short stroll along the attractive waterfront of the Rochdale Canal leads to the Alternative Technology Centre (www.alternativetechnology.org.uk; Hebble End Mill; ◷10am-5pm Mon-Fri, noon-4pm Sat, 1-4pm Sun), which promotes renewable energy, recycling and sustainable lifestyles through a series of intriguing exhibits and workshops.

Above the town is the much older village of Heptonstall, its narrow cobbled street lined with 500-year-old cottages and the ruins of a beautiful 13th-century church. But it's the churchyard of the newer St Thomas' Church that draws literary pilgrims, for here is buried the poet Sylvia Plath (1932–63), wife of another famous poet, Ted Hughes (1930–98), who was born in nearby Mytholmroyd.

The Hebden Bridge Tourist Office & Canal Centre (☎01422-843831; www.hebdenbridge.co.uk; Butlers Wharf, New Rd; ◷9.30am-5.30pm Mon-Fri, 10.30am-5pm Sat & Sun mid-Mar–mid-Oct, shorter hours rest of year) has a good stock of maps and leaflets on local walks, including a saunter to Hardcastle Crags, the local beauty spot, and nearby NT-listed Gibson Mill (www.nationaltrust.org.uk; adult/child £3.80/1.90; ◷11am-4pm Tue-Thu, Sat & Sun Mar-Oct, to 3pm Sat & Sun Nov-Feb), a renovated 19th-century cotton mill. The mill houses a visitor centre with exhibitions covering the industrial and social history of the mill and its former workers.

Sleeping & Eating

Holme House B&B ££

(☎01422-847588; www.holmehousehebdenbridge.co.uk; New Rd; s/d from £62/78; ☃) Holme House is an elegant Victorian villa right in the heart of town, with stylish and spacious bedrooms and fluffy robes and towels in the bathrooms. At breakfast you can choose from smoked haddock with poached egg, fresh fruit and yoghurt, or a fry-up prepared using local produce.

Mankinholes YHA HOSTEL £

(☎0845-371 9751; www.yha.org.uk; dm £19.40; ℗) A converted 17th-century manor house 4 miles southwest of Hebden Bridge, this hostel has limited facilities (no TV room) but is very popular with walkers (the Pennine Way passes only half a mile away). There are buses from New Rd in Hebden to Todmorden every 10 minutes and from there, bus T6/T8 goes to the hostel.

Green's Vegetarian Café   VEGETARIAN ££

(☑01422-843587; www.greensvegetariancafe.co.uk; Old Oxford House, Albert St; mains £10; ☺11am-3pm Wed-Sun, 6.30-9pm Fri & Sat; ☑) One of Yorkshire's best vegetarian restaurants, Green's adopts a gourmet attitude towards veggie and vegan cuisine, serving dishes such as Sicilian *caponata* (aubergines, red pepper, celery, olives and capers) with spaghetti, and Thai green curry with chickpeas, squash and tofu. Best book a table to avoid disappointment, especially for dinner.

Mooch   CAFE, BAR £

(24 Market St; mains £5-8; ☺9am-8pm Mon & Wed-Sat, 10am-7pm Sun) This chilled-out little cafe-bar exemplifies Hebden's alternative atmosphere, with a menu that includes a full-vegan breakfast, brie-and-grape ciabatta, and Mediterranean lunch platters of olives, hummus, stuffed vine leaves, tabouli and more. There's also Krombacher beer on draught, and excellent espresso.

Organic House   CAFE £

(www.organic-house.co.uk; 2 Market St; mains £6-11; ☺9am-5pm Mon-Sat, 10am-5pm Sun; ☎☑⚛) Practically everything on the menu at this busy local caff is organic, locally produced or fair-trade, from the veggie breakfast to the *pâté du jour* (served with toast and chutney). There are outdoor tables in the garden, and a shiatsu and reflexology studio upstairs.

🛈 Getting There & Away

Hebden Bridge is on the Leeds–Manchester train line (£4.80, 50 minutes, every 20 minutes Monday to Saturday, hourly on Sunday). Get off at Todmorden for the Mankinholes YHA.

Haworth

POP 6100

It seems that only Shakespeare himself is held in higher esteem than the beloved Brontë sisters – Emily, Anne and Charlotte – judging by the 8 million visitors a year who trudge up the hill from the train station to pay their respects at the handsome parsonage where the literary classics *Jane Eyre* and *Wuthering Heights* were penned.

Not surprisingly, the whole village is given over to Brontë-linked tourism, but even without the literary associations Haworth is still worth a visit, though you'll be hard pushed not to be overwhelmed by the cottage industry that has grown up around the Brontës and their wonderful creations.

💿 Sights

FREE Haworth Parish Church   CHURCH

(Church St; admission free; ☺9am-5.30pm) Your first stop should be Haworth Parish Church, a lovely old place of worship built in the late 19th century on the site of the older church that the Brontë sisters knew, which was demolished in 1879. In the surrounding churchyard, gravestones are covered in moss or pushed to one side by gnarled tree roots, giving the place a tremendous feeling of age.

Brontë Parsonage Museum   MUSEUM

(www.bronte.info; Church St; adult/child £7/3.60; ☺10am-5.30pm Apr-Sep, 11am-5pm Oct-Mar) Set in a pretty garden overlooking the church and graveyard, the house where the Brontë family lived from 1820 till 1861 is now a museum. The rooms are meticulously furnished and decorated exactly as they were in the Brontë era, including Charlotte's bedroom, her clothes and her writing paraphernalia. There's also an informative exhibition, which includes the fascinating miniature books the Brontës wrote as children.

�, Activities

Above Haworth stretch the bleak moors of the South Pennines – immediately familiar to Brontë fans – and the tourist office has leaflets on local walks to endless Brontë-related places. A 6.5-mile favourite leads to Top Withins, a ruined farm thought to have inspired *Wuthering Heights*, even though a plaque clearly states that the farmhouse bore no resemblance to the one Emily wrote about.

Other walks can be taken around the Brontë Way, a longer route linking Bradford and Colne via Haworth. Alternatively, you can walk or cycle the 8 miles south to Hebden Bridge via the scenic valley of Hardcastle Crags.

BAD-LUCK BRONTËS

The Reverend Patrick Brontë, his wife Maria and six children moved to Haworth Parsonage in 1820. Within four years Maria and the two eldest daughters had died from cancer and tuberculosis. The treble tragedy led the good reverend to keep his remaining family close to him, and for the next few years the children were home-schooled in a highly creative environment.

The children conjured up mythical heroes and fantasy lands, and produced miniature homemade books. It was an auspicious start, at least for the three girls, Charlotte, Emily and Anne. The lone boy, Branwell, was more of a painter, but lacked his sisters' drive and discipline. After a short stint as a professional artist, he ended up spending most of his days in the Black Bull pub, drunk and stoned on laudanum obtained across the street at Rose & Co Apothecary.

While the three sisters were setting the London literary world alight with the publication of three superb novels – *Jane Eyre*, *Wuthering Heights* and *Agnes Grey* – in one extraordinary year (1847), Branwell was fading quickly and died of tuberculosis in 1848. The family was devastated, but things quickly got worse. Emily fell ill with tuberculosis soon after her brother's funeral; she never left the house again, and died on 19 December. Anne, who had also been sick, was next; Charlotte took her to Scarborough to seek a sea cure, but she died on 28 May 1849.

The remaining family never recovered. Despite her growing fame, Charlotte struggled with depression and never quite adapted to her high position in literary society. Despite her misgivings, she eventually married, but died in the early stages of pregnancy on 31 March 1855. All things considered, it's hardly surprising that poor old Patrick Brontë spent the remaining years of his life going steadily insane.

🛏 Sleeping & Eating

Virtually every second house on Main St offers B&B; they're mostly indistinguishable from each other, but some are just that little bit cuter. There are a couple of good restaurants in town, and many of the B&Bs have small cafes that are good for a spot of lunch.

Old Registry   B&B ££
(📞01535-646503; www.theoldregistryhaworth.co.uk; 2-4 Main St; r £75-120; 🛜) This place is a bit special. It's an elegantly rustic guesthouse where each of the carefully themed rooms has a four-poster bed, whirlpool bath and valley view. The Blue Heaven room is just that – at least for fans of Laura Ashley's delphinium blue.

Ye Sleeping House   B&B ££
(📞01535-546992; www.yesleepinghouse.co.uk; 8 Main St; s/d from £29/58) This welcoming B&B has a cosy, country-cottage atmosphere, with just three small rooms and two friendly resident cats. Try to get the one en-suite room, which can sleep a family of four and has great views over the valley.

Aitches   B&B ££
(📞01535-642501; www.aitches.co.uk; 11 West Lane; s/d from £40/60) A classy, stone-built Victorian house with four en-suite rooms, each differently decorated with a pleasantly olde-worlde atmosphere. There's a residents' dining room where a three-course meal will cost £16 (prebooked for a minimum four persons).

Apothecary Guest House   B&B £
(📞01535-643642; www.theapothecaryguesthouse. co.uk; 86 Main St; s/d £35/55; 🛜) Oak beams and narrow, slanted passageways lead to smallish rooms with cheerful decor.

Old White Lion Hotel   INN ££
(📞01535-642313; www.oldwhitelionhotel.com; West Lane; s/d from £70/98; 🛜) Pub-style accommodation, comfortable if not spectacular, above an oak-panelled bar and highly rated restaurant.

Haworth YHA   HOSTEL £
(📞0845-371 9520; www.yha.org.uk; Longlands Dr; dm £19.40; 🅿@) A big old house with a games room, lounge, cycle store and laundry. It's on the northeastern edge of town, off Lees Lane.

Cobbles & Clay   CAFE £
(www.cobblesandclay.co.uk; 60 Main St; mains £5-8; ⊘9am-5pm; 🖋👶) This attractive, child-friendly cafe not only offers fair-trade coffee and healthy salads and snacks – Tuscan bean stew, or hummus with pita bread and raw

veggie sticks – but also provides the opportunity to indulge in a bit of pottery painting.

Weaver's
BRITISH **££**

(☏01535-643822; www.weaversmallhotel.co.uk; 15 West Lane; mains £15-20; ⏱lunch Wed-Fri, dinner Tue-Sat) A stylish and atmospheric restaurant, Weaver's menu features local produce (such as slow-cooked shoulder of Pennine lamb with fennel seed and coriander stuffing), and simple lunches like an Ellison's pork pie with mushy peas and mint sauce (two-course lunch costs £16). Upstairs are three comfy bedrooms, two of which have views towards the moors.

Haworth Old Hall
PUB **££**

(☏01535-642709; www.hawortholdhall.co.uk; Sun St; mains £9-17) A 16th-century pub serving real ale and decent food. If you want to linger longer, two comfortable doubles cost £60 each.

 ## Shopping

Venables & Bainbridge
BOOKS

(111 Main St; ⏱11am-5pm) Secondhand books, including many vintage Brontë volumes.

 ## Information

Post office (98 Main St; ⏱9am-5.30pm Mon-Fri, to 12.30pm Sat)

Tourist office (☏01535-642329; www.haworth-village.org.uk; 2-4 West Lane; ⏱9am-5.30pm Apr-Sep, to 5pm Oct-Mar) The tourist office has an excellent supply of information on the village, the surrounding area and, of course, the Brontës.

Getting There & Away

From Leeds, the easiest approach is via Keighley, which is on the Metro rail network. Bus 500 runs from Keighley bus station to Haworth (15 minutes, hourly) and continues to Todmorden and Hebden Bridge. However, the most interesting way to get from Keighley to Haworth is via the Keighley & Worth Valley Railway.

SOUTH YORKSHIRE

What wool was to West Yorkshire, so steel was to South Yorkshire. A confluence of natural resources – coal, iron ore and ample water – made the region a crucible of the British iron and steel industries. From the 18th to the 20th centuries, the region was the industrial powerhouse of northern England.

Sheffield's and Rotherham's blast furnaces and the coal pits of Barnsley and Doncaster may have closed long ago, but the hulking reminders of that irrepressible Victorian dynamism remain, not only in the old steelworks and pit heads (some of which have been converted into museums and exhibition spaces), but also in the grand civic buildings that grace Sheffield's city centre, fitting testaments to the untrammelled ambitions of their 19th-century patrons.

Sheffield

POP 525,800

Steel is everywhere in Sheffield. Today, however, it's not the steel of the foundries, mills and forges that made the city's fortune, nor the canteens of cutlery that made 'Sheffield Steel' a household name, but the steel of scaffolding and cranes, of modern sculptures and supertrams, and of new steel-framed buildings rising against the skyline.

The steel industry that made the city famous is long since gone, but after many years of decline Sheffield is on the up again – like many of northern England's cities, it has grabbed the opportunities presented by urban renewal with both hands and is working hard to reinvent itself. The new economy is based on services, shopping and the 'knowledge industry' that flows from the city's universities.

 ## Sights

Since 2000 the city centre has been in the throes of a massive redevelopment that will continue into 2020 and beyond, so expect

---

STEAM ENGINES & RAILWAY CHILDREN

Haworth is on the **Keighley & Worth Valley Railway** (www.kwvr.co.uk; adult/child return £10/5, Day Rover £15/7.50), which runs steam and classic diesel engines between Keighley and Oxenhope. It was here, in 1969, that the classic movie *The Railway Children* was shot: Mr Perks was station master at Oakworth, where the Edwardian look has been meticulously maintained. Trains operate about hourly at weekends all year, and in holiday periods they run hourly every day.

building sites and roadworks for several years to come.

Of the parts that are already complete, pride of place goes to the Winter Gardens (Surrey St; ⊙8am-6pm), a wonderfully ambitious public space with a soaring glass roof supported by graceful arches of laminated timber. The 21st-century architecture contrasts sharply with the Victorian town hall nearby, and is further enhanced by the Peace Gardens – complete with fountains, sculptures and lawns full of lunching office workers whenever there's a bit of sun.

Sheffield's cultural revival is spearheaded by the Millennium Gallery (www.museums -sheffield.org.uk; Arundel Gate; ⊙10am-5pm Mon-Sat, 11am-4pm Sun), a collection of four galleries under one roof. Inside, the Ruskin Gallery has an eclectic collection of paintings, drawings and manuscripts established and inspired by Victorian artist, writer, critic and philosopher John Ruskin, while the Metalwork Gallery charts the transformation of Sheffield's steel industry into craft and design – the 'Sheffield Steel' stamp on locally made cutlery and tableware now has the cachet of designer chic.

The nearby Graves Gallery (www.museums -sheffield.org.uk; Surrey St; ⊙10am-5pm Mon-Sat) has a neat and accessible display of British and European modern art. The big names represented include Cézanne, Gauguin, Miró, Klee and Picasso.

In the days before steel mills, metalworking was a cottage industry (just like wool and cotton). For a glimpse of that earlier, more innocent era, explore the restored 18th-century forges, workshops and machines at the Abbeydale Industrial Hamlet (www. simt.co.uk; ⊙10am-4pm Mon-Thu, 11am-4.45pm Sun May-Sep), 4 miles southwest of the centre on the A621 (towards the Peak District).

🍴 Sleeping & Eating

Tourism has not quite taken off yet in Sheffield, and most of the city-centre hotels cater primarily to business travellers. New restaurants are springing up – there are several in the Leopold Sq development on Leopold St – but the main restaurant areas are outside the centre.

There's a mile-long strip of bars, restaurants, cafes and takeaways on Ecclesall Rd, a mile to the southwest of the city centre, while London Rd, a mile south of the central city, has a concentration of good-value ethnic restaurants ranging from Turkish to Thai. To find student bars and eateries, head along Division St and Devonshire St just west of the city centre.

Leopold Hotel   BOUTIQUE HOTEL ££
(☑0845-078 0067; www.leopoldhotel.co.uk; 2 Leopold St; r from £89; ☎) Housed in a former grammar school building, Sheffield's first boutique hotel brings some much-needed style and sophistication to the city's accommodation scene (but without a London-sized price tag). Rooms can suffer late-night noise from the bars on Leopold Sq – ask for a quiet room at the back.

Houseboat Hotels   HOUSEBOAT ££
(☑01909-569393; www.houseboathotels.com; Victoria Quays, Wharf St; d/q from £69/95; Ⓟ) Here's something a bit different: kick off your shoes and relax on board your very own permanently moored houseboat, complete with self-catering kitchen and patio area. Guests are entitled to use the gym and pool facilities at the Hilton across the road.

TOP CHOICE **Gusto**   ITALIAN ££
(☑0114-276 0004; www.gustosheffield.com; 12 Norfolk Row; mains £9-19; ⊙9am-9pm Mon-Sat; ☎) Gusto is a *real* Italian cafe-restaurant, from the Italian owners serving homemade Italian food to the genuine Italian coffee enjoyed by Italian customers reading Italian newspapers...you get the idea. Coffee and home-baked Italian cakes and pastries are served all day, plus a lunch and dinner menu of exquisite Italian cuisine. It's best to book for dinner.

22A   CAFE £
(22a Norfolk Row; mains £5-9; ⊙8am-5pm Mon-Sat) Nice music, nice people, nice place – this homely cafe serves hearty breakfasts with a decent cup of java, and offers a range of inventive dishes at lunchtime – the carrot, leek, cashew and orange stir-fry sounds intriguing...

Blue Moon Cafe   VEGETARIAN £
(2 St James St; mains £6-7; ⊙8am-8pm Mon-Sat; ☑) Tasty veggie and vegan creations, soups and other healthy dishes, all served with the ubiquitous salad, in a very pleasant atmosphere – perfect for a spot of Saturday afternoon lounging.

ℹ Information

Post office (Norfolk Row; ⊙8.30am-5.30pm Mon-Fri, to 3pm Sat)

Tourist office (☎0114-221 1900; www.welcome tosheffield.co.uk; Winter Garden, Surrey St; ⊙9.30am-5pm Mon-Fri, to 4pm Sat, closed 1-1.30pm)

❶ Getting There & Away

For all travel-related info for Sheffield and South Yorkshire, contact **Travel South Yorkshire** (☎01709-515151; www.travelsouthyorkshire. com).

BUS The bus station, called the Interchange, is just east of the centre, about 250m north of the train station. National Express services link Sheffield with most major centres in the north. There are frequent buses to Leeds (£6, one hour, hourly), Manchester (£9, 1½ hours, four daily) and London (£10, 4½ hours, eight daily).

TRAIN Sheffield is served by trains from all directions: Leeds (£10, one hour, twice hourly); London St Pancras (£60, 2½ hours, hourly) via Derby or Nottingham; Manchester Piccadilly (£10, one hour, twice hourly); and York (£10, 1¼ hours, twice hourly).

EAST RIDING OF YORKSHIRE

In command of the East Riding of Yorkshire is the tough old sea dog known as Hull, a no-nonsense port that looks to the North Sea and the broad horizons of the Humber estuary for its livelihood. Just to its north, and in complete contrast to Hull's salt and grit, is East Riding's most attractive town, Beverley, with lots of Georgian character and one of England's finest churches.

Hull

POP 256,200

Tough and uncompromising, Hull is a curmudgeonly English seaport with a proud seafaring tradition. It has long been the principal cargo port of England's east coast, with an economy that grew up around carrying wool out and bringing wine in. It was also a major whaling and fishing port until the trawling industry died out, but it remains a busy cargo terminal and departure point for ferries to the Continent.

◉ Sights & Activities

The Deep   AQUARIUM
(www.thedeep.co.uk; Tower St; adult/child £10.50/8.50; ⊙10am-6pm, last entry 5pm) Hull's biggest tourist attraction is the Deep, a vast aquarium housed in a colossal angular building

that appears to lunge above the muddy waters of the Humber like a giant shark's head. Inside, it's just as dramatic, with echoing commentaries and computer-generated interactive displays that guide you through the formation of the oceans and the evolution of sea life. The largest aquarium is 10m deep, filled with sharks, stingrays and colourful coral fishes, with moray eels draped over rocks like scarves of iridescent slime. A glass elevator plies up and down inside the tank, though you'll get a better view by taking the stairs. Don't miss the cafe on the very top floor, which has a great view of the Humber estuary.

FREE Museum Quarter   MUSEUMS
(☎613902; www.hullcc.gov.uk/museums; 36 High St; admission free; ⊙10am-5pm Mon-Sat, 1.30-4.30pm Sun) Hull has several city-run museums concentrated in an area promoted as the Museum Quarter. All share the same contact details and opening hours, and all are free.

The fascinating Streetlife Museum contains re-created street scenes from Georgian and Victorian times and from the 1930s, with all sorts of historic vehicles to explore, from stagecoaches to bicycles, buses and trams. Behind the museum, marooned in the mud of the River Hull, is the Arctic Corsair (⊙tours 10am-4.30pm Wed & Sat, from 1.30pm Sun). Tours of this Atlantic trawler, a veteran of the 1970s so-called 'Cod Wars', when the UK and Iceland clashed over fishing rights, demonstrate the hardships of fishing north of the Arctic Circle.

Nearby, you'll find the Hull & East Riding Museum, which chronicles local history and archaeology, and Wilberforce House, the birthplace of the politician William Wilberforce, now a museum about the slave trade and its abolition.

FREE Old Town   NEIGHBOURHOOD
Hull's Old Town, whose grand public buildings retain a sense of the prosperity the town once knew, occupies the thumb of land between the River Hull to the east and Princes Quay to the west. The most impressive legacy is the Guildhall (☎01482-300300; Low Gate; ⊙8.30am-4.30pm Mon-Thu, to 3.30pm Fri), a huge neoclassical building that dates from 1916 and houses vast areas of polished marble, and oak and walnut panelling, plus a small collection of sculpture and art. Phone to arrange a free guided tour.

FREE **Spurn Lightship** MUSEUM
(Castle St; ⏰10am-4.30pm Mon-Sat, 1.30-4pm Sun) Built in 1927, Hull's lighthouse-ship once served as a navigation mark for ships entering the notorious Humber estuary. Now safely retired in the marina, it houses an interesting exhibition about its own history, and offers an interesting contrast between the former living quarters of captain and crew.

FREE **Larkin Trail** WALKING TOUR
(www.thelarkintrail.co.uk) Hull's most famous son, the poet Philip Larkin, is commemorated in this self-guided walking tour, which begins beside a bronze statue of the man himself in the railway station. It leads past places mentioned in his poetry, and on to some of his favourite pubs. Pick up a free leaflet at the tourist office.

🎎 Festivals

Hull Literature Festival LITERATURE
(www.humbermouth.co.uk) Besides the Larkin connection, poets Andrew Marvell and Stevie Smith and playwrights Alan Plater and John Godber all hail from Hull. Last two weeks of June.

Hull Jazz Festival JAZZ
(www.hulljazz.org.uk) This week-long festival brings an impressive line-up of jazz musicians to the city in July.

🛏 Sleeping & Eating

Good accommodation in the city centre is pretty thin on the ground and is mostly business-oriented chain hotels and a few mediocre guesthouses. The tourist office will help book accommodation for free.

The best concentration of eating places is found along Princes Ave, from Welbeck St to Blenheim St, a mile northwest of the centre.

Kingston Theatre Hotel HOTEL **££**
(📞01482-225828; www.kingstontheatrehotel.com; 1-2 Kingston Sq; s/d/ste from £50/65/90; 🛜) Overlooking leafy Kingston Sq, close to the New Theatre, this hotel is one of the best options in the city centre, with elegant bedrooms, friendly service and an excellent breakfast.

Fudge CAFE, BRASSERIE **££**
(www.fudgefood.com; 93 Princes Ave; mains £7-16; ⏰breakfast & lunch, also dinner Tue-Thu) This funky cafe serves hearty breakfasts, cakes and coffee all day, but also offers a tempting brasserie menu at lunch and dinner, with dishes that include juicy burgers (beef or veggie), herby crab cakes and roast pork belly with leek and bacon suet pudding.

Hitchcock's Vegetarian Restaurant VEGETARIAN **££**
(📞01482-320233; www.hitchcocksrestaurant.co.uk; 1 Bishop Lane, High St; per person £15; ⏰dinner Tue-Sat; 🖋) The word 'quirky' could have been invented to describe this place. It's an atmospheric maze of small rooms, with an all-you-can-eat vegetarian buffet whose theme – Thai, Indian, Spanish, whatever – is chosen by the first person to book that evening. But, hey, the food is excellent and the welcome is warm. Bookings necessary.

🍷 Drinking & Entertainment

Come nightfall – especially at weekends – Hull can be raucous and often rowdy, especially in the streets around Trinity Sq in the Old Town and on the strip of pubs along Beverley Rd to the north of the city centre.

Minerva PUB
(Nelson St) If you're more into pubbing than clubbing, try a pint of Black Sheep at this lovely 200-year-old pub down by the waterfront. On a sunny day you can sit outdoors and watch the ships go by.

Hull Truck Theatre THEATRE
(www.hulltruck.co.uk; Spring St) Home to acclaimed playwright John Godber, who made his name with the gritty comedies *Bouncers* and *Up 'n' Under* (he is one of the most-performed playwrights in the English-speaking world), Hull Truck presents a lively program of drama, comedy and Sunday jazz. It's just northwest of the Old Town.

Welly Club CLUB
(www.giveitsomewelly.com; 105-107 Beverley Rd; admission £5-12; ⏰10pm-3am Thu-Sat) The East Riding's top nightclub offers two venues – the mainstream Welly:One (which hosts Shuffle, the regular Saturday night dance club) and the more alternative Welly:Two (more house, techno, drum and bass).

Hull New Theatre THEATRE
(www.hullcc.gov.uk; Kingston Sq) A traditional regional theatre hosting popular drama, concerts and musicals.

ℹ Information

Post office (63 Market Pl; ⏰9am-5.30pm Mon-Sat)

Tourist office (☑0844-811 2070; www.visithullandeastyorkshire.com; 1 Paragon St; ☺10am-5pm Mon-Sat, 11am-3pm Sun)

❶ Getting There & Away

BOAT The ferry port is 3 miles east of the centre at King George Dock. A bus connects the train station with the ferries. There are ferry services to Zeebrugge and Rotterdam.

BUS There are buses direct from London (£26, 6½ hours, one daily); Leeds (£8, 1¾ hours, six daily Monday to Friday, eight Saturday, two Sunday); and York (£8, 1¾ hours, one daily).

TRAIN Hull has good rail links north and south to Newcastle (£30, 2½ hours, hourly, change at York or Doncaster) and London King's Cross (£60, 2¾ hours, every two hours); and west to York (£20, 1¼ hours, every two hours) and Leeds (£14, one hour, hourly).

Beverley

POP 29,110

Handsome, unspoilt Beverley is one of the most attractive towns in Yorkshire, largely on account of its magnificent minster – a rival to any cathedral in England – and the tangle of streets that lie beneath it, each brimming with exquisite Georgian and Victorian buildings.

All the sights are a short walk from either train or bus station. There's a large market in the main square on Saturday, and a smaller one on Wednesday on the square called... Wednesday Market.

◉ Sights

Beverley Minster   CHURCH
(www.beverleyminster.org; admission by donation, treadwheel-crane guided tours £5; ☺9am-4pm Mon-Sat, noon-4pm Sun, tours 11.15am, 2.15pm & 3.30pm Mon-Sat) One of the great glories of English religious architecture, Beverley Minster is the most impressive church in the country that is not a cathedral. Construction began in 1220 – the third church to be built on this site, with the first dating from the 7th century – and continued for two centuries, spanning the Early English, Decorated and Perpendicular periods of Gothic style.

The soaring lines of the exterior are imposing, but it is inside that the charm and beauty lie. The 14th-century north aisle is lined with original stone carvings, mostly of musicians. Much of our knowledge of early musical instruments comes from these

images. You'll also see goblins, devils and grotesque figures. Look out for the bagpipe player.

Close to the altar, the elaborate and intricate Percy Canopy (1340), a decorative frill above the tomb of local aristocrat Lady Eleanor Percy, is a testament to the skill of the sculptor and the finest example of Gothic stone carving in England. In complete contrast, in the nearby chancel is the 10th-century Saxon frith stool, a plain and polished stone chair that once gave sanctuary to anyone escaping the law.

In the roof of the tower is a restored treadwheel crane, where workers ground around like hapless hamsters to lift the huge loads necessary to build a medieval church. Access to the roof is by guided tour only.

FREE **St Mary's Church**   CHURCH
(☺9.30am-4.30pm Mon-Fri, 10am-4pm Sat, 2-4pm Sun Apr-Sep, shorter hours Oct-Mar) Doomed to play second fiddle to Beverley Minster, St Mary's Church at the other end of town was built between 1120 and 1530. The west front (early 15th century) is considered one of the finest of any parish church in England. In the north choir aisle there is a carving (c 1330) of a rabbit dressed as a pilgrim, said to have inspired Lewis Carroll's White Rabbit.

🛌 Sleeping & Eating

Friary YHA   HOSTEL £
(☑0845-371 9004; www.yha.org.uk; Friar's Lane; dm £19.40; Ⓟ) In Beverley, the cheapest accommodation also has the best setting and location. This hostel is housed in a beautifully restored 14th-century Dominican friary mentioned in Chaucer's *The Canterbury Tales*, and is only 100m from the minster and a short walk from the train station.

Kings Head   INN ££
(☑01482-868103; www.kingsheadpubbeverley.co.uk; 38 Saturday Market; s/d £70/80; @) A Georgian coaching inn given a modern makeover, the Kings Head is a lively pub with 12 bright and cheerful rooms above the bar. The pub opens late on weekend nights, but earplugs are supplied for those who don't want to join the revelry!

Eastgate Guest House   B&B ££
(☑01482-868464; www.eastgateguesthouse.com; 7 Eastgate; s/d from £60/80; 🛜) A red-brick Victorian town house with comfortable rooms in a central location.

Dine on the Rowe
BRITISH £££

(☎01482-502269; www.dineontherowe.com; 12-14 Butcher Row; mains £15-25; ☺lunch & dinner Tue-Sat, 11am-4.30pm Sun; 🛜) This friendly brasserie rivals the best in its dedication to local produce, but offers an informal atmosphere. Try the signature dish – smoked haddock and salmon fishcake with curry cream – or aged Yorkshire sirloin with black pudding potato cake. Sharing a platter from noon to 6pm, including two glasses of wine, costs £28.

Grant's Bistro
MODERN BRITISH £££

(☎01482-887624; www.grantsbistro.co.uk; 22 North Bar Within; mains £15-24; ☺lunch Fri & Sat, dinner Mon-Sat) A great place for a romantic dinner à deux, with dark-wood tables, fresh flowers and candlelight. The menu makes the most of fresh local beef, game and especially seafood, with dishes such as pan-fried scallops with black pudding. From Monday to Thursday you can get a two-course dinner with a glass of wine for £15.

Café Lempicka
CAFE £

(13 Wednesday Market; mains £5-7) A snug little cafe serving fair-trade coffee and tea, wicked hot chocolate, homemade cakes and daily lunch specials.

ℹ Information

Post office (Register Sq; ☺9am-5.30pm Mon-Fri, to 12.30pm Sat)

Tourist office (☎01482-391672; www.beverley.gov.uk; 34 Butcher Row; ☺9.30am-5.15pm Mon-Fri, 10am-4.45pm Sat year-round, 11am-3pm Sun Jul & Aug)

ℹ Getting There & Away

BUS There are frequent bus services from Hull, including numbers 121, 122, 246 and X46/X47 (30 minutes, every 20 minutes). Bus X46/X47 links Beverley with York (£6.20, 1¼ hours, hourly).

TRAIN Trains run regularly to Scarborough via Filey (£12.80, 1¼ hours, every two hours) and Hull (£6, 15 minutes, twice hourly).

Manchester, Liverpool & Northwest England

Best Places to Eat

» Australasia (p548)

» Monro (p565)

» Mark Addy (p548)

» Upstairs at the Grill (p556)

» Tanroagan (p573)

Best Places to Stay

» Stone Villa (p555)

» Great John Street Hotel (p547)

» Hope Street Hotel (p564)

» Malmaison (p565)

» 62 Castle St (p565)

Why Go?

Music, history and hedonism: just a taster of three good reasons to explore England's once-mighty industrial heartland, the birthplace of the first modern city, the cradle of capitalism and the Age of Englightenment. The industry is, for the most part, gone but among the hulking relics are two of the country's most exciting cities (Manchester and Liverpool), a Tudor postcard-town (Chester) and the sine qua non of traditional holidays-by-the-sea (Blackpool). And, if you fancy a bit of respite from the concrete paw-print of humankind, there's some of the most beautiful countryside in England in northern Lancashire and the Isle of Man.

When to Go

The world's most famous steeplechase, the Aintree Grand National, is run just outside Liverpool over the first weekend in April, while May and June are Tourist Trophy (TT) Festival season on the Isle of Man – beloved of motor enthusiasts the world over. The football (soccer) season runs from late August until May.

In the arts, the highlight is the Manchester International Festival, a biennial showstopper held in July. Music buffs should visit Liverpool in the last week of August for madness at Creamfields dance-fest and the Mathew St Festival, an ode to all things Beatles.

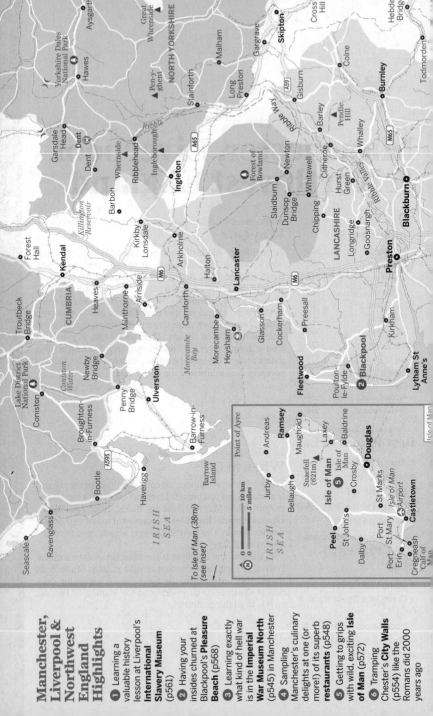

Manchester, Liverpool & Northwest England Highlights

❶ Learning a valuable history lesson at Liverpool's **International Slavery Museum** (p561)

❷ Having your insides churned at Blackpool's **Pleasure Beach** (p568)

❸ Learning exactly what kind of hell war is in the **Imperial War Museum North** (p545) in Manchester

❹ Sampling Manchester's culinary delights at one (or more!) of its superb **restaurants** (p548)

❺ Getting to grips with wild, exciting **Isle of Man** (p572)

❻ Tramping Chester's **City Walls** (p554) like the Romans did 2000 years ago

Activities

Walking & Cycling

In between the urban bits, the northwest is surprisingly good for walking and cycling options, notably in northern Lancashire's Ribble Valley, home to plenty of good walks including the 70-mile Ribble Way. The historic village of Whalley, in the heart of the Ribble Valley, is the meeting point of the two circular routes that make up the 260-mile Lancashire Cycle Way.

The Isle of Man has top-notch walking and cycling opportunities. Regional tourism websites contain walking and cycling information, and tourist offices stock free leaflets as well as maps and guides (usually £1 to £5) that cover walking, cycling and other activities.

Boating

You can explore the historic Peak Forest Canal between Manchester and the Peak District on the Wandering Duck (www.wandering duck.co.uk; 2-night trips per person incl meals from £95), a combined budget hostel and narrowboat tour.

ⓘ Information

Discover England's Northwest (www.visitnorth west.com) is the centralised tourist authority; for the Isle of Man, check out the main **Isle of Man Public Services** (www.gov.im) site.

ⓘ Getting Around

The towns and cities covered are all within easy reach of each other, and are well linked by public transport. The two main cities, Manchester and Liverpool, are only 34 miles apart and are linked by hourly bus and train services. Chester is 18 miles south of Liverpool, but is also easily accessible from Manchester by train or via the M56. Blackpool is 50 miles to the north of Manchester and Liverpool, and is also well connected. See the following for further transport information:

Greater Manchester Passenger Transport Authority (www.gmpte.com) Extensive info on Manchester and its environs.

Merseytravel (www.merseytravel.gov.uk) Taking care of all travel in Merseyside.

National Express (www.nationalexpress.com) Extensive coach services in the northwest; Manchester and Liverpool are major hubs.

MANCHESTER

POP 394,270

Raised on lofty ambition and not afraid to declare its considerable bona fides, Manchester is – by dint of geography and history – England's second city (apologies to Birmingham), although if you were to ask a Mancunian what it's like to be second they might reply: 'Don't know; ask a Londoner.'

Even accounting for northern bluster, the uncrowned capital of the north is well deserving of the title. It has a rich history and culture, easily explored in its myriad museums and galleries. And while history and heritage make the city interesting, its distractions of pure pleasure make Manchester fun: you can dine, drink and dance yourself into happy oblivion in the swirl of hedonism that is one of Manchester's most cherished characteristics.

History

Canals and steam-powered cotton mills were what transformed Manchester from a small disease-infested provincial town into a big disease-infested industrial city. It all happened in the 1760s, with the opening of the Bridgewater Canal between Manchester and the coal mines at Worsley in 1763, and with Richard Arkwright patenting his super cotton mill in 1769. Thereafter Manchester and the world would never be the same again. When the canal was extended to Liverpool and the open sea in 1776, Manchester – dubbed 'Cottonopolis' – kicked into high gear and took off on the coal-fuelled, steam-powered gravy train.

There was plenty of gravy to go around, but the good burghers of 19th-century Manchester made sure that the vast majority of the city's swollen citizenry (with a population of 90,000 in 1801, and 100 years later, two million) who produced most of it never got their hands on any of it. Their reward was life in a new kind of urban settlement: the industrial slum. Working conditions were dire, with impossibly long hours, child labour, work-related accidents and fatalities commonplace. Mark Twain commented that he would like to live here because the 'transition between Manchester and Death would be unnoticeable'. So much for Victorian values.

The wheels started to come off towards the end of the 19th century. The USA had begun to flex its own industrial muscles and was taking over a sizeable chunk of the textile trade; production in Manchester's mills began to slow, and then it stopped altogether. By WWII there was hardly enough cotton produced in the city to make a tablecloth. The postwar years weren't much better: 150,000 manufacturing jobs were lost between 1961 and 1983, and the port – still

MANCHESTER IN...

Two Days

Explore the **Museum of Science & Industry**, visit the **People's History Museum** and come to grips with the beautiful game at the **National Football Museum**. For food, try **The Oast House** before trying one of the bars in the Northern Quarter.

On day two, take the Metrolink to Salford and explore the **Imperial War Museum North**, the **Lowry** and the **Manchester United Museum** at Old Trafford. Take a tour of the BBC spread at **MediaCityUK**. Back in the city, indulge some retail *chi* at the high-end shops of **Spinningfields** or the offbeat boutiques of the **Northern Quarter**. Treat yourself with dinner at **Australasia**.

Four Days

Follow the two-day itinerary and tackle some of the city's lesser-known museums like the **John Rylands Library**. Examine the riches of the **Manchester Art Gallery**. End the evening with a dance at **Fac251**. The next day, take a walking tour – the tourist office has details of a whole host of themed ones – and if you're serious about clubbing, make the pilgrimage to Ancoats for the absolutely fabulous **Sankey's**.

---

the UK's third largest in 1963 – finally closed in 1982 due to declining traffic. The nadir came on 15 June 1996, when an IRA bomb wrecked a chunk of the city centre, but the subsequent reconstruction proved to be the beginning of the glass-and-chrome revolution so much in evidence today.

◉ Sights & Activities

CITY CENTRE

FREE Museum of Science & Industry MUSEUM
(MOSI; ☑0161-832 2244; www.msim.org.uk; Liverpool Rd; charges vary for special exhibitions; ⊙10am-5pm) The city's largest museum comprises 2.8 hectares in the heart of 19th-century industrial Manchester. It's sited in a landscape of enormous, weather-stained brick buildings and rusting cast-iron relics of canals, viaducts, bridges, warehouses and market buildings that make up Castlefield, now deemed an 'urban heritage park'.

If there's anything you want to know about the Industrial (and post-Industrial) Revolution and Manchester's key role in it, you'll find the answers among the collection of steam engines and locomotives, factory machinery from the mills, and the excellent exhibition telling the story of Manchester from the sewers up.

It's an all-ages kind of museum, but the emphasis is on making sure the young 'uns don't get bored – they could easily spend a whole day poking about the place, test-

ing early electric-shock machines here and trying out a printing press there. A unifying theme is that Manchester and Mancunians had a key role to play: did you know that Manchester was home to the world's first computer (a giant contraption called 'the baby') in 1948, or that the world's first submarine was built to the designs of local curate Reverend George Garrett in 1880? Nope, neither did we.

National Football Museum MUSEUM
(☑0161-605 8200; www.nationalfootballmuseum.com; Corporation St, Urbis, Cathedral Gardens; ⊙10am-5pm Mon-Sat, 11am-5pm Sun) It's the world's most popular game and Manchester is home to both the world's most popular and the world's richest teams, so it makes sense that a museum dedicated to the global charms of football should find its home here. Opened in July 2012, the museum is chock-a-block with the world's most extensive collections of memorabilia, trophies and other football keepsakes. Fans won't need convincing, but those unfamiliar with footy's appeal will learn much about the game's development, spread and success, as well as the multitude of names that have graced (and disgraced) its myriad pitches throughout the world. The most interesting bit is Football Plus, a series of interactive stations spread throughout the museum that allow you to test your skills in simulated conditions; buy a token (£2.50) and try your luck – it's recommended for kids over seven.

Manchester

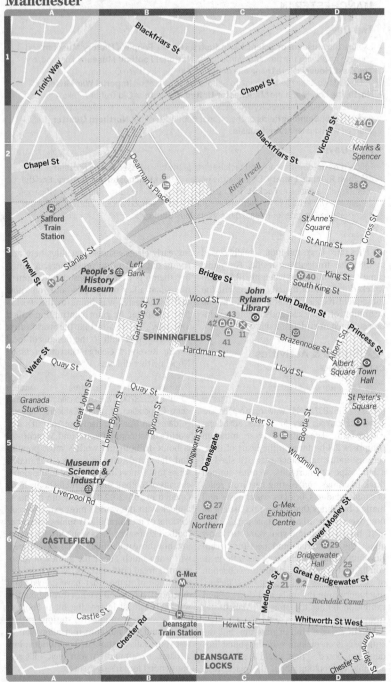

Blackfriars St

Trinity Way

Chapel St

Blackfriars St

Victoria St

34

44

Marks & Spencer

Chapel St

River Irwell

Dearman's Place

6

38

Salford Train Station

St Anne's Square

St Anne St

Cross St

Stanley St

People's History Museum

Left Bank

Bridge St

23

16

King St

40

South King St

Irwell St

14

Gartside St

17

Wood St

John Rylands Library

John Dalton St

Princess St

SPINNINGFIELDS

43

42 11

41

Brazennose St

Albert Sq

Water St

Hardman St

Lloyd St

Albert Square Town Hall

Quay St

Quay St

Peter St

Bootle St

St Peter's Square

1

Granada Studios

Great John St

Lower Byrom St

Byrom St

Longworth St

Deansgate

8

Windmill St

Museum of Science & Industry

Liverpool Rd

27

Great Northern

G-Mex Exhibition Centre

Lower Mosley St

CASTLEFIELD

29

Bridgewater Hall

25

G-Mex

21

2

Great Bridgewater St

Medlock St

Rochdale Canal

Castle St

Chester Rd

Deansgate Train Station

Hewitt St

Whitworth St West

Cambridge St

DEANSGATE LOCKS

Chester St

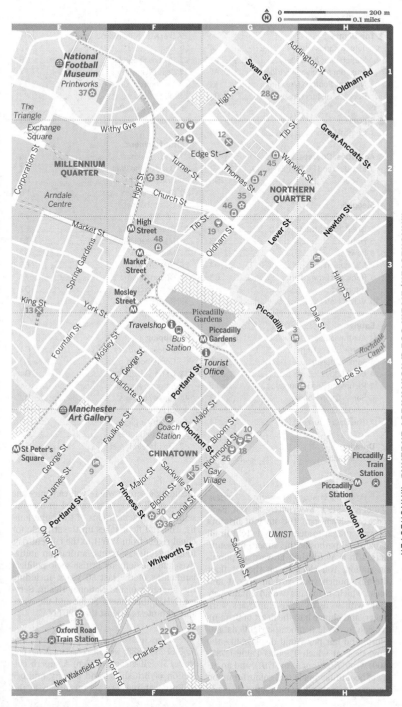

Manchester

FREE **People's History Museum** MUSEUM
(☎0161-838 9190; www.phm.org.uk; Left Bank, Bridge St; ⊙10am-5pm) The story of Britain's 200-year march to democracy is told in all its pain and pathos at this superb museum, housed in a refurbished Edwardian pumping station. You clock in on the 1st floor (literally: punch your card in an old mill clock, which managers would infamously fiddle with so as to make employees work longer) and plunge into the heart of Britain's struggle for basic democratic rights, labour reform and fair pay. Amid displays like the (tiny) desk at which Thomas Paine (1737-1809) wrote *Rights of Man* (1791), and an array of beautifully made and colourful union banners, are compelling interactive displays, including a screen where you can trace the effects of all the events covered in the museum on five generations of the same family. The 2nd floor takes up the struggle for equal rights from WWII to the current day, touching on gay rights, antiracism initiatives and the defining British socio-political landmarks of the last 50 years, including the founding of the National Health Service (NHS), the Miners' Strike and the widespread protests against the Poll Tax.

FREE **Manchester Art Gallery** ART MUSEUM
(☎0161-235 8888; www.manchestergalleries.org; Mosley St; ⊙10am-5pm Tue-Sun) A superb collection of British art and a hefty number of European masters are on display at the

city's top gallery. The older wing, designed by Charles Barry (of Houses of Parliament fame) in 1834, has an impressive collection that includes 37 Turner watercolours, as well as the country's best collection of Pre-Raphaelite art. The newer gallery features a permanent collection of 20th-century British art starring Lucien Freud, Francis Bacon, Stanley Spencer, Henry Moore and David Hockney. Finally, the Gallery of Craft & Design, in the Athenaeum, houses a permanent collection of pre-17th-century art, with works predominantly from the Dutch and early Renaissance masters.

FREE **John Rylands Library**   LIBRARY
(☑0161-306 0555; www.library.manchester.ac .uk; 150 Deansgate; ⊙noon-5pm Sun & Mon, 10am-5pm Tue-Sat) Less a library and more a cathedral to books, Basil Champneys' stunning building is arguably the most beautiful library in Britain and one hell of a way for Rylands' widow to remember her husband, John. It's a breathtaking example of Victorian Gothic, no more so than the Reading Room, complete with high-vaulted ceilings and stained-glass windows. The collection of early printed books and rare manuscripts is equally impressive, and includes a Gutenberg Bible, the earliest extant New Testament text and the country's second-largest assembly of works by Britain's first printer, William Caxton. A £16 million refit has resulted in the addition of a surprisingly tasteful modern annexe with a cafe and a bookshop.

SALFORD QUAYS

Just west of the city centre, and easily reached via Metrolink (£2), is Salford Quays, home to the city's big-ticket attractions and new hub of the BBC's northern HQ. Check out www.thequays.co.uk for more info.

FREE Imperial War Museum North   MUSEUM
(☑0161-836 4000; www.iwm.org.uk/north; Trafford Wharf Rd; ⊙10am-5pm) War museums generally appeal to those with a fascination for military hardware and battle strategy (toy soldiers optional), but Daniel Libeskind's visually stunning Imperial War Museum North takes a radically different approach. War is hell, it tells us, but it's a hell we revisit with tragic regularity.

The exhibits cover the main conflicts of the 20th century through a broad selection of displays, but the really effective bit comes every half-hour when the entire exhibition hall goes dark and one of three 15-minute films (*Children and War, The War at Home* or *Weapons of War*) is projected throughout.

Although the audiovisuals and displays are quite compelling, the extraordinary aluminium-clad building itself is a huge part of the attraction, and the exhibition spaces are genuinely breathtaking. Take the Metrolink to Harbour City or MediaCityUK.

Old Trafford (Manchester United Museum & Tour)   STADIUM
(☑0161-868 8000; www.manutd.com; Sir Matt Busby Way; tours adult/child £15/10, museum adult/child £10.50/8.50; ⊙museum 9.30am-5pm, tours every 10min except match days 9.40am-4.30pm) Home of the world's most famous club, the Old Trafford stadium is both a theatre and a temple for its millions of fans worldwide, many of whom come in pilgrimage to the ground to pay tribute to the minor deities disguised as highly paid footballers that play there. Since 1986 they have been managed by Sir Alex Ferguson, who has brought them unprecedented success, including 12 league titles, five FA Cup titles and two UEFA Champions League trophies – in 2011 they renamed one of the stands in his honour. Yet all that glory doesn't impress at least half

MORE NOTABLE BUILDINGS

Manchester has no shortage of eye-catching architecture, especially from the Victorian Age. Most impressive is the Town Hall (☑0161-234 5000; www.manchester.gov.uk; Albert Sq), crowned by an 85m-high tower and featuring an especially ornate interior. More recent additions to the cityscape include the neoclassical Central Library (☑0161-234 1900; St Peter's Sq), built in 1934 to resemble the Roman Pantheon. It's Britain's largest municipal library and is currently undergoing a major facelift and will re-open sometime in late 2013. The year 1935 saw the opening of Edwin Lutyens' stunning art deco Midland Bank, now home to a branch of Jamie's Italian (p548) – even if you don't eat there it's well worth having a look inside; be sure to go downstairs and peek in at the deposit vaults.

MANCHESTER, LIVERPOOL & NORTHWEST ENGLAND MANCHESTER

the local population, who prefer their less-famous rivals Manchester City. Still, a visit to the stadium is one of the more memorable things you'll do here. We strongly recommend that you take the tour, which includes a seat in the stands, a stop in the changing rooms, a peek at the players' lounge (from which the manager is banned unless invited by the players) and a walk down the tunnel to the pitchside dugout, which is as close to ecstasy as many of the club's fans will ever get. It's pretty impressive stuff. The museum, which is part of the tour but can be visited independently, has a comprehensive history of the club, and a state-of-the-art call-up system that means you can view your favourite goals – as well as a holographic 'chat' with Sir Alex Ferguson. Take the Metrolink to Old Trafford.

Lowry   ARTS CENTRE
(📞0161-876 2020; www.thelowry.com; Pier 8, Salford Quays; ⊙11am-8pm Tue-Fri, 10am-8pm Sat, 11am-6pm Sun & Mon) Looking more like a shiny steel ship than an arts centre, the Lowry is the quays' most notable success. It attracts more than a million visitors a year to its myriad functions, which include everything from performances to bars, restaurants, shops and even weddings. The centre is also home to 300 beautifully humanistic depictions of urban landscapes by LS Lowry (1887–1976), who was born in nearby Stretford, and after whom the complex is named.

MediaCityUK   MEDIA CENTRE
(📞0161-886 5300; www.mediacityuk.co.uk; Salford Quays; adult/student/child £8.50/7.25/5.25; ⊙tours 10.30am, 12.30pm & 3pm Mon-Wed) The BBC's new northern home is but one significant element of this vast, 81-hectare site. Besides hosting six departments of the national broadcaster (BBC Breakfast, Children's, Sport, Radio 5 Live, Learning, and Future Media & Technology), it will also be home to a bespoke set for the world's longest-running soap opera, the perennially popular *Coronation Street* (which broadcasts on ITV). There are no plans as yet to offer tours of the Corrie set, but you can visit the BBC's impressive set-up and see the (new) sets of some of TV's most iconic programs on a guided 90-minute tour that also includes a chance for kids to 'make' a program in an interactive studio. Take the Metrolink here.

Tours
The tourist office sells tickets for guided walks on all aspects of the city, from architecture to radical history, which operate almost daily year-round and cost £6/5 per adult/child.

✨ Festivals & Events

Screenfields   FILM
(www.spinningfieldsonline.com; Spinningfields; admission £2, season ticket £10; ⊙8pm Thu, Apr-Jul) Season of outdoor films, complete with deckchairs and picnics.

FutureEverything   MUSIC, ARTS
(www.futureeverything.org) Superb electronic music and media arts festival that takes place in various venues over a week in mid-May.

Manchester Day   PARADE
(www.themanchesterdayparade.co.uk) Inaugurated in 2010, a parade held in June to celebrate all things Manchester, with music, performances and fireworks.**Manchester International Festival**   ARTS
(📞0161-238 7300; www.mif.co.uk) A three-week-long biennial arts festival of new work across visual arts, performance and popular culture. The next festival is scheduled for July 2013.

Manchester Pride   GAY, LESBIAN
(📞0161-831 7700; www.manchesterpride.com) One of England's biggest celebrations of gay, bisexual and transgender life, held over 10 days in late August.

Manchester Food & Drink Festival   FOOD
(www.foodanddrinkfestival.com) Manchester's superb foodie scene shows off its wares over 10 days in mid-October. Farmers markets, pop-up restaurants and gourmet events are just part of what's on offer.

🛏 Sleeping
Manchester's hotels recognise that the business traveller is their best bet, but in keeping with their capital-of-cool status, they like to throw in more than a bit of style, so you'll find plenty of designer digs around town. Remember that during the football season (August to May), rooms can be almost impossible to find if either of the city's football clubs are playing at home (especially United). If you are having difficulty finding a bed, the tourist office's free accommodation service can help.

CITY CENTRE

Great John Street Hotel
HOTEL **£££**

(📞0161-831 3211; www.greatjohnstreet.co.uk; Great John St; r £85-345; @🛜) Elegant designer luxury? Present. Fabulous rooms with all the usual delights (Egyptian cotton sheets, fabulous toiletries, free-standing baths and lots of high-tech electronics)? Present. A butler to run your bath in the Opus Grand Suite? Present. This former schoolhouse (ah, now you get it) is small but sumptuous – beyond the art deco lobby are the fabulous bedrooms, each an example of style and luxury. If only school left such warm, comfortable memories.

Velvet Hotel
BOUTIQUE HOTEL **££**

(📞0161-236 9003; www.velvetmanchester.com; 2 Canal St; r from £99; 🛜) Nineteen beautiful bespoke rooms each oozing style: there's the sleigh bed in room 24, the double bath of room 34, the saucy framed photographs of a stripped-down David Beckham (this is Gay Village, after all!). But there's substance, too: iPod docking stations in every room, free wi-fi and a well-stocked DVD library. Despite the tantalising decor and location, this is not an exclusive hotel and is as popular with straight visitors as it is with the same-sex crowd.

Abode
HOTEL **££**

(📞0161-247 7744; www.abodehotels.co.uk; 107 Piccadilly St; r from £75; @🛜) Modern British style is the catchphrase at this converted textile factory. The original fittings have been combined successfully with 61 bedrooms divided into four categories of ever-increasing luxury: Comfortable, Desirable, Enviable and Fabulous, the latter being five seriously swanky top-floor suites. Vi-Spring beds, Monsoon showers, LCD-screen TVs and stacks of Aquae Sulis toiletries are standard throughout. In the basement, star chef Michael Caines has a champagne-and-cocktail bar adjacent to his very own restaurant.

Lowry
HOTEL **£££**

(📞0161-827 4000; www.roccofortecollection.com; 50 Dearman's Pl; r £120-950; P@🛜) Simply dripping with designer luxury and five-star comfort, Manchester's top hotel (not to be confused with the arts centre in Salford Quays) has fabulous rooms with enormous beds, ergonomically designed furniture, walk-in wardrobes, and bathrooms finished with Italian porcelain tiles and glass mosaics. You can soothe yourself with a skin-brightening treatment or an aromatherapy head-massage at the health spa.

Roomzzz
SERVICED ACCOMMODATION **££**

(📞0161-236 2121; www.roomzzz.co.uk; 36 Princess St; r £59-169; @🛜) The inelegant name belies the designer digs inside this beautifully restored Grade II building, which features serviced apartments equipped with a kitchen and the latest connectivity gadgetry, including sleek iMac computers and free wi-fi throughout. There's a small pantry with food for sale downstairs. Highly recommended if you're planning a longer stay.

Malmaison
HOTEL **£££**

(📞0161-278 1000; www.malmaison.com; Piccadilly St; r from £109) Drop-dead trendy and full of crushed-red velvet, deep purples, art deco ironwork and signature black-and-white tiles, Malmaison Manchester follows the chain's quirky design style and passion for cool, although rarely at the expense of comfort: the rooms are terrific. The Smoak Grill (📞0161-278 1000; www.smoak-grill.com; mains £13-25) downstairs is hugely popular. Take the Metrolink to Piccadilly Station.

Hatters
HOSTEL **£**

(📞0161-236 9500; www.hattersgroup.com; 50 Newton St; dm/s/d/tr from £15.50/28/52/65; P@🛜) The old-style lift and porcelain sinks are the only leftovers of this former milliner's factory, now one of the best hostels in town, with location to boot – smack in the heart of the Northern Quarter, you won't have to go far to get the best of alternative Manchester.

Radisson Edwardian
HOTEL **££**

(📞0161-835 9929; www.radissonedwardian.com/manchester; Peter St; r from £90; P@🛜) Gladstone, Dickens and Fitzgerald…just some of the names associated with the historic Free Trade Hall, now a sumptuous five-star hotel, all minimalist Zen and luxury (bespoke furnishings, Bang & Olufsen televisions). Sacrilege! scream the purists, but the hotel has done its best to preserve the memories of the building's most famous visitors: suites are named after Bob Dylan and Shirley Bassey, while meeting rooms carry the names of Disraeli, Thackeray and Pankhurst.

Manchester YHA
HOSTEL **£**

(📞0845-371 9647; www.yha.org.uk; Potato Wharf; dm incl breakfast from £16; P@🛜) This purpose-built canalside hostel in the Castlefield area is one of the best in the country. It's a top-class option with four- and six-bed dorms, all with bathroom, as well as three doubles and a host of good facilities. Potato Wharf is just left off Liverpool Rd.

✕ Eating

The choice of restaurants in Manchester is unrivalled outside of London, with something for every palate and every budget. There are good restaurants throughout the city, including a superb selection in China-town and the organic havens of the Northern Quarter, where you'll also find some excellent veggie spots. If you want to dine like an in-the-know Mancunian, you'll have to go to suburbs such as Didsbury (divided into East and West), about 5 miles south of the city centre. The best way to get there is by buses 43 or 143 from Oxford Rd.

CITY CENTRE

TOP CHOICE **Australasia**   MODERN AUSTRALIAN ££

(✆0161-831 0288; www.australasia.uk.com; 1 The Avenue, Spinningfields; mains £13-30, 2-/3-/4-course lunch £11/15/20) What should you do with the dusty old basement archive of the *Manchester Evening News*? Convert it into the city centre's best new restaurant, of course. Descend through an IM Pei–inspired glass triangle into a stunning, beautifully lit space lined with comfortable booths. The menu combines contemporary Australian cuisine with flavours of southeast Asia – the lunchtime selection of fresh sushi is particularly good, as are the specials. A late licence sees it turn into a very cool bar with DJs and dancing in the evenings.

Oast House   INTERNATIONAL ££

(✆0161-829 3830; www.theoasthouse.uk.com; Crown Sq, Spinningfields; mains £9-15) An oast house is a 16th-century kiln used to dry out hops as part of the beer-making process. In Manchester, the Oast House is Tim Bacon's exciting new BBQ restaurant, a slice of medieval charm in the heart of (slightly) po-faced Spinningfields' contemporary designer chic. The kitchen is an outdoor covered grill, so staff have to shuttle the grilled delights (nothing fancy: burgers, kebabs, steaks and rotisserie chickens) to diners inside, but it works brilliantly. The deli boards (lots of cheeses and cured meats) are equally delicious.

Sam's Chop House   BRITISH £

(✆0161-834 3210; www.samschophouse.co.uk; Back Pool Fold, Chapel Walks, off Cross St; mains £6-8) Arguably the city's top gastropub, Sam's is a Victorian classic that serves dishes straight out of a Dickens novel. The highlight is the crispy corned beef hash cake, which is salt-cured for 10 days on the premises. 'There is no such passion in human nature as the passion for gravy among commercial gentlemen', declared Mrs Todgers in *Martin Chuzzlewit*; she would certainly approve of Sam's. The owners also run Mr Thomas' Chop House (p549).

Richmond Tea Rooms   CAFE £

(✆0161-237 9667; www.richmondtearooms.com; Richmond St; mains £5-8) You've never seen Victorian tearooms like this. Or maybe you have – in Tim Burton's *Alice in Wonderland*. Bold, clashing colours, a potpourri of period furniture and a counter painted to resemble the icing on a cake are just some of the features that make the Richmond one of the city's best new additions. Sandwiches and light meals (rarebit, quiche) are the menu's mainstay, but the real treat is the selection of afternoon teas, complete with four-fingered sandwiches, scones, cakes and, of course, your choice of teas.

Mark Addy   MODERN BRITISH ££

(✆0161-832 4080; www.markaddy.co.uk; Stanley St; mains £8.90-12.50; ☽lunch & dinner Wed-Fri, dinner Sat) Another contender for best pub grub in town, the Mark Addy owes its culinary success to Robert Owen Brown, whose loving interpretations of standard British classics – pork hop with honey-roasted bramley apple, pan-fried dab with cockles and spring onion et al (all locally sourced) – have people queuing at the door for a taste. It recently opened a riverside deck, so you can eat by the river where, during the 19th century, local publican Mark Addy rescued 50 people from drowning.

Jamie's Italian   ITALIAN ££

(✆0161-241 3901; www.jamieoliver.com; 100 King St; mains £8-14) The magnificent banking hall of Edwin Lutyens' castle-like art deco Midland Bank (1935) is now home to a branch of Jamie Oliver's fast-expanding gourmet empire. And while the food is perfectly adequate – it's an appealing blend of British staples given the Italian treatment (braised British shin of beef with Parmesan polenta; a South Coast fritto misto of crispy fried fresh fish and shellfish with Italian tartare sauce) – the real treat is the building itself. In the basement, the old deposit vaults have been converted into private dining rooms.

 Drinking

There's every kind of drinking hole in Manchester, from the really grungy ones that smell but have plenty of character to the ones that were designed by a team of architects but have the atmosphere of a freezer. Every neighbourhood in town has its favourites.

Bluu BAR

(☏0161-839 7740; www.bluu.co.uk; Smithfield Market Buildings, Thomas St; ◷noon-midnight Sun-Mon, to 1am Tue-Thu, to 2am Fri & Sat) Our favourite of the Northern Quarter's collection of great bars. Bluu is cool, comfortable and comes with a great terrace on which to enjoy a pint and listen to music selected by folks with really good taste.

Black Dog Ballroom BAR

(www.blackdogballroom.co.uk; 52 Church St) A basement bar with a speakeasy vibe, there's nothing illicit about drinking here: the cocktails are terrific, the atmosphere is always buzzing and the music always good and loud.

Britons Protection PUB

(☏0161-236 5895; 50 Great Bridgewater St; mains £8) Whisky – 200 different kinds of it – is the beverage of choice at this liver-threatening, proper English pub that also does Tudor-style meals (boar, venison and the like). An old-fashioned boozer with open fires in the back rooms and a cosy atmosphere...perfect on a cold evening.

Lass O'Gowrie PUB

(☏0161-273 6932; 36 Charles St; meals £6) A Victorian classic off Princess St that brews its own beer in the basement. It's a favourite with students, old-timers and anyone looking for an authentic pub experience. It also does good-value bar meals.

Odd BAR

(☏0161-833 0070; www.oddbar.co.uk; 30-32 Thomas St; ◷11am-11pm Mon-Sat, to 10.30pm Sun) This eclectic little bar – with its oddball furnishings, wacky tunes and anti-establishment crew of customers – is the perfect antidote to the increasingly similar look of so many modern bars. A slice of Mancuniana to be treasured.

BEST PUBS FOR A PINT IN THE NORTHWEST

» Philharmonic (p566), Liverpool

» Britons Protection (p549), Manchester

» Albion (p557), Chester

» Magnet (p566), Liverpool

Mr Thomas' Chop House PUB

(52 Cross St; mains £10) An old-style boozer that is very popular for a pint as well as a meal.

Peveril of the Peak PUB

(☏0161-236 6364; 127 Great Bridgewater St) An unpretentious pub with wonderful Victorian glazed tilework outside.

☆ **Entertainment**

Nightclubs

There's a constantly changing mixture of club nights, so check the *Manchester Evening News* for details of what's on.

Sankey's CLUB

(☏0161-950 4201; www.sankeys.info; Radium St, Ancoats; admission free-£12; ◷10pm-3am Thu & Fri, to 4am Sat) If you're a fan of techno, electro or any kind of non-mainstream house music, then a pilgrimage to Manchester's best nightclub should on no account be missed. Sankey's has earned itself legendary status for being at the vanguard of dance music (The Chemical Brothers, Daft Punk and others got their start here) and its commitment to top-class DJs is unwavering: these days, you'll hear the likes of Timo Maas, Séb Léger and Thomas Schumacher mix it up with the absolutely superb residents. Choon! The best way to get here is to board the free Disco Bus that picks up at locations throughout the city from Thursday to Saturday night; see the website for details.

Fac251 CLUB

(☏0161-272 7251; www.factorymanchester.com; 112-118 Princess St; admission £1-6; ◷9.30pm-3am Mon-Sat) It might be a paeon to days of yore, but Fac251, located in Tony Wilson's former Factory Records HQ, stands on its own two feet as one of the best venues in town. Three rooms, all with a broad musical appeal, from Monday's Hit & Run (drum and bass, hip hop and dub-step) to Stoned Love on Saturday,

LOCAL KNOWLEDGE

JOHN RYAN: RADIO PRODUCER & GUIDE

John Ryan is the chair of Gaydio 88.4FM, an accredited tour guide and an all-round bon vivant.

Favourite neighbourhood? I love the Northern Quarter, so I based myself there. But Spinningfields is worth a look for its upscale shopping and its wonderful choice of eateries – favourites are Australasia (p548) and the Oast House (p548).

Secret to getting the most from a night out? Mix up the city's offerings for a proper night out. The town is compact, so there really is something for everyone.

John Ryan's ideal night out? I'd start off with a bit of food – at either Home Sweet Home (☑0161-833 1248; www.cheesburgertoastie.co.uk; 49-51 Edge St) or Sam's Chop House (p548). If I'm feeling cultural, I'd take in a play at the Royal Exchange (p550), Manchester's most striking theatre. Afterwards a drink or a reading at Taurus (☑0161-236 4593; www.taurus-bar.co.uk; 1 Canal St) in the Gay Village.

which has indie rock, Motown and techno across three rooms. Something for everybody.

South CLUB
(☑0161-831 7756; 4a South King St; admission £5-8; ☉10pm-3am Fri & Sat) An excellent basement club to kick off the weekend: Friday night is CWord with Strangerways, featuring everything from Ibrahim Ferrer to Northern Soul, and Saturday is the always excellent Disco Rescue with Clint Boon (once of the Inspiral Carpets), which is more of the same eclectic mix of alternative and dance.

Cinemas

Cornerhouse CINEMA
(www.cornerhouse.org; 70 Oxford St) Your only destination for good art-house releases; also has a gallery, bookshop and cafe.

Odeon Cinema CINEMA
(www.odeon.co.uk; The Printworks, Exchange Sq) A 20-screen complex in the middle of the Printworks centre.

AMC Cinemas CINEMA
(www.amccinemas.co.uk; The Great Northern, 235 Deansgate) A 16-screen multiplex in a retail centre that was formerly a goods warehouse for the Northern Railway Company.

Theatre

Green Room THEATRE
(☑0161-236 1677; 54 Whitworth St West) The premier fringe venue in town.

Royal Exchange THEATRE
(☑0161-833 9833; www.royalexchange.co.uk; St Anne's Sq) Interesting contemporary plays are standard at this magnificent, modern theatre-in-the-round.

Live Music
ROCK MUSIC

Band on the Wall BAR, LIVE MUSIC
(☑0161-834 1786; www.bandonthewall.org; 25 Swan St) A top-notch venue that hosts everything from rock to world music, with splashes of jazz, blues and folk thrown in.

MEN Arena CONCERT VENUE
(www.men-arena.com; Great Ducie St) A giant arena north of the centre that hosts rock concerts (as well as being the home of the city's ice-hockey and basketball teams). It's about 300m north of Victoria Station.

Moho Live CONCERT VENUE
(www.moholive.com; 21-31 Oldham St) A new 500-capacity live-music venue that has already proven incredibly popular with its line-up of live music and club nights.

Ruby Lounge BAR, LIVE MUSIC
(☑0161-834 1392; 26-8 High St) Terrific live-music venue in the Northern Quarter that features mostly rock bands.

CLASSICAL MUSIC

Bridgewater Hall CONCERT VENUE
(☑0161-907 9000; www.bridgewater-hall.co.uk; Lower Mosley St) The world-renowned Hallé Orchestra has its home at this enormous and impressive concert hall, which hosts up to 250 concerts and events a year. It has a widespread program that includes opera, folk music, children's shows, comedy and contemporary music.

Lowry THEATRE
(☑0161-876 2020; www.thelowry.com; Pier 8, Salford Quays) Two separate venues in one: the Lyric Theatre, with the country's largest

stage outside the West End, hosts all kinds of performances including Opera North. The smaller Quays hosts more intimate gigs.

Manchester Cathedral CATHEDRAL
(☎0161-833 2220; www.manchestercathedral.org; Victoria St) Hosts a summer season of concerts by the Cantata Choir and ensemble groups.

Royal Northern College of Music MUSIC
(☎0161-907 5555; www.rncm.ac.uk; 124 Oxford Rd) Presents a full program of extremely high-quality classical music and other contemporary offerings.

Sport

For most people, Manchester plus sport equals football, and football means Manchester United (which is why we've included it in the Sights section). But in 2012 its crown was snatched in dramatic fashion by its bitter crosstown rival Manchester City, which, thanks to the investment of an oil-rick sheikh, has established itself as a major presence in world football.

Manchester City FOOTBALL
Perennial underdogs turned 2012 league champions, Manchester City owes its new-found success to Sheikh Mansour of Abu Dhabi, who bought the club in 2008 and transformed it into the world's wealthiest football team. Out went the mediocre players, in came global (highly paid) stars like David Silva, Yaya Touré and Sergio Agüero, who delivered the ultimate prize to the club's

---

THE MADCHESTER SOUND

It is often claimed that Manchester is the engine room of British pop. If this is indeed the case, then the chief engineer was TV presenter and music impresario Tony Wilson (1950–2007), founder of Factory Records. This is the label that in 1983 released New Order's ground-breaking 'Blue Monday', to this day the best-selling 12-inch single in British history, which successfully fused the guitar-driven sound of punk with a pulsating dance beat.

When the money started pouring in, Wilson took the next, all-important step: he opened his own nightclub, which would provide a platform for local bands to perform. The Hacienda opened its doors with plenty of fanfare but just wouldn't take off. Things started to turn around when the club embraced a brand-new sound coming out of Chicago and Detroit: house. DJs Mike Pickering, Graeme Park and Jon Da Silva were the music's most important apostles and, when ecstasy hit the scene late in the decade, it seemed that every kid in town was 'mad for it'.

Heavily influenced by these new arrivals, the city's guitar bands took notice and began shaping their sounds to suit the clubbers' needs. The most successful was the Stone Roses, who in 1989 released 'Fools Gold', a pulsating hit with the rapid shuffle of James Brown's 'Funky Drummer' and a druggie guitar sound that drove dancers wild. Around the same time, Happy Mondays, fronted by the laddish Shaun Ryder and the whacked-out Bez (whose only job was to lead the dancing from the stage), hit the scene with the infectious 'Hallelujah'. The other big anthems of the day were 'The One I Love' by the Charlatans, 'Voodoo Ray' by A Guy Called Gerald, and 'Pacific' by 808 State – all local bands and producers. The party known as Madchester was officially open.

The party ended in 1992. Overdanced and overdrugged, the city woke up with a terrible hangover. The Hacienda went bust, Shaun Ryder's legendary lifestyle stymied his musical creativity and the Stone Roses withdrew in a haze of postparty depression. The latter was not to be heard of again until 1994 when it released *Second Coming,* which just couldn't match its eponymous debut album. The band lasted another two years before breaking up. The fertile crossover scene, which had seen clubbers go mad at rock gigs, and rock bands play the kind of dance sounds that kept the floor thumping until the early hours, virtually disappeared and the two genres withdrew into a more familiar isolation.

Madchester is legendary precisely because it is no more, but it was exciting. If you missed the party, you can get a terrific sense of what it was like by watching Michael Winterbottom's *24-Hour Party People* (2002), which captures the hedonism, extravagance and genius of Madchester's cast of characters; and the superb *Control* (2007) by Anton Corbijn, which tells the story of Ian Curtis, Joy Division's tragic lead singer.

success-starved fans for the first time since 1968. A new era of glory has now begun. In the meantime, you can enjoy the Manchester City Stadium Tour (0161-444 1894; www.mcfc.co.uk; tours adult/child £8.50/6; tours 11am, 1.30pm & 3.30pm Mon-Sat, 11.45am, 1.45pm & 3.30pm Sun except match days), a tour of the ground, dressing rooms and museum before the inevitable steer into the kit shop. Tours must be booked in advance. Take bus 53, 54, 185, 186, 216, 217, 230–37, X36 or X37 from Piccadilly Gardens.

Lancashire County Cricket Club CRICKET
(0161-282 4000; www.lccc.co.uk; Warwick Rd) Cricket is a big deal here and Lancashire, founded in 1816 as the Aurora before changing its name in 1864, is one of the most beloved of England's county teams, despite the fact that it hasn't won the county championship since 1934. Matches are played at Old Trafford (same name, different but adjacent ground to the football stadium) and the key fixture in Lancashire's calendar is the Roses match against Yorkshire, but if you're not around for that, the other games in the county season (admission £11 to £17) are a great day out. The season runs throughout the summer. International test matches are also played here occasionally. Take the Metrolink to Old Trafford.

Shopping

From the boho indie boutiques of the Northern Quarter to the swanky stores of Spinningfields, including Emporio Armani (0161-220 2980; Unit G1 & 2, The Avenue, Spinningfields), Brooks Brothers (0161-834 6649; Unit G19, The Avenue, Spinningfields), DKNY (0161-833 3277; Unit G18, The Avenue, Spinningfields) etc, Manchester's retail credentials are assured. New Cathedral St, part of the Millennium Quarter, and King St also have fancy shops, while the Arndale Centre is the city's equivalent of the English high street.

Oi Polloi BOUTIQUE
(www.oipolloi.com; 70 Tib St) Besides the impressive range of casual footwear, this hip boutique also stocks a range of designers including APC, Lyle & Scott, Nudie Jeans and Fjällräven.

Harvey Nichols DEPARTMENT STORE
(21 New Cathedral St; restaurant mains £8-16; restaurant lunch daily, dinner Tue-Sat) The king of British department stores has an elegant presence on fashionista row. The 2nd-floor restaurant is excellent and even has a wine list of more than 400 different wines.

Tib Street Market MARKET
(0161-234 7357; Tib St; 10am-5pm Sat) Up-and-coming local designers get a chance to display their wares at this relatively new weekly market where you can pick up everything from purses to lingerie and hats to jewellery.

GAY & LESBIAN MANCHESTER

The city's gay scene is unrivalled outside London and caters to every taste. Its healthy heart beats loudest in the Gay Village, centred on handsome Canal St. Here you'll find bars, clubs, restaurants and – crucially – karaoke joints that cater almost exclusively to the pink pound.

The country's biggest gay and lesbian arts festival, Queer Up North, takes place every two years – the next in spring 2013. Manchester Pride (p546) is a 10-day festival from the middle of August each year and attracts more than 500,000 people.

There are bars to suit every taste, but you won't go far wrong in AXM Club (http://axm group.co.uk; 10 Canal St), which is more of a cocktail lounge for the city's flash crowd; or Taurus (p550), which is a little shabbier but equally good fun.

For your clubbing needs, look no further than Club Alter Ego (www.facebook.com/pages/Club-Alter-Ego/116392715108719; 105-107 Princess St; 11pm-5am Thu-Sat).

And then there's karaoke, the ultimate choice for midweek fun. The best of the lot is at the New Union Hotel (0161-228 1492; www.newunionhotel.com; 111 Princess St; r from £40), where you can find your inner Madonna and Cyndi Lauper every Tuesday and Thursday – for a top prize of £50.

For more information, check with the Lesbian & Gay Foundation (0161-235 8035; www.lgf.org.uk; 105-107 Princess St; 4-10pm). Up-to-date information is also available on www.visitmanchester.com under LGBT.

Oxfam Originals
VINTAGE

(Unit 8, Smithfield Bldg, Oldham St) If you're into retro, this terrific store has high-quality gear from the 1960s and '70s. Shop in the knowledge that it's for a good cause.

Rags to Bitches
VINTAGE

(www.rags-to-bitches.co.uk; 60 Tib St) Award-winning vintage boutique with fashions from the 1930s to the '80s. This is the place to go to pick up unusual, individual pieces or that outfit for the fancy-dress ball.

Cornerhouse
BOOKS

(www.cornerhouse.org; 70 Oxford St) Art and film books, specialist magazines and kitschy cards.

ⓘ Information

Emergency
Ambulance (☏0161-436 3999)
Police station (☏0161-872 5050; Bootle St)
Rape Crisis Centre (☏0161-273 4500)
Samaritans (☏0161-236 8000)

Internet Access
L2K Internet Gaming Cafe (32 Princess St; per 30min £2; ☺9am-10pm Mon-Fri, to 9pm Sat & Sun)
Loops Computer (83 Princess St; per 30min £2; ☺9am-10pm Mon-Fri, to 9pm Sat & Sun)

Medical Services
Cameolord Chemist (St Peter's Sq; ☺10am-10pm)
Manchester Royal Infirmary (Oxford Rd)

Post
Post office (Brazennose St; ☺9am-5.30pm Mon-Fri)

Tourist Information
Tourist office (www.visitmanchester.com; Piccadilly Plaza, Portland St; guided tours daily £6/5 per adult/child; ☺10am-5.15pm Mon-Sat, to 4.30pm Sun)

Websites
Manchester City Council (www.manchester .gov.uk) The council's official website, which includes a visitors section.
Manchester Evening News (http://menmedia .co.uk) The city's evening paper in electronic form.
Real Manchester (www.realmanchester.com) Online guide to nightlife.
Restaurants of Manchester (www.restaurants ofmanchester.com) Thorough, reliable and up-to-date reviews of restaurants in the city and suburbs.

Visit Manchester (www.visitmanchester.com) The official website for Greater Manchester.

ⓘ Getting There & Away

Air
Manchester Airport (☏0161-489 3000; www.manchesterairport.co.uk), south of the city, is the largest airport outside London and is served by 13 locations throughout Britain as well as more than 50 international destinations.

Bus
National Express (☏08717 81 81 81; www .nationalexpress.com) serves most major cities almost hourly between the coach station (Chorlton St) in the city centre. Sample destinations:
Leeds £8.40, one hour, hourly
Liverpool £6.30, 1¼ hours, hourly
London £24.40, 3¾ hours, hourly

Train
Manchester Piccadilly (east of the Gay Village) is the main station for trains to and from the rest of the country, although Victoria station (north of the National Football Museum) serves Halifax and Bradford. The two stations are linked by Metrolink. Off-peak fares are considerably cheaper.
Blackpool £13.50, 1¼ hours, half-hourly
Liverpool Lime St £9.80, 45 minutes, half-hourly
London Euston £131, three hours, seven daily
Newcastle £51.20, three hours, six daily

ⓘ Getting Around

To/From the Airport
The airport is 12 miles south of the city. A train to or from Victoria station costs £2, and a coach is £3. A taxi is nearly four times as much in light traffic.

Public Transport
The excellent public transport system can be used with a variety of Day Saver tickets. For enquiries about local transport, including night buses, contact **Travelshop** (☏0161-228 7811; www.gmpte.com; 9 Portland St, Piccadilly Gardens; ☺8am-8pm).

BUS Centreline bus 4 provides a free service around the heart of Manchester every 10 minutes. Pick up a route map from the tourist office. Most local buses start from Piccadilly Gardens.

METROLINK There are frequent **Metrolink** (www.metrolink.co.uk) trams between Victoria and Piccadilly train stations and G-Mex (for Castlefield), as well as further afield to Salford Quays. Buy your tickets from the platform machine.

TRAIN Castlefield is served by Deansgate station with rail links to Piccadilly, Oxford Rd and Salford stations.

CHESHIRE

Generally overshadowed by the loud, busy conurbations of Liverpool and Manchester, Cheshire gets on with life in a quiet, usually bucolic kind of way, happy enough with its reputation as a contemporary version of ye olde Englande – complete with fields of Friesian cows and half-timbered Tudor houses. Interspersed throughout this idyll are the high-walled estates of the region's richest burghers (including many soccer millionaires looking to add a little class to their immense wealth), but for the hoi polloi Cheshire is really just about Chester.

Chester

POP 80,130

Marvellous Chester is one of English history's greatest gifts to the contemporary visitor. Its red-sandstone wall, which today gift-wraps a tidy collection of Tudor and Victorian buildings, was built during Roman times. The town was then called Castra Devana, and was the largest Roman fortress in Britain.

It's hard to believe today, but throughout the Middle Ages Chester made its money as the most important port in the northwest. However, the River Dee silted up over time and Chester fell behind Liverpool in importance.

◉ Sights & Activities

FREE City Walls   LANDMARK
A good way to get a sense of Chester's unique character is to walk the 2-mile circuit along the walls that surround the historic centre. Originally built by the Romans around AD 70, the walls were altered substantially over the following centuries but have retained their current position since around 1200. The tourist office's *Walk Around Chester Walls* leaflet is an excellent guide.

Of the many features along the walls, the most eye-catching is the prominent Eastgate, where you can see the most famous clock in England after London's Big Ben, built for Queen Victoria's Diamond Jubilee in 1897.

At the southeastern corner of the walls are the wishing steps, added in 1785; local legend claims that if you can run up and down these uneven steps while holding your breath your wish will come true. We question the veracity of this claim because our wish was not to twist an ankle.

Just inside Southgate, known here as Bridgegate (as it's located at the northern end of the Old Dee Bridge), is the Bear & Billet (http://bearandbillet.com; Southgate) pub, Chester's oldest timber-framed building, built in 1664, and once a toll gate into the city.

Rows   ARCHITECTURE
Chester's other great draw is the Rows, a series of two-level galleried arcades along the four streets that fan out in each direction from the Central Cross. The architecture is a handsome mix of Victorian and Tudor (original and mock) buildings that house a fantastic collection of individually owned shops. The origin of the Rows is a little unclear, but it is believed that as the Roman walls slowly crumbled, medieval traders built their shops against the resulting rubble banks, while later arrivals built theirs on top.

Chester Cathedral   CATHEDRAL
(☎01244-324756; www.chestercathedral.com; 12 Abbey Sq; adult/child £6/2.50; ☺9am-5pm Mon-Sat, 1-4pm Sun) Originally a Benedictine abbey built on the remains of an earlier Saxon church dedicated to St Werburgh (the city's patron saint), it was shut down in 1540 as part of Henry VIII's dissolution frenzy but reconsecrated as a cathedral the following year. Although the cathedral itself was given a substantial Victorian facelift, the 12th-century cloister and its surrounding buildings are essentially unaltered and retain much of the structure from the early monastic years. Admission includes a 45-minute audio tour of the building.

FREE Grosvenor Museum   MUSEUM
(☎01244-972197; www.grosvenormuseum.co.uk; 27 Grosvenor St; ☺10.30am-5pm Mon-Sat, 2-5pm Sun) Excellent museum with the country's most comprehensive collection of Roman tombstones. At the back of the museum is a preserved Georgian house, complete with kitchen, drawing room, bedroom and bathroom.

Dewa Roman Experience · MUSEUM
(📞01244-343407; www.dewaromanexperience.co
.uk; Pierpoint Lane; adult/child £4.95/3.25; ⊙9am-
5pm Mon-Sat, 10am-5pm Sun) Walk through a
reconstructed Roman street to reveal what
Roman life was like. It's just off Bridge St.

FREE Roman Amphitheatre · RUINS
(Little St John St) Just outside the city walls is
what was once an arena that seated 7000
spectators (making it the country's largest); some historians have suggested that it
may have also been the site of King Arthur's
Camelot and that his knights' 'round table'
was really just this circular construction. Excavations continue; during summer months
there are occasional shows held here.

St John the Baptist Church · CHURCH
(Vicar's Lane; ⊙9.15am-6pm) Built on the site
of an older Saxon church in 1075, it's been
a peaceful ruin since 1581. It includes the
remains of a Norman choir and medieval
chapels.

☞ Tours

Chester Visitor Information Centre (p557)
offers a broad range of walking tours departing from the town hall, including food,
historical and ghost tours. Each lasts between 1½ and two hours. Recommended
are the cruises up and down the Dee run by
Chester Boat (📞01244-325394; www.chester
boat.co.uk; £6.50-14), which include a foray
into the gorgeous Eaton Estate, home of the
duke and duchess of Westminster. All departures are from the riverside along the promenade known as the Groves.

🛏 Sleeping

If you're visiting between Easter and September, you'd better book early if you want
to avoid going over budget or settling for
far less than you bargained for. Except for a
handful of options, most of the accommodation is outside the city walls but within easy
walking distance of the centre.

TOP CHOICE Stone Villa · B&B ££
(📞01244-345014; www.stonevillachester.co.uk; 3
Stone Pl, Hoole Rd; s/d from £45/75; P🐕) Twice
winner of Chester's B&B of the Year in the
last 10 years, this beautiful villa has everything you need for a memorable stay. Elegant
bedrooms, a fabulous breakfast and welcoming, friendly owners all add up to one of the

best lodgings in town. Bus No 9 from town
will get you there in under five minutes (it's
about a mile from the city centre).

Green Bough · BOUTIQUE HOTEL £££
(📞01244-326241; www.chestergreenboughhotel.co
.uk; 60 Hoole Rd; r from £175; P@🐕) The epitome of the boutique hotel, this exclusive,
award-winning Victorian town house has
individually styled rooms dressed in the best
Italian fabrics. The rooms come adorned
with wall coverings, superb antique furniture and period cast-iron and wooden beds,
including a handful of elegant four-posters.
Modern touches include plasma-screen TVs,
mini-stereos and a range of fancy toiletries.
Take bus No 9.

Chester Grosvenor Hotel & Spa · HOTEL £££
(📞01244-324024; www.chestergrosvenor.com; 58
Eastgate St; r from £170; P@🐕) Perfectly located, the Chester Grosvenor has huge, sprawling rooms with exquisite period furnishings
and all mod cons. The spa, which is also
open to nonguests, offers a range of body
treatments, including reiki, LaStone therapy, Indian head massage and four-handed
massage. There's also a Michelin-starred restaurant downstairs.

Chester Backpackers · HOSTEL £
(📞01244-400185; www.chesterbackpackers.co.uk;
67 Boughton; dm from £15.50; 🐕) Comfortable
dorm rooms with nice pine beds in a typically Tudor white-and-black building. It's just
a short walk from the city walls and there's
also a pleasant garden.

🍴 Eating

Chester has great food – it's just not in any of
the tourist-oriented restaurants that line the
Rows. Besides the better restaurants, you'll
find the best grub in some of the pubs.

Joseph Benjamin · MODERN BRITISH ££
(📞01244-344295; www.josephbenjamin.co.uk; 134-
40 Northgate St; mains £13-17; ⊙9am-5pm Tue-
Wed, 9am-midnight Thu & Fri, 10am-5pm Sun) A
bright star in Chester's culinary firmament
is this combo restaurant, bar and deli that
delivers carefully prepared local produce
to take out or sit-in. Excellent sandwiches
and gorgeous salads are the mainstay of the
takeout menu, while the more formal dinner menu features fine examples of modern
British cuisine – the Cajun spiced fillet of
rainbow trout with cuttlefish, couscous, and
mint-and-lime yoghurt is especially good.

Chester

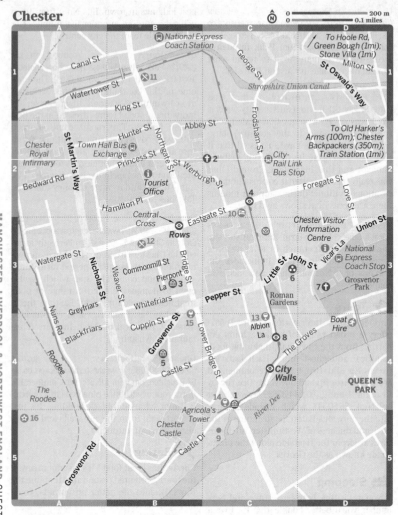

Upstairs at the Grill   STEAKHOUSE £££
(☎01244-344883; www.upstairsatthegrill.co.uk; 70 Watergate St; mains £15-28; ⊗dinner Mon-Sat, lunch & dinner Sun) This Manhattan-style steakhouse, almost hidden on the 2nd floor, is the place to devour every cut of meat from American-style porterhouse to a sauce-sodden chateaubriand. All of the cuts are locally sourced and dry aged for five weeks to guarantee succulence; most cuts are available in 225g or 340g except for the bone-in rib eye, which comes in a daunting racket-sized 680g hunk of meat.

Old Harker's Arms   PUB ££
(☎01244-344525; www.harkersarms-chester.co.uk; 1 Russell St; mains £9-14; ⊗lunch & dinner) An old-style boozer with a gourmet kitchen, this is the perfect place to tuck into Cumberland sausages or a Creole rice salad with sweet potatoes, and then rinse your palate with a pint of local ale, such as Cheshire Cat. It also serves bar snacks and sandwiches. To get here, follow Eastgate St east for 100m and take a left onto Russell St.

Chester

Drinking

Albion　　　　　　　　　　PUB
(4 Albion St) No children, no music and no machines or big screens (but plenty of Union Jacks). This 'family hostile' Edwardian classic pub is a throwback to a time when ale-drinking still had its own rituals. Still, this is one of the finest pubs in northwest England precisely because it doggedly refuses to modernise.

Falcon　　　　　　　　　　PUB
(Lower Bridge St; mains from £5.50) An old-fashioned boozer with a lovely atmosphere, it's great for both a pint and a bite. The surprisingly adventurous menu offers up dishes such as Jamaican peppered beef or spicy Italian sausage casserole.

☆ Entertainment

Roodee　　　　　　　　HORSE RACING
(www.chester-races.co.uk; The Racecourse; ⏲May-Sep) Chester's ancient and very beautiful racetrack, on the western side of the walls, has been hosting races since the 16th century. Highlights of the summer flat season include the two-day July Festival and the August equivalent.

❶ Information

Cheshire Constabulary (☎01244-350000; Town Hall, Northgate St)
Chester visitor information centre (www.visitchester.com; Vicar's Lane; tours £5; ⏲9.30am-5.30pm Mon-Sat, 10am-4pm Sun) Accommodation bookings and walking tours.

Countess of Chester Hospital (☎01244-365000; Health Park, Liverpool Rd)
Post office (2 St John St; ⏲9am-5.30pm Mon-Sat)
Tourist office (☎01244-402111; www.visitchester.com; Town Hall, Northgate St; ⏲9am-5.30pm Mon-Sat, 10am-4pm Sun May-Oct, 10am-5pm Mon-Sat Nov-Apr)

❶ Getting There & Away

Bus

National Express (☎08717 81 81 81; www.nationalexpress.com) coaches stop on Vicar's Lane, just opposite the tourist office by the Roman amphitheatre. Destinations include the following:

Birmingham £12.40, 2¼ hours, four daily
Liverpool £7.20, one hour, four daily
London £24.60, 5½ hours, three daily
Manchester £6.80, 1¼ hours, three daily.

For information on local bus services, ring the **Cheshire Bus Line** (☎01244-602666). Local buses leave from the **Town Hall Bus Exchange** (Princess St).

Train

The train station is about a mile from the city centre via Foregate St and City Rd, or Brook St. City-Rail Link buses are free for people with rail tickets, and operate between the station and **Bus Stop A** (Frodsham St). Destinations:

Liverpool £4.35, 45 minutes, hourly
London Euston £65.20, 2½ hours, hourly
Manchester £12.60, one hour, hourly

ⓘ Getting Around

Much of the city centre is closed to traffic from 10.30am to 4.30pm, so a car is likely to be a hindrance. Anyway, the city is easy to walk around and most places of interest are close to the wall.

City buses depart from the Town Hall Bus Exchange.

Around Chester

The largest of its kind in the country, Chester Zoo (www.chesterzoo.org; Upton-by-Chester; adult/child £16.30/12.60, monorail adult/child £2/1.50, waterbus adult/child £2/1.50; ⊙10am-dusk, last admission 4pm Mon-Fri, to 5pm Sat & Sun) is about as pleasant a place as caged animals in artificial renditions of their natural habitats could ever expect to live. It's so big that there's even a monorail and a waterbus on which to get around. The zoo is on the A41, 3 miles north of Chester's city centre. First bus 1 (every 15 minutes Monday to Saturday, half-hourly Sunday) runs between Chester's Town Hall Bus Exchange and the zoo.

LIVERPOOL

POP 469,020

Few English cities are as shackled by reputation as Liverpool, and none has worked so hard to outgrow the clichés that for so long have been used to define it.

A hardscrabble town with a reputation for wit and an obsessive love of football, Liverpool also has an impressive cultural heritage: it has more listed museums than any other city outside London, has recently undergone an impressive program of urban regeneration and its collection of museums and galleries is easily amongst the best in the country. And then there's the Beatles. Liverpool cherishes them not because it's stuck in the past and hasn't gotten over the fact that they're long gone – it's because their worldwide popularity would make it crazy *not* to do so.

The main attractions are Albert Dock (west of the city centre), and the trendy Ropewalks area (south of Hanover St and west of the two cathedrals). Lime St station, the bus station and the Cavern Quarter – a mecca for Beatles fans – lie just to the north.

History

Liverpool grew wealthy on the back of the triangular trading of slaves, raw materials and finished goods. From 1700 ships carried cotton goods and hardware from Liverpool to West Africa, where they were exchanged for slaves, who in turn were carried to the West Indies and Virginia, where they were exchanged for sugar, rum, tobacco and raw cotton.

As a great port, the city drew thousands of Irish and Scottish immigrants, and its Celtic influences are still apparent. However, between 1830 and 1930 nine million emigrants – mainly English, Scots and Irish, but also Swedes, Norwegians and Russian Jews – sailed from here to the New World.

The start of WWII led to a resurgence of Liverpool's importance. More than one million American GIs disembarked here before D-Day and the port was, once again, hugely important as the western gateway for transatlantic supplies. The GIs brought with them the latest American records, and Liverpool was thus the first European port of call for the new rhythm and blues that would eventually become rock and roll. Within 20 years, the Mersey Beat was *the* sound of British pop, and four mop-topped Scousers had formed a skiffle band...

⊙ Sights

The wonderful Albert Dock is the city's biggest tourist attraction and the key to understanding the city's history, but the city centre is where you'll find most of Liverpool's real day-to-day life.

CITY CENTRE

Liverpool Cathedral   CATHEDRAL
(☎0151-709 6271; www.liverpoolcathedral.org.uk; Upper Duke St; visitor centre & tower admission £5; ⊙8am-6pm) Liverpool's Anglican cathedral is a building of superlatives. Not only is it Britain's largest church, it's also the world's largest Anglican cathedral, and it's all thanks to Sir Giles Gilbert Scott, who made its construction his life's work. Sir Scott also gave us the red telephone box and the Southwark Power Station in London, now the Tate Modern. The central bell is the world's third-largest (with the world's highest and heaviest peal), while the organ, with its 9765 pipes, is likely the world's largest operational model.

The visitor centre features the Great Space; this 10-minute, panoramic high-definition movie about the history of the cathedral is followed by your own audio-visual tour, courtesy of a headset. Your ticket also gives you access to the cathedral's 101m tower, from which there are terrific views of

LIVERPOOL IN...

Two Days

Start at the waterfront's collection of superb museums. Visit the new **Museum of Liverpool** and, just south, the **International Slavery Museum** in Albert Dock.

Pay the Fab Four their due at the **Beatles Story** before heading into town to the Cavern Quarter around Mathew St. The **Monro** is worth a visit for lunch and the **Marco Pierre White Steakhouse & Grill** for dinner. Round off the day with a pint at the marvellous **Philharmonic**, and wrap yourself in the crisp sheets of the **Hotel Indigo**. Night hawks can tear it up in the bars and clubs of the hip **Ropewalks** area. The next day, explore the city's two **cathedrals** and check out the twin delights of the **World Museum** and the **Walker Art Gallery**.

Four Days

Follow the two-day itinerary and make a pilgrimage to **Mendips** and **20 Forthlin Road**, the childhood homes of John Lennon and Paul McCartney respectively. For dinner, try the **Italian Club**. The next day, walk on holy ground at Anfield, home of **Liverpool Football Club**. Race junkies can head to the visitor centre at **Aintree racecourse**, which hosts England's beloved race, the Grand National.

the city and beyond – on a clear day you can see Blackpool Tower.

FREE World Museum   MUSEUM
(☑0151-478 4399; www.liverpoolmuseums.org.uk/wml; William Brown St; ⊙10am-5pm) Natural history, science and technology are the themes of this sprawling museum, whose exhibits range from birds of prey to space exploration. It also includes the country's only free planetarium. This vastly entertaining and educational museum is divided into four major sections: the Human World, one of the top anthropological collections in the country; the Natural World, which includes a new aquarium as well as live insect colonies; Earth, a geological treasure trove; and Space & Time, which includes the planetarium. Highly recommended.

FREE Walker Art Gallery   ART MUSEUM
(☑0151-478 4199; www.liverpoolmuseums.org.uk/walker; William Brown St; ⊙10am-5pm) Touted as the 'National Gallery of the North', the city's foremost gallery is the national gallery for northern England, housing an outstanding collection of art from the 14th to the 21st centuries. Its strong suits are Pre-Raphaelite art, modern British art and sculpture – not to mention the rotating exhibits of contemporary expression. It's a family-friendly place, too: the ground-floor Big Art for Little People gallery is designed especially for under-eights and features interactive exhib-

its and games that will (hopefully) result in a life-long love affair with art.

FREE St George's Hall   CULTURAL CENTRE
(☑0151-707 2391; www.stgeorgesliverpool.co.uk; William Brown St; ⊙10am-5pm Tue-Sat, 1-5pm Sun) Arguably Liverpool's most impressive building is the Grade I–listed St George's Hall, a magnificent example of neoclassical architecture that is as imposing today as it was when it was completed in 1854. Curiously, it was built as law courts *and* a concert hall – presumably a judge could pass sentence and then relax to a string quartet. Today it serves as an all-purpose cultural and civic centre, hosting concerts, corporate gigs and a host of other civic get-togethers; it is also the focal point of any city-wide celebration. Tours (☑0151-225 6909; tours £3.50; ⊙2pm Wed, 11am & 2pm Sat & Sun) of the hall are run in conjunction with the tourist office; the tour route can vary depending on what's going on in the building.

Metropolitan Cathedral of Christ the King   CHURCH
(☑0151-709 9222; www.liverpoolmetrocathedral.org.uk; Brownlow Hill; ⊙8am-6pm Mon-Sat, to 5pm Sun Oct-Mar) Known colloquially as Paddy's Wigwam, Liverpool's Catholic cathedral is a mightily impressive modern building that looks like a soaring concrete teepee, hence its nickname. It was completed in 1967 according to the design of Sir Frederick Gibberd after the original plans by Sir Edwin

MANCHESTER, LIVERPOOL & NORTHWEST ENGLAND LIVERPOOL

Liverpool

200 m
0.1 miles

Pembroke Pl

Brownlow Hill

Mt Pleasant

Oxford St

Everyman Theatre

27

33

Myrtle St

Catherine St

Canning St

5

London Rd

To National Express Coach Station (200m)

29

Russell St

Clarence St

Rodney St

Hardman St

26

Hope Pl

23

Rice St

14

Hope St

Leece St

25

18

Rodney St

Liverpool Cathedral

Brownlow Hill

Mt Pleasant

Renshaw St

Berry St

Great George St

Upper Duke St

William Brown St

Hotham St

Lime St Train Station

Arriva 500

Copperas Hill

Lime St

8

Clayton Square

Ranelagh St

Central

20

Bold St

Wood St

Concert St

Seel St

Slater St

Fleet St

19

21

31

Fair St

Duke St

CHINATOWN

Nelson St

22

32

Duke St

Tabley St

Queen Square

Williamson Square

Victoria St

Church St

School La

Hanover St

Campbell Square

ROPEWALKS

To World Museum Liverpool & Walker Art Gallery (90m)

Cavern Quarter

Paradise St

Lord St

Duke St

Liver St

Paradise St

Park La

Wapping

16

Wapping Dock

To James Monro (150m)

Moorfields

Temple La

28

30

Harrington St

Cook St

34

Merseyside Police Headquarters

35

Strand St

Wapping Basin

Stalhouse Dock

Wapping Basin

Dale St

Castle St

24

13

James St

James St

Strand St

Canning Dock

11

Monarch's Quay

King's

Town Hall

3

Rumford St

Water St

Mersey Tunnel

Chapel St

15

Tithebarn St

To Old Hall St

To Radisson Blu (200m)

Bath St

William Jessop Way

17

New Quay

Goree Piazza

Brunswick St

7

2

6

Mann Island

PIER HEAD

10

Canning Half Tide Basin

Museum of Liverpool

International Slavery Museum

4

Albert Dock

9

1

Beatles Story

12

Princes Dock

Mersey Tunnel

Mersey

Liverpool

Lutyens, whose crypt is inside. The central tower frames the world's largest stained-glass window, created by John Piper and Patrick Reyntiens.

Liverpool War Museum　　　MUSEUM
(www.liverpoolwarmuseum.co.uk; 1 Rumford St; adult/child £6/4; ⊙10.30am-4.30pm Mon-Thu & Sat Mar-Oct) The secret command centre for the Battle of the Atlantic, the Western Approaches, was abandoned at the end of the war with virtually everything left intact. You can get a good glimpse of the labyrinthine nerve centre of Allied operations, including the all-important map room, where you can imagine playing a real-life, full-scale version of Risk.

ALBERT DOCK

Liverpool's biggest tourist attraction is Albert Dock (☑0151-708 8854; www.albertdock .com; admission free), 2.75 hectares of water ringed by enormous cast-iron columns and impressive five-storey warehouses that make up the country's largest collection of protected buildings and are a World Heritage Site. A fabulous development program has really brought the dock to life; here you'll find several outstanding museums and an extension of London's Tate Gallery, as well as a couple of top-class restaurants and bars.

TOP
CHOICE **International Slavery
Museum**　　　MUSEUM
(☑0151-478 4499; www.liverpoolmuseums.org.uk/ ism; Albert Dock; admission free; ⊙10am-5pm) Museums are, by their very nature, like a still of the past, but the extraordinary International Slavery Museum resonates very much in the present. It reveals slavery's unimaginable horrors – including Liverpool's own role in the triangular slave trade – in a clear and uncompromising manner. It does this through a remarkable series of multimedia and other displays, and it doesn't baulk at confronting racism, slavery's shadowy

LIVERPOOL FOR CHILDREN

The waterfront museums are extremely popular with kids, especially the brand-new Museum of Liverpool and the Merseyside Maritime Museum, which has a couple of boats for kids to mess about on. The Yellow Duckmarine Tour (☏0151-708 7799; www .theyellowduckmarine.co.uk; adult/child £14.95/9.95; ☺from 11am) is a sure-fire winner, while a visit to Anfield Rd (p567) is a must if your kids have any kind of interest in football. The Big Art for Little People gallery at the Walker Art Gallery (p559) is perfect for kids who want to find out that art is more than just something adults stare at.

ideological justification for this inhumane practice.

The history of slavery is made real through a series of personal experiences, including a carefully kept ship's log and captain's diary. These tell the story of one slaver's experience on a typical trip, departing Liverpool for West Africa. The ship then purchased or captured as many slaves as it could carry before embarking on the gruesome 'middle passage' across the Atlantic to the West Indies. The slaves that survived the torturous journey were sold for sugar, rum, tobacco and raw cotton, which were then brought back to England for profit. Exhibits include original shackles, chains and instruments used to punish rebellious slaves – each piece of metal is more horrendous than the next.

It's heady, disturbing stuff, but as well as providing an insightful history lesson, we are reminded of our own obligations to humanity and justice throughout the museum, not least in the Legacies of Slavery exhibit, which explores the continuing fight for freedom and equality. A visit to this magnificent museum is unmissable.

Beatles Story   MUSEUM
(☏0151-709 1963; www.beatlesstory.com; Albert Dock; adult/student/child £12.95/9/7, incl Elvis & Us £15.95/12/7; ☺9am-7pm, last admission 5pm) Liverpool's most popular museum won't illuminate any dark, juicy corners in the turbulent history of the world's most famous foursome – there's ne'er a mention of internal discord, drugs or Yoko Ono – but there's plenty of genuine memorabilia to keep a Beatles fan happy. Particularly impressive is the full-size replica Cavern Club (which was actually tiny) and the Abbey Rd studio where the lads recorded their first singles, while George Harrison's crappy first guitar (now worth half a million quid) should inspire budding, penniless musicians to keep the faith. The museum is also the departure

point for the Yellow Duckmarine Tour. You can also get a combo ticket for the Elvis & Us exhibit at the new Beatles Story extension on Pier Head.

FREE Merseyside Maritime Museum   MUSEUM
(☏0151-478 4499; www.liverpoolmuseums.org.uk/maritime; Albert Dock; ☺10am-5pm) The story of one of the world's great ports is the theme of this excellent museum and, believe us, it's a graphic and compelling page-turner. One of the many great exhibits is Emigration to a New World, which tells the story of nine million emigrants and their efforts to get to North America and Australia; the walk-through model of a typical ship shows just how tough conditions on board really were.

FREE Tate Liverpool   ART MUSEUM
(☏0151-702 7400; www.tate.org.uk/liverpool; Albert Dock; special exhibitions adult/child from £5/4; ☺10am-5.50pm Jun-Aug, closed Mon Sep-May) Touted as the home of modern art in the north, this gallery features a substantial checklist of 20th-century artists across its four floors, as well as touring exhibitions from the mother ship on London's Bankside. But it's all a little sparse, with none of the energy we'd expect from the world-famous Tate.

NORTH OF ALBERT DOCK

The area to the north of Albert Dock is known as Pier Head, after a stone pier built in the 1760s. This is still the departure point for ferries across the River Mersey, and was for millions of migrants their final contact with European soil.

The new Museum of Liverpool is an impressive architectural interloper, but pride of place in this part of the dock still goes to the trio of Edwardian buildings known as the 'Three Graces', dating from the days when Liverpool's star was still ascending. The southernmost, with the dome mimicking St Paul's Cathedral, is the Port of Liverpool Building, completed in 1907. Next to it is the Cunard Building, in the style of an Italian palazzo, once HQ to the Cunard Steamship Line. Finally, the Royal Liver Building (pronounced *lie*-ver) was opened in 1911 as the head office of the Royal Liver Friendly Society. It's crowned by Liverpool's symbol, the famous 5.5m copper Liver Bird.

FREE **Museum of Liverpool**   MUSEUM
(☑0151-478 4545; www.liverpoolmuseums.org .uk; Pier Head; ⊙10am-5pm) Liverpool's storied past is explored within the confines of an eye-catching futuristic building designed in typical Scandinavian verve by Danish firm 3XN. Inside, it's all fizz-bang-wallop as you wend your way through an interactive exploration of the cultural and historical milestones of Liverpool – the railroad, poverty, wealth, *Brookside* (a popular '80s TV soap opera set in the city), the Beatles and football (the film on the meaning of the game to the city is worth the 15 minutes). The desire to tell all of the city's rich story means there isn't a huge amount of depth, but the kids will love it, as will anyone who doesn't want a doctoral dissertation on urban development and population growth.

The Beatles Story: Elvis & Us   EXHIBITION
(☑0151-709 1963; www.elvisandus.com; Mersey Ferries Terminal, Pier Head; admission £6; ⊙9am-7pm Apr-Sep, 10am-6pm Oct-Mar) In a near perfect rock and roll symbiosis, the Beatles met Elvis on 27 August 1965 at Elvis' home in Bel Air, California. The meeting of pop music's most iconic figures forms the basis of this exhibit atop the Pier Head ferry terminal. Want to gawk at the white Fender bass Paul played at the meeting? Stare lovingly at the shirt Elvis wore in *Jailhouse Rock*? Look at rare footage and examine a ticket to the '68 comeback special? Then this is the place to do it.

👉 Tours

Beatles Fab Four Taxi Tour   GUIDED TOUR
(☑0151-601 2111; www.thebeatlesfabfourtaxitour .co.uk; 2-/3-hour tours £40/50) Themed tours of the city's mop-top landmarks – there's the three-hour original Lennon tour or the two-hour Epstein express tour. Pick-ups arranged when booking. Up to five people per tour.

Liverpool Beatles Tour   GUIDED TOUR
(☑0151-281 7738; www.beatlestours.co.uk; tours from £50) Your own personalised tour of every bit of Beatles minutiae, from cradle to grave. Tours range from the two-hour Helter Skelter excursion to the all-day There Are Places I Remember, by the end of which, presumably, you'll be convinced you were actually in the band. Pick-ups are arranged upon booking.

(NEVER) LET IT BE

They broke up more than 40 years ago and two of their members are dead, but the Beatles are bigger business than ever in Liverpool.

Most of it centres around tiny Mathew St, site of the original Cavern Club, which is now the main thoroughfare of the 'Cavern Quarter'. Here you can shuck oysters in the Rubber Soul Oyster Bar, buy a George pillowcase in the From Me to You shop and put it on the pillows of the Hard Day's Night Hotel. Ringo may have dissed the city in 2008 by declaring that he missed nothing about it, but the city's tourist authorities continue to exploit Liverpool's ties to the world's most famous group and have done so with enormous success – the Mathew St Festival (p564) attracts over 350,000 fans and generates revenue for the city in excess of £17 million.

Wandering around Mathew St is plenty of fun – and the Beatles Shop is best for memorabilia – but if you really want a bit of Beatles lore, you'll have to visit the National Trust–owned Mendips, the home where John lived with his Aunt Mimi from 1945 to 1963 (which is also the time period covered by Sam Taylor-Wood's superb 2009 biopic of the young Lennon, *Nowhere Boy*) and 20 Forthlin Road, the plain terraced home where Paul grew up; you can only do so by prebooked tour (NT; ☑0151-427 7231; www .nationaltrust.org.uk; pick-up Jury's Inn, 31 Keel Wharf, Wapping Dock; adult/child £20/5; ⊙Wed-Sun Easter-Oct). Tours also leave from Speke Hall (NT; www.nationaltrust.org.uk; house & gardens adult/child £8.10/4, gardens only adult/child £4.95/2.60; ⊙11am-5pm Wed-Sun).

If you'd rather do it yourself, the tourist offices stock the *Discover Lennon's Liverpool* guide and map, and Ron Jones' *The Beatles' Liverpool*.

Magical Mystery Tour   GUIDED TOUR

(☎0151-709 3285; www.beatlestour.org; per person £15.95; ⊙2.30pm year-round, plus noon Sat Jul & Aug) Two-hour tour that takes in all Beatles-related landmarks – their birthplaces, childhood homes, schools and places such as Penny Lane and Strawberry Field – before finishing up in the Cavern Club (which isn't the original). Departs from opposite the tourist office on Albert Dock.

🎪 Festivals & Events

Aintree Festival   HORSE RACING

(www.aintree.co.uk) A three-day race meeting culminating in the world-famous Grand National steeplechase, held on the first Saturday in April.

Creamfields   MUSIC, DANCE

(www.cream.co.uk) An alfresco dance-fest that brings together some of the world's best DJs and dance acts during the last weekend in August. It takes place at the Daresbury Estate near Halton, Cheshire.

Mathew St Festival   MUSIC

(☎0151-239 9091; www.mathewstreetfestival.org) The world's biggest tribute to the Beatles features six days of music, a convention and a memorabilia auction during the last week of August.

🛏 Sleeping

There are some pretty fancy pillows upon which to lay your head, from sexy boutique hotels to stylish upmarket properties. For the rest, it's all about standard business hotels and midrange chains. Beds are rarer than hen's teeth when Liverpool FC are playing at home (it's less of an issue with Everton) and during the mobbed-out Beatles convention in the last week of August. If you fancy self-catering options, the tourist office has all the information you need.

CITY CENTRE

Hope Street Hotel   BOUTIQUE HOTEL £££

(☎0151-709 3000; www.hopestreethotel.co.uk; 40 Hope St; r/ste from £125/170; @🖭) Luxurious Liverpool's pre-eminent flag-waver is this stunning boutique hotel on the city's most elegant street. King-sized beds draped in Egyptian cotton, oak floors with underfloor heating, LCD wide-screen TVs and sleek modern bathrooms (with luxe bath and beauty products) are but the most obvious touches of class at this supremely cool address. Breakfast, taken in the marvellous London Carriage Works, is not included.

Hotel Indigo   HOTEL ££

(☎0151-559 0111; www.hotelindigoliverpool.co.uk; 10 Chapel St; r from £65; @🖭) It's labeled a boutique hotel, but the 151-room Indigo is just too big and part of a franchise, so the feel is more corporate swish than bespoke boutique. Still, the rooms are bright, extremely well-appointed and distinctly modern; downstairs, the Marco Pierre White Steakhouse & Grill (www.mpwsteakhouse liverpool.co.uk; Hotel Indigo, 10 Chapel St; mains £16-25; ⊙lunch & dinner) is full of diners looking for a good night out. An excellent midrange choice.

Radisson Blu   HOTEL ££

(☎0151-966 1500; www.radissonblu.co.uk; 107 Old Hall St; r from £89; @🖭) Funky ergonomic designer furniture in the lobby beneath a soaring nine-story atrium – there's something so appealing about Scandinavian corporate style, at least if you're a fan of contemporary decor. The rooms are divided into 'Ocean', a blue-coloured, wave-themed look with views of the docks and the Mersey; and 'Urban', all luscious reds and other deep colours, with views of the city centre. Each comes with all the designer gadgetry you'd expect: flat-screen TVs, funky see-through minibars and super-hip bathrooms. They're not especially huge, but they're very cool, baby.

THE GRAND NATIONAL

The world's most famous steeplechase – and one of England's most cherished events – takes place on the first Saturday in April across 4.5 miles and over the most difficult fences in world racing. Its protagonists are 40-odd veteran stalwarts of the jumps, ageing bruisers full of the oh-so-English qualities of grit and derring-do.

You can book tickets (☎0151-522 2929; www.aintree.co.uk) for the Grand National, or visit the Grand National Experience (☎0151-523 2600; www.aintree.co.uk; adult/child with tour £11/6, without tour £6/4), a visitor centre that includes a race simulator – those jumps are very steep indeed. Redevelopment work on the centre means you have to book the tour in advance – call to make sure.

62 Castle St
BOUTIQUE HOTEL **££**

(☏0151-702 7898; www.62castlest.com; 62 Castle St; r from £69; P@🖘) This elegant property on (arguably) the city's most handsome street successfully blends the traditional Victorian features of the neoclassical building with a sleek, contemporary style. The 20 fabulously different suites come with high-definition plasma-screen TVs, drench showers and luxe toiletries as standard.

Roscoe House
BOUTIQUE HOTEL **££**

(☏0151-709 0286; www.hotelliverpool.net; 27 Rodney St; r from £50; 🖘) A handsome Georgian home once owned by Liverpool-born writer and historian William Roscoe (1753–1831) has been given the once-over and is now a chic boutique hotel. The elegant rooms combine period touches (original coving, fireplaces and furnishings) with contemporary comforts such as flatscreen TVs and fancy Egyptian cotton sheets.

AROUND ALBERT DOCK

Malmaison
HOTEL **££**

(☏0151-229 5000; www.malmaison.com; 7 William Jessop Way, Princes Dock; r from £69; P@🖘) The Malmaison's preferred colour scheme of plum and black is everywhere in this purpose-built hotel, which gives it an air of contemporary sophistication but sort of makes it hard to see anything very clearly. But you don't really *see* plush, you experience it; and everything about the Liverpool Mal is plush, from the huge beds and the deep baths to the heavy velvet curtains and the excellent buffet breakfast. And, just in case you were in doubt as to which Malmaison property you were in, the sound of the Beatles is heard throughout the bedroom corridors (but thankfully not the bedrooms).

Liverpool YHA
HOSTEL **£**

(☏0845-371 9527; www.yha.org.uk; 25 Tabley St; dm from £16; P🖘) It may have the look of an Eastern European apartment complex, but this award-winning hostel, adorned with plenty of Beatles memorabilia, is one of the most comfortable you'll find anywhere in the country. The dorms with en suite bathrooms even have heated towel rails.

✗ Eating

Top grade international cuisine, the best of British and the greasy spoon...you'll find plenty of choices to satisfy every taste. Best spots include Ropewalks, along Hardman St and Hope St.

Monro
GASTROPUB **££**

(☏0151-707 9933; www.themonro.com; 92 Duke St; 2-course lunch £11.95, dinner mains £14-20; ☺lunch and dinner) The Monro has fast become one of the city's favourite spots for lunch, dinner and, especially, weekend brunch. The constantly changing menu of classic British dishes made with ingredients sourced as locally as possible has transformed this handsome old pub into a superb dining experience. It's tough to find pub grub this good elsewhere, unless you go to its sister pub, the James Monro (☏0151-236 9700; www.thejamesmonro.com; 69 Tithebarn St; ☺lunch & dinner Tue-Sun).

Italian Club
ITALIAN **£**

(☏0151-708 5508; www.theitalianclubliverpool.co.uk; 85 Bold St; mains £6-11; ☺10am-7pm Mon-Sat) The Crolla family must have been homesick for southern Italy, so they opened this fabulous spot, adorned with family pictures and began serving the kind of food relatives visiting from the home country would be glad to tuck into. They've been so successful that they recently opened Italian Club Fish (☏0151-707 2110; 128 Bold St; mains £8-14; ☺Tue-Sun) just down the street, specialising in, erm, fish.

The Noble House
INTERNATIONAL **££**

(☏0151-236 5346; www.thenoblehouse.co.uk; Heywood Bldg, 5 Brunswick St; mains £10-16) The handsome Heywood Building (1799) was once the city's oldest bank. Now it's a classy restaurant with a vaguely Manhattanite feel: if it weren't for the occasional groups of football fans you could imagine yourself surrounded by Wall Streeters tucking into a menu of steaks, burgers and salads. The menu has expanded recently to include North African dishes as well as a handful of Mediterranean options. It's owned by the same crowd that runs the Alma de Cuba (☏0151-709 7097; www.alma-de-cuba.com; St Peter's Church, Seel St; mains £13-25; ☺lunch & dinner).

London Carriage Works
MODERN BRITISH **£££**

(☏0151-705 2222; www.thelondoncarriageworks.co.uk; 40 Hope St; 2-/3-course meals £15/20, mains £15-27) Liverpool's dining revolution is being led by Paul Askew's award-winning restaurant, which successfully blends ethnic influences from around the globe with staunch British favourites and serves up the result in a beautiful dining room – actually more of a bright glass box divided only by a series of sculpted glass shards. Reservations are recommended.

Quarter WINE BAR, BISTRO ££
(☎0151-707 1965; 7-11 Falkner St; mains £9-13; ☻lunch & dinner) A gorgeous little wine bar and bistro with outdoor seating for that elusive summer's day.

🍷 Drinking

Unless specified, all the bars included here open from 11am until 2am Monday to Saturday, and most have a nominal entry charge after 11pm.

Philharmonic PUB
(36 Hope St; ☻to 11.30pm) This extraordinary bar, designed by the shipwrights who built the *Lusitania,* is one of the most beautiful bars in all of England. The interior is resplendent with etched and stained glass, wrought iron, mosaics and ceramic tiling – and if you think that's good, just wait until you see inside the marble men's toilets, the only heritage-listed lav in the country.

Magnet BAR
(www.magnetliverpool.co.uk; 39 Hardman St) Red leather booths, plenty of velvet and a suitably seedy New York–dive atmosphere where Iggy Pop or Tom Waits would feel right at home. The upstairs bar is very cool but totally chilled out, while downstairs the dance floor shakes to the best music in town, spun by up-and-comers and supported with guest slots by some of England's most established DJs.

Rigby's PUB
(21 Dale St) A traditional boozer that serves 'real ale' (a traditional brew with no extraneous carbon dioxide), Rigby's looks, feels and smells like an old-school pub. The perfect antidote to the high-octane noise of the city's newer bars.

Hannah's BAR
(☎0151-708 5959; 2 Leece St) One of the top student bars in town. Try to land yourself a table on the outdoor patio, which is covered in the event of rain. Staying open until late, a friendly, easygoing crowd and some pretty decent music make this one of the better places in which to have a drink.

☆ Entertainment

Nightclubs

Most of the city's clubs are concentrated in Ropewalks, where they compete for customers with a ton of late-night bars; considering the number of punters in the area on a Friday or Saturday night, we're guessing there's plenty of business for everyone.

Masque CLUB
(☎0151-707 6171; www.chibuku.com; 90 Seel St; admission £4-11; ☻Mon-Sat) This converted theatre is home to our favourite club in town. The fortnightly Saturday Chibuku (www.chibuku .com) is one of the best club nights in all of England, led by a mix of superb DJs including Yousef (formerly of Cream nightclub) and superstars such as Dmitri from Paris and Gilles Peterson. The music ranges from hip hop to deep house – if you're in town, get in line. Other nights feature a superb mixed bag of music, from trash to techno.

Nation CLUB
(☎0151-709 1693; 40 Slater St, Wolstenholme Sq; admission £4-13) It looks like an air-raid shelter, but it's the big-name DJs dropping the bombs at the city's premier dance club, formerly the home of Cream. These days, it also hosts live bands as well as pumping techno nights.

Live Music

Philharmonic Hall CLASSICAL MUSIC
(☎0151-709 3789; Hope St) One of Liverpool's most beautiful buildings, the art deco Phil is home to the city's main classical orchestra, but it also stages the work of avant-garde musicians such as John Cage and Nick Cave.

Academy LIVE MUSIC
(☎0151-794 6868; Liverpool University, 11-13 Hotham St) Good spot to see midsize bands on tour.

Cavern Club LIVE MUSIC
(☎0151-236 1965; www.cavernclub.org; 8-10 Mathew St) It's a reconstruction, and not even on the same spot, but the 'world's most famous club' is still a great spot to see local bands.

Sport

Liverpool FC FOOTBALL
(☎0151-263 9199, ticket office 0151-220 2345; www.liverpoolfc.tv; Anfield Rd) Doff o' the cap to Evertonians and Beatle-maniacs, but no single institution represents the Mersey spirit and strong sense of identity more powerfully than Liverpool FC, who won everything in the '70s and '80s but have struggled ever since: they last won the league title in 1990 and in 2011 their bitter rivals Manchester United won their 19th title – one more than Liverpool.

In 2010 the club was bought by US sports investment company Fenway Sports Group, which knows a thing or two about turning longstanding disappointment around – it also owns the Boston Red Sox baseball team, and Liverpool fans have pinned their hopes on Fenway also delivering them to the promised land (although they'd rather not wait the 86 years it took the Red Sox to win the championship).

There are vague plans to redevelop the utterly marvellous Anfield Road ([✆]0151-260 6677; www.liverpoolfc.tv; Anfield Rd; tour & museum adult/child £15/9, museum only £6/4; ⊙hourly 10am-3pm except match days), where the experience of a live match is one of the sporting highlights of an English visit, especially the sound of 40,000 fans singing the club's anthem, 'You'll Never Walk Alone'. Take bus 26 or 27 from Paradise St Interchange or bus 17 or 217 from the Queen St Bus Station.

Everton Football Club   FOOTBALL
([✆]0151-330 2400, ticket office 0151-330 2300; www.evertonfc.com; Goodison Park) Liverpool's blue half consoles itself for existing in the shadow of its more successful neighbour with the historical truth of 'we were there first'. Founded in 1878, Everton FC is the city's first club.

Goodison Park Tours ([✆]0151-530 5212; www.evertonfc.com; adult/child £8.50/5; ⊙11am & 1pm Sun, Mon, Wed & Fri) run throughout the year, except on the Friday before home matches. Take bus 19, 20 or 21 from Paradise St Interchange or Queen St Bus Station.

🛍 Shopping

Sandwiched between Albert Dock, the Cavern Quarter and Ropewalks is the simply enormous Liverpool ONE (www.liverpool-one .com) shopping district ('centre' just feels too small) – 17 hectares of retail and restaurant pleasure.

ℹ Information

Emergency
Merseyside police headquarters ([✆]0151-709 6010; Canning Pl) Opposite Albert Dock.

Internet Access
CafeLatte.net (4 South Hunter St; per 30min £2; ⊙9am-6pm)

Medical Services
Mars Pharmacy (68 London Rd) Open until 10pm every night.
Royal Liverpool University Hospital ([✆]0151-706 2000; Prescot St)

Post
Post office (Ranelagh St; ⊙9am-5.30pm Mon-Sat)

Tourist Information
There is a small **tourist office** ([✆]0151-707 0729; www.visitliverpool.com; Anchor Courtyard; ⊙10am-6pm) in Albert Dock, and a separate **accommodation hotline** ([✆]0845-601 1125; ⊙9am-5.30pm Mon-Fri, 10am-4pm Sat).

Websites
Liverpool Magazine (www.liverpool.com) Insiders' guide to the city, including lots of great recommendations for food and nights out.

Mersey Guide (www.merseyguide.co.uk) Guide to the Greater Mersey area.

Visit Liverpool (www.visitliverpool.com) The official website for the Liverpool city region.

ℹ Getting There & Away

Air
Liverpool John Lennon Airport ([✆]0870-750 8484; www.liverpoolairport.com; Speke Hall Ave) serves a variety of international destinations as well as destinations in the UK (Belfast, London and the Isle of Man).

Bus
The **National Express Coach Station** (www .nationalexpress.com; Norton St) is 300m north of Lime St station. There are services to/from most major towns:
Birmingham £12.40, 2¾ hours, five daily
London £25.60, five to six hours, six daily
Manchester £6.30, 1¼ hours, hourly
Newcastle £21.60, 6½ hours, three daily

Train
Liverpool's main station is Lime St. It has hourly services to almost everywhere, including the following:
Chester £4.35, 45 minutes
London Euston £65.20, 3¼ hours
Manchester £9.80, 45 minutes
Wigan £5.40, 50 minutes

ℹ Getting Around

To/From the Airport
The airport is 8 miles south of the centre. **Arriva Airlink** (www.arriva.co.uk; adult £2; ⊙6am-11pm) buses 80A and 180 depart from Paradise St Interchange, and **Airportxpress 500** (www .arriva.co.uk; adult £2.50; ⊙5.15am-12.15am) buses leave from outside Lime St station. Buses from both stations take half an hour and run every 20 minutes. A taxi to the city centre should cost no more than £18.

Boat

The famous **Mersey ferry** (www.merseyferries .co.uk; adult/child £2.10/1.50) crossing for Woodside and Seacombe departs from Pier Head Ferry Terminal, next to the Royal Liver Building (to the north of Albert Dock).

Car & Motorcycle

You won't really have much use for a car in Liverpool, and it'll no doubt end up costing you plenty in parking fees. If you have to drive, there are parking meters around the city and a number of open and sheltered car parks. Car break-ins are a significant problem, so leave absolutely nothing of value in the car.

Public Transport

Local public transport is coordinated by **Merseytravel** (www.merseytravel.gov.uk). Highly recommended is the Saveaway ticket (adult/child £5/2.50), which allows for one day's off-peak (after 9.30am) travel on all bus, train and ferry services throughout Merseyside. Tickets are available at shops and post offices throughout the city. Paradise St Interchange is in the city centre.

Merseyrail (www.merseyrail.org) is an extensive suburban rail service linking Liverpool with the Greater Merseyside area. There are four stops in the city centre: Lime St, Central (handy for Ropewalks), James St (close to Albert Dock) and Moorfields (for the Liverpool War Museum).

Taxi

Mersey Cabs (☏0151-298 2222) operates tourist taxi services and also has some wheelchair-accessible cabs.

LANCASHIRE

No part of England may be so heavily urbanised as Lancashire, but as you travel north the concrete conurbations break up and bits of green begin to appear. North of Blackpool – the faded queen of beachside holidays – the landscape truly reveals itself in all its undulating, bucolic glory: the Ribble Valley is a gentle and beautiful warm-up for the Lake District that lies beyond the county's northern border. North of the Ribble Valley is the county's handsome Georgian capital, Lancaster.

Blackpool

POP 142,290

The queen bee of England's fun-by-the-sea-type resorts is unquestionably Blackpool. It's bold and brazen in its efforts to cement its position as the country's second-most-visited town after London. Tacky, trashy and tawdry – Blackpool doesn't care because 16 million annual visitors don't either.

The town is famous for its tower, its three piers, its Pleasure Beach and its Illuminations, the latter being a successful ploy to extend the brief summer holiday season. From early September to early November, 5 miles of the Promenade are illuminated with thousands of electric and neon lights.

⦿ Sights

Pleasure Beach   AMUSEMENT PARK
(www.blackpoolpleasurebeach.com; Central Promenade; Pleasure Beach Pass £5, Unlimited Ride wristband 1-day adult/child £27/22, 2-day £45/40, Speedy Pass per person £7.50; ⊙from 10am Feb-Oct, Sat & Sun only Nov) The main reason for Blackpool's immense popularity is the Pleasure Beach, a 16-hectare collection of more than 145 rides that attracts some seven million visitors annually. As amusement parks go, it's easily the best in Britain.

Rides are divided into categories, and once you've gained entry to the park with your Freedom Ticket you can buy tickets for individual categories or for a mixture of them all. Alternatively, an Unlimited Ride wristband includes the £5 entrance fee; there are great discounts if you book your tickets online in advance. A new addition is the Speedy Pass, which saves you the hassle of queuing for rides by allocating you a specific ride time; rent it and add as many people to it as you want.

There are no set times for closing; it depends how busy it is.

Blackpool Tower   ENTERTAINMENT COMPLEX
(☏0844-856 1000; www.theblackpooltower.com; tower admission free, Tower Eye & 4D Experience adult/child £12.60/7.20; ⊙10.30am-4pm) Built in 1894, this 154m-high tower is Blackpool's most recognisable landmark. In 2011 it reopened after a major refurbishment, which saw the addition of the **Blackpool Tower Eye and 4D Experience**, where you watch a film on the town's history (and feel the spray of the sea and smell the donkeys) before taking the elevator 154m up to the new observation deck, which has splendid views and only a (thick) glass floor between you and the ant-sized people below.

Back at ground level, a new dungeon exhibit has opened to sit alongside the old Moorish circus and the magnificent rococo ballroom, with its extraordinary sculptured and gilded plasterwork, murals, chandeliers and couples gliding across the beautifully polished wooden floor to the melodramatic tones of a huge Wurlitzer organ.

Sandcastle Waterpark
AMUSEMENT PARK

(www.sandcastle-waterpark.co.uk; adult/child £12.50/10.50, Hyperzone £5/2.50; ⊙from 10am May-Oct, from 10am Sat & Sun Nov-Feb) Across from Pleasure Beach is this indoor water complex with 15 different slides and rides, including the Hyperzone, which has the complex' most popular slides – Aztec Falls, Montezooma, the Sidewinder and Master Blaster, the world's largest indoor waterslide.

FREE North Pier
LANDMARK

(Promenade) Built in 1862 and opening a year later, the most famous of the three Victorian piers once charged a penny for admission; its plethora of unexciting rides are now free.

🛏 Sleeping

If you want to stay close to the waterfront, prepare for a noisy, boisterous night; accommodation along Albert and Hornby Rds, 300m back from the sea, is that little bit quieter. The tourist office will assist you in finding a bed.

Number One
BOUTIQUE HOTEL ££

(☎01253-343901; www.numberoneblackpool.com; 1 St Lukes Rd; s/d from £70/120; P🐾) Far fancier than anything else around, this stunning boutique guesthouse is all luxury and contemporary style. Everything exudes a kind of discreet elegance, from the dark-wood furniture and high-end mod cons to the top-notch breakfast. It's on a quiet road just set back from the South Promenade near Pleasure Beach amusement park.

Big Blue Hotel
HOTEL ££

(☎01253-400045; www.bigbluehotel.com; Blackpool Pleasure Beach; r from £95; P@🐾) A handsome family hotel with smartly kitted-out rooms. Kids are looked after with DVD players and computer games, while its location at the southern entrance to Pleasure Beach amusement park should ensure that everyone has something to do.

🍴 Eating

Forget gourmet meals – the Blackpool experience is all about stuffing your face with burgers, doughnuts, and fish and chips. Most people eat at their hotels, where roast and three vegetables often costs just £5 per head.

There are a few restaurants around Talbot Sq (near the tourist office) on Queen St, Talbot Rd and Clifton St. Our favourite meal in town is at the Mediterranean Kwizeen (www.kwizeenrestaurant.co.uk; 49 King St; mains £13), which serves a delicious suckling pig in a Sardinian style, topped with a bacon roulade.

ℹ️ Information

Tourist office (☎01253-478222; www.visit blackpool.com; 1 Clifton St; ⊙9am-5pm Mon-Sat)

ℹ️ Getting There & Away

Bus

The central coach station is on Talbot Rd, near the town centre.

London £29, 6½ hours, four daily

Manchester £7.30, 1¾ hours, four daily

Train

The main train station is Blackpool North, about five blocks east of the North Pier on Talbot Rd. There is a direct service from Manchester (£13.50, 1¼ hours, half-hourly) and Liverpool (£14.60, 1½ hours, seven daily), but most other arrivals change in Preston (£6.70, 30 minutes, half-hourly).

ℹ️ Getting Around

A host of travel-card options for trams and buses ranging from one day to a week are available at the tourist office and most newsagents. With more than 14,000 car-parking spaces in Blackpool, you'll have no problem parking. The **land train service** (one way/return £2/3; ⊙from 10.30am Apr-Oct) shuttles funsters between the central corridor car parks and the main entrance to the Pleasure Beach every five minutes or so throughout the day. Otherwise, the town has recently introduced a **bike hire scheme** (www .hourbike.com/blackpool; per 3hr £6) with bikes available for hire from stations along the Promenade and in Stanley Park.

Lancaster

POP 45,960

Lancashire's county seat is genteel, austere and much, much quieter than it was in its 18th-century heyday, when it served as an important trading port for all manner of goods, including people. The city's handsome Georgian architecture was one of the slave trade's ancillary benefits.

◉ Sights

Lancaster Castle & Priory CASTLE
(☑01524-64998; www.lancastercastle.com; Castle Park; adult/child £5/4; ⊙10am-5pm, guided tours every 30min 10.30am-4pm) Lancaster's imposing castle was originally built in 1150. Later additions include the Well Tower, more commonly known as the Witches' Tower because it was used to incarcerate the accused of the famous Pendle Witches Trial of 1612, and the impressive twin-towered gatehouse, both of which were added in the 14th century. However, most of what you see today dates from the 18th and 19th centuries, when the castle was substantially altered to suit its new, and still current, role as a prison. Consequently, you can only visit the castle as part of a 45-minute guided tour, but you do get a chance to experience what it was like to be locked up in the dungeon.

Immediately next to the castle is the equally fine priory church (Priory Cl; admission free; ⊙9.30am-5pm), founded in 1094 but extensively remodelled in the Middle Ages.

Judges' Lodgings MUSEUM
(Church St; adult/child £3/2; ⊙10am-4pm Jun & Jul, 1-4pm Easter-May & Aug-Oct) Once the home of witch-hunter Thomas Covell (he who 'caught' the poor Pendle women), Lancaster's oldest town house, a Grade I–listed Georgian building, is now home to a Museum of Furnishings by master builders Gillows of Lancaster, whose work graces the Houses of Parliament. It also houses a Museum of Childhood, which has memorabilia from the turn of the 20th century.

Williamson Park & Tropical Butterfly House GARDENS
(Tropical Butterfly House adult/child £3.60/2.60; ⊙10am-5pm Apr-Sep, to 4pm Oct-Mar) Lancaster's highest point is the 22-hectare spread of this elegant park, from which there are great views of the town, Morecambe Bay and the Cumbrian fells to the north. In the middle is the Ashton Memorial, a 67m-high baroque folly built by Lord Ashton (the son of the park's founder, James Williamson) for his wife.

More beautiful, however, is the Edwardian Palm House, now the Tropical Butterfly House, full of exotic and stunning species. Take bus 25 or 25A from the station, or else it's a steep, short walk up Moor Lane.

🛏 Sleeping & Eating

Sun Hotel & Bar HOTEL ££
(☑01524-66006; www.thesunhotelandbar.co.uk; 63 Church St; s/d from £75/85; ᵖ🛜) An excellent hotel in a 300-year-old building with a rustic, old-world look that stops at the bedroom door; a recent renovation has resulted in 16 pretty snazzy rooms. The pub downstairs is one of the best in town and a top spot for a bit of grub; the two-course roast of the day is excellent.

Royal King's Arms Hotel HOTEL ££
(☑01524-32451; www.oxfordhotelsandinns.com; Market St; r from £75; ᵖ🛜) Lancaster's swankiest hotel is a period house with modern, comfortable rooms and an all-round businesslike interior. Look out for the beautiful stained-glass windows, one of the only leftovers from the mid-19th century when Charles Dickens frequented the place. The hotel restaurant is an excellent dining choice, with mains around £11.

🌿 Whale Tail Cafe VEGETARIAN £
(www.whaletailcafe.co.uk; 78a Penny St; mains £7-10; ⊙10am-4pm Mon-Fri, to 5pm Sat, to 3pm Sun; 🖉) This gorgeous 1st-floor veggie restaurant has an elegant dining room and a more informal plant-filled courtyard for lunch on a sunny day. The spicy bean burger is particularly good. Food here is locally produced and, where possible, organic.

❶ Information

Post office (85 Market St; ⊙9am-5.30pm Mon-Fri, to 12.30pm Sat)
Tourist office (☑01524-582394; www.citycoastcountryside.co.uk; Storey Creative Industries Centre, Meeting House Lane; ⊙9am-5pm Mon-Sat)

❶ Getting There & Away

Lancaster is on the main west coast railway line and on the Cumbrian coast line. Destinations include Carlisle (£17.40, one hour, hourly), Manchester (£13.90, one hour, hourly) and Morecambe (£2.10, 15 minutes, half-hourly).

Ribble Valley

Known locally as 'Little Switzerland', Lancashire's most attractive landscapes lie east of the brash tackiness of Blackpool and north of the sprawling urban areas of Preston and Blackburn.

The northern half of the valley is dominated by the sparsely populated moorland of the Forest of Bowland, which is a fantastic place for walks, while the southern half features rolling hills, attractive market towns and ruins, with the River Ribble flowing between them.

🏃 Activities

Walking & Cycling

The Ribble Way, a 70-mile footpath that follows the River Ribble from its source at Ribblehead (in the Yorkshire Dales) to the estuary at Preston, is one of the more popular walks in the area and passes through Clitheroe. For online information check out www.visitlancashire.com.

The valley is also well covered by the northern loop of the Lancashire Cycle Way; for more information about routes, safety and so on, contact Blazing Saddles (☏01442-844435; www.blazingsaddles.co.uk; 35 West End, Hebden Bridge, West Yorkshire), a Yorkshire-based bike shop.

CLITHEROE

POP 14,700

Located northeast of Preston, the Ribble Valley's largest market town is best known for its impressive Norman keep (admission free; ☉dawn-dusk), built in the 12th century and now, sadly, standing empty; from it there are great views of the river valley below.

The extensive grounds are home to the newly refurbished Castle Museum (Castle Hill; adult/child £3.75/free; ☉11am-4pm Mar-Oct, noon-4pm Mon, Tue & Fri-Sun Nov-Feb), which explores 350 *million* years of local history.

🛏 Sleeping & Eating

Old Post House Hotel   HOTEL **££**
(☏01200-422025; www.posthousehotel.co.uk; 44-48 King St; s/d from £48/65; 🅿🛜) A former post office is now Clitheroe's most handsome hotel, with 11 superbly decorated rooms.

Halpenny's of Clitheroe   TEAROOM **£**
(Old Toll House, 1-5 Parson Lane; mains £6) A traditional teashop that serves sandwiches, and dishes such as Lancashire hotpot.

ℹ Information

Tourist office (☏01200-425566; www.visit ribblevalley.co.uk; Church Walk; ☉9am-5pm Mon-Sat) Information on the town and surrounding area.

PENDLE HILL

A lovely walk brings you to the top of Pendle Hill (558m) from which there are marvellous views of the surrounding countryside.

In 1612, however, the surrounding villages in the shadow of Pendle Hill were the scene of dramatic witch trials. Ten people, two of them older women who were known locally as 'healers', were accused of practising witchcraft, including murder, and were convicted to hang based on the sole testimony of a nine-year-old child (a legal reference point that would later influence the Salem Witch Trials of the New World). Every Halloween a pseudomystical ceremony is performed here to commemorate their 'activities'. If that's not enough, in 1652 George Fox, the founder of the Quakers, felt compelled to climb Pendle Hill and experienced visions here – an experience that was to add momentum to the growth of the Quaker religion.

FOREST OF BOWLAND

This vast grouse-ridden moorland is somewhat of a misnomer. The use of 'forest' is a throwback to an earlier definition, when it served as a royal hunting ground. Today it is an Area of Outstanding Natural Beauty (AONB), which makes for good walking and cycling. The Pendle Witch Way, a 45-mile walk from Pendle Hill to northeast of Lancaster, cuts right through the area, and the Lancashire Cycle Way runs along the eastern border. The forest's main town is Slaidburn, about 9 miles north of Clitheroe on the B6478.

Other villages worth exploring are Newton, Whitewell and Dunsop Bridge.

🛏 Sleeping & Eating

Inn at Whitewell   INN **££**
(☏01200-448222; www.innatwhitewell.com; s/d from £88/120, mains £10-18) Once the home of Bowland's forest keeper, this is now a superb guesthouse with antique furniture, peat fires and Victorian claw-foot baths. The restaurant specialises in traditional English game dishes.

Hark to Bounty Inn   INN **££**
(☏01200-446246; www.harktobounty.co.uk; Slaidburn; s/d from £42.50/65, mains £9-15) This marvellous 13th-century inn has atmospheric rooms with exposed oak beams. An excellent restaurant downstairs specialises in homemade herb breads.

Slaidburn YHA HOSTEL £
(☎0845-371 9343; www.yha.org.uk; King's House; dm £17; ⊘Apr-Oct) A converted 17th-century village inn that is especially popular with walkers and cyclists.

ℹ Getting There & Away

Clitheroe is served by regular buses from Preston and Blackburn as well as by hourly trains from Manchester (£8.70, 75 minutes) and Preston (£5.90, 50 minutes). Once here, you're better off having your own transport, as there is only a Sunday bus service between Clitheroe and the rest of the valley villages.

ISLE OF MAN

Deliberately different and not-so-ferociously independent, the Isle of Man (Ellan Vannin in Manx, the local lingo) has doggedly held onto its semi-autonomous status (it is home to the world's oldest continuous parliament, the Tynwald) so as to continue doing its own thing, which really means operating as a popular tax haven.

The islanders' rejection of England's warm embrace has led to an oft-quoted prejudice that there's something odd about them, but the only thing that's odd here is the local tailless cat.

Crass commercialism and mass tourism have no place here, except of course for the world-famous summer season of Tourist Trophy (TT) motorbike racing, which attracts around 50,000 punters and bike freaks every May and June, bringing noise and mayhem to the otherwise lush valleys, barren hills and rugged coastlines of this beautiful island. Needless to say, if you want a slice of silence, be sure to avoid the high-rev bike fest.

🏃 Activities

Walking & Cycling
With plenty of great marked trails, the Isle of Man is a firm favourite with walkers and is regularly voted one of the best walking destinations in Britain. Ordnance Survey (OS) Landranger Map 95 (£6.99) covers the whole island, while the free *Walks on the Isle of Man* is available from the tourist office in Douglas. The Millennium Way is a walking path that runs the length of the island amid some spectacular scenery. The most demanding of all the island's walks is the 95-mile Raad ny Foillan (Road of the Gull), a well-marked path that makes a complete circuit of the island and normally takes about five days to complete. The Isle of Man Walking Festival (www.isleofmanwalking.com; ⊘mid-May) takes place over five days in May.

The island has six designated off-road mountain-biking trails, each with varying ranges of difficulty. See www.visitisleofman.com for details.

ℹ Information

Most of the island's historic sites are operated by Manx Heritage, which offers free admission for National Trust or English Heritage members. Unless otherwise indicated, **Manx Heritage** (MH; www.gov.im/mnh) sites are open 10am to 5pm daily, from Easter to October. The Manx Heritage **5 Site Pass** (www.manxheritageshop.com; adult/child/family £18/9/44) grants you entry into five of the island's heritage attractions; pick it up at any of the tourist offices or online.

ℹ Getting There & Away

Air
Ronaldsway Airport (www.iom-airport.com) is 10 miles south of Douglas near Castletown. Airlines that service the region include:

Aer Lingus Regional (www.aerlingus.com; from £25) From Dublin.

Blue Islands (www.blueislands.com; from £167) From Guernsey and Jersey.

Easyjet (www.easyjet.com; from £16) From Liverpool and London Gatwick.

Flybe (www.flybe.com; from £21) From Birmingham, Bristol, Jersey, London Gatwick, Luton, Liverpool, Manchester, Glasgow and Edinburgh.

Manx2 (www.manx2.com; from £20) From Belfast, Blackpool, Leeds-Bradford, Gloucester M5, Newcastle and East Midlands.

Boat
Isle of Man Steam Packet (www.steam-packet.com; foot passenger single/return £19/32.50, car & 2 passengers return from £106) is a car ferry and high-speed catamaran service from Liverpool and Heysham to Douglas. There is also a summer service (mid-April to mid-September) to Dublin (three hours) and Belfast (three hours). It's usually cheaper to buy a return ticket than to pay the single fare.

ℹ Getting Around

Buses link the airport with Douglas every 30 minutes between 7am and 11pm; a taxi should cost you no more than £18.

The island has a comprehensive **bus service** (www.iombusandrail.info); the tourist office in Douglas has timetables and sells tickets. It also sells the **Island Explorer** (1-day adult/child £16/8, 3-day £32/16), which gives you unlimited public transport use, including the tram to Snaefell and Douglas' horse-trams.

Bikes can be hired from **Eurocycles** (www .eurocycles.co.im; 8 Victoria Rd; per day £14-20; ⊗Mon-Sat).

Petrol-heads will love the scenic, sweeping bends that make for some exciting driving – and the fact that outside of Douglas town there's no speed limit. Naturally, the most popular drive is along the TT route. Car-hire operators have desks at the airport, and charge from around £38 per day.

The 19th-century electric and steam **rail services** (☑01624-663366; www.iombusandrail .info; ⊗Mar-Oct) are a thoroughly satisfying way of getting from A to B:

Douglas–Castletown–Port Erin Steam Train (return £10.80)

Douglas–Laxey–Ramsey Electric Tramway (return £10.80)

Laxey–Summit Snaefell Mountain Railway (return £10.80)

Douglas

POP 26.218

Much like Blackpool across the water, Douglas' heyday was in the middle of the 19th century, when it was a favourite destination for Victorian mass tourism. It's not nearly as popular – or as pretty – today, but it still has the best of the island's hotels and restaurants – as well as the bulk of the finance houses that are frequented so regularly by tax-allergic Brits.

The Manx Museum (www.gov.im/mnh; Kingswood Grove; admission free; ⊗10am-5pm Mon-Sat) gives an introduction to everything from the island's prehistoric past to the latest TT race winners.

🛏 Sleeping

The seafront promenade is crammed with B&Bs. Unless you booked back at the beginning of the millennium, however, there's little chance of finding accommodation during TT week and the weeks either side of it. The tourist office's camping information sheet lists sites all around the island.

Sefton Hotel   HOTEL ££
(☑01624-645500; www.seftonhotel.co.im; Harris Promenade; r from £90; P奈) Douglas' best hotel is an upmarket oasis with its own indoor water garden and rooms that range from plain and comfy to elegant and very luxurious. The rooms overlooking the water

garden are superb, even better than the ones with sea views. You save up to 10% if you book online.

Admiral House   B&B ££
(☑01624-629551; www.admiralhouse.com; Loch Promenade; r from £75; P奈) This elegant guesthouse overlooks the harbour near the ferry port. The 23 spotless and modern rooms are a cheerful alternative to the worn look of a lot of other seafront B&Bs.

Hilton Hotel   HOTEL ££
(☑01624-662662; www.hilton.co.uk/isleofman; Central Promenade; r from £75; P@) Tidy, modern rooms, a small gym and a casino – the Hilton takes care of your every need.

✗ Eating & Drinking

There are a few good pubs around, including the trendy Bar George (St George's Chambers, 3 Hill St) and Rover's Return (11 Church St), which specialises in the local brew, Bushy Ales.

Tanroagan   SEAFOOD ££
(☑01624-472411; www.tanroagan.co.uk; 9 Ridgeway St; mains £16-21; ⊗lunch & dinner Tue-Fri, dinner Sat) The place for all things from the sea, this elegant eatery is Douglas' smartest. It serves fresh fish straight off the boats, giving them the merest of Continental twists or just a spell on the hot grill. Reservations are recommended.

14North   MEDITERRANEAN ££
(☑01624-664414; www.14north.im; mains £9-19; ⊗lunch & dinner Mon-Sat, lunch Sun) An old timber merchant's house is now home to this smart eatery serving North African–style flatbreads (basically gourmet pizzas with a variety of toppings) and a selection of fish and meat dishes. The monkfish, with saffron and mussel chowder, is particularly tasty.

❶ Information

Tourist office (☑01624-686766; www.visitisle ofman.com; Sea Terminal Bldg; ⊗9.15am-7pm) Makes free accommodation bookings.

Around Douglas

You can follow the TT circuit up and over the mountain or wind around the coast. The mountain route goes close to the summit of Snaefell (621m), the island's highest point. It's an easy walk up to the summit, or take the electric tram from Laxey, near the coast.

On the edge of Ramsey, on the north of the island, is the Grove Rural Life Museum (MH; Andreas Rd; admission £4.50; ⊙10am-5pm Apr-Oct). The church in the small village of Maughold is on the site of an ancient monastery; a small shelter houses quite a good selection of stone crosses and ancient inscriptions.

It's no exaggeration to describe the Lady Isabella Laxey Wheel (MH; Mines Rd; admission £4.50; ⊙10am-5pm Apr-Oct), built in 1854 to pump water from a mine, as a 'great' wheel; it measures 22m across and can draw 1140L of water per minute from a depth of 550m. The largest wheel of its kind in the world, it's named after the wife of the then lieutenant-governor .

The wheel-headed cross at Lonan Old Church, just north of Douglas, is the island's most impressive early Christian cross.

Castletown & Around

At the southern end of the island is Castletown, a quiet harbour town that was originally the capital of the Isle of Man. The town is dominated by the impressive 13th-century Castle Rushen (MH; Castletown Sq; admission £5.80; ⊙10am-5pm Apr-Oct). The flag tower affords fine views of the town and coast. There's also a small Nautical Museum (MH; Bridge St; admission £4.50; ⊙10am-5pm Easter-Oct) displaying, among other things, its pride and joy, *Peggy,* a boat built in 1791 and still housed in its original boathouse. There is a school dating back to 1570 in St Mary's Church (MH; admission free; ⊙10am-5pm Mar-Nov), behind the castle. The Garrison Tapas Bar (5 Castle St; tapas £5-8; ⊙lunch & dinner Mon-Sat, lunch Sun) brings Iberian flavour to a handsome 17th-century building in the town centre. The paella (£26.50) is fantastic and huge, so is best shared.

Between Castletown and Cregneash, the Iron Age hillfort at Chapel Hill encloses a Viking ship burial site.

On the southern tip of the island, the Cregneash Village Folk Museum (MH; admission £4.50; ⊙10am-5pm Apr-Oct) recalls traditional Manx rural life. The Calf of Man, the small island just off Cregneash, is a bird sanctuary. Calf Island Cruises (☎01624-832339; adult/child £12/6; ⊙10.15am, 11.30am & 1.30pm Apr-Oct, weather permitting) run between Port Erin and the island.

PORT ERIN & PORT ST MARY
Port Erin, another Victorian seaside resort, plays host to the small Railway Museum (Station Rd; adult/child £1/50p; ⊙10am-5pm Apr-Oct), which reveals the history of steam railway on the island.

Port Erin has a good range of accommodation, as does Port St Mary, across the headland and linked by steam train.

Our Port Erin accommodation choice would be the Victorian Falcon's Nest Hotel (☎01624-834077; www.falconsnesthotel.co.uk; Station Rd; r from £42.50; 🛜), once supremely elegant, now just handsome in a nostalgic sort of way. The rooms aren't noteworthy, but the views over the water are superb.

The slightly more splendid Victorian-style Aaron House (☎01624-835702; www.aaronhouse.co.uk; The Promenade; s/d from £35/70) is a B&B that has fussed over every detail, from the gorgeous brass beds and claw-foot baths to the old-fashioned photographs on the walls. The sea views are also sensational.

Peel & Around

The west coast's most appealing town has a fine sandy beach, but its real attraction is the 11th-century Peel Castle (MH; admission £4.50, incl museum £7.70; ⊙10am-5pm Apr-Oct), stunningly positioned atop St Patrick's Island and joined to Peel by a causeway.

The House of Manannan (MH; admission £6, incl castle £7.70; ⊙10am-5pm Apr-Oct) museum uses interactive displays to explain Manx history and its seafaring traditions.

Three miles east of Peel is Tynwald Hill at St John's, where the annual parliamentary ceremony takes place on 5 July.

Peel has several B&Bs, including the Fernleigh Hotel (☎01624-842435; www.isleofman.com/business/f/fernleigh; Marine Pde; r per person incl breakfast from £26; ⊙Feb-Nov), which has 12 decent bedrooms. For a better-than-average bite, head for the Creek Inn (☎01624-842216; www.thecreekinn.co.uk; East Quay; mains around £8, r from £35), opposite the House of Manannan, which serves Manx queenies (scallops served with white cheese sauce) and has self-catering rooms.

The Lake District & Cumbria

Why Go?

For natural splendour, nowhere in England compares to Cumbria. This green, grand, glorious county is a place of nonstop superlatives – home to the nation's longest lake, smallest church, steepest road, highest town and tallest peak. At the heart of the county is the breathtaking Lake District, one of England's oldest and best-loved national parks, still considered by many to be the spiritual heartland of English hiking.

But there's so much more to this region than just fell (mountain) walking and fine views. There's a wealth of historic pubs, literary landmarks, tumbledown castles and stately homes to explore, and the little-explored coastline is ideal if you're looking to escape the crowds. Whether it's cruising across a lake at twilight or surveying the scene from the top of a cloud-capped fell, one thing's for certain: this is one corner of England that definitely knows how to inspire.

Best Places to Eat

» L'Enclume (p605)
» Drunken Duck (p590)
» Punch Bowl Inn (p602)
» Mason's Arms (p582)
» Yanwath Gate Inn (p608)

Best Places to Stay

» The Boundary (p581)
» Wasdale Head Inn (p594)
» Moss Grove Organic (p588)
» Old Dungeon Ghyll (p593)
» Eltermere Inn (p593)

When to Go

Cumbria's largest mountain festival is held in Keswick in mid-May, while the Beer Festival in June welcomes ale aficionados from across the globe. Ambleside's traditional sports day on the last Saturday in July features events such as hound trailing and Cumbrian wrestling; Grasmere's annual sports day takes place on the August Bank Holiday. In November, the world's greatest liars congregate on Santon Bridge for their annual fibbing contest.

The Lake District & Cumbria Highlights

❶ Conquering the top of England's highest mountain, **Scafell Pike** (p594)

❷ Taking a cruise in an antique steam launch on **Coniston Water** (p591)

❸ Wandering round William Wordsworth's homes at **Dove Cottage** and **Rydal Mount** (p587)

❹ Feeling the whiff of wildness around the dramatic valley of **Wasdale** (p594)

❺ Cycling round the wooded trails of **Grizedale Forest** (p590)

❻ Tackling the iconic fell-tops around **Great Langdale** (p593)

❼ Delving the depths of the slate mines around **Honister Pass** (p600)

❽ Catching the miniature steam trains of **La'al Ratty** (p605) into Eskdale

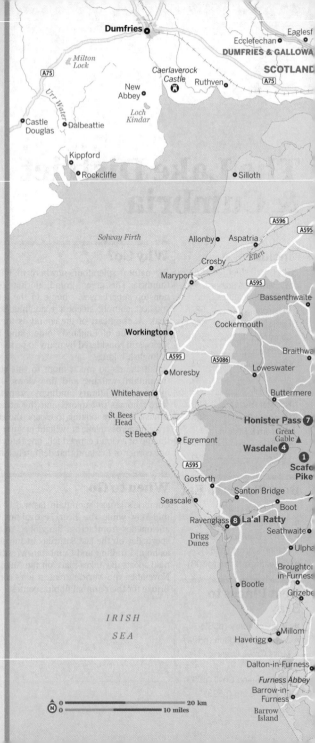

History

Neolithic settlers first quarried flint and stone around Stonethwaite and Seatoller from around 5000 BC. The region was subsequently occupied by Celts, Angles, Vikings and Romans, and during the Dark Ages marked the centre of the ancient kingdom of Rheged.

During the Middle Ages, Cumbria marked the start of 'The Debatable Lands', the wild frontier between England and Scotland. Bands of Scottish raiders, known as Border Reivers, regularly plundered the area, prompting the construction of defensive *pele* towers and castles at Carlisle, Penrith and Kendal.

The area was a centre for the Romantic movement during the 19th century, and writers such as Coleridge, de Quincey and William Wordsworth were among the first to champion the area's beauty. The need to conserve the area's unique environment gathered speed during the late 19th and early 20th centuries, culminating in the creation of the Lake District National Park in 1951.

The new county of Cumbria was formed from the neighbouring districts of Cumberland and Westmorland in 1974.

Activities

Cycling

Cycling is a great way to explore the Lake District and Cumbria, but you're going to have to tackle some hills. For short off-road rides, the dedicated bike trails of Grizedale Forest (p590) and Whinlatter Forest Park (p596) are very popular.

Long-distance routes include the 70-mile Cumbria Way between Ulverston, Keswick and Carlisle; the 140-mile Sea To Sea (C2C) Cycle Route (NCN 7; www.c2c-guide.co.uk), which begins in Whitehaven and cuts east across the northern Pennines to Newcastle; and the 173-mile Reivers Route (NCN 10; www.reivers-route.co.uk) from the River Tyne to Whitehaven.

Most major towns have bike shops that offer hire, supplies and repair.

Walking

For many people, hiking on the fells is the main reason for a Lake District visit. Trails range from low-level rambles to full-blown mountain ascents; all tourist offices and bookshops sell maps and guidebooks, such as Collins' *Lakeland Fellranger*, Ord-nance Survey's *Pathfinder Guides* and Alfred Wainwright's (p604) classic Pictorial Guides.

A good-quality map is essential if you're venturing out on the fells. There are two main publishers: the Ordnance Survey 1:25,000 *Landranger* series maps, which are used by most official bodies, or the hiker-specific Harvey *Superwalker* 1:25,000 maps, which clearly mark major trails and all the official 214 'Wainwright' fells.

Several long distance trails pass through Cumbria. Door-to-door baggage services such as Coast to Coast Packhorse (☎017683-71777; www.c2cpackhorse.co.uk) or Sherpa Van (☎0871-520-0124; www.sherpavan.com) will transport luggage from one destination to the next, meaning you don't have to lug your pack along the whole route.

Allerdale Ramble A 54-mile route from Seathwaite in Borrowdale to Grune Point on the Solway Firth, covering everything from windswept coast to wild hills.

Coast to Coast Conceived by Alfred Wainwright, this 191-mile trail travels from St Bees on the Cumbrian Coast to Robin Hood's Bay in North Yorkshire, via Honister Pass, Grasmere, Patterdale, Kirkby Stephen and Shap.

Cumbria Way It's 70 miles from Ulverston to Carlisle, via Coniston Water, Tarn Hows, Langdale, Borrowdale and Keswick.

Other Activities

Cumbria is a haven for outdoor activities: rock climbing, orienteering, horse-riding, archery, fell-running and ghyll scrambling (a cross between coasteering and river canyoning). Sailing, kayaking and windsurfing are popular too, especially around Windermere, Derwentwater and Coniston.

There are some excellent outdoor activity centres where you can try out several different activities in one day: try Holmescales Activity Centre (☎01539-722147; www.holmescales.com) near Kendal, Rookin House (☎017 684-83561; www.rookinhouse.co.uk) near Ullswater or the Keswick Adventure Centre (☎017687-75687; www.keswickadventurecentre.co.uk; Newlands).

❶ Getting There & Away

TRAIN Carlisle is on the main West Coast line from London Euston to Manchester to Glasgow. To get to the Lake District, you need to change at Oxenholme, where regular trains travel west to Kendal and Windermere. The lines around the

THE LAKE DISTRICT & CUMBRIA

Cumbrian Coast and between Settle and Carlisle are particularly scenic.

BUS National Express coaches run direct from London Victoria and Glasgow to Windermere, Carlisle and Kendal.

ℹ Getting Around

Traveline (📞0871-200 22 33; www.traveline northeast.info) provides comprehensive travel information for the whole of Cumbria and the Lake District. Bus timetables are available from tourist offices.

BOAT There are regular round-the-lake ferry services from Windermere, Coniston Water, Ullswater and Derwentwater.

BUS The main bus operator is **Stagecoach** (www.stagecoachbus.com). Bus suggestions in this chapter are based on summer timetables; most routes run a reduced winter service. You can download timetables from the Stagecoach website or the Cumbria County Council website.

555 (Lakeslink) Lancaster to Keswick, stopping at all the main towns including Windermere and Ambleside.

505 (Coniston Rambler) Kendal, Windermere, Ambleside and Coniston.

X4/X5 Penrith to Workington via Troutbeck, Keswick and Cockermouth.

CAR Traffic can be a serious problem in the Lake District, especially in peak season and on holiday weekends. Many Cumbrian towns use timed parking permits for on-street parking, which you can pick up for free from local shops and tourist offices.

THE LAKE DISTRICT

If you're a lover of the great outdoors, the Lake District is one corner of England where you'll want to linger. This sweeping panorama of slate-capped fells, craggy hilltops, misty mountain tarns and glittering lakes has been pulling in the crowds ever since the Romantics pitched up in the early 19th century, and it remains one of the country's most popular beauty spots. Literary landmarks abound, from Wordsworth's boyhood school to the lavish country estate of John Ruskin at Brantwood, and there are enough hilltop trails, hidden pubs and historic country hotels to fill a lifetime of visits.

ℹ Information

The national park's main visitor centre is at Brockhole (p582), just outside Windermere, and there are efficient tourist offices in Windermere Town, Bowness, Ambleside, Keswick, Carlisle

ℹ BUS PASSES

Several travel passes cover Cumbria.

Lakes Day Ranger (£20.50) is the best-value ticket, allowing unlimited travel for one day on all trains and buses in Cumbria. Also includes a boat cruise on Windermere, 10% discount on the two steam railways and 20% discount on cruise services on Derwentwater, Ullswater and Coniston.

Cumbria Day Ranger (£38.50) provides one day's train travel anywhere in Cumbria extending into parts of Lancashire, North Yorkshire, Northumberland and Dumfries and Galloway.

North West Explorer (one day £10, three days £20) offers bus travel for three days in Cumbria and Lancashire. There's a seven-day version, the Northwest Megarider Gold (£25).

Central Lakes Dayrider (£7) covers Bowness, Ambleside, Grasmere, Langdale and Coniston; includes the 599, 505 and 516.

and several other towns. All carry a wealth of information on local sights, activities, accommodation and public transport, and can help with accommodation bookings.

Windermere & Bowness-on-Windermere

POP 8432

Of all England's lakes, none carries the cachet of Windermere. Stretching for 10.5 silvery miles from Ambleside to Newby Bridge, it's one of the classic Lake District vistas, and has been a centre for tourism since the first steam trains chugged into town in 1847.

The town itself is split between Windermere, 1.5 miles uphill from the lake, and bustling Bowness-on-Windermere (usually shortened to Bowness), with its touristy collection of teashops, ice-cream stalls and cruise boats. On summer days it can feel uncomfortably crowded, but even then it's usually possibly to find some serenity, either by venturing out on the lake itself, or drinking in the views form the surrounding hills.

The two areas of town are linked by Lake Road, lined with hotels and B&Bs. The train and bus stations are both in Windermere town.

Lake District

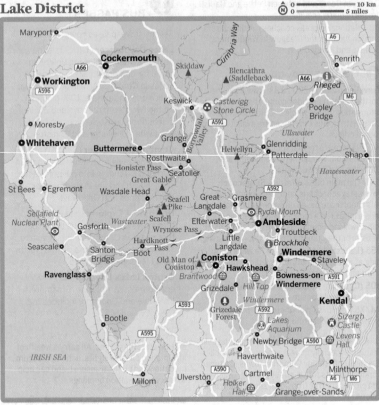

◉ Sights

World of Beatrix Potter   MUSEUM
(www.hop-skip-jump.com; adult/child £6.75/3.50; ◷10am-5.30pm Apr-Sep, to 4.30pm Oct-Mar) This attraction brings to life various scenes from the author's books using a combination of life-size models and decorated rooms. Among the scenes on show are Peter Rabbit's garden, Mr McGregor's greenhouse, Mrs Tiggywinkle's kitchen, Jemima Puddle-Duck's glade; there's even a themed tearoom. Be prepared for long queues in summer.

🏃 Activities

Windermere Lake Cruises   BOAT TOURS
(☏015395-31188; www.windermere-lakecruises.co. uk) Top on the list of things to do in Windermere is to take a lake cruise. The first passenger ferry was launched back in 1845, and cruising on the lake is still a popular pastime: some of the vessels are modern, but

there are a couple of period beauties dating back to the 1930s.

All cruises allow you to jump off at one of the ferry landings (Waterhead/Ambleside, Wray Castle, Brockhole, Bowness, Ferry Landing, Fell Foot Ferry and Lakeside) and catch a later boat back.

Trips include the **Freedom of the Lake Ticket** (adult/child/family £17.75/8.90/48.50), with one day's unlimited travel on all routes; the **Blue Cruise** (adult/child/family £7.20/3.60/19.80), a 45-minute cruise around Windermere's islands and bays; the **Green Cruise** (adult/child/family £7.20/3.60/19.80), a 45-minute cruise from Waterhead/Ambleside via Wray Castle and Brockhole Visitor Centre; the **Red Cruise** (adult/child/family £9.75/5.85/28.25), the North lake cruise from Bowness to Ambleside; the **Yellow Cruise** (adult/child/family £10/6/29), the South cruise from Bowness to Lakeside and the Lakes Aquarium; and **Bowness to Ferry House** (adult/child/family £2.55/1.50/7.35), a cross-lake shuttle service to Ferry House, from where you can catch a bus to Hill Top and Hawkshead.

From April to October, rowing boats can be hired from the lake jetty for £12. Motorboats coast from £18 to £22 for two adults; children under 16 go free. There's a 10mph speed limit on Windermere.

🛏 Sleeping

Windermere's popularity means accommodation tends to be pricier than elsewhere around the Lakes.

TOP CHOICE The Boundary   B&B ££
(☏015394-48978; www.theboundaryonline.co.uk; Lake Rd; d £100-180; P🛜) Not the cheapest sleep in Windermere, but definitely one of the sexiest. Owners Steve and Helen have given this Victorian house a sleek, boutique makeover: chic decor, monochrome colours, quirky furniture and all. Steve's a cricket obsessive, so all the rooms are named after famous batsmen.

Wheatlands Lodge   B&B ££
(☏015394-43789; www.wheatlandslodge-windermere.co.uk; Old College Lane; d £80-150; P🛜) Between Bowness and Windermere, this detached house looks Victorian, but inside you'll find eight elegant, contemporary rooms with either power shower or sit-down jacuzzi. Owner Sarah knows how to spoil her guests, from the welcome coffee-and-cake to the locally-sourced breakfast.

Cranleigh   HOTEL ££
(☏015394-43293; www.thecranleigh.com; Kendal Rd; d £75-180, ste £250-400; P🛜) This heavily refurbed guesthouse is minutes from the Bowness waterfront, and offers a pick-and-mix of rooms: it's worth bumping up to the 'Superior' for space and snazzy bathrooms. The two Suites are fabulously over the top; check out the Sanctuary with its Bose stereo, glass bath and picture-fireplace.

1 Park Road   B&B ££
(www.1parkroad.com; 1 Park Rd; d £76-104; P🛜) It's the little treats that keep this cosy guesthouse a cut above: bath goodies from Pure Lakes and The White Company, iPod docks in every room, and home-made baked beans and marmalade on the breakfast table. Rooms are comfortable, and the rates stay reasonable, even in season.

ℹ THE CROSS LAKES EXPERIENCE

The Cross Lakes Experience (www.lakedistrict.gov.uk/visiting/planning yourvisit/travelandtransport/crosslakes; 🕑Mar-Oct) is a boat, bus and minibus service that enables travel from Windermere to Coniston without a car.

Tickets include travel on the Windermere Ferry from Bowness to Ferry House, from where the Mountain Goat minibus runs to Hill Top and Hawkshead. From Hawkshead, you can catch the X30 bus to Grizedale Forest, or the 505 bus to Coniston, and then travel across the lake on the Coniston Launch. For info and timetables, contact Mountain Goat (☏015394-45161; www.mountain-goat.com; Victoria Rd) or local tourist offices.

A return from Bowness to Coniston costs adult/child £19.10/10.90. Single fares:

» **Ferry House** (£2.55/1.50)
» **Hill Top** (£5.35/3.05)
» **Hawkshead** (£6.35/3.50)
» **Coniston** (£11.25/6.20)

Archway   B&B £
(☏015394-45613; www.the-archway.com; 13 College Rd; d £50-55) A no-nonsense, old-fashioned, great-value B&B, worth a mention for its fell views, knock-down rates and absurdly generous breakfast (choices include Manx kippers, smoked haddock, parma ham omelettes and American-style pancakes).

Number 80 Bed Then Breakfast   B&B ££
(☏015394-43584; www.number80bed.co.uk; 80 Craig Walk; d £80-90; 🛜) This cute Bowness refuge is still off the radar, so keep it under your hats. Just four rooms, but all are up-to-date: room No 1 has a pine four-poster, the other three feel more modern.

Lake District Backpackers Lodge   HOSTEL £
(☏015394-46374; www.lakedistrictbackpackers.co.uk; High St; dm £15; @) Windermere's indie hostel is handy for the station, but it's cramped and showing its age. Dorms and the kitchen are small, but rates include bed linen and breakfast.

✕ Eating

 Mason's Arms PUB, INN ££

(☎015395-68486; www.masonsarmsstrawberry
bank.co.uk; Winster; mains £13-20, d £75-105)
Three miles east of the lake, not far from
Bowlands Bridge, the marvellous Mason's
Arms is a local secret. The rafters, flagstones
and cast-iron range haven't changed in centuries, but the food is up to date, and the
patio has to-die-for views across fields and
fells. In short, a cracker.

 Hooked SEAFOOD ££

(☎015394-48443; www.hookedwindermere.co.uk;
Ellerthwaite Sq; mains £16.95-19.95; ☺dinner Tue-
Sun) It's only been open since 2011, but this
admirably simple seafood restaurant already
has a loyal following. Fish arrives daily from
the Fleetwood docks, and is dished up with
Mediterranean-meets-Asian flair: turbot
with basil pesto, snapper with saffron pasta
and curried monkfish in a creamy sauce.

Francine's BISTRO ££

(☎015394-44088; www.francinesrestaurantwinder
mere.co.uk; 27 Main Rd; 2-/3-course dinner menu
£15.95/18.95, dinner mains £9.95-15.95; ☺lunch &
dinner Tue-Sat) A buzzy place that's as popular with the Windermere locals as with the
tourists (always a good sign). Tiny tables,
potted plants and flowers in jugs lend it a
cosy neighbourhood vibe, and the menu
takes in everything from garlicky mussels to
pot-roast lamb and daube of venison.

Angel Inn GASTROPUB ££

(☎015394-44080; www.the-angelinn.com; Helm
Rd; mains £10.95-16.50) This attractive pub
is set on top of a grassy hummock behind
the Bowness shoreline. It's more big-city-
modern than backcountry-cosy: leather sofas, wooden floors and blackboards, plus a
gastropub menu of pork belly ballotine and
honey-roasted chicken.

Lazy Daisy's Lakeland Kitchen CAFE £

(☎015394-43877; 31-33 Crescent Rd; lunch £4-
10, dinner £10-16; ☺Mon-Sat 10am-9pm) Filling
comfort food is the order of the day at this
trad cafe: Cumberland sausages served with
a giant Yorkshire pudding, or steak-and-
Guinness pie doused in lashings of gravy.
Look out for the regular pudding clubs.

Postilion BISTRO ££

(☎015394-45852; www.postilionrestaurant.co.uk;
Ash St; mains £12-16, set menu £18.95; ☺lunch &
dinner) Reliable bistro tucked away off Ash
St with a good French-Mediterranean menu.

Jericho's at the Waverley Hotel BRITISH £££

(☎015394-42522; www.jerichos.co.uk; College
Rd; dinner mains £15.25-25; ☺dinner Tue-Sun)
A townhouse restaurant run by renowned
local chef Chris Blaydes, who's previously
worked at some of the Lake District's top
hotels. Smart rooms are available upstairs
(£75 to £125).

Lighthouse CAFE £

(Main Rd; mains £8-15; ☺breakfast, lunch & dinner)
This three-storey cafe just downhill from the
station offers a continental-style menu, quality coffee and fresh-baked pastries.

🍷 Drinking

Hole in T' Wall PUB

(Falbarrow Rd) Bowness' best-loved boozer is
also the town's oldest, dating back to 1612,
and offering lashings of rough-beamed, low-
ceilinged atmosphere.

ℹ Information

Bowness tourist office (☎015394-42895;
bownesstic@lake-district.gov.uk; Glebe Rd;
☺9.30am-5.30pm Easter-Oct, 10am-4pm
Fri-Sun Nov-Easter) Beside the waterfront.
Brockhole National Park visitor centre
(☎015394-46601; www.lake-district.gov.uk;
☺10am-5pm Easter-Oct) Installed inside a
19th-century mansion 3 miles north of Windermere on the A591, this is the Lake District's
flagship visitor centre, and also has a teashop,
an adventure playground and gardens.
Library (Broad St; per 30min £1; ☺9am-7pm
Mon, to 5pm Tue, Thu & Fri, to 1pm Sat, closed
Wed & Sun) Internet access.
Windermere tourist office (☎015394-46499;
windermeretic@southlakeland.gov.uk; Victoria
St; ☺9am-5.30pm Mon-Sat, 9.30am-5.30pm
Sun Apr-Oct, shorter hours in winter) Opposite
NatWest Bank.

ℹ Getting There & Away

BOAT The **Windermere Ferry** (car/bike/
pedestrian £4.30/1/50p; ☺6.50am-9.50pm
Mon-Fri, 9.10am-9.50pm Sat & Sun Mar-Oct,
last ferry one hour earlier in winter) carries
vehicles and pedestrians from Ferry Nab, just
south of Bowness, across to Ferry House on the
lake's west side. There's a ferry roughly every
20 minutes, although note that queues can be
horrendous in summer.

BUS There's one daily National Express coach
from London (£30, eight hours) via Lancaster
and Kendal.

WRAY CASTLE & CLAIFE HEIGHTS

Windermere's quieter west side is a good place to escape the crowds. North of the ferry landings at Ferry House, a network of woodland paths winds across Claife Heights, while the nearby National Trust–owned estate of Wray Castle (NT; www.nationaltrust .org.uk/wray-castle; adult/child £6/3; ⊙10.30am-5pm) encompasses 25 hectares of lakeside grounds and a turreted 19th-century mansion, once used as a holiday home by Beatrix Potter's family.

Local buses include the following:

555/556 Lakeslink (half-hourly Monday to Saturday, hourly at weekends) Starts at the train station, stopping at Troutbeck Bridge (five minutes), Brockhole Visitor Centre (seven minutes), Ambleside (15 minutes), Grasmere (30 minutes) and Keswick (one hour). In the opposite direction it continues to Kendal (25 minutes) and Lancaster (1 hour 40 minutes).

505 Coniston Rambler (eight daily Monday to Saturday, six on Sunday) Travels from Windermere to Coniston (50 minutes) via Troutbeck, Brockhole, Ambleside, Skelwith Fold, Hawkshead and Hawkshead Hill. Two buses a day serve Kendal.

599 Lakes Rider (three times hourly Monday to Saturday, hourly on Sunday in summer) Open-top bus between Bowness, Troutbeck, Brockhole, Rydal Church (for Rydal Mount), Dove Cottage and Grasmere. Some buses stop at Windermere train station.

TRAIN Windermere is the only town that's inside the national park and accessible by train. It's on the branch line to Kendal and Oxenholme, from where there are frequent connections north and south.

DESTINATION	FARE (ONE WAY)	DURATION
Edinburgh	£55	2½hr
Glasgow	£43.40	2¾hr
Kendal	£4.20	15min
Lancaster	£12.60	45min
London	£92.10	3¼hr
Manchester Piccadilly	£32.40	1½-2hr
Oxenholme	£4.90	20min

Around Windermere

Blackwell House   HISTORIC BUILDING
(www.blackwell.org.uk; adult/child £7.95/4.40; ⊙10.30am-5pm Apr-Oct, to 4pm Feb-Mar, Nov & Dec) Two miles south of Bowness on the B5360, Blackwell House is one of the finest examples of the 19th-century Arts and Crafts Movement, which championed the importance of handmade goods and high-quality craftsmanship over the mass-produced mentality of the Industrial Revolution.

Designed by Mackay Hugh Baillie Scott for a wealthy brewer, the house has many hallmarks of Arts and Crafts design: light, airy rooms, detailed decor and lots of bespoke craftwork (including wood panelling, stained glass and Delft tiles). Of particular note are the huge wood-panelled Great Hall and the serene White Drawing Room.

FREE **Fell Foot Park**   GARDEN
(NT; www.nationaltrust.org.uk/fell-foot-park; ⊙8am-8pm summer, 9am-5pm winter) Located at the southern end of Windermere, some 7 miles south of Bowness, this 18-acre lakeside estate originally belonged to a manor house. It's now owned by the National Trust, and its shoreline paths and grassy lawns are ideal for a sunny-day picnic. There's also a small cafe (open 10am to 5pm), and rowing boats are available for hire.

Lakes Aquarium   AQUARIUM
(☎015395-30153; www.lakesaquarium.co.uk; Lakeside; adult/child £8.95/5.95; ⊙9am-6pm Apr-Oct) Found at the southern end of the lake near Newby Bridge, this aquarium explores a range of underwater habitats from tropical Africa through to Morecambe Bay. Its highlights inc-lude a simulated diving bell and an underwater tunnel beneath Windermere's lake bed, complete with pike, char and diving ducks. Otter feeding takes place at 10.30am and 3pm.

Windermere Lake Cruises and the Lakeside & Haverthwaite Railway both stop right beside the aquarium, or you could catch bus 618 from Bowness.

There are discounts for tickets purchased online or combination tickets.

ℹ WINDERMERE COMBO TICKETS

Combination tickets cover several Windermere attractions.

Boat & Train (adult/child/family £14.75/8.30/41.25) Includes a Windermere Lake cruise and a trip on the Lakeside & Haverthwaite Steam Railway.

Boat & Aquarium (adult/child/family £16.45/9.45/48.80) Cruise and admission to the Lakes Aquarium.

Boat, Train & Aquarium (adult/child/family £20.95/11.45/59.80)

Boat, Bus, Train & Motor Museum (adult/child/family £20.45/12.10/57.25) Includes a cruise from Bowness, a return trip on the railway to/from Newby Bridge, admission to the Lakeland Motor Museum and a bus back to Bowness.

Lakeside & Haverthwaite Railway
HERITAGE RAILWAY

(☑015395-31594; www.lakesiderailway.co.uk; adult/child/family return £6.30/3.20/16.90; ☉mid-Mar–Oct) Originally built to carry ore, timber and other industrial goods to the ports at Ulverston and Barrow, these vintage steam trains now puff their way between Haverthwaite, near Ulverston, to Newby Bridge and Lakeside. There are between five and seven trains a day depending on the season, handily timed to correspond with the Windermere cruise boats.

Lakeland Motor Museum
MUSEUM

(www.lakelandmotormuseum.co.uk; Backbarrow; adult/child £7.80/5; ☉9.30am-5.30pm Apr-Sep, to 4.30pm Oct-Mar) In a purpose-built new home 2 miles south of Newby Bridge, this car museum houses a wonderful collection of antique cars: classic (Minis, Austin Healeys, MGs), sporty (DeLoreans, Audi Quattros, Aston Martins) and downright odd (Scootacars, Amphicars).

A separate building explores the history of Donald and Malcolm Campbell's record attempts on Coniston Water, with replicas of the original 1935 *Bluebird* car and the 1967 boat, *Bluebird K7*.

The museum is on the A590 from Newby Bridge towards Kendal. The X35 (hourly Monday to Saturday, three on Sunday) from Newby Bridge to Ulverston and Kendal stops nearby.

Troutbeck

Nestled among the fells to the north of Windermere, on the road towards the Kirkstone Pass, this rural hamlet feels a world away from the Bowness bustle.

Apart from the countryside, it's worth a stop for the historic National Trust–owned farmhouse of Townend (NT; ☑01539-432628; www.nationaltrust.org.uk/townend; adult/child £4.70/2.35; ☉1-5pm Wed-Sun Mar-Oct, open daily school holidays), which contains a collection of vintage farming tools and furniture that belonged to the Browne family, who owned the house until 1943. Public visiting hours are from 1pm to 5pm, but you can join hourly guided tours from 11am to 1pm.

Nearby is the excellent Windermere YHA (☑0845-371 9352; www.yha.org.uk/hostel/windermere; Bridge Lane; dm £19.65; ☉reception 7.30-11.30am & 1-11pm; P@), the closest YHA to Windermere. The rooms are modern, and facilities include a well-stocked shop, canteen and gear-drying room. Buses stop about a mile downhill from the village, at the river crossing of Troutbeck Bridge.

ℹ Getting There & Away

Bus 517, the Kirkstone Rambler, travels through Troutbeck en route to Ullswater (one hour, three daily mid-July to August, weekends only other times of year).

Ambleside

POP 3382

Tucked at the northern head of Windermere and backed by a cluster of dramatic fells, Ambleside feels a lot less commercial than its sister towns further to the south, but that doesn't stop it getting jam-packed throughout the summer months. It's a favourite base for hikers, with plenty of quality outdoors shops dotted around town, and it marks the start of several classic fell hikes.

◉ Sights & Activities

The town's best-known landmark is Bridge House, a tiny cottage that spans the clattering brook of Stock Ghyll; now occupied by a National Trust shop, it's thought to have originally been built as an apple store.

Armitt Museum — MUSEUM

(www.armitt.com; Rydal Rd; adult £2.50; ⊙10am-5pm) Artefacts at Ambleside's modest town museum include a lock of John Ruskin's hair, a collection of botanical watercolours by Beatrix Potter and prints by Herbert Bell, the pharmacist turned photographer.

Fell Hikes — WALKING

Ambleside makes a good base for hikes; the tourist office has a good selection of trail leaflets and guidebooks.

The most popular walk is the short half-hour stroll up to the 60ft waterfall of Stock Ghyll Force; the trail is signposted behind the old Market Hall at the bottom of Stock Ghyll Lane.

From the falls, you can hike on across the top of Wansfell (487m/1597ft), which affords a stunning panorama across Windermere, before looping back via Troutbeck, Skelghyll Wood, and the Jenkin's Crag viewpoint. In total, it's a four-hour walk of around 6 miles.

A more formidable proposition is the 10-mile Fairfield Horseshoe, via the summits of Nab Scar, Heron Pike, Fairfield and Dove Crag. It's a full-blown mountain walk, so you'll need boots, a map and supplies.

Low Wood Watersports — BOATING

(☎015394-33441; www.englishlakes.co.uk/watersports) This experienced and well-equipped watersports centre offers water-skiing, sailing and kayaking. Rowboats and motorboats are also available for hire.

🛏 Sleeping

Regent Hotel — HOTEL ££

(☎015394-32254; www.regentlakes.co.uk; Waterhead Bay; d £119-149; P🐾) Recently refurbished and looking much the better for it, this hotel has a near-the-lake location without the sky-high price tag. The rooms offer different settings: some have balconies overlooking the garden, others have bunks for the kids, and a few sneak in views over Windermere.

Lakes Lodge — B&B ££

(☎015394-33240; www.lakeslodge.co.uk; Lake Rd; r £79-129; P🐾) Run by the same team behind the Regent Hotel, this modish mini-hotel offers a touch more luxury than Ambleside's other guesthouses. The 16 rooms are all clean lines, stark walls and zero clutter, and most have a full-size wall mural featuring a local beauty spot. Breakfast is self-serve.

The Gables — B&B ££

(☎015394-33272; www.thegables-ambleside.co.uk; Church Walk; s £45-50, d £90-120; P) One of the best of Ambleside's B&Bs, in a quiet spot overlooking the recreation ground. Spotty cushions and colourful prints keep things cheery, but room sizes are variable (in this instance, bigger is definitely better). Guests receive discounts at the owner's restaurant, Sheila's Cottage.

🌿 Cote How — B&B £££

(☎015394-32765; www.bedbreakfastlakedistrict.com; Rydal, near Ambleside; d £120-160; P🐾) Approved by the Soil Association, this detached house makes a virtue of its sustainable credentials. Food is 100% local and organic, power's sourced from a green supplier, and there's a discount if you don't bring a car. The three rooms are olde Edwardian, with cast-iron beds, roll-top baths and fireplaces. It's in Rydal, 1.5 miles from Ambleside.

Compston House Hotel — B&B £££

(☎015394-32305; www.compstonhouse.co.uk; Compston Rd; d from £80; 🐾) All the rooms are themed after a different American state: sunny Hawaii, bright Florida, maritime Maine, which is perhaps unsurprising, as the owners are ex-New Yorkers. Breakfast includes blueberry muffins and maple pancakes.

Waterhead Hotel — HOTEL £££

(☎08458-504503; www.elh.co.uk/hotels/waterhead; r £125-165; P🐾🐕) Ambleside's main hotel has a super position down beside the lakeshore. The exterior is classic Lakeland, all solid stone and bay windows, but inside it's very much a modern hotel, with spacious rooms stocked with heritage furniture and designer fabrics, and a sophisticated restaurant, the Mountain View.

Low Wray — CAMPSITE £

(NT; ☎bookings 015394-63862; www.ntlakescampsites.org.uk; tents £8.25-12.50 plus £5.50 per extra adult, eco-pods £30-50; ⊙campsite arrivals 3-7pm Sat-Thu, 3-9pm Fri, Mar-Oct) Lakeside camping courtesy of the National Trust – although waterside pitches are extra (£7.50 for a lake view, £10 for the lakeshore). It's 3 miles from town along the B5286; bus 505 stops nearby. Luxury yurts can be booked through Long Valley (☎01539-731089; www.luxury-yurt-holidays.co.uk; per week £335-490) and Wild in Style (☎07909-446381; www.wildinstyle.co.uk; per week £325-495), while 4Winds Lakeland

NATIONAL TRUST CAMPSITE BOOKINGS

The National Trust (☎015394-63862; www.nationaltrust.org.uk; ⏰10am-noon & 2-4pm Mon-Fri) has four Lake District campsites at Low Wray, Wasdale, Great Langdale and Hoathwaite, near Coniston. All accept advance reservations up to 24 hours before your arrival; there's a fee of £5 for booking online, or £7.50 by telephone and email, and stays must be for a minimum of two nights.

Tipis (☎01539-821227; www.4windslakelandtipis.co.uk; tipis per week £290-465) offers 12 Native American–style tipis.

Ambleside YHA HOSTEL £
(☎0845 371 9620; ambleside@yha.org.uk; Windermere Rd; dm/d £23/40, f £99-149; P🅿🛜) One of the YHA's flagship Lake District hostels, this huge lakeside house is a fave for activity holidays (everything from kayaking to ghyll-scrambling). Great facilities (kitchen, bike rental, boat jetty and bar) mean it's heavily subscribed, so book well ahead.

Ambleside Backpackers HOSTEL £
(☎015394-32340; www.englishlakesbackpackers.co.uk; Old Lake Rd; dm £16; P@) Cottage hostel a short walk south from Ambleside's centre.

✘ Eating

Glass House MEDITERRANEAN ££
(☎015394-32137; www.theglasshouserestaurant.co.uk; Rydal Rd; mains £10.25-14.75) Classy dining in a converted fulling mill (with original mill wheels and machinery still in place). It's known for its accomplished Med and French food, so expect plenty of zingy flavours underpinned by quality Lakeland ingredients.

Fellini's VEGETARIAN ££
(☎015394-32487; www.fellinisambleside.com; Church St; mains £11.95; ⏰dinner, closed Mon winter) Fear not, veggies: you might be in the land of the Cumberland sausage and the tattie hotpot, but that doesn't mean you can't indulge. Fellini's turns out fancy 'vegeterranean' food that would tempt even the hardiest of carnivores. It's run by Zeffirelli's owners; a small upstairs screen shows arthouse and opera performances.

Zeffirelli's ITALIAN £
(☎015394-33845; www.zeffirellis.com; Compston Rd; pizzas & mains £8-12; ⏰to 10pm) If it's pizza and pasta you want, Zeff's is the place. Dine on Italian dishes in the basement restaurant, then head next door for a film at the attached cinema. The £17.95 'Double Feature' deal includes two courses and a ticket to the movies. There's a jazz club upstairs.

Sheila's Cottage BISTRO ££
(☎015394-33079; The Slack; mains £9.90-19.95; ⏰lunch & dinner) Rough walls and cottagey furnishings make this a snug place to dine. It serves a mix-and-match menu: chunky sandwiches and salads for lunch, big plates of lamb chump, salmon fillet or squash risotto for dinner. It's in an alley off the main street.

Lucy's on a Plate CAFE, BISTRO ££
(☎015394-31191; www.lucysofambleside.co.uk; Church St; mains £12-20; ⏰breakfast, lunch & dinner) This longstanding bistro has been through turbulent times (original owner went bust in 2011), but it's been rescued from the brink and is back to doing what it does best: quirky bistro food and generous puddings laced with a dash of offbeat imagination. Cooking lessons are available at **Lucy Cooks** (☎015394-32288; www.lucycooks.co.uk; Mill Yard, Staveley) in nearby Staveley, 3 miles from Windermere.

Tarantella ITALIAN ££
(10 Lake Rd; mains £9.95-15.95; ⏰lunch & dinner) Reliable Italian food, with wood-fired pizzas and authentic pastas partnered by unusual regional fare such as duck-and-chilli sausage and roast tuna.

Lucy 4 TAPAS £
(2 St Mary's Lane; tapas £4-10; ⏰5-10.30pm Mon-Fri, noon-10.30pm Sat & Sun) Cosy wine-bar offshoot of Lucy's on a Plate that also does good tapas.

Apple Pie CAFE £
(Rydal Rd; lunches £4-10; ⏰breakfast & lunch) Sunny cafe popular for its sandwiches, buns and hearty pies.

🍺 Drinking & Entertainment

Ambleside has plenty of pubs: locals favour the Golden Rule (Smithy Brow) for its ale selection, while the Royal Oak (Market Pl) packs in the posthike punters.

Ambleside's two-screen Zeffirelli's Cinema (☎015394-33100; Compston Rd) is next to

Zeffirelli's, with extra screens in a converted church down the road.

Shopping

Compston Rd has enough equipment shops to launch an assault on Everest. The largest is **Gaynor Sports** (☑01524-734938; www .gaynors.co.uk; Market Cross), with three floors of outdoor gear by all the top brands, plus sections for camping and footwear.

❶ Information

Hub (☑015394-32582; tic@thehubofamble side.com; Central Buildings, Market Cross; ⊗9am-5pm) The tourist information centre and the post office are both here.

Library (Kelsick Rd; per hr £3; ⊗10am-5pm Mon & Wed, to 7pm Tue & Fri, to 1pm Sat) Internet access.

❶ Getting There & Around

BICYCLE Bikes and gear can be hired from **Biketreks** (☑015394-31505; www.biketreks .net; Compston Rd; per day £20) and **Ghyllside Cycles** (☑015394-33592; www.ghyllside.co.uk; The Slack; per day £18).

BUS Useful routes:

555 to Grasmere and Windermere (hourly, 10 buses on Sunday)

505 to Hawkshead and Coniston (10 daily Monday to Saturday, six on Sunday, mid-March to October)

516 (six daily, five on Sunday) to Elterwater and Langdale.

Around Ambleside

⎡TOP⎤
⎣CHOICE⎦ Rydal Mount   HISTORIC HOME

(www.rydalmount.co.uk; adult/child £6/2.50, gardens only adults £4; ⊗9.30am-5pm Mar-Oct, 11am-4pm Wed-Mon Nov & Feb) William Wordsworth's best-known Lakeland residence is definitely Dove Cottage, but he actually spent much more time at Rydal Mount, a much grander house halfway between Ambleside and Grasmere. This was the Wordsworth family's home from 1813 until the poet's death in 1850, and it's still owned by his descendants.

The house is a treasure trove of Wordsworth memorabilia. Downstairs you can wander around the library, dining room and drawing room (look out in the cabinets for William's pen, inkstand and picnic box, and a famous portrait of the poet by the American painter Henry Inman hanging above the fireplace). Upstairs are the family bedrooms and Wordsworth's attic study, containing his encyclopedia and a sword belonging to his brother John, who was lost in a shipwreck in 1805.

Below the house is **Dora's Field**, which Wordsworth planted with daffodils in memory of his eldest daughter, who died from tuberculosis in 1847.

The house is 1.5 miles northwest of Ambleside, off the A591. Bus 555 (and bus 599 from April to October) stops at the end of the drive.

Grasmere

POP 1458

Even without its Romantic connections, gorgeous Grasmere would still be one of the Lakes' biggest draws. It's one of the prettiest of the Lakeland hamlets, huddled at the base of a sweeping valley dotted with woods, pastures and slate-coloured hills, but most of the thousands of trippers come in search of its famous former residents: opium-eating Thomas de Quincey, unruly Coleridge and grand old man William Wordsworth. With such a rich literary heritage, Grasmere unsurprisingly gets crammed; avoid high summer if you can.

◎ Sights

Dove Cottage   HISTORIC HOME

(☑015394-35544; www.wordsworth.org.uk; adult/child £7.50/4.50; ⊗9.30am-5.30pm) This tiny, creeper-clad cottage, on the edge of the village, famously belonged to William Wordsworth. He arrived here with his sister Dorothy in 1799, before being joined in 1802 by his new wife, Mary, and soon after, three children, John, Dora and Thomas, who were born here in 1803, 1804 and 1806 respectively.

The tiny cottage was a cramped but happy home for the growing family until 1808, when it was subsequently rented by Thomas de Quincey (author of *Confessions of an English Opium Eater*).

Like nearby Rydal Mount, the cottage's cramped rooms are full of artefacts: keep your eyes peeled for the poet's passport, a pair of his spectacles and a portrait of his favourite dog Pepper, given to him by Sir Walter Scott. One upstairs bedroom was lined with newspaper by Wordsworth's sister Dorothy to try and keep out the draughts.

Entry is by timed ticket to avoid over-crowding, and includes a guided tour.

Next door, the **Wordsworth Museum & Art Gallery** houses one of the nation's main collections relating to the Romantic movement, including many original manuscripts.

St Oswald's Church   CHURCH
In the churchyard of this tiny chapel, in the centre of Grasmere, are the graves of many of the Wordsworths, including William, his wife Mary, sister Dorothy, and children Dora, Catherine and Thomas. Samuel Taylor Coleridge's son Hartley is also buried here.

🏃 Activities

Popular **fell hikes** starting from Grasmere include Helm Crag (1328ft), often known as the 'Lion and the Lamb', thanks to its distinctive shape, Silver Howe (1292ft), Loughrigg Fell (1099ft) and the multi-peak circuit known as the Easedale Round (five to six hours, 8.5 to 9 miles).

🛏 Sleeping

TOP CHOICE Moss Grove Organic   HOTEL £££
(☑015394-35251; www.mossgrove.com; r Sun-Thu £114-209, Fri & Sat £129-259; 🅿🖭) This eco-chic hotel champions its green credentials: sheep-wool insulation, organic paints, reclaimed timber beds, but for once, eco also equals elegance. Rooms are enormous, and bathrooms sparkle with sexy showers and underfloor heating. Breakfast is served buffet-style in the kitchen-diner downstairs.

How Foot Lodge   B&B ££
(☑015394-35366; www.howfoot.co.uk; Town End; d from £72; 🅿) Just a stroll from Dove Cottage, this stone house has six rooms finished in fawns and beiges; the nicest are the Deluxe Doubles, one with sun terrace and the other with private sitting room. Rates are an absolute bargain considering the location.

Heidi's Grasmere Lodge   B&B ££
(☑015394-35248; www.heidisgrasmerelodge.co.uk; Red Lion Sq; d £99-135; 🖩) This plush B&B plonked above Heidi's cafe offers six super-feminine rooms full of frilly cushions and Cath Kidston–style patterns. They're quite small but very comfy: room 6 has its own sun patio, reached via a spiral staircase.

Raise View House   B&B ££
(☑015394-35215; www.raiseviewhouse.co.uk; White Bridge; s/d £90/106; 🅿🖩) Fell views unfurl from nearly every room here: Helm Crag,

Easedale and Stone Arthur are particularly impressive. On the edge of Grasmere, the house is smartly appointed: Farrow & Ball paints, Gilchrist & Soames bathstuffs and Wedgwood china on the breakfast table.

Grasmere Hostel   HOSTEL £
(☑015394-35055; www.grasmerehostel.co.uk; Broadrayne Farm; dm £19.50; 🅿@) This independent hostel is in a converted farmhouse on the A591, near the Traveller's Rest pub. There are two kitchens, and each dorm has its own en suite bathroom. There's even a Nordic sauna.

Butharlyp How YHA   HOSTEL £
(☑0845-371 9319; www.yha.org.uk; Easedale Rd; dm £15.50; ⏰reception 7am-10pm Feb-Nov, weekends only Dec & Jan; 🅿@) Grasmere's only remaining YHA (since Thorney How) was sold off is in a large Victorian house set among grassy grounds. There's a good range of different-sized dorms and an unusually good cafe-bar.

Thorney How   HOSTEL £
(☑015394-35597; www.thorneyhow.co.uk; Easedale Rd; dm £21-5) Now independent, this former YHA is in a Grade II–listed farmhouse off Easedale Rd, 15 minutes from Grasmere. Accommodation is in six- to 10-bed dorms, although there are a few doubles, all with fresh carpets and pine furniture. Facilities include a kitchen, cafe and bike shelter, but the showers need renovating.

🍴 Eating & Drinking

TOP CHOICE Jumble Room   MODERN BRITISH £££
(☑015394-35188; Langdale Rd; dinner mains £14.50-26.50; ⏰lunch Fri-Sun, dinner Wed-Sun) Husband-and-wife team Andy and Crissy Hill have turned this village bistro into a much-loved dining landmark. It's a really fun and friendly place to dine. Spotty crockery, cow murals and primary colours set the boho tone, matched by a magpie menu taking in everything from Dithose chicken to cauliflower fritters.

Sara's Bistro   BISTRO ££
(Broadgate; mains £10-16) Hearty homespun cooking is Sarah's raison d'être – big portions of roast chicken, lamb shanks and apple crumble, served without the faintest hint of fuss.

Heidi's of Grasmere   CAFE £
(Red Lion Sq; mains £4-8; ⏰9am-5.30pm) This cute pine-clad cafe makes a welcome refuge

if the weather turns. Thick-cut sandwiches and hot soups are its mainstay, but the house special, 'cheese smokeys', are the choice if you're hungry.

Sarah Nelson's Gingerbread Shop CAKES
(www.grasmeregingerbread.co.uk; Church Stile; 12 pieces of gingerbread £4.95; ⊙9.15am-5.30pm Mon-Sat, 12.30-5pm Sun) In business since 1854, this famous sweetshop makes Grasmere's essential souvenir: traditional gingerbread with a half-biscuit, half-cakey texture, cooked according to a top-secret recipe by ladies in frilly pinafores and starched bonnets.

Rowan Tree CAFE £
(Stocks Lane; mains £3-10, pizzas £6-9) Riverside cafe serving basic pasta and pizzas.

Miller Howe Cafe CAFE ££
(Red Lion Sq; mains £5-14) Smart chrome cafe on the main square.

❶ Getting There & Away

The 555 bus runs from Windermere to Grasmere (15 minutes), via Ambleside, Rydal Church and Dove Cottage.

The open-top 599 (two or three per hour in summer) runs from Grasmere via Ambleside, Troutbeck Bridge, Windermere and Bowness.

Hawkshead

POP 1640

Lakeland villages don't come much more postcard-perfect than Hawkshead, a muddle of whitewashed cottages, cobbled lanes and old pubs lost among bottle-green countryside between Ambleside and Coniston. Throw in connections to both Wordsworth and Beatrix Potter, and you won't be surprised to find Hawkshead awash with visitors in the high summer, although the fact that cars are banned in the village centre keeps things a bit more tranquil.

◉ Sights

Hawkshead Grammar School HISTORIC BUILDING
(www.hawksheadgrammar.org.uk; admission £2; ⊙10am-1pm & 2-5pm Mon-Sat, 1-5pm Sun Apr-Sep, closed Nov-Mar) In centuries past, promising young gentleman were sent to Hawkshead's village school for their educational foundation. Among the former pupils was a certain William Wordsworth, who attended the

school from 1779 to 1787. The curriculum was punishing: 10 hours' study a day, covering weighty subjects such as Latin, Greek, geometry, science and rhetoric. Hardly surprising young Willie felt the urge to carve his name into one of the desks.

Upstairs is a small exhibition exploring the history of the school.

Beatrix Potter Gallery GALLERY
(NT;www.nationaltrust.org.uk/beatrix-potter-gallery; Red Lion Sq; adult/child £4.80/2.40; ⊙11am-5pm Sat-Thu mid-Mar–Oct) As well as being a best-selling children's author, Beatrix Potter was also a talented botanical painter and amateur naturalist. This small gallery (housed in the offices of Potter's husband, solicitor William Heelis) contains a collection of delicate watercolours depicting local flora and fauna. She seems to have been particularly fascinated by mushrooms.

There's discounted admission if you show your ticket from Hill Top.

⌂ Sleeping & Eating

⬥Yewfield B&B ££
(☎015394-36765; www.yewfield.co.uk; Hawkshead Hill; s £49-65, d £98-130; ⓟ⬥) This detached house occupies a hilltop spot near Tarn Hows, halfway between Coniston and Hawkshead. It's run by the owners of Zeffirelli's, and though the building itself is Victorian, it's run along eco-alternative lines: breakfast is veggie and organic, power comes from a wood-mass boiler, and much of the produce comes from the kitchen garden. There are extensive grounds, too.

Hawkshead YHA HOSTEL £
(☎0845-371 9321; hawkshead@yha.org.uk; dm from £14; ⓟ⬥) This hostel occupies a Regency house a mile along the Newby Bridge road. Like many Lakeland YHAs, the period architecture is impressive (cornicing, panelled doors, a verandah) and the big dorms boast big views. There's bike rental and a kitchen, and buses stop outside the door.

Queen's Head PUB ££
(☎015394-36271; www.queensheadhawkshead.co .uk; Main St; mains £14-22) The old Queen's Head brims with oak-panelled appeal. Hale and hearty country food (Esthwaite trout, Winster pork, Gressingham duck) in the bar, partnered by small, prim rooms upstairs (singles £70, doubles £100 to £130). Avoid the lodge annexe if you're staying.

DON'T MISS

GRIZEDALE FOREST

Sprawling across the hills between Coniston Water and Esthwaite Water, Grizedale Forest (from the Old Norse for 'wild boar') is one of the Lake District's most beautiful woodlands – not to mention its largest outdoor art project. More than 90 large-scale artworks and sculptures are sprinkled throughout the forest, from an enormous xylophone to a Tolkienesque 'man of the forest'.

This is also a great place to explore on two wheels: the Grizedale Visitors Centre (☏01229-860010; www.forestry. gov.uk/grizedaleforestpark; ☉10am-5pm, 11am-4pm winter) provides guide leaflets and forest maps detailing the forest's maintained mountain bike trails. You can bring your own bike, or rent one from Grizedale Mountain Bikes (☏01229-860369; www.grizedalemountainbikes. co.uk; adult/child per day from £26/16; ☉9am-5pm, last hire 3pm) next to the visitor centre.

Children (big and little) will also love Go Ape (www.goape.co.uk; adult/child £30/25; ☉9-5pm Mar-Oct, weekends only Nov-Feb), a gravity-defying treetop assault course with a wealth of rope ladders, bridges, platforms and zip-slides to tackle.

TOP CHOICE Drunken Duck   PUB ££
(☏015394-36347; www.drunkenduckinn.co.uk; Barngates; mains £13-25; P⑨) For top-class pub dining, no place beats the Drunken Duck. The menu features whole-roasted duck and beetroot tarte Tatin, and ales come from the Barngates Brewery behind the pub. Rooms (£95 to £275) are stylish. Book weeks in advance for dinner, although lunch is first-come, first-served.

It's tricky to find: follow the B5286 from Hawkshead towards Ambleside, and look out for the brown signs.

Hawkshead Relish Company   DELI £
(☏015394-36614; www.hawksheadrelish.com; The Square; ☉9.30am-5pm winter, 9am-5.30pm summer) This renowned chutney company sells an enormous choice of relishes and jams.

ℹ Getting There & Away

Hawkshead is linked with Windermere, Ambleside and Coniston by bus 505 (eight daily Monday to Saturday, six on Sunday).

Around Hawkshead

TARN HOWS

About 2 miles off the B5285 from Hawkshead, a winding country lane wends its way to Tarn Hows, a famously photogenic man-made lake now owned by the National Trust. Trails wind their way around the lakeshore – keep you eyes peeled for rare red squirrels frolicking in the treetops.

There's a small National Trust car park beside the tarn, but it fills quickly. Several buses, including the 505 and X30, stop nearby; alternatively, you can follow trails up from nearby Hawkshead and Coniston.

HILL TOP

In the tiny village of Near Sawrey, 2 miles south of Hawkshead, the idyllic farmhouse of Hill Top (NT; ☏015394-36269; www.nationaltrust.org.uk/hill-top; adult/child £8/4; ☉10am-5pm Sat-Thu mid-Feb–Oct, shorter hours outside summer) is a must for Beatrix Potter buffs: it was the first house she lived in after moving to the Lake District, and also where she wrote and illustrated many of her famous tales.

Purchased in 1905 (largely on the proceeds of her first bestseller, *The Tale of Peter Rabbit*), Hill Top is crammed with decorative details that fans will recognise from the author's illustrations.

Thanks to its worldwide fame (helped along by the 2006 biopic *Miss Potter*), Hill Top is one of the Lake District's most popular spots. Entry is by timed ticket, and the queues can be seriously daunting during the summer holidays.

ℹ Getting There & Away

Bus **X30 Grizedale Wanderer** (four daily March to November) runs from Haverthwaite to Grizedale via Hawkshead and Moor Top.

Coniston

POP 1948

Hunkered beneath the pockmarked peak of the Old Man (803m), the lakeside village of Coniston was originally established as a centre for the copper-mining industry, but the only remnants of the industry are the many abandoned quarries and mine shafts that now litter the surrounding hilltops.

Coniston's main claim to fame is as the location for a string of world-record speed attempts made here by Sir Malcolm Campbell and his son, Donald, between the 1930s and 1960s. Tragically, after beating the record several times, Donald was killed during an attempt in 1967, when his futuristic jet-boat *Bluebird* flipped at around 320mph. The boat and its pilot were recovered in 2001, and Campbell was buried in the cemetery near St Andrew's church.

Coniston is a fairly quiet village these days, mainly worth a visit for its lovely lake cruises and a trip to the former house of John Ruskin at Brantwood.

◎ Sights

Brantwood   HISTORIC BUILDING

(☑015394-41396; www.brantwood.org.uk; adult/child £6.30/1.35, gardens only £4.50/1.35; ☺10.30am-5pm mid-Mar–mid-Nov, to 4pm Wed-Sun mid-Nov–mid-Mar) John Ruskin (1819–1900), the Victorian polymath, philosopher and critic, was one of the great thinkers of 19th-century society, expounding views on everything from Venetian architecture to the finer points of lace-making.

In 1871 he purchased this impressive house overlooking Coniston and spent the next 20 years expanding and modifying it. The house is a monument to Ruskin's passion for traditional 'Arts and Crafts' over factory-made materials; he helped design everything from the furniture to the garden terraces, and even dreamt up the wallpaper designs. Look out for his shell collection in the downstairs study, and works by JMW Turner (one of Ruskin's favourite artists) in an upstairs bedroom.

The best way to arrive is by boat from Coniston. While you wait, you can have lunch at the Jumping Jenny (lunches £4-8) in the house's former stables.

If you'd prefer to drive, take the B5285 towards Coniston from Hawkshead and follow the signs.

Ruskin Museum   MUSEUM

(www.ruskinmuseum.com; adult/child £5.25/2.50; ☺10am-5.30pm Easter–mid-Nov, 10.30am-3.30pm Wed-Sun other times) Coniston's museum explores the village's history, touching on copper mining, Arthur Ransome and the Campbell story. There's also an extensive section on John Ruskin, with displays of his writings, watercolours and sketchbooks.

The new Bluebird Wing currently houses the recovered engine from Donald Campbell's *Bluebird K7* boat, but it's eventually hoped that the whole boat will be displayed here when (and if) it's finally restored.

⚑ Activities

Boating

Lake Coniston famously inspired Arthur Ransome's classic children's tale *Swallows and Amazons*. Peel Island, towards the southern end of Coniston Water, doubles in the book as Wild Cat Island, while the Gondola steam yacht allegedly gave Ransome the idea for Captain Flint's houseboat.

Coniston Boating Centre (☑015394-41366; Coniston Jetty) hires out rowing boats, Canadian canoes and motorboats, or you can take one of the two cruise services that glide out across the glassy waters.

Steam Yacht Gondola   BOAT TOUR

(☑015394-63850; www.nationaltrust.org.uk/gondola; standard cruise adult/child £9.90/4.90) Built in 1859 and restored in the 1980s by the National Trust, this wonderful steam yacht looks like a cross between a Venetian *vaporetto* and an English houseboat, complete with cushioned saloons and polished wood seats. It's a stately way of seeing the lake, especially if you're visiting Brantwood, and it's even ecofriendly: since 2008 it's been powered by waste-wood.

There are five trips daily from mid-March to October. Longer 'Explorer' cruises covering Ransome, the Campbells and Ruskin run at 2pm Monday and Thursday (adult/child £19.90/9.90). There's also a 'Wild Cat Island' cruise at 2pm Monday (£19.90/9.90). There's a 10% discount available for online bookings.

Coniston Launch   BOAT TOUR

(☑015394-36216; www.conistonlaunch.co.uk; Northern service adult/child return £9.50/4.95, Southern service £14.50/7.25) A more contemporary way to get around the lake is aboard Coniston's two modern launches, which have been solar-powered since 2005.

There are two routes: the 45-minute Northern service calls at the Waterhead Hotel, Torver and Brantwood, while the 105-minute Southern service sails to the jetties at Torver, Water Park, Lake Bank, Sunny Bank and Brantwood via Peel Island. You can break your journey and walk to the next jetty. There are between five and nine daily trips, depending on the time of year.

As with the Gondola, commentated cruises on the Campbell story (adult/child £12/6, 4.40pm Tuesday) and *Swallows and Amazons* (£12.90/6.45, 4.40pm Wednesday). The cruises usually run from May to September depending on demand.

Walking

If you're in Coniston to hike, chances are you've come to conquer the Old Man (7.5 miles, four to five hours). It's a steep but rewarding climb past Coniston's abandoned copper mines to the summit, from where the views stretch to the Cumbrian Coast on a clear day.

The tourist office has leaflets on possible routes up the Old Man and other walks, as well as the annual Coniston Walking Festival (www.conistonwalkingfestival.org), held in September.

🛏 Sleeping

Yew Tree Farm   B&B ££
(☎015394-41433; www.yewtree-farm.com; d £90-124; 🅿) This delightful farmhouse a couple of miles from Coniston has star quality. It was owned by Beatrix Potter and doubled as Hill Top in the biopic *Miss Potter* (starring Renée Zellweger). It's still a working farm, but offers three rustic-chic rooms: Wetherlam and Tarn Hows feature antique furniture and four-posters, while little Holme Fell has valley views.

Bank Ground Farm   B&B ££
(☎015394-41264; www.bankground.com; East of the Lake; d from £90, 2-night minimum; 🅿) This lakeside farmhouse has literary cachet: Arthur Ransome used it as the model for Holly Howe Farm in *Swallows & Amazons*. Parts of the house date back to the 15th century, so the rooms are snug. Some have sleigh beds, others exposed beams. The tearoom is a beauty, too, and there are cottages for longer stays.

Lakeland House   B&B ££
(☎015394-41303; www.lakelandhouse.co.uk; Tilberthwaite Ave; s £40-50, d £78-120) Perched above the village's internet cafe is this no-fuss B&B. Budget doubles border on the utilitarian (a bed, tea-tray and wardrobe is all you get), so it's worth stretching to Superior for space and comfort. The Lookout Suite has its own sitting room.

Coniston Holly How YHA   HOSTEL £
(☎0845-371 9511; conistonhh@yha.org.uk; Far End; dm from £16; ⊙reception 7.30-10am & 5-10pm) Another fine period house offering the usual YHA standards: decent dorms, well-equipped kitchens, organised walks and an inhouse cafe.

Coppermines YHA   HOSTEL £
(☎0845-371 9630; coppermines@yha.org.uk; dm from £16; ⊙reception 7-11am & 5-10pm Easter-Oct) This high-altitude hostel is set among the old copper-workings, along a rough unsealed road 1.5km from Coniston. Facilities are surprisingly good considering the location: a kitchen, showers, a licensed bar and a guests' lounge. It's ideal if you want to get an early start on the Old Man.

Hoathwaite Campsite   CAMPSITE £
(NT; ☎bookings 015394-63862; www.ntlakescampsites.org.uk; sites from £6 for 1 adult, tent & car; ⊙Easter-Nov) This simple National Trust-owned campsite is on the A5394 between Coniston and Torver. There's a toilet block, water taps and not much else – but the views over Coniston Water are super.

Coniston Hall Campsite   CAMPSITE £
(☎015394-41223; sites for 2 adults & car from £12; ⊙Mar-Oct) There are 120 pitches at this busy lakeside campsite a mile from town.

🍴 Eating & Drinking

Sun Hotel   PUB ££
(www.thesunconiston.com; mains £12-20) Dine under solid rafters or in a fell-view conservatory at the Sun, perched on a hill just behind the village, and famously used as an HQ by Donald Campbell during his final fateful campaign.

Harry's   CAFE £
(4 Yewdale Rd; mains £6-14) Part-wine bar, part-cafe, part-bistro, and serving steaks, pizzas, pastas and club sandwiches, along with the prodigious Harry's Big Breakfast.

Bluebird Cafe   CAFE £
(Lake Rd; mains £4-8; ⊙breakfast & lunch) This lakeside cafe does a brisk trade from people waiting for the Coniston launches. The usual salads and sandwiches are on offer, and there are lots of outside tables.

Black Bull   PUB
(www.conistonbrewery.com/black-bull-coniston.htm; Yewdale Rd) Coniston's main meeting spot, the old Black Bull offers a warren of rooms and a popular outside terrace. The

TOP LAKE DISTRICT CAMPSITES

With its unspoilt countryside, majestic scenery and (with a bit of luck) starry skies, the Lake District makes a wonderful place to experience a night under canvas.

In addition to the four great campsites run by the National Trust (near Ambleside, Great Langdale, Wasdale and Coniston), here are five more favourites:

The Quiet Site (☎07768-727016; www.thequietsite.co.uk; sites £15-30, pods £35-50; ⊙year-round; ☎) Spacious site, which is spread across the fells above Ullswater, and has won awards for its ecofriendliness.

Syke Farm (☎01768-770222; sites adult/child £7/3.50; ⊙Easter-Oct) Back-to-basics camping beside the river in Buttermere. Fresh milk and home-made ice cream are available from the farm shop.

Bowkerstead Farm (☎01229-860208; www.grizedale-camping.co.uk; Satterthwaite; adult/child £7/3, camping pods £30, yurts £50-60 Mon-Fri, £60-70 Sat-Sun) Pitch beside the trees of Grizedale Forest, either in your own tent, a luxury yurt or a timber eco-pod.

Seatoller Farm (☎017687-77232; www.seatollerfarm.co.uk; £6/3; ⊙Easter-Oct) A tucked-away site on a 500-year-old farm near Seatoller in Borrowdale, with a choice of either riverside or woodland pitches.

Fisherground Farm (☎019467-23349; www.fishergroundcampsite.co.uk; adult/child £6/3, car £2.50; ⊙Mar-Oct) Family-friendly camping in idyllic Eskdale, handy for the Ravenglass & Eskdale Railway.

grub's good, but it's mainly known for its home-brewed ales: Bluebird Bitter and Old Man Ale are always on tap, and there are seasonal ones too.

ℹ Information

Coniston tourist office (☎015394-41533; www.conistontic.org; Ruskin Ave; ⊙9.30am-5.30pm Easter-Oct, to 4pm Nov-Easter) Sells the Coniston Loyalty Card (£3) offering local discounts.

Hollands Cafe (Tilberthwaite Ave; per hr £5; ⊙9am-5pm) Internet cafe.

ℹ Getting There & Away

Bus 505 runs from Windermere (10 Monday to Saturday, six on Sunday mid-March to October), via Ambleside, with a couple of daily connections to Kendal (1¼ hours).

Elterwater & Great Langdale

Travelling north from Coniston, the road passes into increasingly wild, empty countryside. Barren hilltops loom as you travel north past the old Viking settlement of Elterwater en route to Great Langdale, where the main road comes to an end and many of the Lakes' greatest trails begin.

The most iconic walk in Langdale is the stomp up the **Langdale Pikes**: Pike O'

Stickle (709m), Loft Crag (682m), Harrison Stickle (736m) and Pavey Ark (700m). If you don't fancy taking on the whole thing, you could just walk up to the waterfall of Dungeon Ghyll instead.

🛏 Sleeping & Eating

⌷TOP CHOICE⌷ Eltermere Inn　　HOTEL £££
(☎015394-37207; www.eltermere.co.uk; r £125-225) This recently refurbished inn in Elterwater makes a really delicious place to stay. Rooms mix minimal style with country trappings (go for a lake view), while classy fireside food (mains £14 to £19.50) is served in the downstairs inn. They even serve tea on the lawn when the weather's nice.

⌷TOP CHOICE⌷ Old Dungeon Ghyll　　HOTEL ££
(☎015394-37272; www.odg.co.uk; d from £106, half-board £156; P♠☎) A historic gem awash with Lakeland heritage: countless famous walkers have stayed here, including Prince Charles and Chris Bonington. It's endearingly olde-worlde, with well-worn furniture and furnishings, plus views from every window. The beamed Hiker's Bar is a must for a post-hike pint.

Great Langdale Campsite　　CAMPSITE £
(NT; ☎015394-63862; www.ntlakescampsites.org.uk; tent sites £8.25-12.50, extra adult £5.50, pods £30-50; ⊙arrivals 3-7pm Sat-Thu, 3-9pm Fri; P)

Quite possibly the most spectacularly positioned campsite in the Lake District, spread out over grassy meadows overlooked by Langdale's fells. It gets crowded in season, but around three-quarters of the sites can be booked in advance; the remainder are available on a first-come, first-served basis. Camping pods and yurts are also available for hire.

Elterwater YHA HOSTEL £
(☎0845-371 9017; elterwater@yha.org.uk; dm £14; ☺reception 7.30am-10am & 5-10.30pm Easter-Oct; @) Another pleasant hostel in a former farmhouse, just a stone's throw from Elterwater's village green.

Langdale YHA HOSTEL £
(☎0845-371 9748; langdale@yha.org.uk; High Close, Loughrigg; dm £14; ☺reception 7.30-10am & 5-11pm Mar-Oct; P@) Large hostel in a Victorian house on the road towards Grasmere.

Stickle Barn PUB £
(☎015394-37356; mains £6-12) A walkers' fave, with a lively pub serving filling food such as curries, chillies and hotpots.

ⓘ Getting There & Away

Bus 516 (the Langdale Rambler, six daily, five on Sunday) is the only bus, with stops at Ambleside, Skelwith Bridge, Elterwater, and the Old Dungeon Ghyll Hotel in Great Langdale.

Wasdale

Carving its way for 5 miles from the Cumbrian coast, the craggy, wind-lashed valley of Wasdale is where the Lake District scenery takes a turn for the wild. Ground out by a long-extinct glacier, it's home to the Lake District's highest and wildest peaks, as well as the steely grey expanse of Wastwater, England's deepest and coldest lake.

Wasdale's fells are an irresistible draw for hikers: especially those looking to conquer England's tallest mountain, Scafell Pike (978m/3209ft). The classic route starts from Wasdale Head and is well within the reach of most walkers, although it's long, steep and hard to navigate in bad weather. You're looking at around six to seven hours out on the mountain, so you'll need proper supplies.

The valley is also home to one of England's tiniest chapels, the 16th-century St Olaf's Church. Local legend claims the roof-beams were salvaged from a Viking longboat.

The Barn Door Shop (☎019467-26384; www.wasdaleweb.com), next door to the Wasdale Head Inn, sells camping and walking supplies.

🛏 Sleeping & Eating

Wasdale Head Inn B&B ££
(☎019467-26229; www.wasdale.com; s £59, d £118-130, tr £177; P) If you're looking for the quintessential Lakeland inn, look no longer: the Wasdale Head is the real McCoy, a 19th-century hostelry full of hill-walking heritage. Dog-eared photos and climbing memorabilia are dotted round the inn, and the upstairs rooms are full of times-past charm. The slate-floored bar (mains £9.95 to £16.95) is a hikers' fave, and serves homebrews, including Wasd'ale and Great Gable. Some of the guestbooks date back to the early 1800s.

Wasdale Head Campsite CAMPSITE £
(NT; ☎bookings 015394-63862; www.ntlakescampsites.org.uk; sites £8.25-12.50, extra adult £5.50, pods £30-50; ☺arrivals 8-11am & 5-8pm, year-round) This NT campsite is in a fantastically wild spot, nestled beneath the Scafell range. Facilities are basic (laundry room, showers), but the views are out of this world.

Wastwater YHA HOSTEL £
(☎0845-371 9350; wastwater@yha.org.uk; Wasdale Hall, Nether Wasdale; dm from £14; ☺reception 8-10am & 5-10.30pm) This lakeside hostel on the shores of Wastwater has the kind of location you'd normally pay through the nose for. It's in a 19th-century mansion that still boasts most of its period architecture, including original roof trusses and latticed windows. There's a library full of books to browse and a restaurant serving Cumbrian nosh and ale, and some dorms have lake views.

ⓘ Getting There & Away

The **Wasdale Taxibus** (☎019467-25308) runs between Gosforth and Wasdale twice daily on Thursday, Saturday and Sunday (£3), but you need to ring and book a seat the day before.

Cockermouth

POP 8225

Plonked in flat fields beyond the northerly fells, the Georgian town of Cockermouth was hitherto best known as the birthplace of

WORTH A TRIP

ENNERDALE

Crowds can be a constant headache at the Lakes, but there are some corners of the national park that remain people-free.

The remote valley and lake of Ennerdale just to the north of Wasdale are slowly being returned to nature as part of the innovative Wild Ennerdale project (www .wildennerdale.co.uk). All signs of artifice are slowly being removed, and 1930s conifer plantations are gradually being replaced by native broadleaf species to encourage local wildlife.

Needless to say, the valley is paradise if you prefer your trails quiet, and is also home to one of the Lake District's most isolated hostels, the Black Sail YHA (☎0845 371 9680; www.yha.org.uk/hostel/black-sail; dm £19.40), housed in a shepherd's bothy halfway between Ennerdale and Buttermere.

William Wordsworth and the home base of one of Cumbria's largest beer-makers, Jenning's Brewery. But in November 2009 the town hit the national headlines after flash floods inundated the town centre, causing millions of pounds of damage and forcing the emergency evacuation of many residents by RAF helicopter.

◉ Sights

TOP CHOICE **Wordsworth House**   HISTORIC HOME

(NT; ☎01900-824805; Main St; adult/child £6.15/3.10; ⊙11am-5pm Sat-Thu Mar-Oct) William Wordsworth was born on 7 April 1770 at this handsome Georgian house at the end of Main St. Built around 1745, the house has been painstakingly restored based on accounts from the Wordsworth archive. Costumed guides are on hand to help bring the house to life.

The kitchen garden (mentioned in Wordsworth's autobiographical poem *The Prelude*) was badly damaged during the floods, but has since been carefully replanted.

Jenning's Brewery   BREWERY

(☎01900-821011; www.jenningsbrewery.co.uk; adult/child £8/4; ⊙guided tours 11am & 2pm Mon-Sat Apr-Oct, extra tours Jul & Aug) The town's historic brewer has been in business since 1874 (bar a brief interruption during the 2009 floods). Guided tours include a visit to see the main brewing vats and include a tasting session in the Old Cooperage Bar. Take your pick from golden Cocker Hoop, classic Bitter and the strong, dark, superbly named Sneck Lifter.

⌁ Sleeping

Old Homestead   B&B ££

(☎01900-822223; www.byresteads.co.uk; Byresteads Farm; s £60, d £80-100; P) A sweet farm conversion 2 miles west of Cockermouth, with a stone exterior concealing lavish rooms gleaming with wood floors, restored rafters, leather sofas and rendered walls. The Cruck Rooms and Master's Loft have the most space and luxury.

Croft House   B&B ££

(☎01900-827533; www.croft-guesthouse.com; 6/8 Challoner St; s £45, d £60-80) Gutted by the floods but now fully restored, this swish lemon-yellow B&B is a winner. Rooms are delightfully finished with exposed stone and reclaimed maple-wood floors.

Six Castlegate   B&B ££

(☎01900-826749; www.sixcastlegate.co.uk; 6 Castlegate; s £42, d £65-75; ☎) A Grade II–listed townhouse combining Georgian heritage with a modern twist. Feathery pillows, lofty ceilings and shiny showers make this one of Cockermouth's most attractive B&Bs.

Cockermouth YHA   HOSTEL £

(☎0845-371 9313; cockermouth@yha.org.uk; Double Mills; dm from £14; ⊙reception 7.30-10am & 5-10pm Apr-Oct) A simple hostel in a converted 17th-century watermill, about half a mile's walk from town. Camping space and cycle storage are available.

✗ Eating & Drinking

Quince & Medlar   VEGETARIAN ££

(www.quinceandmedlar.co.uk; 13 Castlegate; mains £12-16; ⊙dinner Tue-Sat; ✓) Imaginative veggie food served in the refined surrounds of one of Castlegate's Georgian houses.

Merienda
CAFE £

(7a Station St; mains £4-8; ⊘breakfast & lunch) The town's best bet for lunch, this bright cafe serves fresh soups and open-face sandwiches.

Bitter End
PUB

(☑01900-828993; www.bitterend.co.uk; 15 Kirkgate; mains £9.50-12.55; ⊘lunch & dinner) This brewpub produces award-winning beers such as Cockermouth Pride, Lakeland Honey Beer and Cuddy Lugs. You can watch the vats at work through a glass partition in the main bar. The food's not at all bad, either.

ℹ Information

Tourist office (☑01900-822634; cocker mouthtic@co-net.com; ⊘10am-4pm Mon-Fri, to 2pm Sat, closed for lunch 12.30-1pm) Inside the town hall.

ℹ Getting There & Away

The X4/X5 (13 to 15 Monday to Saturday, six on Sunday) travels from Workington via Cockermouth to Keswick (35 minutes) and Penrith (1¼ hours).

Keswick

POP 5257

The sturdy slate town of Keswick is nestled alongside one of the region's most idyllic lakes, Derwentwater, a silvery curve studded by wooded islands and criss-crossed by puttering cruise boats.

◉ Sights & Activities

The heart of Keswick is the old Market Place, in the shadow of the town's former prison and meeting rooms at the Moot Hall (now occupied by the tourist office).

Keswick Museum is currently closed for refurbishment, and is due to reopen in 2013. Ask at the tourist office for the latest news.

FREE Castlerigg Stone Circle   MONUMENT
Set on a hilltop a mile east of town, this jaw-dropping stone circle consists of 48 stones that are between 3000 and 4000 years old, surrounded by a dramatic ring of mountain peaks.

Pencil Museum   MUSEUM
(www.pencilmuseum.co.uk; Southy Works; adult/child £4/3; ⊘9.30am-5pm) In the middle of the 17th century, graphite was discovered in the Borrowdale fells, and Keswick became the centre of pencil production. The old Cumberland Pencil Factory now houses this rather odd pencil-themed museum, whose exhibits include the world's longest pencil (measuring 8m from end to end) and a replica of a Borrowdale slate mine. Luxury Derwent colouring pencils are available for you to buy in the museum shop.

Whinlatter Forest Park   FOREST
(www.forestry.gov.uk/whinlatterforestpark) Encompassing 1200 hectares of pine, larch and spruce, Whinlatter is England's only true mountain forest, rising sharply to 790m about 5 miles from Keswick. The forest is a designated red squirrel reserve; you can check out live video feeds from squirrel cams at the visitor centre.

It's also home to two exciting mountain-bike trails and the Go Ape (www.goape.co.uk/days-out/whinlatter; adult/child £30/25; ⊘9am-5pm mid-Mar–Oct) tree-top assault course. You can hire bikes from Cyclewise (☑017687-78711; www.cyclewise.co.uk; ⊘10am-5pm), next to the visitor centre.

Bus 77 (four daily) runs to the visitor centre from Keswick. If you're driving, head towards Cockermouth on the A66 and look out for the brown signs near the turn-off at Braithwaite.

⚡ Activities

Keswick Launch   BOAT TOUR
(☑017687-72263; www.keswick-launch.co.uk; round-the-lake ticket adult/child £9.25/4.50) Derwentwater is one of the Lake District's most attractive lakes, and remained a life-long favourite of Beatrix Potter. The lake jetties are a short stroll south of town, next to the fields of Crow Park. Boats putter out to landing stages at Ashness Gate, Lodore Falls, High Brandlehow, Low Brandlehow, Hawse End and Nichol End. Departures run clockwise and anticlockwise; you can get off and walk to the next stage if you wish. Single fares to each jetty are also available.

There are six daily boats that run from March to November, with a couple of extra afternoon sailings and a twilight cruise in summer. There are only two sailings a day in winter.

Rowboats (£12 per hour) and motorboats (£27 per hour) can be hired next to the launch jetties.

Keswick

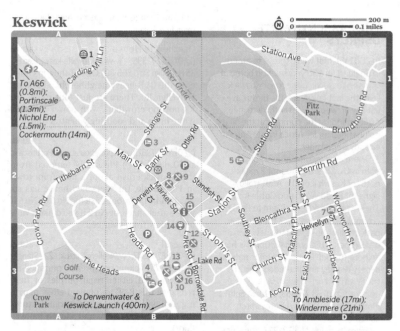

Keswick

◉ Sights
1 Pencil Museum............................A1

⬥ Activities, Courses & Tours
2 Keswick Mountain Bikes A1

🛏 Sleeping
3 Ellergill...............................B2
4 Howe Keld.............................B3
5 Keswick YHA C2
6 Lakeside House.........................B3
7 Oakthwaite House D2

✕ Eating
8 Bryson's.................................B2
9 Lakeland Pedlar Wholefood Cafe B2
10 Mayson's B3
11 Morrel's..............................B3
12 Pumpkin...............................B3

🍷 Drinking
13 Cafe-Bar 26 ....B3
14 Dog & Gun B3

🛍 Shopping
15 Cotswold Outdoor B2
16 George Fisher..........................B3

Fell Walks HIKING

Keswick has a wealth of local walks. The most popular is the family-friendly fell of Catbells (451m), on the lake's west side; the trailhead starts next to the jetty at Hawse End, served by the Keswick Launch.

Hardcore hikers will prefer the more challenging slog up Skiddaw (931m), the huge mountain that looms on Keswick's northern skyline. To the northeast of town near Threlkeld, Blencathra (868m) is an equally challenging proposition.

🎇 Festivals & Events

Keswick Mountain Festival OUTDOORS
(www.keswickmountainfestival.co.uk) This May festival celebrates all things mountainous.

Keswick Beer Festival BEER
(www.keswickbeerfestival.co.uk) Lots and lots of beer is drunk during Keswick's real ale fest in June.

🛏 Sleeping

Keswick is crammed with B&Bs, especially around Stanger St and Helvellyn Rd.

THE BASSENTHWAITE OSPREYS

In 2001 the first wild ospreys to breed in England for 150 years set up home at Bassenthwaite Lake, near Keswick. Over the last few years, the birds have usually arrived at Bassenthwaite in April, spending the summer at the lake before heading for Africa in late August or early September.

There are two official viewpoints, both in Dodd Wood, about 3 miles north of Keswick on the A591 (follow signs for Dodd Wood and Cattle Inn). The lower hide (open 10am to 5pm) is about 15 minutes' walk from the car park at Mirehouse, and the new upper hide (open 10.30am to 4.30pm) is half an hour further. There's an informative osprey display and live video feed at the Whinlatter Forest Park visitor centre (☎01768-778469; ◷10am-5pm). Find out more at www.ospreywatch.co.uk.

From Keswick, the 73/73A bus stops at nearby Mirehouse.

TOP CHOICE Howe Keld
B&B ££

(☎017687-72417; www.howekeld.co.uk; 5-7 The Heads; s £55-58, d £90-130; ☎) This gold-standard B&B pulls out all the stops: goose-down duvets, slate-floored bathrooms, chic colours and locally made furniture. The best rooms have views across Crow Park and the golf course, and the breakfast is a pick-and-mix delight. Free parking is available on the Heads if there's space.

Lakeside House
B&B £££

(☎017687-72868; www.lakesidehouse.co.uk; 40 Lake Rd; d £135-140; ☎) On the corner of Lake Rd, this Victorian house has a top location, with the town centre and Derwentwater both minutes away. It looks fresher thanks to a recent revamp, but rooms are variable: get one with a bay window for park views.

Keswick YHA
HOSTEL £

(☎0845-371 9746; keswick@yha.org.uk; Station Rd; dm £23.40; @) Keswick's YHA is a beauty, lodged inside a converted woollen mill by the clattering River Rothay, and renovated thanks to the benevolence of a generous doctor. Dorms are cosy, there's an excellent cafe, and some rooms even have balconies over Fitz Park.

Oakthwaite House
B&B ££

(☎017687-72398; www.oakthwaite-keswick.co.uk; 35 Helvellyn St; d £66-80) One of the top choices in the B&B-heavy neighbourhood around Helvellyn Rd. There are just four rooms (so it's not too crowded), with power showers, white linen and soothingly neutral tones.

Powe House
B&B ££

(☎017687-73611; www.powehouse.com; Portinscale; s £60, d £80-4; ☎) Pleasantly removed from the Keswick crush about a mile from town in Portinscale, this detached house has six great-value bedrooms: ask for No 3 or No 5 if you're after space, or No 2 if you'd like a view of Skiddaw from your bed.

Ellergill
B&B ££

(☎017687-73347; www.ellergill.co.uk; 22 Stanger St; d £60-75) Velour bedspreads, plumped-up cushions and either regal purples or fiery reds give this B&B an opulent edge, marrying well with the house's Victorian features (including tiled hearths and a lovely hallway floor).

Swinside Lodge
HOTEL ££

(☎017687-72948; www.swinsidelodge-hotel.co.uk; Newlands; d incl dinner £92-136; P) Tucked below Catbells, this fancy number has scooped up awards for its gourmet food and Georgian finery. Supper at the bistro is included in rates. Take the A66 from Keswick towards Cockermouth and look out for signs to Newlands Valley; the hotel is about 2 miles from the turning.

Eating & Drinking

Morrel's
BRITISH ££

(☎017687-72666; www.morrels.co.uk; Lake Rd; 3-course menu £19.95, mains £10.50-16; ◷dinner Tue-Sun) This reliable restaurant is the best address for bistro food in Keswick. Tall windows, leather chairs, spotlights and wood floors provide the perfect setting for sophisticated modern British food. There are two self-catering apartments upstairs (£400 to £700 per week).

Pumpkin
CAFE £

(19 Lake Rd; lunches £3-6; ◷8.30am-5pm Mon-Sat) Deli sandwiches are made to order at this streetside cafe, but it's the counter of cakes and pastries that'll catch your eye. There's seating upstairs, or you can order to go, and the coffee's the best in Keswick.

Mayson's   INTERNATIONAL **£**
(☑017687-74104; 33 Lake Rd; dishes £7-10) Buffet-style dining, cheap prices and generous portions are the modus operandi at this no-fuss diner. Each of the counter-top woks has a different fusion theme (Thai, Chinese, Mexican etc): take your pick, buy a drink, and wait for it to be brought to your table.

Lakeland Pedlar Wholefood Cafe   CAFE **£**
(www.lakelandpedlar.co.uk; Hendersons Yard; mains £4-10; ⊘9am-5pm) This veggie-organic-wholefood emporium has been going for donkey's years, but there's still nowhere better for a chunky sandwich or a bowl of soup. There's a bike shop upstairs.

Bryson's   CAFE **£**
(42 Main St; cakes £2-5) Keswick's renowned bakery is known for its fruit cakes, Battenbergs and chocolately Florentines.

Cafe-Bar 26   CAFE
(26 Lake Rd; tapas £4-10) An attractive corner wine-bar that also serves good tapas.

Dog & Gun   PUB
(2 Lake Rd) Wooden benches, low ceilings, hearths: the old Dog is the picture of a Lakeland pub.

🛍 Shopping

Keswick has plenty of outdoor shops. There's a huge branch of **Cotswold Outdoor** (16 Main St), but the traditionalists' choice is **George Fisher** (2 Borrowdale Rd).

❶ Information

Tourist office (☑017687-72645; keswicktic @lake-district.gov.uk; Moot Hall, Market Pl; ⊘9.30am-5.30pm Apr-Oct, to 4.30pm Nov-Mar) Sells discounted tickets for the Keswick Launch.

U-Compute (48 Main St; per hr £3; ⊘9am-5.30pm) Net access above the post office.

❶ Getting There & Away

BUS The Borrowdale Day Rider (adult/child £7/5) is valid on buses 77/77A and 78 between Keswick and the Borrowdale Valley.
  Buses from Keswick:

555/556 Lakeslink Hourly to Ambleside (40 minutes), Windermere (50 minutes) and Kendal (1½ hours).

X4/X5 Penrith to Workington via Keswick (hourly Monday to Friday, six on Sunday).

73 Caldbeck Rambler (two daily April to November, weekends only in winter) Stops at Mirehouse and Bassenthwaite Lake before continuing to Caldbeck.

77/77A Honister Rambler (four daily) Circular route from Keswick via Portinscale, Catbells, Grange, Seatoller, Honister Pass, Buttermere, Lorton and Whinlatter.

78 Borrowdale Rambler (hourly Monday to Saturday, seven on Sunday) The main Borrowdale bus, with stops at Lodore, Grange, Rosthwaite and Seatoller.

❶ Getting Around

Mountain bikes can be hired from **Keswick Mountain Bikes** (☑017687-75202; www .keswickmountainbikes.co.uk; 133 Main St; adult bikes per day £15-40; ⊘9.30am-5.30pm). Its road-specific shop is above the Lakeland Pedlar Cafe.

Borrowdale

With their patchwork of craggy hills, broad fields, tinkling streams and drystone walls, the side-by-side valleys of **Borrowdale** and **Buttermere** are many people's idea of the quintessential Lakeland landscape. Once a centre for mineral mining (especially for slate, coal and graphite), this is walkers' country these days, and apart from the odd rickety barn or puttering tractor, there's precious little to spoil the view.

The B5289 tracks Derwentwater into the heart of Borrowdale Valley. Past the small village of **Grange-in-Borrowdale**, the valley winds into the jagged ravine of the **Jaws of Borrowdale**, a well-known hiking spot with wonderful views, notably from the summit of **Castle Crag** (290m) at the southern end of Derwentwater.

A mile or so further south from Grange, a turn-off leads up to a National Trust car park and the geological curiosity of the **Bowder Stone**, a 1870-ton lump of rock thought to have been left behind by a retreating glacier. A small stepladder leads up to the top of the rock.

🛏 Sleeping & Eating

TOP
CHOICE **Langstrath Inn**   B&B **££**
(☑017687-77239; www.thelangstrath.com; Stonethwaite; d £100-128; 🅿🛜) Borrowdale's country hotels are expensive, so you'll be better off basing yourself at this out-of-the-way inn in Stonethwaite. The eight rooms feature white walls, crimson throws and pleasant en suites, and the countryside views are to die for. Hearty food (mains from £11.30) and

beers from Hawkshead Brewery are served in the restaurant.

Seatoller House B&B ££
(☎017687-77218; www.seatollerhouse.co.uk; s/d £55/122; P) A tiny hideaway in Seatoller that feels like a Beatrix Potter burrow. It's tucked beneath Honister Pass and all the rooms are named after animals: attic Osprey has skylight views, Rabbit is pine-filled and Badger looks over the garden.

Yew Tree Farm B&B ££
(☎017687-77675; www.borrowdaleherdwick.co.uk; Rosthwaite; d £75; P) There are floral patterns galore at this sturdy Cumbrian farmhouse in rural Rosthwaite, with three rooms snuggled among cob walls and tiny windows. It's run by working sheep farmers, and you'll be able to spot Herdwicks in the nearby fields. Breakfast is huge, and the Flock-In tearoom serves a cracking sticky toffee pudding.

Derwentwater Hostel HOSTEL £
(☎017687-77246; www.derwentwater.org; Barrow House; dm £18.40-20.40, r from £60; P@) With its 17-acre grounds and private waterfall, this listed 19th-century mansion makes a princely location for a hostel. Previously YHA-owned, it's now independently run and offers clean, basic dorms (most have four to eight beds, but one has 22 beds). There's also a kitchen, a cafe and plenty of lounge space, but it's the aristocratic architecture that makes it.

Borrowdale YHA HOSTEL £
(☎0845-371 9624; borrowdale@yha.org.uk; Longthwaite; dm from £16; ⊙Feb-Dec) Purpose-built chalet hostel, specialising in walking and activity trips.

❶ Getting There & Away

Buses 77/77A and 78 connect Borrowdale and Buttermere with Keswick.

Honister Pass

From Borrowdale, a narrow, perilously steep road snakes up the fellside to Honister Pass and Buttermere valley beyond.

Overlooking the top of the pass is the Honister Slate Mine (☎017687-77230; www .honister-slate-mine.co.uk; mine tour adult/child £9.95/4.95, via ferrata £20/15, all-day pass £34/25; ⊙tours 10.30am, 12.30pm & 3.30pm Mar-Oct), where underground tours venture deep into the bowels of the old 'Edge' and 'Kimberley'

mines (a tour into the 'Cathedral' mine runs on Friday by request, but you'll need eight people and it costs £19.75).

Honister is also home to the UK's first Via Ferrata (Iron Way; adult/10-15yr £25/20), a vertiginous system of clifftop ropes and laddersonce used by slate miners. It's exhilarating and great fun, but unsurprisingly you'll need a head for heights.

Buttermere

From the high point of Honister, the road drops sharply into the deep bowl of Buttermere, skirting the lakeshore to Buttermere village, 4 miles from Honister and 9 miles from Keswick. From here, the B5289 cuts past Crummock Water before exiting the valley's northern edge.

Buttermere marks the start of Alfred Wainwright's all-time favourite circuit: up Red Pike (755m), and along High Stile, High Crag and Haystacks (597m). In fact, the great man liked it so much, he stayed here for good: after his death in 1991, his ashes were scattered across the top of Haystacks as requested in his will.

There's limited accommodation in the area. Walkers bunk down at the Buttermere YHA (☎0845-371 9508; buttermere@yha .org.uk; dm from £16; ⊙reception 8.30-10am & 5-10.30pm) or one of the local campsites, a slate-stone house above Buttermere Lake, while those looking for more luxury try one of the valley's two hotels, the Bridge Hotel (☎017687-70252; www.bridge-hotel.com; r £130-150; P) or the Fish Inn (☎017687-70253; www .fishinnbuttermere.co.uk; mains £8-14; P).

❶ Getting There & Away

Bus 77/77A serves Buttermere and Honister Pass.

Ullswater & Around

After Windermere, the second-largest lake in the Lake District is Ullswater, a silvery slash that stretches for 7.5 miles between Pooley Bridge, and Glenridding and Patterdale in the south. Carved out by a long-extinct glacier, the deep valley in which the lake sits is flanked by an impressive string of fells, most notably the razor ridge of Helvellyn, Cumbria's third-highest mountain at 950m.

◉ Sights & Activities

Ullswater 'Steamers'   CRUISE
(☏017684-82229; www.ullswater-steamers.co.uk; round-the-lake ticket adult/child £12.70/6.35) Ullswater's historic steamer service has been running since 1855. There are now four boats, all dressed in the company's distinctive livery; the stately *Lady of the Lake* was launched in 1888, making it the oldest passenger boat still working in the world.

The boats run east–west from Pooley Bridge, stopping at the village of Howtown on the southern shore en route to Glenridding. There's a round-the-lake ticket, or you can buy single fares in each direction.

There are up to 11 sailings a day in summer, dropping to four in winter.

Gowbarrow Park & Aira Force   PARK, WATERFALL
This rolling park stretches out across the lakeshore halfway between Pooley Bridge and Glenridding. Well-marked paths lead up to the impressive waterfall of Aira Force, a 66ft cascade that tumbles down a wooded ravine. Another waterfall, High Force, is further up the hillside. Admission to the park is free, but non-NT members will have to pay for the car park.

A little south of Gowbarrow Park is Glencoyne Bay, where the springtime displays of daffodils inspired Wordsworth to pen the immortal lines: 'I wandered lonely as a cloud/That floats on high over hills and dales/When all at once I saw a crowd/A host of golden daffodils...'. February and March are usually the best months to visit if you want to see the flowers for yourself.

Helvellyn   WALKING
Along with Scafell Pike, this challenging hike is the one everyone wants to do. The classic ascent takes in the twin ridges of Striding and Swirral Edge, which are spectacular but very exposed, and involve some scrambling and dizzyingly steep drops on either side – if you're at all nervous of heights, Helvellyn in probably not the fell for you.

The usual routes climb up through Glenridding or Patterdale. As usual, check the weather forecast and take all the necessary supplies.

🛏 Sleeping

Lowthwaite Farm   B&B ££
(☏017684-82343; www.lowthwaiteullswater.com; Matterdale; d £80-86, 2-night minimum weekends) Lost in the hills around Matterdale, a couple of miles from the lake, this sweet farmhouse is run by a pair of globe-trotters who have filled the place with souvenirs collected on their journeys. Ring ahead for directions, as it's tricky to find.

Waternook   B&B ££
(☏017684-86839; www.waternookonullswater.com; near Howtown; d £90-110) If you really feel like getting away from it all, try this remote house on Ullswater's isolated southern side. The four rooms have White Company linen, duck-down pillows and fantastic lake views, but they're quite small; deluxe Fusedale has the most space. You can even borrow binoculars to spot local wildlife.

Old Water View   B&B ££
(☏017684-82175; www.oldwaterview.co.uk; Patterdale; d £84) Simple B&B with rooms to cover all needs: split-level 'Bothy' is ideal for families, with attic beds for the kids, while 'Little Gem' overlooks a stream and 'Place Fell' is said to have been a favourite of Alfred Wainwright.

Patterdale YHA   HOSTEL £
(☏0845-371 9337; patterdale@yha.org.uk; Patterdale; dm £18.40; ⊙reception 7.30-10am & 5-10.30pm Easter-Oct) This purpose-built hostel lacks the heritage of some Lakeland hostels and has a definite whiff of the 1970s about it, but it boasts the usual YHA trappings (kitchen, cafe, TV lounge) and the lake is a stone's throw away. It's a shame the dorm block looks so much like a prison wing.

Helvellyn YHA   HOSTEL £
(☏0845-371 9742; helvellyn@yha.org.uk; Greenside; dm £20; ⊙Easter-Oct) Saved from the YHA cost-cutting axe, this high-level hostel makes the perfect start for Helvellyn hikers. It's in a converted cottage 274m above the valley at the end of a rough, stony track on the main Helvellyn trail. Dorms are small, clean and cosy, and filling meals are provided by the hostel staff, which is handy, since the nearest cafe or shop is three-quarters of a mile away.

🍴 Eating

Traveller's Rest   PUB ££
(Glenridding; mains £5.50-15) Down a pint with a view of the fells at Traveller's Rest, a Glenridding stalwart. The food might be plain (steaks, pies, prawn cocktails) but the portions are huge.

THE LAKE DISTRICT & CUMBRIA ULLSWATER & AROUND

Fellbites   CAFE **££**

(Glenridding; lunch mains £8-12, evening menus £17.50-23.50; ⊙lunch daily, dinner Thu-Sat) Popular Glenridding cafe that serves a good selection of spuds, sarnies and all-day breakfasts, plus a daily roast.

ℹ️ Information

Ullswater information centre (☑017684-82414; ullswatertic@lake-district.gov.uk; Glenridding; ⊙9am-5.30pm Apr-Oct)

ℹ️ Getting There & Away

The Ullswater Bus-and-Boat Combo ticket (adult/child £14.30/7.75) includes a day's travel on the 108 with a return trip on an Ullswater Steamer; buy the ticket on the bus.

108 Penrith to Patterdale via Pooley Bridge and Glenridding (five daily Monday to Friday, four on weekends).

517 Runs via Glenridding and Patterdale, then crosses the Kirkstone Pass to Troutbeck and Bowness (Kirkstone Rambler; three daily July and August, otherwise weekends only).

Kendal

POP 28,398

Technically Kendal isn't in the Lake District, but it's a major gateway town. Often known as the 'Auld Grey Town' thanks to the sombre grey stone used for many of its buildings, Kendal is a bustling shopping centre with some good restaurants, a funky arts centre and intriguing museums. But it'll forever be synonymous in many people's minds with its famous mint cake, a staple item in the nation's hiking packs ever since Edmund Hillary and Tenzing Norgay munched it during their ascent of Everest in 1953.

◉ Sights

FREE **Kendal Museum**   MUSEUM

(www.kendalmuseum.org.uk; Station Rd; ⊙10.30am-5pm Wed-Sat) Founded in 1796 by the inveterate Victorian collector William Todhunter, this mixed-bag museum features everything from stuffed beasts and transfixed butterflies to medieval coin hoards. There's also a reconstruction of the office of Alfred Wainwright, who served as honorary curator at the museum from 1945 to 1974: look out for his pipe and knapsack.

Abbot Hall Art Gallery   GALLERY

(www.abbothall.org.uk; adult/child £6.85/free; ⊙10.30am-5pm Mon-Sat Apr-Oct, to 4pm Nov-Mar) Kendal's fine art gallery houses one of the northwest's best collections of 18th- and 19th-century art. It's especially strong on portraiture and Lakeland landscapes: look out for works by Constable, John Ruskin and local boy George Romney, a key figure in the Kendal School.

A joint ticket with the Museum of Lakeland Life & Industry costs £8.30.

Museum of Lakeland
Life & Industry   MUSEUM

(www.lakelandmuseum.org.uk; adult/child £5/free; ⊙10.30am-5pm Mon-Sat Mar-Oct, to 4pm Nov-Feb) Directly opposite Abbot Hall, this museum recreates various scenes from Lakeland life during the 18th and 19th centuries, including a farmhouse parlour, a Lakeland kitchen, an apothecary and the study of Arthur Ransome, author of *Swallows and Amazons*.

🎯 Festivals & Events

Kendal Mountain Festival   OUTDOOR ACTIVITIES

(www.mountainfest.co.uk) Annual mountain-themed celebration encompassing films, books and talks in November.

🛏️ Sleeping

Crosthwaite House   B&B **££**

(☑015395-68264; www.crosthwaitehouse.co.uk; d £70-80; P📶) Zingy and zesty, this bright number has lots of imagination: the six rooms are colourfully decorated with swirly wallpapers, funky fabrics and retro furniture, and all named after a type of damson fruit. Breakfast includes tasty options such as blueberry pancakes and *huevos rancheros*.

Beech House   B&B **££**

(☑01539-720385; www.beechhouse-kendal.co.uk; 40 Greenside; s £60-75, d £80-100; P📶) Top Kendal honours go to this extremely elegant B&B at the top of the steep hill of Beast Banks. Rooms are a prim-and-proper treat: some feature sleigh beds and fluffy cushions, others freestanding baths and comfy sofas.

🍴 Eating

TOP CHOICE **Punch Bowl Inn**   PUB **£££**

(☑015395-68237; www.the-punchbowl.co.uk; Crosthwaite; mains £14-28; P) For a top Sunday lunch, this cracking country pub is a fantastic bet. It's in the village of Crosthwaite, about 6 miles from both Kendal and Bowness. The menu has sophisticated fare such as pork tenderloin with damson purée or sea-bass with vanilla beurre blanc. Rooms (£160 to £310) feature reclaimed beams, Roberts Revival radios and underfloor heating. One of Lakeland's poshest pubs.

New Moon   BISTRO ££
(☎01539-729254; www.newmoonrestaurant.co.uk; 129 Highgate; 2-course lunch £9.95, mains £11.95-17; ⊗Tue-Sat) Flavoursome fusion food is the mainstay at this town-centre bistro: think pork loin with dates, chilli-spiced tiger prawns, or confit duck served with ginger, chilli and honey. The dining room is light and contemporary, and the two-course pre-7pm menu is great value at £12.95.

Waterside Wholefoods   CAFE £
(Kent View; light meals £4-10; ⊗8.30am-4.30pm Mon-Sat) Kendal's veggies make a beeline for this riverside cafe, a long-standing staple for filling sandwiches, flapjacks and naughty-but-nice cakes.

Grain Store   BISTRO ££
(pizzas £6.50-10, mains £10-16.50; ⊗10am-11pm Mon-Sat) The Brewery Arts Centre's eatery does a decent line in pub grub and stone-baked pizzas.

1657 Chocolate House   CAFE £
(54 Branthwaite Brow; lunches £3-8) One for chocaholics, this one: handmade chocolates and mint cake in the basement shop, plus umpteen varieties of hot chocolate in the upstairs cafe, served by waitresses in starchy aprons, and flavoured with almond, violet, mint and bitter orange.

☆ Entertainment

Brewery Arts Centre   THEATRE, CINEMA
(☎01539-725133; www.breweryarts.co.uk; Highgate) Lively arts complex with a gallery, a cafe, a theatre and a brace of cinemas.

ℹ Information

Library (75 Stricklandgate; per hr £2; ⊗9.30am-5.30pm Mon & Tue, to 7pm Wed & Fri, to 1pm Thu, 9am-4pm Sat, noon-4pm Sun) Internet access.

ℹ Getting There & Around

BUS Kendal is well-served by buses.
106 To Penrith (80 minutes, six daily Monday to Saturday).

555/556 Regular bus (half-hourly Monday to Saturday, hourly at weekends) to Windermere (30 minutes), Ambleside (40 minutes) and Grasmere (1¼ hours).

505 To Windermere, Ambleside, Hawkshead and Coniston (eight daily Monday to Saturday, six on Sunday).

X35 South to Grange, then westwards via Newby Bridge, Haverthwaite, Ulverston and Barrow (hourly Monday to Saturday, four on Sunday) .

TRAIN The train line from Windermere runs to Kendal (£4.20, 15 minutes, hourly) en route to Oxenholme.

Around Kendal

The countryside around Kendal feels gentler than the dramatic fells and valleys of the rest of the Lakes. It's mainly worth visiting for its stately homes and one of the county's top farm shops.

Sizergh Castle   CASTLE
(NT; ☎015395-60070; www.nationaltrust.org.uk/ sizergh-castle; adult/child £8.15/4.05, gardens only £5.45/2.70; ⊗house 1-5pm Sun-Thu, gardens 11am-5pm daily) Three-and-a-half miles south of Kendal along the A591, this castle is the feudal seat of the Strickland family. Set around a *pele* tower, its finest asset is the lavish wood panelling on display in the Great Hall.

Levens Hall   HISTORIC HOME
(☎015395-60321; www.levenshall.co.uk; adult/child £12/5; ⊗house noon-5pm, gardens 10am-5pm Sun-Thu Mar-Oct) This Elizabethan manor is built around a mid 13th-century *pele* tower, and fine Jacobean furniture litters the house, although the real draw is the 17th-century topiary garden: a surreal riot of pyramids, swirls, curls, pom-poms and peacocks straight out of *Alice in Wonderland*. It's two miles further south from Sizergh Castle along the A6. The 555/556 bus runs past the castle gates.

TOP CHOICE **Low Sizergh Barn**   FARM SHOP
(☎015395-60426; www.lowsizerghbarn.co.uk; ⊗shop 9am-5.30pm, tearoom 9.30am-5.30pm) A prodigious selection of Lakeland goodies are available at this beamed farm shop, one of the Lake District's very best. Breads from Grange Bakery, meats from Mansergh Hall, cheeses from Thornby Moor Dairy and beers from the Coniston Brewery Co are just some of the gourmet treats in store. There's also

a farm trail and woodland walk to follow if the weather's nice. Look out for the signs just outside Kendal on the A590.

CUMBRIAN COAST

While the central lakes and fells pull in a never-ending stream of visitors, surprisingly few ever make the trek west to explore Cumbria's coastline. And that's a shame: while it might not compare to the wild grandeur of Northumberland or the rugged splendour of Scotland's shores, Cumbria's coast is well worth exploring. Less attractive is the nuclear plant of Sellafield, still stirring up controversy some 50 years after its construction.

Holker Hall
HISTORIC HOME

(☏015395-58328; www.holker-hall.co.uk; adult/child £11.50/6, grounds only £7.50/4; ☉house 11am-4pm Sun-Fri, grounds 10.30am-5pm Mar-Oct) Holker Hall has been the family seat of the Cavendish family for nigh on 400 years. Though parts of the house date from the 16th century, the house was almost entirely rebuilt following a devastating fire in 1871.

It's a typically ostentatious Victorian affair, covered with mullioned windows, gables and copper-topped turrets. Of particular note are the drawing room, library and lavish Long Gallery (renowned for its elaborate plasterwork).

Outside, Holker's grounds sprawl for more than 10 hectares, encompassing a rose garden, a woodland, ornamental fountains and a 22m-high lime tree. There's also a food hall (☏015395-59084; www.holkerfoodhall .co.uk) stocking produce from the estate, including venison and saltmarsh lamb.

Laurel & Hardy Museum
MUSEUM

(☏01229-582292; www.laurel-and-hardy.co.uk; Brogden St, Ulverston; adult/child £4/2; ☉10am-5pm Feb-Dec) Founded by avid Laurel and Hardy collector Bill Cubin back in 1983, this eclectic museum in Ulverston (the birthplace of Stan Laurel) has new premises inside the town's old Roxy cinema. It's crammed floor-to-ceiling with cinematic memorabilia, from original posters to film props, and there's a shoebox-sized cinema showing back-to-back Laurel and Hardy classics.

Furness Abbey
ABBEY

(EH; adult/child £12.30/3.90; ☉10am-5pm Thu-Mon) Eight-and-a-half miles southwest of Ulverston, the rosy ruins of Furness Abbey are all that remains of one of northern England's largest and most powerful monasteries. Founded in the 12th century, it met an ignominious end in 1537 during the Dissolution.

You can still make out the abbey's footprint; various arches, windows and some of the south transept walls are still standing, along with the shell of the abbey bell tower. During the recent excavations of a medieval abbot, archaeologists discovered some fascinating treasures including a gold crozier and an ornate gemstone ring, both of which are on display in the abbey museum.

Several buses, including the X35, stop nearby.

ALFRED WAINWRIGHT

Few names are more famous in Lakeland than that of Alfred Wainwright, author of the classic hand-drawn, seven-volume series, *The Pictorial Guides to the Lakeland Fells*, still the guidebook of choice for many walkers, despite the fact that the series is more than 60 years old.

An accountant by training, Wainwright became besotted with the fells following a chance climb up Orrest Head in 1930. He began documenting his walks through journals, hand-drawn maps and illustrations, a project that eventually developed into his groundbreaking fell-walking guides. He began his magnum opus in 1952; the first volume, *The Eastern Fells*, was published in 1955, and the last volume, *The Western Fells*, was completed in 1966.

Part-walking guides, part illustrated artworks and part philosophical memoirs, Wainwright's books have become modern classics, with over two million books sold since their original publication. They've recently been given their first update in 60 years by local hiker and author Chris Jesty.

For more information, contact the Wainwright Society (www.wainwright.org), which keeps a register of all its members who have completed the 214 'official' Wainwright summits.

Ravenglass & Eskdale Railway RAILWAY
(☎01229-717171; www.ravenglass-railway.co.uk;
single fare adult/child £6.60/3.30, day ticket
£11.20/5.60) Built in 1875 to ferry iron ore,
the pocket-size choo-choos of this much-
loved railway (affectionately known as La'al
Ratty) chug for 7 miles from the coastal
town of Ravenglass into the valley of Eskdale and the Lakeland foothills, terminating
at Dalegarth Station, near Boot. There are
up to 17 trips daily in summer, dropping to
just a couple a day in winter.

St Bees Head CLIFFS
(RSPB; stbees.head@rspb.org.uk) Five-and-a-
half miles south of Whitehaven and 1½ miles
north of the tiny town of St Bees, this wind-
battered headland is one of Cumbria's most
important reserves for nesting seabirds. Depending on the season, species nesting here
include fulmars, kittiwakes and razorbills, as
well as Britain's only population of resident
black guillemots. There are over 2 miles of
cliff paths to explore, so remember to bring
some binoculars.

❶ Getting Around

The Furness and Cumbrian Coast railway lines
loop 120 miles from Lancaster to Carlisle, stopping at the coastal resorts of Grange, Ulverston,
Ravenglass, Whitehaven and Workington.

NORTHERN & EASTERN CUMBRIA

Many visitors speed through the northern and eastern reaches of Cumbria in a
headlong dash for the Lake District, but
it's worth taking the time to delve into the
little-explored countryside inland from the
national park.

It might not have the big-name fells and
chocolate-box villages, but it's full of interest
nonetheless: traditional towns, crumbling
castles, abandoned abbeys and sweeping
moors, all set alongside the magnificent Roman engineering project of Hadrian's Wall.

Carlisle

POP 69,527

Carlisle isn't Britain's prettiest city, but it has
history and heritage aplenty. Precariously
perched on the frontier between England
and Scotland, in the area once ominously
dubbed the 'Debatable Lands', Cumbria's

WORTH A TRIP

CARTMEL

Tucked away in the countryside near
Grange, tiny Cartmel is known for three
things: its 12th-century priory (⊙9am-
5.30pm May-Oct, to 3.30pm Nov-Apr), its
miniature racecourse and its world-
famous sticky toffee pudding, sold at
the Cartmel Village Shop (☎015395-
36280; www.stickytoffeepudding.co.uk;
⊙9am-5pm Mon-Sat, 10am-4.30pm Sun).

It's also home to the Lake District's
top gastronomic restaurants, the
Michelin-starred L'Enclume (☎015395-
36362; www.lenclume.co.uk; Cavendish St;
8-/12-course tasting menu £69/89,
d £99-159, ste £179-199; ⊙lunch Wed-Sun,
dinner daily). Head chef Simon Rogan
is known for his artful dishes, wacky
flavour combinations and fondness for
foraged ingredients. There's no à la carte
menu; you choose from an eight-course
or (gulp) 12-course tasting menu.

If the prices are on the steep side, try
Rogan's less formal bistro, Rogan &
Company (☎015395-35917; www
.roganandcompany.co.uk; The Square; mains
£14.50-21; ⊙Wed-Sun), just across the
village.

---

capital is a city with a notoriously stormy
past: sacked by the Vikings, pillaged by the
Scots, and plundered by the Border Reivers,
the city has been on the frontline of England's defences for more than 1000 years.

Reminders of the city's past are still evident in its great crimson castle and cathedral, built from the same rosy red sandstone
as most of the city's houses. It might not
have the wow factor of some of northern
England's other regenerated conurbations,
but Carlisle certainly has enough to justify
at least a couple of days of investigation.

◉ Sights & Activities

TOP CHOICE Carlisle Castle CASTLE
(EH; www.english-heritage.org.uk/daysout/
properties/carlisle-castle; adult/child £5.50/3.30;
⊙9.30am-5pm Apr-Sep, 10am-4pm Oct-Mar) Carlisle's brooding, rust-red castle lurks dramatically on the north side of the city. Founded
around a Celtic and Roman stronghold, the
Norman keep was added in 1092 by William
Rufus, and later refortified by Henry II,

Edward I and Henry VIII (who added the supposedly cannon-proof towers).

The castle has witnessed some dramatic events over the centuries: Mary, Queen of Scots was imprisoned here in 1568, and the castle was the site of a notorious eight-month siege during the English Civil War, when the Royalist garrison survived by eating rats, mice and the castle dogs before finally surrendering in 1645. Look out for the 'licking stones' in the dungeon, which Jacobite prisoners supposedly lapped for moisture.

Admission includes entry to the Kings Own Royal Border Regiment Museum, which details the history of Cumbria's Infantry Regiment. There are guided tours from April to September.

Carlisle Cathedral CHURCH
(www.carlislecathedral.org.uk; 7 The Abbey; suggested donation £5, photography permit £1; ⊘7.30am-6.15pm Mon-Sat, to 5pm Sun;) Built from the same scarlet sandstone as the castle, Carlisle's cathedral began life as a priory church in 1122, and became a cathedral when its first abbot, Athelwold, became the first Bishop of Carlisle. Among its notable features are the 15th-century choir stalls, the barrel-vaulted roof and the 14th-century East Window, one of the largest Gothic windows in England. Surrounding the cathedral are other priory relics, including the 16th-century Fratry and the Prior's Tower.

Tullie House Museum MUSEUM
(www.tulliehouse.co.uk; Castle St; adult/child £5.20/50p; ⊘10am-5pm Mon-Sat, 11am-4pm Sun) This museum ranges through the city's past, from its Celtic foundation through to the development of modern Carlisle. The highlight is the new Roman Frontier Gallery, which opened in 2011 and uses a mix of archaeological exhibits and interactive displays to tell the story of the Roman occupation of Carlisle. There are some particularly fine busts and decorative headstones, as well as a showpiece bronze face-mask dating from the 1st century AD.

Upstairs, the Border Galleries cover the rest of the city's history, from the Bronze Age through to the Border Reivers, the Jacobite Rebellion and the Industrial Revolution. The Carlisle Life Gallery details the city's social history through photos, films and archive recordings, and Old Tullie House has a collection of art, sculpture and porcelain.

Guildhall Museum MUSEUM
(Greenmarket) This tiny museum occupies one of Carlisle's oldest buildings, built for the city's trade guilds during the 15th century. It's currently closed for restoration, but you can still admire the impressive galleried exterior.

☞ Tours

Open Book Visitor Guiding TOUR
(☎01228-670578; www.greatguidedtours.co.uk) Tours of Carlisle and the surrounding area (including Hadrian's Wall) can be arranged through the tourist office.

🛏 Sleeping

Carlisle's accommodation leaves a lot to be desired. Apart from a few chain hotels, the choice in the centre is disappointing. You'll be better off heading to the outskirts.

Willowbeck Lodge B&B ££
(☎01228-513607; www.willowbeck-lodge.com; Lambley Bank, Scotby; d £100-130; P🐾) Escape the city hustle at this uncompromisingly modern house, 3 miles from the centre. Six deluxe rooms are closer to hotel standard than B&B, offering tasteful shades of beige and taupe, luxurious bathrooms and a gabled lounge overlooking a private pond.

Warwick Lodge B&B ££
(☎01228-523796; www.warwicklodgecarlisle.co.uk; 112 Warwick Rd; s/d £40/75) A Brit B&B from the old school, with flouncy rooms, no-frills furnishings and a proper fatty fry-up for breakfast. Luxury is not the word, but it's good value and relatively central.

Cornerways B&B ££
(☎01228-521733; www.cornerwaysguesthouse.co.uk; 107 Warwick Rd; s £30-35, d £55-65; P@🐾) This rambling redbrick is as basic as they come, but offers some of the cheapest B&B rooms in the city.

🍴 Eating

Carlisle has plenty of choice when it comes to pubs and curry houses, but it pays to be a bit more selective when it comes to its fine-dining restaurants.

Holme Bistro BRITISH ££
(☎01228-534343; www.holmebistro.co.uk; 56-58 Denton St; mains £10.95-17.95; ⊘Tue-Sat) The top place to eat in Carlisle, this slick bistro is run by brother-and-sister team Rob Don and Kirsty Robson, and has earned a loyal clien-

tele for its unpretentious cuisine. The two-/
three-course pre-7.30pm menu is a steal.

David's
BISTRO **££**

(01228-523578; www.davidsrestaurant.co.uk; 62
Warwick Rd; 2-/3-course lunch £12.95/15.95, dinner mains £14.95-23.95; ☺Tue-Sat) Town-house
dining with a gentlemanly air. Expect original mantelpieces and overhead chandeliers
in the dining rooms, and a menu of suave
dishes such as 'best-end' of herb-encrusted
lamb, or salmon and crayfish *millefeuille*.

Foxes Cafe Lounge
CAFE **££**

(www.foxescafelounge.co.uk; 18 Abbey St; mains
£4-10; ☺10am-7pm Tue-Thu, to 11pm Fri, to 4.30pm
Sat) This cool cafe-gallery provides a venue
for all kinds of creative happenings, from
open-mic nights and live gigs to photo exhibitions. Count on continental cafe food and
excellent coffee.

Prior's Kitchen Restaurant
CAFE **£**

(Carlisle Cathedral; lunches £4-6; ☺9.45am-4pm
Mon-Sat) Carlisle's best place for traditional
afternoon tea is in the cathedral's fratry,
once used as a monk's mess hall.

Gilded Lily
GASTROPUB **££**

(01228-593600; www.gildedlily.info; 8 Lowther
St; mains £9-15; ☺9am-midnight Mon-Thu, 9am-
1am Fri & Sat, noon-midnight Sun) Once a bank,
this city gastropub turns out reliable food
and is a popular pre-club venue.

Drinking & Entertainment

Botchergate's the place for late-night action,
but it gets notoriously rowdy at kicking-out
time.

Fats
PUB

(48 Abbey St; ☺11am-11pm) A less hectic alternative to Botchergate's pubs. DJs and comedy nights are held regularly.

Brickyard
CONCERT VENUE

(www.thebrickyardonline.com; 14 Fisher St) Carlisle's grungy gig venue, housed in the former
Memorial Hall.

❶ Information

Police station (☎0845-330 0247; English St;
☺8am-midnight)
Tourist office (☎01228-625600; www.historic
-carlisle.org.uk; Greenmarket; ☺9.30am-5pm
Mon-Sat, 10.30am-4pm Sun)

❶ Getting There & Away

BUS National Express coaches depart from the
bus station on Lonsdale St for destinations including London (£34.80, 7½ hours, three direct
daily), Manchester (£25.30 to £27.70, three to
3½ hours, five daily) and Glasgow (£18.70 to
£19.10, two hours, four to six daily).

104 To Penrith (40 minutes, hourly Monday to
Saturday, every two hours on Sunday).

554 To Keswick (70 minutes, four daily).

AD 122 (Hadrian's Wall Bus; three daily April to
September) Runs along the wall, with stops including Brampton, Birdoswald Roman Fort, Haltwhistle, Vindolanda Roman Fort, Housesteads
Roman Fort and Hexham. Three extra buses a
day only run as far as Haltwhistle station.

TRAIN Carlisle is on the main west coast line
from London to Glasgow. It's also the terminus
for the scenic Cumbrian Coast and Tyne Valley
Lines, as well as the historic **Settle to Carlisle
Railway** (www.settle-carlisle.co.uk; single to
Settle £18.90, anytime return £24.40) across
the Yorkshire Dales. Main destinations:

Glasgow £21.80, 1¼ hours
Lancaster £19.50, 45 minutes
London Euston £102.10, 3½ hours
Manchester £50, two hours
Newcastle-upon-Tyne £13, 1½ hours

WORTH A TRIP

BIRDOSWALD ROMAN FORT

Though most of the forts along Hadrian's Wall have long since been plundered for building materials, you can
still visit Birdoswald Roman Fort
(EH; ☎01697-747602; www.birdoswald
romanfort.org; adult/child £5.20/3.10;
☺10am-5.30pm, reduced winter).
Built to replace an earlier timber-and-
turf fort, Birdoswald would have been
the operating base for around 1000 Roman soldiers; excavations have revealed
three of the four gateways, as well as
granary stores, workshops, exterior
walls and a military-drill hall. A visitors
centre explores the fort's history and
the background behind the wall's construction. The AD 122 bus connecting
Carlisle with Hexham passes by the fort.

❶ Getting Around

To book a taxi, call **Radio Taxis** (☎01228-527575), **Citadel Station Taxis** (☎01228-523971) or **County Cabs** (☎01228-596789).

Alston

POP 2227

Surrounded by the bleak hilltops of the Pennines, isolated Alston's main claim to fame is its elevation: at 305m above sea level, it's thought to be the highest market town in England (despite no longer having a market). It's also famous among steam enthusiasts thanks to the South Tynedale Railway (☎01434-381696, timetable 01434-382828; www.strps.org.uk; adult/child return £7.50/3; ☺Apr-Oct), which puffs and clatters through the hilly country between Alston and Kirkhaugh, along a route that originally operated from 1852 to 1976. The return trip takes about an hour; there are up to five daily trains in midsummer.

Penrith

POP 14,882

Traditional butchers, greengrocers and quaint little teashops line the streets of Penrith, a stout, red-brick town that feels closer to the no-nonsense villages of the Yorkshire Dales than to the chocolate-box villages of the Central Lakes.

Cunningly disguised as a Lakeland hill 2 miles west of Penrith, the Rheged visitor centre (www.rheged.com; ☺10am-6pm) houses a large-screen Imax cinema and an exhibition on the history and geology of Cumbria, as well as a retail hall selling Cumbrian goods from handmade paper to chocolate and chutneys. The frequent X4/X5 bus stops at the centre.

🛌 Sleeping

Brooklands   B&B ££

(☎01768-863395; www.brooklandsguesthouse.com; 2 Portland Pl; s £40, d £78-88; 🛜) The town's most elegant B&B is this Victorian red-brick on Portland Place. Rich furnishings and posh extras (such as White Company toiletries, fridges and chocolates on the tea tray) keep it a cut above the competition.

Brandelhow   B&B ££

(☎01768-864470; www.brandelhowguesthouse.co.uk; 1 Portland Pl; s/d £35/70; 🛜) Next door to Brooklands, this family-run establishment is a useful second choice. The rooms are bog-standard B&B, but the little treats make it worth considering, especially the welcome tea, with chunks of Bootle Gingerbread or Lanie's Expedition Flapjack.

George Hotel   HOTEL £££

(☎01768-862696; www.lakedistricthotels.net/george hotel; Devonshire St; d £134-204; 🅿🛜) Penrith's venerable redbrick coaching inn offers classically decorated rooms in prim stripes and country patterns, plus a quaint bar and restaurant. It's right in the heart of town, but rates are pricey.

✗ Eating

TOP CHOICE Yanwath Gate Inn   GASTROPUB ££

(☎01768-862886; Yanwath; mains £16-19) Two miles south of town, the 'Yat' has been named Cumbria's Top Dining Pub for the last three years running in *Good Pub Guide*, and the grub puts many of the county's gastronomic restaurants to shame. The setting is a treat, too, with original A-frame beams, wood panelling and country curios galore.

No 15   CAFE £

(15 Victoria Rd; lunches £6-10; ☺9am-5pm Mon-Sat) Fifteen reasons to visit this cafe-bar-gallery are chalked on the blackboard, but you won't need persuading. It's Penrith's best place for lunch, cakes and coffee, with a light dining room and a gallery annexe displaying local photography and artwork. Lunch options include homemade burgers, spicy falafel salads and great veggie quiches.

❶ Information

Tourist office (☎01768-867466; pen.tic @eden.gov.uk; Middlegate; ☺9.30am-5pm Mon-Sat, 1-4.45pm Sun) Also houses Penrith's tiny museum.

❶ Getting There & Away

BUS The bus station is northeast of the centre, off Sandgate.

104 To Carlisle (40 minutes, hourly Monday to Saturday, every two hours on Sunday)

X4/X5 Via Rheged, Keswick and Cockermouth to the Cumbrian coast (half-hourly Monday to Saturday, six on Sunday)

TRAIN There are frequent connections to Carlisle (£6.70, 15 minutes) and Lancaster (£15.40, one hour).

Newcastle & Northeast England

Best Places to Eat

» Oldfields (p617)
» Jesmond Dene House (p617)
» Bouchon Bistrot (p627)
» Blackfriars (p617)
» The Broad Chare (p617)

Best Places to Stay

» Ashcroft (p631)
» No 1 Sallyport (p638)
» Gadds Townhouse (p623)
» Chillingham (p634)
» Alnwick Lodge (p634)

Why Go?

Ask a Kentish farmer or Cornish fisherman about northeast England and they may describe a forbidding industrial wasteland inhabited by football-mad folk with impenetrable accents. What they may not mention are the untamed landscapes, Newcastle's cultural renaissance, the wealth of Roman sites and the no-nonsense likeability of the locals. Some post-industrial gloom remains, but there's so much more to this frontier country than slag heaps and silenced steelworks.

In fact, if it's silence you are looking for, the northeast is ideal for flits into unpeopled backcountry – from the rounded Cheviot Hills to the brooding Northumberland National Park and the harsh remoteness of the North Pennines, you're spoilt for choice when it comes to fleeing the urban hullabaloo. Spectacular Hadrian's Wall cuts a lonely path through this wild landscape dotted with dramatic castle ruins, haunting reminders of a long and bloody struggle with the Picts and Celts to the north.

When to Go

The best time to discover Northumberland's miles of wide sandy beaches is during the summer (June to August) season. In May you can join the toga party at the Hadrian's Wall spring festival, while September through October is great for losing yourself in the autumnal landscapes of the North Pennines. September is also the month to grab a Newkie Brown ale, or your running shoes, and join the party along the route of Tyneside's Great North Run, one of the world's biggest half marathons.

Newcastle & Northeast England Highlights

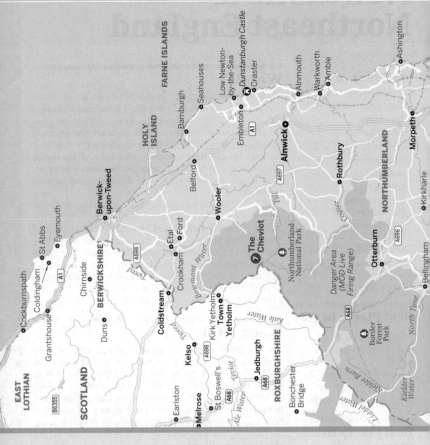

① Viewing cutting-edge modern art and the River Tyne at **BALTIC – Centre for Contemporary Art** (p616)

② Enjoying a thumping **night out** (p618) on the tiles in Newcastle's raucous city centre

③ Hugging the XXL ankles of the **Angel of the North** (p620)

④ Gazing in awe at **Durham Cathedral** (p621), a spectacular Unesco World Heritage Site

⑤ Getting all hands-on with the northeast's industrial past at **Beamish Open-Air Museum** (p621)

⑦ **The Cheviot**

20 km
10 miles

NORTH SEA

FARNE ISLANDS

HOLY ISLAND

EAST LOTHIAN

SCOTLAND

BERWICKSHIRE

ROXBURGHSHIRE

NORTHUMBERLAND

Cockburnspath
St Abbs
Eyemouth
Coldingham
Grantshouse
Chirnside
Duns
Earlston
Melrose
St Boswell's
Kelso
Coldstream
Jedburgh
Bonchester Bridge
Kirk Yetholm
Town Yetholm
Yetholm
Etal
Ford
Crookham
Wooler
Berwick-upon-Tweed
Belford
Bamburgh
Seahouses
Embleton
Low Newton-by-the-Sea
Craster
Dunstanburgh Castle
Alnwick
Rothbury
Kirkharle
Bellingham
Otterburn
Morpeth
Ashington
Amble
Warkworth
Almouth

Northumberland National Park

Danger Area (MOD Live Firing Range)

Border Forest Park

Kielder Water
Kielder Burn
Lewis Water
North Tyne

Tweed
Teviot
Ale Water
Kale Water
Bowmont Water
Till
Coquet

A1
A68
A697
A698
A696
B6355

6 Walking like a Roman – by taking a hike along **Hadrian's Wall** (p625)

7 Clambering to the top of the **Cheviot** (p633), the highest peak in Northumberland National Park

History

Violent history has shaped this region more than any other in England, primarily because of its frontier position. Although Hadrian's Wall didn't serve as a defensive barrier, it nevertheless marked the northern limit of Roman Britain and was the Empire's most heavily fortified line. Following the Romans' departure, the region became part of the Anglian kingdom of Bernicia, which united with the kingdom of Deira (encompassing much of modern-day Yorkshire) to form Northumbria in 604.

The kingdom changed hands and borders shifted several times over the next 500 years as Anglo-Saxons and Danes struggled to seize it. The land north of the River Tweed was finally ceded to Scotland in 1018, while the nascent kingdom of England kept everything below it.

The arrival of the Normans in 1066 added new spice to the mix, as William I was eager to secure his northern borders against the Scots. He commissioned most of the castles you see along the coast, and cut deals with the prince bishops of Durham to ensure their loyalty. The new lords of Northumberland became very powerful because, as Marcher Lords (from the use of 'march' as a synonym of 'border'), they kept the Scots at bay.

Northumberland's reputation as a hotbed of rebellion intensified during the Tudor years, when the largely Catholic north, led by the seventh duke of Northumberland, Thomas Percy, rose up against Elizabeth I in the defeated Rising of the North in 1569. The Border Reivers, raiders from both sides of the border in the 16th century, kept the region in a perpetual state of lawlessness, which only subsided after the Act of Union between England and Scotland in 1707.

The 19th century saw County Durham play a central role in the Industrial Revolution. The region's coalmines were the key to the industrialisation of the northeast, powering steelworks, shipyards and armament works that grew up along the Tyne and Tees. In 1825 the mines also spawned the world's first steam railway, the Stockton & Darlington built by local engineer George Stephenson. However, social strife emerged in the 20th century, the locals' plight most vividly depicted by the Jarrow Crusade in October 1936, which saw 200 men from the shipbuilding town of Jarrow march to London to demand aid for their community devastated by the Great Depression. Decline was the watchword of the postwar years, with mines, shipbuilding, steel production and the railway industry all winding down. Reinventing the northeast has been a mammoth task but regeneration is just beginning to bear fruit.

Activities

With the rugged moors of the Pennines and stunning seascape of the Northumberland coast, there's some good walking and cycling in this region. But be prepared for wind and rain at any time of year and for very harsh conditions in winter. Regional tourism websites all contain walking and cycling information, and tourist offices all stock free leaflets, plus maps and guides covering walking, cycling and other activities.

Cycling

The northeast has some of the most inspiring cycle routes in England. Part of the National Cycle Network (NCN), a long-time favourite is the Coast & Castles Cycle Route (NCN Route 1; www.coast-and-castles.co.uk), which runs south–north along the glorious Northumberland coast between Newcastle-upon-Tyne and Berwick-upon-Tweed, before swinging inland into Scotland to finish at Edinburgh.

The 140-mile Sea to Sea Cycle Route (C2C; www.c2c-guide.co.uk) runs across northern England from Whitehaven or Workington on the Cumbrian coast, through the northern part of the Lake District, and then over the wild hills of the North Pennines to finish at Newcastle-upon-Tyne or Sunderland.

The other coast-to-coast option is the Hadrian's Cycleway (www.cycle-routes.org), a 191-mile route opened in July 2006 that runs from South Shields in Tyneside, west along Hadrian's Wall and down to Ravenglass in Cumbria.

Walking

The North Pennines are billed as 'England's last wilderness', and if you like to walk in quiet and fairly remote areas, these hills – along with the Cheviots further north – are the best in England. Long routes through this area include the famous Pennine Way, which keeps mainly to the high ground as it crosses the region between the Yorkshire Dales and the Scottish border, but also goes through sections of river valley and some tedious patches of plantation. The whole route is over 250 miles, but the 70-mile section between Bowes and Hadrian's Wall would be a fine four-day taster.

Elsewhere in the area, the great Roman ruin of Hadrian's Wall is an ideal focus for walking. There's a huge range of easy loops taking in forts and other historical highlights.

The Northumberland coast has endless miles of open beaches and little in the way of resort towns, so walkers can often enjoy this wild, windswept shore in virtual solitude. One of the finest walks, between the villages of Craster and Bamburgh via Dunstanburgh, includes two of the county's most spectacular castles.

ℹ Getting There & Around

Bus

Bus transport around the region can be difficult, particularly around the more remote reaches of western Northumberland. Contact **Traveline** (✆0871-200 2233; www.travelinenortheast. info) for information on connections, timetables and prices.

Several one-day Explorer tickets are available; always ask if one might be appropriate. The Explorer North East (adult/child £9/8), available on buses, covers from Berwick down to Scarborough, and allows unlimited travel for one day, as well as numerous admission discounts.

Train

The East Coast Main Line runs north from London King's Cross to Edinburgh via Durham, Newcastle and Berwick; Northern Rail operates local and inter-urban services in the north, including west to Carlisle.

There are numerous Rover tickets for single-day travel and longer periods, so ask if one might be worthwhile. For example, the North Country Rover (adult/child £82/41) allows unlimited travel throughout the north (not including Northumberland) any four days out of eight.

NEWCASTLE-UPON-TYNE

POP 189,863

Of all northern England's cities, Newcastle is perhaps the most surprising to the first-time visitor, especially if they come armed with the preconceived notions that have dogged the city's reputation since, well, always. A sooty, industrial wasteland for salt-of-the-earth toughies whose favourite hobby is drinking and braving the elements barechested. Coal slags and cold slags? You may be in for a pleasant surprise.

Welcome to the hipster capital of the northeast, a cool urban centre that knows how to take care of itself and anyone else who comes to visit with an unexpected mix of culture, heritage and sophistication, best exemplified not just by its excellent new art galleries and magnificent concert hall, but by its growing number of fine restaurants, choice hotels and interesting bars.

◉ Sights

CITY CENTRE

Newcastle's Victorian centre, a compact area bordered roughly by Grainger St to the west and Pilgrim St to the east, is supremely elegant and one of the most compelling examples of urban rejuvenation in England. At its heart is the extraordinarily handsome Grey St, lined with fine classical buildings – undoubtedly one of the country's finest thoroughfares, it was voted the UK's third-prettiest street in the Google Street View Awards 2010. Down by the quays are the city's most recognisable attractions – the seven bridges that span the Tyne and some of the striking buildings that flank it.

FREE Great North Museum   MUSEUM
(www.greatnorthmuseum.org; Barras Bridge; ⊙10am-5pm Mon-Sat, from 1pm Sun) This outstanding museum has been created by bringing together the contents of Newcastle University's museums and adding them to the natural history exhibits of the prestigious Hancock Museum in the latter's renovated neoclassical building. The result is a fascinating jumble of dinosaurs, Roman altar stones, Egyptian mummies, Samurai warriors and some impressive taxidermy, all presented in an engaging and easily digestible way. The indisputable highlights are a life-size model of a Tyrannosaurus rex and an interactive model of Hadrian's Wall showing every milecastle and fortress. There's also lots of hands-on stuff for the kids, a planetarium with screenings throughout the day and a decent snack bar.

Life Science Centre   SCIENCE CENTRE
(www.life.org.uk; Times Sq; adult/child £9.95/6.95; ⊙10am-6pm Mon-Sat, from 11am Sun) This excellent science village, part of the soberminded complex of institutes devoted to the study of genetic science, is one of the more interesting attractions in town. Through a series of hands-on exhibits and the latest technology you (or your kids) can discover the incredible secrets of life. The highlight

Newcastle-upon-Tyne

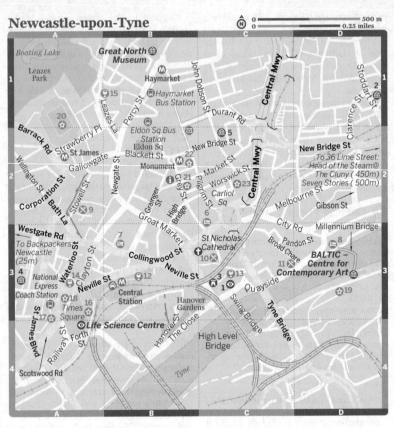

0 | 500 m
0 | 0.25 miles

is the Motion Ride, a motion simulator that lets you 'feel' what it's like to experience things like bungee jumping and other extreme sports (the 3D film changes every year). There are lots of thought-provoking arcade-style games, and if the information sometimes gets lost on the way, never mind, kids will love it.

FREE **Discovery Museum**   MUSEUM
(www.twmuseums.org.uk; Blandford Sq; ⊙10am-5pm Mon-Sat, from 2pm Sun) Tyneside's rich history is uncovered through a fascinating series of exhibits at this unmissable museum. The exhibitions, spread across three floors of the former Co-operative Wholesale Society building, surround the mightily impressive 30m-long *Turbinia,* the fastest ship in the world in 1897. There's an absorbing section dedicated to shipbuilding on the Tyne including a scale model of the river as it was in 1929, a buzzers-and-bells science

maze for the kids and a 'Story of Newcastle' section giving the low-down on the city's history from Pons Aelius (Newcastle's Roman name) to Cheryl Cole.

FREE **Bessie Surtees House**   HISTORIC HOME
(EH; 41-44 Sandhill; ⊙10am-4pm Mon-Fri) The Tyne's northern bank was the hub of commercial Newcastle in the 16th century and on Sandhill a row of leaning merchant houses has survived from that era. One of them is Bessie Surtees House, where three rooms are open to the public. The daughter of a wealthy banker, feisty Bessie annoyed Daddy by falling in love with John Scott (1751–1838), a pauper. It all ended in smiles as John went on to become Lord Chancellor.

Castle Garth Keep   CASTLE
(www.castlekeep-newcastle.org.uk; adult/child £4/free; ⊙10am-4.15pm Mon-Sat, from noon Sun) The stronghold that put both the 'new' and

Newcastle-upon-Tyne

'castle' into Newcastle has been largely swallowed up by the train station, leaving only the square Norman keep as one of the few remaining fragments. Inside you'll discover a fine chevron-covered chapel and an exhibition of architectural models ranging from Hadrian's Wall to 20th-century eyesores. The 360-degree city views from the rooftop are much better than those from the BALTIC's viewing box across the water.

FREE Laing Art Gallery   GALLERY
(www.twmuseums.org.uk; New Bridge St; ⊙10am-5pm Mon-Sat, from 2pm Sun) The exceptional collection at the Laing includes works by Gainsborough, Gauguin and Henry Moore, and an important collection of paintings by Northumberland-born artist John Martin (1789–1854). Free guided tours run Saturdays at 11am.

OUSEBURN VALLEY

About a mile east of the city centre is the much-touted Ouseburn Valley, the 19th-century industrial heartland of Newcastle, now an up-and-coming, semi-regenerated district, dotted with potteries, glass-blowing studios and other creative workspaces, as well as a handful of great bars, clubs and a superb cinema (though much of the area is still an unsightly industrial estate). For more information, check out www.ouseburntrust.org.uk.

Biscuit Factory   COMMERCIAL GALLERY
(www.thebiscuitfactory.com; 16 Stoddart St; ⊙10am-5pm Mon-Fri, 10am-6pm Sat, 11am-5pm Sun) No prizes for guessing what this commercial art gallery used to be. What it is now, though, is the country's biggest art shop, where you can peruse and buy work by artists from near and far in a variety of mediums, including painting, sculpture, glassware and furniture, much of which has a northeast theme. Even if you don't buy, the art is excellent and there's a top-class restaurant too (Brasserie Black Door).

Seven Stories – The Centre for Children's Books   LITERATURE MUSEUM
(www.sevenstories.org.uk; 30 Lime St; adult/child £6.50/5.50; ⊙10am-5pm Mon-Sat, to 4pm Sun) A marvellous conversion of a handsome Victorian mill has resulted in Seven Stories, a very hands-on museum dedicated to the wondrous world of children's literature. Across the seven floors you'll find original manuscripts, a growing collection of artwork from the 1930s onwards, and a constantly changing program of exhibitions, activities and events designed to encourage the AA Milnes of the new millennium.

36 Lime Street   ARTISTS COOPERATIVE
(www.36limestreet.co.uk; Ouseburn Warehouse, 36 Lime St) The artistic, independent spirit of Ouseburn is particularly well represented in this artists cooperative, the largest of its

BRIDGING THE TYNE

The most famous view in Newcastle is the cluster of Tyne bridges, the most famous of these being the **Tyne Bridge** (1925–28). Its resemblance to Australia's Sydney Harbour Bridge is no coincidence as both were built by the same company (Dorman Long of Middlesbrough) around the same time. The quaint little **Swing Bridge** pivots in the middle to let ships through. Nearby, the **High Level Bridge**, designed by Robert Stephenson, was the world's first combined road and railway bridge (1849). The most recent addition is the multiple-award-winning **Millennium Bridge** (aka Blinking Bridge; 2002), which opens like an eyelid to let ships pass.

kind in the northeast, featuring an interesting mix of artists, performers, designers and musicians. They all share a historic building designed by Newcastle's most important architect, John Dobson (1787–1865), who also designed Grey St and Central Station in the neoclassical style. As it's a working studio you can't just wander in, but there are regular exhibitions and open days; check the website for details.

GATESHEAD

You probably didn't realise that the bit of Newcastle south of the Tyne is the 'town' of Gateshead, but local authorities are going to great lengths to put it right, even promoting the whole kit-and-caboodle-on-Tyne as 'NewcastleGateshead', a clumsy piece of marketing indeed.

FREE BALTIC – Centre for
Contemporary Art   ART MUSEUM
(www.balticmill.com; Gateshead Quays; ⊙10am-6pm Wed-Mon, from 10.30am Tue) Once a huge, dirty, yellow grain store overlooking the Tyne, BALTIC is now a huge, dirty, yellow art gallery to rival London's Tate Modern. Unlike the Tate, there are no permanent exhibitions here, but the constantly rotating shows feature the work and installations of some of contemporary art's biggest show-stoppers. The complex has artists in residence, a performance space, a cinema, a bar, a spectacular rooftop restaurant (you'll need to book) and a ground-floor restaurant with riverside

tables. There's also a viewing box for a fine Tyne vista.

🛏 Sleeping

Although the number of city-centre accommodation options is on the increase, they are still generally restricted to the chain variety – either budget or business – that caters conveniently to the party people and business folk that make up the majority of Newcastle's overnight guests. Most of the other accommodations are in the handsome northern suburb of Jesmond, where the forces of gentrification and student power fight it out for territory; Jesmond's main drag, Osborne Rd, is lined with all kinds of bed types as well as bars and restaurants, making it a strong rival with the city centre for the late-night party scene. As the city is a major business destination, most places drop their prices for Friday and Saturday nights.

CITY CENTRE

Hotel Indigo   HOTEL **££**
(☑0191-300 9222; www.hotelindigonewcastle.co.uk; 2-8 Fenkle St; r from £99) Brand new for summer 2012 is this edition of the excellent boutique chain, offering clean lines and pristine rooms equipped with all the mod cons, including rainfall showers and a 'media station' (which really means somewhere to charge and play your iGear). Downstairs is the chain's partner restaurant, Marco Pierre White Steakhouse & Grill.

Greystreethotel   HOTEL **££**
(☑0191-230 6777; www.greystreethotel.com; 2-12 Grey St; r from £99; P) A bit of designer polish along the classiest street in the city centre has been long overdue: the rooms here are gorgeous if a tad poky, all cluttered up with flatscreen TVs, big beds and handsome modern furnishings.

Malmaison   HOTEL **£££**
(☑0191-245 5000; www.malmaison.com; Quayside; r/ste from £99/189; P @ �🕸) The affectedly stylish Malmaison touch has been applied to this former warehouse with considerable success, even down to the French-speaking lifts. Big beds, sleek lighting and designer furniture embellish the bouncy boudoirs and slick chambers.

Backpackers Newcastle   HOSTEL **£**
(☑0191-340 7334; www.backpackersnewcastle.com; 262 Westgate Rd; dm from £17.95; 🕸) This clean, well-run budget flophouse has just 26

beds lending it a bit more of a backpacker vibe than its competitors in the city. Bike storage, a kitchen, a big games room, power-showers and a mild design feel make this a great option on the Tyne.

JESMOND

The shabby-chic suburb of Jesmond is the place to head for budget and midrange accommodation. Catch the Metro to Jesmond or West Jesmond, or catch bus 80A from near Central Station or the 38 from Westgate Rd.

Jesmond Dene House · HOTEL £££
(☑0191-212 3000; www.jesmonddenehouse.co.uk; Jesmond Dene Rd; s/d/ste from £85/120/180; **P@�**) This exquisite property is the perfect marriage between traditional styles and modern luxury. The large, gorgeous bedrooms are furnished in a modern interpretation of the Arts and Crafts style and are bedecked with all manner of technological goodies (flatscreen digital TVs, digital radios) and wonderful bathrooms complete with underfloor heating. The restaurant is not bad either.

Avenue · B&B ££
(☑0191-281 1396; www.avenuenewcastle.co.uk; 2 Manor House Rd; s/d £39.50/60) Buried in a sleepy residential area but just a couple of blocks' walk from the action on Osborne Rd, this well-run, family-friendly B&B goes big on busy floral flounce and faux country style.

Newcastle YHA · HOSTEL £
(☑0845-371 9335; www.yha.org.uk; 107 Jesmond Rd; dm from £18.50) This nice, rambling place has small dorms that are generally full, so book in advance. It's close to the Jesmond Metro stop.

Eating

The Geordie palate is pretty refined these days and there are a host of fine dining options in all price categories that make their mark. Of course for many locals, Geordies plus food equals the legendary Greggs (www.greggs.co.uk; ⊙8am-5pm), a fast-food chain that started in Newcastle in 1951 and now has nearly 1600 stores throughout Britain serving cheap and filling cakes, sandwiches, pastries and drinks. There are 15 locations in the city centre.

CITY CENTRE

TOP CHOICE Blackfriars · BRITISH ££
(☑0191-261 5945; www.blackfriarsrestaurant.co.uk; Friars St; mains £12-21; ⊙lunch & dinner Mon-Sat, lunch Sun) The city centre's top eatery is housed in a 12th-century friary, where chef Troy Terrington serves up a cuisine described as 'modern medieval': beautifully presented, hearty fare sourced locally (check the tablemat map for the provenance of your bream, woodpigeon or roast suckling pygge). Everything else is made from scratch on site, including breads, pastries, ice creams and sausages. Bookings are recommended.

Oldfields · BRITISH ££
(www.oldfieldsrealfood.co.uk; Milburn House, Dean St; mains around £16; ⊙lunch & dinner Mon-Sat, lunch Sun) Oldfields' tasty trade is top-notch, no-nonsense British gourmet fare, using locally sourced ingredients wherever possible. Tuck into rich and satisfying dishes such as Durham rabbit and crayfish pie, mutton hotpot and Eccles cake with custard in the circular wood-panelled dining room, before finishing off with a shot of Wylam gin or a locally brewed ale.

The Broad Chare · GASTROPUB ££
(☑0191-211 2144; www.thebroadchare.co.uk; 25 Broad Chare; mains £11; ⊙lunch & dinner Mon-Sat, lunch Sun) Classic English pub grub – the grilled pork chop with black pudding and cider sauce is divine – and superb cask ales make this gastropub one of the best spots in town for a bite to eat. The Michelin people agreed, and stuck it into their good-pub guide. Recommended.

JESMOND
Jesmond Dene House · REGIONAL CUISINE £££
(☑0191-212 5555; www.jesmonddenehouse.co.uk; Jesmond Dene Rd; mains £14-40) Head chef Pierre Rigothier is the architect of an exquisite menu heavily influenced by the northeast – venison from County Durham, oysters from Lindisfarne and the freshest herbs plucked straight from the garden – all infused with a touch of French sophistication. The result is a gourmet delight and one of the best dining experiences in the northeast.

Pizzeria Francesca · PIZZERIA ££
(134 Manor House Rd; pizzas & pastas £5, other mains £7-15; ⊙Mon-Sat) One of the northeast's best pizza and pasta joints, this chaotic, friendly place is how all Italian restaurants should be. Excitable, happy waiters and

GAY & LESBIAN NEWCASTLE

Newcastle's gay scene is pretty dynamic, with its hub at the 'Pink Triangle' formed by Waterloo, Neville and Collingwood Sts, but stretching as far south as Scotswood Rd. There are plenty of gay bars in the area and a few great clubs.

Camp David (8-10 Westmorland Rd) Mixed bar as trendy with straights as it is with the gay community.

Loft (10a Scotswood Rd) Loud, proud and completely cheesy, this 1st-floor club is open seven nights a week from 11pm.

Powerhouse Nightclub (www.clubph .co.uk; 9-19 Westmorland Rd) Newcastle's brashest queer nightclub, with flashing lights, video screens and lots of suggestive posing.

huge portions of pizza and pasta keep them queuing at the door – get in line and wait because you can't book in advance.

 Drinking

While it's no secret that Geordies love a night on the razzle, the nightlife beyond the coloured cocktails of Bigg Market, the (not so) legendary epicentre of Newcastle's OTT nightlife (just south of Newgate St), is infinitely more interesting and less sloppy. The Ouseburn attracts a mellower crowd, and the western end of Neville St has a decent mix of great bars and is also home to the best of the gay scene.

CITY CENTRE

Centurion Bar   BAR
(Central Station) The former first-class waiting room at Central Station is ideal for a pre-club drink in style or a pre-train brew on the hop. The exquisitely ornate Victorian tile decoration reaching from floor to ceiling is said to be worth £4 million. There's an adjoining cafe and deli platform-side.

Crown Posada   PUB
(31 The Side) An unspoilt, real-ale pub that is a favourite with more seasoned drinkers, be they the after-work or instead-of-work crowd.

Trent House   PUB
(1-2 Leazes Lane) The wall has a simple message: 'Drink Beer. Be Sincere.' This simply unique place is one of the best bars in town because it is all about an ethos rather than a look. Totally relaxed and utterly devoid of pretentiousness, it is an old-school boozer that out-cools every other bar because it isn't trying to. Run by the same folks behind the superb World Headquarters club.

OUSEBURN VALLEY

Cumberland Arms   PUB
(off Byker Bank, Ouseburn) Sitting on a hill at the top of the Ouseburn, this 19th-century bar has a sensational selection of ales and ciders as well as a range of Northumberland meads. There's a terrace outside, where you can read a book from the Bring One, Borrow One library inside.

☆ Entertainment

Are you up for it? You'd better be, because Newcastle's nightlife doesn't mess about. There is action beyond the club scene – you'll just have to wade through a sea of staggering, glassy-eyed clubbers to get to it.

The Crack (www.thecrackmagazine.com) is a free monthly magazine available from clubs, tourist offices and some hotels containing comprehensive club, theatre, music and cinema listings for the northeast's nightlife hotspots.

Nightclubs

Digital   CLUB
(www.yourfutureisdigital.com; Times Sq) A two-floored cathedral to dance music, this mega-club was voted one of the top 20 clubs in the world by DJ Magazine – thanks to the best sound system you're ever likely to hear. Mondays are 'Born in the '80s' nights, Thursdays are the unmissable 'Stonelove' Indie nights and Saturdays are pure 'Love'.

World Headquarters   CLUB
(www.welovewhq.com; Curtis Mayfield House, Carliol Sq) Dedicated to the genius of black music in all its guises – funk, rare groove, dancefloor jazz, northern soul, genuine R&B, lush disco, proper house and reggae – this fabulous club is strictly for true believers, and judging from the numbers, there are thousands of them.

Cinemas

Tyneside Cinema   CINEMA
(www.tynesidecinema.co.uk; Pilgrim St) Opened in 1937 as Newcastle's first newsreel cinema,

this period picture house, all plush red-velvet seats and swish art-deco design, screens a blend of mainstream and offbeat movies as well as archive British Pathé films (11.30am; free). Free guided tours of the building (one hour) run on Tuesday, Wednesday, Friday and Saturday at 11.15am.

Theatre

Theatre Royal THEATRE
(08448-112121; www.theatreroyal.co.uk; 100 Grey St) The winter home of the Royal Shakespeare Company is full of Victorian splendour and has an excellent program of drama.

Live Music

Sage Gateshead MUSIC VENUE
(0191-443 4666; www.thesagegateshead.org; Gateshead Quays) Norman Foster's magnificent chrome-and-glass horizontal bottle distracts most visitors who come to gape and wander, but if you stay long enough you'll hear some excellent live music, from folk to classical orchestras. It is the home of the Northern Sinfonia and Folkworks.

Head of Steam @ the Cluny MUSIC VENUE
(0191-230 4474; www.headofsteam.co.uk; 36 Lime St) This is one of the best-known spots in town to hear live music, attracting all kinds of performers, from experimental prog-rock heads to up-and-coming pop goddesses. Touring acts and local talent fill the bill every night of the week.

Sport

Newcastle United Football Club FOOTBALL
(NUFC; www.nufc.co.uk) NUFC is more than just a football team: it is the collective expression of Geordie hope and pride as well as the release for decades of economic, social and sporting frustration. The club's fabulous ground, St James' Park (Strawberry Pl), is always packed, but you can get a stadium tour (0844-372 1892; adult/child £10/7; 11am & 1.30pm daily, plus 4 hours before kick-off on match days) of the place, including the dugout and changing rooms. Match tickets go on public sale about two weeks before a game or you can try the stadium on the day, but there's no chance for big matches, such as those against arch-rivals Sunderland.

ⓘ Information

City library (33 New Bridge St W; 8.30am-8pm Mon-Thu, to 5.30pm Fri & Sat) Free internet access at Newcastle's stomping new library building. Bring ID.

Newcastle General Hospital (0191-233 6161; Westgate Rd) Has an Accident and Emergency unit.

Police station (03456-043043; cnr Pilgrim & Market Sts)

Post office (36 Northumberland St; 9am-5.30pm Mon-Sat) On the 2nd floor of WH Smith. Has a bureau de change.

Tourist office main branch (0191-277 8000; www.visitnewcastlegateshead.com; Central Arcade, Market St; 9.30am-5.30pm Mon-Sat, 10am-4pm Sun)

ⓘ Getting There & Away

Air

Newcastle International Airport (0871-882 1121; www.newcastleairport.com) Seven miles north of the city off the A696, the airport has direct services to many UK and European cities as well as long-haul flights to Dubai. Tour operators fly charters to the Americas and Africa.

Bus

Local and regional buses leave from Haymarket or Eldon Sq bus stations. National Express buses arrive and depart from the coach station on St James Blvd. For local buses around the northeast, the excellent-value Explorer North East ticket (£8) is valid on most services.

Berwick-upon-Tweed Bus 501/505; £15.30; two hours, five daily

Edinburgh National Express; £17.50, three hours, three daily

London National Express/Megabus; £10–27, seven hours, nine daily

Manchester National Express; £19.50, five hours, five daily

Train

Newcastle is on the main rail line between London and Edinburgh and is the starting point of the scenic Tyne Valley Line west to Carlisle.

Alnmouth (for bus connections to Alnwick) £7.70, 25 minutes, hourly

Berwick £21.50, 45 minutes, hourly

Carlisle £14.50, 1½ hours, hourly

Edinburgh £32, 1½ hours, half-hourly

London King's Cross £105, three hours, half-hourly

York £23.50, one hour, every 20 minutes

ⓘ Getting Around

To/From the Airport

The airport is linked to town by the Metro (£2.90, 20 minutes, every 15 minutes).

Public Transport

There's a large bus network, but the best means of getting around is the excellent Metro, with fares from £1.40. Several saver passes are also available. The tourist office can supply you with route plans for the bus and Metro networks.

The DaySaver (£4.80; £3.90 after 9am) gives unlimited Metro travel for one day, and the Day-Rover (adult/child £6.50/3.50) gives unlimited travel on all modes of transport in Tyne and Wear for one day.

Taxi

On weekend nights taxis can be as rare as covered flesh; try **Noda Taxis** (☑0191-222 1888), which has a kiosk outside the entrance to Central Station.

AROUND NEWCASTLE

If you're in town for a longer stretch there's plenty to keep you entertained even beyond the city limits. All of the following are easily reached on the city's superb public transport system.

Angel of the North

Nicknamed the Gateshead Flasher, this extraordinary 200-tonne, rust-coloured human frame with wings, more soberly known as the *Angel of the North*, has been looming over A1(M) about 5 miles south of Newcastle since 1998. At 20m high and with a wingspan wider than a Boeing 767, Antony Gormley's most successful work is the UK's largest sculpture and the most viewed piece of public art in the country, although Mark Wallinger's *White Horse* in Kent may pinch both titles over the next decade. Buses 21 and 22 from Eldon Sq will take you there.

Tynemouth

One of the most popular Geordie days out is to this handsome seaside resort 6 miles east of Newcastle. Besides being the mouth of the Tyne, this is one of the best surf spots in England, with great all-year breaks off the immense, crescent-shaped Blue Flag beach. The town even occasionally hosts the National Surfing Championships (www.british surfchamps.co.uk).

For all your surfing needs, including lessons, call into the Tynemouth Surf Company (☑0191-258 2496; www.tynemouthsurf. co.uk; Grand Pde), which provides two-hour group lessons for £25 per person or one-hour individual lessons for the same price.

If riding nippy surf is not your thing, the town's other main draw is the 11th-century ruins of Tynemouth Priory (EH; adult/child £5/2.50; ◷10am-5pm Apr-Sep), built by Benedictine monks on a strategic bluff above the mouth of the Tyne, but ransacked during the Dissolution in 1539. The military took over for four centuries, only leaving in 1960, and today the skeletal remains of the priory church sit alongside old military installations, their guns aimed out to sea at an enemy that never came.

From Newcastle city centre take the Metro to Tynemouth or bus 306 from the Haymarket station.

Segedunum

The last strong post of Hadrian's Wall was the fort of Segedunum (www.twmuseums.org .uk; adult/child £4.95/free; ◷10am-5pm Apr-Oct), 6 miles east of Newcastle at Wallsend. Beneath the 35m-high tower, which you can climb for some terrific views, is an absorbing site that includes a reconstructed Roman bathhouse (with steaming pools and frescoes) and a fascinating museum that gives visitors a well-rounded picture of life during Roman times.

Wallsend is located on the Metro line from Newcastle.

COUNTY DURHAM

Spread out across the lonely, rabbit-inhabited North Pennines and the gentle ochre hills of Teesdale, County Durham's star attraction is its county town – home to a magnificent cathedral that is easily one of England's finest. The cathedral and adjoining castle were the seat of the once powerful prince bishops, rulers since 1081 of the Palatinate of Durham, a political entity created by William the Conqueror as a bulwark against rowdy Saxons and uppity Scots.

In more recent times, the county was at the heart of the region's coal-mining industry, a brutal business that saw the last pit close in 1984 and left the landscape with some fast-dissolving yet evocative scarring.

Durham

POP 42,940

Consider the setting: England's most beautiful Romanesque cathedral, a masterpiece of Norman architecture and a resplendent monument to the country's ecclesiastical history; a huge castle; and, surrounding them both, a cobweb of cobbled streets usually full of upper-crust students attending Durham's other big pull, England's third university of choice (after Oxford and Cambridge). Welcome to Durham.

Durham is unquestionably beautiful, but once you've visited the cathedral and walked the old town looking for the best views there isn't much else to do; a day trip from Newcastle or an overnight stop on your way to explore the rest of the county is the best way to see the city of the prince bishops.

◉ Sights

Durham Cathedral CATHEDRAL
(www.durhamcathedral.co.uk; donation requested, guided tours adult/child £4/free; ☉7.30am-6pm, tours 10.30am, 11am & 2pm Mon-Sat, Evensong 5.15pm Mon-Sat & 3.30pm Sun) This exquisite cathedral is the definitive structure of the Anglo-Norman Romanesque style, one of the world's greatest places of worship and, since 1986, a Unesco World Heritage Site.

Beyond the main door – and the famous (and much-reproduced) Sanctuary Knocker, which medieval felons would strike to gain 37 days asylum within the cathedral before standing trial or leaving the country – is a spectacular interior. This was the first

European cathedral to be roofed with stone-ribbed vaulting, which upheld the heavy stone roof and made it possible to build pointed transverse arches – the first in England, and a great architectural achievement. The central tower dates from 1262, but was damaged in a fire caused by lightning in 1429 and unsatisfactorily patched up until it was entirely rebuilt in 1470. The western towers were added in 1217–26.

One of the cathedral's most beautiful parts is the Galilee Chapel, dating from 1175, whose northern side features rare surviving examples of 12th-century wall painting (thought to feature portraits of Sts Cuthbert and Oswald). The chapel also contains the tomb of the Venerable Bede, the 8th-century Northumbrian monk turned historian: his *Ecclesiastical History of the English People* is still the prime source of information on the development of early Christian Britain. Among other things, Bede introduced the numbering of years from the birth of Jesus. He was first buried at Jarrow, but in 1022 a miscreant monk stole his remains and brought them here.

Other highlights include the 14th-century Bishop's Throne; the beautiful stone Neville Screen (1372–80), which separates the high altar from St Cuthbert's tomb; and the mostly 19th-century Cloisters where you'll find the Monk's Dormitory, now a library of 30,000 books and displaying Anglo-Saxon carved stones. There are audiovisual displays on the building of the cathedral and the life of St Cuthbert. Also worthwhile are the guided tours and a visit during Evensong services.

WORTH A TRIP

BEAMISH OPEN-AIR MUSEUM

County Durham's greatest attraction is Beamish (www.beamish.org.uk; adult/child £16/10; ☉10am-5pm Apr-Oct), a living, breathing, working museum that offers a fabulous, warts-and-all portrait of industrial life in the northeast during the 19th and 20th centuries. Instructive and lots of fun to boot, this huge museum spread over 121 hectares will appeal to all ages.

You can go underground, explore mine heads, a working farm, a school, a dentist and a pub, and marvel at how every cramped pit cottage seemed to find room for a piano. Don't miss a ride behind an 1815 Steam Elephant locomotive or a replica of Stephenson's *Locomotion No 1*.

Allow at least three hours to do the place justice. Many elements (such as the railway) aren't open in the winter (when the admission price is lower); check the website for details.

Beamish is about 8 miles northwest of Durham. Buses 28 from Newcastle (one hour, half-hourly) and 720 from Durham (30 minutes, hourly) operate to the museum.

Durham

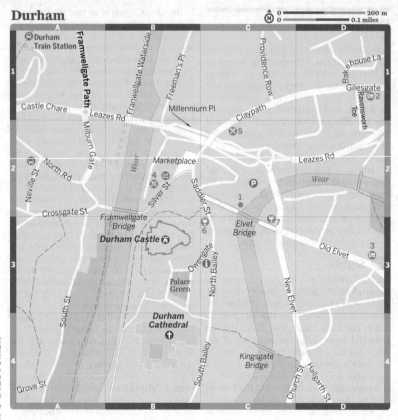

The **tower** (£5) provides show-stopping vistas – if you climb 325 steps to enjoy them.

Durham Castle   CASTLE
(www.dur.ac.uk; admission by guided tour only, adult/child £5/3.50; ⊙tours 2pm, 3pm & 4pm term time, 10am, 11am & noon during university holidays) Built as a standard motte-and-bailey fort in 1072, Durham Castle was the prince bishops' home until 1837, when it became the first college of the newly formed University of Durham. It remains a university hall, and you can stay here.

The castle has been much altered over the centuries, as each successive prince bishop sought to put his particular imprint on the place, but heavy restoration and reconstruction were necessary anyway as the castle is built of soft stone on soft ground. Highlights of the 45-minute tour include the groaning 17th-century **Black Staircase**, the 16th-century and the beautifully preserved Norman chapel (1080).

Activities

Prince Bishop River Cruiser
BOAT TOURS

(☑0191-386 9525; www.princebishoprc.co.uk; Elvet Bridge; adult/child £7/4; ⊘cruises 12.30pm, 2pm & 3pm Jun-Sep) One-hour cruises on the Wear.

Browns Boathouse
BOAT HIRE

(☑0191-386 3779; per hr per person £5) Rowing boats can be hired from below Elvet Bridge.

🛏 Sleeping

TOP CHOICE Gadds Townhouse
BOUTIQUE HOTEL £££

(☑0191-384 1037; www.gaddstownhouse.com; 34 Old Elvet; d from £99) Possibly the northeast's most bizarre digs, the 11 rooms at this fun place leave few indifferent. Each room has a theme, with 'Le Jardin' featuring a shed and garden furniture, the 'Premiere' boasting a huge projection screen and popcorn machine, and the 'Edwardian Express' recreating a night in a yesteryear sleeper compartment. The most 'normal' room is the Garden Lodge, complete with outdoor tub and underfloor heating. The restaurant is superb and some rooms have cathedral views.

Cathedral View
B&B ££

(☑0191-386 9566; www.cathedralview.com; 212 Gilesgate; s/d from £70/85) This anonymous Georgian house has no sign, but inside it does exactly what it says on the tin. Six large rooms decorated with lots of cushions and coordinated bed linen and window dressings make up the numbers, but it's the two at the back that are worth the fuss: the views of the cathedral are fantastic. Breakfast is cooked to order and served on the vista-rich terrace or in the dining room lined with prints by Beryl Cook, the amateur painter who became a national sensation with colourful paintings of larger-than-life figures.

Eating

Oldfields
BRITISH ££

(www.oldfieldsrealfood.co.uk; 18 Claypath; mains £12-19) With strictly seasonal menus that use only local or organic ingredients sourced within a 60-mile radius of Durham, this award-winning restaurant is one of the county's finest, though it's not quite as good as its Newcastle sister. With dishes such as smoked haddock, pan haggerty and wild boar pie on the menu, all served in the old boardroom of the former HQ of the Durham Gas Company (1881), it's still the best meal in town.

Cottons
CAFE £

(32 Silver St; snacks £2.50-5; ⊘9.30am-5.30pm Mon-Sat, 11am-4.30 Sun) Down an inconspicuous flight of steps two doors along from the post office, this junk shop/art gallery/tearoom hides in a brick-and-stone cellar where a range of teas plus sandwiches, jacket potatoes and cakes are served to in-the-know punters.

🍷 Drinking

Shakespeare
PUB

(63 Saddler St) As authentic a traditional bar as you're likely to find in these parts, this is the perfect locals' boozer, complete with dartboard and cosy snugs. Needless to say, the selection of beers and spirits is terrific, and students love it too.

Swan & Three Cygnets
PUB

(Elvet Bridge) This high-ceilinged riverside pub with courtyard tables overlooks the river. It also serves some pretty good food (mains around £8) – usually fancy versions of standard bar fare such as bangers and mash.

ℹ Information

Post office (Silver St)

Public library (Millennium Pl; ⊘9.30am-7pm Mon-Fri, 9am-5pm Sat, 10.30am-4pm Sun) Bring ID to surf the web.

Tourist office (www.thisisdurham.com; Owen Gate; ⊘9.30am-5.30pm Mon-Sat, 11am-4pm Sun) Small but helpful, with all the usual tourist information.

ℹ Getting There & Away

Bus

Darlington Bus 5, 7; one hour, four hourly

London National Express; £29.80, 6½ hours, four daily

Newcastle Bus 21, 44, X2, X41; one hour to 1¾ hours, several hourly

Train

The East Coast Main Line arches over Durham meaning speedy connections to many destinations across the country.

Edinburgh £50.30, two hours, hourly

London King's Cross £103.60, three hours, hourly

Newcastle £5.20, 15 minutes, five hourly

York £21.90, one hour, four hourly

RABY CASTLE

About 7 miles northeast of Barnard Castle is the sprawling, romantic Raby Castle (www.rabycastle.com; adult/child £10/4.50; ☉1-5pm Sun-Wed May, Jun & Sep, Sun-Fri Jul & Aug), a stronghold of the Catholic Neville family until it engaged in some ill-judged plotting (the 'Rising of the North') against the oh-so Protestant Queen Elizabeth in 1569. Most of the interior dates from the 18th and 19th centuries, but the exterior remains true to the original design, built around a courtyard and surrounded by a moat. There are beautiful formal gardens and a deer park. Bus 8 zips between Barnard Castle and Raby (15 minutes, eight daily).

❶ Getting Around

Pratt's (☏0191-386 0700) A trustworthy taxi company.

Barnard Castle

POP 6720

Barnard Castle, or just plain Barney, is anything but: this thoroughly charming market town is a traditionalist's dream, full of antiquarian shops and atmospheric old pubs that serve as a wonderful setting for the town's twin-starred attractions, a daunting ruined castle at its edge and an extraordinary French chateau on its outskirts. If you can drag yourself away, it is also a terrific base for exploring Teesdale and the North Pennines.

◉ Sights

Barnard Castle   CASTLE RUINS
(EH; adult/child £4.40/2.60; ☉10am-6pm Easter-Sep) Partly dismantled in the 16th century, one of northern England's largest castles, built on a cliff above the Tees, still manages to cover more than two very impressive hectares. Founded by Guy de Bailleul and rebuilt around 1150, its occupants spent their time suppressing the locals and fighting off the Scots – on their days off they sat around enjoying the wonderful river views.

Bowes Museum   MUSEUM
(www.thebowesmuseum.org.uk; adult/child £9/free; ☉10am-5pm) About half a mile east of

town stands a Louvre-inspired French chateau containing an extraordinary and wholly unexpected museum. Funded by 19th-century industrialist John Bowes, but largely the brainchild of his Parisienne actress wife Josephine, the museum was built by French architect Jules Pellechet to display a collection the Bowes had travelled the world to assemble. Opened in 1892, this spectacular museum has lavish furniture and paintings by Canaletto, El Greco and Goya as well as 15,000 other objets d'art including 55 paintings by Josephine herself. A new section examines textiles through the ages, with some incredible dresses from the 17th century to the 1970s, while the precious metals exhibition displays clocks, watches and tableware in gold and silver. The museum's star attraction, however, is the marvellous mechanical swan, which performs every day at 2pm. If you miss it or arrive too early, there's now a film showing it in action.

🛏 Sleeping & Eating

Marwood House   B&B ££
(☏01833-637493; www.marwoodhouse.co.uk; 98 Galgate; s/d from £30/60) A handsome Victorian property with tastefully appointed rooms (the owner's tapestries feature in the decor and her homemade biscuits sit on a tray), Marwood House's standout feature is the small fitness room in the basement, complete with a sauna that fits up to four people.

Jersey Farm Country Hotel   HOTEL ££
(☏01833-638223; www.jerseyfarmhotel.co.uk; Darlington Rd; s/d from £72/99; ▣🐾) Another genteel farmhouse conversion, right? Wrong. From the moment you step into the funky reception you know you're not in for the usual frills-and-flowers B&B experience. Although the owners haven't gone the whole design-boutique hog, rooms sport cool retro colour schemes, ultra-sleek bathrooms in several shades of black and gadgets galore. The restaurant is a clean-cut affair. It's a mile east of town just off the A67.

Old Well Inn   HOTEL ££
(☏01833-690130; www.theoldwellinn.co.uk; 21 The Bank; r from £69; 🐾) You won't find larger bedrooms in town than at this old coaching inn, built over a huge well (not visible). Of the 10 rooms, No 9 is the most impressive with its own private entrance, flagstone floors and a bath. The pub has a reputation for excellent, filling pub grub and real ales from Darlington and Yorkshire. The amateur Cas-

tle Players, who perform a different Shakespeare play at the castle every summer, were formed here in early 1980s.

ⓘ Information

Tourist office (☏03000-262626; www.thisis durham.com; Woodleigh, Flatts Rd; ☺9.30am-5pm Mon-Sat, 10am-4pm Sun Easter-Oct) Has information on all the sights.

ⓘ Getting There & Away

Durham Bus 75 and 76 via Darlington; 1½ hours, twice hourly

North Pennines

The North Pennines stretch from western Durham to just short of Hadrian's Wall in the north. In the south is Teesdale, the gently undulating valley of the River Tees; to the north is the much wilder Weardale, carved through by the River Wear. Both dales are marked by ancient quarries and mines – industries that date back to Roman times. The wilds of the North Pennines are also home to the picturesque Derwent and Allen Valleys, north of Weardale.

For online information, check out www.northpennines.org.uk and www.exploretees dale.co.uk.

HADRIAN'S WALL

What exactly have the Romans ever done for us? The aqueducts. Law and order. And this enormous wall, built between AD 122 and 128 to keep 'us' (Romans, subdued Brits) in and 'them' (hairy Pictish barbarians from Scotland) out. Or so the story goes. Hadrian's Wall, named in honour of the emperor who ordered it built, was one of Rome's greatest engineering projects, a spectacular 73-mile testament to ambition and the practical Roman mind. Even today, almost 2000 years after the first stone was laid, the sections that are still standing remain an awe-inspiring sight, proof that when the Romans wanted something done, they just knuckled down and did it.

It wasn't easy. When completed, the mammoth structure ran across the narrow neck of the island, from the Solway Firth in the west almost to the mouth of the Tyne in the east. Every Roman mile (0.95 miles) there was a gateway guarded by a small fort (milecastle) and between each milecastle were two observation turrets. Milecastles are numbered right across the country, starting with Milecastle 0 at Wallsend and ending with Milecastle 80 at Bowness-on-Solway.

A series of forts was developed as bases some distance south (and may predate the wall), and 16 lie astride it. The prime remaining forts on the wall are Cilurnum (Chesters), Vercovicium (Housesteads) and Banna (Birdoswald). The best forts behind the wall are Corstopitum at Corbridge, and Vindolanda, north of Bardon Mill.

Carlisle, in the west, and Newcastle, in the east, are obviously good starting points, but Brampton, Haltwhistle, Hexham and Corbridge all make good bases. The B6318 follows the course of the wall from the outskirts of Newcastle to Birdoswald; from Birdoswald to Carlisle it pays to have a detailed map. The main A69 road and the railway line follow 3 or 4 miles to the south.

Every May there is a spring festival, with lots of recreations of Roman life along the wall (contact tourist offices for details).

🕉 Activities

The Hadrian's Wall Path (www.nationaltrail .co.uk/hadrianswall) is an 84-mile National Trail that runs the length of the wall from Wallsend in the east to Bowness-on-Solway in the west. The entire route should take about seven days on foot, giving plenty of time to explore the rich archaeological heritage along the way. Anthony Burton's *Hadrian's Wall Path – National Trail Guide* (Aurum Press, £12.99), available at most bookshops and tourist offices in the region, is good for history, archaeology and the like, while the *Essential Guide to Hadrian's Wall Path National Trail* (Hadrian's Wall Heritage Ltd, £3.95) by David McGlade is a guide to everyday facilities and services along the walk.

ⓘ Information

Carlisle and Newcastle tourist offices are good places to start gathering information, but there are also tourist offices in Hexham, Haltwhistle, Corbridge and Brampton.

Hadrian's Wall Country (www.hadrians -wall.org) The official portal for the whole of Hadrian's Wall Country. An excellent, easily navigable site.

Hadrian's Wall Information Line (☏01434-322002)

Northumberland National Park visitor centre (☏01434-344396; www.northumberland

Map labels: Melrose, St Boswell's, Selkirk, Kelso, Belford, Kirk Yetholm, Town Yetholm, Morebattle, Wooler, Chatton, Chillingham Castle, Humbleton Hill, SCOTLAND, Jedburgh, Hownam, ROXBURGHSHIRE, The Cheviot (815m), Ingram, Northumberland National Park, Whittingham, Hawick, Bonchester Bridge, Newmill, Teviothead, Byrness, Netherton, Alwinton, Rothbury, Cragside House, Catcleugh Reservoir, Danger Area (MOD Live Firing Range), Rochester, Simonside Hills, Coquet, Deadwater, Border Forest Park, Kielder, Gowanburn, Otterburn, Elsdon, NORTHUMBERLAND, Kielder Water, Falstone, Pennine Way, Newcastleton, Stannersburn, North Tyne, Ridsdale, Kirkharle, Bellingham, Kershopefoot, Wark, Belsay, Catlowdy, Bewcastle, Whygate, Chesters Roman Fort & Museum, Ponteland, Housesteads Roman Fort & Museum, Sewingshields, Chollerford, Low Brunton, Newcastle Airport, CUMBRIA, Roman Army Museum, Once Brewed, Acomb, Corbridge Museum, Kirkcambeck, Corbridge, Birdoswald Roman Fort, Greenhead, Bardon Mill, Haydon Bridge, Hexham, Lanercost Priory, Haltwhistle, Allen Banks, Vindolanda Roman Fort & Museum, Tyne, Brampton, Lambley

nationalpark.org.uk; Once Brewed; ⊙9.30am-5.30pm Apr-Oct) Off the B6318.

ⓘ Getting There & Around

Bus

The AD 122 Hadrian's Wall bus (eight daily, April to October) is a hail-and-ride service that runs between Hexham and Carlisle, with one bus a day starting and ending at Newcastle's Central Station and not all services covering the entire route. Bus 185 zips along the wall the rest of the year (Monday to Saturday only).

West of Hexham the wall runs parallel to the A69, which connects Carlisle and Newcastle. Bus 685 runs along the A69 hourly, passing near the YHA hostels and 2 miles to 3 miles south of the main sites throughout the year.

All these services can be used with the **Hadrian's Wall Rover Ticket** (adult/child one-day £8/5, three-day £16/10), available from bus drivers and tourist offices, where you can also get timetables.

Car & Motorcycle

This is obviously the most convenient method of transport with one fort or garrison usually just a short hop from the next. Parking costs £3 and the ticket is valid at all other sites along the wall.

Train

The railway line between Newcastle and Carlisle (Tyne Valley Line) has stations at Corbridge, Hexham, Haydon Bridge, Bardon Mill, Haltwhistle and Brampton. Trains run hourly but not all services stop at all stations.

Corbridge

POP 2800

The mellow commuter town of Corbridge is a handsome spot above a green-banked curve in the Tyne, its shady, cobbled streets lined with old-fashioned shops. Folks have lived here since Saxon times when there was a substantial monastery, while many of the buildings feature stones nicked from nearby Corstopitum.

Sights

Corbridge Roman Site & Museum
ROMAN GARRISON

(EH; adult/child £4.50/3; ⏰10am-5.30pm Apr-Sep) What's left of the Roman garrison town of Corstopitum lies about half a mile west of Market Pl on Dere St, once the main road from York to Scotland. It is the oldest fortified site in the area, predating the wall itself by some 40 years, when it was used by troops launching retaliation raids into Scotland. Most of what you see here, though, dates from around AD 200, when the fort had developed into a civilian settlement and was the main base along the wall.

You get a sense of the domestic heart of the town from the visible remains, and the Corbridge Museum displays Roman sculpture and carvings, including the amazing 3rd-century Corbridge Lion.

Sleeping & Eating

2 The Crofts
B&B ££

(☎01434-633046; www.2thecrofts.co.uk; B6530; r from £65; 🅿) By far the best place in town to drop your pack, this secluded B&B occupies a beautiful period home around half a mile's walk east of the town centre on Newcastle Rd. The three high-ceilinged, spacious rooms are all en suite and one has impressive carved wardrobes said to be from the *Olympic*, sister ship to the *Titanic*. The energetic owners cook a mean breakfast.

The Black Bull
BRITISH ££

(Middle St; mains £8-16) A menu of British comfort food, such as beef burgers, fish in beer batter and slow-cooked New Zealand lamb, and a series of low-ceilinged, atmospheric dining rooms, make this restaurant-tavern a fine spot to fill the hole.

Information

Tourist office (☎01434-632815; www.thisis corbridge.co.uk; Hill St; ⏰10am-4.30pm Mon-Sat Easter-Oct) Occupies a corner of the library.

Getting There & Away

Bus 685 between Newcastle and Carlisle comes through Corbridge, as does the half-hourly 602 from Newcastle to Hexham, where you can connect with the Hadrian's Wall bus AD 122. Corbridge is also on the Newcastle–Carlisle railway line.

Hexham

POP 10,690

Bustling Hexham is a handsome if somewhat scuffed little market town long famed for its grand Augustinian abbey. Its cobbled alleyways boast more shops and amenities than any other wall town between Carlisle and Newcastle, making it a good place to take on provisions if you're heading out into the windswept wilds beyond.

Sights

Hexham Abbey
MONASTERY

(www.hexhamabbey.org.uk; ⏰9.30am-5pm, Saxon crypt 11am-3.30pm) Dominating tiny Market Pl, Hexham's stately abbey is a marvellous example of Early English architecture. It cleverly escaped the Dissolution of 1537 by rebranding as Hexham's parish church, a role it still has today. The highlight is the 7th-century Saxon crypt, the only surviving element of St Wilifrid's Church, built with inscribed stones from Corstopitum in 674.

Old Gaol
HISTORIC BUILDING

(adult/child £3.95/2.10; ⏰11am-4.30pm Tue-Sat) This strapping stone structure was completed in 1333 as England's first purpose-built prison; today its four floors tell the history of the jail in all its gruesome glory. The history of the Border Reivers – a group of clans who fought, kidnapped, blackmailed and killed each other in an effort to exercise control over a lawless tract of land along the Anglo-Scottish border throughout the 16th century – is also retold, along with tales of the punishments handed out in the prison.

Sleeping & Eating

Hallbank Guest House
B&B ££

(☎01434-605567; www.hallbankguesthouse.com; Hallgate; s/d from £60/80; 🅿🛜) Behind the Old Gaol is this fine Edwardian house with eight stylishly furnished rooms, which combine period elegance with flatscreen TVs and huge beds. It's very popular so book ahead.

TOP CHOICE Bouchon Bistrot
FRENCH ££

(www.bouchonbistrot.co.uk; 4-6 Gilesgate; mains £12-19; ⏰Tue-Sat) Hexham may be an unlikely setting for some true fine dining, but this Gallic affair has an enviable reputation and was voted the UK's best local French restaurant in 2010 by Channel 4 viewers of Gordon Ramsay's *The F Word*. Country-style menus are reassuringly brief, ingredients as

Hadrian's Wall

ROME'S FINAL FRONTIER

Of all Britain's Roman ruins, Emperor Hadrian's 2nd-century wall, cutting across northern England from the Irish Sea to the North Sea, is by far the most spectacular; Unesco awarded it world cultural heritage status in 1987.

We've picked out the highlights, one of which is the prime remaining Roman fort on the wall, Housesteads, which we've reconstructed here.

Housesteads' granaries
Nothing like the clever underground ventilation system, which kept vital supplies of grain dry in Northumberland's damp and drizzly climate, would be seen again in these parts for 1500 years.

Milecastle

North Gate

Interval Tower

Birdoswald Roman Fort
Explore the longest intact stretch of the wall, scramble over the remains of a large fort then head indoors to wonder at a full-scale model of the wall at its zenith. Great fun for the kids.

Housesteads Roman Fort
See Illustration Right

Chesters Roman Fort
Built to keep watch over a bridge spanning the River North Tyne, Britain's best-preserved Roman cavalry fort has a terrific bathhouse, essential if you have months of nippy northern winter ahead.

Hexham Abbey
This may be the finest non-Roman sight near Hadrian's Wall, but the 7th-century parts of this magnificent church were built with stone quarried by the Romans for use in their forts.

Housesteads' hospital
Operations performed at the hospital would have been surprisingly effective, even without anaesthetics; religious rituals and prayers to Aesculapius, the Roman god of healing, were possibly less helpful for a hernia or appendicitis.

Map labels:
0 — 10 km
0 — 5 miles
Birdoswald Roman Fort
Irthing
Roman Army Museum
Harrow Scar Milecastle
Greenhead
Once Brewed
Haltwhistle
South Tyne
Bardon Mill
Sewingshields
Housesteads Roman Fort & Museum
B6318
Vindolanda Roman Fort & Museum
Hadrian's Wall
Chesters Roman Fort & Museum
Chollerford
Low Brunton
Acomb
Haydon Bridge
Hexham
Brampton

Housesteads' latrines
Communal toilets were the norm in Roman times and Housesteads' are remarkably well preserved – fortunately no traces remain of the vinegar-soaked sponges that were used instead of toilet paper.

QUICK WALL FACTS & FIGURES

» **Latin name** Vallum Aelium
» **Length** 73.5 miles (80 Roman miles)
» **Construction date** AD 122–128
» **Manpower for construction**
Three legions (around 16,000 men)
» **Features** at least 16 forts, 80 milecastles, 160 turrets
» **Did you know** Hadrian's wasn't the only wall in Britain – the Antonine Wall was built across what is now central Scotland in the AD 140s, but it was abandoned soon after

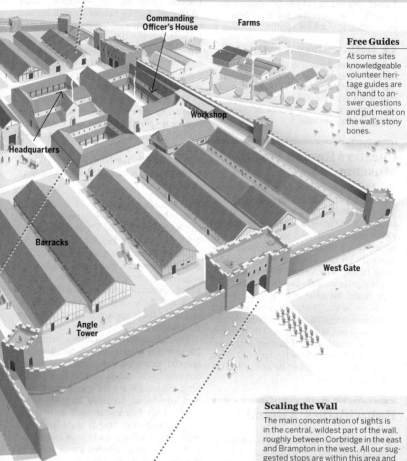

Commanding Officer's House

Farms

Free Guides
At some sites knowledgeable volunteer heritage guides are on hand to answer questions and put meat on the wall's stony bones.

Workshop

Headquarters

Barracks

West Gate

Angle Tower

Housesteads' gatehouses
Unusually at Housesteads neither of the gates faces the enemy, as was the norm at a Roman fort – builders aligned them east-west. Ruts worn by cart wheels are still visible in the stone.

Scaling the Wall

The main concentration of sights is in the central, wildest part of the wall, roughly between Corbridge in the east and Brampton in the west. All our suggested stops are within this area and follow an east-west route. The easiest way to travel is by car, scooting along the B6318, but special bus AD122 will also get you there. Hiking along the designated Hadrian's Wall Path (84 miles) allows you to appreciate the achievement up close.

fresh as nature can provide and the wine list an elite selection of champagnes, reds and whites. The owners have also created a cosy, understated interior in which to enjoy all of the above.

Dipton Mill PUB £

(Dipton Mill Rd; mains £6-10) This superb country pub is 2 miles out on the road to Blanchland, among woodland and by a river. It offers real ploughman's lunches and real ale by real fires – really.

❶ Information

Tourist office (☑01434-652220; Wentworth Car Park; ☉9am-6pm Mon-Sat, 10am-5pm Sun) Northeast of the town centre.

❶ Getting There & Away

Bus 685 between Newcastle and Carlisle comes through Hexham hourly; the AD 122 Hadrian's Wall bus and the winter-service 185 connect with other towns along the wall. Hexham is on the scenic railway line between Newcastle (twice hourly) and Carlisle (hourly).

Chesters Roman Fort & Museum

The best-preserved remains of a Roman cavalry fort in England are at Chesters (EH; ☑01434-681379; Chollerford; adult/child £4.80/2.40; ☉10am-6pm Apr-Sep), set among idyllic green woods and meadows near the village of Chollerford and originally constructed to house a unit of troops from Asturias in northern Spain. They include part of a bridge (beautifully constructed and best appreciated from the eastern bank) across the River North Tyne, four well-preserved gatehouses, an extraordinary bathhouse and an underfloor heating system. The museum has a large collection of Roman sculpture. Take bus 880 or 882 from Hexham (5.5 miles away); it is also on the route of the AD 122 Hadrian's Wall bus.

Haltwhistle & Around

POP 3810

It's one of the more important debates in contemporary Britain: where exactly is the centre of the country? The residents of Haltwhistle, basically one long street just north of the A69, claim that they're the ones. But then so do the folks in Dunsop Bridge, 71 miles to the south. Will we ever know the

truth? In the meantime, Haltwhistle is the spot to get some cash and load up on gear and groceries. Thursday is market day.

◉ Sights

Vindolanda Roman Fort & Museum ROMAN FORT, MUSEUM

(www.vindolanda.com; adult/child £6.25/3.75, with Roman Army Museum £9.50/5.25; ☉10am-6pm Apr-Sep, to 5pm Feb, Mar & Oct) The extensive site of Vindolanda offers a fascinating glimpse into the daily life of a Roman garrison town. The time-capsule museum displays leather sandals, signature Roman toothbrush-flourish helmet decorations, and numerous writing tablets recently returned from the British Library. These include a student's marked work ('sloppy'), and a parent's note with a present of socks and underpants (things haven't changed – in this climate you can never have too many).

The museum is just one part of this large, extensively excavated site, which includes impressive parts of the fort and town (excavations continue) and reconstructed turrets and temple.

It's 1.5 miles north of Bardon Mill between the A69 and B6318 and a mile from Once Brewed.

Housesteads Roman Fort & Museum ROMAN FORT, MUSEUM

(EH; adult/child £6/3.60; ☉10am-6pm Apr-Sep) The wall's most dramatic site – and the best-preserved Roman fort in the whole country – is at Housesteads. From here, high on a ridge and covering 2 hectares, you can survey the moors of Northumberland National Park, and the snaking wall, with a sense of awe at the landscape and the aura of the Roman lookouts.

The substantial foundations bring fort life alive. The remains include an impressive hospital, granaries with a carefully worked out ventilation system and barrack blocks. Most memorable are the spectacularly situated communal flushable latrines, which summon up Romans at their most mundane. Information boards show what the individual buildings would have looked like in their heyday and there's a scale model of the entire fort in the small museum at the ticket office.

Housesteads is 2.5 miles north of Bardon Mill on the B6318, and about 6 miles from Haltwhistle.

Roman Army Museum
MUSEUM

(www.vindolanda.com; adult/child £5/2.75, with Vindolanda £9.50/5.25; ⊙10am-6pm) A mile northeast of Greenhead, near Walltown Crags, this kid-pleasing museum provides lots of colourful background detail to wall life, such as how the soldiers spent their R&R time in this lonely outpost of the empire.

Birdoswald Roman Fort
ROMAN FORT

(EH; ☑016977-47602; adult/child £5.20/3.10; ⊙10am-5.30pm Mar-Oct) *Technically* in Cumbria, the remains of this once-formidable fort on an escarpment overlooking the beautiful Irthing Gorge are on a minor road off the B6318, about 3 miles west of Greenhead; a fine stretch of wall extends from here to Harrow's Scar Milecastle.

Lanercost Priory
PRIORY

(EH; adult/child £3.40/2; ⊙10am-5pm) About 3 miles further west along the A69 from Birdoswald, these peaceful raspberry-coloured ruins are all that remain of a priory founded in 1166 by Augustinian canons. Post-dissolution it became a private house and a priory church was created from the Early English nave. The AD 122 bus drops off at the gate.

🛏 Sleeping

TOP CHOICE Ashcroft
B&B ££

(☑01434-320213; www.ashcroftguesthouse.co.uk; Lanty's Lonnen, Haltwhistle; s/d from £55/85; 🛜) In the world of British B&Bs, things don't get better than this. Picture a large, elegant Edwardian vicarage surrounded by 2 acres of beautifully manicured, layered lawns and gardens from which there are stunning views. Inside, the nine rooms – some with private balconies and terraces – have preposterously high ceilings and are fitted out in an understated style but also contain every gadget 21st-century beings need for survival. The dining room is grander than some snooty hotels and the welcome certainly more genuine. Highly recommended.

Holmhead Guest House
B&B ££

(☑01697-747402; www.bandbhadrianswall.com; Greenhead Brampton; dm/s/d from £12.50/46/65) Built using recycled bits of the wall on whose foundations it stands, this superb farmhouse B&B offers everything from comfy rooms to a basic bunk barn to camping pitches. Both the Pennine Way and the Hadrian's Wall Path pass through the grounds and the jagged ruins of Thirwall Castle loom above the

scene. The owners will gladly show you their piece of 3rd-century Roman graffiti. Half a mile north of Greenhead.

Once Brewed YHA
HOSTEL £

(☑0845-371 9753; www.yha.org.uk; Military Rd, Bardon Mill; dm £14; ⊙Feb-Nov) This modern, well-equipped hostel is central for visiting the Roman forts of Housesteads, 3 miles away, and Vindolanda, 1 mile away. The Hadrian's Wall bus drops you at the door.

Greenhead
HOSTEL £

(☑016977-47411; www.greenheadhotelandhostel.co.uk; Greenhead; dm from £15) No longer affiliated to the YHA, this hostel occupies a converted Methodist chapel by a trickling stream and a pleasant garden, 3 miles west of Haltwhistle. Served by bus AD 122 or 685.

Birdoswald YHA
HOSTEL £

(☑0845-371 9551; www.yha.org.uk; dm £15; ⊙Jul-Sep, call to check other times) Within the grounds of the Birdoswald complex, this hostel has basic facilities, including a self-service kitchen and laundry. The price includes a visit to the fort.

❶ Information

Tourist office (☑01434-322002; Mechanics Institute, Westgate; ⊙9.30am-1pm & 2-5.30pm Mon-Sat, 1-5pm Sun) All the usual info.

NORTHUMBERLAND NATIONAL PARK

England's last great wilderness is the 405 sq miles of natural wonderland that make up Northumberland National Park, spread about the soft swells of the Cheviot Hills, the spiky moors of autumn-coloured heather and gorse, and the endless acres of forest. Even the negligible human influence (this is England's least populated national park with only 2000 inhabitants) has been benevolent: the finest sections of Hadrian's Wall run along the park's southern edge and the landscape is dotted with prehistoric remains and fortified houses – the thick-walled *peles* were the only solid buildings built here until the mid-18th century.

🏃 Activities

The most spectacular stretch of the Hadrian's Wall Path (p625) is between Sewingshields and Greenhead in the south of the park.

There are many fine walks through the Cheviots, frequently passing by prehistoric remnants; the towns of Ingram, Wooler and Rothbury make good bases, and their tourist offices can provide maps, guides and route information.

Though at times strenuous, cycling in the park is a pleasure; the roads are good and the traffic is light. There's off-road cycling in Border Forest Park.

❶ Information

For information, contact **National Park** (☑01434-605555; www.northumberlandnationalpark.org.uk; Eastburn, South Park, Hexham). Besides the tourist offices listed in each town following, there are national park offices in **Once Brewed** (☑01434-344396; Military Rd; ☺9.30am-5pm Apr-Oct) and **Ingram** (☑01665-578890; ☺10am-5pm Apr-Oct). All the tourist offices handle accommodation bookings.

❶ Getting There & Around

Public transport options are limited, aside from buses on the A69. Bus 808 (55 minutes, two daily, Monday to Saturday) runs between Otterburn and Newcastle. Bus 880 (50 minutes, two daily, Tuesday, Friday and Saturday) runs between Hexham and Bellingham. A National Express service calls at Otterburn (£5.70, 50 minutes, daily) on its way from Newcastle to Edinburgh.

Rothbury

POP 1740

The one-time prosperous Victorian resort of Rothbury is an attractive, restful market town on the River Coquet that makes a convenient base for the Cheviots.

◉ Sights

Cragside House, Garden & Estate
HISTORIC BUILDING, GARDENS

(NT; ☑01669-620333; admission £13.90, gardens & estate only £9; ☺house 1-5pm or 11am-5pm Tue-Sun depending on the month, gardens 10.30am-5pm Tue-Sun mid-Mar–Oct) Visitors flock to Rothbury to see Cragside, the quite incredible country retreat of the first Lord Armstrong. In the 1880s the house had hot and cold running water, a telephone and alarm system, and was the first in the world to be lit by electricity, generated through hydropower – the original system has been restored and can be observed in the Power House. The Victorian gardens are also well worth exploring: huge and remarkably varied, they feature lakes, moors and one of Europe's largest rock gardens. Visit late-May to mid-June to see Cragside's famous rhododendrons in bloom.

The estate is 1 mile northeast of town just off the B6341. There's no public transport to the front gates from Rothbury, but you can catch a taxi there.

🛏 Sleeping & Eating

Katerina's Guest House
B&B ££

(☑01669-620691; www.katerinasguesthouse.co.uk; Sun Buildings, High St; r £74; ☎) Beamed ceilings, stone fireplaces and canopied four-posters make Katerina's one of the town's better choices, though the three rooms are a little small for the price.

Haven
B&B ££

(☑01669-620577; www.thehavenrothbury.co.uk; Back Crofts; s/d/ste £40/80/130; Ⓟ) The Haven is a beautiful Edwardian home up on a hill with six comfy bedrooms and one elegant suite.

Sun Kitchen
CAFE £

(High St; snacks & meals £3.60-6.50) There's plenty of pub grub available along High St or you could try Sun Kitchen: it's been serving sandwiches, jacket potatoes and other snacks for four decades.

Rothbury Bakery
BAKERY £

(High St) Come here for great takeaway pies and sandwiches.

❶ Information

Tourist office (☑01669-620887; Church St; ☺10am-5pm Apr-Oct) Has a free exhibition on Northumberland National Park.

❶ Getting There & Around

Bus 144 runs hourly to and from Morpeth (30 minutes) Monday to Saturday. Try **Rothbury Motors** (☑01669-620516) if you need a taxi.

Wooler

POP 1860

A harmonious, stone-terraced town, Wooler owes its sense of unified design to a devastating fire in 1863, which resulted in an almost complete rebuild. It is a wonderful spot in which to catch your breath, especially as it is surrounded by some excellent forays into the nearby Cheviots (including a clamber to the top of the Cheviot, the highest peak in the range). It's also the midway point for the

62.5-mile St Cuthbert's Way, which runs from Melrose in Scotland to Holy Island on the coast.

🏃 Activities

A popular walk from Wooler takes in Humbleton Hill, the site of an Iron Age hill fort and the location of yet another battle (1402) between the Scots and the English. It's immortalised in 'The Ballad of Chevy Chase' and Shakespeare's *Henry IV*. There are great views of the wild Cheviot Hills to the south and plains to the north, merging into the horizon. The well-posted 4-mile trail starts and ends at the bus station (follow the signs to Wooler Common). It takes approximately two hours. Alternatively, the yearly Chevy Chase (www.woolerrunningclub .co.uk) is a classic 20-mile fell run with over 4000ft of accumulated climb, run at the beginning of July.

A more arduous hike leads to the top of the Cheviot (815m), 6 miles southeast. The top is barren and wild, but on a clear day you can see the castle at Bamburgh and as far out as Holy Island. It takes around four hours to reach the top from Wooler. Check with the tourist office for information before setting out.

If you prefer getting around on two wheels, you can rent bikes from Haugh Head Garage (☑01668-281316; per day from £18) in Haugh Head, 1 mile south of Wooler on the A697.

🛏 Sleeping & Eating

Tilldale House   B&B ££
(☑01668-281450; www.tilldalehouse.co.uk; 34-40 High St; s/d from £44/64) One of the houses to survive the fire of 1863 now contains comfortable, spacious rooms that radiate a welcoming golden hue. The five-star breakfast includes veggie and gluten-free options.

Wooler YHA   HOSTEL £
(☑01668-281365; www.yha.org.uk; 30 Cheviot St; dm £16) In a low, red-brick building above the town, the northernmost YHA hostel (at least until the new Berwick hostel opens) contains 46 beds in a variety of rooms, a modern lounge and a small cafe.

Spice Village   INDIAN £
(3 Peth Head; mains from £7; ⊙dinner) There's bog-standard pub grub galore in Wooler, but for a bit more flavour, head for this small takeaway-restaurant that does spicy Indian and Bangladeshi dishes.

ℹ Information

Tourist office (☑01668-282123; www.wooler .org.uk; Cheviot Centre, 12 Padgepool Pl; ⊙10am-4.30pm Easter-Oct) A mine of information on walks in the hills.

ℹ Getting There & Around

Wooler has good bus connections to the major towns in Northumberland. To reach Wooler from Newcastle change at Alnwick.

Alnwick Bus 470, 473; nine daily, Monday to Saturday

Berwick Bus 267, 464; 50 minutes, nine daily, Monday to Saturday

NORTHUMBERLAND COAST

The utterly wild and stunningly beautiful landscapes of Northumberland don't stop with the national park. Hard to imagine an undiscovered wilderness in a country so modern and populated, but as you cast your eye across the rugged interior you will see ne'er a trace of humankind save the fortified houses and lonely villages that dot the horizon.

While the west is covered by the national park, the magnificent and pale sweeping coast to the east is the scene of long, stunning beaches, bookmarked by dramatic wind-worn castles and tiny islands offshore that really do have an air of magic about them. Hadrian's Wall emerges from the national park and slices through the south.

Alnwick

POP 7770

Northumberland's historic ducal town, Alnwick (no tongue gymnastics: just say 'annick') is an elegant maze of narrow cobbled streets spread out beneath the watchful gaze of a colossal medieval castle. England's most perfect bookshop, the northeast's most visited attraction at Alnwick Garden and some olde-worlde emporiums attract secondhand book worms, antique fans, castle junkies and the green-fingered in equal measure, and there's even a little something for *Harry Potter* nerds.

Most of the action takes place around Bondgate Within, Bondgate Without and Clayport St, with the castle to the north overlooking the River Aln.

A MEDIEVAL HAUNT: CHILLINGHAM CASTLE

Recently voted best castle in Europe by readers of the *Independent*, Chillingham (☎01668-215359; www.chillingham-castle.com; adult/child £8.50/4; ⊙noon-5pm Sun-Fri Easter-Sep) is steeped in history, warfare, torture and ghosts: it is said to be one of the country's most haunted places, with ghostly clientele ranging from a phantom funeral to Lady Mary Berkeley in search of her errant husband.

The current owner, Sir Humphrey Wakefield, has gone to great lengths to restore the castle to its eccentric, noble best. This followed a 50-year fallow period when the Grey family (into which Sir Humphrey married) abandoned it, despite having owned it since 1245, because they couldn't afford the upkeep.

Today's visitor is in for a real treat, from the extravagant medieval staterooms that have hosted a handful of kings in their day to the stone-flagged banquet halls. Below ground, Sir Humphrey has gleefully restored the grisly torture chambers, which have a polished rack and the none-too-happy face of an Iron Maiden. There's also a museum with a fantastically jumbled collection of objects.

It's possible to stay at the medieval fortress in the seven apartments designed for guests, where the likes of Henry III and Edward I once snoozed. Prices vary depending on the luxury of the apartment: the Grey Apartment (£170) is the most expensive – it has a dining table to seat 12 – or there's the Tower Apartment (£130), in the Northwest Tower. All of the apartments are self-catering.

Chillingham is 6 miles southeast of Wooler. Bus 470 running between Alnwick and Wooler (three daily, Monday to Saturday) stops at Chillingham.

◉ Sights

Alnwick Castle CASTLE
(www.alnwickcastle.com; adult/child £14/7, with Alnwick Garden £24/10; ⊙10am-6pm Apr-Oct) The outwardly imposing ancestral home of the Duke of Northumberland, and a favourite set for film-makers (it was Hogwarts for the first couple of *Harry Potter* films), has changed little since the 14th century. The interior is sumptuous and extravagant; the six rooms open to the public – staterooms, dining room, guard chamber and library – have an incredible display of Italian paintings, including Titian's *Ecce Homo* and many Canalettos.

A free *Harry Potter* tour runs every day at 2.30pm and includes details of other productions – period drama *Elizabeth* and the British comedy series *Blackadder* to name but two – that have used the castle as a backdrop.

The castle is set in parklands designed by Lancelot 'Capability' Brown. The woodland walk offers some great aspects of the castle, or for a view looking up the River Aln, take the B1340 towards the coast.

Alnwick Garden GARDENS
(www.alnwickgarden.com; adult/child £12/4; ⊙10am-6pm Apr-Oct) As spectacular a bit of green-thumb artistry as you'll see in England,

this is one of the northeast's great success stories. Since the project began in 2000, the 4.8-hectare walled garden has been transformed from a derelict site into a spectacle that easily exceeds the grandeur of the castle's 19th-century gardens, with a series of magnificent green spaces surrounding the breathtaking Grand Cascade – 120 separate jets spurting more than 30,000L of water down 21 weirs for everyone to marvel at and kids to splash around in.

There are half a dozen other gardens, including the Franco-Italian-influenced Ornamental Garden (with more than 15,000 plants), the Rose Garden and the particularly fascinating Poison Garden, home to some of the deadliest – and most illegal – plants in the world, including cannabis, magic mushrooms, belladonna and even tobacco.

🛏 Sleeping

Alnwick packs them in at weekends from Easter onwards so book ahead. B&Bs cluster near the castle.

TOP CHOICE **Alnwick Lodge** B&B ££
(☎01665-604363; www.alnwicklodge.com; West Cawledge Park, A1; s/d from £55/100; P🅿🤶) Is it a B&B? Is it a lonely Victorian farmstead? Is it an antiques gallery? The answer is it's all

of these and more. The never-ending jumble of rooms, each one different and all containing restored antiques; the quirky touches such as free-standing baths with lids; the roaring fire in the Victorian guest lounge; the friendly, flexible owners and the cooked breakfasts around a huge circular banqueting table – all its features make this a truly unique place to stay. The catch: you'll need a car or taxi to get there. It's situated 2 miles south off the A1.

White Swan Hotel HOTEL ££
(☎01665-602109; www.classiclodges.co.uk; Bondgate Within; r from £90; [P][?]) Alnwick's top address is this 300-year-old coaching inn right in the heart of town. Its rooms are all of a pretty good standard (LCD TVs, DVD players and free wi-fi), but this spot stands out for its dining room, filched in its entirety from the *Olympic,* sister ship to the *Titanic,* elaborate panelling, ceiling and stained-glass windows included.

Blackmore's BOUTIQUE HOTEL ££
(☎01665-602395; www.blackmoresofalnwick.com; Bondgate Without; r £100; [P][?]) Trendy Blackmore's motto of 'Eat well, sleep well and party hard' may be a touch incongruous in slow-paced Alnwick, but this takes nothing away from the 14 very comfortable rooms with boutique elements and up-to-the-minute bathrooms. The timber and leather bar-restaurant downstairs is where Alnwick's suited and booted come to booze and get hitched.

 Eating & Drinking

Art House INTERNATIONAL ££
(www.arthouserestaurant.com; 14 Bondgate Within; mains £9-16; ⊙Thu-Mon) Located partially within the 15th-century Hotspur Tower (known locally as the Bondgate Tower), this bright, sharp-edged restaurant/art gallery offers simple but flavoursome combos such as salmon in white wine and pesto sauce, and chicken breast with wild mushrooms and tarragon. Ingredients are locally picked, caught and reared wherever possible. All the art on the walls is for sale.

Market Tavern PUB £
(7 Fenkle St; stottie £6) Near Market Sq, this is the place to go for a traditional giant beef stottie (round loaf) sluiced down with a yard of real ale. B&B available (£30).

Ye Old Cross PUB
Known as 'Bottles', after the dusty bottles in the window, this is another atmospheric stottie-and-pint halt. Legend has it that 150 years ago the owner collapsed and died while trying to move the bottles and no one's dared attempt it since; the irony is that the old window is now behind plexiglass to stop revellers stealing them!

 Shopping

[TOP CHOICE] **Barter Books** SECONDHAND BOOKS
(☎01665-604888; www.barterbooks.co.uk; Alnwick Station; ⊙9am-7pm) If you're familiar with the renaissance of the WWII 'Keep Calm and Carry On' slogan, it's thanks to Barter Books, one of the country's largest and most beautiful secondhand bookshops. When converting the old Victorian railway station, the owner came across a set of posters – and turned it into a successful cottage industry. Coal fires, velvet ottomans and reading rooms make this a place you could spend days in, the silence interrupted only by the tiny rumble of the toy train that runs along the track above your head.

ℹ Information

Tourist office (☎01665-511333; www.visit alnwick.org.uk; 2 The Shambles; ⊙9am-5pm Mon-Sat, 10am-4pm Sun) Located by the marketplace; staff can help find accommodation.

ℹ Getting There & Away

Alnwick's nearest train station is at Alnmouth, connected to Alnwick by bus every 15 minutes.

Berwick-upon-Tweed Bus 501, 505; 50 minutes, 10 daily

Newcastle Bus 501, 505, 518; one hour, two to three hourly

Farne Islands

One of England's most incredible seabird conventions is found on a rocky archipelago of islands about 3 miles offshore from the undistinguished fishing village of Seahouses.

The best time to visit the Farne Islands (NT; admission £6; ⊙depending on island & time of year) is during breeding season (roughly May to July), when you can see feeding chicks of 20 species of seabird, including puffin, kittiwake, Arctic tern, eider duck, cormorant and gull. This is a quite extraordinary experience, for there are few places in the world where you can get so close to nesting seabirds. The islands are also home to a colony of grey seals.

To protect the islands from environmental damage, only two are accessible to the public: Inner Farne and Staple Island. Inner Farne is the more interesting, as it is also the site of a tiny chapel (1370; restored 1848) to the memory of St Cuthbert, who lived here for a spell and died here in 687.

There are various tours, from 1½-hour cruises to all-day specials, and they get going from 10am April to October. Crossings can be rough, and may be impossible in bad weather. Some of the boats have no proper cabin, so make sure you've got warm, waterproof clothing if there's a chance of rain. Also recommended is an old hat – those birds sure can ruin a head of hair!

Of the four operators that sail from the dock in Seahouses, Billy Shiel (☎01665-720308; www.farne-islands.com; 3hr tours adult/child £13/9, all-day tours with landing £30/18) is probably the best known – he even got an MBE for his troubles.

ⓘ Information

The **tourist office** (☎01665-720884; Seafield car park; ☺10am-5pm Apr-Oct) near the harbour in Seahouses and a **National Trust shop** (16 Main St; ☺10am-5pm Apr-Oct) are on hand to provide island-specific information.

ⓘ Getting There & Away

The following buses connect with Seahouses:
Alnwick Bus 501, 505; six daily, one hour
Berwick Bus 501, 505; six daily, 50 minutes

Bamburgh

POP 450

Cute little Bamburgh is dominated by its castle, an imposing structure roosting high up on a basalt crag and a solid contender for England's best. The village itself – a tidy fist of houses around a pleasant green – will be forever associated with the valiant achievements of local lass, Grace Darling.

⊙ Sights

Bamburgh Castle   CASTLE
(www.bamburghcastle.com; adult/child £9/4; ☺10am-5pm mid-Feb–Oct, 11am-4.30pm Sat & Sun Nov–mid-Feb) Northumberland's most dramatic castle was built around a powerful 11th-century Norman keep by Henry II, although its name is a derivative of Bebban-

burgh, after the wife of Anglo-Saxon ruler Aedelfrip, whose fortified home occupied this basalt outcrop 500 years earlier. The castle played a key role in the border wars of the 13th and 14th centuries, and in 1464 was the first English castle to fall as the result of a sustained artillery attack, by Richard Neville, Earl of Warwick, during the Wars of the Roses. It was restored in the 19th century by the great industrialist Lord Armstrong, who died before work was completed. The castle is still home to the Armstrong family.

Once through the gates, head for the museum to view scraps of WWII German bombers washed up on Northumberland's beaches, plus exhibits illustrating just how the Armstrongs raked in their millions (ships, weapons, locomotives), before entering the castle proper. The 12 rooms and chambers inside are crammed with antique furniture, suits of armour, priceless ceramics and works of art, but top billing must go to the King's Hall, a stunning piece of 19th-century neo-Gothic fakery, all wood panelling, leaded windows and hefty beams supporting the roof.

The Bamburgh Castle App (£1.99) is a downloadable audioguide to the castle.

RNLI Grace Darling Museum   MUSEUM
(1 Radcliffe Rd; ☺10am-5pm) Born in Bamburgh, Grace Darling was the lighthouse keeper's daughter on Outer Farne who rowed out to the grounded, flailing SS *Forfarshire* in 1838 and saved its crew in the middle of a dreadful storm. This recently refurbished museum is dedicated to the plucky Victorian heroine and even has the actual coble (rowboat) in which she braved the churning North Sea, as well as a film on the events of that stormy night. Grace was born just three houses down from the museum and is buried in the churchyard opposite, her ornate wrought-iron and sandstone tomb built tall so as to be visible to passing ships.

ⓘ Getting There & Away

Alnwick Bus 401, 501; one hour, four to six daily
Newcastle Bus 501; 2½ hours, three daily Monday to Saturday, two Sunday. Stops at Alnwick and Seahouses.

Holy Island (Lindisfarne)

Holy Island is often referred to as an unearthly place, and while a lot of this talk is just that (and a little bit of bring-'em-in tourist bluster), there *is* something almost other-worldly about this small island (it's only 2 sq miles). It's slightly tricky to reach, as it's connected to the mainland by a narrow causeway that only appears at low tide. It's also fiercely desolate and isolated, barely any different from when St Aidan arrived to found a monastery in 635. As you cross the empty flats to get here, it's not difficult to imagine the marauding Vikings who repeatedly sacked the settlement between 793 and 875, when the monks finally took the hint and left. They carried with them the illuminated *Lindisfarne Gospels* (now in the British Library in London) and the miraculously preserved body of St Cuthbert, who lived here for a couple of years but preferred the hermit's life on Inner Farne. A priory was re-established in the 11th century but didn't survive the Dissolution in 1537.

Pay attention to the crossing-time information, posted at tourist offices and on notice boards throughout the area. Every year a handful of go-it-alone fools are caught midway by the incoming tide and have to abandon their cars.

⊙ Sights

Lindisfarne Priory PRIORY
(EH; adult/child £4.90/2.90; ⊙9.30am-5pm Apr-Sep) The skeletal, red and grey ruins of the priory are an eerie sight and give a fleeting impression of the isolated life lead by the Lindisfarne monks. The later 13th-century St Mary the Virgin Church is built on the site of the first church between the Tees and the Firth of Forth, and the adjacent museum displays the remains of the first monastery and tells the story of the monastic community before and after the Dissolution.

Lindisfarne Heritage Centre MUSEUM
(www.lindisfarne.org.uk; Marygate; adult/child £3/1; ⊙10am-5pm Apr-Oct, according to tides Nov-Mar) Twenty pages of the luminescent *Lindisfarne Gospels* can be flicked through on touch-screens here, though there's normally a queue for the two terminals. While you wait your turn there are fascinating exhibitions on the Vikings and the sacking of Lindisfarne in 793.

Lindisfarne Castle CASTLE
(NT; adult/child £6/3; ⊙10.30am-3pm or noon-4.30pm Tue-Sun Mar-Oct) Half a mile from the village stands this tiny, storybook castle, moulded onto a hunk of rock in 1550, and extended and converted by Sir Edwin Lutyens from 1902 to 1910 for Mr Hudson, the owner of *Country Life* magazine. You can imagine some decadent parties have graced its alluring rooms – Jay Gatsby would have been proud. Its opening times may be extended depending on the tide.

🛏 Sleeping & Eating

It's possible to stay on the island, but you'll need to book well in advance.

Open Gate HOTEL ££
(☑01289-389222; www.aidanandhilda.org; Marygate; s/d £55/70) A Christian retreat in an Elizabethan farmhouse with four en suite rooms.

Manor House Hotel HOTEL ££
(☑01289-389207; www.manorhouselindisfarne.com; s/d £55/95) This pristine hotel in a converted manor home is probably the island's poshest digs.

Ship Inn PUB, B&B ££
(☑01289-389311; www.theshipinn-holyisland.co.uk; Marygate; s/d from £90/110) Four exceptionally comfortable rooms – one with a four-poster – sit above an 18th-century public house known here as the Tavern. There's good local seafood in the bar.

❶ Getting There & Away

Holy Island can be reached by bus 477 from Berwick (Monday to Saturday July and August, Wednesday and Saturday rest of the year). People taking cars across are requested to park in one of the signposted car parks (£4.40 per day). The sea covers the causeway and cuts the island off from the mainland for about five hours each day.

If arriving by car, a **shuttle bus** (£2) runs from the car park to the castle every 20 minutes.

Berwick-upon-Tweed

POP 11,665

The northernmost city in England is a salt-encrusted fortress town and the stubborn holder of two unique honours: it is the most fought-over settlement in European history (between 1174 and 1482 it changed hands 14 times between the Scots and the English); and its football team, Berwick Rangers, is the only English team to play in the Scottish League – albeit in lowly Division Three. Although firmly English since the 15th century, Berwick retains its own peculiar identity, an odd blend of Scottish and English with locals born south of the border very often speaking with a noticeable Scottish whirr.

Sights & Activities

FREE **Berwick's Walls**   WALLS

(EH) You can walk almost the entire length of Berwick's hefty Elizabethan walls, begun in 1558 to reinforce an earlier set built during the reign of Edward II. The mile-long walk is a must, with wonderful, wide-open views. Only a small fragment remains of the once mighty border castle, most of the building having been replaced by the train station.

Berwick Barracks   MUSEUM, GALLERY

(EH; The Parade; adult/child £3.90/2.30; ☺10am-5pm Mon-Fri) Designed by Nicholas Hawksmoor, the oldest purpose-built barracks (1717) in Britain now house an assortment of museums and art galleries, covering a history of the town and British soldiery since the 17th century. The Gymnasium Gallery hosts big-name contemporary art exhibitions.

Cell Block Museum   MUSEUM

(Marygate; adult/child £3/1; ☺tours 10.30am & 2pm Mon-Fri Apr-Sep) The original jail cells in the upper floor of the town hall (1750–61) have been preserved as a museum devoted to crime and punishment. Tours take in the public rooms, museum, jail and belfry.

Sleeping

Church St has a cluster of fairly basic B&Bs.

TOP CHOICE **No 1 Sallyport**   BOUTIQUE B&B £££

(☎01289-308827; www.sallyport.co.uk; 1 Sallyport, off Bridge St; r £150) Not just the best in town, but one of the best B&Bs in England, No 1 Sallyport has only six suites – each carefully appointed to fit a theme. The Manhattan Loft, crammed into the attic, makes the minimalist most of the confined space; the Lowry Room is a country-style Georgian classic; the Smuggler's Suite has a separate sitting room complete with widescreen TV, DVD players and plenty of space to lounge around in. The Tiffany Suite has a grand fireplace and the attic Mulberry Suite has a sexy freestanding bath. The downstairs restaurant is Berwick's finest, serving Cheviot lamb, North Sea fish and homemade cakes and pastries.

Berwick YHA   HOSTEL ££

(☎0845-371 9676; www.yha.org.uk; Dewars Lane; dm/d from £15/48; @) A 240-year-old granary with a distinct 'lean' has been converted into a smart hostel with all the usual facilities: comfortable dorms, a handful of doubles, a TV room, a laundry and internet access. The staff are terrifically friendly and helpful.

Eating & Drinking

Foxton's   CONTINENTAL ££

(26 Hide Hill; mains £9-15; ☺Mon-Sat) This decent brasserie-style restaurant has Continental dishes to complement the local fare, which means there's something for everyone.

Barrels Alehouse   PUB

(56 Bridge St) Berwick's best watering hole attracts a mixed, laid-back crowd who can be found supping real ales and micro-distilled gins and whiskies at all hours. There's regular live music in the atmospherically dingy basement bar.

Information

Berwick library (Walkergate; ☺closed Thu & Sun) Bring ID to access the internet.

Tourist office (☎01289-330733; www.visit northumberland.com; 106 Marygate; ☺10am-5pm Mon-Sat, 11am-3pm Sun Easter-Oct) Can help find accommodation and runs one-hour guided walks at 10am, 11.45am and 2pm on weekdays (£5).

Getting There & Away

Bus

Buses stop on Golden Sq (where Marygate becomes Castlegate).

Edinburgh National Express; £13.70, one hour 20 minutes, twice daily

Holy Island Bus 477; 35 minutes, two services on Wednesday and Saturday (Monday to Saturday in August)

London National Express; £35.30, eight hours, twice daily

Newcastle Bus 505, 501 (via Alnwick); 2½ hours, nine daily

Train

Berwick is almost exactly halfway between Edinburgh (£13.60, 50 minutes, half-hourly) and Newcastle (£19.70, 50 minutes, half-hourly) on the main east-coast London–Edinburgh line.

Wales

Wales Highlights

① Exploring **Cardiff** (p641), the capital, with its fantasy castle, Victorian shopping arcades and lively nightlife

② Catching some breaks or just enjoying the views along the **Gower Peninsula** (p670)

③ Marvelling at the picture-perfect ruins of **Tintern Abbey** (p662) in the Wye Valley

④ Enjoying tiny **St Davids** (p681), with its beautiful cathedral and idyllic setting

⑤ Climbing Wales' highest peak, Snowdon, or enjoying more gentle exercise in **Snowdonia** (p713)

⑥ Buying fish and chips and strolling along the pier in **Llandudno** (p741)

⑦ Seeing **Caernarfon Castle** (p726), arguably the most impressive Welsh fortress

⑧ Wandering through **Hay-on-Wye** (p703), a bookworm's heaven

⑨ Walking in the mountains, then eating in the gastropubs of the **Brecon Beacons** (p693)

Cardiff (Caerdydd)

POP 324,800 / AREA 54 SQ MILES

Best Places to Eat

» Mint & Mustard (p652)

» Riverside Real Foodmarket (p651)

» Woods Bar & Brasserie (p652)

» Cafe Minuet (p651)

» Brava (p652)

Best Places to Stay

» Tŷ Rosa (p651)

» Lincoln House (p650)

» River House Backpackers (p649)

» Park Plaza (p649)

» Beaufort Guest House (p650)

Why Go?

The capital of Wales since only 1955, Cardiff has embraced its new role with vigour, emerging as one of Britain's leading urban centres in the 21st century. Caught between an ancient fort and an ultramodern waterfront, this compact city seems to have surprised even itself with how interesting it has become. Its decline in the middle of last century looked terminal, but Cardiff has entered the new millennium pumped up on steroids, flexing its new architectural muscles as if it's still astonished to have them. This new-found confidence is infectious; people now travel to Cardiff for a good night out, bringing with them a buzz that reverberates through the streets. The city makes a great base for day trips to the surrounding countryside, where you'll find castles, Roman ruins, neolithic stone monuments and beachside amusements.

When to Go

January and February are the coldest months, although Wales' home matches in the Six Nations Rugby Championship warm the spirits of locals and visitors alike during February and March. June is the driest month, and in July the summer-long Cardiff Festival (p649) kicks off, incorporating theatre, comedy, music and a food festival. In August, the warmest month, knights storm the castle, classic cars converge and gay pride takes over the streets. By November, the wettest month, thcoe average daily temperature reaches a high of just 10°C and doesn't scrape back into two digits again until March.

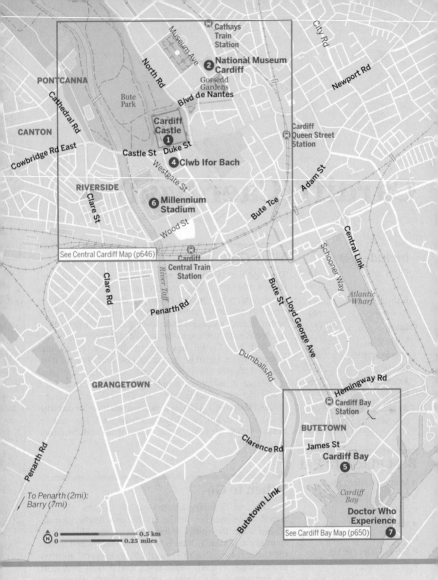

Cardiff Highlights

1 Marvelling at the over-the-top Victorian interiors that add bling to **Cardiff Castle** (p644), the city's ancient citadel

2 Taking an engrossing journey via the big bang, archaeological artefacts and art at the **National Museum Cardiff** (p644)

3 Joining the nighttime revellers hopping between central-city **bars** (p652) as the streets thrum with live music after dark

4 Catching the next big thing on the Welsh music scene at **Clwb Ifor Bach** (p653)

5 Admiring the architectural showpieces that make up the glitzy entertainment precinct at **Cardiff Bay** (p653)

6 Getting swept away by the exhilaration of a fired-up rugby test at **Millennium Stadium** (p645)

7 Coming face to face with a Dalek, without even a couch to hide behind, at the **Doctor Who Experience** (p646)

History

In AD 75 the Romans built a fort where Cardiff Castle now stands. The name 'Cardiff' probably derives from the Welsh Caer Tâf (Fort on the River Taff) or Caer Didi (Didius' Fort), referring to the Roman general Aulus Didius. After the Romans left Britain, the site remained unoccupied until the Norman Conquest. In 1093 a Norman knight named Robert Fitzhamon, conqueror of Glamorgan and later earl of Gloucester, built himself a castle here (the remains stand within the grounds of Cardiff Castle) and a small town grew up around it. Both were damaged during a Welsh revolt in 1183, and the town was sacked in 1404 by Owain Glyndŵr during his unsuccessful rebellion against English domination.

The first of the Tudor Acts of Union in 1536 put the English stamp on Cardiff and brought some stability. But despite Cardiff's importance as a port, market town and bishopric, only 1000 people were living here in 1801.

Cardiff owes its present-day stature to iron and coal mining in valleys to the north. Coal was first exported, on a small scale, as early as 1600. In 1794 the Bute family, which owned much of the land from which Welsh coal was mined, built the Glamorganshire Canal to enable iron to be shipped to Cardiff from Merthyr Tydfil.

In 1840 the canal was superseded by the Taff Vale Railway. A year earlier the second marquess of Bute had completed the first docks at Butetown, just south of Cardiff, getting the jump on other South Wales ports. By the time it dawned on everyone that the valleys held immense reserves of coal, which triggered a kind of black gold rush, the Butes were in a position to insist the coal be shipped from Butetown. Cardiff was off and running.

The docklands expanded rapidly, the Butes grew staggeringly rich, and the town boomed, its population rising to 170,000 by the end of the 19th century and to 227,000 by 1931. A large, multiracial workers' community known as Tiger Bay grew up in the harbourside area of Butetown.

In 1905 Cardiff was officially designated a city, and a year later its elegant Civic Centre was inaugurated. The city's wealth and its hold on the coal trade persuaded Captain Robert Scott to launch his ill-fated expedition to the South Pole from here in 1910. Cardiff became the world's top coal port in 1913, exporting some 13 million tonnes of the stuff.

The slump in the coal trade after WWI and the Great Depression of the 1930s slowed Cardiff's expansion. Bombing in WWII badly damaged the city and claimed more than 350 lives. Shortly afterwards the coal industry was nationalised, prompting the Butes to pack their bags and leave town in 1947.

Wales had no official capital, and the need for one was seen as an important focus for Welsh nationhood. Cardiff had the advantage of being the country's biggest city and boasting the architectural riches of the Civic Centre. A ballot of members of the Welsh authorities gave Cardiff 36 votes against Caernarfon's 11 and Aberystwyth's four, and it was proclaimed the capital of Wales in 1955.

CARDIFF IN...

Two Days

Wander around the central city, stopping to explore **Cardiff Castle** and the **National Museum Cardiff**. Lunch could be a picnic in **Bute Park** with treats acquired at **Cardiff Market** or, if the weather's not cooperating, a meal at any of the reasonably priced central-city eateries. Spend your second day heading back to the future at **Cardiff Bay**, where you can immerse yourself in forward-thinking architecture and have a **Doctor Who Experience**.

Four Days

Spend your third morning steeped in history at **St Fagans: National History Museum**, then check out **Barry Island**. On your last day, head north to explore **Llandaff Cathedral**, then continue on to **Castell Coch** and **Caerphilly Castle**. For your last night in the Welsh capital, blast away the cobwebs in one of the city's live-music venues.

THE BEAUT BUTES

The Butes, an aristocratic Scottish family related to the Stuart monarchy, arrived in Cardiff in 1766 in the shape of John, Lord Mountstuart, who had served briefly as prime minister under King George I. He married a local heiress, Charlotte Jane Windsor, and in the process acquired vast estates and mineral rights in South Wales.

Their grandson, the second marquess of Bute, grew fabulously wealthy from coal mining and then, in 1839, chanced his fortune to create the first docks at Cardiff. The gamble paid off. The coal-export business boomed, and his son, John Patrick Crichton-Stuart, the third marquess of Bute, became one of the richest people on the planet. Not your conventional Victorian aristocrat, John was an intense, scholarly man with a passion for history, architecture, ritual and religion (Catholic). He neither hunted nor fished, but instead supported the antivivisection movement and campaigned for women's right to a university education.

The Butes had interests all over Britain and never spent more than about six weeks at a time in Cardiff. Soon after WWII ended they had sold or given away all of their Cardiff assets, the fifth marquess gifting Cardiff Castle and Bute Park to the city in 1947. The present marquess, the seventh, lives in the family seat at Mount Stuart House on the Isle of Bute in Scotland's Firth of Clyde. Another maverick, he's better known as Johnny Dumfries, the former Formula One racing driver.

⊙ Sights

CENTRAL CARDIFF

Cardiff Castle   CASTLE

(Map p646; www.cardiffcastle.com; Castle St; adult/child £11/8.50, incl guided tour £14/11; ⊗9am-5pm) The grafting of Victorian mock-Gothic extravagance onto Cardiff's most important historical relics makes Cardiff Castle the city's leading attraction. It's far from a traditional Welsh castle, and more a collection of disparate castles scattered around a central green, which encompass practically the entire history of Cardiff. The most conventional castle-like bits are the 12th-century motte-and-bailey **Norman keep** at its centre and the 13th-century **Black Tower**, which forms the entrance gate.

In the 19th century it was discovered that the Normans had built their fortifications on top of the original 1st-century Roman fort. The high walls that surround the castle are largely a Victorian reproduction of the 3m-thick Roman walls from the 3rd century. Also from the 19th century are the towers and turrets on the west side, dominated by the colourful 40m-high **clock tower**.

A 50-minute guided tour takes you through the interiors of this flamboyant fantasy world. Some but not all of these rooms can be accessed with a regular castle entry, which includes an excellent audioguide (also available in a children's edition and a range of languages).

Below the ticket office is **Firing Line**, a small museum devoted to the Welsh soldier.

FREE National Museum Cardiff   MUSEUM

(Map p646; www.museumwales.ac.uk; Gorsedd Gardens Rd; ⊗10am-5pm Tue-Sun) Cardiff's Civic Centre is an early-20th-century complex of neo-baroque buildings in gleaming white Portland stone, set around green lawns and colourful flower beds. They include the **City Hall** (Map p646), police headquarters, law courts, crown offices, Cardiff University and this excellent museum, which is one of Britain's best and covers natural history, archaeology and art.

The *Evolution of Wales* exhibit takes you through 4600 million years of geological history, its rollicking multimedia display placing Wales in a global context. Films of volcanic eruptions and aerial footage of the Welsh landscape explain how its scenery was formed, while woolly mammoths and dinosaur skeletons keep the kids interested.

The natural-history displays range from brightly coloured insects to the 9m-long skeleton of a humpback whale that washed up near Aberthaw in 1982. The world's largest turtle (914kg), found on Harlech Beach on Wales' west coast, is also here.

The art gallery houses an excellent collection, including many impressionist and postimpressionist pieces, and a large new space devoted to contemporary exhibitions. Treasures include works by Monet, Renoir and Van Gogh, along with the more recent luminaries Francis Bacon and David Hockney. Welsh artists such as Ceri Richards,

David Jones, Gwen John and Augustus John are well represented.

Millennium Stadium
STADIUM

(Map p646; ☎029-2082 2228; www.millennium stadium.com; Westgate St; tours adult/child £7.50/4.95; ☺10am-5pm) The spectacular Millennium Stadium squats like a stranded spaceship on the River Taff's east bank. Attendance at international rugby and football matches has increased dramatically since this 72,500-seat, three-tiered stadium with sliding roof was completed in time to host the 1999 Rugby World Cup. The stadium cost £110 million to build and big matches paralyse the city centre, but when the crowd begins to sing, the whole of Cardiff resonates and all is forgiven. It's well worth taking a tour – you get to run through the players' tunnel and sit in the VIP box.

Bute Park
PARK

(Map p646) With Sophia Gardens, Pontcanna Fields and Llandaff Fields, Bute Park forms a green corridor that stretches for 1.5 miles northwest alongside the River Taff to Llandaff. All were once part of the Bute family's vast holdings. The Animal Wall (Map p646), forming the park's southern edge, is topped with stone figures of lions, seals, bears and other creatures. In the 1930s these figures were the subject of a newspaper cartoon strip and many Cardiff kids grew up thinking the animals came alive at night.

Cardiff Story
MUSEUM

(Map p646; ☎029-2078 8334; www.cardiffstory. com; Old Library, The Hayes; ☺10am-5pm) This excellent little museum uses interactive displays, video footage and everyday objects to tell the story of Cardiff's transformation from a small market town into the world's biggest coal port and then into the capital city of today. Check out the original entrance to the library, lined with beautiful Victorian tiles, and head upstairs to see temporary art exhibitions.

St John the Baptist Church
CHURCH

(Map p646; Working St) A graceful Gothic lantern tower rises from this 15th-century church, its delicate stonework looking almost like filigree. A church has stood on this site since at least 1180. Inside are simple, elegant arches. Regular lunchtime organ concerts are held here.

CARDIFF BAY

Cardiff Bay Waterfront
WATERFRONT

(Map p650) Lined with important national institutions, Cardiff Bay is where the modern Welsh nation is put on display in an architect's playground of interesting buildings, large open spaces and public art. It wasn't always this way. By 1913 more than 13 million tonnes of coal was being shipped from Cardiff's docks. After the post-WWI slump, the docklands deteriorated into a wasteland of empty basins, cut off from the city by the railway embankment. The bay outside the docks, which has one of the highest tidal ranges in the world, was ringed for up to 14 hours a day by smelly, sewage-contaminated mudflats.

Since 1987 the area has been completely redeveloped. The turning point came with the completion of a state-of-the-art tidal barrage in 1999, which transformed the mudflats into a freshwater lake by containing the waters at the mouth of the Rivers Taff and Ely. It was a controversial project, as its construction flooded almost 200 hectares of intertidal mudflats, which, despite their unpleasant aspects, were an important habitat for waterfowl. The barrage has sluice gates to control the water flow, three lock gates to allow boats through, and a pass that lets migrating salmon and sea trout swim between river and sea.

Cardiff Bay's main commercial centre is Mermaid Quay (Map p650; www.mermaidquay .co.uk; Harbourside), packed with bars, restaurants and shops. To its east is Roald Dahl Plass (Map p650), a large public space (once a dock basin) named after the Cardiff-born writer, which serves as an open-air performance area, overseen by a soaring, stainless-steel water sculpture.

CARDIFF FOR CHILDREN

Compact and easy to navigate, Cardiff is welcoming to families. Interactive Techniquest (Map p650; www.techni quest.org; Stuart St; adult/child £7/5; ☺10am-4.30pm) is the main attraction for challenging junior brains, while the National Museum Cardiff (p644) is full of weird and wonderful animals and other fascinating exhibits. For a day trip, try the living history of Caerphilly Castle (p658) or Castell Coch (p657).

Central Cardiff

To Caerphilly
(7mi)

Cathays
Train Station

Cardiff
University

Park Pl

Museum Ave

King Edward VII Ave

North Rd

Alexandra
Gardens

National
Museum
Cardiff

PONTCANNA

College Rd

Law
Courts

Gorsedd Gardens Rd

Gorsedd
Gardens

Blvd de Nantes

To Llandaff
(1.7mi)

Cathedral Rd

Bute
Park

Cardiff
Castle

Kingsway

The Friary

Cowbridge Rd East

Lower Cathedral Rd

Castle St

Duke St

Working St

27

15

21

Womanby St

10

26

High St

28

Church St

4

13

Quay St

19

25

2

St Mary St

Wharton St

5

Despenser St

RIVERSIDE

9

River Taff

Fitzhamon Embankment

Guildhall
Pl

12

Millennium
Stadium

Westgate St

Park St

29

30

Great Western La

Clare St

Ninian Park Rd

11

Tudor St

Wood St

Clare Rd

Central
Bus Station

Central Sq

Cardiff Central
Train Station

Penarth Rd

Doctor Who Up Close   EXHIBITION
(Map p650; ☎0844 801 3663; www.doctorwho
exhibitions.com; Porth Teigr; adult/child £15/11;
☺10am-5pm Wed-Mon, daily school holidays) The
huge success of the reinvented classic TV
series *Doctor Who*, produced by BBC Wales,
has brought Cardiff to the attention of sci-fi
fans worldwide. City locations have featured
in many episodes and the first two series of
the spin-off, *Torchwood*, were set in Cardiff

look for the Tardis hovering outside. Perhaps fittingly, given the show's theme, tickets are booked for specific timeslots (you'll save a few pounds by booking online).

Visitors find themselves sucked through a crack in time and thrown into the role of the Doctor's companion. It's great fun, especially when you come face to face with full-sized Daleks in full 'ex-ter-min-ate' mode. But don't blink – there are weeping angels afoot. In reality, it only takes about 20 minutes and afterwards you can wander at your leisure around the displays of props spanning the show's 50-year run.

FREE **Wales Millennium Centre** ARTS CENTRE
(Map p650; ☎029-2063 6464; www.wmc.org.uk; Bute Pl; guided tour adult/child £5.50/4.50; ⊗tours 11am & 2.30pm) The centrepiece and symbol of Cardiff Bay's regeneration, the Millennium Centre is an architectural masterpiece of stacked Welsh slate in shades of purple, green and grey, topped with an overarching bronzed steel shell. Designed by Welsh architect Jonathan Adams, it opened in 2004 as Wales' premier arts complex, housing the Welsh National Opera, National Dance Company, National Orchestra, Academi (Welsh National Literature Promotion Agency), Hi-Jinx Theatre and Ty Cerdd (Music Centre of Wales).

The roof above the main entrance is pierced by 2m-high letter-shaped windows that are spectacularly backlit at night and spell out phrases from the poet Gwyneth Lewis: *Creu Gwir fel Gwydr o Ffwrnais Awen* ('Creating truth like glass from inspiration's furnace') and 'In these stones horizons sing'.

You can wander through the public areas at will, or take a guided tour that leads behind the giant letters, onto the main stage and into the dressing rooms, depending on what shows are on.

FREE **Senedd (National Assembly Building)** NOTABLE BUILDING
(Map p650; ☎0845 010 5500; www.assemblywales.org; ⊗10.30am-4.30pm Fri-Mon, 8am-end of business Tue-Thu) Designed by Lord Richard Rogers (the architect behind London's Lloyd's building and Paris' Pompidou Centre), the Senedd is a striking waterfront structure of concrete, slate, glass and steel, with an undulating canopy roof lined with red cedar. It has won awards for its environmentally

Bay (the hidden lift to their headquarters emerging beneath the water sculpture in Roald Dahl Plass).

Capitalising on Time Lord tourism, this interactive exhibition is located right next to the BBC studios where the series is filmed –

Central Cardiff

friendly design, which includes a huge rotating cowl on the roof for power-free ventilation and a gutter system that collects rainwater for flushing toilets. The lobby and surrounding area are littered with public artworks.

The Welsh National Assembly usually meets in a plenary session from 1.30pm on Tuesday and Wednesday, and seats in the public gallery may be pre-booked, although you can take your chances on the day. There are free tours at 11am daily, with extra tours Thursday to Monday at 2pm and 3pm.

FREE Pierhead   MUSEUM
(Map p650; ☑0845 010 5500; www.pierhead.org; ⊙10.30am-4.30pm Mon-Sat) One of Cardiff Bay's few Victorian remnants, Pierhead is a red-brick and glazed-terracotta French–Gothic Renaissance confection (nicknamed 'Wales' Big Ben'), built in 1897 with Bute family money. Inside, there's an interesting little display on the history of the bay (including a short film and slideshow), some important historical documents and a gallery.

Butetown   NEIGHBOURHOOD
Victorian Butetown, spanning out from Mount Stuart Sq, just northwest of the waterfront, was the heart of Cardiff's coal trade – a multiethnic community that propelled the city to world fame. The old Coal Exchange (Map p650; www.coalexchange.co.uk; Mount Stuart Sq) was the place where international coal prices were set. It was here in March 1908 that a coal merchant wrote the world's first-ever £1 million cheque. It now serves as a function and performance venue.

FREE Butetown History & Arts Centre   GALLLERY
(Map p650; www.bhac.org; Bute St, 4-5 Dock Chambers; ⊙10am-5pm Tue-Sun) This centre is devoted to preserving oral histories, documents and images of the docklands. Displays range from old photographs to contemporary art.

⟨☞ Tours

City Sightseeing   BUS TOURS
(☑029-2047 3432; www.city-sightseeing.com; adult/child £11/5.50) Open-top, hop-on/hop-off bus tours of the city, departing every 30

to 60 minutes from outside Cardiff Castle. Tickets are valid for 24 hours.

☆☆ Festivals & Events

Cardiff Festival   CULTURAL

(www.cardiff-festival.com) Running from June to early September, the Cardiff Festival lineup includes Welsh Proms (two weeks of classical concerts at St David's Hall), Cardiff Carnival, Cardiff International Food & Drink Festival, Grand Medieval Melee, LBGT Mardi Gras, Classic Car & Boat Rally, Everyman Summer Theatre Festival, and lots of crazy one-offs.

Great British Cheese Festival   FOOD

(www.greatbritishcheesefestival.co.uk) You can brush shoulders with the big cheeses at Cardiff Castle in late September.

Cardiff Winter Wonderland   WINTER

(www.cardiffswinterwonderland.com) Festivities here include an outdoor ice-skating rink, Christmas lights, Santa's grotto and family-friendly activities, from mid-November to early January.

🛏 Sleeping

CENTRAL CARDIFF

River House Backpackers   HOSTEL £

(Map p646; ☑029-2039 9810; www.riverhousebackpackers.com; 59 Fitzhamon Embankment; dm/r from £18/35; @🛜) Professionally run by a young brother-and-sister team, the River House is a welcoming place with a well-equipped kitchen, small garden and cosy TV lounge. Free breakfast (cereal and toast) and pizza nights are a nice touch. The private rooms are basically small dorm rooms and share the same bathrooms.

Park Plaza   HOTEL ££

(Map p646; ☑029-2011 1111; www.parkplazacardiff.com; Greyfriars Rd; r from £99) Luxurious without being remotely stuffy, the Plaza has all the facilities you'd expect from an upmarket business-oriented hotel (including a gym, pool and sauna). The snug reception sets the scene, with gas fire blazing along one wall and comfy wingback chairs. The rear rooms have leafy views over the Civic Centre.

Parc Hotel   HOTEL ££

(Map p646; ☑0871 376 9011; www.thistle.com/theparchotel; Park Pl; s/d from £74/79; @🛜) Parc Hotel is a smart contemporary hotel in an elegant French chateau–style shell, situated right in the heart of the main shopping area. It has tastefully decorated rooms, good facilities and helpful staff; use of a neighbouring gym, spa and sauna is included in the rates.

Premier Inn Cardiff City Centre   HOTEL £

(Map p646; ☑0871 527 8196; www.premierinn.com; 10 Churchill Way; r from £45) The Cardiff branch of Britain's biggest chain has 200 beds in a squat, mirror-clad former office tower right in the centre of town. It's certainly not flash, but it's terrific value. All rooms are priced identically, but cheaper if paid in advance, so book early and request a higher floor.

NosDa Budget Hotel   HOTEL £

(Map p646; ☑029-2037 8866; www.nosda.co.uk; 53-59 Despenser St; dm/tw from £19/43; P@🛜) Directly across the river from the Millennium Stadium, NosDa is starting to look a little scuffed – which is a shame, as it was impressively schmick when it first opened. Still, for private budget rooms in a fab location, it's hard to beat, and there's free car parking too.

WORTH A TRIP

LLANDAFF CATHEDRAL

Set in a hollow on the west bank of the River Taff, beautiful Llandaff Cathedral (☑2056 4554; www.llandaffcathedral.org.uk; Cathedral Rd; ⏲10am-4pm) is on the site of a 6th-century monastery. The present cathedral was begun in 1120, but it crumbled throughout the Middle Ages, and during the Reformation and Civil War was used as an alehouse and then an animal shelter. Derelict by the 18th century, it was largely rebuilt in the 19th century and extensively restored after being damaged by a German bomb in 1941. The towers at the western end epitomise the cathedral's fragmented history – one was built in the 15th century, the other in the 19th. Inside, a giant arch supports sculptor Sir Jacob Epstein's huge aluminium work *Majestas*, its modern style a bold contrast in this gracious vaulted space.

Buses 24, 25 and 62 (15 minutes, every 10 to 15 minutes) run along Cathedral Rd to Llandaff, 1.7 miles from the city centre.

CARDIFF (CAERDYDD) FESTIVALS & EVENTS

Cardiff Bay

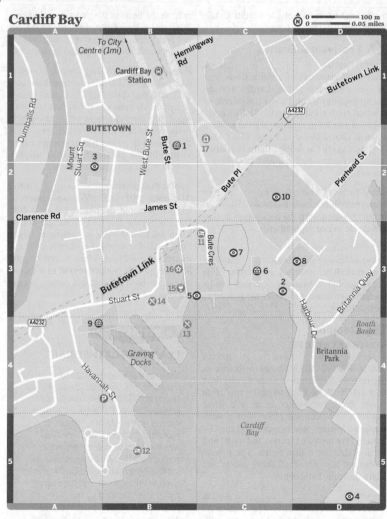

PONTCANNA

Lincoln House

HOTEL ££

(☏029-2039 5558; www.lincolnhotel.co.uk; 118 Cathedral Rd; s/d from £70/90; P🖤) Walking a middle line between a large B&B and a small hotel, Lincoln House is a generously proportioned Victorian property with heraldic emblems in the stained-glass windows of its sitting room, and a separate bar. For added romance, book a four-poster room.

Beaufort Guest House

B&B ££

(☏029-2023 7003; www.beauforthousecardiff.co.uk; 65 Cathedral Rd; s/d from £57/82; 🖤) Despite a thorough refurbishment, the Beaufort retains an old-fashioned Victorian atmosphere, with period-style furniture, gilt mirrors, heavy drapes and even a portrait of the old queen herself. The breakfast room is ready for royalty, with candlesticks and blue-and-white china adding a touch of grandeur.

Town House

B&B ££

(☏029-2023 9399; www.thetownhousecardiff.co.uk; 70 Cathedral Rd; s/d £45/65; P🖤) This elegant, succinctly named Victorian town house on the Cathedral Rd strip has welcoming owners and a relaxed vibe. It retains lots of period features, including a tiled hallway

Cardiff Bay

(with busy wallpaper), original fireplaces and stained-glass windows. The rooms are more restrained.

Saco House   APARTMENTS **££**
(☏0845 122 0405; www.sacoapartments.co.uk; 74-76 Cathedral Rd; apt from £114; P) This Victorian town house has been given a contemporary makeover and converted into serviced apartments, complete with comfortable lounges and fully equipped kitchens. The two-bedroom apartments are good value for families with kids and there's an extra sofa bed in the lounge. It's set up for longer visits, but a two-day stay is the minimum.

GRANGETOWN

Tŷ Rosa   B&B **£**
(☏0845 643 9962; www.tyrosa.com; 118 Clive St; s/d from £39/49; ☎) Half an hour's walk from either the bay or Central Cardiff (follow the river south, turn right on to Penarth Rd and then left after 650m), this wonderful gay-friendly B&B is noted for its sumptuous breakfasts and affable hosts. The thoughtfully equipped rooms are split between the main house and an annexe across the road. Some rooms share bathrooms.

CARDIFF BAY

Jolyons Boutique Hotel   HOTEL **££**
(Map p650; ☏029-2048 8775; www.jolyons.co.uk; 5 Bute Cres; r from £76; ☎) A touch of Georgian elegance in the heart of Cardiff Bay, Jolyon's has six individually designed rooms combining antique furniture with contemporary colours and crisp cotton sheets. The front rooms face out over Roald Dahl Plass to the

Millennium Centre, while one of the rear rooms has its own terrace.

St David's Hotel & Spa   HOTEL **££**
(Map p650; ☏029-2045 4045; www.thestdavidsho tel.com; Havannah St; r from £105; @🤶🏊) Its glassy tower topped with a sail-like flourish, St David's epitomises Cardiff Bay's transformation from wasteland to desirable address. Almost every room has a small private balcony with a bay view. The exterior is already showing signs of wear and tear, but the rooms are still good.

🍴 Eating

CENTRAL CARDIFF

Riverside Real Foodmarket   MARKET **£**
(Map p646; www.riversidemarket.org.uk; Fitzhamon Embankment; ⊙10am-2pm Sun) What it lacks in size, the Riverside market makes up for in sheer yumminess, its stalls heaving with cooked meals, cakes, cheese, organic meat, charcuterie, apple juice and real ale. There are lots of options for vegetarians and the Welsh cakes hot off the griddle are exceptional.

Cafe Minuet   ITALIAN **£**
(Map p646; 42 Castle Arcade; mains £5-8; ⊙lunch Mon-Sat) It may look a little like a greasy spoon from the outside, but this unassuming eatery produces excellent cheap and cheerful Italian food. The menu sports good vegetarian dishes, including lots of pasta options. Get in early at lunchtime or expect to wait for a table.

Goat Major   PUB **£**
(Map p646; www.sabrain.com/goatmajor; 33 High St; pies £7.50; ⊙lunch) A solidly traditional

wood-lined pub with armchairs, fireplace and Brains Dark real ale, the Goat Major's gastronomic contribution takes the form of a selection of homemade pot pies served with chips. Try the Wye Valley pie, a mixture of chicken, leek, asparagus and Tintern Abbey cheese.

Zerodegrees ITALIAN ££

(Map p646; www.zerodegrees.co.uk; 27 Westgate St; mains £8-16) Housed within a big, factory-like space, this microbrewery and restaurant combines all-day food with lip-smacking artisan-crafted beers. The excellent dining options include a United Nations of pizza toppings (including Thai and Mexican), pasta, risotto and kilo pots of mussels, the house speciality.

Madame Fromage DELI, CAFE £

(Map p646; www.madamefromage.co.uk; 18 Castle Arcade; mains £7-11; ⊙lunch) One of Cardiff's best delicatessens, with a wide range of charcuterie and French and Welsh cheeses, the Madame also has a cafe with tables spilling into the arcade. Here, you can read French newspapers and eat a mixture of Breton and Welsh dishes, including rarebit, lamb cawl (a stew-like soup) and bara brith (fruitcake).

Plan CAFE £

(Map p646; 28 Morgan Arcade; mains £4-9; ⊙lunch; ⏂) Serving quite possibly Wales' best coffee (which, admittedly, isn't saying much), this cafe dishes up healthy, organic, locally sourced food, including vegan options. Grab a window seat and a copy of the *Guardian* newspaper and caffeinate to your (racing) heart's content.

PONTCANNA

Brava CAFE ££

(71 Pontcanna St; breakfast £4-8, lunch £6-9, dinner £9-11; ⊙breakfast & lunch daily, dinner Tue-Sat) With local art on the walls and an informal vibe, this cool cafe is our favourite brunch spot on the strength of its eggs Benedict, silky white coffee and attentive service. Tables spill out onto the pavement in summer and in the evening it morphs into a licensed bistro. Brava indeed.

CATHAYS

TOP CHOICE Mint & Mustard INDIAN ££

(☎029-2062 0333; www.mintandmustard.com; 134 Whitchurch Rd; mains £8-18; ⊙lunch Sun-Fri, dinner Mon-Sat) A rewarding short detour to student hub Cathays, north of the city cen-

tre, will bring you to this upmarket Indian eatery, specialising in seafood dishes from Kerala. If you're not enticed by the lobster, crab, prawn and fish dishes, there are plenty of vegetarian options and an excellent crusted lamb biryani.

CARDIFF BAY

Woods Bar & Brasserie MODERN EUROPEAN ££

(Map p650; ☎029-2049 2400; www.knifeandforkfood.co.uk; Stuart St; mains £11-16; ⊙lunch daily, dinner Mon-Sat) The historic Pilotage Building has been given a modern makeover – involving zany wallpaper, exposed stone walls and a floor-to-ceiling glass extension – to accommodate Cardiff Bay's best restaurant. The cuisine is modern European, light and flavoursome, with an emphasis on local ingredients.

Bosphorus TURKISH ££

(Map p650; ☎029-2048 7477; www.bosphorus.co.uk; 31 Mermaid Quay; mains £10-19; ⏂) While the food is good, it's the setting that really distinguishes this upmarket Turkish restaurant. Jutting out over the water on its own private pier, Bosphorus enjoys wonderful all-round views; the best are from the outdoor tables at the end. Early eaters can take advantage of the pre-6.30pm offer: two courses and a drink for £13.50.

🍷 Drinking

You'll find that Cardiff is a prodigiously boozy town. Friday and Saturday nights see the city centre invaded by hordes of generally good-humoured, beered-up lads and ladettes tottering from bar to club to kebab shop, whatever the weather (someone fetch that young woman a coat!). It's not as tacky as it sounds – a lively alternative scene, some swish bars and a swathe of old-fashioned pubs keep things interesting. Try the local Brains SA (meaning Special Ale, Same Again or Skull Attack, depending on how many you've had), brewed by the same family concern since 1882.

CENTRAL CARDIFF

TOP CHOICE Gwdihw BAR

(Map p646; www.gwdihw.co.uk; 6 Guildford Cres) The last word in Cardiff hipsterdom, this cute little bar has an eclectic lineup of entertainment (comedy nights, cake and craft markets, ukelele jams and lots of other live music, including microfestivals that spill over into the car park), but it's a completely

BARTENDER TAG

We asked the bartenders at some of our favourite Cardiff bars for their expert tips on the city's best venues (aside from their own, of course).

Handsome cocktail conjurer at 10 Feet Tall The Welsh Club (Clwb Ifor Bach), of course. Buffalo (and not just because it's our sister bar. Some great bands play upstairs. Moon Bar (Full Moon) is good for live music too. Oh, and try Gwdihw. The name is the Welsh version of an owl's call – you know, 'to-whit-to-woo'.

Dreadhead and Tatts at Full Moon The Club (Clwb Ifor Bach) – that place is legendary. Everyone starts out at Pen & Wig for a cheap beer in the beer garden.

Hip lasses in Bettie Page dresses at Gwdihw If we head out after work, we head to Buffalo – it's open really late. Otherwise, there are some great old pubs along City Rd, east of the city centre.

charming place to stop for a drink at any time. There's a lovely little outdoor space as well.

Buffalo Bar BAR
(Map p646; www.myspace.com/wearebuffalobar; 11 Windsor Pl) A haven for cool kids about town, the laid-back Buffalo features retro furniture, tasty daytime food, life-affirming cocktails and alternative tunes. Upstairs, a roster of cutting-edge indie bands takes to the stage. It's open until at least 3am every day, so staff from other venues kick on here.

10 Feet Tall BAR
(Map p646; www.10feettallcardiff.com; 12 Church St) The sister property to Buffalo Bar, this hip venue over three floors is a cafe, cocktail and tapas bar, and live music venue. Chic barmen swish together two-for-one cocktails between 5pm and 10pm, and all day Sunday.

Full Moon BAR
(Map p646; www.thefullmooncardiff.com; 1/3 Womanby St) Directly opposite Clwb Ifor Bach, this friendly, grungy rock bar is a pretence-free zone. Sample from the large selection of rum, whisky and vodka, or try the 'jar of green shit' if you dare. Upstairs, the Moon Club thrums to live bands.

Pen & Wig PUB
(Map p646; www.penandwigcardiff.co.uk; 1 Park Grove) Legal phrases are printed in Latin on the walls of this solidly traditional pub, but there's nothing stuffy about the large beer garden or the entertainment roster here (open-mic Monday, quiz Tuesday, live-music Saturday). Note: working through the impressive range of ales may induce *mens rea* the morning after.

Pica Pica BAR
(Map p646; www.picapicacardiff.com; 15-23 Westgate St) Housed in a series of low-ceilinged brick vaults, Pica Pica is a cool bar which serves tapas and two-for-one cocktails before 8pm.

CARDIFF BAY
Cwtch BAR
(Map p650; www.jolyons.co.uk; 5 Bute Cres) A *cwtch* is either a warm and safe place or a cuddle. This little bar, below Jolyon's Hotel, is certainly the former and it imparts a cosy feeling that's almost as good as the latter. Sink into a sofa and slip into Cwtch's warm embrace. In summer, head through the Tardis door to the beer garden.

Salt BAR
(Map p650; www.saltcardiff.com; Mermaid Quay) A large bar with plenty of sofas and armchairs for lounging around and a first-floor open-air terrace with views of the yachts out in the bay. DJs spin from Thursday to Saturday night.

☆ Entertainment

Pick up a copy of *Buzz* (www.buzzmag.co.uk), a free monthly magazine with up-to-date entertainment listings, available from the tourist office and venues.

Most of the large arts companies are based at the Wales Millennium Centre (p647), but **St David's Hall** (Map p646; ☎029-2087 8444; www.stdavidshallcardiff.co.uk; The Hayes), the national concert hall, hosts the Welsh Proms in July and a full roster of performances.

Clwb Ifor Bach CLUB
(Map p646; ☎029-2023 2199; www.clwb.net; 11 Womanby St) Truly an independent music great, Y Clwb has launched many a Welsh

GAY & LESBIAN CARDIFF

Cardiff's small gay and lesbian scene is focused on a cluster of venues on Churchill Way and Charles St (for listings, check www.gaycardiff.co.uk). The big event is the annual Mardi Gras (www.cardiffmardigras.co.uk; Coopers Field), held as part of the Cardiff Festival in late August or early September.

Club X (Map p646; www.clubxcardiff.net; 35 Charles St; free before 10pm, £10/5/free Fri/Sat/Sun; ☺8pm-6am Fri-Sun), Cardiff's biggest gay club, has two dance floors, with a chill-out bar and covered beer garden upstairs.

One of the oldest pubs in the city and a long-standing gay venue, the Victorian Golden Cross (Map p646; www.sabrain.com/golden-cross; 283 Hayes Bridge Rd) retains its handsome stained glass, polished wood and ceramic tiles.

band since the early 1980s. It started as a venue for Welsh-language music in Anglophone Cardiff and has survived the Cool Cymru backlash with its reputation as Cardiff's most eclectic and important venue intact. It now hosts bands performing in many tongues and is the best place to catch gigs by up-and-coming new acts, as well as more established artists.

Chapter THEATRE, CINEMA
(☎029-2030 4400; www.chapter.org; Market Rd, Canton) The city's edgiest arts venue, Chapter has a varied rota of contemporary drama, as well as art exhibitions, arthouse cinema, workshops, alternative theatre and dance performances.

Sherman Cymru THEATRE
(Map p646; ☎029-2064 6900; www.shermancymru.co.uk; Senghennydd Rd) South Wales' leading theatre company, Sherman Theatre stages a wide range of material, from classics and children's theatre to works by new playwrights.

Glee Club COMEDY
(Map p650; ☎0871 472 0400; www.glee.co.uk; Mermaid Quay, Cardiff Bay; ☺Thu-Sat) This busy club hosts a well-regarded set of comedy nights.

New Theatre THEATRE
(Map p646; ☎029-2087 8889; www.newtheatrecardiff.co.uk; Park Pl) A restored Edwardian playhouse, New Theatre hosts touring productions, musicals and pantomime.

 Shopping

If you thought Cardiff's 21st-century makeover was all about political edifices, arts centres and sports stadiums, think again. One of the most dramatic developments in the central city is the transformation of the Hayes shopping strip, with the giant, glitzy extension of the St David's shopping centre now eating up its entire eastern flank. The development cost £675 million and is one of Britain's largest shopping centres. Balancing this ultramodern mall is a historic network of Victorian and Edwardian arcades, spreading their dainty tentacles either side of St Mary St.

Craft in the Bay ARTS & CRAFTS
(Map p650; www.makersguildinwales.org.uk; Lloyd George Ave) This retail gallery showcases work by contemporary Welsh artists and craftspeople, with a wide range of ceramics, textiles, woodwork, jewellery, glassware, canvases and ironwork.

St David's MALL
(Map p646; www.stdavidscardiff.com; The Hayes) Immense is the best way to describe this shiny new shopping centre. All the high-street chains you could name have a home here, along with a smorgasbord of eateries, a cinema multiplex and a large branch of the John Lewis department store dominating its southern end.

Spillers Records MUSIC
(Map p646; www.spillersrecords.co.uk; Morgan Arcade) The world's oldest record shop, founded in 1894 (when it sold wax phonograph cylinders), Spillers stocks a large range of CDs and vinyl, prides itself on catering to the non-mainstream end of the market (it's especially good for punk music), and promotes local talent through in-store gigs.

Cardiff Central Market MARKET
(Map p646; www.cardiff-market.co.uk; btwn St Mary & Trinity Sts; ☺8am-5.30pm Mon-Sat) For an age-old shopping experience, head to this Victorian covered market, which is packed with stalls selling everything from fresh fish to mobile phones. Stock up here for a picnic in Bute Park.

Castle Welsh Crafts
SOUVENIRS

(Map p646; www.castlewelshcrafts.co.uk; 1 Castle St) If you're after stuffed dragons, lovespoons or Cardiff T-shirts, this is the city's biggest souvenir shop, conveniently located across the street from the castle.

Royal & Morgan Arcades
SHOPPING ARCADE

(Map p646; www.royalandmorganarcades.co.uk; btwn St Mary St & The Hayes) Cardiff's oldest arcade (1858), the Royal is home to the excellent Wally's Delicatessen. Along with the interconnected Morgan Arcade (Map p646), it forms a shopping precinct called the Morgan Quarter.

High St Arcade
SHOPPING ARCADE

(Map p646; www.cardiffhighstreetarcade.co.uk; btwn High & St John Sts) Divergent points of the music spectrum come together in this arcade: traditional music specialist Telynau Vining Harps (sheet music and instruments) and dance-music gurus Catapult (DJ equipment and records). Stop into the NY Deli for a burger or sandwich, then head on to Hobo's for secondhand 1960s and '70s clothing.

Castle Arcade
SHOPPING ARCADE

(Map p646; www.cardiffcastlearcade.co.uk; btwn Castle & High Sts) The most decorative of the city's arcades, Castle Arcade houses Troutmark Books (secondhand and Welsh-language books), Madame Fromage and Cafe Minuet.

Wyndham Arcade
SHOPPING ARCADE

(Map p646; btwn St Mary St & Mill Lane) Yet another historic arcade, this one has the gloriously old-fashioned Havana House (aka the Bear Shop), a specialist tobacconist from a bygone era.

ⓘ Information

Cardiff tourist office (☏029-2087 3573; www.visitcardiff.com; The Hayes, Old Library; ☺9.30am-5.30pm Mon-Sat, 10am-4pm Sun) Piles of information, an accommodation-booking service and a good stock of Ordnance Survey maps, plus Welsh literature and internet access.

Police (☏0201-2022 2111; King Edward VII Ave)

University Hospital of Wales (☏029-2074 7747; www.cardiffandvaleuhb.wales.nhs.uk; Heath Park) Located 2 miles north of the Civic Centre, with an accident and emergency department.

ⓘ Getting There & Away

Air

Cardiff Airport (☏01446-711111; www.tbicardiff airport.com) is mainly used by budget operators. Aside from summer charters, these are the airlines flying into Cardiff and the destinations they serve:

Aer Lingus (www.aerlingus.com) Dublin.

Eastern Airways (www.easternairways.com) Aberdeen and Newcastle.

Flybe (www.flybe.com) Glasgow, Edinburgh, Jersey, Belfast and Paris.

Helvetic Airways (www.helvetic.com) Zurich.

KLM (www.klm.com) Amsterdam.

Manx2 (www.manx2.com) Anglesey.

Bus

Cardiff's main bus station is on Wood St, next to the train station.

National Express (www.nationalexpress.com) coach destinations include Monmouth (£11, 1¼ hours), Chepstow (£5.40, 45 minutes), Bristol (£9, 1¼ hours), Birmingham (£11, three hours) and London (£11, 3½ hours).

The **First** (www.firstgroup.com) Greyhound service travels regularly between Cardiff and Swansea (peak/off-peak £7/5 return, one hour).

Arriva (www.arrivabus.co.uk) has buses to Carmarthen (1½ hours) and Aberystwyth (3½ hours).

Stagecoach (www.stagecoachbus.com) destinations include Caerphilly (45 minutes), Brecon (1½ hours), Builth Wells (2½ hours), Llandrindod Wells (2¾ hours) and Newtown (3½ hours).

Car

Cardiff is easily reached from the M4 (which runs from London to northwest of Swansea). All major rental car companies have branches in the capital.

Train

Trains from major British cities arrive at Cardiff Central station, on the southern edge of the city centre. **Arriva Trains Wales** (www.arriva trainswales.co.uk) operates all train services in Wales. Direct services from Cardiff include London Paddington (£39, 2¼ hours), Swansea (£7.70, 50 minutes), Fishguard Harbour (£22, three hours), Abergavenny (£12, 40 minutes) and Bangor (£75, 4¼ hours).

ⓘ Getting Around

To/From the Airport

Cardiff Airport is 12 miles southwest of Cardiff, past Barry. A shuttle bus (£1) links the airport terminal to nearby Rhoose Cardiff International Airport train station, with trains to the city (£3.80, 30 minutes) running hourly Monday to

Saturday and more sporadically on Sunday. The X91 bus (£3.90, 35 minutes, every two hours) runs from the airport to the central bus station. A taxi from the airport to the city centre takes 20 to 30 minutes, depending on traffic, and costs about £26.

Public Transport

Local buses are operated by **Cardiff Bus** (☎029-2066 6444; www.cardiffbus.com; trip/day-pass £1.50/3); buy the ticket from the driver (£1.70 to any stop in Cardiff; no change given).

Frequent trains run from Cardiff's Queen St station to Cardiff Bay Station (£1.50, four minutes), which is 500m from the waterfront. From Cathays or Central stations, you have to change at Queen St.

The most appealing way to reach Cardiff Bay is on the **Cardiff Aquabus** (☎2047 2004; www .cardiffaquabus.com) along the River Taff (adult/child £3/2, 25 minutes) (departing on the hour, 11am to 5pm) and Mermaid Quay (returning on the half hour, 10.30am to 4.30pm).

Taxi

Reliable companies include **Capital Cabs** (☎029-2077 7777) and **Dragon Taxis** (☎029-2033 3333). **Checker Cars** (☎01446 711 747; www. checkercars.com) has the airport concession.

AROUND CARDIFF

If you're based in Cardiff, there's a diverting selection of day trips to choose from.

Penarth

POP 24,300

Penarth is an old-fashioned seaside resort stuck somewhere between the 19th and 21st centuries, with a tatty, turquoise Victorian pier staggering out to sea, a rocky shoreline, and a mature population wielding Thermos flasks. It's connected to Cardiff Bay by the freshwater lake formed by the barrage, and there's a busy marina on the lakefront.

Ffoto Gallery (☎029-2034 1667; www.ffoto gallery.org; Plymouth Rd; ☉11am-5pm Tue-Sat) has changing photographic exhibitions and runs summer workshops where kids can do stuff like print making and pinhole photography. It's located in Turner House, a red-brick building a block east of the train station. From the town centre, it's a five-minute walk through pretty, topiary-filled **Alexandra Gardens** to the esplanade.

From June to September, Waverley Excursions (☎0845 130 4647; www.waverleyexcur sions.co.uk) runs cruises on either the *Waverley*, the world's last seagoing paddle steamer, or its sister ship, the *Balmoral*. They depart from Penarth pier for trips across the Bristol Channel to Holm Island, Clevedon, Minehead or Ilfracombe.

Cardiff buses 92, 93 and 94 (£1.70, 20 minutes, every 15 minutes Monday to Saturday, hourly Sunday and evening) run to Penarth, and there are frequent trains from Cardiff Central (£2.40, 15 minutes).

Barry

POP 47,900

Barry is 8 miles southwest of Cardiff, and Barry Island is well signposted at the south end of the town. It stopped being a real island in the 1880s when it was joined to the mainland by a causeway.

Like nearby Penarth, Barry Island is a faded seaside resort, but with a much better

---

FREEWHEELING THROUGH WALES

Cardiff is the start or end point for two of the finest long-distance routes in Wales on the National Cycle Network (NCN). Tackle the routes in their entirety, or pick and mix parts in tandem with your pedalling power and scenery wishlist. End points are linked with the rail network, so you can make your way back to the start by train.

Lôn Las Cymru (Greenways of Wales/Welsh National Route; NCN routes 8 and 42) is the more demanding of the two. The 254-mile route runs from Holyhead through to Hay-on-Wye, then on to Cardiff via Brecon or Chepstow via Abergavenny. Encompassing three mountain ranges, Snowdonia, the Cambrian Mountains and the Brecon Beacons, there's a fair amount of uphill, low-gear huffing and puffing to endure along the way. That said, each peak promises fantastic views and plenty of downhill, freewheeling delights.

Lôn Geltaidd (Celtic Trail; NCN routes 4 and 47) is 337 miles long, snaking from Fishguard through the West Wales hills, the Pembrokeshire Coast and the former coalfields of South Wales, and ending at Chepstow Castle. The glorious, ever-changing landscape provides an engrossing backdrop.

beach and a waterfront lined with amusement arcades and fun parks. The massive popularity of the BBC Wales comedy *Gavin and Stacey* has given it new caché. The staff at Island Leisure (on the Promenade) are used to fans of the show making a pilgrimage to the booth where Nessa (played in the show by co-writer Ruth Jones) works. Other sites include nearby Marco's Cafe, where Stacey works, and Trinity St, where Stacey's mum and Uncle Bryn live.

Cardiff Bus services head to Barry Island every 20 minutes during the day (route 95, £2.40, 55 minutes), but hourly in the evening and two-hourly on Sunday. Frequent trains head here from Cardiff Central (£3, 30 minutes).

St Fagans: National History Museum

Historic buildings from all over the country have been dismantled and rebuilt in a beautiful rural setting at St Fagans (⏀029-2057 3500; www.museumwales.ac.uk/en/stfagans; car-park £3.50; ⏀10am-5pm). More than 40 buildings are on show, including farmhouses of timber and stone, barns, a watermill, a school and an 18th-century Unitarian chapel. Native breeds of livestock graze in the surrounding fields.

St Fagans Castle is no johnny-come-lately construction. This medieval fortress, with a 16th-century manor house at its heart, was donated by the Earl of Plymouth in 1948 and, along with its extensive formal gardens, forms the basis of the museum. You'll need at least half a day to do the whole complex justice and you could easily spend longer, picnicking in the grounds.

Highlights include a farmhouse dating from 1508, imbued with the smells of old timber, beeswax and wood smoke, and a row of six miners' cottages from Merthyr Tydfil, each restored and furnished to represent different periods in the town's history, from the austere minimalism of 1805 to all the mod cons of 1985. It took 20 years to move St Teilo's church here (built 1100–1520), stone by stone. It's been restored to its original look, before Protestants whitewashed the vividly painted interior. Not original but equally fascinating is the reproduction of three circular Celtic houses based on the archaeological remains of actual buildings.

It's a great place for kids, with special events in the summer. You can see craftspeople at work in many of the buildings, showing how blankets, clogs, barrels, tools and cider were once made, and the woollen mill sells its own handmade blankets.

The indoor galleries also hold plenty of interest, exploring the nature of Welshness through traditional costume, farming implements and the accounts of immigrants. Look for the 'Welsh Not', wooden signs that children were forced to wear as punishment if they spoke their native tongue at school.

St Fagans is 5 miles west of central Cardiff. City Sightseeing (p648) buses stop here and are more frequent than the Cardiff Bus services (route 32).

Castell Coch

Cardiff Castle's little brother is perched atop a thickly wooded crag on the northern fringes of the city. Fanciful Castell Coch (Cadw; ⏀029-2081 0101; www.cadw.wales.gov.uk; adult/child £3.80/3.40; ⏀10am-4pm) was the summer retreat of the third marquess of Bute and, like Cardiff Castle, was designed by William Burges in gaudy Victorian Gothic style.

Raised on the ruins of Gilbert de Clare's 13th-century Castell Coch (Red Castle), the Butes' Disneyesque holiday home is a monument to high camp. Lady Bute's huge, circular bedroom is pure fantasy: her bed, with crystal globes on the bedposts, sits beneath an extravagantly decorated and mirrored cupola, with 28 painted panels around the walls depicting monkeys (which were fashionable at the time, apparently, but seem just plain weird now). The corbels are carved with images of birds nesting or feeding their young, and the washbasin is framed between two castle towers.

Lord Bute's bedroom is small and plain by comparison, but the octagonal drawing room is another hallucinogenic tour de force. Its walls are painted with scenes from *Aesop's Fables*, the domed ceiling is a flurry of birds and stars, and the fireplace is topped with figures depicting the three ages of men and women. The tower to the right of the entrance has exhibits explaining the castle's history.

Stagecoach (p655) buses 26 and 132 (27 minutes) stop at Tongwynlais, a 10-minute walk from the castle. Bus 26 continues to Caerphilly Castle, and the two can be combined in a day trip.

THE BIG CHEESE

Any festival that includes a Cheese Olympics and a Tommy Cooper Tent has got to be worth a look. On the last weekend of July, Caerphilly welcomes more than 70,000 people to the Big Cheese (www.caerphilly.gov .uk/bigcheese; admission free), three days of family-oriented fun and games that offer everything from fireworks to falconry, comedy acts and cheese tasting, along with medieval battle re-enactments, food and craft stalls, archery demonstrations, live music and a traditional funfair.

The Cheese Olympics are held on Friday evening, with events including cheese throwing, rolling and stacking. The Tommy Cooper Tent – named after the much-loved British comedian, who was born in Caerphilly and died in 1984 – stages comedy acts, including a Tommy Cooper tribute act. A statue of Cooper, in his trademark fez and with a rabbit at his feet, overlooks the castle near the Tourist Office.

Caerphilly (Caerffili)

POP 31,000

The town of Caerphilly – now almost a suburb of Cardiff – guards the entrance to the Rhymney valley to the north of the capital. Its name is synonymous with a popular variety of hard, slightly crumbly white cheese that originated in the surrounding area.

You could be forgiven for thinking that Caerphilly Castle (Cadw; ☎029-2088 3143; www.cadw.wales.gov.uk; adult/child £3.60/3.20; ⊙9am-5pm Apr-Oct, 9.30am-4pm Mon-Sat & 11am-4pm Sun Nov-Mar), with its profusion of towers and crenellations reflected in a duck-filled lake, was a film set rather than an ancient monument. While it is often used as a film set, it is also one of Britain's finest examples of a 13th-century fortress with water defences.

Unusually, Caerphilly was never a royal castle. Most of the construction was completed between 1268 and 1271 by the powerful English baron Gilbert de Clare, Lord Marcher of Glamorgan (1243–95), in response to the threat of attack by Prince Llywelyn ap Gruffydd, prince of Gwynedd (and the last Welsh Prince of Wales), who had already united most of the country under his control. In the 13th century Caerphilly was state of the art, one of the earliest castles to use lakes, bridges and a series of concentric fortifications for defence. To reach the inner court you had to overcome no fewer than three drawbridges, six portcullises and five sets of double gates.

Edward I's subsequent campaign against the Welsh princes put an end to Llywelyn's ambitions and Caerphilly's short-lived spell on the front line came to an end without ever tasting battle. The famous leaning tower at the southeast corner is a result of subsidence rather than sabotage. In the early 14th century the castle was remodelled as a grand residence and the magnificent Great Hall adapted for entertaining, but from the mid-14th century onward the place began to fall into ruin.

Much of what you see today is the result of restoration from 1928 to 1939 by the fourth marquess of Bute. Work continued after the state bought the castle in 1950. The Great Hall was given a splendid wooden ceiling in the 19th century and its Gothic windows were restored in the 1960s; it is now used to host special events. On the south dam platform you can see reconstructions of medieval siege weapons. These working models lob stone projectiles into the lake during battle re-enactments.

You can buy Caerphilly cheese from the Tourist Office (www.visitcaerphilly.com; Twyn Sq; ⊙10am-5.30pm), just east of the castle, clearly visible 500m north of Caerphilly train station (along Cardiff Rd). The easiest way to reach Caerphilly from Cardiff is by train (£3.80, 19 minutes), or you can catch Stagecoach buses A, B and 26 (45 minutes).

Pembrokeshire & South Wales

Best Places to Eat

» Crown at Whitebrook (p662)

» Cwtch (p683)

» Maes-Yr-Haf (p671)

» The Bell at Skenfrith (p663)

» Joe's Ice Cream Parlour (p668)

Best Places to Stay

» Fronlas (p672)

» Manor Town House (p685)

» Ramsey House (p683)

» Fairyhill (p671)

» St Davids YHA (p683)

Why Go?

Stretching from historic border town Chepstow, via the industrial heritage of the valleys, through to the jagged Pembrokeshire coast in the west, South Wales really packs it in. Hugging the border, the Wye Valley is the birthplace of British tourism. For more than 200 years people have come to explore this tranquil waterway and its winding, wooded vale, where the majestic ruins of Tintern Abbey have inspired generations of poets and artists. In contrast, Blaenavon provides a stark reminder of Wales' contribution to the Industrial Revolution. Reborn Swansea offers something approaching big city sophistication; the Gower Peninsula revels in its coastal beauty; while the fecund heartland of rural Carmarthenshire offers country comfort in abundance. The biggest draw in the south, however, remains Pembrokeshire, where almost 200 miles of magical shoreline has been declared a national park, delineated by craggy cliffs, golden sands, chocolate-box villages and seaside resorts.

When to Go

Average daily temperatures scrape above 10°C in March – spend St David's Day in the saint's city and look out for early daffodils. If you're planning some coastal walking, April to July are the driest months. In late May/early June, Fishguard serenades summer with folk music. Chepstow has a festival in June. July and August are the only months with average highs over 20°C, making them the best for a beach holiday. Swansea Bay's Summer Festival continues right through to September.

South Wales Highlights

1 Exploring **St Davids** (p681), Wales' most beguiling little city

2 Watching the surf break against the great dragon at **Rhossili Bay** (p670)

3 Strolling among romantic ruins on the banks of the Wye at **Tintern Abbey** (p662)

4 Using whiz-bang interactive displays to trace Wales' industrial heritage

at Swansea's **National Waterfront Museum** (p665)

5 Experiencing World Heritage industrial sites and world-class cheese at **Blaenavon** (p663)

6 Viewing Norman Foster's intriguing dome, signalling a monumental garden in the making at the **National Botanic Garden of Wales** (p672)

7 Unearthing some of Britain's most significant Roman remains at **Caerleon** (p664)

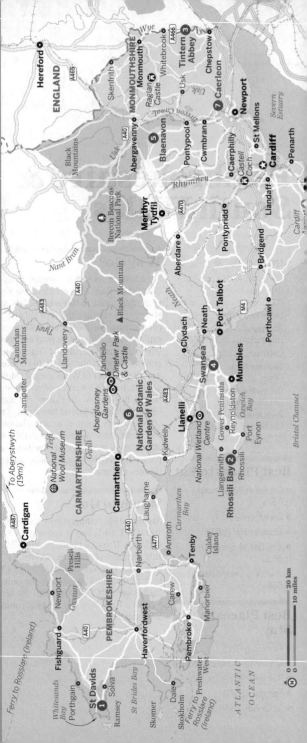

Activities

For outdoor activities, the region's main draw is Pembrokeshire. Walkers love the **Pembrokeshire Coast Path** (http://nt.pcnpa.org.uk), a 186-mile jaunt through some of Britain's most spectacular scenery; while watersports on offer include excellent sea kayaking, surfing and, most thrilling of all, coasteering. Another area popular with surfers and walkers is the Gower Peninsula.

The Celtic Trail cycle route cuts clear across South Wales from the Severn Bridge to Fishguard via Chepstow, Swansea and Carmarthen. Off-road cycling fans should head for the tracks and byways of the Preseli Hills, east of Fishguard, or to the dedicated **Cognation** (www.cognation.co.uk) mountain-bike areas between Cardiff and the Brecon Beacons.

ⓘ Getting There & Around

Frequent train and coach services connect South Wales to England and the rest of Wales; Cardiff and Swansea are main hubs. The main railway continues west to the ferry terminals of Fishguard and Pembroke Dock (both ports for Ireland). Trains trundle through the region on the famously scenic Heart of Wales line (www.heart-of-wales.co.uk) between Swansea and Shrewsbury.

For Wales-wide travel information, see Traveline Cymru (www.traveline-cymru.info).

SOUTHEAST WALES

You need only ponder the preponderance of castles to realise that the pleasantly rural county of Monmouthshire was once a wild frontier. The Norman Marcher lords kept stonemasons extremely busy, erecting mighty fortifications to keep the unruly Welsh at bay. The River Wye forms the Wales–England border before emptying into the River Severn below Chepstow. Much of it is designated an Area of Outstanding Natural Beauty (AONB; www.wyevalleyaonb.org.uk), famous for its limestone gorges and dense broad-leaved woodland.

To the west, the serried South Wales valleys were once the heart of industrial Wales. Although the coal, iron and steel industries have withered, the valleys still evoke a world of tight-knit working-class communities, male voice choirs and rows of neat terraced houses set amid a scarred, coal-blackened landscape. Today, the region is fighting back against decline by creating a tourist industry based on its industrial heritage.

Chepstow (Cas Gwent)

POP 14,200

Chepstow is a market town nestled in a great S-bend in the River Wye, with a splendid Norman castle perched dramatically on a cliff above the water. The town was first developed as a base for the Norman conquest of southeast Wales, later prospering as a port for the timber and wine trades. As river-borne commerce gave way to the railways, Chepstow's importance diminished to reflect its name, which means 'marketplace' in Old English.

◉ Sights

Chepstow Castle   CASTLE

(www.cadw.wales.gov.uk; Bridge St; adult/child £4/3.60; ◷10am-4pm) Magnificent Chepstow Castle perches atop a sheer limestone cliff overhanging the river, guarding the main river crossing from England into South Wales. It is one of the oldest castles in Britain (building began in 1067) and it's remarkably well preserved.

FREE **Chepstow Museum**   MUSEUM

(Bridge St; ◷1am-5pm Mon-Sat, 2-5pm Sun; 🖲) Housed in an 18th-century town house across the road from the castle, this small and kid-friendly museum covers Chepstow's industrial and social history.

✖ Eating

Lime Tree   CAFE, BAR £

(www.facebook.com/limetreecafebar; 24 St Mary St; mains £4-11; ◷8.30am-11pm) The most appealing eatery in Chepstow handles the transition from cosy daytime cafe into trendy gastro bar seamlessly. The vastly varied menu stretches from breakfast into sandwiches, burgers and all the traditional tapas favourites. Grab a newspaper and settle into one of the nooks.

Mythos!   GREEK ££

(☎01291-627222; Welsh St; mains £9-19; ◷lunch Mon-Sat, dinner daily) Exposed beams, stone walls and dramatic lighting make this lively Greek bar and restaurant memorable, but it's the authentic, delicious food that justifies that pretentious exclamation mark in the name: tzatziki, grilled haloumi, spanakopita, lamb souvlaki, moussaka – all served as meze or main-sized portions.

ℹ️ Information

Tourist office (📞01291-623772; www.chepstow towncrier.org.uk; Castle car park, Bridge St; ⊙9.30am-5pm Apr-Oct, 9.30am-3.30pm Nov-Mar) Ask about local walking trails, such as the Tintern & Return path.

ℹ️ Getting There & Away

BUS Route 69 links Chepstow with Monmouth (40 minutes) via Tintern (15 minutes). **National Express** (www.nationalexpress.com) coach destinations include London (£21, three hours), Cardiff (£5.40, one hour), Swansea (£12, two hours), Carmarthen (£17, 2½ hours) and Tenby (£19, 3¼ hours).

TRAIN There are direct **Arriva Trains Wales** (www.arrivatrainswales.co.uk) services from Cardiff (£8.50, 40 minutes) and Gloucester (£8.60, 30 minutes).

Lower Wye Valley

The A466 road follows the snaking, steep-sided valley of the River Wye from Chepstow to Monmouth, passing through the straggling village of Tintern. It's a beautiful drive, rendered particularly mysterious when a twilight mist rises from the river and shrouds the illuminated ruins of Tintern Abbey (Cadw; 📞01291-689251; www.cadw. wales.gov.uk; adult/child £3.60/3.20; ⊙9am-5pm Apr-Oct, 9.30am-4pm Mon-Sat & 11am-4pm Sun Nov-Mar; 🅿️). Founded in 1131 by the Cistercian order, this monastic complex and its riverside setting have inspired poets and artists through the centuries. The huge abbey church was built between 1269 and 1301, the stone shell of which remains surprisingly intact; the finest feature is tracery that once contained the magnificent west windows.

There are plenty of possibilities for riverside walks around Tintern. One of the best begins at the old railway bridge just upstream from the abbey, and leads up to the Devil's Pulpit, a limestone crag on the east side of the river with a spectacular view over the abbey (2.5 miles round trip).

If you take the narrow country lane along the west bank of the Wye, a mile north of the turn-off where the A466 crosses the river into England, and 5 miles north of the abbey, you'll find the Michelin-starred Crown at Whitebrook (📞01600-860254; www.crownat

whitebrook.co.uk; Whitebrook; 2-/3-course lunch £25/28, 3-/6-/9-course dinner £48/55/70; ⊙closed Sun dinner). The food is astonishingly good – inventive, intricately crafted and delicious. If you don't fancy driving afterwards, or the romantic ambience has worked its magic, get a room (single/double from £100/145).

Monmouth (Trefynwy)

POP 9500

The compact market town of Monmouth sits at the confluence of the Rivers Wye and Monnow, and has hopped in and out of Wales over the centuries as the border shifted back and forth. It's famous as the birthplace of Henry V and the home of Charles Stewart Rolls, co-founder of Rolls-Royce. In modern times Monmouth's main claim to fame is the nearby Rockfield recording studio, which has produced a string of hit albums for the likes of Oasis, Coldplay and Super Furry Animals.

Monmouth's main drag, Monnow St, starts at car-free Monnow Bridge, the UK's only complete example of a medieval fortified bridge. It was built in 1270, although much of what you see now was restored in 1705. Before you cross into town, it's worth poking your head into St Thomas the Martyr's Church. Parts of it date from around 1180 – there's an impressive Norman Romanesque arch, as well as pews and a gallery fashioned out of dark wood.

The meagre remains of Monmouth Castle (Castle Hill; no admission), where in 1397 Henry V was born, are set back from Monnow St. Except for the great tower, it was dismantled in the 17th century and the stone used to build Great Castle House next door, now headquarters of the Royal Monmouthshire Regiment.

ℹ️ Information

Tourist office (📞01600-775257; www.shire hallmonmouth.org.uk; Shire Hall, Agincourt Sq; ⊙10am-4pm)

ℹ️ Getting There & Away

Bus 69 runs along the Wye Valley from Monmouth to Chepstow (40 minutes) via Tintern (25 minutes) and route 83 heads to Abergavenny (45 minutes) via Raglan (19 minutes). National Express coaches head to Monmouth from Ross-on-Wye (£4.80, 20 minutes), Birmingham (£20, 1¾ hours) and Cardiff (£11, one hour).

COOL CYMRU

With such a small population and a culture that's been overshadowed by England for centuries, it's something of a surprise that Wales has produced plenty of musical maestros who have hit the big time. Everyone knows perma-tanned warbler Tom Jones, who, together with the likes of Shirley Bassey, has kept Welsh pop on the map since the 1960s.

Along with Lou Reed, valleys-born John Cale was responsible for the experimental edge that made the Velvet Underground one of the most influential bands of all time. He's gone on to become a respected solo performer and producer.

Since then major names have included the Alarm, Manic Street Preachers, Catatonia, Stereophonics, Gorky's Zygotic Mynci, Charlotte Church, Jem, Christopher Rees, Bullet For My Valentine, Kate Le Bon and Duffy. The genre-defying Super Furry Animals produced the biggest-selling Welsh-language album of all time, the dreamy *Mwng*.

The Welsh wave shows no signs of breaking anytime soon, with bands such as Marina & the Diamonds, Kids In Glass Houses, Future of the Left and Lostprophets flying the red dragon flag.

Skenfrith

A chocolate-box village of stone buildings set around a hefty castle and ancient church, and skirted by the River Monnow, Skenfrith encapsulates the essence of the Monmouthshire countryside. Skenfrith Castle was built around 1228 by Hubert de Burgh on the site of earlier Norman fortifications. Its keep and walls are partially intact and there are no barriers to prevent you entering and picnicking on the central lawn. Nearby, a squat tower announces 750-year-old St Bridget's Church, accessed by a low wooden door with a foot-high step.

There are excellent walks in the area – one route leads over the English border to St Michael's Church, Garway, which is adorned with mason's marks from its Knights Templar past.

The riverside village pub, The Bell at Skenfrith (☎01600-750235; www.skenfrith.co.uk; r £110-220; P🖤) , has had a gastronomic makeover and is now an esteemed restaurant serving upmarket country fare (mains £19, 2-/3-course lunch £18/22). Upstairs there are elegant rooms that marry an antique feel with contemporary comfort.

Skenfrith is 8 miles northwest of Monmouth via the B4233, B4347 and B4521. There's no public transport.

Blaenavon (Blaenafon)

POP 6000

Of all the valley towns that were decimated by the demise of heavy industry, the one-time coal and iron town of Blaenavon shows the greenest shoots of regrowth, helped in large part by the awarding of Unesco World Heritage site status in 2000 to its conglomeration of industrial sites. Its proximity to Brecon Beacons National Park and Abergavenny doesn't do it any harm either.

Blaenavon is an interesting town to visit, but not necessarily to stay in; the nearest recommended accommodation is in Abergavenny.

⊙ Sights

FREE Blaenavon World Heritage Centre INTERPRETATION CENTRE (☎01495-742333; www.world-heritage-blaenavon.org.uk; Church Rd; ⊙9am-4pm Tue-Sun) Housed in an artfully converted old school, this centre contains a cafe, tourist office, gallery, gift shop and, more importantly, excellent interactive, audiovisual displays which explore the industrial heritage of the region.

FREE Big Pit: National Coal Museum MINE, MUSEUM (☎029-2057 3650; www.museumwales.ac.uk; ⊙9.30am-5pm, guided tours 10am-3.30pm) Big Pit provides an opportunity to descend 90m into a real coal mine guided by an ex-miner and to get a taste of what life was like for those who worked here. It's cold underground so take extra layers, and wear sturdy shoes. Children must be at least 1m tall. If you don't fancy the descent, there's an interpretative display on the industry in the old Pit Head Baths.

RAGLAN CASTLE

Magnificent Raglan Castle (Cadw; ☑01291-690228; www.cadw.wales.gov.uk; adult/child £3/2.60; ☺9am-5pm Apr-Oct, 9.30am-4pm Mon-Sat & 11am-4pm Sun Nov-Mar; P) was the last great medieval castle to be built in Wales and was designed more as a swaggering declaration of wealth and power than a defensive fortress. A sprawling complex built of dusky pink sandstone, its centrepiece is the lavish Great Tower, a hexagonal keep ringed by a moat, which was badly damaged during the Civil Wars of the 1640s.

Bus 83 from Monmouth (20 minutes) and Abergavenny (25 minutes) stops in Raglan; it's a five-minute walk to the castle.

Blaenavon Ironworks   HISTORIC SITE

(www.cadw.wales.gov.uk; North St; ☺10am-5pm Apr-Oct, 9.30am-4pm Fri & Sat, 11am-4pm Sun Nov-Mar) When it was completed in 1789, Blaenavon Ironworks was one of the most advanced in the world. Today the site is one of the best preserved of all the Industrial Revolution ironworks – although the hulking remains of the kilns and towers are now a home for ravens. Also on display are the ironworkers' tiny terraced cottages.

Pontypool &
Blaenavon Railway   HERITAGE RAILWAY

(☑Heritage Railway; www.pontypool-and-blaenavon. co.uk; adult/child £6/3.50; ☺check online for timetables) Built to haul coal and passengers, this railway has been restored by local volunteers, allowing you to catch a steam train from the town centre to Big Pit and on to Whistle Halt, the highest train station in England and Wales (396m).

🛍 Shopping

Blaenavon Cheddar Company   FOOD

(☑01495-793123; www.chunkofcheese.co.uk; 80 Broad St; bike hire half-/full day £10/20; ☺10am-5pm Mon-Sat) The award-winning cheese company is both a champion for the town and evidence of its gradual resurgence. The shop showcases the company's range of handmade cheese, some of which are matured down in the Big Pit mineshaft. The Pwll Mawr is particularly good, having won a bronze in the British cheese awards, but for extra kick try the chilli-and-ale laced Dragon's Breath. It also stocks a range of Welsh speciality ales, wines and whisky. The same crew offers **bike hire** and small-group cycling and walking **tours**.

❶ Getting There & Away

Bus X24 heads here from Newport (50 minutes).

Caerleon

POP 8700

After the Romans invaded Britain in AD 43, they controlled their new territory through a network of forts and military garrisons. The top tier of military organisation was the legionary fort, of which there were only three in Britain – at Eboracum (York), Deva (Chester) and Isca (Caerleon).

Caerleon ('fort of the legion') was the headquarters of the elite 2nd Augustan Legion for more than 200 years, from AD 75 until the end of the 3rd century. It wasn't just a military camp but a purpose-built township some 9 miles in circumference, complete with a 6000-seat amphitheatre and a state-of-the-art Roman baths complex. Today it is one of the largest and most important Roman settlements in Britain.

Begin with a visit to the excellent National Roman Legion Museum (www.museum wales.ac.uk/en/roman; High St; admission free; ☺10am-5pm Mon-Sat, 2-5pm Sun), which displays a host of intriguing Roman artefacts, from jewellery to armour and teeth to tombstones, and shows what life was like for Roman soldiers in one of the most remote corners of the Empire.

Head next for the Roman Baths (www. cadw.wales.gov.uk; High St; admission free; ☺9.30am-5pm Apr-Oct, 9.30am-5pm Mon-Sat, 11am-4pm Sun Nov-Mar; P), a block to the southeast. Parts of the outdoor swimming pool, *apodyterium* (changing room) and *frigidarium* (cold room) are on show under a protective roof, and give some idea of the scale of the place. Projections of bathers splashing through shimmering water help bring it to life.

The Broadway, the side street opposite the museum, leads to a park on the left where you'll find the turf-covered terraces of the Roman Amphitheatre (admission free; ⊙9.30am-5pm). The oval structure is the only fully excavated Roman amphitheatre in Britain; it lay just outside the old Roman city walls. Follow the signs on the other side of the road to see the foundations of the Barracks.

Two miles to the southeast of Caerleon, in the village of Christchurch, the Old Rectory (☎01633-430700; www.the-oldrectory.co.uk; s/d £50/75; P⊛) offers a warm welcome and three luxurious rooms with views over the Severn Estuary to England.

Caerleon is 4 miles northeast of Newport. Buses 27 and 28 (15 minutes, four per hour) run from Newport bus station to Caerleon High St.

SWANSEA & THE GOWER

Wales' second-largest city sprawls along the 5-mile sweep of Swansea Bay, ending to the southwest in the smart seaside suburb of Mumbles at the head of the beautiful Gower Peninsula.

Swansea (Abertawe)

POP 229,100

Dylan Thomas called Swansea an 'ugly, lovely town' and that remains a fair description today. It's currently in the grip of a Cardiff-esque bout of regeneration that's slowly transforming the drab, postwar city centre into something worthy of its natural assets. A new marina, national museum, waterpark, architecturally tricksy footbridge and transport centre have already opened.

Swansea makes up for its visual shortcomings with a visceral charm. A hefty student population takes to the city's bars with enthusiasm and a few good restaurants have emerged from among all the Chinese and Indian takeaways.

Swansea's Welsh name, Abertawe, describes its location at the mouth of the Tawe, where the river empties into Swansea Bay. The Vikings named the area Sveins Ey (Swein's Island), probably referring to the sandbank in the river mouth.

The Normans built a castle here, but Swansea didn't really get into its stride until the Industrial Revolution, when it developed into an important copper-smelting centre. Ore was first shipped in from Cornwall, across the Bristol Channel, but by the 19th century it was arriving from Chile, Cuba and the USA, in return for Welsh coal.

By the 20th century the city's industrial base had declined, although Swansea's oil refinery and smaller factories were still judged a worthy target by the Luftwaffe, which devastated the city centre in 1941.

⊙ Sights

FREE **National Waterfront Museum** MUSEUM
(www.museumwales.ac.uk/en/swansea; South Dock Marina, Oystermouth Rd, South Dock Marina; ⊙10am-5pm) Housed in a 1901 dockside warehouse with a striking glass and slate extension, the museum's 15 hands-on galleries explore Wales' industrial history and the impact of industrialisation on its people, from 1750 to this day, making much use of interactive computer screens and audiovisual presentations. The effect can be a bit overwhelming, but there's a lot of interesting stuff here, enough to occupy a few hours.

FREE **Swansea Museum** MUSEUM
(www.swansea.gov.uk/swanseamuseum; Victoria Rd; ⊙10am-5pm Tue-Sun) It would be hard to find a more complete contrast to the Waterfront Museum – Dylan Thomas referred to it as 'the museum which should have *been* in a museum'. Founded in 1834, it remains charmingly low-tech, from the eccentric Cabinet of Curiosities to the glass cases of archaeological finds from Gower caves. Pride of place goes to the Mummy of Hor.

FREE **Dylan Thomas Centre** MUSEUM
(www.swansea.gov.uk/dtc; Somerset Pl; ⊙10am-4.30pm) Housed in the former Guildhall, this unassuming museum contains absorbing displays on the Swansea-born poet's life and work. Aside from the collection of memorabilia, what really brings his work to life is a series of recordings, including the booming baritone of Richard Burton performing *Under Milk Wood* and Thomas himself reading *Do Not Go Gentle Into That Good Night,* the celebrated paean to his dying father.

FREE **Egypt Centre** MUSEUM
(www.egypt.swan.ac.uk; Swansea University, Mumbles Rd; ⊙10am-4pm Tue-Sat) Swansea University is in the suburb of Sketty, halfway between the city centre and Mumbles, and displays a fascinating collection of everyday ancient Egyptian artefacts, ranging from a 4000-year-old razor to a mummified

PEMBROKESHIRE & SOUTH WALES SWANSEA (ABERTAWE)

Swansea

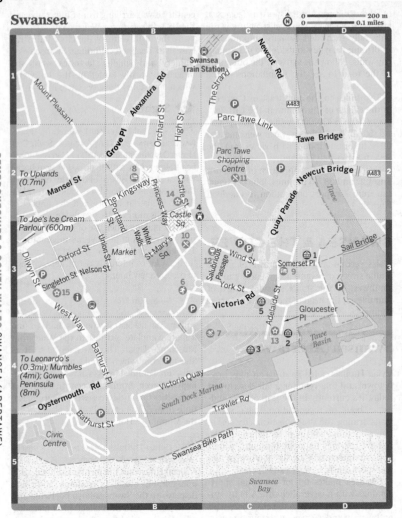

crocodile. The kids can try their hand at 'dummy mummy' mummification.

FREE Mission Gallery   GALLERY
(www.missiongallery.co.uk; Gloucester Pl; ⊙11am-5pm Tue-Sun) Set in a converted 19th-century seamen's chapel, Mission stages Swansea's most striking exhibitions of contemporary art, as well as selling glassware, ceramics, jewellery and art magazines.

Swansea Castle   CASTLE
(Castle Sq) A small pocket of the central city around Wind St and Castle Sq escaped the wartime bombing and retains a remnant of Georgian and Victorian Swansea as well as the ruins of 14th-century Swansea Castle (closed to the public). The castle was mostly destroyed by Cromwell in 1647, but had a brief lease of life as a prison in the 19th century.

🏃 Activities

LC2   SWIMMING
(www.thelcswansea.com; Oystermouth Rd; waterpark adult/child £7/4; ⊙4-8pm Mon-Fri, 9am-8pm Sat & Sun) The Marine Quarter's £32-million

Swansea

⊙ Sights
1 Dylan Thomas Centre D3
2 Mission Gallery C4
3 National Waterfront Museum C4
4 Swansea Castle.......................................B2
5 Swansea Museum C3

⊙ Activities, Courses & Tours
6 Action Bikes..B3
7 LC2..C4

⊙ Sleeping
8 Dragon Hotel B2
9 Morgans..C3

⊗ Eating
10 Hanson at the Chelsea
   Restaurant B3
11 Joe's Ice Cream Parlour C2

⊙ Drinking
12 No Sign Bar C3

⊕ Entertainment
13 Dylan Thomas Theatre..........................C4
14 Monkey B2
15 Swansea Grand Theatre.......................A3

leisure centre includes a toddler's play area, a gym and a 9m indoor climbing wall, but best of all is the waterpark, complete with a wave pool, water slides and the world's first indoor surfing ride.

Action Bikes   CYCLING
(☎01792-464640; www.actionbikesswansea.co.uk; 5 St David's Sq) Rent a bike and hit the section of the Lôn Geltaidd (Celtic Trail; National Cycle Network Route 4) that hugs the bay from downtown Swansea to Mumbles.

⭐ Festivals & Events

Swansea Bay Summer Festival   SUMMER
(www.swanseabayfestival.co.uk) From July to September, the waterfront is taken over by shows, fun fairs, carnivals, music and exhibitions.

Dylan Thomas Festival   CULTURAL
(www.dylanthomas.com) Poetry readings, talks, films and performances; held from 27 October (Thomas' date of birth) to 9 November (the date he died).

🛏 Sleeping

Mirador Town House   B&B ££
(☎01792-466976; www.themirador.co.uk; 14 Mirador Cres, Uplands; s/d from £69/95) Kooky in the extreme, all seven B&B rooms are elaborately themed – Roman, Mediterranean, African, Spanish, Egyptian, Oriental, French – with murals on the walls and sometimes the ceilings as well. They're extremely well kitted out (DVD players, ironing equipment, local maps), and the exuberant hosts are enthusiastic cheerleaders for the area.

Christmas Pie B&B   B&B ££
(☎01792-480266; www.christmaspie.co.uk; 2 Mirador Cres, Uplands; s/d £49/78; P) The name suggests something warm and comforting, and this suburban villa does not disappoint – three tastefully decorated en-suite bedrooms, fresh fruit and an out-of-the-ordinary, vegetarian-friendly breakfast selection. One room is much smaller than the others, but they're all extremely well kept.

Morgans   HOTEL ££
(☎01792-484848; www.morganshotel.co.uk; Somerset Pl; r £65-250; P) The city's first boutique hotel, set in the gorgeous red-brick and Portland stone former Ports Authority building, Morgans combines historic elegance with contemporary design, and a high pamper factor – Egyptian cotton bed linen, suede curtains, big bathrobes, flatscreen TVs. An annexe across the road has lower ceilings but similar standards.

Crescent   B&B ££
(☎01792-465782; www.thecrescentswansea.co.uk; 132 Eaton Cres, Uplands; s £45, d £65-70; 🛜) Perched on a slope with views across the rooftops to Swansea Bay, the Crescent is a grand old Edwardian gent, daringly dressed in powder blue. The bedrooms vary in size, with the larger ones being quite roomy. Bathrooms are small, but they are en suite.

Dragon Hotel   HOTEL ££
(☎01792-657141; www.dragon-hotel.co.uk; The Kingsway; r from £69; P🏊) This 1960s city-centre hotel has been given an expensive upgrade, with dragon-red carpets, orange backlighting and well-turned-out bedrooms.

There's also a gym and an 18m indoor pool. The double-glazing helps combat the noise in this extremely busy location, but you're still better off requesting a higher floor.

Leonardo's GUESTHOUSE **£**
(✆01792-470163; www.leonardosguesthouse.co.uk; 380 Oystermouth Rd; s/d £38/48, without bathroom £26/45; ☎) Leonardo's is the best choice in the long strip of budget seafront guest houses on Oystermouth Rd, with small rooms in bright, sunny colours. Five of the nine bedrooms enjoy views over Swansea Bay and some have en suites. It's much better than you'd expect for the extremely reasonable price.

Eating

Joe's Ice Cream Parlour ICE CREAM **£**
(www.joes-icecream.com; 85 St Helen's Rd; cones/sundaes from £1.15/2.50; ☺noon-8pm) For an ice-cream sundae or a cone, locals love Joe's – a Swansea institution founded in 1922 by Joe Cascarini, son of immigrants from Italy's Abruzzi mountains. There are also branches at **Parc Tawe Shopping Centre** (The Strand, Parc Tawe Shopping Centre; ☺10.30am-5.15pm) and **Mumbles** (✆368212; 524 Mumbles Rd; ☺11am-5.30pm Sun & Mon, 9.30am-5.30pm Tue-Sat).

Hanson at the Chelsea Restaurant MODERN BRITISH **££**
(✆01792-464068; www.hansonatthechelsea.co.uk; 17 St Mary's St; mains £12-20, 2-/3-course lunch £13/17; ☺Mon-Sat) Perfect for a romantic liaison, this elegant little dining room is discreetly tucked away behind the frenzy of Wind St. Seafood's the specialty, although the menu contains plenty of meaty dishes, and blackboard specials are chalked up daily. While the name sounds flash, the prices aren't too bad.

Drinking & Entertainment

In a city synonymous with Dylan Thomas you'd expect some hard drinking to take place…and you'd be right. Swansea's main boozing strip is Wind St (pronounced to rhyme with 'blind', as in drunk) and on weekends it can be a bit of a zoo, full of generally good-natured alcopop-fuelled teens teetering around on high heels.

Buzz magazine (free from the tourist office and bars around town) has its finger on the pulse of the local scene.

No Sign Bar PUB
(www.nosignbar.co.uk; 56 Wind St) Once frequented by Dylan Thomas (it appears as the Wine Vaults in his story *The Followers*), the No Sign stands out as the only vaguely traditional bar left on Wind St. On weekends there's live music downstairs in the Vault. The window seats, looking out over the acres of goose-bumped flesh on the street outside, offer a frisson of schadenfreude.

Uplands Tavern PUB
(www.myspace.com/uplandstavern; 42 Uplands Cres) Yet another Thomas hang-out, Uplands still serves a quiet daytime pint in the Dylan Thomas snug. Come nightfall and it turns into a different beast altogether as the hub of the city's live music scene.

Monkey LIVE MUSIC, CAFE
(www.monkeycafe.co.uk; 13 Castle St) An organic, veggie-friendly cafe-bar by day, with chunky tables, big sofas, modern art and cool tunes, this funky little venue transforms after dark into Swansea's best alternative club, hosting DJs, live musicians and salsa upstairs.

Swansea Grand Theatre THEATRE
(✆01792-475715; www.swanseagrand.co.uk; Singleton St) The city's largest theatre stages a mixed line-up of ballet, opera, musicals, theatre, pantomimes and a comedy club.

THE DYLAN THOMAS TRAIL

The legacy of Dylan Thomas is inescapable in this part of Wales. Whether you're a fan or whether you're just interested to know what all the fuss is about, you'll find plenty of sites in Swansea to stalk the shade of the maverick poet and writer. When you've exhausted them all, you can always head on to Laugharne, northwest of Swansea.

Start at the Dylan Thomas Centre and then check out his statue gazing across the marina outside the Dylan Thomas Theatre. In the nearby suburb of Uplands, a plaque marks Thomas' **birthplace** (5 Cwmdonkin Dr), an unassuming terraced house where he wrote two-thirds of his poetry.

Perhaps the places where you're most likely to feel Thomas' presence are his beloved drinking haunts, which include No Sign Bar and Uplands Tavern.

Taliesin Arts Centre PERFORMING ARTS
(☑01792-602060; www.taliesinartscentre.co.uk;
Swansea University, Mumbles Rd) Part of Swansea University, this vibrant arts centre features live music, theatre, dance and film.

Dylan Thomas Theatre THEATRE
(☑01792-473238; www.dylanthomastheatre.org.uk; Gloucester Pl) Home to Swansea Little Theatre, an amateur dramatic group of which Dylan Thomas was once a member, the company stages a wide repertoire of plays, including regular performances of your man's *Under Milk Wood*.

ⓘ Information

Morriston Hospital (☑01792-702222; Heol Maes Eglwys, Morriston) Accident and emergency department, 5 miles north of centre.

Police station (☑101; Grove Pl)

Swansea tourist office (☑01792-468321; www.visitswanseabay.com; Plymouth St; ☺9.30am-5.30pm Mon-Sat year-round, plus 10am-4pm Sun school holidays)

ⓘ Getting There & Away

BUS Bus 701 links Swansea with Cardiff (1¼ hours), Carmarthen (45 minutes) and Aberystwyth (2¾ hours); and X13 with Llandeilo (1¼ hours). The **First Cymru** (www.firstgroup.com) Greyhound service heads regularly between Cardiff and Swansea (peak/off-peak £7/5 return, one hour). National Express coach destinations include London (£24, five hours), Chepstow (£12, 2¼ hours), Carmarthen (£6.10, 45 minutes), Tenby (£8.10, 1½ hours) and Pembroke (£8.10, 1¾ hours).

TRAIN Direct trains from Swansea head to London Paddington (£42, three hours), Cardiff (£7.80, one hour), Carmarthen (£8.10, 45 minutes), Tenby (£14, 1½ hours) and Llandrindod Wells (£12, 2¼ hours).

ⓘ Getting Around

First Cymru runs local services. A Swansea Bay Day Ticket offers all-day bus travel in the Swansea Bay area (including Mumbles and the Gower Peninsula) for £4.50; buy tickets from the driver.

Mumbles (Y Mwmbwls)

Strung out along the shoreline at the southern end of Swansea Bay, Mumbles has been Swansea's seaside retreat since 1807, when the Oystermouth Railway was opened. Built for transporting coal, the horse-drawn carriages were soon converted for paying customers, and the now defunct Mumbles train

became the first passenger railway service in the world.

Once again fashionable, with restaurants vying for trade along the promenade, Mumbles received a boost to its reputation when its most famous daughter, Hollywood actress Catherine Zeta-Jones, built a £2 million luxury mansion at Limeslade, on the south side of the peninsula. Singer Bonnie Tyler also has a home here.

The origin of Mumbles' unusual name is uncertain, although one theory is that it's a legacy of French seamen who nicknamed the twin rounded rocks at the tip of the headland Les Mamelles ('the breasts').

⊙ Sights

Oystermouth Castle CASTLE
(www.abertawe.gov.uk/oystermouthcastle; Castle Ave; adult/child £2.50/1.50; ☺11am-5pm mid-June–Sep) It wouldn't be Wales without a castle, hence the trendy shops and bars of Newton Rd are guarded by a majestic ruin. Once the stronghold of the Norman lords of Gower it's now the focus of summer Shakespeare performances. There's a fine view over Swansea Bay from the battlements.

Mumbles Pier PIER
(☑365220; www.mumbles-pier.co.uk; Mumbles Rd) At the end of its mile-long strip of pastel-painted houses, pubs and restaurants is a rocky headland abutted by a Victorian pier with a sandy beach below. Built in 1898, it houses the usual amusement arcade and a once-grand cafe, festooned with chandeliers.

🛏 Sleeping

Tides Reach Guest House B&B **££**
(☑01792-404877; www.tidesreachguesthouse.com; 388 Mumbles Rd; s £60-65, d £70-100; @⑦) Delicious eco-conscious breakfasts and stacks of local information are served with a smile at this smart waterfront B&B. Some rooms have sea views; our favourite is suitelike room 9, where the dormer windows open out to create a virtual deck from within the sloping roof.

Patricks with Rooms BOUTIQUE HOTEL **£££**
(☑01792-360199; www.patrickswithrooms.com; 638 Mumbles Rd; r £115-175) Patricks has 16 individually styled designer bedrooms in bold contemporary colours, with art on the walls, fluffy robes and, in some of the rooms, free-standing roll-top baths and sea views. Some are set back in a separate annexe. Downstairs there's an upmarket restaurant and bar.

✗ Eating & Drinking

The famous Mumbles Mile – a pub crawl along Mumbles Rd – is not what it once was; many of the old faithful inns have succumbed to the gastropub bug. Newton Rd does have some rather nice wine bars though, which aren't too bad for a drop of celebrity-spotting.

Jones   PUB

(☎361764; www.jonesbar.co.uk; 61 Newton Rd, Mumbles) Jones buzzes with 40-somethings giving the chandeliers a run for their money in the bling stakes. There's no chance Dylan Thomas ever did, or would, hang out here, but there's a good wine list and a friendly vibe.

❶ Information

Mumbles tourist information (☎01792-361302; www.mumblestic.co.uk; Methodist Church, Mumbles Rd; ⊙10am-5pm Mon-Sat, noon-5pm Sun Jul & Aug, 10am-4pm Mon-Sat Sep-Jun)

❶ Getting There & Away

Buses 1, 2, 3 and 37 head between Swansea and Mumbles (20 minutes).

Gower Peninsula (Y Gwŷr)

With its broad butterscotch beaches, pounding surf, precipitous clifftop walks and rugged, untamed uplands, the Gower Peninsula feels a million miles away from Swansea's urban bustle – yet it's just on the doorstep. This 15-mile-long thumb of land stretching west from Mumbles was designated the UK's first official Area of Outstanding Natural Beauty (AONB) in 1956. The National Trust (NT) owns about three-quarters of the coast, so access for walkers is good. The peninsula also has the best surfing in Wales outside Pembrokeshire.

The main family beaches, patrolled by lifeguards during the summer, are Langland Bay, Caswell Bay and Port Eynon.

◉ Sights

Heading west along the south coast from the family-magnet beach of Port Eynon, the village of Rhossili looks north along the 3-mile sweep of Rhossili Bay at the western tip of the peninsula. The village of Llangennith, at the north of Rhossili Bay, is the infrastructure hub for surfers, with PJ's Surfshop (☎386669; www.pjsurfshop.co.uk), run by former surf champion Peter Jones, the centre of activity.

From Rhossili village follow the 1-mile tidal causeway to rocky, wave-blasted Worm's Head (from Old English *wurm,* meaning dragon) but *only* for a two-hour period either side of low tide. At the Outer Head, look out for choughs, peregrine falcons, razorbills, guillemots and oystercatchers, as well as seals bobbing in the swell.

At the heart of the peninsula is Cefn Bryn, a ruggedly beautiful expanse of moorland that rises to a height of 186m. On a suitably desolate ridge above the village of

---

LOCAL KNOWLEDGE

QUENTIN GRIMLEY, WALES COAST PATH

Fancy a stroll? We asked the Coastal Access Project Officer for the Countryside Council of Wales to tell us about the Wales Coast Path (www.walescoastpath.gov.uk), the first walking track to encompass a country's entire coastline.

Can you tell us about the path? The project started in 2007 with the intention to create a continuous coastal path around all of Wales. It opened in 2012, linking up existing coastal paths like Pembrokeshire, which has been around since 1970, and others such as Ceredigion and Anglesea. If you then walk the Offa's Dyke Path, you can circle the whole of Wales.

How long does it take to walk the whole thing? It's 870 miles long. Walking every day for an average of 13 miles, it would take two months to complete – plus an additional two weeks if you finish with Offa's Dyke Path.

Are there any sections you'd recommend for travellers with only a day or two to spare? Well, places like Pembrokeshire are already well known, so for somewhere a little less obvious, try the Gower Peninsula by Swansea. It's an Area of Outstanding Natural Beauty, it's easy to get to and it's never had a continuous coastal path before now.

Reynoldston stands a mysterious neolithic burial chamber capped by the 25-tonne quartz boulder known as **Arthur's Stone** (Coeten Arthur).

🏃 Activities

Parc-Le-Breos Pony Trekking — HORSE RIDING
(☑01792-371636; www.parc-le-breos.co.uk; Parkmill; half-/full day £35/48) The rural byways and bridleways of Gower are ideal territory for horseback explorations.

Welsh Surfing Federation Surf School — SURFING
(☑01792-386426; www.wsfsurfschool.co.uk; Llangennith) The governing body for surfing in Wales offers initial two-hour surfing lessons for £25.

Sam's Surf Shack — SURFING
(☑01792-390519; www.samssurfshack.com; Rhossili, Rhossili; lesson per hr $25; board & wetsuit hire per day £17) Learn to surf at the Gower's most beautiful beach.

Gower Coast Adventures — CRUISE
(☑07866-250440; www.gowercoastadventures.co.uk) Speedboat trips to Worms Head from Port Eynon (adult/child £34/20) or Mumbles (adult/child £42/26), or from Mumbles to Three Cliffs and Oxwich Bay (adult/child £28/16).

🛏 Sleeping & Eating

Fairyhill — HOTEL £££
(☑01792-390139; www.fairyhill.net; s/d from £160/180; P🐕) Hidden (as any proper fairy place should be) down a narrow lane north of Reynoldston, this Georgian country house has a suitably magical setting. The rooms are excellent and less old-fashioned than the restaurant downstairs, which serves pleasantly Welsh food (two-/three-course lunch £20 to £25, mains £15 to £25) with few surprises.

Maes-Yr-Haf — B&B ££
(☑01792-371000; www.maes-yr-haf.com; Parkmill; s/d from £80/110; P🐕) The restaurant part of this restaurant-with-rooms has a focus on game, seafood and locally farmed meat (mains £17 to £19). The small but stylish rooms are a treat for gadget fans, with iPod docking stations and PlayStations that double as DVD players. Dinner-inclusive rates are available.

King's Head — PUB ££
(☑01792-386212; www.kingsheadgower.co.uk; Llangennith; r from £85; P🐕) The centre of Llangennith's social life is the King's Head, which serves real ales and home-cooked bar meals (mains £9 to £12). Behind it are two custom-made stone blocks, stylishly fitted out with modern bathrooms, pale tiles and underfloor heating.

Culver House — APARTMENTS ££
(☑01792-720300; www.culverhousehotel.co.uk; Port Eynon; apt from £99; @🐕) This renovated 19th-century house offers eight modern self-contained apartments with dishwashers, TVs that double as computers, laundry facilities and continental breakfasts delivered daily to your fridge. The upper apartments have balconies, while those on the ground-floor open onto cute little gardens.

Port Eynon YHA — HOSTEL £
(☑0845 371 9135; www.yha.org.uk; dm/r from £24/57) Worth special mention for its spectacular location, this former lifeboat station is as close as you could come to the sea without sleeping on the beach itself. It's cosier than your average youth hostel, with sea views from the lounge.

Parc-le-Breos House — B&B ££
(☑01792-371636; www.parc-le-breos.co.uk; Parkmill, Parkmill; r from £80; P🐕) Set in a private estate north of the main road, Parc-le-Breos has en-suite B&B accommodation in a Victorian hunting lodge. The majestic lounge and dining room downstairs have grand fireplaces that crackle into action in winter.

King Arthur Hotel — PUB ££
(☑01792-390775; www.kingarthurhotel.co.uk; Higher Green, Reynoldston; s/d from £60/75; P) As traditional as swords in stone and ladies of the lake, the King Arthur serves real ales in a cosy wood-panelled bar and offers a lengthy menu in the neighbouring dining room (mains £8 to £15). The bedrooms above are less atmospheric but clean and comfortable. For true romance, enquire about the stone-walled 18th-century Guinevere's Cottage.

Nicholaston Farm — CAMPSITE £
(☑01792-371209; www.nicholastonfarm.co.uk; Penmaen; sites £15-25; ☀Mar-Oct) Field camping in a working farm overlooking Oxwich Bay. There's a little farm shop/cafe and an excellent ablutions block.

ℹ Information

Rhossili visitor centre (☑01792-390707; www.nationaltrust.org.uk/gower; Coastguard

Cottages, Rhossili; ⊙10.30am-5pm mid-Feb-Dec, 10.30am-4pm Wed-Sun Jan–mid-Feb) The National Trust's centre has information on local walks and wildlife, and an audiovisual display upstairs.

❶ Getting There & Around

The Gower is included in First Cymru's Swansea Bay zone. Buses zip all around the peninsula, with additional services in summer.

CARMARTHENSHIRE (SIR GAERFYRDDIN)

Castle-dotted Carmarthenshire has gentle valleys, deep-green woods and a small, partly sandy coast. Caught between dramatic neighbours – Pembrokeshire to the west and the Brecon Beacons to the east – it remains much quieter and less explored. Yet the appeal of its tranquil countryside hasn't gone entirely unnoticed and charming places like Llandeilo are sprouting upmarket galleries and shops. If your interests stretch to gardens, stately homes and all things green, add this quiet county to your itinerary.

Llandeilo & Around

POP 3000

Set on a hill encircled by the greenest of fields, Llandeilo is little more than a handful of narrow streets lined with grand Georgian and Victorian buildings and centred on a picturesque church and graveyard. The surrounding region was once dominated by large country estates and, though they have long gone, the deer, parkland trees and agricultural character of the landscape are their legacy.

⊙ Sights

National Botanic Garden of Wales   GARDENS
(www.gardenofwales.org.uk; Llanarthne; adult/child £8.50/4.50; ⊙10am-6pm Apr-Oct, 10am-4.30pm Nov-Mar) Concealed in the rolling Tywi valley countryside, this lavish complex opened in 2000 and is still maturing. Formerly an aristocratic estate, the garden has a wide range of plant habitats, from lakes and bogs to woodland and heath, with lots of decorative areas and educational exhibits on plant medicine and organic farming. The centrepiece is the Norman Foster–designed Great Glasshouse, an arresting glass dome sunken into the earth.

The garden is located 8 miles southwest of Llandeilo, signposted from the road to Carmarthen (A40).

Dinefwr Park & Castle   HISTORIC BUILDING
(NT; www.nationaltrust.org.uk; adult/child £6/3; ⊙11am-5pm) At the heart of this large estate, immediately west of Llandeilo, is Newton House, a wonderful 17th-century manor made over with a Victorian facade. It's presented as it was in Edwardian times, focusing particularly on the experience of servants in their downstairs domain. Striking 12th-century Dinefwr Castle is set on a hilltop in the southern corner of the estate. In the 17th century it suffered the indignity of being converted into a picturesque garden feature. There are several marked walking routes around the grounds.

Bus 280 (Carmarthen–Llandeilo) stops here.

Aberglasney Gardens   GARDENS
(www.aberglasney.org; Llangathen; adult/child £8/4; ⊙10am-6pm Apr-Sep, 10.30am-4pm Oct-Mar) Wandering through these formal walled gardens feels a bit like walking into a Jane Austen novel. They date back to the 17th century and contain a unique cloister built solely as a garden decoration. There's also a pool garden, a 250-year-old yew tunnel and a 'wild' garden in the bluebell woods to the west. Several derelict rooms in the central courtyard of Aberglasney House have been converted into a glass-roofed atrium garden full of subtropical plants such as orchids, palms and cycads.

Aberglasney is in the village of Llangathen, just off the A40, 4 miles west of Llandeilo. Bus 280 between Carmarthen and Llandeilo stops on the A40, 500m north of the gardens.

⌷ Sleeping

Fronlas   B&B £££
(☏01558-824733; www.fronlas.com; 7 Thomas St; s/d from £60/80; ⓅⓈ) A Victorian town house given a chic makeover, Fronlas has four rooms dressed in fresh tones, designer wallpaper and marble or slate-floored bathrooms. A similarly well-attired guest lounge has an honesty bar and DVD library. The quiet, town-fringe location affords valley views.

Plough   HOTEL ££
(☏01558-823431; www.ploughrhosmaen.com; s/d from £70/90; ⓅⓈ) On the A40, just north

of Llandeilo, this baby-blue inn offers hip, contemporary rooms, some with country-side views. The standard rooms are spacious enough but the corner-hogging executives have plenty of space and then some. There's a slightly corporate vibe, particularly in the downstairs restaurant.

❶ Getting There & Away

BUS Buses 280 and 281 from Carmarthen (40 minutes) and X13 from Swansea (1½ hours) stop here.

TRAIN Llandeilo is on the Heart of Wales railway line, with direct services to Swansea (£6.40, 59 minutes), Llanwrtyd Wells (£4.50, 44 minutes), Llandrindod Wells (£7, 1¼ hours), Knighton (£9.80, two hours) and Shrewsbury (£12, three hours).

Carmarthen (Caerfyrddin)

POP 14,600

Carmarthenshire's county town is a place of legend and ancient provenance. Though not the kind of place you'll feel inclined to linger in, it's a handy transport and shopping hub. The Romans built a town here, complete with a fort and amphitheatre. A couple of solid walls, a gatehouse and a few crumbling towers are all that remain of Carmarthen's Norman castle, which was largely destroyed in the Civil War.

Most intriguingly, Carmarthen is reputed to be the birthplace of the most famous wizard of them all (no, not Harry Potter) – Myrddin of the Arthurian legends, better known in English as Merlin. An oak tree planted in 1660 for Charles II's coronation came to be called 'Merlin's Tree' and was linked to a prophecy that its death would mean curtains for the town. The tree died in the 1970s, but the town, while a little down at heel, is still standing.

◉ Sights

Carmarthen Market   MARKET
(www.carmarthenmarket.co.uk; Market Way; ⊙9.30am-4.30pm Mon-Sat) There's been a market here since Roman times and in 1180 it was given a royal charter. Housed in an edgy new building, the market sells everything from produce to antiques. On Wednesday and Saturday it spills out onto Red St.

Oriel Myrddin   GALLERY
(Merlin Gallery; ☑222775; www.orielmyrddingallery.co.uk; Church Lane; admission free; ⊙10am-5pm Mon-Sat) Stages changing exhibitions of contemporary art.

King Street Gallery   GALLERY
(www.kingstreetgallery.co.uk; King St; ⊙10am-5pm Mon-Sat) Sells interesting work by a co-operative of 25 local painters, sculptors, ceramicists and potters.

✖ Eating

Carmarthen's contribution to Welsh gastronomy is a salt-cured, air-dried ham. Legend has it that the Romans liked the recipe so much they took it back to Italy (proscuitto). Look for it at Carmarthen market.

Angel Vaults   MODERN WELSH **££**
(☑01267-238305; www.angelvaultsrestaurant.co.uk; 3 Nott Sq; 2-/3-course lunch £12/16, dinner £25/30; ⊙Tue-Sat) For a swanky night out, locals head to Angel Vaults for heavenly food and then finish off across the square at Diablo's for devilish cocktails. A locally focused menu features Carmarthen ham, Gower salt-marsh lamb and Welsh cheeses.

❶ Information

Tourist office (☑01267-231557; www.discovercarmarthenshire.com; Old Castle House; ⊙9.30am-4.30pm Mon-Sat)

PEMBROKESHIRE & SOUTH WALES CARMARTHEN (CAERFYRDDIN)

WORTH A TRIP

NATIONAL WETLAND CENTRE

Covering 97 hectares on the northern shore of the Burry Inlet, across from the Gower Peninsula, the **National Wetland Centre** (☑01554-741087; www.wwt.org.uk/llanelli; Llanelli; adult/child £7.05/3.86; ⊙9.30am-5pm Apr-Sep, 9.30am-4.30pm Oct-Mar; ℗) is one of Wales' most important habitats for waders and waterfowl. Winter is the most spectacular season, when up to 60,000 birds converge on the salt marsh and mudflats. Flashiest of all are the resident flock of nearly fluorescent pink Caribbean flamingos.

There's always plenty on for the littl'uns during the school holidays. Late spring's Duckling Days are filled with downy cuteness, while in the summer months there are canoes and bikes to borrow.

MYTHS & LEGENDS

Wales is awash with sagas inspired by bloody conflict and untamed landscapes. From generation to generation, elaborate tales of enchantment and wizardry have been bequeathed like rich family legacies. As early as the 9th century tales of mystery and heroism were compiled in the *Historia Britonum*. But the finest impressions come from the *Mabinogion*, a 14th-century tome containing occasionally terrifying tales of Celtic magic.

King Arthur is a recurrent character, especially in the *Mabinogion*. One of British legend's most romanticised heroes, he was believed to have been a 5th- or 6th-century cavalry leader who rallied British fighters against the marauding Saxon invaders. Time transformed Arthur into a king of magic deeds, with wise magician Myrddin (Merlin) by his side and a loyal band of followers in support. Arthur went on to slay Rita Gawr, a giant who butchered kings, in an epic battle on Snowdon. Finally, Myrddin delivered the dying hero to Avalon, which may well have been saintly Bardsey Island off the Llŷn Peninsula.

The world of Welsh myths is richly imaginative. For more see Robin Gwyndaf's detailed bilingual *Chwedlau Gwerin Cymru: Welsh Folk Tales*.

❶ Getting There & Away

BUS Bus 701 links Carmarthen with Cardiff (2 hours), Swansea (52 minutes) and Aberystwyth (1¾ hours); 280 and 281 head to Llandeilo (40 minutes); and 460 to Cardigan (1½ hours). National Express destinations include London (£28, six hours), Chepstow (£17, 2¾ hours), Swansea (£6, 45 minutes), Tenby (£5.10, 45 minutes) and Pembroke (£5.10, one hour).

TRAIN The station is 300m south of town across the river. There are direct trains to Cardiff (£17, 1¾ hours), Swansea (£8.10, 45 minutes), Tenby (£8.30, 43 minutes) and Pembroke (£8.30, 1½ hours).

Laugharne (Talacharn)

POP 2900

Sleepy little Laugharne (pronounced 'larn') sits above the tide-washed shores of the Taf Estuary, overlooked by a Norman castle. Dylan Thomas, one of Wales' greatest writers, spent the last four years of his life here, during which he produced some of his most inspired work, including *Under Milk Wood;* the town is one of the inspirations for the play's fictional village of Llareggub (spell it backwards and you'll get the gist).

On Thomas' first visit he described it as the 'strangest town in Wales', but returned repeatedly throughout his restless life. Many Dylan fans make a pilgrimage here to see the Boathouse where he lived, the shed where he wrote, Brown's Hotel where he drank (he used to give the pub telephone number as his contact number) and the churchyard where he's buried.

◉ Sights

Dylan Thomas Boathouse　　　MUSEUM
(www.dylanthomasboathouse.com; Dylan's Walk; adult/child £4/1.95; ⊙10am-5.30pm May-Oct, 10.30am-3.30pm Nov-Apr) Dylan Thomas lived here from 1949 to 1953 with his wife Caitlin and their three children. It's a beautiful setting, looking out over the estuary with its 'heron-priested shore'. The parlour has been restored to its 1950s appearance, with the desk that once belonged to Thomas' schoolmaster father and recordings of the poet reading his own works. Upstairs are photographs, manuscripts, a short video about his life, and his death mask, which once belonged to Richard Burton. Downstairs is a cafe.

Along the lane from the Boathouse is the old shed where Thomas did most of his writing. It looks as if he has just popped out, with screwed-up pieces of paper littered around.

Dylan and Caitlin Thomas are buried in a grave marked by a simple white, wooden cross in the grounds of **St Martin's Church**, on the northern edge of the town.

Laugharne Castle　　　CASTLE
(www.cadw.wales.gov.uk; adult/child £3.20/2.80; ⊙10am-5pm Apr-Oct) Built in the 13th century, Laugharne Castle was converted into a mansion in the 16th century for John Perrot, thought to be the illegitimate son of Henry VIII. It was landscaped with its current lawns and gardens in Victorian times.

🛏 Sleeping & Eating

Boat House　　　B&B ££
(☎01994-427263; www.theboathousebnb.co.uk; 1 Gosport St; s/d from £40/70; @🛜) Friendly,

homely and tastefully decorated, this is the smartest B&B in town. The building was formerly the Corporation Arms pub, where Dylan Thomas told stories in exchange for free drinks. The home-cooked breakfasts would assuage even Thomas' legendary hangovers.

Keepers Cottage B&B ££
(☏01994-427404; www.keepers-cottage.com; s/d £50/75; P⊙) Sitting on the top of the hill by the main approach to town, this white-painted brick cottage has four simply decorated but very comfortable rooms (three doubles and one twin). Complimentary bottled water, chocolates and little bottles of wine are a nice touch.

Hurst House on the Marsh HOTEL £££
(☏01994-427417; www.hurst-house.co.uk; East Marsh; r £225; P⊙⊛) Having had a £5 million makeover, you would expect this converted Georgian farm on the salt-marsh flats south of Laugharne to be luxurious. And it is. Rooms have big beds, bold colours and roll-top baths, there's massage therapy on tap, and a convivial, clubbish lounge bar and restaurant.

🛈 Getting There & Away

Bus 222 runs from Carmarthen to Laugharne (39 minutes).

PEMBROKESHIRE (SIR BENFRO)

The rugged Pembrokeshire coast is what you would imagine the world would look like if God was a geology teacher. There are knobbly hills of volcanic rock, long thin inlets scoured by glacial meltwater, and stratified limestone pushed up vertically and eroded into natural arches, blowholes and sea stacks. Stretches of towering red and grey cliff give way to perfect sandy beaches, only to resume around the headland painted black.

It's a landscape of Norman castles, Iron Age hill forts, holy wells and Celtic saints – including the nation's patron, Dewi Sant (St David). Predating even the ancient Celts are the remnants of an older people, who left behind them dolmens and stone circles – the same people who may have transported their sacred bluestones all the way from the Preseli Hills to form the giant edifice at Stonehenge.

Tenby (Dinbych-y-Pysgod)
POP 4900

Perched on a headland with sandy beaches on either side, Tenby is a postcard-maker's dream. Houses are painted from the pastel palette of a classic fishing village, interspersed with the white elegance of Georgian mansions. The main part of town is still constrained by its Norman-built walls, funnelling holidaymakers through medieval streets lined with pubs, ice-creameries and gift shops. Without the tackiness of the promenade-and-pier beach towns it tastefully returns to being a sleepy little place in the off season. In the summer months it has a boisterous, boozy holiday-resort feel.

Tenby flourished in the 15th century as a centre for the textile trade, exporting cloth in exchange for salt and wine. Clothmaking declined in the 18th century, but the town soon reinvented itself as a fashionable watering place, assisted by the coming of the railway in the 19th century.

◉ Sights & Activities

St Mary's Church CHURCH
(High St) The graceful vaulted roof of this 13th-century church is studded with fascinating wooden bosses, mainly dating from the 15th century, carved into flowers, cheeky

WORTH A TRIP

NATIONAL WOOL MUSEUM

The Cambrian Mills factory, world famous for its high-quality woollen products, closed in 1984 and this interesting museum (☏01559-370929; www.museumwales.ac.uk; admission free; ⊙daily Apr-Sep, 10am-5pm Tue-Sat Oct-Mar) has taken its place. Former mill workers are often on hand to get the machines clickety-clacking, but there's also a working commercial mill next door where you can watch the operations from a viewing platform. There's a cafe onsite and a gift shop selling snug woollen blankets.

The museum is positioned in verdant countryside, 14 miles north of Carmarthen and 14 miles southeast of Cardigan, signposted from the A484.

faces, mythical beasts, fish and even a mermaid holding a comb and mirror. There's a memorial here to Robert Recorde, the 16th-century writer and mathematician who invented the 'equals' sign, along with a confronting cadaver-topped tomb, intended to remind the viewer of their own mortality.

The young Henry Tudor – later to become Henry VII – was hidden here before fleeing to Brittany. It's thought that he left by means of a tunnel into the cellars under Mayor Thomas White's house across the road (where Boots is now).

Caldey Island
ISLAND

(☎01834-844453; www.caldey-island.co.uk; adult/child £11/6; ☺Mon-Sat Apr-Oct) Boat trips run from Tenby harbour to Caldey Island, home to lots of grey seals and seabirds, and a red-topped, whitewashed monastery that houses a community of Cistercian monks. There are guided tours of the monastery and great walks around the island, with good views from the lighthouse.

Tudor Merchant's House
HISTORIC BUILDING

(Quay Hill; adult/child £3.20/1.60; ☺11am-5pm Sun-Fri Easter-Oct) Tenby's handsomely restored 15th-century Tudor house is set up like it would have been in its heyday, with colourful wall hangings, period-style beds and kitchen implements. The curators have drawn the line at recreating the scent of the open cesspit next to the kitchen though.

Tenby Museum & Art Gallery
MUSEUM

(www.tenbymuseum.org.uk; Castle Hill; adult/child £4/2; ☺10am-5pm Mon-Fri Nov-Easter, daily Easter-Oct) Housed within the ruins of a Norman castle, this museum covers local history (summarised in an interesting short film) and includes paintings by Augustus and Gwen John.

Pembrokeshire

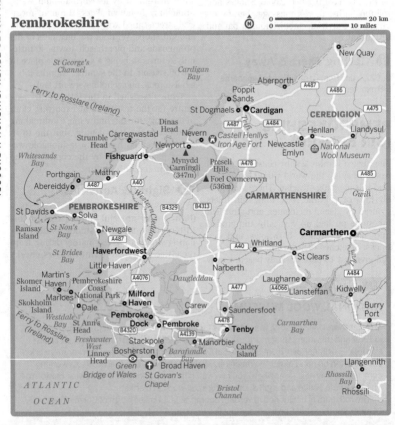

PEMBROKESHIRE COAST NATIONAL PARK

Established in 1952, Pembrokeshire Coast National Park (Parc Cenedlaethol Arfordir Sir Benfro) takes in almost the entire coast and its offshore islands, as well as the Preseli Hills in the north and the inland waters of the Cleddau rivers near Milford Haven. Pembrokeshire's sea cliffs and islands support huge breeding populations of seabirds, while seals, dolphins, porpoises and whales are frequently spotted in coastal waters.

There are three national park information centres – in Tenby, St Davids and Newport – and the local tourist offices scattered across Pembrokeshire are well stocked with park paraphernalia. The free annual newspaper *Coast to Coast* (online at www.pembroke shirecoast.org.uk) has lots of information on park attractions, a calendar of events and details of park-organised activities. It's worth picking it up for the tide tables alone – they're an absolute necessity for many legs of the Pembrokeshire Coast Path, which traverses the entire coast of the park.

🛏 Sleeping

Bay House   B&B **££**
(☎01834-849015; www.tenbybandb.co.uk; 5 Picton Rd; r £80-85) A stylish, modern take on the seaside B&B, Bay House offers a relaxed, friendly atmosphere, airy rooms with flat-screen TVs and DVDs, and an emphasis on local, organic produce. They only have three rooms and they book up well in advance.

Myrtle House   HOTEL **££**
(☎01834-842508; www.myrtlehousehoteltenby. com; St Mary's St; s/d £40/70) Located just a few metres from the steps down to Castle Beach, this late-Georgian house is an attractive place to stay. The eight rooms are spacious and all have en-suite bathrooms. The friendly owners serve up good breakfasts (vegetarians are well catered for).

St Brides Spa Hotel   HOTEL **£££**
(☎01834-812304; www.stbridesspahotel.com; St Brides Hill, Saundersfoot; s/d from £125/150; P ➰) Pembrokeshire's premier spa hotel offers the chance to relax after a massage in the infinity-edge pool overlooking the beach, before dining in the candle-lit Cliff restaurant (mains £16 to 21). The bedrooms are stylish and modern, in colours that evoke the seaside. It's in Saundersfoot, 3 miles north of Tenby.

Lindholme House   B&B **££**
(☎01834-843368; www.lindholmehouse.co.uk; 27 Victoria St; s/d £35/70) A traditional B&B with friendly owners and fry-up breakfasts, salmon-hued Lindholme is a little old-fashioned but clean, comfy and close to the beach and town centre. It doesn't have parking of its own but it's very handy to a large public car park.

🍴 Eating

Blue Ball Restaurant   RESTAURANT **££**
(☎01834-843038; www.theblueballrestaurant.co.uk; Upper Frog St; mains £10-19; ◷dinner Thu-Sun low season, daily summer) Polished wood, old timber beams and exposed brickwork create a cosy, rustic atmosphere in what is Tenby's best restaurant. The menu makes good use of local produce, notably seafood.

D Fecci & Sons   FISH & CHIPS, ICE CREAM **£**
(Lower Frog St; mains £5-9) Eating fish and chips on the beach is a British tradition, and D Fecci & Sons is a Tenby institution, having been in business since 1935. The same family runs the traditional Fecci's Ice Cream Parlour on St George's St and the neighbouring laundromat.

Plantagenet House   RESTAURANT **£££**
(☎01834-842350; Quay Hill; lunch £7-12, dinner £15-40; ◷lunch Sat & Sun, dinner Fri & Sat low season, daily summer) Atmosphere-wise, this place instantly impresses – perfect for a romantic, candle-lit dinner. Tucked down an alley in Tenby's oldest house, it's dominated by an immense 12th-century Flemish hearth. The menu ranges from seafood to organic beef.

ℹ Information

National park centre (☎845040; South Pde; ◷9.30am-5pm daily Apr-Sep, 10am-4.30pm Mon-Sat Oct-Mar)

Police station (Warren St)

Tourist office (☎01834-842402; Upper Park Rd, Tenby; ◷10am-4pm Easter-Oct, Mon-Sat Nov-Easter)

ℹ Getting There & Away

BICYCLE Rental bikes are available from **Tenby Cycles** (☎01834-845573; www.tenbycycles.

co.uk; The Norton; ◷9.30am-5pm Mon-Sat Easter-Sep) for £12 a day.

BUS Routes include 349 to Manorbier (20 minutes), Pembroke (46 minutes) and Haverfordwest (1¾ hours); and 361 to Saundersfoot (10 minutes) and Carew (56 minutes). National Express coach destinations include London (£28, seven hours), Chepstow (£21, 3½ hours), Swansea (£8.10, 90 minutes), Carmarthen (£5.10, 45 minutes) and Haverfordwest (£4.50, 50 minutes).

TRAIN There are direct services from Swansea (£13.20, 1½ hours), Carmarthen (£8.30, 43 minutes), Manorbier (£2.80, nine minutes) and Pembroke (£4.90, 35 minutes).

West of Tenby

Craggy, lichen-spotted Manorbier Castle (☑01834-871394; www.manorbiercastle.co.uk; adult/child £3.50/1.50; ◷10am-6pm Easter-Sep) guards over a little village of leafy, twisting lanes nestled above a lovely sandy beach, 5.5 miles southwest of Tenby. Manorbier YHA (☑0845 371 9031; www.yha.org.uk; dm/d from £16/31; P) occupies a futuristic ex–Ministry of Defence building, 1.5 miles east of the village centre, on a remote clifftop.

Further west, the National Trust's Stackpole Estate takes in 8 miles of coast, including two fine beaches (Barafundle Bay and Broad Haven), a wooded valley and the Bosherston Lily Ponds, a system of artificial ponds famous for their spectacular display of water lilies.

From the car park at the end of the St Govan's Head road, steps hacked into the rock lead down to tiny St Govan's Chapel, wedged into a slot in the cliffs just out of reach of the sea. The chapel dates from the 5th or 6th century, and is named for an itinerant 6th-century Irish preacher. The car park at Stack Rocks, 3 miles to the west, gives access to even more spectacular cliff scenery, including the Green Bridge of Wales, the biggest natural arch in the country.

Wild and windblown Freshwater West, a 2-mile strand of golden sand and silver shingle backed by acres of dunes, is Wales' best surf beach, sitting wide open to the Atlantic rollers. But beware – although great for surfing, its big waves, powerful rips *and* quicksand make it dangerous for swimming; several people have drowned here and the beach has year-round red-flag status. Scenes from *Harry Potter and the Deathly Hallows* and Ridley Scott's *Robin Hood* were filmed here.

At the southern head of the Milford Haven waterway, the village of Angle feels a long way off the beaten track. The main attraction is the tiny beach at West Angle Bay, which has great views across the mouth of Milford Haven to St Ann's Head, and offers good coastal walks with lots of rock pools to explore.

The Coastal Cruiser bus (www.pembroke shiregreenways.co.uk; ◷Mon, Thu & Sat Oct-Apr, daily May-Sep) loops in both directions between Pembroke, Angle, Freshwater West, Bosherston and Stackpole, terminating at Pembroke Dock.

Pembroke (Penfro)

POP 7200

Pembroke is not much more than a single street of neat Georgian and Victorian houses sitting beneath a whopping great castle – the oldest in west Wales and birthplace of Henry VII, the first Tudor king. Spectacular and forbidding Pembroke Castle (☑01646-681510; www.pembrokecastle.co.uk; Main St; adult/child £4.50/3.50; ◷9.30am-6pm Apr-Sep, 10am-5pm Mar & Oct, 10am-4pm Nov-Feb) was the home of the earls of Pembroke for over 300 years. A fort was established here in 1093, but most of the present buildings date from the 12th and 13th centuries. It's a great place for children to explore – wall walks and passages run from tower to tower, and there are vivid exhibitions detailing the castle's history. Guided tours are available from May to August (£1.50; phone for times). Falconry displays and costumed re-enactments are held in summer.

🛏 Sleeping & Eating

Tregenna   B&B ££

(☑01646-621525; www.tregennapembroke.co.uk; 7 Upper Lamphey Rd; s/d £40/65; P🛜) Everything's still modern and shiny in this newly built house on the outskirts of town (900m east of the station). There are lots of treats in the rooms including bottled water and Welsh cakes. Surprisingly, the black carpets and drapes aren't at all oppressive.

Beech House   B&B £

(☑01646-683740; www.beechhousepembroke. com; 78 Main St; s/d/tw £25/45/50) Wearing a garland of ivy over its duck-egg blue walls, this pretty place at the western end of the main street has spick-and-span rooms with period Georgian features and a vibrant front garden. It's convenient for the train station and family-friendly.

High Noon Guest House B&B £
(☎01646-683736; www.highnoon.co.uk; Lower Lamphey Rd; s with/without bathroom £35/25, d £50; P✿) Handy for Pembroke train station, and offering good value rather than atmosphere, this modern house has decent, though smallish rooms with a pleasant garden terrace out back. Some single rooms share bathrooms.

Old King's Arms Hotel PUB £££
(☎01646-683611; www.oldkingsarmshotel.co.uk; Main St; mains £15-23) Dark timber beams, ochre walls and polished copperware lend a country kitchen atmosphere to the restaurant here. The locally sourced protein (Welsh lamb, Carmarthen ham) comes accompanied with enough potatoes and vegetables to fill even a Tudor king.

❶ Information

Tourist office (☎01437-776499; Commons Rd; ⏱10am-4pm Mon-Fri, 10am-1pm Sat Apr-Oct, 10am-1pm Tue-Sat Nov-Mar)

❶ Getting There & Away

BOAT There are two sailings a day serviced by **Irish Ferries** (☎08717-300 500; www.irishferries.co.uk) on the four-hour route between Pembroke Dock and Rosslare in the southeast of Ireland.

BUS The 349 heads to Tenby (46 minutes), Manorbier (26 minutes), Pembroke Dock (14 minutes) and Haverfordwest (54 minutes). National Express destinations include London (£28, 7½ hours), Chepstow (£21, 3¾ hours), Swansea (£8.10, 1¾ hours), Carmarthen (£5.10, one hour) and Tenby (£2.50, 20 minutes).

TRAIN There are direct trains to Swansea (£14, 2¼ hours), Carmarthen (£8.30, 1½ hours), Tenby (£4.90, 35 minutes) and Manorbier (£3.90, 25 minutes).

Haverfordwest (Hwlffordd)

POP 13,400

A workaday town rather than a tourist hot spot, Haverfordwest is Pembrokeshire's main transport and shopping hub. Though it retains some fine Georgian buildings, it lacks the prettiness and historic atmosphere of many of its neighbours. Founded as a fortified Flemish settlement by the Norman Lord Gilbert de Clare in about 1110, its castle became the nucleus for a thriving market and its port remained important until the railway arrived in the mid-19th century.

Today the Riverside Shopping Centre is the main focus of activity and home to an excellent farmers market with organic and local produce stalls every other Friday.

🛏 Sleeping & Eating

College Guest House B&B ££
(☎01437-763710; www.collegeguesthouse.com; 93 Hill St; s/d from £53/76; @✿) Set in a spacious Georgian town house in the town centre, the College offers eight homely rooms with high ceilings and remodelled bathrooms. There's a free car park directly across the road. The owner's little dog is safely locked away but yaps a welcome at each coming and going.

Georges CAFE ££
(☎01437-766683; www.thegeorges.uk.com; 24 Market St; lunch £9-14, dinner £11-20; ⏱lunch Tue-Sat, dinner Fri & Sat; ✿) Gargoyles on leashes guard the door of this trippy, hippy gift shop that doubles as an offbeat cafe. George's has cosy nooks of stained glass and candlelight, lanterns and fairy lights, along with a simple menu of home-cooked food ranging from steak to pasta to curry.

PEMBROKESHIRE & SOUTH WALES HAVERFORDWEST (HWLFFORDD)

WORTH A TRIP

CAREW

Looming romantically over the River Carew, its gaping windows reflected in the glassy water, craggy Carew Castle (☎01646-651782; www.carewcastle.com; adult/child £4.50/3; ⏱10am-5pm Apr-Oct) is an impressive sight. These rambling limestone ruins range from functional 12th-century fortification to Elizabethan country house. Abandoned in 1690, the castle is now inhabited by a large number of bats. A summer program of events includes re-enactments and open-air theatre. The castle ticket also gives you admission to Carew Tidal Mill, the only intact tidal mill in Wales.

Near the castle entrance is the 11th-century Carew Cross, one of the grandest of its kind – around 4m tall and covered in psychedelic Celtic squiggles. Carew is 4 miles northeast of Pembroke and 6 miles northwest of Tenby. Bus 361 heads here from Pembroke Dock (eight minutes), Saundersfoot (34 minutes) and Tenby (56 minutes).

ⓘ PUFFIN SHUTTLE

Between May and September coastal walkers can make use of the local Puffin Shuttle (315/400, fares less than £4), which crawls around the coast three times daily in each direction from Milford Haven to St Davids. Stops include Dale, Marloes, Martin's Haven and Solva. For the rest of the year the route is split, with 315 heading from Milford Haven to Marloes (no Sunday service) and 400 heading from St Davids to Marloes (Monday, Thursday and Saturday only).

ⓘ Information

Police station (Merlin's Hill)
Tourist office (📞01437-763110; 19 Old Bridge St; ◷10am-4pm Mon-Sat)
Withybush General Hospital (📞01437-764545; Fishguard Rd)

ⓘ Getting There & Away

BUS Routes include 322 to Carmarthen (one hour); 349 to Pembroke (54 minutes), Manorbier (1¼ hours) and Tenby (1¾ hours); and 411 to St Davids (50 minutes). National Express destinations include London (£23, eight hours), Chepstow (£21, 4¼ hours), Swansea (£7.90, 2½ hours), Carmarthen (£6.30, 1½ hours) and Tenby (£4.50, 50 minutes).

TRAIN There are direct trains to Cardiff (£20, 2½ hours), Swansea (£12, 1½ hours) and Carmarthen (£7.10, 35 minutes).

Dale & Around

The fishing village of Dale sits on a rugged and remote peninsula, forming the northern head of the Milford Haven waterway. As you round beautiful St Ann's Head, all vestiges of the harbour's heavy industry and, indeed, human habitation disappear from view. Little Westdale Bay follows and then the impressive sweep of Marloes Sands, with views over tidal Gateholm Island – a major Iron Age Celtic settlement where the remains of 130 hut circles have been found. Housed in a group of National Trust–owned farm buildings near the Pembrokeshire Coast Path, Marloes Sands YHA (📞0845 371 9333; www.yha.org.uk; Runwayskiln, Marloes; dm/d from £16/32; ◷Easter-Oct; 🅿) offers a mixture of dorms and private rooms.

Around Wooltack Point is Martin's Haven, the tiny harbour that is the jumping-off point for boat trips to Skomer and Skokholm Islands. An unstaffed information room here has displays on the marine environment, including touchscreen displays of wildlife activity around Skomer. Look for a 7th-century Celtic cross set into the wall outside.

Further around the headland the cliffs change from red to black and Musselwick Sands comes in to view: a large, sandy beach with plenty of craggy inlets to explore.

Skomer, Skokholm & Grassholm Islands

The rocky islands at the south end of St Brides Bay are home to more than half a million seabirds, including guillemots, puffins and Manx shearwaters, as well as grey seals. Skomer and Skokholm Islands are nature reserves run by the Wildlife Trust of South and West Wales (📞01239-621600; www.welsh wildlife.org; dm/s from £30/45), which offers bunkhouse accommodation from April to October on Skomer. Dale Sailing Company (📞01646-603123; www.pembrokeshire-islands.co .uk; adult/child £10/7; ◷10am, 11am & noon Tue-Sun Apr-Oct) runs boats to Skomer on a first-come, first-served basis, departing from Martin's Haven. If you go ashore, there's an additional landing fee (£10).

Eleven miles offshore, Grassholm Island has one of the largest gannet colonies in the northern hemisphere. Grassholm is owned by the Royal Society for the Protection of Birds (RSPB; www.rspb.org.uk) and landing is not permitted, but Dale Sailing Company runs three-hour round-the-island trips (£30); book ahead.

Solva

Lower Solva sits at the head of a peculiar L-shaped harbour, where the water drains away completely at low tide leaving its flotilla of yachts tilted onto the sand. Its single street is lined with brightly painted, flower-laden cottages housing little galleries, pubs and tearooms. If sailing takes your fancy, you can enjoy a cruise aboard a 24ft yacht (up to three passengers) with Solva Sailboats (📞01437-720972; www.solva.net/solvasail boats; 1 Maes-y-Forwen).

The Old Pharmacy (📞01437-720005; 5 Main St; mains £13-19; ◷5.30-10pm) is the village's gastronomic highlight, with a cosy cottage atmosphere, outdoor tables in a riverside garden, and a bistro-style menu that includes Solva lobster and crab, Pembrokeshire duck and Preseli Hills lamb.

Both the Puffin Shuttle and bus 411 between Haverfordwest and St Davids stop here.

St Davids (Tyddewi)

POP 1800

Charismatic St Davids (yes, it has dropped the apostrophe from its name) is Britain's smallest city, its status ensured by the magnificent 12th-century cathedral that marks Wales's holiest site. The birth and burial site of the nation's patron saint, St Davids has been a place of pilgrimage for 1500 years.

The setting itself has a numinous presence. With the sea just beyond the horizon on three sides, you're constantly surprised by glimpses of it at the ends of streets. Then there are those strangely shaped hills in the distance, sprouting from an ancient landscape.

Dewi Sant (St David) founded a monastic community here in the 6th century. In 1124 Pope Calixtus II declared that two pilgrimages to St Davids were the equivalent of one to Rome, and three were equal to one to Jerusalem. The cathedral has seen a constant stream of visitors ever since.

Today St Davids attracts hordes of non-religious pilgrims too, drawn by the town's laid-back vibe and the excellent hiking, surfing and wildlife-watching in the surrounding area.

◉ Sights & Activities

St Davids Cathedral CHURCH
(www.stdavidscathedral.org.uk; suggested donation £3) Hidden in a hollow and behind high walls, St Davids Cathedral is intentionally unassuming. The valley site was chosen in the vain hope that the church would be overlooked by Viking raiders, but it was ransacked at least seven times. Yet once you pass through the gatehouse that separates it from the town and its stone walls come into view, it's as imposing as any of its contemporaries.

Built on the site of a 6th-century chapel, the building dates mainly from the 12th to the 14th centuries. Extensive works were carried out in the 19th century by Sir George Gilbert Scott (architect of the Albert Memorial and St Pancras in London) to stabilise the building. The distinctive west front, with

its four pointed towers of purple stone, dates from this period.

The atmosphere inside is one of great antiquity. As you enter the nave, the oldest surviving part of the cathedral, the first things you notice are the sloping floor and the outward lean of the massive, purplish-grey pillars linked by semicircular Norman Romanesque arches, a result of subsidence. Above is a richly carved 16th-century oak ceiling, adorned with pendants and bosses.

At the far end of the nave is a delicately carved 14th-century Gothic pulpitum (screen), separating it from the magnificent choir. Check out the mischievous carved figures on the 16th-century misericords (under the seats), one of which depicts pilgrims being seasick over the side of a boat. Don't forget to look up at the colourfully painted lantern tower above (those steel tie rods around the walls were installed in the 19th century to hold the structure together).

Between the choir and the high altar is the object of all those religious pilgrimages – a shrine containing the bones of St David and St Justinian. Destroyed in the Reformation, it was restored and rededicated in 2012.

Accessed from the north wall of the nave the Treasury displays vestments and religious paraphernalia crafted from precious metals and stones. Just as valuable are the treasures in the neighbouring Library (admission £1; ◷2-4pm Mon), the oldest of which dates to 1505.

The St Davids Cathedral Festival is 10 days of classical music performances, starting on the Spring Bank Holiday weekend at the end of May. More concerts are performed at the cathedral throughout the year.

Bishop's Palace RUIN
(www.cadw.wales.gov.uk; adult/child £3.20/2.80; ◷10am-4pm) Across the river from the cathedral, this atmospheric ruined palace was begun at the same time as the cathedral, but its final, imposing form owes most to Henry de Gower, bishop from 1327 to 1347.

Its most distinctive feature is the arcaded parapet that runs around the courtyard, decorated with a chequerboard pattern of purple and yellow stone blocks. The corbels that support the arches are richly adorned with a menagerie of carved figures – lions, monkeys, dogs and birds, as well as grotesque mythical creatures and human heads.

The palace courtyard is a spectacular setting for open-air plays in summer.

St Davids

St Davids

⊙ Sights
1 Bishop's Palace......................................A1
2 Oriel y Parc D2
3 St Davids Cathedral.............................A1

⊕ Activities, Courses & Tours
4 Aquaphobia D2
5 Thousand Islands Expeditions B2
6 TYF Adventure B2
Voyages of Discovery ....(see 6)

⊜ Sleeping
7 Alandale B1
8 Y Glennydd C1

⊗ Eating
9 Bench C2
10 Cwtch C2
11 Sampler B1

⊖ Drinking
12 Farmer's Arms B2

St Non's Bay   RUIN, CHURCH
Immediately south of St Davids is this ruggedly beautiful spot, named after St David's mother and traditionally accepted as his birthplace. A path leads down to the 13th-century ruins of St Non's Chapel. Only the base of the walls remains, along with a stone marked with a cross within a circle, believed to date from the 7th century. Standing stones in the surrounding field suggest that the chapel may have been built within an ancient pagan stone circle.

On the approach to the ruins is a pretty little holy well. The spring is said to have emerged at the moment of the saint's birth and the water is believed to have curative powers.

Nearby, the Catholic Chapel of Our Lady and St Non was built in 1935 out of the stones of ruined religious buildings. Its dimensions echo those of the original chapel.

Oriel y Parc   GALLERY
(☎01437-720392; www.orielyparc.co.uk; High St; ⊙10am-4.30pm) In a bold, semicircular, environmentally friendly building on the edge of town, Oriel y Parc (Landscape Gallery) is a winning collaboration between the Pembrokeshire Coast National Park Authority and the National Museum Wales. Not only does it function as a tourist office and national park visitor centre, but also has changing exhibitions from the museum's art collection.

Ramsey Island   WILDLIFE RESERVE
Ramsey Island lies off the headland to the west of St Davids, ringed by dramatic sea cliffs and an offshore armada of rocky islets and reefs. The island is an RSPB reserve famous for its large breeding population of choughs – members of the crow family with glossy black feathers and distinctive red bills and legs – and for its grey seals.

You can reach the island by boat from the tiny harbour at St Justinian's, 2 miles west of St Davids. Longer boat trips run up to 20 miles offshore, to the edge of the Celtic Deep, to spot whales, porpoises and dolphins. What you'll see depends on the weather and the time of year: July to September are the best months. Porpoises are seen on most trips, dolphins on four out of five, and there's a 40% chance of seeing whales. The most common species is the minke, but pilot whales, fin whales and orcas have also been spotted.

Thousand Islands Expeditions (☎01437-721721; www.thousandislands.co.uk; Cross Sq) is the only operator permitted to land day trippers on the island (adult/child £15/7.50). They have a range of other boat trips, including 2½-hour whale- and dolphin-spotting cruises (£60/30) and one-hour jet-boat trips (£25/10).

Voyages of Discovery (☎01437-721911; www.ramseyisland.co.uk; 1 High St) and Aqua-phobia (☎01437-720471; www.aquaphobia-ramsey island.co.uk; Grove Hotel, High St) offer a similar selection of cruises.

🛏 Sleeping

Ramsey House B&B ££
(☎01437-720321; www.ramseyhouse.co.uk; Lower Moor; r £100; P 🛜) The young owners have fashioned a fresh-looking B&B from their new house on the outskirts of town, which is still only a short stroll west from the centre. The six rooms are all different, but it's the kind of place where the chandeliers match the wallpaper.

TOP CHOICE **St Davids YHA** HOSTEL £
(☎0845 371 9141; www.yha.org.uk; Llaethdy, Whitesands; dm £16, tw £42; P 🛜) If you're an enthusiastic walker or have your own transport, this former farmhouse tucked beneath Carn Llidi, 2 miles northwest of town, is a wonderful option. The cow sheds have been made over to house snug dorms and twins, and an inviting communal kitchen.

Alandale B&B ££
(☎01437-720404; www.stdavids.co.uk/guesthouse/ alandale.htm; 43 Nun St; s/d £36/90; @🛜) A neat terraced house built in the 1880s for coastguard officers, Alandale has a bright, cheerful atmosphere – ask for one of the rooms at the back, which are quieter and have sweeping countryside views.

Caerfai Bay Caravan & Tent Park CAMPSITE £
(☎01437-720274; www.caerfaibay.co.uk; sites from £16) A 15-minute walk south of St Davids, this large site has good facilities and great coastal views across St Brides Bay.

Y Glennydd B&B ££
(☎01437-720576; www.yglennydd.co.uk; 51 Nun St; s/d from £40/65; 🛜) Mixing maritime memorabilia and antique oak furniture, this 10-room guesthouse has a traditional, bordering on old-fashioned, feel with smallish, unfussy bedrooms and a cosy lounge bar. The cheapest double room has a private bathroom entered from the corridor.

🍴 Eating & Drinking

Cwtch MODERN WELSH £££
(☎01437-720491; www.cwtchrestaurant.co.uk; 22 High St; 2-/3-courses £24/30; ⏱dinner Tue-Sat, daily summer) Stone walls and wooden beams mark this out as a sense-of-occasion place, as indeed does the price, yet there's a snugness that lives up to its name (*cwtch* means a cosy place or a cuddle). There's an emphasis on local produce, so expect plenty of fresh seafood on the menu.

Sampler TEAHOUSE £
(www.sampler-tearoom.co.uk; 17 Nun St; mains $5-7; ⏱lunch Mon-Thu, extended hours in summer) Named after the embroidery samples blanketing the walls, this may be the perfect exemplar of the traditional Welsh tearoom. Pembrokeshire clotted cream tea comes served with freshly baked scones and *bara brith* (a rich fruit tea-loaf), and there are Welsh cheese platters, jacket potatoes, soups and sandwiches.

Bench CAFE £
(www.bench-bar.co.uk; 11 High St; mains £7-12; ⏱breakfast & lunch; 🛜) A bustling rabbit warren of a cafe with a strong Mediterranean motif, the Bench serves up all-day snacks and ice creams.

Farmer's Arms PUB
(www.farmersstdavids.co.uk; 14 Goat St; mains £8-10) Even though St Davids is a bit of a tourist trap, you'd be hard-pressed finding a more authentic country pub. There's real ale and Guinness on tap, decent pub grub, and it's the place to be when the rugby's playing. The beer garden out back is a pleasant place to watch the sun go down on a summer's evening.

ⓘ Information

The National Park Information Centre & Tourist Office is located at Oriel y Parc (p682).

National Trust visitor centre (☎01437-720385; High St; ⏱10am-5.30pm Mon-Sat, 10am-4pm Sun mid-Mar–Dec, 10am-4pm Mon-Sat Jan–mid-Mar) sells local-interest books and guides to NT properties in Pembrokeshire.

PEMBROKESHIRE & SOUTH WALES ST DAVIDS (TYDDEWI)

COASTEERING

If you fancy a spot of rock climbing, gully scrambling, cave exploration, wave riding and cliff jumping, all rolled together, then try coasteering. More or less conceived on the Pembrokeshire coast, this demanding activity is the mainstay of the local adventure sports scene. It's also risky, so take guidance from an instructor and don't be tempted to take flight from the nearest precipice.

Celtic Quest (☑01348-881530; www.celticquest.co.uk) Coasteering specialists, taking to the cliffs near Abereiddy.

Preseli Venture (☑01348-837709; www.preseliventure.co.uk) Has its own lodge near Mathry, between St Davids and Fishguard. Activities include coasteering, sea kayaking, surfing and coastal hiking.

TYF Adventure (☑01437-721611; www.tyf.com; 1 High St, St David's) Organises coasteering, surfing, sea kayaking and rock-climbing trips from its St Davids base.

ℹ Getting There & Around

Buses include the Puffin Shuttle; 411 to Lower Solva (10 minutes) and Haverfordwest (50 minutes); and 413 to Fishguard (one hour). The Strumble Shuttle (404; Monday, Thursday and Saturday October to April, daily May to September) follows the coast between St Davids and Fishguard, calling at Porthgain.

Porthgain

For centuries the tiny harbour of Porthgain consisted of little more than a few sturdy cottages wedged into a rocky cove. In the mid-19th century it began to prosper as the port for shipping out slate quarried just down the coast at Abereiddy, and by the 1870s its own deposits of granite and fine clay had put it on the map as a source of building stone. The post-WWI slump burst the bubble, and the sturdy stone quays and overgrown brick storage 'bins' are all that remain.

Despite having been an industrial harbour, Porthgain is surprisingly picturesque and today it is home to a couple of art galleries and restaurants. The Strumble Shuttle coastal bus service stops here.

✕ Eating

Shed   SEAFOOD £££

(☑01348-831518; www.theshedporthgain.co.uk; lunch £6-22, dinner £18-22; ⊘daily Apr-Oct, call for hours Nov-Mar) Housed in a converted machine shop right by the little harbour, the Shed has grown into one of Pembrokeshire's finest seafood restaurants; the menu lists Porthgain crab and lobster, and lots of locally caught fish.

Sloop Inn   PUB ££

(☑01348-831449; www.sloop.co.uk; breakfast £4-6, lunch £6-21, dinner £9-21) With wooden tables worn smooth by many a bended elbow, old photos of Porthgain in its industrial heyday and interesting nautical clutter all over the place, the Sloop is a cosy and deservedly popular pub. It dishes up breakfast and hearty home-cooked meals to hungry walkers.

Fishguard (Abergwaun)

POP 3200

Perched on a headland between its modern ferry port and former fishing harbour, Fishguard is often overlooked by travellers, most of them passing through on their way to or from Ireland. It doesn't have any sights as such, but it's an appealing little town and was the improbable setting for the last foreign invasion of Britain.

Fishguard is split into three distinct areas. The main town is centred on Market Sq, where the buses stop. To the east is the picturesque harbour of the Lower Town (Y Cwm), which was used as a setting for the 1971 film version of *Under Milk Wood*. The train station and ferry terminal lie a mile to the northwest of the town centre in Goodwick.

Much that goes on in Fishguard happens in the Town Hall on Market Sq. The tourist office is here, as is the library (handy for free internet access) and the market hall. It hosts a country market on Tuesdays, a town market on Thursdays and a farmers market on Saturdays.

Sights & Activities

FREE **Last Invasion Gallery** GALLERY
(☎01348-776122; ◷9.30am-5pm Mon-Sat Apr-Sep, until 1pm Sat Oct-Mar) Inspired by the Bayeux Tapestry, which recorded the 1066 Norman invasion at Hastings, the Fishguard Tapestry was commissioned in 1997 to commemorate the bicentenary of the failed Fishguard invasion. It uses a similar cartoonish style as Bayeux's (albeit with less rude bits) and tells the story in the course of 37 frames and 30m of cloth. A film about its making demonstrates what a huge undertaking it was.

Mike Mayberry Kayaking KAYAKING
(☎01348-874699; www.mikemayberrykayaking. co.uk) Offers instruction courses (two days £157) and guided kayaking tours for more experienced paddlers.

Sleeping

Manor Town House B&B ££
(☎01348-873260; www.manortownhouse.com; Main St; s £65-75, d £75-105; 🖀) This graceful Georgian house has a lovely garden terrace where you can sit and gaze over the harbour. The young owners are charm personified and the house has been tastefully renovated.

Pentower B&B ££
(☎01348-874462; www.pentower.co.uk; Tower Hill; s £50, d £80-85; 🅿) Built by Sir Evan Jones, the architect who designed the harbour, this rambling home is perched on a hill at the edge of town, overlooking his creation. The house is pretty and unassuming, apart from the grand tiled atrium. Rooms are spacious and romantic.

❶ Information

Fishguard tourist office (☎01437-776636; Market Sq, Town Hall; ◷9.30am-5pm Mon-Fri, 9.30am-4pm Sat Easter-Sep, 10am-4pm Mon-Sat Oct-Easter)

Goodwick tourist office (☎01348-874737; Ocean Lab; ◷10am-4pm; 🚼) Houses an exhibition on marine life and the environment aimed mainly at kids.

❶ Getting There & Away

BOAT Year-round **Stena Line** (☎08447 70 70 70; www.stenaline.co.uk) runs two regular ferries a day (car and driver from £79, additional adult/child £26/15, foot passenger £28, bike £10) between Rosslare in the southeast of Ireland and Fishguard Harbour (3½ hours).

BUS Buses include 412 to Haverfordwest (31 minutes), Newport (16 minutes) and Cardigan (45 minutes); and 413 to St Davids (50 minutes). Services for walkers include the Strumble Shuttle, Poppit Rocket and the Green Dragon Bus (http://greendragonbus.co.uk/).

TRAIN There are direct trains to Fishguard Harbour from Cardiff (£22, 2½ hours), Swansea (£14, 1¾ hours) and Carmarthen (£8.30, 53 minutes).

Newport (Trefdraeth)
POP 1200

In stark contrast to the industrial city of Newport, the Pembrokeshire Newport is a pretty cluster of flower-bedecked cottages huddled beneath a small, privately owned Norman castle. It sits at the foot of Mynydd Carningli (347m), a large bump on the seaward side of the Preseli Hills.

Newport makes a pleasant base for walks along the coastal path or south into the Preseli Hills, but it does get crowded in summer. At the northwest corner of the town is little Parrog Beach, dwarfed by Newport Sands (Traeth Mawr) across the river.

Right in town there's a little dolmen Carreg Coetan Arthur, well signposted from the main road just past the Golden Lion. At first glance it looks like its capstone is

---

THE LAST INVASION OF BRITAIN

While Hastings in 1066 may get all the press, the last invasion of Britain was actually at Carregwastad Point, northwest of Fishguard, on 22 February 1797. The ragtag collection of 1400 French mercenaries and bailed convicts had intended to land at Bristol and march to Liverpool, keeping English troops occupied while France mounted an invasion of Ireland. Bad weather blew them ashore at Carregwastad, where, after scrambling up a steep cliff, they set about looting for food and drink.

The invaders had hoped that the Welsh peasants would rise up to join them in revolutionary fervour but, not surprisingly, their drunken pillaging didn't endear them to the locals. The French were quickly seen off by volunteer 'yeoman' soldiers, with help from the people of Fishguard including, most famously, one Jemima Nicholas who, armed with a pitchfork, single-handedly captured 12 mercenaries.

securely supported by four standing stones. A closer inspection suggests that some old magic has held it together all these thousands of years, as it's balanced on only two of them.

🛏 Sleeping & Eating

Cnapan
B&B ££

(📞01239-820575; www.cnapan.co.uk; East St; s/d £60/90; 🛜) Light-filled rooms and a flower-filled garden are offered at this listed Georgian town house above a popular restaurant (two-/three-course dinner £26/32, closed Tuesday). If you're game enough for the floral wallpaper, ask for room 4 – it's bigger. The somewhat formal dining rooms offer candlelight and crisp white linen tablecloths, but the service is friendly and relaxed.

Llys Meddyg
HOTEL £££

(📞01239-820008; www.llysmeddyg.com; East St; r £100-150; @🛜) This converted doctor's residence takes contemporary big-city cool and plonks it firmly by the seaside. Bedrooms are large and bright, the lounge boasts leather sofas and a fireplace, and there's a secluded back garden. The restaurant (two-/three-course dinner £30/35, Tuesday to Saturday) is superb, with the season-changing menu reflecting the best of local produce.

Golden Lion Hotel
PUB ££

(📞01239-820321; www.goldenlionpembrokeshire.co.uk; East St; s/d £60/85; 🅿🛜) Sunny decor,

---

POPPIT ROCKET

Between May and September, the Poppit Rocket bus (405) heads three times daily in each direction from Fishguard to Cardigan. Stops include Newport, Poppit Sands and St Dogmaels.

---

pine furniture and colourful flower arrangements make for a warm atmosphere in this country pub. In contrast to the modern bedrooms, there's a snug traditional bar with log fire and low ceilings downstairs, serving real ales and meals (mains £11 to £18).

ℹ Information

National park information centre & tourist office (📞01239-820912; Long St; ⏰10am-6pm Mon-Sat Easter-Oct, 10.30am-3pm Mon & Fri, 10.30am-1pm Tue-Thu & Sat Nov-Easter)

ℹ Getting There & Away

BICYCLE The back roads around the Preseli Hills and Cwm Gwaun offer some of the best on-road cycling in southwest Wales. Mountainbikers will find plenty of enjoyment on the ridges and bridleways. You can rent a bike from **Newport Bike Hire** (📞01239-820773; www.newport bikehire.com; East St; per half-/full day £10/15), based in the Carningli Centre antiques store.

BUS Buses include 412 to Haverfordwest (50 minutes), Fishguard (16 minutes) and Cardigan (29 minutes); plus the Poppit Rocket.

WORTH A TRIP

CASTELL HENLLYS IRON AGE FORT

From about 600 BC and right through the Roman occupation there was a thriving Celtic fortified village at what's now Castell Henllys (www.castell henllys.com; Felindre Farchog; adult/child £4.75/3.50; ⏰10am-5pm Easter-Oct, 11am-3pm Nov-Easter). A visit is like travelling back in time. There are reconstructions of the settlement's buildings – four thatched roundhouses, animal pens, a smithy and a grain store – that you can enter and touch. Costumed staff, craft demonstrations, Celtic festivals and other events bring it to life.

Castell Henllys is 4 miles east of Newport.

Preseli Hills

The only upland area in the Pembrokeshire Coast National Park is the Preseli Hills (Mynydd Preseli), rising to 536m at Foel Cwmcerwyn. These hills are at the centre of a fascinating prehistoric landscape, scattered with hill forts, standing stones and burial chambers, and are famous as the source of the mysterious bluestones of Stonehenge. An ancient track called the Golden Road, once part of a 5000-year-old trade route between Wessex and Ireland, runs along the crest of the hills, passing prehistoric cairns and the stone circle of Bedd Arthur.

The largest dolmen in Wales, Pentre Ifan, is a 4500-year-old neolithic burial chamber set on a remote hillside three miles southeast of Newport, signposted from the A487. The huge, 5m-long capstone, weighing more than 16 tonnes, is delicately poised on three upright bluestones.

Hay-on-Wye & Mid-Wales

Best Places to Eat

» Checkers (p709)

» Walnut Tree (p702)

» Felin Fach Griffin (p699)

» Gwesty Cymru (p692)

» Abdul's Tandoori Spice
(p690)

Best Places to Stay

» Checkers (p709)

» Start (p703)

» Bear (p703)

» Hardwick (p702)

» Poppit Sands YHA (p689)

Why Go?

The big draw here is the magnificent upland scenery of Brecon Beacons National Park, with book-loving Hay-on-Wye within its confines and food-loving Abergavenny on its doorstep. By contrast the Ceredigion and Powys countryside is something of a well-kept secret and certainly worthy of a closer look. This is Wales at its most rural – a landscape of lustrous green fields, wooded river valleys and small market towns; it's the part that the Industrial Revolution missed. It's also thoroughly Welsh, with around 40% of people speaking the mother tongue (over 50% in Ceredigion). Apart from exuberant, student-populated Aberystwyth, you won't find a lot of excitement in the urban areas. It's the places in between that are much more interesting, criss-crossed as they are with cycling and walking routes, and plenty of country lanes to tootle about in.

When to Go

If you're planning on walking, you'll get the most rain-free days between April and July. In the midst of spring, in May, the world's intelligentsia gets Hay fever. In August, cap off the Green Man (p700) and Brecon Jazz (p699) music festivals with a spot of bog snorkelling. As the weather starts to cool down, in September, fill up at the Abergavenny Food Festival (p702). July and August are the warmest months, while January and February are the coldest.

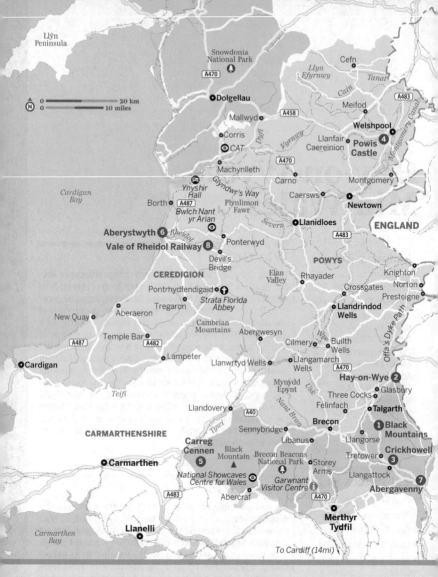

Hay-on-Wye & Mid-Wales Highlights

1 Soaking up the tranquillity of the remote Vale of Ewyas in the **Black Mountains** (p702)

2 Experiencing charming **Hay-on-Wye** (p703), a town surrounded by nature but infatuated with books

3 Settling into village life in Brecon Beacons National Park in **Crickhowell** (p700)

4 Letting the sculptured yew paths of **Powis Castle** (p709) lead you through Welsh history

5 Gazing up at **Carreg Cennen** (p695), Wales' most dramatically positioned fortress

6 Revelling in the high culture and student-inspired high jinks that come

together by the seaside at **Aberystwyth** (p690)

7 Exploring a countryside seasoned with Wales' best restaurants in the fields around **Abergavenny** (p701)

8 Reliving the age of steam with a scenic ride to Devil's Bridge on the **Vale of Rheidol Railway** (p690)

Activities

The main focus for hiking and mountain biking is the Brecon Beacons, but Mid-Wales is chock full of other opportunities for outdoor activities. Walkers can follow the region's main long-distance routes, Offa's Dyke National Trail and Glyndŵr's Way National Trail, for anything between a couple of hours to a couple of weeks. Touring cyclists can enjoy the quiet lanes and back roads that crisscross the countryside, and there are many opportunities for off-road cycling as well.

Rivers for canoeing include the Wye and Usk, while the coast of Cardigan Bay is the place for sailing and sea-kayaking.

ℹ Getting There & Around

Mid-Wales revels in a slower pace of life and there are no motorways; the region's main road artery is the A470 between the Brecon Beacons and Snowdonia. If you're driving on other roads, expect to be stuck behind farm tractors and slow-moving trucks, so just relax, slow down and enjoy the view.

The main railways are the Cambrian Line between Birmingham and Aberystwyth via Shrewesbury and Machynlleth, while the scenic Heart of Wales line (www.heart-of-wales.co.uk) skirts the Brecon Beacons.

Public transport is less frequent than in other regions, especially in more remote areas – check with Traveline Cymru (www.traveline-cymru.info).

CEREDIGION

The Welsh language is stronger in Ceredigion than most other parts of Wales, kept alive in rural communities that escaped the massive population influxes of the coal-mining valleys of the south and the slate-mining towns of the north. That lack of heavy industry has also left Ceredigion with some of Britain's cleanest beaches, and, with no rail access south of Aberystwyth, they tend to be less crowded. Adding to the isolation is the natural barrier known as the Desert of Wales, consisting of the barren uplands of the Cambrian Mountains, which separate Ceredigion from Powys. If any area could be described as off-the-beaten-track in Wales, this is it.

Cardigan (Aberteifi)

POP 4100

While it might not be quite as homespun as its name suggests, neither is Cardigan the most exciting of towns. However, it makes a good base for coastal walkers and for visiting a smattering of interesting sights just across the river in Pembrokeshire.

SIGHTS

Cardigan Castle   CASTLE
(☑01239-615131; www.cardigancastle.com; 2 Green St; tours £3-5) The shored-up and overgrown walls of Cardigan Castle make for a sorry sight. Yet behind the scenes, a team of locals has been beavering away to rescue the crumbling castle since it was purchased by Ceredigion Council in 2003. It's now open for guided tours (call ahead for times) and the occasional event, and it's hoped that a brand spanking new heritage centre will be ready by 2014. The castle holds an important place in Welsh culture, having been the venue for the first competitive National Eisteddfod, held in 1176 under the aegis of Welsh prince Rhys ap Gruffydd.

Guildhall   MARKET
(www.guildhall-cardigan.co.uk; High St) The neo-Gothic Guildhall dates from 1860, and is now home to Cardigan Market. Stalls sell art and craft, and a local producers' market is held on Fridays.

🛏 Sleeping & Eating

TOP CHOICE Poppit Sands YHA   HOSTEL £
(☑01239-612936; www.yha.org.uk; dm £18-20, r with/without bathroom £47/42; ⊙daily Jul & Aug, Tue-Sat Sep-Jun; ℗) Reached by the narrowest road imaginable, this secluded hostel is tucked into a hillside overlooking the sea, four miles northwest of town. A recent renovation has left everything sparkling and new, including a very well appointed kitchen. There are 34 beds in total; book early for the one en-suite room.

fforest   CAMPING ££
(☑01239-623633; www.coldatnight.co.uk; tent per week from £435) Perched on the edge of Teifi Marshes Nature Reserve, fforest's large tents, tepees and geodesic domes challenge the notion that camping means roughing it. They're all kitted out with beds and linen, and a deck with its own BBQ, gas burner and water.

Llety Teifi   HOTEL ££
(☑01239-615566; www.llety.co.uk; Pendre; s/d from £45/70; ℗ 🛜) A renovation a few years back left this bright magenta Georgian house looking extremely schmick, but since then the owners have reverted to unmatched

WORTH A TRIP

STRATA FLORIDA ABBEY

Peaceful countryside surrounds this isolated, ruined Cistercian abbey (www.cadw.wales. gov.uk; adult/child £3.20/2.80; ⊙10am-5pm Apr-Oct, unattended & free in other mths). The best-preserved remnant is an arched doorway, with lines like thick rope. At the rear of the site a roof has been added to protect two chapels that still have some of their 14th-century tiling, including one depicting a man admiring himself in a mirror.

The site is a mile down a rural road from the village of Pontrhydfendigaid; the village is on the B4343, 15 miles southeast of Aberystwyth or 9 miles south of Devil's Bridge.

curtains, thin towels and cheap toiletries. Still, it's more stylish than most and the creamy tiles in the bathrooms still look great. Fry-up breakfasts are served at the much less-hip place next door.

Abdul's Tandoori Spice   INDIAN ££
(☏01239-621416; 2 Royal Oak, Quay St; mains £7-15; ⊙lunch Sat-Thu, dinner daily; 🍴) A cut above your usual curry house, Abdul's has gained a loyal local following with its consistently tasty tandoori dishes and excellent service. Serves are substantial, so resist the urge to over-order. No alcohol is available.

❶ Information

Tourist office (☏01239-613230; www.tourism .ceredigion.gov.uk; Bath House Rd; ⊙10am-5pm Mon-Sat Nov-Feb, daily Mar-Oct) In the lobby of the Theatr Mwldan.

❶ Getting There & Around

BICYCLE You can hire bikes from **New Image Bicycles** (☏01239-621275; www.bikebikebike .co.uk; 29-30 Pendre; per half-day/day £12/18).

BUS Routes include X50 to Aberystwyth (1½ hours); 407 to Poppit Sands (15 minutes); 412 to Newport (29 minutes), Fishguard (45 minutes) and Haverfordwest (1½ hours); and the Poppit Rocket.

Aberystwyth

POP 16,000

Thanks to its status as one of the liveliest university towns in Wales, with an admirable range of options for eating out, drinking and partaking in Welsh culture, Aberystwyth is an essential stop along the Ceredigion coast. Welsh is widely spoken here and locals are proud of their heritage. It's a particularly buzzy town during term time and retains a cosmopolitan feel year-round.

When pub culture and student life get too much, the quintessential Aberystwyth expe-

rience remains soaking up the sunset over Cardigan Bay. Here the trappings of a stately Georgian seaside resort remain, with an impressive promenade skirted by a sweep of pastel-coloured buildings.

◉ Sights

National Library of Wales   LIBRARY
(☏01970-623800; www.llgc.org.uk; ⊙9.30am-5pm Mon-Sat) Sitting proudly on a hilltop half a mile east of town, the National Library is a cultural powerhouse, holding millions of books in many languages. The Hengwrt Room is where it displays all of the really important stuff, such as the 12th-century *Black Book of Carmarthen* (the oldest existing Welsh text) and the 13th-century Tintern Abbey Bible. Other galleries display an everstimulating set of changing exhibitions.

Ceredigion Museum   MUSEUM
(☏01970-633088; http://museum.ceredigion.gov. uk; Terrace Rd; ⊙10am-5pm Mon-Sat Apr-Sep, noon-4.30pm Oct-Mar) This museum houses entertaining displays devoted to Aberystwyth's history – everything from Roman coins to old pharmacy furnishings, and even knitted woollen knickers.

🏃 Activities

Vale of Rheidol Railway   HERITAGE RAILWAY
(☏01970-625819; www.rheidolrailway.co.uk; Park Ave; adult/child return £15/3.75; ⊙Apr-Oct, check online timetable) Old steam locomotives (built between 1923 and 1938) have been lovingly restored by volunteers and chug for almost 12 miles up the valley of the River Rheidol to Devil's Bridge (an hour each way). The line opened in 1902 to bring lead and timber out of the valley.

Cliff Railway   HERITAGE RAILWAY
(☏01970-617642; www.aberystwythcliffrailway. co.uk; adult/child £3/2; ⊙10am-5pm daily Apr-Oct, Wed-Sun mid-Feb–Mar) If your constitution's not up to the climb of Constitution Hill

Aberystwyth

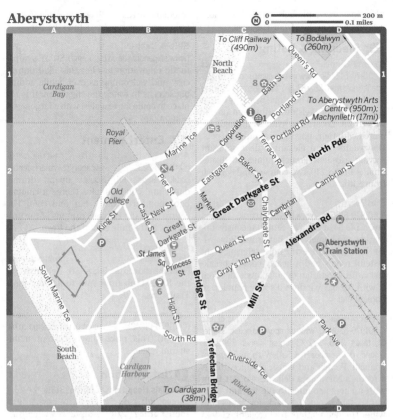

N
0 — 200 m
0 — 0.1 miles

Aberystwyth

◎ Sights
1 Ceredigion Museum C1

❸ Activities, Courses & Tours
2 Vale of Rheidol Railway D3

🛏 Sleeping
3 Gwesty Cymru C2

❌ Eating
4 Ultracomida B2

🍷 Drinking
5 Academy B3
6 Ship & Castle B3

❇ Entertainment
7 Aberystwyth Male Voice Choir C4
8 Commodore Cinema C1

(135m), at the northern end of North Beach, you can catch a lift on the UK's longest (and possibly the slowest, too, at a G-force-busting 4mph) electric funicular (1896). From the windblown balding hilltop there are tremendous coastal views. One relic of the Victorian era is a camera obscura that allows you to see practically into the windows of the houses below.

Ystwyth Trail   CYCLING, WALKING

Suitable for cyclists and walkers, this 20-mile waymarked route mainly follows an old rail line from Aberystwyth southeast to Tregaron, at the foot of the Cambrian Mountains. For the first 12 miles it shadows the River Ystwyth, while at the end it enters the Teifi Valley. At the Aberystwyth end you can pick up the trail from the footbridge on

Riverside Tce; although you'll get more downhills if you start from Tregaron.

🍴 Sleeping & Eating

Gwesty Cymru
HOTEL ££

(☑01970-612252; www.gwestycymru.com; 19 Marine Tce; s/d from £67/87; 🛜) This gem of a hotel is a character-filled boutique property with a strong sense of Welsh identity, right on the waterfront. Local slate features throughout, paired with rich aubergine-coloured carpets. Downstairs is an elegant little restaurant serving excellent French-influenced dishes (mains £16 to £19, two-course Sunday lunch from £13).

Bodalwyn
B&B ££

(☑01970-612578; www.bodalwyn.co.uk; Queen's Ave; s £49-54, d £72; 🛜) Simultaneously upmarket and homely, this handsome Edwardian B&B goes the extra mile, offering eight tasteful rooms and a hearty cooked breakfast (with vegetarian options). Ask for room 3, with the bay window. It's very popular, so book ahead.

Ultracomida
TAPAS, DELI ££

(☑01970-630686; www.ultracomida.co.uk; 31 Pier St; tapas £4-5, 1-/2-/3-course dinner £9/11/13; ⊘lunch daily, dinner Fri & Sat) With its blend of Spanish, French and Welsh produce, this is a foodie's Nirvana: a delicatessen out front with a cheese counter to die for and communal tables out the back for tapas and wine. The deli platters are excellent; choose between meat, cheese or mixed (£9.95).

🍷 Drinking

Thanks to its large student population, during term time Aberystwyth has a livelier nightlife than anywhere else in the northern half of the country, so if you're going to go out bar-hopping anywhere, make it here. It can be a surreal experience when the various university clubs hit the town in costume: one minute you might be sitting in an empty pub and the next minute the whole place may fill up with Kiss impersonators or cross-dressed schoolgirls.

Academy
BAR

(Great Darkgate St) An incongruous setting for a booze palace, perhaps, but a beautiful one. This former chapel has Victorian tiles on the floor, a mezzanine supported by slender cast-iron columns, red lights illuminating a wooden staircase leading to an eagle-fronted pulpit and organ pipes behind the bar.

Ship & Castle
PUB

(www.shipandcastle.co.uk; 1 High St) A sympathetic renovation has left this 1830 pub as cosy and welcoming as ever, while adding big screens to watch the rugger on. It is *the* place to come for real ales, with a large selection on tap.

⭐ Entertainment

Aberystwyth Arts Centre
THEATRE, CINEMA

(☑01970-623232; www.aberystwythartscentre.co.uk; Penglais Rd) Stages opera, drama, dance and concerts, plus there's a cinema, bookshop, art gallery, bar and cafe. The centre is on the Penglais campus of the university, half a mile east of the town.

Aberystwyth Male Voice Choir
TRADITIONAL MUSIC

(www.aberchoir.co.uk; Bridge St) Rehearses at the RAFA Club from 7pm to 8.30pm most Thursdays.

Commodore Cinema
CINEMA

(☑01970-612421; www.commodorecinema.co.uk; Bath St) This place shows current mainstream releases.

ℹ️ Information

Bronglais Hospital (☑01970-623131; Caradoc Rd)

Tourist office (☑01970-612125; www.tourism.ceredigion.gov.uk; cnr Terrace Rd & Bath St; ⊘10am-5pm Mon-Sat, daily school holidays)

ℹ️ Getting There & Away

BUS Routes include X32 to Machynlleth (45 minutes), Dolgellau (1¼ hours), Porthmadog (2¼ hours) and Caernarfon (three hours); and 701 to Carmarthen (1¾ hours), Swansea (2¾ hours) and Cardiff (3½ hours).

A daily National Express coach heads to/from Newtown (£11, 1¼ hours), Welshpool (£12, 1¾ hours), Shrewsbury (£15, 2¼ hours), Birmingham (£29, four hours) and London (£36, 6¾ hours).

TRAIN Aberystwyth is the terminus of the Cambrian line, which crosses Mid-Wales every two hours en route to Birmingham (£27, three hours) via Machynlleth (£5.70, 33 minutes), Newtown (£12, 1¼ hours), Welshpool (£13, 1½ hours) and Shrewsbury (£18, two hours).

YNYSHIR HALL

Tucked away to the south of the River Dovey estuary, just off the main Aberystwyth–Machynlleth road (A487), this grand manor house with a 15th-century core was once kept as a hunting lodge by Queen Victoria. It's now a wonderful boutique hotel (☎01654-781209; www.ynyshirhall.co.uk; Eglwysfach; s/d from £205/275; P🖥) that has hosted Hollywood royalty (Richard Gere stayed in the Vermeer room) and its restaurant (lunch mains £16-19, set dinner £72.50) is one of Wales' finest. The friendly staff are never less than professional.

Bwlch Nant yr Arian

Part of a forestry commission block, Bwlch Nant yr Arian (www.forestry.gov.uk/bwlchnant yrarian; parking 2hrs £1.50) is a picturesque piece of woodland set around a lake, ringed with mountain biking and walking tracks. The main draw, however, is the red-kite feeding, which takes place at 2pm daily (3pm daylight saving time). Even outside of mealtime you'll quite often see the majestic birds of prey circling around. You can watch all the action from the terrace of the attractive turf-roofed visitor centre and cafe.

It's located 9 miles east of Aberystwyth on the A44.

Devil's Bridge

Mysterious Devil's Bridge (www.devilsbridge falls.co.uk; adult/child £3.50/2) spans the Rheidol Valley on the lush western slopes of Plynlimon (Pumlumon Fawr; 752m), source of the Rivers Wye and Severn. Here the Rivers Mynach and Rheidol tumble together in a narrow gorge.

The Mynach is spanned by three stone bridges, stacked on top of each other. The lowest and oldest is believed to have been built by the monks of Strata Florida Abbey (p690) before 1188. It's one of many bridges associated with an arcane legend that involves the devil building the bridge on the condition that he gets the first thing to cross it. An old lady outwits the devil by throwing some food over, which her dog chases and everybody's happy – except the devil and, presumably, the dog.

However it's not the bridges that are the real attraction here. Just above the confluence, the Rheidol drops 90m in a series of spectacular waterfalls. There are two possible walks: one, just to view the three bridges, takes only 10 minutes (£1); the other, a half-hour walk, descends 100 steps (Jacob's Ladder), crosses the Mynach and ascends the other side.

The Vale of Rheidol Railway (p690) heads to Devil's Bridge from Aberystwyth, as does the 18-mile Rheidol Cycle Trail.

BRECON BEACONS NATIONAL PARK

Rippling dramatically for 45 miles from Llandeilo in the west, all the way to the English border, Brecon Beacons National Park (Parc Cenedlaethol Bannau Brycheiniog) encompasses some of the finest scenery in Mid-Wales. High mountain plateaux of grass and heather, their northern rims scalloped with glacier-scoured hollows, rise above wooded, waterfall-splashed valleys and green, rural landscapes. It couldn't be more different than rock-strewn Snowdonia to the north, but it offers comparable thrills.

There are four distinct regions within the park, neatly bounded by main roads: the wild, lonely Black Mountain in the west, with its high moors and glacial lakes; Fforest Fawr, which lies between the A4067 and A470, whose rushing streams and spectacular waterfalls form the headwaters of the Rivers Tawe and Neath; the Brecon Beacons proper, a group of very distinctive, flat-topped hills that includes Pen-y-Fan (886m), the park's highest peak; and, from the A40 northeast to the English border, the rolling heathland ridges of the Black Mountains – don't confuse them with the Black Mountain (singular) in the west.

There are hundreds of walking routes in the park, ranging from gentle strolls to strenuous climbs. The park's staff organise guided walks and other active events throughout the summer. Maps and walk cards are available from the tourist offices of all the towns

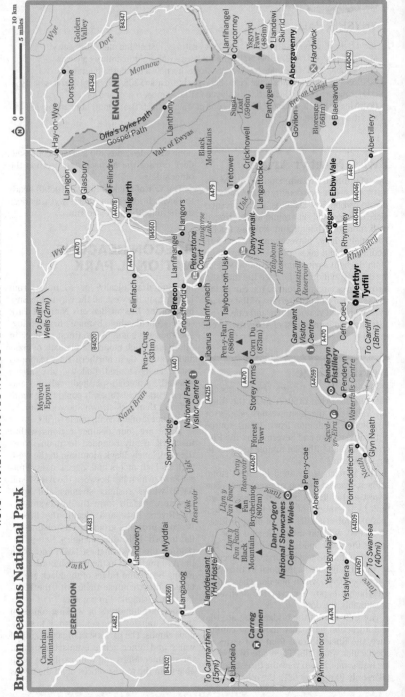

Brecon Beacons National Park

10 km
5 miles

ENGLAND

Offa's Dyke Path
Gospel Path

Vale of Ewyas

Golden Valley

Dore

Monnow

Wye

Dorstone

Hay-on-Wye

Llanigon

Glasbury

Felindre

Talgarth

Llangors

Peterstone Court

Llanfihangel

Brecon

Groesffordd

Llanfrynach

Felinfach

Pen-y-Crug (331m)

Libanus

National Park Visitor Centre

Mynydd Eppynt

Nant Bran

Sennybridge

Usk

Fforest Fawr

Cray Reservoir

Usk Reservoir

Llyn y Fan Fawr

Brycheiniog (802m)

Black Mountain

Llyn y Fan Fach

Llanddeusant YHA Hostel

Myddfai

Llandovery

Llangadog

Tywi

CEREDIGION

Cambrian Mountains

A483

A482

B4302

Llandeilo

Carreg Cennen

To Carmarthen (15mi)

To Swansea (40mi)

Ammanford

Ystalyfera

Ystradgynlais

Pontneddfechan

Glyn Neath

Abercraf

Pen-y-cae

Dan-yr-Ogof National Showcaves Centre for Wales

Pen-y-Fan (886m)

Corn Du (873m)

Storey Arms

Sgwd-yr-Eira

Waterfalls Centre

Penderyn

Penderyn Distillery

Garwnant Visitor Centre

Merthyr Tydfil

Cefn Coed

To Cardiff (18mi)

Talybont-on-Usk

Danywenallt YHA

Talybont Reservoir

Pontsticill Reservoir

Tredegar

Rhymney

Ebbw Vale

Abertillery

Blaenavon

Blorenge (561m)

Govilon

Brecon Canal

Abergavenny

Hardwick

Ysgyryd Fawr (486m)

Llandewi Skirrid

Llanfihangel Crucorney

Llanthony

Black Mountains

Sugar Loaf (596m)

Pantygelli

Crickhowell

Tretower

Llangattock

Usk

A479

A40

A470

B4560

A4078

A470

A4069

B4520

A4215

A4067

A474

A4109

A4059

A470

A467

A4046

A4048

Rhymney

To Builth Wells (2mi)

Wye

B4347

B4348

Llanigon

Wye

Tâf

Neath

Tawe

Llywel

Crai

in and around the park, as well as the main park visitor centre near Libanus.

Likewise, there are many excellent off-road mountain-biking routes, including a series of 14 graded and waymarked trails detailed in a map and guidebook pack (£7.50); see also www.mtbbreconbeacons.co.uk for more information.

Black Mountain & Fforest Fawr

West of the A470, this entire half of the national park is sparsely inhabited, without any towns of note. Black Mountain (Mynydd Du) contains the wildest, loneliest and least-visited walking country. Its finest feature is the sweeping escarpment of Fan Brycheiniog (802m), which rises steeply above the scenic glacial lakes of Llyn y Fan Fach and Llyn y Fan Fawr. It can be climbed from Llanddeusant; the round trip is 12 miles.

Fforest Fawr (Great Forest; www.fforestfawr geopark.org.uk), once a Norman hunting ground, is now a Unesco geopark famous for its varied landscapes, ranging from bleak moorland to flower-flecked limestone pavement and lush, wooded ravines choked with moss and greenery.

⊙ Sights & Activities

Carreg Cennen   CASTLE
(www.carregcennencastle.com; adult/child £4/3.50; ⊙9.30am-6.30pm Apr-Oct, to 4pm Nov-Mar) Perched atop a steep limestone crag high above the River Cennen is Wales' ultimate romantic ruined castle, visible for miles in every direction. The current structure was built at the end of the 13th century in the course of Edward I's conquest of Wales. It was partially dismantled in 1462 during the Wars of the Roses. The most unusual feature is a stone-vaulted passage running along the top of the sheer southern cliff, which leads down to a long, narrow, natural cave; bring a torch or hire one from the ticket office (£1.50).

Carreg Cennen is signposted from the A483, heading south from Llandeilo.

Dan-yr-Ogof National
Showcaves Centre for Wales   CAVES
(☑01639-730284; www.showcaves.co.uk; adult/ child £14/7.75; ⊙10am-4pm Apr-Oct) The limestone plateau of the southern Fforest Fawr, around the upper reaches of the River Tawe, is riddled with some of the largest and most complex cave systems in Britain. Most can

only be visited by experienced cavers, but this set of three caves is well lit, spacious and easily accessible, even to children.

Every effort has been taken to make this natural attraction as unnatural as possible. The entry is through the legs of a fibreglass dinosaur, and there are dozens of others scattered about. The confusion in the space-time continuum continues with a reconstruction of a Iron Age farm.

Dan-yr-Ogof Cave is the first cave you reach; it's part of a 10-mile complex and has interesting limestone formations. Next up is the highlight, Cathedral Cave, a high-domed chamber with a lake fed by two waterfalls that pour from openings in the rock. Nearby is the Bone Cave, where 42 Bronze Age skeletons were discovered and a tableau of cave people is illuminated.

The admission fee also gives entry to a shire-horse centre and petting farm. The complex is just off the A4067 north of Abercraf.

Waterfall Country   WATERFALLS
Between the villages of Pontneddfechan and Ystradfellte is a series of dramatic waterfalls, where the Rivers Mellte, Hepste and Pyrddin pass through steep forested gorges. The Elidir Trail (2½ miles each way) leaves from the Waterfalls Centre and takes in four falls. This can be combined with the Four Falls Trail for a 12-mile loop (allow six hours), which includes Sgwd-yr-Eira (Waterfall of the Snow), where you can actually walk behind the torrent.

Walks on the area are outlined on the national park's *Waterfall Country* publication (£3.50), available from visitor centres.

Penderyn Distillery   DISTILLERY
(☑01685-813300; www.welsh-whisky.co.uk; tours adult/child £6/4; ⊙9.30am-5pm) Before the ascendency of the chapels in the 19th century, the Welsh were as fond of whisky as their Celtic cousins in Scotland and Ireland. This boutique, independently owned distillery released its first malt whisky in 2004, marking the resurgence of Welsh whisky-making after a more than 100-year absence. It's distilled with fresh spring water drawn from directly beneath the distillery, then matured in bourbon casks and finished in rich Madeira wine casks to create a golden-hued drop of liquid fire. It also produces Brecon Gin, Brecon Five Vodka and Merlyn Cream Liqueur.

BEACONS BUSES

The Beacons Buses (☏01873-853254; www.travelbreconbeacons.info; day ticket £9) only run on Sundays and bank holidays from June to September. With a day ticket (buy it on the first bus you board) and a careful analysis of the online timetable you can plan a full day of sightseeing and activities. On the B16 and B17 circular routes you can get on and off at any point (adult/child £5.50/3.50). Some services allow bikes to be transported.

Useful routes include:

» **B1** – Barry, Cardiff, Storey Arms, Libanus, Brecon

» **B2 & B3** – Penderyn, Storey Arms, Libanus, Brecon

» **B4** – Abergavenny, Crickhowell, Tretower, Llanfrynach, Brecon

» **B5** – Cardiff, Caerphilly, Garwnant, Libanus, Brecon

» **B6** – Swansea, Dan-yr-Ogof, Brecon

» **B10** – Carmarthen, National Botanic Garden, Llandeilo, Brecon

» **B11** – Brecon, National Park Visitor Centre

» **B12** – Brecon, Llangorse Lake, Hay-on-Wye

» **B13** (Geopark Circular) – Brecon, National Park Visitor Centre, Dan-yr-Ogof, Penderyn, Storey Arms

» **B15** – Brecon, Talybont-on-Usk, Big Pit, Blaenavon

» **B16** (Taff Trail Roundabout) – Brecon, National Park Visitor Centre, Storey Arms, Brecon Mountain Railway, Llanfrynach

» **B17** (Offa's Dyke Flyer) – Hay-on-Wye, Llanthony Priory, Llanfihangel Crucorney

From the imposing black visitors centre you can watch the spirits being made, and adult tickets include tastings of two products (or a free miniature, if you're driving); it pays to book ahead. Enthusiasts can take a 2½-hour Master Class, which includes a guided tour and tastings (per person £45, bookings essential).

🛏 Sleeping

Llanddeusant Youth Hostel HOSTEL **£**
(☏0845 371 9750; www.yha.org.uk; Old Red Lion; dm/r from £17/49) This is one of Britain's most remote YHAs, occupying a former inn nestled in the western fringes of the Black Mountain.

❶ Information

Garwnant visitor centre (☏01685-723060; www.forestry.gov.uk/garwnant; ⊙10am-5pm) At the head of Llwyn Onn Reservoir, 5 miles north of Merthyr Tydfil on the A470, this is the starting point for a couple of easy forest walks and a mountain-bike park. It also has a cafe, an adventure play area and a ropes course.

Waterfalls centre (☏01639-721795; Pontneathvaughan Rd, Pontneddfechan; ⊙9.30am-5pm Apr-Oct, 9.30am-3pm Sat & Sun Nov-Mar)

❶ Getting There & Away

Bus X63 between Swansea and Brecon stops at Dan-yr-Ogof.

Brecon (Aberhonddu) & Around

POP 7900

The handsome stone market town of Brecon stands at the meeting of the River Usk and the River Honddu. For centuries the town thrived as a centre of wool production and weaving; today it's the main hub of the national park and a natural base for exploring the surrounding countryside. The conical hill of Pen-y-Crug (331m), capped by an Iron Age hill fort, rises to the northwest of the town, and makes a good objective for a short hike (2.5 miles round trip).

◉ Sights & Activities

Brecon Cathedral CHURCH
(www.breconcathedral.org.uk; Cathedral Cl) Perched on a hill above the River Honddu, Brecon Cathedral was founded as part of a Benedictine monastery in 1093, though little remains of the Norman structure except the carved font and parts of the nave. It's a lovely church and very visitor-friendly;

Brecon

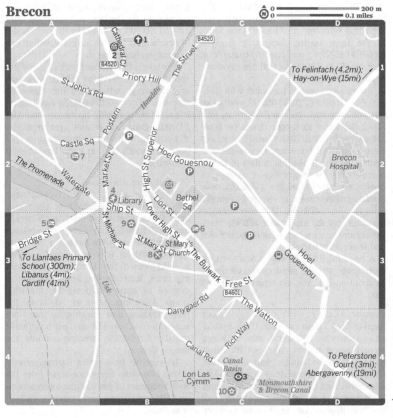

Brecon

seven information points provide details of key features.

In the cathedral grounds is a **Heritage Centre** (admission free; ⊙10am-4.30pm Mon-Sat), cafe and gift shop housed in a restored 15th-century tithe barn.

Monmouthshire & Brecon Canal   CANAL
Brecon is the northern terminus of this canal, built between 1799 and 1812 for the movement of coal, iron ore, limestone and agricultural goods. The 33 miles from Brecon to Pontypool is back in business, transporting a generally less-grimy cargo

of holidaymakers and river-dwellers. The busiest section is around Brecon, with craft departing from the canal basin, 400m south of the town centre. Dragonfly Cruises (☑01874-685222; www.dragonfly-cruises.co.uk; adult/child £7.20/4.50; ☺Mar-Oct) runs 2½-hour narrowboat trips.

You can also take to the water with Beacon Park Boats (☑01873-858277; www.beacon parkboats.com; boats per hour/half-day/day from £16/35/50, up to six people; canoes per hour/half-day/day from £10/20/30), which rents out electric-powered boats and three-seater Canadian canoes. It also has a fleet of luxury narrowboats for longer live-in voyages, as does Cambrian Cruisers (☑665315; www .cambriancruisers.co.uk; Ty Newydd, Pencelli). Backwaters (☑01873-831825; www.backwater shire.co.uk; per day kayak/canoe £28/45) rents kayaks and canoes, including buoyancy aids and waterproof barrels.

A peaceful 8.5-mile walk along the towpath leads to the picturesque village of Talybont-on-Usk. You can return on the X43 bus.

Llangorse Lake   LAKE
Reed-fringed Llangorse Lake (Llyn Syfaddan), to the east of Brecon, may be Wales' second-largest natural lake, but it's barely more than a mile long and half a mile wide. Close to the northern shore is a crannog, a lake dwelling built on an artificial island. Such dwellings or refuges were used from the late Bronze Age until early medieval times. Tree-ring dating shows that this one (of which only the base remains) was built around AD 900, probably by the royal house of Brycheiniog. There's a reconstruction of a crannog house on the shore.

The lake is the national park's main water sports location, used for sailing, windsurfing, canoeing and water-skiing. Lakeside Caravan Park (☑01874-658226; www.llangorse lake.co.uk) rents rowing boats (per hour/day £12/32), Canadian canoes (per hour/day £12/40) and Wayfarer sailing dinghies (per hour £27; you'll need to know how to rig it yourself).

Cantref Adventure Farm
& Riding Centre   HORSE RIDING
(☑01874-665223; www.cantref.com; Llanfrynach, Upper Cantref Farm; height over/under 93cm £8/free; ☺10.30am-5.30pm Easter-Oct, weekends & school holidays only Nov-Easter) In the countryside south of Brecon, Cantref operates a child-focused fun farm, complete with pig races, lamb feeding and unfortunates dressed as horses, dancing for the little troops. More interesting for adults are the pony trekking and hacking (ie more advanced terrain) expeditions (per hour/half-/full day £21/32/58), heading out into the Brecon Beacons.

It's reached by a set of narrow country lanes; follow the horseshoe signs from the A40, southeast of town. Bunkhouse accommodation (£15) and basic camping (£3.50) is available.

CLIMBING PEN-Y-FAN

One of the most popular hikes in the national park is the ascent of Pen-y-Fan (886m), the highest peak in the Brecon Beacons (around 120,000 people make the climb each year). The shortest route to the summit begins at the Pont ar Daf car park on the A470, 10 miles southwest of Brecon. It's a steep but straightforward slog up a deeply eroded path (now paved with natural stone) to the summit of Corn Du (873m), followed by a short dip and final ascent to Pen-y-Fan (4.5 miles round trip; allow three hours). This route has garnered the nickname 'the motorway' – it can be very busy. A slightly longer (5.5 miles round trip), but just as crowded, path starts at the Storey Arms outdoor centre, a mile to the north.

You can avoid the crowds by choosing one of the longer routes on the north side of the mountain, which also have the advantage of more interesting views on the way up. The best starting point is the Cwm Gwdi car park, at the end of a minor road 3.5 miles southwest of Brecon. From here, you follow a path along the crest of the Cefn Cwm Llwch ridge, with great views of the neighbouring peaks and a final steep scramble up to the summit.

Remember that Pen-y-Fan is a serious mountain – the weather can change rapidly, and people have to be rescued here every year. Wear hiking boots and take warm clothes, waterproofs, and a map and compass (particularly for the northern routes). You can get advice and weather forecasts at the National Park Visitor Centre (p700) or from the Met Office (☑0870 900 0100; www.metoffice.gov.uk).

✨ Festivals & Events

Brecon Jazz Festival   MUSIC
(www.breconjazz.co.uk) On the second week-end in August, Brecon hosts one of Europe's leading jazz events, with plenty of free fringe events in the local pubs.

Brecon Beast
(www.breconbeast.co.uk) A gruelling mountain bike challenge over 44 or 68 miles, held in mid-September. The fee covers camping, re-freshments on the route, a 'pasta party' and a brag-worthy T-shirt.

🛏 Sleeping & Eating

BRECON
Cantre Selyf   B&B ££
(☎01874-622904; www.cantreselyf.co.uk; 5 Lion St; s £60, d £80-90; P🖥) This elegant 17th-century town house, right in the middle of Brecon, has atmospheric period decor and furnishings, including plaster mouldings, original fireplaces and cast-iron bedsteads. Surprisingly, for such a central location, there's ample parking and a garden hidden behind the gates.

Castle of Brecon Hotel   HOTEL ££
(☎01874-624611; www.breconcastle.co.uk; Castle Sq; s/d from £65/75; P) Built into the ruined walls of Brecknock Castle, this grand old hotel had been getting a bit creaky but an on-going renovation has left a trail of comfort-able, refurbished rooms. The better rooms are spacious, with views over the Beacons.

Bridge Cafe   B&B £
(☎01874-622024; www.bridgecafe.co.uk; 7 Bridge St; s/d from £45/55) With a particular focus on refuelling weary walkers and mountain bik-ers, Bridge Cafe offers home-cooked meals in cosy surrounds (mains £9 to £13; dinner Thursday to Saturday). Upstairs are three comfortable bedrooms with down-filled duvets and crisp, cotton sheets.

Roberto's   ITALIAN ££
(☎01874-611880; www.robertos.netau.net; St Mary St; mains £9-15; ⊗dinner Mon-Sat) They may be plastic vines hanging from the trellis on the ceiling, but everything else about Roberto's is authentically Italian, from the relaxed atmosphere to the free olives and crostini, to the *carbonara* sauce. Though, of course, that's Welsh beef lurking underneath the gorgonzola.

AROUND BRECON
Peterstone Court   HOTEL ££
(☎01874-665387; www.peterstone-court.com; A40, Llanhamlach; s/d from £105/125; P🖥🐾) An ele-gant Georgian manor house with large com-fortable bedrooms, Peterstone enjoys views across the valley to the Beacons. The excel-lent restaurant (mains £17 to £19) has access to produce straight from the manor's farm. Llanhamlach is 3 miles southeast of Brecon, just off the A40.

Danywenallt Youth Hostel   HOSTEL £
(☎0845 371 9548; www.yha.org.uk; Talybont-on-Usk; dm/r from £15/29) A converted farmhouse in a secluded spot, nestled beneath the dam of Talybont Reservoir, halfway between Bre-con and Crickhowell.

Felin Fach Griffin   RESTAURANT £££
(☎01874-620111; www.felinfachgriffin.co.uk; Fe-linfach; mains £18-19) With a string of awards as long as its extensive wine list, the Griffin offers gourmet dining in a relaxed and un-pretentious setting. Open fires, leather sofas and timber beams create a comfortable at-mosphere, while the kitchen makes the most of local fish, meat and game. Upstairs are a set of comfortable TV-free rooms (single/double from £85/115). The Griffin is 5 miles northeast of Brecon on the A470.

White Swan   PUB ££
(☎01874-665276; www.the-white-swan.com; Llan-frynach; mains £14-19; ⊗Wed-Sun) A traditional village inn that offers a candle-lit dining room with old wooden floors, a bar with comfortably worn leather sofas and arm-chairs, and a beautiful garden terrace. The menu emphasises Welsh lamb, beef and venison. Llanfrynach is 3.5 miles southeast of Brecon off the B4558.

☆ Entertainment

Brecon & District
Male Choir   TRADITIONAL MUSIC
(www.breconchoir.co.uk; Orchard St, Llanfaes Pri-mary School; ⊗7.30-9.30pm Fri) For booming harmonies, head to the practice sessions of the local men's choir; visitors are welcome.

Theatr Brycheiniog   THEATRE
(☎01874-611622; www.theatrbrycheiniog.co.uk; Canal Wharf) This attractive canalside theatre complex is the town's main venue for drama, dance, comedy and music. It often hosts sur-prisingly big-name touring acts.

Coliseum Cinema CINEMA
(☑01874-622501; www.coliseumbrecon.co.uk; Wheat St; tickets £6.50) Screens mainly mainstream films.

ⓘ Information

Brecon War Memorial Hospital (☑01874-622443; Cerrigcochion Rd)

National park visitor centre (☑01874-623366; www.breconbeacons.org; Libanus; ◷9.30am-5pm) The park's main visitor centre, with full details of walks, hiking and biking trails, outdoor activities, wildlife and geology. The centre is off the A470 road 5 miles southwest of Brecon.

Tourist office (☑01874-622485; market car park; ◷9.30am-5.30pm Mon-Sat, 10am-4pm Sun)

ⓘ Getting There & Away

BICYCLE **Biped Cycles** (☑01874-622296; www.bipedcycles.co.uk; 10 Ship St; per half-/full day £18/20) rents bikes and can arrange guided rides. The Taff Trail heads south from here to Cardiff. This forms part of the Lôn Las Cymru national cycling route which also heads north to Builth Wells.

BUS Bus routes include X43 to Crickhowell (26 minutes) and Abergavenny (40 minutes); X63 to Dan-yr-Ogof (32 minutes) and Swansea (1½ hours); and 39 to Hay-on-Wye (41 minutes).

Crickhowell (Crughywel) & Llangattock (Llangatwg)

These prosperous, picturesque, flower-bedecked villages face each across the River Usk, linked by an elegant 17th-century stone bridge famous for having 12 arches on one side, and 13 on the other. Crickhowell is named after the distinctive flat-topped Crug Hywel (Hywel's Rock; 451m), better known as Table Mountain, which rises to the north. A beautiful track leads to the remains of an Iron Age fort at the top (3 miles round trip). The village grew up around a Norman motte (mound) and bailey castle, of which all that remains are a few tumbledown towers.

◉ Sights & Activities

Tretower Court & Castle HISTORIC BUILDING
(www.cadw.wales.gov.uk; Tretower; adult/child £4/3.60; ◷10am-5pm Apr-Oct, 11am-4pm Fri-Sun Nov-Mar) Tretower gives you two historic buildings for the price of one – the sturdy circular tower of a Norman motte-and-bailey castle, and a 15th-century manor house with a fine medieval garden. Together they illustrate the transition from military

stronghold to country house that took place in late medieval times.

Tretower is 3 miles northwest of Crickhowell on the A479.

Golden Castle Riding Stables HORSE RIDING
(☑01873-812649; www.golden-castle.co.uk; per 1½hr/day from £35/55) Offers pony trekking, hacking and trail riding in the surrounding countryside.

✵ Festivals & Events

Green Man Festival MUSIC
(www.greenman.net; Glanusk Park; adult/child £145/5) Staged over an August weekend, 2 miles west of Crickhowell via the B4558, Green Man is a summer music festival which, despite its relatively small size (around 10,000 people), consistently attracts the current 'it' bands of the alternative music firmament and the odd dead-set legend. Tickets include the weekend's camping.

🛏 Sleeping & Eating

Gwyn Deri B&B ££
(☑01873-812494; www.gwynderibedandbreakfast.co.uk; Mill St, Crickhowell; s/d £40/65; P🐕) The friendly couple who run this homely B&B keep its modern rooms immaculately clean, while their little dog provides an enthusiastic welcome. Bonuses include iPod docks, fresh fruit in the rooms and an excellent breakfast selection. Connecting rooms are available for family groups.

Tŷ Gwyn B&B ££
(☑01873-811625; www.tygwyn.com; Brecon Rd, Crickhowell; s/d from £40/68; P@) Once the home of Regency architect John Nash, Tŷ Gwyn is a lovely old Georgian home with three spacious en-suite rooms in the main house and a separate cottage in the garden. A little brook babbles its way through the property.

Gliffaes Hotel HOTEL £££
(☑01874-730371; www.gliffaeshotel.com; s/d from £93/104; P🐕) This Victorian mansion makes quite an impression with its Romanesque towers rising through its thickly wooded grounds on the banks of the Usk. Standard doubles start from £166, but the considerably cheaper 'small doubles' have the same facilities. It's about 4 miles northwest of Crickhowell, off the A40.

Old Rectory HOTEL ££
(☑01873-810373; www.rectoryhotel.co.uk; Llangattock; s/d from £55/85; P🐕) Surprisingly grand

for the price, this partly 16th-century stone mansion was once the home of poet Henry Vaughan. Now it has its own golf course and a clubby atmosphere pervades in the downstairs bar and restaurant. Rooms are chic and comfortable.

Bear Hotel   PUB **££**
(☑01873-810408; www.bearhotel.co.uk; Beaufort St; s/d from £77/95, mains £9-19; [P][?]) The Bear is a fine old coaching inn with low-ceilinged rooms, stone fireplaces, blackened timber beams and antique furniture. Some rooms have four-poster beds and Jacuzzis. The menu ranges from hearty country fare to more exotic dishes (Moroccan lemon chicken; salmon with chilli, lime and coriander).

Number Eighteen   CAFE, BRASSERIE **££**
(☑01873-810337; www.black-mountain.co.uk; 18 High St; lunch £5-7, dinner £9-19; ⊙lunch daily, dinner Wed-Sat) By day it's a bright cafe serving above-average coffee and light lunches, but at night the action shifts to the brasserie upstairs. It's a relaxed spot for a burger, steak or pork chop, with live music serenading the diners on Wednesday evenings.

Nantyffin Cider Mill   MODERN WELSH **££**
(☑01873-810775; www.cidermill.co.uk; lunch £6-20, dinner £16-20; ⊙lunch Tue-Sun, dinner Tue-Sat) This 16th-century drovers' inn uses local produce to create simple, unfussy dishes that allow the quality of the ingredients to shine through. The dining room is a blend of bare stone, exposed roof beams, designer chairs and white table linen, set around the original 19th-century cider press. Nantyffin is a mile northwest of Crickhowell on the A40.

❶ Information

Tourist office (☑01873-811970; www.visit crickhowell.co.uk; Beaufort St; ⊙10am-5pm; [?]) Has leaflets for local walks and an art and craft gallery upstairs.

❶ Getting There & Away

Bus X43 connects Crickhowell with Abergavenny (15 minutes) and Brecon (26 minutes).

Abergavenny (Y Fenni)

POP 14,000

Bustling, workaday Abergavenny makes a fine base for walks, cycling and paragliding in the surrounding hills, but it is as the capital of a burgeoning food scene that the town has really come into its own. Its position at the heart of Wales' new cuisine, which celebrates the best in fresh, local and organic produce, is generating international interest in both its food festival and its acclaimed eateries, the best of which are just out of town in the surrounding countryside.

Abergavenny sits between three impressive protrusions: Blorenge (561m) to the southwest; Ysgyryd Fawr (486m) to the northeast; and Sugar Loaf (596m) to the northwest. Each has rewarding walks and fine views of the Usk Valley and the Black Mountains, of which the last two form the southernmost summits. For more leisurely walks, you can follow easy paths along the banks of the River Usk or explore the towpath of the Monmouthshire and Brecon Canal, which passes a mile southwest of the town.

⊙ Sights

St Mary's Priory Church & Tithe Barn   CHURCH
(www.stmarys-priory.org; Monk St) Relatively modest-looking, St Mary's contains a remarkable treasury of aristocratic tombs within. It was founded at the same time as the castle (1087) as part of a Benedictine priory, but the present building dates mainly from the 14th century, with 15th- and 19th-century additions and alterations. In the northern transept is a monumental 15th-century wooden representation of the biblical figure of Jesse.

The priory's 13th century tithe barn has been restored and converted into an excellent heritage centre and cafe.

[FREE] **Abergavenny Castle & Museum**   MUSEUM
(www.abergavennymuseum.co.uk; Castle St; ⊙11am-5pm Mon-Sat, 2-5pm Sun Mar-Oct, 11am-4pm Mon-Sat Nov-Feb) Not much remains of Abergavenny Castle except for a stretch of curtain wall on either side of the gatehouse. The castle keep was converted into a hunting lodge by the Victorians and now houses a small museum devoted to the history of the castle and the town.

✯ Festivals & Events

South Wales Three Peaks Trial   WALKING
(www.threepeakstrial.co.uk) This annual walking challenge is held in March.

Abergavenny Festival of Cycling   CYCLING
(www.abergavennyfestivalofcycling.co.uk) In Mid-July lycra-enthusiasts' meet incorporating

the Iron Mountain Sportif, a participatory event with 25-mile, 50-mile and 100-mile courses.

Abergavenny Food Festival FOOD
(www.abergavennyfoodfestival.co.uk) The most important gastronomic event in Wales, held on the third weekend in September.

🛏 Sleeping & Eating

Guest House B&B ££
(☎01873-854823; www.theguesthouseabergavenny.co.uk; 2 Oxford St; s/d from £40/75; ☎) This family-friendly B&B with cheerful, eclectically furnished rooms (not all en suite) has a mini-menagerie of pigs, rabbits, chickens and a pair of parrots that can match the gregarious owners in colourful language. It's certainly not lacking in character.

Angel HOTEL ££
(☎01873-857121; www.angelhotelabergavenny.com; 15 Cross St; r from £79; P☎) Abergavenny's top hotel is a fine Georgian building that was once a famous coaching inn. Seemingly in the middle of a never-ending refurbishment, the completed bedrooms and communal areas feel sleek and sophisticated. The menu makes the most of local produce (mains £12 to £20).

Walnut Tree MODERN WELSH £££
(☎01873-852797; www.thewalnuttreeinn.com; Llandewi Skirrid; mains £19-25, 2-/3-course lunch £20/25; ☺Tue-Sat) Established in 1963, the Walnut Tree is one of Wales' finest restaurants, with a Michelin star to prove it. Fresh, local produce dominates, along with a solid selection of seafood. The Walnut Tree is 3 miles northeast of Abergavenny on the B4521.

Hardwick INN £££
(☎01873-854220; www.thehardwick.co.uk; Old Raglan Rd, Abergavenny; mains £18-24, 2-/3-course lunch £17/21) The Hardwick is a traditional inn with an old stone fireplace and low ceiling beams. Ex-Walnut Tree alumnus Stephen Terry has created a gloriously unpretentious menu that celebrates the very best of country cooking. Attached are eight elegant, modern rooms (from £145). The Hardwick is 2 miles south of Abergavenny on the B4598.

Pizzorante ITALIAN £
(☎01873-857777; www.pizzorante.co.uk; Market St; mains £7-9; ☺lunch Tue-Sun, dinner Tue-Sat) If you don't fancy blowing the budget on one of the chichi countryside restaurants, this cheerful family restaurant in the town centre is the perfect alternative. The pizzas are huge, particularly the calzone, with delicious crispy bases.

ℹ Information

Nevill Hall Hospital (☎732732; Brecon Rd; ☺24hr)

Tourist office (☎01873-853254; www.visitabergavenny.co.uk; Swan Meadow, Cross St; ☺10am-4pm) Merged with the Brecon Beacons National Park visitor centre.

ℹ Getting There & Away

BUS Bus routes include 83 to Monmouth (45 minutes) via Raglan (25 minutes); X4 to Cardiff (2½ hours); and X43 to Brecon (40 minutes) via Crickhowell (15 minutes). National Express coaches head to Hereford (£7.50, 40 minutes), Worcester (£13, 1¾ hours) and Birmingham (£13, three hours).

TRAIN There are direct trains from Cardiff (£12, 40 minutes), Hereford (£9.10, 25 minutes), Shrewsbury (£25, 1¼ hours), Bangor (£62, 3½ hours) and Holyhead (£67, 4¼ hours).

Black Mountains (Y Mynyddoedd Duon)

The hills that stretch northward from Abergavenny to Hay-on-Wye, bordered by the A479 road to the west and the English border to the east, are bleak, wild and largely uninhabited, making this a popular walking area. The scenic and secluded Vale of Ewyas runs through the heart of them, from Llanfihangel Crucorney to the 542m-high Gospel Pass, which leads down to Hay-on-Wye. It's a magical place, with only a very narrow, single-track road running along it, best explored on foot, bike or horseback.

◉ Sights & Activities

Llanthony Priory RUIN
(☺10am-4pm) Halfway along the Vale of Ewyas lie these atmospheric 13th-century ruins, set among grasslands and wooded hills by the River Honddu. Though not as grand as Tintern Abbey, the setting is even more romantic; JMW Turner painted it in 1794.

Llanthony Riding and Trekking HORSE RIDING
(☎01873-890359; www.llanthony.co.uk; Court Farm; half-/full day beginners £30/55, experienced £40/65) Apart from pony trekking and hacking, it also offers basic campsites (per per-

son £3) and rents self-catering cottages (per week £370).

🛏 Sleeping & Eating

Llanthony Priory Hotel INN ££

(☏01873-890487; www.llanthonyprioryhotel.co.uk; r from £80) Seemingly growing out of the priory ruins, and incorporating some of the original medieval buildings, the Abbey Hotel is wonderfully atmospheric, with four-poster beds, stone spiral staircases and rooms squeezed into turrets; there are only four rooms and no en suites. It's also a great spot for a beer and snack.

Skirrid Inn PUB ££

(☏01873-890258; www.skirridmountaininn.co.uk; Llanfihangel Crucorney; s/d from £45/75) Those with a taste for the macabre and ghostly will love this place. Wales' oldest inn (dating prior to 1110) once doubled as a court and over 180 people were hung here. Just so you don't forget, a noose dangles from the well-worn hanging beam, directly outside the doors to the spacious bedrooms.

Hay-on-Wye (Y Gelli Gandryll)

POP 1500

This pretty little town on the banks of the River Wye, just inside the Welsh border, has developed a reputation disproportionate to its size. First came the explosion in secondhand bookshops, a charge led by the charismatic and forthright local maverick Richard Booth. He opened his eponymous bookshop in the 1960s and went on to proclaim himself the King of Hay, among other elaborate publicity stunts, while campaigning for an international network of book towns to support failing rural economies. With Hay becoming the world's secondhand book capital, a festival of literature and culture was established in 1988, growing in stature each year to become a major international fixture.

But Hay is not all about book browsing and celebrity spotting – it also makes an excellent base for active pursuits, with the Black Mountains, River Wye and Offa's Dyke Path all within easy access of the superb facilities of the town. The small town centre is made up of narrow sloping lanes, generously peppered with interesting shops, and peopled by the differing types that such individuality and so many books tend to attract. Even outside of festival time, it has a vaguely alternative ambience.

🏃 Activities

Drover Cycles CYCLING, WALKING

(☏01497-821134; www.drovercycles.co.uk; Forest Rd) Rents mountain and touring bikes (per half-day/day/week £25/35/100) and arranges logistics for long-distance cycling or walking expeditions anywhere in Wales.

Paddles & Pedals CANOEING, KAYAKING

(☏01497-820604; www.canoehire.co.uk; 15 Castle St; half-/full day £18/25) Take to the Wye waters at Hay and get collected further downstream.

✦✦ Festivals

Hay Festival BOOKS

(☏822629; www.hayfestival.com) The 10-day Hay Festival in late May has become Britain's leading festival of literature and the arts – a kind of bookworm's Glastonbury or, according to Bill Clinton, 'the Woodstock of the mind'. Like those legendary music festivals, it pulls more than its fair share of internationally famous guest stars. As well as readings, workshops, book signings, concerts and club nights, there's also a very successful children's festival called Hay Fever.

🛏 Sleeping & Eating

Start B&B ££

(☏01497-821391; www.the-start.net; Bridge St; r from £70; P🖤) Peacefully set on the fringes of town, this little three-bedroom place boasts an unbeatable riverside setting with beautiful gardens, homely rooms in a renovated 18th-century house and a flagstone-floored breakfast room. The friendly hosts can advise on local activities and walks.

Bear B&B ££

(☏01497-821302; www.thebearhay.co.uk; 2 Bear St; r £90, s/d without bathroom £50/70; P🖤) Beautifully renovated by its young owners, this 1590 coaching inn retains its historic ambience but combines it with interesting art, sisal floors, modern bathrooms and bright white walls. Home-baked treats are a nice touch and the breakfasts are excellent. Grab a book and while away an hour in the hidden garden out the back.

Old Black Lion PUB ££

(☏01497-820841; www.oldblacklion.co.uk; Lion St; d £90, s with/without bathroom £53/45; P) As traditional and atmospheric as they come, this inn looks 17th-century but parts of it date from the 13th – expect low ceilings and uneven floors. The accumulated weight of centuries of hospitality is cheerfully carried by the current staff. The food is many leagues beyond pub grub: think stuffed Guinea fowl, roast halibut and beef Wellington (mains £13 to £20).

Three Tuns
PUB ££

(☎01497-821855; www.three-tuns.com; Broad St; mains £12-18) Hay's gastronomic heavyweight, this 16th-century pub has a large garden area for alfresco food and a fancier restaurant upstairs. The sophisticated international menu follows that dependable modern mantra: local, organic and sustainable.

Bookshop Cafe
CAFE £

(www.boothbooks.co.uk; 44 Lion St; mains £4-8; ⊙lunch) Tucked into the rear of Richard Booth's Bookshop, this sun-filled cafe offers an adventurous, modern menu with plenty of vegetarian options and greens straight out of their own kitchen garden.

Shepherds Ice Cream Parlour
ICE CREAM £

(www.shepherdsicecream.co.uk; 9 High Town; single scoop £1.50; ⊙9.30am-5.30pm) Nobody should leave Hay without trying the homemade ice cream from Shepherds. It's made from sheep's milk, for a lighter, smoother taste.

🍸 Drinking & Entertainment

Blue Boar
PUB

(Oxford Rd) This cosy, traditional pub is ideal for whiling away a wet afternoon with a pint of Timothy Taylor's ale, a home-cooked lunch of Glamorgan sausage and a good book.

Globe at Hay
CLUB, CAFE

(☎01497-821762; www.globeathay.org; Newport St) Converted from a Methodist chapel and filled with mismatched chairs and sofas, this very cool venue is part cafe, part bar, part club, part theatre and all-round community hub – hosting DJs, live music, comedy, theatre, film, kid's events and political talks.

🔒 Shopping

There are 23 secondhand and antiquarian bookshops in Hay, with hundreds of thousands of tomes stacked floor to ceiling across town. Each store is profiled on a free map, available from the tourist office and from venues around town. There are also excellent stores selling antiques, craft and art.

Richard Booth's Bookshop
BOOKS

(www.boothbooks.co.uk; 44 Lion St) The most famous of the bookstores, and still the best, with an excellent cafe.

Mostly Maps
MAPS

(☎01497-820539; www.mostlymaps.com; 2 Castle St) Specialises in antiquarian maps, with certificates of authenticity dating them as far back as the 17th century.

ℹ Information

Tourist office (☎01497-820144; www.hay-on-wye.co.uk; Oxford Rd; ⊙10am-5pm Apr-Oct, 11am-1pm Nov-Mar)

ℹ Getting There & Away

Bus 39 stops in Hay-on-Wye, en route between Brecon (41 minutes) and Hereford (one hour).

POWYS

By far Wales' biggest county, Powys took the name of an ancient Welsh kingdom when it was formed in 1974 from the historic counties of Montgomeryshire, Radnorshire and Brecknockshire. Overwhelmingly rural, the majority of its 132,000-strong population live in villages and small towns. Newtown is easily the largest, yet even it only just scrapes above the 10,000-person mark. This county isn't just green in a literal sense – Machynlleth has become a focal point for the nation's environmentally friendly aspirations, and all over the county efforts to restore the threatened red kite have been met with outstanding success. The bird is now the very symbol of Powys, the county at Wales' green heart.

Llanwrtyd Wells (Llanwrtyd)

POP 600

Llanwrtyd (khlan-*oor*-tid) Wells is one strange little town: mostly deserted except during one of its oddball festivals when it's packed to the rafters with an influx of crazy contestants and their merry-making supporters. According to the *Guinness Book of Records* it is the UK's smallest town – some local residents even claim that in order to cling onto this status there's a periodic cull.

Apart from its newfound position as the capital of wacky Wales, Llanwrtyd Wells is surrounded by beautiful walking, cycling and riding country, with the Cambrian Mountains to the northwest and the Mynydd Eppynt to the southeast.

LLANWRTYD'S TWISTED EVENTS

While mulling over how to encourage tourism in Llanwrtyd in the dark winter months, some citizens started an inspired roll call of unconventionality. There's something on most months (see www.green-events.co.uk for more details) but these are the wackiest.

Saturnalia Beer Festival & Mountain Bike Chariot Racing Roman-themed festival including a 'best dressed Roman' competition, the devouring of stuffed bulls' testicles and the chariot race.

Man vs Horse Marathon The event that kicked all the craziness off, it's been held every year since 1980 and has resulted in some tense finishes. Two-legged runners have won only twice, the first in 2004.

World Bog Snorkelling Championships The most famous event of all. Competitors are allowed wetsuits, snorkels and flippers to traverse a trench cut out of a peat bog, using no recognisable swimming stroke and surfacing only to navigate. Spin-off events include Mountain Bike Bogsnorkelling ('like trying to ride through treacle') and the Bogsnorkelling Triathlon, both held in July.

Real Ale Wobble & Ramble In conjunction with the Mid-Wales Beer Festival, cyclists and walkers follow waymarked routes (10, 15 or 25 miles, or 35 miles for the wobblers), supping real ales at the 'pintstops' along the way.

Mari Llwyd A revival of the ancient practice of parading a horse's skull from house to house while reciting Welsh poetry.

Sleeping & Eating

Ardwyn House B&B ££

(01591-610768; www.ardwynhouse.co.uk; Station Rd; s/d £60/80; P) The young owners have been busy, restoring the art-nouveau grandeur of this once-derelict house. Some rooms have claw-foot baths and rural views, and there is oak parquet flooring, period wallpaper and a guest lounge with a pool table and bar.

Carlton Riverside B&B ££

(01591-610248; www.carltonriverside.com; Irfon Cres; s £50, d £75-100) This upmarket restaurant-with-rooms has a boutique feel and a mantelpiece that positively groans under the strain of awards for its foodie achievements (mains £17 to £23). The rooms are modern, simple and tasteful, and caters to bon vivants, with late breakfasts and checkouts.

Neuadd Arms Hotel PUB ££

(01591-610236; www.neuaddarmshotel.co.uk; Y Sgwar; s/d £43/75) Like any good village pub should be, the Neuadd Arms is a focal point for the community. During the winter you can join one of the farmers' dogs on the couch in front of the fire. There's also a surprisingly interesting menu (mains £8 to £10) and, upstairs, a set of clean, floral-patterned rooms. It also serves as the tourist office.

Drovers Rest RESTAURANT

(01591-610264; www.food-food-food.co.uk; Y Sgwar; lunch £8-10, dinner £17-20; Tue & Thu-Sun) A well-regarded restaurant-with-rooms, the Drovers has a snug little restaurant serving up the best of local produce. The three-course Sunday lunches are excellent (£14). The owners also run regular cooking classes, including a Welsh Cooking Day (£185).

Getting There & Away

BUS Bus 48 heads to Builth Wells (23 minutes).

TRAIN Llanwrtyd is on the **Heart of Wales** (www.heart-of-wales.co.uk) railway line, with direct services to Swansea (£9.60, two hours), Llandeilo (£4.50, 45 minutes), Llandrindod Wells (£3.70, 31 minutes), Knighton (£6.40, 1¼ hours) and Shrewsbury (£12.10, two hours).

Llandrindod Wells (Llandrindod)

POP 5100

This spa town struck gold in Victorian times by touting its waters to the well-to-do gentry who rolled in for rest and recuperation. The grand architecture of the era remains, but now it's the town that's sleepy – you'd need to prod it with a sharp stick to rouse it on a Wednesday afternoon, when most of the shops close.

WORTH A TRIP

BUILTH WELLS (LLANFAIR-YM-MUALLT)

Builth (pronounced bilth) Wells is by far the liveliest of the former spa towns, with a bustling, workaday feel. Once the playground of the Welsh working classes, it's a handy base for walkers or cyclists tackling any of the long-distance paths that pass through.

The town fills to bursting at the beginning of July, when 230,000 people descend for the Royal Welsh Show (www.rwas.co.uk), which involves everything from livestock judging to lumberjack competitions.

Roman remains at nearby Castell Collen show that it wasn't the Victorians who first discovered the healthy effects of the local spring waters, but it was the arrival of the railway in 1865 that brought visitors en masse.

◉ Sights

National Cycle Collection MUSEUM
(www.cyclemuseum.org.uk; Temple St; adult/child £4/2; ☉10am-4pm Mon-Fri Apr-Oct) The art-nouveau Automobile Palace houses over 250 bikes, tracing the progression from clunky boneshakers to slick modern-day examples. Curios include penny farthings, bamboo bikes from the 1890s and the vertiginous 'Eiffel Tower' of 1899 (used to display billboards).

Rock Park PARK
In 1670 the local spring was given the name the 'Well of the Blacksmith's Dingle', but it was not until the mid-18th century that its therapeutic qualities were discovered. However, the allure of stinky water gradually diminished and it closed in 1972. You can still sup from the rusty-looking (and tasting) Chalybeate Spring beside Arlais Brook as it tinkles through the forested park: apparently the water is good for treating gout, rheumatism, anaemia and more (chalybeate refers to its iron salts).

Llandrindod Lake LAKE
Just southeast of the centre is a sedately pretty, tree-encircled lake, built at the end of the 19th century to allow Victorians to take their exercise without appearing to do so. A metallic dragon spurts water from the middle of the lake.

Radnorshire Museum MUSEUM
(www.powys.gov.uk/radnorshiremuseum; Temple St; adult/child £1/free; ☉10am-4pm Tue-Sat) Small and low-key, rather like the town itself, this museum offers a taste of local history.

✱ Festivals & Events

Victorian Festival VICTORIANA
(www.victorianfestival.co.uk) In the middle of August Llandrindod Wells indulges in nine days of 19th-century costumes and shenanigans.

🛏 Sleeping

Cottage B&B £
(☎01597-825435; www.thecottagebandb.co.uk; Spa Rd; s/d £40/62) This large, appealing Edwardian house, set in a flower-adorned garden, has comfortable rooms with heavy wooden furniture and lots of original features. Not all rooms are en suite and the only TV is in the guest lounge. Expect plenty of wise-cracks from the irrepressibly chatty host.

Metropole Hotel HOTEL £££
(☎01597-823700; www.metropole.co.uk; Temple St; s/d from £98/126; 🅿🛜♨) Dating from the town's Victorian heyday, this turreted hostelry retains an old-fashioned elegance – at least in the lobby, where rose-patterned wallpaper conjures up memories of Great-Aunt Mabel's front parlour. The rooms have been updated but are more functional than they are grand.

ℹ Information

Tourist office (☎01597-822600; www.llandrindod.co.uk; Temple St; ☉10am-4pm Mon-Fri, to 1pm Sat Apr-Sep, to 1pm Mon-Sat Oct-Mar)

ℹ Getting There & Around

BUS Bus routes include T4 to Cardiff (2½ hours), Brecon (one hour), Builth Wells (22 minutes) and Newtown (48 minutes); and 47 to Rhayader (25 minutes).

TRAIN Llandrindod is on the Heart of Wales railway line, with direct services to Swansea (£12, 2¼ hours), Llandeilo (£7, 1¼ hours), Llanwrtyd Wells (£3.70, 31 minutes), Knighton (£4.10, 36 minutes) and Shrewsbury (£11, 1½ hours).

Rhayader (Rhaeadr Gwy)

POP 2100

Life in this small town revolves around its Wednesday livestock market. At other times there are few signs of any life here, especially on Thursdays when businesses trade for only half a day. The main attractions for travellers are the walking and cycling routes in the nearby Elan Valley, the 136-mile Wye Valley Walk which passes through town, and the daily red-kite feeding at a local farm.

◎ Sights & Activities

⬛ Elan Valley   RIVERS

In the early 19th century, dams were built on the River Elan (pronounced ellen), west of Rhayader, with a fourth large dam following in 1952 on the tributary River Claerwen. Together they provide over 264 million litres of water daily for Birmingham and parts of South and Mid-Wales and up to 4.6 megawatts of hydroelectric power. The need to protect the 70-sq-mile watershed has turned it into an important wildlife conservation area.

Located just downstream of the lowest dam is Welsh Water's Elan Valley Visitor Centre (☑01597-810880; www.elanvalley.org.uk; admission free; ◎10am-5.30pm Mar-Oct), with interesting exhibits on the scheme and leaflets on the estate's 80 miles of nature trails. Check the website for details of the frequent guided walks and birdwatching trips, which are mostly free.

The Elan Valley Trail is an 8-mile traffic-free walking, horse-riding and cycling path that mostly follows the line of the long-gone Birmingham Corporation Railway alongside the River Elan and its reservoirs. It starts just west of Rhayader at Cwmdauddwr.

Gigrin Farm Red Kite Feeding Station   BIRDWATCHING

(www.gigrin.co.uk; adult/child £4.50/2; ◎2pm Nov-Mar, 3pm Apr-Oct) Once the most common bird of prey throughout Britain, by the 19th century the red kite was flirting with extinction. Concerted conservation efforts over the last century have meant that red kites are once again a familiar sight in Welsh skies.

Anywhere up to 400 red kites at a time may partake in the daily feeding frenzy at this working farm on the A470, half a mile south of the town centre. Once the meat scraps from a local abattoir are spread on the field the crows descend, then the acrobatically swooping kites – often mugging the crows to get the meat – and later ravens and buzzards.

Clive Powell Mountain Bike Centre   MOUNTAIN BIKING

(☑01597-811343; www.clivepowell-mtb.co.uk; West St) Run by a former cycling champion who offers a roster of 'Dirty Weekends', all-inclusive mountain-biking weekends hitting trails around the Elan Valley. You also can hire a mountain/off-road bike (£20/15 per day), including helmet and puncture kit.

ℹ Getting There & Away

Buses include 46 from Builth Wells (33 minutes); 47 from Llandrindod Wells (25 minutes) and Aberystwyth (1¾ hours); and X75 from Newtown (55 minutes) and Shrewsbury (2¾ hours).

Presteigne (Llanandras)

At the far east of the vanished county of Radnorshire, pressed right up against the English border, is Presteigne (www.presteigne.org.uk), its former county town. It's a quaint little place, lined with attractive old buildings and surrounded by beautiful countryside.

The Judge's Lodging (☑01544-260650; www.judgesloding.org.uk; adult/child £5.95/3.95; ◎10am-5pm Tue-Sun Mar-Oct, 10am-4pm Sat & Sun Nov-Dec) offers an intriguing glimpse into Victorian times via an audioguided wander through the town's 19th-century courthouse, lock-up and judge's apartments. The commentary does tend to ramble on but the displays are interesting. The local tourist office is based here.

In the neighbouring village of Norton, the Old Vicarage (☑01544-260038; www.oldvicarage-nortonrads.co.uk; r £108; ℗) is a three-bedroom, gay-friendly, boutique B&B featuring opulent Victorian fittings and interesting religious art.

Bus 41 heads to Knighton (24 minutes).

Knighton (Tref-Y-Clawdd)

POP 2800

Hilly Knighton (www.visitknighton.co.uk) is so close to the border that its train station is actually in England. It sits midway along the Offa's Dyke Path national trail and at one end of the Glyndŵr's Way national trail, a 132-mile walking route to Welshpool. The two-in-one Tourist Office & Offa's Dyke

OFFA'S DYKE PATH

They say that good fences make good neighbours, but King Offa may have taken the idea a bit far. The 8th-century Mercian king built Offa's Dyke, Britain's longest archaeological monument, to mark the boundary between his kingdom and that of the Welsh princes and even today, though only 80 miles of the dyke remains, the modern Wales–England border roughly follows the line it defined.

The Offa's Dyke Path national trail criss-crosses that border around 30 times in its journey from the Severn Estuary near Chepstow, through the beautiful Wye Valley and Shropshire Hills, to the coast at Prestatyn in North Wales. The dyke itself usually takes the form of a bank next to a ditch, although it's overgrown in some places and built over in others. The trail often strays from the dyke, covering an astonishing range of scenery and vegetation, including river valleys, hill country, oak forests, heathland and bracken, conifer forest, green fields, high moors and the mountainous terrain of the Clwydian range in the north.

While it can be walked in either direction, it's best done south to north, with the wind and sun mainly on your back. Most people take 12 days to complete the 178-mile walk, though it's wise to allow at least two rest days, bringing your adventure to an even two weeks.

The Offa's Dyke Centre in Knighton is the best source of information about the route, stocking maps, guidebooks and pamphlets. Or visit the website http://www.national trail.co.uk/OffasDyke/.

Becky Ohlsen

Centre (☏01547-528753; www.offasdyke.demon .co.uk; West St; ◷10am-5pm Apr-Oct, 10am-4pm Mon-Sat Nov-Mar) is full of information for walkers and interactive displays about the dyke, a section of which runs behind the centre.

The town's best refuelling option is the Horse & Jockey (☏01547-520062; www.the horseandjockeyinn.co.uk; Station Rd; mains bar £4-7, restaurant £6-14), a 14th-century coaching inn. You can eat in the bar or sit down to a more substantial meal in the restaurant; they do an excellent Sunday lunch. The five upmarket en-suite rooms have flatscreen TVs, modern fittings, ancient exposed stone walls and flash bathrooms.

Knighton is one of the stops on the Heart of Wales line; destinations include Swansea (£15, 3¼ hours), Llandeilo (£9.80, two hours), Llanwrtyd Wells (£6.40, 1¼ hours), Llandrindod Wells (£4.10, 36 minutes) and Shrewsbury (£8.60, 50 minutes). Bus 41 heads to Presteigne (24 minutes).

Newtown (Y Drenewydd)

POP 10,400

Newtown's a former mill town with lots of history but, as a destination, it's also a sleepy place these days – absolutely soporific on a Sunday, but waking up for the Tuesday and Saturday markets. Its big claim to fame is

that Robert Owen (1771–1858), the factory reformer, founder of the cooperative movement and 'father of Socialism', was born and died here. Monuments to his esteemed memory abound in the town centre.

Newtown was also once the home of Welsh flannel, and a major UK textile centre. When competition began driving wages down, Wales' first Chartist meeting was held here in October 1838. Pryce Jones, the world's first-ever mail-order firm, got its start here, on the back of the textile trade. By the end of the 19th century Newtown's boom days were over – and they've never been back. There are several small museums devoted to those long-gone salad days.

Newtown is also the home of Laura Ashley, who opened her first shop in Carno, 10 miles west of the centre.

◉ Sights

Robert Owen Museum MUSEUM
(www.robert-owen-museum.org.uk; The Cross; ◷11am-3pm Mon-Fri) If you're not aware of Robert Owen's legacy, you're best to start here. The displays on Owen's life are broken up with mementos and pictures; it's quite text-heavy but it makes fascinating reading. It also serves at the de facto tourist office. Owen's well-tended grave is in the grounds of **St Mary's Old Parish Church** (Old Church St).

Oriel Davies   GALLERY
(www.orieldavies.org; The Park; ☺10am-5pm Mon-Sat) One of Wales' leading contemporary spaces, hosting often edgy exhibitions. Its sunny, glassed-in cafe (mains £5 to £7) is the best place for a light meal, such as home-made soup, quiche or baked potatoes.

🛏 Sleeping

Highgate   B&B ££
(✆01686-623763; www.highgatebandb.co.uk; s £45, d £75-90; 🅿🛜) Fields still surround this heritage-listed half-timbered farmhouse (1651), making it a particularly bucolic retreat. The decor is understated, keeping the focus on the original oak beams and other period features. From Newtown, cross the bridge at the end of the main street, turn right, veer left at All Saints Church and continue for 2.5 miles.

❶ Getting There & Away

BUS Bus routes include X75 to Welshpool (33 minutes), Rhayader (55 minutes) and Shrewsbury (1¼ hours); and T4 to Cardiff (3½ hours) and Brecon (two hours).

The daily National Express coach from Aberystwyth (£11, 1¼ hours) to London (£33, 5½ hours), via Welshpool (£4.60, 25 minutes), Shrewsbury (£8.10, 55 minutes) and Birmingham (£11, 2½ hours), stops here.

TRAIN Newtown is on the Cambrian line, which crosses from Aberystwyth (£12, 1¼ hours) to Birmingham (£18, 1¾ hours) every two hours, via Machynlleth (£8.60, 42 minutes), Welshpool (£4.50, 15 minutes) and Shrewsbury (£6.50, 40 minutes).

Montgomery

Set around a market square lined with Georgian houses in stone and brick, genteel Montgomery is one of the prettiest small towns in the country. This being Wales, there's a castle rising from the craggy outcrop above the town. It's quite ruined, but the views over the chequerboard countryside are beautiful. St Nicholas' Church (13th-century, with add-ons) has a vaulted ceiling decorated with intricate coloured bosses, a carved altar screen and an elaborate Elizabethan tomb.

🛏 Sleeping & Eating

TOP CHOICE Checkers   RESTAURANT £££
(✆01686-669822; www.thecheckersmontgomery.co.uk; Broad St; mains £18-25; ☺lunch Wed-Sun,

dinner Wed-Sat; 🕿) It's no exaggeration to say that one of the main drawcards of Montgomery is this truly excellent restaurant-with-rooms. The modern British menu (the Shropshire pork belly is drool-inducing) and first-rate service has earned it a Michelin star and a loyal fan base. Upstairs, the rooms (single/double from £84/105) are quietly stylish, with extra-comfy beds, L'Occitane products and blissful bathrooms.

❶ Getting There & Away

Bus 71 from Newtown (38 minutes) to Welshpool (26 minutes) stops here.

Machynlleth

POP 2200

It was in little Machynlleth (ma-*hun*-khleth) that nationalist hero Owain Glyndŵr established the country's first Parliament in 1404. But even that legacy is close to being trumped by the town's reinvention as the green capital of Wales – thanks primarily to the Centre for Alternative Technology (CAT).

◉ Sights

⬚CAT   TECHNOLOGY CENTRE
(✆01654-705950; www.cat.org.uk; adult/child £8.50/4; ☺10am-5.30pm) Founded in 1974, CAT is a virtually self-sufficient education

---

DON'T MISS

POWIS CASTLE & GARDEN

Surrounded by magnificent gardens, Powis Castle (www.nationaltrust.org.uk; adult/child castle & gardens £13/6.50, garden only £9.60/4.80; ☺noon-4pm) rises from its terraces as if floating on a fantastical cloud of manicured yew trees. It was originally constructed in the 13th century by Gruffydd ap Gwenwynwyn, prince of Powys, and subsequently enriched by generations of the Herbert and Clive families. The extravagant mural-covered, wood-panelled interior contains one of Wales' finest collections of furniture and paintings, along with curios such as the rosary beads of Mary, Queen of Scots and an exquisite cache of jade, ivory, armour, textiles and other treasures brought back from India by Baron Clive.

The castle is just over a mile south of Welshpool.

centre that acts as an ecologically driven laboratory and information source for alternative technologies. There are more than 3 hectares of displays dealing with topics such as composting, organic gardening, environmentally friendly construction, renewable energy sources, sewage treatment and recycling. It has about 100 on-site workers and five full-time residents. To explore the whole site takes about two hours – take rainwear as it's primarily outdoors. Kids love the interactive displays and adventure playground.

There are workshops and games for children during the main school holidays and an extensive program of residential courses for adults throughout the year. It even offers master's degree courses. Volunteer helpers willing to commit to a six-month stint are welcome, but you'll need to apply.

To get to the CAT from Machynlleth you can take the 32, X32 or 34 bus (six minutes). Arriving by bus or bicycle gets you a discount of £1 on admission.

MOMA Wales GALLERY
(www.momawales.org.uk; Penrallt St; ⊙10am-4pm Mon-Sat) Housed partly in a neoclassical chapel (1880), the Museum of Modern Art exhibits work by contemporary Welsh artists as well as an annual international competition (from mid-July to early September).

Owain Glyndŵr Centre MUSEUM
(www.canolfanglyndwr.org; adult/child £2.50/1; ⊙10am-3pm Tue-Sat Easter-Sep) Housed in a rare example of a late-medieval Welsh town house, the Owain Glyndŵr Centre has somewhat dry displays but nevertheless tells a rip-roaring story of the Welsh hero's fight for independence. Although it's called the Old Parliament Building, it was probably built around 1460, some 50 years after Glyndŵr instituted his parliament on this site, but it's believed to closely resemble the former venue.

🏃 Activities

Dyfi Mountain Biking MOUNTAIN BIKING
(www.dyfimountainbiking.org.uk) Dyfi maintains three waymarked mountain-bike routes from Machynlleth: the Mach 1 (10 miles), 2 (14 miles) and 3 (19 miles), each more challenging than the last. In the Dyfi Forest, near Corris, is the custom-built, 9-mile, Cli-machx loop trail. In May the same crew runs the Dyfi

Enduro, a noncompetitive, long-distance, mountain-bike challenge, limited to 650 riders.

Holey Trail MOUNTAIN BIKING
(✆01654-700411; 31 Maengwyn St; ⊙10am-6pm Mon-Sat) Hires mountain bikes (per day £25), performs repairs, offers bunkhouse accommodation and is a mine of information on the local trails.

🛏️ Sleeping & Eating

Wynnstay Hotel INN ££
(✆01654-702941; www.wynnstay-hotel.com; Maengwyn St; s/d from £59/90, mains £11-18; 🅿️🛜) This erstwhile Georgian coaching inn (1780) has tidy older-style rooms, one with a four-poster bed, and creaky, uneven floors. Downstairs is given over to a rustic bar-eatery. Flying in the face of Machynlleth's veg-warrior image, the Wynnstay's menu revels in local meats.

Quarry Cafe CAFE £
(11 Maengwyn St; mains £3-6; ⊙breakfast & lunch Mon-Sat; 🛜🍴) Run by the same people as the CAT, this popular place dishes up delicious, wholesome, vegetarian lunch specials, using mostly organic ingredients. It's also very baby friendly, with organic baby food on the menu, plus there are changing facilities.

Farmers Market
(Maengwyn St) It's been held for over seven centuries and remains a lively affair.

🛈 Information

Dyfi Craft & Clothing (✆01654-703369; Owain Glyndŵr Centre, Maengwyn St; ⊙10am-4pm Mon-Sat) Following the demise of the official tourist office, this little store stocks brochures, maps and accommodation information.

🛈 Getting There & Away

BUS Routes include X32 to Aberystwyth (35 minutes), Dolgellau (29 minutes), Porthmadog (1¼ hours), Caernarfon (two hours) and Bangor (2½ hours).

TRAIN Machynlleth is on both the Cambrian and Cambrian Coast lines. Destinations include Aberystwyth (£5.70, 37 minutes), Porthmadog (£13, two hours), Pwllheli (£15, 2¼ hours), Newtown (£8.60, 42 minutes) and Birmingham (£20, 2¼ hours).

Snowdonia & North Wales

Best Places to Eat

» Castle Restaurant &
Armoury Bar (p725)

» Fish Tram Chips (p744)

» Gales of Llangollen (p740)

» Ann's Pantry (p734)

Best Places to Stay

» Ffynnon (p722)

» Escape B&B (p743)

» manorhaus (p741)

» Venetia (p730)

Why Go?

From rugged mountain trails and historic train lines to World Heritage castles and rejuvenated seaside towns, North Wales holds its own against arguably more famous attractions down south. The region is dominated by Snowdonia National Park, where mighty peaks scrape moody skies. Protected by such a formidable mountain shield, it's little wonder that the less-visited Llŷn Peninsula and the ancient island enclave of Anglesey have retained their traditional language and culture. In fact, the whole region feels properly Welsh: you'll hear the language on the street, see the Celtic legacy in the landscape and soak up the cultural pride in galleries, museums and attractions, from the beaches of the North Coast to the river-threaded heartland of northeast Wales. In many ways, North Wales distils the very essence of Welshness – just don't mention that to the folks in Cardiff.

When to Go

May is the driest month and Llandudno celebrates the warming weather with much Victorian merriment. In June, as summer kicks in, the Snowdon train can once again make it to the summit. In July you can shuttle between the beaches and Llangollen's International Musical Eisteddfod and Fringe Festival. July and August offer the warmest weather. The north is at its wettest between October and December. Average temperatures rarely scrape into two digits anytime between December and March.

Snowdonia & North Wales Highlights

❶ Exploring the charms of **Beaumaris** (p732), Anglesey's finest town

❷ Climbing Wales's highest peak **Snowdon** (p719)...or cheating by taking the rack-and-pinion train to the top!

❸ Sailing across **Pontcysyllte Aqueduct** (p738), Britain's latest World Heritage site

❹ Disappearing underground into the slate caverns at **Blaenau Ffestiniog** (p717)

❺ Witnessing the Byzantine beauty and strength of **Caernarfon Castle** (p726)

❻ Taking an unforgettable coast-to-coast journey on the narrow-gauge **Welsh Highland Railway** (p731)

❼ Revelling in all things Victorian – pier, promenade and Mr Punch – at the seaside resort of **Llandudno** (p741)

❽ Gazing toward the holy island of Bardsey from end-of-the-world headland **Braich-y-Pwll** (p728)

Activities

North Wales is crammed with adrenaline-pumping activities. The biggest attraction is **Snowdonia National Park** – prime territory for walking, climbing, pony trekking, mountain biking and cycling. **Betws-y-Coed** and **Llanberis** are the key hubs for visitors.

To the west, the **Llŷn Peninsula** and **Isle of Anglesey** are great for water sports, while to the east **Llangollen** and **Bala** are white-water hot spots thanks to dependable rapids on the rivers Dee and Tryweryn.

ⓘ Getting There & Around

Major rail routes in the region include the North Wales Coast Line from Chester to the ferry terminal at Holyhead, the Cambrian Coast Line from Machynlleth to Pwllheli and the Conwy Valley Line from Llandudno to Blaenau Ffestiniog. Snowdonia is well served by buses, but away from the main tourist areas, services are more limited. Check details with **Traveline Cymru** (www.traveline-cymru.info).

SNOWDONIA NATIONAL PARK

Snowdonia National Park (Parc Cenedlaethol Eryri; www.eryri-npa.gov.uk) was founded in 1951 (making it Wales' first national park), primarily to keep the area from being loved to death. This is, after all, Wales' best known and most heavily used slice of nature, with the busiest part around Snowdon (1085m) itself. Around 350,000 people climb, walk or take the train to the summit each year, and all those sturdy shoes make trail maintenance a never-ending task for park staff. Yet the park is so much more than just Snowdon, stretching some 35 miles east to west and over 50 miles north to south and incorporating coastal areas, rivers and Wales' biggest natural lake.

The Welsh name for Snowdonia is Eryri (eh-*ruh*-ree) meaning highlands. The Welsh call Snowdon itself Yr Wyddfa (uhr-*with*-vuh), meaning Great Tomb – according to legend a giant called Rita Gawr was slain here by King Arthur and is buried at the summit.

Like Wales' other national parks, this one is very lived-in, with sizeable towns at Dolgellau, Bala, Harlech and Betws-y-Coed. Two-thirds of the park is privately owned, with over three-quarters used for raising sheep and cattle. While the most popular reason for visiting the park is to walk, you can also go climbing, white-water rafting, kayaking, pony trekking and even windsurfing.

The park authority publishes a free annual visitor newspaper, which includes information on getting around, park-organised walks and other activities. The Met Office keeps the weather conditions constantly updated on its website (www.metoffice.gov.uk/loutdoor/mountainsafety/).

In the alpine reaches you'll need to be prepared to deal with hostile conditions at any time of the year; the sudden appearance of low cloud and mist is common, even on days that start out clear and sunny. Always take food, drink, warm clothing and waterproofs, whatever the weather. Carry *and* know how to read the appropriate map for the area, and carry a compass. Also be aware that even some walks described as easy may follow paths that go near very steep slopes and over loose scree.

Llanberis

POP 1840

While not the most instantly attractive town in the area, Llanberis is a mecca for walkers and climbers, hosting a steady flow of rugged polar fleece wearers year-round, but especially in July and August, when accommodation is at a premium. It's actually positioned just outside the national park but functions as a hub, partly because the Snowdon Mountain Railway leaves from here.

Llanberis straddles the A4086 with nearly all points of interest spread out along the High St, which runs parallel to it. Across the A4086 are the village's two lakes, Llyn Padarn and Llyn Peris.

The town was originally built to house workers in the Dinorwig slate quarry; the massive waste tips are hard to miss as you approach from the east. While tourism is the cornerstone of Llanberis life these days, the town wears its industrial heritage on its sleeve. Indeed, Dinorwig, which once boasted the largest artificial cavern in the world, has now become part of Europe's biggest pumped-storage power station. Some of the old quarry workshops have been reincarnated as a museum of the slate industry, and the narrow-gauge railway that once hauled slate to the coast now tootles along Llyn Padarn.

Snowdonia & Llŷn Peninsula

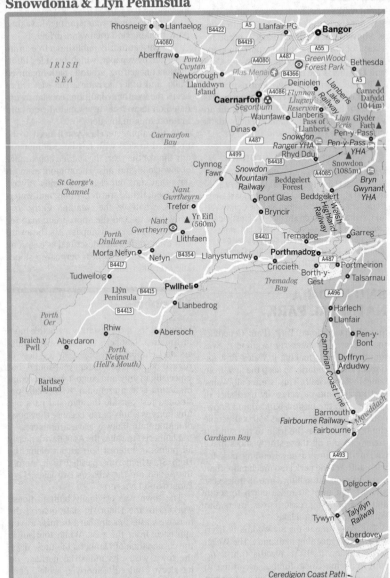

◉ Sights & Activities

FREE **National Slate Museum** MUSEUM
(www.museumwales.ac.uk/en/slate; ⊙10am-5pm
Easter-Oct, to 4pm Sun-Fri Nov-Easter) Even if

you're not all that fussed by industrial museums, this one's well worth a visit. At Llanberis, much of the slate was carved out of the open mountainside – leaving behind a jagged, sculptural cliff face that's fascinat-

Electric Mountain · POWER STATION

(☎01286-870636; www.electricmountain.co.uk; tour adult/child £7.75/3.95; ⊙9.30am-5.30pm Jun-Aug, 10am-4.30pm Sep-May, tours Easter-Oct) Dinorwig Power Station is the largest hydroelectricity scheme of its kind in Europe. It houses the town's tourist office, and runs interesting guided bus tours into the station's guts under the mountain. It's located by the lakeside on the A4086, near the south end of High St. Bookings required.

FREE Dolbadarn Castle · CASTLE

(⊙10am-4pm) Wales is so spoilt for castles that this one gets little attention. Built before 1230 by the Princes of Gwyneth, the keep rises like a perfect chessboard rook from a green hilltop between the two lakes. It's a brief stroll from town, rewarded by wonderful views of the lakes, quarries and Snowdon itself.

🛏 Sleeping

Glyn Afon · B&B ££

(☎01286-872528; www.glyn-afon.co.uk; 72 High St; s/d £40/65; 🅿) Rooms are frill-free but clean, warm and homely, with good information on walks round about, and breakfast will set you up for a day of mountain-striding. Those looking for a peaceful, child-free environment will particularly appreciate this place – the minimum age for guests is 16.

Dolafon · B&B ££

(☎01286-870993; www.dolafon.com; High St; s/d from £50/65; 🅿) Set back from the road, this imposing 19th-century house offers a series of traditional rooms, most of them with en suites. A continental breakfast is included, but it's worth paying extra for the heartier version, including vegetarian options, served in the tearoom downstairs.

Llanberis YHA · HOSTEL £

(☎0845-371-9645; www.yha.org.uk; dm from £15) Former quarry manager's house on the slopes above the town.

🍴 Eating

Peak Restaurant · WELSH, INTERNATIONAL ££

(☎01286-872777; www.peakrestaurant.co.uk; 86 High St; mains £14-18; ⊙from 7pm Wed-Sun) Charming owners and imaginative menus underpin this restaurant's popularity and longevity, and the open kitchen allows you to see the masters at work. Fine local ingredients (Welsh lamb, beef, cheeses) form the

ing if not quite beautiful. The museum occupies the Victorian workshops beside Llyn Padarn, featuring video clips, a huge working water wheel, reconstructed workers' cottages and demonstrations.

SNOWDON SHERPA BUS SERVICE

Walkers may be interested in the Snowdon Sherpa service, a circuit of buses that scurry around the slopes of the mountain, linking up the six main trailheads. This means that you can access trailheads by public transport from nearby towns; or you can walk up the mountain by one path and come down by another, and then hop on a bus to take you back to your starting point. Check timetables carefully first – the S6 service, for example, is extremely limited.

Services S1, S2 and S3 link Llanberis, Pen-y-Pass, Betws-y-Coed and Llanrwst. S4 runs between Caernarfon, Waunfawr and Beddgelert. S6 joins Bangor, Bethesda and Betws y Coed. S97 runs from Porthmadog to Beddgelert and Pen-y-Pass. A day ticket costs adult/child £4/2, but may be a false economy: a ride on services S1, S2 and S6 only costs £1. For up-to-date timetables, see the Gwynedd Council website (www.gwynedd.gov.uk).

basis of the internationally inspired dishes, with tasty veggie options and a good wine list.

Pete's Eats CAFE £
(☎01286-870117; www.petes-eats.co.uk; 40 High St; meals £3-7; ⊙8am-8pm; 🛜) A busy, bright cafe where hikers and climbers swap tips over monster portions in a hostel-like environment. There's bunkhouse accommodation upstairs, a huge noticeboard full of travellers' information, a book exchange, a map and guidebook room, and computers for internet access.

Snowdon Honey Farm & Winery CAFE, STORE £
(www.snowdonhoneyfarmandwinery.co.uk; High St; snacks around £5; ⊙10am-4pm) All manner of honey-related goodies are sold here, including a range of mead. It also functions as a cafe, serving ice cream, cream tea, cakes and sandwiches.

ℹ Information

Tourist office (☎01286-870765; Electric Mountain; ⊙10am-4pm Jun-Aug)

ℹ Getting There & Away

Snowdon Sherpa bus S1 heads to Pen-y-Pass (20 minutes) while S2 continues on to Capel Curig (30 minutes) and Betws-y-Coed (45 minutes). Buses 85 and 86 head to Bangor (45 minutes), while 87, 88 and 89 head to Caernarfon (20 minutes).

Betws-y-Coed

POP 2030

If you're looking for a base with an Alpine feel from which to explore Snowdonia National Park, the bustling little stone village of Betws-y-Coed *(bet-us-ee-koyd)* stands out as a natural option. It boasts a postcard-perfect setting above an inky river, engulfed in the verdant leafiness of the Gwydyr Forest and near the junction of three river valleys: the Llugwy, the Conwy and the Lledr.

The town has been Wales' most popular inland resort since Victorian days when a group of countryside painters founded an artistic community to record the diversity of the landscape. The arrival of the railway in 1868 cemented its popularity and today Betws-y-Coed is as busy with families and coach parties as it is with walkers.

⊙ Sights & Activities

Swallow Falls WATERFALL
(adult/child £1.50/0.50) Betws-y-Coed's main natural tourist trap is located 2 miles west of town alongside the A5. It's a beautiful spot, with the torrent weaving through the rocks into a green pool below.

Gwydyr Forest WALKING, CYCLING
The 28-sq-mile Gwydyr Forest, planted since the 1920s with oak, beech and larch, encircles Betws-y-Coed and is scattered with the crumbling remnants of lead and zinc mine workings. It's ideal for a day's walking, though it gets very muddy in wet weather: *Walks Around Betws-y-Coed* (£4.95), available from the National Park Information Centre, details several circular forest walks. Mountain-bikers are challenged by two mountain biking trails (both waymarked) in the forest north of Betws-y-Coed, as well as the Penmachno loops, 4km south of town near the village of Penmachno.

Beics Betws BICYCLE RENTAL
(☎01690-710766, 07736-903138; www.bikewales.co.uk; ⊙daily Jun-Aug, phone ahead at other times) Can advise on cycling trails, performs re-

pairs and hires mountain bikes from £28 per day.

Gwydir Stables HORSE RIDING
(☎01690-760248; www.horse-riding-wales.co.uk; Penmachno; per hr/half-day/day £22/40/70) Arranges rides through the forest for novice and regular riders alike. It also offers a pub ride for £50, lasting around four hours and stopping off for a pint at a couple of local pubs along the way.

🛏 Sleeping & Eating

Ty Gwyn Hotel HOTEL **££**
(☎01690-710383; www.tygwynhotel.co.uk; r £56-130; P🐾) This ex-coaching inn has been welcoming guests since 1636, its venerable age borne out by misshapen rooms, low ceilings and exposed beams. Predictably, not all rooms have en suites. The restaurant menu focuses on hearty, meaty mains (£13 to £18), but vegetarian choices and lighter bar-style meals are also available. It's located on the A5, just across Waterloo Bridge.

Afon Gwyn BOUTIQUE B&B **££**
(☎01690-710442; www.guest-house-betws-y-coed .com; A470, Coed-y-Celyn; r £80-118; P) Down in the valley, this old stone house has been skilfully converted into a grand boutique guesthouse. The decor is faultlessly tasteful, with white-painted wooden panelling, hushed tones, glittering chandeliers and bathrooms bedecked in Italian tiles and marble. While all the rooms are spacious, the Alice Suite is massive.

Maes-y-Garth B&B **££**
(☎01690-710441; www.maes-y-garth.co.uk; Lon Muriau, off A470; r £60-85; P🐾) Just across the river and a field from the township, this newly built home has earned itself many fans. Inside you'll find a warm welcome and five quietly stylish guest rooms with gorgeous views: perhaps the nicest is Room 4, with its own balcony.

Betws-y-Coed Youth Hostel HOSTEL **£**
(☎01690-710796; www.yha.org.uk; Swallow Falls; dm from £18) A functional hostel that's part of a bustling traveller hub with camping and a pub.

Bistro Betws-y-Coed RESTAURANT **££**
(☎01690-710328; www.bistrobetws-y-coed.com; Holyhead Rd; lunch £6-9, dinner £13-17; ⊗Wed-Sun, daily high season) This cottage-style eatery's statement of intent is 'modern and traditional Welsh'. It gets absolutely packed in summer: book ahead if you want to sample its locally made sausages, pheasant, and haddock-and-chips battered with Llandudno Orme real ale.

WORTH A TRIP

BLAENAU FFESTINIOG

Most of the slate used to roof 19th-century Britain came from Wales, and much of that came from the mines of Blaenau (*blay*-nye) Ffestiniog. However, only about 10% of mined slate is usable, so for every ton that goes to the factory, nine tons are left as rubble. Despite being in the very centre of Snowdonia National Park, the grey mountains of waste that surround Blaenau prevented it from being officially included in the park – a slap in the face for this close-knit but impoverished town in the days before Wales' industrial sites were recognised as part of its heritage.

Blaenau's main attraction, the Llechwedd Slate Caverns (☎01766-830306; www .llechwedd-slate-caverns.co.uk; single tour adult/child £10.25/8.25, both tours £16.50/12.50; ⊗from 10am daily, last tour 5.15pm Apr-Sep, 4.15pm Oct-Mar) offer a chance to descend into a real slate mine. Of the two tours offered, the more evocative Deep Mine Tour includes a descent on the UK's steepest passenger railway and recreates the harsh working conditions of the 19th-century miners – be prepared to duck and scramble around dark tunnels. If you can't manage a lot of steps, go for the Miner's Tramway Tour, a ride through the huge 1846 network of tunnels and caverns.

Blaenau can feel mournful, especially in miserable weather. However, the town centre is currently being smartened up, and there are plans to install zip wires in the hills above it – just what you need to shake off any grey-slate blues! Blaenau makes a great day trip from Porthmadog via the historic Ffestiniog Railway and it's also connected to Betws-y-Coed by the Conwy Valley line.

❶ Information

National park information centre (📞01690-710426; www.betws-y-coed.co.uk; Royal Oak Stables; ⏱9.30am-4.30pm, to 5.30pm Easter-Oct) Sells books and maps and can book accommodation.

Ultimate Outdoors (📞01690-710555; www.ultimateoutdoors.co.uk; Holyhead Rd) An adventure shop with equipment and specialist references for walkers, climbers and cyclists.

❶ Getting There & Away

BUS Snowdon Sherpa buses S2 and S6 stop outside the train station, with services to Swallow Falls (five minutes), Capel Curig (10 minutes), Pen-y-Pass (20 minutes) and Llanberis (30 minutes).

TRAIN Betws-y-Coed is on the **Conwy Valley Line** (www.conwyvalleyrailway.co.uk), with six daily services (three on Sunday) to Llandudno (£5.60, 52 minutes) and Blaenau Ffestiniog (£4.50, 27 minutes).

Beddgelert

POP 500

Charming little Beddgelert is a conservation village of rough grey stone buildings overlooking the trickling River Glaslyn with its ivy-covered bridge. Flowers festoon the village in spring and the surrounding hills are covered in a purple blaze of heather in summer, reminiscent of a Scottish glen.

The name, meaning 'Gelert's Grave', is said to refer to a folk tale concerning 13th-century Welsh prince Llywelyn. Believing that his dog Gelert had savaged his baby son, Llywelyn slaughtered the dog, only to discover that Gelert had fought off the wolf that had attacked the baby. More likely, the name Beddgelert is derived from a 5th-century Irish preacher, Celert, who is believed to have founded a church here. Regardless, the 'grave' of Gelert the dog is a popular attraction, reached by a pretty riverside trail. It was probably constructed by an unscrupulous 19th-century hotelier in an attempt to boost business.

◉ Sights & Activities

Sygun Copper Mine MINE
(www.syguncoppermine.co.uk; adult/child £8.95/6.95; ⏱9.30am-5pm Mar-Oct) A mile east of Beddgelert, this mine dates from Roman times, although extraction was stepped up in the 19th century. Abandoned in 1903, it has since been converted into a museum,

with a short self-guided underground tour containing dioramas that evoke the life of Victorian miners. You can also try your hand at metal-detecting (£2.50) or panning for gold (£2).

Beddgelert Forest MOUNTAIN BIKING
Within this forestry commission block, 2 miles north of Beddgelert along the A4085, is a popular campsite and two mountain bike trails: the 9½km Hir Trail and the easier 4km Byr Trail. **Beics Beddgelert** (📞01766-890434; www.beddgelertbikes.co.uk; per 2/4/8hr £15/21/28), by the West Highland railway station in the village, rents out mountain bikes, tandems and child seats.

🛏 Sleeping & Eating

Plas Tan Y Graig B&B ££
(📞01766-890310; www.plastanygraig.co.uk; d £82; 🛜) This bright, friendly place is the best B&B in the heart of the village. It has seven uncluttered rooms, five with bathrooms, which have been refurbished recently, and a lounge full of maps and books. Minimum two-night stay April to October.

Glaslyn Ices & Cafe Glandwr ICE CREAM ££
(www.glaslynices.co.uk; mains £4-14; ⏱9.30am-5pm Easter-Oct) In summer, this excellent ice-cream parlour is the busiest place in the village. It serves a huge array of homemade flavours and is attached to a family restaurant offering simple meals, especially pizza.

Lyn's Cafe CAFE ££
(meals £5-15; ⏱10am-5.30pm Feb-Oct, plus dinner high season) A family-friendly all-rounder (with a separate children's menu), split between a restaurant serving big breakfasts and Sunday roasts, and a tearoom with riverside seats for simple snacks.

❶ Information

Tourist office & national park information centre (📞01766-890615; Canolfan Hebog; ⏱9.30am-5.30pm daily Easter-Oct, to 4.30pm Fri-Sun Nov-Easter)

❶ Getting There & Away

Beddgelert is a stop on the historic Welsh Highland Railway, which runs between Caernarfon (£25.20 return, 1½ hours) and Porthmadog (£18 return, 50 mins). Snowdon Sherpa bus S4 heads from here to Caernarfon (30 minutes), while S97 heads to Porthmadog (25 minutes) in one direction and Pen-y-Pass (20 minutes) in the other.

TALYLLYN RAILWAY

Famous as the inspiration behind Rev W Awdry's *Thomas the Tank Engine* stories, the narrow-gauge Talyllyn Railway (☎01654-710472; www.talyllyn .co.uk; Wharf Station, Tywyn; adult/child £14/7) was saved from closure in 1950 by the world's first railway-preservation society. It's one of Wales' most enchanting little railways and puffs for 7.3 scenic, steam-powered miles up the Fathew Valley to Nant Gwernol. There are five stations along the way, each with waymarked walking trails. Your ticket entitles you to all-day travel.

At Tywyn's Wharf Station, the Narrow Gauge Railway Museum (www .ngrm.org.uk; admission free; ⊗10am-2pm Apr-Oct, later in peak season) is one for the history buffs, with shiny narrow-gauge steam locomotives and the story of the volunteers who preserved the railway.

Capel Curig

POP 200

Tiny Capel Curig, 5 miles west of Betws-y-Coed, is one of Snowdonia's oldest hill stations, and has long been a magnet for walkers, climbers and other outdoor junkies. The village spreads out along the A5, but the main clump of activity is at the intersection of the A4086. It's a heady setting, ringed by looming mountains.

The Plas y Brenin (☎01690-720214; www .pyb.co.uk), at the western edge of the village, is a multi-activity centre offering an array of residential courses including rock climbing, mountaineering, kayaking and canoeing. Taster days run during school holidays with an introduction to two activities for £35.

The superb five-star Plas Curig Hostel (☎01690-720225; www.snowdoniahostel.co.uk; dm/d/f from £22.50/50/90; P🖻), opened in 2011, offers great views across to the Snowdon Horseshoe.

Snowdon Sherpa buses S2 and S6 stop here.

Snowdon

No Snowdonia experience is complete without coming face-to-face with Snowdon (1085m), one of Britain's most awe-inspiring mountains and the highest in Wales. On a clear day the views stretch to Ireland and the Isle of Man over Snowdon's fine jagged ridges, which drop away in great swoops to sheltered cwms (valleys) and deep lakes. Even on a gloomy day you could find yourself above the clouds. Thanks to the Snowdon Mountain Railway it's extremely accessible – however, the summit and some of the walking trails can get frustratingly crowded.

◉ Activities

Climbing Snowdon

Six paths of varying length and difficulty lead to the summit, all taking around six hours return. Simplest (and dullest) is the Llanberis Path (9 miles return) running beside the railway line. The Snowdon Ranger Path (8 miles), starting at the Snowdon Ranger YHA, is also straightforward and tends to be less busy than Llanberis.

The two options starting from Pen-y-Pass require the least amount of ascent, but are nevertheless tougher walks. The Miner's Track (8 miles) starts off wide and gentle but gets steep beyond Llyn Llydaw; and the more interesting Pyg Track (7 miles) is more rugged still. The classic Snowdon Horseshoe route (7.5 miles, six to seven hours) combines the Pyg Track to the summit (or via the precipitous ridge of Crib Goch if you're very experienced) with a descent over the peak of Llewedd and a final section down the Miner's Track.

The straightforward Rhyd Ddu Path (8 miles) is the least-used route and boasts some stunning views; the trailhead is on the Caernarfon–Beddgelert road (A4085). Most challenging is the Watkin Path (8 miles), involving an ascent of more than 1000m on its southerly approach from Nantgwynant, and finishing with a scramble across a steep-sided scree-covered slope.

Make sure you're well prepared with warm, waterproof clothing and sturdy footwear. Check the weather forecast before setting out.

Snowdon by Rail

Snowdon Mountain Railway   RAILWAY
(☎0844 493 8120; www.snowdonrailway.co.uk; return adult/child £25/18; ⊗9am-5pm mid-Mar–Oct) Those industrious, railway-obsessed Victorians have gifted today's visitors with an alternative to a three-hour mountain walk: the UK's highest and only public rack-and-pinion railway, opened in 1896. Vintage steam and modern diesel locomotives haul

STEAM RIDES AGAIN

Wales' narrow-gauge railways are testament to an industrial heyday of mining and quarrying. Using steam and diesel engines, these railways often crossed terrain that defied standard-gauge trains. By the 20th century, industrial decline and road-building had left many lines defunct and the infamous Beeching report of 1963 closed dozens of rural branch lines. Five years later, British Rail fired up its last steam engine.

Passionate steam enthusiasts formed preservation groups, buying and restoring old locomotives, rolling stock, disused lines and stations – a labour of love financed by offering rides to the public, often with former railway workers helping out.

Ten restored lines around Wales form a group called Great Little Trains of Wales (www.greatlittletrainsofwales.co.uk). A discount card (£10) entitles the holder to a 20% discount for a return trip on each of the 10 railways.

carriages from Llanberis up to Snowdon's very summit in an hour. Return trips involve a scant half-hour at the top before heading back down again. Single tickets can only be booked for the journey up (adult/child £18/15). Thousands of people take the train to the summit each season: make sure you book well in advance or you may miss out. The frequency of departures is based on customer demand. Departures are also weather dependent and from March to May the trains can only head as far as Clogwyn Station (adult/child £19/15) – an altitude of 779m.

🛏 Sleeping

There is no accommodation on top of Snowdon. The following sleeping selections are scattered around the mountain's slopes.

Pen-y-Gwyrd HOTEL £
(☎01286-870211; www.pyg.co.uk; Nant Gwynant; r with/without bathroom £50/42) Eccentric but full of atmosphere, Pen-y-Gwryd was used as a training base by the 1953 Everest team, and memorabilia from their stay includes their signatures on the dining-room ceiling. There's a comfy games room, sauna and a garden pond where you can bathe; tea-lovers might want to bring a travel kettle, though, as there are none in the rooms. You'll find the hotel below Pen-y-Pass, at the junction of the A498 and A4086.

Snowdon Ranger Youth Hostel HOSTEL £
(☎0845 371 9659; www.yha.org.uk; dm from £20) On the A4085, 5 miles north of Beddgelert, at the trailhead for the Snowdon Ranger Path, this former inn is full of character and has its own adjoining lakeside beach.

Pen-y-Pass Youth Hostel HOSTEL £
(☎0845 371 9534; www.yha.org.uk; dm from £12; ☉daily high season) Superbly situated on the slopes of Snowdon, 5.5 miles up the A4086 from Llanberis. See the website for low-season opening hours.

Bryn Gwynant YHA HOSTEL £
(☎0845 371 9108; www.yha.org.uk; Nantgwynant; dm from £15; ☉closed weekdays in winter) Victorian mansion overlooking the lake, 4 miles east of Beddgelert, near the start of the tricky Watkin Path.

❶ Information

Hafod Eryri Just below the cairn that marks Snowdon's summit, this striking piece of architecture opened in 2009 to replace the dilapidated 1930s visitor centre which Prince Charles famously labelled 'the highest slum in Europe'. Clad in granite and curved to blend into the mountain, it's a wonderful building, housing a cafe, toilets and ambient interpretative elements built into the structure itself. A wall of picture windows gazes down towards the west, while a small row faces the cairn. The centre (including the toilets) closes in the winter or if the weather's terrible; it's open whenever the train is running.

❶ Getting There & Away

The Welsh Highland Railway stops at the trailhead of the Rhyd Ddu path, and there is a request stop (Snowdon Ranger Halt) where you can alight for the Snowdon Ranger path. Snowdon Sherpa buses (£1 on buses S1, S2, S6; adult/child day ticket £4/2) stop at all of the trailheads. It's worth considering public transport: car parks can fill up quickly, and Pen-y-Pass costs £10 per day. Another option is to take the Snowdon Mountain Railway to the top and walk back down.

Bala (Y Bala)

POP 2000

Kayakers, canoeists, windsurfers and rafters will appreciate the quiet Welsh-speaking town of Bala. Here you'll find Wales' largest natural lake, four-mile-long Llyn Tegid (Bala Lake), as well as the River Tryweryn, hallowed in whitewater kayaking circles.

Two big watersports centres take advantage of this watery perfection. Canolfan Tryweryn National Whitewater Centre (01678-521083; www.ukrafting.co.uk; Frongoch, 3.5 miles nw of Bala on A4212; 1-/2-hr trip £32/60) runs rafting trips on a 1.5-mile stretch of river that is almost continuous class-III white water with class IV sections. These can be combined with other activities such as rock climbing, mountain biking, pony trekking, bushcraft, canyoning, and quad biking on an adventure-holiday package (from £158 including accommodation). Bala Adventure & Watersports Centre (01678-521059; www.balawatersports.com; Pensarn Rd, lake foreshore) offers similar high jinks (most courses cost £38/75 per half-/full day), as well as renting out kayaks (£12), canoes (£25), rowing boats (£27), pedalos (£15), windsurfers (£18) and wayfarers (£35); all prices are per hour.

The very comfortable Bala Backpackers (01678-521700; www.bala-backpackers.co.uk; 32 Tegid St; dm/tw from £19.50/47) has dorms with a maximum of four single beds, plus smartly decorated twins. Right down at the other end of the lake, the Eagles Inn (Tafarn Yr Eryod) (01678-540278; www.yr-eagles.co.uk; Llanuwchllyn; mains £7.50-15; lunch Sat & Sun, dinner daily) is your consummate North Welsh village pub but with food that's a step above: most of the vegetables and some of the meat comes from its own garden.

The X94 from Dolgellau (35 minutes), Barmouth (1¼ hours) and Llangollen (50 minutes) stops on the High St. For further information, contact Bala tourist office (01678-521021; Pensarn Rd, Leisure Centre; 10am-4pm Fri-Tues Easter-Sep), southwest of the centre by the lake.

Dolgellau

POP 2400

Dolgellau is a charming little market town, steeped in history and boasting the highest concentration of listed buildings in Wales. It was a regional centre for Wales' prosperous wool industry in the 18th and early 19th centuries, and many of its finest buildings, sturdy and unornamented, were built at that time. Pick up the *Dolgellau Town Trail* (£1) brochure from the tourist office to explore the unusual architecture in detail.

Today the town relies heavily on tourism. One of Snowdonia's premier peaks, bulky Cader Idris, rises to the south, the lovely Mawddach Estuary lies to the west and, to the north, the Coed y Brenin Forest offers glorious mountain biking. Most of Dolgellau's accommodation is plush and boutique, making it an appealing (if pricey) base from which to explore the national park.

◎ Sights & Activities

Tŷ Siamas　　　　　　　　　　　EXHIBITION
(01341-421800; www.tysiamas.com; Eldon Sq; phone for opening times) Dolgellau has been an important folk-music hub ever since it held the first Welsh folk festival in 1952. In recognition of that, the town's former market hall has been transformed into the National Centre for Welsh Folk Music, run solely by volunteers. It has a permanent

---

DON'T MISS

TYDDYN LLAN

The glowing reputation of this country restaurant-with-rooms (01490-440264; www.tyddynllan.co.uk; Llandrillo; r £120-190, dinner B&B £175-245; P), located 7½ miles east of Bala on the B4401, was given a boost in 2010 by some Michelin starlight. An elegant property set among gardens in the tranquil Vale of Edeyrnion, it's a cosy bolthole for a rural retreat. The 12 rooms each boast their own individual style, some frou-frou romantic, some shabby-chic modern. On our last visit to the restaurant (2-/3-course lunch £19.50/25.50, dinner £45/55; lunch Fri-Sun, dinner daily) some dishes were extraordinary and some merely good, but overall it was a memorable experience. Proceedings kick off with complementary canapés served in the sitting room before you progress into the elegant dining area.

folk-music exhibition and runs regular workshops and performances.

Cader Idris   MOUNTAIN

Cader Idris (893m), or the 'Seat of Idris' (a legendary giant), is a hulking, menacing-looking mountain with an appropriate mythology attached. It's said that hounds of the underworld fly around its peaks, and strange light effects are often sighted in the area. It's also said that anyone who spends the night on the summit will awake either mad or a poet – although perhaps you'd have to be a little mad or romantic to attempt it in the first place. Regardless of its repute, it's popular with walkers and it's the park's favourite locale for rock climbers.

When tackling Cader Idris, the main route is the Pony Path (6 miles return, five hours), which begins from the Tŷ Nant car park on the A493 southwest of Dolgellau. Round the south side of the mountain is the start of the longest but easiest Tywyn or Llanfihangel y Pennant Path (10 miles, seven hours), northeast from the Talyllyn Railway terminus at Abergynolwyn. The shortest and steepest trail is the Minffordd Path (6 miles, five hours), which begins from the Dôl Idris car park, 6 miles south of Dolgellau at the junction of the A487 and the B4405. At the time of writing, a Cader Idris visitor centre and tearoom was due to open 250 metres from this car park. Whichever route you choose, always carry appropriate clothing and check weather conditions before departure.

Precipice Walk   VIEWPOINT

If you're not up to scaling Cader Idris, this three-mile circular walk through the private Nannau estate is surprisingly varied and has plenty of charm. It leads you through woodland, down lakeside paths, into conifer plantations, and along the brink of a dramatic sheer-sided precipice (keep an eye on kids), with stunning views of Cader Idris, Snowdon and the Mawddach Estuary along the way. The walk starts from Saith Groesffordd car park, Llanfachreth, around 2½ miles from Dolgellau (well signposted).

Coed-y-Brenin
Forest Park   MOUNTAIN BIKING

Covering 3600 hectares, this woodland park is one of the premier locations for mountain biking in Wales. It's laced with 70 miles of purpose-built cycle trails, divided into seven graded routes to suit beginners or guns, and impressively presented by way of old-fashioned waterproof trail cards or downloadable geocaches and MP3 audio files. The park's splendid environmentally-friendly visitor centre (☏01341-440747; www.forestry .gov.uk/wales; ⊙9.30am-4.30pm), 8 miles north of Dolgellau off the A470, has a cafe, toilets and a children's play area, while downstairs you can hire bikes from Beics Brenin (☏01341-440728; www.beicsbrenin.co.uk; per day £25-50). If you prefer to monkey about in the treetops, the park also contains a new Go Ape (☏0845 643 9215; www.goape.co.uk; adult/child from £30/20; ⊙weekends & school hols Easter-Oct) highwires course.

🛏 Sleeping

Ffynnon   BOUTIQUE B&B £££

(☏01341-421774; www.ffynnontownhouse.com; Love Lane; s/d from £100/145; [P][🖥]) With a keen eye for contemporary design and a super-friendly welcome, this first-rate boutique guest house feels both homely and stylish. French antiques are mixed in with modern chandeliers, claw-foot tubs and electronic gadgets, and each room has a seating area so you can admire the views in comfort. Outdoor hot tub.

Bryn Mair House   B&B ££

(☏01341-422640; www.brynmairbedandbreakfast .co.uk; Love Lane; s/d from £75/95; [P][🖥]) On wistfully monikered Love Lane, this is an impressive stone house – a former Georgian rectory no less. Its three comfortable B&B rooms are all kitted out with DVDs and iPod docks; Room 1 has sublime mountain views.

Pandy Isaf   B&B ££

(☏01341-423949; www.pandyisaf-accommodation .co.uk; s/d from £50/80; [P]) This peaceful old mill building provides the perfect place to shake away cares, with spotless rooms, an amazing breakfast, soft green lawns, and a stream running by where otters frolic. Two miles northeast of Dolgellau off the A494.

HYB Bunkhouse   HOSTEL £

(☏01341-421755; www.medi-gifts.com; per person/ rm £20/80; [P]) The only budget accommodation in town. Oak-beamed rooms with handy kitchenettes, each sleeping four people (in bunkbeds). Accommodation rented by the room during busy periods – enquire at the Medi gift shop below.

Eating

T. H. Roberts CAFE £
(Glyndŵr St, Parliament House; mains £4-6;
☺9.30am-5.30pm Mon-Sat; ☎) It's easy to walk
past this atmospheric Grade II-listed coffee
shop, as it still looks exactly like the ironmonger's shop that it once was, with its original counter, glass cabinets, wooden drawers
and other fittings. It's a favourite with locals,
with jolly, if haphazard, service, light meals
(soup, Welsh rarebit, sandwiches, cakes),
newspapers and books to browse, and a
good wi-fi connection.

Y Sospan CAFE, BISTRO ££
(☎01341-423174; Queen's Sq; breakfast & lunch £3-
7, dinner mains £10-14; ☺9am-9.30pm) In a book-
lined and woody 1606 building that once
served as a prison, this relaxed eatery works
very well during the day as a cafe/tearoom,
with fry-up breakfasts, sandwiches, jacket
potatoes, light-cooked meals, and great
homemade cakes. A heavier Welsh bistro
menu comes out at night: lamb and steak
play the starring roles, but veggies have
options too.

**Mawddach Restaurant
& Bar** MODERN WELSH ££
(☎01341-424020; www.mawddach.com; Llanelltyd;
mains £11-17; ☺lunch Wed-Sun, dinner Wed-Sat)
Located 2 miles west of Dolgellau on the
A496, Mawddach brings a touch of urban
style to what was once a barn. Slate floors,
leather seats and panoramic views across
to Cader Idris set the scene. The food is
equally impressive: meat straight from
nearby farms, fresh local fish specials and
traditional Sunday roasts (two/three courses
£14.50/18.50).

Dylanwad Da TAPAS, WELSH ££
(☎01341-422870; www.dylanwad.co.uk; 2 Smithfield
St; mains £14-20; ☺Tue-Sat Easter-Sep) Informal
cafe, wine and tapas bar by day, contemporary restaurant by night, this well-run, low-
lit eatery has been serving up high-quality
food for over 20 years. A long-standing
favourite on the Snowdonia scene, it has a
healthy wine list and an imaginative menu.

ℹ Information

**Tourist office & national park information
centre** (☎01341-422888; Eldon Sq; ☺9.30am-
12.30pm & 1-5.30pm) Very little free information: sells maps, local-history books and trail
leaflets for climbing Cader Idris. Upstairs
there's an interesting little exhibition on the
region's Quaker heritage. Internet access costs
£1.50 for 30 minutes.

ℹ Getting There & Away

BICYCLE **Dolgellau Cycles** (☎01341-423332;
Smithfield St) Rents bikes, performs repairs and
offers advice on local cycle routes. Lôn Las
Cymru, the Welsh National Cycle Route (NCN
route 8), passes through Dolgellau, heading
north to Porthmadog and south to Machynlleth.

BUS All buses stop on Eldon Sq in the heart of
town. Routes include X32 to Machynlleth (35
minutes) and Aberystwyth (1¼ hours), and in
the other direction to Porthmadog (50 minutes),
Caernarfon (1½ hours) and Bangor (two hours);
35 to Blaenau Ffestiniog (50 minutes, Monday to
Saturday); and X94 to Barmouth (20 minutes),
Bala (35 minutes) and Llangollen (1½ hours).

Mawddach Estuary

An important bird habitat, the glorious
Mawddach Estuary is a striking sight –
flanked by woodlands, wetlands and the romantic mountains of southern Snowdonia.
Following its southern edge, the 9½-mile
Mawddach Trail (www.mawddachtrail.co.uk) is
a flat walking and cycling path that follows
an old railway line from the bridge in Dolgellau, through woods and past wetlands,
before crossing over the rail viaduct to Barmouth (where you can grab the bus back).

The Mawddach Way (www.mawddachway
.co.uk) is a 30-mile, two- to three-day track
looping through the hills on either side.
Although the highest point is 346m, by
the end of the undulating path you'll have
climbed 2226m. An A5 booklet can be ordered or downloaded online (booklet/
download £10/5); GPS route data can be
downloaded for free.

Fairbourne

Fairbourne has a lovely, long beach but little
else to offer except the steam-hauled Fairbourne Railway (☎01341-250362; www.fair
bournerailway.com; Beach Rd; adult/child £8.50/5),
Wales' only seaside narrow-gauge railway.
The line heads north along the coast for 2.5
miles to Penrhyn Point, where there are ferries across the mouth of the Mawddach to
Barmouth, timed to meet the trains.

Fairbourne is on the Cambrian Coast line
and bus 28 from Dolgellau (20 minutes)
stops here.

Barmouth (Abermaw)

POP 2250

Despite a Blue Flag beach, the seaside resort of Barmouth has a faded feel to it. In the summer months it becomes a typical kiss-me-quick seaside resort – all chip shops and dodgem cars – catering to the trainloads arriving in their thousands from England's West Midlands. Outside of the brash neon of high summer it's considerably mellower but still has its rough edges.

Wales' only surviving wooden rail viaduct spans the estuary and has a handy pedestrian walkway across it. Behind the town rises rocky Dinas Oleu, the first property ever bequeathed to the National Trust (in 1895) and an irresistible temptation for walkers.

Sleeping & Eating

Richmond House   B&B ££
(☑01341-281366; www.barmouthbedandbreakfast.co.uk; High St; s/d £60/75; P@🛜) This handsome town house has big, contemporary rooms (two with sea views) and an attractive garden area for summer lounging on chunky, wooden furniture. Thoughtful touches include in-room DVD. It's very handy for both the town centre and the beach.

Last Inn   PUB ££
(☑01341-280530; www.lastinn-barmouth.co.uk; Church St; mains £9-14) Dating from the 15th century, this is easily the best place to eat, drink and hang out in. Most unusually, the mountain forms the rear wall, with a spring emerging right inside the pub. Kids are welcome and the menu's full of crowd-pleasers, including a traditional Sunday roast. There's also live music on Tuesday nights.

❶ Information

Tourist office (☑01341-280787; train station, Station Rd; ☉10am-5pm Apr-Oct, 10am-3pm Mon-Sat Nov-Mar)

❶ Getting There & Away

BUS Routes include 38 to Harlech (33 minutes, Monday to Saturday) and X94 to Dolgellau (23 minutes), Bala (one hour) and Llangollen (two hours).

TRAIN Barmouth is on the Cambrian Coast line, with direct trains to Machynlleth (£8.30, 59 minutes), Fairbourne (£2.40, 7 minutes), Harlech (£4.40, 24 minutes), Porthmadog (£6.50, 48 minutes) and Pwllheli (£10.30, 1¼ hours).

Harlech

POP 2000

Hilly Harlech is best known for the mighty, grey-stone towers of its castle, framed by gleaming Tremadog Bay. Some sort of fortified structure has probably surmounted the rock since Iron Age times, but Edward I removed all traces when he commissioned the construction of his castle. Finished in 1289, Harlech Castle is the southernmost of four fortifications included in the Castles and Town Walls of King Edward in Gwynedd Unesco World Heritage site.

Harlech is such a thoroughly pleasant place that it has become one of the more gentrified destinations in Snowdonia – every other shop seems to sell antiques or tea. It makes a great base for a beach holiday or for day trips into the national park; and while it's bustling in summer, it can be deliciously sleepy at other times.

◉ Sights

Harlech Castle   CASTLE
(Cadw; adult/child £3.80/3.40; ☉9.30am-6pm Jul & Aug, 9.30am-5pm Mar-Jun & Sep-Oct, 10am-4pm Mon-Sat, 11am-4pm Sun Nov-Feb) Edward I finished this intimidating building in 1289, the southernmost of his 'iron ring' of fortresses designed to keep the Welsh firmly beneath his boot. Despite its might, the storybook fortress has been called the 'Castle of Lost Causes' because it has been lucklessly defended so many times. Owain Glyndŵr captured it after a long siege in 1404. He was in turn besieged here by the future Henry V.

During the Wars of the Roses the castle is said to have held out against a siege for seven years and was the last Lancastrian stronghold to fall. The siege inspired the popular Welsh hymn *Men of Harlech*, which is still played today in regimental marches and sung with patriotic gusto at rugby matches. The castle was also the last to fall in the Civil War, finally giving in to Cromwell's forces in 1647.

The grey sandstone castle's massive, twin-towered gatehouse and outer walls give the impression of impregnability even now. Cross the drawbridge through the gatehouse into the compact inner ward: four gloomy round towers guard the corners and you can climb onto the ramparts for views in all directions. Some are closed off and partly ruined, but you still get a good feel for what it was once like. The fortress's great natural defence is the seaward cliff face. When it was built, ships could sail supplies right to the base.

🛏 Sleeping & Eating

Maelgwyn House B&B ££
(☑01766-780087; www.maelgwynharlech.co.uk; Ffordd Isaf; r £65-89; 🅿🛜) A model B&B, Maelgwyn has interesting hosts, delicious breakfasts and a small set of elegant rooms stocked with DVD players and tea-making facilities, with tremendous views across the bay. Bridget and Derek can also help arrange bird-watching trips and autumn fungus forays. Full marks.

Castle Cottage BOUTIQUE HOTEL £££
(☑01766-780479; www.castlecottageharlech.co.uk; Ffordd Pen Llech; s/d from £85/130; 🅿🛜) Within arrow's reach of the castle, Castle Cottage has spacious bedrooms in a contemporary style with exposed beams, in-room DVD players and a bowl of fresh fruit for each guest. The award-winning fine-dining restaurant (three-course dinner £39) serves a deliciously patriotic menu, revelling in local produce (Welsh lamb, beef and cod, Ruthin chicken, Menai mussels, wild duck, woodcock and cheeses) and traditional dishes, executed in classical French style, such as bara brith (literally 'speckled bread': a sweet, curranty, almost cake-like bread) and rarebit (melted cheese, sometimes mixed with mustard and beer, poured over toast).

Castle Restaurant &
Armoury Bar CARIBBEAN ££
(☑01766-780416; www.caribbeancrabharlech.com; Castle Sq; mains £14-18; ⊙dinner Tue-Sun Easter-Oct) If this place were transported to London it would have queues out the door, so one has to admire the gumption of opening such a wonderful Caribbean restaurant in Wales, let alone in sleepy Harlech. Upstairs is the coolest cocktail bar in North Wales – red curtains, bauble chandeliers and a smooth soundtrack of Trojan reggae. Downstairs, the locals are switching on to the spicy delights of goat curry, jerk chicken and blackened salmon.

Cemlyn Tea Shop TEAROOM £
(www.cemlyntea.co.uk; High St; snacks around £5; ⊙10.30am-5pm Wed-Sun Easter-Oct) The Coles (Jan and Geoff) may be merry old souls, but it's tea that's king here. There are over 30 varieties on offer, along with a simple range of snacks to accompany them and a slew of Tea Guild Awards of Excellence on the walls. Best of all are the views from the terrace.

ℹ Information

Tourist office (☑01766-780658; High St; ⊙9.30am-5.30pm Apr-Oct)

ℹ Getting There & Away

Harlech is on the Cambrian Coast line, with direct trains to Machynlleth (£11, 1½ hours), Fairbourne (£5.30, 34 minutes), Barmouth (£4.40, 24 minutes), Porthmadog (£3.60, 24 minutes) and Pwllheli (£7.40, 47 minutes). Bus 38 heads to Barmouth (30 minutes, Monday to Saturday), with bus 2 providing a sparse Sunday service.

WEST OF SNOWDONIA

The region between the western fringe of the Snowdonia National Park and the Isle of Anglesey is a staunchly Welsh-speaking area. Indeed, the county of Gwynedd is the traditional heartland of Welsh nationalism; around 70% of people here still use Welsh as their first language.

Caernarfon

POP 9700

Wedged between the gleaming Menai Strait and the deep-purple mountains of Snowdonia, Caernarfon is home to a fantastical castle, its main claim to fame. Given the town's crucial historical importance, its intact medieval walls, its proximity to the national park and its reputation as a centre of Welsh culture (it has the highest percentage of Welsh speakers of anywhere), parts of the town centre are surprisingly down-at-heel. Still, there's a lot of charm in its untouristy air, and a tangible sense of history in the streets around the castle.

The castle was built by Edward I as the last link in his 'iron ring' and is now part of the Castles and Town Walls of King Edward in Gwynedd Unesco World Heritage site. In an attempt by then-Prime Minister David Lloyd George (himself a Welshman) to bring the royals closer to their Welsh constituency, the castle was designated as the venue for the 1911 investiture of the Prince of Wales. In retrospect, linking the modern royals to such a powerful symbol of Welsh subjugation may not have been the best idea. It incensed the largely nationalist local population, and at the next crowning, of Prince

Charles in 1969, the sentiment climaxed in an attempt to blow up his train.

⊙ Sights & Activities

Caernarfon Castle
CASTLE, MUSEUM

(Cadw; adult/child/family £5.25/4.85/15.35; ⊙9.30am-6pm Jul & Aug, 9.30am-5pm Apr-Jun, Sep & Oct, 10am-4pm Mon-Sat & 11am-4pm Sun Nov-Mar) Majestic Caernarfon Castle was built between 1283 and 1330 as a military stronghold, a seat of government and a royal palace. Inspired by the dream of Macsen Wledig recounted in the *Mabinogion,* Caernarfon echoes the 5th-century walls of Constantinople, with colour-banded masonry and polygonal towers, instead of the traditional round towers and turrets.

Despite its fairytale aspect, it is thoroughly fortified. It repelled Owain Glyndŵr's army in 1404 with a garrison of only 28 men, and resisted three sieges during the Civil War before surrendering to Cromwell's army in 1646.

A year after the construction of the building was begun, Edward I's second son was born here, becoming heir to the throne four months later when his elder brother died. To consolidate Edward's power he was made Prince of Wales in 1301, and his mucheroded statue is over the King's Gate.

You exploration of Caernarfon Castle's mass of interconnected walls and towers should start at the Eagle Tower – the one with the flagpoles to the right of the entrance. On the turrets you can spot the weathered eagle from which it gets its name, alongside stone helmeted figures intended to swell the garrison's numbers (they're easier to spot from the quay). Inside is a short film about the castle's history, *The Eagle & The Dragon,* which screens on the half-hour.

There is an exhibition on the investiture of today's Prince of Wales, HRH Prince Charles, in the North East Tower. In the Queen's Tower (named after Edward I's wife Eleanor) is the Regimental Museum of the Royal Welsh Fusiliers.

FREE Segontium Roman Fort
RUIN

(www.segontium.org.uk; Ffordd Cwstenin; ⊙12.30pm-4.30pm Tue-Sun) These stony foundations, dating back to AD 77, represent the westernmost Roman legionary fort of the Roman Empire, which had a crucial strategic position overlooking the Menai Strait. Sadly, the museum is closed for the foreseeable future.

The site is located about half a mile along the A4085 (to Beddgelert).

GreenWood Forest Park
ADVENTURE PARK

(www.greenwoodforestpark.co.uk; Y Felinheli; adult/child £11/9.90; ⊙11am-5pm mid-Mar–Oct) This 7-hectare adventure park makes a brilliant family day out, with a slew of activities for infant-/junior-school-aged kids, all underpinned by a strong green ethos. You'll find mazes, a sledge run, archery, a tree-top playground, den-building, paddle boats, a forest theatre, and the world's first people-powered roller coaster, the Green Dragon. It's signposted from the A487 near Y Felinheli, 4 miles northeast of Caernarfon.

Plas Menai
WATER SPORTS

(⊉01248-670964; www.plasmenai.co.uk) The excellent National Watersports Centre, 3 miles out along the A487 towards Bangor, offers year-round water-based courses for all interests and ability levels (sailing, power-boating, kayaking and windsurfing). Advance reservations are necessary. The centre also offers B&B accommodation (singles/doubles £45/70). Bus 5/5A (Caernarfon to Bangor) stops five minutes' walk away.

Beics Menai
BICYCLE RENTAL

(⊉ 01286-676804; www.beicsmenai.co.uk; 1 Slate Quay; per 2/4/6/8hr £15/17/19/22; ⊙9.30am-4pm Tue-Sat) Hires bikes (including tandems, children's bikes and child seats) and can advise on local cycle routes. Recreational cycle routes include the 12.5-mile Lôn Eifion (starting near the Welsh Highland Railway station and running south to Bryncir) and the four-mile Lôn Las Menai (following the Menai Strait to the village of Y Felinheli).

⊨ Sleeping & Eating

Totters
HOSTEL £

(⊉01286-672963; www.totters.co.uk; 2 High St; dm/d/tr incl breakfast £17/40/54) Modern, clean and very welcoming, this excellent independent hostel is the best-value place to stay in town. In addition to traveller-friendly facilities, the 14th-century arched basement gives a sense of history to guests' breakfasts (and cereal, toast and tea/coffee are included in the price). Unsurprisingly, it fills up quickly – try to book ahead.

Victoria House
B&B ££

(⊉01286-678263; www.thevictoriahouse.co.uk; Church St; d £65-80; ⊛) Victoria House is an exceptional four-bedroom guest house with a homely feel, spacious modern rooms and some nice touches, such as an impressive selection of free toiletries and a DVD on the town's history in each room. Breakfast is a joy – and you can even have pancakes!

Black Boy Inn
B&B ££

(☑01286-673604; www.black-boy-inn.com; Northgate St; s/d from £65/95; P🐾) Dating from 1522, the creaky but atmospheric rooms at this traditional inn have original wooden beams and panelling but a modern sensibility. The public areas are divided into a series of snug rooms and, although the wine might come out of a box, the place serves real ale and excellent hearty meals (mains £9 to £18) such as cassoulet and game pie.

Caer Menai
B&B £

(☑01286-672612; www.caermenai.co.uk; 15 Church St; s/d from £45/57; @🐾) A former county school (1894), this elegant building is on a quiet street nestling against the western wall. The seven en-suite rooms were updated recently, and are fresh, clean and snug; number seven has sunset sea views. Hospitable hosts frequently greet guests with tea and homemade biscuits.

Wal
ITALIAN ££

(☑01286-674383; www.walrestaurant.co.uk; Palace St; pizzas £7-9, mains £8-17; ⊗9.30am-3pm Sun-Tue, 9.30am-9.30pm Wed-Sat) We fell for this convivial little place – first for the cosy interior, bisected by the arches of an ancient wall and packed with merry people; second for its charming staff; and finally for the big, well-presented plates of tasty food. Since it opened in late 2011, it has become a firm town favourite – book ahead for weekend nights.

Stones Bistro
BISTRO ££

(☑01286-676097; 4 Hole in the Wall St; mains £11-18; ⊗dinner Tue-Sat, lunch Sun) Housed in what was a 17th-century temperance house, this place has recently changed owners. The interior is a little dark and odd, but you can't fault the food if you're a meat- or fish-lover: go for catch of the day or lamb shank, and save room for a pudding.

⭐ Entertainment

Galeri Caernarfon
THEATRE, CINEMA

(☑01286-685222; www.galericaernarfon.com; Victoria Dock) This excellent multipurpose arts centre hosts exhibitions, theatre, film and events; check the program online for details. The stylish in-house DOC Cafe Bar serves all-day snacks and pre-event suppers.

ℹ Information

Tourist office (☑01286-672232; Castle Ditch; ⊗9.30am-4.30pm Apr-Oct, 10am-3.30pm Mon-Sat Nov-Mar) Helpful centre opposite the castle's main entrance.

ℹ Getting There & Away

BUS Buses stop at stands along Penllyn, two blocks north of the castle square. Buses include 1/1A to Bangor (25 minutes), Criccieth (40 minutes) and Porthmadog (45 minutes); X5 to Conwy (1¼ hours) and Llandudno (1½ hours); 12 to Pwllheli (45 minutes); and 87/88/89 to Llanberis (30 minutes).

The Snowdon Sherpa bus is run by **Gwynedd Council.** (www.gwynedd.gov.uk). Bus S4 heads to Beddgelert (30 minutes) via the Snowdon Ranger (20 minutes) and Rhyd Ddu (24 minutes) trailheads.

There's a daily National Express service to London (£33, 9½ hours), via Bangor (£6.50, 25 minutes), Llandudno (£8, one hour), Chester (£18, three hours) and Birmingham (£28, 6½ hours). From June to August, there is also a direct service to Manchester (£24, 5¼ hours) via Liverpool (£18.50, four hours).

TRAIN Caernarfon is the northern terminus of the Welsh Highland Railway (p731) tourist train, which runs to Porthmadog (£33 return, 2½ hours) via Dinas, Waunfawr, Snowdon Ranger, Rhd Ddu and Beddgelert. The station is near the river on St Helen's Rd.

Llŷn Peninsula

Jutting out into the Irish Sea from the mountains of Snowdonia, the Llŷn Peninsula (also spelled 'Lleyn') is a green finger of land some 25 miles long and 8 miles wide. It's a peaceful and largely undeveloped region with isolated walking and cycling routes, good beaches, a scattering of small fishing villages and 70 miles of wildlife-rich coastline (much of it in the hands of the National Trust, and almost 80% of it designated an Area of Outstanding Natural Beauty, or AONB). Over the centuries the heaviest footfalls have been those of pilgrims on their way to Bardsey Island.

Welsh is the language of everyday life here. The Llŷn (pronounced 'khlee'en') and the Isle of Anglesey were the last places on the Roman and Norman itineraries, and both have maintained a separate identity, the Llŷn especially so. Isolated physically and culturally, it's been an incubator of Welsh activism. It was the birthplace of David Lloyd George, the first Welsh prime minister of the UK, and of Plaid Cymru (Party of Wales), which was founded in Pwllheli in 1925 and is now the main opposition party in the Welsh Assembly.

With a population of 3900, Pwllheli (poolth-*heh*-lee; meaning 'salt-water pool') is the Llŷn's largest town and the peninsula's public transport hub.

❶ Getting There & Away

Bus

Bus 1 (Porthmadog–Caernarfon–Bangor) stops in Criccieth. All of the peninsula's other bus services originate or terminate at Pwllheli, including bus 3 to Llanystumdwy (20 minutes), Criccieth (24 minutes), Tremadog (40 minutes) and Porthmadog (50 minutes); 12 to Caernarfon (45 minutes); 17/17B to Llanbedrog (10 minutes) and Aberdaron (45 minutes); and 18 to Llanbedrog (10 minutes) and Abersoch (25 minutes). A National Express coach heads between Pwllheli and London (£33, 10½ hours) daily, via Criccieth (£5.70, 17 minutes), Caernarfon (£7.40, one hour), Bangor (£7.80, 1½ hours) and Birmingham (£25, seven hours).

Train

Pwllheli is the terminus of the Cambrian Coast line, with direct trains to Criccieth (£3.10, 13 minutes), Porthmadog (£4.50, 22 minutes), Harlech (£7.40, 45 minutes), Barmouth (£10.30, 1¼ hours), Fairbourne (£10.30, 1¼ hours) and Machynlleth (£14.50, 2½ hours).

PWLLHELI

Pwllheli, a small market town with a shiny new marina, is the gateway to the Llŷn Peninsula. Stop in at **Pwllheli tourist office** (✆01758-613000; Station Sq; ◔9.30am-5pm Apr-Sep) to stock up on information about the area.

Plas Bodegroes   BOUTIQUE HOTEL **£££** (✆01758-612363; www.bodegroes.co.uk; rm£150-180; P🖥) Set in a stately 1780 manor house with immaculately coiffured gardens, this restaurant-with-rooms is a romantic option. Gourmets may be interested in the slick restaurant (dinner £45; open lunch Sunday, dinner Tuesday to Saturday), which is famous for its elegant Michelin-standard dining room with a long wine list; first dibs on its tables go to hotel guests. It's located a mile inland from Pwllheli along the A497.

NANT GWRTHEYRN

The village of Nant Gwrtheyrn was built for workers in the 19th century, but the granite quarries closed after WWII and it was gradually abandoned. In 1978 it was given a new lease of life when it was bought and restored as a residential Welsh Language & Heritage Centre (✆01758-750334; www.nantgwrtheyrn.org; ◔call ahead for times). Even if you don't take a course, it's a magical place – eerily quiet and ideal for a tranquil walk along world's-end cliffs.

The heritage centre has a small but compelling exhibition on the history of the Welsh language, but its main focus is offering Welsh language and literature courses to suit all levels of ability (from £295 for three days including full board). It's reached from the village of Llithfaen (on the B4417) by following a path down a steep valley. If you're driving take it very slowly.

PORTH DINLLAEN

It's hard to believe that this was once a busy cargo, shipbuilding and herring port, the only safe haven on the peninsula's north coast. Today, it's owned in its entirety by the National Trust, which maintains a small information kiosk in its car park (parking £5 in summer, free to NT members).

At the western end of the beach are an isolated cluster of buildings, which include the legendary Tŷ Coch Inn (www.tycoch.co.uk; ◔11am-11pm Mon-Sat, 11am-5pm Sun Jun-Aug, shorter hrs Apr & May), famous for its views and for pints that you can drink while dabbling your toes in the sea.

BRAICH-Y-PWLL, UWCHMYNYYD

While the boats for Bardsey now leave from Porth Meudwy, this rugged National Trust property on the very tip of the Llŷn Peninsula is where the medieval pilgrims set off from – one glimpse of the surf-pounded rocks will reinforce what a terrifying last voyage that would have been. It's an incredibly dramatic, ancient-looking landscape, with Bardsey rising out of the slate-grey sea like the mystical Avalon. A path leads down past the earthworks that are all that remains of St Mary's Abbey to a Neolithic standing stone known as Maen Melyn, bent like a finger towards the island and suggesting this was a holy place long before the Celts or their saints arrived.

ABERDARON

Aberdaron (population 1000) is an ends-of-the-earth kind of place with whitewashed,

THE BARDSEY PILGRIMAGE

At a time when journeys from Britain to Italy were long, perilous and beyond the means of most people, the Pope decreed that three pilgrimages to the holy island of Bardsey would have the same spiritual value as one to Rome. Tens of thousands of penitents took advantage of this get-out-of-purgatory-free (or at least quickly) card and many came here to die. In the 16th century, Henry VIII's ban on pilgrimages put paid to the practice – although a steady trickle of modern-day pilgrims still walk the route.

The traditional path stops at ancient churches and holy wells along the way. It's broken into nine legs on the Edge of Wales Walk (www.edgeofwaleswalk.co.uk) website, run by a cooperative of local residents. They can help to arrange a 47-mile, self-guided walking tour, including five nights' accommodation and baggage transfers (£290 per person). A similar service is also offered for the 95-mile Llŷn Coastal Path, which circumnavigates the peninsula.

windswept houses contemplating Aberdaron Bay. It was traditionally the last resting spot before pilgrims made the treacherous crossing to Bardsey.

Lingering from this time is St Hywyn's Church (◷10am-4pm, to 6pm Apr-Oct), stoically positioned above the pebbly beach. The left half of the church dates from 1100, while the right half was added 400 years later, to cope with the volume of pilgrims. With their spiritual needs sorted, the Bardsey-bound saints could then claim a meal at Y Gegin Fawr (The Big Kitchen; ◷9am-6pm). Dating from 1300, it still dishes up meals.

Right on the beach, the friendly Tŷ Newydd (☎01758-760207; www.gwesty-tynewydd.co.uk; Aberdaron; s/d from £65/100) has fully refurbished, light-drenched, spacious rooms and some truly wonderful sea views. The tide actually comes in right under the terrace off the pub restaurant, which seems designed with afternoon gin and tonics in mind.

BARDSEY ISLAND (YNYS ENLLI)

This rugged island, 2 miles long and 2 miles off the tip of the Llŷn, is a magical place. In the 6th or 7th century the obscure St Cadfan founded a monastery here, giving shelter to Celts fleeing the Saxon invaders, and medieval pilgrims followed in their wake. A Celtic cross amidst the abbey ruins commemorates the pilgrims who came here to die and gave the island its poetic epithet: the Isle of 20,000 Saints. Their bones still periodically emerge from unmarked graves; it's said that in the 1850s they were used as fencing, as there were so many of them. To add to its mythical status, it's one of many candidates for the Isle of Avalon from the

Arthurian legends. It's said that the wizard Merlin is asleep in a glass castle somewhere on the island.

Most modern pilgrims to Bardsey are sea-bird-watchers (the island is home to an important colony of Manx shearwaters). The Bardsey Island Trust (☎0845 811 2233; www.bardsey.org) is Bardsey's custodian and can arrange holiday lets in cottages on the island. In the summer months Bardsey Boat Trips (☎07971-769895; www.bardseyboattrips.com; adult/child £30/20) sails to Bardsey from Porth Meudwy, a little cove outside Aberdaron; and Enlli Charters (☎0845 811 3655; www.enllicharter.co.uk; adult/child £35/20) sails from the marina in Pwllheli.

ABERSOCH

Abersoch (population 1000) comes alive in summer with a 30,000-person influx of boaties, surfers and beachbums. Edged by gentle blue-green hills, the town's main attraction is its beach, one of the most popular on the peninsula. Surfers should head further south around the coast for the Atlantic swell at Porth Neigwl (Hell's Mouth) and Porth Ceiriad. The tourist office (☎01758-712929; www.abersochandllyn.co.uk; High St; ◷10.30am-3pm daily school hols, 10.30am-2pm Fri-Sun rest of year) is open limited hours outside school holidays.

West Coast Surf Shop (www.westcoastsurf.co.uk; Lôn Pen Cei; ◷9.30am-5pm) hires out boards and wetsuits all year around. Its website features daily surf reports. Offaxis (☎01758-713407; www.offaxis.co.uk; Lôn Engan; lessons incl equipment from £30) is another outdoors and surf shop, which specialises in wakeboarding, windsurfing and surfing lessons.

Abersoch Sailing School (☎01758-712963; www.abersochsailingschool.co.uk) offers sailing lessons (from £45), and hires laser fun boats (one/two/three hours £30/45/60), catamarans (one/two/three hours £40/60/80), sea kayaks (per hour single/double £10/20) and skippered day racers and keelboats (per hour £75, minimum two hours). Lucky Abersoch contains one of the region's most sensual places to stay. Venetia (☎01758-713354; www.venetiawales.com; Lôn Sarn Bach, Abersoch; r £108-148; ⓟ) has five beautifully styled rooms decked out with designer lighting and modern art. If you can tear yourself away from their tactile trimmings, there's an excellent Italian restaurant (mains £12 to £20; open Thursday to Sunday low season, daily high season) downstairs, specialising in fresh seafood.

ORIEL PLAS GLYN-Y-WEDDW

Only part of the attraction of this excellent gallery (www.oriel.org.uk; Llanbedrog; entry by donation; ⊙10am-5pm Wed-Mon, daily high season) is the lively collection of work by contemporary Welsh artists, all available for purchase. The gallery is worth visiting just to gape at the flamboyant Victorian Gothic mansion it's housed in, with its flashy exposed beams and stained glass. There's also a nice little cafe and paths through the wooded grounds, which roll down to National Trust-owned Llanbedrog beach.

It's 3 miles from Abersoch and 4 miles west of Pwllheli.

LLANYSTUMDWY

The village of Llanystumdwy is the boyhood home and final resting place of David Lloyd George, one of Wales' finest ever political statesmen, and the British prime minister from 1916 to 1922. There's a small Lloyd George Museum (☎01766-522071; ⊙10.30am-5pm Mon-Fri Apr & May, Mon-Sat Jun, daily Jul-Sep, 11am-4pm Mon-Fri Oct), which gives an impression of the man and to some extent illustrates the tension between his nationality and position, through photos, posters and personal effects. Highgate, the house he grew up in, is 50m away, and his grave is about 150m away on the other side of the car park.

The turn-off to the village is to be found 1.5 miles west of Criccieth on the A497.

CRICCIETH

This genteel slow-moving seaside town (population 1800) sits above a sweep of sand-and-stone beach about 5 miles west of Porthmadog. Its main claim to fame is ruined Criccieth Castle (Cadw; adult/child £3.20/2.80; ⊙10am-5pm Apr-Oct, 11am-4pm Fri-Sun Nov-Mar) perched up on the clifftop and offering views stretching along the southern coast and across Tremadog Bay to Harlech. Constructed by Welsh prince Llywelyn the Great in 1239, it was overrun in 1283 by Edward I's forces and recaptured for the Welsh in 1404 by Owain Glyndŵr, who promptly burnt it. Today there is a small but informative exhibition centre at the ticket office.

Once you've been sandblasted by the rattling winds up at the castle, head for a warming plate of Welsh lamb or fresh monkfish at Tir a Môr (☎01766-523084; www.tiramor-criccieth.co.uk; 1 Mona Terrace, Criccieth; mains £15-20; ⊙dinner Tue-Sat). It's a relaxed restaurant, and popular too – bookings are advised.

Porthmadog & Around

POP 3000

Despite a few rough edges, busy little Porthmadog (port-*mad*-uk) has charm and a conspicuously friendly populace. It straddles both the Llŷn Peninsula and Snowdonia National Park, and is handy for visits to the fantastical village of Portmeirion. Throw in abundant transport connections, and you have found a good place to base yourself for a few days.

The town was founded by (and named after) reforming landowner William Alexander Madocks, who went to work on a grand scale, laying down the mile-long Cob causeway, draining some 400 hectares of wetland habitat, and creating a brand-new harbour. After his death, the causeway became the route for the new Ffestiniog Railway: at its 1873 peak, it transported over 116,000 tons of slate from the mines to the harbour.

Today Porthmadog is a mecca for railway buffs, as it forms the southern terminus for two of Wales' finest narrow-gauge train journeys, the Ffestiniog and Welsh Highland Railways (not to be confused with yet another steam-train line, the tiny Welsh Highland Heritage Railway, at the other end of town!).

◉ Sights & Activities

Ffestiniog & Welsh
Highland Railways   HERITAGE RAILWAY
(☎01766-516024; www.festrail.co.uk) There are 'little trains' all over Wales, a legacy of Victorian industry, but Porthmadog is exceptionally blessed. It is the terminus for both the Ffestiniog and the Welsh Highland narrow-gauge railways, run by the oldest independent railway company in the world. Trains on both lines depart from Harbour Station (near the Cob and the tourist office) in pungent puffs of smoke.

The **Ffestiniog Railway** (Porthmadog; adult/child return £19.60/17.65) is a fantastic, twisting and precipitous line that was built between 1832 and 1836 to haul slate down to Porthmadog from the mines at Blaenau Ffestiniog, 13½ miles away. Horse-drawn wagons were replaced in the 1860s by steam locomotives and the line became a passenger service. Saved after years of neglect, it is one of Wales' most spectacular and beautiful narrow-gauge journeys. Nearly all services are steam-hauled.

Its sibling, the **Welsh Highland Railway** (Porthmadog; adult/child return £33/29.70), is an amalgamation of several late-19th-century slate railways, and runs through equally lovely Snowdonian landscapes. In 2010 the line was extended to Beddgelert and through the outrageously beautiful Aberglaslyn Pass to Pont Croesor, 2 miles from Porthmadog. In 2012, this last small gap was plugged, and the railway now runs the full 25 miles between Porthmadog and Caernarfon. Walkers can hop off at either Rhyd Ddu (£19.60) station or the Snowdon Ranger request stop to follow paths up Snowdon.

Portmeirion Village   TOURIST VILLAGE
(www.portmeirion-village.com; adult/child £10/6; ⊙9.30am-7.30pm) Portmeirion is a uniquely oddball, gingerbread collection of buildings with a heavy Italian influence, masterminded by the Welsh architect Sir Clough Williams-Ellis. Starting in 1926, Clough collected bits and pieces from disintegrating stately mansions to create this weird and wonderful seaside utopia, designing and building many of the structures himself. Fifty years later, and at the ripe old age of 90, Clough deemed the village to be complete. Today the buildings are all listed and the site is a conservation area.

It's more like a stage set than an actual village; and, indeed, it formed the ideally surreal background for cult TV series *The Prisoner*, which was filmed here from 1966 to 1967. Fans of the show still come in droves, with *Prisoner* conventions held annually in March or April.

Several buildings contain cafes and gift shops, including one selling the famously florid Portmeirion pottery (although these days it's made in Stoke-on-Trent). A network of walking paths thread along the coast and through the private forested peninsula; if you want to enjoy them in solitude, most of the village's kooky cottages and mini-mansions are available for holiday lets.

Portmeirion is located 2 miles east of Porthmadog – it's a straightforward walk. Buses aren't great: 98 (five services per day Monday to Saturday) runs nearest, but it's probably easiest to take a taxi (☎01766-514799). Cheapskates can get in for half price after 3.30pm.

Borth-y-Gest   VILLAGE
The best views over the estuary are from Terrace Rd, which becomes Garth Rd above the harbour. At its end a path heads down to Borth-y-Gest, a pretty horseshoe of candy-coloured houses overlooking a sandy bay. At the other end of the crescent the path continues around the cliffs; if you look carefully you should be able to spot Harlech Castle in the distance.

Purple Moose   MICROBREWERY
(www.purplemoose.co.uk; Madoc St, Porthmadog; ⊙9am-5pm Mon-Fri) One of approximately 30 microbreweries across Wales, Purple Moose has grown from humble beginnings into an award-winning company – it picked up a Gold Award at the 2012 CAMRA Champion Beer competition. Tipples include Snowdonia Ale, Madog's Ale, Glaslyn Ale and Dark Side of the Moose. Ale aficionados can arrange a brewery tour (£5; 1pm to 3pm Tuesday to Thursday), including free tastings.

🛏 Sleeping & Eating

Hotel Portmeirion &
Castell Deudraeth   HOTEL, COTTAGES **£££**
(☎01766-770000; www.portmeirion-village.com; Portmeirion; hotel s/d £225/289, castle s/d £199/239, cottage s/d £159/199) You can live the fantasy and stay within the famous fairytale village itself. Hotel Portmeirion (1926), overlooking the estuary, has classic, elegant rooms and a dining room designed by Sir Terence Conran. Up the drive, Castell Deudraeth is, perversely, a more modern

SNOWDONIA & NORTH WALES PORTHMADOG & AROUND

alternative. If you want to dwell like the Prisoner himself, there are also 17 whimsical cottages on site. Prices drop considerably in low season.

Golden Fleece Inn
PUB ££

(☑01766-512421; www.goldenfleeceinn.com; Market Sq, Tremadog; s/d from £45/65; 🛜) An inviting and friendly old inn with hop flowers hanging from the ceilings, real ales, decent pub grub (mains £4 to £12), and an open fire for cold nights. The rooms are comfortable and atmospheric; however, be prepared for noise until closing, or just join the party. Live (acoustic) music on Tuesday nights.

Yr Hen Fecws
INN ££

(☑01766-514625; www.henfecws.com; 16 Lombard St, Porthmadog; s/d £60/75; 🅿) Stylishly restored, this stone cottage has seven simply decorated en-suite rooms with exposed-slate walls and fireplaces. Breakfast is served at the excellent cafe next door.

ℹ Information

Tourist office (☑01766-512981; High St, Porthmadog ; ⊙9.30am-5pm Easter-Oct, 10am-3.30pm Mon-Sat Nov-Easter)

ℹ Getting There & Away

BUS Bus route 1B heads to Blaenau Ffestiniog (27 minutes); 3 to Tremadog (four minutes), Criccieth (13 minutes), Llanystumdwy (16 minutes) and Pwllheli (40 minutes); and X32 to Dolgellau (50 minutes), Machynlleth (1½ hours) and Aberystwyth (2¼ hours), and in the other direction to Caernarfon (40 minutes) and Bangor (one hour). Snowdon Sherpa bus S97 goes to Beddgelert (20 minutes) and Pen-y-Pass (40 minutes). A daily National Express coach heads to London (£33, 10 hours), via Caernarfon (£6.80, 35 minutes), Llandudno (£8, 1½ hour) and Birmingham (£25, 6½ hours).

TRAIN Porthmadog is on the Cambrian Coast line, with direct trains to Harlech (£3, 22 minutes), Barmouth (£6.50, 48 minutes), Fairbourne (£7.30, 58 minutes), Machynlleth (£12.50, 1¾ hours), and in the other direction to Pwllheli (£4.50, 26 minutes). See the Ffestiniog & Welsh Highland Railways (p731) for steam services to Blaenau Ffestiniog, the Snowdon trailheads and Caernarfon.

ISLE OF ANGLESEY

At 276 sq miles, the Isle of Anglesey is the largest island in England and Wales. It's a popular destination for visitors, with miles of inspiring coastline, hidden beaches, chocolate-box villages and Wales' greatest concentration of ancient and prehistoric sites. The new A55 expressway also means that getting round the island by car is now much easier.

Fertile farming land attracted early settlers, while the island was holy to the Celts and the last part of Wales to fall to the Romans around AD 60. Given its outpost status and singular character, Anglesey stakes a fair claim to being the Welsh heartland. Gerald of Wales (admittedly a rather biased commentator!) quoted the ancient name for the island 'Môn mam Cymru' (Mother of Wales) at the end of the 12th century.

The industrial age arrived in 1826 when Thomas Telford established the first permanent link to the mainland. His iconic 174m Menai Suspension Bridge across the Menai Strait has a 30m-high central span, allowing the passage of tall ships. It was joined in 1850 by Robert Stephenson's Britannia Bridge to carry the newly laid railway.

Beaumaris makes the most convenient base on the island, with the best range of infrastructure. Off-the-beaten-track highlights include Cemaes Bay rock pools for crabbing and Church Bay for its idyllic beach.

The two official tourist offices are at Llanfair PG and Holyhead. Menai Bridge is the island's bus hub, with regular local connections across the region.

For more information about the island, see www.visitanglesey.co.uk.

Beaumaris (Biwmares)

POP 1500

Beaumaris was once Wales's largest port, notorious for its smugglers and pirates. It hides its shady past well: today it's a delightfully refined spot, offering a romantic castle and pretty Georgian buildings, an attractive waterfront and newly refurbished pier, and a growing number of boutiques, deli-cafes and galleries. Sailing and walking lure a new generation of Anglesey converts to its smart hotels and chic eateries.

◉ Sights & Activities

Beaumaris Castle
CASTLE

(Cadw; adult/child £3.80/3.40; ⊙9.30am-6pm Jul & Aug, 9.30am-5pm Apr-Jun, Sep & Oct, 10am-4pm Mon-Sat, 11am-4pm Sun Nov-Mar) The last of Edward I's great castles of North Wales, and the largest, Beaumaris is deservedly a World

EXPLORING MORE OF ANGLESEY

Llanfair PG, the small town with the absurdly long name Llanfairpwllgwyngyllgogery chwyrndrobwllllantysiliogogogoch (Llanfair PG for short!), is an unlikely hotspot for visitors. Coach parties jostle for photos of the sign on the train station platform, but more practical is the Llanfair PG tourist office (☏01248-713177; ☺9.30am-5.30pm Mon-Sat, 9.30am-4.30pm Sun), for information, maps and souvenirs.

Anglesey is synonymous with the twin iconic bridges that connect the island to the Welsh mainland. The Menai Heritage Experience (www.menaibridges.co.uk; Menai Bridge; adult/child £3/free; ☺10am-5pm Sun-Thu Jul-Sep) explains the feat of Victoria engineering and explores the ecology of the Menai Strait.

Anglesey's leading arts centre, Oriel Ynys Môn (www.kyffinwilliams.info; Llangefni; admission free; ☺10.30am-5pm) is the lynchpin of Anglesey's visual arts centre. The History Gallery explores Anglesey's past, but the main draw is the Oriel Kyffin Williams Gallery, featuring 400-odd works by Wales' most celebrated artist.

If you only visit one National Trust property in North Wales, make it Plas Newydd (NT; Llanfair PG; adult/child £8.90/4.45; ☺house 1-5pm Sat-Wed, garden 10am-5.30pm Sat-Wed), home to the first Marquess of Anglesey, who commanded the cavalry during the 1815 battle of Waterloo, and famous for its massive Whistler mural in the dining room. Don't confuse this stately property with Llangollen's Plas Newydd.

Although surfers tend to favour South Wales, Anglesey has its moments. Top spots include Rhosneigr on the western coast, also popular with windsurfers. Funsport (☏01407 810899; www.buckys.co.uk; 1 Beach Tce; ☺9am-5pm) rents out wetsuits and equipment, and can arrange two-hour taster courses (£35) in surfing, windsurfing and kitesurfing.

Heritage site. The four successive lines of fortifications and concentric 'walls within walls' make it the most technically perfect castle in Great Britain, even though it was never fully completed. With swans gliding on its water-filled moat, it's definitely the castle with the biggest wow factor.

Beaumaris Courthouse & Gaol
HISTORIC BUILDINGS

(combined ticket adult/child £7.40/5.90; ☺10.30am-5pm Sat-Thu Easter-Sep) Atmospheric and eerie, the courthouse is nearly 400 years old and the Victorian jail contains the last-surviving treadwheel in Britain (for hard-labour prisoners). Admission includes excellent audioguides that really bring both places to life. The courthouse is opposite the castle, and the jail is on Steeple Lane behind the parish church.

Puffin Island Cruises
BOAT TRIP

(☏01248-810746; www.beaumarismarine.com; adult/child £9/7; ☺Apr-Oct) Puffin Island is a hotbed of bird and marine life, designated a Special Protection Area. The (weather-dependent) boat trips take in spectacular views across the Menai Strait to the Snowdonia range and promise encounters with 12 species of sea birds in their natural habitat. Book at the kiosks at the entrance to the pier, or by phone.

🛏 Sleeping

Townhouse
HOTEL ££

(☏01248-810329; www.bullsheadinn.co.uk; Castle St; s/d/ste £80/120/155; ☎) From the team that brought you Beaumaris' stately Ye Olde Bulls Head, this funky little-sister property, located just across the road, provides quite a contrast. While the Bulls Head accommodation is historic and elegant, the Townhouse's is contemporary, high-tech and design driven. Breakfast and drinks are back across the road at its big sister.

Cleifiog
B&B ££

(☏01248-811507; www.cleifiogbandb.co.uk; Townsend; s/d from £60/90) A charmingly dotty little gem, this artistic town house oozes character and history, and boasts superb views of the Menai Strait. Of the three rooms, all stylishly designed, Tapestry is the largest and features the original 18th-century panelling. The owner displays her artworks around the house.

TOP THREE SEASIDE LUNCH SPOTS

Wavecrest Café (☎01407-730650; Church Bay; snacks £5-8; ⊙10.30am-5pm Thu-Mon) Cosy, relaxed cafe with great snack lunches and gigantic scones for afternoon tea.

Ann's Pantry (☎01248-410386; www.annspantry.co.uk; Moelfre; lunch dishes £5-10; ⊙9am-5pm, dinner Thu-Sat) With a delightful garden setting and funky, beach hut–chic interior, Ann's has great homemade food and fair-trade drinks.

Lobster Pot (☎01407-730241; www.lobster-pot.net; Church Bay; mains £14-27; ⊙lunch & dinner Tue-Sat Feb-Nov) For a decadent lobster lunch, try this local institution, famous for its fresh seafood and delightful location.

 ## Eating

Loft at the Ye Olde Bulls Head Inn MODERN WELSH £££
(☎01248-810329; www.bullsheadinn.co.uk; Castle St; 3 courses £41; ⊙dinner Tue-Sat) Compared to the hotel's more pedestrian Brasserie restaurant, the Loft is more of a fine-dining experience. Peruse the menu over aperitifs in the lounge before climbing the stairs for elegant decor, a refined ambience and lovingly crafted food, centring on seasonal Anglesey produce.

Red Boat Ice Cream Parlour ICE CREAM £
(www.redboatgelato.com; 34 Castle St; ⊙10am-6pm) Red Boat is a stylish little parlour, using authentic Italian recipes to prepare the tastiest frozen gelato this side of Florence. Try the exotic strawberry, mascarpone and balsamic vinegar flavour.

Sarah's Delicatessen & the Coffee Shop DELI, CAFE £
(11 Church St; ⊙9am-5pm Mon-Sat) This excellent deli champions local produce, such as cheese and ales, with a well-stocked selection of treats. The owners also run a small cafe round the corner with daily specials (try the Anglesey dressed crab), good coffee and heavenly desserts.

ℹ Information

Tourist office (www.beaumaris.org.uk; Town Hall, Castle St) At the time of writing, the volunteer-run tourist office was undergoing renovation. The next nearest tourist office on Anglesey is in Llangefni (☎01248-713177).

ℹ Getting There & Away

Buses stop on Church St. **Padarn Bus** (☎01286-871347) runs bus 56/57/58 to Bangor (20 to 50 minutes, roughly half-hourly Monday to Saturday, every two hours Sunday) via Menai Bridge for onward connections.

Holyhead (Caergybi)

POP 11,200

Holyhead remains a major travel hub for ferries to Ireland, but the town itself has fallen on hard times. Regeneration funding allowed the impressive Celtic Gateway bridge to be built, linking station and ferry terminal to the main shopping street, and Stena Line has recently proposed a radical waterfront redevelopment; but the town centre is still a rather moribund affair.

Holyhead is divided from the west coast of Anglesey by a narrow channel on Holy Island (Ynys Gybi), a 7-mile stretch of land. It's 'Holy' because this was the domain of St Cybi, a well-travelled monk thought to have lived in the 6th century.

Holyhead is the starting point for the Lôn Las Cymru cycle route (p656) and St Cybi's Church (with beautiful stained-glass windows from William Morris's workshop) marks the official starting point for the Isle of Anglesey Coastal Path.

The **Ucheldre Centre** (☎01407-763361; www.ucheldre.org; ⊙10am-5pm Mon-Sat, 2-5pm Sun), a community arts centre based in a former convent chapel, holds concerts, poetry readings, comedy nights and art exhibitions, and its cinema screens films on Wednesdays, Fridays and Sundays. **Holyhead Maritime Museum** (www.holyhead maritimemuseum.co.uk; Newry Beach; adult/child £3.50/2; ⊙10am-4pm Apr-Sep), housed in one of the oldest lifeboat houses in Wales (c 1858), has model ships and exhibits on Holyhead's maritime history from Roman times onwards.

For an ends-of-the-earth escape, **South Stack Lighthouse** (☎01407-763900, 01248-724444; www.trinityhouse.co.uk; Holyhead; tours adult/child £4.80/2.70; ⊙10.30am-5pm Apr-Sep) and the surrounding **nature reserve** (www.rspb.org.uk/wales; visitor centre; admission free;

⊘10am-5pm Apr-Sep) — run by the Royal Society for the Protection of Birds (RSPB) — is three miles outside Holyhead and feels gloriously remote.

🛏 Sleeping & Eating

Yr Hendre
B&B ££

(☎01407-762929; www.yr-hendre.net; Porth-y-Felin Rd; s/d from £45/60; P @) Yr Hendre remains the best place to stay in Holyhead and a welcome change from the town's recent proliferation of budget chain hotels. Professionally managed and comfortable, the three rooms are elegant; one has sea views. Walkers are welcomed, and there is safe bicycle storage available.

Ucheldre Kitchen
CAFE £

(www.ucheldre.org; Millbank; ⊘10am-4.30pm Mon-Sat, 2-4.30pm Sun) Attached to Holyhead's excellent arts hub, this friendly cafe does lunches and coffees.

Harbourfront Bistro
BISTRO ££

(☎01407-763433; www.harbourfrontbistro.co.uk; Newry Beach; mains £10-14; ⊘10.30am-2.15pm Wed-Sun, 6-9pm Thu-Sat) For super food and sea views, make this cosy little bistro adjoining the maritime museum your first choice.

ℹ Information

Utopia visitor centre (☎01407-762004; www.plascybi.co.uk; 63 Market St; ⊘9am-5pm Mon-Sat) Community-run tourist office/gift shop/fish-pedicure spa on the main shopping street.

ℹ Getting There & Away

Bus

The station is on Summer Hill.

Arriva (www.arrivabus.co.uk) Arriva Bus 4/X4/44 runs to Bangor.

National Express (www.nationalexpress.com) Direct coach destinations include Birmingham (£40, four hours) and London (£90, seven hours).

Ferry

The train station is next to the ferry terminal. The long-stay carpark costs £8 per day.

Irish Ferries (www.irishferries.com) Two daily slow ferries (3¼ hours) and two fast services (one hour 50 minutes) run to Dublin.

Stena Line (www.stenaline.co.uk) Four daily services to Dublin (3¼ hours), only two of which carry foot passengers; one daily service to Dun Laoghaire (two hours).

Train

At the time of writing, the West Coast train service was being run by an interim operator, Virgin trains (www.virgintrains.co.uk): for the latest on

---

WALKING THE ISLE OF ANGLESEY COASTAL PATH

Anglesey is a big draw for walkers thanks to the Isle of Anglesey Coastal Path (www.angleseycoastalpath.co.uk), a 125-mile coastal walking path with clear, yellow waymarking and spectacular views. The full trail takes an average of 12 days and passes through a changing landscape of coastal heath, saltmarsh, beaches and even a National Nature Reserve. Although the path reaches a maximum altitude of just 219m, don't be fooled – its up-and-down nature means your total height gain will be over 4km!

The official trailhead is at St Cybi's Church in Holyhead, but the 12 stages can easily be tackled as individual day hikes, ranging from seven to 13 miles per day. Some of the stages, particularly the far-northern legs from Cemaes Bay to Church Bay, make for bracing strolls against a dramatic backdrop of wild, wind-swept scenery.

A great, introductory day walk from Beaumaris takes in the ancient monastic site of Penmon Priory, Penmon Point with views across to Puffin Island, and Llanddona, a Blue Flag beach for a refreshing dip.

Alternatively, Moelfre is one of the prettiest harbour villages on the east coast. It's home to the tearoom/restaurant Ann's Pantry, as well as the volunteer-run Seawatch Centre (☎01248 410277; admission free; ⊘11am-5pm Tue-Sat, 1-5pm Sun Apr-Sep), with exhibitions on the area's brave lifeboatmen, which is due to reopen in 2013 after a major extension.

OS Explorer Maps 262 (West Coast) and 263 (East Coast) are helpful, as is the Isle of Anglesey Coastal Path – Official Guide by Carl Rogers.

Anglesey Walking Holidays (www.angleseywalkingholidays.com; per person from £435) offers self-guided walking packages, including accommodation, breakfast, luggage transfers and transport between trailheads.

Breathtaking Britain

Britain is best known for the historic capitals of London and Edinburgh, and cultural hotspots like Cardiff and Liverpool. However, beyond the urban sprawl lies another Britain: a landscape of high mountain vistas, dramatic valleys lined with lakes, and – as befitting an island – thousands of miles of spectacular coastline.

Lake District

1 The Lake District (p579) is home to the highest mountains in England, as well as some of the longest and most beautiful lakes. With summits snow-capped in winter, and spectacular at any time of year, this landscape inspired the poet William Wordsworth, and is a major magnet for hikers today.

Snowdonia

2 Wales is crowned with Snowdonia (p713) – a range of rocky peaks and glacier-hewn valleys stretching across the north of the country. The jewel in the crown is the mountain of Snowdon itself – accessible by Swiss-style cog-railway – while surrounding summits offer equally good views and a lot more solitude.

Cornwall's Coast

3 In Britain, you're spoilt for choice when it comes to beautiful coastline, but in the far southwest, the coast of Cornwall (p327) is hard to beat, with its stunning combination of sandy beaches, tranquil coves, picture-postcard fishing ports, adrenaline-pumping surf spots and rugged cliffs carved by Atlantic waves.

Scotland's Northwest Highlands

4 The long journey to the far northwest corner of the Scottish Highlands (p911) is repaid with some of the finest scenery anywhere in Britain. In this wild and remote region, the sheer mountain-sides drop to the sea, while narrow sea lochs cut deep inland, creating a landscape that is almost other-worldly in its beauty.

1. Lake District (p579) 2. Snowdonia (p713), Wales 3. Lusty Glaze beach (p331), Cornwall 4. Cuillin Hills (p921), Isle of Skye, Scotland

ALLAN BAXTER/GETTY IMAGES ©

DEREK CROUCHER/GETTY IMAGES ©

services to/from Holyhead, see www
.nationalrail.co.uk.

Arriva Trains Wales (www.arrivatrainswales
.co.uk) To Chester (£23, 1¾ hours) via Bangor
(£8.30, 30 minutes), and to Birmingham (£16,
four hours).

NORTH COAST & BORDERS

The North Wales coast has both perennial
charms and cultural black spots in equal
measure. Stick with the former and you'll
not be disappointed – they include a glorious, Unesco-listed castle at Conwy and the
Victorian resort of Llandudno, a favourite
family-holiday hub.

Moving southeast towards the English
border, Llangollen has a burgeoning reputation for its adventure sports and cultural
festivals. Most of all, it is known as the
home of the annual International Musical
Eisteddfod.

More details on this region are available
from www.northwalesborderlands.co.uk and
www.visitllandudno.org.uk.

Llangollen

POP 2900

Llangollen (lan-goch-len), huddled in the
fertile Vale of Llangollen around the banks
of the tumbling River Dee, has long been a
scenic gem of North Wales. It was traditionally seen as more of a day-trip destination,
but its appeal has evolved rapidly in recent
years with a slew of smart new places to
eat at, a developing walking and outdoors
scene, and a growing reputation for its arts
festivals.

◎ Sights & Activities

**Horse Drawn Boat Centre &
Pontcysyllte Aqueduct**   LANDMARK
(www.horsedrawnboats.co.uk; adult/child £6.50/
3.5; ⊙11am-4.30pm Apr-Oct) Peace and quiet
are the key features of the 45-minute horse-
drawn excursions along the towpath from
Llangollen Wharf. The company also run
two-hour motorised cruises (adult-child
£12.50/10.50; booking advised) to – and
then across – the Unesco World Heritage
listed Pontcysyllte Aqueduct, a 19th-
century engineering marvel designed by
Thomas Telford. Standing a dizzying 126ft
above the water, it is the tallest navigable
aqueduct in the world.

Castell Dinas Brân   CASTLE
One of North Wales' best-known ancient
sites, the ragged arches and tumbledown
walls of Dinas Brân mark the remnants of
a short-lived 13th-century castle. Its fabulous 360° views are well worth the two-hour
return walk up the steep track (turn uphill
at the taxidermist, cut up the steps on the
other side of the canal, then follow the Offa's
Dyke Path arrows).

Plas Newydd   HISTORIC BUILDING
(☎01978-861314; Hill St; adult/child £5.50/4.50;
⊙10am-5pm Wed-Sun Apr-Oct) Ornate Plas
Newydd was home to Lady Eleanor Butler
and Miss Sarah Ponsonby, two society ladies
who eloped from Ireland to Wales disguised
as men, settling down here to enjoy 'friendship, celibacy and the knitting of stockings'.
High-profile figures of the day, attracted by
the romantic story, came to call on the Ladies of Llangollen: admirers included the
Duke of Wellington and William Wordsworth. There's a good self-guided audio tour
of the house (included in the admission),
and tranquil gardens to explore. Don't confuse it with the National Trust stately home
of the same name on Anglesey.

Valle Crucis Abbey   ABBEY
(Cadw; adult/child £2.80/2.40 Apr-Oct, free Nov-
Mar; ⊙10am-5pm Apr-Oct, 10am-4pm Nov-Mar)
One of the region's ancient treasures, the
dignified ruins of this 13th-century Cistercian abbey are a two-mile walk from
Llangollen. The abbey is remarkably well
preserved, with a beautiful chapter house
and the monks' fishpond on the doorstep;
a small interpretation centre brings the
monks' daily routines to life.

Llangollen Railway   HERITAGE RAILWAY
(www.llangollen-railway.co.uk; adult/child return
£12/6; ⊙daily high season, special services low season) The 7.5-mile jaunt through the Dee Valley via Berwyn (near Horseshoe Falls) and
Carrog on the former Ruabon to Barmouth
line is a superb day out for families and
heritage rail lovers alike.

ProAdventure Activity Centre   OUTDOORS
(☎01978-861912; www.proadventure.co.uk; Parade
St) This not-for-profit company run canyoning, canoeing, rock-climbing, rafting
and bushcraft tasters and trips: prices start
from £45 per person. It also has a dedicated
indoor climbing wall.

Llangollen

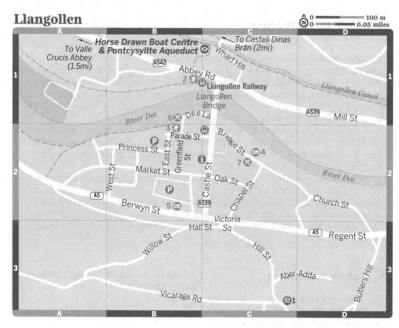

✦ Festivals & Events

Llangollen Fringe Festival ARTS
(www.llangollenfringe.co.uk) This small-town, volunteer-run arts festival, held in July, manages to attract some big names: 2012's line-up included Charlotte Church and Poet Laureate Carol Ann Duffy.

International Musical Eisteddfod MUSIC
(http://international-eisteddfod.co.uk) Staged at the Royal International Pavilion in early July.

☐ Sleeping

Cornerstones Guesthouse B&B ££
(🖰01978-861569; www.cornerstones-guesthouse
.co.uk; 15 Bridge St; r £80-100; 🅿@) This converted 16th-century house, all sloping
floorboards and oak beams, has charm and
history. The River Room is the cosiest of the
five rooms, with the gentle lapping of the
River Dee to send you off to sleep. Rooms
have all kinds of little extras, and free parking
permits are available for the town's carparks.

Llangollen Hostel HOSTEL £
(🖰01978-861773; www.llangollenhostel.co.uk; Berwyn St; dm/d £18/40; 🛜) This excellent independent hostel, based in a former family

Llangollen

home, has friendly owners and a cared-for
feel. It offers various rooms, from private
ensuite doubles to a six-bed dorm, as well
as an orderly kitchen and cosy lounge. It actively welcomes cyclists and canoeists, with
laundry facilities and bike/boat storage.
Prices include a self-service cereal-and-toast
breakfast.

ESSENTIAL EISTEDDFOD

The **National Eisteddfod** (www.eisteddfod.org.uk), pronounced *ey-steth-vot*, an eight-day celebration of Welsh culture, is Europe's largest festival of competitive music-making and poetry. Descended from ancient Bardic tournaments, it is conducted in Welsh, but the festival welcomes all entrants and visitors. Many people come in search of Welsh ancestry, while musical fringe events featuring local bands lend a slight Glastonbury-style atmosphere. It's generally held in early August, and the venue swings annually between north and south Wales.

Urdd Eisteddfod (www.urdd.org) is a separate young people's festival – *urdd* (pronounced *irth*) is Welsh for 'youth' – held in late May/early June at changing venues. The format resembles its bigger brother, although any self-respecting teenager prefers to hang out on the fringe at the main event.

Most famous of all is the International Musical Eisteddfod (p739), established after WWII to promote international harmony. Held over six days in early July, it attracts participants from around 50 countries, transforming the town of Llangollen into a global village. In addition to daily folk music and dancing competitions, gala concerts at the Royal International Pavilion feature international stars. It was nominated for the Nobel Peace Prize in 2004.

Eating & Drinking

TOP CHOICE **Gales of Llangollen** WINE BAR **££**
(www.galesofllangollen.co.uk; 18 Bridge St; mains £9-16; ⊙noon-2pm & 6-9.30pm Mon-Sat, 11am-3pm Sun) Gales wine bar/restaurant, a Llangollen institution, is consistently one of the best places to eat – turn up early, as it's not possible to reserve a table. It boasts a daily-changing menu best enjoyed with a good glass of plonk from the 100-strong wine list. The owners also run the **Wine Shop** (⊙10am-5.30pm Mon-Sat, to 4pm Sun) next door.

Corn Mill GASTROPUB **££**
(☎01978-869555; Dee Lane; light meals £7-10; mains £10-16; ⊙noon-9.30pm) The water wheel still turns at the heart of this converted mill, now a cheerful, bustling pub and all-day eatery. The deck is the best spot in town for an unfussy alfresco lunch, with views over the River Dee to the steam railway.

ℹ Information

Llangollen tourist office (☎01978-860828; The Chapel, Castle St; ⊙9.30am-5.30pm high season, to 5pm low season) Helpful well-stocked tourist office, in the same building as the library.

ℹ Getting There & Away

Bus
Bus services 5/5A/X94 run to Wrexham (up to 38 minutes, every 15 minutes Monday to Saturday, hourly Sunday) and the X94 also goes to Barmouth (two hours, every two hours Monday to Saturday, five daily on Sunday). Most buses stop on Parade St.

Car
Short-stay car park (Market St; per 3hrs £1)

Train
The nearest mainline station is at Ruabon, 6 miles east on the Shrewsbury–Chester line. Buses run from the station to Llangollen every 15 minutes until 6pm, then hourly.

Around Llangollen

It might be a little off the beaten track, but the stately home of **Erddig** (NT; ☎01978-355314; www.nationaltrust.org.uk; adult/child £9.90/4.95, grounds only £6.30/3.15; ⊙house 12.30-4.30pm Mar-Nov, 11am-3.30pm Dec-Feb, grounds 11am-5.30pm Mar-Nov, 11am-4pm Dec-Feb, last admission 1hr before closing) is truly worth seeking out. This splendid National Trust property offers an illuminating glimpse into 18th-century upper-class life: original artwork and furniture is on display in the fine staterooms, while a formal, walled garden has been restored in Victorian style, and informative tours run twice daily. There's plenty to keep kids and adults busy, with history trails, bike hire, shire horses, and a full events program (including 'Mob Cap Monday', when visitors can try their hand at Victorian crafts).

Erddig lies 12 miles northeast of Llangollen on the A483 in the village of Rhostyllen.

Llandudno

POP 14,900

Llandudno is a master of reinvention. Developed as an upmarket Victorian holiday town, it still retains much of its 19th-century grandeur, yet continues to find new fans with its booming boutique accommodation, big-name retail outlets, and Welsh art and performance. No wonder the American travel writer Bill Bryson was moved to describe Llandudno as his 'favourite seaside resort'.

The dominating feature is the Great Orme (207m), a spectacular 2-mile-long limestone headland jutting into the Irish Sea. Old-school tramway and cable-car rides go to the summit, providing breathtaking views of the Snowdonia range. On the seafront, traditional delights include strolling along the pier and catching Professor Codman's historic Punch and Judy show.

The opening of arts hub Venue Cymru has boosted the town's cultural life, and a major new retail park, Parc Llandudno, located at the east end of town, has brought big-name shops to the resort.

The town straddles its own peninsula, with Llandudno Bay and North Shore Beach to the northeast and Conwy Bay and West Shore Beach to the southwest.

◉ Sights & Activities

Great Orme
Country Park   INTERPRETATION CENTRE
From sea level it's difficult to gauge the sheer scale of the Great Orme, designated a Site of Special Scientific Interest (SSSI). The peak is home to several Neolithic sites, a cornucopia of flowers, butterflies and sea birds, a gang of wild goats, three waymarked summit trails (of which the Haulfre Gardens Trail is the easiest stroll to negotiate) and its own visitor centre. (www.conwy.gov.uk/greatorme; ◎10am-5.30pm Easter-Oct)

You can walk to the summit; take a ride on the Great Orme Tramway (www.great ormetramway.co.uk; adult/child return £5.90/4.10; ◎10am-6pm Apr-Sep, to 5pm Mar & Oct), a masterpiece of Victorian engineering which leaves every 20 minutes from Church Walks; or ride Britain's longest cable car from the Happy Valley Gardens above the pier – departures are weather dependent.

Archaeology fans might want to stop halfway up the limestone headland at the Great Orme Ancient Mine (www.greatormemines .info; adult/child £6.50/4.50; ◎10am-4.30pm mid-Mar–Oct), from which Bronze-Age people extracted around 200 tons of copper using only tools of bone and stone.

Llandudno Promenade & Pier   WATERFRONT
(◎pier 9am-6pm) A trip to Llandudno isn't complete until you've strolled along the majestic sweep of the promenade, eating ice cream and shooing away seagulls. Queen Victoria herself watched Professor Codman's Punch & Judy Show (◎2pm & 4pm Easter–mid-Sep), performed by the same family since 1860 – we hope she was amused. Mr Punch's iconic red-and-white-striped tent sits by the entrance to the 1878-built Victorian pier, the longest in Wales at 670m. A small amusement hall at the far end contains slot machines and twopenny-falls.

WORTH A TRIP

RUTHIN

Tucked away in the quiet Clwyd valley, well off any tourist route, Ruthin (www.visitruthin .com) is the town that time forgot. But it's worth a jaunt: Offa's Dyke Path national trail passes through the nearby Clwydian Range Area of Outstanding Natural Beauty (AONB) and the town is packed with history. The 15th-century Nantclwyd y Dre (adult/child £3.60/2.50; ◎10am-5pm Fri-Sun Apr-Sep) is the oldest timber-framed building in Wales, with rooms restored to various eras and an attic full of bats. More grisly is the audio-guided tour around Ruthin Gaol (adult/child £3.50/2.50; ◎10am-5pm Wed-Sun Apr-Oct), a sombre Victorian construction.

Ruthin Craft Centre (www.ruthincraftcentre.org.uk; Park Rd; admission free; ◎10am-5.30pm; P) is the town's arts hub, with a decent cafe. The place to stay is the town's boutique restaurant-with-rooms, manorhaus (☏01824-704830; www.manorhaus.com; Well St; s/d from £82/115; ☎), with eight gorgeously styled bedrooms, each showcasing the works of different local and national artists.

Llandudno

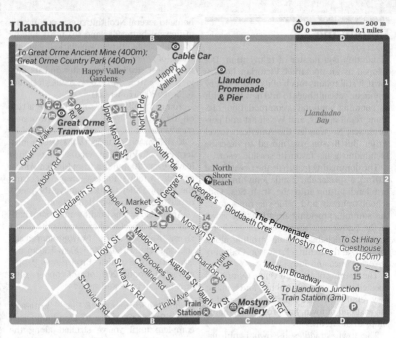

Llandudno

FREE Mostyn Gallery   GALLERY
(www.mostyn.org; 12 Vaughan St; ⊙10.30am-5pm)
A listed 1901 exterior hides the fabulous
award-winning innards of Wales' leading
contemporary art gallery. Its five galleries –
the result of an imaginative three-year expansion program – house changing exhibitions. Call in to explore the shop or grab a

coffee upstairs at Café Lux even if you're not
a modern-art fan.

City Sightseeing   BUS TOUR
(www.city-sightseeing.com; adult/child £7.50/3;
⊙Mar-Oct) Departs the pier half-hourly for a
hop-on/hop-off bus tour of Llandudno and
Conwy; tickets are valid for 24 hours.

Llandudno Land Train   BUS TOUR
(☉Apr-Oct) Runs a regular loop shuttle from the pier to the quieter West Shore and back (£2.50 each way).

⭐ Festivals & Events

Victorian Extravaganza   PERFORMING ARTS
(www.victorian-extravaganza.co.uk) Llandudno's biggest annual event, held over the early-May Bank Holiday weekend – book ahead for accommodation.

🛏 Sleeping

Escape B&B   BOUTIQUE B&B ££
(☎01492-877776; www.escapebandb.co.uk; 48 Church Walks; r £99-140; P🐾) Escape, Llandudno's first boutique B&B, has nine five-star rooms decorated in designer style and including a host of energy-saving and trend-setting features. It's hard to choose a favourite, but The Loft, with its split-level accommodation and retro vibe, does it for us. All rooms come with Blu-Ray players and Bose iPod docks, tasty breakfasts and an atmosphere of indulgence.

St Hilary Guesthouse   B&B ££
(☎01492-875551; www.sthilaryguesthouse.co.uk; The Promenade, 16 Craig-y-don Parade; s/d from £45/69; 🐾) Slap-bang on the Promenade, this lovely guest house provides a friendly welcome and clean, bright rooms with modern-but-neutral trappings. Thoughtful touches include iPod docks, fair-trade tea/coffee, and telescopes or binoculars in the sea-view rooms. One of those places where you feel nothing is too much trouble.

Osborne House   HOTEL £££
(☎01492-860330; www.osbornehouse.com; 17 North Pde; ste £145-175; P@) All marble, antique furniture and fancy drapes, the lavish Osbourne House takes a classical approach to aesthetics, and the results are impressive. All rooms are suites, with the best on the 1st floor with Victorian-style sitting rooms and sea views. Guests have use of spa facilities at nearby sister property the Empire Hotel.

Plas Madoc   B&B ££
(☎01492-876514; www.plasmadocguesthouse.co.uk; 60 Church Walks; s/d from £40/65; P) Formerly a fully vegetarian and vegan guest house, the new owners have widened the remit to non-vegetarian guests, but maintained the soya milk and free-range eggs tradition for those who request it. The five cosy rooms are light and airy with lots of homely touches.

Abbey Lodge   B&B ££
(☎01492-878042; 14 Abbey Rd; s/d £45/80; P🐾) The owners of Abbey Lodge keep this four-room property fresh and provide some homely touches, such as a small collection of local-interest books in each room. Hang out in the garden on a sunny day or read in the cosy lounge.

Llandudno Hostel   HOSTEL £
(☎01492-877430; www.llandudnohostel.co.uk; 14 Charlton St; dm £20, tw £48-52, f £65-120; 🐾) This family-run, Victorian-pile independent hostel close to the train station is rather an odd fish: ancient decor, cavernous rooms and the lack of a communal kitchen/dining area create a rather soulless atmosphere. On the plus side, rooms are clean and contain tea-/coffee-making facilities, and a continental breakfast is included. It's cheap and central.

SNOWDONIA & NORTH WALES LLANDUDNO

WORTH A TRIP

BODNANT GARDEN

Green-fingered visitors must drop in to Bodnant Garden (NT; www.bodnantgarden.co.uk; adult/child £8/4; ☉10am-5pm daily Mar-Oct, 11am-3pm daily early Nov), one of Wales's most beautiful gardens, 10km south of Llandudno off the A470. Laid out in 1875, its 80 lush acres unfurl around picturesque Bodnant Hall (closed to the public). Formal Italianate terraces and rectangular ponds creep away from the house into orderly disorder, transforming themselves into a picturesque wooded valley and wild garden, complete with rushing stream. Key features are the 55m laburnum tunnel, a hair-raising howl of yellow when it blooms in late May/early June; fragrant rose gardens; great banks of azaleas and rhododendrons; and some of the tallest giant redwoods in Britain. Spring is probably the best time to visit; but there's something to see in every season.

✕ Eating & Drinking

Fish Tram Chips
CAFE £

(Old Rd; fish & chips £7; ⏰noon-2pm & 5-7.30pm Tue-Sat, noon-2.15pm Sun low season, noon-3pm & 4.30-7.30pm daily high season) One of the tastiest and best-value fish suppers in North Wales, Fish Tram Chips is a pretty low-frills place but big on tasty, fresh fish and home-made side dishes with views across to the Great Orme Tramway station. Probably the best bargain in town.

Ham Bone Food Hall & Brasserie
DELI, CAFE ££

(Lloyd St; sandwiches £4-7, mains £8-12; ⏰8am-8pm) The best deli-cafe in Llandudno, the Hambone has a huge range of freshly made sandwiches, perfect for a picnic on the promenade. At night it becomes a brasserie, with great food made from scratch: pork-and-apple burgers, haddock-and-smoked-ham fishcakes, huge pizzas, and an ever-changing range of specials.

Seahorse
SEAFOOD £££

(☎01492-875315;www.the-seahorse.co.uk;7 Church Walks; mains £19, 2-course menu from £25.50; ⏰5pm-late Tue-Sat) Puzzlingly for a coastal resort, this is Llandudno's only proper sea-food restaurant – thankfully it's a good 'un! The chef is a keen fisherman, and the menu reflects his passion for the local catch (although there are meat and veggie options too). The restaurant itself is a split-level af-fair: upstairs is decorated with large murals, while the more intimate cellar room has a cosier feel.

Cottage Loaf
PUB ££

(☎01492-870762; www.the-cottageloaf.co.uk; Mar-ket St; mains £9-14; ⏰food served noon-8pm; 🌐) Tucked down an alleyway off Mostyn St, this homey pub makes staunchly traditional meals using high-quality local ingredients: black pudding, Conwy mussels, slow-roasted pork belly, beef-and-ale pie (veggie options exist, but are tame in comparison). Good beer, smiling service and a flower-filled beer garden enhance the experience.

Candles
MEDITERRANEAN ££

(☎01492-874422; www.candlesllandudno.com; 29 Lloyd St; mains £15-20, 4-course menu £20; ⏰din-ner; 🍴) A popular place among locals for cel-ebration meals, this cosy family-run cellar restaurant is a relaxing place to spend the evening. Staff are friendly, the set menus are good value, and there's even a four-course vegetarian alternative available.

King's Head
PUB ££

(Old Rd; mains £7-12) For a quiet pint and pub grub at a Victorian pub overlooking the tramway station.

Badgers Tearooms
CAFE

(Mostyn St, Victoria Shopping Centre; ⏰9.30am-5pm Mon-Sat, 11am-4pm Sun) A traditional tea-room, best known for its creamy afternoon teas and gooey cakes. The Victorian attire of the staff adds a frisson of genteel nostalgia.

☆ Entertainment

Venue Cymru
THEATRE

(☎01472-872000; www.venuecymru.co.uk; The Promenade; ⏰box office 10am-7pm Mon-Sat, plus 1hr before performances) The town's leading arts venue for shows and events from rock gigs to highbrow classical performances.

St John's Methodist Church
MUSIC

(Mostyn St; tickets £6; ⏰8pm Tue & Thu Jul-Oct) Summer season of choir concerts.

❶ Information

Llandudno Hospital (☎01492-860066) One mile south of the centre of town.

Llandudno tourist office (☎01492-577577; www.visitllandudno.org.uk; Mostyn St; ⏰9am-5.30pm Mon-Sat, 9.30am-4.30pm Sun Apr-Oct, 9am-5pm Mon-Sat Nov-Mar) In the library building, with helpful staff and an accommoda-tion booking service.

❶ Getting There & Away

Bus

Buses stop on the corner of Upper Mostyn St and Gloddaeth St. Bus 5 runs to Bangor (one hour, around two per hour Monday to Saturday, and one per hour Sunday) and Caernarfon (1½ hours, half-hourly Monday to Saturday, hourly Sunday). Bus 19 runs to Llanrwst (40 minutes, hourly Monday to Saturday, seven buses Sunday).

Bus

National Express runs a direct long-distance service to London (£32, 8½ hours); and another to Liverpool (£12, 2½ hours) and Manchester (£15, 3½ hours).

Car

Parking on the Promenade is at a premium. For easiest parking, head for the large number of spaces within the Parc Llandudno complex and its accompanying Asda supermarket, located just off the A470 close to the railway station.

Train

Llandudno's train station, the subject of a long-awaited and much-needed regeneration plan, is located three blocks south of Mostyn St; taxis wait by the station.

Arriva Trains (www.arrivatrainswales.co.uk) Runs services to Holyhead (£12.80, 1½ hours), with a change of train necessary at nearby Llandudno Junction station. Also runs direct services from Llandudno to Blaenau Ffestiniog (£7.70, 1¼ hours) via Betws-y-Coed (£5.60, 40 minutes) on the Conwy Valley line.

Virgin Trains (www.virgintrains.co.uk) The West Coast rail franchise was under review at the time of writing. It was being held temporarily by Virgin, with several direct services from Llandudno Junction to London Euston (six Monday to Friday, four on weekends).

Conwy

POP 3800

Unesco-designated Conwy Castle dominates the walled town: approaching from the east, three bridges span the river and add a further theatrical flourish to the splendid sight of its turrets and towers. Conwy Quay at the castle's feet has been newly regenerated – stroll along the waterside to see the smallest house in Britain, a tiny 10' by 4'2".

A highlight of the year is the Gwledd Conwy Feast (www.gwleddconwyfeast.co.uk), a food festival with additional arts events, held annually in late October – book accommodation well in advance. If you're out of luck, nearby Llandudno has more sleeping and eating options.

◎ Sights

Conwy Castle & Town Wall　　CASTLE
(Cadw; adult/child £4.80/4.30; ⊙9.30am-6pm Jul & Aug, 9.30am-5pm Mar-Jun, Sep & Oct, 10am-4pm Mon-Sat, 11am-4pm Sun Nov-Feb) Probably the most stunning of all Edward I's Welsh fortresses, built between 1277 and 1307, Conwy Castle rises from a rocky outcrop with commanding views across the estuary and Snowdonia National Park. Exploring the castle's nooks and crannies makes for a superb, living-history visit. Best of all, head to the battlements for panoramic views and an overview of Conwy's majestic complexity.

The survival of the 1200m-long Conwy town wall, built simultaneously with the castle, makes this one of the UK's prime medieval sites. You can walk part-way round the wall; the best views are to be had from Upper Gate.

Plas Mawr　　HISTORIC BUILDING
(Cadw; High St; adult/child £5.20/4.80; ⊙9am-5pm Tue-Sun Apr-Sep, 9.30am-4pm Tue-Sun Oct, last admission 45 minutes before closing) Plas Mawr, one of Britain's finest surviving Elizabethan town houses, was built in 1585 and is well worth a visit. The tall, whitewashed exterior is an indication of the owner's status, but gives no clue to the vivid interior, with its colourful friezes and plasterwork ceilings. The admission price includes a helpful audioguide; and weekly in summer, Blodwen the maid leads a spooky evening tour (tickets £6) to discover the resident ghosts.

Aberconwy House　　HISTORIC BUILDING
(NT; Castle St; adult/child £3.40/1.70; ⊙11am-5pm daily Jul & Aug, 11am-4pm Wed-Mon Sep, Oct & Mar-Jun, noon-3pm weekends Nov-Feb) This timber-and-plaster building is the town's oldest medieval merchant's house, dating from around 1300.

FREE **Royal Cambrian Academy**　　GALLERY
(www.rcaconwy.org; Crown Lane; ⊙11am-5pm Tue-Sat Mar-Oct, 11am-4pm Wed-Sat Nov-Feb) The twin white-walled galleries host a full program of exhibitions by members, plus visiting shows from the National Museum of Wales and elsewhere. The academy also hosts the excellent Annual Summer Exhibition from July to September, featuring the cream of fine art in Wales under one roof.

🛏 Sleeping

Whinward House　　B&B ££
(☏01492-573275; www.whinwardhouse.co.uk; Whinacres Morfa; s/d £70/80; P🖕) This three-room B&B, located just outside Conwy's city walls at the end of a country lane, is a cosy, homely affair. A conservatory and outside decking area for summer nights, the latter with a maritime theme, add to the overall appeal. Book ahead.

Castle Hotel　　HOTEL £££
(☏01492-582800; www.castlewales.co.uk; High St; s/d/ste from £70/120/160; P) Following a major refit, the new-look rooms feature purple and gold decor and Bose sound systems; higher-priced rooms boast castle views and freestanding baths. The hotel's Dawson's Restaurant has also gained a new lease of life, serving tasty brasserie-style meals in elegant surroundings: one of the finest places to dine in the area (snacks £6 to £9, mains £14 to £19).

Conwy

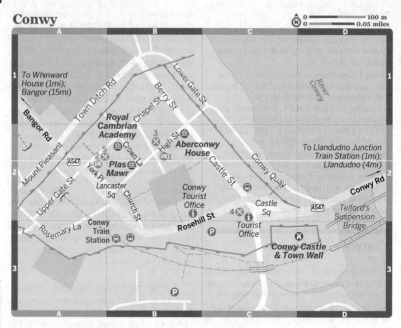

Conwy

◎ Top Sights

🛏 Sleeping

⊗ Eating

Gwynfryn   B&B **££**

(☎01492-576733; www.gwynfrynbandb.co.uk; 4 York Pl; r £60-80; 🛜) The owners of this family B&B – set in a refurbished, five-bedroom Victorian property just off the main square – have created clean, brightly-coloured rooms with thoughtful touches: fridges, biscuits and chocolates, and books and DVDs to borrow. Breakfast is served in the conservatory.

✕ Eating

Watson's Bistro   WELSH **££**

(☎01492-596326; www.watsonsbistroconwy.co.uk; Chapel St; lunch mains around £10, dinner mains £15-18; ☺lunch Tue-Sun, dinner daily) For modern Welsh food in an intimate bistro setting, Watson's is the smartest option in town. Everything is homemade, from the chicken-liver pate at the start of the meal to the delicate sorbets at the end. Sandwiches and lighter mains grace the lunchtime menu; at night, go for the bistro's most popular dish, slow-roast shoulder of lamb.

Amelies   FRENCH **££**

(☎01492-583142; 10 High St; mains £10-18; ☺11am-2pm & 6-9pm Tue-Sat; 🌿) Named after the Audrey Tautou film, Amelies is a welcoming French-motif bistro with wood floors and flowers on the tables. Tasty mains include vegetarian options – and make sure you leave room for dessert. It's a relaxed place, popular for an easygoing lunch, right in the heart of town.

Press Room Café   CAFE **£**

(☎01492-592242; 3 Rosehill St; mains £4-8.50; ☺10am-4.30pm; 🌿) Located by the entrance to the castle and with an outdoor courtyard, this arty cafe/health-food shop is a useful spot for light (mainly vegetarian) lunches and fair-trade coffees.

Information

Conwy tourist office (☎01492-577566; www.visitllandudno.org.uk; Rosehill St; ⏲9.30am-5pm daily Apr-Oct, 9.30am-4pm Mon-Sat, 11am-4pm Sun Nov-Mar)

Getting There & Away

Bus

Most buses stop by the train station.

Arriva (www.arrivabus.co.uk) Runs buses 5/X5 to Caernarfon (1¼ hours) and Llandudno (22 minutes, every 15 minutes Monday to Saturday, half-hourly Sunday). Buses 14 and 15 also go to Llandudno. Arriva bus 19 stops on Castle St for Llanrwst (40 minutes) and Betws y Coed (45 minutes, hourly Monday to Saturday, eight buses Sunday).

Train

The West Coast rail franchise was under review at the time of writing, and was being held temporarily by Virgin Trains (www.virgintrains.co.uk). For the latest on services to/from Conwy, see www.nationalrail.co.uk.

Bangor

POP 15,300

St Deiniol established a monastery here in AD 525, which grew up into Bangor's sweet little cathedral. Bangor's glory days have rather faded since then – today, it's a quiet university town, huddled around the Deiniol Shopping Centre. Exciting plans are afoot, though: work has just begun on an ambitious new £44m arts centre, which is due to open in 2014, fuelling hopes for a kind of cultural renaissance. Bangor is also a major transport hub with a raft of onward connections to Anglesey and Snowdonia. The nearest tourist office is in Caernarfon.

Sights

Penrhyn Castle CASTLE

(NT; adult/child £10/5; ⏲11am-5pm Jul & Aug, noon-5pm Wed-Mon Easter-Jun, Sep & Oct) Edward I's medieval masterpieces get the glory in these parts, but this 19th-century fantasy Norman castle should not be missed. Its extravagant rooms, complete with intricately carved ceilings, stained-glass windows, opulent furniture and even early flushing toilets, are a gothic wonder. Beautiful grounds include a Victorian walled garden, a bog garden, and a railway museum, along with epic views of Snowdonia. The castle is 1½ miles outside Bangor: buses to Llandudno and Caernarfon stop at the gate.

FREE **Gwynedd Museum & Art Gallery** MUSEUM

(Ffordd Gwynedd; ⏲12.30-4.30pm Tue-Fri, 10.30am-4.30pm Sat) Has a section devoted to tracing the evolution of the Welsh identity.

Sleeping & Eating

Management Centre HOTEL ££

(☎01248-365900; www.themanagementcentre.co.uk; College Rd; rm from £65; P 📶) Bangor isn't exactly blessed with accommodation options, but this university business centre has 57 small en-suite rooms and makes for a comfortable (if slightly impersonal) stay. There's an onsite restaurant and bar if you don't fancy the steep walk down into town and back.

Blue Sky Cafe CAFE £

(☎01248-355444; www.blueskybangor.co.uk; Ambassador Hall, 236 High St; mains £7; ⏲9.30am-5.30pm Mon-Sat) Easy to miss, the Blue Sky Cafe hides itself down an alleyway off the high street. It's worth seeking out: locally-sourced ingredients go into its breakfasts, soups, sandwiches, burgers and salads, and rich wood and red walls make for a cosy ambience. We can recommend the Blue Sky Platter (£12.25), a selection of Welsh nibbles made for sharing.

Kyffin CAFE £

(☎01248-355161; 129 High St; lunch mains £5, evening menu £13; ⏲9.30am-5.30pm Mon-Sat; 🖉) Hidden-gem, fair-trade, vegetarian and vegan cafe with jazz music, a cosy lounge and antique-shop fittings, plus a deli counter with organic goodies. The menu is small – just four items – but tasty.

Information

Gwynedd Hospital (☎01248-384384; Penrhos Rd) Located 2 miles southwest of the centre, this is the regional hub for medical emergencies.

Getting There & Away

Bus

The station is located behind the Deiniol Shopping Centre; some buses also stop just outside the station.

Arriva (www.arrivabus.co.uk) Bus 4/X4/44 runs to Holyhead (1¼ hours, two per hour Monday to Saturday, seven buses Sunday); bus 5/X5 runs to Caernarfon (30 minutes)

and Llandudno (one hour, every 15 minutes
Monday to Saturday, half-hourly Sunday).

National Express (www.nationalexpress.com)
Runs daily to London (£34, nine hours).

Padarn Bus (☑01286-871347) Bus 56/57/58
runs to Beaumaris (20 to 50 minutes, roughly
half-hourly Monday to Saturday, every two
hours Sunday).

Train

The West Coast rail franchise was under review
at the time of writing, and was being held temporarily by Virgin Trains (www.virgintrains.co.uk).
For the latest on services to/from Bangor, see
www.nationalrail.co.uk.

Scotland

Scotland Highlights

1 Exploring the capital, **Edinburgh** (p751), one of the world's most fascinating cities

2 Enjoying glorious Victorian architecture, great nightlife and friendly locals in **Glasgow** (p786)

3 Getting permanent jawdrop along the **northwest Highlands coast** (p911)

4 Experiencing the romantic ruins of the **Border Abbeys** (p807)

5 Uncovering beauty and tragic history at **Glen Coe** (p899)

6 Capturing the brooding beauty of Skye's **Cuillin Hills** (p921)

7 Climbing **Ben Nevis** (p903), the highest point in Britain

8 Admiring the forests and lochs in **Perthshire** (p862)

9 Finding 5000-year-old neolithic sites on **Orkney** (p933)

Edinburgh

POP 430,000 / AREA 116 SQ KM

Best Places to Eat

» Tower (p775)

» The Dogs (p776)

» Ondine (p775)

» Porto & Fi (p775)

» Café Marlayne (p777)

Best Places to Stay

» Hotel Missoni (p773)

» Sheridan Guest House (p775)

» Southside Guest House (p774)

» B+B Edinburgh (p774)

» Ardmor House (p775)

Why Go?

Edinburgh is a city that begs to be explored. From the vaults and wynds (narrow lanes) that riddle the Old Town to the urban villages of Stockbridge and Cramond, it's filled with quirky come-hither nooks that tempt you to walk just a little bit further. And every corner turned reveals sudden views and unexpected vistas – green sunlit hills, a glimpse of rust-red crags, a blue flash of distant sea.

But there's more to Edinburgh than sightseeing – there are top shops, world-class restaurants and a bacchanalia of bars to enjoy. This is a city of pub crawls and impromptu music sessions, mad-for-it clubbing and all-night parties, overindulgence, late nights and wandering home through cobbled streets at dawn.

All these superlatives come together in August at festival time, when it seems as if half the world descends on Edinburgh for one enormous party. If you can possibly manage it, join them.

When to Go

In May there's good weather (usually), flowers and cherry blossom everywhere, and (gasp!) no crowds. August is festival time – crowded and mad, but unmissable. In December there are Christmas decorations, cosy pubs with open fires and ice skating in Princes Street Gardens.

Edinburgh Highlights

❶ Taking in the views from the battlements of **Edinburgh Castle** (p754)

❷ Feasting on steak and oysters at the **Tower** (p775) restaurant as the sun sets over the city

❸ Nosing around the Queen's private quarters on the former **Royal Yacht Britannia** (p766) at Leith

❹ Listening to live folk music at **Sandy Bell's** (p778)

❺ Trying to decipher the Da Vinci code at mysterious **Rosslyn Chapel** (p767)

❻ Exploring Edinburgh's subterranean history in the haunted vaults of **South Bridge** (p761) and **Real Mary King's Close** (p759)

❼ Climbing to the summit of the city's miniature mountain, **Arthur's Seat** (p761)

History

Back in the 7th century the Castle Rock was called Dun Eiden (meaning 'Fort on the Hill Slope'). When invaders from the kingdom of Northumbria in northeast England captured it in 638, they took the existing Gaelic name 'Eiden' and tacked it onto their own Old English word for fort, 'burh', to create the name Edinburgh.

Originally a purely defensive site, Edinburgh began to expand in the 12th century when King David I held court at the castle and founded the abbey at Holyrood. The city's first effective town wall was constructed around 1450, enclosing the Old Town; this overcrowded area became a medieval Manhattan, forcing its inhabitants to build tenements five and six storeys high.

The capital played an important role in the Reformation (1560–1690), led by the firebrand John Knox. Mary, Queen of Scots held court in the Palace of Holyroodhouse for six brief years, but when her son James VI succeeded to the English throne in 1603 he moved his court to London. The Act of Union in 1707 further reduced Edinburgh's importance.

Nevertheless, cultural and intellectual life flourished during the Scottish Enlightenment (roughly 1740–1830), and Edinburgh became known as 'a hotbed of genius'. In the second half of the 18th century the New Town was built, and in the 19th century the population quadrupled to 400,000 as suburbs of Victorian tenements spread to the north and south.

In the 1920s the city's borders expanded again to encompass Leith in the north, Cramond in the west and the Pentland Hills in the south. Following WWII, the city's cultural life blossomed, stimulated by the Edinburgh International Festival and its fellow traveller the Fringe, both held for the first time in 1947 and now recognised as world-class arts festivals.

Edinburgh entered a new era following the 1997 referendum vote in favour of a devolved Scottish parliament, which first convened in July 1999. The parliament is housed in a controversial new building in Holyrood at the foot of the Royal Mile, where the 2007 elections saw the Scottish National Party – whose long-term aim is independence for Scotland – take power for the first time.

◉ Sights

Edinburgh's main attractions are concentrated in the city centre – on and around the Old Town's Royal Mile between the castle and Holyrood, and in New Town. A major exception is the Royal Yacht *Britannia,* which is in the redeveloped docklands district of Leith, 2 miles northeast of the centre.

OLD TOWN

Edinburgh's Old Town stretches along a ridge to the east of the castle, and tumbles down Victoria St to the broad expanse of the Grassmarket. It's a jagged and jumbled

---

EDINBURGH IN...

Two Days

A two-day trip to Edinburgh should start at **Edinburgh Castle**, followed by a stroll down the **Royal Mile** to the **Scottish Parliament Building** and the **Palace of Holyroodhouse**. You can work up an appetite by climbing **Arthur's Seat**, then satisfy your hunger with dinner at **Ondine** or the **Tower**. On day two spend the morning in the **National Museum of Scotland** then catch the bus to **Leith** for a visit to the **Royal Yacht Britannia**. In the evening have dinner at one of Leith's many excellent restaurants, or scare yourself silly on a guided **ghost tour**.

Four Days

Two more days will give you time for a morning stroll around the **Royal Botanic Garden**, followed by an afternoon spent exploring the enigmatic and beautiful **Rosslyn Chapel**, which famously appeared in the book and film *The Da Vinci Code*. Dinner at **The Dogs** could be before or after your sunset walk to the summit of **Calton Hill**. On day four, admire the art in the **Scottish National Gallery** and the **Scottish National Portrait Gallery**, hit the shops in **Cockburn** and **Victoria streets**, and round off your trip with the **Edinburgh Literary Pub Tour**.

THE STONE OF DESTINY

On St Andrew's Day 1996 a block of sandstone – 26.5in x 16.5in x 11in in size, with rusted iron hoops at either end – was installed with much pomp and ceremony in Edinburgh Castle. For the previous 700 years it had lain in London, beneath the Coronation Chair in Westminster Abbey. Almost all English, and later British, monarchs from Edward II in 1307 to Elizabeth II in 1953 have parked their backsides firmly over this stone during their coronation ceremony.

The legendary Stone of Destiny – said to have originated in the Holy Land, and on which Scottish kings placed their feet during their coronation (not their bums; the English got that bit wrong) – was stolen from Scone Abbey near Perth by King Edward I of England in 1296. It was taken to London and there it remained for seven centuries – except for a brief removal to Gloucester during WWII air raids, and a three-month sojourn in Scotland after it was stolen by Scottish Nationalist students at Christmas in 1950 – an enduring symbol of Scotland's subjugation by England.

The Stone of Destiny returned to the political limelight in 1996, when the then Scottish Secretary and Conservative Party MP, Michael Forsyth, arranged for the return of the sandstone block to Scotland. A blatant attempt to boost the flagging popularity of the Conservative Party in Scotland prior to a general election, Forsyth's publicity stunt failed miserably. The Scots said thanks very much for the stone and then, in May 1997, voted every Conservative MP in Scotland into oblivion.

Many people, however, believe that Edward I was fobbed off with a shoddy imitation in 1296 and that the true Stone of Destiny remains safely hidden somewhere in Scotland. This is not impossible – some descriptions of the original stone state that it was made of black marble and decorated with elaborate carvings. Interested parties should read *Scotland's Stone of Destiny* by Nick Aitchison, which details the history and cultural significance of Scotland's most famous lump of rock.

maze of masonry riddled with closes (alleys) and wynds (narrow lanes), stairs and vaults, and cleft along its spine by the cobbled ravine of the Royal Mile.

Until the founding of New Town in the 18th century, old Edinburgh was an overcrowded and insanitary hive of humanity squeezed between the boggy ground of the Nor' Loch (North Loch, now drained and occupied by Princes Street Gardens) to the north and the city walls to the south and east. The only way for the town to expand was upwards, and the five- and six-storey tenements that were raised along the Royal Mile in the 16th and 17th centuries were the skyscrapers of their day, remarked upon with wonder by visiting writers such as Daniel Defoe. All classes of society, from beggars to magistrates, lived cheek by jowl in these urban ants' nests, the wealthy occupying the middle floors – high enough to be above the noise and stink of the streets, but not so high that climbing the stairs would be too tiring – while the poor squeezed into attics, basements, cellars and vaults amid the rats, rubbish and raw sewage.

THE ROYAL MILE

This mile-long street earned its regal nickname in the 16th century when it was used by the king to travel between the castle and the Palace of Holyroodhouse. There are five sections – the Castle Esplanade, Castlehill, Lawnmarket, High St and Canongate – whose names reflect their historical origins.

Edinburgh Castle   CASTLE

(Map p758; www.edinburghcastle.gov.uk; adult/child incl audioguide £16/9.20; ⊙9.30am-6pm Apr-Sep, to 5pm Oct-Mar, last admission 45min before closing) The brooding, black crags of Castle Rock rising above the western end of Princes St are the very reason for Edinburgh's existence. This rocky hill was the most easily defended hilltop on the invasion route between England and central Scotland, a route followed by countless armies from the Roman legions of the 1st and 2nd centuries AD to the Jacobite troops of Bonnie Prince Charlie in 1745.

Edinburgh Castle has played a pivotal role in Scottish history, both as a royal residence – King Malcolm Canmore (r 1058–93) and Queen Margaret first made their home here in the 11th century – and as a military stronghold. The castle last saw military action in 1745; from then until the 1920s it served as the British army's main base in Scotland. Today it is one of Scotland's most atmospheric, most popular – and most expensive – tourist attractions.

The Entrance Gateway, flanked by statues of Robert the Bruce and William Wallace, opens to a cobbled lane that leads up beneath the 16th-century Portcullis Gate to the cannons ranged along the Argyle and Mills Mount batteries. The battlements here have great views over New Town to the Firth of Forth.

At the far end of Mills Mount Battery is the famous One O'Clock Gun, where crowds gather to watch a gleaming WWII 25-pounder fire an ear-splitting time signal at exactly 1pm (every day except Sundays, Christmas Day and Good Friday).

South of Mills Mount, the road curls up leftwards through Foog's Gate to the highest part of Castle Rock, crowned by the tiny, Romanesque St Margaret's Chapel, the oldest surviving building in Edinburgh. It was probably built by David I or Alexander I in memory of their mother, Queen Margaret, sometime around 1130 (she was canonised in 1250). Beside the chapel stands Mons Meg, a giant 15th-century siege gun built at Mons (in what is now Belgium) in 1449.

The main group of buildings on the summit of Castle Rock are ranged around Crown Sq, dominated by the shrine of the Scottish National War Memorial. Opposite is the Great Hall, built for James IV (r 1488–1513) as a ceremonial hall and used as a meeting place for the Scottish parliament until 1639. Its most remarkable feature is the original, 16th-century hammer-beam roof.

The Castle Vaults beneath the Great Hall (entered from Crown Sq via the Prisons of War exhibit) were used variously as storerooms, bakeries and a prison. The vaults have been renovated to resemble 18th- and early-19th-century prisons, where graffiti carved by French and American prisoners can be seen on the ancient wooden doors.

On the eastern side of the square is the Royal Palace, built during the 15th and 16th centuries, where a series of historical tableaux leads to the highlight of the castle – a strongroom housing the Honours of Scotland (the Scottish crown jewels), the oldest surviving crown jewels in Europe. Locked away in a chest following the Act of Union in 1707, the crown (made in 1540 from the gold of Robert the Bruce's 14th-century coronet), sword and sceptre lay forgotten until they were unearthed at the instigation of the novelist Sir Walter Scott in 1818. Also on display here is the Stone of Destiny.

Among the neighbouring Royal Apartments is the bedchamber where Mary, Queen of Scots gave birth to her son James VI, who was to unite the crowns of Scotland and England in 1603.

Scotch Whisky Experience   EXHIBITION
(Map p758; www.scotchwhiskyexperience.co.uk; 354 Castlehill; adult/child incl tour & tasting £12.50/6.50; ⊘10am-6.30pm Jun-Aug, to 6pm Sep-May) A former school houses this multimedia centre explaining the making of whisky from barley to bottle in a series of exhibits, demonstrations and tours that combine sight, sound and smell, including the world's largest collection of malt whiskies; look out for Peat, the distillery cat! There's also a restaurant that serves traditional Scottish dishes with, where possible, a dash of whisky thrown in. It's a short distance downhill from the Castle Esplanade.

Camera Obscura   CAMERA OBSCURA
(Map p758; www.camera-obscura.co.uk; Castlehill; adult/child £10.95/7.95; ⊘9.30am-9pm Jul & Aug, 9.30am-7pm Apr-Jun & Sep-Oct, 10am-6pm Nov-Mar) Edinburgh's 'camera obscura' is a curious 19th-century device – in constant use since 1853 – that uses lenses and mirrors to throw a live image of the city onto a large horizontal screen. The accompanying commentary is entertaining and the whole experience has a quirky charm, complemented by an intriguing exhibition dedicated to illusions of all kinds. Stairs lead up through various displays to the Outlook Tower, which offers great views over the city.

DON'T MISS

CASTLE HIT LIST

If you're pushed for time, here's a list of the top things to see at Edinburgh Castle:

» Views from Argyle Battery

» One O'Clock Gun

» Great Hall

» Honours of Scotland

» Prisons of War

Royal Mile

A GRAND DAY OUT

Planning your own procession along the Royal Mile involves some tough decisions – it would be impossible to see everything in a single day, so it's wise to decide in advance what you don't want to miss and shape your visit around that. Remember to leave time for lunch, for exploring some of the Mile's countless side alleys and, during festival time, for enjoying the street theatre that is bound to be happening in High St.

The most pleasant way to reach the Castle Esplanade at the start of the Royal Mile is to hike up the zigzag path from the footbridge behind the Ross Bandstand in Princes Street Gardens (in springtime you'll be knee-deep in daffodils). Starting at **Edinburgh Castle** 1 means that the rest of your walk is downhill. For a superb view up and down the length of the Mile, climb the **Camera Obscura's Outlook Tower** 2 before visiting **Gladstone's Land** 3 and **St Giles**

LONELY PLANET / GETTY IMAGES ©

Royal Visits to the Royal Mile

1561: Mary, Queen of Scots arrives from France and holds an audience with John Knox.
1745: Bonnie Prince Charlie fails to capture Edinburgh Castle, and instead sets up court in Holyroodhouse.
2004: Queen Elizabeth II officially opens the Scottish Parliament building.

Edinburgh Castle
If you're pushed for time, visit the Great Hall, the Honours of Scotland and the Prisons of War exhibit. Head for the Half Moon Battery for a photo looking down the length of the Royal Mile.

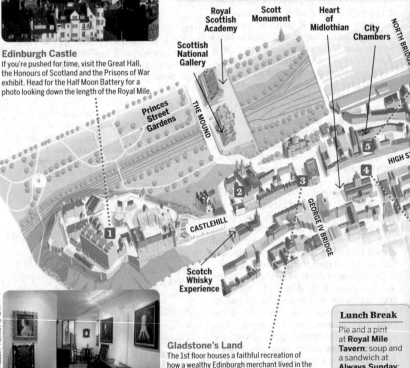

Royal Scottish Academy

Scott Monument

Heart of Midlothian

City Chambers

NORTH BRIDGE

Scottish National Gallery

Princes Street Gardens

THE MOUND

5

HIGH ST

2

3

4

GEORGE IV BRIDGE

CASTLEHILL

1

Scotch Whisky Experience

KARL BLACKWELL / GETTY IMAGES ©

Gladstone's Land
The 1st floor houses a faithful recreation of how a wealthy Edinburgh merchant lived in the 17th century. Check out the beautiful Painted Bedchamber, with its ornately decorated walls and wooden ceilings.

Lunch Break
Pie and a pint at **Royal Mile Tavern**; soup and a sandwich at **Always Sunday**; bistro nosh at **Café Marlayne**.

Cathedral 4. If history's your thing, you'll want to add **Real Mary King's Close 5**, **John Knox House 6** and the **Museum of Edinburgh 7** to your must-see list.

At the foot of the mile, choose between modern and ancient seats of power – the **Scottish Parliament 8** or the **Palace of Holyroodhouse 9**. Round off the day with an evening ascent of Arthur's Seat or, slightly less strenuously, Calton Hill. Both make great sunset viewpoints.

TAKING YOUR TIME

Minimum time needed for each attraction:

» **Edinburgh Castle:** two hours
» **Gladstone's Land:** 45 minutes
» **St Giles Cathedral:** 30 minutes
» **Real Mary King's Close:** one hour (tour)
» **Scottish Parliament:** one hour (tour)
» **Palace of Holyroodhouse:** one hour

Real Mary King's Close
The guided tour is heavy on ghost stories, but a highlight is standing in an original 17th-century room with tufts of horsehair poking from the crumbling plaster, and breathing in the ancient scent of stone, dust and history.

Canongate Kirk

CANONGATE

ST MARY'S ST

SOUTH BRIDGE

Our Dynamic Earth

Palace of Holyroodhouse
Find the secret staircase joining Mary, Queen of Scots' bedchamber with that of her husband, Lord Darnley, who restrained the queen while his henchmen stabbed to death her secretary (and possible lover), David Rizzio.

Scottish Parliament
Don't have time for the guided tour? Pick up a 'Discover the Scottish Parliament Building' leaflet from reception and take a self-guided tour of the exterior, then hike up to Salisbury Crags for a great view of the complex.

St Giles Cathedral
Look out for the Burne-Jones stained-glass window (1873) at the west end, showing the crossing of the River Jordan, and the bronze memorial to Robert Louis Stevenson in the Moray Aisle.

COLIN PALMER PHOTOGRAPHY/ALAMY ©

JEAN-CHRISTOPHE GODET/ALAMY ©

Gladstone's Land
HISTORIC BUILDING

(NTS; Map p758; www.nts.org.uk; 477 Lawnmarket; adult/child £6/5; ☺10am-6.30pm Jul & Aug, to 5pm Apr-Jun & Sep-Oct) One of Edinburgh's most prominent 17th-century merchants was Thomas Gledstanes, who in 1617 purchased the tenement later known as Gladstone's Land. It contains fine painted ceilings, walls and beams, and some splendid furniture from the 17th and 18th centuries. The volunteer guides provide a wealth of anecdotes and a detailed history.

St Giles Cathedral
CHURCH

(Map p758; www.stgilescathedral.org.uk; High St; suggested donation £3; ☺9am-7pm Mon-Fri, 9am-5pm Sat, 1-5pm Sun May-Sep, 9am-5pm Mon-Sat, 1-5pm Sun Oct-Apr) Dominating the high street is the great grey bulk of St Giles Cathedral. Properly called the High Kirk of Edinburgh (it was only a true cathedral – the seat of a bishop – from 1633 to 1638 and from 1661 to 1689), St Giles Cathedral was named after the patron saint of cripples and beggars. A Norman-style church was built here in 1126 but was destroyed by English invaders in 1385; the only substantial remains are the central piers that support the tower.

The present church dates largely from the 15th century – the beautiful crown spire was completed in 1495 – but much of it was restored in the 19th century. The interior lacks grandeur but is rich in history: St Giles was at the heart of the Scottish Reformation, and John Knox served as minister here from 1559 to 1572. One of the most interesting corners of the kirk is the Thistle Chapel, built in 1911 for the Knights of the Most Ancient & Most Noble Order of the Thistle. The elaborately carved Gothic-style stalls have canopies topped with the helms and arms of the 16 knights – look out for the bagpipe-playing angel amid the vaulting.

By the side of the street, outside the western door of St Giles, is the Heart of Midlothian, set into the cobblestone paving. This marks the site of the Tolbooth. Built in the 15th century and demolished in the early

Edinburgh Old Town

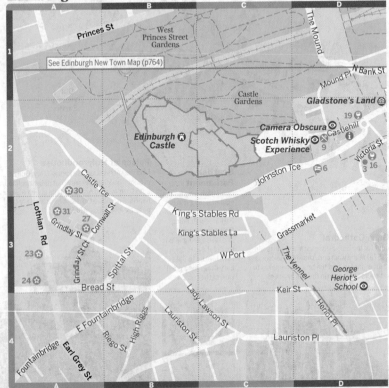

19th century, the Tolbooth served variously as a meeting place for parliament, the town council and the General Assembly of the Reformed Kirk, before becoming law courts and, finally, a notorious prison and place of execution. Passers-by traditionally spit on the heart for luck (don't stand downwind!).

At the other end of St Giles is the **Mercat Cross**, a 19th-century copy of the 1365 original, where merchants and traders met to transact business and royal proclamations were read.

Real Mary King's Close   HISTORIC BUILDING

(Map p758; ☏0845 070 6244; www.realmarykings close.com; 2 Warriston's Close, High St; adult/child £12.95/7.45; ◷10am-9pm Apr-Oct, to 11pm Aug, 10am-5pm Sun-Thu & 10am-9pm Fri & Sat Nov-Mar) Across from St Giles is the City Chambers, originally built by John Adam (brother of Robert) between 1753 and 1761 to serve as the Royal Exchange – a covered meeting place for city merchants. However, the merchants preferred their old stamping ground

in the street and the building became the city council offices in 1811.

Part of the Royal Exchange was built over the sealed-off remains of Mary King's Close, and the lower levels of this medieval Old Town alley have survived almost unchanged in the foundations of the City Chambers for 250 years. Now open to the public as the Real Mary King's Close, this spooky, subterranean labyrinth gives a fascinating insight into the daily life of 16th- and 17th-century Edinburgh. Costumed characters give tours through a 16th-century town house and the plague-stricken home of a 17th-century gravedigger. Advance booking recommended.

FREE **Museum of Edinburgh**   MUSEUM

(www.edinburghmuseums.org.uk; 142 Canongate; ◷10am-5pm Mon-Sat year-round, 2-5pm Sun Aug) You can't miss the colourful facade of Huntly House, newly renovated in bright red and yellow ochre, opposite the Tolbooth

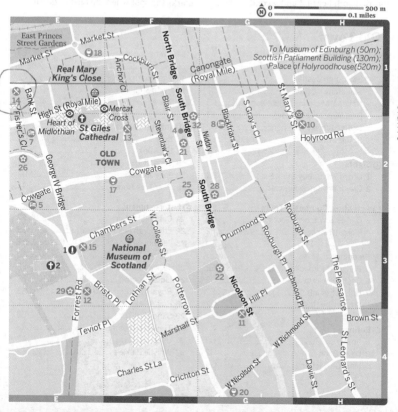

EDINBURGH SIGHTS

clock. Built in 1570, it houses a museum covering Edinburgh from its prehistory to the present. Exhibits of national importance include an original copy of the National Covenant of 1638, but the big crowd-pleaser is the dog collar and feeding bowl that once belonged to Greyfriars Bobby (p762), the city's most famous canine citizen.

HOLYROOD

Palace of Holyroodhouse   PALACE
(www.royalcollection.org.uk; adult/child £10.75/6.50; ☺9.30am-6pm Apr-Oct, to 4.30pm Nov-Mar)
This palace is the royal family's official residence in Scotland, but is more famous as the 16th-century home of the ill-fated Mary, Queen of Scots. The palace developed from a guesthouse, attached to Holyrood Abbey, which was extended by King James IV in 1501. The oldest surviving part of the building, the northwestern tower, was built in 1529 as a royal apartment for James V and his wife, Mary of Guise. Mary, Queen of Scots spent six turbulent years here, during which time she debated with John Knox, married both her first and second husbands, and witnessed the murder of her secretary David Rizzio. The palace is closed to the public when the royal family is visiting and during state functions (usually in mid-May, and mid-June to early July; check the website for exact dates).

The self-guided audio tour leads you through a series of impressive royal apartments, ending in the Great Gallery. The 89 portraits of Scottish kings were commissioned by Charles II and supposedly record his unbroken lineage from Scota, the Egyptian pharaoh's daughter who discovered the infant Moses in a reed basket on the banks of the Nile.

But the highlight of the tour is Mary, Queen of Scots' Bed Chamber, home to the unfortunate Mary from 1561 to 1567, and connected by a secret stairway to her husband's bedchamber. It was here that her jealous first husband, Lord Darnley, restrained the pregnant queen while his henchmen murdered her secretary – and favourite – Rizzio. A plaque in the neighbouring room marks the spot where he bled to death.

Old Town

UNDERGROUND EDINBURGH

As Edinburgh expanded in the late 18th and early 19th centuries, many old tenements were demolished and new bridges were built to link the Old Town to the newly built areas to its north and south. South Bridge (built between 1785 and 1788) and George IV Bridge (built between 1829 and 1834) lead southwards from the Royal Mile over the deep valley of Cowgate, but so many buildings have been built closely around them that you can hardly tell they are bridges – George IV Bridge has a total of nine arches but only two are visible; South Bridge has no less than 18 hidden arches.

These subterranean vaults were originally used as storerooms, workshops and drinking dens. But as early-19th-century Edinburgh's population was swelled by an influx of penniless Highlanders cleared from their lands, and Irish refugees from the potato famine, the dark, dripping chambers were given over to slum accommodation and abandoned to poverty, filth and crime.

The vaults were eventually cleared in the late 19th century, then lay forgotten until 1994 when the South Bridge Vaults were opened to guided tours. Certain chambers are said to be haunted and one particular vault was investigated by paranormal researchers in 2001.

Nevertheless, the most ghoulish aspect of Edinburgh's hidden history dates from much earlier – from the plague that struck the city in 1645. Legend has it that the disease-ridden inhabitants of Mary King's Close (a lane on the northern side of the Royal Mile on the site of the City Chambers – you can still see its blocked-off northern end from Cockburn St) were walled up in their houses and left to perish. When the lifeless bodies were eventually cleared from the houses, they were so stiff that workmen had to hack off limbs to get them through the small doorways and narrow, twisting stairs.

From that day on, the close was said to be haunted by the spirits of the plague victims. The few people who were prepared to live there reported seeing apparitions of severed heads and limbs, and the largely abandoned close fell into ruin. When the Royal Exchange (now the City Chambers) was constructed between 1753 and 1761, it was built over the lower levels of Mary King's Close, which were left intact and sealed off beneath the building.

Interest in the close revived in the 20th century when Edinburgh's city council began to allow occasional guided tours to enter. Visitors have reported many supernatural experiences – the most famous ghost is 'Sarah', a little girl whose sad tale has prompted people to leave gifts of dolls in a corner of one of the rooms. In 2003 the close was opened to the public as the Real Mary King's Close (p759).

Holyrood Park
PARK

In Holyrood Park Edinburgh is blessed with a little bit of wilderness in the heart of the city. The former hunting ground of Scottish monarchs, the park covers 263 hectares of varied landscape, including crags, moorland and loch. The highest point is the 251m summit of Arthur's Seat, the deeply eroded remnant of a long-extinct volcano. Holyrood Park can be circumnavigated by car or bike along Queen's Dr, and you can hike from Holyrood to the summit in around 45 minutes.

SOUTH OF THE ROYAL MILE

FREE National Museum
of Scotland
MUSEUM

(Map p758; www.nms.ac.uk; Chambers St; fee for special exhibitions; ◉10am-5pm) Broad, elegant Chambers St is dominated by the long facade of the National Museum of Scotland. Its extensive collections are spread between two buildings, one modern, one Victorian. The museum reopened to the public in 2011 after two years of major renovation and reconstruction.

The golden stone and striking modern architecture of the museum's new building, opened in 1998, is one of the city's most distinctive landmarks. The five floors of the museum trace the history of Scotland from geological beginnings to the 1990s, with many imaginative and stimulating exhibits – audioguides are available in several languages.

The new building connects with the original Victorian museum, dating from 1861, the stolid, grey exterior of which gives way to a bright and airy, glass-roofed hall. The museum houses an eclectic collection covering natural history, archaeology, scientific and industrial technology, and the decorative arts of ancient Egypt, Islam, China, Japan, Korea and the West.

SCOTTISH PARLIAMENT BUILDING

The Scottish Parliament Building ([icon]0131-348 5200; www.scottish.parliament.uk; admission free; ⊙9am-6.30pm Tue-Thu, 10am-5.30pm Mon & Fri in session, 10am-6pm Mon-Fri in recess Apr-Oct, 10am-4pm in recess Nov-Mar), built on the site of a former brewery close to the Palace of Holyroodhouse, was officially opened by HM the Queen in October 2005.

The public areas of the parliament building – the Main Hall, where there is an exhibition, a shop and a cafe, and the public gallery in the Debating Chamber – are open to visitors (tickets needed for public gallery; see website for details). You can also take a free, one-hour guided tour (advance booking recommended) that includes a visit to the Debating Chamber, a committee room, the Garden Lobby and, when possible, the office of an MSP (Member of the Scottish Parliament). If you want to see the parliament in session, check the website to see when it will be sitting – business days are normally Tuesday to Thursday year-round.

Enric Miralles (1955–2000), the architect who conceived the Scottish Parliament Building, believed that a building could be a work of art. However, the weird concrete confection that has sprouted at the foot of Salisbury Crags has left the good people of Edinburgh staring and scratching their heads in confusion. What does it all mean? The strange forms of the exterior are all symbolic in some way, from the oddly shaped windows on the west wall (inspired by the silhouette of the *Reverend Robert Walker Skating on Duddingston Loch,* one of Scotland's most famous paintings), to the ground plan of the whole complex, which represents a 'flower of democracy rooted in Scottish soil' (best seen looking down from Salisbury Crags).

The Main Hall, inside the public entrance, has a low, triple-arched ceiling of polished concrete, like a cave, or cellar, or castle vault. It is a dimly lit space, the starting point for a metaphorical journey from this relative darkness up to the Debating Chamber (sitting directly above the Main Hall), which is, in contrast, a palace of light – the light of democracy. This magnificent chamber is the centrepiece of the parliament, designed not to glorify but to humble the politicians who sit within it. The windows face Calton Hill, allowing MSPs to look up to its monuments (reminders of the Scottish Enlightenment), while the massive, pointed oak beams of the roof are suspended by steel threads above the MSPs' heads like so many Damoclean swords.

FREE Greyfriars Kirk & Kirkyard   CHURCH, CEMETERY
(Map p758; www.greyfriarskirk.com; Candlemaker Row; ⊙10.30am-4.30pm Mon-Fri & 11am-2pm Sat Apr-Oct, 1.30-3.30pm Thu only Nov-Mar) One of Edinburgh's most famous churches, Greyfriars Kirk was built on the site of a Franciscan friary and opened for worship on Christmas Day 1620. In 1638 the National Covenant was signed here, rejecting Charles I's attempts to impose episcopacy and a new English prayer book on the Scots, and affirming the independence of the Scottish Church. Many who signed were later executed at the Grassmarket and, in 1679, 1200 Covenanters were held prisoner in terrible conditions in the southwestern corner of the kirkyard. There's a small exhibition inside the church.

Surrounding the church, hemmed in by high walls and overlooked by the brooding presence of the castle, Greyfriars Kirkyard is one of Edinburgh's most evocative cemeteries, a peaceful green oasis dotted with elaborate monuments. Many famous Edinburgh names are buried here, including poet Allan Ramsay (1686–1758), architect William Adam (1689–1748) and William Smellie (1740–95), editor of the first edition of the *Encyclopædia Britannica.*

If you want to experience the graveyard at its scariest – inside a burial vault, in the dark, at night – go on one of Black Hart Storytellers (p767) guided tours.

Greyfriars Bobby Statue   MONUMENT
(Map p758) The memorials inside Greyfriars Kirkyard are interesting, but the one that draws the biggest crowds is outside, opposite the pub beside the kirkyard gate. It's the tiny statue of Greyfriars Bobby, a Skye terrier who, from 1858 to 1872, maintained a vigil over the grave of his master, an Edinburgh police officer. The story was immortalised in a novel by Eleanor Atkinson

in 1912, and in 1963 was made into a movie by – who else? – Walt Disney. Bobby's own grave, marked by a small, pink granite stone, is just inside the entrance to the kirkyard. You can see his original collar and bowl in the Museum of Edinburgh.

NEW TOWN

Edinburgh's New Town lies north of the Old Town, on a ridge running parallel to the Royal Mile and separated from it by the valley of Princes Street Gardens. Its regular grid of elegant, neoclassical terraces is the world's most complete and unspoilt example of Georgian architecture and town planning. Along with the Old Town, it was declared a Unesco World Heritage Site in 1995.

PRINCES STREET

Princes St is one of the world's most spectacular shopping streets. Built up on the north side only, it catches the sun in summer and allows expansive views across Princes Street Gardens to the castle and the crowded skyline of the Old Town.

Princes Street Gardens lie in a valley that was once occupied by the Nor' Loch, a boggy depression that was drained in the early 19th century. The gardens are split in the middle by The Mound, which was created by around two million cart-loads of earth excavated from the foundations of New Town being dumped here to provide a road link across the valley to the Old Town. It was completed in 1830.

Scott Monument   MONUMENT
(Map p764; www.edinburghmuseums.org.uk; East Princes Street Gardens; admission £3; ☉10am-7pm Mon-Sat Apr-Sep, 9am-4pm Mon-Sat Oct-Mar, 10am-6pm Sun year-round) The eastern half of Princes Street Gardens is dominated by the massive Gothic spire of the Scott Monument, built by public subscription in memory of the novelist Sir Walter Scott after his death in 1832. The exterior is decorated with carvings of characters from his novels; inside you can see an exhibition on Scott's life, and climb the 287 steps to the top for a superb view of the city.

FREE Scottish National Gallery   GALLERY
(Map p764; www.nationalgalleries.org; The Mound; fee for special exhibitions; ☉10am-5pm Fri-Wed, to 7pm Thu) Designed by William Playfair, this imposing classical building with its Ionic porticoes dates from the 1850s. Its octagonal rooms, lit by skylights, have been restored to their original Victorian decor of deep-green carpets and dark-red walls.

The gallery houses an important collection of European art from the Renaissance to post-Impressionism, with works by Verrocchio (Leonardo da Vinci's teacher), Tintoretto, Titian, Holbein, Rubens, Van Dyck, Vermeer, El Greco, Poussin, Rembrandt, Gainsborough, Turner, Constable, Monet, Pissarro, Gauguin and Cézanne; each year in January the gallery exhibits its collection of Turner watercolours, bequeathed by Henry Vaughan in 1900. Room X is graced by Antonio Canova's white marble sculpture The Three Graces; it is owned jointly with London's Victoria and Albert Museum.

The upstairs galleries house portraits by Sir Joshua Reynolds and Sir Henry Raeburn, and a clutch of Impressionist paintings including Monet's luminous *Haystacks,* Van Gogh's demonic *Olive Trees* and Gauguin's hallucinatory *Vision After the Sermon.* But the painting that really catches your eye is the gorgeous portrait of *Lady Agnew of Lochnaw* by John Singer Sargent.

The basement galleries dedicated to Scottish art include glowing portraits by Allan Ramsay and Sir Henry Raeburn, rural scenes by Sir David Wilkie and impressionistic landscapes by William MacTaggart. Look out for Raeburn's iconic *Reverend Robert Walker Skating on Duddingston Loch,* and Sir George Harvey's hugely entertaining *A Schule Skailin* (A School Emptying) – a stern dominie (teacher) looks on as the boys stampede for the classroom door, one reaching for a spinning top confiscated earlier. Kids will love the fantasy paintings of Sir Joseph Noel Paton in Room B5; the incredibly detailed canvases are crammed with hundreds of tiny fairies, goblins and elves.

GEORGE STREET & AROUND

Until the 1990s George St – the major axis of New Town – was the centre of Edinburgh's financial industry and Scotland's equivalent of Wall St. Today the big financial firms have moved to premises in the Exchange office district west of Lothian Rd, and George St's former banks and offices house upmarket shops, pubs and restaurants.

At the western end of George St is Charlotte Square, the architectural jewel of New Town, designed by Robert Adam shortly before his death in 1791. The northern side of the square is Adam's masterpiece and one of the finest examples of Georgian architecture anywhere. Bute House, in the

Edinburgh New Town

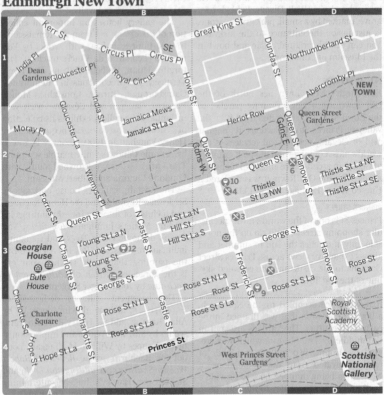

New Town

centre at No 6, is the official residence of Scotland's first minister.

Not as architecturally distinguished as its sister at the opposite end of George St, **St Andrew Square** is dominated by the fluted column of the Melville Monument, commemorating Henry Dundas, 1st Viscount Melville (1742–1811).

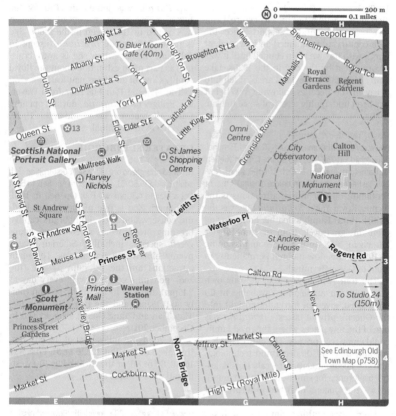

Georgian House   HISTORIC BUILDING

(NTS; Map p764; 7 Charlotte Sq; adult/child £6/5; ⊙10am-6pm Jul & Aug, 10am-5pm Apr-Jun & Sep-Oct, 11am-4pm Mar, 11am-3pm Nov) The National Trust for Scotland's Georgian House has been beautifully restored and furnished to show how Edinburgh's wealthy elite lived at the end of the 18th century. The walls are decorated with paintings by Allan Ramsay, Sir Henry Raeburn and Sir Joshua Reynolds.

FREE Scottish National
Portrait Gallery   GALLERY

(Map p764; www.nationalgalleries.org; 1 Queen St; ⊙10am-5pm Fri-Wed, to 7pm Thu) The Venetian Gothic palace of the Scottish National Portrait Gallery reopened its doors in 2011 after a two-year renovation, emerging as one of the city's top attractions. Its galleries illustrate Scottish history through paintings, photographs and sculptures, putting faces to famous names from Scotland's past and present, from Robert Burns, Mary, Queen of Scots and Bonnie Prince Charlie to Sean Connery, Billy Connolly and poet Jackie Kay.

CALTON HILL

Calton Hill (100m), rising dramatically above the eastern end of Princes St, is Edinburgh's acropolis, its summit scattered with grandiose memorials mostly dating from the first half of the 19th century. It is also one of the best viewpoints in Edinburgh, with a panorama that takes in the castle, Holyrood, Arthur's Seat, the Firth of Forth, New Town and the full length of Princes St.

Looking a bit like an upturned telescope – the similarity is intentional – and offering even better views, the Nelson Monument (Map p764; admission £3; ⊙10am-7pm Mon-Sat & noon-5pm Sun Apr-Sep, 10am-3pm Mon-Sat Oct-Mar; ⊡all Leith St buses) was built to commemorate Admiral Lord Nelson's victory at Trafalgar in 1805.

LEITH

Two miles northeast of the city centre, Leith has been Edinburgh's seaport since the 14th century and remained an independent burgh with its own town council until it was incorporated by the city in the 1920s. Like many of Britain's dockland areas, it fell into decay in the decades following WWII but has been undergoing a revival since the late 1980s.

Royal Yacht Britannia   HISTORIC VESSEL

(www.royalyachtbritannia.co.uk; Ocean Terminal; adult/child £11.75/7.50; ⊘9.30am-4.30pm Jul-Sep, 9.30am-4pm Apr-Jun & Oct, 10am-3.30pm Nov-Mar, last admission 90min before closing) One of Scotland's biggest tourist attractions is the former Royal Yacht *Britannia*. She was the British Royal Family's floating home during their foreign travels from the time of her launch in 1953 until her decommissioning in 1997, and is now moored permanently in front of Ocean Terminal.

The tour, which you take at your own pace with an audioguide (available in 20 languages), gives an intriguing insight into the Queen's private tastes – *Britannia* was one of the few places where the royal family could enjoy true privacy. The entire ship is a monument to 1950s decor and technology, and the accommodation reveals Her Majesty's preference for simple, unfussy surroundings – the Queen's own bed is surprisingly tiny and plain.

There was nothing simple or unfussy, however, about the running of the ship. When the Queen travelled, along with her went 45 members of the royal household, five tonnes of luggage and a Rolls-Royce that was carefully squeezed into a specially built garage on the deck. The ship's company consisted of an admiral, 20 officers and 220 yachtsmen. The decks (of Burmese teak) were scrubbed daily, but all work near the royal accommodation was carried out in complete silence and had to be finished by 8am. A thermometer was kept in the Queen's bathroom to make sure that the water was the correct temperature, and when in harbour one yachtsman was charged with ensuring that the angle of the gangway never exceeded 12 degrees. And note the mahogany windbreak that was added to the balcony deck in front of the bridge. It was put there to stop wayward breezes from blowing up skirts and inadvertently revealing the royal undies.

Britannia was joined in 2010 by the 1930s racing yacht Bloodhound, which was owned by the Queen in the 1960s. She is moored alongside *Britannia* (except in July and August, when she is away cruising) as part of an exhibition about the Royal Family's love of all things nautical.

The Majestic Tour bus runs from Waverley Bridge to *Britannia* during opening times. Alternatively, take Lothian Bus 11, 22, or 35 to Ocean Terminal.

GREATER EDINBURGH

Edinburgh Zoo   ZOO

(www.edinburghzoo.org.uk; 134 Corstorphine Rd; adult/child £15.50/11; ⊘9am-6pm Apr-Sep, to 5pm Oct & Mar, to 4.30pm Nov-Feb) Opened in 1913, Edinburgh Zoo is one of the world's leading conservation zoos. Edinburgh's captive breeding program has saved many endangered species, including Siberian tigers, pygmy hippos and red pandas. The main attractions are the penguin parade (the zoo's penguins go for a walk every day at 2.15pm), the sea lion training session (daily at 11.15am), and the two giant pandas, Tian Tian and Yang Guang, who arrived in December 2011.

The zoo is 2.5 miles west of the city centre; take Lothian Bus 12, 26 or 31, First Bus 16, 18, 80 or 86, or the Airlink Bus 100 westbound from Princes St.

FREE Royal Botanic Garden   GARDEN

(www.rbge.org.uk; 20a Inverleith Row; admission to glasshouses £4.50; ⊘10am-6pm Mar-Sep, to 5pm Feb & Oct, to 4pm Nov-Jan) Just north of Stockbridge is the lovely Royal Botanic Garden. Twenty-eight beautifully landscaped hectares include splendid Victorian palm houses, colourful swathes of rhododendron and azalea, and a world-famous rock garden. The Terrace Cafe offers good views towards the city centre.

Take Lothian Bus 8, 17, 23 or 27 to the East Gate, or the Majestic Tour bus.

Activities

Edinburgh is lucky to have several good walking areas within the city boundary, including Arthur's Seat, Calton Hill, Blackford Hill, Hermitage of Braid, Corstorphine Hill, and the coast and river at Cramond.

You can follow the Water of Leith Walkway from the city centre to Balerno (8 miles), and continue across the Pentlands to Silverburn (6.5 miles) or Carlops (8 miles),

ROSSLYN CHAPEL

The success of Dan Brown's novel *The Da Vinci Code* and the subsequent Hollywood film has seen a flood of visitors descend on Scotland's most beautiful and enigmatic church – Rosslyn Chapel (Collegiate Church of St Matthew; www.rosslynchapel.org.uk; adult/child £9/free; ⊙9.30am-6pm Mon-Sat, noon-4.45pm Sun). The chapel was built in the mid-15th century for William St Clair, third earl of Orkney, and the ornately carved interior – at odds with the architectural fashion of its time – is a monument to the mason's art, rich in symbolic imagery. As well as flowers, vines, angels and biblical figures, the carved stones include many examples of the pagan 'Green Man'; other figures are associated with Freemasonry and the Knights Templar. Intriguingly, there are also carvings of plants from the Americas that predate Columbus' voyage of discovery. The symbolism of these images has led some researchers to conclude that Rosslyn is some kind of secret Templar repository, and it has been claimed that hidden vaults beneath the chapel could conceal anything from the Holy Grail or the head of John the Baptist to the body of Christ himself. The chapel is owned by the Episcopal Church of Scotland and services are still held here on Sunday mornings.

The chapel is on the eastern edge of the village of Roslin, 7 miles south of Edinburgh's centre. Lothian Bus 15 (not 15A) runs from the west end of Princes St in Edinburgh to Roslin (£1.40, 30 minutes, every 30 minutes) via Penicuik (it may be faster to catch any bus to Penicuik, then the 15 to Roslin).

A refreshing alternative to the mainstream tours is offered by Celtic Trails (www.celtic trails.co.uk), whose knowledgeable owner Jackie Queally leads guided tours of Rosslyn Chapel and other ancient and sacred sites covering subjects such as Celtic mythology, geomancy, sacred geometry and the Knights Templar. A half-day tour of the chapel and surrounding area cost £130 for up to three people, plus £33 per person thereafter, not including admission fees.

and return to Edinburgh by bus. Another good walk is along the towpath of the Union Canal, which begins in Fountainbridge and runs all the way to Falkirk (31 miles).

☞ Tours

Walking Tours

There are plenty of organised walks around Edinburgh, many of them related to ghosts, murders and witches. For starting times of individual walks, check the tour websites.

Black Hart Storytellers   WALKING TOUR
(www.blackhart.uk.com; adult/concession £10/5) Not suitable for young children. The 'City of the Dead' tour of Greyfriars Kirkyard is probably the scariest of Edinburgh's 'ghost' tours. Many people have reported encounters with the 'McKenzie Poltergeist', the ghost of a 17th-century judge who persecuted the Covenanters, and now haunts their former prison in a corner of the kirkyard.

Cadies & Witchery Tours   WALKING TOUR
(Map p758; www.witcherytours.com; adult/child £8.50/6) The becloaked and pasty-faced Adam Lyal (deceased) leads a 'Murder & Mystery' tour of the Old Town's darker corners. These tours are famous for their 'jumper-ooters' – meaning costumed actors who 'jump oot' when you least expect it.

Edinburgh Literary Pub Tour   WALKING TOUR
(www.edinburghliterarypubtour.co.uk; adult/student £10/8) An enlightening two-hour trawl through the city's literary history – and its associated howffs (pubs) – in the entertaining company of Messrs Clart and McBrain. One of the city's best walking tours.

Mercat Tours   WALKING TOUR
(Map p758; www.mercattours.com; adult/child £10/5) Mercat offers a wide range of fascinating tours including history walks in the Old Town and Leith, 'Ghosts & Ghouls' tours and visits to haunted underground vaults.

Rebus Tours   WALKING TOUR
(www.rebustours.com; adult/student £10/9) Tours of the 'hidden Edinburgh' frequented by novelist Ian Rankin's fictional detective John Rebus. Not recommended for children under 10.

Bus Tours

Open-topped buses leave from Waverley Bridge outside the main train station and

Rosslyn Chapel

DECIPHERING ROSSLYN

Rosslyn Chapel is a small building, but the density of decoration inside can be overwhelming. It's well worth buying the official guidebook by the Earl of Rosslyn first; find a bench in the gardens and have a skim through before going into the chapel – the background information will make your visit all the more interesting. The book also offers a useful self-guided tour of the chapel, and explains the legend of the Master Mason and the Apprentice.

Entrance is through the north door **1**. Take a pew and sit for a while to allow your eyes to adjust to the dim interior; then look up at the ceiling vault, decorated with engraved roses, lilies and stars, (Can you spot the sun and the moon?). Walk left along the north aisle to reach the Lady Chapel, separated from the rest of the church by the **Mason's Pillar 2** and the **Apprentice Pillar 3**. Here you'll find carvings of **Lucifer 4**, the Fallen Angel, and the **Green Man 5**. Nearby are carvings **6** that appear to resemble Indian corn (maize). Finally, go to the western end and look up at the wall – in the left corner is the head of the **Apprentice 7**; to the right is the (rather worn) head of the **Master Mason 8**.

ROSSLYN CHAPEL & THE DA VINCI CODE

» Dan Brown was referencing Rosslyn Chapel's alleged links to the Knights Templar and the Freemasons – unusual symbols found among the carvings, and the fact that a descendant of its founder, William St Clair, was a Grand Master Mason – when he chose it as the setting for his novel's denouement. Rosslyn is indeed a coded work, written in stone, but its meaning depends on your point of view. See *The Rosslyn Hoax?* by Robert LD Cooper (www.rosslynhoax.com) for an alternative interpretation of the chapel's symbolism.

SANDRO VANNINI/CORBIS ©

Explore Some More

After visiting the chapel, head downhill to see the spectacularly sited ruins of Roslin Castle, then take a walk along leafy Roslin Glen.

Lucifer, the Fallen Angel

At head height, to the left of the second window from the left, is an upside-down angel bound with rope, a symbol often associated with Freemasonry. The arch above is decorated with the Dance of Death.

The Apprentice

High in the corner, beneath an empty statue niche, is the head of the murdered Apprentice, with a deep wound in his forehead above the right eye. Legend says the Apprentice was murdered in a jealous rage by the Master Mason. The worn head on the side wall to the left of the Apprentice is that of his mother.

The Master Mason

8

Baptistery

Practical Tips

Buy your tickets in advance through the chapel's website (except in August, when no bookings are taken). No photography is allowed inside the chapel.

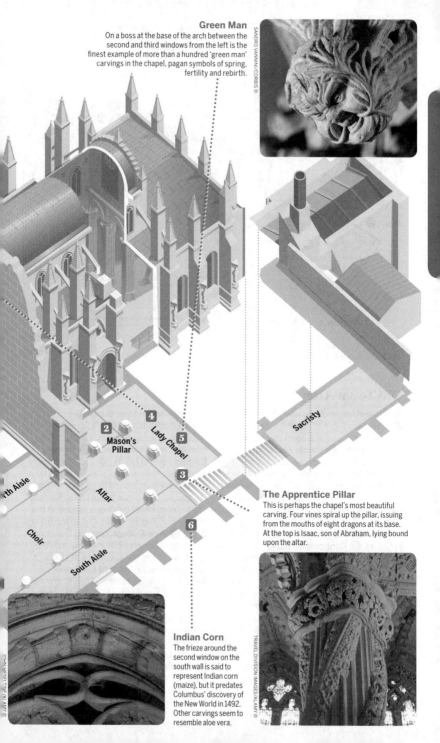

Green Man
On a boss at the base of the arch between the second and third windows from the left is the finest example of more than a hundred 'green man' carvings in the chapel, pagan symbols of spring, fertility and rebirth.

SANDRO VANNINI/CORBIS ©

2 Mason's Pillar

4

5 Lady Chapel

3

Sacristy

North Aisle

Altar

Choir

South Aisle

6

The Apprentice Pillar
This is perhaps the chapel's most beautiful carving. Four vines spiral up the pillar, issuing from the mouths of eight dragons at its base. At the top is Isaac, son of Abraham, lying bound upon the altar.

TRAVEL DIVISION IMAGES/ALAMY ©

Indian Corn
The frieze around the second window on the south wall is said to represent Indian corn (maize), but it predates Columbus' discovery of the New World in 1492. Other carvings seem to resemble aloe vera.

JOHN WEST LTD/ALAMY ©

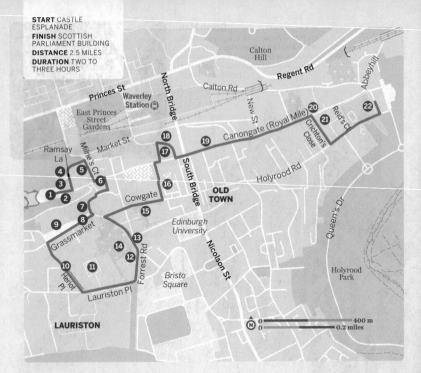

Walking Tour
Old Town Alleys

❯ This walk explores the alleys and side streets around the Royal Mile, and involves a bit of climbing up and down steep stairs.

Begin on the ① **Castle Esplanade**, which provides a grandstand view south over the Grassmarket; the prominent quadrangular building with all the turrets is George Heriot's School, which you'll be passing later on. Head towards Castlehill and the start of the Royal Mile.

The 17th-century house on the right is known as ② **Cannonball House** because of the iron ball lodged in the wall (look between, and slightly below, the two largest windows on the wall facing the castle). It was not fired in anger, but marks the gravitation height to which water would flow naturally from the city's first piped water supply.

The low, rectangular building across the street (now a touristy tartan-weaving mill) was originally the reservoir that held the Old Town's water supply. On its west wall is the ③ **Witches Well**, where a bronze fountain commemorates around 4000 people (mostly women) who were executed between 1479 and 1722 on suspicion of witchcraft.

Go past the reservoir and turn left down Ramsay Lane. Take a look at ④ **Ramsay Garden** – one of Edinburgh's most desirable addresses – where late 19th-century apartments were built around the octagonal Ramsay Lodge, once home to poet Allan Ramsay. The cobbled street continues around to the right below student residences, to the towers of the ⑤ **New College**, home to Edinburgh University's Faculty of Divinity. Nip into the courtyard to see the statue of John Knox (a firebrand preacher who led the Protestant Reformation in Scotland and was instrumental in the creation of the Church of Scotland in 1560).

Just past New College turn right and climb the stairs into Milne's Court, a student residence belonging to Edinburgh University. Exit into Lawnmarket, cross the street (bearing slightly left) and duck into ⑥ **Riddell's Court** at No 322-328, a typical Old Town close. You'll find yourself in a small courtyard, but the house in front of you (built in 1590) was originally the edge of the street (the building you just walked under was added in 1726 – look for the inscription in the doorway on the right). The arch with the inscription *Vivendo discimus* (we live and learn) leads into the original 16th-century courtyard.

Go back into the street, turn right and right again down Fisher's Close, which leads to the delightful Victoria Tce, strung above the cobbled curve of shop-lined Victoria St. Wander right, enjoying the view – **7** **Maxie's Bistro**, at the far end of the terrace, is a great place to stop for a drink – then descend the stairs at the foot of Upper Bow and continue downhill to the Grassmarket. At the east end, outside Maggie Dickson's pub, is the **8** **Covenanters Monument**, which marks the site of the gallows where more than 100 Covenanters were martyred in the 17th century.

If you're peckish, the Grassmarket has several places to eat and a couple of good pubs – poet Robert Burns once stayed at the **9** **White Hart Inn**. Go to the west end of the Grassmarket and turn left up the stairs known as The Vennel. At the top, on the left, you'll find the **10** **Flodden Wall**, one of the few surviving fragments of the city wall that was built in the early 16th century as protection against a feared English invasion. Follow its extension, the Telfer Wall, to Lauriston Pl and turn left along the impressive facade of **11** **George Heriot's School**, built in the 17th century with funds bequeathed by George Heriot (goldsmith and banker to King James VI). It was originally a school and home for orphaned children, but became a fee-paying public school in 1886. Note this is the back of the building – the front was designed to face the castle and impress the inhabitants of the Grassmarket.

Turn left at Forrest Rd, and if it's a Sunday afternoon pop into **12** **Sandy Bell's** for a pint and some Scottish folk music; otherwise, pause for a photo opportunity with the statue of **13** **Greyfriars Bobby**, then take a stroll through atmospheric **14** **Greyfriars Kirkyard**. Descend Candlemakers Row and turn right at the bottom into the Cowgate.

Pass under the arch of George IV Bridge – the buildings to your right are the new Law Courts, while high up to the left are the complex of buildings behind Parliament Sq. Past the courts on the right is **15** **Tailors Hall** (built 1621, extended 1757), now a hotel and bar but formerly the meeting place of the Companie of Tailzeours (Tailors' Guild).

Turn left and climb Old Fishmarket Close, and perhaps stop for lunch at the little brasserie, **16** **Passepartout**. Emerge once more onto the Royal Mile – across the street and slightly downhill is **17** **Anchor Close**, named for a tavern that once stood there. It hosted the Crochallan Fencibles, an 18th-century drinking club that provided its patrons with an agreeable blend of intellectual debate and intoxicating liquor. The club was founded by William Smellie, editor of the first edition of the *Encyclopædia Britannica;* its best-known member was Robert Burns.

Go down Anchor Close, which leads to Cockburn St, one of the city's coolest shopping streets, lined with record shops and clothes boutiques. The street was cut through the Old Town tenements in the 1850s to provide an easy route between Waverley Station and the Royal Mile. Turn right and head uphill. Look up high above **18** **55-57 Cockburn St** (on the left) – on either side of the gable are the carved figures of an owl and a grotesque cat-like creature with huge claws and fangs. Their origin and meaning are unknown.

At the top of Cockburn St turn left along the Royal Mile, and pause at **19** **Paisley Close**, beneath a protruding castellated window. Above the entrance is a carving of a young man's head, and the words 'Heave awa' chaps, I'm no dead yet'. This is a monument to a young man who survived a tenement collapse in 1861; his rescuers heard him yell these words from beneath a pile of debris.

Continue down the Royal Mile and look for the first alley on the left after Canongate Kirk. This is **20** **Dunbar's Close**, which leads to a hidden garden laid out in 17th-century style. Across the street and slightly downhill (beside Starbucks) follow Crichton's Close past the **21** **Scottish Poetry Library**, an architectural-award-winning modern building, to Holyrood Rd. Turn left to finish outside the **22** **Scottish Parliament Building**, beneath the imposing skyline of Salisbury Crags.

offer hop-on/hop-off tours of the main sights, taking in New Town, the Grassmarket and the Royal Mile. They're a good way to get your bearings, although with a bus map and a Day Saver bus ticket (£3) you could do much the same thing but without the commentary. Tours run daily, year-round, except for 24 and 25 December.

Tickets for the following two tours remain valid for 24 hours.

City Sightseeing

BUS TOUR

(www.edinburghtour.com; adult/child £12/5) Bright-red open-top buses depart every 20 minutes from Waverley Bridge.

Majestic Tour

BUS TOUR

(www.edinburghtour.com; adult/child £12/5) Runs every 30 minutes (every 20 minutes in July and August) from Waverley Bridge to the Royal Yacht *Britannia* at Ocean Terminal via the New Town, Royal Botanic Garden and Newhaven, returning via Leith Walk, Holyrood and the Royal Mile.

★ Festivals & Events

April

Edinburgh International Science Festival

SCIENCE

(www.sciencefestival.co.uk) First held in 1987, this festival hosts a wide range of events including talks, lectures, exhibitions, demonstrations, guided tours and interactive experiments designed to stimulate, inspire and challenge. From dinosaurs to ghosts to alien life forms, there's something to interest everyone. The festival runs over two weeks in April.

May

Imaginate Festival

ARTS

(www.imaginate.org.uk) This is Britain's biggest festival of performing arts for children, with events suitable for kids from three to 12. Groups from around the world perform classic tales like *Hansel and Gretel* as well as new material written specially for children. The festival takes place annually in the last week of May.

June

Scottish Real Ale Festival

FOOD & DRINK

(www.scottishbeerfestival.org.uk) A celebration of all things fermented and yeasty, Scotland's biggest beer-fest gives you the opportunity to sample a wide range of traditionally brewed beers from Scotland and around the world. Froth-topped bliss. The festival is held over a weekend in June.

Royal Highland Show

AGRICULTURAL SHOW

(www.royalhighlandshow.org; Royal Highland Centre) Scotland's hugely popular national agricultural show is a four-day feast of all things rural, with everything from show-jumping and tractor-driving to sheep-shearing and falconry. Countless pens are filled with coiffed show-cattle and pedicured prize ewes. The show is held over a long weekend (Thursday to Sunday) in late June.

Edinburgh International Film Festival

FILM

(www.edfilmfest.org.uk) One of the original Edinburgh Festival trinity, having first been staged in 1947 along with the International Festival and the Fringe, this two-week film festival is a major international event, serving as a showcase for new British and European films, and staging the European premieres of one or two Hollywood blockbusters.

July

Edinburgh International Jazz & Blues Festival

MUSIC FESTIVAL

(www.edinburghjazzfestival.com) Held annually since 1978, the Jazz & Blues Festival pulls in top talent from all over the world. The festival runs for nine days, beginning on a Friday, a week before the Fringe and Tattoo begin. The first weekend sees a Mardi Gras–style festival in the Grassmarket on Saturday, and a Sunday carnival on Princes St and in Princes Street Gardens, with an afternoon of free open-air music.

August

Half a dozen world-class events run simultaneously. See boxed text opposite.

December

Edinburgh's Christmas

CHRISTMAS

(www.edinburghchristmas.com) The youngest of the Scottish capital's festivals, first held in 2000, the Christmas bash includes a big street parade, a fairground and Ferris wheel, and an open-air ice rink in Princes Street Gardens. The celebrations are held over the three weeks before Christmas Day.

Edinburgh's Hogmanay

WINTER

(www.edinburghshogmanay.com) Edinburgh's Hogmanay is the biggest winter festival in Europe. Events run from 29 December to 1 January, and include a torchlight procession, a huge street party and a New Year's Day triathlon. To get into the main party area in the city centre after 8pm on

FESTIVAL CITY

August in Edinburgh sees a frenzy of festivals, with half a dozen world-class events running at the same time.

Edinburgh Festival Fringe (☎0131-226 0026; www.edfringe.com; 180 High St) When the first Edinburgh Festival was held in 1947, there were eight theatre companies who didn't make it onto the main program. Undeterred, they grouped together and held their own mini-festival, on the fringe, and an Edinburgh institution was born. Today the Edinburgh Festival Fringe is the biggest festival of the performing arts anywhere in the world. The Fringe takes place over 3½ weeks in August, the last two weeks overlapping with the first two of the Edinburgh International Festival.

Edinburgh International Festival (☎0131-473 2099; www.eif.co.uk) First held in 1947 to mark a return to peace after the ordeal of WWII, the Edinburgh International Festival is festooned with superlatives – the oldest, the biggest, the most famous, the best in the world. The original was a modest affair, but today hundreds of the world's top musicians and performers congregate in Edinburgh for three weeks of diverse and inspirational music, opera, theatre and dance. The festival takes place over the three weeks ending on the first Saturday in September; the program is usually available from April. Tickets for popular events – especially music and opera – sell out quickly, so it's best to book as far in advance as possible. You can buy tickets in person at the **Hub** (☎0131-473 2000; www.thehub-edinburgh.com; Castlehill; admission free; ⊙ticket center 10am-5pm Mon-Sat), by phone or over the internet.

Edinburgh Military Tattoo (☎0131-225 1188; www.edintattoo.co.uk; Tattoo Office, 32 Market St) The month kicks off with the Edinburgh Military Tattoo, a spectacular display of military marching bands, massed pipes and drums, acrobats, cheerleaders and motorcycle display teams, all played out in front of the magnificent backdrop of the floodlit castle. The Tattoo takes place over the first three weeks of August (from a Friday to a Saturday); there's one show at 9pm Monday to Friday and two (at 7.30pm and 10.30pm) on Saturday, but no performance on Sunday.

Edinburgh International Book Festival (☎0845 373 5888; www.edbookfest.co.uk) Held in a little village of marquees in the middle of Charlotte Sq, the Edinburgh International Book Festival is a fun fortnight of talks, readings, debates, lectures, book signings and meet-the-author events, with a cafe and tented bookshop thrown in. The festival lasts for two weeks in August (usually the first two weeks of the Edinburgh International Festival).

31 December you'll need a ticket – book well in advance.

Sleeping

Edinburgh is not short of accommodation, but you can guarantee the city will be packed to the gills during the festival period (August) and over Hogmanay (New Year). If you want a room during these periods, book as far in advance as possible. In general, it's best to book ahead for accommodation at Easter and from mid-May to mid-September.

OLD TOWN

TOP CHOICE **Hotel Missoni** BOUTIQUE HOTEL £££
(Map p758; ☎0131-220 6666; www.hotelmissoni .com; 1 George IV Bridge; r £90-225; ☎) The Italian fashion house has established a style icon in the heart of the medieval Old Town with this bold statement of a hotel: modernistic architecture, black-and-white decor with well-judged splashes of colour, impeccably mannered staff and – most importantly – very comfortable bedrooms and bathrooms with lots of nice touches, from fresh milk in the minibar to plush bathrobes.

Smart City Hostel HOSTEL £
(Map p758; ☎0870 892 3000; www.smartcity hostels.com; 50 Blackfriars St; dm from £22, tr £107; @☎) A big (620 beds), bright, modern hostel that feels more like a hotel, with a convivial cafe where you can buy breakfast, and mod cons such as keycard access and secure charging stations for mobile phones, MP3 players and laptops. Lockers in every room, a huge bar and a central location just off the Royal Mile make this a favourite place to

stay for the young, party-mad crowd - don't expect a quiet night!

Castle Rock Hostel HOSTEL £

(Map p758; ☎0131-225 9666; www.scotlands-top-hostels.com; 15 Johnston Tce; dm/d £22/50; @🛜) With its bright, spacious, single-sex dorms, superb views and friendly staff, the 200-bed Castle Rock has lots to like. It has a great location (the only way to get closer to the castle would be to pitch a tent on the esplanade), a games room, a reading lounge and big-screen video nights.

Budget Backpackers HOSTEL £

(Map p758; ☎0131-226 6351; www.budgetbackpackers.com; 9 Cowgate; dm from £16, tw £54; @) This fun spot piles on the extras, with bike storage, pool tables, a laundry and a colourful chill-out lounge. You'll pay a little more for four-bunk dorms, but larger dorms are great value. The only downside is that prices increase at weekends, but otherwise it's a brilliant spot to doss.

NEW TOWN & AROUND

B+B Edinburgh HOTEL ££

(☎0131-225 5084; www.bb-edinburgh.com; 3 Rothesay Tce; s/d £99/140; 🛜) Built in 1883 as a grand home for the proprietor of the *Scotsman* newspaper, this Victorian extravaganza of carved oak, parquet floors, stained glass and elaborate fireplaces was given a designer makeover in 2011 to create a striking contemporary hotel. Rooms on the 2nd floor are the most spacious, but the smaller top-floor rooms enjoy the finest views – those at the front can see Edinburgh Castle, those at the back look across the Water of Leith to the Firth of Forth.

Tigerlily BOUTIQUE HOTEL £££

(Map p764; ☎0131-225 5005; www.tigerlilyedinburgh.co.uk; 125 George St; r from £175; 🛜) Georgian meets gorgeous at this glamorous, glittering boutique hotel (complete with its own nightclub) decked out in mirror mosaics, beaded curtains, swirling Timorous Beasties textiles and wall coverings, and atmospheric pink uplighting. Book the Georgian Suite (from £310) for a truly special romantic getaway.

Dene Guest House B&B ££

(☎0131-556 2700; www.deneguesthouse.com; 7 Eyre Pl; per person £25-50) The Dene is a friendly and informal place, set in a charming Georgian town house, with a welcoming owner and spacious bedrooms. The inex-

pensive single rooms make it ideal for solo travellers; children under 10 staying in their parents' room pay half price.

West End Hostel HOSTEL £

(☎0131-202 6107; www.hosteledinburgh.co.uk; 3 Clifton Tce; dm £18-22; 🛜) This relatively new hostel is still clean and bright, with six- to 16-bed dorms (including female-only ones), a coffee lounge with pool table, and a pleasant garden terrace out back. Handy for train travellers (Edinburgh Haymarket station is across the road), it's just a 10-minute walk from Princes St.

SOUTH EDINBURGH

TOP CHOICE Southside Guest House B&B ££

(☎0131-668 4422; www.southsideguesthouse.co.uk; 8 Newington Rd; s/d £70/90; 🛜) Though set in a typical Victorian terrace, the Southside transcends the traditional guesthouse category and feels more like a modern boutique hotel. Its eight stylish rooms ooze interior design, standing out from other Newington B&Bs through the clever use of bold colours and modern furniture.

45 Gilmour Rd B&B ££

(☎0131-667 3536; www.edinburghbedbreakfast.com; 45 Gilmour Rd; s/d £70/140) A peaceful setting, large garden and friendly owners contribute to the appeal of this Victorian terraced house, which overlooks the local bowling green. The decor is a blend of 19th- and 20th-century influences, with bold Victorian reds, pine floors and period fireplace in the lounge, a rocking horse and art-nouveau lamp in the hallway, and a 1930s vibe in the three spacious bedrooms. Located 1 mile southeast of the city centre.

Aonach Mor Guest House B&B ££

(☎0131-667 8694; www.aonachmor.com; 14 Kilmaurs Tce; r per person £33-70; @🛜) This elegant Victorian terraced house is located on a quiet back street and has seven bedrooms, beautifully decorated, with many original period features. Our favourite is the four-poster bedroom with polished mahogany furniture and period fireplace. Located 1 mile southeast of the city centre.

Sherwood Guest House B&B ££

(☎0131-667 1200; www.sherwood-edinburgh.com; 42 Minto St; s £65-85, d £75-100; P🛜) One of the most attractive guesthouses on Minto St's B&B strip, the Sherwood is a refurbished Georgian terraced house decked out with hanging baskets and shrubs. Inside are six en-suite rooms that combine Regency-style striped wallpaper with modern fabrics and pine furniture.

Argyle Backpackers HOSTEL £
(☑0131-667 9991; www.argyle-backpackers.co.uk; 14 Argyle Pl; dm £17-22, d & tw £45-65; ☎) The Argyle, spread across three adjacent terraced houses, is a quiet and relaxed hostel offering double and twin rooms as well as four- to 10-bed dorms (mixed sex). There is a comfortable TV lounge, an attractive little conservatory, and a pleasant walled garden at the back where you can sit outside in summer.

NORTHEAST EDINBURGH

TOP CHOICE **Sheridan Guest House** B&B ££
(☑0131-554 4107; www.sheridanedinburgh.co.uk; 1 Bonnington Tce, Newhaven Rd; s/d from £55/70; ☎) Flowerpots filled with colourful blooms line the steps of this little haven hidden away to the north of the New Town. The eight bedrooms (all en suite) blend crisp colours with contemporary furniture, stylish lighting and colourful paintings, which complement the house's clean-cut Georgian lines, while the breakfast menu adds omelettes, pancakes with maple syrup, and scrambled eggs with smoked salmon to the usual offerings. Take bus 11 from the city centre.

Ardmor House B&B ££
(☑0131-554 4944; www.ardmorhouse.com; 74 Pilrig St; s £60-85, d £85-170; ☎) The 'gay-owned, straight-friendly' Ardmor is a stylishly renovated Victorian house with five en-suite bedrooms, and all those little touches that make a place special – an open fire, thick towels, crisp white bed linen and free newspapers at breakfast.

Edinburgh Central Youth Hostel HOSTEL £
(SYHA; ☑0131-524 2090; www.edinburghcentral .org; 9 Haddington Pl, Leith Walk; dm/s/tw £25/49/74; @☎) This modern, purpose-built hostel, about half a mile north of Waverley train station, is a big (300 beds), flashy, five-star establishment with its own cafe-bistro as well as self-catering kitchen, smart and comfortable eight-bed dorms and private rooms, and mod cons including keycard entry and plasma TVs.

Millers 64 B&B ££
(☑0131-454 3666; www.millers64.com; 64 Pilrig St; s from £80, d £90-150; ☎) Luxury textiles, colourful cushions, stylish bathrooms and fresh flowers added to a warm Edinburgh

welcome make this Victorian town house a highly desirable address. There are just two bedrooms (and a minimum three-night stay during festival periods) so book well in advance.

 Eating

In the last decade there has been a boom in the number of restaurants in Edinburgh – the city now has more restaurants per head of population than any other UK city.

For good-value eats, head for the student-populated areas south of the city centre: Bruntsfield, Marchmont and Newington. Fine dining is concentrated in the New Town, Stockbridge and Leith.

OLD TOWN

TOP CHOICE **Ondine** SEAFOOD £££
(Map p758; ☑0131-226 1888; www.ondinerestaurant .co.uk; 2 George IV Bridge; mains £15-25; ☺lunch & dinner) Ondine is one of Edinburgh's finest seafood restaurants, with a menu based on sustainably sourced fish. Take an octopus-inspired seat at the curved Crustacean Bar and tuck into oysters Kilpatrick, lobster thermidor, a roast shellfish platter, or just good old haddock and chips (with minted pea purée, just to keep things posh). The two-course lunch (noon to 2.30pm) and pre-theatre (5pm to 6.30pm) menu costs £17.

TOP CHOICE **Porto & Fi** CAFE £
(Map p758; www.portofi.com; 9 North Bank St; mains £4-8; ☺10am-11pm Mon-Sat, 10am-9pm Sun) With its designer decor, a prime location overlooking The Mound, and a suprisingly sophisticated menu built around quality Scottish produce, this cafe is hard to beat for a breakfast of eggs Benedict or Stornoway black pudding (served till noon, all day Sunday) or lunch of smoked salmon cannelloni or roast fig and asparagus salad.

TOP CHOICE **Tower** SCOTTISH £££
(Map p758; ☑0131-225 3003; www.tower-restaurant .com; National Museum of Scotland, Chambers St; mains £16-30; ☺noon-11pm) Chic and sleek, with a great view of the castle, Tower is perched in a turret atop the National Museum of Scotland building. A star-studded guest list of celebrities has enjoyed its menu of quality Scottish food, simply prepared – try half a dozen oysters followed by roast partridge with chestnut stuffing. A two-/three-course pre-theatre menu (£16/22) is

BEST VALUE BISTROS

Many restaurants in Edinburgh offer good-value lunches. Here are a few suggestions from various parts of the city:

Urban Angel (Map p764; ☎0131-225 6215; www.urban-angel.co.uk; 121 Hanover St; mains £8-14; ☺9am-10pm Mon-Sat, 10am-5pm Sun; ☒☟) A wholesome deli that puts the emphasis on fair-trade, organic and locally sourced produce, Urban Angel also has a delightfully informal cafe-bistro that serves all-day brunch (porridge with honey, French toast, eggs Benedict), tapas, and a wide range of light, snacky meals.

La P'tite Folie (Map p764; ☎0131-225 7983; www.laptitefolie.co.uk; 61 Frederick St; mains £16-25; ☺lunch & dinner) This is a delightful little restaurant with a Breton owner whose menu includes French classics – onion soup, *moules marinières* – alongside steaks, seafood and a range of *plats du jour*. The two-course lunch is a bargain at £9.

First Coast (☎0131-313 4404; www.first-coast.co.uk; 99-101 Dalry Rd; mains £10-19; ☺lunch & dinner Mon-Sat) This neighbourhood bistro near Haymarket train station has a short and simple menu offering hearty comfort food such as Thai marinated chicken salad or glazed ham hough with mustard mash. At lunch, and from 5pm to 6.30pm, you can have an excellent two-course meal for £12.

available from 5pm to 6.30pm, and afternoon tea (£16) is served from 3pm to 5pm.

Mums   CAFE £
(Map p758; www.monstermashcafe.co.uk; 4a Forrest Rd; mains £6-9; ☺9am-10pm Mon-Sat, 10am-10pm Sun) This nostalgia-fuelled cafe serves up classic British comfort food that wouldn't look out of place on a 1950s menu – bacon and eggs, bangers and mash, shepherd's pie, fish and chips. But there's a twist – the food is all top-quality nosh freshly prepared from local produce, including Crombie's gourmet sausages. There's even a wine list, though we prefer the real ales and Scottish-brewed cider.

Passepartout   INTERNATIONAL £
(Map p758; ☎0131-629 0252; 7 Old Fishmarket Close; platters for two £12-13) Hidden down a steep cobbled alley off the Royal Mile, with three indoor seating areas (including a 'cinema room' screening old movies) and a lovely little sun-trap of an outdoor terrace, this French-owned, Indian-inspired bistro offers an eclectic menu of dishes – from lobster with mussels to chickpea curry to kebabs – served as sharing platters for two, which you eat with your fingers. Great fun and good value.

Mosque Kitchen   INDIAN £
(Map p758; www.mosquekitchen.com; 31 Nicolson Sq; mains £3-6; ☺11.30am-12.50pm & 1.50-11pm; ☒) Sophisticated it ain't – expect shared tables and disposable plates – but this is the place to go for cheap, authentic and delicious homemade curries, kebabs, pakora

and naan bread washed down with lassi or mango juice. Caters to Edinburgh's Central Mosque, but welcomes all – local students have taken to it big time. No alcohol.

David Bann   VEGETARIAN ££
(Map p758; ☎0131-556 5888; www.davidbann.com; 56-58 St Mary's St; mains £9-13; ☺noon-10pm Mon-Fri, 11am-10pm Sat & Sun; ☒) If you want to convince a carnivorous friend that cuisine à la veg can be as tasty and inventive as a meat-muncher's menu, take them to David Bann's stylish restaurant – dishes such as beetroot, apple and Dunsyre blue cheese pudding, and Thai fritter of spiced broccoli and smoked tofu are guaranteed to win converts.

Amber   SCOTTISH ££
(Map p758; ☎0131-477 8477; www.amber-restaurant .co.uk; 354 Castlehill; mains £10-25; ☺lunch daily, dinner Tue-Sat) You've got to love a place where the waiter greets you with the words, 'My name is Craig, and I'll be your whisky adviser for this evening'. Located in the Scotch Whisky Experience, this whisky-themed restaurant manages to avoid the tourist clichés and creates genuinely interesting and flavoursome dishes such as mussels in a cream, leek and Islay whisky sauce, and sirloin steak with thyme-roasted potatoes and whisky butter.

NEW TOWN

The Dogs   BRITISH ££
TOP CHOICE
(Map p764; ☎0131-220 1208; www.thedogsonline .co.uk; 110 Hanover St; mains £9-13; ☺noon-4pm

& 5-10pm) One of the coolest tables in town, this bistro-style place uses cheaper cuts of meat and less well known, more sustainable species of fish to create hearty, no-nonsense dishes such as lamb sweetbreads on toast, and baked coley with *skirlie* (fried oatmeal and onion), and devilled liver with bacon and onions.

Café Marlayne
FRENCH **££**
(Map p764; 0131-226 2230; www.cafemarlayne.com; 76 Thistle St; mains £12-15; noon-10pm) All weathered wood and candlelit tables, Café Marlayne is a cosy nook offering French farmhouse cooking – *brandade de morue* (salt cod) with green salad, slow roast rack of lamb, *boudin noir* (black pudding) with scallops and sautéed potato – at very reasonable prices. Booking recommended.

Mussel Inn
SEAFOOD **££**
(Map p764; www.mussel-inn.com; 61-65 Rose St; mains £9-23; noon-10pm;) Owned by west-coast shellfish farmers, the Mussel Inn provides a direct outlet for fresh Scottish seafood. The busy restaurant, decorated with bright beechwood indoors, spills out onto the pavement in summer. A kilogram pot of mussels with a choice of sauces – try leek, Dijon mustard and cream – is £12.20.

Blue Moon Cafe
CAFE **£**
(0131-556 2788; 1 Barony St; mains £7-10; 11am-10pm Mon-Fri, 10am-10pm Sat & Sun) The Blue Moon is the focus of Broughton St's gay social life, always busy, always friendly, and serving up delicious nachos, salads, sandwiches and baked potatoes. It's famous for its homemade burgers (beef, chicken or felafel), which come with a range of toppings, and delicious daily specials.

LEITH

Fishers Bistro
TOP CHOICE
SEAFOOD **££**
(0131-554 5666; www.fishersbistros.co.uk; 1 The Shore; mains £10-23; noon-10.30pm Mon-Sat, 12.30-10pm Sun) This cosy little restaurant, tucked beneath a 17th-century signal tower, is one of the city's best seafood places. The menu ranges widely in price, from cheaper dishes such as classic fishcakes with lemon and chive mayonnaise, to more expensive delights such as North Berwick lobster thermidor.

Chop Chop
CHINESE **£**
(0131-553 1818; www.chop-chop.co.uk; 76 Commercial St; mains £8-10; dinner daily, lunch Sat & Sun) Chop Chop is a Chinese restaurant with a difference, in that it serves dishes popular in China rather than Britain; as the slogan says, 'Can a billion people be wrong?' No sweet and sour pork here, but a range of delicious dumplings filled with pork and coriander, beef and chilli, or lamb and leek, and unusual vegetarian dishes such as aubergine fried with garlic and Chinese spices.

Drinking
Edinburgh has more than 700 bars, which are as varied as the population – everything from Victorian palaces to rough-and-ready drinking dens, and from bearded, real-ale howffs to trendy cocktail bars.

OLD TOWN

Bow Bar
PUB
(Map p758; 80 West Bow) One of the city's best traditional-style pubs (it's not as old as it looks) serving a range of excellent real ales and a vast selection of malt whiskies, the Bow Bar often has standing-room only on Friday and Saturday evenings.

Jolly Judge
PUB
(Map p758; www.jollyjudge.co.uk; 7a James Ct;) A snug little howff tucked away down a close, the Judge exudes a cosy 17th-century atmosphere (low, timber-beamed painted ceilings) and has the added attraction of a cheering open fire in cold weather. No music or gaming machines, just the buzz of conversation.

BrewDog
BAR
(Map p758; www.brewdog.com; 143 Cowgate;) A new bar from Scotland's self-styled 'punk brewery', BrewDog stands out among the grimy, sticky-floored dives that line the Cowgate, with its cool, industrial-chic designer look. As well as its own highly rated beers, there's a choice of four guest real ales.

Ecco Vino
WINE BAR
(Map p758; www.eccovinoedinburgh.com; 19 Cockburn St;) With outdoor tables on sunny afternoons, and cosy candlelit intimacy in the evenings, this comfortably cramped Tuscan-style wine bar offers a tempting range of Italian wines, though not all are available by the glass – best to share a bottle.

Pear Tree House
PUB
(Map p758; www.pear-tree-house.co.uk; 38 West Nicolson St;) Set in an 18th-century house with cobbled courtyard, the Pear Tree is a student favourite with an open fire in

winter, comfy sofas and board games inside, plus the city's biggest and most popular beer garden in summer.

NEW TOWN

Oxford Bar
PUB

(Map p764; www.oxfordbar.co.uk; 8 Young St) The Oxford is that rarest of things these days, a real pub for real people, with no 'theme', no music, no frills and no pretensions. 'The Ox' has been immortalised by Ian Rankin, author of the Inspector Rebus novels, whose fictional detective is a regular here.

Bramble
COCKTAIL BAR

(Map p764; www.bramblebar.co.uk; 16a Queen St) One of those places that easily earns the so-briquet 'best kept secret', Bramble is an un-marked cellar bar where a maze of stone and brick hideaways conceals what is arguably the city's best cocktail bar. No beer taps, no fuss, just expertly mixed drinks.

Cumberland Bar
PUB

(www.cumberlandbar.co.uk; 1-3 Cumberland St; ☎) Immortalised as the stereotypical New Town pub in Alexander McCall-Smith's serialised novel *44 Scotland Street,* the Cumberland has an authentic, traditional wood-brass-and-mirrors look (despite being relatively new), and serves well-looked-after, cask-conditioned ales and a wide range of malt whiskies. There's also a pleasant little beer garden outside.

Amicus Apple
COCKTAIL BAR

(Map p764; www.amicusapple.com; 15 Frederick St; ☎) This laid-back cocktail lounge is the hip-pest hang-out in the New Town. The drinks menu ranges from retro classics such as Bloody Marys and mojitos, to original and unusual concoctions such as the Cuillin Martini (Tanqueray No 10 gin, Talisker malt whisky and smoked rosemary).

LEITH

Teuchter's Landing
PUB

(www.aroomin.co.uk; 1 Dock Pl; ☎) A cosy warren of timber-lined nooks and crannies housed in a single-storey red-brick building (once a waiting room for ferries across the Firth of Forth), this real-ale and malt-whisky bar also has outdoor tables on a floating terrace in the dock.

Port O'Leith
PUB

(www.portoleithpub.com; 58 Constitution St) This is a good, old-fashioned, friendly local boozer, swathed with flags and cap bands left behind by visiting sailors – Leith docks are just down the road. Pop in for a pint and you'll probably stay until closing time.

 Entertainment

The comprehensive source for what's-on info is *The List* (www.list.co.uk), an excel-lent listings magazine covering both Edin-burgh and Glasgow. It's available from most newsagents, and is published fortnightly on a Thursday.

Live Music

Henry's Cellar
LIVE MUSIC

(Map p758; www.musicglue.com/theraft; 8a Morri-son St) One of Edinburgh's most eclectic live-music venues, Henry's has something going on most nights of the week, from rock and indie to 'Balkan-inspired folk', funk to hip-hop to hardcore, staging both local bands and acts from around the world. Open till 3am at weekends.

Whistle Binkie's
LIVE MUSIC

(Map p758; www.whistlebinkies.com; 4-6 South Bridge) This crowded cellar-bar just off the Royal Mile has live music every night till 3am, from rock and blues to folk and jazz. Open-mic night on Monday and breaking bands on Tuesday are showcases for new talent.

Jazz Bar
JAZZ

(Map p758; www.thejazzbar.co.uk; 1a Chambers St; ☎) This atmospheric cellar bar, with its pol-ished parquet floors, bare stone walls, can-dlelit tables and stylish steel-framed chairs is owned and operated by jazz musicians. There's live music every night from 9pm to 3am, and on Saturday from 3pm.

Sandy Bell's
TRADITIONAL MUSIC

(Map p758; 25 Forrest Rd) This unassuming pub is a stalwart of the traditional music scene (the founder's wife sang with The Corries). There's music almost every evening at 9pm, and from 3pm Saturday and Sunday, plus lots of impromptu sessions.

Royal Oak
TRADITIONAL MUSIC

(Map p758; www.royal-oak-folk.com; 1 Infirmary St) This popular folk pub is tiny, so get there early (9pm start weekdays, 2.30pm Saturday) if you want to be sure of a place. Sundays from 4pm to 7pm is open session – bring your own instruments (or a good singing voice).

Nightclubs

Bongo Club
MULTI-ARTS VENUE

(www.thebongoclub.co.uk; Moray House, Paterson's Land, 37 Holyrood Rd) The weird and wonderful Bongo Club boasts a long history of hosting everything from wild club nights to performance art to kids comedy shows, and is open as a cafe and exhibition space during the day. It may shift to new premises in 2013 – check the website for latest news.

Cabaret Voltaire
CLUB, LIVE MUSIC

(Map p758; www.thecabaretvoltaire.com; 36 Blair St) An atmospheric warren of stone-lined vaults houses Edinburgh's most 'alternative' club, which eschews huge dance floors and egotistical DJ worship in favour of a 'creative crucible' hosting an eclectic mix of DJs, live acts, comedy, theatre, visual arts and the spoken word. Well worth a look.

Liquid Room
CLUB, LIVE MUSIC

(Map p758; www.liquidroom.com; 9c Victoria St) Set in a subterranean vault deep beneath Victoria St, the Liquid Room is a superb club venue with a thundering sound system.

There are regular club nights Wednesday to Saturday as well as live bands.

Studio 24
CLUB

(www.studio24.me; 24 Calton Rd) Studio 24 is the dark heart of Edinburgh's underground music scene, with a program that covers all bases, from house to nu metal via punk, ska, reggae, crossover, tribal, electro, techno and dance.

Cinemas

Cameo
CINEMA

(www.picturehouses.co.uk; 38 Home St) The three-screen, independently owned Cameo is a good, old-fashioned cinema showing an imaginative mix of mainstream and art-house movies. There is a good program of midnight movies and Sunday matinees, and the seats in Screen 1 are big enough to get lost in.

Filmhouse
CINEMA

(Map p758; www.filmhousecinema.com; 88 Lothian Rd; ☎) The Filmhouse is the main venue for the annual Edinburgh International Film

---

TOP FIVE TRADITIONAL PUBS

Edinburgh is blessed with a large number of traditional 19th- and early-20th-century pubs, which have preserved much of their original Victorian or Edwardian decoration and serve cask-conditioned real ales and a staggering range of malt whiskies.

Athletic Arms (Diggers; 1-3 Angle Park Tce) Nicknamed after the cemetery across the street – the gravediggers used to nip in and slake their thirst after a hard day's interring – the Diggers dates from the 1890s. It's still staunchly traditional – the decor has barely changed in 100 years – and has recently revived its reputation as a real-ale drinker's mecca by serving locally brewed Diggers' 80-shilling ale. Packed to the gills with football and rugby fans on match days.

Abbotsford (Map p764; www.theabbotsford.com; 3 Rose St) Dating from 1902, and named after Sir Walter Scott's country house, the Abbotsford is one of the few pubs in Rose St that has retained its Edwardian splendour. It has long been a hang-out for writers, actors, journalists and media people, and has many loyal regulars. The pub's centrepiece is a splendid, mahogany island bar with a good selection of Scottish and English real ales.

Bennet's Bar (8 Leven St) Situated beside the King's Theatre, Bennet's has managed to hang on to almost all of its beautiful Victorian fittings, from the leaded, stained-glass windows and ornate mirrors to the wooden gantry and the brass water taps on the bar (for your whisky – there are over 100 malts to choose from).

Cafe Royal Circle Bar (Map p764; www.caferoyal.org.uk; 17 West Register St) Perhaps the classic Edinburgh bar, the Cafe Royal's main claims to fame are its magnificent oval bar and the series of Doulton tile portraits of famous Victorian inventors. Check out the bottles on the gantry – staff line them up to look like there's a mirror there, and many a drink-befuddled customer has been seen squinting and wondering why he can't see his reflection.

Sheep Heid (www.sheepheid.co.uk; 43-45 The Causeway) Possibly the oldest inn in Edinburgh – with a licence dating back to 1360 – the Sheep Heid feels more like a country pub than an Edinburgh bar. Set in the semi-rural shadow of Arthur's Seat, it's famous for its 19th-century skittles alley and the lovely little beer garden.

Festival and screens a full program of art-house, classic, foreign and second-run films, with lots of themes, retrospectives and 70mm screenings. It has wheelchair access to all three screens.

Classical Music, Opera & Ballet

Edinburgh Festival Theatre
BALLET, OPERA

(Map p758; www.edtheatres.com/festival; 13-29 Nicolson St; ☉box office 10am-6pm Mon-Sat, to 8pm show nights, 4pm-showtime Sun) A beautifully restored art-deco theatre with a modern frontage, the Festival is the city's main venue for opera, dance and ballet, but also stages musicals, concerts, drama and children's shows.

Usher Hall
CLASSICAL MUSIC

(Map p758; www.usherhall.co.uk; Lothian Rd; ☉box office 10.30am-5.30pm, to 8pm show nights) The architecturally impressive Usher Hall hosts concerts by the Royal Scottish National Orchestra (RSNO) and performances of popular music.

Sport

Edinburgh is home to two rival football (soccer) teams playing in the Scottish Premier League. Heart of Midlothian (aka Hearts) has its home ground at Tynecastle Stadium (www.heartsfc.co.uk; Gorgie Rd), while the Hibernian (aka Hibs) home ground is at Easter Road Stadium (www.hibernianfc.co.uk; 12 Albion Pl).

Each year, from January to March, Scotland's national rugby team takes part in the Six Nations Rugby Union Championship. Murrayfield Stadium (www.scottishrugby.org; 112 Roseburn St), about 1.5 miles west of the city centre, is the venue for international matches.

Theatre, Musicals & Comedy

Royal Lyceum Theatre
DRAMA, MUSICALS

(Map p758; www.lyceum.org.uk; 30b Grindlay St; ☉box office 10am-6pm Mon-Sat, to 8pm show nights; ☝) A grand Victorian theatre located beside the Usher Hall, the Lyceum stages drama, concerts, musicals and ballet.

Traverse Theatre
DRAMA, DANCE

(Map p758; www.traverse.co.uk; 10 Cambridge St; ☉box office 10am-6pm Mon-Sat, to 8pm show nights) The Traverse is the main focus for new Scottish writing and stages an adventurous program of contemporary drama and dance. The box office is only open on Sunday (from 4pm) when there's a show on.

King's Theatre
DRAMA, MUSICALS

(www.edtheatres.com/kings; 2 Leven St; ☉box office open 1hr before show) King's is a traditional theatre with a program of musicals, drama, comedy and its famous Christmas pantomimes.

Stand Comedy Club
COMEDY

(Map p764; www.thestand.co.uk; 5 York Pl) The Stand, founded in 1995, is Edinburgh's main independent comedy venue. It's an intimate cabaret bar with performances every night and a free Sunday lunchtime show.

🛍 Shopping

Princes St is Edinburgh's principal shopping street, lined with all the big high-street stores, with many smaller shops along pedestrianised Rose St and more expensive designer boutiques on George St. There are also two big shopping centres in the New Town – Princes Mall, at the eastern end of Princes St, and the nearby St James Shopping Centre at the top of Leith St, plus Multrees Walk, a designer shopping complex with a flagship Harvey Nichols store on the eastern side of St Andrew Sq. The huge Ocean Terminal in Leith is the biggest shopping centre in the city.

For more off-beat shopping – including fashion, music, crafts, gifts and jewellery – head for the cobbled lanes of Cockburn, Victoria and St Mary's Sts, all near the Royal Mile in the Old Town; William St in the western part of New Town; and the Stockbridge district, immediately north of the New Town.

ℹ Information

Emergency

Edinburgh Rape Crisis centre (☎08088 01 03 02; www.rapecrisisscotland.org.uk)

Lothian & Borders Police HQ (☎non-emergency 0131-311 3131; www.lbp.police.uk; Fettes Ave)

Lothian & Borders Police information centre (☎0131-226 6966; 188 High St; ☉10am-1pm & 2-5.30pm, to 9.30pm during Fringe Festival) Report a crime or make lost-property enquiries here.

Internet Access

There are several internet-enabled telephone boxes (10p a minute, 50p minimum) scattered around the city centre, and countless wi-fi hot spots – search on www.jiwire.com. Internet cafes are spread around the city. Some convenient ones include the following:

Coffee Home (www.coffeehome.co.uk; 28 Crighton Pl, Leith Walk; per 20min 60p; ☉10am-10pm Mon-Sat, noon-10pm Sun)

e-corner (www.e-corner.co.uk; 54 Blackfriars St; per 20min £1; ⊙7.30am-9pm Mon-Fri, 8am-9pm Sat & Sun; 🕿)

G-Tec (www.grassmarket-technologies.com; 67 Grassmarket; per 20min £1; ⊙10am-6pm Mon-Fri, to 5.30pm Sat)

Internet Resources

Edinburgh & Lothians tourist board (www .edinburgh.org) Official tourist-board site, with listings of accommodation, sights, activities and events.

Edinburgh Architecture (www.edinburgh architecture.co.uk) Informative site dedicated to the city's modern architecture.

Edinburgh festival guide (www.edinburgh festivals.co.uk) Everything you need to know about Edinburgh's many festivals.

Events Edinburgh (www.eventsedinburgh.org .uk) The city council's official events guide.

The List (www.list.co.uk) Listings of restaurants, pubs, clubs and nightlife.

Medical Services

For urgent medical advice you can call the **NHS 24 Helpline** (☑08454 24 24 24; www.nhs24. com). Chemists (pharmacists) can advise you on minor ailments. At least one local chemist remains open round the clock – its location will be displayed in the windows of other chemists.

For urgent dental treatment you can visit the walk-in **Chalmers Dental Centre** (3 Chalmers St; ⊙9am-4.45pm Mon-Thu, to 4.15pm Fri). In the case of a dental emergency in the evenings or at weekends, call **Lothian dental advice line** (☑0131-536 4800).

Royal Infirmary of Edinburgh (☑0131-536 1000; www.nhslothian.scot.nhs.uk; 51 Little France Cres, Old Dalkeith Rd) Edinburgh's main general hospital; has a 24-hour accident and emergency department.

Post

Main post office (St James Shopping Centre, Leith St; ⊙8.30am-5.30pm Mon-Fri, to 6pm Sat) Hidden away inside a shopping centre.

Tourist Information

Edinburgh information centre (☑0131-473 3868; www.edinburgh.org; Princes Mall, 3 Princes St; ⊙9am-9pm Mon-Sat, 10am-8pm Sun Jul & Aug, 9am-7pm Mon-Sat, 10am-7pm Sun May-Jun & Sep, 9am-5pm Mon-Wed, 9am-6pm Thu-Sun Oct-Apr) Includes an accommodation booking service, currency exchange, a gift and bookshop, internet access, and counters selling tickets for Edinburgh city tours and Scottish Citylink bus services.

Edinburgh Airport information centre (☑0131-344 3120; Main Concourse, Edinburgh Airport; ⊙7.30am-9pm)

❶ Getting There & Away

Air

Edinburgh Airport (☑0131-333 1000; www.edinburghairport.com) Eight miles west of the city; has numerous flights to other parts of Scotland and the UK, Ireland and mainland Europe.

FlyBe/Loganair (☑0871 700 2000; www .loganair.co.uk) Operates daily flights to Inverness, Wick, Orkney, Shetland and Stornoway.

Bus

Edinburgh bus station is at the northeast corner of St Andrew Sq, with pedestrian entrances from the square and from Elder St. For timetable information, call **Traveline** (☑0871 200 22 33; www.travelinescotland.com).

Scottish Citylink (☑0871 266 3333; www .citylink.co.uk) buses connect Edinburgh with all of Scotland's cities and major towns. The following are sample one-way fares departing from Edinburgh.

DESTINATION	FARE	DURATION (HR)	FREQUENCY
Aberdeen	£28	3¼	3 daily
Dundee	£15	2	hourly
Fort William	£33	4-5	8 daily
Glasgow	£6.80	1¼	every 15 min
Inverness	£28	4	hourly
Portree	£47	7	1 daily
Stirling	£7.50	1	hourly

EDINBURGH GETTING THERE & AWAY

THE FORTH BRIDGES

At Queensferry, west of Edinburgh, the narrowest part of the Firth of Forth is spanned by two spectacular bridges. Ferries have crossed to Fife here from the earliest times – the village takes its name from Queen Margaret (1046–93), who gave pilgrims free passage across the firth on their way to St Andrews. Ferries continued to operate until 1964 when the graceful **Forth Road Bridge** was opened. Construction has started on a second road bridge, scheduled to open in 2016.

Predating the road bridge by 74 years, the magnificent **Forth Bridge** – only outsiders ever call it the Forth Rail Bridge – is one of the finest engineering achievements of the 19th century. Completed in 1890 after seven years' work, its three huge cantilevers span 1447m and took 59,000 tonnes of steel, eight million rivets and the lives of 58 men to build.

It's also worth checking with **Megabus** (☎0900 160 0900; www.megabus.com) for cheap inter-city bus fares (from as little as £5) from Edinburgh to Aberdeen, Dundee, Glasgow, Inverness and Perth.

There are various buses to Edinburgh from London and the rest of the UK.

Train

The main terminus in Edinburgh is Waverley train station, located in the heart of the city. Trains arriving from, and departing for, the west also stop at Haymarket station, which is more convenient for the West End.

You can buy tickets, make reservations and get travel information at the **Edinburgh rail travel centre** (⊙4.45am-12.30am Mon-Sat, 7am-12.30am Sun) in Waverley station. For fare and timetable information, phone the **National Rail enquiry service** (☎08457 48 49 50; www.nationalrail.co.uk) or use the Journey Planner on the website.

First ScotRail operates a regular shuttle service between Edinburgh and Glasgow (£12.90, 50 minutes, every 15 minutes), and frequent daily services to all Scottish cities including Aberdeen (£45, 2½ hours), Dundee (£23, 1¼ hours) and Inverness (£40, 3½ hours).

ⓘ Getting Around

To/From the Airport

The Lothian Buses **Airlink** (www.flybybus.com) service 100 runs from Waverley Bridge, outside the train station, to the airport (£3.50/6 one-way/return, 30 minutes, every 10 to 15 minutes) via the West End and Haymarket.

An airport taxi to the city centre costs around £16 and takes about 20 minutes. Both buses and taxis depart from outside the arrivals hall; go out through the main doors and turn left.

Car & Motorcycle

Though useful for day trips beyond the city, a car in central Edinburgh is more of a liability than a convenience. There is restricted access on Princes St, George St and Charlotte Sq, many streets are one-way, and finding a parking place is like striking gold. Queen's Dr around Holyrood Park is closed to motorised traffic on Sunday.

All the big international car-rental agencies have offices in Edinburgh, but there are many smaller local agencies that offer better rates. **Arnold Clark** (☎0131-657 9120; www.arnoldclark rental.co.uk; 20 Seafield Rd East) near Portobello, charges from £30 a day, or £180 a week for a small car, including VAT and insurance.

Public Transport

Edinburgh's public transport system currently consists entirely of buses (a tram network is under construction, due to come into operation in 2014). The main operators are **Lothian Buses** (www.lothianbuses.com) and **First** (☎0131-663 9233; www.firstedinburgh.co.uk); for timetable information contact Traveline (p781).

Adult fares are £1.40; children under five travel free and those aged five to 15 pay a flat fare of 70p. Purchase from the driver; on Lothian Buses you must pay the exact fare, but First buses will give change. Lothian Bus drivers also sell a Day-saver ticket (£3.50) that gives unlimited travel (on Lothian Buses only, excluding night buses) for a day. **Night-service buses** (www.night buses.com), which run hourly between midnight and 5am, charge a flat fare of £3.

Taxi

Central Taxis (☎0131-229 2468)

City Cabs (☎0131-228 1211)

ComCab (☎0131-272 8000)

Glasgow & Southern Scotland

Best Places to Eat

» The Ubiquitous Chip (p799)

» Stravaigin (p799)

» The Brodick Bar (p814)

» Coltman's (p811)

Best Places to Stay

» Brunswick Hotel (p795)

» Malmaison (p795)

» Corsewall Lighthouse Hotel (p823)

» Kildonan Hotel (p815)

» Knockinaam Lodge (p823)

» Hotel du Vin (p797)

Why Go?

For many, southern Scotland is what you drive through on the way to big cities Glasgow or Edinburgh, or even points further north. Big mistake. But it means plenty of peaceful corners here. The south's proximity to England brought strife, but the ruins of Borders castles and the abbeys they protected make wonderfully atmospheric historic sites. The hillier west enjoys extensive forest cover; hills cascade down to sandy coasts blessed with Scotland's sunniest weather. Visible offshore, Arran is an island jewel offering top cycling and walking.

The region's premier attraction, however, is urban. Glasgow, Scotland's biggest city, is a fascinatingly vital place. Glaswegians are proud of their working-class background, black humour and leftist traditions, and their city combines art, architecture, great food and nightlife, style, edgy urbanity and the people's legendary friendliness in a captivating blend that will leave you wanting more.

When to Go

June sees music festivals in Glasgow, and spectacular gardens in bloom at the region's numerous castles and stately homes.

Glasgow is super-friendly at any time, but in the August sunshine there's no happier city in Britain.

In autumn, hit Galloway's forests to see red deer, high on stag testosterone, battle it out in the rutting season.

Glasgow & Southern Scotland Highlights

1 Gazing at Glasgow's fabulous wealth of paintings in the **Burrell Collection** (p792), the **Kelvingrove** (p792) and the **Hunterian Art Gallery** (p792)

2 Hiking or cycling between the noble ruins of the **Border Abbeys** (p808)

3 Catching a **Celtic** (p804) or **Rangers** (p804) match at their massive football stadiums

4 Deciding just which one of Glasgow's excellent West End **restaurants** (p799) you are going to dine at next

5 Discovering the work of **Charles Rennie Mackintosh**

(p791) – 'genius' is an overused word, but few would argue here

6 Marvelling at the radical social reform instituted in the mill community of **New Lanark** (p806)

7 Plunging into Glasgow's legendary and diverse **music and nightclub scene** (p802)

8 Blowing away the cobwebs on the scenic, activity-packed **Isle of Arran** (p812)

9 Learning some Lallans words from the Scottish Bard's verses at the **Robert Burns Birthplace Museum** (p817)

10 Whooshing down forest trails at the **7stanes mountain-biking hubs** (p822)

Activities

For walkers and hikers, the hills of the Southern Uplands provide endless opportunities, including the 212-mile Southern Upland Way (p808). For a shorter sample, one of the best bits is between St John's Town of Dalry and Beattock. Other walking routes in the region include St Cuthbert's Way (p808) and the Border Abbeys Way (p808). The Isle of Arran has some great walking, too, as does the Glasgow area, with the Clyde Walkway and the beginning of the West Highland Way.

This is an ideal region for touring cyclists, thanks to the beauty of the countryside and light traffic on the roads (except the main north–south A roads and the A75 to Stranraer). The Tweed Cycle Way (p808) is a waymarked route running 62 miles along the scenic Tweed Valley. Off-road fans can head for one of the highly rated mountain bike centres across the region, grouped together under the banner of the 7stanes (p811).

❶ Getting There & Around

Train services are limited. There are stations at Berwick-upon-Tweed on the main Edinburgh–London line (in Northumberland on the English side of the border, but a natural jumping-off point for the Tweed Valley); at Dumfries on the main Glasgow–London line; and at Stranraer and Ayr, which are linked to Glasgow.

Bus transport is excellent around the Borders, Ayrshire and Lanarkshire, and reasonable on the main north–south routes and the A75 to Stranraer, but limited elsewhere in Dumfries & Galloway.

Check details with **Traveline Scotland** (☎0871 200 22 33; www.travelinescotland.com).

GLASGOW

POP 634,700

Displaying a disarming blend of sophistication and earthiness, Scotland's biggest city has regenerated and evolved over the last couple of decades to become one of Britain's most intriguing metropolises.

Its Victorian architectural legacy is now swamped with stylish bars and top-notch restaurants, and a hedonistic club culture to bring out your nocturnal instincts. Glasgow's pounding live-music scene is one of the best in Britain.

Yet nightlife is only the beginning. Top-drawer museums and galleries abound, and the city's proud industrial and artistic heritage is innovatively displayed. Charles Rennie Mackintosh's sublime works dot the town, while the River Clyde, traditionally associated with Glasgow's earthier side, is now a symbol of the city's renaissance.

History

Glasgow grew around the cathedral founded by St Kertigan, later to become St Mungo, in the 6th century. Unfortunately, with the exception of the cathedral, virtually nothing of the medieval city remains. It was swept away by the energetic people of a new age – the age of capitalism, the Industrial Revolution and the British Empire.

GLASGOW IN...

Two Days

On your first day, hit the East End for **Glasgow Cathedral**, **St Mungo's Museum** and a wander through the hillside necropolis. Later take on one of the city's top museums: either the **Burrell Collection** or the **Kelvingrove**. As evening falls, head to upbeat **Merchant City** for a stroll and dinner – **Café Gandolfi** maybe, or the latest trendy newcomer. Make sure you head to **Artá** for a pre- or post-meal drink. The next day, visit whichever museum you missed yesterday, and then it's Mackintosh time. **Glasgow School of Art** is his finest work: if you like his style, head to the West End for **Mackintosh House**. Hungry? Thirsty? Some of the city's best restaurants and bars are up this end of town, so you could make a night of it. Make sure to check out one of the numerous excellent music venues around the city.

Four Days

A four-day stay gives much better scope for getting to know the city in some depth. Spend a day along the Clyde – the **Riverside Museum** and the **Science Centre**. Plan your weekend around a night out at **Arches** or the legendary **Sub Club**, a day strolling the stylish city-centre clothing emporia, earthier shopping at the **Barras** flea market and a football match. Don't miss trying at least one of the city's classic curry houses.

In the 18th century much of the tobacco trade between Europe and the USA was routed through Glasgow and provided a great source of wealth. In the 19th century the city continued to prosper as a centre of textile manufacturing, shipbuilding and the coal and steel industries. The outward appearance of prosperity, however, was tempered by the dire working conditions in the factories.

In the first half of the 20th century, Glasgow was the centre of Britain's munitions industry, supplying arms and ships for the two world wars. In the postwar years, however, the port and heavy industries began to dwindle. Working-class Glasgow had few alternatives when recession hit and the city became synonymous with unemployment, economic depression and urban violence. More recently development and a booming cultural sector have injected style and confidence into the city; though the standard of living remains low for Britain and life continues to be tough for many, the ongoing regeneration process gives grounds for optimism.

◉ Sights

CITY CENTRE

Glasgow School of Art MACKINTOSH BUILDING
(☑0141-353 4526; www.gsa.ac.uk/tours; 167 Renfrew St; adult/child/family £8.75/7/24; ⊙9.30am-6.30pm Apr-Sep, 10.30am-5pm Oct-Mar) Mackintosh's greatest building, the Glasgow School of Art, still fulfils its original function, so just follow the steady stream of eclectically dressed students up the hill to find it. It's hard not to be impressed by the thoroughness of the design; the architect's pencil seems to have shaped everything inside and outside the building. The interior design is strikingly austere, with simple colour combinations and those high-backed chairs for which Mackintosh is famous. The library, designed as an addition in 1907, is a masterpiece. The visitor entrance is at the side of the building on Dalhousie St; here there's a shop with a useful interpretative display. Excellent hour-long guided tours (roughly hourly summer; 11am, 1pm and 3pm winter) run by architecture students leave from here; this is the only way (apart from enrolling) you can visit the building's interior. They're worth booking by phone at busy times. Multilingual translations available.

FREE Gallery of Modern Art GALLERY
(GoMA; www.glasgowmuseums.com; Royal Exchange Sq; ⊙10am-5pm Mon-Wed & Sat, to 8pm Thu, 11am-5pm Fri & Sun) Scotland's most popular contemporary art gallery features modern works from artists worldwide in a graceful neoclassical building. The original interior is used to make a daring, inventive art display. Social issues are a focal point of the museum but it's not all heavy going: there's a big effort made to keep the kids entertained.

FREE Willow Tearooms MACKINTOSH BUILDING
(www.willowtearooms.co.uk; 217 Sauchiehall St; ⊙9am-5pm Mon-Sat, 11am-5pm Sun) Admirers of the great Mackintosh will love the Willow Tearooms, an authentic reconstruction of tearooms Mackintosh designed and furnished in the early 20th century for restaurateur Kate Cranston. Relive the original splendour and admire the architect's stroke in just about everything. He had a free rein and even the teaspoons were given his distinctive touch.

FREE Lighthouse MACKINTOSH BUILDING
(☑0141-221 6362; www.thelighthouse.co.uk; 11 Mitchell Lane; ⊙10.30am-5pm Mon-Sat, noon-5pm Sun) Mackintosh's first building, designed in 1893, was a striking new headquarters for the *Glasgow Herald*. Tucked up a narrow lane off Buchanan St, it now serves as Scotland's Centre for Architecture & Design, with fairly technical temporary exhibitions (sometimes admission is payable for these), as well as the Mackintosh Interpretation Centre, a detailed if dryish overview of his life and work. On the top floor of the 'lighthouse', drink in great views over the rooftops and spires of the city centre.

EAST END

The oldest part of the city, given a facelift in the 1990s, is concentrated around Glasgow Cathedral, to the east of the modern city centre. It takes 15 to 20 minutes to walk from

Central Glasgow

George Sq, but numerous buses pass nearby, including buses 11, 12, 36, 37, 38 and 42.

Glasgow Cathedral CATHEDRAL
(HS; www.historic-scotland.gov.uk; Cathedral Sq; ⊙9.30am-5.30pm Mon-Sat, 1-5pm Sun Apr-Sep, closes 4.30pm Oct-Mar) An attraction that shouldn't be missed, Glasgow Cathedral has a rare timelessness. The dark, imposing interior conjures up medieval might and can send a shiver down the spine. It's a shining example of Gothic architecture, and, unlike

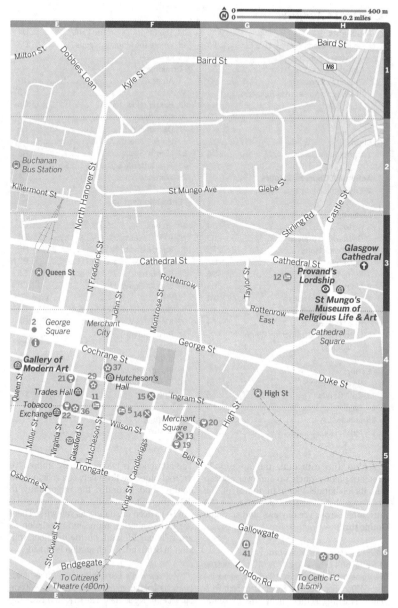

nearly all of Scotland's cathedrals, survived the turmoil of the Reformation mobs almost intact. Most of the current building dates from the 15th century.

The most interesting part of the cathedral, the **lower church**, is reached by a stairway. Its forest of pillars creates a powerful atmosphere around St Mungo's tomb (St Mungo founded a monastic community here in the 5th century), the focus of a famous medieval pilgrimage that was believed to be as meritorious as a visit to Rome.

Central Glasgow

Behind the cathedral, the **necropolis** stretches picturesquely up and over a green hill. Its elaborate Victorian tombs of the city's wealthy industrialists make for an intriguing stroll, great views and a vague Gothic thrill.

TOP CHOICE **St Mungo's Museum of Religious Life & Art** MUSEUM
(www.glasgowmuseums.com; 2 Castle St; admission free; ⊙10am-5pm Tue-Thu & Sat, 11am-5pm Fri & Sun) A startling achievement, this museum, set in a reconstruction of the bishop's palace that once stood here in the cathedral forecourt, is an audacious attempt to capture the world's major religions in an artistic nutshell, while presenting the similarities and differences in how they approach common themes such as birth, marriage and death.

The attraction is twofold: firstly, impressive art that blurs the lines between religion and culture; and secondly, the opportunity to delve into different faiths, an experience that can be as deep or shallow as you wish. There are three galleries, representing religion as art, religious life and, on the top floor, religion in Scotland. A Zen garden is outside.

FREE **Provand's Lordship** HISTORIC HOUSE
(www.glasgowmuseums.com; 3 Castle St; ⊙10am-5pm Tue-Thu & Sat, 11am-5pm Fri & Sun) Near the cathedral is Provand's Lordship, the oldest house in Glasgow. A rare example of 15th-century domestic Scottish architecture, it was built in 1471 as a manse for the chaplain of St Nicholas Hospital. The ceilings and doorways are low, and the rooms are sparsely furnished with period artefacts, except

for an upstairs room, which has been furnished to reflect the living space of an early-16th-century chaplain. The building's best feature is its authentic feel – if you ignore the tacky imitation-stone linoleum covering the ground floor.

THE CLYDE

Once a thriving shipbuilding area, the Clyde sank into dereliction during the post-war era, but is being rejuvenated.

FREE **Riverside Museum** MUSEUM
(www.glasgowmuseums.com; 100 Pointhouse Pl; ⏱10am-5pm Mon-Thu & Sat, 11am-5pm Fri & Sun) The latest development along the Clyde is the building of this visually impressive new museum, whose striking curved facades are the work of Iraqi architect Zaha Hadid. The main part of the collection is a transport museum; an atmospherically re-created Glasgow shopping street from the early 20th century puts the vintage vehicles into a social context. The **Tall Ship Glenlee** (www.thetallship.com; adult/child £5/3; ⏱10am-5pm Mar-Oct, till 4pm Nov-Feb), a beautiful three-master launched in 1896, is berthed alongside the museum. On board are displays about her history, restoration and shipboard life. The Riverside is west of the city centre at Glasgow Harbour; you can reach it on bus 100 from the north side of George Sq, or via the Clyde Clippers boat service. There's a cafe here.

Glasgow Science Centre MUSEUM
(☎0141-420 5000; www.gsc.org.uk; 50 Pacific Quay; Science Mall adult/child £9.95/7.95, IMAX, tower or planetarium £2.50; ⏱10am-5pm Wed-Sun) Scotland's flagship millennium project, this superb museum will keep the kids entertained for hours (that's middle-aged kids, too!). It brings science and technology alive through hundreds of interactive exhibits on four floors. It consists of an egg-shaped titanium-covered **IMAX** theatre (phone for current screenings) and an interactive **Science Mall** with floor-to-ceiling windows – a bounty of discovery for young, inquisitive minds. There's also a rotating **observation tower**, 127m high. And check out the planetarium, where the **Scottish Power Space Theatre** brings the night sky to life and a **Virtual Science Theatre** treats visitors to a 3D molecular journey. To get here take bus 24 from Renfield St or bus 89 or 90 from Union St. It closes earlier in winter, and doesn't open Monday or Tuesday.

WEST END

With its expectant buzz, trendy bars and cafes and nonchalant swagger, the bohemian West End is great for people-watching. From the city centre, buses 9, 16 and 23 run towards Kelvingrove, buses 8, 11 and 16 to the university, and buses 20, 44 and 66 to Byres Rd (among others).

THE GENIUS OF CHARLES RENNIE MACKINTOSH

Great cities have great artists, designers and architects contributing to the cultural and historical roots of their urban environment while expressing its soul and individuality. Charles Rennie Mackintosh was all of these. His quirky, linear and geometric designs have had almost as much influence on the city as have Gaudí's on Barcelona. Many of the buildings Mackintosh designed in Glasgow are open to the public, and you'll see his tall, thin, art nouveau typeface repeatedly reproduced.

Born in 1868, Mackintosh studied at the Glasgow School of Art. In 1896, when he was aged only 27, he won a competition for his design of the School of Art's new building. The first section was opened in 1899 and is considered to be the earliest example of art nouveau in Britain, as well as Mackintosh's supreme architectural achievement. This building demonstrates his skill in combining function and style.

Although Mackintosh's genius was quickly recognised on the Continent, he did not receive the same encouragement in Scotland. His architectural career here lasted only until 1914, when he moved to England to concentrate on furniture design. He died in 1928, and it is only fairly recently that Mackintosh's genius has been widely recognised. For more about the man and his work, contact the **Charles Rennie Mackintosh Society** (☎0141-946 6600; www.crmsociety.com; 870 Garscube Rd, Mackintosh Church).

If you're planning to go CRM crazy, the **Mackintosh Trail ticket** (£16), available at the tourist office or any Mackintosh building, gives you a day's free admission to all his creations as well as unlimited bus and subway travel.

TOP CHOICE Kelvingrove Art
Gallery & Museum   MUSEUM, GALLERY
(www.glasgowmuseums.com; Argyle St; admission
free; ⊙10am-5pm Mon-Thu & Sat, 11am-5pm Fri
& Sun; 🚗) In a magnificent stone building,
this grand Victorian cathedral of culture
has been revamped into a fascinating and
unusual museum, with a bewildering variety of exhibits, but not so tightly packed
as to overwhelm. Here you'll find fine art
alongside stuffed animals, and Microne-
sian shark-tooth swords alongside a Spitfire
plane, but it's not mix 'n' match: rooms are
carefully and thoughtfully themed, and the
collection is a manageable size. There's an
excellent room of Scottish art, a room of
fine French Impressionist works, and quality Renaissance paintings from Italy and
Flanders. Salvador Dalí's superb *Christ of
St John of the Cross* is also here. Best of all,
nearly everything – including the paintings –
has an easy-reading paragraph of interpretation next to it: you can learn a lot about
art and more here, and it's excellent for the
children, with plenty for them to do and displays aimed at a variety of ages. There are
free hour-long guided tours leaving at 11am
and 2.30pm. Bus 17, among many others,
runs here from Renfield St.

FREE Hunterian Museum   MUSEUM
(www.hunterian.gla.ac.uk; University Ave; ⊙10am-
5pm Tue-Sat, 11am-4pm Sun) Housed in the
glorious sandstone main building of the
university, which is in itself reason enough
to pay a visit, this quirky museum contains
the collection of renowned one-time student
of the university, William Hunter (1718–83).
Hunter was primarily an anatomist and
physician but, as one of those gloriously
well-rounded Enlightenment figures, he
interested himself in everything the world
had to offer. Pickled organs in glass jars take
their place alongside geological phenom-
ena, potsherds gleaned from ancient brochs,
dinosaur skeletons and a creepy case of deformed animals. The main halls of the exhibition, with their high vaulted roofs, are
magnificent in themselves. A highlight is the
1674 'Map of the Whole World' in the World
Culture section.

FREE Hunterian Art Gallery   GALLERY, MUSEUM
(www.hunterian.gla.ac.uk; 82 Hillhead St; ⊙10am-
5pm Tue-Sat, 11am-4pm Sun) Across the road
from the Hunterian Museum, the bold tones
of the Scottish Colourists (Samuel Peploe,

Francis Cadell, JD Fergusson) are well represented in this gallery, which also forms
part of Hunter's bequest to the university.
There are also Sir William MacTaggart's impressionistic Scottish landscapes and a gem
by Thomas Millie Dow. There's a special collection of James McNeill Whistler's limpid
prints, drawings and paintings. Upstairs, in
a section devoted to late-19th-century Scottish art, you can see works by several of the
Glasgow Boys.

TOP CHOICE Mackintosh House   MACKINTOSH BUILDING
(www.hunterian.gla.ac.uk; 82 Hillhead St; adult/
concession £5/3; ⊙10am-5pm Tue-Sat, 11am-4pm
Sun) Attached to the Hunterian Art Gallery,
this is a reconstruction of the first home
that Charles Rennie Mackintosh bought
with his wife, noted artist and designer
Mary Macdonald. It's fair to say that interior
decoration was one of their strong points;
the Mackintosh House is startling even today. The quiet elegance of the hall and dining room on the ground floor give way to a
stunning drawing room. There's something
otherworldly about the very mannered style
of the beaten silver panels, the long-backed
chairs and the surface decorations echoing Celtic manuscript illuminations. You
wouldn't have wanted to be the guest that
spilled a glass of red on this carpet.

SOUTH SIDE

FREE Burrell Collection   GALLERY
(www.glasgowmuseums.com; Pollok Country Park;
⊙10am-5pm Mon-Thu & Sat, 11am-5pm Fri & Sun)
One of Glasgow's top attractions is this collection amassed by wealthy industrialist Sir
William Burrell before being donated to the
city and housed in an outstanding museum,
3 miles south of the city centre. Burrell collected all manner of art from his teens to
his death at 97, and this idiosyncratic collection of treasure includes everything from
Chinese porcelain and medieval furniture to
paintings by Degas and Cézanne. It's not so
big as to be overwhelming, and the stamp of
the collector lends an intriguing coherence.

Within the spectacular interior, carved-
stone Romanesque doorways are incorporated into the structure so you actually walk
through them. Floor-to-ceiling windows
admit a flood of light, and enable the surrounding landscape outside to enhance the
effect of the exhibits. It feels as if you're wandering in a huge tranquil greenhouse.

MUSEUM ITINERARY – KELVINGROVE

There are over a million objects in the museum's collection, but fortunately they've pared things down so you won't feel overwhelmed. Enter from either side and first admire the building's interior, with its high central hall, elaborate lamps and organ (recitals at 1pm). The itinerary we've outlined should take approximately three hours.

There are two sides to the museum, Life (history, archaeology and natural history) and Expression (art). Start with the art: upstairs in the hall with the hanging heads. The Dutch room has Rembrandt's magnificent *Man in Armour,* with chiaroscuro techniques learned from Caravaggio. Hit the interactive screen and decide whom you think the painting represents.

The adjacent French gallery holds a fine Renoir portrait of his pupil Valentine Fray, and an early Van Gogh depicting his Glaswegian flatmate Alexander Reid. Nearby, Monet's *Vétheuil* could define both Impressionism and the French countryside. Contrast it with Cézanne's less ethereal landscape alongside. Dufy's famous canvas of *The Jetty at Trouville* also inhabits this room, as do works by many other masters.

The Scottish landscape gallery has some jaw-dropping depictions of Highland scenes. Standing in front of Gustave Doré's *Glen Massan* you can almost feel the drizzle and smell the heather. David Wilkie's *The Cottar's Saturday Night* is based on a Robert Burns poem of the same name.

While you're up here, don't miss the paintings around the arcade. The collection's highlight, however, sits upstairs in the central atrium. Based on dreams, Salvador Dalí's *Christ of St John of the Cross* is his greatest work. Forget ridiculous moustaches and Surrealist frippery: this is a serious, awesomely powerful painting. A sinewy man-god looks down through an infinity of sky and darkness to a simple fishing boat in Galilee, or Catalunya in this case. You could spend a while in front of this.

Downstairs, the **Art Discovery Centre** is aimed at kids but well worth a stroll, then head for the large room devoted to the Glasgow Boys. Inspired by Whistler, these artists broke with romanticism to pioneer a more modern style. Compare William Kennedy's grounded *Stirling Station* or the realism of James Guthrie's *A Funeral Service in the Highlands* with those misty Scottish landscapes upstairs. Also noteworthy in this space are John Lavery's famous theatrical portrait of Anna Pavlova, and EA Hornel's much-reproduced *The Coming of Spring.*

You've seen most of the paintings now, but there's plenty left to discover if you're not done yet. There's a room dedicated to interiors and designs of art deco and the Glasgow style. 'Margaret has genius, I have only talent', said Charles Rennie Mackintosh of his wife, and there's a good display of her work here, as well as that of her sister, Frances Macdonald.

The other side of the museum, dominated by a hanging Spitfire, has rooms with impressive carved stones from the Viking era, Egyptian grave goods and other archaeological finds. Suits of armour are cleverly placed in an exhibition of the human consequences of war and the Holocaust and there are some fine social history displays. The stuffed animals downstairs are a reminder of the museum's Victorian past. Don't miss John Fulton's elaborate orrery, a working model of the solar system: you'll find it near the much-loved elephant, who is called Sir Roger if you want to be introduced.

In springtime, it's worth making a full day of your trip here and spending some time wandering in the beautiful park, studded with flowers. Once part of the estates of Pollok House, which can be visited, the grounds have numerous enticing picnic spots; if you're not heading further north, here's the place to see shaggy Highland cattle, as well as heavy horses.

Many buses pass the park gates (including buses 45, 47, 48 and 57 from the city centre), and there's a twice-hourly bus service between the gallery and the gates (a pleasant 10-minute walk). Alternatively catch a train to Pollokshaws West from Central station (four per hour; you want the second station on the line for East Kilbride or Kilmarnock).

 Activities

Walking & Cycling

The **Clyde Walkway** extends from Glasgow upriver to the Falls of Clyde near New Lanark, some 40 miles away. The tourist office has a good leaflet pack detailing different sections of this walk. The 10-mile section through Glasgow has interesting parts, though modern buildings have replaced most of the old shipbuilding works.

The well-trodden West Highland Way footpath begins in Milngavie, 8 miles north of Glasgow (you can walk to Milngavie from Glasgow along the River Kelvin), and runs for 95 spectacular miles to Fort William.

There are several long-distance pedestrian/cycle routes that begin in Glasgow and follow off-road routes for most of the way. Check www.sustrans.org.uk for more details.

Tours

City Sightseeing BUS TOUR
(☑0141-204 0444; www.citysightseeingglasgow.co.uk; adult/child £11/5) These double-decker tourist buses run a circuit along the main sightseeing routes, starting near the tourist office on George Sq. You get on and off as you wish. A ticket, bought from the driver or in the tourist office, is valid for two consecutive days. All buses have wheelchair access and multilingual commentary.

Seaforce BOAT TOUR
(☑0141-221 1070; www.seaforce.co.uk; Riverside Museum) Departing from the Riverside Museum, Seaforce offers speedy all-weather powerboat jaunts along the Clyde. There's a variety of trips, including a half-hour ride around central Glasgow (adult/child £12/6), an hour trip to the Erskine Bridge (£15/10) or four-hour rides to local wildlife hot spots (£50/35).

✦☆ Festivals & Events

Not to be outdone by Edinburgh, Glasgow has some kicking festivals of its own.

Glasgow Jazz Festival JAZZ
(☑0141-552 3552; www.jazzfest.co.uk) Excellent festival held in June.

**Glasgow International
Festival of Visual Art** VISUAL ART
(☑0141-276 8384; www.glasgowinternational.org) Held in late April in even years, this features

---

MUSEUM ITINERARY – BURRELL COLLECTION

The Burrell collection is of a manageable size, but the surrounding parkland is so lovely, you should come equipped for strolling and, if it's a fine day, with a picnic. The itinerary we've outlined should take approximately two hours.

In the museum itself, start in the luminous main courtyard, which is dignified by Rodin bronzes, including an 1880 version of *The Thinker,* and the fabulous *Eve After the Fall* and *Age of Bronze*. Next, pass through the ornate portal; this 16th-century work was originally part of Hornby Castle in Yorkshire and is appropriate preparation for the eclectic nature of the collection.

As you pass through, you are thrown back millennia in time to ancient Egypt. Admire the fine carvings and the delicate faience shawabtis, mummy-like figures that accompanied the deceased to the afterlife. Attic black- and red-figure vases are next; continuing along the windows you jump forward via Chinese porcelain to religious sculpture; look for the noteworthy *Lamentation over the Crucified Christ,* an early-16th-century German work by that most versatile and prolific of artists, Anonymous.

Also on the ground floor are re-created interiors of Hutton Castle, in a French medieval style, a small section on Islamic art, and the Burrell's superb collection of tapestries, which get regularly rotated.

Retrace your steps to the Greek vases, and head up the stairs to the small suite of rooms that make this gallery a must-see for art lovers. First up are some wonderful 15th- and 16th-century Flemish paintings, mostly on wood, and beautifully restored. *Rest on the Flight into Egypt* stands out here, the title belied by the very European landscape in the background.

The rest of this assemblage of art is French. Burrell was an important patron of Edgar Degas, whose series of ballet paintings, snapshot-like *Woman With a Parasol,* and masterful portrait of his friend Edmond Duranty are highlights. A series of Manets shows that artist's versatility, while Géricault's horses are also to be admired. You can feel the French summer sun in Alfred Sisley's *Church at Noisy-le-Roi;* compare it with the more dreamlike landscape of Cézanne's almost tropical *Château de Médan*.

Pleasingly, there's good information on all the canvases here and, downstairs, computers where you can browse the database of the collection.

a range of innovative installations, performances and exhibitions around town.

West End Festival   ARTS
(☏0141-341 0844; www.westendfestival.co.uk) This music and arts event is Glasgow's biggest festival, running for three weeks in June.

🛏 Sleeping

The city centre gets very rowdy on weekends, and accommodation options fill up fast, mostly with groups who will probably roll in boisterously some time after 3am. If you prefer an earlier appointment with your bed, you'll be better off in a smaller, quieter lodging or in the West End. Booking ahead is essential anywhere on weekends and in July and August.

CITY CENTRE

TOP CHOICE Brunswick Hotel   HOTEL **££**
(☏0141-552 0001; www.brunswickhotel.co.uk; 106 Brunswick St; d £50-95; 🛜🍽) Some places have dour owners threatening lockouts if you break curfew. Then there's the Brunswick, which every now and then converts the whole hotel into a party venue, with DJs in the lifts and art installations in the rooms. You couldn't ask for a more relaxed and friendly Merchant City base. The rooms are all stylish with a mixture of minimalism and rich, sexy colours. Compact and standard doubles will do if you're here for a night out, but king-size rooms are well worth the £10 upgrade. There's an excellent restaurant downstairs and occasional nightclub in the basement.

Malmaison   HOTEL **£££**
(☏0141-572 1000; www.malmaison.com; 278 West George St; r/ste £160/345; 🛜🍽) Heavenly Malmaison is the ultimate in seductive urban accommodation. Cutting-edge but decadent and plush living at its best, this sassy sister of hospitality is super slinky and a cornerstone of faith in Glaswegian accommodation. Stylish rooms with their moody lighting have a dark, brooding tone, opulent furnishings and a designer touch. It's best to book online, as it's cheaper, and various suite offers can be mighty tempting.

Blythswood Square   HOTEL **£££**
(☏0141-248 8888; www.blythswoodsquare.com; 11 Blythswood Sq; r £150-290; 🛜🍽🍽🍽) In a gorgeous Georgian terrace, this elegant five-star offers plenty of inner-city luxury, with grey and cerise tweeds providing casual soft-toned style throughout. Grades of rooms go from standard to penthouse with corresponding increases in comfort; it's hard to resist the traditional 'classic' ones with windows onto the delightful square, but on weekends you'll have a quieter sleep in the new wing at the back. There's an excellent bar and superb restaurant, as well as a very handsome floorboarded and colonnaded salon space on the 1st floor that functions as an evening spot for cocktails. Other facilities include valet parking and a seductive spa complex.

Citizen M   HOTEL **££**
(☏0141-4049485; www.citizenm.com; 60 Renfrew St; r £70-120; @🛜) This modern chain does away with some of the accoutrements of the standard hotel in favour of self-check-in terminals and minimalist, plasticky modern rooms with just two features: a big, comfortable king-sized bed and a decent shower with mood lighting. The idea is that guests make liberal use of the public areas, and why wouldn't you, with upbeat and super-comfortable designer furniture, a 24-hour cafe, and a table full of Macs to use. Prices vary widely according to demand.

Rab Ha's   INN **££**
(☏0141-572 0400; www.rabhas.com; 83 Hutcheson St; r £69-89; 🛜) This Merchant City favourite is an atmospheric pub-restaurant with four stylish upstairs rooms. They are all quite distinct and colourful. Room 1 is the best and largest, but all are comfortable, and the location is great. The personal touches like fresh flowers, iPod docks, a big welcome and anytime breakfast make you feel special.

Artto   HOTEL **££**
(☏0141-248 2480; www.arttohotel.com; 37 Hope St; s/d £75/90; 🛜) Right by the train station, this modish but affordable hotel has soft white, fawn and burgundy tones in its compact but attractive rooms above a popular bar and eatery. Large windows make staying at the front appealing but, though the double glazing does a good job of subduing the street noise, light sleepers will be happier at the rear. Rates vary widely by the day, and there are room-only prices available.

🛜 Pipers Tryst Hotel   HOTEL **££**
(☏0141-353 5551; www.thepipingcentre.co.uk; 30-34 McPhater St; s/d £50/65; 🛜) The name is no strategy to lure tartan tourists; this intimate, cosy hotel is in a noble building actually run by the adjacent bagpiping centre, with all profits going to maintain it. Cheery

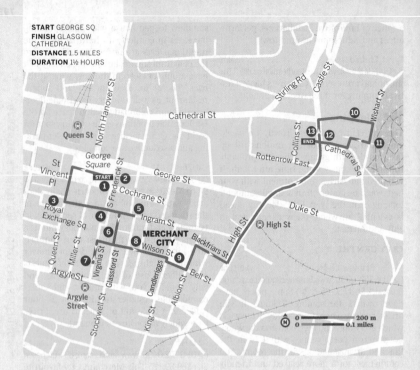

Walking Tour

Walking Tour Glasgow

❯ This stroll takes you to Glasgow Cathedral through trendy Merchant City, once headquarters for Glasgow industrialists.

The tourist office on **❶ George Sq** is a good starting point. The square is surrounded by imposing Victorian architecture: the old post office, the Bank of Scotland and the grandiose **❷ City Chambers**. Statues include Robert Burns, James Watt, and, atop a Doric column, Sir Walter Scott.

Walk one block south down Queen St to the **❸ Gallery of Modern Art**. This striking colonnaded building was once the Royal Exchange and now hosts some of the country's best contemporary art displays.

The gallery faces Ingram St, which you should cross and then follow east four blocks to **❹ Hutcheson's Hall**. Built in 1805, this elegant building is now maintained by the National Trust for Scotland (NTS). On your way, duck into the former Court House cells now housing the **❺ Corinthian** pub/club for a glimpse of the extravagant interior. Retrace your steps one block and continue south

down Glassford St past **❻ Trades Hall**, designed by Robert Adam in 1791 to house the trades guild. The exterior is best viewed from Garth St. Turn right into Wilson St and left along Virginia St, lined with the old warehouses of the Tobacco Lords; many of these have been converted into posh flats. The **❼ Tobacco Exchange** became the Sugar Exchange in 1820.

Back on Wilson St, the **❽ Sheriff Court** fills a whole block and was originally Glasgow's town hall. Continue east on Wilson St past Ingram Sq to **❾ Merchant Sq**, a covered courtyard that was once the city's fruit market but now bustles with cafes and bars.

Head up Albion St, then right into Blackfriars St. Emerging onto High St, turn left and follow it up to the **❿ cathedral**. Behind the cathedral wind your way up through the **⓫ Necropolis**, which offers great city views. On your way back check out the fabulous **⓬ St Mungo's Museum of Religious Life & Art** and **⓭ Provand's Lordship**.

staff, great value and a prime city-centre location make this a cut above other places. Of the eight well-appointed rooms, Nos 6 and 7 are our faves; you won't have far to migrate after a night of Celtic music and fine single malts in the snug bar-restaurant downstairs.

Euro Hostel
HOSTEL £

(☎0141-222 2828; www.euro-hostels.co.uk; 318 Clyde St; dm £17-20, s £29-40, d £36-52; @🛜) With hundreds of beds, this mammoth hostel is handily close to the train station and city centre. While it feels a bit institutional, it has excellent facilities, with en-suite dorms with lockers, internet, a compact kitchen, breakfast available, and laundry. Dorms range in size from four to 14 beds, and price varies on a daily basis. It's very popular with groups and has an instant social life, with snooker, pool, and a great downstairs bar on-site.

McLay's Guesthouse
B&B £

(☎0141-332 4796; www.mclays.com; 260 Renfrew St; s/d £36/56, without bathroom £28/48; @🛜) The string of cheapish guest houses along the western end of Renfrew St are a mixed bag but offer a tempting location right by the Sauchiehall nightlife and a block or so from the College of Art. This is among the best of them; a solid choice with decent warm rooms and fair prices. It's sometimes a little cheaper via online booking agencies.

EAST END

University of Strathclyde

Campus Village
UNIVERSITY ACCOMMODATION ££

(☎0141-553 4148; www.rescat.strath.ac.uk; Rottenrow East; s £42, without bathroom £33, d £57; ⊗mid-Jun–mid-Sep; 🛜) This uni opens its halls of residence to tourists over summer. The Campus Village, opposite Glasgow Cathedral, offers B&B accommodation in single rooms (there may be a few doubles available on request) at good prices. Cheaper, self-catering prices are also available.

WEST END

Hotel Du Vin
HOTEL £££

(One Devonshire Gardens; ☎0141-339 2001; www .hotelduvin.com; 1 Devonshire Gardens; r/ste from £160/425; P@🛜🐾) This is traditionally Glasgow's favoured hotel of the rich and famous, and the patriarch of sophistication and comfort. A study in elegance, it's sumptuously decorated and occupies three classical sandstone terrace houses. There's a bewildering array of room types, all different in style and size. The hospitality is old-school courteous, and there's an excellent restaurant on-site

with a wine selection exceeding 600 varieties. Breakfast is extra.

Glasgow SYHA
HOSTEL £

(☎0141-332 3004; www.syha.org.uk; 8 Park Tce; dm/tw £23/62; @🛜) Perched on a hill overlooking Kelvingrove Park in a charming town house, this place is simply fabulous and one of Scotland's best official hostels. Dorms are mostly four to six beds with padlock lockers and all have their own en suite – very posh. The common rooms are spacious, plush and good for lounging about. There's no curfew, it has a good kitchen and meals are available. The prices listed reflect maximums and are usually cheaper.

Embassy Apartments
APARTMENT ££

(☎0141-946 6698; www.glasgowhotelsand apartments.co.uk; 8 Kelvin Dr; 1-/2-/4-person flat per night £60/80/99; 🛜) If you're after a self-catering option, it's hard to go past this elegant place both for facilities and location. Situated in the leafy West End on a quiet, exclusive street right on the edge of the Botanical Gardens, it sleeps one to seven in studio-style apartments that have fully equipped kitchens and are sparkling clean. It's a particularly good option for couples and families with older kids. They are available by the day, but prices drop for three- and seven-day rentals. Prices vary extensively according to demand; the rates listed are guides only.

Alamo Guest House
B&B ££

(☎0141-339 2395; www.alamoguesthouse.com; 46 Gray St; d/superior d £95/145, s/d without bathroom £55/74; @🛜) The Alamo may not sound like a quiet, peaceful spot, but that's exactly what this great little place is. Opposite Kelvingrove Park, it feels miles from the hustle of the city, but the city centre and West End are within walking distance, and several of the best museums and restaurants in town are close by. The decor is an enchanting mix of antique furnishings and modern design, with excellent bathrooms, and the breezy owners will make you very welcome. All rooms have DVD players and there's an extensive collection to borrow from. Breakfast is abundant but there's no full Scottish option.

Kirklee Hotel
HOTEL ££

(☎0141-334 5555; www.kirkleehotel.co.uk; 11 Kensington Gate; s/d £65/80; 🛜) Want to spoil someone special? In a leafy neighbourhood, Kirklee is a quiet little gem that combines the luxury of a classy hotel with the warmth of staying in someone's home. The rooms are simply gorgeous, beautifully furnished and mostly looking onto lush gardens. For families there is an excellent downstairs room with an enormous en suite. It's located on possibly Glasgow's most beautiful street.

Amadeus Guest House
B&B £

(☎0141-339 8257; www.amadeusguesthouse.co.uk; 411 North Woodside Rd; s £26-36, d £48-60; ☞) Just off the bustle of Great Western Road, a minute's walk from the subway but on a quiet street by the riverside pathway, this has compact bright rooms with cheerful cushions on the comfortable beds. There's a variety of room types, but prices are very good for all of them. Breakfast is continental.

Bunkum Backpackers
HOSTEL £

(☎0141-581 4481; www.bunkumglasgow.co.uk; 26 Hillhead St; dm/tw £14/36; P⃝☞) A tempting budget headquarters for assaults on the eateries and pubs of the West End, Bunkum Backpackers occupies a noble old Victorian terrace on a quiet street. The dorms are spacious – one exaggeratedly so – and the common room and kitchen are also large. There's no curfew but it's not a party hostel. Watch the street numbers; the place isn't well signposted. Slightly cheaper midweek.

✕ Eating

Glasgow is the best place to eat in Scotland, with an excellent range of eateries. The West End is the culinary centre of the city, with Merchant City also boasting an incredible concentration of quality restaurants and cafes.

CITY CENTRE

Café Gandolfi
CAFE, BISTRO ££

(☎0141-552 6813; 64 Albion St; mains £11-15; ☺9am-11.30pm) In the fashionable Merchant City, this cafe was once part of the old cheese market. It's been pulling in the punters for years and packs an interesting clientele: diehard Gandolfers, the upwardly mobile and tourists. It's an excellent, friendly bistro and upmarket coffee shop. Book a Tim Stead-designed, medieval-looking table in advance for well-prepared Scottish and continental food. There's an expansion, specialising in fish, next door.

Brutti Ma Buoni
MEDITERRANEAN £

(☎0141-552 0001; www.brunswickhotel.co.uk; 106 Brunswick St; mains £7-11; ☺11am-10pm; ☗) If you like dining in a place that has a sense of fun, Brutti delivers – it's the antithesis of some of the pretentious places around the Merchant City. With dishes such as 'ugly but good' pizza and 'angry or peaceful' prawns, Brutti's menu draws a smile for its quirkiness and its prices. The Italian and Spanish influences give rise to tapaslike servings or full-blown meals, which are imaginative, fresh and frankly delicious.

🖉 Mussel Inn
SEAFOOD ££

(☎0141-572 1405; www.mussel-inn.com; 157 Hope St; mains £10-18) Airy and easygoing, this two-level eatery – a longtime Rose St favourite in Edinburgh – has recently opened in Scotland's largest city. It specialises in sustainable scallops, oysters and mussels at affordable prices, served with a smile in a comfortable atmosphere.

Lunch@Lily's
CAFE, CHINESE £

(103 Ingram St; mains £3-6; ☺9.30am-4pm Mon-Sat) Don't be put off by the slightly sterile feel: Lily's is a top lunch spot fusing a creative blend of East and West. It's a unique cross between a Chinese bistro and chic cafe with made-to-order Chinese food (such as dumpling buns and mandarin-duck wraps) and standards like burgers and baked potatoes that are tarted up almost beyond recognition. The Chinese food is outstanding – fresh, lively and served with fruits and salad.

Dakhin
INDIAN ££

(☎0141-553 2585; www.dakhin.com; 89 Candleriggs; mains £7-19) This south Indian restaurant breathes fresh air into the city's curry scene. Dishes are from all over the south, and include dosas – thin rice-based crêpes – and a yummy variety of fragrant coconut-based curries. If you're really hungry, try a thali: an assortment of Indian 'tapas'.

🖉 The Chippy Doon The Lane
FISH & CHIPS £

(www.thechippyglasgow.com; McCormick Lane, 84 Buchanan St; meals £6-11; ☺noon-9.30pm) Don't be put off by this down-at-heel alleyway off the shopping precinct, for this is a cut above your average chip shop. Sustainable seafood is served in a rather chic space, all old-time brick, metal archways and jazz. Otherwise, chow down on your takeaway at the wooden tables in the lane or out on Buchanan St itself.

Where the Monkey Sleeps
CAFE £

(www.monkeysleeps.com; 182 West Regent St; dishes £4-7; ☺7am-5pm Mon-Fri) This funky little number in the middle of the business district is just what you need to get away from the ubiquitous coffee chains. Laid-back and a little hippy, the bagels and panini, with names like Burn the Witch or Meathammer, are highlights, as are some very inventive dishes, such as the 'nuclear' beans, dripping with cayenne and Tabasco.

WEST END
There are numerous excellent restaurants in the West End. They cluster along Byres Rd, and, just off it, on Ashton Lane and Ruthven Lane. Gibson St and Great Western Rd also have plenty to offer.

The Ubiquitous Chip SCOTTISH £££

`TOP CHOICE`

(☎0141-334 5007; www.ubiquitouschip.co.uk; 12 Ashton Lane; 2-/3-course dinner £35/40, brasserie mains lunch £7-12, dinner £12-15) The original champion of Scottish produce, The Ubiquitous Chip has won lots of awards for its unparalleled Scottish cuisine, and for its lengthy wine list. Named to poke fun at Scotland's perceived lack of finer cuisine, it offers a French touch but resolutely Scottish ingredients, carefully selected and following sustainable principles. The elegant courtyard space offers some of Glasgow's highest-quality dining, while above and in the atmospheric pub, the cheaper brasserie menu doesn't skimp on quality but keeps things affordable. The cute 'Wee Pub' down the side alley offers plenty of drinking pleasure. There's always something going on here – check the website for upcoming events.

Stravaigin SCOTTISH ££

(☎0141-334 2665; www.stravaigin.co.uk; 28 Gibson St; mains £10-18; ☺9am-11pm) Stravaigin is a serious foodie's delight, with a menu constantly pushing the boundaries of originality and offering creative culinary excellence. The cool contemporary dining space in the basement has booth seating, and helpful, laid-back waiting staff to assist in deciphering the audacious menu. Entry level has a buzzing two-level bar; you can also eat here. There are always plenty of menu deals and special culinary nights.

Mother India INDIAN ££

(☎0141-221 1663; www.motherindia.co.uk; 28 Westminster Tce, Sauchiehall St; mains £8-14; ☺lunch Fri-Sun, dinner daily; ☝🚼) Glasgow curry buffs are forever debating the merits of the city's numerous excellent south Asian restaurants, and Mother India features in every discussion. It may lack the trendiness of some of the up-and-comers but it's been a stalwart

for years and the quality and innovation on show is superb. It also makes a real effort for kids, with a separate menu.

Wau Cafe MALAY £

(27 Old Dumbarton Rd; dishes £4-7; ☺1-10pm Mon-Thu & Sat, 2.30-10pm Fri) The Wau factor at this hole-in-the-wall Malaysian diner comes not just from the incredibly low prices but also the quality and authenticity of the dishes, which include noodles, laksas and curries as well as lesser-known delights.

The Left Bank BISTRO ££

(☎0141-339 5969; www.theleftbank.co.uk; 33 Gibson St; mains £12-18; ☺9am-10pm Mon-Fri, 10am-10pm Sat & Sun; ☝🚼) Huge windows fronting the street greet patrons to this outstanding eatery specialising in gastronomic delights and lazy afternoons. There are lots of little spaces filled with couches and chunky tables reflecting a sense of intimacy. The large starter menu can be treated like tapas, making it good for sharing plates. There are lots of delightful creations that use seasonal and local produce, with an eclectic variety of influences.

Heart Buchanan CAFE, DELI £

(www.heartbuchanan.co.uk; 380 Byres Rd; light meals £6-10; ☺9am-4pm Mon-Sat, 10am-6pm Sun) The famous West End deli – give your nose a treat and drop in – has a small cafe space next door. Break any or all of the 10 commandments to bag a table, then enjoy some of Glasgow's best breakfasts, all with an exquisite quality of produce, a refreshing juice or milkshake, or regularly changing light-lunch options. If you failed in the table quest, the deli also does some of these meals to take away.

Bay Tree Café CAFE £

(www.baytreecafe.com; 403 Great Western Rd; mains £6-10; ☺9am-10pm Mon-Sat, to 9pm Sun; 🛜☝) There are many good cafes in the two or three blocks around here, but the Bay Tree is still our favourite. With lots of vegan and vegetarian options, it has smiling staff, filling mains (mostly Middle Eastern and Greek), generous salads and a good range of hot drinks. The cafe is famous for its all-day breakfasts.

Drinking
Some of Scotland's best nightlife is found in the din and sometimes roar of Glasgow's pubs and bars. There are as many different styles of bar as there are punters to guzzle in them; a month of solid drinking wouldn't get you past the halfway mark.

Flavour of Britain

Food fans know that Britain has finally shaken off its reputation for bland meals. Wherever you go it's easy to find quality dishes, celebrating tradition – often with a modern twist – with local ingredients.

For many visitors, the culinary day begins in a hotel or B&B with the 'Full English Breakfast' – also available as the Full Welsh, Full Scottish, Full Yorkshire etc – a plate full of mainly fried meat that might shock, but there's enough fuel here for several hours of energetic sightseeing.

Lunch or dinner is the time to try regional specialities such as haggis or salmon in Scotland, lamb or laver bread in Wales, Cumberland sausage in northern England, Stilton cheese in the Midlands, curry in Birmingham's Balti Triangle or London's Brick Lane, and seafood just about anywhere on the coast.

And if you're feeling peckish in between meals, look out for country cafes serving cream teas: scones, jam and cream, with that other British classic, a hot cup of tea.

BRITISH CLASSICS

» **Fish and chips** Long-standing favourite, best sampled in coastal towns.

» **Haggis** Scottish icon, mainly offal and oatmeal, traditionally served with 'tatties and neeps' (potatoes and turnips).

» **Sandwich** Global snack today, but an English 'invention' from the 18th century.

» **Laver bread** Laver is a type of seaweed. It's mixed with oatmeal and fried to create this traditional Welsh speciality.

» **Ploughman's lunch** Bread and cheese – pub menu regular, perfect with a pint.

» **Roast beef & Yorkshire pudding** Traditional lunch on Sunday for the English.

» **Cornish pasty** Savoury pastry, southwest speciality, now available country-wide.

Clockwise from top left
1 Cornish pasties 2 Fish and chips
3 Full English Breakfast 4 Haggis with 'tatties and neeps'

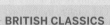

CITY CENTRE

TOP CHOICE Artà
BAR

(www.arta.co.uk; 62 Albion St; ⊙5pm-3am Thu-Sat)
This extraordinary place is so baroque that
when you hear a Mozart concerto over the
sound system, it wouldn't surprise you to
see the man himself at the other end of the
bar. Set in a former cheese market, it really
does have to be seen to be believed. Behind
the door, an opulent, cavernous candle-lit
interior features floor-to-ceiling velvet and
red curtains revealing a staircase to the
tapas bar and restaurant above in a show
of decadence that the Romans would have
appreciated. Despite the luxury, it's got a relaxed, chilled vibe and a mixed crowd. The
big cocktails are great.

Horse Shoe
PUB

(www.horseshoebar.co.uk; 17 Drury St) This legendary city pub and popular meeting place
dates from the late 19th century and is largely unchanged. It's a picturesque spot, with
the longest continuous bar in the UK, but its
main attraction is what's served over it – real
ale and good cheer. Upstairs in the lounge
is some of the best-value pub food (three-
course lunch £4.25) in town.

Corinthian
BAR

(www.thecorinthianclub.co.uk; 191 Ingram St; ☜)
A breathtaking domed ceiling and majestic
chandeliers make Corinthian an awesome
venue. Originally a bank and later Glasgow's
High Court, this regal building's main bar
has to be seen to be believed. Cosy wraparound seating and extra space are complemented by a snug downstairs wine bar and a
plush club downstairs in old court cells.

The Butterfly & The Pig
PUB

(www.thebutterflyandthepig.com; 153 Bath St) One
of many appealing basement bars along this
stretch of Bath St, the piggery is a little offbeat. The decor is eclectic with a retro feel
and this adds to its familiarity. There's a sizeable menu of pub grub, and more refined
fare in the tearoom upstairs.

Babbity Bowster
PUB

(16-18 Blackfriars St) In a quiet corner of Merchant City, this handsome spot is perfect for
a tranquil daytime drink, particularly in the
adjoining beer garden. Service is attentive,
and the smell of sausages may tempt you to
lunch; there's also accommodation. This is
one of the city centre's most charming pubs,
in one of its noblest buildings.

Arches
BAR

(www.thearches.co.uk; 253 Argyle St) A one-stop
culture/entertainment fix, Arches doubles
as a theatre showing contemporary, avant-
garde productions and there's also a club.
The hotel-like entrance belies the deep interior, which makes you feel as though you've
discovered Hades' bohemian underworld.
The crowd is mixed – hiking boots are as
welcome as Versace.

Nice 'n' Sleazy
BAR, CLUB

(www.nicensleazy.com; 421 Sauchiehall St) Students from the nearby School of Art make
the buzz here reliably friendly on the rowdy
Sauchiehall strip. If you're over 35 you'll feel
like a professor not a punter, but retro decor,
a big selection of tap and bottled beers, 3am
closing, and nightly alternative live music
downstairs followed by a club on weekends
make this a winner. There's also popular,
cheap Tex-Mex food (dishes £5 to £7).

WEST END

Hillhead Bookclub
BAR

(www.hillheadbookclub.com; 17 Vinicombe St) Atmosphere in spades is the callsign of this easygoing West End bar. An ornate wooden ceiling
overlooks two levels of well-mixed cocktails,
seriously cheap drinks, comfort food and numerous intriguing decorative touches. There's
even a pingpong table in a cage.

Òran Mór
BAR

(www.oran-mor.co.uk; 731 Great Western Rd) Now
some may be a little uncomfortable with
the thought of drinking in a church. But we
say: the Lord giveth. Praise be and let's give
thanks – a converted church and an almighty
one at that is now a bar, restaurant and club
venue. The bar feels like it's been here for
years – all wood and thick, exposed stone
giving it warmth and a celestial air. There's
an excellent array of whiskies. The only thing
missing is holy water on your way in.

Brel
BAR

(www.brelbarrestaurant.com; 39 Ashton Lane) Perhaps the best on Ashton Lane, this bar can
seem tightly packed, but there's a conservatory out the back so you can pretend you're
sitting outside when it's raining, and when
the sun comes out there's a beer garden. It's
got a huge range of Belgian beers, and serves
mussels and other Lowlands favourites.

☆ Entertainment

Glasgow is Scotland's entertainment city,
from classical music, fine theatres and ballet; to cracking nightclubs pumping out

LOCAL KNOWLEDGE

CINDY-LOU RAMSAY: TV CAMERA OPERATOR & PHOTOGRAPHER

Top photography spot? Pollok Park. The park itself is gorgeous and full of lots of good walks for walkers and cyclists to explore. It also takes you to the famous Burrell Collection, which may not look like much from the outside, but it's a really calming, beautiful building on the inside and jam-packed with exhibits from all over the world.

Favourite spots for live music? Barrowland and King Tut's Wah Wah Hut. Barrowland is an old, tired-looking ballroom badly in need of a bit of a wee facelift, but you're guaranteed to get an unforgettable atmosphere; this is the reason that the biggest bands in the world continue to grace its stage. King Tut's is a much smaller venue for getting 'up close and personal' with some great bands.

Pub for a pint and read of the paper? Blackfriars in the Merchant City.

Typical local words? Blethering (chatting)! Glaswegians tend to do a lot of it, especially if you decide to ask them about their city!

state-of-the-art hip-hop, electro or techno; to cheesy chart tunes and Scottish bands at the cutting edge of contemporary music.

For theatre tickets book directly with the venue. For concerts, a useful booking centre is Tickets Scotland (☑0141-204 5151; www.tickets-scotland.com; 237 Argyle St).

Nightclubs

Sub Club   CLUB
(www.subclub.co.uk; 22 Jamaica St) Saturdays at the Sub Club are one of Glasgow's legendary nights, offering serious clubbing with a sound system that aficionados usually rate the city's best. The claustrophobic, last-one-in vibe is not for those faint of heart.

Arches   CLUB
(www.thearches.co.uk; 253 Argyle St) The Godfather of Glaswegian clubs, it has a design based around hundreds of arches slammed together, and is a must for funk and hip-hop freaks. It is one of the city's biggest, pulling top DJs, and you'll also hear some of the UK's up-and-coming turntable spinners. The club entrance is off Jamaica St.

Cathouse   CLUB
(www.cathouse.co.uk; 15 Union St; ☉Thu-Sun) Mostly rock, emo and metal at this longstanding indie, Goth and alternative venue. There are two dance floors: upstairs is pretty intense with lots of metal and hard rock, downstairs is a little more tranquil.

Live Music

Glasgow is the king of Scotland's live-music scene. Pick up a copy or check the The Gig Guide (www.gigguide.co.uk), available free in most pubs and venues for the latest listings.

One of the city's premier live-music pub venues, the excellent King Tut's Wah Wah Hut (☑0141-221 5279; www.kingtuts.co.uk; 272a St Vincent St) hosts bands every night of the week. Oasis was signed after playing here.

Two bars to see the best, and worst, of Glasgow's newest bands are Brunswick Cellars (239 Sauchiehall St) and Classic Grand (www.classicgrand.com; 18 Jamaica St). Several of the bars mentioned earlier are great for live music, including Nice 'n' Sleazy (opposite).

ABC   CLUB
(O2 ABC; www.o2abcglasgow.co.uk; 300 Sauchiehall St) Both nightclub and venue, this star of Sauchiehall has two large concert spaces and several attractive bars. It's a good all-rounder, with a variety of DJs playing every Thursday to Saturday. Punters scrub up fairly well here.

Barrowland   CONCERT VENUE
(www.glasgow-barrowland.com; 244 Gallowgate) An exceptional old dancehall catering for some of the larger acts that visit the city.

The Captain's   LIVE MUSIC
(www.captainsrest.co.uk; 185 Great Western Rd) Variety of indie bands. Gigs nearly every night, and a Monday open-mic session.

Clyde Auditorium   AUDITORIUM
(☑0844 395 4000; www.secc.co.uk; Finnieston Quay) Also known as the Armadillo because of its bizarre shape, the Clyde adjoins the SECC auditorium, both catering for big national and international acts.

The Hydro   AUDITORIUM
(☑0141-248 3000; www.thehydro.com; Finnieston Quay) This slick new venue will provide a

high-capacity Colosseum-shaped space for big-name bands.

Theatres & Concert Halls

Theatre Royal
OPERA HOUSE

(☑0844 871 7627; www.atgtickets.com; 282 Hope St) This is the home of Scottish Opera, and the Scottish Ballet often has performances here.

Glasgow Royal Concert Hall
CONCERT VENUE

(☑0141-353 8000; www.glasgowconcerthalls.com; 2 Sauchiehall St) A feast of classical music is showcased at this concert hall, the modern home of the Royal Scottish National Orchestra.

Citizens' Theatre
THEATRE

(☑0141-429 0022; www.citz.co.uk; 119 Gorbals St) This is one of the top theatres in Scotland and it's well worth trying to catch a performance here.

Sport

Two football clubs dominate the sporting scene in Scotland, having vastly more resources than other clubs and a long history (and rivalry). This rivalry is also along partisan lines, with Rangers representing Protestant supporters, and Celtic, Catholic. It's worth going to a game; both play in magnificent arenas with great atmosphere. Rangers are currently working their way back up after a financial meltdown led to them reforming in Division 3, the fourth tier of Scottish football.

Celtic FC
FOOTBALL

(☑0871 226 1888; www.celticfc.net; Celtic Park, Parkhead) There are daily stadium tours (adult/child £8.50/5.50). Get bus 61 or 62 from outside St Enoch centre.

Rangers FC
FOOTBALL

(☑0871 702 1972; www.rangers.co.uk; Ibrox Stadium, 150 Edmiston Dr) Tours of the stadium and trophy room run Friday to Sunday (£8/5.50 per adult/child). Get the subway to Ibrox station.

🛍 Shopping

Boasting the UK's largest retail phalanx outside London, Glasgow is a shopaholic's paradise. The 'Style Mile' around Buchanan and Argyle Sts and Merchant City (particularly upmarket Ingram St) is a fashion hub, while the West End has quirkier, more bohemian shopping options: Byres Rd is great for vintage clothing.

Barras
FLEA MARKET

(www.glasgow-barrowland.com; btwn Gallowgate & London Rd; ☺10am-5pm Sat & Sun) Glasgow's flea market, the Barras on Gallowgate, is the living, breathing heart of this city in many respects. It has almost a thousand stalls and people come here just for a wander as much as for their shopping, which gives the place a holiday air. The Barras is notorious for selling designer frauds, so be cautious. Watch your wallet, too.

ℹ Information

The List (www.list.co.uk; £2.20), available from newsagents, is Glasgow and Edinburgh's invaluable fortnightly guide to films, theatre, cabaret, music, clubs – the works. The excellent Eating & Drinking Guide (£5.95), published by The List every April, covers Glasgow and Edinburgh.

Internet Access

Gallery of Modern Art (☑0141-229 1996; Royal Exchange Sq; ☺10am-5pm Mon-Wed & Sat, 10am-8pm Thu, 11am-5pm Fri & Sun) Basement library; free internet access. Bookings recommended.

iCafe (www.icafe.uk.com; 250 Woodlands Rd; per hr £2; ☺10am-11pm) Sip a coffee and munch on a pastry while you check your emails on super-fast connections. Wi-fi too.

Mitchell Library (☑0141-287 2999; www .glasgowlife.org.uk; North St; ☺9am-8pm Mon-Thu, to 5pm Fri & Sat) Free internet access; bookings recommended.

Yeeh@ (48 West George St; per hr £2; ☺9.30am-7pm Mon-Fri, 11am-6pm Sat & Sun)

Medical Services

Glasgow Royal Infirmary (☑0141-211 4000; www.nhsggc.org.uk; 84 Castle St) Medical emergencies and outpatients facilities.

Money

There are numerous ATMs around the city centre. The post office and the tourist office have bureaux de change.

Tourist Information

Airport tourist office (☑0141-848 4440; Glasgow International Airport; ☺7.30am-5pm Mon-Sat, to 3.30pm Sun)

Glasgow information centre (☑0141-204 4400; www.seeglasgow.com; 11 George Sq; ☺9am-5pm Mon-Sat) Excellent tourist office; makes local and national accommodation bookings (£4). Closes later and opens Sundays in summer.

ℹ Getting There & Away

Air

Ten miles west of the city, Glasgow International Airport (GLA; www.glasgowairport.com) handles domestic traffic and international flights. Glasgow Prestwick Airport (PIK; www.glasgow

prestwick.com), 30 miles southwest of Glasgow, is used by **Ryanair** (www.ryanair.com) and some other budget airlines, with many connections to the rest of Britain and Europe.

Bus

All long-distance buses arrive at and depart from **Buchanan bus station** (☏0141-333 3708; www.spt.co.uk; Killermont St), which has pricey lockers, ATMs, and a cafe with wi-fi.

Your first port of call if you're looking for the cheapest fare should be **Megabus** (www .megabus.com), which offers very cheap demand-dependent prices on many major bus routes, including Edinburgh and London. The fare to London can be as little as £12 if you're lucky.

Scottish Citylink (p902) has buses to most major towns in Scotland, including the following ones:

Edinburgh £6.80, 1¼ hours, every 15 minutes

Fort William £22, three hours, seven daily

Inverness £27.50, 3½ hours, eight daily

Oban £17.50, three hours, four direct daily

Stirling £7.30, 45 minutes, at least hourly

Some of the longer distance services are

designated Gold, with onboard service and more amenities.

As well as Megabus, **National Express** (☏08717 81 81 81; www.nationalexpress.com) and **Greyhound** (☏0900 096 0000; www .greyhounduk.com) also run to London (£23 to £36, eight hours). National Express also runs daily to several English cities. Check Megabus and the National Express websites for heavily discounted fares on these routes.

Car & Motorcycle

There are numerous car-rental companies; the big names have offices at Glasgow International and Glastgow Prestwick airports. Companies include the following:

Arnold Clark (☏0141-423 9559; www.arnold clarkrental.com; 43 Allison St)

Avis (☏0844 544 6064; www.avis.co.uk; 70 Lancefield St)

Europcar (☏0141-204 1072; www.europcar .co.uk; 1 Waterloo St)

Train

As a general rule, **Glasgow Central station** serves southern Scotland, England and Wales,

---

GAY & LESBIAN GLASGOW

Glasgow has a vibrant gay scene, with the gay quarter found in and around the Merchant City (particularly Virginia, Wilson and Glassford Sts). The city's gay community has a reputation for being very friendly.

To tap into the scene, check out the *List*, and the free *Scots Gay* (www.scotsgay.co.uk) magazine and website.

Many straight clubs and bars have gay and lesbian nights. The following are just a selection of gay and lesbian pubs and clubs in the city:

AXM (www.axmgroup.co.uk; 80 Glassford St; ⊙10pm-3am Wed-Sun) This popular Manchester club has recently opened up in Glasgow with a makeover of what used to be Bennet's, a Pink Triangle legend. It's a cheery spot, not too scene-y, with all welcome.

Delmonica's (☏0141-552 4803; 68 Virginia St; ⊙noon-midnight) In the heart of the Pink Triangle, this is a popular bar with a bit of a predatory feeling of people on the pull. It's packed on weekday evenings. Drop in here before heading on to the adjacent Polo Lounge, as it often gives out free passes.

FHQ (www.fhqbar.co.uk; 10 John St) In-fashion women-only location in the heart of the Pink Triangle.

Polo Lounge (84 Wilson St; admission £3-6; ⊙to 3am Tue-Sun) Staff claim 'the city's best talent' is found here; a quick glance at the many glamour pusses – male and female – proves their claim. The downstairs club is packed on weekends; just the main bars open on other nights.

Underground (www.underground-glasgow.com; 6a John St) Downstairs on cosmopolitan John St, this sports a relaxed crowd and, crucially, a free jukebox. You'll be listening to indie rather than Abba here.

Speakeasy (www.speakeasyglasgow.co.uk; 10 John St; ⊙4pm-2am Mon-Thu, 4pm-3am Fri, noon-3am Sat, 12.30pm-2am Sun) Relaxed and friendly bar that starts out pub-like and gets louder with gay-anthem DJs as the night progresses. Serves food until very late.

Waterloo Bar (306 Argyle St) This is a traditional pub that's Scotland's oldest gay bar. It attracts punters of all ages. It's very friendly and, with a large group of regulars, a good place to meet people away from the scene.

and **Queen St station** serves the north and east. There are buses every 10 minutes between them. There are direct trains from London's Euston station; they're much quicker (advance purchase single £28 to £105, full fare £162, 4½ hours, more than hourly) and more comfortable than the bus.

Scotrail (☑08457 55 00 33; www.scotrail .co.uk) runs Scottish trains. Destinations include: Edinburgh (£12.90, 50 minutes, every 15 minutes), Oban (£21.60, three hours, three to four daily), Fort William (£26.30, 3¾ hours, four to five daily), Dundee (£25.30, 1½ hours, hourly), Aberdeen (£45.20, 2½ hours, hourly) and Inverness (£79, 3½ hours, 10 daily, four on Sunday).

❶ Getting Around

To/From the Airport

There are buses every 10 or 15 minutes from Glasgow International Airport to Buchanan bus station via Central and Queen St stations (single/return £5/7.50). This is a 24-hour service. Another bus, the 747, heads to the West End. A taxi costs £20 to £25.

Bicycle

There are several places to hire a bike; the tourist office has a full list.

Gear Bikes (☑0141-339 1179; www.gearbikes .com; 19 Gibson St; half-/1/2 days £15/20/35) Decent hybrids. Open daily.

Public Transport

BUS City bus services, mostly run by First Glasgow (p840), are frequent. You can buy tickets when you board buses but on most you must have the exact change. Short journeys in town cost £1.85; a day ticket (£4.50) is good value and is valid until 1am, when a night network starts. A weekly is £15.50. The tourist office hands out the highly complicated SPT Bus Map, detailing all routes in and around the city.

TRAIN & UNDERGROUND There's an extensive suburban network of trains in and around Glasgow; tickets should be bought before travel if the station is staffed, or from the conductor if it isn't. There's also an underground line, the Subway, that serves 15 stations in the city centre, west and south of the city (single £1.20, 10-ride pass £11). The train network connects with the Subway at Buchanan St station. The Discovery Ticket (£3.50) gives unlimited travel on the Subway for a day, while the Roundabout ticket gives a day's unlimited train and Subway travel for £6.

COMBINED TICKET The Daytripper ticket gives you a day's unlimited travel on buses, the Subway, rail and some ferries in the Glasgow region. It costs £10.70 for one or £19 for two. Two kids per adult are included free.

AROUND GLASGOW

Other appealing destinations within easy reach of Glasgow are covered elsewhere, such as Loch Lomond (p838).

Lanark & New Lanark

POP 8300

Below the market town of Lanark, in an attractive gorge by the River Clyde, is the World Heritage site of New Lanark – an intriguing collection of restored mill buildings and warehouses.

Once the largest cotton-spinning complex in Britain, it was better known for the pioneering social experiments of Robert Owen, who managed the mill from 1800. New Lanark is really a memorial to this enlightened capitalist. You'll need at least half a day to explore this site, as there's plenty to see, and appealing walks along the riverside.

◉ Sights & Activities

TOP CHOICE New Lanark Visitor Centre MUSEUM (www.newlanark.org; adult/child/family £8.50/6/24; ⊙10am-5pm Apr-Oct, 10am-4pm Nov-Mar) You need to buy a ticket to enter the main attractions. These include a huge working spinning mule, producing woollen yarn, the Historic Schoolhouse, which contains an innovative, high-tech journey to New Lanark's past via a 3D hologram of the spirit of Annie McLeod, a 10-year-old mill girl who describes life here in 1820. The kids will love it as it's very realistic, although the 'do good for all mankind' theme is a little overbearing.

Also included in your admission is a millworker's house, Robert Owen's home and exhibitions on 'saving New Lanark'. There's also a 1920s-style village store.

Falls of Clyde EXHIBITION, WALK The **Falls of Clyde Wildlife Centre** (www .scottishwildlifetrust.co.uk; adult/child £2/1; ⊙10am-5pm Apr-Sep, 11am-5pm Oct-Mar) is also by the river in New Lanark. This place has child-friendly displays focused on badgers, bats, peregrine falcons and other prominent species. In season, there's a live video feed of peregrines nesting nearby. Outside is a bee tree, where you can see honey being made.

From the centre, you can walk up to Corra Linn and Bonnington Linn (one hour), two of the Falls of Clyde that inspired Turner and Wordsworth, through the beautiful nature reserve managed by the Scottish Wildlife Trust.

🛌 Sleeping

New Lanark makes a very relaxing, attractive place to stay.

TOP CHOICE **New Lanark Mill Hotel** HOTEL **££**
(☎01555-667200; www.newlanarkmillhotel.co.uk; s/d £75/119; 🅿@🛜🏊🐕) Cleverly converted from an 18th-century mill, this hotel is full of character and is a stone's throw from the major attractions. It has luxury rooms (only £10 extra for a spacious superior room), with contemporary art on the walls and views of the churning Clyde below, as well as self-catering accommodation in charming cottages (from £67 a night). There are good facilities for the disabled here. The hotel also serves toothsome meals (bar meals £10 to £17, restaurant mains £15 to £20).

New Lanark SYHA HOSTEL **£**
(☎01555-666710; www.syha.org.uk; dm/tw £18/45; ⊙mid-Mar–mid-Oct; 🅿@🛜) This hostel has a great location in an old mill building by the River Clyde in the heart of the New Lanark complex. It has comfortable en-suite dormitories, and a really good downstairs common area. It serves breakfasts and dinners and will also make a packed lunch. Closed between 10am and 4pm.

ℹ️ Information

Lanark information centre (☎01555-661661; lanark@visitscotland.com; Ladyacre Rd; ⊙10am-5pm) Close to the bus and train stations. Closed Sundays October to March.

ℹ️ Getting There & Around

Lanark is 25 miles southeast of Glasgow. Express buses from Glasgow make the hourly run from Monday to Saturday (one hour).

Trains also run daily between Glasgow Central station and Lanark (£6.20, 55 minutes, half-hourly, hourly on Sundays).

It's a pleasant walk to New Lanark, but there's also a half-hourly bus service from the train station (daily).

BORDERS REGION

The Borders is a distinctive region – centuries of war and plunder have left a battle-scarred landscape, encapsulated by the remnants of the great Border abbeys. Their wealth was an irresistible magnet during the Border wars, and were destroyed and rebuilt numerous times. The monasteries met their scorched end in the 16th century and were never reconstructed. Today these massive stone shells are the region's finest attraction.

Kelso

POP 5100

Kelso, a prosperous market town with a broad, cobbled square flanked by Georgian buildings, has a French feel to it and an historic appeal. During the day it's a busy little place, but after 8pm you'll have the streets to yourself. The town has a lovely site at the junction of the Rivers Tweed and Teviot, and is one of the most enjoyable places in the Borders.

👁️ Sights

Floors Castle CASTLE
(www.floorscastle.com; adult/child £8/4; ⊙11am-5pm May-Oct) Grandiose Floors Castle is Scotland's largest inhabited mansion, home to the Dukes of Roxburghe, and overlooks the River Tweed about a mile west of Kelso. Built by William Adam in the 1720s, the original Georgian simplicity was 'improved' in the 1840s with the addition of rather ridiculous battlements and turrets. Inside, view the vivid colours of the 17th-century Brussels tapestries in the drawing room and the intricate oak carvings in the ornate ballroom. It opens at 10.30am from June to September and is also open over Easter.

FREE **Kelso Abbey** RUIN
(HS; www.historic-scotland.gov.uk; Bridge St; ⊙9.30am-6.30pm Apr-Sep, 9.30am-4.30pm Sat-Wed Oct-Mar) Once one of the richest abbeys in southern Scotland, Kelso Abbey was built by the Tironensians, an order founded at Tiron in Picardy and brought to the Borders around 1113 by David I. English raids in the 16th century reduced it to ruins, though what remains today is some of the finest surviving Romanesque architecture in Scotland.

🛌 Sleeping

TOP CHOICE **Old Priory** B&B **££**
(☎01573-223030; www.theoldpriorykelso.com; 33 Woodmarket St; s/d £50/80; 🅿🛜) The doubles in this atmospheric place are fantastic and the family room has to be seen to be believed; rooms are sumptuous and debonair with gorgeous dark polished wood pieces. The good news extends to the garden – perfect for a coffee in the morning – and a most comfortable sitting room. The huge

BORDERS WALKING & CYCLING

The region's most famous walk is the challenging 212-mile Southern Upland Way (www.southernuplandway.gov.uk). Another long-distance walk is the 62-mile St Cuthbert's Way (www.stcuthbertsway.info), inspired by the travels of St Cuthbert (a 7th-century saint who worked in Melrose Abbey), which crosses some superb scenery between Melrose and Lindisfarne (in England).

The Borders Abbeys Way (www.bordersabbeysway.com) links all the great Border abbeys in a 65-mile circuit. For shorter walks and especially circular loops in the hills, the towns of Melrose, Jedburgh and Kelso all make ideal bases.

The Tweed Cycle Way is a waymarked 62-mile route along the beautiful Tweed Valley, following minor roads from Biggar to Peebles (13 miles), Melrose (16 miles), Coldstream (19 miles) and Berwick-upon-Tweed (14 miles). Jedburgh tourist office has details.

windows are another feature, flooding the rooms with natural light.

 Edenbank House　　　B&B **££**

(☑01573-226734; www.edenbank.co.uk; Stichill Rd; s/d £40/80; Ⓟⓢⓢ) Half a mile down the road to Stichill, this grand Victorian house (no sign) sits in spacious grounds where only the bleating of lambs in the green fields and birds in the garden break the silence. It's a fabulous place, with huge opulent rooms, lovely views over the fields and incredibly warm, generous hospitality. Breakfast features home-made produce and there's a laissez-faire attitude that makes for an utterly relaxing stay. Call ahead.

Ednam House Hotel　　　HOTEL **££**

(☑01573-224168; www.ednamhouse.com; Bridge St; s/d from £85/125; Ⓟⓢⓢ) The genteel, Georgian Ednam House, touched with a quiet dignity, contains many of its original features and is the top place in town, with fine gardens overlooking the river and an excellent restaurant, as well as a deli-bistro by the gates. It's very popular with fisher folk and during salmon season, from the end of August until November, the hotel is very busy. Rooms have charming old furniture; those with a river view cost more.

✘ Eating & Drinking

The Cobbles　　　PUB **££**

(☑01573-223548; www.thecobblesinn.co.uk; 7 Bowmont St; bar mains £9-13; ⊙meals Tue-Sun) We've included the phone number for a reason: this inn off the main square is so popular you should book for a meal on weekends. Why does it pack out? Because it's cheery, very welcoming, warm, and serves excellent upmarket pub food in generous portions.

Choose from the bar menu or the more upmarket dinner list (£21 for two courses). There's a decent wine selection and proper coffee, but the wise leave room for dessert too. The bar always has an interesting guest ale or two as well. A cracking place.

❶ Information

Kelso library (Bowmont St; ⊙Mon-Sat) Free internet access.

Kelso information centre (☑01573-223464; www.visitscottishborders.com; The Square; ⊙10am-4pm Mon-Sat Apr-Oct, plus 10am-2pm Sun late Jun-early Sep)

❶ Getting There & Away

There are nine buses daily (four on Sunday) to Berwick-upon-Tweed (40 minutes to one hour). Buses run to/from Jedburgh (25 minutes, up to 10 daily Monday to Saturday, four Sunday) and on to Hawick (one hour). There are also frequent services to Edinburgh (£6.90, two hours).

Around Kelso

SMAILHOLM TOWER

Perched on a rocky knoll above a small lake, the narrow, stone Smailholm Tower (HS; www.historic-scotland.gov.uk; adult/child £4.50/2.70; ⊙9.30am-5.30pm daily Apr-Sep, 9.30am-4.30pm Sat & Sun only Oct-Mar) provides one of the most evocative sights in the Borders and keeps the bloody uncertainties of its history alive. Although the displays inside are sparse, the panoramic view from the top is worth the climb.

The nearby farm, Sandyknowe, was owned by Sir Walter Scott's grandfather. As Scott himself recognised, his imagination was fired by the ballads and stories he heard as a child at Sandyknowe, and by the ruined tower a stone's throw away.

The tower is 6 miles west of Kelso, a mile south of Smailholm village on the B6397. You pass through the farmyard to get to the tower. Munro's bus 65 between Melrose and Kelso stops in Smailholm village.

Melrose
POP 1700

Tiny, charming Melrose is a polished village running on the well-greased wheels of tourism. This little enclave is a complete contrast with overbearing Galashiels, whose urban sprawl laps at its western edges. Sitting at the feet of the three heather-covered Eildon Hills, Melrose has a classic market square and one of the great abbey ruins.

⊙ Sights

Melrose Abbey RUIN
(HS; www.historic-scotland.gov.uk; adult/child £5.50/3.30; ⊙9.30am-5.30pm Apr-Sep, to 4.30pm Oct-Mar) Perhaps the most interesting of all the great Border abbeys, the red-sandstone Melrose Abbey was repeatedly destroyed by the English in the 14th century. The remaining broken shell is pure Gothic and the ruins are famous for their decorative stonework – see if you can glimpse the pig gargoyle playing the bagpipes on the roof. You can climb to the top for tremendous views.

The abbey was founded by David I in 1136 for Cistercian monks from Rievaulx in Yorkshire. It was rebuilt by Robert the Bruce, whose heart is buried here. The ruins date from the 14th and 15th centuries, and were repaired by Sir Walter Scott in the 19th century.

The adjoining museum has many fine examples of 12th- to 15th-century stonework and pottery found in the area. Note the impressive remains of the 'great drain' outside – a medieval sewerage system.

✯✯ Festivals & Events

Melrose Rugby Sevens RUGBY
(www.melrose7s.com) In mid-April rugby followers fill the town to see the week-long competition.

Borders Book Festival BOOKS
(www.bordersbookfestival.org) Stretching over four days in late June.

⊨ Sleeping

TOP
CHOICE **Townhouse** HOTEL **££**
(☎01896-822645; www.thetownhousemelrose.co. uk; Market Sq; s/d £90/126; P ☜) The classy Townhouse, exuding warmth and professionalism, has some of the best rooms in town – tastefully furnished with attention to detail. There are two superior rooms (£140) that are enormous in size with lavish furnishings; the one on the ground floor in particular has an excellent en suite, which includes a Jacuzzi. It's well worth the price.

TOP
CHOICE **Old Bank House** B&B **£**
(☎01896-823712; www.oldbankhousemelrose. co.uk; 27 Buccleuch St; s/d £45/60; ☜☀) Right in the middle of town, this is a superb B&B option in a characterful old building. Art on the walls, spacious rooms and a sumptuous breakfast room are complemented by a generous can-do attitude. A great Borders base.

✕ Eating

Townhouse SCOTTISH **££**
(☎01896-822645; www.thetownhousemelrose.co .uk; Market Sq; mains £10-15) The brasserie and restaurant here turn out just about the best gourmet cuisine in town – the sister hotel Burt's, opposite, comes a close second – and offers decent value. There's some rich, elaborate, beautifully presented fare here, but you can always opt for the range of creative lunchtime sandwiches for a lighter feed.

Marmion's Brasserie SCOTTISH **££**
(☎01896-822245; www.marmionsbrasserie.co.uk; 5 Buccleuch St; mains £11-18; ⊙lunch & dinner Mon-Sat; ☝) This atmospheric, oak-panelled niche serves snacks all day, but the lunch and dinner menus include gastronomic delights, featuring things like local lamb, venison steaks or pan-seared cod. The spicy bean lasagne is one of several more-than-token offerings for vegetarians. For lunch the focaccias with creative fillings are a good choice.

ⓘ Information

Melrose information centre (☎01896-822283; www.visitscottishborders.com; Abbey St; ⊙10am-4pm Mon-Sat, noon-4pm Sun Apr-Oct) By the abbey.

Melrose library (18 Market Sq; ⊙Mon-Fri) Free internet access.

ⓘ Getting There & Away

First buses run to/from Edinburgh (£6.80, 2¼ hours, hourly) via Peebles. Change in Galashiels (20 minutes, frequent) for more frequent Edinburgh services and for other Borders destinations.

Around Melrose

DRYBURGH ABBEY

The most beautiful, complete Border abbey is Dryburgh Abbey (HS; www.historic-scotland.gov.uk; adult/child £5/3; ⊙9.30am-5.30pm Apr-Sep, 9.30am-4.30pm Oct-Mar), partly because the neighbouring town of Dryburgh no longer exists (another victim of the wars) and partly because it has a lovely site in a sheltered valley by the River Tweed, accompanied only by a symphony of birdsong. The abbey conjures up images of 12th-century monastic life more successfully than its counterparts in nearby towns. Dating from about 1150, it belonged to the Premonstratensians, a religious order founded in France. The pink-hued stone ruins were chosen as the burial place for Sir Walter Scott.

The abbey is 5 miles southeast of Melrose on the B6404, which passes famous Scott's View overlooking the valley. You can hike there along the southern bank of the River Tweed, or take a bus to the nearby village of Newtown St Boswells.

ABBOTSFORD

Fans of Sir Walter Scott should visit his former residence, Abbotsford (www.scotts abbotsford.co.uk; adult/child £8/4; ⊙9.30am-5pm Mon-Sat, 9.30am-5pm Sun Jun-Sep, 11am-4pm Sun Mar-Oct). The inspiration he drew from the surrounding 'wild' countryside influenced many of his most famous works. A collection of Scott memorabilia is on display, including many personal possessions.

The mansion is about 2 miles west of Melrose between the River Tweed and the B6360. Frequent buses run between Galashiels and Melrose; alight at the Tweed bank roundabout and follow the signposts (it's a 15-minute walk). You can also walk from Melrose to Abbotsford in an hour along the southern bank of the Tweed.

Jedburgh

POP 4100

Attractive Jedburgh, where many old buildings and wynds (narrow alleys) have been intelligently restored, invites exploration by foot. It's constantly busy with domestic tourists, but wander into some of the pretty side streets and you won't hear a pin drop.

◎ Sights

Jedburgh Abbey RUIN

(HS; www.historic-scotland.gov.uk; Abbey Rd; adult/child £5.50/3.30; ⊙9.30am-5.30pm Apr-Sep, 9.30am-4.30pm Oct-Mar) Dominating the town skyline, Jedburgh Abbey was the first great Border abbey to be passed into state care, and it shows – audio and visual presentations telling the abbey's story are scattered throughout the carefully preserved ruins (good for the kids). The red-sandstone ruins are roofless but relatively intact, and the ingenuity of the master mason can be seen in some of the rich (if somewhat faded) stone carvings in the nave. The abbey was founded in 1138 by David I as a priory for Augustinian canons.

FREE **Mary, Queen of Scots House** HISTORIC HOUSE

(Queen St; ⊙10am-4.30pm Mon-Sat, 11am-4.30pm Sun Mar-Nov) Mary stayed at this beautiful 16th-century tower house in 1566 after her famous ride to visit the injured earl of Bothwell, her future husband, at Hermitage Castle. The interesting displays evoke the sad saga of Mary's life.

⌶ Sleeping

Maplebank B&B £

(☑01835-862051; maplebank3@btinternet.com; 3 Smiths Wynd; s/d £25/40; [P]) It's very pleasing to come across places like this, where it really feels like you're staying in someone's home. That someone in this case is like your favourite aunt: friendly and chaotic and generous. There's lots of clutter and it's very informal. The rooms are comfortable and large, and share a good bathroom. Breakfast (particularly if you like fruit, yoghurts, home-made jams and a selection of everything) is much better than you get at most posher places.

Willow Court B&B ££

(☑01835-863702; www.willowcourtjedburgh.co.uk; The Friars; d £80-86; [P][⊚]) It seems inadequate to call this impressive option a B&B; it's more like a boutique hotel. Three impeccable rooms with elegant wallpaper, showroom bathrooms and great beds are complemented by a courteous professional welcome. Breakfast can include a grapefruit medley or smoked salmon, while you could spend hours in the conservatory lounge admiring the views over the garden and town.

✕ Eating

The Clock Tower BISTRO **££**
(☎01835-869788; www.clocktowerbistro.co.uk; Abbey Pl; mains £9-15; ☺Tue-Sat) Opposite the skeleton of the abbey, this place will put meat on your bones with an eclectic menu of upmarket bistro fare, drizzling truffle oil or Rioja jus over ingredients like tuna steaks, duck confit or west-coast scallops. Prices are good for this level of food, though some of the flavours could be more adventurous.

ℹ Information

There's a free wi-fi zone around the town centre.

Jedburgh information centre (☎01835-863170; jedburgh@visitscotland.com; Murray's Green; ☺9.15am-5pm Mon-Sat, 10am-4pm Sun) Head tourist office for the Borders region. Very helpful. Extended hours in summer. Closed Sunday November to March.

Jedburgh library (Castlegate; ☺Mon-Fri) Free internet.

ℹ Getting There & Away

Jedburgh has good bus connections to Hawick (25 minutes, roughly hourly, four on Sunday), Melrose (30 minutes, at least hourly Monday to Saturday, every two hours Sunday) and Kelso (25 minutes, at least hourly Monday to Saturday, four Sunday). Munro's runs from Jedburgh to Edinburgh (£7.10, two hours, at least hourly Monday to Saturday, five Sunday).

Peebles

POP 8100

With a picturesque main street set on a ridge between the River Tweed and the Eddleston Water stream, Peebles is one of the most handsome of the Border towns. Though it lacks a major sight, the agreeable atmosphere and good walking options in the rolling, wooded hills hereabouts will entice you to linger for a couple of days.

Two miles east of town off the A72, in Glentress forest, is one of the 7stanes (www.7stanesmountainbiking.com) mountain-biking hubs (see boxed text, p822). It also has osprey viewing and marked walking trails.

⌖ Sleeping & Eating

Rowanbrae B&B **££**
(☎01721-721630; www.aboutscotland.co.uk/peebles/rowanbrae.html; 103 Northgate; s/d £40/63; ☞) A marvellously hospitable couple runs this great B&B in a quiet cul-de-sac not far from the main street; you'll soon feel like you're staying with friends. There are three upstairs bedrooms, two with en suite, and an excellent guest lounge for relaxation.

Tontine Hotel HOTEL, SCOTTISH **££**
(☎01721-720892; www.tontinehotel.com; High St; s/d £60/110; P☞☺) Glorious is the only word to describe the Georgian dining room here, complete with musicians' gallery, fireplace, and windows the like of which we'll never see again. It'd be worth it even if it served catfood on mouldy bread, but luckily the meals (mains £8 to £14) – ranging from pub classics like steak-and-ale pie to more ambitious fare – are tasty and backed up by very welcoming service. Rooms are decent too: there's a small supplement for river views.

TOP CHOICE **Coltman's** BISTRO, DELI **££**
(www.coltmans.co.uk; 71 High St; mains £10-14; ☺10am-5pm Mon-Wed, to 10pm Thu-Sat, to 4pm Sun) This main street deli has numerous temptations, such as excellent cheeses and Italian smallgoods, as well as perhaps Scotland's tastiest sausage roll – buy two to avoid the trip back for another one. Behind the shop, the good-looking dining area serves confident bistro fare and light snacks with a variety of culinary influences, using top-notch local ingredients.

Sunflower Restaurant FUSION **££**
(☎01721-722420; www.thesunflower.net; 4 Bridgegate; lunches £6-9, dinner mains £12-16; ☺lunch Mon-Sat, dinner Thu-Sat; ✔) The Sunflower, with its warm yellow dining room, is in a quiet spot off the main drag and has a reputation that brings lunchers from all over southern Scotland. It serves good salads for lunch and has an admirable menu in the evenings, with creative and elegant dishes that always include some standout vegetarian fare.

ℹ Information

Peebles information centre (☎01721-723159; www.visitscottishborders.com; High St; ☺9am-5pm Mon-Sat) Open to 6pm in summer (April to September).

ℹ Getting There & Away

The bus stop is beside the post office on Eastgate. Bus 62 runs half-hourly (hourly on Sundays) to Edinburgh (£7, one hour) and Melrose (one hour).

WORTH A TRIP

HERMITAGE CASTLE

The 'guardhouse of the bloodiest valley in Britain', Hermitage Castle (HS; www.historic
-scotland.gov.uk; adult/child £4/2.40; ⊙9.30am-5.30pm Apr-Sep) embodies the brutal history
of the Scottish Borders. Desolate but proud with its massive squared stone walls, it looks
more like a lair for orc raiding parties than a home for Scottish nobility, and is one of the
bleakest and most stirring of Scottish ruins.

Strategically crucial, the castle was the scene of many a dark deed and dirty deal with
the English invaders, all of which rebounded heavily on the perfidious Scottish lord in
question. Here, in 1338, Sir William Douglas imprisoned his enemy Sir Alexander Ramsay
and deliberately starved him to death. Ramsay survived for 17 days by eating grain that
trickled into his pit (which can still be seen) from the granary above. In 1566 Mary Queen
of Scots famously visited the wounded tenant of the castle, Lord Bothwell, here. Fortified,
he recovered to (probably) murder her husband, marry her himself, then abandon her
months later and flee into exile.

The castle is about 12 miles south of Hawick on the B6357.

AYRSHIRE & ARRAN

Ayrshire is synonymous with golf and with
Robert Burns – and there's plenty on offer
here to satisfy both of these pursuits. Troon
has six golf courses for starters, and plenty of
yachties, and there's enough Burns memorabilia in the region to satisfy his most fanatic
admirers.

This region's main drawcard, though, is
the irresistible Isle of Arran. With the most
varied and scenic countryside of the southern Hebridean islands, this easily accessible
island shouldn't be missed.

Isle of Arran

POP 4800

Enchanting Arran is a jewel in Scotland's
scenic crown. The island is a visual feast,
and boasts culinary delights, cosy pubs (as
well as its own brewery and distillery) and
stacks of accommodation. The variations
in Scotland's dramatic landscape can all be
experienced on this one small island, best
explored by pulling on the hiking boots or
jumping on a bicycle. Arran offers some
challenging walks in the mountainous
north, often compared to the Highlands,
while the island's circular road is very
popular with cyclists.

ⓘ Information

In Brodick (and a couple of other places) there
are ATMs.

Arran library (⌨01770-302835; Brodick Hall,
Brodick; ⊙10am-5pm Tue, 10am-7.30pm Thu &
Fri, 10am-1pm Sat) Free internet access.

Brodick information centre (⌨01770-303774;
www.ayrshire-arran.com; Brodick; ⊙9am-5pm
Mon-Sat) Efficient. Located by Brodick ferry
pier; also open Sundays in July and August.

ⓘ Getting There & Away

CalMac runs a car ferry between Ardrossan and
Brodick (passenger/car return £10.75/66, 55
minutes, four to six daily), and from April to late
October runs services between Claonaig on the
Kintyre peninsula and Lochranza (passenger/car
return £9.75/44, 30 minutes, seven to nine daily).

ⓘ Getting Around

BICYCLE Several places hire out bicycles in
Brodick, including **Arran Adventure Company**
(⌨01770-302244; www.arranadventure.com;
Auchrannie Rd, Brodick; day/week £15/60)
and the **Boathouse** (⌨01770-302868; Brodick
Beach; day/week £14/48).

CAR For car hire try **Arran Transport** (⌨01770-
302839; car rental half-/full day from £25/32)
at the service station near the ferry pier.

PUBLIC TRANSPORT Three to six buses daily
go from Brodick pier to Lochranza (45 minutes),
and many daily go from Brodick to Lamlash and
Whiting Bay (30 minutes), then on to Kildonan
and Blackwaterfoot. Pick up a timetable from
the tourist office. An Arran Day Rider ticket costs
£4.90 and permits travel anywhere on the island
for a day (buy it from the driver).

BRODICK & AROUND

Most visitors arrive in Brodick, the heartbeat of the island.

⊙ Sights

Brodick Castle & Park　　　　　　　CASTLE
(NTS; www.nts.org.uk; adult/child castle & park
£11.50/8.50, park only £6.50/5.50; ⊙castle 11am-

Isle of Arran

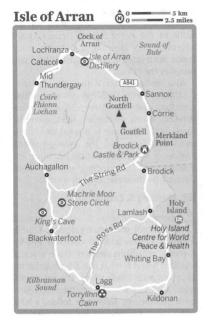

4.30pm Apr-Oct, park 9.30am-sunset year-round) The first impression of this estate 2.5 miles north of Brodick is that of an animal morgue – you enter via the hunting gallery, which is wallpapered with deer heads. On your way to the formal dining room (with its peculiar table furnishings), note the intricacy of the fireplace in the library. The castle has more of a lived-in feel than some National Trust for Scotland (NTS) properties. Only a small portion is open to visitors. The extensive grounds, now a country park with trails among the rhododendrons, justify the steep entry fee.

Activities

Drop into the tourist office for walking and cycling suggestions around the island. The 55-mile circuit on the coastal road is popular with cyclists and has few serious hills – more in the south than the north. There are plenty of walking booklets and maps available and walking trails clearly signposted around the island. Several leave from Lochranza, including the spectacular walk to the island's northeast tip, Cock of Arran, and finishing in the village of Sannox (8 miles one way).

The walk up and down Goatfell takes up to eight hours return, starting in Brodick. If the weather's fine, there are superb views to Ben Lomond and the coast of Northern Ireland. It can, however, be very cold and windy up there; take the appropriate maps (available at the tourist office), waterproof gear and a compass.

Arran Adventure Company OUTDOORS
(01770-302244; www.arranadventure.com; Auchrannie Rd; adult/teen/child £50/40/30; Easter-Oct) Offers loads of activities, running a different one each day (such as gorge walking, sea kayaking, climbing, abseiling and mountain biking). All activities run for about three hours. Drop in to see what's available while you're around.

Festivals & Events

Arran Folk Festival FOLK MUSIC
(www.arranfolkfestival.com) A four-day festival in mid-June.

Sleeping

TOP CHOICE **Kilmichael Country House Hotel** HOTEL £££
(01770-302219; www.kilmichael.com; s £95, d £163-204; Apr-Oct;) The island's best hotel, the Kilmichael is also the oldest building – it has a glass window dating from 1650. The hotel is a luxurious, tastefully decorated spot, a mile outside Brodick but a seemingly a world away in deep countryside. It has just eight rooms and excellent set dinners (open to nonguests; four-course dinner £45). It's an ideal, utterly relaxing hideaway, and feels very classy without being overly formal.

The Douglas HOTEL £££
(01770-302968; www.thedouglashotel.co.uk; d/superior d £135/165) Opposite the ferry, this hotel has been reborn as a smart, stylish, haven of island hospitality. The views were already there, but the luxurious rooms make the most of them. There are numerous thoughtful touches like binoculars to admire the vistas, and the bathrooms are great. The downstairs bar and bistro are also recommended. Prices drop midweek and in winter.

Glenartney B&B ££
(01770-302220; www.glenartney-arran.co.uk; Mayish Rd; s/d £50/80; late Mar-Sep;) Uplifting bay views and genuine, helpful hosts make this a cracking option. Airy, stylish rooms make the most of the natural light available here at the top of the town. Cyclists will appreciate the bike wash, repair and storage facilities, while hikers can benefit from the drying rooms and expert trail advice. The owners make big efforts to be sustainable too.

ℹ️ ARDROSSAN

This unremarkable coastal town is the main ferry port for Arran. Trains leave Glasgow Central station (£6.70, 40 to 50 minutes, half-hourly) to connect with ferries.

Glen Rosa Farm
CAMPING £

(☎01770-302380; www.arrancamping.co.uk; sites per adult/child £4/2; 🐾P) In a lush glen by a river, 2 miles from Brodick, this large place has plenty of nooks and crannies to pitch a tent. It's remote camping with cold water and toilets only. To get there from Brodick head north, take String Rd, then turn right almost immediately on the road signed to Glen Rosa. After 400m, on the left is a white house where you book in; the campground is further down the road.

🍴 Eating

TOP CHOICE / The Brodick Bar
BRASSERIE ££

(Alma Rd; mains £9-19) Don't leave Brodick without dropping in here. The regularly changing menu chalked up on a blackboard brings a modern French flair to this Arran pub, with great presentation, efficient service and delicious flavour combinations. It's very buzzy on weekend evenings.

Creelers
SEAFOOD

(☎01770-302810; www.creelers.co.uk; mains £12-20; ⊙Wed-Sun Apr-Sep) Creelers has been threatening to close for years, but seems to keep on opening every season so you might be lucky. Situated 1.5 miles north of Brodick, it's Arran's top choice for fresh seafood. It's rather no-frills inside, but the dishes – cured salmon, fish soup, fresh oysters, daily fish special – are delicious. It's not licensed, so bring a bottle.

Eilean Mòr
CAFE ££

(www.eileanmorarran.com; Shore Rd; mains £9-12; ⊙meals 10am-9.30pm; 🛜) Upbeat and modern, this likeable little cafe-bar does tasty meals through the day, featuring pizzas and pastas. But it's not afraid to give them a Scottish twist; try the haggis ravioli.

LOCHRANZA

The village of Lochranza is in a stunning location in a small bay at the north of the island. On a promontory stand the ruins of the 13th-century Lochranza Castle (HS; www.historic-scotland.gov.uk; admission free; ⊙24hr), said to be the inspiration for the castle in *The Black Island*, Hergé's Tintin adventure. It's basically a draughty shell inside, with interpretative signs to help you decipher the layout.

Also in Lochranza is the Isle of Arran Distillery (☎01770-830264; www.arranwhisky .com; tours adult/child £6/free; ⊙10am-6pm mid-Mar–Oct), which produces a light, aromatic single malt. The tour is a good one; it's a small distillery, and the whisky-making process is thoroughly explained. More expensive tours (£15) include extra tastings. Opening hours are reduced in winter.

🛏️ Sleeping & Eating

🏅 Lochranza SYHA
HOSTEL £

(☎01770-830631; www.syha.org.uk; dm/d £19/50; ⊙mid Mar–Oct plus Sat & Sun year-round; P@🛜) A recent refurbishment has made a really excellent hostel of what was always a charming place, with lovely views. The rooms are great, with chunky wooden furniture, keycards and lockers. Rainwater toilets, a heat exchange system and an excellent disabled room shows the thought that's gone into the redesign, while plush lounging areas, a kitchen you could run a restaurant out of, laundry, drying room, red deer in the garden and welcoming management make this a top option. Internet unreliable and expensive.

Apple Lodge
B&B ££

(☎01770-830229; s/d/ste £54/78/90; P) Once the village manse, this rewarding choice is most dignified and hospitable. Rooms are individually furnished, and very commodious. One has a four-poster bed, while another is a self-contained suite in the garden. The guest lounge is perfect for curling up with a good book, and courteous hosts mean you should book this one well ahead in summer. Dinner is available (£25).

Catacol Bay Hotel
PUB £

(☎01770-830231; www.catacol.co.uk; r per person £30; P@🛜) Genially run, and with a memorable position overlooking the water, this no-frills pub 2 miles south of Lochranza offers comfortable-enough rooms with shared bathroom and views to lift the heaviest heart. No-frills bar food comes out in generous portions, there's a Sunday lunch buffet (£13.25), and the beer garden is worth a contemplative pint or two as you gaze off across the water into the west.

WEST COAST

On the western side of the island is the Machrie Moor Stone Circle, a pleasant 20- to 30-minute stroll from the parking area on the coastal road. There are actually several separate groups of stones of varying sizes, erected around 4000 years ago. You pass a Bronze Age burial cairn along the path.

SOUTH COAST

The landscape in the southern part of the island is much gentler; the road drops into little wooded valleys, and it's particularly lovely around Lagg. There's a 10-minute walk from Lagg Hotel to Torrylinn Cairn, a chambered tomb over 4000 years old where at least eight bodies were found. Kildonan has pleasant sandy beaches, a gorgeous water outlook, a hotel, a campground and an ivy-clad ruined castle.

🛏 Sleeping & Eating

`TOP CHOICE` **Kildonan Hotel**   HOTEL ££

(☑01770-820207; www.kildonanhotel.com; Kildonan; s/d/ste £75/99/135; P@🖤🐾) Luxurious rooms and a grounded attitude – dogs and kids are made very welcome – combine to make this one of Arran's best options. Oh,

and it's right by the water, with fabulous views and seals basking on the rocks. The standard rooms are beautifully furnished and spotless, but the suites – with private terrace or small balcony – are superb. Other amenities include great staff, a bar serving good grub, a restaurant doing succulent seafood, an ATM, book exchange and laptops lent to guests if you didn't bring one. Applause.

Royal Arran Hotel   B&B ££

(☑01770-700286; www.royalarran.co.uk; Shore Rd, Whiting Bay; s £55, d £95-110; P🖤) This personalised, intimate spot has just four rooms. The double upstairs is our idea of accommodation heaven – four-poster bed, big heavy linen, a huge room and gorgeous water views. Room 1 downstairs is a great size and has a private patio. The hosts couldn't be more welcoming (except to kids under 12, who aren't allowed).

Sealshore Campsite   CAMPGROUND £

(☑01770-820320; www.campingarran.com; sites per adult/child £6/3, per tent £1-4; 🐾P) Living up to its name, this excellent small campground is right by sea (and, happily, the

---

DON'T MISS

TRAQUAIR HOUSE

One of Scotland's great country houses, Traquair House (www.traquair.co.uk; adult/child/family £7.70/4/21; ⊙11am-5pm Easter-Sep, 11am-4pm Oct, 11am-3pm Sat & Sun Nov) has a powerful ethereal beauty, and an exploration here is like time travel. Odd, sloping floors and a musty odour bestow a genuine feel, and parts of the building are believed to have been constructed long before the first official record of its existence in 1107. The massive tower house was gradually expanded over the next 500 years but has remained virtually unchanged since the 17th century.

Since the 15th century, the house has belonged to various branches of the Stewart/Stuart family, and the family's unwavering Catholicism and loyalty to the Stuart cause led to famous visitors like Mary, Queen of Scots and Bonnie Prince Charlie, but also to numerous problems after the deposing of James II of England in 1688. The family's estate, wealth and influence were gradually whittled away, as life as a Jacobite became a furtive, clandestine affair.

One of Traquair's most interesting places is the concealed room where priests secretly lived and performed Mass – up until 1829 when the Catholic Emancipation Act was finally passed. Other beautiful, time-worn rooms hold fascinating relics, including the cradle used by Mary for her son, James VI of Scotland (who also became James I of England), and fascinating letters from the Jacobite Earls of Traquair and their families, including one particularly moving one written from death row in the Tower of London.

The main gates to the house were locked by one earl in the 18th century until the day a Stuart king reclaimed the throne in London, so meanwhile you'll have to enter by a side gate.

In addition to the house, there's a garden maze, a small brewery producing the tasty Bear Ale, and a series of craft workshops.

Traquair is 1.5 miles south of Innerleithen, about 6 miles southeast of Peebles. Bus 62 runs from Edinburgh via Peebles to Innerleithen and on to Galashiels and Melrose.

Kildonan Hotel) with one of Arran's finest views from its grassy camping area. There's a good washroom area with heaps of showers, kitchen facilities, and the breeze keeps the midges away.

LAMLASH

Lamlash is in a dazzling setting, strung along the beachfront. The bay was used as a safe anchorage by the navy during WWI and WWII.

Just off the coast is Holy Island, owned by the Samye Ling Tibetan Centre and with retreat-style accommodation (☑01770-601100; www.holyisle.org; dm/s/d £28/47/72) available. Day visits are allowed. Depending on tides, the ferry (☑01770-600998; tomin10@btinternet.com; adult/child return £11/6) makes around seven trips a day (15 minutes) from Lamlash and runs between May and September. The same folk also run fun mackerel-fishing expeditions (£20 per person).

⌷ Sleeping & Eating

Glenisle Hotel HOTEL, PUB ££
(www.glenislehotel.com; Shore Rd; s/d £78/113; 🛜) This stylish hotel in the heart of town offers plush rooms and cordial service. Upgrade to a superior for the best views over the water. Downstairs is excellent pub food, with Scottish classics such as Cullen skink (soup made with smoked haddock, potato, onion and milk) and a good wine list.

Ayrshire

AYR
POP 46,400

Ayr, whose long sandy beach has made it a popular family seaside resort since Victorian times, makes a convenient base for exploring this section of coast and the area's Robbie Burns heritage.

⊙ Sights

Most things to see in Ayr are Robert Burns–related. The bard was baptised in the **Auld Kirk** (Old Church) off High St. Several of his poems are set here in Ayr; in *Twa Brigs,* Ayr's old and new bridges argue with one another. The **Auld Brig** (Old Bridge) was built in 1491 and spans the river just north of the church. **St John's Tower** (Eglinton Tce) is the only remnant of a church where a parliament was held in 1315, the year after the celebrated victory at Bannockburn.

✤ Festivals & Events

Burns an' a' That CULTURAL
(www.burnsfestival.com) Held in late May, this festival has a bit of everything, from wine-tasting to horseracing to concerts, some of it Burns-related.

⌷ Sleeping

TOP CHOICE 26 The Crescent B&B ££
(☑01292-287329; www.26crescent.co.uk; 26 Bellevue Cres; s £53, d £75-93; 🛜) When the blossoms are out, Bellevue Cres is Ayr's prettiest street, and this is an excellent place to stay on it. The rooms are impeccable – an upgrade to the spacious four-poster room is a sound investment – but it's the warm welcome given by the hosts that makes this special. Numerous little extras, like iPod docks, Arran toiletries, bottled water in the rooms and silver cutlery at breakfast, add appeal. B&B at its best.

Eglinton Guest House B&B ££
(☑01292-264623; www.eglintonguesthouse.com; 23 Eglinton Tce; r per person £28; 🛜🐾) A short walk west of the bus station, this friendly family-run Georgian property is in a quiet cul-de-sac and has a range of traditional, tidy rooms. The location is brilliant – between the beach and the town – and it offers plenty of value, with comfortable beds and compact en suite bathrooms.

✕ Eating & Drinking

TOP CHOICE Beresford BISTRO ££
(☑01292-280820; www.theberesfordayr.co.uk; 22 Beresford Tce; mains £11-15; ⊘meals 9am-9pm) Style and fun go hand in hand at this upbeat establishment serving afternoon martinis in teapots and luring churchgoing ladies with artisanal chocolates. The food is a creative fusion of influences based on solid local produce, with Ayrshire pork, west-coast oysters and Scottish lamb often featuring. Some dishes hit real heights, and are solidly backed by a wide choice of wines, with 10 available by the glass. Upstairs does pizzas and other Italian dishes. Stays open as a bar after the kitchen closes. Top service seals the deal.

Tam O'Shanter PUB
(☑01292 611684; 230 High St; mains £7-9) Opened in the mid-18th century and featured in the Burns poem whose name it now bears, this is an atmospheric old pub with traditional pub grub (served noon to 9pm).

ℹ Information

Ayr information centre (☎01292-290300; www.ayrshire-arran.com; 22 Sandgate; ☺9am-5pm Mon-Sat year-round, 10am-5pm Sun Easter-Aug; 🖳) In the centre of town.

Carnegie library (12 Main St; ☺Mon-Sat) Free internet access.

ℹ Getting There & Around

Ayr is 33 miles from Glasgow and is Ayrshire's major transport hub. There are very frequent express services to Glasgow (£5.60, one hour) via Prestwick Airport, and also serves Stranraer (£7.80, two hours, four to eight daily), other Ayrshire destinations, and Dumfries (£6.20, 2¼ hours, five to seven daily).

There are at least two trains an hour that run to/from Glasgow Central station (£7.50, 50 minutes), and some trains continue south from Ayr to Stranraer (£14.60, 1½ hours).

ALLOWAY

The pretty, lush village of Alloway (3 miles south of Ayr) should be on the itinerary of every Robert Burns fan – he was born here on 25 January 1759.

☉ Sights

Robert Burns Birthplace Museum   MUSEUM
(NTS; www.nts.org.uk; adult/child £8/6; ☺10am-5pm Oct-Mar, to 5.30pm Apr-Sep; 🖳) This impressive new museum has collected a solid range of Burnsiana, including manuscripts and possessions of the poet like the pistols he packed in order to carry out his daily work – as a taxman. There's good biographical information, and a series of displays that bring to life individual poems via background snippets, translations, and audiophones with recitations. Appropriately, it doesn't take itself too seriously: there's plenty of humour that the man himself surely would have approved of, and entertaining audio and visual performances will keep the kids amused.

The admission ticket also covers the atmospheric **Burns Cottage**, connected by a walkway from the Birthplace Museum. Born in the little box-bed in this cramped thatched dwelling, the poet spent the first seven years of his life here. It's an attractive display that gives you a context for reading plenty of his verse. Much-needed translation of some of the more obscure Scots farming terms he loved to use decorate the walls.

Alloway Auld Kirk   CHURCH
Near the Birthplace Museum are the ruins of the kirk, the setting for part of 'Tam o'Shanter'. Burns' father, William Burnes (his son dropped the 'e' from his name), is

buried in the kirkyard; read the poem on the back of the gravestone.

Burns Monument & Gardens   GARDEN
The monument was built in 1823; the gardens afford a view of the 13th-century Brig o'Doon.

ℹ Getting There & Away

Various buses (including bus 58) operate regularly between Alloway and Ayr (10 minutes). Otherwise, walk or rent a bike and cycle here.

TROON
POP 14,800

Troon, a major sailing centre on the coast 7 miles north of Ayr, has excellent sandy beaches and six golf courses. The demanding championship Old Course at **Royal Troon** (☎01292-311555; www.royaltroon.com; Craigend Rd) is a classic of links golf. There are offers on its website; the standard green fee is £175, which includes a complimentary round at the Portland course.

ℹ Getting There & Away

There are half-hourly trains to Ayr (10 minutes) and Glasgow (£6.90, 40 minutes).

P&O (☎0871 66 44 777; www.poirishsea.com) sails twice daily to Larne (£33 for passengers, up to £142 for a car and driver, two hours) in Northern Ireland.

CULZEAN CASTLE & COUNTRY PARK

The Scottish National Trust's flagship property, magnificent **Culzean** (NTS; ☎01655-884400; www.culzeanexperience.org; adult/child/family £15/11/36, park only adult/child £9.50/7; ☺castle 10.30am-5pm Apr-Oct, park 9.30am-sunset year round) is one of the most impressive of Scotland's great stately homes. The entrance to Culzean (kull-ANE) is a converted viaduct, and on approach the castle appears like a mirage, floating into view. Designed by Robert Adam, who was encouraged to exercise his romantic genius in its design, this 18th-century mansion is perched dramatically on the edge of the cliffs. Robert Adam was the most influential architect of his time, renowned for his meticulous attention to detail and the elegant classical embellishments with which he decorated his ceilings and fireplaces.

ℹ Getting There & Away

Culzean is 12 miles south of Ayr; Maybole is the nearest train station, but since it's 4 miles away it's best to come by bus from Ayr (30 minutes, 11 daily Monday to Saturday). Buses pass the park gates, from where it's a

THE SCOTTISH BARD

Best remembered for penning the words of *Auld Lang Syne*, Robert Burns (1759–96) is Scotland's most famous poet and a popular hero whose birthday (25 January) is celebrated as Burns Night by Scots around the world.

Burns was born in 1759 in Alloway to a poor family, who scraped a living gardening and farming. At school he soon showed an aptitude for literature and a fondness for folk songs. He later began to write his own songs and satires. When the problems of his arduous farming life were compounded by the threat of prosecution from the father of Jean Armour, with whom he'd had an affair, he decided to emigrate to Jamaica. He gave up his share of the family farm and published his poems to raise money for the journey.

The poems were so well reviewed in Edinburgh that Burns decided to remain in Scotland and devote himself to writing. He went to Edinburgh in 1787 to publish a second edition, but the financial rewards were not enough to live on and he had to take a job as an excise man in Dumfriesshire. Though he worked well, he wasn't a taxman by nature, and described his job as 'the execrable office of whip-person to the blood-hounds of justice'. He contributed many songs to collections published by Johnson and Thomson in Edinburgh, and a third edition of his poems was published in 1793. To give an idea of the prodigious writings of the man, Robert Burns composed more than 28,000 lines of verse over 22 years. Burns died of rheumatic fever in Dumfries in 1796, aged 37.

Burns wrote in Lallans, the Scottish Lowland dialect of English that is not very accessible to an English person or other foreigners; perhaps this is part of his appeal. He was also very much a man of the people, satirising the upper classes and the church for their hypocrisy.

The Burns connection in southern Scotland is milked for all it's worth and tourist offices have a *Burns Heritage Trail* leaflet leading you to every place that can claim some link with the bard. Burns fans should have a look at www.robertburns.org.

20-minute walk through the grounds to the castle.

DUMFRIES & GALLOWAY

Some of the region's finest attractions lie in the gentle hills and lush valleys of Dumfries & Galloway. Ideal for families, there's plenty on offer for the kids. Galloway Forest is a highlight, with its sublime views, mountain-biking and walking trails, red deer, kites and other wildlife, as are the dreamlike ruins of Caerlaverock Castle. Adding to the appeal of this enticing region is a string of southern Scotland's most idyllic towns, charming when the sun shines. And shine it does. Warmed also by the Gulf Stream, this is the mildest region in Scotland, a phenomenon that has allowed the development of some famous gardens.

Dumfries

POP 31,100

Lovely, red-hued sandstone bridges criss-cross pleasant Dumfries, bisected by the wide River Nith, with pleasant grassed areas along the river bank. Historically, Dumfries held a strategic position in the path of vengeful English armies. Consequently, although it has existed since Roman times, the oldest standing building dates from the 17th century. Plenty of famous names have passed through here: Robert Burns lived here and worked as a tax collector; JM Barrie, creator of Peter Pan, was schooled here; and the former racing driver David Coulthard hails from here.

◉ Sights

The red-sandstone bridges arching over the River Nith are the most attractive features of the town: **Devorgilla Bridge** (1431) is one of the oldest bridges in Scotland. You can download a multilingual MP3 audio tour of the town at www.dumgal.gov.uk/audiotour.

FREE **Burns House**   MUSEUM
(www.dumgal.gov.uk/museums; Burns St; ⊙10am-5pm Mon-Sat & 2-5pm Sun Apr-Sep, 10am-1pm & 2-5pm Tue-Sat Oct-Mar) This is a place of pilgrimage for Burns enthusiasts. It's here that the poet spent the last years of his life, and there are various items of his possessions in glass cases, as well as manuscripts and,

entertainingly, letters: make sure you have a read.

FREE **Robert Burns Centre** MUSEUM
(www.dumgal.gov.uk/museums; Mill Rd; audiovisual presentation £2.20; ⊙10am-5pm Mon-Sat & 2-5pm Sun Apr-Sep, 10am-1pm & 2-5pm Tue-Sat Oct-Mar) A worthwhile Burns exhibition in an old mill on the banks of the River Nith. It tells the story of the poet and Dumfries in the 1790s. The optional audiovisual presentations give more background on Dumfries, and explain the exhibition's contents.

You'll find Robert Burns' mausoleum (St Michael's Kirk) in the graveyard at St Michael's Kirk; there's a grisly account of his reburial on the information panel. At the top of High St is a statue of the bard.

🛏 Sleeping

Merlin B&B £
(☏01387-261002; 2 Kenmure Tce; s/d £35/60; 🛜) Beautifully located on the riverbank across a pedestrian bridge from the town centre, this is a top place to hole up in Dumfries. So much work goes on behind the scenes here that it seems effortless: numerous small details and a friendly welcome make this a very impressive set-up. Rooms share a bathroom, and have super-comfy beds; the breakfast table is also quite a sight.

Ferintosh Guest House B&B ££
(☏01387-252262; www.ferintosh.net; 30 Lovers Walk; s £30-40, d £50-66; 🛜🐾) A Victorian villa, opposite the train station, Ferintosh has sumptuous rooms done in individual themes. The whisky room is our fave – no matter which you choose, there'll probably be a free dram awaiting you on arrival. These people have the right attitude towards hospitality. The owner's original artwork complements the decor, and cyclists are welcomed with a shed and washing facilities out the back for bikes.

🍴 Eating & Drinking

Cavens Arms PUB £
(20 Buccleuch St; mains £7-13; ⊙food Tue-Sun, pub daily) Engaging staff, 10 real ales on tap and a warm contented buzz make this a legendary Dumfries pub. Generous portions of typical pub nosh backed up by a long list of more adventurous daily specials make it one of the town's most enjoyable places to eat too. If you were going to move to Dumfries, you'd make sure you were within a block or two of here.

ℹ Information

Dumfries information centre (☏01387-253862; www.visitdumfriesandgalloway.co.uk; 64 Whitesands; ⊙9.30am-5pm Mon-Sat year-round, plus 11am-4pm Sun Jul–mid-Oct) Plenty of information on the region.

Ewart library (☏01387-253820; Catherine St; ⊙9.15am-7.30pm Mon-Wed & Fri, 9.15am-5pm Thu & Sat) Free internet access.

ℹ Getting There & Away

Bus
Local buses run regularly to Kirkcudbright (one hour, roughly hourly Monday to Saturday, six on Sunday) and Stranraer (£7.80, 2¼ hours, eight daily Monday to Saturday, three on Sunday).

Bus 100/101 runs to/from Edinburgh (£7.50, 2¾ hours, four to seven daily).

Train
There are trains between Carlisle and Dumfries (£9.70, 35 minutes, every hour or two), and direct trains between Dumfries and Glasgow (£14.50, 1¾ hours, eight daily Monday to Saturday). Services are reduced on Sundays.

South Of Dumfries

CAERLAVEROCK
The ruins of Caerlaverock Castle (HS; www.historic-scotland.gov.uk; adult/child £5.50/3.30; ⊙9.30am-5.30pm Apr-Sep, 9.30am-4.30pm Oct-Mar), by Glencaple on a beautiful stretch of the Solway coast, are among the loveliest in Britain. Surrounded by a moat, lawns and stands of trees, the unusual pink-stoned triangular castle looks impregnable. In fact, it fell several times, most famously when it was attacked in 1300 by Edward I: the siege became the subject of an epic poem, *The Siege of Caerlaverock*. The current castle dates from the late 13th century but, once defensive purposes were no longer a design necessity, it was refitted as a luxurious Scottish Renaissance mansion house in 1634. Ironically, the rampaging Covenanter militia sacked it a few years later. With nooks and crannies to explore, passageways and remnants of fireplaces, this castle is great for the whole family.

From Dumfries, bus 6A runs several times a day (just twice on Sunday) to Caerlaverock Castle. By car take the B725 south.

NEW ABBEY
The small, picturesque village of New Abbey lies 7 miles south of Dumfries and contains the remains of the 13th-century Cistercian

Sweetheart Abbey (HS; www.historic-scotland.gov.uk; adult/child £4/2.40; ⌚9.30am-5.30pm Apr-Sep, to 4.30pm Oct, to 4.30pm Sat-Wed Nov-Mar). The shattered, red-sandstone remnants of the abbey are impressive and stand in stark contrast to the manicured lawns surrounding them. The abbey, the last of the major monasteries to be established in Scotland, was founded by Devorgilla of Galloway in 1273 in honour of her dead husband John Balliol (with whom she had founded Balliol College, Oxford). On his death, she had his heart embalmed and carried it with her until she died 22 years later. She and the heart were buried by the altar – hence the name.

Bus 372 from Dumfries travels to New Abbey.

Kirkcudbright

POP 3400

Kirkcudbright (kirk-*coo*-bree), with its dignified streets of 17th- and 18th-century merchants' houses and its appealing harbour, is the ideal base from which to explore the south coast. Look out for the nook-and-cranny wynds in the elbow of beautifully restored High St. With its architecture and setting, it's easy to see why Kirkcudbright has been an artists' colony since the late 19th century.

Sights & Activities

Broughton House GALLERY

(NTS; www.nts.org.uk; 12 High St; adult/child £6/5; ⌚noon-5pm Apr-Oct) The 18th-century Broughton House displays paintings by EA Hornel (he lived and worked here), one of the Glasgow Boys group of painters. Behind the house is a lovely Japanese-style garden (also open Monday to Friday in February and March). The library with its wood panelling and stone carvings is probably the most impressive room.

MacLellan's Castle CASTLE

(HS; www.historic-scotland.gov.uk; Castle St; adult/child £4/2.40; ⌚9.30am-1pm & 2-5.30pm Apr-Sep) Near the harbour, this is a large, atmospheric ruin built in 1577 by Thomas MacLellan, then provost of Kirkcudbright, as his town residence. Inside look for the 'lairds' lug', a 16th-century hidey-hole designed for the laird to eavesdrop on his guests.

FREE **Tolbooth Art Centre** EXHIBITION, GALLERY

(High St; ⌚11am-5pm Mon-Sat, 2-5pm Sun) As well as catering for today's local artists, this centre has an exhibition on the history of the town's artistic development. The place is as interesting for the building itself as for the artistic works on display. It's one of the oldest and best-preserved tollbooths in Scotland and interpretative signboards reveal its past. Reduced hours in winter.

Sleeping & Eating

Kirkcudbright has a swathe of good B&Bs.

TOP CHOICE **Selkirk Arms Hotel** HOTEL ££

(☎01557-330402; www.selkirkarmshotel.co.uk; High St; s/d/superior d £84/110/130; P@🛜) What a haven of good hospitality this is. Superior rooms are excellent – wood furnishings and views over the back garden give them a rustic appeal. The bistro (mains £11 to £18) serves pricey but tasty pub nosh – the fish and chips come wrapped in the hotel newsletter – and the restaurant, Artistas, serves similar fare in a more refined atmosphere. The staff is happy to be here, and you will be too.

Greengate B&B ££

(☎01557-331895; www.thegreengate.co.uk; 46 High St; s/d £60/80; 🛜) The artistically inclined should snap up the one double room in this lovely place, with both historic and current painterly connections.

Number One B&B ££

(☎01557-330540; www.number1bedandbreakfast.co.uk; 1 Castle Gdns; s/d £65/80; 🛜) Right by the castle, this tasteful spot offers high-end B&B with two very smart rooms, one with a great view of the fortress itself. In keeping with the town's artistic nature, there's a fine variety of canvases and watercolours on the walls. Solicitous hosts prepare great breakfasts and are happy to advise about walks in the area.

Castle Restaurant RESTAURANT ££

(☎01557-330569; www.thecastlerestaurant.net; 5 Castle St; mains £12-15; ⌚dinner Mon-Sat; 👪) The Castle Restaurant is the best place to eat in town and uses organic produce where possible. It covers a few bases with chicken, beef and seafood dishes, as well as tempting morsels for vegetarians.

ℹ Information

Check out www.kirkcudbright.co.uk and www .artiststown.org.uk for heaps of information on the town.

Kirkcudbright information centre (☑01557-330494; www.visitdumfriesandgalloway. co.uk; Harbour Sq; ☺9.30am-5pm Mon-Sat, 11am-3pm Sun mid-Feb–Nov) Handy office with useful brochures detailing walks and road tours in the surrounding district. Extended hours in July and August.

ℹ Getting There & Away

Kirkcudbright is 28 miles southwest of Dumfries. Buses run hourly to Dumfries (one hour). Change at Gatehouse of Fleet for Stranraer.

Galloway Forest Park

South and northwest of the small town of New Galloway is 300-sq-mile Galloway Forest Park, with numerous lochs and great whale-backed, heather- and pine-covered mountains. The highest point is Merrick (843m). The park is criss-crossed by off-road bike routes and some superb signposted walking trails, from gentle strolls to long-distance paths, including the Southern Upland Way. The park is very family focused; look out for the booklet of annual events in tourist offices.

The park is also great for stargazing; it's been named a Dark Sky Park by the International Dark-Sky Association.

The scenic 19-mile A712 (Queen's Way) between New Galloway and Newton Stewart slices through the southern section of the park.

On the shore of Clatteringshaws Loch, 6 miles west of New Galloway, is Clatteringshaws Visitor Centre (☑01671-402420; www.forestry.gov.uk/scotland; ☺10.30am-4.30pm Apr–Oct, to 5.30pm Jul & Aug), with an exhibition on the area's flora and fauna. Pick up a copy of the *Galloway Red Kite Trail* leaflet here, which details a circular route through impressive scenery that offers a good chance to spot one of these majestic reintroduced birds. From the visitor centre you can walk to a replica of a Romano-British homestead, and to Bruce's Stone, where Robert the Bruce is said to have rested after defeating the English at the Battle of Rapploch Moss (1307).

About a mile west of Clatteringshaws, Raiders Rd is a 10-mile drive through the forest with various picnic spots, child-friendly activities, and short walks marked along the way. It costs £2 per vehicle; drive slowly as there's plenty of wildlife about.

Further west is the Galloway Red Deer Range where you can observe Britain's largest land-based beast. During rutting season in autumn it's a bit like watching a bullfight as snorting, charging stags compete for the harem. During summer there are guided ranger-led walks (adult/child £4/3).

Walkers and cyclists head for Glentrool in the park's west, accessed by the forest road east from Bargrennan off the A714, north of Newton Stewart. Located just over a mile from Bargrennan is the Glentrool Visitor Centre (☺10.30am-4.30pm Apr–Oct, to 5.30pm Jul & Aug), which has a cafe and stocks information on activities, including mountain biking. The road then winds and climbs up to Loch Trool, where there are magnificent views.

The Machars

The Galloway Hills give way to the softly rolling pastures of the triangular peninsula known as the Machars. The south has many early Christian sites and the loping 25-mile Pilgrims Way.

Buses running between Stranraer and Dumfries stop in Newtown Stewart, from where you can get a bus to Wigtown and Whithorn.

WIGTOWN
POP 1000

Little Wigtown, officially Scotland's National Book Town, has more than a dozen bookshops offering an astonishingly wide selection of volumes, giving book enthusiasts the opportunity to get lost here for days. A major book festival (www.wigtownbookfestival .com) is held here in late September.

The Bookshop (www.the-bookshop.com; 17 North Main St; ☺9am-5pm Mon-Sat) claims to be Scotland's largest secondhand bookshop, and has a great collection of Scottish and regional titles.

A noble stone building in a quiet part of town, Hillcrest House (☑01988-402018; www.hillcrest-wigtown.co.uk; Station Rd; s £40-45, d £68-78; P☎) features high ceilings and huge windows; spend the extra for one of the superior rooms, which have stupendous views overlooking rolling green hills and the sea beyond. This is all complemented by a ripper breakfast involving fresh local produce. **ReadingLasses Bookshop Café** (www.reading-lasses.com; 17 South Main St; mains £6.50; ⊙10am-5pm Mon-Sat, plus noon-5pm Sun May-Oct; ☑) sells caffeine to prolong your reading time and does simple but scrumptious comfort food with several vegetarian options. It specialises in books on the social sciences and women's studies.

WHITHORN
POP 900

Whithorn has a broad, attractive High St, which is virtually closed at both ends (it was designed to enclose a medieval market). In 397, while the Romans were still in Britain, St Ninian established the first Christian mission beyond Hadrian's Wall in Whithorn. After his death, Whithorn Priory, the earliest recorded church in Scotland, was built to house his remains, and Whithorn became the focus of an important medieval pilgrimage.

Today the ruined priory is part of the excellent **Whithorn Trust Discovery Centre** (www.whithorn.com; 45 George St; adult/child £4.50/2.25; ⊙10.30am-5pm Apr-Oct), which introduces you to the history of the place with a good audiovisual and very informative exhibition. There's ongoing archaeological investigation here, and a museum with some fascinating early Christian stone sculptures, including the Latinus Stone (c 450), reputedly Scotland's oldest Christian artefact. Learn about the influences their carvers drew from around the British Isles and beyond.

Stranraer
POP 10900

The friendly but somewhat ramshackle port of Stranraer has seen its mainstay, the ferry traffic to Northern Ireland, move up the road to Cairnryan. The town's still wondering what to do with itself, but there's lots to explore in the surrounding area.

🛏 Sleeping & Eating

TOP CHOICE **Balyett Farm**   B&B, HOSTEL ££
(☑01776-703395; www.balyettbb.co.uk; Cairnryan Rd; dm/s £20/55, d £65-75; 🅿🛜) A mile north of town on the A77, Balyett has a super-welcoming host and lovely relaxing rooms in a tranquil setting; they are light, bright, clean as a whistle and boast lovely views over the surrounding country. Out the back is a self-catering cabin that sleeps five; it's a great space for a family but can also be used for beds on a dorm basis.

Ivy House   B&B £
(☑01776-704176; www.ivyhouse-ferrylink.co.uk; 3 Ivy Pl; s/d £30/50, s without bathroom £25; 🛜) This is a great guest house and does Scottish hospitality proud, with excellent facilities, tidy en-suite rooms and a smashing breakfast. Nothing is too much trouble for the genial host, who always has a smile for guests. The room at the back overlooking the churchyard is particularly light and quiet.

L'Aperitif   BISTRO ££
(☑01776-702991; www.laperitifstranraer.co.uk; London Rd; mains £10-14; ⊙Tue-Sat; 🛜) Purgatory at dinnertime can look uncannily like Stranraer at times, so thank the powers that be for this cheerful local. It's definitely the town's best restaurant and is close to being its best pub too. Despite the name, dishes are more Italian than French, with great pastas alongside roasts and saltimbocca, and delicious appetisers featuring items like smoked salmon or greenlip mussels.

MOUNTAIN-BIKING HEAVEN

A brilliant way to experience southern Scotland's forests is by pedal power. The **7stanes** (stones) are seven mountain-biking centres around the region with trails through some of the finest forest scenery you'll find in the country.

Glentrool is one of these centres and the **Blue Route** here is 5.6 miles in length and a lovely ride climbing up to Green Torr Ridge overlooking Loch Trool. If you've more serious intentions, the **Big Country Route** is 36 miles of challenging ascents and descents that afford magnificent views of the Galloway Forest. It takes a full day and is not for wimps.

Another of the trailheads is at **Kirroughtree Visitor Centre**, 3 miles southeast of Newton Stewart. This offers plenty of singletrack at four different skill levels. You can hire bikes here (www.thebreakpad.com). For more information on routes see www.7stanesmountainbiking.com.

WORTH A TRIP

Corsewall Lighthouse Hotel (☎01776-853220; www.lighthousehotel.co.uk; d incl 5-course dinner £180-290; P☎) It's just you and the cruel sea out here at this fabulously romantic 200-year-old lighthouse, right at the northwest tip of the peninsula, 13 miles northwest of Stranraer. On a sunny day, the water shimmers with light, and you can see Ireland, Kintyre, Arran and Ailsa Craig. But when the wind and rain beat in, it's just great to be cosily holed up in the snug bar-restaurant or snuggling under the covers in your room. Rooms in the lighthouse building itself are attractive if necessarily compact; chalets are also available.

ⓘ Information

Library (North Strand St; ⏰9.15am-7.30pm Mon-Wed & Fri, to 5pm Thu & Sat) Free internet access.

Stranraer information centre (☎01776-702595; www.visitdumfriesandgalloway.com; 28 Harbour St; ⏰10am-4pm Mon-Sat) Efficient and friendly.

ⓘ Getting There & Away

Boat

Cairnryan is 6 miles north of Stranraer on the eastern side of Loch Ryan. Bus 358 runs frequently between Stranraer and Ayr, stopping in Cairnryan. For a taxi to Cairnryan (around £11), contact **McLean's Taxis** (☎01776-703343; 21 North Strand St; ⏰24hr), just up from the tourist office.

P&O (☎0871 66 44 777; www.poferries.com) Runs six to eight fast ferries a day from Cairnryan to Larne (Northern Ireland). The crossing takes two hours; there's one Express service that takes just one hour.

Stena Line (☎08445-762762; www.stenaline .co.uk; passenger/car £28/110) Runs four to six ferries from Cairnryan to Belfast (2¾ hours).

Bus

Scottish Citylink buses run to Glasgow (£17.50, 2½ hours, three daily) and Edinburgh (£20, four hours, three daily).

There are also several daily local buses to Kirkcudbright and the towns along the A75, such as Dumfries (£7.40, 2¼ hours, nine daily Monday to Saturday, three on Sunday).

Train

First Scotrail runs to/from Glasgow (£21.60, 2¼ hours, two to seven trains daily); it may be necessary to change at Ayr.

Around Stranraer

Magnificent **Castle Kennedy Gardens** (www. castlekennedygardens.co.uk; adult/child £5/1.50; ⏰10am-5pm daily Apr-Oct, Sat & Sun only Feb-Mar), 3 miles east of Stranraer, are among the most famous in Scotland. They cover 30 hectares and are set on an isthmus between two lochs and two castles (Castle Kennedy, burnt in 1716, and Lochinch Castle, built in 1864). The landscaping was undertaken in 1730 by the Earl of Stair, who used unoccupied soldiers to do the work. Buses heading east from Stranraer stop here; it's a most pleasant 20-minute stroll from here to the entrance.

Portpatrick

POP 600

Portpatrick is a charming port on the rugged west coast of the Rhinns of Galloway peninsula. It is a good base from which to explore the south of the peninsula, and it's the starting point for the Southern Upland Way. You can follow part of the way to Stranraer (9 miles). It's a clifftop walk, followed by sections of farmland and heather moor.

Harbour House Hotel (☎01776-810456; www.theharbourhousehotel.co.uk; 53 Main St; s/d £60/100; ☎☎) was formerly the customs house but is now a popular, friendly old pub. Some of the beautifully refurbished rooms have brilliant views over the harbour; there are also self-catering apartments out the back. The hotel is also a warm nook for a traditional bar meal (£7 to £10). There are various other hotels, seafood eateries and B&Bs along the harbourfront.

For a real dose of luxury, head 5 miles southeast to **Knockinaam Lodge** (☎01776-810471; www.knockinaamlodge.com; dinner, bed & breakfast s £215-340, d £340-440; P☎☎), a former hunting lodge in a dramatic, secluded location with grassy lawns rolling down to a sandy cove. It's where Churchill plotted the endgame of WWII – you can stay in his suite – and it's a very romantic place to get away from it all. The excellent French-influenced cuisine (lunch/dinner £40/58) is backed up by a great range of wines and single malts, and breakfast features home-made jams.

Bus 367 runs to Stranraer (20 minutes, more than hourly Monday to Saturday, three Sunday).

Stirling & Central Scotland

Includes »

Best Places to Eat

» Café Fish (p851)

» Breizh (p864)

» Moulin Hotel (p867)

» Café 52 (p876)

Best Places to Stay

» Monachyle Mhor (p838)

» George Hotel (p840)

» Argyll Hotel (p853)

» Globe Inn (p875)

Why Go?

Covering everything from the green pastures of the northeast to the mountain landscapes of Glen Lyon, from urban Dundee to the far Mull of Kintyre, central Scotland is less a geographical region than a catch-all term for everything between the Lowlands and the northern Highlands. Anything you ever dreamed about Scotland can be found here: lochs aplenty, from romantic Lomond to the picturesque Trossachs; castles, ranging from royal Balmoral to noble Stirling; whiskies, from the honeyed lotharios of Speyside to the peaty clan chiefs of Islay; and islands, from brooding, deer-studded Jura to emerald Iona, birthplace of Scottish Christianity.

The active are well catered for, with a welter of hills to climb and some of Britain's best long-distance trails to hike. Cyclists and walkers are spoiled for choice, with scenery ranging from mighty Perthshire forests to the rugged Argyll hills; from fishing hamlets of Fife to the epic landscapes of Mull.

When to Go

If the weather is kind, May is a magical time for exploring before the summer crowds arrive. August is the best month of the year for whale-watching off the west coast. In September there are the Braemar Gathering (Highland games) and the Spirit of Speyside whisky and music festival in Dufftown.

Activities

CYCLING

Long-distance routes include much of the northern section of the 214-mile Lochs & Glens Cycle Way (NCN route 7). Starting in Glasgow, it winds its way through the region's heart via Pitlochry to Inverness, and includes some wonderful traffic-free sections in the Trossachs and Cairngorms. NCN route 77 crosses picturesque Perthshire heading west from Dundee to Pitlochry (54 miles). NCN route 78 is a 120-mile ride between Oban and Campbeltown, while part of NCN route 1 bisects Fife then follows the coast to Dundee, Aberdeen and on to Inverness. Browse www.sustrans.org.uk for details and maps of these routes.

For shorter rides, the Trossachs and the islands of Islay and Mull are ideal for a day or more's exploration by bike; cycle hire is available.

A great two-week tour could start by circling Arran. From here, take a ferry to the Kintyre Peninsula and loop down to Campbeltown. Then cross to Islay and Jura, timing your trip so you can take the Wednesday-only ferry from Islay to Oban and crossing by ferry to Mull. From Mull, you can cross to remote Kilchoan, and head north to Mallaig.

Fife takes cycling very seriously, and produces several maps and leaflets detailing cycle routes in this area (www.fife-cycleways .co.uk). There are only a few steep hills here, and the country roads are fairly quiet.

Check out http://active.visitscotland.com for details and further routes in the region.

WALKING

One of Britain's best-known long-distance walks, the West Highland Way (www.west -highland-way.co.uk), starts just outside Glasgow and finishes at Fort William. It covers 96 miles through mountains and glens via Loch Lomond and Rannoch Moor.

The route begins in the Lowlands but the greater part of the trail is among the mountains, lochs and fast-flowing rivers of the western Highlands. After following the eastern shore of Loch Lomond and passing Crianlarich and Tyndrum, the route crosses the vast wilderness of Rannoch Moor and reaches Fort William via Glen Nevis, in the shadow of Britain's highest peak, Ben Nevis.

The path is easy to follow, making use of old drovers' roads (along which Highland cattle were once driven to Lowland markets), an old military road (built by troops to help subdue the Highlands in the 18th century) and disused railway lines.

Best done from south to north, the walk takes about six or seven days, and is completed by about 30,000 hikers each year.

The 65-mile Speyside Way (www.spey sideway.org) is a picturesque route running from Buckie on the northeast coast, through lush green whisky country, and finishing at Aviemore in the Cairngorms (or vice versa). Much of the route is along a peaceful disused railway line well away from traffic.

Both of these routes have baggage-carrying services available.

ⓘ Getting Around

BOAT Most ferries to the west-coast islands are run by **CalMac** (CalMac; ☎0800 066 5000; www.calmac.co.uk). Car space on busier routes should be reserved by phone ahead of your trip.

If you plan to island-hop, you'll save money with an Island Hopscotch ticket, which offers 30 combinations that can save you more than 20% off the normal fares.

Island Rover Passes (passengers £55/79, vehicles £259/388; consecutive days 8/15) cover the whole system and are good value if you want to see a lot of islands fast. Bicycles travel free on this pass.

BUS Citylink (☎0871 266 33 33; www.citylink .co.uk) is the major intercity bus operator. Most local bus transport is operated by **Stagecoach** (www.stagecoachbus.com).

TRAIN Scotrail (☎08457 55 00 33; www .scotrail.co.uk) runs three north–south lines, including the spectacular West Highland line, running from Glasgow to Fort William with a branch to Oban. Another line runs from Glasgow and Edinburgh (via Stirling) to Perth, Pitlochry and Inverness; the third line goes from Perth to Dundee and Aberdeen, then northwest via Elgin to Inverness. Fife also has a rail network. See individual towns for transport details.

The **Central Scotland Rover** pass allows unlimited travel (for three days out of seven) between Edinburgh and Glasgow and the Fife and Stirling areas. It costs £35 and is available from all train stations. Similarly, the **Highland Rover** pass (£79) allows travel on four days out of eight and includes Oban, Aberdeen and buses on Mull.

STIRLING REGION

Covering Scotland's wasplike waist, this region has always been a crucial strategic point dividing the Lowlands from the Highlands. For this reason, Scotland's two most important independence battles were

Stirling & Central Scotland Highlights

1 Gazing in amazement at the epic splendour of **Glen Lyon** (p868), gateway to a faerie land

2 Admiring the views from magnificent **Stirling Castle** (p828), overlooking ancient independence battlefields

3 Scoffing at critics of British cuisine as you sample the super seafood in **Tobermory** (p851), **Oban** (p847) or **Loch Fyne** (p840)

4 Strolling the verdant **Speyside Way** (p825) and sauntering into distilleries for a sly dram along the way

5 Unwinding totally on delightful tiny **Iona** (p852), holy island and tomb of Scottish kings

6 Experiencing the astonishing hospitality of **Islay** (p842), whisky and bird paradise and Scotland's friendliest island

7 Exploring the castles, villages, forests and hills of **Royal Deeside** (p879), home to the Queen's Balmoral Castle

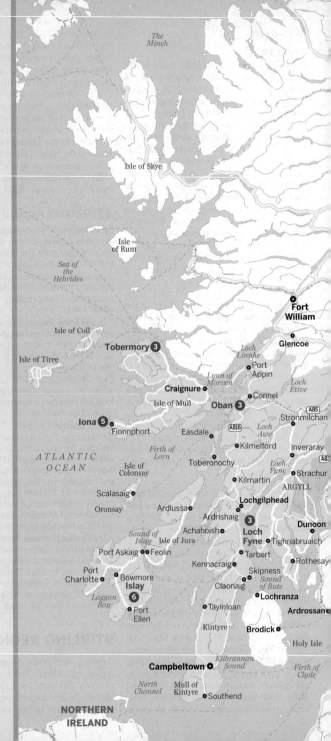

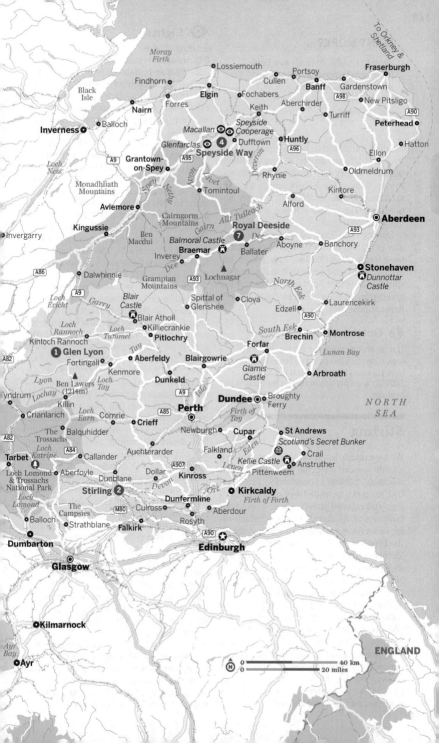

STIRLING & CENTRAL SCOTLAND STIRLING

WANT MORE?

Head to Lonely Planet (www.lonely planet.com/scotland/central-scotland/ stirling) for planning advice, author recommendations, traveller reviews and insider tips.

fought here, within sight of Stirling's hilltop stronghold. Separated by 17 years, William Wallace's victory over the English at Stirling Bridge, followed by Robert Bruce's triumph at Bannockburn, established Scottish nationhood. The region remains a source of much national pride.

Stirling's Old Town perches on a spectacular crag, and the castle is among Britain's most fascinating. Within easy reach, the dreamy Trossachs, home to Rob Roy and inspiration to Walter Scott, offer great walking and cycling in the eastern half of Scotland's first national park.

❶ Getting Around

Trains service Stirling but not the rest of the region, so you'll be relying on buses if you don't have your own transport. **First** (☑01324-602200; www.firstgroup.com) is the main operator.

Stirling

POP 32,673

With an utterly impregnable position atop a mighty wooded crag (the plug of an extinct volcano), Stirling's beautifully preserved Old Town is a treasure-trove of noble buildings and cobbled streets winding up to the ramparts of its dominant castle, which offer views for miles around. Clearly visible is the brooding Wallace Monument, a strange Victorian Gothic creation honouring the legendary freedom fighter of *Braveheart* fame. Nearby is Bannockburn, scene of Robert the Bruce's major triumph over the English.

The castle makes a fascinating visit, but make sure you spend time exploring the Old Town and the picturesque path that encircles it. Near the castle are a couple of snug pubs in which to toast Scotland's hoary heroes. Below the Old Town, retail-minded modern Stirling doesn't offer the same appeal; stick to the high ground as much as possible and you'll love the place.

◉ Sights

Stirling Castle   CASTLE
(HS; www.historic-scotland.gov.uk; adult/child £13/ 6.50; ⊙9.30am-6pm Apr-Sep, to 5pm Oct-Mar) Hold Stirling and you control Scotland. This maxim has ensured that a fortress of some kind has existed here since prehistoric times. You cannot help drawing parallels with Edinburgh castle, but many find Stirling's fortress more atmospheric; the location, architecture, historical significance and utterly commanding views combine to make it a grand and memorable sight. This means it draws plenty of visitors, so visiting in the afternoon is advisable; many tourists come on day trips, so you may have the castle to yourself by about 4pm.

The current castle dates from the late 14th to the 16th century, when it was a residence of the Stuart monarchs. The undisputed highlight of a visit is the fabulous recently restored Royal Palace. The idea was that it should look brand new, just as when it was constructed by French masons under the orders of James V in the mid-16th century with the aim of impressing his new (also French) bride and other crowned heads of Europe. The suite of six rooms – three for the king, three for the queen – is a sumptuous riot of colour. Particularly notable are the fine fireplaces, the re-created painted oak discs in the ceiling of the king's audience chamber, and the fabulous series of tapestries that have been painstakingly woven over many years. Based on originals in New York's Metropolitan Museum, they depict the hunting of a unicorn – an event ripe with Christian metaphor – and are utterly beautiful. Don't miss the exterior of the palace, studded with beautiful sculptures, nor the Stirling Heads Gallery above the royal chambers. This has the original oak roundels – a real rogue's gallery of royals, courtiers and classical personalities. In the vaults beneath the palace is a kid-friendly exhibition on various aspects of castle life.

The other buildings surrounding the main castle courtyard are the vast Great Hall, built by James IV; the Royal Chapel, remodelled in the early 17th-century by James VI and with the colourful original mural painting intact; and the King's Old Building. This is now home to the Museum of the Argyll & Sutherland Highlanders (admission free, donations encouraged), which traces the history of this famous regiment from 1794, including their famous defensive action in the Battle of Balaclava in 1854. Make sure you read the moving letters from WWI and WWII.

Stirling

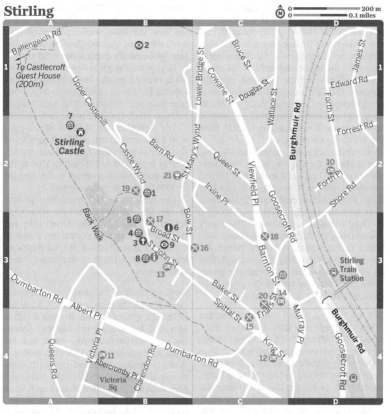

STIRLING & CENTRAL SCOTLAND STIRLING

Until the last tapestry is completed, probably in late 2013, you can watch the weavers at work in the Tapestry Studio at the far end of the castle. It's fascinating to see. Other displays include the Great Kitchens, bringing to life the bustle and scale of the enterprise of cooking for the king and, near the entrance, the Castle Exhibition, which gives good background information on the Stuart kings and updates on current archaeological investigations. The magnificent vistas from the ramparts are stirring.

Admission includes an audioguide, and free guided tours leave regularly from near the entrance. Tours (£2 extra, free for HS members) also run to Argyll's Lodging (Castle Wynd), at the top of Castle Wynd. Complete with turrets, this spectacular lodge is Scotland's most impressive 17th-century town house, former home of William Alexander, Earl of Stirling and noted literary figure. It has been tastefully restored and gives an insight into lavish, 17th-century aristocratic life. There are four or five tours daily (you can't enter by other means).

Old Town   HISTORIC DISTRICT
Below the castle, the steep Old Town has a remarkably different feel to modern Stirling, its cobblestone streets packed with 15th- to 17th-century architectural gems. Its growth began when Stirling became a royal burgh (about 1124), and in the 15th and 16th centuries rich merchants built their houses here.

Stirling has the best surviving town wall in Scotland. It was built around 1547 when Henry VIII of England began the 'Rough Wooing' – attacking the town in order to force Mary, Queen of Scots to marry his son so that the two kingdoms could be united. The wall can be explored on the Back Walk, which follows the line of the wall from Dumbarton Rd to the castle. You pass the town cemeteries (check out the Star Pyramid, an outsized affirmation of Reformation values dating from 1863), then the path continues around the back of the castle to Gowan Hill where you can see the Beheading Stone, now encased in iron bars to prevent contemporary use.

Mar's Wark, on Castle Wynd at the head of the Old Town, is the ornate facade of a Renaissance town house commissioned in 1569 by the wealthy Earl of Mar, regent of Scotland during James VI's minority.

The Church of the Holy Rude (www.holyrude.org; St John St; admission free; 11am-4pm May-Sep) has been the town's parish church for 600 years and James VI was crowned here in 1567. The nave and tower date from 1456, and the church has one of the few surviving medieval open-timber roofs. Stunning stained-glass windows and huge stone pillars create a powerful effect.

Behind the church is Cowane's Hospital (49 St John St; admission free; 10.30am-3.30pm Apr-Oct), built as an almshouse in 1637 by the merchant John Cowane. The high vaulted hall was much modified in the 19th century.

The Mercat Cross, in Broad St, is topped with a unicorn (known as 'The Puggie'), and was once surrounded by a bustling market. Nearby is the Tolbooth, built in 1705 as the town's administrative centre and renovated in 2001 to become an arts venue.

The Old Town Jail (www.oldtownjail.com; St John St; adult/child £6.75/4.25; 10am-5pm Apr-Oct) is great for kids: actors take you through the complex, portraying a cast of characters that illustrate the hardships of Victorian prison life in an innovative, entertaining style.

National Wallace Monument   MONUMENT
(www.nationalwallacemonument.com; adult/child £8.25/5.25; 10am-5pm Apr-Jun, Sep & Oct, to 6pm Jul & Aug, 10.30am-5pm Nov-Mar) Towering over Scotland's narrow waist, this nationalist memorial is so Victorian Gothic it deserves circling bats and ravens. It commemorates the bid for Scottish independence depicted in the film *Braveheart*. From the visitor centre below, walk or shuttle bus up the hill to the building itself. Once there, break the climb up the narrow staircase inside to admire Wallace's 168cm of broadsword and see the man himself re-created in a 3D audiovisual display. More staid is the marble pantheon of lugubrious Scottish heroes, but the view from the top over the flat, green gorgeousness of the Forth Valley, including the site of Wallace's 1297 victory over the English at Stirling Bridge, almost justifies the steep entry fee.

Buses 62 and 63 run from Murray Pl in Stirling to the visitor centre, otherwise it's a half-hour walk from central Stirling. There's a cafe here.

Bannockburn   HISTORIC SITE
Though Wallace's heroics were significant, it was Robert the Bruce's defeat of the English on 24 June 1314 at Bannockburn, just outside Stirling, that eventually established lasting Scottish nationhood. Exploiting the marshy ground, Bruce won a great tactical victory against a much larger and better-

equipped force, and sent Edward II 'homeward, tae think again', as the song 'Flower of Scotland' commemorates.

The Bannockburn Heritage Centre (NTS; www.nts.org.uk) is due to reopen in spring 2014 after a big refurbishment, in time for the 700th anniversary of the battle.

The battlefield itself (which never closes) will hopefully receive a bit of work too; at present, apart from a statue of the victor astride his horse and a misbegotten flag memorial, there's nothing to see. Bannockburn is 2 miles south of Stirling; you can reach it on bus 51 from Murray Pl in the town centre.

🛏 Sleeping

TOP CHOICE Castlecroft Guest House B&B ££

(☎01786-474933; www.castlecroft-uk.com; Ballengeich Rd; s/d £50/65; P@🕾) Nestling into the hillside under the back of the castle, this great hideaway feels like a rural retreat but is a short, spectacular walk from the heart of historic Stirling. The fabulous lounge and deck area boasts extravagant views over green fields to the hills that gird the town, the rooms have excellent modern bathrooms, and the welcome couldn't be more hospitable. Breakfast features home-made bread among other delights.

Neidpath B&B £

(☎01786-469017; www.neidpath-stirling.co.uk; 24 Linden Ave; s/d £40/58; P🕾) Offering excellent value and a genuine welcome, this is a fine choice and easily accessed by car. A particularly appealing front room is one of three excellent modernised chambers with fridges and good bathrooms. The owners also run various self-catering options around town; details are on the website.

Willy Wallace Backpackers Hostel HOSTEL £

(☎01786-446773; www.willywallacehostel.com; 77 Murray Pl; dm/tw £16/36; @🕾) This highly convenient central hostel is friendly, roomy and sociable. The colourful, spacious dormitories are clean and light, there's free tea and coffee, a good kitchen and a laissez-faire atmosphere. Other amenities include cycle hire, a laundry service and free internet and wi-fi.

Linden Guest House B&B ££

(☎01786-448850; www.lindenguesthouse.co.uk; 22 Linden Ave; d £60-80; P@🕾) The warm welcome and easy parking here offer understandable appeal. The rooms, two of which are great for families, have fridges and posh TVs with DVD and an iPod dock, and the

gleaming bathrooms could feature in ads for cleaning products. Breakfast features fresh fruit and kippers, among other choices.

Stirling SYHA HOSTEL £

(☎01786-473442; www.syha.org.uk; St John St; dm/tw £18.75/48; P🕾) Right in the Old Town, this hostel has an unbeatable location and great facilities. Though its facade is that of a former church, the interior is modern and efficient. The dorms are compact but comfortable, with lockers and en suite bathrooms; other highlights include a pool table, a bike shed and, at busy times, cheap meals on offer. Lack of atmosphere can be the only problem.

Sruighlea B&B ££

(☎01786-471082; www.sruighlea.com; 27 King St; s/d £40/60; 🕾) This place feels like a secret hideaway – there's no sign – but it's conveniently located smack bang in the centre of town. You'll feel like a local staying here, and there are eating and drinking places practically on the doorstep. It's a B&B that welcomes guests with the kind of warmth that keeps them returning.

Garfield Guesthouse B&B ££

(☎01786-473730; www.garfieldgh.com; 12 Victoria Sq; small/large d £65/70) Though close to the town centre, Victoria Sq is a quiet oasis, with noble Victorian buildings surrounding a verdant swathe of lawn. The Garfield's huge rooms, bay windows, ceiling roses and other period features make it a winner. There's a great family room, and some rooms have views to the castle towering above.

Forth Guest House B&B ££

(☎01786-471020; www.forthguesthouse.co.uk; 23 Forth Pl; s/d £50/60; P🕾) Just a couple of minutes' walk from town on the other side of the railway, this noble Georgian terrace offers attractive and stylish accommodation at a fair price. The rooms are very commodious, particularly the cute garret rooms with their coombed ceilings and good modern bathrooms. Substantially cheaper in the low season.

🍴 Eating & Drinking

The Kitchen BISTRO ££

(☎01786-448833; www.thekitchenstirling.co.uk; 3 Friars St; mains £11-15) Likeable and laid-back on a central pedestrian street, this Stirling newcomer is doing things right. The small slate-floored dining area offers – in particular – excellent fish and seafood options with

Stirling Castle

PLANNING YOUR ATTACK

Stirling's a sizeable fortress, but not so huge that you'll have to decide what to leave out – there's time to see it all. Unless you've got a working knowledge of Scottish monarchs, head to the **Castle Exhibition 1** first: it'll help you sort one James from another. That done, take on the sights at leisure. First, stop and look around you from the **ramparts 2**; the views high over this flat valley, a key strategic point in Scotland's history, are magnificent.

Next, head through to the back of the castle to the **Tapestry Studio 3**, if it is still functioning; seeing these skilful weavers at work is a highlight.

Track back towards the citadel's heart, stopping for a quick tour through the **Great Kitchens 4**; looking at all that fake food might make you seriously hungry, though. Then enter the main courtyard. Around you are the principal castle buildings. During summer there are events (such as Renaissance dancing) in the **Great Hall 5** – get details at the entrance. The **Museum of the Argyll & Sutherland Highlanders 6** is a treasure trove if you're interested in regimental history, but missable if you're not. Leave the best for last – crowds thin in the afternoon – and enter the sumptuous **Royal Palace 7**.

THE WAY UP & DOWN

If you have time, take the atmospheric Back Walk, a peaceful, shady stroll around the Old Town's fortifications and up to the castle's imposing crag-top position. Afterwards, wander down through the Old Town to admire its facades.

TOP TIPS

» **Admission** Entrance is free for Historic Scotland members. If you'll be visiting several Scottish castles and ruins, a membership will save you plenty.

» **Vital Statistics** First constructed: before 1110; number of sieges: at least nine; last besieger: Bonnie Prince Charlie (unsuccessful); money spent refurbishing the Royal Palace: £12 million.

DAVID ROBERTSON/ALAMY ©

Museum of the Argyll & Sutherland Highlanders
The history of one of Scotland's legendary regiments – now subsumed into the Royal Regiment of Scotland – is on display here, featuring memorabilia, weapons and uniforms.

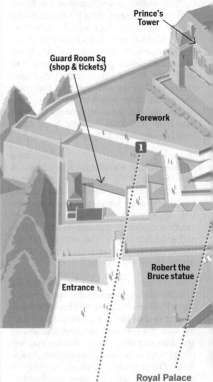

Prince's Tower

Guard Room Sq (shop & tickets)

Forework

Robert the Bruce statue

Entrance

Castle Exhibition
A great overview of the Stewart dynasty here will get your facts straight, and also offers the latest archaeological titbits from the ongoing excavations under the citadel. Analysis of skeletons has revealed surprising amounts of biographical data.

Royal Palace
The impressive new highlight of a visit to the castle is this recreation of the royal lodgings originally built by James V. The finely worked ceiling, ornate furniture and sumptuous unicorn tapestries dazzle.

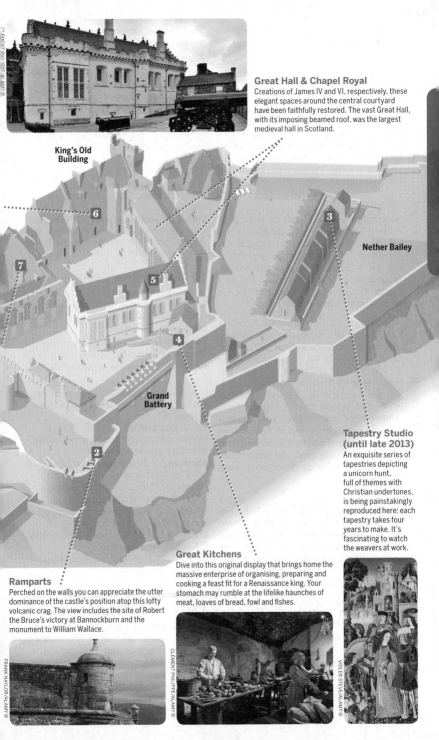

Great Hall & Chapel Royal

Creations of James IV and VI, respectively, these elegant spaces around the central courtyard have been faithfully restored. The vast Great Hall, with its imposing beamed roof, was the largest medieval hall in Scotland.

King's Old Building

6

3

Nether Bailey

7

5

4

Grand Battery

2

Tapestry Studio (until late 2013)

An exquisite series of tapestries depicting a unicorn hunt, full of themes with Christian undertones, is being painstakingly reproduced here: each tapestry takes four years to make. It's fascinating to watch the weavers at work.

Great Kitchens

Dive into this original display that brings home the massive enterprise of organising, preparing and cooking a feast fit for a Renaissance king. Your stomach may rumble at the lifelike haunches of meat, loaves of bread, fowl and fishes.

Ramparts

Perched on the walls you can appreciate the utter dominance of the castle's position atop this lofty volcanic crag. The view includes the site of Robert the Bruce's victory at Bannockburn and the monument to William Wallace.

willing, if slow, service. It's worth booking ahead on weekends.

Portcullis
PUB ££

(☎01786-472290; www.theportcullishotel.com; Castle Wynd; bar meals £8-12) Built in stone as solid as the castle that it stands below, this former school is just the spot for a pint and a pub lunch after your visit. With bar meals that would have had even William Wallace loosening his belt a couple of notches, a little beer garden and a cosy buzz indoors, it's well worth a visit; there are also rooms here (single/double £69/89).

Breá
CAFE £

(www.breastirling.co.uk; 5 Baker St; mains £7-13; ☉10am-9.30pm Tue-Sun; 🌱) Bringing a bohemian touch to central Stirling, this has pared-back contemporary decor and a short menu showcasing carefully sourced Scottish produce. Best in show is perhaps the pork burger with apple and black pudding – a huge thing with home-made bread.

Hermann's
AUSTRIAN, SCOTTISH ££

(☎01786-450632; www.hermanns.co.uk; 58 Broad St; 2-course lunch/3-course dinner £13/22, mains £16-20; 🌱) Solidly set on a corner above the Mercat Cross and below the castle, this elegant Scottish-Austrian restaurant is a reliable and popular choice. The solid, conservative decor is weirdly offset by magazine-style skiing photos, but the food doesn't miss a beat and ranges from Scottish favourites to gourmet schnitzel and Spätzle noodles. Vegetarian options are good, and quality Austrian wines provide an out-of-the-ordinary accompaniment.

Ibby's East India Company
INDIAN £

(www.eastindiastirling.co.uk; 7 Viewfield Pl; mains £7-10; ☉5-11pm) This basement Indian restaurant is sumptuously decorated to resemble a ship's stateroom, with portraits of tea barons on the wall to conjure images of the days of the clippers. It offers dishes from all parts of India and you can BYO wine.

Darnley Coffee House
CAFE £

(☎01786-474468; www.darnley.connectfree.co.uk; 18 Bow St; snacks £4-7; ☉breakfast & lunch) Just down the hill from the castle, beyond the end of Broad St, this is a good pit stop for home baking and speciality coffees during a walk around the Old Town. The cafe is in the vaulted cellars of an historic 16th-century house where Darnley, lover and later hus-band of Mary, Queen of Scots, once stayed while visiting her.

Settle Inn
PUB

(☎01786-474609; 91 St Mary's Wynd; 🛜) A warm welcome is guaranteed at Stirling's oldest pub (1733), a spot redolent with atmosphere, what with its log fire, vaulted back room and low-slung ceilings. Guest ales, atmospheric nooks for settling in for the night and a blend of local characters make it a classic of its kind.

ℹ Information

Stirling Community Hospital (☎01786-434000; Livilands Rd) South of the town centre.

Stirling information centre (☎01786-475019; www.visitscottishheartlands.com; St John St; ☉10am-5pm) At the entrance to the Old Town Jail below the castle.

ℹ Getting There & Away

BUS The **bus station** (☎01786-446474) is on Goosecroft Rd. Citylink (p825) offers a number of services to/from Stirling:

Dundee £13, 1½ hours, hourly

Edinburgh £7.50, one hour, hourly

Glasgow £7, 40 minutes, hourly

Perth £8.30, 50 minutes, at least hourly

Some buses continue to Aberdeen, Inverness and Fort William; more frequently a change will be required.

TRAIN **First ScotRail** (www.scotrail.co.uk) has services to/from a number of destinations, including the following:

Aberdeen £43.30, 2¼ hours, hourly weekdays, every two hours Sunday

Dundee £17.70, one hour, hourly weekdays, every two hours Sunday

Edinburgh £7.70, 55 minutes, twice hourly Monday to Saturday, hourly Sunday

Glasgow £8, 40 minutes, twice hourly Monday to Saturday, hourly Sunday

Perth £11.70, 30 minutes, hourly weekdays, every two hours Sunday

The Trossachs

The Trossachs region has long been a favourite weekend getaway, offering outstanding natural beauty and excellent walking and cycling routes within easy reach of the southern population centres. With thickly forested hills, romantic lochs and an increasingly interesting selection of places to stay and eat, its popularity is sure to continue, protected by its national park status.

The Trossachs first gained popularity as a tourist destination in the early 19th century, when curious visitors came from all over Britain, drawn by the romantic language of Walter Scott's poem *The Lady of the Lake*, inspired by Loch Katrine, and *Rob Roy*, about the derring-do of the region's most famous son.

In summer the Trossachs can be overburdened with coach tours, but many of these are day trippers – peaceful, long evenings gazing at the reflections in the nearest loch are still possible. It's worth timing your visit not to coincide with a weekend.

ABERFOYLE & AROUND
POP 576

Crawling with visitors on most weekends and dominated by a huge car park, little Aberfoyle is a fairly uninteresting place, easily overwhelmed by day trippers. Instead of staying here, we recommend Callander or other Trossachs towns.

Half a mile north of Aberfoyle on the A821 is the David Marshall Lodge Visitor Centre (www.forestry.gov.uk; car park £1-3; ⊙10am-4pm Oct-Mar, to 5pm Apr-Sep, to 6pm Jul & Aug) in the Queen Elizabeth Forest Park, which has info about the many walks and cycle routes in and around the park. The Royal Society for the Protection of Birds (RSPB) has a display here on local bird life, the highlight being a live video link to the resident osprey family. The visitor centre is worth visiting solely for the views.

Three miles east is the Lake of Menteith (called lake not loch due to a mistranslation from Gaelic). A ferry takes visitors to the substantial ruins of Inchmahome Priory (HS; www.historic-scotland.gov.uk; adult/child incl ferry £5/3; ⊙9.30am-5.30pm Apr-Sep, to 4.30pm Oct, last ferry to island 1hr before closing). Mary, Queen of Scots was kept safe here as a child during Henry VIII's 'Rough Wooing'. Henry attacked Stirling in an attempt to force Mary to marry his son so the kingdoms could be united.

🏃 Activities
Several picturesque but busy waymarked trails start from the David Marshall Lodge Visitor Centre in the forest park. These range from an easy 20-minute stroll to a nearby waterfall to a hilly 4-mile circuit. Also here, Go Ape! (www.goape.co.uk; adult/child £30/20; ⊙daily Apr-Oct, Wed-Mon Feb-Jun, Sep & Oct) will bring out the monkey in you on its exhilarating adventure course of long ziplines, swings and rope bridges through the forest.

An excellent 20-mile circular cycle route links with the boat at Loch Katrine. From Aberfoyle, join the Lochs & Glens Cycle Way on the forest trail, or take the A821 over Duke's Pass. Following the southern shore of Loch Achray, you reach the pier on Loch Katrine. The ferry can take you to Stronachlachar (one way with bike £16) on the western shore, from where you can follow the beautiful B829 via Loch Ard back to Aberfoyle.

🍴 Sleeping & Eating
Forth Inn   PUB ££
(☑01877-382372; www.forthinn.com; Main St; mains £8-12; P🐾📶🐕) In the middle of the village, the solid Forth Inn is the lifeblood of the town, with locals and visitors alike queuing up for good, honest pub fare – the best bar meal in Aberfoyle. It also provides accommodation and beer, with drinkers spilling outside into the sunny courtyard. Rooms are available (single £55, double £80 to £90), but they can be noisy on weekends.

❶ Information
Aberfoyle information centre (☑01877-382352; www.visitscottishheartlands.com; Main St; ⊙10am-5pm Apr-Oct, 10am-4pm Nov-Mar) Large office, with good selection of walking information.

❶ Getting There & Away
First (www.firstgroup.com) has six daily buses (Monday to Saturday) from Stirling (40 minutes); you'll have to connect at Balfron on Sundays. There are also three Monday to Saturday buses from Glasgow.

CALLANDER
POP 2754

Callander has been pulling in the tourists for over 150 years, and has a laid-back ambience along its main thoroughfare. It's a far better place than Aberfoyle to spend time in, quickly lulling visitors into lazy pottering. There's also an excellent array of accommodation options here.

The Trossachs is a lovely area to cycle around. The excellent Wheels Cycling Centre (☑01877-331100; www.wheelscyclingcentre.com) has a wide range of hire bikes starting from £10/15 per half-/full day.

🍴 Sleeping
TOP CHOICE Roman Camp Hotel   HOTEL ££
(☑01877-330003; www.romancamphotel.co.uk; Main St; s/d/superior £100/155/195; P🐾📶🐕)

TROSSACHS TRANSPORT

In a bid to cut public transport costs, Demand Responsive Transport (DRT) now covers the Trossachs area. Sounds complex, but basically it means you get a taxi to where you want to go, for the price of a bus. There are various zones; taxis run Monday to Saturday and should preferably be booked 24 hours in advance; call or text ☏0844 567 5670 between 7am and 7pm Monday to Saturday, or book online at www.aberfoylecoaches.com.

Callander's best hotel is centrally located but feels rural, set by the river in its own beautiful grounds with birdsong the only sound. Its endearing features include a lounge with a blazing fire, and a library with a tiny secret chapel. It's an old-fashioned rabbit warren of a place with three grades of room; the standards are certainly luxurious, but the superior ones are even more appealing, with period furniture, excellent bathrooms, armchairs and a fireplace. The upmarket restaurant is open to the public. Reassuringly, the name refers not to toga parties but to a ruin in the adjacent fields.

Abbotsford Lodge   B&B **££**
(☏01877-330066; www.abbotsfordlodge.com; Stirling Rd; s/d £50/85; ☉mid-Feb–mid-Dec; **P**🐾🛜) This friendly Victorian house offers something different to the norm, with tartan and florals consigned to the bonfire, replaced by stylish comfortable contemporary design that enhances the building's original features. Ruffled fabrics and ceramic vases with flower arrangements characterise the renovated rooms. There are fabulous superiors with bathrobes and big beds with great mattresses (£125) as well as cheaper top-floor rooms that share a bathroom (doubles £55), but have lovably offbeat under-roof designs. It's on the main road on the eastern side of town.

Roslin Cottage   B&B **££**
(☏01877-339787; www.roslincottage.co.uk; Stirling Rd; s £40-50, d £60-70; **P**🛜) A characterful cottage that's a haven of good hospitality holds three snug en suite rooms that make an enticing Trossachs base. They all have charm: we love the Kirtle room with the original 17th-century wall exposed. Other delights include a lovely big back garden, a log fire in the lounge and sociable chef-cooked breakfasts. It's on the right as you enter Callander from the east, before the petrol station.

Arden House   B&B **££**
(☏01877-330235; www.ardenhouse.org.uk; Bracklinn Rd; s/d £45/75; **P**🛜) This elegant home has a woodsy, hillside location close to the town centre but far from the crowds. The commodious rooms include a suite (£90) with great views. New owners will be in place by the time you read this, but it should definitely still be worth a look.

White Shutters   B&B **£**
(☏01877-330442; www.incallander.co.uk/white shutters.htm; 6 South Church St; s/d £24/42) A cute little house just off the main street, White Shutters offers pleasing rooms with shared bathroom and a friendly welcome. The mattresses aren't exactly new, but it's comfortable and offers great value for this part of the world.

Linley Guest House   B&B **££**
(☏01877-330087; www.linleyguesthouse.co.uk; 139 Main St; s/d £33/46, d en suite £50) A spick-and-span B&B with bright rooms and helpful owners. The double en suite is worth the extra: it's beautifully appointed, with a large window that draws in lots of natural light. Room-only rate is available.

🍴 Eating & Drinking

Callander Meadows   SCOTTISH **££**
(☏01877-330181; www.callandermeadows.co.uk; 24 Main St; lunch £8.95, mains £11-18; ☉Thu-Sun) Informal but smart, this well-loved restaurant in the centre of Callander occupies the two front rooms of a house on the main street. There's a contemporary flair for presentation and unusual flavour combinations, but a solidly British base underpins the cuisine, with mackerel, red cabbage, salmon and duck making regular and welcome appearances. There's a great daytime beer/coffee garden out the back, and the restaurant is also open on Monday from April to September, and daily in high summer.

🐟 Mhor Fish   SEAFOOD **££**
(☏01877-330213; www.mhor.net; 75 Main St; fish supper £6, mains £8-14; ☉noon-9pm Tue-Sun) Both chip shop and fish restaurant, but wholly different, this endearing black-and-white-tiled cafe displays the day's fresh catch. You can choose how you want it

cooked, whether pan-seared and accompanied by one of many good wines, or fried and wrapped in paper with chips to take away. The fish and seafood come from sustainable stock, and includes oysters and other goodies. If it runs out of fresh fish, it shuts, so opening hours can be a bit variable.

Lade Inn   PUB
(www.theladeinn.com; Kilmahog; 🅿) Callander's best pub isn't in Callander – it's a mile west of town. It pulls a good pint (the real ales here are brewed to a house recipe), and next door the owners run a shop with a dazzling selection of Scottish beers. There's low-key live music here on weekends, but it shuts early midweek. The food at last visit was overpriced and mediocre.

ℹ️ Information

Loch Lomond & the Trossachs National Park visitor centre (☑01389-722600; www.loch lomond-trossachs.org; 52 Main St; ⊙9.30am-3.30pm Mon, Wed & Thu, 9.30am-4.30pm Tue & Fri) This place is a useful centre for specific information on the park. Closes half an hour for lunch.

Rob Roy & Trossachs information centre (☑01877-330342; www.visitscottishheart lands.com; Ancaster Sq; ⊙10am-5pm Apr-Oct, 10am-4pm Nov-Mar) This centre has heaps of info on the area. There's a 20-minute film on Rob Roy that costs £1.50.

ℹ️ Getting There & Away

First (☑0871 200 2233; www.firstgroup.com) operates buses from Stirling (45 minutes, hourly Monday to Saturday, two-hourly Sunday), while **Kingshouse** (☑01877-384768; www.king shousetravel.com) buses run from Killin (45 minutes, two to six daily). For Aberfoyle, get off a Stirling-bound bus at Blair Drummond safari park and cross the road. There are also **Citylink** (www.citylink.co.uk) buses from Edinburgh to Oban or Fort William via Callander (£15.60, 1¾ hours, two daily).

LOCH KATRINE

This rugged area, 6 miles north of Aberfoyle and 10 miles west of Callander, is the heart of the Trossachs. From April to October two boats (☑01877-376315; www.lochkatrine.com; Trossachs Pier;) run cruises (one-hour adult/child £12/8) from Trossachs Pier at the eastern tip of Loch Katrine. One of these is *Sir Walter Scott,* the fabulous centenarian steamship; check the website for boat departures. From Stronachlachar (also accessible by car via Aberfoyle), you can reach the eastern shore of Loch Lomond at isolated

Inversnaid. A tarmac path links Trossachs Pier with Stronachlachar, so you can also take the boat out and walk/cycle back (12.5 miles). At Trossachs Pier, you can hire good bikes from **Katrinewheelz** (www.wheelscycling centre.com; hire per half-/full day from £8/12; ⊙daily Apr-Oct). It even has electric buggies for the less mobile or inclined (from £20).

KILLIN
POP 666

A fine base for the Trossachs or Perthshire, this lovely village sits at the western end of Loch Tay and has a spread-out, relaxed sort of a feel, particularly around the scenic **Falls of Dochart**, which tumble through the town centre. On a sunny day people sprawl over the rocks by the bridge, with a pint or picnic in hand. Killin offers some fine walking around the town, and mighty mountains and glens close at hand.

🏃 Activities

Five miles northeast of Killin, **Ben Lawers** rises above Loch Tay. Other routes abound; one rewarding **circular walk** heads up into the Acharn forest south of town, emerging above the treeline to great views of Loch Tay and Ben Lawers. The tourist office has stacks of walking leaflets and maps covering the area.

Killin is on the Lochs & Glens cycle route from Glasgow to Inverness. Hire bikes at **Killin Outdoor Centre** (☑01567-820652; www .killinoutdoor.co.uk; Main St; bike hire per 24hr £20; ⊙daily). It also rents out canoes and kayaks.

🛌 Sleeping & Eating

There are numerous good guesthouses strung along the road through town, and a couple of supermarkets for trail supplies.

High Creagan   CAMPGROUND £
(☑01567-820449; Aberfeldy Rd; tent/caravan site per person £5/8; ⊙Mar-Oct) This place has a well-kept, sheltered campground with plenty of grass set high on the slopes overlooking sparkling Loch Tay, three miles east of Killin. Kids under five years aren't allowed in the tent area as there's a stream running through it.

TOP CHOICE Falls of Dochart Inn   PUB ££
(☑01567-820270; www.falls-of-dochart-inn.co.uk; mains £10-13; 🅿🛜) In a prime position overlooking the falls, this is a terrific pub, a snug, atmospheric space with a roaring fire, personable service and really satisfying greatvalue food, ranging from light meals to tasty, tender steaks and a couple of more advanced

WORTH A TRIP

MONACHYLE MHOR

Monachyle Mhor (☎01877-384622; www.mhor.net; d £195-265; ⊗Feb-Dec; Ｐ🛜🐾) Monachyle Mhor is a luxury hideaway with a fantastically peaceful location overlooking two lochs. It's a great fusion of country Scotland and contemporary attitudes to design and food. The rooms and suites are superb and feature quirkily original decor. The restaurant offers set lunch (£20 for two courses) and dinner (£46) menus, which are high in quality, sustainably sourced and deliciously innovative.

Enchantment lies in its successful combination of top-class hospitality with a relaxed rural atmosphere; dogs and kids happily romp on the lawns, and no one looks askance if you come in flushed and muddy after a day's fishing or walking.

creations. The rooms (singles/doubles from £60/80) are handsome but a few glitches, such as poor heating, let some of them down.

ⓘ Getting There & Away

Two daily **Citylink** (www.citylink.co.uk) buses between Edinburgh and Oban/Fort William stop here; two buses from Dundee to Oban also pass through. These buses stop in Crianlarich among other places. Kingshouse (p837) runs buses to Callander, where you can change to a Stirling service.

ARGYLL

An ancient and disparate area, Argyll comprises a series of peninsulas and islands along Scotland's ragged southwestern coast, pierced by long sea lochs knifing their way into the hilly, moody landscape. Because of its dramatic geography, places such as the Mull of Kintyre – not so far from Glasgow as the crow flies – can seem impossibly remote.

The islands offer great diversity. Romantic Mull is the gateway to sacred Iona, whereas cheery Islay reverberates with the names of the heavyweights of the whisky world and Jura's wild hillscapes show nature's ultimate mastery and majesty. Meanwhile, the banks of Loch Lomond, the oysters of Loch Fyne and the prehistoric sites of Kilmartin Glen – all within easy striking distance of Glasgow – mean the mainland has nothing to envy.

Loch Lomond & Around

The 'bonnie banks' and 'bonnie braes' of Loch Lomond have long been Glasgow's rural retreat – a scenic region of hills, lochs and healthy fresh air within easy reach of Scotland's largest city. Since the 1930s Glaswegians have made a regular weekend exodus to the hills – by car, by bike and on foot – and

today the loch's popularity shows no sign of decreasing (Loch Lomond is within an hour's drive of 70% of Scotland's population).

The main tourist focus is along the A82 on the loch's western shore, and at the southern end, around Balloch, which can occasionally be a nightmare of jet skies and motorboats. The eastern shore, which is followed by the West Highland Way long-distance footpath, is a little quieter.

The region's importance was recognised when it became the heart of Loch Lomond & the Trossachs National Park (www.loch lomond-trossachs.org) – Scotland's first national park, created in 2002; for info on the Trossachs, see p834.

🏃 Activities

Walking

The big walk around here is the West Highland Way (p825), which runs along the eastern shore of the loch. There are shorter lochside walks at Firkin Point on the western shore and at several other places around the loch.

Rowardennan is the starting point for an ascent of Ben Lomond (974m), a popular and relatively straightforward (if strenuous) five-to six-hour round trip. The route starts at the car park just past the Rowardennan Hotel.

Boat Trips & Canoeing

The main centre for boat trips is Balloch, where Sweeney's Cruises (☎01389-752376; www.sweeneyscruises.com; Balloch Rd, Ballock) offers a range of trips including a one-hour cruise to Inchmurrin and back (adult/child £8.50/5, departs hourly).

Cruise Loch Lomond (www.cruiseloch lomond.co.uk) is based in Tarbet and offers trips to Inversnaid and Rob Roy MacGregor's Cave. You can also be dropped off at Rowardennan and picked up at Inversnaid after a 9-mile hike along the West Highland Way (£14.50).

Lomond Adventure (☎01360-870218; www.lomondadventure.co.uk), in Balmaha, rents out Canadian canoes (£30 per day) and kayaks (£25).

Can You Experience (☎01389-756251; www.canyouexperience.com; Loch Lomond Shores, Balloch) rents out canoes (£12/17 per half-/full hour) and bicycles (£13/17 per three hours/full day), and offers a full-day guided canoe safari on the loch (adult/child £65/55).

🛏️ Sleeping & Eating

Loch Lomond SYHA   HOSTEL £
(☎01360-850226; www.syha.org.uk; dm £19; ☺Mar-Oct; P@🛜) Forget about roughing it, this is one of the most impressive hostels in the country – an imposing 19th-century country house set in beautiful grounds overlooking the loch. It's 2 miles north of Balloch and very popular, so book in advance in summer. And yes, it *is* haunted.

Oak Tree Inn   INN ££
(☎01360-870357; www.oak-tree-inn.co.uk; Balmaha; dm/s/d £30/60/75; P🛜) An attractive traditional inn built in slate and timber, the Oak Tree offers luxurious guest bedrooms for pampered hikers, and two four-bed bunk rooms for hardier souls. The rustic restaurant dishes up hearty lunches and dinners (mains £9 to £12) such as steak-and-mushroom pie, and roast Arctic char with lime and chive butter, and cooks an excellent bowl of Cullen skink (soup made with smoked haddock, potato, onion and milk).

Rowardennan SYHA   HOSTEL £
(☎01360-870259; www.syha.org.uk; Rowardennan; dm £17.50; ☺Mar-Oct) Housed in an attractive Victorian lodge, this hostel has a superb setting right on the loch shore, beside the West Highland Way.

Cashel Campsite   CAMPGROUND £
(☎01360-870234; www.campingintheforest.co.uk; Rowardennan; sites incl car £19, backpackers per person £6; ☺Mar-Oct) The most attractive campground in the area is 3 miles north of Balmaha, on the loch shore.

Drover's Inn TOP CHOICE   INN ££
(☎01301-704234; www.thedroversinn.co.uk; bar meals £7-12; ☺lunch & dinner; P) This is one howff (drinking den) you shouldn't miss – a low-ceilinged place with smoke-blackened stone, bare wooden floors spotted with candle wax, barmen in kilts, and walls festooned with moth-eaten stags' heads and stuffed birds. There's even a stuffed bear and the desiccated husk of a basking shark.

The bar serves hearty hill-walking fuel such as steak-and-Guinness pie with mustard mash, and hosts live folk music on Friday and Saturday nights. We recommend this inn more as an atmospheric place to eat and drink than somewhere to stay – accommodation (singles/doubles from £42/83) varies from eccentric, old-fashioned and rather run-down rooms in the old building (including a ghost in room 6), to more comfortable rooms (with en suite bathrooms) in the modern annexe across the road. Ask to see your room before taking it.

ℹ️ Information

Balloch tourist office (☎0870 720 0607; Balloch Rd, Balloch; ☺9.30am-6pm Jun-Aug, 10am-6pm Apr & Sep)
Balmaha National Park centre (☎01389-722100; Balmaha; ☺9.30am-4.15pm Apr-Sep)
National park gateway centre (☎01389-751035; www.lochlomondshores.com; Loch

ROB ROY

Nicknamed 'Red' ('ruadh' in Gaelic, anglicised to 'roy') for his ginger locks, Robert MacGregor (1671–1734) was the wild leader of the wildest of Scotland's clans. Although they had rights to the lands the clan occupied, these estates stood between powerful neighbours who had the MacGregors outlawed, hence their sobriquet 'Children of the Mist'. Incognito, Rob became a prosperous livestock trader, before a dodgy deal led to a warrant for his arrest.

A legendary swordsman, the fugitive from justice then became notorious for his daring raids into the Lowlands to carry off cattle and sheep. He was forever hiding from potential captors; he was twice imprisoned, but escaped dramatically on both occasions. He finally turned himself in, and received his liberty and a pardon from the King. He lies buried in the churchyard at Balquhidder; his uncompromising epitaph reads 'MacGregor despite them'. His life has been glorified over the years due to Walter Scott's novel and the 1995 film. Many Scots see his life as a symbol of the struggle of the common folk against the inequable ownership of vast tracts of the country by landed aristocrats.

Lomond Shores, Balloch; ⊙10am-6pm Apr-Sep, to 5pm Oct-Mar; 🐸)

Tarbet tourist office (🖉0870-720 0623; Tarbet; ⊙10am-6pm Jul & Aug, to 5pm Easter-Jun, Sep & Oct) At the junction of the A82 and the A83.

🛈 Getting There & Away

BUS **First Glasgow** (🖉0141-423 6600; www .firstglasgow.com) buses 204 and 215 run from Argyle St in central Glasgow to Balloch and Loch Lomond shores (1½ hours, at least two per hour).

Scottish Citylink (www.citylink.co.uk) coaches from Glasgow to Oban and Fort William stop at Luss (£8.20, 55 minutes, six daily), Tarbet (£8.20, 65 minutes) and Ardlui (£14.30, 1¼ hours).

TRAIN Train services include the following:

Glasgow to Balloch £4.70, 45 minutes, every 30 minutes

Glasgow to Arrochar & Tarbet £11, 1¼ hours, three or four daily

Glasgow to Ardlui £14, 1½ hours, three or four daily, continuing to Oban and Fort William

Inveraray

POP 700

You can spot Inveraray long before you get here – its neat, whitewashed buildings stand out from a distance on the shores of Loch Fyne. It's a planned town, built by the Duke of Argyll in Georgian style when he revamped his nearby castle in the 18th century. The tourist office (🖉0845 225 5121; Front St; ⊙9am-6pm Jul & Aug, 10am-5pm Mon-Sat Apr-Jun, Sep & Oct, 10am-3pm Mon-Sat Nov-Mar) is on the seafront.

⊙ Sights

Inveraray Castle CASTLE
(🖉01499-302203; www.inveraray-castle.com; adult/child £10/6.50; ⊙10am-5.45pm Apr-Oct) Inveraray Castle has been the seat of the Dukes of Argyll – chiefs of Clan Campbell – since the 15th century. The 18th-century building, with its fairy-tale turrets and fake battlements, houses an impressive armoury hall, its walls patterned with a collection of more than 1000 pole arms, dirks, muskets and Lochaber axes. The castle is 500m north of town, entered from the A819 Dalmally road.

Inveraray Jail MUSEUM
(🖉01499-302381; www.inverarayjail.co.uk; Church Sq; adult/child £8.95/4.95; ⊙9.30am-6pm Apr-Oct, 10am-5pm Nov-Mar) At this award-winning, in-

teractive tourist attraction you can sit in on a trial, try out a cell and discover the harsh tortures that were meted out to unfortunate prisoners. The attention to detail – including a life-sized model of an inmate squatting on a 19th-century toilet – more than makes up for the sometimes tedious commentary.

🛏 Sleeping & Eating

TOP
CHOICE **George Hotel** HOTEL ££
(🖉01499-302111; www.thegeorgehotel.co.uk; Main St E; d from £75; P) The George Hotel boasts a magnificent choice of opulent rooms complete with four-poster beds, period furniture, Victorian roll-top baths and private Jacuzzis (superior double rooms cost £140 to £165). The cosy wood-panelled bar, with its rough stone walls, flagstone floor and peat fires, is a delightful place for a bar meal (mains £8 to £16, open for lunch and dinner).

Inveraray SYHA HOSTEL £
(🖉01499-302454; www.syha.org.uk; Dalmally Rd; dm £17; ⊙Apr-Oct; @) To get to this hostel, housed in a comfortable, modern bungalow, go through the arched entrance on the seafront – it's set back on the left of the road about 100m further on.

Loch Fyne Oyster Bar SEAFOOD ££
(🖉01499-600236; www.lochfyne.com; Clachan, Cairndow; mains £11-22; ⊙9am-8pm) Six miles northeast of Inveraray, this rustic-themed restaurant serves excellent seafood, though the service can be a bit hit and miss. It's housed in a converted byre, and the menu includes locally farmed oysters, mussels and salmon. The neighbouring shop sells packaged seafood and other deli goods to take away, as well as bottled beer from the nearby Fyne Ales microbrewery.

🛈 Getting There & Away

Scottish Citylink (www.citylink.co.uk) buses run from Glasgow to Inveraray (£11, 1¾ hours, six daily Monday to Saturday, two Sunday). Three of these buses continue to Lochgilphead and Campbeltown (£12, 2½ hours); the others continue to Oban (£10, 1¼ hours).

Kilmartin Glen

In the 6th century, Irish settlers arrived in this part of Argyll and founded the kingdom of Dalriada, which eventually united with the Picts in 843 to create the first Scottish kingdom. Their capital was the hill fort of Dunadd, on the plain to the south of Kilmartin Glen.

This magical glen is the focus of one of the biggest concentrations of prehistoric sites in Scotland. Burial cairns, standing stones, stone circles, hill forts and cup-and-ring-marked rocks litter the countryside. Within a 6-mile radius of Kilmartin village there are 25 sites with standing stones and over 100 rock carvings.

◉ Sights

Your first stop should be **Kilmartin House Museum** (☑01546-510278; www.kilmartin.org; adult/child £5/2; ◷10am-5.30pm Mar-Oct, 11am-4pm Nov-23 Dec), in Kilmartin village, a fascinating interpretive centre that provides a context for the ancient monuments you can go on to explore, alongside displays of artefacts recovered from various sites. The project was partly funded by midges – the curator exposed his body in Temple Wood on a warm summer's evening and was sponsored per midge bite!

The oldest monuments at Kilmartin date from 5000 years ago and comprise a linear cemetery of **burial cairns** that runs south from Kilmartin village for 1.5 miles. There are also ritual monuments (two stone circles) at **Temple Wood**, 0.75 miles southwest of Kilmartin. The museum bookshop sells maps and guides.

Kilmartin Churchyard contains some 10th-century Celtic crosses and medieval grave slabs with carved effigies of knights. Some researchers have surmised that these were the tombs of the Knights Templar who fled persecution in France in the 14th century.

The hill fort of **Dunadd**, 3.5 miles south of Kilmartin village, was the seat of power of the first kings of Dalriada, and may have been where the **Stone of Destiny** was originally located. The faint rock carvings of a wild boar and two footprints with an Ogham inscription may have been used in some kind of inauguration ceremony. A slippery path leads to the summit where you can gaze out on much the same view that the kings of Dalriada enjoyed 1300 years ago.

🛏 Sleeping & Eating

Kilmartin Hotel INN **££**
(☑01546-510250; www.kilmartin-hotel.com; s/d £40/65; P) Though the rooms here are a bit on the small side, this attractively old-fashioned hotel is full of atmosphere. There's

a restaurant (mains £8 to £15) here too, and a whisky bar with real ale on tap where you can enjoy live folk music on weekends.

[TOP CHOICE] **Glebe Cairn Café** CAFE **£**
(☑01546-510278; mains £5-8; ◷10am-5pm Mar-Oct, 11am-4pm Nov-Dec, closed Jan & Feb) The cafe in the Kilmartin House Museum has a lovely conservatory with a view across fields to a prehistoric cairn. Dishes include homemade Cullen skink, a Celtic cheese platter and hummus with sweet-and-sour beetroot relish. The drinks menu ranges from espresso to elderflower wine by way of Fraoch heather-scented ale.

❶ Getting There & Away

Bus 423 between Oban and Ardrishaig (four daily Monday to Friday, two on Saturday) stops at Kilmartin (£5, one hour 20 minutes).

You can walk or cycle along the Crinan Canal from Ardrishaig, then turn north at Bellanoch on the minor B8025 road to reach Kilmartin (12 miles one way).

Kintyre

Almost an island, the 40-mile-long Kintyre Peninsula has only a narrow isthmus at Tarbert connecting it to the rest of Scotland. Magnus Barefoot the Viking, who could claim any island he circumnavigated, made his people drag their longship across this strand to validate his claim to Kintyre.

TARBERT
POP 1500

The attractive fishing village and yachting centre of Tarbert is the gateway to Kintyre, and well worth a stopover for lunch or dinner. There's a tourist office (p924) here.

The picturesque harbour is overlooked by the crumbling, ivy-covered ruins of **Tarbert Castle**, built by Robert the Bruce in the 14th century. You can hike up to it via a signposted footpath beside the **Loch Fyne Gallery** (www.lochfynegallery.com; Harbour St; ◷10am-5pm), which showcases the work of local artists.

There are plenty of B&Bs and hotels here, but be sure to book ahead during festivals and major events. The **Knap Guest House** (☑01880-820015; www.knapguesthouse .co.uk; Campbeltown Rd; s/d from £50/70; 🛜) has three spacious en suite bedrooms sporting an attractive blend of Scottish and Far Eastern decor. The welcome is warm, and there are great harbour views from the residents lounge (leather sofas, a log fire and a small library) and the breakfast room.

It's worth a trip to Tarbert just to eat at the Starfish (☑01880-820733; wwwstarfish tarbert.com; Castle St; mains £10-20; ⊗lunch & dinner Tue-Sun), a simple but stylish place that serves 'Scotch egg' scallops (wrapped in smoked salmon mousse and coated with crunchy crumbs) – who'd have thought of that? And local languostines with garlic butter and homebaked bread are finger-lickingly scrumptious. Best to book.

CAMPBELTOWN
POP 6000

Campbeltown, with its ranks of grey council houses, feels a bit like an Ayrshire mining town that's been placed incongruously on the shores of a beautiful Argyllshire harbour. It was once a thriving fishing port and whisky-making centre, but industrial decline and the closure of the former airforce base at nearby Machrihanish saw Campbeltown's fortunes wane.

But renewal is in the air – the spruced-up seafront, with its flower beds, smart Victorian buildings and restored art-deco cinema, lends the town a distinctly optimistic air. The tourist office (☑01586-552056; The Pier; ⊗9am-5.30pm Mon-Sat) is beside the harbour.

There were once no fewer than 32 distilleries in the Campbeltown area, but most closed down in the 1920s. Today Springbank Distillery (☑01586-551710, ext 1; www.the-tasting room.com; 85 Longrow; tours from £6.50; ⊗tours 10am & 2pm Mon-Sat) is one of only three that now operates in town. It is also one of the very few distilleries in Scotland that distils, matures and bottles all its whisky on the one site.

Opened in 2009, the nearby Machrihanish Dunes (www.machrihanishdunes.com) golf resort has won accolades around the world for the quality of its two golf courses and associated hotels.

Mull of Kintyre Seatours (☑07785-542811; www.mull-of-kintyre.co.uk; adult/child from £35/£25) operates two-hour, high-speed boat trips out of Campbeltown harbour to look for wildlife: seals, porpoises, minke whales, golden eagles and peregrine falcons live in the turbulent tidal waters and on the spectacular sea cliffs of the Mull of Kintyre. Book in advance by phone or at the tourist office.

Loganair/FlyBe (www.loganair.co.uk) operates two flights daily, Monday to Friday, from Glasgow to Campbeltown (£51, 35 minutes). Citylink (www.citylink.co.uk) buses run from Campbeltown to Glasgow (£18.50, four hours, three daily) via Tarbert, Invera-ray, Arrochar and Loch Lomond.

Kintyre Express (☑01856-555895; www .kintyreexpress.com) operates a small, high-speed passenger ferry from Campbeltown to Ballycastle in Northern Ireland (one way £35, two hours, three daily May to September, twice weekly October to April). Tickets must be booked in advance.

MULL OF KINTYRE

A narrow winding road, about 18 miles long, leads south from Campbeltown to the Mull of Kintyre, passing some good sandy beach-es near Southend. The name of this remote headland was immortalised in Paul Mc-Cartney's famous song – the former Beatle owns a farmhouse in the area. A lighthouse marks the spot closest to Northern Ireland, whose coastline, only 12 miles away, is visible across the North Channel.

Isle of Islay
POP 3400

The home of the world's greatest and peati-est whiskies, whose names reverberate on the tongue like a pantheon of Celtic deities, Islay (eye-lah) is a wonderfully friendly place whose warmly welcoming inhabitants offset its lack of majestic scenery. Even if you're not into your drams, the birdlife, fine sea-food, turquoise bays and basking seals are ample reason to visit this island. There are currently eight working distilleries; perhaps this is why the locals are so genial. A wave or cheerio to passersby is mandatory, and you'll soon find yourself slowing down to Islay's relaxing pace.

Fèis Ìle (Islay Festival; www.theislayfestival .co.uk) is a week-long celebration of tradi-tional Scottish music and whisky at the end of May. Events include ceilidhs (informal entertainment and dance), pipe-band per-formances, distillery tours, barbecues and whisky tastings.

❶ Information

Islay service point (☑01496-810332; Jamie-son St; ⊗9am-12.30pm & 1.30-5pm Mon-Fri) Free internet access.

Islay tourist office (☑01496-810254; The Square, Bowmore; ⊗10am-5pm Mon-Sat, 2-5pm Sun Apr-Aug, shorter hours Sep-Mar)

Islay, Jura & Colonsay

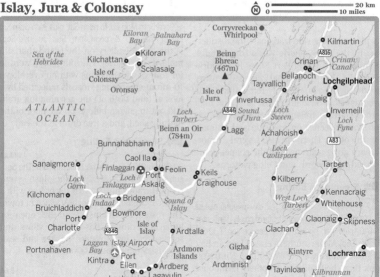

MacTaggart Community CyberCafé
(☏01496-302693; www.islaycybercafe.co.uk;
30 Mansfield Pl, Port Ellen; per 30min £1;
⊙9am-10pm Mon & Wed-Sat, to 5pm Tue & Sun;
☏) Internet access.

① Getting There & Away

There are two ferry terminals on the island, both served by ferries from Kennacraig in West Loch Tarbert – Port Askaig on the east coast and Port Ellen in the south. Islay airport lies midway between Port Ellen and Bowmore.

AIR **Loganair/FlyBe** (www.loganair.co.uk) flies from Glasgow to Islay (one way £62, 45 minutes, two or three flights daily Monday to Friday, one or two Saturday and Sunday).

Hebridean Air Services (☏0845 805 7465; www.hebrideanair.co.uk) operates flights (one way £65, twice daily Tuesday and Thursday) from Connel Airfield (near Oban) to Colonsay (30 minutes) and Islay (40 minutes).

BOAT **CalMac** (www.calmac.co.uk) runs ferries from Kennacraig in West Loch Tarbert to Port Ellen (passenger/car £10.20/55, 2¼ hours, one to three daily) and Port Askaig (£10.20/55, two hours, one to three daily). On Wednesday only in summer the ferry continues from Port Askaig to Colonsay (£5.45/28, 1¼ hours) and on to Oban (£14.65/73, four hours).

① Getting Around

BICYCLE You can hire bikes from **Bowmore post office** (£10 per day), and from the house opposite the Port Charlotte Hotel.

BUS A bus service links Ardbeg, Port Ellen, Bowmore, Port Charlotte, Portnahaven and Port Askaig (limited service on Sunday). Pick up a copy of the *Islay & Jura Public Transport Guide* from the tourist office.

CAR **D & N MacKenzie** (☏01496-302300; Islay Airport) Car hire from £32 a day.

TAXI **Bowmore** (☏01496-810449); **Port Ellen** (☏01496-302155).

PORT ELLEN & AROUND

Port Ellen is the main point of entry for Islay. While there's nothing to see in the town itself, the coast stretching northeast from Port Ellen is one of the loveliest parts of the island.

There are three whisky distilleries in close succession (see websites for tour times):

Laphroaig (www.laphroaig.com; tours £4.80; ⊙9.30am-5.30pm Mon-Fri, also 10am-4pm Sat & Sun Mar-Dec)

Lagavulin (www.discovering-distilleries.com; tours £6; ⊙9am-5pm Mon-Fri Apr-Oct, to 12.30pm Nov-Mar, plus 9am-5pm Sat & 12.30-4pm Sun Jul & Aug)

Ardbeg (www.ardbeg.com; tours from £4; ⊙10am-5pm Jun-Aug, 10am-4pm Mon-Fri Sep-May)

A pleasant bike ride leads past the distilleries to the atmospheric Kildalton Chapel, 8 miles northeast of Port Ellen. In the kirkyard is the exceptional late-8th-century Kildalton Cross, the only remaining Celtic high cross in Scotland (most surviving high crosses are in Ireland). There are carvings of biblical scenes on one side and animals on the other. There are also several extraordinary grave slabs around the chapel, some carved with swords and Celtic patterns.

🛏 Sleeping & Eating

TOP CHOICE **Kintra Farm** CAMPGROUND, B&B ££
(☎01496-302051; www.kintrafarm.co.uk; tent sites £4-10, plus per person £3, r per person £30-38; ⊙Apr-Sep) At the southern end of Laggan Bay, 3.5 miles northwest of Port Ellen, Kintra offers three bedrooms in a homely farmhouse B&B. There's also a basic but beautiful campground on buttercup-sprinkled turf amid the dunes, with a sunset view across the beach.

Oystercatcher B&B B&B ££
(☎01496-300409; www.islay-bedandbreakfast.com; 63 Frederick Cres; r per person £40; @🕿) If you like your breakfasts fishy, then this welcoming waterfront house is the place for you – there's smoked haddock, smoked salmon and kippers on the menu, as well as the usual fry up. Bedrooms are small but comfortable and nicely decorated.

TOP CHOICE **Old Kiln Café** CAFE £
(☎01496-302244; mains £5-10; ⊙10am-4pm daily Jun-Aug, Mon-Fri only Sep-Jun, lunch served from noon) Housed in the former malting kiln at Ardbeg distillery, this well-run cafe serves hearty home-made soups, tasty light meals (try a panini sandwich with haggis and apple chutney, or a platter of smoked Islay beef, venison and pastrami); and a range of home-baked desserts, including traditional clootie dumpling (a rich steamed pudding filled with currants and raisins) with ice cream.

BOWMORE

The attractive Georgian village of Bowmore was built in 1768 to replace the village of Kilarrow, which just had to go – it was spoiling the view from the laird's house. Its centrepiece is the distinctive Round Church at the top of Main St, built in circular form to ensure that the devil had no corners to hide in.

Bowmore Distillery (☎01496-810671; www.bowmore.co.uk; School St; tours adult/child £6/free; ⊙9am-5pm Mon-Fri, to noon Sat, plus 9am-5pm Sat Easter–mid-Sep & noon-4pm Sun Jul–mid-Sep) is the only distillery on the island that still malts its own barley. The tour (check website for times), which begins with an overblown 10-minute marketing video, is redeemed by a look at (and taste of) the germinating grain laid out in golden billows on the floor of the malting shed, and a free dram at the end.

🛏 Sleeping & Eating

Harbour Inn INN £££
(☎01496-810330; www.harbour-inn.com; The Square; s/d from £100/135; @🕿) The plush seven-room Harbour Inn, smartly decorated with a nautical theme, is the poshest place in town. The restaurant (mains £18 to £25, open for lunch and dinner) has harbour views and serves fresh local oysters, lobster and scallops, Islay lamb and Jura venison.

Lambeth House B&B ££
(☎01496-810597; lambethguesthouse@tiscali.co.uk; Jamieson St; s/d £60/90; @) A short stroll from the harbour, the Lambeth is a simple, good-value guesthouse with comfy en suite bedrooms. Breakfasts are excellent, and it also offers a two-course evening meal for £12.

PORT CHARLOTTE

Eleven miles from Bowmore, on the opposite shore of Loch Indaal, is the attractive village of Port Charlotte. It has a general store (⊙9am-12.30pm & 1.30-5.30pm Mon-Sat, 11.30am-1.30pm Sun) and post office.

Islay's long history is lovingly recorded in the Museum of Islay Life (☎01496-850358; www.islaymuseum.org; adult/child £3/1; ⊙10am-5pm Mon-Sat, 2-5pm Sun Easter-Oct), housed in the former Free Church. Prize exhibits include an illicit still, 19th-century crofters' furniture, and a set of leather boots once worn by the horse that pulled the lawnmower at Islay House (so it wouldn't leave hoof prints on the lawn!). There are also touchscreen computers displaying archive photos of Islay in the 19th and early 20th centuries.

The Bruichladdich Distillery (☎01496-850190; www.bruichladdich.com; tours £5; ⊙9am-5pm Mon-Fri, 10am-4pm Sat), at the northern edge of the village, reopened in 2001 with all of its original Victorian equipment restored to working condition. Independently owned and independently minded, Bruichladdich (brook-*lah*-day) produces an intriguing range of distinctive, very peaty whiskies. Call ahead to book a tour.

Sleeping & Eating

TOP CHOICE Port Charlotte Hotel   HOTEL **£££**
(☎01496-850360; www.portcharlottehotel.co.uk;
s/d £105/180; ☺restaurant 6.30-9pm, bar meals
noon-2pm & 5.30-8.30pm; ℗🔊) This lovely old
Victorian hotel has stylish, individually decorated bedrooms with sea views, and a candlelit restaurant (mains £16 to £27) serving
local seafood (such as seared scallops with
braised leeks and truffle cream sauce), Islay
beef, venison and duck. The bar (meals £9 to
£14) is well stocked with Islay malts and real
ales, and has a nook at the back with a view
over the loch towards the Paps of Jura.

Port Mor Campsite   CAMPGROUND **£**
(☎01496-850441; www.islandofislay.co.uk; tent sites
per adult/child £8/4; @🔊) The sports field to
the south of the village doubles as a campground – there are toilets, showers, a laundry
and a children's play area in the main building. Open year-round.

Islay SYHA   HOSTEL **£**
(☎01496-850385; www.syha.org.uk; dm £17.50;
☺Apr-Oct; @🔊) This modern and comfortable hostel is housed in a former distillery
building with views over the loch.

Debbie's Minimarket   CAFE **£**
(☎01496-850319; ☺9am-5.30pm Mon-Sat; 🖉)
The village shop and post office at Bruichladdich doubles as a deli that stocks good wine
and posh picnic grub, and also serves the
best coffee on Islay – sit at one of the outdoor tables and enjoy an espresso with a sea
view.

FINLAGGAN
Lush meadows swathed in buttercups and dai-
sies slope down to reed-fringed Loch Finlaggan, the medieval capital of the Lords of the
Isles. This bucolic setting, 3 miles southwest
of Port Askaig, was once the most important
settlement in the Hebrides, the central seat of
power of the Lords of the Isles from the 12th
to the 16th centuries. From the little island at
the northern end of the loch the descendants
of Somerled administered their island territories and entertained visiting chieftains in
their great hall. Little remains now except the
tumbled ruins of houses and a chapel, but the
setting is beautiful and the history fascinating.
A wooden walkway leads over the reeds and
water lilies to the island, where information
boards describe the remains.

The **Finlaggan Visitor Centre** (www
.finlaggan.com; adult/child £3/1; ☺10.30am-

4.30pm Mon-Sat, 1.30-4.30pm Sun Apr-Sep), in a
nearby cottage (plus modern extension), explains the site's history and archaeology. The
island itself is open at all times.

Buses from Port Askaig stop at the road-
end, from where it's a 15-minute walk to the
loch.

Isle of Jura
POP 170

Jura lies off the coast of Argyll – long, dark
and low like a vast Viking longship, its billowing sail the distinctive triple peaks of
the Paps of Jura. A magnificently wild and
lonely island, Jura is the perfect place for
getting away from it all – as George Orwell
did in 1948. Orwell wrote his masterpiece
1984 while living at the remote farmhouse of
Barnhill in the north of the island. Jura takes
its name from the Old Norse *dyr-a* (deer island) – an apt appellation, as the island supports a population of around 6000 red deer,
who outnumber their human cohabitants by
about 35 to one.

Apart from the superb wilderness walking
and wildlife-watching, there's not a whole
lot to do on the island apart from visit the
Isle of Jura Distillery (☎01496-820385; www
.isleofjura.com; Craighouse; tours free; ☺10am-4pm
Mon-Fri, 10am-2pm Sat Apr-Sep, 10am-2pm Mon-Fri
Oct-Mar) or attend the **Jura Music Festival**
(www.juramusicfestival.com) in late September,
a convivial weekend of traditional Scottish
folk music.

You can hire bikes from **Jura Bike Hire**
(☎07768-450000; per day £12.50) at Bramble Cottage in Keils, a mile northeast of
Craighouse.

Sleeping & Eating

Places to stay on the island are very limited,
so book ahead. Most of Jura's accommodation is in self-catering cottages that are let by
the week (see www.juradevelopment.co.uk).
You can camp for free in the field below the
Jura Hotel.

Jura Hotel   HOTEL **££**
(☎01496-820243; www.jurahotel.co.uk; Craighouse;
s/d from £50/78; ℗) The 18-room Jura is the
most comfortable place to stay on the island; ask for a room at the front with a view
of the bay. The hotel also serves decent bar
meals (£8 to £12; food served noon to 2pm
and 6.30pm to 9pm) and the bar itself is a
very sociable place to spend the evening.

Antlers BISTRO ££

(☑01496-820496; Craighouse; mains £5-9, 2-/3-course dinner £25/29; ☺10am-6pm & 7-10pm Mon-Sat, 10am-4pm Sun Mar-Oct; ☎) This bistro makes the most of locally sourced produce, offering coffee, cakes, sandwiches and burgers during the day, and an unexpectedly classy menu at dinner time (booking essential) with dishes such as grilled local langoustines, and scallops with black pudding. Not licensed – £3 corkage.

❶ Getting There & Away

A car ferry shuttles between Port Askaig on Islay and Feolin on Jura (passenger/car/bicycle £1.35/7.60/free, five minutes, hourly Monday to Saturday, every two hours Sunday). There is no direct car-ferry connection to the mainland.

From April to September **Jura Passenger Ferry** (☑07768-450000; www.jurapassenger ferry.com) runs from Tayvallich on the mainland to Craighouse on Jura (£20, one hour, one or two daily except Wednesday). Booking recommended.

Oban

POP 8120

Oban is a peaceful waterfront town on a delightful bay, with sweeping views to Kerrera and Mull. OK, that first bit about peaceful is true only in winter; in summer the town centre is a heaving mass of humanity, its streets jammed with traffic and crowded with holidaymakers, day trippers and travellers headed for the islands. But the setting is still lovely.

There's not a huge amount to see in the town itself, but it's an appealingly busy place with some excellent restaurants and lively pubs, and it's the main gateway to the islands of Mull, Iona, Colonsay, Barra, Coll and Tiree.

◉ Sights

McCaig's Tower HISTORIC BUILDING

(cnr Laurel & Duncraggan Rds; ☺24hr) Crowning the hill above the town centre sits the Victorian folly known as McCaig's Tower. Its construction was commissioned in 1890 by local worthy John Stuart McCaig, an art critic, philosophical essayist and banker, with the philanthropic intention of providing work for unemployed stonemasons.

To reach it on foot, make the steep climb up Jacob's Ladder (a flight of stairs) from Argyll St and then follow the signs. The views over the bay are worth the effort.

Oban Distillery DISTILLERY

(☑01631-572004; www.discovering-distilleries.com; Stafford St; tours £7; ☺9.30am-5pm Mon-Sat Easter-Oct, plus noon-5pm Sun Jul-Sep, closed Sat & Sun Nov, Dec & Feb-Easter, closed Jan) This distillery has been producing Oban single malt whisky since 1794. There are guided tours available (last tour begins one hour before closing time), but even without a tour, it's still worth a look at the small exhibition in the foyer.

FREE **War & Peace Museum** MUSEUM

(☑01631-570007; www.obanmuseum.org.uk; Corran Esplanade; ☺10am-6pm Mon-Sat, to 4pm Sun May-Sep, to 4pm daily Mar, Apr, Oct & Nov) Military buffs will enjoy the little War & Peace Museum, which chronicles Oban's role in WWII as a base for Catalina seaplanes and as a marshalling area for Atlantic convoys.

Dunollie Castle & 1745 House CASTLE

(☑01631-570550; www.dunollie.org; Dunollie Rd; adult/child £3/free; ☺11am-4pm Tue-Sat, 1-4pm Sun) A pleasant 1-mile stroll along the coast road north of Corran Esplanade leads to Dunollie Castle, built by the MacDougalls of Lorn in the 13th century and unsuccessfully besieged for a year during the 1715 Jacobite rebellion. It's very much a ruin, but the nearby 1745 House, the seat of Clan MacDougall, is now a fascinating museum of local and clan history.

⛹ Activities

A tourist-office leaflet lists local bike rides, which include a 7-mile Gallanach circular tour, a 16-mile route to the Isle of Seil and routes to Connel, Glenlonan and Kilmore. You can hire mountain bikes from Nevis Cycles (☑01631-566033; www.neviscycles.com; 87 George St; per half-/full day £12/20; ☺10am-5.30pm Tue-Sat).

Sea Kayak Oban (☑01631-565310; www.sea kayakoban.com; Argyll St; ☺9am-5pm Mon, Tue, Sat & Sun, 10am-5pm Wed & Fri) has a well-stocked shop, and offers sea-kayaking courses, including a two-day intro for beginners (£160 per person).

Various operators offer boat trips to spot seals and other marine wildlife, departing from the North Pier slipway (adult/child £8/5.50); ask for details at the tourist office.

🛏 Sleeping

Despite having lots of B&B accommodation, Oban's beds can still fill up quickly in July and August so try to book ahead. If you can't find a bed in Oban, consider staying at Connel, 4 miles to the north.

Barriemore Hotel
B&B **££**

(☏01631-566356; www.barriemore-hotel.co.uk; Corran Esplanade; s/d from £70/99; [P][☎]) The Barriemore enjoys a grand location, overlooking the entrance to Oban Bay. It has 13 spacious rooms (ask for one with a sea view), plus a guest lounge with magazines and newspapers, and plump Loch Fyne kippers on the breakfast menu.

Heatherfield House
B&B **££**

(☏01631-562806; www.heatherfieldhouse.co.uk; Albert Rd; s/d from £38/88; [P][@][☎]) The welcoming Heatherfield House occupies a converted 1870s rectory set in extensive grounds and has six spacious rooms. If possible, ask for room 1, which comes complete with fireplace, sofa and a view over the garden to the harbour.

Old Manse Guest House
B&B **££**

(☏01631-564886; www.obanguesthouse.co.uk; Dalriach Rd; s/d from £65/80; [P][☎]) Set on a hillside above the town, the Old Manse commands great views over to Kerrera and Mull. The sunny, brightly decorated bedrooms have some nice touches (a couple of wine glasses and a corkscrew), and kids are made welcome with Balamory books, toys and DVDs.

Kathmore Guest House
B&B **££**

(☏01631-562104; www.kathmore.co.uk; Soroba Rd; s £45-65, d £55-75; [P][☎]) Warm and welcoming, the Kathmore combines traditional Highland hospitality and hearty breakfasts with a wee touch of boutique flair in its stylish bedspreads and colourful artwork. There's a comfortable lounge and outdoor deck where you can enjoy a pre- or post-prandial glass of wine on those long summer evenings.

Oban Backpackers Plus
HOSTEL **£**

(☏01631-567189; www.backpackersplus.com; Breadalbane St; dm/tw £20/49; [@][☎]) This is a friendly place with a good vibe and a large and attractive communal lounge with lots of sofas and armchairs. Buffet breakfast is included in the price, plus there's free tea and coffee, a laundry service (£2.50) and powerful showers. Private rooms available in a separate building just around the corner.

Oban Caravan & Camping Park
CAMPGROUND **£**

(☏01631-562425; www.obancaravanpark.com; Gallanachmore Farm; tent/campervan sites £15/17; ☺Apr-Oct; [☸]) This spacious campground has a superb location overlooking the Sound of Kerrera, 2.5 miles south of Oban (bus twice daily). The quoted rate includes up to two people and a car; extra people stay for £2 each. A one-person tent with no car is £8. No prebooking – it's first come, first served.

Jeremy Inglis Hostel
HOSTEL **£**

(☏01631-565065; www.jeremyinglishostel.co.uk; 21 Airds Cres; dm/s from £15/22; [☎]) More of an eccentric B&B than a hostel – most 'dorms' have only two or three beds, and are decorated with original artwork, books, flowers and cuddly toys.

Sand Villa Guest House
B&B **££**

(☏01631-562803; www.holidayoban.co.uk; Breadalbane St; r per person £28-33; [P][☎]) Smart and stylish bedrooms. No credit cards.

Roseneath Guest House
B&B **££**

(☏01631-562929; www.roseneathoban.com; Dalriach Rd; s/d £45/74; [P]) Peaceful location with sea views.

Eating

TOP CHOICE / Waterfront Fishhouse Restaurant
SEAFOOD **££**

(☏01631-563110; www.waterfrontoban.co.uk; Railway Pier; mains £11-20; ☺lunch & dinner; [☷]) Housed on the top floor of a converted seamen's mission, the Waterfront's stylish, unfussy decor in burgundy and brown, with dark wooden furniture, does little to distract from the superb seafood freshly landed at the quay just a few metres away. The menu ranges from classic haddock and chips to fresh oysters, scallops and langoustines.

The lunch and early evening menu (5.30pm to 6.45pm) offers two courses for £10. Best to book for dinner.

TOP CHOICE / Shellfish Bar
SEAFOOD **£**

(Railway Pier; mains £3-13; ☺9am-6pm) If you want to savour superb Scottish seafood without the expense of an upmarket restaurant, head for Oban's famous seafood stall – it's the green shack on the quayside near the ferry terminal. Here you can buy fresh and cooked seafood to take away – excellent prawn sandwiches (£2.95), dressed crab (£4.95), and fresh oysters for only 75p each.

Seafood Temple
SEAFOOD **£££**

(☏01631-566000; www.obanseafood.com; Gallanach Rd; mains £16-35; ☺lunch & dinner) Locally sourced seafood is the god that's worshipped at this tiny temple – a former park pavilion with glorious views over the bay. Oban's smallest restaurant serves up whole lobster cooked to order, baked crab with cheese-and-herb crust, plump langoustines, and the 'Taste of Argyll' seafood platter (£70 for two persons), which offers a taste of everything. Dinner is in two sittings, at 6.15pm and 8.30pm; booking essential.

Cuan Mor BISTRO **££**
(☎01631-565078; www.cuanmor.co.uk; 60 George St; mains £9-14; ☺10am-midnight; 🔊🍴) This always busy bar and bistro brews its own beer, and sports a no-nonsense menu of old favourites – from haddock and chips or home-made lasagne to sausage and mash with onion gravy – spiced with a few more-sophisticated dishes, such as squat lobster carbonara, and a decent range of vegetarian dishes. And the sticky toffee pudding is not to be missed!

Ee'usk SEAFOOD **££**
(☎01631-565666; www.eeusk.com; North Pier; mains £13-20; ☺lunch & dinner) Bright and modern Ee'usk (it's how you pronounce *iasg*, the Gaelic word for fish) occupies Oban's prime location on the North Pier. Floor-to-ceiling windows allow diners on two levels to enjoy views over the harbour to Kerrera and Mull, while sampling a menu of locally caught seafood ranging from fragrant Thai fishcakes to langoustines with chilli and ginger.

A little pricey, perhaps, but both food and location are first class.

Kitchen Garden CAFE **£**
(☎01631-566332; www.kitchengardenoban.co.uk; 14 George St; mains £5-8; ☺9am-5.30pm Mon-Sat, 10am-4.30pm Sun) A deli packed with delicious picnic food. Also has a great little cafe above the shop – good coffee, scones, cakes, home-made soups and sandwiches.

ℹ Information

Fancy That (☎01631-562996; 112 George St; per 20min £1; ☺9.30am-7pm Mon-Sat, 10am-5pm Sun) Internet access.

Lorn & Islands District General Hospital (☎01631-567500; Glengallan Rd) Southern end of town.

Main post office (☎01631-510450; Lochside St; ☺8am-6pm Mon-Sat, 10am-1pm Sun) Inside Tesco supermarket.

Tourist office (☎01631-563122; www.oban .org.uk; 3 North Pier; ☺9am-7pm Mon-Sat, 10am-6pm Sun May-Sep, 9am-5.30pm Mon-Sat Oct-Apr)

ℹ Getting There & Away

The bus, train and ferry terminals are conveniently grouped next to the harbour on the southern edge of the bay.

BOAT CalMac (www.calmac.co.uk) ferries link Oban with the islands of Mull, Coll, Tiree, Lismore, Colonsay, Barra and Lochboisdale (South Uist). See the relevant island sections for details. Information and reservations for all CalMac ferry services are available at the **ferry terminal** (☎01631-562244; Railway Pier; ☺9am-6pm Mar-Oct) near the train station.

BUS Scottish Citylink (www.citylink.co.uk) operates intercity coaches to Oban, while **West Coast Motors** (www.westcoastmotors.co.uk) runs local and regional services. The bus terminal is outside the train station. Destinations include the following:

Cambeltown (change at Inveraray) £19, four hours, three daily

Fort William (via Appin and Balluchulish) £9.40, 1½ hours, three daily Monday to Saturday

Glasgow (via Inveraray and Arrochar) £18, three hours, four daily

Perth (via Tyndrum and Killin) £16, three hours, twice daily

TRAIN Oban is at the terminus of a scenic route that branches off the West Highland line at Crianlarich. The train isn't much use for travelling north from Oban – to reach Fort William requires a detour via Crianlarich (3¾ hours). Take the bus instead. Destinations from Oban include the following:

Glasgow £22, three hours, three daily

Tyndrum £10, one hour, three daily

Isle of Mull

POP 2600

From the rugged ridges of Ben More and the black basalt crags of Burg to the blinding white sand, rose-pink granite and emerald waters that fringe the Ross, Mull can lay claim to some of the finest and most varied scenery in the Inner Hebrides. Add in two impressive castles, a narrow-gauge railway, the sacred island of Iona and easy access from Oban and you can see why it's sometimes impossible to find a spare bed on the island.

The waters to the west of Mull provide some of the best whale-spotting opportunities in Scotland, with several operators offering whale-watching cruises.

Mull, Iona & Staffa

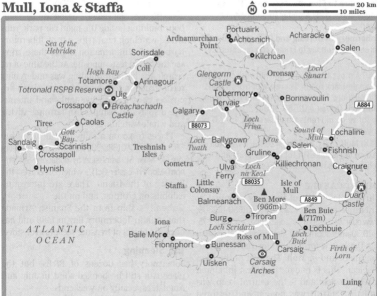

☞ Tours

Bowman's Tours   COACH TOUR

(☏01631-566809; www.bowmanstours.co.uk; 1 Queens Park Pl) From April to October, Bowman's offers a Three Isles day-trip (adult/child £55/27.50, 10 hours, daily) from Oban that visits Mull, Iona and Staffa. Note that the crossing to Staffa is weather dependent. Bowman's also runs a circular coach tour around Mull (adult/child £20/10).

ℹ Information

Clydesdale Bank (Main St; ⊙9.15am-4.45pm Mon-Fri) The island's only bank and 24-hour ATM. You can get cash using a debit card from the post offices in Salen and Craignure, or get cash back with a purchase from Co-op food stores.

Craignure tourist office (☏01680-812377; ⊙8.30am-5pm Mon-Sat, 10.30am-5pm Sun)

Dunaros Hospital (☏01680-300392) Has a minor injuries unit; the nearest casualty department is in Oban.

Mull visitor & information centre (☏01688-302875; Ledaig, Tobermory; ⊙9am-5pm)

Post office (Main St; ⊙9am-1pm & 2-5.30pm Mon, Tue, Thu & Fri, 9am-1pm Wed & Sat) There are also post-office counters in Salen, Craignure and Fionnphort.

ℹ Getting There & Away

There are three **CalMac** (www.calmac.co.uk) car ferries linking Mull with the mainland.

Oban to Craignure (passenger/car £5.25/46.50, 40 minutes, every two hours) The shortest and busiest route – booking advised for cars.

Lochaline to Fishnish (£3.10/13.65, 15 minutes, at least hourly) On the east coast of Mul.

Tobermory to Kilchoan (£5/25.50, 35 minutes, seven daily Monday to Saturday) Links to the Ardnamurchan peninsula; from May to August there are also five sailings on Sunday.

ℹ Getting Around

BICYCLE You can hire bikes for around £10 to £15 per day from the following places.

Brown's Hardware Shop (☏01688-302020; www.brownstobermory.co.uk; Main St, Tobermory)

On Yer Bike (☏01680-300501; Salen) Easter to October only. Also has an outlet by the ferry terminal at Craignure.

BUS Public transport on Mull is fairly limited.

Bowman's Tours (☏01680-812313; www.bowmanstours.co.uk) The main operator, connecting the ferry ports and the island's main villages.

Craignure to Tobermory (return £7.30, one hour, four to seven daily Monday to Friday, three to five Saturday and Sunday)

Craignure to Fionnphort (return £11, 1¼ hours, three daily Monday to Saturday, one Sunday)

Tobermory to Dervaig and Calgary (return £4, three daily Monday to Friday, two on Saturday)

CAR Almost all of Mull's road network consists of single-track roads. There are petrol stations at Craignure, Fionnphort, Salen and Tobermory. **Mull Self Drive** (☎01680-300402; www.mull selfdrive.co.uk) rents small cars for £45/237 per day/week.

TAXI **Mull Taxi** (☎07760-426351; www.mull taxi.co.uk) is based in Tobermory, and has a vehicle that is wheelchair accessible.

DUART CASTLE

Three miles south of the ferry terminal at Cragnure is **Duart Castle** (☎01680-812309; www.duartcastle.com; adult/child £5.50/2.75; ☻10.30am-5.30pm daily May–mid-Oct, 11am-4pm Sun-Thu Apr), a formidable fortress dominating the Sound of Mull. The seat of the Clan Maclean, this is one of the oldest inhabited castles in Scotland – the central keep was built in 1360. It was bought and restored in 1911 by Sir Fitzroy Maclean and has damp dungeons, vast halls and bathrooms equipped with ancient fittings. A bus to the castle meets the 9.50am, 11.55am and 2pm ferries from Oban to Craignure.

TOBERMORY
POP 750

Tobermory, the island's main town, is a picturesque little fishing port and yachting centre with brightly painted houses arranged around a sheltered harbour, with a grid-patterned 'upper town'. The village was the setting for the children's TV program *Balamory*, and while the series stopped filming in 2005 regular repeats mean that the town still swarms in summer with toddlers towing parents around looking for their favourite TV characters (frazzled parents can get a *Balamory* booklet from the tourist offices in Oban and Tobermory).

◉ Sights & Activities

The Hebridean Whale & Dolphin Trust's **Marine Discovery Centre** (☎01688-302620; www.whaledolphintrust.co.uk; 28 Main St; admission free; ☻10am-5pm Mon-Fri, 11am-4pm Sun Apr-Oct, 11am-5pm Mon-Fri Nov-Mar) has displays, videos and interactive exhibits on whale and dolphin biology and ecology, and is a great place for kids to learn about sea mammals. It also provides information about volunteering and reporting sightings of whales and dolphins.

Sea Life Surveys (☎01688-302916; www .sealifesurveys.com; Ledaig), based in the harbour building beside the main car park, runs whale-watching boat trips out of Tobermory harbour; for information about these trips, see the boxed text, opposite. At the time of research, the harbour building was undergoing reconstruction to house a new **marine education centre**, with live tanks and interactive displays on fishing, fish farming, diving and whale watching.

Places to go on a rainy day include **Mull Museum** (☎01688-302603; www.mullmuseum .org.uk; Main St; admission by donation; ☻10am-4pm Mon-Fri Easter-Oct), which records the history of the island. There are interesting exhibits on crofting, and on the **Tobermory Galleon**, a ship from the Spanish Armada that sank in Tobermory Bay in 1588 and has been the object of treasure seekers ever since.

🛏 Sleeping

Tobermory has dozens of B&Bs, but the place can still be booked solid in July and August, especially on weekends.

Sonas House   B&B ££

(☎01688-302304; www.sonashouse.co.uk; The Fairways, Erray Rd; s/d £110/125, apt from £90; ⓟ☎☎) Here's a first: a B&B with a 10m heated, indoor swimming pool! Sonas is a large, modern house that offers luxury B&B in a beautiful setting with superb views over Tobermory Bay; ask for the Blue Poppy bedroom, which has its own balcony. There's also a self-contained studio apartment with double bed.

Cuidhe Leathain   B&B ££

(☎01688-302504; www.cuidhe-leathain.co.uk; Salen Rd; r per person £40; ☎) A handsome 19th-century house in the upper town, Cuidhe Leathain (coo-*lane*), which means Maclean's Corner, exudes a cosily cluttered Victorian atmosphere. The breakfasts will set you up for the rest of the day, and the owners are a fount of knowledge about Mull and its wildlife. Minimum two-night stay.

Harbour View   B&B ££

(☎01688-301111; www.tobermorybandb.com; 1 Argyll Tce; r per person £40-45; ☎) This beautifully renovated fisherman's cottage is perched on the edge of Tobermory's 'upper town'. Exposed patches of original stone walls add a touch of character, while a new extension provides the family suite (two adjoining rooms with shared bathroom, sleeps four) with an outdoor terrace that enjoys breathtaking views across the harbour.

THAR SHE BLOWS!

The North Atlantic Drift, a swirling tendril of the Gulf Stream, carries warm water into the cold, nutrient-rich seas off the Scottish coast, resulting in huge blooms of plankton. Small fish feed on the plankton, and bigger fish feed on the smaller fish... This huge seafood smorgasbord attracts large numbers of marine mammals, from harbour porpoises and dolphins to minke whales and even – though sightings are rare – humpback and sperm whales.

In contrast to Iceland and Norway, Scotland has cashed in on the abundance of minke whales off its coast by embracing whale watching rather than whaling. There are now dozens of operators around the coast offering whale-watching boat trips lasting from a couple of hours to all day; some have whale-sighting success rates of 95% in summer.

While seals, porpoises and dolphins can be seen year-round, minke whales are migratory. The best time to see them is from June to August, with August being the peak month for sightings. The website of the Hebridean Whale & Dolphin Trust (www .whaledolphintrust.co.uk) has lots of information on the species you are likely to see, and how to identify them.

A booklet titled *Is It a Whale?* is available from tourist offices and bookshops, and provides tips on identifying the various species of marine mammal that you're likely to see.

Tobermory Campsite   CAMPGROUND £
(01688-302624; www.tobermorycampsite.co.uk; Newdale, Dervaig Rd; tent sites per adult/child £7/3; Mar-Oct) A quiet, family-friendly campground a mile west of town on the road to Dervaig. Credit/debit cards not accepted.

Tobermory SYHA   HOSTEL £
(01688-302481; www.syha.org.uk; Main St; dm £17.50; Mar-Oct; @🛜) Great location in a Victorian house right on the waterfront. Bookings recommended.

Eating & Drinking

TOP CHOICE Café Fish   SEAFOOD ££
(01688-301253; www.thecafefish.com; The Pier; mains £10-22; lunch & dinner) Seafood doesn't come much fresher than the stuff served at this warm and welcoming little restaurant overlooking Tobermory harbour – as its motto says, 'The only thing frozen here is the fisherman'! Langoustines and squat lobsters go straight from boat to kitchen to join rich Tuscan-style seafood stew, fat scallops, fish pie and catch-of-the-day on the daily-changing menu.

Also has freshly baked bread, home-made desserts and a range of Scottish cheeses on offer.

Fish & Chip Van   FISH & CHIPS £
(01688-301109; www.tobermoryfishandchipvan .co.uk; Main St; mains £3-8; 12.30-9pm Mon-Sat Apr-Dec, plus Sun Jun-Sep, 12.30-7pm Mon-Sat Jan-

Mar) If it's a takeaway you're after, you can tuck into some of Scotland's best gourmet fish and chips down on the waterfront. And where else will you find a chip van selling freshly cooked prawns and scallops?

MacGochan's   PUB ££
(01688-302350; www.macgochans-tobermory.co .uk; Ledaig; mains £9-20; lunch & dinner) A lively pub beside the car park at the southern end of the waterfront, MacGochan's does good bar meals (haddock and chips, steak pie, vegetable lasagne), and often has outdoor barbecues on summer evenings. There's a beer garden out the front, and live music in the bar on weekends.

Mishnish Hotel   PUB ££
(01688-302009; www.mishnish.co.uk; Main St; mains £11-20; lunch & dinner; 🛜) 'The Mish' is a favourite hang-out for visiting yachties and a good place for a pint, or a meal at the pub's Mish-Dish restaurant. Wood-panelled and flag-draped, this is a good old traditional pub where you can listen to live folk music, toast your toes by the open fire or challenge the locals to a game of pool.

NORTH MULL

The road from Tobermory west to Calgary cuts inland, leaving most of the north coast of Mull wild and inaccessible. Just outside Tobermory, a long, single-track road leads north for 4 miles to majestic Glengorm Castle (01688-302321; www.glengormcastle.co.uk;

Glengorm; ◷10am-5pm Easter–mid-Oct), with views across the sea to Ardnamurchan, Rum and the Outer Hebrides. The castle outbuildings house an art gallery, a farm shop and an excellent coffee shop. The castle itself is not open to the public, but you're free to explore its beautiful grounds.

Mull's best (and busiest) silver-sand beach, flanked by cliffs and with views out to Coll and Tiree, is at Calgary, about 12 miles west of Tobermory. And yes – this is the place from which the more famous Calgary in Alberta, Canada, takes its name.

🛏 Sleeping & Eating

Bellachroy   HOTEL **££**

(☎01688-400314; www.bellachroyhotel.co.uk; Dervaig; s/d £75/100; P🐾🛜) The Bellachroy is an atmospheric 17th-century droving inn with six plain but comfortable bedrooms. The bar is a focus for local social life and serves excellent meals (mains £11 to £19, plus there's a kids' menu) based on fresh local produce: pork from a local Dervaig farm, lamb from Ulva, mutton from Iona, mussels from Inverlussa and Mull-landed seafood.

🍽 Calgary Farmhouse   APARTMENTS **££**

(☎01688-400256; www.calgary.co.uk; Calgary; 2-person apt per 3 nights £195; P🛜) This farmhouse complex offers eight fantastic self-catering properties (including apartments, cottages and a farmhouse, sleeping from two to eight people), beautifully designed and fitted out with timber furniture and wood-burning stoves. The Hayloft (sleeps eight, £1200 a week in high season) includes a spectacular lounge/dining room with curved oak frames and locally produced art work.

Dervaig Village Hall Hostel   HOSTEL **£**

(☎01688-400491; www.mull-hostel-dervaig.co.uk; Dervaig; dm/q £15/55; P) Basic but very comfortable bunkhouse accommodation in Dervaig's village hall, with self-catering kitchen and sitting room.

FREE **Calgary Bay Campsite**   CAMPGROUND **£**

(Calgary) You can camp for free at the southern end of the beach at Calgary Bay – keep to the area south of the stream. There are no facilities other than the public toilets across the road; water comes from the stream.

🍽 Glengorm Coffee Shop   CAFE **£**

(www.glengormcastle.co.uk; Glengorm; mains £5-8; ◷10am-5pm Easter-Oct) Set in a cottage courtyard in the grounds of Glengorm Castle, this cafe serves superb lunches (from noon to 4.30pm) – the menu changes daily, but includes sandwiches and salads (much of the salad veg is grown on the Glengorm estate), soups and specials, such as curry-flavoured salmon fishcakes with mint and cucumber salad.

Calgary Farmhouse Tearoom   CAFE **£**

(www.calgary.co.uk; mains £5-8; ◷10.30am-5.30pm Jul & Aug, to 4.30pm rest of year; P🛜) Just a few minutes' walk from the sandy beach at Calgary Bay, this tearoom serves soups, sandwiches, coffee and cake using fresh local produce as much as possible. There's also an art gallery and craft shop here.

SOUTH MULL

The road from Craignure to Fionnphort climbs through some wild and desolate scenery before reaching the southwestern part of the island, which consists of a long peninsula called the Ross of Mull. The Ross has a spectacular south coast lined with black basalt cliffs that give way further west to white-sand beaches and pink granite crags.

At the western end of the Ross, 38 miles from Craignure, is Fionnphort (*finn*-a-fort) and the ferry to Iona. The coast here is a beautiful blend of pink granite rocks, white sandy beaches and vivid turquoise sea.

Isle of Iona

POP 130

There are few more uplifting sights on Scotland's west coast than the view of Iona from Mull on a sunny day – an emerald island set in a sparkling turquoise sea. From the moment you step off the ferry you begin to appreciate the hushed, spiritual atmosphere that pervades this sacred island.

St Columba sailed from Ireland and landed on Iona in 563 before setting out to spread Christianity throughout Scotland. He established a monastery on the island and it was here that the *Book of Kells* – the prize attraction of Dublin's Trinity College – is believed to have been transcribed. It was taken to Kells in Ireland when Viking raids drove the monks from Iona.

The monks returned and the monastery prospered until its destruction during the Reformation. The ruins were given to the Church of Scotland in 1899, and by 1910 a group of enthusiasts called the Iona Community (www.iona.org.uk) had reconstructed the abbey. It's still a flourishing spiritual community that holds regular courses and retreats.

Sights & Activities

Head uphill from the ferry pier and turn right through the grounds of a ruined 13th-century nunnery with fine cloistered gardens, and exit at the far end. Across the road is the Iona Heritage Centre (☑01681-700576; adult/child £2/free; ☺10.30am-5pm Mon-Sat Apr-Oct), which covers the history of Iona, crofting and lighthouses; the centre's coffee shop serves delicious home baking.

Turn right here and continue along the road to Reilig Oran, an ancient cemetery that holds the graves of 48 of Scotland's early kings, including Macbeth, and a tiny Romanesque chapel. Beyond rises the spiritual heart of the island, Iona Abbey (HS; ☑01681-700512; adult/child £5.50/3.30; ☺9.30am-5.30pm Apr-Sep, to 4.30pm Oct-Mar). The spectacular nave, dominated by Romanesque and early Gothic vaults and columns, contains the elaborate, white marble tombs of the 8th duke of Argyll and his wife. A door on the left leads to the beautiful Gothic cloister, where medieval grave slabs sit alongside modern religious sculptures. A replica of the intricately carved St John's Cross stands just outside the abbey – the massive 8th-century original is in the Infirmary Museum (around the far side of the abbey) along with many other fine examples of early Christian and medieval carved stones.

Continue past the abbey and look for a footpath on the left signposted Dun I (dunee). An easy walk of about 15 to 20 minutes leads to the highest point on Iona, with fantastic views in all directions.

Sleeping & Eating

TOP
CHOICE Argyll Hotel HOTEL ££

(☑01681-700334; www.argyllhoteliona.co.uk; s/d from £66/99; ☺Mar-Oct; @☎) This cute little hotel has 16 snug rooms (a sea view costs rather a bit more – £140 for a double) and a country-house restaurant (mains £12 to £17, open 8am to 10am, 12.30pm to 1.20pm and 7pm to 8pm) with wooden fireplace and antique tables and chairs. The kitchen is supplied by a huge organic garden around the back, and the menu includes home-grown salads, local seafood and Scottish beef and lamb.

TOP
CHOICE Iona Hostel HOSTEL £

(☑01681-700781; www.ionahostel.co.uk; dm per adult/child £20/17; ☺check-in 4-7pm) This hostel is set in an attractive, modern timber building on a working croft, with stunning views out to Staffa and the Treshnish Isles. Rooms are clean and functional, and the well-equipped lounge/kitchen area has an open fire. It's at the northern end of the island; to get here, continue along the road past the abbey for 1.5 miles (a 20- to 30-minute walk).

Cnoc-Oran Campsite CAMPGROUND £

(☑01681-700112; www.ionaselfcateringaccommodation.co.uk; tent sites per adult/child £5/2.50; ☺Apr-Oct) Basic campground about a mile west of the ferry.

Getting There & Away

The passenger ferry from Fionnphort to Iona (return £4.80, five minutes, hourly) runs daily. There are also various day trips available from Oban to Iona.

FIFE

Protruding like a serpent's head from Scotland's east coast, Fife (www.visitfife.com) is a spit of land between the Firths of Forth and Tay. A royal history and atmosphere distinct from the rest of Scotland leads it to style itself as 'The Kingdom of Fife'.

Though overdeveloped southern Fife is commuter-belt territory, the eastern region's rolling green farmland and quaint fishing villages are prime turf for exploration and crab crunching, and the fresh sea air feels like it's doing a power of good. Elsewhere in the county, little Falkland makes a great stop, and dignified Culross is a superbly preserved 17th-century burgh.

Fife's biggest attraction, St Andrews, has Scotland's most venerable university and a wealth of historic buildings. It's also, of course, the headquarters of golf and draws professionals and keen slashers alike to take on the Old Course – the classic links experience.

Activities

The Fife Coastal Path (www.fifecoastalpath.co.uk) runs more than 80 miles following the entire Fife coastline from the Forth Road Bridge to the Tay Bridge and beyond. It's well waymarked, picturesque and not too

ISLE OF STAFFA

Felix Mendelssohn, who visited the uninhabited island of Staffa in 1829, was inspired to compose the *Hebrides Overture* after hearing waves echoing in the impressive and cathedral-like Fingal's Cave. The cave walls and surrounding cliffs are composed of vertical, hexagonal basalt columns that look like pillars (Staffa is Norse for 'Pillar Island'). You can land on the island and walk into the cave via a causeway. Nearby Boat Cave can be seen from the causeway, but you can't reach it on foot. Staffa also has a sizeable puffin colony, north of the landing place.

Unless you have your own boat, the only way to reach Staffa and the Treshnish Isles is on an organised boat trip.

rigorous, though winds can buffet. It's easily accessed for shorter sections or day walks, and long stretches of it can be tackled on a mountain bike too.

❶ Getting Around

The main bus operator here is **Stagecoach Fife** (☑ 0871 200 2233; www.stagecoachbus.com). For £7.50 you can buy a Fife Dayrider ticket, which gives unlimited travel around Fife on Stagecoach buses.

If you are driving from the Forth Road Bridge to St Andrews, a slower but much more scenic route along the M90/A91 is along the signposted **Fife Coastal Tourist Route**.

St Andrews

POP 14,209

For a small place, St Andrews made a big name for itself, firstly as religious centre, then as Scotland's oldest university town. But its status as the home of golf has propelled it to even greater fame, and today's pilgrims arrive with a set of clubs. But it's a lovely place to visit even if you've no interest in the game, with impressive medieval ruins, stately university buildings, idyllic white sands, and excellent accommodation and eating options.

The Old Course, the world's most famous, has a striking seaside location at the western end of town. Although it's difficult to get a game, it's still a thrilling experience to stroll the hallowed turf.

History

St Andrews is said to have been founded by St Regulus, who arrived from Greece in the 4th century bringing the bones of St Andrew, Scotland's patron saint. The town soon grew into a major pilgrimage centre and St Andrews developed into the ecclesiastical capital of the country. The university was founded in 1410, the first in Scotland.

Golf has been played here for more than 600 years; the Royal & Ancient Golf Club, the game's governing body, was founded in 1754 and the imposing clubhouse was built a hundred years later. The British Open Championship takes place here every few years in July.

⊙ Sights

St Andrews Cathedral   RUIN
(HS; www.historic-scotland.gov.uk; The Pends; adult/child £4.50/2.70, incl castle £7.60/4.60; ⊙9.30am-5.30pm Apr-Sep, to 4.30pm Oct-Mar) The ruins of this cathedral are all that's left of one of Britain's most magnificent medieval buildings. You can appreciate the scale and majesty of the edifice from the small sections that remain standing. Although founded in 1160, it was not consecrated until 1318, but stood as the focus of this important pilgrimage centre until 1559 when it was pillaged during the Reformation.

St Andrew's supposed bones lie under the altar; until the cathedral was built, they had been enshrined in the nearby Church of St Regulus (Rule). All that remains of this church is St Rule's Tower, worth the climb for the view across St Andrews. There's also a museum with a collection of Celtic crosses and gravestones found on the site. The entrance fee only applies for the tower and museum; you can wander freely around the atmospheric ruins, a fine picnic spot.

St Andrews Castle   CASTLE
(HS; www.historic-scotland.gov.uk; The Scores; adult/child £5.50/3.30, incl cathedral £7.60/4.60; ⊙9.30am-5.30pm Apr-Sep, to 4.30pm Oct-Mar) With dramatic coastline views, the castle is mainly in ruins, but the site itself is evocative. It was founded around 1200 as the bishop's fortified home. After the execution of Protestant reformers in 1545, other reformers retaliated by murdering Cardinal Beaton and taking over the castle. They spent

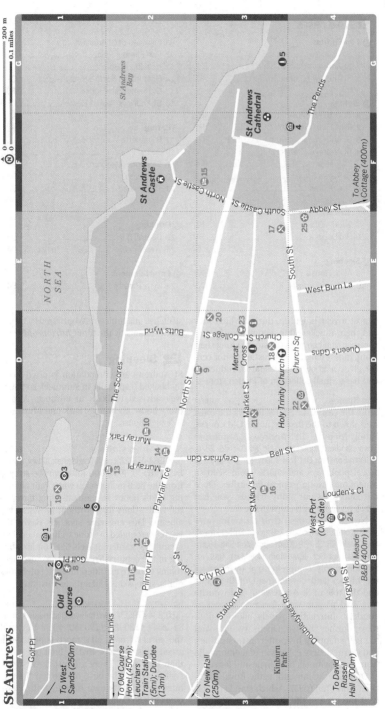

St Andrews

North Sea

St Andrews Bay

St Andrews Castle

St Andrews Cathedral

Old Course

The Scores

North St

Market St

South St

Butts Wynd

College St

Church St

Mercat Cross

Holy Trinity Church

Church Sq

Queen's Gdns

West Burn La

Abbey St

North Castle St

South Castle St

The Pends

Golf Pl

The Links

Pilmour Pl

Playfair Tce

Murray Pl

Murray Park

Greyfriars Gdn

Bell St

St Mary's Pl

Hope St

City Rd

Station Rd

West Port (Old Gate)

Louden's Cl

Argyle St

Doubleykes Rd

Kinburn Park

To West Sands (250m)

To Old Course Hotel (450m); Leuchars Train Station (5mi); Dundee (13mi)

To New Hall (250m)

To David Russell Hall (700m)

To Meade B&B (400m)

To Abbey Cottage (400m)

200 m
0.1 miles

St Andrews

almost a year holed up, during which they and their attackers dug a complex of siege tunnels; you can walk (or stoop) along their damp mossy lengths. The castle's visitor centre gives a good audiovisual introduction and has a small collection of Pictish stones.

The Scores   STREET
From the castle, the Scores follows the coast west down to the first tee at the Old Course. Family-friendly St Andrews Aquarium (www.standrewsaquarium.co.uk; adult/child £8/6; ☺10am-5pm Mar-Oct, to 4.30pm Nov-Feb; ⛩) has a seal pool, rays and sharks from Scottish waters and exotic tropical favourites. Once introduced to our finny friends, you can snack on them with chips in the cafe.

Nearby, the British Golf Museum (www.britishgolfmuseum.co.uk; Bruce Embankment; adult/child £6/3; ☺9.30am-5pm Mon-Sat, 10am-5pm Sun Apr-Oct, 10am-4pm Nov-Mar) has an extraordinarily comprehensive overview of the history and development of the game and the role of St Andrews in it. Favourite fact: bad players were formerly known as 'foozlers'. Interactive panels allow you to relive former British Opens (watch Paul Azinger snapping his putter in frustration), and there's a large collection of memorabilia from Open winners both male and female.

Opposite the museum is the Royal & Ancient Golf Club (p857), which stands proudly at the head of the Old Course. Beside it

stretches magnificent West Sands beach, made famous by the film *Chariots of Fire*.

🛌 Sleeping

St Andrews accommodation is often heavily booked (especially in summer), so you're well advised to book in advance. Almost every house on Murray Park and Murray Pl is a guesthouse.

TOP CHOICE Abbey Cottage   B&B ££
(☎01334-473727; coull@lineone.net; Abbey Walk; s £45, d £65-70; ⓟ⛩) You know you've strayed from the B&B mainstream when your charming host's hobby is photographing tigers in the wild – don't leave without browsing her albums. This engaging spot sits below the town, surrounded by stone walls that enclose a rambling garden; it feels like you are staying in the country. There are three excellent rooms that are all different, with patchwork quilts, sheepskins and antique furniture.

Fairways of St Andrews   B&B ££
(☎01334-479513; www.fairwaysofstandrews.co.uk; 8a Golf Pl; s £80-120, d £90-150; ⛩) Just around the corner from golf's most famous 18th green, this is more in the boutique hotel than B&B class. There are just three super-stylish rooms; the best, on the top floor, is huge and has its own balcony with views over the Old Course.

Hazelbank Hotel
HOTEL ££

(☎01334-472466; www.hazelbank.com; 28 The Scores; s £69-89, d £99-151; @🤶) Offering a genuine welcome, the family-run Hazelbank is the most likeable of the pleasingly old-fashioned hotels along the Scores. The front rooms have marvellous views along the beach and out to sea; those at the back are cheaper. Prices drop significantly outside the height of summer. There's a thoughtful hospitality that's particularly endearing and a good portent if you are playing a round – Bobby Locke won the Open in 1957 while a guest here.

Five Pilmour Place
B&B £££

(☎01334-478665; www.5pilmourplace.com; 5 Pilmour Pl; s £78, d £120-160; @🤶) Just around the corner from the Old Course, this luxurious and intimate spot offers stylish, compact rooms with an eclectic range of styles as well as modern conveniences such as flatscreen TV and a DVD player. The king-size beds are especially comfortable, and the lounge area is a stylish treat.

Aslar House
B&B ££

(☎01334-473460; www.aslar.com; 120 North St; s/d/ste £50/96/100; ☺Feb–mid-Nov; 🤶) The rooms are so impeccable at this place that it's frightening to imagine how much work goes on behind the scenes. The modern comforts don't detract from the house's historical features (including a whimsical turret room) but certainly add value. DVD players, iPod docks and hair straighteners in every room are complemented by fabulous new bathrooms. The master suite is very spacious and worth the extra investment. No under 16-year-olds.

Cameron House
B&B ££

(☎01334-472306; www.cameronhouse-sta.co.uk; 11 Murray Park; s/d £45/90; 🤶) Beautifully decorated rooms and warm, cheerful hosts make this a real home away from home on this guesthouse-filled street. The two single rooms share a bathroom. Prices drop £10 per person outside high season.

Meade B&B
B&B ££

(☎01334-477350; annmeade10@hotmail.com; 6 Livingstone Cres; d £60-70; 🤶🐾) This welcoming gem in a quiet street south of the town centre is run by a friendly family and their pets, including a portly marmalade cat and feisty black lab. There's just one double room and it's lovely, light and comfortable. You'll feel right at home.

PLAYING THE OLD COURSE

Golf has been played at St Andrews since the 15th century. By 1457 it was so popular that James II banned it because it interfered with his troops' archery practice. Although it lies beside the exclusive, all-male-membership Royal & Ancient Golf Club, the Old Course (☎01334-466666; www.standrews.org.uk; Reservations Office, St Andrews Links Trust) is public.

You'll need to book in advance to play via St Andrews Links Trust (☎01334-466666; www.standrews.org.uk). Reservations open on the first Wednesday in September the year before you wish to play. No bookings are taken for Saturdays or the month of September.

Unless you've booked months in advance, getting a tee-off time is literally a lottery; enter the ballot at the caddie office (☎01334-466666) before 2pm two days before you wish to play (there's no Sunday play). Be warned that applications by ballot are normally heavily oversubscribed, and green fees are £150 in summer. Singles are not accepted in the ballot and should start queuing as early as possible on the day – 5am is good – in the hope of joining a group. You'll need a handicap certificate (24/36 for men/women). If your number doesn't come up, there are six other public courses in the area (book up to seven days in advance on ☎01334-466718, no handicap required), including the prestigious Castle Course (£120). Other summer green fees: New £70, Jubilee £70, Eden £40, Strathtyrum £25 and Balgove (nine-holer for beginners and kids) £12. There are various multiple-day tickets available. A caddie for your round costs £45 plus tip. If you play on a windy day, expect those scores to balloon: Nick Faldo famously stated, 'When it blows here, even the seagulls walk.'

Guided walks (£2.50) of the Old Course run Tuesdays to Sundays in July and August, and hit famous landmarks such as the Swilcan Bridge and the Road Hole bunker. They run from outside the shop by the 18th green at 11am and 1.30pm and last 50 minutes. On Sundays, a three-hour walk (£5) takes you around the whole course. You are free to walk over the course on Sundays, or follow the footpaths around the edge at any time.

Old Fishergate House
B&B ££

(☑01334-470874; www.oldfishergatehouse.co.uk; North Castle St; s/d £80/110; 🛜) This historic 17th-century town house, furnished with period pieces, is in a great location – the oldest part of town, close to the cathedral and castle. The two twin rooms are very spacious and even have their own sitting room and cushioned ledges on their window sills. On a scale of one to 10 for quaintness, we'd rate it about a 9.5. Cracking breakfasts feature fresh fish and pancakes.

St Andrews Tourist Hostel
HOSTEL £

(☑01334-479911; www.standrewshostel.com; St Marys Pl; dm £11-13; 🛜) Laid-back and central, this hostel is a little bit hard to spot. Occupying a stately old building, it has high corniced ceilings, especially in the huge lounge, and a laissez-faire approach. The dorms could use new mattresses, but are clean and bright. There's a supermarket close by. Reception closed between 2pm and 5pm

Ogstons on North Street
HOTEL £££

(☑01334-473387; www.ogstonsonnorthst.com; 127 North St; r £120-180; 🛜) If you want to eat, drink and sleep in the same stylish place then this classy inn could be for you. Smartened-up rooms feature elegant contemporary styling and coolly beautiful bathrooms, some with Jacuzzi. There are also DVD players, iPod docks, crisp white linen and large windows that give the rooms an airy feel. The Oak Rooms (serving lunch and dinner) is the place for meals and a read of the paper. The bar is perfect for a snug tipple, and the Lizard Lounge in the basement is a late-night bar that cranks up with live gigs and regular DJs.

✕ Eating

TOP CHOICE Vine Leaf
SCOTTISH £££

(☑01334-477497; www.vineleafstandrews.co.uk; 131 South St; 2-course dinner £26.50; ⊙dinner Tue-Sat; 🍴) Classy, comfortable and well-established, the friendly Vine Leaf offers a changing menu of sumptuous Scottish seafood, game and vegetarian dishes. There's a huge selection within the set-price menu, all well presented, and an interesting, mostly old-world wine list. It's down a close (alley) off South St.

Seafood Restaurant
SEAFOOD £££

(☑01334-479475; www.theseafoodrestaurant.com; The Scores; lunch/dinner £22/45) The Seafood Restaurant occupies a stylish glass-walled room, built out over the sea, with plush navy carpet, crisp white linen, an open kitchen and panoramic views of St Andrews Bay. It offers top seafood and an excellent wine list. Look out for its special winter deals.

Doll's House
SCOTTISH ££

(☑01334-477422; www.dolls-house.co.uk; 3 Church Sq; mains £13-15) With its high-backed chairs, bright colours and creaky wooden floor, the Doll's House blends a Victorian child's bedroom with modern stylings. The result is a surprising warmth and no pretensions. The menu makes the most of local fish and other Scottish produce, and the two-course lunch for £6.95 is unbeatable value. The early-evening two-course deal for £12.95 isn't bad either.

The Glass House
ITALIAN, SCOTTISH ££

(www.glasshouse-restaurant.co.uk; 80 North St; mains £7-15; ⊙noon-9pm) Casual but comfortable, this mostly Italian restaurant offers plenty of light in its split-level, open kitchen dining area. The menu is basically Italian, with attractively presented pizzas and pastas popular with students. But a handful of daily specials offer more Scottish meat and game choices of notable quality.

🐟 The Tailend
SEAFOOD £

(www.tailendfishbar.co.uk; 130 Market St; fish & chips takeaway/eat in £6/10.50; ⊙11.30am-10pm) Delicious fresh fish sourced from Arbroath just up the coast puts this a class above most chippies. It fries to order and it's worth the wait. The array of exquisite smoked delicacies at the counter will have you planning a picnic or fighting for a table in the licensed cafe out the back.

B Jannetta
ICE CREAM £

(☑01334-473285; www.jannettas.co.uk; 31 South St; 1/2 scoop cone £1.40/2; ⊙Mon-Sat) B Jannetta is a St Andrews institution, offering 52 varieties of ice cream from the weird (Irn-Bru sorbet) to the decadent (strawberries and champagne).

🍷 Drinking

Central Bar
PUB

(www.taylor-walker.co.uk; 77 Market St) Rather staid compared to some of the wilder student-driven drinking options, this likeable pub keeps it real with traditional features, an island bar, lots of Scottish beers, decent service and filling (if uninspiring) pub grub.

West Port PUB

(www.maclay.com; 170 South St; 🐦) Just by the gateway of the same name, this sleek, modernised pub has several levels, and a great beer garden out the back. Cheap cocktails rock the uni crowd, mixed drinks are above average, and there's some OK bar food.

☆ Entertainment

Byre Theatre THEATRE

(📞01334-475000; www.byretheatre.com; Abbey St) This theatre company started life in a converted cow byre in the 1930s, and now occupies a flashy premises making clever use of light and space.

ℹ Information

J&G Innes (www.jg-innes.co.uk; 107 South St) Plenty of local-interest books, such as Fife's history of burning witches.

Library (Church Sq; ⊘9.30am-5pm Mon, Fri & Sat, to 7pm Tue-Thu) Free internet access – drop-in only; no bookings.

St Andrews Community Hospital (📞01334-465656; www.nhsfife.org; Largo Rd)

St Andrews information centre (📞01334-472021; www.visit-standrews.co.uk; 70 Market St; ⊘9.15am-6pm Mon-Sat, 10am-5pm Sun Jul & Aug, 9.15am-5pm Mon-Sat Sep-Jun, plus 11am-4pm Sun Apr-Jun, Sep & Oct) Helpful staff with good knowledge of St Andrews and Fife.

ℹ Getting There & Away

BUS All buses leave from the bus station on Station Rd. There are frequent services to the following:

Anstruther 40 minutes, regularly

Crail 30 minutes, regularly

Dundee 30 minutes, half-hourly

Edinburgh £9.50, two hours, hourly

Glasgow £9.95, 2½ hours, hourly

Stirling £7.45, two hours, every two hours, Monday to Saturday

TRAIN There is no train station in St Andrews itself, but you can take a train from Edinburgh (grab a seat on the right-hand side of the carriage for great firth views) to Leuchars, 5 miles to the northwest (£12.60, one hour, hourly). From here, buses leave regularly for St Andrews.

ℹ Getting Around

To order a cab, call **Golf City Taxis** (📞01334-477788). A taxi between Leuchars train station and St Andrews town centre costs around £12.

Spokes (📞01334-477835; www.spokescycles.com; 37 South St; per half-/full day/week £8.50/13.50/60; ⊘9am-5.30pm Mon-Sat) hires out mountain bikes.

East Neuk

This charming stretch of coast runs south from St Andrews to the point at Fife Ness, then west to Leven. Neuk is an old Scots word for corner, and it's certainly an appealing nook of the country to investigate, with picturesque fishing villages, some great restaurants and pretty coastal walks; the Fife Coastal Path's most scenic stretches are in this area. It's easily visited from St Andrews, but also makes a very pleasant place to stay.

CRAIL
POP 1695

Pretty and peaceful, little Crail has a much-photographed stone-sheltered harbour surrounded by wee cottages with red-tiled roofs. You can buy lobster and crab from a kiosk (⊘lunch Sat & Sun) there. The benches in the nearby grassed area are perfectly placed for munching your alfresco crustaceans while admiring the view across to the Isle of May.

The village's history and involvement with the fishing industry is outlined in the Crail Museum (www.crailmuseum.org.uk; 62 Marketgate; admission free; ⊘10am-1pm & 2-5pm Mon-Sat, 2-5pm Sun Jun-Sep, Sat & Sun only Apr & May), which also offers tourist information.

Eighteenth-century Selcraig House (📞01333-450697; www.selcraighouse.co.uk; 47 Nethergate; s/d £35/70; 🐦🐦) is a characterful, well-run B&B with a variety of rooms. Across the road from the museum, a lot of work has gone into making Hazelton Guest House (📞01333-450250; www.thehazelton.co.uk; 29 Marketgate North; s £45-50, d £70-85; ⊘Mar-Oct; 🐦) what it is. Attractively remodelled rooms make full use of the abundant natural light in this lovely old building.

Crail is 10 miles southeast of St Andrews. Stagecoach (www.stagecoachbus.com) bus 95 between Leven, Anstruther, Crail and St Andrews passes through Crail hourly every day (30 minutes to St Andrews).

ANSTRUTHER
pop 3442

Once among Scotland's busiest ports, cheery Anstruther has ridden the tribulations of the fishing industry better than some, and now has a very pleasant mixture of bobbing boats, historic streets, and visitors ambling around the harbour grazing on fish and chips or contemplating a trip to the Isle of May.

⊙ Sights

The displays at the excellent Scottish Fisheries Museum (www.scotfishmuseum .org; adult/child £6/free; ◷10am-5.30pm Mon-Sat, 11am-5pm Sun Apr-Sep, 10am-4.30pm Mon-Sat, noon-4.30pm Sun Oct-Mar) include the Zulu Gallery, which houses the huge, partly restored hull of a traditional Zulu-class fishing boat, redolent with the scent of tar and timber. Afloat in the harbour outside the museum lies the *Reaper*, a fully restored Fifie-class fishing boat built in 1902.

The mile-long Isle of May, 6 miles southeast of Anstruther, is a stunning nature reserve. Between April and July the intimidating cliffs are packed with breeding kittiwakes, razorbills, guillemots, shags and around 40,000 puffins.

The five-hour trip to the island on the May Princess (◷01333-311808; www.anstru therpleasurecruises.co.uk; adult/child £22/11), including two to three hours ashore, sails almost daily from April to September; check times by phone or via the website. There's also a faster boat, the 12-seater rigid-hull inflatable *Osprey*, which makes nonlanding circuits of the island (adult/child £20/12.50) as well as longer visits (£25/15).

⎰ Sleeping & Eating

TOP CHOICE The Spindrift   B&B **££**

(◷01333-310573; www.thespindrift.co.uk; Pittenweem Rd; s/d £60/80; 🅿🛜🐾) Arriving from the west, there's no need to go further than Anstruther's first house on the left, a redoubt of Scottish cheer and warm hospitality. The rooms are elegant, classy and extremely comfortable – some have views across to Edinburgh and one is like a ship's cabin, courtesy of the sea captain who once owned the house. There are DVD players and teddies for company, an honesty-bar with characterful ales and malts, and fine company from your hosts. Breakfast includes porridge once voted the best in the kingdom. Dinner (£23) is also available.

Dreel Tavern   PUB **£**

(16 High St W; mains £8-11; 🍽) This charming old pub on the banks of the Dreel Burn has bucketloads of character and serves reliably tasty bar meals. Chow down in the outdoor beer garden in summer. There are also some top-quality cask ales here.

Wee Chippy   FISH & CHIPS **£**

(4 Shore St; fish supper £5.50) The Anstruther Fish Bar is one of Britain's best chippies, but we – and plenty of locals – reckon this one might be even better. The fish is of a very high quality and there's less of a queue too. Eat your catch by the water.

Cellar Restaurant   SEAFOOD **£££**

(◷01333-310378; www.cellaranstruther.co.uk; 24 East Green; 2-/3-course set dinner £35/40; ◷lunch Fri & Sat, dinner Tue-Sat) Tucked away in an alley behind the museum, the Cellar is famous for its seafood and fine wines. Try the local crab, lobster or whatever delicacies have been caught that day. Inside it's elegant and upmarket. Advance bookings are essential.

ⓘ Information

Anstruther information centre (◷01333-311073; www.visitfife.com; Harbourhead; ◷10am-5pm Mon-Sat, 11am-4pm Sun Apr-Oct) The best tourist office in East Neuk.

ⓘ Getting There & Away

Stagecoach (www.stagecoachbus.com) bus 95 runs daily from Leven (more departures from St Monans) to Anstruther and on to St Andrews (40 minutes, hourly) via Crail.

Falkland

POP 1183

Below the soft ridges of the Lomond Hills in the centre of Fife is the charming village of Falkland. Rising majestically out of the town centre is the outstanding 16th-century Falkland Palace (NTS; www.nts.org.uk; adult/child £11.50/8.50; ◷11am-5pm Mon-Sat, 1-5pm Sun Mar-Oct), a country residence of the Stuart monarchs. Mary, Queen of Scots is said to have spent the happiest days of her life 'playing the country girl in the woods and parks' at Falkland. The palace was built between 1501 and 1541 to replace a castle dating from the 12th century; French and Scottish craftspeople were employed to create a masterpiece of Scottish Gothic architecture. The King's bedchamber and the chapel, with its beautiful painted ceiling, have both been restored. Don't miss the prodigious 17th-century Flemish hunting tapestries in the hall. One feature of the royal leisure centre still exists: the oldest royal tennis court in Britain, built in 1539 for James V. It's in the grounds and still in use.

Falkland is 11 miles north of Kirkcaldy. Bus 36 travels between Glenrothes and Auchtermuchty via Falkland. From either of those two places there are regular connections to St Andrews and other Fife destinations. Buses continue on to Perth (one hour) more or less hourly.

Dunfermline

POP 39,229

Historic, monastic Dunfermline is Fife's largest population centre, sprawling eastwards through once-distinct villages. Its noble history is centred on evocative Dunfermline Abbey (HS; www.historic-scotland.gov.uk; St Margaret St; adult/child £3.70/2.20; ⊗9.30am-5.30pm daily Apr-Sep, to 4.30pm Oct, 9.30am-4.30pm Sat-Wed Nov-Mar), founded by David I in the 12th century as a Benedictine monastery. Dunfermline was already favoured by religious royals; Malcolm III married the exiled Saxon princess Margaret here in the 11th century, and both chose to be interred here. There were many more royal burials, none more notable than Robert the Bruce, whose remains were discovered here in 1818.

What's left of the abbey are the ruins of the impressive three-tiered refectory building, and the atmosphere-laden nave of the church, endowed with geometrically patterned columns and fine Romanesque and Gothic windows. It adjoins the 19th-century church (⊗May-Sep) in which Robert the Bruce now lies under the ornate pulpit.

Next to the refectory (and included in your abbey admission price) is Dunfermline Palace. Once the abbey guesthouse, it was converted for James VI, whose son, the ill-fated Charles I, was born here in 1600. Below stretches the bosky, strollable Pittencrieff Park.

Dunfermline is a culinary desert, but the good folk at Fresh (2 Kirkgate; light meals £4-7; ⊗9am-5pm Mon-Sat, 10.30am-5pm Sun; ⌨), just up from the abbey, do decent sandwiches and coffee, as well as tasty daily specials based on deli produce. There's also wine, internet access, a gallery and a book exchange.

There are frequent bus services running between Dunfermline and Edinburgh (£5.05, 40 minutes), Stirling (£9.95, 1¼ hours) and St Andrews (£9.95, 1¼ hours), and trains to/from Edinburgh (30 minutes).

Culross

POP 500

An enchanting little town, Culross (koo-ross) is Scotland's best-preserved example of a 17th-century Scottish burgh: the National Trust for Scotland (NTS) owns 20 of the town's buildings, including the palace. Small, red-tiled, whitewashed buildings line the cobbled streets, and the winding Back Causeway to the abbey is embellished with whimsical stone cottages.

As birthplace of St Mungo, Glasgow's patron saint, Culross was an important religious centre from the 6th century. The burgh developed, under laird George Bruce, by mining coal through extraordinary underwater tunnels. When mining was ended by flooding of the tunnels, the town switched to making linen and shoes.

Culross Palace (NTS; www.nts.org.uk; adult/child £9.50/7; ⊗noon-5pm Thu-Mon Apr, May & Sep, noon-5pm daily Jun-Aug, noon-4pm Fri-Mon Oct) is more a large house than a palace, and features extraordinary decorative painted woodwork, barrel-vaulted ceilings and an interior largely unchanged since the early 17th century. The Town House (tourist office downstairs) and the Study, also completed in the early 17th century, are open to the public (via guided tour included in palace admission), but the other NTS properties can only be viewed from the outside.

Ruined Culross Abbey (HS; www.historic-scotland.gov.uk; admission free; ⊗9.30am-7pm Mon-Sat, 2-7pm Sun Apr-Sep, 9.30am-4pm Mon-Sat, 2-4pm Sun Oct-Mar), founded by the Cistercians in 1217, is on the hill in a lovely peaceful spot with vistas of the firth. Part of the ruins were converted into the parish church in the 16th century; it's worth a peek inside for the stained glass and the Gothic Argyll tomb.

Above a pottery workshop near the palace, Biscuit Café (www.culrosspottery.com; light meals £3-6; ⊗10am-5pm Mon-Sat, 11am-5pm Sun) has a tranquil little garden and sells coffee, tempting organic cakes and scones, and tasty light meals.

Culross is 12 miles west of the Forth Road Bridge. Stagecoach (www.stagecoachbus.com) bus 78 runs to Culross from Dunfermline (25 minutes, hourly daily) and to Stirling (50 minutes, hourly Monday to Saturday).

PERTHSHIRE

For sheer scenic variety, Perthshire is the pick of Scotland's regions and a place where everyone will find a special, personal spot – whether it's a bleak moor, snaking loch, post-card-perfect village or magnificent forest. Highlights are many: the enchanting valley of Glen Lyon strikes visitors dumb with its wild and remote beauty; stunning Loch Tay is nearby (the base for ascending Ben Lawers); and the River Tay runs east from here towards Dunkeld, whose cathedral is among the most beautifully situated in the country.

Things begin sedately in the southeast corner with Perth itself, a fine country town with a fabulous attraction in lavish Scone Palace, and get gradually wilder as you move northwards and westwards, moving through wooded slopes and river-blessed valleys and culminating in the bleak expanse of Rannoch Moor.

Perth

POP 43,450

Sedately arranged along the banks of the Tay, this former capital of Scotland is a most liveable place with large tracts of enticing parkland surrounding an easily managed town centre. On its outskirts lies Scone Palace, a country house of staggering luxury built alongside the mound that was the crowning place of Scotland's kings. It's a must-see, but the town itself, ennobled by stately architecture, fine galleries and a few excellent restaurants, merits exploration, and is within easy striking distance of Edinburgh and Glasgow.

◉ Sights

Scone Palace PALACE

(www.scone-palace.co.uk; adult/child/family £10/7/30; ⊙9.30am-5pm Apr-Oct, closed 4.30pm Sat) 'So thanks to all at once and to each one, whom we invite to see us crowned at Scone.' This line from *Macbeth* indicates the importance of this place (pronounced 'skoon'), 2 miles north of Perth. The palace itself was built in 1580 on a site intrinsic to Scottish history. Here in 838, Kenneth MacAlpin became the first king of a united Scotland and brought the Stone of Destiny, on which Scottish kings were ceremonially invested, to Moot Hill. In 1296 Edward I of England carted the talisman off to Westminster Abbey, where it remained for 700 years before being returned to Scotland.

These days, however, Scone doesn't really conjure up ye olde days of bearded warrior-kings swearing oaths in the mist because the palace, rebuilt in the early 19th century, is a Georgian mansion of extreme elegance and luxury.

The visit takes you through a succession of sumptuous rooms filled with fine French furniture and noble artworks. There's an astonishing collection of porcelain and portraits, as well as a series of exquisite Vernis Martin papier-mâché. Scone has belonged for centuries to the Murray family, Earls of Mansfield, and many of the objects have fascinating history attached to them (friendly guides are on hand). Each room has comprehensive multilingual information; there are also panels relating histories of some of the Scottish kings crowned at Scone.

Outside, peacocks – all named after a monarch – strut around the magnificent grounds, which incorporate woods, a butterfly garden and a maze.

Ancient kings were crowned atop Moot Hill, topped by a chapel, next to the palace. It's said that the hill was created by bootfuls of earth, brought by nobles attending the coronations as an acknowledgment of the king's rights over their lands, although it's more likely the site of an ancient motte-and-bailey castle.

From Perth's centre, cross the bridge, turn left and keep bearing left until you reach the gates of the estate (15 to 20 minutes' walking). From here, it's a half-mile to the palace. Various buses from town stop here roughly every hour; the tourist office has a printout. There's a good cafe at the palace, too.

FJD Fergusson Gallery GALLERY

(www.pkc.gov.uk; cnr Marshall Pl & Tay St; ⊙10am-5pm Mon-Sat, plus 1-4.30pm Sun May-Sep) Beautifully set in the round waterworks building, this gallery exhibits much of the work of the Scottish Colourist JD Fergusson in a most impressive display. Fergusson spent time in Paris, and the influence of artists such as Matisse on his work is evident; his voluptuous female portraits against a tropical-looking Riviera background are memorable, as is the story of his lifelong relationship with noted Scottish dancer Margaret Morris.

FREE **St John's Kirk** CHURCH

(www.st-johns-kirk.co.uk; St John's St; ⊙10am-4pm Mon-Sat, to 1pm Sun May-Sep) Daunting St John's Kirk, founded in 1126, is surrounded by cobbled streets and is still the centrepiece

Perth

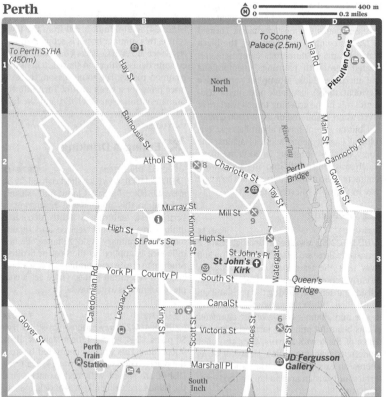

STIRLING & CENTRAL SCOTLAND PERTH

of the town. In 1559 John Knox preached a powerful sermon here that helped begin the Reformation, inciting a frenzied destruction of Scone abbey and other religious sites. Perth used to be known as St John's Town after this church; the football team here is still called St Johnstone.

FREE **Perth Museum** MUSEUM
(www.pkc.gov.uk; cnr George & Charlotte Sts; ⊙10am-5pm Mon-Sat) The city's main museum is worth wandering through for the elegant neoclassical interior alone. There's a varied shower of exhibits, ranging from portraits of dour lairds to interesting local social history. A geological room provides more entertainment for the young, while there are often excellent temporary exhibitions.

Black Watch Museum MUSEUM
(www.theblackwatch.co.uk; Hay St; adult/child £5/2.50; ⊙9.30am-5pm Mon-Sat, plus 10am-4pm Sun

Apr-Oct) Housed in a mansion on the edge of North Inch, this museum honours what was once Scotland's foremost regiment. Formed in 1725 to combat rural banditry, the Black Watch fought in numerous campaigns, re-created here with paintings, memorabilia and anecdotes. Little attempt at perspective is evident: there's justifiable pride in the regiment's role in the gruelling trench warfare of WWI, where it suffered nearly 30,000 casualties, but no sheepishness about less glorious colonial engagements, such as against the 'Fuzzy Wuzzies' of Sudan. In 2006 the Black Watch was subsumed into the new Royal Regiment of Scotland. There should be a cafe here by the time you read this.

🛏 Sleeping

Parklands   HOTEL ££

(☑01738-622451; www.theparklandshotel.com; 2 St Leonard's Bank; s/d £93/123; P@🖥) Tucked away near the train station, this relaxing, recently renovated hotel sits amid a lush hillside garden overlooking the parklands of South Inch. While the rooms – which vary in size and shape – conserve the character of this beautiful building, formerly the residence of the town's mayors, they also offer modern conveniences and plenty of style. There's an excellent restaurant and a great terrace and garden area to lap up the Perthshire sun.

Pitcullen Guest House   B&B ££

(☑01738-626506; www.pitcullen.co.uk; 17 Pitcullen Cres; s/d £50/70; P🖥) New owners have given this excellent place a much more contemporary look than other guesthouses on this strip. Great-looking fabrics and modern styling give the light rooms an upbeat feel. Lots of thought has gone into making your stay more comfortable, resulting in features such as fridges with free drinks in the rooms, plenty of plugs to make recharging easy, and maps on the walls to help you plan the next stage of your journey.

Comely Bank Cottage   B&B ££

(☑01738-631118; www.comelybankcottage.co.uk; 19 Pitcullen Cres; d £60-70; P🖥) Pitcullen Cres is bristling with upmarket, flowery B&Bs. This is one of our favourites, a perfectly maintained family home offering large and commodious rooms with spacious bathrooms, and a solicitous owner who doesn't disappoint come breakfast time.

Perth SYHA   HOSTEL £

(☑01738-877800; www.syha.org.uk; Crieff Rd; dm/tw £15/34) A 20-minute stroll from the town centre, this summer hostel is set in a student residence at Perth College. The rooms are all en suite twins, with good share kitchens and common rooms. For some reason, there's a price jump for a week in July. Turn into the Brahan entrance on Crieff Rd and the hostel is by the large carpark. Numerous buses stop outside.

✖ Eating & Drinking

TOP CHOICE 63 Tay Street   SCOTTISH ££

(☑01738-441451; www.63taystreet.com; 63 Tay St; mains £13.50; ⊙Tue-Sat) Classy and warmly welcoming, this understated restaurant is Perth's best, featuring a lightly decorated dining area, excellent service and quality food. In a culinary Auld Alliance, French influence is applied to the best of Scottish produce to create memorable game, seafood, beef and vegetarian plates. There are a couple of set menus available.

TOP CHOICE Breizh   BISTRO ££

(☑01738-444427; www.cafebreizh.co.uk; 28 High St; mains £8-14; ⊙9am-9.30pm Mon-Sat, 11am-9.30pm Sun) This warmly decorated bistro – the place could define the word – is a treat. Dishes are served with real panache, and the salads, featuring all sorts of delicious ingredients, are a feast of colour, texture and subtle flavours. The blackboard meat and fish specials offer great value and a real taste of northwest France: breakfasts, *galettes* (Breton buckwheat crêpes), tasty wines... If you like quality food served in an unpretentious way, you'll love it here.

Deans@Let's Eat   SCOTTISH ££

(☑01738-643377; www.letseatperth.co.uk; 77 Kinnoull St; mains £15-20; ⊙Tue-Sat) A Perth favourite for splashing out on a special meal, this busy corner restaurant has a can-do attitude and an excellent line in fresh Scottish produce. Juicy scallops, fine Orkney beef, local venison or lamb may feature, but you can't really go wrong whatever you select. Browse the menu on the comfy couches with aperitif in hand before being shown to your table. Recession-busting lunch and dinner set menus are a good way to graze here on a budget.

Paco's   INTERNATIONAL ££

(www.pacos.co.uk; 3 Mill St; mains £8-14; ⊙4.30-10pm Sun-Thu, to 11pm Fri, noon-11pm Sat; 🖥) Something of an institution, Paco's keeps Perthers coming back over and over, perhaps because it would take dozens of visits to even try half of the menu. There's something for everyone: steaks, seafood, pizza, pasta and Mexican, all served in generous portions. The fountain-tinkled terrace is the place for a sunny day.

Twa Tams PUB
(www.myspace.com/thetwatams; 79 Scott St) Perth's best pub has a strange outdoor space with windows peering out onto the street, an ornate entrance gate and a large, cosy interior. There are regular events, including live music every Friday and Saturday night; it has a sound reputation for attracting talented young bands.

ℹ Information

AK Bell Library (York Pl; ⊙9.30am-5pm Mon, Wed & Fri, to 8pm Tue & Thu, to 4pm Sat) Free internet; lots of terminals.

Perth information centre (☑01738-450600; www.perthshire.co.uk; West Mill St; ⊙daily Apr-Oct, Mon-Sat Nov-Mar) Efficiently run tourist office.

Perth Royal Infirmary (☑01738-623311; www .nhstayside.scot.nhs.uk; Taymount Tce) West of the town centre.

ℹ Getting There & Away

Bus

From the bus station, **Citylink** (www.citylink .co.uk) operate buses to/from these cities:

Dundee £7, 40 minutes, hourly
Edinburgh £11, 1½ hours, hourly
Glasgow £11.20, 1¾ hours, hourly
Inverness £20, 2¾ hours, at least five daily
Stirling £8.30, 55 mintutes, hourly

Further buses run from the Broxden Park & Ride on Glasgow Rd; this is connected regularly with the bus station by shuttle bus. These include **Megabus** (www.megabus.com) discount services to Aberdeen, Edinburgh, Glasgow, Dundee and Inverness.

Stagecoach (www.stagecoachbus.com) buses serve Perthshire destinations regularly, with reduced Sunday service. A Tayside Megarider ticket gives you seven days travel in Perth & Kinross and Dundee & Angus for £22. It also operates a Stirling service.

Train

Trains run between Perth and various destinations, including the following:

Edinburgh £14.50, 1¼ hours, at least hourly Monday to Saturday, every two hours Sunday

Glasgow £14.50, one hour, at least hourly Monday to Saturday, every two hours Sunday
Pitlochry £12.30, 40 minutes, two hourly, fewer on Sunday
Stirling £11.70, 30 minutes, one or two per hour

Perth to Blair Castle

There are a number of major sights strung along the busy but scenic A9, the main route north to the Cairngorms and Inverness.

DUNKELD & BIRNAM
POP 1005

Ever been to a feel-good town? Well, Dunkeld and Birnam, with their enviable location nestled in the heart of Perthshire's big-tree country, await. The River Tay runs like a storybook river between the two. As well as Dunkeld's lovely cathedral, there's much walking to be done in this area of magnificent forested hills. These same walks inspired Beatrix Potter to create her children's tales.

◉ Sights & Activities

Situated between open grassland between the River Tay on one side and rolling hills on the other, **Dunkeld Cathedral** (HS; www .historic-scotland.gov.uk; High St; admission free; ⊙9.30am-6.30pm Mon-Sat, 2-4.30pm Sun Apr-Sep, 9.30am-4pm Mon-Sat, 2-4pm Sun Oct-Mar) is one of the most beautifully sited cathedrals in Scotland. Don't miss it on a sunny day, as there are few lovelier places to be. Half the cathedral is still in use as a church; the rest is in ruins, and you can explore it all. It partly dates from the 14th century; the cathedral was damaged during the Reformation and burnt in the battle of Dunkeld (Jacobites versus Government) in 1689.

Across the bridge is Birnam, made famous by *Macbeth*. There's not much left of Birnam Wood, but there is a small, leafy **Beatrix Potter Park** (the children's author, who wrote *The Tale of Peter Rabbit*, spent childhood holidays in the area). Next to the park, in the Birnam Arts Centre, is a small **exhibition** (www.birnamarts.com; Station Rd; admission £1.50; ⊙10am-4.30pm Oct-Mar, to 5pm Apr-Sep) on Potter and her characters.

🛏 Sleeping & Eating

Birnam Hotel HOTEL ££
(☑01350-728030; www.birnamhotel.com; Perth Rd; s/d/f £80/100/138; P🐾🐕) This grand-looking place with crow-stepped gables has tastefully fitted rooms – superiors (double £133)

are substantially larger than the standards. Service is very welcoming. There's a fairly formal restaurant, as well as a livelier pub alongside, serving creative bar meals.

TOP CHOICE Taybank

PUB £

(☎01350-727340; www.thetaybank.com; Tay Tce; mains £5-9) Top choice for a sun-kissed pub lunch by the river is the Taybank, a regular meeting place and performance space for musicians of all creeds and a wonderfully open and welcoming bar. There's live music of some kind nightly, and the menu runs to burgers and various incarnations of stovies (stewed potato and onion with meat or other ingredients).

ℹ Information

Dunkeld's **tourist office** (☎01350-727688; www.perthshire.co.uk; The Cross; ⊙daily Apr-Oct, Fri-Sun Nov-Mar) has information on local trails and paths.

ℹ Getting There & Away

Dunkeld is 15 miles north of Perth. Trains and buses between Glasgow/Edinburgh and Inverness stop here. **Stagecoach** (www.stagecoachbus.com) also runs 10 buses daily (only one on Sunday) between Perth and Aberfeldy via Dunkeld. There are also services to Blairgowrie (30 minutes), twice daily Monday to Friday only.

PITLOCHRY
POP 2564

Pitlochry, with its air already smelling of the Highlands, is a popular stop on the way north and convenient base for exploring northern Central Scotland. On a quiet spring evening it's a pretty place with salmon jumping in the Tummel and good things brewing at the Moulin Hotel. In summer the main street can be a conga line of tour groups, but get away from that and it'll still charm you.

◉ Sights

One of Pitlochry's attractions is its beautiful riverside; the River Tummel is dammed here, and you can watch salmon swimming (not jumping) up a fish ladder to the loch above.

FREE Edradour Distillery

DISTILLERY

(☎01796-472095; www.edradour.co.uk; ⊙daily) This is proudly Scotland's smallest distillery and a great one to visit: you can see the whole process, easily explained, in one room. It's 2.5 miles east of Pitlochry along the Moulin road, and it's a pleasant walk.

Explorers Garden

GARDEN

(☎01796-484600; www.explorersgarden.com; Foss Rd; adult/child £4/1; ⊙10am-5pm Apr-Oct) At the Pitlochry Festival Theatre, this excellent garden commemorates 300 years of plant collecting and those who hunted down 'new' species. The whole collection is based on plants brought back to Scotland by Scottish explorers.

🛏 Sleeping

TOP CHOICE Craigatin House

B&B ££

(☎01796-472478; www.craigatinhouse.co.uk; 165 Atholl Rd; s £75, d deluxe/ standard £85/95; ⊙mid-Jan–Oct; P@⑨) Several times more tasteful than the average Pitlochry lodging, this noble house and garden is set back from the main road. Chic contemporary fabrics covering expansive beds offer a standard of comfort above and beyond the reasonable price; the rooms in the converted stable block are particularly inviting. A fabulous breakfast and lounge area gives perspectives over the lush garden. Breakfast choices include whisky-laced porridge, smoked-fish omelettes and apple pancakes. Kids not allowed.

Ashleigh

B&B £

(☎01796-470316; www.realbandbpitlochry.co.uk; 120 Atholl Rd; s/d £30/50; ⑨) Genuine welcomes don't come much better than Nancy's, and her place on the main street makes a top Pitlochry pitstop. Three comfortable rooms share an excellent bathroom, and there's an open kitchen stocked with goodies where you make your own breakfast in the morning. A home away from home and standout budget choice. She also has a good self-catering apartment with great views available by the night.

Pitlochry Backpackers Hotel

HOSTEL £

(☎01796-470044; www.scotlands-top-hostels.com; 134 Atholl Rd; dm/tw/d £18/47/52; P@⑨) Friendly, laid-back and very comfortable, this is a cracking hostel smack-bang in the middle of town, with three- to eight-bed dorms that are in mint condition. There are also good-value en suite twins and doubles, with beds, not bunks. Cheap breakfast and a pool table add to the convivial party atmosphere. No extra charge for linen.

Tir Aluinn

B&B ££

(☎01796-473811; www.tiraluinn.co.uk; 10 Higher Oakfield Rd; s/d £35/70; P⑨) Tucked away above the main street, this is a little gem of a place, with bright rooms with easy-on-the-eye furniture, and an excellent personal welcome. Breakfasts are excellent.

Pitlochry SYHA
HOSTEL £

(☏01796-472308; www.syha.org.uk; Knockard Rd; dm £18.50; ⊗Mar-Oct; P@☞) Great location overlooking the town centre. Popular with families and walkers.

✕ Eating & Drinking

TOP CHOICE Moulin Hotel
PUB ££

(☏01796-472196; www.moulinhotel.co.uk; bar mains £9-12) A mile away but a world apart, this atmospheric hotel was trading centuries before the tartan tack came to Pitlochry. With its romantic low ceilings, ageing wood and booth seating, the inn is a wonderfully atmospheric spot for a house-brewed ale or a portion of Highland comfort food: try the filling haggis or venison stew. A more formal restaurant (mains £12 to £16) serves equally delicious traditional fare, with excellent game and meat options. The hotel also has a variety of rooms (single/double £62/77) as well as a self-catering annexe. The best way to get here from Pitlochry is by walking: it's a pretty uphill stroll through green fields, and an easy roll down the slope afterwards.

Port-na-Craig Inn
BISTRO ££

(☏01796-472777; www.portnacraig.com; Port Na Craig; mains £12-17; ⊗11am-8.30pm) Right on the river, this top little spot sits in what was once a separate hamlet. Delicious main meals are prepared with confidence and panache; there are also simpler sandwiches, kids' meals and light lunches. Or you could just sit out by the river with a pint and watch the anglers.

☆ Entertainment

Pitlochry Festival Theatre
THEATRE

(☏01796-484626; www.pitlochry.org.uk; Foss Rd; tickets £26-35) This well-known and loved theatre has a summer season of several different plays performed daily except Sunday, from May to mid-October.

ⓘ Information

Computer Services Centre (www.computer servicescentre.co.uk; 23 Atholl Rd; ⊗9.30am-5.30pm Mon-Fri, to 12.30pm Sat; ☞) Internet access opposite the tourist office.

Pitlochry information centre (☏01796-472215; www.perthshire.co.uk; 22 Atholl Rd; ⊗daily Mar-Oct, Mon-Sat Nov-Feb) Good information on local walks.

ⓘ Getting There & Away

Citylink (www.citylink.co.uk) buses run roughly hourly to Inverness (£15.50, two hours), Perth (£10, 40 minutes), Edinburgh (£15.50, two to 2½ hours) and Glasgow (£15.70, 2¼ hours). **Megabus** (☏0871 266 3333; www.megabus.com) discount services also run these routes.

Stagecoach (www.stagecoachbus.com) runs to Aberfeldy (30 minutes, hourly Monday to Saturday, three Sunday), Dunkeld (25 minutes, up to 10 daily Monday to Saturday) and Perth (one hour, up to 10 daily Monday to Saturday).

Pitlochry is on the main railway from Perth (£12.30, 30 minutes, nine daily Monday to Saturday, five on Sunday) to Inverness.

BLAIR CASTLE

One of the most popular tourist attractions in Scotland, magnificent Blair Castle (☏01796-481207; www.blair-castle.co.uk; adult/child/family £9.50/5.70/25.75; ⊗9.30am-5.30pm Apr-Oct, 10am-4pm Sat & Sun Nov-Mar) and the 108 sq miles it sits on, is the seat of the Duke of Atholl, head of the Murray clan. It's an impressive white building set beneath forested slopes above the River Garry.

The original tower was built in 1269, but the castle has undergone significant remodelling since. Thirty rooms are open to the public and they present a wonderful picture of upper-class Highland life from the 16th century on. The dining room is sumptuous – check out the 9-pint wine glasses – and the ballroom is a vaulted chamber that's a virtual stag cemetery.

The current duke visits the castle every May to review the Atholl Highlanders, Britain's only private army.

Blair Atholl is 6 miles northwest of Pitlochry, and the castle a further mile beyond it. Local buses run between Pitlochry and Blair Atholl (25 minutes, three to seven daily). Four buses daily (Monday to Saturday) go directly to the castle. There's a train station in the village, but not all trains stop here.

For a continuation of this route north up the A9, see the Cairngorms (p895).

West Perthshire

The jewel in central Scotland's crown, West Perthshire achieves a Scottish ideal with rugged, noble hills reflected in some of the nation's most beautiful lochs. Bring your hiking boots and camera and prepare for a stay of a few days.

LOCH TAY

Serpentine and picturesque, long Loch Tay reflects the powerful forests and mountains around it. The bulk of mighty Ben Lawers (1214m) looms above and is part of a National Nature Reserve that includes the nearby Tarmachan Range.

The main access point for the ascent of Ben Lawers is the now-defunct tourist office, a mile off the A827 five miles east of Killin. An easier nature trail also leaves from here.

There's good accommodation in Kenmore and Killin, as well as Culdees Bunkhouse (☎01887-830519; www.culdeesbunkhouse.co.uk; dm/tw/f £18/46/69; P@ 🛜🐾), a wonderfully offbeat hostel with utterly majestic vistas: the whole of the loch stretches out before and below you. It's half a mile above the village of Fearnan, four miles west from Kenmore.

KENMORE

Pretty Kenmore lies at Loch Tay's eastern end, 6 miles west of Aberfeldy, and is dominated by a church, a clock tower and the striking archway of privately owned Taymouth Castle. Just outside town on the loch is the fascinating Scottish Crannog Centre (☎01887-830583; www.crannog.co.uk; tours adult/child £7/5; ☻10am-5.30pm Apr-Oct, to 4pm Sat & Sun Nov). A crannog, perched on stilts in the water, was a favoured form of defence-minded dwelling in Scotland from the 3rd millennium BC onwards. This one has been superbly reconstructed, and the guided tour includes an impressive demonstration of fire making. It's an excellent attraction.

The heart of the village, Kenmore Hotel (☎01887-830205; www.kenmorehotel.com; The Square; s/d £84/135; P@ 🛜🐾) has a bar with a roaring fire and some verses by Robert Burns scribbled on the chimneypiece in 1787, when the inn was already a couple of centuries old. There's also a riverbank beer garden and a wide variety of rooms, some across the road. They sport modern conveniences; the nicest have bay windows and river views. Prices plummet in the low season and midweek.

Regular buses link Aberfeldy with Kenmore, some continuing to Killin via the turnoff to the trailhead for Ben Lawers.

FORTINGALL

Fortingall is one of the prettiest villages in Scotland, with 19th-century thatched cottages in a very tranquil setting. The church has impressive wooden beams and a 7th-century monk's bell. In the churchyard, there's a 2000-year-old yew, probably the oldest tree in Europe. This tree was around when the Romans camped in the meadows by the River Lyon: popular, if unlikely, tradition says that Pontius Pilate was born here. Today the tree is a shell of its former self – at its zenith it had a girth of over 17m! But souvenir hunters have reduced it to two much smaller trunks.

Fortingall Hotel (☎01887-830367; www.fortingall.com; s/d £90/120; P🛜🐾) is a peaceful, old-fashioned country hotel with polite service and furnished with quiet good taste.

GLEN LYON

This remote and stunningly beautiful glen runs for some 34 unforgettable miles of rickety stone bridges, Caledonian pine forest and sheer heather-splashed peaks poking through swirling clouds. It becomes wilder and more uninhabited as it snakes its way west, and is proof that hidden treasures still exist in Scotland. The ancients believed it to be a gateway to Faerieland, and even the most sceptical of people will be entranced by the valley's magic.

From Fortingall, a narrow road winds up the glen – another road from Loch Tay crosses the hills and reaches the glen halfway in, at Bridge of Balgie. The glen continues up to a dam (past a memorial to explorer Robert Campbell; bearing left here you can actually continue over a wild and remote road (unmarked on maps) to isolated Glen Lochay and down to Killin. Cycling through Glen Lyon is a wonderful way to experience this special place.

There's little in the way of attractions in the valley – the majestic and lonely scenery is the reason to be here – but at Glenlyon Gallery (www.glenlyongallery.co.uk; admission free; ☻10am-5pm Thu-Tue), in Bridge of Balgie, a selection of fine handmade pieces are for sale. Adjacent is the Bridge of Balgie post office (light meals £3-4; ☻8am-6pm Apr-Oct, closed Tue-Thu Nov-Mar, food served until 4pm), the best – the only – spot for supplies (limited), or sandwiches and soups (very tasty).

There is no public transport in the glen.

LOCHS TUMMEL & RANNOCH

The route along Lochs Tummel and Rannoch is worth doing any way you can – by foot, bicycle or car – just don't miss it! Hills of ancient birch and forests of spruce, pine and larch make up the Tay Forest Park – the king of Scotland's forests. It's the product of a brilliant bit of forward thinking: the replanting of Tay Forest 300 years ago. These

BAG A MUNRO: BEN LAWERS

The ascent of Ben Lawers can take up to five hours return: pack wet-weather gear, water and food. From the car park (£2), where a stone enclosure should have route maps, cross the road and follow the trail just uphill from you. After the boardwalk protecting a bog, cross a stile then fork left and ascend along the Edramucky burn (to the right). At the next rise, fork right and cross the burn. A few minutes later ignore the nature trail's right turn and continue ascending parallel to the burn's left bank for just over half a mile. Leave the protected zone by another stile and steeply ascend Beinn Ghlas' shoulder. Reaching a couple of large rocks, ignore a northbound footpath and continue zigzagging uphill. The rest of the ascent is a straightforward succession of three false summits. The last and steepest section alternates between erosion-sculpted rock and a meticulously crafted cobbled trail. Long views of majestic hillscapes, and even the North Sea and Atlantic, are your reward on a clear day.

wooded hills roll into the glittering waters of the lochs; a visit in autumn is recommended, when the birch trees are at their finest.

Far beyond, the road ends at romantic, isolated Rannoch train station, which is on the Glasgow–Fort William line. Beyond is desolate, intriguing Rannoch Moor, a windy, vaguely threatening peat bog stretching as far as the A82 and Glen Coe. There's a tearoom on the platform, and a welcoming small hotel alongside the station.

DUNDEE & ANGUS

Angus is a region of fertile farmland stretching north from Dundee – Scotland's fourth-largest city – to the Highland border. It's an attractive area of broad straths (valleys) and low, green hills contrasting with the rich, red-brown soil of freshly ploughed fields. Romantic glens finger their way into the foothills of the Grampian Mountains, while the scenic coastline ranges from the red-sandstone cliffs of Arbroath to the long, sandy beaches around Montrose. This was the Pictish heartland of the 7th and 8th centuries, and many interesting Pictish symbol stones survive here.

Apart from the crowds visiting Discovery Point in newly confident Dundee and the coach parties shuffling through Glamis Castle, Angus is a bit of a tourism backwater and a good place to escape the hordes.

Dundee

POP 144,000

London's Trafalgar Sq has Nelson on his column, Edinburgh's Princes St has its monument to Sir Walter Scott and Belfast has a statue of Queen Victoria outside City Hall. Dundee's City Sq, on the other hand, is graced – rather endearingly – by the bronze figure of Desperate Dan. Familiar to generations of British school children, Dan is one of the best-loved cartoon characters from the children's comic *The Dandy,* published by Dundee firm DC Thomson from 1937 to 2012.

Dundee is often called the city of the 'Three Js' – jute, jam and journalism. According to legend, it was a Dundee woman named Janet Keillor who invented marmalade in the late 18th century; her son founded the city's famous Keillor jam factory. Jute is no longer produced, and when the Keillor factory was taken over in 1988 production was transferred to England. Journalism still thrives, however, led by the family firm of DC Thomson. Best known for children's comics, such as *The Beano,* Thomson is now the city's largest employer.

Dundee enjoys perhaps the finest location of any Scottish city, spreading along the northern shore of the Firth of Tay, and can boast tourist attractions of national importance in Discovery Point and the Verdant Works museum. Add in the attractive seaside suburb of Broughty Ferry, some lively nightlife and the Dundonians themselves – among the friendliest, most welcoming and most entertaining people you'll meet – and Dundee is definitely worth a stopover.

◉ Sights

Discovery Point   MUSEUM
(www.rrsdiscovery.com; Discovery Quay; adult/child £8.25/5; ⊙10am-6pm Mon-Sat, 11am-6pm Sun Apr-Oct, to 5pm Nov-Mar) The three masts of Captain Robert Falcon Scott's famous polar expedition vessel the RRS Discovery dominate the riverside to the south of the

city centre. The ship was built in Dundee in 1900, with a wooden hull at least half a metre thick to survive the pack ice, and sailed for the Antarctic in 1901 where it spent two winters trapped in the ice. From 1931 on it was laid up in London where its condition steadily deteriorated, until it was rescued by the efforts of Peter Scott (son of Robert) and the Maritime Trust, and restored to its 1925 condition. In 1986 the ship was given a berth in its home port of Dundee, where it became a symbol of the city's regeneration.

Exhibitions and audiovisual displays in the main building provide a fascinating history of both the ship and Antarctic exploration, but *Discovery* itself – afloat in a protected dock – is the star attraction. You can visit the bridge, the galley and the mahogany-panelled officers' wardroom, and poke your nose into the cabins used by Scott and his crew.

A joint ticket that gives entry to both Discovery Point and the Verdant Works costs £13.50/8.50 per adult/child.

Verdant Works   MUSEUM
(www.verdantworks.com; West Henderson's Wynd; adult/child £8.25/5; ⊙10am-6pm Mon-Sat, 11am-6pm Sun Apr-Oct, 10:30am-4.30pm Wed-Sun Nov-Mar) One of the finest industrial museums in Europe, the Verdant Works explores the history of Dundee's jute industry. Housed in a restored jute mill, complete with original machinery still in working condition, the museum's interactive exhibits and computer displays follow the raw material from its origins in India through to the manufacture of a wide range of finished products, from sacking to rope to wagon covers for the pioneers of the American West. The mill is 250m west of the city centre.

A joint ticket that gives entry to both Discovery Point and the Verdant Works costs £13.50/8.50 per adult/child.

FREE **McManus Galleries**   MUSEUM
(www.mcmanus.co.uk; Albert Sq; ⊙10am-5pm Mon-Sat, 12.30-4.30pm Sun) Housed in a solid Victorian Gothic building designed by Gilbert Scott in 1867, the McManus Galleries is a city museum on a human scale – you can see everything there is to see, without feeling rushed or overwhelmed. The exhibits cover the history of the city from the Iron Age to the present day, including relics of the Tay Bridge Disaster and the Dundee

whaling industry. Computer geeks will enjoy the Sinclair ZX81 and Spectrum (pioneering personal computers with a whole 16K of memory!), which were made in Dundee in the early 1980s.

FREE Dundee
Contemporary Arts   ARTS CENTRE
(www.dca.org.uk; Nethergate; ⊙11am-6pm Tue, Wed, Fri & Sat, 11am-8pm Thu, noon-6pm Sun) The focus for the city's emerging Cultural Quarter is Dundee Contemporary Arts, a centre for modern art, design and cinema. The galleries here exhibit work by contemporary UK and international artists, and there are printmakers' studios where you can watch artists at work, or even take part in craft demonstrations and workshops. There's also the Jute Cafe-Bar (www.jute cafebar.co.uk; 152 Nethergate; lunch mains £8-12, dinner £10-19; ⊙10.30am-midnight Mon-Sat, noon-midnight Sun).

🛏 Sleeping

Balgowan House   B&B ££
(☎01382-200262; www.balgowanhouse.co.uk; 510 Perth Rd; s/d from £55/80; P🛜) Built in 1900 and perched in a prime location with stunning views over the Firth of Tay, Balgowan is a wealthy merchant's mansion converted into a luxurious guesthouse with three sumptuous en suite bedrooms. It's 2 miles west of the city centre, overlooking the university botanic gardens.

Apex City Quay Hotel   HOTEL ££
(☎0845 365 0000; www.apexhotels.co.uk; 1 West Victoria Dock Rd; r from £72; P🛜☄) Though it looks plain and boxy from the outside, the Apex overlooks the city's redeveloping waterfront and sports the sort of stylish, spacious, sofa-equipped rooms that make you want to lounge around all evening munching chocolate in front of the TV. If you can drag yourself away from your room, there are spa treatments, saunas and Japanese hot tubs to enjoy. The hotel is just east of the city centre, close to the Frigate Unicorn.

Errolbank Guest House   B&B ££
(☎01382-462118; www.errolbank-guesthouse.com; 9 Dalgleish Rd; s/d £49/69; P) A mile east of the city centre, just north of the road to Broughty Ferry, Errolbank is a lovely Victorian family home with small but beautifully decorated en suite rooms set on a quiet street.

Dundee Backpackers · HOSTEL £

(☏01382-224646; www.hoppo.com; 71 High St; dm £18.50, s/tw from £25/40; @) Set in a beautifully converted historic building, with a clean, modern kitchen, a pool room and an ideal location right in the city centre. Can get a bit noisy at night, but that's because it's close to pubs and nightlife.

Aabalree · B&B £

(☏01382-223867; www.aabalree.com; 20 Union St; s/d £24/40) This is a pretty basic B&B – there are no en suites – but the owners are welcoming (don't be put off by the dark entrance) and it couldn't be more central, close to both train and bus stations. This makes it popular, so book ahead.

✗ Eating

TOP CHOICE Metro · BRASSERIE ££

(☏0845 365 0002; www.apexhotels.co.uk/eat; Apex City Quay Hotel, 1 West Victoria Dock Rd; mains £11-22; ☺lunch & dinner) Sleek, slate-blue banquettes, white linen napkins, black-clad staff and a view of Victoria Dock lend an air of sophistication to this stylish hotel brasserie, with a menu that ranges from steaks and burgers to Indian butter chicken curry. There's a three-course dinner menu for £22.50 (before 7pm).

Blue Marlin · SEAFOOD £££

(☏01382-221397; www.thebluemarlin.co.uk; City Quay; mains £20-25; ☺lunch & dinner Mon-Sat) The ongoing redevelopment of Dundee's former docks means that the setting for the city's best fish restaurant doesn't look too promising. But once inside, there is sleek and understated nautical-themed decor, and the chance to feast on the best of Scottish seafood.

Playwright · BISTRO £££

(☏01382-223113; www.theplaywright.co.uk; 11 Tay Sq; mains £23-26; ☺10am-midnight) Next door to the Dundee Rep Theatre, and decorated with photos of Scottish actors, this innovative cafe-bar and bistro serves a set lunch (two course £13) and pre-theatre menu (two/three courses £17/20, 5pm to 6.30pm) and a gourmet à la carte menu that concentrates on fine Scottish produce, with dishes such as saddle of lamb with celeriac dauphinoise.

Encore Bar & Brasserie · CAFE, BAR ££

(☏01382-206699; www.encoredundee.co.uk; Tay Sq; mains £10-16; ☺bar 11am-late, brasserie noon-3pm & 5-9pm Mon-Sat) The city's arty types hang out in this continental-style cafe-bar and restaurant in the foyer at the Dundee Rep Theatre.

The menu ranges from crayfish salad to wild mushroom-and-blue-cheese puff pastry.

ℹ Information

Dundee tourist office (☏01382-527527; www.angusanddundee.co.uk; Discovery Point; ☺10am-5pm Mon-Sat, noon-4pm Sun Jun-Sep, 10am-4pm Mon-Sat Oct-May)

Ninewells Hospital (☏01382-660111; ☺casualty 24hr) At Menzieshill, west of the city centre.

ℹ Getting There & Around

AIR Two and a half miles west of the city centre, **Dundee Airport** (www.hial.co.uk) has daily scheduled services to London City airport, Birmingham and Belfast. A taxi from the city centre to the airport takes five to 10 minutes and costs £3.80.

BUS The bus station is northeast of the city centre. Some Aberdeen buses travel via Arbroath, others via Forfar.

Aberdeen £16, 1½ hours, hourly
Edinburgh £15, two hours, hourly; some change at Perth
Glasgow £15, two hours, hourly
London National Express; £40, 11 hours
Oban £23, 3½ hours, two daily
Perth £7, 35 minutes, hourly

TRAIN Trains from Dundee to Aberdeen travel via Arbroath and Stonehaven.

Aberdeen £27, 1¼ hours, twice hourly
Edinburgh £23, 1¼ hours, at least hourly
Glasgow £25, 1½ hours, hourly

Arbroath

POP 22,800

Arbroath is an old-fashioned seaside resort and fishing harbour, home of the famous Arbroath smokie (a form of smoked haddock). The humble smokie achieved EU 'Protected Geographical Indication' status in 2004 – the term 'Arbroath smokie' can be only used legally to describe haddock smoked in the traditional manner within an 8km radius of Arbroath. No visit is complete without buying a pair of smokies from one of the many fish shops and eating them with your fingers while sitting beside the harbour. Yum.

◉ Sights

Arbroath Abbey · ABBEY

(HS; Abbey St; adult/child £5.50/3.30; ☺9.30am-5.30pm Apr-Sep, to 4.30pm Oct-Mar) The magnificent, red-sandstone ruins of Arbroath

WORTH A TRIP

GLAMIS CASTLE

Looking every inch the archetypal Scottish Baronial castle, with its roofline sprouting a forest of pointed turrets and battlements, Glamis Castle (www.glamis-castle.co.uk; adult/child £9.75/7.25; ⊙10am-6pm Mar–Oct, 10.30am-4.30pm Nov & Dec, closed Jan & Feb) claims to be the legendary setting for Shakespeare's *Macbeth* (his character is the Thane of Glamis at the start of the play). A royal residence since 1372, it is the family home of the earls of Strathmore and Kinghorne: the Queen Mother (born Elizabeth Bowes-Lyon; 1900–2002) spent her childhood at Glamis (pronounced 'glams') and Princess Margaret (the Queen's sister; 1930–2002) was born here. The one-hour guided tours depart every 15 minutes (last tour at 4.30pm, or 3.30pm in winter).

Glamis Castle is 12 miles north of Dundee. There are two to four buses a day from Dundee (35 minutes) to Glamis; some continue to Kirriemuir.

Abbey, founded in 1178 by King William the Lion, dominate the town centre. It is thought that Bernard of Linton, the abbot here in the early 14th century, wrote the famous Declaration of Arbroath in 1320, asserting Scotland's right to independence from England. You can climb to the top of one of the towers for a grand view over the town.

FREE **Signal House Museum** MUSEUM (Ladyloan; ⊙10am-5pm Mon-Sat year-round, plus 2-5pm Sun Jul & Aug) This museum is housed in the elegant Signal Tower that was once used to communicate with the construction team working on the Bell Rock Lighthouse 12 miles offshore. There are displays dedicated to Arbroath's maritime heritage and the Bell Rock lighthouse, which was built between 1807 and 1811 by the famous engineer Robert Stevenson (grandfather of writer Robert Louis Stevenson).

🛏 Sleeping & Eating

Harbour Nights Guest House B&B ££ (☎01241-434343; www.harbournights-scotland .com; 4 The Shore; s/d from £45/60) With a superb location overlooking the harbour, five stylishly decorated bedrooms and a gourmet breakfast menu, Harbour Nights Guest House is our favourite place to stay in Arbroath. Rooms 2 and 3, with harbour views, are a bit more expensive (doubles £70 to £80), but well worth asking for when booking.

But'n'Ben Restaurant SCOTTISH ££ (☎01241-877223; www.butnbenauchmithie.co.uk; 1 Auchmithie; mains £8-17; ⊙lunch & dinner Wed-Mon; 🖈) Above the harbour in Auchmithie, this cosy cottage restaurant with open fire-

place, rustic furniture and sea-themed art serves the best of local seafood – the Arbroath smokie pancakes are recommended – plus great home-made cakes and desserts. Best to book.

❶ Getting There & Away

Bus 140 runs from Arbroath to Auchmithie (15 minutes, six daily Monday to Friday, three daily Saturday and Sunday).

Trains from Dundee to Arbroath (£5, 20 minutes, twice hourly) continue to Aberdeen (£21, 55 minutes) via Montrose and Stonehaven.

ABERDEENSHIRE & MORAY

Since medieval times Aberdeenshire and its northwestern neighbour Moray have been the richest and most fertile regions of the Highlands. Aberdeenshire is famed for its Aberdeen Angus beef cattle, its many fine castles and the prosperous 'granite city' of Aberdeen. Moray's main attractions are the Speyside whisky distilleries that line the valley of the River Spey and its tributaries.

Aberdeen

POP 197,300

Aberdeen is the powerhouse of the northeast, fuelled by the North Sea petroleum industry. Oil money has made the city as expensive as London and Edinburgh, and there are hotels, restaurants and clubs with prices to match the depth of oil-wealthy pockets. Fortunately, most of the cultural attractions, such as the excellent Maritime Museum and the Aberdeen Art Gallery, are free.

The name Aberdeen is a combination of two Pictish-Gaelic words, *aber* and *devana*, meaning 'the meeting of two waters'. Known throughout Scotland as the granite city, much of the town was built using silvery grey granite hewn from the now abandoned Rubislaw Quarry, at one time the biggest artificial hole in the ground in Europe. On a sunny day the granite lends an attractive glitter to the city, but when low, grey rain clouds scud in off the North Sea it can be hard to tell where the buildings stop and the sky begins.

Royal Deeside is easily accessible to the west, Dunnottar Castle to the south, sandy beaches to the north and whisky country to the northwest.

◉ Sights

CITY CENTRE

FREE **Provost Skene's House** HISTORIC BUILDING

(www.aagm.co.uk; ⊙10am-5pm Mon-Sat) Surrounded by concrete and glass office blocks in what was once the worst slum in Aberdeen is this late-medieval turreted town house occupied in the 17th century by the provost (the Scottish equivalent of a mayor) Sir George Skene. It was also occupied for six weeks by the Duke of Cumberland on his way to Culloden in 1746. The tempera ceiling of the Painted Gallery with its religious symbolism, dating from 1622, is unusual for having survived the depredations of the Reformation. It's a period gem featuring earnest-looking angels, soldiers and St Peter with crowing cockerels.

FREE **Marischal College & Museum** MUSEUM

(www.abdn.ac.uk/marischal_museum; Marischal College, Broad St; ⊙10am-5pm Mon-Fri, 2-5pm Sun) Marischal College, founded in 1593 by the 5th Earl Marischal, merged with King's College (founded 1495) in 1860 to create the modern University of Aberdeen. The huge and impressive facade in Perpendicular Gothic style – unusual in having such elaborate masonry hewn from notoriously hard-to-work granite – dates from 1906 and is the world's second-largest granite structure (after L'Escorial near Madrid). A recent renovation project saw the facade returned to it original silvery grey glory, and the building now houses Aberdeen City Council's new headquarters.

Founded in 1786, the **Marischal Museum** houses a fascinating collection of material donated by graduates and friends of the university over the centuries. In one room, the history of northeastern Scotland is depicted through its myths, customs, famous people, architecture and trade. The other gallery gives an anthropological overview of the world, incorporating objects from vastly different cultures, arranged thematically (Polynesian wooden masks alongside gas masks and so on). There are the usual Victorian curios, an Inuit kayak found in the local river estuary in the 18th century and Inuit objects collected by whalers. At the time of research the museum was still closed to the public following renovation work; check the website for notice of its reopening.

FREE **Aberdeen Art Gallery** MUSEUM

(☎01224-523700; www.aagm.co.uk; Schoolhill; ⊙10am-5pm Tue-Sat, 2-5pm Sun) Behind the grand facade of Aberdeen Art Gallery is a cool, marble-lined space exhibiting the work of contemporary Scottish and English painters, such as Gwen Hardie, Stephen Conroy, Trevor Sutton and Tim Ollivier. There are also several landscapes by Joan Eardley, who lived in a cottage on the cliffs near Stonehaven in the 1950s and '60s and painted oils of the tempestuous North Sea and poignant portraits of slum children. Among the Pre-Raphaelite works upstairs, look out for the paintings of Aberdeen artist William Dyce (1806–64), ranging from religious works to rural scenes.

ABERDEEN HARBOUR

Aberdeen has a busy, working harbour crowded with survey vessels and supply ships servicing the offshore oil installations, and car ferries bound for Orkney and Shetland.

FREE **Aberdeen Maritime Museum** MUSEUM

(☎01224-337700; www.aagm.co.uk; Shiprow; ⊙10am-5pm Tue-Sat, noon-3pm Sun) Overlooking the nautical bustle of Aberdeen harbour is the Maritime Museum. Centred on a three-storey replica of a North Sea oil production platform, its exhibits explain all you ever wanted to know about the petroleum industry. Other galleries, some situated in **Provost Ross's House**, the oldest building in the city and part of the museum, cover the shipbuilding, whaling and fishing industries. Sleek and speedy Aberdeen clippers were a 19th-century shipyard speciality, used by British merchants for the importation of tea, wool and exotic goods (opium, for instance) to Britain, and, on the return journey, the transportation of emigrants to Australia.

Aberdeen

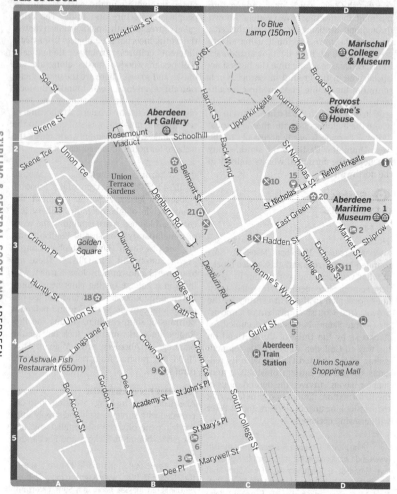

ABERDEEN BEACH

Just 800m east of Castlegate is a spectacular 2-mile sweep of clean, golden sand stretching between the mouths of the Rivers Dee and Don. At one time Aberdeen Beach was a good, old-fashioned British seaside resort, but the availability of cheap package holidays has lured Scottish holidaymakers away from its somewhat chilly delights. On a warm summer's day, though, it's still an excellent beach. When the waves are right, a small group of dedicated surfers ride the breaks at the southern end.

OLD ABERDEEN

Just over a mile north of the city centre is the district called Old Aberdeen. The name is misleading – although Old Aberdeen is certainly old, the area around Castlegate is older still. This part of the city was originally called Aulton, from the Gaelic for 'village by the pool', and this was anglicised in the 17th century to Old Town.

FREE **St Machar's Cathedral** CATHEDRAL (www.stmachar.com; The Chanonry; ⊙9am-5pm Mon-Sat Apr-Oct, 10am-4pm Nov-Mar) The 15th-century St Machar's Cathedral, with

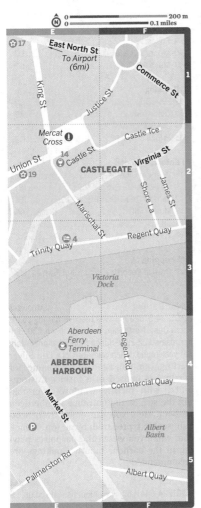

which are found 400m southwest of the train station) and along Great Western Rd (the A93, a 25-minute walk southwest of the city centre. Prices tend to be lower on weekends.

TOP CHOICE Globe Inn
B&B ££

(01224-624258; www.the-globe-inn.co.uk; 13-15 North Silver St; s/d £70/75) This popular pub has seven appealing and comfortable guest bedrooms upstairs, done out in dark wood with burgundy bedspreads. There's live music in the pub on weekends so it's not a place for early-to-bed types, but the price-versus-location factor can't be beaten. No dining room, so breakfast is continental, served on a tray in your room.

City Wharf Apartments
APARTMENTS ££

(0845 094 2424; www.citywharfapartments.co.uk; 19-20 Regent Quay; d from £105;) You can watch the bustle of Aberdeen's commercial harbour as you eat breakfast in one of these luxury serviced apartments, complete with stylish, fully equipped kitchen, champagne-stocked minibar and daily cleaning service. Available by the night or the week, with discounts for longer stays.

Butler's Guest House
B&B ££

(01224-212411; www.butlersguesthouse.com; 122 Crown St; s/d from £58/65; @) Butler's is a cosy place with a big breakfast menu that includes fresh fruit salad, kippers and kedgeree as alternatives to the traditional fry-up (rates include a continental breakfast – cooked breakfast is £5 extra per person). There are cheaper rooms with shared bathrooms.

Aberdeen Douglas Hotel
HOTEL £££

(01224-582255; www.aberdeendouglas.com; 43-45 Market St; s/d Mon-Fri from £145/155, Sat & Sun from £65/75;) You can't miss the grand Victorian facade of this historic landmark, which first opened its doors as a hotel in 1853. Now renovated, it offers classy modern rooms with polished woodwork and crisp white bed linen, and is barely a minute's walk from the train station.

Royal Crown Guest House
B&B ££

(01224-586461; www.royalcrown.co.uk; 111 Crown St; s £35-70, d £60-80; P) The Royal Crown has eight small but nicely furnished bedrooms, and has a top location only five minutes' walk from the train station (though up a steep flight of stairs).

its massive twin towers, is a rare example of a fortified cathedral. According to legend, St Machar was ordered to establish a church where the river takes the shape of a bishop's crook, which it does just here. The cathedral is best known for its impressive heraldic ceiling, dating from 1520, which has 48 shields of kings, nobles, archbishops and bishops. Sunday services are held at 11am and 6pm.

Sleeping

There are clusters of B&Bs along Bon Accord St and Springbank Tce (both of

Aberdeen

◎ Top Sights
Aberdeen Maritime Museum	D3
Aberdeen Art Gallery	B2
Marischal College & Museum	D1
Provost Skene's House	D2

◎ Sights
1	Provost Ross's House	D3

🛏 Sleeping
2	Aberdeen Douglas Hotel	D3
3	Butler's Guest House	B5
4	City Wharf Apartments	E3
	Globe Inn	(see 13)
5	Jurys Inn	C4
6	Royal Crown Guest House	B5

🍴 Eating
7	Beautiful Mountain	C3
8	Café 52	C3
9	Foyer	B4
10	Moonfish Café	C2
11	Musa Art Cafe	D3

🍷 Drinking
12	BrewDog	D1
13	Globe Inn	A3
14	Old Blackfriars	E2
15	Prince of Wales	C2

🎭 Entertainment
16	Belmont Cinema	B2
	Box Office	(see 18)
17	Lemon Tree Theatre	E1
18	Music Hall	A4
19	Snafu	E2
20	Tunnels	D2

🛍 Shopping
21	One Up Records	B3

Aberdeen Youth Hostel HOSTEL £
(SYHA; 🖉01224-646988; 8 Queen's Rd; dm £21; @🛜) This hostel, set in a granite Victorian villa, is a mile west of the train station. Walk west along Union St and take the right fork along Albyn Pl until you reach a roundabout; Queen's Rd continues on the western side of the roundabout.

Jurys Inn HOTEL ££
(🖉01224-381200; www.jurysinns.com; Union Sq, Guild St; r £75-155; 🛜) Stylish and comfortable hotel right next to the train station.

Adelphi Guest House B&B ££
(🖉01224-583078; www.adelphiguesthouse.com; 8 Whinhill Rd; s/d from £45/60; 🛜) Located 400m south from the western end of Union St.

🍴 Eating

TOP CHOICE Café 52 BISTRO ££
(🖉01224-590094; www.cafe52.net; 52 The Green; mains £12; ◐noon-midnight Mon-Sat, to 6pm Sun; 🛜) This little haven of laid-back industrial chic – a high, narrow space lined with bare stonework, rough plaster and exposed ventilation ducts – serves some of the finest and most inventive cuisine in the northeast. Try starters such as baked black pudding with wine-poached pear, or mains like beef casserole with red wine and Moroccan spices.

Silver Darling SEAFOOD £££
(🖉01224-576229; www.thesilverdarling.co.uk; Pocra Quay, North Pier; 2-course lunch £20, dinner mains £22-29; ◐lunch Mon-Fri, dinner Mon-Sat year-round, lunch Sun Apr-Oct) The Silver Darling (an old Scottish nickname for herring) is housed in a former Customs office, with picture windows overlooking the sea, at the entrance to Aberdeen harbour. Here you can enjoy fresh Scottish seafood prepared by a top French chef while you watch the porpoises playing in the harbour mouth. Bookings are recommended.

Moonfish Café FRENCH £££
(🖉01224-644166; www.moonfishcafe.co.uk; 9 Correction Wynd; 2-/3-course dinner £24/29; ◐lunch & dinner Tue-Sat) The menu of this funky little eatery tucked away on a back street concentrates on good quality Scottish produce cooked with an international flair that draws its influences from cuisines all around the world, from simple smoked haddock with pea risotto, to nut-crusted skate wing with Peruvian potatoes (with chilli, onion and hard-boiled egg).

Foyer FUSION ££
(🖉01224-582277; www.foyerrestaurant.com; 82a Crown St; mains £12-18; ◐11am-10pm Tue-Sat; 🖉) A light, airy space filled with blonde wood and bold colours, Foyer is an art gallery as

well as a restaurant and is run by a charity that fights youth homelessness and unemployment. The seasonal menu is a fusion of Scottish, Mediterranean and Asian influences, with lots of good vegetarian (and gluten- or dairy-free) options.

Musa Art Cafe
MODERN SCOTTISH ££

(☑01224-571771; www.musaaberdeen.com; 33 Exchange St; lunch mains £8-10, dinner £13-23; ⊘noon-11pm Tue-Sat; ☑) The bright paintings on the walls match the vibrant furnishings and smart gastronomic creations at this great cafe-restaurant, set in a former church. As well as a menu that focuses on quality local produce cooked in a quirky way – think haggis-and-coriander spring rolls with chilli jam – there are Brewdog beers from Fraserburgh, and interesting music, sometimes live.

Beautiful Mountain
CAFE £

(www.thebeautifulmountain.com; 11-13 Belmont St; mains £4-10; ⊘7.30am-3.30pm Mon-Fri, 8am-4.30pm Sat, 10.30am-3.30pm Sun) This cosy cafe is squeezed into a couple of tiny rooms (seating upstairs), but serves all-day breakfasts and tasty sandwiches (smoked salmon, Thai chicken, pastrami) on sourdough, bagels, ciabatta and lots of other breads, along with exquisite espresso and consummate cappuccino. Also opens for dinner Thursday to Saturday, when the menu changes to tapas.

Sand Dollar Café
CAFE, BISTRO £

(☑01224-572288; www.sanddollarcafe.com; 2 Beach Esplanade; mains £4-10; ⊘9am-9pm daily, closed 4-6pm Thu-Sat) A cut above your usual seaside cafe – on sunny days you can sit at the wooden tables outside and share a bottle of chilled white wine, and there's a tempting menu that includes pancakes with maple syrup, home-made burgers, and chocolate brownie with Orkney ice cream. An evening bistro menu (mains £12 to £24, served from 6pm Thursday to Saturday) offers steak and seafood dishes. The cafe is on the esplanade, 800m northeast of the city centre.

Drinking

Globe Inn
PUB

(www.the-globe-inn.co.uk; 13-15 North Silver St) This lovely Edwardian-style pub with wood panelling, marble-topped tables and walls decorated with old musical instruments is a great place for a quiet lunchtime or afternoon drink. It serves good coffee as well as real ales

and malt whiskies, and has live music (rock, blues, soul) Friday to Sunday. And probably the poshest pub toilets in the country.

Prince of Wales
PUB

(7 St Nicholas Lane) Tucked down an alley off Union St, Aberdeen's best-known pub boasts the longest bar in the city, and a great range of real ales and good-value pub grub. Quiet in the afternoons, but standing-room only in the evenings.

Old Blackfriars
PUB

(www.old-blackfriars.co.uk; 52 Castlegate; ☎) One of the most attractive traditional pubs in the city, with a lovely stone and timber interior, stained-glass windows and a relaxed atmosphere – a great place for an afternoon pint.

BrewDog
BAR

(www.brewdog.com/bars/aberdeen; 17 Gallowgate) The flagship bar of northeast Scotland's most innovative craft brewery brings a bit of designer chic to Aberdeen's pub scene along with a vast range of guest beers from around the world.

⭐ Entertainment

Cinemas

Belmont Cinema
CINEMA

(www.picturehouses.co.uk; 49 Belmont St) The Belmont is a great little art-house cinema, with a lively program of cult classics, director's seasons, foreign films and mainstream movies.

Clubs & Live Music

Check out what's happening in the club and live music scene at local record shops – try One Up Records (www.oneupmusic.co.uk; 17 Belmont St).

Snafu
CLUB, MUSIC

(www.clubsnafu.com; 1 Union St) Aberdeen's coolest club – though admittedly there isn't much competition – cosy Snafu offers a wide range of rotating club nights and guest DJs, as well as a Tuesday night comedy club and live music gigs.

Tunnels
LIVE MUSIC

(www.thetunnels.co.uk; Carnegie's Brae) This cavernous, subterranean club – the entrance is in a road tunnel beneath Union St – is a great live music venue, with a packed program of up-and-coming Scottish bands. It also hosts regular DJ nights – check the website for the latest program.

Theatre & Concerts

You can book tickets for most concerts and other events at the Box Office (www.boxoffice aberdeen.com; ☺9.30am-6pm Mon-Sat) next to the Music Hall (Union St), the main venue for classical music concerts.

Lemon Tree Theatre   PERFORMING ARTS
(www.boxofficeaberdeen.com; 5 West North St) An interesting program of dance, music and drama, and often has live rock, jazz and folk bands playing. There are also children's shows, ranging from comedy to drama to puppetry.

❶ Information

Aberdeen Royal Infirmary (☎01224-681818; www.nhsgrampian.org; Foresterhill) Medical services. About a mile northwest of the western end of Union St.

Aberdeen tourist office (☎01224-288828; www.aberdeen-grampian.com; 23 Union St; ☺9am-6.30pm Mon-Sat, 10am-4pm Sun Jul & Aug, 9.30am-5pm Mon-Sat Sep-Jun) Handy for general information; has internet access too.

Books & Beans (www.booksandbeans.co.uk; 22 Belmont St; per 15min £1; ☺8am-6pm) Internet access; also Fairtrade coffee and secondhand books.

Main post office (St Nicholas Shopping Centre, Upperkirkgate; ☺9am-5.30pm Mon-Sat)

❶ Getting There & Away

AIR **Aberdeen Airport** (ABZ; www.aberdeen airport.com) is at Dyce, 6 miles northwest of the city centre. There are regular flights to numerous Scottish and UK destinations, including Orkney and Shetland, and international flights to the Netherlands, Norway, Denmark, Germany and France.

BOAT Car ferries from Aberdeen to Orkney and Shetland are run by **Northlink Ferries** (www .northlinkferries.co.uk). The ferry terminal is a short walk east of the train and bus stations.

BUS The bus station is next to Jurys Inn, close to the train station.

Braemar £10, 2¼ hours, twice hourly; via Ballater and Balmoral

Dundee £16, 1½ hours, hourly

Edinburgh £28, 3¼ hour, hourly; change at Perth

Glasgow £28, three hours, hourly

Inverness £9, 3¾ hours, hourly; via Huntly, Keith, Fochabers, Elgin and Nairn

London National Express; £46, 12 hours, twice daily

Perth £22, two hours, hourly

TRAIN The train station is south of the city centre, next to the massive Union Sq shopping mall.

Dundee £27, 1¼ hours, twice hourly

Edinburgh £45, 2½ hours, hourly

Glasgow £45, 2¾ hours, hourly

Inverness £28, 2¼ hour, eight daily

London King's Cross £140, eight hours, hourly; some direct, most change at Edinburgh

❶ Getting Around

TO/FROM THE AIRPORT Stagecoach Jet bus 727 runs regularly from Aberdeen bus station to the airport (single £2.70, 35 minutes). A taxi from the airport to the city centre takes 25 minutes and costs £15.

BUS The main city bus operator is **First Aberdeen** (www.firstaberdeen.com). Local fares cost £1.10 to £2.40; pay the driver as you board the bus.

The most useful services for visitors are buses 16A and 19 from Union St to Great Western Rd (for B&Bs); bus 27 from the bus station to Aberdeen Youth Hostel and the airport; and bus 20 from Marischal College to Old Aberdeen.

CAR Car-rental companies include the following:

Arnold Clark (☎01224-249159; www.arnold clarkrental.com; Girdleness Rd)

Enterprise Car Hire (☎01224-642642; www.enterprise.co.uk; 80 Skene Sq)

TAXI The main city-centre taxi ranks are at the train station and on Back Wynd, off Union St. To order a taxi, phone **ComCab** (☎01224-353535) or **Rainbow City Taxis** (☎01224-878787).

Dunottar Castle

A pleasant, 15-minute walk along the clifftops south of Stonehaven harbour leads to the spectacular ruins of Dunnottar Castle (☎01569-762173; www.dunnottarcastle.co.uk; adult/child £5/2; ☺9am-6pm Apr-Oct, 10.30am-dusk Nov-Mar), spread out across a grassy promontory rising 50m above the sea. As dramatic a film set as any director could wish for, it provided the backdrop for Franco Zeffirelli's *Hamlet,* starring Mel Gibson. The original fortress was built in the 9th century; the keep is the most substantial remnant, but the drawing room (restored in 1926) is more interesting.

Stonehaven is 15 miles south of Aberdeen and is served by a number of frequent buses travelling between Aberdeen (45 minutes, hourly) and Dundee (1½ hours). Trains to

Dundee are faster (£12, 55 minutes, hourly) and offer a more scenic journey.

Deeside

The valley of the River Dee – often called Royal Deeside because of the royal family's long association with the area – stretches west from Aberdeen to Braemar, closely paralleled by the A93 road. From Deeside north to Strathdon is serious castle country – there are more examples of fanciful Scottish Baronial architecture here than anywhere else in the country.

BALLATER
POP 1450

The attractive little village of Ballater owes its 18th-century origins to the curative waters of nearby Pannanich Springs (now bottled commercially as Deeside Natural Mineral Water) and its prosperity to nearby Balmoral Castle.

When Queen Victoria travelled to Balmoral Castle she would alight from the royal train at Ballater's Old Royal Station (☏01339-755306; Station Sq; admission £2; ☺9am-6pm Jul & Aug, 10am-5pm Sep-Jun). The station has been beautifully restored and now houses the tourist office, a cafe and a museum with a replica of Victoria's royal coach. Note the crests on the shop fronts along the main street proclaiming 'By Royal Appointment' – the village is a major supplier of provisions to Balmoral.

You can hire bikes from CycleHighlands (www.cyclehighlands.com; The Pavilion, Victoria Rd; bicycle hire per day £16; ☺9am-6pm), which also offers guided bike rides and advice on local trails, and Cabin Fever (☏01339-54004; Station Sq; bicycle hire per 2hr £8; ☺9am-6pm), which can also arrange pony-trekking, quad-biking, clay-pigeon shooting or canoeing.

The tourist office (☏01339-755306; Station Sq; ☺9am-6pm Jul & Aug, 10am-5pm Sep-Jun) is in the Old Royal Station.

Bus 201 runs from Aberdeen to Ballater (£9.60, 1¾ hours, hourly Monday to Saturday, six on Sunday) via Crathes Castle, and continues to Braemar (30 minutes) every two hours.

BALMORAL CASTLE

Eight miles west of Ballater lies Balmoral Castle (☏01339-742334; www.balmoralcastle.com; adult/child £9/5; ☺10am-5pm Apr-Jul, last admission 4pm), the Queen's Highland holiday home, screened from the road by a thick curtain of trees. Built for Queen Victoria in 1855 as a private residence for the royal family, it kicked off the revival of the Scottish Baronial style of architecture that characterises so many of Scotland's 19th-century country houses.

The admission fee includes an interesting and well-thought-out audioguide, but the tour is very much an outdoor one through garden and grounds; as for the castle itself, only the ballroom, which displays a collection of Landseer paintings and royal silver, is open to the public. Don't expect to see the Queen's private quarters! The main attraction is learning about Highland estate management, rather than royal revelations. Guided tours are available on Saturday from October to December – check the website for details.

Balmoral is beside the A93 at Crathie and it can be reached on the Aberdeen to Braemar bus.

BRAEMAR
POP 400

Braemar is a pretty little village with a grand location on a broad plain ringed by mountains where the Dee valley and Glen Clunie meet. In winter this is one of the coldest places in the country – temperatures as low as minus 29°C have been recorded – and during spells of severe cold hungry deer wander the streets looking for a bite to eat. Braemar is an excellent base for hill walking, and there's skiing at nearby Glenshee.

BRAEMAR GATHERING

There are Highland games in many towns and villages throughout summer, but the best known is the Braemar Gathering (☏01339-755377; www.braemargathering.org; adult/child from £10/2), which takes place on the first Saturday in September. It's a major occasion, organised every year since 1817 by the Braemar Royal Highland Society. Events include highland dancing, pipers, tug-of-war, a hill race up Morrone, tossing the caber, hammer- and stone-throwing and the long jump. International athletes are among those who take part.

Just north of the village, turreted Braemar Castle (www.braemarcastle.co.uk; adult/child £6/3; ⊙10am-4pm Sat & Sun Easter-Oct, also Wed Jul–mid-Sep) dates from 1628 and served as a government garrison after the 1745 Jacobite rebellion. It was taken over by the local community in 2007, and now offers guided tours of the historic castle apartments.

Five miles west of Braemar is the tiny settlement of Inverey. Numerous mountain walks start from here, including the adventurous walk through the Lairig Ghru pass to Aviemore (for experienced and well-equipped hikers only).

A good short walk (3 miles, 1½ hours) begins at the Linn of Quoich – a waterfall that thunders through a narrow slot in the rocks. Head uphill on a footpath on the east bank of the stream, past the impressive rock scenery of the Punch Bowl (a giant pothole), to a modern bridge that spans the narrow gorge and return via an unsurfaced road on the far bank.

Sleeping

TOP CHOICE Rucksacks Bunkhouse HOSTEL £

(☑01339-741517; 15 Mar Rd; bothy £7, dm £12-15, tw £36; P@) An appealing cottage with a comfy dorm, and cheaper beds in an alpine-style bothy (shared sleeping platform for 10 people; bring your own sleeping bag). Extras include a drying room (for wet-weather gear), laundry and even a sauna (£10 per hour). Nonguests are welcome to use the internet (£3 per hour, from 10.30am to 4.30pm), laundry and even the showers (£2). The friendly owner is a fount of knowledge about the local area.

Craiglea B&B ££

(☑01339-741641; www.craigleabraemar.com; Hillside Dr; d £72; P🐾) Craiglea is a homely B&B set in a pretty stone cottage with three en suite bedrooms. Vegetarian breakfasts are available and the owners can give advice on local walks.

Braemar SYHA HOSTEL £

(☑01339-741659; 21 Glenshee Rd; dm £18; ⊙Feb-Oct; @) This hostel is housed in a grand former shooting lodge just south of Braemar viilage centre on the A93 to Perth. It has a comfy lounge with a pool table, and a barbecue in the garden.

St Margarets B&B ££

(☑01339-741697; 13 School Rd; s/tw £32/54; 🐾) Grab this place if you can, but there's only one room – a twin with a serious sunflower theme. The genuine warmth of the welcome is heart-warming.

Eating

TOP CHOICE Gathering Place BISTRO ££

(☑01339-741234; www.the-gathering-place.co.uk; 9 Invercauld Rd; mains £15-19; ⊙dinner Tue-Sat) This bright and breezy bistro is an unexpected corner of culinary excellence, with a welcoming dining room and sunny conservatory, tucked below the main road junction at the entrance to Braemar village.

Taste CAFE £

(☑01339-741425; www.taste-braemar.co.uk; Airlie House, Mar Rd; mains £3-6; ⊙10am-5pm Mon-Sat; 🐾) Taste is a relaxed little cafe with armchairs in the window, serving soups, snacks, coffee and cakes.

Getting There & Away

Bus 201 runs from Aberdeen to Braemar (£9, 2¼ hours, eight daily Monday to Saturday, five on Sunday). The 50-mile drive from Perth to Braemar is beautiful, but there's no public transport on this route.

WORTH A TRIP

DUFF HOUSE

Duff House (☑01261-818181; www.duffhouse.org.uk; adult/child £6.90/4.10; ⊙11am-5pm Apr-Oct, 11am-4pm Thu-Sun Nov-Mar) is an impressive baroque mansion on the southern edge of Banff (upstream from the bridge, and across from the tourist office), 35 miles east of Elgin. Built between 1735 and 1740 as the seat of the earls of Fife, it was designed by William Adam and bears similarities to that Adam masterpiece, Hopetoun House. Since being gifted to the town in 1906 it has served as a hotel, a hospital and a POW camp, but is now an art gallery. One of Scotland's hidden gems, it houses a superb collection of Scottish and European art, including important works by Raeburn and Gainsborough.

BLAZE YOUR OWN WHISKY TRAIL

Visiting a distillery can be memorable, but only hardcore malthounds will want to go to more than two or three. Some are great to visit; others are depressingly corporate. The following are some recommendations.

Aberlour (☑01340-881249; www.aberlour.com; tours £12; ☺10am & 2pm daily Apr-Oct, by appointment Mon-Fri Nov-Mar) Has an excellent, detailed tour with a proper tasting session. It's on the main street in Aberlour.

Glenfarclas (☑01807-500257; www.glenfarclas.co.uk; admission £5; ☺10am-4pm Mon-Fri Oct-Mar, to 5pm Mon-Fri Apr-Sep, plus to 4pm Sat Jul-Sep) Small, friendly and independent, Glenfarclas is 5 miles south of Aberlour on the Grantown road. The last tour leaves 1½ hours before closing. The in-depth Connoisseur's Tour (Friday only, July to September) is £20.

Glenfiddich (www.glenfiddich.com; admission free; ☺9.30am-4.30pm daily year-round, closed Christmas & New Year) It's big and busy, but handiest for Dufftown and foreign languages are available. The standard tour starts with an overblown video, but it's fun, informative and free. An in-depth Connoisseur's Tour (£20) must be prebooked. Glenfiddich kept single malt alive during the dark years.

Macallan (☑01340-872280; www.themacallan.com; ☺9.30am-4.30pm Mon-Sat Easter-Oct, 11am-3pm Mon-Fri Nov-Mar) Excellent sherry-casked malt. Several small-group tours are available (last tour at 3.30pm), including an expert one (£20); all should be prebooked. Lovely location 2 miles northwest of Craigellachie.

Speyside Cooperage (☑01340-871108; www.speysidecooperage.co.uk; adult/child £3.50/2; ☺9am-4pm Mon-Fri) Here you can see the fascinating art of barrel-making in action. It's a mile from Craigellachie on the Dufftown road.

Spirit of Speyside (www.spiritofspeyside.com) This biannual whisky festival in Dufftown has a number of great events. It takes place in early May and late September; both accommodation and events should be booked well ahead.

Moray

The old county of Moray (*murr*-ree), centred on the county town of Elgin, lies at the heart of an ancient Celtic earldom and is famed for its mild climate and rich farmland – the barley fields of the 19th century once provided the raw material for the Speyside whisky distilleries, one of the region's main attractions for present-day visitors.

ELGIN

POP 21,000

Elgin has been the provincial capital of Moray for over eight centuries and was an important town in medieval times. Dominated by a hilltop monument to the 5th duke of Gordon, Elgin's main attraction is its impressive ruined cathedral, where the tombs of the duke's ancestors lie.

◉ Sights

Elgin Cathedral CATHEDRAL
(HS; King St; adult/child £5/3, incl Spynie Palace £6.70/4; ☺9.30am-5.30pm Apr-Sep, 9.30am-4.30pm Oct, 9.30am-4.30pm Sat-Wed Oct-Mar) Many people think that the ruins of Elgin Cathedral, known as the 'lantern of the

north', are the most beautiful and evocative in Scotland. Consecrated in 1224, the cathedral was burned down in 1390 by the infamous Wolf of Badenoch, the illegitimate son of Robert II, following his excommunication by the Bishop of Moray. The octagonal chapter house is the finest in the country.

Elgin Museum MUSEUM
(www.elginmuseum.org.uk; 1 High St; adult/child £4/1.50; ☺10am-5pm Mon-Fri, 11am-4pm Sat Apr-Oct) Palaeontologists and Pict lovers will enjoy Elgin Museum, where the highlights are its collections of fossil fish and Pictish carved stones.

⊫ Sleeping & Eating

Croft Guesthouse B&B ££
(☑01343-546004; www.thecroftelgin.co.uk; 10 Institution Rd; s/d from £55/70; P) The Croft offers a taste of Victorian high society, set in a spacious mansion built for a local lawyer back in 1848. The house is filled with period features – check out the cast-iron and tile fireplaces – and the three large bedrooms are equipped with easy chairs and crisp bed linen.

Southbank Guest House
B&B ££

(☑01343-547132; www.southbankguesthouse.co
.uk; 36 Academy St; s/d £55/75; ℗) The family-
run, 12-room Southbank is set in a large
Georgian town house in a quiet street south
of Elgin's centre, just five minutes' walk
from the cathedral and other sights.

Johnstons Coffee Shop
CAFE £

(Newmill; mains £5-7; ⊙10am-5pm Mon-Sat,
11am-4.30pm Sun; 🛜🚷) The coffee shop at
Johnstons woollen mill is the best place to
eat in town, serving breakfast till 11.45am,
hot lunches from noon to 3pm (crêpes with
a range of fillings, including smoked salmon with cream cheese and dill), and
cream teas.

❶ Getting There & Away

BUS Elgin is a stop on the hourly Stagecoach
bus 10 service between Inverness (£9.50, one
hour) and Aberdeen (£13, two hours). Bus 305
goes from Elgin to Banff and Macduff (£9, one
hour), continuing to Aberdeen via Fyvie. Bus 336
goes to Dufftown (£4.30, 30 minutes, hourly
Monday to Saturday).

TRAIN Trains run to the following destinations:

Aberdeen £17, 1½ hours, five daily

Inverness £12, 50 minutes, five daily

DUFFTOWN
POP 1450

Rome may be built on seven hills, but Dufftown's built on seven stills, say the locals.
Founded in 1817 by James Duff, 4th earl
of Fife, Dufftown is 17 miles south of Elgin
and lies at the heart of the Speyside whisky-
distilling region.

With seven working distilleries nearby,
Dufftown has been dubbed Scotland's malt
whisky capital. Ask at the tourist office for
a Malt Whisky Trail (www.maltwhiskytrail.com)
booklet, a self-guided tour around the seven
stills plus the Speyside Cooperage.

The tourist office (☑01340-820501;
⊙10am-1pm & 2-5.30pm Mon-Sat, 11am-3pm Sun
Easter-Oct) is in the clock tower in the main
square; the adjoining museum contains
some interesting local items.

Buses link Dufftown to Elgin (50 minutes,
hourly), Huntly, Aberdeen and Inverness.

On summer weekends, you can take a
train from Aberdeen or Inverness to Keith,
and then ride the Keith and Dufftown
Railway (☑01340-821181; www.keith-dufftown
-railway.co.uk; Dufftown Station; adult/child return
£10/5) to Dufftown.

Inverness & the Northern Highlands & Islands

Best Places to Eat

» Albannach (p913)

» Three Chimneys (p923)

» Contrast Brasserie (p888)

» Lime Tree (p902)

Best Places to Stay

» The Torridon (p917)

» Toravaig House Hotel (p921)

» Rocpool Reserve (p888)

» West Manse (p944)

» Brinkies Guest House (p940)

» Shetland Lighthouse Cottages (p947)

Why Go?

Scotland's vast melancholy soul is here, an epic land whose stark beauty indelibly imprints upon the hearts of those who see it. Mist, peat, whisky, heather... and long, sunblessed summer evenings that repay the many days of horizontal drizzle.

The region's capital, Inverness, is backed by the craggy Cairngorms, which draw skiers and walkers to its slopes. Further north, ancient stones are testament left by prehistoric builders in Caithness, and across the water on the magical Orkney and remote Shetland Islands – where wind keeps the vegetation at a minimum – isolation makes it a haven for sea birds and more.

The most epic scenery – you really need an orchestra to do it justice – is in the far northwest, and it continues on to Skye, where the mighty Cuillin Ridge towers jaggedly in the setting sun. Beyond here, the Outer Hebrides offer the nation's best beaches and a glimpse of traditional life.

When to Go

In January hit the Cairngorms for skiing or the Shetland Islands for Up Helly Aa, a fiery Viking festival.

The long, long evenings in June up here bathe heartachingly sublime landscapes in a dreamlike light.

September is the ideal time for hiking and hill walking – midges are dying off, but the weather is still reasonably good.

Inverness & the Northern Highlands & Islands Highlights

1 Hiking among the hills, lochs and forests of beautiful **Glen Affric** (p891)

2 Dipping your toes in the water at the beautiful beaches on **Harris** (p928) and **Barra** (p931)

3 Shouldering the challenge of the **Cuillin Hills** (p921), whose rugged silhouettes brood over the skyscape of Skye

4 Picking your jaw up off the floor as you marvel at the Highland scenery of the **far northwest** (p911)

5 Launching into a **sea-kayak** (p918) to explore the waters around the Isle of Skye

6 Shaking your head in astonishment at extraordinary **Skara Brae** (p939) and **Maes Howe** (p938), prehistoric perfection that predates the pyramids

7 Island-hopping Orkney's **Northern Islands** (p933), where crystal azure waters lap against glittering white-sand beaches

8 Capering with puffins or spotting orcas in the Shetland Islands' **nature reserves** (p945)

9 Soaking up the scenery in magnificent **Glen Coe** (p899)

10 Making it to the summit of **Ben Nevis** (p903) – and being able to see the view

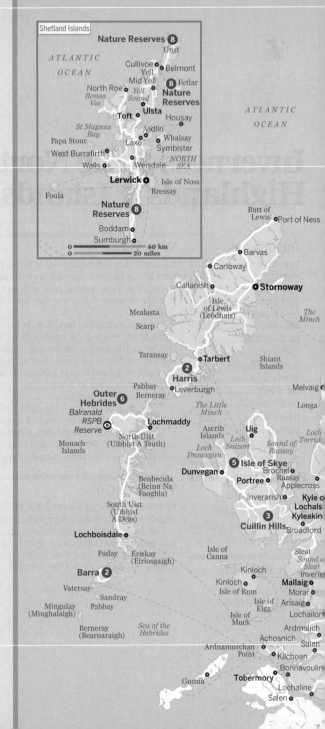

Activities

For outdoor fans, especially hikers and hill-walkers, the Highlands are heaven. Famous spots like Ben Nevis, Glen Coe, Skye and the Cairngorms offer endless opportunities for experienced walkers – and several options for strollers too. Long-distance walking routes include the Great Glen Way (www.greatglenway.com), while the West Highland Way and Speyside Way are nearby (covered in the Stirling & Central Scotland chapter).

For touring cyclists, the roads of the Highlands are enjoyable, as car traffic is often fairly light. The islands are also ideal: Skye is ever-popular, as is the end-to-end tour of the Outer Hebrides, where south-to-north (Barra to Lewis) gives you the best chance of a following wind. Gateways for mountain-biking include Fort William and Laggan. The Great Glen Way is also suitable for off-road bikes.

Other activities include fishing in rivers and the sea, scuba diving (notably at Scapa Flow in the Orkney Islands) and mountaineering on Ben Nevis or the Cairngorms. The main skiing and snowboarding areas include the Cairngorms and the Nevis Range near Fort William.

ⓘ Getting There & Around

For train travel in the region, Inverness is the main hub, with connections south to England and the rest of Scotland, and lines north to Thurso and west to Kyle of Lochalsh – both passing through fabulous scenery. The West Highland line from Glasgow to Fort William and Mallaig is similarly scenic. Inverness is also the main hub for bus travel. Check details with **Traveline Scotland** (www.travelinescotland.com).

Ferries to/from the Western islands are mostly run by **Caledonian MacBrayne** (www.calmac.co.uk), with mainland ports including Mallaig and Ullapool (plus Uig on Skye), while ferries to Orkney and Shetland depart mainly from Scrabster and Aberdeen respectively.

INVERNESS & THE GREAT GLEN

Inverness, one of the fastest growing towns in Britain, is the capital of the Highlands. It's a transport hub and jumping-off point for the central, western and northern Highlands, the Moray Firth coast and the Great Glen.

The Great Glen is a geological fault running in an arrow-straight line, filled by a series of lochs, across Scotland from Fort William to Inverness. In 1822 the various lochs were linked by the Caledonian Canal to create a cross-country waterway. The modern A82 road along the glen was completed in 1933 – a date that coincides neatly with the first modern sightings of the Loch Ness Monster.

Inverness

POP 55,000

Inverness, the primary city and shopping centre of the Highlands, has a great location astride the River Ness at the northern end of the Great Glen. In summer it overflows with visitors intent on monster hunting at nearby Loch Ness, but it's worth a visit in its own right for a stroll along the picturesque River Ness, a cruise on Loch Ness, and a meal in one of the city's excellent restaurants.

◉ Sights

Ness Islands PARK
The main attraction in Inverness is a leisurely stroll along the river to the Ness Islands. Planted with mature Scots pine, fir, beech and sycamore, and linked to the river banks and each other by elegant Victorian footbridges, the islands make an appealing picnic spot.

They're a 20-minute walk south of the castle (Castle St) – head upstream on either side of the river (the start of the Great Glen Way), and return on the opposite bank. On the way you'll pass the red-sandstone towers of St Andrew's Cathedral, dating from 1869, and the modern Eden Court Theatre, which hosts regular art exhibits, both on the west bank.

☞ Tours

Jacobite Cruises BOAT TOUR
(☏01463-233999; www.jacobite.co.uk; Glenurquhart Rd; adult/child £29/22; ⊙twice daily Jun-Sep, once daily Apr-May) Boats depart from Tomnahurich Bridge for a 1½-hour cruise along Loch Ness, followed by a visit to Urquhart Castle (admission fee included in tour price) and a return to Inverness by coach. You can buy tickets at the tourist office and catch a free minibus to the boat. Other cruises and combined cruise/coach tours, from one to 6½ hours, are also available.

Inverness

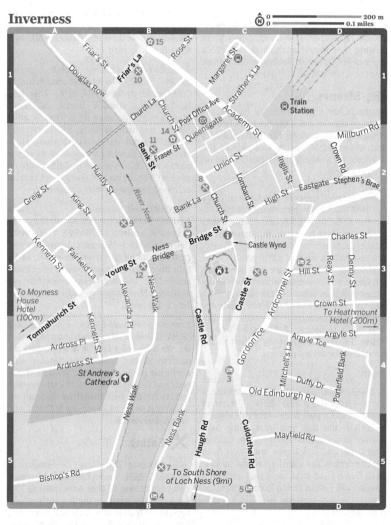

N 0 —————— 200 m
0 —————— 0.1 miles

Inverness

◉ Sights
1 Inverness Castle	C3

🛏 Sleeping
2 Ardconnel House	D3
3 Bazpackers Backpackers Hotel	C4
4 MacRae Guest House	B5
5 Rocpool Reserve	C5

✕ Eating
6 Café 1	C3
7 Contrast Brasserie	B5
8 Joy of Taste	C2
9 Kitchen	B3
10 Leakey's	B1
11 Mustard Seed	B2
12 Rocpool	B3

🍷 Drinking
13 Johnny Foxes	B3

🎭 Entertainment
14 Hootananny	B2
15 Ironworks	B1

John O'Groats Ferries BUS TOUR

(☏01955-611353; www.jogferry.co.uk; ⊘departs 7.30am) From May to September, daily tours (lasting 13½ hours; adult/child £57/28.50) are run by bus and passenger ferry from Inverness bus station to Orkney.

🛏 Sleeping

Inverness has a good range of backpacker accommodation, and there are lots of guesthouses and B&Bs along Old Edinburgh Rd and Ardconnel St on the east side of the river, and on Kenneth St and Fairfield Rd on the west bank.

TOP CHOICE Rocpool Reserve BOUTIQUE HOTEL £££

(☏01463-240089; www.rocpool.com; Culduthel Rd; s/d from £175/210; P♠) Boutique chic meets the Highlands in this slick and sophisticated little hotel, where an elegant Georgian exterior conceals an oasis of contemporary cool. A gleaming white entrance hall lined with red carpet and contemporary art leads to designer rooms in shades of chocolate, cream and gold; expect lots of high-tech gadgetry in the more expensive rooms, ranging from iPod docks to balcony hot tubs with aquavision TV. A restaurant by Albert Roux completes the luxury package.

TOP CHOICE Trafford Bank B&B ££

(☏01463-241414; www.traffordbankguesthouse.co.uk; 96 Fairfield Rd; d £110-125; P♠) Lots of word-of-mouth rave reviews for this elegant Victorian villa that was once home to a bishop, just a mitre-toss from the Caledonian Canal and 10 minutes' walk west from the city centre. The luxurious rooms include fresh flowers and fruit, bathrobes and fluffy towels – ask for the Tartan Room, which has a wrought-iron king-size bed and a Victorian roll-top bath.

Ardconnel House B&B ££

(☏01463-240455; www.ardconnel-inverness.co.uk; 21 Ardconnel St; r per person £35-40; ♠) The six-room Ardconnel is one of our favourites – a terraced Victorian house with comfortable en-suite rooms, a dining room with crisp white table linen, and a breakfast menu that includes Vegemite for homesick Antipodeans. Kids under 10 not allowed.

Ach Aluinn B&B ££

(☏01463-230127; www.achaluinn.com; 27 Fairfield Rd; r per person £25-35; P) This large, detached Victorian house is bright and homely, and offers all you might want from a guesthouse –

private bathroom, TV, reading lights, comfy beds with two pillows each, and an excellent breakfast. Less than 10 minutes' walk west from the city centre.

Bazpackers Backpackers Hotel HOSTEL £

(☏01463-717663; www.bazpackershostel.co.uk; 4 Culduthel Rd; dm/tw £17/44; @♠) This may be Inverness' smallest hostel (30 beds), but it's hugely popular. It's a friendly, quiet place – the main building has a convivial lounge centred on a wood-burning stove and a small garden and great views (some rooms are in a separate building with no garden). The dorms and kitchen can be a bit cramped, but the showers are great.

MacRae Guest House B&B ££

(☏01463-243658; joycemacrae@hotmail.com; 24 Ness Bank; s/d from £45/64; P) This pretty, flower-bedecked Victorian house on the eastern bank of the river has smart, tastefully decorated bedrooms (one is wheelchair accessible), and vegetarian breakfasts are available. Minimum two-night bookings in July and August.

Inverness Millburn SYHA HOSTEL £

(SYHA; ☏01463-231771; wwwsyha.org.uk; Victoria Dr; dm £18; ⊘Apr-Dec; P@♠) Inverness' modern 166-bed hostel is 10 minutes' walk northeast of the city centre. With its comfy beds and flashy stainless-steel kitchen, some reckon it's the best hostel in the country. Booking is essential, especially at Easter, and in July and August.

🍴 Eating

TOP CHOICE Contrast Brasserie BRASSERIE ££

(☏01463-227889; www.glenmoristontownhouse.com/contrast.html; 22 Ness Bank; mains £13-20) Book early for what we think is the best restaurant in Inverness – a dining room that drips designer style, smiling professional staff, and truly delicious food. Try scallops with chorizo bolognaise, or pork belly with mange tout salad and lemongrass purée; 10 out of 10. And at £10 for a two-course lunch, or £15 for three-course early-bird dinner (5pm to 6.30pm), the value is unbeatable.

TOP CHOICE Café 1 BISTRO ££

(☏01463-226200; www.cafe1.net; 75 Castle St; mains £10-23; ⊘noon-9.30pm Mon-Fri, noon-2.30pm & 6-9.30pm Sat) Café 1 is a friendly and appealing bistro with candlelit tables amid elegant blonde-wood and wrought-iron decor. There is an international menu based on quality Scottish produce, from Aberdeen Angus steaks to crisp sea bass with velvet crab risotto and chilli jam. Early-bird menu (one/two courses for £9/12.50) is served noon to 6.45pm weekdays, and noon to 2.30pm Saturday.

Rocpool
MEDITERRANEAN ££

(☑01463-717274; www.rocpoolrestaurant.com; 1 Ness Walk; mains £17-24; ⊘Mon-Sat) Lots of polished wood, navy-blue leather and crisp white linen lend a nautical air to this relaxing bistro, which offers a Mediterranean-influenced menu that makes the most of quality Scottish produce, especially seafood. The two-course lunch is £14.

Mustard Seed
BISTRO ££

(☑01463-220220; www.mustardseedrestaurant.co.uk; 16 Fraser St; mains £11-16) The menu at this bright and bustling bistro changes weekly, but focuses on Scottish and French cuisine with a modern twist. Grab a table on the upstairs balcony if you can – it's the best outdoor lunch spot in Inverness, with a great view across the river. And a two-course lunch for £7 – yes, that's right – is hard to beat.

Kitchen
MODERN SCOTTISH ££

(☑01463-259119; www.kitchenrestaurant.co.uk; 15 Huntly St; mains £11-16; 🛜🍽) This spectacular glass-fronted restaurant is under the same management as the Mustard Seed (with same bargain lunch deal), and offers a great menu and a view of the River Ness – try to get a table upstairs.

Joy of Taste
BRITISH ££

(☑01463-241459; www.thejoyoftaste.co.uk; 25 Church St; mains £12-17) Here's a novel concept – a restaurant run by a head chef and 25 volunteers who work a shift a week just for 'the love of creating a beautiful restaurant' (plus a share of the profits). And a very good job they're making of it, with a menu of classic British cuisine – from broccoli and stilton soup to lemon posset via Scottish sirloin – and a growing fan club of satisfied customers.

Leakey's
CAFE £

(Greyfriars Hall, Church St; mains £3-5; ⊘10am-5.30pm Mon-Sat) Cosy cafe in an excellent secondhand bookshop.

Drinking

Clachnaharry Inn
PUB

(☑01463-239806; www.clachnaharryinn.co.uk; 17-19 High St) Just over a mile northwest of the city centre, on the bank of the Caledonian Canal just off the A862, this is a delightful old coaching inn (with beer garden out back) serving an excellent range of real ales and good pub grub.

Johnny Foxes
BAR

(☑01463-236577; www.johnnyfoxes.co.uk; 26 Bank St) Stuck beneath the ugliest building on the riverfront, Johnny Foxes is a big and boisterous Irish bar with a wide range of food served all day and live music nightly. Part of the premises, the Den, is a smart cocktail bar and club.

☆ Entertainment

Hootananny
LIVE MUSIC

(☑01463-233651; www.hootananny.com; 67 Church St) Hootananny is the city's best live-music venue, with traditional folk- and/or rock-music sessions nightly, including big-name bands from all over Scotland (and, indeed, the world). The bar is well stocked with a range of beers from the local Black Isle Brewery.

Ironworks
LIVE MUSIC, COMEDY

(☑0871 789 4173; www.ironworksvenue.com; 122 Academy St) With live bands (rock, pop, tribute) and comedy shows two or three times a week, the Ironworks is the town's main venue for big-name acts.

ℹ Information

ClanLAN (22 Baron Taylor's St; per 30 minutes £1.50; ⊘10am-8pm Mon-Fri, 11am-8pm Sat, noon-5pm Sun)

Inverness tourist office (☑01463-252401; www.visithighlands.com; Castle Wynd; internet access per 20min £1; ⊘9am-6pm Mon-Sat, 9.30am-5pm Sun Jul & Aug, 9am-5pm Mon-Sat, 10am-4pm Sun Jun, Sep & Oct, 9am-5pm Mon-Sat Apr & May) Bureau de change and accommodation booking service; also sells tickets for tours and cruises. Opening hours limited November to March.

ℹ Getting There & Away

Air

Inverness Airport (INV; ☑01667-464000; www.hial.co.uk) At Dalcross, 10 miles east of the city off the A96 towards Aberdeen. There are scheduled flights to Amsterdam, Düsseldorf, London, Bristol, Manchester, Belfast, Stornoway, Benbecula, Orkney, Shetland and several other British airports.

Stagecoach Jet (www.stagecoachbus.com) Buses run from the airport to Inverness bus station (£3.30, 20 minutes, every 30 minutes).

Bus

Buses depart from Inverness **bus station** (Margaret St). Services include:

Aberdeen (£9, 3¾ hours, hourly)

Aviemore (£5.50, 1¾ hours, three daily Monday to Friday) Via Grantown-on-Spey.

Edinburgh (£28, 3½ to 4½ hours, hourly)

Glasgow (£28, 3½ to 4½ hours, hourly)

Fort William (£12, two hours, five daily)

London (£45, 13 hours, one daily) More frequent services requiring a change at Glasgow. Operated by National Express.

Portree (£23, 3½ hours, four daily)

Thurso (£18.50, 3½ hours, two daily)

Ullapool (£12, 1½ hours, two daily except Sunday)

If you book far enough in advance, **Megabus** (☑0871 266 3333; www.megabus.com) offers fares from as little as £5.50 for buses from Inverness to Glasgow and Edinburgh, and £17 to London.

Train

The train station is on Academy St. Services include:

Aberdeen (£28, 2¼ hours, eight daily)

Edinburgh (£40, 3½ hours, eight daily)

Glasgow (£40, 3½ hours, eight daily)

Kyle of Lochalsh (£13, 2½ hours, four daily Monday to Saturday, two Sunday) One of Britain's great scenic train journeys.

London (£100, eight hours, one daily) One daily direct; other services require a change at Edinburgh.

Wick (£13, four hours, four daily Monday to Saturday, one or two on Sunday) Via Thurso.

❶ Getting Around

Bicycle

Ticket to Ride (☑01463-419160; www.ticket toridehighlands.co.uk; Bellfield Park; per day from £20) Hires mountain bikes, hybrids and tandems. Will deliver bikes free to local hotels and B&Bs.

Bus

City services and buses to places around Inverness, including the Culloden battlefield, are operated by Stagecoach. A City Dayrider ticket costs £3.30 and gives unlimited travel for a day on buses throughout the city.

Car

Focus Vehicle Rental (☑01667-461212; www.focusvehiclerental.co.uk; Inverness Airport) The big boys charge from around £50 per day, but Focus has cheaper rates starting at £35 per day.

Around Inverness

CULLODEN BATTLEFIELD

The Battle of Culloden in 1746, the last pitched battle ever fought on British soil, saw the defeat of Bonnie Prince Charlie and the end of the Jacobite dream when 1200 Highlanders were slaughtered by government forces in a 68-minute rout. The duke of Cumberland, son of the reigning king George II and leader of the Hanoverian army, earned the nickname 'Butcher' for his brutal treatment of the defeated Scottish forces. The battle sounded the death knell for the old clan system, and the horrors of the Clearances soon followed. The sombre moor where the conflict took place has scarcely changed in the ensuing 260 years.

The impressive visitor centre (NTS; www .nts.org.uk/culloden; adult/child £10/7.50; ☺9am-6pm Apr-Sep, 9am-5pm Oct, 10am-4pm Nov-Mar) presents detailed information about the battle, with perspectives from both sides. An innovative film puts you on the battlefield in the middle of the mayhem. The admission fee includes an audioguide for a self-guided tour of the battlefield itself.

Culloden is 6 miles east of Inverness. Bus No 1 runs from Queensgate in Inverness to Culloden battlefield (30 minutes, hourly).

FORT GEORGE

The headland guarding the narrows in the Moray Firth opposite Fortrose is occupied by the magnificent and virtually unaltered 18th-century artillery fortification of Fort George (HS; ☑01667-462777; adult/child £6.90/4.10; ☺9.30am-5.30pm Apr-Sep, to 4.30pm Oct-Mar). One of the finest examples of its kind in Europe, it was established in 1748 as a base for George II's army of occupation in the Highlands – by the time of its completion in 1769 it had cost the equivalent of around £1 billion in today's money. The mile-plus walk around the ramparts offers fine views out to sea and back to the Great Glen. Given its size, you'll need at least two hours to do the place justice. The fort is off the A96, about 11 miles northeast of Inverness.

CAWDOR CASTLE

Built in the 14th century, Cawdor Castle (☑01667-404615; www.cawdorcastle.com; adult/child £9.50/6; ☺10am-5.30pm May–Sep) was the home of the Thanes of Cawdor, one of the titles prophesied by the three witches for the eponymous character of Shakespeare's *Macbeth*. Macbeth couldn't have moved in, though, since the central tower dates from the 14th century (the wings were 17th-century additions), and he died in 1057.

BRODIE CASTLE

Set in 70 hectares of parkland, Brodie Castle (NTS; ☑01309-641371; adult/child £9.50/7; ⊘10.30am-5pm daily Jul & Aug, 10.30am-4.30pm Apr, 10.30am-4.30pm Sun-Thu May-Jun & Sep-Oct) has several highlights, including a library with more than 6000 peeling, dusty volumes. There are wonderful clocks, a huge Victorian kitchen and a 17th-century dining room with wildly extravagant moulded plaster ceilings depicting mythological scenes. The Brodies have been living here since 1160, but the present structure dates mostly from 1567, with many additions over the years.

Stagecoach bus 10A or 11 from Inverness to Elgin stops at Brodie (35 minutes, hourly Monday to Saturday). The castle is 23 miles northeast of Inverness.

GLEN AFFRIC

The broad valley of Strathglass extends about 18 miles inland from the town of Beauly, followed by the A831 road to Cannich, the only village in the area, where there's a grocery store and a post office.

Glen Affric (www.glenaffric.org), one of the most beautiful glens in Scotland, extends deep into the hills beyond Cannich. The upper reaches of the glen, now designated as Glen Affric National Nature Reserve, is a scenic wonderland of shimmering lochs, rugged mountains and native Scots pine, home to pine marten, wildcat, otter, red squirrel and golden eagle.

It's possible to walk all the way from Cannich to Glen Shiel on the west coast (35 miles) in two days, spending the night at the remote Glen Affric Youth Hostel.

🛏 **Sleeping**

Kerrow House   B&B ££
(☑01456-415243; www.kerrow-house.co.uk; Cannich; per person £35-43; ℗) This wonderful Georgian hunting lodge has bags of old-fashioned character – it was once the home of Highland author Neil Gunn – and has spacious grounds with 3.5 miles of private trout fishing. It's a mile south of Cannich on the minor road along the east side of the River Glass.

Glen Affric SYHA   HOSTEL £
(☑bookings 0845 293 7373; www.syha.org.uk; Allt Beithe; dm £21.50; ⊘Apr–mid-Sep) This remote and rustic hostel is set amid magnificent scenery at the halfway point of the cross-country walk from Cannich to Glen Shiel, 8 miles from the nearest road. Facilities are basic and you'll need to take all supplies with you. Book in advance. There is no phone at the hostel.

❶ **Getting There & Away**

Stagecoach bus 17 runs from Inverness to Cannich (one hour, three a day Monday to Saturday) via Drumnadrochit.

BLACK ISLE

The Black Isle – a peninsula rather than an island – is linked to Inverness by the Kessock Bridge.

At Fortrose Cathedral you'll find the vaulted crypt of a 13th-century chapter house and sacristy, and the ruinous 14th-century south aisle and chapel. In Rosemarkie, the Groam House Museum (☑01381-620961; www.groamhouse.org.uk; High St; admission free; ⊘11am-4.30pm Mon-Fri, 2-4.30pm Sat Apr-Oct, 2-4pm Sat only Nov) has a superb collection of Pictish stones engraved with designs similar to those on Celtic Irish stones.

The pretty village of Cromarty at the northeastern tip of the Black Isle has lots of 18th-century red-sandstone houses. The 18th-century Cromarty Courthouse (☑01381-600418; www.cromarty-courthouse.org.uk; Church St; admission free; ⊘noon-4pm Sun-Thu Apr-Sep) details the town's history using contemporary references. Kids will love the talking mannequins.

From Cromarty harbour, Ecoventures (☑01381-600323; www.ecoventures.co.uk; Cromarty Harbour; adult/child £24/18) runs 2½-hour boat trips (adult/child £22/16) into the Moray Firth to see bottlenose dolphins and other wildlife.

Stagecoach buses 26 and 26A run from Inverness to Fortrose and Rosemarkie (30 to 40 minutes, twice hourly Monday to Saturday); half of them continue to Cromarty (one hour).

Loch Ness

Deep, dark and narrow, Loch Ness stretches for 23 miles between Inverness and Fort Augustus. Its bitterly cold waters have been extensively explored in search of Nessie, the elusive Loch Ness monster, but most visitors see her only in cardboard-cutout form at the monster exhibitions. The busy A82 road runs along the northwestern shore, while the more tranquil and picturesque B862 follows the southeastern shore. A complete circuit of the loch is about 70 miles – travel anticlockwise for the best views.

🏃 Activities

The 73-mile **Great Glen Way** (www.greatglen way.com) long-distance footpath stretches from Inverness to Fort William, where walkers can connect with the **West Highland Way**. The Great Glen Way footpath shares some sections with the 80-mile **Great Glen Mountain Bike Trail**, a waymarked mountain-bike route that follows canal towpaths and gravel tracks through forests, avoiding roads where possible.

The new **South Loch Ness Trail** (www .visitlochness.com/south-loch-ness-trail) links a series of footpaths and minor roads along the less-frequented southern side of the loch. The 28 miles from Loch Tarff near Fort Augustus to Torbreck on the fringes of Inverness can be done on foot, by bike or on horseback.

There's also the option of the **Great Glen Canoe Trail** (www.greatglencanoetrail.info), a series of access points, waymarks and informal campsites that allow you to travel the length of the glen by canoe or kayak.

DRUMNADROCHIT
POP 800

Seized by monster madness, its gift shops bulging with Nessie cuddly toys, Drumnadrochit is a hotbed of beastie fever, with two monster exhibitions battling it out for the tourist dollar.

👁 SIGHTS & ACTIVITIES

Urquhart Castle   CASTLE
(HS; ☑01456-450551; adult/child £7.40/4.50; ⊙9.30am-6pm Apr-Sep, to 5pm Oct, to 4.30pm Nov-Mar) Commanding a brilliant location 1.5 miles east of Drumnadrochit, with outstanding views (on a clear day), Urquhart Castle is a popular Nessie-watching hotspot. A huge visitor centre includes a video theatre and displays of medieval items discovered in the castle.

The castle was repeatedly sacked and rebuilt over the centuries; in 1692 it was blown up to prevent the Jacobites from using it. The five-storey tower house at the northern point is the most impressive remaining fragment and offers wonderful views across the water. The site includes a huge gift shop and a restaurant, and is often very crowded in summer.

Loch Ness Centre & Exhibition   EXHIBITION
(☑01456-450573; www.lochness.com; adult/child £6.95/4.95; ⊙9am-6pm Jul & Aug, to 5.30pm Jun, 9.30am-5pm Easter-May & Sep-Oct, 10am-3.30pm Nov-Easter) The better of the two Nessie-themed exhibitions in Drumnadrochit, this adopts a scientific approach that allows you to weigh the evidence for yourself. You'll find out about hoaxes and optical illusions, as well as learning a lot about the ecology of Loch Ness – is there enough food in the loch to support even one 'monster', let alone a breeding population?

Nessie Hunter   BOAT TRIP
(☑01456-450395; www.lochness-cruises.com; adult/child £15/10; ⊙Easter-Oct) One-hour monster-hunting cruises, complete with sonar and underwater cameras. Cruises depart from Drumnadrochit hourly (except 1pm) from 9am to 6pm daily.

🛏 Sleeping & Eating

Loch Ness Inn   INN ££
(☑01456-450991; www.staylochness.co.uk; Lewiston; s/d/f £89/102/145; ℗🖼) The Loch Ness Inn ticks all the weary traveller's boxes, with comfortable bedrooms (the family suite sleeps two adults and two children), a cosy bar pouring real ales from the Cairngorm and Isle of Skye breweries, and a rustic restaurant (mains £9 to £18) serving hearty, wholesome fare such as whisky-flambéed haggis, and roast rump of Scottish lamb.

It's conveniently located in the quiet hamlet of Lewiston, between Drumnadrochit and Urquhart Castle.

Drumbuie Farm   B&B ££
(☑01456-450634; www.loch-ness-farm.co.uk; Drumnadrochit; per person from £30; ⊙Mar-Oct; ℗) Drumbuie is a B&B in a modern house on a working farm – the surrounding fields are full of sheep and highland cattle – with views over Urquhart Castle and Loch Ness. Walkers and cyclists are welcome.

Loch Ness Backpackers Lodge   HOSTEL £
(☑01456-450807; www.lochness-backpackers .com; Coiltie Farmhouse, East Lewiston; per person from £16; ℗) This snug, friendly hostel housed in a cottage and barn has six-bed dorms, one double and a large barbecue area. It's about 0.75 miles from Drumnadrochit, along the A82 towards Fort William; turn left where

STRANGE SPECTACLE ON LOCH NESS

Highland folklore is filled with tales of strange creatures living in lochs and rivers, notably the kelpie (water horse) that lures unwary travellers to their doom. The use of the term 'monster', however, is a relatively recent phenomenon whose origins lie in an article published in the *Inverness Courier* on 2 May 1933, entitled 'Strange Spectacle on Loch Ness'.

The article recounted the sighting of a disturbance in the loch by Mrs Aldie Mackay and her husband: 'There the creature disported itself, rolling and plunging for fully a minute, its body resembling that of a whale, and the water cascading and churning like a simmering cauldron'.

The London newspapers couldn't resist. In December 1933 the *Daily Mail* sent Marmaduke Wetherall, a film director and big-game hunter, to Loch Ness to track down the beast. Within days he found 'reptilian' footprints in the shoreline mud (soon revealed to have been made with a stuffed hippopotamus foot, possibly an umbrella stand). Then in April 1934 came the famous 'long-necked monster' photograph taken by the seemingly reputable Harley St surgeon Colonel Kenneth Wilson. The press went mad and the rest, as they say, is history.

In 1994, however, Christian Spurling – Wetherall's stepson, by then 90 years old – revealed that the most famous photo of Nessie ever taken was in fact a hoax, perpetrated by his stepfather with Wilson's help. Today, of course, there are those who claim that Spurling's confession is itself a hoax. And, ironically, the researcher who exposed the surgeon's photo as a fake still believes wholeheartedly in the monster's existence.

Hoax or not, there's no denying that the bizarre mini-industry that has grown up around Loch Ness, and its mysterious monster since that eventful summer 80 years ago, is the strangest spectacle of all.

you see the sign for Loch Ness Inn, just before the bridge.

ⓘ Getting There & Away

Scottish Citylink and Stagecoach buses from Inverness to Fort William run along the shores of Loch Ness (six to eight daily, five on Sunday); those headed for Skye turn off at Invermoriston. There are bus stops at Drumnadrochit (£6.20, 30 minutes) and Urquhart Castle (£6.60, 35 minutes).

Fort Augustus

POP 500

Fort Augustus, at the junction of four old military roads, was originally a government garrison and the headquarters of General George Wade's road-building operations in the early 18th century. Today it's a neat and picturesque little place, often overrun by tourists in summer.

⊙ Sights & Activities

Caledonian Canal CANAL

At Fort Augustus, boats using the Caledonian Canal are raised and lowered 13m by a 'ladder' of five consecutive locks. It's fun to watch, and the neatly landscaped canal banks are a great place to soak up the sun or compare accents with fellow tourists.

The Caledonian Canal Heritage Centre (☑01320-366493; admission free; ⊗10am-5pm Apr-Oct), beside the lowest lock, showcases the history of the canal.

🛏 Sleeping & Eating

Lovat ⟨TOP CHOICE⟩ HOTEL £££

(☑01456-459250; www.thelovat.com; Main Rd; d from £121; P✿) A boutique-style makeover has transformed this former huntin'-and-shootin' hotel into a luxurious but ecoconscious retreat set apart from the tourist crush around the canal. The bedrooms are spacious and stylishly furnished, while the lounge is equipped with a log fire, comfy armchairs and grand piano.

There's an informal brasserie and a highly acclaimed restaurant (five-course dinner £45) which serves top quality cuisine.

Morag's Lodge HOSTEL £

(☑01320-366289; www.moragslodge.com; Bunoich Brae; dm/tw/f from £20/48/66; P@✿) This large and well-run hostel is based in a big Victorian house with great views of Fort Augustus' hilly surrounds, and has a convivial bar with open fire. It's hidden away in the trees up the steep side road just north of the tourist office car park.

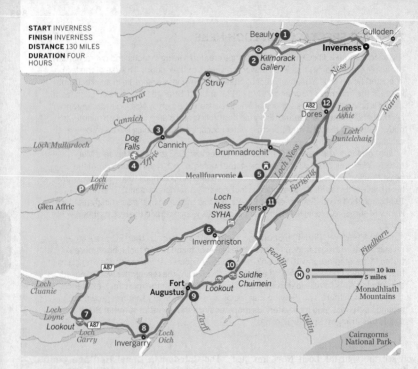

Beauly ● ❶
Culloden
Inverness ◉
❷ *Kilmorack Gallery*
Struy
Farrar
Ness
Cannich
[A82] ⓬
Dores *Loch Ashie*
❸ Cannich
Dog Falls
Loch Mullardoch
❹
Affric
Drumnadrochit
Loch Ness
Loch Duntelchaig
Meallfuarvonie ▲ ❺
Ⓟ *Affric*
Glen Affric
Farigaig
Loch Ness SYHA
Foyers ⓫
❻
Invermoriston
Fechlin
Findhorn
[A87]
⓾ *Suidhe Chuimein*
Ⓟ *Lookout*
0 — 10 km
0 — 5 miles
Ⓝ
Loch Cluanie
Fort Augustus ❾
Lookout
Monadhliath Mountains
Loch Loyne Lookout
[A87] ❼
❽ *Loch Oich*
Tarff
Cairngorms National Park
Loch Garry
Invergarry
Killin

Driving Tour
A Loch Ness Circuit

❯ Head out of Inverness on the A862 to Beauly, arriving in time for breakfast at ❶ **Corner on the Square** in Beauly. Backtrack a mile and turn right on the A831 to Cannich, passing ❷ **Kilmorack Gallery**, which exhibits contemporary art in a converted church. The scenery gets wilder as you approach ❸ **Cannich**; turn right and follow the singletrack road to the car park at ❹ **Dog Falls**. Take a stroll along the rushing river, or hike to the viewpoint (one-hour round trip) for a glimpse of remote Glen Affric.

Return to Cannich and turn right on the A831 to Drumnadrochit, then right on the A82 past picturesque ❺ **Urquhart Castle** and along the shores of Loch Ness. At ❻ **Invermoriston**, pause to look at the old bridge, built by Telford in 1813, then head west on the A897 towards Kyle of Lochalsh; after 16 miles go left on the A87 towards Invergarry. You are now among some of the

finest mountain scenery in the Highlands; as the road turns east above Loch Garry, stop at the famous ❼ **viewpoint** (layby on right, not signposted). By a quirk of perspective, the lochs to the west appear to form the map outline of Scotland.

At ❽ **Invergarry**, turn left on the A82 to reach ❾ **Fort Augustus** for a late lunch at the Lovat or Lock Inn. Take the B862 out of town, following the line of General Wade's 18th-century military road, to another viewpoint at ⓾ **Suidhe Chuimein**. A short (800m) walk up the well-worn path to the summit affords an even better panorama.

Ahead, you can choose the low road via the impressive ⓫ **Falls of Foyers**, or stay on the high road (B862) for more views; both converge on Loch Ness at the ⓬ **Dores Inn**, where you can sip a pint with a view along Loch Ness, and even stay for dinner before returning to Inverness.

Lock Inn   PUB **££**

(Canal Side; mains £9-14; ☺meals noon-8pm) A superb little pub right on the canal bank, the Lock Inn has a vast range of malt whiskies and a tempting menu of bar meals, which includes Orkney salmon, Highland venison and daily seafood specials; the house speciality is beer-battered haddock and chips.

ⓘ Information

There's an ATM and bureau de change (in the post office) beside the canal.

Fort Augustus tourist office (☎01320-366367; ☺9am-6pm Mon-Sat & 9am-5pm Sun Easter-Oct) In the central car park.

ⓘ Getting There & Away

Scottish Citylink and Stagecoach buses from Inverness to Fort William stop at Fort Augustus (£10.20, one hour, six to eight daily Monday to Saturday, five on Sunday).

THE CAIRNGORMS

The Cairngorms National Park (www .cairngorms.co.uk) encompasses the highest landmass in Britain – a broad mountain plateau, riven only by the deep valleys of the Lairig Ghru and Loch Avon, with an average altitude of over 1000m, and including five of the six highest summits in the UK. This wild mountain landscape of granite and heather has a sub-Arctic climate and supports rare alpine tundra vegetation and high-altitude bird species, such as snow bunting, ptarmigan and dotterel.

The harsh mountain environment gives way lower down to scenic glens softened by beautiful open forests of native Caledonian pine, home to rare animals and birds such as pine marten, wildcat, red squirrel, osprey, capercaillie and crossbill.

This is prime hill-walking territory, but even couch potatoes can enjoy a taste of the high life by taking the Cairngorm Mountain Railway up to the edge of the Cairngorm plateau.

Aviemore

POP 2400

Aviemore is the gateway to the Cairngorms, the region's main centre for transport, accommodation, restaurants and shopping. It's not the prettiest town in Scotland by a long stretch – the main attractions are in the surrounding area.

The Cairngorm skiing area and mountain railway lie 9 miles east of Aviemore along the B970 (Ski Rd) and its continuation through Coylumbridge and Glenmore.

◉ Sights & Activities

Strathspey Steam Railway   HERITAGE RAILWAY

(☎01479-810725; www.strathspeyrailway.co.uk; Station Sq; return ticket per adult/child £11.50/5.75) Strathspey Steam Railway runs steam trains on a section of restored line between Aviemore and Broomhill, 10 miles to the northeast, via Boat of Garten. There are four or five trains daily from June to September, and a more limited service in April, May, October and December.

An extension to Grantown-on-Spey is planned (see www.railstograntown.org); in the meantime, you can continue from Broomhill to Grantown-on-Spey by bus.

Rothiemurchus Estate   FOREST

(www.rothiemurchus.net) The Rothiemurchus Estate, which extends from the River Spey at Aviemore to the Cairngorm summit plateau, is famous for having Scotland's largest remnant of Caledonian forest, the ancient forest of Scots pine that once covered most of the country. The forest is home to a large population of red squirrels, and is one of the last bastions of the Scottish wildcat.

The Rothiemurchus visitor centre (☎01479-812345; admission free; ☺9am-5.30pm), a mile southeast of Aviemore along the B970, sells an Explorer Map detailing more than 50 miles of footpaths and cycling trails, including the wheelchair-accessible 4-mile trail around Loch an Eilein, with its ruined castle and peaceful pine woods.

Cairngorm Mountain   WINTER SPORTS

(www.cairngormmountain.org) Aspen or Val d'Isere it ain't, but with 19 runs and 23 miles of piste Cairngorm is Scotland's biggest ski area. A ski pass for one day is £31.50/19 for adults/under 16s. Ski or snowboard hire is around £22.50/16.50 per adult/child per day; there are lots of hire outlets at Coire Cas, Glenmore and Aviemore.

When the snow is at its best and the sun is shining you can close your eyes and imagine you're in the Alps; sadly, low cloud, high winds and horizontal sleet are more common. The season usually runs from December until the snow melts, which may be as late as the end of April, but snowfall here

INVERNESS & THE NORTHERN HIGHLANDS & ISLANDS AVIEMORE

The Cairngorms

is unpredictable – in some years the slopes can be open in November, but closed for lack of snow in February. During the season the tourist office displays snow conditions and avalanche warnings. You can check the latest snow conditions at http://ski.visitscotland.com and www.winterhighland.info.

🛏 Sleeping

Old Minister's House   B&B **££**
(☎01479-812181; www.theoldministershouse.co.uk; Rothiemurchus; s/d £70/110; [P][🛜]) This former manse dates from 1906 and has four rooms with a homely, country-farmhouse feel. It's in a lovely setting amid Scots pines on the banks of the River Druie, just 0.75 miles southeast of Aviemore.

Ardlogie Guest House   B&B **££**
(☎01479-810747; www.ardlogie.co.uk; Dalfaber Rd; s/d from £40/60, bothy per 3 nights £165; [P][🛜]) Handy for the train station, the five-room Ardlogie has great views over the River Spey towards the Cairngorms. There's also self-catering accommodation in the Bothy, a cosy, two-person timber cabin. Facilities include a boules pitch in the garden, and guests can get free use of the local country club's pool, spa and sauna.

Aviemore Bunkhouse   HOSTEL **£**
(☎01479-811181; www.aviemore-bunkhouse.com; Dalfaber Rd; dm/tw/f £17/55/65; [P][@][🛜]) This independent hostel provides accommodation in bright, modern six- or eight-bed dorms, each with private bathroom, and one twin/family room. There's a drying room, secure bike storage and wheelchair-accessible dorms. From the train station, cross the pedestrian bridge over the tracks, turn right and walk south on Dalfaber Rd.

Ravenscraig Guest House   B&B **££**
(☎01479-810278; www.aviemoreonline.com; Grampian Rd; r per person £35-42; [P][🛜]) Ravenscraig is a large, flower-bedecked Victorian villa with six spacious en-suite rooms, plus another six in a modern chalet at the back (one wheelchair accessible). It serves traditional and veggie breakfasts in an attractive conservatory dining room.

Aviemore SYHA   HOSTEL **£**
(☎01479-810345; www.syha.org.uk; 25 Grampian Rd; dm £18; [P][@][🛜]) Upmarket hostelling in a spacious, well-equipped building, five minutes' walk south of the village centre. There are four- and six-bed rooms, and a comfortable lounge with views of the mountains.

Rothiemurchus Camp
& Caravan Park
CAMPGROUND £

(☏01479-812800; www.rothiemurchus.net; Coylumbridge; sites per adult/child £9/2) The nearest camping ground to Aviemore is this year-round park set among Scots pines at Coylumbridge, 1.5 miles along the B970.

 Eating & Drinking

TOP CHOICE **Mountain Cafe**
CAFE £

(www.mountaincafe-aviemore.co.uk; 111 Grampian Rd; mains £4-10; ⊙8.30am-5pm Tue-Thu, to 5.30pm Fri-Mon; 🖳) The Mountain Cafe offers freshly prepared local produce with a Kiwi twist (owner is from NZ) – healthy breakfasts of muesli, porridge and fresh fruit (till 11.30am), hearty lunches of seafood chowder, burgers and imaginative salads, and home-baked breads, cakes and biscuits. Vegan, coeliac and nut-allergic diets are also catered for here.

Old Bridge Inn
PUB

(☏01479-811137; www.oldbridgeinn.co.uk; 23 Dalfaber Rd; 🛜) The Old Bridge has a snug bar, complete with roaring log fire in winter, and a cheerful, chalet-style restaurant (mains £9 to £18) at the back serving quality Scottish cuisine.

Café Mambo
CAFE, BAR

(The Mall, Grampian Rd; 🛜) The Mambo is a popular chill-out cafe in the afternoon, and turns into a clubbing and live-band venue in the evenings.

ℹ️ **Information**

Aviemore tourist office (☏01479-810363; www.visitaviemore.com; The Mall, Grampian Rd; ⊙9am-6pm Mon-Sat, 9.30am-5pm Sun Jul & Aug, 9am-5pm Mon-Sat, 10am-4pm Sun Easter-Jun, Sep & Oct) Hours are limited from October to Easter.

Caffe Bleu (www.caffebleu.com; Grampian Rd; per 30min £1; 🛜) Free wi-fi. Next door to the tourist office.

ℹ️ **Getting There & Away**

BUS Buses stop on Grampian Rd opposite the train station; buy tickets at the tourist office. Services include:

Edinburgh (£24.40, 3¾ hours, three daily)
Glasgow (£24.40, 3¾ hours, three daily)
Inverness (£5.50, 1¾ hours, three daily Monday to Friday) Via Grantown-on-Spey.
Perth (£18, two hours, five daily)

TRAIN Services include:
Glasgow/Edinburgh £44, three hours, six daily
Inverness £11, 40 minutes, 12 daily

ℹ️ **Getting Around**

BICYCLE Several places in Aviemore, Rothiemurchus Estate and Glenmore have mountain bikes for hire.

Bothy Bikes (☏01479-810111; www.bothybikes.co.uk; Ski Rd; ⊙9am-5.30pm) Charges £20 a day for a quality bike with front suspension and disc brakes.

BUS Bus 34 links Aviemore to Cairngorm car park (45 minutes, hourly) via Coylumbridge and Glenmore. A Strathspey Dayrider/Megarider ticket gives one/seven days unlimited bus travel (£6.40/16) from Aviemore as far as Cairngorm, Carrbridge and Kingussie (buy from the bus driver).

Around Aviemore

CAIRNGORM MOUNTAIN RAILWAY
Aviemore's most popular attraction is the Cairngorm Mountain Railway (☏01479-861261; www.cairngormmountain.org; adult/child return £9.95/6.50; ⊙10.20am-4pm May-Nov, 9am-4.30pm Dec-Apr) that will whisk you to the edge of Cairngorm plateau (1085m) in just eight minutes. The bottom station is at the Coire Cas car park at the end of Ski Rd; at the top is an exhibition, a shop (of course) and a restaurant. Unfortunately, for environmental and safety reasons, you're not allowed out of the top station in summer, not even to walk down – you must return to the car park on the funicular. However, a trial project launched in 2010 offers 90-minute guided walks to the summit (adult/child £13/10) four times a day from mid-July to October. Check the website for details.

LOCH MORLICH
Six miles east of Aviemore, Loch Morlich is surrounded by some 8 sq miles of pine and spruce forest that make up the Glenmore Forest Park. Its attractions include a sandy beach (at the east end) and a visitor centre with a small exhibition on the Caledonian forest.

👁️ **Sights & Activities**

Cairngorm Reindeer Centre
WILDLIFE PARK

(www.cairngormreindeer.co.uk; adult/child £10/5) The warden here will take you on a tour to see and feed Britain's only herd of reindeer, who are very tame and will even eat out of

INVERNESS & THE NORTHERN HIGHLANDS & ISLANDS AROUND AVIEMORE

MOUNTAIN WALKS IN THE CAIRNGORMS

The climb from the car park at the Coire Cas ski area to the summit of Cairn Gorm (1245m) takes about two hours (2 miles, one way). From there, you can continue south across the high-level plateau to Ben Macdui (1309m), Britain's second-highest peak another 3.5 miles). This takes eight to 10 hours return from the car park and is a serious undertaking; for experienced and well-equipped walkers only.

The Lairig Ghru trail, which can take eight to 10 hours, is a demanding 24-mile walk from Aviemore through the Lairig Ghru pass (840m) to Braemar. An alternative to doing the full route is to make the six-hour return hike up to the summit of the pass and back to Aviemore. The path starts from Ski Rd, a mile east of Coylumbridge, and involves some very rough going.

Warning – the Cairngorm plateau is a sub-Arctic environment where navigation is difficult and weather conditions can be severe, even in midsummer. Hikers must have proper hill-walking equipment, and know how to use a map and compass. In winter it is a place for experienced mountaineers only.

your hand. Walks take place at 11am, plus another at 2.30pm from May to September, and 3.30pm Monday to Friday in July and August.

Loch Morlich
Watersports Centre   WATERSPORTS
(www.lochmorlich.com; ⊙9am-5pm May-Oct) This popular outfit rents out Canadian canoes (£19 an hour), kayaks (£7.50), windsurfers (£16.50), sailing dinghies (£23) and rowing boats (£19), and also offers instruction.

TOP CHOICE Glenmore Lodge   ADVENTURE SPORTS
(www.glenmorelodge.org.uk) One of Britain's leading adventure sports training centres, offering courses in hill walking, rock climbing, ice climbing, canoeing, mountain biking and mountaineering. The centre's comfortable B&B accommodation (twin rooms £54 to £74) is available to all, even if you're not taking a course, as is the indoor-climbing wall, gym and sauna.

🛏 Sleeping

Cairngorm Lodge SYHA   HOSTEL £
(☏01479-861238; dm £18; ⊙closed Nov & Dec; @🛜) Set in a former shooting lodge that enjoys a great location at the east end of Loch Morlich; prebooking is essential.

Glenmore Caravan &
Camping Site   CAMPGROUND £
(☏01479-861271; www.campingintheforest.co.uk; tent & campervan sites £23; ⊙year-round) Campers can set up base at this attractive lochside site with pitches amid the Scots pines; rates include up to four people per tent/campervan.

BOAT OF GARTEN
Boat of Garten is known as the Osprey Village because these rare and beautiful birds of prey nest nearby at the RSPB Loch Garten Osprey Centre (☏01479-831694; www.rspb.org.uk/lochgarten; Tulloch; adult/child £4/2.50; ⊙10am-6pm Apr-Aug). The ospreys migrate here each spring from Africa and nest in a tall pine tree – you can watch from an upmarket hide via telescopes and videolink as the birds feed their young. The centre is signposted about 2 miles east of the village.

Boat of Garten is 6 miles northeast of Aviemore. The most interesting way to get here is on the Strathspey Steam Railway (p895).

Kingussie & Newtonmore

The gracious old Speyside towns of Kingussie (kin-*yew*-see) and Newtonmore, 2.5 miles apart, sit at the foot of the great heather-clad humps known as the Monadhliath Mountains. Newtonmore is best known as the home of the excellent Highland Folk Museum.

⊙ Sights & Activities

FREE **Highland Folk Museum**   MUSEUM
(☏01540-673551; www.highlandfolk.museum; Kingussie Rd, Newtonmore; ⊙10.30am-5.30pm Apr-Aug, 11am-4.30pm Sep & Oct) The open-air Highland Folk Museum comprises a collection of historical buildings and relics revealing many aspects of Highland culture and lifestyle. Laid out like a farming township, it has a community of traditional thatch-roofed cottages, a sawmill, a schoolhouse, a shepherd's bothy (hut) and a rural post

office. Actors in period costume give demonstrations of woodcarving, spinning and peat-fire baking. You'll need at least two to three hours to make the most of a visit here.

FREE Laggan Wolftrax   MOUNTAIN BIKING
(www.forestry.gov.uk/WolfTrax; Strathmashie Forest; ⊘10am-6pm Mon, 9.30am-5pm Tue, Thu & Fri, 9.30am-6pm Sat & Sun) Ten miles southwest of Newtonmore, on the A86 road towards Spean Bridge, this is one of Scotland's top mountain-biking centres with purpose-built trails ranging from open-country riding to black-diamond downhills with rock slabs and drop-offs. Bike hire is available on site from £25 a day for a hardtail mountain bike to £50 for a full-suspension bike.

🛏 Sleeping & Eating

TOP CHOICE Eagleview Guest House   B&B ££
(✆01540-673675;www.eagleviewguesthouse.co.uk; Perth Rd, Newtonmore; r per person £36-38; P@🛜) The family-friendly Eagleview is one of the nicest places to stay in the area, with beautifully decorated bedrooms, super-king-size beds, spacious bathrooms with power showers, and nice little touches like wall-mounted flatscreen TVs, cafetières with real coffee on your hospitality tray and real milk rather than that yucky UHT stuff.

Homewood Lodge   B&B ££
(✆01540-661507; www.homewood-lodge-kingussie .co.uk; Newtonmore Rd, Kingussie; r per person £25-30; P) This elegant Victorian lodge on the western outskirts of Kingussie offers double rooms with exquisite views of the Cairngorms – a nice way to wake up in the mornings! The owners are committed to recycling and energy efficiency, and have created a mini-nature reserve in the garden.

TOP CHOICE Cross   SCOTTISH £££
(✆01540-661166; www.thecross.co.uk; Tweed Mill Brae, off Ardbroilach Rd, Kingussie; 3-course dinner £55; ⊘dinner Tue-Sat, closed Jan; P) Housed in a converted water mill beside the Allt Mor burn, the Cross is one of the finest restaurants in the Highlands. The intimate, low-raftered dining room has an open fire and a patio overlooking the stream, and serves a daily-changing menu of fresh Scottish produce accompanied by a superb wine list.

If you want to stay the night, there are eight stylish rooms (double or twin £110 to £140) to choose from.

🛈 Getting There & Away

BUS Kingussie is served by Scottish Citylink buses:
Aviemore £7.20, 25 minutes, five to seven daily
Inverness £12.50, one hour, six to eight Monday to Saturday, three Sunday
Perth £15.20, 1¾ hours, five daily

TRAIN Kingussie's train station is at the southern end of town:
Edinburgh £44, 2½ hours, seven a day Monday to Saturday, two Sunday
Inverness £11, one hour, eight a day Monday to Saturday, four Sunday

CENTRAL WESTERN HIGHLANDS

This area extends from the bleak blanket-bog of the Moor of Rannoch to the west coast beyond Glen Coe and Fort William, and includes the southern reaches of the Great Glen. The scenery is grand, with high and wild mountains dominating the glens. Great expanses of moor alternate with lochs and patches of commercial forest. Fort William, at the inner end of Loch Linnhe, is the only sizable town in the area.

Since 2007 the region has been promoted as Lochaber Geopark (www.lochabergeopark .org.uk), an area of outstanding geology and scenery.

Glencoe

Scotland's most famous glen is also one of the grandest and, in bad weather, the grimmest. The southern side is dominated by three massive, brooding spurs, known as the Three Sisters, while the northern side is enclosed by the continuous steep wall of the knife-edged Aonach Eagach ridge. The main road threads its lonely way through the middle of all this mountain grandeur.

Glencoe village was written into the history books in 1692 when the resident MacDonalds were murdered by Campbell soldiers in what became known as the Glencoe Massacre.

🏃 Activities

There are several short, pleasant walks around Glencoe Lochan, near the village. A more strenuous hike, but well worth the effort on a fine day, is the climb to the Lost

Valley, a magical mountain sanctuary still haunted by the ghosts of the murdered Mac-Donalds (only 2.5 miles round trip, but allow three hours). A rough path from the car park at Allt na Reigh (on the A82, 6 miles east of Glencoe village) climbs up the wooded valley between Beinn Fhada and Gearr Aonach (the first and second of the Three Sisters) before emerging – quite unexpectedly – into a broad, open valley with an 800m-long meadow as flat as a football pitch.

A few miles east of Glencoe proper, on the south side of the A82, is the car park and base station for the Glencoe Mountain Resort (www.glencoemountain.com). The chairlift (adult/child £10/5; ⊗9.30am-4.30pm Thu-Mon) continues to operate in summer – there's a grand view over the Moor of Rannoch from the top station – and provides access to a downhill mountain-biking track. In winter a lift pass costs £30 a day and equipment hire is £25 a day.

GLENCOE VILLAGE
POP 360

The little village of Glencoe stands on the south shore of Loch Leven at the western end of the glen.

◉ Sights

Glencoe Folk Museum MUSEUM
(☑01855-811664; www.glencoemuseum.com; adult/child £3/free; ⊗10am-4.30pm Mon-Sat Easter-Oct) This small, thatched museum houses a varied collection of military memorabilia, farm equipment, and tools of the woodworking, blacksmithing and slate-quarrying trades.

Glencoe Visitor Centre VISITOR CENTRE
(NTS; ☑01855-811307; www.glencoe-nts.org.uk; adult/child £6/5; ⊗9.30am-5.30pm Easter-Oct, 10am-4pm Thu-Sun Nov-Easter) About 1.5 miles east of Glencoe village is this modern facility with an ecotourism angle. It provides comprehensive information on the geological, environmental and cultural history of Glencoe via high-tech interactive and audiovisual displays, charts the history of mountaineering in the glen, and tells the story of the Glencoe Massacre in all its gory detail.

🛏 Sleeping & Eating

TOP CHOICE Clachaig Inn HOTEL, PUB ££
(☑01855-811252; www.clachaig.com; s/d from £70/92; P🐾) The Clachaig has long been a favourite haunt of hill walkers and climbers. As well as comfortable en-suite accommodation, there's a smart, wood-panelled lounge bar with lots of sofas and armchairs, moun-

taineering photos, and climbing magazines to leaf through.

Climbers usually head for the lively Boots Bar on the other side of the hotel – it has log fires, serves real ale and good pub grub (mains £9 to £18), and has live Scottish, Irish and blues music on Friday and Saturday nights.

Glencoe Independent Hostel HOSTEL £
(☑01855-811906; www.glencoehostel.co.uk; dm £13-16.50, bunkhouse £11.50-13.50; P@🐾) This handily located hostel, just 10 minutes' walk from the Clachaig Inn, is set in an old farmhouse with six- and eight-bed dorms, and a bunkhouse with 16 more bed spaces in communal, Alpine-style bunks. There's also a cute little wooden cabin that sleeps up to three (£20 to £24 per person per night).

❶ Getting There & Away

Scottish Citylink buses run between Fort William and Glencoe (£7.50, 30 minutes, eight daily) and from Glencoe to Glasgow (£20, 2½ hours, eight daily). Buses stop at Glencoe village, Glencoe Visitor Centre, and Glencoe Mountain Resort.

Stagecoach bus 44 links Glencoe village with Fort William (35 minutes, hourly Monday to Saturday, three on Sunday) and Kinlochleven (25 minutes).

Kinlochleven
POP 900

Kinlochleven is hemmed in by high mountains at the head of the beautiful fjordlike Loch Leven, about 7 miles east of Glencoe village.

🏃 Activities

The final section of the West Highland Way stretches for 14 miles from Kinlochleven to Fort William. The village is also the starting point for easier walks up the glen of the River Leven, through pleasant woods to the Grey Mare's Tail waterfall, and harder mountain hikes into the Mamores.

If you fancy trying your hand at ice-climbing, even in the middle of summer, head for Ice Factor (☑01855-831100; www.ice-factor.co.uk; Leven Rd; ⊗9am-10pm Tue & Thu, to 7pm Mon, Wed & Fri-Sun; 🖶), the world's biggest indoor ice-climbing wall; a one-hour beginner's 'taster' session costs £30.

🛏 Sleeping & Eating

Blackwater Hostel HOSTEL, CAMPGROUND £
(☑01855-831253; www.blackwaterhostel.co.uk; Lab Rd; dm/tw £15/35, sites per person £7) This

40-bed hostel has spotless dorms with en-suite bathrooms and TV, and a level, well-sheltered camping ground.

 Lochleven Seafood Cafe   RESTAURANT **££**
(☎01855-821048; www.lochlevenseafoodcafe.co.uk; mains £10-22; ☺noon-9pm Wed-Sun) This outstanding place serves superb shellfish freshly plucked live from tanks – oysters on the half shell, razor clams, scallops, lobster and crab – plus a daily fish special and some nonseafood dishes. For warm days, there's an outdoor terrace with a view across the loch to the Pap of Glencoe, a distinctive conical mountain.

❶ Getting There & Away

Stagecoach bus 44 runs from Fort William to Kinlochleven (50 minutes, hourly Monday to Saturday, three on Sunday) via Ballachulish and Glencoe village.

Fort William

POP 9900

Basking on the shores of Loch Linnhe amid magnificent mountain scenery, Fort William has one of the most enviable settings in Scotland. If it wasn't for the busy dual carriageway crammed between the town centre and the loch, and one of the highest rainfall records in the country, it would be almost idyllic. Even so, the Fort has carved out a reputation as 'Outdoor Capital of the UK' (www.outdoorcapital.co.uk), and its easy rail and bus access makes it a good base for exploring the surrounding mountains and glens.

◉ Sights

West Highland Museum   MUSEUM
(☎01397-702169; www.westhighlandmuseum.org.uk; Cameron Sq; ☺10am-5pm Mon-Sat Apr-Oct, to 4pm Mar & Oct-Dec, closed Jan & Feb) This fascinating museum is packed with Highland memorabilia. Look out for the secret portrait of Bonnie Prince Charlie – after the Jacobite rebellions all things Highland were banned, including pictures of the exiled leader, and this tiny painting looks like a smear of paint until viewed in a cylindrical mirror, which reflects a credible likeness of the prince.

☞ Tours

Crannog Cruises   WILDLIFE CRUISE
(☎01397-700714; adult/child £10/5; ☺four daily) Operates 1½-hour wildlife cruises on Loch Linnhe, visiting a seal colony and a salmon farm.

 Festivals & Events

UCI Mountain Bike World Cup   MOUNTAIN BIKING
(www.fortwilliamworldcup.co.uk) In June, Fort William pulls in crowds of more than 18,000 spectators for this World Cup downhill mountain-biking event. The gruelling downhill course is at nearby Nevis Range ski area.

⌐ Sleeping

It's best to book well ahead in summer, especially for hostels.

Lime Tree   HOTEL **££**
(☎01397-701806; www.limetreefortwilliam.co.uk; Achintore Rd; s/d from £80/110; ℗) Much more interesting than your average guesthouse, this former Victorian manse overlooking Loch Linnhe is an 'art gallery with rooms', decorated with the artist-owner's atmospheric Highland landscapes. Foodies rave about the restaurant, and the gallery space – a triumph of sensitive design – stages everything from serious exhibitions (works by David Hockney and Andy Goldsworthy have appeared) to folk concerts.

Grange   B&B **££**
(☎01397-705516; www.grangefortwilliam.com; Grange Rd; r per person £58-63; ℗) An exceptional 19th-century villa set in its own landscaped grounds, the Grange is crammed with antiques and fitted with log fires, chaise longues and Victorian roll-top baths. The Turret Room, with its window seat in the turret overlooking Loch Linnhe, is our favourite. It's 500m southwest of the centre.

St Andrew's Guest House   B&B **££**
(☎01397-703038; www.standrewsguesthouse.co.uk; Fassifern Rd; r per person £24-30; ℗☏) Set in a lovely 19th-century building that was once a rectory and choir school, St Andrew's retains period features, such as carved masonry, wood panelling and stained-glass windows. It has six spacious bedrooms, some with stunning views.

Fort William Backpackers   HOSTEL **£**
(☎01397-700711; www.scotlands-top-hostels.com; Alma Rd; dm/tw £18/47; ℗@☏) A 10-minute walk from the bus and train stations, this lively and welcoming hostel is set in a grand Victorian villa, perched on a hillside with great views over Loch Linnhe.

INVERNESS & THE NORTHERN HIGHLANDS & ISLANDS FORT WILLIAM

Bank Street Lodge   HOSTEL £

(☎01397-700070; www.bankstreetlodge.co.uk; Bank St; dm/tw £16/52) Part of a modern hotel and restaurant complex, the Bank Street Lodge offers the most central budget beds in town, only 250m from the train station. It has kitchen facilities and a drying room.

✖ Eating & Drinking

Lime Tree   SCOTTISH £££

(☎01397-701806; www.limetreefortwilliam.co.uk; Achintore Rd; 2-/3-course dinner £28/30; ⊙dinner daily, lunch Sun) Fort William is not over-endowed with great places to eat, but the restaurant at this small hotel and art gallery has put the UK's Outdoor Capital on the gastronomic map. The chef won a Michelin star in his previous restaurant, and turns out delicious dishes built around fresh Scottish produce, such as seared saddle of Glenfinnan venison with red wine and rosemary jus.

Crannog Seafood Restaurant   SEAFOOD ££

(☎01397-705589; www.crannog.net; Town Pier; mains £16-20) The Crannog wins the prize for best location in town – perched on the Town Pier, giving window-table diners an uninterrupted view down Loch Linnhe. Informal and unfussy, it specialises in fresh seafood – there are three or four daily fish specials plus the main menu – though there are beef, poultry and vegetarian dishes, too. Two-course lunch £13.

Sugar and Spice   CAFE £

(☎01397-705005; 147 High St; mains £7-9; ⊙10am-5pm Mon-Sat, 6-9pm Thu-Sat; 🌱🍴) Enjoy what is probably the best coffee in town at this colourful cafe, just a few paces from the official finishing line of the West Highland Way. In the evening it serves authentic Thai dishes.

Grog & Gruel   PUB

(☎01397-705078; www.grogandgruel.co.uk; 66 High St; ⊙bar meals noon-9pm) The Grog & Gruel is a traditional-style, wood-panelled pub with an excellent range of cask ales from regional Scottish and English microbreweries.

ⓘ Information

Fort William tourist office (☎01397-703781; www.visithighlands.com; 15 High St; internet per 20min £1; ⊙9am-6pm Mon-Sat, 10am-5pm Sun Apr-Sep, limited hours Oct-Mar) Tourist info and internet access.

ⓘ Getting There & Away

Bus

Both bus and train station are next to the huge Morrisons supermarket, reached from the town centre via an underpass next to the Nevisport shop.

Scottish Citylink (☎0871 266 3333; www.citylink.co.uk) buses link Fort William with other major towns and cities. **Shiel Buses** (www.shielbuses.co.uk) service No. 500 runs to Mallaig (1½ hours, three daily Monday to Friday only) via Glenfinnan (30 minutes) and Arisaig (one hour). Other services:

Edinburgh (£33, 4½ hours, one daily direct, seven with a change at Glasgow) Via Glencoe and Crianlarich.

Glasgow (£22, three hours, eight daily)

Inverness (£12, two hours, five daily)

Oban (£9.40, 1½ hours, three daily)

Portree (£28.60, three hours, four daily)

Train

The spectacular **West Highland line** runs from Glasgow to Mallaig via Fort William. The overnight **Caledonian Sleeper** service connects Fort William and London Euston (£103 sharing a twin-berth cabin, 13 hours).

There's no direct rail connection between Oban and Fort William – you have to change at Crianlarich, so it's faster to use the bus.

Edinburgh (£44, five hours, three daily) Change at Glasgow's Queen St station.

Glasgow (£26.30, 3¾ hours, three daily, two on Sunday)

Mallaig (£11, 1½ hours, four daily, three on Sunday)

ⓘ Getting Around

Bicycle

Alpine Bikes (☎01397-704008; www.alpinebikes.com; 117 High St; ⊙9am-5.30pm Mon-Sat, 10am-5.30pm Sun) Rents out mountain bikes for £12/20 for a half-/day.

Bus

The Fort Dayrider ticket (£3) gives unlimited travel for one day on Stagecoach bus services in the Fort William area. Buy from the bus driver.

Around Fort William

GLEN NEVIS

You can walk the 3 miles from Fort William to scenic Glen Nevis in about an hour or so. The Glen Nevis visitor centre (☎01397-705922; www.bennevisweather.co.uk; ⊙9am-5pm Apr-Oct, shorter hours in winter) is situated 1.5 miles up the glen, and provides informa-

CLIMBING BEN NEVIS

As the highest peak in the British Isles, Ben Nevis (1344m) attracts many would-be ascensionists who would not normally think of climbing a Scottish mountain – a staggering (often literally) 100,000 people reach the summit each year.

Although anyone who is reasonably fit should have no problem hiking to the summit of Ben Nevis on a fine summer's day, an ascent should not be undertaken lightly. Every year people have to be rescued from the mountain. You will need proper walking boots (the path is rough and stony, and there may be soft, wet snowfields on the summit), warm clothing, waterproofs, a map and compass, and plenty of food and water. And don't forget to check the weather forecast (see www.bennevisweather.co.uk).

In thick cloud, visibility at the summit can be 10m or less; and in such conditions the only safe way off the mountain requires careful use of a map and compass to avoid walking over 700m cliffs.

There are three possible starting points for the tourist track (the walkers' route) ascent – Achintee Farm; the footbridge at Glen Nevis Youth Hostel; and the car park at Glen Nevis Visitor Centre. The path climbs gradually to the shoulder at Lochan Meall an t-Suidhe (known as the Halfway Lochan), then zigzags steeply up beside the Red Burn to the summit plateau.

The total distance to the summit and back is 8 miles; allow at least four or five hours to reach the top, and another 2½ to three hours for the descent. Afterwards, as you celebrate in the pub with a pint, consider the fact that the record time for the annual Ben Nevis Hill Race is just under 1½ hours – up *and* down. Then have another pint.

tion on walking as well as specific advice on climbing Ben Nevis.

From the car park at the far end of the road along Glen Nevis, there is an excellent 1.5-mile walk through the spectacular Nevis Gorge to Steall Meadows, a verdant valley dominated by a 100m-high bridal-veil waterfall. You can reach the foot of the falls by crossing the river on a wobbly, three-cable wire bridge – one cable for your feet and one for each hand – a real test of balance!

Sleeping & Eating

TOP CHOICE Ben Nevis Inn
HOSTEL £

(✆01397-701227; www.ben-nevis-inn.co.uk; Achintee; dm £15.50; ☺noon-11pm daily Apr-Oct, Thu-Sun only Nov-Mar; P) This great barn of a pub (real ale and tasty bar meals available; mains £9 to £16), has a comfy 24-bed hostel downstairs. It's at the Achintee start of the path up Ben Nevis, and only a mile from the end of the West Highland Way. Food served noon to 9pm.

Achintee Farm
B&B, HOSTEL £

(✆01397-702240; www.achinteefarm.com; Achintee; B&B s/d £60/78, hostel dm/tw £17/38; P🐾) This attractive farmhouse offers excellent B&B accommodation and also has a small hostel attached. It's just 100m from the Ben Nevis Inn, and ideally positioned for climbing Ben Nevis.

Glen Nevis Caravan & Camping Park
CAMPGROUND £

(✆01397-702191; www.glen-nevis.co.uk; tent sites £7, tent & car sites £11, campervan £11.90, per person £3.20; ☺mid-Mar–Oct) This big, well-equipped site is a popular base camp for Ben Nevis and the surrounding mountains.

❶ Getting There & Away

Bus 41 runs from Fort William bus station up Glen Nevis (10 minutes, two daily year round, five daily Monday to Saturday June to September). Check at the tourist office for the latest timetable, which is liable to alteration.

NEVIS RANGE

The Nevis Range ski area (✆01397-705825; www.nevisrange.co.uk; gondola return trip per adult/child £11.25/6.50; ☺10am-5pm summer, 9am-5pm winter), 6 miles north of Fort William, spreads across the northern slopes of Aonach Mor (1221m). The gondola that gives access to the bottom of the ski area at 655m operates year-round from 10am to 5pm; a return trip costs £10.50/6 for an adult/child (15 minutes each way). At the top there's a restaurant and a couple of walking routes through nearby Leanachan Forest. During the ski season a one-day lift pass costs £28/16.50 per adult/child; a one-day package, including equipment hire, lift pass and two hours' instruction, costs £62.

A world championship downhill mountain-bike trail (⊙11am-3pm mid-May–mid-Sep) – for experienced riders only – runs from the Snowgoose restaurant to the base station; bikes are carried on a rack on the gondola cabin. A single trip with your own bike costs £12; full-suspension bike hire costs from £40/70 per half-/full day depending on the bike. There are also 25 miles of waymarked mountain-bike trails in the nearby forest.

Bus 41 runs from Fort William bus station to Nevis Range (15 minutes, five daily Monday to Saturday, three on Sunday, limited service October to April). Check at the tourist office for the latest timetable, which is liable to alteration.

ROAD TO THE ISLES
The 46-mile A830 from Fort William to Mallaig is traditionally known as the Road to the Isles, as it leads to the jumping-off point for ferries to the Small Isles and Skye, itself a stepping stone to the Outer Hebrides.

GLENFINNAN
POP 100
Glenfinnan is hallowed ground for fans of Bonnie Prince Charlie; the monument here marks where he raised his Highland army. It is also a place of pilgrimage for Harry Potter fans – the famous railway viaduct features in the films.

By the monument, the Glenfinnan Visitor Centre (NTS; adult/child £3.50/2.50; ⊙9.30am-5.30pm Jul & Aug, 10am-5pm Easter-Jun, Sep & Oct) recounts the story of the '45, as the Jacobite rebellion of 1745 is known, when the prince's loyal clansmen marched and fought from Glenfinnan south to Derby, then back north to final defeat at Culloden.

WORTH A TRIP

GLENUIG INN

Set on a peaceful bay on the Arisaig coast, halfway between Lochailort and Acharacle on the A830 road, the recently renovated Glenuig Inn (☎01687-470219; www.glenuig.com; B&B s/d/q from £60/95/125, bunkhouse per person £25; P☎) is a great place to get away from it all. As well as offering comfortable accommodation, good food (mains £9 to £19), and real ale on tap, it's a great base for exploring Arisaig, Morar and the Loch Shiel area.

ARISAIG & MORAR
The 5 miles of coast between Arisaig and Morar is a fretwork of rocky islets, inlets and gorgeous silver-sand beaches backed by dunes and machair, with stunning sunset views across the sea to the silhouetted peaks of Eigg and Rum. The Silver Sands of Morar, as they are known, draw crowds of bucket-and-spade holidaymakers in July and August, when the many camping grounds scattered along the coast are filled to overflowing.

Built as a hunting lodge in 1840, Garramore House (☎01687-450268; r per person £25-35; ❀P) served as a Special Operations Executive HQ during WWII. Today it's a wonderfully atmospheric, child- and pet-friendly guesthouse set in lovely woodland gardens with resident peacocks and great views to the Small Isles and Skye.

MALLAIG
POP 800
If you're travelling between Fort William and Skye, you may find yourself overnighting in the bustling fishing and ferry port of Mallaig. The village's rainy-day attractions are limited to the Mallaig Heritage Centre (☎01687-462085; www.mallaigheritage.org.uk; Station Rd; adult/child £2/free; ⊙9.30am-4.30pm Mon-Fri, noon-4pm Sat & Sun) which covers the archaeology and history of the region, including the heart-rending tale of the Highland Clearances in Knoydart (p912).

🛏 Sleeping & Eating
Seaview Guest House   B&B ££
(☎01687-462059; www.seaviewguesthousemallaig.com; Main St; r per person £28-35; ⊙Mar-Nov; P) Just beyond the tourist office, this comfortable three-bedroom B&B has grand views over the harbour, not only from the upstairs bedrooms but also from the breakfast room. There's also a cute little cottage next door that offers self-catering accommodation (www.selfcateringmallaig.com; one double and one twin room) for £350 to £450 a week.

TOP CHOICE Fish Market Restaurant   SEAFOOD ££
(☎01687-462299; Station Rd; mains £9-21) At least half-a-dozen signs in Mallaig advertise 'seafood restaurant', but this bright, modern, bistro-style place next to the harbour is our favourite, serving simply prepared scallops with smoked salmon and savoy cabbage, grilled langoustines with garlic butter, and fresh Mallaig haddock fried in breadcrumbs, as well as the tastiest Cullen skink on the west coast.

Upstairs is a coffee shop (mains £5-6; ⊙11am-5pm) that serves delicious hot roast-beef rolls with horseradish sauce, and scones with clotted cream and jam.

Tea Garden   CAFE £

(☎01687-462764; www.mallaigbackpackers.co.uk; Harbour View; mains £6-12; ⊙9am-6pm) On a sunny day the Tea Garden's terrace cafe, with its flowers, greenery and cosmopolitan backpacker staff, can feel more like the Med than Mallaig. The coffee is good, and the speciality of the house is a pint glass full of Mallaig prawns with dipping sauce (£12.50). From late May to September the cafe opens in the evening with a bistro menu.

❶ Getting There & Away

BOAT Ferries run from Mallaig to the Isle of Skye; see the transport info for Skye for more (p920).

BUS Shiel Buses (www.shielbuses.co.uk) bus 500 runs from Fort William to Mallaig (1½ hours, three daily Monday to Friday, one on Saturday) via Glenfinnan (30 minutes) and Arisaig (one hour).

TRAIN The West Highland line runs between Fort William and Mallaig (£11, 1½ hours) four times a day (three on Sunday).

NORTHEAST COAST

In both landscape and character, the east coast is where the real barrenness of the Highlands begins to unfold. While the interior is dominated by the vast and mournful Sutherland mountain range, along the coast great heather-covered hills heave themselves out of the wild North Sea. Rolling farmland drops suddenly into the icy waters, and small, historic towns are moored precariously on the coast's edge.

Tain

POP 3500

Scotland's oldest royal burgh, Tain is a proud sandstone town that rose to prominence as pilgrims descended to venerate the relics of St Duthac.

◉ Sights

Tain Through Time   MUSEUM

(☎01862-894089; www.tainmuseum.org.uk; Tower St; adult/child £3.50/2.50; ⊙10am-5pm Mon-Fri Apr-Oct, also Sat Jun-Aug) Set in the grounds of St Duthus Church is Tain Through Time, an entertaining heritage centre with a colourful and educational display on St Duthac, King James IV and key moments in Scottish history. Another building focuses on the town's fine silversmithing tradition. Admission includes an audio-guided walk around town.

Glenmorangie Distillery   DISTILLERY

(www.glenmorangie.com; tours £2.50; ⊙10am-5pm Mon-Fri, plus 10am-4pm Sat & noon-4pm Sun Jun-Aug) Located on Tain's northern outskirts, the distillery Glenmorangie (emphasis on the second syllable) produces a fine light malt, which is subjected to a number of different cask finishes for variation. The tour is less in-depth than some but finishes with a free dram.

🛏 Sleeping & Eating

Golf View House   B&B ££

(☎01862-892856; www.bedandbreakfasttain.co.uk; 13 Knockbreck Rd; s/d £50/70; P🅿🛜) Set in an old manse in a secluded location just off the main road through town, this spot offers magnificent views over fields and water. The impeccable rooms are very cheerful and bright, and there's an upbeat feel, with delicious breakfasts and welcoming hospitality. It's worth the extra fiver for a room with a view.

Royal Hotel   HOTEL ££

(☎01862-892013; www.royalhoteltain.co.uk; High St; s/d £50/85; 🛜🛁) So much the heart of town that the main street has to detour around it, the Royal Hotel has undergone a refurbishment that has left its good-sized rooms looking very spruce. For only a tenner more, you get a four-poster room in the old part of the hotel. The restaurant is the best in town and bar meals are also decent.

❶ Getting There & Away

Stagecoach buses run to Tain (£8.50, 50 minutes, roughly hourly) from Inverness; three daily continue north as far as Thurso.

There are up to three trains daily to Inverness (£12.60, 1¼ hours) and Thurso (£15.40, 2¾ hours).

Bonar Bridge & Around

The A9 crosses the Dornoch Firth, on a bridge and causeway, near Tain. An alternative route goes around the firth via the tiny settlements of Ardgay and Bonar Bridge, where the A836 to Lairg branches west.

From Ardgay, a single-track road leads 10 miles up Strathcarron to Croick, the scene of notorious evictions during the 1845 Clearances. You can still see the evocative messages scratched by refugee crofters from Glencalvie on the eastern windows of Croick Church.

Opulent Carbisdale Castle SYHA (☏01549-421232; www.syha.org.uk; dm/s/d £21/26/52; ☺mid-Mar–Oct; 🅿@🛜), 10 minutes' walk north of Culrain train station, was built in 1914 for the dowager duchess of Sutherland, but is now Scotland's biggest and most luxurious hostel, its halls studded with statues and dripping with opulence (advance bookings are highly recommended). Kick back in the super-elegant library room or cook up a feast in the kitchen; catered meals (£12 for a three-course dinner) are also available. There are mountain-biking trails alongside. At time of research the hostel was closed for extensive refurbishment.

Trains running from Inverness to Thurso stop at Culrain (£15.20, 1½ hours, four Monday to Saturday, one Sunday), half a mile from Carbisdale Castle.

Dornoch

POP 1200

On the north shore of the Dornoch Firth, 2 miles from the A9, this attractive market town is one of the most pleasant settlements on the east coast. Dornoch is best known for its championship golf course, but there are some fine old buildings, including Dornoch Cathedral. Among other historical oddities, the last witch to be executed in Scotland was boiled alive in hot tar here in 1722.

◉ Sights

If you've struck Dornoch on a sunny day make sure you have a walk along its golden sand beach, which stretches for miles.

FREE Dornoch Cathedral CHURCH
(www.dornoch-cathedral.com; St Gilbert St; ☺9am–7pm or later) Consecrated in the 13th century, Dornoch Cathedral is an elegant Gothic edifice with an interior softly illuminated through modern stained-glass windows. By the western door is the sarcophagus of Sir Richard de Moravia, who died fighting the Danes at the battle of Embo in the 1260s. Until he met his maker, the battle had been going rather well for him; he'd managed to slay the Danish commander with the unattached leg of a horse that was to hand.

🛏 Sleeping & Eating

TOP CHOICE Dornoch Castle Hotel HOTEL ££
(☏01862-810216; www.dornochcastlehotel.com; Castle St; s/d £73/123, superior/deluxe d £169/250;

🅿🛜) This 16th-century former bishop's palace makes a wonderful place to stay, particularly if you upgrade to one of the superior rooms, which have views, space, malt whisky and chocolates on the welcome tray, and, in some cases, four-poster beds; the deluxe rooms are unforgettable. Cheaper rooms (s/d £50/65) are also available in adjoining buildings. In the evening, toast your toes in the cosy bar before dining in style at the first-rate restaurant (three-course dinner £32.50) tucking into dishes featuring plenty of game and seasonal produce. The restaurant's open for lunch and dinner; bar meals are also available during the day.

Trevose Guest House B&B ££
(☏01862-810269; jamackenzie@tiscali.co.uk; Cathedral Sq; s/d £30/60; ☺Mar–Sep; 🛜🐾) First impressions deceive at Trevose Guest House, a lovely stone cottage right by the cathedral. It looks compact but actually boasts very spacious rooms with significant comfort and well-loved old wooden furnishings. Character oozes from every pore of the place and a benevolent welcome is a given.

ℹ Information

The **tourist office** (☏01862-810594; Castle St; ☺9am-12.30pm & 1.30-5pm Mon-Fri, also 10am-4pm Sat May-Aug & 10am-4pm Sun Jul-Aug) is in the Highland Council Building next to Dornoch Castle Hotel.

ℹ Getting There & Away

There are buses roughly hourly from Inverness to Dornoch, with some services continuing north to Wick or Thurso.

Dunrobin Castle

Mighty Dunrobin Castle (☏01408-633177; www.dunrobincastle.co.uk; adult/child £9.50/5.50; ☺10.30am-4.30pm Mon-Sat, noon-4.30pm Sun Apr, May & Sep–mid-Oct, 10.30am-5.30pm Jun-Aug) is the largest house in the Highlands (187 rooms). Although it dates back to around 1275, most of what you see today was built in French style between 1845 and 1850. One of the homes of the earls and dukes of Sutherland, it's richly furnished and offers an intriguing insight into their opulent lifestyle. The pitiless first Duke of Sutherland cleared 15,000 people from the north of Scotland while residing here.

Only 22 rooms are on display, with hunting trophies much to the fore. The museum offers an eclectic mix of archaeological finds, natural-history exhibits, more non-PC animal remains and an excellent collection of Pictish stones found in Sutherland. The formal gardens host impressive falconry displays two or three times a day.

Buses between Inverness and Thurso stop in Golspie, one mile to the south of the castle. There are also trains from Inverness (£16.90, 2¼ hours, two or three daily) to Golspie and to Dunrobin Castle.

Helmsdale

POP 900

Surrounded by hills whose gorse explodes mad yellow in springtime, this sheltered fishing town, like many spots on this coast, was a major emigration point during the Clearances and also a booming herring port. It's surrounded by stunning, undulating coastline and the River Helmsdale is one of the best salmon rivers in the Highlands.

In the centre of town, Timespan (www .timespan.org.uk; Dunrobin St; adult/child £4/2; ☉10am-5pm Mon-Sat, noon-5pm Sun Mar-Oct, 11am-4pm Sat & Sun, 2-4pm Tue Nov-Feb) has an impressive display covering local history (including the 1869 gold rush) and Barbara Cartland, late queen of romance novels, who was a Helmsdale regular. There are also local art exhibitions, a geology garden and a cafe.

🛏 Sleeping & Eating

TOP CHOICE Bridge Hotel   HOTEL ££
(☎01431-821100; www.bridgehotel.net; Dunrobin St; s/d £77/117; 🐾🅿) Ideally located and exceptionally welcoming, this early-19th-century coaching inn is the smartest place to stay and the best place to eat in town. It's proud of its Highland heritage, and displays a phalanx of antlers. The guest lounge has to be seen to be believed: it's a Who's Who of the dead-deer world, but they all have their backstory: ask at reception. The rooms don't have the expected patina of age; they have wonderfully plush fabrics and a smart contemporary feel; there's a handsome suite that's ideal for families. The downstairs bar, with impressive whisky selection, and restaurant (April to mid-October only, closed Mondays) hum with good cheer and relaxed hospitality.

Helmsdale Hostel   HOSTEL £
(☎01431-821636; www.helmsdalehostel.co.uk; Stafford St; dm/tw/f £17.50/40/60; ☉Apr-Sep; 🐾) This caringly run hostel is in very good nick and makes a cheerful, comfortable budget base for exploring Caithness. The dorm berths are mostly cosy single beds rather than bunks, and the en suite rooms are great for families. The lofty kitchen-lounge space has a wood stove and good kitchen.

La Mirage   BISTRO £
(☎01431-821615; www.lamirage.org; 7 Dunrobin St; mains £7-12; ☉11am-8.45pm Mon-Sat, from noon Sun) Created in homage to Barbara Cartland by the larger-than-life late owner, this minor legend is a medley of pink flamboyance, faded celebrity photos and show tunes. The meals aren't gourmet – think chicken Kiev – but portions are huge and very tasty, especially the excellent fish and chips (also available to take away: eat 'em down on the pretty harbour).

❶ Getting There & Away

Buses from Inverness (£10.80, 2¾ hours, six daily) and Thurso (£12.50, 1¼ hours, six daily) stop in Helmsdale as do trains (from Inverness £16.90, 2½ hours, two to three daily).

CAITHNESS

Once you pass Helmsdale, you are entering Caithness, a place of jagged gorse-and-grass-topped cliffs hiding tiny fishing harbours. This top corner of Scotland was Viking territory, historically more connected to Orkney and Shetland than to the rest of the mainland. It's a magical and mystical land with an ancient aura, peopled by wise folk with long memories who are fiercely proud of their corner of Scotland.

Helmsdale to Wick

Lybster is a purpose-built fishing village dating from 1810, with a stunning harbour area surrounded by grassy cliffs. In its heyday, it was Scotland's third busiest port.

There are several interesting prehistoric sites near Lybster. Five miles to the northwest, on the minor road to Achavanich, just south of Loch Stemster, are the unsigned 30 Achavanich Standing Stones. In a desolate setting, these crumbling monuments of the distant past still capture the imagination with their evocative location.

A mile east of Lybster on the A99, a turn-off leads 4 miles north to the Grey Cairns of Camster. Dating from between 4000

BC and 2500 BC, these burial chambers are hidden in long, low mounds rising from an evocatively desolate stretch of moor.

Back on the A99, the Hill o'Many Stanes, 2 miles beyond the Camster turn-off, is a curious, fan-shaped arrangement of 22 rows of small stones that probably date from around 2000 BC.

Stagecoach buses between Thurso and Inverness run via Lybster (one hour, up to four daily). There's also a coastal service from Wick to Helmsdale stopping here.

Wick

POP 7300

More gritty than pretty, Wick has been down on its luck since the collapse of the herring industry. It was once the world's largest fish port for the 'silver darlings', but when the market dropped off after WWII, job losses were huge and the town hasn't totally recovered. It's worth a look, particularly for its excellent museum, which puts everything in context, and its attractive spruced-up harbour area.

SIGHTS & ACTIVITIES

TOP CHOICE Wick Heritage Centre   MUSEUM
(☑01955-605393; www.wickheritage.org; 20 Bank Row; adult/child £4/50p; ☺10am-5pm Mon-Sat Apr-Oct, last entry 3.45pm) Tracking the rise and fall of the herring industry, this great town museum displays everything from fishing equipment to complete herring boats. It's absolutely huge inside, crammed with memorabilia and extensive displays describing Wick's heyday in the mid-19th century.

The Johnston photographic collection is the museum's star exhibit. From 1863 to 1977, three generations of Johnstons photographed everything that happened around Wick, and the 70,000 photographs are an amazing portrait of the town's life.

Caithness Seacoast   BOAT TOUR
(☑01955-609200; www.caithness-seacoast.co.uk) Wick's a boat town, and this outfit will take you out to sea to inspect the rugged coastline of the northeast. There are various options, from a half-hour jaunt (adult/child £17/11) to a three-hour trip down to Lybster and back (adult/child £45/35).

Sleeping & Eating

Quayside   B&B £
(☑01955-603229; www.quaysidewick.co.uk; 25 Harbour Quay; s/d without breakfast £30/55; P 🕲)

Quayside should be your first port of call for guesthouse accommodation.The owners couldn't be more helpful – they've been in the business for many years and know what they're doing. Right by the harbour, it's handy for everything worth seeing in town. Spruce rooms have kitchenettes and can be taken at B&B or bed-only rates. There's a handy family room, and self-catering flats available too, plus good facilities for cyclists and motorcyclists. Book ahead.

Mackays Hotel   HOTEL ££
(☑01955-602323; www.mackayshotel.co.uk; Union St; s/d £89/119; 🕲) The renovated Mackays is Wick's best hotel. Rooms vary in layout and size, so ask to see a few; prices drop if you're staying more than one night, and walk-up prices are usually quite a bit lower than the rack rates we list here. On-site No 1 Bistro (Union St; mains £12-18) is a fine option for lunch or dinner. The 2.06m-long Ebenezer Pl, the world's shortest street, runs past one end of the hotel.

Bord de l'Eau   FRENCH ££
(☑01955-604400; 2 Market St; mains £14-18; ☺lunch Tue-Sat, dinner Tue-Sun) This serene, relaxed French restaurant is the best place to eat in Wick. It overlooks the river and serves a changing menu of mostly meat and game French classics, backed up by daily fish specials. Starters are great value, and the pricier mains come with a huge assortment of vegetables, so you won't go hungry here. The conservatory dining room overlooking the river is lovely on a sunny evening.

ⓘ Information

Wick information centre (www.visithighlands.com; 66 High St; ☺9am-5.30pm Mon-Sat) Good selection of information; upstairs in McAllans Clothing Store.

Wick Carnegie Library (☑01955-602864; www.highland.gov.uk; Sinclair Tce; ☺Mon-Sat; 🕲) Free internet access.

ⓘ Getting There & Away

Wick is a transport gateway to the region.

AIR Flybe (☑0871 700 2000; www.flybe.com) flies between Edinburgh and Wick airport once daily except Saturday. Eastern Airways (☑0870 366 9989; www.easternairways.com) flies to Aberdeen (three Monday to Friday).

BUS Stagecoach (www.stagecoachbus.com) and Citylink (☑0871 266 33 33; www.citylink.co.uk) operate buses to/from Inverness (£18.30, three hours, six daily) and Thurso (30 minutes, hourly). There's also connecting service to John O'Groats (40 minutes, two to three daily) for the passenger ferry to Burwick, Orkney, and to the Gills Bay ferry to St Margaret's Hope, Orkney.

TRAIN Trains service Wick from Inverness (£18, 4¼ hours, four daily).

John O'Groats

POP 500

Though it's not the northernmost point of the British mainland (that's Dunnet Head), John O'Groats still serves as the end-point of the mammoth cross-country trek from Land's End in Cornwall, a popular if arduous route for cyclists and walkers, many of whom raise money for charitable causes. There's a passenger ferry from here to Orkney, and the settlement's spectacular setting is some consolation for the disappointment of finding that this famous destination is basically a car park surrounded by tourist shops.

Two miles east, Duncansby Head provides a more solemn end-of-Britain moment with a small lighthouse and 60m cliffs sheltering nesting fulmars. From here a 15-minute walk through a sheep paddock yields spectacular views of the sea-surrounded monoliths known as Duncansby Stacks.

The tourist office (☏01955-611373; www.visithighlands.com; ◷10am-5pm Apr-Oct) has a fine selection of local novels and books about Caithness and the Highland Clearances.

SLEEPING & EATING

There's a campsite and several B&Bs in and around John O'Groats. At time of research, a series of wooden holiday chalets offering sensational views were being built, and the hotel, long in need of a loving hand, was being redeveloped into upmarket self-catering accommodation. Hit www.naturalretreats.co.uk to book. A licensed cafe has opened as part of the development; while the hotel at the main-road intersection that serves meals and has a pub.

ⓘ Getting There & Away

Stagecoach runs buses between John O'Groats and Wick (40 minutes, two to three daily). There are also three to eight services Monday to Saturday to/from Thurso.

From May to September, a passenger ferry (p933) shuttles across to Burwick in Orkney. Ninety-minute wildlife cruises to the island of Stroma or Duncansby Head cost £17 (late June to August).

Mey

The Castle of Mey (www.castleofmey.org.uk; adult/child £10/5.50; ◷10.20am-5pm May-Sep, last admission to castle 4pm), a big crowd-puller for its Queen Mother connections, is about 6 miles west of John O'Groats, off the A836 to Thurso. The exterior may seem grand but inside it feels domestic and everything is imbued with the character of the late Queen Mum: from a surprisingly casual lounge area with a TV showing her favourite show (*Dad's Army*, since you asked) to a photo of the corgis' evening meal – they didn't dine badly. The highlight is the genteel guided tour, with various anecdotes recounted by staff who once worked for her. Outside in the castle grounds there's a farm zoo, an unusual walled garden that's worth a stroll and lovely views over the Pentland Firth. The castle normally closes for a couple of weeks at the end of July for royal visits.

Dunnet Head

Turn off 8 miles east of Thurso to reach the most northerly point on the British mainland, dramatic Dunnet Head, which banishes tacky pretenders with its majestic cliffs dropping into Pentland Firth. There are inspiring views of the Orkney Islands, flopping seals and nesting seabirds below, and a lighthouse built by Robert Louis Stevenson's granddad.

Just west, Dunnet Bay offers one of Scotland's finest beaches, backed by high dunes.

Thurso & Scrabster

POP 7700

Britain's most northerly mainland town, Thurso makes a handy overnight stop if you're heading west or across to Orkney. There's a pretty town beach, riverbank strolls and a good museum. Ferries cross from Scrabster, 2.5 miles west of Thurso, to Orkney.

◉ Sights

FREE Caithness Horizons   MUSEUM
(www.caithnesshorizons.co.uk; High St; ◷10am-6pm Mon-Sat, also 11am-4pm Sun Apr-Sep) This museum brings much of the history and lore of Caithness to life through its excellent displays. A couple of fine Pictish cross-slabs greet the visitor downstairs; the main exhibition is a wide-ranging look at local history using plenty of audiovisuals – check out the

wistful account of the now-abandoned island of Stroma for an emotional slice of social history. There's also a gallery space, an exhibition on the Dounreay nuclear reactor and a cafe.

🛏 Sleeping

TOP CHOICE **Pennyland House** B&B ££

(📞01847-891194; www.pennylandhouse.co.uk; s/d £60/70; 🅿🛜) A super conversion of an historic house once lived in by the founder of the Boys' Brigade, this is Thurso's standout B&B choice. It offers phenomenal value for this level of accommodation, with huge rooms named after golf courses: we especially loved St Andrews – so spacious, with a great chessboard-tiled bathroom. The hospitality is enthusiastic and most helpful, and there's an inviting breakfast space and terraced area with views over the water to Hoy.

Forss House Hotel HOTEL ££

(📞01847-861201; www.forsshousehotel.co.uk; s/d superior d £97/130/165; 🅿🛜🐕) Tucked into a thicket of trees 4 miles west of Thurso is an old Georgian 4 mansion offering elegant accommodation that has both character and style. Sumptuous upstairs rooms are preferable to basement rooms as they have lovely views of the garden. There are also separate, beautifully appointed suites in the garden itself, which provide both privacy and a sense of tranquillity. Thoughtful extras like a selection of CDs and books in every room add appeal. It's right alongside a beautiful salmon river – the hotel can sort out permits and equipment – and if you've had a chilly day in the waders, some 300 malt whiskies await in the hotel bar.

Waterside House B&B £

(📞01847-894751; www.watersidehouse.org; 3 Janet St; s £30, d £50-60; 🛜🐕) Easy to find, and easy to park outside, this guesthouse (turn left just after the bridge coming into town) offers very spruce, recently made-over rooms with good en suites. There's a range of sizes, and the price is very reasonable. Breakfast choices include egg-and-bacon rolls or takeaway if you've got an early ferry. No credit cards.

Sandra's Hostel HOSTEL £

(📞01847-894575; www.sandras-backpackers.co.uk; 24 Princes St; dm/d/f £16/38/60; 🅿@🛜) In the heart of town above a chip shop, this reliable backpacker option offers appealing en-suite dorms, mostly four-berthers, a spacious

kitchen, and traveller-friendly facilities like free internet and help-yourself cereals and toast.

✕ Eating

TOP CHOICE **Captain's Galley** SEAFOOD £££

(📞01847-894999; www.captainsgalley.co.uk; Scrabster; 5-course dinner £47; ⏰dinner Tue-Sat) Right by the ferry terminal in Scrabster, Captain's Galley is a classy but friendly place offering a short, seafood-based menu that features local and sustainably sourced produce prepared in relatively simple ways, letting the natural flavours shine through. The chef picks the best fish off the local boats every day, and the menu describes exactly what boat and fishing grounds your morsel came from. Most rate it the best eatery in Caithness.

Holborn BISTRO, PUB ££

(📞01847-892771; www.holbornhotel.co.uk; 16 Princes St; bar meals £8-11, restaurant mains £12-20; 🛜) A trendy, comfortable place decked out in light wood, the Holborn contrasts starkly with more traditional Thurso watering holes. Quality seafood – including delicious home-smoked salmon – is the mainstay of a short but solid menu at its Red Pepper restaurant, where desserts are excellent too. Its bar, Bar 16, is a modern space with couches and comfy chairs where bar meals are uncomplicated but decent.

ℹ Information

Thurso information centre (📞01847-893155; www.visithighlands.com; Riverside Rd; ⏰daily Apr-Sep, Mon-Sat Oct) The future of Sunday opening was in doubt at time of research.

Thurso library (📞01847-893237; Davidson's Lane; ⏰10am-6pm Mon & Wed, to 8pm Tue & Fri, to 1pm Thu & Sat) Free internet.

ℹ Getting There & Around

It's a 2-mile walk from Thurso train station to the ferry port at Scrabster or there are buses from Olrig St.

BUS From Inverness, Stagecoach/Citylink run to Thurso/Scrabster (£18.30, 3 hours, six daily). From Thurso, there are buses roughly hourly to Wick, as well as services every couple of hours to John O'Groats (one hour, Monday to Saturday). There's one bus on Tuesdays and Fridays westwards to Tongue via Bettyhill; it also runs some Saturdays.

TRAIN There are four daily train services from Inverness (£18, 3¾ hours), with connecting bus to Scrabster. Space for bicycles is limited, so book ahead.

NORTH & NORTHWEST COAST

Quintessential Highland country such as this, marked by single-track roads, breathtaking emptiness and a wild, fragile beauty, is a rarity on the modern, crowded, highly urbanised island of Britain. The north and northwest coastline is a feast of deep inlets, forgotten beaches and surging peninsulas. Within the rugged confines, the deep interior is home to vast, empty spaces, enormous lochs and some of Scotland's highest peaks.

Thurso to Durness

It's 80 winding, often spectacular, coastal miles from Thurso to Durness.

BETTYHILL

POP 500

The panorama of a sweeping, sandy beach backed by velvety green hills with bulbous, rocky outcrops makes a sharp contrast to the sad history of this area. Bettyhill is a crofting community of resettled tenant farmers kicked off their land during the Clearances. Just west of town, an enormous stretch of white sand flanks the River Naver as it meets the sea.

Strathnaver Museum (☏01641-521418; www.strathnavermuseum.org.uk; adult/child £2/50p; ⊙10am-5pm Mon-Sat Apr-Oct), housed in an old church, tells the sad story of the Strathnaver Clearances through posters written by local kids. Outside the back door of the church is the Farr Stone, a fine carved Pictish cross-slab.

Bettyhill tourist office (☏01641-521244; www.visithighlands.com; ⊙10.30am-4.30pm Mon-Thu, 10.30am-7.30pm Fri-Sat Apr-Oct) has information on the area and the cafe (☏01641-521244; mains £5-9; ⊙10.30am-4.30pm Mon-Thu, 10.30am-7.30pm Fri-Sat Apr-Sep, 5-7.30pm Fri & Sat Oct-Mar) here serves home baking and light meals.

COLDBACKIE & TONGUE

POP 500

Coldbackie has outstanding views over sandy beaches, turquoise waters and offshore islands. Only 2 miles further on is Tongue, with the evocative 14th-century ruins of Castle Varrich, once a Mackay stronghold. To get to the castle, take the trail next to the Royal Bank of Scotland, near Ben Loyal Hotel – it's an easy stroll. Tongue has a shop, post office, bank and petrol station.

🍴 Sleeping & Eating

TOP CHOICE Tongue SYHA HOSTEL £
(☏01847-611789; www.syha.org.uk; dm/tw £19/45; ⊙Apr-Sep; P) In a wonderful spot right by the causeway across the Kyle of Tongue, a mile west of town, Tongue SYHA is the top budget option in the area, with clean, comfortably refitted dorms – some with views – a decent kitchen and cosy lounge. It's bright and helpful, and there's a lockable shed for bikes.

Cloisters B&B ££
(☏01847-601286; www.cloistertal.demon.co.uk; s/d £35/60; P🛜🐾) Vying for the position of best-located B&B in Scotland, Cloisters has three en-suite twin rooms and brilliant views over the Kyle of Tongue and offshore islands. Breakfast is in the artistically converted church alongside, and they can do evening meals at weekends. To get here from Tongue, cross the causeway and take the first turning on the right to Melness; Cloisters is a couple of miles down this road.

Tigh-nan-Ubhal B&B ££
(☏01847-611281; www.tigh-nan-ubhal.com; Main St; d £55-70; P🛜🐾) At the junction of the A836 and A838 and within stumbling distance of two pubs is this charming B&B. There are snug, loft-style rooms here with plenty of natural light, but the basement double with spa is the pick of the bunch – it's the biggest en suite we've seen in northern Scotland. There's also accommodation in a caravan in the garden.

Tongue Hotel HOTEL ££
(☏01847-611206; www.tonguehotel.co.uk; s/d/superior d £75/110/120; P🛜) Tongue Hotel is a welcoming spot that offers attractive, roomy chambers in a former hunting lodge. It has a restaurant and bar meals in the snug Brass Tap bar in the basement, a good spot to chat with locals or shelter from the weather.

Craggan Hotel SCOTTISH ££
(☏01847-601278; www.thecraggan.co.uk; mains £11-20; ⊙11am-9.15pm) On the side road to Melness, across the causeway from Tongue village, the Craggan Hotel doesn't look much from outside, but go in and you'll find smart, formal service and a menu ranging from exquisite burgers to classy game and seafood dishes, presented beautifully. It also does pizzas and curries to take away and the wine list's not bad for a pub either.

CROFTING & THE CLEARANCES

The wild and empty spaces up in these parts of the Highlands are among Europe's least populated zones, but this wasn't always so. Ruins of cottages in the most desolate areas are mute witnesses to one of the most heartless episodes of Scottish history: the Highland Clearances.

Up until the 19th century the most common form of farming settlement here was the *baile*, a group of a dozen or so families who farmed the land granted to them by the local chieftain in return for military service and a portion of the harvest.

After Culloden, however, the king banned private armies and new laws made the clan chiefs actual owners of their traditional lands, often vast tracts of territory. With the prospect of unimagined riches allied to a depressing failure of imagination, the lairds decided that sheep were more profitable than agriculture and proceeded to evict tens of thousands of farmers from their lands. The Clearances forced these desperate folk to head for the cities in the hope of finding work or to emigrate to the Americas or Southern Hemisphere. Those not moving eked a living from narrow plots of marginal agricultural land. This was a form of smallholding that became known as crofting. The small patch of land barely provided a living and had to be supplemented by other work such as fishing and kelp-gathering. It was always precarious, as rights were granted on a year-by-year basis, so at any moment a crofter could lose not only the farm but also the house they'd built on it.

The economic depression of the late 19th century meant many couldn't pay their rent. This time, however, they resisted expulsion, instead forming the Highland Land Reform Association and their own political party. Their resistance led to several of their demands being acceded to by the government, including security of tenure, fair rents and eventually the supply of land for new crofts. Crofters now have the right to purchase their farmland and recent laws have abolished the feudal system, which created so much misery.

Durness

POP 400

The scattered village of Durness (www .durness.org) is strung out along cliffs, which rise from a series of pristine beaches. It has one of the finest locations in Scotland. When the sun shines the effects of blinding white sand, the cry of sea birds and the lime-coloured seas combine in a magical way.

There are shops, an ATM, petrol and lots of accommodation options in Durness.

◉ Sights & Activities

Walking around the sensational sandy coastline is a highlight here, as is a visit to Cape Wrath. Durness's beautiful beaches, include Rispond to the east, Sargo Sands below town and Balnakeil to the west; the sea offers scuba-diving sites complete with wrecks, caves, seals and whales. At Balnakeil, less than a mile beyond Durness, a craft village occupies what was once an early warning radar station. A walk along the beach to the north leads to Faraid Head, where you can see puffin colonies in early summer.

A mile east of the village centre is a path down to Smoo Cave. From the vast main chamber, you can head through to a smaller flooded cavern where a waterfall sometimes cascades from the roof. From here you can take a boat trip (adult/child £4/2.50; ⊗Apr-Sep) to explore further into the interior.

🛏 Sleeping & Eating

Mackays   HOTEL ££
(☎01971-511202; www.visitdurness.com; d standard/deluxe £125/135; ⊗Easter-Oct; 🛜😮) You really feel you're at the furthest corner of Scotland here, where the road turns through 90 degrees. But whether you're heading south or east, you'll go far before you find a better place to stay than this haven of Highland hospitality. With big beds and soft fabrics it's a romantic spot, and the restaurant presents local seafood and robust meat dishes. The same owners run Croft 103 (☎01971-511202; www.croft103.com; Port na Con, Laid; wk £1400; P🛜), a stunning modern self-catering option for couples 6 miles east right on Loch Eriboll.

Lazy Crofter Bunkhouse   HOSTEL £
(☎01971-511202; www.durnesshostel.com; dm £16.50; 🛜) Lazy Crofter Bunkhouse is Durness' best budget accommodation. A bothy vibe gives it a Highland feel. The inviting dorms

have plenty of room and lockers, and there's also a sociable shared table for meals and board games, and a great wooden deck with sea views, perfect for midge-free evenings.

Sango Sands Oasis CAMPGROUND £
(☑01971-511222; www.sangosands.com; sites per adult/child £6.50/4; 🐾 P) You couldn't imagine a better location for a campground: great grassy areas on the edge of cliffs descend to two lovely sandy beaches. Facilities are good and very clean and there's a pub next door. You can camp here free from November to March but don't complain about the cold.

Sango Sands Oasis PUB £
(www.sangosands.com; mains £8-13) On the clifftops in the centre of town, this pub by the campsite offers some great views from its window tables. A cosy restaurant area does decent bar food in generous quantities.

Loch Croispol Bookshop CAFE £
(www.scottish-books.net; light meals £5-9; ⊙10am-5pm Mon-Sat, 10am-4pm Sun) At this place you can feed your body and your mind. Set among books featuring all things Scottish are a few tables where you can enjoy an all-day breakfast, sandwiches and other scrumptious fare at lunch, such as fresh Achiltibuie salmon.

ℹ️ Information

Durness community building (1 Bard Tce; per 30min £1; 🛜) Coin-op internet access, opposite Mackays.

Durness information centre (☑01971-511368; www.visithighlands.com; ⊙9am-5pm daily Apr-Oct, 10am-12.30pm Tue & Thu Nov-Mar)

Durness to Ullapool

Perhaps Scotland's most spectacular road trip, the 69 miles connecting Durness to Ullapool is a smorgasbord of dramatic scenery, almost too much to take in. From Durness to Rhiconich the road is almost all singletrack, passing through a broad heathered valley with the looming grey bulk of Foinaven and Arkle to the southeast. Heather gives way to a rockier landscape of Lewisian gneiss pockmarked with hundreds of small lochans, and gorse-covered hills prefacing the magnificent Torridonian sandstone mountains of Assynt and Coigach, including ziggurat-like Quinag, the distinctive sugarloaf of Suilven and pinnacled Stac Pollaidh. It's no wonder the area has been dubbed the Northwest Highlands Geopark (www.northwest-highlands-geopark.co.uk).

KYLESKU & LOCH GLENCOUL

Cruises (☑07955 188352; www.kyleskucruises.co.uk; adult/child £20/10, short cruise £10/5; ⊙May-Sep) on Loch Glencoul take you past treacherous-looking mountains, seal colonies and the 213m-drop of Eas a'Chual Aulin, Britain's highest waterfall.

By the boat dock, the **Kylesku Hotel** (☑01971-502231; www.kyleskuhotel.co.uk; s £60-73, d £90-108, mains £10-19; ⊙Mar-Oct, food served noon-9pm; 🛜🐾), run with pride and enthusiasm, is a great place to stay, or to gorge yourself on delicious sustainable seafood in the convivial bar. Local langoustines and mussels are a speciality. There's a variety of rooms; the small extra charge for loch views is well worthwhile.

LOCHINVER & ASSYNT

With its otherworldly scenery of isolated peaks rising above a sea of crumpled, lochan-spattered gneiss, Assynt epitomises the wild magnificence of the northwest Highlands. The glaciers of the last Ice Age have sculpted the hills of Suilven (731m), Canisp (846m), Quinag (808m) and Ben More Assynt (998m) into strange and wonderful silhouettes.

Lochinver is the main settlement in the Assynt region, a busy little fishing port that's a popular port of call for tourists, with its laid-back atmosphere, good facilities, striking scenery and range of accommodation.

🛏️ Sleeping & Eating

There are several B&Bs; for magnificent vistas head a mile around the bay to Baddidarrach, which looks back at Lochinver and the magnificent bulk of Suilven behind.

TOP CHOICE Albannach HOTEL £££
(☑01571-844407; www.thealbannach.co.uk; s/d/ste incl dinner £220/290/370; ⊙Tue-Sun Mar-Dec; P🛜) One of the Highlands' top places to stay and eat, this combines old-fashioned country house elements – steep creaky stairs, stuffed animals, fireplaces, and noble antique furniture – with strikingly handsome rooms that range from a sumptuous four-poster to more modern spaces with things like underfloor heating and, in one case, a private deck with outdoor Jacuzzi. The restaurant serves a table d'hôte (they'll tailor it to your needs) that's famed throughout Scotland (£61 for nonresidents); the welcoming owners grow lots of their own produce and focus on organic and local ingredients. Glorious views, spacious grounds,

and great walks in easy striking distance make this a perfect base.

Achmelvich Beach SYHA
HOSTEL £

(☏01571-844480; www.syha.org.uk; dm/tw £18/44; ⊙Apr–mid-Sep) A whitewashed cottage set beside a great beach at the end of a side road four miles from Lochinver, this has simple dorms and a sociable common kitchen/eating area. There's a basic shop at the adjacent campsite.

TOP CHOICE Lochinver Larder & Riverside Bistro
CAFE, BISTRO ££

(☏01571-844356; www.lochinverlarder.co.uk; 3 Main St; pies £5, mains £10-16; ⊙10am-8.30pm) Serving as coffee shop, bistro and takeaway, the Larder offers an outstanding menu of inventive food made with local produce. The bistro turns out delicious seafood dishes in the evening, while the takeaway counter (open till 7pm) sells delicious Lochinver pies with a wide range of gourmet fillings: try the smoked haddock, or wild boar and apricot – very tasty indeed.

❶ Information

There's a supermarket in town, as well as a post office, bank (with an ATM) and petrol station.

Assynt visitor centre (☏01571-844654; www.assynt.info; Main St; ⊙10am-5pm Mon-Sat Easter-Oct, also 10am-3pm Sun Jun-Aug) Has leaflets on hill walks in the area and a display on the story of Assynt, from wildlife and geology to clans, conflict and controversy.

ULLAPOOL
POP 1300

The pretty port of Ullapool, on the shores of Loch Broom, is the largest settlement in Wester Ross and one of the most alluring spots in the Highlands, a wonderful destination in itself as well as a gateway to the Western Isles. Offering a row of white-washed cottages arrayed along the harbour and special views of the loch and its flanking hills, the town has a very distinctive appeal. The harbour served as an emigration point during the Clearances, with thousands of Scots watching the loch recede behind them as the diaspora cast them across the world.

◉ Sights & Activities

Ullapool Museum
MUSEUM

(www.ullapoolmuseum.co.uk; 7 West Argyle St; adult/child £3.50/free; ⊙10am-5pm Mon-Sat Apr-Oct) Housed in a converted Telford Parliamentary church, this museum relates the pre-historic, natural and social history of the town and Lochbroom area, with a particular focus on the emigration to Nova Scotia and other places. There's also a genealogy section if you want to trace your Scottish roots.

Seascape
BOAT TOUR

(☏01854-633708; www.sea-scape.co.uk; adult/child £32/22) Runs two-hour tours out to the Summer Isles in an orange rigid inflatable boat (RIB).

Summer Queen
BOAT TOUR

(☏07713-257219; www.summerqueen.co.uk; ⊙Mon-Sat May-Sep) The stately *Summer Queen* takes you out (weather permitting) around Isle Martin (adult/child £20/10, 2hrs) or to the Summer Isles (adult/child £30/15, 4hrs), with a stop on Tanera Mor.

⎚ Sleeping

Note that during summer Ullapool is very busy and finding accommodation can be tricky – the answer: book ahead.

WORTH A TRIP

CAPE WRATH

Though its name comes from the Norse word for 'turning point', there's something daunting and primal about Cape Wrath, the northwesternmost point of the British mainland. It is crowned by a lighthouse (built by Robert Stevenson in 1828) and stands close to the seabird colonies of Clo Mor, Britain's highest coastal cliffs. Getting to Cape Wrath involves a boat ride (☏01971-511246; return adult/child £6/4, bicycle £2; ⊙Easter-Oct) – passengers and bikes only – across the Kyle of Durness (return £5.50, 10 minutes), connecting with an optional minibus (☏07742-670196, 01971-511284; www.capewrath.org.uk; single/return £6/10; ⊙Easter-Oct) running 12 miles to the cape (return £10, 40 minutes). This is a friendly but eccentric, sometimes shambolic, service, so plan on waiting in high season, and ring before going to make sure the ferry is running. The ferry leaves from Keoldale pier, a couple of miles southwest of Durness, and runs two or more times daily from Easter to September. It's a spectacular ride or hike to Cape Wrath over bleak scenery sometimes used by the Ministry of Defence as a firing range. There's a cafe at the lighthouse serving soup and sandwiches.

West House TOP CHOICE B&B **££**

(☑01854-613126; www.ullapoolaccommodation .net; West Argyle St; d £60-80; P🖥) Slap bang in the centre of Ullapool, this solid white house that was once a manse offers excellent rooms with contemporary style and great bathrooms. Breakfast is continental style: rooms come with a fridge stocked with fresh fruit salad, and quality cheeses, yoghurts, bread and juice so you can eat at your leisure in your own chamber. Most rooms have great views, as well as iPod docks and other conveniences. The owners also have tempting self-catering options in the Ullapool area.

Ceilidh Place HOTEL **££**

(☑01854-612103; www.theceilidhplace.com; 14 West Argyle St; s £55-68, d £136-158; P🖥🅿) Ceilidh Place is one of the more unusual and delightful places to stay in the Highlands. Rooms pleasingly go for character rather than modern conveniences, and, rather than television, come with a selection of books chosen by Scottish literati, eclectic artwork and nice little touches like hot-water bottles. Best of all is the sumptuous lounge, with sofas, chaises longues and an honesty bar. The hotel, which includes a bookshop, is also a celebration of Scottish culture, with a capital C – we're talking literature and traditional music, not tartan and Nessie dolls. A great place.

Tamarin Lodge B&B **££**

(☑01854-612667; www.tamarinullapool.com; The Braes; s/d £40/80; P🖥🅿) The effortlessly elegant modern architecture in this hilltop house is noteworthy in its own right, but the glorious vistas over the hills opposite and water far below are unforgettable. All the rooms face the view – some have a balcony to admire it from – and are very spacious, quiet, and utterly relaxing, with unexpected features and gadgets. A great lounge with telescope and terrace provides another inviting space, while the benevolent hosts are a delight. Follow the sign for Braes a mile outside of town on the Inverness road.

Ullapool SYHA HOSTEL **£**

(☑01854-612254; www.syha.org.uk; Shore St; dm £19; ☉Apr-Oct; 🖥) You've got to hand it to the SYHA; they've chosen some very sweet locations for their hostels. This is as close to the water as it is to the town's best pub: about four seconds' walk. The front rooms have harbour views but the busy dining area and little lounge are also good spots for contemplating the water.

Point Cottage B&B **££**

(☑01854-613702; www.ullapoolbedandbreakfast.co .uk; 22 West Shore St; d £70; P🖥) If you've just arrived by ferry, you've probably already admired Ullapool's line of shorefront cottages; this is one of them. Under keen new owners, this sports appealing renovated rooms with modern bathrooms and a very kindly welcome. It's got an optimistic, upbeat feel that chimes with the super views from all the chambers. Breakfast features blueberry pancakes, vegetarian sausages or smoked haddock among other choices.

Ceilidh Clubhouse HOSTEL **£**

(☑01854-612103; West Lane; s/tw/f £22/38/66; P🖥) Opposite the Ceilidh Place, and under the same management, this annex offers no-frills accommodation for walkers, journey-people and staff. A big building, it has hostel-style rooms with sturdy bunks and basins. Though showers and toilets are a little institutional, the big bonus is that rooms are private: if you're woken by snores, at least they'll be familiar ones.

Broomfield Holiday Park CAMPSITE **£**

(☑01854-612664; www.broomfieldhp.com; West Lane; tent sites £13-17; ☉Apr-Sep; P🖥🅿) Great grassy headland location very close to the centre. Midge-busting machines in action.

✗ **Eating & Drinking**

Ceilidh Place SCOTTISH **££**

(☑01854-612103; 14 West Argyle St; mains £10-16; ☉8am-9pm) The restaurant at the Ceilidh Place serves up inventive dishes that focus on fresh local seafood backed up by stews, pies and burgers. Presentation and quality are high here, and it's an atmospheric place, with a cosy atmosphere, outdoor seating, good wines by the glass and regular live music and events.

Ferry Boat Inn PUB **££**

(☑01854-612366; www.ferryboat-inn.com; Shore St; mains £11-14) Known as the FBI, this character-laden waterfront inn is a little less traditional-looking these days with its bleached wood and nonstained carpet, but it's still the place where locals and visitors mingle. Some dishes on the menu are a little bland, but a well-run dining room, quality ingredients and great presentation compensate.

ℹ **Information**

Ullapool library (☑01854-612543; Mill St; ☉9am-5pm Mon-Fri, plus 6-8pm Tue & Thu, closed Mon & Wed during holidays) Free internet.

Ullapool information centre (☎01854-612486; ullapool@visitscotland.com; Argyle St; ☺daily Apr-Sep, Mon-Sat Oct)

❶ Getting There & Away

Citylink has one to three daily buses from Inverness to Ullapool (£11.90, 1½ hours), connecting with the Lewis ferry.

Ullapool to Kyle of Lochalsh

Although it's less than 50 miles as the crow flies from Ullapool to Kyle of Lochalsh, it's more like 150 miles along the circuitous coastal road – but don't let that put you off. It's a deliciously remote region and there are fine views of beaches and bays backed by mountains all the way along.

The A832 doubles back to the coast from the A835, 12 miles from Ullapool. Just after the junction, the **Falls of Measach** spill 45m into the spectacularly deep and narrow Corrieshalloch Gorge. You can cross from side to side on a wobbly suspension bridge; the thundering falls and misty vapours rising from the gorge are very impressive.

If you're in a hurry to get to Skye, head inland on the A835 (towards Inverness) and catch up with the A832 further down, near Garve.

GAIRLOCH
POP 1100

Gairloch is a group of villages (comprising Achtercairn, Strath and Charlestown) around the inner end of a loch of the same name. The surrounding area has beautiful sandy beaches, good trout-fishing and birdwatching. Hill walkers also use Gairloch as a base for the Torridon hills and An Teallach.

◉ Sights & Activities

FREE **Gairloch Marine Wildlife Centre** NATURE DISPLAY
(☎01445-712636; www.porpoise-gairloch.co.uk; Pier Rd; ☺10am-4pm Easter-Oct) Has displays, lots of charts and photos, and knowledgeable staff. **Cruises** (☎01445-712636; www.porpoise-gairloch.co.uk; adult/child £20/15) run from the centre and sail up to three times daily (weather permitting); during the two-hour trips you may see basking sharks, porpoises and minke whales. The crew collects data on water temperature and conditions, and monitor cetacean populations, so your fare is subsidising an important research project.

Inverewe Garden GARDENS
(NTS; www.nts.org.uk; adult/concession £9.50/7; ☺10am-3pm Nov-Mar, to 6pm Apr-Aug, to 4pm Sep & Oct) Six miles north of Gairloch, this splendid garden is a welcome splash of colour on an otherwise bleak stretch of coast. The climate here is warmed by the waters of the Gulf Stream, which allowed Osgood MacKenzie, a son of the laird of Gairloch, to create this exotic woodland garden in 1862. There are free guided tours on weekdays at 1.30pm (March to October). The cafe has great cakes.

🛏 Sleeping & Eating

Rua Reidh Lighthouse Hostel HOSTEL £
(☎01445-771263; www.ruareidh.co.uk; dm/d £13.50/38; P) Beyond Melvaig, 13 miles north of Gairloch (at the end of the road), this is an excellent hostel and will give you a taste of a lighthouse-keeper's life. Buses from Gairloch run as far as Melvaig, then it's a 3-mile walk along the road to the lighthouse. En-suite twins and doubles (£42 to £48) and family rooms are also available, as are breakfasts and dinners.

Wayside Guest House B&B ££
(☎01445-712008; issmith@msn.com; s/d £40/60; 🖭) Cosy and compact, this place offers comfortable and welcoming accommodation in Strath, the spiritual heart of Gairloch. The spotless rooms either come with en-suite bathroom or fabulous view; you decide what's more important to you.

TOP CHOICE **Badachro Inn** PUB ££
(☎01445-741255; www.badachroinn.com; light meals £5-8, mains £11-16; P) Set in an enchanting location overlooking a sheltered yacht harbour at Badachro, 5 miles southwest of Gairloch, this old Highland inn serves real ales from the An Teallach brewery on Loch Broom, and platters of fresh local seafood: crab, scallops and langoustines, some landed at the pier right beside the inn. There are also tasty panini and sandwiches; eating out on the deck on a sunny day here is a real treat. The bar staff will recommend the potato wedges as a side dish – say yes!

❶ Information
Gairloch information centre (☎01445-712071; ☺10am-4pm Mon-Sat mid-Sep–Jun, 10am-5pm Mon-Sat, 11am-4pm Sun Jun–mid-Sep) Set in the smart new wooden Gale Centre, on the main road through town, this has good walking pamphlets.

LOCH MAREE & KINLOCHEWE

Stretching for 12 miles southeast of Gairloch, Loch Maree is often regarded as one of the most beautiful lochs in Scotland. At the southern end of the loch, tiny Kinlochewe makes a good base for outdoor activities. Kinlochewe Hotel (☎01445-760253; www.kinlochewehotel.co.uk; dm £14.50, s £50, d £90-98; P🅿️🛜🐕) is a well-run, welcoming place that's very walker-friendly. As well as comfortable, spotless, new-looking rooms, there are nice features like a handsome lounge well stocked with books, a great bar with several real ales on tap and a thoughtful menu of locally sourced food. There's also a bunkhouse with one no-frills 12-bed dorm (BYO sleeping bag and towels), a decent kitchen and clean bathrooms.

TORRIDON

Southwest from Kinlochewe, the A896 follows Glen Torridon, overlooked by multiple peaks, including Beinn Eighe (1010m) and Liathach (1055m). The drive along Glen Torridon is one of the most breathtaking in Scotland. Mighty, brooding mountains, often partly obscured by clumps of passing clouds, seemingly drawn to their peaks like magnets, loom over the tiny, winding, single-track road.

The road reaches the sea at spectacularly sited Torridon village, where there is a Countryside Centre (NTS; donation £3; ⏰10am-5pm Sun-Fri Easter-Sep) offering information on flora, fauna and walks in the rugged area. There's a camping ground (☎01445-791368; sites free) here.

Modern, squat Torridon SYHA (☎01445-791284; www.syha.org.uk; dm £18; ⏰Mar-Oct, plus weekends Nov-Feb; P🅿️@🛜) is in a magnificent location surrounded by spectacular mountains. It's a very popular walking base so book ahead in summer.

If you prefer the lap of luxury to the sound of rain beating on your tent, head for The Torridon (☎01445-791242; www.thetorridon.com; r standard/superior/master £220/275/425; ⏰closed Jan, closed Mon & Tue Nov, Dec, Feb & Mar; P🅿️@🛜🐕), a lavish Victorian shooting lodge with a romantic lochside location. Service is excellent, with muddy boots positively welcomed, and dinners are sumptuous affairs, also open to nonresidents (£55). Part of the same set-up, adjacent Torridon Inn (☎01445-791242; www.thetorridon.com; s/d/q £89/99/165; ⏰daily May-Oct, Thu-Sun Nov, Dec, Mar & Apr, closed Jan & Feb; P🅿️🛜🐕) offers excellent modern rooms that vary substantially in size and layout, and a sociable bar offering all-day food.

APPLECROSS

POP 200

The remote settlement of Applecross feels like an island retreat, partly because of its isolation, and partly because of the magnificent views of Raasay and the hills of Skye that set the pulse racing, particularly at sunset. On a clear day it's an unforgettable place, but the tranquil atmosphere isn't quite the same when the campsite and pub fill to the brim in school holidays.

A long side trip abandons the A896 to follow the coast road here, or you can continue a bit further down the A896 to one of the best drives in the country (best in terms of the remote and incredibly rugged and spectacular scenery, not the actual road, which winds and twists and balances on sheer precipices). The road climbs steeply to the Bealach na Ba pass (626m), then drops dramatically to the village. This drive is pure magic and a must if you're in the area.

You can pitch your tent at the Applecross Campsite (☎01520-744268; www.applecross.uk.com; sites per adult/child £8/4, 2-person hut £38; ⏰Mar-Oct; P🅿️), which offers green grassy plots, cute little wooden cabins and a good cafe.

The hub of the spread-out community here is the Applecross Inn (☎01520-744262; www.applecross.uk.com; Shore St; s/d £80/120, mains £9-17; ⏰food noon-9pm; P🅿️🛜🐕), the perfect shoreside location for a sunset pint. The inn is famous for its food, mostly daily blackboard specials that concentrate on local seafood and venison, and sports seven snug bedrooms, all with a view of the Skye hills and the sea.

PLOCKTON

POP 500

There's something distinctly tropical about idyllic little Plockton, a filmset-like village with palm trees, whitewashed houses and a small bay dotted with islets and hemmed in by green-fuzzed mountains.

Calum's Seal Trips (☎01599-544306; www.calums-sealtrips.com; adult/child £9/5; ⏰Apr-Oct) runs seal-watching cruises. There are swarms of the slippery fellas just outside the harbour and the trip comes with an excellent commentary.

Airily set in the one-time train station (it's now opposite), Plockton Station Bunkhouse (☎01599-544235; mickcoe@btInternet.com; dm £14; P🅿️🛜) has cosy four-bed dorms, a garden and kitchen-lounge with plenty of light and good perspectives over the frenetic comings and goings (OK, that last bit's a lie) of the platforms below.

The black-painted Plockton Hotel (☎01599-544274; www.plocktonhotel.co.uk; 41 Harbour St; s/d £90/130, cottage s/d £55/80, mains £8-16; ☎) is one of those classic Highland spots that manages to make everyone happy, whether it's thirst, hunger, or fatigue that brings you knocking. The assiduously tended rooms are a delight, with excellent facilities and thoughtful touches like bathrobes. The cosy bar (or wonderful beer garden on a sunny day) are memorable places for a pint, and food ranges from sound-value bar meals to seafood platters and local langoustines brought in on the afternoon boat.

KYLE OF LOCHALSH
POP 740

Before the controversial bridge, Kyle of Lochalsh was Skye's main ferry-port. Visitors now tend to buzz through town. The tourist office (☎01599-534276; ☺daily Easter-Oct), beside the main seafront car park, stocks information on Skye. Next to it is one of Scotland's most lavishly decorated public toilets.

From the pier below, glass-hulled Seaprobe Atlantis (☎0800 980 4846; www.seaprobeatlantis.com; adult/child from £13/7; ☺Easter-Oct) takes you on a spin around the kyle to spot seabirds, seals and maybe an otter or two. The basic trip includes an entertaining guided tour and plenty of beautiful jellyfish; longer trips also take in a WWII shipwreck. Book at the tourist office.

Citylink runs to Kyle three times daily from Inverness (£19.20, two hours), and Glasgow (£34.90, 5¾ hours).

The train route between Inverness and Kyle of Lochalsh (£20.50, 2½ hours, up to four daily) is one of Scotland's most scenic.

EILEAN DONAN CASTLE

Photogenically sited at the entrance to Loch Duich, near Dornie village, Eilean Donan Castle (☎01599-555202; www.eileandonancastle.com; adult/child £6/5; ☺9.30am-6pm Mar-Oct) is one of Scotland's most evocative castles, and must be represented in millions of photo albums. It's on an offshore islet, magically linked to the mainland by an elegant, stone-arched bridge. It's very much a re-creation inside with an excellent introductory exhibition. Keep an eye out for the photos of scenes from the movie Highlander.

Citylink buses from Fort William and Inverness to Portree will stop at the castle.

ISLE OF SKYE

POP 9900

The Isle of Skye (an t-Eilean Sgiathanach in Gaelic) takes its name from the old Norse sky-a, meaning 'cloud island', a Viking reference to the often mist-enshrouded Cuillin Hills. It's the biggest of Scotland's islands, a 50-mile-long smorgasbord of velvet moors, jagged mountains, sparkling lochs and towering sea cliffs. The stunning scenery is the main attraction, but when the mist closes in there are plenty of castles, crofting museums and cosy pubs and restaurants to retire to.

🏃 Activities

Walking

Skye offers some of the finest – and in places the roughest and most difficult – walking in Scotland. There are many detailed guidebooks available. You'll need Ordnance Survey (OS) 1:50,000 maps 23 and 32. Don't attempt the longer walks in bad weather or in winter.

Skye Walking Holidays   WALKING
(☎01470-552213; www.skyewalks.co.uk; Duntulm Castle Hotel, Trotternish) Organises three-day guided walking holidays for £400 per person, including four nights of hotel accommodation.

Climbing

The Cuillin Hills is a playground for rock climbers, and the two-day traverse of the Cuillin Ridge is the finest mountaineering expedition in the British Isles. There are several mountain guides who can provide instruction and safely introduce inexperienced climbers to the harder routes.

Skye Guides   ROCK CLIMBING
(☎01471-822116; www.skyeguides.co.uk) A two-day introduction to rock-climbing course costs around £360, and a private mountain guide can be hired for around £200 a day (both rates apply for up to two clients).

Sea Kayaking

The sheltered coves and sea lochs around the coast of Skye provide magnificent sea-kayaking opportunities. The following centres provide kayaking instruction, guiding and equipment hire for beginners and experts. It costs around £35 for a half-day kayak hire with instruction.

Whitewave Outdoor Centre   KAYAKING
(☎01470-542414; www.white-wave.co.uk; 19 Linicro, Kilmuir; ☺Mar-Oct) Provides kayaking in-

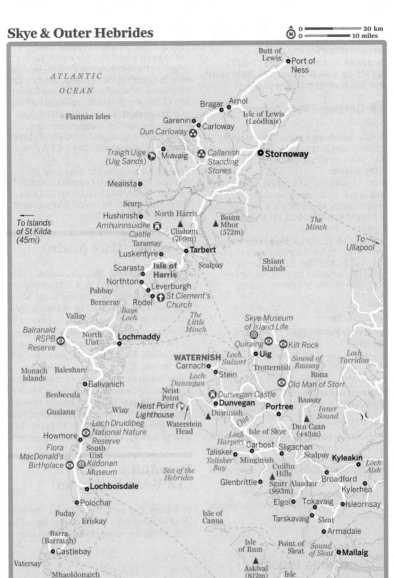

struction, guiding and equipment hire for both beginners and experts.

Skyak Adventures KAYAKING
(☏01471-820002; www.skyakadventures.com; 29 Lower Breakish, Breakish) Expeditions and courses to take both beginners and expe-

rienced paddlers to otherwise inaccessible places.

❶ Information

Portree information centre (☏01478-612137; Bayfield Rd, Portree; internet per 20min £1;

⊙9am-6pm Mon-Sat, 10am-4pm Sun Jun-Aug, 9am-5pm Mon-Fri, 10am-4pm Sat Apr, May & Sep, limited opening hrs Oct-Mar)

Broadford information centre (☑01471-822361; car park, Broadford; ⊙9.30am-5pm Mon-Sat, 10am-4pm Sun Apr-Oct)

ⓘ Getting There & Away

Boat

Despite there being a bridge, there are still a couple of ferry links between Skye and the mainland. There are ferries from Uig on Skye to the Outer Hebrides.

MALLAIG–ARMADALE CalMac operates the Mallaig to Armadale **ferry** (www.calmac.co.uk; per person/car £4.35/22.60). It's very popular in July and August, so book ahead if you're travelling by car.

GLENELG–KYLERHEA **Skye Ferry** (www .skyeferry.com; foot passenger/car with passengers £3/14; ⊙10am-6pm Easter–mid-Oct) runs a tiny vessel (six cars only) on the very worthwhile Glenelg to Kylerhea crossing.

Bus

Services include:

Glasgow to Portree (£40, seven hours, four daily)

Glasgow to Uig (£40, 7½ hours, two daily) Via Crianlarich, Fort William and Kyle of Lochalsh.

Inverness to Portree (£23, 3½ hours, three daily)

Car & Motorcycle

The Isle of Skye became permanently tethered to the Scottish mainland when the Skye Bridge opened in 1995. The controversial bridge tolls were abolished in 2004 and the crossing is now free.

There are **petrol stations** at Broadford (open 24 hours), Armadale, Portree, Dunvegan and Uig.

ⓘ Getting Around

Getting around the island by public transport can be a pain, especially if you want to explore away from the main Kyleakin–Portree–Uig road. Here, as in much of the Highlands, there are only a few buses on Saturdays, and only one Sunday service (between Kyle of Lochalsh and Portree).

BUS **Stagecoach** (www.stagecoachbus.com) operates the main bus routes on the island, linking all the main villages and towns. Its **Skye Dayrider** ticket gives unlimited bus travel for one day for £7.50.

TAXI & CAR HIRE You can order a taxi or rent a car from **Kyle Taxi Company** (☑01599-534323). Rentals cost from around £38 a day, and you can arrange for the car to be waiting at Kyle of Lochalsh train station.

Kyleakin (Caol Acain)

POP 100

Poor wee Kyleakin had the carpet pulled from under it when the Skye Bridge opened – it went from being the gateway to the island to a backwater bypassed by the main road. It's now a pleasant, peaceful little place, with a harbour used by yachts and fishing boats.

The homely Dun Caan Independent Hostel (☑01599-534087; www.skyerover.co.uk; Castle View; dm from £15), in a fine, old, pine-panelled house overlooking the harbour, has the most attractive location of several nearby hostels.

A shuttle bus runs half-hourly between Kyle of Lochalsh and Kyleakin (five minutes), and there are eight to 10 buses daily (except Sunday) to Broadford and Portree.

Broadford (An T-Ath Leathann)

POP 1100

Broadford is a service centre for the scattered communities of southern Skye. The long, straggling village has a tourist office, a

---

MADDENING MIDGES

Forget Nessie; the Highlands have a real monster – a voracious bloodsucking female 3mm-long, known as the Highland midge. The bane of campers and as much a symbol of Scotland as the kilt or dram, they drive sane folk to distraction as they descend in biting clouds.

Though normally vegetarian, the female midge needs a dose of blood in order to lay her eggs. And, like it or not, if you're in the Highlands between June and August, you just volunteered as a donor. Midges especially congregate near water, and are most active in the early morning, though squadrons also patrol in the late evening, around 10pm.

Repellents and creams are reasonably effective, though some walkers favour midge veils. Light-coloured clothing also helps. Pubs and campsites increasingly have midge-zapping machines. Check www.midgeforecast.co.uk for activity levels by area, but don't blame us: we've been eaten alive when the forecast said moderate too.

24-hour petrol station, a large Co-op super-market (⊘8am-10pm Mon-Sat, 9am-6pm Sun), a laundrette and a bank with an ATM.

There are lots of B&Bs in and around Broadford and the village is well placed for exploring southern Skye by car.

Sleeping & Eating

Tigh an Dochais
B&B ££

(☏01471-820022; www.skyebedbreakfast.co.uk; 13 Harrapool; per person from £40; P) A cleverly de-signed modern building, Tigh an Dochais is one of Skye's best B&Bs – a little footbridge leads to the front door, which is on the first floor. Here you'll find the breakfast room and lounge with a stunning view of sea and hills; the bedrooms (downstairs) have spa-cious en suites and open onto an outdoor deck with that same wonderful view.

Creelers
SEAFOOD ££

(☏01471-822281; www.skye-seafood-restaurant.co.uk; Lower Harrapool; mains £12-17; ⊘noon-9.30pm Mon-Sat Mar-Nov;) Broadford has several places to eat but one really stands out: Creel-ers is a small, bustling, no-frills restaurant that serves some of the best seafood on Skye. The house speciality is a rich, spicy seafood gumbo. Best to book ahead. If you can't get a table then nip around to the back door, where you'll find Ma Doyle's Takeaway, for fish and chips (£6) to go.

Sleat

If you cross over the sea to Skye on the ferry from Mallaig you arrive in Armadale, at the southern end of the long, low-lying peninsula known as Sleat (pronounced 'slate'). There are six or seven buses a day (Monday to Saturday) from Armadale to Broadford and Portree.

Sights & Activities

Museum of the Isles
MUSEUM

(☏01471-844305; www.clandonald.com; adult/child £6.95/4.95; ⊘9.30am-5.30pm Apr-Oct) Just along the road from the ferry pier is the part-ruined Armadale Castle, former seat of Lord MacDonald of Sleat. The neighbour-ing museum will tell you all you ever want-ed to know about Clan Donald, as well as providing an easily digestable history of the Lordship of the Isles.

Prize exhibits include rare portraits of clan chiefs, and a wine glass that was once used by Bonnie Prince Charlie. The ticket also gives admission to the lovely castle gardens.

Sleeping

TOP CHOICE Toravaig House Hotel
HOTEL ££

(☏01471-820200; www.skyehotel.co.uk; d £95-120; P) This hotel, 3 miles south of Isleorn-say, is one of those places where the owners know a thing or two about hospitality – as soon as you arrive you'll feel right at home, whether relaxing on the sofas by the log fire in the lounge or admiring the view across the Sound of Sleat from the garden lawn chairs.

The spacious bedrooms – ask for room 1 (Eriskay), with its enormous sleigh bed – are luxuriously equipped, from the rich and heavy bed linen to the huge, high-pressure shower heads. The elegant Islay restaurant serves the best of local fish, game and lamb.

Cuillin Hills

The Cuillin Hills are Britain's most spectacu-lar mountain range. Though small in stature (Sgurr Alasdair, the highest summit, is only 993m), the peaks are near-alpine in charac-ter, with knife-edge ridges, jagged pinnacles, scree-filled gullies and acres of naked rock. While they are a paradise for experienced mountaineers, the higher reaches of the Cuil-lin are off limits to the majority of walkers.

The good news is that there are also plen-ty of good, low-level hikes within the ability of most. One of the best (on a fine day) is the steep climb from Glenbrittle camping ground to Coire Lagan (6 miles round trip; allow at least three hours).

There are two main bases for exploring the Cuillin – Sligachan to the north, and Glenbrittle to the south.

Sleeping

Sligachan Hotel
HOTEL ££

(☏01478-650204; www.sligachan.co.uk; per per-son £65-75; P@) The Slig, as it has been known to generations of climbers, is a near village in itself, encompassing a luxurious hotel, a microbrewery, self-catering cottages, a bunkhouse (☏01478-650458; www.sligachan selfcatering.co.uk; dm £16), a campsite (sites per person £5.50; ⊘Apr-Oct), a big barn of a pub (all-day bar meals £8 to £10) and an adventure playground.

ⓘ Getting There & Away

Bus 53 runs five times a day Monday to Friday (once on Saturday) from Portree to Carbost via Sligachan (50 minutes); for Glenbrittle, you'll have to hitch or walk the remaining 8 miles.

Minginish

Loch Harport, to the north of the Cuillin, divides the Minginish Peninsula from the rest of Skye. On its southern shore lies the village of Carbost, home to the smooth, sweet and smoky Talisker malt whisky, produced at Talisker Distillery (☏01478-614308; www.discovering-distilleries.com; guided tour £6; ☺9.30am-5pm Mon-Sat Apr-Oct, 11am-5pm Sun Jul & Aug, 10am-4.30pm Mon-Fri Nov-Mar) This is the only distillery on Skye; the guided tour includes a free dram. Magnificent Talisker Bay, 5 miles west of Carbost, has a sandy beach, sea stack and waterfall.

There are five buses a day on weekdays (one on Saturday) from Portree to Carbost via Sligachan.

Portree (Port Righ)

POP 1900

Portree is Skye's largest and liveliest town. It has a pretty harbour lined with brightly painted houses, and there are great views of the surrounding hills. Its name (from the Gaelic for King's Harbour) commemorates James V, who came here in 1540 to pacify the local clans.

⌂ Sleeping

Portree is well supplied with B&Bs but many of them are in bland, modern bungalows that, though comfortable, often lack character. Accommodation fills up fast in July and August, so be sure to book ahead.

Ben Tianavaig B&B
B&B ££
(☏01478-612152; www.ben-tianavaig.co.uk; 5 Bosville Tce; r £70-80; ☐ি) A warm welcome awaits from the Irish-Welsh couple who run this appealing B&B bang in the centre of town. All four bedrooms have a view across the harbour to the hill that gives the house its name and breakfasts include free-range eggs and vegetables grown in the garden.

Peinmore House
B&B ££
(☏01478-612574; www.peinmorehouse.co.uk; r £130-140; ☐ি) Signposted off the main road about

2 miles south of Portree, this former manse has been cleverly converted into a guesthouse that is more stylish and luxurious than most hotels. The bedrooms and bathrooms are huge (one bathroom has an armchair in it!), as is the choice of breakfast (kippers and smoked haddock on the menu), and there are panoramic views to the old Man of Storr.

Bosville Hotel
HOTEL ££
(☏01478-612846; www.bosvillehotel.co.uk; 9-11 Bosville Tce; s/d from £130/138; ি) The Bosville brings a little bit of metropolitan style to Portree with its designer fabrics and furniture, flatscreen TVs, fluffy bathrobes and bright, spacious bathrooms. It's worth splashing out a bit for the 'premier' rooms, with leather recliner chairs from which you can lap up the view over the town and harbour.

Bayfield Backpackers
HOSTEL £
(☏01478-612231; www.skyehostel.co.uk; Bayfield; dm £17; @ি) Clean, central and modern, this hostel provides the best backpacker accommodation in town. The owner really makes you feel welcome, and is a fount of advice on what to do and where to go in Skye.

✕ Eating

TOP CHOICE Harbour View
Seafood Restaurant
SEAFOOD ££
(☏01478-612069; www.harbourviewskye.co.uk; 7 Bosville Tce; mains £14-19; ☺noon-3pm & 5.30-11pm Tue-Sun) The Harbour View is Portree's most congenial place to eat. It has a homely dining room with a log fire in winter, books on the mantelpiece and bric-a-brac on the shelves. And on the table, superb Scottish seafood, such as fresh Skye oysters, seafood chowder, succulent king scallops, langoustines and lobster. The platters are enormous and great value. Book ahead. Restricted hours October to April.

Café Arriba
CAFE £
(☏01478-611830; www.cafearriba.co.uk; Quay Brae; mains £4-8; ☺7am-10pm May-Sep, 8am-5.30pm Oct-Apr; ☑) Arriba is a funky little cafe, brightly decked out in primary colours and offering delicious flatbread melts (bacon, leek and cheese is our favourite) as well as the best choice of vegetarian grub on the island, ranging from a veggie breakfast fry-up to Indian-spiced bean cakes with mint yoghurt. Also serves excellent coffee.

❶ Getting There & Around

BICYCLE **Island Cycles** (☏01478-613121; www.islandcycles-skye.co.uk; The Green; ⊙9am-5pm Mon-Sat) You can hire bikes here for £8.50/15 per half-/full day.

BUS The main bus stop is in Somerled Sq. There are seven Scottish Citylink buses a day, including Sundays, from Kyle of Lochalsh to Portree (£6, one hour) and on to Uig.

Local buses (Monday to Saturday only) run from Portree to Broadford (40 minutes, at least hourly) via Sligachan (15 minutes); to Armadale (1¼ hours, connecting with the ferries to Mallaig); to Carbost (40 minutes, four daily); to Uig (30 minutes, six daily) and to Dunvegan Castle (40 minutes, five daily Monday to Friday, three on Saturday). There are also five or six buses a day on a circular route around Trotternish (in both directions) taking in Flodigarry (20 minutes), Kilmuir (1¼ hours) and Uig (30 minutes). Buses from the mainland also come through Portree.

Dunvegan (Dun Bheagain) & Around

Skye's most famous historic building, and one of its most popular tourist attractions, is **Dunvegan Castle** (☏01470-521206; www .dunvegancastle.com; adult/child £9.50/5; ⊙10am-5pm Apr–mid-Oct), seat of the chief of Clan MacLeod. It has played host to Samuel Johnson, Sir Walter Scott and, most famously, Flora MacDonald. The oldest parts are the 14th-century keep and dungeon but most of it dates from the 17th to 19th centuries.

There are some interesting artefacts, most famous being the **Fairy Flag**, a diaphanous silk banner that dates from some time between the 4th and 7th centuries.

🛏 Sleeping & Eating

⎡TOP⎤
⎣CHOICE⎦ **Three Chimneys**　MODERN SCOTTISH **£££**
(☏01470-511258; www.threechimneys.co.uk; Colbost; 3-course lunch/dinner £37/60; ⊙lunch Mon-Sat mid-Mar–Oct, dinner daily year-round; P) Halfway between Dunvegan and Waterstein, the Three Chimneys is a superb romantic retreat combining a gourmet restaurant in a candlelit crofter's cottage with sumptuous five-star rooms (double £295, dinner/ B&B including dinner per couple £415) in the modern house next door. Book well in advance, and note that children are not welcome in the restaurant in the evenings.

Trotternish

The Trotternish Peninsula to the north of Portree has some of Skye's most beautiful – and bizarre – scenery. On the eastern coast, the 50m-high, potbellied pinnacle of crumbling basalt known as the **Old Man of Storr**, is prominent above the road 6 miles north of Portree. North again is spectacular **Kilt Rock**, a stupendous cliff of columnar basalt whose vertical ribbing is fancifully compared to the pleats of a kilt, and the Quiraing, an impressive land-slipped escarpment bristling with crags and pinnacles. At Flodigarry, **Dun Flodigarry Hostel** (☏01470-552212; www.hostelflodigarry.co.uk; Flodigarry; dm/tw £17/38, sites per person £9; P@) enjoys a stunning location above the sea, with views across Raasay to the mainland mountains. A nearby hiking trail leads to the Quiraing (2.5 miles away), and there's a hotel bar barely 100m from the door. You can also camp here.

On the western side of the peninsula, the peat-reek of crofting life in the 18th and 19th centuries is preserved in thatched cottages at **Skye Museum of Island Life** (☏01470-552206; www.skyemuseum.co.uk; adult/child £2.50/50p; ⊙9.30am-5pm Mon-Sat Easter-Oct). Behind the museum is Kilmuir Cemetery, where a tall Celtic cross marks the grave of Flora MacDonald.

Whichever way you arrive at **Uig** (oo-ig), the picture-perfect bay, ringed by steep hills, rarely fails to impress. There's a cluster of B&Bs as well as the **Uig SYHA** (☏01470-542746; Uig; dm £17.50; ⊙Apr-Sep; P@).

Isle Of Raasay

POP 200

Raasay is the rugged, 10-mile-long island that lies off Skye's east coast. There are several good walks here, including one to the flat-topped conical hill of **Dun Caan** (443m). The extraordinary ruin of **Brochel Castle** was home to Calum Garbh MacLeod, an early 16th-century pirate.

Set in a rustic cottage high on the hill overlooking Skye, **Raasay SYHA** (☏01478-660240; Creachan Cottage; dm £18; ⊙mid-May–Aug) is a fair walk from the ferry pier (2.5 miles) but is a good base for exploring the island.

See www.raasay.com for a full listing of accommodation.

FLORA MACDONALD

Flora MacDonald, who became famous for helping Bonnie Prince Charlie escape after his defeat at the Battle of Culloden, was born in 1722 at Milton in South Uist, where a memorial cairn marks the site of one of her early childhood homes.

In 1746, she helped Bonnie Prince Charlie make his way from Benbecula to Skye disguised as her Irish maidservant. With a price on the prince's head, their little boat was fired on but they managed to land safely and Flora escorted the prince to Portree where he gave her a gold locket containing his portrait before setting sail for Raasay.

Waylaid on the way home, the boatmen admitted everything. Flora was arrested and imprisoned in the Tower of London. She never saw or heard from the prince again.

In 1747, she returned to Skye, marrying Allan MacDonald and having nine children. Dr Samuel Johnson stayed with her in 1773 during his trip to the Western Isles, but later poverty forced her family to emigrate to North Carolina. There her husband was captured by rebels. Flora returned to Kingsburgh on Skye where she died in 1790. She was buried in Kilmuir churchyard, wrapped in the sheet on which both Bonnie Prince Charlie and Dr Johnson had slept.

A CalMac **ferry** (www.calmac.co.uk; return passenger/car £7.25/39) runs from Sconser, between Portree and Broadford, to Raasay (15 minutes, hourly Monday to Saturday, twice daily Sunday). There are no petrol stations on the island.

OUTER HEBRIDES

POP 26,500

The Outer Hebrides – also known as the Western Isles, or Na h-Eileanan an Iar in Gaelic – are a 130-mile-long string of islands lying off the northwest coast of Scotland. There are 119 islands in total, of which the five main inhabited islands are: Lewis and Harris (two parts of a single island, although often described as if they are separate islands), North Uist, Benbecula, South Uist and Barra. The middle three (often referred to simply as 'the Uists') are connected by road-bearing causeways.

The ferry crossing from Ullapool or Uig to the Western Isles marks an important cultural divide – more than a third of Scotland's registered crofts are in the Outer Hebrides, and no less than 60% of the population are Gaelic speakers. The rigours of life in the old island blackhouses are still within living memory.

The name Hebrides is likely a corruption of the Roman name for the islands. But the alternative derivation from the Norse *hav-bredey* – 'isles at the edge of the sea' – has a much more poetic ring, alluding to the broad vistas of sky and sea that characterise the islands' often bleak and treeless landscapes. But there is beauty here too, in the machair (grassy, wildflower-speckled dunes) and dazzling white-sand beaches, majesty in the rugged hills and sprawling lochs, and mystery in the islands' fascinating past. It's a past signalled by Neolithic standing stones, Viking place names, deserted crofts and folk memories of the Clearances.

① Information

Tourist Information

Castlebay information centre (☑01871-810336; Main St, Castlebay; ☺9am-1pm & 2-5pm Mon-Sat, noon-4pm Sun Apr-Oct)

Lochboisdale information centre (☑01878-700286; Pier Rd, Lochboisdale; ☺9am-1pm & 2-5pm Fri-Mon & Wed, 9am-9.30pm Tue & Thu Apr-Oct)

Stornoway information centre (☑01851-703088; www.visithebrides.com; 26 Cromwell St, Stornoway; ☺9am-6pm & 8-9pm Mon, Tue & Thu, 9am-8pm Wed & Fri, 9am-5.30pm & 8-9pm Sat year-round)

Tarbert information centre (☑01880-820429; Harbour St, Tarbert; ☺9am-5pm Mon-Sat Apr-Oct)

① Getting There & Away

AIR There are airports at Stornoway (Lewis), Benbecula and Barra. There are flights to Stornoway from Edinburgh, Inverness, Glasgow and Aberdeen. There are also two flights a day (weekdays only) between Stornoway and Benbecula.

There are daily flights from Glasgow to Barra and Benbecula, and from Inverness to Benbecula. At Barra, the planes land on the hard-sand beach at low tide, so the timetable depends on the tides.

Airlines serving the Western Isles:
FlyBe/Loganair (☑01857-873457; www.loganair.co.uk)

Eastern Airways (☏0870 366 9100; www
.easternairways.com)

BOAT Standard one-way fares:

CROSSING	DURATION (HOURS)	CAR	DRIVER/ PASSENGER
Ullapool– Stornoway	2¾	£43	£8.40
Uig– Lochmaddy	1¾	£26	£5.70
Uig–Tarbet	1½	£26	£5.70
Oban– Castlebay	4¾	£57	£12.60
Oban– Lochboisdale	6¾	£57	£12.60

There are two to three ferries a day to Stornoway, one to two a day to Tarbert (not Sunday) and Lochmaddy, one a day to Castlebay and four a week to Lochboisdale. You can also take the ferry from Lochboisdale to Castlebay (car/passenger £21.65/7.50, 1½ hours, one daily Monday, Tuesday and Thursday) and from Castlebay to Lochboisdale (one daily Wednesday, Friday and Sunday).

Advance booking for cars is essential in July and August; foot and bicycle passengers should have no problems. Bicycles are carried for free.

❶ Getting Around

Despite their separate names, Lewis and Harris are actually one island. Berneray, North Uist, Benbecula, South Uist and Eriskay are all linked by road bridges and causeways. There are car ferries between Leverburgh (Harris) and Berneray; Tarbert (Harris) and Lochmaddy (North Uist); Eriskay and Castlebay (Barra); and Lochboisdale (South Uist) and Castlebay (Barra).

The local council publishes timetables of all bus, ferry and air services in the Outer Hebrides, available at tourist offices. Timetables can also be found online at www.cne-siar.gov.uk/travel.

BICYCLE Many visiting cyclists plan to cycle the length of the archipelago, but if you're one of them, remember that the wind is often strong, so south to north is usually the easier direction. Bikes can be hired for around £15 a day or £60 to £80 a week in Stornoway (Lewis), Leverburgh (Harris), Howmore (South Uist) and Castlebay (Barra).

BUS The bus network covers almost every village in the islands, with around four to six buses a day on all the main routes; however, there are no buses at all on Sundays.

CAR & MOTORCYCLE Cars can be hired from around £30 per day. One option:

Lewis Car Rentals (☏01851-703760; www
.lewis-car-rental.co.uk; 52 Bayhead St, Stornoway; ⊙Mon-Sat)

Lewis (Leodhais)
POP 18,600

The northern part of Lewis is dominated by the desolate expanse of the Black Moor, a vast, undulating peat bog dimpled with glittering lochans, seen clearly from the Stornoway–Barvas road. But Lewis' finest scenery is on the west coast. The Outer Hebrides' most evocative historic sites – Callanish Standing Stones, Dun Carloway, and Arnol Blackhouse Museum – are also to be found here.

STORNOWAY (STEORNABHAGH)
POP 6000

Stornoway is the bustling 'capital' of the Outer Hebrides and the only real town in the whole archipelago. It's a surprisingly busy little place, with cars and people swamping the centre on weekdays. Though set on a beautiful natural harbour, the town isn't going to win any prizes for beauty or atmosphere, but it's a pleasant enough introduction to this remote corner of the country.

◎ Sights

FREE An Lanntair Art Centre ARTS CENTRE
(☏01851-703307; www.lanntair.com; Kenneth St; ⊙10am-9pm Mon-Wed, to 10pm Thu, to midnight Fri & Sat) The modern, purpose-built An Lanntair Art Centre, complete with art gallery, theatre, cinema and restaurant, is the centre of the town's cultural life; it hosts changing exhibitions of contemporary art and is a good source of information on cultural events.

FREE Museum nan Eilean MUSEUM
(☏01851-703773; Francis St; ⊙10am-5.30pm Mon-Sat, shorter hrs in winter) This museum strings together a loose history of the Outer Hebrides from the earliest human settlements some 9000 years ago to the 20th century, exploring traditional island life and the changes brought by progress and technology.

☆ Festivals

Hebridean Celtic Festival MUSIC
(www.hebceltfest.com) A four-day extravaganza of folk/rock/Celtic music held in the second half of July.

KEEPING THE SABBATH

The Protestants of the Outer Hebrides have succeeded in maintaining a distinctive fundamentalist approach to their religion, with Sunday being devoted largely to religious services, prayer and Bible reading. On Lewis and Harris, the last bastion of Sabbath observance in the UK, almost everything closes down on a Sunday. In fact, Stornoway must be the only place in the UK to suffer a Sunday rush hour as people drive to church around 10.30am; it's then a ghost town for an hour and a half until the services are over. But a few cracks have begun to appear.

There was outrage when British Airways/Loganair introduced Sunday flights from Edinburgh and Inverness to Stornoway in 2002, with members of the Lord's Day Observance Society spluttering that this was the thin end of the wedge. They were probably right – in 2003 a Stornoway petrol station began to open on a Sunday, and now does a roaring trade in Sunday papers and takeaway booze. Then in 2006, CalMac ferries between Leverburgh and Berneray began operating on Sundays, followed in 2009 by the Ullapool to Stornoway crossing, despite strong opposition from the residents (ironically, they were unable to protest at the ferries' arrival, as that would have meant breaking the Sabbath).

🛏 Sleeping

Hal o' the Wynd   B&B ££
(☎01851-706073; www.halothewynd.com; 2 Newton St; s/d from £45/60) Touches of tartan and Harris tweed lend a tradtional air to this welcoming B&B, conveniently located directly opposite the ferry pier. Most rooms have views over the harbour to Lews Castle.

Braighe House   B&B ££
(☎01851-705287; www.braighehouse.co.uk; 20 Braighe Rd; s/d from £95/130; P) This spacious and comfortable guesthouse, 3 miles east of the centre on the A866, has stylish, modern bedrooms and a great seafront location. Good bathrooms with powerful showers, hearty breakfasts and genuinely hospitable owners round off the perfect package.

Park Guest House   B&B ££
(☎01851-702485; www.theparkguesthouse.co.uk; 30 James St; s/d from £58/110; @) A charming Victorian villa with a conservatory and eight luxurious rooms (mostly en suite), the Park Guest House is comfortable and central and has the advantage of an excellent restaurant specialising in Scottish seafood, beef and game (plus one or two vegetarian dishes). Rooms overlooking the main road can be noisy on weekday mornings.

Royal Hotel   HOTEL ££
(☎01851-702109; www.royalstornoway.co.uk; Cromwell St; s/d £87/133; P🛜) The 19th-century Royal is the most appealing of Stornoway's hotels – the rooms at the front retain period features such as wood panelling, and enjoy a view across the harbour to Lews Castle. Ask to see your room first, though, as some are a bit cramped.

Heb Hostel   HOSTEL £
(☎01851-709889; www.hebhostel.co.uk; 25 Kenneth St; dm £16; @🛜) The Heb is a friendly, easygoing hostel close to the ferry, with comfy wooden bunks, a convivial living room with peat fire and a welcoming owner who can provide all kinds of advice on what to do and where to go.

🍴 Eating

TOP CHOICE Digby Chick   BISTRO £££
(☎01851-700026; www.digbychick.co.uk; 5 Bank St; mains £18-24, 2-course lunch £12.50; ⊗Mon-Sat) A modern restaurant that dishes up bistro cuisine such as haddock and chips, slow roast pork belly or spiced cauliflower and spinach fritter at lunchtime, the Digby Chick metamorphoses into a candlelit gourmet restaurant in the evening, serving dishes such as grilled langoustines, seared scallops, venison and steak. There is a three-course early-bird menu for £18 (5.30pm to 6.30pm).

Thai Café   THAI £
(☎01851-701811; www.thai-cafe-stornoway.co.uk; 27 Church St; mains £5-8; ⊗noon-2.30pm & 5.30-11pm Mon-Sat) Here's a surprise – authentic, inexpensive Thai food in the heart of Stornoway. This spick-and-span little restaurant has a genuine Thai chef, and serves some of the most delicious, best-value Asian food in the Hebrides. If you can't get a table, it does takeaway too.

🛍 Shopping

Sandwick Rd Petrol Station FOOD & DRINK
(☑01851-702304; Sandwick Rd) The only shop in town that's open on a Sunday (from 10am to 4pm); the Sunday papers arrive around 2pm.

ℹ Getting There & Around

The bus station is on the waterfront, next to the ferry terminal (left luggage desk, 90p per piece). Bus W10 runs from Stornoway to Tarbert (£4.30, one hour, four or five daily Monday to Saturday) and Leverburgh (£6, two hours).

The Westside Circular bus W2 runs a circular route from Stornoway through Callanish, Carloway, Garenin and Arnol; the timetable means you can visit one or two of the sites in a day.

ARNOL

One of Scotland's most evocative historic buildings, the **Arnol Blackhouse** (HS; ☑01851-710395; adult/child £3.25/free; ⊙9.30am-5.30pm Mon-Sat Apr-Sep, to 4.30pm Mon-Sat Oct-Mar, last admission 30min before closing) is not so much a museum as a perfectly preserved fragment of a lost world. Built in 1885, this traditional blackhouse – a combined byre, barn and home – was inhabited until 1964 and has not been changed since the last inhabitant moved out. The staff faithfully rekindle the central peat fire every morning so you can experience the distinctive peat-reek; there's no chimney, and the smoke finds its own way out through the turf roof, windows and door – spend too long inside and you might feel like you've been kippered! The museum is just off the A858, about 3 miles west of Barvas.

GARENIN (NA GEARRANNAN)

The picturesque and fascinating **Gearrannan Blackhouse Village** is a cluster of nine restored thatch-roofed blackhouses perched above the exposed Atlantic coast. One of the cottages is home to the **Blackhouse Museum** (☑01851-643416; www.gearrannan.com; adult/child £2.70/1; ⊙9.30am-5.30pm Mon-Sat Apr-Sep), a traditional 1955 blackhouse with displays on the village's history, while another houses the **Taigh an Chocair Cafe** (mains £3-6; ⊙9.30am-5.30pm Mon-Sat).

The other blackhouses in the village are let out as self-catering **holiday cottages** (☑01851-643416; www.gearrannan.com; 2-person cottage £199 for 3 nights) offering the chance to stay in a unique and luxurious modernised blackhouse with attached kitchen and lounge. There's a minimum five-night let from June to August.

CARLOWAY (CARLABAGH)

Dun Carloway (Dun Charlabhaigh) is a 2000-year-old, dry-stone broch, perched defiantly above a beautiful loch with views to the mountains of North Harris. The site is clearly signposted along a minor road off the A858, a mile southwest of Carloway village. One of the best-preserved brochs in Scotland, its double walls (with internal staircase) still stand to a height of 9m and testify to the engineering skills of its Iron Age architects.

The tiny, turf-roofed **Doune Broch Centre** (☑01851-643338; admission free; ⊙10am-5pm Mon-Sat Apr-Sep) nearby has interpretative displays and exhibitions about the history of the broch and the life of the people who lived there.

CALLANISH (CALANAIS)

The **Callanish Standing Stones**, 15 miles west of Stornoway on the A858 road, form one of the most complete stone circles in

---

FOR PEAT'S SAKE

In the Outer Hebrides, where trees are few and far between and coal is absent, peat has been the main source of domestic fuel for many centuries. Although oil-fired central heating is now the norm, many houses have held on to their peat fires for nostalgia's sake.

Peat in its raw state is extremely wet and can take a couple of months to dry out. It is cut from roadside bogs, where the cuttings are at least a metre deep. Rectangular blocks of peat are cut using a long-handled tool called a *tairsgeir* (peat-iron) and carefully assembled into a *cruach-mhonach* (peat stack), each balanced on top of the other in a grid pattern thus creating maximum air space. Once the peat has dried out it is stored in a shed.

Peat burns much more slowly than wood or coal and produces a not unpleasant smell, but in the old blackhouses (which had no chimney) it permeated every corner of the dwelling, not to mention the inhabitants' clothes and hair, hence the expression 'peat-reek' – the ever-present smell of peat smoke that was long associated with island life.

SUNDAY EATS

Most restaurants in Stornoway are closed on Sundays. The few options for a sit-down meal include:

HS-1 Cafe-Bar (☑01851-702109; Royal Hotel, Cromwell St; mains £8-11; ☺noon-4pm & 5-9pm)

Stornoway Balti House (☑01851-706116; 24 South Beach; mains £8-13; ☺noon-2.30pm & 6-11pm)

Britain. It is one of the most atmospheric prehistoric sites anywhere; its ageless mystery, impressive scale and undeniable beauty leave a lasting impression. Sited on a wild and secluded promontory overlooking Loch Roag, 13 large stones of beautifully banded gneiss are arranged, as if in worship, around a 4.5m-tall central monolith. Some 40 smaller stones radiate from the circle in the shape of a cross, with the remains of a chambered tomb at the centre. Dating from 3800 to 5000 years ago, the stones are roughly contemporary with the pyramids of Egypt.

The nearby Calanais Visitor Centre (☑01851-621422; www.callanishvisitorcentre.co.uk; admission free, exhibition £2.50; ☺10am-9pm Mon-Sat Apr-Sep, to 4pm Wed-Sat Oct-Mar; 🅿) is a tour de force of discreet design. Inside is a small exhibition that speculates on the origins and purpose of the stones, and an excellent cafe (mains £5 to £7).

If you plan to stay the night, you have a choice of Eshcol Guest House (☑01851-621357; www.eshcol.com; 21 Breascleit; r per person £43; 🅿) and neighbouring Loch Roag Guest House (☑01851-621357; www.lochroag.com; 22a Breascleit; r per person £40-55; 🅿), half a mile north of Callanish. Both are modern bungalows with the same friendly owner, who is very knowledgeable about the local area.

Harris (Na Hearadh)

POP 2000

Harris, to the south of Lewis, is the scenic jewel in the necklace of islands that comprise the Outer Hebrides. It has a spectacular blend of rugged mountains, pristine beaches, flower-speckled machair and barren rocky landscapes. The isthmus at Tarbert splits Harris neatly in two: North Harris is dominated by mountains that rise forbiddingly above the peat moors to the south of

Stornoway – Clisham (799m) is the highest point. South Harris is lower-lying, fringed by beautiful white-sand beaches on the west and a convoluted rocky coastline to the east.

Harris is famous for Harris Tweed, a high-quality woollen cloth still hand-woven in islanders' homes. The industry employs around 400 weavers; staff at Tarbert tourist office can tell you about weavers and workshops that you can visit.

TARBERT (AN TAIRBEART)

POP 480

Tarbert is a harbour village with a spectacular location, tucked into the narrow neck of land that links North and South Harris. It has ferry connections to Uig on Skye.

Village facilities include a petrol station, bank, ATM and two general stores.

🛌 Sleeping & Eating

Hotel Hebrides　　　　　　　HOTEL ££
(☑01859-502364; www.hotel-hebrides.com; Pier Rd; s/d from £50/130; 🕿) The location and setting don't look promising – a nondescript new-build squeezed between ferry pier and car park – but this modern establishment brings a dash of urban glamour to Harris, with flashy fabrics and wall coverings, luxurious towels and toiletries, and a stylish restaurant and lounge bar.

Harris Hotel　　　　　　　　HOTEL ££
(☑01859-502154; www.harrishotel.com; s/d from £65/98; 🅿@🕿) Run since 1903 by four generations of the Cameron family, Harris Hotel is a 19th-century sporting hotel, originally built for deer-stalkers visiting the North Harris Estates. It has spacious, comfy rooms and a good restaurant; look out for JM Barrie's initials scratched on the dining-room window (the author of Peter Pan visited in the 1920s).

The hotel is on the way out of the village, on the road north towards Stornoway.

SOUTH HARRIS

The west coast of South Harris has some of the most beautiful beaches in Scotland. The blinding white sands and turquoise waters of Luskentyre and Scarasta would be major holiday resorts if they were transported to somewhere with a warm climate; as it is, they're usually deserted.

The culture and landscape of the Hebrides are celebrated in the fascinating exhibition at Seallam! Visitor Centre (www.seallam.com; Northton; adult/child £2.50/2; ☺10am-5pm Mon-Sat). The centre, which is in

Northton, just south of Scarasta, also has a genealogical research centre for people who want to trace their Hebridean ancestry.

The east coast is a complete contrast to the west – a strange, rocky moonscape of naked gneiss pocked with tiny lochans, the bleakness lightened by the occasional splash of green around the few crofting communities.

The village of Leverburgh (An t-Ob; www .leverburgh.co.uk) has a post office with an ATM, a general store and a petrol station.

Sleeping & Eating

Carminish Guest House
B&B ££

(☏01859-520400; www.carminish.com; 1a Strond, Leverburgh; s/d £55/75; P🛜) One of the few B&Bs in Harris that is open all year, the welcoming Carminish is a modern house with three comfy bedrooms. There's a view of the ferry from the dining room, and lots of nice little touches such as handmade soaps, a carafe of drinking water in the bedroom and individual reading lamps above the beds.

Sorrel Cottage
B&B ££

(☏01859-520319; www.sorrelcottage.co.uk; 2 Glen, Leverburgh; s/d from £45/70; 🕾) Sorrel Cottage is a pretty crofter's house, 1.5 miles west of the ferry at Leverburgh. Evening meals can be provided (£18); vegetarians and vegans are happily catered for. Bike hire available.

Am Bothan
HOSTEL £

(☏01859-520251; www.ambothan.com; Ferry Rd, Leverburgh; dm £20; P🛜) An attractive, chalet-style hostel, Am Bothan has small, neat dorms and a great porch where you can enjoy morning coffee with views over the creek. The hostel offers bike hire and can arrange wildlife-watching boat trips.

❶ Getting There & Around

A **CalMac** (www.calmac.co.uk) car ferry zig-zags through the reefs of the Sound of Harris from Leverburgh to Berneray (pedestrian/car £6.95/31.50, 1¼ hours, three or four daily Monday to Saturday).

There are two to four buses a day (except Sunday) from Tarbert to Leverburgh.

Berneray (Bearnaraigh)
POP 140

Berneray (www.isleofberneray.com) was linked to North Uist by a causeway in October 1998, but that hasn't altered the peace and beauty of the island. The beaches on its

west coast are some of the most beautiful and unspoilt in Britain, and seals and otters can be seen in Bays Loch on the east coast.

The basic but atmospheric Gatliff Hostel (www.gatliff.org.uk; dm adult/child £12/7, sites per person £7), housed in a pair of restored blackhouses right by the sea, is the place to stay. You can camp outside, or on the grass above the gorgeous white-sand beach just to the north.

Bus W19 runs from Berneray (Gatliff Hostel and Harris ferry) to Lochmaddy (30 minutes, six daily Monday to Saturday). There are ferries to Leverburgh (Harris).

North Uist (Uibhist A Tuath)
POP 1550

North Uist, an island half-drowned by lochs, is famed for its trout fishing but also has some magnificent beaches on its north and west coasts. For birdwatchers this is an earthly paradise, with regular sightings of waders and wildfowl ranging from red-shank to red-throated diver to red-necked phalarope. The landscape is less wild and mountainous than Harris but it has a sleepy, subtle appeal.

Little Lochmaddy is the first village you hit after arriving on the ferry from Skye. There's a tourist office, a couple of stores, a bank with an ATM, a petrol station, a post office and a pub.

SIGHTS & ACTIVITIES

Balranald RSPB Reserve
WILDLIFE RESERVE

Birdwatchers flock to this Royal Society for the Protection of Birds (RSPB) nature reserve, 18 miles west of Lochmaddy, in the hope of spotting the rare red-necked phalarope or hearing the distinctive call of the corncrake. There's a visitors centre (admission free; ☺9am-6pm Apr-Aug) with a resident warden who offers 1½-hour guided walks (£5, 10am on Tuesdays, May to August).

Taigh Chearsabhagh
ARTS CENTRE, MUSEUM

(☏01876-500293; http://taigh-chearsabhagh.org; Lochmaddy; arts centre free, museum £3; ☺10am-4pm Mon-Sat) Taigh Chearsabhagh is a museum and arts centre that preserves and displays the history and culture of the Uists, and is also a thriving community centre, post office and meeting place. The centre's cafe (mains £3 to £7) dishes up homemade soups, sandwiches and cakes.

🛏 Sleeping & Eating

Tigh Dearg Hotel   HOTEL ££
(📞01876-500700; www.tighdearghotel.co.uk; Lochmaddy; s/d from £99/110; 🅿🛜) It looks a little like a hostel from the outside but the 'Red House' (as the name means) is actually Lochmaddy's most luxurious accommodation, with nine designer bedrooms, a lounge with leather sofas around an open fire, a gym and even a sauna. There's a good restaurant too, with sea views from the terrace.

Old Courthouse   B&B ££
(📞01876-500358; oldcourthouse@googlemail.com; Lochmaddy; r per person from £30; 🅿) This Georgian-style villa is within walking distance of the ferry, on the road that leads to Uist Outdoor Centre. It's a bit worn around the edges but full of character, with traditional porridge for breakfast, homemade marmalade, and kippers on the menu too.

Benbecula (Beinn Na Faoghla)

POP 1200

Benbecula is a low-lying island whose flat, lochan-studded landscape is best appreciated from the summit of Rueval (124m), the island's highest point. There's a path around the south side of the hill (signposted from the main road; park beside the landfill site) that is said to be the route taken to the coast by Bonnie Prince Charlie and Flora MacDonald during the prince's escape in 1746.

The control centre for the British army's Hebrides Missile Range (located on the northwestern tip of South Uist) is the island's main source of employment, and Balivanich (Baile a'Mhanaich) – looking like a corner of a Glasgow housing estate planted incongruously on the machair – is the commercial centre serving the troops and their families. The village has an airport, bank with an ATM, a post office, a large Co-op supermarket (⊙8am-8pm Mon-Sat, 11am-6pm Sun) and a petrol station (open on Sundays).

South Uist (Uibhist A Deas)

POP 1900

South Uist is the second-largest island in the Outer Hebrides and saves its choicest corners for those who explore away from the main north–south road. The low-lying west coast is an almost unbroken stretch of white-sand beach and flower-flecked mach-

air – a new waymarked hiking trail, the Machair Way, follows the coast – while the multitude of inland lochs provide excellent trout fishing. The east coast, riven by four large sea lochs, is hilly and remote, with spectacular Beinn Mhor (620m) the highest point.

Driving south from Benbecula you cross from the predominantly Protestant northern half of the Outer Hebrides into the mostly Roman Catholic south, a religious transition marked by the granite statue of Our Lady of the Isles on the slopes of Rueval (the hill with the military radomes on its summit), and the presence of many roadside shrines.

The ferry port of Lochboisdale is the island's largest settlement, with a tourist office, a bank with an ATM, a grocery store and a petrol station. There's a Co-op supermarket (⊙8am-8pm Mon-Sat, 12.30-6pm Sun) at Daliburgh, 3 miles west of the village.

SIGHTS & ACTIVITIES

Loch Druidibeg National Nature Reserve   WILDLIFE RESERVE
The northern part of the island is mostly occupied by the watery expanses of Loch Bee and Loch Druidibeg. Loch Druidibeg National Nature Reserve is an important breeding ground for birds such as dunlin, redshank, ringed plover, greylag goose and corncrake; you can take a 5-mile self-guided walk through the reserve.

Pick up a leaflet from the Scottish Natural Heritage office on the main road beside Loch Druidiberg.

Kildonan Museum   MUSEUM
(📞01878-710343; www.kildonanmuseum.co.uk; Kildonan; adult/child £2/free; ⊙10am-5pm Apr-Oct) Six miles south of Howmore, Kildonan Museum explores the lives of local crofters through its collection of artefacts – an absorbing exhibition of black-and-white photography and first-hand accounts of harsh Hebridean conditions.

There's also an excellent tearoom (mains £3-8; ⊙11am-4pm) and craft shop.

Amid Milton's ruined blackhouses, half a mile south of the museum, a cairn marks the site of Flora MacDonald's birthplace.

🛏 Sleeping & Eating

🏆 Polochar Inn   INN ££
(📞01878-700215; www.polocharinn.com; Polochar; s/d from £70/90; 🅿) Run by local sisters

Morag McKinnon and Margaret Campbell, this 18th-century inn has been transformed into a stylish, welcoming hotel with a stunning location looking out across the sea to Barra. The excellent restaurant and bar menu (mains £8 to £17) includes fish chowder, haddock and chips, local salmon and Uist lamb.

Polochar is 7 miles southwest of Lochboisdale, on the way to Eriskay.

Wireless Cottage   B&B £

(☏01878-700660; www.wirelesscottage.co.uk; Lochboisdale; per person £25) This pretty little cottage that once housed the local telephone exchange is now a welcoming and good-value B&B a short (300m) walk from the ferry, with just two bedrooms (one double, one family).

Tobha Mor Crofters' Hostel   HOSTEL £

(www.gatliff.org.uk; Howmore; dm adult/child £12/7) Atmospheric hostel housed in a restored thatched blackhouse, about six miles south of Loch Druidibeg.

Eriskay (Eiriosgaigh)

POP 170

In 1745 Bonnie Prince Charlie first set foot in Scotland on the west coast of Eriskay, on the sandy beach (immediately north of the ferry terminal) still known as Prince's Strand (Coilleag a'Phrionnsa).

More recently the SS *Politician* sank just off the island in 1941. The islanders salvaged much of its cargo of around 250,000 bottles of whisky and, after a binge of dramatic proportions, the police intervened and a number of the islanders landed in jail. The story was immortalised by Sir Compton Mackenzie in his comic novel *Whisky Galore*, later made into a famous film.

A CalMac (p929) car ferry links Eriskay with Ardmhor at the northern end of Barra (pedestrian/car £7.50/21.65, 40 minutes, four or five daily).

Barra (Barraigh)

POP 1150

With its beautiful beaches, wildflower-clad dunes, rugged little hills and strong sense of community, diminutive Barra – just 14 miles in circumference – is the Outer Hebrides in miniature. For a great view of the island, walk up to the top of Heaval (383m), a mile northeast of Castlebay.

Castlebay (Bagh a'Chaisteil), in the south, is the largest village. There's a tourist office (p924), a bank with an ATM, a post office and two grocery stores.

⊙ Sights & Activities

Kisimul Castle   CASTLE

(HS; ☏01871-810313; Castlebay; adult/child incl ferry £5/3; ⊙9.30am-5.30pm Apr-Sep) Castlebay takes its name from the island fortress of Kisimul Castle, first built by the MacNeil clan in the 11th century. A short boat trip (weather permitting) takes you out to the island, where you can explore the fortifications and soak up the view from the battlements.

The castle was restored in the 20th century by American architect Robert MacNeil, who became the 45th clan chief; he gifted the castle to Historic Scotland in 2000 for an annual rent of £1 and a bottle of whisky (Talisker single malt, if you're interested).

🛏 Sleeping & Eating

Wild camping (on foot or by bike) is allowed almost anywhere.

Castlebay Hotel   HOTEL ££

(☏01871-810223; www.castlebayhotel.com; Castlebay; s/d from £60/102; 🅿) The Castlebay Hotel offers spacious bedrooms decorated with a subtle tartan motif – it's worth paying a bit extra for a sea view – and there's a comfy lounge and conservatory with grand views across the harbour to the islands south of Barra.

The hotel bar is the hub of island social life, with regular sessions of traditional music, and the restaurant specialises in local seafood and game (rabbit is often on the menu).

Dunard Hostel   HOSTEL £

(☏01871-810443; www.dunardhostel.co.uk; Castlebay; dm/tw from £16/36; 🅿) This is a friendly, family-run hostel just five minutes' walk from the ferry terminal. The owners can organise sea-kayaking tours for £35/65 for a half-/full day.

❶ Getting There & Around

BICYCLE You can hire bikes from **Island Adventures** (☏01871-810284; Castlebay; per day £12).

BOAT There are CalMac ferries from Castlebay to Oban and Lochboisdale (South Uist) and flights to the Scottish mainland; there is also a ferry from Ardmhor, at the northern end of Barra, to Eriskay.

BUS Bus W32 makes a regular (not Sundays) circuit of the island and also connects with flights.

Orkney Islands

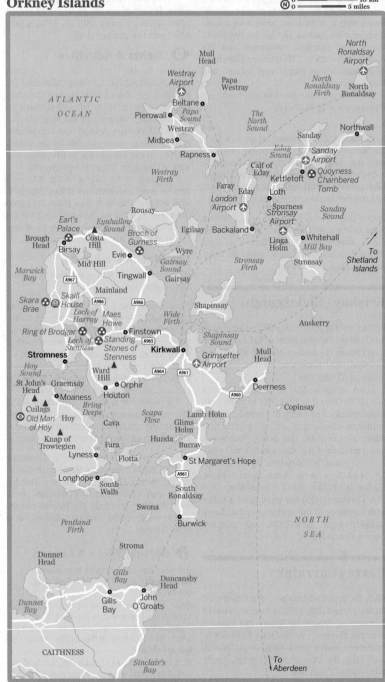

ORKNEY ISLANDS

There's a magic to the Orkney Islands that you'll begin to feel as soon as the Scottish mainland slips away astern. Consisting of 70 flat, green-topped islands stripped bare of trees by the wind, it's a place of ancient standing stones and prehistoric villages, an archipelago of old-style hospitality and Viking heritage narrated in the *Orkneyinga Saga* and still strong today, a region whose ports tell of lives led with the blessings and rough moods of the sea, and a destination where seekers can find melancholy wrecks of warships and the salty clamour of remote seabird colonies.

The principal island, confusingly called Mainland, has the two major settlements – bustling market-town Kirkwall, and Stromness with its grey-flagged streets – and the standout ancient sites. Ferries and flights give access to the other 15 inhabited islands.

Tours

Wildabout Orkney GUIDED TOUR
(☑01856-877737; www.wildaboutorkney.com) Operates tours covering Orkney's history, ecology, folklore and wildlife. Day-trips operate year-round and cost £49, with pick-ups in Stromness and Kirkwall.

John O'Groats Ferries BUS TOUR
(☑01955-611353; www.jogferry.co.uk; ⊗May-Sep) If you're in a hurry, this operator runs a one-day tour of the main sites for £52, including the ferry from John O'Groats. You can do the whole thing as a long day-trip from Inverness.

Getting There & Away
Air
Flybe (☑0871 700 2000; www.flybe.com) flies daily from Kirkwall to Aberdeen, Edinburgh, Glasgow, Inverness and Sumburgh (Shetland). In summer it also serves Bergen (Norway).

Boat
During summer, book car spaces ahead. Fares vary according to season (low to peak fares are quoted here).

FROM SCRABSTER, SHETLANDS & ABERDEEN Northlink Ferries (☑0845 6000 449; www.northlinkferries.co.uk) operates ferries from Scrabster to Stromness (passenger £16 to £19, car £50 to £55, 1½ hours, two to three daily), from Aberdeen to Kirkwall (passenger £20 to £30, car £75 to £104, six hours, three or four weekly) and from Kirkwall to Lerwick (passenger one way £16 to £23, car one way £58 to £96, six to eight hours, three or four a week) on the Shetland Islands.

FROM GILLS BAY Pentland Ferries (☑0800 688 8998, 01856-831226; www.pentlandferries.co.uk) boats leave from Gills Bay, about 3 miles west of John O'Groats, and head to St Margaret's Hope on South Ronaldsay (passenger/car £14/33, one hour). There are three to four crossings daily.

FROM JOHN O'GROATS From May to September, **John O'Groats Ferries** (☑01955-611353; www.jogferry.co.uk) operates a passenger-only service from John O'Groats to Burwick, on the southern tip of South Ronaldsay (one way/return £20/30). A bus to Kirkwall meets the ferry (all-included return from John O'Groats to Kirkwall is £32). There are two to three departures daily.

Bus
John O'Groats Ferries operates the summer-only Orkney bus service from Inverness to Kirkwall. Tickets (one way/return £38/52, five hours) include bus-ferry-bus travel from Inverness to Kirkwall. There are two buses daily from June to early September.

Getting Around

The *Orkney Transport Guide*, a detailed schedule of all bus, ferry and air services around and to/from Orkney, is available free from tourist offices.

The largest island, Mainland, is linked by causeways to Burray and South Ronaldsay; other islands are reached by air and ferry.

Air
Loganair (☑01856-873457; www.loganair.co.uk) operates interisland flights from Kirkwall. See individual islands for details.

Bicycle
Various locations on Mainland hire bikes, including **Cycle Orkney** (☑01856-875777; www.cycleorkney.com; Tankerness Lane, Kirkwall; per day £15; ⊗Mon-Sat; 🚲) and **Orkney Cycle Hire** (☑01856-850255; www.orkneycyclehire.co.uk; 54 Dundas St, Stromness; per day £8.50-10).

Boat
Orkney Ferries (☑01856-872044; www.orkneyferries.co.uk) operates car ferries from Mainland to the islands. See individual islands for details.

Bus
Stagecoach (☑01856-870555; www.stagecoachbus.com) Runs buses on Mainland and connecting islands. Most don't operate on Sunday. Dayrider (£7.75) and 7-Day Megarider (£17) tickets allow unlimited travel.

Car
Small-car rates begin at around £34/175 per day/week, although there are specials for as low as £28 per day.

INVERNESS & THE NORTHERN HIGHLANDS & ISLANDS ORKNEY ISLANDS

Kirkwall

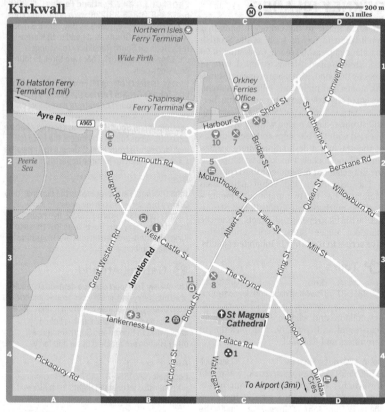

Kirkwall

⊚ Top Sights
St Magnus Cathedral C4

⊚ Sights
1 Earl's Palace & Bishop's Palace C4
2 Orkney Museum B4

⊕ Activities, Courses & Tours
3 Cycle Orkney B4

⊜ Sleeping
4 2 Dundas Crescent D4
5 Albert Hotel C2
6 Peedie Hostel B2

⊗ Eating
7 Kirkwall Hotel C2
8 Reel C3
9 Shore C2

⊜ Drinking
10 Helgi's C2

⊜ Shopping
11 Longship B3

Drive Orkney (☎01856-877551; www.drive
orkney.com; Garrison Rd, Kirkwall)
Norman Brass Car Hire (☎01856-850850;
www.stromnesscarhire.co.uk; North End Rd,
Stromness) At the Blue Star Garage.

Orkney Car Hire (☎01856-872866; www
.orkneycarhire.co.uk; Junction Rd, Kirkwall)
WR Tullock (☎01856-875500; www.orkney
carrental.co.uk; Castle St, Kirkwall)

Kirkwall

POP 6200

The capital of Orkney is a bustling market town, set back from a wide bay. Kirkwall's long, winding, paved main street and twisting wynds (lanes) are very atmospheric, and the town has a magnificent cathedral. Founded in the early 11th century, when Earl Rognvald Brusson established his kingdom here, the original part of Kirkwall is one of the best examples of an ancient Norse town.

◉ Sights

FREE **St Magnus Cathedral**   CATHEDRAL
(☑01856-874894; www.stmagnus.org; Broad St; ⊙9am-6pm Mon-Sat, 2-6pm Sun Apr-Sep, 9am-1pm & 2-5pm Mon-Sat Oct-Mar) Founded in 1137 and constructed from local red sandstone, fabulous St Magnus Cathedral is Kirkwall's centrepiece. The powerful atmosphere of an ancient faith pervades the impressive interior. Lyrical and melodramatic epitaphs of the dead line the walls and emphasise the serious business of 17th- and 18th-century bereavement.

Earl Rognvald Brusason commissioned the cathedral in the name of his martyred uncle, Magnus Erlendsson, who was killed by Earl Hakon Paulsson on Egilsay in 1117. Work began in 1137, but the building is actually the result of 300 years of construction and alteration.

Earl's Palace & Bishop's Palace   RUIN
(HS; ☑01856-871918; www.historic-scotland.gov.uk; Watergate; adult/child £4.50/2.70; ⊙9.30am-5.30pm Apr-Sep, to 4.30pm Oct) These two ruined palaces are worth poking around. The more intriguing, the Earl's Palace, was once known as the finest example of French Renaissance architecture in Scotland. One room features an interesting history of its builder, Earl Patrick Stewart, who was executed in Edinburgh for treason. He started construction in about 1600, but ran out of money and it was never completed.

The Bishop's Palace was built in the mid-12th century to provide comfortable lodgings for Bishop William the Old. There's a good view of the cathedral from the tower, and a plaque showing the different phases of the cathedral's construction.

FREE **Orkney Museum**   MUSEUM
(☑01856-873191; www.orkney.gov.uk; Broad St; ⊙10.30am-5pm Mon-Sat May-Sep, 10.30am-12.30pm & 1.30-5pm Mon-Sat Oct-Apr) Opposite St Magnus Cathedral, in a former merchant's house, is this labyrinthine display. It has an overview of Orcadian history and prehistory, including Pictish carvings and a display on the Ba'. Most engaging are the last rooms, covering 19th- and 20th-century social history.

TOP CHOICE **Highland Park Distillery**   DISTILLERY
(☑01856 874619; www.highlandpark.co.uk; Holm Rd; tour adult/child £6/free; ⊙daily May-Aug, Mon-Fri Sep-Apr) This distillery, where they malt their own barley, is great to visit. You can see the barley and the peat kiln used to dry it on the excellent, well-informed hourlong tour (hourly when open, and weekdays at 2pm and 3pm in winter).The standard 12-year-old is a soft, balanced malt, great for novices and aficionados alike; the 18-year-old is among the world's finest drams. This and older whiskies can be tasted on more specialised tours (£35 and £75), which you can prearrange.

✦ Festivals & Events

St Magnus Festival   ARTS, MUSIC
(☑01856-871445; www.stmagnusfestival.com) A colourful celebration of music and the arts in June.

⌁ Sleeping

TOP CHOICE **Albert Hotel**   HOTEL ££
(☑01856-876000; www.alberthotel.co.uk; Mounthoolie Lane; s/d £96/133; ☎) Stylishly refurbished in plum and grey, this central but peaceful hotel is Kirkwall's finest address. Comfortable contemporary rooms in a variety of categories sport super-inviting beds and smart bathrooms. A great Orkney base, but you may end up spending more time in the excellent Bothy Bar downstairs. Walk-in prices are usually somewhat lower than these rack rates.

Lynnfield Hotel   HOTEL ££
(☑01856-872505; www.lynnfieldhotel.co.uk; Holm Rd; s £85-95, d £110-150; ☎) Within whiffing distance of the Highland Park distillery, this sizeable yet intimate hotel is run with a professional, but warmly personal, touch. Rooms are individually decorated, and feature extremely handsome furniture

and plenty of character. Deluxe rooms feature enormous bathrooms and opulent four-poster beds; others might showcase a Jacuzzi or antique writing desk. The public areas include a cosy dark-wood drawing room and a large, well-regarded restaurant (dinner mains £16 to £19).

Orcades Hostel
HOSTEL £

(☎01856-873745; www.orcadeshostel.com; Muddisdale Rd; dm/s/d £18/40/50; P@⑤) Book ahead to get a bed in this cracking hostel near the campground on the western edge of town. It's a guesthouse conversion so there's a very smart kitchen and lounge area, and great-value doubles. Comfortable dorms with just four bunks make for sound sleeping, and young, enthusiastic owners give the place plenty of spark.

2 Dundas Crescent
B&B ££

(☎01856-874805; www.twodundas.co.uk; 2 Dundas Cres; s/d £40/75; P⑤) This former manse is a magnificent building that has four enormous rooms blessed with large windows and sizeable beds. There are plenty of period features, but the en-suite bathrooms are not among them: they're sparklingly new, and one has a free-standing bathtub. Both the welcome and the breakfast will leave you more than satisfied.

Peedie Hostel
HOSTEL £

(☎01856-875477; www.peediehostel.yolasite.com; Ayre Rd; dm/s/d £15/20/30) Nestling into a corner at the end of the Kirkwall waterfront, this cute hostel set in former fisherfolk's cottages squeezes in all the necessary features for a comfortable stay. Despite the compact appearance, the dorms actually have plenty of room – and there are three tiny kitchens so you should find some elbow room. A separate 'bothy' sleeps four and costs £60.

Pickaquoy Caravan & Camping Park
CAMPGROUND £

(☎01856-879900; www.pickaquoy.co.uk; Muddisdale Rd; sites per person £6.95, 2-3 people £13.50; ⊙Apr-Oct; P⑤⑧) No view, but plenty of grass and excellent modern facilities. If the office is unattended, check in at the nearby Pickaquoy leisure centre.

✕ Eating & Drinking

TOP CHOICE Foveran
ORCADIAN ££

(☎01856-872389; www.thefoveran.com; St Ola; mains £14-23; ⊙dinner) Three miles from Kirkwall on the Orphir road, this is one of Orkney's best dining options, but surprisingly affordable for the quality on offer. In a tranquil location with a cosy eating area overlooking the sea, it's at its best presenting classic Orcadian ingredients – the steak with haggis and whisky sauce is feted throughout the region, while the North Ronaldsay lamb comes with meat from four different cuts and is deliciously tender. A medley of toothsome vegetables accompanies the mains, and interesting wines complement the dishes. If you like the spot – and why wouldn't you? – there are rooms available (single/double £78/116).

Reel
CAFE £

(www.wrigleyandthereel.com; Albert St; sandwiches £3-4; ⊙9am-6pm) Part music shop and part cafe, Kirkwall's best coffee-stop is alongside St Magnus Cathedral, and bravely puts tables outside at the slightest threat of sunshine. It's a relaxed spot that's good for a morning-after debriefing, as well as a lunchtime panini and musically named sandwiches (as well as their cheese one: Skara Brie). It's a centre for local folk musicians, with regular evening sessions.

Shore
GASTROPUB ££

(www.theshore.co.uk; 6 Shore St; restaurant mains £12-18; ⊙food 8am-9.30pm; ⑤) This popular harbourside eatery brings the gastropub concept to Kirkwall, offering bar meals combined with more adventurous fare in the restaurant section. It's run with a customer-comes-first attitude, and the seafood is especially good.

Kirkwall Hotel
PUB, SCOTTISH ££

(☎01856-872232; www.kirkwallhotel.com; Harbour St; mains £8-16) This grand old hotel on the waterfront is one of Kirkwall's best dining places. The elegant bar and eating area packs out; it's a favourite spot for an evening out with the clan. There's a fairly standard pub-food list that's complemented by a seasonal menu featuring local seafood and meat – the lamb is delicious.

Helgi's
PUB

(www.helgis.co.uk; 14 Harbour St; ⑤) There's a traditional cosiness about this place, but the decor has moved beyond the time-honoured beer-soaked carpet to a comfortable contemporary slate floor and quotes from the *Orkneyinga Saga* plastering the walls. It's more find-a-table than jostle-at-the-bar and serves cheerful, well-priced comfort food (mains

£7 to £10). Take your pint upstairs for quiet harbour contemplation.

Shopping

Kirkwall has some gorgeous jewellery and crafts along Albert St. Try Longship (01856-888790; 7 Broad St; 9am-5.30pm Mon-Sat) for Orkney-made crafts and gifts, and exquisite designer jewellery.

Information

Kirkwall information centre (01856-872856; www.visitorkney.com; West Castle St; 9am-6pm daily May-Sep, 9am-5pm Mon-Fri & 10am-4pm Sat Oct-Apr) Has a good range of publications on Orkney.

Orkney library (01856-873166; 44 Junction Rd; 9.15am-5pm Tue-Sat, to 7pm Mon & Thu) Free Internet.

Getting There & Away

AIR Flybe (p933) and Loganair (p933) services use **Kirkwall Airport** (www.hial.co.uk), located 2.5 miles east of town.

BOAT Ferries to the North Isles depart from the town harbour; however, ferries to Aberdeen and Shetland use the Hatston terminal, 1 mile northwest.

BUS The bus station is on the west side of town behind the tourist office. From here, bus X1 runs direct from Kirkwall to Stromness (30 minutes, hourly, seven Sunday); bus 2 runs to Orphir and Houton (20 minutes, four or five Monday to Saturday); bus 6 runs from Kirkwall to Evie (30 minutes, three to five daily Monday to Saturday) and to Tingwall to connect with the ferry to Rousay.

Mainland to South Ronaldsay

After the sinking of the battleship HMS *Royal Oak* by a German U-boat in 1939, Winston Churchill had vast causeways of concrete blocks erected across the channels on the eastern side of Scapa Flow, linking Mainland to the islands of Lamb Holm, Burray and South Ronaldsay. The Churchill Barriers, as they became known, flanked by the rusting wrecks of blockships, now support the main road from Kirkwall to Burwick.

Getting There & Away

There are buses from Kirkwall to South Ronaldsay's St Margaret's Hope (30 minutes, almost hourly Monday to Saturday).

THE BA'

Every Christmas Day and New Year's Day, Kirkwall holds a staggering spectacle: a crazy ball game known as the Ba'. Two enormous teams, the Uppies and the Doonies, fight their way, no holds barred, through the streets, trying to get a leather ball to the other end of town. Violence, skulduggery and other stunts are common and the event, fuelled by plenty of strong drink, can last hours.

LAMB HOLM

On the tiny island of Lamb Holm, the Italian Chapel (01865-781268; admission free; 9am-dusk) is all that remains of a POW camp that housed the Italian soldiers who worked on the Churchill Barriers. They built the chapel in their spare time, using two Nissen huts, scrap metal and their considerable artistic and decorative skills. One of the artists returned in 1960 to restore the paintwork. It's quite extraordinary inside and definitely worth seeing.

SOUTH RONALDSAY

South Ronaldsay's main village, pristine St Margaret's Hope was named after the Maid of Norway, who died here in 1290 on the way from her homeland to marry Edward II of England (strictly a political affair: Margaret was only seven years old). The ferry from Gills Bay on mainland Scotland docks here, while the passenger ferry from John O'Groats lands at Burwick, at the island's southern tip.

Sights

Tomb of the Eagles ARCHAEOLOGICAL SITE (01865-831339; www.tomboftheeagles.co.uk; Liddel; adult/child £6.80/2; 9.30am-5.30pm Apr-Oct, 10am-noon Mar, by arrangement Nov-Feb) Near Burwick, this is the result of a local farmer finding two significant archaeological sites on his land. The first is a Bronze Age stone building with a firepit, indoor well, and plenty of seating; a communal cooking site or the original Orkney pub? Beyond, in a spectacular clifftop position, the Neolithic tomb (wheel yourself in prone on a trolley) is an elaborate stone construction which held the remains of up to 340 people who died some five millennia ago. Before you head out to the sites, an excellent personal explanation is given to you at the visitor centre; you meet a few spooky skulls and can handle some of the artefacts found. It's about a mile's airy walk to the tomb from the centre.

Banks Chambered Tomb ARCHAEOLOGICAL SITE
(Tomb of the Otters; www.bankschamberedtomb. co.uk; Cleat; adult/child £5/free; ⊙10am-5pm Apr-Oct) Accidentally discovered recently while making a carpark for the adjacent bistro, this 5000-year-old chambered tomb is still being investigated but has yielded a vast quantity of human bones, well preserved thanks to the saturation of the earth. The tomb is dug into bedrock and makes for an atmospheric if claustrophobic visit. The guided tour from the guy who found it mixes homespun archaeological theories with astute observations. You can handle stones and bones that have been found, including the remains of otters, who presumably used this as a den in between burial ceremonies. Follow signs for Tomb of the Eagles, until you see this tomb signposted.

🛏 Sleeping & Eating

TOP CHOICE **Bankburn House** B&B ££
(☎01856-831310; www.bankburnhouse.co.uk; s/d £45/70, without bathroom £40/59; 🅿@🛜🐾) This large rustic house does everything right, with smashing rooms of a great size, and engaging owners who put on quality breakfasts and take pride in thinking of new innovations to further improve guests' comfort levels. There's a huge stretch of lawn out the front, which overlooks the town and bay – perfect for sunbathing on shimmering Orkney summer days. Listed prices are for one-night stays; things drop substantially after that, so for example, for three nights you'll only pay £52 per night for the double ensuite: an absolute bargain. It's on the A961, just outside St Margaret's Hope.

St Margaret's Hope Backpackers HOSTEL £
(☎01856-831225; www.orkneybackpackers.com; dm £14; 🅿) Just a stroll from the ferry, this hostel is a lovely stone cottage offering small, simple rooms with up to four berths – great for families. There's a lounge, kitchen, laundry and good, hot showers. It's an excellent set-up and you can use the adjacent cafe's wi-fi. Book in at the Trading Post shop next door.

TOP CHOICE **Creel** SEAFOOD £££
(☎01856-831311; www.thecreel.co.uk; Front Rd, St Margaret's Hope; 2-/3-course dinner £33/40; ⊙dinner Wed-Sun Apr–mid-Oct; 🛜) On the water-

front in an unassuming house, on unpretentious wooden tables, some of Scotland's best seafood has been served up for well over 20 years. Upstairs, three most comfortable rooms (singles/doubles £75/110) face the spectacular sunset over the water. Wooden ceilings and plenty of space give them an airy feel. It was up for sale at the time of research, so fingers crossed.

West & North Mainland

This part of the island is sprinkled with outstanding prehistoric monuments: the journey up to Orkney is worth it for these alone.

A short walk to the east are the excavated remains of Barnhouse Neolithic Village, thought to have been inhabited by the builders of Maes Howe.

MAES HOWE

Egypt has the pyramids, Scotland has Maes Howe (HS; ☎01856-761606; www.historic-scotland.gov.uk; adult/child £5.50/3.30; ⊙tours hourly 10am-4pm). Constructed about 5000 years ago, it's an extraordinary place, a Stone Age tomb built from enormous sandstone blocks, some of which weighed many tons and were brought from several miles away. Creeping down the long stone passageway to the central chamber, you feel the indescribable gulf of years that separate us from the architects of this mysterious place. Though nothing is known about who and what was interred here, the scope of the project suggests it was a structure of real significance.

In the 12th century, the tomb was broken into by Vikings searching for treasure. Later another group sought shelter in the chamber from a blizzard that lasted three days. While they waited out the storm, they carved runic graffiti on the walls. As well as the some-things-never-change 'Olaf was 'ere' and 'Thorni bedded Helga', there are also more intricate carvings, including a particularly fine dragon and a knotted serpent.

Buy tickets in Tormiston Mill, on the other side of the road. Entry is by 45-minute guided tours that leave on the hour. Be sure to reserve your tour-slot ahead by phone. Due to the oversized groups, guides tend to only show a couple of the Viking inscriptions, but they'll happily show more if asked.

STANDING STONES OF STENNESS

Within sight of Maes Howe, four mighty stones (HS; www.historic-scotland.gov.uk; admission free; ⊙24hr) remain of what was once a circle of 12. Recent research suggests they were perhaps erected as long ago as 3300 BC, and they impose by their sheer size; the tallest measures 5.7m in height. This narrow strip of land, the Ness of Brodgar, separates the Harray and Stenness lochs and was the site of a large settlement, inhabited during the Neolithic period (3500–1800 BC).

A short walk to the east are the excavated remains of Barnhouse Neolithic Village, thought to have been inhabited by the builders of Maes Howe. Don't skip this: it brings the area to life.

RING OF BRODGAR

A mile north of Stenness is this wide circle of standing stones (HS; www.historic-scotland .gov.uk; admission free; ⊙24hr), some over 5m tall. The last of the three Stenness monuments to be built (2500–2000 BC), it remains a most atmospheric location. Twenty-one of the original 60 stones still stand among the heather. On a grey day with dark clouds thudding low across the sky, the stones are a spine-tingling sight. Free guided tours leave from the carpark at 1pm from June to August (Thursdays only rest of year).

SKARA BRAE & SKAILL HOUSE

A visit to extraordinary Skara Brae (HS; www.historic-scotland.gov.uk; joint ticket with Skaill House adult/child £6.90/4.10; ⊙9.30am-5.30pm Apr-Sep, to 4.30pm Oct-Mar), one of the world's most evocative prehistoric sites, offers the best opportunity in Scotland for a glimpse of Stone Age life. Idyllically situated by a sandy bay 8 miles north of Stromness, and predating Stonehenge and the pyramids of Giza, Skara Brae is northern Europe's best-preserved prehistoric village.

Even the stone furniture – beds, boxes and dressers – has survived the 5000 years since a community lived and breathed here. It was hidden until 1850, when waves whipped up by a severe storm eroded the sand and grass above the beach, exposing the houses underneath. There's an excellent interactive exhibit and short video, arming visitors with facts and theory, which will enhance the impact of the site. You then enter a reconstructed house, giving the excavation, which you head on to next, more meaning. The official guidebook, available from the visitors centre, includes a good self-guided tour.

The joint ticket also gets you into Skaill House (HS; ⊙Apr-Sep), a mansion built for the bishop in 1620. It's a bit anticlimactic catapulting straight from the Neolithic to 1950s decor, but you can see a smart hidden compartment in the library and the bishop's original 17th century four-poster bed.

Buses run to Skara Brae from Kirkwall and Stromness a few times weekly in summer, but not all are useful to visit the site. It's possible to walk along the coast from Stromness to Skara Brae via Yesnaby Sea Stacks and the Broch of Borwick (9 miles).

BIRSAY

The small village of Birsay is 6 miles north of Skara Brae. The ruins of the Earl's Palace (⊙24hr), built in the 16th century by the despotic Robert Stewart, earl of Orkney, dominate the village centre. Today it's a mass of half walls and crumbling columns, the latter climbing like dilapidated chimney stacks.

At low tide (check tide times at the shop in Earl's Palace) you can walk out to the Brough of Birsay (HS; www.historic-scotland .gov.uk; adult/child £4/2.40; ⊙9.30am-5.30pm mid-Jun–Sep), you'll find the extensive ruins of a Norse settlement and the 12th-century St Peter's Church.

Birsay makes a lovely, peaceful place to stay amid the Orkney countryside. Birsay Hostel (⊙after hrs 01856-721470, office hrs 01856-873535; www.orkney.gov.uk; sites per 4 people £6.25-9.95, dm/tw £15.60/43; 🅿️) is a former activity centre and school that now has dorms that vary substantially in spaciousness – go for one of the two- or four-bedded ones. There's a big kitchen and a grassy camping area.

One of Orkney's most charming B&Bs is Linkshouse (⊙01856-721221; www.ewaf.co.uk; Birsay village; s/d £55/90; ⊙Mar-Oct; 🅿️🛜), a most welcoming stone house near the sea. The beautiful rooms – one with comforting sloping ceiling, one with a toilet that has wonderful vistas – have been recently renovated and it's all looking fabulous. Original art and handsome furniture grace them and the lounge. Breakfast is a treat, served on gorgeous crockery with standout fish and vegetarian options changing daily – pancakes with blueberries and crème fraiche, anyone?

EVIE

On an exposed headland at Aikerness, a 1.5-mile walk northeast from the straggling village of Evie, you'll find the Broch of Gurness (HS; www.historic-scotland.gov. uk; adult/child £5/3; ⊙9.30am-12.30pm & 1.30-5.30pm Apr-Sep, to 4.30pm Oct), a fine example of these drystone fortified towers that were both status symbol for powerful farmers and useful protection from raiders some 2200 years ago. The imposing entranceway and sturdy stone walls – originally 10m high – impress; inside you can see the hearth and where a mezzanine floor would have fitted. Around the broch are the remains of the settlement centred on it.

Stromness

POP 1600

This appealing grey-stone port has a narrow, elongated, flagstone-paved main street and tiny alleys leading down to the waterfront between tall stone houses. It lacks Kirkwall's size but makes up for that with bucketloads of character, having changed little since its heyday in the 18th century. Stromness is ideally located for trips to Orkney's major prehistoric sites.

◉ Sights

Stromness Museum   MUSEUM
(☑01856-850025; www.orkneycommunities.co.uk/stromnessmuseum; 52 Alfred St; adult/child £4.50/1; ⊙10am-5pm Apr-Sep, 11am-3.30pm Mon-Sat Oct-Mar) A superb museum full of knick-knacks from maritime and natural-history exhibitions covering whaling, the Hudsons Bay Company and the sunk German fleet. You can happily nose around for a couple of hours. Across the street is the house where local poet and novelist George Mackay Brown lived.

FREE Pier Arts Centre   GALLERY
(☑01856-850209; www.pierartscentre.com; 30 Victoria St; ⊙10.30am-5pm Tue-Sat) Resplendently redesigned, this gallery has really rejuvenated the Orkney modern-art scene with its sleek lines and upbeat attitude. It's worth a look as much for the architecture as its high-quality collection of 20th-century British art and the changing exhibitions.

✯ Festivals & Events

Orkney Folk Festival   MUSIC
(☑01856-851331; www.orkneyfolkfestival.com) A four-day event in late May, with folk concerts, *ceilidhs* and casual pub sessions. Stromness packs out, and late-night buses from Kirkwall are laid on. Book ahead for event tickets and accommodation.

🛏 Sleeping

TOP CHOICE Brinkies Guest House   B&B ££
(☑01856-851881; www.brinkiesguesthouse.co.uk; s/d £60/70; P🐾🛇🛈) Just a short walk from the centre, but with a lonely, king-of-the-castle position overlooking the town and bay, this exceptional place offers five-star islander hospitality. Compact modern rooms are handsome, stylish and comfortable, public areas are done out most attractively in wood, but above all it's the charming owner's flexibility and can-do attitude that makes this so special. Breakfast is 'continental Orcadian' - a stupendous array of quality local cheese, smoked fish, and homemade bere bannocks. Want a lie-in? No problem, saunter down at 10am. Don't want breakfast? How about packed lunch instead? Take Outertown Rd off Back Rd, turn right on to Brownstown Rd, and keep going.

Miller's House   B&B ££
(☑01856-851969; www.millershouseorkney.com; 13 John St; s/d from £50/65; ⊙Easter-Oct) Miller's House is a historic Stromness residence with a wonderful 1716 stone doorway. There are two delightful en suite bedrooms where you can smell the cleanliness, and there's plenty of light and an optimistic feel. Showers hit the spot, there are fridges in the rooms, and exceptional breakfasts include vegetarian options and daily baked bread.

Hamnavoe Hostel   HOSTEL £
(☑01856-851202; www.hamnavoehostel.co.uk; 10a North End Rd; dm/s/tw £17/20/34; 🛈) This well-equipped hostel is efficiently run and boasts excellent facilities, including a fine kitchen and a lounge room with great perspectives over the water. The dorms are very commodious, with duvets, decent mattresses and reading lamps, and the showers are good. Ring ahead as the owner lives off-site.

Brown's Hostel   HOSTEL £
(☑01856-850661; www.brownsorkney.com; 45 Victoria St; dm £16, s & d per person £18-20; @🛈) On the main street, this handy, sociable place has cramped but cosy and homelike dorms (the upstairs ones are a pound more but have more space) as well as small private rooms. Life centres on its inviting common area, where you can browse the internet for free or swap pasta recipes in the open kitchen. There are overflow rooms in a house up

the street, with self-catering options available. There's a bike shed available for cyclists.

Ness Caravan & Camping Park
CAMPGROUND £

(☎01856-873535; www.orkney.gov.uk; Ness Rd; sites for 4 people £7-10.85; ☺Apr-Sep; ℗) This breezy, fenced-in campground overlooks the bay at the southern end of town and is as neat as a pin.

✗ Eating & Drinking

Hamnavoe Restaurant
SEAFOOD ££

(☎01856-850606; 35 Graham Pl; mains £15-22; ☺dinner Tue-Sun Apr-Oct) Tucked away off the main street, this Stromness favourite specialises in excellent local seafood backed up by professional service. There's always something good off the boats, and the chef prides himself on his lobster. Booking is a must. It usually opens weekends in the winter months.

Ferry Inn
PUB £

(☎01856-850280; www.ferryinn.com; 10 John St; mains £8-18; ☺food 7.15am-9.30pm; ⊚) Every port has its pub, and in Stromness it's the Ferry. Convivial and central, it warms the cockles with folk music, local beers and characters, and pub food that's unsophisticated but generously proportioned and good value. At time of research, you were better sticking to the bar menu rather than the overpriced dinner offerings..

❶ Information

Stromness information centre (☎01856-850716; www.visitorkney.com; Ferry Rd; ☺10am-4pm Mon-Sat Apr-May & Sep-Oct, 9am-5pm daily Jun-Aug) In the ferry terminal. Also open on Sunday in summer.

Stromness library (☎01856-850907; Alfred St; ☺2-7pm Mon-Thu, 2-5pm Fri, 11am-5pm Sat) Free internet access.

❶ Getting There & Away

Northlink Ferries (p933) runs services from Stromness to Scrabster on the mainland.

Bus X1 runs regularly to Kirkwall (30 minutes) and on to St Margaret's Hope.

Hoy

Orkney's second-largest island, Hoy (meaning 'High Island'), got the lion's share of the archipelago's scenic beauty. Shallow turquoise bays lace the east coast and massive seacliffs guard the west, while peat and moorland cover Orkney's highest hills. Much of the north is a bird reserve, with breeding seabirds. The ferry service from Mainland gets very busy over summer – book ahead.

◉ Sights

Scapa Flow Visitor Centre
MUSEUM

(☎01856-791300; www.orkney.gov.uk; admission by donation; ☺9am-4.30pm Mon-Fri Mar-Oct, Sat May-Oct, Sun May-Sep) Lyness, on the eastern side of Hoy, was an important naval base during both world wars, when the British Grand Fleet was based in Scapa Flow. This fascinating museum and photographic display, located in an old pumphouse that once fed fuel to the ships, is a must-see for anyone interested in Orkney's military history.

Old Man of Hoy
ROCK FORMATION

Hoy's best-known sight is this spectacular 137m-high rock stack that juts improbably from the ocean off the tip of an eroded headland. It's a tough ascent for experienced climbers only but a great walk from Moaness or Rackwick. You can see the Old Man as you pass on the Scrabster–Stromness ferry.

⌸ Sleeping & Eating

Stromabank Hotel
HOTEL, PUB ££

(☎01856-701494; www.stromabank.co.uk; s/d £42/64; ☺lunch Sat & Sun, dinner Fri-Wed Jun-Aug, lunch Sun, dinner Sat & Sun Sep-May) Perched on the hill above Longhope, the small atmospheric Stromabank has very acceptable, refurbished en suite rooms, as well as an attractive bar, offering tasty home-cooked meals (£6 to £10) using lots of local produce.

Hoy Centre
HOSTEL £

(☎office hrs only 01856-873535; www.orkney.gov.uk; dm/f £17/41; ℗) This clean, bright hostel has an enviable location, around 15 minutes' walk from Moaness Pier, at the base of the rugged Cuilags. Rooms are all en suite and include family options.

❶ Getting There & Away

Orkney Ferries (p933) runs a passenger and bike ferry (adult £4.15, 30 minutes, two to six daily) between Stromness and Moaness at the north end of Hoy.

There's also a frequent car ferry to Lyness (on Hoy) from Houton on Mainland (passenger/car £4.15/13.20, 40 minutes, up to seven daily Monday to Friday, two or three Saturday and Sunday); cars must be booked in advance. Sunday service is May to September only.

DIVING SCAPA FLOW'S WRECKS

One of the world's largest natural harbours, Scapa Flow, the sheltered bay enclosed by the archipelago's main islands, has been in near-constant use by various fleets from the Vikings onwards. After WWI, 74 German ships were interned here; when the terms of the armistice included a severely reduced German navy, Admiral von Reuter, who was in charge of the fleet, decided to take matters into his own hands. A secret signal was passed from ship to ship and the British watched incredulously as every German ship began to sink. Fifty-two of them went to the bottom, with the rest left aground in shallow water.

Most were salvaged, but seven vessels remain to attract divers. There are three battleships – the *König*, the *Kronprinz Wilhelm* and the *Markgraf* – all of which weigh over 25,000 tonnes. The first two were subjected to blasting for scrap metal, but the *Markgraf* is undamaged and considered one of Scotland's best dives.

Numerous other ships rest on the sea bed in Scapa Flow. HMS *Royal Oak*, sunk by a German U-boat in October 1939 with the loss of 833 crew, is an official war grave – diving here is prohibited.

It's worth prebooking your diving excursion far in advance. Scapa Scuba (☎01856-851218; www.scapascuba.co.uk; Dundas St, Stromness; 2 guided dives £140) is an excellent operator.

Getting Around

There's no public transport to Rackwick Bay, where there's a hostel and trailhead for the Old Man of Hoy, so if you don't feel like walking call Rendall's (☎01856-791262) or North Hoy Transport (☎01856-791315) for a minibus taxi service.

Northern Islands

The group of windswept islands north of Mainland provides a refuge for migrating birds and a nesting ground for seabirds. Some of the islands are also rich in archaeological sites, but it's the beautiful scenery, with wonderful white-sand beaches and azure seas, that's the main attraction. Most islands are home to traditional Orcadian communities that give a real sense of what Orkney was like before the modern world infringed upon island life.

The tourist offices in Kirkwall and Stromness on Mainland have the useful *Islands of Orkney* brochure with maps and details of these islands. Note that the 'ay' at the end of each island name (from the Old Norse for 'island') is pronounced 'ee' (Shapinsay is pronounced 'shap-in-see').

ROUSAY

Off the north coast of Mainland, Rousay makes a great day trip, but you'll feel like staying longer. This hilly island is famous for its numerous archaeological sites, earning it the nickname 'Egypt of the North' (perhaps pushing it a *bit* too far).

Sights & Activities

Rousay Tours (☎01856-821234; www.rousaytours.co.uk; adult/child £17.50/5.50) offers taxi service and guided tours of the island, including wildlife-spotting (seals and otters) and visits to the prehistoric sites.

FREE Prehistoric Sites ARCHAEOLOGICAL SITE (HS; www.historic-scotland.gov.uk; ⊙24hr) The major archaeological sites are clearly labelled from the road ringing the island. Heading west from the ferry, you soon come to Taversoe Tuick, an intriguing burial cairn constructed on two levels, with separate entrances – perhaps a joint tomb for different families; a semi-detached solution in posthumous housing. Squeeze into the cairn to explore both levels, but there's not much space. Not far beyond are two other significant cairns; Blackhammer, then Knowe of Yarso, the latter a fair walk up the hill but with majestic views.

Six miles from the ferry, mighty Midhowe Cairn has been dubbed the 'Great Ship of Death'. Built around 3500 BC and enormous in size, it's divided into compartments, in which the remains of 25 people were found. Covered by a protective stone building, it's nevertheless a memorable sight. Next to it, Midhowe Broch, the sturdy stone lines of which echo the striations of the rocky shoreline, is a muscular Iron Age fortified compound with a mezzanine floor. The sites are by the water, a 10-minute walk downhill from the main road.

Sleeping & Eating

Taversoe Hotel   HOTEL **££**
(☎01856-821325; www.taversoehotel.co.uk; s/d
£45/75; **P**) About 2 miles west from the pier,
the island's only hotel is a low-key place,
with neat, simple doubles with water vistas that share a bathroom and a twin with
en-suite bathroom but no view. The best
views, however, are from the dining room,
which serves good-value meals. The friendly
owners will pick you up from the ferry.

Trumland Farm Hostel   HOSTEL **£**
(☎01856-821252; trumland@btopenworld.com;
sites £5, dm £10, bedding £2; **P**) An easy stroll
from the ferry, this organic farm has a wee
hostel with rather cramped six-bed dorms
and a pretty little kitchen and common
area. You can pitch tents outside and use the
facilities; there's also a well-equipped self-
catering cottage that can sleep three (£60
to 100).

Getting There & Around

A small **ferry** (☎01856-751360; www.orkney
ferries.co.uk) connects Tingwall on Mainland
with Rousay (passenger/bicycle/car return
£9.30/2/26.40, 30 minutes, up to six daily) and
the nearby islands of Egilsay and Wyre. Vehicle
bookings are compulsory. A bus from Kirkwall
connects with some ferries.

Bikes can be hired for £7 per day from Trumland Farm.

STRONSAY

Stronsay attracts walkers and cyclists for
its lack of serious inclines and the beautiful
landscapes of its four curving bays. You can
spot wildlife here: chubby seals basking on
the rocks, puffins and other seabirds.

Sights & Activities

There are good coastal walks and, in the
east, the Vat o'Kirbister is a fine example of
a gloup (natural arch). At the southern end
of the island, you can visit the seal-watch
hide on the beach. There's also a chance to
see otters at nearby Loch Lea-shun.

Sleeping & Eating

Stronsay Hotel   HOTEL **££**
(☎01857-616213; www.stronsayhotelorkney.co.uk;
s/d £38/76; 🛜🍽) The island's watering hole
is near the ferry and has immaculate refurbished rooms. There's also recommended
pub grub (mains from £7) in the bar, with
excellent seafood (including paella and lobster) in particular. There are good deals for
multinight stays.

Getting There & Away

Loganair (☎01857-873457; www.loganair.co
.uk) flies from Kirkwall to Stronsay (£37 one
way, 20 minutes, one or two daily Monday to
Saturday).

A **ferry** (☎01856-872044; www.orkney
ferries.co.uk) links Kirkwall with Stronsay
(passenger/car £8.10/19.15, 1½ hours, two
to three daily) and Eday.

EDAY

This slender island was extensively cut for
peat to supply the surrounding islands. The
interior is hilly and covered in peat bog,
while the coast and the north of the island
are low-lying and green.

Eday Heritage & Visitor Centre (☎01857-
622283; www.visiteday.com; ⊙9am-5.30pm daily
May-Sep, 10am-5pm Sat Oct-Apr) has a range
of local history exhibits, as well as an audiovisual about tidal energy initiatives. The
early-17th-century Carrick House (☎01857-
622260; adult/child £3/1; ⊙by appointment), with
its floor bloodstained from a pirate skirmish,
is worth a visit; tours of the house run in
summer with advance notice.

Eday Minibus Tour (☎01857-622206; adult/
child £13.50/11.50) offers 2¼-hour guided tours
from the ferry pier on Monday, Wednesday
and Friday from May to August. It also operates as a taxi service.

Sleeping & Eating

Eday Hostel   HOSTEL **£**
(☎07977-281084; dm £15; **P@**) Four miles
north of the ferry pier, this recently renovated, community-run hostel is an excellent place to stay. You can camp alongside
it too.

Getting There & Around

There are two flights from Kirkwall (one way £37,
30 minutes) to London airport – that's London,
Eday – on Wednesday only.

Ferries sail from Kirkwall, usually via Stronsay
or Sanday (passenger/car £8.10/19.15, two
hours, two to three daily).

SANDAY

Aptly named, blissfully quiet flat Sanday is
ringed by Orkney's best beaches – with daz-
zling-white sand of the sort you'd expect in
the Caribbean.

At the tip of the headland east of the main
village of Kettletoft is Quoyness chambered tomb, similar to Maes Howe and
dating from the 3rd millennium BC. It has
triple walls, a main chamber and six smaller
cells.

Beyond the loch at the northeastern tip is Tofts Ness, a largely unexcavated funerary complex with some 500 prehistoric burial mounds and the remains of an Iron Age roundhouse.

🛏 Sleeping

Belsair
B&B, PUB £

(☎01857-600206; www.belsairsanday.co.uk; r per person £30; 🛜) Overlooks the harbour with tidy en-suite rooms that are good value. Bar meals all day feature Orcadian produce.

Ayre's Rock Hostel & Campsite
HOSTEL, CAMPGROUND £

(☎01857-600410; www.ayres-rock-sanday-orkney.co.uk; 1-/2-person tent sites £5/7, huts £20, dm/s £13.50/18; P@) Cosy hostel sleeping eight in the outbuildings of a farm. There's a craft shop and chip shop on site, breakfasts and dinners are available, and you can also pitch a tent or sleep in a camping hut. It's on the west coast, 6 miles north of the ferry pier. Car and bike hire can be organised.

❶ Getting There & Around

There are flights from Kirkwall to Sanday (one way £37, 20 minutes, once or twice daily Monday to Saturday).

Ferries run from Kirkwall (passenger/car £8.10/19.15, 1½ hours), with a link to Eday. A bus meets the boat.

WESTRAY

If you've time to visit only one of Orkney's northern islands, make Westray the one. The largest of the group, it has rolling farmland, handsome sandy beaches, great coastal walks and several appealing places to stay.

◎ Sights & Activities

FREE Noup Head
NATURE RESERVE

The RSPB reserve at Noup Head, at Westray's northwestern tip is a dramatic area of sea cliffs with vast numbers of breeding seabirds from April to July.

Westray Heritage Centre
HERITAGE CENTRE

(☎01857-677414; www.westrayheritage.co.uk; Pierowall; adult/child £2.50/50p; ⊙11.30am-5pm Mon, 10am-noon & 2-5pm Tue-Sat, 1.30-5.30pm Sun May-Sep) This has displays on local history, nature dioramas, and archaeological finds, including the famous 5000-year-old 'Westray Wife'. The sandstone figurine is the oldest depiction of the human form yet found in Scotland.

Westraak
GUIDED TOUR

(☎01857-677777; www.westraak.co.uk; Quarry Rd, Pierowall) Runs informative and engaging trips around the island, covering everything from Viking history to puffin mating habits.

🛏 Sleeping & Eating

TOP CHOICE West Manse
B&B £

(☎01857-677482; www.westmanse.co.uk; Westside; r per person £20; 🐕P) No timetables reign at this imposing house with arcing coastal vistas; make your own breakfast when you feel like it. Your welcoming hosts have introduced a raft of green solutions for heating, fuel and more. Kids will love this unconventional place, while art exhibitions, cooking classes, venerably comfortable furniture and clean air are drawcards for parents.

Barn
HOSTEL, CAMPGROUND £

(☎01857-677214; www.thebarnwestray.co.uk; Pierowall; sites £5, per person £1.50, dm £17; P) This excellent, intimate, modern 13-bed hostel is an Orcadian gem. It's heated throughout and has an inviting lounge, complete with DVD collection. The price includes bed linen, shower and pristine kitchen facilities; local advice comes free. There's also a campground on site, complete with laundry and campers' kitchen.

Pierowall Hotel
PUB £

(☎01857-677472; www.pierowallhotel.co.uk; mains £8-10) The heart of this island community, the local pub is famous throughout Orkney for its popular fish and chips – whatever has turned up in the day's catch by the hotel's boats is displayed on the blackboard. There are also some curries available, but the sea is the way to go here.

❶ Getting There & Away

There are daily flights from Kirkwall to Westray (one way £37, 20 minutes).

A ferry (p933) links Kirkwall with Rapness (passenger/car £8.10/19.15, 1½ hours, daily). A bus to the main town Pierowall meets the ferry.

PAPA WESTRAY

Known locally as Papay, this exquisitely peaceful, tiny island (4 miles by one) attracts superlatives. It is home to Europe's oldest domestic building, the Knap of Howar (built about 5500 years ago), and to Europe's largest colony of Arctic terns. Even the two-minute hop from Westray airfield is featured in *Guinness World Records* as the world's shortest scheduled air service. The island was the cradle of Christianity in Orkney –

St Boniface's Church was founded in the 8th century, but most of it is 12th century.

Beltane Guest House & Hostel (☎01857-644224; www.papawestray.co.uk; dm/s/d £15/25/35; 🅿), owned by the local community co-op, comprises a 20-bed hostel and a guest house with four rooms with en suite.

❶ Getting There & Away

There are daily flights to Papa Westray (£18, 15 minutes) from Kirkwall, and a special £21 return fare if you stay overnight.

A passenger-only ferry runs from Pierowall to Papa Westray (£4.05, 25 minutes, three to six daily in summer); the crossing is free if you go direct from the Rapness ferry from Westray.

NORTH RONALDSAY

North Ronaldsay is a real outpost surrounded by rolling seas and big skies. Delicious peace-and-quiet and excellent birdwatching lure visitors. There are enough semi-feral sheep to seize power, but a 13-mile drystone wall running around the island keeps them off the grass; they make do with seaweed, which gives their meat a unique flavour.

◉ Sights

North Ronaldsay Tour   GUIDED TOUR
(☎07703-112224; lighthouse or mill adult/child £4/2, combined £6/4) Offers excellent tours of one of North Ronaldsay's two lighthouses and the **Woollen Mill** (adult/child £4/2, combined lighthouse & mill ticket £6/3).

⌂ Sleeping & Eating

Observatory Guest House   HOSTEL, CAMPGROUND ££
(☎01857-633200; www.nrbo.co.uk; sites £4.50, dm/s/d £15.50/36/72; 🅿@🛜) Powered by wind and solar energy, this offers first-rate accommodation and ornithological activities next to the ferry pier. There's a cafe-bar with lovely coastal views and convivial communal dinners (£13.50) in a sun-kissed (sometimes) conservatory; if you're lucky, local lamb might be on the menu. You can also camp here.

❶ Getting There & Away

There are two or three daily flights to North Ronaldsay (£18, 20 minutes) from Kirkwall. The £21 return offer is great value.

A ferry runs from Kirkwall on Tuesday and Friday (passenger/car £8.10/19.15, 2½ hours).

SHETLAND ISLANDS

Adrift in the North Sea and close enough to Norway geographically and historically to make nationality an ambiguous concept here, the Shetland Islands are Britain's most northerly outpost. There's a Scandinavian lilt to the local accent, and streets named King Haakon or St Olaf reminds that Shetland was under Norse rule until 1469, when it was gifted to Scotland in lieu of the dowry of a Danish princess. The setting of this archipelago of mighty, wind-ravaged clumps of brown and green earth rising from the frigid waters of the North Sea is still uniquely Scottish though, with deep, naked glens flanked by steep hills, twinkling, sky-blue lochs and (of course) sheep on the roads.

There are 16 inhabited islands here, of which Mainland, the principal one, is by far the largest and busiest.

NATURE-WATCHING IN SHETLAND

For birdwatchers, Shetland is paradise – a stopover for migrating Arctic species, it hosts vast seabird breeding colonies.

Of the 24 seabird species that nest in the British Isles, 21 are found here; June is the height of the breeding season. Every bird has its own name here: rain geese are red-throated divers, bonxies are great skuas, and alamooties are storm petrels. The RSPB (RSPB; ☎01950-460800; www.rspb.org.uk) maintains several reserves around the islands. There are National Nature Reserves at Hermaness (where you can't fail to be entertained by the clownish antics of the almost tame puffins), Keen of Hamar and Noss. Fair Isle also supports large seabird populations.

But keep an eye on the sea itself: killer whales are regularly sighted (as are other cetaceans), as well as sea otters. A useful website for all species is www.nature-shetland.co.uk, which details latest sightings.

Held over a week in early July, the Shetland Nature Festival (www.shetlandnaturefestival.co.uk) has guided walks, talks, boat trips, open days and art and photography workshops celebrating Shetland's wildlife and geology.

Shetland Islands

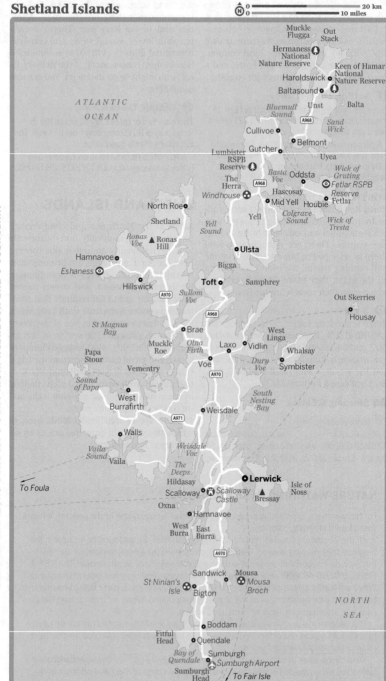

0 — 20 km
0 — 10 miles

Muckle Flugga
Out Stack
Hermaness National Nature Reserve
Haroldswick
Baltasound
Keen of Hamar National Nature Reserve

ATLANTIC OCEAN

Bluemull Sound
Unst
Balta
Sand Wick

Cullivoe
Belmont
Gutcher
Uyea

Lumbister RSPB Reserve
Basta Voe
Oddsta
Wick of Gruting
Fetlar RSPB Reserve
Fetlar

The Herra
Windhouse
Hascosay
Mid Yell
Houbie

North Roe
Yell
Colgrave Sound
Wick of Tresta

Shetland
Yell Sound

Ronas Voe
Ronas Hill

Hamnavoe
Eshaness
Hillswick
Ulsta

Bigga
Toft
Samphrey

Out Skerries
Housay

St Magnus Bay
Sullom Voe
A970
A968

Brae
West Linga

Papa Stour
Muckle Roe
Olna Firth
Laxo
Vidlin
Whalsay

Vementry
Voe
A970
Dury Voe
Symbister

Sound of Papa
South Nesting Bay

West Burrafirth
Weisdale
A971

Walls
Weisdale Voe

Vaila Sound
Vaila
The Deeps

Hildasay
Scalloway
Scalloway Castle
Lerwick
Isle of Noss
Bressay

Oxna
Hamnavoe

West Burra
East Burra
A970

Sandwick
Mousa
Mousa Broch

St Ninian's Isle
Bigton

NORTH SEA

To Foula

Boddam

Fitful Head
Quendale

Bay of Quendale
Sumburgh
Sumburgh Airport
Sumburgh Head
To Fair Isle

A LIGHT IN THE NORTH

Shetland offers intriguing options for getting off the beaten accommodation track. There's a great network of *böds* – simple rustic cottages or huts with peat fires. They cost £10 per person, or £8 for the ones without electricity, and are available from March to October. Contact and book via Shetland Amenity Trust (☑01595-694688; www .camping-bods.com).

The same organisation runs three Lighthouse Cottages (☑01595-694688; www .shetlandlighthouse.com), commanding dramatic views of rugged coastline: one at Sumburgh (under renovation until 2014), one on the island of Bressay near Lerwick, and one at Eshaness. Sleeping six to seven, the cottages cost from £190 to £290 for a three-night booking in high season.

One of the great attractions of Shetland is the birdlife; it's worth packing binoculars even if you're not fanatical about it.

⊙ Getting There & Around

Air

The oil industry ensures that air connections are good. The main **airport** (LSI; ☑01950-461000; www.hial.co.uk) is at Sumburgh, 25 miles south of Lerwick. **Flybe** (☑0871 700 2000; www .flybe.com) runs daily services to Aberdeen, Kirkwall, Inverness, Edinburgh and Glasgow, and also twice-weekly summer services to Bergen (Norway).

Bicycle

You can hire bikes from several places, including Grantfield Garage (p947) (per day/week £12.50/50) in Lerwick.

Boat

Northlink Ferries (☑0845 600 0449; www .northlinkferries.co.uk; ☎) runs daily overnight car ferries between Aberdeen and Lerwick (passenger one-way £25 to £38, car £101 to £136, 12 to 15 hours), stopping three to four times a week at Kirkwall, Orkney. With a basic ticket you can sleep in recliner chairs or in the bar area. It's £31 for a berth in a shared cabin, up to £129 for a comparatively luxurious double cabin. There's a cafe, bar, restaurant and cinema on-board as well as slow wi-fi.

Car & Motorcycle

Shetland's broad, well-made roads (think 'oil money') seem like motorways after Orkney's winding lanes. Car hire is fuss-free, and they'll bring your vehicle to whatever transport terminal you arrive at. Prices start at around £20/110 for a day/week but are more usually around £30 a day.

Bolts Car Hire (☑01595-693636; www.bolt-scarhire.co.uk; 26 North Rd, Lerwick) Also has an office at Sumburgh airport.

Grantfield Garage (☑01595-692709; www .grantfieldgarage.co.uk; North Rd, Lerwick)

The cheapest. A short walk towards town from the Lerwick ferry.

Star Rent-a-Car (☑01595-692075; www .starrentacar.co.uk; 22 Commercial Rd, Lerwick) Opposite the bus station. Has an office at Sumburgh airport.

Lerwick

POP 6800

Built on the herring trade, Lerwick is Shetland's only real town, home to a third of the islands' population and dug into the hills overlooking Bressay Sound. It has a solidly maritime feel, with aquiline oilboats competing for space in the superb natural harbour with the dwindling fishing fleet. The water's clear blue tones makes wandering along atmospheric Commercial St a delight, and the excellent museum provides all the cultural background.

⊙ Sights

FREE Shetland Museum   MUSEUM
(☑01595-695057; www.shetland-museum.org.uk; Hay's Dock; admission free; ⊙10am-5pm Mon-Sat, noon-5pm Sun) This modern museum is an impressive recollection of 5000 years' worth of culture, people and their interaction with this ancient landscape. Comprehensive but never dull, the display covers everything from the archipelago's geology to its fishing industry, via a great section on local mythology – find out about the scary *nyuggles* (ghostly horses), or use the patented machine for detecting *trows* (fairies). Pictish carvings and replica jewellery are among the finest pieces here; the museum also includes a working lighthouse mechanism, small art gallery, and a boatbuilding workshop, where you can watch carpenters restoring and re-creating traditional Shetland fishing ves-

Lerwick

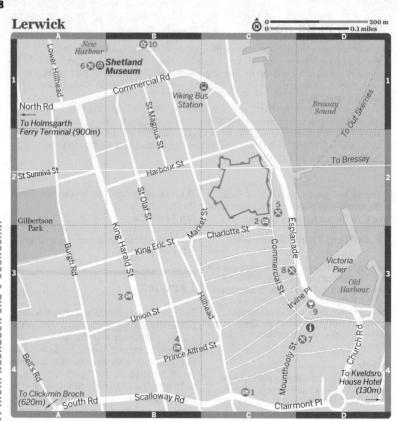

sels. There's also an archive here for tracing your Shetland ancestry.

FREE Clickimin Broch   ARCHEOLOGICAL SITE

This fortified site, just under a mile southwest of the town centre, was occupied from the 7th century BC to the 6th century AD. It's impressively large, and its setting on a small loch gives it a feeling of being removed from the present day.

FREE Böd of Gremista   MUSEUM

(☏01595-695057; www.shetlandtextilemuseum
.com; Gremista Rd; ☉noon-4pm Tue-Sat May–
mid-Sep) This house was once a fish-curing station, and also the birthplace of Arthur Anderson, who founded P&O. The friendly custodian will show you around two rooms restored to how they were 200 years ago, as well as an exhibit on the history of the whitefish industry. The building also houses

displays on the knitted and woven textiles and patterns that take their name from the islands. The *böd* is a mile north of the town centre.

✯ Festivals & Events

Shetland Folk Festival   MUSIC

(www.shetlandfolkfestival.com) Held in late April or early May.

🛌 Sleeping

TOP CHOICE Alder Lodge Guest House   B&B ££

(☏01595-695705; www.alderlodgeguesthouse
.com; 6 Clairmont Pl; s £40-50, d £75; **P**🛇) This stone former bank is a delightful place to stay. Imbued with a sense of space and light, the rooms are large and very well furnished, with good en suites, fridges, and DVD player. Excellent hosts really make the effort to make you feel at home, and do a great breakfast, with a smoked fish option and special

Lerwick

◎ Top Sights
    Shetland Museum............................A1

⌂ Sleeping
    1 Alder Lodge Guest House..................C4
    2 Fort Charlotte Guesthouse...............C2
    3 Isleburgh House Hostel.....................B3
    4 Woosung..B4

⊗ Eating
    5 Fort Café...C2

    6 Hay's Dock.......................................A1
    7 Monty's Bistro..................................D4
    8 Peerie Shop Cafe.............................C3

☺ Drinking
    9 Captain Flint's..................................D3

☻ Entertainment
    10 Mareel...B1

---

diets catered for. There is also a self-catering house nearby.

TOP CHOICE Fort Charlotte Guesthouse   B&B ££

(☎01595-692140; www.fortcharlotte.co.uk; 1 Charlotte St; s £30-35, d £65; ❀☻) Sheltering under the fortress walls, this friendly place offers summery en-suite rooms, including great singles. Views down the pedestrian street are on offer in some; sloping ceilings and oriental touches add charm to others. There's a bike shed and local salmon for breakfast. Very popular; book ahead.

Isleburgh House Hostel   HOSTEL £

(☎01595-745100; www.isleburgh.org.uk; King Harald St; dm/tw £17/34; ☀Apr-Sep; ₱@❀) This typically grand Lerwick mansion houses an excellent hostel, with comfortable dorms, a shop, a laundry, a cafe and an industrial kitchen. Electronic keys offer excellent security and no curfew. It's wise to book ahead; ask about winter availability as it sometimes opens for groups.

Woosung   B&B £

(☎01595-693687; conroywoosung@hotmail.com; 43 St Olaf St; s £25-35, d £46-50; ❀☻) A budget gem in the heart of Lerwick B&B-land, this has a wise and welcoming host, and comfortable, clean, good-value rooms that share a bathroom. The solid stone house dates from the 19th century, built by a clipper captain who traded tea out of the Chinese port it's named after.

Kveldsro House Hotel   HOTEL ££

(☎01595-692195; www.shetlandhotels.com; Greenfield Pl; s/d £105/130; ₱❀) Lerwick's best hotel overlooks the harbour and has a quiet but central setting. It's a dignified small set-up that will appeal to older visitors or couples. All doubles cost the same, but some

are markedly better than others, with four-poster beds or water views. Rooms 415 and 417 have striking harbour vistas, if after a twin, try lovely 413. All boast new stylish bathrooms and Ipod docks.

Clickimin Caravan & Camp Site   CAMPGROUND £

(☎01595-741000; www.srt.org.uk; South Lochside; sites per small/large tent £8.80/11.90; ₱❀☒☻) Clickimin is a small and tidy park with good grassy sites overlooking a small loch. There's a laundry and shower block, and you've got a leisure centre with pool and more as part of the complex.

✗ Eating

TOP CHOICE Hay's Dock   CAFE, RESTAURANT ££

(☎01595-741569; www.haysdock.co.uk; Hay's Dock; mains lunch £6-11, dinner £11-20; ☀lunch daily, dinner Tue-Sat; ❀) The upstairs cafe-restaurant in the Shetland Museum sports a wall of picture windows and a fairweather balcony that overlooks the harbour. Clean lines and pale wood recall Scandinavia, but the menu relies on carefully selected local and Scottish produce. Lunch ranges from delicious fish 'n' chips to chowder, while the evening menu concentrates on seafood and steak.

Monty's Bistro   BRITISH ££

(☎01595-696555; www.montys-shetland.co.uk; 5 Mounthooly St; mains lunch £8-9, dinner £14-17; ☀lunch Tue-Sat, dinner Mon-Sat) Though well hidden away behind the tourist office, Monty's is far from a secret and Shetlanders descend on its wee wooden tables with alacrity. The upstairs dining room is fragrant with aromas of things like Gressingham duck and local mussels from the short, quality menu, and the wine list has some welcome old friends.

UP HELLY AA!!!

Shetland's long Viking history has rubbed off in more ways than just street names and square-shouldered locals. Most villages have a fire festival, a continuation of Viking midwinter celebrations of the rebirth of the sun. The most spectacular happens in Lerwick.

Up Helly Aa (www.uphellyaa.org) takes place on the last Tuesday in January. Squads of *guizers*, people dressed in Viking costume, march through the streets with blazing torches, dragging a replica longship, which they then surround and burn, bellowing out Viking songs from behind bushy beards.

Peerie Shop Cafe   CAFE £
(☑01595-692816; www.peerieshopcafe.com; Esplanade; light meals £2-7; ☺9am-6pm Mon-Sat) If you've been craving proper espresso since leaving the mainland, head to this gem, with art exhibitions, wire-mounted halogens and industrial-gantry chic. Newspapers, scrumptious cakes and sandwiches, hot chocolate that you deserve after that blasting wind outside, and – more rarely – outdoor seating give everyone a reason to be here.

Fort Café   CAFE £
(☑01595-693125; 2 Commercial St; fish & chips £6-8; ☺11am-10.30pm Mon-Fri, 11am-7pm Sat, 4-10.30pm Sun) Lerwick's salty air often creates fish-and-chip cravings. Eat in (until 8pm), or munch down on the pier if you don't mind the seagulls' envious stares.

🍷 Drinking & Entertainment

Shetland Fiddlers Society plays around town, and it's worth attending a session – enquire at the tourist office. Look out for Mareel (www.shetlandarts.org), a new arts venue near the museum.

Captain Flint's   PUB
(2 Commercial St; ☺11am-1am) This lively bar – by some distance Lerwick's best – throbs with happy conversation and has a distinctly nautical, creaky-wooden feel. There's a cross-section of young 'uns, tourists, boat folk and older locals. There's live music some nights and a pool table upstairs.

ℹ️ Information

Lerwick tourist office (cnr Commercial St & Mounthooly St) Helpful, with a good range of books and maps and a comprehensive brochure selection.
Shetland library (☑01595-693868; Lower Hillhead; ☺9am-8pm Mon & Thu, to 5pm Tue, Wed, Fri & Sat) Free internet.

ℹ️ Getting There & Around

Buses service various corners of the archipelago, including regular services to/from Sumburgh Airport.

Northlink Ferries (p947) services dock at **Holmsgarth terminal**, a 15-minute walk from the town centre.

Bressay & Noss

POP 350

These islands lie across Bressay Sound just east of Lerwick. Bressay (*bress*-ah) has some interesting seals, especially along the cliffs and up Ward Hill (226m), which has good views of the islands. Much smaller Noss, east of Bressay, is a nature reserve.

👁️ Sights & Activities

Isle of Noss   NATURE RESERVE
(☑0800-107 7818; www.nnr-scotland.org.uk/noss; boat adult/child £3/1.50; ☺10am-5pm Tue, Wed & Fri-Sun May-Aug) Little Noss, 1.5 miles wide, lies 150m east of Bressay. The high seacliffs on its east coast provide nesting sites for more than 100,000 pairs of breeding seabirds, while the inland heath supports 400 pairs of great skua.

Access is by dinghy from Bressay; if you see a red flag on Noss from the carpark above the boat dock, it's not running. Phone in advance to check. Walking anticlockwise around Noss is an easier hike with better cliff viewing. There's a small visitor centre by the boat dock.

Seabirds & Seals   CRUISE
(☑07595-540224; www.seabirds-and-seals.com; adult/child £45/25; ☺10am & 2pm mid-Apr–mid-Sep) Runs three-hour wildlife cruises (10am and 2pm) around Bressay and Noss, departing from Lerwick. It includes an underwater viewing session. Trips run year-round, weather permitting; book by phone or at Lerwick tourist office.

ℹ️ Getting There & Away

Ferries (passenger/car return £4.30/10, seven minutes, frequent) link Lerwick and Bressay. It's then a 2.5-mile walk or bike ride across the island to reach the crossing point to Noss.

Central & West Mainland

SCALLOWAY

POP 812

Surrounded by bare, rolling hills, Scalloway (pronounced '*scall*-o-wah') – Shetland's former capital – is a busy fishing and yachting harbour with a thriving seafood-processing industry. It's on the west coast 6 miles from Lerwick.

◎ Sights & Activities

Scalloway Museum   MUSEUM
(www.shetlandheritageassociation.com; Castle St; adult/child £3/1; ⊙11am-4pm Mon-Sat, 2-4pm Sun May-Sep; ⊕) This enthusiastic new museum by the castle has an excellent display on Scalloway life and history, with prehistoric finds, witch-burnings and locat lore all featuring. There's a detailed section on the Shetland Bus, and a fun area for kids.

FREE Scalloway Castle   CASTLE
(HS; www.historic-scotland.co.uk) The town's most prominent landmark is Scalloway Castle, built around 1600 by Earl Patrick Stewart. The turreted and corbelled tower house is fairly well preserved. If it's locked, get keys from the museum or Scalloway Hotel.

🛏️ Sleeping & Eating

TOP CHOICE Scalloway Hotel   HOTEL **££**
(✆01595-880444; www.scallowayhotel.com; Main St; s/d/superior d £75/110/150; P🅟🛜) One of Shetland's best, this energetically-run waterfront place has very stylish rooms featuring sheepskins, local tweeds and other fabrics and views over the harbour. Some are larger than others; the best is the fabulous superior, with handmade furniture, artworks and a top-of-the-line mattress on its four-poster bed. The restaurant (mains £14 to £23) is especially good for quality seafood. Excellent Scottish cheeses round off your meal.

ℹ️ Getting There & Away

Buses run from Lerwick (25 minutes, roughly hourly Monday to Saturday, two Sunday) to Scalloway.

South Mainland

From Lerwick, the main road south winds 25 miles down the eastern side of this long, narrow, hilly tail of land to Sumburgh Head.

SANDWICK & AROUND

Opposite the scattered village of Sandwick, where you pass the 60-degree latitude line, is the small isle of Mousa, an RSPB reserve protecting some 7000 breeding pairs of nocturnal storm petrels. Mousa is also home to rock-basking seals as well as impressive Mousa Broch, the best preserved of these northern fortifications. Rising to 13m, it's an imposing structure, typically double-walled, and with a spiral staircase to access a second floor. It features in two Viking sagas as a hide-out for eloping couples.

From April to mid-September, Mousa Boat Trips (✆07901-872339; www.mousa.co.uk) runs daily boat trips to Mousa (adult/child return £15.50/7, 15 minutes) from Sandwick, allowing three hours ashore on the island. It also offers night trips to view the petrels (see website for dates).

There are buses between Lerwick and Sandwick (25 minutes, four to eleven daily).

SUMBURGH

With sea cliffs, and grassy headlands jutting out into sparkling blue waters, Sumburgh is one of the most scenic places to stay on the island. There's a tourist office open daily at Sumburgh airport.

◎ Sights

Jarlshof   ARCHAEOLOGICAL SITE
(HS; ✆01950-460112; www.historic-scotland.gov.uk; adult/child £5.30/3.30; ⊙9.30am-5.30pm Apr-Sep, 9.30am-4.30pm Oct-Mar) Old and new collide here, as Sumburgh airport lies only a few metres from this picturesque and instructive archaeological site. Various periods of occupation from 2500 BC to AD 1500 can be seen, and the complete change that occurred upon the Vikings' arrival is obvious: their rectangular longhouses present a marked contrast to the brochs, roundhouses, and wheelhouses that preceded them.

Atop the site is the 16th century Old House, named 'Jarlshof' in a novel by Sir Walter Scott. There's an informative audio tour included with admission.

TOP CHOICE Old Scatness   ARCHAEOLOGICAL SITE
(✆01950-461869; www.shetland-heritage.co.uk; adult/child £5/4; ⊙10am-5pm Sun-Thu late

May-Aug; 🚹) This dig brings Shetland's prehistoric past vividly to life; it's a must-see for archaeology buffs, but fun for kids, too. Clued-up guides in Iron Age clothes show you around the site, which is still being excavated – it has provided important clues on the Viking takeover and the dating of these northern Scottish sites.

There's an impressive broch from around 300 BC, roundhouses and later wheelhouses. Best of all is the reconstruction of one of these, complete with smoky peat fire and working loom.

Sumburgh Head   BIRDWATCHING

(www.rspb.org.uk) At the end of the island, these spectacular cliffs offer a good chance to get up close to puffins, and see huge nesting colonies of fulmars, guillemots and razorbills. If you're lucky, you might spot dolphins or orcas; the car-park noticeboard documents recent sightings.

🛏 Sleeping & Eating

Other options are atmospheric Sumburgh Lighthouse cottage and a camping *böd* (rustic cottage) behind Old Scatness.

Sumburgh Hotel   HOTEL **££**

(✆01950-460201; www.sumburghhotel.com; s/d £75/90; 🅿@🛜) Next to Jarlshof is this reliable country-style hotel. Rooms have been recently renovated and feature soft duvets, attractive colour schemes and big towels. Larger sea-view rooms looking out to Fair Isle cost a tenner more. This is a great location for birdwatching at Sumburgh Head or for convenience to the airport, though the food has dipped. A mile up the road is a cheaper lodge (single/double £45/65) with simpler en-suite rooms.

❶ Getting There & Away

To get to Sumburgh from Lerwick, take the airport bus (45 minutes, four to seven daily).

North Mainland

The north of Mainland is very photogenic. Around Hillswick, there's stunning scenery and several good places to stay; this makes one of the best bases in the Shetland Islands.

BRAE & AROUND

Just outside Brae and built in 1588, luxurious, genteel **Busta House Hotel** (✆01806-522506; www.bustahouse.com; s/d £99/115; 🅿🛜🐾) has a long, sad history and inevitable rumours of a (friendly) ghost. Built in

the late 18th century (though the oldest part dates from 1588), its refurbished rooms – all individually decorated and named after islands in Shetland – are compact but retain a classy but homely charm. Rooms with sea views and/or four-poster bed cost a bit more. There are excellent dinners with local produce for £35.

Buses from Lerwick to Eshaness and North Roe stop in Brae (35 minutes, four to six daily Monday to Saturday).

ESHANESS & HILLSWICK

Eleven miles northwest of Brae the road ends at the red basalt cliffs of Eshaness, which form some of the most impressive, wild coastal scenery in Shetland. When the wind subsides there is superb walking and panoramic views from the lighthouse on the headland.

A mile east, a side road leads to **Tangwick Haa Museum** (✆01806-503389; admission free; ⏲11am-5pm mid-Apr–Sep), in a restored 17th-century house. The wonderful collection of ancient black-and-white photos capture the sense of community here.

At **Hamnavoe**, which you reach from another side road heading north, about 3.5 miles east of Eshaness, is **Johnny Notions Camping Böd** (✆01595-694688; www.camping-bods.co.uk; dm £8; ⏲Apr-Sep), offering four spacious berths in a cute wee stone cottage with a challengingly low door.

Decent tent pitches and tasty light meals served in a cafe (Thursday to Monday, dishes £3 to £10) with stunning views over St Magnus Bay and its weird and wonderful rock formations, are on offer at **Braewick Cafe & Caravan Park** (✆01806-503345; www.eshaness.shetland.co.uk; sites for 1/2/wigwams £5/7/36; ⏲10am-5pm Mar-Oct; 🛜). Much of the food is sourced from the owners' croft next door. It also has 'wigwams' – wooden huts with fridge and kettle that sleep four (six at a pinch).

Follow the puffin signpost a mile short of Hillswick to **Almara B&B** (✆01806-503261; www.almara.shetland.co.uk; s/d £30/60; 🅿🛜) and the most wonderful welcome in the Shetland Islands. With sweeping views over the bay, this house has a great lounge, a few unusual features in the excellent rooms and bathrooms, and a good eye on the environment. You'll feel completely at home and appreciated; this is B&B at its best.

Buses from Lerwick run (evenings only) to Hillswick (1¼ hours) and Eshaness (1½ hours).

return £4.30, car and driver return £10, 20 minutes, frequent). It's wise to book in summer.

Three buses run Monday to Saturday from Lerwick to Yell and on to Unst, crossing on the ferries. Connecting buses serve other parts of the island.

The North Isles

Yell, Unst and Fetlar make up the North Isles, connected to each other by ferry.

YELL
POP 1100

Yell if you like but nobody will hear; the desolate peat moors here are typical Shetland scenery. Though many folk fire on through to Unst, Yell offers several good hill walks, especially around the Herra peninsula, about halfway up the west coast.

Across Whale Firth from the peninsula is Lumbister RSPB Reserve, where red-throated divers (called rain geese in Shetland), merlins, skuas and other bird species breed. The area is home to a large otter population, too, best viewed around Whale Firth, where you may also spot common and grey seals.

South of Lumbister, on the hillside above the main road, stand the reputedly haunted ruins of Windhouse, dating from 1707.

🛏 Sleeping & Eating

There are lots of excellent self-catering cottages dotted around the island: check www .visitshetland.com for options.

Pinewood House B&B £
(www.pinewoodhouseshetland.co.uk; Aywick; s/d £30/60; P🐾) Next to Aywick shop, this three-roomer boasts glorious water views from the lounge and bedrooms, and offers a warm welcome and optional evening meals.

Windhouse Lodge Camping Böd BÖD £
(☎01957-702475; www.camping-bods.co.uk; dm £10) Below the haunted ruins of Windhouse, and on the A968, you'll find this well-kept, clean, snug camping böd with power and a pot-belly stove to warm your toes. It's unstaffed and locked, so you have to book in advance.

Wind Dog Café CAFE £
(☎01957-744321; www.winddogcafe.co.uk; Gutcher; mains £2-5; ⊙9am-6pm; 🐾) This eclectic cafe offers a warm atmosphere and good-value homemade nosh: cheap burgers, baked potatoes, soups, and all-day fry-ups. Books to read and jigsaws to finish are great if the rain is pelting down.

ℹ Getting There & Away

Yell is connected with Mainland by **ferries** (☎01595-745804; www.shetland.gov.uk/ferries) between Toft and Ulsta (passenger

UNST
POP 1100

You're fast running out of Scotland once you cross to Unst, a rugged island of ponies and seabirds. Britain's most northerly inhabited island is prettier than Yell, with bare, velvety-smooth hills and clusters of settlements that cling to their waterside locations, fiercely resisting the buffeting winds.

◎ Sights & Activities

TOP CHOICE Hermaness
Nature Reserve NATURE RESERVE
Unst's stellar attraction is marvellous Hermaness headland, where a 4.5-mile round walk from the reserve entrance takes you to cliffs where gannets, fulmars, and guillemots nest and numerous puffins frolic. The path is guarded by a small army of great skuas who nest in the nearby heather, and dive-bomb at will if they feel threatened. They're damn solid birds too, but don't usually make contact. From the cliffs, you can see Britain's most northerly point, the rocks of Out Stack, and Muckle Flugga, with its lighthouse built by Robert Louis Stevenson's uncle. For tips on wildlife-watching duck into Hermaness Visitor Centre (☎01595-711278; admission free; ⊙9am-5pm Apr–mid-Sep), near the reserve's entrance, with its poignant story about long-time resident Albert Ross. From here, boat trips (☎01806-522447; www.muckleflugga.co.uk; ⊙Tue, Thu, Sat Jun-Sep) run to Muckle Flugga.

TOP CHOICE Unst Bus Shelter LANDMARK
(www.unstbusshelter.shetland.co.uk) At the turn-off from the main road to Littlehamar, just past Baltasound, is Britain's most impressive bus stop. Enterprising locals, tired of waiting in discomfort, have installed armchair, novels, flowers, a telly, and a visitors' book to sign. The colour scheme changes yearly.

Unst Heritage Centre HERITAGE CENTRE
(☎01957-711528; Haroldswick; adult/child £3/free, combined ticket with Unst Boat Haven £5; ⊙11am-5pm May-Sep) This heritage centre houses a modern museum with a history of the Shetland pony and a re-creation of a croft house.

Unst Boat Haven
MUSEUM

(☎01957-711528; Haroldswick; adult/child £3/ free, combined ticket with Unst Heritage Centre £5; ☺11am-5pm May-Sep) This large shed is a boaty's delight, packed with a beautifully cared for collection of Shetland rowing and sailing boats, all with a backstory. Old photos and maritime artefacts speak of the glory days of Unst fishing.

🛏 Sleeping & Eating

TOP CHOICE Gardiesfauld Hostel
HOSTEL £

(☎01957-755279; www.gardiesfauld.shetland.co.uk; 2 East Rd, Uyeasound; tent & 2 people £6, dm £13; ☺Apr-Sep; P) This 35-bed hostel is very clean, has most spacious dorms with lockers, family rooms, a garden, an elegant lounge and a wee conservatory dining area with great bay views. You can camp here too. The bus stops right outside. Bring 20p pieces for the shower.

Saxa Vord
HOSTEL £

(☎01957-711711; www.saxavord.com; Haroldswick; s/d £19.50/39; ☺late May-early Sep; P🖧) This former RAF base is not the most atmospheric lodging, but the barracks-style rooms offer great value. The restaurant dishes out reasonable local food, and there's a bar – Britain's northernmost, by our reckoning – and a friendly, helpful atmosphere. Self-catering holiday houses (£485 per week) are good for families and available year-round.

Baltasound Hotel
HOTEL, PUB ££

(☎01957-711334; www.baltasound-hotel.shetland .co.uk; Baltasound; s/d £52.50/85; P🖧) Brightly decorated, commodious rooms – some bigger than others – inside the building are complemented by wooden chalets arrayed around the lawn. There's also a lovely country outlook, and bar meals in a dining room dappled by the evening sun.

ℹ Getting There & Away

Unst is connected with Yell by a small car **ferry** (☎01957-722259; www.shetland.gov.uk/ ferries; free, 10 minutes, frequent).

Three buses a day (except Sunday) run from Lerwick to Unst (2½ hours), via the ferries. There are also services around Unst itself.

FETLAR
POP 90

Fetlar is the smallest but most fertile of the North Isles. There's great birdwatching here, and the 705 hectares of grassy moorland around Vord Hill (159m) in the north form the Fetlar RSPB Reserve. Common and grey seals can also be seen on the shores. Much of the reserve is off-limits in the summer breeding season but it's still the best time to see birds, including the red-necked phalarope.

Five to 10 daily free ferries (p953) connect Fetlar with Yell and Unst.

Understand
Great Britain

population per sq km

† ≈ 30 people

Great Britain Today

For Britain and the British, the first dozen years of the 21st century has been a time of change, conflict, controversy and national soul-searching. And it doesn't look like settling down any time soon…

Change at the Top

A key milestone in Britain's current story was the general election of May 2010. The Labour government was ousted after 13 years, and an agreement between the Conservative and Liberal-Democrat parties created the first coalition government in modern British history.

» Population: 60 million

» Total number of active mobile phones (UK): 80 million

» Average number of texts (SMS) sent per person per month: 200

The 'Con-Lib' alignment was unexpected, but under the helm of Prime Minister David Cameron (the Conservative leader) and Deputy PM Nick Clegg (the Liberal-Democrat leader), the new government got down to work and initially impressed most observers with laudable displays of collaboration, despite coming from opposite sides of the centre ground.

National Treasures

Through the rest of 2010 and much of 2011, the coalition's foundation policies were based around the tenets of 'fairness' and 'choice'. The most notable, and controversial, plans included major reforms of hospital and medical funding to give more flexibility to doctors and patients, and new laws allowing parents to set up their own schools.

Education is always a political hot potato in Britain, while the National Health Service is often regarded as a national treasure by politicians and public alike (it was famously celebrated as part of the London 2012 Olympic opening ceremony), so any changes in these areas are always heavily scrutinised and fiercely debated.

Manners

Queues The British are notoriously polite, especially when it comes to queuing; do not 'jump the queue'.

Bargaining In markets, haggling over the price of goods (but not food) is OK, but very rare in shops.

Escalators Stand on the right, so people in a hurry can pass on the left.

Best Brit Flicks

» *Brief Encounter* (1945)
» *Under Milk Wood* (1972)
» *Trainspotting* (1996)
» *Sense & Sensibility* (1996)
» *The Full Monty* (1997)
» *Elizabeth: The Golden Age* (2007)
» *War Horse* (2011)

belief systems
(% of population)

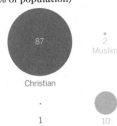

87

Christian

2
Muslim

1
Hindu

10
Other

if Britain were 100 people

85 would be Caucasian
4 would be South Asian
2 would be African & Afro Caribbean
9 would be other

Home & Away

Some cracks in the coalition appeared in late 2011, further strained in 2012, when Conservative 'rebels' blocked Lib-Dem moves to reform the House of Lords, which would have transformed the British parliament's second chamber into a fully elected body.

But beyond home politics, it is the impact of the global financial crisis, and Britain's own levels of debt, that remain the biggest issue for most people in Britain today. This has been addressed by the coalition government with an austerity package including tax increases and public spending cuts, while the Labour opposition espouses increased public spending, and points to slow economic growth and rising unemployment (especially for young adults) as failures of government policies. Which side is correct remains to be seen.

» Inflation (consumer price index): 2.5%

» Per capita GDP: £24,000 (US$38,000)

» Number of railway stations: 2500

Greece is the Word

The global economic crisis has also exposed weaknesses in the euro-zone countries, especially in Greece, with the Governor of the Bank of England, the UK's central bank, stating in May 2012 that UK recovery was hampered by the poor health of Europe's single currency. On the up-side, the Bank of England also predicted that the Olympic Games coming to London in August 2012 would benefit the national economy - meaning the British at least have one reason to thank the Greeks.

Rule Britannia

Meanwhile, away from political battles, there are deeper schisms at work. Where once the state of Great Britain (or, to use its full official name, the United Kingdom of Great Britain and Northern Ireland) was

Top Tunes

» 'God Save The Queen' by The Sex Pistols

» 'Take Me Out' by Franz Ferdinand

» 'Town Called Malice' by The Jam

» 'Sultans of Swing' by Dire Straits

» 'Waterloo Sunset' by The Kinks

» 'Country House' by Blur

» 'Ghost Town' by The Specials

» 'Rock n Roll Star' by Oasis

» 'This Charming Man' by The Smiths

» 'A Design for Life' by Manic Street Preachers

» 'I Predict a Riot' by Kaiser Chiefs

» 'Common People' by Pulp

» 'Our House' by Madness

» 'Shipbuilding' by Elvis Costello

a single entity, it's now anything but united. The process of devolution has seen the constituent countries of Scotland and Wales get their own independent ruling bodies – the Welsh Assembly in Cardiff and the Scottish Parliament in Edinburgh – while a referendum scheduled for 2014 on Scottish independence means Great Britain may cease to exist in its current form as a political entity.

» Area: 88,500 sq miles (230,000 sq km)

» Total number of TVs (UK): 60 million

» Average number of cups of tea per person per day: three

This rebalancing of power across Britain has led to an ongoing reassessment – by politicians and the people themselves – of what it actually means to be British. This occurred especially in England (where the difference between British and English has been hazy for centuries), while the Welsh and Scots are much more aware of the institutions that bind the countries together – and keep them apart.

And while moves towards devolution and autonomy continue, these were perhaps countered slightly in 2012, as the multiple successes of Team GB's athletes at the London Olympics and Paralympics helped install a sense of (definitely British) national pride.

So as Britain and the British continue their journey, the future is anything but certain. Wars are raging, the economy is dicey and national identity is under the glass. But if there's one thing the people of Britain have displayed through the centuries, it's resilience – as long as there's a nice hot mug of tea to hand, of course.

Travelogue Britain

» *Notes from a Small Island* by Bill Bryson. An American's fond and astute take on Britain.

» *Two Degrees West* by Nicholas Crane. A revealing walk (in a perfectly straight line) across Britain.

» *Slow Coast Home* by Josie Drew. The chatty tale of a 5000-mile cycle tour through England and Wales.

» *Great British Bus Journeys* by David McKie. Witty observations of towns off the beaten track but on the bus route.

» *B-road Britain* by Robbie Coltrane. An 'under-the-skin' drive around Britain away from main roads and motorways.

» *On the Slow Train* by Michael Williams. A paean to the pleasure of British rail travel.

History

Britain may be a small country on the edge of Europe, but it has never been on the sidelines of history. For thousands of years, invaders and incomers have arrived, settled and made their mark. The result is Britain's fascinating mix of landscape, culture and language – a dynamic pattern that shaped the nation and continues to evolve today.

Among the earliest migrants were neolithic peoples; thanks to lower sea levels they crossed the land bridge between Britain and the continent of Europe. Much later the Celts arrived, and then the Romans left a legacy of spectacular ruins that can still be seen.

After the Romans, the Anglo-Saxon migration was a key period, laying the foundations for the modern state we now call England. At the same time, the Celtic peoples established their own territories that would become the nations of Wales and Scotland.

Next came 1066, a pivotal date in British history, when the country was invaded by the army of William the Conqueror. This led to the great constructions of the medieval period – the sturdy castles and graceful cathedrals – that are such a feature on tourist itineraries today.

By the 18th century, the aristocrats no longer needed castles, so instead they built great country mansions, and these 'stately homes', another major attraction, dot the British landscape.

Today, Britain's rich historic legacy – everything from Stonehenge to Glen Coe, via Hadrian's Wall, Canterbury Cathedral, Caernarfon Castle and the Tower of London – is one of the country's main attractions for visitors.

> Great Britain consists of the countries of England, Wales and Scotland. The United Kingdom (UK) is Great Britain plus Northern Ireland. The British Isles is a *geographical* term for the islands that make up the UK and the Republic of Ireland, plus others such as the Channel Islands.

First Arrivals

Stone tools discovered near the town of Lowestoft in Suffolk, East Anglia show that human habitation in Britain stretches back at least 700,000 years, although exact dates depend on your definition of 'human'. As the centuries rolled on, ice ages came and went, sea levels rose and fell,

TIMELINE	4000 BC	c 500 BC	c 55 BC
	Neolithic peoples migrate from continental Europe. They differ significantly from previous arrivals: instead of hunting and moving on, they settle in one place and start farming.	The Celts, a group originally from Central Europe, arrive in Britain, and by the middle of the 1st millennium BC have settled across much of the island, absorbing the indigenous people.	Relatively small groups of Roman invaders under the command of Julius Caesar make forays into southern England from the northern coast of Gaul (today's France).

STONEHENGE

and the island now called Britain was frequently joined to the European mainland. Hunter-gatherers crossed the land bridge, moving north as the ice melted and retreating to warmer climes when the glaciers advanced once again.

Around 4000 BC a group of migrants arrived from Europe, differing significantly from previous groups: instead of hunting and moving on, they settled in one place and started farming, most notably in open chalky hill areas such as the South Downs and Salisbury Plain in southern England.

Alongside the fields, Britain's Stone Age people used rocks and turf to build massive burial mounds, and the remains of many of these can still be seen, including West Kennet Long Barrow in Wiltshire, Pentre Ifan in Pembrokeshire and Maes Howe, in Orkney.

But perhaps the most enduring, and certainly the most impressive, legacy left by these nascent Britons was the great stone circles such as Callanish on Lewis in Scotland, and, most famously, the elaborate and enigmatic great stone circles of Avebury and Stonehenge.

Iron & Celts

Move on a millennium or two, and it's the Iron Age. The population expanded and began to divide into specific groups or tribes. Across the whole island the forests were cleared with increasing efficiency as more land was used for farming. This led to a patchwork pattern of fields, woods and small villages that still exists in many parts of rural lowland Britain. As the population grew, territorial defence became an issue, so the Iron Age people left another legacy; the great 'earthwork' castles of southern England, stone forts in northern England and *brochs* (defensive towers) in Wales and Scotland.

As landscapes altered, this was also a time of cultural change. The Celts, a people who originally migrated from Central Europe, had settled across much of the island of Britain by around 500 BC. (Historians are not clear if the new arrivals absorbed the indigenous people, or vice versa.) A Celtic-British population developed (sometimes known as the 'Ancient Britons' to distinguish them from contemporary natives), separated into about 20 tribes, including the Cantiaci (in today's county of Kent), the Iceni (Norfolk), the Brigantes (northwest England), the Picts and Caledonii (Scotland), the Ordivices (parts of Wales) and the Scotti (much of Ireland).

You noticed the Latin-sounding names? That's because the tribal tags were first handed out by the next arrivals on Britain's shores...

Probably built around 3000 BC, Stonehenge has stood on Salisbury Plain for more than 5000 years and is older than the famous Great Pyramids of Egypt.

AD 43	60	c 108	122
Emperor Claudius leads the first proper Roman invasion of England. His army wages a ruthless campaign, and the Romans control most of southern England by AD 50.	Warrior-queen Boudica leads an army against the Romans, destroys the Roman town of Colchester and gets as far as Londinium, the Roman port on the present site of London.	According to legend, Roman soldiers of the ninth legion sent to fight the Picts in Scotland mysteriously disappear. In reality the regiment is probably simply disbanded.	Rather than conquer wild north British tribes, Emperor Hadrian settles for building a coast-to-coast barricade. For nearly 300 years, Hadrian's Wall marks the northernmost limit of the Roman Empire.

Enter the Romans

Think of the Romans, and you think of legions, centurions and aqueducts. They were all here, as Britain and much of Europe came under the power (or the yoke, for those on the receiving end) of the classical period's greatest military empire.

Julius Caesar, the ruler everyone remembers, made forays to the island of Britain from what is now France in 55 BC. But the real Roman invasion happened a century later, when Emperor Claudius led a ruthless campaign resulting in the Romans controlling pretty much everywhere in southern England by AD 50.

Much of the occupation was straightforward: several Celtic-British tribal kings realised collaboration was more profitable than battle. For example, King Togidbnus of the Regnenses tribe changed his name to Tiberius Cogidubnus and built a Roman-style villa, which can still be seen today at Fishbourne near the town of Chichester; and a historian called Nennius suggests in his *Historia Britonum* (written around AD 800) that the people of Wales revered their Roman governors so much that one governor, Magnus Maximus, was transformed into a mythical hero called Maxen Wledig.

It wasn't all plain sailing, though, and some locals fought back. The most famous freedom fighter was warrior-queen Boudica, who led an army as far as Londinium, the Roman port on the present site of London.

However, opposition was mostly sporadic and no real threat to the legions' military might. By around AD 80 the new province of Britannia (much of today's England and Wales) was firmly under Roman rule. And although it's tempting to imagine noble natives battling courageously against occupying forces, in reality Roman control and stability was probably welcomed by a general population tired of feuding chiefs and insecure tribal territories.

Exit the Romans

Settlement by the Romans in Britain lasted almost four centuries. Intermarriage was common between locals and incomers (many from other parts of the empire, including today's Belgium, Spain and Syria, rather than Rome itself), and a Romano-British population evolved, particularly in the towns, while indigenous Celtic-British culture remained in rural areas.

Along with stability and wealth, the Romans introduced another cultural facet: a new religion called Christianity, after it was recognised by Emperor Constantine in AD 313. Although Romano-British culture was thriving by this time, back in its Mediterranean heartland the empire was already in decline.

Christianity was introduced to Britain by the Romans and adopted by the Celts, but the Anglo-Saxons were pagans, and their invasion of Britain forced the Christian religion, along with other aspects of Celtic culture, to the edges of the British Isles – today's Wales, Scotland and Ireland.

Boudica was queen of the Iceni, a Celtic-British tribe whose territory was invaded by the Romans around AD 60. A year later, she led an army against the Roman settlements of Camulodunum (now Colchester) and Londinium (London), but was eventually defeated at the Battle of Watling Street (in today's Shropshire).

200	c 410	5th century	Late 5th century
The Romans build a defensive wall around the city of London with four main entrance gates, still remembered today by the districts of Aldgate, Ludgate, Newgate and Bishopsgate.	As the classical world's greatest empire finally declines after more than three centuries of relative peace and prosperity, Roman rule ends in Britain with more of a whimper than a bang.	Teutonic tribes (known today as the Anglo-Saxons) from the area now called Germany migrate to England and quickly spread across much of the country.	The Scotti people (from today's Ireland) invade the land of the Picts (today's Scotland). In today's Argyll they establish the kingdom of Dalriada.

It was an untidy finale. The Romans were not driven out by the Ancient Britons (Romano-British culture was so established that there was nowhere for the 'invaders' to go 'home' to). In reality, Britannia was simply dumped by the rulers in Rome, and the colony slowly fizzled out of existence. But historians are neat folk, and the end of Roman power in Britain is generally dated at AD 410.

The Emergence of England

When Roman power faded, the province of Britannia went downhill. Coins were no longer minted, so the use of money dwindled and long-distance trade declined. Some Romano-British towns in England and Wales were abandoned (most of Scotland had escaped Roman control in the first place), and some rural areas became no-go zones as local warlords fought over fiefdoms.

Britain's post-Roman vacuum didn't go unnoticed and once again invaders crossed from the European mainland. Angles and Saxons (Teutonic tribes from the land we now call Germany) advanced across the former Roman turf.

Historians disagree on exactly what happened next. Either the Anglo-Saxons largely overcame, replaced or absorbed the Romano-British and Celts, or the indigenous tribes simply adopted the Anglo-Saxon language and culture. Either way, by the late 6th century much of the area we now call England was dominated by the Anglo-Saxons and divided into three separate kingdoms: Wessex (in today's southern England), Mercia (today's Midlands) and Northumbria (today's northern England).

In many areas the original inhabitants lived alongside the Anglo-Saxons and remained unaffected by the incomers (records show that the Celtic language was still being spoken in parts of southern England when the Normans invaded 500 years later), but the overall impact was immense: today the core of the English language is Anglo-Saxon, many place names have Anglo-Saxon roots, and the very term 'Anglo-Saxon' has become a (much-abused and factually incorrect) byword for 'pure English'.

Meanwhile, back in reality, Northumbria was initially the dominant Anglo-Saxon kingdom, covering much of today's northern England and extending its power into Scotland. In the 8th century, the kingdom of Mercia became stronger and its ruler, King Offa, marked a clear border between England and Wales; a defensive ditch called Offa's Dyke that can still be seen today. A century later, at the top of the league was the kingdom Wessex, covering today's southern England and ruled by King Egbert, grandfather of the future King Alfred.

The best place to see Roman remains is Hadrian's Wall, a giant barrier across northern England, built from AD 122 to control wild Caledonian tribes, and mark the limit of the Roman Empire. The best-preserved section is in Northumberland, near Haltwhistle.

6th century	597	7th century	685
St David is born, going on to establish a sacred place of worship in Pembrokeshire and becoming the patron saint of Wales.	Pope Gregory sends missionary St Augustine to southern England to revive interest in Christianity among the southern Anglo-Saxons. His colleague St Aidan similarly converts many people in northern England.	Anglo-Saxons from the expanding English kingdom of Northumbria attempt to colonise southeast Alba (today's southern Scotland) and are met by the Scotti.	The Pictish king Bridei defeats the Northumbrians at Nechtansmere in Angus, an against-the-odds victory that sets the foundations for Scotland as a separate entity.

The Waking of Wales

Away from the emerging kingdoms of England, the Celts on the outer fringes of the British Isles (particularly in Ireland) kept alive their own distinct yet Roman-influenced culture, along with the ideals of Christianity. And while the Anglo-Saxons took advantage of the post-Roman void in eastern Britain, towards the end of the 5th century others played the same game on the west side of the island: the Scotti people (from today's Ireland) invaded the land of the Picts (today's Wales and Scotland).

In response to the invasion, people from the kingdom of Gododdin (in today's Scotland) came to northwest Wales. Their initial plan was to drive out the invaders, but they stayed and settled in the area, which became the kingdom of Gwynedd. (The modern county in northern Wales still proudly bears this name.)

The struggle between Welsh settlers and Irish raiders along the coast carried on for the rest of the Dark Ages. At the same time, more settlers came to Wales from today's Cornwall and western France, and Christian missionaries arrived from Ireland in the 6th and 7th centuries.

While these newcomers arrived from the west and south, the people of Wales were also under pressure to the east, harassed by the Anglo-Saxons of England pretty much constantly for hundreds of years. In response, by the 8th century the disparate tribes of Wales had started to band together and sow the seeds of nationhood. They called themselves *cymry* (fellow countrymen), and today Cymru is the Welsh word for Wales.

LEGACY OF THE LEGIONS

To control the territory they'd occupied, the Romans built castles and garrisons across Britain, especially in Wales and England. Many of these developed into towns, later called 'chesters' and today remembered by names such as Winchester, Manchester, Cirencester and Chester. The Romans are also well known for the roads they built, initially so the legions could march quickly from place to place, and later so that trade could develop. Wherever possible the roads were built in straight lines (because it was efficient and not, as the old joke goes, to stop the Ancient Britons hiding around corners) and included Ermine Street between London and York, Watling Street between London and Chester, and the Fosse Way between Exeter and Lincoln. As you travel around Britain today, you'll notice many ruler-straight Roman roads still followed by modern highways, and in a country better known for old lanes and turnpike routes winding through the landscape, they clearly stand out on the map.

8th century	8th century	850	872
King Offa of Mercia orders the construction of a clear border between his kingdom and Wales – a defensive ditch called Offa's Dyke, still visible today.	The disparate tribes of Wales start to band together and sow the seeds of nationhood, calling themselves *cymry* (fellow countrymen).	Vikings come from today's Denmark and conquer east and northeast England. They establish their capital at Jorvik, today's city of York.	The King of Norway creates an earldom in Orkney; Shetland is also governed from here. These island groups become a Viking base for raids and colonisation into Scotland and northern England.

The Stirring of Scotland

While Wales was becoming established in the west of the island of Britain, similar events were taking place to the north, in the land the Romans had called Caledonia. The Picts were the region's dominant indigenous tribe and named their kingdom Alba, which still today is the Gaelic word for Scotland.

In the power vacuum that followed the fizzle-out of Roman rule in Britannia, Alba was invaded from two sides: first, towards the end of the 5th century, the Scotti crossed the sea from today's Ireland and established the kingdom of Dalriada (in today's Argyll), then in the 7th century Anglo-Saxons from the expanding English kingdom of Northumbria moved in to colonise southeast Alba. But by this time the Scotti were well dug in alongside the Picts, foreshadowing the time when yet another name – Scotland – would be applied to northern Britain.

> The best place to see Viking remains is the city of York in northern England, once the Viking capital of Jorvik.

The Viking Era

in the 9th century, just as the new territories of England, Wales and Scotland were becoming established, Britain was yet again invaded by a bunch of pesky continentals. This time, it was the Vikings – Nordic people from today's Scandinavia.

It's another classic historical image: blonde hair, horned helmets, big swords, square-sailed longboats, raping and pillaging. Tradition has it that Vikings turned up, killed everyone, took everything and left. There's *some* truth in that, but in reality many Vikings settled in Britain, and their legacy is especially evident in today's northern England.

BRITAIN'S MYTHICAL MONARCH

It was during the Dark Ages that a particularly powerful leader, whose name just may have been Arthur, came to prominence. He may have been a Romano-Briton or he may have been a Celt. He may have come from southern England or he may have been born in Wales. Or maybe Scotland. He might have fought against the Anglo-Saxons or against pagan Celts. In truth, virtually nothing is known about this mythical figure from the mists of time, but King Arthur has nevertheless become the focus of many legends. Along with Merlin the magician and the Knights of the Round Table, Arthur has inspired a huge body of literature, not least by the Welsh in the epic tale *Mabinogion,* and by Thomas Malory in his masterpiece *Morte d'Arthur.* Numerous sites in Britain, from Tintagel in Cornwall to Arthur's Seat in Edinburgh, via Snowdonia, Glastonbury and Pembrokeshire, claim Arthurian links that you'll undoubtedly come across as you travel around Britain today.

9th century	9th century	927	1018
King Rhodri Mawr of Wales defeats a Viking force and begins the Welsh unification process. His grandson Hywel the Good draws up a set of laws.	Kenneth MacAilpin, the king of the Scotti, declares himself ruler of both the Scots *and* the Picts, thus uniting Scotland north of the Firth of Forth into a single kingdom.	Athelstan, grandson of Alfred the Great, son of Edward the Elder, is the first monarch to be specifically crowned King of England, building on his ancestors' success in regaining Viking territory.	Scottish King Malcolm II defeats the Northumbrians at the battle of Carham and gains the Lothian region, thus expanding the size of Scotland.

After conquering northern and eastern areas, the Vikings started to expand into central England. Blocking their route were the Anglo-Saxon armies heading north, led by Alfred the Great, the king of Wessex and one of English history's best-known characters.

The battles that followed were seminal to the foundation of the nation-state of England, but the fighting didn't all go Alfred's way. For a few months he was on the run, wading through swamps, hiding in peasant hovels and famously burning cakes. It was the stuff of legend, which is just what you need when the chips are down, and by 886 Alfred had gathered his strength, garnered his forces and pushed the Vikings back to the north.

The Year 1000 by Robert Lacey and Danny Danziger looks long and hard at English life a millennium ago. Apparently it was cold and damp then, too.

United England?

Thus England was divided in two: north and east was Viking 'Danelaw', while south and west was Anglo-Saxon territory. Alfred was hailed as king of the English – the first time the Anglo-Saxons regarded themselves as a truly united people.

Alfred's son and successor was Edward the Elder. After more battles, he gained control of the Danelaw, and thus became the first king to rule the whole of England. His son, Athelstan, took the process a stage further and was specifically crowned King of England in 927. But it was hardly cause for celebration: the Vikings were still around, and later in the 10th century more raids from Scandinavia threatened this fledgling English unity. Over the following decades, control swung from Saxon (King Edgar) to Dane (King Knut) and back to Saxon again (King Edward the Confessor). As England came to the end of the 1st millennium AD, the future was anything but certain.

Highs & Lows in Wales

Meanwhile, as England fought off the Viking threat, Wales was also dealing with the Nordic intruders. Building on the initial cooperation forced upon them by Anglo-Saxon oppression, in the 9th and 10th centuries the small kingdoms of Wales began cooperating, through necessity, to repel the Vikings.

King Rhodri Mawr (who died in 878) defeated a Viking force off the Isle of Anglesey and began the unification process. His grandson Hywel the Good is thought to have been responsible for drawing up a set of laws to bind the disparate Welsh tribes. Things were going well, but just as Wales was becoming a recognisable entity, the young country was faced with more destructive onslaughts than it could handle and in 927 the Welsh kings recognised the Anglo-Saxon King Athelstan as their overlord, in exchange for an anti-Viking alliance.

A History of Britain by historian and TV star Simon Schama is a highly accessible set of three books, examining events from 3000 BC to AD 2000 from a modern context.

1040	1066	1085–86	1095
Macbeth takes the Scottish throne after defeating Duncan in battle. This, and the fact that he was later killed by Duncan's son Malcolm, are the only parallels with the Shakespeare play.	Battle of Hastings – a crucial date in English history. Incumbent King Harold is defeated by an invading Norman army, and England has a new monarch: William the Conqueror.	The new Norman rulers establish the Domesday Book census. Within three years they have a snapshot of England's current stock and future potential.	The start of the First Crusade – a campaign of Christian European armies against the Muslim occupation of Jerusalem and the 'Holy Land'. A series of crusades continues until 1272.

Scotland Becomes a Kingdom

While the Welsh were forming their own nation, similar events were being played out in Alba. In the 9th century, the king of the Scotti of Dalriada was one Kenneth MacAilpin (usually anglicised to MacAlpin). His father was a Scotti, but his mother was a Pict princess, so MacAilpin took advantage of the Pictish custom of matrilineal succession to declare himself ruler of both the Scots *and* the Picts, and therefore king of all Alba.

In a surprisingly short time, the Scots gained cultural and political ascendancy. The Picts were absorbed, and Pictish culture simply, and quite suddenly, came to an end. As part of this process, Alba became known as Scotia.

In the 11th century, Scottish nation building was further consolidated by King Malcolm III (whose most famous act was the 1057 murder of Macbeth, immortalised by William Shakespeare). With his English queen, Margaret, he founded the Canmore dynasty that would rule Scotland for the next two centuries.

Myths and Legends of the British Isles by Richard Barber is an ideal read if you want a break from firm historical facts. Learn about King Arthur and the Knights of the Round Table, plus much more from the mists of time.

MYTHS & LEGENDS

1066 & All That

While Wales and Scotland laid the foundations of nationhood, back in England things were unsettled, as the royal pendulum was still swinging between Saxon and Danish-Viking monarchs. When King Edward the Confessor died, the crown passed to Harold, his brother-in-law. That should've settled things, but Edward had a cousin in Normandy (the northern part of today's France) called William, who thought that *he* should have succeeded to the throne of England.

The result was the Battle of Hastings in 1066, the most memorable of dates for anyone who's studied English history – or for anyone who hasn't. William sailed from Normandy with an army of Norman soldiers, the Saxons were defeated and Harold was killed (according to tradition, by an arrow in the eye).

Norman Wisdom

William became king of England, earning himself the prestigious title William the Conqueror. It was no idle nickname. To control the Anglo-Saxons, the Norman invaders wisely built castles across their newly won territory, and by 1085–86 the Domesday Book provided a census of England's current stock and future potential.

William the Conqueror was followed by William II, but he was mysteriously assassinated during a hunting trip and succeeded by Henry I, another Norman ruler and the first of a long line of kings called Henry.

In the years after the invasion, the French-speaking Normans and the English-speaking Anglo-Saxons kept pretty much to themselves. A strict hierarchy of class developed, known as the feudal system.

1124–53	12th century	1215
The rule of David I of Scotland – the Scottish aristocracy adopts the Norman feudal system, and the king grants land to great Norman families.	Oxford University is founded. There's evidence of teaching in the area since 1096, but King Henry II's 1167 ban on students attending the University of Paris solidified Oxford's importance.	King John signs Magna Carta, limiting the monarch's power for the first time in English history in an early step along the path towards constitutional rule.

DAVID SILVERMAN/GETTY IMAGES ©

» Radcliffe Camera, Oxford

Intermarriage was not completely unknown, however. Henry himself married a Saxon princess. Nonetheless, such unifying moves stood for nothing after Henry's death: a bitter struggle for succession followed, finally won by Henry II, who took the throne as the first king of the House (or dynasty) of Plantagenet.

Post-Invasion Wales & Scotland

By the time the Normans invaded England, the Welsh no longer needed anti-Viking protection and had returned to their independent ways – but not if William the Conqueror had anything to do with it. To secure his new kingdom, and keep the Welsh in theirs, William built castles and appointed feudal barons along the border. The Lords Marcher, as they were known, became massively rich and powerful, and the parts of western England along the Welsh border are still called the Marches today.

In Scotland, King Malcolm III and Queen Margaret were more accommodating to Norman ways, or at least they liked the way the Normans ran a country. Malcolm's successor, David I (1124–53), was impressed too, and adopted the Norman feudal system, as well as granting land to great Norman families. By 1212 a courtier called Walter of Coventry remarked that the Scottish court was 'French in race and manner of life, in speech and in culture'.

But while the French-Norman effect changed England and lowland Scotland over the following centuries, further north the Highland clans remained inaccessible in their glens; they were a law unto themselves for another 600 years.

> At the top of the feudal system came the monarch, followed by nobles (barons and baronesses, dukes and duchesses, plus bishops), then earls, knights, lords and ladies. At the bottom were peasants or 'serfs'. This strict hierarchy became the basis of a class system that still exists in Britain today.

Royal & Holy Squabbling

In England the rule of Henry I had come to an end, and the fight to take his place continued the enduring English habit of competition for the throne, and introduced an equally enduring tendency for bickering between royalty and the church. Things came to a head in 1170 when Henry II had 'turbulent priest' Thomas Becket murdered in Canterbury

LOOKING SOUTH

The arrival of William the Conqueror was a watershed event, as it marked the end of Britain's century-old ties to the Nordic countries (only in Orkney and Shetland did the Viking presence continue until the 15th century). The perspective turned to France, Western Europe and the Mediterranean, giving rise to massive cultural implications that were to last into our own time. In addition, the Norman landing capped an era of armed invasion. Since 1066, in the near-on thousand years to the present day, Britain has never again been seriously invaded by a foreign power.

1295	1296	1298–1305	1314
John Balliol of Scotland and Philip IV of France sign a mutual defence treaty that establishes the 'Auld Alliance' – this predominantly anti-English agreement remains in place for several centuries.	King Edward I marches on Scotland with an army of 30,000 men and in a brutal invasion captures the castles of Berwick, Edinburgh, Roxburgh and Stirling.	William Wallace is proclaimed Guardian of Scotland in 1298. After Edward's army defeats the Scots at the Battle of Falkirk, Wallace goes into hiding but is betrayed and executed in 1305.	An army under Robert the Bruce wins against the English at the Battle of Bannockburn – a victory that consolidated Scottish independence for the next 400 years.

Cathedral. (The stunning cathedral is still an important shrine and a major destination for visitors to Britain today.)

Perhaps the next king, Richard I, wanted to make amends for his forebears' unholy sentiments by leading a crusade (a Christian 'holy war') to liberate Jerusalem and the Holy Land (the area at the eastern end of the Mediterranean, today known as Israel and the Palestinian Territories, plus parts of Syria, Jordan and Lebanon) from occupation by Muslim 'heathens' under their leader Saladin. The campaign became known as the Third Crusade, and although the Christian armies under Richard captured the cities of Acre and Jaffa, they did not take Jerusalem.

Unfortunately, Richard's overseas activities meant he was too busy crusading to bother about governing England and in his absence the country fell into disarray, although his bravery and ruthlessness earned him the sobriquet Richard the Lionheart.

Richard was succeeded by his brother John, but under his harsh rule things got even worse for the general population. According to legend, during this time a nobleman called Robert of Loxley, better known as Robin Hood, hid in Sherwood Forest and engaged in a spot of wealth redistribution.

Expansionist Edward

The next king was Henry III, followed in 1272 by Edward I, a skilled ruler and ambitious general. During a busy 35-year reign, he expounded English nationalism and was unashamedly expansionist in his outlook, leading campaigns into Wales and Scotland.

Some decades earlier, the Welsh king Llywelyn the Great (who died in 1240) had attempted to set up a state in Wales along the lines of the new feudal system in England, and his grandson Llywelyn (Llywelyn the Last) was recognised by Henry III as the first Prince (but not King) of Wales.

Historic Websites

» www.royal
.gov.uk

» www.bbc.co.uk
/history

» www.english
monarchs.co.uk

» www.victorian
web.org

HELL OF A JOB

The story of Britain's ruling dynasties clearly shows that life was never dull for the folk at the top. Despite immense power and privilege, the position of monarch (or, perhaps worse, *potential* monarch) probably ranks as one of history's least safe occupations. English kings have been killed in battle (Harold), beheaded (Charles I), assassinated (William II), murdered by a wicked uncle (Edward V) and knocked off by their queen and her lover (Edward II). Similarly, life was just as uncertain for the rulers of Wales and Scotland; threats came from rival warlords or ambitious clan chiefs (think of Shakespeare's *Macbeth*) and often from the English king next door. As you visit the castles and battlefields of Britain, you may feel a touch of sympathy – but only a touch – for those all-powerful figures continually looking over their shoulder.

1328	1337–1453	1348	1371
Continuing raids by the Scots into northern England force the English to sue for peace; the Treaty of Northampton gives Scotland its independence, with Robert I, the Bruce, as king.	England battles France in a long conflict known as the Hundred Years' War. It was actually a series of small conflicts. And it lasted for more than a century, too...	The bubonic plague (called the Black Death) arrives, ultimately killing more than a third of the population. For peasant labourers who survived, an upside was a rise in wages.	The last of the Bruce dynasty dies, succeeded by the Stewards (Stewarts), who rule Scotland and then Britain for the next three centuries.

KING JOHN CALLED TO BOOK

In 1215 the barons found King John's erratic rule increasingly hard to swallow and forced him to sign a document called Magna Carta (the Great Charter), limiting the monarch's power for the first time in British history. Although originally intended as a set of handy ground rules, Magna Carta was a fledgling bill of human rights that eventually led to the creation of parliament – a body to rule the country, independent of the throne. The signing took place at Runnymede, near Windsor, and you can still visit the site today.

But Edward I had no time for such niceties, and descended on Wales in a bloody invasion that lasted much of the 1270s. In the end, Wales became a dependent principality, owing allegiance to England. There were no more Welsh kings, and just to make it clear who was boss, Edward made his own son Prince of Wales. Ever since, the British sovereign's eldest son has been automatically given the title. (Most recently, Prince Charles was formally proclaimed Prince of Wales at Caernarfon Castle in 1969, much to the displeasure of Welsh nationalists.)

Edward I then looked north. For 200 years, Scotland had been ruled by the Canmores, but the dynasty effectively ended in 1286 with the death of Alexander III. He was succeeded by his four-year-old grand-daughter Margaret ('the Maid of Norway'), who was engaged to the son of Edward I, but she died in 1290 before the wedding could take place.

There followed a dispute for the Scottish throne in which there were 13 *tanists* (contestants), but in the end it came down to two: John Balliol and Robert Bruce of Annandale. Arbitration was needed and Edward I was called in: he chose Balliol. But, having finished the job, Edward then sought to formalise his feudal overlordship and travelled through Scotland forcing clan leaders to swear allegiance. In a final blow to Scottish pride, Edward removed the Stone of Scone (also known as the Stone of Destiny or Fatal Stone), on which the kings of Scotland had been crowned for centuries, and sent it to London.

That was too much. In response, Balliol got in touch with Edward's old enemy, France, and arranged a treaty of cooperation, the start of an anti-English partnership 'the Auld Alliance', which was to last for many centuries (and to the present day when it comes to rugby or football).

Edward wasn't the sort of bloke to brook opposition, though. In 1296 the English army defeated Balliol, forcing the Scottish barons to accept Edward's rule, and his ruthless retaliation earned him the title 'Hammer of the Scots'. But still the Scottish people refused to lie down; in 1297, at the Battle of Stirling Bridge, the English were defeated by a Scots army

Iconic Historical Sights

» **Stonehenge** (ancient circle)

» **Battle**, near Hastings (1066 invasion)

» **Bannock-burn** (Scottish independence milestone)

» **Caernarfon Castle** (Welsh-versus-English focal point)

» **Runnymede** (Magna Carta signed here)

» **Westminster Abbey** (crowning site for monarchs)

» **Hadrian's Wall** (symbol of Roman rule)

1381	1399	1400	1459–71
Richard II is confronted by the Peasants' Revolt. This attempt by commoners to overthrow the feudal system is brutally suppressed, further injuring an already deeply divided country.	Richard II, the last of the Plantagenet dynasty, is ousted by a powerful baron called Henry Bolingbroke, who becomes Henry IV – the first monarch of the House of Lancaster.	Welsh nationalist hero Owain Glyndŵr leads the Welsh in rebellion, declaring a parliament in Machynlleth, but his rebellion is short-lived and victory fleeting.	The Wars of the Roses takes place – an ongoing conflict between two competing dynasties, the Houses of Lancaster and York. The Yorkists are eventually successful, enabling King Edward IV to gain the throne.

under the leadership of William Wallace. Over 700 years later, Wallace is still remembered as the epitome of Scottish patriots.

Dominating the Landscape

If you're travelling through Wales, it won't take you long to notice the country's most striking architectural asset: castles. There are about 600 in all, giving Wales the dubious honour of being Europe's most densely fortified country. Most were built in medieval times, first by William the Conqueror and then by other Anglo-Norman kings, to keep the Welsh in check. In the late 13th century Edward I built spectacular castles at Caernarfon, Harlech, Conwy and Beaumaris, now jointly listed as a Unesco World Heritage Site. Other castles to see include Rhuddlan, Denbigh, Cricceith, Raglan, Pembroke, Kidwelly, Chepstow and Caerphilly. While undeniably great for visitors, the castles are a sore point for patriotic Welsh; the writer Thomas Pennant called them 'the magnificent badge of our subjection'.

The story of William Wallace is told in the Mel Gibson epic *Braveheart*. In devolution debates of the 1990s, the patriotic pride engendered by this movie did more for Scottish nationalism than any politician's speech.

Hard Times

In England, Edward I was succeeded by Edward II, but the new model lacked the military success of his forebear, and his favouring of personal friends over barons didn't help. Edward failed in the marriage department too, and his rule came to a grisly end when his wife, Isabella, and her lover, Roger Mortimer, had him murdered. Fans of (reputedly) grisly ends can visit the very spot where it happened – Berkeley Castle.

By this time, Robert the Bruce (grandson of Robert Bruce of Annandale) had crowned himself king of Scotland (1290), been beaten in battle, gone on the run and, while hiding in a cave, been famously inspired to renew his efforts by a spider persistently spinning its web. Bruce's army went on to defeat Edward II and the English at the Battle of Bannockburn in 1314, another milestone in Scotland's long fight to remain independent.

Next in line was Edward III. Highlights (actually, lowlights) of his reign include the start of the Hundred Years' War with France in 1337 and the arrival of a plague called the Black Death about a decade later, which eventually carried off 1.5 million people, more than a third of the country's population.

Another change of king didn't improve things either. Richard II had barely taken the throne when the Peasants' Revolt erupted in 1381. This attempt by commoners to overthrow the feudal system was brutally suppressed, further injuring an already deeply divided country.

WILLIAM WALLACE

1468–69	1485	1509–47	1536 & 1543
Orkney and then Shetland are mortgaged to Scotland as part of a dowry from Danish King Christian I, whose daughter is to marry the future King James III of Scotland.	Henry Tudor defeats Richard III at the Battle of Bosworth to become King Henry VII, establishing the Tudor dynasty and ending York-Lancaster rivalry for the throne.	The reign of King Henry VIII. The Pope's disapproval of Henry's serial marriage and divorce results in the English Reformation – the founding of the Church of England.	English authority is exerted over Wales; the Laws in Wales Acts, also known as the Acts of Union, formally tie the two countries as a single political entity.

Stewarts Enter the Scene

While the Hundred Years' War raged (or rather, rumbled) between England and France, things weren't much better in Scotland. After the death of Robert the Bruce in 1329, the country was ravaged by endless internal conflicts and plague epidemics.

Bruce's son became David II of Scotland, but he was soon caught up in battles against fellow Scots disaffected by his father and aided by England's Edward III. So when David died in 1371, the Scots quickly crowned Robert Stewart (Robert the Bruce's grandson) as king, marking the start of the House of Stewart, which was to crop up again in England a bit later down the line.

Houses of York & Lancaster

In 1399 the ineffectual Richard II was ousted by a powerful baron called Henry Bolingbroke, who became Henry IV, the first monarch of the House of Lancaster. Less than a year later, his rule was disrupted by a final cry of resistance from the downtrodden Welsh, led by royal descendant Owain Glyndŵr (Owen Glendower to the English). It wasn't a good result for Wales: the rebellion was crushed, vast areas of farmland were destroyed, Glyndŵr died an outlaw and the Welsh elite were barred from public life for many years.

Henry IV was followed, neatly, by Henry V, who decided it was time to stir up the dormant Hundred Years' War. He defeated France at the Battle of Agincourt and the patriotic speech penned by Shakespeare for him in *Henry V* ('Cry "God for Harry, England, and St George!"') has ensured his position among the most famous English kings of all time.

Still keeping things neat, Henry V was followed by Henry VI. Interspersed with bouts of insanity, his main claim to fame was overseeing the building of great places of worship (King's College Chapel in Cambridge and Eton Chapel near Windsor), architectural wonders that can still be explored and admired today.

When the Hundred Years' War finally ground to a halt in 1453, you'd have thought things would be calm for a while, but no. The English forces returning from France threw their energies into another battle: a civil war dubbed the Wars of the Roses.

Briefly it went like this: Henry VI of the House of Lancaster (whose emblem was a red rose) was challenged by Richard, Duke of York (emblem, a white rose). Henry was weak and it was almost a walkover for Richard. But Henry's wife, Margaret of Anjou, was made of sterner mettle and her forces defeated the challenger. It didn't rest there. Richard's son Edward entered the scene with an army, turned the tables and finally

Shakespeare's *Henry V* was filmed most recently in 1989. It's a superb epic starring Kenneth Branagh as the eponymous king. Also worth catching is the earlier movie of the same name starring Laurence Olivier, made in 1944 as a patriotic rallying cry.

1560	1588	1558–1603
The Scottish Parliament creates a Protestant Church that is independent of Rome and the monarchy, as a result of the Reformation. The Latin Mass is abolished and the pope's authority denied.	The first complete translation of the Bible into Welsh helps the cause of Protestantism and also helps the survival of the neglected Welsh language.	The reign of Queen Elizabeth I, a period of boundless English optimism. Enter stage right playwright William Shakespeare. Exit due west navigators Walter Raleigh and Francis Drake.

» Tomb of Elizabeth I

HENRY VIII

drove out Henry. He became King Edward IV, the first monarch of the House of York.

Dark Deeds in the Tower

Life was never easy for the guy at the top. Edward IV hardly had time to catch his breath before facing a challenger to his own throne. Enter scheming Richard Neville, Earl of Warwick, who liked to be billed as 'the kingmaker'. In 1470 he teamed up with the energetic Margaret of Anjou to shuttle Edward into exile and bring Henry VI to the throne. But a year later Edward IV came bouncing back, and this time there was no messing about: he killed Warwick, captured Margaret and had Henry snuffed out in the Tower of London.

Although Edward IV's position seemed secure, he ruled for only a decade before being succeeded by his 12-year-old son, now Edward V. But the boy-king's reign was even shorter than his dad's. In 1483 he was mysteriously murdered, along with his brother, and once again the Tower of London was the scene of the crime.

With the 'little princes' dispatched, this left the throne open for their dear old Uncle Richard. Whether he was the princes' killer is still the subject of debate, but his rule as Richard III was short-lived. Despite being given another famous posthumous Shakespearean sound bite ('A horse, a horse! My kingdom for a horse!'), few tears were shed in 1485 when he was tumbled from the top job by a nobleman from Wales called Henry Tudor, who became King Henry VII.

Moves Towards Unity

There hadn't been a Henry on the throne for a while, and this new incumbent harked back to the days of his namesakes with a skilful reign. After the Wars of the Roses, his Tudor neutrality was important. He also diligently mended fences with his northern neighbours by marrying off his daughter to James IV of Scotland, thereby linking the Tudor and Stewart lines.

On top of his family links with Scotland, Henry was also half-Welsh. He withdrew many of the anti-Welsh restrictions imposed after the Glyndŵr uprising, and his countrymen were only too grateful to enjoy new-found preferential treatment at the English court and career opportunities in English public life.

Matrimony may have been more useful than warfare for Henry VII, but the multiple marriages of his successor, Henry VIII, were a very different story. Fathering a male heir was his problem, hence the famous six wives, but the pope's disapproval of divorce and remarriage led to a split with the Roman Catholic Church. Parliament made Henry the head of the Protestant Church of England – the beginning of a pivotal

Six Wives: The Queens of Henry VIII, by historian David Starkey, is an accessible modern study of the multi-marrying monarch.

1603	1605	1642–49	1688
James VI of Scotland inherits the English throne in the so-called Union of the Crowns, becoming James I of England and James VI of Scotland.	King James' attempts to smooth religious relations are set back by an anti-Catholic outcry following the infamous Gunpowder Plot, an attempt to blow up parliament led by Guy Fawkes.	English Civil War between the king's Cavaliers and Oliver Cromwell's Roundheads establishes the Commonwealth of England.	William of Orange and his wife, Mary, daughter of King James II, jointly ascend the throne after William defeats his father-in-law in the Glorious Revolution.

division between Catholics and Protestants that still exists in some areas of Britain.

In 1536 Henry followed this up by 'dissolving' many monasteries in Britain and Ireland, a blatant takeover of their land and wealth rather than a symptom of the struggle between church and state. Nonetheless, the general populace felt little sympathy for the wealthy (and often corrupt) abbeys, and in 1539–40 another monastic land grab swallowed the larger ones as well.

At the same time, Henry signed the Acts of Union (1536 and 1543), formally uniting England and Wales for the first time. This was welcomed by the aspiring Welsh gentry, as it meant English law and parliamentary representation for Wales, plus plenty of trade opportunities. The Welsh language, however, ceased to be recognised in the law courts.

Meanwhile, in Scotland, James IV had been succeeded by James V, who died in 1542, broken-hearted, it is said, after yet another defeat at the hands of the English. His baby daughter Mary became queen and Scotland was ruled by regents.

The Elizabethan Age

Henry VIII died in 1547, succeeded by his son Edward VI, then by his daughter Mary I, but their reigns were short. So, unexpectedly, the third child, Elizabeth, came to the throne.

As Elizabeth I, she inherited a nasty mess of religious strife and divided loyalties, but after an uncertain start she gained confidence and turned the country around. Refusing marriage, she borrowed biblical imagery and became known as the Virgin Queen, making her perhaps the first British monarch to create a cult image.

It paid off. Her 45-year reign was a period of boundless optimism, characterised by the naval defeat of the Spanish Armada, the expansion of trade due to the global explorations of seafarers such as Walter Raleigh and Francis Drake, not to mention a cultural flourishing thanks to writers such as William Shakespeare and Christopher Marlowe.

Mary, Queen of Scots

During Elizabeth's reign, her cousin Mary (the Catholic daughter of Scottish King James V) had become known as Mary, Queen of Scots. She'd spent her childhood in France and had married the French *dauphin* (crown prince), thereby becoming queen of France as well. Why stop at two? After her husband's death, Mary returned to Scotland, from where she ambitiously claimed the English throne as well, on the grounds that Elizabeth I was illegitimate.

However, Mary's plans failed. She was imprisoned and forced to abdicate in favour of her son (a Protestant, who became James VI of

The 1998 film *Elizabeth*, directed by Shekhar Kapur and starring Cate Blanchett, covers the early years of the Virgin Queen's rule, as she graduates from princess to commanding monarch – a time of forbidden love, unwanted suitors, intrigue and death.

1692	1707	1721–42	1745–46
The Massacre of Glencoe causes further rifts between those clans loyal to the British crown and those loyal to the old ways.	The Act of Union brings England and Scotland under one parliament, one sovereign and one flag.	Violent struggles for the throne seem a thing of the past and the Hanoverian kings increasingly rely on parliament to govern the country. Robert Walpole becomes Britain's first prime minister.	The culmination of the Jacobite uprisings sees Bonnie Prince Charlie land in Scotland, gather an army and march southwards, to be eventually defeated at the Battle of Culloden.

THE ROUGH WOOING

When the child Mary, daughter of James V, became queen of Scotland, the English king Henry VIII sent a proposal that Mary should marry his son. But Mary's regents rejected his offer and (not forgetting the 'Auld Alliance' treaty with the French) Mary was sent to France instead. Henry was furious and sent his armies to ravage southern Scotland and sack Edinburgh in an (unsuccessful) attempt to force an agreement to the wedding. With typical irony and understatement, the Scots dubbed it 'the Rough Wooing'.

Mary, Queen of Scots, Slept Here

» **Carlisle Castle**, Cumbria

» **Bolton Castle**, Yorkshire

» **Tutbury Castle**, Staffordshire

» **Chatsworth House**, Derbyshire

» **Fotheringhay Castle**, Northamptonshire

» **St Mary's Guildhall**, Warwickshire

Scotland), but she escaped to England and appealed to Elizabeth for help. This could have been a rookie error, or she might have been advised by courtiers with their own agenda. Either way, it was a bad move. Mary was seen, not surprisingly, as a security risk and imprisoned once again. In an uncharacteristic display of indecision, Elizabeth held Mary under arrest for 19 years before finally ordering her execution. As a prisoner, Mary was frequently moved from house to house, so that today England has many stately homes (and even a few pubs) claiming 'Mary, Queen of Scots slept here'.

United & Disunited Britain

Elizabeth I died in 1603. Despite a bountiful reign, she had failed to provide an heir, and was succeeded by her closest relative James, the safely Protestant son of the executed Mary. He became James I of England and James VI of Scotland, the first English monarch of the House of Stuart (Mary's time in France had Gallicised the Stewart name). Most importantly, James united England, Wales and Scotland into one kingdom for the first time in history – another step towards British unity, at least on paper – although the terms 'Britain' and 'British' were still not yet widely used in this context.

James' attempts to smooth religious relations were set back by the anti-Catholic outcry that followed the infamous Guy Fawkes Gunpowder Plot, a terrorist attempt to blow up parliament in 1605. The event is still celebrated every 5 November with fireworks, bonfires and burning effigies of Guy himself.

Alongside the Catholic-Protestant rift, the divide between king and parliament continued to smoulder. The power struggle worsened during the reign of the next king, Charles I, and eventually degenerated into the Civil War of 1644–49. The antiroyalist (or 'parliamentarian') forces were led by Oliver Cromwell, a Puritan who preached against the excesses of the monarchy and established Church. His army (known as the Roundheads) was pitched against the king's forces (the Cavaliers) in a conflict

1749	1776–83	1799–1815	1858 & 1860
Author and magistrate Henry Fielding founds the Bow Street Runners, cited as London's first professional police force. A 1792 Act of Parliament allows the Bow Street model to spread across England.	The American War of Independence is the British Empire's first major reverse, a fact not missed by French ruler Napoleon.	In the Napoleonic Wars, Napoleon threatens invasion on a weakened Britain, but his ambitions are curtailed by Nelson and Wellington at the famous battles of Trafalgar (1805) and Waterloo (1815).	The first modern national eisteddfods are held in Llangollen and Denbigh – although earlier ones had been organised from the end of the 18th century as part of a Welsh cultural revival.

that tore England apart, although it was the final civil war in English history. It ended with victory for the Roundheads, with the king executed, England declared a republic and Cromwell hailed as 'Protector'.

The Civil War had been a bitter conflict, but it failed to exhaust Cromwell's appetite for mayhem; a devastating rampage to gain control of Ireland (the first British colony) followed quickly in its wake. Meanwhile, the Scots suffered their own parallel civil war between the royalists and radical 'Covenanters', who sought freedom from state interference in church government.

The Return of the King

By 1653 Cromwell was finding parliament too restrictive and he assumed dictatorial powers, much to his supporters' dismay. On his death in 1658, he was followed half-heartedly by his son, but in 1660 parliament decided to re-establish the monarchy, as republican alternatives were proving far worse.

Charles II (the exiled son of Charles I) came to the throne, and his rule, known as 'the Restoration', saw scientific and cultural activity bursting forth after the straitlaced ethics of Cromwell's time. Exploration and expansion were also on the agenda. Backed by the army and navy (modernised, ironically, by Cromwell), English colonies stretched down the American coast, while the East India Company set up headquarters in Bombay (now Mumbai), laying foundations for what was to become the British Empire.

The next king, James II, had a harder time. Attempts to ease restrictive laws on Catholics ended with his defeat at the Battle of the Boyne by William III, the Protestant king of Holland, better known as William of Orange. William was married to James' own daughter Mary, but it didn't stop him having a bash at his father-in-law.

William and Mary came to the throne as King and Queen, each in their own right (Mary had more of a claim, but William would not agree to be a mere consort), and their joint accession in 1688 was known as the Glorious Revolution.

Killiecrankie & Glen Coe

In Scotland things weren't quite so glorious. Anti-English (essentially anti-William and anti-Protestant) feelings ran high, as did pro-James ('Jacobite') support. In 1689 Jacobite leader Graham of Claverhouse, better known as 'Bonnie Dundee', raised a Highlander army and routed English troops at Killiecrankie.

Then in 1692 came the infamous Massacre of Glen Coe, in which members of the MacDonald clan were killed ostensibly as punishment for failing to swear allegiance to William, although there were deeper

On the chilly day of his execution, dethroned King Charles I reputedly wore two shirts to avoid shivering and being regarded as a coward.

Walks Through Britain's History (published by the Automobile Association) guides you on foot to castles, battlefields and hundreds of other sites with a link to the past. Take the air. Breathe in history!

1837–1901	1847	1900	1914
The reign of Queen Victoria, during which the British Empire – 'on which the sun never sets' – expands from Canada through Africa and India to Australia and New Zealand.	Publication of a government report, dubbed the 'Treason of the Blue Books', suggests the Welsh language is detrimental to education in Wales, and fuels the Welsh-language struggle.	James Keir Hardie (usually known as just Keir Hardie) becomes the first Labour MP, winning a seat in the Welsh mining town of Merthyr Tydfyl.	Archduke Franz Ferdinand of Austria is assassinated in the Balkan city of Sarajevo – the final spark in a decade-long crisis that starts the Great War, now called WWI.

conspiracies at work. This atrocity further fuelled Catholic-Protestant divisions and tightened English domination of Britain, although Jacobite sentiment surfaced in two more rebellions before finally succumbing to history.

Full Final Unity

In 1694 Mary died, leaving William as sole monarch. He died a few years later and was succeeded by his sister-in-law Anne (the second daughter of James II). In 1707, during Anne's reign, the Act of Union was passed, bringing an end to the independent Scottish Parliament and finally linking the countries of England, Wales and Scotland under one parliament (based in London) for the first time. The nation of Britain was now established as a single state, with a bigger, better and more powerful parliament, and a constitutional monarchy with clear limits on the power of the king or queen.

At its height, the British Empire covered 20% of the land area of the earth and contained a quarter of the world's population.

The new-look parliament didn't wait long to flex its muscles. The Act of Union banned any Catholic, or anyone married to a Catholic, from ascending the throne – a rule still in force today. Although the Glorious Revolution was relatively painless in Britain, the impact on Ireland (where the Protestant ascendancy dates from William III's victory in the Battle of Boyne) sowed the seeds for division that continues to the present day.

In 1714 Anne died without leaving an heir, marking the end of the Stuart line. The throne was then passed to distant (but still safely Protestant) German relatives: the House of Hanover.

The Jacobite Rebellions

Despite, or perhaps because of, the 1707 Act of Union, anti-English feeling in Scotland refused to disappear. The Jacobite rebellions, most notably those of 1715 and 1745, were attempts to overthrow the Hanoverian monarchy and bring back the Stuarts. Although these are iconic events in Scottish history, in reality there was never much support for the Jacobite cause outside the Highlands: the people of the lowlands were mainly Protestant, and feared a return to the Catholicism that the Stuarts represented.

The 1715 rebellion was led by James Edward Stuart (the Old Pretender), the son of the exiled James II of England (James VII of Scotland), but when the attempt failed he fled to France, and to impose control on the Highlands, roads were build into many previously inaccessible glens.

In 1745 James' son Charles Edward Stuart (Bonnie Prince Charlie, the Young Pretender) landed in Scotland to claim the crown for his father. He was initially successful, moving south into England as far as Derby, but the prince and his Highland supporters suffered a catastrophic

1916	1925	1926	1939–45
The Welsh Liberal MP David Lloyd George becomes the British prime minister in an alliance with the Conservative Party, having built a reputation for championing the poor and needy.	Plaid (Cenedlaethol) Cymru, the Welsh Nationalist Party, is formed, initiating the struggle for Welsh self-governance and laying the foundations for the modern-day party.	Increasing mistrust of the government, fuelled by soaring unemployment, leads to the General Strike. Millions of workers – train drivers, miners, ship builders – down tools and bring the country to a halt.	WWII rages across Europe, and much of Africa and Asia. Britain and Allies including America, Russia, Australia, India and New Zealand eventually defeat the armies of Germany, Japan and Italy.

defeat at the Battle of Culloden in 1746, and his legendary escape to the western isles is eternally remembered in 'The Skye Boat Song'. And in a different way, General Wade is remembered too, as many of the roads his troops built are still in use today.

The Empire Strikes Out

By the mid-18th century, struggles for the British throne seemed a thing of the past, and the Hanoverian kings increasingly relied on parliament to govern the country. As part of the process, from 1721 to 1742 a senior parliamentarian called Sir Robert Walpole effectively became Britain's first prime minister.

Meanwhile, the British Empire continued to grow in America, Canada and India. The first claims were made to Australia after Captain James Cook's epic voyage in 1768.

The empire's first major reverse came when the American colonies won the War of Independence (1776–83). This setback forced Britain to withdraw from the world stage for a while, a gap not missed by French ruler Napoleon. He threatened to invade Britain and hinder the power of the British overseas, before his ambitions were curtailed by navy hero Viscount Horatio Nelson and military hero the Duke of Wellington at the famous battles of Trafalgar (1805) and Waterloo (1815).

The Industrial Age

While the empire expanded abroad, at home Britain had become the crucible of the Industrial Revolution. Steam power (patented by James Watt in 1781) and steam trains (launched by George Stephenson in 1830) transformed methods of production and transport, and the towns of the English Midlands became the first industrial cities.

This population shift in England was mirrored in Scotland. From about 1750, much of the Highlands region had been emptied of people, as landowners casually expelled entire farms and villages to make way for more profitable sheep farming, a seminal event in Scotland's history known as the Clearances. Industrialisation just about finished the job. Although many of the dispossessed left for the New World, others came from the glens to the burgeoning factories of the lowlands. The tobacco trade with America boomed, and then gave way to textile and engineering industries, as the cotton mills of Lanarkshire and the Clyde shipyards around Glasgow expanded rapidly.

The same happened in Wales. By the early 19th century, copper, iron and slate were being extracted in the Merthyr Tydfil and Monmouth areas. The 1860s saw the Rhondda valleys opened up for coal mining, and Wales soon became a major exporter of coal, as well as the world's leading producer of tin plate.

CAPTAIN COOK

Captain Cook's voyage to the southern hemisphere was primarily a scientific expedition. His objectives included monitoring the transit of Venus, an astronomical event that happens only twice every 180 years or so (most recently in 2004 and 2008). 'Discovering' Australia was just a sideline.

1945	1946–48	1948	1952
WWII ends, and in the immediate postwar election the Labour Party under Clement Attlee defeats the Conservatives under Winston Churchill, despite the latter's pivotal rule in Britain's WWII victory.	The Labour Party nationalises key industries such as shipyards, coal mines and steel foundries. Britain's 'big four' train companies are combined into British Railways.	Aneurin Bevan, the health minister in the Labour government, launches the National Health Service – the core of Britain as a 'welfare state'.	Princess Elizabeth becomes Queen Elizabeth II when her father, George VI, dies. Her coronation takes place in Westminster Abbey in June 1953.

Across Britain, industrialisation meant people were on the move as never before. People left the land and villages their families had occupied for generations. They often went to the nearest factory, but not always. People from rural Dorset migrated to the Midlands, for example, while farmers from Scotland and England settled in South Wales and became miners. The rapid change from rural to urban society caused great dislocation, and although knowledge of science and medicine also improved alongside industrial advances, for many people the adverse side effects of Britain's economic blossoming were poverty and deprivation.

Despite the social turmoil of the early 19th century, by the time Queen Victoria took the throne in 1837, Britain's factories dominated world trade and Britain's fleets dominated the oceans. The rest of the 19th century was seen as Britain's Golden Age, a period of confidence not enjoyed since the days of the last great queen, Elizabeth I.

Victoria ruled a proud nation at home and great swaths of territories abroad, from Canada through much of Africa and India to Australia and New Zealand, trumpeted as 'the empire on which the sun never sets'. In a final move of PR genius, the queen's chief spin doctor and most effective prime minister, Benjamin Disraeli, had Victoria crowned Empress of India. She'd never even been to India, but the British people simply loved the idea.

The times were optimistic, but it wasn't all tub-thumping jingoism. Disraeli and his successor William Gladstone also introduced social reforms to address the worst excesses of the Industrial Revolution. Education became universal, trade unions were legalised and the right to vote was extended to commoners – well, to male commoners. Women didn't get the vote for another few decades. Disraeli and Gladstone may have been enlightened gentlemen, but there *were* limits.

BIRDSONG

One of the finest novels about WWI is *Birdsong* by Sebastian Faulks. Understated, perfectly paced and intensely moving, it tells of passion, fear, waste, incompetent generals and the poor bloody infantry.

World War I

When Queen Victoria died in 1901, it seemed Britain's energy fizzled out too. The new king, Edward VII, ushered in the relaxed new Edwardian era – and a long period of decline.

Meanwhile, in continental Europe, other states were more active: four restless military powers (Russia, Austria-Hungary, Turkey and Germany) focused their sabre-rattling on the Balkan states, and the assassination of Archduke Ferdinand at Sarajevo in 1914 finally sparked a clash that became the 'Great War' we now call WWI. When German forces entered Belgium on their way to invade France, soldiers from Britain and Allied countries were drawn into a conflict of horrendous slaughter, most infamously on the killing fields of Flanders and the beaches of Gallipoli.

By the war's weary end in 1918, over a million Britons had died (not to mention millions more from many other countries) and there was hardly

» Queen Elizabeth II

1955 & 1959	1960s	1960s
Cardiff is declared the Welsh capital in 1955, and Wales gets its own official flag (the red dragon on a green and white field) in 1959.	It's the era of African and Caribbean independence, including Nigeria (1960), Tanzania (1961), Jamaica and Trinidad & Tobago (1962), Kenya (1963), Malawi (1964), The Gambia (1965) and Barbados (1966).	At home, it's the era of Beatlemania. Successful songs such as 'Please, Please Me' ensure the Beatles become household names in Britain, then America – then the world.

OLI SCARFF/GETTY IMAGES ©

a street or village untouched by death, as the sobering lists of names on war memorials all over Britain still show.

Disillusion & Depression

For the soldiers that did return from WWI, the war had created disillusion and a questioning of the social order. Many supported the ideals of a new political force, the Labour Party, to represent the working class, thereby upsetting the balance long enjoyed by the Liberal and Conservative Parties since the days of Walpole. The first Labour leader was Keir Hardie, a Scottish politician representing a Welsh constituency (the coal-mining town of Merthyr Tydfil) in the London-based parliament.

Meanwhile, Britain and Ireland fought the bitter Anglo-Irish War, which ended in mid-1921 with most of Ireland achieving full independence (although six counties in the north remained British). The new political entity may have been billed as the United Kingdom of Great Britain and Northern Ireland, but the decision to divide the island of Ireland in two was to have long-term repercussions that still dominate political agendas in both the UK and the Republic of Ireland today.

The Labour Party won for the first time in the 1923 election, in coalition with the Liberals. James Ramsay MacDonald was the first Labour prime minister, but by the mid-1920s the Conservatives were back. The world economy was in decline and industrial unrest had become widespread. The situation worsened in the 1930s as the Great Depression meant another decade of misery and political upheaval. Even the royal family took a knock when Edward VIII abdicated in 1936 in order to marry Wallis Simpson, a woman twice divorced and – horror of horrors – American.

World War II

The throne was taken by Edward's less-than-charismatic brother George VI and Britain dithered through the rest of the decade, with governments failing to confront the country's deep-set social and economic problems.

In 1933 Adolf Hitler came to power in Germany and in 1939 Germany invaded Poland, drawing Britain once again into war. The German army swept through Europe and pushed back British forces to the beaches of Dunkirk (northern France) in June 1940. An extraordinary flotilla of rescue vessels turned total disaster into a brave defeat, and Dunkirk Day is still remembered with pride and sadness every year in Britain.

By mid-1940 most of Europe was controlled by Germany. In Russia, Stalin had negotiated a peace agreement. The USA was neutral, leaving Britain virtually isolated. Into this arena came a new prime minister, Winston Churchill.

Between September 1940 and May 1941, the German air force launched the Blitz, a series of (mainly night-time) bombing raids on London and

1971	1970s	1970s	1972
Britain adopts the 'decimal' currency (one pound equals 100 pence) and drops the ancient system of one pound equals 20 shillings or 240 pennies, the centuries-old bane of school maths lessons.	Much of the decade is characterised by inflation, inept government (on the left and right), trade-union disputes, strikes, shortages and blackouts, culminating in the 1978–79 'Winter of Discontent'.	The discovery of oil and gas in the North Sea brings new prosperity to Aberdeen in Scotland and the surrounding area, and also to the Shetland Islands.	In Uganda, East Africa, the dictator Idi Amin expels all people of Asian origin. Many have British passports and migrate to Britain, settling predominantly in London and the cities of the Midlands.

other cities. Despite this, morale in Britain remained strong, thanks partly to Churchill's regular radio broadcasts. In late 1941 the USA entered the war, and the tide began to turn.

By 1944 Germany was in retreat. Russia pushed back from the east, and Britain, the USA and other Allies were again on the beaches of France. The Normandy landings (or D-Day, as they are better remembered) marked the start of the liberation of Europe's western side. By 1945 Hitler was dead and the war was finally over.

Swinging & Sliding

Despite victory in WWII, there was an unexpected swing on the political front in 1945. An electorate tired of war and hungry for change tumbled Churchill's Conservatives, in favour of the Labour Party.

Normandy Landings

» Largest military armada in history

» More than 5000 ships

» Approximately 150,000 Allied troops landed

» Campaign time: four days

CHURCHILL: LIFE & LEGACY

Although he was from an aristocratic family, Churchill's early years were not auspicious; he was famously a 'dunce' at school (an image he actively cultivated in later life).

As a young man Churchill joined the British Army, and in 1901 he was elected as a Conservative member of Parliament (MP). In 1904 he defected to the Liberals, the main opposition party at the time. A year later, after a Liberal election victory, he became a government minister.

Churchill rejoined the Conservatives in 1922, and held various ministerial positions through the rest of the 1920s. Notable statements during this period included calling Mussolini a 'genius' and Gandhi 'a half-naked fakir'.

The 1930s Churchill criticised Prime Minister Neville Chamberlain's 'appeasement' of Hitler and called for British rearmament to face a growing German threat, but his political life was generally quiet, so he concentrated on writing. His multivolume *History of the English-Speaking Peoples* was drafted during this period. Although biased and flawed by modern standards, it remains his best-known work.

In 1939 Britain entered WWII, and by 1940 Churchill was prime minister, taking additional responsibility as minister of defence. Hitler had expected an easy victory, but Churchill's extraordinary dedication, not to mention his radio speeches (most famously offering 'nothing but blood, toil, tears and sweat' and promising to 'fight on the beaches'), inspired the British people to resist.

Between July and October 1940 the Royal Air Force withstood Germany's aerial raids to win what became known as the Battle of Britain, a major turning point in the war and a chance for land forces to rebuild their strength. It was an audacious strategy, but it paid off and Churchill was lauded as a national hero – praise that continued to the end of the war, and beyond his death in 1965.

1979	1982	1990	1992
A Conservative government led by Margaret Thatcher wins the national election, a major milestone of Britain's 20th-century history, ushering in a decade of dramatic political and social change.	Britain is victorious in a war against Argentina over the invasion of the Falkland Islands, leading to a rise in patriotic sentiment.	Mrs Thatcher ousted as leader and the Conservative Party enters a period of decline but remains in power thanks to inept Labour opposition.	Labour remains divided between traditionalists and modernists. The Conservatives, under their new leader John Major, confound the pundits and unexpectedly win the general election.

There was change abroad too, as parts of the British Empire became independent, including India and Pakistan in 1947 and Malaya in 1957, followed by much of Africa and the Caribbean.

But while the empire's sun may have been setting, Britain's royal family was still going strong. In 1952 George VI was succeeded by his daughter Elizabeth II and, following the trend set by earlier queens Elizabeth I and Victoria, she has remained on the throne for over six decades, overseeing a period of massive social and economic change.

By the late 1950s, recovery was strong enough for Prime Minister Harold Macmillan to famously remind the British people they had 'never had it so good'. Some saw this as a boast for a confident future, others as a warning about difficult times ahead, but most probably forgot all about it, because by this time the 1960s had started and grey old Britain was suddenly more fun and lively than it had been for generations, especially if you were over 10 and under 30.

Although the 1960s were swinging, the 1970s saw an economic slide thanks to a grim combination of inflation, the oil crisis and international competition. The rest of the decade was marked by strikes, disputes and all-round gloom, especially when the electricity supply was cut because power stations were short of fuel or labour.

The economic situation improved slightly when reserves of oil were discovered in the North Sea, off the Scottish coast. However, nationalist sentiment in Scotland was fuelled when oil revenues were spent across Britain rather than ring-fenced north of the border.

Neither the Conservatives (also known as the Tories), under Edward Heath, nor Labour, under Harold Wilson and Jim Callaghan, proved capable of controlling the strife. The British public had had enough, and in the elections of 1979 the Conservatives won a landslide victory, led by a little-known politician named Margaret Thatcher.

The Thatcher Years

Soon everyone had heard of Margaret Thatcher. Love her or hate her, no one could argue that her methods weren't dramatic. Looking back from a 21st-century vantage point, most commentators agree that by economic measures the Thatcher government's policies were largely successful, but by social measures they were a failure and created a polarised Britain: on one side were the people who gained from the prosperous wave of opportunities in the 'new' industries, while on the other side were the unemployed and dispossessed as the 'old' industries such as coal-mining and steel production became an increasingly small part of the country's economic picture.

Despite, or perhaps thanks to, policies that were frequently described as uncompromising, Margaret Thatcher was, by 1988, the longest-serving British prime minister of the 20th century, although her repeated

For detail on the 1980s, read *No Such Thing as Society* by Andy McSmith. Drawing on Margaret Thatcher's famous quotation, this book studies the era dominated by the Iron Lady.

electoral victories were helped considerably by the Labour Party's ineffective campaigns and destructive internal struggles.

New Labour, New Millennium, New Government

For a full-colour review of the 2012 Games, from the early construction to the grand finale, read *London 2012 Olympic & Paralympic Games: The Official Commemorative Book*, by Tom Knight and Sybil Ruscoe.

The political pendulum started to swing again in the early 1990s. Margaret Thatcher was replaced as leader by John Major, but voters still regarded Labour with suspicion, allowing the Conservatives to unexpectedly win the 1992 election. The turning point came in 1997, when 'New' Labour swept to power, with leader Tony Blair declared the new Prime Minister.

The Labour Party enjoyed an extended honeymoon period, and the next election (in 2001) was another walkover. The Conservative Party continued to struggle, allowing Labour to win a historic third term in 2005, and a year later Tony Blair became the longest-serving Labour prime minister in British history.

In May 2010, a record 13 years of Labour rule came to an end, and a new coalition between the Conservative and Liberal-Democrat Parties became the new government.

2003	2005	2007	2010
Britain joins America and other countries in the invasion of Iraq, initially with some support from parliament and public, despite large anti-war street demonstrations in London and other cities.	Public support for the Iraq War wanes, and the Labour government faces several internal crises but still wins the general election for a historic third term.	The Government of Wales Bill heralds the largest transfer of power from Westminster to Cardiff since the founding of the National Assembly.	Labour is narrowly defeated in the general election as the minority Liberal-Democrats align with the Conservatives to form the first coalition government in Britain's postwar history.

The British Table

Once upon a time, British food was highly regarded. In the later medieval period and 17th century, many people – especially the wealthy – ate a varied diet. Then along came the Industrial Revolution, with mass migration from the country to the city, and food quality took a nosedive, a legacy that means there's still no English equivalent for the phrase *bon appétit*.

Today the tide has turned once again. A culinary landmark came in 2005, when food bible *Gourmet* magazine famously singled out London as having the best collection of restaurants in the world. In the years since then the choice for food lovers – whatever their budget – has continued to improve. London is now regarded as a global gastronomic capital, and it's increasingly easy to find decent food in other cities, towns and rural areas across Britain.

Having said that, a culinary heritage of ready-sliced white bread, fatty meats and vegetables boiled to death, all washed down by tea with four sugars, remains firmly in place in many parts of the country. But wherever you travel in Britain, for each greasy spoon or fast-food joint, there's a local pub or restaurant serving up enticing home-grown specialities. Epicures can splash out big bucks on fine dining, while shoestringers can also enjoy tasty eating that definitely won't break the bank.

Eating in Britain

The infamous outbreaks of 'mad cow' disease in the 1990s are ancient history now, and British beef is once again exported to the world, but an upside of the bad press at the time was a massive surge in demand for good-quality food. That means wherever you go in Britain today, you'll find a plethora of organic, natural, unadulterated, chemical-free, free-range, hand-reared, locally farmed, nonintensive foods available in shops, markets, cafes and restaurants.

Alongside this greater awareness of quality and provenance, there have been other changes to British food thanks to outside influences. For decades most towns have boasted Chinese and Indian restaurants, so a chow mein or a vindaloo is no longer considered exotic, but in more recent times dishes from Japan, Korea or Thailand and other Asian countries have become available.

From influences elsewhere in the world, there's been a growth in restaurants serving up South American, Middle Eastern, African and Caribbean cuisine. Closer to home, a wide range of Mediterranean dishes – from countries as diverse as Morocco and Greece – are commonplace, not only in smarter restaurants but also in everyday eateries.

The overall effect of these foreign influences has been the introduction to 'traditional' British cuisine of new techniques (such as steaming), new condiments (for example, chilli sauce), new implements (such as woks) and even revolutionary ingredients (such as fresh vegetables). So now we have 'modern British cuisine', where even humble bangers and mash

In 2009 Phaidon Press published a book called *Coco, 10 World-Leading Masters Choose 100 Contemporary Chefs*. Of the up-and-coming culinary stars selected by the experts, 13 were based in London – presumably much to the chagrin of food fans in New York (eight chefs selected) and Paris (just five).

EATING PRICE RANGES

In this book's restaurant reviews, we've given an indication of their price range:

£ means a budget place where a main dish is less than £9

££ means midrange; mains are £9 to £18

£££ means top end; mains are more than £18

rises to new heights when handmade pork, apple and thyme-flavoured sausages are paired with lightly chopped fennel and new potatoes, and 'fusion' dishes in which native ingredients get new flavours from adding, for example, Asian spices.

But beware the hype. While some restaurants in Britain experiment with new ideas and are undeniably excellent, others are not. Only a few months after *Gourmet* magazine called the capital 'the best place in the world to eat right now', one of the country's most respected food critics, the *Evening Standard*'s Fay Maschler, decried the domination of style over substance, and accused several top eateries of offering poor value for money, reiterating what any food fan will tell you: you're often better spending £5 on a top-notch curry in Birmingham or a homemade steak-and-ale pie in a country pub in Devon than forking out £30 in a restaurant for a 'modern European' concoction that tastes like it came from a can.

> Perhaps the best example of fusion cuisine – though purist foodies will wince – is chicken tikka masala, the UK's favourite 'Indian' dish created specifically for the British palate and unheard of in India itself.

Meanwhile, away from the cafes and restaurants, many British people still have an odd attitude to eating at home. They love to sit on the sofa and watch TV food shows. Then, inspired, they rush out and buy recipe books. On the way back, they pop into the supermarket and buy a stack of ready-made meals. Homemade food sounds great in theory, but in reality the recipe for dinner is more likely to be something like this: open freezer, take out package, throw in microwave, ping, eat.

So without doubt, you can definitely find great food in Britain. It's just that not all the British seem to like eating it.

The Full British

Although grazing on a steady supply of snacks is increasingly commonplace in Britain, as it is in many other industrialised nations, the British culinary day is still punctuated by the three traditional meals of breakfast, lunch and dinner. And just to keep you on your toes, those later meals are also called dinner and tea or lunch and supper – depending on social class and geographical location.

Breakfast

Many people in Britain make do with toast or a bowl of cereal before dashing to work, but visitors staying in hotels and B&Bs will undoubtedly encounter a phenomenon called the 'Full English Breakfast' – or one of its regional equivalents. This usually consists of bacon, sausages, eggs, tomatoes, mushrooms, baked beans and fried bread, In Scotland the 'full Scottish breakfast' might include oatcakes instead of fried bread. In Wales you may be offered *lavabread,* which is not a bread at all but seaweed – a tasty speciality often served with oatmeal and bacon on toast. In northern England you may get black pudding. And just in case you thought this insufficient, it's still preceded by cereal, and followed by toast and marmalade.

> In Yorkshire, the eponymous pudding is traditionally a *starter,* a reminder of days when food was scarce and the pudding was a pre-meal stomach-filler.

If you don't feel like eating half a farmyard first thing in the morning, most places offer a lighter alternative or local speciality such as kippers (smoked fish) or a 'continental breakfast', which completely omits the cooked stuff and may even add something exotic such as croissants.

Lunch

One of the many great inventions that England gave the world is the sandwich, often eaten as a midday meal. Slapping a slice of cheese or ham between two bits of bread may seem a simple concept, but no one apparently thought of it until the 18th century, when the Earl of Sandwich (his title comes from the southeast England town of Sandwich that originally got its name from the Viking word for sandy beach) ordered his servants to bring cold meat between bread so he could keep working at his desk, or, as some historians claim, keep playing cards late at night.

Another lunch classic that perhaps epitomises British food more than any other – especially in pubs – is the ploughman's lunch. Basically it's bread and cheese, and although hearty yokels probably did carry such food to the fields (no doubt wrapped in a red-spotted handkerchief) in the days of yore, the meal is actually a modern phenomenon. It was invented in the 1960s by the marketing chief of the national cheesemakers' organisation as a way to boost consumption, neatly cashing in on public nostalgia and fondness for tradition.

You can still find a basic ploughman's lunch offered in some pubs – and it undeniably goes well with a pint or two of local ale at lunchtime – but these days the meal has usually been smartened up to include butter, salad, pickle, pickled onion and dressings. At some pubs you get a selection of cheeses. You'll also find other variations, such as a farmer's lunch (bread and chicken), stockman's lunch (bread and ham), Frenchman's lunch (brie and baguette) and fisherman's lunch (you guessed it, with fish).

For cheese and bread in a different combination, try Welsh rarebit – a sophisticated variation of cheese on toast, seasoned and flavoured with butter, milk and sometimes a little beer. For a takeaway lunch in Scotland, look out for *stovies* (tasty pies of meat, mashed onion and fried potato).

Dinner

For generations, a typical British dinner has been 'meat and two veg'. The meat is pork, beef or lamb, one of the vegetables is potatoes and the other inevitably carrots, cabbage or cauliflower – and just as inevitably cooked long and hard. Although tastes and diets are changing, this classic combination still graces the tables of many British families several times a week.

And when the British say beef, they usually mean roast beef – a dish that's become a symbol of the nation, and the reason why the French call the British *les rosbifs*. Perhaps the most famous beef comes from Scotland's Aberdeen Angus cattle, while the best-known meat from Wales is lamb (although a lowly vegetable, the leek, is Wales' national emblem).

ORGANIC FOOD

According to the Soil Association (www.soilassociation.org), the leading organic-food campaign group, more than 85% of people in Britain want pesticide-free food. See www.whyorganic.org for more.

THE PIG, THE WHOLE SHEEP & NOTHING BUT THE COW

One of the many trends enjoyed by modern British cuisine is the revival of 'nose to tail' cooking – that is, using the whole animal, not just the more obvious cuts such as chops and fillet steaks. This does not mean boiling or grilling a pig or sheep all in one go – although spit-roasts are popular. It means utilising the parts that may at first seem unappetising or, frankly, inedible. So as well as dishes involving liver, heart, chitterlings (intestines) and other offal, traditional delights such as bone marrow on toast or tripe (stomach) served with onions once again grace the menus of fashionable restaurants. The movement has been spearheaded by chef Fergus Henderson at his St John restaurant in London, and via his influential recipe book, *Nose to Tail Eating: A Kind of British Cooking* (1999), and its follow-up *Beyond Nose To Tail* (2007).

Venison – usually from red deer – is readily available in Scotland, as well as in parts of Wales and England, most notably in the New Forest.

With beef – especially at Sunday lunches – comes another British classic: Yorkshire pudding. It's simply roast batter, but very tasty when cooked properly. Yet another classic British dish brings together Yorkshire pudding and sausages to create the delightfully named 'toad-in-the-hole'.

Yorkshire pudding also turns up at dinner in another guise, especially in pubs and cafes in northern England, where menus may offer a big bowl-shaped Yorkshire pudding filled with meat stew, beans, vegetables or – in these multicultural times – curry.

North of the border, at dinner time you may be introduced to haggis, Scotland's national dish. It's essentially a large sausage made from a sheep's stomach filled with minced meat and oatmeal, and often available in restaurants, and also deep-fried at takeaways. If you're wary, search the menu for Highland chicken, a meal that stuffs portions of haggis into baked chicken – that way you can sample a small serving.

Scottish salmon is also well known, and available (smoked or poached) everywhere in Britain, but there's a big difference between bland fatty salmon from fish farms and the lean tasty wild version. The latter is more expensive, but as well as the taste, there are sound environmental reasons for preferring the nonfarmed variety. Herring, trout and haddock are other examples of British seafood. In Scotland haddock is enjoyed with potato and cream in the old-style soup called *cullen skink*.

Another traditional soup is Scotch broth (a thick mix of barley, lentils and mutton stock), while in Wales a favourite is *cawl*, a broth that comes in many variations with ingredients including (but not limited to) bacon, lamb, leeks and potatoes.

Perhaps the best-known British meal is fish and chips, often bought from the 'chippie', wrapped in paper to carry home – it's especially popular with families on Friday evening. Late at night, epicures may order their fish and chips 'open' to eat immediately while walking back from the pub. It has to be said that quality varies outrageously across the country; sometimes the chips are limp and soggy, and the fish greasy and tasteless, especially once you get away from the sea, but in towns with salt in the air, this classic deep-fried delight is always worth trying.

Puddings & Desserts

After the main course – usually at an evening meal, or if you're enjoying a hearty lunch – comes dessert (pudding). In British English, 'pudding' has two meanings: the course that comes after the main course; and a

---

Britain's most popular takeaway food is curry, outstripping even fish and chips.

Sherry trifle was considered the height of sophistication at dinner parties during the 1970s, but then fell out of fashion. A few decades later this combination of custard, fruit, sponge cake, whipped cream, and – of course – sherry is back in style, and enjoying a renaissance in many English restaurants.

CAFES & RESTAURANTS – STANDARD HOURS

» Standard hours for cafes are 9am to 5pm. Most cafes open daily.

» In this book, where we specify 'breakfast & lunch' we mean open 9am to 5pm.

» In cities, some cafes open at 7am for breakfast, then shut at 6pm or later.

» In country areas, some cafes open until 7pm or later in the summer.

» In winter months, country cafe hours are reduced; some close completely from October to Easter.

» Standard hours for restaurants are: noon to 3pm for lunch, and 6pm to 11pm (to midnight or later in cities) for dinner. Most restaurants open daily; some are closed Sunday evening or all day Monday.

» Some restaurants open only for lunch, or only for dinner.

» A few restaurants open for breakfast (usually at 9am); cafes usually do.

type of food that might be sweet (such as Bakewell pudding) or savoury (such as Yorkshire pudding).

A classic British dessert is rhubarb crumble: the juicy stem of a large-leafed garden plant, stewed and sweetened, then topped with a crunchy mix of flour, butter and more sugar, and served with custard or ice cream.

Moving onto another sweet option, Bakewell pudding blundered into the recipe books around 1860 when a cook at the Rutland Arms Hotel in the Derbyshire town of Bakewell was making a strawberry tart, but mistakenly (some stories say drunkenly) spread the egg mixture on top of the jam instead of stirring it into the pastry. Especially in northern England, the Bakewell pudding (pudding, mark you, not 'Bakewell tart' as it's sometimes erroneously called) features regularly on local dessert menus and is certainly worth sampling.

More of a cake than a pudding, the Welsh speciality *bara brith* (spicy fruit loaf) is a delight, while Scottish bakeries usually offer milk scones and griddle scones as well as plain varieties. Other sweet temptations include *bannocks* (half-scone, half-pancake), shortbread (a sweet biscuit) and Dundee cake (a rich fruit mix topped with almonds).

Other favourite British puddings include treacle sponge, bread-and-butter pudding and plum pudding, a dome-shaped cake with fruit, nuts and brandy or rum, traditionally eaten at Christmas, when it's called – surprise, surprise – Christmas pudding. This pudding is steamed (rather than baked), cut into slices and served with brandy butter.

While key ingredients of most puddings are self-explanatory, they are perhaps not so obvious for another well-loved favourite: spotted dick. But fear not. The origin of 'dick' in this context is unclear (it may be a corruption of 'dough' or derived from the German *dicht,* meaning 'thick' or even from 'spotted dog') but the ingredients are easy: it's just a white suet pudding dotted with black currants. Plus sugar, of course. Most British puddings have loads of butter or loads of sugar, preferably both. Light, subtle and healthy? No chance!

Like meat, but not battery pens? Go to the Royal Society for the Prevention of Cruelty to Animals (www.rspca.org.uk) and follow the links to Freedom Food.

THE BRITISH TABLE

Regional Specialities

With Britain's lengthy coastline, it's no surprise that seafood is a speciality in many parts of the country. Yorkshire's seaside resorts are particularly famous for huge servings of cod, despite it becoming an endangered species thanks to overfishing. Other local seafood you may encounter elsewhere on your travels includes Norfolk crab and Northumberland kippers, while restaurants in Scotland, West Wales and southwest England regularly conjure up prawns, lobsters, oysters, mussels and scallops.

Meat-based specialities in northern and central England include Cumberland sausage – a tasty mix of minced pork and herbs, so large it has to be spiralled to fit on your plate. Look out too for Melton Mowbray pork pies – cooked ham compressed in a casing of pastry and always eaten cold, ideally with pickle. A legal victory in 2005 ensured that only pies made in the eponymous Midlands town could carry the Melton Mowbray moniker – in the same way that only fizzy wine from the Champagne region of France can carry that name.

Another British speciality that enjoys the same protection is Stilton – a strong white cheese, either plain or blue vein. Only five dairies in all of Britain (four of which are in Derbyshire) are allowed to name the cheese they produce Stilton. Bizarrely, the cheese cannot be made in the village of Stilton in Cambridgeshire, although this is where it was first sold – hence the name.

Perhaps less appealing is black pudding, effectively a large sausage made from ground meat, offal, fat and blood, and traditionally served for breakfast. It's known in other countries as 'blood sausage', but the British

Rick Stein is a TV chef, energetic restaurateur and good-food evangelist. His books *Food Heroes* and *Food Heroes: Another Helping* extol small-scale producers and top-notch local food, from organic vegetable to wild boar sausages.

version has a high content of oatmeal so that it doesn't fall apart in the pan when fried.

Eating Out

In Britain, 'eating out' means simply going to a restaurant or cafe – anywhere away from home. There's a huge choice across the country.

Picnics & Self-Catering

Eggs, Bacon, Chips & Beans by Russell Davies showcases 50 of the UK's finest traditional cafes, with tongue-in-cheek taster's notes on their various versions of the traditional fry-up.

When shopping for food, as well as the more obvious chain stores and corner shops, markets can be a great place for bargains – everything from dented tins of tomatoes to home-baked cakes and organic goat's cheese. Farmers markets are always worth a browse; they're a great way for producers to sell good food direct to consumers.

Cafes & Teashops

The traditional British cafe is nothing like its continental European namesake. For a start, asking for a brandy with your coffee may cause confusion, as cafes in Britain rarely serve alcohol. Most are simple places serving simple meals such as a meat pie, beans on toast, baked potato or omelette with chips (costing around £3 to £4) and sandwiches, cakes and other snacks (£1 to £2). Quality varies enormously: some cafes definitely earn their 'greasy spoon' handle, while others are neat and clean.

In London and some other cities, a rearguard of classic cafes – with formica tables, seats in booths and decor unchanged from the their 1950s glory days – stand against the onslaught of the international chains.

In rural areas, many market towns and villages have cafes catering for tourists, walkers, cyclists and other outdoor types, and in summer they're open every day. Whether you're in town or the country, good British cafes are a wonderful institution and always worth a stop during your travels.

Smarter cafes are called teashops – and more often found in country areas – where you might pay a bit more for extras such as quaint decor and table service. Teashops are your best bet for sampling a 'cream tea' – a plate of scones, clotted cream and jam, served with a pot of tea. This is known as a Devonshire tea in some other English-speaking countries, but not in Britain (except of course in the county of Devon, where it's a well-known – and much-hyped – local speciality).

As well as the traditional establishments, in most cities and towns you'll also find coffee shops – independents and international chains – and a growing number of Euro-style cafe-bars, serving decent lattes and espressos, and offering bagels or ciabattas rather than beans on toast (you'll probably be able to get that brandy, too). Some of these modern places even have outdoor chairs and tables – rather brave considering the narrow pavements and inclement weather much of Britain enjoys.

NAME THAT PASTY

A favourite speciality in southwest England is the Cornish pasty. Originally a mix of cooked vegetables wrapped in pastry, it's often available in meat varieties (much to the scorn of the Cornish people) and now sold everywhere in Britain. Invented long before Tupperware, the pasty was an all-in-one-lunch pack that tin miners carried underground and left on a ledge ready for mealtime. So that pasties weren't mixed up, they were marked with their owner's initials – always at one end, so the miner could eat half and safely leave the rest to snack on later without it mistakenly disappearing into the mouth of a workmate. Before going back to the surface, the miners traditionally left the last few crumbs of the pasty as a gift for the spirits of the mine, known as 'knockers', to ensure a safe shift the next day.

WHERE THERE'S SMOKE...

All restaurants and cafes in Britain are nonsmoking throughout. Virtually all pubs have the same rule, which is why there's often a small crowd of smokers standing on the pavement outside. Some pubs provide specific outdoor smoking areas, ranging from a simple yard to elaborate gazebos with canvas walls and the full complement of lighting, heating, piped music and TV screens – where you'd never need to know you were 'outside' at all, apart from the pungent clouds of burning tobacco. Smoking is permitted in pub gardens, so nonsmokers sometimes need to go *inside* to escape the fumes.

Restaurants

London has scores of excellent restaurants that could hold their own in major cities worldwide, while eating places in Bath, Cardiff, Manchester and Edinburgh can give the capital a fair run for its money (often for rather less money).

Prices vary considerably across the country, with a main course in a basic restaurant costing around £9 or less, and anywhere between £10 and £18 at midrange places. Utterly excellent food, service and surroundings can be enjoyed for around £20 to £50 – although in London you can pay double this, if you want.

For vegetarians, Britain is not too bad. Many restaurants and pubs have at least one token vegetarian dish, while better places offer much more imaginative choices. Vegans will find the going trickier, except of course at dedicated veggie/vegan restaurants.

Pubs & Gastropubs

Not so many years ago, a pub was the place to go for a drink. And that was it. If you felt peckish, your choice might be a ham or cheese roll, with pickled onions if you were lucky. Today it's totally different. Many pubs sell a wide range of food, and it's often a good-value option, whether you want a toasted sandwich between museum visits in London, or a three-course meal in the evening after touring the castles of Wales.

While the food in many pubs is decent quality and good value, some have raised the bar to such a degree that there is now a whole new genre of eatery – the gastropub. The finest gastropubs are almost restaurants (with smart decor, neat menus and uniformed table service) but others have gone for a more relaxed atmosphere where you'll find mismatched cutlery, no tablecloths, waiters in T-shirts and the day's choices chalked up on a blackboard. The key for each, though, is top-notch no-frills food. For visitors relaxing after a hard day doing the sights, nothing beats the luxury of a wholesome shepherd's pie washed down with a decent ale, without the worry of guessing which fork to use.

Drinking in Britain

The drinks most associated with Britain are probably tea, beer and whisky. The first two are unlike drinks of the same name found elsewhere in the world, and all three are well worth sampling on your travels around the country.

Tea & Coffee

In Britain, if a local asks 'Would you like a drink?', don't automatically expect a gin and tonic. They may well mean a 'cuppa' – a cup of tea – Britain's best-known beverage. It's usually made with dark tea leaves to produce a strong, brown drink, more bitter in taste than tea served in

Many towns and cities in England hold regular farmers markets – a chance for food producers large and small to sell direct to the public. For more info and a list, see www.farmers markets.net.

In the 16th century, Queen Elizabeth I decreed that mutton could only be served with bitter herbs – intended to stop people eating sheep in order to help the wool trade – but her subjects discovered mint sauce improved the taste, and it's been the favourite condiment for roast lamb ever since.

EARLY DOORS, LATE NIGHTS

Pubs in towns and country areas usually open daily from 11am to 11pm Sunday to Thursday, and sometimes until midnight on Friday and Saturday. A few pubs shut from 3pm to 6pm. We don't list pub opening and closing times unless they vary significantly from these hours.

In cities, some pubs stay open until midnight or later, but it's mostly bars and clubs that take advantage of new licensing laws ('the provision of late-night refreshment', as it's officially and charmingly called) to stay open until 1am, 2am or later. As each place is different, we list opening hours for all bars and clubs.

some other Western countries, which is partly why it's usually served with a dash of milk.

Although tea is sometimes billed as the national drink, coffee is equally popular these days; the Brits consume 165 million cups a day and the British coffee market is worth almost £700 million a year – but with the prices some coffee shops charge, maybe that's not surprising.

A final word of warning: when you're ordering a coffee and the server says 'white or black', don't panic. It simply means 'Do you want milk in it?'

Beer, Wine & Whisky

As you travel around Britain, you should definitely try some local brew. British beer typically ranges from dark brown to bright orange in colour, and is often served at room temperature. Technically it's called ale and is more commonly called 'bitter'. This is to distinguish it from lager – the drink that most of the rest of the word calls 'beer', which is generally yellow and served cold.

Good Beer Guide to Great Britain, by the Campaign for Real Ale, and *Good Pub Guide*, by Alisdair Aird and Fiona Stapley.

Bitter that's brewed and served traditionally is called 'real ale' to distinguish it from mass-produced brands, and there are many different regional varieties. But be ready! If you're used to the 'amber nectar' or 'king of beers', a traditional British brew may come as a shock – a warm, flat and expensive shock. This is partly to do with Britain's climate, and partly to do with the beer being served by hand pump rather than gas pressure. Most important, though, is the integral flavour: traditional British beer doesn't need to be chilled or fizzed to make it palatable.

Another key feature is that real ale must be looked after, which usually means a willingness on the part of the pub manager or landlord to put in extra effort. This often translates into extra effort on food, atmosphere, cleanliness and so on, too. But the extra effort is why many pubs don't serve real ale, so beware of places where bar staff give the barrels as much care as they give the condom machine in the toilets. There's honestly nothing worse than a bad pint of real ale.

If beer doesn't tickle your palate, try cider – available in sweet and dry varieties. In western parts of England, notably Herefordshire and the southwestern counties such as Devon and Somerset, you could try 'scrumpy', a very strong dry cider traditionally made from local apples. Many pubs serve it straight from the barrel.

On hot summer days, you could go for shandy – beer and lemonade mixed in equal quantities. You'll usually need to specify 'lager shandy' or 'bitter shandy'. To outsiders, it may seem an astonishing combination, but it's very refreshing and, of course, not very strong.

Many visitors are surprised to learn that wine is produced in Britain, and has been since the time of the Romans. Today, more than 400 vineyards and wineries produce around two million bottles a year – many highly regarded and frequently winning major awards. English white sparkling wines have been a particular success story, especially those produced in southeast England where the chalky soil and climatic conditions are similar to those of the Champagne region in France.

Moving on to something stronger, the usual arrays of gin, vodka, rum and so on are served in pubs and bars, but the spirit most visitors associate with Britain – and especially Scotland – is whisky (note the spelling – it's Irish whiskey that has an 'e'). More than 2000 brands are produced, but the two main kinds are single malt, made from malted barley, and blended whisky, made from unmalted grain blended with malts. Single malts are rarer (there are only about 100 brands) and more expensive.

If you're bemused by the wide choice, ask to try a local whisky – although if your budget is low, you might want to check the price first. A measure of blended whisky costs around £2, a straightforward single malt around £3, while a rare classic could be £10 or more. And a final word of warning: when ordering a dram in Scotland remember to ask for whisky – only the English and other foreigners say 'Scotch'. What else would you be served in Scotland?

Bars & Pubs

In Britain the difference between a bar and a pub is sometimes vague, but generally bars are smarter, larger and louder than pubs, possibly with a younger crowd. Drinks are more expensive too, unless there is a gallon-of-vodka-and-Red-Bull-for-a-fiver promotion – which there often is.

As well as beer, cider and wine, pubs and bars offer the usual choice of spirits, often served with a 'mixer', producing English favourites such as gin and tonic, rum and coke or vodka and lime. These drinks are served in measures called 'singles' and 'doubles'. A single is 35mL – just over one US fluid ounce. A double is, of course, 70mL – still disappointingly small when compared with measures in other countries. To add further to your disappointment, the vast array of cocktail options, as found in America, is generally restricted to more upmarket city bars in Britain.

And while we're serving up warnings, here are two more: first, if you see a pub calling itself a 'free house', it's simply a place that doesn't belong to a brewery or pub company, and thus is 'free' to sell any brand of beer. Unfortunately, it doesn't mean the booze is free of charge. Second, remember that drinks in English pubs are ordered and paid for at the bar. You can always spot the freshly arrived tourists – they're the ones sitting forlornly at an empty table hoping to spot a waiter.

When it comes to gratuities, it's not usual to tip pub and bar staff. However, if you're ordering a large round, or the service has been good all

REAL ALE

The Campaign for Real Ale promotes the understanding of traditional British beer. Look for endorsement stickers on pub windows, and for more info see www.camra .org.uk.

THE OLDEST PUB IN BRITAIN?

Many drinkers are often surprised to learn that the word 'pub', short for 'public house', although apparently steeped in history, dates only from the 19th century. But places selling beer have been around for much longer, and the 'oldest pub in Britain' is a hotly contested title.

One of the country's oldest pubs, with the paperwork to prove it, is Ye Olde Trip to Jerusalem (p443) in Nottingham, which was serving ale to departing crusaders in the 12th century.

Other contenders sniff that Ye Trip is a mere newcomer. A fine old inn called the Royalist Hotel in Stow-on-the-Wold (Gloucestershire) claims to have been selling beer since around AD 947, while another pub called Ye Olde Fighting Cocks in St Albans (Hertfordshire) claims to date back to the 8th century – although the 13th is more likely.

But then back comes Ye Olde Trip with a counter-claim: one of its bars is a cave hollowed out of living rock, and that's more than a million years old.

evening, you can say to the person behind the bar '...and one for yourself' when ordering. They may not have a drink, but they'll add the monetary equivalent to the total you pay and keep it as a tip.

Apart from great service, what makes a good pub? It's often surprisingly hard to pin down, but in our opinion the best pubs follow a remarkably simple formula: they offer a welcoming atmosphere, pleasant surroundings, a range of hand-pulled beers and a decent menu of snacks and meals – cooked on the premises, not shipped in by the truckful and defrosted in the microwave.

After months of painstaking research, this is the type of pub we recommend. But, of course, there are many more pubs in Britain than even we could sample, and nothing beats the fun of doing your own research. So we urge you to get out there and tickle your taste buds.

Food & Drink Glossary

aubergine	large purple-skinned vegetable; 'eggplant' in the USA and Australia
bangers	sausages (colloquial)
bap	a large, wide, flat, soft bread roll
bevvy	drink (slang, mainly used in northern England)
bill	the total you need to pay after eating in a restaurant ('check' to Americans)
bitter	ale; a type of beer
black pudding	type of sausage made from dried blood and other ingredients
bun	bread roll, usually sweet, eg currant bun, cream bun
BYO	bring your own (usually in the context of bringing your own drink to a restaurant)
caff	abbreviated form of cafe
candy floss	light sugar-based confectionery; called 'cotton candy' in the US and 'fairy floss' in Australia
chips	sliced, deep-fried potatoes, eaten hot (what Americans call 'fries')
cider	beer made from apples
clotted cream	cream so heavy or rich that it's become almost solid (but not sour)
corkage	a small charge levied by the restaurant when you *BYO*
courgette	green vegetable; 'zucchini' in America and Australia
cream cracker	white, unsalted savoury biscuit
cream tea	pot of tea and a scone loaded with jam and *clotted cream*
crisps	thin slices of fried potato bought in a packet, eaten cold; called 'chips' or 'potato chips' in the US and Australia
crumpet	circular piece of doughy bread, toasted before eating and usually covered with butter

double cream	heavy or thick cream
dram	whisky measure
fish fingers	strips of fish pieces covered in bread-crumbs, usually bought frozen and cooked by frying or grilling
greasy spoon	basic cafe (colloquial)
ice lolly	flavoured ice on a stick; called 'popsicle' in the US and 'icy pole' in Australia
icing	thick, sweet and solid covering on a cake
jam	fruit conserve often spread on bread; called 'jelly' in the US
jelly	sweet dessert of flavoured gelatine; called 'jello' in the US
joint	cut of meat used for roasting
kippers	salted and smoked fish, traditionally herring
pickle	a thick, vinegary vegetable-based condiment
Pimms	popular English spirit mixed with lemonade, mint and fresh fruit
pint	measure of beer; also means beer itself (as in 'let me buy you a pint')
salad cream	creamy vinegary salad dressing, much sharper than mayonnaise
scrumpy	a type of strong dry cider
shandy	beer and lemonade mixed together in equal quantities
shepherd's pie	two-layered oven dish with a ground beef and onion mixture on the bottom and mashed potato on the top, cooked in an oven
shout	to buy a group of people drinks, usually reciprocated (colloquial)
single cream	light cream (to distinguish from *double cream* and *clotted cream*)
snug	usually a small separate room in a pub
squash	fruit drink concentrate mixed with water
stout	dark, full-bodied beer made from malt; Guinness is the most famous variety
swede	large root vegetable; sometimes called 'yellow turnip' or 'rutabaga' in the US
sweets	what Americans call 'candy' and Australians call 'lollies'
tipple	an old-fashioned word for drink, often used ironically, eg 'Do you fancy a tipple?'; a tippler is a drinker
treacle	molasses or dark syrup

Architecture in Britain

With an architectural heritage that stretches back more than three millennia, Britain's many different buildings, from simple cottages to grand cathedrals, are an obvious highlight of any visit.

The Callanish Standing Stones on Scotland's Isle of Lewis, dating from 3800 to 5000 years ago, are even older than those at Stonehenge and Avebury.

Early Foundations

The oldest buildings in the country are the grass-covered mounds of earth called 'tumuli' or 'barrows', used as burial sites by Britain's prehistoric residents. These mounds, measuring anything from a rough hemisphere just 2m high to oval domes around 5m high and 10m long, are dotted across the countryside and are especially common in areas of chalk such as Salisbury Plain and the Wiltshire Downs in southern England.

Perhaps the most famous barrow, and certainly the largest and most mysterious, is Silbury Hill near Marlborough. Historians are not sure exactly why this huge conical mound was built – there's no evidence of it actually being used for burials. Theories include the possibility it was used at cultural ceremonies or in the worship of deities in the style of South American pyramids. Whatever the original purpose, it's still awe inspiring today, many centuries after it was built.

Even more impressive than the giant tumuli are another legacy of the neolithic era – menhirs, or standing stones. These are especially well known when they're set out in rings, such as the iconic stone circle of Stonehenge and even larger Avebury Stone Circle, both in Wiltshire.

Organisations protecting Britain's architecture:

» National Trust (www.national trust.org.uk)

» National Trust for Scotland (www.nts.org .uk)

» English Heritage (www .english-herit age.org.uk)

» Cadw (http://cadw .wales.gov.uk)

» Historic Scotland (www .historic-scot land.gov.uk)

Bronze Age & Iron Age

After the neolithic era's large stone circles, the Bronze Age architecture we can see today is more domestic in scale. Hut circles from this period can still be seen in parts of Britain, most notably on Dartmoor in Devon. The Scottish islands hold many of Europe's best surviving Bronze and Iron Age remains, in places like the stone villages of Skara Brae in Orkney and Jarlshof in Shetland.

During the Iron Age, the early peoples of Britain began organising themselves into clans or tribes. Their legacy includes forts built to defend territory and protect from rival tribes or other invaders. Most forts consisted of a steep mound of earth behind a large circular or oval ditch. A famous example is Maiden Castle in Dorset.

The Roman Era

Remains of the Roman Empire are found in many towns and cities (mostly in England and Wales, as the Romans didn't colonise Scotland). There are impressive remains in Chester, Exeter and St Albans, as well as in the lavish Roman spa and bath house complex in Bath. Britain's largest and most impressive Roman relic is the 73-mile-long sweep of Hadrian's Wall, built in the 2nd century as a defensive line stretching from coast to coast across the country. Originally intended to separate marauding Pictish warriors north of the wall (in what is now Scotland) from the Empire's territories in the south, it became as much a symbol of Roman power as a fortification.

Medieval Masterpieces

In the centuries following the Norman Conquest of 1066, there was an explosion of architecture, inspired by the two most pressing concerns of the day: worship and defence. Churches, abbeys and monasteries sprang up during the early Middle Ages, along with many cathedrals that remain modern landmarks, such as Salisbury, Winchester, Canterbury and York.

As for castles in Britain, you're spoilt for choice. Castles range from the atmospheric ruins of Tintagel and Dunstanburgh, and the sturdy ramparts of Conwy and Beaumaris, to the stunning crag-top fortresses of Stirling and Edinburgh. And then there's the most impressive of them all: the Tower of London, guarding the capital for more than 900 years.

Stately Homes

The medieval period was tumultuous, but by about 1600 life had become more settled and the nobility had less need for castles. While they were excellent for keeping out rivals or the riff-raff, castles were often too cold and draughty to be comfortable.

Many castles underwent the home improvements of the day, with larger windows, wider staircases and better drainage installed. Others were simply abandoned for a brand-new dwelling next door – an example of this is Hardwick Hall in Derbyshire.

Following the Civil War the trend away from castles gathered pace, and throughout the 17th century the landed gentry developed a taste for fine 'country houses' designed by famous architects of the day. Many became the stately homes that are a major feature of the British landscape and a major attraction for visitors today. Among the most extravagant are Chatsworth House and Blenheim Palace in England, Powis Castle in Wales and Hopetoun House in Scotland.

The great stately homes all display the proportion, symmetry and architectural harmony in vogue during the 17th and 18th centuries. These styles were later reflected in the fashionable town houses of the Georgian era, most notably in the city of Bath, where the stunning Royal Crescent is the ultimate example of the genre.

Victoriana

The Victorian era was a time of great building activity. A style called Victorian Gothic developed, echoing the towers and spires featured in the original Gothic cathedrals. The most famous example of this style

Britain's Best Castles

» Alnwick
» Balmoral
» Beaumaris
» Berkeley
» Carlisle
» Caernarfon
» Caerphilly
» Chepstow
» Conwy
» Edinburgh
» Eilean Donan
» Glamis
» Harlech
» Ludlow
» Pembroke
» Raglan
» Richmond
» Skipton
» Stirling
» Tintagel

CHALK FIGURES

As you travel around Britain, look out for the chalk figures gracing many hilltops. They are created in areas where the underlying rock is pale limestone by cutting through turf and soil to reveal the white chalk below, and are most notably found in southwest England, especially the counties of Dorset and Wiltshire. Some figures, such as the Uffington White Horse, date from the Bronze Age, but most are more recent. The formidably endowed Cerne Abbas Giant is often thought to be an ancient pagan figure, but recent research suggests it was etched some time in the 17th century.

is London's Houses of Parliament and the clock tower that everyone knows as Big Ben (although technically this is the name of the large bell that strikes the hour), which was officially renamed Elizabeth Tower in 2012 to celebrate the Queen's diamond jubilee. Other Victorian–Gothic highlights in England's capital include the Natural History Museum and St Pancras train station. The style was copied all around the country, especially for civic buildings, with the finest examples including Manchester Town Hall and Glasgow City Chambers.

> As well as many grand cathedrals, Britain has thousands of parish churches, many with historical or architectural significance, especially in rural areas.

Industrialisation

Through the late 19th and early 20th centuries, as Britain's cities grew in size and stature, the newly moneyed middle classes built smart town houses in streets and squares. Elsewhere, the first town planners oversaw the construction of endless terraces of 'back-to-back' and 'two-up-two-down' houses to accommodate the massive influx of workers required for the country's factories. In South Wales, similar, though often single-storeyed houses were built for the burgeoning numbers of coal miners. The industrial areas of Scotland saw the construction of tenements, usually three or four storeys high, with a central communal staircase and two dwellings on each floor. In many cases the terraced houses and basic tenements are not especially scenic, but they are perhaps the most enduring mark on the British architectural landscape.

Postwar Pains & Pride

During WWII bombing damaged many of Britain's cities and the rebuilding that followed showed little regard for the overall look of the cities or for the lives of people who lived in them. Rows of terraces were swept away in favour of high-rise tower blocks, while the brutalist architecture of the 1950s and '60s embraced the modern and efficient building materials of steel and concrete.

Perhaps this is why the British are largely conservative in their architectural tastes. They often resent ambitious or experimental designs, especially applied to public buildings or when a building's form appears more important than its function. However, a familiar pattern unfolds: after a few years of resentment the building is given a nickname, then it gains grudging acceptance, and finally it becomes a source of pride and affection. The British just don't like to be rushed, that's all.

With this attitude in mind, over the past few decades modern British architecture has begun to redeem itself and many big cities have contemporary buildings their residents can enjoy and be proud of. Highlights in London's financial district include the bulging cone at the official address of 30 St Mary Axe (better known by its nickname, 'the Gherkin')

ROYAL GRANDEUR

> The stunning Royal Crescent in Bath, with its magnificent curved facade of grand town houses and perfect harmonious design, is the epitome of Georgian-era architecture.

HOUSE & HOME

In Britain, it's not all about big houses. Alongside the stately homes, ordinary domestic architecture can still be seen in rural areas. Black-and-white 'half-timbered' houses characterise counties such as Worcestershire, brick-and-flint buildings pepper Suffolk and Sussex, and hardy, centuries-old cottages and farm buildings of slate and local stone are a feature of North Wales. In northern Scotland, the blackhouse is a classic basic dwelling, with walls of dry, unmortared stone packed with earth and a roof of straw and turf.

DOMINATING THE LANDSCAPE

If you're travelling through Wales, it won't take you long to notice the country's most striking architectural asset: castles. There are about 600 in all, giving Wales the dubious honour of being Europe's most densely fortified country. Most were built in medieval times, first by William the Conqueror and then by other Anglo-Norman kings, to keep the Welsh in check. In the late 13th century Edward I built spectacular castles at Caernarfon, Harlech, Conwy and Beaumaris, now jointly listed as a Unesco World Heritage Site. Other castles to see include Rhuddlan, Denbigh, Cricceith, Raglan, Pembroke, Kidwelly, Chepstow and Caerphilly. While undeniably great for visitors, the castles are a sore point for patriotic Welsh; the writer Thomas Pennant called them 'the magnificent badge of our subjection'.

and the former Millennium Dome now rebranded as 'the O2' (the name is sponsored by the O2 mobile phone network), which has been transformed from a source of national embarrassment into one of the capital's leading live-music venues.

21st Century

During the first decade of this century, many areas of Britain placed new importance on having progressive, popular architecture as part of a wider regeneration. Top examples include Manchester's Imperial War Museum North, Birmingham's chic new Bullring shopping centre, the Welsh National Assembly building and the Wales Millennium Centre (both on the Cardiff waterfront), the interlocking arches of Glasgow's Scottish Exhibition & Conference Centre (affectionately called 'the Armadillo') and The Sage concert hall in Gateshead in northeast England.

From about 2010, development slowed and some plans were shelved in response to the global economic slowdown. Several significant projects that have reached completion include the Turner Contemporary Gallery in Margate and the futuristic Library of Birmingham (scheduled to open in 2013).

Britain's largest and highest-profile architectural project of recent times was the Olympic Park, the centrepiece of the 2012 Olympic Games. Situated in the London suburb of Stratford, it was renamed the Queen Elizabeth Olympic Park after the games. The main Olympic Stadium and other arenas, including the Velodrome and Aquatics Centre, were built using cutting-edge techniques and are all dramatic structures in their own right.

Meanwhile, in the centre of the capital, the London Bridge Tower (its tall and jagged shape quickly earning it the nickname of 'the Shard') dominates the South Bank; at 306m, it's one of Europe's tallest buildings. On the other side of the River Thames, two more giant skyscrapers are due for completion in 2014: 20 Fenchurch St (thanks to its shape, already nicknamed 'the Walkie-Talkie') and the slanting-walled Leadenhall Building (dubbed, inevitably, 'the Cheese Grater').

London continues to grow upwards and British architecture continues to push new boundaries of style and technology. The buildings may look a little different, but they're still iconic and impressive, so it's great to see the spirit of Stonehenge alive and well after all these years.

Perhaps the best-known example of 1950/60s brutalist architecture is London's Southbank Centre. A building of its time, it was applauded when finished, then reviled for its ugliness, and is now regarded by Londoners with something close to pride and affection.

Glossary of British Architecture

aisle	passageway or open space along either side of a church *nave*
apse	area for clergy, traditionally at the east end of a church
bailey	outermost wall of a castle
bar	gate (York, and in some other northern cities)
barrel vault	semicircular arched roof
boss	covering for the meeting point of ribs in a *vaulted* roof
brass	memorial consisting of a brass plate set into the side or lid of a tomb, or into the floor of a church to indicate a burial place below
buttress	vertical support for a wall; see also *flying buttress*
campanile	free-standing belfry or bell tower
chancel	eastern end of the church, usually reserved for choir and clergy
chantry	*chapel* established by a donor for use in their name after death
chapel	small church; shrine or area of worship off the main body of a cathedral
chapel of ease	*chapel* built for those who lived far from a parish church
choir	area in a church where the choir is seated
cloister	covered walkway linking a church with adjacent monastic buildings
close	buildings grouped around a cathedral
cob	mixture of mud and straw for building
corbel	stone or wooden projection from a wall supporting a beam or arch
crossing	intersection of a church *nave* and *transepts*
flying buttress	supporting *buttress* in the form of one side of an open arch
font	basin used for baptisms, often in a separate baptistry
frater	common or dining room in a medieval monastery
lady chapel	*chapel* dedicated to the Virgin Mary
lancet	pointed window in Early English style
lierne vault	*vault* containing many tertiary ribs
Martello tower	small circular tower used for coastal defence
minster	church connected to a monastery

misericord	hinged choir seat with a bracket (often elaborately carved)
nave	main body of a church at the western end, where a congregation gathers
oast house	building containing a kiln for drying hops
pargeting	decorative stucco plasterwork
pele	fortified house
precinct	see *close*
presbytery	eastern area of *chancel* beyond the choir, where the clergy operates
priory	religious house governed by a prior or prioress (a senior monk or nun)
pulpit	raised box where the priest gives sermons
quire	medieval term for *choir*
refectory	monks' dining room
reredos	literally 'behind the back'; backdrop to an altar
rood	archaic word for a cross in a church
rood screen	screen carrying a *rood* or crucifix, separating the *nave* from the *chancel*
squint	angled opening in a wall or pillar allowing a view of an altar
transepts	north–south projections from a church's *nave,* creating a cruciform (cross-shaped layout)
undercroft	vaulted underground room or cellar
vault	roof with arched ribs, usually in a decorative pattern
vestry	priest's changing room

The Arts in Britain

Britain's contributions to the worlds of literature, drama, cinema and pop are celebrated around the world, thanks in no small part to the global dominance of the English language. As you travel around Britain today you'll see landscapes made famous as movie sets and literary locations, or mentioned in songs, so for this chapter we've picked some major milestones and focused on works with a connection to real places where you can experience something of your favourite artist or even walk in the footsteps of their characters.

Literature

The roots of Britain's literary heritage stretch back to Norse sagas and Early English epics such as *Beowulf*, but most scholars agree that modern English-language literature starts in the late 14th century: yes, that counts as 'modern' in history-soaked Britain.

First Stars

For extra insight while travelling, the *Oxford Literary Guide to Great Britain & Ireland*, edited by Daniel Hahn and Nicholas Robins, gives details of towns, villages and the countryside immortalised by writers, from Chaucer's Canterbury and Austen's Bath to Scott's Highlands.

The first big name in Britain's literary canon is Geoffrey Chaucer, best known for *The Canterbury Tales*. This mammoth collection of fables, stories and morality tales, using travelling pilgrims (the Knight, the Wife of Bath, the Nun's Priest and so on) as a narrative hook is considered an essential of the canon.

After Chaucer, two centuries passed before Britain's next major literary figure rose to prominence: enter stage left William Shakespeare. Best known for his plays (discussed in the Theatre section) he was also a prolific and influential poet. 'Shall I compare thee to a summer's day?' is just one of his famous lines still widely quoted today.

The 17th & 18th Centuries

The 17th century saw the publication of John Milton's epic blank verse poem *Paradise Lost*, a literary landmark inspired by the biblical tale of Adam and Eve's expulsion from the Garden of Eden. This was followed a few years later by the equally seminal *Pilgrim's Progress* by John Bunyan, an allegorical tale of the everyday Christian struggle. For mere mortals, reading these books in their entirety can be hard going, but they're worth dipping into for a taste of the rich language.

More familiar to most British people are the words of *Auld Lang Syne*, penned by 18th-century poet and lyricist Robert Burns, and traditionally sung at New Year. His more unusual *Address to a Haggis* is also still recited annually at Burns Night, a Scottish celebration held on 25 January.

Another milestone literary work of this period is Daniel Defoe's *Robinson Crusoe*. On one level it's an adventure story about a man shipwrecked on an uninhabited island, but it's also a discussion on

BEST-LOVED LIT: AUSTEN & THE BRONTËS

The beginning of the 19th century saw the emergence of some of English literature's best-loved writers: Jane Austen and the Brontë sisters.

Austen's fame stems from her exquisite observations of love, friendship, intrigues and passions boiling under the stilted reserve of middle-class social convention. These observations have spawned countless films and TV costume dramas based on her works. The location now most associated with Austen is the city of Bath – a beautiful place even without such a literary link. As one of her heroines said, 'Oh! Who can ever be tired of Bath?'.

Of the Brontë sisters' prodigious output, Emily Brontë's *Wuthering Heights* is the best known, an epic tale of obsession and revenge, where the dark and moody landscape plays a role as great as any human character, while Charlotte Brontë's *Jane Eyre* and Anne Brontë's *The Tenant of Wildfell Hall* are classics of passion, mystery and love. Visitors still flock to the former Brontë home in the Yorkshire town of Haworth, perched on the edge of the wild Pennine moors that inspired so many of their books.

civilisation, colonialism and faith, and is regarded by many scholars as the first English-language novel. It's also been an armchair travellers' favourite since its publication in 1719.

The Romantic Era

As industrialisation began to take hold in Britain during the late 18th and early 19th century, a new generation of writers, including William Blake, John Keats, Percy Bysshe Shelley, Lord Byron and Samuel Taylor Coleridge, drew inspiration from human imagination and the natural world (in some cases aided by a healthy dose of laudanum). Known as the 'Romantics', perhaps the best known of all was William Wordsworth; his famous line from the poem commonly known as *Daffodils*, 'I wandered lonely as a cloud', were inspired by a hike in the hills of the Lake District.

Victoriana

During the reign of Queen Victoria (1837–1901), key novels of the time explored social themes. Charles Dickens is the best-known writer of the period: *Oliver Twist* is a tale of young thieves in the London slums, while *Hard Times* is a critique of the excess of capitalism.

At around the same time, but choosing a rural setting, George Eliot (the pen name of Mary Anne Evans) wrote *The Mill on the Floss*, whose central character, Maggie Tulliver, searches for true love and struggles against society's expectations.

Meanwhile, Thomas Hardy's classic *Tess of the D'Urbervilles* deals with the peasantry's decline, and *The Trumpet Major* paints a picture of idyllic English country life interrupted by war and encroaching modernity. Many of Hardy's works are in the fictionalised county of Wessex, largely based on today's Dorset and surrounding counties, where towns such as Dorchester are popular stops on tourist itineraries today.

With similarly close links to the landscape is *Waverley* by Sir Walter Scott. Written in the early 19th century and set in the mountains and glens of Scotland during the time of the Jacobite rebellion, it is usually regarded as the first historical novel in the English language.

The Modern World

Britain – and its literature – changed forever following WWI and the social disruption of the period. This fed into the modernist movement, with DH Lawrence perhaps its finest exponent; *Sons and Lovers* follows

Burning Bright

The painter, writer, poet and visionary William Blake (1757–1827) mixed fantastical landscapes and mythological scenes with motifs drawn from classical art, religious iconography and legend. For more see www .blakearchive.org.

the lives and loves of generations in the English Midlands as the country changes from rural idyll to an industrial landscape, while his controversial exploration of sexuality in *Lady Chatterley's Lover* was banned until 1960 because of its 'obscenity'.

Other highlights of this period included Daphne du Maurier's romantic suspense novel *Rebecca*, with close connections to Cornwall, Evelyn Waugh's *Brideshead Revisited*, an exploration of moral and social disintegration among the English aristocracy, and Richard Llewellyn's Welsh classic *How Green Was My Valley*. A decade or so later, after WWII, Compton Mackenzie lifted postwar spirits with *Whisky Galore,* a comic novel about a cargo of booze washed up from a sinking ship onto a Scottish island.

In the 1950s, the poet Dylan Thomas found fame with his *Portrait of The Artist As A Young Dog,* although his most celebrated work is a radio play *Under Milk Wood* (1954), exposing the tensions of small-town Wales.

Then came the swinging '60s. Liverpool poet Roger McGough and friends determined to make art relevant to daily life and produced *The Mersey Sound* – landmark pop poetry for the streets. Other new writers included Muriel Spark, who introduced the world to a highly unusual Edinburgh school mistress in *The Prime of Miss Jean Brodie.*

The 1970s saw the arrival of two novelists who went on to become prolific through the rest of the century and beyond. Martin Amis published *The Rachel Papers,* followed by a string of novels whose common themes include the absurdity and unappealing nature of modern life, such as *London Fields* (1989) and *Lionel Asbo: State of England* (2012). Ian McEwan made his debut with *The Cement Garden* (1978), and earned critical acclaim for finely observed studies of the English character in works such as *The Child in Time* (1987), *Atonement* (2001) and *On Chesil Beach* (2007).

Contemporary novels in a different vein include 1993's *Trainspotting* by Irvine Welsh, a dark look at Edinburgh's drug culture, and the start of a new genre coined 'Tartan Noir'. Ian Rankin, best known for his Edinburgh-set *Inspector Rebus* novels, is another writer often associated with this genre, while perhaps the most successful modern Scottish novelist is Iain Banks (who also writes sci-fi under the cunning pseudonym of Iain M Banks); his early works include *The Crow Road* (1992), while more recent publications include *Stonemouth* (2012), set near Aberdeen.

New Millennium

As the 20th century came to a close, and the new millennium dawned, Britain's multicultural landscape proved a rich inspiration for contemporary novelists. Hanif Kureishi sowed the seeds with his ground-breaking 1990 novel *The Buddha of Suburbia,* examining the hopes and fears of a group of Anglo-Asians in London. This was followed by Zadie Smith's

---

Graham Greene's novel *Brighton Rock* (1938) is a classic account of wayward English youth. For an even more shocking take, try *A Clockwork Orange* by Anthony Burgess, later infamously filmed by Stanley Kubrick in 1971.

BRITISH ENGLISH

The language of most of Britain's literature is English, the main 'indigenous' language of Britain, and known as British English, to distinguish it from American English, Australian English and so on.

But English is not the only language of Great Britain. Others include Welsh (spoken in Wales) and Cornish (in Cornwall). In Scotland, two other languages are spoken: Lowland Scots (also known as Lallans) and the distinct Scottish Gaelic (spoken mainly in the northwest). The Isle of Man and Channel Islands also have their own languages.

Wherever you go in Britain, though, even if Welsh or Gaelic is the first language in the area, nearly everyone speaks English as well.

FIFTY SHADES OF GREY

In 2012, British author EL James's *Fifty Shades of Grey*, renowned for its scenes of sado-masochistic eroticism, became a global best-seller and the fastest-selling paperback ever. Journalists were delighted to report on the beating and outstripping of previous record-holder *Harry Potter*.

acclaimed debut *White Teeth* (2000) and a string of bestsellers including her most recent novel, *NW* (2012). Andrea Levy found acclaim with *Small Island* (2004), about a Jamaican couple settled in postwar London, and Monica Ali's *Brick Lane* was shortlisted for the 2003 Man Booker Prize, a high-profile literary award.

Other big-name writers of the current era include Will Self, known for his surreal, satirical novels that include *The Book of Dave*, and Nick Hornby, whose most recent novel is *Juliet, Naked* (2009), although he's still best known for *Fever Pitch*, a study of the insecurities of English blokishness and re-released by the publisher as a 'modern classic' in 2012.

Also popular is Julian Barnes, whose book *England, England* is a darkly ironic study of nationalism and tourism, while *The Sense of Ending* won the 2011 Man Booker Prize. Hilary Mantel, author of many novels on an astoundingly wide range of themes and subjects, including *Wolf Hall* (another Man Booker Prize winner) about Henry VIII and his ruthless advisor Thomas Cromwell, followed by the sequels *Bring Up the Bodies*, which won the 2012 Man Booker Prize, and the forthcoming *The Mirror and the Light*.

A new name on the literary scene is Stephen Kelman, whose debut novel *Pigeon English*, about gang culture and multicultural tensions, was nominated ('gatecrashed' in the words of the author) for the Man Booker Prize in 2011. Other names and books to look out for include: David Mitchell (*Cloud Atlas*), Kazuo Ishiguro (*Never Let Me Go*), Alan Hollinghurst (*The Line Of Beauty*), Sarah Waters (*The Little Stranger*).

Britain's greatest literary phenomenon of the 21st century is JK Rowling's *Harry Potter* series, a set of other-worldly adventures that have entertained millions of children (and many grown-ups too) since the first book was published in 1996. The magical tales are the latest in a long line of British children's classics enjoyed by adults, stretching back to the works of Lewis Carroll *(Alice's Adventures in Wonderland)*, E Nesbit *(The Railway Children)*, AA Milne *(Winnie-the-Pooh)* and CS Lewis *(The Chronicles of Narnia)*.

Alongside the work of British poets and novelists, it's impossible to overlook the current trend for celebrity autobiographies – penned by everyone from footballers to reality TV also-rans – a reminder of the increasing importance of hype over merit in the modern book market. But whatever you make of the literary qualities of these memoirs, it's hard to argue with the figures – the British public buys them by the bucket load.

For a taste of surreal humour, try two of Britain's funniest (and most successful) writers: Douglas Adams (*The Hitchhiker's Guide to the Galaxy* plus sequels) and Terry Pratchett (the *Discworld* series).

Helen Fielding's *Bridget Jones's Diary* is a fond look at the heartache of a modern single girl's blundering search for love and epitomised the late-1990s 'chick lit' genre.

Cinema

British cinema has a long history, with many early directors cutting their teeth in the silent-film industry. Perhaps the best-known of these was Alfred Hitchcock, who directed *Blackmail*, one of the first British 'talkies' in 1929, and who went on to direct a string of films during the 1930s, before migrating to Hollywood in the early 1940s.

Patriot Games

During WWII, British films were dominated by patriotic stories designed to raise morale: *Went the Day Well?* (1942), *In Which We Serve* (1942) and *We Dive at Dawn* (1943) are prime examples of the genre. During this period David Lean directed the classic tale of buttoned-up passion, *Brief Encounter* (1945), before graduating to Hollywood epics, including *Lawrence of Arabia* and *Doctor Zhivago*.

Another great film of the 1940s is *How Green Was My Valley,* a tale of everyday life in the coal-mining villages of Wales. Perhaps the best-known Welsh film, it manages to annoy more Welsh people than any other, with its stereotypical characters, absence of Welsh actors, and the fact that it was shot in a Hollywood studio. It's worth seeing, though, for a taste of the period.

The British Film Institute (BFI) is dedicated to promoting film and cinema in Britain, and publishes the monthly academic journal *Sight & Sound*. For more, see www.bfi.org .uk and www .screenonline.org. uk for complete coverage of Britain's film and TV industry.

After the War

Following the hardships of the war, British audiences were in the mood for escape and entertainment. During the late 1940s and early '50s, the domestic film industry specialised in eccentric British comedies epitomised by the output of Ealing Studios: notable titles include *Passport to Pimlico* (1949), *Kind Hearts and Coronets* (1949) and *The Titfield Thunderbolt* (1953).

Dramatic box-office hits of the time included *Hamlet* (the first British film to win an Oscar in the Best Picture category), starring Laurence Olivier and Carol Reed's *The Third Man*. In a post-war Britain still struggling with rationing and food shortages, tales of heroic derring-do such as *The Dam Busters* (1955) and *Reach for the Sky* (1956) helped lighten the national mood.

The Ladykillers (1955) is a classic Ealing comedy about a band of hapless bank robbers holed up in a London guest house, and features Alec Guinness sporting quite possibly the most outrageous set of false teeth ever committed to celluloid.

Swinging Sixties

In the late 1950s, 'British New Wave' and 'Free Cinema' explored the gritty realities of life in an intimate, semidocumentary style, with Lindsay Anderson and Tony Richardson crystallising the movement with films such as *This Sporting Life* (1961) and *A Taste of Honey* (1961).

At the other end of the spectrum were the *Carry On* films, packed with bawdy gags and double entendres, and starring a troupe of 'national treasures' including Barbara Windsor, Sid James and Kenneth Williams.

The 1960s saw the birth of another classic British icon: super-spy James Bond, adapted from the Ian Fleming novels and first played by Sean Connery in *Dr No* (1962). Since then over 20 Bond movies have been made, with Bond played by other British actors including Roger Moore and Daniel Craig.

HAMMER HORROR

The British company Hammer Film Productions produced low-budget horror films in the 1950s and '60s, still revered by fans around the globe. Early flicks included *The Quatermass Xperiment* (1955) and *The Curse of Frankenstein* (1957). The stars of the latter – Peter Cushing as Dr Frankenstein and Christopher Lee as the Monster – would feature in many of Hammer's best films over the next 20 years, including a string of nine *Dracula* films (most of which star Lee as Dracula and Cushing as Van Helsing or his descendants) and six *Frankenstein* sequels.

The studio also launched the careers of several other notable actors (including Oliver Reed, who made his debut in *The Curse of the Werewolf*, 1961) and even spawned its very own spoof, *Carry On Screaming* – the ultimate British seal of approval.

Burning Gold

After the boom of the 1960s, British cinema entered troubled waters for a decade or so, but was revived in the 1980s thanks partly to David Puttnam's *Chariots of Fire*, the Oscar-winning tale of two British runners competing at the 1924 Olympics. Not surprisingly, the film's famous theme featured in the opening ceremony and at numerous victory parades of the London 2012 Olympics.

The newly established (1982) Channel 4 invested in edgy films such as *My Beautiful Laundrette* (1985), while the British producing duo of Ismail Merchant and James Ivory played Hollywood at its own game with period films such as *Heat and Dust* (1983) and *A Room With A View* (1986), capitalising on the success of Richard Attenborough's big-budget *Gandhi* (1982), which bagged eight Academy Awards.

Brit Flicks

In the 1990s, the massively successful *Four Weddings and a Funeral*, which introduced Hugh Grant in his trademark role as the likeable, self-deprecating Englishman (an archetype he reprised in subsequent hits *Notting Hill* and *Love, Actually*) spearheaded the the 'Brit-flick' genre. These included *Brassed Off*, relating the trials of a struggling colliery band. *The Full Monty* (1997), about a troupe of laid-off steel workers turned male strippers, became Britain's most successful film ever and *The Englishman Who Went Up a Hill and Came Down a Mountain*, an affectionate story about a hill in North Wales deemed too low.

Grittier films of the 1990s included *Trainspotting*, a visually innovative, hard-hitting film about Edinburgh's drugged-out underbelly, which launched the careers of Scottish actors Ewan McGregor and Robert Carlyle, while Mike Leigh's *Secrets and Lies*, a Palme d'Or winner at Cannes, tells the story of an adopted black woman who seeks out her white mother.

Other landmark films of the decade included gangster movie *Lock, Stock and Two Smoking Barrels*, which spawned a host of copycats, *Breaking the Waves*, a perfect study of culture clash in 1970s Scotland, *Human Traffic*, an edgy romp through Cardiff's clubland, and the Oscar-winning Austen adaptation *Sense and Sensibility* starring English doyennes Emma Thompson and Kate Winslet as the Dashwood sisters, with Hugh Grant as (you guessed it) a likeable and self-deprecating Englishman.

Award-winning Welsh-language films of the time include *Hedd Wynn*, a heartbreaking story of a poet killed in WWI, and *Solomon and Gaenor*, a passionate tale of forbidden love at the turn of the 20th century, staring Ioan Gruffudd and filmed twice; once in the Welsh language and once in English.

The decade ended with films such as *East Is East* (1999), a beautifully understated study of the clash between first- and second-generation immigrant Pakistanis in Britain, and *Billy Elliott* (2000), about a boy's quest to learn ballet and escape the slag-heaps of post-industrial northern England.

WITHNAIL AND I

Withnail and I (1987) is one of the great cult British comedies. Directed by Bruce Robinson, it stars Paul McGann and Richard E Grant as a pair of hapless out-of-work actors on a disastrous holiday to the Lake District.

The 21st Century

In the early part of the 21st century, literature continued to provide the richest seam mined by the British film industry. Hits of this genre include the blockbuster *Harry Potter* franchise (based on the books of the same name, and the most financially successful film series of all time) staring Daniel Radcliffe, as well as 2005's *The Constant Gardener* (based on a John Le Carré novel), 2008's *Atonement* (based on Ian McEwan's novel), 2011's *War Horse* (directed by Stephen Spielberg and based on

A GRAND SUCCESS

One of the great success stories of British television and cinema has been Bristol-based animator Nick Park and the production company Aardman Animations, best known for the award-winning series starring the man-and-dog duo Wallace and Gromit. This lovable pair first appeared in Park's graduation film, *A Grand Day Out* (1989) and went on to star in *The Wrong Trousers* (1993), *A Close Shave* (1995) and their full-length feature debut, *The Curse of the Were-Rabbit* (2005).

Known for their intricate plots, film homages and amazingly realistic animation, the Wallace and Gromit films have netted Nick Park four Oscars. Other Aardman films include *Chicken Run* (2000), *Flushed Away* (2006) and *The Pirates! – In an Adventure with Scientists* (2012).

Michael Morpurgo's novel), and 2012's *Anna Karenina*, directed by Joe Wright and staring Keira Knightley.

After the outstanding success of the *Lord of the Rings* trilogy of films (based on the books by British author JRR Tolkien), the first of the films in *The Hobbit* trilogy – also based on a book by Tolkien – was released in late 2012. Produced by Peter Jackson and starring Martin Freeman as Bilbo Baggins, it features many of the original cast from the *Lord of the Rings* series including Christopher Lee, Orlando Bloom and Elijah Wood.

Biopics are a perennial favourite, especially, it seems, of famous females, with recent highlights including: Queen Elizabeth I (*Elizabeth: The Golden Age*, 2007), Queen Elizabeth II (*The Queen*, 2006) and Margaret Thatcher (*The Iron Lady*, 2011). A film about Diana, Princess of Wales is due to be released in 2013.

Comedy continues to thrive: building on the success of films such as zombie-spoof *Shaun of the Dead* (2004), recent releases include smutty coming-of-age story *The Inbetweeners* (2011) and *Johnny English Reborn* (2012), the further adventures of the hapless sleuth.

Meanwhile, the oldest of British film franchises rolls on, with James Bond now a tough, toned and occasionally fallible character played by Daniel Craig in *Casino Royale (2006)*, *Quantum of Solace* (2008) and *Skyfall* (2012), while his boss 'M' is played by one of Britain's best-known screen names, Dame Judi Dench.

Television

Since the earliest days of TV broadcasting, Britain has produced some of the world's finest shows and programmes, from classic comedy to ground-breaking drama. Many of the world's most popular formats have their origins in British broadcasting, including the phenomenon known as reality TV.

The main broadcasters are BBC and ITV, each with several channels. Others include channels 4 and 5. The BBC is a national institution, especially famous for its news and natural-history programming, epitomised by landmark series such as *Planet Earth* and *The Blue Planet* (reassuringly helmed by Sir David Attenborough, a similarly precious national institution since the 1970s).

The big-budget costume drama is British staple; BBC viewers have been treated to adaptations of practically every Dickens, Bronte and Thackeray novel, while ITV has entered the same territory, notably with Jane Austen's *Munsfield Park* and *Northanger Abbey*.

Reality TV has dominated many channels in recent years, although the popularity of shows such as *Big Brother* and *I'm a Celebrity, Get Me Out of Here!* seems to be on the wane. On the flipside, variety has made a big comeback, with programs like *Britain's Got Talent* and *Strictly Come*

The BBC is a public-service broadcaster, financed by the licence fee of £145, paid annually by every house in Britain with a TV set, rather than by advertising. This means shows are not interrupted by commercial breaks.

Dancing (the latter under the brand of *Dancing with the Stars*) syndicated the world over. Game shows are another success story, with British inventions such as *Who Wants to be a Millionaire?* and *The Weakest Link* spawning countless foreign versions.

Comedy is strong point for British TV, with classics such as *Monty Python*, *Steptoe and Son* and *Only Fools and Horses* continuing to enjoy cult status. More-recent additions in comedy's hall of fame are *Mr Bean*, *Ali G* and *The Office*.

Britain's main broadcasters are known for their long-running 'soaps' such as Eastenders (BBC), Emmerdale and Coronation Street (both ITV), which have collectively been running on British screens for well over a century.

THE ARTS IN BRITAIN

Pop & Rock Music

Britain's been putting the world through its musical paces ever since a mop-haired four-piece from Liverpool tuned up their Rickenbackers and created The Beatles. And while some may claim that Elvis invented rock 'n' roll, it was the Fab Four who transformed it into a global phenomenon, backed by the other bands of the 1960s 'British Invasion' – The Rolling Stones, The Who, Cream, The Kinks and soul man Tom Jones.

Glam to Punk

In the 1970s, glam rock swaggered onto the stage, led by the likes of Marc Bolan and David Bowie in their tight-fitting jumpsuits and chameleon guises, succeeded by early boy-band Bay City Rollers, art-rockers Roxy Music, outrageously-costumed Elton John and anthemic popsters Queen. In a different genre, Led Zeppelin, Deep Purple and Black Sabbath laid down the blueprint for heavy metal, while the psychedelia of the previous decade morphed into the spacey noodlings of prog rock, epitomised by Pink Floyd, Genesis and Yes.

By the late '70s, glam and prog bands were looking out of touch in a Britain wracked by rampant unemployment and industrial unrest, and punk rock exploded onto the scene, summing up the air of doom with nihilistic lyrics and three-chord tunes. The Sex Pistols remain the best-known band of the era, while other punk pioneers included The Clash, The Damned, The Buzzcocks and The Stranglers.

Punk begat New Wave, with acts such as The Jam and Elvis Costello blending spiky tunes and sharp lyrics into a more radio-friendly sound. A little later, along came bands like The Specials and baggy-trousered rude boys Madness, mixing punk, reggae and ska sounds. Meanwhile, another punk-and-reggae-influenced band called The Police – fronted by bassist Sting – became one of the biggest names of the decade.

Mode, Metal & Miserabilism

The conspicuous consumption of Britain in the early 1980s were reflected in the decade's pop scene. Big hair and shoulder pads became the uniform of New Romantics such as Spandau Ballet, Duran Duran and Culture Club, while the increased use of synthesizers led to the development of a new electronic sound in the music of Depeche Mode and The Human League. More hits and highlights were supplied by Texas, Eurythmics and Wham! – a boyish duo headed by a bright young fellow named George Michael.

Away from the glitz, fans enjoyed the doom-laden lyrics of The Cure, Bauhaus and Siouxsie & the Banshees, while Britain's heavy rock heritage inspired acts such as Iron Maiden. In a different tone entirely, the disaffection of mid-1980s Britain was summed up by the arch-priests of 'miserabilism', The Smiths, fronted by quiffed wordsmith Morrissey.

Raves, Indie & Britpop

The beats and bleeps of 1980s electronica fuelled the burgeoning dance-music scene of the early '90s. Pioneering artists such as New Order (risen from the ashes of Joy Division) created the soundtrack for an ecstasy-saturated rave culture, centred on famous clubs like Manchester's Haçienda and London's Ministry of Sound. Subgenres such as trip-hop, jungle, house and big-beat were created in other UK cities, with key acts including Massive Attack, Portishead and The Chemical Brothers.

Manchester was also a focus for the burgeoning British 'indie' scene, driven by guitar-based bands such as The Charlatans, The Stone Roses, James, and Happy Mondays.

Indie grew up in the mid- to late-1990s, and the term 'Britpop' was coined, with Oasis at the forefront and covering a wide range of bands including Blur, Elastica, Suede, Supergrass, Ocean Colour Scene, The Verve, Pulp, Travis, Feeder, Super Furry Animals, Stereophonics, Catatonia and the Manic Street Preachers.

This distinctively British music chimed with the country's new sense of optimism following the landslide election of 'New Labour' in 1997. Noel Gallagher of Oasis famously drinking tea with Prime Minister Tony Blair at No 10 Downing St in 1997 was regarded by many as a defining moment of the 'Cool Britannia' era, but the phenomenon was short-lived and well and truly over by the end of the '90s.

Around Britain, buildings associated with notable people are marked with a (usually blue) plaque. In early 2012, a plaque was placed at 23 Heddon St in London to commemorate fictional pop character Ziggy Stardust.

Pop Today, Gone Tomorrow

The new millennium saw no let-up in the British music scene's shape-shifting and reinvention. Jazz, soul, R&B and hip-hop have fused into an 'urban' sound epitomised by artists like Dizzee Rascal, Tinie Tempah and Plan B.

In a totally different genre, British folk and roots music, and folk-influenced acoustic music, is enjoying its biggest revival since the 1960s, with major names including Eliza Carthy and Mumford & Sons.

Meanwhile, the singer-songwriter, exemplified by Katie Melua, Ed Sheeran, the late Amy Winehouse and the all-conquering Adele, has made a comeback, and the spirit of British punk and indie stays alive thanks to the likes of Snow Patrol, Florence & the Machine, Coldplay, Muse, Kasabian, Radiohead and The Horrors.

By the time you read this, half of the 'best new bands' of last year will have sunk without trace, and a fresh batch of unknowns will have risen to dominate the airwaves and download sites. One thing's for sure, the

ROCK 'N' ROLL LOCATIONS

Fans buy the music, then the T-shirt. However, true fans visit the locations featured on album covers. Here are some favourites, many in London, plus a few others around the country:

» **Abbey Rd**, St John's Wood, London – *Abbey Road*, The Beatles

» **Battersea Power Station**, London – *Animals*, Pink Floyd

» **Berwick St**, Soho, London – *(What's the Story) Morning Glory*, Oasis

» **Big Ben**, London – *My Generation* (US version), The Who.

» **Camden Market**, London – *The Clash*, The Clash

» **Heddon St**, off Regent St, London – *The Rise and Fall of Ziggy Stardust & the Spiders from Mars*, David Bowie

» **Porthmadog** (Black Rock Sands) – *This is My Truth Tell Me Yours*, Manic Street Preachers

» **Salford Boys Club**, Manchester – *The Queen is Dead*, The Smiths

» **Thor's Cave**, Manifold Valley, near Ashbourne, Peak District National Park – *A Storm In Heaven*, The Verve

» **Yes Tor**, Dartmoor, Devon – *Tomato*, Yes

POP ON FILM

If you want to combine British pop music with British cinema, try some of these films: *Backbeat* (1994), a look at the early days of The Beatles; *Sid and Nancy* (1986), following The Sex Pistols bassist and his American girlfriend; *Velvet Goldmine* (1998), a tawdry glimpse of the glam-rock scene; *24 Hour Party People* (2002), a totally irreverent and suitably chaotic film about the 1990s Manchester music scene; *Control* (2007), a biopic about Joy Divsion singer Ian Curtis; *and Nowhere Boy* (2009) about John Lennon in his pre-Beatles days.

British music scene has never stood still, and it doesn't look like settling down any time soon.

Painting & Sculpture

For many centuries, continental Europe – especially Holland, Spain, France and Italy – set the artistic agenda. The first artist with a truly British style and sensibility was arguably William Hogarth, whose riotous canvases exposed the vice and corruption of 18th-century London. His most celebrated work is *A Rake's Progress*, which kick-started a long tradition of British caricatures that can be traced right through to the work of modern-day cartoonists such as Gerald Scarfe and Steve Bell. It's displayed at Sir John Soane's Museum in London.

One of the most famous pop creations of the 1990s was the Spice Girls, later becoming the world's best-selling all-female group. Sporty, Scary, Baby, Ginger and Posh famously reunited in 2012 to perform at the London Olympics closing ceremony.

Portraits & Landscapes

While Hogarth was busy satirising society, other artists were hard at work showing it in its best light. The leading figures of 18th-century British portraiture were Sir Joshua Reynolds, Thomas Gainsborough and George Romney, while George Stubbs is best known for his intricate studies of animals (particularly horses). Works by these artists are displayed at Tate Britain or the National Gallery in London.

In the 19th century, leading painters favoured the landscape. John Constable's best-known works include *Salisbury Cathedral* and *The Haywain*, depicting a mill in Suffolk (and now on show in the National Gallery, London), while JMW Turner was fascinated by the effects of light and colour, with his works becoming almost entirely abstract by the 1840s – vilified at the time but prefiguring the Impressionist movement that was to follow 50 years later.

Fables & Flowers

In the mid- to late 19th century, the Pre-Raphaelite movement harked back to the figurative style of classical Italian and Flemish art, tying in with the prevailing Victorian taste for fables, myths and fairy tales. Key members of the movement included Sir John Everett Millais and William Holman Hunt. Millais's *Ophelia,* showing the damsel picturesquely drowned in a river, is an excellent example of their style, and can be seen the Tate Britain. However, one of the best collections of Pre-Raphaelite art is in the Birmingham Museum and Art Gallery.

A good friend of the Pre-Raphaelites was William Morris; he saw late-19th-century furniture and interior design as increasingly vulgar, and with Dante Gabriel Rossetti and Edward Burne-Jones founded the Arts and Crafts movement to encourage the revival of a decorative approach to features such as wallpaper, tapestries and windows. Many of his designs are still used today.

North of the border, Charles Rennie Mackintosh, fresh from the Glasgow School of Art, fast became a renowned artist, designer and architect. He is still Scotland's greatest art nouveau exponent, and much of his

SCULPTURE

work remains in this city. He also influenced a group of artists from the 1890s that became known as the Glasgow School (often divided into two groups: the Glasgow Boys and the Glasgow Girls), among them Margaret and Frances MacDonald, James Guthrie and EA Walton. Much of their work can be seen in the Kelvingrove Art Gallery in Glasgow.

Stone & Sticks

In the tumultuous 20th century, British art became increasingly experimental, with key painters including Francis Bacon, whose work was influenced by Freudian psychoanalysis, and the group known as the Scottish Colourists – Francis Cadell, SJ Peploe, Leslie Hunter and JD Ferguson. Meanwhile, pioneering sculptors such as Henry Moore and Barbara Hepworth experimented with natural forms in stone and new materials.

The Scottish Colourists were followed in the interwar years by a group known as the Edinburgh School. This group included William MacTaggart, who was much influenced by the French expressionists and became one of Scotland's best-known painters. His rich and colourful landscapes can be seen in London's National Gallery and the Hunterian Art Gallery in Glasgow.

At around the same time, Welsh artist Gwen John painted introspective portraits of women friends, cats and nuns (and famously became the model and lover of French artist Rodin), while her brother Augustus John became Britain's leading portrait painter, with famous sitters such as Thomas Hardy and George Bernard Shaw. One place to admire the Johnses' works is at the Glynn Vivian Art Gallery in Swansea.

After WWII, Howard Hodgkin and Patrick Heron developed a British version of American abstract expressionism. At the same time, but in great contrast, Manchester artist LS Lowry was painting his much-loved 'matchstick men' figures set in an urban landscape of narrow streets and smoky factories. A good place to see his work is in the Lowry centre, Manchester.

The works of Henry Moore and Barbara Hepworth can be seen at the Yorkshire Sculpture Park, between Sheffield and Leeds, in northern England. Hepworth is also forever associated with St Ives in Cornwall.

Pop Art

The mid-1950s and early '60s saw an explosion of British artists plundering TV, music, advertising and popular culture for inspiration. Leaders of this new 'pop art' movement included David Hockney, who used bold colours and simple lines to depict his dachshunds and swimming pools, and Peter Blake, who designed the collage cover for the Beatles' landmark *Sgt Pepper* album.

The '60s also saw the rise of sculptor Anthony Caro, who held his first groundbreaking exhibition at the Whitechapel Art Gallery in 1963. Creating large abstract works in steel and bronze, he remains one of Britain's most influential sculptors.

Britart & Beyond

Thanks partly to the support (and money) of advertising tycoon Charles Saatchi, a new wave of British artists came to the fore in the 1990s. The movement was dubbed, inevitably, 'Britart'; its leading members included Damien Hirst, initially famous (or infamous) for works involving pickled sharks, semi-dissected human figures and, more recently, a diamond-encrusted skull entitled *For the Love of God*.

A contemporary is Tracey Emin. Once considered an enfant terrible, she incurred the wrath of the tabloids for works such as *My Bed*, a messed-up bedroom scene, but is now a respected figure and patron of the new Turner Gallery in Margate, named for the famous English artist JMW Turner.

ANISH KAPOOR, OLYMPIAN SCULPTOR

Sculptor Anish Kapoor has been based in London since the 1970s, and his work appears around the world. He is best known for his large outdoor installations, which often feature curved shapes and reflective materials, such as highly polished steel. His recent works include a major new installation at Olympic Park in London, called *ArcelorMittal Orbit*, to celebrate the 2012 Olympic Games. Its sinuous shapes are inspired by the five Olympic rings, and at over 110m high it is the largest piece of public art in Britain.

Turner also gives his name to the Turner Prize, a high-profile (and frequently controversial) annual award for British visual artists. As well as Hirst, other winners have included Martin Creed (his work was a room with lights going on and off), Mark Wallinger (a collection of anti-war objects), Simon Starling (a shed converted to a boat and back again), Rachel Whiteread (a plaster cast of a house) and Antony Gormley (best known for his gigantic *Angel of the North*).

The winner of the Turner prize in 2011 was Martin Boyce, for his *Do Words Have Voices*, a room with angular installations representing an urban park in autumn. Thousands of people came to see the work on display at the Baltic Centre in Gateshead, proving that contemporary art in Britain can attract the crowds, even if it remains controversial.

Theatre

Theatre in Britain has its roots in medieval morality plays, court jesters and travelling storytellers. Its origins can possibly be traced all the way back to dramas during Roman times in amphitheatres, a few of which still remain at places such as Chester and Cirencester. Most scholars agree that the key milestone in the story is the opening of England's first theatre, called simply The Theatre, in London in 1576. A few years later, two more theatres appeared, the Rose and the Globe, and the stage was set for the entrance of Britain's best-known playwright.

Shakespeare

For most visitors to Britain (and for most locals) drama means just one name: Shakespeare. Born in 1564, in the Midlands town of Stratford-upon-Avon, William Shakespeare made his name in London, where most of his plays were performed at the Globe Theatre.

He started writing plays around 1585, and his early theatrical works are grouped together as 'comedies' and 'histories', many of which are household names today – such as *All's Well that Ends Well, The Taming of the Shrew, A Midsummer Night's Dream, Richard III* and *Henry V.* Later in his career Shakespeare wrote many of the famous plays, known collectively as the 'tragedies', such as *Romeo and Juliet, Macbeth, Julius Caesar, Hamlet* and *King Lear.* His brilliant plots and spectacular use of language, plus the sheer size of his canon of work have turned him into a national – and international – icon.

Today, almost 400 years after he shuffled off his mortal coil, the Bard's plays still pull in big crowds, and can be enjoyed at the rebuilt Globe on London's South Bank or at the Royal Shakespeare Company's own theatre in his original hometown of Stratford-upon-Avon.

Antony Gormley's *Angel of the North* is one of the most viewed works of art in the world. Standing beside the busy A1 London to Edinburgh road, millions of drivers each year can't help but see it.

British Theatre Today

However you budget your time and money during your visit to Britain, be sure to see some theatre. It easily lives up to its reputation as the finest in the world, especially in London (whatever New Yorkers may say), while other big cities around the country boast their own top-class

WHAT A PANTOMIME

If any British tradition is guaranteed to bemuse outsiders, it's the pantomime. This over-the-top Christmas spectacle graces stages throughout the land throughout December and January, and traces its roots back to Celtic legends, medieval morality plays and the British music hall. The modern incarnation is usually based on a classic fairy tale and features a mix of saucy dialogue, comedy skits, song-and-dance routines and plenty of custard-pie humour, mixed in with topical gags for the grown-ups. Tradition dictates that the leading 'boy' is played by a woman, and the leading lady, or 'dame', is played by a chap. B-list celebrities, struggling actors and soap stars famously make a small fortune hamming it up for Christmas panto, and there are always a few staple routines that everyone knows and joins in. The hero (or villain) asks 'Where's that dragon/wizard/pirate/lion?' and the audience shouts back 'He's behind you!' It's cheesy, daft and frequently rather surreal, but guaranteed to be great fun for the family. Oh, no it isn't! Oh, yes it is! Oh, no it isn't!

venues, such as the Birmingham Repertory Theatre, the Bristol Old Vic, the Chichester Festival Theatre, the Playhouse in Nottingham, the New Theatre in Cardiff and the Royal Lyceum in Edinburgh.

Many accomplished British actors, including Judi Dench, Ralph Fiennes, Brenda Blethyn, Toby Stephens and Simon Callow, juggle high-paying Hollywood roles with appearances on the British stage, while over the last decade or so several American stars have taken hefty pay cuts to tread the London boards – including Glenn Close, Kevin Spacey, Gwyneth Paltrow, Macaulay Culkin, Christian Slater and Danny DeVito.

Other options in London include the Donmar Warehouse and Royal Court Theatre, best known for new and experimental works. For big names, most people head for the West End, where famous spots include the Shaftsbury, Adelphi and Theatre Royal at Drury Lane. These venues are mostly the preserve of classic plays, with top shows in 2012 including *War Horse*, the play that inspired the Spielberg movie of the same name, and *39 Steps*, also well known as an Alfred Hitchcock movie in the 1930s, as well as *The Mousetrap*, the legendary whodunnit and world's longest-running play; 2012 was its 60th year.

In 2012, the massively successful musical *Matilda*, based on the novel by Roald Dahl, broke records by winning seven Olivier Awards, the most prestigious prize in British theatre, and the equivalent of America's Tony Awards.

WEST END MUSICALS

As well as drama, London's West End means big musicals, with a long history of crowd-pullers such as *Cats*, *The Wizard of Oz*, *Les Misérables*, *Sweeney Todd*, *The Phantom of the Opera* and *The Lion King*, with many of today's shows raiding the pop world for material, such as *We Will Rock You*, inspired by the music of Queen.

For details of other top shows and venues, and how to buy tickets, see the Entertainment section of the London chapter (p133). Details of major theatres in other cities around Britain are also given in the relevant chapters.

The British Landscape

Britain may be small, but even a relatively short journey takes you through a surprising mix of landscapes. Seeing the change – subtle in some areas, dramatic in others – as you travel is one of this country's great drawcards.

Location, Location, Location

The island of Britain sits on the eastern edge of the North Atlantic and consists of three nations: England in the south and centre, Scotland in the north and Wales in the west – together making up the state of Great Britain. Farther west lies the island of Ireland. The islands of Ireland and Britain, plus several smaller islands, together make up the archipelago of the British Isles. Looking southeast, France is just 20 miles away, while to the northeast lie the countries of Scandinavia.

Geologically at least, Britain is part of Europe. It's on the edge of the Eurasian landmass, separated from the mother continent by the shallow English Channel. (The French are not so proprietorial, and call it La Manche – 'the sleeve'.) About 10,000 years ago, Britain was physically part of Europe, but then sea levels rose and created the island we know today. Only in more recent times has there been a reconnection, in the form of the Channel Tunnel.

When it comes to topology, Britain is not a place of extremes; there are no Himalayas or Lake Baikals here. But there's plenty to keep you enthralled.

Southern England is covered in a mix of cities, towns and gently undulating countryside. Eastern England (especially the area called East Anglia) is almost entirely low and flat, while southwest England has wild

Landscape & Environment Online

» www.aonb
.org.uk

» www.environ
ment-agency.
gov.uk

» www.national
parks.gov.uk

» www.wildabout
britain.co.uk

COMPARING COVERAGE

Statistics can be boring, but these essential measurements may be handy for planning or perspective as you travel around:

» Wales: 8000 sq miles
» Scotland: 30,500 sq miles
» England: 50,000 sq miles
» Great Britain (England, Scotland, Wales): 88,500 sq miles
» UK (Great Britain and Northern Ireland): 95,000 sq miles
» British Isles (UK, Ireland and other smaller islands): 123,000 sq miles

For comparison, France is about 210,000 sq miles, Texas 260,000 sq miles, Australia nearly 3 million sq miles and the USA over 3.5 million sq miles. When Britain is compared with these giants, it's amazing that such a small island can make so much noise.

moors, granite outcrops and rich pastures (Devon's cream is world famous), plus a rugged coast with sheltered beaches, making it a favourite holiday destination.

In the north of England, farmland remains interspersed with towns and cities, but the landscape is noticeably more bumpy. A line of large hills called the Pennines (fondly tagged 'the backbone of England') runs from Derbyshire to the Scottish border, and includes the peaty plateaus of the Peak District, the wild moors around Haworth (immortalised in Brontë novels), the delightful valleys of the Yorkshire Dales and the frequently windswept but ruggedly beautiful hills of Northumberland.

Perhaps England's best-known landscape is the Lake District, a small but spectacular cluster of mountains in the northwest, where Scafell Pike (a towering 978m) is England's highest peak.

The landscape of Wales is also defined by hills and mountains: notably the rounded Black Mountains and Brecon Beacons in the south, and the spiky peaks of Snowdonia in the north, with Snowdon (1085m) the highest summit in Wales. In between lie the wild Cambrian Mountains of central Wales, rolling to the west coast of spectacular cliffs and shimmering river estuaries.

For real mountains, you need to head to Scotland, especially the wild, remote and thinly populated northwest Highlands – separated from the rest of the country by a diagonal gash in the earth's crust called the Boundary Fault. Ben Nevis (1343m) is Scotland's – and Britain's – highest mountain, but there are many more to choose from. The Highlands are further enhanced by the vast cluster of beautiful islands that lie off the loch-indented west coast.

South of the Scottish Highlands is the relatively flat Central Lowlands, home to the bulk of Scotland's population. Further south, down to the border with England, things get hillier again; this is the Southern Uplands, a fertile farming area.

National Parks

Back in 1810, English poet and outdoor fan William Wordsworth suggested that the wild landscape of the Lake District in Cumbria, northwest England, should be 'a sort of national property, in which every man has a right'. More than a century later the Lake District did become a national park, along with Brecon Beacons, Cairngorms, Dartmoor, Exmoor, Loch Lomond & the Trossachs, New Forest, Norfolk and Suffolk Broads, Northumberland, North York Moors, Peak District, Pembrokeshire Coast, Snowdonia, South Downs and Yorkshire Dales.

Combined, Britain's national parks cover over 10% of its area, but the term 'national park' can cause confusion. First, these areas are not state owned: nearly all land in Britain is private, belonging to farmers, estates

Top Protected National Scenic Areas (Scotland)

» Ben Nevis & Glencoe

» Cuillin Hills (Skye)

» Glen Affric

» Isle of Mull

» North Arran

» River Tay (Dunkeld)

» Shetland

BRITAIN'S BEST BEACHES

Britain has a great many beaches, each with their own distinct character, from tiny hidden coves in Cornwall and Pembrokeshire to vast neon-lined strands in resorts such as Brighton or Blackpool. Favourite spots line the entire southwest peninsula and much of the south coast. Other great beaches can be found in Suffolk, Norfolk, Lancashire, Yorkshire and Northumberland in England, and pretty much anywhere on the Welsh coast between the Gower Peninsula and Llandudno. Scotland offers even more choice, from the rocky bays on the west coast to the flat sands of the east. Britain's best resort beaches earn the coveted international Blue Flag (www.blueflag.org) award, meaning sand and water are clean and unpolluted. Other parameters include the presence of lifeguards, litter bins and recycling facilities – meaning some wild beaches may not earn the award, but are still stunning nonetheless.

BRITAIN'S NATIONAL PARKS

NATIONAL PARK	FEATURES	ACTIVITIES	BEST TIME TO VISIT	PAGE
Brecon Beacons	great green ridgelines, waterfalls; mountain ponies, otters, red kites, peregrine falcons,	horse riding, cycling, caving, canoeing, hang-gliding	Mar-Apr (spring lambs on the hills)	p693
Cairngorms	snowy peaks, pine forests; ospreys, pine martens, wild-cats, grouse, capercaillies	skiing, birdwatching, walking	Feb (for the snow)	p895
Dartmoor	rolling hills, rocky outcrops, serene valleys; wild ponies, deer, peregrine falcons	walking, mountain biking, horse riding	May-Jun (wildflowers in bloom)	p319
Exmoor	moors, sea cliffs; red deer, wild ponies, horned sheep	horse riding, walking	Sep (heather in bloom)	p296
Lake District	majestic fells, rugged mountains, lakes; red squirrels, osprey, golden eagles	water sports, walking, mountaineering, climbing	Sep-Oct (summer crowds depart, autumn colours abound)	p579
Loch Lomond & the Trossachs	sparkling lochs, mountains; deer, squirrels, badgers, foxes, otters, buzzards	climbing, walking, cycling	Sep-Oct (after the summer rush)	p838
New Forest	woods, heathland; wild ponies, otters, Dartford warblers, southern damselflies	walking, cycling, horse riding	Apr-Sep (lush vegetation)	p237
Norfolk & Suffolk Broads	lakes, rivers, marshlands, water lilies; otters, wildfowl	walking, cycling, boating	Apr-May (birds most active)	p381
North York Moors	heather-clad hills, valleys; merlins, curlews, plovers	walking, mountain biking	Aug-Sep (heather flowering)	p504
Northumberland	wild rolling moors, heather, gorse; red squirrels, black grouse; Hadrian's Wall	walking, cycling, climbing	Apr-May (lambs) & Sep (heather flowering)	p631
Peak District	high moors, tranquil dales, limestone caves; badgers, kestrels, grouse	walking, cycling, hang-gliding, climbing	Apr-May (even more lambs)	p467
Pembrokeshire Coast	wave-ravaged shorelines, cliffs, beaches; puffins, fulmars, shearwaters, grey seals, dolphins, porpoises	walking, kayaking, coasteering, mountain biking, horse riding	Apr-May (lambs again)	p675
Snowdonia	mountain ranges, lakes, estuaries, Snowdon lilies; wild goats, polecats, curlews, choughs, red kites, buzzards	walking, kayaking, climbing, mountain biking, horse riding	May-Sep (better weather)	p713
South Downs	rolling chalky hills, farmland, sheer white sea-cliffs, bastard toadflax; Adonis Blue butterflies, buzzards, red kites, peregrine falcons	walking, mountain biking, cycling, horse riding	any time of year (thanks to mild climate)	p169
Yorkshire Dales	rugged hills, lush valleys, limestone pavements; red squirrels, hares, curlews, lapwings, buzzards	walking, cycling, climbing	Apr-May (you guessed it, lambs)	p512

and conservation organisations. Second, they are not areas of wilderness as in many other countries. In Britain's national parks you'll see crop-fields in lower areas and grazing sheep on the uplands, as well as roads, railways and villages. Some national parks even contain towns, quarries and factories. It's a reminder of the balance that needs to be struck in this crowded country between protecting the natural environment and catering for the people who live in it.

But don't be put off. Despite these apparent anomalies, Britain's national parks still contain mountains, hills, downs, moors, woods, river valleys and other areas of quiet countryside, all ideal for long walks, easy rambles, cycle rides, sightseeing or just lounging around. To help you get the best from the parks, they all have information centres, and all provide various recreational facilities (trails, car parks, campsites etc) for visitors.

Finally, it's worth noting also that there are many beautiful parts of Britain that are *not* national parks (such as central Wales, the North Pennines in England, and many parts of Scotland). These can be just as good for outdoor activities or simply exploring by car or foot, and are often less crowded than the popular national parks.

Wildlife

For a small country, Britain has a diverse range of plants and animals. Many native species are hidden away, but there are some undoubted gems, from lowland woods carpeted in shimmering bluebells to stately herds of deer on the high moors. Taking the time to have a closer look will enhance your trip greatly, especially if you have the time and inclination to enjoy some walking or cycling through the British landscape.

Farmland

In farmland areas, rabbits are everywhere, but if you're hiking through the countryside be on the lookout for brown hares, an increasingly rare species. They're related to rabbits but much larger. Males who battle for territory by boxing on their hind legs in early spring are, of course, as 'mad as a March hare'.

Although hare numbers are on the decline, otters are making a comeback. In southern Britain they inhabit the banks of rivers and lakes, and in Scotland they frequently live on the coast. Although their numbers are growing, they are mainly nocturnal, but keep your eyes peeled in daytime and you might be lucky.

You're much more likely to see a red fox. This classic British mammal was once seen only in the countryside, but these wily beasts adapt well

Wildlife on the Web

» National Trust (England & Wales; www.national trust.org.uk)

» National Trust for Scotland (www.nts.org.uk)

» Royal Society for the Protection of Birds (www .rspb.org.uk)

» Wildlife Trusts (www.wildlife trusts.org)

» Woodland Trust (www.woodland trust.org.uk)

WILDLIFE IN YOUR POCKET

Is it a rabbit or a hare? A gull or a tern? Buttercup or cowslip? If you need to know a bit more about Britain's plant and animal kingdoms the following field guides are ideal for entry-level naturalists:

Complete Guide to British Wildlife by Paul Sterry is portable and highly recommended, covering mammals, birds, fish, plants, snakes, insects and even fungi, with brief descriptions and excellent photos.

If feathered friends are enough, the *Complete Guide to British Birds* by Paul Sterry combines clear photos and descriptions, plus when and where each species may be seen.

Wildlife of the North Atlantic by world-famous film-maker Tony Soper beautifully covers the animals seen from beach, boat and clifftop in the British Isles and beyond.

Collins Gem series includes handy little books on wildlife topics such as *Birds, Trees, Fish* and *Wild Flowers.*

'THE UNSPEAKABLE IN PURSUIT OF THE INEDIBLE'

For centuries, fox hunting – complete with packs of hounds, horse-riders in red coats and the famous sound of the hunting horn – has been a traditional English countryside activity (according to its supporters) or a savage blood sport (according to its opponents). The practice was banned in 2005 by a controversial law, but as this kind of hunting killed only a small proportion of the total fox population, opinion is still divided on its impact on overall numbers.

to any situation, so these days you're just as likely to see them scavenging in towns and even in city suburbs.

Elsewhere, another British classic, the black-and-white striped badger, is under threat from farmers who believe they transmit bovine tuberculosis to cattle, although conservationists say the case is far from proven.

Common birds of farmland and similar landscapes (and urban gardens) include: the robin, with its instantly recognisable red breast and cheerful whistle; the wren, whose loud trilling song belies its tiny size; and the yellowhammer, with a song that sounds like (if you use your imagination) 'a-little-bit-of-bread-and-no-cheese'. In open fields, the warbling cry of a skylark is another classic, but now threatened, sound of the English outdoors. You're more likely to see a pheasant, a large bird originally introduced from Russia to the nobility's shooting estates, but now considered naturalised.

Between the fields, hedges provide cover for flocks of finches, but these seed-eaters must watch out for sparrowhawks – birds of prey that come from nowhere at tremendous speed. Other predators include barn owls, a wonderful sight as they fly silently along hedgerows listening for the faint rustle of a vole or shrew. In rural Wales or Scotland you may see a buzzard, Britain's most common large raptor.

Woodland

In woodland areas, mammals include the small white-spotted fallow deer and the even smaller roe deer. Woodlands are full of birds too, but you'll hear them more than see them. Listen out for willow warblers (which, as the name suggests, have a warbling song with a descending cadence) and chiffchaffs (once again, the clues in the name: they make a repetitive 'chiff chaff' noise).

If you hear rustling among the fallen leaves it might be a hedgehog – a cute-looking, spiny-backed insect eater – but it's an increasingly rare sound these days; conservationists say they'll be extinct in Britain by 2025, due to insecticides in farming, increased building in rural areas and hedgehogs' notoriously poor ability to safely cross roads.

In no such danger are grey squirrels, originally introduced from North America. They have proved very adaptable, to the extent that native red squirrels are severely endangered because the greys eat all the food. Pockets of red squirrels survive in the English Lake District and in various parts of Scotland, notably the Isle of Arran.

Much larger than squirrels are pine martens, which are seen in some forested regions, especially in Scotland. With beautiful brown coats, they were once hunted for their fur, but are now fully protected.

Mountain & Moorland

On mountains and high moors – including Exmoor, Dartmoor, the Lake District, Northumberland and much of Scotland – the most visible mammal is the red deer. Males of the species grow their famous large antlers between April and July, and shed them again in February.

Top Areas of Outstanding Natural Beauty (AONBs) in England & Wales

» Anglesey
» Chilterns
» Cornwall
» Cotswolds
» Gower Peninsula
» Isles of Scilly
» Llŷn Peninsula
» North Pennines
» Northumberland Coast
» Suffolk Coast
» Wye Valley

Britain's most wooded county is Surrey, despite its proximity to London. The soil is too poor for agriculture, and while woodland areas elsewhere in Britain were cleared, Surrey's trees were spared.

Britain is home to herds of wild goats who've gambolled on the moorland in Devon for almost 1000 years. The Great Orme peninsula in North Wales also features wild goats, but these are new kids on the block, having been introduced only a century ago.

GOATS

Also on the high ground, well known and easily recognised birds include the red grouse, which often hides in the heather until almost stepped on then flies away with a loud warning call. On the high peaks of Scotland you may see the grouse's northern cousin, the ptarmigan, dappled brown in the summer but white in the winter.

Look out, too, for the curlew, with its stately long legs and elegant curved bill. With luck you may see beautifully camouflaged golden plovers, while the spectacular aerial displays of lapwings are impossible to miss.

Other mountain birds include red kites (there have been various successful projects around the country to reintroduce these spectacular fork-tailed raptors). Also in the Scottish mountains, keep an eye peeled for golden eagles, Britain's largest birds of prey, as they glide and soar along ridges.

Rivers & Coasts

If you're near inland water, you have a chance of spotting an osprey; the best places in Britain to see this magnificent bird include Rutland Water in the English Midlands and the Cairngorms in Scotland. You could also look along the riverbanks for signs of water voles, endearing rodents that were once very common but have been all but wiped out by wild mink (fur farm escapees first introduced from America).

On the coasts of Britain, particularly in Cornwall, Pembrokeshire and northwest Scotland, the dramatic cliffs are a marvellous sight in early summer (around May), when they are home to hundreds of thousands of breeding seabirds. Guillemots, razorbills and kittiwakes, among others, fight for space on impossibly crowded rock ledges. The cliffs become white with droppings and the air is filled with their shrill calls. Even if you're not into bird spotting, this is one of Britain's finest wildlife spectacles.

Another bird to look out for in coastal areas is the comical puffin (especially common in Shetland), with its distinctive rainbow beak and 'nests' burrowed in sandy soil. In total contrast, gannets are one of the largest seabirds and make dramatic dives for fish, often from a great height.

Estuaries and mudflats are feeding grounds for numerous migrant wading birds; easily spotted are black-and-white oystercatchers with their long red bills, while flocks of small ringed plovers skitter along the sand.

And finally, the sea mammals. There are two species of seal that frequent British waters; the larger grey seal is more often seen than the (misnamed) common seal. Boat trips to see their offshore colonies are available at various points around the coast, and are especially popular when the seal pups are born.

Dolphins, porpoises and minke whales can all be seen off the west coast of Britain, particularly off Scotland, and especially from May to September when viewing conditions are better. Whale-watching trips (also good for seeing other marine wildlife such as basking sharks) are available from several harbour towns, especially in Scotland.

Britain's Best Wildlife by Mike Dilger and Chris Packham is a 'Top 40' countdown of favourites compiled by experts and the public, with details on when and where to see wildlife at its finest.

Plants

In any part of Britain, the best places to see wildflowers are areas that evade large-scale farming. In the chalky downs of southern England and in limestone areas such as the Peak District and Yorkshire Dales, for example, many fields erupt with great profusions of cowslips and primroses in April and May.

Some flowers prefer woodland and, again, the best time to visit is April and May. This is because the leaf canopy of the woods is not yet fully developed, allowing sunlight to break through to encourage plants such as bluebells (a beautiful and internationally rare species). Another classic British plant is gorse – you can't miss the swathes of this spiky bush in heath areas, most notably in the New Forest in southern England.

In contrast, the blooming season for heather is quite short. On the Scottish mountains, the Pennine moors of northern England, and Dartmoor in the south, the landscape is covered in a riot of purple in August and September.

Britain's natural deciduous trees include oak, ash, hazel and rowan, with seeds and leaves supporting a vast range of insects and birds. The New Forest in southern England and the Forest of Dean on the Wales–England border are good examples of this type of habitat. In some parts of Scotland, most notably Glen Affric, stands of indigenous Caledonian pine can still be seen. As you travel through Britain you're also likely to see non-native pines, often in vast plantations empty of wildlife, although an increasing number of deciduous trees are also planted these days.

Environmental Issues

With Britain's long history, it's not surprising that the country's appearance is almost totally the result of human interaction with the environment. Since the earliest times, people have been chopping down trees and creating fields for crops or animals, but the most dramatic changes in rural areas came in the late 1940s, continuing into the '50s and '60s, when a postwar drive to be self-reliant in food meant new and intensive large-scale farming methods. The result was lowland Britain's ancient patchwork of small meadows becoming a landscape of vast fields, as walls were demolished, woodlands felled, ponds filled, wetlands drained and, most notably, hedgerows ripped out.

In most cases the hedgerows were lines of dense bushes, shrubs and trees forming a network that stretched across the countryside, protecting fields from erosion, supporting a varied range of flowers, and providing shelter for numerous insects, birds and small mammals. But in the rush to improve farm yields, thousands of miles of hedgerows were destroyed in the postwar decades, and between the mid-1980s and the early 2000s another 25% disappeared.

Hedgerows have come to symbolise many other environmental issues in rural areas, and in recent years the destruction has abated, partly because farmers recognise their anti-erosion qualities, and partly because they're encouraged – with financial incentives from UK or European agencies – to 'set aside' such areas as wildlife havens.

In addition to hedgerow clearance, other farming techniques remain hot environmental issues. Studies have shown that the use of pesticides and intensive irrigation results in rivers running dry or being poisoned by run-off. Meanwhile, monocropping means vast fields with one type of grass, dubbed 'green deserts' by conservationists as they support no insects, causing wild bird populations to plummet. This is not a case of wizened old peasants recalling the idyllic days of their forebears; you only have to be over about 40 in Britain to remember a countryside where birds such as skylarks or lapwings were visibly much more numerous.

But despite the loss of habitats and species, Britain still boasts great biodiversity, and some of the best wildlife areas are protected (to a greater or lesser extent) by the creation of national parks and similar sites or private reserves owned by conservation campaign groups such as the Wildlife Trusts, Woodland Trust and the Royal Society for the Protection of Birds. Many of these areas are open to the public – ideal spots for walking, birdwatching or simply enjoying the peace and beauty of the countryside – and well worth a visit as you travel around.

Britain's new 'hedgerows' are the long strips of grass and bushes alongside motorways and major roads. Rarely trod by humans, they support rare flowers and thousands of insect species, plus mice, shrews and other small mammals – hence kestrels are often seen hovering nearby.

Wildlife of Britain by George McGavin et al is subtitled 'the definitive visual guide'. Although too heavy to carry around, this beautiful photographic book is great for pre-trip inspiration or post-trip memories.

Sporting Britain

The British invented many of the world's favourite team sports – or at least codified the modern rules – including cricket, tennis, rugby, golf and football (soccer) although, it has to be said, the national teams in the high-profile sports aren't always very good at playing them. This applies especially to the male teams, whereas the British women's national teams have a better record of success, with the England women's national football team reaching the quarter finals in the FIFA Women's World Cup on three occasions, and the England women's cricket team winning the World Cup in 2009.

But whether the British 'home teams' are winning or losing – be they individual teams of the separate countries of England, Wales and Scotland, or national teams representing Great Britain or the whole of the UK – nothing dulls the enthusiasm of the fans. Every weekend, thousands of people turn out to cheer their favourite football or rugby team, while annual sporting highlights such as the FA Cup, Wimbledon or the Derby keep the entire nation enthralled. During your travels around Britain, taking the opportunity to watch a match and mingle with the fans is a sure-fire way to learn about Britain and the British.

But away from the high-profile competitions of individual sports, the highlight of the nation's entire sporting history was the outstanding achievements by Team GB at the 2012 Olympic and Paralympic Games in London. The team (which represented the whole of the UK – with athletes from Northern Ireland choosing to compete for the UK or Irish team) won 65 medals, including 29 golds, and third place overall on the medals table behind China and the USA. The British Paralympic athletes exceeded even this impressive total by winning 120 medals, and notching up another third place in the medals table behind China and Russia.

The nation's sports stars and spectators now look towards the 2014 Commonwealth Games in Glasgow, when it's hoped the Olympian performances will once again be repeated on the world stage.

Football (Soccer)

Despite what the football fans may say in Madrid or Sao Paulo, the English Premier League has some of the finest teams in the world,

---

SPORTING COVERAGE

Perhaps surprisingly, unlike many countries, Britain has no dedicated large circulation sports newspaper (apart from perhaps *The Sportsman*, which concentrates mainly on the betting angle). But read the excellent coverage in the back pages of the *Daily Telegraph*, the *Times* and the *Guardian* and you'll see there's no need for one. The tabloid newspapers also cover sport, especially if a star has been caught with their pants down. Talking of which, the *Daily Sport* is not a sports newspaper, despite the name, unless photos of glamour models wearing only a pair of Arsenal socks count as 'sport'.

THE SWEET FA CUP

The Football Association held its first interclub knockout tournament in 1871. Fifteen clubs took part, playing for a nice piece of silverware called the FA Cup – then worth about £20.

Nowadays, around 600 clubs compete for this legendary and priceless trophy. It differs from many other competitions in that every team – from the lowest-ranking part-timers to the stars of the Premier League – is in with a chance. The preliminary rounds begin in August, and the world-famous Cup Final is held in May at the iconic Wembley Stadium in London.

The team with the most FA Cup victories is Manchester United, but public attention, and affection, is invariably focused on the 'giant-killers' – minor clubs that claw their way up through the rounds, unexpectedly beating higher-ranked competitors. The best-known giant-killing event occurred in 1992, when Wrexham, then ranked 24th in Division 3, famously beat league champions Arsenal. Other shocks include non-league Kidderminster Harriers defeat of big boys Birmingham City in 1994, and Oldham Athletic beating premier leaguers Manchester City in 2005.

In recent years, the FA Cup has become one football competition among many. The Premier League and Champions League (against European teams) have a higher profile, bigger kudos and simply more money to play with. But, just as a country gets behind their national side, nothing raises community spirit more than a town team doing better than expected. Perhaps the FA Cup will one day be consigned to history – but what a sweet and glorious history it's been!

---

dominated in recent years by the four top teams – Arsenal, Liverpool, Chelsea and Manchester United – joined in 2012 by a fifth big player in the shape of Manchester City.

Down from the Premier League, 72 other teams play in the English divisions called the Championship, League One and League Two.

The Scottish football scene has a similar pattern: best teams in the Scottish Premier League, the rest in the Scottish Football League. The top flight has long been dominated by Glasgow Celtic and Glasgow Rangers (although in 2012 the latter went into financial adminstration and was relegated to a lower division).

In Wales football is less popular (rugby is the national sport) and the main Welsh football teams such as Wrexham, Cardiff and Swansea play in lower English leagues.

The football season is the same for all divisions (August to May), so seeing a match can easily be tied into most visitors' itineraries. However, tickets for Premier League matches are like gold dust – your chances of bagging one are pretty much zilch unless you're a club member or know someone who is – you're better off buying tickets for a lower-division game, which are cheaper. You can often buy tickets on the spot at stadiums, or go to club websites or online agencies such as www.ticketmaster.co.uk and www.myticketmarket.com.

Sometimes known as 'soccer' outside Britain, the name derives from 'association' (football is officially called Association Football) or from 'sock' – a leather foot-cover worn in medieval times, ideal for kicking a pig's bladder around the park on a Saturday afternoon.

Rugby

A wit once said that football was a gentlemen's game played by hooligans, while rugby was the other way around. That may be true, but rugby is very popular, especially since England became world champions in 2004 (and nearly did it again in 2008). It's worth catching a game for the display of skill (OK, and brawn), and the fun atmosphere in the grounds. Tickets for games cost around £15 to £40 depending on the club's status and fortunes.

There are two versions of the game in Britain: Rugby Union (www.rfu.com) is played more in southern England, Wales and Scotland, and is traditionally the game of the middle and upper classes, while Rugby League (www.therfl.co.uk) is played predominantly in northern England, traditionally by the working classes – although these days there's a lot of crossover.

Both rugby codes trace their roots to a football match in 1823 at Rugby School, in Warwickshire. A player called William Ellis, frustrated at the limitations of mere kicking, reputedly picked up the ball and ran with it towards the opponents' goal. True to the British tradition of fair play, rather than Ellis being dismissed from the game, a whole new sport was developed around his tactic, and the Rugby Football Union was formally inaugurated in 1871. Today, the Rugby World Cup is named the Webb Ellis trophy after this enterprising young tearaway.

> For the dates and details of major football and cricket matches, horse racing and other sporting fixtures across Britain, a great place to start is the sports pages of www.britevents.com.

The highlight of rugby union's international calendar is the annual Six Nations Championship (www.rbs6nations.com), between teams from England, Wales, Scotland, Ireland, France and Italy. A simple points system sees teams compete to win the Grand Slam or Triple Crown, or at least avoid the Wooden Spoon award for coming last.

The Rugby League World Cup (www.rlwc2013.com) will be held in Britain in late 2013, with matches at various venues around England and Wales (plus some neighbouring countries), with the final played in Manchester.

An even bigger event on the horizon is the Rugby Union World Cup to be hosted by England in 2015, with the final played at Twickenham. For details see www.rugbyworldcup.com.

Cricket

One of the most popular sports in Britain, cricket remains a predominantly English activity at home, although it became an international game during Britain's colonial era, when it was exported to the countries of the Commonwealth. Australia, the Caribbean and the Indian subcontinent took to the game with gusto, and a century on the former colonies delight in giving the old country a good spanking on the cricket pitch.

> Causing ructions in the cricket world, the fast-paced Twenty20 format emphasises big-batting scores, rather than slow and careful run-building. Traditionalists say it's changing the character of the game, but there's no doubting its popularity – many Twenty20 matches are sell-outs.

While many English people follow cricket like a religion, to the uninitiated it's an impenetrable spectacle. Spread over one-day games or five-day test matches, progress seems so *slow* (surely, say the unbelievers, this is the game for which TV highlights were invented) and dominated by arcane terminology such as innings, over, googlie, out-swinger, leg-bye and silly-mid-off. Nonetheless, at least one cricket match should feature in your travels. If you're patient and learn the intricacies, you could find cricket as enriching and enticing as all the fans who remain glued to their radio or computer all summer, 'just to see how England's getting on'.

One-day games and international tests are played at grounds including Lord's in London, Edgbaston in Birmingham and Headingley in Leeds. Tickets cost from £30 to well over £200. The County Championship pits together the best teams from around the country; tickets cost £15 to £25, and only the most crucial games tend to sell out. Details are on the website of the English Cricket Board (www.ecb.co.uk).

The easiest way to watch cricket – and often the most enjoyable – is stumbling across a local game on a village green as you travel around the country. There's no charge for spectators, and no one will mind if you nip into the pub during a quiet period.

Horse Racing

The tradition of horse racing in Britain stretches back centuries, and there's a 'meeting' somewhere pretty much every day. For all but the major events you should be able to get a ticket on the day, or buy in advance from the British Horse Racing Authority's website (www.lovetheraces.com), which

THE ASHES

The historic test cricket series between England and Australia known as the Ashes has been played every other year since 1882 (bar a few interruptions during wartime). It is played alternately in England and Australia with each of the five matches in the series held at a different cricket ground, always in the summer in the host location.

The contest's name dates back to the landmark test match of 1882, won (for the very first time) by the Australians. Defeat of the mother country by the colonial upstarts was a source of profound national shock: a mock obituary in the *Sporting Times* lamented the death of English cricket and referred to the game's ashes being taken to Australia.

Later the name was given to a terracotta urn presented the following year to the English captain Ivo Bligh, purportedly containing the cremated ashes of a stump or bail used in this landmark match. Since 1953 this hallowed relic has resided at the Marylebone Cricket Club (MCC) Museum at Lord's Cricket Ground. Despite the vast importance given to winning the series, the urn itself is a diminutive 6in high.

The recent history of the Ashes is not without drama. After eight straight defeats, England won the series in 2005, then handed the prize straight back to the Aussies after a humiliating thrashing in 2007, before 'regaining the Ashes' once again in 2009. In the 2010–11 series England thrashed Australia, winning on Australian turf for the first time since the 1986–87 series.

also has lots of information about social events such as music festivals that coincide with the races.

The top event in the calendar is Royal Ascot (p223) at Ascot Racecourse in mid-June, where the rich and famous come to see and be seen, and the fashion is almost as important as the nags. Even the Queen turns up to put a fiver each way on Lucky Boy in the 3.15.

Other highlights include the Grand National steeplechase at Aintree (p564) in early April; and the Derby at Epsom (www.epsomdowns.co.uk) on the first Saturday in June. The latter is especially popular with the masses so, unlike at Ascot, you won't see many morning suits and outrageous hats.

Tennis

Tennis is widely played in Britain, but the best known tournament for spectators is the All England Championships – known to everyone as Wimbledon – when tennis fever sweeps through Britain in the last week of June and first week of July. There's something quintessentially English (yes, more English than British) about the combination of grass courts, polite applause and umpires in boaters.

Demand for seats at Wimbledon always outstrips supply, but to give everyone an equal chance tickets are sold through a public ballot. You can also take your chance on the spot; about 6000 tickets are sold each day (excluding the final four days), but you'll need to be an early riser: dedicated fans start queuing before dawn. For more information, see www.wimbledon.org.

Over 27 tonnes of strawberries and 7000L of cream are consumed every year during the two weeks of the Wimbledon Tennis Championships.

Survival Guide

Directory A–Z

Accommodation

Accommodation in Britain is as varied as the sights you visit. From hip hotels to basic barns, the wide choice is all part of the attraction.

B&Bs

The B&B (bed and breakfast) is a great British institution. At smaller places it's pretty much a room in somebody's house; larger places may be called a 'guesthouse' (halfway between a B&B and a full hotel). Prices start from around £20 per person for a simple bedroom and shared bathroom; for around £25 to £30 per person you get a private bathroom – either down the hall or en suite.

B&B prices are usually quoted per person, based on two people sharing a room. Single rooms for solo travellers are harder to find, and

have a 20% to 50% premium. Some B&Bs simply won't take single people (unless you pay the full double-room price), especially in summer.

Advance reservations are preferred at B&Bs and are essential during popular periods. You can book many B&Bs via online agencies but rates may be cheaper if you book direct. If you haven't booked in advance, most towns have a main drag of B&Bs; those with spare rooms hang up a 'Vacancies' sign.

Many B&Bs require a minimum two-night stay at weekends. Some places reduce rates for longer stays (two or three nights) mid-week. If a B&B is full, owners may recommend another place nearby (possibly a private house taking occasional guests, not in tourist listings).

In cities, some B&Bs are for long-term residents or people on welfare; they don't

take passing tourists. In country areas, most B&Bs cater for walkers and cyclists, but some don't, so let them know if you'll be turning up with dirty boots or wheels.

Most B&Bs serve enormous breakfasts; some offer packed lunches (around £5) and evening meals (around £12 to £15).

When booking, check where your B&B actually is. In country areas, postal addresses include the nearest town, which may be 20 miles away – important if you're walking! Some B&B owners will pick you up by car for a small charge.

Bunkhouses

A bunkhouse in Britain is a simple place to stay, usually in country areas, with a communal sleeping area and bathroom, plus stoves for self-catering. You provide a sleeping bag and possibly cooking gear. Most charge around £10 per person per night.

Some basic places are called 'camping barns' – usually converted farm buildings. Take everything you'd need to camp except the tent. Charges are from around £5 per person.

Camping

The opportunities for camping in Britain range from farmers' fields with a tap and basic toilet, costing from £3 per person per night, to smarter affairs with hot showers and many other facilities, charging up to £10. You usually need all your own kit.

Britain doesn't have huge sites of permanent tents, as found in France and some other countries, but a few campsites also offer self-catering accommodation in chalets, caravans, tepees and yurts. Some options are very stylish – dubbed 'glamping'.

If you're touring Britain with a tent or campervan (motorhome), it's worth joining the **Camping & Caravanning Club** (www .campingandcaravanningclub

.co.uk). The club owns almost 100 campsites and lists thousands more in the invaluable Big Sites Book (free to members).

Hostels

There are two types of hostel in Britain: those run by the **Youth Hostels Association** (YHA; www.yha.org.uk) and **Scottish Youth Hostels Association** (SYHA; www.syha.org.uk); and independent hostels, most listed in the **Independent Hostel Guide** (www.independenthostelguide.co.uk).

Hostels can be found in rural areas, towns and cities, and are aimed at all types of traveller, young and old. Some hostels are converted cottages, country houses and even castles – often in wonderful locations. Sleeping is usually in dormitories; some hostels also have twin or four-bed rooms.

YHA & SYHA HOSTELS

The simplest YHA and SYHA hostels cost around £10 per person per night. Larger hostels with more facilities are £15 to £20. London's YHA hostels cost from £25. Advance bookings and payments with credit card are usually possible.

You don't have to be a member of the YHA or SYHA (or another Hostelling International organisation) to stay, but most hostels charge extra if you're not a member (£3 at YHA hostels; £1 at SYHA hostels), so it's usually worth joining. Annual YHA membership costs £16; annual SYHA membership costs £10; younger people and families get discounts.

Most hostel prices vary according to demand and season. Book early for a Tuesday night in May and you'll get the best rate. Book late for a weekend in August and you'll pay top price – if there's space at all. We have generally quoted the cheaper rates (in line with those listed on the YHA's website); you may find yourself paying more.

YHA hostels tend to have complicated opening times and days, especially in remote locations or out of tourist season, so check before turning up.

FLEXIBLE HOTEL RATES

There's no such thing as a 'standard' hotel rate in Britain. Many hotels, especially larger places or chains, vary prices according to demand – or have different rates for online, phone or walk-in bookings – just like airlines and train operators. So if you book early for a night when the hotel is likely to be quiet, rates are cheap. If you book late, or aim for a public holiday weekend, you'll pay a lot. But wait until the very last minute, and you can *sometimes* get a bargain as rates drop again. The end result: you can pay anything from £19 to £190 for the very same hotel room. With that in mind, the hotel rates we quote are often guide prices only. (In contrast, B&B prices tend to be much more consistent.)

INDEPENDENT HOSTELS

In rural areas some independent hostels are little more than simple bunkhouses (charging around £7), or almost up to B&B standard (£15 or more). In cities, independent backpacker hostels are usually aimed at young budget travellers. Most are open 24 hours, with a lively atmosphere, range of rooms (doubles or dorms), bar, cafe, wi-fi and laundry. Prices go from around £15 for a dorm bed to £35 for a bed in a private room.

Hotels

There's a massive choice of hotels in Britain, from small town houses to grand country mansions, from no-frills locations to boutique hideaways. At the bargain end, single/double rooms cost from £30/40. Move up the scale

---

PRACTICALITIES

» **Newspapers** Tabloids include the *Sun* and *Mirror,* and *Daily Record* (in Scotland); quality 'broadsheets' include (from right to left, politically) the *Telegraph, Times, Independent* and *Guardian.*

» **TV** All TV in the UK is digital. Leading broadcasters include BBC, ITV and Channel 4. Satellite and cable TV providers include Sky and Virgin Media.

» **Radio** Main BBC stations and wavelengths are Radio 1 (98–99.6MHz FM), Radio 2 (88–92MHz FM), Radio 3 (90–92.2 MHz FM), Radio 4 (92–94.4MHz FM) and Radio 5 Live (909 or 693 AM). National commercial stations include Virgin Radio (1215Hz MW) and nonhighbrow classical specialist Classic FM (100–102MHz FM). All are available on digital.

» **DVD** PAL format (incompatible with NTSC and Secam).

» **Weights & Measures** Britain uses a mix of metric and imperial measures (eg petrol is sold by the litre but beer by the pint; mountain heights are in metres but road distances in miles).

PRICE RANGES

Reviews of places to stay use the following price ranges, all based on double room with private bathroom in high season. Hotels in London are more expensive than the rest of the country, so have different price ranges.

BUDGET	LONDON	ELSEWHERE
£	<£90	<£60
££	£90–180	£60–130
£££	>£180	>£130

and you'll pay £100/150 or beyond.

If all you want is a place to put your head down, budget chain hotels can be a good option. Most are lacking in ambience, but who cares? You'll only be there for eight hours, and six of them you'll be asleep. Prices vary on demand: at quiet times twin-bed rooms start from £20; at the height of the tourist season you'll pay £45 or more. Options include:

Etap Hotels (www.etaphotel .com)

Hotel Formule 1 (www.hotel formule1.com)

Premier Inn (www.premierinn .com)

Travelodge (www.travelodge .co.uk)

Houseboats

A popular English holiday option is renting a houseboat on one of England's picturesque waterways, combining accommodation and transport for a few days or a week.

UK Boat Hire (www.ukboat hire.com)

Hoseasons (www.hoseasons .co.uk)

Wandering Duck (www .wanderingduck.co.uk; 2-night trips incl meals from per person £95) 'Floating hostels' for budget travellers.

Pubs & Inns

As well as selling drinks, many pubs and inns offer lodging, particularly in country areas. For bed and breakfast, you'll pay around £20 per person for a basic

room, around £35 for something better. An advantage for solo tourists: pubs often have single rooms.

Rental Accommodation

If you want to stay in place, renting for a week can be ideal. Choose from neat apartments in cities or quaint old houses (always called 'cottages', whatever the size) in country areas. Cottages for four people cost between £200 and £600 in high season. Rates fall at quieter times and you may be able to rent for a long weekend. Handy websites include the following:

Bed & Breakfast Nationwide (www.bedandbreakfast nationwide.com)

Cottages & Castles (www .cottages-and-castles.co.uk)

Cottages4U (www.cottages4u .co.uk)

Hoseasons (www.hoseasons .co.uk)

National Trust (www.national trust.org.uk/holidays)

Stilwell's (www.stilwell.co.uk)

University Accommodation

During vacations, many universities offer accommodation to visitors. You usually get a functional single bedroom, and self-catering flats are also available. Prices range from £20 to £50 per person. A handy portal is www.universityrooms.co.uk.

Business Hours

Banks

» Monday to Friday, 9.30am to 4pm or 5pm.

» Saturday, main branches 9.30am to 1pm.

Bars, Pubs & Clubs

» Standard hours for pubs: 11am to 11pm Monday to Sunday. Some pubs shut from 3pm to 6pm; some open to midnight or 1am Friday and Saturday.

» Standard hours for bars: 11am until midnight, often later, especially at weekends.

» Clubs open any time from 8pm to 10pm, until 2am or beyond.

Cafes & Restaurants

Most restaurants and cafes are open for lunch or dinner or both, so precise opening times and days are given in reviews only if they differ markedly from the pattern outlined here.

» Standard hours for cafes: 9am to 5pm. Most cafes open daily.

» Where we specify 'breakfast & lunch' in reviews we mean open 9am to 5pm.

SOMETHING DIFFERENT FOR THE WEEKEND?

For some more unusual accommodation options, the **Landmark Trust** (☏01628-825925; www.landmarktrust.org .uk) rents historic buildings; your options include ancient cottages, medieval castles, Napoleonic forts and 18th-century follies. Or try **Distinctly Different** (www.distinctly different.co.uk), specialising in unusual and bizarre places to stay.

EMBASSIES & CONSULATES IN LONDON

COUNTRY	PHONE	WEBSITE	ADDRESS
Australia	☎020-7887 5776	www.australia.org.uk	The Strand, WC2B 4LA
Canada	☎020-7258 6600	www.canada.org.uk	1 Grosvenor Sq, W1X 0AB
China	☎020-7299 4049	www.chinese-embassy.org.uk	Portland Pl, W1B 4JL
France	☎020-7073 1000	www.ambafrance-uk.org	58 Knightsbridge, SW1 7JT
Germany	☎020-7824 1300	www.london.diplo.de	23 Belgrave Sq, SW1X 8PX
Ireland	☎020-7235 2171	www.embassyofireland.co.uk	17 Grosvenor Pl, SW1X 7HR
Japan	☎020-7465 6500	www.uk.emb-japan.go.jp	101 Piccadilly, W1J 7JT
Netherlands	☎020-7590 3200	www.netherlands-embassy.org.uk	38 Hyde Park Gate, SW7 5DP
New Zealand	☎020-7930 8422	www.nzembassy.com/uk	80 Haymarket, SW1Y 4TQ
Poland	☎020-7291 3520	www.londyn.polemb.net	47 Portland Pl, W1B 1HQ
USA	☎020-7499 9000	www.usembassy.org.uk	24 Grosvenor Sq, W1A 1AE

» In cities, some cafes open at 7am for breakfast, then shut at 6pm or later.

» In country areas, some cafes open until 7pm or later in the summer. In winter months, hours are reduced; some cafes close completely from October to Easter.

» Standard hours for restaurants: lunch noon to 3pm, dinner 6pm to 11pm (to midnight or later in cities). Most restaurants open daily; some close Sunday evening or all day Monday.

» A few restaurants open for breakfast (usually 9am), but mainly cafes do this.

Museums & Sights

» Large museums and sights usually open daily.

» Some smaller places open Saturday and Sunday but close Monday and/or Tuesday.

» Smaller places open daily in high season but operate weekends only or completely close in low season.

Post Offices

» Monday to Friday, 9am to 5pm (5.30pm or 6pm in cities).

» Saturday, 9am to 12.30pm; main branches to 5pm.

Shops

» Monday to Friday, 9am to 5pm (5.30pm or 6pm in cities).

» Saturday, 9am to 5pm.

» Sunday, larger shops open 10am to 4pm. London and other cities have convenience stores open 24/7.

» In smaller towns and country areas shops often shut for lunch (normally 1pm to 2pm) and on Wednesday or Thursday afternoon.

Customs Regulations

Britain has a two-tier customs system: one for goods bought duty-free outside the EU; the other for goods bought in another EU country where tax and duty is

paid. Below is a summary of the rules; for more details go to www.hmce.gov.uk and search for 'Customs Allowances'.

Duty-Free

The duty-free limits for goods from outside the EU include 200 cigarettes or equivalent in cigars, 4L of wine, 1L of spirits, 60cc of perfume, and other goods worth up to £390.

Tax & Duty Paid

There is no limit on goods from within the EU (if taxes have been paid), but customs officials use the following guidelines to distinguish personal use from commercial imports: 800 cigarettes, 200 cigars, 10L of spirits, 90L of wine and 110L of beer. Still enough to have one hell of a party.

Discount Cards

There's no specific discount card for visitors to Britain, although travel cards are discounted for younger and older people.

Electricity

230V/50Hz

Embassies & Consulates

The table on p1029 gives a selection of embassies, consulates and high commissions in London. For a complete list of embassies in Britain, see the website of the **Foreign & Commonwealth Office** (www.fco.gov.uk), which also lists Britain's diplomatic missions overseas.

Gay & Lesbian Travellers

Britain is a generally tolerant place for gays and lesbians. London, Manchester and Brighton have flourishing gay scenes, and in other sizeable cities (even some small towns) you'll find communities not entirely in the closet. That said, you'll still find pockets of homophobic hostility in some areas. Resources include the following:

Diva (www.divamag.co.uk)
Gay Times (www.gaytimes .co.uk)

Climate

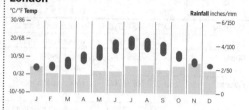

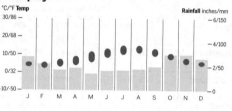

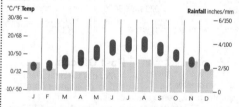

London Lesbian & Gay Switchboard (☎0300 330 0630; www.llgs.org.uk)
Pink Paper (www.pinkpaper .com)

Health

No immunisations are mandatory for visiting Britain. For more information, check with your health or medical provider in your own country before you travel.

Regardless of nationality, everyone receives free emergency treatment at accident and emergency (A&E) departments of state-run National Health Service (NHS) hospitals. European Economic Area (EEA) nationals get free nonemergency treatment (ie the same service British citizens receive) with a European Health Insurance Card (EHIC) validated in their home country. Reciprocal

arrangements between Britain and some other countries (including Australia) allow free medical treatment at hospitals and surgeries, and subsidised dental care.

If you don't need hospital treatment, chemists (pharmacies) can advise on minor ailments such as sore throats and earaches. In large cities, there's always at least one 24-hour chemist.

Heritage Organisations

A highlight of a journey through Britain is visiting the numerous castles and historic sites that pepper the country. Membership of a heritage organisation gets you free admission (usually a good saving) as well as information handbooks and so on.

Cardiff

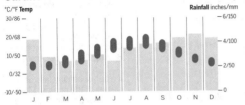

Inverness

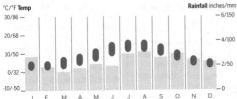

Edinburgh

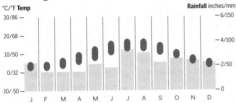

The **National Trust** (NT; www.nationaltrust.org.uk) is a charity protecting historic buildings and land with scenic importance across England and Wales. Annual membership costs £53 (with discounts for under-26s and families). A Touring Pass allows free entry to NT properties for one/two weeks (£23/28 per person); families and couples get cheaper rates. The **National Trust for Scotland** (NTS; www.nts .org.uk) is similar.

English Heritage (EH; www.english-heritage.org.uk) is a state-funded organisation responsible for numerous historic sites. Annual membership costs £47 (couples and seniors get discounts). An Overseas Visitors Pass allows free entry to most sites for 9/16 days for £23/27 (with cheaper rates for couples and families). In Wales and Scotland the equivalent organisations are **Cadw** (www.cadw.wales.gov.uk) and **Historic Scotland** (HS; www.historic-scotland.gov.uk).

You can join at the first site you visit. If you join an English heritage organisation, it covers you for Wales and Scotland, and vice versa.

Insurance

Although everyone receives free emergency treatment, regardless of nationality, travel insurance is still highly recommended. It will usually cover medical and dental consultation and treatment at private clinics, which can be quicker than NHS places – as well as the cost of any emergency flights – plus all the usual stuff like loss of baggage. Worldwide travel insurance is available at www.lonelyplanet.com/ travel_services. You can buy, extend and claim online any-

time, even if you're already on the road.

Internet Access

Internet cafes are surprisingly rare in Britain, especially away from big cities and tourist spots. Most charge from £1 per hour, but out in the sticks you can pay up to £5 per hour.

Public libraries often have computers with free internet access, but only for 30-minute slots, and demand is high. All the usual warnings apply about keystroke-capturing software and other security risks.

If you'll be using your laptop to get online, an increasing number of hotels, hostels, stations and coffee shops (even some trains) have wi-fi access, charging anything from nothing to £5 per hour.

Legal Matters

You must be over 18 to buy alcohol and cigarettes. You usually have to be 18 to enter a pub or bar, although rules are different for under-18s if eating. Some bars and clubs are over-21 only.

Illegal drugs are widely available, especially in clubs. Cannabis possession is a criminal offence; punishment for carrying a small amount may be a warning, a fine or imprisonment. Dealers face stiffer penalties, as do people caught with other drugs.

On buses and trains (including the London Underground), people without a valid ticket are fined on the spot – usually around £20.

Money

The currency of Britain is the pound sterling (£). Paper money ('notes') comes in £5, £10, £20 and £50 denominations. Some shops don't accept £50 notes because fakes circulate.

Other currencies are very rarely accepted, except at some gift shops in London, which may take euros, US dollars, yen and other major currencies.

Exchange rates are given in the Need to Know chapter.

ATMs

ATMs (usually called 'cash machines' in Britain) are common in cities and even small towns. Watch out for tampered ATMs; a common ruse is to attach a card-reader or minicamera.

Changing Money

Cities and larger towns have banks and exchange bureaux for changing your money into pounds. Check rates first; some bureaux offer poor rates or levy outrageous commissions. You can also change money at some post offices – very handy in country areas, and exchange rates are fair.

SCOTTISH POUNDS

Scotland issues its own currency (including a £1 note) that's interchangeable with the money used in the rest of Britain, although in reality you'll find shops more readily accept them in the north of England than in the south. Banks will always change them.

Credit & Debit Cards

Visa and MasterCard credit and debit cards are widely accepted in Britain. Most businesses will assume your card is 'Chip and PIN' enabled (using a PIN instead of signing). If it isn't, you should be able to sign instead, but some places may not accept your card. Some smaller country B&Bs don't take cards, so you'll need to pay with cash.

Tipping

In Britain you're not obliged to tip if the service or food was unsatisfactory (even if it's been automatically added to your bill as a 'service charge').

» **Restaurants** Around 10%. Also at teashops and smarter cafes with full table service. At smarter restaurants waiters expect tips nearer 12% or 15%.

» **Taxis** 10%, or rounded up to the nearest pound, especially in London. It's less usual to tip minicab drivers.

» **Toilet attendants** Around 50p.

» **Pubs** Around 10% if you order food at the table and your meal is brought to you. If you order and pay at the bar (food or drinks), tips are not expected.

Public Holidays

Holidays for the whole of Britain:

New Year's Day 1 January
Easter March/April (Good Friday to Easter Monday inclusive)
May Day First Monday in May
Spring Bank Holiday Last Monday in May
Summer Bank Holiday Last Monday in August
Christmas Day 25 December
Boxing Day 26 December

If a public holiday falls on a weekend, the nearest Monday is usually taken instead. In England and Wales most businesses and banks close on official public holidays (hence the quaint term 'bank holiday'). In Scotland, bank holidays are just for the banks, and many businesses stay open. Many Scottish towns normally have a spring and autumn holiday, but the dates vary.

On public holidays, some small museums and places of interest close, but larger attractions have their busiest times. If a place closes on Sunday, it'll probably be shut on bank holidays as well.

Virtually everything – attractions, shops, banks, offices – closes on Christmas Day, although pubs are open at lunchtime. There's usually no public transport on Christmas Day, and a very minimal service on Boxing Day.

Safe Travel

Britain is a remarkably safe country, but crime is not unknown in London and other cities. Watch out for pickpockets and hustlers in crowded areas popular with tourists such as around Westminster Bridge in London. When travelling by tube, tram or urban train services at night, choose a carriage containing other people.

Unlicensed minicabs – a bloke with a car earning money on the side – operate in large cities, and are worth avoiding unless you know what you're doing. Some have been known to drive round in circles, then charge an enormous fare. There have also been cases of robbery or rape. To avoid this, use a metered taxi or phone a reputable minicab company and get an up-front quote for the ride.

Telephone

Area Codes

Area codes in Britain do not have a standard format or length, eg ☎020 for London, ☎0161 for Manchester, ☎01225 for Bath, ☎029 for Cardiff, ☎0131 for Edinburgh, ☎015394 for Ambleside, followed as usual by the individual number.

National Codes

☎**0500 or** ☎**0800** Free calls
☎**0845** Calls at local rate, wherever you're dialling from within the UK
☎**087** Calls at national rate
☎**089** or ☎**09** Premium rate
☎**07** Mobile phones, more expensive than calling a landline

International Codes

To call outside the UK dial 00, then the country code (1 for USA, 61 for Australia etc), the area code (you usually drop the initial zero) and the number.

The international code for Britain (and the rest of the UK) is 44.

Operator

For help and reverse-charge (collect) calls:
☎ **100** National operator
☎ **155** International operator

Directory

For directory enquiries, a host of agencies compete for your business and charge from 10p to 40p; numbers include 118 192, 118 118, 118 500 and 118 811.

Time

In winter (late October to late March) Britain is on GMT/UTC 0. In summer (late March to late October) it uses daylight saving so the time is GMT/UTC +1. In summer, if it's noon in London, it's 9pm in Melbourne (Australia) and 7am in New York (USA).

Tourist Information

All British cities and towns, and some villages, have a tourist information centre or visitor information centre – for ease we've called all these places 'tourist offices'. Such places have helpful staff, books and maps for sale, leaflets to give away, and advice on things to see or do. Some can also assist with booking accommodation. Some are run by national parks and often have small exhibits about the area.

Most tourist offices keep regular business hours; in quiet areas they close from October to March, while in popular areas they open daily year-round.

Before leaving home, check the comprehensive website of Britain's official tourist board, **Visit Britain** (www.visitbritain.com), covering all the angles of national tourism, with links to numerous other sites.

Travellers with Disabilities

All new buildings have wheelchair access, and even hotels in grand old country houses often have lifts, ramps and other facilities. Smaller B&Bs are often harder to adapt, so you'll have less choice here.

Getting around in cities, new buses have low floors for easy access, but few have conductors who can lend a hand when you're getting on or off. Many taxis take wheelchairs, or just have more room in the back.

For long-distance travel, coaches may present problems if you can't walk, but the main operator, **National Express** (www.nationalexpress.com) has wheelchair-friendly coaches on many routes. For details, see the website or ring their dedicated Disabled Passenger Travel Helpline on ☎0121-423 8479.

On most intercity trains there's more room and better facilities, compared with travel by coach, and usually station staff around; just have a word and they'll be happy to help. A **Disabled Person's Railcard** (www.disabledpersons-railcard.co.uk) costs £20 and gets you 33% off most train fares.

Useful organisations:
Disability Rights UK (www.disabilityrightsuk.org) Published titles include a Holiday Guide. Other services include a key for 7000 public disabled toilets across the UK.
Good Access Guide (www.goodaccessguide.co.uk)
Tourism for All (www.tourismforall.org.uk)

Visas

If you're a European Economic Area (EEA) national, you don't need a visa to visit (or work in) Britain. Citizens of Australia, Canada, New Zealand, South Africa and the USA are given leave to enter the UK at their point of arrival for up to six months (three months for some nationalities), but are prohibited from working without a visa. For more info see www.ukba.homeoffice.gov.uk.

Work

Nationals of most European countries don't need a permit to work in Britain, but everyone else does. Exceptions include most Commonwealth citizens with a UK-born parent: the 'Right of Abode' allows you to live and work in Britain and the rest of the UK.

Most Commonwealth citizens under 31 are eligible for a Working Holidaymaker Visa. It's valid for two years, you can work for a total of 12 months, and it must be obtained in advance.

Useful websites include www.ukba.homeoffice.gov.uk and www.workpermit.com. Also very handy is the 'Living & Working Abroad' thread on the Thorntree forum at www.lonelyplanet.com.

Transport

GETTING THERE & AWAY

Most visitors reach Britain by air. As London is a global transport hub, it's easy to fly to Britain from just about anywhere. In recent years, the massive growth of budget ('no-frills') airlines has increased the number of routes – and reduced the fares – between Britain and other countries in Europe.

The other main option for travel between Britain and mainland Europe is ferry, either port-to-port or combined with a long-distance bus trip, although journeys can be long and financial savings not huge compared with budget airfares.

International trains are much more comfortable and a 'green' option; the Channel Tunnel allows direct rail services between Britain, France and Belgium, with onward connections to many other European destinations.

Flights, cars and rail tickets can be booked online at lonelyplanet.com/bookings.

Air

London Airports

London's main airports are listed following. For details of getting from the airports into the city, see p142.

Heathrow (LHR; www.heathrowairport.com) Britain's main airport for international flights; often chaotic and crowded. About 15 miles west of central London.

Gatwick (LGW; www.gatwickairport.com) Britain's number-two airport, mainly for international flights, 30 miles south of central London.

Stansted (STN; www.stanstedairport.com) About 35 miles northeast of central London, mainly handling charter and budget European flights.

Luton (LTN; www.london-luton.co.uk) Some 35 miles north of central London, well known as a holiday-flight airport.

London City (LCY; www.londoncityairport.com) A few miles east of central London, specialising in flights to/from European and other UK airports.

Regional Airports

Some planes on European and long-haul routes avoid London and use major regional airports including Manchester and Glasgow. Smaller regional airports such as Southampton, Cardiff and Birmingham are served by flights to and from continental Europe and Ireland.

Land

Bus & Coach

You can easily get between Britain and other European countries via long-distance bus or coach. The international network **Eurolines**

CLIMATE CHANGE & TRAVEL

Every form of transport that relies on carbon-based fuel generates CO_2, the main cause of human-induced climate change. Modern travel is dependent on aeroplanes, which might use less fuel per kilometre per person than most cars but travel much greater distances. The altitude at which aircraft emit gases (including CO_2) and particles also contributes to their climate change impact. Many websites offer 'carbon calculators' that allow people to estimate the carbon emissions generated by their journey and, for those who wish to do so, to offset the impact of the greenhouse gases emitted with contributions to portfolios of climate-friendly initiatives throughout the world. Lonely Planet offsets the carbon footprint of all staff and author travel.

PASSPORT CHECK

Travelling between Britain's three nations of England, Scotland and Wales is easy. The bus and train systems are fully integrated and in most cases you won't even know you've crossed the border. Passports are not required – although some Scots and Welsh may think they should be!

(www.eurolines.com) connects a huge number of destinations; you can buy tickets online via one of the national operators.

Services to/from Britain are operated by **National Express** (www.national express.com). Some sample journey times to/from London:

» Amsterdam, 12 hours
» Barcelona, 24 hours
» Dublin, 12 hours
» Paris, eight hours

If you book early, and can be flexible with timings (ie travel when few other people want to), you can get some very good deals. For example, between London and Paris or Amsterdam from about £10 one-way (although paying nearer £30 is more usual).

Train
CHANNEL TUNNEL PASSENGER SERVICE
High-speed **Eurostar** (www .eurostar.com) passenger services shuttle at least 10 times daily between London and Paris (2½ hours) or Brussels (two hours). Buy tickets from travel agencies, major train stations or the Eurostar website.

The normal one-way fare between London and Paris/ Brussels costs £150 to £180; advance booking and off-peak travel gets cheaper fares as low as £40 one-way.

CHANNEL TUNNEL CAR SERVICE
Drivers use **Eurotunnel** (www.eurotunnel.com). At Folkestone in England or Calais in France, you drive onto a train, get carried through the tunnel and drive off at the other end.

Trains run about four times an hour from 6am to 10pm, then hourly through the night. Loading and unloading takes an hour; the journey lasts 35 minutes.

Book in advance online or pay on the spot. One way for a car and passengers costs from £70 to £150 depending on time of day; promotional fares often bring it nearer £50.

Sea
Ferry Routes
The main ferry routes between Britain and other European countries include the following:

GREAT BRITAIN	REST OF EUROPE
Dover	Calais (France)
Dover	Boulogne (France)
Newhaven	Dieppe (France)
Harwich	Hook of Holland (Netherlands)
Hull	Zeebrugge (Belgium)
Hull	Rotterdam (Netherlands)
Portsmouth	Santander (Spain)
Portsmouth	Bilbao (Spain)
Holyhead	Dun Laoghaire (Ireland)
Fishguard	Roddlare (Ireland)

Ferry Fares
Most ferry operators offer flexible fares, meaning great bargains at quiet times of day or year. For example, short cross-channel routes such as Dover to Calais or Boulogne can be as low as £20 for a car plus up to five passengers, although around £50 is more likely. If you're a foot passenger, or cycling, there's less need to book ahead; cheap fares on short crossings start from about £10 each way.

Ferry Bookings
Book direct with one of the operators listed following, or use the very handy www .ferrybooker.com – a single site covering all sea-ferry routes, plus Eurotunnel.

Brittany Ferries (www.brittany-ferries.com)
DFDS Seaways (www.dfdseaways.co.uk)
Irish Ferries (www.irishferries.com)
P&O Ferries (www.poferries.com)
Stena Line (www.stenaline.com)
Transmanche (www.transmancheferries.com)

GETTING AROUND
For getting around Britain your first main choice is going by car or public transport.

TRAIN & FERRY CONNECTIONS

As well as Eurostar, many 'normal' trains run between Britain and mainland Europe. You buy one ticket, but get off the train at the port, walk onto a ferry, then get another train on the other side. Routes include Amsterdam–London (via Hook of Holland and Harwich). Travelling between Ireland and Britain, the main train-ferry-train route is Dublin to London, via Dun Laoghaire and Holyhead. Ferries also run between Rosslare and Fishguard or Pembroke (Wales), with train connections on either side.

INFORMATION SERVICE

Traveline (☑0871 200 2233; www.traveline.org.uk) is a very useful information service covering bus, coach, taxi and train services nationwide, with numerous links to help plan your journey. By phone, you get transferred automatically to an adviser in the region you're phoning *from;* for details on another part of the country, you need to key in a code number (81 for London, 874 for Cumbria etc) – for a full list of codes, go to the Traveline website.

Having your own car makes the best use of time, and helps reach remote places, but rental and fuel costs can be expensive for budget travellers (while traffic jams in major cities hit everyone) – public transport is often the better way to go. As long as you have time, using a mix of train, bus, taxi, walking and occasionally hiring a bike, you can get almost anywhere in Britain without having to drive.

The main public transport options are train and long-distance bus (called coach in Britain). Services between major towns and cities are generally good, although at peak times you must book in advance to be sure of getting a ticket. If you book ahead early or travel at off-peak periods – ideally both – train and coach tickets can be very cheap.

Air

Britain's domestic air companies include British Airways, EasyJet and Ryanair. If you're really pushed for time, flights on longer routes across Britain (eg Exeter or Southampton to Newcastle, Edinburgh or Inverness) are handy, although you miss the glorious scenery in between. On some shorter routes (eg London to Newcastle, or Manchester to Newquay) trains compare favourably with planes on time, once airport downtime is factored

in. On costs, you might get a bargain airfare, but trains can be cheaper if you buy tickets in advance.

Bicycle

Britain is a compact country, and hiring a bike – for an hour or two, or a week or longer – is a great way to really see the country if you've got time to spare.

Rental in London

London is famous for its Barclays Cycle Hire Scheme (p143; known as 'Boris bikes' after the mayor that introduced them to the city). Bikes can be hired on the spot from automatic docking stations. For more information visit the **Transport for London** (www.tfl.gov.uk) website. Other rental options in the capital are listed at www.lcc.org.uk.

Rental Elsewhere

Tourist towns such as Oxford and Cambridge have plentiful bike rental options, and bikes can also be hired in national parks or forestry sites now primarily used for leisure activities, such as Kielder Water in Northumberland, Grizedale Forest in the Lake District and the Elan Valley in Mid-Wales. In some areas, disused railway lines are now bike routes, notably the Peak District in Derbyshire. Rental rates start at about £10 per day, or £20 for something half decent.

Bus & Coach

If you're on a tight budget, long-distance buses (called coaches in Britain) are nearly always the cheapest way to get around, although they're also the slowest – sometimes by a considerable margin. Many towns have separate stations for local buses and long-distance coaches; make sure you go to the right one!

National Express is the main coach operator, with a wide network and frequent services between main centres. North of the border, services tie in with those of **Scottish Citylink** (☑0871 266 3333; www.citylink.co.uk), Scotland's leading coach company. Fares vary: they're cheaper if you book in advance and travel at quieter times, and more expensive if you buy your ticket on the spot and it's Friday afternoon. As a guide, a 200-mile trip (eg London to York) will cost £15 to £20 if you book a few days in advance.

Megabus (www.megabus .com) operates a budget coach service between about 30 destinations around the country. Go at a quiet time, book early and your ticket will be very cheap. Book later, for a busy time and... You get the picture.

Passes & Discounts

National Express offers discount passes to full-time students and under-26s,

POSTBUS SERVICES

In remote areas, vans on mail services also carry passengers, an especially useful service for walkers and backpackers. For more info go to www.royal mail.com/personal then search for 'postbus'.

BIKES ON TRAINS

Bicycles can be taken free of charge on most local urban trains (although they may not be allowed at peak times when the trains are crowded with commuters) and on shorter trips in rural areas, on a first-come, first-served basis – though there may be space limits.

Bikes can be carried on long-distance train journeys free of charge, but advance booking is required for most conventional bikes. (Folding bikes can be carried on pretty much any train at any time.) In theory, this shouldn't be too much trouble as most long-distance rail trips are best bought in advance anyway, but you have to go a long way down the path of booking your seat before you start booking your bike – only to find space isn't available. A better course of action is to buy in advance at a major rail station, where the booking clerk can help you through the options.

A final warning: when railways are repaired, cancelled trains are replaced by buses – and they won't take bikes.

A very useful leaflet called *National Rail Cycling by Train* is available at major stations or downloadable from www.nationalrail.co.uk (from the homepage follow links to 'Stations & On-train' then 'Cyclists').

called Young Persons Coach-cards. They cost £10 and give you 30% off standard adult fares. Also available are coachcards for people over 60, families and disabled travellers.

For touring the country, National Express offers Brit Xplorer passes, allowing unlimited travel for 7/14/28 days (£79/139/219). You don't need to book journeys in advance: if the coach has a spare seat, you can take it.

Car & Motorcycle

Travelling by car or motorbike around Britain means you can be independent and flexible, and reach remote places. Downsides for drivers include traffic jams and high parking costs in cities.

HOW MUCH TO...?

When travelling by long-distance bus, coach or train in Britain, it's important to realise that there's no such thing as a standard fare. Prices vary according to demand and when you buy your ticket. Book long in advance and travel on Tuesday mid-morning and it's cheap. Buy your ticket on the spot late Friday afternoon and it'll be a lot more expensive. Ferries use similar systems. We have generally quoted sample fares somewhere in between the very cheapest and most expensive options. The price you pay will almost certainly be different.

Car Hire

Compared with many countries (especially the USA), hire rates are expensive in Britain; the smallest cars start from about £120 per week, and it's around £250 per week for a medium car. All rates include insurance and unlimited mileage, and can rise at busy times (or drop at quiet times).

Some main players:
Avis (www.avis.co.uk)
Budget (www.budget.co.uk)
Europcar (www.europcar.co.uk)
Sixt (www.sixt.co.uk)
Thrifty (www.thrifty.co.uk)

Another option is to look online for small local car-hire companies in Britain that can undercut the international franchises. Generally those in cities are cheaper than in rural areas. Using a rental-broker site such as **UK Car Hire** (www.ukcarhire.net) can also help find bargains.

Motorhome Rental

Hiring a motorhome or campervan is more expensive than hiring a car, but saves on accommodation costs and gives almost unlimited freedom. Sites to check include the following:
Just Go (www.justgo.uk.com)
Wild Horizon (www.wildhorizon.co.uk)

Insurance

It's illegal to drive a car or motorbike in Britain without (at least) third-party insurance. This will be included with all rental cars. If you're bringing a car from Europe you'll need to arrange it.

Parking

Many cities have short-stay and long-stay car parks; the latter are cheaper though may be less convenient. 'Park & Ride' systems allow you to park on the edge of the city then ride to the centre on frequent nonstop buses for an all-in-one price.

Yellow lines (single or double) along the edge of the road indicate restrictions. Nearby signs spell out when you can and can't park. In London and other big cities, traffic wardens operate with efficiency; if you park on the yellow lines at the wrong time, your car will be clamped or towed away, and it'll cost you £100 or more to get driving again. In some cities there are also red lines, which mean no stopping at all. Ever.

Roads

Motorways and main A-roads deliver you quickly from one end of the country to another. Lesser A-roads, B-roads and minor roads are much more scenic – ideal for car or motorcycle touring. You can't travel fast, but you won't care.

Speed limits are usually 30mph (48km/h) in built-up areas, 60mph (96km/h) on main roads and 70mph (112km/h) on motorways and most (but not all) dual carriageways.

Road Rules

A foreign driving licence is valid in Britain for up to 12 months.

Drink driving is taken very seriously; you're allowed a maximum blood-alcohol level of 80mg/100mL (0.08%) – campaigners want it reduced to 50mg/100mL (0.05%).

Some other important rules:

» drive on the left (!)
» wear fitted seat belts in cars
» wear helmets on motorcycles
» give way to your right at junctions and roundabouts
» always use the left lane on motorways and dual carriageways unless overtaking (although so many people ignore this rule, you'd think it didn't exist)
» don't use a mobile phone while driving unless it's fully hands-free (another rule frequently flouted)

Hitching

Hitching is not as common as it used to be in Britain: maybe because more

people have cars and maybe because few drivers give lifts any more. It's perfectly possible, however, if you don't mind long waits, although travellers should understand they're taking a small but potentially serious risk, and we don't recommend it. If you decide to go by thumb, note that it's illegal to hitch on motorways; you must use approach roads or service stations.

However, it's all different in remote rural areas such as Mid-Wales or northwest Scotland, where hitching is a part of getting around – especially if you're a walker heading back to base after a hike on the hills. On some Scottish islands, local drivers may stop and offer a lift without you even asking.

Local Transport

British cities usually have good public transport systems – a combination of bus, train and tram – often run by a confusing number of separate companies. Tourist offices can provide maps and information.

Local Bus

There are good local bus networks year-round in cities and towns. Buses also run in some rural areas year-round, although timetables are designed to serve schools and businesses, so there aren't many midday and weekend services (and they may stop running during school holidays), or buses may link local villages to a market town on only one day each week.

In tourist areas (especially national parks) there are frequent services from Easter to September. However, it's always worth double-checking at a tourist office before planning your day's activities around a bus that may not actually be running.

In this book, along with the local bus route number, frequency and duration, we have provided indicative prices if the fare is over £5. If it's less than this, we have generally omitted the fare.

LOCAL BUS PASSES
If you're taking a few local bus rides in one area, day passes (with names like Day Rover, Wayfarer or Explorer) are cheaper than buying several single tickets. Often they can be bought on your first bus, and may include local rail services. It's always worth asking ticket clerks or bus drivers about your options.

Local Ferry

Local ferries are another option when travelling around Britain; for example, from the mainland to the Isle of Wight or the Scottish islands.

Taxi

There are two sorts of taxi in England: those with meters that can be hailed in the street; and minicabs, which are cheaper but can only be called by phone. Unlicensed minicabs operate in some cities; see p1032 for advice about safe travel.

In London, most taxis are the famous 'black cabs' (some with advertising livery in other colours) which charge by distance and time. Depending on the time of day, a 1-mile journey takes five to 10 minutes and cost £5 to £9. Longer journeys are proportionally cheaper.

Black cabs also operate in some other large cities around Britain, with rates usually lower than in London.

In London, taxis are best flagged down in the street; a 'for hire' light on the roof indicates availability. In other cities, you can flag down a cab if you see one, but it's usually easier to go to a taxi rank.

In rural areas, taxis need to be called by phone; the best place to find the local taxi's phone number is the local pub. Fares are £2 to £3 per mile.

Handy resources:

National Cabline (☑0800 123444) Call from a landline phone; the service pinpoints your location and transfers you to an approved local taxi company.

Train-Taxi (www.traintaxi .co.uk) Portal site to help 'bridge the final gap' between the train station and your hotel or other final destination.

Train

For long-distance travel around Britain, trains are generally faster and more comfortable than coaches but can be more expensive, although with discount tickets they're competitive – and often take you through beautiful countryside. The British like to moan about their trains, but around 85% run on time. The other 15% that get delayed or cancelled mostly impact commuter services rather than long-distance journeys.

Information

Your first stop should be **National Rail Enquiries** (☑08457 48 49 50; www .nationalrail.co.uk), the nationwide timetable and fare information service. Its website advertises special offers and

has real-time links to station departure boards and downloadable maps of the rail network.

Operators

About 20 different companies operate train services in Britain, while Network Rail operates track and stations. For some passengers this system can be confusing at first, but information and ticket-buying services are mostly centralised. If you have to change trains, or use two or more train operators, you still buy one ticket – valid for the whole journey. The main railcards and passes are also accepted by all train operators.

Tickets & Reservations

BUYING TICKETS

Once you've found the journey you need on the National Rail Enquiries website, links take you to the relevant train operator to buy the ticket. This can be posted (UK addresses only) or collected at the station on the day of travel from automatic machines. There's usually no booking fee on top of the ticket price.

You can also use a centralised ticketing service to buy your train ticket. These cover all train services in a single site, and make a small

booking fee on top of every ticket price. The main players include:

QJump (www.qjump.co.uk)
Rail Easy (www.raileasy.co.uk)
Train Line (www.thetrainline .com)

To use operator or centralised ticketing websites you always have to state a preferred time and day of travel, even if you don't mind when you go, but you can change it as you go through the process, and with a little delving around you can find some real bargains.

You can also buy train tickets on the spot at stations, which is fine for short journeys (under about 50 miles), but discount tickets for longer trips are usually not available and must be bought in advance by phone or online.

COSTS

For longer journeys, on-the-spot fares are always available, but tickets are much cheaper if bought in advance. The earlier you book, the cheaper it gets. You can also save if you travel off-peak. Advance purchase usually gets a reserved seat, too.

Whichever operator you travel with and wherever you buy tickets, these are the three main fare types:

» **Anytime** Buy anytime, travel anytime – usually the most expensive option

---

STATION NAMES

London has several mainline train stations, such as Victoria, Paddington, King's Cross, Waterloo, Charing Cross and Liverpool St, positioned in a rough circle around the city's central area (and mostly linked by the Circle underground line). The stations' proper names are London Victoria, London Paddington, London King's Cross and so on, and this is how you'll see them on official timetables, information boards and booking websites – although the British never use the full names in everyday speech.

In this guide, for clarity, we have used the full name for London stations. This is also to help distinguish the London stations from stations in some other British cities that also share names such as Victoria and Charing Cross.

» **Off-peak** Buy ticket any time, travel off-peak

» **Advance** Buy ticket in advance, travel only on specific trains – usually the cheapest option

For an idea of the price difference, an Anytime single ticket from London to York will cost £100 or more, an Off-peak around £80, with an Advance around £20, and even less if you book early enough or don't mind arriving at midnight.

The cheapest fares are nonrefundable, so if you miss your train you'll have to buy a new ticket.

ONWARD TRAVEL

If train doesn't get you all the way to your destination, when making your reservation you can add a **PlusBus** (www.plusbus.info) supplement to validate your train ticket for onward travel by bus. This is more convenient, and usually cheaper, than buying a separate bus ticket.

Train Classes

There are two classes of rail travel: first and standard. First class costs around 50% more than standard fare (up to double at busy periods) and gets you bigger seats, more leg-room, and usually a more peaceful business-like atmosphere, plus extras such as complimentary drinks and newspapers. At weekends some train operators offer 'upgrades' to first class for an extra £10 to £15 on top of your standard class fare, payable on the spot.

Train Passes

DISCOUNT PASSES

If you're staying in Britain for a while, passes known as **Railcards** (www.railcard.co.uk) are available:

» **16-25 Railcard** For those aged 16 to 25, or a full-time UK student

» **Senior Railcard** For anyone over 60

» **Family & Friends Railcard** Covers up to four adults and four children travelling together

Railcards cost around £28 (valid for one year, available from major stations or online) and get 33% discount on most train fares, except those already heavily discounted. With the Family card, adults get 33% and children get 60% discounts, so the fee is easily repaid in a couple of journeys.

LOCAL & REGIONAL PASSES

Local train passes usually cover rail networks around a city (many include bus travel too) and are detailed in the relevant sections throughout this guide.

If you're concentrating your travels on southeast England (eg London to Dover, Weymouth, Cambridge or Oxford) a **Network Railcard** (www.railcard.co.uk/network; per year £28) covers up to four adults and up to four children travelling together outside peak times.

NATIONAL PASSES

For country-wide travel, **BritRail** (www.britrail.com) passes are available for visitors from overseas. They must be bought in your country of origin (not in Britain) from a specialist travel agency. Available in three different versions (England only; all Britain; UK and Ireland) for periods from four to 30 days.

Glossary

almshouse – accommodation for the aged or needy

ap – prefix in a Welsh name meaning 'son of'

bag – originally to 'catch' – a shooting term – now used to mean 'reach the top of' (as in to 'bag a couple of peaks' or 'Munro bagging')

bailey – outermost wall of a castle

bar – gate (York, and some other northern cities)

beck – stream (northern England)

bill – the total you need to pay after eating in a restaurant ('check' to Americans)

billion – the British billion is a million million (unlike the American billion – a thousand million)

blackhouse – traditional low-walled stone cottage with thatch or turf roof and earth floors; shared by both humans and cattle and typical of the Outer Hebrides until the early 20th century (Scotland)

bloke – man (colloquial)

Blue Flag – an award given to beaches for their unpolluted sand and water

böd – once a simple trading booth used by fishing communities, today it refers to basic accommodation for walkers etc (used only in Shetland)

bothy – very simple hut or shelter, usually in mountain or wilderness area, used by walkers and hikers

brae – hill (Scotland)

bridleway – track for horse riders that can be also used by walkers and cyclists

broch – ancient defensive tower

burgh – town

burn – stream

bus – local bus; see also *coach*

Cadw – the Welsh historic monuments agency

cairn – pile of stones marking path, junction of paths or the summit of a mountain

CalMac – Caledonian MacBrayne, the main Scottish island ferry operator

canny – good, great, wise (northern England)

castell – castle (Welsh)

ceilidh – (*kay*-lee) a session of traditional music, song and dance; originally Scottish, now more widely used across Britain

Celtic high cross – a large, elaborately carved stone cross decorated with biblical scenes and Celtic interlace designs dating from the 8th to 10th centuries

cheers – goodbye; thanks (colloquial); also a drinking toast

chemist – pharmacist

chine – valley-like fissure leading to the sea (southern England)

chippy – fish-and-chip shop

circus – junction of several city streets, usually circular, and usually with a green or other feature at the centre

Clearances – eviction of Highland farmers from their land by *lairds* wanting to use it for grazing sheep

close – entrance to an alley

coach – long-distance bus

coasteering – adventurous activity that involves making your way around a rocky coastline by climbing, scrambling, jumping or swimming

cob – mixture of mud and straw for building

corrie – circular hollow on a hillside

cot – small bed for a baby ('crib' to Americans)

court – courtyard

craic – lively conversation; pronounced, and sometimes spelt, 'crack'

craig – exposed rock

crannog – an artificial island in a loch built for defensive purposes

croft – smallholding, usually in marginal agricultural area (Scotland); the activity is known as 'smallholding'

Cymraeg – Welsh language (Welsh); also Gymraeg

Cymru – Welsh word for Wales

dene – valley

dirk – dagger

DIY – do-it-yourself, ie home improvements

dram – a measure of whisky

dodgy – suspect, bad, dangerous (colloquial)

dolmen – chambered tomb (Wales)

dough – money (colloquial)

downs – rolling upland, characterised by lack of trees

duvet – quilt replacing sheets and blankets ('doona' to Australians)

EH – English Heritage; state-funded organisation responsible for historic sites

en suite room – hotel room with private attached bathroom (ie shower, basin and toilet)

eisteddfod – literally a gathering or session; festival in which competitions are held in music, poetry, drama and the fine arts; plural eisteddfodau (Welsh)

Evensong – daily evening service (Church of England)

fell race – tough running race through hills or moors

fen – drained or marshy low-lying flat land

firth – estuary

fiver – £5 note (colloquial)

flat – single dwelling in a larger building ('apartment' to Americans)

flip-flops – plastic sandals with a single strap over toes ('thongs' to Australians)

footpath – path through countryside and between houses, not beside a road (that's called a 'pavement')

gate – street (York, and some other northern cities)

graft – work (not corruption, as in American English; colloquial)

grand – 1000 (colloquial)

gutted – very disappointed (colloquial)

guv, guvner – from governor, a respectful term of address for owner or boss; can sometimes be used ironically

hart – deer

HI – Hostelling International (organisation)

hire – rent

Hogmanay – Scottish celebration of New Year's Eve

howff – pub or shelter (Scotland)

HS – Historic Scotland; organisation that manages historic sites in Scotland

inn – pub with accommodation

jumper – woollen item of clothing worn on torso ('sweater' to Americans)

ken – Scottish term for 'understand' or 'know', as in 'do you ken' = 'do you know'

kirk – church (northern England and Scotland)

knowe – burial mound (Scotland)

kyle – strait or channel (Scotland)

laird – estate owner (Scotland)

lass – young woman (northern England and Scotland)

lift – machine for carrying people up and down in large buildings ('elevator' to Americans)

linn – waterfall (Scotland)

loch – lake (Scotland)

lochan – small loch

lock – part of a canal or river that can be closed off and the water levels changed to raise or lower boats

lolly – money (colloquial); candy on a stick (possibly frozen)

lorry (s), lorries (pl) – truck

Mabinogion – key source of Welsh folk legends

machair – grass- and wildflower-covered sand dunes

mad – insane (not angry, as in American English)

Marches – borderlands (ie between England and Wales or Scotland) after the Anglo-Saxon word mearc, meaning 'boundary'

menhir – standing stone

Mercat Cross – a symbol of the trading rights of a market town or village, usually found in the centre of town and usually a focal point for the community

mere – a body of water, usually shallow; technically a lake that has a large surface area relative to its depth

merthyr – burial place of a saint (Welsh)

midge – mosquito-like insect

motorway – major road linking cities (equivalent to 'interstate' or 'freeway')

motte – early Norman fortification consisting of a raised, flattened mound with a keep on top; when attached to a bailey it is known as a motte-and-bailey

Munro – hill or mountain 3000ft (914m) or higher, especially in Scotland; those over 2500ft are called Corbetts

Munro bagger – a hill walker who tries to climb all the Munros in Scotland

naff – inferior, in poor taste (colloquial)

NCN – National Cycle Network

newydd – new (Welsh)

NNR – National Nature Reserve, managed by the Scottish Natural Heritage (SNH)

NT – National Trust; organisation that protects historic buildings and land with scenic importance in England and Wales

NTS – National Trust for Scotland; organisation dedicated to the preservation of historic sites and the environment in Scotland

oast house – building containing a kiln for drying hops

ogham – ancient Celtic script

oriel – gallery (Welsh)

OS – Ordnance Survey

p – (pronounced pee) pence; ie 2p is 'two p' not 'two pence' or 'tuppence'

pele – fortified house

Picts – early inhabitants of north and east Scotland (from Latin pictus, or 'painted', after their body-paint decorations)

pile – large imposing building (colloquial)

pissed – slang for drunk (not angry)

pissed off – angry (slang)

pitch – playing field

postbus – minibus delivering the mail, also carrying passengers in remote areas

provost – mayor

punter – customer (colloquial)

quid – pound (colloquial)

ramble – short easy walk

reiver – warrior or raider (historic term; northern England)

return ticket – round-trip ticket

RIB – rigid inflatable boat

rood – an old Scots word for a cross

RSPB – Royal Society for the Protection of Birds

RSPCA – Royal Society for the Prevention of Cruelty to Animals

sarsen – boulder, a geological remnant usually found in chalky areas (sometimes used in neolithic constructions, eg Stonehenge and Avebury)

Sassenach – from Gaelic 'Sasannach': anyone who is not a Highlander (including Lowland Scots)

sheila-na-gig – Celtic fertility symbol of a woman with exaggerated genitalia, often carved in stone on churches and castles; rare in England, found mainly in the Marches, along the border with Wales

single ticket – one-way ticket

SMC – Scottish Mountaineering Club

SNH – Scottish Natural Heritage, a government organisation directly responsible for safeguarding and improving Scotland's natural heritage

snickelway – narrow alley (York)

snug – usually a small separate room in a pub

sporran – purse worn around waist with the kilt (Scotland)

SSSI – Site of Special Scientific Interest

Sustrans – sustainable transport charity encouraging people to walk, cycle and use public transport; also responsible for instigating and developing the National Cycle Network (NCN)

SYHA – Scottish Youth Hostel Association

tarn – a small lake or pool, usually in mountain areas in England, often in a depression caused by glacial erosion

tenner – £10 note (colloquial)

TIC – Tourist Information Centre

ton – 100 (colloquial)

tor – pointed hill

torch – flashlight

Tory – Conservative (political party)

towpath – path running beside a river or canal, where horses once towed barges

twitcher – obsessive birdwatcher

Tube, the – London's underground railway system (colloquial)

Underground, the – London's underground railway system

wolds – open, rolling countryside

wynd – lane or narrow street (northern England and Scotland)

YHA – Youth Hostels Association

behind the scenes

SEND US YOUR FEEDBACK

We love to hear from travellers – your comments keep us on our toes and help make our books better. Our well-travelled team reads every word on what you loved or loathed about this book. Although we cannot reply individually to postal submissions, we always guarantee that your feedback goes straight to the appropriate authors, in time for the next edition. Each person who sends us information is thanked in the next edition – the most useful submissions are rewarded with a selection of digital PDF chapters.

Visit **lonelyplanet.com/contact** to submit your updates and suggestions or to ask for help. Our award-winning website also features inspirational travel stories, news and discussions.

Note: We may edit, reproduce and incorporate your comments in Lonely Planet products such as guidebooks, websites and digital products, so let us know if you don't want your comments reproduced or your name acknowledged. For a copy of our privacy policy visit lonelyplanet.com/privacy.

OUR READERS

Many thanks to the travellers who used the last edition and wrote to us with helpful hints, useful advice and interesting anecdotes:

Bente Benedict, Mary Louise Brown, David Clark, John Deuchars, Tony Dobson, James Fairman, Caroline Hall, Glen Kilday, Valeria Lamelas, Garrick Larkin, Piet Liebenberg, Carla Malcolm, Peter Martin, Terry Phippen, Lindsay Radford, Jeannie Scown, Thomas Simpson, Stacie Sullivan, Nick Thomson, Jon Turner

AUTHOR THANKS

David Else

As always, massive appreciation goes to my wife, Corinne, for joining me on many of my research trips around Britain, and for not minding when I locked myself away for 12 hours at a time to write this book – and for bringing coffee when it got nearer 18 hours. Thanks also to the co-authors of this book – my name goes down as coordinating author, but I couldn't have done it without this team; and to Cliff Wilkinson, my commissioning editor at Lonely Planet London, and to all the friendly faces in the production departments at Lonely Planet Melbourne who helped bring this book to final fruition.

Oliver Berry

Thanks to Cliff Wilkinson for the England gig, David Else for keeping us on course, Belinda Dixon for co-authoring and moral support, and David Carroll, Dan Corbett and the rest of the SPP team for being there whenever we needed you! Special thanks to Susie, Molly and Gracie Berry, and to all the people I met out on the road.

Fionn Davenport

A huge thanks to John Ryan, Emma Fox, Andy Parkinson, Louise Latham, Andrew Stokes, Erica Dillon, Sylvia O'Malley, Tina Snowball and Andy Hook. As always, thanks to Caroline for putting up with me.

Marc Di Duca

A huge 'ta' goes to all the staff at tourist offices across the Southeast (those that haven't been axed, that is) but especially the helpful guys in Brighton, Hastings, Canterbury and Rye. Also thanks to David Else for his guidance throughout, Therese at Canterbury Cathedral and my Kyiv parents-in-law, Mykola and Vira, for looking after son Taras while I was on the road. And last, but certainly not least, heartfelt gratitude must go to my wife, Tanya, for all those long days we spend apart.

Belinda Dixon

Huge thanks go to: Lonely Planet's behind-the-scenes team who magic the words from my battered notebooks onto the shelves (technical wizards, take an oh-so-hard-earned bow); Cliff for the gig; everyone encountered on the road for tips, facts and countless kindnesses; and JL for (still) making me smile.

Peter Dragicevich

Thanks to Becky Ohlsen for use of her description of the Offa's Dyke Path, originally written for Lonely Planet's *Walking In Britain* book. Thanks also to Kerri Tyler for a memorable time in Hay-on-Wye. Many thanks to Vanessa Irvine and Paul Sajewicz for the writing retreat, and to my long-suffering travel agent David Inglis.

Damian Harper

My hat is off to a long list of helpful people, including Daniel Hands, Bill Moran, Matthew Scudamore, Daisy Harper, George Whitman, Jane Egginton, Richard Samuels and the helpful staff at Waterstone's (Piccadilly). A slap on the back for the folk of the West Midlands and London for unflagging chirpiness in the face of driving rain would not go amiss, while big thanks are further extended to the staff at Lonely Planet for helping in the production of this book.

Anna Kaminski

I'm grateful for all the great advice from friends, family, locals and tourism staff. In particular, I'd like to thank the Cambridge crew – Subo, Dawn, Sara, Sarah, Steve and my parents; the Oxford crew – Nicolas, Bill and Georgia; Colin in Cheltenham; Joanna and Gabriel Dick in Ely; Sonia and Matt – my fellow gourmets; and Genie in Southend-on-Sea. A big thank you to the CA – David Else – and editors Clifton Wilkinson and Katie O'Connell.

Catherine Le Nevez

Cheers first and foremost to Julian, to my co-author Damian Harper for his contribution to the Birmingham, the Midlands & the Marches chapter, and to Ade Andrews for the interview, as well as all of the locals, tourism professionals and fellow travellers who provided insights, inspiration and good times. Thanks also to David Else, Cliff Wilkinson, Katie O'Connell, Angela Tinson, Mandy Sierp and everyone at Lonely Planet. As ever, *merci encore* to my parents, brother and *belle-sœur*.

Fran Parnell

A big thank you to all the tourist-office staff who answered questions even during the busiest times, especially at Harlech, Caernarvon and Porthmadog. Thanks to David Else for his coordinating and patience, and to the inhouse Lonely Planet team. Gratitude to Stuart Cooper for his knowledge of Snowdonian hiking: I'm sorry I didn't get to see your Welsh wood!

Andy Symington

Many thanks are due, but particularly to Jenny Neil, and Juliette and David Paton for guaranteed warm hospitality. Gratitude also to my mother for visiting, to Jose Eliseo Vázquez González for navigational assistance, to Harry Wycherley for audiovisuals, to Cindy-Lou Ramsay, helpful tourist-office staff and cabbies, to David for coordinating, and to Cliff and the Lonely Planet team for a top organising job. And to Elena Vázquez Rodríguez, at my side even when I'm far away: *gracias profundas amor*.

Neil Wilson

Many thanks to all the helpful and enthusiastic staff at TICs throughout the country, and to the many travellers I met on the road who chipped in with advice and recommendations. Thanks also to my co-authors and to the ever-helpful and patient editors and cartographers at Lonely Planet.

ACKNOWLEDGMENTS

Climate Map Data Climate map data adapted from Peel MC, Finlayson BL & McMahon TA (2007) 'Updated World Map of the Köppen-Geiger Climate Classification', *Hydrology and Earth System Sciences*, 11, 163344.

Illustrations: pp76-7, pp86-7, pp628-9, pp756-7, pp768-9 and pp832-3 by Javier Zarracina.

Cover photograph: Broadway Tower and deer, the Cotswolds, Paul Fawcett/Getty Images.

This Book

This 10th edition of Lonely Planet's *Great Britain* guidebook was researched and written by David Else, Oliver Berry, Fionn Davenport, Marc Di Duca, Belinda Dixon, Peter Dragicevich, Damian Harper, Anna Kaminski, Catherine Le Nevez, Fran Parnell, Andy Symington and Neil Wilson. This guidebook was commissioned in Lonely Planet's London office, and produced by the following:

Commissioning Editors Katie O'Connell, Clifton Wilkinson

Coordinating Editor Nigel Chin

Coordinating Cartographer Peter Shields

Coordinating Layout Designers Sandra Helou, Clara Monitto

Managing Editors Barbara Delissen, Angela Tinson

Managing Cartographer Diana Von Holdt

Managing Layout Designer Chris Girdler

Assisting Editors Michelle Bennett, Kate Daly, Carly Hall, Victoria Harrison, Kellie Langdon, Rosemary Neilson, Sally O'Brien, Kristin Odijk, Gabrielle Stefanos, Jeanette Wall

Assisting Cartographers Valeska Cañas, Mick Garrett, Joelene Kowalski, Gabriel Lindquist, Brendan Streager

Assisting Layout Designer Frank Deim

Cover Research Naomi Parker

Thanks to Andrea Dobbin, Ryan Evans, Justin Flynn, Larissa Frost, Jane Hart, Andi Jones, Jouve India, Katherine Marsh, Catherine Naghten, Trent Paton, Martine Power, Raphael Richards, Luna Soo, Branislava Vladisavljevic, Gerard Walker

NOTES

index

000 Map pages
000 Photo pages

how to use this book

These symbols will help you find the listings you want:

👁 Sights   ☞ Tours   🍷 Drinking

🏊 Beaches   🎆 Festivals & Events   ☆ Entertainment

🏃 Activities   🛏 Sleeping   🛍 Shopping

🎓 Courses   🍴 Eating   ℹ Information/Transport

Look out for these icons:

TOP CHOICE — Our author's recommendation

FREE — No payment required

🍃 — A green or sustainable option

Our authors have nominated these places as demonstrating a strong commitment to sustainability – for example by supporting local communities and producers, operating in an environmentally friendly way, or supporting conservation projects.

These symbols give you the vital information for each listing:

📞 Telephone Numbers   🛜 Wi-Fi Access   🚌 Bus
🕐 Opening Hours   🏊 Swimming Pool   ⛴ Ferry
🅿 Parking   🥗 Vegetarian Selection   Ⓜ Metro
🚭 Nonsmoking   📖 English-Language Menu   Ⓢ Subway
❄ Air-Conditioning   👪 Family-Friendly   ⊖ London Tube
@ Internet Access   🐾 Pet-Friendly   🚊 Tram
  🚆 Train

Reviews are organised by author preference.

Map Legend

Sights
Beach, Buddhist, Castle, Christian, Hindu, Islamic, Jewish, Monument, Museum/Gallery, Ruin, Winery/Vineyard, Zoo, Other Sight

Activities, Courses & Tours
Diving/Snorkelling, Canoeing/Kayaking, Skiing, Surfing, Swimming/Pool, Walking, Windsurfing, Other Activity/Course/Tour

Sleeping
Sleeping, Camping

Eating
Eating

Drinking
Drinking, Cafe

Entertainment
Entertainment

Shopping
Shopping

Information
Post Office, Tourist Information

Transport
Airport, Border Crossing, Bus, Cable Car/Funicular, Cycling, Ferry, Monorail, Parking, S-Bahn, Taxi, Train/Railway, Tram, Tube Station, U-Bahn, Underground Train Station, Other Transport

Routes
Tollway, Freeway, Primary, Secondary, Tertiary, Lane, Unsealed Road, Plaza/Mall, Steps, Tunnel, Pedestrian Overpass, Walking Tour, Walking Tour Detour, Path

Boundaries
International, State/Province, Disputed, Regional/Suburb, Marine Park, Cliff, Wall

Population
Capital (National), Capital (State/Province), City/Large Town, Town/Village

Geographic
Hut/Shelter, Lighthouse, Lookout, Mountain/Volcano, Oasis, Park, Pass, Picnic Area, Waterfall

Hydrography
River/Creek, Intermittent River, Swamp/Mangrove, Reef, Canal, Water, Dry/Salt/Intermittent Lake, Glacier

Areas
Beach/Desert, Cemetery (Christian), Cemetery (Other), Park/Forest, Sportsground, Sight (Building), Top Sight (Building)

Catherine Le Nevez

Birmingham, the Midlands & the Marches Catherine first roadtripped around Great Britain aged four and she's been roadtripping here at every opportunity since, completing her Doctorate of Creative Arts in Writing, Masters in Professional Writing, and post-grad qualifications in Editing and Publishing along the way, as well as dozens of Lonely Planet guidebooks and newspaper, magazine and online articles covering the UK, Europe and beyond. Roaming castle ruins and corridors of stately homes were highlights of researching this book, as was discovering idyllic countryside pubs.

Fran Parnell

Snowdonia & North Wales Early family holidays in Wales ignited Fran's love of the country, undimmed even after being dismissed from a B&B for sneaking in fish and chips. Studying for a Masters degree in Anglo-Saxon, Norse and Celtic fanned the flames: the romance of the medieval Welsh stories and poems has never left her. A particular highlight of this research trip was watching the sun set from the lofty ruins of Castell Dinas Brân.

Andy Symington

Inverness & the Northern Highlands & Islands; Glasgow & Southern Scotland Andy's Scottish forebears make their presence felt in a love of malt, a debatable ginger colour to his facial hair and a love of wild places. From childhood slogs up the M1 he graduated to making dubious road trips around the firths in a disintegrating Mini Metro and thence to peddling whisky in darkest Leith. Whilst living there, he travelled widely around the country in search of the perfect dram, and, now resident in Spain, continues to visit very regularly.

Read more about Andy at:
lonelyplanet.com/memebers/andy_symington

Neil Wilson

Inverness & the Northern Highlands & Islands; Edinburgh; Stirling & Central Scotland; Yorkshire Neil has made many cross-border forays into 'God's own country' from his home in Edinburgh, as well as regular expeditions to every corner of Scotland. It's a toss-up whether the hiking, mountain-biking and beer is better in Yorkshire or north of the border. Neil is a full-time travel writer based in Edinburgh, and has written around 60 guidebooks for various publishers.

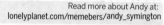

Belinda Dixon

Southwest England Belinda made a gleeful bolt for the sunny southwest for her post-grad, having been drawn there by the palm trees on campus. Like the best Westcountry limpets she's proved hard to shift since and now writes and broadcasts in the region. Research highlights for this book included kayaking up (and riding the tide down) the River Dart, hugging sarsen stones at Avebury, tasting freedom on the Isle of Wight, and oh-so-diligently testing the pick of Plymouth's newest eateries.

Peter Dragicevich

Cardiff (Caerdydd); Hay-on-Wye & Mid-Wales; Pembrokeshire & South Wales Wales has held a fascination for Peter ever since he was sent to write about Welsh castles for one of his first ever newspaper travel features. Since then he's co-authored dozens of Lonely Planet titles, including the stand-alone *Wales* guidebook and *Walking in Britain*, where he got to trek around the entirety of the beautiful Pembrokeshire coast. And while his name may not be Welsh, it does have more than half a dragon in it.

Damian Harper

London Born in London and growing up in Notting Hill, Damian went to school in Hampshire for a decade, cultivating a sense of affection for both city and country. Writing for Lonely Planet for more than 15 years, Damian recently turned his attention from far-flung cultures to his lush and well-watered homeland, revelling in England's diversity, good looks, insular charms, awe-inspiring sense of history and entirely intelligible local tongue (in the main).

Anna Kaminski

Cambridge & East Anglia; Oxford, the Cotswolds & Around Anna's love affair with England began in 1991 once she got over the shock of moving from the Soviet Union to Cambridge – her home for the next 20 years. Since budget flights hadn't been invented at the time, her parents tirelessly tried to instil some culture in her by taking her to every museum, castle, church and stately home in a 250-mile radius, most of which she revisited with great pleasure during this research trip. Memorable moments from her most recent trip include slurping fresh oysters in Aldeburgh, driving along some impossibly narrow country lanes in the Cotswolds and getting acquainted with Oxford's ghosts.

OUR STORY

A beat-up old car, a few dollars in the pocket and a sense of adventure. In 1972 that's all Tony and Maureen Wheeler needed for the trip of a lifetime – across Europe and Asia overland to Australia. It took several months, and at the end – broke but inspired – they sat at their kitchen table writing and stapling together their first travel guide, *Across Asia on the Cheap*. Within a week they'd sold 1500 copies. Lonely Planet was born.

Today, Lonely Planet has offices in Melbourne, London and Oakland, with more than 600 staff and writers. We share Tony's belief that 'a great guidebook should do three things: inform, educate and amuse'.

OUR WRITERS

David Else

Coordinating Author As a professional writer, David has authored more than 40 books, including several editions of Lonely Planet's *England* and *Great Britain* guides. His knowledge comes from a lifetime of travel around the country – often on foot – a passion dating from university years, when heading for the hills was always more attractive than visiting the library. Originally from London, David has lived in Yorkshire, Wales and Derbyshire, and is now a resident of the Cotswolds. For this current edition of *Great Britain*, David's research took him from the Isle of Wight in the south to the Isle of Skye in the north – via most of the bits in between.

Read more about David at:
lonelyplanet.com/members/davidelse

Oliver Berry

Southwest England; The Lake District & Cumbria Oliver is a writer and photographer based in Cornwall. Among many other projects for Lonely Planet, Oliver has written the first editions of *Devon, Cornwall & Southwest England* and *The Lake District*, and worked on several previous editions of the *England* and *Great Britain* guides. You can see some of his latest work at www.oliverberry.com and follow him at www.twitter.com/olivertomberry.

Read more about Oliver at:
lonelyplanet.com/members/oliverberry

Fionn Davenport

Manchester, Liverpool & Northwest England; Newcastle & Northeast England Fionn has been traipsing about Northern England's bigger burgs for over a decade and has found that the cities of the north are simply fantastic; a rich repository of culture, fine museums, terrific restaurants, bucolic landscapes and – most importantly – peopled by a few million lovable gruffs that exude a no-nonsense warmth. Fionn is a full-time travel writer and broadcaster based in Dublin, Ireland – you can catch him on Newstalk 106-108 (www.newstalk.ie).

Marc Di Duca

Canterbury & Southeast England Originally from Darlington, County Durham, Marc has been a northerner-gone-south since 2000 and covered his adopted corner of weald and down for the past two editions of Lonely Planet's *England* and *Great Britain*. A travel author for eight years, Marc has updated and written the Lonely Planet guides of Ukraine, Russia, Trans-Siberian Railway, Poland and Germany, though he can usually be found in Sandwich, Kent, where he lives with his Kievite wife Tanya and their two sons.

Read more about Marc at:
lonelyplanet.com/members/madidu

OVER PAGE | MORE WRITERS

Published by Lonely Planet Publications Pty Ltd
ABN 36 005 607 983
10th edition – May 2013
ISBN 978 1 74220 411 6
© Lonely Planet 2013   Photographs © as indicated 2013
10 9 8 7 6 5 4 3 2 1
Printed in China